P9-AQC-280

INDEX OF ECONOMIC ARTICLES
In Journals and Collective Volumes

Index of Economic Articles

IN JOURNALS AND COLLECTIVE VOLUMES

Volume XXV · 1983

Part One—Subject Index

Prepared under the auspices of

THE JOURNAL OF ECONOMIC LITERATURE

of the

AMERICAN ECONOMIC ASSOCIATION

Distributed by
RICHARD D. IRWIN, INC.
1818 RIDGE ROAD
HOMEWOOD, ILLINOIS 60430
1986

Student Classifiers: Jang-Bong Choi; A'Amer Farooqi; Tat P. Fong; Nayyer Hussain; Edgar L. Zamalloa, and Lorena M. Zamalloa.

Executive Office
1313 21st Avenue South, Nashville, Tennessee 37212

Library of Congress Catalog Card Number: 61–8020
International Standard Book Number: 0–917290–14–3
International Standard Standard Serial Number: 0536–647X
Printed in the United States of America

TABLE OF CONTENTS

INTRODUCTORY DISCUSSION

This volume of the *Index* lists, both by subject category and by author, articles in major economic journals and in collective volumes published during the year 1983. The articles listed include all articles published in English or with English summaries in the journals and books listed below (p. x). Part one includes the Subject Index of Articles in Journals and Collective Volumes, and Part Two consists of an alphabetical Author Index of all the articles indexed in Part One.

Relationship to JEL

This *Index* is prepared largely as an adjunct to the bibliographic activities of the *Journal of Economic Literature (JEL)*. Economies of joint production are pursued throughout the production process. Journals included are those indexed in the *JEL* quarterly; collective volumes are selected from the annotated 1983 books; the classification system is a more detailed version of the *JEL* system.

Journals Included

The 279 journals listed represent, in general, those journals that we believe will be most helpful to research workers and teachers of economics. These journals are listed below on p. x.

Generally, articles, notes, communications, comments, replies, rejoinders, as well as papers and formal discussions in proceedings and review articles in the included journals have been indexed. There are some exceptions; only articles in English or with English summaries are included—this practice results in a slightly reduced coverage compared with the *JEL* quarterly. Articles lacking author identification are omitted, as are articles without economic content. Identical articles appearing in two different journals in 1983 are listed from both sources. The journal issues included usually fall within a single volume. When a volume of a journal overlaps two calendar years, for example, Fall 1982 to Summer 1983, we include the issues from the two volumes relating to 1983 as best we can determine.

Collective Volumes

The collective volumes consist of the following:

1. *Festschriften*
2. Conference publications with individual papers
3. Collected essays, original, by one or more authors
4. Collected essays, reprinted, by one or more authors
5. Proceedings volumes with individual papers not included among the journal listings
6. Books of readings

All original articles in English are indexed with the exception of unsigned articles or articles without economic content. Reprinted articles are included on the basis that a researcher would be interested in knowing about another source of the article. The original publication dates are shown in italics on the citations of reprinted articles. Excerpts are not included. The same article appearing for the first time in different collective volumes in the same year is cited from both publications.

In the article citation, reference to the book in which the article appears is by author or editor of the volume. If the same person or persons wrote or edited more than one book included in the 1983 *Index,* it is indicated by a I or II appearing in both the source given in the article citation and the bibliographic reference in the book listing. If the same person wrote one book and edited another in 1983, the specification of "ed" in the reference indicates which book is being cited.

The collective volumes are listed alphabetically by author or editor beginning on p. xvi and include a full bibliographic reference. If there is more than one edition, the publisher cited is the one on the copy the *JEL* received, usually the American publisher.

Arrangement

The *Index* consists of two parts:

1. A Subject Index in which the articles are arranged by subject.
2. An Author Index.

Subject Index

In Part One, all articles are listed alphabetically by first author under each 4-digit subject category. Joint authors are listed up to three; beyond that, only the first author is listed, followed by *et al.*

There is one exception to the alphabetical author arrangement. In the 0322 category, a subdivision of **History of Thought** entitled **Individuals,** the arrangement is first alphabetical by the individual discussed in the article and then alphabetical by the article's author.

Articles with empirical content or discussing a particular geographic area carry a geographic descriptor (see discussion below).

Author Index

In the alphabetical Author Index in Part Two citations appear under each author (up to three) of an article. Wherever possible the full first name and middle initial or middle name(s) are used. Wherever it could be definitely ascertained, articles by the same person are grouped together with only one listing of the name. Authors' first names and initials are listed differently in various journals and books; for example, an individual may be identified as John L. Smith, J. L. Smith, or John Smith. Thus, despite our best efforts, we were left in doubt in several instances. Joint authors are listed up to three; beyond that, only the first author is listed, followed by *et al.* Under each author, articles are listed alphabetically. Names carrying prefixes are alphabetized according to the first *capitalized* letter, with occasional exceptions following national practices. Thus, van Arkadie would appear under A and D'Alabro under D.

Geographic Descriptors

Geographic descriptors appear in brackets at the end of any article entry in the Subject Index where the article cites data from or refers to a particular country or area. Research workers interested in these countries thus are made aware of the empirical content in the article. The descriptors used are countries or broader areas, such as southeast Asia (S.E. Asia); articles referring to cities or regions within a country are classified under the country. In general, the country name is written out in full with some adaptations and abbreviations, *e.g.,* U.S. is used for United States, U.K. for United Kingdom, and U.S.S.R. for Union of Soviet Socialist Republics. Abbreviations include: W. for West, E. for East, S. for South, N. for North. A shortened name such as W. Germany is used rather than the correct, but longer, Federal Republic of Germany. When broader regions are used as descriptors, the article may or may not refer to the full unit. For example, OECD has been used at times when most, but not all, of the OECD member countries are referred to.

Index volumes prior to 1979 sometimes did not include geographic descriptors on articles listed under subject categories 1210, 1211, 1220, 1221, 1230, 1240, and 1241, involving general or comparative economic country studies. In the 1979 *Index* and later volumes, these articles carry geographic descriptors in order to facilitate online identification in the ECONOMIC LITERATURE INDEX on DIALOG. Because the descriptor fields are limited to five, very general descriptors, such as LDCs (developing countries) and MDCs (developed countries), are often used on articles.

The fact that an article carries a geographic descriptor does not necessarily preclude its being primarily theoretical in nature. Any theoretical article drawing on empirical data to demonstrate its findings will carry a geographic descriptor.

Classification System

The classification system is an expansion of the 3-digit classification system used in the *Journal of Economic Literature* to a 4-digit system with slightly over 300 subcategories. The classification system, itself, is shown beginning on p. xxxiv (Part One). In most cases the classification heading is self-explanatory; however, in some cases notes have been added to clarify the coverage or indicate alternative subject classifications. The basic approach in classification is from the point of view of the researcher rather than the teacher; course content does not necessarily coincide with subfields of our classification system. In all cases where there are two or more 4-digit classifications under a 3-digit category, there is a zero classification; in most instances this is labeled "General." The zero or general category has been used both as an inclusive and a residual category; thus, when the subject matter of an article covers all or most of the subcategories, that article appears in the zero or general category. For example, an article discussing *all* aspects of international trade theory appears in the general category. There are also some articles that do not fall in any of the individual subcategories, and these, too, are classified in the general or zero category.

The criterion used in the classifying process is whether persons interested in this topic would wish to have the article drawn to their attention. With the advent of the online ECONOMIC LITERATURE INDEX on DIALOG, the interpretation of "interest" has broadened slightly to include cross-classifications that indicate the subject matter, particularly in such categories as industry studies or occupational designations. Over half of the articles are classified in more than one subcategory. From time to time, we find it desirable to add subject classifications as particular topics become prominent or to change subject headings to make them more descriptive of the contents of the category.

Topical Guide to the Classification System

At the end of Part One there is an alphabetical listing of standard economic terms and concepts. References are to the appropriate 4-digit classification numbers, not to page numbers.

LIST OF JOURNALS INDEXED 1983

Accounting Review, Vol. 58.

Acta Oeconomica, Vol. 30; Vol. 31.

L'Actualité Economique, Vol. 59.

African Economic History, No. 12, 1983.

Agricultural Economics Research, Vol. 35.

American Economic Review, Vol. 73.
Includes American Economic Association **Papers and Proceedings** of the annual meeting in *73*(2).

American Economist, Vol. 27.

American Historical Review, Vol. 88.

American Journal of Agricultural Economics, Vol. 65.
Title changed from **Journal of Farm Economics** in 1968.

American Journal of Economics and Sociology, Vol. 42.

American Political Science Review, Vol. 77.

American Real Estate and Urban Economics Association Journal, Vol. 11.

Annales de l'INSEE, Issue nos. 49–52.

Annales de Sciences Économiques Appliquées, Vol. 39.

Annals of the American Academy of Political and Social Science, Vol. 465.

Annals of Public and Co-operative Economy, Vol. 54.

Antitrust Bulletin, Vol. 28.

Applied Economics, Vol. 15.

ACES Bulletin (Association for Comparative Economic Studies Bulletin), Vol. 25.

Atlantic Economic Journal, Vol. 11.

Aussenwirtschaft, Vol. 38.

Australian Bulletin of Labor, Vol. 9, Issue nos. 2–4; Vol. 10, Issue no. 1.

Australian Economic History Review, Vol. 23.
Title changed from **Business Archives and History** in 1967; prior to 1962 entitled **Bulletin of the Business Archives Council of Australia.**

Australian Economic Papers, Vol. 22.

Australian Economic Review, Issue nos. 61–64.

Australian Journal of Agricultural Economics, Vol. 27.

Australian Journal of Management, Vol. 8, Issue no. 1.

Banca Nazionale del Lavoro—Quarterly Review, Issue nos. 144–147.

Bancaria, Vol. 39.

Bell Journal of Economics, Vol. 14.

British Journal of Industrial Relations, Vol. 21.

British Review of Economic Issues, Vol. 5.

Brookings Papers on Economic Activity, Issue nos. 1–2, 1983.

Bulletin of Economic Research, Vol. 35.
Title changed from **Yorkshire Bulletin of Economic and Social Research** in 1971.

Bulletin of Indonesian Economic Studies, Vol. 19.

Bulletin for International Fiscal Documentation, Vol. 37.

Business Economics, Vol. 18.

Business History Review, Vol. 57.
Title changed from **Bulletin of the Business Historical Society** in 1954.

Cahiers Économiques de Bruxelles, Issue nos. 97–100.

California Management Review, Vol. 25, Issue no. 2.

Cambridge Journal of Economics, Vol. 7.

Canadian Journal of Agricultural Economics, Vol. 31.

Canadian Journal of Economics, Vol. 16.

Canadian Public Policy, Vol. 9.

Carnegie–Rochester Conference Series on Public Policy, Vols. 18–19.
Vols. 1–17 were listed as supplements to the **Journal of Monetary Economics.**

Cato Journal, Vol. 3.

Cepal Review, Issue nos. 19–21.

Challenge, Vol. 25, Issue no. 6; Vol. 26, Issue nos. 1–5.

Chinese Economic Studies, Vol. 16; Issue nos. 2–4; Vol. 17, Issue no. 1.

Conflict Management and Peace Science, Vol. 7, Issue no. 1.
Title changed from **Journal of Peace Science** in 1979–80.

Consommation, Vol. 30.

Contemporary Policy Issues, Issue nos. 2–3, 1983.

Cuadernos de Economia, Vol. 20.

Czechoslovak Economic Digest, Issue nos. 1–8, 1983.

Czechoslovak Economic Papers, Issue no. 21, 1983.

Demography, Vol. 20.

Desarrollo Economico, Vol. 22, Issue no. 88; Vol. 23, Issue nos. 89–91.

Eastern Economic Journal, Vol. 9.

Eastern European Economics, Vol. 21, Issue no. 3; Vol. 22, Issue nos. 1–2.

Econometric Reviews, Vol. 2.

Econometrica, Vol. 51.

Economia, Vol. 7.

Economia Internazionale, Vol. 36.

Economic Affairs, Vol. 28.

Economic Analysis and Workers' Management, Vol. 17.

Economic Computation and Economic Cybernetics Studies and Research, Vol. 18.
Title changed from **Studii şi Cercetări Economicè** in 1974. Changed from issue numbers to volume numbers in 1978.

Economic Development and Cultural Change, Vol. 31, Issue nos. 2–4; Vol. 32, Issue no. 1.

Economic Forum, Vol. 13—Supplement; Vol. 14.
Title changed from **Intermountain Economic Review** in 1979.

Economic Geography, Vol. 59.

Economic History Review, Vol. 36.

Economic Inquiry, Vol. 21.
Title changed from **Western Economic Journal** in 1974.

Economic Journal, Vol. 93, Issue nos. 369–372, Supplement.

Economic Notes, Issue nos. 1–3, 1983.

Economic Record, Vol. 59.

Economic and Social Review, Vol. 14, Issue nos. 2–4; Vol. 15, Issue no. 1.

Economic Studies Quarterly, Vol. 34.

Economica, Vol. 50.
Title changed from **Economica, N.S.** in 1974.

Económica, Vol. 29, Issue no. 1.

Économie Appliquée, Vol. 36.

Economies et Sociétés, Vol. 17.

Economisch en Sociaal Tijdschrift, Vol. 37.

De Economist, Vol. 131.

Ekonomiska Samfundets Tidskrift, Vol. 36.

Empirica, Issue nos. 1–2, 1983.

Empirical Economics, Vol. 8.

Energy Economics, Vol. 5.

Energy Journal, Vol. 4, Supplement.

European Economic Review, Vol. 20; Vol. 21; Vol. 22; Vol. 23.

European Review of Agricultural Economics, Vol. 10.

Explorations in Economic History, Vol. 20.
Title changed from **Explorations in Entrepreneurial History** in 1969–70.

Federal Reserve Bank of Dallas Economic Review, January, March, May, July, September, November, 1983.

Federal Reserve Bank of Minneapolis Quarterly Review, Spring, Summer, Fall, Winter, Vol. 7.

Federal Reserve Bank of New York Quarterly Review, Vol. 8.

Federal Reserve Bank of San Francisco Economic Review, Issue nos. 1–4, 1983.

Federal Reserve Bank of St. Louis Review, Vol. 65.

Federal Reserve Bulletin, Vol. 69.

Finance and Development, Vol. 20.

Food Research Institute Studies, Vol. 19, Issue no. 1.

Foreign Affairs, Vol. 61, Issue nos. 2–5; Vol. 62, Issue no. 1.

Giornale degli Economisti e Annali di Economia, Vol. 42.

Greek Economic Review, Vol. 5.

Growth and Change, Vol. 14.

History of Political Economy, Vol. 15.

Hitotsubashi Journal of Economics, Vol. 23, Issue no. 2; Vol. 24, Issue nos. 1–2.

Housing Finance Review, Vol. 2, Issue no. 4.

Ifo-Studien, Vol. 29.

L'Impresa, Vol. 25, Issue nos. 1–2, 4–6.

Indian Economic Journal, Vol. 30, Issue nos. 3–4; Vol. 31, Issue nos. 1–2.

Indian Economic Review, Vol. 18.

Industrial and Labor Relations Review, Vol. 36, Issue nos. 2–4; Vol. 37, Issue no. 1.

Industrial Relations, Vol. 22.

Information Economics and Policy, Vol. 1, Issue nos. 1–2.

Inquiry, Vol. 20.

International Economic Review, Vol. 24.

International Journal of Industrial Organization, Vol. 1.

International Journal of Social Economics, Vol. 10.

International Labour Review, Vol. 122.

International Monetary Fund, Staff Papers, Vol. 30.

International Regional Science Review, Vol. 8.

International Social Science Journal, Vol. 35.

Irish Banking Review, March, June, September, December, 1983.

Irish Journal of Agricultural Economics and Rural Sociology, Vol. 9, Issue no. 2.

Jahrbücher für Nationalökonomie und Statistik, Vol. 198.

Journal of Accounting and Economics, Vol. 5.

Journal of Accounting Research, Vol. 21.

Journal of the American Statistical Association, Vol. 78.

Journal of Bank Research, Vol. 13, Issue no. 4; Vol. 14, Issue nos. 1–3.

Journal of Banking and Finance, Vol. 7.

Journal of Behavioral Economics, Vol. 12.

Journal of Business, Vol. 56.

Journal of Business and Economic Statistics, Vol. 1.

Journal of Common Market Studies, Vol. 21, Issue nos. 3–4; Vol. 22, Issue nos. 1–2.

Journal of Comparative Economics, Vol. 7.

Journal of Consumer Research, Vol. 9, Issue no. 4; Vol. 10, Issue nos. 1–3.

Journal of Cultural Economics, Vol. 7.

Journal of Developing Areas, Vol. 17, Issue nos. 2–4; Vol. 18, Issue no. 1.

Journal of Development Economics, Vol. 12; Vol. 13.

Journal of Development Studies, Vol. 19, Issue nos. 2–4; Vol. 20, Issue no. 1.

Journal of Econometrics, Vol. 21; Vol. 22; Vol. 23.

Journal of Economic Behavior and Organization, Vol. 4.

Journal of Economic Development, Vol. 8.

Journal of Economic Dynamics and Control, Vol. 5; Vol. 6.

Journal of Economic Education, Vol. 14.

Journal of Economic History, Vol. 43.

Journal of Economic Issues, Vol. 17.

Journal of Economic Literature, Vol. 21.

Journal of Economic Studies, Vol. 10.

Journal of Economic Theory, Vol. 29; Vol. 30; Vol. 31.

Journal of Economics and Business, Vol. 35.
Title changed from Economics and Business Bulletin in 1972–73.

Journal of Energy and Development, Vol. 8, Issue no. 2; Vol. 9, Issue no. 1.

Journal of Environmental Economics and Management, Vol. 10.

Journal of European Economic History, Vol. 12.

Journal of Finance, Vol. 38.

Journal of Financial Economics, Vol. 11; Vol. 12.

Journal of Financial and Quantitative Analysis, Vol. 18.

Journal of Financial Research, Vol. 6.

Journal of Futures Markets, Vol. 3.

Journal of Health Economics, Vol. 2.

Journal of Human Resources, Vol. 18.

Journal of Industrial Economics, Vol. 31, Issue nos. 3–4; Vol. 32, Issue nos. 1–2.

Journal of International Business Studies, Vol. 14.

Journal of International Economics, Vol. 14; Vol. 15.

Journal of International Money and Finance, Vol. 2.

Journal of Labor Economics, Vol. 1.

Journal of Labor Research, Vol. 4.

Journal of Law and Economics, Vol. 26.

Journal of Macroeconomics, Vol. 5.

Journal of Mathematical Economics, Vol. 11; Vol. 12.

Journal of Monetary Economics, Vol. 11; Vol. 12.

Journal of Money, Credit and Banking, Vol. 15.

Journal of Policy Analysis and Management, Vol. 2, Issue nos. 2–4; Vol. 3, Issue no. 1.

Journal of Policy Modeling, Vol. 5.

Journal of Political Economy, Vol. 91.

Journal of Portfolio Management, Vol. 9, Issue nos. 2–4; Vol. 10, Issue no. 1.

Journal of Post Keynesian Economics, Vol. 5, Issue nos. 2–4; Vol. 6, Issue no. 1.

Journal of Public Economics, Vol. 20; Vol. 21; Vol. 22.

Journal of Regional Science, Vol. 23.

Journal of Research in Islamic Economics, Vol. 1, Issue no. 1.

Journal of Risk and Insurance, Vol. 50.

Journal of the Royal Statistical Society, Series A, Vol. 146.

Journal for Studies in Economics and Econometrics, Issue nos. 16–17, 1983.

Journal of Transport Economics and Policy, Vol. 17.

Journal of Urban Economics, Vol. 13; Vol. 14.

Journal of World Trade Law, Vol. 17.

Kansantaloudellinen Aikakauskirja, Vol. 79.

Kobe Economic and Business Review, Vol. 29.

Kobe University Economic Review, Issue no. 29, 1983.

Konjunkturpolitik, Vol. 29.

Kredit und Kapital, Vol. 16.

Kyklos, Vol. 36.

Kyoto University Economic Review, Vol. 53.

Labor History, Vol. 24.

Land Economics, Vol. 59.

Law and Contemporary Problems, Vol. 46.

Liiketaloudellinen Aikakauskirja, Vol. 32.

Lloyds Bank Review, Issue nos. 147–150, 1983.

Logistics and Transportation Review, Vol. 19.

Malayan Economic Review.
See **Singapore Economic Review.**

Managerial and Decision Economics, Vol. 4.

Manchester School of Economics and Social Studies, Vol. 51.
Title changed from **The Manchester School** in 1939; prior to 1932 entitled **The Manchester School of Economics, Commerce and Administration.**

Margin, Vol. 15, Issue nos. 3–4; Vol. 16, Issue no. 1.

Matekon, Vol. 19, Issue nos. 3–4; Vol. 20, Issue nos. 1–2.
Title changed from **Mathematical Studies in Economics and Statistics in the USSR and Eastern Europe** in 1969.

Mathematical Social Sciences, Vol. 4; Vol. 5; Vol. 6.

Metroeconomica, Vol. 35, Issue nos. 1–3.

METU—Studies in Development, Vol. 10.

Michigan Law Review, Vol. 81, Issue nos. 5–6; Vol. 82, Issue nos. 1, 3.

Mondo Aperto, Vol. 37.

Monthly Labor Review, Vol. 106.

National Institute Economic Review, Issue nos. 103–106, 1983.

National Tax Journal, Vol. 36.

National Westminster Bank Quarterly Review, Issue nos. 1–4, 1983.

Nationaløkonomisk Tidsskrift, Vol. 121.

Natural Resources Journal, Vol. 23.

Nebraska Journal of Economics and Business, Vol. 22, Issue nos. 1–3.
See also **Quarterly Journal of Business and Economics.**

New England Economic Review, January/February, March/April, May/June, July/August, September/October, November/December, 1983.

OECD Economic Studies, Issue no. 1, 1983.

Osaka Economic Papers, Vol. 32, Issue no. 4; Vol. 33, Issue no. 1.

Oxford Bulletin of Economics and Statistics, Vol. 45.
Title changed from **Bulletin Oxford University Institute of Economics and Statistics** in 1973. Prior to 1972 entitled **Bulletin of the Institute of Economics and Statistics.**

Oxford Economic Papers, N. S., Vol. 35, Supplement.

Pakistan Development Review, Vol. 22.

Pakistan Journal of Applied Economics, Vol. 2, Issue no. 1.

Philippine Economic Journal, Vol. 22, Issue nos. 1–2.

Policy Review, Issue nos. 23–26, 1983.

Political Science Quarterly, Vol. 98.

Population and Development Review, Vol. 9.

Population Studies, Vol. 37.

Problems of Economics, Vol. 25, Issue nos. 9–12; Vol. 26, Issue nos. 1–8.

Public Budgeting and Finance, Vol. 3.

Public Choice, Vol. 40; Vol. 41.

Public Finance, Vol. 38.

Public Finance Quarterly, Vol. 11.

Quarterly Journal of Business and Economics, Vol. 22, Issue no. 4.
Title changed from **Nebraska Journal of Economics and Business** in 1983.

Quarterly Journal of Economics, Vol. 98. Supplement.

Quarterly Review of Economics and Business, Vol. 23.

Regional Science Perspectives, Vol. 13.

Regional Science and Urban Economics, Vol. 13.

Regional Studies, Vol. 17.

Review of Black Political Economy, Vol. 12, Issue nos. 2–3.

Review of Business and Economic Research, Vol. 18, Issue nos. 2–3; Vol. 19, Issue no. 1.
Title changed from **Mississippi Valley Journal of Business and Economics** in 1975.

Review of Economic Conditions in Italy, Issue nos. 1–3, 1983.

Review of Economic Studies, Vol. 50.

Review of Economics and Statistics, Vol. 65.
Title changed from **The Review of Economic Statistics** in 1948.

Review of Income and Wealth, Vol. 29.

Review of Marketing and Agricultural Economics, Vol. 51.

Review of Public Data Use, Vol. 11.

Review of Radical Political Economics, Vol. 15.

Review of Social Economy, Vol. 41.

Revue d'Economie Industrielle, Issue nos. 23–26, 1983.

Revue d'Economie Politique, Vol. 93.

Revue Économique, Vol. 34.

Rivista Internazionale di Scienze Economiche e Commerciali, Vol. 30.

Rivista di Politica Economica, Vol. 73, Supplement—Selected Papers.

Scandinavian Economic History Review, Vol. 31.

Scandinavian Journal of Economics, Vol. 85. Title changed from **Swedish Journal of Economics** in 1976; prior to 1965 entitled **Ekonomisk Tidskrift.**

Schweizerische Zeitschrift für Volkswirtschaft und Statistik, Vol. 119.

Science and Society, Vol. 47.

Scottish Journal of Political Economy, Vol. 30.

Singapore Economic Review, Vol. 28. Title changed from **Malayan Economic Review** in 1983.

Sloan Management Review, Vol. 24, Issue nos. 2–4; Vol. 25, Issue no. 1.

Social and Economic Studies, Vol. 32.

Social Research, Vol. 50.

Social Science Quarterly, Vol. 64.

Social Security Bulletin, Vol. 46.

South African Journal of Economics, Vol. 51.

Southern Economic Journal, Vol. 49, Issue nos. 3–4; Vol. 50, Issue nos. 1–2.

Southern Journal of Agricultural Economics, Vol. 15.

Soviet and Eastern European Foreign Trade, Vol. 19, Issue nos. 3–4.

Statistica, Vol. 43.

Statistical Journal, Vol. 1, Issue nos. 3–4.

Studi Economici, Vol. 38.

Survey of Current Business, Vol. 63.

Tijdschrift Voor Economie en Management, Vol. 28. Title changed from **Tijdschrift voor Economie** in 1975.

Urban Studies, Vol. 20.

Water Resources Research, Vol. 19.

Weltwirtschaftliches Archiv, Vol. 119.

World Development, Vol. 11.

Yale Journal on Regulation, Vol. 1, Issue no. 1.

Yale Law Journal, Vol. 92, Issue nos. 4–8; Vol. 93, Issue nos. 1–2.

Zeitschrift für die gesamte Staatswissenschaft, Vol. 139.

Zeitschrift für Nationalökonomie, Vol. 43, Supplement.

Zeitschrift für Wirtschafts-und Socialwissenschaften, Vol. 103.

LIST OF COLLECTIVE VOLUMES INDEXED 1983

ADAMS, F. GERARD AND KLEIN, LAWRENCE R., eds. *Industrial Policies for Growth and Competitiveness: An Economic Perspective.* Wharton Econometric Studies series. Lexington, Mass., and Toronto: Heath, Lexington Books, 1983.

ADELMAN, M. A., ET AL. *Energy Resources in an Uncertain Future: Coal, Gas, Oil, and Uranium Supply Forecasting.* Cambridge, Mass.: Harper and Row; Ballinger, 1983.

AHMED, ZIAUDDIN; IQBAL, MUNAWAR AND KHAN, M. FAHIM, eds. *Money and Banking in Islam.* Islamabad, Pakistan: Institute of Policy Studies for International Centre for Research in Islamic Economics, King Abdul Aziz University, Jeddah, Saudi Arabia, 1983.

AKAO, NOBUTOSHI, ed. *Japan's Economic Security.* New York: St. Martin's Press for the Royal Institute of International Affairs, 1983.

AKRASANEE, NARONGCHAI, ed. *ASEAN–Japan Relations: Trade and Development. Proceedings of a Workshop and a Conference.* Singapore: Institute of Southeast Asian Studies, 1983.

ALKIN, MARVIN C. AND SOLMON, LEWIS C., eds. *The Costs of Evaluation.* Sage Focus editions, no. 60. Beverly Hills; London and New Delhi: Sage, 1983.

ANDERSON, MALCOLM, ed. *Frontier Regions in Western Europe.* London and Totowa, N.J.: Cass, 1983.

ANDERSON, TERRY L., ed. *Water Rights: Scarce Resource Allocation, Bureaucracy, and the Environment.* Foreword by JACK HIRSHLEIFER. Pacific Studies in Public Policy series. San Francisco: Pacific Institute for Public Policy Research; Cambridge, Mass.: Harper and Row, Ballinger, 1983.

ARCHER, STEPHEN H. AND D'AMBROSIA, CHARLES A. *The Theory of Business Finance: A Book of Readings.* Third edition. New York: Macmillan; London: Collier Macmillan, [1967, 1976] 1983.

ARMBRUSTER, WALTER J.; HENDERSON, DENNIS R. AND KNUTSON, RONALD D., eds. *Federal Marketing Programs in Agriculture: Issues and Options.* Danville, Ill.: Interstate, 1983.

ARMELLA, PEDRO ASPE; DORNBUSCH, RUDIGER AND OBSTFELD, MAURICE, eds. *Financial Policies and the World Capital Market: The Problem of Latin American Countries.* NBER Conference Report. Chicago and London: University of Chicago Press, 1983.

ARONSON, JONATHAN DAVID AND COWHEY, PETER F., eds. *Profit and the Pursuit of Energy: Markets and Regulation.* Westview Special Studies in International Economics and Business. Boulder, Colo.: Westview Press, 1983.

ARROW, KENNETH J. *Collected Papers of Kenneth J. Arrow. Volume 1: Social Choice and Justice.* Cambridge, Mass.: Harvard University Press, Belknap Press, 1983.

ARROW, KENNETH J. *Collected Papers of Kenneth J. Arrow. Volume 2: General Equilibrium.* Cambridge, Mass.: Harvard University Press, Belknap Press, 1983.

ATKINSON, A. B. *Social Justice and Public Policy.* Cambridge: MIT Press, 1983.

AUERBACH, ALAN J. *The Taxation of Capital Income.* Harvard Economic Studies, vol. 153. Cambridge, Mass., and London: Harvard University Press, 1983.

AV, REDIGERT, ET AL., eds. *Analysis of Supply and Demand of Electricity in the Norwegian Economy.* Samfunnsokonomiske Studier, no. 53. Oslo: Central Bureau of Statistics of Norway; distributed in U.S. and Canada by Columbia University Press, 1983.

BACHARACH, SAMUEL B., ed. *Research in the Sociology of Organizations.* A Research Annual, vol. 2. Greenwich, Conn., and London: JAI Press, 1983.

BACKMAN, JULES, ed. *Entrepreneurship and the Outlook for America.* New York: Macmillan, Free Press; London: Collier Macmillan, 1983.

BAHL, ROY AND MILLER, BARBARA D., eds. *Local Government Finance in the Third World: A Case Study of the Philippines.* New York: Praeger, 1983.

BALL, NICOLE AND LEITENBERG, MILTON, eds. *The Structure of the Defense Industry: An International Survey.* New York: St. Martin's Press, 1983.

BALLARD, STEVEN C. AND JAMES, THOMAS E., eds. *The Future of the Sunbelt: Managing Growth and Change.* New York: Praeger, 1983.

BARBASH, JACK, ET AL., eds. *The Work Ethic--A Critical Analysis.* Industrial Relations Research Association Series. Madison, Wisc.: Industrial Relations Research Association, 1983.

BARKER, MICHAEL, ed. *Financing State and Local Economic Development.* Foreword by ROBERT N. WISE. Duke Press Policy Studies series. Durham, N.C.: Duke University Press in cooperation with the Council of State Planning Agencies, 1983.(I)

BARKER, MICHAEL, ed. *State Employment Policy in Hard Times.* Foreword by ROBERT N. WISE. Duke Press Policy Studies series. Durham, N.C.: Duke University Press in cooperation with the Council of State Planning Agencies, 1983.(II)

BARKIN, SOLOMON, ed. *Worker Militancy and Its Consequences: The Changing Climate of Western Industrial Relations.* Second edition. New York: Praeger, [1975] 1983.

BARNES, CLARENCE H., ed. *Alternative Futures: Energy, the Economy and the Quality of Life.* Foreword by RAND V. ARASKOG. ITT Key Issues Lecture Series. New York: KCG Productions, 1983.

BASAGNI, FABIO, ed. *International Debt, Financial Stability and Growth.* The Atlantic Papers, no. 51. Paris: The Atlantic Institute for International Affairs; distributed in the U.S. by Allanheld, Osmun, Totowa, N.J., 1983.

BAUM, KENNETH H. AND SCHERTZ, LYLE P., eds. *Modeling Farm Decisions for Policy Analysis.* Westview Special Studies in Agriculture Science and Policy series. Boulder, Colo.: Westview Press, in cooperation with the Farm Foundation and the Economic Research Service, U.S. Dept. of Agriculture, 1983.

BECKER, ABRAHAM S., ed. *Economic Relations with the USSR: Issues for the Western Alliance.* Policy Study of the California Seminar on International Security and Foreign Policy series, Lexington, Mass. and Toronto: Heath, Lexington Books, 1983.

BENSTON, GEORGE J., ed. *Financial Services: The Changing Institutions and Government Policy.* Columbia University, The American Assembly series. Englewood Cliffs, N.J.: Prentice-Hall, Spectrum, 1983.

BERG, SANFORD V., ed. *Innovative Electric Rates: Issues in Cost-Benefit Analysis.* Lexington, Mass., and Toronto: Heath, Lexington Books, 1983.

BERGESEN, ALBERT, ed. *Crises in the World-System.* Political Economy of the World-System Annuals, vol. 6. Beverly Hills; London and New Delhi: Sage, 1983.

BERGSON, ABRAM AND LEVINE, HERBERT S., eds. *The Soviet Economy: Toward the Year 2000.* Boston; London and Sydney: Allen & Unwin, 1983.

BERGSTEN, C. FRED. *The United States in the World Economy: Selected Papers of C. Fred Bergsten, 1981-1982.* Lexington, Mass., and Toronto: Heath, Lexington Books, 1983.

BÉTEILLE, ANDRE, ed. *Equality and Inequality: Theory and Practice.* Delhi; New York; London and Toronto: Oxford University Press, 1983.

BHAGWATI, JAGDISH. *Essays in International Economic Theory. Volume 1. The Theory of Commercial Policy.* Edited by ROBERT C. FEENSTRA. Cambridge, Mass., and London: MIT Press, 1983.

BHAGWATI, JAGDISH. *Essays in International Economic Theory. Volume 2. International Factor Mobility.* Edited by ROBERT C. FEENSTRA. Cambridge, Mass., and London: MIT Press, 1983.

BHANDARI, JAGDEEP S. AND PUTNAM, BLUFORD H., eds. *Economic Interdependence and Flexible Exchange Rates.* With JAY H. LEVIN. Foreword by RUDIGER DORNBUSCH. Cambridge, Mass., and London: MIT Press, 1983.

BIEHL, DIETER; ROSKAMP, KARL W. AND STOLPER, WOLFGANG F., eds. *Public Finance and Economic Growth: Proceedings of the 37th Congress of the International Institute of Public Finance, Tokyo, 1981.* Detroit: Wayne State University Press, 1983.

BIGMAN, DAVID AND TAYA, TEIZO, eds. *Exchange Rate and Trade Instability: Causes, Consequences, and Remedies.* Cambridge, Mass.: Harper and Row, Ballinger, 1983.

BLACK, JOHN AND WINTERS, L. ALAN, eds. *Policy and Performance in International Trade: Papers of the Sixth Annual Conference of the International Economics Study Group.* New York: St. Martin's Press, 1983.

BLANDY, RICHARD AND COVICK, OWEN, eds. *Understanding Labour Markets in Australia.* Sydney; London and Boston: Allen & Unwin, 1983.

BODIE, ZVI AND SHOVEN, JOHN B., eds. *Financial Aspects of the United States Pension System.* National Bureau of Economic Research Project Report. Chicago and London: University of Chicago Press, 1983.

[BONBRIGHT, JAMES C.]. *Current Issues in Public-Utility Economics: Essays in Honor of James C. Bonbright.* Edited by ALBERT L. DANIELSEN AND DAVID R. KAMERSCHEN. Lexington, Mass., and Toronto: Heath, Lexington Books, 1983.

BORUS, MICHAEL E., ed. *Tomorrow's Workers.* With Contributions by JOHN E. CROWLEY ET AL. Lexington, Mass., and Toronto: Heath, Lexington Books, 1983.

BREAK, GEORGE F., ed. *State and Local Finance: The Pressures of the 1980s.* TRED series, no. 12. Madison and London: University of Wisconsin Press for the Committee on Taxation, Resources and Economic Development, Lincoln Institute of Land Policy, 1983.

BRECHER, CHARLES AND HORTON, RAYMOND D., eds. *Setting Municipal Priorities, 1984.* New York and London: New York University Press; distributed by Columbia University Press, New York, 1983.

BRENNER, MENACHEM, ed. *Option Pricing: Theory and Applications.* Lexington Books/Salomon Brothers Center Series on Financial Institutions and Markets. Lexington, Mass., and Toronto: Heath, Lexington Books, 1983.

BREWSTER, DAVID E.; RASMUSSEN, WAYNE D. AND YOUNGBERG, GARTH, eds. *Farms in Transition: Interdisciplinary Perspectives on Farm Structure.* Ames: Iowa State University Press, 1983.

BRITTAN, SAMUEL. *The Role and Limits of Government: Essays in Political Economy.* London: Temple Smith, 1983.

BRITTON, ANDREW, ed. *Employment, Output and Inflation: The National Institute Model of the British Economy.* London and Exeter, N.H.: Heinemann, 1983.

BROWN, E. CARY AND SOLOW, ROBERT M., eds. *Paul Samuelson and Modern Economic Theory.* New York; London; Toronto and Sydney: McGraw-Hill, 1983.

BROWN, GORDON AND COOK, ROBIN, eds. *Scotland: The Real Divide: Poverty and Deprivation in Scotland.* Edinburgh: Mainstream; distributed in the U.S. by Humanities Press, Atlantic Highlands, N.J., 1983.

BROWN, HOWARD J., ed. *Decentralizing Electricity Production.* With TOM RICHARD STRUMOLO. New Haven and London: Yale University Press, 1983.

BROWN, PETER G. AND SHUE, HENRY, eds. *The Border That Joins: Mexican Migrants and U.S. Responsibility.* Maryland Studies in Public Philosophy series. Totowa, N.J.: Rowman and Littlefield, 1983.

BRUNNER, KARL AND MELTZER, ALLAN H., eds. *Theory, Policy, Institutions: Papers from the Carnegie-Rochester Conferences on Public Policy.* Amsterdam; New York and Oxford: North-Holland; distributed in the U.S. and Canada by Elsevier Science, New York, 1983.

BULATAO, RODOLFO A. AND LEE, RONALD D., eds. *Determinants of Fertility in Developing Countries. Volume 1: Supply and Demand for Children.* With PAULA E. HOLLERBACH AND JOHN BONGAARTS. Studies in Population series. New York; London; Sydney and Toronto: Harcourt Brace Jovanovich, Academic Press, 1983.

BULATAO, RODOLFO A. AND LEE, RONALD D., eds. *Determinants of Fertility in Developing Countries. Volume 2: Fertility Regulation and Institutional Influences.* With PAULA E. HOLLERBACH AND JOHN BONGAARTS. Studies in Population series. New York; London; Sydney and Toronto: Harcourt Brace Jovanovich, Academic Press, 1983.

CARAVALE, GIOVANNI, ed. *The Crisis in Economic Theories.* Seminari di economia, vol. 1. Milan: Franco Angeli, 1983.

CARLSSON, JERKER, ed. *Recession in Africa: Background Papers to the Seminar, 'Africa--Which Way Out of the Recession?' Uppsala, September 1982.* Uppsala, Sweden: Scandinavian Institute of African Studies, 1983.

CARR, JAMES H. AND DUENSING, EDWARD E., eds. *Land Use Issues of the 1980s.* New Brunswick, N.J.: Rutgers University, Center for Urban Policy Research, 1983.

CASSON, MARK, ed. *The Growth of International Business.* Boston; London and Sydney: Allen & Unwin, 1983.

DE CECCO, MARCELLO, ed. *International Economic Adjustment: Small Countries and the European Monetary System.* New York: St. Martin's Press in cooperation with European University Institute, Florence, 1983.

CHEN, PETER S. J., ed. *Singapore Development Policies and Trends.* Singapore; New York; Oxford and Melbourne: Oxford University Press; Hamburg: Institute of Asian Affairs, 1983.

CH'EN, YUN. *Ch'en Yun's Strategy for China's Development: A Non-Maoist Alternative.* Edited with an introduction by NICHOLAS R. LARDY AND KENNETH LIEBERTHAL. Translated by MAO TONG AND DU ANXIA. Armonk, N.Y. and London: Sharpe, 1983.

CLAASSEN, E. AND SALIN, P., eds. *Recent Issues in the Theory of Flexible Exchange Rates: Fifth Paris-Dauphine Conference on Money and International Monetary Problems, June 15-17, 1981.* Studies in Monetary Economics series, vol. 8. New York; Amsterdam and Oxford: North-Holland; distributed in the U.S. and Canada by Elsevier Science, New York, 1983.

CLEGG, STEWART; DOW, GEOFF AND BOREHAM, PAUL, eds. *The State, Class and the Recession.* New York: St. Martin's Press; London and Canberra: Croom Helm, 1983.

CLINE WILLIAM R., ed. *Trade Policy in the l980s.* Washington, D.C.: Institute for International Economics; distributed by the MIT Press, Cambridge, Mass., and London, 1983.

[COCHRAN, THOMAS C.]. *Business and Its Environment: Essays for Thomas C. Cochran.* Edited by HAROLD ISSADORE SHARLIN. Contributions in American Studies, no. 63. Westport, Conn., and London: Greenwood Press, 1983.

CONKLIN, DAVID W. AND COURCHENE, THOMAS J., eds. *Deficits: How Big and How Bad?* Special Research Report series. Toronto: Ontario Economic Council; distributed by Ontario Government Bookstore, Publications Section, 1983.

CONNOR, JOHN M. AND WARD, RONALD W., eds. *Advertising and the Food System: Proceedings of a Symposium Held at Airlie House, Virginia on November 6 & 7, 1980.* With the assistance of ROSANNA MENTZER MORRISON. North Central Regional Research Project NC 117, Monograph no. 14. Madison: University of Wisconsin, College of Agricultural and Life Sciences, Research Division, 1983.

CORNER, DESMOND AND MAYES, DAVID G., eds. *Modern Portfolio Theory and Financial Institutions.* London: Macmillan; New York: Holmes & Meier, 1983.

COURVILLE, LEON; DE FONTENAY, ALAIN AND DOBELL, RODNEY, eds. *Economic Analysis of Telecommunications: Theory and Applications.* Amsterdam; New York and Oxford: North-Holland; distributed in the U.S. and Canada by Elsevier Science, New York, 1983.

CRAVEN, JOHN V., ed. *Industrial Organization, Antitrust, and Public Policy.* Middlebury College Conference Series on Economic Issues. Boston; The Hague and London: Kluwer-Nijhoff, 1983.

CULYER, A. J., ed. *Health Indicators: An International Study for the European Science Foundation.* Oxford: Robertson, 1983.

CUMMINGS, L. L. AND STAW, BARRY M., eds. *Research in Organizational Behavior: An Annual Series of Analytical Essays and Critical Reviews.* Volume 5. Greenwich, Conn., and London: JAI Press, 1983.

CZINKOTA, MICHAEL R., ed. *Export Promotion: The Public and Private Sector Interaction.* In cooperation with JUAN LUIS COLAIACOVO, ROBERTO DE MORAES SARMENTO, AND ELIZABETH M. CHANT. New York: Praeger, 1983.(I)

CZINKOTA, MICHAEL R., ed. *U.S. & Latin American Trade Relations: Issues and Concerns.* New York: Praeger, 1983.(II)

DALTON, GEORGE, ed. *Research in Economic Anthropology.* A Research Annual, vol. 5. Greenwich, Conn., and London: JAI Press, 1983.

DARBY, MICHAEL P. AND LOTHIAN, JAMES R., ET AL. *The International Transmission of Inflation.* National Bureau of Economic Research Monograph series. Chicago and London: University of Chicago Press, 1983.

DEBRAAL, J. PETER AND WUNDERLICH, GENE, eds. *Rents and Rental Practices in U.S. Agriculture: Proceedings of a Workshop on Agricultural Rents.* Washington: Farm Foundation in cooperation with the U.S. Department of Agriculture, Economic Research Service, 1983.

DEBREU, GERARD. *Mathematical Economics: Twenty Papers of Gerard Debreu.* Introduction by WERNER HILDENBRAND. Econometric Society Monographs in Pure Theory series, no. 4. Cambridge; New York and Sydney: Cambridge University Press, 1983.

DE GRAUWE, PAUL AND PEETERS, THEO, eds. *Exchange Rates in Multicountry Econometric Models.* New York: St. Martin's Press; London: Macmillan Press, 1983.

DEVINE, T. M. AND DICKSON, DAVID, eds. *Ireland and Scotland, 1600-1850: Parallels and Contrasts in Economic and Social Development.* Edinburgh: Donald; distributed in the U.S. by Humanities Press, Atlantic Highlands, N.J., 1983.

DEWEES, DONALD N., ed. *The Regulation of Quality: Products, Services, Workplaces, and the Environment.* Studies in Law and Economics series. Toronto: Butterworths, 1983.

DICKSON, DOUGLAS N., ed. *Managing Effectively in the World Marketplace.* The Harvard Business Review Executive Book series. New York; Chichester, England; Toronto and Brisbane:

DIEWERT, W. E. AND MONTMARQUETTE, C., eds. *Price Level Measurement: Proceedings from a Conference Sponsored by Statistics Canada.* Ottawa: Minister of Supply and Services Canada, 1983.

DORAN, CHARLES F.; MODELSKI, GEORGE AND CLARK, CAL, eds. *North/South Relations: Studies of Dependency Reversal.* New York: Praeger, 1983.

DORNBUSCH, RUDIGER AND SIMONSEN, MARIO HENRIQUE, eds. *Inflation, Debt, and Indexation.* Cambridge, Mass., and London: MIT Press, 1983.

DUNCAN, GREG J., AND MORGAN, JAMES N., eds. *Five Thousand American Families--Patterns of Economic Progress. Volume X. Analyses of the First Thirteen Years of the Panel Study of Income Dynamics.* Ann Arbor: University of Michigan, Institute for Social Research, Survey Research Center, 1983.

DUNKERLEY, HAROLD B., ed. *Urban Land Policy: Issues and Opportunities.* Assisted by CHRISTINE M. E. WHITEHEAD. Oxford; New York; Toronto and Tokyo: Oxford University Press for the World Bank, 1983.

DUTTA, MANORANJAN; HARTLINE, JESSIE C. AND LOEB, PETER D., eds. *Essays in Regional Economic Studies.* Acorn Economic Communication Series, no. 1. Durham, N.C.: Acorn Press, 1983.

DYSON, KENNETH AND WILKS, STEPHEN, eds. *Industrial Crisis: A Comparative Study of the State and Industry.* New York: St. Martin's Press, 1983.

EARL, MICHAEL J., ed. *Perspectives on Management: A Multidisciplinary Analysis.* London; New York; Toronto and Tokyo: Oxford University Press, 1983.

EASTON, BRIAN, ed. *Studies in the Labour Market.* Research Paper no. 29. Wellington: New Zealand Institute of Economic Research, 1983.

EATWELL, JOHN AND MILGATE, MURRAY, eds. *Keynes's Economics and the Theory of Value and Distribution.* New York: Oxford University Press, 1983.

EICHNER, ALFRED S., ed. *Why Economics is not yet a Science.* Armonk, N.Y.: Sharpe, 1983.

EL-AGRAA, ALI M., ed. *Britain within the European Community: The Way Forward.* London: Macmillan Press; distributed in the United States by Crane, Russak, New York, 1983.

ELIASSON, GUNNAR; SHAREFKIN, MARK AND YSANDER, BENGT-CHRISTER, eds. *Policy Making in a Disorderly World Economy.* IUI Conference Reports, 1983:1. Energy and Economic Structure Research Report, no. 3. Stockholm: Industrial Institute for Economic and Social Research; distributed by Almqvist & Wiksell International, 1983.

ENGELBRECHT-WIGGANS, RICHARD; SHUBIK, MARTIN AND STARK, ROBERT M., EDS. *Auctions, Bidding, and Contracting: Uses and Theory.* Studies in Game Theory and Mathematical Economics series. New York: New York University Press; distributed by Columbia University Press, 1983.

[ERLICH, ALEXANDER]. *Marxism, Central Planning, and the Soviet Economy: Economic Essays in Honor of Alexander Erlich.* Edited by PADMA DESAI. Cambridge, Mass., and London: MIT Press, 1983.

EVANS, DAVID S., ed. *Breaking up Bell: Essays on Industrial Organization and Regulation.* A CERA Research Study. New York; Amsterdam and Oxford: North-Holland; Distributed by Elsevier Science New York, 1983.

FARRIS, PAUL L., ed. *Future Frontiers in Agricultural Marketing Research.* Ames: Iowa State University Press, 1983.

FEDERAL RESERVE BANK OF ATLANTA. *Growth Industries in the 1980s: Conference Proceedings.* Westport, Conn., and London: Greenwood Press, Quorum, 1983.

FEDERAL RESERVE BANK OF BOSTON. *The Economics of Large Government Deficits: Proceedings of a Conference Held at Melvin Village, New Hampshire, October, 1983.* Federal Reserve Bank of Boston Conference Series, no. 27. Boston: Author, 1983.

FEINSTEIN, CHARLES, ed. *The Managed Economy: Essays in British Economic Policy and Performance since 1929.* Edited for THE ECONOMIC HISTORY SOCIETY. Oxford; New York; Toronto and Tokyo: Oxford University Press, 1983.

FELDSTEIN, MARTIN, ed. *Behavioral Simulation Methods in Tax Policy Analysis.* NBER Project Report Series. Chicago and London: University of Chicago Press, 1983.

FELDSTEIN, MARTIN. *Capital Taxation.* Cambridge, Mass., and London: Harvard University Press, 1983.(I)

FELDSTEIN, MARTIN. *Inflation, Tax Rules, and Capital Formation.* NBER Monograph series. Chicago and London: University of Chicago Press, 1983.(II)

FEUCHTWANG, STEPHAN AND HUSSAIN, ATHAR, eds. *The Chinese Economic Reforms.* London and Canberra: Croom Helm; New York: St. Martin's Press, 1983.

FIACCO, A. V. AND KORTANEK, K. O., eds. *Semi-Infinite Programming and Applications: An International Symposium, Austin, Texas, September 8-10, 1981.* Lecture Notes in Economics and Mathematical Systems series, no. 215. New York; Berlin and Tokyo: Springer, 1983.

FIELD, FRANK, ed. *The Wealth Report - 2.* Inequality in Society series. Boston; London and Melbourne: Routledge and Kegan Paul, 1983.

FINN, JAMES, ed. *Global Economics and Religion.* New Brunswick, N.J., and London: Transaction Books, 1983.

FINSINGER, JORG, ed. *Public Sector Economics.* Foreword by BERNHARD GAHLEN. New York: St. Martin's Press, 1983.

FITOUSSI, JEAN-PAUL, ed. *Modern Macroeconomic Theory.* Totowa, N.J.: Barnes and Noble Books in cooperation with the European University Institute, Florence, 1983.

FODELLA, GIANNI, ed. *Japan's Economy in a Comparative Perspective.* Tenterden, Kent, England: Norbury, 1983.

FOSS, MURRAY F., ed. *The U.S. National Income and Product Accounts: Selected Topics.* NBER Studies in Income and Wealth, vol. 47. Chicago and London: University of Chicago Press, 1983.

FRANCIS, ARTHUR; TURK, JEREMY AND WILLMAN, PAUL, eds. *Power, Efficiency and Institutions: A Critical Appraisal of the 'Markets and Hierarchies' Paradigm.* London; Exeter, N.H., and Melbourne: Heinemann Educational Books, 1983.

FRENKEL, JACOB A., ed. *Exchange Rates and International Macroeconomics.* National Bureau of Economic Research Conference Report. Chicago and London: University of Chicago Press, 1983.

FRIEDMAN, JOSEPH AND WEINBERG, DANIEL H., eds. *The Great Housing Experiment.* Urban Affairs Annual Reviews, Volume 24. Beverly Hills; London and New Delhi: Sage, 1983.

FROOMKIN, JOSEPH, ed. *The Crisis in Higher Education: Proceedings of the Academy of Political Science, vol. 35, no. 2.* New York: The Academy of Political Science, 1983.

FRYDMAN, ROMAN AND PHELPS, EDMUND S., eds. *Individual Forecasting and Aggregate Outcomes: "Rational Expectations" Examined.* Cambridge; New York and Sydney: Cambridge University Press, 1983.

VON FURSTENBERG, GEORGE M., ed. *International Money and Credit: The Policy Roles.* Washington, D.C.: International Monetary Fund, 1983.

GALBRAITH, JOHN KENNETH. *The Voice of the Poor: Essays in Economic and Political Persuasion.* Cambridge, Mass., and London: Harvard University Press, 1983.

GAU, GEORGE W. AND GOLDBERG, MICHAEL A., eds. *North American Housing Markets into the Twenty-first Century.* Cambridge, Mass.: Harper and Row, Ballinger, 1983.

GAUHAR, ALTAF, ed. *The Rich and the Poor: Development, Negotiations and Cooperation—An Assessment.* London: Third World Foundation for Social and Economic Studies; Boulder, Colo.: Westview Press, 1983.(I)

GAUHAR, ALTAF, ed. *Third World Strategy: Economic and Political Cohesion in the South.* New York: Praeger in cooperation with the Third World Foundation, London, 1983.(II)

GEORGE, ABRAHAM M. AND GIDDY, IAN H., eds. *International Finance Handbook. Volume 1.* New York; Chichester, England; Brisbane and Toronto: Wiley, Wiley-Interscience, 1983.

GEORGE, ABRAHAM M. AND GIDDY, IAN H., eds. *International Finance Handbook. Volume 2.* New York; Chichester, England; Brisbane and Toronto: Wiley, Wiley-Interscience, 1983.

GHAI, DHARAM AND RADWAN, SAMIR, eds. *Agrarian Policies and Rural Poverty in Africa.* A World Employment Programme Study. Geneva: International Labour Office, 1983.

GIERSCH, HERBERT, ed. *Reassessing the Role of Government in the Mixed Economy: Symposium 1982.* Tubingen: Mohr (Paul Siebeck), 1983.

[GIERSCH, HERBERT]. *Reflections on a Troubled World Economy: Essay in Honor of Herbert Giersch.* Edited by FRITZ MACHLUP, GERHARD FELS, AND HUBERTUS MULLER-GROELING. New York: St. Martin's Press, 1983.

GLASSNER, MARTIN I., ed. *Global Resources: Challenges of Interdependence.* New York: Praeger for the Foreign Policy Association, 1983.

GOLDBERG, WALTER H., ed. *Governments and Multinationals: The Policy of Control versus Autonomy.* In cooperation with ANANT R. NEGANDHI. Cambridge, Mass.: Oelgeschlager, Gunn & Hain, 1983.

GOLDSTEIN, RICHARD AND SACHS, STEPHEN M., eds. *Applied Poverty Research.* Totowa, N.J.: Littlefield, Adams; Rowman & Allanheld, 1983.

[GOODE, RICHARD]. *Comparative Tax Studies: Essays in Honor of Richard Goode.* Edited by SIJBREN CNOSSEN. Contributions to Economic Analysis, no. 144. New York; Amsterdam and Oxford: North-Holland; distributed in the U.S. and Canada by Elsevier Science, New York, 1983.

GOODWIN, R. M. *Essays in Linear Economic Structures.* London: Macmillan Press; distributed in the U.S. by Humanities Press, Atlantic Highlands, N.J., 1983.

GOWLAND, D. H., ed. *Modern Economic Analysis 2.* London; Boston and Toronto: Butterworths, 1983.

GRIESON, RONALD E., ed. *The Urban Economy and Housing.* Lexington, Mass., and Toronto: Heath, Lexington Books, 1983.

GRILICHES, ZVI AND INTRILIGATOR, MICHAEL D., eds. *Handbook of Econometrics. Volume 1.* Handbooks in Economics Series, Book 2. New York; Amsterdam and Oxford: North-Holland; distributed in U.S. and Canada by Elsevier Science, New York, 1983.

GROENEWEGEN, PETER AND HALEVI, JOSEPH, eds. *Altro Polo: Italian Economics Past and Present.* Sydney: University of Sydney, Frederick May Foundation for Italian Studies, 1983.

GRUBER, JOSEF, ed. *Econometric Decision Models: Proceedings of a Conference Held at the University of Hagen, West Germany, June 19-20, 1981.* Lecture Notes in Economics and Mathematical Systems, no. 208. New York; Berlin and Tokyo: Springer, 1983.

GUROFF, GREGORY AND CARSTENSEN, FRED V., eds. *Entrepreneurship in Imperial Russia and the Soviet Union.* Princeton, N.J.: Princeton University Press, 1983.

HAMILTON, F. E. IAN AND LINGE, G. J. R., eds. *Spatial Analysis, Industry and the Industrial Environment: Progress in Research and Applications. Volume 3. Regional Economies and Industrial Systems.* Chichester, England; New York; Brisbane and Toronto: Wiley, 1983.

HANSEN, PIERRE, ed. *Essays and Surveys on Multiple Criteria Decision Making: Proceedings of the Fifth International Conference on Multiple Criteria Decision Making, Mons, Belgium, August 9-13, 1982.* Lecture Notes in Economics and Mathematical Systems, no. 209. New York and Berlin: Springer, 1983.

HARRISS, C. LOWELL, ed. *The Property Tax and Local Finance: Proceedings of the Academy of Political Science.* Vol. 35, no. 1. New York: Academy of Political Science, 1983.

HAWKINS, ROBERT G.; LEVICH, RICHARD M. AND WIHLBORG, CLAS G., eds. *Research in Interna-*

tional Business and Finance. Volume 3. The Internationalization of Financial Markets and National Economic Policy. A Research Annual. Greenwich, Conn., and London: JAI Press, 1983.

HEAD, BRIAN W., ed. *State and Economy in Australia.* Oxford; Melbourne; Auckland and New York: Oxford University Press, 1983.

HEADY, EARL O. AND BHIDE, SHASHANKA, eds. *Livestock Response Functions.* Ames: Iowa State University Press, 1983.

HECHTER, MICHAEL, ed. *The Microfoundations of Macrosociology.* Philadelphia: Temple University Press, 1983.

HEERTJE, ARNOLD, ed. *Investing in Europe's Future.* Preface by YVES LE PORTZ. New York: St. Martin's Press for the European Investment Bank, 1983.

HELD, DAVID, ET AL., eds. *States and Societies.* New York and London: New York University Press; distributed by Columbia University Press, 1983.

HELPMAN, ELHANAN; RAZIN, ASSAF AND SADKA, EFRAIM, eds. *Social Policy Evaluation: An Economic Prespective.* New York; London; Toronto and Sydney: Harcourt Brace Jovanovich, Academic Press, 1983.

HENDERSON, J. VERNON, ed. *Research in Urban Economics. Volume 3. COUPE Papers on Public Economics.* A Research Annual. Greenwich, Conn., and London: JAI Press, 1983.

HENDON, WILLIAM S. AND SHANAHAN, JAMES L., eds. *Economics of Cultural Decisions.* Introduction by ALAN PEACOCK. Cambridge, Mass.: Abt Books, 1983.

HERRING, RICHARD J., ed. *Managing Foreign Exchange Risk: Essays Commissioned in Honor of the Centenary of the Wharton School, University of Pennsylvania.* Cambridge; New York and Sydney: Cambridge University Press, 1983.

HICKMAN, BERT G., ed. *Global International Economic Models: Selected Papers from an IIASA Conference.* Contributions to Economic Analysis Series, no. 147. Amsterdam; New York and Oxford: North-Holland; distributed in U.S. and Canada by Elsevier Science, New York, 1983.

HICKS, JOHN. *Collected Essays on Economic Theory: Volume III: Classics and Moderns.* Cambridge, Mass.: Harvard University Press, 1983.

HILL, STEPHEN AND JOHNSTON, RON, eds. *Future Tense? Technology in Australia.* St. Lucia; London and New York: University of Queensland Press, 1983.

HINDLEY, BRIAN, ed. *State Investment Companies in Western Europe: Picking Winners or Backing Losers?* New York: St. Martin's Press and London: Macmillan Press, for the Trade Policy Research Centre, London, 1983.

HIRSCH, WERNER Z., ed. *The Economics of Municipal Labor Markets.* Monograph and Research Series, no. 33. Los Angeles: University of California, Institute of Industrial Relations, 1983.

HODGMAN, DONALD R., ed. *The Political Economy of Monetary Policy: National and International Aspects: Proceedings of a Conference Held at Perugia, Italy, July 1983.* Conference Series, no. 26. Boston: Federal Reserve Bank of Boston, 1983.

HOLZNER, B.; KNORR, K. D. AND STRASSER, H., eds. *Realizing Social Science Knowledge: The Political Realization of Social Science Knowledge and Research: Toward New Scenarios: A Symposium in Memoriam Paul F. Lazarsfeld.* Institute for Advanced Studies, no. 3. Vienna and Wurzberg, West Germany: Physica, 1983.

HOOKE, A. W., ed. *The Fund and China in the International Monetary System: Papers Presented at a Colloquium Held in Beijing, China, October 20-28, 1982.* Washington, D.C.: International Monetary Fund, 1983.

INGHAM, KEITH P. D. AND LOVE, JAMES, eds. *Understanding the Scottish Economy.* Oxford: Martin Robertson, 1983.

INTERNATIONAL FISCAL ASSOCIATION. *International Problems in the Field of General Taxes on Sales of Goods and Services.* Studies on International Fiscal Law, vol. 68b. Hingham, Mass.; Deventer, The Netherlands; London and Frankfurt: Kluwer for the International Fiscal Association, 1983.(I)

INTERNATIONAL FISCAL ASSOCIATION. *Tax Avoidance/Tax Evasion.* Studies on International Fis-

KHAN, AZIZUR RAHMAN AND LEE, EDDY, eds. *Poverty in Rural Asia.* Bangkok: International Labour Organisation and Asian Employment Programme, 1983.

KIELMANN, ARNFRIED, A., ET AL. *Child and Maternal Health Services in Rural India: The Narangwal Experiment. Volume I. Integrated Nutrition and Health Care.* World Bank Research Publication. Baltimore and London: Johns Hopkins University Press for the World Bank, 1983.

KINDLEBERGER, CHARLES P. AND AUDRETSCH, DAVID B., eds. *The Multinational Corporation in the 1980s.* Cambridge and London: MIT Press, 1983.

KLAMER, ARJO. *Conversations with Economists: New Classical Economists and Opponents Speak Out on the Current Controversy in Macroeconomics.* Totowa, N.J.: Littlefield, Adams; Rowman & Allanheld, 1983.

[KLEIN, LAWRENCE R.]. *Global Econometrics: Essays in Honor of Lawrence R. Klein.* Edited by F. GERARD ADAMS AND BERT G. HICKMAN. Cambridge, Mass., and London: MIT Press, 1983.

KOMLOS, JOHN, ed. *Economic Development in the Habsburg Monarchy in the Nineteenth Century: Essays.* East European Monographs, no. 128. Boulder, Colo.: East European Monographs; distributed by Columbia University Press, New York, 1983.

KRASNER, STEPHEN D., ed. *International Regimes.* Cornell Studies in Political Economy. Ithaca and London: Cornell University Press, 1983.

KREGEL, J. A., ed. *Distribution, Effective Demand and International Economic Relations: Proceedings of a Conference Held by the Centro di Studi Economici Avanzati, Trieste, at Villa Manin de Passariano, Udine.* New York: St. Martin's Press, 1983.

KRISTOL, IRVING. *Reflections of a Neoconservative: Looking Back, Looking Ahead.* New York: Basic Books, 1983.

KUMAR, DHARMA, ed. *The Cambridge Economic History of India. Volume 2: c. 1757–c. 1970.* With the Editorial Assistance of MEGHNAD DESAI. Cambridge; New York and Sydney: Cambridge University Press, 1983.

KUPERBERG, MARK AND BEITZ, CHARLES, eds. *Law, Economics, and Philosophy: A Critical Introduction, with Applications to the Law of Torts.* Totowa, N.J.: Littlefield, Adams; Rowman and Allanheld, 1983.

LAKE, ROBERT W., ed. *Readings in Urban Analysis: Perspectives on Urban Form and Structure.* New Brunswick, N.J.: Rutgers University, Center for Urban Policy Research, 1983.

LALL, SANJAYA. *The New Multinationals: The Spread of Third World Enterprises.* Foreword by PAUL STREETEN. In Collaboration with Edward Chen et al. Wiley/IRM Series on Multinationals. Chichester, England; New York; Brisbane and Toronto: Wiley, 1983.

LANGLAND, ELIZABETH AND GOVE, WALTER, eds. *A Feminist Perspective in the Academy: The Difference It Makes.* Chicago and London: University of Chicago Press, 1983.

LEFCOE, GEORGE, ed. *Urban Land Policy for the 1980s: The Message for State and Local Government.* A Lincoln Institute of Land Policy Book. Lexington, Mass., and London: Heath, Lexington Books, 1983.

LENEL, HANS OTTO; WILLGERODT, HANS AND MOLSBERGER, JOSEF. *ORDO: Jahrbuch fur die Ordnung von Wirtschaft und Gesellschaft.* Vol. 34. Stuttgart and New York: Fischer, 1983.

LERNER, ABBA P. *Selected Economic Writings of Abba P. Lerner.* Edited by DAVID C. COLANDER. New York University Series in Selected Economic Writings. New York: New York University Press; distributed by Columbia University Press, 1983.

LETWIN, WILLIAM, ed. *Against Equality: Readings on Economic and Social Policy.* London: Macmillan Press in association with the Foundation for Education in Economics; distributed in the U.S. by Humanities Press, Atlantic Highlands, N.J., 1983.

LEV, BENJAMIN, ed. *Energy Models and Studies.* Studies in Management Science and Systems Series, vol. 9. New York; Amsterdam and Oxford: North-Holland; distributed in U.S. and Canada by Elsevier Science, New York, 1983.

LEVIN, HENRY M. AND SCHÜTZE, HANS G., eds. *Financing Recurrent Education: Strategies for Increasing Employment, Job Opportunities, and Productivity.* Beverly Hills; London and New Delhi: Sage, in cooperation with the Institute for Research on Educational Finance and Governance, Stanford University, and the Organization for Economic Cooperation and Development, 1983.

LEVY, HAIM, ed. *Research in Finance. Volume 4. A Research Annual.* Greenwich, Conn., and London: JAI Press, 1983.

LEWIS, JOHN P. AND KALLAB, VALERIANA, eds. *U.S. Foreign Policy and the Third World: Agenda 1983.* New York: Praeger for the Overseas Development Council, 1983.

LEWIS, W. ARTHUR. *Selected Economic Writings of W. Arthur Lewis.* Edited by MARK GERSOVITZ. New York University Series in Selected Economic Writings. New York: New York University Press; distributed by Columbia University Press, New York, 1983.

LIEBER, ROBERT J., ed. *Will Europe Fight for Oil? Energy Relations in the Atlantic Area.* New York: Praeger in cooperation with the Committee on Atlantic Studies, Washington, D.C., 1983.

LIM, DAVID, ed. *Further Readings on Malaysian Economic Development.* Oxford in Asia University readings. Kuala Lumpur; Oxford; New York and Melbourne: Oxford University Press, 1983.

LIM, LINDA Y. C. AND GOSLING, L. A. PETER, eds. *The Chinese in Southeast Asia. Volume 1: Ethnicity and Economic Activity.* Singapore: Maruzen Asia, 1983.

LIMQUECO, PETER AND MCFARLANE, BRUCE, eds. *Neo-Marxist Theories of Development.* New York: St. Martin's Press; London and Canberra: Croom Helm, 1983.

LITTRELL, W. BOYD; SJOBERG, GIDEON AND ZURCHER, LOUIS A., eds. *Bureaucracy as a Social Problem.* Contemporary Studies in Applied Behavioral Science, vol. 1. Greenwich, Conn., and London: JAI Press, 1983.

LUNDAHL, MATS. *The Haitian Economy: Man, Land and Markets.* New York: St. Martin's Press, 1983.

MACDONALD, STUART; LAMBERTON, DONALD MCLEAN AND MANDEVILLE, THOMAS, eds. *The Trouble with Technology: Explorations in the Process of Technological Change.* New York: St. Martin's Press, 1983.

MACHAN, TIBOR R. AND JOHNSON, M. BRUCE, eds. *Rights and Regulation: Ethical, Political, and Economic Issues.* Foreword by AARON WILDAVSKY. Pacific Studies in Public Policy series. San Francisco: Pacific Institute for Public Policy Research; Cambridge, Mass.: Harper and Row, Ballinger, 1983.

The Malthus Library Catalogue: The Personal Collection of Thomas Robert Malthus at Jesus College, Cambridge. New York; Oxford; Toronto and Sydney: Pergamon Press, 1983.

MARR, WILLIAM L. AND RAJ, BALDEV, eds. *How Economists Explain: A Reader in Methodology.* Lanham, Md., and London: University Press of America, 1983.

MARTIN, T. R., ed. *Stewardship: The Corporation and the Individual.* Foreword by RAND V. ARASKOG. ITT Key Issues Lecture Series. New York: KCG Productions, 1983.

MCCLINTOCK, CYNTHIA AND LOWENTHAL, ABRAHAM F., eds. *The Peruvian Experiment Reconsidered.* Princeton, N.J.: Princeton University Press, 1983.

MCLURE, CHARLES E., JR., ed. *Tax Assignment in Federal Countries.* Canberra; London; New York and Tokyo: Australian National University, Centre for Research on Federal Financial Relations, in association with the International Seminar in Public Economics; distributed by ANU Press, 1983.

MCLURE, CHARLES E., JR. AND MIESZKOWSKI, PETER, eds. *Fiscal Federalism and the Taxation of Natural Resources.* Lincoln Institute of Land Policy series. Lexington, Mass., and Toronto: Heath, Lexington Books, 1983.

MEEK, PAUL, ed. *Central Bank Views on Monetary Targeting: Papers Presented at a Conference Held at the Federal Reserve Bank of New York, May 1982.* New York: Federal Reserve Bank of New York, 1983.

MEYER, JACK A., ed. *Market Reforms in Health Care: Current Issues, New Directions, Strategic Decisions.* AEI Symposia, no. 82F. Washington, D.C., and London: American Enterprise Institute for Public Policy Research, 1983.

MIGLIARO, A. AND JAIN, C. L., eds. *An Executive's Guide to Econometric Forecasting: A Book of Readings.* Flushing, N.Y.: Graceway, 1983.

MILLER, G. WILLIAM, ed. *Regrowing the American Economy.* Columbia University, American Assembly series. Englewood Cliffs, N.J.: Prentice-Hall, Spectrum Books, 1983.

MITCHELL, EDWARD J., ed. *The Deregulation of Natural Gas.* AEI Symposia, no. 83B. Washington and London: American Enterprise Institute for Public Policy Research, 1983.

MODIGLIANI, FRANCO AND HEMMING, RICHARD, eds. *The Determinants of National Saving and Wealth: Proceedings of a Conference Held by the International Economic Association at Bergamo, Italy.* New York: St. Martin's Press, 1983.

MOORE, GEOFFREY H. *Business Cycles, Inflation, and Forecasting.* Second edition. National Bureau of Economic Research Studies in Business Cycles, no. 24. Cambridge, Mass.: Harper and Row, Ballinger, for the National Bureau of Economic Research, [1980] 1983.

MORRISON, PETER A., ed. *Population Movements: Their Forms and Functions in Urbanization and Development.* Liege, Belgium: Ordina Editions, 1983.

MÖTTÖLÄ, KARI; BYKOV, O. N. AND KOROLEV, I. S., eds. *Finnish-Soviet Economic Relations.* New York: St. Martin's Press; London: Macmillan Press, 1983.

MUELLER, DENNIS C., ed. *The Political Economy of Growth.* New Haven and London: Yale University Press, 1983.

MURPHY, D. J., ed. *The Big Strikes: Queensland 1889-1965.* St. Lucia; London and New York: University of Queensland Press, 1983.

NATIONAL SCIENCE FOUNDATION, NATIONAL SCIENCE BOARD. *University-Industry Research Relationships: Selected Studies.* Washington, D.C.: Author; available from U.S.G.P.O., 1983.

NELSON, JAMES C. *Regulation and Competition in Transportation: Selected Works of James C. Nelson.* Edited by JOHN W. FULLER. Centre Transportation Series. Vancouver: University of British Columbia, Centre for Transportation Studies, 1983.

NINCIC, MIROSLAV AND WALLENSTEEN, PETER, eds. *Dilemmas of Economic Coercion: Sanctions in World Politics.* New York: Praeger, 1983.

NOLL, ROGER G. AND OWEN, BRUCE M. *The Political Economy of Deregulation: Interest Groups in the Regulatory Process.* AEI Studies in Government Regulation, no. 379. Washington, D.C., and London: American Enterprise Institute for Public Policy Research, 1983.

OBERAI, A. S., ed. *State Policies and Internal Migration: Studies in Market and Planned Economies.* London and Canberra: Croom Helm; New York: St. Martin's Press, 1983.

O'BRIEN, RITA CRUISE, ed. *Information, Economics and Power: The North-South Dimension.* London; Sydney; Auckland and Toronto: Hodder and Stoughton, 1983.

ODDEN, ALLAN AND WEBB, L. DEAN, eds. *School Finance and School Improvement: Linkages for the 1980s.* Fourth Annual Yearbook of the American Education Finance Association. Cambridge, Mass.: Harper and Row, Ballinger, 1983.

OKUN, ARTHUR M. *Economics for Policymaking : Selected Essays of Arthur M. Okun.* Edited by JOSEPH A. PECHMAN. Cambridge and London: MIT Press, 1983.

ORTIZ, SUTTI, ed. *Economic Anthropology: Topics and Theories.* Monographs in Economic Anthropology, no. 1. Lanham, Md., and London: University Press of America and Society for Economic Anthropology, 1983.

OXMAN, BERNARD H.; CARON, DAVID D. AND BUDERI, CHARLES L. O., eds. *Law of the Sea: U.S. Policy Dilemma.* San Francisco: ICS Press, 1983.

PAGAN, A. R. AND TRIVEDI, P. K., eds. *The Effects of Inflation: Theoretical Issues and Australian Evidence.* Canberra: Australian National University, Centre for Economic Policy Research, 1983.

PARKINSON, J. R., ed. *Poverty and Aid.* New York: St. Martin's Press, 1983.

PARNES, HERBERT S., ed. *Policy Issues in Work and Retirement.* Kalamazoo, Mich.: W. E. Upjohn Institute for Employment Research, 1983.

PATIENCE, ALLAN AND SCOTT, JEFFREY, eds. *Australian Federalism: Future Tense.* Melbourne; Oxford and New York: Oxford University Press, 1983.

PATTANAIK, PRASANTA K. AND SALLES, MAURICE, eds. *Social Choice and Welfare.* Contributions to Economic Analysis, no. 145. New York; Amsterdam and Oxford: North-Holland; distributed in U.S. and Canada by Elsevier Science, New York, 1983.

PECHMAN, JOSEPH A., ed. *Setting National Priorities: The 1984 Budget.* Washington, D.C.: Brookings Institution, 1983.

PEJOVICH, SVETOZAR, ed. *Philosophical and Economic Foundations of Capitalism.* Lexington, Mass., and Toronto: Heath, Lexington Books, 1983.

PENNER, RUDOLPH G., ed. *Taxing the Family.* AEI Symposia, no. 83A. Washington, D.C. and London: American Enterprise Institute for Public Policy Research, 1983.

PIPER, DON C. AND TERCHEK, RONALD J., eds. *Interaction: Foreign Policy and Public Policy.* AEI Studies in Foreign Policy, no. 381. Washington and London: American Enterprise Institute for Public Policy Research, 1983.

PRICHARD, J. ROBERT S., ed. *Crown Corporations in Canada: The Calculus of Instrument Choice.* Studies in Law and Economic series. Toronto and London: Butterworths, 1983.

QUEEN'S UNIVERSITY, INDUSTRIAL RELATIONS CENTRE. *Termination of Employment: Proceedings of a Symposium Held at Queen's University, October 3 and 4, 1981.* Kingston, Ont.: Author, 1983.

QUEEN'S UNIVERSITY, INDUSTRIAL RELATIONS CENTRE AND THE JOHN DEUTSCH MEMORIAL FOR THE STUDY OF ECONOMIC POLICY. *Canadian Labour Markets in the 1980s: Proceedings of a Conference Held at Queen's University February 25-26, 1983.* Kingston, Ont.: Queen's University, Industrial Relations Centre, 1983.

QUIGLEY, JOHN M., ed. *Perspectives on Local Public Finance and Public Policy.* A Research Annual, Volume 1. Greenwich, Conn., and London: JAI Press, 1983.

[RAMANADHAM, V. V.]. *Government and Public Enterprise: Essays in Honour of Professor V. V. Ramanadham.* Edited by G. RAM REDDY. London: Cass; distributed in the U.S. by Biblio Distribution Centre, Totowa, N.J., 1983.

REID, JOSEPH D., JR., ed. *New Approaches to Labor Unions.* Research in Labor Economics: A Research Annual, supplement 2. Greenwich, Conn., and London: JAI Press, 1983.

REIN, MARTIN. *From Policy to Practice.* Armonk, N.Y.: Sharpe, 1983.

REUBENS, BEATRICE G., ed. *Youth at Work: An International Survey.* Foreword by ELI GINZBERG. Conservation of Human Resources series, no. 22. LandMark Studies. Totowa, N.J.: Littlefield, Adams; Rowman & Allanheld, 1983.

REYNOLDS, CLARK W. AND TELLO, CARLOS, eds. *U.S.-Mexico Relations: Economic and Social Aspects.* Revised, updated, and supplemented translation. Stanford, Calif.: Stanford University Press, [1981] 1983.

RICH, DANIEL, ET AL., eds. *The Solar Energy Transition: Implementation and Policy Implications.* AAAS Selected Symposium, no. 74. Boulder, Colo.: Westview Press for the American Association for the Advancement of Science, Washington, D.C., 1983.

RITTER, ARCHIBALD R. M. AND POLLOCK, DAVID H., eds. *Latin American Prospects for the 1980s: Equity, Democratization, and Development.* New York: Praeger, 1983.

ROBINSON, DEREK AND MAYHEW, KEN, eds. *Pay Policies for the Future.* London; New York; Toronto and Melbourne: Oxford University Press, 1983.

RONEN, JOSHUA, ed. *Entrepreneurship.* Lexington, Mass., and Toronto: Heath, Lexington Books, 1983.

ROTBERG, ROBERT I., ed. *Namibia: Political and Economic Prospects.* Lexington, Mass., and Toronto: Heath, Lexington Books, 1983.

ROWE, ROBERT D. AND CHESTNUT, LAURAINE G., eds. *Managing Air Quality and Scenic Resources at National Parks and Wilderness Areas.* Foreword by RUSSELL E. DICKENSON. Boulder, Colo.: Westview Press, 1983.

RUBIN, SEYMOUR J. AND GRAHAM, THOMAS R., eds. *Managing Trade Relations in the 1980s: Issues Involved in the GATT Ministerial Meeting of 1982.* Published under the auspices of the American Society of International Law. Totowa, N.J.: Littlefield, Adams; Rowman & Allanheld, 1983.

RUBIN, SEYMOUR J. AND HUFBAUER, GARY CLYDE, eds. *Emerging Standards of International Trade and Investment: Multinational Codes and Corporate Conduct.* Totowa, N.J.: Littlefield, Adams; Rowman & Allanheld, 1983.

RUGGIE, JOHN GERARD, ed. *The Antinomies of Interdependence: National Welfare and the International Division of Labor.* The Political Economy of International and Change series. New York and Guildford, Surrey, England: Columbia University Press, 1983.

SALKEVER, DAVID; SIRAGELDIN, ISMAIL AND SORKIN, ALAN, eds. *Research in Human Capital and Development. Volume 3. Health and Development.* A Research Annual. Greenwich, Conn., and London: JAI Press, 1983.

SAMPEDRO, JOSE LUIS AND PAYNO, JUAN ANTONIO, eds. *The Enlargement of the European Community: Case-Studies of Greece, Portugal and Spain.* English version edited by LYN GORMAN AND MARJA-LIISA KILJUNEN. Studies in the Integration of Western Europe series. London: Macmillan Press; distributed in the U.S. by Humanities Press, Atlantic Highlands, N.J., 1983.

SANFORD, TERRY, ed. *The Interest Rate Dilemma.* Foreword by RAND V. ARASKOG. ITT Key Issues Lecture series. New York: KCG Productions, 1983.

SAUNDERS, CHRISTOPHER T., ed. *Regional Integration in East and West.* East-West European Economic Interaction Workshop Papers, vol. 7. New York: St. Martin's Press, 1983.

[SAUNDERS, CHRISTOPHER THOMAS]. *Controlling Industrial Economies: Essays in Honour of Christopher Thomas Saunders.* Edited by STEPHEN F. FROWEN. New York: St. Martin's Press, 1983.

SCHELLING, THOMAS C., ed. *Incentives for Environmental Protection.* MIT Press Series on the Regulation of Economic Activity, no. 5. Cambridge, Mass., and London: MIT Press, 1983.

SCHICK, ALLEN, ed. *Making Economic Policy in Congress.* AEI Studies in Political and Social Processes, no. 391. Washington, D.C., and London: American Enterprise Institute for Public Policy Research, 1983.

SCHMUKLER, NATHAN AND MARCUS, EDWARD, eds. *Inflation through the Ages: Economic, Social, Psychological and Historical Aspects.* Social Science Monographs. New York: Brooklyn College Press; distributed by Columbia University Press for East European Quarterly, 1983.

SCHURR, SAM H.; SONENBLUM, SIDNEY AND WOOD, DAVID O., eds. *Energy, Productivity, and Economic Growth: A Workshop Sponsored by the Electric Power Research Institute.* Cambridge, Mass.: Oelgeschlager, Gunn & Hain, 1983.

SEERS, DUDLEY AND ÖSTRÖM, KJELL, eds. *The Crises of the European Regions.* New York: St. Martin's Press, 1983.

SELDON, ARTHUR, ET AL. *Agenda for Social Democracy: Essays on the Prospects for New Economic Thinking and Policy in the Changing British Political Scene.* Hobart Paperback, no. 15. London: Institute of Economic Affairs; distributed in the U.S. by Transatlantic Arts, Albuquerque, N.M., 1983.

SHADOW OPEN MARKET COMMITTEE. *Policy Statement and Position Papers.* Rochester: University of Rochester, Graduate School of Management, Center for Research in Government Policy and Business, 1983.

SHAW, LOIS BANFILL, ed. *Unplanned Careers: The Working Lives of Middle-aged Women.* Lexington, Mass., and Toronto: Heath, Lexington Books, 1983.

SHEPHERD, DAVID; TURK, JEREMY AND SILBERSTON, AUBREY, eds. *Microeconomic Efficiency and Macroeconomic Performance.* Oxford: Allan; distributed in the U.S. by Humanities Press, Atlantic Highlands, N.J., 1983.

SHEPHERD, GEOFFREY; DUCHÊNE, FRANÇOIS AND SAUNDERS, CHRISTOPHER, EDS. *Europe's Industries: Public and Private Strategies for Change.* Cornell Studies in Political Economy. Ithaca, N.Y.: Cornell University Press, 1983.

SHIHATA, IBRAHIM F. I., ET AL. *The OPEC Fund for International Development: The Formative Years.* New York: St. Martin's Press; London and Canberra: Croom Helm, 1983.

SIDDIQI, MUHAMMAD NEJATULLAH. *Issues in Islamic Banking: Selected Papers.* Islamic Economics series, no. 4. Leicester: Islamic Foundation, 1983.

SIRAGELDIN, ISMAIL; SALKEVER, DAVID AND OSBORN, RICHARD W., eds. *Evaluating Population Programs: International Experience with Cost-Effectiveness Analysis and Cost-Benefit Analysis.* With Assistance of D. CEBULA ET AL. New York: St. Martin's Press; London and Canberra: Croom Helm, 1983.

SKURSKI, ROGER, ed. *New Directions in Economic Justice.* Notre Dame, Ind., and London: University of Notre Dame Press, 1983.

SNOEYENBOS, MILTON; ALMEDER, ROBERT AND HUMBER, JAMES, eds. *Business Ethics: Corporate Values and Society.* Buffalo: Prometheus Books, 1983.

SÖDERSTRÖM, LARS, ed. *Social Insurance: Papers Presented at the 5th Arne Ryde Symposium, Lund, Sweden, 1981.* Contributions to Economic Analysis Series, no. 148. Amsterdam; New York and Oxford: North-Holland; distributed in U.S. and Canada by Elsevier Science, New York, 1983.

SOHLMAN, ASA M., ed. *Energy Demand Analysis: Report from the French-Swedish Energy Conference, Stockholm, 30 June-2 July, 1982.* Energy Systems Studies, AES 1983:2, Project Results. Stockholm: Energy Research Commision, 1983.

STANSKY, PETER, ed. *On Nineteen Eighty-four.* New York: Freeman, 1983.

STARR, JOYCE R., ed. *A Shared Destiny: Near East Regional Development and Cooperation.* Assisted by ADDEANE S. CAELLEIGH. New York: Praeger in cooperation with Georgetown University, Center for Strategic and International Studies, 1983.

STEINBRUNER, JOHN D. AND SIGAL LEON V., eds. *Alliance Security: NATO and the No-First-Use Question.* Studies in Defense Policy series. Washington, D.C.: Brookings Institution, 1983.

STEWART, FRANCES, ed. *Work, Income and Inequality: Payments Systems in the Third World.* New York: St. Martin's Press, 1983.

STIGLER, GEORGE J. *Essays in the History of Economics.* Reprint. Chicago and London: University of Chicago Press, [1965] 1983.

STIGUM, BERNT P. AND WENSTØP, FRED, eds. *Foundations of Utility and Risk Theory with Applications.* Theory and Decision Library series, vol. 37. Dordrecht, Holland; Boston and Lancaster: Kluwer Academic, Reidel; distributed in the U.S. and Canada by Kluwer Academic, Hingham, Mass., 1983.

STOREY, DAVID J., ed. *The Small Firm: An International Survey.* New York: St. Martin's Press; London and Canberra: Croom Helm, 1983.

STREETEN, PAUL AND MAIER, HARRY, eds. *Human Resources, Employment and Development. Volume 1. Concepts, Measurement and Long-run Perspective: Proceedings of the Sixth World Congress of the International Economic Association Held in Mexico City, 1980.* New York: St. Martin's Press, 1983.

STUART, ROBERT C., ed. *The Soviet Rural Economy.* Totowa, N.J.: Littlefield, Adams; Rowman & Allanheld, 1983.

STUBBLEBINE, WM. CRAIG AND WILLETT, THOMAS D., eds. *Reaganomics: A Midterm Report.* San Francisco: ICS Press, 1983.

SUSSKIND, LAWRENCE E. AND SERIO, JANE FOUNTAIN, eds. *Proposition 2 1/2: Its Impact on Massachusetts: A Report from the Impact: 2 1/2 Project at the Massachusetts Institute of Technology.* Cambridge, Mass.: Oelgeschlager, Gunn & Hain, 1983.

TAHIR-KHELI, SHIRIN AND AYUBI, SHAHEEN, eds. *The Iran-Iraq War: New Weapons, Old Conflicts.* Foreign Policy Issues, a Foreign Policy Research Institute series. New York: Praeger, 1983.

TAYLOR, CARL E., ET AL. *Child and Maternal Health Services in Rural India: The Narangwal Experiment. Volume 2. Integrated Family Planning and Health Care.* World Bank Research Publication. Baltimore and London: Johns Hopkins University Press for the World Bank, 1983.

TEICHOVA, ALICE AND COTTRELL, P. L., eds. *International Business and Central Europe, 1918-1939.* New York: St. Martin's Press; Leicester: Leicester University, 1983.

TEMPEST, PAUL, ed. *International Energy Markets.* Cambridge, Mass.: Oelgeschlager, Gunn and Hain; London: Graham and Trotman, 1983.

THARAKAN, P. K. M., ed. *Intra-industry Trade: Empirical and Methodological Aspects.* Advanced Series in Management, vol. 4. New York; Amsterdam and Oxford: North-Holland; distributed in the U.S. by Elsevier Science, New York, 1983.

THISSE, JACQUES-FRANCOIS AND ZOLLER, HENRY G., eds. *Locational Analysis of Public Facilities.* Studies in Mathematical and Managerial Economics series, vol. 31. Amsterdam; New York

and Oxford: North-Holland; distributed in the U.S. and Canada by Elsevier Science, New York, 1983.

THOMPSON, W. SCOTT, ed. *The Third World: Premises of U.S. Policy.* Revised Edition. San Francisco: Institute for Contemporary Studies, ICS Press, [1978] 1983.

THRALL, ROBERT M.; THOMPSON, RUSSELL G. AND HOLLOWAY, MILTON L., eds. *Large-scale Energy Models: Prospects and Potential.* AAAS Selected Symposia series, no. 73. Boulder, Colo.: Westview Press for the American Association for the Advancement of Science, 1983.

THURLEY, KEITH AND WOOD, STEPHEN, eds. *Industrial Relations and Management Strategy.* Management and Industrial Relations series, no. 4. Cambridge; New York and Sydney: Cambridge University Press, 1983.

TIETZ, REINHARD, ed. *Aspiration Levels in Bargaining and Economic Decision Making: Proceedings of the Third Conference on Experimental Economics, Winzenhohl, Germany, August 29–September 3, 1982.* Lecture Notes in Economics and Mathematical Systems, no. 213. New York; Berlin and Tokyo: Springer, 1983.

TOBIN, JAMES, ed. *Macroeconomics, Prices, and Quantities: Essays in Memory of Arthur M. Okun.* Washington, D.C.: Brookings Institution, 1983.

TODARO, MICHAEL P., ed. *The Struggle for Economic Development: Readings in Problems and Policies.* New York and London: Longman, 1983.

TRATTNER, WALTER I., ed.. *Social Welfare or Social Control? Some Historical Reflections on "Regulating the Poor."* Knoxville: University of Tennessee Press, 1983.

TREBILCOCK, MICHAEL J., ET AL., eds. *Federalism and the Canadian Economic Union.* Toronto; Buffalo and London: University of Toronto Press for the Ontario Economic Council, 1983.

TRIPLETT, JACK E., ed. *The Measurement of Labor Cost.* NBER Studies in Income and Wealth, vol. 48. Chicago and London: University of Chicago Press, 1983.

TSIPIS, KOSTA AND PHILLIPS, SHEENA. *Annual Review of Military Research and Development: 1982.* New York: Praeger in cooperation with the Program in Science & Technology for International Security, Massachusetts Institute of Technology, 1983.

TSOUKALIS, LOUKAS, ed. *The European Community: Past, Present and Future.* Oxford and New York: Blackwell, 1983.

TSURU, SHIGETO, ed. *Human Resources, Employment and Development. Volume 1: The Issues: Proceedings of the Sixth World Congress of the International Economic Association Held in Mexico City, 1980.* New York: St. Martin's Press, 1983.

TUCKER, RICHARD P. AND RICHARDS, J. F., eds. *Global Deforestation and the Nineteenth-Century World Economy.* Duke Press Policy Studies. Durham, N.C.: Duke University Press, 1983.

DE ULHOA CANTO, GILBERTO; DA SILVA MARTINS, IVES GANDRA AND VAN HOORN, J., JR., eds. *Monetary Indexation in Brazil.* International Bureau of Fiscal Documentation, no. 34. Amsterdam: International Bureau of Fiscal Documentation, 1983.

URQUIDI, VICTOR L. AND REYES, SAUL TREJO, eds. *Human Resources, Employment and Development. Volume 4. Latin America: Proceedings of the Sixth World Congress of the International Economic Association Held in Mexico City, 1980.* New York: St. Martin's Press, 1983.

U.S. DEPARTMENT OF COMMERCE, NATIONAL OCEANIC AND ATMOSPHERIC ADMINISTRATION, NATIONAL OCEAN SERVICE. *Assessing the Social Costs of Oil Spills: The AMOCO CADIZ Case Study.* Rockville, Md.: Author, 1983.

UUSITALO, LIISA, ed. *Consumer Behavior and Environmental Quality: Trends and Prospects in the Ways of Life: Proceedings of a Symposium Organized by the International Institute for Environment and Society of the Science Center Berlin, November 1980.* New York: St. Martin's Press, 1983.

VOGEL, RONALD J. AND PALMER, HANS C., eds. *Long-term Care: Perspectives from Research and Demonstration.* Baltimore: U.S. Department of Health and Human Services, Health Care Financing Administration; distributed by the National Technical Information Service, Springfield, Va., 1983.

VON PISCHKE, J. D.; ADAMS, DALE W. AND DONALD, GORDON, eds. *Rural Financial Markets in Developing Countries: Their Use and Abuse.* EDI series in Economic Development. Baltimore and London: Johns Hopkins University Press for the Economic Development Institute of the World Bank, 1983.

WALKER, CHARLES A.; GOULD, LEROY C. AND WOODHOUSE, EDWARD J., eds. *Too Hot to Handle? Social and Policy Issues in the Management of Radioactive Wastes.* New Haven and London: Yale University Press, 1983.

WALKER, CHARLS E. AND BLOOMFIELD, MARK E., eds. *New Directions in Federal Tax Policy for the 1980s.* Cambridge, Mass.: Harper & Row, Ballinger, for the American Council for Capital Formation, Center for Policy Research, 1983.

WANG, JAW-KAI, ed. *Taro: A Review of "Colocasia Esculenta" and Its Potentials.* Assisted by SALLY HIGA. Honolulu: University of Hawaii Press, 1983.

WEDDERBURN OF CHARLTON [LORD]; LEWIS, ROY AND CLARK, JON, eds. *Labour Law and Industrial Relations: Building on Kahn-Freund.* Oxford; New York; Toronto and Tokyo: Oxford University Press, Clarendon Press, 1983.

WEINTRAUB, SIDNEY AND GOODSTEIN, MARVIN, eds. *Reaganomics in the Stagflation Economy.* Post Keynesian Economics series. Philadelphia: University of Pennsylvania Press, 1983.

WEISBROD, BURTON AND HUGHES, HELEN, eds. *Human Resources, Employment and Development. Volume 3. The Problems of Developed Countries and the International Economy: Proceedings of the Sixth World Congress of the International Economics Association Held in Mexico City, 1980.* New York: St. Martin's Press, 1983.

WHYTE, WILLIAM FOOTE AND BOYNTON, DAMON, eds. *Higher-yielding Human Systems for Agriculture.* Ithaca and London: Cornell University Press, 1983.

WILD, TREVOR, ed. *Urban and Rural Change in West Germany.* Totowa, N.J.: Barnes and Noble Books; London and Canberra: Croom Helm, 1983.

WILLIAMSON, JOHN, ed. *IMF Conditionality.* Washington, D.C.: Institute for International Economics; distributed by MIT Press, Cambridge, London, and Tokyo, 1983.

WILSON, B.; BERG, C. C. AND FRENCH, D., eds. *Efficiency of Manufacturing Systems.* NATO Conference series, Series II: Systems Science, vol. 14. New York and London: Plenum Press in cooperation with NATO Scientific Affairs Division, 1983.

WISEMAN, JACK, ed. *Beyond Positive Economics? Proceedings of Section F (Economics) of the British Association for the Advancement of Science, York 1981.* New York: St. Martin's Press, 1983.

WITHERS, GLENN, ed. *Bigger or Smaller Government? Papers from the Sixth Symposium of the Academy of the Social Sciences in Australia, 1982.* Canberra: Academy of Social Sciences in Australia; distributed by Australian National University Press, Canberra, 1983.

WOOD, W. D. AND KUMAR, PRADEEP, eds. *The Current Industrial Relations Scene in Canada, 1983.* Kingston, Ont.: Queen's University, Industrial Relations Centre, 1983.

WORSWICK, DAVID AND TREVITHICK, JAMES, eds. *Keynes and the Modern World: Proceedings of the Keynes Centenary Conference, King's College, Cambridge.* New York; London and Sydney: Cambridge University Press, 1983.

[YAMADA, ISAMU]. *Technology, Organization and Economic Structure: Essays in Honor of Professor Isamu Yamada.* Edited by RYUZO SATO AND MARTIN J. BECKMANN. Lecture Notes in Economics and Mathematical Systems series, no. 210. New York and Heidelberg: Springer, 1983.

YOUNG, KEN, ed. *National Interests and Local Government.* Joint Studies in Public Policy Series, no. 7. London; Exeter, N.H., and Melbourne, 1983.

YOUNGSON, A. J., ed. *China and Hong Kong: The Economic Nexus.* Hong Kong; Oxford; New York and Melbourne: Oxford University Press, 1983.

YSANDER, BENGT-CHRISTER, ed. *Energy in Swedish Manufacturing.* Energy and Economic Structure Research Report, no. 5. Stockholm: Industrial Institute for Economic and Social Research; Stockholm School of Economics, Economic Research Institute; and University of Stockholm, Energy Systems Research Group; distributed by Almqvist and Wiksell International, 1983.

Zartman, I. William, ed. *The Political Economy of Nigeria.* A SAIS Study on Africa. New York: Praeger, 1983.

Zeckhauser, Richard J. and Leebaert, Derek, eds. *What Role for Government? Lessons from Policy Research.* Duke Press Policy Studies series. Durham, N.C.: Duke University Press, 1983.

Zodrow, George R., ed. *Local Provision of Public Services: The Tiebout Model after Twenty-five Years.* Studies in Urban Economics series. New York; London; Toronto and Sydney: Harcourt Brace Jovanovich, Academic Press, 1983.

Zysman, John and Tyson, Laura, eds. *American Industry in International Competition: Government Policies and Corporate Strategies.* Cornell Studies in Political Economy series. Ithaca and London: Cornell University Press, 1983.

CLASSIFICATION SYSTEM

Editor's note: Notes on the *Classification System* further clarify the subject matter covered under specific categories or point out specific topics included. They also may contain cross references to other categories. In addition, the *Topical Guide* at the end of this volume provides an index to classification numbers appropriate for specific topics. Please note that "General" categories may include *both* detailed articles covering all subcategories and very general articles falling into no subcategory.

Subject Index of Articles in Current Periodicals and Collective Volumes

Abbreviated titles for journals are the same as those used in the *Journal of Economic Literature.* Full titles of journals may be found on pages x–xv.

Books have been identified by author or editor (noted *ed.*). In rare cases where two books by the same author appear, volumes are distinguished by I or II after the name. In some cases there appear two books by the same person, once as author, once as editor. These may be distinguished by *ed.* noted for the edited volume. Full titles and bibliographic references for books may be found on pages xvi–xxxiii.

Geographic Descriptors when appropriate appear in brackets at the end of the article citation.

000 General Economics; Theory; History; Systems

010 General Economics

011 General Economics

0110 General

Abrams, Burton A. An Economic Analysis of the Language Market. *J. Econ. Educ.*, Summer 1983, *14*(3), pp. 40–47.

Arrow, Kenneth J. The Economics of *Nineteen Eighty-Four.* **In** *Stansky, P., ed.*, 1983, pp. 43–47.

Arrow, Kenneth J. The Future and the Present in Economic Life. **In** *Arrow, K. J., Vol. 2*, 1983, *1978*, pp. 275–89.

Baumol, William J. On the Career of a Microeconomist. *Banca Naz. Lavoro Quart. Rev.*, December 1983, (147), pp. 311–35.

Bell, Wendell. An Introduction to Futuristics: Assumptions, Theories, Methods, and Research Topics. *Soc. Econ. Stud.*, June 1983, *32*(2), pp. 1–64.

Bodkin, Ronald G. and West, Edwin G. Conjectural Nobel Prizes in Economics: 1770 to 1890. *Eastern Econ. J.*, July–September 1983, *9*(3), pp. 151–65.

Briefs, Goetz A. A Challenge to Western Civilization. *Rev. Soc. Econ.*, December 1983, *41*(3), pp. 317–29.

Christ, Carl F. The Founding of the Econometric Society and *Econometrica. Econometrica*, January 1983, *51*(1), pp. 3–6.

Coats, A. W. The First Decade of *HOPE* (1968–79). *Hist. Polit. Econ.*, Fall 1983, *15*(3), pp. 303–19. **[G: U.K.; U.S.]**

Coe, Robert K. and Weinstock, Irwin. Evaluating the Finance Journals: The Department Chairperson's Perspective. *J. Finan. Res.*, Winter 1983, *6*(4), pp. 345–49. **[G: U.S.]**

Danner, Richard A. Federal Regulation of Non-Nuclear Hazardous Wastes: A Research Bibliography. *Law Contemp. Probl.*, Summer 1983, *46*(3), pp. 285–305.

Drăgănescu, M. Information Economy. *Econ. Computat. Cybern. Stud. Res.*, 1983, *18*(3), pp. 11–21. **[G: Romania; U.S.]**

Eichner, Alfred S. Why Economics Is Not Yet a Science: Introduction. **In** *Eichner, A. S., ed.*, 1983, pp. 3–14.

Frey, Bruno S., et al. Consensus, Dissension and Ideology among Economists in Various European Countries and in the United States. *Europ. Econ. Rev.*, September 1983, *23*(1), pp. 59–69. **[G: Belgium; France; W. Germany; Switzerland; U.S.]**

Ginting, Meneth. The Seventh National Conference on Agricultural Economics. *Bull. Indonesian Econ. Stud.*, April 1983, *19*(1), pp. 97–99.

Gómez, Manuel Aguilera. Human Resources, Employment and Development: Address to Final Session. **In** *Tsuru, S., ed.*, 1983, pp. 149–51.

Groenewegen, Peter D. and Halevi, Joseph. Altro Polo: Italian Economics Past and Present: Preface and Introduction. **In** *Groenewegen, P. and Halevi, J., eds.*, 1983, pp. 7–16.

Hague, Douglas. Discussion and Conclusion: A Global Perspective on the World Economy. *Int. Soc. Sci. J.*, 1983, *35*(3), pp. 535–47. **[G: Global]**

Harrison, John. The Malthus Library Catalogue: Introductory Essay. **In** *Malthus Library Catalogue*, 1983, pp. xv–xxxi.

Heller, Walter W. What's Right with Economics? **In** *Marr, W. L. and Raj, B., eds.*, 1983, pp. 337–74. **[G: U.S.]**

Horton, Joseph. The Eastern Economic Association: The First Decade. *Eastern Econ. J.*, July–September 1983, *9*(3), pp. 147–50.

Howard, Thomas P. and Nikolai, Loren A. Attitude Measurement and Perceptions of Accounting Faculty Publication Outlets. *Accounting Rev.*, October 1983, *58*(4), pp. 765–76. **[G: U.S.]**

Hutchison, Terence. From 'Dismal Science' to 'Positive Economics'—A Century-and-a-Half of Progress? **In** *Wiseman, J., ed.*, 1983, pp. 192–211.

Jones, R. J. Barry. Political Economy: Contrasts, Commonalities, Criteria and Contributions. **In** *Jones, R. J. B., ed.*, 1983, pp. 3–13.

Joyce, Patrick and Merz, Tom. On the Long-run Effects of Manuscript Submission Fees: A Comment. *Amer. Econ.*, Fall 1983, *27*(2), pp. 80–81.

Katouzian, Homa. Towards the Progress of Economic Knowledge. **In** *Wiseman, J., ed.*, 1983, pp. 50–64.

Kau, James B. and Johnson, Linda L. Regional Science Programs: A Ranking Based on Publication Performance. *J. Reg. Sci.*, May 1983, *23*(2), pp. 177–86. **[G: U.S.]**

011 General Economics

Kern, William. Returning to the Aristotelian Paradigm: Daly and Schumacher. *Hist. Polit. Econ.*, Winter 1983, *15*(4), pp. 501–12.

Kilby, Peter. An Entrepreneurial Problem. *Amer. Econ. Rev.*, May 1983, *73*(2), pp. 107–11. **[G: LDCs]**

Klamer, Arjo. Conversations with Economists: New Classical Economists and Opponents Speak Out on the Current Controversy in Macroeconomics: An Interpretation of the Conversations. **In** *Klamer, A.*, 1983, pp. 237–54.

Koch, James V. and Cebula, Richard J. On the Long-Run Effects of Manuscript Submission Fees—Reply. *Amer. Econ.*, Fall 1983, *27*(2), pp. 82.

Lavoie, Marc. Bilinguisme, langue dominante et réseaux d'information. (Bilingualism, Dominant Languages and Information Network. With English summary.) *L'Actual. Econ.*, March 1983, *59*(1), pp. 38–62.

Litzenberg, Kerry K.; Gorman, William D. and Schneider, Vernon E. Academic and Professional Programs in Agribusiness. *Amer. J. Agr. Econ.*, December 1983, *65*(5), pp. 1060–64. **[G: U.S.]**

Lucas, Robert E., Jr. Conversations with New Classical Economists [Interview]. **In** *Klamer, A.*, 1983, pp. 29–57.

Lux, Kenneth and Lutz, Mark A. Creative vs. Mechanical Evolutionism: A Commentary [Economic Evolution and Economic Policy: Is Reaganomics a Sustainable Force?] [Creationism versus Evolutionism in Economics: Societal Consequences of Economic Doctrine]. *J. Econ. Issues*, December 1983, *17*(4), pp. 1113–17. **[G: U.S.]**

Machlup, Fritz. Are the Social Sciences Really Inferior? **In** *Marr, W. L. and Raj, B., eds.*, 1983, *1961*, pp. 3–23.

de Marchi, Neil B. and Lodewijks, John. *HOPE* and the Journal Literature in the History of Economic Thought. *Hist. Polit. Econ.*, Fall 1983, *15*(3), pp. 321–43. **[G: U.S.]**

McAfee, R. Preston. American Economic Growth and the Voyage of Columbus. *Amer. Econ. Rev.*, September 1983, *73*(4), pp. 735–40. **[G: U.S.]**

McDowell, John M. and Melvin, Michael. The Determinants of Co-Authorship: An Analysis of the Economics Literature. *Rev. Econ. Statist.*, February 1983, *65*(1), pp. 155–60.

McIvor, R. Craig. A Note on the University of Chicago's "Academic Scribblers." *J. Polit. Econ.*, October 1983, *91*(5), pp. 888–93.

Moore, William J., et al. A Quality-Adjustment Model of the Academic Labor Market: The Case of Economists. *Econ. Inquiry*, April 1983, *21*(2), pp. 241–54. **[G: U.S.]**

North, Douglass C. A Theory of Institutional Change and the Economic History of the Western World. **In** *Hechter, M., ed.*, 1983, pp. 190–215.

Nyilas, András. Empirical Research in Hungarian Economics. *Acta Oecon.*, 1983, *30*(2), pp. 255–67. **[G: Hungary]**

Petr, Jerry L. Rejoinder to Lux and Lutz [Economic Evolution and Economic Policy: Is Reaganomics a Sustainable Force?] [Creationism versus Evolutionism in Economics: Societal Consequences of Economic Doctrine]. *J. Econ. Issues*, December 1983, *17*(4), pp. 1118–20. **[G: U.S.]**

Robertson, H. M. Fifty Years of the South African Journal of Economics. *S. Afr. J. Econ.*, March 1983, *51*(1), pp. 174–231. **[G: S. Africa]**

Rohrlich, George F. Employment Security and World Peace: An Autobiographical Splinter. *Int. J. Soc. Econ.*, 1983, *10*(6/7), pp. 9–11.

Rugina, Anghel N. Toward a Third Revolution in Economic Thinking: The Concept of Balanced (Equilibrium) Growth and Social Economics. *Int. J. Soc. Econ.*, 1983, *10*(1), pp. 3–46.

Salda, Anne C. M. The International Monetary Fund, 1982: A Selected Bibliography. *Int. Monet. Fund Staff Pap.*, September 1983, *30*(3), pp. 619–49.

Samuelson, Paul A. My Life Philosophy. *Amer. Econ.*, Fall 1983, *27*(2), pp. 5–12.

Sargent, Thomas J. Conversations with New Classical Economists [Interview]. **In** *Klamer, A.*, 1983, pp. 58–80.

Schneider, Friedrich; Pommerehne, Werner W. and Frey, Bruno S. Relata Referimus: Ergebnisse und Analyse einer Befragung deutscher Ökonomen. (Relata Referimus: Results and Analysis of a Survey among German Economists. With English summary.) *Z. ges. Staatswiss.*, March 1983, *139*(1), pp. 19–66. **[G: W. Germany]**

Schroyer, Trent. Critique of the Instrumental Interest in Nature. *Soc. Res.*, Spring 1983, *50*(1), pp. 158–84.

Schumpeter, Joseph A. American Institutions and Economic Progress. *Z. ges. Staatswiss.*, June 1983, *139*(2), pp. 191–96.

Schweser, Carl. The Economics of Academic Publishing. *J. Econ. Educ.*, Winter 1983, *14*(1), pp. 60–64. **[G: U.S.]**

Shubik, Martin; Heim, Peggy and Baumol, William J. On Contracting with Publishers: Author's Information Updated. *Amer. Econ. Rev.*, May 1983, *73*(2), pp. 365–81. **[G: U.S.]**

Siegfried, John J. and Wilkinson, James T. The Economics and Business Economics Majors in the United States. *J. Econ. Educ.*, Winter 1983, *14*(1), pp. 50–59. **[G: U.S.]**

Solow, Robert M. Conversations with Neo-Keynesian Economists: The "Older Generation" [Interview]. **In** *Klamer, A.*, 1983, pp. 127–48.

Solow, Robert M. Economic Development and the Development of Economics: Discussion. *World Devel.*, October 1983, *11*(10), pp. 891–93.

Stanfield, J. Ron. The Affluent Society after Twenty-Five Years. *J. Econ. Issues*, September 1983, *17*(3), pp. 589–607.

Stein, Herbert. Conservatives, Economists and Neckties. *Bus. Econ.*, January 1983, *18*(1), pp. 5–9. **[G: U.S.]**

Stigler, George J. Nobel Lecture: The Process and Progress of Economics. *J. Polit. Econ.*, August 1983, *91*(4), pp. 529–45.

Stigler, George J. The Nature and Role of Originality in Scientific Progress. **In** *Stigler, G. J.*, 1983, *1955*, pp. 1–15.

Stolz, Peter. Das wiedererwachte Interesse der Ökonomie an rechtlichen und politischen Institutionen. (The Renewed Interest of Economics in Legal and Political Institutions. With English summary.) *Schweiz. Z. Volkswirtsch. Statist.*,

March 1983, *119*(1), pp. 49–67.

Stone, Kenneth E. Agribusiness Management and Food Marketing: Discussion. *Amer. J. Agr. Econ.*, December 1983, *65*(5), pp. 1073–74. **[G: U.S.]**

Street, James H. The Reality of Power and the Poverty of Economic Doctrine. *J. Econ. Issues*, June 1983, *17*(2), pp. 294–313. **[G: Chile; Argentina; Paraguay; Uruguay]**

Tobin, James. Conversations with Neo-Keynesian Economists: The "Older Generation" [Interview]. **In** *Klamer, A.*, 1983, pp. 97–113.

Townsend, Robert M. Conversations with New Classical Economists [Interview]. **In** *Klamer, A.*, 1983, pp. 81–94.

Ulmer, Melville J. The Economic Civil War. *Atlantic Econ. J.*, September 1983, *11*(3), pp. 44–48. **[G: U.S.]**

Ulrich, Peter. Sozialökonomische Entwicklungs-perspektiven aus dem Blickwinkel der Lebenswelt. (Prospects of Socio-Economic Development from a Life-Practical Point of View. With English summary.) *Schweiz. Z. Volkswirtsch. Statist.*, September 1983, *119*(3), pp. 237–59.

Urquidi, Victor L. Human Resources, Employment and Development: Address to Final Session. **In** *Tsuru, S., ed.*, 1983, pp. 143–48.

Weintraub, Sidney. A Jevonian Seditionist: A Mutiny to Enhance the Economic Bounty? *Banca Naz. Lavoro Quart. Rev.*, September 1983, (146), pp. 215–34.

0112 Role of Economics; Role of Economists

Canterbery, E. Ray and Burkhardt, Robert J. What Do We Mean by Asking Whether Economics Is a Science? **In** *Eichner, A. S., ed.*, 1983, pp. 15–40.

Coddington, Alan. Economists and Policy. **In** *Marr, W. L. and Raj, B., eds.*, 1983, *1973*, pp. 229–38.

Conlan, Don R. In This Autumn of Our Discontent, a Word to the Wise; Otherwise . . . *Bus. Econ.*, January 1983, *18*(1), pp. 10–14. **[G: U.S.]**

Deane, Phyllis. The Scope and Method of Economic Science. *Econ. J.*, March 1983, *93*(369), pp. 1–12.

Delhaye, Guy and Sturbois Georges. Les politiques de relance. Perceptions de jeunes économistes en situation d'insertion professionnelles. (The Revival Policies' Perception by Young Economists. With English summary.) *Ann. Sci. Écon. Appl.*, 1983, *39*(2), pp. 53–80. **[G: France]**

Earl, Peter E. A Behavioral Theory of Economists' Behavior. **In** *Eichner, A. S., ed.*, 1983, pp. 90–125.

Eichner, Alfred S. Why Economics Is Not Yet a Science. **In** *Eichner, A. S., ed.*, 1983, pp. 205–41.

Gamble, Andrew. Critical Political Economy. **In** *Jones, R. J. B., ed.*, 1983, pp. 64–89.

Harl, Neil E. Agriculture Economics: Challenges to the Profession. *Amer. J. Agr. Econ.*, December 1983, *65*(5), pp. 845–54.

Heilbroner, Robert L. Economics as a "Value-free" Science. **In** *Marr, W. L. and Raj, B., eds.*, 1983, *1973*, pp. 27–38.

Hicks, John. A Discipline Not a Science. **In** *Hicks, J.*, 1983, pp. 365–75.

Hoffman, Dennis L. and Low, Stuart A. Rationality and the Decision to Invest in Economics. *J. Human Res.*, Fall 1983, *18*(4), pp. 480–96. **[G: U.S.]**

Leontief, Wassily W. Why Economics Is Not Yet a Science: Foreword. **In** *Eichner, A. S., ed.*, 1983, pp. vii–xi.

Lerner, Abba P. Economics and the Control of Man. **In** *Lerner, A. P.*, 1983, *1960*, pp. 619–27.

Mayer, Thomas. Economics as a Hard Science: Realistic Goal or Wishful Thinking? **In** *Marr, W. L. and Raj, B., eds.*, 1983, *1980*, pp. 49–66.

McCloskey, Donald N. The Rhetoric of Economics. *J. Econ. Lit.*, June 1983, *21*(2), pp. 481–517.

McDaniel, Bruce A. and Silvia, John E. Economic Stabilization, Supply Side Economics, and the Social Economist. *Rev. Soc. Econ.*, October 1983, *41*(2), pp. 109–23.

McKinney, George W., Jr. The Need for Militant Moderatism. *Challenge*, March/April 1983, *26*(1), pp. 39–42.

Mendels, R. P. The Economist as a Consultant: A Note. *Amer. Econ.*, Fall 1983, *27*(2), pp. 86–88.

Ng, Yew-Kwang. Value Judgments and Economists' Role in Policy Recommendation. **In** *Marr, W. L. and Raj, B., eds.*, 1983, *1972*, pp. 39–47.

Okun, Arthur M. Political Economy: Some Lessons of Recent Experience. **In** *Okun, A. M.*, 1983, *1972*, pp. 450–70. **[G: U.S.]**

Okun, Arthur M. The Economist and Presidential Leadership. **In** *Okun, A. M.*, 1983, *1970*, pp. 577–83. **[G: U.S.]**

Pommerehne, Werner W.; Schneider, Friedrich and Frey, Bruno S. *Quot Homines, Tot Sententiae?* A Survey among Austrian Economists. *Empirica*, 1983, (2), pp. 93–127. **[G: Austria]**

Rao, B. Sarveswara. Some Issues of Relevance in Mainstream Economics—A Few Comments. *Indian Econ. J.*, April-June 1983, *30*(4), pp. 1–18.

Stanfield, J. Ron. Institutional Analysis: Toward Progress in Economic Science. **In** *Eichner, A. S., ed.*, 1983, pp. 187–204.

Stigler, George J. Statistical Studies in the History of Economic Thought. **In** *Stigler, G. J.*, 1983, pp. 31–50.

Stigler, George J. The Case, If Any, for Economic Literacy. *J. Econ. Educ.*, Summer 1983, *14*(3), pp. 60–66.

Stigler, George J. The Politics of Political Economists. **In** *Stigler, G. J.*, 1983, *1959*, pp. 51–65.

Vaughan, Roger J. Economists, Economics, and State Economic Policy. *Amer. Econ. Rev.*, May 1983, *73*(2), pp. 169–71. **[G: U.S.]**

Weber, Max. Economy and Society. **In** *Held, D., et al., eds.*, 1983, *1978*, pp. 113–16.

Whitman, Marina v.N. Economics from Three Perspectives. *Bus. Econ.*, January 1983, *18*(1), pp. 20–24. **[G: U.S.]**

0113 Relation of Economics to Other Disciplines

Barker, Randolph and Whyte, William Foote. Reorienting the Social Sciences. **In** *Whyte, W. F. and Boynton, D., eds.*, 1983, pp. 264–94.

Bennett, John W. and Kanel, Don. Agricultural Economics and Economic Anthropology: Confrontation and Accommodation. **In** *Ortiz, S., ed.*, 1983, pp. 201–47.

011 General Economics

Berdan, Frances F. The Reconstruction of Ancient Economies: Perspectives from Archaeology and Ethnohistory. **In** *Ortiz, S., ed.,* 1983, pp. 83–95.

Blanton, Richard E. Factors Underlying the Origin and Evolution of Market Systems. **In** *Ortiz, S., ed.,* 1983, pp. 51–66.

Blatt, John M. How Economists Misuse Mathematics. **In** *Eichner, A. S., ed.,* 1983, pp. 166–86.

Bolin, Meb. The Independent, Simultaneous Development of Instrumental Thoughts in Various Disciplines. *J. Econ. Issues,* June 1983, *17*(2), pp. 345–52.

Burkitt, Brian and Spiers, M. The Economic Theory of Politics: A Re-Appraisal. *Int. J. Soc. Econ.,* 1983, *10*(2), pp. 12–21.

Chanier, P. Trinitarisme, unitarisme et physique économique. (Trinitarism, Unitarism and Economic Physics. With English summary.) *Écon. Soc.,* June 1983, *17*(6), pp. 1003–55.

Dunlap, Riley E. Ecologist versus Exemptionalist: The Ehrlich-Simon Debate. *Soc. Sci. Quart.,* March 1983, *64*(1), pp. 200–203.

Gowler, Dan and Legge, Karen. The Meaning of Management and the Management of Meaning: A View from Social Anthropology. **In** *Earl, M. J., ed.,* 1983, pp. 197–233.

Gross, Daniel R. The Ecological Perspective in Economic Anthropology. **In** *Ortiz, S., ed.,* 1983, pp. 155–81.

Hakansson, Nils H. Accounting and Economics: Comment. *Accounting Rev.,* April 1983, *58*(2), pp. 381–84.

Hart, Keith. The Contribution of Marxism to Economic Anthropology. **In** *Ortiz, S., ed.,* 1983, pp. 105–44.

Hechter, Michael. Karl Polanyi's Social Theory: A Critique. **In** *Hechter, M., ed.,* 1983, pp. 158–89.

Hodgson, Dennis. Demography as Social Science and Policy Science. *Population Devel. Rev.,* March 1983, *9*(1), pp. 1–34. **[G: Global]**

Kornai, János. The Health of Nations: Reflections on the Analogy between the Medical Science and Economics. *Kyklos,* 1983, *36*(2), pp. 191–212.

Lerner, Abba P. Economics, Politltics, and Administration. **In** *Lerner, A. P.,* 1983, *1951,* pp. 315–30.

Lindenberg, Siegwart. Utility and Morality. *Kyklos,* 1983, *36*(3), pp. 450–68.

Neale, Walter C. and Mayhew, Anne. Polanyi, Institutional Economics, and Economic Anthropology. **In** *Ortiz, S., ed.,* 1983, pp. 11–20.

Ortiz, Sutti. Economic Anthropology: Topics and Theories: Introduction. **In** *Ortiz, S., ed.,* 1983, pp. vii–xvi.

Ross, Stephen A. Accounting and Economics. *Accounting Rev.,* April 1983, *58*(2), pp. 375–80.

Salisbury, Richard F. Anthropological Economic and Development Planning. **In** *Ortiz, S., ed.,* 1983, pp. 399–419.

Snoeyenbos, Milton; Almeder, Robert and Humber, James. Business Ethics: Introduction. **In** *Snoeyenbos, M.; Almeder, R. and Humber, J., eds.,* 1983, pp. 13–39.

Stanfield, J. Ron. Toward an Ecological Economics. *Int. J. Soc. Econ.,* 1983, *10*(5), pp. 27–37.

Tietzel, Manfred. Ökonomie und Soziobiologie oder: We kann was von wem lernen? (Economics and Sociobiology or: Who Can Learn from Whom and What? With English summary.) *Z. Wirtschaft. Sozialwissen.,* 1983, *103*(2), pp. 107–27.

Voge, Jean. The Political Economics of Complexity: From the Information Economy to the 'Complexity' Economy. *Info. Econ. Policy,* 1983, *1*(2), pp. 97–114.

0114 Relation of Economics to Social Values

Ahmad, Kabir U. An Empirical Study of Politico-Economic Interaction in the United States: A Comment. *Rev. Econ. Statist.,* February 1983, *65*(1), pp. 173–78. **[G: U.S.]**

Akerlof, George A. Loyalty Filters. *Amer. Econ. Rev.,* March 1983, *73*(1), pp. 54–63.

Anderson, Raymond L. Ethical Issues in Resource Economics: Discussion. *Amer. J. Agr. Econ.,* December 1983, *65*(5), pp. 1035–36.

Arrow, Kenneth J. The Place of Moral Obligation in Preference Systems. **In** *Arrow, K. J., Vol. 1,* 1983, *1967,* pp. 78–80.

Bauer, Peter T. The Grail of Equality. **In** *Letwin, W., ed.,* 1983, pp. 360–82.

Beeman, William O. Patterns of Religion and Economic Development in Iran from the Qajar Era to the Islamic Revolution of 1978–79. **In** *Finn, J., ed.,* 1983, pp. 73–103. **[G: Iran]**

Bennett, Douglas C. Catholicism, Capitalism, and the State in the Development of Mexico. **In** *Finn, J., ed.,* 1983, pp. 125–41. **[G: Mexico]**

Bienen, Henry S. Religion and Economic Change in Nigeria. **In** *Finn, J., ed.,* 1983, pp. 201–27. **[G: Nigeria]**

Blaug, Mark. Justifications for Subsidies to the Arts: A Reply to F. F. Ridley, "Cultural Economics and the Culture of Economists." *J. Cult. Econ.,* June 1983, *7*(1), pp. 19–22.

Boulding, Kenneth E. The Stability of Inequality. **In** *Letwin, W., ed.,* 1983, *1975,* pp. 261–75. **[G: U.S.]**

Brunner, Karl. The Perception of Man and Justice and the Conception of Political Institutions. **In** *[Giersch, H.],* 1983, pp. 327–55.

Burness, H. Stuart; Gorman, William D. and Lansford, Robert L. Economics, Ethics, and the Quantification of Indian Water Rights. *Amer. J. Agr. Econ.,* December 1983, *65*(5), pp. 1027–32. **[G: U.S.]**

Buultjens, Ralph. India: Values, Visions, and Economic Development. **In** *Finn, J., ed.,* 1983, pp. 17–34.

Choudhury, Masudul Alam. Insurance and Investment in Islamic Perspective. *Int. J. Soc. Econ.,* 1983, *10*(5), pp. 14–26.

Debertin, David L. Value Judgments and Efficiency in Publicly Supported Research: Discussion. *Southern J. Agr. Econ.,* July 1983, *15*(1), pp. 9–10.

Diskin, I. Socioeconomic Problems in the Development of the Cultural Infrastructure. *Prob. Econ.,* October 1983, *26*(6), pp. 3–22. **[G: U.S.S.R.]**

Dwyer, Larry. 'Value Freedom' and the Scope of Economic Inquiry: II. The Fact/Value Continuum and the Basis for Scientific and Humanistic

Policy. *Amer. J. Econ. Soc.*, July 1983, *42*(3), pp. 353–68.

Finn, James. Global Economics and Religion: Introduction. **In** *Finn, J., ed.*, 1983, pp. 1–9.

Frankel, Francine R. Religio-cultural Values, Political Gradualism, and Economic Development in India. **In** *Finn, J., ed.*, 1983, pp. 35–65. **[G: India]**

Goulet, Denis. Obstacles to World Development: An Ethical Reflection. *World Devel.*, July 1983, *11*(7), pp. 609–24.

Goulet, Denis. Overcoming Injustice: Possibilities and Limits. **In** *Skurski, R., ed.*, 1983, pp. 113–58.

van den Haag, Ernest. Against Natural Rights. *Policy Rev.*, Winter 1983, (23), pp. 143–75.

Hamlin, Alan P. Procedural Individualism and Outcome Liberalism. *Scot. J. Polit. Econ.*, November 1983, *30*(3), pp. 251–63.

Hasan, Zubair. Theory of Profit: The Islamic Viewpoint. *J. Res. Islamic Econ.*, Summer 1983, *1*(1), pp. 1–16.

von Hayek, Friedrich August. The Constitution of Liberty. **In** *Held, D., et al., eds.*, 1983, *1960*, pp. 127–29.

Heilbroner, Robert L. Economics as a "Value-free" Science. **In** *Marr, W. L. and Raj, B., eds.*, 1983, *1973*, pp. 27–38.

Hopkin, John A. Moral Responsibility in Agricultural Research: Discussion. *Southern J. Agr. Econ.*, July 1983, *15*(1), pp. 81–82. **[G: U.S.]**

Johnson, Harry G. Equality and Economic Theory. **In** *Letwin, W., ed.*, 1983, *1975*, pp. 276–93.

Kirsch, G. Ordnungspolitik zwischen Freiheit, Gleichheit, Brüderlichkeit. (Economic Policy and Liberty, Equality, Solidarity. With English summary.) *Schweiz. Z. Volkswirtsch. Statist.*, September 1983, *119*(3), pp. 357–80.

Koslowski, Peter F. The Ethics of Capitalism. **In** *Pejovich, S., ed.*, 1983, pp. 33–64.

Kristol, Irving. Business Ethics and Economic Man. **In** *Kristol, I.*, 1983, *1979*, pp. 219–23.

Ladd, George W. Value Judgments and Efficiency in Publicly Supported Research. *Southern J. Agr. Econ.*, July 1983, *15*(1), pp. 1–7.

Lerner, Abba P. Economics and the Control of Man. **In** *Lerner, A. P.*, 1983, *1960*, pp. 619–27.

Lerner, Abba P. Economics, Polilitics, and Administration. **In** *Lerner, A. P.*, 1983, *1951*, pp. 315–30.

Lindenberg, Siegwart. Utility and Morality. *Kyklos*, 1983, *36*(3), pp. 450–68.

Mannan, M. A. Islamic Economics as a Social Science: Some Methodological Issues. *J. Res. Islamic Econ.*, Summer 1983, *1*(1), pp. 49–61.

McQueen, David. Alternative Scenarios in Broadcasting. *Can. Public Policy*, March 1983, *9*(1), pp. 129–34. **[G: Canada]**

Mott, Tracy and Singell, Larry D. The Positive Treatment of Social Values: State of the Art. *J. Behav. Econ.*, Summer 1983, *12*(1), pp. 71–87.

Napier, Ron. Interrelationships of the Economic and Social Systems in Japan. **In** *Finn, J., ed.*, 1983, pp. 179–94. **[G: Japan]**

Norton, David L. Good Government, Justice, and Self-fulfilling Individuality. **In** *Skurski, R., ed.*, 1983, pp. 33–52.

Okun, Arthur M. Equal Rights but Unequal Incomes. **In** *Okun, A. M.*, 1983, *1976*, pp. 595–605. **[G: U.S.]**

Okun, Arthur M. Further Thoughts on Equality and Efficiency. **In** *Okun, A. M.*, 1983, *1977*, pp. 606–31. **[G: U.S.]**

Peacock, Alan. The Politics of Culture and the Ignorance of Political Scientists: A Reply to F. F. Ridley. *J. Cult. Econ.*, June 1983, *7*(1), pp. 23–26.

Pomerleau, Claude. Religion and Values in the Formation of Modern Mexico: Some Economic and Political Considerations. **In** *Finn, J., ed.*, 1983, pp. 143–60. **[G: Mexico]**

Ray, Benjamin C. Economic Values and Traditional Religion among the Yoruba of Nigeria. **In** *Finn, J., ed.*, 1983, pp. 229–39. **[G: Nigeria]**

Ridley, F. F. Cultural Economics and the Culture of Economists. *J. Cult. Econ.*, June 1983, *7*(1), pp. 1–18.

Ruttan, Vernon W. Moral Responsibility in Agricultural Research. *Southern J. Agr. Econ.*, July 1983, *15*(1), pp. 73–80. **[G: U.S.]**

Schmitz, Wolfgang. Economic and Social Partnership and Incomes Policy and the Social Doctrine of the Church. *Economia*, May 1983, *7*(2), pp. 307–29.

Schneider, Friedrich and Frey, Bruno S. An Empirical Study of Politico-Economic Interaction in the United States: A Reply. *Rev. Econ. Statist.*, February 1983, *65*(1), pp. 178–82. **[G: U.S.]**

Shinohara, Koichi. Religion and Economic Development in Japan: An Exploration Focusing on the Institution of *Ie*. **In** *Finn, J., ed.*, 1983, pp. 167–78. **[G: Japan]**

Tilman, Rick. Social Value Theory, Corporate Power, and Political Elites: Appraisals of Lindblom's *Politics and Markets*. *J. Econ. Issues*, March 1983, *17*(1), pp. 115–31.

Tisdell, Clem A. Dissent from Value, Preference and Choice Theory in Economics. *Int. J. Soc. Econ.*, 1983, *10*(2), pp. 32–43.

Tobin, James. The Conservative Counter-Revolution in Economic Policy. *J. Econ. Educ.*, Winter 1983, *14*(1), pp. 30–39. **[G: U.S.]**

Tool, Marc R. Equational Justice and Social Value. *J. Econ. Issues*, June 1983, *17*(2), pp. 335–44.

Ulmer, Melville J. Ideologies and Economic Science. *Atlantic Econ. J.*, March 1983, *11*(1), pp. 17–23.

Worland, Stephen T. Adam Smith: Economic Justice and the Founding Father. **In** *Skurski, R., ed.*, 1983, pp. 1–32.

0115 Methods Used by Economists

Blatt, John M. How Economists Misuse Mathematics. **In** *Eichner, A. S., ed.*, 1983, pp. 166–86.

Brookins, O. T. Economics as a Science: Some Theoretical Aspects. *Amer. Econ.*, Spring 1983, *27*(1), pp. 58–60.

Giarini, Orio. La notion de valeur économique dans la société post-industrielle: éléments pour la recherche de nouveaux paradigmes de l'économique. (The Notion of Economic Value in Post-Industrial Society: Elements towards Research on New Paradigms for Economics. With English summary.) *Écon. Soc.*, February 1983, *17*(2), pp. 299–334.

Hill, Lewis E. The Pragmatic Alternative to Positive Economics. *Rev. Soc. Econ.*, April 1983, *41*(1), pp. 1–11.

Leontief, Wassily W. Academic Economics. **In** *Marr, W. L. and Raj, B., eds.*, 1983, *1982*, pp. 331–35.

Leontief, Wassily W. Theoretical Assumptions and Nonobserved Facts. **In** *Marr, W. L. and Raj, B., eds.*, 1983, *1971*, pp. 321–30.

Machlup, Fritz. The Problem of Verification in Economics. **In** *Marr, W. L. and Raj, B., eds.*, 1983, *1955*, pp. 157–83.

Rich, Robert F. Making, Relaying, and Using Knowledge. **In** *Holzner, B.; Knorr, K. D. and Strasser, H., eds.*, 1983, pp. 220–35.

012 Teaching of Economics

0120 Teaching of Economics

Armento, Beverly J. A Study of the Basic Economic Concepts Presented in DEEP Curriculum Guides, Grades 7–12. *J. Econ. Educ.*, Summer 1983, *14*(3), pp. 22–27.

Bach, G. L. Above and Beyond the Call of Duty—A Tribute to Henry Villard. *J. Econ. Educ.*, Winter 1983, *14*(1), pp. 7–8. **[G: U.S.]**

Becker, William E., Jr. Economic Education Research: Part II, New Directions in Theoretical Model Building. *J. Econ. Educ.*, Spring 1983, *14*(2), pp. 4–10.

Becker, William E., Jr. Economic Education Research: Part III, Statistical Estimation Methods. *J. Econ. Educ.*, Summer 1983, *14*(3), pp. 4–15.

Becker, William E., Jr. Economic Education Research: Part I, Issues and Questions. *J. Econ. Educ.*, Winter 1983, *14*(1), pp. 10–17.

Blackwell, J. Lloyd. A Statistical Interpretation of Student Evaluation Feedback: A Comment. *J. Econ. Educ.*, Summer 1983, *14*(3), pp. 28–31. **[G: U.S.]**

Brandao, Antonio Salazar P. The U.S. Graduate Training in Agricultural Economics: The Perspective of a Former Foreign Student. *Amer. J. Agr. Econ.*, December 1983, *65*(5), pp. 1149–52. **[G: U.S.]**

Branson, William H. Macroeconomic Theory: Income Determination: Princeton University. *Amer. Econ.*, Spring 1983, *27*(1), pp. 79–86.

Buckles, Stephen and Freeman, Vera. Male–Female Differences in the Stock and Flow of Economic Knowledge. *Rev. Econ. Statist.*, May 1983, *65*(2), pp. 355–58. **[G: U.S.]**

Chizmar, John F. and Halinski, Ronald S. Performance in the *Basic Economics Test* (BET) and "Trade-offs." *J. Econ. Educ.*, Winter 1983, *14*(1), pp. 18–29. **[G: U.S.]**

Chizmar, John F. and Zak, Thomas A. Modeling Multiple Outputs in Educational Production Functions. *Amer. Econ. Rev.*, May 1983, *73*(2), pp. 17–22. **[G: U.S.]**

Dabysing, S. and Jones, D. I. H. A Simplified Post-Keynesian Model of Inflation for Teaching Purposes. *Brit. Rev. Econ. Issues*, Autumn 1983, *5*(13), pp. 87–105.

Darby, Michael R. A Syllabus for Macrodynamics: University of California, Los Angeles. *Amer. Econ.*, Spring 1983, *27*(1), pp. 71–78.

Dilley, Steven C.; Hayes, Randall B. and Steinbart, Paul. Development of a Paradigm for Applied Accounting Research: A Way of Coping with Subject-Matter Complexity. *Accounting Rev.*, April 1983, *58*(2), pp. 405–16.

Drèze, Jacques H. Nonspecialist Teaching of Econometrics: A Personal Comment and Personalistic Lament [University Teaching of Econometrics: A Personal View]. *Econometric Rev.*, 1983, *2*(2), pp. 291–99.

Ferber, Marianne A.; Birnbaum, Bonnie G. and Green, Carole A. Gender Differences in Economic Knowledge: A Reevaluation of the Evidence. *J. Econ. Educ.*, Spring 1983, *14*(2), pp. 24–37. **[G: U.S.]**

Frenzel, K. A. and McCready, D. J. Introductory Economics Texts: A Conflict between What Economists Do and Teach? *Eastern Econ. J.*, April–June 1983, *9*(2), pp. 111–17.

Friedman, Milton. A Monetarist View. *J. Econ. Educ.*, Fall 1983, *14*(4), pp. 44–55. **[G: U.S.; U.K.; Japan]**

Gay, David E. R. A Note on Professor Simmons and Teaching Law and Economics. *Atlantic Econ. J.*, December 1983, *11*(4), pp. 77. **[G: U.S.]**

Hansen, W. Lee. Improving Classroom Discussion in Economics Courses. *J. Econ. Educ.*, Winter 1983, *14*(1), pp. 40–49. **[G: U.S.]**

Hogan, Lloyd L. The Political Economy of Black Americans: Perspectives on Curriculum Development. *Rev. Black Polit. Econ.*, Winter 1983, *12*(2), pp. 145–61. **[G: U.S.]**

Howe, Keith R. and Baldwin, Bruce A. The Effects of Evaluative Sequencing on Performance, Behavior, and Attitudes. *Accounting Rev.*, January 1983, *58*(1), pp. 135–42.

Howells, P. G. A. and Bain, K. The Derivation of the LM Schedule—A Pedagogical Note. *Brit. Rev. Econ. Issues*, Spring 1983, *5*(12), pp. 57–65.

Johnson, Glenn L. The Relevance of U.S. Graduate Curricula in Agricultural Economics for the Training of Foreign Students. *Amer. J. Agr. Econ.*, December 1983, *65*(5), pp. 1142–48. **[G: U.S.]**

Karns, James M. L.; Burton, Gene E. and Martin, Gerald D. Learning Objectives and Testing: An Analysis of Six Principles of Economics Textbooks, Using Bloom's Taxonomy. *J. Econ. Educ.*, Summer 1983, *14*(3), pp. 16–20.

Kelley, Allen C. The Newspaper Can Be an Effective Teaching Tool. *J. Econ. Educ.*, Fall 1983, *14*(4), pp. 56–58.

Kourilsky, Marilyn and Kehret-Ward, Trudy. Determinants of Economic Reasoning in Monetary and Time-Allocation Decisions: An Exploratory Study. *J. Econ. Educ.*, Fall 1983, *14*(4), pp. 23–31. **[G: U.S.]**

Kregel, J. A. Post-Keynesian Theory: An Overview. *J. Econ. Educ.*, Fall 1983, *14*(4), pp. 32–43.

La Ferney, Preston E. An Administrative Perspective on Microcomputers for Agricultural Research and Education. *Southern J. Agr. Econ.*, July 1983, *15*(1), pp. 53–55. **[G: U.S.]**

Lord, Blair M. University Insurance Instructor: It

Is Time to Teach Problem Solving. *J. Risk Ins.*, June 1983, *50*(2), pp. 315–22.

Lumsden, Keith G. and Scott, Alex. The Efficacy of Innovative Teaching Techniques in Economics: The U.K. Experience. *Amer. Econ. Rev.*, May 1983, *73*(2), pp. 13–17. **[G: U.K.]**

Manahan, Jerry. An Educational Production Function for Principles of Economics. *J. Econ. Educ.*, Spring 1983, *14*(2), pp. 11–16. **[G: U.S.]**

Mazodier, Pascal. University Teaching of Econometrics: A Personal View: Comment. *Econometric Rev.*, 1983, *2*(2), pp. 301–06.

McConnell, Campbell. Readability: Blind Faith in Numbers? *J. Econ. Educ.*, Winter 1983, *14*(1), pp. 65–71.

O'Donnell, Margaret G. Harriet Martineau: A Popular Early Economics Educator. *J. Econ. Educ.*, Fall 1983, *14*(4), pp. 59–64.

Orpin, Christopher. Repeatable Testing as a Technique for Improving Management Education: A Research Note. *Australian J. Manage.*, June 1983, *8*(1), pp. 93–95. **[G: Australia]**

Outslay, Edmund; Robinson, John R. and Boley, Richard. A Framework for Utilizing Individual Return Problems in Introductory Tax Courses. *Accounting Rev.*, April 1983, *58*(2), pp. 428–38.

Owen, Wyn F. and Cross, Larry R. Foreign Students in Agricultural Economics from the Perspective of the Economics Institute. *Amer. J. Agr. Econ.*, December 1983, *65*(5), pp. 1136–41. **[G: U.S.]**

Phillips, P. C. B. On University Education in Econometrics. *Econometric Rev.*, 1983, *2*(2), pp. 307–15.

Reeve, James M. The Five-Year Accounting Program as a Quality Signal. *Accounting Rev.*, July 1983, *58*(3), pp. 639–46. **[G: U.S.]**

Reid, Roger. A Note on the Environment as a Factor Affecting Student Performance in Principles of Economics. *J. Econ. Educ.*, Fall 1983, *14*(4), pp. 18–22. **[G: U.S.]**

Robinson, J. Nicholas. A Macroeconomic Stabilization Game: Design, Development, and Testing. *J. Econ. Educ.*, Summer 1983, *14*(3), pp. 67–74.

Sawa, Takamitsu. University Teaching of Econometrics: A Personal View: Comment. *Econometric Rev.*, 1983, *2*(2), pp. 317–22.

Schmidt, Robert M. Who Maximizes What? A Study in Student Time Allocation. *Amer. Econ. Rev.*, May 1983, *73*(2), pp. 23–28. **[G: U.S.]**

Scott, Charles E. and Breeden, Charles H. Behavioral Style and Group Performance: An Empirical Study. *J. Behav. Econ.*, Summer 1983, *12*(1), pp. 99–119. **[G: U.S.]**

Seiver, Daniel A. Evaluations and Grades: A Simultaneous Framework. *J. Econ. Educ.*, Summer 1983, *14*(3), pp. 32–38. **[G: U.S.]**

Seiver, Daniel A. Fredonia: A Simulation Model for Teaching Undergraduate Development Economics. *J. Devel. Econ.*, Aug.–Oct. 1983, *13*(1–2), pp. 103–07.

Siegfried, John J. and Wilkinson, James T. The Business Economics Major in the United States. *Bus. Econ.*, January 1983, *18*(1), pp. 31–37. **[G: U.S.]**

Siegfried, John J. and Wilkinson, James T. The Economics and Business Economics Majors in the United States. *J. Econ. Educ.*, Winter 1983, *14*(1), pp. 50–59. **[G: U.S.]**

Solow, Robert M. Teaching Economics in the 1980s. *J. Econ. Educ.*, Spring 1983, *14*(2), pp. 65–68. **[G: U.S.]**

Soper, John C. and Walstad, William B. On Measuring Economic Attitudes. *J. Econ. Educ.*, Fall 1983, *14*(4), pp. 4–17. **[G: U.S.]**

Sowey, Eric R. The Teaching of Econometrics: Several Personal Views. *Econometric Rev.*, 1983, *2*(2), pp. 329–33.

Sowey, Eric R. University Teaching of Econometrics: A Personal View. *Econometric Rev.*, 1983, *2*(2), pp. 255–89.

Sterrett, Jack and Barr, Saul. Graduate Economics Programs in the United States. *J. Econ. Educ.*, Fall 1983, *14*(4), pp. 65–67. **[G: U.S.]**

Stigler, George J. The Case, If Any, for Economic Literacy. *J. Econ. Educ.*, Summer 1983, *14*(3), pp. 60–66.

Sussman, Jeffrey. A Note on Independent Study in Introductory Microeconomics. *J. Econ. Educ.*, Spring 1983, *14*(2), pp. 69–73. **[G: U.S.]**

Sweeney, M. Jane Barr, et al. The Structure of the Introductory Economics Course in United States Colleges. *J. Econ. Educ.*, Fall 1983, *14*(4), pp. 68–75. **[G: U.S.]**

Thomas, Arthur L. Use of Microcomputer Spreadsheet Software in Preparing and Grading Complex Accounting Problems. *Accounting Rev.*, October 1983, *58*(4), pp. 777–86.

Tinsley, W. A. Teaching with the Microcomputer: Adoption of a New Technology. *Southern J. Agr. Econ.*, July 1983, *15*(1), pp. 57–59. **[G: U.S.]**

Walstad, William B. and Buckles, Stephen. The New Economics Tests for the College and Pre-College Levels: A Comment. *J. Econ. Educ.*, Spring 1983, *14*(2), pp. 17–23. **[G: U.S.]**

Zellner, Arnold. University Teaching of Econometrics: A Personal View: Comment. *Econometric Rev.*, 1983, *2*(2), pp. 323–27.

020 General Economic Theory

0200 General Economic Theory

Albin, Peter S. Structural Theory and Structural Formations. *Math. Soc. Sci.*, November 1983, *6*(2), pp. 133–52.

Albin, Peter S. and Gottinger, Hans W. Structure and Complexity in Economic and Social Systems. *Math. Soc. Sci.*, September 1983, *5*(3), pp. 253–68.

Albin, Peter S. and Hormozi, Farrokh Z. Theoretical Reconciliation of Equilibrium and Structural Approaches. *Math. Soc. Sci.*, November 1983, *6*(2), pp. 261–84.

Ames, Edward. Automaton and Group Structures in Certain Economic Adjustment Mechanisms. *Math. Soc. Sci.*, November 1983, *6*(2), pp. 247–60.

d'Arcy, P. Le pluralisme dans la logique économique. (Pluralism and Economic Logic. With English summary.) *Écon. Soc.*, June 1983, *17*(6), pp. 959–82.

Arrow, Kenneth J. The Future and the Present in Economic Life. In *Arrow, K. J., Vol. 2*, 1983, *1978*,

pp. 275–89.

Arrow, Kenneth J. The Genesis of Dynamic Systems Governed by Metzler Matrices. **In** *Arrow, K. J., Vol. 2,* 1983, *1976,* pp. 245–64.

Arrow, Kenneth J. Tullock and an Existence Theorem. **In** *Arrow, K. J., Vol. 1,* 1983, *1969,* pp. 81–87.

Balasko, Yves. Extrinsic Uncertainty Revisited. *J. Econ. Theory,* December 1983, *31* (2), pp. 203–10.

Barucci, Piero. Economic Theory and Economic Policy in Historical Evolution of Economic Thought. *Rivista Polit. Econ.,* Supplement Dec. 1983, *73* (12), pp. 3–22.

Bausor, Randall. Time and the Structure of Economic Analysis. *J. Post Keynesian Econ.,* Winter 1982–83, *5* (2), pp. 163–79.

Bhagwati, Jagdish N. DUP Activities and Rent Seeking [Rent Seeking: A Survey]. *Kyklos,* 1983, *36* (4), pp. 634–37.

Blatt, John M. How Economists Misuse Mathematics. **In** *Eichner, A. S., ed.,* 1983, pp. 166–86.

Boland, Lawrence A. The Neoclassical Maximization Hypothesis: Reply. *Amer. Econ. Rev.,* September 1983, *73* (4), pp. 828–30.

Botha, D. J. J. Some Thoughts around the *General Theory* (Review Article). *S. Afr. J. Econ.,* September 1983, *51* (3), pp. 426–45.

Brahmananda, P. R. Joan Robinson, 1904–1983. *Indian Econ. J.,* July–September 1983, *31* (1), pp. 1–24.

Brittan, Samuel. Two Cheers for Utilitarianism. *Oxford Econ. Pap.,* November 1983, *35* (3), pp. 331–50.

Brittan, Samuel. Two Cheers for Utilitarianism. **In** *Brittan, S.,* 1983, pp. 22–47.

Caldwell, Bruce J. The Neoclassical Maximization Hypothesis: Comment. *Amer. Econ. Rev.,* September 1983, *73* (4), pp. 824–27.

Caravale, Giovanni. The Crisis in Economic Theories: Introduction. **In** *Caravale, G., ed.,* 1983, pp. 32–54.

Cass, David and Shell, Karl. Do Sunspots Matter? *J. Polit. Econ.,* April 1983, *91* (2), pp. 193–227.

Coddington, A. Positive Economics. **In** *Marr, W. L. and Raj, B., eds.,* 1983, *1972,* pp. 69–88.

De Alessi, Louis. Property Rights and X-Efficiency: Reply. *Amer. Econ. Rev.,* September 1983, *73* (4), pp. 843–45.

De Alessi, Louis. Property Rights, Transaction Costs, and X-Efficiency: An Essay in Economic Theory. *Amer. Econ. Rev.,* March 1983, *73* (1), pp. 64–81.

Demaria, Giovanni. Teoria economica dell'energia partenogenetica. (The Economics of Parthenogenetic Energy. With English summary.) *Rivista Int. Sci. Econ. Com.,* January 1983, *30* (1), pp. 5–40.

Dow, Sheila C. Substantive Mountains and Methodological Molehills: A Rejoinder [Weintraub and Wiles: The Methodological Basis of Policy Conflict]. *J. Post Keynesian Econ.,* Winter 1982–83, *5* (2), pp. 304–08.

Earl, Peter E. A Behavioral Theory of Economists' Behavior. **In** *Eichner, A. S., ed.,* 1983, pp. 90–125.

Eichner, Alfred S. Why Economics Is Not Yet a Science: Introduction. **In** *Eichner, A. S., ed.,* 1983, pp. 3–14.

Eichner, Alfred S. Why Economics Is Not Yet a Science. **In** *Eichner, A. S., ed.,* 1983, pp. 205–41.

Epstein, Larry G. and Hynes, J. Allan. The Rate of Time Preference and Dynamic Economic Analysis. *J. Polit. Econ.,* August 1983, *91* (4), pp. 611–35.

Gram, Harvey and Walsh, Vivian. Joan Robinson's Economics in Retrospect. *J. Econ. Lit.,* June 1983, *21* (2), pp. 518–50.

Heiner, Ronald A. The Origin of Predictable Behavior. *Amer. Econ. Rev.,* September 1983, *73* (4), pp. 560–95.

Hicks, John. Myrdal. **In** *Hicks, J.,* 1983, *1954,* pp. 343–46.

Hicks, John. Positive Economics? **In** *Hicks, J.,* 1983, *1965,* pp. 347–48.

Hildenbrand, Werner. Mathematical Economics: Twenty Papers of Gerard Debreu: Introduction. **In** *Debreu, G.,* 1983, pp. 1–29.

Kindleberger, Charles P. Standards as Public, Collective and Private Goods. *Kyklos,* 1983, *36* (3), pp. 377–96.

Kornai, János. Equilibrium as a Category of Economics. *Acta Oecon.,* 1983, *30* (2), pp. 145–59.

Kregel, J. A. Conceptions of Equilibrium, Conceptions of Time and Conceptions of Economic Interaction. **In** *Caravale, G., ed.,* 1983, *1975,* pp. 55–101.

Kristol, Irving. Rationalism in Economics. **In** *Kristol, I.,* 1983, *1980,* pp. 177–93.

Leibenstein, Harvey. Property Rights and X-Efficiency: Comment. *Amer. Econ. Rev.,* September 1983, *73* (4), pp. 831–42.

Leontief, Wassily W. Theoretical Assumptions and Nonobserved Facts. **In** *Marr, W. L. and Raj, B., eds.,* 1983, *1971,* pp. 321–30.

Mickwitz, Gösta. Kriser i ekonomi och teori. (Crises in Economic Environment and Theory. With English summary.) *Ekon. Samfundets Tidskr.,* 1983, *36* (4), pp. 139–50.

Mincer, Jacob. George Stigler's Contributions to Economics. *Scand. J. Econ.,* 1983, *85* (1), pp. 65–75.

Mirowski, Philip. An Evolutionary Theory of Economics Change: A Review Article. *J. Econ. Issues,* September 1983, *17* (3), pp. 757–68.

Rao, B. Sarveswara. Some Issues of Relevance in Mainstream Economics—A Few Comments. *Indian Econ. J.,* April-June 1983, *30* (4), pp. 1–18.

Ricossa, Sergio. Scarcity or Producibility. An Inexistant Dilemma. *Rivista Polit. Econ.,* Supplement Dec. 1983, *73* (12), pp. 133–45.

Ritschard, Gilbert. Computable Qualitative Comparative Static Techniques. *Econometrica,* July 1983, *51* (4), pp. 1145–68.

Roy, Subroto. Economic Theory and Development Economics: A Comment. *World Devel.,* October 1983, *11* (10), pp. 901–03.

Rugina, Anghel N. Toward a Third Revolution in Economic Thinking: The Concept of Balanced (Equilibrium) Growth and Social Economics. *Int. J. Soc. Econ.,* 1983, *10* (1), pp. 3–46.

Schotter, Andrew. Why Take a Game Theoretical Approach to Economics? Institutions, Economics and Game Theory. *Écon. Appl.*, 1983, *36*(4), pp. 673–95.

Sen, Amartya K. The Profit Motive. *Lloyds Bank Rev.*, January 1983, (147), pp. 1–20.

Shackle, George L. S. Review Article: Decisions, Process and the Market. *J. Econ. Stud.*, 1983, *10*(3), pp. 56–66.

Shackle, George L. S. Time and the Structure of Economic Analysis: Comment. *J. Post Keynesian Econ.*, Winter 1982–83, *5*(2), pp. 180–81.

Sonnenschein, Hugo. The Economics of Incentives: An Introductory Account. **In** *[Yamada, I.]*, 1983, pp. 79–92.

Stanfield, J. Ron. Institutional Analysis: Toward Progress in Economic Science. **In** *Eichner, A. S., ed.*, 1983, pp. 187–204.

Stigler, George J. Nobel Lecture: The Process and Progress of Economics. *J. Polit. Econ.*, August 1983, *91*(4), pp. 529–45.

Suzumura, Kotaro. Perron–Frobenius Theorem on Non-Negative Square Matrices: An Elementary Proof. *Hitotsubashi J. Econ.*, December 1983, *24*(2), pp. 137–41.

Troub, Roger M. General Adjustment Theory and Institutional Adjustment Processes. *J. Econ. Issues*, June 1983, *17*(2), pp. 315–24. [G: U.S.]

Weintraub, E. Roy. Substantive Mountains and Methodological Molehills: Comment [Weintraub and Wiles: The Methodological Basis of Policy Conflict]. *J. Post Keynesian Econ.*, Winter 1982–83, *5*(2), pp. 295–303.

Wilkinson, Frank. Productive Systems. *Cambridge J. Econ.*, September/December 1983, *7*(3/4), pp. 413–29.

Wiseman, Jack. Beyond Positive Economics—Dream and Reality. **In** *Wiseman, J., ed.*, 1983, pp. 13–27.

Young, Jeffrey T. Entropy, Scarcity, and Neo-Ricardianism. *J. Post Keynesian Econ.*, Fall 1983, *6*(1), pp. 82–88.

021 General Equilibrium and Disequilibrium Theory

0210 General

Aliprantis, Charalambos D. and Brown, Donald J. Equilibria in Markets with a Riesz Space of Commodities. *J. Math. Econ.*, April 1983, *11*(2), pp. 189–207.

Allen, Beth. Expectations Equilibria with Dispersed Information: Existence with Approximate Rationality in a Model with a Continuum of Agents and Finitely Many States of the World. *Rev. Econ. Stud.*, April 1983, *50*(2), pp. 267–85.

Arrow, Kenneth J. Alternative Proof of the Substitution Theorem for Leontief Models in the General Case. **In** *Arrow, K. J., Vol. 2*, 1983, *1951*, pp. 1–12.

Arrow, Kenneth J. An Extension of the Basic Theorems of Classical Welfare Economics. **In** *Arrow, K. J., Vol. 2*, 1983, *1951*, pp. 13–45.

Arrow, Kenneth J. Cost-theoretical and Demand-theoretical Approaches to the Theory of Price Determination. **In** *Arrow, K. J., Vol. 2*, 1983, *1973*, pp. 227–44.

Arrow, Kenneth J. Economic Equilibrium. **In** *Arrow, K. J., Vol. 2*, 1983, *1968*, pp. 107–32.

Arrow, Kenneth J. Existence of an Equilibrium for a Competitive Economy. **In** *Arrow, K. J., Vol. 2*, 1983, *1954*, pp. 58–91.

Arrow, Kenneth J. General Economic Equilibrium: Purpose, Analytic Techniques, Collective Choice. **In** *Arrow, K. J., Vol. 2*, 1983, *1972*, pp. 199–226.

Arrow, Kenneth J. Import Substitution in Leontief Models. **In** *Arrow, K. J., Vol. 2*, 1983, *1954*, pp. 92–106.

Arrow, Kenneth J. Quantity Adjustments in Resource Allocation: A Statistical Interpretation. **In** *Arrow, K. J., Vol. 2*, 1983, *1976*, pp. 265–74.

Arrow, Kenneth J. The Firm in General Equilibrium Theory. **In** *Arrow, K. J., Vol. 2*, 1983, *1971*, pp. 156–98.

Arrow, Kenneth J. The Organization of Economic Activity: Issues Pertinent to the Choice of Market versus Nonmarket Allocation. **In** *Arrow, K. J., Vol. 2*, 1983, *1969*, pp. 133–55.

Arrow, Kenneth J. The Role of Securities in the Optimal Allocation of Risk Bearing. **In** *Arrow, K. J., Vol. 2*, 1983, *1963*, pp. 46–57.

Arrow, Kenneth J. and Debreu, Gerard. Existence of an Equilibrium for a Competitive Economy. **In** *Debreu, G.*, 1983, *1954*, pp. 68–97.

Aubin, Jean-Pierre. Exemples de mécanismes décentralisés de régulation par les prix dans un contexte de déséquilibre. (Example of Decentralized Price Regulation Mechanism in a Disequilibrium Framework. With English summary.) *Écon. Appl.*, 1983, *36*(2–3), pp. 333–47.

Beato, Paulina and Mas-Colell, Andreu. Gestion au coût marginal et efficacité de la production agrégée: un exemple. (Marginal Cost Management and Efficiency of Aggregate Production: An Example. With English summary.) *Ann. INSEE*, July–September 1983, (51), pp. 39–46.

Becker, Robert A. A Simple Dynamic Equilibrium Model with Adjustment Costs. *J. Econ. Dynam. Control*, September 1983, *6*(1/2), pp. 79–98.

Bergstrom, Theodore C.; Simon, Carl P. and Titus, Charles J. Counting Groves–Ledyard Equilibria via Degree Theory. *J. Math. Econ.*, October 1983, *12*(2), pp. 167–84.

Bewley, Truman. A Difficulty with the Optimum Quantity of Money. *Econometrica*, September 1983, *51*(5), pp. 1485–504.

Bliss, Christopher. Consistent Temporary Equilibrium. **In** *Fitoussi, J.-P., ed.*, 1983, pp. 141–52.

Bowers, Patricia F. A Theoretical Analysis of the Exchange Process and Inflation. **In** *Schmukler, N. and Marcus, E., eds.*, 1983, pp. 120–32.

Brown, Donald J. and Heal, Geoffrey M. Marginal vs. Average Cost Pricing in the Presence of a Public Monopoly. *Amer. Econ. Rev.*, May 1983, *73*(2), pp. 189–93.

Calvo, Guillermo A. and Phelps, Edmund S. A Model of Non-Walrasian General Equilibrium. **In** *Tobin, J., ed.*, 1983, pp. 135–50.

Champsaur, Paul and Rochet, Jean-Charles. On Planning Procedures Which Are Locally Strategy Proof. *J. Econ. Theory*, August 1983, *30*(2), pp. 353–69.

Chander, Parkash. On the Information Efficiency of

the Competitive Resource Allocation Process. *J. Econ. Theory,* October 1983, *31* (1), pp. 54–67.

Chander, Parkash. The Nonlinear Input–Output Model. *J. Econ. Theory,* August 1983, *30*(2), pp. 219–29.

Chang, Winston W.; Kemp, Murray C. and Long, Ngo Van. Dynamic Properties of a Simple Overlapping-Generations Model. *Oxford Econ. Pap.,* November 1983, *35*(3), pp. 366–72.

Cheng, Hsueh-Cheng. A Uniform Core Convergence Result for Non-convex Economies. *J. Econ. Theory,* December 1983, *31* (2), pp. 269–82.

Cheng, Hsueh-Cheng. The Best Rate of Convergence of the Core. *Int. Econ. Rev.,* October 1983, *24*(3), pp. 629–36.

Cheng, Leonard and Hart, David. The Local Stability of an Open-Loop Nash Equilibrium in a Finite Horizon Differential Game. *J. Math. Econ.,* October 1983, *12*(2), pp. 139–47.

Cohen, Avi J. and Cohen, Jon S. Classical and Neoclassical Theories of General Equilibrium [A Review Article]. *Australian Econ. Pap.,* June 1983, *22*(40), pp. 180–200.

Conn, David. Comparative Economic Systems Theory: Progress and Prospects. *ACES Bull. (See Comp. Econ. Stud. after 8/85),* Summer 1983, *25*(2), pp. 61–80.

Cornet, Bernard. Neutrality of Planning Procedures. *J. Math. Econ.,* April 1983, *11* (2), pp. 141–60.

Cowen, Tyler. The Rate of Return in General Equilibrium—A Critique. *J. Post Keynesian Econ.,* Summer 1983, *5* (4), pp. 608–17.

Debreu, Gerard. A Classical Tax-Subsidy Problem. **In** *Debreu, G.,* 1983, *1954,* pp. 59–67.

Debreu, Gerard. A Social Equilibrium Existence Theorem. **In** *Debreu, G.,* 1983, *1952,* pp. 50–58.

Debreu, Gerard. Economies with a Finite Set of Equilibria. **In** *Debreu, G.,* 1983, *1970,* pp. 179–85.

Debreu, Gerard. Four Aspects of the Mathematical Theory of Economic Equilibrium. **In** *Debreu, G.,* 1983, *1974,* pp. 217–31.

Debreu, Gerard. Market Equilibrium. **In** *Debreu, G.,* 1983, *1956,* pp. 111–14.

Debreu, Gerard. New Concepts and Techniques for Equilibrium Analysis. **In** *Debreu, G.,* 1983, *1962,* pp. 133–50.

Debreu, Gerard. Smooth Preferences. **In** *Debreu, G.,* 1983, *1972,* pp. 186–201.

Debreu, Gerard. The Application to Economics of Differential Topology and Global Analysis: Regular Differentiable Economies. **In** *Debreu, G.,* 1983, *1976,* pp. 232–41.

Debreu, Gerard. The Rate of Convergence of the Core of an Economy. **In** *Debreu, G.,* 1983, *1975,* pp. 210–16.

Debreu, Gerard. Valuation Equilibrium and Pareto Optimum. **In** *Debreu, G.,* 1983, *1954,* pp. 98–104.

Debreu, Gerard and Scarf, Herbert. A Limit Theorem on the Core of an Economy. **In** *Debreu, G.,* 1983, *1963,* pp. 151–62.

Denzau, Arthur T. and Parks, Robert P. Existence of Voting-Market Equilibria. *J. Econ. Theory,* August 1983, *30*(2), pp. 243–65.

Donaldson, John B. A Note on Value Maximization for Consumption Sets in *l*. *J. Econ. Theory,* June 1983, *30*(1), pp. 191–200.

Eden, Benjamin. On Competitive Price Adjustment for a Storable Good and Abstention from Trade. *J. Polit. Econ.,* December 1983, *91* (6), pp. 1028–44.

Ellickson, Bryan. Indivisibility, Housing Markets, and Public Goods. **In** *Henderson, J. V., ed.,* 1983, pp. 91–116.

Ellis, Christopher J. A Note on Walrasian Equilibria in Non-Walrasian Models. *Europ. Econ. Rev.,* September 1983, *23*(1), pp. 55–58.

Escude, Guillermo. Equilibrio General Walrasiano y no-Walrasiano en una Economía de Leontief. (General Walrasian and Non-Walrasian Equilibrium in a Leontief Economy. With English summary.) *Económica,* May–December 1983, *29*(2–3), pp. 217–39.

Filippini, Luigi. Price and Quantity Adjustment in a Dynamic Closed Model: The Dual Stability Theorem. *J. Macroecon.,* Spring 1983, *5*(2), pp. 185–96.

Flaschel, Peter. Actual Labor Values in a General Model of Production. *Econometrica,* March 1983, *51* (2), pp. 435–54.

Florenzano, Monique. On the Existence of Equilibria in Economies with an Infinite Dimensional Commodity Space. *J. Math. Econ.,* December 1983, *12*(3), pp. 207–19.

Fuchs, Gérard and Guesnerie, Roger. Structure of Tax Equilibria. *Econometrica,* March 1983, *51* (2), pp. 403–34.

Fujimoto, Takao; Herrero, Carmen and Villar, Antonia. Technical Changes and Their Effects on the Price Structure. *Metroecon.,* February–June 1983, *35*(1–2), pp. 123–27.

Gardner, Roy. λ-transfer Value and Fixed-Price Equilibrium in Two-Sided Markets. **In** *Pattanaik, P. K. and Salles, M., eds.,* 1983, pp. 301–23.

Ginsburgh, Victor and Waelbroeck, Jean. Generalized Tâtonnement and the Solution of Economic Models. *Econ. Rec.,* June 1983, *59*(165), pp. 111–17.

Goodwin, R. M. Static and Dynamic Linear General Equilibrium Models. **In** *Goodwin, R. M.,* 1983, *1953,* pp. 75–120.

Gordon, Wendell C. Errata [Welfare Maxima in Economics]. *J. Econ. Issues,* September 1983, *17*(3), pp. 585.

Gordon, Wendell C. Welfare Maxima in Economics. *J. Econ. Issues,* March 1983, *17*(1), pp. 1–6.

Gourieroux, Christian; Laffont, Jean-Jacques and Monfort, Alain. Révision adaptative des anticipations et convergence vers les anticipations rationnelles. (Adaptative Revision of Expectations and Convergence towards Rational Expectations. With English summary.) *Écon. Appl.,* 1983, *36*(1), pp. 9–26.

Greenberg, Joseph. Local Public Goods with Mobility: Existence and Optimality of a General Equilibrium. *J. Econ. Theory,* June 1983, *30*(1), pp. 17–33.

Greenberg, Joseph and Weber, Shlomo. A Core Equivalence Theorem with an Arbitrary Communication Structure. *J. Math. Econ.,* January 1983, *11* (1), pp. 43–55.

Haga, Hanjiro and Matsumoto, Akio. Economic

Equilibrium under Price Rigidities and Quantity Constraints. In *[Yamada, I.]*, 1983, pp. 93–102.

Hahn, F. H. On General Equilibrium and Stability. In *Brown, E. C. and Solow, R. M., eds.*, 1983, pp. 31–53.

Hands, Douglas W. Stability in a Discrete Time Model of the Walrasian Tâtonnement. *J. Econ. Dynam. Control,* December 1983, *6*(4), pp. 399–411.

Hicks, John. Linear Theory. In *Hicks, J.*, 1983, *1960,* pp. 246–91.

Hildenbrand, Werner. Mathematical Economics: Twenty Papers of Gerard Debreu: Introduction. In *Debreu, G.*, 1983, pp. 1–29.

Homma, Masaaki and Osano, Hiroshi. The Structural Stability of an Implicit Labor Contract System. (In Japanese. With English summary.) *Econ. Stud. Quart.*, August 1983, *34*(2), pp. 133–46.

Ichiishi, Tatsuro and Quinzii, Martine. Decentralization for the Core of a Production Economy with Increasing Returns. *Int. Econ. Rev.*, June 1983, *24*(2), pp. 397–412.

Ichiishi, Tatsuro and Schäffer, Juan Jorge. The Topological Core of a Game Without Sidepayments. *Econ. Stud. Quart.*, April 1983, *34*(1), pp. 1–8.

Imai, Haruo. Voting, Bargaining, and Factor Income Distribution. *J. Math. Econ.*, July 1983, *11*(3), pp. 211–33.

Jaffé, William. Another Look at Léon Walras's Theory of *Tâtonnement.* In *Jaffé, W.*, 1983, *1981,* pp. 244–66.

Jaffé, William. The Normative Bias of the Walrasian Model: Walras versus Gossen. In *Jaffé, W.*, 1983, *1977,* pp. 326–42.

Jaffé, William. Walras's Economics as Others See It. In *Jaffé, W.*, 1983, *1980,* pp. 343–70.

Jaffé, William. Walras's Theory of *Tâtonnement:* A Critique of Recent Interpretations. In *Jaffé, W.*, 1983, *1967,* pp. 221–43.

John, Andrew. The Major-General Theory. *J. Post Keynesian Econ.*, Fall 1983, *6*(1), pp. 122–24.

John, Kose and Majthay, Antal. Structural Stability of Market Models. *Math. Soc. Sci.*, August 1983, *5*(1), pp. 89–95.

Jones, Larry E. Existence of Equilibria with Infinitely Many Consumers and Infinitely Many Commodities: A Theorem Based on Models of Commodity Differentiation. *J. Math. Econ.*, October 1983, *12*(2), pp. 119–38.

Jordan, J. S. Locally Stable Price Mechanisms. *J. Math. Econ.*, July 1983, *11*(3), pp. 235–59.

Jorgenson, Dale W. Modeling Production for General Equilibrium Analysis. *Scand. J. Econ.*, 1983, *85*(2), pp. 101–12. **[G: U.S.]**

Kehoe, Timothy J. Regularity and Index Theory for Economies with Smooth Production Technologies. *Econometrica,* July 1983, *51*(4), pp. 895–917.

Kim, Oliver. Balanced Equilibrium in a Consumption Loans Model. *J. Econ. Theory,* April 1983, *29*(2), pp. 339–46.

Kuboniwa, Masaaki. A Comparison of Convergence Speed of Old and New Iterative Processes for an Input–Output System. *Hitotsubashi J. Econ.*, December 1983, *24*(2), pp. 143–48.

van der Laan, G. Note on the Optimality of Unemployment Equilibria. *J. Math. Econ.*, October 1983, *12*(2), pp. 185–90.

Laroque, Guy and Rochet, Jean-Charles. Myopic versus Intertemporal Manipulation in Decentralized Planning Procedures. *Rev. Econ. Stud.*, January 1983, *50*(1), pp. 187–95.

Mainwaring, L. A Reconsideration of Exchange and Accumulation in Marx [Marxian Economics as General Equilibrium Theory]. *Australian Econ. Pap.*, December 1983, *22*(41), pp. 454–66.

Makowski, Louis. Competitive Stock Markets. *Rev. Econ. Stud.*, April 1983, *50*(2), pp. 305–30.

Mas-Colell, Andreu. Walrasian Equilibria as Limits of Noncooperative Equilibria. Part I: Mixed Strategies. *J. Econ. Theory,* June 1983, *30*(1), pp. 153–70.

McKenzie, Lionel W. Turnpike Theory, Discounted Utility, and the von Neumann Facet. *J. Econ. Theory,* August 1983, *30*(2), pp. 330–52.

Muench, Thomas and Walker, Mark. Are Groves–Ledyard Equilibria Attainable? [Optimal Allocation of Public Goods: A Solution to the "Free Rider" Problem]. *Rev. Econ. Stud.*, April 1983, *50*(2), pp. 393–96.

Myerson, Roger B. A Dynamic Microeconomic Model with Durable Goods and Adaptive Expectations. *J. Econ. Behav. Organ.*, December 1983, *4*(4), pp. 309–51.

Nagatani, Keizo. Macroeconomic Foundations of Macroeconomics. In *[Yamada, I.]*, 1983, pp. 51–63.

Nicola, Piercarlo. Pareto Optimality When Production Is Lagged. *Giorn. Econ.*, November–December 1983, *42*(11–12), pp. 719–23.

Nielsen, Lars Tyge. Pareto Optima, Non-Convexities and Regulated Market Equilibria. *J. Math. Econ.*, January 1983, *11*(1), pp. 57–63.

Novshek, William and Sonnenschein, Hugo. Walrasian Equilibria as Limits of Noncooperative Equilibria. Part II: Pure Strategies. *J. Econ. Theory,* June 1983, *30*(1), pp. 171–87.

Okuno, Masahiro and Zilcha, Itzhak. Optimal Steady-State in Stationary Consumption-Loan Type Models. *J. Econ. Theory,* December 1983, *31*(2), pp. 355–63.

Peters, Michael and Winter, Ralph A. Market Equilibrium and the Resolution of Uncertainty. *Can. J. Econ.*, August 1983, *16*(3), pp. 381–90.

Polemarchakis, Heraklis M. On the Transer Paradox. *Int. Econ. Rev.*, October 1983, *24*(3), pp. 749–60.

Polterovich, V. M. and Spivak, V. A. Erratum [Gross Substitutability of Point-to-Set Correspondences]. *J. Math. Econ.*, October 1983, *12*(2), pp. 191.

Polterovich, V. M. and Spivak, V. A. Gross Substitutability of Point-to-Set Correspondences. *J. Math. Econ.*, April 1983, *11*(2), pp. 117–40.

Pomery, John. Restricted Stock Markets in Simple General Equilibrium Models with Production Uncertainty. *J. Int. Econ.*, November 1983, *15*(3/4), pp. 253–76.

Rouzaud, Catherine. Anticipations rationnelles et information révélée par les prix: une introduction. (Rational Expectations and Information Revealed by Prices: An Introduction. With English summary.) *Revue Écon.*, November 1983, *34*(6), pp. 1116–44.

Safra, Zvi. Manipulation by Reallocating Initial Endowments. *J. Math. Econ.*, September 1983, *12*(1), pp. 1–17.

Samuelson, Paul A. Durable Capital Inputs: Conditions for Price Ratios to Be Invariant to Profit–Rate Changes. *Z. Nationalökon.*, 1983, *43*(1), pp. 1–20.

Scapparone, Paolo. Esistenza dell'equilibrio economico generale con preferenze non complete. (On the Existence of General Economic Equilibrium with Incomplete Preferences. With English summary.) *Giorn. Econ.*, May-June 1983, *42*(5–6), pp. 347–68.

Scheinkman, José A. and Schechtman, Jack. A Simple Competitive Model with Production and Storage. *Rev. Econ. Stud.*, July 1983, *50*(3), pp. 427–41.

Schulz, Norbert. On the Global Uniqueness of Fix-Price Equilibria. *Econometrica,* January 1983, *51*(1), pp. 47–68.

Schweizer, Urs. Efficient Exchange with a Variable Number of Consumers. *Econometrica,* May, 1983, *51*(3), pp. 575–84.

Shitovitz, Benyamin. The Proportion of Blocking Coalitions in Atomless Economies. *J. Math. Econ.*, December 1983, *12*(3), pp. 247–55.

Shubik, Martin and Wooders, Myrna Holtz. Approximate Cores of Replica Games and Economies. Part I: Replica Games, Externalities, and Approximate Cores. *Math. Soc. Sci.,* October 1983, *6*(1), pp. 27–48.

Shubik, Martin and Wooders, Myrna Holtz. Approximate Cores of Replica Games and Economies. Part II: Set-Up Costs and Firm Formation in Coalition Production Economies. *Math. Soc. Sci.*, December 1983, *6*(3), pp. 285–306.

Silvestre, Joaquim. Fixprice Analysis in Productive Economies. *J. Econ. Theory,* August 1983, *30*(2), pp. 401–09.

Silvestre, Joaquim. Fixprice Analysis with Intermediate Goods. *Int. Econ. Rev.*, June 1983, *24*(2), pp. 485–92.

Spence, A. Michael. A Model of Non-Walrasian General Equilibrium: Comment. **In** *Tobin, J., ed.*, 1983, pp. 150–55.

Stephan, Gunter. Roundaboutness, Nontightness and Malinvaud Prices in Multisector Models with Infinite Horizon. *Z. ges. Staatswiss.*, December 1983, *139*(4), pp. 660–77.

Svensson, Lars-Gunnar. Large Indivisibles: An Analysis with Respect to Price Equilibrium and Fairness. *Econometrica,* July 1983, *51*(4), pp. 939–54.

Thorlund-Petersen, Lars. Existence of Proportional Distribution Schemes: A Note. *J. Math. Econ.*, January 1983, *11*(1), pp. 77–79.

Tillmann, Georg. Existence of a Temporary Equilibrium in a Three-Commodity Model. *Rev. Econ. Stud.*, July 1983, *50*(3), pp. 573–79.

Tillmann, Georg. Stability in a Simple Pure Consumption Loan Model. *J. Econ. Theory,* August 1983, *30*(2), pp. 315–29.

Townsend, Robert M. Financial Structure and Economic Activity. *Amer. Econ. Rev.*, December 1983, *73*(5), pp. 895–911.

Tressler, J. H. and Menezes, C. F. Constant Returns to Scale and Competitive Equilibrium under Uncertainty. *J. Econ. Theory,* December 1983, *31*(2), pp. 383–91.

Vind, Karl. Equilibrium with Coordination. *J. Math. Econ.*, December 1983, *12*(3), pp. 275–85.

Weddepohl, Claus. Developments in the Theory of General Equilibrium. *De Economist,* 1983, *131*(3), pp. 373–99.

Weintraub, E. Roy. On the Existence of a Competitive Equilibrium: 1930–1954. *J. Econ. Lit.*, March 1983, *21*(1), pp. 1–39.

Winter, Sidney G. A Model of non-Walrasian General Equilibrium: Comment. **In** *Tobin, J., ed.*, 1983, pp. 155–57.

Wooders, Myrna Holtz. The Epsilon Core of a Large Replica Game. *J. Math. Econ.*, July 1983, *11*(3), pp. 277–300.

Yamazaki, Akira. Competitive Firm Structures and Equilibria in a Coalition Production Economy. *Hitotsubashi J. Econ.*, June 1983, *24*(1), pp. 69–94.

Yamazaki, Akira. Continuous Preference Relations Which Are Observable in Markets. *Hitotsubashi J. Econ.*, February 1983, *23*(2), pp. 40–47.

Yamazaki, Akira. On Open Preferences. *Hitotsubashi J. Econ.*, December 1983, *24*(2), pp. 149–52.

Yannelis, Nicholas C. Existence and Fairness of Value Allocation without Convex Preferences. *J. Econ. Theory,* December 1983, *31*(2), pp. 283–92.

Yannelis, Nicholas C. and Prabhakar, N. D. Existence of Maximal Elements and Equilibria in Linear Topological Spaces. *J. Math. Econ.*, December 1983, *12*(3), pp. 233–45.

Zikry, Emad. A Note on the Stability Requirements in Disequilibrium States. *Amer. Econ.*, Fall 1983, *27*(2), pp. 77–79.

022 Microeconomic Theory

0220 General

Ackley, Gardner. Commodities and Capital: Prices and Quantities. *Amer. Econ. Rev.*, March 1983, *73*(1), pp. 1–16.

Araujo, A. and Scheinkman, José A. Maximum Principle and Transversality Condition for Concave Infinite Horizon Economic Models. *J. Econ. Theory,* June 1983, *30*(1), pp. 1–16.

Arrow, Kenneth J. Cost-theoretical and Demand-theoretical Approaches to the Theory of Price Determination. **In** *Arrow, K. J., Vol. 2,* 1983, *1973,* pp. 227–44.

Arrow, Kenneth J. Rawls's Principle of Just Saving. **In** *Arrow, K. J., Vol. 1,* 1983, *1973,* pp. 133–46.

Becker, Robert A. A Simple Dynamic Equilibrium Model with Adjustment Costs. *J. Econ. Dynam. Control,* September 1983, *6*(1/2), pp. 79–98.

Biswas, Tapan. A Note on the Generalised Measures of Risk Aversion. *J. Econ. Theory,* April 1983, *29*(2), pp. 347–52.

Bowbrick, Peter. The Economics of Superstars: Comment. *Amer. Econ. Rev.*, June 1983, *73*(3), pp. 459.

Boyer, Marcel and Dionne, Georges. Variations in the Probability and Magnitude of Loss: Their Impact on Risk. *Can. J. Econ.*, August 1983, *16*(3), pp. 411–19.

Brambilla, Francesco. Un modello economico della professione medica. (An Economic Model of the Physician's Profession. With English summary.) *Giorn. Econ.*, May-June 1983, *42*(5–6), pp. 289–94.

Carruth, Alan. On the Quantitative Significance of Imperfect Information. *Europ. Econ. Rev.*, January 1983, *20*(1–3), pp. 365–79.

Champsaur, Paul and Rochet, Jean-Charles. On Planning Procedures Which Are Locally Strategy Proof. *J. Econ. Theory*, August 1983, *30*(2), pp. 353–69.

Chenault, Larry A. and Flueckiger, Gerald E. An Information Theoretic Model of Bounded Rationality. *Math. Soc. Sci.*, November 1983, *6*(2), pp. 227–46.

Cornides, Thomas. Karl Menger's Contributions to Social Thought. *Math. Soc. Sci.*, October 1983, *6*(1), pp. 1–11.

Davidson, Paul. Rational Expectations: A Fallacious Foundation for Studying Crucial Decision-Making Processes. *J. Post Keynesian Econ.*, Winter 1982–83, *5*(2), pp. 182–98.

Debreu, Gerard. Neighboring Economic Agents. **In** *Debreu, G.*, 1983, *1969*, pp. 173–78.

Debreu, Gerard. Smooth Preferences. **In** *Debreu, G.*, 1983, *1972*, pp. 186–201.

Dolton, Peter J. Lemons and Supergames. *Bull. Econ. Res.*, May 1983, *35*(1), pp. 55–64.

Eeckhoudt, Louis and Hansen, Pierre. Micro-Economic Applications of Marginal Changes in Risk. *Europ. Econ. Rev.*, July 1983, *22*(2), pp. 167–76.

Elbadawi, Ibrahim; Gallant, A. Ronald and Souza, Geraldo. An Elasticity Can Be Estimated Consistently without A Priori Knowledge of Functional Form. *Econometrica*, November 1983, *51*(6), pp. 1731–51.

Epstein, Larry G. and Hynes, J. Allan. The Rate of Time Preference and Dynamic Economic Analysis. *J. Polit. Econ.*, August 1983, *91*(4), pp. 611–35.

Fishburn, Peter C. Research in Decision Theory: A Personal Perspective. *Math. Soc. Sci.*, September 1983, *5*(2), pp. 129–48.

Fishburn, Peter C. Transitive Measurable Utility. *J. Econ. Theory*, December 1983, *31*(2), pp. 293–317.

Flament, Claude. On Incomplete Preference Structures. *Math. Soc. Sci.*, August 1983, *5*(1), pp. 61–72.

Francis, Arthur; Turk, Jeremy and Willman, Paul. Power, Efficiency & Institutions: Introduction. **In** *Francis, A.; Turk, J. and Willman, P., eds.*, 1983, pp. 1–12.

Fudenberg, Drew and Levine, David K. Subgame-Perfect Equilibria of Finite- and Infinite-Horizon Games. *J. Econ. Theory*, December 1983, *31*(2), pp. 251–68.

Gabszewicz, Jean Jaskold. Blue and Red Cars, or Blue Cars Only? A Note on Product Variety. *Economica*, May 1983, *50*(198), pp. 203–06.

Ganssmann, Heiner. Marx without the Labor Theory of Value? *Soc. Res.*, Summer 1983, *50*(2), pp. 278–304.

Giarini, Orio. La notion de valeur économique dans la société post-industrielle: éléments pour la recherche de nouveaux paradigmes de l'économique. (The Notion of Economic Value in Post-Industrial Society: Elements towards Research on New Paradigms for Economics. With English summary.) *Écon. Soc.*, February 1983, *17*(2), pp. 299–334.

Gourieroux, Christian; Laffont, Jean-Jacques and Monfort, Alain. Révision adaptative des anticipations et convergence vers les anticipations rationnelles. (Adaptative Revision of Expectations and Convergence towards Rational Expectations. With English summary.) *Écon. Appl.*, 1983, *36*(1), pp. 9–26.

Hammond, Peter J. Overlapping Expectations and Hart's Conditions for Equilibrium in a Securities Model. *J. Econ. Theory*, October 1983, *31*(1), pp. 170–75.

Harvey, Philip. Marx's Theory of the Value of Labor Power: An Assessment. *Soc. Res.*, Summer 1983, *50*(2), pp. 305–44.

Heilbroner, Robert L. The Problem of Value in the Constitution of Economic Thought. *Soc. Res.*, Summer 1983, *50*(2), pp. 253–77.

Hicks, John. Micro and Macro. **In** *Hicks, J.*, 1983, *1979*, pp. 349–52.

Hirayama, Asazi. Quality Uncertainty, Commerce and Money. *Econ. Stud. Quart.*, December 1983, *34*(3), pp. 249–58.

Hunt, E. K. Joan Robinson and the Labour Theory of Value. *Cambridge J. Econ.*, September/December 1983, *7*(3/4), pp. 331–42.

Kariya, Takeaki. Optimal Rational Expectations. *Hitotsubashi J. Econ.*, December 1983, *24*(2), pp. 101–08.

Karni, Edi. On the Correspondence between Multivariate Risk Aversion and Risk Aversion with State-Dependent Preferences. *J. Econ. Theory*, August 1983, *30*(2), pp. 230–42.

Karni, Edi. Risk Aversion for State-Dependent Utility Functions: Measurement and Applications. *Int. Econ. Rev.*, October 1983, *24*(3), pp. 637–47.

Karni, Edi; Schmeidler, David and Vind, Karl. On State Dependent Preferences and Subjective Probabilities. *Econometrica*, July 1983, *51*(4), pp. 1021–31.

Leonard, Herman B. Elicitation of Honest Preferences for the Assignment of Individuals to Positions. *J. Polit. Econ.*, June 1983, *91*(3), pp. 461–79.

Lerner, Abba P. Marginal Cost Pricing in the 1930's. **In** *Lerner, A. P.*, 1983, *1977*, pp. 187–91.

Loasby, Brian. Knowledge, Learning and Enterprise. **In** *Wiseman, J., ed.*, 1983, pp. 104–21.

Loury, Glenn C. The Welfare Effects of Intermittent Interruptions of Trade. *Amer. Econ. Rev.*, May 1983, *73*(2), pp. 272–77.

Meyer, Jack and Ormiston, Michael B. The Comparative Statics of Cumulative Distribution Function Changes for the Class of Risk Averse Agents. *J. Econ. Theory*, October 1983, *31*(1), pp. 153–69.

Morrison, Clarence C. and Pfouts, Ralph W. Hotelling's Proof of the Marginal Cost Pricing Theorem: A Correction. *Atlantic Econ. J.*, March 1983, *11*(1), pp. 113.

Murray, Michael P. Mythical Demands and Mythical

Supplies for Proper Estimation of Rosen's Hedonic Price Model. *J. Urban Econ.*, November 1983, *14*(3), pp. 326–37.

Myerson, Roger B. A Dynamic Microeconomic Model with Durable Goods and Adaptive Expectations. *J. Econ. Behav. Organ.*, December 1983, *4*(4), pp. 309–51.

Myerson, Roger B. and Satterthwaite, Mark A. Efficient Mechanisms for Bilateral Trading. *J. Econ. Theory,* April 1983, *29*(2), pp. 265–81.

Nalebuff, Barry J. and Stiglitz, Joseph E. Prizes and Incentives: Towards a General Theory of Compensation and Competition. *Bell J. Econ. (See Rand J. Econ. after 4/85),* Spring 1983, *14*(1), pp. 21–43.

Polemarchakis, Heraklis M. Observable Probabilistic Beliefs. *J. Math. Econ.*, January 1983, *11*(1), pp. 65–75.

ten Raa, Thijs. Supportability and Anonymous Equity. *J. Econ. Theory,* October 1983, *31*(1), pp. 176–81.

Reichlin, Pietro and Siconolfi, Paolo. Aspettative razionali, mercato atomistico e principio del costo marginale. (Rational Expectations, the Atomistic Market and the Marginal Cost Issue. With English summary.) *Giorn. Econ.*, November–December 1983, *42*(11–12), pp. 769–79.

Rosen, Sherwin. The Economics of Superstars: Reply. *Amer. Econ. Rev.*, June 1983, *73*(3), pp. 460–62.

Schmalensee, Richard. George Stigler's Contributions to Economics. *Scand. J. Econ.*, 1983, *85*(1), pp. 77–86.

Sen, Amartya K. Carrots, Sticks and Economics: Perception Problems in Incentives. *Indian Econ. Rev.*, January–June 1983, *18*(1), pp. 1–16.

Smith, V. Kerry. Option Value: A Conceptual Overview. *Southern Econ. J.*, January 1983, *49*(3), pp. 654–68.

Stiglitz, Joseph E. and Weiss, Andrew. Incentive Effects of Terminations: Applications to the Credit and Labor Markets. *Amer. Econ. Rev.*, December 1983, *73*(5), pp. 912–27.

Szpiro, George G. The Aggregation of Risk Aversions. *Math. Soc. Sci.*, August 1983, *5*(1), pp. 55–59.

Thomson, William. Equity in Exchange Economies. *J. Econ. Theory,* April 1983, *29*(2), pp. 217–44.

Tillmann, Georg. Stability in a Simple Pure Consumption Loan Model. *J. Econ. Theory,* August 1983, *30*(2), pp. 315–29.

West, Edwin G. and McKee, Michael. De Gustibus *Est* Disputandum: The Phenomenon of "Merit Wants" Revisited. *Amer. Econ. Rev.*, December 1983, *73*(5), pp. 1110–21. **[G: U.K.]**

Wiggins, Steven N. and Lane, W. J. Quality Uncertainty, Search, and Advertising. *Amer. Econ. Rev.*, December 1983, *73*(5), pp. 881–94.

Williamson, Oliver E. and Ouchi, William G. The Markets and Hierarchies Programme of Research: Origins, Implications, Prospects. **In** *Francis, A.; Turk, J. and Willman, P., eds.*, 1983, *1981*, pp. 13–34.

Wintrobe, Ronald. Taxing Altruism. *Econ. Inquiry,* April 1983, *21*(2), pp. 255–70.

Wolinsky, Asher. Prices as Signals of Product Quality. *Rev. Econ. Stud.*, October 1983, *50*(4), pp. 647–58.

Ziemer, Rod F. Tolerance Limits and Expected Utility Analysis. *Amer. J. Agr. Econ.*, August 1983, *65*(3), pp. 611–14.

0222 Theory of the Household (consumer demand)

Ahrens, Heinz. A New Look at Giffen's Paradox. *Jahr. Nationalökon. Statist.*, January 1983, *198*(1), pp. 37–47.

Akerlof, George A. Loyalty Filters. *Amer. Econ. Rev.*, March 1983, *73*(1), pp. 54–63.

Arrow, Kenneth J. Behavior under Uncertainty and Its Implications for Policy. **In** *Stigum, B. P. and Wenstøp, F., eds.*, 1983, pp. 19–32.

Atkinson, Anthony B. Inheritance and the Redistribution of Wealth. **In** *Atkinson, A. B.*, 1983, pp. 171–96.

Atkinson, Scott E. The Implications of Homothetic Separability for Share Equation Price Elasticities [The Bias in Price Elasticity Estimates under Homothetic Separability: Implications for Analysis of Peak-Load Electricity Pricing]. *J. Bus. Econ. Statist.*, July 1983, *1*(3), pp. 211–14. **[G: U.S.]**

Baldwin, Michael A.; Hadid, M. and Phillips, G. D. A. The Estimation and Testing of a System of Demand Equations for the UK. *Appl. Econ.*, February 1983, *15*(1), pp. 81–90. **[G: U.K.]**

Barnett, William A. The Recent Reappearance of the Homotheticity Restriction on Preferences [The Bias in Price Elasticity Estimates under Homothetic Separability: Implications for Analysis of Peak-Load Electricity Pricing]. *J. Bus. Econ. Statist.*, July 1983, *1*(3), pp. 215–18. **[G: U.S.]**

Basmann, R. L.; Molina, Daniel J. and Slottje, D. J. Budget Constraint Prices as Preference Changing Parameters of Generalized Fechner-Thurstone Direct Utility Functions. *Amer. Econ. Rev.*, June 1983, *73*(3), pp. 411–13.

Basu, Kaushik. Cardinal Utility, Utilitarianism, and a Class of Invariance Axioms in Welfare Analysis. *J. Math. Econ.*, December 1983, *12*(3), pp. 193–206.

Bell, Edward B.; Bodenhorn, Diran and Taub, Allan J. Ranking Alternative Taxable Income Streams. *Nat. Tax J.*, June 1983, *36*(2), pp. 225–31.

Bergstrom, Theodore C. and Cornes, Richard C. Independence of Allocative Efficiency from Distribution in the Theory of Public Goods. *Econometrica,* November 1983, *51*(6), pp. 1753–65.

Berndt, Ernst R. Quality Adjustment, Hedonics, and Modern Empirical Demand Analysis. **In** *Diewert, W. E. and Montmarquette, C., eds.*, 1983, pp. 817–63.

Bigman, David and Shalit, Haim. Applied Welfare Analysis for Consumers with Commodity Income. *De Economist,* 1983, *131*(1), pp. 31–45.

Blackorby, Charles and Donaldson, David. Preference Diversity and Aggregate Economic Cost-of-Living Indexes. **In** *Diewert, W. E. and Montmarquette, C., eds.*, 1983, pp. 373–409.

Blanciforti, Laura and Green, Richard. An Almost Ideal Demand System Incorporating Habits: An Analysis of Expenditures on Food and Aggregate

Commodity Groups. *Rev. Econ. Statist.,* August 1983, *65*(3), pp. 511–15. [G: U.S.]

Blatt, John M. Expected Utility Theory Does *Not* Apply to All Rational Men. **In** *Stigum, B. P. and Wenstøp, F., eds.,* 1983, pp. 107–16.

Bloch, Laurence. Le Modèle de cycle de vie. Application aux données individuelles tirées de l'enquête épargne 1973–1975, INSEE. (The Life-Cycle Hypothesis. An Application to a Cross-Section Drawn from the INSEE 1973–1975 Survey of Households Savings. With English summary.) *Ann. INSEE,* October–December 1983, (52), pp. 123–61. [G: France]

Bockstael, Nancy E. and McConnell, Kenneth E. Welfare Measurement in the Household Production Framework. *Amer. Econ. Rev.,* September 1983, *73*(4), pp. 806–14.

Bodily, Samuel E. and White, Chelsea C., III. Optimal Consumption and Portfolio Strategies in a Continuous-Time Model with Summary-Dependent Preferences. **In** *Hansen, P., ed.,* 1983, pp. 1–7.

Bond, Eric W. Trade in Used Equipment with Heterogeneous Firms. *J. Polit. Econ.,* August 1983, *91*(4), pp. 688–705. [G: U.S.]

Bopp, Anthony E. The Demand for Kerosene: A Modern Giffen Good. *Appl. Econ.,* August 1983, *15*(4), pp. 459–67. [G: U.S.]

Bossons, John. Leisure Time and the Measurement of Economic Welfare: Comment. **In** *Diewert, W. E. and Montmarquette, C., eds.,* 1983, pp. 368–72. [G: Canada]

Boyer, Marcel. Rational Demand and Expenditures Patterns under Habit Formation. *J. Econ. Theory,* October 1983, *31*(1), pp. 27–53.

Boyer, Marcel and Dionne, Georges. Riscophobie et étalement à moyenne constante: analyse et applications. (Risk Aversion and Mean-Preserving Spread; Analysis and Application. With English summary.) *L'Actual. Econ.,* June 1983, *59*(2), pp. 208–29.

Bridges, Douglas S. A Numerical Representation of Preferences with Intransitive Indifference. *J. Math. Econ.,* January 1983, *11*(1), pp. 25–42.

Bridges, Douglas S. Numerical Representation of Intransitive Preferences on a Countable Set. *J. Econ. Theory,* June 1983, *30*(1), pp. 213–17.

Buchanan, James M. Rent Seeking, Noncompensated Transfers, and Laws of Succession. *J. Law Econ.,* April 1983, *26*(1), pp. 71–85.

Bucovetsky, Sam. Price Dispersion and Stockpiling by Consumers. *Rev. Econ. Stud.,* July 1983, *50*(3), pp. 443–65.

Burbridge, John B. Government Debt in an Overlapping-Generations Model with Bequests and Gifts. *Amer. Econ. Rev.,* March 1983, *73*(1), pp. 222–27. [G: U.S.]

Camacho, A. Cardinal Utility and Decision Making under Uncertainty. **In** *Stigum, B. P. and Wenstøp, F., eds.,* 1983, pp. 347–70.

Carlson, John A. and Gieseke, Robert J. Price Search in a Product Market. *J. Cons. Res.,* March 1983, *9*(4), pp. 357–65. [G: U.S.]

Caves, Douglas W. and Christensen, Laurits R. The Bias in Price Elasticity Estimates under Homothetic Separability: Implications for Analysis of Peak-Load Electricity Pricing: Discussion. *J. Bus. Econ. Statist.,* July 1983, *1*(3), pp. 219–20. [G: U.S.]

Chambers, Robert G. and McConnell, Kenneth E. Decomposition and Additivity in Price-Dependent Demand Systems. *Amer. J. Agr. Econ.,* August 1983, *65*(3), pp. 596–602. [G: U.S.]

Chapman, Randall G. and Palda, Kristian S. Electoral Turnout in Rational Voting and Consumption Perspectives. *J. Cons. Res.,* March 1983, *9*(4), pp. 337–46. [G: Canada]

Chichilnisky, Graciela and Heal, Geoffrey M. Community Preferences and Social Choice. *J. Math. Econ.,* September 1983, *12*(1), pp. 33–61.

Cooper, Lee G. and Nakanishi, Masao. Standardizing Variables in Multiplicative Choice Models. *J. Cons. Res.,* June 1983, *10*(1), pp. 96–108.

Cooper, Russel J. and McLaren, Keith R. Modelling Price Expectations in Intertemporal Consumer Demand Systems: Theory and Application. *Rev. Econ. Statist.,* May 1983, *65*(2), pp. 282–88. [G: Australia]

Cressy, Robert C. Goodwill, Intertemporal Price Dependence and the Repurchase Decision. *Econ. J.,* December 1983, *93*(372), pp. 847–61.

Crouzeix, J.-P. Duality between Direct and Indirect Utility Functions: Differentiability Properties. *J. Math. Econ.,* October 1983, *12*(2), pp. 149–65.

Dalal, Ardeshir J. Comparative Statics and Asset Substitutability/Complementarity in a Portfolio Model: A Dual Approach. *Rev. Econ. Stud.,* April 1983, *50*(2), pp. 355–67.

Daniel, Coldwell, III. The Roles of Time in the Specification of Market Conditions. *Rev. Bus. Econ. Res.,* Winter, 1983, *18*(2), pp. 51–59.

Debreu, Gerard. Continuity Properties of Paretian Utility. **In** *Debreu, G.,* 1983, *1964,* pp. 163–72.

Debreu, Gerard. Excess Demand Functions. **In** *Debreu, G.,* 1983, *1974,* pp. 203–09.

Debreu, Gerard. Least Concave Utility Functions. **In** *Debreu, G.,* 1983, *1976,* pp. 242–50.

Debreu, Gerard. Representation of a Preference Ordering by a Numerical Function. **In** *Debreu, G.,* 1983, *1954,* pp. 105–10.

Debreu, Gerard. Smooth Preferences: A Corrigendum. **In** *Debreu, G.,* 1983, *1976,* pp. 201–02.

Debreu, Gerard. Topological Methods in Cardinal Utility Theory. **In** *Debreu, G.,* 1983, *1960,* pp. 120–32.

DeGroot, Morris H. Decision Making with an Uncertain Utility Function. **In** *Stigum, B. P. and Wenstøp, F., eds.,* 1983, pp. 371–84.

Diewert, W. Erwin. The Theory of the Cost-of-Living Index and the Measurement of Welfare Change. **In** *Diewert, W. E. and Montmarquette, C., eds.,* 1983, pp. 163–233.

Dodgson, J. S. Compensating and Equivalent Variation Measures of Investment Benefits with Multiple Price Changes. *Public Finance,* 1983, *38*(1), pp. 16–26. [G: U.K.]

Dooley, Peter C. Slutsky's Equation Is Pareto's Solution. *Hist. Polit. Econ.,* Winter 1983, *15*(4), pp. 513–17.

Driffill, E. John and Rosen, Harvey S. Taxation and Excess Burden: A Life Cycle Perspective. *Int. Econ. Rev.,* October 1983, *24*(3), pp. 671–83.

Dybvig, Philip H. Recovering Additive Utility Functions. *Int. Econ. Rev.*, June 1983, *24*(2), pp. 379–96.

Dybvig, Philip H. and Lippman, Steven A. An Alternative Characterization of Decreasing Absolute Risk Aversion. *Econometrica*, January 1983, *51*(1), pp. 223–24.

Earl, Peter E. The Consumer in His/Her Social Setting—A Subjectivist View. **In** *Wiseman, J., ed.*, 1983, pp. 176–91.

Encarnación, José, Jr. Positive Time Preference: A Comment. *J. Polit. Econ.*, August 1983, *91*(4), pp. 706–08.

Epstein, Larry G. Decreasing Absolute Risk Aversion and Utility Indices Derived from Cake-Eating Problems. *J. Econ. Theory*, April 1983, *29*(2), pp. 245–64.

Epstein, Larry G. Erratum: Integrability of Incomplete Systems of Demand Functions. *Rev. Econ. Stud.*, July 1983, *50*(3), pp. 581.

Epstein, Larry G. Stationary Cardinal Utility and Optimal Growth under Uncertainty. *J. Econ. Theory*, October 1983, *31*(1), pp. 133–52.

Fallis, George B. Housing Tenure in a Model of Consumer Choice: A Simple Diagrammatic Analysis. *Amer. Real Estate Urban Econ. Assoc. J.*, Spring 1983, *11*(1), pp. 30–44.

Farquhar, Peter H. Research Directions in Multiattribute Utility Analysis. **In** *Hansen, P., ed.*, 1983, pp. 63–85.

Farquhar, Peter H. and Fishburn, Peter C. Indifference Spanning Analysis. **In** *Stigum, B. P. and Wenstøp, F., eds.*, 1983, pp. 443–59.

Feldstein, Martin S. The Rate of Return, Taxation, and Personal Savings. **In** *Feldstein, M. (I)*, 1983, *1978*, pp. 29–35.

Fine, Ben. The Order of Acquisition of Consumer Durables: A Social Choice Theoretic Approach. *J. Econ. Behav. Organ.*, June–September 1983, *4*(2–3), pp. 239–48.

Fishburn, Peter C. Utility Functions on Ordered Convex Sets. *J. Math. Econ.*, December 1983, *12*(3), pp. 221–32.

Friedman, Milton and Savage, Leonard J. The Utility Analysis of Choices Involving Risk. **In** *Archer, S. H. and D'Ambrosia, C. A.*, 1983, *1948*, pp. 16–45.

Fuchs-Seliger, Susanne. Budget Preferences and Direct Utility. *J. Econ. Theory*, June 1983, *30*(1), pp. 188–90.

Fuchs-Seliger, Susanne. On Continuous Utility Functions Derived from Demand Functions. *J. Math. Econ.*, September 1983, *12*(1), pp. 19–32.

Gal-Or, Esther. "Sales" and Risk-Averse Consumers. *Economica*, November 1983, *50*(200), pp. 477–83.

Goux, Jean-François. La dynamique de l'accumulation réelle des ménages. (The Dynamics of Household Real Estate Accumulation. With English summary.) *Revue Écon.*, January 1983, *34*(1), pp. 182–235. **[G: France]**

Graham, Daniel A. Estimating the "State Dependent" Utility Function. *Natural Res. J.*, July 1983, *23*(3), pp. 649–56.

Green, Robert T., et al. Societal Development and Family Purchasing Roles: A Cross-National Study. *J. Cons. Res.*, March 1983, *9*(4), pp. 436–42. **[G: Venezuela; U.S.; France; Gabon; Netherlands]**

Gregory, Paul R. Soviet Theories of Economic Demography: A Survey. *J. Compar. Econ.*, June 1983, *7*(2), pp. 105–13. **[G: U.S.S.R.]**

Grether, David M. and Wilde, Louis L. Consumer Choice and Information: New Experimental Evidence. *Info. Econ. Policy*, 1983, *1*(2), pp. 115–44. **[G: U.S.]**

Grout, Paul. Welfare Aspects of Naive and Sophisticated Decision-making. **In** *Pattanaik, P. K. and Salles, M., eds.*, 1983, pp. 207–24.

Hagen, Ole. Paradoxes and Their Solutions. **In** *Stigum, B. P. and Wenstøp, F., eds.*, 1983, pp. 5–17.

Harwitz, Mitchell; Lentnek, Barry and Narula, Subhash C. Do I Have to Go Shopping Again? A Theory of Choice with Movement Costs. *J. Urban Econ.*, March 1983, *13*(2), pp. 165–80.

Hey, John D. Towards Double Negative Economics. **In** *Wiseman, J., ed.*, 1983, pp. 160–75.

Hicks, John. Direct and Indirect Additivity. **In** *Hicks, J.*, 1983, *1969*, pp. 308–11.

Hildenbrand, Werner. On the "Law of Demand." *Econometrica*, July 1983, *51*(4), pp. 997–1019.

Hjorth-Anderson, Christian. Lancaster's Principle of Efficient Choice: An Empirical Note. *Int. J. Ind. Organ.*, September 1983, *1*(3), pp. 287–95. **[G: U.S.]**

Holland, Thomas E. The Periodic Table of the Neoclassical Paradigm. *Amer. Econ.*, Spring 1983, *27*(1), pp. 30–36.

Hoskin, Robert E. Opportunity Cost and Behavior. *J. Acc. Res.*, Spring 1983, *21*(1), pp. 78–95. **[G: U.S.]**

Houthakker, Hendrik S. On Consumption Theory. **In** *Brown, E. C. and Solow, R. M., eds.*, 1983, pp. 55–68.

Huang, Kuo S. The Family of Inverse Demand Systems. *Europ. Econ. Rev.*, December 1983, *23*(3), pp. 329–37.

Jaffé, William. The Walras–Poincaré Correspondence on the Cardinal Measurability of Utility. **In** *Jaffé, W.*, 1983, *1977*, pp. 213–20.

James, Jeffrey. The New Household Economics, General X-Efficiency Theory, and Developing Countries. *J. Devel. Stud.*, July 1983, *19*(4), pp. 485–503.

Jessen, Franz. Addictive Goods and the Growth of Government. *Public Choice*, 1983, *40*(1), pp. 101–03.

Johnson, Glenn L. Ethical Issues in Resource Economics: Discussion. *Amer. J. Agr. Econ.*, December 1983, *65*(5), pp. 1033–34.

Katz, Eliakim. Wealth, Rank, Risk Aversion and the Friedman–Savage Utility Function. *Australian Econ. Pap.*, December 1983, *22*(41), pp. 487–90.

Kesenne, Stefan. Substitution in Consumption: An Application to the Allocation of Time. *Europ. Econ. Rev.*, November 1983, *23*(2), pp. 231–39. **[G: Belgium]**

Kessler, Denis. Les politiques sociales modifient-elles le comportement des individus? Le cas du système de retraite. (With English summary.) *Revue Écon. Polit.*, May–June 1983, *93*(3), pp. 328–44.

Kohler, Daniel F. The Bias in Price Elasticity Estimates under Homothetic Separability: Implications for Analysis of Peak-Load Electricity Pricing. *J. Bus. Econ. Statist.*, July 1983, *1* (3), pp. 202–10. **[G: U.S.]**

Kohler, Daniel F. The Bias in Price Elasticity Estimates under Homothetic Separability: Implications for Analysis of Peak-Load Electricity Pricing: Response. *J. Bus. Econ. Statist.*, July 1983, *1* (3), pp. 226–28. **[G: U.S.]**

Kolosnitsyn, I. V. and Makarchuk, N. I. On Constructing an Objective Function in Consumption. *Matekon*, Summer 1983, *19* (4), pp. 21–44.

Krzysztofowicz, Roman. Risk Attitude Hypotheses of Utility Theory. **In** *Stigum, B. P. and Wenstøp, F., eds.*, 1983, pp. 201–16.

Kuniansky, Anna. Soviet Fertility, Labor-Force Participation, and Marital Instability. *J. Compar. Econ.*, June 1983, *7* (2), pp. 114–30. **[G: U.S.S.R.]**

Labulwa, A. S. G. Commodity Characteristics and Intertemporal Inconsistency. *Scot. J. Polit. Econ.*, February 1983, *30* (1), pp. 80–87.

Laferrière, Richard. Une étude sélective des mesures de bien-être d'un individu. (A Study of Welfare Measurements for an Individual. With English summary.) *L'Actual. Econ.*, June 1983, *59* (2), pp. 325–43.

Lakshmanan, T. R. and Hua, Chang-i. A Temporal–Spatial Theory of Consumer Behavior. *Reg. Sci. Urban Econ.*, August 1983, *13* (3), pp. 341–61.

Lee, Maw Lin and Hu, Teh-wei. Socioeconomic Factors and Consumption Theories. *Math. Soc. Sci.*, August 1983, *5* (1), pp. 17–32.

Lerner, Abba P. A Note on the Diminishing Marginal Utility of Income. **In** *Lerner, A. P.*, 1983, pp. 53–56.

Lerner, Abba P. Consumer's Surplus and Micro–Macro. **In** *Lerner, A. P.*, 1983, *1963*, pp. 47–52.

Lerner, Abba P. The Analysis of Demand. **In** *Lerner, A. P.*, 1983, *1962*, pp. 31–45.

Lerner, Abba P. The Diagrammatical Representation of Elasticity of Demand. **In** *Lerner, A. P.*, 1983, *1933*, pp. 1–6.

Levhari, David. The Effects of Government Intermediation in the Indexed Bonds Market on Consumer Behavior. **In** *Dornbusch, R. and Simonsen, M. H., eds.*, 1983, pp. 281–307.

Levikson, Benny and Rabinovitch, Ramon. Optimal Consumption—Saving Decisions with Uncertain but Dependent Incomes. *Int. Econ. Rev.*, June 1983, *24* (2), pp. 341–60.

Lin, Tzong-biau. Some Features of the General Demand System. *Z. Nationalökon.*, 1983, *43* (1), pp. 45–61.

Lollivier, Stefan and Rochet, Jean-Charles. Bunching and Second-Order Conditions: A Note on Optimal Tax Theory. *J. Econ. Theory*, December 1983, *31* (2), pp. 392–400.

Loomes, Graham and Sugden, Robert. A Rationale for Preference Reversal. *Amer. Econ. Rev.*, June 1983, *73* (3), pp. 428–32.

Machina, Mark J. Generalized Expected Utility Analysis and the Nature of Observed Violations of the Independence Axiom. **In** *Stigum, B. P. and Wenstøp, F., eds.*, 1983, pp. 263–93.

Martin, Robert E. Petrol Supplies and Consumer Expectations. *Energy Econ.*, January 1983, *5* (1), pp. 16–26.

Mason, R. S. The Economic Theory of Conspicuous Consumption. *Int. J. Soc. Econ.*, 1983, *10* (3), pp. 3–17.

Masson, Paul R. Les effets à long terme de différentes règles de financement du gouvernement. (Long Term Effects of Different Financing Methods of Government. With English summary.) *L'Actual. Econ.*, June 1983, *59* (2), pp. 266–82. **[G: Canada]**

McClennen, Edward F. Sure-thing Doubts. **In** *Stigum, B. P. and Wenstøp, F., eds.*, 1983, pp. 117–36.

McCord, Mark and de Neufville, Richard. Empirical Demonstration That Expected Utility Decision Analysis Is Not Operational. **In** *Stigum, B. P. and Wenstøp, F., eds.*, 1983, pp. 181–99.

McCormick, Ken. Duesenberry and Veblen: The Demonstration Effect Revisited. *J. Econ. Issues*, December 1983, *17* (4), pp. 1125–29.

McKean, John R. and Keller, Robert R. The Shaping of Tastes, Pareto Efficiency and Economic Policy. *J. Behav. Econ.*, Summer 1983, *12* (1), pp. 23–41.

Mehta, Granshyam. Recent Developments in Utility Theory. *Indian Econ. J.*, April-June 1983, *30* (4), pp. 103–24.

Merz, Joachim. Der Einfluss sozioökonomischer Grössen auf die individuelle private Nachfrage nach dauerhaften Konsumgütern: Eine Anwendung der diskreten Entscheidungsmodelle LOGIT und TOBIT. (Socioeconomic Influence on Individual Private Demand for Durable Goods. An Application of the Discrete Choice Models LOGIT and TOBIT. With English summary.) *Z. Wirtschaft. Sozialwissen.*, 1983, *103* (3), pp. 225–53. **[G: W. Germany]**

Miller, Michael S. Methodology and the Theory of Consumer Behavior. *Rev. Soc. Econ.*, April 1983, *41* (1), pp. 39–51.

Minabe, Shigeo. The Utility Analysis of Choices Involving Risk Revisited. *Public Finance*, 1983, *38* (1), pp. 98–109.

Moore, James C. Measurable Triples and Cardinal Measurement. *J. Econ. Theory*, February 1983, *29* (1), pp. 120–60.

Morrill, John E. A Mathematician's Brief Excursion into Economic History—The Concept of Arc Elasticity of Demand. *Amer. Econ.*, Spring 1983, *27* (1), pp. 47–53.

Muellbauer, John. Surprises in the Consumption Function. *Econ. J.*, Supplement March 1983, pp. 34–50. **[G: U.K.]**

Múnera, Héctor A. and de Neufville, Richard. A Decision Analysis Model When the Substitution Principle Is Not Acceptable. **In** *Stigum, B. P. and Wenstøp, F., eds.*, 1983, pp. 247–62.

Nickols, Sharon Y. and Fox, Karen D. Buying Time and Saving Time: Strategies for Managing Household Production. *J. Cons. Res.*, September 1983, *10* (2), pp. 197–208. **[G: U.S.]**

Ortiz, Sutti. What Is Decision Analysis About? The Problems of Formal Representations. **In** *Ortiz, S., ed.*, 1983, pp. 249–97.

Page, Talbot and MacLean, Douglas. Risk Conservatism and the Circumstances of Utility Theory.

Amer. J. Agr. Econ., December 1983, *65*(5), pp. 1021–26.

Parks, Richard W. The Bias in Price Elasticity Estimates under Homothetic Separability: Implications for Analysis of Peak-Load Electricity Pricing: Discussion. *J. Bus. Econ. Statist.*, July 1983, *1*(3), pp. 221–25. **[G: U.S.]**

Phillips, Ronnie J. and Slottje, Daniel J. The Importance of Relative Prices in Analyzing Veblen Effects. *J. Econ. Issues*, March 1983, *17*(1), pp. 197–206. **[G: U.S.]**

Polemarchakis, Heraklis M. Disaggregation of Excess Demand under Additive Separability. *Europ. Econ. Rev.*, January 1983, *20*(1–3), pp. 311–18.

Polemarchakis, Heraklis M. Expectations, Demand, and Observability. *Econometrica*, May, 1983, *51*(3), pp. 565–74.

Polemarchakis, Heraklis M. Homotheticity and the Aggregation of Consumer Demands. *Quart. J. Econ.*, May 1983, *98*(2), pp. 363–69.

Polemarchakis, Heraklis M. On the Disaggregation of Excess Demand Functions When Prices and Aggregate Income Vary Independently. *Europ. Econ. Rev.*, January 1983, *20*(1–3), pp. 217–29.

Pollak, Robert A. The Theory of the Cost-of-Living Index. **In** *Diewert, W. E. and Montmarquette, C., eds.*, 1983, pp. 87–161.

Poncet, Patrice. Optimum Consumption and Portfolio Rules with Money as an Asset. *J. Banking Finance*, June 1983, *7*(2), pp. 231–52.

Pope, Robin. The Pre-outcome Period and the Utility of Gambling. **In** *Stigum, B. P. and Wenstøp, F., eds.*, 1983, pp. 137–77.

Pratt, John W. Risk Aversion in the Small and in the Large. **In** *Archer, S. H. and D'Ambrosia, C. A.*, 1983, *1964*, pp. 46–60.

Ram, Rati. Some Direct Estimates of "Discount Rates" and Consumer "Horizon" from Kendrick's Data. *Southern Econ. J.*, January 1983, *49*(3), pp. 860–66. **[G: U.S.]**

Ray, Ranjan. Measuring the Costs of Children: An Alternative Approach. *J. Public Econ.*, October 1983, *22*(1), pp. 89–102. **[G: U.K.]**

Rettig, Rudi. Ein vollständiges Nachfragesystem für den privaten Verbrauch. (A Complete Demand System for Private Consumption. With English summary.) *Z. Wirtschaft. Sozialwissen.*, 1983, *103*(3), pp. 205–24. **[G: W. Germany]**

Riddell, W. Craig. Leisure Time and the Measurement of Economic Welfare. **In** *Diewert, W. E. and Montmarquette, C., eds.*, 1983, pp. 337–67. **[G: Canada]**

Russell, R. Robert. The Theory of the Cost-of-Living Index and the Measurement of Welfare Change: Comments. **In** *Diewert, W. E. and Montmarquette, C., eds.*, 1983, pp. 234–39.

Sanghvi, Arun P. Household Welfare Loss Due to Electricity Supply Disruptions. *Energy J.*, Supplement 1983, *4*, pp. 33–54. **[G: U.S.]**

Sarin, Rakesh Kumar. Measurable Value Function Theory: Survey and Open Problems. **In** *Hansen, P., ed.*, 1983, pp. 337–46.

Sasaki, Komei. A Household Production Approach to the Evaluation of Transportation System Change. *Reg. Sci. Urban Econ.*, August 1983, *13*(3), pp. 363–82.

Schokkaert, Erik. The Introduction of Sociological Variables in Engle Curve Analysis. *Tijdschrift Econ. Manage.*, 1983, *28*(4), pp. 409–36. **[G: Belgium]**

Schwartz, Aba and Pines, David. Portfolio Choice, Consumption and Welfare When Rate of Return Are Related to Prices of Consumer Goods. *J. Public Econ.*, June 1983, *21*(1), pp. 53–77.

Schweizer, Urs. Reducing Distortions under the Revealed Preference Hypothesis. *Z. Nationalökon.*, 1983, *43*(1), pp. 31–43.

Segal, Uzi. A Theorem on the Additivity of the Quasi-Concave Closure of an Additive Convex Function. *J. Math. Econ.*, July 1983, *11*(3), pp. 261–66.

Sekulović, Slobodan. Segmentiranje tržišta lične potrošnje funkcijom jakosti preferiranja jedne marke nad drugom. (Segmentation of the Market of Consumer Goods by the Function of the Strength of Preferences for One Brand over the Other. With English summary.) *Econ. Anal. Worker's Manage.*, 1983, *17*(4), pp. 383–402.

Shapiro, Edward. Leisure–Income Indifference Curves and the Laffer Curve. *Amer. Econ.*, Spring 1983, *27*(1), pp. 37–39.

Sherry, John F., Jr. Gift Giving in Anthropological Perspective. *J. Cons. Res.*, September 1983, *10*(2), pp. 157–68.

Sheshinski, Eytan and Weiss, Yoram. Inequality within and between Families. **In** *Helpman, E.; Razin, A. and Sadka, E., eds.*, 1983, pp. 255–77.

Slovic, Paul and Lichtenstein, Sarah. Preference Reversals: A Broader Perspective. *Amer. Econ. Rev.*, September 1983, *73*(4), pp. 596–605.

Spiro, Rosann L. Persuasion in Family Decision-Making. *J. Cons. Res.*, March 1983, *9*(4), pp. 393–402.

Stahl, Dale O., II. A Note on the Consumer Surplus Path-of-Integration Problem. *Economica*, February 1983, *50*(197), pp. 95–98.

Stahl, Dale O., II. On Benefit–Cost Analysis with Quality Attributes. *Z. Nationalökon.*, 1983, *43*(3), pp. 273–87.

Stark, Oded. A Note on Modelling Labour Migration in LDCs. *J. Devel. Stud.*, July 1983, *19*(4), pp. 539–43.

Stigler, George J. Notes on the History of the Giffen Paradox. **In** *Stigler, G. J.*, 1983, *1947*, pp. 374–84. **[G: U.K.]**

Stigler, George J. The Development of Utility Theory. **In** *Stigler, G. J.*, 1983, *1950*, pp. 66–155.

Stroyan, K. D. Myopic Utility Functions on Sequential Economies. *J. Math. Econ.*, July 1983, *11*(3), pp. 267–76.

Tanaka, Osamu. A Theory of the Supplies of Labor and Homemakers' Services. *Kobe Univ. Econ.*, 1983, (29), pp. 1–14.

Thore, Sten. Hotelling Utility Functions. **In** *Stigum, B. P. and Wenstøp, F., eds.*, 1983, pp. 329–46.

Triplett, Jack E. Quality Adjustment, Hedonics, and Modern Empirical Demand Analysis: Comment. **In** *Diewert, W. E. and Montmarquette, C., eds.*, 1983, pp. 864–75.

Val'toukh, K. K. Dynamique des dépenses privées des consommateurs français: Analyse avec utilisation d'une fonction théorique d'utilité. (Dynamics of Private Consumer Expenditures in France: An

Analysis Using a Theoretical Utility Function. With English summary.) *Ann. INSEE*, Jan.–Mar. 1983, (49), pp. 89–112. [G: France]

Varian, Hal R. Non-Parametric Tests of Consumer Behaviour. *Rev. Econ. Stud.*, January 1983, *50*(1), pp. 99–110.

Vartia, Yrjö O. Efficient Methods of Measuring Welfare Change and Compensated Income in Terms of Ordinary Demand Functions. *Econometrica*, January 1983, *51*(1), pp. 79–98.

Watts, Martin J. and Gaston, Noel G. The "Reswitching" of Consumption Bundles: A Parallel to the Capital Controversies? *J. Post Keynesian Econ.*, Winter 1982–83, *5*(2), pp. 281–88.

Weber, M. O. An Empirical Investigation on Multiattribute Decision Making. **In** *Hansen, P., ed.*, 1983, pp. 379–88.

Wold, Herman. Utility Analysis from the Point of View of Model Building. **In** *Stigum, B. P. and Wenstøp, F., eds.*, 1983, pp. 87–93.

Wolf, Charles and Pohlman, Larry. The Recovery of Risk Preferences from Actual Choices. *Econometrica*, May, 1983, *51*(3), pp. 843–50. [G: U.S.]

Wu, Mickey T. C. and Monahan, Dennis. An Experimental Study of Consumer Demand Using Rats. *J. Behav. Econ.*, Summer 1983, *12*(1), pp. 121–38.

Yamazaki, Akira. Continuous Preference Relations Which Are Observable in Markets. *Hitotsubashi J. Econ.*, February 1983, *23*(2), pp. 40–47.

Yamazaki, Akira. On Open Preferences. *Hitotsubashi J. Econ.*, December 1983, *24*(2), pp. 149–52.

0223 Theory of Production

Abel, Andrew B. Energy Price Uncertainty and Optimal Factor Intensity: A Mean-Variance Analysis. *Econometrica*, November 1983, *51*(6), pp. 1839–45.

Abel, Andrew B. Market Structure and the Durability of Goods. *Rev. Econ. Stud.*, October 1983, *50*(4), pp. 625–37.

Abel, Andrew B. Optimal Investment under Uncertainty. *Amer. Econ. Rev.*, March 1983, *73*(1), pp. 228–33.

Abel, Andrew B. Tax Neutrality in the Presence of Adjustment Costs. *Quart. J. Econ.*, November 1983, *98*(4), pp. 705–12.

Akyüz, Yilmaz. Value and Exploitation under Joint Production. *Australian Econ. Pap.*, June 1983, *22*(40), pp. 171–79.

Alam, M. Shahid. Intrafirm Productivity: Comment [The Prisoners' Dilemma in the Visible Hand: An Analysis of Intrafirm Productivity]. *Amer. Econ. Rev.*, September 1983, *73*(4), pp. 817–21.

Alberts, William W. and Hite, Gailen L. The Modigliani–Miller Leverage Equation Considered in a Product Market Context. *J. Finan. Quant. Anal.*, December 1983, *18*(4), pp. 425–37.

Albrecht, James W. and Hart, Albert G. A Putty-Clay Model of Demand Uncertainty and Investment. *Scand. J. Econ.*, 1983, *85*(3), pp. 393–402.

Alperovich, Gershon and Katz, Eliakim. Transport Rate Uncertainty and the Optimal Location of the Firm. *J. Reg. Sci.*, August 1983, *23*(3), pp. 389–96.

Amihud, Yakov and Mendelson, Haim. Multiperiod Sales-Production Decisions under Uncertainty. *J. Econ. Dynam. Control*, May 1983, *5*(2/3), pp. 249–65.

Amihud, Yakov and Mendelson, Haim. Price Smoothing and Inventory. *Rev. Econ. Stud.*, January 1983, *50*(1), pp. 87–98.

Anderson, Richard K. and Ormiston, Michael B. A Full-Pricing Analysis of the Owner-Managed Firm. *Southern Econ. J.*, July 1983, *50*(1), pp. 57–70.

Aoki, Masahiko. Managerialism Revisited in the Light of Bargaining-Game Theory. *Int. J. Ind. Organ.*, 1983, *1*(1), pp. 1–21.

Apostolakis, Bobby. Une fonction translog de demande d'importation: le cas de la France. (A Translog Import Demand Function: The French Case. With English summary.) *L'Actual. Econ.*, March 1983, *59*(1), pp. 8–19. [G: France]

Arestis, P.; Karakitsos, Elias and Sarantis, N. Real Money Balances as a Factor of Production in the United Kingdom. *Rivista Int. Sci. Econ. Com.*, December 1983, *30*(12), pp. 1171–86. [G: U.K.]

Arnott, Richard J.; Davidson, Russell and Pines, David. Housing Quality, Maintenance and Rehabilitation. *Rev. Econ. Stud.*, July 1983, *50*(3), pp. 467–94.

Arvan, Lanny and Moses, Leon N. Inventory Investment and the Theory of the Firm: Errata. *Amer. Econ. Rev.*, March 1983, *73*(1), pp. 251.

Atkinson, Anthony B. Capital-Growth-Sharing Schemes and the Behaviour of the Firm. **In** *Atkinson, A. B.*, 1983, *1972*, pp. 383–95.

Auerbach, Alan J. Efficient Design of Investment Incentives. **In** *Auerbach, A. J.*, 1983, *1981*, pp. 51–57.

Auerbach, Alan J. Taxation, Corporate Financial Policy and the Cost of Capital. *J. Econ. Lit.*, September 1983, *21*(3), pp. 905–40.

Austin, Mark. The Theory of the Firm. **In** *Gowland, D. H., ed.*, 1983, pp. 157–70.

Azariadis, Costas. Employment with Asymmetric Information. *Quart. J. Econ.*, Supplement 1983, *98*(3), pp. 157–72.

Azariadis, Costas and Stiglitz, Joseph E. Implicit Contracts and Fixed Price Equilibria. *Quart. J. Econ.*, Supplement 1983, *98*(3), pp. 1–22.

Bailey, R. E. and Scarth, William M. Macroeconomic Implications of Adjustment Costs: A Further Note [Adjustment Costs and Aggregate Demand Theory]. *Economica*, August 1983, *50*(199), pp. 365–69.

Baldone, Salvatore. Dalle funzioni surrogate alle pseudo funzioni di produzione. (From Surrogate to Pseudo Production Functions. With English summary.) *Giorn. Econ.*, January–February 1983, *42*(1–2), pp. 55–78.

Barron, John M.; Black, Dan A. and Loewenstein, Mark A. Adjustment Costs and Aggregate Demand Theory: A Note. *Economica*, August 1983, *50*(199), pp. 361–64.

Batlin, Carl Alan. Production under Price Uncertainty with Imperfect Time Hedging Opportunities in Futures Markets. *Southern Econ. J.*, January 1983, *49*(3), pp. 681–92.

Beato, Paulina and Mas-Colell, Andreu. Gestion au

coût marginal et efficacité de la production agrégée: un exemple. (Marginal Cost Management and Efficiency of Aggregate Production: An Example. With English summary.) *Ann. INSEE,* July–September 1983, (51), pp. 39–46.

Beckmann, Martin J. Production Functions in the Analysis of Organizational Structure. In *[Yamada, I.],* 1983, pp. 2–14.

Bernanke, Ben S. Irreversibility, Uncertainty, and Cyclical Investment. *Quart. J. Econ.,* February 1983, *98* (1), pp. 85–106.

Bernanke, Ben S. The Determinants of Investment: Another Look. *Amer. Econ. Rev.,* May 1983, *73* (2), pp. 71–75. **[G: U.S.]**

Bernstein, Jeffrey I. Investment, Labour Skills, and Variable Factor Utilization in the Theory of the Firm. *Can. J. Econ.,* August 1983, *16* (3), pp. 463–79.

Blackorby, Charles and Schworm, William E. Aggregating Heterogeneous Capital Goods in Adjustment-Cost Technologies. *Scand. J. Econ.,* 1983, *85* (2), pp. 207–22.

Blaug, Mark. The Cambridge Debate on the Theory of Capital and Distribution. In *Caravale, G., ed.,* 1983, *1976,* pp. 102–230.

Blitch, Charles P. Allyn Young on Increasing Returns. *J. Post Keynesian Econ.,* Spring 1983, *5* (3), pp. 359–72.

Blümle, Ernst-Bernd and Dewarrat, Gérard. Expériences en matière de mesure de l'efficience dans les coopératives. (Experiments with Efficiency Measurement in Cooperatives. With English summary.) *Ann. Pub. Co-op. Econ.,* April–June 1983, *54* (2), pp. 173–83.

Bonin, John P. Innovation in a Labor-Managed Firm: A Membership Perspective. *J. Ind. Econ.,* March 1983, *31* (3), pp. 313–29.

Booth, Laurence D. Total Price Uncertainty and the Theory of the Competitive Firm. *Economica,* May 1983, *50* (198), pp. 183–91.

Borjas, George J.; Frech, H. E., III and Ginsburg, Paul B. Property Rights and Wages: The Case of Nursing Homes. *J. Human Res.,* Spring 1983, *18* (2), pp. 231–46. **[G: U.S.]**

Bosshardt, Donald I. Spanning, Pareto Optimality, and the Mean-Variance Model. *Int. Econ. Rev.,* October 1983, *24* (3), pp. 649–69.

Bosworth, Derek and Pugh, Clive. Production and Maintenance: Joint Activities of the Firm. *Scand. J. Econ.,* 1983, *85* (2), pp. 267–82.

Braulke, Michael. Price Responsiveness and Market Conditions. *Econometrica,* July 1983, *51* (4), pp. 971–80.

Breslaw, J. A. and Smith, J. Barry. Des observations empiriques encourageantes pour la théorie dualiste. (Some Encouraging Firm Level Evidence for Duality Theory. With English summary.) *L'Actual. Econ.,* June 1983, *59* (2), pp. 230–39. **[G: Canada]**

Brown, Elba K. and Smith, William Doyle. Is Perfect Competition an Empirically Inadequate Model? A Comment. *Econ. Inquiry,* October 1983, *21* (4), pp. 593–94. **[G: U.S.]**

Browning, M. J. Efficient Decentralisation with a Transferable Good. *Rev. Econ. Stud.,* April 1983, *50* (2), pp. 375–81.

Browning, M. J. Necessary and Sufficient Conditions for Conditional Cost Functions. *Econometrica,* May, 1983, *51* (3), pp. 851–56.

Brueckner, Jan K. and Raymon, Neil. Optimal Production with Learning by Doing. *J. Econ. Dynam. Control,* September 1983, *6* (1/2), pp. 127–35.

Buck, Trevor and Chiplin, Brian. Risk Bearing and Self Management. *Kyklos,* 1983, *36* (2), pp. 270–84.

Cantor, David G. and Lippman, Steven A. Investment Selection with Imperfect Capital Markets. *Econometrica,* July 1983, *51* (4), pp. 1121–44.

Cette, Gilbert. Degrés d'utilisation des facteurs et demande d'investissement et de travail. (Factors Utilisation Levels and Capital Labour Demands. With English summary.) *Revue Écon.,* July 1983, *34* (4), pp. 756–93.

Chambers, Robert G. Scale and Productivity Measurement under Risk. *Amer. Econ. Rev.,* September 1983, *73* (4), pp. 802–05.

Chamley, Christophe. Entrepreneurial Abilities and Liabilities in a Model of Self-Selection. *Bell J. Econ. (See Rand J. Econ. after 4/85),* Spring 1983, *14* (1), pp. 70–80.

Chan, M. W. Luke and Mountain, Dean C. Economies of Scale and the Tornqvist Discrete Measure of Productivity Growth. *Rev. Econ. Statist.,* November 1983, *65* (4), pp. 663–67. **[G: Canada]**

Chander, Parkash. The Nonlinear Input–Output Model. *J. Econ. Theory,* August 1983, *30* (2), pp. 219–29.

Chari, V. V. Involuntary Unemployment and Implicit Contracts. *Quart. J. Econ.,* Supplement 1983, *98* (3), pp. 107–22.

Chauveau, Thierry. L'inflation et les entreprises. (About Firms and Inflation. With English summary.) *Revue Écon.,* September 1983, *34* (5), pp. 897–925. **[G: France]**

Cheung, Steven N. S. The Contractual Nature of the Firm. *J. Law Econ.,* April 1983, *26* (1), pp. 1–21. **[G: Hong Kong]**

Clark, Kim B. and Freeman, Richard. How Elastic Is the Demand for Labor? A Reply. *Rev. Econ. Statist.,* November 1983, *65* (4), pp. 694. **[G: U.S.]**

Clarke, Frank H. and Darrough, Masako N. Optimal Employment Contracts in a Principal–Agent Relationship. *J. Econ. Behav. Organ.,* June–September 1983, *4* (2–3), pp. 69–90.

Clarke, Harry R. and Shrestha, Ram M. Location and Input Mix Decisions for Energy Facilities. *Reg. Sci. Urban Econ.,* November 1983, *13* (4), pp. 487–504.

Clarke, Richard N. Collusion and the Incentives for Information Sharing. *Bell J. Econ. (See Rand J. Econ. after 4/85),* Autumn 1983, *14* (2), pp. 383–94.

Cohen, Avi J. "The Laws of Returns under Competitive Conditions": Progress in Microeconomics since Sraffa (1926)? *Eastern Econ. J.,* July–September 1983, *9* (3), pp. 213–20.

Cohen, Wesley M. Investment and Industrial Expansion: A Corporate Variables Framework. *J. Econ. Behav. Organ.,* June–September 1983, *4* (2–3), pp. 91–111.

Conrad, Klaus. Cost Prices and Partially Fixed Factor Proportions in Energy Substitution. *Europ. Econ. Rev.*, May 1983, *21* (3), pp. 299–312. [G: U.S.]

Cornes, Richard C. and Sandler, Todd. On Commons and Tragedies. *Amer. Econ. Rev.*, September 1983, *73* (4), pp. 787–92.

Correa, Hector. The Firm's Administrative Structure: Theory, Measurement and Applications to Growth Accounting and Income Distribution. *Empirical Econ.*, 1983, *8* (2), pp. 93–109. [G: U.S.]

Crouzeix, J.-P. Duality between Direct and Indirect Utility Functions: Differentiability Properties. *J. Math. Econ.*, October 1983, *12* (2), pp. 149–65.

Dalal, Ardeshir J. A Third-Order Translog Cost Function. *Rivista Int. Sci. Econ. Com.*, April-May 1983, *30* (4–5), pp. 355–61.

Danziger, Leif. On the Frequency of Wage Indexation. *Europ. Econ. Rev.*, August 1983, *22* (3), pp. 297–304.

Demsetz, Harold. The Structure of Ownership and the Theory of the Firm. *J. Law Econ.*, June 1983, *26* (2), pp. 375–90.

DeVany, Arthur S. and Saving, Thomas R. The Economics of Quality. *J. Polit. Econ.*, December 1983, *91* (6), pp. 979–1000.

Devine, James N. and Reich, Michael. The Microeconomics of Conflict and Hierarchy under Capitalist Production: A Reply. *Rev. Radical Polit. Econ.*, Summer 1983, *15* (2), pp. 133–35.

Dholakia, Ravindra H. A Comment on "The Firm's Long-Run Average Cost Curve Revisited." *Indian Econ. J.*, April-June 1983, *30* (4), pp. 125–27.

Dormont, Brigitte. Substitution et coûts des facteurs: une approche en termes de modèles à erreurs sur les variables. (On the Use of a Theoretical Constraint to Eliminate Error-in-Variables Biases. With English summary.) *Ann. INSEE*, April–June 1983, (50), pp. 73–92. [G: France]

Duesing, Erick C. Multiple Objective Linear Programming and the Theory of the Firm: I. Substitution and Sensitivity Analysis. **In** *Hansen, P., ed.*, 1983, pp. 43–52.

Duménil, G. and Lévy, D. Prix et quantités: le cas des productions jointes. (Prices and Quantities: The Joint Production Model. With English summary.) *Écon. Appl.*, 1983, *36* (2–3), pp. 411–45.

Durand, David. The Cost of Capital, Corporation Finance, and the Theory of Investment: Comment. **In** *Archer, S. H. and D'Ambrosia, C. A.*, 1983, *1959*, pp. 386–402.

Dybvig, Philip H. Duality, Interest Rates, and the Theory of Present Value. *J. Econ. Theory*, June 1983, *30* (1), pp. 98–114.

Dyckhoff, Harald. Economically Essential Factors of Production. *Jahr. Nationalökon. Statist.*, July 1983, *198* (4), pp. 362–68.

Dyckhoff, Harald. Inada-Bedingungen und Eigenschaften der neoklassischen Produktionsfunktion. (Inada-Derivative Conditions and Properties of the Neoclassical Production Function. With English summary.) *Z. ges. Staatswiss.*, March 1983, *139* (1), pp. 146–54.

Easley, David and O'Hara, Maureen. The Economic Role of the Nonprofit Firm. *Bell J. Econ. (See Rand J. Econ. after 4/85)*, Autumn 1983, *14* (2), pp. 531–38.

Eichenbaum, Martin. A Rational Expectations Equilibrium Model of Inventories of Finished Goods and Employment. *J. Monet. Econ.*, August 1983, *12* (2), pp. 259–77.

Eichner, Alfred S. The Micro Foundations of the Corporate Economy. *Managerial Dec. Econ.*, September 1983, *4* (3), pp. 136–52.

Epstein, Larry G. Aggregating Quasi-Fixed Factors. *Scand. J. Econ.*, 1983, *85* (2), pp. 191–205.

Epstein, Larry G. Intertemporal Price Indices for the Firm. *J. Econ. Dynam. Control*, September 1983, *6* (1/2), pp. 109–26.

Epstein, Larry G. and Denny, Michael G. S. The Multivariate Flexible Accelerator Model: Its Empirical Restrictions and an Application to U.S. Manufacturing. *Econometrica*, May, 1983, *51* (3), pp. 647–74. [G: U.S.]

Estrin, Saul and Connock, Michael. Ideas of Industrial Democracy in Eastern Europe: A Comment from the Yugoslav Perspective. *ACES Bull. (See Comp. Econ. Stud. after 8/85)*, Spring 1983, *25* (1), pp. 67–74.

Färe, Rolf G. and Grosskopf, Shawna P. Measuring Congestion in Production. *Z. Nationalökon.*, 1983, *43* (3), pp. 257–71.

Färe, Rolf G.; Grosskopf, Shawna P. and Lovell, C. A. Knox. The Structure of Technical Efficiency. *Scand. J. Econ.*, 1983, *85* (2), pp. 181–90.

Färe, Rolf G. and Logan, James. The Rate-of-Return Regulated Firm: Cost and Production Duality. *Bell J. Econ. (See Rand J. Econ. after 4/85)*, Autumn 1983, *14* (2), pp. 405–14.

Fayolle, Jacky. Emploi et prix: Un Modèle de court terme construit sur des variables d'opinion. (Manpower and Prices: A Short Term Model Based on Business Surveys. With English summary.) *Ann. INSEE*, October–December 1983, (52), pp. 87–121.

Feldstein, Martin S. and Rothschild, Michael. Toward an Economic Theory of Replacement Investment. **In** *Feldstein, M. (I)*, 1983, *1974*, pp. 295–330.

Fisher, Franklin M. On the Simultaneous Existence of Full and Partial Capital Aggregates. *Rev. Econ. Stud.*, January 1983, *50* (1), pp. 197–208.

Flacco, Paul R. Output, Entry, and Competitive Production under Price Uncertainty. *Southern Econ. J.*, October 1983, *50* (2), pp. 565–71.

Fraser, R. W. and Van Noorden, R. J. Extraction of an Exhaustible Resource: The Effects on Investment of Several Parameters Being Subject to Uncertainty. *Econ. Rec.*, December 1983, *59* (167), pp. 365–74.

Freixas, Xavier and Laffont, Jean-Jacques. Tarification au coût marginal ou équilibre budgétaire? (Pricing Marginal Cost or Budgetary Equilibrium? With English summary.) *Ann. INSEE*, July–September 1983, (51), pp. 65–88.

Fudenberg, Drew and Tirole, Jean. Capital as a Commitment: Strategic Investment to Deter Mobility. *J. Econ. Theory*, December 1983, *31* (2), pp. 227–50.

Fudenberg, Drew and Tirole, Jean. Learning-by-Doing and Market Performance. *Bell J. Econ. (See*

Rand J. Econ. after 4/85), Autumn 1983, *14*(2), pp. 522–30.

Fujimoto, Takao. Inventions and Technical Change: A Curiosum. *Manchester Sch. Econ. Soc. Stud.,* March 1983, *51*(1), pp. 16–20.

Fukuda, Wataru. On the Output and Employment Decisions of an Egalitarian Labor-managed Firm. *Kobe Univ. Econ.,* 1983, (29), pp. 51–67.

Fusfeld, Daniel R. Labor-Managed and Participatory Firms: A Review Article. *J. Econ. Issues,* September 1983, *17*(3), pp. 769–89.

Gaudet, Gérard. Investissement optimal et coûts d'adjustement dans la théorie économique de la mine. (Optimal Investment and Adjustment Costs in the Economic Theory of the Mine. With English summary.) *Can. J. Econ.,* February 1983, *16*(1), pp. 39–51.

Gilligan, Thomas W. and Smirlock, Michael L. Predation and Cross-Subsidization in the Value Maximizing Multiproduct Firm. *Southern Econ. J.,* July 1983, *50*(1), pp. 37–42.

Gray, R. S. and Furtan, W. Harley. Risk Analysis in the Theory of the Firm: An Old Problem Revisited. *Can. J. Agr. Econ.,* March 1983, *31*(1), pp. 27–44.

Green, Jerry R. and Kahn, Charles M. Wage–Employment Contracts. *Quart. J. Econ.,* Supplement 1983, *98*(3), pp. 173–87.

Greenberg, Edward; Marshall, William J. and Yawitz, Jess B. Firm Behavior under Conditions of Uncertainty and the Theory of Finance. *Quart. Rev. Econ. Bus.,* Summer 1983, *23*(2), pp. 6–22.

Grossman, Sanford J. and Hart, Oliver D. Implicit Contracts under Asymmetric Information. *Quart. J. Econ.,* Supplement 1983, *98*(3), pp. 123–56.

Grossman, Sanford J.; Hart, Oliver D. and Maskin, Eric S. Unemployment with Observable Aggregate Shocks. *J. Polit. Econ.,* December 1983, *91*(6), pp. 907–28.

Groves, Theodore. The Usefulness of Demand Forecasts for Team Resource Allocation in a Dynamic Environment. *Rev. Econ. Stud.,* July 1983, *50*(3), pp. 555–71.

Guasch, J. Luis and Sobel, Joel. Breeding and Raiding: A Theory of Strategic Production of Skills. *Europ. Econ. Rev.,* June 1983, *22*(1), pp. 97–115.

Hamlen, William A., Jr. and Jen, Frank. An Alternative Model of Interruptible Service Pricing and Rationing. *Southern Econ. J.,* April 1983, *49*(4), pp. 1108–21.

Hamlin, Alan P. and Heathfield, David F. Shiftwork and the Choice of Technique under Alternative Maximands. *Scand. J. Econ.,* 1983, *85*(2), pp. 283–94.

Hammes, David L. Is Perfect Competition an Empirically Too-Adequate Model? *Econ. Inquiry,* October 1983, *21*(4), pp. 591–92. **[G: U.S.]**

Hands, Douglas W. "Testing" Perfect Competition: A Comment [Is Perfect Competition an Empirically Inadequate Model?]. *Econ. Inquiry,* October 1983, *21*(4), pp. 588–90. **[G: U.S.]**

Hanseman, Dennis J. A Further Note on Factor Substitution and Efficiency. *Rev. Econ. Statist.,* February 1983, *65*(1), pp. 153–55.

Hansson, Bjorn. Wicksell's Critique of Ricardo's Chapter "On Machinery." *J. Econ. Stud.,* 1983, *10*(3), pp. 49–55.

Hawawini, Gabriel A. and Michel, Pierre A. The Effect of Production Uncertainty on the Labor-Managed Firm. *J. Compar. Econ.,* March 1983, *7*(1), pp. 25–42.

Heertje, Arnold. The Economic Theorist's Dilemma. **In** *Macdonald, S.; Lamberton, D. M. and Mandeville, T., eds.,* 1983, pp. 37–49.

Hicks, John. A Note on the Elasticity of Supply. **In** *Hicks, J.,* 1983, *1934,* pp. 237–45.

Hicks, John. Elasticity of Substitution Reconsidered. **In** *Hicks, J.,* 1983, pp. 312–26.

Hicks, John. Limited Liability: Pros and Cons. **In** *Hicks, J.,* 1983, *1982,* pp. 179–88.

Hicks, John. Linear Theory. **In** *Hicks, J.,* 1983, *1960,* pp. 246–91.

Hicks, John. The Austrian Theory of Capital and Its Re-birth in Modern Economics. **In** *Hicks, J.,* 1983, *1973,* pp. 96–112.

Hiebert, L. Dean. Self Insurance, Self Protection and the Theory of the Competitive Firm. *Southern Econ. J.,* July 1983, *50*(1), pp. 160–68.

Hirshleifer, Jack. Investment Decision under Uncertainty: Choice—Theoretic Approaches. **In** *Archer, S. H. and D'Ambrosia, C. A.,* 1983, *1965,* pp. 61–85.

Hirshleifer, Jack. On the Theory of Optimal Investment Decision. **In** *Archer, S. H. and D'Ambrosia, C. A.,* 1983, *1958,* pp. 321–50.

Hoel, Michael and Vislie, Jon. Supply Functions for Outputs and Demand Functions for Inputs in the Short and Long Run under Uncertainty. *Scand. J. Econ.,* 1983, *85*(1), pp. 53–60.

Holland, Thomas E. The Periodic Table of the Neoclassical Paradigm. *Amer. Econ.,* Spring 1983, *27*(1), pp. 30–36.

Holtmann, Alphonse G. A Theory of Non-Profit Firms. *Economica,* November 1983, *50*(200), pp. 439–49.

Holtmann, Alphonse G. Uncertainty, Organizational Form, and X-Efficiency. *J. Econ. Bus.,* 1983, *35*(1), pp. 131–37.

Honda, Yuzo. Risk, Risk Aversion and Many Control Variables. *Z. Nationalökon.,* 1983, *43*(4), pp. 405–22.

Hori, Kaname. Shutdown Decision and the Supply Curve of a Firm under Uncertainty. (In Japanese. With English summary.) *Osaka Econ. Pap.,* March 1983, *32*(4), pp. 32–46.

Hübler, Olaf. Lohn- und Beschäftigungsstrukturbewegungen unter Unsicherheit. (Uncertainty and Changes of Wage and Employment Structure. With English summary.) *Konjunkturpolitik,* 1983, *29*(2), pp. 67–88.

Ilmakunnas, Pekka. Elasticities of Derived Demand under Different Objectives of the Firm. *Atlantic Econ. J.,* December 1983, *11*(4), pp. 6–13.

Ireland, Norman J. and Law, Peter J. A Cournot-Nash Model of the Consumer Cooperative. *Southern Econ. J.,* January 1983, *49*(3), pp. 706–16.

Jensen, Richard. Innovation Adoption and Diffusion When There Are Competing Innovations. *J. Econ. Theory,* February 1983, *29*(1), pp. 161–71.

Jordan, W. John. Heterogeneous Users and the Peak Load Pricing Model. *Quart. J. Econ.,* February 1983, *98*(1), pp. 127–38.

Katz, Eliakim. Relative Risk Aversion in Comparative Statics. *Amer. Econ. Rev.*, June 1983, *73*(3), pp. 452–53.

Kawai, Masahiro. Price Volatility of Storable Commodities under Rational Expectations in Spot and Futures Markets. *Int. Econ. Rev.*, June 1983, *24*(2), pp. 435–59.

Kawasaki, Seiichi; McMillan, John and Zimmermann, Klaus F. Inventories and Price Inflexibility. *Econometrica*, May, 1983, *51* (3), pp. 599–610. [G: W. Germany]

Kay, N. M. Optimal Size of Firm as a Problem in Transaction Costs and Property Rights. *J. Econ. Stud.*, 1983, *10*(2), pp. 29–41.

Khan, M. Ali. Public Inputs and the Pure Theory of Trade. *Z. Nationalökon.*, 1983, *43*(2), pp. 131–56.

Kihlstrom, Richard E. and Laffont, Jean-Jacques. Implicit Labor Contracts and Free Entry. *Quart. J. Econ.*, Supplement 1983, *98*(3), pp. 55–105.

Kihlstrom, Richard E. and Laffont, Jean-Jacques. Taxation and Risk Taking in General Equilibrium Models with Free Entry. *J. Public Econ.*, July 1983, *21* (2), pp. 159–81.

Kohli, Ulrich R. Non-joint Technologies. *Rev. Econ. Stud.*, January 1983, *50*(1), pp. 209–19.

Kohn, Robert E. Returns to Scale in Welfare Economics. *Atlantic Econ. J.*, March 1983, *11* (1), pp. 54–57.

Kokkelenberg, Edward C. Interrelated Factor Demands Revisited. *Rev. Econ. Statist.*, May 1983, *65*(2), pp. 342–47. [G: U.S.]

Kon, Yoshinori. Capital Input Choice under Price Uncertainty: A Putty–Clay Technology Case. *Int. Econ. Rev.*, February 1983, *24*(1), pp. 183–97.

Kopp, Raymond J. and Smith, V. Kerry. Neoclassical Modeling of Nonneutral Technological Change: An Experimental Appraisal. *Scand. J. Econ.*, 1983, *85*(2), pp. 127–46.

Kornai, János and Weibull, Jörgen W. Paternalism, Buyers' and Sellers' Market. *Math. Soc. Sci.*, November 1983, *6*(2), pp. 153–69.

Kushman, John E. A Modified Minkowski Theorem and Applications. *Atlantic Econ. J.*, September 1983, *11* (3), pp. 114.

Larsen, Odd I. Marginal Cost Pricing of Scheduled Transport Services. *J. Transp. Econ. Policy*, September 1983, *17*(3), pp. 315–17.

Laussel, Didier. Le stock de capital optimal en déséquilibre: introduction de l'incertitude et de la substituabilité des facteurs. (With English summary.) *Revue Écon. Polit.*, November-December 1983, *93*(6), pp. 871–81.

Lawrence, Colin and Spiller, Pablo T. Product Diversity, Economies of Scale, and International Trade. *Quart. J. Econ.*, February 1983, *98*(1), pp. 63–83.

Leban, Raymond and Lesourne, Jacques. Adaptive Strategies of the Firm through a Business Cycle. *J. Econ. Dynam. Control*, May 1983, *5*(2/3), pp. 201–34.

Leibenstein, Harvey. Intrafirm Productivity: Reply [The Prisoners' Dilemma in the Invisible Hand: An Analysis of Intrafirm Productivity]. *Amer. Econ. Rev.*, September 1983, *73*(4), pp. 822–23.

Lerner, Abba P. On the Marginal Product of Capital and the Marginal Efficiency of Investment. In *Lerner, A. P.*, 1983, *1953*, pp. 531–44.

Lerner, Abba P. On Some Recent Developments in Capital Theory. In *Lerner, A. P.*, 1983, *1965*, pp. 551–62.

Lerner, Abba P. Paleo-Austrian Capital Theory. In *Lerner, A. P.*, 1983, pp. 563–79.

Lerner, Abba P. The Diagrammatical Representation of Elasticity of Substitution. In *Lerner, A. P.*, 1983, *1933*, pp. 27–30.

Lesourne, Jacques and Dominguez, A. Employment Policy of a Self-Financing Firm Facing a Risk of Bankruptcy. *J. Econ. Dynam. Control*, July 1983, *5*(4), pp. 325–58.

Lilja, Kari. Yrityksen teoria, työpaikan työelämän suhteet ja työntekijöiden työpaikkaorganisaation käsite. (The Theory of the Firm, Workplace Industrial Relations, and the Concept of Workers' Workplace Organisation. With English summary.) *Liiketaloudellinen Aikak.*, 1983, *32*(4), pp. 389–98.

Lioukas, Spyros K. Peak Load Pricing under Periodic and Stochastic Supply. *Europ. Econ. Rev.*, January 1983, *20*(1–3), pp. 13–21. [G: U.K.]

von der Lippe, Peter and Westerhoff, Horst-Dieter. Ein ökonometrisches Modell des Investitionsprozesses in der Volksrepublik Polen—Empirische Ergebnnisse und wirtschaftspolitische Folgerungen. (An Econometric Model of the Investment Process in Poland. With English summary.) *Jahr. Nationalökon. Statist.*, May 1983, *198*(3), pp. 211–36. [G: Poland]

Lloyd, Peter J. Why Do Firms Produce Multiple Outputs? *J. Econ. Behav. Organ.*, March 1983, *4*(1), pp. 41–51.

Lovell, C. A. Knox and Sickles, Robin C. Testing Efficiency Hypotheses in Joint Production: A Parametric Approach. *Rev. Econ. Statist.*, February 1983, *65*(1), pp. 51–58. [G: U.S.]

Lowenstein, Mark A. Worker Heterogeneity, Hours Restrictions, and Temporary Layoffs. *Econometrica*, January 1983, *51* (1), pp. 69–78.

MacMinn, Richard D. and Holtmann, Alphonse G. Technological Uncertainty and the Theory of the Firm. *Southern Econ. J.*, July 1983, *50*(1), pp. 120–36.

Makowski, Louis. Competition and Unanimity Revisited. *Amer. Econ. Rev.*, June 1983, *73*(3), pp. 329–39.

Makowski, Louis. Competitive Stock Markets. *Rev. Econ. Stud.*, April 1983, *50*(2), pp. 305–30.

Maloney, Kevin J.; Marshall, William J. and Yawitz, Jess B. The Effect of Risk on the Firm's Optimal Capital Stock: A Note. *J. Finance*, September 1983, *38*(4), pp. 1279–84.

Maloney, Michael T. and McCormick, Robert E. A Theory of Cost and Intermittent Production. *J. Bus.*, April 1983, *56*(2), pp. 139–53.

Mathur, Vijay K. Location Theory of the Firm under Price Uncertainty. *Reg. Sci. Urban Econ.*, August 1983, *13*(3), pp. 411–28.

McGuinness, Tony. Efficiency and Industrial Organisation. In *Shepherd, D.; Turk, J. and Silberston, A., eds.*, 1983, pp. 8–29.

McIntosh, James. Dynamic Interrelated Factor Demand Systems: The United Kingdom, 1950-78.

Econ. J., Supplement March 1983, pp. 79–86. [G: U.K.]

McKay, Lloyd; Lawrence, Denis and Vlastuin, Chris. Profit, Output Supply, and Input Demand Functions for Multiproduct Firms: The Case of Australian Agriculture. *Int. Econ. Rev.*, June 1983, *24*(2), pp. 323–39. [G: Australia]

de Meza, David. A Growth Model for a Tenured-Labor-Managed Firm: Comment. *Quart. J. Econ.*, August 1983, *98*(3), pp. 539–42.

Mirman, Leonard J. and Neyman, Abraham. Prices for Homogeneous Cost Functions. *J. Math. Econ.*, December 1983, *12*(3), pp. 257–73.

Mirman, Leonard J.; Samet, Dov and Tauman, Yair. An Axiomatic Approach to the Allocation of a Fixed Cost through Prices. *Bell J. Econ. (See Rand J. Econ. after 4/85)*, Spring 1983, *14*(1), pp. 139–51.

Miyazaki, Hajime and Neary, Hugh M. The Illyrian Firm Revisited. *Bell J. Econ. (See Rand J. Econ. after 4/85)*, Spring 1983, *14*(1), pp. 259–70.

Mizon, Grayham E. and Nickell, S. J. Vintage Production Models of U.K. Manufacturing Industry. *Scand. J. Econ.*, 1983, *85*(2), pp. 295–310. [G: U.K.]

Modigliani, Franco and Miller, Merton H. Corporate Income Taxes and the Cost of Capital: A Correction. In *Archer, S. H. and D'Ambrosia, C. A.*, 1983, *1963*, pp. 418–28.

Modigliani, Franco and Miller, Merton H. The Cost of Capital, Corporation Finance, and the Theory of Investment: Reply. In *Archer, S. H. and D'Ambrosia, C. A.*, 1983, *1959*, pp. 403–17.

Modigliani, Franco and Miller, Merton H. The Cost of Capital, Corporation Finance, and the Theory of Investment. In *Archer, S. H. and D'Ambrosia, C. A.*, 1983, *1958*, pp. 351–85.

Mohtadi, A. Negative Labor Values and the Joint Production Technique: Erratta. *Rev. Radical Polit. Econ.*, Spring 1983, *15*(1), pp. 67.

Nalebuff, Barry J. and Stiglitz, Joseph E. Information, Competition, and Markets. *Amer. Econ. Rev.*, May 1983, *73*(2), pp. 278–83.

Nell, Edward J. On Monetary Circulation and the Rate of Exploitation. *Econ. Forum*, Spring 1983 Supplement, *13*, pp. 1–38.

Nerlove, Marc. Expectations, Plans, and Realizations in Theory and Practice. *Econometrica*, September 1983, *51*(5), pp. 1251–79. [G: France; W. Germany]

Niho, Yoshio and Musacchio, Robert A. Effects of Regulation and Capital Market Imperfections on the Dynamic Behavior of a Firm. *Southern Econ. J.*, January 1983, *49*(3), pp. 625–36.

Niho, Yoshio and Mussachio, Robert A. Revenue Maximization and Optimal Capital Policies of a Regulated Firm. In *[Yamada, I.]*, 1983, pp. 15–26.

Ogawa, Haruo. The Behavior of Resource Explorating Firm under Stochastic World. In *[Yamada, I.]*, 1983, pp. 115–21.

Ohtani, Kazuhiro. A Bayesian Analysis of the Generalized Production Function with Heteroscedasticity. *Econ. Stud. Quart.*, August 1983, *34*(2), pp. 171–78. [G: U.S.]

Oi, Walter Y. Heterogeneous Firms and the Organization of Production. *Econ. Inquiry*, April 1983, *21*(2), pp. 147–71.

Peters, Michael. Labour Contracts in a Stock Market Economy. *J. Econ. Theory*, August 1983, *30*(2), pp. 296–314.

Pindyck, Robert S. and Rotemberg, Julio J. Dynamic Factor Demands and the Effects of Energy Price Shocks. *Amer. Econ. Rev.*, December 1983, *73*(5), pp. 1066–79. [G: U.S.]

Pindyck, Robert S. and Rotemberg, Julio J. Dynamic Factor Demands under Rational Expectations. *Scand. J. Econ.*, 1983, *85*(2), pp. 223–38. [G: U.S.]

Pinheiro, António Cipriano Afonso. Intervalos de confiança para a função de produção e para equações dela derividas. (With English summary.) *Economia*, October 1983, *7*(3), pp. 531–42.

Plessner, Yakir and Yitzhaki, Shlomo. Unemployment and Wage Rigidity: The Demand Side. *Oxford Econ. Pap.*, July 1983, *35*(2), pp. 202–12.

Plott, Charles R. Externalities and Corrective Policies in Experimental Markets. *Econ. J.*, March 1983, *93*(369), pp. 106–27.

Pryor, Frederic L. The Economics of Production Cooperatives: A Reader's Guide. *Ann. Pub. Co-op. Econ.*, April–June 1983, *54*(2), pp. 133–72.

Puccinelli, Pietro. A Cyclical Model of Large Firms. *Econ. Notes*, 1983, (2), pp. 65–83.

Quandt, Richard E. Complexity in Regulation. *J. Public Econ.*, November 1983, *22*(2), pp. 199–214.

Raboy, David G. Capital Composition Changes: Effects of Changing Haig–Simons Income Tax Rates. *Public Finance Quart.*, January 1983, *11*(1), pp. 67–78.

Reynolds, R. Larry. Policy Choices and Economies of Scale. *J. Econ. Issues*, December 1983, *17*(4), pp. 1067–74.

Ricardo-Campbell, Rita. Comments on the Structure of Ownership and the Theory of the Firm. *J. Law Econ.*, June 1983, *26*(2), pp. 391–93.

Riley, John G. and Zeckhauser, Richard J. Optimal Selling Strategies: When to Haggle, When to Hold Firm. *Quart. J. Econ.*, May 1983, *98*(2), pp. 267–89.

Rosser, J. Barkley, Jr. Reswitching as a Cusp Catastrophe. *J. Econ. Theory*, October 1983, *31*(1), pp. 182–93.

Salant, Stephen W.; Eswaran, Mukesh and Lewis, Tracy R. The Length of Optimal Extraction Programs When Depletion Affects Extraction Costs. *J. Econ. Theory*, December 1983, *31*(2), pp. 364–74.

Salinger, Michael A. and Summers, Lawrence H. Tax Reform and Corporate Investment: A Microeconometric Simulation Study. In *Feldstein, M., ed.*, 1983, pp. 247–81. [G: U.S.]

Salop, Steven C. and Scheffman, David T. Raising Rivals' Costs. *Amer. Econ. Rev.*, May 1983, *73*(2), pp. 267–71.

Sapir, André. A Growth Model for a Tenured-Labor-Managed Firm: Reply. *Quart. J. Econ.*, August 1983, *98*(3), pp. 543.

Scazzieri, Roberto. The Production Process: General Characteristics and Taxonomy. *Rivista Int. Sci. Econ. Com.*, July 1983, *30*(7), pp. 597–611.

Schefold, Bertram. Straffas Theorie der Kuppelproduktion: Ein Überblick. (Sraffa's Theory of Joint

Production: A Survey. With English summary.) *Z. Wirtschaft. Sozialwissen.*, 1983, *103*(4), pp. 315–40.

Scherer, F. M. R&D and Declining Productivity Growth. *Amer. Econ. Rev.*, May 1983, *73*(2), pp. 215–18. **[G: U.S.]**

Schmalensee, Richard. Product Differentiation Advantages of Pioneering Brands: Errata. *Amer. Econ. Rev.*, March 1983, *73*(1), pp. 250.

von der Schulenberg, J.-Mattias Graf. A Note on Activity-Level and Uncertainty. *Z. Wirtschaft. Sozialwissen.*, 1983, *103*(5), pp. 485–96.

Scott, Robert C. and Sattler, Edward L. Catastrophe Theory in Economics. *J. Econ. Educ.*, Summer 1983, *14*(3), pp. 48–59.

Seoka, Yoshihiko. Steady State Growth of the Long-Run Sales-Maximizing Firm: Comment. *Quart. J. Econ.*, November 1983, *98*(4), pp. 713–19.

Sertel, Murat R. Technological Preferences of Capitalist and Workers' Enterprises. *Econ. Anal. Worker's Manage.*, 1983, *17*(3), pp. 273–77.

Shapiro, Alan C. Nominal Contracting in a World of Uncertainty. *J. Banking Finance*, March 1983, *7*(1), pp. 69–82.

Shapiro, Carl. Premiums for High Quality Products as Returns to Reputations. *Quart. J. Econ.*, November 1983, *98*(4), pp. 659–79.

Shapiro, Nina. An Economic Theory of Business Strategy: A Review Article. *J. Post Keynesian Econ.*, Spring 1983, *5*(3), pp. 483–88.

Sherali, Hanif D. and Soyster, Allen L. Analysis of Network Structured Models for Electric Utility Capacity Planning and Marginal Cost Pricing Problems. **In** *Lev, B., ed.*, 1983, pp. 113–34.

Shieh, Yeung-nan. Location and Bid Price Curves of the Urban Firm. *Urban Stud.*, November 1983, *20*(4), pp. 491–94.

Shieh, Yeung-nan. The Moses–Predöhl Pull and the Neoclassical Location Theory: An Alternative Approach. *Reg. Sci. Urban Econ.*, November 1983, *13*(4), pp. 517–24.

Shieh, Yeung-nan and Mai, Chao-cheng. A Firm's Bid Price Curve and the Neoclassical Theory of Production: A Correction and Further Analysis. *Southern Econ. J.*, July 1983, *50*(1), pp. 230–33.

Shilony, Yuval. Surplus May Measure Waste [On the Equivalence of Input and Output Market Marshallian Surplus Measures]. *J. Public Econ.*, December 1983, *22*(3), pp. 363–74.

Siebert, Horst. Extraction, Fixed Costs and the Hotelling Rule. *Z. ges. Staatswiss.*, June 1983, *139*(2), pp. 259–68.

Silberston, Aubrey. Efficiency and the Individual Firm. **In** *Shepherd, D.; Turk, J. and Silberston, A., eds.*, 1983, pp. 30–45.

Silvestre, Joaquim. Fixprice Analysis with Intermediate Goods. *Int. Econ. Rev.*, June 1983, *24*(2), pp. 485–92.

Smiley, Robert H. and Ravid, S. Abraham. The Importance of Being First: Learning Price and Strategy. *Quart. J. Econ.*, May 1983, *98*(2), pp. 353–62.

Solow, Robert M. Leif Johansen (1930–1982): A Memorial. *Scand. J. Econ.*, 1983, *85*(4), pp. 445–59.

de Sousa, Alfredo. Interest Rate and Capital Intensity. *Economia*, October 1983, *7*(3), pp. 519–30.

Spulber, Daniel F. and Becker, Robert A. Regulatory Lag and Deregulation with Imperfectly Adjustable Capital. *J. Econ. Dynam. Control*, September 1983, *6*(1/2), pp. 137–51.

Stamatis, Georgios. On Negative Labor Values. *Rev. Radical Polit. Econ.*, Winter 1983, *15*(4), pp. 81–91.

Stapleton, David C. How Elastic Is the Demand for Labor? A Comment. *Rev. Econ. Statist.*, November 1983, *65*(4), pp. 692–93. **[G: U.S.]**

Steigum, Erling, Jr. A Financial Theory of Investment Behavior. *Econometrica*, May, 1983, *51*(3), pp. 637–45.

Stiegler, Harald. Assessment of the Expedience of Subsidies for the Restoration of Financial Soundness under Operational Analysis Aspects. *Rivista Int. Sci. Econ. Com.*, June 1983, *30*(6), pp. 531–39.

Stoneman, P. and Ireland, Norman J. The Role of Supply Factors in the Diffusion of New Process Technology. *Econ. J.*, Supplement March 1983, pp. 66–78.

Taylor, John B. Equilibrium Theory with Learning and Disparate Expectations: Some Issues and Methods: Comment. **In** *Frydman, R. and Phelps, E. S., eds.*, 1983, pp. 198–202.

Tonks, Ian. Bayesian Learning and the Optimal Investment Decision of the Firm. *Econ. J.*, Supplement March 1983, pp. 87–98.

Townsend, Robert M. Equilibrium Theory with Learning and Disparate Expectations: Some Issues and Methods. **In** *Frydman, R. and Phelps, E. S., eds.*, 1983, pp. 169–98.

Townsend, Robert M. Forecasting the Forecasts of Others. *J. Polit. Econ.*, August 1983, *91*(4), pp. 546–88.

Tressler, J. H. and Menezes, C. F. Constant Returns to Scale and Competitive Equilibrium under Uncertainty. *J. Econ. Theory*, December 1983, *31*(2), pp. 383–91.

Trueman, Brett. Motivating Management to Reveal Inside Information. *J. Finance*, September 1983, *38*(4), pp. 1253–69. **[G: U.S.]**

Viallet, Claude. Resolution of Conflicts of Interest in the Ownership of a Firm: The Case of Mixed Firms. *Ann. Pub. Co-op. Econ.*, July–September 1983, *54*(3), pp. 255–69.

Vislie, Jon. On the Dynamics of Production under Cost Uncertainty. *Scand. J. Econ.*, 1983, *85*(2), pp. 249–66.

Wan, Fu Chi. Elasticities and Effects of Price Change on Revenue. *Atlantic Econ. J.*, September 1983, *11*(3), pp. 115.

Wang, Leonard F. S. Input Price Uncertainty and the Optimal Input Demand of the Imperfectly Competitive Firm. *Econ. Notes*, 1983, (3), pp. 180–83.

Watson, Harry. A Note on Pensions in a Neoclassical Model of the Firm. *J. Econ. Dynam. Control*, September 1983, *6*(1/2), pp. 41–54.

Watts, Martin J. Microeconomic Theory: Should Radicals Steal the Neoclassicals' Clothes? [The Microeconomics of Conflict and Hierarchy under Capitalist Production: A Reply to Watts]. *Rev. Radical Polit. Econ.*, Winter 1983, *15*(4), pp. 100–103.

Watts, Ross L. and Zimmerman, Jerold L. Agency

Problems, Auditing, and the Theory of the Firm: Some Evidence. *J. Law Econ.*, October 1983, *26*(3), pp. 613–33. **[G: U.S.; U.K.]**

Weiss, Nitzan. Leverage, Risk-Adjusted Discount Rate and Industry Equilibrium. *Amer. Econ.*, Spring 1983, *27*(1), pp. 5–12.

Williamson, Oliver E. Organizational Innovation: The Transaction-Cost Approach. **In** *Ronen, J., ed.*, 1983, pp. 101–33.

Wolinsky, Asher. Retail Trade Concentration Due to Consumers' Imperfect Information. *Bell J. Econ. (See Rand J. Econ. after 4/85)*, Spring 1983, *14*(1), pp. 275–82.

Woods, J. E. Prices of Production and Fixed Capital. *Z. ges. Staatswiss.*, June 1983, *139*(2), pp. 306–18.

Yamazaki, Akira. Competitive Firm Structures and Equilibria in a Coalition Production Economy. *Hitotsubashi J. Econ.*, June 1983, *24*(1), pp. 69–94.

Zafiris, Nicos. The Form of the Maximand of the Inegalitarian Workers' Co-operative. *Brit. Rev. Econ. Issues*, Autumn 1983, *5*(13), pp. 39–61.

Zieschang, Kimberly D. A Note on the Decomposition of Cost Efficiency into Technical and Allocative Components. *J. Econometrics*, December 1983, *23*(3), pp. 401–05.

Zwiener, Rudolf. "Crowding-out" durch öffentliche Investitionen? Eine Diskussion der Modellergebnisse der Deutschen Bundesbank und eine Gegenüberstellung mit den Ergebnissen der DIW-Version des ökonometrischen Konjunkturmodells der Wirtschaftsforschungsinstitute. ("Crowding-Out" through Public Investment. With English summary.) *Konjunkturpolitik*, 1983, *29*(3), pp. 121–40. **[G: W. Germany]**

0224 Theory of Factor Distribution and Distributive Shares

Baumol, William J. Toward Operational Models of Entrepreneurship. **In** *Ronen, J., ed.*, 1983, pp. 29–48.

Bental, Benjamin and Wenig, Alois. Will All People Become Alike if They Are Alike? *Z. Nationalökon.*, 1983, *43*(3), pp. 289–300.

Braeutigam, Ronald R. A Dynamic Analysis of Second-best Pricing. **In** *Finsinger, J., ed.*, 1983, pp. 103–16.

Casale, Giuseppe. Capitale, interesse, profitto ed equa tassazione. (Capital, Interest and Fiscal Equity. With English summary.) *Giorn. Econ.*, March-April 1983, *42*(3–4), pp. 153–78.

Cowen, Tyler. The Rate of Return in General Equilibrium—A Critique. *J. Post Keynesian Econ.*, Summer 1983, *5*(4), pp. 608–17.

Cubbin, John S. and Hall, Graham. Directors' Remuneration in the Theory of the Firm: Specification and Testing of the Null Hypothesis. *Europ. Econ. Rev.*, January 1983, *20*(1–3), pp. 333–48. **[G: U.K.]**

D'Agata, A. The Existence and Unicity of Cost-Minimizing Systems in Intensive Rent Theory. *Metroecon.*, February-June 1983, *35*(1–2), pp. 147–58.

Dixon, Robert J. A Mark-Up Approach to the Distribution of Aggregate Profits. *Australian Econ. Pap.*, December 1983, *22*(41), pp. 448–53.

Duménil, G. and Lévy, D. Prix et quantités: le cas des productions jointes. (Prices and Quantities: The Joint Production Model. With English summary.) *Écon. Appl.*, 1983, *36*(2–3), pp. 411–45.

Encarnación, José, Jr. Positive Time Preference: A Comment. *J. Polit. Econ.*, August 1983, *91*(4), pp. 706–08.

Gibson, Bill and McLeod, Darryl. Non-Produced Means of Production in Sraffa's System: Basics, Non-Basics and Quasi-Basics. *Cambridge J. Econ.*, June 1983, *7*(2), pp. 141–50.

Hatiboglu, Z. An Unconventional Approach to the Analysis of Growth in Developing Countries and Its Application in Turkey. *S. Afr. J. Econ.*, June 1983, *51*(2), pp. 297–309. **[G: Turkey]**

Hicks, John. Is Interest the Price of a Factor of Production? **In** *Hicks, J.*, 1983, *1979*, pp. 113–28.

Hicks, John. The Austrian Theory of Capital and Its Re-birth in Modern Economics. **In** *Hicks, J.*, 1983, *1973*, pp. 96–112.

Hicks, John. The Concept of Business Income. **In** *Hicks, J.*, 1983, *1979*, pp. 189–203.

Lau, Lawrence J. Socially Optimal Income Distributions. **In** *[Klein, L. R.]*, 1983, pp. 68–83.

Linde, Robert. Prämienlohn und Grenzproduktivitätstheorie der Einkommensverteilung. (Premium Pay and Marginal Productivity Theory of Income Distribution. With English summary.) *Z. Wirtschaft. Sozialwissen.*, 1983, *103*(4), pp. 351–68.

Mutti, John H. and Morgan, William E. Changing Energy Prices and Economic Rents: The Case of Western Coal. *Land Econ.*, May 1983, *59*(2), pp. 163–76. **[G: U.S.]**

Rainelli, Michel. Entrepreneur et profits dans les "Principes" de John Stuart Mill et d'Alfred Marshall. (Entrepreneur and Profits in Mill's and Marshall's *Principles.* With English summary.) *Revue Écon.*, July 1983, *34*(4), pp. 794–810.

Salvadori, Neri. On a New Variety of Rent. *Metroecon.*, February-June 1983, *35*(1–2), pp. 73–85.

Shapiro, Harold N. Entrepreneurial Concepts, Definitions, and Model Formulations. **In** *Ronen, J., ed.*, 1983, pp. 75–99.

Siddiqi, Muhammad Nejatullah. Economics of Profit-sharing. **In** *Siddiqi, M. N.*, 1983, pp. 97–123.

Stoneman, P. Diffusion, Technology Transfer and Trade. **In** *Macdonald, S.; Lamberton, D. M. and Mandeville, T., eds.*, 1983, pp. 93–103.

Wessel, Robert H. The Advantages of a Concept of Negative Rent. *Rivista Int. Sci. Econ. Com.*, June 1983, *30*(6), pp. 520–30.

0225 Theory of Firm and Industry under Competitive Market Structure

Abel, Andrew B. Market Structure and the Durability of Goods. *Rev. Econ. Stud.*, October 1983, *50*(4), pp. 625–37.

Adachi, Hideyuki. Innovations under Monopoly and Competition. *Kobe Univ. Econ.*, 1983, (29), pp. 41–50.

Arrow, Kenneth J. The Firm in General Equilibrium

Theory. In *Arrow, K. J., Vol. 2*, 1983, *1971*, pp. 156–98.

Baumol, William J.; Panzar, John C. and Willig, Robert D. Contestable Markets: An Uprising in the Theory of Industry Structure: Reply. *Amer. Econ. Rev.*, June 1983, *73*(3), pp. 491–96.

Brock, William A. Contestable Markets and the Theory of Industry Structure: A Review Article. *J. Polit. Econ.*, December 1983, *91*(6), pp. 1055–66.

Brown, Elba K. and Smith, William Doyle. Is Perfect Competition an Empirically Inadequate Model? A Comment. *Econ. Inquiry*, October 1983, *21*(4), pp. 593–94. **[G: U.S.]**

Brown, James N. Structural Estimation in Implicit Markets. In *Triplett, J. E., ed.*, 1983, pp. 123–51. **[G: U.S.]**

Cottle, Rex L. and Wallace, Myles S. Economic Effects of Non-Binding Price Constraints. *J. Ind. Econ.*, June 1983, *31*(4), pp. 469–74.

Daniel, Coldwell, III. The Roles of Time in the Specification of Market Conditions. *Rev. Bus. Econ. Res.*, Winter, 1983, *18*(2), pp. 51–59.

DeVany, Arthur S. and Saving, Thomas R. The Economics of Quality. *J. Polit. Econ.*, December 1983, *91*(6), pp. 979–1000.

Donnenfeld, Shabtai and Strebel, Paul J. Industry Structure and Trade Policy under Fluctuating Import Prices. *Europ. Econ. Rev.*, November 1983, *23*(2), pp. 203–15.

Eden, Benjamin. On Competitive Price Adjustment for a Storable Good and Abstention from Trade. *J. Polit. Econ.*, December 1983, *91*(6), pp. 1028–44.

Fixler, Dennis J. Uncertainty, Market Structure and the Incentive to Invent. *Economica*, November 1983, *50*(200), pp. 407–23.

Fudenberg, Drew, et al. Preemption, Leapfrogging and Competition in Patent Races. *Europ. Econ. Rev.*, June 1983, *22*(1), pp. 3–31.

Hammes, David L. Is Perfect Competition an Empirically Too-Adequate Model? *Econ. Inquiry*, October 1983, *21*(4), pp. 591–92. **[G: U.S.]**

Hands, Douglas W. "Testing" Perfect Competition: A Comment [Is Perfect Competition an Empirically Inadequate Model?]. *Econ. Inquiry*, October 1983, *21*(4), pp. 588–90. **[G: U.S.]**

Hicks, John. Scitovsky on Competition. In *Hicks, J.*, 1983, *1952*, pp. 153–62.

Hiebert, L. Dean. Self Insurance, Self Protection and the Theory of the Competitive Firm. *Southern Econ. J.*, July 1983, *50*(1), pp. 160–68.

Lerner, Abba P. An Alternative Formulation of the Welfare Equations, Equality and Proportionality. In *Lerner, A. P.*, 1983, *1944*, pp. 153–62.

Lerner, Abba P. Simple Production II (under Perfect Competition) the Welfare Equations. In *Lerner, A. P.*, 1983, *1970*, pp. 147–52.

Lunn, John. Market Structure and the Incentive to Invent. *Eastern Econ. J.*, October–December 1983, *9*(4), pp. 333–36.

Raymon, Neil. Price Ceilings in Competitive Markets with Variable Quality. *J. Public Econ.*, November 1983, *22*(2), pp. 257–64.

Scheinkman, José A. and Schechtman, Jack. A Simple Competitive Model with Production and Storage. *Rev. Econ. Stud.*, July 1983, *50*(3), pp. 427–41.

Schwartz, Marius and Reynolds, Robert J. Contestable Markets: An Uprising in the Theory of Industry Structure: Comment. *Amer. Econ. Rev.*, June 1983, *73*(3), pp. 488–90.

Shapiro, Carl. Premiums for High Quality Products as Returns to Reputations. *Quart. J. Econ.*, November 1983, *98*(4), pp. 659–79.

Shepherd, A. Ross. Factor Price, Optimum Scale and the Structure of Industry [The Comparative Statics of the Competitive, Increasing-Cost Industry]. *Southern Econ. J.*, April 1983, *49*(4), pp. 1169–73.

Spence, A. Michael. *Contestable Markets and the Theory of Industry Structure:* A Review Article. *J. Econ. Lit.*, September 1983, *21*(3), pp. 981–90.

Stigler, George J. Perfect Competition, Historically Contemplated. In *Stigler, G. J.*, 1983, *1957*, pp. 234–67.

Taylor, John B. Equilibrium Theory with Learning and Disparate Expectations: Some Issues and Methods: Comment. In *Frydman, R. and Phelps, E. S., eds.*, 1983, pp. 198–202.

Townsend, Robert M. Equilibrium Theory with Learning and Disparate Expectations: Some Issues and Methods. In *Frydman, R. and Phelps, E. S., eds.*, 1983, pp. 169–98.

Ushio, Yoshiaki. Cournot Equilibrium with Free Entry: The Case of Decreasing Average Cost Functions. *Rev. Econ. Stud.*, April 1983, *50*(2), pp. 347–54.

Wang, Leonard F. S. Price Constraints, Forward Markets and the Competitive Firm under Price Uncertainty. *Bull. Econ. Res.*, May 1983, *35*(1), pp. 47–54.

Weiss, Nitzan. Leverage, Risk-Adjusted Discount Rate and Industry Equilibrium. *Amer. Econ.*, Spring 1983, *27*(1), pp. 5–12.

Weitzman, Martin L. Contestable Markets: An Uprising in the Theory of Industry Structure: Comment. *Amer. Econ. Rev.*, June 1983, *73*(3), pp. 486–87.

0226 Theory of Firm and Industry under Imperfectly Competitive Market Structure

Abel, Andrew B. Market Structure and the Durability of Goods. *Rev. Econ. Stud.*, October 1983, *50*(4), pp. 625–37.

Adachi, Hideyuki. Innovations under Monopoly and Competition. *Kobe Univ. Econ.*, 1983, (29), pp. 41–50.

Afxentiou, Panayiotis C. Some Thoughts on the Theory of Monopolistic Competition. *Greek Econ. Rev.*, April 1983, *5*(1), pp. 55–64.

Allsbrook, Ogden O., Jr. and Gilliam, Kenneth P. An Industrial Interpretation of Inflationary Unemployment. *Kredit Kapital*, 1983, *16*(4), pp. 479–87.

Arrow, Kenneth J. The Firm in General Equilibrium Theory. In *Arrow, K. J., Vol. 2*, 1983, *1971*, pp. 156–98.

Arvan, Lanny and Moses, Leon N. Inventory Investment and the Theory of the Firm: Errata. *Amer. Econ. Rev.*, March 1983, *73*(1), pp. 251.

d'Aspremont, Claude, et al. On the Stability of Collusive Price Leadership. *Can. J. Econ.*, February 1983, *16*(1), pp. 17–25.

Balcer, Yves. F.O.B. Pricing versus Uniform Delivered Pricing: A Welfare Analysis in a Stochastic Environment. *J. Econ. Theory*, June 1983, *30*(1), pp. 54–73.

Baldwin, Carliss Y. Administered Prices Fifty Years Later: A Comment of Gardiner C. Means: Corporate Power in the Marketplace. *J. Law Econ.*, June 1983, *26*(2), pp. 487–96. **[G: U.S.]**

Baumol, William J. Minimum and Maximum Pricing Principles for Residual Regulation. **In** *[Bonbright, J. C.]*, 1983, pp. 177–96.

Baumol, William J.; Panzar, John C. and Willig, Robert D. Contestable Markets: An Uprising in the Theory of Industry Structure: Reply. *Amer. Econ. Rev.*, June 1983, *73*(3), pp. 491–96.

Bhagwati, Jagdish N. Oligopoly Theory, Entry-Prevention, and Growth. **In** *Bhagwati, J. N., Vol. 2*, 1983, *1973*, pp. 296–309.

Bishop, William. Oligopoly Pricing: A Proposal. *Antitrust Bull.*, Summer 1983, *28*(2), pp. 311–36. **[G: U.K.]**

Bittlingmayer, George. A Model of Vertical Restriction and Equilibrium in Retailing. *J. Bus.*, October 1983, *56*(4), pp. 477–96.

Bohm, Volker, et al. Monopolistic Quantity Rationing. *Quart. J. Econ.*, Supplement 1983, *98*(3), pp. 189–97.

Bös, Dieter and Tillmann, Georg. Cost-Axiomatic Regulatory Pricing. *J. Public Econ.*, November 1983, *22*(2), pp. 243–56.

Boyer, Marcel and Moreaux, Michel. Conjectures, Rationality, and Duopoly Theory. *Int. J. Ind. Organ.*, 1983, *1*(1), pp. 23–41.

Boyer, Marcel and Moreaux, Michel. Consistent versus Non-Consistent Conjectures in Doupoly Theory: Some Examples. *J. Ind. Econ.*, September 1983, *32*(1), pp. 97–110.

Boyer, Marcel and Moreaux, Michel. Théorie de l'oligopole, conjectures autoréalisantes et contraintes de rationalité. (Oligolopy Theory, Self-Fulfilling Conjectures and the Constraints of Rationality. With English summary.) *Écon. Appl.*, 1983, *36*(1), pp. 99–127.

Bradburd, Ralph M. and Over, A. Mead, Jr. The Notion of a Critical Region of Concentration: Theory and Evidence. **In** *Craven, J. V., ed.*, 1983, pp. 109–28.

Brander, James A. and Spencer, Barbara J. Strategic Commitment with R&D: The Symmetric Case. *Bell J. Econ. (See Rand J. Econ. after 4/85)*, Spring 1983, *14*(1), pp. 225–35.

Braverman, Avishay; Guasch, J. Luis and Salop, Steven C. Defects in Disneyland: Quality Control as a Two-Part Tariff. *Rev. Econ. Stud.*, January 1983, *50*(1), pp. 121–31.

Brazelton, W. Robert. Price Adjustments during Inflation in Non-Competitive Markets: A Micro-Macro Comment. *Jahr. Nationalökon. Statist.*, November 1983, *198*(6), pp. 557–61.

Brennan, Geoffrey and Buchanan, James M. Predictive Power and the Choice among Regimes. *Econ. J.*, March 1983, *93*(369), pp. 89–105.

Brennan, Geoffrey; Buchanan, James M. and Lee, Dwight R. On Monopoly Price. *Kyklos*, 1983, *36*(4), pp. 531–47.

Brennan, Geoffrey; Lee, Dwight R. and Walsh, Cliff. Monopoly Markets in Public Goods: The Case of the Uniform All-or-None Price. *Public Finance Quart.*, October 1983, *11*(4), pp. 465–90.

Bresnahan, Timothy F. Duopoly Models with Consistent Conjectures: Reply. *Amer. Econ. Rev.*, March 1983, *73*(1), pp. 240–41.

Bresnahan, Timothy F. Existence of Consistent Conjectures: Reply. *Amer. Econ. Rev.*, June 1983, *73*(3), pp. 457–58.

Brock, William A. Contestable Markets and the Theory of Industry Structure: A Review Article. *J. Polit. Econ.*, December 1983, *91*(6), pp. 1055–66.

Brock, William A. Pricing, Predation, and Entry Barriers in Regulated Industries. **In** *Evans, D. S., ed.*, 1983, pp. 191–229.

Brock, William A. and Scheinkman, José A. Free Entry and the Sustainability of Natural Monopoly: Bertrand Revisited by Cournot. **In** *Evans, D. S., ed.*, 1983, pp. 231–52.

Brown, Donald J. and Heal, Geoffrey M. Marginal vs. Average Cost Pricing in the Presence of a Public Monopoly. *Amer. Econ. Rev.*, May 1983, *73*(2), pp. 189–93.

Buccola, Steven T. Risk Preferences and Short-Run Pricing Efficiency. *Amer. J. Agr. Econ.*, August 1983, *65*(3), pp. 587–91.

Bucovetsky, Sam. Price Dispersion and Stockpiling by Consumers. *Rev. Econ. Stud.*, July 1983, *50*(3), pp. 443–65.

Burdett, Kenneth and Judd, Kenneth L. Equilibrium Price Dispersion. *Econometrica*, July 1983, *51*(4), pp. 955–69.

Carlson, John A. and McAfee, R. Preston. Discrete Equilibrium Price Dispersion. *J. Polit. Econ.*, June 1983, *91*(3), pp. 480–93.

Carlton, Dennis W. A Reexamination of Delivered Pricing Systems. *J. Law Econ.*, April 1983, *26*(1), pp. 51–70. **[G: U.S.]**

Casson, Mark and Norman, George. Pricing and Sourcing Strategies in a Multinational Oligopoly. **In** *Casson, M., ed.*, 1983, pp. 63–83.

Clarke, Richard N. Collusion and the Incentives for Information Sharing. *Bell J. Econ. (See Rand J. Econ. after 4/85)*, Autumn 1983, *14*(2), pp. 383–94.

Comanor, William. Commentary [Theoretical Approaches to the Economics of Advertising] [Advertising and Brand Loyalty as Barriers to Entry]. **In** *Connor, J. M. and Ward, R. W., eds.*, 1983, pp. 71–73.

Conlisk, John. Competitive Approximation of a Cournot Market. *Rev. Econ. Stud.*, October 1983, *50*(4), pp. 597–607.

Conrad, Cecilia A. The Advantage of Being First and Competition between Firms. *Int. J. Ind. Organ.*, December 1983, *1*(4), pp. 353–64.

Crampes, Claude. Subventions et régulation d'une entreprise privée. (Subsidies and Regulation of a Private Entreprise. With English summary.) *Ann. INSEE*, July–September 1983, (51), pp. 47–64.

Crössmann, H. Jürgen and Tietz, Reinhard. Market Behavior Based on Aspiration Levels. **In** *Tietz,*

R., ed., 1983, pp. 170–85.

Cubbin, John. Apparent Collusion and Conjectural Variations in Differentiated Oligopoly. *Int. J. Ind. Organ.*, June 1983, *1* (2), pp. 155–63.

Daniel, Coldwell, III. Duopoly Models with Consistent Conjectures: Comment. *Amer. Econ. Rev.*, March 1983, *73* (1), pp. 238–39.

Danziger, Leif. Price Adjustments with Stochastic Inflation. *Int. Econ. Rev.*, October 1983, *24* (3), pp. 699–707.

DeVany, Arthur S. and Saving, Thomas R. The Economics of Quality. *J. Polit. Econ.*, December 1983, *91* (6), pp. 979–1000.

Dixit, Avinash. Vertical Integration in a Monopolistically Competitive Industry. *Int. J. Ind. Organ.*, 1983, *1* (1), pp. 63–78.

Donnenfeld, Shabtai. Market Uncertainty and the Monopolist Incentive to Innovate. *Int. J. Ind. Organ.*, December 1983, *1* (4), pp. 379–86.

Donnenfeld, Shabtai and Strebel, Paul J. Industry Structure and Trade Policy under Fluctuating Import Prices. *Europ. Econ. Rev.*, November 1983, *23* (2), pp. 203–15.

Evans, David S. and Heckman, James J. Multiproduct Cost Function Estimates and Natural Monopoly Tests for the Bell System. **In** *Evans, D. S., ed.*, 1983, pp. 253–82. **[G: U.S.]**

Fane, G. and Sieper, E. Preference Revelation and Monopsony. *J. Public Econ.*, April 1983, *20* (3), pp. 357–72.

Fershtman, Chaim and Spiegel, Uriel. Monopoly versus Competition: The Learning by Doing Case. *Europ. Econ. Rev.*, November 1983, *23* (2), pp. 217–22.

Finsinger, Jörg and Vogelsang, Ingo. Reply to Professor Gravelle's Comments [Alternative Institutional Frameworks for Price Incentive Mechanisms]. *Kyklos*, 1983, *36* (1), pp. 121–22.

Fixler, Dennis J. Uncertainty, Market Structure and the Incentive to Invent. *Economica*, November 1983, *50* (200), pp. 407–23.

Flacco, Paul R. Output, Entry, and Competitive Production under Price Uncertainty. *Southern Econ. J.*, October 1983, *50* (2), pp. 565–71.

Folsom, Roger Nils and Greer, Douglas F. Advertising and Brand Loyalty as Barriers to Entry. **In** *Connor, J. M. and Ward, R. W., eds.*, 1983, pp. 47–70.

Forchheimer, Karl. Imperfect Monopoly: Some Theoretical Considerations. *Nebr. J. Econ. Bus.*, Spring 1983, *22* (2), pp. 65–77.

Formby, John P.; Layson, Stephen K. and Smith, W. James. Price Discrimination, 'Adjusted Concavity,' and Output Changes under Conditions of Constant Elasticity. *Econ. J.*, December 1983, *93* (372), pp. 892–99.

Freixas, Xavier and Laffont, Jean-Jacques. Tarification au coût marginal ou équilibre budgétaire? (Pricing Marginal Cost or Budgetary Equilibrium? With English summary.) *Ann. INSEE*, July–September 1983, (51), pp. 65–88.

Friedman, James W. Advertising and Oligopolistic Equilibrium. *Bell J. Econ. (See Rand J. Econ. after 4/85)*, Autumn 1983, *14* (2), pp. 464–73.

Friedman, James W. Limit Price Entry Prevention When Complete Information Is Lacking. *J. Econ. Dynam. Control*, May 1983, *5* (2/3), pp. 187–99.

Friedman, James W. Low Information Nash Equilibria for Oligopolistic Markets. *Info. Econ. Policy*, 1983, *1* (1), pp. 37–53.

Fudenberg, Drew and Tirole, Jean. Capital as a Commitment: Strategic Investment to Deter Mobility. *J. Econ. Theory*, December 1983, *31* (2), pp. 227–50.

Fudenberg, Drew, et al. Preemption, Leapfrogging and Competition in Patent Races. *Europ. Econ. Rev.*, June 1983, *22* (1), pp. 3–31.

Furlong, William J. and Slotsve, George A. "Will That Be Pickup or Delivery?" An Alternative Spatial Pricing Strategy. *Bell J. Econ. (See Rand J. Econ. after 4/85)*, Spring 1983, *14* (1), pp. 271–74.

Gal-Or, Esther. "Sales" and Risk-Averse Consumers. *Economica*, November 1983, *50* (200), pp. 477–83.

Gal-Or, Esther. Quality and Quantity Competition. *Bell J. Econ. (See Rand J. Econ. after 4/85)*, Autumn 1983, *14* (2), pp. 590–600.

Gallini, Nancy T. and Winter, Ralph A. On Vertical Control in Monopolistic Competition. *Int. J. Ind. Organ.*, September 1983, *1* (3), pp. 275–86.

Gelman, Judith R. and Salop, Steven C. Judo Economics: Capacity Limitation and Coupon Competition. *Bell J. Econ. (See Rand J. Econ. after 4/85)*, Autumn 1983, *14* (2), pp. 315–25.

Gilligan, Thomas W. and Smirlock, Michael L. Predation and Cross-Subsidization in the Value Maximizing Multiproduct Firm. *Southern Econ. J.*, July 1983, *50* (1), pp. 37–42.

Gowland, D. H. Market Failure and State Intervention. **In** *Gowland, D. H., ed.*, 1983, pp. 171–99.

Gravelle, H. S. E. Alternative Institutional Frameworks for Price Incentive Mechanisms: Some Comments. *Kyklos*, 1983, *36* (1), pp. 115–20.

Green, Jerry R. and Honkapohja, Seppo. Bilateral Contracts. *J. Math. Econ.*, April 1983, *11* (2), pp. 171–87.

Grillo, Michele. Equilibri di congetture in un modello di duopolio. (Conjectural Equilibria in a Model of Duopoly. With English summary.) *Giorn. Econ.*, November–December 1983, *42* (11–12), pp. 781–93.

Guttman, Joel M. and Miller, Michael. Endogenous Conjectural Variations in Oligopoly. *J. Econ. Behav. Organ.*, June–September 1983, *4* (2–3), pp. 249–64.

Hamilton, Neil W. and Hamilton, Peter R. Duopoly in the Distribution of Electricity: A Policy Failure. *Antitrust Bull.*, Summer 1983, *28* (2), pp. 281–309. **[G: U.S.]**

Hannesson, Rögnvaldur. A Note on Socially Optimal versus Monopolistic Exploitation of a Renewable Resource. *Z. Nationalökon.*, 1983, *43* (1), pp. 63–70.

Harris, Milton. Pricing Schemes When Demand Is Unobservable. **In** *Engelbrecht-Wiggans, R.; Shubik, M. and Stark, R. M., eds.*, 1983, pp. 195–203.

Helpman, Elhanan and Razin, Assaf. Increasing Returns, Monopolistic Competition, and Factor Movements: A Welfare Analysis. *J. Int. Econ.*, May 1983, *14* (3/4), pp. 263–76.

Hicks, John. Scitovsky on Competition. **In** *Hicks, J.*, 1983, *1952,* pp. 153–62.

Hicks, John. Stickers and Snatchers. **In** *Hicks, J.*, 1983, *1954,* pp. 163–78.

Hicks, John. The Theory of Monopoly: A Survey. **In** *Hicks, J.*, 1983, *1935,* pp. 131–52.

Hill, Martyn and Waterson, Michael. Labor-Managed Cournot Oligopoly and Industry Output. *J. Compar. Econ.*, March 1983, *7*(1), pp. 43–51.

Hoel, Michael. Monopoly Resource Extractions under the Presence of Predetermined Substitute Production. *J. Econ. Theory,* June 1983, *30*(1), pp. 201–12.

Horowitz, Ira. Entry Inclinations under Uncertainty. *J. Econ. Bus.*, 1983, *35*(1), pp. 1–10.

Hsu, Song-ken. Monopoly Output and Economic Welfare under Third-Degree Price Discrimination. *Southern Econ. J.*, July 1983, *50*(1), pp. 234–39.

Hsu, Song-ken. Social Optimal Pricing in a Spatial Market. *Reg. Sci. Urban Econ.*, August 1983, *13*(3), pp. 401–10.

Ireland, Norman J. A Note on Conglomerate Merger and Behavioural Response to Risk. *J. Ind. Econ.*, March 1983, *31*(3), pp. 283–89.

Ireland, Norman J. Monopolistic Competition and a Firm's Product Range. *Int. J. Ind. Organ.*, September 1983, *1*(3), pp. 239–52.

Itoh, Motoshige. Monopoly, Product Differentiation and Economic Welfare. *J. Econ. Theory,* October 1983, *31*(1), pp. 88–104.

Jenny, Frédéric and Weber, André-Paul. Aggregate Welfare Loss Due to Monopoly Power in the French Economy: Some Tentative Estimates. *J. Ind. Econ.*, December 1983, *32*(2), pp. 113–30. **[G: France]**

Johnson, Frederick I. On the Stability of Commodity Cartels. *Amer. Econ.*, Fall 1983, *27*(2), pp. 34–36. **[G: LDCs]**

Joyce, Patrick. Information and Behavior in Experimental Markets. *J. Econ. Behav. Organ.*, December 1983, *4*(4), pp. 411–24.

Kamien, Morton I. and Schwartz, Nancy L. Conjectural Variations. *Can. J. Econ.*, May 1983, *16*(2), pp. 191–211.

Katz, Michael L. Non-Uniform Pricing, Output and Welfare under Monopoly. *Rev. Econ. Stud.*, January 1983, *50*(1), pp. 37–56.

Kawashima, Yasuo. Product Differentiation, Prices, and Market Structure. *Europ. Econ. Rev.*, June 1983, *22*(1), pp. 75–96.

Kay, J. A. A General Equilibrium Approach to the Measurement of Monopoly Welfare Loss. *Int. J. Ind. Organ.*, December 1983, *1*(4), pp. 317–31.

Kreps, David M. and Scheinkman, José A. Quantity Precommitment and Bertrand Competition Yield Cournot Outcomes. *Bell J. Econ. (See Rand J. Econ. after 4/85),* Autumn 1983, *14*(2), pp. 326–37.

Kuran, Timur. Asymmetric Price Rigidity and Inflationary Bias. *Amer. Econ. Rev.*, June 1983, *73*(3), pp. 373–82.

LaCroix, Sumner J. Marketing, Price Discrimination, and Welfare. *Southern Econ. J.*, January 1983, *49*(3), pp. 847–52.

Laffont, Jean-Jacques and Moreaux, Michel. The Nonexistence of a Free Entry Cournot Equilibrium in Labor-Managed Economies. *Econometrica,* March 1983, *51*(2), pp. 455–62.

Lerner, Abba P. The Concept of Monopoly and the Measurement of Monopoly Power. **In** *Lerner, A. P.*, 1983, *1934,* pp. 7–25.

Lewis, Tracy R. Preemption, Divestiture, and Forward Contracting in a Market Dominated by a Single Firm. *Amer. Econ. Rev.*, December 1983, *73*(5), pp. 1092–1101.

Liebermann, Yehoshua and Syrquin, M. On the Use and Abuse of Rights: An Economic View. *J. Econ. Behav. Organ.*, March 1983, *4*(1), pp. 25–40.

Liebowitz, S. J. Tie-In Sales and Price Discrimination. *Econ. Inquiry,* July 1983, *21*(3), pp. 387–99.

Lunn, John. Market Structure and the Incentive to Invent. *Eastern Econ. J.*, October–December 1983, *9*(4), pp. 333–36.

Maoz, Ilan. The Cournot Duopoly Model Reconsidered in the Presence of Costly Communication and Enforcement Agreements. *J. Econ. Behav. Organ.*, December 1983, *4*(4), pp. 395–410.

Mathewson, G. Frank and Winter, Ralph A. The Incentives for Resale Price Maintenance under Imperfect Information. *Econ. Inquiry,* July 1983, *21*(3), pp. 337–48.

Mathewson, G. Frank and Winter, Ralph A. Vertical Integration by Contractual Restraints in Spatial Markets. *J. Bus.*, October 1983, *56*(4), pp. 497–517.

Matthews, Steven A. Selling to Risk Averse Buyers with Unobservable Tastes. *J. Econ. Theory,* August 1983, *30*(2), pp. 370–400.

Matthews, Steven A. and Mirman, Leonard J. Equilibrium Limit Pricing: The Effects of Private Information and Stochastic Demand. *Econometrica,* July 1983, *51*(4), pp. 981–96.

Means, Gardiner C. Corporate Power in the Marketplace. *J. Law Econ.*, June 1983, *26*(2), pp. 467–85. **[G: U.S.]**

de Meza, David. The Simple Welfare Economics of Monopolistic Competition. *J. Econ. Stud.*, 1983, *10*(1), pp. 60–62.

Morrison, Clarence C. Ownership Dispersion as a Second-Best Counterstrategy against Monopoly. *J. Econ. Bus.*, June 1983, *35*(2), pp. 159–68.

Nakao, Takeo. Profitability, Market Share, Product Quality, and Advertising in Oligopoly. *J. Econ. Dynam. Control,* September 1983, *6*(1/2), pp. 153–71.

Norman, George. Spatial Competition and Spatial Price Discrimination: A Correction. *Rev. Econ. Stud.*, October 1983, *50*(4), pp. 755–56.

Norman, George. Spatial Pricing with Differentiated Products. *Quart. J. Econ.*, May 1983, *98*(2), pp. 291–310.

O'Brien, D. P. Research Programmes in Competitive Structure. *J. Econ. Stud.*, 1983, *10*(4), pp. 29–51.

Okada, Akira. Coalition Formation of Oligopolistic Firms for Information Exchange. *Math. Soc. Sci.*, December 1983, *6*(3), pp. 337–51.

Okuguchi, Koji. Equilibria in an Industry with a Cartel and a Competitive Fringe. *Econ. Stud. Quart.*, April 1983, *34*(1), pp. 38–43.

Okuguchi, Koji. Price Discrimination in Related Markets: Comment. *Econ. Inquiry,* July 1983,

21(3), pp. 439–40.

Oren, Shmuel S.; Smith, Stephen A. and Wilson, Robert B. Competitive Nonlinear Tariffs. *J. Econ. Theory,* February 1983, *29*(1), pp. 49–71.

Osborne, Martin J. and Pitchik, Carolyn. Profit-Sharing in a Collusive Industry. *Europ. Econ. Rev.,* June 1983, *22*(1), pp. 59–74.

Otani, Kiyoshi. The Price Determination in the Inventory Stock Market: A Disequilibrium Analysis. *Int. Econ. Rev.,* October 1983, *24*(3), pp. 709–19.

Palfrey, Thomas R. Bundling Decisions by a Multiproduct Monopolist with Incomplete Information. *Econometrica,* March 1983, *51*(2), pp. 463–83.

Perrakis, Stylianos and Warskett, George. Capacity and Entry under Demand Uncertainty. *Rev. Econ. Stud.,* July 1983, *50*(3), pp. 495–511.

Phillips, Owen R. and Battalio, Raymond C. Two-Part Tariffs and Monopoly Profits When Visits Are Variable [A Disneyland Dilemma: Two-Part Tariffs for a Mickey Mouse Monopoly]. *Bell J. Econ. (See Rand J. Econ. after 4/85),* Autumn 1983, *14*(2), pp. 601–04.

Plott, Charles R. and Agha, Gul. Intertemporal Speculation with a Random Demand in an Experimental Market. In *Tietz, R., ed.,* 1983, pp. 201–16.

Porter, Robert H. Optimal Cartel Trigger Price Strategies. *J. Econ. Theory,* April 1983, *29*(2), pp. 313–38.

Reinganum, Jennifer F. Uncertain Innovation and the Persistence of Monopoly. *Amer. Econ. Rev.,* September 1983, *73*(4), pp. 741–48.

Reynolds, Peter J. Kalecki's Degree of Monopoly. *J. Post Keynesian Econ.,* Spring 1983, *5*(3), pp. 493–503.

Rheaume, G. C. Welfare Optimal Subsidy-free Prices under a Regulated Monopoly. In *Courville, L.; de Fontenay, A. and Dobell, R., eds.,* 1983, pp. 319–40.

Robson, Arthur J. Existence of Consistent Conjectures: Comment. *Amer. Econ. Rev.,* June 1983, *73*(3), pp. 454–56.

Salant, Stephen W.; Switzer, Sheldon and Reynolds, Robert J. Losses from Horizontal Merger: The Effects of an Exogenous Change in Industry Structure on Cournot–Nash Equilibrium. *Quart. J. Econ.,* May 1983, *98*(2), pp. 185–99.

Sappington, David. Optimal Regulation of a Multiproduct Monopoly with Unknown Technological Capabilities. *Bell J. Econ. (See Rand J. Econ. after 4/85),* Autumn 1983, *14*(2), pp. 453–63.

Schmalensee, Richard. Advertising and Entry Deterrence: An Exploratory Model. *J. Polit. Econ.,* August 1983, *91*(4), pp. 636–53.

Schöler, Klaus. Alternative Preistechniken im räumlichen Monopol: Ein einzelwirtschaftlicher und wohlfahrtstheoretischer Vergleich. (Alternative Pricing Techniques in Spatial Monopoly. With English summary.) *Z. ges. Staatswiss.,* June 1983, *139*(2), pp. 289–305.

Schöler, Klaus. Preisbildung bei räumlichem Wettbewerb. (Pricing under Spatial Competition. With English summary.) *Jahr. Nationalökon. Statist.,* March 1983, *198*(2), pp. 145–60.

Schutte, David P. Inventories and Sticky Prices: Note. *Amer. Econ. Rev.,* September 1983, *73*(4), pp. 815–16.

Schwartz, Marius and Reynolds, Robert J. Contestable Markets: An Uprising in the Theory of Industry Structure: Comment. *Amer. Econ. Rev.,* June 1983, *73*(3), pp. 488–90.

Scott, Frank A., Jr. A Note on Uncertain Input Prices, Profit Risk, and the Rate-of-Return Regulated Firm. *Land Econ.,* August 1983, *59*(3), pp. 337–41.

Selten, Reinhard. A Model of Oligopolistic Size Structure and Profitability. *Europ. Econ. Rev.,* June 1983, *22*(1), pp. 33–57.

Semmler, Willi. Competition, Monopoly, and Differentials of Profit Rates: A Reply. *Rev. Radical Polit. Econ.,* Winter 1983, *15*(4), pp. 92–99. **[G: U.S.]**

Sengupta, Jati K.; Leonard, John E. and Vanyo, James P. A Limit Pricing Model for U.S. Computer Industry: An Application. *Appl. Econ.,* June 1983, *15*(3), pp. 297–308. **[G: U.S.]**

Shaffer, Sherrill. Demand-Side Determinants of Natural Monopoly. *Atlantic Econ. J.,* December 1983, *11*(4), pp. 71–73.

Shaked, Avner and Sutton, John. Natural Oligopolies. *Econometrica,* September 1983, *51*(5), pp. 1469–83.

Shapiro, Carl. Optimal Pricing of Experience Goods. *Bell J. Econ. (See Rand J. Econ. after 4/85),* Autumn 1983, *14*(2), pp. 497–507.

Sherman, Howard J. Monopoly Power and Profit Rates [Competition, Monopoly and Differentials of Profit Rates: Theoretical Considerations and Empirical Evidence]. *Rev. Radical Polit. Econ.,* Summer 1983, *15*(2), pp. 125–33. **[G: U.S.]**

Sheshinski, Eytan and Weiss, Yoram. Optimum Pricing Policy under Stochastic Inflation. *Rev. Econ. Stud.,* July 1983, *50*(3), pp. 513–29.

Silberston, Aubrey. Efficiency and the Individual Firm. In *Shepherd, D.; Turk, J. and Silberston, A., eds.,* 1983, pp. 30–45.

da Silva, Amado and Santos, Aníbal. Uma digressão pela economia industrial: de Harvard a Chicago passando pela Europa. *Economia,* January 1983, *7*(1), pp. 87–110.

Skinner, Andrew S. E. H. Chamberlin: The Origins and Development of Monopolistic Competition. *J. Econ. Stud.,* 1983, *10*(4), pp. 52–67.

Smiley, Robert H. and Ravid, S. Abraham. The Importance of Being First: Learning Price and Strategy. *Quart. J. Econ.,* May 1983, *98*(2), pp. 353–62.

Spatt, Chester S. Imperfect Price Discrimination and Variety. *J. Bus.,* April 1983, *56*(2), pp. 203–16.

Spence, A. Michael. *Contestable Markets and the Theory of Industry Structure:* A Review Article. *J. Econ. Lit.,* September 1983, *21*(3), pp. 981–90.

Stewart, Marion B. Noncooperative Oligopoly and Preemptive Innovation without Winner-Take-All. *Quart. J. Econ.,* November 1983, *98*(4), pp. 681–94.

Thépot, Jacques. Marketing and Investment Policies of Duopolists in a Growing Industry. *J. Econ. Dynam. Control,* July 1983, *5*(4), pp. 387–404.

Tisdell, Clem A. Workable Competition, Deadweight Losses, and Demand Elasticities. *Man-*

chester Sch. Econ. Soc. Stud., June 1983, *51* (2), pp. 152–58.

Turnovsky, Stephen J. The Determination of Spot and Futures Prices with Storable Commodities. *Econometrica,* September 1983, *51* (5), pp. 1363–87.

Ulph, David. Rational Conjectures in the Theory of Oligopoly. *Int. J. Ind. Organ.,* June 1983, *1* (2), pp. 131–54.

d'Ursel, Laurent. Politiques de "non-prix": équilibre et optimum: essai de synthèse. (Nonprice Competition: Equilibrium and Optimum. With English summary.) *Revue Écon.,* November 1983, *34* (6), pp. 1057–88.

Ushio, Yoshiaki. Cournot Equilibrium with Free Entry: The Case of Decreasing Average Cost Functions. *Rev. Econ. Stud.,* April 1983, *50* (2), pp. 347–54.

Vaughan, Michael B. A Note on the Allocative Differences between Contracting and Regulation. *Atlantic Econ. J.,* March 1983, *11* (1), pp. 117.

Vind, Karl. Equilibrium with Coordination. *J. Math. Econ.,* December 1983, *12* (3), pp. 275–85.

Vogelsang, Ingo. Effort Rewarding Incentive Mechanisms for Public Enterprise Managers. *Int. J. Ind. Organ.,* September 1983, *1* (3), pp. 253–73.

Vogelsang, Ingo. Public Interest Firms as Leaders in Oligopolistic Industries. **In** *Finsinger, J., ed.,* 1983, pp. 86–99. **[G: W. Germany]**

Waagstein, Thorbjørn. A Dynamic Model of Entry Deterrence. *Scand. J. Econ.,* 1983, *85* (3), pp. 325–37.

Wahlroos, Björn. Regulation of "Administered" Prices: An Empirical Analysis of the Microeconomics of Price Movement in Finland, 1972–77. *J. Ind. Econ.,* June 1983, *31* (4), pp. 363–81. **[G: Finland]**

Wang, Leonard F. S. Input Price Uncertainty and the Optimal Input Demand of the Imperfectly Competitive Firm. *Econ. Notes,* 1983, (3), pp. 180–83.

Waterson, Michael. Economies of Scope within Market Frameworks. *Int. J. Ind. Organ.,* June 1983, *1* (2), pp. 223–37.

Weitzman, Martin L. Contestable Markets: An Uprising in the Theory of Industry Structure: Comment. *Amer. Econ. Rev.,* June 1983, *73* (3), pp. 486–87.

Wied-Nebbeling, Susanne. Zur Preis-Absatz-Funktion beim Oligopol auf dem unvollkommenen Markt: Empirische Evidenz und theoretisch-analytische Probleme der Gutenberg-Funktion. (The Demand Function on Oligopolistic Imperfect Markets: Some Evidence and Problems of Theory and Analysis Concerning the Gutenberg Function. With English summary.) *Jahr. Nationalökon. Statist.,* March 1983, *198* (2), pp. 123–44.

0227 Theory of Auction Markets

Bazerman, Max H. and Samuelson, William F. The Winner's Curse: An Empirical Investigation. **In** *Tietz, R., ed.,* 1983, pp. 186–200.

Coursey, Don L. and Smith, Vernon L. Price Controls in a Posted Offer Market. *Amer. Econ. Rev.,* March 1983, *73* (1), pp. 218–21.

Cox, James C.; Smith, Vernon L. and Walker, James M. A Test That Discriminates between Two Models of the Dutch-First Auction Non-Isomorphism. *J. Econ. Behav. Organ.,* June–September 1983, *4* (2–3), pp. 205–19.

DeBrock, Larry M. and Smith, James L. Joint Bidding, Information Pooling, and the Performance of Petroleum Lease Auctions. *Bell J. Econ. (See Rand J. Econ. after 4/85),* Autumn 1983, *14* (2), pp. 395–404.

Engelbrecht-Wiggans, Richard. An Introduction to the Theory of Bidding for a Single Object. **In** *Engelbrecht-Wiggans, R.; Shubik, M. and Stark, R. M., eds.,* 1983, pp. 53–103.

Englebrecht-Wiggans, Richard; Milgrom, Paul R. and Weber, Robert J. Competitive Bidding and Proprietary Information. *J. Math. Econ.,* April 1983, *11* (2), pp. 161–69.

Güth, Werner; Schmittberger, Rolf and Schwarze, Bernd. A Theoretical and Experimental Analysis of Bidding Behavior in Vickrey-Auction Games. *Z. ges. Staatswiss.,* June 1983, *139* (2), pp. 269–88.

Güth, Werner and Schwarze, Bernd. Auctioning Strategic Roles to Observe Aspiration Levels for Conflict Situations. **In** *Tietz, R., ed.,* 1983, pp. 217–30.

Harris, Milton. Pricing Schemes When Demand Is Unobservable. **In** *Engelbrecht-Wiggans, R.; Shubik, M. and Stark, R. M., eds.,* 1983, pp. 195–203.

Holt, Charles A., Jr. and Sherman, Roger. When a Queue Is Like an Auction. **In** *Engelbrecht-Wiggans, R.; Shubik, M. and Stark, R. M., eds.,* 1983, pp. 255–82.

Kuhlman, John M. and Johnson, Stanley R. The Number of Competitors and Bid Prices. *Southern Econ. J.,* July 1983, *50* (1), pp. 213–20. **[G: U.S.]**

Lohrenz, John and Waller, Ray A. Federal Mineral-Lease Bidding Data Bases and the Real World. **In** *Engelbrecht-Wiggans, R.; Shubik, M. and Stark, R. M., eds.,* 1983, pp. 335–61. **[G: U.S.]**

Maskin, Eric S. and Riley, John G. The Gains to Making Losers Pay in High-Bid Auctions. **In** *Engelbrecht-Wiggans, R.; Shubik, M. and Stark, R. M., eds.,* 1983, pp. 205–29.

Milgrom, Paul R. Private Information in an Auction-like Securities Market. **In** *Engelbrecht-Wiggans, R.; Shubik, M. and Stark, R. M., eds.,* 1983, pp. 137–47.

Monash, Curt A. Efficient Allocation of a Stochastic Supply: Auction Mechanisms. **In** *Engelbrecht-Wiggans, R.; Shubik, M. and Stark, R. M., eds.,* 1983, pp. 231–54. **[G: U.S.]**

Muto, Shigeo. Sequential Auctions on Böhm–Bawerk's Horse Market. *Math. Soc. Sci.,* April 1983, *4* (2), pp. 117–30.

Myerson, Roger B. The Basic Theory of Optimal Auctions. **In** *Engelbrecht-Wiggans, R.; Shubik, M. and Stark, R. M., eds.,* 1983, pp. 149–63.

Palfrey, Thomas R. Bundling Decisions by a Multiproduct Monopolist with Incomplete Information. *Econometrica,* March 1983, *51* (2), pp. 463–83.

Ramsey, James B. Empirical Analysis on Lease Bidding Using Historical Data. **In** *Engelbrecht-Wig-*

gans, R.; Shubik, M. and Stark, R. M., eds., 1983, pp. 285–306. [G: U.S.]

Rothkopf, Michael H. Bidding Theory: The Phenomena to Be Modeled. **In** *Engelbrecht-Wiggans, R.; Shubik, M. and Stark, R. M., eds.*, 1983, pp. 105–20.

Samuelson, William F. Competitive Bidding for Defense Contracts. **In** *Engelbrecht-Wiggans, R.; Shubik, M. and Stark, R. M., eds.*, 1983, pp. 389–419.

Schweizer, Urs and von Ungern-Sternberg, Thomas R. Sealed Bid Auctions and the Search for Better Information. *Economica*, February 1983, *50*(197), pp. 79–85.

Shubik, Martin. Auctions, Bidding, and Markets: An Historical Sketch. **In** *Engelbrecht-Wiggans, R.; Shubik, M. and Stark, R. M., eds.*, 1983, pp. 33–52.

Shubik, Martin. On Auctions, Bidding, and Contracting. **In** *Engelbrecht-Wiggans, R.; Shubik, M. and Stark, R. M., eds.*, 1983, pp. 3–31.

Smith, Charles H. Evaluation of Competitive Alternatives for Weapon System Production. **In** *Engelbrecht-Wiggans, R.; Shubik, M. and Stark, R. M., eds.*, 1983, pp. 421–35.

Smith, James L. Joint Bidding, Collusion, and Bid Clustering in Competitive Auctions. *Southern Econ. J.*, October 1983, *50*(2), pp. 355–68.

Smith, Vernon L. and Williams, Arlington W. An Experimental Comparison of Alternative Rules for Competitive Market Exchange. **In** *Engelbrecht-Wiggans, R.; Shubik, M. and Stark, R. M., eds.*, 1983, pp. 307–34.

Stark, Robert M. and Varley, Thomas C. Bidding, Estimating, and Engineered Construction Contracting. **In** *Engelbrecht-Wiggans, R.; Shubik, M. and Stark, R. M., eds.*, 1983, pp. 121–33.

Weber, Robert J. Multiple-Object Auctions. **In** *Engelbrecht-Wiggans, R.; Shubik, M. and Stark, R. M., eds.*, 1983, pp. 165–91.

Wilson, Robert. On Competitive Bidding Applied. **In** *Engelbrecht-Wiggans, R.; Shubik, M. and Stark, R. M., eds.*, 1983, pp. 363–68.

0228 Agent Theory

Baiman, Stanley and Evans, John H., III. Pre-Decision Information and Participative Management Control Systems. *J. Acc. Res.*, Autumn 1983, *21*(2), pp. 371–95.

Ben-Zion, Uri and Spiegel, Menahem. The Agency Problem and Behavior toward Risk. *Atlantic Econ. J.*, March 1983, *11*(1), pp. 68–70.

Bishop, William. Oligopoly Pricing: A Proposal. *Antitrust Bull.*, Summer 1983, *28*(2), pp. 311–36. [G: U.K.]

Carmichael, H. Lorne. The Agent–Agents Problem: Payment by Relative Output. *J. Lab. Econ.*, January 1983, *1*(1), pp. 50–65.

Clarke, Frank H. and Darrough, Masako N. Optimal Employment Contracts in a Principal–Agent Relationship. *J. Econ. Behav. Organ.*, June–September 1983, *4*(2–3), pp. 69–90.

Crawford, Vincent P. and Guasch, J. Luis. The Theory of Contracts and Agency. *Amer. J. Agr. Econ.*, May 1983, *65*(2), pp. 373–79.

Demski, Joel S. Comments on Wilson and Jensen [Auditing: Perspectives from Multi-person Decision Theory] [Organization Theory and Methodology]. *Accounting Rev.*, April 1983, *58*(2), pp. 347–49.

Dye, Ronald A. Communication and Post-Decision Information. *J. Acc. Res.*, Autumn 1983, *21*(2), pp. 514–33.

Easterbrook, Frank H. and Fischel, Daniel R. Voting in Corporate Law. *J. Law Econ.*, June 1983, *26*(2), pp. 395–427. [G: U.S.]

Fama, Eugene F. and Jensen, Michael C. Agency Problems and Residual Claims. *J. Law Econ.*, June 1983, *26*(2), pp. 327–49.

Fama, Eugene F. and Jensen, Michael C. Separation of Ownership and Control. *J. Law Econ.*, June 1983, *26*(2), pp. 301–25.

Fershtman, Chaim and Spiegel, Uriel. Monopoly versus Competition: The Learning by Doing Case. *Europ. Econ. Rev.*, November 1983, *23*(2), pp. 217–22.

Gordon, Lawrence A. and Hamer, Michelle. GASB's Survival Potential: An Agency Theory Perspective. *Public Budg. Finance*, Spring 1983, *3*(1), pp. 103–12. [G: U.S.]

Granick, David. Institutional Innovation and Economic Management: The Soviet Incentive System, 1921 to the Present. **In** *Guroff, G. and Carstensen, F. V., eds.*, 1983, pp. 223–57. [G: U.S.S.R.]

Green, Jerry R. and Stokey, Nancy L. A Comparison of Tournaments and Contracts. *J. Polit. Econ.*, June 1983, *91*(3), pp. 349–64.

Grossman, Sanford J. and Hart, Oliver D. An Analysis of the Principal–Agent Problem. *Econometrica*, January 1983, *51*(1), pp. 7–45.

Jensen, Michael C. Organization Theory and Methodology. *Accounting Rev.*, April 1983, *58*(2), pp. 319–39.

Kaplan, Robert S. Comments on Wilson and Jensen [Auditing: Perspectives from Multi-person Decision Theory] [Organization Theory and Methodology]. *Accounting Rev.*, April 1983, *58*(2), pp. 340–46.

Klein, Benjamin. Contracting Costs and Residual Claims: The Separation of Ownership and Control. *J. Law Econ.*, June 1983, *26*(2), pp. 367–74.

Kornhauser, Lewis A. Control of Conflicts of Interest in Class-Action Suits. *Public Choice*, 1983, *41*(1), pp. 145–75.

Lambert, Richard A. Long-term Contracts and Moral Hazard. *Bell J. Econ. (See Rand J. Econ. after 4/85)*, Autumn 1983, *14*(2), pp. 441–52.

Luckhardt, C. G. Duties of Agent to Principal. **In** *Snoeyenbos, M.; Almeder, R. and Humber, J., eds.*, 1983, pp. 115–21.

Myerson, Roger B. Mechanism Design by an Informed Principal. *Econometrica*, November 1983, *51*(6), pp. 1767–97.

Rubinstein, Ariel and Yaari, Menahem E. Repeated Insurance Contracts and Moral Hazard. *J. Econ. Theory*, June 1983, *30*(1), pp. 74–97.

Sappington, David. Limited Liability Contracts between Principal and Agent. *J. Econ. Theory*, February 1983, *29*(1), pp. 1–21.

Spatt, **Chester S.** Control of Conflicts of Interest in Class-Action Suits: A Comment. *Public Choice,* 1983, *41*(1), pp. 177–79.

023 Macroeconomic Theory

0230 General

Abel, Andrew B. and Blanchard, Olivier J. An Intertemporal Model of Saving and Investment. *Econometrica,* May, 1983, *51*(3), pp. 675–92.

Abel, Andrew B. and Mishkin, Frederic S. An Integrated View of Tests of Rationality, Market Efficiency and the Short-Run Neutrality of Monetary Policy. *J. Monet. Econ.*, January 1983, *11*(1), pp. 3–24.

Ackley, Gardner. Commodities and Capital: Prices and Quantities. *Amer. Econ. Rev.*, March 1983, *73*(1), pp. 1–16.

Aiginger, Karl. Die Wirkung von asymmetrischen Verlusten auf die Bildung von rationalen ökonomischen Erwartungen. (The Incorporation of Asymmetric Losses into the Formation of Economically Rational Expectations (Forecasts, Plans) With English summary.) *Ifo-Studien,* 1983, *29*(3), pp. 175–215. **[G: EEC; U.S.; Japan; Austria]**

Akyüz, Yilmaz. Value and Exploitation under Joint Production. *Australian Econ. Pap.*, June 1983, *22*(40), pp. 171–79.

Alesina, Alberto. Inflazione, indicizzazione e stabilità macroeconimica. (Inflation, Indexation, and Macroeconomic Stability. With English summary.) *Giorn. Econ.*, January–February 1983, *42*(1–2), pp. 91–112.

Alogoskoufis, George S. and Pissarides, Christopher A. A Test of Price Sluggishness in the Simple Rational Expectations Model: U.K. 1950–1980. *Econ. J.*, September 1983, *93*(371), pp. 616–28. **[G: U.K.]**

Andersen, Ellen. Erfaringer med keynesianske makromodeller. (With English summary.) *Nationaløkon. Tidsskr.*, 1983, *121*(3), pp. 323–31.

Andersen, Ellen. Opbrud i makroteorien—en oversigt. (Recent Trends in Macroeconomic Theory—A Survey Article. With English summary.) *Nationaløkon. Tidsskr.*, 1983, *121*(1), pp. 1–16.

Ando, Albert. Equilibrium Business-Cycle Models: An Appraisal. **In** *[Klein, L. R.],* 1983, pp. 39–67. **[G: U.S.]**

Asimakopulos, A. The Role of the Short Period: Comment [On Effective Demand: Certain Recent Critiques]. **In** *Kregel, J. A., ed.*, 1983, pp. 28–34.

Atesoglu, H. Sonmez. Inflation and Unemployment Models. *Nebr. J. Econ. Bus.*, Summer 1983, *22*(3), pp. 53–65. **[G: U.S.]**

Auernheimer, Leonardo. The Revenue-Maximizing Inflation Rate and the Treatment of the Transition to Equilibrium. *J. Money, Credit, Banking,* August 1983, *15*(3), pp. 368–76.

d'Autume, Antoine. Processus d'ajustement et croissance. (Adjustment Process and Growth. With English summary.) [Une maquette représentative des modèles macroeconomiques]. *Ann. INSEE,* Jan.–Mar. 1983, (49), pp. 113–22. **[G: France]**

Azam, J. P. Money, Growth and Disequilibrium. *Economica,* August 1983, *50*(199), pp. 325–35.

Baumgarten, Klaus. Adjustment to Variations in Prices of Imported Inputs: The Role of Economic Structure—A Comment. *Weltwirtsch. Arch.*, 1983, *119*(3), pp. 575–78.

Bausor, Randall. The Rational-Expectations Hypothesis and the Epistemics of Time. *Cambridge J. Econ.*, March 1983, *7*(1), pp. 1–10.

Benassy, Jean-Pascal. The Three Regimes of the IS-LM Model: A Non-Walrasian Analysis. *Europ. Econ. Rev.*, September 1983, *23*(1), pp. 1–17.

Benedetti, G. and Gui, Benedetto. Keynesian State of Expectation and Rational Expectations. *Metroecon.*, February–June 1983, *35*(1–2), pp. 177–94.

Bhaduri, Amit. Multimarket Classification of Unemployment: A Sceptical Note. *Cambridge J. Econ.*, September/December 1983, *7*(3/4), pp. 235–41.

Bharadwaj, Krishna. On Effective Demand: Certain Recent Critiques. **In** *Kregel, J. A., ed.*, 1983, pp. 3–27.

Bini Smaghi, Lorenzo and Tardini, Pietro. The Effectiveness of Monetary Policy: An Empirical Investigation for Italy (1966–1981). *Giorn. Econ.*, September–October 1983, *42*(9–10), pp. 679–90. **[G: Italy]**

Blanchard, Olivier J. Methods of Solution and Simulation for Dynamic Rational Expectations Models. *Écon. Appl.*, 1983, *36*(1), pp. 27–46.

Blinder, Alan S. Conversations with Neo-Keynesian Economists: The "Younger Generation" [Interview]. **In** *Klamer, A.*, 1983, pp. 151–69.

Bliss, Christopher. Consistent Temporary Equilibrium. **In** *Fitoussi, J.-P., ed.*, 1983, pp. 141–52.

Bliss, Christopher. Two Views of Macroeconomics. *Oxford Econ. Pap.*, March 1983, *35*(1), pp. 1–12.

Block, Walter. Who Speaks for the Free Market: Monetarists or Supply-Siders? [What's Wrong with Supply-Side Economics] [The Trouble with Monetarism]. *Policy Rev.*, Spring 1983, (24), pp. 9–12. **[G: U.S.]**

Boltho, Andrea. Is Western Europe Caught in an 'Expectations Trap'? *Lloyds Bank Rev.*, April 1983, (148), pp. 1–13. **[G: W. Europe]**

Booth, Alan. The "Keynesian Revolution" in Economic Policy-Making. *Econ. Hist. Rev., 2nd Ser.*, February 1983, *36*(1), pp. 103–23. **[G: U.K.]**

Boschen, John and Grossman, Herschel I. Monetary Information and Macroeconomic Fluctuations. **In** *Fitoussi, J.-P., ed.*, 1983, pp. 173–84.

Bossons, John. What Can Macroeconomic Theory Tell Us about the Way Deficits Should Be Measured? Comment. **In** *Conklin, D. W. and Courchene, T. J., eds.*, 1983, pp. 181–86.

Bray, Margaret. Convergence to Rational Expectations Equilibrium. **In** *Frydman, R. and Phelps, E. S., eds.*, 1983, pp. 123–32.

Brockway, George P. On Speculation: A Footnote to Keynes. *J. Post Keynesian Econ.*, Summer 1983, *5*(4), pp. 515–22.

Brunner, Karl. Conversation with a Monetarist [Interview]. **In** *Klamer, A.*, 1983, pp. 179–99.

Brunner, Karl; Cukierman, Alex and Meltzer, Allan H. Money and Economic Activity, Inventories and Business Cycles. *J. Monet. Econ.*, May 1983, *11*(3), pp. 281–319.

Bryant, John. A Simple Rational Expectations Keynes-Type Model. *Quart. J. Econ.*, August 1983, *98* (3), pp. 525–28.

Bryant, John. Government Irrelevance Results: A Simple Exposition. *Amer. Econ. Rev.*, September 1983, *73* (4), pp. 758–61.

Bryant, John. The Role of Overlapping-Generations Models in Monetary Economics: A Comment. *Carnegie-Rochester Conf. Ser. Public Policy*, Spring 1983, *18*, pp. 45–50.

Buiter, Willem H. Expectations and Control Theory. *Écon. Appl.*, 1983, *36* (1), pp. 129–56.

Bull, Clive. Expectations of Others' Expectations and the Transitional Nonneutrality of Fully Believed Systematic Monetary Policy: Comment. **In** *Frydman, R. and Phelps, E. S., eds.*, 1983, pp. 66–68.

Burmeister, Edwin; Flood, Robert P. and Garber, Peter M. On the Equivalence of Solutions in Rational Expectations Models. *J. Econ. Dynam. Control*, May 1983, *5* (2/3), pp. 311–21.

Burton, David. Devaluation, Long-Term Contracts and Rational Expectations. *Europ. Econ. Rev.*, September 1983, *23* (1), pp. 19–32.

den Butter, Frank A. G. Choice of Monetary Policy Instruments in a Stochastic IS–LM Model: Some Empirical Remarks for the Netherlands. *De Economist*, 1983, *131* (1), pp. 46–54. **[G: Netherlands]**

Cagan, Phillip. The Roles of Money and Credit in Macroeconomic Analysis: Comment. **In** *Tobin, J., ed.*, 1983, pp. 189–93. **[G: U.S.]**

Cagan, Phillip. The Trouble with "Rational Expectations" and the Problem of Inflation Stabilization: Comment. **In** *Frydman, R. and Phelps, E. S., eds.*, 1983, pp. 41–45.

Calmfors, Lars. Output, Inflation and the Terms of Trade in a Small Open Economy. *Kyklos*, 1983, *36* (1), pp. 40–65.

Calvo, Guillermo A. Staggered Prices in a Utility–Maximizing Framework. *J. Monet. Econ.*, September 1983, *12* (3), pp. 383–98.

Calvo, Guillermo A. The Stability of Rational Expectations in Macroeconomic Models: Comment. **In** *Frydman, R. and Phelps, E. S., eds.*, 1983, pp. 94–96.

Cansier, Dieter. Einperioden-Multiplikatoren gegebener Haushaltsdefizite nach dem Blinder–Solow-Modell: Erwiderung. (Single-Period Multipliers of Given Budget Deficits in Accordance with the Blinder–Solow Model: Reply. With English summary.) *Kredit Kapital*, 1983, *16* (1), pp. 54–61.

Carraro, Carlo. Ottimalità della politica economica nei modelli con aspettative razionali. (The Optimality of Economic Policy in the Rational Expectations Models. With English summary.) *Giorn. Econ.*, September–October 1983, *42* (9–10), pp. 643–65.

Chase, Richard X. The Development of Contemporary Mainstream Macroeconomics: Vision, Ideology, and Theory. **In** *Eichner, A. S., ed.*, 1983, *1981*, pp. 126–65.

Cherry, Robert. A Marxist Critique of Natural Unemployment Rate Theories. **In** *Schmukler, N. and Marcus, E., eds.*, 1983, pp. 133–43.

Chetty, V. K. and Lahiri, Ashok K. On the Effectiveness of Monetary and Fiscal Policies in a Keynesian Model. *Europ. Econ. Rev.*, September 1983, *23* (1), pp. 33–54.

Chevallier, François. Prévisions rationnelles: prévisions d'équilibre? (Rational Expectations: Equilibrium Expectations? With English summary.) *Écon. Appl.*, 1983, *36* (1), pp. 47–73.

Chick, Victoria. A Question of Relevance: The *General Theory* in Keynes's Time and Ours. *S. Afr. J. Econ.*, September 1983, *51* (3), pp. 380–406. **[G: U.K.]**

Chiesa, Gabriella. Disturbi di offerta, natura della disoccupazione ed interventi di riassorbimento in un'economia aperta. (Supply Shocks, the Nature of Unemployment and Policies for Internal and External Balance in an Open Economy. With English summary.) *Giorn. Econ.*, September–October 1983, *42* (9–10), pp. 617–41.

Claassen, Emil-Maria. The Keynesian and Classical Determination of the Exchange Rate. *Weltwirtsch. Arch.*, 1983, *119* (1), pp. 19–35.

Coleman, W. O. Wicksell and the Akerman Axe Model: A Re-Examination. *Australian Econ. Pap.*, December 1983, *22* (41), pp. 467–76.

Collard, David A. Pigou on Expectations and the Cycle. *Econ. J.*, June 1983, *93* (370), pp. 411–14.

Conway, Roger K. and Barth, James R. New Developments in Microeconomic Theory: A Prospectus and Appraisal. *Agr. Econ. Res.*, July 1983, *35* (3), pp. 23–39.

Covi, Antonio. Keynes e la critica di Lucas. (Keynes and Lucas' Criticism. With English summary.) *Rivista Int. Sci. Econ. Com.*, December 1983, *30* (12), pp. 1115–31.

Craine, Roger and Hardouvelis, Gikas A. Are Rational Expectations for Real? *Greek Econ. Rev.*, April 1983, *5* (1), pp. 5–32. **[G: U.S.]**

Crotty, James R. On Keynes and Capital Flight [Keynes's *General Theory:* A Different Perspective]. *J. Econ. Lit.*, March 1983, *21* (1), pp. 59–65.

Currie, Lauchlin. The "Multiplier" in Economic Literature. *J. Econ. Stud.*, 1983, *10* (3), pp. 42–48.

Darity, William A., Jr. and Horn, Bobbie L. Involuntary Unemployment Reconsidered. *Southern Econ. J.*, January 1983, *49* (3), pp. 717–33.

Davenport, Paul. Unemployment, Demand Restraint, and Endogenous Capacity. *Eastern Econ. J.*, July–September 1983, *9* (3), pp. 258–71.

Davidson, Paul. Rational Expectations: A Fallacious Foundation for Studying Crucial Decision-Making Processes. *J. Post Keynesian Econ.*, Winter 1982–83, *5* (2), pp. 182–98.

Davidson, Paul. The Dubious Labor Market Analysis in Meltzer's Restatement of Keynes' *Theory. J. Econ. Lit.*, March 1983, *21* (1), pp. 52–56.

Devine, James N. Underconsumption, Over-Investment and the Origins of the Great Depression. *Rev. Radical Polit. Econ.*, Summer 1983, *15* (2), pp. 1–27. **[G: U.S.]**

Di Tata, Juan Carlos. Expectations of Others' Expectations and the Transitional Nonneutrality of Fully Believed Systematic Monetary Policy. **In** *Frydman, R. and Phelps, E. S., eds.*, 1983, pp. 47–66.

Ditz, Gerhard W. Demand-Side, Supply-Side, Marketing Philosophy, and Beyond. *Econ. Notes,* 1983, (1), pp. 112–29.

Dixon, Robert J. On the New Cambridge School. *J. Post Keynesian Econ.,* Winter 1982–83, *5*(2), pp. 289–94.

Dow, Sheila C. Schools of Thought in Macroeconomics: The Method Is the Message. *Australian Econ. Pap.,* June 1983, *22*(40), pp. 30–47.

Driscoll, Michael J.; Ford, J. L. and Mullineux, A. W. The Gains and Losses to Predicting Nominal Income by Disaggregating via the New Classical Aggregate Supply and Rational Expectations Hypotheses. *Empirical Econ.,* 1983, *8*(1), pp. 47–58. **[G: U.S.]**

Driscoll, Michael J., et al. Testing of the Rational Expectations and Structural Neutrality Hypotheses. *J. Macroecon.,* Summer 1983, *5*(3), pp. 353–60. **[G: U.S.]**

Driver, Ciaran. The Macroeconomic Theory of A. S. Eichner. *Brit. Rev. Econ. Issues,* Autumn 1983, *5*(13), pp. 63–85. **[G: U.K.]**

Duck, Nigel W. The Effects of Uncertainty about the Money Supply Process in a Rational Expectations Macroeconomic Model. *Scot. J. Polit. Econ.,* June 1983, *30*(2), pp. 142–52.

Dumas, Lloyd J. Resource Diversion and the Failure of Conventional Macrotheory. *J. Econ. Issues,* June 1983, *17*(2), pp. 555–64.

Eatwell, John. Theories of Value, Output and Employment. **In** *Eatwell, J. and Milgate, M., eds.,* 1983, pp. 93–128.

Eatwell, John. Theories of Value, Output and Employment. **In** *Caravale, G., ed.,* 1983, *1978,* pp. 276–322.

Eatwell, John and Milgate, Murray. Keynes's Economics and the Theory of Value and Distribution: Introduction. **In** *Eatwell, J. and Milgate, M., eds.,* 1983, pp. 1–17.

Eddé, Richard. Keynes' Basic Error. *Rivista Int. Sci. Econ. Com.,* April-May 1983, *30*(4–5), pp. 375–92.

Eden, Benjamin. Competitive Price Setting, Price Flexibility, and Linkage to the Money Supply. *Carnegie-Rochester Conf. Ser. Public Policy,* Autumn 1983, *19,* pp. 253–99.

Eden, Benjamin. Competitive Price Setting, Price Flexibility, and Linkage to the Money Supply: Reply. *Carnegie-Rochester Conf. Ser. Public Policy,* Autumn 1983, *19,* pp. 313–16.

Eichengreen, Barry J. Protection, Real Wage Resistance and Employment. *Weltwirtsch. Arch.,* 1983, *119*(3), pp. 429–52.

Eichner, Alfred S. The Micro Foundations of the Corporate Economy. *Managerial Dec. Econ.,* September 1983, *4*(3), pp. 136–52.

Eichner, Alfred S. Why Economics Is Not Yet a Science. *J. Econ. Issues,* June 1983, *17*(2), pp. 507–20.

Ellis, Christopher J. A Note on Walrasian Equilibria in Non-Walrasian Models. *Europ. Econ. Rev.,* September 1983, *23*(1), pp. 55–58.

Eltis, Walter. *A Neoclassical Analysis of Macroeconomic Policy:* A Review Essay. *J. Money, Credit, Banking,* November 1983, *15*(4), pp. 519–26.

Enders, Klaus and Herberg, Horst. The Dutch Disease: Causes, Consequences, Cures and Calmatives. *Weltwirtsch. Arch.,* 1983, *119*(3), pp. 473–97.

Evans, George. The Stability of Rational Expectations in Macroeconomic Models. **In** *Frydman, R. and Phelps, E. S., eds.,* 1983, pp. 69–94.

Evans, Owen J. Tax Policy, the Interest Elasticity of Saving, and Capital Accumulation: Numerical Analysis of Theoretical Models. *Amer. Econ. Rev.,* June 1983, *73*(3), pp. 398–410. **[G: U.S.]**

Fase, M. M. G. The 1930 Correspondence between Koopmans, Robertson and Gregory. *De Economist,* 1983, *131*(3), pp. 305–43.

Faxén, Karl-Olof. Stability in Economic Growth under Uncertainty—Growth of Knowledge, Decision Processes and Contingency Contracts. **In** *Eliasson, G.; Sharefkin, M. and Ysander, B.-C., eds.,* 1983, pp. 375–417. **[G: OECD]**

Feldstein, Martin S. Tax Incentives, Corporate Saving, and Capital Accumulation in the United States. **In** *Feldstein, M. (I),* 1983, *1973,* pp. 123–34. **[G: U.S.]**

Ferguson, J. David and Hart, William R. Income Determination in Market Disequilibrium: The Implications of Spillover for the Design of Monetary Policy. *J. Macroecon.,* Summer 1983, *5*(3), pp. 317–33.

Ferri, Piero. The Consumption-Wage Gap. *J. Post Keynesian Econ.,* Summer 1983, *5*(4), pp. 579–89. **[G: Developed Countries]**

Fischer, Stanley. Macroconfusion: The Dilemmas of Economic Policy: Comment. **In** *Tobin, J., ed.,* 1983, pp. 267–76.

Fitoussi, Jean-Paul. Modern Macroeconomic Theory: An Overview. **In** *Fitoussi, J.-P., ed.,* 1983, pp. 1–46.

Flood, Robert P. and Garber, Peter M. Process Consistency and Monetary Reform: Some Further Evidence. *J. Monet. Econ.,* August 1983, *12*(2), pp. 279–95. **[G: Europe]**

Foley, Duncan K. Money and Effective Demand in Marx's Scheme of Expanded Reproduction. **In** *[Erlich, A.],* 1983, pp. 19–33.

Friedman, Benjamin M. The Roles of Money and Credit in Macroeconomic Analysis. **In** *Tobin, J., ed.,* 1983, pp. 161–89. **[G: U.S.]**

Frydman, Roman. A Distinction between the Unconditional Expectational Equilibrium and the Rational Expectations Equilibrium. **In** *Frydman, R. and Phelps, E. S., eds.,* 1983, pp. 139–46.

Frydman, Roman. Individual Rationality, Decentralization, and the Rational Expectations Hypothesis. **In** *Frydman, R. and Phelps, E. S., eds.,* 1983, pp. 97–122.

Frydman, Roman and Phelps, Edmund S. Individual Forecasting and Aggregate Outcomes: "Rational Expectations" Examined: Introduction. **In** *Frydman, R. and Phelps, E. S., eds.,* 1983, pp. 1–30.

Fujimoto, Takao and Leslie, Derek. A Two-class Model of Keynesian Unemployment. *Metroecon.,* February-June 1983, *35*(1–2), pp. 53–71.

Gale, Douglas. Competitive Models with Keynesian Features. *Econ. J.,* Supplement March 1983, pp. 17–33.

Gallestegui, M. C. and Urrutia, J. Crisis, teoria economica y margen de maniobra. (Crisis, Economic

Theory and Margin for "Manoeuvre." With English summary.) *Écon. Soc.*, September–October–November 1983, *17*(9–10–11), pp. 1345–81. **[G: OECD]**

Garner, C. Alan. 'Uncertainty' in Keynes' *General Theory:* A Comment. *Hist. Polit. Econ.*, Spring 1983, *15*(1), pp. 83–86.

Girão, José António. Aspectos da política económica em países em desenvolvimento: o caso de Portugal. (With English summary.) *Economia*, January 1983, *7*(1), pp. 51–69. **[G: Portugal]**

Gleting, Jørgen H. Om fastprismodellernes forklaring af arbejdsløsheden. (Some Critical Comments on Macroeconomic Fixprice Models. With English summary.) *Nationaløkon. Tidsskr.*, 1983, *121*(1), pp. 17–19.

Godley, Wynne. Keynes and the Management of Real National Income and Expenditure. **In** *Worswick, D. and Trevithick, J., eds.*, 1983, pp. 135–57.

Goodhart, Charles A. E. On Keynes and Monetarism: Comment. **In** *Worswick, D. and Trevithick, J., eds.*, 1983, pp. 75–81.

Gordon, David M. Conversations with Nonconventional Economists [Interview]. **In** *Klamer, A.*, 1983, pp. 203–17.

Gourlaouen, Jean-Pierre. Une analyse économétrique des liens entre l'inflation, le chomage et la nature des anticipations. (An Econometric Analysis of Inflation, Unemployment and the Nature of Expectations. With English summary.) *Revue Écon.*, September 1983, *34*(5), pp. 971–86. **[G: France]**

Gowland, D. H. Issues in Macroeconomics. **In** *Gowland, D. H., ed.*, 1983, pp. 57–87.

Graziani, Augusto. The Macroeconomic Theory of Vera C. Lutz. *Banca Naz. Lavoro Quart. Rev.*, March 1983, (144), pp. 3–27. **[G: Italy]**

Green, Jerry R. On Mistaken Beliefs and Resultant Equilibria: Comment. **In** *Frydman, R. and Phelps, E. S., eds.*, 1983, pp. 166–68.

Green, Jerry R. and Honkapohja, Seppo. Variance-Minimizing Monetary Policies with Lagged Price Adjustment and Rational Expectations. *Europ. Econ. Rev.*, January 1983, *20*(1–3), pp. 123–41.

Grinols, Earl and Bhagwati, Jagdish N. Foreign Capital, Savings and Dependence. **In** *Bhagwati, J. N., Vol. 2,* 1983, *1976,* pp. 493–501.

Grossman, Herschel I. The Natural-Rate Hypothesis, the Rational-Expectations Hypothesis, and the Remarkable Survival of Non-Market-Clearing Assumptions. *Carnegie-Rochester Conf. Ser. Public Policy,* Autumn 1983, *19,* pp. 225–45.

Gylfason, Thorvaldur and Schmid, Michael. Does Devaluation Cause Stagflation? *Can. J. Econ.*, November 1983, *16*(4), pp. 641–54. **[G: Selected Countries]**

Hahn, F. H. On Keynes and Monetarism: Comment. **In** *Worswick, D. and Trevithick, J., eds.*, 1983, pp. 72–75.

Hahn, Frank. Keynesianism, Monetarism, and Rational Expectations: Some Reflections and Conjectures: Comment. **In** *Frydman, R. and Phelps, E. S., eds.*, 1983, pp. 223–30.

Halevi, Joseph. Employment and Planning. *Soc. Res.*, Summer 1983, *50*(2), pp. 345–58.

Hall, Robert E. Rational Expectations and the Invisible Handshake: Comment. **In** *Tobin, J., ed.*, 1983, pp. 77–79.

Haraf, William S. Tests of a Rational Expectations-Structural Neutrality Model with Persistent Effects of Monetary Disturbances. *J. Monet. Econ.*, January 1983, *11*(1), pp. 103–16.

Harris, Milton and Holmstrom, Bengt. Microeconomic Developments and Macroeconomics. *Amer. Econ. Rev.*, May 1983, *73*(2), pp. 223–27.

Hart, Oliver D. Economic Fluctuations with an Imperfectly Competitive Labour Market. **In** *Fitoussi, J.-P., ed.*, 1983, pp. 153–70.

Hazari, Bharat R. The IS-LM Curves Revisited with the Aid of Geometry of International Trade. *Indian Econ. J.*, January-March 1983, *30*(3), pp. 17–24.

Hénin, Pierre-Yves. L'impact macro-économique d'un choc pétrolier. (The Macroeconomic Impact of an Oil Shock. With English summary.) *Revue Écon.*, September 1983, *34*(5), pp. 865–96.

Hénin, Pierre-Yves and Zylberberg, André. Sur l'efficacité de la politique monétaire dans des modèles de prévisions rationnelles avec ajustement partiel des prix. (On the Efficiency of the Monetary Policy in Rational Expectations Models with Partial Price Adjustment. With English summary.) *Écon. Appl.*, 1983, *36*(1), pp. 157–74.

Hicks, John. IS-LM: An Explanation. **In** *Fitoussi, J.-P., ed.*, 1983, pp. 49–63.

Hicks, John. Micro and Macro. **In** *Hicks, J.*, 1983, *1979,* pp. 349–52.

Honkapohja, Seppo and Ito, Takatoshi. Stability and Regime Switching. *J. Econ. Theory,* February 1983, *29*(1), pp. 22–48.

Hotson, John H. What's Wrong with Mainstream Macroeconomics? *Eastern Econ. J.*, July–September 1983, *9*(3), pp. 246–57. **[G: U.S.]**

Howells, P. G. A. and Bain, K. The Derivation of the LM Schedule—A Pedagogical Note. *Brit. Rev. Econ. Issues,* Spring 1983, *5*(12), pp. 57–65.

Ioannides, Yannis M. Endogenous Trading Uncertainty and Macroeconomic Equilibrium. *Econ. J.*, Supplement March 1983, pp. 99–105.

Iša, Jan. The Crisis of Keynesianism and Economic Neo-Conservatism. *Czech. Econ. Digest.*, November 1983, (7), pp. 68–87.

Jaeger, Klaus. Diskrete und stetige Analyse im IS-LM Modell. (Discrete and Continuous Time Analysis in the IS-LM Model. With English Summary.) *Z. ges. Staatswiss.*, June 1983, *139*(2), pp. 229–44.

Jha, Raghbendra and Lächler, Ulrich. Inflation and Economic Growth in a Competitive Economy with Exhaustible Resources. *J. Econ. Behav. Organ.*, June–September 1983, *4*(2–3), pp. 113–29.

Kahn, Richard F. Malinvaud on Keynes. **In** *Eatwell, J. and Milgate, M., eds.*, 1983, *1977,* pp. 214–28.

Kaldor, Nicholas. Keynesian Economics after Fifty Years. **In** *Worswick, D. and Trevithick, J., eds.*, 1983, pp. 1–28.

Kang, Heejoon. The Effect of Monetary Changes on Interest Rates: A Comment. *Rev. Econ. Statist.*, May 1983, *65*(2), pp. 360–62. **[G: U.S.]**

Katseli, Louka T. and Marion, Nancy P. Adjustment to Variations in Prices of Imported Inputs: The

Role of Economic Structure—A Reply. *Weltwirtsch. Arch.*, 1983, *119*(3), pp. 579–80.

Keller, Robert R. Keynesian and Institutional Economics: Compatibility and Complementarity? *J. Econ. Issues,* December 1983, *17*(4), pp. 1087–95.

Kennally, Gerald F. Some consequences of Opening a Neo-Keynesian Model. *Econ. J.*, June 1983, *93*(370), pp. 390–410.

Kenway, Peter. Marx, Keynes and the Possibility of Crisis. **In** *Eatwell, J. and Milgate, M., eds.*, 1983, *1980*, pp. 149–66.

Kirman, Alan. On Mistaken Beliefs and Resultant Equilibria. **In** *Frydman, R. and Phelps, E. S., eds.*, 1983, pp. 147–66.

Klamer, Arjo. Conversations with Economists: New Classical Economists and Opponents Speak Out on the Current Controversy in Macroeconomics: An Interpretation of the Conversations. **In** *Klamer, A.*, 1983, pp. 237–54.

Klamer, Arjo. Conversations with Economists: New Classical Economists and Opponents Speak Out on the Current Controversy in Macroeconomics: A Background for the Conversations. **In** *Klamer, A.*, 1983, pp. 1–25.

Klamer, Arjo. Empirical Arguments in New Classical Economics. *Écon. Appl.*, 1983, *36*(1), pp. 229–54.

Kloten, Norbert. Zyklus und Politik: Zu den Ursachen der wirtschaftlichen Stagnation. (Cycle and Policy: About the Reasons for the Economic Stagnation. With English summary.) *Kredit Kapital,* 1983, *16*(1), pp. 1–15. **[G: MDCs]**

van de Klundert, Theo. The Energy Problem in a Small Open Economy. *J. Macroecon.*, Spring 1983, *5*(2), pp. 211–22.

Korliras, Panayotis G. Conjectural Stock and Flow Responses to Market Rationing: An Analysis of Output and Employment Multipliers in Non-Walrasian Equilibria. **In** *Fitoussi, J.-P., ed.*, 1983, pp. 115–37.

Kornai, János and Weibull, Jörgen W. Paternalism, Buyers' and Sellers' Market. *Math. Soc. Sci.*, November 1983, *6*(2), pp. 153–69.

Kregel, J. A. Post-Keynesian Theory: An Overview. *J. Econ. Educ.*, Fall 1983, *14*(4), pp. 32–43.

Kregel, J. A. The Microfoundations of the 'Generalisation of *The General Theory*' and 'Bastard Keynesianism': Keynes's Theory of Employment in the Long and the Short Period. *Cambridge J. Econ.*, September/December 1983, *7*(3/4), pp. 343–61.

Kurz, H. What Is Wrong with Keynesian Economics?: Comment [On Effective Demand: Certain Recent Critiques]. **In** *Kregel, J. A., ed.*, 1983, pp. 35–42.

Lächler, Ulrich. A Macrotheoretic Analysis of Inflation, Taxes, and the Price of Equity. *J. Macroecon.*, Summer 1983, *5*(3), pp. 281–301.

Lad, Frank. A Subjectivist View of the Rational Expectations Hypothesis: Critique and Development. *Metroecon.*, February–June 1983, *35*(1–2), pp. 29–51. **[G: U.S.]**

Laidler, David and Bentley, Brian. A Small Macro-Model of the Post-War United States. *Manchester Sch. Econ. Soc. Stud.*, December 1983, *51*(4), pp. 317–40. **[G: U.S.]**

Lavoie, Marc. Loi de Minsky et loi d'entropie. (Minsky Law and Entropy Law. With English summary.) *Écon. Appl.*, 1983, *36*(2–3), pp. 287–331.

Leach, John. A Comment on the Foundations of the Precautionary Demand for Money. *J. Monet. Econ.*, March 1983, *11*(2), pp. 273–80.

Lee, S. Y. and Li, W. K. Money, Income and Prices and Their Lead-Lag Relationships in Singapore. *Singapore Econ. Rev.*, April 1983, *28*(1), pp. 73–87. **[G: Singapore]**

Leijonhufvud, Axel. Keynesianism, Monetarism, and Rational Expectations: Some Reflections and Conjectures. **In** *Frydman, R. and Phelps, E. S., eds.*, 1983, pp. 203–23.

Leijonhufvud, Axel. What Was the Matter with IS-LM? **In** *Fitoussi, J.-P., ed.*, 1983, pp. 64–90.

Leijonhufvud, Axel. What Would Keynes Have Thought of Rational Expectations? **In** *Worswick, D. and Trevithick, J., eds.*, 1983, pp. 179–205.

Lerner, Abba P. Alternative Formulations of the Theory of Interest. **In** *Lerner, A. P.*, 1983, *1938*, pp. 507–26.

Lerner, Abba P. From the Treatise on Money to the General Theory. **In** *Lerner, A. P.*, 1983, *1974*, pp. 393–97.

Lerner, Abba P. From Pre-Keynes to Post-Keynes. **In** *Lerner, A. P.*, 1983, *1977*, pp. 399–427.

Lerner, Abba P. Keynesianism: Alive, if Not So Well, at Forty. **In** *Lerner, A. P.*, 1983, *1978*, pp. 429–39.

Lerner, Abba P. Mr. Keynes' "General Theory of Employment, Interest and Money." **In** *Lerner, A. P.*, 1983, *1936*, pp. 251–70.

Lerner, Abba P. On Generalizing the General Theory: Review Article. **In** *Lerner, A. P.*, 1983, *1960*, pp. 351–73.

Lerner, Abba P. On Keynes, Policy, and Theory—A Grumble. **In** *Lerner, A. P.*, 1983, pp. 441–51.

Lerner, Abba P. Some Swedish Stepping Stones in Economic Theory: Review Article. **In** *Lerner, A. P.*, 1983, *1940*, pp. 333–50.

Lerner, Abba P. The Economist's Can Opener. **In** *Lerner, A. P.*, 1983, *1968*, pp. 647–49.

Levine, A. L. Price and Incomes Policy: A 'Sraffian' Perspective. *Math. Soc. Sci.*, November 1983, *6*(2), pp. 215–25.

Lucas, Robert E., Jr. Conversations with New Classical Economists [Interview]. **In** *Klamer, A.*, 1983, pp. 29–57.

Lucas, Robert E., Jr. Econometric Policy Evaluation: A Critique. **In** *Brunner, K. and Meltzer, A. H., eds.*, 1983, *1976*, pp. 257–84.

Lucas, Robert E., Jr. Expectations and the Neutrality of Money. *J. Econ. Theory,* October 1983, *31*(1), pp. 197–99.

Lucas, Robert E., Jr. Understanding Business Cycles. **In** *Brunner, K. and Meltzer, A. H., eds.*, 1983, *1977*, pp. 1–23.

Machlup, Fritz. The Rationality of 'Rational Expectations.' *Kredit Kapital,* 1983, *16*(2), pp. 172–83.

Magnani, Marco. 'Keynesian Fundamentalism': A Critique. **In** *Eatwell, J. and Milgate, M., eds.*, 1983, pp. 247–59.

Makinen, Gail E. Recent Developments in Macroeconomic Theory and Policy. *Atlantic Econ. J.*, December 1983, *11*(4), pp. 84–88.

Malinvaud, Edmond. Keynes and the Management of Real National Income and Expenditure: Comment. **In** *Worswick, D. and Trevithick, J., eds.*, 1983, pp. 157–62.

Malinvaud, Edmond. Notes on Growth Theory with Imperfectly Flexible Prices. **In** *Fitoussi, J.-P., ed.*, 1983, pp. 93–114.

Marty, Alvin L. Indexing to the Money Supply: Pros and Cons: A Comment [Competitive Price Setting, Price Flexibility, and Linkage to the Money Supply]. *Carnegie-Rochester Conf. Ser. Public Policy*, Autumn 1983, *19*, pp. 301–11.

Mashiyama, Koichi. An Inventory Stock Market in a Business Cycle Model and Rational Expectations. *Econ. Stud. Quart.*, December 1983, *34*(3), pp. 211–24.

McCallum, Bennett T. On Non-Uniqueness in Rational Expectations Models: An Attempt at Perspective. *J. Monet. Econ.*, March 1983, *11*(2), pp. 139–68.

McCallum, Bennett T. Reply to Bryant and Wallace [The Role of Overlapping-Generations Models in Monetary Economics]. *Carnegie-Rochester Conf. Ser. Public Policy*, Spring 1983, *18*, pp. 57–58.

McCallum, Bennett T. The Liquidity Trap and the Pigou Effect: A Dynamic Analysis with Rational Expectations. *Economica*, November 1983, *50*(200), pp. 395–405.

McCallum, Bennett T. The Role of Overlapping-Generations Models in Monetary Economics. *Carnegie-Rochester Conf. Ser. Public Policy*, Spring 1983, *18*, pp. 9–44.

McCallum, Bennett T. The Role of Overlapping-Generations Models in Monetary Economics. **In** *Brunner, K. and Meltzer, A. H., eds.*, 1983, *1983*, pp. 129–64.

McDonald, John. A Solution to an Estimation Problem Involving Models with Rational Expectations. *J. Monet. Econ.*, May 1983, *11*(3), pp. 381–86.

McElroy, F. W. A Simple Supply-Side Model. *Econ. Int.*, May–August–November 1983, *36*(2–3–4), pp. 192–98.

Meade, James. A New Keynesian Approach to Full Employment. *Lloyds Bank Rev.*, October 1983, (150), pp. 1–18.

Meade, James. A New Keynesian Approach to Full Employment. *Nationaløkon. Tidsskr.*, 1983, *121*(3), pp. 299–316.

Medio, Alfredo and Muso, Ignazio. Changes in Money Wages and Employment in a Keynesian Analysis. *Econ. Notes*, 1983, (1), pp. 5–23.

Mehta, Granshyam. Comments on Professor Minoguchi's Interpretation of the *Treatise* and the *General Theory*. *Hitotsubashi J. Econ.*, December 1983, *24*(2), pp. 153–58.

Meltzer, Allan H. Interpreting Keynes [Keynes's *General Theory:* A Different Perspective]. *J. Econ. Lit.*, March 1983, *21*(1), pp. 66–78.

Meltzer, Allan H. On Keynes and Monetarism. **In** *Worswick, D. and Trevithick, J., eds.*, 1983, pp. 49–72.

Merrick, John J., Jr. Financial Market Efficiency, the Decomposition of "Anticipated" versus "Unanticipated" Money Growth, and Further Tests of the Relation between Money and Real Output: A Note. *J. Money, Credit, Banking*, May 1983, *15*(2), pp. 222–32. **[G: U.S.]**

Meyer, Paul A. Money Multipliers and the Slopes of IS-LM. *Southern Econ. J.*, July 1983, *50*(1), pp. 226–29.

Michel, Philippe. Indétermination et détermination des prix en prévisions rationnelles. (Price Indeterminacy in Rational Expectations Models. With English summary.) *Écon. Appl.*, 1983, *36*(1), pp. 77–97.

Milgate, Murray. The 'New' Keynes Papers. **In** *Eatwell, J. and Milgate, M., eds.*, 1983, pp. 187–99.

Milgate, Murray and Eatwell, John. Unemployment and the Market Mechanism. **In** *Eatwell, J. and Milgate, M., eds.*, 1983, pp. 260–80.

Minford, A. P. L. and Peel, David A. Some Implications of Partial Current Information Sets in Macroeconomic Models Embodying Rational Expectations. *Manchester Sch. Econ. Soc. Stud.*, September 1983, *51*(3), pp. 235–49.

Minford, Patrick; Ioannidis, Christos and Marwaha, Satwant. Rational Expectations in a Multilateral Macro-Model. **In** *De Grauwe, P. and Peeters, T., eds.*, 1983, pp. 239–66.

Minoguchi, Takeo. Reply [The Process of Writing the *General Theory* as a 'Monetary Theory of Production'] [Some Questions about IS-LM Interpretation of the *General Theory*]. *Hitotsubashi J. Econ.*, December 1983, *24*(2), pp. 159.

Minsky, Hyman P. Notes on Effective Demand: Comment [On Effective Demand: Certain Recent Critiques]. **In** *Kregel, J. A., ed.*, 1983, pp. 43–49.

Mishkin, Frederic S. The Remarkable Survival of Non-Market-Clearing Assumptions: A Comment. *Carnegie-Rochester Conf. Ser. Public Policy*, Autumn 1983, *19*, pp. 247–51.

Mitchell, Douglas W. Inventories and Macrodynamics. *Quart. Rev. Econ. Bus.*, Summer 1983, *23*(2), pp. 40–44.

Modigliani, Franco. Conversations with Neo-Keynesian Economists: The "Older Generation" [Interview]. **In** *Klamer, A.*, 1983, pp. 114–26.

Molins-Ysal, Georges. Malinvaud et la théorie macroéconomique (partie I). (Malinvaud and the *Théorie Macroéconomique* [Vol. 1]: A Review Article. With English summary.) *L'Actual. Econ.*, March 1983, *59*(1), pp. 89–107.

Monissen, Hans G. Preisniveau- und Outputbestimmung in einem einfachen gesamtwirtschaftlichen Modell. (The Determination of Output and Price Level in a Simple Macro-Economic Model. With English summary.) *Jahr. Nationalökon. Statist.*, July 1983, *198*(4), pp. 289–310.

Moosa, Suleman A. The Double Whammy of Stagflation and Uncertainty. *Kredit Kapital*, 1983, *16*(3), pp. 297–315. **[G: U.S.]**

Moosa, Suleman A. The Treatment of Uncertainty in the Application of Rational Expectations to the Analysis of Economic Policy. *Appl. Econ.*, August 1983, *15*(4), pp. 451–58.

Myerson, Roger B. A Dynamic Microeconomic Model with Durable Goods and Adaptive Expectations. *J. Econ. Behav. Organ.*, December 1983, *4*(4), pp. 309–51.

Nagatani, Keizo. Macroeconomic Foundations of

Macroeconomics. **In** *[Yamada, I.]*, 1983, pp. 51–63.

Nell, Edward J. On the Conception of the State in Macroeconomic Theory. *Soc. Res.*, Summer 1983, *50*(2), pp. 401–28.

Ng, Yew-Kwang and McGregor, L. Macroeconomics with Non-Perfect Competition: Tax Cuts and Wage Increases. *Australian Econ. Pap.*, December 1983, *22*(41), pp. 431–47.

Nordhaus, William D. Macroconfusion: The Dilemmas of Economic Policy. **In** *Tobin, J., ed.*, 1983, pp. 247–67. **[G: OECD]**

Okun, Arthur M. Rational-Expectations-with-Misperceptions as a Theory of the Business Cycle. **In** *Okun, A. M.*, 1983, *1980*, pp. 131–41.

Ormerod, Paul. Alternative Models of Inflation in the United Kingdom under the Assumption of Rational Expectations. **In** *Schmukler, N. and Marcus, E., eds.*, 1983, pp. 643–58. **[G: U.K.]**

Parkin, Michael. What Can Macroeconomic Theory Tell Us about the Way Deficits Should Be Measured? **In** *Conklin, D. W. and Courchene, T. J., eds.*, 1983, pp. 150–77.

Parkin, Michael. What Can Macroeconomic Theory Tell Us about the Way Deficits Should be Measured? Reply. **In** *Conklin, D. W. and Courchene, T. J., eds.*, 1983, pp. 186–88.

Pasinetti, Luigi L. The Accumulation of Capital. *Cambridge J. Econ.*, September/December 1983, *7*(3/4), pp. 405–11.

Pasinetti, Luigi L. What Would Keynes Have Thought of Rational Expectations? Comment. **In** *Worswick, D. and Trevithick, J., eds.*, 1983, pp. 205–11.

Patinkin, Don. New Perspectives or Old Pitfalls? Some Comments on Allan Meltzer's Interpretation of the *General Theory*. *J. Econ. Lit.*, March 1983, *21*(1), pp. 47–51.

Peden, G. C. Sir Richard Hopkins and the "Keynesian Revolution" in Employment Policy, 1929–1945. *Econ. Hist. Rev., 2nd Ser.*, May 1983, *36*(2), pp. 281–96. **[G: U.K.]**

Pemberton, James. A New Model of Inflation Expectations in a Simple Macroeconomic Model. *Economica*, August 1983, *50*(199), pp. 281–89.

Pen, Jan. Keynesology à la Leijonhufvud: False Signals. *De Economist*, 1983, *131*(1), pp. 16–30.

Perry, George L. Rational Expectations and the Invisible Handshake: Comment. **In** *Tobin, J., ed.*, 1983, pp. 79–82.

Persson, Torsten and Svensson, Lars E. O. Is Optimism Good in a Keynesian Economy? *Economica*, August 1983, *50*(199), pp. 291–300.

Phelps, Edmund S. The Trouble with "Rational Expectations" and the Problem of Inflation Stabilization. **In** *Frydman, R. and Phelps, E. S., eds.*, 1983, pp. 31–41.

Picard, Pierre. Inflation and Growth in a Disequilibrium Macroeconomic Model. *J. Econ. Theory*, August 1983, *30*(2), pp. 266–95.

Pohl, Rüdiger. Nicht-neutrale Inflation. (Non-neutral Inflation. With English summary.) *Kredit Kapital*, 1983, *16*(4), pp. 458–78.

Raboy, David G. Who Speaks for the Free Market: Monetarists or Supply-Siders? [What's Wrong with Supply-Side Economics] [The Trouble with Monetarism]. *Policy Rev.*, Spring 1983, (24), pp. 13–16. **[G: U.S.]**

Radner, Roy. Convergence to Rational Expectations Equilibria: Comment. **In** *Frydman, R. and Phelps, E. S., eds.*, 1983, pp. 133–37.

Rapping, Leonard A. Conversations with Nonconventional Economists [Interview]. **In** *Klamer, A.*, 1983, pp. 218–34.

Ratner, Jonathan B. A Doubtful Post Keynesian Unemployment Model. *J. Post Keynesian Econ.*, Spring 1983, *5*(3), pp. 474–82.

Redslob, Alain. Rationalité des anticipations et théorie de la politique monétaire: une note critique. (Rational Expectations Hypothesis and the Theory of Monetary Policy: A Critical Note. With English summary.) *Écon. Soc.*, July-August 1983, *17*(7–8), pp. 1259–75.

Reichlin, Pietro and Siconolfi, Paolo. Aspettative razionali, mercato atomistico e principio del costo marginale. (Rational Expectations, the Atomistic Market and the Marginal Cost Issue. With English summary.) *Giorn. Econ.*, November–December 1983, *42*(11–12), pp. 769–79.

Reynolds, Alan. Who Speaks for the Free Market: Monetarists or Supply-Siders? [The Trouble with Monetarism]. *Policy Rev.*, Spring 1983, (24), pp. 16–18. **[G: U.S.]**

Rogers, Colin. Neo–Walrasian Macroeconomics, Microfoundations and Pseudo–Production Models. *Australian Econ. Pap.*, June 1983, *22*(40), pp. 201–20.

Rustichini, Aldo. Equilibrium Points and "Strange Trajectories" in Keynesian Dynamics Models. *Econ. Notes*, 1983, (3), pp. 161–79.

Samuelson, Paul A. Rigorous Observational Positivism: Klein's Envelope Aggregation; Thermodynamics and Economic Isomorphisms. **In** *[Klein, L. R.]*, 1983, pp. 1–38.

Samuelson, Paul A. What Would Keynes Have Thought of Rational Expectations? Comment. **In** *Worswick, D. and Trevithick, J., eds.*, 1983, pp. 212–17.

Santacoloma, J.-F. Open Economy Macroeconomics: An Overview. *Écon. Soc.*, July-August 1983, *17*(7–8), pp. 1097–1148.

Sargent, Thomas J. Conversations with New Classical Economists [Interview]. **In** *Klamer, A.*, 1983, pp. 58–80.

Scarfe, Brian L. What Can Macroeconomic Theory Tell Us about the Way Deficits Should Be Measured? Comment. **In** *Conklin, D. W. and Courchene, T. J., eds.*, 1983, pp. 177–81.

Scarth, William M. Tax-Related Incomes Policies and Macroeconomic Stability. *J. Macroecon.*, Winter 1983, *5*(1), pp. 91–103.

Scheele, Erwin. Vermögensrestriktion, Budgetrestriktionen, Wirkungen der Staatsverschuldung und die Budget-Multiplikatoren von Dieter Cansier. (Wealth Restriction, Budget Restriction, Effects of Public Debt and D. Cansier's Budget Multipliers. With English summary.) *Kredit Kapital*, 1983, *16*(1), pp. 36–53.

Schefold, Bertram. Kahn on Malinvaud. **In** *Eatwell, J. and Milgate, M., eds.*, 1983, pp. 229–46.

Schott, Kerry. The Rise of Keynesian Economics: Britain 1940–64. **In** *Held, D., et al., eds.*, 1983,

1982, pp. 338–62. **[G: U.K.]**

Seccareccia, Mario S. A Reconsideration of the Underlying Structuralist Explanation of Price Movements in Keynes' 'Treatise on Money.' *Eastern Econ. J.,* July–September 1983, *9*(3), pp. 272–83. **[G: Canada]**

Shackle, George L. S. Levels of Simplicity in Keynes's Theory of Money and Employment. *S. Afr. J. Econ.,* September 1983, *51*(3), pp. 357–67.

Shah, Anup R. K. Rational Expectations Macro Models with Possible Steady-State Inflation and Unemployment. *J. Macroecon.,* Fall 1983, *5*(4), pp. 461–71.

Shaller, Douglas R. Working Capital Finance Considerations in a National Income Theory. *Amer. Econ. Rev.,* March 1983, *73*(1), pp. 156–65.

Shiller, Robert J. The Roles of Money and Credit in Macroeconomic Analysis: Comment. **In** *Tobin, J., ed.,* 1983, pp. 193–99. **[G: U.S.]**

Silvestre, Joaquim. Fixprice Analysis in Productive Economies. *J. Econ. Theory,* August 1983, *30*(2), pp. 401–09.

Sinclair, P. J. N. How Does an Energy Price Shock Affect Aggregate Output and Employment? *Greek Econ. Rev.,* August 1983, *5*(2), pp. 123–46.

Sinn, Hans-Werner. International Capital Movements, Flexible Exchange Rates, and the IS-LM Model: A Comparison between the Portfolio-Balance and the Flow Hypotheses. *Weltwirtsch. Arch.,* 1983, *119*(1), pp. 36–63.

Sjaastad, Larry A. Macroconfusion: The Dilemmas of Economic Policy: Comment. **In** *Tobin, J., ed.,* 1983, pp. 276–79. **[G: Chile; Argentina]**

Sleeman, Allen G. and Cebula, Barbara A. A Relevant Alternative to *IS-LM* Analysis: A Note. *Rivista Int. Sci. Econ. Com.,* February 1983, *30*(2), pp. 187 92.

Smyth, David J. Taxes and Inflation. **In** *Schmukler, N. and Marcus, E., eds.,* 1983, pp. 326–39.

Smyth, David J. The Effect of an Autonomous Expenditure Increase on the Excess Demand for Money. *Atlantic Econ. J.,* March 1983, *11*(1), pp. 64–67.

Sneessens, H. R. A Macroeconomic Rationing Model of the Belgian Economy. *Europ. Econ. Rev.,* January 1983, *20*(1–3), pp. 193–215. **[G: Belgium]**

Snower, Dennis J. Imperfect Competition, Underemployment and Crowding-Out. *Oxford Econ. Pap.,* Supplement November 1983, *35,* pp. 245–70.

Solow, Robert M. Conversations with Neo-Keynesian Economists: The "Older Generation" [Interview]. **In** *Klamer, A.,* 1983, pp. 127–48.

Solow, Robert M. Keynes and the Management of Real National Income and Expenditure: Comment. **In** *Worswick, D. and Trevithick, J., eds.,* 1983, pp. 162–68.

Solow, Robert M. Macroconfusion: The Dilemmas of Economic Policy: Comment. **In** *Tobin, J., ed.,* 1983, pp. 279–84. **[G: U.S.]**

Stohs, Mark. 'Uncertainty' in Keynes' *General Theory:* A Rejoinder. *Hist. Polit. Econ.,* Spring 1983, *15*(1), pp. 87–91.

Stokes, Houston H. and Neuburger, Hugh. The Effect of Monetary Changes on Interest Rates: A Reply. *Rev. Econ. Statist.,* May 1983, *65*(2), pp. 362. **[G: U.S.]**

Svindland, Eirik. Konjunkturtheoretische Implikationen der Hypothese rationaler Erwartungen. (Implications of the "Rational Expectations" Hypothesis with Respect to Business Cycle Theory. With English summary.) *Kredit Kapital,* 1983, *16*(3), pp. 331–50.

Tarantelli, Ezio. Foundations of a Likelihood Theory of Employment and Inflation. **In** *Fitoussi, J.-P., ed.,* 1983, pp. 185–203.

Targetti, Ferdinando. Nota sulle crisi in Roemer. (A Note on the Economic Crisis in a Roemer's Model. With English summary.) *Giorn. Econ.,* July–August 1983, *42*(7–8), pp. 527–35.

Taylor, John B. Conversations with Neo-Keynesian Economists: The "Younger Generation" [Interview]. **In** *Klamer, A.,* 1983, pp. 170–76.

Taylor, John B. Rational Expectations and the Invisible Handshake. **In** *Tobin, J., ed.,* 1983, pp. 63–77.

Thirlwall, Anthony P. Keynesian Economics after Fifty Years: Comment. **In** *Worswick, D. and Trevithick, J., eds.,* 1983, pp. 37–44.

Thirlwall, Anthony P. What Are Estimates of the Natural Rate of Unemployment Measuring? *Oxford Bull. Econ. Statist.,* May 1983, *45*(2), pp. 173–79.

Thygesen, Niels. Praktisk relevans af keynesiansk teori i dag. (With English summary.) *Nationaløkon. Tidsskr.,* 1983, *121*(3), pp. 332–44.

Tobin, James. Conversations with Neo-Keynesian Economists: The "Older Generation" [Interview]. **In** *Klamer, A.,* 1983, pp. 97–113.

Tobin, James. Financial Structure and Monetary Rules. *Kredit Kapital,* 1983, *16*(2), pp. 155–71. **[G: U.S.]**

Tobin, James. Keynes' Policies in Theory and Practice. *Challenge,* November/December 1983, *26*(5), pp. 5–11.

Tobin, James. Keynesian Economics after Fifty Years: Comment. **In** *Worswick, D. and Trevithick, J., eds.,* 1983, pp. 28–37.

Tobin, James. Macroeconomics and Fiscal Policy. **In** *Brown, E. C. and Solow, R. M., eds.,* 1983, pp. 189–201.

Townsend, Robert M. Conversations with New Classical Economists [Interview]. **In** *Klamer, A.,* 1983, pp. 81–94.

Tronzano, Marco. La nuova macroeconomia classica: una rassegna critica. (New Classical Macroeconomics: A Critical Survey. With English summary.) *Rivista Int. Sci. Econ. Com.,* July 1983, *30*(7), pp. 625–53.

Turnovsky, Stephen J. Wage Indexation and Exchange Market Interventions in a Small Open Economy. *Can. J. Econ.,* November 1983, *16*(4), pp. 574–92.

Vanderhoff, James. Support for Rational Expectations Models with U.S. Data. *J. Monet. Econ.,* August 1983, *12*(2), pp. 297–308. **[G: U.S.]**

Vedel, Claude. Politique Monétaire et Politique Budgétaire dans un Modèle Dynamique Synthétique d'une Economie en Croissance. **In** *Biehl, D.; Roskamp, K. W. and Stolper, W. F., eds.,* 1983, pp. 101–26.

023 Macroeconomic Theory

Wallace, Neil. A Comment on McCallum [The Role of Overlapping-Generations Models in Monetary Economics]. *Carnegie-Rochester Conf. Ser. Public Policy,* Spring 1983, *18,* pp. 51–56.

Walliser, Bernard. Equilibres avec anticipations et représentations autoréalisatrices. (Expectational Equilibria and Self-Fulfilling Realizations. With English summary.) *Écon. Appl.,* 1983, *36*(1), pp. 177–205.

Watanabe, Ken-ichi. An Adaptation of Weintraub's Model. *J. Post Keynesian Econ.,* Winter 1982–83, *5*(2), pp. 228–44.

Weddepohl, Claus. Developments in the Theory of General Equilibrium. *De Economist,* 1983, *131*(3), pp. 373–99.

Weddepohl, Claus. Fixed Price Equilibria in a Multifirm Model. *J. Econ. Theory,* February 1983, *29*(1), pp. 95–108.

Weintraub, Sidney. A Macro-Distributive Theory Dispelling the Econometric Fog. *Banca Naz. Lavoro Quart. Rev.,* March 1983, (144), pp. 69–80.

Weintraub, Sidney. Comment on Allan Meltzer's "Keynes's *General Theory.*" *J. Econ. Lit.,* March 1983, *21*(1), pp. 57–58.

Wells, Paul. A Post Keynesian View of Liquidity Preference and the Demand for Money. *J. Post Keynesian Econ.,* Summer 1983, *5*(4), pp. 523–36.

Wible, James R. The Rational Expectations Tautologies. *J. Post Keynesian Econ.,* Winter 1982–83, *5*(2), pp. 199–207.

Wilcox, James A. Why Real Interest Rates Were So Low in the 1970's. *Amer. Econ. Rev.,* March 1983, *73*(1), pp. 44–53. **[G: U.S.]**

Williams, Edward G. Analyzing the World's Money. *J. Post Keynesian Econ.,* Summer 1983, *5*(4), pp. 625–34.

Wren-Lewis, Simon. Labour Supply and Wealth: Some Macroeconomic Policy Implications. *Manchester Sch. Econ. Soc. Stud.,* March 1983, *51*(1), pp. 1–15. **[G: U.K.]**

Zikry, Emad. A Note on the Stability Requirements in Disequilibrium States. *Amer. Econ.,* Fall 1983, *27*(2), pp. 77–79.

0232 Theory of Aggregate Demand: Consumption

Anstie, Roslyn K.; Gray, M. R. and Pagan, A. R. Inflation and the Consumption Ratio. **In** *Pagan, A. R. and Trivedi, P. K., eds.,* 1983, pp. 322–49. **[G: Australia]**

Anyadike-Danes, Michael. A 'Comment' on Chrystal [The 'New Cambridge' Aggregate Expenditure Function]. *J. Monet. Econ.,* January 1983, *11*(1), pp. 133–35. **[G: U.K.]**

Auerbach, Alan J. and Kotlikoff, Laurence J. An Examination of Empirical Tests of Social Security and Savings. **In** *Helpman, E.; Razin, A. and Sadka, E., eds.,* 1983, pp. 161–79. **[G: U.S.]**

Bladen-Hovell, R. C. and Richards, G. M. Inflation and Australian Savings Behaviour, 1959–1981. *Australian Econ. Pap.,* December 1983, *22*(41), pp. 290–301. **[G: Australia]**

Blinder, Alan S.; Gordon, Roger H. and Wise, Donald E. Social Security, Bequests and the Life Cycle Theory of Saving: Cross-sectional Tests. **In** *Modigliani, F. and Hemming, R., eds.,* 1983, pp. 89–122. **[G: U.S.]**

Chatterji, Monojit. On Forecasting U.K. Consumption. *Appl. Econ.,* June 1983, *15*(3), pp. 417–23. **[G: U.K.]**

Chrystal, K. Alec. The New Cambridge Aggregate Expenditure Function: Reply. *J. Monet. Econ.,* January 1983, *11*(1), pp. 137–38. **[G: U.K.]**

Cuthbertson, K. Consumer Spending. **In** *Britton, A., ed.,* 1983, pp. 16–27. **[G: U.K.]**

Danziger, Sheldon, et al. The Life-Cycle Hypothesis and the Consumption Behavior of the Elderly. *J. Post Keynesian Econ.,* Winter 1982–83, *5*(2), pp. 208–27. **[G: U.S.]**

Davidson, Russell and MacKinnon, James G. Inflation and the Savings Rate. *Appl. Econ.,* December 1983, *15*(6), pp. 731–43. **[G: U.S.; Canada]**

Deaton, Angus. Savings and Inflation: Theory and British Evidence. **In** *Modigliani, F. and Hemming, R., eds.,* 1983, pp. 125–39. **[G: U.K.]**

Eisner, Robert. Government Policy, Saving and Investment. *J. Econ. Educ.,* Spring 1983, *14*(2), pp. 38–49. **[G: U.S.]**

Feldstein, Martin S. Social Security Benefits and the Accumulation of Pre-retirement Wealth. **In** *Modigliani, F. and Hemming, R., eds.,* 1983, pp. 3–23. **[G: U.S.]**

Feldstein, Martin S. and Fane, George. Taxes, Corporate Dividend Policy, and Personal Savings: The British Postwar Experience. **In** *Feldstein, M. (I),* 1983, *1973,* pp. 135–55. **[G: U.K.]**

Friend, Irwin and Hasbrouck, Joel. Saving and After-Tax Rates of Return. *Rev. Econ. Statist.,* November 1983, *65*(4), pp. 537–43. **[G: U.S.]**

Garegnani, Pierangelo. Notes on Consumption, Investment and Effective Demand. **In** *Eatwell, J. and Milgate, M., eds.,* 1983, *1978,* pp. 21–69.

Garegnani, Pierangelo. Notes on Consumption, Investment and Effective Demand: Reply. **In** *Eatwell, J. and Milgate, M., eds.,* 1983, *1979,* pp. 72–78.

Gleting, Jørgen H. Om fastprismodellernes forklaring af arbejdsløsheden. (Some Critical Comments on Macroeconomic Fixprice Models. With English summary.) *Nationaløkon. Tidsskr.,* 1983, *121*(1), pp. 17–19.

Goodwin, R. M. Does the Matrix Multiplier Oscillate? **In** *Goodwin, R. M.,* 1983, *1950,* pp. 22–29. **[G: U.S.]**

Goodwin, R. M. The Multiplier as Matrix. **In** *Goodwin, R. M.,* 1983, *1949,* pp. 1–21.

Gowland, D. H. Consumption, Saving and Inflation. **In** *Gowland, D. H., ed.,* 1983, pp. 119–39. **[G: U.K.]**

Grieves, Robin. The Demand for Consumer Durables. *J. Money, Credit, Banking,* August 1983, *15*(3), pp. 316–26. **[G: U.S.]**

Hendry, David F. Econometric Modelling: The "Consumption Function" in Retrospect. *Scot. J. Polit. Econ.,* November 1983, *30*(3), pp. 193–220. **[G: U.K.]**

Johnson, Paul. Life-Cycle Consumption under Rational Expectations: Some Australian Evidence. *Econ. Rec.,* December 1983, *59*(167), pp. 345–50. **[G: Australia]**

Kormendi, Roger C. Government Debt, Government Spending, and Private Sector Behavior. *Amer. Econ. Rev.*, December 1983, *73*(5), pp. 994–1010. [G: U.S.]

Koskela, Erkki and Virén, Matti. National Debt Neutrality: Some International Evidence. *Kyklos*, 1983, *36*(4), pp. 575–88. [G: Selected OECD]

Krzyzaniak, Marian. The Dynamic Incidence of the Levy on Income, Government Expenditures Wasteful. *Public Finance*, 1983, *38*(3), pp. 339–61.

L'Hardy, Philippe. Le comportement de l'épargnant a la lumière de la crise. (Savings Patterns in the Light of the Economic Crisis. With English summary.) *Revue Écon.*, January 1983, *34*(1), pp. 124–51. [G: France]

Laumas, Prem S. and Bausch, James. On the Proper Specification of the Permanent Income Hypothesis. *Econ. Notes*, 1983, (2), pp. 152–60. [G: U.S.]

Lee, Maw Lin and Hu, Teh-wei. Socioeconomic Factors and Consumption Theories. *Math. Soc. Sci.*, August 1983, *5*(1), pp. 17–32.

Lyon, Kenneth S. Intertemporal Consumption Theory and the Balanced Budget Multiplier. *Southern Econ. J.*, July 1983, *50*(1), pp. 206–12.

Masson, André. Profils d'accumulation patrimoniale et modèles de cycle de vie. (Wealth Accumulation Profiles and Life-Cycle Models. With English summary.) *Revue Écon.*, January 1983, *34*(1), pp. 10–63. [G: France]

Mellin, Ilkka and Virén, Matti. Real Wages, Inflation and Household Consumption Behavior. *Liiketaloudellinen Aikak.*, 1983, *32*(3), pp. 267–85. [G: Finland]

Menchik, Paul L. and David, Martin H. Income Distribution, Lifetime Savings, and Bequests. *Amer. Econ. Rev.*, September 1983, *73*(4), pp. 672–90. [G: U.S.]

Modigliani, Franco and Sterling, Arlie. Determinants of Private Saving with Special Reference to the Role of Social Security—Cross-country Tests. **In** *Modigliani, F. and Hemming, R., eds.*, 1983, pp. 24–55. [G: Selected OECD]

Molho, Lazaros E. On Testing the Efficacy of Selective Credit Controls. *J. Money, Credit, Banking*, February 1983, *15*(1), pp. 120–22. [G: U.S.]

Muellbauer, John. Surprises in the Consumption Function. *Econ. J.*, Supplement March 1983, pp. 34–50. [G: U.K.]

Nevile, J. W. Inflation and the Consumption Ratio: Discussion. **In** *Pagan, A. R. and Trivedi, P. K., eds.*, 1983, pp. 356–61. [G: Australia]

Peek, Joe. Capital Gains and Personal Saving Behavior. *J. Money, Credit, Banking*, February 1983, *15*(1), pp. 1–23. [G: U.S.]

Penner, Rudolph G. Public Policy and Aggregate Saving. *Bus. Econ.*, March 1983, *18*(2), pp. 1–10. [G: U.S.]

Polemarchakis, Heraklis M. Homotheticity and the Aggregation of Consumer Demands. *Quart. J. Econ.*, May 1983, *98*(2), pp. 363–69.

Ram, Rati. Some Direct Estimates of "Discount Rates" and Consumer "Horizon" from Kendrick's Data. *Southern Econ. J.*, January 1983, *49*(3), pp. 860–66. [G: U.S.]

Robinson, Joan. Notes on Consumption, Investment and Effective Demand: Comment. **In** *Eatwell, J. and Milgate, M., eds.*, 1983, *1979*, pp. 70–71.

Russell, Thomas. Notes on Exact Aggregation. **In** *[Yamada, I.]*, 1983, pp. 171–76.

Schröder, Jürgen. Social Security and the Macroeconomic Saving–Income Ratio. *Weltwirtsch. Arch.*, 1983, *119*(3), pp. 554–68.

Seidman, Laurence S. Taxes in a Life Cycle Growth Model with Bequests and Inheritances. *Amer. Econ. Rev.*, June 1983, *73*(3), pp. 437–41.

Strauss-Kahn, Dominique. Explaining the Composition of Household Saving Flows and Their Relationship to Aggregate Saving in France. **In** *Modigliani, F. and Hemming, R., eds.*, 1983, pp. 180–200. [G: France]

Thys-Clement, Françoise; Van Regemorter, Denise and Vuchelen, Josef. La consommation privée: Cycle de vie et rationalité, une analyse empirique. (With English summary.) *Cah. Écon. Bruxelles*, Third Trimestre 1983, (99), pp. 327–60. [G: Belgium]

Williams, Ross A. and Ouliaris, Sam. Inflation and the Consumption Ratio: Comments. **In** *Pagan, A. R. and Trivedi, P. K., eds.*, 1983, pp. 350–55. [G: Australia]

0233 Theory of Aggregate Demand: Investment

Akhtar, M. A. Effects of Interest Rates and Inflation on Aggregate Inventory Investment in the United States. *Amer. Econ. Rev.*, June 1983, *73*(3), pp. 319–28. [G: U.S.]

Anyadike-Danes, Michael. A 'Comment' on Chrystal [The 'New Cambridge' Aggregate Expenditure Function]. *J. Monet. Econ.*, January 1983, *11*(1), pp. 133–35. [G: U.K.]

Asimakopulos, A. Kalecki and Keynes on Finance, Investment and Saving. *Cambridge J. Econ.*, September/December 1983, *7*(3/4), pp. 221–33.

Auerbach, Alan J. Efficient Design of Investment Incentives. **In** *Auerbach, A. J.*, 1983, *1981*, pp. 51–57.

Baden Fuller, Charles. The Implications of the 'Learning Curve' for Firm Strategy and Public Policy. *Appl. Econ.*, August 1983, *15*(4), pp. 541–51. [G: U.K.]

Bailey, R. E. and Scarth, William M. Macroeconomic Implications of Adjustment Costs: A Further Note [Adjustment Costs and Aggregate Demand Theory]. *Economica*, August 1983, *50*(199), pp. 365–69.

Barron, John M.; Black, Dan A. and Loewenstein, Mark A. Adjustment Costs and Aggregate Demand Theory: A Note. *Economica*, August 1983, *50*(199), pp. 361–64.

Bernanke, Ben S. Irreversibility, Uncertainty, and Cyclical Investment. *Quart. J. Econ.*, February 1983, *98*(1), pp. 85–106.

Bernanke, Ben S. The Determinants of Investment: Another Look. *Amer. Econ. Rev.*, May 1983, *73*(2), pp. 71–75. [G: U.S.]

Blackorby, Charles and Schworm, William E. Aggregating Heterogeneous Capital Goods in Adjustment-Cost Technologies. *Scand. J. Econ.*, 1983, *85*(2), pp. 207–22.

Chrystal, K. Alec. The New Cambridge Aggregate Expenditure Function: Reply. *J. Monet. Econ.*,

January 1983, *11*(1), pp. 137–38. [G: U.K.]

Costrell, Robert M. Profitability and Aggregate Investment under Demand Uncertainty. *Econ. J.*, March 1983, *93*(369), pp. 166–81.

Dickson, Harald. How Did Keynes Conceive of Entrepreneurs' Motivation? Notes on Patinkin's Hypothesis. *Hist. Polit. Econ.*, Summer 1983, *15*(2), pp. 229–47.

Eisner, Robert. Government Policy, Saving and Investment. *J. Econ. Educ.*, Spring 1983, *14*(2), pp. 38–49. [G: U.S.]

Eisner, Robert. Tax Policy and Investment. **In** *Biehl, D.; Roskamp, K. W. and Stolper, W. F., eds.*, 1983, pp. 167–80.

Feldstein, Martin S. Fiscal Policies, Inflation, and Capital Formation. **In** *Feldstein, M. (II)*, 1983, *1980*, pp. 61–80.

Feldstein, Martin S. Inflation, Tax Rules, and Investment: Some Econometric Evidence. **In** *Feldstein, M. (I)*, 1983, *1982*, pp. 331–73. [G: U.S.]

Feldstein, Martin S. Inflation, Tax Rules, and Investment: Some Econometric Evidence. **In** *Feldstein, M. (II)*, 1983, *1982*, pp. 243–85. [G: U.S.]

Feldstein, Martin S. Tax Incentives, Corporate Saving, and Capital Accumulation in the United States. **In** *Feldstein, M. (I)*, 1983, *1973*, pp. 123–34. [G: U.S.]

Feldstein, Martin S. and Flemming, John. Tax Policy, Corporate Saving, and Investment Behavior in Britain. **In** *Feldstein, M. (I)*, 1983, *1971*, pp. 269–94. [G: U.K.]

Feldstein, Martin S. and Rothschild, Michael. Toward an Economic Theory of Replacement Investment. **In** *Feldstein, M. (I)*, 1983, *1974*, pp. 295–330.

Garegnani, Pierangelo. Notes on Consumption, Investment and Effective Demand: Reply. **In** *Eatwell, J. and Milgate, M., eds.*, 1983, *1979*, pp. 72–78.

Garegnani, Pierangelo. Notes on Consumption, Investment and Effective Demand. **In** *Eatwell, J. and Milgate, M., eds.*, 1983, *1978*, pp. 21–69.

Garegnani, Pierangelo. Two Routes to Effective Demand: Comment [Effective Demand: Origins and Development of the Notion]. **In** *Kregel, J. A., ed.*, 1983, pp. 69–80.

Harcourt, Geoffrey C. Keynes's College Bursar View of Investment: Comment [Effective Demand: Origins and Development of the Notion]. **In** *Kregel, J. A., ed.*, 1983, pp. 81–84.

Henry, S. G. B. and Wren-Lewis, S. Investment and Stockbuilding. **In** *Britton, A., ed.*, 1983, pp. 28–39. [G: U.K.]

Izenson, Mark Steven. A Brief Note on the Relationship between Investment and the Interest Rate in the United States, 1970–1979. *Econ. Notes*, 1983, (1), pp. 135–39. [G: U.S.]

Jüttner, D. Johannes. Rates of Return, Investment Behaviour and Monetary Policy. *Kredit Kapital*, 1983, *16*(1), pp. 16–35.

Kotlikoff, Laurence J. National Savings and Economic Policy: The Efficacy of Investment vs. Savings Incentives. *Amer. Econ. Rev.*, May 1983, *73*(2), pp. 82–87. [G: U.S.]

Kregel, J. A. Effective Demand: Origins and Development of the Notion. **In** *Kregel, J. A., ed.*, 1983, pp. 50–68.

Lerner, Abba P. On the Marginal Product of Capital and the Marginal Efficiency of Investment. **In** *Lerner, A. P.*, 1983, *1953*, pp. 531–44.

LeRoy, Stephen F. Keynes's Theory of Investment. *Hist. Polit. Econ.*, Fall 1983, *15*(3), pp. 397–421.

Miles, James A. Taxes and the Fisher Effect: A Clarifying Analysis. *J. Finance*, March 1983, *38*(1), pp. 67–77.

Mitchell, Douglas W. Inventories and Macrodynamics. *Quart. Rev. Econ. Bus.*, Summer 1983, *23*(2), pp. 40–44.

Naggl, Walter. Prediction of Inventory Investment with the Use of Business Survey Data. *Konjunkturpolitik*, 1983, *29*(2), pp. 89–99. [G: W. Germany]

Nell, Edward J. Keynes after Sraffa: The Essential Properties of Keynes's Theory of Interest and Money: Comment [Effective Demand: Origins and Development of the Notion]. **In** *Kregel, J. A., ed.*, 1983, pp. 85–103.

de la Peunte, F. and de Ullivarri, Fdez. La intensidad de la crisis actual a la luz de la teoría de los ciclos económicos. (Intensity of the Present Crisis under the Economic Cycle Theory. With English summary.) *Écon. Soc.*, September–October–November 1983, *17*(9–10–11), pp. 1403–19.

Poterba, James M. and Summers, Lawrence H. Dividend Taxes, Corporate Investment, and *'Q.'*. *J. Public Econ.*, November 1983, *22*(2), pp. 135–67. [G: U.K.]

Robinson, Joan. Notes on Consumption, Investment and Effective Demand: Comment. **In** *Eatwell, J. and Milgate, M., eds.*, 1983, *1979*, pp. 70–71.

Schiantarelli, Fabio. Investment Models and Expectations: Some Estimates for the Italian Industrial Sector. *Int. Econ. Rev.*, June 1983, *24*(2), pp. 291–312. [G: Italy]

Sinai, Allen and Eckstein, Otto. Tax Policy and Business Fixed Investment Revisited. *J. Econ. Behav. Organ.*, June–September 1983, *4*(2–3), pp. 131–62. [G: U.S.]

Tarkka, Juha and Pikkarainen, Pentti. Hinnat, palkat ja avoimen sektorin kasvu. (Prices, Wages and Open Sector Growth. With English summary.) *Kansant. Aikak.*, 1983, *79*(2), pp. 180–93. [G: Finland]

Tobin, James. Liquidity Preference as Behaviour towards Risk. **In** *Archer, S. H. and D'Ambrosia, C. A.*, 1983, *1958*, pp. 101–25.

Weintraub, Sidney. Effective Demand and Income Distribution. **In** *Kregel, J. A., ed.*, 1983, pp. 104–11.

Weintraub, Sidney. The Supply Price in the Marginal Efficiency of Capital. *J. Post Keynesian Econ.*, Summer 1983, *5*(4), pp. 618–24.

0234 Theory of Aggregate Supply

Allsbrook, Ogden O., Jr. and Gilliam, Kenneth P. An Industrial Interpretation of Inflationary Unemployment. *Kredit Kapital*, 1983, *16*(4), pp. 479–87.

Apostolakis, Bobby. Money Balances as Factor Inputs: An Empirical Evidence Based on Translog Specification. *Europ. Econ. Rev.*, November 1983,

23(2), pp. 149–60. **[G: Greece]**

Artis, M. J. The Capital Constraint on Employment. **In** *[Saunders, C. T.]*, 1983, pp. 109–26. **[G: U.K.]**

Attfield, Clifford L. F. An Analysis of the Implications of Omitting Variables from the Monetary Growth Equation in a Model of Real Output and Unanticipated Money Growth. *Europ. Econ. Rev.*, December 1983, *23*(3), pp. 281–90.

Azariadis, Costas and Stiglitz, Joseph E. Implicit Contracts and Fixed Price Equilibria. *Quart. J. Econ.*, Supplement 1983, *98*(3), pp. 1–22.

Baldone, Salvatore. Dalle funzioni surrogate alle pseudo funzioni di produzione. (From Surrogate to Pseudo Production Functions. With English summary.) *Giorn. Econ.*, January–February 1983, *42*(1–2), pp. 55–78.

Bean, Charles R. Targeting Nominal Income: An Appraisal. *Econ. J.*, December 1983, *93*(372), pp. 806–19.

Benavie, Arthur. Optimal Monetary Policy under Rational Expectations with a Micro-Based Supply Function. *J. Macroecon.*, Spring 1983, *5*(2), pp. 149–66.

Blackorby, Charles and Schworm, William E. Aggregating Heterogeneous Capital Goods in Adjustment-Cost Technologies. *Scand. J. Econ.*, 1983, *85*(2), pp. 207–22.

Blanchard, Olivier J. Dynamic Effects of a Shift in Savings; The Role of Firms. *Econometrica*, September 1983, *51*(5), pp. 1583–91.

Blitch, Charles P. Allyn Young on Increasing Returns. *J. Post Keynesian Econ.*, Spring 1983, *5*(3), pp. 359–72.

Brazelton, W. Robert. A Further Note on the Aggregate Supply Function. *Amer. Econ.*, Spring 1983, *27*(1), pp. 69–70.

Brodbeck, Karl-Heinz. Neue Kapitalgüter, unvollkommene Konkurrenz und Profitrate. (New Capital Goods, Imperfect Competition and the Rate of Profit. With English summary.) *Z. ges. Staatswiss.*, March 1983, *139*(1), pp. 131–45.

Bull, Clive and Frydman, Roman. The Derivation and Interpretation of the Lucas Supply Function. *J. Money, Credit, Banking*, February 1983, *15*(1), pp. 82–95.

Bulow, Jeremy and Polemarchakis, Heraklis M. Retroactive Money. *Economica*, August 1983, *50*(199), pp. 301–10.

Calvo, Guillermo A. and Peel, David A. Growth and Inflationary Finance: Variations on a Mundellian Theme. *J. Polit. Econ.*, October 1983, *91*(5), pp. 880–87.

Caselli, Paola. Exchange Rate and Current Account Dynamics with Imperfect Flexible Real Wages. *Stud. Econ.*, 1983, *38*(19), pp. 73–121.

Chatterji, Monojit and Wickens, Michael R. Verdoorn's Law and Kaldor's Law: A Revisionist Interpretation? *J. Post Keynesian Econ.*, Spring 1983, *5*(3), pp. 397–413. **[G: OECD]**

Costrell, Robert M. Profitability and Aggregate Investment under Demand Uncertainty. *Econ. J.*, March 1983, *93*(369), pp. 166–81.

Cothren, Richard D. Monetary Shocks and Labor Market Equilibrium. *Southern Econ. J.*, October 1983, *50*(2), pp. 346–54.

Darby, Michael R. Actual versus Unanticipated Changes in Aggregate Demand Variables: A Sensitivity Analysis of the Real-Income Equation. **In** *Darby, M. P. and Lothian, J. R., et al.*, 1983, pp. 273–88. **[G: OECD]**

Davidson, Paul. The Marginal Product Curve Is Not the Demand Curve for Labor and Lucas's Labor Supply Function Is Not the Supply Curve for Labor in the Real World. *J. Post Keynesian Econ.*, Fall 1983, *6*(1), pp. 105–17.

Day, Richard H. The Emergence of Chaos from Classical Economic Growth. *Quart. J. Econ.*, May 1983, *98*(2), pp. 201–13.

Diewert, W. Erwin. The Theory of the Output Price Index and the Measurement of Real Output Change. **In** *Diewert, W. E. and Montmarquette, C., eds.*, 1983, pp. 1049–1113.

Driscoll, Michael J., et al. Money, Output, Rational Expectations and Neutrality: Some Econometric Results for the UK. *Economica*, August 1983, *50*(199), pp. 259–68. **[G: U.K.]**

Driscoll, Michael J., et al. Testing the Rational Expectations and Structural Neutrality Hypotheses: Some Econometric Results for Austria 1965(1)–1979(4). *Empirica*, 1983, (1), pp. 3–13. **[G: Austria]**

Dyckhoff, Harald. Economically Essential Factors of Production. *Jahr. Nationalökon. Statist.*, July 1983, *198*(4), pp. 362–68.

Eatwell, John. The Long-Period Theory of Employment. *Cambridge J. Econ.*, September/December 1983, *7*(3/4), pp. 269–85.

van Eijk, Cornelis J. Possible Policy Implications of Modern Underemployment Equilibrium Theory. *De Economist*, 1983, *131*(3), pp. 344–72. **[G: Netherlands]**

Eisner, Robert. Social Security, Saving, and Macroeconomics. *J. Macroecon.*, Winter 1983, *5*(1), pp. 1–19. **[G: U.S.]**

Evans, Paul. Price-Level Instability and Output in the U.S. *Econ. Inquiry*, April 1983, *21*(2), pp. 172–87.

Feige, Edgar L. and McGee, Robert T. Sweden's Laffer Curve: Taxation and the Unobserved Economy. *Scand. J. Econ.*, 1983, *85*(4), pp. 499–519. **[G: Sweden]**

Fisher, Franklin M. On the Simultaneous Existence of Full and Partial Capital Aggregates. *Rev. Econ. Stud.*, January 1983, *50*(1), pp. 197–208.

Fitzgerald, M. Desmond and Pollio, Gerald. Money, Activity and Prices: Some Inter-Country Evidence. *Europ. Econ. Rev.*, December 1983, *23*(3), pp. 299–314. **[G: Selected OECD]**

Frank, Jeff L. Uncertain Vacancies and Unemployment Equilibria. *J. Econ. Theory*, June 1983, *30*(1), pp. 115–38.

Gibson, Bill and Esfahani, Hadi. Nonproduced Means of Production: Neo-Ricardians vs. Fundamentalists. *Rev. Radical Polit. Econ.*, Summer 1983, *15*(2), pp. 83–105.

Gomulka, Stanislaw. Industrialization and the Rate of Growth: Eastern Europe, 1955–75. *J. Post Keynesian Econ.*, Spring 1983, *5*(3), pp. 388–96. **[G: E. Europe]**

Grossman, Sanford J.; Hart, Oliver D. and Maskin, Eric S. Unemployment with Observable Aggregate Shocks. *J. Polit. Econ.*, December 1983,

91(6), pp. 907–28.

Gunning, Jan Willem. Rationing in an Open Economy: Fix-Price Equilibrium and Two-Gap Models. *Europ. Econ. Rev.*, September 1983, *23*(1), pp. 71–98.

Hercowitz, Zvi. Anticipated Inflation, the Frequency of Transactions, and the Slope of the Phillips Curve. *J. Money, Credit, Banking,* May 1983, *15*(2), pp. 139–54.

Hicks, John. A Note on the Elasticity of Supply. **In** *Hicks, J.*, 1983, *1934,* pp. 237–45.

Hicks, John. Elasticity of Substitution Reconsidered. **In** *Hicks, J.*, 1983, pp. 312–26.

Hodgson, Geoffrey M. Worker Participation and Macroeconomic Efficiency. *J. Post Keynesian Econ.*, Winter 1982–83, *5*(2), pp. 266–75.

Johnson, Ronald. Supply-Side Economics: The Rise to Prominence. *Rev. Black Polit. Econ.*, Winter 1983, *12*(2), pp. 189–202. **[G: U.S.]**

Kataoka, Haruo. On the Local Conservation Laws in the Von Neumann Model. **In** *[Yamada, I.]*, 1983, pp. 156–63.

Klein, Lawrence R. Supply-side Modeling. **In** *Thrall, R. M.; Thompson, R. G. and Holloway, M. L., eds.*, 1983, pp. 55–75.

Kotlikoff, Laurence J. National Savings and Economic Policy: The Efficacy of Investment vs. Savings Incentives. *Amer. Econ. Rev.*, May 1983, *73*(2), pp. 82–87. **[G: U.S.]**

Krelle, Wilhelm E. The Aggregate Production Function and the Representative Firm. **In** *[Klein, L. R.]*, 1983, pp. 175–87.

Lawrence, Colin. Rational Expectations, Supply Shocks and the Stability of the Inflation–Output Tradeoff: Some Time Series Evidence for the United Kingdom, 1957–1977. *J. Monet. Econ.*, March 1983, *11*(2), pp. 225–45. **[G: U.K.]**

Lerner, Abba P. Paleo-Austrian Capital Theory. **In** *Lerner, A. P.*, 1983, pp. 563–79.

Lewis, W. Arthur. Economic Development with Unlimited Supplies of Labour. **In** *Lewis, W. A.*, 1983, *1954,* pp. 311–63.

Lewis, W. Arthur. Reflections on Unlimited Labor. **In** *Lewis, W. A.*, 1983, *1972,* pp. 421–42.

Lewis, W. Arthur. Unlimited Labour: Further Notes. **In** *Lewis, W. A.*, 1983, *1958,* pp. 365–96.

McCombie, John S. L. Kaldor's Laws in Retrospect. *J. Post Keynesian Econ.*, Spring 1983, *5*(3), pp. 414–29. **[G: U.S.]**

McCombie, John S. L. and de Ridder, John R. Increasing Returns, Productivity, and Output Growth: The Case of the United States. *J. Post Keynesian Econ.*, Spring 1983, *5*(3), pp. 373–87. **[G: U.S.]**

McGee, Robert T. Some Implications of the Natural Rate Hypotheses. *J. Macroecon.*, Summer 1983, *5*(3), pp. 303–16.

McIntosh, James. Dynamic Interrelated Factor Demand Systems: The United Kingdom, 1950-78. *Econ. J.*, Supplement March 1983, pp. 79–86. **[G: U.K.]**

Michel, Philippe and Padoa Schioppa, Fiorella. A Dynamic Macroeconomic Model with Monopolistic Behavior in the Labor Market. *Europ. Econ. Rev.*, August 1983, *22*(3), pp. 331–50.

Mork, Knut Anton. Comment on "Optimal Oil Producer Behavior Considering Macrofeedbacks." *Energy J.*, October 1983, *4*(4), pp. 29–31.

Muysken, Joan. The Distribution Approach to the Aggregation of Putty–Clay Production Functions. *Europ. Econ. Rev.*, August 1983, *22*(3), pp. 351–62. **[G: Japan]**

Neary, J. Peter and Stiglitz, Joseph E. Toward a Reconstruction of Keynesian Economics: Expectations and Constrained Equilibria. *Quart. J. Econ.*, Supplement 1983, *98*(3), pp. 199–228.

Phelps, Edmund S. Implicit Contracts and the Social Contract: Toward a Welfare Economics without Costless Mobility. **In** *Dornbusch, R. and Simonsen, M. H., eds.*, 1983, pp. 46–53.

Ranson, Baldwin. The Unrecognized Revolution in the Theory of Capital Formation. *J. Econ. Issues,* December 1983, *17*(4), pp. 901–13.

Rogers, Colin. Neo–Walrasian Macroeconomics, Microfoundations and Pseudo–Production Models. *Australian Econ. Pap.*, June 1983, *22*(40), pp. 201–20.

Rotemberg, Julio J. Supply Shocks, Sticky Prices, and Monetary Policy. *J. Money, Credit, Banking,* November 1983, *15*(4), pp. 489–98.

Sato, Ryuzo and Nôno, Takayuki. Invariance Principle and "G-Neutral" Types of Technical Change. **In** *[Yamada, I.]*, 1983, pp. 177–86.

Saunders, Harry D. Optimal Oil Producer Behavior Considering Macrofeedbacks. *Energy J.*, October 1983, *4*(4), pp. 1–27.

Saunders, Harry D. Optimal Oil Producer Behavior Considering Macrofeedbacks: Reply. *Energy J.*, October 1983, *4*(4), pp. 31–35.

Schutte, David P. Inventories and Sticky Prices: Note. *Amer. Econ. Rev.*, September 1983, *73*(4), pp. 815–16.

Shaller, Douglas R. The Tax-Cut-But-Revenue-Will-Not-Decline Hypothesis and the Classical Macromodel. *Southern Econ. J.*, April 1983, *49*(4), pp. 1147–54. **[G: U.S.]**

Singleton, Kenneth J. Real and Nominal Factors in the Cyclical Behavior of Interest Rates, Output, and Money. *J. Econ. Dynam. Control,* May 1983, *5*(2/3), pp. 289–309. **[G: U.S.]**

Soubeyran, Antoine. La théorie de la captation. (The Capturing Theory. With English summary.) *Écon. Appl.*, 1983, *36*(2–3), pp. 447–507.

Steigum, Erling, Jr. Capital Shortage and Classical Unemployment. *Int. Econ. Rev.*, June 1983, *24*(2), pp. 461–73.

Strebel, Paul J. Contract Revision and Price Quantity Adjustment: A Catastrophe Model. *Atlantic Econ. J.*, March 1983, *11*(1), pp. 24–35.

Sullivan, Sherman R. Implications of Production Functions: Yugoslav Economic Growth—1952–1974. *Amer. Econ.*, Fall 1983, *27*(2), pp. 67–73.

Thirlwall, Anthony P. A Plain Man's Guide to Kaldor's Growth Laws. *J. Post Keynesian Econ.*, Spring 1983, *5*(3), pp. 345–58.

Turner, R. E. A Re-examination of Verdoorn's Law and Its Application to the Manufacturing Industries of the UK, West Germany and the USA. *Europ. Econ. Rev.*, September 1983, *23*(1), pp. 141–48. **[G: U.K.; U.S.; W. Germany]**

Weitzman, Martin L. On the Meaning of Comparative Factor Productivity. **In** *[Erlich, A.]*, 1983,

pp. 166–70.

Winston, Gordon C. Productivity-Reducing Supply-Side Policies. *J. Post Keynesian Econ.*, Winter 1982–83, *5*(2), pp. 257–65.

Woods, J. E. Prices of Production and Fixed Capital. *Z. ges. Staatswiss.*, June 1983, *139*(2), pp. 306–18.

Yoo, Jang H. and Kim, In Kie. Aggregate Supply and the Productivity of Money—A Transaction Cost Approach. *J. Econ. Devel.*, December 1983, *8*(2), pp. 25–44.

0235 Theory of Aggregate Distribution

Adelman, Irma and Cheng, Leonard. A Dynamic Model of Personal Wealth and Income Distribution in a Growing Closed Economy. *Jahr. Nationalökon. Statist.*, November 1983, *198*(6), pp. 481–504.

Asimakopulos, A. A Kaleckian Profits Equation and the United States Economy, 1950–82. *Metroecon.*, February-June 1983, *35*(1–2), pp. 1–27. **[G: U.S.]**

Asimakopulos, A. Profit and Paper Profit: Some Kaleckian Evolution: A Comment. *J. Post Keynesian Econ.*, Fall 1983, *6*(1), pp. 125–32.

Blaug, Mark. The Cambridge Debate on the Theory of Capital and Distribution. **In** *Caravale, G., ed.*, 1983, *1976*, pp. 102–230.

Brodbeck, Karl-Heinz. Neue Kapitalgüter, unvollkommene Konkurrenz und Profitrate. (New Capital Goods, Imperfect Competition and the Rate of Profit. With English summary.) *Z. ges. Staatswiss.*, March 1983, *139*(1), pp. 131–45.

Brosnan, Peter. The Wage Share in an Open Economy. *J. Post Keynesian Econ.*, Fall 1983, *6*(1), pp. 65–72.

Burkitt, Brian. Post-Keynesian Distribution Theory and Employee Investment Funds. *Econ. Stud. Quart.*, August 1983, *34*(2), pp. 124–32.

Cawley, Leo. Scarcity, Distribution and Growth: Notes on Classical Rent Theory. *Rev. Radical Polit. Econ.*, Fall 1983, *15*(3), pp. 143–58.

Chiodi, Guglielmo and Velupillai, Kumaraswamy. A Note on Lindahl's Theory of Distribution. *Kyklos*, 1983, *36*(1), pp. 103–11.

Cogoy, Mario. Lavoro eterogeneo, sovrappiù e crescita nel modello di von Neumann. (Heterogeneous Labour, Surplus and Growth in the von Neumann Model. With English summary.) *Giorn. Econ.*, May-June 1983, *42*(5–6), pp. 295–306.

Cowen, Tyler. The Rate of Return in General Equilibrium—A Critique. *J. Post Keynesian Econ.*, Summer 1983, *5*(4), pp. 608–17.

Dixon, Robert J. A Mark-Up Approach to the Distribution of Aggregate Profits. *Australian Econ. Pap.*, December 1983, *22*(41), pp. 448–53.

Duménil, G. Beyond the Transformation Riddle: A Labor Theory of Value. *Sci. Soc.*, Winter 1983–1984, *47*(4), pp. 427–50.

Eatwell, John. Theories of Value, Output and Employment. **In** *Caravale, G., ed.*, 1983, *1978*, pp. 276–322.

Encarnación, José, Jr. Positive Time Preference: A Comment. *J. Polit. Econ.*, August 1983, *91*(4), pp. 706–08.

Erdös, Peter and Molnár, Ferenc. An Answer to Asimakopulos's Comment [Profit and Paper Profit: Some Kaleckian Evolution]. *J. Post Keynesian Econ.*, Fall 1983, *6*(1), pp. 133–39.

Fan, Yiu-Kwan. On the Rate of Profit in the Ricardo–Dmitrief–Sraffa Models. *Atlantic Econ. J.*, July 1983, *11*(2), pp. 97.

Ferri, Piero. The Consumption–Wage Gap. *J. Post Keynesian Econ.*, Summer 1983, *5*(4), pp. 579–89. **[G: Developed Countries]**

Flaschel, Peter. Actual Labor Values in a General Model of Production. *Econometrica*, March 1983, *51*(2), pp. 435–54.

Fujimoto, Takao. Duality in Capital Theory with Variable Consumption: A Comment. *Z. Nationalökon.*, 1983, *43*(2), pp. 213–17.

Garegnani, Pierangelo. On a Change in the Notion of Equilibrium in Recent Work on Value and Distribution. **In** *Eatwell, J. and Milgate, M., eds.*, 1983, *1976*, pp. 129–45.

Gibson, Bill and Esfahani, Hadi. Nonproduced Means of Production: Neo-Ricardians vs. Fundamentalists. *Rev. Radical Polit. Econ.*, Summer 1983, *15*(2), pp. 83–105.

Gibson, Bill and McLeod, Darryl. Non-Produced Means of Production in Sraffa's System: Basics, Non-Basics and Quasi-Basics. *Cambridge J. Econ.*, June 1983, *7*(2), pp. 141–50.

Glombowski, Jörg. A Marxian Model of Long Run Capitalist Development. *Z. Nationalökon.*, 1983, *43*(4), pp. 363–82.

Goodwin, R. M. Capital Theory in Orthogonalised General Co-ordinates. **In** *Goodwin, R. M.*, 1983, *1977*, pp. 153–72.

Goodwin, R. M. Use of Normalised General Co-ordinates in Linear Value and Distribution Theory. **In** *Goodwin, R. M.*, 1983, *1976*, pp. 130–52.

Harris, Donald J. Accumulation of Capital and the Rate of Profit in Marxian Theory. *Cambridge J. Econ.*, September/December 1983, *7*(3/4), pp. 311–30.

Hasan, Zubair. Theory of Profit: The Islamic Viewpoint. *J. Res. Islamic Econ.*, Summer 1983, *1*(1), pp. 1–16.

Hausmann, Ricardo and Lipietz, Alain. Marx et la divergence entre production en valeur et revenus nominaux. (With English summary.) *Revue Écon. Polit.*, March–April 1983, *93*(2), pp. 270–300.

Hedlund, Jeffrey D. Distribution Theory Revisited: An Empirical Examination of the Weintraub Synthesis. *J. Post Keynesian Econ.*, Fall 1983, *6*(1), pp. 73–81. **[G: U.S.]**

Hicks, John. Is Interest the Price of a Factor of Production? **In** *Hicks, J.*, 1983, *1979*, pp. 113–28.

Hicks, John. The Austrian Theory of Capital and Its Re-birth in Modern Economics. **In** *Hicks, J.*, 1983, *1973*, pp. 96–112.

Hunt, Ian. An Obituary or a New Life for the Tendency of the Rate of Profit to Fall? *Rev. Radical Polit. Econ.*, Spring 1983, *15*(1), pp. 131–48.

Jaffé, William. Léon Walras's Theory of Capital Accumulation. **In** *Jaffé, W.*, 1983, *1942*, pp. 139–50.

Jüttner, D. Johannes and Murray, John H. Notes and Numbers on Marx's Falling Rate of Profit.

Econ. Rec., December 1983, *59*(167), pp. 375–83. [G: Australia]

Lerner, Abba P. On the Marginal Product of Capital and the Marginal Efficiency of Investment. **In** *Lerner, A. P.*, 1983, *1953*, pp. 531–44.

Lerner, Abba P. On Some Recent Developments in Capital Theory. **In** *Lerner, A. P.*, 1983, *1965*, pp. 551–62.

Lerner, Abba P. Paleo-Austrian Capital Theory. **In** *Lerner, A. P.*, 1983, pp. 563–79.

Mainwaring, L. A Reconsideration of Exchange and Accumulation in Marx [Marxian Economics as General Equilibrium Theory]. *Australian Econ. Pap.*, December 1983, *22*(41), pp. 454–66.

Nikaido, Hukukane. Marx on Competition. *Z. Nationalökon.*, 1983, *43*(4), pp. 337–63.

Pasinetti, Luigi L. Conditions of Existence of a Two Class Economy in the Kaldor and More General Models of Growth and Income Distribution. *Kyklos*, 1983, *36*(1), pp. 91–102.

van der Ploeg, Frederick. Economic Growth and Conflict over the Distribution of Income. *J. Econ. Dynam. Control*, November 1983, *6*(3), pp. 253–79.

Ranson, Baldwin. The Unrecognized Revolution in the Theory of Capital Formation. *J. Econ. Issues*, December 1983, *17*(4), pp. 901–13.

Reynolds, Peter J. Kalecki's Degree of Monopoly. *J. Post Keynesian Econ.*, Spring 1983, *5*(3), pp. 493–503.

Rivera-Batiz, Francisco L. Trade Theory, Distribution of Income, and Immigration. *Amer. Econ. Rev.*, May 1983, *73*(2), pp. 183–87.

Samuelson, Paul A. Marx without Matrices: Understanding the Rate of Profit. **In** *[Erlich, A.]*, 1983, pp. 3–18.

Solow, Robert M. Modern Capital Theory. **In** *Brown, E. C. and Solow, R. M., eds.*, 1983, pp. 169–87.

Soubeyran, Antoine. La théorie de la captation. (The Capturing Theory. With English summary.) *Écon. Appl.*, 1983, *36*(2–3), pp. 447–507.

de Sousa, Alfredo. A Dual for Pasinetti's Paradox. *Economia*, May 1983, *7*(2), pp. 407–13.

Steedman, Ian. Three Lectures on Marx after Sraffa. **In** *Caravale, G., ed.*, 1983, *1979*, pp. 323–42.

Szlajfer, Henryk. Economic Surplus and Surplus Value: An Attempt at Comparison. *Rev. Radical Polit. Econ.*, Spring 1983, *15*(1), pp. 107–30.

Twomey, Michael J. Devaluations and Income-Distribution in Latin America. *Southern Econ. J.*, January 1983, *49*(3), pp. 804–21. [G: Latin America]

Van Parijs, Philippe. Why Marxist Economics Needs Microfoundations: Postscript to an Obituary [The Falling-Rate-of-Profit Theory of Crisis: A Rational Reconstruction by Way of Obituary]. *Rev. Radical Polit. Econ.*, Summer 1983, *15*(2), pp. 111–24.

Velupillai, Kumaraswamy. A Neo-Cambridge Model of Income Distribution and Unemployment. *J. Post Keynesian Econ.*, Spring 1983, *5*(3), pp. 454–73.

Weintraub, Sidney. Effective Demand and Income Distribution. **In** *Kregel, J. A., ed.*, 1983, pp. 104–11.

Weitzman, Martin L. Some Macroeconomic Implications of Alternative Compensation Systems. *Econ. J.*, December 1983, *93*(372), pp. 763–83.

024 Welfare Theory

0240 General

Araujo, A. and Scheinkman, José A. Maximum Principle and Transversality Condition for Concave Infinite Horizon Economic Models. *J. Econ. Theory*, June 1983, *30*(1), pp. 1–16.

Arrow, Kenneth J. A Difficulty in the Concept of Social Welfare. **In** *Arrow, K. J., Vol. 1*, 1983, *1950*, pp. 1–29.

Arrow, Kenneth J. Contributions to Welfare Economics. **In** *Brown, E. C. and Solow, R. M., eds.*, 1983, pp. 15–30.

Arrow, Kenneth J. Extended Sympathy and the Possibility of Social Choice. **In** *Arrow, K. J., Vol. 1*, 1983, *1977*, pp. 147–61.

Arrow, Kenneth J. Formal Theories of Social Welfare. **In** *Arrow, K. J., Vol. 1*, 1983, *1973*, pp. 115–32.

Arrow, Kenneth J. Little's Critique of Welfare Economics. **In** *Arrow, K. J., Vol. 1*, 1983, *1951*, pp. 30–44.

Arrow, Kenneth J. Nozick's Entitlement Theory of Justice. **In** *Arrow, K. J., Vol. 1*, 1983, *1978*, pp. 175–89.

Arrow, Kenneth J. Optimal and Voluntary Income Distribution. **In** *Arrow, K. J., Vol. 1*, 1983, *1981*, pp. 201–24.

Arrow, Kenneth J. Rawls's Principle of Just Saving. **In** *Arrow, K. J., Vol. 1*, 1983, *1973*, pp. 133–46.

Arrow, Kenneth J. Some Ordinalist-Utilitarian Notes on Rawls's Theory of Justice. **In** *Arrow, K. J., Vol. 1*, 1983, *1973*, pp. 96–114.

Arrow, Kenneth J. Values and Collective Decision Making. **In** *Arrow, K. J., Vol. 1*, 1983, *1967*, pp. 59–77.

d'Aspremont, Claude and Gérard-Varet, Louis-André. Regional Externalities and Efficient Decentralization under Incomplete Information. **In** *Thisse, J.-F. and Zoller, H. G., eds.*, 1983, pp. 207–20.

Atkinson, Anthony B. Income Distribution and Inequality of Opportunity. **In** *Atkinson, A. B.*, 1983, *1980*, pp. 77–92.

Atkinson, Anthony B. Introduction to Part I: Inequality and Mobility. **In** *Atkinson, A. B.*, 1983, pp. 3–13.

Atkinson, Anthony B. On the Measurement of Inequality. **In** *Atkinson, A. B.*, 1983, *1970*, pp. 15–36. [G: MDCs; LDCs]

Atkinson, Anthony B. The Measurement of Economic Mobility. **In** *Atkinson, A. B.*, 1983, *1981*, pp. 61–75.

Atkinson, Anthony B. and Bourguignon, François. The Comparison of Multi-dimensioned Distributions of Economic Status. **In** *Atkinson, A. B.*, 1983, pp. 37–59.

Atkinson, Anthony B. and Stern, Nicholas H. Pigou, Taxation and Public Goods. **In** *Atkinson, A. B.*, 1983, pp. 259–70.

Bandyopadhyay, Taradas. On a Pareto Optimal and Rational Choice. *Econ. J.*, Supplement March

1983, pp. 115–22.

Barberá, Salvador. Pivotal Voters: A Simple Proof of Arrow's Theorem. **In** *Pattanaik, P. K. and Salles, M., eds.,* 1983, pp. 31–35.

Barberá, Salvador. Strategy-Proofness and Pivotal Voters: A Direct Proof of the Gibbard–Satterthwaite Theorem. *Int. Econ. Rev.,* June 1983, *24* (2), pp. 413–17.

Barthelemy, J.-P. Arrow's Theorem: Unusual Domains and Extended Co-domains. **In** *Pattanaik, P. K. and Salles, M., eds.,* 1983, pp. 19–30.

Basu, Kaushik. Cardinal Utility, Utilitarianism, and a Class of Invariance Axioms in Welfare Analysis. *J. Math. Econ.,* December 1983, *12* (3), pp. 193–206.

Beckmann, Martin J. On Optimal Spacing under Exponential Distance Effect. **In** *Thisse, J.-F. and Zoller, H. G., eds.,* 1983, pp. 117–25.

Bénard, Jean. Colloque de Paris, juin 1981: les progrès récents de l'analyse économique des dépenses publiques. (With English summary.) *Revue Écon. Polit.,* July–August 1983, *93* (4), pp. 509–50.

Bental, Benjamin and Wenig, Alois. Will All People Become Alike if They Are Alike? *Z. Nationalökon.,* 1983, *43* (3), pp. 289–300.

Bergson, Abram. Pareto on Social Welfare. *J. Econ. Lit.,* March 1983, *21* (1), pp. 40–46.

Bhagwati, Jagdish N. and Rodriguez, Carlos. Welfare-Theoretical Analyses of the Brain Drain. **In** *Bhagwati, J. N., Vol. 2,* 1983, *1975,* pp. 75–102.

Bicchieri, Maria Cristina. Economic Welfare and the Distribution of Economic Advantages: Individual Rights versus Common Goals. *Econ. Notes,* 1983, (1), pp. 58–79.

Bigman, David and Shalit, Haim. Applied Welfare Analysis for Consumers with Commodity Income. *De Economist,* 1983, *131* (1), pp. 31–45.

Blair, Douglas H. and Muller, Eitan. Essential Aggregation Procedures on Restricted Domains of Preferences. *J. Econ. Theory,* June 1983, *30* (1), pp. 34–53.

Blaug, Mark. Justifications for Subsidies to the Arts: A Reply to F. F. Ridley, "Cultural Economics and the Culture of Economists." *J. Cult. Econ.,* June 1983, *7* (1), pp. 19–22.

Bohanon, Cecil E. McCaleb on Lindahl: A Comment [A Reconsideration of the Lindahl Model]. *Public Finance,* 1983, *38* (2), pp. 326–31.

Border, Kim C. Social Welfare Functions for Economic Environments with and without the Pareto Principle. *J. Econ. Theory,* April 1983, *29* (2), pp. 205–16.

Bös, Dieter. Public Pricing with Distributional Objectives. **In** *Finsinger, J., ed.,* 1983, pp. 171–88.

Braulke, Michael. An Approximation to the Gini Coefficient for a Population Based on Sparse Information for Sub-Groups. *J. Devel. Econ.,* February/April 1983, *12* (1/2), pp. 75–81. **[G: LDCs]**

Brittan, Samuel. Two Cheers for Utilitarianism. *Oxford Econ. Pap.,* November 1983, *35* (3), pp. 331–50.

Brittan, Samuel. Two Cheers for Utilitarianism. **In** *Brittan, S.,* 1983, pp. 22–47.

Brookshire, David S.; Eubanks, Larry S. and Randall, Alan. Estimating Option Prices and Existence Values for Wildlife Resources. *Land Econ.,* February 1983, *59* (1), pp. 1–15. **[G: U.S.]**

Brown, Eleanor. Comment: Bequests and Horizontal Equity under a Consumption Tax [The Incidence of a Lifetime Consumption Tax]. *Nat. Tax J.,* December 1983, *36* (4), pp. 511–13. **[G: U.S.]**

Brown, William S. and Shaw, W. Doug, Jr. Neoclassical and Post Keynesian Environmental Economics: An Addendum. *J. Post Keynesian Econ.,* Fall 1983, *6* (1), pp. 140–42.

Brunner, Karl. The Perception of Man and Justice and the Conception of Political Institutions. **In** *[Giersch, H.],* 1983, pp. 327–55.

Chakrabarty, Gurupada. Sen's Welfare Measure and Sources of Income. *Margin,* April 1983, *15* (3), pp. 73–78.

Chakravarty, Satya Ranjan. A New Index of Poverty. *Math. Soc. Sci.,* December 1983, *6* (3), pp. 307–13.

Chakravarty, Satya Ranjan. Ethically Flexible Measures of Poverty. *Can. J. Econ.,* February 1983, *16* (1), pp. 74–85.

Chew, Soo Hong. A Generalization of the Quasilinear Mean with Applications to the Measurement of Income Inequality and Decision Theory Resolving the Allais Paradox. *Econometrica,* July 1983, *51* (4), pp. 1065–92.

Christiansen, Vidar. Some Important Properties of the Social Marginal Utility of Income. *Scand. J. Econ.,* 1983, *85* (3), pp. 359–71.

Coleman, Jules L. The Economic Analysis of Law. **In** *Kuperberg, M. and Beitz, C., eds.,* 1983, *1982,* pp. 102–22.

Collard, David A. Economics of Philanthropy: A Comment. *Econ. J.,* September 1983, *93* (371), pp. 637–38.

Conn, David. The Scope of Satisfactory Mechanisms for the Provision of Public Goods. *J. Public Econ.,* March 1983, *20* (2), pp. 249–63.

Cooter, Robert D. Justice and Mathematics: Two Simple Ideas. **In** *Skurski, R., ed.,* 1983, pp. 198–231.

Cullis, John G. and Jones, Philip R. The Welfare State and Private Alternatives: Towards an Existence Proof. *Scot. J. Polit. Econ.,* June 1983, *30* (2), pp. 97–113.

Dean, James M. Public Good Benefits and Interdependence. *Econ. Notes,* 1983, (1), pp. 130–34.

Debertin, David L. Value Judgments and Efficiency in Publicly Supported Research: Discussion. *Southern J. Agr. Econ.,* July 1983, *15* (1), pp. 9–10.

Debreu, Gerard. Continuity Properties of Paretian Utility. **In** *Debreu, G.,* 1983, *1964,* pp. 163–72.

Dodgson, John S. On the Accuracy and Appropriateness of Alternative Measures of Excess Burden. *Econ. J.,* Supplement March 1983, pp. 106–14. **[G: U.K.]**

Donaldson, David and Weymark, John A. Ethically Flexible Gini Indices for Income Distributions in the Continuum. *J. Econ. Theory,* April 1983, *29* (2), pp. 353–58.

Dworkin, Ronald. Why Efficiency? **In** *Kuperberg, M. and Beitz, C., eds.,* 1983, *1980,* pp. 123–40.

Eisman, Deborah E. Product Liability: Who Should Bear the Burden? *Amer. Econ.,* Spring 1983,

27(1), pp. 54–57.

Ellickson, Bryan. Is a Local Public Good Different from Any Other? **In** *Grieson, R. E., ed.*, 1983, pp. 143–70.

Enbar, Michael. Equity in the Social Sciences. **In** *Kasperson, R. E., ed.*, 1983, pp. 3–23.

Fölscher, G. C. K. A Note on the Social Discount Rate—(SDR). *J. Stud. Econ. Econometrics*, July 1983, (16), pp. 50–62.

Foster, James E. An Axiomatic Characterization of the Theil Measure of Income Inequality. *J. Econ. Theory*, October 1983, *31*(1), pp. 105–21.

Fourgeaud, Claude; Lenclup, Bernard and Michel, Pierre. Taux d'actualisation et prix de l'énergie. (On the Social Rate of Discount and the Energy Price. With English summary.) *Revue Écon.*, March 1983, *34*(2), pp. 253–76. **[G: France]**

Friesen, Peter H. and Miller, Danny. Annual Inequality and Lifetime Inequality. *Quart. J. Econ.*, February 1983, *98*(1), pp. 139–55. **[G: U.S.]**

Gaertner, Wulf. Equity- and Inequity-Type Borda Rules. *Math. Soc. Sci.*, April 1983, *4*(2), pp. 137–54.

Gärdenfors, Peter. On the Information about Individual Utilities Used in Social Choice. *Math. Soc. Sci.*, July 1983, *4*(3), pp. 219–28.

Goff, Edwin L. Justice as Fairness: The Practice of Social Science in a Rawlsian Model. *Soc. Res.*, Spring 1983, *50*(1), pp. 81–97.

Gordon, Wendell C. Errata [Welfare Maxima in Economics]. *J. Econ. Issues*, September 1983, *17*(3), pp. 585.

Gordon, Wendell C. Welfare Maxima in Economics. *J. Econ. Issues*, March 1983, *17*(1), pp. 1–6.

Gowland, D. H. Market Failure and State Intervention. **In** *Gowland, D. H., ed.*, 1983, pp. 171–99.

Grootaert, Christiaan. The Conceptual Basis of Measures of Household Welfare and Their Implied Survey Data Requirements. *Rev. Income Wealth*, March 1983, *29*(1), pp. 1–21.

Hagen, Kåre P. Optimal Shadow Prices and Discount Rates for Budget-Constrained Public Firms. *J. Public Econ.*, October 1983, *22*(1), pp. 27–48.

Halpern, Jonathan and Maimon, Oded. Accord and Conflict among Several Objectives in Locational Decisions on Tree Networks. **In** *Thisse, J.-F. and Zoller, H. G., eds.*, 1983, pp. 301–14.

Hansen, Pierre; Peeters, D. and Thisse, Jacques-François. Public Facility Location Models: A Selective Survey. **In** *Thisse, J.-F. and Zoller, H. G., eds.*, 1983, pp. 223–62.

Heiner, Ronald A. and Pattanaik, P. K. The Structure of General Probabilistic Group Decision Rules. **In** *Pattanaik, P. K. and Salles, M., eds.*, 1983, pp. 37–54.

van Herwaarden, F. G. and de Kam, C. A. An Operational Concept of the Ability to Pay Principle (with an Application for the Netherlands, 1973). *De Economist*, 1983, *131*(1), pp. 55–64. **[G: Netherlands]**

Hirayama, Asazi. Interpersonal Comparison and Criteria of Justice. *Econ. Stud. Quart.*, August 1983, *34*(2), pp. 156–70.

Hirshleifer, Jack. From Weskest-Link to Best-Shot: The Voluntary Provision of Public Goods. *Public Choice*, 1983, *41*(3), pp. 371–86.

Holub, Hans Werner. Some Critical Reflections on Measures of Net Economic Welfare [A Theoretical Framework for the Measurement of Well-Being]. *Rev. Income Wealth*, September 1983, *29*(3), pp. 317–21.

Hosomatsu, Yasu. A Necessary and Sufficient Condition for a Continuously Rational Social Choice. **In** *[Yamada, I.]*, 1983, pp. 103–14.

Hyde, William F. The Federal Preserve in the West: Environmental Champion or Economic Despoiler. *J. Policy Anal. Manage.*, Summer 1983, *2*(4), pp. 605–14. **[G: U.S.]**

Jaffé, William. The Normative Bias of the Walrasian Model: Walras versus Gossen. **In** *Jaffé, W.*, 1983, *1977*, pp. 326–42.

Johnson, Harry G. Equality and Economic Theory. **In** *Letwin, W., ed.*, 1983, *1975*, pp. 276–93.

Johnson, M. Bruce. Regulation and Justice: An Economist's Perspective. **In** *Machan, T. R. and Johnson, M. B., eds.*, 1983, pp. 127–34.

Kelman, Steven. Limited Government: An Incoherent Concept. *J. Policy Anal. Manage.*, Fall 1983, *3*(1), pp. 31–44.

Kemp, Murray C. and Ng, Yew-Kwang. Individualistic Social Welfare Functions under Ordinalism: A Reply to Mayston. *Math. Soc. Sci.*, July 1983, *4*(3), pp. 305–07.

King, Mervyn A. An Index of Inequality: With Applications to Horizontal Equity and Social Mobility. *Econometrica*, January 1983, *51*(1), pp. 99–115. **[G: U.K.]**

Kohn, Robert E. Returns to Scale in Welfare Economics. *Atlantic Econ. J.*, July 1983, *11*(2), pp. 91–95.

van de Kragt, Alphons J. C.; Orbell, John M. and Dawes, Robyn M. The Minimal Contributing Set as a Solution to Public Goods Problems. *Amer. Polit. Sci. Rev.*, March 1983, *77*(1), pp. 112–22.

Ladd, George W. Value Judgments and Efficiency in Publicly Supported Research. *Southern J. Agr. Econ.*, July 1983, *15*(1), pp. 1–7.

Lea, Anthony C. Some Lessons from the Theory of Public and Impure Goods for Public Facility Location-Allocation Models. **In** *Thisse, J.-F. and Zoller, H. G., eds.*, 1983, pp. 263–300.

Lerner, Abba P. Consumer's Surplus and Micro-Macro. **In** *Lerner, A. P.*, 1983, *1963*, pp. 47–52.

Lerner, Abba P. Marginal Cost Pricing in the 1930's. **In** *Lerner, A. P.*, 1983, *1977*, pp. 187–91.

Lerner, Abba P. On Optimal Taxes with an Untaxable Sector. **In** *Lerner, A. P.*, 1983, *1970*, pp. 193–203.

Lerner, Abba P. Utilitarian Marginalism (Nozick, Rawls, Justice, and Welfare). **In** *Lerner, A. P.*, 1983, *1978*, pp. 227–41.

Lévy, Emile. La mesure de l'efficacité dans l'évaluation des politiques sociales: L'exemple de la santé. (With English summary.) *Revue Écon. Polit.*, May–June 1983, *93*(3), pp. 377–87. **[G: France]**

Lott, John R. A Note on Law, Property Rights, and Air Pollution. *Cato J.*, Winter 1983/84, *3*(3), pp. 875–78.

Lotz, Jørgen R. The Role of Local Government Taxation: The Tiebout Effect and Equalization. **In** *[Goode, R.]*, 1983, pp. 279–93.

Lundahl, Mats. Insuring against Risk in Primitive

Economies: The Role of Prestige Goods. **In** *Söderström, L., ed.*, 1983, pp. 35–51.

McCaleb, Thomas S. Economic Paradigms of Government and the Market: A Further Look at the Lindahl Model. *Public Finance*, 1983, *38*(2), pp. 332–37.

McMillan, Melville L. A Further Consideration of Coalitions under the Demand-Revealing Process. *Public Choice*, 1983, *40*(2), pp. 227–30.

McMorris, F. R. and Neumann, Dean. Consensus Functions Defined on Trees. *Math. Soc. Sci.*, April 1983, *4*(2), pp. 131–36.

Melvin, J. R. Political Structure and the Pursuit of Economic Objectives. **In** *Trebilcock, M. J., et al., eds.*, 1983, pp. 111–58. **[G: Canada]**

Menchik, Paul L. and David, Martin H. Reply and Comment [The Incidence of a Lifetime Consumption Tax]. *Nat. Tax J.*, December 1983, *36*(4), pp. 515–20. **[G: U.S.]**

Mott, Tracy and Singell, Larry D. The Positive Treatment of Social Values: State of the Art. *J. Behav. Econ.*, Summer 1983, *12*(1), pp. 71–87.

Moulin, Hervé. Choix social cardinal: résultats récents. (Cardinal Social Choices: Recent Results. With English summary.) *Ann. INSEE*, July–September 1983, (51), pp. 89–124.

Musgrave, Richard A. Public Goods. **In** *Brown, E. C. and Solow, R. M., eds.*, 1983, pp. 141–56.

Nakayama, Mikio. Truthful Revelation of Preferences for a Public Good. *Math. Soc. Sci.*, August 1983, *5*(1), pp. 47–54.

Ng, Yew-Kwang. Some Broader Issues of Social Choice. **In** *Pattanaik, P. K. and Salles, M., eds.*, 1983, pp. 151–73.

Parikh, Ashok and Das, Tarun. Inequality Index with Differences in Inequality Aversion for Income and Population Groups. *Rivista Int. Sci. Econ. Com.*, April-May 1983, *30*(4–5), pp. 362–74. **[G: U.S.]**

Pattanaik, P. K. and Salles, Maurice. Social Choice and Welfare: Introduction. **In** *Pattanaik, P. K. and Salles, M., eds.*, 1983, pp. 1–15.

Peacock, Alan. The Politics of Culture and the Ignorance of Political Scientists: A Reply to F. F. Ridley. *J. Cult. Econ.*, June 1983, *7*(1), pp. 23–26.

Pen, Jan. A Very Cultural Economist's Ideas about the Locus of Decision-making. **In** *Hendon, W. S. and Shanahan, J. L., eds.*, 1983, pp. 16–30.

Poole, Robert W., Jr. Objections to Privatization. *Policy Rev.*, Spring 1983, (24), pp. 105–19. **[G: U.S.]**

Pope, Rulon; Chavas, Jean-Paul and Just, Richard E. Economic Welfare Evaluations for Producers under Uncertainty. *Amer. J. Agr. Econ.*, February 1983, *65*(1), pp. 98–107.

Randall, Alan. The Problem of Market Failure. *Natural Res. J.*, January 1983, *23*(1), pp. 131–48. **[G: U.S.]**

Randall, Alan; Hoehn, John P. and Brookshire, David S. Contingent Valuation Surveys for Evaluating Environmental Assets. *Natural Res. J.*, July 1983, *23*(3), pp. 635–48. **[G: U.S.]**

Rao, T. V. S. Ramamohan. Public Goods and Disequilibrium Growth. *Rivista Int. Sci. Econ. Com.*, April-May 1983, *30*(4–5), pp. 321–38.

Rein, Martin and Peattie, Lisa. Claims, Claiming, and Claims Structures. **In** *Rein, M.*, 1983, pp. 23–39.

Renas, Stephen M., et al. Toward an Economic Theory of Defamation, Liability, and the Press. *Southern Econ. J.*, October 1983, *50*(2), pp. 451–60.

Ridley, F. F. Cultural Economics and the Culture of Economists. *J. Cult. Econ.*, June 1983, *7*(1), pp. 1–18.

Ritz, Zvi. Restricted Domains, Arrow-Social Welfare Functions and Noncorruptible and Nonmanipulable Social Choice Correspondences: The Case of Private Alternatives. *Math. Soc. Sci.*, April 1983, *4*(2), pp. 155–79.

Saposnik, Rubin. On Evaluating Income Distributions: Rank Dominance, the Suppes-Sen Grading Principle of Justice, and Pareto Optimality. *Public Choice*, 1983, *40*(3), pp. 329–36.

Sato, Kimitoshi. On Compatibility between Neutrality and Aggregate Correction Revelation for Public Goods. *Econ. Stud. Quart.*, August 1983, *34*(2), pp. 97–109.

Sato, Toshihiro. On the MDP Procedure with Non-Myopic Agents. *Econ. Stud. Quart.*, August 1983, *34*(2), pp. 110–23.

Sawicki, David S. On the Virtues of the Policy of Doing Nothing. *J. Policy Anal. Manage.*, Spring 1983, *2*(3), pp. 454–57. **[G: U.S.]**

Schokkaert, Erik and Lagrou, Leo. An Empirical Approach to Distributive Justice. *J. Public Econ.*, June 1983, *21*(1), pp. 33–52. **[G: Belgium]**

Schweizer, Urs. Edgeworth and the Henry George Theorem: How to Finance Local Public Projects. **In** *Thisse, J.-F. and Zoller, H. G., eds.*, 1983, pp. 79–93.

Schweizer, Urs. Grundsätzliche Überlegungen zur Projektbewertung am Beispiel des Strassenbaus. (Some Thoughts on Expenditure Evaluation: The Case of Highway Construction. With English summary.) *Z. Wirtschaft. Sozialwissen.*, 1983, *103*(4), pp. 369–88.

Schweizer, Urs. Reducing Distortions under the Revealed Preference Hypothesis. *Z. Nationalökon.*, 1983, *43*(1), pp. 31–43.

Sen, Amartya K. Poor, Relatively Speaking. *Oxford Econ. Pap.*, July 1983, *35*(2), pp. 153–69.

Shilony, Yuval. More Methodological Notes on Welfare Calculus. *J. Transp. Econ. Policy*, January 1983, *17*(1), pp. 95–98.

Shorrocks, Anthony F. Ranking Income Distributions. *Economica*, February 1983, *50*(197), pp. 3–17.

Shoup, Carl S. Collective Goods and Population Growth. **In** *Biehl, D.; Roskamp, K. W. and Stolper, W. F., eds.*, 1983, pp. 55–68.

Slivinski, Alan D. Income Distribution Evaluation and the Law of One Price. *J. Public Econ.*, February 1983, *20*(1), pp. 103–12.

Solow, Robert M. Leif Johansen (1930–1982): A Memorial. *Scand. J. Econ.*, 1983, *85*(4), pp. 445–59.

Staaf, Robert J. Privatization of Public Goods. *Public Choice*, 1983, *41*(3), pp. 435–40.

Stahl, Dale O., II. A Note on the Consumer Surplus Path-of-Integration Problem. *Economica*, February 1983, *50*(197), pp. 95–98.

Stahl, Dale O., II. Quasi-Homothetic Preferences, the Generalized Divisia Quantity Index, and Aggregation. *Economica,* February 1983, *50*(197), pp. 87–93.

Stiglitz, Joseph E. Public Goods in Open Economics with Heterogeneous Individuals. **In** *Thisse, J.-F. and Zoller, H. G., eds.,* 1983, pp. 55–78.

Stiglitz, Joseph E. The Theory of Local Public Goods Twenty-Five Years after Tiebout: A Perspective. **In** *Zodrow, G. R., ed.,* 1983, pp. 17–53.

Stiglitz, Joseph E. and Weiss, Andrew. Alternative Approaches to Analyzing Markets with Asymmetric Information: Reply [The Theory of 'Screening,' Education, and the Distribution of Income]. *Amer. Econ. Rev.,* March 1983, *73*(1), pp. 246–49.

Sturgess, N. H. and Wijaya, Hesti. Rice Havesting: A View from the Theory of Common Property. *Bull. Indonesian Econ. Stud.,* August 1983, *19*(2), pp. 27–45. **[G: Indonesia]**

Sugden, Robert. On the Economics of Philanthropy: Reply. *Econ. J.,* September 1983, *93*(371), pp. 639.

Suzumura, Kotaro. Resolving Conflicting Views of Justice in Social Choice. **In** *Pattanaik, P. K. and Salles, M., eds.,* 1983, pp. 125–49.

Tendulkar, Suresh D. Economic Inequality in an Indian Perspective. **In** *Béteille, A., ed.,* 1983, pp. 71–128. **[G: India]**

Thisse, Jacques-François and Zoller, Henri G. Some Notes on Public Facility Location. **In** *Thisse, J.-F. and Zoller, H. G., eds.,* 1983, pp. 1–8.

Thon, Dominique. A Note on a Troublesome Axiom for Poverty Indices [On Indices for the Measurement of Poverty]. *Econ. J.,* March 1983, *93*(369), pp. 199–200.

Tideman, T. Nicolaus. An Experiment in the Demand-Revealing Process. *Public Choice,* 1983, *41*(3), pp. 387–401.

Tisdell, Clem A. Allocation of Public Funds to Projects Reducing Risk with Special Reference to Medical Research. *Rivista Int. Sci. Econ. Com.,* June 1983, *30*(6), pp. 555–60.

Tisdell, Clem A. Dissent from Value, Preference and Choice Theory in Economics. *Int. J. Soc. Econ.,* 1983, *10*(2), pp. 32–43.

Tool, Marc R. Equational Justice and Social Value. *J. Econ. Issues,* June 1983, *17*(2), pp. 335–44.

Tulkens, Henry and Kiabantu, Tomasikila Kioni. A Planning Process for the Efficient Allocation of Resources to Transportation Infrastructure. **In** *Thisse, J.-F. and Zoller, H. G., eds.,* 1983, pp. 127–52.

Vartia, Yrjö O. Efficient Methods of Measuring Welfare Change and Compensated Income in Terms of Ordinary Demand Functions. *Econometrica,* January 1983, *51*(1), pp. 79–98.

Wansbeek, Tom and Kapteyn, Arie. Tackling Hard Questions by Means of Soft Methods: The Use of Individual Welfare Functions in Socio-Economic Policy. *Kyklos,* 1983, *36*(2), pp. 249–69.

Ward, J. E. and Wendell, Richard E. Characterizing Efficient Points in Location Problems under the One-Infinity Norm. **In** *Thisse, J.-F. and Zoller, H. G., eds.,* 1983, pp. 413–29.

Wintrobe, Ronald. Taxing Altruism. *Econ. Inquiry,* April 1983, *21*(2), pp. 255–70.

Wiseman, Jack. Public Finance and the Cultural Factor in Economic Growth. **In** *Biehl, D.; Roskamp, K. W. and Stolper, W. F., eds.,* 1983, pp. 419–27.

Yabushita, Shiro. Theory of Screening and the Behavior of the Firm: Comment. *Amer. Econ. Rev.,* March 1983, *73*(1), pp. 242–45.

Yamada, Masatoshi. A Reconciliation between Equity and Efficiency in Public Goods Economy. *Z. Nationalökon.,* 1983, *43*(1), pp. 71–79.

Yitzhaki, Shlomo. On an Extension of the Gini Inequality Index. *Int. Econ. Rev.,* October 1983, *24*(3), pp. 617–28.

Yoshida, Tateo. The Lorenz Partial Ordering and Lerner's Probabilistic Egalitarianism. *Econ. Stud. Quart.,* December 1983, *34*(3), pp. 225–36.

Zagier, Don. Inequalities for the Gini Coefficient of Composite Populations. *J. Math. Econ.,* October 1983, *12*(2), pp. 103–18.

0242 Allocative Efficiency Including Theory of Cost/Benefit

Adelman, Irma and Cheng, Leonard. The Lack of Pareto Superiority of Unegalitarian Wealth Distribution. *Metroecon.,* February–June 1983, *35*(1–2), pp. 105–22.

Alm, James. Intergovernmental Grants and Social Welfare. *Public Finance,* 1983, *38*(3), pp. 376–97.

Arrow, Kenneth J. An Extension of the Basic Theorems of Classical Welfare Economics. **In** *Arrow, K. J., Vol. 2,* 1983, *1951,* pp. 13–45.

Arrow, Kenneth J. Behavior under Uncertainty and Its Implications for Policy. **In** *Stigum, B. P. and Wenstøp, F., eds.,* 1983, pp. 19–32.

Arrow, Kenneth J. Pareto Efficiency with Costly Transfers. **In** *Arrow, K. J., Vol. 2,* 1983, *1981,* pp. 290–302.

Arrow, Kenneth J. Rawls's Principle of Just Saving. **In** *Arrow, K. J., Vol. 1,* 1983, *1973,* pp. 133–46.

Arrow, Kenneth J. Team Theory and Decentralized Resource Allocation: An Example. **In** *[Erlich, A.],* 1983, pp. 63–76.

Arrow, Kenneth J. The Organization of Economic Activity: Issues Pertinent to the Choice of Market versus Nonmarket Allocation. **In** *Arrow, K. J., Vol. 2,* 1983, *1969,* pp. 133–55.

Arrow, Kenneth J. The Trade-off between Growth and Equity. **In** *Arrow, K. J., Vol. 1,* 1983, *1979,* pp. 190–200.

Bandyopadhyay, Taradas. Coalitional Manipulation and the Pareto Rule. *J. Econ. Theory,* April 1983, *29*(2), pp. 359–63.

Baumol, William J. Applied Fairness Theory: Reply. *Amer. Econ. Rev.,* December 1983, *73*(5), pp. 1161–62.

Beato, Paulina and Mas-Colell, Andreu. Gestion au coût marginal et efficacité de la production agrégée: un exemple. (Marginal Cost Management and Efficiency of Aggregate Production: An Example. With English summary.) *Ann. INSEE,* July–September 1983, (51), pp. 39–46.

Bergstrom, Theodore C. and Cornes, Richard C. Independence of Allocative Efficiency from

Distribution in the Theory of Public Goods. *Econometrica,* November 1983, *51* (6), pp. 1753–65.

Bergstrom, Theodore C.; Simon, Carl P. and Titus, Charles J. Counting Groves–Ledyard Equilibria via Degree Theory. *J. Math. Econ.,* October 1983, *12* (2), pp. 167–84.

Bhagwati, Jagdish N. Directly Unproductive, Profit-seeking (DUP) Activities. **In** *Bhagwati, J. N., Vol. 1,* 1983, *1982,* pp. 259–73.

Bhagwati, Jagdish N. Lobbying and Welfare. **In** *Bhagwati, J. N., Vol. 1,* 1983, *1980,* pp. 365–73.

Bhagwati, Jagdish N. Lobbying, DUP Activities and Welfare: A Response. **In** *Bhagwati, J. N., Vol. 1,* 1983, *1982,* pp. 374–80.

Bhagwati, Jagdish N. The Generalized Theory of Distortions and Welfare. **In** *Bhagwati, J. N., Vol. 1,* 1983, *1971,* pp. 73–94.

Bhagwati, Jagdish N. and Srinivasan, T. N. On Reanalyzing the Harris–Todaro Model: Policy Rankings in the Case of Sector-specific Sticky Wages. **In** *Bhagwati, J. N., Vol. 1,* 1983, *1974,* pp. 498–504.

Bhagwati, Jagdish N. and Srinivasan, T. N. Smuggling and Trade Policy. **In** *Bhagwati, J. N., Vol. 1,* 1983, *1973,* pp. 302–14.

Bhagwati, Jagdish N. and Srinivasan, T. N. The General Equilibrium Theory of Effective Protection and Resource Allocation. **In** *Bhagwati, J. N., Vol. 1,* 1983, *1973,* pp. 215–37.

Bhagwati, Jagdish N. and Srinivasan, T. N. The Welfare Consequences of Directly-Unproductive Profit-seeking (DUP) Lobbying Activities. **In** *Bhagwati, J. N., Vol. 1,* 1983, *1982,* pp. 274–85.

Bhagwati, Jagdish N. and Wan, Henry, Jr. The "Stationarity" of Shadow Prices of Factors in Project Evaluation, with and without Distortions. **In** *Bhagwati, J. N., Vol. 1,* 1983, *1979,* pp. 558–70.

Blewett, Robert A. and Congleton, Roger D. Non-Global Social Contracts: A Note on Inefficient Social Institutions. *Public Choice,* 1983, *41* (3), pp. 441–48.

Bosshardt, Donald I. Spanning, Pareto Optimality, and the Mean-Variance Model. *Int. Econ. Rev.,* October 1983, *24* (3), pp. 649–69.

Braeutigam, Ronald R. A Dynamic Analysis of Second-best Pricing. **In** *Finsinger, J., ed.,* 1983, pp. 103–16.

Breton, Albert. Federalism versus Centralism in Regional Growth. **In** *Biehl, D.; Roskamp, K. W. and Stolper, W. F., eds.,* 1983, pp. 251–63.

Browning, M. J. Efficient Decentralisation with a Transferable Good. *Rev. Econ. Stud.,* April 1983, *50* (2), pp. 375–81.

Brueckner, Jan K. and Raymon, Neil. Optimal Production with Learning by Doing. *J. Econ. Dynam. Control,* September 1983, *6* (1/2), pp. 127–35.

Chamley, Christophe. Optimal Fiscal and Monetary Policies in Neoclassical Dynamic Models. **In** *Biehl, D.; Roskamp, K. W. and Stolper, W. F., eds.,* 1983, pp. 69–87.

Champsaur, Paul and Rochet, Jean-Charles. On Planning Procedures Which Are Locally Strategy Proof. *J. Econ. Theory,* August 1983, *30* (2), pp. 353–69.

Chander, Parkash. On the Information Efficiency of the Competitive Resource Allocation Process. *J. Econ. Theory,* October 1983, *31* (1), pp. 54–67.

Chander, Parkash. On the Informational Size of Message Spaces for Efficient Resource Allocation Processes. *Econometrica,* July 1983, *51* (4), pp. 919–38.

Choudhury, Masudul Alam. Towards an Evaluative Study of Joint Venture Projects with Socio-economic Indicators. *Singapore Econ. Rev.,* October 1983, *28* (2), pp. 59–78. **[G: Mauritania]**

Christainsen, Gregory B. Using Donor Preferences in Evaluating Public Expenditures: A Suggested Procedure. *Public Finance Quart.,* July 1983, *11* (3), pp. 283–98. **[G: U.S.]**

Cornes, Richard C. and Sandler, Todd. On Commons and Tragedies. *Amer. Econ. Rev.,* September 1983, *73* (4), pp. 787–92.

Cornet, Bernard. Neutrality of Planning Procedures. *J. Math. Econ.,* April 1983, *11* (2), pp. 141–60.

Cremer, Jacques. The Discrete Heal Algorithm with Intermediate Goods. *Rev. Econ. Stud.,* April 1983, *50* (2), pp. 383–91.

Dasgupta, Swapan and Mitra, Tapan. Intergenerational Equity and Efficient Allocation of Exhaustible Resources. *Int. Econ. Rev.,* February 1983, *24* (1), pp. 133–53.

Debreu, Gerard. The Coefficient of Resource Utilization. **In** *Debreu, G.,* 1983, *1951,* pp. 30–49.

Debreu, Gerard. Valuation Equilibrium and Pareto Optimum. **In** *Debreu, G.,* 1983, *1954,* pp. 98–104.

Desai, Meghnad J. and Shah, Anup R. K. Bequest and Inheritance in Nuclear Families and Joint Families. *Economica,* May 1983, *50* (198), pp. 193–202.

Desai, Padma and Martin, Ricardo. Measuring Resource-Allocational Efficiency in Centrally Planned Economies: A Theoretical Analysis. **In** *[Erlich, A.],* 1983, pp. 91–109.

Diewert, W. Erwin. Cost–Benefit Analysis and Project Evaluation: A Comparison of Alternative Approaches. *J. Public Econ.,* December 1983, *22* (3), pp. 265–302.

Diewert, W. Erwin. The Measurement of Waste within the Production Sector of an Open Economy. *Scand. J. Econ.,* 1983, *85* (2), pp. 159–79.

Dodgson, J. S. Compensating and Equivalent Variation Measures of Investment Benefits with Multiple Price Changes. *Public Finance,* 1983, *38* (1), pp. 16–26. **[G: U.K.]**

Dominique, C-René. Labor-Surplus Project Appraisal Methods: Didactic and Operational Differences, and Value Judgements between OECD and UNIDO. *J. Econ. Devel.,* July 1983, *8* (1), pp. 59–88.

Donaldson, John B. A Note on Value Maximization for Consumption Sets in *l*. *J. Econ. Theory,* June 1983, *30* (1), pp. 191–200.

Ericson, Richard E. On an Allocative Role of the Soviet Second Economy. **In** *[Erlich, A.],* 1983, pp. 110–32. **[G: U.S.S.R.]**

Erlenkotter, Donald. On the Choice of Models for Public Facility Location. **In** *Thisse, J.-F. and Zoller, H. G., eds.,* 1983, pp. 385–93.

Foster, Edward. Rents and Pecuniary Externalities in Cost–Benefit Analysis: Reply. *Amer. Econ. Rev.,* December 1983, *73* (5), pp. 1171–72.

Grant, Douglas L. Reasonable Groundwater Pumping Levels under the Appropriation Doctrine: Underlying Social Goals. *Natural Res. J.*, January 1983, *23*(1), pp. 53–75. **[G: U.S.]**

Greenberg, Joseph and Weber, Shlomo. A Core Equivalence Theorem with an Arbitrary Communication Structure. *J. Math. Econ.*, January 1983, *11*(1), pp. 43–55.

Grout, Paul. Welfare Aspects of Naive and Sophisticated Decision-making. **In** *Pattanaik, P. K. and Salles, M., eds.*, 1983, pp. 207–24.

Hansen, Pierre; Peeters, D. and Thisse, Jacques-François. Public Facility Location Models: A Selective Survey. **In** *Thisse, J.-F. and Zoller, H. G., eds.*, 1983, pp. 223–62.

Henry, Claude. Some Inconsistencies in Public Land-Use Choices. **In** *Thisse, J.-F. and Zoller, H. G., eds.*, 1983, pp. 183–205.

Hicks, John. Scitovsky on Competition. **In** *Hicks, J.*, 1983, *1952*, pp. 153–62.

Hildenbrand, Werner. Mathematical Economics: Twenty Papers of Gerard Debreu: Introduction. **In** *Debreu, G.*, 1983, pp. 1–29.

Holcombe, Randall G. Applied Fairness Theory: Comment. *Amer. Econ. Rev.*, December 1983, *73*(5), pp. 1153–56.

Holmström, Bengt and Myerson, Roger B. Efficient and Durable Decision Rules with Incomplete Information. *Econometrica*, November 1983, *51*(6), pp. 1799–819.

Hsu, Song-ken. Monopoly Output and Economic Welfare under Third-Degree Price Discrimination. *Southern Econ. J.*, July 1983, *50*(1), pp. 234–39.

Kim, Oliver. Balanced Equilibrium in a Consumption Loans Model. *J. Econ. Theory*, April 1983, *29*(2), pp. 339–46.

Krutilla, John V., et al. Public versus Private Ownership: The Federal Lands Case. *J. Policy Anal. Manage.*, Summer 1983, *2*(4), pp. 548–58. **[G: U.S.]**

van der Laan, G. Note on the Optimality of Unemployment Equilibria. *J. Math. Econ.*, October 1983, *12*(2), pp. 185–90.

LaCroix, Sumner J. Marketing, Price Discrimination, and Welfare. *Southern Econ. J.*, January 1983, *49*(3), pp. 847–52.

Laffont, Jean-Jacques and Maskin, Eric S. A Characterization of Strongly Locally Incentive Compatible Planning Procedures with Public Goods. *Rev. Econ. Stud.*, January 1983, *50*(1), pp. 171–86.

Laroque, Guy and Rochet, Jean-Charles. Myopic versus Intertemporal Manipulation in Decentralized Planning Procedures. *Rev. Econ. Stud.*, January 1983, *50*(1), pp. 187–95.

Lea, Anthony C. Some Lessons from the Theory of Public and Impure Goods for Public Facility Location-Allocation Models. **In** *Thisse, J.-F. and Zoller, H. G., eds.*, 1983, pp. 263–300.

Léonard, Daniel and Manning, Richard. Advantageous Reallocations: A Constructive Example. *J. Int. Econ.*, November 1983, *15*(3/4), pp. 291–95.

Leonard, Herman B. Elicitation of Honest Preferences for the Assignment of Individuals to Positions. *J. Polit. Econ.*, June 1983, *91*(3), pp. 461–79.

Lerner, Abba P. An Alternative Formulation of the Welfare Equations, Equality and Proportionality. **In** *Lerner, A. P.*, 1983, *1944*, pp. 153–62.

Lerner, Abba P. Principles of Efficient Economic Policy. **In** *Lerner, A. P.*, 1983, *1975*, pp. 163–69.

Lerner, Abba P. Simple Production II (under Perfect Competition) the Welfare Equations. **In** *Lerner, A. P.*, 1983, *1970*, pp. 147–52.

Lerner, Abba P. The Optimum Division of Income. **In** *Lerner, A. P.*, 1983, *1944*, pp. 207–24.

Lerner, Abba P. Welfare Economics and the Scitovsky Paradox. **In** *Lerner, A. P.*, 1983, pp. 243–47.

Liebermann, Yehoshua and Syrquin, M. On the Use and Abuse of Rights: An Economic View. *J. Econ. Behav. Organ.*, March 1983, *4*(1), pp. 25–40.

Marx, Thomas G. The Cost of Living: Life, Liberty, and Cost–Benefit Analysis. *Policy Rev.*, Summer 1983, (25), pp. 53–58. **[G: U.S.]**

McKean, John R. and Keller, Robert R. The Shaping of Tastes, Pareto Efficiency and Economic Policy. *J. Behav. Econ.*, Summer 1983, *12*(1), pp. 23–41.

McKenzie, Lionel W. Turnpike Theory, Discounted Utility, and the von Neumann Facet. *J. Econ. Theory*, August 1983, *30*(2), pp. 330–52.

Mills, David E. Resource Allocation and Welfare with Risky Production. *Southern Econ. J.*, October 1983, *50*(2), pp. 551–59.

Mitra, Tapan and Ray, Debraj. Efficient and Optimal Programs When Investment Is Irreversible: A Duality Theory. *J. Math. Econ.*, January 1983, *11*(1), pp. 81–113.

Mitsui, Toshihide. Asymptotic Efficiency of the Pivotal Mechanism with General Project Space. *J. Econ. Theory*, December 1983, *31*(2), pp. 318–31.

Morisugi, Hisayoshi. Welfare Implications of Cost-Benefit Analysis. **In** *Isard, W. and Nagao, Y., eds.*, 1983, pp. 161–85.

Morrison, Clarence C. Ownership Dispersion as a Second-Best Counterstrategy against Monopoly. *J. Econ. Bus.*, June 1983, *35*(2), pp. 159–68.

Muench, Thomas and Walker, Mark. Are Groves–Ledyard Equilibria Attainable? [Optimal Allocation of Public Goods: A Solution to the "Free Rider" Problem]. *Rev. Econ. Stud.*, April 1983, *50*(2), pp. 393–96.

Ng, Yew-Kwang. Rents and Pecuniary Externalities in Cost–Benefit Analysis: Comment. *Amer. Econ. Rev.*, December 1983, *73*(5), pp. 1163–70.

Nicola, Piercarlo. Pareto Optimality When Production Is Lagged. *Giorn. Econ.*, November–December 1983, *42*(11–12), pp. 719–23.

Nielsen, Lars Tyge. Pareto Optima, Non-Convexities and Regulated Market Equilibria. *J. Math. Econ.*, January 1983, *11*(1), pp. 57–63.

Oates, Wallace E. The Regulation of Externalities: Efficient Behavior by Sources and Victims. *Public Finance*, 1983, *38*(3), pp. 362–75.

Okamura, Makoto. Public Goods Supply and Incentive Compatibility: A Survey. (In Japanese. With English summary.) *Osaka Econ. Pap.*, March 1983, *32*(4), pp. 61–78.

Okun, Arthur M. Further Thoughts on Equality and Efficiency. **In** *Okun, A. M.*, 1983, *1977*, pp. 606–31. **[G: U.S.]**

Okuno, Masahiro and Zilcha, Itzhak. Optimal Steady-State in Stationary Consumption-Loan

Type Models. *J. Econ. Theory,* December 1983, *31* (2), pp. 355–63.

P'ng, I. P. L. Strategic Behavior in Suit, Settlement, and Trial. *Bell J. Econ. (See Rand J. Econ. after 4/85),* Autumn 1983, *14* (2), pp. 539–50. **[G: U.S.]**

Pagano, U. Profit Maximization, Industrial Democracy and the Allocation of Labour. *Manchester Sch. Econ. Soc. Stud.,* June 1983, *51* (2), pp. 159–83.

Parish, R. M. Government and Economic Management. **In** *Withers, G., ed.,* 1983, pp. 83–94.

Peacock, Alan. Welfare Economics, Public Finance and Selective Aid Policies. **In** *[Giersch, H.],* 1983, pp. 238–53. **[G: U.K.]**

Peters, Michael and Winter, Ralph A. Market Equilibrium and the Resolution of Uncertainty. *Can. J. Econ.,* August 1983, *16* (3), pp. 381–90.

Pethig, Rüdiger. On the Production and Distribution of Information. *Z. Nationalökon.,* 1983, *43* (4), pp. 383–403.

Philpotts, Geoffrey. Applied Fairness Theory: Comment. *Amer. Econ. Rev.,* December 1983, *73* (5), pp. 1157–60.

Rheaume, G. C. Welfare Optimal Subsidy-free Prices under a Regulated Monopoly. **In** *Courville, L.; de Fontenay, A. and Dobell, R., eds.,* 1983, pp. 319–40.

Safra, Zvi. Manipulation by Reallocating Initial Endowments. *J. Math. Econ.,* September 1983, *12* (1), pp. 1–17.

Sandmo, Agnar. Ex Post Welfare Economics and the Theory of Merit Goods. *Economica,* February 1983, *50* (197), pp. 19–33.

Saraydar, Edward. Bargaining Power, Dissimulation, and the Coase Theorem. *Z. ges. Staatswiss.,* December 1983, *139* (4), pp. 599–611.

Scafuri, Allen J. An Overlapping Generations Model of Exhaustible Natural Resources. *Reg. Sci. Persp.,* 1983, *13* (1), pp. 55–59.

Schwartz, Aba and Pines, David. Portfolio Choice, Consumption and Welfare When Rate of Return Are Related to Prices of Consumer Goods. *J. Public Econ.,* June 1983, *21* (1), pp. 53–77.

Schweizer, Urs. Efficient Exchange with a Variable Number of Consumers. *Econometrica,* May, 1983, *51* (3), pp. 575–84.

Scriven, Michael. Costs in Evaluation: Concept and Practice. **In** *Alkin, M. C. and Solmon, L. C., eds.,* 1983, pp. 27–44.

Shavell, Steven. Strict Liability versus Negligence. **In** *Kuperberg, M. and Beitz, C., eds.,* 1983, *1980,* pp. 210–34.

Söderbaum, Peter. Ezra Mishan on Economic Evaluation: A Comment. *J. Econ. Issues,* March 1983, *17* (1), pp. 206–13.

Spencer, Barbara J. and Brander, James A. Second Best Pricing of Publicly Produced Inputs: The Case of Downstream Imperfect Competition. *J. Public Econ.,* February 1983, *20* (1), pp. 113–19.

Stahl, Dale O., II. On Benefit–Cost Analysis with Quality Attributes. *Z. Nationalökon.,* 1983, *43* (3), pp. 273–87.

Stephan, Gunter. Roundaboutness, Nontightness and Malinvaud Prices in Multisector Models with Infinite Horizon. *Z. ges. Staatswiss.,* December 1983, *139* (4), pp. 660–77.

Stern, Nicholas. Taxation for Efficiency. **In** *Shepherd, D.; Turk, J. and Silberston, A., eds.,* 1983, pp. 77–107. **[G: OECD]**

Sussangkarn, Chal and Goldman, Steven M. Dealing with Envy. *J. Public Econ.,* October 1983, *22* (1), pp. 103–12.

Svensson, Lars-Gunnar. Large Indivisibles: An Analysis with Respect to Price Equilibrium and Fairness. *Econometrica,* July 1983, *51* (4), pp. 939–54.

Svensson, Lars-Gunnar. On the Existence of Fair Allocations. *Z. Nationalökon.,* 1983, *43* (3), pp. 301–08.

Thomson, William. Equity in Exchange Economies. *J. Econ. Theory,* April 1983, *29* (2), pp. 217–44.

Thomson, William. Problems of Fair Division and the Egalitarian Solution. *J. Econ. Theory,* December 1983, *31* (2), pp. 211–26.

Thomson, William and Lensberg, Terje. Guarantee Structures for Problems of Fair Division. *Math. Soc. Sci.,* July 1983, *4* (3), pp. 205–18.

Thorlund-Petersen, Lars. Existence of Proportional Distribution Schemes: A Note. *J. Math. Econ.,* January 1983, *11* (1), pp. 77–79.

Tisdell, Clem A. Law, Economics and Risk–Taking. *Kyklos,* 1983, *36* (1), pp. 3–20.

Trueman, Brett. Optimality of the Disclosure of Private Information in a Production-Exchange Economy. *J. Finance,* June 1983, *38* (3), pp. 913–24.

Warr, Peter G. Private Benevolence and Distributional Weights for Benefit–Cost Analysis. *Public Finance,* 1983, *38* (2), pp. 293–308.

Withers, Glenn A. Government and Economic Management: Discussion. **In** *Withers, G., ed.,* 1983, pp. 95–105.

Yannelis, Nicholas C. Existence and Fairness of Value Allocation without Convex Preferences. *J. Econ. Theory,* December 1983, *31* (2), pp. 283–92.

Zusman, Pinhas. Collective Choice, Pareto Optimality and the Organization of Cooperatives: The Case of Agricultural Credit Associations. *J. Econ. Behav. Organ.,* June–September 1983, *4* (2–3), pp. 185–204.

0243 Redistribution Analyses

Adelman, Irma and Cheng, Leonard. The Lack of Pareto Superiority of Unegalitarian Wealth Distribution. *Metroecon.,* February–June 1983, *35* (1–2), pp. 105–22.

Adelman, Irma and Cheng, Leonard. A Dynamic Model of Personal Wealth and Income Distribution in a Growing Closed Economy. *Jahr. Nationalökon. Statist.,* November 1983, *198* (6), pp. 481–504.

Arrow, Kenneth J. A Utilitarian Approach to the Concept of Equality in Public Expenditures. **In** *Arrow, K. J., Vol. 1,* 1983, *1971,* pp. 88–95.

Arrow, Kenneth J. Nozick's Entitlement Theory of Justice. **In** *Arrow, K. J., Vol. 1,* 1983, *1978,* pp. 175–89.

Arrow, Kenneth J. Some Ordinalist-Utilitarian Notes on Rawls's Theory of Justice. **In** *Arrow, K. J., Vol. 1,* 1983, *1973,* pp. 96–114.

024 Welfare Theory

Atkinson, Anthony B. Capital Taxes, the Redistribution of Wealth and Individual Savings. In *Atkinson, A. B.*, 1983, *1971*, pp. 147–69.

Atkinson, Anthony B. Horizontal Equity and the Distribution of the Tax Burden. **In** *Atkinson, A. B.*, 1983, *1980*, pp. 93–105.

Atkinson, Anthony B. How Progressive Should Income Tax Be? **In** *Atkinson, A. B.*, 1983, *1973*, pp. 295–314.

Atkinson, Anthony B. Inheritance and the Redistribution of Wealth. **In** *Atkinson, A. B.*, 1983, pp. 171–96.

Atkinson, Anthony B. Introduction to Part III: Design of Taxation. **In** *Atkinson, A. B.*, 1983, pp. 199–203.

Balcer, Yves and Sadka, Efraim. Horizontal Equity in Models of Self-selection with Applications to Income Tax and Signaling Cases. **In** *Helpman, E.; Razin, A. and Sadka, E., eds.*, 1983, pp. 235–53.

Becker, Irene. Umverteilungswirkungen monetärer Transfers—Eine empirische Analyse von Steuern, Sozialabgaben und Sozialleistungen. (Redistributive Effects of Monetary Transfers—An Empirical Analysis of Taxes, Payroll Taxes and Social Transfers in the Federal Republic of Germany. With English summary.) *Ifo-Studien*, 1983, *29*(4), pp. 273–98. **[G: W. Germany]**

Beckerman, Wilfred. Human Resources: Are They Worth Preserving? **In** *Streeten, P. and Maier, H., eds.*, 1983, pp. 8–28.

Beenstock, Michael. Social Policy for Social Democracy. **In** *Seldon, A., et al.*, 1983, pp. 73–86. **[G: U.K.]**

Ben-Zion, Uri and Spiegel, Uriel. Philanthropic Motives and Contribution Policy. *Public Choice*, 1983, *40*(2), pp. 117–33.

Bhagwati, Jagdish N.; Ramaswami, V. K. and Srinivasan, T. N. Domestic Distortions, Tariffs, and the Theory of Optimum Subsidy: Some Further Results. **In** *Bhagwati, J. N., Vol. 1*, 1983, *1969*, pp. 245–50.

Bicchieri, Maria Cristina. Economic Welfare and the Distribution of Economic Advantages: Individual Rights versus Common Goals. *Econ. Notes*, 1983, (1), pp. 58–79.

Brennan, Geoffrey. Estate Gift Duty and the Family: Prolegomena to a Theory of the Family Unit. **In** *Penner, R. G., ed.*, 1983, pp. 109–26.

Brennan, Geoffrey and Pincus, Jonathan J. Government Expenditure Growth and Resource Allocation: The Nebulous Connection. *Oxford Econ. Pap.*, November 1983, *35*(3), pp. 351–65.

Brittan, Samuel. Hayek, Freedom and Interest Groups. **In** *Brittan, S.*, 1983, *1980*, pp. 48–79.

Buchanan, James M. Fairness, Hope, and Justice. **In** *Skurski, R., ed.*, 1983, pp. 53–89.

Buchanan, James M. Rent Seeking, Noncompensated Transfers, and Laws of Succession. *J. Law Econ.*, April 1983, *26*(1), pp. 71–85.

Coleman, Jules L. The Economic Analysis of Law. **In** *Kuperberg, M. and Beitz, C., eds.*, 1983, *1982*, pp. 102–22.

Cordes, Joseph J.; Goldfarb, Robert S. and Barth, James R. Compensating When the Government Harms. **In** *Zeckhauser, R. J. and Leebaert, D., eds.*, 1983, pp. 295–309.

Debreu, Gerard. A Classical Tax-Subsidy Problem. **In** *Debreu, G.*, 1983, *1954*, pp. 59–67.

Dipert, Randall R. Reflections on the Rights of Future Generations. **In** *Machan, T. R. and Johnson, M. B., eds.*, 1983, pp. 203–13.

Fishburn, Geoffrey F. Normative Aspects of Indexation Schemes. *Public Finance*, 1983, *38*(1), pp. 27–37.

Foulon, A. Les différents aspects de l'efficacité redistributive des politiques sociales. (With English summary.) *Revue Écon. Polit.*, May–June 1983, *93*(3), pp. 316–27.

Gardner, Bruce L. Efficient Redistribution through Commodity Markets. *Amer. J. Agr. Econ.*, May 1983, *65*(2), pp. 225–34.

Gustafson, Charles. Estate Gift Duty and the Family: Prolegomena to a Theory of the Family Unit: Commentary. **In** *Penner, R. G., ed.*, 1983, pp. 133–36.

Hartle, D. G. The Theory of 'Rent Seeking': Some Reflections. *Can. J. Econ.*, November 1983, *16*(4), pp. 539–54.

Hendershott, Patric H. The Distribution of Gains and Losses from Changes in the Tax Treatment of Housing: Comment. **In** *Feldstein, M., ed.*, 1983, pp. 133–37. **[G: U.K.]**

Hilley, John L. The Distributive Impact of Education Finance Reform. *Nat. Tax J.*, December 1983, *36*(4), pp. 503–09. **[G: U.S.]**

Hochman, Harold M. Contractarian Theories of Income Redistribution. **In** *Helpman, E.; Razin, A. and Sadka, E., eds.*, 1983, pp. 211–34.

Ioannides, Yannis M. and Sato, Ryuzo. Taxation and the Distribution of Income and Wealth. **In** *Biehl, D.; Roskamp, K. W. and Stolper, W. F., eds.*, 1983, pp. 367–86.

Jones, Philip R. Aid to Charities. *Int. J. Soc. Econ.*, 1983, *10*(2), pp. 3–11. **[G: U.K.]**

Keyfitz, Nathan. Can Inequality Be Cured? **In** *Letwin, W., ed.*, 1983, *1973*, pp. 313–27.

King, Mervyn A. The Distribution of Gains and Losses from Changes in the Tax Treatment of Housing. **In** *Feldstein, M., ed.*, 1983, pp. 109–32. **[G: U.K.]**

King, Mervyn A. Welfare Analysis of Tax Reforms Using Household Data. *J. Public Econ.*, July 1983, *21*(2), pp. 183–214. **[G: U.K.]**

Lau, Lawrence J. Socially Optimal Income Distributions. **In** *[Klein, L. R.]*, 1983, pp. 68–83.

Lerner, Abba P. Distributional Equality and Aggregate Utility: Reply. **In** *Lerner, A. P.*, 1983, *1970*, pp. 225–26.

Letwin, William. The Case Against Equality. **In** *Letwin, W., ed.*, 1983, pp. 1–70. **[G: U.K.]**

Lewis, W. Arthur. Development and Distribution. **In** *Lewis, W. A.*, 1983, *1976*, pp. 443–59.

Musgrave, Richard A. Private Labor and Common Land. **In** *Break, G. F., ed.*, 1983, pp. 185–200.

Pasour, E. C., Jr. A Limited Defense of Pareto Optimal Redistribution: Comment. *Public Choice*, 1983, *41*(3), pp. 451–54.

Polemarchakis, Heraklis M. On the Transer Paradox. *Int. Econ. Rev.*, October 1983, *24*(3), pp. 749–60.

Posner, Richard A. Economic Justice and the Economist. In *Letwin, W., ed.*, 1983, *1973*, pp. 345–59. [G: U.S.]

Posner, Richard A. The Ethical and Political Basis of the Efficiency Norm in Common Law Adjudication. In *Kuperberg, M. and Beitz, C., eds.*, 1983, *1980*, pp. 81–101.

Quinn, Timothy H. Distributive Consequences and Political Concerns: On the Design of Feasible Market Mechanisms for Environmental Control. In *Joeres, E. F. and David, M. H., eds.*, 1983, pp. 39–54. [G: U.S.]

Sartorius, Rolf. Government Regulation and Intergenerational Justice. In *Machan, T. R. and Johnson, M. B., eds.*, 1983, pp. 177–201.

Sheshinski, Eytan and Weiss, Yoram. Inequality within and between Families. In *Helpman, E.; Razin, A. and Sadka, E., eds.*, 1983, pp. 255–77.

Srinivasan, T. N. and Bhagwati, Jagdish N. Shadow Prices for Project Selection in the Presence of Distortions: Effective Rates of Protection and Domestic Resource Costs. In *Bhagwati, J. N., Vol. 1*, 1983, *1978*, pp. 523–42.

Tullock, Gordon. The Charity of the Uncharitable. In *Letwin, W., ed.*, 1983, *1971*, pp. 328–44.

Wagner, Richard E. Estate Gift Duty and the Family: Prolegomena to a Theory of the Family Unit: Commentary. In *Penner, R. G., ed.*, 1983, pp. 127–33.

Wagner, Richard E. The Egalitarian Imperative. In *Letwin, W., ed.*, 1983, *1977*, pp. 297–312.

Wickström, Bengt-Arne. Income Redistribution and the Demand for Social Insurance. In *Söderström, L., ed.*, 1983, pp. 21–33.

Wilson, L. S. and Katz, Michael L. The Socialization of Commodities [The Welfare Economics of the Socialization of Commodities]. *J. Public Econ.*, April 1983, *20*(3), pp. 347–56.

Yunker, James A. Optimal Redistribution with Interdependent Utility Functions: A Simulation Study. *Public Finance*, 1983, *38*(1), pp. 132–55.

0244 Externalities

Anderson, Terry L. and Hill, Peter J. Privatizing the Commons: An Improvement? *Southern Econ. J.*, October 1983, *50*(2), pp. 438–50.

d'Aspremont, Claude and Gérard-Varet, Louis-André. Regional Externalities and Efficient Decentralization under Incomplete Information. In *Thisse, J.-F. and Zoller, H. G., eds.*, 1983, pp. 207–20.

Atkinson, Anthony B. Smoking and the Economics of Government Intervention. In *Atkinson, A. B.*, 1983, *1974*, pp. 371–82. [G: U.K.; U.S.]

Bamford, Shaun C. and Hughes, Joseph P. The Uncertain Case for Controlling Pollution by Taxes on Emissions. In *Dutta, M.; Hartline, J. C. and Loeb, P. D., eds.*, 1983, pp. 259–68.

Barrese, James T. Efficiency and Equity Considerations in the Operation of Transfer of Development Rights Plans. *Land Econ.*, May 1983, *59*(2), pp. 235–41.

Barton, Stephen E. Property Rights and Human Rights: Efficiency and Democracy as Criteria for Regulatory Reform. *J. Econ. Issues*, December 1983, *17*(4), pp. 915–30.

Brown, Stephen P. A. A Note on Environmental Risk and the Rate of Discount [Environmental Externalities and the Arrow–Lind Public Investment Theorem]. *J. Environ. Econ. Manage.*, September 1983, *10*(3), pp. 282–86.

Calabresi, Guido and Melamed, A. Douglas. Property Rules, Liability Rules, and Inalienability: One View of the Cathedral. In *Kuperberg, M. and Beitz, C., eds.*, 1983, *1972*, pp. 41–80.

Coase, R. H. The Problem of Social Cost. In *Kuperberg, M. and Beitz, C., eds.*, 1983, *1960*, pp. 13–40.

Collinge, Robert A. and Bailey, Martin J. Optimal Quasi-Market Choice in the Presence of Pollution Externalities. *J. Environ. Econ. Manage.*, September 1983, *10*(3), pp. 221–32.

Crone, Theodore M. Elements of an Economic Justification for Municipal Zoning. *J. Urban Econ.*, September 1983, *14*(2), pp. 168–83. [G: U.S.]

Dodds, Daniel and Bishop, Richard C. On the Role of Information in Mineral Exploration. *Land Econ.*, November 1983, *59*(4), pp. 411–19.

Dragun, Andrew K. Externalities, Property Rights, and Power. *J. Econ. Issues*, September 1983, *17*(3), pp. 667–80.

Dworkin, Ronald. Why Efficiency? In *Kuperberg, M. and Beitz, C., eds.*, 1983, *1980*, pp. 123–40.

Dybvig, Philip H. and Spatt, Chester S. Adoption Externalities as Public Goods. *J. Public Econ.*, March 1983, *20*(2), pp. 231–47.

Gisser, Micha. Groundwater: Focusing on the Real Issue. *J. Polit. Econ.*, December 1983, *91*(6), pp. 1001–27. [G: U.S.]

Grieson, Ronald E. and Wittman, Donald A. Regulation May Be No Worse Than Its Alternatives. In *Grieson, R. E., ed.*, 1983, pp. 171–91.

Hahn, Robert W. Designing Markets in Transferable Property Rights: A Practitioner's Guide. In *Joeres, E. F. and David, M. H., eds.*, 1983, pp. 83–97.

Harford, Jon D. and Karp, Gordon. The Effects and Efficiencies of Different Pollution Standards. *Eastern Econ. J.*, April–June 1983, *9*(2), pp. 79–89. [G: U.S.]

Hughes, Joseph P. Controlling a Firm's Emission of a Pollutant from Many Sources. In *Dutta, M.; Hartline, J. C. and Loeb, P. D., eds.*, 1983, pp. 253–58.

Kay, N. M. Optimal Size of Firm as a Problem in Transaction Costs and Property Rights. *J. Econ. Stud.*, 1983, *10*(2), pp. 29–41.

Kelly, Jerry S. Externalities and the Possibility of Pareto-Satisfactory Decentralization. *Math. Soc. Sci.*, September 1983, *5*(3), pp. 241–51.

Oates, Wallace E. The Regulation of Externalities: Efficient Behavior by Sources and Victims. *Public Finance*, 1983, *38*(3), pp. 362–75.

Plott, Charles R. Externalities and Corrective Policies in Experimental Markets. *Econ. J.*, March 1983, *93*(369), pp. 106–27.

Prud'homme, Rémy. Le Rôle de la Fiscalité dans la Lutte contre les Encombrements et les Pollutions. In *Biehl, D.; Roskamp, K. W. and Stolper, W. F., eds.*, 1983, pp. 387–98.

Randall, Alan. The Problem of Market Failure. *Natural Res. J.*, January 1983, *23*(1), pp. 131–48. [G: U.S.]

024 Welfare Theory

Rolph, Elizabeth S. Government Allocation of Property Rights: Who Gets What? *J. Policy Anal. Manage.*, Fall 1983, *3*(1), pp. 45–61. [G: U.S.]

Saraydar, Edward. Bargaining Power, Dissimulation, and the Coase Theorem. *Z. ges. Staatswiss.*, December 1983, *139*(4), pp. 599–611.

Schelling, Thomas C. Prices as Regulatory Instruments. **In** *Schelling, T. C., ed.*, 1983, pp. 1–40.

Schwartz, Alan. The Enforceability of Security Interests in Consumer Goods. *J. Law Econ.*, April 1983, *26*(1), pp. 117–62. [G: U.S.]

Scott, Anthony. Property Rights and Property Wrongs. *Can. J. Econ.*, November 1983, *16*(4), pp. 555–73.

Shibata, Hirofumi. Fiscal Measures against Pollution: Are Effluent Taxes and Abatement Subsidies Equivalent? **In** *Biehl, D.; Roskamp, K. W. and Stolper, W. F., eds.*, 1983, pp. 399–418.

Shibata, Hirofumi and Winrich, J. Steven. Control of Pollution when the Offended Defend Themselves. *Economica*, November 1983, *50*(200), pp. 425–37.

Wiegard, Wolfgang. Environmental Externalities and Corrective Input and Output Taxes. *Atlantic Econ. J.*, March 1983, *11*(1), pp. 36–41.

025 Social Choice

0250 Social Choice

Abramovitz, Moses. Notes on International Differences in Productivity Growth Rates. **In** *Mueller, D. C., ed.*, 1983, pp. 79–89. [G: OECD]

Ahmad, Kabir U. An Empirical Study of Politico-Economic Interaction in the United States: A Comment. *Rev. Econ. Statist.*, February 1983, *65*(1), pp. 173–78. [G: U.S.]

Aldrich, John H. A Spatial Model with Party Activists: Implications for Electoral Dynamics. *Public Choice*, 1983, *41*(1), pp. 63–100.

Aldrich, John H. A Spatial Model with Party Activists: Implications for Electoral Dynamics: Response. *Public Choice*, 1983, *41*(1), pp. 103–05.

Alt, James E. The Evolution of Tax Structures. *Public Choice*, 1983, *41*(1), pp. 181–222.

Amershi, Amin H. and Stoeckenius, Jan H. W. The Theory of Syndicates and Linear Sharing Rules. *Econometrica*, September 1983, *51*(5), pp. 1407–16.

Ancot, J. P. and Hughes Hallett, A. J. The Determination of Collective Preferences in Economic Decision Models: With an Application to Soviet Economic Policy. **In** *Gruber, J., ed.*, 1983, pp. 263–304. [G: U.S.S.R.]

Anselin, Luc. A Simulation Framework for Modeling Dynamics in Policy Space. *Conflict Manage. Peace Sci.*, Fall 1983, *7*(1), pp. 25–38.

Arrow, Kenneth J. A Difficulty in the Concept of Social Welfare. **In** *Arrow, K. J., Vol. 1*, 1983, *1950*, pp. 1–29.

Arrow, Kenneth J. Contributions to Welfare Economics. **In** *Brown, E. C. and Solow, R. M., eds.*, 1983, pp. 15–30.

Arrow, Kenneth J. Current Developments in the Theory of Social Choice. **In** *Arrow, K. J., Vol. 1*, 1983, *1977*, pp. 162–74.

Arrow, Kenneth J. Extended Sympathy and the Possibility of Social Choice. **In** *Arrow, K. J., Vol. 1*, 1983, *1977*, pp. 147–61.

Arrow, Kenneth J. Formal Theories of Social Welfare. **In** *Arrow, K. J., Vol. 1*, 1983, *1973*, pp. 115–32.

Arrow, Kenneth J. General Economic Equilibrium: Purpose, Analytic Techniques, Collective Choice. **In** *Arrow, K. J., Vol. 2*, 1983, *1972*, pp. 199–226.

Arrow, Kenneth J. Optimal and Voluntary Income Distribution. **In** *Arrow, K. J., Vol. 1*, 1983, *1981*, pp. 201–24.

Arrow, Kenneth J. The Place of Moral Obligation in Preference Systems. **In** *Arrow, K. J., Vol. 1*, 1983, *1967*, pp. 78–80.

Arrow, Kenneth J. The Principle of Rationality in Collective Decisions. **In** *Arrow, K. J., Vol. 1*, 1983, *1952*, pp. 45–58.

Arrow, Kenneth J. Tullock and an Existence Theorem. **In** *Arrow, K. J., Vol. 1*, 1983, *1969*, pp. 81–87.

Arrow, Kenneth J. Values and Collective Decision Making. **In** *Arrow, K. J., Vol. 1*, 1983, *1967*, pp. 59–77.

d'Aspremont, Claude and Gérard-Varet, Louis-André. Regional Externalities and Efficient Decentralization under Incomplete Information. **In** *Thisse, J.-F. and Zoller, H. G., eds.*, 1983, pp. 207–20.

Asselain, Jean-Charles and Morrisson, Christian. Economic Growth and Interest Groups: The French Experience. **In** *Mueller, D. C., ed.*, 1983, pp. 157–75. [G: France]

Atkinson, Glen W. Political Economy: Public Choice or Collective Action? *J. Econ. Issues*, December 1983, *17*(4), pp. 1057–65.

Aumann, R. J.; Kurz, Mordecai and Neyman, Abraham. Voting for Public Goods. *Rev. Econ. Stud.*, October 1983, *50*(4), pp. 677–93.

Auster, Richard. Institutional Entropy, Again [Property Rights in Bureaucracies and Bureaucratic Efficiency]. *Public Choice*, 1983, *40*(2), pp. 211–16.

Bandyopadhyay, Taradas. Coalitional Manipulation and the Pareto Rule. *J. Econ. Theory*, April 1983, *29*(2), pp. 359–63.

Bandyopadhyay, Taradas. Limited Resoluteness and Strategic Voting: The Case of Linear Sincere Preference Orderings. *Math. Soc. Sci.*, October 1983, *6*(1), pp. 109–17.

Bandyopadhyay, Taradas. On a Class of Strictly Nonmanipulable Collective Choice Rules. *Math. Soc. Sci.*, February 1983, *4*(1), pp. 79–86.

Bandyopadhyay, Taradas. On a Pareto Optimal and Rational Choice. *Econ. J.*, Supplement March 1983, pp. 115–22.

Bandyopadhyay, Taradas and Deb, Rajat. Strategic Voting for Weakly Binary Group Decision Functions: The Case of Linear Individual Orderings. **In** *Pattanaik, P. K. and Salles, M., eds.*, 1983, pp. 227–38.

Barberá, Salvador. Pivotal Voters: A Simple Proof of Arrow's Theorem. **In** *Pattanaik, P. K. and Salles, M., eds.*, 1983, pp. 31–35.

Barberá, Salvador. Strategy-Proofness and Pivotal Voters: A Direct Proof of the Gibbard–Satterthwaite Theorem. *Int. Econ. Rev.*, June 1983, *24*(2), pp. 413–17.

Barberá, Salvador and Valenciano, Federico. Collective Probabilistic Judgements. *Econometrica,* July 1983, *51*(4), pp. 1033–46.

Barthelemy, J.-P. Arrow's Theorem: Unusual Domains and Extended Co-domains. **In** *Pattanaik, P. K. and Salles, M., eds.,* 1983, pp. 19–30.

Bauer, Peter T. The Grail of Equality. **In** *Letwin, W., ed.,* 1983, pp. 360–82.

Becker, Gary S. A Theory of Competition among Pressure Groups for Political Influence. *Quart. J. Econ.,* August 1983, *98*(3), pp. 371–400.

Ben-Zion, Uri and Spiegel, Uriel. Philanthropic Motives and Contribution Policy. *Public Choice,* 1983, *40*(2), pp. 117–33.

Bénard, Jean. Colloque de Paris, juin 1981: les progrès récents de l'analyse économique des dépenses publiques. (With English summary.) *Revue Écon. Polit.,* July–August 1983, *93*(4), pp. 509–50.

Bennett, James T. and DiLorenzo, Thomas J. Public Employee Unions and the Privatization of "Public" Services. *J. Lab. Res.,* Winter 1983, *4*(1), pp. 33–45. **[G: U.S.]**

Bennett, James T. and Orzechowski, William P. The Voting Behavior of Bureaucrats: Some Empirical Evidence. *Public Choice,* 1983, *41*(2), pp. 271–83. **[G: U.S.]**

Benson, Bruce L. "High Demand" Legislative Committees and Bureaucratic Output. *Public Finance Quart.,* July 1983, *11*(3), pp. 259–81.

Benson, Bruce L. Logrolling and High Demand Committee Review. *Public Choice,* 1983, *41*(3), pp. 427–34.

Berg, Sven and Bjurulf, Bo H. A Note on the Paradox of Voting: Anonymous Preference Profiles and May's Formula. *Public Choice,* 1983, *40*(3), pp. 307–16.

Bergstrom, Theodore C. and Cornes, Richard C. Independence of Allocative Efficiency from Distribution in the Theory of Public Goods. *Econometrica,* November 1983, *51*(6), pp. 1753–65.

Bhagwati, Jagdish N. Directly Unproductive, Profit-seeking (DUP) Activities. **In** *Bhagwati, J. N., Vol. 1,* 1983, *1982,* pp. 259–73.

Bhagwati, Jagdish N. Lobbying and Welfare. **In** *Bhagwati, J. N., Vol. 1,* 1983, *1980,* pp. 365–73.

Bhagwati, Jagdish N. Lobbying, DUP Activities and Welfare: A Response. **In** *Bhagwati, J. N., Vol. 1,* 1983, *1982,* pp. 374–80.

Bhagwati, Jagdish N. and Srinivasan, T. N. The Welfare Consequences of Directly-Unproductive Profit-seeking (DUP) Lobbying Activities. **In** *Bhagwati, J. N., Vol. 1,* 1983, *1982,* pp. 274–85.

Blair, Douglas H. and Muller, Eitan. Essential Aggregation Procedures on Restricted Domains of Preferences. *J. Econ. Theory,* June 1983, *30*(1), pp. 34–53.

Blankart, Charles B. The Contribution of Public Choice to Public Utility Economics—A Survey. **In** *Finsinger, J., ed.,* 1983, pp. 151–70.

Blewett, Robert A. Fiscal Externalities and Residential Growth Controls: A Theory-of-Clubs Perspective. *Public Finance Quart.,* January 1983, *11*(1), pp. 3–20.

Blewett, Robert A. and Congleton, Roger D. Non-Global Social Contracts: A Note on Inefficient Social Institutions. *Public Choice,* 1983, *41*(3), pp. 441–48.

Bohanon, Cecil E. and Van Cott, T. Norman. A Note on the Political Economy of Indexation. *Public Finance Quart.,* January 1983, *11*(1), pp. 121–27. **[G: U.S.]**

Bolle, Friedel. Towards a Theory of Yes-No-Voting: A Comment. *Public Choice,* 1983, *40*(2), pp. 231–32.

Borcherding, Thomas E. Toward a Positive Theory of Public Sector Supply Arrangements. **In** *Prichard, J. R. S., ed.,* 1983, pp. 99–184. **[G: Canada; Selected Countries]**

Border, Kim C. Social Welfare Functions for Economic Environments with and without the Pareto Principle. *J. Econ. Theory,* April 1983, *29*(2), pp. 205–16.

Border, Kim C. and Jordan, J. S. Straightforward Elections, Unanimity and Phantom Voters. *Rev. Econ. Stud.,* January 1983, *50*(1), pp. 153–70.

Bordes, Georges. On the Possibility of Reasonable Consistent Majoritarian Choice: Some Positive Results. *J. Econ. Theory,* October 1983, *31*(1), pp. 122–32.

Boute, Serge and Praet, Jean-Claude. Testing Coalition Theories in Belgian Local Governments. *Cah. Écon. Bruxelles,* 4th Trimester 1983, (100), pp. 561–93.

Brand, Donald R. Corporatism, the NRA, and the Oil Industry. *Polit. Sci. Quart.,* Spring 1983, *98*(1), pp. 99–118. **[G: U.S.]**

Brennan, Geoffrey and Buchanan, James M. Normative Tax Theory for a Federal Polity: Some Public Choice Preliminaries. **In** *McLure, C. E., Jr., ed.,* 1983, pp. 52–65.

Brennan, Geoffrey and Buchanan, James M. Predictive Power and the Choice among Regimes. *Econ. J.,* March 1983, *93*(369), pp. 89–105.

Brittan, Samuel. Hayek, Freedom and Interest Groups. **In** *Brittan, S.,* 1983, *1980,* pp. 48–79.

Broder, Josef M. and Schmid, A. Allan. Public Choice in Local Judicial Systems. *Public Choice,* 1983, *40*(1), pp. 7–19. **[G: U.S.]**

Brubaker, Earl R. On the Margolis 'Thought Experiment,' and the Applicability of Demand-Revealing Mechanisms to Large-Group Decisions [A Thought Experiment on Demand-Revealing Mechanisms]. *Public Choice,* 1983, *41*(2), pp. 315–19.

Buchanan, James M. Fairness, Hope, and Justice. **In** *Skurski, R., ed.,* 1983, pp. 53–89.

Buchanan, James M. Social Security Survival: A Public-Choice Perspective. *Cato J.,* Fall 1983, *3*(2), pp. 339–53. **[G: U.S.]**

Burkitt, Brian and Spiers, M. The Economic Theory of Politics: A Re-Appraisal. *Int. J. Soc. Econ.,* 1983, *10*(2), pp. 12–21.

Burris, Val. Who Opposed the ERA? An Analysis of the Social Bases of Antifeminism. *Soc. Sci. Quart.,* June 1983, *64*(2), pp. 305–17. **[G: U.S.]**

Carter, Richard. Séparation, annexion, et fédéralisme: au-delà des préceptes normatifs usuels. (Separation, Annexation, Federalism: Beyond the Usual Normative Precepts. With English summary.) *L'Actual. Econ.,* September 1983, *59*(3), pp. 596–619. **[G: Canada]**

025 Social Choice

Cebula, Richard J. A Note on Voter Participation Rates in the United States. *Public Choice,* 1983, *41*(3), pp. 449–50. [G: U.S.]

Cebula, Richard J. and Kafoglis, Milton Z. In Search of Optimum 'Relative Unanimity.' *Public Choice,* 1983, *40*(2), pp. 195–210.

Chandler, Marsha A. The Politics of Public Enterprise. **In** *Prichard, J. R. S., ed.,* 1983, pp. 185–218. [G: Canada]

Chapman, Randall G. and Palda, Kristian S. Electoral Turnout in Rational Voting and Consumption Perspectives. *J. Cons. Res.,* March 1983, *9*(4), pp. 337–46. [G: Canada]

Chappell, Henry W., Jr. Presidential Popularity and Macroeconomic Performance: Are Voters Really So Naive? *Rev. Econ. Statist.,* August 1983, *65*(3), pp. 385–92. [G: U.S.]

Chappell, Henry W., Jr. and Keech, William R. Welfare Consequences of the Six-Year Presidential Term Evaluated in the Context of a Model of the U.S. Economy. *Amer. Polit. Sci. Rev.,* March 1983, *77*(1), pp. 75–91. [G: U.S.]

Chichilnisky, Graciela. Social Choice and Game Theory: Recent Results with a Topological Approach. **In** *Pattanaik, P. K. and Salles, M., eds.,* 1983, pp. 79–102.

Chichilnisky, Graciela and Heal, Geoffrey M. Community Preferences and Social Choice. *J. Math. Econ.,* September 1983, *12*(1), pp. 33–61.

Chichilnisky, Graciela and Heal, Geoffrey M. Necessary and Sufficient Conditions for a Resolution of the Social Choice Paradox. *J. Econ. Theory,* October 1983, *31*(1), pp. 68–87.

Choi, Kwang. A Statistical Test of Olson's Model. **In** *Mueller, D. C., ed.,* 1983, pp. 57–78. [G: OECD]

Clarke, Clifford J. The End of Bureaucratization? Recent Trends in Cross-National Evidence. *Soc. Sci. Quart.,* March 1983, *64*(1), pp. 127–35. [G: Selected MDCs; Selected LDCs]

Clement, Werner. Comprehensive Models for Financing Recurrent Education: Intermediate ("Parafiscal") Financing Schemes. **In** *Levin, H. M. and Schütze, H. G., eds.,* 1983, pp. 81–98.

Coleman, James S. Recontracting, Trustworthiness, and the Stability of Vote Exchanges. *Public Choice,* 1983, *40*(1), pp. 89–94.

Cooter, Robert D. Justice and Mathematics: Two Simple Ideas. **In** *Skurski, R., ed.,* 1983, pp. 198–231.

Cooter, Robert D. The Objectives of Private and Public Judges. *Public Choice,* 1983, *41*(1), pp. 107–32.

Coughlin, Peter J. Social Utility Functions for Strategic Decisions in Probabilistic Voting Models. *Math. Soc. Sci.,* July 1983, *4*(3), pp. 275–93.

Coughlin, Peter J. and Nitzan, Shmuel. Directional and Local Electoral Equilibria with Probabilistic Voting. **In** *Pattanaik, P. K. and Salles, M., eds.,* 1983, pp. 285–99.

Craven, John. Social Choice and Telling the Truth. *J. Public Econ.,* August 1983, *21*(3), pp. 359–75.

Crosby, Lawrence A. and Taylor, James R. Psychological Commitment and Its Effects on Post-Decision Evaluation and Preference Stability among Voters. *J. Cons. Res.,* March 1983, *9*(4), pp. 413–31. [G: U.S.]

Dean, James W. Polyarchy and Economic Growth. **In** *Mueller, D. C., ed.,* 1983, pp. 231–57. [G: U.S.]

Deb, Rajat. Binariness and Rational Choice. *Math. Soc. Sci.,* August 1983, *5*(1), pp. 97–105.

Demange, Gabrielle. Spatial Models of Collective Choice. **In** *Thisse, J.-F. and Zoller, H. G., eds.,* 1983, pp. 153–82.

Denzau, Arthur T. and Parks, Robert P. Existence of Voting-Market Equilibria. *J. Econ. Theory,* August 1983, *30*(2), pp. 243–65.

Di Tella, Torcuato S. "Partidos del pueblo" en América Latina. Revisión teórica y reseña de tendencias recientes. (With English summary.) *Desarrollo Econ.,* January–March 1983, *22*(88), pp. 451–83. [G: Latin America]

DiLorenzo, Thomas J. Economic Competition and Political Competition: An Empirical Note. *Public Choice,* 1983, *40*(2), pp. 203–09. [G: U.S.]

Dobra, John L. An Approach to Empirical Studies of Voting Paradoxes: An Update and Extension [Why So Much Stability?]. *Public Choice,* 1983, *41*(2), pp. 241–50.

Dobra, John L. Property Rights in Bureaucracies and Bureaucratic Efficiency. *Public Choice,* 1983, *40*(1), pp. 95–99.

Dragun, Andrew K. Externalities, Property Rights, and Power. *J. Econ. Issues,* September 1983, *17*(3), pp. 667–80.

Dutta, Bhaskar. Further Results on Voting with Veto. **In** *Pattanaik, P. K. and Salles, M., eds.,* 1983, pp. 239–50.

Enbar, Michael. Equity in the Social Sciences. **In** *Kasperson, R. E., ed.,* 1983, pp. 3–23.

Encarnación, José, Jr. Social Values and Individual Choices. *J. Econ. Behav. Organ.,* June–September 1983, *4*(2–3), pp. 265–75.

Enelow, James M. and Hinich, Melvin J. On Plott's Pairwise Symmetry Condition for Majority Rule Equilibrium. *Public Choice,* 1983, *40*(3), pp. 317–21.

Epple, Dennis; Filimon, Radu and Romer, Thomas. Housing, Voting, and Moving: Equilibrium in a Model of Local Public Goods with Multiple Jurisdictions. **In** *Henderson, J. V., ed.,* 1983, pp. 59–90.

Esty, Daniel C. and Caves, Richard E. Market Structure and Political Influence: New Data on Political Expenditures, Activity, and Success. *Econ. Inquiry,* January 1983, *21*(1), pp. 24–38. [G: U.S.]

Feenstra, Robert C. and Bhagwati, Jagdish N. Tariff Seeking and the Efficient Tariff. **In** *Bhagwati, J. N., Vol. 1,* 1983, *1982,* pp. 381–95.

Feeny, David H. Extensive versus Intensive Agricultural Development: Induced Public Investment in Southeast Asia, 1900–1940. *J. Econ. Hist.,* September 1983, *43*(3), pp. 687–704. [G: Asian LDCs]

Ferejohn, John. Congress and Redistribution. **In** *Schick, A., ed.,* 1983, pp. 131–57. [G: U.S.]

Ferejohn, John A. and McKelvey, Richard D. Von Neumann-Morgenstern Solution Social Choice Functions: An Impossibility Theorem. *J. Econ.*

Theory, February 1983, *29*(1), pp. 109–19.

Ferejohn, John A. and Packel, Edward W. Continuous Social Decision Procedures. *Math. Soc. Sci.,* October 1983, *6*(1), pp. 65–73.

Ferris, James M. Demands for Public Spending: An Attitudinal Approach. *Public Choice,* 1983, *40*(2), pp. 135–54. **[G: U.S.]**

Findlay, Ronald and Wellisz, Stanislaw. Some Aspects of the Political Economy of Trade Restrictions. *Kyklos,* 1983, *36*(3), pp. 469–81.

Fine, Ben. The Order of Acquisition of Consumer Durables: A Social Choice Theoretic Approach. *J. Econ. Behav. Organ.,* June–September 1983, *4*(2–3), pp. 239–48.

Fishburn, Peter C. Research in Decision Theory: A Personal Perspective. *Math. Soc. Sci.,* September 1983, *5*(2), pp. 129–48.

Fortune, Peter. A Test of the Cobb-Douglas Assumption for Local Governments. *Nat. Tax J.,* June 1983, *36*(2), pp. 233–36.

Gaertner, Wulf. Equity- and Inequity-Type Borda Rules. *Math. Soc. Sci.,* April 1983, *4*(2), pp. 137–54.

Gamble, Andrew. Critical Political Economy. **In** *Jones, R. J. B., ed.,* 1983, pp. 64–89.

Gärdenfors, Peter. On the Information about Individual Utilities Used in Social Choice. *Math. Soc. Sci.,* July 1983, *4*(3), pp. 219–28.

Gardner, Roy. Variation of the Electorate: Veto and Purge. *Public Choice,* 1983, *40*(3), pp. 237–47.

Gauglhofer-Witzig, Margrit and Loeffel, Hans. Ein Beitrag aus formal-logischer Sicht zur Diskussion des Abstimmungsproblems bei Initiative und Gegenvorschlag. (A Contribution from the Viewpoint of Formal Logic to the Discussion of the Problem of Voting on Initiatives and Counter-Proposals. With English summary.) *Schweiz. Z. Volkswirtsch. Statist.,* March 1983, *119*(1), pp. 23–48. **[G: Switzerland]**

Gehrlein, William V. and Fishburn, Peter C. Scoring Rule Sensitivity to Weight Selection. *Public Choice,* 1983, *40*(3), pp. 249–61.

Ginsburgh, Victor and Michel, Philippe. Random Timing of Elections and the Political Business Cycle. *Public Choice,* 1983, *40*(2), pp. 155–64.

Gintis, Herbert. Social Contradictions and the Liberal Theory of Justice. **In** *Skurski, R., ed.,* 1983, pp. 90–112.

Goles, E. and Tchuente, M. Iterative Behaviour of Generalized Majority Functions. *Math. Soc. Sci.,* July 1983, *4*(3), pp. 197–204.

Goodin, Robert E. Voting through the Looking Glass. *Amer. Polit. Sci. Rev.,* June 1983, *77*(2), pp. 420–34.

Gormley, William; Hoadley, John and Williams, Charles. Potential Responsiveness in the Bureaucracy: Views of Public Utility Regulation. *Amer. Polit. Sci. Rev.,* September 1983, *77*(3), pp. 704–17. **[G: U.S.]**

Grofman, Bernard. Models of Voter Turnout: A Brief Idiosyncratic Review: A Comment. *Public Choice,* 1983, *41*(1), pp. 55–61.

Grosskopf, Shawna P. and Hayes, Kathy. Do Local Governments Maximize Anything? *Public Finance Quart.,* April 1983, *11*(2), pp. 202–16. **[G: U.S.]**

Guesnerie, Roger. La théorie de la fiscalité sur les transactions entre les ménages et les entreprises: Une présentation synthétique de travaux récents. (Taxing Transactions between Households and Firms: A Synthetical Presentation of Recent Theoretical Work. With English summary.) *Ann. INSEE,* July–September 1983, (51), pp. 7–38.

Haas, Hansjorg. Conflict, Cooperation and Social Preference Functions. **In** *Gruber, J., ed.,* 1983, pp. 148–69. **[G: U.S.]**

Hamlin, Alan P. Procedural Individualism and Outcome Liberalism. *Scot. J. Polit. Econ.,* November 1983, *30*(3), pp. 251–63.

Hammond, Peter J. Ex-post Optimality as a Dynamically Consistent Objective for Collective Choice under Uncertainty. **In** *Pattanaik, P. K. and Salles, M., eds.,* 1983, pp. 175–205.

Handler, Joel F. Discretion in Social Welfare: The Uneasy Position in the Rule of Law. *Yale Law J.,* June 1983, *92*(7), pp. 1270–286.

Hartle, D. G. The Theory of 'Rent Seeking': Some Reflections. *Can. J. Econ.,* November 1983, *16*(4), pp. 539–54.

Hartley, Keith and Lynk, Edward L. Budget Cuts and Public Sector Employment: The Case of Defence. *Appl. Econ.,* August 1983, *15*(4), pp. 531–40. **[G: U.K.]**

Heal, Geoffrey M. Contractibility and Public Decision-making. **In** *Pattanaik, P. K. and Salles, M., eds.,* 1983, pp. 103–22.

Heiner, Ronald A. and Pattanaik, P. K. The Structure of General Probabilistic Group Decision Rules. **In** *Pattanaik, P. K. and Salles, M., eds.,* 1983, pp. 37–54.

Hibbs, Douglas A. Comment on Beck [Parties, Administrations, and American Macroeconomic Outcomes]. *Amer. Polit. Sci. Rev.,* June 1983, *77*(2), pp. 447–51. **[G: U.S.]**

Hibbs, Douglas A. Errata: Economic Outcomes and Political Support for British Governments among Occupational Classes: A Dynamic Analysis. *Amer. Polit. Sci. Rev.,* March 1983, *77*(1), pp. 195. **[G: U.K.]**

Hibbs, Douglas A. Performance économique et fonction de popularité des Présidents Pompidou et Giscard d'Estaing. *Revue Écon. Polit.,* January–February 1983, *93*(1), pp. 44–61. **[G: France]**

Hill, David B. Women State Legislators and Party Voting on the ERA. *Soc. Sci. Quart.,* June 1983, *64*(2), pp. 318–26. **[G: U.S.]**

Hillman, Arye L. and Swan, Peter L. Participation Rules for Pareto-Optimal Clubs. *J. Public Econ.,* February 1983, *20*(1), pp. 55–76.

Hinich, Melvin J. A Spatial Model with Party Activists: Implications for Electoral Dynamics: Comment. *Public Choice,* 1983, *41*(1), pp. 101–02.

Hirayama, Asazi. Interpersonal Comparison and Criteria of Justice. *Econ. Stud. Quart.,* August 1983, *34*(2), pp. 156–70.

Hjern, Benny and Porter, David O. Implementation Structures: A New Unit of Administrative Analysis. **In** *Holzner, B.; Knorr, K. D. and Strasser, H., eds.,* 1983, pp. 265–77.

Hochman, Harold M. Contractarian Theories of Income Redistribution. **In** *Helpman, E.; Razin, A. and Sadka, E., eds.,* 1983, pp. 211–34.

Hockley, G. C. and Harbour, G. Revealed Preferences between Public Expenditures and Taxation Cuts: Public Sector Choice [A New Approach to the Demand for Public Goods]. *J. Public Econ.*, December 1983, *22*(3), pp. 387–99. **[G: U.K.]**

Hoenack, Stephen A. On the Stability of Legislative Outcomes [Why So Much Stability?]. *Public Choice*, 1983, *41*(2), pp. 251–60.

Hoffman, Elizabeth and Plott, Charles R. Pre-Meeting Discussions and the Possibility of Coalition-Breaking Procedures in Majority Rule Committees. *Public Choice*, 1983, *40*(1), pp. 21–39.

Holcombe, Randall G. and Zardkoohi, Asghar. On the Distribution of Federal Taxes and Expenditures, and the New War between the States. *Public Choice*, 1983, *40*(2), pp. 165–74. **[G: U.S.]**

Holler, Manfred J. and Packel, Edward W. Power, Luck and the Right Index. *Z. Nationalökon.*, 1983, *43*(1), pp. 21–29.

Hosomatsu, Yasu. A Necessary and Sufficient Condition for a Continuously Rational Social Choice. **In** *[Yamada, I.]*, 1983, pp. 103–14.

Hunt, Janet C. and White, Rudolph A. The Legal Status of Collective Bargaining by Public School Teachers. *J. Lab. Res.*, Summer 1983, *4*(3), pp. 213–24. **[G: U.S.]**

Hunter, William J. Tax Structure and Bureaucratic Bargaining. *Public Finance Quart.*, July 1983, *11*(3), pp. 347–64.

Imai, Haruo. Voting, Bargaining, and Factor Income Distribution. *J. Math. Econ.*, July 1983, *11*(3), pp. 211–33.

Jacobson, Arthur J. Democratic Participation and the Legal Structure of the Economy of Firms. *Soc. Res.*, Winter 1983, *50*(4), pp. 803–49.

Jessen, Franz. Addictive Goods and the Growth of Government. *Public Choice*, 1983, *40*(1), pp. 101–03.

Johnson, Linda L. The Impact of Real Estate Political Action Committees on Congressional Voting and Elections. *Amer. Real Estate Urban Econ. Assoc. J.*, Winter 1983, *11*(4), pp. 462–75. **[G: U.S.]**

Jurion, Bernard J. A Theory of Public Services with Distance-Sensitive Utility. **In** *Thisse, J.-F. and Zoller, H. G., eds.*, 1983, pp. 95–116.

Kane, N. Stephan. Reassessing the Bureaucratic Dimension of Foreign Policy Making: A Case Study of the Cuban Sugar Quota Decision, 1954–56. *Soc. Sci. Quart.*, March 1983, *64*(1), pp. 46–65. **[G: U.S.]**

Kearl, J. R. Rules, Rule Intermediaries and the Complexity and Stability of Regulation. *J. Public Econ.*, November 1983, *22*(2), pp. 215–26.

Kelman, Steven. Limited Government: An Incoherent Concept. *J. Policy Anal. Manage.*, Fall 1983, *3*(1), pp. 31–44.

Kemp, D. A. The National Economic Summit: Authority, Persuasion and Exchange. *Econ. Rec.*, September 1983, *59*(166), pp. 209–19. **[G: Australia]**

Kenney, Patrick J. The Effect of State Economic Conditions on the Vote for Governor. *Soc. Sci. Quart.*, March 1983, *64*(1), pp. 154–62. **[G: U.S.]**

Keohane, Robert O. The Demand for International Regimes. **In** *Krasner, S. D., ed.*, 1983, *1982*, pp. 141–71.

Kiel, Lisa J. and McKenzie, Richard B. The Impact of Tenure on the Flow of Federal Benefits to SMSA's. *Public Choice*, 1983, *41*(2), pp. 285–93. **[G: U.S.]**

Kirchgässner, Gebhard. An Application of Optimal Control to a Small Model of Politico-economic Interaction. **In** *Gruber, J., ed.*, 1983, pp. 55–80. **[G: W. Germany]**

Kirchgässner, Gebhard. The Political Business Cycle if the Government Is Not Myopic: An Integration of the Long-Run and Short-Run Models of the Political Business Cycle. *Math. Soc. Sci.*, July 1983, *4*(3), pp. 243–60.

Kirk, Richard M. Political Terrorism and the Size of Government: A Positive Institutional Analysis of Violent Political Activity. *Public Choice*, 1983, *40*(1), pp. 41–52.

Kornhauser, Lewis A. Control of Conflicts of Interest in Class-Action Suits. *Public Choice*, 1983, *41*(1), pp. 145–75.

Kramer, Gerald H. Is There a Demand for Progressivity?: A Comment. *Public Choice*, 1983, *41*(1), pp. 223–28.

Kramer, Gerald H. The Ecological Fallacy Revisited: Aggregate- versus Individual-Level Findings on Economics and Elections, and Sociotropic Voting. *Amer. Polit. Sci. Rev.*, March 1983, *77*(1), pp. 92–111. **[G: U.S.]**

Kraus, Richard. Bureaucratic Privilege as an Issue in Chinese Politics. *World Devel.*, August 1983, *11*(8), pp. 673–82. **[G: China]**

Kydland, Finn E. Implications of Dynamic Optimal Taxation for the Evolution of Tax Structures: A Comment. *Public Choice*, 1983, *41*(1), pp. 229–35.

Laband, David N. Federal Budget Cuts: Bureaucrats Trim the Meat, Not the Fat. *Public Choice*, 1983, *41*(2), pp. 311–14. **[G: U.S.]**

Ladd, Helen F. and Wilson, Julie Boatright. Who Supports Tax Limitations: Evidence from Massachusetts' Proposition 2½ *J. Policy Anal. Manage.*, Winter 1983, *2*(2), pp. 256–79. **[G: U.S.]**

Laing, James D.; Nakabayashi, Sampei and Slotznick, Benjamin. Winners, Blockers, and the Status Quo: Simple Collective Decision Games and the Core. *Public Choice*, 1983, *40*(3), pp. 263–79.

Laney, Leroy O. and Willett, Thomas D. Presidential Politics, Budget Deficits, and Monetary Policy in the United States; 1960–1976. *Public Choice*, 1983, *40*(1), pp. 53–69. **[G: U.S.]**

Lecaillon, Jacques. Aspects conjoncturels et électoraux des fluctuations de la répartition. *Revue Écon. Polit.*, January–February 1983, *93*(1), pp. 29–43. **[G: France]**

Lee, Dwight R. Conflicting Analysis of a 'Conflicting Commons': Comment. *Public Choice*, 1983, *41*(2), pp. 327–31.

Lee, Dwight R. The Effectiveness of Supply-Side Tax Cuts under Alternative Political Models. *Atlantic Econ. J.*, September 1983, *11*(3), pp. 49–55.

Lehner, Franz. Pressure Politics and Economic Growth: Olson's Theory and the Swiss Experience. **In** *Mueller, D. C., ed.*, 1983, pp. 203–14. **[G: Switzerland]**

Letwin, William. The Case Against Equality. **In** *Letwin, W., ed.*, 1983, pp. 1–70. **[G: U.K.]**

Levi, Margaret. The Predatory Theory of Rule. **In** *Hechter, M., ed.*, 1983, pp. 216–49.

Levin, Henry M. Educational Choice and the Pains of Democracy. **In** *James, T. and Levin, H. M., eds.*, 1983, pp. 17–38. **[G: U.S.]**

Lewis, Gordon H. The Day Care Tangle: Unexpected Outcomes When Programs Interact. *J. Policy Anal. Manage.*, Summer 1983, *2*(4), pp. 531–47. **[G: U.S.]**

Lipset, Seymour Martin and Schneider, William. The Decline of Confidence in American Institutions. *Polit. Sci. Quart.*, Fall 1983, *98*(3), pp. 379–402. **[G: U.S.]**

Lovell, Michael C. The Collective Allocation of Commodities in a Democratic Society. **In** *Dutta, M.; Hartline, J. C. and Loeb, P. D., eds.*, 1983, *1975*, pp. 35–50.

Mackay, Robert J. and Weaver, Carolyn L. Commodity Bundling and Agenda Control in the Public Sector. *Quart. J. Econ.*, November 1983, *98*(4), pp. 611–35.

Magee, Stephen P. and Brock, William A. A Model of Politics, Tariffs and Rentseeking in General Equilibrium. **In** *Weisbrod, B. and Hughes, H., eds.*, 1983, pp. 497–523.

Magee, Stephen P. and Young, Leslie. Multinationals, Tariffs, and Capital Flows with Endogenous Politicians. **In** *Kindleberger, C. P. and Audretsch, D. B., eds.*, 1983, pp. 21–37.

Mann, Bruce D. and Veseth, Michael. Moderate Rent Controls: A Microeconomic and Public Choice Analysis. *Amer. Real Estate Urban Econ. Assoc. J.*, Fall 1983, *11*(3), pp. 333–43. **[G: U.S.]**

Margolis, Howard. A Note on Demand-Revealing. *Public Choice*, 1983, *40*(2), pp. 217–25.

Margolis, Howard. Reply to Brubaker and Tullock [A Thought Experiment on Demand-Revealing Mechanisms]. *Public Choice*, 1983, *41*(2), pp. 321–25.

Marks, Denton. Public Choice and Rent Control. *Atlantic Econ. J.*, September 1983, *11*(3), pp. 63–69. **[G: U.S.]**

McKelvey, Richard D. and Ordeshook, Peter C. Some Experimental Results That Fail to Support the Competitive Solution. *Public Choice*, 1983, *40*(3), pp. 281–91.

McManus, Maurice. Positive Association and Its Relatives. **In** *Pattanaik, P. K. and Salles, M., eds.*, 1983, pp. 55–71.

McMillan, Melville L. A Further Consideration of Coalitions under the Demand-Revealing Process. *Public Choice*, 1983, *40*(2), pp. 227–30.

Megdal, Sharon Bernstein. The Determination of Local Public Expenditures and the Principal and Agent Relation: A Case Study. *Public Choice*, 1983, *40*(1), pp. 71–87. **[G: U.S.]**

Meier, Kenneth J. and Copeland, Gary W. Interest Groups and Public Policy. *Soc. Sci. Quart.*, September 1983, *64*(3), pp. 641–46. **[G: U.S.]**

de Melo, A. Barbosa. Introdução às formas de concertação social. (With English summary.) *Economia*, May 1983, *7*(2), pp. 255–306. **[G: Portugal]**

Meltzer, Allan H. and Richard, Scott F. Further Tests of a Rational Theory of the Size of Government: Rejoinder. *Public Choice*, 1983, *41*(3), pp. 423–26. **[G: U.S.]**

Meltzer, Allan H. and Richard, Scott F. Tests of a Rational Theory of the Size of Government. *Public Choice*, 1983, *41*(3), pp. 403–18. **[G: U.S.]**

Merkies, A. H. Q. M. and Nijman, Th.E. The Measurement of Quadratic Preference Functions with Small Samples. **In** *Gruber, J., ed.*, 1983, pp. 242–62. **[G: Netherlands]**

Miller, Gary J. and Moe, Terry M. Bureaucrats, Legislators, and the Size of Government. *Amer. Polit. Sci. Rev.*, June 1983, *77*(2), pp. 297–322.

Miller, Nicholas R. Pluralism and Social Choice. *Amer. Polit. Sci. Rev.*, September 1983, *77*(3), pp. 734–47.

Mitsui, Toshihide. Asymptotic Efficiency of the Pivotal Mechanism with General Project Space. *J. Econ. Theory*, December 1983, *31*(2), pp. 318–31.

Molitor, Bruno. Schwäche der Demokratie. **In** *Lenel, H. O.; Willgerodt, H. and Molsberger, J.*, 1983, pp. 17–38. **[G: OECD]**

Monjardet, Bernard. On the Use of Ultrafilters in Social Choice Theory. **In** *Pattanaik, P. K. and Salles, M., eds.*, 1983, pp. 73–78.

Moulin, Hervé. Aspects stratégiques des procédures de vote: Introduction au livre *The Strategy of Social Choice*. *Écon. Appl.*, 1983, *36*(4), pp. 711–19.

Mueller, Dennis C. The Political Economy of Growth and Redistribution. **In** *Mueller, D. C., ed.*, 1983, pp. 261–76. **[G: OECD]**

Murnane, Richard J. How Clients' Characteristics Affect Organization Performance: Lessons from Education. *J. Policy Anal. Manage.*, Spring 1983, *2*(3), pp. 403–17. **[G: U.S.]**

Murrell, Peter. The Comparative Structure of the Growth of the West German and British Manufacturing Industries. **In** *Mueller, D. C., ed.*, 1983, pp. 109–31. **[G: W. Germany; U.K.]**

Muto, Shigeo. Power Indices in a Discretely Proportional Representative System with a Large Number of Voters. *Math. Soc. Sci.*, October 1983, *6*(1), pp. 93–98.

Nadel, Mark V. Making Regulatory Policy. **In** *Schick, A., ed.*, 1983, pp. 221–56. **[G: U.S.]**

Nakayama, Mikio. Truthful Revelation of Preferences for a Public Good. *Math. Soc. Sci.*, August 1983, *5*(1), pp. 47–54.

Nelson, Glenn L. A Critique of Executive Branch Decision-Making Processes. *Amer. J. Agr. Econ.*, December 1983, *65*(5), pp. 901–07. **[G: U.S.]**

Netter, Jeffry M. Political Competition and Advertising as a Barrier to Entry. *Southern Econ. J.*, October 1983, *50*(2), pp. 510–20. **[G: U.S.]**

Ng, Yew-Kwang. Some Broader Issues of Social Choice. **In** *Pattanaik, P. K. and Salles, M., eds.*, 1983, pp. 151–73.

Niemi, Richard G. An Exegesis of Farquharson's *Theory of Voting*. *Public Choice*, 1983, *40*(3), pp. 323–28.

Niemi, Richard G. Why So Much Stability?: Another Opinion. *Public Choice*, 1983, *41*(2), pp. 261–70.

Niemi, Richard G.; Bjurulf, Bo H. and Blewis, Gordon. The Power of the Chairman. *Public Choice*, 1983, *40*(3), pp. 293–305.

Noll, Roger G. The Political Foundations of Regulatory Policy. *Z. ges. Staatswiss.*, October 1983,

139(3), pp. 377–404.

Norton, David L. Good Government, Justice, and Self-fulfilling Individuality. **In** *Skurski, R., ed.*, 1983, pp. 33–52.

Norton, Eleanor Holmes. Public Assistance, Post-New Deal Bureaucracy, and the Law: Learning from Negative Models. *Yale Law J.*, June 1983, *92*(7), pp. 1287–99.

Olson, Mancur. "Social Security Survival": A Comment [Social Security Survival: A Public-Choice Perspective]. *Cato J.*, Fall 1983, *3*(2), pp. 355–59. **[G: U.S.]**

Olson, Mancur. The Ideal Environment for Nuturing Growth. **In** *Federal Reserve Bank of Atlanta*, 1983, pp. 3–13. **[G: U.S.]**

Olson, Mancur. The Political Economy of Comparative Growth Rates. **In** *Mueller, D. C., ed.*, 1983, pp. 7–52. **[G: U.S.]**

Oppenheimer, Joe A. and Russell, Clifford. A Tempest in a Teapot: The Analysis and Evaluation of Environmental Groups Trading in Markets for Pollution Permits. **In** *Joeres, E. F. and David, M. H., eds.*, 1983, pp. 131–48.

Ovchinnikov, S. V. Convex Geometry and Group Choice. *Math. Soc. Sci.*, August 1983, *5*(1), pp. 1–16.

Palfrey, Thomas R. and Rosenthal, Howard. A Strategic Calculus of Voting. *Public Choice*, 1983, *41*(1), pp. 7–53.

Palmer, Jan. Senate Confirmation of Appointments to the U.S. Supreme Court. *Rev. Soc. Econ.*, October 1983, *41*(2), pp. 152–62. **[G: U.S.]**

Panda, Santosh C. On Non-Binary Social Choice. *Math. Soc. Sci.*, February 1983, *4*(1), pp. 73–78.

Parish, R. M. Government and Economic Management. **In** *Withers, G., ed.*, 1983, pp. 83–94.

Pattanaik, P. K. and Salles, Maurice. Social Choice and Welfare: Introduction. **In** *Pattanaik, P. K. and Salles, M., eds.*, 1983, pp. 1–15.

Peleg, Bezalel. On Simple Games and Social Choice Correspondences. **In** *Pattanaik, P. K. and Salles, M., eds.*, 1983, pp. 251–68.

Pollard, Walker A. Presidential Elections: Cyclical and Distributional Economic Effects. *Public Finance Quart.*, April 1983, *11*(2), pp. 217–36.

Quandt, Richard E. Complexity in Regulation. *J. Public Econ.*, November 1983, *22*(2), pp. 199–214.

Raab, Raymond L. Market Structure and Corporate Power Investment: An Empirical Investigation of Campaign Contributions of the 1972 Federal Elections. *Nebr. J. Econ. Bus.*, Winter, 1983, *22*(1), pp. 59–65. **[G: U.S.]**

Ray, Dipankar. Hare's Voting Scheme and Negative Responsiveness. *Math. Soc. Sci.*, July 1983, *4*(3), pp. 301–03.

Rein, Martin and Peattie, Lisa. Claims, Claiming, and Claims Structures. **In** *Rein, M.*, 1983, pp. 23–39.

Rein, Martin and Rabinovitz, Francine. Implementation: A Theoretical Perspective. **In** *Rein, M.*, 1983, pp. 113–37.

Ricketts, Martin. Local Authority Housing Investment and Finance: A Test of the Theory of Regulation. *Manchester Sch. Econ. Soc. Stud.*, March 1983, *51*(1), pp. 45–62. **[G: U.K.]**

Ritz, Zvi. Restricted Domains, Arrow-Social Welfare Functions and Noncorruptible and Nonmanipulable Social Choice Correspondences: The Case of Private Alternatives. *Math. Soc. Sci.*, April 1983, *4*(2), pp. 155–79.

Roberts, Kevin W. Social Choice Rules and Real-Valued Representations. *J. Econ. Theory*, February 1983, *29*(1), pp. 72–94.

Rose-Ackerman, Susan. Beyond Tiebout: Modeling the Political Economy of Local Government. **In** *Zodrow, G. R., ed.*, 1983, pp. 55–83.

Rose-Ackerman, Susan. Tiebout Models and the Competitive Ideal: An Essay on the Political Economy of Local Government. **In** *Quigley, J. M., ed.*, 1983, pp. 23–46.

Rottenberg, Simon. National Commissions: Preaching the Garb of Analysis. *Policy Rev.*, Winter 1983, (23), pp. 217–41. **[G: U.S.]**

Rowland, C. K. and Carp, Robert A. Presidential Effects on Federal District Court Policy Decisions: Economic Liberalism, 1960–77. *Soc. Sci. Quart.*, June 1983, *64*(2), pp. 386–92. **[G: U.S.]**

Rowley, Charles K. The Failure of Government to Perform Its Proper Task. **In** *Lenel, H. O.; Willgerodt, H. and Molsberger, J.*, 1983, pp. 39–58. **[G: OECD]**

Rowley, Charles K. The Political Economy of the Public Sector. **In** *Jones, R. J. B., ed.*, 1983, pp. 17–63. **[G: U.K.]**

Rowley, Charles K. The Post-war Economic Failure of British Government: A Public Choice Perspective. **In** *Seldon, A., et al.*, 1983, pp. 131–48. **[G: U.K.]**

Roy, John R. and Lesse, Paul F. Planning Models for Non-Cooperative Situations: A Two-Player Game Approach. *Reg. Sci. Urban Econ.*, May 1983, *13*(2), pp. 195–211.

Rubin, Paul H. The Objectives of Private and Public Judges: A Comment. *Public Choice*, 1983, *41*(1), pp. 133–37.

Rubinfeld, Daniel L. Normative Tax Theory for a Federal Polity: Some Public Choice Preliminaries: Comment. **In** *McLure, C. E., Jr., ed.*, 1983, pp. 67–69.

Rudder, Catherine E. Tax Policy: Structure and Choice. **In** *Schick, A., ed.*, 1983, pp. 196–220. **[G: U.S.]**

Salant, David. Existence of Vote Maximizing Equilibrium in One Dimension. *Math. Soc. Sci.*, August 1983, *5*(1), pp. 73–87.

Salles, Maurice. Jeux simples d'agrégation. (With English summary.) *Écon. Appl.*, 1983, *36*(4), pp. 697–710.

Sandler, Todd; Cauley, Jon and Tschirhart, John. Toward a Unified Theory of Nonmarket Institutional Structures. *Australian Econ. Pap.*, June 1983, *22*(40), pp. 233–54.

Sato, Kimitoshi. On Compatibility between Neutrality and Aggregate Correction Revelation for Public Goods. *Econ. Stud. Quart.*, August 1983, *34*(2), pp. 97–109.

Sawicki, David S. On the Virtues of the Policy of Doing Nothing. *J. Policy Anal. Manage.*, Spring 1983, *2*(3), pp. 454–57. **[G: U.S.]**

Schick, Allen. The Distributive Congress. **In** *Schick, A., ed.*, 1983, pp. 257–73. **[G: U.S.]**

Schneider, Friedrich and Frey, Bruno S. An Empirical Study of Politico-Economic Interaction in the United States: A Reply. *Rev. Econ. Statist.*, February 1983, *65*(1), pp. 178–82. **[G: U.S.]**

Schneider, Friedrich and Pommerehne, Werner W. Macroeconomia della crescita in disequilibrio e settore pubblico in espansione: il peso delle differenze istituzionali. (The Macroeconomics of Unbalanced Growth and the Expanding Public Sector: The Influence of Institutional Differences. With English summary.) *Rivista Int. Sci. Econ. Com.*, April-May 1983, *30*(4–5), pp. 306–19. **[G: Switzerland]**

Schneider, Friedrich and Pommerehne, Werner W. Private Demand for Public Subsidies to the Arts: A Study in Voting and Expenditure Theory. **In** *Hendon, W. S. and Shanahan, J. L., eds.*, 1983, pp. 192–206. **[G: Switzerland]**

Schofield, Norman. Equilibria in Simple Dynamic Games. **In** *Pattanaik, P. K. and Salles, M., eds.*, 1983, pp. 269–84.

Schofield, Norman. Generic Instability of Majority Rule. *Rev. Econ. Stud.*, October 1983, *50*(4), pp. 695–705.

Schokkaert, Erik and Lagrou, Leo. An Empirical Approach to Distributive Justice. *J. Public Econ.*, June 1983, *21*(1), pp. 33–52. **[G: Belgium]**

Sen, Manimay. Implementable Social Choice Rules: Characterization and Correspondence Theorems under Strong Nash Equilibrium. *J. Math. Econ.*, January 1983, *11*(1), pp. 1–24.

Shughart, William F., II and Tollison, Robert D. Preliminary Evidence on the Use of Inputs by the Federal Reserve System. *Amer. Econ. Rev.*, June 1983, *73*(3), pp. 291–304.

Shull, Steven A. Identifying Presidents' Domestic Agendas. *Soc. Sci. Quart.*, March 1983, *64*(1), pp. 163–72. **[G: U.S.]**

Simon, William H. Legality, Bureaucracy, and Class in the Welfare System. *Yale Law J.*, June 1983, *92*(7), pp. 1198–1269.

Skaggs, Neil T. The Federal Reserve System and Congressional Demands for Information. *Soc. Sci. Quart.*, September 1983, *64*(3), pp. 566–81. **[G: U.S.]**

Skaggs, Neil T. and Wasserkrug, Cheryl L. Banking Sector Influence on the Relationship of Congress to the Federal Reserve System. *Public Choice*, 1983, *41*(2), pp. 295–306. **[G: U.S.]**

Spatt, Chester S. Control of Conflicts of Interest in Class-Action Suits: A Comment. *Public Choice*, 1983, *41*(1), pp. 177–79.

Spatt, Chester S. The Objectives of Private and Public Judges: A Comment. *Public Choice*, 1983, *41*(1), pp. 139–43.

Stein, Arthur A. Coordination and Collaboration: Regimes in an Anarchic World. **In** *Krasner, S. D., ed.*, 1983, *1982*, pp. 115–40.

Stiglitz, Joseph E. Public Goods in Open Economics with Heterogeneous Individuals. **In** *Thisse, J.-F. and Zoller, H. G., eds.*, 1983, pp. 55–78.

Sufrin, Sidney C. The Ethics of Administration. *Rivista Int. Sci. Econ. Com.*, September 1983, *30*(9), pp. 829–39. **[G: U.S.]**

Suzumura, Kotara. Resolving Conflicting Views of Justice in Social Choice. **In** *Pattanaik, P. K. and Salles, M., eds.*, 1983, pp. 125–49.

Thomson, William. Equity in Exchange Economies. *J. Econ. Theory*, April 1983, *29*(2), pp. 217–44.

Thomson, William. Problems of Fair Division and the Egalitarian Solution. *J. Econ. Theory*, December 1983, *31*(2), pp. 211–26.

Thomson, William and Lensberg, Terje. Guarantee Structures for Problems of Fair Division. *Math. Soc. Sci.*, July 1983, *4*(3), pp. 205–18.

Tideman, T. Nicolaus. A Collective Conception of Collective Value. **In** *Quigley, J. M., ed.*, 1983, pp. 3–22.

Tideman, T. Nicolaus. An Experiment in the Demand-Revealing Process. *Public Choice*, 1983, *41*(3), pp. 387–401.

Tilman, Rick. Social Value Theory, Corporate Power, and Political Elites: Appraisals of Lindblom's *Politics and Markets*. *J. Econ. Issues*, March 1983, *17*(1), pp. 115–31.

Toma, Eugenia Froedge. Institutional Structures, Regulation, and Producer Gains in the Education Industry. *J. Law Econ.*, April 1983, *26*(1), pp. 103–16. **[G: U.S.]**

Tucci, Ginarocco. Razionalità sostanziale e funzionale nella programmazione regionale dei trasporti in Italia. (Substantial and Functional Rationality in Regional Planning of Transportation in Italy. With English summary.) *Rivista Int. Sci. Econ. Com.*, June 1983, *30*(6), pp. 540–54. **[G: Italy]**

Tullock, Gordon. Further Tests of a Rational Theory of the Size of Government. *Public Choice*, 1983, *41*(3), pp. 419–21. **[G: U.S.]**

von Ungern-Sternberg, Thomas R. A Model of the Political Process with Party Loyalty. *J. Public Econ.*, August 1983, *21*(3), pp. 389–96.

Wallace, Myles S. and Warner, John T. A Note: Presidential Elections and Federal Reserve Policy. *J. Post Keynesian Econ.*, Spring 1983, *5*(3), pp. 489–92.

Waste, Robert J. The Early Years in the Life Cycle of City Councils: A Downsian Analysis. *Urban Stud.*, February 1983, *20*(1), pp. 73–81. **[G: U.S.]**

Weatherford, M. Stephen. Economic Voting and the "Symbolic Politics" Argument: A Reinterpretation and Synthesis. *Amer. Polit. Sci. Rev.*, March 1983, *77*(1), pp. 158–74. **[G: U.S.]**

Weingast, Barry R. and Moran, Mark J. Bureaucratic Discretion or Congressional Control? Regulatory Policymaking by the Federal Trade Commission. *J. Polit. Econ.*, October 1983, *91*(5), pp. 765–800. **[G: U.S.]**

Weller, Barry R. The Political Business Cycle: A Discriminating Analysis. *Soc. Sci. Quart.*, June 1983, *64*(2), pp. 398–403. **[G: U.S.]**

Weymark, John A. Quasitransitive Rationalization and the Superset Property. *Math. Soc. Sci.*, October 1983, *6*(1), pp. 105–08.

Widmaier, Hans Peter. Human Resources and Social Policy. **In** *Streeten, P. and Maier, H., eds.*, 1983, pp. 295–309.

Wilson, H. T. Technocracy and Late Capitalist Society: Reflections on the Problem of Rationality and Social Organisation. **In** *Clegg, S.; Dow, G. and Boreham, P., eds.*, 1983, pp. 152–238.

Wilson, L. S. and Katz, Michael L. The Socialization

of Commodities [The Welfare Economics of the Socialization of Commodities]. *J. Public Econ.*, April 1983, *20*(3), pp. 347–56.

Winer, Stanley L. Some Evidence on the Effect of the Separation of Spending and Taxing Decisions. *J. Polit. Econ.*, February 1983, *91*(1), pp. 126–40. **[G: Canada]**

Withers, Glenn A. Government and Economic Management: Discussion. **In** *Withers, G., ed.*, 1983, pp. 95–105.

Yandle, T. Bruce. Conflicting Analysis of a 'Conflicting Commons': Reply. *Public Choice*, 1983, *41*(2), pp. 333–35.

Yeager, Leland B. Is There a Bias Toward Overregulation? **In** *Machan, T. R. and Johnson, M. B., eds.*, 1983, pp. 99–126. **[G: U.S.]**

Zeckhauser, Richard J. and Leebaert, Derek. Introduction: What Role for Government? **In** *Zeckhauser, R. J. and Leebaert, D., eds.*, 1983, pp. 3–15.

Zusman, Pinhas. Collective Choice, Pareto Optimality and the Organization of Cooperatives: The Case of Agricultural Credit Associations. *J. Econ. Behav. Organ.*, June–September 1983, *4*(2–3), pp. 185–204.

026 Economics of Uncertainty and Information; Game Theory and Bargaining Theory

0260 Economics of Uncertainty and Information; Game Theory and Bargaining Theory

Amershi, Amin H. and Stoeckenius, Jan H. W. The Theory of Syndicates and Linear Sharing Rules. *Econometrica*, September 1983, *51*(5), pp. 1407–16.

Clarke, Richard N. Collusion and the Incentives for Information Sharing. *Bell J. Econ. (See Rand J. Econ. after 4/85)*, Autumn 1983, *14*(2), pp. 383–94.

Correa, Hector. The Firm's Administrative Structure: Theory, Measurement and Applications to Growth Accounting and Income Distribution. *Empirical Econ.*, 1983, *8*(2), pp. 93–109. **[G: U.S.]**

Debreu, Gerard. Economics under Uncertainty. **In** *Debreu, G.*, 1983, pp. 115–19.

Demski, Joel S. Comments on Wilson and Jensen [Auditing: Perspectives from Multi-person Decision Theory] [Organization Theory and Methodology]. *Accounting Rev.*, April 1983, *58*(2), pp. 347–49.

Faxén, Karl-Olof. Stability in Economic Growth under Uncertainty—Growth of Knowledge, Decision Processes and Contingency Contracts. **In** *Eliasson, G.; Sharefkin, M. and Ysander, B.-C., eds.*, 1983, pp. 375–417. **[G: OECD]**

Frydman, Roman and Phelps, Edmund S. Individual Forecasting and Aggregate Outcomes: "Rational Expectations" Examined: Introduction. **In** *Frydman, R. and Phelps, E. S., eds.*, 1983, pp. 1–30.

Kaplan, Robert S. Comments on Wilson and Jensen [Auditing: Perspectives from Multi-person Decision Theory] [Organization Theory and Methodology]. *Accounting Rev.*, April 1983, *58*(2), pp. 340–46.

Myerson, Roger B. Mechanism Design by an Informed Principal. *Econometrica*, November 1983, *51*(6), pp. 1767–97.

Reinganum, Jennifer F. Nash Equilibrium Search for the Best Alternative. *J. Econ. Theory*, June 1983, *30*(1), pp. 139–52.

Saraydar, Edward. Transaction Costs and the Solution to Captain MacWhirr's Problem. *J. Polit. Econ.*, April 1983, *91*(2), pp. 312–15.

Schepanski, Albert and Uecker, Wilfred. Toward a Positive Theory of Information Evaluation. *Accounting Rev.*, April 1983, *58*(2), pp. 259–83.

Schweizer, Urs and von Ungern-Sternberg, Thomas R. Sealed Bid Auctions and the Search for Better Information. *Economica*, February 1983, *50*(197), pp. 79–85.

Sonnenschein, Hugo. The Economics of Incentives: An Introductory Account. **In** *[Yamada, I.]*, 1983, pp. 79–92.

0261 Theory of Uncertainty and Information

Allais, Maurice. Frequency, Probability and Chance. **In** *Stigum, B. P. and Wenstøp, F., eds.*, 1983, pp. 35–86.

Allen, Beth. Expectations Equilibria with Dispersed Information: Existence with Approximate Rationality in a Model with a Continuum of Agents and Finitely Many States of the World. *Rev. Econ. Stud.*, April 1983, *50*(2), pp. 267–85.

Allen, Beth. Neighboring Information and Distributions of Agents' Characteristics under Uncertainty. *J. Math. Econ.*, September 1983, *12*(1), pp. 63–101.

Andersen, Torben M. Price and Quantity Signals in Financial Markets. *Z. Nationalökon.*, 1983, *43*(2), pp. 109–29.

Arrow, Kenneth J. Behavior under Uncertainty and Its Implications for Policy. **In** *Stigum, B. P. and Wenstøp, F., eds.*, 1983, pp. 19–32.

Arrow, Kenneth J. Team Theory and Decentralized Resource Allocation: An Example. **In** *[Erlich, A.]*, 1983, pp. 63–76.

Arrow, Kenneth J. The Role of Securities in the Optimal Allocation of Risk Bearing. **In** *Arrow, K. J., Vol. 2*, 1983, *1963*, pp. 46–57.

d'Aspremont, Claude and Gérard-Varet, Louis-André. Regional Externalities and Efficient Decentralization under Incomplete Information. **In** *Thisse, J.-F. and Zoller, H. G., eds.*, 1983, pp. 207–20.

Baiman, Stanley and Evans, John H., III. Pre-Decision Information and Participative Management Control Systems. *J. Acc. Res.*, Autumn 1983, *21*(2), pp. 371–95.

Balcer, Yves and Sadka, Efraim. Horizontal Equity in Models of Self-selection with Applications to Income Tax and Signaling Cases. **In** *Helpman, E.; Razin, A. and Sadka, E., eds.*, 1983, pp. 235–53.

Bausor, Randall. The Rational-Expectations Hypothesis and the Epistemics of Time. *Cambridge J. Econ.*, March 1983, *7*(1), pp. 1–10.

Bazerman, Max H. and Samuelson, William F. The

Winner's Curse: An Empirical Investigation. **In** *Tietz, R., ed.*, 1983, pp. 186–200.

Benhabib, Jess and Bull, Clive. Job Search: The Choice of Intensity. *J. Polit. Econ.*, October 1983, *91*(5), pp. 747–64.

Bernoulli, Daniel. Exposition of a New Theory on the Measurement of Risk. **In** *Archer, S. H. and D'Ambrosia, C. A.*, 1983, *1954*, pp. 2–15.

Bhattacharya, Sudipto and Ritter, Jay R. Innovation and Communication: Signalling with Partial Disclosure. *Rev. Econ. Stud.*, April 1983, *50*(2), pp. 331–46.

Biswas, Tapan. A Note on the Generalised Measures of Risk Aversion. *J. Econ. Theory*, April 1983, *29*(2), pp. 347–52.

Blatt, John M. Expected Utility Theory Does *Not* Apply to All Rational Men. **In** *Stigum, B. P. and Wenstøp, F., eds.*, 1983, pp. 107–16.

Boyer, Marcel and Dionne, Georges. Riscophobie et étalement à moyenne constante: analyse et applications. (Risk Aversion and Mean-Preserving Spread; Analysis and Application. With English summary.) *L'Actual. Econ.*, June 1983, *59*(2), pp. 208–29.

Boyer, Marcel and Dionne, Georges. Variations in the Probability and Magnitude of Loss: Their Impact on Risk. *Can. J. Econ.*, August 1983, *16*(3), pp. 411–19.

Browning, M. J. Efficient Decentralisation with a Transferable Good. *Rev. Econ. Stud.*, April 1983, *50*(2), pp. 375–81.

Bucovetsky, Sam. Price Dispersion and Stockpiling by Consumers. *Rev. Econ. Stud.*, July 1983, *50*(3), pp. 443–65.

Burdett, Kenneth and Judd, Kenneth L. Equilibrium Price Dispersion. *Econometrica*, July 1983, *51*(4), pp. 955–69.

Camacho, A. Cardinal Utility and Decision Making under Uncertainty. **In** *Stigum, B. P. and Wenstøp, F., eds.*, 1983, pp. 347–70.

Carlson, John A. and McAfee, R. Preston. Discrete Equilibrium Price Dispersion. *J. Polit. Econ.*, June 1983, *91*(3), pp. 480–93.

Carruth, Alan. On the Quantitative Significance of Imperfect Information. *Europ. Econ. Rev.*, January 1983, *20*(1–3), pp. 365–79.

Chamley, Christophe. Entrepreneurial Abilities and Liabilities in a Model of Self-Selection. *Bell J. Econ. (See Rand J. Econ. after 4/85)*, Spring 1983, *14*(1), pp. 70–80.

Chander, Parkash. On the Information Efficiency of the Competitive Resource Allocation Process. *J. Econ. Theory*, October 1983, *31*(1), pp. 54–67.

Chateau, John-Peter D. Credit Rationing as a (Temporary) Suboptimal Equilibrium with Imperfect Information. *Europ. Econ. Rev.*, November 1983, *23*(2), pp. 195–201.

Chenault, Larry A. and Flueckiger, Gerald E. An Information Theoretic Model of Bounded Rationality. *Math. Soc. Sci.*, November 1983, *6*(2), pp. 227–46.

Chew, Soo Hong. A Generalization of the Quasilinear Mean with Applications to the Measurement of Income Inequality and Decision Theory Resolving the Allais Paradox. *Econometrica*, July 1983, *51*(4), pp. 1065–92.

Cox, Samuel H., Jr. and Martin, John D. Abandonment Value and Capital Budgeting under Uncertainty. *J. Econ. Bus.*, August 1983, *35*(3/4), pp. 331–41.

Cozzolino, John M. The Evaluation of Loss Control Options. *J. Risk Ins.*, September 1983, *50*(3), pp. 404–16.

Crawford, Vincent P. and Guasch, J. Luis. The Theory of Contracts and Agency. *Amer. J. Agr. Econ.*, May 1983, *65*(2), pp. 373–79.

Crocker, Keith J. Vertical Integration and the Strategic Use of Private Information. *Bell J. Econ. (See Rand J. Econ. after 4/85)*, Spring 1983, *14*(1), pp. 236–48.

DeGroot, Morris H. Decision Making with an Uncertain Utility Function. **In** *Stigum, B. P. and Wenstøp, F., eds.*, 1983, pp. 371–84.

Doherty, Neil A. Stochastic Choice in Insurance and Risk Sharing: A Reply. *J. Finance*, June 1983, *38*(3), pp. 1037–38.

Doherty, Neil A. and Schlesinger, Harris. Optimal Insurance in Incomplete Markets. *J. Polit. Econ.*, December 1983, *91*(6), pp. 1045–54.

Doherty, Neil A. and Schlesinger, Harris. The Optimal Deductible for an Insurance Policy When Initial Wealth Is Random. *J. Bus.*, October 1983, *56*(4), pp. 555–65.

Don, F. J. Henk. Uncertainty and the Vigour of Policy: A Stronger Result [Uncertainty and the Vigour of Policy: Some Implications of Quadratic Preferences]. *J. Econ. Dynam. Control*, September 1983, *6*(1/2), pp. 187–91.

Driscoll, Michael J. and Ford, J. L. Protection and Optimal Trade-Restricting Policies under Uncertainty. *Manchester Sch. Econ. Soc. Stud.*, March 1983, *51*(1), pp. 21–32.

Dybvig, Philip H. and Lippman, Steven A. An Alternative Characterization of Decreasing Absolute Risk Aversion. *Econometrica*, January 1983, *51*(1), pp. 223–24.

Dye, Ronald A. Communication and Post-Decision Information. *J. Acc. Res.*, Autumn 1983, *21*(2), pp. 514–33.

Easley, David and Jarrow, Robert A. Consensus Beliefs Equilibrium and Market Efficiency. *J. Finance*, June 1983, *38*(3), pp. 903–11.

Eden, Benjamin. On Competitive Price Adjustment for a Storable Good and Abstention from Trade. *J. Polit. Econ.*, December 1983, *91*(6), pp. 1028–44.

Englebrecht-Wiggans, Richard; Milgrom, Paul R. and Weber, Robert J. Competitive Bidding and Proprietary Information. *J. Math. Econ.*, April 1983, *11*(2), pp. 161–69.

Epstein, Larry G. Decreasing Absolute Risk Aversion and Utility Indices Derived from Cake-Eating Problems. *J. Econ. Theory*, April 1983, *29*(2), pp. 245–64.

Farquhar, Peter H. Research Directions in Multiattribute Utility Analysis. **In** *Hansen, P., ed.*, 1983, pp. 63–85.

Fishburn, Peter C. Research in Decision Theory: A Personal Perspective. *Math. Soc. Sci.*, September 1983, *5*(2), pp. 129–48.

Frank, Jeff L. Uncertain Vacancies and Unemployment Equilibria. *J. Econ. Theory*, June 1983,

30(1), pp. 115–38.

Friedman, James W. Low Information Nash Equilibria for Oligopolistic Markets. *Info. Econ. Policy,* 1983, *1* (1), pp. 37–53.

Friedman, Milton and Savage, Leonard J. The Utility Analysis of Choices Involving Risk. **In** *Archer, S. H. and D'Ambrosia, C. A.*, 1983, *1948*, pp. 16–45.

Garner, C. Alan. 'Uncertainty' in Keynes' *General Theory:* A Comment. *Hist. Polit. Econ.*, Spring 1983, *15*(1), pp. 83–86.

Giran, Jean-Pierre. Production d-information et accumulation de capital. (Information Production and Capital Accumulation. With English summary.) *Écon. Appl.*, 1983, *36*(2–3), pp. 389–409.

Green, Jerry R. On Mistaken Beliefs and Resultant Equilibria: Comment. **In** *Frydman, R. and Phelps, E. S., eds.*, 1983, pp. 166–68.

Grether, David M. and Wilde, Louis L. Consumer Choice and Information: New Experimental Evidence. *Info. Econ. Policy,* 1983, *1* (2), pp. 115–44. **[G: U.S.]**

Grossman, Sanford J. and Hart, Oliver D. An Analysis of the Principal–Agent Problem. *Econometrica,* January 1983, *51* (1), pp. 7–45.

Hagen, Ole. Paradoxes and Their Solutions. **In** *Stigum, B. P. and Wenstøp, F., eds.*, 1983, pp. 5–17.

Hammond, Peter J. Ex-post Optimality as a Dynamically Consistent Objective for Collective Choice under Uncertainty. **In** *Pattanaik, P. K. and Salles, M., eds.*, 1983, pp. 175–205.

Hart, Oliver D. Optimal Labour Contracts under Asymmetric Information: An Introduction. *Rev. Econ. Stud.*, January 1983, *50*(1), pp. 3–35.

Hartwick, John M. Learning about and Exploiting Exhaustible Resource Deposits of Uncertain Size. *Can. J. Econ.*, August 1983, *16*(3), pp. 391–410.

Hey, John D. Towards Double Negative Economics. **In** *Wiseman, J., ed.*, 1983, pp. 160–75.

Hey, John D. Whither Uncertainty? *Econ. J.*, Supplement March 1983, pp. 130–39.

Hirshleifer, Jack. Investment Decision under Uncertainty: Choice—Theoretic Approaches. **In** *Archer, S. H. and D'Ambrosia, C. A.*, 1983, *1965*, pp. 61–85.

Holmström, Bengt and Myerson, Roger B. Efficient and Durable Decision Rules with Incomplete Information. *Econometrica,* November 1983, *51* (6), pp. 1799–819.

Honda, Yuzo. Risk, Risk Aversion and Many Control Variables. *Z. Nationalökon.*, 1983, *43*(4), pp. 405–22.

Huberman, Gur; Mayers, David and Smith, Clifford W., Jr. Optimal Insurance Policy Indemnity Schedules. *Bell J. Econ. (See Rand J. Econ. after 4/85),* Autumn 1983, *14*(2), pp. 415–26.

Huberman, Gur and Ross, Stephen A. Portfolio Turnpike Theorems, Risk Aversion, and Regularly Varying Utility Functions. *Econometrica,* September 1983, *51* (5), pp. 1345–61.

Jefferson, Michael. Economic Uncertainty and Business Decision-making. **In** *Wiseman, J., ed.*, 1983, pp. 122–59.

Jennings, Robert H. and Barry, Christopher B. Information Dissemination and Portfolio Choice. *J. Finan. Quant. Anal.*, March 1983, *18*(1), pp. 1–19.

Johnson, Glenn L. Ethical Issues in Resource Economics: Discussion. *Amer. J. Agr. Econ.*, December 1983, *65*(5), pp. 1033–34.

Jonscher, Charles. Information Resources and Economic Productivity. *Info. Econ. Policy,* 1983, *1* (1), pp. 13–35. **[G: U.S.]**

Joyce, Patrick. Information and Behavior in Experimental Markets. *J. Econ. Behav. Organ.*, December 1983, *4*(4), pp. 411–24.

Karni, Edi. On the Correspondence between Multivariate Risk Aversion and Risk Aversion with State-Dependent Preferences. *J. Econ. Theory,* August 1983, *30*(2), pp. 230–42.

Karni, Edi. Risk Aversion for State-Dependent Utility Functions: Measurement and Applications. *Int. Econ. Rev.*, October 1983, *24*(3), pp. 637–47.

Karni, Edi. Risk Aversion in the Theory of Health Insurance. **In** *Helpman, E.; Razin, A. and Sadka, E., eds.*, 1983, pp. 97–106.

Karni, Edi; Schmeidler, David and Vind, Karl. On State Dependent Preferences and Subjective Probabilities. *Econometrica,* July 1983, *51* (4), pp. 1021–31.

Katz, Eliakim. Relative Risk Aversion in Comparative Statics. *Amer. Econ. Rev.*, June 1983, *73*(3), pp. 452–53.

Kirman, Alan. On Mistaken Beliefs and Resultant Equilibria. **In** *Frydman, R. and Phelps, E. S., eds.*, 1983, pp. 147–66.

Kroll, Yoram. Stochastic Choice in Insurance and Risk Sharing: A Comment. *J. Finance,* June 1983, *38*(3), pp. 1033–35.

Krzysztofowicz, Roman. Risk Attitude Hypotheses of Utility Theory. **In** *Stigum, B. P. and Wenstøp, F., eds.*, 1983, pp. 201–16.

Lamberton, D. McL. Information Economics and Technological Change. **In** *Macdonald, S.; Lamberton, D. M. and Mandeville, T., eds.*, 1983, pp. 75–92.

Machina, Mark J. Generalized Expected Utility Analysis and the Nature of Observed Violations of the Independence Axiom. **In** *Stigum, B. P. and Wenstøp, F., eds.*, 1983, pp. 263–93.

Maloney, Kevin J.; Marshall, William J. and Yawitz, Jess B. The Effect of Risk on the Firm's Optimal Capital Stock: A Note. *J. Finance,* September 1983, *38*(4), pp. 1279–84.

Manove, Michael. Provider Insurance. *Bell J. Econ. (See Rand J. Econ. after 4/85),* Autumn 1983, *14*(2), pp. 489–96.

Matthews, Steven A. and Mirman, Leonard J. Equilibrium Limit Pricing: The Effects of Private Information and Stochastic Demand. *Econometrica,* July 1983, *51* (4), pp. 981–96.

McClennen, Edward F. Sure-thing Doubts. **In** *Stigum, B. P. and Wenstøp, F., eds.*, 1983, pp. 117–36.

McCord, Mark and de Neufville, Richard. Empirical Demonstration That Expected Utility Decision Analysis Is Not Operational. **In** *Stigum, B. P. and Wenstøp, F., eds.*, 1983, pp. 181–99.

Meyer, Jack and Ormiston, Michael B. The Comparative Statics of Cumulative Distribution Function Changes for the Class of Risk Averse Agents. *J.*

Econ. Theory, October 1983, *31*(1), pp. 153–69.

Milne, Frank and Shefrin, H. M. Welfare Losses Arising from Increased Public Information, and/or the Opening of New Securities Markets: Examples of the General Theory of the Second Best. **In** *Stigum, B. P. and Wenstøp, F., eds.,* 1983, pp. 385–95.

Minabe, Shigeo. The Utility Analysis of Choices Involving Risk Revisited. *Public Finance,* 1983, *38*(1), pp. 98–109.

Moosa, Suleman A. The Treatment of Uncertainty in the Application of Rational Expectations to the Analysis of Economic Policy. *Appl. Econ.,* August 1983, *15*(4), pp. 451–58.

Morgan, Peter B. Search and Optimal Sample Sizes. *Rev. Econ. Stud.,* October 1983, *50*(4), pp. 659–75.

Múnera, Héctor A. and de Neufville, Richard. A Decision Analysis Model When the Substitution Principle Is Not Acceptable. **In** *Stigum, B. P. and Wenstøp, F., eds.,* 1983, pp. 247–62.

Nalebuff, Barry J. and Stiglitz, Joseph E. Information, Competition, and Markets. *Amer. Econ. Rev.,* May 1983, *73*(2), pp. 278–83.

Nalebuff, Barry J. and Stiglitz, Joseph E. Prizes and Incentives: Towards a General Theory of Compensation and Competition. *Bell J. Econ. (See Rand J. Econ. after 4/85),* Spring 1983, *14*(1), pp. 21–43.

Nalebuff, Barry J. and Varian, Hal R. Some Aspects of Risk Sharing in Nonclassical Environments. **In** *Söderström, L., ed.,* 1983, pp. 7–19.

Okada, Akira. Coalition Formation of Oligopolistic Firms for Information Exchange. *Math. Soc. Sci.,* December 1983, *6*(3), pp. 337–51.

Okamura, Makoto. Public Goods Supply and Incentive Compatibility: A Survey. (In Japanese. With English summary.) *Osaka Econ. Pap.,* March 1983, *32*(4), pp. 61–78.

Page, Talbot and MacLean, Douglas. Risk Conservatism and the Circumstances of Utility Theory. *Amer. J. Agr. Econ.,* December 1983, *65*(5), pp. 1021–26.

Perloff, Jeffrey M. and Rausser, Gordon C. The Effect of Asymmetrically Held Information and Market Power in Agricultural Markets. *Amer. J. Agr. Econ.,* May 1983, *65*(2), pp. 366–72.

Peters, Michael and Winter, Ralph A. Market Equilibrium and the Resolution of Uncertainty. *Can. J. Econ.,* August 1983, *16*(3), pp. 381–90.

Pethig, Rüdiger. On the Production and Distribution of Information. *Z. Nationalökon.,* 1983, *43*(4), pp. 383–403.

Plott, Charles R. and Agha, Gul. Intertemporal Speculation with a Random Demand in an Experimental Market. **In** *Tietz, R., ed.,* 1983, pp. 201–16.

Pope, Robin. The Pre-outcome Period and the Utility of Gambling. **In** *Stigum, B. P. and Wenstøp, F., eds.,* 1983, pp. 137–77.

Pratt, John W. Risk Aversion in the Small and in the Large. **In** *Archer, S. H. and D'Ambrosia, C. A.,* 1983, *1964,* pp. 46–60.

Reilly, Robert J. Some Evidence on the Reliability of Variance as a Proxy for Risk. *J. Risk Ins.,* December 1983, *50*(4), pp. 697–702.

Riordan, Michael H. Contracting in an Idiosyncratic Market. *Bell J. Econ. (See Rand J. Econ. after 4/85),* Autumn 1983, *14*(2), pp. 338–50.

Rouzaud, Catherine. Anticipations rationnelles et information révélée par les prix: une introduction. (Rational Expectations and Information Revealed by Prices: An Introduction. With English summary.) *Revue Écon.,* November 1983, *34*(6), pp. 1116–44.

Sappington, David. Limited Liability Contracts between Principal and Agent. *J. Econ. Theory,* February 1983, *29*(1), pp. 1–21.

Schneider, H. Mitbestimmung, unvollständige Information und Leistungsanreize: Überlegungen zu einer funktionsfähigen Unternehmensverfassung. (Codetermination, Incomplete Information, and Incentives. With English summary.) *Schweiz. Z. Volkswirtsch. Statist.,* September 1983, *119*(3), pp. 337–55.

von der Schulenberg, J.-Mattias Graf. A Note on Activity-Level and Uncertainty. *Z. Wirtschaft. Sozialwissen.,* 1983, *103*(5), pp. 485–96.

Schwartz, Alan and Wilde, Louis L. Warranty Markets and Public Policy. *Info. Econ. Policy,* 1983, *1*(1), pp. 55–67.

Shackle, George L. S. The Bounds of Unknowledge. **In** *Wiseman, J., ed.,* 1983, pp. 28–37.

Sheshinski, Eytan and Weiss, Yoram. Optimum Pricing Policy under Stochastic Inflation. *Rev. Econ. Stud.,* July 1983, *50*(3), pp. 513–29.

Stiglitz, Joseph E. and Weiss, Andrew. Alternative Approaches to Analyzing Markets with Asymmetric Information: Reply [The Theory of 'Screening,' Education, and the Distribution of Income]. *Amer. Econ. Rev.,* March 1983, *73*(1), pp. 246–49.

Stiglitz, Joseph E. and Weiss, Andrew. Incentive Effects of Terminations: Applications to the Credit and Labor Markets. *Amer. Econ. Rev.,* December 1983, *73*(5), pp. 912–27.

Stohs, Mark. 'Uncertainty' in Keynes' *General Theory:* A Rejoinder. *Hist. Polit. Econ.,* Spring 1983, *15*(1), pp. 87–91.

Streit, M. E. Heterogene Erwartungen, Preisbildung und Informationseffizienz auf spekulativen Märkten. (Heterogenous Expectations, Price Formation, and Informational Efficiency in Speculative Markets. With English summary.) *Z. ges. Staatswiss.,* March 1983, *139*(1), pp. 67–79.

Szpiro, George G. The Aggregation of Risk Aversions. *Math. Soc. Sci.,* August 1983, *5*(1), pp. 55–59.

Tannery, Frederick J. Search Effort and Unemployment Insurance Reconsidered. *J. Human Res.,* Summer 1983, *18*(3), pp. 432–40. **[G: U.S.]**

Tapiero, Charles S. and Desplas, Maurice. Optimal Location of Two Competing Facilities under Uncertainty. **In** *Thisse, J.-F. and Zoller, H. G., eds.,* 1983, pp. 315–30.

Taylor, John B. Equilibrium Theory with Learning and Disparate Expectations: Some Issues and Methods: Comment. **In** *Frydman, R. and Phelps, E. S., eds.,* 1983, pp. 198–202.

Tietz, Reinhard. Aspiration-oriented Decision Making—In Memoriam Heinz Sauermann. **In** *Tietz, R., ed.,* 1983, pp. 1–7.

Tisdell, Clem A. Allocation of Public Funds to Projects Reducing Risk with Special Reference to Medical Research. *Rivista Int. Sci. Econ. Com.*, June 1983, *30*(6), pp. 555–60.

Toland, Anne and O'Neill, Patrick. A Test of Prospect Theory. *J. Econ. Behav. Organ.*, March 1983, *4*(1), pp. 53–56.

Townsend, Robert M. Equilibrium Theory with Learning and Disparate Expectations: Some Issues and Methods. **In** *Frydman, R. and Phelps, E. S., eds.*, 1983, pp. 169–98.

Trueman, Brett. Optimality of the Disclosure of Private Information in a Production-Exchange Economy. *J. Finance,* June 1983, *38*(3), pp. 913–24.

Turnbull, S. M. Additional Aspects of Rational Insurance Purchasing. *J. Bus.*, April 1983, *56*(2), pp. 217–29.

Verrecchia, Robert E. Discretionary Disclosure. *J. Acc. Econ.*, December 1983, *5*(3), pp. 179–94.

Voge, Jean. The Political Economics of Complexity: From the Information Economy to the 'Complexity' Economy. *Info. Econ. Policy,* 1983, *1*(2), pp. 97–114.

Wang, Leonard F. S. Price Constraints, Forward Markets and the Competitive Firm under Price Uncertainty. *Bull. Econ. Res.*, May 1983, *35*(1), pp. 47–54.

Wiggins, Steven N. and Lane, W. J. Quality Uncertainty, Search, and Advertising. *Amer. Econ. Rev.*, December 1983, *73*(5), pp. 881–94.

Wold, Herman. Utility Analysis from the Point of View of Model Building. **In** *Stigum, B. P. and Wenstøp, F., eds.*, 1983, pp. 87–93.

Wolinsky, Asher. Retail Trade Concentration Due to Consumers' Imperfect Information. *Bell J. Econ. (See Rand J. Econ. after 4/85)*, Spring 1983, *14*(1), pp. 275–82.

Yabushita, Shiro. Theory of Screening and the Behavior of the Firm: Comment. *Amer. Econ. Rev.*, March 1983, *73*(1), pp. 242–45.

Yilmaz, Mustafa R. The Use of Risk and Return Models for Multiattribute Decisions with Decomposable Utilities. *J. Finan. Quant. Anal.*, September 1983, *18*(3), pp. 279–85.

Ziemer, Rod F. Tolerance Limits and Expected Utility Analysis. *Amer. J. Agr. Econ.*, August 1983, *65*(3), pp. 611–14.

Zweifel, Peter. Identifizierung kommt vor Optimierung: Eine Kritik neuerer Entwicklungen in der mikroökonomischen Theorie. (Identification Precedes Optimization: A Critique of Recent Developments in Microeconomics. With English summary.) *Z. Wirtschaft. Sozialwissen.*, 1983, *103*(1), pp. 1–26.

0262 Game Theory and Bargaining Theory

Albers, Wulf and Albers, Gisela. Prominence and Aspiration Adjustment in Location Games. **In** *Tietz, R., ed.*, 1983, pp. 243–58.

Aoki, Masahiko. Managerialism Revisited in the Light of Bargaining-Game Theory. *Int. J. Ind. Organ.*, 1983, *1*(1), pp. 1–21.

Armbruster, Walter and Böge, Werner. Efficient, Anonymous, and Neutral Group Decision Procedures. *Econometrica*, September 1983, *51*(5), pp. 1389–405.

Aumann, R. J.; Kurz, Mordecai and Neyman, Abraham. Voting for Public Goods. *Rev. Econ. Stud.*, October 1983, *50*(4), pp. 677–93.

Auray, Jean Paul and Duru, Gérard. Sur un processus de formation des coalitions. (With English summary.) *Écon. Appl.*, 1983, *36*(4), pp. 649–56.

Bartos, Otomar J.; Tietz, Reinhard and McLean, Carolyn. Toughness and Fairness in Negotiation. **In** *Tietz, R., ed.*, 1983, pp. 35–51.

Bennett, Elaine. Characterization Results for Aspirations in Games with Sidepayments. *Math. Soc. Sci.*, July 1983, *4*(3), pp. 229–41.

Bigoness, William J. and Grigsby, David W. The Effects of Need for Achievement and Alternative Forms of Arbitration upon Bargaining Behavior. **In** *Tietz, R., ed.*, 1983, pp. 122–35.

Brandstätter, Hermann; Kette, Gerhard and Sageder, Josef. Expectations, Attributions, and Behavior in Bargaining with Liked and Disliked Partners. **In** *Tietz, R., ed.*, 1983, pp. 136–52.

Buiter, Willem H. Expectations and Control Theory. *Écon. Appl.*, 1983, *36*(1), pp. 129–56.

Cheng, Leonard and Hart, David. The Local Stability of an Open-Loop Nash Equilibrium in a Finite Horizon Differential Game. *J. Math. Econ.*, October 1983, *12*(2), pp. 139–47.

Chichilnisky, Graciela. Social Choice and Game Theory: Recent Results with a Topological Approach. **In** *Pattanaik, P. K. and Salles, M., eds.*, 1983, pp. 79–102.

Cole, Steven G. and Nail, Paul. Social Learning vs. Direct Experience as Determinants of Aspiration Level and Bargaining Behavior. **In** *Tietz, R., ed.*, 1983, pp. 231–42.

Coleman, James S. Recontracting, Trustworthiness, and the Stability of Vote Exchanges. *Public Choice,* 1983, *40*(1), pp. 89–94.

Crössmann, H. Jürgen and Tietz, Reinhard. Market Behavior Based on Aspiration Levels. **In** *Tietz, R., ed.*, 1983, pp. 170–85.

Crott, Helmut W.; Luhr, Rudolf and Rombach, Cornelia. The Effects of the Level of Aspiration and Experience in Three-person Bargaining Games. **In** *Tietz, R., ed.*, 1983, pp. 276–90.

Druckman, Daniel; Karis, Demetrios and Donchin, Emanuel. Information-processing in Bargaining: Reactions to an Opponent's Shift in Concession Strategy. **In** *Tietz, R., ed.*, 1983, pp. 153–69.

Engelbrecht-Wiggans, Richard. An Introduction to the Theory of Bidding for a Single Object. **In** *Engelbrecht-Wiggans, R.; Shubik, M. and Stark, R. M., eds.*, 1983, pp. 53–103.

Forman, Robin and Laing, James D. Game-Theoretic Expectations, Interest Groups, and Salient Majorities in Committees. **In** *Tietz, R., ed.*, 1983, pp. 321–36.

Friedman, James W. Limit Price Entry Prevention When Complete Information Is Lacking. *J. Econ. Dynam. Control,* May 1983, *5*(2/3), pp. 187–99.

Fudenberg, Drew and Levine, David K. Subgame-Perfect Equilibria of Finite- and Infinite-Horizon Games. *J. Econ. Theory,* December 1983, *31*(2), pp. 251–68.

Fudenberg, Drew and Tirole, Jean. Sequential Bargaining with Incomplete Information. *Rev. Econ. Stud.*, April 1983, *50*(2), pp. 221–47.

Gardner, Roy. λ-transfer Value and Fixed-Price Equilibrium in Two-Sided Markets. **In** *Pattanaik, P. K. and Salles, M., eds.*, 1983, pp. 301–23.

Green, Jerry R. and Honkapohja, Seppo. Bilateral Contracts. *J. Math. Econ.*, April 1983, *11*(2), pp. 171–87.

Güth, Werner and Schwarze, Bernd. Auctioning Strategic Roles to Observe Aspiration Levels for Conflict Situations. **In** *Tietz, R., ed.*, 1983, pp. 217–30.

Guttman, Joel M. and Miller, Michael. Endogenous Conjectural Variations in Oligopoly. *J. Econ. Behav. Organ.*, June–September 1983, *4*(2–3), pp. 249–64.

Haas, Hansjorg. Conflict, Cooperation and Social Preference Functions. **In** *Gruber, J., ed.*, 1983, pp. 148–69. **[G: U.S.]**

Harnett, Donald L. and Wall, James A., Jr. Aspiration/Competitive Effects on the Mediation of Bargaining. **In** *Tietz, R., ed.*, 1983, pp. 8–21.

Harsanyi, John C. Use of Subjective Probabilities in Game Theory. **In** *Stigum, B. P. and Wenstøp, F., eds.*, 1983, pp. 297–310.

Hart, Sergiu and Kurz, Mordecai. Endogenous Formation of Coalitions. *Econometrica*, July 1983, *51*(4), pp. 1047–64.

Holler, Manfred J. and Packel, Edward W. Power, Luck and the Right Index. *Z. Nationalökon.*, 1983, *43*(1), pp. 21–29.

Hughes Hallett, A. J. and Brandsma, Andries S. How Effective Could Sanctions against the Soviet Union Be? *Weltwirtsch. Arch.*, 1983, *119*(3), pp. 498–522. **[G: U.S.S.R.]**

Ichiishi, Tatsuro and Quinzii, Martine. Decentralization for the Core of a Production Economy with Increasing Returns. *Int. Econ. Rev.*, June 1983, *24*(2), pp. 397–412.

Ichiishi, Tatsuro and Schäffer, Juan Jorge. The Topological Core of a Game Without Sidepayments. *Econ. Stud. Quart.*, April 1983, *34*(1), pp. 1–8.

Imai, Haruo. Individual Monotonicity and Lexicographic Maxmin Solution. *Econometrica*, March 1983, *51*(2), pp. 389–401.

Imai, Haruo. Voting, Bargaining, and Factor Income Distribution. *J. Math. Econ.*, July 1983, *11*(3), pp. 211–33.

Isard, Walter and Smith, Christine. A Dynamical Systems Approach to Learning Processes in Conflict Mediation and Interaction. **In** *Isard, W. and Nagao, Y., eds.*, 1983, pp. 11–31.

Johansen, Leif. Mechanistic and Organistic Analogies in Economics: The Place of Game Theory: Some Notes on H. Thoben's Article. *Kyklos*, 1983, *36*(2), pp. 304–07.

Jordan, J. S. Acceptable versus Straightforward Game Forms: An Example. *Rev. Econ. Stud.*, April 1983, *50*(2), pp. 369–73.

Karp, Larry S. and McCalla, Alex F. Dynamic Games and International Trade: An Application to the World Corn Market. *Amer. J. Agr. Econ.*, November 1983, *65*(4), pp. 641–50.

Kim, Ki Hang and Roush, Fred W. A Dynamic Solution in *N*-Person Cooperative Game Theory. *Math. Soc. Sci.*, October 1983, *6*(1), pp. 49–63.

Kim, Ki Hang and Roush, Fred W. Social Systems Analysis II. *Math. Soc. Sci.*, April 1983, *4*(2), pp. 87–102.

Komorita, Samuel; Lange, Rense and Hamilton, Thomas. The Effects of Level of Aspiration in Coalition Bargaining. **In** *Tietz, R., ed.*, 1983, pp. 291–305.

de Koster, R., et al. Risk Sensitivity, Independence of Irrelevant Alternatives and Continuity of Bargaining Solutions. *Math. Soc. Sci.*, July 1983, *4*(3), pp. 295–300.

Kravitz, David A. and Dobson, Mickie. Motivations and Cognitions in Coalition Formation. **In** *Tietz, R., ed.*, 1983, pp. 306–20.

Kwon, Young K. and Yu, P. L. Conflict Dissolution by Reframing Game Payoffs: Introduction. **In** *Hansen, P., ed.*, 1983, pp. 214–20.

Laroque, Guy and Rochet, Jean-Charles. Myopic versus Intertemporal Manipulation in Decentralized Planning Procedures. *Rev. Econ. Stud.*, January 1983, *50*(1), pp. 187–95.

Leung, Yee. A Value-based Approach to Conflict Resolution Involving Multiple Objectives and Multiple Decision-making Units. **In** *Isard, W. and Nagao, Y., eds.*, 1983, pp. 55–71.

Maoz, Ilan. The Cournot Duopoly Model Reconsidered in the Presence of Costly Communication and Enforcement Agreements. *J. Econ. Behav. Organ.*, December 1983, *4*(4), pp. 395–410.

McKelvey, Richard D. and Ordeshook, Peter C. Some Experimental Results That Fail to Support the Competitive Solution. *Public Choice*, 1983, *40*(3), pp. 281–91.

Midgaard, Knut. Bargaining and Rationality: A Discussion of Zeuthen's Principle and Some Other Decision Rules. **In** *Stigum, B. P. and Wenstøp, F., eds.*, 1983, pp. 311–25.

Mueller, Guenter F. and Galinat, Withold H. Bargaining Efficiency in Real-Life Buyer–Seller-Interaction: A Fieldexperiment. **In** *Tietz, R., ed.*, 1983, pp. 80–90.

Muto, Shigeo. Sequential Auctions on Böhm–Bawerk's Horse Market. *Math. Soc. Sci.*, April 1983, *4*(2), pp. 117–30.

Myerson, Roger B. and Satterthwaite, Mark A. Efficient Mechanisms for Bilateral Trading. *J. Econ. Theory*, April 1983, *29*(2), pp. 265–81.

Nagao, Yoshimi; Kuroda, Katsuhiko and Wakai, Ikujiro. Decisionmaking under Conflict in Project Evaluation. **In** *Isard, W. and Nagao, Y., eds.*, 1983, pp. 73–90.

Neilsen, Lars Tyge. Ordinal Interpersonal Comparisons in Bargaining. *Econometrica*, January 1983, *51*(1), pp. 219–21.

Paelinck, J. H. P. and Vossen, P. H. Axiomatics of Conflict Analysis. **In** *Isard, W. and Nagao, Y., eds.*, 1983, pp. 33–51.

Pohjola, Matti. Nash and Stackelberg Solutions in a Differential Game Model of Capitalism. *J. Econ. Dynam. Control*, September 1983, *6*(1/2), pp. 173–86.

Porter, Robert H. Optimal Cartel Trigger Price Strategies. *J. Econ. Theory*, April 1983, *29*(2), pp. 313–38.

Pruitt, Dean G., et al. Incentives for Cooperation in Integrative Bargaining. **In** *Tietz, R., ed.*, 1983,

pp. 22–34.

Rapoport, Amnon and Kahan, James P. Standards of Fairness in 3-quota, 4-person Games. In *Tietz, R., ed.*, 1983, pp. 337–51.

Roth, Alvin E. and Murnighan, J. Keith. Information and Aspirations in Two-person Bargaining. In *Tietz, R., ed.*, 1983, pp. 91–103.

Roth, Alvin E. and Schoumaker, Francoise. Expectations and Reputations in Bargaining: An Experimental Study. *Amer. Econ. Rev.*, June 1983, *73*(3), pp. 362–72.

Samuelson, William F. Competitive Bidding for Defense Contracts. In *Engelbrecht-Wiggans, R.; Shubik, M. and Stark, R. M., eds.*, 1983, pp. 389–419.

Saraydar, Edward. Bargaining Power, Dissimulation, and the Coase Theorem. *Z. ges. Staatswiss.*, December 1983, *139*(4), pp. 599–611.

Schleicher, Heinz. A Value for a Class of Cooperative L-Games with Side Payments. *Écon. Appl.*, 1983, *36*(4), pp. 657–72.

Scholz, Roland W.; Fleischer, Andreas and Bentrup, Andreas. Aspiration Forming and Predictions Based on Aspiration Levels Compared between Professional and Nonprofessional Bargainers. In *Tietz, R., ed.*, 1983, pp. 104–21.

Schotter, Andrew. Why Take a Game Theoretical Approach to Economics? Institutions, Economics and Game Theory. *Écon. Appl.*, 1983, *36*(4), pp. 673–95.

Selten, Reinhard. Equal Division Payoff Bounds for 3-Person Characteristic Function Experiments. In *Tietz, R., ed.*, 1983, pp. 265–75.

Selten, Reinhard. Evolutionary Stability in Extensive Two-Person Games. *Math. Soc. Sci.*, September 1983, *5*(3), pp. 269–363.

Selten, Reinhard and Krischker, Wilhelm. Comparison of Two Theories for Characteristic Function Experiments. In *Tietz, R., ed.*, 1983, pp. 259–64.

Selten, Reinhard and Leopold, Ulrike. Equilibrium Point Selection in a Bargaining Situation with Opportunity Costs. *Écon. Appl.*, 1983, *36*(4), pp. 611–48.

Shubik, Martin. On Auctions, Bidding, and Contracting. In *Engelbrecht-Wiggans, R.; Shubik, M. and Stark, R. M., eds.*, 1983, pp. 3–31.

Shubik, Martin and Wooders, Myrna Holtz. Approximate Cores of Replica Games and Economies. Part II: Set-Up Costs and Firm Formation in Coalition Production Economies. *Math. Soc. Sci.*, December 1983, *6*(3), pp. 285–306.

Shubik, Martin and Wooders, Myrna Holtz. Approximate Cores of Replica Games and Economies. Part I: Replica Games, Externalities, and Approximate Cores. *Math. Soc. Sci.*, October 1983, *6*(1), pp. 27–48.

Sobel, Joel and Takahashi, Ichiro. A Multistage Model of Bargaining. *Rev. Econ. Stud.*, July 1983, *50*(3), pp. 411–26.

Spencer, Barbara J. and Brander, James A. International R & D Rivalry and Industrial Strategy. *Rev. Econ. Stud.*, October 1983, *50*(4), pp. 707–22.

Stoecker, Rolf. Das erlernte Schlussverhalten—eine experimentelle Untersuchung. (Behavior of Experienced Subjects at the End of Finite Supergames. With English summary.) *Z. ges. Staatswiss.*, March 1983, *139*(1), pp. 100–121.

Thomson, William. Equity in Exchange Economies. *J. Econ. Theory*, April 1983, *29*(2), pp. 217–44.

Thomson, William and Lensberg, Terje. Guarantee Structures for Problems of Fair Division. *Math. Soc. Sci.*, July 1983, *4*(3), pp. 205–18.

Tietz, Reinhard and Bartos, Otomar J. Balancing of Aspiration Levels as Fairness Principle in Negotiations. In *Tietz, R., ed.*, 1983, pp. 52–66.

Tirole, Jean. Jeux dynamiques: un guide de l'utilisateur. (With English summary.) *Revue Écon. Polit.*, July–August 1983, *93*(4), pp. 551–75.

Ville, Jean A. Théorie des jeux, dualité, développement. (With English summary.) *Écon. Appl.*, 1983, *36*(4), pp. 593–609.

Wagner, R. Harrison. The Theory of Games and the Problem of International Cooperation. *Amer. Polit. Sci. Rev.*, June 1983, *77*(2), pp. 330–46.

Weintraub, E. Roy. On the Existence of a Competitive Equilibrium: 1930–1954. *J. Econ. Lit.*, March 1983, *21*(1), pp. 1–39.

Werner, Thomas and Tietz, Reinhard. The Search Process in Bilateral Negotiations. In *Tietz, R., ed.*, 1983, pp. 67–79.

Wooders, Myrna Holtz. The Epsilon Core of a Large Replica Game. *J. Math. Econ.*, July 1983, *11*(3), pp. 277–300.

027 Economics of Centrally Planned Economies

0270 Economics of Centrally Planned Economies

Bulgaru, M. Consideration Concerning the National Economy Potential Reproduction. *Econ. Computat. Cybern. Stud. Res.*, 1983, *18*(3), pp. 23–33.

Chander, Parkash. On the Informational Size of Message Spaces for Efficient Resource Allocation Processes. *Econometrica*, July 1983, *51*(4), pp. 919–38.

Christensen, Peer Møller. The Shanghai School and Its Rejection. In *Feuchtwang, S. and Hussain, A., eds.*, 1983, pp. 74–90. **[G: China]**

Clausen, Søren. Chinese Economic Debates after Mao and the Crisis of Official Marxism. In *Feuchtwang, S. and Hussain, A., eds.*, 1983, pp. 53–73. **[G: China]**

Conn, David. Comparative Economic Systems Theory: Progress and Prospects. *ACES Bull. (See Comp. Econ. Stud. after 8/85)*, Summer 1983, *25*(2), pp. 61–80.

Desai, Padma and Bhagwati, Jagdish N. Three Alternative Concepts of Foreign Exchange Difficulties in Centrally Planned Economies. In *Bhagwati, J. N., Vol. 2*, 1983, *1979*, pp. 536–46.

Drabek, Zdenek. Changes in Relative World Prices and Their Transmission into Economies Protected by Foreign Trade Monopoly. *Econ. Int.*, February 1983, *36*(1), pp. 20–34. **[G: CMEA]**

Ellman, Michael. Changing Views on Central Economic Planning: 1958–1983. *ACES Bull. (See Comp. Econ. Stud. after 8/85)*, Spring 1983, *25*(1), pp. 11–34. **[G: U.S.S.R.]**

Ericson, Richard E. A Difficulty with the "Command" Allocation Mechanism. *J. Econ. Theory*, October 1983, *31*(1), pp. 1–26.

Focşăneanu, Gr. and Stroe, R. Cybernetic Modelling of Intercorrelations in Territorial Selfmanagement. *Econ. Computat. Cybern. Stud. Res.*, 1983, *18*(3), pp. 47–61. **[G: Romania]**

Fröhlich, Gerhard. A Theoretical Problem of Foreign Trade Effectiveness. *Soviet E. Europ. Foreign Trade,* Fall 1983, *19*(3), pp. 3–31. **[G: CMEA; OECD]**

Hewett, Edward A. Research on East European Economies: The Last Quarter Century. *ACES Bull. (See Comp. Econ. Stud. after 8/85),* Summer 1983, *25*(2), pp. 1–21. **[G: E. Europe]**

Hüttl, Antónia; Losonczy, I. and Örszigety, G. The Financial Regulator Model. *Matekon,* Summer 1983, *19*(4), pp. 3–20. **[G: Hungary]**

Iasin, E. G. Distributional Relations in the Structure of the Economic Mechanism. *Matekon,* Winter 1983–84, *20*(2), pp. 24–54.

Khachaturov, Tigran S. Once Again on the Effectiveness of Capital Investments. *Prob. Econ.*, November 1983, *26*(7), pp. 3–23. **[G: U.S.S.R.]**

Koriagin, A. Socialist Reproduction and the Comparison of Labor Inputs. *Prob. Econ.*, July 1983, *26*(3), pp. 53–71. **[G: U.S.S.R.]**

Kozma, Ferenc. Unkarin talouspolitiikka ja taloudenohjaus: vaatimuksia, periaatteita ja tehtäviä. (The Hungarian Economic Policy and Economic Management: Requirements, Principles, Tasks. With English summary.) *Kansant. Aikak.*, 1983, *79*(4), pp. 394–401. **[G: Hungary]**

Lerner, Abba P. Economic Theory and Socialist Economy: A Rejoinder. **In** *Lerner, A. P.*, 1983, *1935,* pp. 143–45.

Lerner, Abba P. Economic Theory and Socialist Economy. **In** *Lerner, A. P.*, 1983, *1934,* pp. 131–41.

McFarlane, Bruce. Political Economy of Class Struggle and Economic Growth in China, 1950–1982. *World Devel.*, August 1983, *11*(8), pp. 659–72. **[G: China]**

Milenkovitch, Deborah Duff. Self Management and Thirty Years of Yugoslav Experience. *ACES Bull. (See Comp. Econ. Stud. after 8/85),* Fall 1983, *25*(3), pp. 1–26. **[G: Yugoslavia]**

Niculescu-Mizil, E. Cybernetic Peculiarities of the Development of Social-Economical Systems. *Econ. Computat. Cybern. Stud. Res.*, 1983, *18*(4), pp. 5–14. **[G: Romania]**

Petrakov, N. Ia. On Reflecting Relative Planned Inputs in the Price System. *Matekon,* Fall 1983, *20*(1), pp. 3–28. **[G: U.S.S.R.]**

Podkaminer, Leon. Estimates of the Disequilibria in Poland's Consumer Markets (1965–1978). **In** *Kelley, A. C.; Sanderson, W. C. and Williamson, J. G., eds.*, 1983, pp. 167–84. **[G: Poland; Italy; Ireland]**

Subotskii, Iu. V. Branch Production and Departmental Disconnectedness. *Prob. Econ.*, February 1983, *25*(10), pp. 71–91. **[G: U.S.S.R.]**

Tardos, Márton. Enterprise Supply and the Market. *Eastern Europ. Econ.*, Spring–Summer 1983, *21*(3–4), pp. 8–25. **[G: Hungary]**

Wang, Linsheng. On the Role of Foreign Trade under Socialism. *Chinese Econ. Stud.*, Spring 1983, *16*(3), pp. 48–65. **[G: U.S.S.R.; China]**

Wiles, Peter. Methodology: In Praise of Ourselves. *ACES Bull. (See Comp. Econ. Stud. after 8/85),* Spring 1983, *25*(1), pp. 1–10. **[G: U.S.S.R.]**

Yue, Wei. Production, Distribution, and Allocation of the National Economy. *Chinese Econ. Stud.*, Winter 1982/83, *16*(2), pp. 3–19. **[G: China]**

Zakharov, S. N. and Shagalov, G. L. Methods for Determining the Efficiency of Foreign Economic Relations. *Matekon,* Fall 1983, *20*(1), pp. 57–77.

Zalai, Ernö. A Nonlinear Multisectoral Model for Hungary: General Equilibrium versus Optimal Planning Approaches. **In** *Kelley, A. C.; Sanderson, W. C. and Williamson, J. G., eds.*, 1983, pp. 185–222. **[G: Hungary]**

Zalai, Ernö. Adaptability of Nonlinear Equilibrium Models to Central Planning. *Acta Oecon.*, 1983, *30*(3–4), pp. 433–45.

0271 Microeconomic Theory

Arrow, Kenneth J. Team Theory and Decentralized Resource Allocation: An Example. **In** *[Erlich, A.],* 1983, pp. 63–76.

Bergson, Abram. Entrepreneurship under Labor Participation: The Yugoslav Case. **In** *Ronen, J., ed.*, 1983, pp. 177–233. **[G: Yugoslavia]**

Bonin, John P. Innovation in a Labor-Managed Firm: A Membership Perspective. *J. Ind. Econ.*, March 1983, *31*(3), pp. 313–29.

Desai, Padma and Martin, Ricardo. Measuring Resource-Allocational Efficiency in Centrally Planned Economies: A Theoretical Analysis. **In** *[Erlich, A.],* 1983, pp. 91–109.

Ericson, Richard E. On an Allocative Role of the Soviet Second Economy. **In** *[Erlich, A.],* 1983, pp. 110–32. **[G: U.S.S.R.]**

Feltenstein, Andrew. The Allocation of Badly Needed Goods to Low-Income Consumers: A System of Central Planning without Redistributive Taxation. *J. Compar. Econ.*, March 1983, *7*(1), pp. 52–70.

Fukuda, Wataru. On the Output and Employment Decisions of an Egalitarian Labor-managed Firm. *Kobe Univ. Econ.*, 1983, (29), pp. 51–67.

Fusfeld, Daniel R. Labor-Managed and Participatory Firms: A Review Article. *J. Econ. Issues,* September 1983, *17*(3), pp. 769–89.

Granick, David. Institutional Innovation and Economic Management: The Soviet Incentive System, 1921 to the Present. **In** *Guroff, G. and Carstensen, F. V., eds.*, 1983, pp. 223–57. **[G: U.S.S.R.]**

Groves, Theodore. The Usefulness of Demand Forecasts for Team Resource Allocation in a Dynamic Environment. *Rev. Econ. Stud.*, July 1983, *50*(3), pp. 555–71.

Gui, Benedetto. Struttura finanziaria e "Moral Risk" in imprese non quotate nel mercato azionario. (Financial Structure and Moral Risk When Firms' Shares Are Not Traded. With English summary.) *Rivista Int. Sci. Econ. Com.*, February 1983, *30*(2), pp. 125–42.

Hannesson, Rögnvaldur. A Note on Socially Optimal versus Monopolistic Exploitation of a Renewable Resource. *Z. Nationalökon.*, 1983, *43*(1), pp. 63–70.

Hartulari, Carmen and Popescu, Angela. A Cybernetic Mode for Solving the Assembly Line-Balancing Problem. *Econ. Computat. Cybern. Stud. Res.*, 1983, *18*(1), pp. 43–50.

Hawawini, Gabriel A. and Michel, Pierre A. The Effect of Production Uncertainty on the Labor-Managed Firm. *J. Compar. Econ.*, March 1983, *7*(1), pp. 25–42.

Hill, Martyn and Waterson, Michael. Labor-Managed Cournot Oligopoly and Industry Output. *J. Compar. Econ.*, March 1983, *7*(1), pp. 43–51.

Keren, Michael; Miller, Jeffrey and Thornton, James R. The Ratchet: A Dynamic Managerial Incentive Model of the Soviet Enterprise. *J. Compar. Econ.*, December 1983, *7*(4), pp. 347–67. **[G: U.S.S.R.]**

Laffont, Jean-Jacques and Moreaux, Michel. The Nonexistence of a Free Entry Cournot Equilibrium in Labor-Managed Economies. *Econometrica*, March 1983, *51*(2), pp. 455–62.

Lipovetskii, S. S. Variational Analysis of the Breakdown of an Increase between Factors. *Matekon*, Fall 1983, *20*(1), pp. 93–104.

Martynov, G. V. and Pitelin, A. K. A Two-Stage System for Optimizing the Development and Location of a Multibranch Complex Which Uses Variants for the Branch Models. *Matekon*, Winter 1983–84, *20*(2), pp. 55–73.

de Meza, David. A Growth Model for a Tenured-Labor-Managed Firm: Comment. *Quart. J. Econ.*, August 1983, *98*(3), pp. 539–42.

Milanovic, Branko. The Investment Behaviour of the Labour-Managed Firm: A Property-Rights Approach. *Econ. Anal. Worker's Manage.*, 1983, *17*(4), pp. 327–40. **[G: Yugoslavia]**

Ohlson, James A. Price–Earnings Ratios and Earnings Capitalization under Uncertainty. *J. Acc. Res.*, Spring 1983, *21*(1), pp. 141–54.

Pairault, Thierry. Chinese Market Mechanism: A Controversial Debate. *World Devel.*, August 1983, *11*(8), pp. 639–45. **[G: China]**

Prašnikar, Janez. The Role of the Enterprise in the Self-Managed Organization of Labor. *Eastern Europ. Econ.*, Winter 1983–84, *22*(2), pp. 44–77. **[G: Yugoslavia]**

Prašnikar, Janez. The Yugoslav Self-Managed Firm and Its Behavior. *Eastern Europ. Econ.*, Winter 1983–84, *22*(2), pp. 3–43. **[G: Yugoslavia]**

Pryor, Frederic L. The Economics of Production Cooperatives: A Reader's Guide. *Ann. Pub. Co-op. Econ.*, April–June 1983, *54*(2), pp. 133–72.

Putterman, Louis. Incentives and the Kibbutz: Toward an Economics of Communal Work Motivation. *Z. Nationalökon.*, 1983, *43*(2), pp. 157–88.

Sapir, André. A Growth Model for a Tenured-Labor-Managed Firm: Reply. *Quart. J. Econ.*, August 1983, *98*(3), pp. 543.

Sertel, Murat R. Technological Preferences of Capitalist and Workers' Enterprises. *Econ. Anal. Worker's Manage.*, 1983, *17*(3), pp. 273–77.

Steinherr, Alfred. The Labour-managed Economy: A Survey of the Economics Literature. **In** *Kennedy, L., ed.*, 1983, *1978*, pp. 123–50.

Stephen, Frank H. Review Article: The Economics of Labour-Managed Firms. *J. Econ. Stud.*, 1983, *10*(2), pp. 66–71.

Stoica, M. Stochastic Splitors Used in Scheduling. *Econ. Computat. Cybern. Stud. Res.*, 1983, *18*(1), pp. 63–71.

Toms, Miroslav. Disequilibrium, Price System and Value. *Czech. Econ. Pap.*, 1983, (21), pp. 31–54.

Travaglini, Guido. Jugoslavia: un miracolo economico mancato, ovvero un paradosso nella teoria della crescita. (Yugoslavia: The End of an Economic Miracle: A Paradox in the Theory of Growth. With English summary.) *Giorn. Econ.*, September–October 1983, *42*(9–10), pp. 667–78. **[G: Yugoslavia]**

Wilhelm, J. From the Achieved Level: A Microeconomic Analysis. *ACES Bull. (See Comp. Econ. Stud. after 8/85)*, Spring 1983, *25*(1), pp. 75–88. **[G: U.S.S.R.]**

Yoshikawa, Tomomichi. Some Additional Results on the New Soviet Incentive Model and Its Generalization. *Econ. Stud. Quart.*, December 1983, *34*(3), pp. 276–79. **[G: U.S.S.R.]**

0272 Macroeconomic Theory

Ancot, J. P. and Hughes Hallett, A. J. The Determination of Collective Preferences in Economic Decision Models: With an Application to Soviet Economic Policy. **In** *Gruber, J., ed.*, 1983, pp. 263–304. **[G: U.S.S.R.]**

Brabec, František. Method for the Transition from Retrospective Analyses of the National Economy to Concepts of Future Development. *Czech. Econ. Pap.*, 1983, (21), pp. 19–29.

Bródy, András. About Investment Cycles and Their Attenuation. *Acta Oecon.*, 1983, *31*(1–2), pp. 37–51. **[G: Hungary]**

Bulgaru, M. Cybernetic Systems and Monetary Balance. *Econ. Computat. Cybern. Stud. Res.*, 1983, *18*(2), pp. 5–17.

Chen, Fu-Sen and Cheung, Tow. On Some Problems of Modelling Chinese Economic Growth. **In** *Youngson, A. J., ed.*, 1983, pp. 226–81. **[G: China]**

Ellman, Michael. Monetarism and the State Socialist World. **In** *Jansen, K., ed.*, 1983, pp. 96–109. **[G: CMEA]**

Hodgson, Geoffrey M. Worker Participation and Macroeconomic Efficiency. *J. Post Keynesian Econ.*, Winter 1982–83, *5*(2), pp. 266–75.

Hrnčíř, Miroslav. External Balance in Planned Economy. *Czech. Econ. Pap.*, 1983, (21), pp. 71–87. **[G: Czechoslovakia]**

Kazakevich, G. D. Experience in Developing and Using a Nonlinear Econometric Model of the Economy of the RSFSR. *Matekon*, Summer 1983, *19*(4), pp. 62–78. **[G: U.S.S.R.]**

Kornai, János and Weibull, Jörgen W. Paternalism, Buyers' and Sellers' Market. *Math. Soc. Sci.*, November 1983, *6*(2), pp. 153–69.

Krasovskii, V. Intensification of the Economy and the Time Factor. *Prob. Econ.*, February 1983, *25*(10), pp. 34–50. **[G: U.S.S.R.]**

Liu, Guoguang. Some Issues Concerning the National Economic Overall Balance. *Chinese Econ. Stud.*, Winter 1982/83, *16*(2), pp. 85–106. **[G: China]**

Livshits, V. N. and Tarakanova, I. A. On the Effect of Changes in Resource Costs on Branch Development Strategy. *Matekon*, Summer 1983, *19*(4),

pp. 79–95.

Maksimovic, Ivan. Social Ownership in the Yugoslav Self-Management System. *Econ. Anal. Worker's Manage.*, 1983, *17*(2), pp. 155–75. **[G: Yugoslavia]**

Mănescu, Manea. The National Wealth System. *Econ. Computat. Cybern. Stud. Res.*, 1983, *18*(1), pp. 3–13.

Melkov, A. The Effectiveness of Bank Credit. *Prob. Econ.*, January 1983, *25*(9), pp. 71–87. **[G: U.S.S.R.]**

Nasilowski, Mieczyslaw. Accumulation in a Socialist Economy: The Case of Poland. **In** *Modigliani, F. and Hemming, R., eds.*, 1983, pp. 235–54. **[G: Poland]**

Pick, Miloš. Criteria of Effectiveness of Structural Changes of Production. *Czech. Econ. Pap.*, 1983, (21), pp. 55–69. **[G: Czechoslovakia]**

Portes, Richard. Central Planning and Monetarism: Fellow Travelers? **In** *[Erlich, A.]*, 1983, pp. 149–65.

Rutgaizer, V.; Bokov, A. and Orlov, V. Forecasting the Population's Monetary Savings. *Prob. Econ.*, January 1983, *25*(9), pp. 52–70. **[G: U.S.S.R.; E. Germany]**

Soós, Károly Attila. The Problem of Time Lags in the Short-Term Control of Macroeconomic Processes. *Acta Oecon.*, 1983, *30*(3–4), pp. 369–79. **[G: Hungary]**

Sorokin, G. Patterns of Socialist Intensification. *Prob. Econ.*, July 1983, *26*(3), pp. 3–21. **[G: U.S.S.R.]**

Stroe, R. National Wealth in National-Territorial Connexion. *Econ. Computat. Cybern. Stud. Res.*, 1983, *18*(1), pp. 15–22.

Tyson, Laura D'Andrea. Investment Allocation: A Comparison of the Reform Experiences of Hungary and Yugoslavia. *J. Compar. Econ.*, September 1983, *7*(3), pp. 288–303. **[G: Hungary; Yugoslavia]**

Wang, Da'an. A Comprehensive Balance Should Mean Overall Balance in the Process of Social Reproduction. *Chinese Econ. Stud.*, Winter 1982/83, *16*(2), pp. 51–66. **[G: China]**

Xue, Muqiao. Readjust the National Economy and Strike an Overall Balance. *Chinese Econ. Stud.*, Winter 1982/83, *16*(2), pp. 67–84. **[G: China]**

030 History of Thought; Methodology

031 History of Economic Thought

0310 General

Barucci, Piero. Economic Theory and Economic Policy in Historical Evolution of Economic Thought. *Rivista Polit. Econ.*, Supplement Dec. 1983, *73*(12), pp. 3–22.

Caravale, Giovanni. The Crisis in Economic Theories: Introduction. **In** *Caravale, G., ed.*, 1983, pp. 32–54.

Cesarano, Filippo. On the Role of the History of Economic Analysis. *Hist. Polit. Econ.*, Spring 1983, *15*(1), pp. 63–82.

Coats, A. W. Is There a "Structure of Scientific Revolutions" in Economics? **In** *Marr, W. L. and Raj, B., eds.*, 1983, *1969*, pp. 273–79.

Coats, A. W. The First Decade of *HOPE* (1968–79). *Hist. Polit. Econ.*, Fall 1983, *15*(3), pp. 303–19. **[G: U.K.; U.S.]**

Groenewegen, Peter D. and Halevi, Joseph. Altro Polo: Italian Economics Past and Present: Preface and Introduction. **In** *Groenewegen, P. and Halevi, J., eds.*, 1983, pp. 7–16.

Heilbroner, Robert L. The Problem of Value in the Constitution of Economic Thought. *Soc. Res.*, Summer 1983, *50*(2), pp. 253–77.

Henderson, James P. The Oral Tradition in British Economics: Influential Economists in the Political Economy Club of London. *Hist. Polit. Econ.*, Summer 1983, *15*(2), pp. 149–79. **[G: U.K.]**

Hicks, John. 'Revolutions' in Economics. **In** *Hicks, J.*, 1983, *1976*, pp. 3–16.

Karsten, Siegfried G. Dialectics, Functionalism, and Structuralism in Economic Thought. *Amer. J. Econ. Soc.*, April 1983, *42*(2), pp. 179–92.

de Marchi, Neil B. and Lodewijks, John. *HOPE* and the Journal Literature in the History of Economic Thought. *Hist. Polit. Econ.*, Fall 1983, *15*(3), pp. 321–43. **[G: U.S.]**

Rugina, Anghel N. Toward a Third Revolution in Economic Thinking: The Concept of Balanced (Equilibrium) Growth and Social Economics. *Int. J. Soc. Econ.*, 1983, *10*(1), pp. 3–46.

Stanley, Charles E. Schumpeter's 1947 Course in the History of Economic Thought. *Hist. Polit. Econ.*, Spring 1983, *15*(1), pp. 25–37.

Stigler, George J. Perfect Competition, Historically Contemplated. **In** *Stigler, G. J.*, 1983, *1957*, pp. 234–67.

Stigler, George J. The Influence of Events and Policies on Economic Theory. **In** *Stigler, G. J.*, 1983, *1960*, pp. 16–30.

Thweatt, William O. Origins of the Terminology "Supply and Demand." *Scot. J. Polit. Econ.*, November 1983, *30*(3), pp. 287–94.

0311 Ancient, Medieval

Bales, Kevin B. Nicole Oresme and Medieval Social Science: The 14th Century Debunker of Astrology Wrote an Early Monetary Treatise. *Amer. J. Econ. Soc.*, January 1983, *42*(1), pp. 101–12.

Campbell, William F. Pericles and the Sophistication of Economics. *Hist. Polit. Econ.*, Spring 1983, *15*(1), pp. 122–35.

Kern, William. Returning to the Aristotelian Paradigm: Daly and Schumacher. *Hist. Polit. Econ.*, Winter 1983, *15*(4), pp. 501–12.

0312 Pre-Classical Except Mercantilist

Gordon, Kenneth. Consumption and Expenditure in the *Tableau Economique* [The Historical Bases of Physiocracy: An Analysis of the *Tableau Economique*]. *Sci. Soc.*, Winter 1983–1984, *47*(4), pp. 483–84.

Hicks, John. The Social Accounting of Classical Models. **In** *Hicks, J.*, 1983, pp. 17–31.

0314 Classical

Bhagwati, Jagdish N. and Johnson, Harry G. Notes on Some Controversies in the Theory of International Trade. **In** *Bhagwati, J. N., Vol. 2,* 1983, *1960,* pp. 433–52.

Bharadwaj, Krishna. On a Controversy over Ricardo's Theory of Distribution. *Cambridge J. Econ.,* March 1983, *7*(1), pp. 11–36.

Bradley, Michael E. Mill on Proprietorship, Productivity, and Population: A Theoretical Reappraisal. *Hist. Polit. Econ.,* Fall 1983, *15*(3), pp. 423–49.

Cesarano, Filippo. The Rational Expectations Hypothesis in Retrospect. *Amer. Econ. Rev.,* March 1983, *73*(1), pp. 198–203.

Costabile, Lilia. Natural Prices, Market Prices and Effective Demand in Malthus. *Australian Econ. Pap.,* June 1983, *22*(40), pp. 144–70.

Dugger, William M. Classical Economists and the Corporation. *Int. J. Soc. Econ.,* 1983, *10*(2), pp. 22–31.

Duménil, G. Beyond the Transformation Riddle: A Labor Theory of Value. *Sci. Soc.,* Winter 1983–1984, *47*(4), pp. 427–50.

Eatwell, John. Theories of Value, Output and Employment. **In** *Eatwell, J. and Milgate, M., eds.,* 1983, pp. 93–128.

Eatwell, John. Theories of Value, Output and Employment. **In** *Caravale, G., ed.,* 1983, *1978,* pp. 276–322.

Fan, Yiu-Kwan. On the Rate of Profit in the Ricardo–Dmitrief–Sraffa Models. *Atlantic Econ. J.,* July 1983, *11*(2), pp. 97.

Fay, Margaret. The Influence of Adam Smith on Marx's Theory of Alienation. *Sci. Soc.,* Summer 1983, *47*(2), pp. 129–51.

Foley, Duncan K. Money and Effective Demand in Marx's Scheme of Expanded Reproduction. **In** *[Erlich, A.],* 1983, pp. 19–33.

Gamble, Andrew. Critical Political Economy. **In** *Jones, R. J. B., ed.,* 1983, pp. 64–89.

Ganssmann, Heiner. Marx without the Labor Theory of Value? *Soc. Res.,* Summer 1983, *50*(2), pp. 278–304.

Garegnani, Pierangelo. Notes on Consumption, Investment and Effective Demand. **In** *Eatwell, J. and Milgate, M., eds.,* 1983, *1978,* pp. 21–69.

Garegnani, Pierangelo. Notes on Consumption, Investment and Effective Demand: Reply. **In** *Eatwell, J. and Milgate, M., eds.,* 1983, *1979,* pp. 72–78.

Garegnani, Pierangelo. Ricardo's Early Theory of Profits and Its 'Rational Foundation': A Reply to Professor Hollander [On Hollander's Interpretation of Ricardo's Early Theory of Profits]. *Cambridge J. Econ.,* June 1983, *7*(2), pp. 175–78.

Garegnani, Pierangelo. The Classical Theory of Wages and the Role of Demand Schedules in the Determination of Relative Prices. *Amer. Econ. Rev.,* May 1983, *73*(2), pp. 309–13.

Grieve, Roy H. Adam Smith's *Wealth of Nations:* The Legacy of a Great Scottish Economist. **In** *Ingham, K. P. D. and Love, J., eds.,* 1983, pp. 41–54.

Groenewegen, Peter D. Turgot, Beccaria and Smith. **In** *Groenewegen, P. and Halevi, J., eds.,* 1983, pp. 31–78.

Groenewegen, Peter D. Turgot's Place in the History of Economic Thought: A Bicentenary Estimate. *Hist. Polit. Econ.,* Winter 1983, *15*(4), pp. 585–616.

Harris, Donald J. Accumulation of Capital and the Rate of Profit in Marxian Theory. *Cambridge J. Econ.,* September/December 1983, *7*(3/4), pp. 311–30.

Harvey, David. Population, Resources, and the Ideology of Science. **In** *Glassner, M. I., ed.,* 1983, *1974,* pp. 97–103.

Henry, John F. Comment: Ideology in the Ricardo Debate. *J. Post Keynesian Econ.,* Winter 1982–83, *5*(2), pp. 314–17.

Hicks, John. From Classical to Post-classical: The Work of J. S. Mill. **In** *Hicks, J.,* 1983, pp. 60–70.

Hicks, John. Ricardo's Theory of Distribution. **In** *Hicks, J.,* 1983, *1972,* pp. 32–38.

Hicks, John and Hollander, Samuel. Ricardo and the Moderns. **In** *Hicks, J.,* 1983, *1977,* pp. 39–59.

Hollander, Samuel. On the Interpretation of Ricardian Economics: The Assumption Regarding Wages. *Amer. Econ. Rev.,* May 1983, *73*(2), pp. 314–18.

Hollander, Samuel. Professor Garegnani's Defence of Sraffa on the Material Rate of Profit [On Hollander's Interpretation of Ricardo's Early Theory of Profits]. *Cambridge J. Econ.,* June 1983, *7*(2), pp. 167–74.

Jaffé, William. A Centenarian on a Bicentenarian: Léon Walras's *Eléments* on Adam Smith's *Wealth of Nations.* **In** *Jaffé, W.,* 1983, *1977,* pp. 93–107.

King, John E. Utopian or Scientific? A Reconsideration of the Ricardian Socialists. *Hist. Polit. Econ.,* Fall 1983, *15*(3), pp. 345–73.

Kregel, J. A. Conceptions of Equilibrium, Conceptions of Time and Conceptions of Economic Interaction. **In** *Caravale, G., ed.,* 1983, *1975,* pp. 55–101.

Kristol, Irving. Adam Smith and the Spirit of Capitalism. **In** *Kristol, I.,* 1983, *1976,* pp. 139–76.

Mainwaring, L. A Reconsideration of Exchange and Accumulation in Marx [Marxian Economics as General Equilibrium Theory]. *Australian Econ. Pap.,* December 1983, *22*(41), pp. 454–66.

Miranda, Armindo. The Demographic Perspective. **In** *Parkinson, J. R., ed.,* 1983, pp. 40–51. **[G: Selected Countries]**

Parrinello, Sergio. Exhaustible Natural Resources and the Classical Method of Long-Period Equilibrium. **In** *Kregel, J. A., ed.,* 1983, pp. 186–99.

Perelman, Michael. Classical Political Economy and Primitive Accumulation: The Case of Smith and Steuart. *Hist. Polit. Econ.,* Fall 1983, *15*(3), pp. 451–94.

Platteau, Jean-Philippe. Classical Economics and Agrarian Reforms in Underdeveloped Areas: The Radical Views of the Two Mills. *J. Devel. Stud.,* July 1983, *19*(4), pp. 435–60.

Porta, Pier Luigi. Ricardo on Economics and Policy. *Rivista Int. Sci. Econ. Com.,* September 1983, *30*(9), pp. 840–48.

Robinson, Joan. Notes on Consumption, Investment and Effective Demand: Comment. **In** *Eatwell, J. and Milgate, M., eds.,* 1983, *1979,* pp. 70–71.

Salanti, Andrea. Sraffa's Views about Non-Basics and Ricardo's "Corn-Model." *Econ. Notes,* 1983, (2), pp. 145–51.

Samuelson, Paul A. Marx without Matrices: Understanding the Rate of Profit. **In** *[Erlich, A.]*, 1983, pp. 3–18.

Samuelson, Paul A. 1983: Marx, Keynes and Schumpeter. *Eastern Econ. J.*, July–September 1983, *9*(3), pp. 166–79.

Stigler, George J. Sraffa's Ricardo. **In** *Stigler, G. J.*, 1983, *1953,* pp. 302–25.

Stigler, George J. The Development of Utility Theory. **In** *Stigler, G. J.*, 1983, *1950,* pp. 66–155.

Stigler, George J. The Ricardian Theory of Value and Distribution. **In** *Stigler, G. J.*, 1983, *1952,* pp. 156–97.

von Weizsäcker, C. C. On Ricardo and Marx. **In** *Brown, E. C. and Solow, R. M., eds.*, 1983, pp. 203–10.

Winch, Donald. Science and the Legislator: Adam Smith and After. *Econ. J.*, September 1983, *93*(371), pp. 501–20.

Winkel, Harald. Johann Heinrich von Thünen und die Rezeption der englischen Klassik. (Johann von Thünen and English Classical Economic Theory. With English summary.) *Z. Wirtschaft. Sozialwissen.*, 1983, *103*(6), pp. 543–59.

Worland, Stephen T. Adam Smith: Economic Justice and the Founding Father. **In** *Skurski, R., ed.*, 1983, pp. 1–32.

Young, Jeffrey T. Comment on "Hollander's Ricardo." *J. Post Keynesian Econ.*, Winter 1982–83, *5*(2), pp. 309–13.

0315 Austrian, Marshallian, Neoclassical

Bartoli, Gloria. Programma positivista e rivoluzione marginalista in economia. (Positivistic Programme and Marginalistic Revolution in Economics. With English summary.) *Giorn. Econ.*, November–December 1983, *42*(11–12), pp. 749–68.

Brodbeck, Karl-Heinz. Zins und technischer Wandel in Planungssystemen. Ein Vergleich neo-österreichischer Modelle mit der Arbeitswertlehre. (Interest and Technical Change in a Planned Economy: A Comparison between Neo-Austrian Capital Theory and the Labour Theory of Value. With English summary.) *Z. Wirtschaft. Sozialwissen.*, 1983, *103*(1), pp. 27–41.

Cornides, Thomas. Karl Menger's Contributions to Social Thought. *Math. Soc. Sci.*, October 1983, *6*(1), pp. 1–11.

Dooley, Peter C. Consumer's Surplus: Marshall and His Critics. *Can. J. Econ.*, February 1983, *16*(1), pp. 26–38.

Eatwell, John. Theories of Value, Output and Employment. **In** *Eatwell, J. and Milgate, M., eds.*, 1983, pp. 93–128.

Eatwell, John. Theories of Value, Output and Employment. **In** *Caravale, G., ed.*, 1983, *1978,* pp. 276–322.

Eichner, Alfred S. Why Economics Is Not Yet a Science. *J. Econ. Issues,* June 1983, *17*(2), pp. 507–20.

Garegnani, Pierangelo. Notes on Consumption, Investment and Effective Demand. **In** *Eatwell, J. and Milgate, M., eds.*, 1983, *1978,* pp. 21–69.

Garegnani, Pierangelo. Notes on Consumption, Investment and Effective Demand: Reply. **In** *Eatwell, J. and Milgate, M., eds.*, 1983, *1979,* pp. 72–78.

Garegnani, Pierangelo. Two Routes to Effective Demand: Comment [Effective Demand: Origins and Development of the Notion]. **In** *Kregel, J. A., ed.*, 1983, pp. 69–80.

Harcourt, Geoffrey C. Keynes's College Bursar View of Investment: Comment [Effective Demand: Origins and Development of the Notion]. **In** *Kregel, J. A., ed.*, 1983, pp. 81–84.

Hechter, Michael. Karl Polanyi's Social Theory: A Critique. **In** *Hechter, M., ed.*, 1983, pp. 158–89.

Henry, John F. Comment: Ideology in the Ricardo Debate. *J. Post Keynesian Econ.*, Winter 1982–83, *5*(2), pp. 314–17.

Henry, John F. John Bates Clark and the Marginal Product: An Historical Inquiry into the Origins of Value-Free Economic Theory. *Hist. Polit. Econ.*, Fall 1983, *15*(3), pp. 375–89.

Hicks, John. Edgeworth, Marshall and the 'Indeterminateness' of Wages. **In** *Hicks, J.*, 1983, *1930,* pp. 71–84.

Hicks, John. Is Interest the Price of a Factor of Production? **In** *Hicks, J.*, 1983, *1979,* pp. 113–28.

Hicks, John. The Austrian Theory of Capital and Its Re-birth in Modern Economics. **In** *Hicks, J.*, 1983, *1973,* pp. 96–112.

Hirayama, Asazi. Quality Uncertainty, Commerce and Money. *Econ. Stud. Quart.*, December 1983, *34*(3), pp. 249–58.

Hunt, E. K. Joan Robinson and the Labour Theory of Value. *Cambridge J. Econ.*, September/December 1983, *7*(3/4), pp. 331–42.

Jaffé, William. Léon Walras's Role in the "Marginal Revolution" of the 1870s. **In** *Jaffé, W.*, 1983, *1972,* pp. 288–310.

Jaffé, William. Menger, Jevons and Walras De-homogenized. **In** *Jaffé, W.*, 1983, *1976,* pp. 311–25.

Jensen, Hans E. J. M. Keynes as a Marshallian. *J. Econ. Issues,* March 1983, *17*(1), pp. 67–94.

Kærgård, Niels. Marginalismens gennembrud i Danmark og mændene bag. (The Penetration of Marginalism in Denmark. With English summary.) *Nationaløkon. Tidsskr.*, 1983, *121*(1), pp. 20–42. **[G: Denmark]**

Kregel, J. A. Conceptions of Equilibrium, Conceptions of Time and Conceptions of Economic Interaction. **In** *Caravale, G., ed.*, 1983, *1975,* pp. 55–101.

Kregel, J. A. Effective Demand: Origins and Development of the Notion. **In** *Kregel, J. A., ed.*, 1983, pp. 50–68.

Krohn, Claus-Dieter. An Overlooked Chapter of Economic Thought: The "New School's" Effort to Salvage Weimar's Economy. *Soc. Res.*, Summer 1983, *50*(2), pp. 452–68. **[G: Germany]**

Lachmann, L. M. John Maynard Keynes: A View from an Austrian Window. *S. Afr. J. Econ.*, September 1983, *51*(3), pp. 368–79.

Lerner, Abba P. Paleo-Austrian Capital Theory. **In** *Lerner, A. P.*, 1983, pp. 563–79.

Levine, A. L. Marshall: A Reply [Marshall and the Classical Tradition]. *J. Post Keynesian Econ.*, Summer 1983, *5*(4), pp. 667–68.

Levine, A. L. Marshall's *Principles* and the "Biological Viewpoint": A Reconsideration. *Manchester Sch. Econ. Soc. Stud.*, September 1983, *51* (3), pp. 276–93.

Morrill, John E. A Mathematician's Brief Excursion into Economic History—The Concept of Arc Elasticity of Demand. *Amer. Econ.*, Spring 1983, *27* (1), pp. 47–53.

Murrell, Peter. Did the Theory of Market Socialism Answer the Challenge of Ludwig von Mises? A Reinterpretation of the Socialist Controversy. *Hist. Polit. Econ.*, Spring 1983, *15* (1), pp. 92–105.

Nell, Edward J. Keynes after Sraffa: The Essential Properties of Keynes's Theory of Interest and Money: Comment [Effective Demand: Origins and Development of the Notion]. **In** *Kregel, J. A., ed.*, 1983, pp. 85–103.

Robinson, Joan. Notes on Consumption, Investment and Effective Demand: Comment. **In** *Eatwell, J. and Milgate, M., eds.*, 1983, *1979*, pp. 70–71.

Simpson, David. Joseph Schumpeter and the Austrian School of Economics. *J. Econ. Stud.*, 1983, *10* (4), pp. 15–28.

Stigler, George J. Notes on the History of the Giffen Paradox. **In** *Stigler, G. J.*, 1983, *1947*, pp. 374–84. **[G: U.K.]**

Stigler, George J. Stuart Wood and the Marginal Productivity Theory. **In** *Stigler, G. J.*, 1983, *1947*, pp. 287–301.

Stigler, George J. The Development of Utility Theory. **In** *Stigler, G. J.*, 1983, *1950*, pp. 66–155.

Streissler, Erich. Schumpeter and Hayek: On Some Similarities in Their Thought. **In** *[Giersch, H.]*, 1983, pp. 356–64.

Walker, Lance W. A Comment on "Marshall and the Classical Tradition." *J. Post Keynesian Econ.*, Summer 1983, *5* (4), pp. 664–66.

Wiles, Peter. Ideology, Methodology, and Neoclassical Economics. **In** *Eichner, A. S., ed.*, 1983, *1979–80*, pp. 61–89.

Young, Jeffrey T. Comment on "Hollander's Ricardo." *J. Post Keynesian Econ.*, Winter 1982–83, *5* (2), pp. 309–13.

0316 General Equilibrium until 1945

Cohen, Avi J. and Cohen, Jon S. Classical and Neoclassical Theories of General Equilibrium [A Review Article]. *Australian Econ. Pap.*, June 1983, *22* (40), pp. 180–200.

Hicks, John. Leon Walras. **In** *Hicks, J.*, 1983, *1934*, pp. 85–95.

Jaffé, William. A Centenarian on a Bicentenarian: Léon Walras's *Eléments* on Adam Smith's *Wealth of Nations*. **In** *Jaffé, W.*, 1983, *1977*, pp. 93–107.

Jaffé, William. A. N. Isnard, Progenitor of the Walrasian General Equilibrium Model. **In** *Jaffé, W.*, 1983, *1969*, pp. 55–77.

Jaffé, William. Another Look at Léon Walras's Theory of *Tâtonnement*. **In** *Jaffé, W.*, 1983, *1981*, pp. 244–66.

Jaffé, William. Léon Walras. **In** *Jaffé, W.*, 1983, *1968*, pp. 131–35.

Jaffé, William. Léon Walras and His Conception of Economics. **In** *Jaffé, W.*, 1983, *1956*, pp. 121–30.

Jaffé, William. Léon Walras's Role in the "Marginal Revolution" of the 1870s. **In** *Jaffé, W.*, 1983, *1972*, pp. 288–310.

Jaffé, William. New Light on an Old Quarrel: Barone's Unpublished Review of Wicksteed's "Essay on the Coordination of the Laws of Distribution" and Related Documents. **In** *Jaffé, W.*, 1983, *1964*, pp. 176–212.

Jaffé, William. Reflections on the Importance of Léon Walras. **In** *Jaffé, W.*, 1983, *1971*, pp. 269–87.

Jaffé, William. The Birth of Léon Walras's *Eléments*. **In** *Jaffé, W.*, 1983, *1977*, pp. 78–92.

Jaffé, William. The Normative Bias of the Walrasian Model: Walras versus Gossen. **In** *Jaffé, W.*, 1983, *1977*, pp. 326–42.

Jaffé, William. Walras's Economics as Others See It. **In** *Jaffé, W.*, 1983, *1980*, pp. 343–70.

Jaffé, William. Walras's Theory of *Tâtonnement:* A Critique of Recent Interpretations. **In** *Jaffé, W.*, 1983, *1967*, pp. 221–43.

Jaffé, William. Walras's Theory of Capital Formation in the Framework of His Theory of General Equilibrium. **In** *Jaffé, W.*, 1983, *1953*, pp. 151–75.

Rugina, Anghel N. Toward a Third Revolution in Economic Thinking: The Concept of Balanced (Equilibrium) Growth and Social Economics. *Int. J. Soc. Econ.*, 1983, *10* (1), pp. 3–46.

Samuelson, Paul A. Thünen at Two Hundred. *J. Econ. Lit.*, December 1983, *21* (4), pp. 1468–88.

Semmler, Willi. On the Classical Theory of Taxation. An Analysis of Tax Incidence in a Linear Production Model. *Metroecon.*, February–June 1983, *35* (1–2), pp. 129–46.

Weintraub, E. Roy. On the Existence of a Competitive Equilibrium: 1930–1954. *J. Econ. Lit.*, March 1983, *21* (1), pp. 1–39.

0317 Socialist and Marxian until 1945

Amato, Sergio. The Debate between Marxists and Legal Populists on the Problems of Market and Industrialization in Russia (1882–1899) and Its Classical Foundations. *J. Europ. Econ. Hist.*, Spring 1983, *12* (1), pp. 119–43. **[G: U.S.S.R.]**

Bologh, Roslyn Wallach. Economic Problems and Proposed Solutions in the Mid-Nineteenth Century: Marx's Analysis and Critique. **In** *Schmukler, N. and Marcus, E., eds.*, 1983, pp. 246–62.

Brodbeck, Karl-Heinz. Zins und technischer Wandel in Planungssystemen. Ein Vergleich neo-österreichischer Modelle mit der Arbeitswertlehre. (Interest and Technical Change in a Planned Economy: A Comparison between Neo-Austrian Capital Theory and the Labour Theory of Value. With English summary.) *Z. Wirtschaft. Sozialwissen.*, 1983, *103* (1), pp. 27–41.

Brus, Wlodzimierz and Kowalik, Tadeusz. Socialism and Development. *Cambridge J. Econ.*, September/December 1983, *7* (3/4), pp. 243–55.

Clawson, Patrick. A Comment on Van Parijs' Obituary [The Falling-Rate-of-Profit Theory of Crisis: A Rational Reconstruction by Way of Obituary]. *Rev. Radical Polit. Econ.*, Summer 1983, *15* (2), pp. 107–10.

Eatwell, John. Theories of Value, Output and Employment. **In** *Eatwell, J. and Milgate, M., eds.*, 1983, pp. 93–128.

Falkinger, Josef and Laski, Kazimierz. Marx's Theory of Exploitation and Technical Progress. *Metro-*

econ., February–June 1983, *35*(1–2), pp. 159–76.

Foley, Duncan K. Money and Effective Demand in Marx's Scheme of Expanded Reproduction. **In** *[Erlich, A.]*, 1983, pp. 19–33.

Goldstick, Danny. Objectivity and Moral Commitment in the World-View of Marx and Engels. *Sci. Soc.*, Spring 1983, *47*(1), pp. 84–91.

Hacken, Richard D. Scandinavian Social Economics 1850–1930: A Bibliographic Note. *Rev. Soc. Econ.*, October 1983, *41*(2), pp. 137–51. **[G: Scandinavia]**

Hart, Keith. The Contribution of Marxism to Economic Anthropology. **In** *Ortiz, S., ed.*, 1983, pp. 105–44.

Hunt, E. K. Joan Robinson and the Labour Theory of Value. *Cambridge J. Econ.*, September/December 1983, *7*(3/4), pp. 331–42.

Johnson, Carol. Philosophy and Revolution in the Young Marx. *Sci. Soc.*, Spring 1983, *47*(1), pp. 66–83.

Kenway, Peter. Marx, Keynes and the Possibility of Crisis. **In** *Eatwell, J. and Milgate, M., eds.*, 1983, *1980*, pp. 149–66.

Kesselman, Mark. From State Theory to Class Struggle and Compromise: Contemporary Marxist Political Study. *Soc. Sci. Quart.*, December 1983, *64*(4), pp. 826–45.

King, John E. Utopian or Scientific? A Reconsideration of the Ricardian Socialists. *Hist. Polit. Econ.*, Fall 1983, *15*(3), pp. 345–73.

Lad, Frank. The Construction of Probability Theory: A Marxist Discussion. *Sci. Soc.*, Fall 1983, *47*(3), pp. 285–99.

Lerner, Abba P. From Vulgar Political Economy to Vulgar Marxism. **In** *Lerner, A. P.*, 1983, *1939*, pp. 583–93.

Matthaei, Julie A. Freedom and Unfreedom in Marxian Economics. *Eastern Econ. J.*, April–June 1983, *9*(2), pp. 71–78.

Nell, Edward J. On Monetary Circulation and the Rate of Exploitation. *Econ. Forum*, Spring 1983 Supplement, *13*, pp. 1–38.

Panico, Carlo. Marx's Analysis of the Relationship between the Rate of Interest and the Rate of Profits. **In** *Eatwell, J. and Milgate, M., eds.*, 1983, *1980*, pp. 167–86.

Samuelson, Paul A. Marx without Matrices: Understanding the Rate of Profit. **In** *[Erlich, A.]*, 1983, pp. 3–18.

Steedman, Ian. Three Lectures on Marx after Sraffa. **In** *Caravale, G., ed.*, 1983, *1979*, pp. 323–42.

Stigler, George J. Bernard Shaw, Sidney Webb, and the Theory of Fabian Socialism. **In** *Stigler, G. J.*, 1983, *1959*, pp. 268–86.

Sylos Labini, Paolo. The Problem of Economic Growth in Marx and Schumpeter. **In** *Groenewegen, P. and Halevi, J., eds.*, 1983, pp. 129–66.

Tool, Marc R. Social Value Theory of Marxists: An Instrumental Review and Critique: Part Two. *J. Econ. Issues*, March 1983, *17*(1), pp. 155–73.

0318 Historical and Institutional

Blanton, Richard E. Factors Underlying the Origin and Evolution of Market Systems. **In** *Ortiz, S., ed.*, 1983, pp. 51–66.

Bush, Paul D. An Exploration of the Structural Characteristics of a Veblen–Ayres–Foster Defined Institutional Domain. *J. Econ. Issues*, March 1983, *17*(1), pp. 35–66.

Bush, Paul D. Errata [An Exploration of the Structural Characteristics of a Veblen–Ayres–Foster Defined Institutional Domain]. *J. Econ. Issues*, September 1983, *17*(3), pp. 585.

Chase, Richard X. Adolph Lowe's Paradigm Shift for a Scientific Economics: An Interpretive Perspective. *Amer. J. Econ. Soc.*, April 1983, *42*(2), pp. 167–77.

Dalton, George and Köcke, Jasper. The Work of the Polanyi Group: Past, Present, and Future. **In** *Ortiz, S., ed.*, 1983, pp. 21–50.

Dugger, William M. The Transaction Cost Analysis of Oliver E. Williamson: A New Synthesis? *J. Econ. Issues*, March 1983, *17*(1), pp. 95–114.

Etherington, Norman. The Capitalist Theory of Capitalist Imperialism. *Hist. Polit. Econ.*, Spring 1983, *15*(1), pp. 38–62.

Head, Brian W. State and Economy: Theories and Problems. **In** *Head, B. W., ed.*, 1983, pp. 22–54.

Hickerson, Steven R. Planning for Institutional Change in a Complex Environment: An Approach and an Application. *J. Econ. Issues*, September 1983, *17*(3), pp. 631–65.

Junker, Louis. Institutionalism and the Criteria of Development. *Econ. Forum*, Summer 1983, *14*(1), pp. 27–56.

Junker, Louis. The Conflict between the Scientific-Technological Process and Malignant Ceremonialism. *Amer. J. Econ. Soc.*, July 1983, *42*(3), pp. 341–52.

Keller, Robert R. Keynesian and Institutional Economics: Compatibility and Complementarity? *J. Econ. Issues*, December 1983, *17*(4), pp. 1087–95.

Klein, Philip A. Reagan's Economic Policies: An Institutional Assessment. *J. Econ. Issues*, June 1983, *17*(2), pp. 463–74. **[G: U.S.]**

Klein, Philip A. The Neglected Institutionalism of Wesley Clair Mitchell: The Theoretical Basis for Business Cycle Indicators. *J. Econ. Issues*, December 1983, *17*(4), pp. 867–99. **[G: U.S.]**

Lux, Kenneth and Lutz, Mark A. Creative vs. Mechanical Evolutionism: A Commentary [Economic Evolution and Economic Policy: Is Reaganomics a Sustainable Force?] [Creationism versus Evolutionism in Economics: Societal Consequences of Economic Doctrine]. *J. Econ. Issues*, December 1983, *17*(4), pp. 1113–17. **[G: U.S.]**

Marshall, Ray. Comments of the Institutional View of Reaganomics. *J. Econ. Issues*, June 1983, *17*(2), pp. 503–06. **[G: U.S.]**

Millar, James R. A Natural Science Version of Socioeconomic Evolution: Copeland's Essays Are His First Sustained Attempt to Apply His Approach to Economic History. *Amer. J. Econ. Soc.*, January 1983, *42*(1), pp. 117–19.

Minsky, Hyman P. Institutional Roots of American Inflation. **In** *Schmukler, N. and Marcus, E., eds.*, 1983, pp. 265–77. **[G: U.S.]**

Neale, Walter C. and Mayhew, Anne. Polanyi, Institutional Economics, and Economic Anthropology. **In** *Ortiz, S., ed.*, 1983, pp. 11–20.

Petr, Jerry L. Creationism versus Evolutionism in

Economics: Societal Consequences of Economic Doctrine. *J. Econ. Issues,* June 1983, *17*(2), pp. 475–83. [G: U.S.]

Petr, Jerry L. Rejoinder to Lux and Lutz [Economic Evolution and Economic Policy: Is Reaganomics a Sustainable Force?] [Creationism versus Evolutionism in Economics: Societal Consequences of Economic Doctrine]. *J. Econ. Issues,* December 1983, *17*(4), pp. 1118–20. [G: U.S.]

Phillips, Ronnie J. and Slottje, Daniel J. The Importance of Relative Prices in Analyzing Veblen Effects. *J. Econ. Issues,* March 1983, *17*(1), pp. 197–206. [G: U.S.]

Rutherford, Malcolm H. Ayres's Instrumentalism: A Reply. *J. Econ. Issues,* September 1983, *17*(3), pp. 750–53.

Rutherford, Malcolm H. J. R. Commons's Institutional Economics. *J. Econ. Issues,* September 1983, *17*(3), pp. 721–44.

Simich, J. L. and Tilman, Rick. On the Use and Abuse of Thorstein Veblen in Modern American Sociology, I: David Riesman's Reductionist Interpretation and Talcott Parsons' Pluralist Critique. *Amer. J. Econ. Soc.,* October 1983, *42*(4), pp. 417–29.

Sobel, Irvin. Joseph Spengler: The Institutionalist Approach to Our Profession and Its Ideas. *Eastern Econ. J.,* October–December 1983, *9*(4), pp. 337–50.

Stanfield, J. Ron. Institutional Analysis: Toward Progress in Economic Science. **In** *Eichner, A. S., ed.,* 1983, pp. 187–204.

Stolz, Peter. Das wiedererwachte Interesse der Ökonomie an rechtlichen und politischen Institutionen. (The Renewed Interest of Economics in Legal and Political Institutions. With English summary.) *Schweiz. Z. Volkswirtsch. Statist.,* March 1983, *119*(1), pp. 49–67.

Troub, Roger M. General Adjustment Theory and Institutional Adjustment Processes. *J. Econ. Issues,* June 1983, *17*(2), pp. 315–24. [G: U.S.]

Weinel, Ivan. Clarence Ayres's Instrumental Value Theory: A Rejoinder. *J. Econ. Issues,* September 1983, *17*(3), pp. 753–55.

Wilber, Charles K. and Harrison, Robert S. The Methodological Basis of Institutional Economics: Pattern Model, Storytelling, and Holism. **In** *Marr, W. L. and Raj, B., eds.,* 1983, *1978,* pp. 243–72.

Wood, John Cunningham. J. A. Hobson and British Imperialism. *Amer. J. Econ. Soc.,* October 1983, *42*(4), pp. 483–500. [G: U.K.]

032 History of Economic Thought (continued)

0321 Other Schools Since 1800

Ditz, Gerhard W. Demand-Side, Supply-Side, Marketing Philosophy, and Beyond. *Econ. Notes,* 1983, (1), pp. 112–29.

Duncan, Colin A. M. Under the Cloud of *Capital:* History vs. Theory. *Sci. Soc.,* Fall 1983, *47*(3), pp. 300–322.

Kerr, Clark. The Intellectual Role of the Neorealists in Labor Economics. *Ind. Relat.,* Spring 1983, *22*(2), pp. 298–318. [G: U.S.]

Krohn, Claus-Dieter. An Overlooked Chapter of Economic Thought: The "New School's" Effort to Salvage Weimar's Economy. *Soc. Res.,* Summer 1983, *50*(2), pp. 452–68. [G: Germany]

Parrini, Carl P. and Sklar, Martin J. New Thinking about the Market, 1896–1904: Some American Economists on Investment and the Theory of Surplus Capital. *J. Econ. Hist.,* September 1983, *43*(3), pp. 559–78. [G: U.S.]

Rotwein, Eugene. Jacob Viner and the Chicago Tradition. *Hist. Polit. Econ.,* Summer 1983, *15*(2), pp. 265–80.

Stigler, George J. Nobel Lecture: The Process and Progress of Economics. *J. Polit. Econ.,* August 1983, *91*(4), pp. 529–45.

0322 Individuals

Ayres, Clarence

Bolin, Meb. The Independent, Simultaneous Development of Instrumental Thoughts in Various Disciplines. *J. Econ. Issues,* June 1983, *17*(2), pp. 345–52.

Rutherford, Malcolm H. Ayres's Instrumentalism: A Reply. *J. Econ. Issues,* September 1983, *17*(3), pp. 750–53.

Weinel, Ivan. Clarence Ayres's Instrumental Value Theory: A Rejoinder. *J. Econ. Issues,* September 1983, *17*(3), pp. 753–55.

Bauer, Otto

Orzech, Ze'ev B. and Groll, Shalom. Otto Bauer's Scheme of Expanded Reproduction: An Early Harrodian Growth Model. *Hist. Polit. Econ.,* Winter 1983, *15*(4), pp. 529–48.

Baumol, William J.

Baumol, William J. On the Career of a Microeconomist. *Banca Naz. Lavoro Quart. Rev.,* December 1983, (147), pp. 311–35.

Beccaria, Cesare

Groenewegen Peter D. Turgot, Beccaria and Smith. **In** *Groenewegen, P. and Halevi, J., eds.,* 1983, pp. 31–78.

Bernstein, Eduard

Fletcher, R. A. Cobden as Educator: The Free-Trade Internationalism of Eduard Bernstein, 1899–1914. *Amer. Hist. Rev.,* June 1983, *88*(3), pp. 561–78. [G: Germany]

Bonbright, James C.

Trebing, Harry M. James C. Bonbright's Contributions to Public-Utility Economics and Regulation. **In** *[Bonbright, J. C.],* 1983, pp. 3–21.

Boulding, Kenneth

Harcourt, Geoffrey C. A Man for All Systems: Talking with Kenneth Boulding. *J. Post Keynesian Econ.,* Fall 1983, *6*(1), pp. 143–54.

Briefs, Goetz A.

Briefs, Henry W. Goetz Briefs on Capitalism and Democracy: An Introduction. *Rev. Soc. Econ.,* December 1983, *41*(3), pp. 212–27.

Hermens, Ferdinand A. . . . And Now the Future. *Rev. Soc. Econ.,* December 1983, *41*(3), pp. 330–55.

Cantillon, Richard

Bordo, Michael David. Some Aspects of the Monetary Economics of Richard Cantillon. *J. Monet. Econ.,* August 1983, *12*(2), pp. 235–58.

Brems, Hans J. Richard Cantillon: Resources and

Population. *Écon. Appl.*, 1983, *36*(2–3), pp. 277–86.

Chamberlain, Neil W.

Kuhn, James W.; Lewin, David and McNulty, Paul J. Neil W. Chamberlain: A Retrospective Analysis of His Scholarly Work and Influence. *Brit. J. Ind. Relat.*, July 1983, *21*(2), pp. 143–60.

Chamberlin, Edward H.

O'Brien, D. P. Research Programmes in Competitive Structure. *J. Econ. Stud.*, 1983, *10*(4), pp. 29–51.

Skinner, Andrew S. E. H. Chamberlin: The Origins and Development of Monopolistic Competition. *J. Econ. Stud.*, 1983, *10*(4), pp. 52–67.

Chen, Yun

Lardy, Nicholas R. and Lieberthal, Kenneth. Chen Yun's Strategy for China's Development: A Non-Maoist Alternative: Introduction. **In** *Ch'en, Y.*, 1983, pp. xi–xliii. **[G: China]**

Clark, John Bates

Henry, John F. John Bates Clark and the Marginal Product: An Historical Inquiry into the Origins of Value-Free Economic Theory. *Hist. Polit. Econ.*, Fall 1983, *15*(3), pp. 375–89.

Cochran, Thomas C.

Sharlin, Harold Issadore. Business and Its Environment: Essays for Thomas C. Cochran: Introduction. **In** *[Cochran, T. C.]*, 1983, pp. 3–21.

Copeland, Morris A.

Millar, James R. A Natural Science Version of Socioeconomic Evolution: Copeland's Essays Are His First Sustained Attempt to Apply His Approach to Economic History. *Amer. J. Econ. Soc.*, January 1983, *42*(1), pp. 117–19.

Copleston, Edward

Rashid, Salim. Edward Copleston, Robert Peel, and Cash Payments. *Hist. Polit. Econ.*, Summer 1983, *15*(2), pp. 249–59. **[G: U.K.]**

Daly, Herman E.

Kern, William. Returning to the Aristotelian Paradigm: Daly and Schumacher. *Hist. Polit. Econ.*, Winter 1983, *15*(4), pp. 501–12.

Debreu, Gerard

Hildenbrand, Werner. Mathematical Economics: Twenty Papers of Gerard Debreu: Introduction. **In** *Debreu, G.*, 1983, pp. 1–29.

Del Vecchio, Gustav

Caffè, Federico. Il pensiero di Gustavo Del Vecchio nel centenario della nascita. (Gustav Del Vecchio's Thought in the Centennial Anniversary of His Birth. With English summary.) *Giorn. Econ.*, November–December 1983, *42*(11–12), pp. 705–17.

Dupuit, Jules

Hicks, John. Dupuit. **In** *Hicks, J.*, 1983, *1935*, pp. 329–30.

Edgeworth, Francis Ysidro

Creedy, John. F. Y. Edgeworth's Mathematical Training. *J. Roy. Statist. Soc.*, 1983, *146*(2), pp. 158–62.

Engels, Frederick

Goldstick, Danny. Objectivity and Moral Commitment in the World-View of Marx and Engels. *Sci. Soc.*, Spring 1983, *47*(1), pp. 84–91.

Fisher, R. A.

Geary, R. C. R. A. Fisher: A Memoir. *Econ. Soc. Rev.*, April 1983, *14*(3), pp. 167–71.

Forchheimer, Karl

Forchheimer, Karl. Imperfect Monopoly: Some Theoretical Considerations. *Nebr. J. Econ. Bus.*, Spring 1983, *22*(2), pp. 65–77.

Geary, Robert Charles

Spencer, John E. Robert Charles Geary—An Appreciation. *Econ. Soc. Rev.*, April 1983, *14*(3), pp. 161–64.

George, Henry

Fuller, Aaron B., III. Selected Elements of Henry George's Legitimacy as an Economist. *Amer. J. Econ. Soc.*, January 1983, *42*(1), pp. 45–61.

Samuels, Warren J. Henry George's Challenge to the Economics Profession. *Amer. J. Econ. Soc.*, January 1983, *42*(1), pp. 63–66.

Samuels, Warren J. The Progress and Poverty Centenary: Advocates and Opponents Will Enjoy and Learn from the Papers Given at One Celebration. *Amer. J. Econ. Soc.*, April 1983, *42*(2), pp. 247–54.

Gide, Charles

Pénin, Marc. Charles Gide, économiste: pour une action en réhabilitation. (With English summary.) *Revue Écon. Polit.*, November-December 1983, *93*(6), pp. 816–46.

Schmidt, Christian. De Charles Gide à Mark Blaug: éléments pour une histoire de l'Histoire de la pensée économique. (With English summary.) *Revue Écon. Polit.*, November–December 1983, *93*(6), pp. 847–68.

Giersch, Herbert

Machlup, Fritz. Herbert Giersch: Scholar, Policy Adviser and Public Figure. **In** *[Giersch, H.]*, 1983, pp. xxvii–xxxvii.

Gray, Lewis C.

Crabbé, Philippe J. The Contribution of L. C. Gray to the Economic Theory of Exhaustible Natural Resources and Its Roots in the History of Economic Thought. *J. Environ. Econ. Manage.*, September 1983, *10*(3), pp. 195–220.

Gregory, T. E.

Fase, M. M. G. The 1930 Correspondence between Koopmans, Robertson and Gregory. *De Economist*, 1983, *131*(3), pp. 305–43.

Hamilton, Robert

Mepham, Michael J. Robert Hamilton's Contribution to Accounting. *Accounting Rev.*, January 1983, *58*(1), pp. 43–57.

von Hayek, Friedrich A.

Brittan, Samuel. Hayek, Freedom and Interest Groups. **In** *Brittan, S.*, 1983, *1980*, pp. 48–79.

Lerner, Abba P. A Keynesian on Hayek. **In** *Lerner, A. P.*, 1983, *1980*, pp. 651–53.

Streissler, Erich. Schumpeter and Hayek: On Some Similarities in Their Thought. **In** *[Giersch, H.]*, 1983, pp. 356–64.

Hicks, John R.

Hicks, John. The Formation of an Economist. **In** *Hicks, J.*, 1983, *1979*, pp. 355–64.

Hobson, John A.

Etherington, Norman. The Capitalist Theory of

Capitalist Imperialism. *Hist. Polit. Econ.*, Spring 1983, *15*(1), pp. 38–62.

Wood, John Cunningham. J. A. Hobson and British Imperialism. *Amer. J. Econ. Soc.*, October 1983, *42*(4), pp. 483–500. **[G: U.K.]**

Holden, Edward [Sir]

Kamitake, Yoshiro. Some Notes on the Life and Works of Sir Edward Holden. *Hitotsubashi J. Econ.*, February 1983, *23*(2), pp. 48–56. **[G: U.K.]**

Isnard, Achille-Nicolas

Jaffé, William. A. N. Isnard, Progenitor of the Walrasian General Equilibrium Model. **In** *Jaffé, W.*, 1983, *1969*, pp. 55–77.

Jaffé, William

Walker, Donald A. William Jaffé's Essays on Walras: Introduction. **In** *Jaffé, W.*, 1983, pp. 1–14.

Jevons, William Stanley

Hicks, John. Jevons. **In** *Hicks, J.*, 1983, *1978*, pp. 331–32.

Jaffé, William. Menger, Jevons and Walras Dehomogenized. **In** *Jaffé, W.*, 1983, *1976*, pp. 311–25.

Johansen, Leif

Sandmo, Agnar. Leif Johansen's Contribution to Public Economics. *J. Public Econ.*, August 1983, *21*(3), pp. 317–24.

Solow, Robert M. Leif Johansen (1930–1982): A Memorial. *Scand. J. Econ.*, 1983, *85*(4), pp. 445–59.

Kahn-Freund, Otto

Clark, Jon. Towards a Sociology of Labour Law: An Analysis of the German Writings of Otto Kahn-Freund. **In** *Wedderburn of Charlton [Lord]; Lewis, R. and Clark, J., eds.*, 1983, pp. 81–106.

Lewis, Roy. Method and Ideology in the Labour Law Writings of Otto Kahn-Freund. **In** *Wedderburn of Charlton [Lord]; Lewis, R. and Clark, J., eds.*, 1983, pp. 107–26.

Kaldor, Nicholas

Chatterji, Monojit and Wickens, Michael R. Verdoorn's Law and Kaldor's Law: A Revisionist Interpretation? *J. Post Keynesian Econ.*, Spring 1983, *5*(3), pp. 397–413. **[G: OECD]**

McCombie, John S. L. Kaldor's Laws in Retrospect. *J. Post Keynesian Econ.*, Spring 1983, *5*(3), pp. 414–29. **[G: U.S.]**

McCombie, John S. L. and de Ridder, John R. Increasing Returns, Productivity, and Output Growth: The Case of the United States. *J. Post Keynesian Econ.*, Spring 1983, *5*(3), pp. 373–87. **[G: U.S.]**

Pasinetti, Luigi L. Nicholas Kaldor: A Few Personal Notes. *J. Post Keynesian Econ.*, Spring 1983, *5*(3), pp. 333–40.

Thirlwall, Anthony P. A Plain Man's Guide to Kaldor's Growth Laws. *J. Post Keynesian Econ.*, Spring 1983, *5*(3), pp. 345–58.

Kalecki, Michal

Asimakopulos, A. Kalecki and Keynes on Finance, Investment and Saving. *Cambridge J. Econ.*, September/December 1983, *7*(3/4), pp. 221–33.

Kaldor, Nicholas. Gemeinsamkeiten und Unterschiede in den Theorien von Keynes, Kalecki und Rüstow. (Common Features and Controversial Issues in the Theories of Keynes, Kalecki, and Rüstow. With English summary.) *Ifo-Studien*, 1983, *29*(1), pp. 1–10.

Keynes, John Maynard

Asimakopulos, A. Anticipations of Keynes's General Theory? *Can. J. Econ.*, August 1983, *16*(3), pp. 517–30.

Asimakopulos, A. Kalecki and Keynes on Finance, Investment and Saving. *Cambridge J. Econ.*, September/December 1983, *7*(3/4), pp. 221–33.

Benedetti, G. and Gui, Benedetto. Keynesian State of Expectation and Rational Expectations. *Metroecon.*, February–June 1983, *35*(1–2), pp. 177–94.

Booth, Alan. The "Keynesian Revolution" in Economic Policy-Making. *Econ. Hist. Rev., 2nd Ser.*, February 1983, *36*(1), pp. 103–23. **[G: U.K.]**

Botha, D. J. J. Some Thoughts around the *General Theory* (Review Article). *S. Afr. J. Econ.*, September 1983, *51*(3), pp. 426–45.

Braithwaite, Richard. Impressions of Maynard Keynes. **In** *Worswick, D. and Trevithick, J., eds.*, 1983, pp. 261–63.

Brown, A. J. The Demand-Side Economics of Inflation: Comment. **In** *Worswick, D. and Trevithick, J., eds.*, 1983, pp. 238–44.

Cate, Tom. Keynes and Thurow: The Socialization of Investment. *Eastern Econ. J.*, July–September 1983, *9*(3), pp. 205–12.

Chase, Richard X. The Development of Contemporary Mainstream Macroeconomics: Vision, Ideology, and Theory. **In** *Eichner, A. S., ed.*, 1983, *1981*, pp. 126–65.

Chua, Jess H. and Woodward, Richard S. J. M. Keynes's Investment Performance: A Note. *J. Finance*, March 1983, *38*(1), pp. 232–35. **[G: U.K.]**

Crotty, James R. On Keynes and Capital Flight [Keynes's *General Theory:* A Different Perspective]. *J. Econ. Lit.*, March 1983, *21*(1), pp. 59–65.

Cuyvers, Ludo. Keynes's Collaboration with Erwin Rothbarth. *Econ. J.*, September 1983, *93*(371), pp. 629–36.

Darity, William A., Jr. and Horn, Bobbie L. Involuntary Unemployment Reconsidered. *Southern Econ. J.*, January 1983, *49*(3), pp. 717–33.

Davidson, Paul. The Dubious Labor Market Analysis in Meltzer's Restatement of Keynes' *Theory. J. Econ. Lit.*, March 1983, *21*(1), pp. 52–56.

Dell, Sidney. Keynes and the International Economic Order: Comment. **In** *Worswick, D. and Trevithick, J., eds.*, 1983, pp. 119–27.

Dickson, Harald. How Did Keynes Conceive of Entrepreneurs' Motivation? Notes on Patinkin's Hypothesis. *Hist. Polit. Econ.*, Summer 1983, *15*(2), pp. 229–47.

Dornbusch, Rudiger. Keynes and the International Economic Order: Comment. **In** *Wors-*

wick, D. and Trevithick, J., eds., 1983, pp. 113–19.

Eatwell, John and Milgate, Murray. Keynes's Economics and the Theory of Value and Distribution: Introduction. **In** *Eatwell, J. and Milgate, M., eds.*, 1983, pp. 1–17.

Eddé, Richard. Keynes' Basic Error. *Rivista Int. Sci. Econ. Com.*, April-May 1983, *30*(4–5), pp. 375–92.

Fleming, J. The Demand-Side Economics of Inflation: Comment. **In** *Worswick, D. and Trevithick, J., eds.*, 1983, pp. 244–47.

Garner, C. Alan. 'Uncertainty' in Keynes' *General Theory:* A Comment. *Hist. Polit. Econ.*, Spring 1983, *15*(1), pp. 83–86.

Gelting, Jørgen H. Keynes' samfundsopfattelse. (With English summary.) *Nationaløkon. Tidsskr.*, 1983, *121*(3), pp. 317–22.

Godley, Wynne. Keynes and the Management of Real National Income and Expenditure. **In** *Worswick, D. and Trevithick, J., eds.*, 1983, pp. 135–57.

Goodhart, Charles A. E. On Keynes and Monetarism: Comment. **In** *Worswick, D. and Trevithick, J., eds.*, 1983, pp. 75–81.

Hahn, F. H. On Keynes and Monetarism: Comment. **In** *Worswick, D. and Trevithick, J., eds.*, 1983, pp. 72–75.

Harrod, R. F. Keynes and the Macmillan Committee: Proposals for Public Works and Protection. **In** *Feinstein, C., ed.*, 1983, *1951*, pp. 31–46. **[G: U.K.]**

Hixon, William F. A New Perspective on the Economic Crisis. *Eastern Econ. J.*, July–September 1983, *9*(3), pp. 221–31. **[G: U.S.]**

Jensen, Hans E. J. M. Keynes as a Marshallian. *J. Econ. Issues*, March 1983, *17*(1), pp. 67–94.

Kafka, Alexandre. John Maynard Keynes. *Finance Develop.*, December 1983, *20*(4), pp. 37–38.

Kaldor, Nicholas. Gemeinsamkeiten und Unterschiede in den Theorien von Keynes, Kalecki und Rüstow. (Common Features and Controversial Issues in the Theories of Keynes, Kalecki, and Rüstow. With English summary.) *Ifo-Studien*, 1983, *29*(1), pp. 1–10.

Kaldor, Nicholas. Keynesian Economics after Fifty Years. **In** *Worswick, D. and Trevithick, J., eds.*, 1983, pp. 1–28.

Kenway, Peter. Marx, Keynes and the Possibility of Crisis. **In** *Eatwell, J. and Milgate, M., eds.*, 1983, *1980*, pp. 149–66.

Labia, J. F. Keynes's Impact on Monetary Economics (Review Article). *S. Afr. J. Econ.*, September 1983, *51*(3), pp. 446–56.

Lachmann, L. M. John Maynard Keynes: A View from an Austrian Window. *S. Afr. J. Econ.*, September 1983, *51*(3), pp. 368–79.

Leijonhufvud, Axel. What Would Keynes Have Thought of Rational Expectations? **In** *Worswick, D. and Trevithick, J., eds.*, 1983, pp. 179–205.

Lerner, Abba P. From the Treatise on Money to the General Theory. **In** *Lerner, A. P.*, 1983, *1974*, pp. 393–97.

Lerner, Abba P. On Keynes, Policy, and Theory—A Grumble. **In** *Lerner, A. P.*, 1983, pp. 441–51.

LeRoy, Stephen F. Keynes's Theory of Investment. *Hist. Polit. Econ.*, Fall 1983, *15*(3), pp. 397–421.

Littleboy, B. and Mehta, Granshyam. The Scientific Method of Keynes. *J. Econ. Stud.*, 1983, *10*(4), pp. 3–14.

Malinvaud, Edmond. Keynes and the Management of Real National Income and Expenditure: Comment. **In** *Worswick, D. and Trevithick, J., eds.*, 1983, pp. 157–62.

Marsh, James Barney. Keynes on the Supply of Gold: A Statistical Test. *Eastern Econ. J.*, January–March 1983, *9*(1), pp. 7–12. **[G: S. Africa]**

Mátyás, Antal. Similarities between the Economic Theories of Marx and Keynes. *Acta Oecon.*, 1983, *31*(3–4), pp. 155–73.

Meade, James. Impressions of Maynard Keynes. **In** *Worswick, D. and Trevithick, J., eds.*, 1983, pp. 263–66.

Mehta, Granshyam. Comments on Professor Minoguchi's Interpretation of the *Treatise* and the *General Theory. Hitosubashi J. Econ.*, December 1983, *24*(2), pp. 153–158.

Meltzer, Allan H. Interpreting Keynes [Keynes's *General Theory:* A Different Perspective]. *J. Econ. Lit.*, March 1983, *21*(1), pp. 66–78.

Meltzer, Allan H. On Keynes and Monetarism. **In** *Worswick, D. and Trevithick, J., eds.*, 1983, pp. 49–72.

Milgate, Murray. Keynes on the 'Classical' Theory of Interest. **In** *Eatwell, J. and Milgate, M., eds.*, 1983, *1977*, pp. 79–92.

Milgate, Murray. The 'New' Keynes Papers. **In** *Eatwell, J. and Milgate, M., eds.*, 1983, pp. 187–99.

Milgate, Murray and Eatwell, John. Unemployment and the Market Mechanism. **In** *Eatwell, J. and Milgate, M., eds.*, 1983, pp. 260–80.

Minoguchi, Takeo. Reply [The Process of Writing the *General Theory* as a 'Monetary Theory of Production'] [Some Questions about IS-LM Interpretation of the *General Theory*] *Hitotsubashi J. Econ.*, December 1983, *24*(2), p. 159.

Minsky, Hyman P. The Legacy of Keynes. *Metroecon.*, February–June 1983, *35*(1–2), pp. 87–103.

Parsons, R. W. K. Keynes and South Africa. *S. Afr. J. Econ.*, September 1983, *51*(3), pp. 419–25.

Pasinetti, Luigi L. What Would Keynes Have Thought of Rational Expectations? Comment. **In** *Worswick, D. and Trevithick, J., eds.*, 1983, pp. 205–11.

Patinkin, Don. New Perspectives or Old Pitfalls? Some Comments on Allan Meltzer's Interpretation of the *General Theory. J. Econ. Lit.*, March 1983, *21*(1), pp. 47–51.

Pen, Jan. Keynesology à la Leijonhufvud: False Signals. *De Economist*, 1983, *131*(1), pp. 16–30.

Robertson, H. M. J. M. Keynes and Cambridge in the 1920s. *S. Afr. J. Econ.*, September 1983, *51*(3), pp. 407–18.

Robinson, Austin [Sir]. Impressions of Maynard

Keynes. **In** *Worswick, D. and Trevithick, J., eds.,* 1983, pp. 255–61.

Samuelson, Paul A. What Would Keynes Have Thought of Rational Expectations? Comment. **In** *Worswick, D. and Trevithick, J., eds.,* 1983, pp. 212–17.

Samuelson, Paul A. 1983: Marx, Keynes and Schumpeter. *Eastern Econ. J.,* July–September 1983, *9*(3), pp. 166–79.

Shackle, George L. S. Levels of Simplicity in Keynes's Theory of Money and Employment. *S. Afr. J. Econ.,* September 1983, *51*(3), pp. 357–67.

Solow, Robert M. Keynes and the Management of Real National Income and Expenditure: Comment. **In** *Worswick, D. and Trevithick, J., eds.,* 1983, pp. 162–68.

Stohs, Mark. 'Uncertainty' in Keynes' *General Theory:* A Rejoinder. *Hist. Polit. Econ.,* Spring 1983, *15*(1), pp. 87–91.

Thirlwall, Anthony P. Keynesian Economics after Fifty Years: Comment. **In** *Worswick, D. and Trevithick, J., eds.,* 1983, pp. 37–44.

Thweatt, William O. Note: Keynes on Marx's *Das Kapital. Hist. Polit. Econ.,* Winter 1983, *15*(4), pp. 617–20.

Tobin, James. Keynes' Policies in Theory and Practice. *Challenge,* November/December 1983, *26*(5), pp. 5–11.

Tobin, James. Keynesian Economics after Fifty Years: Comment. **In** *Worswick, D. and Trevithick, J., eds.,* 1983, pp. 28–37.

Travaglini, Guido. La natura parascientifica del pensiero di Keynes. (The Pseudo-Scientific Foundations of Keynes' Thought. With English summary.) *Rivista Int. Sci. Econ. Com.,* April-May 1983, *30*(4–5), pp. 393–97.

Weintraub, Sidney. Comment on Allan Meltzer's "Keynes's *General Theory.*" *J. Econ. Lit.,* March 1983, *21*(1), pp. 57–58.

Williamson, John. Keynes and the International Economic Order. **In** *Worswick, D. and Trevithick, J., eds.,* 1983, pp. 87–113.

Wulwick, Nancy J. Can Keynesian Economics Be Scientific? An Historical Reconstruction. *Eastern Econ. J.,* July–September 1983, *9*(3), pp. 190–204. **[G: U.K.]**

Klein, Lawrence R.

Samuelson, Paul A. Rigorous Observational Positivism: Klein's Envelope Aggregation; Thermodynamics and Economic Isomorphisms. **In** *[Klein, L. R.],* 1983, pp. 1–38.

Koopmans, Johan Gerbrand

Fase, M. M. G. The 1930 Correspondence between Koopmans, Robertson and Gregory. *De Economist,* 1983, *131*(3), pp. 305–43.

Leijonhufvud, Axel

Pen, Jan. Keynesology à la Leijonhufvud: False Signals. *De Economist,* 1983, *131*(1), pp. 16–30.

Lerner, Abba P.

Bronfenbrenner, Martin. Abba, 1903–1982. *Atlantic Econ. J.,* March 1983, *11*(1), pp. 1–5.

Sobel, Irvin. Abba Petachya Lerner, 1903–1982: Six Decades of Achievement, *J. Post Keynesian Econ.,* Fall 1983, *6*(1), pp. 3–19.

Sobel, Irvin. Selected Economic Writings of Abba P. Lerner: Foreword. **In** *Lerner, A. P.,* 1983, pp. vii–xii.

Lindahl, Erik

Chiodi, Guglielmo and Velupillai, Kumaraswamy. A Note on Lindahl's Theory of Distribution. *Kyklos,* 1983, *36*(1), pp. 103–11.

Lösch, August

Arcangeli, Fabio. Un riesame dell' "ordine spaziale dell'economia" di August Lösch. (Lösch's "Spatial Order of Economics." With English summary.) *Giorn. Econ.,* July–August 1983, *42*(7–8), pp. 483–506.

Lowe, Adolph

Chase, Richard X. Adolph Lowe's Paradigm Shift for a Scientific Economics: An Interpretive Perspective. *Amer. J. Econ. Soc.,* April 1983, *42*(2), pp. 167–77.

Halevi, Joseph. Employment and Planning. *Soc. Res.,* Summer 1983, *50*(2), pp. 345–58.

Lutz, Vera C.

Graziani, Augusto. The Macroeconomic Theory of Vera C. Lutz. *Banca Naz. Lavoro Quart. Rev.,* March 1983, (144), pp. 3–27. **[G: Italy]**

Masera, Rainer S. Inflation, Stabilization and Economic Recovery in Italy after the War: Vera Lutz's Assessment. *Banca Naz. Lavoro Quart. Rev.,* March 1983, (144), pp. 29–50. **[G: Italy]**

Machlup, Fritz

Haberler, Gottfried. Fritz Machlup: In Memoriam. *Cato J.,* Spring 1983, *3*(1), pp. 11–14.

Malthus, Thomas Robert

Costabile, Lilia. Natural Prices, Market Prices and Effective Demand in Malthus. *Australian Econ. Pap.,* June 1983, *22*(40), pp. 144–70.

Harrison, John. The Malthus Library Catalogue: Introductory Essay. **In** *Malthus Library Catalogue,* 1983, pp. xv–xxxi.

Harvey, David. Population, Resources, and the Ideology of Science. **In** *Glassner, M. I., ed.,* 1983, *1974,* pp. 97–103.

James, Patricia. The Malthus Library Catalogue: Introductory Remarks. **In** *Malthus Library Catalogue,* 1983, pp. xxxix–xlvii.

Ménard, Claude. Régulation et direction le projet économique de Malthus. (With English summary.) *Revue Écon. Polit.,* March–April 1983, *93*(2), pp. 233–47.

Minami, Ryozaburo. T. R. Malthus as Population Scientist. **In** *Malthus Library Catalogue,* 1983, pp. xxxiii–xxxvii.

Petersen, William. The Malthus Library Catalogue: Introductory Remarks. **In** *Malthus Library Catalogue,* 1983, pp. xlviii–liii.

Pullen, John. The Malthus Library Catalogue: Introductory Remarks. **In** *Malthus Library Catalogue,* 1983, pp. liv–lxii.

Schmidt, Christian. Malthus et la semantique économique. (With English summary.) *Revue Écon. Polit.,* March–April 1983, *93*(2), pp. 248–69.

Silver, Morris. A Non-Neo Malthusian Model of English Land Value, Wages, and Grain Yield before the Black Death. *J. Europ. Econ. Hist.,* Winter 1983, *12*(3), pp. 631–50. **[G: U.K.]**

Marshall, Alfred

Dooley, Peter C. Consumer's Surplus: Marshall and His Critics. *Can. J. Econ.*, February 1983, *16*(1), pp. 26–38.

Dugger, William M. Classical Economists and the Corporation. *Int. J. Soc. Econ.*, 1983, *10*(2), pp. 22–31.

Gee, J. M. A. Marshall's Views on 'Short Period' Value Formation. *Hist. Polit. Econ.*, Summer 1983, *15*(2), pp. 181–205.

Hicks, John. Marshall. **In** *Hicks, J.*, 1983, *1976*, pp. 335–37.

Levine, A. L. Marshall: A Reply [Marshall and the Classical Tradition]. *J. Post Keynesian Econ.*, Summer 1983, *5*(4), pp. 667–68.

Levine, A. L. Marshall's *Principles* and the "Biological Viewpoint": A Reconsideration. *Manchester Sch. Econ. Soc. Stud.*, September 1983, *51*(3), pp. 276–93.

Rainelli, Michel. Entrepreneur et profits dans les "Principes" de John Stuart Mill et d'Alfred Marshall. (Entrepreneur and Profits in Mill's and Marshall's *Principles.* With English summary.) *Revue Écon.*, July 1983, *34*(4), pp. 794–810.

Walker, Lance W. A Comment on "Marshall and the Classical Tradition." *J. Post Keynesian Econ.*, Summer 1983, *5*(4), pp. 664–66.

Martineau, Harriet

O'Donnell, Margaret G. Harriet Martineau: A Popular Early Economics Educator. *J. Econ. Educ.*, Fall 1983, *14*(4), pp. 59–64.

Marx, Karl

Anderson, Kevin. The "Unknown" Marx's *Capital,* Volume I: The French Edition of 1872–75, 100 Years Later. *Rev. Radical Polit. Econ.*, Winter 1983, *15*(4), pp. 71–80.

Baumol, William J. Marx and the Iron Law of Wages. *Amer. Econ. Rev.*, May 1983, *73*(2), pp. 303–08.

Bologh, Roslyn Wallach. Economic Problems and Proposed Solutions in the Mid-Nineteenth Century: Marx's Analysis and Critique. **In** *Schmukler, N. and Marcus, E., eds.*, 1983, pp. 246–62.

Cawley, Leo. Scarcity, Distribution and Growth: Notes on Classical Rent Theory. *Rev. Radical Polit. Econ.*, Fall 1983, *15*(3), pp. 143–58.

Darity, William A., Jr. Contemporary Marxism: Ideology or Science? A Review Essay on: *Research in Political Economy. Rev. Radical Polit. Econ.*, Winter 1983, *15*(4), pp. 136–48.

Duménil, G. Beyond the Transformation Riddle: A Labor Theory of Value. *Sci. Soc.*, Winter 1983–1984, *47*(4), pp. 427–50.

Elliott, John E. Schumpeter and Marx on Capitalist Transformation. *Quart. J. Econ.*, May 1983, *98*(2), pp. 333–36.

Fay, Margaret. The Influence of Adam Smith on Marx's Theory of Alienation. *Sci. Soc.*, Summer 1983, *47*(2), pp. 129–51.

Foster, John Bellamy. Theories of Capitalist Transformation: Critical Notes on the Comparison of Marx and Schumpeter. *Quart. J. Econ.*, May 1983, *98*(2), pp. 327–31.

Glombowski, Jörg. A Marxian Model of Long Run Capitalist Development. *Z. Nationalökon.*, 1983, *43*(4), pp. 363–82.

Goldstick, Danny. Objectivity and Moral Commitment in the World-View of Marx and Engels. *Sci. Soc.*, Spring 1983, *47*(1), pp. 84–91.

Harvey, David. Population, Resources, and the Ideology of Science. **In** *Glassner, M. I., ed.*, 1983, *1974*, pp. 97–103.

Harvey, Philip. Marx's Theory of the Value of Labor Power: An Assessment. *Soc. Res.*, Summer 1983, *50*(2), pp. 305–44.

Hausmann, Ricardo and Lipietz, Alain. Marx et la divergence entre production en valeur et revenus nominaux. (With English summary.) *Revue Écon. Polit.*, March–April 1983, *93*(2), pp. 270–300.

Houston, David B. Capitalism without Capitalists: A Comment on "Classes in Marxian Theory." *Rev. Radical Polit. Econ.*, Spring 1983, *15*(1), pp. 153–56.

Hunt, Ian. An Obituary or a New Life for the Tendency of the Rate of Profit to Fall? *Rev. Radical Polit. Econ.*, Spring 1983, *15*(1), pp. 131–48.

Johnson, Carol. Philosophy and Revolution in the Young Marx. *Sci. Soc.*, Spring 1983, *47*(1), pp. 66–83.

Kenway, Peter. Marx, Keynes and the Possibility of Crisis. **In** *Eatwell, J. and Milgate, M., eds.*, 1983, *1980*, pp. 149–66.

Kieve, Ronald A. The Hegelian Inversion: On the Possibility of a Marxist Dialectic. *Sci. Soc.*, Spring 1983, *47*(1), pp. 37–65.

Lavoie, Don C. Some Strengths in Marx's Disequilibrium Theory of Money. *Cambridge J. Econ.*, March 1983, *7*(1), pp. 55–68.

Lindsey, J. K. Classes in Marxist Theory. *Rev. Radical Polit. Econ.*, Spring 1983, *15*(1), pp. 149–52.

Machalek, Richard. Karl Marx: "A Swarthy Fellow from *Trier*" *Soc. Sci. Quart.*, December 1983, *64*(4), pp. 778–85.

Mănescu, Manea. The Systemic Outlook in the Works of Karl Marx. *Econ. Computat. Cybern. Stud. Res.*, 1983, *18*(3), pp. 5–10.

Matthaei, Julie A. Freedom and Unfreedom in Marxian Economics. *Eastern Econ. J.*, April–June 1983, *9*(2), pp. 71–78.

Mátyás, Antal. Similarities between the Economic Theorics of Marx and Keynes. *Acta Oecon.*, 1983, *31*(3–4), pp. 155–73.

Nell, Edward J. On Monetary Circulation and the Rate of Exploitation. *Econ. Forum*, Spring 1983 Supplement, *13*, pp. 1–38.

Nikaido, Hukukane. Marx on Competition. *Z. Nationalökon.*, 1983, *43*(4), pp. 337–63.

Panico, Carlo. Marx's Analysis of the Relationship between the Rate of Interest and the Rate of Profits. **In** *Eatwell, J. and Milgate, M., eds.*, 1983, *1980*, pp. 167–86.

Rugina, Anghel N. There Are Two Karl Marxes! *Eastern Econ. J.*, July–September 1983, *9*(3), pp. 232–45.

Rugina, Anghel N. What Is the Alternative for the East? Neither Orthodox Marxism nor Capitalism but "Liberal Socialism." *Int. J. Soc.*

Econ., 1983, *10*(4), pp. 3–67.

Samuelson, Paul A. 1983: Marx, Keynes and Schumpeter. *Eastern Econ. J.*, July–September 1983, *9*(3), pp. 166–79.

Světlý, Jiří. Marx's Method of Political Economy and the Present Time. *Czech. Econ. Digest.*, June 1983, (4), pp. 20–35.

Sylos Labini, Paolo. The Problem of Economic Growth in Marx and Schumpeter. **In** *Groenewegen, P. and Halevi, J., eds.*, 1983, pp. 129–66.

Tarascio, Vincent J. Pareto's *Trattato. Eastern Econ. J.*, April–June 1983, *9*(2), pp. 119–31.

Thweatt, William O. Note: Keynes on Marx's *Das Kapital. Hist. Polit. Econ.*, Winter 1983, *15*(4), pp. 617–20.

Waitzman, Norman J. Moments, Spheres and Levels: Which Is of Value? *Econ. Forum*, Summer 1983, *14*(1), pp. 111–25.

Walton, John. Marx for the Late Twentieth Century: Transnational Capital and Disenfranchised Labor. *Soc. Sci. Quart.*, December 1983, *64*(4), pp. 786–809. **[G: U.S.]**

West, Edwin G. Marx's Hypotheses on the Length of the Working Day. *J. Polit. Econ.*, April 1983, *91*(2), pp. 266–81.

Wolff, Richard and Resnick, Stephen. Capitalism without Capitalists: Reply [Classes in Marxian Theory]. *Rev. Radical Polit. Econ.*, Spring 1983, *15*(1), pp. 157–59.

Meli, Anton

Senglet, J.-J. Dr. h.c. Anton Meli zum achtzigsten Geburtstag. *Schweiz. Z. Volkswirtsch. Statist.*, September 1983, *119*(3), pp. 209–10.

Menger, Carl

Hicks, John. Menger. **In** *Hicks, J.*, 1983, *1951*, pp. 333–34.

Jaffé, William. Menger, Jevons and Walras Dehomogenized. **In** *Jaffé, W.*, 1983, *1976*, pp. 311–25.

Menger, Karl

Cornides, Thomas. Karl Menger's Contributions to Social Thought. *Math. Soc. Sci.*, October 1983, *6*(1), pp. 1–11.

Mill, James

Platteau, Jean-Philippe. Classical Economics and Agrarian Reforms in Underdeveloped Areas: The Radical Views of the Two Mills. *J. Devel. Stud.*, July 1983, *19*(4), pp. 435–60.

Mill, John Stuart

Bradley, Michael E. Mill on Proprietorship, Productivity, and Population: A Theoretical Reappraisal. *Hist. Polit. Econ.*, Fall 1983, *15*(3), pp. 423–49.

Hicks, John. From Classical to Post-classical: The Work of J. S. Mill. **In** *Hicks, J.*, 1983, pp. 60–70.

Hollander, Samuel. On John Stuart Mill's Defence of Ricardian Economics. *Revue Écon. Polit.*, November-December 1983, *93*(6), pp. 894–99.

Platteau, Jean-Philippe. Classical Economics and Agrarian Reforms in Underdeveloped Areas: The Radical Views of the Two Mills. *J. Devel. Stud.*, July 1983, *19*(4), pp. 435–60.

Rainelli, Michel. Entrepreneur et profits dans les "Principes" de John Stuart Mill et d'Alfred Marshall. (Entrepreneur and Profits in Mill's and Marshall's *Principles.* With English summary.) *Revue Écon.*, July 1983, *34*(4), pp. 794–810.

von Mises, Ludwig

Murrell, Peter. Did the Theory of Market Socialism Answer the Challenge of Ludwig von Mises? A Reinterpretation of the Socialist Controversy. *Hist. Polit. Econ.*, Spring 1983, *15*(1), pp. 92–105.

Mitchell, Wesley Clair

Klein, Philip A. The Neglected Institutionalism of Wesley Clair Mitchell: The Theoretical Basis for Business Cycle Indicators. *J. Econ. Issues,* December 1983, *17*(4), pp. 867–99. **[G: U.S.]**

Moore, Henry

Stigler, George J. Henry L. Moore and Statistical Economics. **In** *Stigler, G. J.*, 1983, *1962*, pp. 343–73.

Myrdal, Gunnar

Hicks, John. Myrdal. **In** *Hicks, J.*, 1983, *1954*, pp. 343–46.

Ohlin, Bertil

Löfgren, Karl G. The Faustmann–Ohlin Theorem: A Historical Note. *Hist. Polit. Econ.*, Summer 1983, *15*(2), pp. 261–64. **[G: Sweden]**

Okun, Arthur

Tobin, James. Okun on Macroeconomic Policy: A Final Comment. **In** *Tobin, J., ed.*, 1983, pp. 297–300.

Oresme, Nicole

Bales, Kevin B. Nicole Oresme and Medieval Social Science: The 14th Century Debunker of Astrology Wrote an Early Monetary Treatise. *Amer. J. Econ. Soc.*, January 1983, *42*(1), pp. 101–12.

Pareto, Vilfredo

Cirillo, Renato. Was Vilfredo Pareto Really a 'Precursor' of Facism? *Amer. J. Econ. Soc.*, April 1983, *42*(2), pp. 235–45.

Hicks, John. Pareto. **In** *Hicks, J.*, 1983, *1961*, pp. 338–42.

Tarascio, Vincent J. Pareto's *Trattato. Eastern Econ. J.*, April–June 1983, *9*(2), pp. 119–31.

Patinkin, Don D.

Dickson, Harald. How Did Keynes Conceive of Entrepreneurs' Motivation? Notes on Patinkin's Hypothesis. *Hist. Polit. Econ.*, Summer 1983, *15*(2), pp. 229–47.

Pesch, Heinrich

Briefs, Goetz A. Pesch and His Contemporaries: *Nationalokonomie* vs. Contemporary Economic Theories. *Rev. Soc. Econ.*, December 1983, *41*(3), pp. 235–45.

Rugina, Anghel N. About the Doctrine of "Solidarism" in Social Economics. *Int. J. Soc. Econ.*, 1983, *10*(2), pp. 62–71.

Petty, William

Kaji, Naoki. A Religious Background of Petty's Economic Thought. (In Japanese. With English summary.) *Osaka Econ. Pap.*, March 1983, *32*(4), pp. 21–31.

Pigou, A. C.

Collard, David A. Pigou on Expectations and the

Cycle. *Econ. J.*, June 1983, *93*(370), pp. 411–14.

Poincaré, Jules Henri

Jaffé, William. The Walras-Poincaré Correspondence on the Cardinal Measurability of Utility. In *Jaffé, W.*, 1983, *1977*, pp. 213–20.

Polanyi, Karl

Dalton, George and Köcke, Jasper. The Work of the Polanyi Group: Past, Present, and Future. In *Ortiz, S., ed.*, 1983, pp. 21–50.

Hechter, Michael. Karl Polanyi's Social Theory: A Critique. In *Hechter, M., ed.*, 1983, pp. 158–89.

Silver, Morris. Karl Polanyi and Markets in the Ancient Near East: The Challenge of the Evidence. *J. Econ. Hist.*, December 1983, *43*(4), pp. 795–829. **[G: Middle East]**

Popper, Karl

Faludi, Andreas. Critical Rationalism and Planning Methodology. *Urban Stud.*, August 1983, *20*(3), pp. 265–78.

Prebisch, Rául

Gurrieri, Adolfo. Technical Progress and Its Fruits: The Idea of Development in the Works of Rául Prebisch. *J. Econ. Issues,* June 1983, *17*(2), pp. 389–96.

Quesnay, François

de Gaudemar, Jean-Paul. La régulation despotique un commentaire du tableau économique de Quesnay. (With English summary.) *Revue Écon. Polit.*, March–April 1983, *93*(2), pp. 177–96.

Gordon, Kenneth. Consumption and Expenditure in the *Tableau Economique* [The Historical Bases of Physiocracy: An Analysis of the *Tableau Economique*]. *Sci. Soc.*, Winter 1983–1984, *47*(4), pp. 483–84.

Ricardo, David

Bharadwaj, Krishna. On a Controversy over Ricardo's Theory of Distribution. *Cambridge J. Econ.*, March 1983, *7*(1), pp. 11–36.

Cawley, Leo. Scarcity, Distribution and Growth: Notes on Classical Rent Theory. *Rev. Radical Polit. Econ.*, Fall 1983, *15*(3), pp. 143–58.

Courtois, Claude. Ricardo et la population. (With English summary.) *Revue Écon. Polit.*, March–April 1983, *93*(2), pp. 197–210.

Eagly, Robert V. Tax Incidence in Ricardian Analysis. *Public Finance,* 1983, *38*(2), pp. 217–31.

Fine, Ben. The Historical Approach to Rent and Price Theory Reconsidered. *Australian Econ. Pap.*, June 1983, *22*(40), pp. 132–43.

Garegnani, Pierangelo. Ricardo's Early Theory of Profits and Its 'Rational Foundation': A Reply to Professor Hollander [On Hollander's Interpretation of Ricardo's Early Theory of Profits]. *Cambridge J. Econ.*, June 1983, *7*(2), pp. 175–78.

Gordon, Kenneth. Hicks and Hollander on Ricardo: A Mathematical Note. *Quart. J. Econ.*, November 1983, *98*(4), pp. 721–26.

Hansson, Bjorn. Wicksell's Critique of Ricardo's Chapter "On Machinery." *J. Econ. Stud.*, 1983, *10*(3), pp. 49–55.

Henry, John F. Comment: Ideology in the Ricardo Debate. *J. Post Keynesian Econ.*, Winter 1982–83, *5*(2), pp. 314–17.

Hicks, John and Hollander, Samuel. Ricardo and the Moderns. In *Hicks, J.*, 1983, *1977*, pp. 39–59.

Hollander, Samuel. On the Interpretation of Ricardian Economics: The Assumption Regarding Wages. *Amer. Econ. Rev.*, May 1983, *73*(2), pp. 314–18.

Hollander, Samuel. Professor Garegnani's Defence of Sraffa on the Material Rate of Profit [On Hollander's Interpretation of Ricardo's Early Theory of Profits]. *Cambridge J. Econ.*, June 1983, *7*(2), pp. 167–74.

Ong, Nai-Pew. Ricardo's Invariable Measure of Value and Sraffa's 'Standard Commodity.' *Hist. Polit. Econ.*, Summer 1983, *15*(2), pp. 207–27.

Porta, Pier Luigi. Ricardo on Economics and Policy. *Rivista Int. Sci. Econ. Com.*, September 1983, *30*(9), pp. 840–48.

Salanti, Andrea. Sraffa's Views about Non-Basics and Ricardo's "Corn-Model." *Econ. Notes,* 1983, (2), pp. 145–51.

Stigler, George J. Ricardo and the 93 Per Cent Labor Theory of Value. In *Stigler, G. J.*, 1983, *1958*, pp. 326–42.

Stigler, George J. Sraffa's Ricardo. In *Stigler, G. J.*, 1983, *1953*, pp. 302–25.

Stigler, George J. The Ricardian Theory of Value and Distribution. In *Stigler, G. J.*, 1983, *1952*, pp. 156–97.

Young, Jeffrey T. Comment on "Hollander's Ricardo." *J. Post Keynesian Econ.*, Winter 1982–83, *5*(2), pp. 309–13.

Robertson, Dennis H.

Fase, M. M. G. The 1930 Correspondence between Koopmans, Robertson and Gregory. *De Economist,* 1983, *131*(3), pp. 305–43.

Robinson, Joan

Brahmananda, P. R. Joan Robinson, 1904–1983. *Indian Econ. J.*, July–September 1983, *31*(1), pp. 1–24.

Brus, Wlodzimierz and Kowalik, Tadeusz. Socialism and Development. *Cambridge J. Econ.*, September/December 1983, *7*(3/4), pp. 243–55.

Gram, Harvey and Walsh, Vivian. Joan Robinson's Economics in Retrospect. *J. Econ. Lit.*, June 1983, *21*(2), pp. 518–50.

Narasimhan, Sita. Joan Robinson: In the Radical Vein. A Laywoman's Homage. *Cambridge J. Econ.*, September/December 1983, *7*(3/4), pp. 213–19.

O'Brien, D. P. Research Programmes in Competitive Structure. *J. Econ. Stud.*, 1983, *10*(4), pp. 29–51.

Rosenstein-Rodan, Paul

Chakravarty, Sukhamoy. Paul Rosenstein-Rodan: An Appreciation. *World Devel.*, January 1983, *11*(1), pp. 73–75.

Rostow, Walt W.

Caire, Guy. Histoire recetter ou histoire méthode: A propos de la problématique rostowienne et des paradigmes dominants de l'économie du développement. (History as Receipts or History as Method: Concerning the Problems Raised by Rostow and the Dominant Paradigmes of Economy of Development. With English summary.) *Écon. Soc.*, February 1983, *17*(2), pp. 261–88.

Rothbarth, Erwin

Cuyvers, Ludo. Keynes's Collaboration with Erwin Rothbarth. *Econ. J.*, September 1983, *93*(371), pp. 629–36.

Rüstow, Hans-Joachim

Kaldor, Nicholas. Gemeinsamkeiten und Unterschiede in den Theorien von Keynes, Kalecki und Rüstow. (Common Features and Controversial Issues in the Theories of Keynes, Kalecki, and Rüstow. With English summary.) *Ifo-Studien*, 1983, *29*(1), pp. 1–10.

Samuelson, Paul A.

Arrow, Kenneth J. Contributions to Welfare Economics. **In** *Brown, E. C. and Solow, R. M., eds.*, 1983, pp. 15–30.

Hahn, F. H. On General Equilibrium and Stability. **In** *Brown, E. C. and Solow, R. M., eds.*, 1983, pp. 31–53.

Houthakker, Hendrik S. On Consumption Theory. **In** *Brown, E. C. and Solow, R. M., eds.*, 1983, pp. 55–68.

Jones, Ronald W. International Trade Theory. **In** *Brown, E. C. and Solow, R. M., eds.*, 1983, pp. 69–103.

Merton, Robert C. Financial Economics. **In** *Brown, E. C. and Solow, R. M., eds.*, 1983, pp. 105–40.

Musgrave, Richard A. Public Goods. **In** *Brown, E. C. and Solow, R. M., eds.*, 1983, pp. 141–56.

Patinkin, Don. Monetary Economics. **In** *Brown, E. C. and Solow, R. M., eds.*, 1983, pp. 157–67.

Samuelson, Paul A. Economics in a Golden Age: A Personal Memoir. **In** *Brown, E. C. and Solow, R. M., eds.*, 1983, *1972*, pp. 1–14.

Samuelson, Paul A. My Life Philosophy. *Amer. Econ.*, Fall 1983, *27*(2), pp. 5–12.

Solow, Robert M. Modern Capital Theory. **In** *Brown, E. C. and Solow, R. M., eds.*, 1983, pp. 169–87.

Tobin, James. Macroeconomics and Fiscal Policy. **In** *Brown, E. C. and Solow, R. M., eds.*, 1983, pp. 189–201.

von Weizsäcker, C. C. On Ricardo and Marx. **In** *Brown, E. C. and Solow, R. M., eds.*, 1983, pp. 203–10.

Sauermann, Heinz

Tietz, Reinhard. Aspiration-oriented Decision Making—In Memoriam Heinz Sauermann. **In** *Tietz, R., ed.*, 1983, pp. 1–7.

Schumacher, E. F.

Kern, William. Returning to the Aristotelian Paradigm: Daly and Schumacher. *Hist. Polit. Econ.*, Winter 1983, *15*(4), pp. 501–12.

Schumpeter, Joseph A.

Backhaus, Juergen. Economic Theories and Political Interests: Scholarly Economics in Pre-Hitler Germany: Review Article. *J. Europ. Econ. Hist.*, Winter 1983, *12*(3), pp. 661–67. **[G: Germany]**

Brahmananda, P. R. Joseph Alois Schumpeter: A Centennial Appraisal. *Indian Econ. J.*, October–December 1983, *31*(2), pp. 1–26.

Elliott, John E. Schumpeter and the Theory of Capitalist Economic Development. *J. Econ. Behav. Organ.*, December 1983, *4*(4), pp. 277–308.

Elliott, John E. Schumpeter and Marx on Capitalist Transformation. *Quart. J. Econ.*, May 1983, *98*(2), pp. 333–36.

Foster, John Bellamy. Theories of Capitalist Transformation: Critical Notes on the Comparison of Marx and Schumpeter. *Quart. J. Econ.*, May 1983, *98*(2), pp. 327–31.

Giersch, Herbert. The World Economy at Century's End: Comment. **In** *Tsuru, S., ed.*, 1983, pp. 78–88.

Samuelson, Paul A. The World Economy at Century's End. **In** *Tsuru, S., ed.*, 1983, pp. 58–77.

Samuelson, Paul A. 1983: Marx, Keynes and Schumpeter. *Eastern Econ. J.*, July–September 1983, *9*(3), pp. 166–79.

Simpson, David. Joseph Schumpeter and the Austrian School of Economics. *J. Econ. Stud.*, 1983, *10*(4), pp. 15–28.

Stanley, Charles E. Schumpeter's 1947 Course in the History of Economic Thought. *Hist. Polit. Econ.*, Spring 1983, *15*(1), pp. 25–37.

Streissler, Erich. Schumpeter and Hayek: On Some Similarities in Their Thought. **In** *[Giersch, H.]*, 1983, pp. 356–64.

Sylos Labini, Paolo. The Problem of Economic Growth in Marx and Schumpeter. **In** *Groenewegen, P. and Halevi, J., eds.*, 1983, pp. 129–66.

Talamona, Mario. Sviluppo, moneta e credito: la "visione" di Schumpeter e il caso italiano. (Schumpeter's View on Growth, Money and Credit, and the "Italian Case." With English summary.) *Giorn. Econ.*, July–August 1983, *42*(7–8), pp. 405–29. **[G: Italy]**

Zinn, Karl Georg. Zyklus, Stabilität und Geldneutralität. Ein lehrgeschichtliche Ergänzung zum Problem der potentialorientierten Geldpolitik auf der Grundlage von Schumpeters Entwicklungstheorie. (Business Cycle, Stability, and Neutral Money. With English summary.) *Konjunkturpolitik*, 1983, *29*(6), pp. 329–47.

Shackle, George L. S.

Shackle, George L. S. A Student's Pilgrimage. *Banca Naz. Lavoro Quart. Rev.*, June 1983, (145), pp. 107–16.

Simons, Henry C.

Gay, David E. R. A Note on Professor Simmons and Teaching Law and Economics. *Atlantic Econ. J.*, December 1983, *11*(4), pp. 77. **[G: U.S.]**

Sismondi, Charles Leonard

Beaugrand, Philippe. Sismondi, théoricien a-monétaire. *Revue Écon. Polit.*, March–April 1983, *93*(2), pp. 301–07.

Smith, Adam

Dugger, William M. Classical Economists and the Corporation. *Int. J. Soc. Econ.*, 1983, *10*(2), pp. 22–31.

Fine, Ben. The Historical Approach to Rent and Price Theory Reconsidered. *Australian Econ. Pap.*, June 1983, *22*(40), pp. 132–43.

Grieve, Roy H. Adam Smith's *Wealth of Nations:* The Legacy of a Great Scottish Economist. **In** *Ingham, K. P. D. and Love, J., eds.*, 1983, pp. 41–54.

Groenewegen, Peter D. Turgot, Beccaria and Smith. **In** *Groenewegen, P. and Halevi, J., eds.*, 1983, pp. 31–78.

Jaffé, William. A Centenarian on a Bicentenarian: Léon Walras's *Eléments* on Adam Smith's *Wealth of Nations.* **In** *Jaffé, W.*, 1983, *1977*, pp. 93–107.

Kristol, Irving. Adam Smith and the Spirit of Capitalism. **In** *Kristol, I.*, 1983, *1976*, pp. 139–76.

Perelman, Michael. Classical Political Economy and Primitive Accumulation: The Case of Smith and Steuart. *Hist. Polit. Econ.*, Fall 1983, *15*(3), pp. 451–94.

Winch, Donald. Science and the Legislator: Adam Smith and After. *Econ. J.*, September 1983, *93*(371), pp. 501–20.

Worland, Stephen T. Adam Smith: Economic Justice and the Founding Father. **In** *Skurski, R., ed.*, 1983, pp. 1–32.

Sombart, Werner

Backhaus, Juergen. Economic Theories and Political Interests: Scholarly Economics in Pre-Hitler Germany: Review Article. *J. Europ. Econ. Hist.*, Winter 1983, *12*(3), pp. 661–67. **[G: Germany]**

Somermeyer, Willem Hendrik

van Daal, J. and Kloek, T. In Memoriam: W. H. Somermeyer (1919–1982). *De Economist*, 1983, *131*(1), pp. 1–15.

Spengler, Jospeh J.

Sobel, Irvin. Joseph Spengler: The Institutionalist Approach to Our Profession and Its Ideas. *Eastern Econ. J.*, October–December 1983, *9*(4), pp. 337–50.

Spiethoff, Arthur

Backhaus, Juergen. Economic Theories and Political Interests: Scholarly Economics in Pre-Hitler Germany: Review Article. *J. Europ. Econ. Hist.*, Winter 1983, *12*(3), pp. 661–67. **[G: Germany]**

Sproul, Allan

Lucia, Joseph L. Allan Sproul and the Treasury–Federal Reserve Accord, 1951. *Hist. Polit. Econ.*, Spring 1983, *15*(1), pp. 106–21.

Sraffa, Piero

Cohen, Avi J. "The Laws of Returns under Competitive Conditions": Progress in Microeconomics since Sraffa (1926)? *Eastern Econ. J.*, July–September 1983, *9*(3), pp. 213–20.

Garegnani, Pierangelo. Ricardo's Early Theory of Profits and Its 'Rational Foundation': A Reply to Professor Hollander [On Hollander's Interpretation of Ricardo's Early Theory of Profits]. *Cambridge J. Econ.*, June 1983, *7*(2), pp. 175–78.

Harcourt, Geoffrey C. On Piero Sraffa's Contributions to Economics. **In** *Groenewegen, P. and Halevi, J., eds.*, 1983, pp. 117–28.

Hollander, Samuel. Professor Garegnani's Defence of Sraffa on the Material Rate of Profit [On Hollander's Interpretation of Ricardo's Early Theory of Profits]. *Cambridge J. Econ.*, June 1983, *7*(2), pp. 167–74.

Roncaglia, Alessandro. Piero Sraffa and the Reconstruction of Political Economy. *Banca Naz. Lavoro Quart. Rev.*, December 1983, (147), pp. 337–50.

Samuelson, Paul A. Durable Capital Inputs: Conditions for Price Ratios to Be Invariant to Profit–Rate Changes. *Z. Nationalökon.*, 1983, *43*(1), pp. 1–20.

Schefold, Bertram. Straffas Theorie der Kuppelproduktion: Ein Überblick. (Sraffa's Theory of Joint Production: A Survey. With English summary.) *Z. Wirtschaft. Sozialwissen.*, 1983, *103*(4), pp. 315–40.

Watts, Martin J. Sraffa after Marx: A Correction. *Australian Econ. Pap.*, June 1983, *22*(40), pp. 255–57.

Steuart, James [Sir]

Perelman, Michael. Classical Political Economy and Primitive Accumulation: The Case of Smith and Steuart. *Hist. Polit. Econ.*, Fall 1983, *15*(3), pp. 451–94.

Stigler, George

Mincer, Jacob. George Stigler's Contributions to Economics. *Scand. J. Econ.*, 1983, *85*(1), pp. 65–75.

Schmalensee, Richard. George Stigler's Contributions to Economics. *Scand. J. Econ.*, 1983, *85*(1), pp. 77–86.

da Silva, Amado and Santos, Aníbal. Uma digressão pela economia industrial: de Harvard a Chicago passando pela Europa. *Economia*, January 1983, *7*(1), pp. 87–110.

Sun, Yefang

Bertinelli, Roberto. Sun Yefang. (In Italian. With English summary.) *Rivista Int. Sci. Econ. Com.*, August 1983, *30*(8), pp. 779–91.

Süssmilch, Johann P.

Süssmilch, Johann Peter. On Removing Obstacles to Population Growth. *Population Devel. Rev.*, September 1983, *9*(3), pp. 521–29. **[G: Germany]**

von Thünen, Johann Heinrich

Beckmann, Martin J. Der "isolirte Staat" im räumlichen Gleichgewicht. (The "Isolirte Staat" in the General Spatial Equilibrium. With English summary.) *Z. Wirtschaft. Sozialwissen.*, 1983, *103*(6), 629–39.

Engelhardt, Werner Wilhelm. Zum Situations- und Problembezug von Entscheidungsmodellen bei Johann Heinrich von Thünen. (Relevance of Decision-Oriented Models by Johann Heinrich von Thünen. With English summary.) *Z. Wirtschaft. Sozialwissen.*, 1983, *103*(6), pp. 561–88.

Samuelson, Paul A. 1983: Marx, Keynes and Schumpeter. *Eastern Econ. J.*, July–September 1983, *9*(3), pp. 166–79.

Samuelson, Paul A. Thünen at Two Hundred. *J. Econ. Lit.*, December 1983, *21*(4), pp. 1468–88.

Schmitt, Günther. Johann Heinrich von Thünen und die Agrarökonomie heute. (Johann Heinrich von Thünen and the Present State of Agricultural Economics. With English summary.) *Z. Wirtschaft. Sozialwissen.*, 1983, *103*(6), pp. 641–59.

Winkel, Harald. Johann Heinrich von Thünen und die Rezeption der englischen Klassik. (Johann von Thünen and English Classical Economic Theory. With English summary.) *Z. Wirtschaft. Sozialwissen.*, 1983, *103*(6), pp. 543–59.

Thurow, Lester

Cate, Tom. Keynes and Thurow: The Socialization of Investment. *Eastern Econ. J.*, July–September 1983, *9*(3), pp. 205–12.

Turgot, Anne Robert Jacques

Groenewegen, Peter D. Turgot, Beccaria and Smith. **In** *Groenewegen, P. and Halevi, J., eds.*, 1983, pp. 31–78.

Groenewegen, Peter D. Turgot's Place in the History of Economic Thought: A Bicentenary Estimate. *Hist. Polit. Econ.*, Winter 1983, *15*(4), pp. 585–616.

Ulman, Lloyd

Brown, Clair; Flanagan, Robert J. and Strauss, George. In Honor of Lloyd Ulman. *Ind. Relat.*, Spring 1983, *22*(2), pp. 135–40.

Uno, Kozo

Duncan, Colin A. M. Under the Cloud of *Capital:* History vs. Theory. *Sci. Soc.*, Fall 1983, *47*(3), pp. 300–322.

Valois, Georges

Douglas, Allen. Georges Valois and the Franc—Or: A Right-Wing Reaction to Inflation. **In** *Schmukler, N. and Marcus, E., eds.*, 1983, pp. 226–45.

Veblen, Thorstein

Simich, J. L. and Tilman, Rick. On the Use and Abuse of Thorstein Veblen in Modern American Sociology, I: David Riesman's Reductionist Interpretation and Talcott Parsons' Pluralist Critique. *Amer. J. Econ. Soc.*, October 1983, *42*(4), pp. 417–29.

Vico, Giambattista

Haddad, Louis. The Evolutionary Economics of Giambattista Vico. **In** *Groenewegen, P. and Halevi, J., eds.*, 1983, pp. 17–30.

Villard, Henry

Bach, G. L. Above and Beyond the Call of Duty—A Tribute to Henry Villard. *J. Econ. Educ.*, Winter 1983, *14*(1), pp. 7–8. **[G: U.S.]**

Viner, Jacob

Rotwein, Eugene. Jacob Viner and the Chicago Tradition. *Hist. Polit. Econ.*, Summer 1983, *15*(2), pp. 265–80.

Walras, Léon

Hall, S. G. F. Money and the Walrasian Utility Function. *Oxford Econ. Pap.*, July 1983, *35*(2), pp. 247–53.

Hicks, John. Leon Walras. **In** *Hicks, J.*, 1983, *1934*, pp. 85–95.

Jaffé, William. A Centenarian on a Bicentenarian: Léon Walras's *Eléments* on Adam Smith's *Wealth of Nations*. **In** *Jaffé, W.*, 1983, *1977*, pp. 93–107.

Jaffé, William. A. N. Isnard, Progenitor of the Walrasian General Equilibrium Model. **In** *Jaffé, W.*, 1983, *1969*, pp. 55–77.

Jaffé, William. Léon Walras. **In** *Jaffé, W.*, 1983, *1968*, pp. 131–35.

Jaffé, William. Léon Walras and His Conception of Economics. **In** *Jaffé, W.*, 1983, *1956*, pp. 121–30.

Jaffé, William. Léon Walras and His Relations with American Economists. **In** *Jaffé, W.*, 1983, *1960*, pp. 108–18.

Jaffé, William. Léon Walras, an Economic Adviser *Manque*. **In** *Jaffé, W.*, 1983, *1975*, pp. 36–52.

Jaffé, William. Menger, Jevons and Walras Dehomogenized. **In** *Jaffé, W.*, 1983, *1976*, pp. 311–25.

Jaffé, William. Reflections on the Importance of Léon Walras. **In** *Jaffé, W.*, 1983, *1971*, pp. 269–87.

Jaffé, William. The Birth of Léon Walras's *Eléments*. **In** *Jaffé, W.*, 1983, *1977*, pp. 78–92.

Jaffé, William. The Walras–Poincaré Correspondence on the Cardinal Measurability of Utility. **In** *Jaffé, W.*, 1983, *1977*, pp. 213–20.

Jaffé, William. Unpublished Papers and Letters of Léon Walras. **In** *Jaffé, W.*, 1983, *1935*, pp. 17–35.

Jaffé, William. Walras's Economics as Others See It. **In** *Jaffé, W.*, 1983, *1980*, pp. 343–70.

Weintraub, Sidney

Davidson, Paul. An Appraisal of Weintraub's Work. *Eastern Econ. J.*, October–December 1983, *9*(4), pp. 291–94.

Seidman, Laurence S. Sidney Weintraub, the Man and His Ideas. *Challenge*, November/December 1983, *26*(5), pp. 22–28.

Weintraub, Sidney. A Jevonian Seditionist: A Mutiny to Enhance the Economic Bounty? *Banca Naz. Lavoro Quart. Rev.*, September 1983, (146), pp. 215–34.

Whewell, William

Porta, Pier Luigi. A Comment on Dr. Campanelli's Article on W. Whewell's Contribution to Economic Analysis. *Rivista Int. Sci. Econ. Com.*, April-May 1983, *30*(4–5), pp. 398–400.

Wicksell, Knut

Coleman, W. O. Wicksell and the Akerman Axe Model: A Re-Examination. *Australian Econ. Pap.*, December 1983, *22*(41), pp. 467–76.

Goodwin, R. M. Capital Theory in Orthogonalised General Co-ordinates. **In** *Goodwin, R. M.*, 1983, *1977*, pp. 153–72.

Hansson, Bjorn. Wicksell's Critique of Ricardo's Chapter "On Machinery." *J. Econ. Stud.*, 1983, *10*(3), pp. 49–55.

Spengler, Joseph. Knut Wicksell, Father of the Optimum. *Atlantic Econ. J.*, December 1983, *11*(4), pp. 1–5.

Williams, John H.

Malamud, Bernard. John H. Williams on the German Inflation: The International Amplification of Monetary Disturbances. **In** *Schmukler, N. and Marcus, E., eds.*, 1983, pp. 417–34. **[G: Germany]**

Wilson, James

Boot, H. M. James Wilson and the Commercial Crisis of 1847. *Hist. Polit. Econ.*, Winter 1983, *15*(4), pp. 567–83. **[G: U.K.]**

Wood, Stuart

Stigler, George J. Stuart Wood and the Marginal Productivity Theory. **In** *Stigler, G. J.*, 1983, *1947*, pp. 287–301.

Young, Allyn Abbott

Blitch, Charles P. Allyn A. Young: A Curious Case of Professional Neglect. *Hist. Polit. Econ.*, Spring 1983, *15*(1), pp. 1–24.

Blitch, Charles P. Allyn A. Young on Increasing Returns. *J. Post Keynesian Econ.*, Spring 1983, *5*(3), pp. 359–79.

0329 Other Special Topics

Andersen, Peder. 'On Rent of Fishing Grounds': A Translation of Jens Warming's 1911 Article, with an Introduction. *Hist. Polit. Econ.*, Fall 1983, *15*(3), pp. 391–96.

Asimakopulos, A. Anticipations of Keynes's General Theory? *Can. J. Econ.*, August 1983, *16*(3), pp. 517–30.

Backhaus, Juergen. Economic Theories and Political Interests: Scholarly Economics in Pre-Hitler Germany: Review Article. *J. Europ. Econ. Hist.*, Winter 1983, *12*(3), pp. 661–67. **[G: Germany]**

Bartoli, Henri. Le problème des régions dans la pensée économique italienne. (The Problem of Regions in the Italian Economic Thought. With English summary.) *Giorn. Econ.*, September–October 1983, *42*(9–10), pp. 561–99. **[G: Italy]**

Bodkin, Ronald G. and West, Edwin G. Conjectural Nobel Prizes in Economics: 1770 to 1890. *Eastern Econ. J.*, July–September 1983, *9*(3), pp. 151–65.

Botha, D. J. J. Some Thoughts around the *General Theory* (Review Article). *S. Afr. J. Econ.*, September 1983, *51*(3), pp. 426–45.

Briefs, Goetz A. Catholic Social Doctrine, *Laissez-Faire* Liberalism, and Social Market Economy. *Rev. Soc. Econ.*, December 1983, *41*(3), pp. 246–58.

Briefs, Goetz A. Marginal Ethics in the Pluralistic Society. *Rev. Soc. Econ.*, December 1983, *41*(3), pp. 259–70.

Briefs, Goetz A. Pesch and His Contemporaries: *Nationalokonomie* vs. Contemporary Economic Theories. *Rev. Soc. Econ.*, December 1983, *41*(3), pp. 235–45.

Buchanan, James M. 'La Scienza delle Finanze': The Italian Tradition in Fiscal Theory. **In** *Groenewegen, P. and Halevi, J., eds.*, 1983, pp. 79–115.

Cawley, Leo. Scarcity, Distribution and Growth: Notes on Classical Rent Theory. *Rev. Radical Polit. Econ.*, Fall 1983, *15*(3), pp. 143–58.

Collins, Randall. The Weberian Revolution of the High Middle Ages. **In** *Bergesen, A., ed.*, 1983, pp. 205–25.

Currie, Lauchlin. The "Multiplier" in Economic Literature. *J. Econ. Stud.*, 1983, *10*(3), pp. 42–48.

Dooley, Peter C. Slutsky's Equation Is Pareto's Solution. *Hist. Polit. Econ.*, Winter 1983, *15*(4), pp. 513–17.

Elliott, John E. Schumpeter and the Theory of Capitalist Economic Development. *J. Econ. Behav. Organ.*, December 1983, *4*(4), pp. 277–308.

Fine, Ben. The Historical Approach to Rent and Price Theory Reconsidered. *Australian Econ. Pap.*, June 1983, *22*(40), pp. 132–43.

Hacken, Richard D. Scandinavian Social Economics 1850–1930: A Bibliographic Note. *Rev. Soc. Econ.*, October 1983, *41*(2), pp. 137–51. **[G: Scandinavia]**

Hicks, John. Is Interest the Price of a Factor of Production? **In** *Hicks, J.*, 1983, *1979*, pp. 113–28.

Jaffé, William. Léon Walras and His Relations with American Economists. **In** *Jaffé, W.*, 1983, *1960*, pp. 108–18.

Jaffé, William. Léon Walras's Role in the "Marginal Revolution" of the 1870s. **In** *Jaffé, W.*, 1983, *1972*, pp. 288–310.

Jaffé, William. Léon Walras's Theory of Capital Accumulation. **In** *Jaffé, W.*, 1983, *1942*, pp. 139–50.

Jaffé, William. Menger, Jevons and Walras De-homogenized. **In** *Jaffé, W.*, 1983, *1976*, pp. 311–25.

Jaffé, William. New Light on an Old Quarrel: Barone's Unpublished Review of Wicksteed's "Essay on the Coordination of the Laws of Distribution" and Related Documents. **In** *Jaffé, W.*, 1983, *1964*, pp. 176–212.

Jaffé, William. The Walras–Poincaré Correspondence on the Cardinal Measurability of Utility. **In** *Jaffé, W.*, 1983, *1977*, pp. 213–20.

Jaffé, William. Unpublished Papers and Letters of Léon Walras. **In** *Jaffé, W.*, 1983, *1935*, pp. 17–35.

Jaffé, William. Walras's Theory of Capital Formation in the Framework of His Theory of General Equilibrium. **In** *Jaffé, W.*, 1983, *1953*, pp. 151–75.

Kuran, Timur. Behavioral Norms in the Islamic Doctrine of Economics: A Critique. *J. Econ. Behav. Organ.*, December 1983, *4*(4), pp. 353–79.

Lerner, Abba P. From Vulgar Political Economy to Vulgar Marxism. **In** *Lerner, A. P.*, 1983, *1939*, pp. 583–93.

Lerner, Abba P. Marginal Cost Pricing in the 1930's. **In** *Lerner, A. P.*, 1983, *1977*, pp. 187–91.

Marotta, Gary. The Academic Mind and the Rise of U.S. Imperialism: Historians and Economists as Publicists for Ideas of Colonial Expansion. *Amer. J. Econ. Soc.*, April 1983, *42*(2), pp. 217–34. **[G: U.S.]**

Mathias, Peter. Entrepreneurship and Economic History: The State of the Debate. **In** *Earl, M. J., ed.*, 1983, pp. 40–54.

Mátyás, Antal. Similarities between the Economic Theories of Marx and Keynes. *Acta Oecon.*, 1983, *31*(3–4), pp. 155–73.

Musgrave, Richard A. Private Labor and Common Land. **In** *Break, G. F., ed.*, 1983, pp. 185–200.

Ranson, Baldwin. The Unrecognized Revolution in the Theory of Capital Formation. *J. Econ. Issues*, December 1983, *17*(4), pp. 901–13.

Rogers, Colin. Neo-Walrasian Macroeconomics, Microfoundations and Pseudo-Production Models. *Australian Econ. Pap.*, June 1983, *22*(40), pp. 201–20.

Rugina, Anghel N. About the Doctrine of "Solidarism" in Social Economics. *Int. J. Soc. Econ.*, 1983, *10*(2), pp. 62–71.

Schmitz, Wolfgang. Economic and Social Partnership and Incomes Policy and the Social Doctrine of the Church. *Economia,* May 1983, *7*(2), pp. 307–29.

Stigler, George J. Henry L. Moore and Statistical Economics. **In** *Stigler, G. J.*, 1983, *1962*, pp. 343–73.

Stigler, George J. Statistical Studies in the History of Economic Thought. **In** *Stigler, G. J.*, 1983, pp. 31–50.

036 Economic Methodology

0360 Economic Methodology

Albin, Peter S. Structural Theory and Structural Formations. *Math. Soc. Sci.*, November 1983, *6*(2), pp. 133–52.

Andersen, Ellen. Erfaringer med keynesianske makromodeller. (With English summary.) *Nationaløkon. Tidsskr.*, 1983, *121*(3), pp. 323–31.

Archibald, G. C. The State of Economic Science. **In** *Marr, W. L. and Raj, B., eds.*, 1983, *1959,* pp. 185–98.

d'Arcy, P. Le pluralisme dans la logique économique. (Pluralism and Economic Logic. With English summary.) *Écon. Soc.*, June 1983, *17*(6), pp. 959–82.

Bartoli, Gloria. Programma positivista e rivoluzione marginalista in economia. (Positivistic Programme and Marginalistic Revolution in Economics. With English summary.) *Giorn. Econ.*, November–December 1983, *42*(11–12), pp. 749–68.

Black, Philip A. Participant Observation and Logical Positivism in the Social Sciences: A Note. *World Devel.*, April 1983, *11*(4), pp. 389–90.

Boland, Lawrence A. A Critique of Friedman's Critics. **In** *Marr, W. L. and Raj, B., eds.*, 1983, *1979,* pp. 101–30.

Bolin, Meb. The Independent, Simultaneous Development of Instrumental Thoughts in Various Disciplines. *J. Econ. Issues,* June 1983, *17*(2), pp. 345–52.

Brennan, Geoffrey and Buchanan, James M. Predictive Power and the Choice among Regimes. *Econ. J.*, March 1983, *93*(369), pp. 89–105.

Brookins, O. T. Economics as a Science: Some Theoretical Aspects. *Amer. Econ.*, Spring 1983, *27*(1), pp. 58–60.

Campbell, William F. Pericles and the Sophistication of Economics. *Hist. Polit. Econ.*, Spring 1983, *15*(1), pp. 122–35.

Canterbery, E. Ray and Burkhardt, Robert J. What Do We Mean by Asking Whether Economics Is a Science? **In** *Eichner, A. S., ed.*, 1983, pp. 15–40.

Cesarano, Filippo. On the Role of the History of Economic Analysis. *Hist. Polit. Econ.*, Spring 1983, *15*(1), pp. 63–82.

Chanier, P. Trinitarisme, unitarisme et physique économique. (Trinitarism, Unitarism and Economic Physics. With English summary.) *Écon. Soc.*, June 1983, *17*(6), pp. 1003–55.

Chase, Richard X. Adolph Lowe's Paradigm Shift for a Scientific Economics: An Interpretive Perspective. *Amer. J. Econ. Soc.*, April 1983, *42*(2), pp. 167–77.

Chase, Richard X. The Kuhnian Paradigm Thesis as a Dialectical Process and Its Application to Economics. *Rivista Int. Sci. Econ. Com.*, September 1983, *30*(9), pp. 809–28.

Coats, A. W. Is There a "Structure of Scientific Revolutions" in Economics? **In** *Marr, W. L. and Raj, B., eds.*, 1983, *1969,* pp. 273–79.

Coats, A. W. The Revival of Subjectivism in Economics. **In** *Wiseman, J., ed.*, 1983, pp. 87–103.

Coddington, A. Positive Economics. **In** *Marr, W. L. and Raj, B., eds.*, 1983, *1972,* pp. 69–88.

Covi, Antonio. Keynes e la critica di Lucas. (Keynes and Lucas' Criticism. With English summary.) *Rivista Int. Sci. Econ. Com.*, December 1983, *30*(12), pp. 1115–31.

Crossland, Philip P. and Weinel, Ivan. Modern Empiricism and Quantum Leap Theorizing in Economics: A Comment. *J. Econ. Issues,* December 1983, *17*(4), pp. 1129–38.

Deane, Phyllis. The Scope and Method of Economic Science. *Econ. J.*, March 1983, *93*(369), pp. 1–12.

Dow, Sheila C. Schools of Thought in Macroeconomics: The Method Is the Message. *Australian Econ. Pap.*, June 1983, *22*(40), pp. 30–47.

Dow, Sheila C. Substantive Mountains and Methodological Molehills: A Rejoinder [Weintraub and Wiles: The Methodological Basis of Policy Conflict]. *J. Post Keynesian Econ.*, Winter 1982–83, *5*(2), pp. 304–08.

Dugger, William M. Two Twists in Economic Methodology: Positivism and Subjectivism. *Amer. J. Econ. Soc.*, January 1983, *42*(1), pp. 75–91.

Dwyer, Larry. 'Value Freedom' and the Scope of Economic Inquiry: II. The Fact/Value Continuum and the Basis for Scientific and Humanistic Policy. *Amer. J. Econ. Soc.*, July 1983, *42*(3), pp. 353–68.

Earl, Peter E. The Consumer in His/Her Social Setting—A Subjectivist View. **In** *Wiseman, J., ed.*, 1983, pp. 176–91.

Eichner, Alfred S. Why Economics Is Not Yet a Science. *J. Econ. Issues,* June 1983, *17*(2), pp. 507–20.

Eichner, Alfred S. Why Economics Is Not Yet a Science. **In** *Eichner, A. S., ed.*, 1983, pp. 205–41.

Engelhardt, Werner Wilhelm. Zum Situations- und Problembezug von Entscheidungsmodellen bei Johann Heinrich von Thünen. (Relevance of Decision-Oriented Models by Johann Heinrich von Thünen. With English summary.) *Z. Wirtschaft. Sozialwissen.*, 1983, *103*(6), pp. 561–88.

Faludi, Andreas. Critical Rationalism and Planning Methodology. *Urban Stud.*, August 1983, *20*(3), pp. 265–78.

Fellner, William. Entrepreneurship in Economic Theory: The "Scientific Method" and Vicarious Introspection. **In** *Backman, J., ed.*, 1983, pp. 25–53.

Frazer, William J., Jr. and Boland, Lawrence A. An Essay on the Foundations of Friedman's Methodology. *Amer. Econ. Rev.*, March 1983, *73*(1), pp. 129–44.

Giarini, Orio. La notion de valeur économique dans la société post-industrielle: éléments pour la recherche de nouveaux paradigmes de l'économique. (The Notion of Economic Value in Post-Industrial Society: Elements towards Research on New Paradigms for Economics. With English summary.) *Écon. Soc.*, February 1983, *17*(2), pp. 299–334.

Gould, Peter and Straussfogel, Debra. Revolution and Structural Disconnection: A Note on Portugal's International Trade. *Economia,* October 1983, *7*(3), pp. 435–53. **[G: Portugal]**

Gowdy, John M. Biological Analogies in Economics: A Comment [Marshall Revisited in the Age of DNA]. *J. Post Keynesian Econ.*, Summer 1983, *5*(4), pp. 676–78.

Greenfield, Robert L. and Salerno, Joseph T. Another Defense of Methodological Apriorism. *Eastern Econ. J.*, January–March 1983, *9*(1), pp. 45–56.

Helm, Dieter. Three Views of Methodology. *Greek Econ. Rev.*, December 1983, *5*(3), pp. 278–85.

Hicks, John. 'Revolutions' in Economics. **In** *Hicks, J.*, 1983, *1976,* pp. 3–16.

Hill, Lewis E. The Pragmatic Alternative to Positive Economics. *Rev. Soc. Econ.*, April 1983, *41* (1), pp. 1–11.

Hutchison, Terence. From 'Dismal Science' to 'Positive Economics'—A Century-and-a-Half of Progress? **In** *Wiseman, J., ed.*, 1983, pp. 192–211.

Johansen, Leif. Mechanistic and Organistic Analogies in Economics: The Place of Game Theory: Some Notes on H. Thoben's Article. *Kyklos,* 1983, *36*(2), pp. 304–07.

Johnson, L. E. Economic Paradigms: A Missing Dimension. *J. Econ. Issues,* December 1983, *17*(4), pp. 1097–1111.

Karsten, Siegfried G. Dialectics, Functionalism, and Structuralism in Economic Thought. *Amer. J. Econ. Soc.*, April 1983, *42*(2), pp. 179–92.

Katouzian, Homa. Towards the Progress of Economic Knowledge. **In** *Wiseman, J., ed.*, 1983, pp. 50–64.

Klamer, Arjo. Empirical Arguments in New Classical Economics. *Écon. Appl.*, 1983, *36*(1), pp. 229–54.

Kornai, János. The Health of Nations: Reflections on the Analogy between the Medical Science and Economics. *Kyklos,* 1983, *36*(2), pp. 191–212.

Koslowski, Peter F. Mechanistische und organistische Analogien in der Wirtschaftswissenschaft—eine verfehlte Alternative [Mechanistic and Organistic Analogies in Economics Reconsidered]. *Kyklos,* 1983, *36*(2), pp. 308–12.

Kristol, Irving. Rationalism in Economics. **In** *Kristol, I.*, 1983, *1980,* pp. 177–93.

Leontief, Wassily W. Academic Economics. **In** *Marr, W. L. and Raj, B., eds.*, 1983, *1982,* pp. 331–35.

Lerner, Abba P. Professor Samuelson on Theory and Realism: Comment. **In** *Lerner, A. P.*, 1983, *1965,* pp. 643–45.

Lindenberg, Siegwart. Utility and Morality. *Kyklos,* 1983, *36*(3), pp. 450–68.

Littleboy, B. and Mehta, Granshyam. The Scientific Method of Keynes. *J. Econ. Stud.*, 1983, *10*(4), pp. 3–14.

Littlechild, Stephen. Subjectivism and Method in Economics. **In** *Wiseman, J., ed.*, 1983, pp. 38–49.

Machlup, Fritz. The Problem of Verification in Economics. **In** *Marr, W. L. and Raj, B., eds.*, 1983, *1955,* pp. 157–83.

McCloskey, Donald N. The Rhetoric of Economics. *J. Econ. Lit.*, June 1983, *21* (2), pp. 481–517.

Miller, Michael S. Methodology and the Theory of Consumer Behavior. *Rev. Soc. Econ.*, April 1983, *41* (1), pp. 39–51.

Mott, Tracy and Singell, Larry D. The Positive Treatment of Social Values: State of the Art. *J. Behav. Econ.*, Summer 1983, *12*(1), pp. 71–87.

Nuccio, Oscar. Medieval and Italian Sources of Economic Rationalism: A Critique and Indications of Historical Methodology. *Rivista Polit. Econ.*, Supplement Dec. 1983, *73*(12), pp. 69–131.

Nurmi, Hannu. The F-Twist and the Evaluation of Political Institutions. *Z. Wirtschaft. Sozialwissen.*, 1983, *103*(2), pp. 143–59.

Pope, David and Pope, Robin. In Defense of Predictionism. **In** *Marr, W. L. and Raj, B., eds.*, 1983, *1972,* pp. 89–100.

Ricci, F. Paradoxes logiques et temporalité. (Logical Paradoxes and Temporality. With English summary.) *Écon. Soc.*, June 1983, *17*(6), pp. 983–1002.

Rich, Robert F. Making, Relaying, and Using Knowledge. **In** *Holzner, B.; Knorr, K. D. and Strasser, H., eds.*, 1983, pp. 220–35.

Ricossa, Sergio. Scarcity or Producibility. An Inexistant Dilemma. *Rivista Polit. Econ.*, Supplement Dec. 1983, *73*(12), pp. 133–45.

Rotwein, Eugene. Empiricism and Economic Method: Several Views Considered. **In** *Marr, W. L. and Raj, B., eds.*, 1983, *1973,* pp. 133–56.

Schmidt, Christian. De Charles Gide à Mark Blaug: éléments pour une histoire de l'Histoire de la pensée économique. (With English summary.) *Revue Écon. Polit.*, November-December 1983, *93*(6), pp. 847–68.

Schmidt, Christian. Malthus et la semantique économique. (With English summary.) *Revue Écon. Polit.*, March–April 1983, *93*(2), pp. 248–69.

Schroyer, Trent. Critique of the Instrumental Interest in Nature. *Soc. Res.*, Spring 1983, *50*(1), pp. 158–84.

Shackle, George L. S. Review Article: Decisions, Process and the Market. *J. Econ. Stud.*, 1983, *10*(3), pp. 56–66.

Shackle, George L. S. The Bounds of Unknowledge. **In** *Wiseman, J., ed.*, 1983, pp. 28–37.

Shearmur, Jeremy. Subjectivism, Falsification, and Positive Economics. **In** *Wiseman, J., ed.*, 1983, pp. 65–86.

Simpson, David. Joseph Schumpeter and the Austrian School of Economics. *J. Econ. Stud.*, 1983, *10*(4), pp. 15–28.

Söderbaum, Peter. Ezra Mishan on Economic Evaluation: A Comment. *J. Econ. Issues,* March 1983, *17*(1), pp. 206–13.

Stigler, George J. Nobel Lecture: The Process and Progress of Economics. *J. Polit. Econ.*, August 1983, *91* (4), pp. 529–45.

Stigler, George J. The Nature and Role of Originality in Scientific Progress. **In** *Stigler, G. J.*, 1983, *1955,* pp. 1–15.

Swaney, James A. and Premus, Robert. Modern Empiricism and Quatum-Leap Theorizing in Economics. **In** *Eichner, A. S., ed.*, 1983, *1982*, pp. 41–60.

Swaney, James A. and Premus, Robert. Practice, Logic, and Problem Solving: A Reply. *J. Econ. Issues,* December 1983, *17*(4), pp. 1138–42.

Tarascio, Vincent J. Pareto's *Trattato. Eastern Econ. J.*, April–June 1983, *9*(2), pp. 119–31.

Tarascio, Vincent J. The Problem of Progress in Economic Science. *Atlantic Econ. J.*, July 1983, *11*(2), pp. 29–34.

Tietzel, Manfred. Erkenntnisfortschritt und Konjunkturtheorie. (Progress of Knowledge and the Theory of the Trade Cycle. With English summary.) *Ifo-Studien,* 1983, *29*(1), pp. 11–30.

Tilman, Rick. Social Value Theory, Corporate Power, and Political Elites: Appraisals of Lindblom's *Politics and Markets. J. Econ. Issues,* March 1983, *17*(1), pp. 115–31.

Tisdell, Clem A. Dissent from Value, Preference and Choice Theory in Economics. *Int. J. Soc. Econ.*, 1983, *10*(2), pp. 32–43.

Weintraub, E. Roy. Substantive Mountains and Methodological Molehills: Comment [Weintraub and Wiles: The Methodological Basis of Policy Conflict]. *J. Post Keynesian Econ.*, Winter 1982–83, *5*(2), pp. 295–303.

Wilber, Charles K. and Harrison, Robert S. The Methodological Basis of Institutional Economics: Pattern Model, Storytelling, and Holism. **In** *Marr, W. L. and Raj, B., eds.*, 1983, *1978*, pp. 243–72.

Wiles, Peter. Ideology, Methodology, and Neoclassical Economics. **In** *Eichner, A. S., ed.*, 1983, *1979–80*, pp. 61–89.

Wiles, Peter. Methodology: In Praise of Ourselves. *ACES Bull. (See Comp. Econ. Stud. after 8/85)*, Spring 1983, *25*(1), pp. 1–10. **[G: U.S.S.R.]**

Wiseman, Jack. Beyond Positive Economics? Introduction. **In** *Wiseman, J., ed.*, 1983, pp. 1–12.

Wiseman, Jack. Beyond Positive Economics—Dream and Reality. **In** *Wiseman, J., ed.*, 1983, pp. 13–27.

Wulwick, Nancy J. Can Keynesian Economics Be Scientific? An Historical Reconstruction. *Eastern Econ. J.*, July–September 1983, *9*(3), pp. 190–204. **[G: U.K.]**

Zaltman, Gerald. Construing Knowledge Use. **In** *Holzner, B.; Knorr, K. D. and Strasser, H., eds.*, 1983, pp. 236–51.

040 Economic History

041 Economic History: General

0410 General

Chase-Dunn, Christopher. Inequality, Structural Mobility, and Dependency Reversal in the Capitalist World Economy. **In** *Doran, C. F.; Modelski, G. and Clark, C., eds.*, 1983, pp. 73–95. **[G: Selected Countries]**

Engerman, Stanley L. Contract Labor, Sugar, and Technology in the Nineteenth Century. *J. Econ. Hist.*, September 1983, *43*(3), pp. 635–59. **[G: Europe; U.S.]**

Jones, Geoffrey. Some Recent Histories of International Oil. *J. Econ. Hist.*, December 1983, *43*(4), pp. 993–96. **[G: France; Latin America; U.K.]**

Lewis, W. Arthur. The Rate of Growth of World Trade, 1830–1973. **In** *Lewis, W. A.*, 1983, *1981*, pp. 293–308.

Othick, John. Development Indicators and the Historical Study of Human Welfare: Towards a New Perspective. *J. Econ. Hist.*, March 1983, *43*(1), pp. 63–70.

Piven, Frances Fox and Cloward, Richard A. Humanitarianism in History: A Response to the Critics. **In** *Trattner, W. I., ed..*, 1983, pp. 114–48.

Trattner, Walter I. Social Welfare or Social Control? Some Historical Reflections: Introduction. **In** *Trattner, W. I., ed..*, 1983, pp. 3–14.

0411 Development of the Discipline

Braeman, John. The New Left and American Foreign Policy during the Age of Normalcy: A Re-Examination. *Bus. Hist. Rev.*, Spring 1983, *57*(1), pp. 73–104. **[G: U.S.]**

Caire, Guy. Histoire recetter ou histoire méthode: A propos de la problématique rostowienne et des paradigmes dominants de l'économie du développement. (History as Receipts or History as Method: Concerning the Problems Raised by Rostow and the Dominant Paradigmes of Economy of Development. With English summary.) *Écon. Soc.*, February 1983, *17*(2), pp. 261–88.

Galambos, Louis. Technology, Political Economy, and Professionalization: Central Themes of the Organizational Synthesis. *Bus. Hist. Rev.*, Winter 1983, *57*(4), pp. 471–93. **[G: U.S.]**

Hannah, Leslie. New Issues in British Business History. *Bus. Hist. Rev.*, Summer 1983, *57*(2), pp. 165–74. **[G: U.K.]**

Jacobson, Jon. Is There a New International History of the 1920s? *Amer. Hist. Rev.*, June 1983, *88*(3), pp. 617–45. **[G: Europe]**

Lindert, Peter H. Remodeling British Economic History: A Review Article. *J. Econ. Hist.*, December 1983, *43*(4), pp. 986–92. **[G: U.K.]**

North, Douglass C. A Theory of Institutional Change and the Economic History of the Western World. **In** *Hechter, M., ed.*, 1983, pp. 190–215.

Zieger, Robert H. Industrial Relations and Labor History in the Eighties. *Ind. Relat.*, Winter 1983, *22*(1), pp. 58–70. **[G: U.S.]**

0412 Comparative Intercountry or Intertemporal Economic History

Alexander, Malcolm L. Australia in the Capitalist World Economy. **In** *Head, B. W., ed.*, 1983, pp. 55–76. **[G: Australia; Canada; Latin America]**

Aujac, Henri. Culture nationale et aptitude á l'industrialisation (1). *Revue Écon. Polit.*, January–February 1983, *93*(1), pp. 1–28. **[G: France; Japan; Brazil; Ivory Coast]**

Balán, Jorge. Comment [The Integration of Italian Immigrants into the United States and Argentina: A Comparative Analysis]. *Amer. Hist. Rev.*, April 1983, *88*(2), pp. 330–34. **[G: U.S.; Argentina]**

Bosworth, Barry P. A Century of Evidence on Wage and Price Stickiness in the United States, the United Kingdom and Japan: Comment. **In** *Tobin,*

J., ed., 1983, pp. 121–24. **[G: U.S.; U.K.; Japan]**

Capie, Forrest. Tariff Protection and Economic Performance in the Nineteenth Century. **In** *Black, J. and Winters, L. A., eds.*, 1983, pp. 1–24. **[G: Europe; U.S.]**

Destanne de Bernis, Gérard. De l'existence de points de passage obligatoires pour une politique de développement. (On the Existence of Obligatory Passage Points for Development Policy. With English summary.) *Écon. Soc.*, February 1983, *17* (2), pp. 213–59.

Dunning, John H. Changes in the Level and Structure of International Production: The Last One Hundred Years. **In** *Casson, M., ed.*, 1983, pp. 84–139. **[G: Global]**

Dunning, John H. Market Power of the Firm and International Transfer of Technology: A Historical Excursion. *Int. J. Ind. Organ.*, December 1983, *1* (4), pp. 333–51. **[G: U.S.; Europe; LDCs]**

Field, Alexander James. Land Abundance, Interest/Profit Rates, and Nineteenth-Century American and British Technology. *J. Econ. Hist.*, June 1983, *43* (2), pp. 405–31. **[G: U.K.; U.S.]**

Fontana, Josep. Economic Development of the Mediterranean Countries in Historical Perspective. **In** *Sampedro, J. L. and Payno, J. A., eds.*, 1983, pp. 41–54. **[G: Italy; Greece; Portugal; Spain]**

Goldfrank, Walter L. The Limits of Analogy: Hegemonic Decline in Great Britain and the United States. **In** *Bergesen, A., ed.*, 1983, pp. 143–54. **[G: U.K.; U.S.]**

Gordon, Robert J. A Century of Evidence on Wage and Price Stickiness in the United States, the United Kingdom, and Japan. **In** *Tobin, J., ed.*, 1983, pp. 85–121. **[G: U.S.; Japan; U.K.]**

Gould, John D. Comment [The Integration of Italian Immigrants into the United States and Argentina: A Comparative Analysis]. *Amer. Hist. Rev.*, April 1983, *88* (2), pp. 334–38. **[G: U.S.; Argentina]**

Gross, Nachum. Austria–Hungary in the World Economy. **In** *Komlos, J., ed.*, 1983, pp. 1–45. **[G: Austria; Hungary; Europe]**

Halperin-Donghi, Tulio. Comment [The Integration of Italian Immigrants into the United States and Argentina: A Comparative Analysis]. *Amer. Hist. Rev.*, April 1983, *88* (2), pp. 338–42. **[G: U.S.; Argentina]**

Heinsohn, Gunnar and Steiger, Otto. Private Property, Debts and Interest or: The Origin of Money and the Rise and Fall of Monetary Economies. *Stud. Econ.*, 1983, *38* (21), pp. 3–56.

Klein, Herbert S. Reply [The Integration of Italian Immigrants into the United States and Argentina: A Comparative Analysis]. *Amer. Hist. Rev.*, April 1983, *88* (2), pp. 343–46. **[G: U.S.; Argentina]**

Klein, Herbert S. The Integration of Italian Immigrants into the United States and Argentina: A Comparative Analysis. *Amer. Hist. Rev.*, April 1983, *88* (2), pp. 306–29. **[G: U.S.; Argentina]**

Leiby, James. Social Control and Historical Explanation: Historians View the Piven and Cloward Thesis. **In** *Trattner, W. I., ed..*, 1983, pp. 90–113.

Lewis, W. Arthur. Aspects of Tropical Trade. **In** *Lewis, W. A.*, 1983, *1969*, pp. 235–81. **[G: OECD; LDCs]**

Lewis, W. Arthur. International Economics: International Competition in Manufactures. **In** *Lewis, W. A.*, 1983, *1969*, pp. 225–34. **[G: U.K.]**

Lewis, W. Arthur. Trade Drives. **In** *Lewis, W. A.*, 1983, *1957*, pp. 209–23. **[G: U.K.; Germany; U.S.; Japan]**

Lewis, W. Arthur. World Production, Prices and Trade, 1870–1960. **In** *Lewis, W. A.*, 1983, *1954*, pp. 175–208.

Maddison, Angus. A Comparison of Levels of GDP Per Capita in Developed and Developing Countries, 1700–1980. *J. Econ. Hist.*, March 1983, *43* (1), pp. 27–41. **[G: MDCs; LDCs]**

Martin, Geoffrey J. Global Resources in Historical Perspective. **In** *Glassner, M. I., ed.*, 1983, pp. 35–50. **[G: Global]**

Morris, Cynthia Taft and Adelman, Irma. Institutional Influences on Poverty in the Nineteenth Century: A Quantitative Comparative Study. *J. Econ. Hist.*, March 1983, *43* (1), pp. 43–55. **[G: MDCs; LDCs]**

Morris, Cynthia Taft and Adelman, Irma. Institutional Influences on Poverty in the Nineteenth Century: A Quantitative Comparative Study: Reply to Williamson. *J. Econ. Hist.*, March 1983, *43* (1), pp. 61–62. **[G: MDCs; LDCs]**

Olson, Mancur. Public Choice and Growth: Barriers to Trade, Factor Mobility, and Growth. **In** *Biehl, D.; Roskamp, K. W. and Stolper, W. F., eds.*, 1983, pp. 15–40. **[G: OECD]**

Reynolds, Lloyd G. The Spread of Economic Growth to the Third World: 1850–1980. *J. Econ. Lit.*, September 1983, *21* (3), pp. 941–80. **[G: LDCs]**

Salop, Steven C. A Century of Evidence on Wage and Price Stickiness in the United States, the United Kingdom, and Japan: Comment. **In** *Tobin, J., ed.*, 1983, pp. 124–33. **[G: U.S.; U.K.; Japan]**

Schaeffer, Robert K. Crises of Supply: Two Cases of the Shortage of Seafaring Labor. **In** *Bergesen, A., ed.*, 1983, pp. 253–62. **[G: Europe]**

Stigler, George J. The Early History of Empirical Studies of Consumer Behavior. **In** *Stigler, G. J.*, 1983, *1954*, pp. 198–233. **[G: U.K.; U.S.; Belgium]**

Teichova, Alice. A Comparative View of the Inflation of the 1920s in Austria and Czechoslovakia. **In** *Schmukler, N. and Marcus, E., eds.*, 1983, pp. 531–67. **[G: Austria; Czechoslovakia]**

Twomey, Michael J. The 1930s Depression in Latin America: A Macro Analysis. *Exploration Econ. Hist.*, July 1983, *20* (3), pp. 221–47. **[G: Latin America; Europe; N. America]**

Williamson, Jeffrey G. Institutional Influences on Poverty in the Nineteenth Century: A Quantitative Comparative Study: Discussion. *J. Econ. Hist.*, March 1983, *43* (1), pp. 56–60. **[G: MDCs; LDCs]**

042 Economic History: United States and Canada

0420 General

Atack, Jeremy and Brueckner, Jan K. Steel Rails and American Railroads, 1867–1880: Reply to Harley. *Exploration Econ. Hist.*, July 1983, *20* (3), pp. 258–62. **[G: U.S.]**

Bailis, Stanley. Modernization and Habitual Change: A Model Explored through American Autobiography. **In** *[Cochran, T. C.]*, 1983, pp. 117–43. **[G: U.S.]**

Baily, Samuel L. The Adjustment of Italian Immigrants in Buenos Aires and New York, 1870–1914. *Amer. Hist. Rev.*, April 1983, *88*(2), pp. 281–305. **[G: U.S.; Argentina]**

Braeman, John. The New Left and American Foreign Policy during the Age of Normalcy: A Re-Examination. *Bus. Hist. Rev.*, Spring 1983, *57*(1), pp. 73–104. **[G: U.S.]**

Brody, David. On the Failure of U.S. Radical Politics: A Farmer-Labor Analysis. *Ind. Relat.*, Spring 1983, *22*(2), pp. 141–63. **[G: U.S.]**

Bularzik, Mary J. The Bonds of Belonging: Leonora O'Reilly and Social Reform. *Labor Hist.*, Winter 1983, *24*(1), pp. 60–83. **[G: U.S.]**

Burns, Malcolm R. An Empirical Analysis of Stockholder Injury under § 2 of the Sherman Act. *J. Ind. Econ.*, June 1983, *31*(4), pp. 333–62. **[G: U.S.]**

Cain, Louis P. To Annex or Not? A Tale of Two Towns: Evanston and Hyde Park. *Exploration Econ. Hist.*, January 1983, *20*(1), pp. 58–72. **[G: U.S.]**

Chandler, Alfred D., Jr. The Place of the Modern Industrial Enterprise in Three Economies. **In** *Teichova, A. and Cottrell, P. L., eds.*, 1983, pp. 3–29. **[G: U.S.; U.K.; Germany]**

Clemens, Paul G. E. Levels of Living in Colonial America: Discussion. *J. Econ. Hist.*, March 1983, *43*(1), pp. 118–19. **[G: U.S.]**

Craine, Roger and Hardouvelis, Gikas A. Are Rational Expectations for Real? *Greek Econ. Rev.*, April 1983, *5*(1), pp. 5–32. **[G: U.S.]**

Devine, Warren D., Jr. From Shafts to Wires: Historical Perspective on Electrification. *J. Econ. Hist.*, June 1983, *43*(2), pp. 347–72. **[G: U.S.]**

Diebold, William, Jr. The United States in the World Economy: A Fifty Year Perspective. *Foreign Aff.*, Fall 1983, *62*(1), pp. 81–104. **[G: U.S.]**

Eltis, David. Free and Coerced Transatlantic Migrations: Some Comparisons. *Amer. Hist. Rev.*, April 1983, *88*(2), pp. 251–80. **[G: U.S.; S. America]**

Fabricant, Solomon. The Productivity-Growth Slowdown—A Review of the "Facts." **In** *Schurr, S. H.; Sonenblum, S. and Wood, D. O., eds.*, 1983, pp. 47–70. **[G: U.S.]**

Foner, Philip S. A Martyr to His Cause: The Scenario of the First Labor Film in the United States. *Labor Hist.*, Winter 1983, *24*(1), pp. 103–11. **[G: U.S.]**

Foner, Philip S. Alexander von Humboldt on Slavery in America. *Sci. Soc.*, Fall 1983, *47*(3), pp. 330–42. **[G: U.S.]**

Galambos, Louis. Technology, Political Economy, and Professionalization: Central Themes of the Organizational Synthesis. *Bus. Hist. Rev.*, Winter 1983, *57*(4), pp. 471–93. **[G: U.S.]**

Gendreau, Brian C. The Implicit Return on Bankers' Balances. *J. Money, Credit, Banking*, November 1983, *15*(4), pp. 411–24. **[G: U.S.]**

Gordon, Robert B. Cost and Use of Water Power during Industrialization in New England and Great Britain: A Geological Interpretation. *Econ. Hist. Rev., 2nd Ser.*, May 1983, *36*(2), pp. 240–59. **[G: U.K.; U.S.]**

Harley, C. Knick. Steel Rails and American Railroads 1867–1880: Cost Minimizing Choice: A Comment on the Analysis of Atack and Brueckner. *Exploration Econ. Hist.*, July 1983, *20*(3), pp. 248–57. **[G: U.S.]**

Keohane, Robert O. Associative American Development, 1776–1860: Economic Growth and Political Disintegration. **In** *Ruggie, J. G., ed.*, 1983, pp. 43–90. **[G: U.S.]**

King, Robert G. On the Economics of Private Money. *J. Monet. Econ.*, July 1983, *12*(1), pp. 127–58. **[G: U.S.]**

MacDonald, Ronald. Tests of Efficiency and the Impact of 'News' in Three Foreign Exchange Markets: The Experience of the 1920's. *Bull. Econ. Res.*, November 1983, *35*(2), pp. 123–44. **[G: France; U.K.; U.S.]**

Main, Gloria L. The Standard of Living in Colonial Massachusetts. *J. Econ. Hist.*, March 1983, *43*(1), pp. 101–08. **[G: U.S.]**

Main, Jackson Turner. Standards of Living and the Life Cycle in Colonial Connecticut. *J. Econ. Hist.*, March 1983, *43*(1), pp. 159–65. **[G: U.S.]**

Margo, Robert A. and Steckel, Richard H. Heights of Native-Born Whites during the Antebellum Period. *J. Econ. Hist.*, March 1983, *43*(1), pp. 167–74. **[G: U.S.]**

Marotta, Gary. The Academic Mind and the Rise of U.S. Imperialism: Historians and Economists as Publicists for Ideas of Colonial Expansion. *Amer. J. Econ. Soc.*, April 1983, *42*(2), pp. 217–34. **[G: U.S.]**

McAfee, R. Preston. American Economic Growth and the Voyage of Columbus. *Amer. Econ. Rev.*, September 1983, *73*(4), pp. 735–40. **[G: U.S.]**

McDean, Harry C. "Reform" Social Darwinists and Measuring Levels of Living on American Farms, 1920–1926. *J. Econ. Hist.*, March 1983, *43*(1), pp. 79–85. **[G: U.S.]**

Mohl, Raymond A. The Abolition of Public Outdoor Relief, 1870–1900: A Critique of the Piven and Cloward Thesis. **In** *Trattner, W. I., ed..*, 1983, pp. 35–50. **[G: U.S.]**

Monroy, Douglas. Anarquismo y Comunismo: Mexican Radicalism and the Communist Party in Los Angeles during the 1930s. *Labor Hist.*, Winter 1983, *24*(1), pp. 34–59. **[G: U.S.]**

Moore, Geoffrey H. Cyclical Fluctuations and Secular Inflation. **In** *Moore, G. H.*, 1983, pp. 237–44. **[G: U.S.]**

Moore, Geoffrey H. Recession or Depression? **In** *Moore, G. H.*, 1983, *1982*, pp. 19–22. **[G: U.S.]**

Moore, Geoffrey H. Security Markets and Business Cycles. **In** *Moore, G. H.*, 1983, *1975*, pp. 139–60. **[G: U.S.]**

Moore, Geoffrey H. When Lagging Indicators Lead: The History of an Idea. **In** *Moore, G. H.*, 1983, *1978*, pp. 361–67. **[G: U.S.]**

Mowery, David C. The Relationship between Intrafirm and Contractual Forms of Industrial Research in American Manufacturing, 1900–1940. *Exploration Econ. Hist.*, October 1983, *20*(4), pp.

351–74. [G: U.S.]

Nordhaus, William D. Energy Productivity and Total Productivity: Comment. **In** *Schurr, S. H.; Sonenblum, S. and Wood, D. O., eds.*, 1983, pp. 215–19. [G: U.S.]

Ó Gráda, Cormac. Across the Briny Ocean: Some Thoughts on Irish Emigration to America, 1800–1850. **In** *Devine, T. M. and Dickson, D., eds.*, 1983, pp. 118–30. [G: U.S.; Ireland]

Officer, Lawrence H. Dollar–Sterling Mint Parity and Exchange Rates, 1791-1834. *J. Econ. Hist.*, September 1983, *43*(3), pp. 579–616. [G: U.K.; U.S.]

Parrini, Carl P. and Sklar, Martin J. New Thinking about the Market, 1896–1904: Some American Economists on Investment and the Theory of Surplus Capital. *J. Econ. Hist.*, September 1983, *43*(3), pp. 559–78. [G: U.S.]

Pegrum, Dudley, F. Changes in Freight Traffic among the Modes of Transport Past and Future. **In** *Khachaturov, T. S. and Goodwin, P. B., eds.*, 1983, pp. 22–33. [G: U.S.]

Peterson, Richard L. Consumer Finance. **In** *Benston, G. J., ed.*, 1983, pp. 185–212. [G: U.S.]

Power, Marilyn. From Home Production to Wage Labor: Women as a Reserve Army of Labor. *Rev. Radical Polit. Econ.*, Spring 1983, *15*(1), pp. 71–91. [G: U.S.]

Redish, Angela. The Economic Crisis of 1837–1839 in Upper Canada: Case Study of a Temporary Suspension of Specie Payments. *Exploration Econ. Hist.*, October 1983, *20*(4), pp. 402–17. [G: U.S.; Canada]

Rolnick, Arthur J. and Weber, Warren E. New Evidence on the Free Banking Era. *Amer. Econ. Rev.*, December 1983, *73*(5), pp. 1080–91. [G: U.S.]

Rosenberg, Nathan. The Effects of Energy Supply Characteristics on Technology and Economic Growth. **In** *Schurr, S. H.; Sonenblum, S. and Wood, D. O., eds.*, 1983, pp. 279–305. [G: U.S.]

Schurr, Sam H. Energy Efficiency and Economic Efficiency: An Historical Perspective. **In** *Schurr, S. H.; Sonenblum, S. and Wood, D. O., eds.*, 1983, pp. 203–14. [G: U.S.]

Shlomowitz, Ralph. New and Old Views on the Rural Economy of the Postbellum South: A Review Article. *Australian Econ. Hist. Rev.*, September 1983, *23*(2), pp. 258–75. [G: U.S.]

Smith, Timothy J. Wampum as Primitive Valuables. **In** *Dalton, G., ed.*, 1983, pp. 225–46. [G: U.S.]

de Sola Pool, Ithiel. Communications Technology and Land Use. **In** *Carr, J. H. and Duensing, E. E., eds.*, 1983, *1980*, pp. 291–303. [G: U.S.]

Soltow, James H. Structure and Strategy: The Small Manufacturing Enterprise in the Modern Industrial Economy. **In** *[Cochran, T. C.]*, 1983, pp. 81–99. [G: U.S.]

Soltow, Lee. Kentucky Wealth at the End of the Eighteenth Century. *J. Econ. Hist.*, September 1983, *43*(3), pp. 617–33. [G: U.S.]

Soltow, Lee. Land Fragmentation as an Index of History in the Virginia Military District of Ohio. *Exploration Econ. Hist.*, July 1983, *20*(3), pp. 263–73. [G: U.S.]

Sonenblum, Sidney. Energy Productivity and Total Productivity: Comment. **In** *Schurr, S. H.; Sonenblum, S. and Wood, D. O., eds.*, 1983, pp. 219–45. [G: U.S.]

Stabile, Donald. The New Class and Capitalism: A Three-and-Three-Thirds-Class Model. *Rev. Radical Polit. Econ.*, Winter 1983, *15*(4), pp. 45–70. [G: U.S.]

Ståhl, Ingemar. Sweden at the End of the Middle Way. **In** *Pejovich, S., ed.*, 1983, pp. 119–39. [G: Sweden; OECD]

Steckel, Richard H. The Economic Foundations of East-West Migration during the 19th Century. *Exploration Econ. Hist.*, January 1983, *20*(1), pp. 14–36. [G: U.S.]

Stricker, Frank. Affluence for Whom?—Another Look at Prosperity and the Working Classes in the 1920s. *Labor Hist.*, Winter 1983, *24*(1), pp. 5–33. [G: U.S.]

Stricker, Frank. Causes of the Great Depression, or What Reagan Doesn't Know about the 1920s. *Econ. Forum*, Winter 1983-84, *14*(2), pp. 41–58. [G: U.S.]

Summers, Lawrence H. On the Economics of Private Money: Comments. *J. Monet. Econ.*, July 1983, *12*(1), pp. 159–62. [G: U.S.]

Temin, Peter. Monetary Trends and Other Phenomena. *J. Econ. Hist.*, September 1983, *43*(3), pp. 729–39. [G: U.S.]

Tonveronachi, Mario. Friedman and Schwartz on Monetary Trends in the USA and the UK from 1867 to 1975: A First Assessment. *Banca Naz. Lavoro Quart. Rev.*, June 1983, (145), pp. 117–42. [G: U.S.; U.K.]

Walsh, Lorena S. Urban Amenities and Rural Sufficiency: Living Standards and Consumer Behavior in the Colonial Chesapeake, 1643–1777. *J. Econ. Hist.*, March 1983, *43*(1), pp. 109–17. [G: U.S.]

Webber, M. J. Location of Manufacturing and Operational Urban Models. **In** *Hamilton, F. E. I. and Linge, G. J. R., eds.*, 1983, pp. 141–202. [G: U.S.; U.K.; Australia; Netherlands]

Wood, John H. Familiar Developments in Bank Loan Markets. *Fed. Res. Bank Dallas Econ. Rev.*, November 1983, pp. 1–13. [G: U.S.]

Wood, John H. Interest Rates and Inflation: An Old and Unexplained Relationship. *Fed. Res. Bank Dallas Econ. Rev.*, January 1983, pp. 11–23. [G: U.S.]

Woodruff, A. M. The Property Tax in Periods of Instable Prices. **In** *Harriss, C. L., ed.*, 1983, pp. 123–32. [G: U.S.]

Woods, Thomas J. Energy Productivity and Total Productivity: Comment. **In** *Schurr, S. H.; Sonenblum, S. and Wood, D. O., eds.*, 1983, pp. 253–57. [G: U.S.]

Wren, Daniel A. American Business Philanthropy and Higher Education in the Nineteenth Century. *Bus. Hist. Rev.*, Autumn 1983, *57*(3), pp. 321–46. [G: U.S.]

Zanjani, Sally Springmeyer. The Mike Smith Case: A Note on High Grading in Goldfield, Nevada, 1910. *Labor Hist.*, Fall 1983, *24*(4), pp. 580–87. [G: U.S.]

Zucker, Lynne G. Organizations as Institutions. **In**

Bacharach, S. B., ed., 1983, pp. 1–47. [G: U.S.]

Zuckerman, Michael. Fate, Flux, and Good Fellowship: An Early Virginia Design for the Dilemma of American Business. **In** *[Cochran, T. C.]*, 1983, pp. 161–84. [G: U.S.]

0421 History of Product Prices and Markets

Abernathy, William J. and Wayne, Kenneth. Limits of the Learning Curve. **In** *Kantrow, A. M., ed.*, 1983, pp. 114–31. [G: U.S.]

Allen, Robert C. Collective Invention. *J. Econ. Behav. Organ.*, March 1983, *4*(1), pp. 1–24. [G: U.S.; U.K.]

Alston, Lee J. Farm Foreclosures in the United States during the Interwar Period. *J. Econ. Hist.*, December 1983, *43*(4), pp. 885–903. [G: U.S.]

Armstrong, Robert. Le développement des droits miniers au Québec à la fin du XIXe siècle. (The Development of Mining Rights in Quebec at the End of the 19th Century. With English summary.) *L'Actual. Econ.*, September 1983, *59*(3), pp. 576–95. [G: Canada]

Bernanke, Ben S. Nonmonetary Effects of the Financial Crisis in Propagation of the Great Depression. *Amer. Econ. Rev.*, June 1983, *73*(3), pp. 257–76. [G: U.S.]

Bornholz, Robert and Evans, David S. The Early History of Competition in the Telephone Industry. **In** *Evans, D. S., ed.*, 1983, pp. 7–40. [G: U.S.]

Burns, Malcolm R. Economies of Scale in Tobacco Manufacture, 1897–1910. *J. Econ. Hist.*, June 1983, *43*(2), pp. 461–74. [G: U.S.]

Chew, Sing C. Capital in Crisis: Stagnation and Timber Company Operations, Canada, 1873–1896. **In** *Bergesen, A., ed.*, 1983, pp. 287–308. [G: Canada]

Cox, Thomas R. Trade, Development, and Environmental Change: The Utilization of North America's Pacific Coast Forests to 1914 and Its Consequences. **In** *Tucker, R. P. and Richards, J. F., eds.*, 1983, pp. 14–29. [G: U.S.]

Devine, James N. Underconsumption, Over-Investment and the Origins of the Great Depression. *Rev. Radical Polit. Econ.*, Summer 1983, *15*(2), pp. 1–27. [G: U.S.]

Doerflinger, Thomas M. Commercial Specialization in Philadelphia's Merchant Community, 1750–1791. *Bus. Hist. Rev.*, Spring 1983, *57*(1), pp. 20–49. [G: U.S.]

Fraser, Steven. Combined and Uneven Development in the Men's Clothing Industry. *Bus. Hist. Rev.*, Winter 1983, *57*(4), pp. 522–47. [G: U.S.]

Haines, Walter W. The Myth of Continuous Inflation: United States Experience, 1700–1980. **In** *Schmukler, N. and Marcus, E., eds.*, 1983, pp. 183–204. [G: U.S.]

Hanson, John R., II. Export Earnings Instability before World War II: Price, Quantity, Supply, Demand? *Econ. Develop. Cult. Change*, April 1983, *31*(3), pp. 621–37.

James, John A. Structural Change in American Manufacturing, 1850–1890. *J. Econ. Hist.*, June 1983, *43*(2), pp. 433–59. [G: U.S.]

Lipartito, Kenneth J. The New York Cotton Exchange and the Development of the Cotton Futures Market. *Bus. Hist. Rev.*, Spring 1983, *57*(1), pp. 50–72. [G: U.S.]

MacDonald, James M. Merger Statistics Revisited: A Comment [Mergers, External Growth, and Finance in the Development of Large-Scale Enterprise in Germany, 1880–1913]. *J. Econ. Hist.*, June 1983, *43*(2), pp. 483–85. [G: U.S.; U.K.]

Manchester, Alden C. The Role and Dimensions of Food Advertising for 100 Years. **In** *Connor, J. M. and Ward, R. W., eds.*, 1983, pp. 105–30. [G: U.S.]

McEvoy, Arthur F. Law, Public Policy, and Industrialization in the California Fisheries, 1900–1925. *Bus. Hist. Rev.*, Winter 1983, *57*(4), pp. 494–521. [G: U.S.]

Mowery, David C. Industrial Research and Firm Size, Survival, and Growth in American Manufacturing, 1921–1946: An Assessment. *J. Econ. Hist.*, December 1983, *43*(4), pp. 953–80. [G: U.S.]

Porter, Robert H. A Study of Cartel Stability: The Joint Executive Committee, 1880–1886. *Bell J. Econ. (See Rand J. Econ. after 4/85)*, Autumn 1983, *14*(2), pp. 301–14. [G: U.S.]

Read, Robert. The Growth and Structure of Multinationals in the Banana Export Trade. **In** *Casson, M., ed.*, 1983, pp. 180–213. [G: Caribbean; Central America; U.S.]

Rothenberg, Winifred B. The Market and Massachusetts Farmers: Reply. *J. Econ. Hist.*, June 1983, *43*(2), pp. 479–80. [G: U.S.]

Schaefer, Donald F. The Effect of the 1859 Crop Year upon Relative Productivity in the Antebellum Cotton South. *J. Econ. Hist.*, December 1983, *43*(4), pp. 851–65. [G: U.S.]

Temin, Peter. Patterns of Cotton Agriculture in Post-Bellum Georgia. *J. Econ. Hist.*, September 1983, *43*(3), pp. 661–74. [G: U.S.]

Thompson, Alexander M., III. Technological Change and the Control of Work: The U.S. Bituminous Coal Industry 1865–1930. *Econ. Forum*, Winter 1983-84, *14*(2), pp. 1–18. [G: U.S.]

Tilly, Richard. Reply [Mergers, External Growth, and Finance in the Development of Large-Scale Enterprises in Germany, 1880–1913]. *J. Econ. Hist.*, June 1983, *43*(2), pp. 486. [G: U.S.; U.K.]

Weiss, Rona S. The Market and Massachusetts Farmers, 1750–1850: Comment. *J. Econ. Hist.*, June 1983, *43*(2), pp. 475–78. [G: U.S.]

0422 History of Factor Prices and Markets

Baily, Martin Neil. The Labor Market in the 1930's. **In** *Tobin, J., ed.*, 1983, pp. 21–61. [G: U.S.]

Berlin, Ira and Gutman, Herbert G. Natives and Immigrants, Free Men and Slaves: Urban Workingmen in the Antebellum American South. *Amer. Hist. Rev.*, December 1983, *88*(5), pp. 1175–1200. [G: U.S.]

Bogue, Allan G. Changes in Mechanical and Plant Technology: The Corn Belt, 1910–1940. *J. Econ. Hist.*, March 1983, *43*(1), pp. 1–25. [G: U.S.]

Cain, Louis P. Incomes in the Twentieth Century United States: Discussion. *J. Econ. Hist.*, March 1983, *43*(1), pp. 241–42. [G: U.S.]

Chew, Sing C. Capital in Crisis: Stagnation and Timber Company Operations, Canada, 1873–1896.

In *Bergesen, A., ed.*, 1983, pp. 287–308. [G: Canada]

Diamond, Peter A. The Labor Market in the 1930's: Comment. **In** *Tobin, J., ed.*, 1983, pp. 61–62. [G: U.S.]

Erlich, Mark. Peter J. McGuire's Trade Unionism: Socialism of a Trades Union Kind? *Labor Hist.*, Spring 1983, *24*(2), pp. 165–97. [G: U.S.]

Ficken, Robert E. The Wobbly Horrors: Pacific Northwest Lumbermen and the Industrial Workers of the World, 1917–1918. *Labor Hist.*, Summer 1983, *24*(3), pp. 325–41. [G: U.S.]

Fulton, Ralph Thomas. Workers in the Fields: Historical Perspectives on U.S. Farm Structure and Agricultural Labor. **In** *Brewster, D. E.; Rasmussen, W. D. and Youngberg, G., eds.*, 1983, pp. 125–33. [G: U.S.]

García y Griego, Manuel. The Importation of Mexican Contract Laborers to the United States, 1942–1964: Antecedents, Operation, and Legacy. **In** *Brown, P. G. and Shue, H., eds.*, 1983, pp. 49–98. [G: Mexico; U.S.]

Ginger, Ann Fagan. Workers' Self-Defense in the Courts. *Sci. Soc.*, Fall 1983, *47*(3), pp. 257–84. [G: U.S.]

Golin, Steve. Defeat Becomes Disaster: The Paterson Strike of 1913 and the Decline of the IWW. *Labor Hist.*, Spring 1983, *24*(2), pp. 223–48. [G: U.S.]

Graves, Philip E.; Sexton, Robert L. and Vedder, Richard K. Slavery, Amenities, and Factor Price Equilization: A Note on Migration and Freedom. *Exploration Econ. Hist.*, April 1983, *20*(2), pp. 156–62. [G: U.S.]

Greenwald, Bruce C. and Glasspiegel, Robert R. Adverse Selection in the Market for Slaves: New Orleans, 1830–1860. *Quart. J. Econ.*, August 1983, *98*(3), pp. 479–99. [G: U.S.]

Haines, Walter W. The Myth of Continuous Inflation: United States Experience, 1700–1980. **In** *Schmukler, N. and Marcus, E., eds.*, 1983, pp. 183–204. [G: U.S.]

Jacoby, Sanford M. Industrial Labor Mobility in Historical Perspective. *Ind. Relat.*, Spring 1983, *22*(2), pp. 261–82. [G: U.S.]

Jacoby, Sanford M. Union–Management Cooperation in the United States: Lessons from the 1920s. *Ind. Lab. Relat. Rev.*, October 1983, *37*(1), pp. 18–33. [G: U.S.]

Kearl, J. R. and Pope, Clayne L. The Life Cycle in Economic History. *J. Econ. Hist.*, March 1983, *43*(1), pp. 149–58. [G: U.S.]

Kessler-Harris, Alice. "Rosie the Riveter": Who Was She? *Labor Hist.*, Spring 1983, *24*(2), pp. 249–53. [G: U.S.]

Klehr, Harvey. American Communism and the United Auto Workers: New Evidence on an Old Controversy. *Labor Hist.*, Summer 1983, *24*(3), pp. 404–13. [G: U.S.]

McFarlane, Larry A. British Investment and the Land: Nebraska, 1877–1946. *Bus. Hist. Rev.*, Summer 1983, *57*(2), pp. 258–72. [G: U.K.; U.S.]

Moscovitch, Allan. Les sociétés de construction au Canada avant 1867: préliminaries à une analyse. (Building Societies in Canada before 1867: Prolegomena to the Analysis. With English summary.) *L'Actual. Econ.*, September 1983, *59*(3), pp. 514–30. [G: Canada]

Ouellet, Fernand. L'accroissement naturel de la population catholique québécoise avant 1850: aperçus historiographiques et quantitatifs. (The Natural Increase of the Roman Catholic Quebec Population before 1850: Historiographical and Quantitative Snapshots. With English summary.) *L'Actual. Econ.*, September 1983, *59*(3), pp. 402–22. [G: Canada]

Paquet, Gilles and Smith, Wayne R. L'émigration des Canadiens français vers les États-Unis, 1790–1940; problématique et coups de sonde. (The Emigration of French Canadians to the United States, 1790–1940: A Conceptual Framework and Some Quantitative Guesstimates. With English summary.) *L'Actual. Econ.*, September 1983, *59*(3), pp. 423–53. [G: Canada; U.S.]

Paquet, Gilles and Wallot, Jean-Pierre. Le système financier bas-canadien au tournant du XIXe siècle. (The Lower Canadian Financial System at the Turn of the 19th Century. With English summary.) *L'Actual. Econ.*, September 1983, *59*(3), pp. 456–513. [G: Canada]

Preston, Jo Anne. "To Learn Me the Whole of the Trade": Conflict between a Female Apprentice and a Merchant Tailor in Ante-Bellum New England. *Labor Hist.*, Spring 1983, *24*(2), pp. 259–73. [G: U.S.]

Rosenzweig, Roy. "United Action Means Victory": Militant Americanism on Film. *Labor Hist.*, Spring 1983, *24*(2), pp. 274–88. [G: U.S.]

Rozen, Marvin E. Segmented Work and Divided Workers: A Review Article. *J. Econ. Issues*, March 1983, *17*(1), pp. 215–24. [G: U.S.]

Schmitz, Mark and Fishback, Price V. The Distribution of Income in the Great Depression: Preliminary State Estimates. *J. Econ. Hist.*, March 1983, *43*(1), pp. 217–30. [G: U.S.]

Shiells, Martha and Wright, Gavin. Night Work as a Labor Market Phenomenon: Southern Textiles in the Interwar Period. *Exploration Econ. Hist.*, October 1983, *20*(4), pp. 331–50. [G: U.S.]

Smiley, Gene. Did Incomes for Most of the Population Fall from 1923 through 1929? *J. Econ. Hist.*, March 1983, *43*(1), pp. 209–16. [G: U.S.]

Smiley, Gene. Recent Unemployment Rate Estimates for the 1920s and 1930s. *J. Econ. Hist.*, June 1983, *43*(2), pp. 487–93. [G: U.S.]

Stricker, Frank. Affluence for Whom?—Another Look at Prosperity and the Working Classes in the 1920s. *Labor Hist.*, Winter 1983, *24*(1), pp. 5–33. [G: U.S.]

Stromquist, Shelton. Enginemen and Shopmen: Technological Change and the Organization of Labor in an Era of Railroad Expansion. *Labor Hist.*, Fall 1983, *24*(4), pp. 485–99. [G: U.S.]

Swanson, Dorothy. Annual Bibliography on American Labor History 1982: Periodicals, Dissertations, and Research in Progress. *Labor Hist.*, Fall 1983, *24*(4), pp. 526–45. [G: U.S.]

Whatley, Warren C. Labor for the Picking: The New Deal in the South. *J. Econ. Hist.*, December 1983, *43*(4), pp. 905–29. [G: U.S.]

Williams, Michael. Ohio: Microcosm of Agricultural Clearing in the Midwest. **In** *Tucker, R. P. and Richards, J. F., eds.*, 1983, pp. 3–13. [G: U.S.]

042 Economic History: United States and Canada

Wrege, Charles D. Medical Men and Scientific Management: A Forgotten Chapter in Management History. *Rev. Bus. Econ. Res.*, Spring 1983, *18*(3), pp. 32–47. **[G: U.S.]**

Zieger, Robert H. Industrial Relations and Labor History in the Eighties. *Ind. Relat.*, Winter 1983, *22*(1), pp. 58–70. **[G: U.S.]**

0423 History of Public Economic Policy (all levels)

Achenbaum, W. Andrew. The Formative Years of Social Security: A Test Case of the Piven and Cloward Thesis. **In** *Trattner, W. I., ed.*., 1983, pp. 67–89. **[G: U.S.]**

Alexander, John K. The Functions of Public Welfare in Late-Eighteenth-Century Philadelphia: Regulating the Poor? **In** *Trattner, W. I., ed.*., 1983, pp. 15–34. **[G: U.S.]**

Anderson, Terry L. and Hill, Peter J. Privatizing the Commons: An Improvement? *Southern Econ. J.*, October 1983, *50*(2), pp. 438–50.

Asher, Robert. Failure and Fulfillment: Agitation for Employers' Liability Legislation and the Origins of Workmen's Compensation in New York State, 1876–1910. *Labor Hist.*, Spring 1983, *24*(2), pp. 198–222. **[G: U.S.]**

Baack, Bennett D. and Ray, Edward John. The Political Economy of Tariff Policy: A Case Study of the United States. *Exploration Econ. Hist.*, January 1983, *20*(1), pp. 73–93. **[G: U.S.]**

Borins, Sandford F. World War II Crown Corporations: Their Functions and Their Fate. **In** *Prichard, J. R. S., ed.*, 1983, pp. 447–75. **[G: Canada]**

Brand, Donald R. Corporatism, the NRA, and the Oil Industry. *Polit. Sci. Quart.*, Spring 1983, *98*(1), pp. 99–118. **[G: U.S.]**

Breimyer, Harold F. Agricultural Marketing Policy in Perspective. **In** *Armbruster, W. J.; Henderson, D. R. and Knutson, Ronald D., eds.*, 1983, pp. 1–20. **[G: U.S.]**

Breimyer, Harold F. Conceptualization and Climate for New Deal Farm Laws of the 1930s. *Amer. J. Agr. Econ.*, December 1983, *65*(5), pp. 1153–57. **[G: U.S.]**

Browning, Edgar K. "The Economics and Politics of the Emergence of Social Security": A Comment. *Cato J.*, Fall 1983, *3*(2), pp. 381–84. **[G: U.S.]**

Canto, Victor A. U.S. Trade Policy: History and Evidence. *Cato J.*, Winter 1983/84, *3*(3), pp. 679–96. **[G: U.S.]**

Carstensen, Fred V. and Werking, Richard Hume. International Harvester in Russia: The Washington–St. Petersburg Connection? *Bus. Hist. Rev.*, Autumn 1983, *57*(3), pp. 347–66. **[G: U.S.; U.S.S.R.]**

Chisholm, Derek. La Banque du Canada était-elle nécessaire? (Was the Bank of Canada Really Necessary? With English summary.) *L'Actual. Econ.*, September 1983, *59*(3), pp. 551–74.

Cuzán, Alfred G. Appropriators versus Expropriators: The Political Economy of Water in the West. **In** *Anderson, T. L., ed.*, 1983, pp. 13–43. **[G: U.S.]**

Dublin, Thomas. A Personal Perspective on the Ten Hour Movement in New England. *Labor Hist.*, Summer 1983, *24*(3), pp. 398–403. **[G: U.S.]**

Eisenbeis, Robert A. What Is the Role of Government in a Major Restructuring of Financial Institutions in the 80s?: Discussant's Comments. *J. Bank Res.*, Spring 1983, *14*(1), pp. 33–36. **[G: U.S.]**

Elliott, James V. What Is the Role of Government in a Major Restructuring of Financial Institutions in 1980s? *J. Bank Res.*, Spring 1983, *14*(1), pp. 25–32. **[G: U.S.]**

Epstein, Richard A. A Common Law for Labor Relations: A Critique of the New Deal Labor Legislation. *Yale Law J.*, July 1983, *92*(8), pp. 1357–1408. **[G: U.S.]**

Epstein, Richard A. Common Law, Labor Law, and Reality: A Rejoinder [A Common Law for Labor Relations: A Critique of the New Deal Labor Legislation]. *Yale Law J.*, July 1983, *92*(8), pp. 1435–41. **[G: U.S.]**

Farrell, Kenneth R. and Runge, Carlisle Ford. Institutional Innovation and Technical Change in American Agriculture: The Role of the New Deal. *Amer. J. Agr. Econ.*, December 1983, *65*(5), pp. 1168–73. **[G: U.S.]**

Fellner, William. Gold and the Uneasy Case for Responsibly Managed Fiat Money. **In** *[Giersch, H.]*, 1983, pp. 91–116. **[G: U.S.; OECD]**

Flink, James J. The National Parks: The Business of the Environment. **In** *[Cochran, T. C.]*, 1983, pp. 23–48. **[G: U.S.]**

Getman, Julius G. and Kohler, Thomas C. The Common Law, Labor Law, and Reality: A Response [A Common Law for Labor Relations: A Critique of the New Deal Labor Legislation]. *Yale Law J.*, July 1983, *92*(8), pp. 1415–34. **[G: U.S.]**

Haggard, Thomas R. Government Regulation of the Employment Relationship. **In** *Machan, T. R. and Johnson, M. B., eds.*, 1983, pp. 13–41. **[G: U.S.]**

Harpham, Edward J. Social Security: Political History and Prospects for Reform [The Economics and Politics of the Emergence of Social Security: Some Implications for Reform]. *Cato J.*, Fall 1983, *3*(2), pp. 385–91. **[G: U.S.]**

Huertas, Thomas F. The Regulation of Financial Institutions: A Historical Perspective on Current Issues. **In** *Benston, G. J., ed.*, 1983, pp. 6–27. **[G: U.S.]**

James, Thomas. Questions about Educational Choice: An Argument from History. **In** *James, T. and Levin, H. M., eds.*, 1983, pp. 55–70. **[G: U.S.]**

Mayhew, Anne. Ideology and the Great Depression: Monetary History Rewritten. *J. Econ. Issues*, June 1983, *17*(2), pp. 353–60. **[G: U.S.]**

Mergen, Bernard. The Government as Manager: Emergency Fleet Shipbuilding, 1917–1919. **In** *[Cochran, T. C.]*, 1983, pp. 49–80. **[G: U.S.]**

Nelson, James C. New Concepts in Transportation Regulation. **In** *Nelson, J. C.*, 1983, *1942*, pp. 178–230. **[G: U.S.]**

Nelson, Paul Gunnar. What Is the Role of Government in a Major Restructuring of Financial Institutions in the 80s?: Discussant's Comments. *J. Bank Res.*, Spring 1983, *14*(1), pp. 36–38. **[G: U.S.]**

O'Hara, Maureen. Tax-Exempt Financing: Some Lessons from History. *J. Money, Credit, Banking,*

November 1983, *15*(4), pp. 425–41. **[G: U.S.]**

Ojeda, Mario. The Future of Relations between Mexico and the United States. **In** *Reynolds, C. W. and Tello, C., eds.*, 1983, pp. 315–30. **[G: U.S.; Mexico]**

Paarlberg, Don. Effects of New Deal Farm Programs on the Agricultural Agenda a Half Century Later and Prospect for the Future. *Amer. J. Agr. Econ.*, December 1983, *65*(5), pp. 1163–67.

Paavonen, Tapani. Reformist Programmes in the Planning for Post-War Economic Policy during World War II. *Scand. Econ. Hist. Rev.*, 1983, *31*(3), pp. 178–200. **[G: OECD]**

Pastor, Robert. The Cry-and-Sigh Syndrome: Congress and Trade Policy. **In** *Schick, A., ed.*, 1983, pp. 158–95. **[G: U.S.]**

Pumphrey, Muriel W. and Pumphrey, Ralph E. The Widows' Pension Movement, 1900–1930: Preventive Child-saving or Social Control? **In** *Trattner, W. I., ed..*, 1983, pp. 51–66. **[G: U.S.]**

Randall, Stephen J. Harold Ickes and United States Foreign Petroleum Policy Planning, 1939–1945. *Bus. Hist. Rev.*, Autumn 1983, *57*(3), pp. 367–87. **[G: U.S.]**

Rasmussen, Wayne D. The New Deal Farm Programs: What They Were and Why They Survived. *Amer. J. Agr. Econ.*, December 1983, *65*(5), pp. 1158–62. **[G: U.S.]**

Reynolds, Alan. Why Gold? *Cato J.*, Spring 1983, *3*(1), pp. 211–32. **[G: U.S.; U.K.]**

Sautter, Udo. North American Government Labor Agencies before World War One: A Cure for Unemployment? *Labor Hist.*, Summer 1983, *24*(3), pp. 366–93. **[G: Canada; U.S.]**

Sharlin, Harold Issadore. New York's Electricity: Establishing a Technological Paradigm. **In** *[Cochran, T. C.]*, 1983, pp. 101–16. **[G: U.S.]**

Sivachev, Nikolai. The Rise of Statism in 1930s America: A Soviet View of the Social and Political Effects of the New Deal. *Labor Hist.*, Fall 1983, *24*(4), pp. 500–525. **[G: U.S.]**

Tracy, Ronald L. and Trescott, Paul B. Monetary Policy and Inflation in the United States, 1912–1978: Evidence from Monthly Data. **In** *Schmukler, N. and Marcus, E., eds.*, 1983, pp. 205–25. **[G: U.S.]**

Tripp, Joseph F. Progressive Jurisprudence in the West: The Washington Supreme Court, Labor Law, and the Problem of Industrial Accidents. *Labor Hist.*, Summer 1983, *24*(3), pp. 342–65. **[G: U.S.]**

Vallières, Marc. Le gouvernement du Québec et les milieux financiers de 1867 à 1920. (The Quebec Government and Its Financial Environment from 1867 to 1920. With English summary.) *L'Actual. Econ.*, September 1983, *59*(3), pp. 531–50. **[G: Canada]**

Verkuil, Paul R. Whose Common Law for Labor Relations? [A Common Law for Labor Relations: A Critique of the New Deal Labor Legislation]. *Yale Law J.*, July 1983, *92*(8), pp. 1409–14. **[G: U.S.]**

Weaver, Carolyn L. On the Lack of a Political Market for Compulsory Old-Age Insurance Prior to the Great Depression: Insights from Economic Theories of Government. *Exploration Econ. Hist.*, July 1983, *20*(3), pp. 294–328. **[G: U.S.]**

Weaver, Carolyn L. The Economics and Politics of the Emergence of Social Security: Some Implications for Reform. *Cato J.*, Fall 1983, *3*(2), pp. 361–79. **[G: U.S.]**

West, Robert Craig. The Evolution and Devolution of Bank Regulations in the United States. *J. Econ. Issues*, June 1983, *17*(2), pp. 361–67. **[G: U.S.]**

Wilson, Thomas F. Institutional Change as a Source of Excessive Monetary Expansion. **In** *Schmukler, N. and Marcus, E., eds.*, 1983, pp. 79–93. **[G: U.S.]**

043 Economic History: Ancient and Medieval (until 1453)

0430 General

Berdan, Frances F. The Reconstruction of Ancient Economies: Perspectives from Archaeology and Ethnohistory. **In** *Ortiz, S., ed.*, 1983, pp. 83–95.

Brucker, Gene. Tale of Two Cities: Florence and Venice in the Renaissance. *Amer. Hist. Rev.*, June 1983, *88*(3), pp. 599–616. **[G: Italy]**

Carrasco, Pedro. Some Theoretical Considerations about the Role of the Market in Ancient Mexico. **In** *Ortiz, S., ed.*, 1983, pp. 67–82.

Collins, Randall. The Weberian Revolution of the High Middle Ages. **In** *Bergesen, A., ed.*, 1983, pp. 205–25.

Lui, Francis T. Cagan's Hypothesis and the First Nationwide Inflation of Paper Money in World History. *J. Polit. Econ.*, December 1983, *91*(6), pp. 1067–74. **[G: China]**

McDougall, E. Ann. The Sahara Reconsidered: Pastoralism, Politics and Salt from the Ninth through the Twelfth Centuries. *African Econ. Hist.*, 1983, (12), pp. 263–86. **[G: Sahara]**

Mundy, John Hine. The Financing of the Cistercian Order. *J. Europ. Econ. Hist.*, Spring 1983, *12*(1), pp. 203–09. **[G: Europe]**

Nuccio, Oscar. Medieval and Italian Sources of Economic Rationalism: A Critique and Indications of Historical Methodology. *Rivista Polit. Econ.*, Supplement Dec. 1983, *73*(12), pp. 69–131.

Peragallo, Edward. Development of the Compound Entry in the 15th Century Ledger of Jachomo Badoer, a Venetian Merchant. *Accounting Rev.*, January 1983, *58*(1), pp. 98–104.

Shubik, Martin. Auctions, Bidding, and Markets: An Historical Sketch. **In** *Engelbrecht-Wiggans, R.; Shubik, M. and Stark, R. M., eds.*, 1983, pp. 33–52.

Silver, Morris. Karl Polanyi and Markets in the Ancient Near East: The Challenge of the Evidence. *J. Econ. Hist.*, December 1983, *43*(4), pp. 795–829. **[G: Middle East]**

Thornton, M. K. and Thornton, R. L. Manpower Needs for the Public Works Programs for the Julio–Claudian Emperors. *J. Econ. Hist.*, June 1983, *43*(2), pp. 373–78. **[G: Italy]**

0431 History of Product Prices and Markets

Ashtor, Eliyahu and Cevidalli, Guidobaldo. Levantine Alkali Ashes and European Industries. *J. Eu-*

rop. Econ. Hist., Winter 1983, *12*(3), pp. 475–522. **[G: Europe]**

Braunstein, Philippe. Innovations in Mining and Metal Production in Europe in the Late Middle Ages. *J. Europ. Econ. Hist.*, Winter 1983, *12*(3), pp. 573–91. **[G: Europe]**

Campbell, Bruce M. S. Agricultural Progress in Medieval England: Some Evidence from Eastern Norfolk. *Econ. Hist. Rev., 2nd Ser.*, February 1983, *36*(1), pp. 26–46. **[G: U.K.]**

Campbell, Bruce M. S. Arable Productivity in Medieval England: Some Evidence from Norfolk. *J. Econ. Hist.*, June 1983, *43*(2), pp. 379–404. **[G: U.K.]**

Josefsson, Märtha and Örtengren, Johan. Crises, Inflation and Relative Prices: Investigations into Price Structure Stability in Swedish Industry 1913–80. **In** *Eliasson, G.; Sharefkin, M. and Ysander, B.-C., eds.*, 1983, pp. 53–110. **[G: Sweden]**

Leone, Alfonso. Some Preliminary Remarks on the Study of Foreign Currency Exchange in the Medieval Period. *J. Europ. Econ. Hist.*, Winter 1983, *12*(3), pp. 619–29.

Shoshan, Boaz. Money Supply and Grain Prices in Fifteenth-Century Egypt. *Econ. Hist. Rev., 2nd Ser.*, February 1983, *36*(1), pp. 47–67. **[G: Egypt]**

Silver, Morris. A Non-Neo Malthusian Model of English Land Value, Wages, and Grain Yield before the Black Death. *J. Europ. Econ. Hist.*, Winter 1983, *12*(3), pp. 631–50. **[G: U.K.]**

Van Cauwenberghe, E. H. G. Inflation in the Southern Low Countries, from the Fourteenth to the Seventeenth Century: A Record of Some Significant Periods of High Prices. **In** *Schmukler, N. and Marcus, E., eds.*, 1983, pp. 147–56. **[G: U.K.; Low Countries]**

0432 History of Factor Prices and Markets

Jacobsen, Grethe. Women's Work and Women's Role: Ideology and Reality in Danish Urban Society, 1300–1550. *Scand. Econ. Hist. Rev.*, 1983, *31*(1), pp. 3–20. **[G: Denmark]**

0433 History of Public Economic Policy (all levels)

Hadwin, J. F. The Medieval Lay Subsidies and Economic History. *Econ. Hist. Rev., 2nd Ser.*, May 1983, *36*(2), pp. 200–217. **[G: U.K.]**

044 Economic History: Europe

0440 General

Allcock, John B. Tourism and Social Change in Dalmatia. *J. Devel. Stud.*, October 1983, *20*(1), pp. 34–55. **[G: Yugoslavia]**

Alter, G. Plague and the Amsterdam Annuitant: A New Look at Life Annuities as a Source for Historial Demography. *Population Stud.*, March 1983, *37*(1), pp. 23–41. **[G: Netherlands]**

Amato, Sergio. The Debate between Marxists and Legal Populists on the Problems of Market and Industrialization in Russia (1882–1899) and Its Classical Foundations. *J. Europ. Econ. Hist.*, Spring 1983, *12*(1), pp. 119–43. **[G: U.S.S.R.]**

Andersson, Bertil. Early History of Banking in Gothenburg Discount House Operations, 1783–1818. *Scand. Econ. Hist. Rev.*, 1983, *31*(1), pp. 50–67. **[G: Sweden]**

Armstrong, John A. Socializing for Modernization in a Multiethnic Elite. **In** *Guroff, G. and Carstensen, F. V., eds.*, 1983, pp. 84–103. **[G: U.S.S.R.]**

Asselain, Jean-Charles and Morrisson, Christian. Economic Growth and Interest Groups: The French Experience. **In** *Mueller, D. C., ed.*, 1983, pp. 157–75. **[G: France]**

Balderston, T. The Beginning of the Depression in Germany, 1927–30: Investment and the Capital Market. *Econ. Hist. Rev., 2nd Ser.*, August 1983, *36*(3), pp. 395–415. **[G: Germany]**

Baron, Samuel H. Entrepreneurs and Entrepreneurship in Sixteenth/Seventeenth-Century Russia. **In** *Guroff, G. and Carstensen, F. V., eds.*, 1983, pp. 27–58. **[G: U.S.S.R.]**

Bartoli, Henri. Le problème des régions dans la pensée économique italienne. (The Problem of Regions in the Italian Economic Thought. With English summary.) *Giorn. Econ.*, September–October 1983, *42*(9–10), pp. 561–99. **[G: Italy]**

Batchelder, Ronald W. and Freudenberger, Herman H. On the Rational Origins of the Modern Centralized State. *Exploration Econ. Hist.*, January 1983, *20*(1), pp. 1–13. **[G: W. Europe]**

Beaud, C. The Interests of the Union Européenne in Central Europe. **In** *Teichova, A. and Cottrell, P. L., eds.*, 1983, pp. 375–97. **[G: Central Europe]**

Birdsall, Nancy. Fertility and Economic Change in Eighteenth and Nineteenth Century Europe: A Comment [Fertility, Economy, and Household Formation in England over Three Centuries]. *Population Devel. Rev.*, March 1983, *9*(1), pp. 111–23. **[G: U.K.]**

Black, Cyril E. Russian and Soviet Entrepreneurship in a Comparative Context. **In** *Guroff, G. and Carstensen, F. V., eds.*, 1983, pp. 3–10. **[G: U.S.S.R.]**

Blackwell, William. The Russian Entrepreneur in the Tsarist Period: An Overview. **In** *Guroff, G. and Carstensen, F. V., eds.*, 1983, pp. 13–26. **[G: U.S.S.R.]**

Boot, H. M. James Wilson and the Commercial Crisis of 1847. *Hist. Polit. Econ.*, Winter 1983, *15*(4), pp. 567–83. **[G: U.K.]**

Boswell, Jonathan. The Informal Social Control of Business in Britain: 1880–1939. *Bus. Hist. Rev.*, Summer 1983, *57*(2), pp. 237–57. **[G: U.K.]**

Butt, John. Belfast and Glasgow: Connections and Comparisons, 1790–1850. **In** *Devine, T. M. and Dickson, D., eds.*, 1983, pp. 193–203. **[G: U.K.; Ireland]**

Cage, R. A. The Standard of Living Debate: Glasgow, 1800–1850. *J. Econ. Hist.*, March 1983, *43*(1), pp. 175–82. **[G: U.K.]**

Campbell, R. H. The Influence of Religion on Economic Growth in Scotland in the Eighteenth Century. **In** *Devine, T. M. and Dickson, D., eds.*, 1983, pp. 220–34. **[G: U.K.]**

Capie, Forrest. Tariff Protection and Economic Performance in the Nineteenth Century. **In** *Black,*

J. and Winters, L. A., eds., 1983, pp. 1–24. [G: Europe; U.S.]

Capie, Forrest and Webber, Alan. Total Coin and Coin in Circulation in the United Kingdom, 1868–1914. *J. Money, Credit, Banking,* February 1983, *15*(1), pp. 24–39. [G: U.K.]

Carstensen, Fred V. Foreign Participation in Russian Economic Life: Notes on British Enterprise, 1865–1914. **In** *Guroff, G. and Carstensen, F. V., eds.,* 1983, pp. 140–58. [G: U.S.S.R.]

Carstensen, Fred V. and Guroff, Gregory. Economic Innovation in Imperial Russia and the Soviet Union: Observations. **In** *Guroff, G. and Carstensen, F. V., eds.,* 1983, pp. 347–60. [G: U.S.S.R.]

Cassese, Sabino. The "Division of Labour in Banking." The Functional and Geographical Distribution of Credit from 1936 to Today. *Rev. Econ. Cond. Italy,* October 1983, (3), pp. 381–411. [G: Italy]

de Cecco, Marcello. The Vicious/Virtuous Circle Debate in the Twenties and the Seventies. *Banca Naz. Lavoro Quart. Rev.,* September 1983, (146), pp. 285–303. [G: Europe]

Chandler, Alfred D., Jr. The Place of the Modern Industrial Enterprise in Three Economies. **In** *Teichova, A. and Cottrell, P. L., eds.,* 1983, pp. 3–29. [G: U.S.; U.K.; Germany]

Chick, Victoria. A Question of Relevance: The *General Theory* in Keynes's Time and Ours. *S. Afr. J. Econ.,* September 1983, *51*(3), pp. 380–406. [G: U.K.]

Coleman, D. C. Proto-Industrialization: A Concept Too Many. *Econ. Hist. Rev., 2nd Ser.,* August 1983, *36*(3), pp. 435–48.

Connolly, S. J. Religion, Work-Discipline and Economic Attitudes: The Case of Ireland. **In** *Devine, T. M. and Dickson, D., eds.,* 1983, pp. 235–45. [G: Ireland]

Crafts, N. F. R. British Economic Growth, 1700–1831: A Review of the Evidence. *Econ. Hist. Rev., 2nd Ser.,* May 1983, *36*(2), pp. 177–99. [G: U.K.]

Crafts, N. F. R. Gross National Product in Europe 1870–1910: Some New Estimates. *Exploration Econ. Hist.,* October 1983, *20*(4), pp. 387–401. [G: Europe]

Crawford, W. H. Ulster as a Mirror of the Two Societies. **In** *Devine, T. M. and Dickson, D., eds.,* 1983, pp. 60–69. [G: Ireland; U.K.]

Crouzet, François. Comment [The Interests of the Union Européenne in Central Europe] [The Interests of the Banque de l'Union Parisienne in Czechoslovakia, Hungary and the Balkans, 1919–30]. **In** *Teichova, A. and Cottrell, P. L., eds.,* 1983, pp. 411–13. [G: Central Europe; France]

Cullen, L. M. Incomes, Social Classes and Economic Growth in Ireland and Scotland, 1600–1900. **In** *Devine, T. M. and Dickson, D., eds.,* 1983, pp. 248–60. [G: U.K.; Ireland]

Devine, T. M. The English Connection and Irish and Scottish Development in the Eighteenth Century. **In** *Devine, T. M. and Dickson, D., eds.,* 1983, pp. 12–29. [G: U.K.; Ireland]

Devine, T. M. The Social Composition of the Business Class in the Larger Scottish Towns, 1680–1740. **In** *Devine, T. M. and Dickson, D., eds.,* 1983, pp. 163–76. [G: U.K.]

Devine, T. M. and Dickson, David. In Pursuit of Comparative Aspects of Irish and Scottish Development: A Review of the Symposium. **In** *Devine, T. M. and Dickson, D., eds.,* 1983, pp. 261–72. [G: U.K.; Ireland]

Dickson, David. The Place of Dublin in the Eighteenth-Century Irish Economy. **In** *Devine, T. M. and Dickson, D., eds.,* 1983, pp. 177–92. [G: Ireland]

Digby, Anne. Changes in the Asylum: The Case of York, 1777–1815. *Econ. Hist. Rev., 2nd Ser.,* May 1983, *36*(2), pp. 218–39. [G: U.K.]

Douglas, Allen. Georges Valois and the Franc—Or: A Right-Wing Reaction to Inflation. **In** *Schmukler, N. and Marcus, E., eds.,* 1983, pp. 226–45.

Dutton, H. I. and Jones, S. R. H. Invention and Innovation in the British Pin Industry, 1790–1850. *Bus. Hist. Rev.,* Summer 1983, *57*(2), pp. 175–93. [G: U.K.]

Egge, Åsmund. Transformation of Bank Structures in the Industrial Period: The Case of Norway 1830–1914. *J. Europ. Econ. Hist.,* Fall 1983, *12*(2), pp. 271–94. [G: Norway]

Eichengreen, Barry J. *The Economic History of Britain since 1700:* Review Article. *J. Europ. Econ. Hist.,* Fall 1983, *12*(2), pp. 437–43. [G: U.K.]

Eichengreen, Barry J. The Causes of British Business Cycles, 1833–1913. *J. Europ. Econ. Hist.,* Spring 1983, *12*(1), pp. 145–61. [G: U.K.]

Ekelund, Robert B., Jr. and Tollison, Robert D. Tradeable Shares and the Supply-Side of Corporate Development: Reply [Mercantilist Origins of the Corporation]. *Bell J. Econ. (See Rand J. Econ. after 4/85),* Spring 1983, *14*(1), pp. 298–300. [G: U.K.]

Fakiolas, Tasos. Targets and Results of Soviet Economic Policy. *Rivista Int. Sci. Econ. Com.,* January 1983, *30*(1), pp. 41–56. [G: U.S.S.R.]

Flood, Robert P. and Garber, Peter M. Process Consistency and Monetary Reform: Some Further Evidence. *J. Monet. Econ.,* August 1983, *12*(2), pp. 279–95. [G: Europe]

Fontana, Josep. Economic Development of the Mediterranean Countries in Historical Perspective. **In** *Sampedro, J. L. and Payno, J. A., eds.,* 1983, pp. 41–54. [G: Italy; Greece; Portugal; Spain]

Fox, Alan. British Management and Industrial Relations: The Social Origins of a System. **In** *Earl, M. J., ed.,* 1983, pp. 6–39. [G: U.K.]

Freudenberger, Herman H. An Industrial Momentum Achieved in the Habsburg Monarchy. *J. Europ. Econ. Hist.,* Fall 1983, *12*(2), pp. 339–50. [G: Austria; E. Europe]

Freudenberger, Herman H. Levels of Living of European Peasantry: Discussion. *J. Econ. Hist.,* March 1983, *43*(1), pp. 146–47. [G: Czechoslovakia; U.S.S.R.]

Friedlander, Dov. Demographic Responses and Socioeconomic Structure: Population Processes in England and Wales in the Nineteenth Century. *Demography,* August 1983, *20*(3), pp. 249–72. [G: U.K.]

Fure, Eli. Are Children Poor Men's Riches? *Scand. Econ. Hist. Rev.,* 1983, *31*(3), pp. 161–77. [G: Norway]

de Gaudemar, Jean-Paul. La régulation despotique un commentaire du tableau économique de Quesnay. (With English summary.) *Revue Écon. Polit.*, March–April 1983, *93*(2), pp. 177–96.

George, C. H. A Century of Marxist Historical Writing about the English: A Critical Retrospect. *Soc. Sci. Quart.*, December 1983, *64*(4), pp. 810–25. **[G: U.K.]**

Glazier, Ira A. Levels of Living of European Peasantry: Discussion. *J. Econ. Hist.*, March 1983, *43*(1), pp. 145–46. **[G: U.S.S.R.; France]**

Golini, Antonio. Present Relationships between Migration and Urbanization: The Italian Case. **In** *Morrison, P. A., ed.*, 1983, pp. 187–209. **[G: Italy]**

Good, David F. Economic Union and Uneven Development in the Habsburg Monarchy. **In** *Komlos, J., ed.*, 1983, *1981*, pp. 65–80. **[G: Austria; Hungary]**

Gordon, Robert B. Cost and Use of Water Power during Industrialization in New England and Great Britain: A Geological Interpretation. *Econ. Hist. Rev., 2nd Ser.*, May 1983, *36*(2), pp. 240–59. **[G: U.K.; U.S.]**

Gray, Malcolm. Migration in the Rural Lowlands of Scotland, 1750–1850. **In** *Devine, T. M. and Dickson, D., eds.*, 1983, pp. 104–17. **[G: U.K.]**

Gregory, Paul R. The Russian Agrarian Crisis Revisited. **In** *Stuart, R. C., ed.*, 1983, pp. 21–31. **[G: U.S.S.R.]**

Gross, Nachum. Austria–Hungary in the World Economy. **In** *Komlos, J., ed.*, 1983, pp. 1–45. **[G: Austria; Hungary; Europe]**

Guroff, Gregory. The Red-expert Debate: Continuities in the State-Entrepreneur Tension. **In** *Guroff, G. and Carstensen, F. V., eds.*, 1983, pp. 201–22. **[G: U.S.S.R.]**

Hannah, Leslie. New Issues in British Business History. *Bus. Hist. Rev.*, Summer 1983, *57*(2), pp. 165–74. **[G: U.K.]**

Harrison, Joseph. The Inter-War Depression and the Spanish Economy. *J. Europ. Econ. Hist.*, Fall 1983, *12*(2), pp. 295–321. **[G: Spain]**

Hartwell, R. M. Growth and Equity: Discussion. *J. Econ. Hist.*, March 1983, *43*(1), pp. 203–06. **[G: U.K.; Australia]**

Henderson, James P. The Oral Tradition in British Economics: Influential Economists in the Political Economy Club of London. *Hist. Polit. Econ.*, Summer 1983, *15*(2), pp. 149–79. **[G: U.K.]**

Hennart, Jean-François. The Political Economy of Comparative Growth Rates: The Case of France. **In** *Mueller, D. C., ed.*, 1983, pp. 176–202. **[G: France]**

Inkster, Ian. Technology as the Cause of the Industrial Revolution: Some Comments. *J. Europ. Econ. Hist.*, Winter 1983, *12*(3), pp. 651–57. **[G: U.K.]**

Jonung, Lars. Monetization and the Behavior of Velocity in Sweden, 1871–1913. *Exploration Econ. Hist.*, October 1983, *20*(4), pp. 418–39. **[G: Sweden]**

Kahan, Arcadius. Notes on Jewish Entrepreneurship in Tsarist Russia. **In** *Guroff, G. and Carstensen, F. V., eds.*, 1983, pp. 104–24. **[G: U.S.S.R.]**

Kamitake, Yoshiro. Some Notes on the Life and Works of Sir Edward Holden. *Hitotsubashi J. Econ.*, February 1983, *23*(2), pp. 48–56. **[G: U.K.]**

Katus, László. Transport Revolution and Economic Growth in Hungary. **In** *Komlos, J., ed.*, 1983, pp. 183–204. **[G: Hungary]**

Kendrick, Stephen. Social Change in Scotland. **In** *Brown, G. and Cook, R., eds.*, 1983, pp. 40–65. **[G: U.K.]**

Kiesling, H. J. Nineteenth-Century Education According to West: A Comment [Resource Allocation and Growth in Early Nineteenth-Century British Education]. *Econ. Hist. Rev., 2nd Ser.*, August 1983, *36*(3), pp. 416–25. **[G: U.K.]**

Klima, Arnost. Industrial Growth and Entrepreneurship in the Early Stages of Industrialization in the Czech Lands. **In** *Komlos, J., ed.*, 1983, *1977*, pp. 81–99. **[G: Czechoslovakia]**

Komlos, John. The Diffusion of Financial Technology into the Austro-Hungarian Monarchy toward the End of the Nineteenth Century. **In** *Komlos, J., ed.*, 1983, pp. 137–63. **[G: Austria; Hungary]**

Komlos, John H. Poverty and Industrialization at the End of the "Phase-Transition" in the Czech Crown Lands. *J. Econ. Hist.*, March 1983, *43*(1), pp. 129–35. **[G: Czechoslovakia]**

Krantz, Olle. Historical National Accounts—Some Methodological Notes. *Scand. Econ. Hist. Rev.*, 1983, *31*(2), pp. 109–31. **[G: Europe]**

Krohn, Claus-Dieter. An Overlooked Chapter of Economic Thought: The "New School's" Effort to Salvage Weimar's Economy. *Soc. Res.*, Summer 1983, *50*(2), pp. 452–68. **[G: Germany]**

Kunitz, Stephen J. Speculations on the European Mortality Decline. *Econ. Hist. Rev., 2nd Ser.*, August 1983, *36*(3), pp. 349–64. **[G: Europe]**

Lampe, John R. Debating the Balkan Potential for Pre-1914 Development. *J. Europ. Econ. Hist.*, Spring 1983, *12*(1), pp. 187–96. **[G: Serbia; Bulgaria]**

Lazonick, William. Industrial Organization and Technological Change: The Decline of the British Cotton Industry. *Bus. Hist. Rev.*, Summer 1983, *57*(2), pp. 195–236. **[G: U.K.]**

Lee, R. and Lam, D. Age Distribution Adjustments for English Censuses, 1821 to 1931. *Population Stud.*, November 1983, *37*(3), pp. 445–64. **[G: U.K.]**

Leone, Alfonso. Maritime Insurance as a Source for the History of International Credit in the Middle Ages. *J. Europ. Econ. Hist.*, Fall 1983, *12*(2), pp. 363–69. **[G: W. Europe]**

Lesthaeghe, Ron. A Century of Demographic and Cultural Change in Western Europe: An Exploration of Underlying Dimensions. *Population Devel. Rev.*, September 1983, *9*(3), pp. 411–35. **[G: W. Europe]**

Levitt, Ian. Scottish Poverty: The Historical Background. **In** *Brown, G. and Cook, R., eds.*, 1983, pp. 66–75. **[G: U.K.]**

Lindert, Peter H. English Living Standards, Population Growth, and Wrigley-Schofield. *Exploration Econ. Hist.*, April 1983, *20*(2), pp. 131–55. **[G: U.K.]**

Lindert, Peter H. Remodeling British Economic History: A Review Article. *J. Econ. Hist.*, December 1983, *43*(4), pp. 986–92. **[G: U.K.]**

Lindert, Peter H. and Williamson, Jeffrey G. Erratum [Revising England's Social Tables, 1688–1812] [Reinterpreting Britain's Social Tables, 1688–1913]. *Exploration Econ. Hist.*, July 1983, *20*(3), pp. 329–30. **[G: U.K.]**

Lindert, Peter H. and Williamson, Jeffrey G. Reinterpreting Britain's Social Tables, 1688–1913. *Exploration Econ. Hist.*, January 1983, *20*(1), pp. 94–109. **[G: U.K.]**

Lockhart, D. G. Planned Village Development in Scotland and Ireland, 1700–1850. **In** *Devine, T. M. and Dickson, D., eds.*, 1983, pp. 132–45. **[G: Ireland; U.K.]**

Lutfalla, Michel. La désinflation en Occident: sommes-nous en 1815? *Revue Écon. Polit.*, March–April 1983, *93*(2), pp. 211–32. **[G: France]**

MacDonald, Ronald. Tests of Efficiency and the Impact of 'News' in Three Foreign Exchange Markets: The Experience of the 1920's. *Bull. Econ. Res.*, November 1983, *35*(2), pp. 123–44. **[G: France; U.K.; U.S.]**

März, Eduard and Weber, Fritz. The Antecedents of the Austrian Financial Crash of 1931. *Z. Wirtschaft. Sozialwissen.*, 1983, *103*(5), pp. 497–519. **[G: Austria]**

Mathias, Peter. The Machine: Icon of Economic Growth. **In** *Macdonald, S.; Lamberton, D. M. and Mandeville, T., eds.*, 1983, pp. 11–25. **[G: U.K.]**

Matis, Herbert. Disintegration and Multi-national Enterprises in Central Europe during the Post-war Years (1918–23). **In** *Teichova, A. and Cottrell, P. L., eds.*, 1983, pp. 72–96. **[G: Central Europe]**

McNulty, Paul J. and Pontecorvo, Giulio. Mercantilist Origins of the Corporation: Comment. *Bell J. Econ. (See Rand J. Econ. after 4/85)*, Spring 1983, *14*(1), pp. 294–97. **[G: U.K.]**

Meyering, Anne C. Did Capitalism Lead to the Decline of the Peasantry? The Case of the French Combraille. *J. Econ. Hist.*, March 1983, *43*(1), pp. 121–28. **[G: France]**

Mitchison, Rosalind. Ireland and Scotland: The Seventeenth-Century Legacies Compared. **In** *Devine, T. M. and Dickson, D., eds.*, 1983, pp. 2–11. **[G: Ireland; U.K.]**

Mokyr, Joel. Uncertainty and Prefamine Irish Agriculture. **In** *Devine, T. M. and Dickson, D., eds.*, 1983, pp. 89–101. **[G: Ireland]**

Mosser, A. Concentration and the Finance of Austrian Industrial Combines, 1880-1914. **In** *Teichova, A. and Cottrell, P. L., eds.*, 1983, pp. 57–71. **[G: Austria]**

Munn, Charles W. The Coming of Joint-Stock Banking in Scotland and Ireland, c. 1820–1845. **In** *Devine, T. M. and Dickson, D., eds.*, 1983, pp. 204–18. **[G: U.K.; Ireland]**

Nakamura, James I. Growth and Equity: Discussion. *J. Econ. Hist.*, March 1983, *43*(1), pp. 206–08. **[G: Japan; Australia]**

Newsinger, John. James Connolly and the Easter Rising. *Sci. Soc.*, Summer 1983, *47*(2), pp. 152–77. **[G: Ireland]**

Nicholas, Stephen J. Agency Contracts, Institutional Modes, and the Transition to Foreign Direct Investment by British Manufacturing Multinationals before 1939. *J. Econ. Hist.*, September 1983, *43*(3), pp. 675–86. **[G: U.K.]**

Nygren, Ingemar. Transformation of Bank Structures in the Industrial Period. The Case of Sweden 1820–1913. *J. Europ. Econ. Hist.*, Spring 1983, *12*(1), pp. 29–68. **[G: Sweden]**

O'Brien, Patrick. European Economic Development: A Reply. *Econ. Hist. Rev., 2nd Ser.*, November 1983, *36*(4), pp. 548–85. **[G: W. Europe]**

Ó Gráda, Cormac. Across the Briny Ocean: Some Thoughts on Irish Emigration to America, 1800–1850. **In** *Devine, T. M. and Dickson, D., eds.*, 1983, pp. 118–30. **[G: U.S.; Ireland]**

Oddy, D. J. Urban Famine in Nineteenth-Century Britain: The Effect of the Lancashire Cotton Famine on Working-Class Diet and Health. *Econ. Hist. Rev., 2nd Ser.*, February 1983, *36*(1), pp. 68–86. **[G: U.K.]**

Officer, Lawrence H. Dollar–Sterling Mint Parity and Exchange Rates, 1791–1834. *J. Econ. Hist.*, September 1983, *43*(3), pp. 579–616. **[G: U.K.; U.S.]**

Olney, Martha L. Fertility and the Standard of Living in Early Modern England: In Consideration of Wrigley and Schofield. *J. Econ. Hist.*, March 1983, *43*(1), pp. 71–77. **[G: U.K.]**

Orton, Keith. Finland and Mexico: A Comparative Historical Analysis. **In** *Doran, C. F.; Modelski, G. and Clark, C., eds.*, 1983, pp. 187–204. **[G: Finland; Mexico]**

Owen, Thomas C. Entrepreneurship and the Structure of Enterprise in Russia, 1800–1880. **In** *Guroff, G. and Carstensen, F. V., eds.*, 1983, pp. 59–83. **[G: U.S.S.R.]**

Palairet, Michael. Land, Labour and Industrial Progress in Bulgaria and Serbia before 1914. *J. Europ. Econ. Hist.*, Spring 1983, *12*(1), pp. 163–85. **[G: Bulgaria; Serbia]**

Peaker, Antony. New Found Wealth and Economic Decline in Sixteenth Century Spain. *Nat. Westminster Bank Quart. Rev.*, February 1983, pp. 46–54. **[G: Spain]**

Phelps Brown, Henry. Egalitarianism and the Distribution of Wealth and Income in the U.K. *Ind. Relat.*, Spring 1983, *22*(2), pp. 186–202. **[G. U.K.]**

Pick, John. The Compulsion towards Inefficiency. **In** *Hendon, W. S. and Shanahan, J. L., eds.*, 1983, pp. 110–20. **[G: U.K.]**

Pond, Chris. Wealth and the Two Nations. **In** *Field, F., ed.*, 1983, pp. 9–33. **[G: U.K.]**

Ránki, György. On the Development of the Austro-Hungarian Monarchy. **In** *Komlos, J., ed.*, 1983, pp. 47–63. **[G: Austria; Hungary]**

Richards, Toni. Weather, Nutrition, and the Economy: Short-Run Fluctuations in Births, Deaths, and Marriages, France, 1740–1909. *Demography*, May 1983, *20*(2), pp. 197–212. **[G: France]**

Riley, James C. and McCusker, John J. Money Supply, Economic Growth, and the Quantity Theory of Money: France, 1650–1788. *Exploration Econ. Hist.*, July 1983, *20*(3), pp. 274–93. **[G: France]**

Rudolph, Richard L. Economic Revolution in Austria? The Meaning of 1848 in Austrian Economic History. **In** *Komlos, J., ed.*, 1983, pp. 165–82. **[G: Austria]**

Samura, Terutoshi. The Economic Movements of North France in the Latter Half of the Seventeenth Century. *Osaka Econ. Pap.*, September 1983, *33*(1–2), pp. 30–49. **[G: France]**

Schwarz, L. D. and Jones, L. J. Wealth, Occupations, and Insurance in the Late Eighteenth Century: The Policy Registers of the Sun Fire Office. *Econ. Hist. Rev., 2nd Ser.*, August 1983, *36*(3), pp. 365–73. **[G: U.K.]**

Shammas, Carole. Food Expenditures and Economic Well-Being in Early Modern England. *J. Econ. Hist.*, March 1983, *43*(1), pp. 89–100. **[G: U.K.]**

Siegenthaler, Hansjörg. Konsens, Erwartungen und Entschlusskraft: Erfahrungen der Schweiz in der Überwindung der Grossen Depression vor hundert Jahren. (On the Swiss Experience in Overcoming the Great Depression of the Years 1876–1885. With English summary.) *Schweiz. Z. Volkswirtsch. Statist.*, September 1983, *119*(3), pp. 213–35. **[G: Switzerland]**

Smith, Richard M. On Putting the Child before the Marriage: Reply to Birdsall [Fertility, Economy, and Household Formation in England over Three Centuries]. *Population Devel. Rev.*, March 1983, *9*(1), pp. 124–35. **[G: U.K.]**

Solar, Peter M. Agricultural Productivity and Economic Development in Ireland and Scotland in the Early Nineteenth Century. **In** *Devine, T. M. and Dickson, D., eds.*, 1983, pp. 70–88. **[G: Ireland; U.K.]**

Ståhl, Ingemar. Sweden at the End of the Middle Way. **In** *Pejovich, S., ed.*, 1983, pp. 119–39. **[G: Sweden; OECD]**

Süssmilch, Johann Peter. On Removing Obstacles to Population Growth. *Population Devel. Rev.*, September 1983, *9*(3), pp. 521–29. **[G: Germany]**

Sylos Labini, Paolo. Some Aspects of Economic Development in an Advanced Capitalist Country (Great Britain). *Soc. Res.*, Summer 1983, *50*(2), pp. 429–51. **[G: U.K.]**

Taylor, Michael and Thrift, Nigel. The Role of Finance in the Evolution and Functioning of Industrial Systems. **In** *Hamilton, F. E. I. and Linge, G. J. R., eds.*, 1983, pp. 359–85. **[G: U.K.; U.S.]**

Teichova, Alice and Cottrell, P. L. Industrial Structures in West and East Central Europe during the Inter-war Period. **In** *Teichova, A. and Cottrell, P. L., eds.*, 1983, pp. 31–55. **[G: Austria; Hungary; U.K.; Czechoslovakia]**

Temin, Peter. Monetary Trends and Other Phenomena. *J. Econ. Hist.*, September 1983, *43*(3), pp. 729–39. **[G: U.S.]**

Tonveronachi, Mario. Friedman and Schwartz on Monetary Trends in the USA and the UK from 1867 to 1975: A First Assessment. *Banca Naz. Lavoro Quart. Rev.*, June 1983, (145), pp. 117–42. **[G: U.S.; U.K.]**

Trebilcock, C. Comment [Concentration and the Finance of Austrian Industrial Combines, 1880–1914] [Disintegration and Multi-national Enterprises in Central Europe during the Post-war Years (1918–23)]. **In** *Teichova, A. and Cottrell, P. L., eds.*, 1983, pp. 96–100. **[G: Central Europe; Austria]**

Van Roon, Ger. 'Long Wave' Economic Trends and Economic Policies in the Netherlands in the XIXth and XXth Century. *J. Europ. Econ. Hist.*, Fall 1983, *12*(2), pp. 323–37. **[G: Netherlands]**

Wallerstein, Immanuel. European Economic Development: A Comment. *Econ. Hist. Rev., 2nd Ser.*, November 1983, *36*(4), pp. 580–83. **[G: W. Europe]**

Weissbach, Lee Shai. Entrepreneurial Traditionalism in Nineteenth-Century France: A Study of the *Patronage industriel des enfants de l'ébénisterie. Bus. Hist. Rev.*, Winter 1983, *57*(4), pp. 548–65. **[G: France]**

West, Edwin G. Nineteenth-Century Educational History: The Kiesling Critique [Resource Allocation and Growth in Early Nineteenth-Century British Education]. *Econ. Hist. Rev., 2nd Ser.*, August 1983, *36*(3), pp. 426–34. **[G: U.K.]**

Whyte, I. D. and Whyte, K. A. Some Aspects of the Structure of Rural Society in Seventeenth-Century Lowland Scotland. **In** *Devine, T. M. and Dickson, D., eds.*, 1983, pp. 32–45. **[G: U.K.]**

Wilbur, Elvira M. Was Russian Peasant Agriculture Really That Impoverished? New Evidence from a Case Study from the "Impoverished Center" at the End of the Nineteenth Century. *J. Econ. Hist.*, March 1983, *43*(1), pp. 137–44. **[G: U.S.S.R.]**

Woods, R. and Smith, C. W. The Decline of Marital Fertility in the Late Nineteenth Century: The Case of England and Wales. *Population Stud.*, July 1983, *37*(2), pp. 207–25. **[G: U.K.]**

Wrigley, E. A. and Schofield, R. S. English Population History from Family Reconstitution: Summary Results 1600–1799. *Population Stud.*, July 1983, *37*(2), pp. 157–84. **[G: U.K.]**

Wyrobisz, Andrej. Functional Types of Polish Towns in the XVI–XVIIIth Centuries. *J. Europ. Econ. Hist.*, Spring 1983, *12*(1), pp. 69–103. **[G: Poland]**

0441 History of Product Prices and Markets

Allen, Robert C. Collective Invention. *J. Econ. Behav. Organ.*, March 1983, *4*(1), pp. 1–24. **[G: U.S.; U.K.]**

Anderson, B. L. and Richardson, David R. Market Structure and Profits of the British African Trade in the Late Eighteenth Century: A Comment. *J. Econ. Hist.*, September 1983, *43*(3), pp. 713–21. **[G: U.K.]**

Anderson, Gary M.; McCormick, Robert E. and Tollison, Robert D. The Economic Organization of the English East India Company. *J. Econ. Behav. Organ.*, June–September 1983, *4*(2–3), pp. 221–38. **[G: U.K.]**

Ashtor, Eliyahu. The Wool Guild in Medieval Florence. *J. Europ. Econ. Hist.*, Spring 1983, *12*(1), pp. 197–201. **[G: Italy]**

Ashtor, Eliyahu and Cevidalli, Guidobaldo. Levantine Alkali Ashes and European Industries. *J. Europ. Econ. Hist.*, Winter 1983, *12*(3), pp. 475–522. **[G: Europe]**

Black, Jeremy. Grain Exports and Neutrality. A Speculative Note on British Neutrality in the War of the Polish Succession. *J. Europ. Econ. Hist.*, Winter 1983, *12*(3), pp. 593–600. **[G: U.K.; Poland]**

Childers, Thomas. Inflation and Electoral Politics in Germany 1919–29. **In** *Schmukler, N. and Marcus,*

E., eds., 1983, pp. 373–85. [G: Germany]

Cieślak, Edmund. Aspects of Baltic Sea-Borne Trade in the Eighteenth Century: The Trade Relations between Sweden, Poland, Russia and Prussia. *J. Europ. Econ. Hist.*, Fall 1983, *12*(2), pp. 239–70. **[G: Germany; Poland; Sweden; U.S.S.R.]**

Cochran, Laura E. Scottish–Irish Trade in the Eighteenth Century. **In** *Devine, T. M. and Dickson, D., eds.*, 1983, pp. 151–59. **[G: U.K.; Ireland]**

Corley, T. A. B. Strategic Factors in the Growth of a Multinational Enterprise: The Burmah Oil Company 1886–1928. **In** *Casson, M., ed.*, 1983, pp. 214–35. **[G: U.K.]**

Cuddy, Michael and Curtin, Chris. Commercialisation in West of Ireland Agriculture in the 1890s. *Econ. Soc. Rev.*, April 1983, *14*(3), pp. 173–84. **[G: Ireland]**

Davies, Timothy. Changes in the Structure of the Wheat Trade in Seventeenth-Century Sicily and the Building of New Villages. *J. Europ. Econ. Hist.*, Fall 1983, *12*(2), pp. 371–405. **[G: Italy]**

Dodgshon, Robert A. Agricultural Change and Its Social Consequences in the Southern Uplands of Scotland, 1600–1780. **In** *Devine, T. M. and Dickson, D., eds.*, 1983, pp. 46–59. **[G: U.K.]**

Feldman, Gerald D. The Historian and the German Inflation. **In** *Schmukler, N. and Marcus, E., eds.*, 1983, pp. 386–99. **[G: Germany]**

Fischer, P. G. The Österreichisch-Alpine Montangesellschaft, 1918–38. **In** *Teichova, A. and Cottrell, P. L., eds.*, 1983, pp. 253–67. **[G: Austria]**

Flynn, Dennis O. Sixteenth-Century Inflation from a Production Point of View. **In** *Schmukler, N. and Marcus, E., eds.*, 1983, pp. 157–69. **[G: Europe; U.S.]**

Forsyth, Peter J. and Nicholas, Stephen J. The Decline of Spanish Industry and the Price Revolution: A Neoclassical Analysis. *J. Europ. Econ. Hist.*, Winter 1983, *12*(3), pp. 601–10. **[G: Spain]**

Gøbel, Erik. Danish Trade to the West Indies and Guinea, 1671–1754. *Scand. Econ. Hist. Rev.*, 1983, *31*(1), pp. 21–49. **[G: Denmark; West Indies; Guinea]**

Gullickson, Gay L. Agriculture and Cottage Industry: Redefining the Causes of Proto-Industrialization. *J. Econ. Hist.*, December 1983, *43*(4), pp. 831–50. **[G: France]**

Hannah, L. German Concerns in Eastern Europe: Commentary. **In** *Teichova, A. and Cottrell, P. L., eds.*, 1983, pp. 192–96. **[G: Europe]**

Hanson, John R., II. Export Earnings Instability before World War II: Price, Quantity, Supply, Demand? *Econ. Develop. Cult. Change*, April 1983, *31*(3), pp. 621–37.

Harrison, Joseph. Heavy Industry, the State, and Economic Development in the Basque Region, 1876–1936. *Econ. Hist. Rev., 2nd Ser.*, November 1983, *36*(4), pp. 535–51. **[G: Spain]**

Hatton, T. J.; Lyons, John S. and Satchell, S. E. Eighteenth-Century British Trade: Homespun or Empire Made? *Exploration Econ. Hist.*, April 1983, *20*(2), pp. 163–82. **[G: U.K.]**

Heim, Carol E. Industrial Organization and Regional Development in Interwar Britain. *J. Econ. Hist.*, December 1983, *43*(4), pp. 931–52. **[G: U.K.]**

Holtfrerich, Carl-Ludwig. Political Factors of the German Inflation 1914–23. **In** *Schmukler, N. and Marcus, E., eds.*, 1983, pp. 400–416. **[G: Germany]**

Inikori, J. E. Market Structure and the Profits of the British African Trade in the Late Eighteenth Century: A Rejoinder. *J. Econ. Hist.*, September 1983, *43*(3), pp. 723–28. **[G: U.K.]**

Isarescu, Mugur. Inflation in Romania during the Post-World War I Period. **In** *Schmukler, N. and Marcus, E., eds.*, 1983, pp. 500–509. **[G: Romania]**

Jennings, Robert M. and Trout, Andrew P. The Irish Tontine (1777) and Fifty Genevans: An Essay on Comparative Mortality. *J. Europ. Econ. Hist.*, Winter 1983, *12*(3), pp. 611–18. **[G: Ireland]**

Jones, S. R. H. Technology and the Organization of Work: A Reply. *J. Econ. Behav. Organ.*, March 1983, *4*(1), pp. 63–66.

Jónsson, Sigfús. The Icelandic Fisheries in the Pre-Mechanization Era, c. 1800–1905: Spatial and Economic Implications of Growth. *Scand. Econ. Hist. Rev.*, 1983, *31*(2), pp. 132–50. **[G: Iceland]**

Jonung, Lars. Money and Prices in Sweden, 1871–1970: A Comment. *Scand. J. Econ.*, 1983, *85*(3), pp. 433–36.

Landau, Zbigniew. Inflation in Poland after World War I. **In** *Schmukler, N. and Marcus, E., eds.*, 1983, pp. 510–23. **[G: Poland]**

MacDonald, James M. Merger Statistics Revisited: A Comment [Mergers, External Growth, and Finance in the Development of Large-Scale Enterprise in Germany, 1880–1913]. *J. Econ. Hist.*, June 1983, *43*(2), pp. 483–85. **[G: U.S.; U.K.]**

Malamud, Bernard. John H. Williams on the German Inflation: The International Amplification of Monetary Disturbances. **In** *Schmukler, N. and Marcus, E., eds.*, 1983, pp. 417–34. **[G: Germany]**

März, Eduard. The Österreichisch-Alpine Montangesellschaft, 1918–38: Commentary. **In** *Teichova, A. and Cottrell, P. L., eds.*, 1983, pp. 267–68. **[G: Austria]**

März, Eduard. The Austrian Credit Mobilier in a Time of Transition. **In** *Komlos, J., ed.*, 1983, pp. 117–35. **[G: Austria]**

O'Flanagan, Patrick. Settlement Development and Trading in Ireland, 1600–1800: A Preliminary Investigation. **In** *Devine, T. M. and Dickson, D., eds.*, 1983, pp. 146–50. **[G: Ireland]**

Pohl, Hans. German Concerns in Eastern Europe: Commentary. **In** *Teichova, A. and Cottrell, P. L., eds.*, 1983, pp. 203–06. **[G: Europe]**

Pollard, Sidney. Capitalism and Rationality: A Study of Measurements in British Coal Mining, ca. 1750–1850. *Exploration Econ. Hist.*, January 1983, *20*(1), pp. 110–29. **[G: U.K.]**

Ránki, György. Inflation in Hungary. **In** *Schmukler, N. and Marcus, E., eds.*, 1983, pp. 524–30. **[G: Hungary]**

Ránki, György. Inflation in Post-World War I East Central Europe. **In** *Schmukler, N. and Marcus, E., eds.*, 1983, pp. 475–87. **[G: E. Europe]**

Ray, George F. Energy and the Long Cycles. *Energy Econ.*, January 1983, *5*(1), pp. 3–8. **[G: Austro-Hungary; Sweden; EEC]**

Schröter, Harm. Siemens and Central and South-

East Europe between the Two World Wars. **In** *Teichova, A. and Cottrell, P. L., eds.*, 1983, pp. 173–92. **[G: Europe]**

Schröter, Verena. The IG Farbenindustrie AG in Central and South-East Europe, 1926–38. **In** *Teichova, A. and Cottrell, P. L., eds.*, 1983, pp. 139–72. **[G: Europe]**

Stein, Robert. The State of French Colonial Commerce on the Eve of the Revolution. *J. Europ. Econ. Hist.*, Spring 1983, *12*(1), pp. 105–17. **[G: France]**

Stigler, George J. Notes on the History of the Giffen Paradox. **In** *Stigler, G. J.*, 1983, *1947*, pp. 374–84. **[G: U.K.]**

Takeoka, Yukiharu. A Study on the History of a French Firm of Machine-Tool Industry. (In Japanese. With English summary.) *Osaka Econ. Pap.*, March 1983, *32*(4), pp. 1–10. **[G: France]**

Teichova, Alice. A Comparative View of the Inflation of the 1920s in Austria and Czechoslovakia. **In** *Schmukler, N. and Marcus, E., eds.*, 1983, pp. 531–67. **[G: Austria; Czechoslovakia]**

Teichova, Alice. The Mannesmann Concern in East Central Europe in the Inter-war Period. **In** *Teichova, A. and Cottrell, P. L., eds.*, 1983, pp. 103–37. **[G: Austria]**

Tilly, Richard. Reply [Mergers, External Growth, and Finance in the Development of Large-Scale Enterprises in Germany, 1880–1913]. *J. Econ. Hist.*, June 1983, *43*(2), pp. 486. **[G: U.S.; U.K.]**

Van Cauwenberghe, E. H. G. Inflation in the Southern Low Countries, from the Fourteenth to the Seventeenth Century: A Record of Some Significant Periods of High Prices. **In** *Schmukler, N. and Marcus, E., eds.*, 1983, pp. 147–56. **[G: U.K.; Low Countries]**

Van der Wee, Herman. A Contribution to the Study of Inflation in the Interwar Period. **In** *Schmukler, N. and Marcus, E., eds.*, 1983, pp. 677–85. **[G: Belgium]**

Wells, Curt. A Reconsideration of the Causal Relationship between Money and Prices in Sweden, 1871–1970. *Scand. J. Econ.*, 1983, *85*(3), pp. 425–32. **[G: Sweden]**

Wendt, Bernd-Jürgen. German Concerns in Eastern Europe: Commentary. **In** *Teichova, A. and Cottrell, P. L., eds.*, 1983, pp. 196–203. **[G: Europe]**

Wheatcroft, S. G. A Reevaluation of Soviet Agricultural Production in the 1920s and the 1930s. **In** *Stuart, R. C., ed.*, 1983, pp. 32–62. **[G: U.S.S.R.]**

Wikander, Ulla. The Swedish Match Company in Central Europe between the Wars: 'Internal Power Struggle' between Former Competitors—Solo v. Swedish Match. **In** *Teichova, A. and Cottrell, P. L., eds.*, 1983, pp. 209–25. **[G: Sweden; Europe]**

Wyntjes, Sherrin Marshall. Raising Hell or Raising the Rent: The Gentry's Response to Inflation in Sixteenth-Century Holland and Utrecht. **In** *Schmukler, N. and Marcus, E., eds.*, 1983, pp. 170–82. **[G: Netherlands]**

0442 History of Factor Prices and Markets

Almquist, Eric L. Labour Specialization and the Irish Economy in 1841: An Aggregate Occupational Analysis. *Econ. Hist. Rev., 2nd Ser.*, November 1983, *36*(4), pp. 506–17. **[G: Ireland]**

Angeli, Aurora. Strutture familiari nella pianura e nella montagna bolognesi a meta' del XIX secolo. Confronti territoriali. (The Family Structures in the Plain and Mountain of Bologna's Area in the XIX Century. With English summary.) *Statistica*, October–December 1983, *43*(4), pp. 727–41. **[G: Italy]**

Berend, Iván T. German Capital in Silesian Industry in Poland between the Two World Wars: Commentary. **In** *Teichova, A. and Cottrell, P. L., eds.*, 1983, pp. 251. **[G: Poland; Selected Countries]**

Breen, Richard. Farm Servanthood in Ireland, 1900–40. *Econ. Hist. Rev., 2nd Ser.*, February 1983, *36*(1), pp. 87–102. **[G: Ireland]**

Broadberry, S. N. Unemployment in Interwar Britain: A Disequilibrium Approach. *Oxford Econ. Pap.*, November 1983, *35*(3), pp. 463–85. **[G: U.K.]**

Bussière, Eric. The Interests of the Banque de I'Union Parisienne in Czechoslovakia, Hungary and the Balkans, 1919–30. **In** *Teichova, A. and Cottrell, P. L., eds.*, 1983, pp. 399–410. **[G: France; Central Europe]**

Collins, Michael. Long-term Growth of the English Banking Sector and Money Stock, 1844–80. *Econ. Hist. Rev., 2nd Ser.*, August 1983, *36*(3), pp. 374–94. **[G: U.K.]**

Cottrell, P. L. Aspects of Western Equity Investment in the Banking Systems of East Central Europe. **In** *Teichova, A. and Cottrell, P. L., eds.*, 1983, pp. 309–47. **[G: Austria; Czechoslovakia; Hungary]**

Cottrell, P. L. The Hungarian General Credit Bank in the 1920s: Commentary. **In** *Teichova, A. and Cottrell, P. L., eds.*, 1983, pp. 374. **[G: Hungary]**

Di Comite, Luigi. L'emigrazione italiana nella prima fase dell processo transizionale. (Italian Migrations in the First Phase of the Transitional Process. With English summary.) *Giorn. Econ.*, July–August 1983, *42*(7–8), pp. 507–17. **[G: Italy]**

Dtugorborski, Waclaw. German Capital in Silesian Industry in Poland between the Two World Wars: Commentary. **In** *Teichova, A. and Cottrell, P. L., eds.*, 1983, pp. 247–50. **[G: Poland; Selected Countries]**

Eddie, Scott M. Agriculture as a Source of Supply: Conjectures from the History of Hungary, 1870–1913. **In** *Komlos, J., ed.*, 1983, pp. 101–15. **[G: Hungary]**

Fenoaltea, Stefano. The Organization of Serfdom in Eastern Europe: A Comment. *J. Econ. Hist.*, September 1983, *43*(3), pp. 705–08. **[G: E. Europe]**

Glynn, Sean and Booth, Alan. Unemployment in Interwar Britain: A Case for Re-learning the Lessons of the 1930s? *Econ. Hist. Rev., 2nd Ser.*, August 1983, *36*(3), pp. 329–48. **[G: U.K.]**

Gospel, Howard F. The Development of Management Organization in Industrial Relations: A Historical Perspective. **In** *Thurley, K. and Wood, S., eds.*, 1983, pp. 91–110. **[G: U.K.]**

Hatton, T. J. Unemployment Benefits and the Macroeconomics of the Interwar Labour Market: A Further Analysis. *Oxford Econ. Pap.*, November 1983, *35*(3), pp. 486–505. **[G: U.K.]**

Hirsch, Barry T. and Hausman, William J. Labour Productivity in the British and South Wales Coal Industry, 1874–1914. *Economica,* May 1983, *50*(198), pp. 145–57. **[G: U.K.]**

Jacobsen, Grethe. Women's Work and Women's Role: Ideology and Reality in Danish Urban Society, 1300–1550. *Scand. Econ. Hist. Rev.,* 1983, *31*(1), pp. 3–20. **[G: Denmark]**

Krengel, Jochen. Der Beschäftigungseffekt von Arbeitszeitverkürzungen im sekundären Sektor Deutschlands 1871 bis 1913—ein historisches Beispiel. (The Effect of Shorter Working Hours on Employment within the Secondary Sector of the German Economy between 1871 and 1913—An Historical Example. With English summary.) *Konjunkturpolitik,* 1983, *29*(5), pp. 314–28. **[G: W. Germany]**

Lévy-Leboyer, M. Aspects of Western Equity Investment in the Banking Systems of East Central Europe: Commentary. **In** *Teichova, A. and Cottrell, P. L., eds.,* 1983, pp. 347–49. **[G: Austria; Czechoslovakia; Hungary]**

Lindert, Peter H. and Williamson, Jeffrey G. English Workers' Living Standards during the Industrial Revolution: A New Look. *Econ. Hist. Rev., 2nd Ser.,* February 1983, *36*(1), pp. 1–25. **[G: U.K.]**

März, Eduard and Weber, Fritz. The Reconstruction of the Credit-Anstalt: Commentary. **In** *Teichova, A. and Cottrell, P. L., eds.,* 1983, pp. 430–36. **[G: Austria]**

McFarlane, Larry A. British Investment and the Land: Nebraska, 1877–1946. *Bus. Hist. Rev.,* Summer 1983, *57*(2), pp. 258–72. **[G: U.K.; U.S.]**

Michel, B. Aspects of Western Equity Investment in the Banking Systems of East Central Europe: Commentary. **In** *Teichova, A. and Cottrell, P. L., eds.,* 1983, pp. 350–53. **[G: Austria; Czechoslovakia; Hungary]**

Millward, Robert. The Organization of Serfdom in Eastern Europe: A Reply. *J. Econ. Hist.,* September 1983, *43*(3), pp. 709–12. **[G: E. Europe]**

Modest, David M. and Smith, Bruce D. The Standard of Living Debate, Rational Expectations, and Neutrality: Some Evidence from the Industrial Revolution. *J. Monet. Econ.,* November 1983, *12*(4), pp. 571–93. **[G: U.K.]**

Mokyr, Joel. Three Centuries of Population Change. *Econ. Develop. Cult. Change,* October 1983, *32*(1), pp. 183–92. **[G: U.K.]**

Nash, Gary B.; Smith, Billy G. and Hoerder, Dirk. Labor in the Era of the American Revolution: An Exchange: Laboring Americans and the American Revolution. *Labor Hist.,* Summer 1983, *24*(3), pp. 414–39. **[G: U.S.]**

Nicholas, Stephen J. Agency Contracts, Institutional Modes, and the Transition to Foreign Direct Investment by British Manufacturing Multinationals before 1939. *J. Econ. Hist.,* September 1983, *43*(3), pp. 675–86. **[G: U.K.]**

Nielsen, Peter Bøegh. Aspects of Industrial Financing in Denmark 1890–1914. *Scand. Econ. Hist. Rev.,* 1983, *31*(2), pp. 79–108. **[G: Denmark]**

Penn, Roger. The Course of Wage Differentials between Skilled and Nonskilled Manual Workers in Britain between 1856 and 1964. *Brit. J. Ind. Relat.,* March 1983, *21*(1), pp. 69–90. **[G: U.K.]**

Ránki, György. The Hungarian General Credit Bank in the 1920s. **In** *Teichova, A. and Cottrell, P. L., eds.,* 1983, pp. 355–73. **[G: Hungary]**

Reid, Donald W. The Origins of Industrial Labor Management in France: The Case of the Decazeville Ironworks during the July Monarchy. *Bus. Hist. Rev.,* Spring 1983, *57*(1), pp. 1–19. **[G: France]**

Schaeffer, Robert K. Crises of Supply: Two Cases of the Shortage of Seafaring Labor. **In** *Bergesen, A., ed.,* 1983, pp. 253–62. **[G: Europe]**

Smyth, David J. The British Labor Market in Disequilibrium: Did the Dole Reduce Employment in Interwar Britain? *J. Macroecon.,* Winter 1983, *5*(1), pp. 41–51. **[G: U.K.]**

Stiefel, Dieter. The Reconstruction of the Credit-Anstalt. **In** *Teichova, A. and Cottrell, P. L., eds.,* 1983, pp. 415–30. **[G: Austria]**

Sullivan, Rodney J. and Sullivan, Robyn A. The London Dock Strike, the Jondaryan Strike and the Brisbane Bootmakers' Strike, 1889–1890. **In** *Murphy, D. J., ed.,* 1983, pp. 47–64. **[G: Australia; U.K.]**

Tomaszewski, Jerzy. German Capital in Silesian Industry in Poland between the Two World Wars. **In** *Teichova, A. and Cottrell, P. L., eds.,* 1983, pp. 227–47. **[G: Poland; Selected Countries]**

Wedderburn [Lord]. Otto Kahn-Freund and British Labour Law. **In** *Wedderburn of Charlton [Lord]; Lewis, R. and Clark, J., eds.,* 1983, pp. 29–80. **[G: U.K.]**

Wellenreuther, Hermann. Rejoinder [Labor in the Era of the American Revolution: A Discussion of Recent Concepts and Theories]. *Labor Hist.,* Summer 1983, *24*(3), pp. 440–54. **[G: U.S.]**

Williamson, Oliver E. Technology and the Organization of Work: A Reply. *J. Econ. Behav. Organ.,* March 1983, *4*(1), pp. 57–62.

Williamson, Oliver E. Technology and the Organization of Work: A Rejoinder. *J. Econ. Behav. Organ.,* March 1983, *4*(1), pp. 67–68.

Wordie, J. R. The Chronology of English Enclosure, 1500–1914. *Econ. Hist. Rev., 2nd Ser.,* November 1983, *36*(4), pp. 483–505. **[G: U.K.]**

0443 History of Public Economic Policy (all levels)

Anan'ich, Boris V. The Economic Policy of the Tsarist Government and Enterprise in Russia from the End of the Nineteenth through the Beginning of the Twentieth Century. **In** *Guroff, G. and Carstensen, F. V., eds.,* 1983, pp. 125–39. **[G: U.S.S.R.]**

Anderson, Gary M. and Tollison, Robert D. Apologiae for Chartered Monopolies in Foreign Trade, 1600–1800. *Hist. Polit. Econ.,* Winter 1983, *15*(4), pp. 549–66. **[G: U.K.]**

Anderson, R. D. Education and the State in Nineteenth-Century Scotland. *Econ. Hist. Rev., 2nd Ser.,* November 1983, *36*(4), pp. 518–34. **[G: Scotland]**

Backhaus, Juergen. Economic Theories and Political Interests: Scholarly Economics in Pre-Hitler Germany: Review Article. *J. Europ. Econ. Hist.,* Winter 1983, *12*(3), pp. 661–67. **[G: Germany]**

Berov, Ljuben. Inflation and Deflation Policy in Bulgaria during the Period between World War I and World War II. **In** *Schmukler, N. and Marcus, E., eds.*, 1983, pp. 488–99. **[G: Bulgaria]**

Berti, Gian Luigi. Il sistema monetario e la moneta d'oro di San Marino. (The Monetary System and the Gold Coin of San Marino. With English summary.) *Bancaria,* March 1983, *39*(3), pp. 259–78. **[G: Italy; San Marino]**

Black, Jeremy. Grain Exports and Neutrality. A Speculative Note on British Neutrality in the War of the Polish Succession. *J. Europ. Econ. Hist.*, Winter 1983, *12*(3), pp. 593–600. **[G: U.K.; Poland]**

Booth, Alan. The "Keynesian Revolution" in Economic Policy-Making. *Econ. Hist. Rev., 2nd Ser.*, February 1983, *36*(1), pp. 103–23. **[G: U.K.]**

Capie, Forrest. The British Tariff and Industrial Protection in the 1930s. **In** *Feinstein, C., ed.*, 1983, *1978,* pp. 93–106. **[G: U.K.]**

Davis, Lance E. and Huttenback, Robert A. The Social Rate of Return: A Note on a Note [The Political Economy of British Imperialism: Measures of Benefits and Support]. *J. Econ. Hist.*, December 1983, *43*(4), pp. 983–95. **[G: U.K.]**

Dtugorborski, Waclaw. Göring's 'Multi-national Empire': Commentary. **In** *Teichova, A. and Cottrell, P. L., eds.*, 1983, pp. 298–302. **[G: Germany; Europe]**

Fletcher, R. A. Cobden as Educator: The Free-Trade Internationalism of Eduard Bernstein, 1899–1914. *Amer. Hist. Rev.*, June 1983, *88*(3), pp. 561–78. **[G: Germany]**

Flynn, Dennis O. and St. Clair, David J. The Social Returns to Empire: A Note [The Political Economy of British Imperialism: Measures of Benefits and Support]. *J. Econ. Hist.*, December 1983, *43*(4), pp. 981–82. **[G: U.K.]**

Granick, David. Institutional Innovation and Economic Management: The Soviet Incentive System, 1921 to the Present. **In** *Guroff, G. and Carstensen, F. V., eds.*, 1983, pp. 223–57. **[G: U.S.S.R.]**

Grissa, Abdessatar. The French Monetary and Exchange Rate Experience in the 1920s. **In** *Claassen, E. and Salin, P., eds.*, 1983, pp. 261–80. **[G: France]**

Halaga, Ondrej R. A Mercantilist Initiative to Compete with Venice: Kaschau's Fustian Monopoly (1411). *J. Europ. Econ. Hist.*, Fall 1983, *12*(2), pp. 407–35. **[G: Czechoslovakia]**

Hardach, Karl. Wheat, Rye, and the Sources of German Protection: A Comment on Webb's Article [Agricultural Protection in Wilhelminian Germany: Forging an Empire with Pork and Rye]. *J. Econ. Hist.*, June 1983, *43*(2), pp. 481. **[G: Germany]**

Harrison, Mark. Why Was NEP Abandoned? **In** *Stuart, R. C., ed.*, 1983, pp. 63–78. **[G: U.S.S.R.]**

Herlitz, Lars. Landlords' Agrarian Reforms? *Scand. Econ. Hist. Rev.*, 1983, *31*(1), pp. 68–73. **[G: Denmark]**

Hindley, Brian. Trade Policy, Economic Performance, and Britain's Economic Problems. **In** *Black, J. and Winters, L. A., eds.*, 1983, pp. 25–42. **[G: U.K.]**

Hodges, Richard and Cherry, John F. Cost-Control and Coinage: An Archaeological Approach to Economic Change in Anglo-Saxon England. **In** *Dalton, G., ed.*, 1983, pp. 131–83. **[G: U.K.]**

Hunter, Holland. The New Tasks of Soviet Planning in the Thirties. **In** *[Erlich, A.]*, 1983, pp. 173–97. **[G: U.S.S.R.]**

Jennings, Robert M. and Trout, Andrew P. The Irish Tontine (1777) and Fifty Genevans: An Essay on Comparative Mortality. *J. Europ. Econ. Hist.*, Winter 1983, *12*(3), pp. 611–18. **[G: Ireland]**

Leite, J. Costa. A Portuguese Contrast: Agrarian System and Common Lands in Two Freguesias. *Economia,* January 1983, *7*(1), pp. 1–50. **[G: Portugal]**

Overy, R. F. Göring's 'Multi-national Empire.' **In** *Teichova, A. and Cottrell, P. L., eds.*, 1983, pp. 269–98. **[G: Germany; Europe]**

Paavonen, Tapani. Reformist Programmes in the Planning for Post-War Economic Policy during World War II. *Scand. Econ. Hist. Rev.*, 1983, *31*(3), pp. 178–200. **[G: OECD]**

Peden, G. C. Sir Richard Hopkins and the "Keynesian Revolution" in Employment Policy, 1929–1945. *Econ. Hist. Rev., 2nd Ser.*, May 1983, *36*(2), pp. 281–96. **[G: U.K.]**

Rashid, Salim. Edward Copleston, Robert Peel, and Cash Payments. *Hist. Polit. Econ.*, Summer 1983, *15*(2), pp. 249–59. **[G: U.K.]**

Reynolds, Alan. Why Gold? *Cato J.*, Spring 1983, *3*(1), pp. 211–32. **[G: U.S.; U.K.]**

Richardson, H. W. Fiscal Policy in the 1930s. **In** *Feinstein, C., ed.*, 1983, *1967,* pp. 68–92. **[G: U.K.]**

Roosa, Ruth AmEnde. Russian Industrialists during World War I: The Interaction of Economics and Politics. **In** *Guroff, G. and Carstensen, F. V., eds.*, 1983, pp. 159–87. **[G: U.S.S.R.]**

Sayers, R. S. 1941—The First Keynesian Budget. **In** *Feinstein, C., ed.*, 1983, *1956,* pp. 107–17. **[G: U.K.]**

Selden, Mark. Imposed Collectivization and the Crisis of Agrarian Development in the Socialist States. **In** *Bergesen, A., ed.*, 1983, pp. 227–51. **[G: Yugoslavia; China; U.S.S.R.]**

Siebrand, Jan C. and van der Windt, Nico. Economic Crisis and Economic Policy in the Thirties and the Seventies. *De Economist,* 1983, *131*(4), pp. 517–47. **[G: Netherlands]**

Thomas, Mark. Rearmament and Economic Recovery in the Late 1930s. *Econ. Hist. Rev., 2nd Ser.*, November 1983, *36*(4), pp. 552–79. **[G: U.K.]**

Waller, Robert. Göring's 'Multi-national Empire': Commentary. **In** *Teichova, A. and Cottrell, P. L., eds.*, 1983, pp. 302–06. **[G: Europe; Germany]**

Walsh, Brendan M. Ireland in the European Monetary System: The Effects of a Change in Exchange Rate Regime. **In** *de Cecco, M., ed.*, 1983, pp. 160–88. **[G: Ireland]**

Webb, Steven B. Reply [Agricultural Protection in Wilhelminian Germany: Forging an Empire with Pork and Rye]. *J. Econ. Hist.*, June 1983, *43*(2), pp. 482. **[G: Germany]**

Winch, Donald. Britain in the 'Thirties: A Managed Economy? **In** *Feinstein, C., ed.*, 1983, *1969,* pp. 47–67. **[G: U.K.]**

Witt, Peter-Christian. Tax Policies, Tax Assessment and Inflation; Toward a Sociology of Public Finances in the German Inflation 1914–23. **In** *Schmukler, N. and Marcus, E., eds.*, 1983, pp. 450–72. **[G: Germany]**

Wordie, J. R. The Chronology of English Enclosure, 1500–1914. *Econ. Hist. Rev., 2nd Ser.,* November 1983, *36*(4), pp. 483–505. **[G: U.K.]**

Yamaji, Hidetoshi. Two Types of Railroad Regulation by States in the 19th Century of the U.S.—Search for the Social Foundation of Modern Corporate Financial Reporting. *Kobe Econ. Bus. Rev.,* 1983, (29), pp. 33–42. **[G: U.S.]**

Zaleski, Eugène. The Collectivization Drive and Agricultural Planning in the Soviet Union. **In** *Stuart, R. C., ed.,* 1983, pp. 79–106. **[G: U.S.S.R.]**

045 Economic History: Asia

0450 General

Adams, John. Financial Subinfeudation and the Penchant for Real Investment. *J. Econ. Issues,* June 1983, *17*(2), pp. 485–94. **[G: India]**

Beeman, William O. Patterns of Religion and Economic Development in Iran from the Qajar Era to the Islamic Revolution of 1978–79. **In** *Finn, J., ed.,* 1983, pp. 73–103. **[G: Iran]**

Buultjens, Ralph. India: Values, Visions, and Economic Development. **In** *Finn, J., ed.,* 1983, pp. 17–34.

Chaudhuri, K. N. Foreign Trade and Balance of Payments (1757–1947). **In** *Kumar, D., ed.,* 1983, pp. 804–77. **[G: India]**

Hanley, Susan B. A High Standard of Living in Nineteenth-Century Japan: Fact or Fantasy? *J. Econ. Hist.,* March 1983, *43*(1), pp. 183–92. **[G: Japan]**

Hanley, Susan B. Economic Growth and Population Control in Preindustrial Japan. **In** *Dalton, G., ed.,* 1983, pp. 185–223. **[G: Japan]**

Heston, Alan W. National Income. **In** *Kumar, D., ed.,* 1983, pp. 376–462. **[G: India]**

Hugo, Graeme J. New Conceptual Approaches to Migration in the Context of Urbanization: A Discussion Based on the Indonesian Experience. **In** *Morrison, P. A., ed.,* 1983, pp. 69–113. **[G: Indonesia]**

Kessinger, Tom G., et al. Regional Economy (1757–1857). **In** *Kumar, D., ed.,* 1983, pp. 242–375. **[G: India]**

Martin, Linda G. and Culter, Suzanne. Mortality Decline and Japanese Family Structure. *Population Devel. Rev.,* December 1983, *9*(4), pp. 633–49. **[G: Japan]**

McAlpin, Michelle B. Price Movements and Fluctuations in Economic Activity (1860–1947). **In** *Kumar, D., ed.,* 1983, pp. 878–904. **[G: India]**

Miyamoto, Mataji. Money Exchange Business of the Sumitomo in the Late Tokugawa Period. *Osaka Econ. Pap.,* September 1983, *33*(1–2), pp. 1–18. **[G: Japan]**

Morris, Morris D. The Growth of Large-Scale Industry to 1947. **In** *Kumar, D., ed.,* 1983, pp. 553–676. **[G: India]**

Nakamura, James I. Growth and Equity: Discussion. *J. Econ. Hist.,* March 1983, *43*(1), pp. 206–08. **[G: Japan; Australia]**

Onitiri, H. M. A. Economic Development and Human Resources: Japan's Experience: Comments. **In** *Tsuru, S., ed.,* 1983, pp. 120–23. **[G: Japan]**

Osaka, Masako M. Forest Preservation in Tokugawa Japan. **In** *Tucker, R. P. and Richards, J. F., eds.,* 1983, pp. 129–45. **[G: Japan]**

Raychaudhuri, Tapan. The Mid-Eighteenth-Century Background. **In** *Kumar, D., ed.,* 1983, pp. 3–35. **[G: India]**

Sathyamurthy, T. V. The Political Economy of Poverty: The Case of India. **In** *Parkinson, J. R., ed.,* 1983, pp. 90–113. **[G: India]**

Shishido, Hisanobu. Modeling Dualism in Japan. **In** *Kelley, A. C.; Sanderson, W. C. and Williamson, J. G., eds.,* 1983, pp. 103–38. **[G: Japan]**

Soltow, Lee. Long-Run Wealth Inequality in Malaysia. *Singapore Econ. Rev.,* October 1983, *28*(2), pp. 79–97. **[G: Malaysia]**

Stokes, Eric, et al. Agrarian Relations. **In** *Kumar, D., ed.,* 1983, pp. 36–241. **[G: India]**

Thomson, James T. The Precolonial Woodstock in Sahelien West Africa: The Example of Central Niger (Damagaram, Damergu, Aïr). **In** *Tucker, R. P. and Richards, J. F., eds.,* 1983, pp. 167–77. **[G: W. Africa]**

Tsuru, Shigeto. Economic Development and Human Resources: Japan's Experience. **In** *Tsuru, S., ed.,* 1983, pp. 95–119. **[G: Japan]**

Tucker, Richard P. The British Colonial System and the Forests of the Western Himalayas, 1815–1914. **In** *Tucker, R. P. and Richards, J. F., eds.,* 1983, pp. 146–66. **[G: India]**

Visaria, Leela and Visaria, Pravin. Population (1757–1947). **In** *Kumar, D., ed.,* 1983, pp. 463–532. **[G: India]**

Whitcombe, Elizabeth and Hurd, John M. Irrigation and Railways. **In** *Kumar, D., ed.,* 1983, pp. 677–761. **[G: India]**

Wright, Tim. Economic Development in China during the Nineteenth and Twentieth Centuries: A Review Article. *J. Econ. Hist.,* June 1983, *43*(2), pp. 494–500. **[G: China]**

Zarfaty, Joseph. The Moshav in Israel: Possibilities for Its Application in Developing Countries. **In** *Stewart, F., ed.,* 1983, pp. 189–214. **[G: Israel]**

0451 History of Product Prices and Markets

Adas, Michael. Colonization, Commercial Agriculture, and the Destruction of the Deltaic Rainforests of British Burma in the Late Nineteenth Century. **In** *Tucker, R. P. and Richards, J. F., eds.,* 1983, pp. 95–110. **[G: Burma]**

Hafner, James A. Market Gardening in Thailand: The Origins of an Ethnic Chinese Monopoly. **In** *Lim, L. Y. C. and Gosling, L. A. P., eds.,* 1983, pp. 30–45. **[G: Thailand]**

Latham, A. J. H. and Neal, Larry. The International Market in Rice and Wheat, 1868–1914. *Econ. Hist. Rev., 2nd Ser.,* May 1983, *36*(2), pp. 260–80. **[G: Selected LDCs; Selected MDCs]**

Minami, Ryoshin and Makino, Fumio. Conditions for Technological Diffusion: Case of Power Looms. *Hitotsubashi J. Econ.,* February 1983, *23*(2), pp. 1–20. **[G: Japan]**

Molteni, Corrado. The Development of the Silk Reeling Industry in the Process of Japanese Industrialization (1868–1930) *Rivista Int. Sci. Econ. Com.,* August 1983, *30*(8), pp. 735–58. **[G: Japan]**

Murphey, Rhoads. Deforestation in Modern China. **In** *Tucker, R. P. and Richards, J. F., eds.,* 1983, pp. 111–28. [G: China]

Richards, J. F. and McAlpin, Michelle B. Cotton Cultivating and Land Clearing in the Bombay Deccan and Karnatak: 1818–1920. **In** *Tucker, R. P. and Richards, J. F., eds.,* 1983, pp. 68–94. [G: India]

Roth, Dennis M. Philippine Forests and Forestry: 1565–1920. **In** *Tucker, R. P. and Richards, J. F., eds.,* 1983, pp. 30–49. [G: Philippine]

Twomey, Michael J. Employment in Nineteenth Century Indian Textiles. *Exploration Econ. Hist.,* January 1983, *20*(1), pp. 37–57. [G: India]

Uemura, Masahiro. The Development of the Shipping Business in the Shiwaku Islands under the Ninmyo System. *Osaka Econ. Pap.,* September 1983, *33*(1–2), pp. 50–70. [G: Japan]

0452 History of Factor Prices and Markets

Chandavarkar, A. G. Money and Credit (1858–1947). **In** *Kumar, D., ed.,* 1983, pp. 762–803. [G: India]

Krishnamurty, J. The Occupational Structure. **In** *Kumar, D., ed.,* 1983, pp. 533–50. [G: India]

0453 History of Public Economic Policy (all levels)

Feeny, David H. Extensive versus Intensive Agricultural Development: Induced Public Investment in Southeast Asia, 1900–1940. *J. Econ. Hist.,* September 1983, *43*(3), pp. 687–704. [G: Asian LDCs]

Kumar, Dharma. The Fiscal System. **In** *Kumar, D., ed.,* 1983, pp. 905–44. [G: India]

Linhart, Sepp. Social Security versus Family Ideology. The State's Reaction to the Consequences of Early Industrialization in Japan. *Rivista Int. Sci. Econ. Com.,* August 1983, *30*(8), pp. 703–15. [G: Japan]

046 Economic History: Africa

0460 General

Fetter, Bruce. The Union Miniere and its Hinterland: A Demographic Reconstruction. *African Econ. Hist.,* 1983, (12), pp. 67–81. [G: Congo]

Geschiere, Peter. European Planters, African Peasants, and the Colonial State: Alternatives in the *Mise en Valeur* of Makaland, Southeast Cameroun, During the Interbellum. *African Econ. Hist.,* 1983, (12), pp. 83–108. [G: Cameroun]

Gluckman, Max. Essays on Lozi Land and Royal Property. **In** *Dalton, G., ed.,* 1983, *1943,* pp. 1–94. [G: S. Africa]

Harms, Robert. The World Abir Made: The Maringa-Lopori Basin, 1885–1903. *African Econ. Hist.,* 1983, (12), pp. 125–39. [G: Congo]

Rodney, Walter. Africa's Contribution to the Capitalist Development of Europe—The Colonial Period. **In** *Glassner, M. I., ed.,* 1983, *1972,* pp. 369–80. [G: Africa; Europe]

Terray, E. Gold Production, Slave Labor, and State Intervention in Precolonial Akan Societies: A Reply to Raymond Dumett. **In** *Dalton, G., ed.,* 1983, pp. 95–129. [G: W. Africa]

Viljoen, S. P. The Industrial Achievement of South Africa. *S. Afr. J. Econ.,* March 1983, *51*(1), pp. 29–57. [G: S. Africa]

0461 History of Product Prices and Markets

Eickelman, Dale F. Religion and Trade in Western Morocco. **In** *Dalton, G., ed.,* 1983, pp. 335–48. [G: Morocco]

van der Laan, H. Laurens. A Swiss Family Firm in West Africa: A. Brunnschweiler & Co., 1929–1959. *African Econ. Hist.,* 1983, (12), pp. 287–97. [G: W. Africa]

van der Laan, H. Laurens. Trading in the Congo: The NAHV from 1918 to 1955. *African Econ. Hist.,* 1983, (12), pp. 241–59. [G: Congo]

Shoshan, Boaz. Money Supply and Grain Prices in Fifteenth-Century Egypt. *Econ. Hist. Rev., 2nd Ser.,* February 1983, *36*(1), pp. 47–67. [G: Egypt]

Stürzinger, Ulrich. The Introduction of Cotton Cultivation in CHAD: The Role of the Administration, 1920–1936. *African Econ. Hist.,* 1983, (12), pp. 213–25. [G: CHAD]

de Swardt, S. J. J. Agricultural Marketing Problems in the Nineteen Thirties. *S. Afr. J. Econ.,* March 1983, *51*(1), pp. 1–28. [G: S. Africa]

0462 History of Factor Prices and Markets

Curtin, Patricia Romero. Laboratory for the Oral History of Slavery: The Island of Lamu on the Kenya Coast. *Amer. Hist. Rev.,* October 1983, *88*(4), pp. 858–82. [G: Africa]

Derksen, Richard. Forminiere in the Kasai, 1906–1939. *African Econ. Hist.,* 1983, (12), pp. 49–65. [G: Congo]

Hansen, Bent. Interest Rates and Foreign Capital in Egypt under British Occupation. *J. Econ. Hist.,* December 1983, *43*(4), pp. 867–84. [G: Egypt]

Katzenellenbogen, Simon E. Financial Links between the Congo and Its Southern Neighbors. *African Econ. Hist.,* 1983, (12), pp. 183–93. [G: Congo]

Manning, Patrick. Contours of Slavery and Social Change in Africa. *Amer. Hist. Rev.,* October 1983, *88*(4), pp. 835–57. [G: Africa]

Steenkamp, W. F. J. Labour Problems and Policies of Half a Century. *S. Afr. J. Econ.,* March 1983, *51*(1), pp. 58–87. [G: S. Africa]

0463 History of Public Economic Policy (all levels)

Franzsen, D. G. Monetary Policy in South Africa, 1932–82. *S. Afr. J. Econ.,* March 1983, *51*(1), pp. 88–133. [G: S. Africa]

Obdeijn, Herman. The New Africa Trading Company and the Struggle for Import Duties in the Congo Free State, 1886–1894. *African Econ. Hist.,* 1983, (12), pp. 195–212. [G: Congo]

047 Economic History: Latin America and Caribbean

0470 General

Baily, Samuel L. The Adjustment of Italian Immigrants in Buenos Aires and New York, 1870–1914.

Amer. Hist. Rev., April 1983, *88* (2), pp. 281–305. **[G: U.S.; Argentina]**

Bazant, Jan. The Basques in the History of Mexico. *J. Europ. Econ. Hist.*, Spring 1983, *12* (1), pp. 5–27. **[G: Mexico]**

Bennett, Douglas C. Catholicism, Capitalism, and the State in the Development of Mexico. **In** *Finn, J., ed.*, 1983, pp. 125–41. **[G: Mexico]**

Cardoso, Eliana A. Exchange Rates in Nineteenth-Century Brazil: An Econometric Model. *J. Devel. Stud.*, January 1983, *19* (2), pp. 170–78. **[G: Brazil]**

Cotler, Julio. Democracy and National Integration in Peru. **In** *McClintock, C. and Lowenthal, A. F., eds.*, 1983, pp. 3–38. **[G: Peru]**

Díaz-Alejandro, Carlos F. Stories of the 1930s for the 1980s. **In** *Armella, P. A.; Dornbusch, R. and Obstfeld, M., eds.*, 1983, pp. 5–35. **[G: Latin America]**

Eltis, David. Free and Coerced Transatlantic Migrations: Some Comparisons. *Amer. Hist. Rev.*, April 1983, *88* (2), pp. 251–80. **[G: U.S.; S. America]**

Gaudio, Ricardo and Pilone, Jorge. El desarrollo de la negociación colectiva durante la etapa de modernización industrial en la Argentina. 1935–1943. (With English summary.) *Desarrollo Econ.*, July–September 1983, *23* (90), pp. 255–86. **[G: Argentina]**

Herold, Marc W. Finanzkapital in El Salvador, 1900–1980. *Econ. Forum*, Summer 1983, *14* (1), pp. 79–94. **[G: El Salvador]**

Higonnet, Rene P. Latin American Debt: More Rescheduling? **In** *Jorge, A.; Salazar-Carillo, J. and Higonnet, R. P., eds.*, 1983, pp. 61–76. **[G: Latin America]**

Hollist, W. Ladd. Dependency Transformed: Brazilian Agriculture in Historical Perspective. **In** *Doran, C. F.; Modelski, G. and Clark, C., eds.*, 1983, pp. 157–86. **[G: Brazil]**

Lundahl, Mats. Co-operative Structures in the Haitian Economy. **In** *Lundahl, M.*, 1983, pp. 211–36. **[G: Haiti]**

Lundahl, Mats. Population Pressure and Agrarian Property Rights in Haiti. **In** *Lundahl, M.*, 1983, *1980*, pp. 67–82. **[G: Haiti]**

Mancera, Miguel. Stories of the 1930s for the 1980s: Comment. **In** *Armella, P. A.; Dornbusch, R. and Obstfeld, M., eds.*, 1983, pp. 36–40. **[G: Latin America]**

Orton, Keith. Finland and Mexico: A Comparative Historical Analysis. **In** *Doran, C. F.; Modelski, G. and Clark, C., eds.*, 1983, pp. 187–204. **[G: Finland; Mexico]**

Pregger-Román, Charles G. Dependence, Underdevelopment, and Imperialism in Latin America: A Reappraisal. *Sci. Soc.*, Winter 1983–1984, *47* (4), pp. 406–26. **[G: Latin America]**

Stone, Carl. Patterns of Insertion into the World Economy: Historical Profile and Contemporary Options. *Soc. Econ. Stud.*, September 1983, *32* (3), pp. 1–34. **[G: Caribbean]**

Tandeter, Enrique and Wachtel, Nathan. Precios y producción agraria. Potosí y charcas en el siglo XVIII. (With English summary.) *Desarrollo Econ.*, July–September 1983, *23* (90), pp. 197–232. **[G: Bolivia]**

0471 History of Product Prices and Markets

Dean, Warren. Deforestation in Southeastern Brazil. **In** *Tucker, R. P. and Richards, J. F., eds.*, 1983, pp. 50–67. **[G: Brazil]**

Read, Robert. The Growth and Structure of Multinationals in the Banana Export Trade. **In** *Casson, M., ed.*, 1983, pp. 180–213. **[G: Caribbean; Central America; U.S.]**

0472 History of Factor Prices and Markets

Balán, Jorge. Agrarian Structures and Internal Migration in a Historical Perspective: Latin American Case Studies. **In** *Morrison, P. A., ed.*, 1983, pp. 151–85. **[G: Latin America]**

Barrow, Christine. Ownership and Control of Resources in Barbados: 1834 to the Present. *Soc. Econ. Stud.*, September 1983, *32* (3), pp. 83–120. **[G: Barbados]**

Fraginals, Manuel Moreno; Klein, Herbert S. and Engerman, Stanley L. The Level and Structure of Slave Prices on Cuban Plantations in the Mid-Nineteenth Century: Some Comparative Perspectives. *Amer. Hist. Rev.*, December 1983, *88* (5), pp. 1201–18. **[G: Cuba]**

García y Griego, Manuel. The Importation of Mexican Contract Laborers to the United States, 1942–1964: Antecedents, Operation, and Legacy. **In** *Brown, P. G. and Shue, H., eds.*, 1983, pp. 49–98. **[G: Mexico; U.S.]**

Lundahl, Mats. A Note on Haitian Migration to Cuba, 1890–1934. **In** *Lundahl, M.*, 1983, *1982*, pp. 94–110. **[G: Cuba; Haiti]**

Lundahl, Mats and Vargas, Rosemary. Haitian Migration to the Dominican Republic. **In** *Lundahl, M.*, 1983, pp. 111–150. **[G: Dominican Republic; Haiti]**

Weinberg, Gregorio. A Historical Perspective of Latin American Education. *Cepal Rev.*, December 1983, (21), pp. 39–55. **[G: Latin America]**

0473 History of Public Economic Policy (all levels)

Duncan, Tim. La política fiscal durante el gobierno de Juárez Celman, 1886–1890: Una audaz estrategia financiera internacional. (With English summary.) *Desarrollo Econ.*, April–June 1983, *23* (89), pp. 11–34. **[G: Argentina]**

Ojeda, Mario. The Future of Relations between Mexico and the United States. **In** *Reynolds, C. W. and Tello, C., eds.*, 1983, pp. 315–30. **[G: U.S.; Mexico]**

048 Economic History: Oceania

0480 General

Butlin, Noel G. Trends in Public/Private Relations, 1901–75. **In** *Head, B. W., ed.*, 1983, pp. 79–97. **[G: Australia]**

Butlin, Noel G. Yo, Ho, Ho and How Many Bottles of Rum? *Australian Econ. Hist. Rev.*, March 1983, *23* (1), pp. 1–27. **[G: Australia]**

Davies, Mel. Copper and Credit: Commission Agents and the South Australian Mining Association

1845–77. *Australian Econ. Hist. Rev.*, March 1983, *23*(1), pp. 58–77. **[G: Australia]**

Hartwell, R. M. Growth and Equity: Discussion. *J. Econ. Hist.*, March 1983, *43*(1), pp. 203–06. **[G: U.K.; Australia]**

Macintyre, Stuart F. Labour, Capital and Arbitration, 1890–1920. **In** *Head, B. W., ed.*, 1983, pp. 98–114. **[G: Australia]**

Matthews, Trevor V. Business Associations and the State, 1850–1979. **In** *Head, B. W., ed.*, 1983, pp. 115–49. **[G: Australia]**

McLean, Ian W. and Pincus, Jonathan J. Did Australian Living Standards Stagnate between 1890 and 1940? *J. Econ. Hist.*, March 1983, *43*(1), pp. 193–202. **[G: Australia]**

Nakamura, James I. Growth and Equity: Discussion. *J. Econ. Hist.*, March 1983, *43*(1), pp. 206–08. **[G: Japan; Australia]**

0482 History of Factor Prices and Markets

Armstrong, John. The Sugar Strike, 1911. **In** *Murphy, D. J., ed.*, 1983, pp. 100–116. **[G: Australia]**

Carter, Michael and Maddock, Rodney. Working Hours in Australia: Some Issues. **In** *Blandy, R. and Covick, O., eds.*, 1983, pp. 222–45. **[G: Australia]**

Costar, Brian. Two Depression Strikes, 1931. **In** *Murphy, D. J., ed.*, 1983, pp. 186–201. **[G: Australia]**

Forster, C. and Harris, P. A Note on Engineering Wages in Melbourne 1892–1929. *Australian Econ. Hist. Rev.*, March 1983, *23*(1), pp. 50–57. **[G: Australia]**

Haig, Bryan D. and Cain, Neville G. Industrialization and Productivity: Australian Manufacturing in the 1920s and 1950s. *Exploration Econ. Hist.*, April 1983, *20*(2), pp. 183–98. **[G: Australia]**

Hunt, Doug. The Townsville Meatworkers' Strike, 1919. **In** *Murphy, D. J., ed.*, 1983, pp. 144–61. **[G: Australia]**

Kennedy, K. H. The South Johnstone Strike, 1927. **In** *Murphy, D. J., ed.*, 1983, pp. 174–85. **[G: Australia]**

Menghetti, Diane. The Weil's Disease Strike, 1935. **In** *Murphy, D. J., ed.*, 1983, pp. 201–16. **[G: Australia]**

Murphy, D. J. The Big Strikes: Queensland 1889–1965: Trade Unions. **In** *Murphy, D. J., ed.*, 1983, pp. 33–44. **[G: Australia]**

Murphy, D. J. The North Queensland Railway Strike, 1917. **In** *Murphy, D. J., ed.*, 1983, pp. 132–43. **[G: Australia]**

Murphy, D. J. The Tramway and General Strike, 1912. **In** *Murphy, D. J., ed.*, 1983, pp. 117–31. **[G: Australia]**

Smith, Anne. The Railway Strike, 1925. **In** *Murphy, D. J., ed.*, 1983, pp. 162–73. **[G: Australia]**

Sullivan, Rodney J. The Maritime Strike, 1890. **In** *Murphy, D. J., ed.*, 1983, pp. 65–79. **[G: Australia]**

Sullivan, Rodney J. and Sullivan, Robyn A. The London Dock Strike, the Jondaryan Strike and the Brisbane Bootmakers' Strike, 1889–1890. **In** *Murphy, D. J., ed.*, 1983, pp. 47–64. **[G: Australia; U.K.]**

Sullivan, Rodney J. and Sullivan, Robyn A. The Pastoral Strikes, 1891 and 1894. **In** *Murphy, D. J., ed.*, 1983, pp. 80–99. **[G: Australia]**

0483 History of Public Economic Policy (all levels)

Cain, Neville G. Recovery Policy in Australia 1930–33: Certain Native Wisdom. *Australian Econ. Hist. Rev.*, September 1983, *23*(2), pp. 193–218. **[G: Australia]**

Groenewegen, Peter D. Tax Assignment and Revenue Sharing in Australia: Reply. **In** *McLure,!bm C. E., Jr., ed.*, 1983, pp. 327. **[G: Australia]**

Groenewegen, Peter D. Tax Assignment and Revenue Sharing in Australia. **In** *McLure, C. E., Jr., ed.*, 1983, pp. 293–318. **[G: Australia]**

Groenewegen, Peter D. The Political Economy of Federalism, 1901–81. **In** *Head, B. W., ed.*, 1983, pp. 169–95. **[G: Australia]**

Hall, D. R. Strike Law in Queensland. **In** *Murphy, D. J., ed.*, 1983, pp. 15–32. **[G: Australia]**

Head, John G. Tax Assignment and Revenue Sharing in Australia: Comment. **In** *McLure, C. E., Jr., ed.*, 1983, pp. 319–22. **[G: Australia]**

Maddock, Rodney and Penny, Janet. Economists at War: The Financial and Economic Committee 1939–44. *Australian Econ. Hist. Rev.*, March 1983, *23*(1), pp. 28–49. **[G: Australia]**

Musgrave, Peggy B. Tax Assignment and Revenue Sharing in Australia: Comment. **In** *McLure, C. E., Jr., ed.*, 1983, pp. 323–26. **[G: Australia; Canada; U.S.; W. Germany]**

Richmond, W. H. S. M. Bruce and Australian Economic Policy 1923–29. *Australian Econ. Hist. Rev.*, September 1983, *23*(2), pp. 238–57. **[G: Australia]**

050 Economic Systems

0500 General

Ames, Edward. Automaton and Group Structures in Certain Economic Adjustment Mechanisms. *Math. Soc. Sci.*, November 1983, *6*(2), pp. 247–60.

Briefs, Goetz A. Marginal Ethics in the Pluralistic Society. *Rev. Soc. Econ.*, December 1983, *41*(3), pp. 259–70.

Briefs, Goetz A. The Roots of Totalism. *Rev. Soc. Econ.*, December 1983, *41*(3), pp. 300–316.

Espinosa, Juan Guillermo. Worker Participation in the Management of Enterprises and the Ownership and Financing of the Means of Production: A Transition Strategy. *Econ. Anal. Worker's Manage.*, 1983, *17*(2), pp. 99–121.

Horvat, Branko. The World Economy from the Socialist Viewpoint. *Econ. Anal. Worker's Manage.*, 1983, *17*(1), pp. 1–25.

Isard, Walter. Social System Framework and Causal History: Part III, Interdependent Multi-Role Behavior and Operationality. *Conflict Manage. Peace Sci.*, Fall 1983, *7*(1), pp. 87–110.

Pejovich, Svetozar. Basic Institutions of Capitalism and Socialism. **In** *Pejovich, S., ed.*, 1983, pp. 1–9.

Worsley, Peter. One World or Three? A Critique

of the World-System Theory of Immanuel Wallerstein. **In** *Held, D., et al., eds.*, 1983, *1980*, pp. 504–25.

051 Capitalist Economic Systems

0510 Market Economies

Abel-Smith, Brian. The Attacks on Welfare: A European Viewpoint. *Int. J. Soc. Econ.*, 1983, *10*(6/7), pp. 67–75. **[G: OECD]**

Ackerman, Bruce A. Forward: Law in an Activist State. *Yale Law J.*, June 1983, *92*(7), pp. 1083–1128.

Ahmed, Ziauddin; Iqbal, Munawar and Khan, M. Fahim. Money and Banking in Islam: Introduction. **In** *Ahmed, Z.; Iqbal, M. and Khan, M. F., eds.*, 1983, pp. 1–25.

Akyüz, Yilmaz. Value and Exploitation under Joint Production. *Australian Econ. Pap.*, June 1983, *22*(40), pp. 171–79.

Al-Jarhi, Ma'bid Ali. A Monetary and Financial Structure for an Interest-Free Economy: Institutions, Mechanism and Policy. **In** *Ahmed, Z.; Iqbal, M. and Khan, M. F., eds.*, 1983, pp. 69–87.

Albert, Michael and Hahnel, Robin. The Resurrection of Utopian Socialism: Reply. *Rev. Radical Polit. Econ.*, Winter 1983, *15*(4), pp. 126–35.

Albrecht, Sandra L. Politics, Bureaucracy, and Worker Participation: The Swedish Case. **In** *Littrell, W. B.; Sjoberg, G. and Zurcher, L. A., eds.*, 1983, pp. 55–71. **[G: Sweden]**

Alexander, Charles P. Dalla tecnologia la "nuova economia" USA. (The New Economy. With English summary.) *Mondo Aperto*, November-December 1983, *37*(6), pp. 341–54. **[G: U.S.]**

Alexander, Malcolm L. Australia in the Capitalist World Economy. **In** *Head, B. W., ed.*, 1983, pp. 55–76. **[G: Australia; Canada; Latin America]**

Alexander, Robert J. Contributions of the Galbraith "Technostructure" to the Growing Crisis of the U.S. Economy. *J. Econ. Issues*, June 1983, *17*(2), pp. 495–502. **[G: U.S.]**

Anderson, Terry L. and Hill, Peter J. Privatizing the Commons: An Improvement? *Southern Econ. J.*, October 1983, *50*(2), pp. 438–50.

Andreff, Wladimir. Where Has All the Socialism Gone? Post-Revolutionary Society versus State Capitalism: Review Article. *Rev. Radical Polit. Econ.*, Summer 1983, *15*(2), pp. 137–52. **[G: E. Europe]**

Apple, Nixon. The Historical Foundations of Class Struggle in Late Capitalist Liberal Democracies. **In** *Clegg, S.; Dow, G. and Boreham, P., eds.*, 1983, pp. 72–128. **[G: OECD]**

Ariff, Mohamed. Monetary Policy in an Islamic Economy: Comment. **In** *Ahmed, Z.; Iqbal, M. and Khan, M. F., eds.*, 1983, pp. 47–52.

Atkinson, Glen W. Political Economy: Public Choice or Collective Action? *J. Econ. Issues*, December 1983, *17*(4), pp. 1057–65.

Backman, Jules. Entrepreneurship: An Overview. **In** *Backman, J., ed.*, 1983, pp. 1–24. **[G: U.S.]**

Baldwin, Carliss Y. Administered Prices Fifty Years Later: A Comment of Gardiner C. Means: Corporate Power in the Marketplace. *J. Law Econ.*, June 1983, *26*(2), pp. 487–96. **[G: U.S.]**

Baron, Samuel H. Entrepreneurs and Entrepreneurship in Sixteenth/Seventeenth-Century Russia. **In** *Guroff, G. and Carstensen, F. V., eds.*, 1983, pp. 27–58. **[G: U.S.S.R.]**

Barone, Charles A. Dependency, Marxist Theory, and Salvaging the Idea of Capitalism in South Korea. *Rev. Radical Polit. Econ.*, Spring 1983, *15*(1), pp. 43–67. **[G: S. Korea]**

Barton, Stephen E. Property Rights and Human Rights: Efficiency and Democracy as Criteria for Regulatory Reform. *J. Econ. Issues*, December 1983, *17*(4), pp. 915–30.

Baumol, William J. Entrepreneurship and the Sociopolitical Climate. **In** *Backman, J., ed.*, 1983, pp. 173–92.

Bell, Wendell. An Introduction to Futuristics: Assumptions, Theories, Methods, and Research Topics. *Soc. Econ. Stud.*, June 1983, *32*(2), pp. 1–64.

Bennett, Douglas C. Catholicism, Capitalism, and the State in the Development of Mexico. **In** *Finn, J., ed.*, 1983, pp. 125–41. **[G: Mexico]**

Bergesen, Albert. Crises in the World-System: An Introduction. **In** *Bergesen, A., ed.*, 1983, pp. 9–17.

Bergesen, Albert. Modeling Long Waves of Crisis in the World-System. **In** *Bergesen, A., ed.*, 1983, pp. 73–92.

Berliner, Joseph S. Entrepreneurship in the Soviet Period: An Overview. **In** *Guroff, G. and Carstensen, F. V., eds.*, 1983, pp. 191–200. **[G: U.S.S.R.]**

Bhagwati, Jagdish N. The Latin-American Periphery in the Global System of Capitalism: Comment. **In** *Tsuru, S., ed.*, 1983, pp. 46–51.

del Bianco, Lucio. Efficienza, partecipazione e controllo sociale: un equilibrio difficile. (Efficiency, Participation and Control: A Difficult Balance. With English summary.) *L'Impresa*, 1983, *25*(5), pp. 63–69. **[G: Italy]**

Black, Cyril E. Russian and Soviet Entrepreneurship in a Comparative Context. **In** *Guroff, G. and Carstensen, F. V., eds.*, 1983, pp. 3–10. **[G: U.S.S.R.]**

Blackwell, William. The Russian Entrepreneur in the Tsarist Period: An Overview. **In** *Guroff, G. and Carstensen, F. V., eds.*, 1983, pp. 13–26. **[G: U.S.S.R.]**

Blümle, Ernst-Bernd and Dewarrat, Gérard. Expériences en matière de mesure de l'efficience dans les coopératives. (Experiments with Efficiency Measurement in Cooperatives. With English summary.) *Ann. Pub. Co-op. Econ.*, April–June 1983, *54*(2), pp. 173–83.

Bowles, Samuel and Eatwell, John. Between Two Worlds: Interest Groups, Class Structure, and Capitalist Growth. **In** *Mueller, D. C., ed.*, 1983, pp. 217–30.

Bricall, Josep M. Algunos aspectos monetarios y financieros de la crisis. (Some Monetary and Financial Aspects of the Crisis. With English summary.) *Écon. Soc.*, September–October–November 1983, *17*(9–10–11), pp. 1611–30.

Briefs, Goetz A. A Challenge to Western Civilization. *Rev. Soc. Econ.*, December 1983, *41*(3), pp. 317–29.

Briefs, Goetz A. The Ethos Problem in the Present

Pluralistic Society. *Rev. Soc. Econ.*, December 1983, *41*(3), pp. 271–99.

Briefs, Henry W. Goetz Briefs on Capitalism and Democracy: An Introduction. *Rev. Soc. Econ.*, December 1983, *41*(3), pp. 212–27.

Brunner, Karl. The Perception of Man and Justice and the Conception of Political Institutions. **In** *[Giersch, H.]*, 1983, pp. 327–55.

Buchanan, James M. Constitutional Contract in Capitalism. **In** *Pejovich, S., ed.*, 1983, pp. 65–69.

Buck, Trevor and Chiplin, Brian. Risk Bearing and Self Management. *Kyklos*, 1983, *36*(2), pp. 270–84.

Bulgarelli, Marco. Una mappa delle cooperative in Italia. (An Atlas of Cooperatives. With English summary.) *L'Impresa*, 1983, *25*(5), pp. 81–84. **[G: Italy]**

Burkitt, Brian. Post-Keynesian Distribution Theory and Employee Investment Funds. *Econ. Stud. Quart.*, August 1983, *34*(2), pp. 124–32.

Burkitt, Brian and Spiers, M. The Economic Theory of Politics: A Re-Appraisal. *Int. J. Soc. Econ.*, 1983, *10*(2), pp. 12–21.

Butlin, Noel G. Trends in Public/Private Relations, 1901–75. **In** *Head, B. W., ed.*, 1983, pp. 79–97. **[G: Australia]**

Campbell, C. Co-Operatives in Scotland: The Role of The Scottish Co-Operatives Development Committee. *Reg. Stud.*, August 1983, *17*(4), pp. 281–83. **[G: U.K.]**

Carter, Stephen L. Separatism and Skepticism. *Yale Law J.*, June 1983, *92*(7), pp. 1334–41.

Cate, Tom. Keynes and Thurow: The Socialization of Investment. *Eastern Econ. J.*, July–September 1983, *9*(3), pp. 205–12.

Chapra, M. Umer. Elimination of Interest from the Economy: Report: Comment. **In** *Ahmed, Z.; Iqbal, M. and Khan, M. F., eds.*, 1983, pp. 212–23. **[G: Pakistan]**

Chapra, M. Umer. Monetary Policy in an Islamic Economy. **In** *Ahmed, Z.; Iqbal, M. and Khan, M. F., eds.*, 1983, pp. 27–46.

Choudhury, Masudul Alam. Insurance and Investment in Islamic Perspective. *Int. J. Soc. Econ.*, 1983, *10*(5), pp. 14–26.

Clawson, Patrick. A Comment on Van Parijs' Obituary [The Falling-Rate-of-Profit Theory of Crisis: A Rational Reconstruction by Way of Obituary]. *Rev. Radical Polit. Econ.*, Summer 1983, *15*(2), pp. 107–10.

Clegg, Stewart; Dow, Geoff and Boreham, Paul. Politics and Crisis: The State of the Recession. **In** *Clegg, S.; Dow, G. and Boreham, P., eds.*, 1983, pp. 1–50.

Collins, Randall. The Weberian Revolution of the High Middle Ages. **In** *Bergesen, A., ed.*, 1983, pp. 205–25.

Condominas, S. La crisis economica contemporanea: algunas consideraciones generales. (The Present Economic Crisis. With English summary.) *Écon. Soc.*, September–October–November 1983, *17*(9–10–11), pp. 1383–1401.

Coomans, G. Coûts sociaux de l'accumulation et genèse de la crise du capital. (Special Costs of Accumulation and Genesis of the Crisis of Capital. With English summary.) *Écon. Soc.*, September–October–November 1983, *17*(9–10–11), pp. 1487–1516.

Cottle, Rex L.; Macaulay, Hugh H. and Yandle, T. Bruce. Codetermination: Union Style. *J. Lab. Res.*, Spring 1983, *4*(2), pp. 125–35. **[G: U.S.]**

Crouch, Colin. The State, Capital, and Liberal Democracy. **In** *Held, D., et al., eds.*, 1983, *1979*, pp. 320–29.

Cullis, John G. and Jones, Philip R. The Welfare State and Private Alternatives: Towards an Existence Proof. *Scot. J. Polit. Econ.*, June 1983, *30*(2), pp. 97–113.

Dahl, Robert. Comment on Manley: Neo-Pluralism: A Class Analysis of Pluralism I and Pluralism II. *Amer. Polit. Sci. Rev.*, June 1983, *77*(2), pp. 386–89. **[G: U.S.]**

Damaška, Mirjan. Activism in Perspective. *Yale Law J.*, June 1983, *92*(7), pp. 1189–197.

Deaglio, Mario. L'economia capitalista in mezzo al guado. (The Capitalist Economy in Deep Water. With English summary.) *L'Impresa*, 1983, *25*(6), pp. 41–46. **[G: OECD]**

Defourny, Jacques. L'autofinancement des coopératives de travailleurs et la théorie économique. (Self-Financing in Workers' Cooperatives and Economic Theory. With English summary.) *Ann. Pub. Co-op. Econ.*, April–June 1983, *54*(2), pp. 201–24.

Demsetz, Harold. The Neglect of the Entrepreneur. **In** *Ronen, J., ed.*, 1983, pp. 271–80.

Destanne de Bernis, G. De quelques questions concernant la théorie des crises. (Some Questions on the Theory of Crisis. With English summary.) *Écon. Soc.*, September–October–November 1983, *17*(9–10–11), pp. 1277–1329.

Devine, James N. Underconsumption, Over-Investment and the Origins of the Great Depression. *Rev. Radical Polit. Econ.*, Summer 1983, *15*(2), pp. 1–27. **[G: U.S.]**

Dickman, A. B. Market-Orientated Policies and Financial Markets. *S. Afr. J. Econ.*, December 1983, *51*(4), pp. 467–85. **[G: S. Africa]**

Donnithorne, Audrey. Hong Kong as an Economic Model for the Great Cities of China. **In** *Youngson, A. J., ed.*, 1983, pp. 282–310. **[G: Hong Kong]**

Dugger, William M. Classical Economists and the Corporation. *Int. J. Soc. Econ.*, 1983, *10*(2), pp. 22–31.

Duvall, Raymond D. and Freeman, John R. The Techno-Bureaucratic Elite and the Entrepreneurial State in Dependent Industrialization. *Amer. Polit. Sci. Rev.*, September 1983, *77*(3), pp. 569–87. **[G: LDCs]**

Dyson, Kenneth. Industrial Crisis: The Cultural, Ideological and Structural Context. **In** *Dyson, K. and Wilks, S., eds.*, 1983, pp. 26–66. **[G: U.S.; W. Europe]**

Ehlers, Eckart. Rent-Capitalism and Unequal Development in the Middle East: The Case of Iran. **In** *Stewart, F., ed.*, 1983, pp. 32–61. **[G: Iran]**

Eichner, Alfred S. The Micro Foundations of the Corporate Economy. *Managerial Dec. Econ.*, September 1983, *4*(3), pp. 136–52.

Ekelund, Robert B., Jr. and Tollison, Robert D. Tradeable Shares and the Supply-Side of Corporate Development: Reply [Mercantilist Origins of the Corporation]. *Bell J. Econ. (See Rand J. Econ. after 4/85),* Spring 1983, *14*(1), pp. 298–300. **[G: U.K.]**

Ellerman, David P. A Model Structure for Cooperatives: Worker Co-ops and Housing Co-ops. *Rev. Soc. Econ.,* April 1983, *41*(1), pp. 52–67.

Elliott, John E. Schumpeter and the Theory of Capitalist Economic Development. *J. Econ. Behav. Organ.,* December 1983, *4*(4), pp. 277–308.

Elliott, John E. Schumpeter and Marx on Capitalist Transformation. *Quart. J. Econ.,* May 1983, *98*(2), pp. 333–36.

Fanning, Connell and McCarthy, Thomas. Hypotheses Concerning the Non-Viability of Labour-Directed Firms in Capitalist Economies. *Econ. Anal. Worker's Manage.,* 1983, *17*(2), pp. 123–54.

Fellner, William. Entrepreneurship in Economic Theory: The "Scientific Method" and Vicarious Introspection. **In** *Backman, J., ed.,* 1983, pp. 25–53.

Foglesong, Richard E. Business against the Welfare State. *Challenge,* November/December 1983, *26*(5), pp. 38–45. **[G: U.S.]**

Foster, John Bellamy. Theories of Capitalist Transformation: Critical Notes on the Comparison of Marx and Schumpeter. *Quart. J. Econ.,* May 1983, *98*(2), pp. 327–31.

Frug, Gerald E. Why Neutrality? [Regulation in a Liberal State: The Role of Non-commodity Values]. *Yale Law J.,* July 1983, *92*(8), pp. 1591–1601. **[G: U.S.]**

Galbraith, John Kenneth. Historical Process and the Rich. **In** *Galbraith, J. K.,* 1983, pp. 65–82. **[G: U.S.]**

Galbraith, John Kenneth. The Anatomy of Power: Interview. *Challenge,* July/August 1983, *26*(3), pp. 26–33. **[G: U.S.]**

García, Alvaro and Wells, John. Chile: A Laboratory for Failed Experiments in Capitalist Political Economy. *Cambridge J. Econ.,* September/December 1983, *7*(3/4), pp. 287–304. **[G: Chile]**

Gasparotti, Giorgio. Un sistema di valori da salvare. (A Value System to Be Saved. With English summary.) *L'Impresa,* 1983, *25*(5), pp. 77–80.

Gelting, Jørgen H. Keynes' samfundsopfattelse. (With English summary.) *Nationaløkon. Tidsskr.,* 1983, *121*(3), pp. 317–22.

Gerbier, B. Le thatcherisme: vers une économie mondiale anglo-américaine? (Thatcherism: Towards an Anglo-Saxon World Economy. With English summary.) *Écon. Soc.,* September–October–November 1983, *17*(9–10–11), pp. 1763–95. **[G: U.K.]**

Gibson, Katherine D. and Horvath, Ronald J. Global Capital and the Restructuring Crisis in Australian Manufacturing. *Econ. Geogr.,* April 1983, *59*(2), pp. 178–94. **[G: Australia]**

Giersch, Herbert. Socialist Elements as Limits to Economic Growth. **In** *Lenel, H. O.; Willgerodt, H. and Molsberger, J.,* 1983, pp. 3–12. **[G: OECD]**

Giersch, Herbert. The World Economy at Century's End: Comment. **In** *Tsuru, S., ed.,* 1983, pp. 78–88.

Gillies, Grazia Ietto. Monopoly Capitalism and the UK Economy: A Review Article. *Stud. Econ.,* 1983, *38*(21), pp. 57–75. **[G: U.K.]**

Glombowski, Jörg. A Marxian Model of Long Run Capitalist Development. *Z. Nationalökon.,* 1983, *43*(4), pp. 363–82.

Goldfrank, Walter L. The Limits of Analogy: Hegemonic Decline in Great Britain and the United States. **In** *Bergesen, A., ed.,* 1983, pp. 143–54. **[G: U.K.; U.S.]**

Goldman, Paul. The Labor Process and the Sociology of Organizations. **In** *Bacharach, S. B., ed.,* 1983, pp. 49–81. **[G: U.S.]**

Gordon, Avery and Herman, Andrew. The Resurrection of Utopian Socialism: Review Article. *Rev. Radical Polit. Econ.,* Winter 1983, *15*(4), pp. 104–25.

Gowland, D. H. Market Failure and State Intervention. **In** *Gowland, D. H., ed.,* 1983, pp. 171–99.

Gülalp, Haldun. Frank and Wallerstein Revisited: A Contribution to Brenner's Critique. **In** *Limqueco, P. and McFarlane, B., eds.,* 1983, pp. 114–36.

Handler, Joel F. Discretion in Social Welfare: The Uneasy Position in the Rule of Law. *Yale Law J.,* June 1983, *92*(7), pp. 1270–286.

Hartwell, R. M. The Origins of Capitalism: A Methodological Essay. **In** *Pejovich, S., ed.,* 1983, pp. 11–23.

Harvey, David. The Urban Process under Capitalism: A Framework for Analysis. **In** *Lake, R. W., ed.,* 1983, *1978,* pp. 197–227. **[G: U.S.; U.K.]**

Hasan, Zubair. Theory of Profit: The Islamic Viewpoint. *J. Res. Islamic Econ.,* Summer 1983, *1*(1), pp. 1–16.

Hausmann, Ricardo and Lipietz, Alain. Marx et la divergence entre production en valeur et revenus nominaux. (With English summary.) *Revue Écon. Polit.,* March–April 1983, *93*(2), pp. 270–300.

Head, Brian W. State and Economy: Theories and Problems. **In** *Head, B. W., ed.,* 1983, pp. 22–54.

Head, Brian W. The Australian Political Economy: Introduction. **In** *Head, B. W., ed.,* 1983, pp. 3–21. **[G: Australia]**

Hechter, Michael. Karl Polanyi's Social Theory: A Critique. **In** *Hechter, M., ed.,* 1983, pp. 158–89.

Heineman, Ben W., Jr. The Law Schools' Failing Grade on Federalism. *Yale Law J.,* June 1983, *92*(7), pp. 1349–56.

Heinsohn, Gunnar and Steiger, Otto. Private Property, Debts and Interest or: The Origin of Money and the Rise and Fall of Monetary Economies. *Stud. Econ.,* 1983, *38*(21), pp. 3–56.

Hermens, Ferdinand A. . . . And Now the Future. *Rev. Soc. Econ.,* December 1983, *41*(3), pp. 330–55.

Hill, Richard Child. Capital Accumulation and Urbanization in the United States. **In** *Lake, R. W., ed.,* 1983, *1977,* pp. 228–49. **[G: U.S.]**

Hixon, William F. A New Perspective on the Economic Crisis. *Eastern Econ. J.,* July–September 1983, *9*(3), pp. 221–31. **[G: U.S.]**

Houston, David B. Capitalism without Capitalists: A Comment on "Classes in Marxian Theory." *Rev. Radical Polit. Econ.,* Spring 1983, *15*(1), pp. 153–56.

Hunt, Ian. An Obituary or a New Life for the Tendency of the Rate of Profit to Fall? *Rev. Radical Polit. Econ.*, Spring 1983, *15*(1), pp. 131–48.

Iqbal, Munawar. Monetary Policy in an Islamic Economy: Comment. **In** *Ahmed, Z.; Iqbal, M. and Khan, M. F., eds.*, 1983, pp. 52–57.

Ireland, Norman J. and Law, Peter J. A Cournot-Nash Model of the Consumer Cooperative. *Southern Econ. J.*, January 1983, *49*(3), pp. 706–16.

Iša, Jan. The Crisis of Keynesianism and Economic Neo-Conservatism. *Czech. Econ. Digest.*, November 1983, (7), pp. 68–87.

Jacobson, Arthur J. Democratic Participation and the Legal Structure of the Economy of Firms. *Soc. Res.*, Winter 1983, *50*(4), pp. 803–49.

Jones, Derek C. Producer Co-operatives in Industrialised Western Economies. **In** *Kennedy, L., ed.*, 1983, *1980*, pp. 31–60. **[G: OECD]**

Jones, R. J. Barry. Perspectives on International Political Economy. **In** *Jones, R. J. B., ed.*, 1983, pp. 169–208.

Jüttner, D. Johannes and Murray, John H. Notes and Numbers on Marx's Falling Rate of Profit. *Econ. Rec.*, December 1983, *59*(167), pp. 375–83. **[G: Australia]**

Kahan, Arcadius. Notes on Jewish Entrepreneurship in Tsarist Russia. **In** *Guroff, G. and Carstensen, F. V., eds.*, 1983, pp. 104–24. **[G: U.S.S.R.]**

Katzenstein, Peter J. The Small European States in the International Economy: Economic Dependence and Corporatist Politics. **In** *Ruggie, J. G., ed.*, 1983, pp. 91–130. **[G: W. Europe]**

Kendrick, John W. Entrepreneurship, Productivity, and Economic Growth. **In** *Backman, J., ed.*, 1983, pp. 111–48. **[G: OECD]**

Kenway, Peter. Marx, Keynes and the Possibility of Crisis. **In** *Eatwell, J. and Milgate, M., eds.*, 1983, *1980*, pp. 149–66.

Kesselman, Mark. From State Theory to Class Struggle and Compromise: Contemporary Marxist Political Study. *Soc. Sci. Quart.*, December 1983, *64*(4), pp. 826–45.

Khachaturov, Tigran S. The World Economy at Century's End: Comments. **In** *Tsuru, S., ed.*, 1983, pp. 89–94.

Khan, Mahmood Hasan. Classes and Agrarian Transition in Pakistan. *Pakistan Devel. Rev.*, Autumn 1983, *22*(3), pp. 129–62. **[G: Pakistan]**

Kim, Ki Hang and Roush, Fred W. Asymptotic Inequality of the Market System. *Math. Soc. Sci.*, December 1983, *6*(3), pp. 325–35.

Kipnis, Baruch A. and Meir, Avinoam. The Kibbutz Industrial System: A Unique Rural-industrial Community in Israel. **In** *Hamilton, F. E. I. and Linge, G. J. R., eds.*, 1983, pp. 463–84. **[G: Israel]**

Kirzner, Israel M. Entrepreneurs and the Entrepreneurial Function: A Commentary. **In** *Ronen, J., ed.*, 1983, pp. 281–90.

Kirzner, Israel M. Entrepreneurship and the Future of Capitalism. **In** *Backman, J., ed.*, 1983, pp. 149–71.

Koslowski, Peter F. The Ethics of Capitalism. **In** *Pejovich, S., ed.*, 1983, pp. 33–64.

Kristol, Irving. Adam Smith and the Spirit of Capitalism. **In** *Kristol, I.*, 1983, *1976*, pp. 139–76.

Kristol, Irving. On Corporate Capitalism in America. **In** *Kristol, I.*, 1983, *1976*, pp. 202–18. **[G: U.S.]**

Kurz, Mordecai. Entrepreneurial Activity in a Complex Economy. **In** *Ronen, J., ed.*, 1983, pp. 291–300.

Laibman, David. Capitalism and Immanent Crisis: Broad Strokes for a Theoretical Foundation. *Soc. Res.*, Summer 1983, *50*(2), pp. 359–400.

Landa, Janet T. The Political Economy of the Ethnically Homogeneous Chinese Middleman Group in Southeast Asia: Ethnicity and Entrepreneurship in a Plural Society. **In** *Lim, L. Y. C. and Gosling, L. A. P., eds.*, 1983, pp. 86–116. **[G: Malaysia; Singapore]**

Lange, Oscar and Lerner, Abba P. Strengthening the Economic Foundations of Democracy. **In** *Lerner, A. P.*, 1983, *1944*, pp. 171–86. **[G: U.S.]**

Lavoie, Marc. Loi de Minsky et loi d'entropie. (Minsky Law and Entropy Law. With English summary.) *Écon. Appl.*, 1983, *36*(2–3), pp. 287–331.

Leon, Paola. Impresa cooperativa e impresa capitalistica. (Cooperative and Capitalistic Business. With English summary.) *L'Impresa*, 1983, *25*(5), pp. 55–61.

Lerner, Abba P. Economic Democracy (or, the Market and the Ballot). **In** *Lerner, A. P.*, 1983, *1961*, pp. 629–37.

Lerner, Abba P. Planning and Freedom. **In** *Lerner, A. P.*, 1983, *1945*, pp. 595–606.

Levin, Henry M. Raising Employment and Productivity with Producer Co-operatives. **In** *Streeten, P. and Maier, H., eds.*, 1983, pp. 310–28. **[G: Spain]**

Lindblom, Charles E. Comment on Manley: Neo-Pluralism: A Class Analysis of Pluralism I and Pluralism II. *Amer. Polit. Sci. Rev.*, June 1983, *77*(2), pp. 384–86. **[G: U.S.]**

Lindsey, J. K. Classes in Marxist Theory. *Rev. Radical Polit. Econ.*, Spring 1983, *15*(1), pp. 149–52.

Lux, Kenneth and Lutz, Mark A. Creative vs. Mechanical Evolutionism: A Commentary [Economic Evolution and Economic Policy: Is Reaganomics a Sustainable Force?] [Creationism versus Evolutionism in Economics: Societal Consequences of Economic Doctrine]. *J. Econ. Issues*, December 1983, *17*(4), pp. 1113–17. **[G: U.S.]**

Madeuf, Bernadette and Ominami, Carlos. Crise et investissement international. (Crisis and International Investment. With English summary.) *Revue Écon.*, September 1983, *34*(5), pp. 926–70. **[G: OECD]**

Mandel, Ernest. The Nation-State and Imperialism. **In** *Held, D., et al., eds.*, 1983, *1975*, pp. 526–39.

Mandel, Ernest. World Crisis and the Monetarist Answer. **In** *Jansen, K., ed.*, 1983, pp. 79–95. **[G: OECD]**

Mändle, Eduard. Die Entwicklung der gesamtwirtschaftlichen Rahmenbedingungen und ihre Auswirkungen auf die genossenschaftlichen Strukturen. (Macroeconomic Trends and Their Effect on Co-Operative Structures. With English summary.) *Ann. Pub. Co-op. Econ.*, October-December 1983, *54*(4), pp. 397–424.

Manley, John F. Neo-Pluralism: A Class Analysis of Pluralism I and Pluralism II. *Amer. Polit. Sci. Rev.*, June 1983, *77*(2), pp. 368–83. **[G: U.S.]**

Mannan, M. A. Islamic Economics as a Social Science: Some Methodological Issues. *J. Res. Islamic Econ.*, Summer 1983, *1*(1), pp. 49–61.

Mansfield, Edwin. Entrepreneurship and the Management of Innovation. **In** *Backman, J., ed.*, 1983, pp. 81–109. **[G: U.S.]**

Mariti, P. and Smiley, Robert H. Co-Operative Agreements and the Organization of Industry. *J. Ind. Econ.*, June 1983, *31*(4), pp. 437–51.

Marshall, Ray. Comments of the Institutional View of Reaganomics. *J. Econ. Issues,* June 1983, *17*(2), pp. 503–06. **[G: U.S.]**

Mashaw, Jerry L. "Rights" in the Federal Administrative State. *Yale Law J.*, June 1983, *92*(7), pp. 1129–173.

Mason, Kenneth. A Philosophical Rationale for Contemporary Capitalism (II). **In** *Martin, T. R., ed.*, 1983, pp. 34–42.

Mathias, Peter. Entrepreneurship and Economic History: The State of the Debate. **In** *Earl, M. J., ed.*, 1983, pp. 40–54.

Matthaei, Julie A. Freedom and Unfreedom in Marxian Economics. *Eastern Econ. J.*, April–June 1983, *9*(2), pp. 71–78.

Mátyás, Antal. Similarities between the Economic Theories of Marx and Keynes. *Acta Oecon.*, 1983, *31*(3–4), pp. 155–73.

McNulty, Paul J. and Pontecorvo, Giulio. Mercantilist Origins of the Corporation: Comment. *Bell J. Econ. (See Rand J. Econ. after 4/85)*, Spring 1983, *14*(1), pp. 294–97. **[G: U.K.]**

Means, Gardiner C. Corporate Power in the Marketplace. *J. Law Econ.*, June 1983, *26*(2), pp. 467–85. **[G: U.S.]**

de Melo, A. Barbosa. Introdução às formas de concertação social. (With English summary.) *Economia,* May 1983, *7*(2), pp. 255–306. **[G: Portugal]**

Mestmäcker, Ernst-Joachim. Socialist Elements as Limits to Economic Growth: Comment. **In** *Lenel, H. O.; Willgerodt, H. and Molsberger, J.*, 1983, pp. 13–15. **[G: OECD]**

Middlemas, Keith. Corporate Bias. **In** *Held, D., et al., eds.*, 1983, *1979*, pp. 330–37.

Molitor, Bruno. Schwäche der Demokratie. **In** *Lenel, H. O.; Willgerodt, H. and Molsberger, J.*, 1983, pp. 17–38. **[G: OECD]**

Morawetz, David. The Kibbutz as a Model for Developing Countries: On Maintaining Full Economic Equality in Practice. **In** *Stewart, F., ed.*, 1983, pp. 215–42. **[G: Israel]**

Morris, Jacob. Underconsumption and the General Crisis: Gillman's Theory. *Sci. Soc.*, Fall 1983, *47*(3), pp. 323–29.

Mukasa, R. Les conditions de travail au Japon: Leur aspect global après la Seconde Guerre mondiale. (Labour Conditions in Japan: The Overall Post-War Picture. With English summary.) *Écon. Soc.*, March–April 1983, *17*(3–4), pp. 481–516. **[G: Japan]**

Munkirs, John R. Centralized Private Sector Planning: An Institutionalist's Perspective on the Contemporary U.S. Economy. *J. Econ. Issues,* December 1983, *17*(4), pp. 931–67. **[G: U.S.]**

Munkirs, John R. and Ayers, Michael. Political and Policy Implications of Centralized Private Sector Planning. *J. Econ. Issues,* December 1983, *17*(4), pp. 969–84.

Nadri, M. Ishaq. A Monetary and Financial Structure for an Interest-Free Economy: Institutions, Mechanism and Policy: Comment. **In** *Ahmed, Z.; Iqbal, M. and Khan, M. F., eds.*, 1983, pp. 88–90.

North, Douglass C. A Theory of Institutional Change and the Economic History of the Western World. **In** *Hechter, M., ed.*, 1983, pp. 190–215.

North, Liisa L. Problems of Democratization in Peru and Ecuador. **In** *Ritter, A. R. M. and Pollock, D. H., eds.*, 1983, pp. 214–39. **[G: Peru; Ecuador]**

Norton, Eleanor Holmes. Public Assistance, Post-New Deal Bureaucracy, and the Law: Learning from Negative Models. *Yale Law J.*, June 1983, *92*(7), pp. 1287–99.

Nutzinger, Hans G. Empirical Research into German Codetermination: Problems and Perspectives. *Econ. Anal. Worker's Manage.*, 1983, *17*(4), pp. 361–82. **[G: Germany]**

Offe, Claus. Competitive Party Democracy and the Keynesian Welfare State: Some Reflections on Their Historical Limits. **In** *Clegg, S.; Dow, G. and Boreham, P., eds.*, 1983, pp. 51–71.

Okun, Arthur M. Our Blend of Democracy and Capitalism: It Works, but Is in Danger. **In** *Okun, A. M.*, 1983, *1979*, pp. 632–44. **[G: U.S.]**

Opp, Karl-Dieter. Problems of Defining and Explaining Capitalism. **In** *Pejovich, S., ed.*, 1983, pp. 25–31.

Osadchaia, I. The Theoretical Platform of Contemporary U.S. Conservatism. *Prob. Econ.*, August 1983, *26*(4), pp. 73–93. **[G: U.S.]**

Owen, Thomas C. Entrepreneurship and the Structure of Enterprise in Russia, 1800–1880. **In** *Guroff, G. and Carstensen, F. V., eds.*, 1983, pp. 59–83. **[G: U.S.S.R.]**

Paderni, Enio. I punti di forza dell'impresa cooperativa. (The Strengths of the Cooperative Business. With English summary.) *L'Impresa,* 1983, *25*(5), pp. 71–75.

Pakistan Council of Islamic Ideology. Elimination of Interest from the Economy: Report. **In** *Ahmed, Z.; Iqbal, M. and Khan, M. F., eds.*, 1983, pp. 103–211. **[G: Pakistan]**

Pejovich, Svetozar. Codetermination in the West: The Case of Germany. **In** *Pejovich, S., ed.*, 1983, pp. 101–17. **[G: W. Germany]**

Pelinka, Anton. The Austrian Experience of Social and Economic Cooperation. *Economia,* May 1983, *7*(2), pp. 239–53. **[G: Austria]**

Petr, Jerry L. Creationism versus Evolutionism in Economics: Societal Consequences of Economic Doctrine. *J. Econ. Issues,* June 1983, *17*(2), pp. 475–83. **[G: U.S.]**

Petr, Jerry L. Rejoinder to Lux and Lutz [Economic Evolution and Economic Policy: Is Reaganomics a Sustainable Force?] [Creationism versus Evolutionism in Economics: Societal Consequences of Economic Doctrine]. *J. Econ. Issues,* December 1983, *17*(4), pp. 1118–20. **[G: U.S.]**

Petras, James F. New Perspectives on Imperialism and Social Classes in the Periphery. **In** *Limqueco, P. and McFarlane, B., eds.*, 1983, pp. 198–220.

Pimentel, J. M. Rocha. Concertação social e política

de rendimentos em Portugal: Experiência recente e perspectivas para a década de 80. (With English summary.) *Economia,* May 1983, *7*(2), pp. 357–94. **[G: Portugal]**

Pinto, Mário. Doutrina social de Igreja e concertação social. (With English summary.) *Economia,* May 1983, *7*(2), pp. 331–55.

Pohjola, Matti. Nash and Stackelberg Solutions in a Differential Game Model of Capitalism. *J. Econ. Dynam. Control,* September 1983, *6*(1/2), pp. 173–86.

Pohjola, Matti. Workers' Investment Funds and the Dynamic Inefficiency of Capitalism. *J. Public Econ.,* March 1983, *20*(2), pp. 271–79.

Prebisch, Raúl. Capitalism: The Second Crisis. **In** *Gauhar, A., ed. (II),* 1983, pp. 1–8.

Prebisch, Raúl. The Crisis of Capitalism and International Trade. *Cepal Rev.,* August 1983, (20), pp. 51–74. **[G: Latin America]**

Prebisch, Raúl. The Latin-American Periphery in the Global System of Capitalism. **In** *Tsuru, S., ed.,* 1983, pp. 30–45.

Pryor, Frederic L. The Economics of Production Cooperatives: A Reader's Guide. *Ann. Pub. Co-op. Econ.,* April–June 1983, *54*(2), pp. 133–72.

Rabin, Robert L. Legitimacy, Discretion, and the Concept of Rights. *Yale Law J.,* June 1983, *92*(7), pp. 1174–188.

Ramaekers, Roger. Analyse critique des principes coopératifs. (A Critical Analysis of Co-Operative Principles. With English summary.) *Ann. Pub. Co-op. Econ.,* October-December 1983, *54*(4), pp. 425–32.

Ray, John. An Empirical Study of the Political Business Cycle: Government Fiscal Policy and the Business Cycle in the United States. *Econ. Forum,* Winter 1983-84, *14*(2), pp. 19–40. **[G: U.S.]**

Remus, Jean. Financial Participation of Employees: An Attempted Classification and Major Trends. *Int. Lab. Rev.,* January–February 1983, *122*(1), pp. 1–21. **[G: Selected MDCs]**

Rodney, Walter. Africa's Contribution to the Capitalist Development of Europe—The Colonial Period. **In** *Glassner, M. I., ed.,* 1983, *1972,* pp. 369–80. **[G: Africa; Europe]**

Ronen, Joshua. Some Insights into the Entrepreneurial Process. **In** *Ronen, J., ed.,* 1983, pp. 137–73.

Rooney, Patrick M. Worker Control: Greater Efficiency and Job Satisfaction. *Econ. Forum,* Winter 1983-84, *14*(2), pp. 97–123. **[G: U.S.]**

Roosa, Ruth AmEnde. Russian Industrialists during World War I: The Interaction of Economics and Politics. **In** *Guroff, G. and Carstensen, F. V., eds.,* 1983, pp. 159–87. **[G: U.S.S.R.]**

Rosen, Sherwin. Economics and Entrepreneurs. **In** *Ronen, J., ed.,* 1983, pp. 301–10.

Ross, Robert J. S. Facing Leviathan: Public Policy and Global Capitalism. *Econ. Geogr.,* April 1983, *59*(2), pp. 144–60. **[G: U.S.; U.K.]**

Rozen, Marvin E. Segmented Work and Divided Workers: A Review Article. *J. Econ. Issues,* March 1983, *17*(1), pp. 215–24. **[G: U.S.]**

Ruiz, G.; Narvaez, A. and Gallego, J.-A. Crisis económica, desarrollo y medio ambiente. (Economic Crisis, Development and Environment. With English summary.) *Écon. Soc.,* September–October–November 1983, *17*(–10–11), pp. 1647–69.

Samuelson, Paul A. The World Economy at Century's End. **In** *Tsuru, S., ed.,* 1983, pp. 58–77.

Sapelli, Giulio. Come gestire una "cooperativa ereditaria." (The Management of "Inherited Cooperatives." With English summary.) *L'Impresa,* 1983, *25*(4), pp. 37–43. **[G: Italy]**

Schatz, Sayre P. Socializing Adaptation: A Perspective on World Capitalism. *World Devel.,* January 1983, *11*(1), pp. 1–10. **[G: Global]**

Schmitz, Wolfgang. Economic and Social Partnership and Incomes Policy and the Social Doctrine of the Church. *Economia,* May 1983, *7*(2), pp. 307–29.

Schuck, Peter H. Regulation, Non-market Values, and the Administrative State: A Comment [Regulation in a Liberal State: The Role of Non-commodity Values]. *Yale Law J.,* July 1983, *92*(8), pp. 1602–13. **[G: U.S.]**

Schumpeter, Joseph A. American Institutions and Economic Progress. *Z. ges. Staatswiss.,* June 1983, *139*(2), pp. 191–96.

Scott, Anthony. Property Rights and Property Wrongs. *Can. J. Econ.,* November 1983, *16*(4), pp. 555–73.

Seldon, Arthur. New Hope for Economic Policy in a Changing Polity. **In** *Seldon, A., et al.,* 1983, pp. 3–12. **[G: U.K.]**

Sen, Amartya K. The Profit Motive. *Lloyds Bank Rev.,* January 1983, (147), pp. 1–20.

Shapiro, Moses. The Entrepreneurial Individual in the Large Organization. **In** *Backman, J., ed.,* 1983, pp. 55–80.

Sherman, Howard J. Realization Crisis Theory and the Labor Theory of Value [A Note on the Underconsumptionist Theory and the Labor Theory of Value]. *Sci. Soc.,* Summer 1983, *47*(2), pp. 205–13.

Siddiqi, Muhammad Nejatullah. Banking in an Islamic Framework. **In** *Siddiqi, M. N.,* 1983, pp. 51–65.

Siddiqi, Muhammad Nejatullah. Economics of Profit-sharing. **In** *Siddiqi, M. N.,* 1983, pp. 97–123.

Siddiqi, Muhammad Nejatullah. Islamic Approaches to Money, Banking and Monetary Policy. **In** *Siddiqi, M. N.,* 1983, pp. 15–50.

Siddiqi, Muhammad Nejatullah. Issues in Islamisation of Banking. **In** *Siddiqi, M. N.,* 1983, pp. 133–45. **[G: Pakistan]**

Siddiqi, Muhammad Nejatullah. Monetary Theory of Islamic Economics. **In** *Siddiqi, M. N.,* 1983, pp. 125–31.

Siddiqi, Muhammad Nejatullah. Rationale of Islamic Banking. **In** *Siddiqi, M. N.,* 1983, pp. 67–96.

Siddiqi, Nejatullah. Elimination of Interest from the Economy: Report: Comment. **In** *Ahmed, Z.; Iqbal, M. and Khan, M. F., eds.,* 1983, pp. 223–32. **[G: Pakistan]**

Simms, Marian. State Interventionism and Coalition Governments, 1949–66. **In** *Head, B. W., ed.,* 1983, pp. 150–68. **[G: Australia]**

Simon, Herbert A. What Is Industrial Democracy?

Challenge, January/February 1983, *25*(6), pp. 30–39. **[G: U.S.]**

Simon, William H. Legality, Bureaucracy, and Class in the Welfare System. *Yale Law J.,* June 1983, *92*(7), pp. 1198–1269.

Sirc, Ljubo. Employee Participation and the Promotion of Employee Ownership. **In** *Seldon, A., et al.,* 1983, pp. 113–27. **[G: W. Germany; Yugoslavia]**

Sivachev, Nikolai. The Rise of Statism in 1930s America: A Soviet View of the Social and Political Effects of the New Deal. *Labor Hist.,* Fall 1983, *24*(4), pp. 500–525. **[G: U.S.]**

Smith, Louis P. Economists, Economic Theory, and Co-operatives. **In** *Kennedy, L., ed.,* 1983, pp. 95–121. **[G: Selected Countries]**

Södersten, Bo. The Latin-American Periphery in the Global System of Capitalism: Comments. **In** *Tsuru, S., ed.,* 1983, pp. 52–57. **[G: Sweden]**

Stabile, Donald. The New Class and Capitalism: A Three-and-Three-Thirds-Class Model. *Rev. Radical Polit. Econ.,* Winter 1983, *15*(4), pp. 45–70. **[G: U.S.]**

Stamos, Stephen C., Jr. A Critique of James and Street's "Technology, Institutions, and Public Policy in the Age of Energy Substitution: The Case of Latin America." *J. Econ. Issues,* September 1983, *17*(3), pp. 745–50. **[G: Latin America]**

Stanfield, J. Ron. The Affluent Society after Twenty-Five Years. *J. Econ. Issues,* September 1983, *17*(3), pp. 589–607.

Stanfield, J. Ron. The Institutional Crisis of the Corporate Welfare State. *Int. J. Soc. Econ.,* 1983, *10*(6/7), pp. 45–66.

Stefanelli, Renzo. Forze sociali e cooperazione. (Sociopolitical Forces and the Cooperative Movement. With English summary.) *L'Impresa,* 1983, *25*(4), pp. 21–26. **[G: Italy]**

Stephen, Frank H. Understanding the Scottish Economy: Producers' Cooperatives. **In** *Ingham, K. P. D. and Love, J., eds.,* 1983, pp. 94–104. **[G: U.K.]**

Stewart, Richard B. Regulation in a Liberal State: The Role of Non-commodity Values. *Yale Law J.,* July 1983, *92*(8), pp. 1537–90. **[G: U.S.]**

Stigler, George J. Luci ed ombre del capitalismo moderno. (The Pleasures and Pains of Modern Capitalism. With English summary.) *Bancaria,* September 1983, *39*(9), pp. 806–15.

Stricker, Frank. Causes of the Great Depression, or What Reagan Doesn't Know about the 1920s. *Econ. Forum,* Winter 1983-84, *14*(2), pp. 41–58. **[G: U.S.]**

Strümpel, Burkhard. Postmaterial Values and Their Institutional Inertia. **In** *Uusitalo, L., ed.,* 1983, pp. 74–87.

Sturgeon, James I. Micro–Macro Literature and the Implications of Centralized Private Sector Planning. *J. Econ. Issues,* December 1983, *17*(4), pp. 985–1009. **[G: U.S.]**

Susman, Paul and Schutz, Eric. Monopoly and Competitive Firm Relations and Regional Development in Global Capitalism. *Econ. Geogr.,* April 1983, *59*(2), pp. 161–77. **[G: U.S.]**

Sutcliffe, B. Unas observaciones sobre la teorización de la crisis económica actual. (Observations on the Theorization of the Present Economic Crisis. With English summary.) *Écon. Soc.,* September–October–November 1983, *17*(9–10–11), pp. 1331–43.

Svensson, Claes. Consumer Co-Operation and the Federative Form of Organization. *Ann. Pub. Co-op. Econ.,* April–June 1983, *54*(2), pp. 185–200. **[G: Sweden]**

Swaney, James A. Rival and Missing Interpretations of Market Society: A Comment. *J. Econ. Lit.,* December 1983, *21*(4), pp. 1489–93.

Szlajfer, Henryk. Economic Surplus and Surplus Value: An Attempt at Comparison. *Rev. Radical Polit. Econ.,* Spring 1983, *15*(1), pp. 107–30.

Talamona, Mario. Sviluppo, moneta e credito: la "visione" di Schumpeter e il caso italiano. (Schumpeter's View on Growth, Money and Credit, and the "Italian Case." With English summary.) *Giorn. Econ.,* July–August 1983, *42*(7–8), pp. 405–29. **[G: Italy]**

Targetti, Ferdinando. Nota sulle crisi in Roemer. (A Note on the Economic Crisis in a Roemer's Model. With English summary.) *Giorn. Econ.,* July–August 1983, *42*(7–8), pp. 527–35.

Taylor, A. The Expansion of Worker Co-Operatives: the Role of Local Authorities. *Reg. Stud.,* August 1983, *17*(4), pp. 276–81. **[G: U.K.]**

Taylor, Ryland A. The Credit Union as a Co-operative Institution. **In** *Kennedy, L., ed.,* 1983, *1971,* pp. 61–75. **[G: U.S.]**

Thangamuthu, C. and Iyyampillai, S. A Social Profile of Entrepreneurship. *Indian Econ. J.,* October–December 1983, *31*(2), pp. 107–15. **[G: India]**

Travaglini, Guido. La natura parascientifica del pensiero di Keynes. (The Pseudo-Scientific Foundations of Keynes' Thought. With English summary.) *Rivista Int. Sci. Econ. Com.,* April-May 1983, *30*(4–5), pp. 393–97.

Tulloch, Patricia. The Welfare State and Social Policy. **In** *Head, B. W., ed.,* 1983, pp. 252–71. **[G: Australia]**

Van Parijs, Philippe. Why Marxist Economics Needs Microfoundations: Postscript to an Obituary [The Falling-Rate-of-Profit Theory of Crisis: A Rational Reconstruction by Way of Obituary]. *Rev. Radical Polit. Econ.,* Summer 1983, *15*(2), pp. 111–24.

Vanberg, Viktor. Libertarian Evolutionism and Contractarian Constitutionalism. **In** *Pejovich, S., ed.,* 1983, pp. 71–87.

Viviani, Mario. Quale futuro per l'impresa cooperativa? (The Future Cooperatives. With English summary.) *L'Impresa,* 1983, *25*(4), pp. 45–52. **[G: Italy]**

Vogelsang, Ingo. Public Interest Firms as Leaders in Oligopolistic Industries. **In** *Finsinger, J., ed.,* 1983, pp. 86–99. **[G: W. Germany]**

Wahlroos, Björn. Regulation and Free-Enterprise Economy. *Ekon. Samfundets Tidskr.,* 1983, *36*(4), pp. 177–84.

Wallerstein, Immanuel. Crises: The World-Economy, the Movements, and the Ideologies. **In** *Bergesen, A., ed.,* 1983, pp. 21–36.

Walton, Clarence C. A Philosophical Rationale for

Contemporary Capitalism (I). In *Martin, T. R., ed.*, 1983, pp. 8–33. **[G: U.S.]**

Watts, Martin J. Sraffa after Marx: A Correction. *Australian Econ. Pap.*, June 1983, *22*(40), pp. 255–57.

Weede, Erich. The Impact of Democracy on Economic Growth: Some Evidence from Cross-National Analysis. *Kyklos*, 1983, *36*(1), pp. 21–39.

Weeks, John. On the Issue of Capitalist Circulation and the Concepts Appropriate to Its Analysis [Realization Crisis Theory and the Labor Theory of Value]. *Sci. Soc.*, Summer 1983, *47*(2), pp. 214–25.

Weissbach, Lee Shai. Entrepreneurial Traditionalism in Nineteenth-Century France: A Study of the *Patronage industriel des enfants de l'ébénisterie. Bus. Hist. Rev.*, Winter 1983, *57*(4), pp. 548–65. **[G: France]**

Whyatt, A. Developments in the Structure and Organization of the Co-Operative Movement: Some Policy Considerations. *Reg. Stud.*, August 1983, *17*(4), pp. 273–76. **[G: U.K.]**

Wildavsky, Aaron. An Immodest Agenda for Rebuilding America: A Review Essay. *Polit. Sci. Quart.*, Winter 1983–84, *98*(4), pp. 681–85. **[G: U.S.]**

Wilson, H. T. Technocracy and Late Capitalist Society: Reflections on the Problem of Rationality and Social Organisation. In *Clegg, S.; Dow, G. and Boreham, P., eds.*, 1983, pp. 152–238.

Wolff, Richard and Resnick, Stephen. Capitalism without Capitalists: Reply [Classes in Marxian Theory]. *Rev. Radical Polit. Econ.*, Spring 1983, *15*(1), pp. 157–59.

Yellin, Joel. Science, Technology, and Administrative Government: Institutional Designs for Environmental Decisionmaking. *Yale Law J.*, June 1983, *92*(7), pp. 1300–1333.

Zafiris, Nicos. The Form of the Maximand of the Inegalitarian Workers' Co-operative. *Brit. Rev. Econ. Issues*, Autumn 1983, *5*(13), pp. 39–61.

Zan, Stefano. Tipologia delle cooperative. (Classifying Coops. With English summary.) *L'Impresa*, 1983, *25*(4), pp. 13–19. **[G: Italy]**

Zarfaty, Joseph. The Moshav in Israel: Possibilities for Its Application in Developing Countries. In *Stewart, F., ed.*, 1983, pp. 189–214. **[G: Israel]**

Zusman, Pinhas. Collective Choice, Pareto Optimality and the Organization of Cooperatives: The Case of Agricultural Credit Associations. *J. Econ. Behav. Organ.*, June–September 1983, *4*(2–3), pp. 185–204.

052 Socialist and Communist Economic Systems

0520 Socialist and Communist Economic Systems

Albert, Michael and Hahnel, Robin. The Resurrection of Utopian Socialism: Reply. *Rev. Radical Polit. Econ.*, Winter 1983, *15*(4), pp. 126–35.

Andreff, Wladimir. Where Has All the Socialism Gone? Post-Revolutionary Society versus State Capitalism: Review Article. *Rev. Radical Polit. Econ.*, Summer 1983, *15*(2), pp. 137–52. **[G: E. Europe]**

Armstrong, John A. Socializing for Modernization in a Multiethnic Elite. In *Guroff, G. and Carstensen, F. V., eds.*, 1983, pp. 84–103. **[G: U.S.S.R.]**

Bácskai, Tamás and Várhegyi, Éva. Monetization of the Hungarian Economy. *Acta Oecon.*, 1983, *31*(1–2), pp. 13–22. **[G: Hungary]**

Balassa, Bela. Reforming the New Economic Mechanism in Hungary. *J. Compar. Econ.*, September 1983, *7*(3), pp. 253–76. **[G: Hungary]**

Balassa, Bela. The Hungarian Economic Reform, 1968–82. *Banca Naz. Lavoro Quart. Rev.*, June 1983, (145), pp. 163–84. **[G: Hungary]**

Bauer, Tamás. The Hungarian Alternative to Soviet-Type Planning. *J. Compar. Econ.*, September 1983, *7*(3), pp. 304–16. **[G: U.S.S.R.; Hungary]**

Berend, Iván T. The First Phase of Economic Reform in Hungary: 1956–1957. *J. Europ. Econ. Hist.*, Winter 1983, *12*(3), pp. 523–71. **[G: Hungary]**

Bergson, Abram. Entrepreneurship under Labor Participation: The Yugoslav Case. In *Ronen, J., ed.*, 1983, pp. 177–233. **[G: Yugoslavia]**

Berliner, Joseph S. Entrepreneurship in the Soviet Period: An Overview. In *Guroff, G. and Carstensen, F. V., eds.*, 1983, pp. 191–200. **[G: U.S.S.R.]**

Bhagwati, Jagdish N. and Grinols, Earl. Foreign Capital, Dependence, Destabilisation and Feasibility of Transition to Socialism. In *Bhagwati, J. N., Vol. 2*, 1983, *1975*, pp. 479–92. **[G: Ghana; Israel; S. Korea; Philippines; India]**

Black, Cyril E. Russian and Soviet Entrepreneurship in a Comparative Context. In *Guroff, G. and Carstensen, F. V., eds.*, 1983, pp. 3–10. **[G: U.S.S.R.]**

Bourmeyster, A. Révolution scientifique et technique et société socialiste avancée. (With English summary.) *Écon. Soc.*, January 1983, *17*(1), pp. 179–201. **[G: U.S.S.R.]**

Brhlovič, Gerhard. Technical Progress—Transformations of Labour—Development of Personality. *Czech. Econ. Digest.*, May 1983, (3), pp. 19–31.

Briefs, Goetz A. A Challenge to Western Civilization. *Rev. Soc. Econ.*, December 1983, *41*(3), pp. 317–29.

Bromlei, Iu. and Shkaratan, O. National Traditions in a Socialist Economy. *Prob. Econ.*, November 1983, *26*(7), pp. 24–39. **[G: U.S.S.R.]**

Brus, Wlodzimierz and Kowalik, Tadeusz. Socialism and Development. *Cambridge J. Econ.*, September/December 1983, *7*(3/4), pp. 243–55.

Carstensen, Fred V. and Guroff, Gregory. Economic Innovation in Imperial Russia and the Soviet Union: Observations. In *Guroff, G. and Carstensen, F. V., eds.*, 1983, pp. 347–60. **[G: U.S.S.R.]**

Červinka, Antonín. Investments That Are Certain to Return. *Czech. Econ. Digest.*, August 1983, (5), pp. 54–60. **[G: Czechoslovakia]**

Changrong, Chen. An Experiment Attracting World-Wide Attention. *Econ. Anal. Worker's Manage.*, 1983, *17*(1), pp. 43–54. **[G: China]**

Chen, Yun. Manage Commercial Work Well. In *Ch'en, Y.*, 1983, *1956*, pp. 39–46. **[G: China]**

Chen, Yun. New Issues since the Basic Completion of the Socialist Transformation. In *Ch'en, Y.*, 1983, *1956*, pp. 7–22. **[G: China]**

Chen, Yun. Regulation on the Improvement of the Industrial Management System. In *Ch'en, Y.*, 1983, *1957*, pp. 76–83. **[G: China]**

Chen, Yun. Speech at the Enlarged Ministerial Affairs Conference. **In** *Ch'en, Y.*, 1983, *1956*, pp. 30–38. **[G: China]**

Chen, Yun. The Scale of Construction Should Be Compatible with National Strength. **In** *Ch'en, Y.*, 1983, *1957*, pp. 47–57. **[G: China]**

Christensen, Peer Møller. The Shanghai School and Its Rejection. **In** *Feuchtwang, S. and Hussain, A., eds.*, 1983, pp. 74–90. **[G: China]**

Clausen, Søren. Chinese Economic Debates after Mao and the Crisis of Official Marxism. **In** *Feuchtwang, S. and Hussain, A., eds.*, 1983, pp. 53–73. **[G: China]**

Colombatto, Enrico. CMEA, Money and Ruble Convertibility. *Appl. Econ.*, August 1983, *15*(4), pp. 479–506. **[G: CMEA]**

Csikós-Nagy, Béla and Gadó, Otto. Effective Monetary and Fiscal Policy to Promote Economic Growth—A Socialist Approach. **In** *Biehl, D.; Roskamp, K. W. and Stolper, W. F., eds.*, 1983, pp. 149–66.

Daněček, Jiří. The Basic Relationships between Foreign Exchange Instruments, Prices, and the Plan. *Soviet E. Europ. Foreign Trade*, Fall 1983, *19*(3), pp. 50–79. **[G: Czechoslovakia]**

Darity, William A., Jr. Contemporary Marxism: Ideology or Science? A Review Essay on: *Research in Political Economy. Rev. Radical Polit. Econ.*, Winter 1983, *15*(4), pp. 136–48.

Diskin, I. Socioeconomic Problems in the Development of the Cultural Infrastructure. *Prob. Econ.*, October 1983, *26*(6), pp. 3–22. **[G: U.S.S.R.]**

Drach, Marcel and Revuz, Christine. La brigade de travail sous contrat dans l'industrie soviétique et la réforme de juillet 1979. (With English summary.) *Écon. Soc.*, January 1983, *17*(1), pp. 115–78. **[G: U.S.S.R.]**

Durgin, Frank A., Jr. The Relationship of the Death of Stalin to the Economic Change of the Post-Stalin Era or Was Stalin's Departure Really Necessary? **In** *Stuart, R. C., ed.*, 1983, pp. 118–42. **[G: U.S.S.R.]**

Ellman, Michael. Monetarism and the State Socialist World. **In** *Jansen, K., ed.*, 1983, pp. 96–109. **[G: CMEA]**

Ericson, Richard E. On an Allocative Role of the Soviet Second Economy. **In** *[Erlich, A.]*, 1983, pp. 110–32. **[G: U.S.S.R.]**

Estrin, Saul and Connock, Michael. Ideas of Industrial Democracy in Eastern Europe: A Comment from the Yugoslav Perspective. *ACES Bull. (See Comp. Econ. Stud. after 8/85)*, Spring 1983, *25*(1), pp. 67–74.

Fakiolas, Tasos. Targets and Results of Soviet Economic Policy. *Rivista Int. Sci. Econ. Com.*, January 1983, *30*(1), pp. 41–56. **[G: U.S.S.R.]**

Ferge, Zsuzsa. Cooperation and Conflict between Researchers and Planners in Social Policy. *Acta Oecon.*, 1983, *30*(3–4), pp. 425–32. **[G: Hungary]**

Feuchtwang, Stephan and Hussain, Athar. The Chinese Economic Reforms: Introduction. **In** *Feuchtwang, S. and Hussain, A., eds.*, 1983, pp. 1–50. **[G: China]**

Focşăneanu, Gr. and Stroe, R. Cybernetic Modelling of Intercorrelations in Territorial Selfmanagement. *Econ. Computat. Cybern. Stud. Res.*, 1983, *18*(3), pp. 47–61. **[G: Romania]**

Gács, János. Planning and Adjustment Policy Changes in the Development of the Building Materials Industry. *Eastern Europ. Econ.*, Spring–Summer 1983, *21*(3–4), pp. 105–24. **[G: Hungary]**

Ge, Zhida. On the Issue of Balancing the State Budget. *Chinese Econ. Stud.*, Winter 1982/83, *16*(2), pp. 107–23. **[G: China]**

Gönczi, Iván. Division of Labour and Work Organization in the Hungarian Large-Scale Agricultural Production. *Acta Oecon.*, 1983, *31*(1–2), pp. 71–86. **[G: Hungary]**

Gordon, Avery and Herman, Andrew. The Resurrection of Utopian Socialism: Review Article. *Rev. Radical Polit. Econ.*, Winter 1983, *15*(4), pp. 104–25.

Gowdy, John M. The Economics of Entropy: Reply to Stehle [Radical Economics and Resource Scarcity]. *Rev. Soc. Econ.*, October 1983, *41*(2), pp. 183–85.

Gowdy, John M. Toward a Sustainable Radical Economy: Reply to Stanfield [Radical Economics and Resource Scarcity]. *Rev. Soc. Econ.*, April 1983, *41*(1), pp. 72–73.

Granick, David. Institutional Innovation and Economic Management: The Soviet Incentive System, 1921 to the Present. **In** *Guroff, G. and Carstensen, F. V., eds.*, 1983, pp. 223–57. **[G: U.S.S.R.]**

Granick, David. The Ministry and the Ratchet: Response to Keren. *J. Compar. Econ.*, December 1983, *7*(4), pp. 432–43. **[G: E. Germany; U.S.S.R.]**

Grinev, Vladimir Sergeevich. The Management of the USSR's Economic Relations with the CMEA Countries. *Soviet E. Europ. Foreign Trade*, Fall 1983, *19*(3), pp. 80–89. **[G: CMEA; U.S.S.R.]**

Grossman, Gregory. Economics of Virtuous Haste: A View of Soviet Industrialization and Institutions. **In** *[Erlich, A.]*, 1983, pp. 198–216. **[G: U.S.S.R.]**

Grossman, Gregory. The Party as Manager and Entrepreneur. **In** *Guroff, G. and Carstensen, F. V., eds.*, 1983, pp. 284–305. **[G: U.S.S.R.]**

Guroff, Gregory. The Red-expert Debate: Continuities in the State-Entrepreneur Tension. **In** *Guroff, G. and Carstensen, F. V., eds.*, 1983, pp. 201–22. **[G: U.S.S.R.]**

Hewett, Edward A. Research on East European Economies: The Last Quarter Century. *ACES Bull. (See Comp. Econ. Stud. after 8/85)*, Summer 1983, *25*(2), pp. 1–21. **[G: E. Europe]**

Hošková, Adéla. Uniform Principles for Evaluating the Economic Effect of International Specialization and Cooperation in Industry. *Soviet E. Europ. Foreign Trade*, Winter 1983–84, *19*(4), pp. 62–72.

Hussain, Athar. Economic Reforms in Eastern Europe and Their Relevance to China. **In** *Feuchtwang, S. and Hussain, A., eds.*, 1983, pp. 91–120. **[G: China; E. Europe]**

Ishikawa, Shigeru. China's Economic System Reform: Underlying Factors and Prospects. *World Devel.*, August 1983, *11*(8), pp. 647–58. **[G: China; E. Europe]**

Kay, W. D. Toward a Theory of Cultural Policy in Non-Market, Ideological Societies. *J. Cult. Econ.*, December 1983, *7*(2), pp. 1–24. **[G: U.S.S.R.; E. Europe; China; Germany; CMEA]**

Keren, Michael. The Ministry and the Ratchet: A Rejoinder to Granick. *J. Compar. Econ.*, December 1983, *7*(4), pp. 444–48. **[G: E. Germany; U.S.S.R.]**

Khachaturov, Tigran S. The World Economy at Century's End: Comments. **In** *Tsuru, S., ed.*, 1983, pp. 89–94.

Khan, Azizur Rahman and Ghai, Dharam. Collective Agriculture in Soviet Central Asia. **In** *Stewart, F., ed.*, 1983, pp. 279–305. **[G: U.S.S.R.]**

Kheifets, L. State Regulation of Wages. *Prob. Econ.*, July 1983, *26*(3), pp. 39–52. **[G: U.S.S.R.]**

Kornai, János. Comments on the Present State and the Prospects of the Hungarian Economic Reform. *J. Compar. Econ.*, September 1983, *7*(3), pp. 225–52. **[G: Hungary]**

Kristol, Irving. Socialism: An Obituary for an Idea. **In** *Kristol, I.*, 1983, *1976*, pp. 114–22.

Kulagin, G. On Ways to Intensify (From an Economist's Notebook). *Prob. Econ.*, December 1983, *26*(8), pp. 45–58. **[G: U.S.S.R.]**

Kvěš, Václav. Topical Tasks of the Political Economy of Socialism. *Czech. Econ. Digest.*, May 1983, (3), pp. 49–70. **[G: Czechoslovakia]**

Laco, Karol. To Observe the Principles of Socialist Legality and Discipline (Problems of Dishonest Material Gains). *Czech. Econ. Digest.*, August 1983, (5), pp. 18–35. **[G: Czechoslovakia]**

Laird, Roy D. and Laird, Betty A. The Soviet Farm Manager as an Entrepreneur. **In** *Guroff, G. and Carstensen, F. V., eds.*, 1983, pp. 258–83. **[G: U.S.S.R.]**

Lardy, Nicholas R. and Lieberthal, Kenneth. Chen Yun's Strategy for China's Development: A Non-Maoist Alternative: Introduction. **In** *Ch'en, Y.*, 1983, pp. xi–xliii. **[G: China]**

Levine, Herbert S. On the Nature and Location of Entrepreneurial Activity in Centrally Planned Economies: The Soviet Case. **In** *Ronen, J., ed.*, 1983, pp. 235–67.

Lewis, W. Arthur. Socialism and Economic Growth. **In** *Lewis, W. A.*, 1983, *1971*, pp. 669–82.

Luke, Timothy W. The Proletarian Ethic and Soviet Industrialization. *Amer. Polit. Sci. Rev.*, September 1983, *77*(3), pp. 588–601. **[G: U.S.S.R.]**

Luo, Gengmo. An Analysis of the Development of China's Planned Economy and the Tortuous Course It Has Trudged: A Few Issues Concerning Socialist Planned Economy That Need to Be Clarified, Part 2. *Chinese Econ. Stud.*, Winter 1982/83, *16*(2), pp. 29–50. **[G: China]**

Mach, Miloš. Mechanism of Functioning of the Economy. *Czech. Econ. Digest.*, 1983, (8), pp. 53–68.

Maksimovic, Ivan. Social Ownership in the Yugoslav Self-Management System. *Econ. Anal. Worker's Manage.*, 1983, *17*(2), pp. 155–75. **[G: Yugoslavia]**

Maslova, I. Improving the Manpower Redistribution Mechanism. *Prob. Econ.*, July 1983, *26*(3), pp. 72–93. **[G: U.S.S.R.]**

Milenkovitch, Deborah Duff. Self Management and Thirty Years of Yugoslav Experience. *ACES Bull. (See Comp. Econ. Stud. after 8/85)*, Fall 1983, *25*(3), pp. 1–26. **[G: Yugoslavia]**

Millar, James R. Views on the Economics of Soviet Collectivization of Agriculture: The State of the Revisionist Debate. **In** *Stuart, R. C., ed.*, 1983, pp. 109–17. **[G: U.S.S.R.]**

Nagovitsin, A. The Management Structure of a Production Association. *Prob. Econ.*, May 1983, *26*(1), pp. 57–73. **[G: U.S.S.R.]**

Nekrasov, O.; Rutgaizer, V. and Kovaleva, N. Territorial Planning of Social Development. *Prob. Econ.*, March 1983, *25*(11), pp. 70–88. **[G: U.S.S.R.]**

Niculescu-Mizil, E. Cybernetic Peculiarities of the Development of Social-Economical Systems. *Econ. Computat. Cybern. Stud. Res.*, 1983, *18*(4), pp. 5–14. **[G: Romania]**

Nolan, Peter and White, Gordon. Economic Distribution and Rural Development in China: The Legacy of the Maoist Era. **In** *Stewart, F., ed.*, 1983, pp. 243–78. **[G: China]**

Nyers, Rezsö. Interrelations between Policy and the Economic Reform in Hungary. *J. Compar. Econ.*, September 1983, *7*(3), pp. 211–24. **[G: Hungary]**

Oblomskaia, I.; Strakhov, A. and Umanets, L. The Social and Economic Homogeneity of Labor. *Prob. Econ.*, December 1983, *26*(8), pp. 75–94. **[G: U.S.S.R.]**

Osipenkov, P. The Social Infrastructure and Stimuli in Territorial Economic Management. *Prob. Econ.*, October 1983, *26*(6), pp. 40–54. **[G: U.S.S.R.]**

Pairault, Thierry. Chinese Market Mechanism: A Controversial Debate. *World Devel.*, August 1983, *11*(8), pp. 639–45. **[G: China]**

Pineye, Daniel. The Bases of Soviet Power in the Third World. *World Devel.*, December 1983, *11*(12), pp. 1083–95. **[G: LDCs; U.S.S.R.]**

Prašnikar, Janez. The Role of the Enterprise in the Self-Managed Organization of Labor. *Eastern Europ. Econ.*, Winter 1983–84, *22*(2), pp. 44–77. **[G: Yugoslavia]**

Prašnikar, Janez. The Yugoslav Self-Managed Firm and Its Behavior. *Eastern Europ. Econ.*, Winter 1983–84, *22*(2), pp. 3–43. **[G: Yugoslavia]**

Průcha, Václav. The Economic Strategy of the Communist Party of Czechoslovakia after February 1948 and at the Present Stage of Development. *Czech. Econ. Digest.*, May 1983, (3), pp. 32–48. **[G: Czechoslovakia]**

Putterman, Louis. A Modified Collective Agriculture in Rural Growth-with-Equity: Reconsidering the Private, Unimodal Solution. *World Devel.*, February 1983, *11*(2), pp. 77–100. **[G: China; Tanzania]**

Rugina, Anghel N. What Is the Alternative for the East? Neither Orthodox Marxism nor Capitalism but "Liberal Socialism." *Int. J. Soc. Econ.*, 1983, *10*(4), pp. 3–67.

Rusmich, Ladislav. Value Aspects of the Development of Socialist Integration. *Acta Oecon.*, 1983, *31*(3–4), pp. 241–59. **[G: CMEA]**

Selden, Mark. Imposed Collectivization and the Crisis of Agrarian Development in the Socialist States. **In** *Bergesen, A., ed.*, 1983, pp. 227–51. **[G: Yugoslavia; China; U.S.S.R.]**

Selden, Mark. The Logic—and Limits—of Chinese

Socialist Development. *World Devel.*, August 1983, *11*(8), pp. 631–37. **[G: China]**

Sirc, Ljubo. Employee Participation and the Promotion of Employee Ownership. **In** *Seldon, A., et al.*, 1983, pp. 113–27. **[G: W. Germany; Yugoslavia]**

Sit, Victor F. S. The Informal Sector within a Communist Industrial Structure: The Case of the People's Republic of China. **In** *Hamilton, F. E. I. and Linge, G. J. R., eds.*, 1983, pp. 551–80. **[G: China]**

Smirnov, V. The Plan and the Increase in the Consumer's Influence on Production. *Prob. Econ.*, July 1983, *26*(3), pp. 22–38. **[G: U.S.S.R.]**

Šolcová, Miroslava. Existential and Social Certainties and Their Realization. *Czech. Econ. Digest.*, March 1983, (2), pp. 80–96.

Stanfield, J. Ron. Radical Economics and Resource Scarcity: A Comment. *Rev. Soc. Econ.*, April 1983, *41*(1), pp. 68–71.

Stehle, John F. The Economics of Entropy [Radical Economics and Resource Scarcity]. *Rev. Soc. Econ.*, October 1983, *41*(2), pp. 179–82.

Stuart, Robert C. Perspectives on the Russian and Soviet Rural Economy. **In** *Stuart, R. C., ed.*, 1983, pp. 1–17. **[G: U.S.S.R.]**

Stuart, Robert C. Russian and Soviet Agriculture: The Western Perspective. *ACES Bull. (See Comp. Econ. Stud. after 8/85),* Fall 1983, *25*(3), pp. 43–52. **[G: U.S.S.R.]**

Sziraczki, G. The Development and Functioning of an Enterprise Labour Market in Hungary. *Écon. Soc.*, March–April 1983, *17*(3–4), pp. 517–47. **[G: Hungary]**

Tardos, Márton. Enterprise Supply and the Market. *Eastern Europ. Econ.*, Spring–Summer 1983, *21*(3–4), pp. 8–25. **[G: Hungary]**

Tardos, Márton. The Increasing Role and Ambivalent Reception of Small Enterprises in Hungary. *J. Compar. Econ.*, September 1983, *7*(3), pp. 277–87. **[G: Hungary]**

Tímár, János. Problems of Full Employment. *Acta Oecon.*, 1983, *31*(3–4), pp. 209–24. **[G: Hungary]**

Turgeon, Lynn. A Quarter Century of Non-Soviet East European Agriculture. *ACES Bull. (See Comp. Econ. Stud. after 8/85),* Fall 1983, *25*(3), pp. 27–41. **[G: E. Europe]**

Vissi, Ferenc. Major Questions of the Improvement of Economic Control and Management in Hungary in the Mid-Eighties. *Acta Oecon.*, 1983, *30*(3–4), pp. 325–39. **[G: Hungary]**

Wang, Kaike. Tie Industry with Trade: An Important Way to Develop Foreign Trade. *Chinese Econ. Stud.*, Summer 1983, *16*(4), pp. 70–77. **[G: China]**

Weisskopf, Thomas E. Economic Development and the Development of Economics: Some Observations from the Left. *World Devel.*, October 1983, *11*(10), pp. 895–99.

Westoby, Adam. Conceptions of Communist States. **In** *Held, D., et al., eds.*, 1983, pp. 219–40.

Whitehorn, Alan. Alienation and Socialism: An Analysis of Yugoslav Workers' Self-Management. *Econ. Anal. Worker's Manage.*, 1983, *17*(3), pp. 245–71. **[G: Yugoslavia; Canada]**

Wyzan, Michael L. The Kolkhoz and the Sovkhoz: Relative Performance as Measured by Productive Technology. **In** *Stuart, R. C., ed.*, 1983, pp. 173–98. **[G: U.S.S.R.]**

Xu, Riqing. A Preliminary Discussion of Comprehensive Public Finance. *Chinese Econ. Stud.*, Winter 1982/83, *16*(2), pp. 20–28. **[G: China]**

Yoshikawa, Tomomichi. Some Additional Results on the New Soviet Incentive Model and Its Generalization. *Econ. Stud. Quart.*, December 1983, *34*(3), pp. 276–79. **[G: U.S.S.R.]**

Yu, Guangyuan. On the Theory of Reform of the Economic Management System. *Chinese Econ. Stud.*, Fall 1983, *17*(1), pp. 65–73. **[G: China]**

Yue, Wei. Production, Distribution, and Allocation of the National Economy. *Chinese Econ. Stud.*, Winter 1982/83, *16*(2), pp. 3–19. **[G: China]**

Zaitsev, A. P. The State Bank and the Enterprise: Is the Influence of Bank Credit Effective? *Prob. Econ.*, September 1983, *26*(5), pp. 43–56. **[G: U.S.S.R.]**

Zakharov, V. Credit and Banks in the Economic Management System. *Prob. Econ.*, May 1983, *26*(1), pp. 3–19. **[G: U.S.S.R.]**

Zhang, Li. Reform Blazes a New Path for Foreign Trade. *Chinese Econ. Stud.*, Summer 1983, *16*(4), pp. 17–26. **[G: China]**

Ziegler, Charles E. Worker Participation and Worker Discontent in the Soviet Union. *Polit. Sci. Quart.*, Summer 1983, *98*(2), pp. 235–53. **[G: U.S.S.R.]**

Zotov, M. Financial Problems in Managing the Investment Process. *Prob. Econ.*, September 1983, *26*(5), pp. 25–42. **[G: U.S.S.R.]**

053 Comparative Economic Systems

0530 Comparative Economic Systems

Conn, David. Comparative Economic Systems Theory: Progress and Prospects. *ACES Bull. (See Comp. Econ. Stud. after 8/85),* Summer 1983, *25*(2), pp. 61–80.

Devine, James N. and Reich, Michael. The Microeconomics of Conflict and Hierarchy under Capitalist Production: A Reply. *Rev. Radical Polit. Econ.*, Summer 1983, *15*(2), pp. 133–35.

Dumas, André. Economic Systems and Participation: An Essay on the Practical Experiences of Participation. *Econ. Anal. Worker's Manage.*, 1983, *17*(2), pp. 177–200. **[G: Yugoslavia; France; W. Germany]**

Ehrenreich, John H. Socialism, Nationalism and Capitalist Development. *Rev. Radical Polit. Econ.*, Spring 1983, *15*(1), pp. 1–42.

Galtung, Johan. Buts et processus du développement: une vue intégrée. (Goals and Process of Development: An Integrated View. In English.) *Écon. Soc.*, February 1983, *17*(2), pp. 335–63.

Hella, Karl N. Basic Needs and Economic Systems: Notes on Data, Methodology, and Interpretation. *Rev. Soc. Econ.*, October 1983, *41*(2), pp. 172–77. **[G: LDCs]**

Kuran, Timur. Behavioral Norms in the Islamic Doctrine of Economics: A Critique. *J. Econ. Behav. Organ.*, December 1983, *4*(4), pp. 353–79.

Lavigne, Marie. EEC and CMEA, General Comparisons: Comment. **In** *Saunders, C. T., ed.*, 1983, pp.

60–62. [G: CMEA; EEC]

Mandle, Jay R. Reply to Karl N. Hella [Basic Needs and Economic Systems]. *Rev. Soc. Econ.*, October 1983, *41* (2), pp. 178. [G: LDCs]

Maximova, Margarita. Socialist and Capitalist Integration: A Comparative Analysis. **In** *Saunders, C. T., ed.*, 1983, pp. 27–39. [G: CMEA; EEC]

Murrell, Peter. Did the Theory of Market Socialism Answer the Challenge of Ludwig von Mises? A Reinterpretation of the Socialist Controversy. *Hist. Polit. Econ.*, Spring 1983, *15* (1), pp. 92–105.

Sakakibara, Eisuke and Feldman, Robert A. The Japanese Financial System in Comparative Perspective. *J. Compar. Econ.*, March 1983, *7* (1), pp. 1–24. [G: U.S.; Japan]

Stewart, Frances. Inequality, Technology and Payments Systems. **In** *Stewart, F., ed.*, 1983, pp. 1–31. [G: Selected LDCs; Selected MDCs]

Stewart, Frances. Payments Systems and Third World Development: Some Conclusions. **In** *Stewart, F., ed.*, 1983, pp. 306–23.

Watts, Martin J. Microeconomic Theory: Should Radicals Steal the Neoclassicals' Clothes? [The Microeconomics of Conflict and Hierarchy under Capitalist Production: A Reply to Watts]. *Rev. Radical Polit. Econ.*, Winter 1983, *15* (4), pp. 100–103.

Weisskopf, Thomas E. Alternative Models of Economic Development. *Écon. Soc.*, February 1983, *17* (2), pp. 451–78.

100 Economic Growth; Development; Planning; Fluctuations

110 Economic Growth; Development; and Planning Theory and Policy

111 Economic Growth Theory and Models

1110 Growth Theories

Arrow, Kenneth J. The Trade-off between Growth and Equity. **In** *Arrow, K. J., Vol. 1*, 1983, *1979*, pp. 190–200.

Baumol, William J. Toward Operational Models of Entrepreneurship. **In** *Ronen, J., ed.*, 1983, pp. 29–48.

Blaug, Mark. The Cambridge Debate on the Theory of Capital and Distribution. **In** *Caravale, G., ed.*, 1983, *1976*, pp. 102–230.

Burbridge, John B. Government Debt in an Overlapping-Generations Model with Bequests and Gifts. *Amer. Econ. Rev.*, March 1983, *73* (1), pp. 222–27. [G: U.S.]

Chatterji, Monojit and Wickens, Michael R. Verdoorn's Law and Kaldor's Law: A Revisionist Interpretation? *J. Post Keynesian Econ.*, Spring 1983, *5* (3), pp. 397–413. [G: OECD]

Dasgupta, Swapan and Mitra, Tapan. Intergenerational Equity and Efficient Allocation of Exhaustible Resources. *Int. Econ. Rev.*, February 1983, *24* (1), pp. 133–53.

Day, Richard H. The Emergence of Chaos from Classical Economic Growth. *Quart. J. Econ.*, May 1983, *98* (2), pp. 201–13.

Dyckhoff, Harald. Inada-Bedingungen und Eigenschaften der neoklassischen Produktionsfunktion. (Inada-Derivative Conditions and Properties of the Neoclassical Production Function. With English summary.) *Z. ges. Staatswiss.*, March 1983, *139* (1), pp. 146–54.

Epstein, Larry G. Stationary Cardinal Utility and Optimal Growth under Uncertainty. *J. Econ. Theory*, October 1983, *31* (1), pp. 133–52.

Gigliotti, Gary Anthony. Total Utility, Overlapping Generations and Optimal Population. *Rev. Econ. Stud.*, January 1983, *50* (1), pp. 71–86.

Goodwin, R. M. Economic Growth Planning. **In** *Goodwin, R. M.*, 1983, *1956*, pp. 121–29.

Grinols, Earl and Bhagwati, Jagdish N. Foreign Capital, Savings and Dependence. **In** *Bhagwati, J. N., Vol. 2*, 1983, *1976*, pp. 493–501.

Kuznets, Simon. Modern Economic Growth: Findings and Reflections. **In** *Todaro, M. P., ed.*, 1983, *1973*, pp. 56–67.

Lerner, Abba P. On Some Recent Developments in Capital Theory. **In** *Lerner, A. P.*, 1983, *1965*, pp. 551–62.

Lewis, W. Arthur. Industrialization and Social Peace. **In** *Lewis, W. A.*, 1983, *1963*, pp. 623–37.

Malinvaud, Edmond. Notes on Growth Theory with Imperfectly Flexible Prices. **In** *Fitoussi, J.-P., ed.*, 1983, pp. 93–114.

McCombie, John S. L. Kaldor's Laws in Retrospect. *J. Post Keynesian Econ.*, Spring 1983, *5* (3), pp. 414–29. [G: U.S.]

McCombie, John S. L. and de Ridder, John R. Increasing Returns, Productivity, and Output Growth: The Case of the United States. *J. Post Keynesian Econ.*, Spring 1983, *5* (3), pp. 373–87. [G: U.S.]

Mitra, Tapan. Limits on Population Growth under Exhaustible Resource Constraints. *Int. Econ. Rev.*, February 1983, *24* (1), pp. 155–68.

Mitra, Tapan. Sensitivity of Optimal Programs with Respect to Changes in Target Stocks: The Case of Irreversible Investment. *J. Econ. Theory*, February 1983, *29* (1), pp. 172–84.

Parrinello, Sergio. Exhaustible Natural Resources and the Classical Method of Long-Period Equilibrium. **In** *Kregel, J. A., ed.*, 1983, pp. 186–99.

Picard, Pierre. Inflation and Growth in a Disequilibrium Macroeconomic Model. *J. Econ. Theory*, August 1983, *30* (2), pp. 266–95.

Rosser, J. Barkley, Jr. Reswitching as a Cusp Catastrophe. *J. Econ. Theory*, October 1983, *31* (1), pp. 182–93.

Rugina, Anghel N. Toward a Third Revolution in Economic Thinking: The Concept of Balanced (Equilibrium) Growth and Social Economics. *Int. J. Soc. Econ.*, 1983, *10* (1), pp. 3–46.

Samuel, Judita. A Stochastic Model of Economic Growth with Markovian Dependence. *Econ. Computat. Cybern. Stud. Res.*, 1983, *18* (3), pp. 63–76.

Sathaye, Deepak. Primitive Accumulation and Optimum Development in the Dual Economy. *Brit. Rev. Econ. Issues*, Autumn 1983, *5* (13), pp. 1–22.

Scazzieri, Roberto. Economic Dynamics and Structural Change: A Comment on Pasinetti. *Rivista Int. Sci. Econ. Com.*, January 1983, *30* (1), pp. 73–90.

Shapiro, Harold N. Entrepreneurial Concepts, Definitions, and Model Formulations. **In** *Ronen, J., ed.*, 1983, pp. 75–99.

de Sousa, Alfredo. A Dual for Pasinetti's Paradox. *Economia,* May 1983, *7*(2), pp. 407–13.

Sylos Labini, Paolo. The Problem of Economic Growth in Marx and Schumpeter. **In** *Groenewegen, P. and Halevi, J., eds.*, 1983, pp. 129–66.

Thirlwall, Anthony P. A Plain Man's Guide to Kaldor's Growth Laws. *J. Post Keynesian Econ.*, Spring 1983, *5*(3), pp. 345–58.

Zinn, Karl Georg. Zyklus, Stabilität und Geldneutralität. Ein lehrgeschichtliche Ergänzung zum Problem der potentialorientierten Geldpolitik auf der Grundlage von Schumpeters Entwicklungstheorie. (Business Cycle, Stability, and Neutral Money. With English summary.) *Konjunkturpolitik,* 1983, *29*(6), pp. 329–47.

1112 One and Two Sector Growth Models and Related Topics

Abel, Andrew B. and Blanchard, Olivier J. An Intertemporal Model of Saving and Investment. *Econometrica,* May, 1983, *51*(3), pp. 675–92.

Adelman, Irma and Cheng, Leonard. A Dynamic Model of Personal Wealth and Income Distribution in a Growing Closed Economy. *Jahr. Nationalökon. Statist.*, November 1983, *198*(6), pp. 481–504.

Araujo, A. and Scheinkman, José A. Maximum Principle and Transversality Condition for Concave Infinite Horizon Economic Models. *J. Econ. Theory,* June 1983, *30*(1), pp. 1–16.

Becker, Robert A. Comparative Dynamics in the One-Sector Optimal Growth Model. *J. Econ. Dynam. Control,* September 1983, *6*(1/2), pp. 99–107.

Bertrand, Hugues. Accumulation, régulation, crise: un modèle seclectionnel théorique et appliqué. (Accumulation, Regulation, Crisis: A Theoretical and Applied Bi-Sectorial Model. With English summary.) *Revue Écon.*, March 1983, *34*(2), pp. 305–43. **[G: France]**

Cooper, Charles M. Extensions of the Raj–Sen Model of Economic Growth. *Oxford Econ. Pap.*, July 1983, *35*(2), pp. 170–85.

Danthine, Jean-Pierre; Donaldson, John B. and Mehra, Rajnish. On the Impact of Shock Persistence on the Dynamics of a Recursive Economy. *Europ. Econ. Rev.*, July 1983, *22*(2), pp. 147–66.

Davenport, Paul. Embodied Technical Change: A New Approach. *Can. J. Econ.*, February 1983, *16*(1), pp. 139–49.

Dechert, W. Davis and Nishimura, Kazuo. A Complete Characterization of Optimal Growth Paths in an Aggregated Model with a Non-Concave Production Function. *J. Econ. Theory,* December 1983, *31*(2), pp. 332–54.

Donaldson, John B. and Mehra, Rajnish. Stochastic Growth with Correlated Production Shocks. *J. Econ. Theory,* April 1983, *29*(2), pp. 282–312.

Feldstein, Martin S. Inflation, Income Taxes, and the Rate of Interest: A Theoretical Analysis. **In** *Feldstein, M. (I)*, 1983, *1976,* pp. 448–64.

Fourgeaud, Claude; Lenclup, Bernard and Michel, Pierre. Taux d'actualisation et prix de l'énergie. (On the Social Rate of Discount and the Energy Price. With English summary.) *Revue Écon.*, March 1983, *34*(2), pp. 253–76. **[G: France]**

Gehrels, Franz. Optimal Private and Collective Consumption in a Growing Economy. *Public Finance,* 1983, *38*(2), pp. 202–16.

Kuipers, S. K. and van Zon, A. H. Substitution and Technical Progress: A Putty–Clay Model for the Netherlands. **In** *Biehl, D.; Roskamp, K. W. and Stolper, W. F., eds.*, 1983, pp. 181–206. **[G: Netherlands]**

Lewis, W. Arthur. Reflections on Unlimited Labor. **In** *Lewis, W. A.*, 1983, *1972,* pp. 421–42.

Lewis, W. Arthur. Unlimited Labour: Further Notes. **In** *Lewis, W. A.*, 1983, *1958,* pp. 365–96.

Marrelli, Massimo and Salvadori, Neri. Tax Incidence and Growth Models. *Public Finance,* 1983, *38*(3), pp. 409–18.

Mehmet, Ozay. Growth and Impoverishment in a Dual Economy with Capital Imports. *Australian Econ. Pap.*, June 1983, *22*(40), pp. 221–32.

Nguyen, Dung. A Remark on the Graphical Exposition of Neo-Classical Two-Sector Growth Models. *Eastern Econ. J.*, January–March 1983, *9*(1), pp. 37–43.

Orzech, Ze'ev B. and Groll, Shalom. Otto Bauer's Scheme of Expanded Reproduction: An Early Harrodian Growth Model. *Hist. Polit. Econ.*, Winter 1983, *15*(4), pp. 529–48.

van der Ploeg, Frederick. Economic Growth and Conflict over the Distribution of Income. *J. Econ. Dynam. Control,* November 1983, *6*(3), pp. 253–79.

van der Ploeg, Frederick. Predator–Prey and Neo-Classical Modes of Cyclical Growth. *Z. Nationalökon.*, 1983, *43*(3), pp. 235–56.

Rao, T. V. S. Ramamohan. Public Goods and Disequilibrium Growth. *Rivista Int. Sci. Econ. Com.*, April-May 1983, *30*(4–5), pp. 321–38.

Seidman, Laurence S. Social Security and Demographics in a Life Cycle Growth Model. *Nat. Tax J.*, June 1983, *36*(2), pp. 213–24. **[G: U.S.]**

Simon, Julian L. The Present Value of Population Growth in the Western World. *Population Stud.*, March 1983, *37*(1), pp. 5–21.

Smith, Paul E. and Wisley, Thomas O. On a Model of Economic Growth Using Factors of Production to Extract an Exhaustible Resource. *Southern Econ. J.*, April 1983, *49*(4), pp. 966–74.

Srinivasan, T. N. and Bhagwati, Jagdish N. Trade and Welfare in a Steady State. **In** *Bhagwati, J. N., Vol. 1,* 1983, *1980,* pp. 136–48.

Takekuma, Shin-ichi. On Existence of Optimal Programs of Capital Accumulation with Exhaustible Resources. *Hitotsubashi J. Econ.*, December 1983, *24*(2), pp. 109–18.

Vicary, Simon J. R. Endogenous Population Growth in an Overlapping Generations Model with International Lending and Borrowing. *Bull. Econ. Res.*, May 1983, *35*(1), pp. 1–24. **[G: LDCs]**

Withagen, Cees. The Optimal Exploitation of a Natural Resource When There Is Full Complementarity. *J. Econ. Dynam. Control,* November 1983, *6*(3), pp. 239–52.

111 Economic Growth Theory and Models

1113 Multisector Growth Models and Related Topics

Brosnan, Peter. The Wage Share in an Open Economy. *J. Post Keynesian Econ.*, Fall 1983, *6*(1), pp. 65–72.

de Castro, Steve. Comparison of Turnpikes with Consumption Maximising Sectoral Growth Paths for Jamaica, 1957–1971. *J. Devel. Econ.*, Aug.–Oct. 1983, *13*(1–2), pp. 175–95. **[G: Jamaica]**

Craven, John. Input–Output Analysis and Technical Change. *Econometrica,* May, 1983, *51*(3), pp. 585–98.

Donaldson, John B. A Note on Value Maximization for Consumption Sets in *l*. *J. Econ. Theory,* June 1983, *30*(1), pp. 191–200.

Hicks, John. Prices and the Turnpike: The Story of a Mare's Nest. **In** *Hicks, J.*, 1983, *1961*, pp. 292–307.

Kataoka, Haruo. On the Local Conservation Laws in the Von Neumann Model. **In** *[Yamada, I.]*, 1983, pp. 156–63.

Majumdar, Mukul K. and Mitra, Tapan. Dynamic Optimization with a Non-Convex Technology: The Case of a Linear Objective Function. *Rev. Econ. Stud.*, January 1983, *50*(1), pp. 143–51.

Majumdar, Mukul K. and Radner, Roy. Stationary Optimal Policies with Discounting in a Stochastic Activity Analysis Model. *Econometrica,* November 1983, *51*(6), pp. 1821–37.

McKenzie, Lionel W. Turnpike Theory, Discounted Utility, and the von Neumann Facet. *J. Econ. Theory,* August 1983, *30*(2), pp. 330–52.

Mitra, Tapan and Ray, Debraj. Efficient and Optimal Programs When Investment Is Irreversible: A Duality Theory. *J. Math. Econ.*, January 1983, *11*(1), pp. 81–113.

Nishimura, Kiyohiko G. A New Concept of Stability and Dynamical Economic Systems. *J. Econ. Dynam. Control,* September 1983, *6*(1/2), pp. 25–40.

Polterovich, V. M. Equilibrium Trajectories of Economic Growth. *Econometrica,* May, 1983, *51*(3), pp. 693–729.

Solow, Robert M. Modern Capital Theory. **In** *Brown, E. C. and Solow, R. M., eds.*, 1983, pp. 169–87.

1114 Monetary Growth Models

Asako, Kazumi. The Utility Function and the Superneutrality of Money on the Transition Path [Capital Accumulation on the Transition Path in a Monetary Optimizing Model]. *Econometrica,* September 1983, *51*(5), pp. 1593–96.

Auerbach, Alan J. Inflation and the Choice of Asset Life. **In** *Auerbach, A. J.*, 1983, *1979*, pp. 100–117.

Azam, J. P. Money, Growth and Disequilibrium. *Economica,* August 1983, *50*(199), pp. 325–35.

Boggess, Trent E. A Generalized Keynes–Wicksell Model with Variable Labor Force Growth. *J. Macroecon.*, Spring 1983, *5*(2), pp. 197–209.

Drabicki, John Z. and Takayama, Akira. An Optimal Monetary Policy in an Aggregate Neoclassical Model of Economic Growth. *J. Macroecon.*, Winter 1983, *5*(1), pp. 53–74.

Feldstein, Martin S. Fiscal Policies, Inflation, and Capital Formation. **In** *Feldstein, M. (II)*, 1983, *1980*, pp. 61–80.

Feldstein, Martin S. Inflation, Income Taxes, and the Rate of Interest: A Theoretical Analysis. **In** *Feldstein, M. (II)*, 1983, *1976*, pp. 28–43.

Feldstein, Martin S.; Green, Jerry R. and Sheshinski, Eytan. Inflation and Taxes in a Growing Economy with Debt and Equity Finance. **In** *Feldstein, M. (II)*, 1983, *1978*, pp. 44–60. **[G: U.S.]**

Fischer, Stanley. Inflación y crecimiento. (With English summary.) *Cuadernos Econ.*, December 1983, *20*(61), pp. 267–78. **[G: LDCs]**

Hayakawa, Hiroaki. Rationality of Liquidity Preferences and the Neoclassical Monetary Growth Model. *J. Macroecon.*, Fall 1983, *5*(4), pp. 495–501.

Jha, Raghbendra and Lächler, Ulrich. Inflation and Economic Growth in a Competitive Economy with Exhaustible Resources. *J. Econ. Behav. Organ.*, June–September 1983, *4*(2–3), pp. 113–29.

Kumar, Ramesh C. Money in Development: A Monetary Growth Model à la McKinnon. *Southern Econ. J.*, July 1983, *50*(1), pp. 18–36.

Long, Millard. A Note on Financial Theory and Economic Development. **In** *Von Pischke, J. D.; Adams, D. W. and Donald, G., eds.*, 1983, pp. 22–28.

112 Economic Development Models and Theories

1120 Economic Development Models and Theories

Afxentiou, Panayiotis C. Economic Development and Government Revenue and Expenditure Theorizing: A Critical Appraisal. *Econ. Notes,* 1983, (1), pp. 98–111.

Agmon, Tamir and Deitrich, J. KImball. International Lending and Income Redistribution: An Alternative View of Country Risk. *J. Banking Finance,* 1983, *7*(4), pp. 483–95. **[G: LDCs]**

Ahmed, Salehuddin; Feeny, David H. and Mestelman, Stuart. Implications of a Neoclassical Dual Economy Model of Bangladesh. *J. Devel. Areas,* April 1983, *17*(3), pp. 319–36. **[G: Bangladesh]**

Alam, M. Shahid. Efficiency Differentials Favouring Resource-Based Industries. *J. Devel. Econ.*, December 1983, *13*(3), pp. 361–66. **[G: LDCs]**

Alam, M. Shahid. The Nature of Mass Poverty: A Review Article. *Pakistan J. Appl. Econ.*, Summer 1983, *2*(1), pp. 85–92.

Amano, Masanori. On the Harris–Todaro Model with Intersectoral Migration of Labour. *Economica,* August 1983, *50*(199), pp. 311–23. **[G: LDCs]**

Amsden, Alice H. 'De-Skilling,' Skilled Commodities, and the NICs' Emerging Competitive Advantage. *Amer. Econ. Rev.*, May 1983, *73*(2), pp. 333–37.

Arndt, H. W. The "Trickle-Down" Myth. *Econ. Develop. Cult. Change,* October 1983, *32*(1), pp. 1–10.

Aujac, Henri. Culture nationale et aptitude á l'industrialisation (1). *Revue Écon. Polit.*, January–February 1983, *93*(1), pp. 1–28. **[G: France; Japan; Brazil; Ivory Coast]**

Bacha, Edmar Lisboa. Crecimiento con Oferta Limitada de Divisas: Una Reevaluación del Modelo de dos Brechas. (Growth with Limited Supplies of Foreign Exchange: A Reappraisal of the Two-Gap Model. With English summary.) *Económica,* May–December 1983, *29*(2–3), pp. 241–66.

Banaji, Jairus. Gunder Frank in Retreat? **In** *Limqueco, P. and McFarlane, B., eds.,* 1983, pp. 97–113.

Bardhan, Pranab K. Labor-Tying in a Poor Agrarian Economy: A Theoretical and Empirical Analysis. *Quart. J. Econ.,* August 1983, *98*(3), pp. 501–14. **[G: India]**

Barone, Charles A. Dependency, Marxist Theory, and Salvaging the Idea of Capitalism in South Korea. *Rev. Radical Polit. Econ.,* Spring 1983, *15*(1), pp. 43–67. **[G: S. Korea]**

Bartlett, William. On the Dynamic Instability of Induced-Migration Unemployment in a Dual Economy. *J. Devel. Econ.,* Aug.–Oct. 1983, *13*(1–2), pp. 85–96.

Bates, Robert H. Some Core Assumptions in Development Economics. **In** *Ortiz, S., ed.,* 1983, pp. 361–98.

Behrman, Jere R. Developing-Country Perspective on Industrial Policy. **In** *Adams, F. G. and Klein, L. R., eds.,* 1983, pp. 153–85. **[G: Selected Countries]**

Bell, Clive and Devarajan, Shantayanan. Shadow Prices for Project Evaluation under Alternative Macroeconomic Specifications. *Quart. J. Econ.,* August 1983, *98*(3), pp. 457–77.

Bennett, John and Phelps, Michael. A Model of Employment Creation in an Open Developing Economy. *Oxford Econ. Pap.,* November 1983, *35*(3), pp. 373–98.

Bequela, Assefa and Freedman, David H. Employment and Basic Needs: An Overview. **In** *Todaro, M. P., ed.,* 1983, *1979,* pp. 153–64.

Berberoglu, Berch. Industrialization, Employment, and Class Formation in the Periphery. *Econ. Forum,* Summer 1983, *14*(1), pp. 131–41. **[G: Brazil; S. Korea; Mexico; Taiwan]**

Bhagwati, Jagdish N. The Latin-American Periphery in the Global System of Capitalism: Comment. **In** *Tsuru, S., ed.,* 1983, pp. 46–51.

Bhagwati, Jagdish N. and Grinols, Earl. Foreign Capital, Dependence, Destabilisation and Feasibility of Transition to Socialism. **In** *Bhagwati, J. N., Vol. 2,* 1983, *1975,* pp. 479–92. **[G: Ghana; Israel; S. Korea; Philippines; India]**

Bhagwati, Jagdish N. and Srinivasan, T. N. On Reanalyzing the Harris–Todaro Model: Policy Rankings in the Case of Sector-specific Sticky Wages. **In** *Bhagwati, J. N., Vol. 1,* 1983, *1974,* pp. 498–504.

Bharat-Ram, Vinay. Import Substitution, Exchange Rates and Growth in the Context of a Developing Economy. *Greek Econ. Rev.,* August 1983, *5*(2), pp. 147–57. **[G: LDCs; India]**

Bhatt, V. V. A Note on Financial Innovations and Development. *Rivista Int. Sci. Econ. Com.,* October–November 1983, *30*(10–11), pp. 1064–72.

Bhatt, V. V. Financial Innovations and Development. **In** *Von Pischke, J. D.; Adams, D. W. and Donald, G., eds.,* 1983, pp. 43–49.

Bornschier, Volker. World Economy, Level Development and Income Distribution: An Integration of Different Approaches to the Explanation of Income Inequality. *World Devel.,* January 1983, *11*(1), pp. 11–20. **[G: Global; LDCs]**

Bos, Henk C. Some Simple Thoughts on Model Building for Developing Countries. *Pakistan Devel. Rev.,* Summer 1983, *22*(2), pp. 63–71.

Bourguignon, François; Michel, G. and Miqueu, D. Short–Run Rigidities and Long–Run Adjustments in a Computable General Equilibrium Model of Income Distribution and Development. *J. Devel. Econ.,* Aug.–Oct. 1983, *13*(1–2), pp. 21–43. **[G: Venezuela]**

Braulke, Michael. A Note on Kuznets' U. *Rev. Econ. Statist.,* February 1983, *65*(1), pp. 135–39.

Bresson, Yoland and Sinsou, J. Paul. L'intégration de la répartition des revenus dans l'analyse des projets d'investissements: une mesure des avantages collectifs à partir du seuil de pauvreté. (A Renewal of Investment Project Appraisal by Integration of Income Distribution and Evaluation of a "Poverty Threshold." With English summary.) *Écon. Appl.,* 1983, *36*(2–3), pp. 509–33.

Browett, John. Out of the Dependency Perspective. **In** *Limqueco, P. and McFarlane, B., eds.,* 1983, pp. 181–97.

Byerlee, Derek, et al. Employment-Output Conflicts, Factor-Price Distortions, and Choice of Technique: Empirical Results from Sierra Leone. *Econ. Develop. Cult. Change,* January 1983, *31*(2), pp. 315–36. **[G: Sierra Leone]**

Caire, Guy. Histoire recetter ou histoire méthode: A propos de la problématique rostowienne et des paradigmes dominants de l'économie du développement. (History as Receipts or History as Method: Concerning the Problems Raised by Rostow and the Dominant Paradigmes of Economy of Development. With English summary.) *Écon. Soc.,* February 1983, *17*(2), pp. 261–88.

Caire, Guy. Plaidoyer et agenda pour la prise en compte des ressources humaines dans la recherche relative aux pays sous-développés. (Defense and Agenda for Taking Human Resources into Account in Research Regarding Underdeveloped Countries. With English summary.) *Consommation,* October–December 1983, *30*(4), pp. 3–21.

Casar, José I. and Ros, Jaime. Trade and Capital Accumulation in a Process of Import Substitution. *Cambridge J. Econ.,* September/December 1983, *7*(3/4), pp. 257–67. **[G: Mexico]**

de Castillo, J. Reestructuraciones sectoriales y regionales en la crisis. (Sectorial and Regional Restructurizations on the Crisis. With English summary.) *Écon. Soc.,* September–October–November 1983, *17*(9–10–11), pp. 1551–68.

Chakravarty, Sukhamoy. Trade and Development: Some Basic Issues. *Int. Soc. Sci. J.,* 1983, *35*(3), pp. 424–40. **[G: Global]**

Chase-Dunn, Christopher. Inequality, Structural Mobility, and Dependency Reversal in the Capitalist World Economy. **In** *Doran, C. F.; Modelski, G. and Clark, C., eds.,* 1983, pp. 73–95. **[G: Selected Countries]**

Chenery, Hollis B. Interaction between Theory and Observation in Development. *World Devel.,* October 1983, *11*(10), pp. 853–61.

Chenery, Hollis B. Poverty and Progress—Choices

for the Developing World. In *Todaro, M. P., ed.*, 1983, *1980*, pp. 86–94.

Choudhury, Masudul Alam. How Effective Is Human Resource Planning in Developing the Third World? *METU*, 1983, *10*(3), pp. 249–69. **[G: Libya; Ghana; Gambia]**

Choudhury, Masudul Alam. Towards an Evaluative Study of Joint Venture Projects with Socio-economic Indicators. *Singapore Econ. Rev.*, October 1983, *28*(2), pp. 59–78. **[G: Mauritania]**

Clark, Cal; Doran, Charles F. and Modelski, George. North/South Relations: Studies of Dependency Reversal: Introduction. In *Doran, C. F.; Modelski, G. and Clark, C., eds.*, 1983, pp. ix–xx.

Clifton, Eric V. The Effects of Increased Interest-Rate Volatility on LDCs. *J. Int. Money Finance*, April 1983, *2*(1), pp. 67–74.

Clifton, Eric V. The Maximin Objective Function and Less Developed Countries. *Atlantic Econ. J.*, March 1983, *11*(1), pp. 71–72. **[G: LDCs]**

Cong, Li. Strategies for a Social–Economic Development of Developing Countries and Their Adjustment. In *Gauhar, A., ed. (I)*, 1983, pp. 3–15.

Cooper, Charles M. Extensions of the Raj–Sen Model of Economic Growth. *Oxford Econ. Pap.*, July 1983, *35*(2), pp. 170–85.

Darity, William A., Jr. Contemporary Marxism: Ideology or Science? A Review Essay on: *Research in Political Economy. Rev. Radical Polit. Econ.*, Winter 1983, *15*(4), pp. 136–48.

Davis, Lance E. and Huttenback, Robert A. The Social Rate of Return: A Note on a Note [The Political Economy of British Imperialism: Measures of Benefits and Support]. *J. Econ. Hist.*, December 1983, *43*(4), pp. 983–95. **[G: U.K.]**

De Janvry, Alain and Sadoulet, Elisabeth. Social Articulation as a Condition for Equitable Growth. *J. Devel. Econ.*, December 1983, *13*(3), pp. 275–303. **[G: Brazil; Mexico; LDCs]**

Dellaportas, George. Classification of Nations as Developed and Less Developed: An Arrangement by Discriminant Analysis of Socioeconomic Data. *Amer. J. Econ. Soc.*, April 1983, *42*(2), pp. 153–66. **[G: Global; LDCs; MDCs]**

Dervis, Kemal. Foreign Protectionism and Resource Allocation in a Developing Economy: A General Equilibrium Analysis. In *Kelley, A. C.; Sanderson, W. C. and Williamson, J. G., eds.*, 1983, pp. 43–56.

Destanne de Bernis, Gérard. De l'existence de points de passage obligatoires pour une politique de dévéloppement. (On the Existence of Obligatory Passage Points for Development Policy. With English summary.) *Écon. Soc.*, February 1983, *17*(2), pp. 213–59.

Di Tella, Torcuato S. "Partidos del pueblo" en América Latina. Revisión teórica y reseña de tendencias recientes. (With English summary.) *Desarrollo Econ.*, January–March 1983, *22*(88), pp. 451–83. **[G: Latin America]**

Dominique, C-René. Labor-Surplus Project Appraisal Methods: Didactic and Operational Differences, and Value Judgements between OECD and UNIDO. *J. Econ. Devel.*, July 1983, *8*(1), pp. 59–88.

Donges, Juergen B. Re-appraisal of Foreign Trade Strategies for Industrial Development. In *[Giersch, H.]*, 1983, pp. 279–301. **[G: LDCs]**

Doran, Charles F. Structuring the Concept of Dependency Reversal. In *Doran, C. F.; Modelski, G. and Clark, C., eds.*, 1983, pp. 1–27.

Dos Santos, Theotonio. The Structure of Dependence. In *Todaro, M. P., ed.*, 1983, *1970*, pp. 68–75.

Dowidar, Mohamed. Conception du développement et conception corrélative du sous-développement. (The Concept of Development and Its Correlate, the Concepts of Under-Development. With English summary.) *Écon. Soc.*, February 1983, *17*(2), pp. 289–98.

Driscoll, Michael J. and Lahiri, Ashok K. Income-Velocity of Money in Agricultural Developing Economies. *Rev. Econ. Statist.*, August 1983, *65*(3), pp. 393–401. **[G: Selected LDCs]**

Duvall, Raymond D. and Freeman, John R. The Techno-Bureaucratic Elite and the Entrepreneurial State in Dependent Industrialization. *Amer. Polit. Sci. Rev.*, September 1983, *77*(3), pp. 569–87. **[G: LDCs]**

Edwards, Sebastian. The Short-Run Relation between Growth and Inflation in Latin America: Comment. *Amer. Econ. Rev.*, June 1983, *73*(3), pp. 477–82. **[G: Latin America]**

Ehrenreich, John H. Socialism, Nationalism and Capitalist Development. *Rev. Radical Polit. Econ.*, Spring 1983, *15*(1), pp. 1–42.

Elliott, John E. Schumpeter and the Theory of Capitalist Economic Development. *J. Econ. Behav. Organ.*, December 1983, *4*(4), pp. 277–308.

Espinosa, Juan Guillermo. Worker Participation in the Management of Enterprises and the Ownership and Financing of the Means of Production: A Transition Strategy. *Econ. Anal. Worker's Manage.*, 1983, *17*(2), pp. 99–121.

Feder, Gershon. On Exports and Economic Growth. *J. Devel. Econ.*, February/April 1983, *12*(1/2), pp. 59–73.

Finn, James. Global Economics and Religion: Introduction. In *Finn, J., ed.*, 1983, pp. 1–9.

Fitzgerald, Frank T. Sociologies of Development. In *Limqueco, P. and McFarlane, B., eds.*, 1983, pp. 12–28.

Flynn, Dennis O. and St. Clair, David J. The Social Returns to Empire: A Note [The Political Economy of British Imperialism: Measures of Benefits and Support]. *J. Econ. Hist.*, December 1983, *43*(4), pp. 981–82. **[G: U.K.]**

Frank, Charles R., Jr. and Webb, Richard. Policy Choices and Income Distributions in Less Developed Countries. In *Todaro, M. P., ed.*, 1983, *1978*, pp. 102–18. **[G: LDCs]**

Frankel, Francine R. Religio-cultural Values, Political Gradualism, and Economic Development in India. In *Finn, J., ed.*, 1983, pp. 35–65. **[G: India]**

Fuà, Giorgio. Problems of Lagged Development in OECD Europe: A Study of Six Countries. *Rivista Int. Sci. Econ. Com.*, March 1983, *30*(3), pp. 228–43. **[G: Selected European]**

von Furstenberg, George M. The Uncertain Effects

of Inflationary Finance on Growth in Developing Countries. *Public Finance,* 1983, *38*(2), pp. 232–66. **[G: U.S.]**

Galbraith, John Kenneth. The Constraints of Historical Process. **In** *Galbraith, J. K.,* 1983, pp. 6–24.

Galtung, Johan. Buts et processus du développement: une vue intégrée. (Goals and Process of Development: An Integrated View. In English.) *Écon. Soc.,* February 1983, *17*(2), pp. 335–63.

Gersovitz, Mark. Savings and Nutrition at Low Incomes. *J. Polit. Econ.,* October 1983, *91*(5), pp. 841–55.

Ghosh, Dipak. Planning for Employment in a Developing Economy. *Acta Oecon.,* 1983, *31*(3–4), pp. 287–96. **[G: LDCs]**

Ghosh, Ranen. Analytical Implications of Time Series Economic Variable Data: Re—Economic Development. *Econ. Aff.,* April–June 1983, *28*(2), pp. 664–74, 681. **[G: Nigeria; LDCs]**

Giovannini, Alberto. The Interest Elasticity of Savings in Developing Countries: The Existing Evidence. *World Devel.,* July 1983, *11*(7), pp. 601–07. **[G: Selected LDCs]**

Godfrey, Martin. Surplus Labour as a Source of Foreign Exchange? *World Devel.,* November 1983, *11*(11), pp. 945–56. **[G: LDCs]**

Goulet, Denis. Obstacles to World Development: An Ethical Reflection. *World Devel.,* July 1983, *11*(7), pp. 609–24.

Goulet, Denis. Overcoming Injustice: Possibilities and Limits. **In** *Skurski, R., ed.,* 1983, pp. 113–58.

Goulet, Denis. The Shock of Underdevelopment. **In** *Todaro, M. P., ed.,* 1983, *1971,* pp. 3–9.

Gouri, Getta. Skill-Formation in Export-Led Industrial Strategy. *Indian Econ. J.,* January-March 1983, *30*(3), pp. 87–102. **[G: Korea]**

Gow, David D. and VanSant, Jerry. Beyond the Rhetoric of Rural Development Participation: How Can It Be Done? *World Devel.,* May 1983, *11*(5), pp. 427–46. **[G: Guatemala; Indonesia]**

Graziani, Augusto. The Macroeconomic Theory of Vera C. Lutz. *Banca Naz. Lavoro Quart. Rev.,* March 1983, (144), pp. 3–27. **[G: Italy]**

Green, Reginald Herbold. African Economies in the Mid-1980's—"Naught for Your Comfort but That the Waves Grow Higher and the Storms Grow Wilder." **In** *Carlsson, J., ed.,* 1983, pp. 173–203. **[G: Sub-Saharan Africa]**

Grinols, Earl and Bhagwati, Jagdish N. Foreign Capital, Savings and Dependence. **In** *Bhagwati, J. N., Vol. 2,* 1983, *1976,* pp. 493–501.

Gülalp, Haldun. Frank and Wallerstein Revisited: A Contribution to Brenner's Critique. **In** *Limqueco, P. and McFarlane, B., eds.,* 1983, pp. 114–36.

Gunning, Jan Willem. Rationing in an Open Economy: Fix-Price Equilibrium and Two-Gap Models. *Europ. Econ. Rev.,* September 1983, *23*(1), pp. 71–98.

Gupta, Kanhaya L. and Islam, M. Anisul. Income Distribution and Economic Growth: Some Empirical Evidence. *J. Econ. Devel.,* July 1983, *8*(1), pp. 25–44. **[G: Selected Countries]**

Gurrieri, Adolfo. Technical Progress and Its Fruits: The Idea of Development in the Works of Rául Prebisch. *J. Econ. Issues,* June 1983, *17*(2), pp. 389–96.

Gurrieri, Adolfo and Sáinz, Pedro. Is There a Fair and Democratic Way Out of the Crisis? Some Proposals in the Light of the ECLA Philosophy. *Cepal Rev.,* August 1983, (20), pp. 127–48. **[G: Latin America]**

Hamilton, Carl and Svensson, Lars E. O. On the Choice between Capital Import and Labor Export. *Europ. Econ. Rev.,* January 1983, *20*(1–3), pp. 167–92.

Hansen, Bent. LDC Labor Markets: Applications of Internal Labor Market Theory. *Ind. Relat.,* Spring 1983, *22*(2), pp. 238–60. **[G: Egypt; LDCs]**

Hanson, James A. The Short-Run Relation between Growth and Inflation in Latin America: Reply. *Amer. Econ. Rev.,* June 1983, *73*(3), pp. 483–85. **[G: Latin America]**

Harberger, Arnold C. The Cost–Benefit Approach to Development Economics. *World Devel.,* October 1983, *11*(10), pp. 863–73. **[G: LDCs]**

Hart, Jeffrey A. The Constraints on Associative Development in a Privileged Developing Country: The Case of Venezeula. **In** *Ruggie, J. G., ed.,* 1983, pp. 191–238. **[G: Venezuela]**

Hatiboglu, Z. An Unconventional Approach to the Analysis of Growth in Developing Countries and Its Application in Turkey. *S. Afr. J. Econ.,* June 1983, *51*(2), pp. 297–309. **[G: Turkey]**

He, Xinhoa. Exploit the Role of Foreign Trade and Accelerate the Rate of China's Economic Development. *Chinese Econ. Stud.,* Summer 1983, *16*(4), pp. 37–50. **[G: China]**

Henriot, Peter J. A. Development Alternatives: Problems, Strategies, and Values. **In** *Todaro, M. P., ed.,* 1983, *1981,* pp. 26–40.

Henríquez, Pedro. Beyond Dependency Theory. *Int. Soc. Sci. J.,* 1983, *35*(2), pp. 391–400.

Hicks, Norman L. Is There a Tradeoff between Growth and Basic Needs? **In** *Todaro, M. P., ed.,* 1983, *1980,* pp. 95–101.

Hotz, M. C. B. Resources and Development: Trying to Close the Gap Responsibly. **In** *Glassner, M. I., ed.,* 1983, *1981,* pp. 108–17. **[G: LDCs]**

Hveem, Helge. Selective Dissociation in the Technology Sector. **In** *Ruggie, J. G., ed.,* 1983, pp. 273–316. **[G: Algeria; India; LDCs]**

Iglesias, Enrique V. The Brandt Report and Latin American Development in the 1980s. **In** *Ritter, A. R. M. and Pollock, D. H., eds.,* 1983, pp. 22–39. **[G: Latin America]**

Ionescu, V. and Berar, U. Cybernetic Model for Optimizing the Agro-Economic Development Plan of the Irrigated Zone Balikh (Northern Syria). *Econ. Computat. Cybern. Stud. Res.,* 1983, *18*(4), pp. 15–24. **[G: Syria]**

Islam, Nurul. Lessons of Experience: Development Policy and Practice. **In** *Parkinson, J. R., ed.,* 1983, pp. 79–89.

Jansen, Karel. Monetarism: Economic Crisis and the Third World: An Introduction. **In** *Jansen, K., ed.,* 1983, pp. 1–42.

Junker, Louis. Institutionalism and the Criteria of

Development. *Econ. Forum,* Summer 1983, *14*(1), pp. 27–56.

Kader, Ahmad. Sources of Growth with Domestic Factor Shift and Foreign Factor Transfer: The Case of Libya. *J. Econ. Devel.,* July 1983, *8*(1), pp. 89–108. **[G: Libya]**

Kapp, K. William. Social Costs in Economic Development. **In** *Kapp, K. W.,* 1983, *1965,* pp. 1–38. **[G: LDCs; Philippines]**

Kapur, Basant K. A Short-Term Analytical Model of the Singapore Economy. *J. Devel. Econ.,* June 1983, *12*(3), pp. 355–76. **[G: Singapore]**

Kapur, Basant K. Optimal Financial and Foreign-Exchange Liberalization of Less Developed Economies. *Quart. J. Econ.,* February 1983, *98*(1), pp. 41–62.

Kelley, Allen C. and Williamson, Jeffrey G. A Computable General Equilibrium Model of Third-World Urbanization and City Growth: Preliminary Comparative Statics. **In** *Kelley, A. C.; Sanderson, W. C. and Williamson, J. G., eds.,* 1983, pp. 3–41. **[G: LDCs]**

Khan, M. Ali and Naqvi, Syed Nawab Haider. Capital Markets and Urban Unemployment. *J. Int. Econ.,* November 1983, *15*(3/4), pp. 367–85.

Khan, Mohsin S. and Zahler, Roberto. The Macroeconomic Effects of Changes in Barriers to Trade and Capital Flows: A Simulation Analysis. *Int. Monet. Fund Staff Pap.,* June 1983, *30*(2), pp. 223–82.

Kilby, Peter. An Entrepreneurial Problem. *Amer. Econ. Rev.,* May 1983, *73*(2), pp. 107–11. **[G: LDCs]**

Kofi, Tetteh A. and Hansen, Emmanuel. Ghana—A History of an Endless Recession. **In** *Carlsson, J., ed.,* 1983, pp. 48–79. **[G: Ghana]**

Kovács, János. Labour Planning and Economic Development Strategy. **In** *Streeten, P. and Maier, H., eds.,* 1983, pp. 395–404.

Krueger, Anne O. The Effects of Trade Strategies on Growth. *Finance Develop.,* June 1983, *20*(2), pp. 6–8. **[G: Selected LDCs]**

Kubo, Yuji, et al. Modelos de equilibrio general para el análisis de estrategias alternativas de comercio exterior: una aplicación a Corea. (With English summary.) *Cuadernos Econ.,* December 1983, *20*(61), pp. 313–43. **[G: S. Korea]**

Kumar, Ramesh C. Money in Development: A Monetary Growth Model à la McKinnon. *Southern Econ. J.,* July 1983, *50*(1), pp. 18–36.

Kuran, Timur. Behavioral Norms in the Islamic Doctrine of Economics: A Critique. *J. Econ. Behav. Organ.,* December 1983, *4*(4), pp. 353–79.

Kwon, Jene K. Toward Incentive Transfers, Global Tax and Welfare Indices. *J. Econ. Devel.,* December 1983, *8*(2), pp. 71–87. **[G: LDCs; MDCs]**

Labra, Armando. Basing Development Strategy on the Human Factor: Comments. **In** *Tsuru, S., ed.,* 1983, pp. 25–29.

Lahera, Eugenio and Nochteff, Hugo. Microelectronics and Latin American Development. *Cepal Rev.,* April 1983, (19), pp. 167–81. **[G: Latin America]**

Landell-Mills, Pierre. Management: A Limiting Factor in Development. *Finance Develop.,* September 1983, *20*(3), pp. 11–15. **[G: LDCs]**

Lanyi, Anthony and Saracoglu, Rüşdü. The Importance of Interest Rates in Developing Economies. *Finance Develop.,* June 1983, *20*(2), pp. 20–23. **[G: Selected LDCs]**

Leaver, Richard. Samir Amin on Underdevelopment. **In** *Limqueco, P. and McFarlane, B., eds.,* 1983, pp. 58–72.

Leaver, Richard. The Debate on Underdevelopment: "On Situating Gunder Frank." **In** *Limqueco, P. and McFarlane, B., eds.,* 1983, pp. 87–96.

Lewis, W. Arthur. Aspects of Economic Development. **In** *Dalton, G., ed.,* 1983, *1969,* pp. 247–310. **[G: LDCs]**

Lewis, W. Arthur. Development and Distribution. **In** *Lewis, W. A.,* 1983, *1976,* pp. 443–59.

Lewis, W. Arthur. Economic Development with Unlimited Supplies of Labour. **In** *Lewis, W. A.,* 1983, *1954,* pp. 311–63.

Lewis, W. Arthur. Employment Policy in an Underdeveloped Area. **In** *Lewis, W. A.,* 1983, *1958,* pp. 397–409. **[G: Caribbean]**

Lewis, W. Arthur. Objectives and Prognostications. **In** *Lewis, W. A.,* 1983, *1972,* pp. 697–706.

Lewis, W. Arthur. Reflections on Unlimited Labor. **In** *Lewis, W. A.,* 1983, *1972,* pp. 421–42.

Lewis, W. Arthur. The Dual Economy Revisited. **In** *Lewis, W. A.,* 1983, *1979,* pp. 461–79.

Lewis, W. Arthur. The Slowing Down of the Engine of Growth. **In** *Lewis, W. A.,* 1983, *1980,* pp. 283–92.

Lewis, W. Arthur. Unlimited Labour: Further Notes. **In** *Lewis, W. A.,* 1983, *1958,* pp. 365–96.

Leys, Colin. Underdevelopment and Dependency: Critical Notes. **In** *Limqueco, P. and McFarlane, B., eds.,* 1983, pp. 29–49.

Lim, Chong Yah. Development Economics by R. M. Sundrum: A Review Article. *Singapore Econ. Rev.,* April 1983, *28*(1), pp. 88–103.

Lim, David. Government Recurrent Expenditure and Economic Growth in Less Developed Countries. *World Devel.,* April 1983, *11*(4), pp. 377–80. **[G: LDCs]**

Limqueco, Peter and McFarlane, Bruce. Neo-marxist Theories of Development: Introduction. **In** *Limqueco, P. and McFarlane, B., eds.,* 1983, pp. 1–11.

Lisk, Franklyn. Conventional Development Strategies and Basic-Needs Fulfilment. **In** *Todaro, M. P., ed.,* 1983, *1977,* pp. 41–54.

Long, Millard. A Note on Financial Theory and Economic Development. **In** *Von Pischke, J. D.; Adams, D. W. and Donald, G., eds.,* 1983, pp. 22–28.

Long, Ngo Van. The Effects of a Booming Export Industry on the Rest of the Economy. *Econ. Rec.,* March 1983, *59*(164), pp. 57–60.

Lopes, Francisco L. and Bacha, Edmar L. Inflation, Growth and Wage Policy: A Brazilian Perspective. *J. Devel. Econ.,* Aug.–Oct. 1983, *13*(1–2), pp. 1–20. **[G: Brazil]**

Lundahl, Mats. Intergenerational Sharecropping in Haiti: A Re-interpretation of the Murray Thesis. **In** *Lundahl, M.,* 1983, *1982,* pp. 83–93. **[G: Haiti]**

Lundahl, Mats. Teknologiska förändringar och ekonomisk tillväxt i u-länder. (Technological Change and Economic Growth in the Developing Countries. With English summary.) *Ekon. Samfundets Tidskr.*, 1983, *36*(3), pp. 91–106. [G: LDCs; MDCs]

Maillet, Pierre. Basing Development Strategy on the Human Factor: Comments. **In** *Tsuru, S., ed.*, 1983, pp. 20–24.

Mamalakis, Markos. Overall Employment and Income Strategies. **In** *Urquidi, V. L. and Reyes, S. T., eds.*, 1983, pp. 111–30.

Maneschi, Andrea. The Prebisch-Singer Thesis and the 'Widening Gap' between Developed and Developing Countries. *Can. J. Econ.*, February 1983, *16*(1), pp. 104–08.

Mansur, Ahsan H. Determining the Appropriate Levels of Exchange Rates for Developing Economies: Some Methods and Issues. *Int. Monet. Fund Staff Pap.*, December 1983, *30*(4), pp. 784–818. [G: LDCs]

Mawuli, Agogo. Balance of Payments Problem as a Consequence of Rapid Capital Accumulation in Developing Countries. *Indian Econ. J.*, January-March 1983, *30*(3), pp. 39–64. [G: LDCs]

Mazumdar, Dipak. The Rural–Urban Wage Gap Migration and the Working of Urban Labor Market: An Interpretation Based on a Study of the Workers of Bombay City. *Indian Econ. Rev.*, July–December 1983, *18*(2), pp. 169–98. [G: India]

McCarthy, F. Desmond. General Equilibrium Model for Egypt. **In** *Kelley, A. C.; Sanderson, W. C. and Williamson, J. G., eds.*, 1983, pp. 71–102. [G: Egypt]

Mehmet, Ozay. Growth and Impoverishment in a Dual Economy with Capital Imports. *Australian Econ. Pap.*, June 1983, *22*(40), pp. 221–32.

Méndez, José A. Immiserisation and the Emergence of Multinational Firms in a Less Developed Country: A General Equilibrium Analysis. *J. Devel. Stud.*, October 1983, *20*(1), pp. 22–23.

Mendez, Sofia. Problems of Labour Utilisation in the Long Term. **In** *Streeten, P. and Maier, H., eds.*, 1983, pp. 289–94.

Mihailov, Boris. Modeling Alternative Socioeconomic Mechanisms. **In** *Kelley, A. C.; Sanderson, W. C. and Williamson, J. G., eds.*, 1983, pp. 141–65.

Mkandawire, P. Thandika. Accumulation on a World Scale. **In** *Limqueco, P. and McFarlane, B., eds.*, 1983, pp. 50–57.

Modelski, George. Dependency Reversal in the Modern State System: A Long Cycle Perspective. **In** *Doran, C. F.; Modelski, G. and Clark, C., eds.*, 1983, pp. 49–72.

Myrdal, Gunnar. The Beam in Our Eyes. **In** *Glassner, M. I., ed.*, 1983, *1968*, pp. xv–xxii. [G: LDCs]

Nabe, Oumar. Military Expenditures and Industrialization in Africa. *J. Econ. Issues*, June 1983, *17*(2), pp. 575–87. [G: Africa]

Newfarmer, Richard S. Multinationals and Marketplace Magic in the 1980s. **In** *Kindleberger, C. P. and Audretsch, D. B., eds.*, 1983, pp. 162–97. [G: Global]

Norton, Roger D.; Santaniello, Vittorio and Echevarria, Julio A. Economic Evaluation of an Agricultural Sector Investment Program: A Case Study for Peru. *J. Policy Modeling*, June 1983, *5*(2), pp. 149–77. [G: Peru]

Nugent, Jeffrey B. An Alternative Source of Measurement Error as an Explanation for the Inverted-U Hypothesis. *Econ. Develop. Cult. Change*, January 1983, *31*(2), pp. 385–96. [G: Mexico]

O'Brien, Patrick. European Economic Development: A Reply. *Econ. Hist. Rev., 2nd Ser.*, November 1983, *36*(4), pp. 548–85. [G: W. Europe]

Onitiri, H. M. A. Economics and Development Policy. *Int. Soc. Sci. J.*, 1983, *35*(3), pp. 507–16.

Oshima, Harry T. The Industrial and Demographic Transitions in East Asia. *Population Devel. Rev.*, December 1983, *9*(4), pp. 583–607. [G: E. Asia]

Othick, John. Development Indicators and the Historical Study of Human Welfare: Towards a New Perspective. *J. Econ. Hist.*, March 1983, *43*(1), pp. 63–70.

Packenham, Robert A. The Dependency Perspective and Analytic Dependency. **In** *Doran, C. F.; Modelski, G. and Clark, C., eds.*, 1983, pp. 29–47. [G: Brazil]

Pajestka, Józef. Basing Development Strategy on the Human Factor. **In** *Tsuru, S., ed.*, 1983, pp. 3–19.

Papanek, Gustav F. Economic Development Theory: The Earnest Search for a Mirage. **In** *Todaro, M. P., ed.*, 1983, *1977*, pp. 17–26.

Park, Se-Hark and Kubursi, Atif A. The Energy Constraint and Development: Consistency and Optimality over Time. *Energy Econ.*, January 1983, *5*(1), pp. 9–15. [G: LDCs]

Peel, David A. On Inflation and Economic Growth. *Singapore Econ. Rev.*, April 1983, *28*(1), pp. 53–58. [G: LDCs]

de la Peña, H. Flores. Economic Development in the Coming Years. **In** *Tsuru, S., ed.*, 1983, pp. 131–35.

Petras, James F. New Perspectives on Imperialism and Social Classes in the Periphery. **In** *Limqueco, P. and McFarlane, B., eds.*, 1983, pp. 198–220.

Pfeffermann, Guy and Webb, Richard. Poverty and Income Distribution in Brazil. *Rev. Income Wealth*, June 1983, *29*(2), pp. 101–24. [G: Brazil]

Platteau, Jean-Philippe. Classical Economics and Agrarian Reforms in Underdeveloped Areas: The Radical Views of the Two Mills. *J. Devel. Stud.*, July 1983, *19*(4), pp. 435–60.

Pollock, David H. A Latin American Strategy to the Year 2000. **In** *Ritter, A. R. M. and Pollock, D. H., eds.*, 1983, pp. 3–21. [G: Latin America]

Prebisch, Raúl. The Latin-American Periphery in the Global System of Capitalism. **In** *Tsuru, S., ed.*, 1983, pp. 30–45.

Pregger-Román, Charles G. Dependence, Underdevelopment, and Imperialism in Latin America: A Reappraisal. *Sci. Soc.*, Winter 1983–1984, *47*(4), pp. 406–26. [G: Latin America]

Quizon, Jaime B. and Binswanger, Hans P. Income Distribution in Agriculture: A Unified Approach. *Amer. J. Agr. Econ.*, August 1983, *65*(3), pp. 526–38.

Ray, Edward John. Impact of General Economic Policies on the Performance of Rural Financial Markets. In *Von Pischke, J. D.; Adams, D. W. and Donald, G., eds.*, 1983, pp. 67–71.

Repetto, Robert and Holmes, Thomas. The Role of Population in Resource Depletion in Developing Countries. *Population Devel. Rev.*, December 1983, *9*(4), pp. 609–32. **[G: LDCs]**

Reynolds, Lloyd G. The Spread of Economic Growth to the Third World: 1850–1980. *J. Econ. Lit.*, September 1983, *21*(3), pp. 941–80. **[G: LDCs]**

Rodgers, Gerry. Population Growth, Inequality and Poverty. *Int. Lab. Rev.*, July-August 1983, *122*(4), pp. 443–60. **[G: LDCs]**

Rondinelli, Dennis A. and Evans, Hugh. Integrated Regional Development Planning: Linking Urban Centres and Rural Areas in Bolivia. *World Devel.*, January 1983, *11*(1), pp. 31–53. **[G: Bolivia; S. America]**

Rosier, Bernard. Le développement économique, processus univoque ou produit spécifique d'un système économique? une approche en termes de type de développement. (Universal process of specific product? An Approach to Economic Development in Terms of Typology. With English summary.) *Écon. Soc.*, February 1983, *17*(2), pp. 365–403.

Ross, Howard N. and Thomadakis, Stavros. Rate of Return, Firm Size and Development Subsidies: The Case of Greece. *J. Devel. Econ.*, February/April 1983, *12*(1/2), pp. 5–18. **[G: Greece]**

Roy, Subroto. Economic Theory and Development Economics: A Comment. *World Devel.*, October 1983, *11*(10), pp. 901–03.

Ruane, Frances P. Trade Policies and the Spatial Distribution of Development: A Two-Sector Analysis. *Int. Reg. Sci. Rev.*, June 1983, *8*(1), pp. 47–58. **[G: LDCs]**

Ruggie, John Gerard. International Interdependence and National Welfare. In *Ruggie, J. G., ed.*, 1983, pp. 1–39. **[G: LDCs; MDCs]**

Ruiz, G.; Narvaez, A. and Gallego, J.-A. Crisis económica, desarrollo y medio ambiente. (Economic Crisis, Development and Environment. With English summary.) *Écon. Soc.*, September–October–November 1983, *17*(–10–11), pp. 1647–69.

Sachs, Ignacy. Le potentiel de développement endogène. (The Potential for Endogenous Development. With English summary.) *Écon. Soc.*, February 1983, *17*(2), pp. 405–26. **[G: India; Brazil; Japan]**

Saith, Ashwani. Development and Distribution: A Critique of the Cross-Country U-Hypothesis. *J. Devel. Econ.*, December 1983, *13*(3), pp. 367–82. **[G: LDCs]**

Salisbury, Richard F. Anthropological Economic and Development Planning. In *Ortiz, S., ed.*, 1983, pp. 399–419.

Salvatore, Dominick. A Simultaneous Equations Model of Trade and Development with Dynamic Policy Simulations. *Kyklos*, 1983, *36*(1), pp. 66–90.

Sathaye, Deepak. Primitive Accumulation and Optimum Development in the Dual Economy. *Brit. Rev. Econ. Issues*, Autumn 1983, *5*(13), pp. 1–22.

Schmidt, Robert M. Incorporating Demography into General Equilibrium Modeling. In *Kelley, A. C.; Sanderson, W. C. and Williamson, J. G., eds.*, 1983, pp. 317–37.

Seers, Dudley. Structuralism vs Monetarism in Latin America: A Reappraisal of a Great Debate, with Lessons for Europe in the 1980s. In *Jansen, K., ed.*, 1983, pp. 110–26. **[G: Latin America]**

Sen, Amartya K. Development: Which Way Now? *Econ. J.*, December 1983, *93*(372), pp. 742–62. **[G: LDCs]**

Sen, Amartya K. Economic Development: Some Strategic Issues. In *Gauhar, A., ed. (I)*, 1983, pp. 43–54. **[G: LDCs]**

Şen, Asim. Lessons for Development from the Japanese Experience. *J. Econ. Issues*, June 1983, *17*(2), pp. 415–22. **[G: Japan]**

Shoazhi, Su. Socialism; China's Conditions; Modern Science and Technology; Democratization; Development Strategies: A Tentative Discourse on the Chinese Road to Modernization. *Econ. Notes*, 1983, (1), pp. 24–41. **[G: China]**

Sideri, Sandro. Crisi mondiale, crisi dei modelli di sviluppo latino-americani e ralazioni economiche della Comunità Europea con l'America Latina. (The World Crisis, the Crisis of Latin American Development Models and the Economic Relations of the European Community with Latin America. With English summary.) *Giorn. Econ.*, September–October 1983, *42*(9–10), pp. 601–16. **[G: EEC; Latin America]**

Silber, Jacques. ELL (The Equivalent Length of Life) or Another Attempt at Measuring Development. *World Devel.*, January 1983, *11*(1), pp. 21–29. **[G: Global]**

Simmons, John. Education for Development, Reconsidered. In *Todaro, M. P., ed.*, 1983, *1979*, pp. 262–76. **[G: Sri Lanka; Colombia; China; Pakistan]**

Singer, Hans W. The Role of Human Capital in Development. *Pakistan J. Appl. Econ.*, Summer 1983, *2*(1), pp. 1–11. **[G: S. Korea]**

Smith, Carol A. Regional Analysis in World-System Perspective: A Critique of Three Structural Theories of Uneven Development. In *Ortiz, S., ed.*, 1983, pp. 307–59. **[G: Guatemala]**

Smith, Sheila. Class Analysis versus World Systems: Critique of Samir Amin's Typology of Underdevelopment. In *Limqueco, P. and McFarlane, B., eds.*, 1983, pp. 73–86.

Smith, Sheila and Toye, John. Trade Theory, Industrialization and Commercial Policies. In *Todaro, M. P., ed.*, 1983, *1979*, pp. 289–300.

Smith, Tony. The Case of Dependency Theory. In *Thompson, W. S., ed.*, 1983, pp. 203–22.

Södersten, Bo. The Latin-American Periphery in the Global System of Capitalism: Comments. In *Tsuru, S., ed.*, 1983, pp. 52–57. **[G: Sweden]**

Solow, Robert M. Economic Development and the Development of Economics: Discussion. *World Devel.*, October 1983, *11*(10), pp. 891–93.

Steel, William F. and Takagi, Yasuoki. Small Enterprise Development and the Employment-Output Trade-Off. *Oxford Econ. Pap.*, November 1983, *35*(3), pp. 423–46. **[G: LDCs]**

Stein, Leslie. Emmanuel's Unequal Exchange Thesis: A Critique. *Econ. Int.*, February 1983, *36*(1), pp. 70–88.

Stern, Ernest. The Challenge of Development Today. *Finance Develop.*, September 1983, *20*(3), pp. 2–5. **[G: LDCs]**

Stewart, Frances and Streeten, Paul. Conflicts between Output and Employment Objectives in Developing Countries. **In** *Todaro, M. P., ed.*, 1983, *1971*, pp. 164–81.

Stolper, Wolfgang F. Fiscal and Monetary Policy in the Context of Development: A Schumpeterian Approach. **In** *Biehl, D.; Roskamp, K. W. and Stolper, W. F., eds.*, 1983, pp. 127–47.

Stone, Carl. Patterns of Insertion into the World Economy: Historical Profile and Contemporary Options. *Soc. Econ. Stud.*, September 1983, *32*(3), pp. 1–34. **[G: Caribbean]**

Streeten, Paul. Development Dichotomies. *World Devel.*, October 1983, *11*(10), pp. 875–89.

Tanaka, Osamu. A Theory of the Supplies of Labor and Homemakers' Services. *Kobe Univ. Econ.*, 1983, (29), pp. 1–14.

Teilhet-Waldorf, Saral and Waldorf, William H. Earnings of Self-Employed in an Informal Sector: A Case Study of Bangkok. *Econ. Develop. Cult. Change*, April 1983, *31*(3), pp. 587–607. **[G: Thailand]**

Thirlwall, Anthony P. Confusion over Measuring the Relative Worth of Trade and Aid. *World Devel.*, January 1983, *11*(1), pp. 71–72. **[G: Sudan]**

Thirlwall, Anthony P. Foreign Trade Elasticities in Centre-Periphery Models of Growth and Development. *Banca Naz. Lavoro Quart. Rev.*, September 1983, (146), pp. 249–61.

Thorsson, Inga. Guns and Butter: Can the World Have Both? *Int. Lab. Rev.*, July–August 1983, *122*(4), pp. 397–410. **[G: Global]**

Tiano, André. The Dialectics of Dependency Reversal: Technology Transfer. **In** *Doran, C. F.; Modelski, G. and Clark, C., eds.*, 1983, pp. 129–55.

Tinbergen, Jan. Développement optimal et facteurs exogènes. (Optimal Development and Exogenous Factors. With English summary.) *Écon. Soc.*, February 1983, *17*(2), pp. 427–50.

Tisdell, Clem A. Dissent from Value, Preference and Choice Theory in Economics. *Int. J. Soc. Econ.*, 1983, *10*(2), pp. 32–43.

Togan, Sübidey. Effects of Alternative Policy Regimes on Foreign-Payments Imbalances. *Pakistan Devel. Rev.*, Winter 1983, *22*(4), pp. 239–60. **[G: Turkey]**

Tokman, Victor E. The Influence of the Urban Informal Sector on Economic Inequality. **In** *Stewart, F., ed.*, 1983, pp. 108–37. **[G: Mexico; Chile]**

Townsend, Robert M. Financial Structure and Economic Activity. *Amer. Econ. Rev.*, December 1983, *73*(5), pp. 895–911.

Toye, John. The Disparaging of Development Economics: A Review Article. *J. Devel. Stud.*, October 1983, *20*(1), pp. 87–107.

Urquidi, Victor L. Major Problems Affecting the Process of Development, with Special Reference to Latin America. **In** *Gauhar, A., ed. (I)*, 1983, pp. 17–41. **[G: Latin America]**

Venieris, Yiannis P. and Gupta, Dipak K. Sociopolitical and Economic Dimensions of Development: A Cross-Section Model. *Econ. Develop. Cult. Change*, July 1983, *31*(4), pp. 727–56. **[G: Selected MDCs; Selected LDCs]**

Ville, Jean A. Théorie des jeux, dualité, développement. (With English summary.) *Écon. Appl.*, 1983, *36*(4), pp. 593–609.

Vink, N. and Kassier, W. E. A Paradigm for a Micro-Level Rural Development Strategy. *S. Afr. J. Econ.*, June 1983, *51*(2), pp. 283–96. **[G: S. Africa]**

Wallerstein, Immanuel. European Economic Development: A Comment. *Econ. Hist. Rev.*, *2nd Ser.*, November 1983, *36*(4), pp. 580–83. **[G: W. Europe]**

Warr, Peter G. Domestic Resource Cost as an Investment Criterion. *Oxford Econ. Pap.*, July 1983, *35*(2), pp. 302–06.

Weede, Erich. The Impact of Democracy on Economic Growth: Some Evidence from Cross-National Analysis. *Kyklos*, 1983, *36*(1), pp. 21–39.

Weisskopf, Thomas E. Alternative Models of Economic Development. *Écon. Soc.*, February 1983, *17*(2), pp. 451–78.

Weisskopf, Thomas E. Economic Development and the Development of Economics: Some Observations from the Left. *World Devel.*, October 1983, *11*(10), pp. 895–99.

Wiarda, Howard J. Toward a Nonethnocentric Theory of Development: Alternative Conceptions from the Third World. *J. Devel. Areas*, July 1983, *17*(4), pp. 433–52.

van Wijnbergen, Sweder. Credit Policy, Inflation and Growth in a Financially Repressed Economy. *J. Devel. Econ.*, Aug.–Oct. 1983, *13*(1–2), pp. 45–65.

van Wijnbergen, Sweder. Interest Rate Management in LDCs. *J. Monet. Econ.*, September 1983, *12*(3), pp. 433–52. **[G: LDCs]**

Winston, Gordon C. Productivity-Reducing Supply-Side Policies. *J. Post Keynesian Econ.*, Winter 1982–83, *5*(2), pp. 257–65.

von Witzke, Harald. Growth and Equity in Agricultural Development: A Survey of the 18th International Conference of Agricultural Economists, Jakarta, Indonesia, August 24 to September 2, 1982. *Europ. Rev. Agr. Econ.*, 1983, *10*(2), pp. 151–63. **[G: Global]**

Wolfe, Marshall. Styles of Development and Education: A Stocktaking of Myths, Prescriptions and Potentialities. *Cepal Rev.*, December 1983, (21), pp. 157–73. **[G: Latin America]**

Xu, Shiwei. On the Development of China's Foreign Trade. *Chinese Econ. Stud.*, Summer 1983, *16*(4), pp. 3–16. **[G: China]**

Yotopoulos, Pan A. A Micro Economic-Demographic Model of the Agricultural Household in the Philippines. *Food Res. Inst. Stud.*, 1983, *19*(1), pp. 1–24. **[G: Philippines]**

Yuan, Wenqi and Wang, Jianmin. We Must Review and Reevaluate the Role of Foreign Trade in the Development of the National Economy. *Chinese Econ. Stud.*, Spring 1983, *16*(3), pp. 24–39. **[G: China]**

Zerby, J. A. and Khan, M. Habibullah. Quantitative Analysis of World Development: A Cluster Analytic Approach. *Pakistan J. Appl. Econ.*, Summer 1983, *2*(1), pp. 39–63.

Zhou, Shulian. Seriously Study the Strategy of Our Economic Development from a Historical Viewpoint. *Chinese Econ. Stud.*, Fall 1983, *17*(1), pp. 88–95. **[G: China]**

Zonnoor, S. H. Maximization over a Set of Competitive Equilibria: A Planning Application. *J. Econ. Dynam. Control,* December 1983, *6*(4), pp. 351–69. **[G: Iran]**

Zuberi, Habib A. Institutional Credit and Balanced Growth: A Case Study of Pakistan. *J. Econ. Devel.*, December 1983, *8*(2), pp. 167–84. **[G: Pakistan]**

113 Economic Planning Theory and Policy

1130 Economic Planning Theory and Policy

Ancot, J. P. and Hughes Hallett, A. J. The Determination of Collective Preferences in Economic Decision Models: With an Application to Soviet Economic Policy. **In** *Gruber, J., ed.*, 1983, pp. 263–304. **[G: U.S.S.R.]**

Andréani, Edgard. Quantification sociale et évaluation des politiques sociales. (With English summary.) *Revue Écon. Polit.*, May–June 1983, *93*(3), pp. 362–76. **[G: France]**

Anonsen, Carl. Is Planning in Developing Countries Worth the Price? **In** *Parkinson, J. R., ed.*, 1983, pp. 114–22.

Antal, László. Conflicts of Financial Planning and Regulation in Hungary (The "Nature" of Restrictions). *Acta Oecon.*, 1983, *30*(3–4), pp. 341–67. **[G: Hungary]**

Balassa, Bela. The Hungarian Economic Reform, 1968–82. *Banca Naz. Lavoro Quart. Rev.*, June 1983, (145), pp. 163–84. **[G: Hungary]**

Bánhidi, Ferenc and Gábor, László. The Price Model. *Matekon,* Spring 1983, *19*(3), pp. 18–35. **[G: Hungary]**

Bauer, Tamás. The Hungarian Alternative to Soviet-Type Planning. *J. Compar. Econ.*, September 1983, *7*(3), pp. 304–16. **[G: U.S.S.R.; Hungary]**

Bhagwati, Jagdish N. and Wan, Henry, Jr. The "Stationarity" of Shadow Prices of Factors in Project Evaluation, with and without Distortions. **In** *Bhagwati, J. N., Vol. 1,* 1983, *1979,* pp. 558–70.

Blecher, Marc. 'The New Course in China': Summing-Up Speeches at Oxford Conference, Contemporary China Centre, September 1982. *World Devel.*, August 1983, *11*(8), pp. 769. **[G: China]**

Chen, Yun. A Letter to Comrades in the Central Finance and Economics Small Group. **In** *Ch'en, Y.*, 1983, *1959,* pp. 112–16. **[G: China]**

Chen, Yun. Regulation on the Improvement of the Commercial Management System. **In** *Ch'en, Y.*, 1983, *1957,* pp. 84–87. **[G: China]**

Csikós-Nagy, Béla. Liquidity Troubles and Economic Consolidation in Hungary. *Acta Oecon.*, 1983, *31*(1–2), pp. 1–11. **[G: Hungary]**

Csikós-Nagy, Béla and Gadó, Otto. Effective Monetary and Fiscal Policy to Promote Economic Growth—A Socialist Approach. **In** *Biehl, D.; Roskamp, K. W. and Stolper, W. F., eds.*, 1983, pp. 149–66.

Dvořák, Jiří. On the Main Theoretical Foundations of the Improvement in the Management System of the Czechoslovak Economy. *Czech. Econ. Pap.*, 1983, (21), pp. 7–17. **[G: Czechoslovakia]**

Ellman, Michael. Changing Views on Central Economic Planning: 1958–1983. *ACES Bull. (See Comp. Econ. Stud. after 8/85),* Spring 1983, *25*(1), pp. 11–34. **[G: U.S.S.R.]**

Ericson, Richard E. A Difficulty with the "Command" Allocation Mechanism. *J. Econ. Theory,* October 1983, *31*(1), pp. 1–26.

Faluvégi, Lajos. Actual Concerns and Responsibility of the Hungarian Planners. *Acta Oecon.*, 1983, *30*(3–4), pp. 285–90. **[G: Hungary]**

Fel'zenbaum, V.; Efimova, E. and Farbirovich, V. The Effectiveness of Scientific and Technical Programs. *Prob. Econ.*, June 1983, *26*(2), pp. 41–60. **[G: U.S.S.R.]**

Ferge, Zsuzsa. Cooperation and Conflict between Researchers and Planners in Social Policy. *Acta Oecon.*, 1983, *30*(3–4), pp. 425–32. **[G: Hungary]**

Feuchtwang, Stephan and Hussain, Athar. The Chinese Economic Reforms: Introduction. **In** *Feuchtwang, S. and Hussain, A., eds.*, 1983, pp. 1–50. **[G: China]**

Focşăneanu, Gr. and Stroe, R. Cybernetic Modelling of Intercorrelations in Territorial Selfmanagement. *Econ. Computat. Cybern. Stud. Res.*, 1983, *18*(3), pp. 47–61. **[G: Romania]**

Gács, János. Planning and Adjustment Policy Changes in the Development of the Building Materials Industry. *Eastern Europ. Econ.*, Spring–Summer 1983, *21*(3–4), pp. 105–24. **[G: Hungary]**

Gavrilov, R. Rates, Factors, and New Indicators of the Growth of Labor Productivity. *Prob. Econ.*, March 1983, *25*(11), pp. 3–18. **[G: U.S.S.R.]**

Ghosh, Dipak. Planning for Employment in a Developing Economy. *Acta Oecon.*, 1983, *31*(3–4), pp. 287–96. **[G: LDCs]**

Goodwin, R. M. Economic Growth Planning. **In** *Goodwin, R. M.*, 1983, *1956,* pp. 121–29.

Granick, David. The Ministry and the Ratchet: Response to Keren. *J. Compar. Econ.*, December 1983, *7*(4), pp. 432–43. **[G: E. Germany; U.S.S.R.]**

Grieger, Ignác, et al. Plan-Based Management and Channeling of Social Development. *Czech. Econ. Digest.*, June 1983, (4), pp. 69–88. **[G: Czechoslovakia]**

Harberger, Arnold C. The Cost-Benefit Approach to Development Economics. *World Devel.*, October 1983, *11*(10), pp. 863–73. **[G: LDCs]**

Hinchliffe, Keith and Allan, Bill. Public Expenditure Planning in Papua New Guinea: An Evaluation of Innovation. *World Devel.*, November 1983, *11*(11), pp. 957–69. **[G: Papua New Guinea]**

Hussain, Athar. Economic Reforms in Eastern Europe and Their Relevance to China. **In** *Feuchtwang, S. and Hussain, A., eds.*, 1983, pp. 91–120. **[G: China; E. Europe]**

Hüttl, Antónia; Losonczy, I. and Örszigety, G. The Financial Regulator Model. *Matekon,* Summer 1983, *19*(4), pp. 3–20. **[G: Hungary]**

Iasin, E. G. Distributional Relations in the Structure of the Economic Mechanism. *Matekon,* Winter 1983–84, *20*(2), pp. 24–54.

Ishikawa, Shigeru. China's Economic System Reform: Underlying Factors and Prospects. *World Devel.*, August 1983, *11*(8), pp. 647–58. **[G: China; E. Europe]**

Kádár, Béla. World Economic Situation of the 1980s and Conclusions on the Development of the Hungarian Economy. *Acta Oecon.*, 1983, *30*(3–4), pp. 291–312. **[G: Hungary; OECD; CMEA]**

Kemp, D. A. The National Economic Summit: Authority, Persuasion and Exchange. *Econ. Rec.*, September 1983, *59*(166), pp. 209–19. **[G: Australia]**

Keren, Michael. The Ministry and the Ratchet: A Rejoinder to Granick. *J. Compar. Econ.*, December 1983, *7*(4), pp. 444–48. **[G: E. Germany; U.S.S.R.]**

Khachaturov, Tigran S. Once Again on the Effectiveness of Capital Investments. *Prob. Econ.*, November 1983, *26*(7), pp. 3–23. **[G: U.S.S.R.]**

King, Richard A. Relation to Global Modeling to Development Planning. *Amer. J. Agr. Econ.*, May 1983, *65*(2), pp. 438–44.

Koriagin, A. Socialist Reproduction and the Comparison of Labor Inputs. *Prob. Econ.*, July 1983, *26*(3), pp. 53–71. **[G: U.S.S.R.]**

Kotov, V. Planning Prices, Proportions, and the Effectiveness of Production. *Prob. Econ.*, December 1983, *26*(8), pp. 3–17. **[G: U.S.S.R.]**

Lardy, Nicholas R. and Lieberthal, Kenneth. Chen Yun's Strategy for China's Development: A Non-Maoist Alternative: Introduction. **In** *Ch'en, Y.*, 1983, pp. xi–xliii. **[G: China]**

Lerner, Abba P. Planning and Freedom. **In** *Lerner, A. P.*, 1983, *1945*, pp. 595–606.

Lewis, W. Arthur. Aspects of Economic Development. **In** *Dalton, G., ed.*, 1983, *1969*, pp. 247–310. **[G: LDCs]**

Liu, Guoguang. Some Issues Concerning the National Economic Overall Balance. *Chinese Econ. Stud.*, Winter 1982/83, *16*(2), pp. 85–106. **[G: China]**

McFarlane, Bruce. Political Economy of Class Struggle and Economic Growth in China, 1950–1982. *World Devel.*, August 1983, *11*(8), pp. 659–72. **[G: China]**

Nielsen, Richard P. Should a Country Move toward International Strategic Market Planning? *Calif. Manage. Rev.*, January 1983, *25*(2), pp. 34–44. **[G: U.S.]**

Nolan, Peter. 'The New Course in China': Summing-Up Speeches at Oxford Conference, Contemporary China Centre, September 1982. *World Devel.*, August 1983, *11*(8), pp. 769–70. **[G: China]**

Opie, Roger. Economic Planning and Growth. **In** *Feinstein, C., ed.*, 1983, *1972*, pp. 147–68. **[G: U.K.]**

Paavonen, Tapani. Reformist Programmes in the Planning for Post-War Economic Policy during World War II. *Scand. Econ. Hist. Rev.*, 1983, *31*(3), pp. 178–200. **[G: OECD]**

Petrakov, N. Ia. On Reflecting Relative Planned Inputs in the Price System. *Matekon*, Fall 1983, *20*(1), pp. 3–28. **[G: U.S.S.R.]**

Roca, Sergio. Economic Policy and Institutional Change in Socialist Cuba. *J. Econ. Issues*, June 1983, *17*(2), pp. 405–13. **[G: Cuba]**

Sen, Chandra. A New Approach for Multiobjective Rural Development Planning. *Indian Econ. J.*, April-June 1983, *30*(4), pp. 91–96. **[G: India]**

Solow, Robert M. Leif Johansen (1930–1982): A Memorial. *Scand. J. Econ.*, 1983, *85*(4), pp. 445–59.

Sturgeon, James I. Micro–Macro Literature and the Implications of Centralized Private Sector Planning. *J. Econ. Issues*, December 1983, *17*(4), pp. 985–1009. **[G: U.S.]**

Tardos, Márton. Enterprise Supply and the Market. *Eastern Europ. Econ.*, Spring–Summer 1983, *21*(3–4), pp. 8–25. **[G: Hungary]**

Tikidzhiev, R. Balance in the Reproduction of Fixed Capital and Labor Resources. *Prob. Econ.*, March 1983, *25*(11), pp. 19–35. **[G: U.S.S.R.]**

Vietorisz, Thomas. Planning and Political Economy. *Soc. Res.*, Summer 1983, *50*(2), pp. 469–84. **[G: Mexico; Greece]**

Vissi, Ferenc. Major Questions of the Improvement of Economic Control and Management in Hungary in the Mid-Eighties. *Acta Oecon.*, 1983, *30*(3–4), pp. 325–39. **[G: Hungary]**

Watts, Nita. Inflation in the USSR and Eastern Europe. **In** *[Saunders, C. T.]*, 1983, pp. 127–55. **[G: E. Europe; U.S.S.R.]**

Wiedemann, Paul. Policy Modeling, Planning, and Flexibility. *Jahr. Nationalökon. Statist.*, March 1983, *198*(2), pp. 161–72.

Wilhelm, J. From the Achieved Level: A Microeconomic Analysis. *ACES Bull. (See Comp. Econ. Stud. after 8/85)*, Spring 1983, *25*(1), pp. 75–88. **[G: U.S.S.R.]**

Xue, Muqiao. Readjust the National Economy and Strike an Overall Balance. *Chinese Econ. Stud.*, Winter 1982/83, *16*(2), pp. 67–84. **[G: China]**

Zalai, Ernö. A Nonlinear Multisectoral Model for Hungary: General Equilibrium versus Optimal Planning Approaches. **In** *Kelley, A. C.; Sanderson, W. C. and Williamson, J. G., eds.*, 1983, pp. 185–222. **[G: Hungary]**

Zalai, Ernö. Adaptability of Nonlinear Equilibrium Models to Central Planning. *Acta Oecon.*, 1983, *30*(3–4), pp. 433–45.

Zhou, Shulian. Seriously Study the Strategy of Our Economic Development from a Historical Viewpoint. *Chinese Econ. Stud.*, Fall 1983, *17*(1), pp. 88–95. **[G: China]**

1132 Economic Planning Theory

Anandalingam, G. Planning Studies with an Optimal Control Multisectoral Dynamic Economic Model: The Case of Sri Lanka. *J. Policy Modeling*, June 1983, *5*(2), pp. 179–205. **[G: Sri Lanka]**

Anandalingam, G. Project Impact Analysis as an Optimal Control Problem. *J. Econ. Dynam. Control*, November 1983, *6*(3), pp. 207–37. **[G: Sri Lanka]**

Arrow, Kenneth J. Team Theory and Decentralized Resource Allocation: An Example. **In** *[Erlich, A.]*, 1983, pp. 63–76.

Batten, David F. International Conflict Management via Adaptive Learning and Multistage Compromises. *Conflict Manage. Peace Sci.*, Fall 1983, *7*(1), pp. 1–24.

Berliner, Joseph S. Planning and Management. **In** *Bergson, A. and Levine, H. S., eds.*, 1983, pp. 350–90. **[G: U.S.S.R.]**

Bos, Henk C. Some Simple Thoughts on Model Building for Developing Countries. *Pakistan*

Devel. Rev., Summer 1983, *22*(2), pp. 63–71.

Brabec, František. Method for the Transition from Retrospective Analyses of the National Economy to Concepts of Future Development. *Czech. Econ. Pap.*, 1983, (21), pp. 19–29.

Brodbeck, Karl-Heinz. Zins und technischer Wandel in Planungssystemen. Ein Vergleich neo-österreichischer Modelle mit der Arbeitswertlehre. (Interest and Technical Change in a Planned Economy: A Comparison between Neo-Austrian Capital Theory and the Labour Theory of Value. With English summary.) *Z. Wirtschaft. Sozialwissen.*, 1983, *103*(1), pp. 27–41.

Champsaur, Paul and Rochet, Jean-Charles. On Planning Procedures Which Are Locally Strategy Proof. *J. Econ. Theory*, August 1983, *30*(2), pp. 353–69.

Chen, Fu-Sen and Cheung, Tow. On Some Problems of Modelling Chinese Economic Growth. **In** *Youngson, A. J., ed.*, 1983, pp. 226–81. **[G: China]**

Cherevan', V. Coordinating the Reproduction of Workplaces with Labor Resources. *Prob. Econ.*, May 1983, *26*(1), pp. 38–56. **[G: U.S.S.R.]**

Cornet, Bernard. Neutrality of Planning Procedures. *J. Math. Econ.*, April 1983, *11*(2), pp. 141–60.

Cremer, Jacques. The Discrete Heal Algorithm with Intermediate Goods. *Rev. Econ. Stud.*, April 1983, *50*(2), pp. 383–91.

Ezhov, A. Improving the Mechanism of Planned Price Control. *Prob. Econ.*, May 1983, *26*(1), pp. 20–37. **[G: U.S.S.R.]**

Faludi, Andreas. Critical Rationalism and Planning Methodology. *Urban Stud.*, August 1983, *20*(3), pp. 265–78.

Fedorenko, N. and L'vov, D. Economic Strategy and Scientific and Technical Progress. *Prob. Econ.*, April 1983, *25*(12), pp. 30–50. **[G: U.S.S.R.]**

Feltenstein, Andrew. The Allocation of Badly Needed Goods to Low-Income Consumers: A System of Central Planning without Redistributive Taxation. *J. Compar. Econ.*, March 1983, *7*(1), pp. 52–70.

Fölscher, G. C. K. A Note on the Social Discount Rate—(SDR). *J. Stud. Econ. Econometrics*, July 1983, (16), pp. 50–62.

Groves, Theodore. The Usefulness of Demand Forecasts for Team Resource Allocation in a Dynamic Environment. *Rev. Econ. Stud.*, July 1983, *50*(3), pp. 555–71.

Hare, Paul. China's System of Industrial Economic Planning. **In** *Feuchtwang, S. and Hussain, A., eds.*, 1983, pp. 185–223. **[G: China]**

Hickerson, Steven R. Planning for Institutional Change in a Complex Environment: An Approach and an Application. *J. Econ. Issues*, September 1983, *17*(3), pp. 631–65.

Killick, Tony. The Possibilities of Development Planning. **In** *Todaro, M. P., ed.*, 1983, *1976*, pp. 351–69.

Köszegi, László. Planning the Production Sphere in Hungary under the New Conditions. *Acta Oecon.*, 1983, *30*(3–4), pp. 413–24. **[G: Hungary]**

Kotouč, Václav. Coordination of National Economic Plans of the CMEA Countries. *Czech. Econ. Digest.*, March 1983, (2), pp. 43–60. **[G: CMEA]**

Kulagin, G. On Ways to Intensify (From an Economist's Notebook). *Prob. Econ.*, December 1983, *26*(8), pp. 45–58. **[G: U.S.S.R.]**

Livshits, V. N. and Tarakanova, I. A. On the Effect of Changes in Resource Costs on Branch Development Strategy. *Matekon*, Summer 1983, *19*(4), pp. 79–95.

Maier, V.; Rutgaizer, V. and Chernikov, D. The Substantiation of Long-Range Plans for the Country's Economic and Social Development. *Prob. Econ.*, December 1983, *26*(8), pp. 59–74. **[G: U.S.S.R.]**

Mihailov, Boris. Modeling Alternative Socioeconomic Mechanisms. **In** *Kelley, A. C.; Sanderson, W. C. and Williamson, J. G., eds.*, 1983, pp. 141–65.

Nagovitsin, A. The Management Structure of a Production Association. *Prob. Econ.*, May 1983, *26*(1), pp. 57–73. **[G: U.S.S.R.]**

O'Brien, Mike J. Optimal Macroeconomic Policy with Constrained Instruments. *J. Econ. Dynam. Control*, September 1983, *6*(1/2), pp. 193–200.

Orlov, A. V. Assigning Top Priority to Demand and Coordination. *Prob. Econ.*, January 1983, *25*(9), pp. 36–51. **[G: U.S.S.R.]**

Potáč, Svatopluk. On the State Plan of Economic and Social Development. *Czech. Econ. Digest.*, February 1983, (1), pp. 3–46. **[G: Czechoslovakia]**

Reade, Eric. If Planning Is Anything, Maybe It Can Be Identified. *Urban Stud.*, May 1983, *20*(2), pp. 159–71.

Soós, Károly Attila. The Problem of Time Lags in the Short-Term Control of Macroeconomic Processes. *Acta Oecon.*, 1983, *30*(3–4), pp. 369–79. **[G: Hungary]**

Wang, Da'an. A Comprehensive Balance Should Mean Overall Balance in the Process of Social Reproduction. *Chinese Econ. Stud.*, Winter 1982/83, *16*(2), pp. 51–66. **[G: China]**

Wohltmann, Hans-Werner and Krömer, W. A Note on Buiter's Sufficient Condition for Perfect Output Controllability of a Rational Expectations Model. *J. Econ. Dynam. Control*, September 1983, *6*(1/2), pp. 201–05.

Zonnoor, S. H. Maximization over a Set of Competitive Equilibria: A Planning Application. *J. Econ. Dynam. Control*, December 1983, *6*(4), pp. 351–69. **[G: Iran]**

Zou, Siyi. The Problem of Export Strategy. *Chinese Econ. Stud.*, Spring 1983, *16*(3), pp. 10–23. **[G: China]**

1136 Economic Planning Policy

Ansari, M. M. Variations in Plan Expenditure and Physical Achievement among the Indian States: An Empirical Analysis. *Margin*, April 1983, *15*(3), pp. 49–58. **[G: India]**

Asselain, Jean-Charles. La répartition des revenus en Hongrie: Deuxième partie: les incertitudes des années 70. (With English summary.) *Écon. Soc.*, January 1983, *17*(1), pp. 43–88. **[G: Hungary]**

Augustinovics, Mária. Macroeconomic Models for the Sixth Five-Year Plan. *Matekon*, Spring 1983, *19*(3), pp. 3–17. **[G: Hungary]**

Balassa, Bela. Reforming the New Economic Mechanism in Hungary. *J. Compar. Econ.*, September 1983, *7*(3), pp. 253–76. **[G: Hungary]**

Berend, Iván T. The Renewal Cycle of Fixed Assets under the Conditions of the 1980s in Hungary. *Acta Oecon.*, 1983, *30*(3–4), pp. 401–11. **[G: Hungary]**

Blazyca, G. Polish Economic Management 1970–81. **In** *[Saunders, C. T.]*, 1983, pp. 157–73. **[G: Poland]**

Bond, Daniel L. and Green, Donald W. Prospects for Soviet Agriculture in the Eleventh Five-year Plan: Econometric Analysis and Projections. **In** *Stuart, R. C., ed.*, 1983, pp. 296–319. **[G: U.S.S.R.]**

Brada, Josef C.; King, Arthur E. and Schlagenhauf, Don E. The Benefits of Long-Term Developmental Planning: An Estimate. *World Devel.*, November 1983, *11*(11), pp. 971–79. **[G: Czechoslovakia]**

Chen, Yun. Talk at a Meeting of the Central Finance and Economics Small Group. **In** *Ch'en, Y.*, 1983, *1962*, pp. 202–11. **[G: China]**

Cima, Ján. Step by Step along the Path of Savings. *Czech. Econ. Digest.*, 1983, (8), pp. 69–81. **[G: Czechoslovakia]**

Croll, Elisabeth J. Production versus Reproduction: A Threat to China's Developing Strategy. *World Devel.*, June 1983, *11*(6), pp. 467–81. **[G: China]**

Csikós-Nagy, Béla. Hungary's Adjustment to the New World Market Relations. *Acta Oecon.*, 1983, *30*(1), pp. 77–88. **[G: Hungary]**

Eisner, Robert. Which Way for France? *Challenge*, July/August 1983, *26*(3), pp. 34–41. **[G: France]**

Estrin, Saul and Holmes, Peter. How Far Is Mitterrand from Barre? *Challenge*, November/December 1983, *26*(5), pp. 46–50. **[G: France]**

Ffrench-Davis, Ricardo. The Monetarist Experiment in Chile: A Critical Survey. *World Devel.*, November 1983, *11*(11), pp. 905–26. **[G: Chile]**

Gasparetto, Marialuisa Manfredini. Turchia—l'economia reale e la programmazione. (Turkey: Real Economy and Planning. With English summary.) *Rivista Int. Sci. Econ. Com.*, April-May 1983, *30*(4–5), pp. 452–73. **[G: Turkey]**

Gorlin, Alice C. and Doane, David P. Plan Fulfillment and Growth in Soviet Ministries. *J. Compar. Econ.*, December 1983, *7*(4), pp. 415–31. **[G: U.S.S.R.]**

Greffe, Xaviere. Les entreprises publiques dans la politique de l'État. (Public Enterprises in National Public Policies. With English summary.) *Revue Écon.*, May 1983, *34*(3), pp. 496–535. **[G: France]**

Hare, Paul. China's System of Industrial Economic Planning. **In** *Feuchtwang, S. and Hussain, A., eds.*, 1983, pp. 185–223. **[G: China]**

Harrison, Mark. Why Was NEP Abandoned? **In** *Stuart, R. C., ed.*, 1983, pp. 63–78. **[G: U.S.S.R.]**

Hunter, Holland. The New Tasks of Soviet Planning in the Thirties. **In** *[Erlich, A.]*, 1983, pp. 173–97. **[G: U.S.S.R.]**

Jakeš, Miloš. Report of the Presidium of the Central Committee of the Communist Party of Czechoslovakia on Speeding Up the Practical Application of the Results of Scientific and Technical Research. *Czech. Econ. Digest.*, September 1983, (6), pp. 3–57. **[G: Czechoslovakia]**

Korovkin, V. Scientific and Technical Programs in Commercial Trade. *Prob. Econ.*, October 1983, *26*(6), pp. 55–70. **[G: U.S.S.R.]**

Köszegi, László. Planning the Production Sphere in Hungary under the New Conditions. *Acta Oecon.*, 1983, *30*(3–4), pp. 413–24. **[G: Hungary]**

Lisk, Franklyn. Conventional Development Strategies and Basic-Needs Fulfilment. **In** *Todaro, M. P., ed.*, 1983, *1977*, pp. 41–54.

Lockett, Martin. Enterprise Management—Moves towards Democracy? **In** *Feuchtwang, S. and Hussain, A., eds.*, 1983, pp. 224–56. **[G: China]**

Luo, Gengmo. An Analysis of the Development of China's Planned Economy and the Tortuous Course It Has Trudged: A Few Issues Concerning Socialist Planned Economy That Need to Be Clarified, Part 2. *Chinese Econ. Stud.*, Winter 1982/83, *16*(2), pp. 29–50. **[G: China]**

Markish, Yuri and Malish, Anton F. The Soviet Food Program: Prospects for the 1980s. *ACES Bull. (See Comp. Econ. Stud. after 8/85)*, Spring 1983, *25*(1), pp. 47–65. **[G: U.S.S.R.]**

Perkins, F. C. Technology Choice, Industrialisation and Development Experiences in Tanzania. *J. Devel. Stud.*, January 1983, *19*(2), pp. 213–43. **[G: Tanzania]**

Potáč, Svatopluk. The Year of a Turn Towards a More Dynamic Rate of Economic and Social Development. *Czech. Econ. Digest.*, May 1983, (3), pp. 3–18. **[G: Czechoslovakia]**

Rogovskii, N. The Effectiveness of Labor under the Eleventh Five-Year Plan. *Prob. Econ.*, April 1983, *25*(12), pp. 51–66. **[G: U.S.S.R.]**

Sabolčík, Michal. The Plan, Prices and Mobilization of Reserves in Czechoslovak Economy. *Czech. Econ. Digest.*, August 1983, (5), pp. 36–53. **[G: Czechoslovakia]**

Şenses, Fikret. Beşinci Beş Yillik Kalkinma Plani (1985–89). (Turkey's Fifth Five-Year Plan, 1985-89. *METU*, 1983, *10*(4), pp. 387–407. **[G: Turkey]**

Shiriaev, P. Cooperation in Investments: A Factor in the Intensification of Production in CMEA Member Nations. *Prob. Econ.*, May 1983, *26*(1), pp. 74–89.

Smirnov, V. The Plan and the Increase in the Consumer's Influence on Production. *Prob. Econ.*, July 1983, *26*(3), pp. 22–38. **[G: U.S.S.R.]**

Sorokin, G. Patterns of Socialist Intensification. *Prob. Econ.*, July 1983, *26*(3), pp. 3–21. **[G: U.S.S.R.]**

Stefani, Giorgio. Special Economic Zones and Economic Policy in China. *Ann. Pub. Co-op. Econ.*, July–September 1983, *54*(3), pp. 289–312. **[G: China]**

Štrougal, Lubomír. Statement on the Implementation of the Czechoslovakian Program Statement Delivered by Premier Lubomír Štrougal on March 16, 1983. *Czech. Econ. Digest.*, June 1983, (4), pp. 3–19. **[G: Czechoslovakia]**

Štrougal, Lubomír. The Pressing Tasks of Further Economic Development. *Czech. Econ. Digest.*, 1983, (8), pp. 3–52. **[G: Czechoslovakia]**

Tilak, Jandhyala B. G. On Allocating Plan Resources for Education in India. *Margin*, October 1983, *16*(1), pp. 92–102. **[G: India]**

Val'tukh, K. K. The Investment Complex and the Intensification of Production. *Prob. Econ.*, April 1983, *25*(12), pp. 3–29. [G: U.S.S.R.]

Wangwe, Samuel M. Industrialization and Resource Allocation in a Developing Country: The Case of Recent Experiences in Tanzania. *World Devel.*, June 1983, *11*(6), pp. 483–92. [G: Tanzania]

Weiss, Dieter. Überlegungen zur jordanischen Entwicklungsplanung. (Reflections on Development Planning in Jordan. With English summary.) *Konjunkturpolitik*, 1983, *29*(1), pp. 33–66. [G: Jordan]

Zaleski, Eugène. The Collectivization Drive and Agricultural Planning in the Soviet Union. **In** *Stuart, R. C., ed.*, 1983, pp. 79–106. [G: U.S.S.R.]

114 Economics of War, Defense, and Disarmament

1140 Economics of War, Defense, and Disarmament

Albrecht, Ulrich. Military R&D Communities. *Int. Soc. Sci. J.*, 1983, *35*(1), pp. 7–23. [G: Selected MDCs]

Anton, Thomas J. The Regional Distribution of Federal Expenditures, 1971–1980. *Nat. Tax J.*, December 1983, *36*(4), pp. 429–42. [G: U.S.]

Ash, J. Colin K.; Udis, Bernard and McNown, Robert F. Enlistments in the All-Volunteer Force: A Military Personnel Supply Model and Its Forecasts. *Amer. Econ. Rev.*, March 1983, *73*(1), pp. 145–55. [G: U.S.]

Ayres, Ron. Arms Production as a Form of Import-Substituting Industrialization: The Turkish Case. *World Devel.*, September 1983, *11*(9), pp. 813–23. [G: Turkey]

Ball, Nicole. Defense and Development: A Critique of the Benoit Study. *Econ. Develop. Cult. Change*, April 1983, *31*(3), pp. 507–24.

Ball, Nicole. Military Expenditure and Socio-Economic Development. *Int. Soc. Sci. J.*, 1983, *35*(1), pp. 81–97. [G: LDCs]

Ball, Nicole. The Structure of the Defense Industry: Appendix 1: The United Kingdom. **In** *Ball, N. and Leitenberg, M., eds.*, 1983, pp. 344–60. [G: U.K.]

Bell, Carolyn Shaw. On DeGrasse and Military Spending [Military Spending and Jobs]. *Challenge*, Sept.–Oct. 1983, *26*(4), pp. 49–51. [G: U.S.]

Berger, Mark C. and Hirsch, Barry T. The Civilian Earnings Experience of Vietnam-Era Veterans. *J. Human Res.*, Fall 1983, *18*(4), pp. 455–79. [G: U.S.]

Bergson, Abram. On the Measurement of Soviet Real Defense Outlays. **In** *[Erlich, A.]*, 1983, pp. 77–90. [G: U.S.S.R.]

Black, Jeremy. Grain Exports and Neutrality. A Speculative Note on British Neutrality in the War of the Polish Succession. *J. Europ. Econ. Hist.*, Winter 1983, *12*(3), pp. 593–600. [G: U.K.; Poland]

Blackaby, Frank. Introduction: The Military Sector and the Economy. **In** *Ball, N. and Leitenberg, M., eds.*, 1983, pp. 6–20.

Borins, Sandford F. World War II Crown Corporations: Their Functions and Their Fate. **In** *Prichard, J. R. S., ed.*, 1983, pp. 447–75. [G: Canada]

Brzoska, Michael. The Structure of the Defense Industry: The Federal Republic of Germany. **In** *Ball, N. and Leitenberg, M., eds.*, 1983, pp. 111–39. [G: W. Germany]

Dale, Charles and Gilroy, Curtis. The Effects of the Business Cycle on the Size and Composition of the U.S. Army. *Atlantic Econ. J.*, March 1983, *11*(1), pp. 42–53. [G: U.S.]

Deese, David A. The Vulnerability of Modern Nations: Economic Diplomacy in East–West Relations. **In** *Nincic, M. and Wallensteen, P., eds.*, 1983, pp. 155–81. [G: OECD; CMEA]

Deger, Saadet and Sen, Somnath. Military Expenditure, Spin-Off and Economic Development. *J. Devel. Econ.*, Aug.–Oct. 1983, *13*(1–2), pp. 67–83. [G: LDCs]

DeGrasse, Robert W., Jr. Helping Those Who Need It Least [Military Spending and Jobs]. *Challenge*, Sept.–Oct. 1983, *26*(4), pp. 51–52. [G: U.S.]

DeGrasse, Robert W., Jr. Military Spending and Jobs. *Challenge*, July/August 1983, *26*(3), pp. 4–15. [G: U.S.]

DeMayo, Peter. Bidding on New Ship Construction. **In** *Engelbrecht-Wiggans, R.; Shubik, M. and Stark, R. M., eds.*, 1983, pp. 371–87. [G: U.S.]

Deshingkar, Giri. Military Technology and the Quest for Self-Reliance: India and China. *Int. Soc. Sci. J.*, 1983, *35*(1), pp. 99–123. [G: China; India]

Domke, William K.; Eichenberg, Richard C. and Kelleher, Catherine M. The Illusion of Choice: Defense and Welfare in Advanced Industrial Democracies, 1948–1978. *Amer. Polit. Sci. Rev.*, March 1983, *77*(1), pp. 19–35. [G: U.S.; U.K.; W. Germany; France]

Dror, Yehezkel. The Politics of Defense Allocations in Western Europe. *Public Budg. Finance*, Spring 1983, *3*(1), pp. 3–22. [G: W. Europe]

Duchin, Faye. Economic Consequences of Military Spending. *J. Econ. Issues*, June 1983, *17*(2), pp. 543–53. [G: U.S.]

Faramazjan, Rachik. The Role of the Scientific Community in the Conversion of the Arms Industry. *Int. Soc. Sci. J.*, 1983, *35*(1), pp. 185–99.

Galtung, Johan. On the Effects of International Economic Sanctions. **In** *Nincic, M. and Wallensteen, P., eds.*, 1983, pp. 17–60. [G: Rhodesia]

Garrison, Charles B. and Mayhew, Anne. The Alleged Vietnam War Origins of the Current Inflation: A Comment. *J. Econ. Issues*, March 1983, *17*(1), pp. 175–86. [G: U.S.]

Gordon, David F. The Politics of International Sanctions: A Case Study of South Africa. **In** *Nincic, M. and Wallensteen, P., eds.*, 1983, pp. 183–210. [G: S. Africa]

Gottheil, Fred M. Establishing the Preconditions to Long-run Development: Egypt after the Treaty. **In** *Starr, J. R., ed.*, 1983, pp. 35–45. [G: Egypt]

Green, Jerrold D. Strategies for Evading Economic Sanctions. **In** *Nincic, M. and Wallensteen, P., eds.*, 1983, pp. 61–85. [G: U.S.; Rhodesia; Cuba]

Hammon, Colin P. and Graham, David R. A Method for Estimating the Cost of Changes for Navy Shipbuilding Programs. **In** *Engelbrecht-Wiggans, R.; Shubik, M. and Stark, R. M., eds.*, 1983, pp. 437–71. [G: U.S.]

Hartley, Keith. EC Defence Policy. **In** *El-Agraa, A. M., ed.*, 1983, pp. 299–316. **[G: EEC; U.K.]**

Hartley, Keith and Lynk, Edward L. Budget Cuts and Public Sector Employment: The Case of Defence. *Appl. Econ.*, August 1983, *15*(4), pp. 531–40. **[G: U.K.]**

Henze, Arno. Nutzen-kosten-theoretische Überlegungen zur Sicherstellung der Versorgung für Krisenzeiten. (Theoretical Cost-Benefit-Considerations on Supply Security for Times of Crisis. With English summary.) *Z. Wirtschaft. Sozialwissen.*, 1983, *103*(2), pp. 129–42.

Holloway, David. The Structure of the Defense Industry: The Soviet Union. **In** *Ball, N. and Leitenberg, M., eds.*, 1983, pp. 50–80. **[G: U.S.S.R.]**

Holmström, Per and Olsson, Ulf. The Structure of the Defense Industry: Sweden. **In** *Ball, N. and Leitenberg, M., eds.*, 1983, pp. 140–80. **[G: Sweden]**

Hughes Hallett, A. J. and Brandsma, Andries S. How Effective Could Sanctions against the Soviet Union Be? *Weltwirtsch. Arch.*, 1983, *119*(3), pp. 498–522. **[G: U.S.S.R.]**

Jammes, Sydney. The Structure of the Defense Industry: China. **In** *Ball, N. and Leitenberg, M., eds.*, 1983, pp. 257–77. **[G: China]**

Kaldor, Mary. Military R&D: Cause or Consequence of the Arms Race? *Int. Soc. Sci. J.*, 1983, *35*(1), pp. 25–45. **[G: U.S.; U.S.S.R.; Japan; EEC]**

Kastler, Alfred. Burdens of Militarization: Introduction. *Int. Soc. Sci. J.*, 1983, *35*(1), pp. 3–5.

Katz, Claudio J.; Mahler, Vincent A. and Franz, Michael G. The Impact of Taxes on Growth and Distribution in Developed Capitalist Countries: A Cross-National Study. *Amer. Polit. Sci. Rev.*, December 1983, *77*(4), pp. 871–86. **[G: Selected OECD]**

Kaufmann, William W. Nonnuclear Deterrence. **In** *Steinbruner, J. D. and Sigal, L. V., eds.*, 1983, pp. 43–90. **[G: NATO]**

Kaufmann, William W. The Defense Budget. **In** *Pechman, J. A., ed.*, 1983, pp. 39–79. **[G: U.S.]**

Kennedy, Gavin. How Much is Enough? Defence in Scotland. **In** *Ingham, K. P. D. and Love, J., eds.*, 1983, pp. 117–26. **[G: U.K.]**

Kick, Edward L. and Conaty, Joseph. African Economic Development: The Effects of East, West, and Chinese Penetration. **In** *Bergesen, A., ed.*, 1983, pp. 263–86. **[G: Africa]**

Kolodziej, Edward A. The Structure of the Defense Industry: France. **In** *Ball, N. and Leitenberg, M., eds.*, 1983, pp. 81–110. **[G: France]**

Lee, Sang M.; Brisch, Hans and Snyder, Charles A. Demilitarized Zone Planning: A Multiobjective Approach. *Math. Soc. Sci.*, August 1983, *5*(1), pp. 33–46.

Leitenberg, Milton. The Structure of the Defense Industry: Appendix 2: Use of Raw Materials for Military Purposes. **In** *Ball, N. and Leitenberg, M., eds.*, 1983, pp. 361–62.

Leitenberg, Milton and Ball, Nicole. The Structure of the Defense Industry: Preface. **In** *Ball, N. and Leitenberg, M., eds.*, 1983, pp. 1–5.

Lerner, Abba P. How to Keep the Peace . . . An Analysis and a Proposal. **In** *Lerner, A. P.*, 1983, *1946*, pp. 657–60.

Lerner, Abba P. Nuclear Symmetry as a Framework for Coexistence. **In** *Lerner, A. P.*, 1983, *1964*, pp. 671–84.

Lerner, Abba P. The President Addresses the World. **In** *Lerner, A. P.*, 1983, *1947*, pp. 661–69.

Lim, David. Another Look at Growth and Defense in Less Developed Countries. *Econ. Develop. Cult. Change*, January 1983, *31*(2), pp. 377–84. **[G: LDCs]**

Linz, Susan J. Measuring the Carryover Cost of WWII to the Soviet People: 1945–1953. *Exploration Econ. Hist.*, October 1983, *20*(4), pp. 375–86. **[G: U.S.S.R.]**

Maddock, Rodney and Penny, Janet. Economists at War: The Financial and Economic Committee 1939–44. *Australian Econ. Hist. Rev.*, March 1983, *23*(1), pp. 28–49. **[G: Australia]**

Majeski, Stephen J. Dynamic Properties of the U.S. Military Expenditure Decision-Making Process. *Conflict Manage. Peace Sci.*, Fall 1983, *7*(1), pp. 65–86.

Manser, Marilyn E. Deflation of Defense Purchases: Comment. **In** *Foss, M. F., ed.*, 1983, pp. 199–203. **[G: U.S.]**

McCormick, William. Military Transactions in the U.S. International Accounts, 1976–82. *Surv. Curr. Bus.*, May 1983, *63*(5), pp. 18–24. **[G: U.S.]**

Mergen, Bernard. The Government as Manager: Emergency Fleet Shipbuilding, 1917–1919. **In** *[Cochran, T. C.]*, 1983, pp. 49–80. **[G: U.S.]**

de Mesquita, Bruce Bueno. The Costs of War: A Rational Expectations Approach. *Amer. Polit. Sci. Rev.*, June 1983, *77*(2), pp. 347–57.

Mossavar-Rahmani, Bijan. Economic Implications for Iran and Iraq. **In** *Tahir-Kheli, S. and Ayubi, S., eds.*, 1983, pp. 51–64. **[G: Iran; Iraq]**

Munnell, Alicia H. Wars Are Expensive: Veterans and the Budget. *New Eng. Econ. Rev.*, March/April 1983, pp. 46–64. **[G: U.S.]**

Nabe, Oumar. Military Expenditures and Industrialization in Africa. *J. Econ. Issues*, June 1983, *17*(2), pp. 575–87. **[G: Africa]**

Nawaz, Shuja. Economic Impact of Defense Expenditures. *Finance Develop.*, March 1983, *20*(1), pp. 34–35. **[G: Global]**

Nincic, Miroslav and Wallensteen, Peter. Economic Coercion and Foreign Policy. **In** *Nincic, M. and Wallensteen, P., eds.*, 1983, pp. 1–15.

Nzimiro, Ikenna. Militarization in Nigeria: Its Economic and Social Consequences. *Int. Soc. Sci. J.*, 1983, *35*(1), pp. 125–39. **[G: Nigeria]**

Paarlberg, Robert L. Using Food Power: Opportunities, Appearances, and Damage Control. **In** *Nincic, M. and Wallensteen, P., eds.*, 1983, *1982*, pp. 131–53. **[G: U.S.]**

Phillips, Sheena. Cruise Missiles. **In** *Tsipis, K. and Phillips, S.*, 1983, pp. 148–71.

Phillips, Sheena. Laser Weapons. **In** *Tsipis, K. and Phillips, S.*, 1983, pp. 111–47.

Phillips, Sheena. Trends in U.S. Military R&D Funding. **In** *Tsipis, K. and Phillips, S.*, 1983, pp. 1–48. **[G: U.S.]**

Ponssard, Jean-Pierre. Military Procurement in France: Regulation and Incentive Contracts. **In** *Engelbrecht-Wiggans, R.; Shubik, M. and Stark, R. M., eds.*, 1983, pp. 499–545. **[G: France]**

Quester, Aline and Nakada, Michael. The Military's Monopsony Power. *Eastern Econ. J.*, October–December 1983, *9*(4), pp. 295–308. [G: U.S.]

Ramphal, Shridath S. North–South Cooperation: Why and How the South Must Persist. In *Gauhar, A., ed. (I)*, 1983, pp. 101–38. [G: LDCs; MDCs]

Ravenal, Earl C. The Economic Claims of National Security [U.S. Trade Policy and National Security]. *Cato J.*, Winter 1983/84, *3*(3), pp. 729–41. [G: U.S.]

Reppy, Judith. The Structure of the Defense Industry: The United States. In *Ball, N. and Leitenberg, M., eds.*, 1983, pp. 21–49. [G: U.S.]

Rossi, Sergio A. The Structure of the Defense Industry: Italy. In *Ball, N. and Leitenberg, M., eds.*, 1983, pp. 214–56. [G: Italy]

Sabolo, Yves. Disarmament and Employment: Background for a Research Programme. *Int. Lab. Rev.*, May–June 1983, *122*(3), pp. 263–77. [G: Selected MDCs; Selected LDCs]

Sachs, Abner and Ziemer, Richard C. Implicit Price Deflators for Military Construction. *Surv. Curr. Bus.*, November 1983, *63*(11), pp. 14–18. [G: U.S.]

Samuelson, William F. Competitive Bidding for Defense Contracts. In *Engelbrecht-Wiggans, R.; Shubik, M. and Stark, R. M., eds.*, 1983, pp. 389–419.

Šelešovský, Jan and Staníček, Jiří. To Ensure Security Is Also an Economic Task. *Czech. Econ. Digest.*, May 1983, (3), pp. 71–84.

Smith, Charles H. Evaluation of Competitive Alternatives for Weapon System Production. In *Engelbrecht-Wiggans, R.; Shubik, M. and Stark, R. M., eds.*, 1983, pp. 421–35.

Sovereign, Michael G. Application of the Conceptual Model for Setting Design-to-Cost Goals: The FFG-7. In *Engelbrecht-Wiggans, R.; Shubik, M. and Stark, R. M., eds.*, 1983, pp. 473–98. [G: U.S.]

Steinberg, Gerald. The Structure of the Defense Industry: Israel. In *Ball, N. and Leitenberg, M., eds.*, 1983, pp. 278–309. [G: Israel]

Sylvan, David J. Ideology and the Concept of Economic Security. In *Nincic, M. and Wallensteen, P., eds.*, 1983, pp. 211–41.

Thee, Marek. Swords into Ploughshares: The Quest for Peace and Human Development. *Int. Lab. Rev.*, Sept.–Oct. 1983, *122*(5), pp. 535–48. [G: W. Europe]

Thomas, Mark. Rearmament and Economic Recovery in the Late 1930s. *Econ. Hist. Rev., 2nd Ser.*, November 1983, *36*(4), pp. 552–79. [G: U.K.]

Thorsson, Inga. Guns and Butter: Can the World Have Both? *Int. Lab. Rev.*, July–August 1983, *122*(4), pp. 397–410. [G: Global]

Tiedtke, Stephen. The Structure of the Defense Industry: Czechoslovakia. In *Ball, N. and Leitenberg, M., eds.*, 1983, pp. 181–213. [G: Czechoslovakia]

Tsipis, Kosta. Fundamental Technologies with Extensive Military Applications. In *Tsipis, K. and Phillips, S.*, 1983, pp. 49–88.

Ullman, John E. The Arms Race and the Decline of U.S. Technology. *J. Econ. Issues*, June 1983, *17*(2), pp. 565–74. [G: U.S.]

Varas, Augusto and Bustamante, Fernando. The Effect of R&D on the Transfer of Military Technology to the Third World. *Int. Soc. Sci. J.*, 1983, *35*(1), pp. 141–62. [G: Selected MDCs; Selected LDCs]

Väyrynen, Raimo. Military R&D and Science Policy. *Int. Soc. Sci. J.*, 1983, *35*(1), pp. 61–79. [G: U.S.; U.S.S.R.; France]

Verner, Joel G. Budgetary Trade-Offs between Education and Defense in Latin America: A Research Note. *J. Devel. Areas*, October 1983, *18*(1), pp. 77–91. [G: Latin America]

Wagner, R. Harrison. The Theory of Games and the Problem of International Cooperation. *Amer. Polit. Sci. Rev.*, June 1983, *77*(2), pp. 330–46.

Walinsky, Louis J. Coherent Defense Strategy: The Case for Economic Denial. *Foreign Aff.*, Winter 1982/83, *61*(2), pp. 272–91.

Walker, John F. and Vatter, Harold G. Demonstrating the Undemonstrable: A Reply to Garrison and Mayhew [The Princess and the Pea; or, The Alleged Vietnam War Origins of the Current Inflation]. *J. Econ. Issues*, March 1983, *17*(1), pp. 186–96. [G: U.S.]

Wallensteen, Peter. Economic Sanctions: Ten Modern Cases and Three Important Lessons. In *Nincic, M. and Wallensteen, P., eds.*, 1983, pp. 87–129. [G: Selected Countries]

Wängborg, Manne. Some Problems of Measuring Military R&D. *Int. Soc. Sci. J.*, 1983, *35*(1), pp. 47–59. [G: Selected MDCs]

Watkins, John. Military Spending and the Contemporary American Crises: A Comment. *Econ. Forum*, Winter 1983-84, *14*(2), pp. 125–28. [G: U.S.]

Weidenbaum, Murray L. Let's Examine National Defense Spending. *Challenge*, January/February 1983, *25*(6), pp. 50–53. [G: U.S.]

Willett, Thomas D. and Jalalighajar, Mehrdad. U.S. Trade Policy and National Security. *Cato J.*, Winter 1983/84, *3*(3), pp. 717–27. [G: U.S.]

Wright, Claudia. Neutral or Neutralized? Iraq, Iran, and the Superpowers. In *Tahir-Kheli, S. and Ayubi, S., eds.*, 1983, pp. 172–92. [G: Iraq; Iran]

Wulf, Herbert. The Structure of the Defense Industry: Developing Countries. In *Ball, N. and Leitenberg, M., eds.*, 1983, pp. 310–43. [G: LDCs]

Ziemer, Richard C. and Galbraith, Karl D. Deflation of Defense Purchases. In *Foss, M. F., ed.*, 1983, pp. 147–99. [G: U.S.]

Zimmerman, William and Palmer, Glenn. Words and Deeds in Soviet Foreign Policy: The Case of Soviet Military Expenditures. *Amer. Polit. Sci. Rev.*, June 1983, *77*(2), pp. 358–67. [G: U.S.S.R.]

120 Country Studies

121 Economic Studies of Developing Countries

1210 General

Adelman, Irma and Hihn, Jairus M. The Political Economy of Investment in Human Capital. In *Streeten, P. and Maier, H., eds.*, 1983, pp. 117–46. [G: LDCs]

Almark, Barry and Alvarado, S. S. Dependent Development in the Third World in the Decade of Oil. *Rev. Radical Polit. Econ.*, Fall 1983, *15*(3), pp. 97–114. [G: LDCs]

Ball, Nicole. Defense and Development: A Critique of the Benoit Study. *Econ. Develop. Cult. Change*, April 1983, *31*(3), pp. 507–24.

Ball, Nicole. Military Expenditure and Socio-Economic Development. *Int. Soc. Sci. J.*, 1983, *35*(1), pp. 81–97. [G: LDCs]

Baneth, Jean. The Role of the World Bank as an International Institution: Comment on the Krueger Paper. *Carnegie-Rochester Conf. Ser. Public Policy*, Spring 1983, *18*, pp. 313–23.

Bird, Graham. Low Income Countries as a Special Case in the International Financial System: An Analysis of Some Proposals for Reform. *Econ. Notes*, 1983, (2), pp. 5–22. [G: Selected LDCs]

Chenery, Hollis B. Interaction between Theory and Observation in Development. *World Devel.*, October 1983, *11*(10), pp. 853–61.

Chenery, Hollis B. Poverty and Progress—Choices for the Developing World. **In** *Todaro, M. P., ed.*, 1983, *1980*, pp. 86–94.

Feder, Gershon. On Exports and Economic Growth. *J. Devel. Econ.*, February/April 1983, *12*(1/2), pp. 59–73.

Fieleke, Norman S. International Lending on Trial. *New Eng. Econ. Rev.*, May/June 1983, pp. 5–13. [G: U.S.; Non-OPEC; LDCs]

Ghosh, Ranen. Analytical Implications of Time Series Economic Variable Data: Re—Economic Development. *Econ. Aff.*, April–June 1983, *28*(2), pp. 664–74, 681. [G: Nigeria; LDCs]

Gow, David D. and VanSant, Jerry. Beyond the Rhetoric of Rural Development Participation: How Can It Be Done? *World Devel.*, May 1983, *11*(5), pp. 427–46. [G: Guatemala; Indonesia]

Hoffmann, Lutz. Impact of the Energy Crisis on the Third World and the Prospects for Adjustment. **In** *[Giersch, H.]*, 1983, pp. 302–24. [G: LDCs]

Kelley, Allen C. and Williamson, Jeffrey G. A Computable General Equilibrium Model of Third-World Urbanization and City Growth: Preliminary Comparative Statics. **In** *Kelley, A. C.; Sanderson, W. C. and Williamson, J. G., eds.*, 1983, pp. 3–41. [G: LDCs]

Krueger, Anne O. The Role of the World Bank as an International Institution. *Carnegie-Rochester Conf. Ser. Public Policy*, Spring 1983, *18*, pp. 281–311.

Lewis, W. Arthur. Richard T. Ely Lecture: A Review of Economic Development. **In** *Lewis, W. A.*, 1983, *1965*, pp. 653–68. [G: LDCs]

Lewis, W. Arthur. The Slowing Down of the Engine of Growth. **In** *Lewis, W. A.*, 1983, *1980*, pp. 283–92.

Love, James. Concentration, Diversification and Earnings Instability: Some Evidence on Developing Countries' Exports of Manufactures and Primary Products. *World Devel.*, September 1983, *11*(9), pp. 787–93. [G: Selected LDCs]

Meerman, Jacob. Minimizing the Burden of Recurrent Costs. *Finance Develop.*, December 1983, *20*(4), pp. 41–43. [G: Africa]

Onida, Fabrizio and Perasso, Giancarlo. Oil Export and Economic Development: OPEC Strategies and Opportunities for Western Economic Cooperation. *Rivista Int. Sci. Econ. Com.*, March 1983, *30*(3), pp. 293–303. [G: OPEC; OECD]

Peel, David A. On Inflation and Economic Growth. *Singapore Econ. Rev.*, April 1983, *28*(1), pp. 53–58. [G: LDCs]

Rice, Gerard; Corr, James and Fennell, Susan. Maintaining Financing for Adjustment and Development. *Finance Develop.*, December 1983, *20*(4), pp. 44–47. [G: LDCs]

Saith, Ashwani. Development and Distribution: A Critique of the Cross-Country U-Hypothesis. *J. Devel. Econ.*, December 1983, *13*(3), pp. 367–82. [G: LDCs]

Salvatore, Dominick. A Simultaneous Equations Model of Trade and Development with Dynamic Policy Simulations. *Kyklos*, 1983, *36*(1), pp. 66–90.

Singer, Hans W. North–South Multipliers. *World Devel.*, May 1983, *11*(5), pp. 451–54. [G: LDCs]

Stewart, Frances. Macro–Policies for Appropriate Technology: An Introductory Classification. *Int. Lab. Rev.*, May–June 1983, *122*(3), pp. 279–93. [G: LDCs]

Weiss, Thomas G. and Jennings, Anthony. What Are the Least Developed Countries and What Benefits May Result from the Paris Conference? *World Devel.*, April 1983, *11*(4), pp. 337–57. [G: MDCs; LDCs]

1211 Comparative Country Studies

Baer, Werner. Import Substitution and Industrialization in Latin America: Experiences and Interpretations. **In** *Todaro, M. P., ed.*, 1983, *1972*, pp. 301–15. [G: Latin America]

Bhagwati, Jagdish N. and Grinols, Earl. Foreign Capital, Dependence, Destabilisation and Feasibility of Transition to Socialism. **In** *Bhagwati, J. N., Vol. 2*, 1983, *1975*, pp. 479–92. [G: Ghana; Israel; S. Korea; Philippines; India]

Eckstein, Susan. Revolution and Redistribution in Latin America. **In** *McClintock, C. and Lowenthal, A. F., eds.*, 1983, pp. 347–86. [G: Latin America]

Lim, David. Another Look at Growth and Defense in Less Developed Countries. *Econ. Develop. Cult. Change*, January 1983, *31*(2), pp. 377–84. [G: LDCs]

Ranis, Gustav. Alternative Patterns of Distribution and Growth in the Mixed Economy: The Philippines and Taiwan. **In** *Stewart, F., ed.*, 1983, pp. 83–107. [G: Philippines; Taiwan]

Sheahan, John. The Economics of the Peruvian Experiment in Comparative Perspective. **In** *McClintock, C. and Lowenthal, A. F., eds.*, 1983, pp. 387–414. [G: Latin America]

1213 European Countries

Balassa, Bela. Economic Policies in Portugal. *Economia*, January 1983, *7*(1), pp. 111–34. [G: Portugal]

Ceyhun, Fikret. Economic Development in Turkey since 1960: A Critique. *Econ. Forum*, Summer 1983, *14*(1), pp. 57–77. [G: Turkey]

Erdilek, Asim. Inequity Based on Inefficiency: The Turkish Case [A Review Article]. *Weltwirtsch. Arch.*, 1983, *119*(4), pp. 754–62. **[G: Turkey]**

Fuà, Giorgio. Problems of Lagged Development in OECD Europe: A Study of Six Countries. *Rivista Int. Sci. Econ. Com.*, March 1983, *30*(3), pp. 228–43. **[G: Selected European]**

Gasparetto, Marialuisa Manfredini. La turchia nell'economia mediterranea e della CEE. (Turkey as an Associate Member of the EEC within the Mediterranean Economy. With English summary.) *Rivista Int. Sci. Econ. Com.*, March 1983, *30*(3), pp. 268–92. **[G: Turkey]**

Gasparetto, Marialuisa Manfredini. Turchia—l'economia reale e la programmazione. (Turkey: Real Economy and Planning. With English summary.) *Rivista Int. Sci. Econ. Com.*, April-May 1983, *30*(4–5), pp. 452–73. **[G: Turkey]**

Gasparetto, Marialuisa Manfredini. Turchia: l'attività economica e l'interscambio. (Turkey: Economic Activity and Interexchange. With English summary.) *Rivista Int. Sci. Econ. Com.*, June 1983, *30*(6), pp. 566–88. **[G: Turkey]**

Kondonassis, A. J.; Malliaris, A. G. and Robinson, N. S. Political Instability and Economic Development: An Economic History Case Study of Greece, 1948–1966. *J. Europ. Econ. Hist.*, Fall 1983, *12*(2), pp. 351–62. **[G: Greece]**

Marques, A. and Romao, A. Croissance et crise de l'économie portugaise (1960–1982). (Growth and Crisis of the Portuguese Economy. With English summary.) *Écon. Soc.*, September–October–November 1983, *17*(9–10–11), pp. 1701–40. **[G: Portugal]**

Payno, Juan Antonio. Characteristics and Motives for Entry. **In** *Sampedro, J. L. and Payno, J. A., eds.*, 1983, pp. 187-209. **[G: Spain; EEC]**

Payno, Juan Antonio. The Second Enlargment from the Perspective of the New Members. **In** *Sampedro, J. L. and Payno, J. A., eds.*, 1983, pp. 1–37. **[G: Greece; Portugal; Spain; EEC]**

Ross, Howard N. and Thomadakis, Stavros. Rate of Return, Firm Size and Development Subsidies: The Case of Greece. *J. Devel. Econ.*, February/April 1983, *12*(1/2), pp. 5–18. **[G: Greece]**

Şenses, Fikret. An Assessment of Turkey's Liberalization Attempts since 1980 against the Background of Her Stabilization Program. *METU*, 1983, *10*(3), pp. 271–321. **[G: Turkey]**

Siotis, Jean. Characteristics and Motives for Entry. **In** *Sampedro, J. L. and Payno, J. A., eds.*, 1983, pp. 57–69. **[G: Greece]**

Togan, Sübidey. Effects of Alternative Policy Regimes on Foreign-Payments Imbalances. *Pakistan Devel. Rev.*, Winter 1983, *22*(4), pp. 239–60. **[G: Turkey]**

1214 Asian Countries

Aggarwal, Mangat Ram. Trade: An Engine of Economic Development in ASEAN Countries. *Rivista Int. Sci. Econ. Com.*, September 1983, *30*(9), pp. 861–72. **[G: S.E. Asia]**

Ahmed, Salehuddin; Feeny, David H. and Mestelman, Stuart. Implications of a Neoclassical Dual Economy Model of Bangladesh. *J. Devel. Areas*, April 1983, *17*(3), pp. 319–36. **[G: Bangladesh]**

Anandalingam, G. Planning Studies with an Optimal Control Multisectoral Dynamic Economic Model: The Case of Sri Lanka. *J. Policy Modeling*, June 1983, *5*(2), pp. 179–205. **[G: Sri Lanka]**

Barone, Charles A. Dependency, Marxist Theory, and Salvaging the Idea of Capitalism in South Korea. *Rev. Radical Polit. Econ.*, Spring 1983, *15*(1), pp. 43–67. **[G: S. Korea]**

Beeman, William O. Patterns of Religion and Economic Development in Iran from the Qajar Era to the Islamic Revolution of 1978–79. **In** *Finn, J., ed.*, 1983, pp. 73–103. **[G: Iran]**

Bose, Swadesh R. The Pakistan Economy since Independence (1947–70). **In** *Kumar, D., ed.*, 1983, pp. 995–1026. **[G: Pakistan]**

Browning, John. Ombre sullo sviluppo economico della penisola araba. (Shadows on the Economic Development in the Arabian Peninsula. With English summary.) *Mondo Aperto*, September-October 1983, *37*(5), pp. 255–85. **[G: Middle East]**

Chaudhry, Kiren Aziz and McDonough, Peter. State, Society, and Sin: The Political Beliefs of University Students in Pakistan. *Econ. Develop. Cult. Change*, October 1983, *32*(1), pp. 11–44. **[G: Pakistan]**

Chen, Edward K. Y. The Impact of China's Four Modernizations on Hong Kong's Economic Development. **In** *Youngson, A. J., ed.*, 1983, pp. 77–103. **[G: China; Hong Kong]**

Chen, Yun. The Current Financial and Economic Situation and Some Methods for Overcoming Difficulties. **In** *Ch'en, Y.*, 1983, *1962*, pp. 185–201. **[G: China]**

David, Cristina C. Economic Policies and Agricultural Incentives. *Philippine Econ. J.*, 1983, *22*(2), pp. 154–82. **[G: Philippine]**

Estanislao, Jesus P. Philippine Economic Setting in a Turbulent World Economy. *Philippine Econ. J.*, 1983, *22*(2), pp. 107–18. **[G: Philippine]**

Feuchtwang, Stephan and Hussain, Athar. The Chinese Economic Reforms: Introduction. **In** *Feuchtwang, S. and Hussain, A., eds.*, 1983, pp. 1–50. **[G: China]**

Glassburner, Bruce and Poffenberger, Mark. Survey of Recent Developments. *Bull. Indonesian Econ. Stud.*, December 1983, *19*(3), pp. 1–27. **[G: Indonesia]**

Haggard, Stephan and Moon, Chung-in. The South Korean State in the International Economy: Liberal, Dependent, or Mercantile? **In** *Ruggie, J. G., ed.*, 1983, pp. 131–89. **[G: S. Korea]**

Hamilton, Clive. Capitalist Industrialization in the Four Little Tigers of East Asia. **In** *Limqueco, P. and McFarlane, B., eds.*, 1983, pp. 137–80. **[G: Korea; Taiwan; Hong Kong; Singapore]**

Heston, Alan W. National Income. **In** *Kumar, D., ed.*, 1983, pp. 376–462. **[G: India]**

Hiemenz, Ulrich. Export Growth in Developing Asian Countries: Past Trends and Policy Issues. *Weltwirtsch. Arch.*, 1983, *119*(4), pp. 686–708. **[G: Hong Kong; S. Korea; Taiwan; S.E. Asia]**

Hsaio, Frank S. T. and Hsaio, Mei-Chu Wang. Some Development Indicators of Taiwan: A Comparative Study. *J. Econ. Devel.*, July 1983, *8*(1), pp. 45–58. **[G: Taiwan]**

Kalirajan, K. P. South–South Co-operation: Trade Relations between Indonesia and South Asia. *Pakistan Devel. Rev.*, Winter 1983, *22*(4), pp. 261–82. **[G: Indonesia; S. Asia]**

Kapur, Basant K. A Short-Term Analytical Model of the Singapore Economy. *J. Devel. Econ.*, June 1983, *12*(3), pp. 355–76. **[G: Singapore]**

Kincaid, G. Russell. Korea's Major Adjustment Effort. *Finance Develop.*, December 1983, *20*(4), pp. 20–23. **[G: S. Korea]**

Kwack, Sung Y. Developments in and Prospects for External Debt Position and Burden of Developing Countries: The Case of Korea. *J. Policy Modeling*, November 1983, *5*(3), pp. 443–59. **[G: S. Korea]**

Lim, Chong Yah. Singapore's Economic Development: Retrospect and Prospect. **In** *Chen, P. S. J., ed.*, 1983, pp. 89–104. **[G: Singapore]**

Lim, David. The Political Economy of the New Economic Policy in Malaysia. **In** *Lim, D., ed.*, 1983, pp. 3–22. **[G: Malaysia]**

Looney, Robert E. Absorptive Capacity of the Prerevolutionary Iranian Economy. *J. Energy Devel.*, Spring 1983, *8*(2), pp. 319–40. **[G: Iran]**

McCawley, Peter. Survey of Recent Developments. *Bull. Indonesian Econ. Stud.*, April 1983, *19*(1), pp. 1–31. **[G: Indonesia]**

Oshima, Harry T. On the Coming Pacific Century: Perspectives and Prospects. *Singapore Econ. Rev.*, October 1983, *28*(2), pp. 6–21. **[G: OECD; E. Asia]**

Oshima, Harry T. The Industrial and Demographic Transitions in East Asia. *Population Devel. Rev.*, December 1983, *9*(4), pp. 583–607. **[G: E. Asia]**

Rice, Robert C. The Origins of Basic Economic Ideas and Their Impact on 'New Order' Policies. *Bull. Indonesian Econ. Stud.*, August 1983, *19*(2), pp. 60–82. **[G: Indonesia]**

Sicat, Gerardo P. National Economic Strategy in a Sluggish World Setting. *Philippine Econ. J.*, 1983, *22*(2), pp. 183–94. **[G: Philippine]**

Vaidyanathan, A. The Indian Economy since Independence (1947–70). **In** *Kumar, D., ed.*, 1983, pp. 947–94. **[G: India]**

Weiss, Dieter. Überlegungen zur jordanischen Entwicklungsplanung. (Reflections on Development Planning in Jordan. With English summary.) *Konjunkturpolitik*, 1983, *29*(1), pp. 33–66. **[G: Jordan]**

Wu, Yuan-li. Chinese Entrepreneurs in Southeast Asia. *Amer. Econ. Rev.*, May 1983, *73*(2), pp. 112–17. **[G: S.E. Asia]**

Youngson, A. J. China and Hong Kong: The Economic Nexus: Introduction. **In** *Youngson, A. J., ed.*, 1983, pp. 1–11. **[G: Hong Kong]**

Zuberi, Habib A. Institutional Credit and Balanced Growth: A Case Study of Pakistan. *J. Econ. Devel.*, December 1983, *8*(2), pp. 167–84. **[G: Pakistan]**

1215 African Countries

Abedian, I. A Quantitative Review of the Economy of Transkei. *S. Afr. J. Econ.*, June 1983, *51*(2), pp. 252–69. **[G: S. Africa]**

Balassa, Bela. Policy Responses to External Shocks in Sub-Saharan African Countries. *J. Policy Modeling*, March 1983, *5*(1), pp. 75–105. **[G: Africa]**

Bequele, Assefa. Stagnation and Inequality in Ghana. **In** *Ghai, D. and Radwan, S., eds.*, 1983, pp. 219–47. **[G: Ghana]**

Bienen, Henry S. Religion and Economic Change in Nigeria. **In** *Finn, J., ed.*, 1983, pp. 201–27. **[G: Nigeria]**

Bruton, Henry J. Egypt's Development in the Seventies. *Econ. Develop. Cult. Change*, July 1983, *31*(4), pp. 679–704. **[G: Egypt]**

Byerlee, Derek, et al. Employment-Output Conflicts, Factor-Price Distortions, and Choice of Technique: Empirical Results from Sierra Leone. *Econ. Develop. Cult. Change*, January 1983, *31*(2), pp. 315–36. **[G: Sierra Leone]**

Clarence-Smith, W. G. Business Empires in Equatorial Africa. *African Econ. Hist.*, 1983, (12), pp. 3–11. **[G: Africa]**

Dick, Hermann, et al. The Short-Run Impact of Fluctuating Primary Commodity Prices on Three Developing Economies: Colombia, Ivory Coast and Kenya. *World Devel.*, May 1983, *11*(5), pp. 405–16. **[G: Colombia; Ivory Coast; Kenya]**

Dickman, A. B. Market-Orientated Policies and Financial Markets. *S. Afr. J. Econ.*, December 1983, *51*(4), pp. 467–85. **[G: S. Africa]**

Egerö, Bertil and Torp, Jens Erik. What Kind of Socialist Transition in Capitalist Recession? The Case of Mozambique. **In** *Carlsson, J., ed.*, 1983, pp. 141–72. **[G: Mozambique]**

Ghai, Dharam and Radwan, Samir. Growth and Inequality: Rural Development in Malawi, 1964–78. **In** *Ghai, D. and Radwan, S., eds.*, 1983, pp. 71–97. **[G: Malawi]**

Green, Reginald Herbold. "No Worst There Is None"? Tanzanian Political Economic Crises 1978–???? **In** *Carlsson, J., ed.*, 1983, pp. 108–40. **[G: Tanzania]**

Green, Reginald Herbold. African Economies in the Mid-1980's—"Naught for Your Comfort but That the Waves Grow Higher and the Storms Grow Wilder." **In** *Carlsson, J., ed.*, 1983, pp. 173–203. **[G: Sub-Saharan Africa]**

Kader, Ahmad. Sources of Growth with Domestic Factor Shift and Foreign Factor Transfer: The Case of Libya. *J. Econ. Devel.*, July 1983, *8*(1), pp. 89–108. **[G: Libya]**

Kick, Edward L. and Conaty, Joseph. African Economic Development: The Effects of East, West, and Chinese Penetration. **In** *Bergesen, A., ed.*, 1983, pp. 263–86. **[G: Africa]**

Kofi, Tetteh A. and Hansen, Emmanuel. Ghana—A History of an Endless Recession. **In** *Carlsson, J., ed.*, 1983, pp. 48–79. **[G: Ghana]**

Marcussen, Henrik Secher. The Ivory Coast Facing the Economic Crisis. **In** *Carlsson, J., ed.*, 1983, pp. 1–27. **[G: Ivory Coast]**

McCarthy, D. M. P. Measurement of Levels of Living in the People's Republic of the Congo since 1950: Discussion. *J. Econ. Hist.*, March 1983, *43*(1), pp. 272–73. **[G: Congo]**

McCarthy, F. Desmond. General Equilibrium Model for Egypt. **In** *Kelley, A. C.; Sanderson, W. C. and Williamson, J. G., eds.*, 1983, pp. 71–102. **[G: Egypt]**

Mkandawire, P. Thandika. Economic Crisis in Malawi. **In** *Carlsson, J., ed.*, 1983, pp. 28–47. **[G: Malawi]**

Nzimiro, Ikenna. Militarization in Nigeria: Its Economic and Social Consequences. *Int. Soc. Sci. J.*, 1983, *35*(1), pp. 125–39. **[G: Nigeria]**

Olofin, S. and Iyaniwura, J. O. From Oil Shortage to Oil Glut: Simulation of Growth Prospects in the Nigerian Economy. *J. Policy Modeling*, November 1983, *5*(3), pp. 363–78. **[G: Nigeria]**

Rotberg, Robert I. Political and Economic Realities in a Time of Settlement. **In** *Rotberg, R. I., ed.*, 1983, pp. 29–40. **[G: Namibia]**

Sanders, Margaret. Measurement of Levels of Living in the People's Republic of the Congo since 1950. *J. Econ. Hist.*, March 1983, *43*(1), pp. 243–50. **[G: Congo]**

Seidman, Ann. Debt and the Development Options in Central Southern Africa: The Case of Zambia and Zimbabwe. **In** *Carlsson, J., ed.*, 1983, pp. 80–107. **[G: Zambia; Zimbabwe]**

Srivastava, R. K. and Livingstone, I. Growth and Distribution: The Case of Mozambique. **In** *Ghai, D. and Radwan, S., eds.*, 1983, pp. 249–80. **[G: Mozambique]**

Thomas, Wolfgang H. The Economy in Transition to Independence. **In** *Rotberg, R. I., ed.*, 1983, pp. 41–91. **[G: Namibia]**

Zartman, William and Schatz, Sayre P. The Political Economy of Nigeria: Introduction. **In** *Zartman, I. W., ed.*, 1983, pp. 1–24.

1216 Latin American and Caribbean Countries

Bacha, Edmar L. A Critique of Southern Cone Monetarism. *Int. Soc. Sci. J.*, 1983, *35*(3), pp. 413–23. **[G: Argentina; Chile; Uruguay]**

Balassa, Bela. Trade Policy in Mexico. *World Devel.*, September 1983, *11*(9), pp. 795–811. **[G: Mexico]**

Bernal, Richard L. Economic Growth and External Debt of Jamaica. **In** *Jorge, A.; Salazar-Carillo, J. and Higonnet, R. P., eds.*, 1983, pp. 89–108. **[G: Jamaica]**

Bocco, Arnaldo. Ecuador. Política económica y estilos de desarrollo en la fase de auge petrolero (1972–78). (With English summary.) *Desarrollo Econ.*, January–March 1983, *22*(88), pp. 485–510. **[G: Ecuador]**

Casar, José I. and Ros, Jaime. Trade and Capital Accumulation in a Process of Import Substitution. *Cambridge J. Econ.*, September/December 1983, *7*(3/4), pp. 257–67. **[G: Mexico]**

Corbo, Vittorio. Desarrollos macroeconomicos recientes en la economia chilena. (With English summary.) *Cuadernos Econ.*, April 1983, *20*(59), pp. 5–20. **[G: Chile]**

Cortázar, René. Chile: Resultados distributivos 1973–82. (With English summary.) *Desarrollo Econ.*, October-December 1983, *23*(91), pp. 369–94. **[G: Chile]**

Cotler, Julio. Democracy and National Integration in Peru. **In** *McClintock, C. and Lowenthal, A. F., eds.*, 1983, pp. 3–38. **[G: Peru]**

Cullen, Andrew. Structural Economic Domination and World Trade with Reference to Latin America: A Marxist Approach. *Soc. Econ. Stud.*, September 1983, *32*(3), pp. 35–81. **[G: Latin America]**

Dick, Hermann, et al. The Short-Run Impact of Fluctuating Primary Commodity Prices on Three Developing Economies: Colombia, Ivory Coast and Kenya. *World Devel.*, May 1983, *11*(5), pp. 405–16. **[G: Colombia; Ivory Coast; Kenya]**

Eckstein, Susan. Revolution and Redistribution in Latin America. **In** *McClintock, C. and Lowenthal, A. F., eds.*, 1983, pp. 347–86. **[G: Latin America]**

Eckstein, Susan and Hagopian, Frances. The Limits of Industrialization in the Less Developed World: Bolivia. *Econ. Develop. Cult. Change*, October 1983, *32*(1), pp. 63–95. **[G: Bolivia]**

Edwards, Sebastian. The Short-Run Relation between Growth and Inflation in Latin America: Comment. *Amer. Econ. Rev.*, June 1983, *73*(3), pp. 477–82. **[G: Latin America]**

Ffrench-Davis, Ricardo. The Monetarist Experiment in Chile: A Critical Survey. *World Devel.*, November 1983, *11*(11), pp. 905–26. **[G: Chile]**

FitzGerald, E. V. K. State Capitalism in Peru: A Model of Economic Development and Its Limitations. **In** *McClintock, C. and Lowenthal, A. F., eds.*, 1983, pp. 65–93. **[G: Peru]**

Foxley, Alejandro. Towards a Free Market Economy: Chile 1974–1979. **In** *Todaro, M. P., ed.*, 1983, *1982*, pp. 369–83.

García, Alvaro and Wells, John. Chile: A Laboratory for Failed Experiments in Capitalist Political Economy. *Cambridge J. Econ.*, September/December 1983, *7*(3/4), pp. 287–304. **[G: Chile]**

Gillespie, Fran. Comprehending the Slow Pace of Urbanization in Paraguay between 1950 and 1972. *Econ. Develop. Cult. Change*, January 1983, *31*(2), pp. 355–75. **[G: Paraguay]**

Glade, William. The Levantines in Latin America. *Amer. Econ. Rev.*, May 1983, *73*(2), pp. 118–22. **[G: Latin America]**

Gurrieri, Adolfo and Sáinz, Pedro. Is There a Fair and Democratic Way Out of the Crisis? Some Proposals in the Light of the ECLA Philosophy. *Cepal Rev.*, August 1983, (20), pp. 127–48. **[G: Latin America]**

Hanson, James A. The Short-Run Relation between Growth and Inflation in Latin America: Reply. *Amer. Econ. Rev.*, June 1983, *73*(3), pp. 483–85. **[G: Latin America]**

Hart, Jeffrey A. The Constraints on Associative Development in a Privileged Developing Country: The Case of Venezeula. **In** *Ruggie, J. G., ed.*, 1983, pp. 191–238. **[G: Venezuela]**

Irvin, George. Nicaragua: Establishing the State as the Centre of Accumulation. *Cambridge J. Econ.*, June 1983, *7*(2), pp. 125–39. **[G: Nicaragua]**

Jorge, Antonio and Salazar-Carrillo, Jorge. External Debt and Development in Latin America: A Background Paper. **In** *Jorge, A.; Salazar-Carillo, J. and Higonnet, R. P., eds.*, 1983, pp. 1–35. **[G: Latin America]**

Leven, Ronald and Roberts, David L. Latin America's Prospects for Recovery. *Fed. Res. Bank New York Quart. Rev.*, Autumn 1983, *8*(3), pp. 6–13. **[G: Latin America]**

López, Julio. The Mexican Economy: Present Situation, Perspectives and Alternatives. *World Devel.*, May 1983, *11* (5), pp. 455–65. **[G: Mexico]**

Lowenthal, Abraham F. The Peruvian Experiment Reconsidered. **In** *McClintock, C. and Lowenthal, A. F., eds.*, 1983, pp. 415–30. **[G: Peru]**

Lundahl, Mats. Intergenerational Sharecropping in Haiti: A Re-interpretation of the Murray Thesis. **In** *Lundahl, M.*, 1983, *1982*, pp. 83–93. **[G: Haiti]**

Neffa, Julio César. Development and Employment Models in Argentina: A Long-term View of Their Relations. **In** *Urquidi, V. L. and Reyes, S. T., eds.*, 1983, pp. 362–86. **[G: Argentina]**

Nugent, Jeffrey B. An Alternative Source of Measurement Error as an Explanation for the Inverted-U Hypothesis. *Econ. Develop. Cult. Change*, January 1983, *31* (2), pp. 385–96. **[G: Mexico]**

Parkin, Vincent. Economic Liberalism in Chile, 1973–82: A Model for Growth and Development or a Recipe for Stagnation and Impoverishment. *Cambridge J. Econ.*, June 1983, *7*(2), pp. 101–24. **[G: Chile]**

Pfeffermann, Guy and Webb, Richard. Poverty and Income Distribution in Brazil. *Rev. Income Wealth*, June 1983, *29*(2), pp. 101–24. **[G: Brazil]**

Pregger-Román, Charles G. Dependence, Underdevelopment, and Imperialism in Latin America: A Reappraisal. *Sci. Soc.*, Winter 1983–1984, *47* (4), pp. 406–26. **[G: Latin America]**

Quiñones, Fernando Gonzáles. Employment and Development in Latin America. **In** *Urquidi, V. L. and Reyes, S. T., eds.*, 1983, pp. 406–23. **[G: Latin America]**

Ranis, Gustav. Employment and Income Distribution Constraints in Latin America. **In** *Urquidi, V. L. and Reyes, S. T., eds.*, 1983, pp. 131–50. **[G: Taiwan; Colombia; Mexico]**

Schydlowsky, Daniel M. and Wicht, Juan J. The Anatomy of an Economic Failure. **In** *McClintock, C. and Lowenthal, A. F., eds.*, 1983, pp. 94–143. **[G: Peru]**

Sheahan, John. The Economics of the Peruvian Experiment in Comparative Perspective. **In** *McClintock, C. and Lowenthal, A. F., eds.*, 1983, pp. 387–414. **[G: Latin America]**

Stone, Carl. Patterns of Insertion into the World Economy: Historical Profile and Contemporary Options. *Soc. Econ. Stud.*, September 1983, *32* (3), pp. 1–34. **[G: Caribbean]**

Street, James H. Institutional Reform and Manpower Development in Mexico. *J. Econ. Issues*, March 1983, *17*(1), pp. 17–33. **[G: Mexico]**

Thorp, Rosemary. The Evolution of Peru's Economy. **In** *McClintock, C. and Lowenthal, A. F., eds.*, 1983, pp. 39–61. **[G: Peru]**

Tokman, Victor E. Wages and Employment in International Recessions: Recent Latin American Experience. *Cepal Rev.*, August 1983, (20), pp. 113–26. **[G: Latin America]**

Twomey, Michael J. Devaluations and Income Distribution in Latin America. *Southern Econ. J.*, January 1983, *49*(3), pp. 804–21. **[G: Latin America]**

Witter, Michael. Exchange Rate Policy in Jamaica: A Critical Assessment. *Soc. Econ. Stud.*, December 1983, *32* (4), pp. 1–50. **[G: Jamaica]**

1217 Oceanic Countries

Knapman, Bruce and Schiavo-Campo, Salvatore. Growth and Fluctuations of Fiji's Exports, 1875–1978. *Econ. Develop. Cult. Change*, October 1983, *32* (1), pp. 97–119. **[G: Fiji]**

122 Economic Studies of Developed Countries

1220 General

Barkin, Solomon. The Postwar Decades: Growth and Activism Followed by Stagnancy and Malaise. **In** *Barkin, S., ed.*, 1983, pp. 1–38. **[G: OECD]**

Eliasson, Gunnar; Sharefkin, Mark and Ysander, Bengt-Christer. Stability and Macroeconomic Policy: The Lesson of the 1970s. **In** *Eliasson, G.; Sharefkin, M. and Ysander, B.-C., eds.*, 1983, pp. 11–49. **[G: OECD]**

1221 Comparative Country Studies

Baily, Martin Neil. Productivity Trends: Comment. **In** *Schurr, S. H.; Sonenblum, S. and Wood, D. O., eds.*, 1983, pp. 121–26. **[G: OECD; U.S.]**

Batten, Dallas S. and Hafer, R. W. The Relative Impact of Monetary and Fiscal Actions on Economic Activity: A Cross-Country Comparison. *Fed. Res. Bank St. Louis Rev.*, January 1983, *65* (1), pp. 5–12.

Böhm, Bernhard and Clemenz, Gerhard. The Development of Factor Productivity in an International Comparison. *Empirica*, 1983, (1), pp. 41–66. **[G: Selected OECD]**

Boltho, Andrea. Italian and Japanese Postwar Growth: Some Similarities and Differences. **In** *Fodella, G., ed.*, 1983, pp. 48–63. **[G: Japan]**

Coe, David T. and Holtham, Gerald. Output Responsiveness and Inflation: An Aggregate Study. *OECD Econ. Stud.*, Autumn 1983, (1), pp. 93–145. **[G: OECD]**

Fodella, Gianni. Economic Performance in Japan and Italy. **In** *Fodella, G., ed.*, 1983, pp. 1–30. **[G: Japan; Italy]**

Furuki, Toshiaki. The Post-war Development of Capitalism and Regional Problems: A Comparison of Italy and Japan. **In** *Fodella, G., ed.*, 1983, pp. 179–92. **[G: Italy; Japan]**

Hulsman, W.; Suyker, W. B. C. and van Welzenis, G. Recent Economic Performances and Policies of Smaller European Countries. An Assessment for Austria, Belgium, Denmark and Switzerland. *De Economist*, 1983, *131* (4), pp. 609–33. **[G: Austria; Belgium; Denmark; Switzerland]**

Kendrick, John W. International Comparisons of Recent Productivity Trends. **In** *Schurr, S. H.; Sonenblum, S. and Wood, D. O., eds.*, 1983, pp. 71–120. **[G: OECD]**

Kregel, J. A. The Interaction of United States and

European Policies. **In** *Weintraub, S. and Goodstein, M., eds.*, 1983, pp. 192–204. **[G: U.S.; EEC]**

Lombardo, Antonio. Japan's and Italy's Political Systems: Developmental and Comparative Perspectives. **In** *Fodella, G., ed.*, 1983, pp. 193–214. **[G: Japan; Italy]**

Moore, Geoffrey H. and Cullity, John P. Trends and Cycles in Productivity, Unit Costs, and Prices: An International Perspective. **In** *Moore, G. H.*, 1983, *1982*, pp. 245–80. **[G: Japan; U.K.; U.S.; W. Germany]**

Onida, Fabrizio. Japan and Italy: Old and Newly Emerging Roles in the International Division of Labour. **In** *Fodella, G., ed.*, 1983, pp. 125–57. **[G: Japan; Italy]**

1223 European Countries

Argy, Victor. France's Experience with Monetary and Exchange Rate Management: March 1973 to End-1981. *Banca Naz. Lavoro Quart. Rev.*, December 1983, (147), pp. 387–411. **[G: France]**

Atkinson, F. J.; Brooks, Simon J. and Hall, S. G. F. The Economic Effects of North Sea Oil. *Nat. Inst. Econ. Rev.*, May 1983, (104), pp. 38–44. **[G: U.K.]**

Batchelor, R. A. British Economic Policy under Margaret Thatcher: A Mid Term Examination: A Comment on Darby and Lothian. *Carnegie-Rochester Conf. Ser. Public Policy,* Spring 1983, *18*, pp. 209–19. **[G: U.K.]**

Bizaquet, Armand. L'importance des entreprises publiques dans l'économie française et européenne après les nationalisations de 1982. (The French Public Sector after the 1982 Nationalizations: An Assessment of Its Relative Size in the Context of the French and European Economies. With English summary.) *Revue Écon.*, May 1983, *34*(3), pp. 434–65. **[G: France]**

Black, W. Northern Ireland after the Recession. *Irish Banking Rev.*, December 1983, pp. 3–12. **[G: U.K.]**

Boltho, Andrea. Is Western Europe Caught in an 'Expectations Trap'? *Lloyds Bank Rev.*, April 1983, (148), pp. 1–13. **[G: W. Europe]**

Brandsma, Andries S.; Hughes Hallett, A. J. and van der Windt, Nico. Optimal Control of Large Nonlinear Models: An Efficient Method of Policy Search Applied to the Dutch Economy. *J. Policy Modeling,* June 1983, *5*(2), pp. 253–70. **[G: Netherlands]**

Brittan, Samuel. How British Is the British Sickness? **In** *Brittan, S.*, 1983, *1978*, pp. 219–38.

Buiter, Willem H. and Miller, Marcus H. Changing the Rules: Economic Consequences of the Thatcher Regime. *Brookings Pap. Econ. Act.*, 1983, (2), pp. 305–79. **[G: U.K.]**

Claassen, Emil-Maria. Against Pessimism: The Annual Report 1982/83 of the German Council of Economic Experts. *Z. ges. Staatswiss.*, June 1983, *139*(2), pp. 331–44. **[G: W. Germany]**

Craven, Barrie M. and Wright, Grahame A. The Thatcher Experiment. *J. Macroecon.*, Winter 1983, *5*(1), pp. 21–40. **[G: U.K.]**

Darby, Michael R. and Lothian, James R. British Economic Policy under Margaret Thatcher: A Midterm Examination. *Carnegie-Rochester Conf. Ser. Public Policy,* Spring 1983, *18*, pp. 157–207. **[G: U.K.]**

De Grauwe, Paul. Symptoms of an Overvalued Currency: The Case of the Belgian Franc. **In** *de Cecco, M., ed.*, 1983, pp. 99–116. **[G: Belgium]**

Del Monte, Alfredo. Dualism and Economic Development in a Peripheral Economy: The Italian Case. **In** *Groenewegen, P. and Halevi, J., eds.*, 1983, pp. 183–217. **[G: Italy]**

El-Agraa, Ali M. Has Membership of the EC Been a Disaster for Britain? **In** *El-Agraa, A. M., ed.*, 1983, pp. 319–33. **[G: EEC; U.K.]**

Faini, Riccardo. Cumulative Processes of De-Industrialisation in an Open Region: The Case of Southern Italy, 1951-1973. *J. Devel. Econ.*, June 1983, *12*(3), pp. 277–301. **[G: Italy]**

Feinstein, Charles. The Managed Economy: Essays in British Economic Policy and Performance since 1929: Introduction. **In** *Feinstein, C., ed.*, 1983, pp. 1–30. **[G: U.K.]**

Fels, Gerhard. The Supply-Side Approach to Macroeconomic Policy: The West German Experience. **In** *[Giersch, H.]*, 1983, pp. 224–37. **[G: W. Germany]**

Frisch, Helmut. Stabilization Policy in Austria, 1970–80. **In** *de Cecco, M., ed.*, 1983, pp. 117–40. **[G: Austria]**

Gillies, Grazia Ietto. Monopoly Capitalism and the UK Economy: A Review Article. *Stud. Econ.*, 1983, *38*(21), pp. 57–75. **[G: U.K.]**

Grassman, Sven and Olsson, Hans. The Productivity Link between Exports and Domestic Demand: Sweden. **In** *de Cecco, M., ed.*, 1983, pp. 34–48. **[G: Sweden]**

Halttunen, Hannu and Korkman, Sixten. External Shocks and Adjustment Policies in Finland, 1973–80. **In** *de Cecco, M., ed.*, 1983, pp. 7–33. **[G: Finland]**

Isachsen, Arne Jon. Norwegian Economic Policy in the Past Decade and Some Thoughts on Policy in the Present One. **In** *de Cecco, M., ed.*, 1983, pp. 49–64. **[G: Norway]**

Kaldor, Nicholas. Conflicts in National Economic Objectives. **In** *Feinstein, C., ed.*, 1983, *1971*, pp. 169–84. **[G: U.K.]**

Kästli, René. The New Economic Environment in the 1970s: Market and Policy Response in Switzerland. **In** *de Cecco, M., ed.*, 1983, pp. 141–59. **[G: Switzerland]**

Katseli, Louka T. Macroeconomic Adjustment and Exchange-Rate Policy in Middle-Income Countries: Greece, Portugal and Spain in the 1970s. **In** *de Cecco, M., ed.*, 1983, pp. 189–211. **[G: Greece; Portugal; Spain]**

Katzenstein, Peter J. The Small European States in the International Economy: Economic Dependence and Corporatist Politics. **In** *Ruggie, J. G., ed.*, 1983, pp. 91–130. **[G: W. Europe]**

Kjaer, Jørn H. International Adjustment, the EMS and Small European Countries: The Danish Experience. **In** *de Cecco, M., ed.*, 1983, pp. 65–73. **[G: Denmark]**

Majmudar, Madhavi G. Government and the Scottish Economic Performance: 1954–1978. *Scot. J.*

Polit. Econ., June 1983, *30*(2), pp. 153–69. **[G: U.K.]**

Mayes, David G. Industrial Production. *Nat. Inst. Econ. Rev.*, November 1983, (106), pp. 49–55. **[G: U.K.]**

McAleese, Dermot. Competitiveness and Economic Performance: The Irish Experience. **In** *Black, J. and Winters, L. A., eds.*, 1983, pp. 65–91. **[G: Ireland; OECD]**

Mehrling, Perry. Has Mrs. Thatcher Exorcised the Demons? *Challenge*, January/February 1983, *25*(6), pp. 57–60. **[G: U.K.]**

Mendizabal Gorostiaga, A. La crisis económica: su incidencia en el País Vasco. (The Economic Crisis: Its Incidence in the Basque Country. With English summary.) *Écon. Soc.*, September–October–November 1983, *17*(9–10–11), pp. 1595–1609. **[G: Spain]**

O'Cleireacain, Seamus C. M. Northern Ireland and Irish Integration: The Role of the European Communities. *J. Common Market Stud.*, December 1983, *22*(2), pp. 107–24. **[G: Ireland; EEC; U.K.]**

Pelinka, Anton. The Austrian Experience of Social and Economic Cooperation. *Economia*, May 1983, *7*(2), pp. 239–53. **[G: Austria]**

Posthumus, Godert. The Netherlands: Financial-Economic Adjustment Policies in the 1970s. **In** *de Cecco, M., ed.*, 1983, pp. 74–98. **[G: Netherlands]**

Reddaway, W. Brian. Problems and Prospects for the UK Economy. *Econ. Rec.*, September 1983, *59*(166), pp. 220–31. **[G: U.K.]**

Seton, Francis. Thatcherism in Britain. **In** *Weintraub, S. and Goodstein, M., eds.*, 1983, pp. 180–91. **[G: U.K.]**

Singh, Ajit. U.K. Industry and the World Economy: A Case of De-industrialisation? **In** *Feinstein, C., ed.*, 1983, *1977*, pp. 226–57. **[G: U.K.]**

Sylos Labini, Paolo. Some Aspects of Economic Development in an Advanced Capitalist Country (Great Britain). *Soc. Res.*, Summer 1983, *50*(2), pp. 429–51. **[G: U.K.]**

Winch, Donald. Britain in the 'Thirties: A Managed Economy? **In** *Feinstein, C., ed.*, 1983, *1969*, pp. 47–67. **[G: U.K.]**

1224 Asian Countries

Akao, Nobutoshi. Japan's Economic Security: Introduction. **In** *Akao, N., ed.*, 1983, pp. 1–13. **[G: Japan]**

Akao, Nobutoshi. Japan's Search for Economic Security. **In** *Akao, N., ed.*, 1983, pp. 245–72. **[G: U.S.; Selected Countries]**

Akao, Nobutoshi. Resources and Japan's Security. **In** *Akao, N., ed.*, 1983, pp. 15–44. **[G: Japan]**

Ariki, Soichiro. Japan's Economy at the Crossroads: An Analysis of Conditions for Her Survival. **In** *Fodella, G., ed.*, 1983, pp. 90–106. **[G: Japan]**

Halliday, Jon. The Specificity of Japan's Re-integration into the World Capitalist Economy after 1945: Notes on Some Myths and Misconceptions. **In** *Fodella, G., ed.*, 1983, pp. 31–47. **[G: Japan]**

Kagami, N. Maturing of the Japanese Economy in the 1980s. *Nat. Westminster Bank Quart. Rev.*, November 1983, pp. 18–28. **[G: Japan]**

Mendl, Wolf. Japan–China: The Economic Nexus. **In** *Akao, N., ed.*, 1983, pp. 217–44. **[G: Japan; China]**

Napier, Ron. Interrelationships of the Economic and Social Systems in Japan. **In** *Finn, J., ed.*, 1983, pp. 179–94. **[G: Japan]**

Shishido, Hisanobu. Modeling Dualism in Japan. **In** *Kelley, A. C.; Sanderson, W. C. and Williamson, J. G., eds.*, 1983, pp. 103–38. **[G: Japan]**

1225 African Countries

Carlsson, Jerker. Recession in Africa: Introduction. **In** *Carlsson, J., ed.*, 1983, pp. iii–xi. **[G: Sub-Saharan Africa]**

Viljoen, S. P. The Industrial Achievement of South Africa. *S. Afr. J. Econ.*, March 1983, *51*(1), pp. 29–57. **[G: S. Africa]**

1226 Latin American and Caribbean Countries

Ffrench-Davis, Ricardo. El experimento monetarista en Chile: una síntesis crítica. (With English summary.) *Desarrollo Econ.*, July–September 1983, *23*(90), pp. 163–96. **[G: Chile]**

1227 Oceanic Countries

Arndt, H. W. Statement No. 2 and Reserve Bank Annual Report: A Comment. *Econ. Rec.*, June 1983, *59*(165), pp. 186–87. **[G: Australia]**

McGuinness, P. P. Statement No. 2 and Reserve Bank Annual Report: Rejoinder. *Econ. Rec.*, June 1983, *59*(165), pp. 188. **[G: Australia]**

Norton, W. E. and McDonald, R. The Decline in Australia's Economic Performance in the 1970s: An Analysis of Annual Data. *Australian Econ. Pap.*, June 1983, *22*(40), pp. 1–29. **[G: Australia]**

1228 North American Countries

Alexander, Robert J. Contributions of the Galbraith "Technostructure" to the Growing Crisis of the U.S. Economy. *J. Econ. Issues*, June 1983, *17*(2), pp. 495–502. **[G: U.S.]**

Denison, Edward F. The Interruption of Productivity Growth in the United States. *Econ. J.*, March 1983, *93*(369), pp. 56–77. **[G: U.S.]**

Dungan, D. P. and Wilson, T. A. Deficits and the Economy to 1990: Projections and Alternatives. **In** *Conklin, D. W. and Courchene, T. J., eds.*, 1983, pp. 116–48. **[G: Canada]**

Hunt, Lacy H. The Causes of the 1981–82 Recession. **In** *Weintraub, S. and Goodstein, M., eds.*, 1983, pp. 84–91. **[G: U.S.]**

Keyserling, Leon H. U.S. Economy, Performance and Prospects, and Needed Corrective Policies. *Atlantic Econ. J.*, September 1983, *11*(3), pp. 9–43. **[G: U.S.]**

Kumar, Pradeep. The Current Industrial Relations Scene in Canada, 1983: The Economy: Summary Outline. **In** *Wood, W. D. and Kumar, P., eds.*, 1983, pp. 3–27. **[G: Canada]**

Martellaro, Joseph A. Alcuni aspetti dell'economia politica americana attuale: base storica, ragioni e metodi. (A Few Aspects of the Present American Economic Policy: Historical Grounds, Reasons and Methods. With English summary.)

Rivista Int. Sci. Econ. Com., September 1983, *30*(9), pp. 873–85. **[G: U.S.]**

Minsky, Hyman P. Pitfalls Due to Financial Fragility. **In** *Weintraub, S. and Goodstein, M., eds.*, 1983, pp. 104–19. **[G: U.S.]**

Nichols, Donald A. The Prospects for Economic Growth in the United States, 1980–2000. **In** *Reynolds, C. W. and Tello, C., eds.*, 1983, pp. 109–32. **[G: U.S.]**

Okun, Arthur M. Achieving Sustained Prosperity. **In** *Okun, A. M.*, 1983, *1970*, pp. 424–49. **[G: U.S.]**

Rousseas, Stephen. The Ideology of Supply-Side Economics. **In** *Weintraub, S. and Goodstein, M., eds.*, 1983, pp. 21–33. **[G: U.S.]**

Scitovsky, Tibor. The Prospects for Economic Growth in the United States, 1980–2000: Comments. **In** *Reynolds, C. W. and Tello, C., eds.*, 1983, pp. 133–35. **[G: U.S.]**

123 Comparative Economic Studies of Developing, Developed, and/or Centrally Planned Economies

1230 Comparative Economic Studies of Developing, Developed, and/or Centrally Planned Economies

Berry, Albert; Bourguignon, François and Morrisson, Christian. Changes in the World Distribution of Income between 1950 and 1977. *Econ. J.*, June 1983, *93*(370), pp. 331–50.

Brittan, Samuel. How British Is the British Sickness? **In** *Brittan, S.*, 1983, *1978*, pp. 219–38.

Choi, Kwang. A Statistical Test of Olson's Model. **In** *Mueller, D. C., ed.*, 1983, pp. 57–78. **[G: OECD]**

Clements, Kenneth W. and Semudram, Muthi. An International Comparison of the Price of Nontraded Goods. *Weltwirtsch. Arch.*, 1983, *119*(2), pp. 356–63. **[G: Selected LDCs; Selected MDCs]**

Gemmell, Norman. International Comparisons of the Effects of Nonmarket-Sector Growth. *J. Compar. Econ.*, December 1983, *7*(4), pp. 368–81. **[G: Selected MDCs; Selected LDCs]**

Glezakos, Constantine. Instability and the Growth of Exports: A Misinterpretation of the Evidence from the Western Pacific Countries. *J. Devel. Econ.*, February/April 1983, *12*(1/2), pp. 229–36. **[G: E. Asia; S. Asia]**

Goodwin, R. M. The World Matrix Multiplier. **In** *Goodwin, R. M.*, 1983, pp. 30–56.

Hanseman, Dennis J. A Further Note on Factor Substitution and Efficiency. *Rev. Econ. Statist.*, February 1983, *65*(1), pp. 153–55.

Heston, Alan W. A Different Perspective of Pakistan's Economy: The Structure of Expenditures and Prices, 1975–81. *Pakistan Devel. Rev.*, Autumn 1983, *22*(3), pp. 163–77. **[G: Pakistan; LDCs; MDCs]**

Koo, Anthony Y. C.; Quan, Nguyen and Rasche, Robert H. Identification of the Lorenz Curve by Lorenz Coefficient: A Reply. *Weltwirtsch. Arch.*, 1983, *119*(2), pp. 368–69. **[G: Selected Countries]**

Kravis, Irving B.; Heston, Alan W. and Summers, Robert. The Share of Services in Economic Growth. **In** *[Klein, L. R.]*, 1983, pp. 188–218. **[G: U.S.; U.K.; France]**

Kurabayashi, Yoshimasa and Sakuma, Itsuo. Alternative Matrix Consistent Methods of Multilateral Comparisons for Real Product and Prices. **In** *[Yamada, I.]*, 1983, pp. 127–41. **[G: Selected LDCs; Selected MDCs]**

Kuznets, Simon. Modern Economic Growth: Findings and Reflections. **In** *Todaro, M. P., ed.*, 1983, *1973*, pp. 56–67.

Lewis, W. Arthur. The Slowing Down of the Engine of Growth. **In** *Lewis, W. A.*, 1983, *1980*, pp. 283–92.

Lim, Chong Yah. Development Economics by R. M. Sundrum: A Review Article. *Singapore Econ. Rev.*, April 1983, *28*(1), pp. 88–103.

Maddison, Angus. A Comparison of Levels of GDP Per Capita in Developed and Developing Countries, 1700–1980. *J. Econ. Hist.*, March 1983, *43*(1), pp. 27–41. **[G: MDCs; LDCs]**

Maddison, Angus. Economic Stagnation since 1973, Its Nature and Causes: A Six Country Survey. *De Economist*, 1983, *131*(4), pp. 585–608. **[G: Selected OECD]**

Marsden, Keith. Taxes and Growth. *Finance Develop.*, September 1983, *20*(3), pp. 40–43. **[G: Selected Countries]**

McIntire, John. International Farm Prices and the Social Cost of Cheap Food Policies: Comment. *Amer. J. Agr. Econ.*, November 1983, *65*(4), pp. 823–26. **[G: LDCs]**

Mihaljek, Dubravko. Osvrt na kretanje privrednog rasta u zemljama južne Evrope i nekim vanevropskim zemljama u razdoblju 1952–1981. (A Review on the Course of Economic Growth in South European and Some Non-European Countries 1952–1981. With English summary.) *Econ. Anal. Worker's Manage.*, 1983, *17*(3), pp. 279–308. **[G: Selected Countries]**

Mueller, Dennis C. The Political Economy of Growth and Redistribution. **In** *Mueller, D. C., ed.*, 1983, pp. 261–76. **[G: OECD]**

Onishi, Akira. North–South Relations: Alternative Policy Simulations for the World Economy in the 1980s. *J. Policy Modeling*, March 1983, *5*(1), pp. 55–74. **[G: Global]**

Oshima, Harry T. On the Coming Pacific Century: Perspectives and Prospects. *Singapore Econ. Rev.*, October 1983, *28*(2), pp. 6–21. **[G: OECD; E. Asia]**

Peterson, Willis L. International Farm Prices and the Social Cost of Cheap Food Policies: Reply. *Amer. J. Agr. Econ.*, November 1983, *65*(4), pp. 827–28. **[G: LDCs]**

Pryor, Frederic L. A Quasi-test of Olson's Hypotheses. **In** *Mueller, D. C., ed.*, 1983, pp. 90–105. **[G: Selected Countries]**

Quiñones, Fernando Gonzáles. Employment and Development in Latin America. **In** *Urquidi, V. L. and Reyes, S. T., eds.*, 1983, pp. 406–23. **[G: Latin America]**

Ram, Rati. Comparison of the Actual and Projected Cross-Country Inequality in the Mid-1970's. *Atlantic Econ. J.*, December 1983, *11*(4), pp. 79. **[G: Global]**

Salazar-Carrillo, Jorge. Real Product and Price Comparisons for Latin America and Other World Countries. *Econ. Develop. Cult. Change,* July 1983, *31* (4), pp. 757–73. **[G: Latin America; Selected LDCs; Selected MDCs]**

Tan, Gerald. Export Instability, Export Growth and *GDP* Growth. *J. Devel. Econ.,* February/April 1983, *12* (1/2), pp. 219–27. **[G: OECD; E. Asia; S. Asia]**

Thon, Dominique. Lorenz Curves and Lorenz Coefficients: A Sceptical Note. *Weltwirtsch. Arch.,* 1983, *119* (2), pp. 364–67. **[G: Selected Countries]**

Venieris, Yiannis P. and Gupta, Dipak K. Sociopolitical and Economic Dimensions of Development: A Cross-Section Model. *Econ. Develop. Cult. Change,* July 1983, *31* (4), pp. 727–56. **[G: Selected MDCs; Selected LDCs]**

Zerby, J. A. and Khan, M. Habibullah. Quantitative Analysis of World Development: A Cluster Analytic Approach. *Pakistan J. Appl. Econ.,* Summer 1983, *2* (1), pp. 39–63.

124 Economic Studies of Centrally Planned Economies

1240 General

Bogomolov, Oleg. New Integration Strategies for the CMEA Countries. **In** *Saunders, C. T., ed.,* 1983, pp. 193–210. **[G: CMEA]**

Conn, David. Comparative Economic Systems Theory: Progress and Prospects. *ACES Bull. (See Comp. Econ. Stud. after 8/85),* Summer 1983, *25* (2), pp. 61–80.

Hewett, Edward A. Research on East European Economies: The Last Quarter Century. *ACES Bull. (See Comp. Econ. Stud. after 8/85),* Summer 1983, *25* (2), pp. 1–21. **[G: E. Europe]**

Lukaszewicz, Aleksander. Specific Programmes of EEC and CMEA: Comment. **In** *Saunders, C. T., ed.,* 1983, pp. 212–14. **[G: CMEA]**

1243 European Countries

Abalkin, L. Conversion of the Economy to the Intensive Path of Development. *Prob. Econ.,* February 1983, *25* (10), pp. 51–70. **[G: U.S.S.R.]**

Balassa, Bela. Reforming the New Economic Mechanism in Hungary. *J. Compar. Econ.,* September 1983, *7* (3), pp. 253–76. **[G: Hungary]**

Balassa, Bela. The Hungarian Economic Reform, 1968–82. *Banca Naz. Lavoro Quart. Rev.,* June 1983, (145), pp. 163–84. **[G: Hungary]**

Bauer, Tamás. The Hungarian Alternative to Soviet-Type Planning. *J. Compar. Econ.,* September 1983, *7* (3), pp. 304–16. **[G: U.S.S.R.; Hungary]**

Berend, Iván T. The First Phase of Economic Reform in Hungary: 1956–1957. *J. Europ. Econ. Hist.,* Winter 1983, *12* (3), pp. 523–71. **[G: Hungary]**

Blazyca, G. Polish Economic Management 1970–81. **In** *[Saunders, C. T.],* 1983, pp. 157–73. **[G: Poland]**

Bomberger, William A. and Makinen, Gail E. The Hungarian Hyperinflation and Stabilization of 1945–1946. *J. Polit. Econ.,* October 1983, *91* (5), pp. 801–24. **[G: Hungary]**

Bond, Daniel L. and Levine, Herbert S. The Soviet Economy: Toward the Year 2000: An Overview. **In** *Bergson, A. and Levine, H. S., eds.,* 1983, pp. 1–33. **[G: U.S.S.R.]**

Brada, Josef C.; King, Arthur E. and Schlagenhauf, Don E. The Benefits of Long-Term Developmental Planning: An Estimate. *World Devel.,* November 1983, *11* (11), pp. 971–79. **[G: Czechoslovakia]**

Burkett, John P. The Impact of Economic Reform on Macroeconomics Policy in Yugoslavia: Some Econometric Evidence. *Econ. Anal. Worker's Manage.,* 1983, *17* (3), pp. 213–43. **[G: Yugoslavia]**

Csikós-Nagy, Béla. Hungary's Adjustment to the New World Market Relations. *Acta Oecon.,* 1983, *30* (1), pp. 77–88. **[G: Hungary]**

Csikós-Nagy, Béla. Liquidity Troubles and Economic Consolidation in Hungary. *Acta Oecon.,* 1983, *31* (1–2), pp. 1–11. **[G: Hungary]**

Durgin, Frank A., Jr. More on the New Model of Soviet Growth. *ACES Bull. (See Comp. Econ. Stud. after 8/85),* Spring 1983, *25* (1), pp. 35–46. **[G: U.S.S.R.]**

Fakiolas, Tasos. Targets and Results of Soviet Economic Policy. *Rivista Int. Sci. Econ. Com.,* January 1983, *30* (1), pp. 41–56. **[G: U.S.S.R.]**

Furgeri, Italo and Betlen, János. The Past, Present, and Future of the East-European Economies: The Hungarian Case: An Interview with Rezso-Nyers. *Acta Oecon.,* 1983, *31* (3–4), pp. 297–326. **[G: Hungary]**

Gomulka, Stanislaw. Industrialization and the Rate of Growth: Eastern Europe, 1955–75. *J. Post Keynesian Econ.,* Spring 1983, *5* (3), pp. 388–96. **[G: E. Europe]**

Grossman, Gregory. Economics of Virtuous Haste: A View of Soviet Industrialization and Institutions. **In** *[Erlich, A.],* 1983, pp. 198–216. **[G: U.S.S.R.]**

Jakeš, Miloš. Report of the Presidium of the Central Committee of the Communist Party of Czechoslovakia on Speeding Up the Practical Application of the Results of Scientific and Technical Research. *Czech. Econ. Digest.,* September 1983, (6), pp. 3–57. **[G: Czechoslovakia]**

Kornai, János. Comments on the Present State and the Prospects of the Hungarian Economic Reform. *J. Compar. Econ.,* September 1983, *7* (3), pp. 225–52. **[G: Hungary]**

Krasovskii, V. The Nation's Investment Potential. *Prob. Econ.,* September 1983, *26* (5), pp. 57–76. **[G: U.S.S.R.]**

Leontief, Wassily W.; Mariscal, Jorge and Sohn, Ira. Prospects for the Soviet Economy to the Year 2000. *J. Policy Modeling,* March 1983, *5* (1), pp. 1–18. **[G: U.S.S.R.]**

Major, Iván. The Years 1978–1981 and the "Long Stages" in the Development of the Hungarian Economy. *Acta Oecon.,* 1983, *30* (3–4), pp. 381–99. **[G: Hungary]**

Matits, Ágnes and Temesi, József. Changes in Economic Regulators and Enterprise Reactions. *Acta Oecon.,* 1983, *31* (3–4), pp. 197–208. **[G: Hungary]**

Nyers, Rezsö. Interrelations between Policy and the Economic Reform in Hungary. *J. Compar. Econ.*, September 1983, *7*(3), pp. 211–24. **[G: Hungary]**

Nyitrai, Vera. Industrial Structure and Structural Change in Hungary. *Acta Oecon.*, 1983, *31* (3–4), pp. 175–95. **[G: Hungary]**

Osipenkov, P. The Social Infrastructure and Stimuli in Territorial Economic Management. *Prob. Econ.*, October 1983, *26*(6), pp. 40–54. **[G: U.S.S.R.]**

Právo, Rude. Accelerating Rate of Development: Report on the Development of the National Economy and Fulfilment of the Plan in Czechoslovakia in the First Six Months of 1983. *Czech. Econ. Digest.*, November 1983, (7), pp. 3–21. **[G: Czechoslovakia]**

Průcha, Václav. The Economic Strategy of the Communist Party of Czechoslovakia after February 1948 and at the Present Stage of Development. *Czech. Econ. Digest.*, May 1983, (3), pp. 32–48. **[G: Czechoslovakia]**

Štrougal, Lubomír. The Pressing Tasks of Further Economic Development. *Czech. Econ. Digest.*, 1983, (8), pp. 3–52. **[G: Czechoslovakia]**

Valenta, František. Structure of Innovations in the Process of Intensification of the Economy. *Czech. Econ. Digest.*, June 1983, (4), pp. 36–52. **[G: Czechoslovakia]**

Zalai, Ernö. A Nonlinear Multisectoral Model for Hungary: General Equilibrium versus Optimal Planning Approaches. **In** *Kelley, A. C.; Sanderson, W. C. and Williamson, J. G., eds.*, 1983, pp. 185–222. **[G: Hungary]**

1244 Asian Countries

Blecher, Marc. Peasant Labour for Urban Industry: Temporary Contract Labour, Urban–Rural Balance and Class Relations in a Chinese County. *World Devel.*, August 1983, *11*(8), pp. 731–45. **[G: China]**

Byrd, William. Enterprise-Level Reforms in Chinese State-Owned Industry. *Amer. Econ. Rev.*, May 1983, *73*(2), pp. 329–32. **[G: China]**

Changrong, Chen. An Experiment Attracting World-Wide Attention. *Econ. Anal. Worker's Manage.*, 1983, *17*(1), pp. 43–54. **[G: China]**

Fodella, Gianni. China towards a High Rate of Economic Growth: Similarities with Post-War Japan. *Rivista Int. Sci. Econ. Com.*, August 1983, *30*(8), pp. 792–97. **[G: China]**

Griffin, Keith and Griffin, Kimberley. Institutional Change and Income Distribution in the Chinese Countryside. *Oxford Bull. Econ. Statist.*, August 1983, *45*(3), pp. 223–48. **[G: China]**

Ishikawa, Shigeru. China's Economic System Reform: Underlying Factors and Prospects. *World Devel.*, August 1983, *11*(8), pp. 647–58. **[G: China; E. Europe]**

Kraus, Richard. Bureaucratic Privilege as an Issue in Chinese Politics. *World Devel.*, August 1983, *11*(8), pp. 673–82. **[G: China]**

Luo, Yuanzheng. The Chinese Economy and Its Role in the World. **In** *Hooke, A. W. ed.*, 1983, pp. 85–93. **[G: China]**

McFarlane, Bruce. 'The New Course in China': Summing-Up Speeches at Oxford Conference, Contemporary China Centre, September 1982. *World Devel.*, August 1983, *11*(8), pp. 767–69. **[G: China]**

McFarlane, Bruce. Political Economy of Class Struggle and Economic Growth in China, 1950–1982. *World Devel.*, August 1983, *11*(8), pp. 659–72. **[G: China]**

Pairault, Thierry. Chinese Market Mechanism: A Controversial Debate. *World Devel.*, August 1983, *11*(8), pp. 639–45. **[G: China]**

Rawski, Thomas G. New Sources for Studying China's Economy. *J. Econ. Hist.*, December 1983, *43*(4), pp. 997–1002. **[G: China]**

Reynolds, Bruce L. Economic Reforms and External Imbalance in China, 1978–81. *Amer. Econ. Rev.*, May 1983, *73*(2), pp. 325–28. **[G: China]**

Selden, Mark. The Logic—and Limits—of Chinese Socialist Development. *World Devel.*, August 1983, *11*(8), pp. 631–37. **[G: China]**

Shoazhi, Su. Socialism; China's Conditions; Modern Science and Technology; Democratization; Development Strategies: A Tentative Discourse on the Chinese Road to Modernization. *Econ. Notes*, 1983, (1), pp. 24–41. **[G: China]**

Wiegersma, Nancy. Regional Differences in Socialist Transformation in Vietnam. *Econ. Forum*, Summer 1983, *14*(1), pp. 95–109. **[G: Vietnam]**

Wright, Tim. Economic Development in China during the Nineteenth and Twentieth Centuries: A Review Article. *J. Econ. Hist.*, June 1983, *43*(2), pp. 494–500. **[G: China]**

1246 Latin American and Caribbean Countries

Ray, James Lee. The Cuban Path to Dependency Reversal. **In** *Doran, C. F.; Modelski, G. and Clark, C., eds.*, 1983, pp. 223–38. **[G: Cuba]**

Roca, Sergio. Economic Policy and Institutional Change in Socialist Cuba. *J. Econ. Issues*, June 1983, *17*(2), pp. 405–13. **[G: Cuba]**

130 Economic Fluctuations; Forecasting; Stabilization; and Inflation

131 Economic Fluctuations

1310 Economic Fluctuations: General

Alogoskoufis, George S. The Labour Market in an Equilibrium Business Cycle Model. *J. Monet. Econ.*, January 1983, *11*(1), pp. 117–28.

Ando, Albert. Equilibrium Business-Cycle Models: An Appraisal. **In** *[Klein, L. R.]*, 1983, pp. 39–67. **[G: U.S.]**

Beenstock, Michael and Dicks, G. R. An Aggregate Monetary Model of the World Economy. *Europ. Econ. Rev.*, May 1983, *21*(3), pp. 261–85.

Bergesen, Albert. Modeling Long Waves of Crisis in the World-System. **In** *Bergesen, A., ed.*, 1983, pp. 73–92.

Blatt, John M. Economic Policy and Endogenous Cycles. *J. Post Keynesian Econ.*, Summer 1983, *5*(4), pp. 635–47.

Boot, H. M. James Wilson and the Commercial Crisis of 1847. *Hist. Polit. Econ.*, Winter 1983, *15*(4), pp. 567–83. **[G: U.K.]**

Brunner, Karl; Cukierman, Alex and Meltzer, Allan H. Money and Economic Activity, Inventories and Business Cycles. *J. Monet. Econ.*, May 1983, *11*(3), pp. 281–319.

Clegg, Stewart; Dow, Geoff and Boreham, Paul. Politics and Crisis: The State of the Recession. **In** *Clegg, S.; Dow, G. and Boreham, P., eds.*, 1983, pp. 1–50.

Cohen, Morris. The GNP Data Improvement Project (The Creamer Report): Overview and Business Cycle Perspective. **In** *Foss, M. F., ed.*, 1983, pp. 384–97. **[G: U.S.]**

Cole, Rosanne. The GNP Data Improvement Project (The Creamer Report): Overview and Business Cycle Perspective: Comment. **In** *Foss, M. F., ed.*, 1983, pp. 397–402. **[G: U.S.]**

Collard, David A. Pigou on Expectations and the Cycle. *Econ. J.*, June 1983, *93*(370), pp. 411–14.

Copeland, Laurence S. Public Sector Prices and the Real Exchange-Rate in the UK Recession. *Bull. Econ. Res.*, November 1983, *35*(2), pp. 97–121. **[G: U.K.]**

Day, Richard H. The Emergence of Chaos from Classical Economic Growth. *Quart. J. Econ.*, May 1983, *98*(2), pp. 201–13.

Destanne de Bernis, G. De quelques questions concernant la théorie des crises. (Some Questions on the Theory of Crisis. With English summary.) *Écon. Soc.*, September–October–November 1983, *17*(9–10–11), pp. 1277–1329.

Donovan, Donal. Measuring Macroeconomic Performance. *Finance Develop.*, June 1983, *20*(2), pp. 2–5.

Driehuis, Wim and Klant, Jan J. The Nature and Causes of the World Depression. *De Economist*, 1983, *131*(4), pp. 474–97.

Edel, Matthew. Energy and the Long Swing. *Rev. Radical Polit. Econ.*, Fall 1983, *15*(3), pp. 115–30. **[G: U.S.]**

Eichengreen, Barry J. The Causes of British Business Cycles, 1833–1913. *J. Europ. Econ. Hist.*, Spring 1983, *12*(1), pp. 145–61. **[G: U.K.]**

Feldstein, Martin S. Shifting Sands of Recovery. *Challenge*, May/June 1983, *26*(2), pp. 26–33. **[G: U.S.]**

Felmingham, B. S. The Market Integration of Large and Small Economies: Australia, the U.S., and Japan. *J. Macroecon.*, Summer 1983, *5*(3), pp. 335–51. **[G: Australia; Japan; U.S.]**

Forrester, Jay W. Price Behavior and Economic Prospects. **In** *Diewert, W. E. and Montmarquette, C., eds.*, 1983, pp. 1137–69.

Gallestegui, M. C. and Urrutia, J. Crisis, teoria economica y margen de maniobra. (Crisis, Economic Theory and Margin for "Manoeuvre." With English summary.) *Écon. Soc.*, September–October–November 1983, *17*(9–10–11), pp. 1345–81. **[G: OECD]**

Gärtner, Manfred and Heri, Erwin W. Konjunktur und realer Wechselkurs. Eine Kausalitätsanalyse für neum OECD-Länder. (The Trade Cycle and Real Exchange Rates: A Causality Analysis for Nine OECD Countries. With English summary.) *Kredit Kapital*, 1983, *16*(1), pp. 98–116. **[G: OECD]**

Ginsburgh, Victor and Michel, Philippe. Random Timing of Elections and the Political Business Cycle. *Public Choice*, 1983, *40*(2), pp. 155–64.

Glastetter, Werner. Einige Überlegungen zum Wachstumspfad der Bundesrepublik Deutschland. (Some Reflections on the Path of Real Growth in the Federal Republic of Germany. With English summary.) *Kredit Kapital*, 1983, *16*(3), pp. 316–30. **[G: W. Germany]**

Goodwin, R. M. A Note on Wages, Profits and Fluctuating Growth Rates. *Cambridge J. Econ.*, September/December 1983, *7*(3/4), pp. 305–09.

Gordon, David M.; Weisskopf, Thomas E. and Bowles, Samuel. Long Swings and the Nonreproductive Cycle. *Amer. Econ. Rev.*, May 1983, *73*(2), pp. 152–57. **[G: U.S.]**

Grossman, Herschel I. The Natural-Rate Hypothesis, the Rational-Expectations Hypothesis, and the Remarkable Survival of Non-Market-Clearing Assumptions. *Carnegie-Rochester Conf. Ser. Public Policy*, Autumn 1983, *19*, pp. 225–45.

Kimbrough, Kent P. The Information Content of the Exchange Rate and the Stability of Real Output under Alternative Exchange-Rate Regimes. *J. Int. Money Finance*, April 1983, *2*(1), pp. 27–38.

King, Robert G. Interest Rates, Aggregate Information, and Monetary Policy. *J. Monet. Econ.*, August 1983, *12*(2), pp. 199–234.

Kirchgässner, Gebhard. The Political Business Cycle if the Government Is Not Myopic: An Integration of the Long-Run and Short-Run Models of the Political Business Cycle. *Math. Soc. Sci.*, July 1983, *4*(3), pp. 243–60.

Laibman, David. Capitalism and Immanent Crisis: Broad Strokes for a Theoretical Foundation. *Soc. Res.*, Summer 1983, *50*(2), pp. 359–400.

Langfeldt, Enno. Kann eine monetäre Schätzgleichung zur Verbessrung der Konjunkturprognosen beitragen? (Can a Monetary Estimating Equation Contribute to Improvement of Trade Cycle Forecasts? With English summary.) *Kredit Kapital*, 1983, *16*(2), pp. 205–19. **[G: W. Germany]**

Leban, Raymond and Lesourne, Jacques. Adaptive Strategies of the Firm through a Business Cycle. *J. Econ. Dynam. Control*, May 1983, *5*(2/3), pp. 201–34.

Liu, Guoguang and Shen, Liren. How to Transform Cyclical Economic Fluctuations into Smooth, Expanded Reproduction. *Chinese Econ. Stud.*, Fall 1983, *17*(1), pp. 96–104. **[G: China]**

Long, John B., Jr. and Plosser, Charles I. Real Business Cycles. *J. Polit. Econ.*, February 1983, *91*(1), pp. 39–69. **[G: U.S.]**

Lucas, Robert E., Jr. Understanding Business Cycles. **In** *Brunner, K. and Meltzer, A. H., eds.*, 1983, *1977*, pp. 1–23.

Mashiyama, Koichi. An Inventory Stock Market in a Business Cycle Model and Rational Expectations. *Econ. Stud. Quart.*, December 1983, *34*(3), pp. 211–24.

McCallum, Bennett T. The Liquidity Trap and the Pigou Effect: A Dynamic Analysis with Rational Expectations. *Economica*, November 1983,

50(200), pp. 395–405.

Mickwitz, Gösta. En behavioristisk stagflationsteori. (A Behavioral theory of Stagflation. With English summary.) *Ekon. Samfundets Tidskr.*, 1983, *36*(1), pp. 19–24.

Mishkin, Frederic S. The Remarkable Survival of Non-Market-Clearing Assumptions: A Comment. *Carnegie-Rochester Conf. Ser. Public Policy*, Autumn 1983, *19*, pp. 247–51.

Moore, Geoffrey H. What Is a Recession? **In** *Moore, G. H.*, 1983, *1967*, pp. 3–9. **[G: U.S.]**

Okun, Arthur M. Rational-Expectations-with-Misperceptions as a Theory of the Business Cycle. **In** *Okun, A. M.*, 1983, *1980*, pp. 131–41.

Öller, Lars-Erik. Suhdanteet Suomessa vuosina 1948–81 BKT:n neljännesvuosisarjan valossa. (Recessions and Recoveries in Finland 1948–81—Time Series Analysis of Quarterly GDP. With English summary.) *Kansant. Aikak.*, 1983, *79*(2), pp. 194–202. **[G: Finland]**

Pen, Jan. Stagnation Explained? *De Economist*, 1983, *131*(4), pp. 457–73.

van der Ploeg, Frederick. Predator–Prey and Neo-Classical Modes of Cyclical Growth. *Z. Nationalökon.*, 1983, *43*(3), pp. 235–56.

Puccinelli, Pietro. A Cyclical Model of Large Firms. *Econ. Notes*, 1983, (2), pp. 65–83.

Roberts, Charles C. Kann eine monetäre Schätzgleichung zuar Verbesserung der Geldpolitik beitragen?—Kommentar zum Beitrag von Enno Langfeldt. (Can a Monetary Estimating Equation Contribute to Improvement of Monetary Policy? Comment on the Article by E. Langfeldt. With English summary.) *Kredit Kapital*, 1983, *16*(2), pp. 220–30. **[G: W. Germany]**

Rosenberg, Nathan and Frischtak, Claudio R. Long Waves and Economic Growth: A Critical Appraisal. *Amer. Econ. Rev.*, May 1983, *73*(2), pp. 146–51.

Rostow, W. W. Technology and Unemployment in the Western World. *Challenge*, March/April 1983, *26*(1), pp. 6–17. **[G: MDCs]**

Schui, Herbert. Arbeitsproduktivität, Verteilung und Stabilität des Konjunkturaufschwunges. Einige Überlegungen zu einem aktuellen Problem (Productivity, Distribution and Stability of the Economic Upswing: Some Notes on a Present-Day Problem. With English summary.) *Konjunkturpolitik*, 1983, *29*(4), pp. 229–47. **[G: W. Germany]**

Sellekaerts, Willy. Coping with Stagflation. *Atlantic Econ. J.*, December 1983, *11*(4), pp. 14–19. **[G: U.S.]**

Sherman, Howard J. Realization Crisis Theory and the Labor Theory of Value [A Note on the Underconsumptionist Theory and the Labor Theory of Value]. *Sci. Soc.*, Summer 1983, *47*(2), pp. 205–13.

Siebrand, Jan C. and van der Windt, Nico. Economic Crisis and Economic Policy in the Thirties and the Seventies. *De Economist*, 1983, *131*(4), pp. 517–47. **[G: Netherlands]**

Sims, Christopher A. Is There a Monetary Business Cycle? *Amer. Econ. Rev.*, May 1983, *73*(2), pp. 228–33.

Sutcliffe, B. Unas observaciones sobre la teorización de la crisis económica actual. (Observations on the Theorization of the Present Economic Crisis. With English summary.) *Écon. Soc.*, September–October–November 1983, *17*(9–10–11), pp. 1331–43.

Svindland, Eirik. Konjunkturtheoretische Implikationen der Hypothese rationaler Erwartungen. (Implications of the "Rational Expectations" Hypothesis with Respect to Business Cycle Theory. With English summary.) *Kredit Kapital*, 1983, *16*(3), pp. 331–50.

Tietzel, Manfred. Erkenntnisfortschritt und Konjunkturtheorie. (Progress of Knowledge and the Theory of the Trade Cycle. With English summary.) *Ifo-Studien*, 1983, *29*(1), pp. 11–30.

Ueda, Kazuo. Trade Balance Adjustment with Imported Intermediate Goods: The Japanese Case. *Rev. Econ. Statist.*, November 1983, *65*(4), pp. 618–25. **[G: Japan]**

Watson, Mark W. Imperfect Information and Wage Inertia in the Business Cycle: A Comment. *J. Polit. Econ.*, October 1983, *91*(5), pp. 876–79.

Weber, Robert Philip. Cyclical Theories of Crises in the World-System. **In** *Bergesen, A., ed.*, 1983, pp. 37–55. **[G: U.S.; U.K.]**

Weeks, John. On the Issue of Capitalist Circulation and the Concepts Appropriate to Its Analysis [Realization Crisis Theory and the Labor Theory of Value]. *Sci. Soc.*, Summer 1983, *47*(2), pp. 214–25.

Weller, Barry R. The Political Business Cycle: A Discriminating Analysis. *Soc. Sci. Quart.*, June 1983, *64*(2), pp. 398–403. **[G: U.S.]**

Zinn, Karl Georg. Zyklus, Stabilität und Geldneutralität. Ein lehrgeschichtliche Ergänzung zum Problem der potentialorientierten Geldpolitik auf der Grundlage von Schumpeters Entwicklungstheorie. (Business Cycle, Stability, and Neutral Money. With English summary.) *Konjunkturpolitik*, 1983, *29*(6), pp. 329–47.

Zwintz, Richard. Probleme einer komparativ-dynamischen Analyse in einem einfachen Zwei-Regionen-Konjunkturmodell. (Some Problems of Comparative Dynamic Analysis in a Two-Region Business Cycle Model. With English summary.) *Jahr. Nationalökon. Statist.*, September 1983, *198*(5), pp. 409–24.

1313 Economic Fluctuations: Studies

Barr, G. D. I. and Kantor, B. S. A Rational Expectations Analysis of the South African Business Cycles. *J. Stud. Econ. Econometrics*, July 1983, (16), pp. 5–16. **[G: S. Africa]**

Bednarzik, Robert W. Short Workweeks during Economic Downturns. *Mon. Lab. Rev.*, June 1983, *106*(6), pp. 3–11. **[G: U.S.]**

Bergsten, C. Fred. Can We Prevent a World Economic Crisis? *Challenge*, January/February 1983, *25*(6), pp. 4–13. **[G: U.S.]**

Bernanke, Ben S. Nonmonetary Effects of the Financial Crisis in Propagation of the Great Depression. *Amer. Econ. Rev.*, June 1983, *73*(3), pp. 257–76. **[G: U.S.]**

Bono Martínez, E.; Jordán Galduf, J. M. and Tomás Carpi, J.-A. Notas sobre crisis de legitimación, déficit público y transición politíca en España. (Notes on the Crisis of Legitimacy, the Public

Deficit and Transitional Politics in Spain. With English summary.) *Écon. Soc.*, September–October–November 1983, *17*(9–10–11), pp. 1741–61. [G: Spain]

Booth, G. Geoffrey and Koveos, Peter E. Employment Fluctuations: An R/S Analysis. *J. Reg. Sci.*, February 1983, *23*(1), pp. 19–31. [G: U.S.]

Borsu-Bilande, A. Application des méthodes de Box et Jenkins à la construction d'un indice de conjoncture. (With English summary.) *Cah. Écon. Bruxelles,* 4th Trimester 1983, (100), pp. 594–620.

Bródy, András. About Investment Cycles and Their Attenuation. *Acta Oecon.*, 1983, *31* (1–2), pp. 37–51. [G: Hungary]

Bruce, Neil and Purvis, Douglas D. Fiscal Policy and Recovery from the Great Recession. *Can. Public Policy,* March 1983, *9*(1), pp. 53–67. [G: Canada]

Cain, Neville G. Recovery Policy in Australia 1930–33: Certain Native Wisdom. *Australian Econ. Hist. Rev.*, September 1983, *23*(2), pp. 193–218. [G: Australia]

Cripps, Francis and Ward, Terry. Government Policies, European Recession and Problems of Recovery. *Cambridge J. Econ.*, March 1983, *7*(1), pp. 85–99. [G: W. Europe]

Dailami, Mansoor. Cyclical Economic Fluctuations and Oil Consumption Behavior. *Energy Econ.*, July 1983, *5*(3), pp. 157–63. [G: OECD]

De Nicola, Eugenio. Early Signals of Economic Change Coming from a Group of International Business Climate Indicators. *Econ. Notes,* 1983, (3), pp. 184–98. [G: Italy; Germany; France; U.K.]

Devine, James N. Underconsumption, Over-Investment and the Origins of the Great Depression. *Rev. Radical Polit. Econ.*, Summer 1983, *15*(2), pp. 1–27. [G: U.S.]

Driver, Ciaran. The Macroeconomic Theory of A. S. Eichner. *Brit. Rev. Econ. Issues,* Autumn 1983, *5*(13), pp. 63–85. [G: U.K.]

Duncan, Joseph W. Private Sector Data on Business Failures. *Rev. Public Data Use (See J. Econ. Soc. Meas. after 4/85),* March 1983, *11*(1), pp. 29–35. [G: U.S.]

Dupriez, L. H. The Long Wave Theory Confirmed by the Present Crisis. **In** *[Saunders, C. T.],* 1983, pp. 51–59. [G: Global]

Fernandez Arufe, J. E. La actual crisis económica y políticas de empleo: la situación española. (The Economic Crisis and Employment Policies: The Case of Spain. With English summary.) *Écon. Soc.*, September–October–November 1983, *17*(9–10–11), pp. 1517–35. [G: Spain]

Førsund, Finn R. and Jansen, Eilev S. Analysis of Energy Intensive Industries—The Case of Norwegian Aluminium Production 1966–1978. **In** *Av, R., et al., eds.*, 1983, pp. 221–59. [G: Norway]

Gay, Robert S. and Hedlund, Jeffrey D. The Labor Market in Recession and Recovery. *Fed. Res. Bull.*, July 1983, *69*(7), pp. 477–88. [G: U.S.]

Goodwin, R. M. Does the Matrix Multiplier Oscillate? **In** *Goodwin, R. M.*, 1983, *1950,* pp. 22–29. [G: U.S.]

Graham, Alan K. The Long Wave. **In** *Migliaro, A. and Jain, C. L., eds.*, 1983, pp. 69–74. [G: U.S.]

Hamilton, James D. Oil and the Macroeconomy since World War II. *J. Polit. Econ.*, April 1983, *91*(2), pp. 228–48. [G: U.S.]

Hill, C. W. L. Conglomerate Performance over the Economic Cycle. *J. Ind. Econ.*, December 1983, *32*(2), pp. 197–211. [G: U.K.]

Hoffman, Joan. Urban Squeeze Plays: New York City Crises of the 1930s and 1970s. *Rev. Radical Polit. Econ.*, Summer 1983, *15*(2), pp. 29–57. [G: U.S.]

Hunt, Lacy H. The Causes of the 1981–82 Recession. **In** *Weintraub, S. and Goodstein, M., eds.*, 1983, pp. 84–91. [G: U.S.]

Klein, Philip A. The Neglected Institutionalism of Wesley Clair Mitchell: The Theoretical Basis for Business Cycle Indicators. *J. Econ. Issues,* December 1983, *17*(4), pp. 867–99. [G: U.S.]

Korteweg, Pieter. The Economics of Inflation and Output Fluctuations in the Netherlands, 1954–1975: A Test of Some Implications of the Dominant Impulse-cum-Rational Expectations Hypothesis. **In** *Brunner, K. and Meltzer, A. H., eds.*, 1983, *1978,* pp. 25–79. [G: Netherlands]

Labys, Walter C. and Afrasiabi, A. Cyclical Disequilibrium in the U.S. Copper Market. *Appl. Econ.*, August 1983, *15*(4), pp. 437–49. [G: U.S.]

Lackman, Conway Lee. Gallaway's Labor Force Participation Studies Revisited. *Econ. Notes,* 1983, (1), pp. 140–52. [G: U.S.]

Laidler, David. The Consumer Price Index and Signals of Recession and Recovery: Comment. **In** *Diewert, W. E. and Montmarquette, C., eds.*, 1983, pp. 1133–35. [G: U.S.]

Lecaillon, Jacques. Aspects conjoncturels et électoraux des fluctuations de la répartition. *Revue Écon. Polit.*, January–February 1983, *93*(1), pp. 29–43. [G: France]

Leeuw, Frank and de Holloway, Thomas M. Cyclical Adjustment of the Federal Budget and Federal Debt. *Surv. Curr. Bus.*, December 1983, *63*(12), pp. 25–40. [G: U.S.]

Leiderman, Leonardo. The Response of Real Wages to Unanticipated Money Growth. *J. Monet. Econ.*, January 1983, *11*(1), pp. 73–88. [G: U.S.]

Lissner, Will. A Major Contribution to Business Cycle Research. *Amer. J. Econ. Soc.*, October 1983, *42*(4), pp. 429–30. [G: U.K.; U.S.; Japan; Australia]

Loeb, Peter D. Leading and Coincident Indicators of Recession and Recovery in New Jersey. **In** *Dutta, M.; Hartline, J. C. and Loeb, P. D., eds.*, 1983, pp. 151–72. [G: U.S.]

Maddison, Angus. Economic Stagnation since 1973, Its Nature and Causes: A Six Country Survey. *De Economist,* 1983, *131*(4), pp. 585–608. [G: Selected OECD]

Mansfield, Edwin. Long Waves and Technological Innovation. *Amer. Econ. Rev.*, May 1983, *73*(2), pp. 141–45. [G: U.S.]

McAlpin, Michelle B. Price Movements and Fluctuations in Economic Activity (1860–1947). **In** *Kumar, D., ed.*, 1983, pp. 878–904. [G: India]

McDonald, John. The Emergence of Countercyclical U.S. Fertility: A Reassessment of the Evidence. *J. Macroecon.*, Fall 1983, *5*(4), pp. 421–36. [G: U.S.]

Michaely, Michael. Trade in a Changed World Economy. *World Devel.*, May 1983, *11*(5), pp.

397–403. [G: OECD]

Moore, Geoffrey H. A New Leading Index of Employment and Unemployment. **In** *Moore, G. H.,* 1983, *1981,* pp. 353–60. [G: U.S.]

Moore, Geoffrey H. A New Weekly Leading Index. *Bus. Econ.,* May 1983, *18*(3), pp. 5–12. [G: U.S.]

Moore, Geoffrey H. Cyclical Fluctuations and Secular Inflation. **In** *Moore, G. H.,* 1983, pp. 237–44. [G: U.S.]

Moore, Geoffrey H. Employment, Unemployment, and the Inflation–Recession Dilemma. **In** *Moore, G. H.,* 1983, *1976,* pp. 211–32. [G: U.S.]

Moore, Geoffrey H. Five Little-known Facts about Inflation. **In** *Moore, G. H.,* 1983, *1977,* pp. 171–74. [G: U.S.]

Moore, Geoffrey H. Forecasting Short-term Economic Change. **In** *Moore, G. H.,* 1983, *1969,* pp. 401–32. [G: U.S.]

Moore, Geoffrey H. Growth Cycles: A New–Old Concept. **In** *Moore, G. H.,* 1983, *1979,* pp. 61–64. [G: U.S.]

Moore, Geoffrey H. Presenting Employment and Unemployment Statistics in a Business Cycle Context. **In** *Moore, G. H.,* 1983, *1978,* pp. 93–125. [G: U.S.]

Moore, Geoffrey H. Recession or Depression? **In** *Moore, G. H.,* 1983, *1982,* pp. 19–22. [G: U.S.]

Moore, Geoffrey H. Recession Slows Inflation. **In** *Moore, G. H.,* 1983, *1979,* pp. 233–36. [G: Japan; U.K.; U.S.; W. Germany]

Moore, Geoffrey H. Security Markets and Business Cycles. **In** *Moore, G. H.,* 1983, *1975,* pp. 139–60. [G: U.S.]

Moore, Geoffrey H. Some Secular Changes in Business Cycles. **In** *Moore, G. H.,* 1983, *1974,* pp. 161–68. [G: U.S.]

Moore, Geoffrey H. The Consumer Price Index and Signals of Recession and Recovery. **In** *Diewert, W. E. and Montmarquette, C., eds.,* 1983, pp. 1117–32. [G: U.S.]

Moore, Geoffrey H. The Cyclical Behavior of Prices. **In** *Moore, G. H.,* 1983, *1971,* pp. 175–210. [G: U.S.]

Moore, Geoffrey H. The Federal Deficit as a Business Cycle Stabilizer. **In** *Moore, G. H.,* 1983, *1976,* pp. 127–37. [G: U.S.]

Moore, Geoffrey H. The Forty-second Anniversary of the Leading Indicators. **In** *Moore, G. H.,* 1983, *1979,* pp. 369–400. [G: U.S.]

Moore, Geoffrey H. When Lagging Indicators Lead: The History of an Idea. **In** *Moore, G. H.,* 1983, *1978,* pp. 361–67. [G: U.S.]

Moore, Geoffrey H. Why the Leading Indicators Really Do Lead. **In** *Moore, G. H.,* 1983, *1978,* pp. 339–51. [G: U.S.]

Moore, Geoffrey H. and Cullity, John P. Trends and Cycles in Productivity, Unit Costs, and Prices: An International Perspective. **In** *Moore, G. H.,* 1983, *1982,* pp. 245–80. [G: Japan; U.K.; U.S.; W. Germany]

Moore, Geoffrey H. and Moore, Melita H. An Introduction to International Economic Indicators. **In** *Moore, G. H.,* 1983, pp. 65–91. [G: OECD]

Nermuth, Manfred. Insolvencies and the Business Cycle in Austria. *Empirica,* 1983, (2), pp. 159–82. [G: Austria]

Neumann, Manfred; Böbel, Ingo and Haid, Alfred. Business Cycle and Industrial Market Power: An Empirical Investigation for West German Industries, 1965–1977. *J. Ind. Econ.,* December 1983, *32*(2), pp. 187–96. [G: W. Germany]

Niemira, Michael P. Sequential Signals of Recession and Recovery: Revisited. *Bus. Econ.,* January 1983, *18*(1), pp. 51–53. [G: U.S.]

Okun, Arthur M. A Postmortem of the 1974 Recession. **In** *Okun, A. M.,* 1983, *1975,* pp. 482–95. [G: U.S.]

Okun, Arthur M. Achieving Sustained Prosperity. **In** *Okun, A. M.,* 1983, *1970,* pp. 424–49. [G: U.S.]

Okun, Arthur M. On the Appraisal of Cyclical Turning-Point Predictors. **In** *Okun, A. M.,* 1983, *1960,* pp. 525–52. [G: U.S.]

Okun, Arthur M. Postwar Macroeconomics: The Evolution of Events and Ideas. **In** *Okun, A. M.,* 1983, *1981,* pp. 496–504. [G: U.S.]

de la Peunte, F. and de Ullivarri, Fdez. La intensidad de la crisis actual a la luz de la teoría de los ciclos económicos. (Intensity of the Present Crisis under the Economic Cycle Theory. With English summary.) *Écon. Soc.,* September–October–November 1983, *17*(9–10–11), pp. 1403–19.

Pollard, Walker A. Presidential Elections: Cyclical and Distributional Economic Effects. *Public Finance Quart.,* April 1983, *11*(2), pp. 217–36.

Ray, George F. Energy and the Long Cycles. *Energy Econ.,* January 1983, *5*(1), pp. 3–8. [G: Austro-Hungary; Sweden; EEC]

Ray, John. An Empirical Study of the Political Business Cycle: Government Fiscal Policy and the Business Cycle in the United States. *Econ. Forum,* Winter 1983-84, *14*(2), pp. 19–40. [G: U.S.]

Renshaw, Edward F. The Anatomy of Stock Market Cycles. *J. Portfol. Manage.,* Fall 1983, *10*(1), pp. 53–57. [G: U.S.]

Rice, G. Randolph and Lozada, Gabriel A. The Effects of Unemployment and Inflation on the Income Distribution: A Regional View. *Atlantic Econ. J.,* July 1983, *11*(2), pp. 12–21. [G: U.S.]

Samura, Terutoshi. The Economic Movements of North France in the Latter Half of the Seventeenth Century. *Osaka Econ. Pap.,* September 1983, *33*(1–2), pp. 30–49. [G: France]

Sannucci, Valeria. L'andamento dei profitti bancari rispetto al ciclo economico. (The Trend of Banking Profits Relative to the Business Cycle. With English summary.) *Bancaria,* November 1983, *39*(11), pp. 1080–091. [G: U.S.; Italy]

Santoni, G. J. Business Cycles and the Eighth District. *Fed. Res. Bank St. Louis Rev.,* December 1983, *65*(10), pp. 14–21. [G: U.S.]

Schoonbeek, L. On the Number of Non-Zero Eigenvalues of a Dynamic Linear Econometric Model: A Note. *Empirical Econ.,* 1983, *8*(2), pp. 119–23. [G: W. Germany]

Sherman, Howard J. Cyclical Behavior of Government Fiscal Policy. *J. Econ. Issues,* June 1983, *17*(2), pp. 379–88. [G: U.S.]

Sideri, Sandro. Crisi mondiale, crisi dei modelli di sviluppo latino-americani e ralazioni economiche della Comunità Europea con l'America Latina. (The World Crisis, the Crisis of Latin American

Development Models and the Economic Relations of the European Community with Latin America. With English summary.) *Giorn. Econ.*, September–October 1983, *42*(9–10), pp. 601–16. **[G: EEC; Latin America]**

Siegenthaler, Hansjörg. Konsens, Erwartungen und Entschlusskraft: Erfahrungen der Schweiz in der Überwindung der Grossen Depression vor hundert Jahren. (On the Swiss Experience in Overcoming the Great Depression of the Years 1876–1885. With English summary.) *Schweiz. Z. Volkswirtsch. Statist.*, September 1983, *119*(3), pp. 213–35. **[G: Switzerland]**

Stricker, Frank. Causes of the Great Depression, or What Reagan Doesn't Know about the 1920s. *Econ. Forum,* Winter 1983-84, *14*(2), pp. 41–58. **[G: U.S.]**

Strong, John S. Regional Variations in Industrial Performance. *Reg. Stud.*, December 1983, *17*(6), pp. 429–44. **[G: U.S.]**

Talamona, Mario. Sviluppo, moneta e credito: la "visione" di Schumpeter e il caso italiano. (Schumpeter's View on Growth, Money and Credit, and the "Italian Case." With English summary.) *Giorn. Econ.*, July–August 1983, *42*(7–8), pp. 405–29. **[G: Italy]**

Taylor, C. T. Why Is Britain in a Recession? **In** *Feinstein, C., ed.*, 1983, *1978*, pp. 185–206. **[G: U.K.]**

Tokman, Victor E. Wages and Employment in International Recessions: Recent Latin American Experience. *Cepal Rev.*, August 1983, (20), pp. 113–26. **[G: Latin America]**

Twomey, Michael J. The Cyclical Relationship between Output and Real Wages in LDC's. *Quart. Rev. Econ. Bus.*, Spring 1983, *23*(1), pp. 79–84. **[G: Latin America]**

Twomey, Michael J. The 1930s Depression in Latin America: A Macro Analysis. *Exploration Econ. Hist.*, July 1983, *20*(3), pp. 221–47. **[G: Latin America; Europe; N. America]**

Tyson, Laura D'Andrea. Investment Allocation: A Comparison of the Reform Experiences of Hungary and Yugoslavia. *J. Compar. Econ.*, September 1983, *7*(3), pp. 288–303. **[G: Hungary; Yugoslavia]**

Vaciago, Giacomo. Re dollaro contro tutti. (King Dollar: One against Everybody. With English summary.) *L'Impresa,* 1983, *25*(6), pp. 59–62. **[G: Italy; U.S.]**

Van Roon, Ger. 'Long Wave' Economic Trends and Economic Policies in the Netherlands in the XIXth and XXth Century. *J. Europ. Econ. Hist.*, Fall 1983, *12*(2), pp. 323–37. **[G: Netherlands]**

Westerhoff, Horst-Dieter. Wirkungsverzögerungen in der Konjunkturpolitik. Eine empirische Messung für die Bauwirtschaft. (Time-Lags in Trade Cycle Policy: Empirical Measurement for the Building Industry. With English summary.) *Ifo-Studien,* 1983, *29*(1), pp. 31–71. **[G: W. Germany]**

Zarnowitz, Victor and Moore, Geoffrey H. Sequential Signals of Recession and Recovery. **In** *Moore, G. H.*, 1983, *1982*, pp. 23–59. **[G: U.S.]**

Zarnowitz, Victor and Moore, Geoffrey H. The Timing and Severity of the 1980 Recession. **In** *Moore, G. H.*, 1983, *1981*, pp. 11–17. **[G: U.S.]**

132 Forecasting; Econometric Models

1320 General

Britton, Andrew. Employment, Output and Inflation: Introduction. **In** *Britton, A., ed.*, 1983, pp. 1–15. **[G: U.K.]**

Dantzig, George B. Concerns about Large-scale Models. **In** *Thrall, R. M.; Thompson, R. G. and Holloway, M. L., eds.*, 1983, pp. 15–20.

Evans, Michael K. Macroeconomic Forecasting in the 1980s. *Bus. Econ.*, September 1983, *18*(4), pp. 5–10. **[G: U.S.]**

Gass, Saul I. and Parikh, Shailendra C. Credible Analysis for Public Policy Studies. **In** *Lev, B., ed.*, 1983, pp. 85–98.

Gilli, Manfred; Ritschard, Gilbert and Royer, Daniel. Pour une approche structurale en économie. (Towards a Structural Approach in Economics. With English summary.) *Revue Écon.*, March 1983, *34*(2), pp. 277–304.

Hirshfield, D.S. and Rapoport, L. A. Evaluation of U.S. Energy Policy Impacts on Energy Supplies and Costs. **In** *Lev, B., ed.*, 1983, pp. 445–63. **[G: U.S.]**

Hogan, William W. Alternatives to Transfer of Large-scale Models. **In** *Thrall, R. M.; Thompson, R. G. and Holloway, M. L., eds.*, 1983, pp. 173–89.

Holaday, Bart. Conditions for Effective Model Utilization in Policy Decision-making. **In** *Thrall, R. M.; Thompson, R. G. and Holloway, M. L., eds.*, 1983, pp. 21–24.

Holt, Charles C. Quantitative Modeling: Needs and Shortfalls for Energy Analysis. **In** *Thrall, R. M.; Thompson, R. G. and Holloway, M. L., eds.*, 1983, pp. 219–30.

Hüttl, Antónia; Losonczy, I. and Örszigety, G. The Financial Regulator Model. *Matekon,* Summer 1983, *19*(4), pp. 3–20. **[G: Hungary]**

Klein, Lawrence R. Supply-side Modeling. **In** *Thrall, R. M.; Thompson, R. G. and Holloway, M. L., eds.*, 1983, pp. 55–75.

Migliaro, A. The National Econometric Model—A Layman's Guide. **In** *Migliaro, A. and Jain, C. L., eds.*, 1983, pp. 5–8.

Mihailov, Boris. Modeling Alternative Socioeconomic Mechanisms. **In** *Kelley, A. C.; Sanderson, W. C. and Williamson, J. G., eds.*, 1983, pp. 141–65.

Moore, Geoffrey H. Using a Leading Employment Index to Forecast Unemployment in 1983. *Mon. Lab. Rev.*, May 1983, *106*(5), pp. 30–32. **[G: U.S.]**

Moses, Lincoln E. Energy Models: Complexity, Documentation, and Simplicity. **In** *Thrall, R. M.; Thompson, R. G. and Holloway, M. L., eds.*, 1983, pp. 5–14.

Okun, Arthur M. A Review of Some Economic Forecasts for 1955–57. **In** *Okun, A. M.*, 1983, *1959*, pp. 507–24. **[G: U.S.]**

Okun, Arthur M. Uses of Models for Policy Formulation. **In** *Okun, A. M.*, 1983, *1975*, pp. 562–74.

Reischauer, Robert D. Getting, Using, and Misusing Economic Information. **In** *Schick, A., ed.*, 1983, pp. 38–68. **[G: U.S.]**

Savage, David and Payne, Judith. The Assessment of the National Institute's Forecasts of GDP, 1959–82. *Nat. Inst. Econ. Rev.,* August 1983, (105), pp. 29–35. **[G: U.S.]**

Sohlman, Åsa. Using Quantified General Equilibrium Models for Cost-benefit Analysis of Alternative Energy Policies. **In** *Sohlman, A. M., ed.,* 1983, pp. 306–27. **[G: Sweden]**

Weintraub, Sidney. A Macro-Distributive Theory Dispelling the Econometric Fog. *Banca Naz. Lavoro Quart. Rev.,* March 1983, (144), pp. 69–80.

1322 General Forecasts and Models

Adams, F. Gerard and Marquez, Jaime R. The Impact of Petroleum and Commodity Prices in a Model of the World Economy. **In** *Hickman, B. G., ed.,* 1983, pp. 203–16. **[G: LDCs; MDCs]**

Anandalingam, G. Planning Studies with an Optimal Control Multisectoral Dynamic Economic Model: The Case of Sri Lanka. *J. Policy Modeling,* June 1983, *5*(2), pp. 179–205. **[G: Sri Lanka]**

Anderson, Evan E. An Analysis of NABE Multiperiod Quarterly Forecasts. *Bus. Econ.,* September 1983, *18*(4), pp. 11–17. **[G: U.S.]**

Andreassen, Arthur J.; Saunders, Norman C. and Su, Betty W. Economic Outlook for the 1990's: Three Scenarios for Economic Growth. *Mon. Lab. Rev.,* November 1983, *106*(11), pp. 11–23. **[G: U.S.]**

Arestis, P.; Holly, S. and Karakitsos, Elias. Optimal Stabilisation Policies in West Germany and the Netherlands. **In** *[Saunders, C. T.],* 1983, pp. 309–38. **[G: Netherlands; W. Germany]**

Augustinovics, Mária. Macroeconomic Models for the Sixth Five-Year Plan. *Matekon,* Spring 1983, *19*(3), pp. 3–17. **[G: Hungary]**

Barker, K. M. World Economy Forecast Post-Mortems: 1978–82. *Nat. Inst. Econ. Rev.,* May 1983, (104), pp. 32–37. **[G: OECD; Global]**

Batten, Dallas S. and Thornton, Daniel L. Polynomial Distributed Lags and the Estimation of the St. Louis Equation. *Fed. Res. Bank St. Louis Rev.,* April 1983, *65*(4), pp. 13–25. **[G: U.S.]**

Beenstock, Michael and Dicks, G. R. An Aggregate Monetary Model of the World Economy. *Europ. Econ. Rev.,* May 1983, *21*(3), pp. 261–85.

Bergman, Lars. A Model of Multisectoral Economic Growth in a Small Open Economy. **In** *Kelley, A. C.; Sanderson, W. C. and Williamson, J. G., eds.,* 1983, pp. 225–36. **[G: Sweden]**

Bergman, Lars. General Equilibrium Modeling of Trade-Liberalization Issues among Major World Trade Blocs: Comment. **In** *Hickman, B. G., ed.,* 1983, pp. 137–38. **[G: OECD; Global]**

Brandsma, Andries S.; Hughes Hallett, A. J. and van der Windt, Nico. Optimal Control of Large Nonlinear Models: An Efficient Method of Policy Search Applied to the Dutch Economy. *J. Policy Modeling,* June 1983, *5*(2), pp. 253–70. **[G: Netherlands]**

Brooks, S. and Henry, S. G. B. A Tracking Exercise. **In** *Britton, A., ed.,* 1983, pp. 133–42. **[G: U.K.]**

Brooks, S. and Henry, S. G. B. Simulation Exercises with the Complete Model. **In** *Britton, A., ed.,* 1983, pp. 121–32. **[G: U.K.]**

Brooks, Simon J. and Henry, Brian. Re-Estimation of the National Institute Model. *Nat. Inst. Econ. Rev.,* February 1983, (103), pp. 62–70. **[G: U.K.]**

Brooks, Simon J.; Henry, Brian and Karakitsos, Elias. Policy Trade-Offs in the NIESR Model: Exercises Using Optimal Control. *Nat. Inst. Econ. Rev.,* August 1983, (105), pp. 36–45. **[G: U.K.]**

Burkett, John P. The Impact of Economic Reform on Macroeconomics Policy in Yugoslavia: Some Econometric Evidence. *Econ. Anal. Worker's Manage.,* 1983, *17*(3), pp. 213–43. **[G: Yugoslavia]**

Carlson, Keith M. and Hein, Scott E. Four Econometric Models and Monetary Policy: The Longer-Run View. *Fed. Res. Bank St. Louis Rev.,* January 1983, *65*(1), pp. 13–24. **[G: U.S.]**

Carrin, G.; Gunning, Jan Willem and Waelbroeck, Jean. A General Equilibrium Model for the World Economy: Some Preliminary Results. **In** *Hickman, B. G., ed.,* 1983, pp. 99–117. **[G: LDCs; Global]**

Caton, Christopher N. and Probyn, Christopher J. The DRI Model. **In** *Migliaro, A. and Jain, C. L., eds.,* 1983, pp. 37–40. **[G: U.S.]**

Challen, D. W. and Hagger, A. J. Macro-Econometric Models: A Taxonomy. *Australian Econ. Rev.,* 3rd Quarter 1983, (63), pp. 26–33.

Chappell, Henry W., Jr. and Keech, William R. Welfare Consequences of the Six-Year Presidential Term Evaluated in the Context of a Model of the U.S. Economy. *Amer. Polit. Sci. Rev.,* March 1983, *77*(1), pp. 75–91. **[G: U.S.]**

Coen, Robert M. Long-term Forecasts and Policy Implications: Simulations with a World Econometric Model (T-FAIS IV): Comment. **In** *Hickman, B. G., ed.,* 1983, pp. 66–68. **[G: Global]**

Costa, Antonio Maria. DYNAMICO: A Multilevel Programming Model of World Trade and Development. **In** *Hickman, B. G., ed.,* 1983, pp. 259–76. **[G: Global]**

Cumby, Robert E.; Huizinga, John and Obstfeld, Maurice. Two-Step Two-Stage Least Squares Estimation in Models with Rational Expectations. *J. Econometrics,* April 1983, *21*(3), pp. 333–55. **[G: U.S.]**

Darby, Michael R. International Transmission of Monetary and Fiscal Shocks under Pegged and Floating Exchange Rates: Simulation Experiments. **In** *Darby, M. P. and Lothian, J. R., et al.,* 1983, pp. 162–231. **[G: OECD]**

Darby, Michael R. The Importance of Oil Price Changes in the 1970s World Inflation. **In** *Darby, M. P. and Lothian, J. R., et al.,* 1983, pp. 232–72. **[G: OECD]**

Darby, Michael R. and Stockman, Alan C. The Mark III International Transmission Model: Specification. **In** *Darby, M. P. and Lothian, J. R., et al.,* 1983, pp. 85–112. **[G: OECD]**

Darby, Michael R. and Stockman, Alan C. The Mark III International Transmission Model: Estimates. **In** *Darby, M. P. and Lothian, J. R., et al.,* 1983, pp. 113–61. **[G: OECD]**

Driscoll, Michael J.; Ford, J. L. and Mullineux, A. W. The Gains and Losses to Predicting Nominal Income by Disaggregating via the New Classical Aggregate Supply and Rational Expectations Hypotheses. *Empirical Econ.*, 1983, *8*(1), pp. 47–58. **[G: U.S.]**

Drud, Arne and Grais, Wafik M. Macroeconomic Adjustment in Thailand: Demand Management and Supply Conditions. *J. Policy Modeling*, June 1983, *5*(2), pp. 207–31. **[G: Thailand]**

Fair, Ray C. An Outline of a Multicountry Econometric Model. **In** *Hickman, B. G., ed.*, 1983, pp. 85–92. **[G: Global]**

Filatov, Victor; Hickman, Bert G. and Klein, Lawrence R. Long-term Simulations with the Project LINK System, 1978–85. **In** *Hickman, B. G., ed.*, 1983, pp. 29–51. **[G: Global]**

Fischer, J. and Uebe, Gotze. The "Optimal" Control of the RWI-Model. **In** *Gruber, J., ed.*, 1983, pp. 10–20. **[G: W. Germany]**

Forrester, Jay W. Price Behavior and Economic Prospects. **In** *Diewert, W. E. and Montmarquette, C., eds.*, 1983, pp. 1137–69.

Friedrich, D. and Termin, J. Ökonometrische Modellprognose versus univariate Zeitreihenprojektion: Eine Fallstudie mit dem F & T-Modell. (Econometric Model Forecasts versus Prediction with an Univariate Time Series Method: A Case Study with the F & T-Model. With English summary.) *Jahr. Nationalökon. Statist.*, September 1983, *198*(5), pp. 437–57. **[G: W. Germany]**

Frommholz, H. and Wolters, J. A Control-theoretic Analysis for a Small Econometric Model of the Federal Republic of Germany. **In** *Gruber, J., ed.*, 1983, pp. 116–30. **[G: W. Germany]**

Garganas, Nicholas C. An Evaluation of the Predictive Accuracy of the Bank of Greece Model of the Greek Economy. *Greek Econ. Rev.*, August 1983, *5*(2), pp. 101–22. **[G: Greece]**

Grimm, Bruce T. and Hirsch, Albert A. The Impact of the 1976 NIPA Benchmark Revision on the Structure and Predictive Accuracy of the BEA Quarterly Econometric Model. **In** *Foss, M. F., ed.*, 1983, pp. 333–80. **[G: U.S.]**

Gustely, Richard D. and Ireland, Timothy C. Developing a Quarterly Counterpart to an Existing Annual Regional Econometric Model. *Reg. Sci. Persp.*, 1983, *13*(1), pp. 25–47. **[G: U.S.]**

Heike, Hans-Dieter and Rossa, Harald. Optimal Stabilization with a Quarterly Model of the Federal Republic of Germany. **In** *Gruber, J., ed.*, 1983, pp. 21–47. **[G: W. Germany]**

Hickman, Bert G. A Cross Section of Global International Economic Models. **In** *Hickman, B. G., ed.*, 1983, pp. 3–26.

Hickman, Bert G. and Filatov, Victor. A Decomposition of International Income Multipliers. **In** *[Klein, L. R.]*, 1983, pp. 340–67. **[G: OECD]**

Hirsch, Albert A. Macroeconomic Effects of Price Shocks: A Simulation Study. *Surv. Curr. Bus.*, February 1983, *63*(2), pp. 30–43. **[G: U.S.]**

Hoffman, Dennis L. and Schlagenhauf, Don E. Rationality, Specification Tests, and Macroeconomic Models. *J. Econometrics*, April 1983, *21*(3), pp. 367–86. **[G: U.S.]**

Holly, S. and Zarrop, M. B. On Optimality and Time Consistency When Expectations Are Rational. *Europ. Econ. Rev.*, January 1983, *20*(1–3), pp. 23–40. **[G: Netherlands]**

Howe, Howard J. and Guill, Gene D. The Wharton Model. **In** *Migliaro, A. and Jain, C. L., eds.*, 1983, pp. 44–49.

Hymans, Saul H. The Deficit and the Fiscal and Monetary Policy Mix: Discussion. **In** *Federal Reserve Bank of Boston*, 1983, pp. 195–98. **[G: U.S.]**

Hymans, Saul H. The Impact of the 1976 NIPA Benchmark Revision on the Structure and Predictive Accuracy of the BEA Quarterly Econometric Model: Comment. **In** *Foss, M. F., ed.*, 1983, pp. 380–82. **[G: U.S.]**

Ichimura, Shinichi. Project FUGI and the Future of ESCAP Developing Countries: Comment. **In** *Hickman, B. G., ed.*, 1983, pp. 254–57. **[G: Global]**

Kaya, Yoichi; Onishi, Akira and Suzuki, Yutaka. Project FUGI and the Future of ESCAP Developing Countries. **In** *Hickman, B. G., ed.*, 1983, pp. 237–54. **[G: Global]**

Kazakevich, G. D. Experience in Developing and Using a Nonlinear Econometric Model of the Economy of the RSFSR. *Matekon*, Summer 1983, *19*(4), pp. 62–78. **[G: U.S.S.R.]**

Kehoe, Timothy J. and Serra-Puche, Jaime. A Computational General Equilibrium Model with Endogenous Unemployment: An Analysis of the 1980 Fiscal Reform in Mexico. *J. Public Econ.*, October 1983, *22*(1), pp. 1–26. **[G: Mexico]**

Kenen, Peter B. Perspective: Problems in Modeling International Risks [Modeling Exchange Rate Fluctuations and International Disturbances]. **In** *Herring, R. J., ed.*, 1983, pp. 109–13. **[G: Global]**

Kim, Dae Sik. Monetary Accommodations under External Supply Shocks in Korea: Some Empirical Results. *J. Econ. Devel.*, July 1983, *8*(1), pp. 161–80. **[G: S. Korea]**

Klein, Lawrence R. Modeling Exchange Rate Fluctuations and International Disturbances. **In** *Herring, R. J., ed.*, 1983, pp. 85–109. **[G: Global]**

Klein, Lawrence R. The Deficit and the Fiscal and Monetary Policy Mix. **In** *Federal Reserve Bank of Boston*, 1983, pp. 174–94. **[G: U.S.]**

Klein, Lawrence R.; Friedman, Edward and Able, Stephen. Money in the Wharton Quarterly Model. *J. Money, Credit, Banking*, May 1983, *15*(2), pp. 237–59. **[G: U.S.]**

Knight, Malcolm D. and Mathieson, Donald J. Economic Change and Policy Response in Canada under Fixed and Flexible Exchange Rates. **In** *Bhandari, J. S. and Putnam, B. H., eds.*, 1983, pp. 500–529. **[G: Canada]**

Knoester, Anthonie. Stagnation and the Inverted Haavelmo Effect: Some International Evidence. *De Economist*, 1983, *131*(4), pp. 548–84. **[G: U.S.; U.K.; Netherlands; W. Germany]**

Kopcke, Richard W. Will Big Deficits Spoil the Recovery? **In** *Federal Reserve Bank of Boston*, 1983, pp. 141–68. **[G: U.S.]**

Krelle, Wilhelm E. An Outline of a Multicountry Econometric Model: Comment. **In** *Hickman, B. G., ed.*, 1983, pp. 93–95. **[G: Global]**

Kuipers, S. K. and van Zon, A. H. Substitution and Technical Progress: A Putty–Clay Model for the Netherlands. **In** *Biehl, D.; Roskamp, K. W. and Stolper, W. F., eds.*, 1983, pp. 181–206. **[G: Netherlands]**

Kurihara, Shiro. Macroeconomic Policy Alternatives

for Higher Oil Prices in the Japanese Economy. *Econ. Stud. Quart.*, April 1983, *34*(1), pp. 44–69. **[G: Japan]**

Kwack, Sung Y., et al. The Structure and Properties of the Multicountry Model. **In** *Hickman, B. G., ed.*, 1983, pp. 69–84. **[G: OECD; Global]**

Laidler, David and Bentley, Brian. A Small Macro-Model of the Post-War United States. *Manchester Sch. Econ. Soc. Stud.*, December 1983, *51*(4), pp. 317–40. **[G: U.S.]**

Laidler, David, et al. A Small Macroeconomic Model of an Open Economy: The Case of Canada. **In** *Claassen, E. and Salin, P., eds.*, 1983, pp. 149–71. **[G: Canada]**

Langohr, Herwig. A Small Macroeconomic Model of an Open Economy: The Case of Canada: Comment. **In** *Claassen, E. and Salin, P., eds.*, 1983, pp. 172–77. **[G: Canada]**

Law, I. A. and Lewis, P. E. T. A Bayesian Approach to Expectations Formation. *Brit. Rev. Econ. Issues*, Spring 1983, *5*(12), pp. 46–56. **[G: U.K.]**

Looney, Robert E. and Frederiksen, P. C. The Feasibility of Alternative IMF-Type Stabilization Programs in Mexico, 1983–87. *J. Policy Modeling*, November 1983, *5*(3), pp. 461–70. **[G: Mexico]**

Lundgren, Stefan. Computing Equilibria in Mixed Neoclassical and Activity Analysis Models. **In** *Sohlman, A. M., ed.*, 1983, pp. 172–89.

Macfarlane, I. J. and Hawkins, J. R. Economic Forecasts and Their Assessment. *Econ. Rec.*, December 1983, *59*(167), pp. 321–31. **[G: Australia; U.S.]**

Maki, Wilbur R.; del Ninno, Carlo and Stenberg, Peter L. Forecasting State Economic Growth in Recession and Recovery. *Reg. Sci. Persp.*, 1983, *13*(2), pp. 39–50. **[G: U.S.]**

Manne, Alan S. A Three-Region Model of Energy, International Trade, and Economic Growth. **In** *Hickman, B. G., ed.*, 1983, pp. 141–62. **[G: LDCs; OECD; OPEC]**

Marwah, Kanta and Klein, Lawrence R. A Model of Foreign Exchange Markets: Endogenising Capital Flows and Exchange Rates. *Z. Nationalökon.*, Supplement 3, 1983, *43*, pp. 61–95. **[G: Canada; Germany; France; U.K.; U.S.]**

Mayer, Thomas. Effects of Export Diversification in a Primary Commodity Export Country: Colombia. *J. Policy Modeling*, June 1983, *5*(2), pp. 233–52. **[G: Colombia]**

McCarthy, F. Desmond. General Equilibrium Model for Egypt. **In** *Kelley, A. C.; Sanderson, W. C. and Williamson, J. G., eds.*, 1983, pp. 71–102. **[G: Egypt]**

McKees, Stephen K. and Ries, John. The Track Record of Macroeconomic Forecasts. *New Eng. Econ. Rev.*, November/December 1983, pp. 5–18. **[G: U.S.]**

Miller, Preston J. Will Big Deficits Spoil the Recovery? Discussion. **In** *Federal Reserve Bank of Boston*, 1983, pp. 169–73. **[G: U.S.]**

Minford, Patrick; Ioannidis, Christos and Marwaha, Satwant. Rational Expectations in a Multilateral Macro-Model. **In** *De Grauwe, P. and Peeters, T., eds.*, 1983, pp. 239–66.

Moore, Geoffrey H. Forecasting Short-term Economic Change. **In** *Moore, G. H.*, 1983, *1969*, pp. 401–32. **[G: U.S.]**

Moore, Geoffrey H. The Forty-second Anniversary of the Leading Indicators. **In** *Moore, G. H.*, 1983, *1979*, pp. 369–400. **[G: U.S.]**

Moore, Geoffrey H. The President's Economic Report: A Forecasting Record. **In** *Moore, G. H.*, 1983, *1977*, pp. 433–51. **[G: U.S.]**

Olofin, S. and Iyaniwura, J. O. From Oil Shortage to Oil Glut: Simulation of Growth Prospects in the Nigerian Economy. *J. Policy Modeling*, November 1983, *5*(3), pp. 363–78. **[G: Nigeria]**

Onishi, Akira. North–South Relations: Alternative Policy Simulations for the World Economy in the 1980s. *J. Policy Modeling*, March 1983, *5*(1), pp. 55–74. **[G: Global]**

Parmenter, Brian R. The IMPACT Macro Package and Export Demand Elasticities. *Australian Econ. Pap.*, December 1983, *22*(41), pp. 411–17. **[G: Australia]**

Peach, James T. and Webb, James L. Randomly Specified Macroeconomic Models: Some Implications for Model Selection. *J. Econ. Issues*, September 1983, *17*(3), pp. 697–720. **[G: U.S.]**

Personick, Valerie A. The Job Outlook through 1995: Industry Output and Employment Projections. *Mon. Lab. Rev.*, November 1983, *106*(11), pp. 24–36. **[G: U.S.]**

Prausello, Franco. L'economia eurpea alle soglie degli anni 2000: lineamenti di analisi prospettiva. (With English summary.) *Econ. Int.*, May–August–November 1983, *36*(2–3–4), pp. 199–254. **[G: Europe]**

Ranuzzi, Paolo. Some Evidence for European Monetary Union from Eurolink Simulations. *Econ. Notes*, 1983, (2), pp. 23–48. **[G: EEC]**

Savage, David. The Use of the Model for Forecasting. **In** *Britton, A., ed.*, 1983, pp. 111–20. **[G: U.K.]**

Sawyer, J. A.; Dungan, D. P. and Jump, G. V. The Transmission of World Economic Expansion to an Open Economy: Some Experiments for Canada. **In** *[Klein, L. R.]*, 1983, pp. 368–92. **[G: Canada]**

Sheikh, M. A.; Grady, P. and Lapointe, P.-H. The Effectiveness of Fiscal Policy in a Keynesian–Monetarist Model of Canada. *Empirical Econ.*, 1983, *8*(3–4), pp. 139–68. **[G: Canada]**

Shishido, Hisanobu. Modeling Dualism in Japan. **In** *Kelley, A. C.; Sanderson, W. C. and Williamson, J. G., eds.*, 1983, pp. 103–38. **[G: Japan]**

Shishido, Shuntaro. Long-term Forecasts and Policy Implications: Simulations with a World Econometric Model (T-FAIS IV). **In** *Hickman, B. G., ed.*, 1983, pp. 53–66. **[G: Global]**

Sickles, Robin C. and Thurman, Stephan S. Consistent Price Determination of Income and Production: A Singular Equation System Applied to the MPS Model. *J. Policy Modeling*, March 1983, *5*(1), pp. 125–48. **[G: U.S.]**

Simunek, Vladimir J. and Switzer, Brian C. The Kent Model. **In** *Migliaro, A. and Jain, C. L., eds.*, 1983, pp. 41–43.

Sneessens, H. R. A Macroeconomic Rationing Model of the Belgian Economy. *Europ. Econ. Rev.*, January 1983, *20*(1–3), pp. 193–215. **[G: Belgium]**

Snower, Dennis J. DYNAMICO: A Multilevel Programming Model of World Trade and Development: Comment. In *Hickman, B. G., ed.*, 1983, pp. 276–79. **[G: Global]**

Spinelli, Franco. Fixed Exchange Rates and Adaptive Expectations Monetarism: The Italian Case. *Rev. Econ. Cond. Italy*, February 1983, (1), pp. 97–124. **[G: Italy]**

Tindall, Michael L. and Atkins, Joseph C. Monetarism: The St. Louis Model and a Recent Monetarist Forecasting Model: A Reply. *Bus. Econ.*, January 1983, *18*(1), pp. 46–47. **[G: U.S.]**

Togan, Sübidey. A Macroeconometric Model of the Turkish Economy: A Comment. *METU*, 1983, *10*(3), pp. 323–28. **[G: Turkey]**

Trzeciakowski, W. General Equilibrium Modelling of Trade-Liberalization Issues among Major World Trade Blocs: Comment. In *Hickman, B. G., ed.*, 1983, pp. 138–40. **[G: OECD; Global]**

Waelbroeck, Jean and De Roo, D. How Do European Short-term Forecasters Predict? An Evaluation of Two Sets of GNP Forecasts. In *[Klein, L. R.]*, 1983, pp. 393–413. **[G: EEC]**

Weinberg, Carl B.; Nadiri, M. I. and Choi, J. An Evaluation of the Effects of Commodity-Price Indexation on Developed and Developing Economies: An Application of the Rempis Model. In *Hickman, B. G., ed.*, 1983, pp. 219–34. **[G: Global]**

Whalley, John. General Equilibrium Modeling of Trade-Liberalization Issues among Major World Trade Blocs. In *Hickman, B. G., ed.*, 1983, pp. 121–36. **[G: OECD; Global]**

Worswick, G. D. N. National Institute Forecasting. In *[Saunders, C. T.]*, 1983, pp. 339–56. **[G: U.K.]**

Yağci, Fahrettin. A Macroeconometric Model of the Turkish Economy. *METU*, 1983, *10*(1), pp. 1–44. **[G: Turkey]**

Yağci, Fahrettin. On Tagan's Comments [A Macroeconometric Model of the Turkish Economy]. *METU*, 1983, *10*(3), pp. 329–30. **[G: Turkey]**

Young, Richard M. The Chase Model: An Interview. In *Migliaro, A. and Jain, C. L., eds.*, 1983, pp. 33–36. **[G: U.S.]**

Zalai, Ernö. A Nonlinear Multisectoral Model for Hungary: General Equilibrium versus Optimal Planning Approaches. In *Kelley, A. C.; Sanderson, W. C. and Williamson, J. G., eds.*, 1983, pp. 185–222. **[G: Hungary]**

1323 Specific Forecasts and Models

Abele, Hanns. A Model of Trade and Exchange Rates: Comment. In *Hickman, B. G., ed.*, 1983, pp. 311–13. **[G: OECD; Global]**

Adams, F. Gerard and Marquez, Jaime R. A Global Model of Oil-Price Impacts. In *[Klein, L. R.]*, 1983, pp. 317–39. **[G: Global]**

d'Alcantara, Gonzales. Exchange Rates in Project LINK: Comment. In *De Grauwe, P. and Peeters, T., eds.*, 1983, pp. 134–38. **[G: OECD]**

Amano, Akihiro. Exchange-Rate Modelling in the EPA World Economic Model. In *De Grauwe, P. and Peeters, T., eds.*, 1983, pp. 139–71. **[G: Japan; W. Germany; U.K.; U.S.]**

Andrikopoulos, Andreas A. and Brox, James A. Short-Run Forecasts of Consumer Expenditures Based on the Linear Expenditure Systems. *Atlantic Econ. J.*, December 1983, *11*(4), pp. 20–33. **[G: Canada]**

Avi-Itzhak, Benjamin; Iusem, Alfredo and Dantzig, George B. The Consumers Energy Services Model of the Pilot System. In *Lev, B., ed.*, 1983, pp. 195–220. **[G: U.S.]**

Babbel, David F. Duration and the Term Structure of Interest Rate Volatility. In *Kaufman, G. G.; Bierwag, G. O. and Toevs, A., eds.*, 1983, pp. 239–65. **[G: U.S.]**

Ballard, Kenneth P. The Structure of a Large-Scale Small-Area Multiregional Model of California: Modelling an Integrated System of Urban, Suburban and Rural Growth. *Reg. Stud.*, October 1983, *17*(5), pp. 327–38. **[G: U.S.]**

Bánhidi, Ferenc and Gábor, László. The Price Model. *Matekon*, Spring 1983, *19*(3), pp. 18–35. **[G: Hungary]**

Bauwens, Luc and d'Alcantara, Gonzague. An Export Model for the Belgian Industry. *Europ. Econ. Rev.*, August 1983, *22*(3), pp. 265–76. **[G: Belgium]**

Bergendahl, Per Anders. Energy and the Economy—A Vintage Approach to the Analysis of Adaptation Inertia. In *Sohlman, A. M., ed.*, 1983, pp. 221–33.

de Bever, Leo. Deficits and the Economy to 1990: Projections and Alternatives: Comment. In *Conklin, D. W. and Courchene, T. J., eds.*, 1983, pp. 148–49. **[G: Canada]**

Bilson, John F. O. The Evaluation and Use of Foreign Exchange Rate Forecasting Services. In *Herring, R. J., ed.*, 1983, pp. 149–79. **[G: OECD]**

Bjerkholt, Olav and Rinde, Jon. Consumption Demand in the MSG Model. In *Av, R., et al., eds.*, 1983, pp. 84–107. **[G: Norway]**

Braschler, Curtis. The Changing Demand Structure for Pork and Beef in the 1970s: Implications for the 1980s. *Southern J. Agr. Econ.*, December 1983, *15*(2), pp. 105–10. **[G: U.S.]**

Brillet, Jean-Louis and d'Hose, Claire. The Mini-DMS Energy Model: Some Simulation Results. In *Sohlman, A. M., ed.*, 1983, pp. 274–305. **[G: France]**

Brooks, S. Exports and Imports. In *Britton, A., ed.*, 1983, pp. 40–51. **[G: U.K.]**

Burch, Susan Weller. The Aging U.S. Auto Stock: Implications for Demand. *Bus. Econ.*, May 1983, *18*(3), pp. 22–26. **[G: U.S.]**

Cherif, M'hamed. Sensibilité du bilan énergétique belge par rapport à une tarification optimale. (With English summary.) *Cah. Écon. Bruxelles*, 1983, *97*(1), pp. 38–60. **[G: Belgium]**

Chirinko, Robert S. and Eisner, Robert. Tax Policy and Investment in Major U.S. Macroeconomic Econometric Models. *J. Public Econ.*, March 1983, *20*(2), pp. 139–66. **[G: U.S.]**

Collins, Glenn S. and Taylor, C. Robert. TECHSIM: A Regional Field Crop and National Livestock Econometric Simulation Model. *Agr. Econ. Res.*, April 1983, *35*(2), pp. 1–18. **[G: U.S.]**

Corneil, Jim. Labour Market Projections in Canada: A Progress Report: Comment. In *Queen's Univ. Indust. Relat. Centre and John Deutsch Mem.*, 1983, pp. 106–09. **[G: Canada]**

Criqui, P. Impacts of the First Oil Crisis, International Comparisons from the Sibilin Data Base. **In** *Sohlman, A. M., ed.,* 1983, pp. 13–37. **[G: France; U.K.; U.S.; Japan; W. Germany]**

Criqui, P. Price Effects and Demand Forecasting. The Sibilin Model. **In** *Sohlman, A. M., ed.,* 1983, pp. 149–71. **[G: U.K.; France; Japan; U.S.; W. Germany]**

Cuthbertson, K. Consumer Spending. **In** *Britton, A., ed.,* 1983, pp. 16–27. **[G: U.K.]**

Cuthbertson, K. The Monetary Sector. **In** *Britton, A., ed.,* 1983, pp. 98–110. **[G: U.K.]**

Daniel, Terrence E. and Goldberg, Henry M. Modeling Key Canadian Energy Policy Issues. **In** *Lev, B., ed.,* 1983, pp. 483–91. **[G: Canada]**

Dantzig, George B. and Iusem, Alfredo. Analyzing Labor Productivity Growth with the PILOT Model. **In** *Schurr, S. H.; Sonenblum, S. and Wood, D. O., eds.,* 1983, pp. 347–66. **[G: U.S.]**

Darby, Michael R. International Transmission under Pegged and Floating Exchange Rates: An Empirical Comparison. **In** *Bhandari, J. S. and Putnam, B. H., eds.,* 1983, pp. 427–71. **[G: OECD]**

Dargay, Joyce M. The Demand for Energy in Swedish Engineering: Factor Substitution, Technical Change and Scale Effects. **In** *Sohlman, A. M., ed.,* 1983, pp. 80–96. **[G: Sweden]**

Dargay, Joyce M. The Demand for Energy in Swedish Manufacturing. **In** *Ysander, B.-C., ed.,* 1983, pp. 57–128. **[G: Sweden]**

Dickens, Paul F., III, et al. Net Effects of Government Intervention in Energy Markets. *Energy J.,* April 1983, *4*(2), pp. 135–49. **[G: U.S.]**

Dixon, Peter B., et al. The Agricultural Sector of Orani 78: Theory, Data, and Application. **In** *Kelley, A. C.; Sanderson, W. C. and Williamson, J. G., eds.,* 1983, pp. 237–74. **[G: Australia]**

Dombrecht, Michel. Exchange-Rate Modelling in the EPA World Economic Model: Comment. **In** *De Grauwe, P. and Peeters, T., eds.,* 1983, pp. 172–74. **[G: Japan; U.S.; U.K.; W. Germany]**

Duan, Naihua, et al. A Comparison of Alternative Models for the Demand for Medical Care. *J. Bus. Econ. Statist.,* April 1983, *1*(2), pp. 115–26. **[G: U.S.]**

Dungan, D. P. and Wilson, T. A. Deficits and the Economy to 1990: Projections and Alternatives. **In** *Conklin, D. W. and Courchene, T. J., eds.,* 1983, pp. 116–48. **[G: Canada]**

de Falleur, Richard. Les perspectives de la sécurité sociale dans les projections à moyen terme du Bureau du Plan. (With English summary.) *Cah. Écon. Bruxelles,* 1983, *97*(1), pp. 115–60. **[G: Belgium]**

Figlewski, Stephen and Urich, Thomas. Optimal Aggregation of Money Supply Forecasts: Accuracy, Profitability and Market Efficiency. *J. Finance,* June 1983, *38*(3), pp. 695–710. **[G: U.S.]**

Fildes, Robert A. and Fitzgerald, M. Desmond. The Use of Information in Balance of Payments Forecasting. *Economica,* August 1983, *50*(199), pp. 249–58. **[G: U.K.]**

Fox, Glenn and Ruttan, Vernon W. A Guide to LDC Food Balance Projections. *Europ. Rev. Agr. Econ.,* 1983, *10*(4), pp. 325–56. **[G: Selected Countries; LDCs]**

Freedman, David; Rothenberg, Thomas and Sutch, Richard. On Energy Policy Models. *J. Bus. Econ. Statist.,* January 1983, *1*(1), pp. 24–32. **[G: U.S.]**

Freedman, David; Rothenberg, Thomas and Sutch, Richard. On Energy Policy Models: Rejoinder. *J. Bus. Econ. Statist.,* January 1983, *1*(1), pp. 36. **[G: U.S.]**

Gehr, Adam K., Jr. and Berry, Thomas. FNMA Auction Results as a Forecaster of Residential Mortgage Yields: A Comment. *J. Money, Credit, Banking,* February 1983, *15*(1), pp. 116–19. **[G: U.S.]**

Girod, J. L'élasticité-prix dans les modèles économétriques. (Elasticity Price in the Econometric Models. With English summary.) *Écon. Soc.,* December 1983, *17*(12), pp. 1847–868.

Glassey, C. Roger. Large-scale Model Transplants from the Donor's Point of View. **In** *Thrall, R. M.; Thompson, R. G. and Holloway, M. L., eds.,* 1983, pp. 165–71. **[G: U.S.]**

Goettle, Richard J., IV and Hudson, Edward A. Macroeconomic Effects of Natural Gas Price Decontrol. **In** *Lev, B., ed.,* 1983, pp. 183–93. **[G: U.S.]**

Gorbet, Frederick W. The Energy Outlook. **In** *Lieber, R. J., ed.,* 1983, pp. 17–32. **[G: OECD]**

Gordon, Richard L. The Evolution of Coal Market Models and Coal Policy Analysis. **In** *Lev, B., ed.,* 1983, pp. 65–84. **[G: U.S.]**

Gough, Robert A., Jr. The Future Constraints on Interest Rates. **In** *Sanford, T., ed.,* 1983, pp. 56–78. **[G: U.S.]**

Gramlich, Edward M. Models of Inflation Expectations Formation: A Comparison of Household and Economist Forecasts. *J. Money, Credit, Banking,* May 1983, *15*(2), pp. 155–73. **[G: U.S.]**

Grassini, Maurizio. A System of Demand Equations for Medium-to-Long-Term Forecasting with Input–Output Econometric Models. *Econ. Notes,* 1983, (2), pp. 84–98. **[G: Italy]**

Grilli, Enzo R. and Yang, Maw-cheng. Real and Monetary Determinants of Non-oil Primary Commodity Price Movements. **In** *Kregel, J. A., ed.,* 1983, pp. 115–41. **[G: OECD]**

Hall, S. G. F. North Sea Oil. **In** *Britton, A., ed.,* 1983, pp. 91–97. **[G: U.K.]**

Hall, S. G. F. The Exchange Rate. **In** *Britton, A., ed.,* 1983, pp. 79–90. **[G: U.K.]**

Hall, S. G. F.; Henry, S. G. B. and Trinder, Chris. Wages and Prices. **In** *Britton, A., ed.,* 1983, pp. 65–78. **[G: U.K.]**

Harris, Carl M. Oil and Gas Supply Modeling under Uncertainty: Putting DOE Midterm Forecasts in Perspective. *Energy J.,* October 1983, *4*(4), pp. 53–65. **[G: U.S.]**

Hashimoto, Hideo. A World Iron and Steel Economy Model: A Projection for 1980–95. *J. Policy Modeling,* November 1983, *5*(3), pp. 379–96. **[G: Global]**

Henry, S. G. B. and Wren-Lewis, S. Investment and Stockbuilding. **In** *Britton, A., ed.,* 1983, pp. 28–39. **[G: U.K.]**

Hickman, Bert G. Exchange Rates in Project LINK. **In** *De Grauwe, P. and Peeters, T., eds.,* 1983, pp. 103–33. **[G: OECD]**

Hoffmann, Lutz and Jarass, Lorenz. The Impact of Rising Oil Prices of Oil-Importing Developing

Countries and the Scope for Adjustment. *Weltwirtsch. Arch.*, 1983, *119*(2), pp. 297–316. [G: India; Brazil; Kenya]

Hogan, William W. On Energy Policy Models: Comment. *J. Bus. Econ. Statist.*, January 1983, *1*(1), pp. 33. [G: U.S.]

Hooper, Peter; Haas, Richard D. and Symansky, Steven A. Revision of Exchange-Rate Determination in the MCM. **In** *De Grauwe, P. and Peeters, T., eds.*, 1983, pp. 210–35. [G: U.S.]

Horne, Jocelyn. The Money Formation Table Approach to Forecasting: An Evaluation of the Institute of Money Supply Forecasts. *Australian Econ. Rev.*, 1983, (64), pp. 69–77. [G: Australia]

Houghton, John C. Uranium: Estimates of U.S. Reserves and Resources. **In** *Adelman, M. A., et al.*, 1983, pp. 333–84. [G: U.S.]

Huang, Wen-yuan; Heady, Earl O. and Weisz, Reuben N. Linkage of a National Recursive Econometric Model and an Interregional Programming Model for Agricultural Policy Analysis. **In** *Thrall, R. M.; Thompson, R. G. and Holloway, M. L., eds.*, 1983, pp. 77–99. [G: U.S.]

Hubbard, R. Glenn and Weiner, Robert. The 'Sub-Trigger' Crisis: An Economic Analysis of Flexible Stock Policies. *Energy Econ.*, July 1983, *5*(3), pp. 178–89. [G: U.S.]

Hultkrantz, Lars. Energy Substitution in the Forest Industry. **In** *Ysander, B.-C., ed.*, 1983, pp. 209–26. [G: Sweden]

Jacoby, Henry D. and Paddock, James L. World Oil Prices and Economic Growth in the 1980s. *Energy J.*, April 1983, *4*(2), pp. 31–47. [G: U.S.]

Jansson, Leif. A Vintage Model for the Swedish Iron and Steel Industry. **In** *Ysander, B.-C., ed.*, 1983, pp. 129–69. [G: Sweden]

Kain, John F. Impacts of Higher Petroleum Prices on Transportation Patterns and Urban Development. **In** *Keeler, T. E., ed.*, 1983, pp. 1–26. [G: U.S.]

Kaliski, Steve F. Labour Market Projections in Canada: A Progress Report: Comment. **In** *Queen's Univ. Indust. Relat. Centre and John Deutsch Mem.*, 1983, pp. 105–06. [G: Canada]

Kaufman, Gordon. Oil and Gas: Estimation of Undiscovered Resources. **In** *Adelman, M. A., et al.*, 1983, pp. 83–294. [G: U.S.]

Kimbell, Larry J. and Shulman, David. Reaganomics: Implications for California Governments. **In** *Lefcoe, G., ed.*, 1983, pp. 3–14. [G: U.S.]

Kröger, Jürgen. Devisenkurse, Leistungsbilanz und interne Anpassungsprozesse. (Exchange Rates, the Current Account Balance, and Internal Adjustment Processes. With English summary.) *Konjunkturpolitik*, 1983, *29*(1), pp. 1–20. [G: W. Germany]

Lapillonne, B. and Château, B. The Medee 3 Model. **In** *Sohlman, A. M., ed.*, 1983, pp. 124–48.

Leclercq, Claudie. Le demande d'énergie de l'industrie pour les principaux pays de la CEE. (With English summary.) *Cah. Écon. Bruxelles*, 1983, *97*(1), pp. 14–37. [G: EEC]

Leontief, Wassily W.; Mariscal, Jorge and Sohn, Ira. Prospects for the Soviet Economy to the Year 2000. *J. Policy Modeling*, March 1983, *5*(1), pp. 1–18. [G: U.S.S.R.]

Leontief, Wassily W. and Sohn, Ira. Population, Food, Energy and Growth. **In** *Tempest, P., ed.*, 1983, pp. 241–46. [G: LDCs; MDCs]

Levich, Richard M. Exchange Rate Forecasting Techniques. **In** *George, A. M. and Giddy, I. H., eds., Vol. 2*, 1983, pp. 8.1:1–30.

Litterman, Robert B. and Supel, Thomas M. Using Vector Autoregressions to Measure the Uncertainty in Minnesota's Revenue Forecasts. *Fed. Res. Bank Minn. Rev.*, Spring 1983, *7*(2), pp. 10–22. [G: U.S.]

Liu, Ben-chieh. Helium Conservation and Supply and Demand Projections in the USA. *Energy Econ.*, January 1983, *5*(1), pp. 58–64. [G: U.S.]

Lombra, Raymond E. and Moran, Michael. Policy Advice and Policymaking at the Federal Reserve. **In** *Brunner, K. and Meltzer, A. H., eds.*, 1983, *1980*, pp. 385–444. [G: U.S.]

Longva, Svein; Lorentsen, Lorents and Olsen, Øystein. Energy in the Multi-sectoral Growth Model MSG. **In** *Av, R., et al., eds.*, 1983, pp. 27–51. [G: Norway]

Longva, Svein and Olsen, Øystein. Producer Behaviour in the MSG Model. **In** *Av, R., et al., eds.*, 1983, pp. 52–83. [G: Norway]

Longva, Svein and Olsen, Øystein. The Specification of Electricity Flows in the MSG Model. **In** *Av, R., et al., eds.*, 1983, pp. 108–33. [G: Norway]

Longva, Svein; Olsen, Øystein and Rinde, Jon. Energy Price Sensitivity of the Norwegian Economy. **In** *Av, R., et al., eds.*, 1983, pp. 161–79. [G: Norway]

Longva, Svein, et al. Use of the MSG Model in Forecasting Electricity Demand. **In** *Av, R., et al., eds.*, 1983, pp. 180–94. [G: Norway]

Louviere, Jordan J. and Hensher, David A. Using Discrete Choice Models with Experimental Design Data to Forecast Consumer Demand for a Unique Cultural Event. *J. Cons. Res.*, December 1983, *10*(3), pp. 348–61. [G: Australia]

Lundgren, Stefan. A Model of Energy Demand in the Swedish Iron and Steel Industry. **In** *Ysander, B.-C., ed.*, 1983, pp. 171–208. [G: Sweden]

Lyckeborg, Håkan. A Box–Jenkins Approach to Short-term Energy Consumption Forecasting in Sweden: Univariate Models. **In** *Sohlman, A. M., ed.*, 1983, pp. 98–123. [G: Sweden]

May, Doug. Labour Market Projections in Canada: A Progress Report: Comment. **In** *Queen's Univ. Indust. Relat. Centre and John Deutsch Mem.*, 1983, pp. 109–11. [G: Canada]

Mayes, David G. and Savage, David. The Contrast between Portfolio Theory and Econometric Models of the U.K. Monetary Sector. **In** *Corner, D. and Mayes, D. G., eds.*, 1983, pp. 211–44. [G: U.K.]

McColl, G. D. and Gallagher, D. R. Market Price and Resource Cost in Australia. **In** *Tempest, P., ed.*, 1983, pp. 179–87. [G: Australia]

Meese, Richard A. and Rogoff, Kenneth S. The Out-of-Sample Failure of Empirical Exchange Rate Models: Sampling Error or Misspecification? **In** *Frenkel, J. A., ed.*, 1983, pp. 67–105. [G: Japan; U.K.; U.S.; W. Germany]

Mills, Terence C. The Information Content of the UK Monetary Components and Aggregates. *Bull.*

Econ. Res., May 1983, *35*(1), pp. 25–46. **[G: U.K.]**

Motaman, H. Macroeconomic Planning of Oil Revenue in Industrialised Countries: The British Case. **In** *[Saunders, C. T.]*, 1983, pp. 231–57. **[G: U.K.]**

Murphy, Frederic H. Design Strategies for Energy Market Models. **In** *Lev, B., ed.*, 1983, pp. 45–64.

Nabli, Mustapha K. Revision of Exchange-Rate Determination in the MCM: Comment. **In** *De Grauwe, P. and Peeters, T., eds.*, 1983, pp. 236–38. **[G: U.S.]**

Nagy, András. Structural Changes and Development Alternatives in International Trade. **In** *Hickman, B. G., ed.*, 1983, pp. 283–95. **[G: Global]**

Nakamura, Jiro. The Role of the Labor Market for Solving the Problem of Stagflation. *Econ. Stud. Quart.*, August 1983, *34*(2), pp. 147–55. **[G: Japan]**

Narasimham, Gorti V. L. A Comparison of Three Methods of Modelling Energy Outlooks in a Global Setting. **In** *Lev, B., ed.*, 1983, pp. 99–110.

Nerlove, Marc. Expectations, Plans, and Realizations in Theory and Practice. *Econometrica*, September 1983, *51*(5), pp. 1251–79. **[G: France; W. Germany]**

Niemira, Michael P. Sequential Signals of Recession and Recovery: Revisited. *Bus. Econ.*, January 1983, *18*(1), pp. 51–53. **[G: U.S.]**

Oettinger, Christina. Long-term Simulation of the Effects of Different Energy Policy Measures. **In** *Sohlman, A. M., ed.*, 1983, pp. 190–220. **[G: Sweden]**

Okun, Arthur M. On the Appraisal of Cyclical Turning-Point Predictors. **In** *Okun, A. M.*, 1983, *1960*, pp. 525–52. **[G: U.S.]**

Okun, Arthur M. The Predictive Value of Surveys of Business Intentions. **In** *Okun, A. M.*, 1983, *1962*, pp. 553–61. **[G: U.S.]**

Park, Se-Hark and Kubursi, Atif A. The Energy Constraint and Development: Consistency and Optimality over Time. *Energy Econ.*, January 1983, *5*(1), pp. 9–15. **[G: LDCs]**

Pearce, Douglas K. and Wisley, Thomas O. Sales Expectations and Inventory Changes in Retail Trade. *J. Econ. Bus.*, 1983, *35*(1), pp. 109–21. **[G: U.S.]**

Perazzelli, P. A. and Perrin, J. R. Investment—Inflation Linkages in the NIF-10 Model. **In** *Pagan, A. R. and Trivedi, P. K., eds.*, 1983, pp. 283–310. **[G: Australia]**

Platt, Harlan D. An Integrated Approach to Electricity Demand Forecasting. *Energy J.*, Supplement 1983, *4*, pp. 75–91. **[G: U.S.]**

Powell, Alan A. Aspects of the Design of Bachuroo, an Economic–Demographic Model of Labor Supply. **In** *Kelley, A. C.; Sanderson, W. C. and Williamson, J. G., eds.*, 1983, pp. 277–300. **[G: Australia]**

Powell, Alan A. Aspects of Labour Market Theory and Behaviour Highlighted by IMPACT Project Studies. **In** *Blandy, R. and Covick, O., eds.*, 1983, pp. 137–65. **[G: Australia]**

Quadrio-Curzio, Alberto. Alternative Explanations: [Real and Monetary Determinants of Non-oil Primary Commodity Price Movements]. **In** *Kregel, J. A., ed.*, 1983, pp. 142–52. **[G: OECD]**

Razavi, Hossein. Optimal Adjustment of Manpower-Requirement Forecasts: A Case Study of Iran. *Math. Soc. Sci.*, December 1983, *6*(3), pp. 315–23. **[G: Iran]**

Rochon, Michel. Labour Market Projections in Canada: A Progress Report. **In** *Queen's Univ. Indust. Relat. Centre and John Deutsch Mem.*, 1983, pp. 81–104. **[G: Canada]**

Rødseth, Asbjørn. An Expenditure System for Energy Planning. **In** *Av, R., et al., eds.*, 1983, pp. 195–220. **[G: Norway]**

Rushinek, Avi, et al. The Construction of an International Investor's Perception Model for Corporate Published Forecasted Financial Reports for the USA, the UK and New Zealand. *Managerial Dec. Econ.*, December 1983, *4*(4), pp. 258–65. **[G: New Zealand; U.K.; U.S.]**

Sachs, Jeffrey D. Energy and Growth under Flexible Exchange Rates: A Simulation Study. **In** *Bhandari, J. S. and Putnam, B. H., eds.*, 1983, pp. 191–220. **[G: OPEC]**

Saïdi, Nasser. The Out-of-Sample Failure of Empirical Exchange Rate Models: Sampling Error or Misspecification? Comment. **In** *Frenkel, J. A., ed.*, 1983, pp. 105–09. **[G: Japan; U.K.; U.S.; W. Germany]**

Saito, Mitsuo. Finance and Economic Growth: The Japanese Experience. **In** *[Klein, L. R.]*, 1983, pp. 296–313. **[G: Japan]**

Salemi, Michael K. The Out-of-Sample Failure of Empirical Exchange Rate Models: Sampling Error or Misspecification? Comment. **In** *Frenkel, J. A., ed.*, 1983, pp. 110–12. **[G: Japan; U.K.; U.S.; W. Germany]**

Samouilidis, J-Emmanuel and Mitropoulos, Costas S. Energy Investment and Economic Growth: A Simplified Approach. *Energy Econ.*, October 1983, *5*(4), pp. 237–46. **[G: U.K.]**

Sarma, K. S. An Examination of the Impact of Changes in the Prices of Fuels and Primary Metals on Nordic Countries Using a World Econometric Model. **In** *Eliasson, G.; Sharefkin, M. and Ysander, B.-C., eds.*, 1983, pp. 245–68. **[G: Nordic Countries; OECD]**

Sathaye, Jayant and Ruderman, Henry. The Role of Renewables in Hawaii's Energy Future. *Energy J.*, April 1983, *4*(2), pp. 121–34. **[G: U.S.]**

Saunders, Peter. A Disaggregate Study of the Rationality of Australian Producers' Price Expectations. *Manchester Sch. Econ. Soc. Stud.*, December 1983, *51*(4), pp. 380–98. **[G: Australia]**

Shaikh, A. Hafeez and Zaman, Asad. Forecasting without Theory: Pakistan's Export of Cotton and Rice. *Pakistan J. Appl. Econ.*, Summer 1983, *2*(1), pp. 65–84. **[G: Pakistan]**

Sharefkin, Mark. Stabilization and Growth Policy with Uncertain Oil Prices: Some Rules of Thumb. **In** *Eliasson, G.; Sharefkin, M. and Ysander, B.-C., eds.*, 1983, pp. 327–74.

Smith, Wray. On Energy Policy Models: Comment. *J. Bus. Econ. Statist.*, January 1983, *1*(1), pp. 34–35. **[G: U.S.]**

Sohlman, Asa and Launay, Didier. Energy Demand Analysis: A Survey and Introduction. **In** *Sohlman,*

A. M., ed., 1983, pp. 1–12.

Speare, Alden, Jr. Methods of Projecting Rural-to-Urban Migration, with Reference to Southeast Asia. In *Morrison, P. A., ed.*, 1983, pp. 261–78. **[G: Southeast Asia]**

Sweeney, James L. Energy Model Comparison: An Overview. In *Thrall, R. M.; Thompson, R. G. and Holloway, M. L., eds.*, 1983, pp. 191–217. **[G: U.S.]**

Switzer, Brian C.; Simunek, Vladimir J. and Mathews, H. Lee. Sociometrics. In *Migliaro, A. and Jain, C. L., eds.*, 1983, pp. 55–65. **[G: U.S.]**

Sylos Labini, Paolo. Secular Movements in Primary and Manufactured Goods' Prices: Comment [Real and Monetary Determinants of Non-oil Primary Commodity Price Movements]. In *Kregel, J. A., ed.*, 1983, pp. 153–55.

Thimrén, Claes. Potential Benefits from Isolating the Domestic Oil Price Level during Short-run Oil Price Booms. In *Sohlman, A. M., ed.*, 1983, pp. 234–73. **[G: Sweden]**

Thompson, Russell G., et al. Input–Output Modeling from the Bottom Up Rather Than from the Top Down. In *Thrall, R. M.; Thompson, R. G. and Holloway, M. L., eds.*, 1983, pp. 101–40. **[G: U.S.]**

Trivedi, P. K. Investment—Inflation Linkages in the NIF-10 Model: Discussion. In *Pagan, A. R. and Trivedi, P. K., eds.*, 1983, pp. 311–17. **[G: Australia]**

Tullio, Giuseppe. The Role of Savings and Investment in Current Account Determination: The Case of the Federal Republic of Germany (1973–1979). *Kredit Kapital*, 1983, *16*(3), pp. 351–70. **[G: W. Germany]**

Valentine, T. J. Investment—Inflation Linkages in the NIF-10 Model: Discussion. In *Pagan, A. R. and Trivedi, P. K., eds.*, 1983, pp. 318–20. **[G: Australia]**

Viscio, Albert J., Jr. United States Energy Demand: Conservation and Recession Effects, 1973 to 1982. *J. Energy Devel.*, Spring 1983, *8*(2), pp. 231–46. **[G: U.S.]**

Warner, Dennis L. A Model of Trade and Exchange Rates. In *Hickman, B. G., ed.*, 1983, pp. 297–311. **[G: OECD; Global]**

Werbos, Paul J. Solving and Optimizing Complex Systems: Lessons from the EIA Long-term Energy Model. In *Lev, B., ed.*, 1983, pp. 163–80.

Wilkinson, Jack W. The Supply, Demand, and Average Price of Natural Gas under Free-Market Conditions. *Energy J.*, January 1983, *4*(1), pp. 99–123. **[G: U.S.]**

Wren-Lewis, S. Employment. In *Britton, A., ed.*, 1983, pp. 52–64. **[G: U.K.]**

Ysander, Bengt-Christer and Nordström, Tomas. Energy in Swedish Manufacturing 1980–2000. In *Ysander, B.-C., ed.*, 1983, pp. 229–60. **[G: Sweden]**

Zarnowitz, Victor and Moore, Geoffrey H. Sequential Signals of Recession and Recovery. In *Moore, G. H.*, 1983, *1982*, pp. 23–59. **[G: U.S.]**

Zweifel, Peter. Inflation in the Health Care Sector and the Demand for Insurance: A Micro Study. In *Söderström, L., ed.*, 1983, pp. 105–35. **[G: Switzerland]**

Zwiener, Rudolf. "Crowding-out" durch öffentliche Investitionen? Eine Diskussion der Modellergebnisse der Deutschen Bundesbank und eine Gegenüberstellung mit den Ergebnissen der DIW-Version des ökonometrischen Konjunkturmodells der Wirtschaftsforschungsinstitute. ("Crowding-Out" through Public Investment. With English summary.) *Konjunkturpolitik*, 1983, *29*(3), pp. 121–40. **[G: W. Germany]**

1324 Forecasting and Econometric Models: Theory and Methodology

Aiginger, Karl. Die Wirkung von asymmetrischen Verlusten auf die Bildung von rationalen ökonomischen Erwartungen. (The Incorporation of Asymmetric Losses into the Formation of Economically Rational Expectations (Forecasts, Plans) With English summary.) *Ifo-Studien*, 1983, *29*(3), pp. 175–215. **[G: EEC; U.S.; Japan; Austria]**

Andersen, Ellen. Erfaringer med keynesianske makromodeller. (With English summary.) *Nationaløkon. Tidsskr.*, 1983, *121*(3), pp. 323–31.

Anderson, Donald W. Development of Product-Specific Output Projections Using an Input–Output Model. *Empirical Econ.*, 1983, *8*(1), pp. 1–8. **[G: U.S.]**

Ando, Albert. Equilibrium Business-Cycle Models: An Appraisal. In *[Klein, L. R.]*, 1983, pp. 39–67. **[G: U.S.]**

Ang, James S.; Chua, Jess H. and Fatemi, Ali M. A Comparison of Econometric, Times Series, and Composite Forecasting Methods in Predicting Accounting Variables. *J. Econ. Bus.*, August 1983, *35*(3/4), pp. 301–11. **[G: U.S.]**

Ansley, Craig F. Forecasting Economic Time Series with Structural and Box–Jenkins Models: A Case Study: Comment. *J. Bus. Econ. Statist.*, October 1983, *1*(4), pp. 307–09. **[G: France; U.S.]**

d'Autume, Antoine. Processus d'ajustement et croissance. (Adjustment Process and Growth. With English summary.) [Une maquette représentative des modèles macroeconomiques]. *Ann. INSEE*, Jan.–Mar. 1983, (49), pp. 113–22. **[G: France]**

Bos, Henk C. Some Simple Thoughts on Model Building for Developing Countries. *Pakistan Devel. Rev.*, Summer 1983, *22*(2), pp. 63–71.

Brandon, Charles; Fritz, Richard and Xander, James. Econometric Forecasts: Evaluation and Revision. *Appl. Econ.*, April 1983, *15*(2), pp. 187–201.

Conerly, William B. A Program to Improve Forecast Accuracy. *Bus. Econ.*, September 1983, *18*(4), pp. 18–25. **[G: U.S.]**

De Nicola, Eugenio. Early Signals of Economic Change Coming from a Group of International Business Climate Indicators. *Econ. Notes*, 1983, (3), pp. 184–98. **[G: Italy; Germany; France; U.K.]**

Duncan, Marvin. Macro–Micro Relationships: Modeling and Evaluating Policy and Institutional Impacts on Farm Firms: Discussion. In *Baum, K. H. and Schertz, L. P., eds.*, 1983, pp. 96–99. **[G: U.S.]**

Eliasson, Gunnar. On the Optimal Rate of Structural Adjustment. In *Eliasson, G.; Sharefkin, M. and*

Ysander, B.-C., eds., 1983, pp. 269–323. **[G: Sweden]**

Figlewski, Stephen. Optimal Price Forecasting Using Survey Data. *Rev. Econ. Statist.*, February 1983, *65*(1), pp. 13–21. **[G: U.S.]**

Figlewski, Stephen and Urich, Thomas. Optimal Aggregation of Money Supply Forecasts: Accuracy, Profitability and Market Efficiency. *J. Finance*, June 1983, *38*(3), pp. 695–710. **[G: U.S.]**

Findley, David F. Forecasting Economic Time Series with Structural and Box–Jenkins Models: A Case Study: Comment. *J. Bus. Econ. Statist.*, October 1983, *1*(4), pp. 309–11.

Francis, Jack Clark. Financial Planning and Forecasting Models: An Overview. *J. Econ. Bus.*, August 1983, *35*(3/4), pp. 285–300.

Friedrich, D. and Termin, J. Ökonometrische Modellprognose versus univariate Zeitreihenprojektion: Eine Fallstudie mit dem F & T-Modell. (Econometric Model Forecasts versus Prediction with an Univariate Time Series Method: A Case Study with the F & T–Model. With English summary.) *Jahr. Nationalökon. Statist.*, September 1983, *198*(5), pp. 437–57. **[G: W. Germany]**

Harvey, A. C. and Todd, P. H. J. Forecasting Economic Time Series with Structural and Box–Jenkins Models: A Case Study: Response. *J. Bus. Econ. Statist.*, October 1983, *1*(4), pp. 313–15. **[G: U.S.]**

Harvey, A. C. and Todd, P. H. J. Forecasting Economic Time Series with Structural and Box–Jenkins Models: A Case Study. *J. Bus. Econ. Statist.*, October 1983, *1*(4), pp. 299–307. **[G: U.K.]**

Hendry, David F. On Keynesian Model Building and the Rational Expectations Critique: A Question of Methodology. *Cambridge J. Econ.*, March 1983, *7*(1), pp. 69–75.

Hertford, Reed. Issues in International Agricultural Development: Discussion. *Amer. J. Agr. Econ.*, May 1983, *65*(2), pp. 455–57.

Holloway, Milton L. The Importance of Transfer in Understanding Large-scale Models. **In** *Thrall, R. M.; Thompson, R. G. and Holloway, M. L., eds.*, 1983, pp. 145–63. **[G: U.S.]**

Holt, Charles C. and Olson, Jerome A. How to Detect and Correct Structural Changes in Historical Relationships. **In** *Migliaro, A. and Jain, C. L., eds.*, 1983, pp. 22–26.

Kariya, Takeaki. Optimal Rational Expectations. *Hitotsubashi J. Econ.*, December 1983, *24*(2), pp. 101–08.

Kaufman, Roger T. and Woglom, Geoffrey. Estimating Models with Rational Expectations. *J. Money, Credit, Banking*, August 1983, *15*(3), pp. 275–85.

King, Richard A. Relation to Global Modeling to Development Planning. *Amer. J. Agr. Econ.*, May 1983, *65*(2), pp. 438–44.

Larson, Don. Summary Statistics and Forecasting Performance. *Agr. Econ. Res.*, July 1983, *35*(3), pp. 11–22. **[G: U.S.]**

Lawson, Tony. Different Approaches to Economic Modelling [On Keynesian Model Building and the Rational Expectations Critique]. *Cambridge J. Econ.*, March 1983, *7*(1), pp. 77–84.

Le Van, Cuong. Étude de la stabilité du sentier d'équilibre d'une maquette dynamique d'économie ouverte. (A Study of the Stability of the Equilibrium Path of a Dynamic Maquette of an Open Economy. With English summary.) *Ann. INSEE*, April–June 1983, (50), pp. 93–111. **[G: France]**

Lucas, Robert E., Jr. Econometric Policy Evaluation: A Critique. **In** *Brunner, K. and Meltzer, A. H., eds.*, 1983, *1976*, pp. 257–84.

Madden, M. and Batey, P. W. J. Linked Population and Economic Models: Some Methodological Issues in Forecasting, Analysis, and Policy Optimization. *J. Reg. Sci.*, May 1983, *23*(2), pp. 141–64.

Mayer, Francine. Les modèles de répartition des revenus de type intégré: quelques éléments de comparaison. (Integrated Income Distribution Models: Some Comparisons. With English summary.) *L'Actual. Econ.*, March 1983, *59*(1), pp. 121–34.

McClements, L. D. Some Aspects of Model Building. **In** *Marr, W. L. and Raj, B., eds.*, 1983, *1973*, pp. 203–27.

McDonald, John. A Solution to an Estimation Problem Involving Models with Rational Expectations. *J. Monet. Econ.*, May 1983, *11*(3), pp. 381–86.

Migliaro, A. The Five Economic Theories Underlying Econometric Models. **In** *Migliaro, A. and Jain, C. L., eds.*, 1983, pp. 10–14.

Miller, Thomas A. Macro–Micro Relationships: Understanding and Human Capital as Outputs of the Modeling Process: Discussion. **In** *Baum, K. H. and Schertz, L. P., eds.*, 1983, pp. 91–95.

Moore, Geoffrey H. Why the Leading Indicators Really Do Lead. **In** *Moore, G. H.*, 1983, *1978*, pp. 339–51. **[G: U.S.]**

Moore, Geoffrey H. and Moore, Melita H. An Introduction to International Economic Indicators. **In** *Moore, G. H.*, 1983, pp. 65–91. **[G: OECD]**

Newbold, Paul. Forecasting Economic Time Series with Structural and Box–Jenkins Models: A Case Study: Comment. *J. Bus. Econ. Statist.*, October 1983, *1*(4), pp. 311–12.

Peach, James T. and Webb, James L. Randomly Specified Macroeconomic Models: Some Implications for Model Selection. *J. Econ. Issues*, September 1983, *17*(3), pp. 697–720. **[G: U.S.]**

Ray, Jean-Claude. La fiabilité des pronostics conjoncturels en France. (The Accuracy of Macroeconomic Forecasts in France. With English summary.) *L'Actual. Econ.*, March 1983, *59*(1), pp. 62–73. **[G: France]**

Resek, Robert W. Comparative Performance of Multiple Reaction Function Equations Estimated by Canonical Methods. **In** *Hodgman, D. R., ed.*, 1983, pp. 336–52. **[G: W. Germany; U.K.; Italy; France]**

Rogovskii, E. A. Problems in Developing Dynamic Models to Forecast the Input–Output Structure of the Economy. *Matekon*, Spring 1983, *19*(3), pp. 52–73.

Schleicher, Stefan. Forecasting Theory for Hierarchical Systems with Applications to Multicountry Models. **In** *[Klein, L. R.]*, 1983, pp. 153–71.

Singh, Inderjit. Issues in International Agricultural Development: Discussion. *Amer. J. Agr. Econ.*, May 1983, *65*(2), pp. 452–54.

Taylor, C. Robert. Complementarities between Micro- and Macro-Systems Simulation and Analysis. In *Baum, K. H. and Schertz, L. P., eds.*, 1983, pp. 63–72.

Uebe, Götze. A Nonlinear Difference Equation of Malgrange. *Ann. INSEE*, Jan.–Mar. 1983, (49), pp. 123–31.

Visco, Ignazio. Comparative Performance of Multiple Reaction Function Equations Estimated by Canonical Methods: Discussion. In *Hodgman, D. R., ed.*, 1983, pp. 353–58.

Wallenius, Hannele and Wallenius, Jyrki. A Methodology for Solving the Multiple Criteria Macroeconomic Policy Problem. In *Gruber, J., ed.*, 1983, pp. 310–33. [G: Finland]

Winkler, Robert L. and Makridakis, Spyros. The Combination of Forecasts. *J. Roy. Statist. Soc.*, 1983, *146*(2), pp. 150–57. [G: U.S.]

Worswick, G. D. N. National Institute Forecasting. In *[Saunders, C. T.]*, 1983, pp. 339–56. [G: U.K.]

133 General Outlook and Stabilization Theories and Policies

1330 General Outlook

Ahtiala, Pekka. Uuden hallituksen talouspolitiikka: haasteita ja mahdollisuuksia. (Challenges and Possibilities for the Economic Policy of the New Cabinet. With English summary.) *Kansant. Aikak.*, 1983, *79*(3), pp. 264–69. [G: Finland]

Albert, Michel. Growth, Investment and Employment in Europe in the 1980s. In *Heertje, A., ed.*, 1983, pp. 41–55. [G: EEC]

Alzamora, Carlos and Iglesias, Enrique V. Bases for a Latin American Response to the International Economic Crisis. *Cepal Rev.*, August 1983, (20), pp. 17–46. [G: Latin America]

Amuzegar, Jahangir. Managing Oil Wealth. *Finance Develop.*, September 1983, *20*(3), pp. 19–22. [G: OPEC; U.K.; Norway]

Andreassen, Arthur J.; Saunders, Norman C. and Su, Betty W. Economic Outlook for the 1990's: Three Scenarios for Economic Growth. *Mon. Lab. Rev.*, November 1983, *106*(11), pp. 11–23. [G: U.S.]

Arndt, H. W. Statement No. 2 and Reserve Bank Annual Report: A Comment. *Econ. Rec.*, June 1983, *59*(165), pp. 186–87. [G: Australia]

Baguley, Robert W. Government Deficits: Historical Analysis and Present Policy Alternatives: Comment. In *Conklin, D. W. and Courchene, T. J., eds.*, 1983, pp. 317–19. [G: Canada]

Balassa, Bela. Policy Responses to External Shocks in Sub-Saharan African Countries. *J. Policy Modeling*, March 1983, *5*(1), pp. 75–105. [G: Africa]

Bandeen, Robert A. International Effects of High Interest Rates. In *Sanford, T., ed.*, 1983, pp. 157–66. [G: U.S.; Canada]

Bartel, Richard D. Reflections and Speculations. *Challenge*, March/April 1983, *26*(1), pp. 3–5. [G: U.S.]

Bautista, Romeo M. The "Turbulent World Economy" and Industrial Development Strategy in the Philippines. *Philippine Econ. J.*, 1983, *22*(2), pp. 130–36. [G: Philippine]

Bergsten, C. Fred. Can We Prevent a World Economic Crisis? *Challenge*, January/February 1983, *25*(6), pp. 4–13. [G: U.S.]

Bergsten, C. Fred. The United States and the World Economy. In *Bergsten, C. F.*, 1983, *1982*, pp. 3–12. [G: U.S.]

Black, W. Northern Ireland after the Recession. *Irish Banking Rev.*, December 1983, pp. 3–12. [G: U.K.]

Bluestone, Barry. Deindustrialization and Unemployment in America. *Rev. Black Polit. Econ.*, Spring 1983, *12*(3), pp. 27–42. [G: U.S.]

Bognár, József. Is It Possible to Recover from the World Economic Crisis? (Economic Dependence in an Age of Interdependence). *Acta Oecon.*, 1983, *30*(1), pp. 1–12. [G: Global]

Bowles, Samuel. The Zero-Sum Illusion: Interview. *Challenge*, November/December 1983, *26*(5), pp. 29–37. [G: U.S.]

Brittan, Samuel. A Very Painful World Adjustment. *Foreign Aff.*, 1982, *61* (3), pp. 541–68. [G: Global]

Brittan, Samuel. Economic Stresses in the West. In *Brittan, S.*, 1983, pp. 186–215. [G: Global]

Bronfenbrenner, Martin. Notes on Reaganomics. In *[Yamada, I.]*, 1983, pp. 64–77. [G: U.S.]

Cagan, Phillip. Alcuni aspetti della politica economica degli Stati Uniti. (Current Issues in United States Macro Policy. With English summary.) *Bancaria*, February 1983, *39*(2), pp. 131–38. [G: U.S.]

Capra, James R. Federal Deficits and Private Credit Demands: Economic Impact Analysis. *Fed. Res. Bank New York Quart. Rev.*, Summer 1983, *8*(2), pp. 29–44. [G: U.S.]

Catley, Robert. The Politics of Inflation and Unemployment, 1970–82. In *Head, B. W., ed.*, 1983, pp. 272–93. [G: Australia]

Ciampi, Carlo Azeglio. La via obbligata per il risanamento dell'economia. (The Obligatory Path for Rehabilitation of the Economy. With English summary.) *Bancaria*, August 1983, *39*(8), pp. 683–89. [G: Italy]

Cordera, Rolando and Tello, Carlos. Prospects and Options for Mexican Society. In *Reynolds, C. W. and Tello, C., eds.*, 1983, pp. 47–81. [G: Mexico]

Darity, William A., Jr. Reaganomics and the Black Community. In *Weintraub, S. and Goodstein, M., eds.*, 1983, pp. 59–77. [G: U.S.]

Davidson, Paul. Monetarism and Reaganomics. In *Weintraub, S. and Goodstein, M., eds.*, 1983, pp. 92–103. [G: U.S.]

Donner, Arthur. Perspective on Canada's Stagflation Economy. In *Weintraub, S. and Goodstein, M., eds.*, 1983, pp. 205–13. [G: Canada]

Drud, Arne and Grais, Wafik M. Macroeconomic Adjustment in Thailand: Demand Management and Supply Conditions. *J. Policy Modeling*, June 1983, *5*(2), pp. 207–31. [G: Thailand]

Englander, A. Steven and Los, Cornelis A. Recovery without Accelerating Inflation? *Fed. Res. Bank New York Quart. Rev.*, Summer 1983, *8*(2), pp. 19–28. [G: U.S.]

Estanislao, Jesus P. Philippine Economic Setting in a Turbulent World Economy. *Philippine Econ. J.*, 1983, *22*(2), pp. 107–18. [G: Philippine]

Feinstein, Charles. The Managed Economy: Essays in British Economic Policy and Performance since 1929: Introduction. **In** *Feinstein, C., ed.,* 1983, pp. 1–30. **[G: U.K.]**

Feldstein, Martin S. Shifting Sands of Recovery. *Challenge,* May/June 1983, *26*(2), pp. 26–33. **[G: U.S.]**

Feldstein, Martin S. Sulla politica economica degli Stati Uniti. (The United States Economic Policy. With English summary.) *Bancaria,* July 1983, *39*(7), pp. 577–80. **[G: U.S.]**

Fels, Gerhard. The Supply-Side Approach to Macroeconomic Policy: The West German Experience. **In** *[Giersch, H.],* 1983, pp. 224–37. **[G: W. Germany]**

Fendt, Robert, Jr. Growth and Debt: Issues and Prospects for the Brazilian Economy in the Eighties. **In** *Jorge, A.; Salazar-Carillo, J. and Higonnet, R. P., eds.,* 1983, pp. 125–37. **[G: Brazil]**

FitzGerald, E. V. K. Mexico–United States Economic Relations and the World Cycle: A European View. **In** *Reynolds, C. W. and Tello, C., eds.,* 1983, pp. 349–67. **[G: U.S.; Mexico]**

Glynn, Leonard. America Latina: un continente alle corde. (Latin America on the Ropes. With English summary.) *Mondo Aperto,* March-April 1983, *37*(2), pp. 93–100. **[G: Latin America]**

Haberler, Gottfried. Economic Malaise and a Positive Programme for a Benevolent and Enlightened Dictator. **In** *[Giersch, H.],* 1983, pp. 211–23. **[G: OECD]**

Hague, Douglas. Discussion and Conclusion: A Global Perspective on the World Economy. *Int. Soc. Sci. J.,* 1983, *35*(3), pp. 535–47. **[G: Global]**

Hamilton, David B. The Cure May Be the Cancer: Remarks upon Receipt of the Veblens–Commons Award. *J. Econ. Issues,* June 1983, *17*(2), pp. 287–93. **[G: U.S.]**

von Hayek, Friedrich August. The Muddle of the Middle. **In** *Pejovich, S., ed.,* 1983, pp. 89–100. **[G: U.K.]**

Heller, Walter W. What's Right with Economics? **In** *Marr, W. L. and Raj, B., eds.,* 1983, pp. 337–74. **[G: U.S.]**

Hermens, Ferdinand A. . . . And Now the Future. *Rev. Soc. Econ.,* December 1983, *41*(3), pp. 330–55.

Hibbs, Mark Danser. Changing the Guard in Germany. *Challenge,* May/June 1983, *26*(2), pp. 50–57. **[G: W. Germany]**

Hong, Junyan. Some Comments on the Current Economic Situation in the West. **In** *Hooke, A. W., ed.,* 1983, pp. 74–82.

Hood, William C. The Current World Economic Situation and the Problem of Global Payments Imbalances. **In** *Hooke, A. W., ed.,* 1983, pp. 56–70.

Horvat, Branko. The World Economy from the Socialist Viewpoint. *Int. Soc. Sci. J.,* 1983, *35*(3), pp. 469–92. **[G: Global]**

Horvat, Branko. The World Economy from the Socialist Viewpoint. *Econ. Anal. Worker's Manage.,* 1983, *17*(1), pp. 1–25.

Iglesias, Enrique V. Reflections on the Latin American Economy in 1982. *Cepal Rev.,* April 1983, (19), pp. 7–49. **[G: Latin America]**

Ingham, Keith P. D. and Love, James. Understanding the Scottish Economy: Conclusion—The Future: An Open Question. **In** *Ingham, K. P. D. and Love, J., eds.,* 1983, pp. 297–99. **[G: U.K.]**

Isachsen, Arne Jon. Norwegian Economic Policy in the Past Decade and Some Thoughts on Policy in the Present One. **In** *de Cecco, M., ed.,* 1983, pp. 49–64. **[G: Norway]**

Jayawardena, Lal. International Keynesianism—A Solution to the World Crisis? **In** *Jansen, K., ed.,* 1983, pp. 149–74.

Jowell, Kate. Economic Priorities for an Independent Namibia. **In** *Rotberg, R. I., ed.,* 1983, pp. 93–99. **[G: Namibia]**

Kagami, N. Maturing of the Japanese Economy in the 1980s. *Nat. Westminster Bank Quart. Rev.,* November 1983, pp. 18–28. **[G: Japan]**

Kaldor, Nicholas. Conflicts in National Economic Objectives. **In** *Feinstein, C., ed.,* 1983, *1971,* pp. 169–84. **[G: U.K.]**

Kaldor, Nicholas. The World Economic Outlook. **In** *Tsuru, S., ed.,* 1983, pp. 136–40.

Keatley, Robert. East Asia: The Recession Arrives. *Foreign Aff.,* 1982, *61*(3), pp. 692–713. **[G: E. Asia]**

Kemp, D. A. The National Economic Summit: Authority, Persuasion and Exchange. *Econ. Rec.,* September 1983, *59*(166), pp. 209–19. **[G: Australia]**

Keyserling, Leon H. U.S. Economy, Performance and Prospects, and Needed Corrective Policies. *Atlantic Econ. J.,* September 1983, *11*(3), pp. 9–43. **[G: U.S.]**

Kindleberger, Charles P. 1929: Ten Lessons for Today. *Challenge,* March/April 1983, *26*(1), pp. 58–61.

Kirchgässner, Gebhard. An Application of Optimal Control to a Small Model of Politico-economic Interaction. **In** *Gruber, J., ed.,* 1983, pp. 55–80. **[G: W. Germany]**

Kissinger, Henry A. Salvare l'economia del mondo. (Saving the World Economy. With English summary.) *Mondo Aperto,* September-October 1983, *37*(5), pp. 245–54. **[G: OECD]**

Kjaer, Jørn H. International Adjustment, the EMS and Small European Countries: The Danish Experience. **In** *de Cecco, M., ed.,* 1983, pp. 65–73. **[G: Denmark]**

Kumar, Pradeep. The Current Industrial Relations Scene in Canada, 1983: The Economy: Summary Outline. **In** *Wood, W. D. and Kumar, P., eds.,* 1983, pp. 3–27. **[G: Canada]**

Laffer, Arthur B. Supply-Side Economics and the Reagan Program: Response: Not Enough Incentives. **In** *Stubblebine, Wm. C. and Willett, T. D., eds.,* 1983, pp. 71–76. **[G: U.S.]**

Lawrence, Robert Z. The Myth of U.S. Deindustrialization. *Challenge,* November/December 1983, *26*(5), pp. 12–21. **[G: U.S.; OECD]**

Lee, Dwight R. Constitutional Reform: A Prerequisite for Supply-Side Economics. *Cato J.,* Winter 1983/84, *3*(3), pp. 793–810. **[G: U.S.]**

van Lennep, Emile. The Outlook for Europe's Economic Development. **In** *Heertje, A., ed.,* 1983, pp. 1–40.

Lerner, Abba P. Principles of Efficient Economic Policy. **In** *Lerner, A. P.,* 1983, *1975,* pp. 163–69.

Leven, Ronald and Roberts, David L. Latin America's Prospects for Recovery. *Fed. Res. Bank New York Quart. Rev.*, Autumn 1983, *8*(3), pp. 6–13. **[G: Latin America]**

Lim, Chong Yah. Singapore's Economic Development: Retrospect and Prospect. **In** *Chen, P. S. J., ed.*, 1983, pp. 89–104. **[G: Singapore]**

Liu, Guoguang and Shen, Liren. How to Transform Cyclical Economic Fluctuations into Smooth, Expanded Reproduction. *Chinese Econ. Stud.*, Fall 1983, *17*(1), pp. 96–104. **[G: China]**

Llewellyn, John. Resource Prices and Macroeconomic Policies: Lessons from Two Oil Price Shocks. *OECD Econ. Stud.*, Autumn 1983, (1), pp. 197–212. **[G: OECD]**

Ma, Hong. Economic Adjustment and the Rate of Growth. *Chinese Econ. Stud.*, Fall 1983, *17*(1), pp. 74–87. **[G: China]**

Magnifico, Giovanni. Problems of the World Economy Today. *Econ. Notes*, 1983, (2), pp. 49–64. **[G: Global]**

Maira, Luis. Prospects and Options for United States Society. **In** *Reynolds, C. W. and Tello, C., eds.*, 1983, pp. 83–107. **[G: U.S.]**

Martin, Preston. Statement to the Subcommittee on Domestic Monetary Policy, U.S. House Committee on Banking, Finance, and Urban Affairs, June 1, 1983. *Fed. Res. Bull.*, June 1983, *69*(6), pp. 411–15. **[G: U.S.]**

Matthews, R. C. O. Why Has Britain Had Full Employment since the War? **In** *Feinstein, C., ed.*, 1983, *1968*, pp. 118–32. **[G: U.K.]**

Mayes, David G. Industrial Production. *Nat. Inst. Econ. Rev.*, November 1983, (106), pp. 49–55. **[G: U.K.]**

McCallum, John. Government Deficits: Historical Analysis and Present Policy Alternatives. **In** *Conklin, D. W. and Courchene, T. J., eds.*, 1983, pp. 284–317. **[G: Canada]**

McCawley, Peter. Survey of Recent Developments. *Bull. Indonesian Econ. Stud.*, April 1983, *19*(1), pp. 1–31. **[G: Indonesia]**

McClure, J. Harold and Willett, Thomas D. Understanding the Supply-Siders. **In** *Stubblebine, Wm. C. and Willett, T. D., eds.*, 1983, pp. 59–69. **[G: U.S.]**

McGuinness, P. P. Statement No. 2 and Reserve Bank Annual Report: Rejoinder. *Econ. Rec.*, June 1983, *59*(165), pp. 188. **[G: Australia]**

McMahon, C. W. Financial Aspects of the International Economic Situation. *Nationaløkon. Tidsskr.*, 1983, *121*(1), pp. 74–82. **[G: OECD]**

McNamara, Robert S. U.S. Foreign Policy and the Third World: Agenda 1983: Introduction. **In** *Lewis, J. P. and Kallab, V., eds.*, 1983, pp. 1–4. **[G: LDCs; OECD]**

Meltzer, Allan H. Present and Future in an Uncertain World. **In** *Sanford, T., ed.*, 1983, pp. 37–55. **[G: U.S.]**

Nakagawa, Yukitsugu. What Should Be the Future Role of Japan in Today's International Scene? *Ann. Sci. Écon. Appl.*, 1983, *39*(3), pp. 187–96. **[G: Japan]**

Nichols, Donald A. The Prospects for Economic Growth in the United States, 1980–2000. **In** *Reynolds, C. W. and Tello, C., eds.*, 1983, pp. 109–32. **[G: U.S.]**

Nordhaus, William D. Reflections on Monetarism, Stagnation and Other North American Exports. *Int. Soc. Sci. J.*, 1983, *35*(3), pp. 493–506. **[G: U.S.]**

Okun, Arthur M. Conflicting National Goals. **In** *Okun, A. M.*, 1983, *1976*, pp. 221–49. **[G: U.S.]**

Okun, Arthur M. Political Economy: Some Lessons of Recent Experience. **In** *Okun, A. M.*, 1983, *1972*, pp. 450–70. **[G: U.S.]**

Okun, Arthur M. Potential GNP: Its Measurement and Significance. **In** *Okun, A. M.*, 1983, *1962*, pp. 145–58. **[G: U.S.]**

Okun, Arthur M. The Conduct of Monetary Policy. **In** *Okun, A. M.*, 1983, *1975*, pp. 471–81. **[G: U.S.]**

Okun, Arthur M. The Formulation of National Economic Policy. **In** *Okun, A. M.*, 1983, *1968*, pp. 584–91. **[G: U.S.]**

Okun, Arthur M. The Full Employment Surplus Revisited. **In** *Okun, A. M.*, 1983, *1970*, pp. 304–37. **[G: U.S.]**

Ollila, Esko. Kvalitativa faktorer vid utveckling av vår konkurrenskraft. (Qualitative Factors in the Development of Our International Competitiveness. With English summary.) *Ekon. Samfundets Tidskr.*, 1983, *36*(2), pp. 55–60. **[G: Finland]**

Oshima, Harry T. On the Coming Pacific Century: Perspectives and Prospects. *Singapore Econ. Rev.*, October 1983, *28*(2), pp. 6–21. **[G: OECD; E. Asia]**

Pekkala, Ahti. Vuoden 1984 tulo- ja menoarvioesitys. (The Budget for 1984. With English summary.) *Kansant. Aikak.*, 1983, *79*(4), pp. 405–11. **[G: Finland]**

Plassard, Jacques. Les équilibres économiques généraux en France et la politique conduite depuis mai 1981. (With English summary.) *Revue Écon. Polit.*, September–October 1983, *93*(5), pp. 659–68. **[G: France]**

Rabeau, Yves. Quelques perspectives de la conjoncture au cours des prochaines années (revues et corrigées). (Economic Conjuncture for the Next Years: A Reassessment. With English summary.) *L'Actual. Econ.*, March 1983, *59*(1), pp. 135–43. **[G: Canada]**

Rahn, Richard W. Supply-Side Economics: The U.S. Experience. **In** *Stubblebine, Wm. C. and Willett, T. D., eds.*, 1983, pp. 43–57. **[G: U.S.]**

Rangel, Charles B. Interest Rates: Impact on the Budget. **In** *Sanford, T., ed.*, 1983, pp. 91–102. **[G: U.S.]**

Reddaway, W. Brian. Problems and Prospects for the UK Economy. *Econ. Rec.*, September 1983, *59*(166), pp. 220–31. **[G: U.K.]**

Rousseas, Stephen. The Ideology of Supply-Side Economics. **In** *Weintraub, S. and Goodstein, M., eds.*, 1983, pp. 21–33. **[G: U.S.]**

Rozen, Marvin E. The Administration's Dodecalogue: A Dozen Handy Explanations if Recovery Aborts. *Challenge*, May/June 1983, *26*(2), pp. 46–48. **[G: U.S.]**

Scitovsky, Tibor. The Prospects for Economic Growth in the United States, 1980–2000: Comments. **In** *Reynolds, C. W. and Tello, C., eds.*, 1983, pp. 133–35. **[G: U.S.]**

Seton, Francis. Thatcherism in Britain. **In** *Weintraub, S. and Goodstein, M., eds.*, 1983, pp. 180–91. **[G: U.K.]**

Shaw, Timothy M. Nigeria in the International System. **In** *Zartman, I. W., ed.*, 1983, pp. 207–36. **[G: Nigeria]**

Sicat, Gerardo P. National Economic Strategy in a Sluggish World Setting. *Philippine Econ. J.*, 1983, *22*(2), pp. 183–94. **[G: Philippine]**

Six, Jean Michel. Ripresa internazionale più lenta ma più sana. (Slow but Healthy World Recovery. With English summary.) *L'Impresa*, 1983, *25*(6), pp. 21–24. **[G: OECD]**

Steindl, Josef. The Control of the Economy. *Banca Naz. Lavoro Quart. Rev.*, September 1983, (146), pp. 235–48.

Stubblebine, Wm. Craig and Willett, Thomas D. Future Directions. **In** *Stubblebine, Wm. C. and Willett, T. D., eds.*, 1983, pp. 205–08. **[G: U.S.]**

Stubblebine, Wm. Craig and Willett, Thomas D. The Reagan Program: An Overview. **In** *Stubblebine, Wm. C. and Willett, T. D., eds.*, 1983, pp. 3–8. **[G: U.S.]**

Syren, Jean-Louis. États-Unis: l'année de la reprise. (With English summary.) *Revue Écon. Polit.*, September–October 1983, *93*(5), pp. 781–93. **[G: U.S.]**

Tantazzi, Angelo. Azienda Italia: un recupero difficile. (The Italian Economic Scenario. With English summary.) *L'Impresa*, 1983, *25*(6), pp. 17–19. **[G: Italy]**

Thurow, Lester C. America in a Competitive Economic World. **In** *Miller, G. W., ed.*, 1983, pp. 36–51. **[G: U.S.]**

Ulmer, Melville J. The Economic Civil War. *Atlantic Econ. J.*, September 1983, *11*(3), pp. 44–48. **[G: U.S.]**

Uys, Stanley. SWAPO and the Postindependence Era. **In** *Rotberg, R. I., ed.*, 1983, pp. 101–14. **[G: Namibia]**

Vatter, Harold G. and Walker, John F. Can the Good Performance of the 1960s Be Repeated in the 1980s? *J. Econ. Issues*, June 1983, *17*(2), pp. 369–78. **[G: U.S.]**

Volcker, Paul A. Monetary Policy for the 1980s. **In** *Walker, C. E. and Bloomfield, M. E., eds.*, 1983, pp. 35–43. **[G: U.S.]**

Volcker, Paul A. Statement to the Joint Economic Committee, October 20, 1983. *Fed. Res. Bull.*, November 1983, *69*(11), pp. 842–46. **[G: U.S.]**

Volcker, Paul A. Statement to the U.S. House Committee on the Budget, March 8, 1983. *Fed. Res. Bull.*, March 1983, *69*(3), pp. 187–93. **[G: U.S.]**

Volcker, Paul A. Statement to the U.S. Senate Committee on Banking, Housing, and Urban Affairs, February 16, 1983. *Fed. Res. Bull.*, March 1983, *69*(3), pp. 167–74. **[G: U.S.]**

Volcker, Paul A. Statement to the U.S. Senate Committee on the Budget, February 24, 1983. *Fed. Res. Bull.*, March 1983, *69*(3), pp. 181–86. **[G: U.S.]**

Volcker, Paul A. Statement to U.S. Congress Joint Economic Committee, January 27, 1983. *Fed. Res. Bull.*, February 1983, *69*(2), pp. 75–80. **[G: U.S.]**

Wahlroos, Björn. Avreglering och industripolitik [Kvalitativa faktorer vid utveckling av vår konkurrenskraft]. (Lifting Controls and Industrial Policy. With English summary.) *Ekon. Samfundets Tidskr.*, 1983, *36*(2), pp. 61–63. **[G: Finland]**

Weidenbaum, Murray L. Lessons in Economic Policy since January 1981 and Current Applications. *Bus. Econ.*, January 1983, *18*(1), pp. 15–19. **[G: U.S.]**

1331 Stabilization Theories and Policies

Abel, Andrew B. Financing Private Business in an Inflationary Context: The Experience of Argentina between 1967 and 1980: Comment. **In** *Armella, P. A.; Dornbusch, R. and Obstfeld, M., eds.*, 1983, pp. 183–85. **[G: Argentina]**

Aghevli, Bijan B. Economic Structure and Policy for External Balance: Comment. *Int. Monet. Fund Staff Pap.*, March 1983, *30*(1), pp. 67–70. **[G: U.S.; W. Europe]**

Allen, Polly Reynolds. Policies to Correct Cyclical Imbalance within a Monetary Union. *J. Common Market Stud.*, March 1983, *21*(3), pp. 313–27.

Apple, Nixon. The Historical Foundations of Class Struggle in Late Capitalist Liberal Democracies. **In** *Clegg, S.; Dow, G. and Boreham, P., eds.*, 1983, pp. 72–128. **[G: OECD]**

Arestis, P. and Driver, Ciaran. U.K. Unemployment and Post-Keynesian Remedies. *Metroecon.*, October 1983, *35*(3), pp. 275–91. **[G: U.K.]**

Arestis, P.; Holly, S. and Karakitsos, Elias. Optimal Stabilisation Policies in West Germany and the Netherlands. **In** *[Saunders, C. T.]*, 1983, pp. 309–38. **[G: Netherlands; W. Germany]**

Ashenfelter, Orley. The Withering away of a Full Employment Goal. *Can. Public Policy*, March 1983, *9*(1), pp. 114–25. **[G: Canada]**

Bacha, Edmar L. A Critique of Southern Cone Monetarism. *Int. Soc. Sci. J.*, 1983, *35*(3), pp. 413–23. **[G: Argentina; Chile; Uruguay]**

Bacha, Edmar L. Vicissitudes of Recent Stabilization Attempts in Brazil and the IMF Alternative. **In** *Williamson, J., ed.*, 1983, pp. 323–40. **[G: Brazil]**

Balabkins, Nicholas W. Repressed Inflation and Uncertainty in Postwar Germany. **In** *Schmukler, N. and Marcus, E., eds.*, 1983, pp. 353–72. **[G: U.S.; Germany]**

Balassa, Bela. Economic Policies in Portugal. *Economia*, January 1983, *7*(1), pp. 111–34. **[G: Portugal]**

Balassa, Bela. The Adjustment Experience of Developing Economies after 1973. **In** *Williamson, J., ed.*, 1983, pp. 145–74. **[G: LDCs]**

Ball, R. J. Economic Management and Aggregate Supply. **In** *[Klein, L. R.]*, 1983, pp. 239–61. **[G: OECD]**

Bator, Francis M. America's Inflation. **In** *Weintraub, S. and Goodstein, M., eds.*, 1983, pp. 3–14. **[G: U.S.]**

Batten, Dallas S. and Hafer, R. W. The Relative Impact of Monetary and Fiscal Actions on Economic Activity: A Cross-Country Comparison. *Fed. Res. Bank St. Louis Rev.*, January 1983, *65*(1), pp. 5–12.

Baum, Christopher F. Evaluating Macroeconomic

Policy: Optimal Control Solutions versus Suboptimal Alternatives. **In** *Gruber, J., ed.*, 1983, pp. 81–109. **[G: U.S.]**

Bean, Charles R. Targeting Nominal Income: An Appraisal. *Econ. J.*, December 1983, *93*(372), pp. 806–19.

Benavie, Arthur. Achieving External and Internal Targets with Exchange-Rate and Interest-Rate Intervention. *J. Int. Money Finance*, April 1983, *2*(1), pp. 75–85.

Bergsten, C. Fred. The Costs of Reaganomics. **In** *Bergsten, C. F.*, 1983, *1981*, pp. 37–46. **[G: U.S.]**

Berov, Ljuben. Inflation and Deflation Policy in Bulgaria during the Period between World War I and World War II. **In** *Schmukler, N. and Marcus, E., eds.*, 1983, pp. 488–99. **[G: Bulgaria]**

de Bever, Leo. Deficits and the Economy to 1990: Projections and Alternatives: Comment. **In** *Conklin, D. W. and Courchene, T. J., eds.*, 1983, pp. 148–49. **[G: Canada]**

Bhandari, Jagdeep S. Indexation, Deficit Finance and the Inflationary Process. *Southern Econ. J.*, April 1983, *49*(4), pp. 1077–93.

Blackaby, F. Post-mortem on British Economic Policy 1960–76. **In** *[Saunders, C. T.]*, 1983, pp. 259–70. **[G: U.K.]**

Blatt, John M. Economic Policy and Endogenous Cycles. *J. Post Keynesian Econ.*, Summer 1983, *5*(4), pp. 635–47.

Bockelmann, Horst. 'Exchange Rates, Inflation, and the Sterilization Problem: Germany, 1975–1981' by M. Obstfeld: Comment. *Europ. Econ. Rev.*, March/April 1983, *21*(1/2), pp. 191–95. **[G: W. Germany]**

Bogdanowicz-Bindert, Christine A. Portugal, Turkey and Peru: Three Successful Stabilization Programmes under the Auspices of the IMF. *World Devel.*, January 1983, *11*(1), pp. 65–70. **[G: Portugal; Turkey; Peru]**

Boltho, Andrea. Is Western Europe Caught in an 'Expectations Trap'? *Lloyds Bank Rev.*, April 1983, (148), pp. 1–13. **[G: W. Europe]**

Bomberger, William A. and Makinen, Gail E. The Hungarian Hyperinflation and Stabilization of 1945–1946. *J. Polit. Econ.*, October 1983, *91*(5), pp. 801–24. **[G: Hungary]**

Bomhoff, Edward J. Permanent and Transitory Changes in Monetary Policy: A Comment. *Carnegie-Rochester Conf. Ser. Public Policy*, Autumn 1983, *19*, pp. 211–23. **[G: Switzerland; U.S.; W. Germany]**

Borchert, Manfred. Einige aussenwirtschaftliche Aspekte staatlicher Verschuldung. (Some International Economic Aspects of Public Debt. With English summary.) *Kredit Kapital*, 1983, *16*(4), pp. 513–27. **[G: W. Germany]**

Bossons, John. Rapporteur's Remarks: Discussion. **In** *Conklin, D. W. and Courchene, T. J., eds.*, 1983, pp. 358–60.

Branson, William H. Economic Structure and Policy for External Balance. *Int. Monet. Fund Staff Pap.*, March 1983, *30*(1), pp. 39–66. **[G: U.S.; W. Europe]**

Branson, William H. Fighting Stagflation: Macroeconomics under Reagan: Responses: The Problem Is Not Credibility. **In** *Stubblebine, Wm. C. and Willett, T. D., eds.*, 1983, pp. 27–29. **[G: U.S.]**

Branson, William H. and Buiter, Willem H. Monetary and Fiscal Policy with Flexible Exchange Rates. **In** *Bhandari, J. S. and Putnam, B. H., eds.*, 1983, pp. 251–85.

Bricall, Josep M. Algunos aspectos monetarios y financieros de la crisis. (Some Monetary and Financial Aspects of the Crisis. With English summary.) *Écon. Soc.*, September–October–November 1983, *17*(9–10–11), pp. 1611–30.

Brittan, Samuel. Breaking the Mould. **In** *Brittan, S.*, 1983, pp. 239–63. **[G: U.K.]**

Brittan, Samuel. Jobs, Output and Prices. **In** *Brittan, S.*, 1983, pp. 105–24. **[G: U.K.; U.S.]**

Brittan, Samuel. Money in Longer Perspective. **In** *Brittan, S.*, 1983, pp. 143–55. **[G: U.S.]**

Brittan, Samuel. The Argument Summarised. **In** *Brittan, S.*, 1983, pp. 83–104. **[G: U.K.]**

Brittan, Samuel. The Case for Money GDP. **In** *Brittan, S.*, 1983, pp. 125–42. **[G: U.K.; U.S.]**

Brooks, Simon J.; Henry, Brian and Karakitsos, Elias. Policy Trade-Offs in the NIESR Model: Exercises Using Optimal Control. *Nat. Inst. Econ. Rev.*, August 1983, (105), pp. 36–45. **[G: U.K.]**

Brothwell, John F. Wages and Employment: A Reply to Maynard and Rose [Monetarism, Wages, and Employment Policy in the United Kingdom]. *J. Post Keynesian Econ.*, Fall 1983, *6*(1), pp. 101–04.

Brown, Clair. Unemployment Theory and Policy, 1946–1980. *Ind. Relat.*, Spring 1983, *22*(2), pp. 164–85. **[G: U.S.]**

Bruce, Neil and Purvis, Douglas D. Fiscal Discipline and Rules for Controlling the Deficit: Some Unpleasant Keynesian Arithmetic. **In** *Conklin, D. W. and Courchene, T. J., eds.*, 1983, pp. 323–40.

Bruce, Neil and Purvis, Douglas D. Fiscal Policy and Recovery from the Great Recession. *Can. Public Policy*, March 1983, *9*(1), pp. 53–67. **[G: Canada]**

Brunner, Karl. The Politics of Myopia and Its Ideology. **In** *Shadow Open Market Committee.*, 1983, pp. 7–17. **[G: U.S.]**

Buiter, Willem H. Measurement of the Public Sector Deficit and Its Implications for Policy Evaluation and Design. *Int. Monet. Fund Staff Pap.*, June 1983, *30*(2), pp. 306–49.

Buiter, Willem H. and Miller, Marcus H. Changing the Rules: Economic Consequences of the Thatcher Regime. *Brookings Pap. Econ. Act.*, 1983, (2), pp. 305–79. **[G: U.K.]**

Burton, David. Flexible Exchange Rates and Perfect Foresight: The Implications of Domestic Monetary Policy for Foreign Prices and Stabilization Policy. *Weltwirtsch. Arch.*, 1983, *119*(2), pp. 201–13.

Butlin, Noel G. Trends in Public/Private Relations, 1901–75. **In** *Head, B. W., ed.*, 1983, pp. 79–97. **[G: Australia]**

Büttler, Hans-Jürg and Schiltknecht, Kurt. Transitory Changes in Monetary Policy and Their Implications in Money-Stock Control. *Carnegie-Rochester Conf. Ser. Public Policy*, Autumn 1983, *19*, pp. 171–209.

Cagan, Phillip. The Trouble with "Rational Expectations" and the Problem of Inflation Stabilization: Comment. **In** *Frydman, R. and Phelps, E. S., eds.*, 1983, pp. 41–45.

Calvo, Guillermo A. Trying to Stabilize: Some Theoretical Reflections Based on the Case of Argentina. **In** *Armella, P. A.; Dornbusch, R. and Obstfeld, M., eds.*, 1983, pp. 199–216. **[G: Argentina]**

Campbell, Robert B. Cost Function Bias and Linear Quadratic Stabilisation. *Australian Econ. Pap.*, December 1983, *22*(41), pp. 495–98.

Canarella, Giorgio and Garston, Neil. Monetary and Public Debt Shocks: Tests and Efficient Estimates. *J. Money, Credit, Banking*, May 1983, *15*(2), pp. 199–211. **[G: U.S.]**

Carlsson, Bo A. W. Industrial Subsidies in Sweden: Macro-Economic Effects and an International Comparison. *J. Ind. Econ.*, September 1983, *32*(1), pp. 1–23. **[G: Sweden; W. Germany; U.K.; Norway; Italy]**

Cavallo, Domingo F. and Petrei, A. Humberto. Financing Private Business in an Inflationary Context: The Experience of Argentina between 1967 and 1980. **In** *Armella, P. A.; Dornbusch, R. and Obstfeld, M., eds.*, 1983, pp. 153–80. **[G: Argentina]**

de Cecco, Marcello. Political Factors in Monetary Policy: Discussion. **In** *Hodgman, D. R., ed.*, 1983, pp. 204–05. **[G: U.K.; France; W. Germany]**

de Cecco, Marcello. The Vicious/Virtuous Circle Debate in the Twenties and the Seventies. *Banca Naz. Lavoro Quart. Rev.*, September 1983, (146), pp. 285–303. **[G: Europe]**

Chambers, Robert G. Impact of Federal Fiscal–Monetary Policy on Farm Structure: Discussion. *Southern J. Agr. Econ.*, July 1983, *15*(1), pp. 69–71. **[G: U.S.]**

Chamley, Christophe. Optimal Fiscal and Monetary Policies in Neoclassical Dynamic Models. **In** *Biehl, D.; Roskamp, K. W. and Stolper, W. F., eds.*, 1983, pp. 69–87.

Chand, Sheetal K. and Otani, Ichiro. Some Criteria to Evaluate Demand Management Policies in Asian Countries. *J. Policy Modeling*, March 1983, *5*(1), pp. 107–23. **[G: Asia]**

Chappell, Henry W., Jr. and Keech, William R. Welfare Consequences of the Six-Year Presidential Term Evaluated in the Context of a Model of the U.S. Economy. *Amer. Polit. Sci. Rev.*, March 1983, *77*(1), pp. 75–91. **[G: U.S.]**

Christ, Carl F. An Evaluation of the Economic Policy Proposals of the Joint Economic Committee of the 92nd and 93rd Congresses. **In** *Brunner, K. and Meltzer, A. H., eds.*, 1983, *1977*, pp. 349–83. **[G: U.S.]**

Ciampi, Carlo Azeglio. Le scelte da compiere per una ripresa nella stabilità. (Choices for Achievement of Recovery with Stability. With English summary.) *Bancaria*, February 1983, *39*(2), pp. 115–30. **[G: Italy]**

Clegg, Stewart; Dow, Geoff and Boreham, Paul. Politics and Crisis: The State of the Recession. **In** *Clegg, S.; Dow, G. and Boreham, P., eds.*, 1983, pp. 1–50.

Cline, William R. Economic Stabilization in Developing Countries: Theory and Stylized Facts. **In** *Williamson, J., ed.*, 1983, *1981*, pp. 175–208.

Conklin, David and Sayeed, Adil. Overview of the Deficit Debate. **In** *Conklin, D. W. and Courchene, T. J., eds.*, 1983, pp. 12–54. **[G: Canada]**

Connolly, Michael B. Exchange Rates, Real Economic Activity and the Balance of Payments: Evidence from the 1960s. **In** *Claassen, E. and Salin, P., eds.*, 1983, pp. 129–43. **[G: Selected Countries]**

Cortázar, René. Chile: Resultados distributivos 1973–82. (With English summary.) *Desarrollo Econ.*, October-December 1983, *23*(91), pp. 369–94. **[G: Chile]**

Cortés Douglas, Hernán. Políticas de estabilización en Chile: inflación, desempleo y depresión 1975–1982. (With English summary.) *Cuadernos Econ.*, August 1983, *20*(60), pp. 149–75. **[G: Chile]**

Cripps, Francis. What Is Wrong with Monetarism? **In** *Jansen, K., ed.*, 1983, pp. 55–68.

Cripps, Francis and Ward, Terry. Government Policies, European Recession and Problems of Recovery. *Cambridge J. Econ.*, March 1983, *7*(1), pp. 85–99. **[G: W. Europe]**

Dell, Sidney. Stabilization: The Political Economy of Overkill. **In** *Williamson, J., ed.*, 1983, pp. 17–45.

Demopoulos, George D.; Katsimbris, George M. and Miller, Stephen M. Do Macroeconomic Policy Decisions Affect the Private Sector Ex Ante?—The EEC Experience with Crowding Out. **In** *Hodgman, D. R., ed.*, 1983, pp. 246–67. **[G: EEC]**

Dewald, William G. Fast and Gradual Anti-inflation Policies: Evidence for Germany, Italy, and the United States. **In** *Schmukler, N. and Marcus, E., eds.*, 1983, pp. 689–706. **[G: W. Germany; Italy; France]**

Diaz-Alejandro, Carlos F. IMF Conditionality: Country Studies: Comments, Chapters 11–14. **In** *Williamson, J., ed.*, 1983, pp. 341–46.

Dornbusch, Rudiger. Flexible Exchange Rates and Interdependence. *Int. Monet. Fund Staff Pap.*, March 1983, *30*(1), pp. 3–30. **[G: U.S.]**

Dornbusch, Rudiger. Issues Related to Conditionality: Comments, Chapters 7–10. **In** *Williamson, J., ed.*, 1983, pp. 223–30.

Dreyer, Jacob. Fighting Stagflation: Macroeconomics under Reagan: Response: Some International Aspects of U.S. Macroeconomic Policy. **In** *Stubblebine, Wm. C. and Willett, T. D., eds.*, 1983, pp. 36–40. **[G: U.S.]**

Duesenberry, James S. The Political Economy of Central Banking in the United States or Quis Custodiet Ipsos Custodes. **In** *Hodgman, D. R., ed.*, 1983, pp. 123–40. **[G: U.S.]**

Dungan, D. P. and Wilson, T. A. Deficits and the Economy to 1990: Projections and Alternatives. **In** *Conklin, D. W. and Courchene, T. J., eds.*, 1983, pp. 116–48. **[G: Canada]**

van Eijk, Cornelis J. Possible Policy Implications of Modern Underemployment Equilibrium Theory. *De Economist*, 1983, *131*(3), pp. 344–72. **[G: Netherlands]**

Eliasson, Gunnar; Sharefkin, Mark and Ysander, Bengt-Christer. Stability and Macroeconomic Policy: The Lesson of the 1970s. **In** *Eliasson, G.;*

Sharefkin, M. and Ysander, B.-C., eds., 1983, pp. 11–49. [G: OECD]

Eltis, Walter. *A Neoclassical Analysis of Macroeconomic Policy:* A Review Essay. *J. Money, Credit, Banking,* November 1983, *15*(4), pp. 519–26.

Fand, David I. Monetary-Fiscal Policy for Promoting Growth: The Merits and Shortcomings of the Keynesian Approach. **In** *Biehl, D.; Roskamp, K. W. and Stolper, W. F., eds.*, 1983, pp. 89–100. [G: U.S.]

Feldstein, Martin S. Fiscal Policy for the 1980s. **In** *Walker, C. E. and Bloomfield, M. E., eds.*, 1983, pp. 23–34. [G: U.S.]

Ffrench-Davis, Ricardo. El experimento monetarista en Chile: una síntesis crítica. (With English summary.) *Desarrollo Econ.*, July–September 1983, *23*(90), pp. 163–96. [G: Chile]

Ffrench-Davis, Ricardo. Trying to Stabilize: Some Theoretical Reflections Based on the Case of Argentina: Comment. **In** *Armella, P. A.; Dornbusch, R. and Obstfeld, M., eds.*, 1983, pp. 217–20. [G: Argentina]

Fischer, Stanley. Macroconfusion: The Dilemmas of Economic Policy: Comment. **In** *Tobin, J., ed.*, 1983, pp. 267–76.

Fougstedt, Gunnar. Ekonomisk stagnation och arbetslöshet. (Economic Stagnation and Unemployment. With English summary.) *Ekon. Samfundets Tidskr.*, 1983, *36*(1), pp. 15–17. [G: Finland]

Frenkel, Jacob A. 'Exchange Rates, Inflation, and the Sterilization Problem: Germany, 1975–1982' by M. Obstfeld: Comment. *Europ. Econ. Rev.*, March/April 1983, *21*(1/2), pp. 197–202. [G: W. Germany]

Frenkel, Jacob A. Turbulence in the Foreign Exchange Markets and Macroeconomic Policies. **In** *Bigman, D. and Taya, T., eds.*, 1983, pp. 3–27. [G: U.S.; France; U.K.; W. Germany]

Frey, Bruno S.; Pommerehne, Werner W. and Schneider, Friedrich. Are We All Monetarists Now? An Empirical Inquiry. *J. Post Keynesian Econ.*, Fall 1983, *6*(1), pp. 89–96.

Friedman, Benjamin M. Monetary Policy Management. **In** *Miller, G. W., ed.*, 1983, pp. 72–99. [G: U.S.]

Friedmann, Ralph. The Asymptotic Distribution of Optimal Policy Feedback Coefficients. **In** *Gruber, J., ed.*, 1983, pp. 131–47. [G: U.S.]

Frisch, Helmut. Stabilization Policy in Austria, 1970–80. **In** *de Cecco, M., ed.*, 1983, pp. 117–40. [G: Austria]

Frommholz, H. and Wolters, J. A Control-theoretic Analysis for a Small Econometric Model of the Federal Republic of Germany. **In** *Gruber, J., ed.*, 1983, pp. 116–30. [G: W. Germany]

Galbraith, John Kenneth. Historical Process and the Rich. **In** *Galbraith, J. K.*, 1983, pp. 65–82. [G: U.S.]

Gallestegui, M. C. and Urrutia, J. Crisis, teoria economica y margen de maniobra. (Crisis, Economic Theory and Margin for "Manoeuvre." With English summary.) *Écon. Soc.*, September–October–November 1983, *17*(9–10–11), pp. 1345–81. [G: OECD]

Garrison, Charles B. and Kort, John R. Regional Impact of Monetary and Fiscal Policy: A Comment. *J. Reg. Sci.*, May 1983, *23*(2), pp. 249–61. [G: U.S.]

Godley, Wynne. Keynes and the Management of Real National Income and Expenditure. **In** *Worswick, D. and Trevithick, J., eds.*, 1983, pp. 135–57.

Goodhart, Charles A. E. 'Inflation, Financial and Fiscal Structure, and the Monetary Mechanism' by L. Papademos and F. Modigliani: Comment. *Europ. Econ. Rev.*, March/April 1983, *21*(1/2), pp. 251–56.

Green, Reginald Herbold. Political–Economic Adjustment and IMF Conditionality: Tanzania 1974–81. **In** *Williamson, J., ed.*, 1983, pp. 347–80.

Hall, Peter. Patterns of Economic Policy: An Organizational Approach. **In** *Held, D., et al., eds.*, 1983, pp. 363–94. [G: U.K.; W. Germany]

Harrington, R. L. Monetarisms: Real and Imaginary: A Review Article. *Manchester Sch. Econ. Soc. Stud.*, March 1983, *51*(1), pp. 63–71.

Harris, Ralph. Thatcherissima: The Economics of Thatcherism. *Policy Rev.*, Fall 1983, (26), pp. 35–37. [G: U.K.]

Harris, Ralph. The Mould to Be Broken. **In** *Seldon, A., et al.*, 1983, pp. 15–31. [G: U.K.]

Heertje, Arnold. Monetarism: Is the Debate Closed? **In** *Jansen, K., ed.*, 1983, pp. 69–78.

Heike, Hans-Dieter and Rossa, Harald. Optimal Stabilization with a Quarterly Model of the Federal Republic of Germany. **In** *Gruber, J., ed.*, 1983, pp. 21–47. [G: W. Germany]

Hénin, Pierre-Yves and Zylberberg, André. Sur l'efficacité de la politique monétaire dans des modèles de prévisions rationnelles avec ajustement partiel des prix. (On the Efficiency of the Monetary Policy in Rational Expectations Models with Partial Price Adjustment. With English summary.) *Écon. Appl.*, 1983, *36*(1), pp. 157–74.

Hibbs, Douglas A. Performance économique et fonction de popularité des Présidents Pompidou et Giscard d'Estaing. *Revue Écon. Polit.*, January–February 1983, *93*(1), pp. 44–61. [G: France]

Holly, S. and Zarrop, M. B. On Optimality and Time Consistency When Expectations Are Rational. *Europ. Econ. Rev.*, January 1983, *20*(1–3), pp. 23–40. [G: Netherlands]

Holzmann, Robert and Winckler, Georg. Austrian Economic Policy: Some Theoretical and Critical Remarks on "Austro-Keynesianism." *Empirica*, 1983, (2), pp. 183–203. [G: Austria]

Hotson, John H. What's Wrong with Mainstream Macroeconomics? *Eastern Econ. J.*, July–September 1983, *9*(3), pp. 246–57. [G: U.S.]

Howard, Michael. Control of Inflation in a Small, Open Economy: A Comment. *Amer. Econ.*, Fall 1983, *27*(2), pp. 83–85.

Irvin, George. Nicaragua: Establishing the State as the Centre of Accumulation. *Cambridge J. Econ.*, June 1983, *7*(2), pp. 125–39. [G: Nicaragua]

Irvine, Reed J. and Emery, Robert F. Interest Rates as an Anti-inflationary Instrument in Taiwan. **In** *Von Pischke, J. D.; Adams, D. W. and Donald, G., eds.*, 1983, pp. 393–97. [G: Taiwan]

Jansen, Karel. Monetarism: Economic Crisis and the Third World: An Introduction. **In** *Jansen, K., ed.*,

1983, pp. 1–42.

Johnson, Ronald. Supply-Side Economics: The Rise to Prominence. *Rev. Black Polit. Econ.,* Winter 1983, *12*(2), pp. 189–202. **[G: U.S.]**

Jonung, Lars. Lessons from Swedish Stabilization Policy in the 1970s. *Nat. Westminster Bank Quart. Rev.,* February 1983, pp. 21–34. **[G: Sweden]**

Jordan, Jerry L. Monetary Policy Options and the Economic Outlook. **In** *Shadow Open Market Committee.,* 1983, pp. 29–34. **[G: U.S.]**

Kaldor, Nicholas. The Role of Commodity Prices in Economic Recovery. *Lloyds Bank Rev.,* July 1983, (149), pp. 21–34.

Karjalainen, Ahti. Keskuspankkipolitiikan mahdollisuudet ja rajoitukset. (The Scope for and Limits to Central Bank Policy. With English summary.) *Kansant. Aikak.,* 1983, *79*(2), pp. 149–54. **[G: Finland]**

Kästli, René. The New Economic Environment in the 1970s: Market and Policy Response in Switzerland. **In** *de Cecco, M., ed.,* 1983, pp. 141–59. **[G: Switzerland]**

Killick, Tony. Kenya, the IMF, and the Unsuccessful Quest for Stabilization. **In** *Williamson, J., ed.,* 1983, pp. 381–413. **[G: Kenya]**

Kim, Dae Sik. Monetary Accommodations under External Supply Shocks in Korea: Some Empirical Results. *J. Econ. Devel.,* July 1983, *8*(1), pp. 161–80. **[G: S. Korea]**

Kimbell, Larry J. and Shulman, David. Reaganomics: Implications for California Governments. **In** *Lefcoe, G., ed.,* 1983, pp. 3–14. **[G: U.S.]**

Kincaid, G. Russell. Korea's Major Adjustment Effort. *Finance Develop.,* December 1983, *20*(4), pp. 20–23. **[G: S. Korea]**

Klamer, Arjo. Conversations with Economists: New Classical Economists and Opponents Speak Out on the Current Controversy in Macroeconomics: A Background for the Conversations. **In** *Klamer, A.,* 1983, pp. 1–25.

Klein, Philip A. Reagan's Economic Policies: An Institutional Assessment. *J. Econ. Issues,* June 1983, *17*(2), pp. 463–74. **[G: U.S.]**

Kloten, Norbert. Zyklus und Politik: Zu den Ursachen der wirtschaftlichen Stagnation. (Cycle and Policy: About the Reasons for the Economic Stagnation. With English summary.) *Kredit Kapital,* 1983, *16*(1), pp. 1–15. **[G: MDCs]**

Komiya, Ryutaro. Economic Structure and Policy for External Balance: Comment. *Int. Monet. Fund Staff Pap.,* March 1983, *30*(1), pp. 70–74. **[G: U.S.; W. Europe]**

Kopcke, Richard W. Do Macroeconomic Policy Decisions Affect the Private Sector Ex Ante?—The EEC Experience with Crowding Out: Discussion. **In** *Hodgman, D. R., ed.,* 1983, pp. 268–72. **[G: EEC]**

Kurihara, Shiro. Macroeconomic Policy Alternatives for Higher Oil Prices in the Japanese Economy. *Econ. Stud. Quart.,* April 1983, *34*(1), pp. 44–69. **[G: Japan]**

Laidler, David. Rapporteur's Remarks. **In** *Conklin, D. W. and Courchene, T. J., eds.,* 1983, pp. 346–58.

Lanyi, Anthony and Saracoglu, Rüşdü. The Importance of Interest Rates in Developing Economies. *Finance Develop.,* June 1983, *20*(2), pp. 20–23. **[G: Selected LDCs]**

Leibinger, Hans-Bodo and Rohwer, Bernd. Was kann die Fiskalpolitik noch leisten? (What Can Fiscal Policy Still Accomplish? With English summary.) *Konjunkturpolitik,* 1983, *29*(3), pp. 141–62.

Lekachman, Robert. Remedies Available, Good Sense Lacking. *Challenge,* March/April 1983, *26*(1), pp. 42–44. **[G: U.S.]**

LeLoup, Lance T. Congress and the Dilemma of Economic Policy. **In** *Schick, A., ed.,* 1983, pp. 6–37. **[G: U.S.]**

Lerner, Abba P. From Pre-Keynes to Post-Keynes. **In** *Lerner, A. P.,* 1983, *1977,* pp. 399–427.

Lerner, Abba P. On Keynes, Policy, and Theory—A Grumble. **In** *Lerner, A. P.,* 1983, pp. 441–51.

Lerner, Abba P. The Economic Steering Wheel: The Story of the People's New Clothes. **In** *Lerner, A. P.,* 1983, *1941,* pp. 271–77.

Levin, Jay H. A Model of Stabilization Policy in a Jointly Floating Currency Area. **In** *Bhandari, J. S. and Putnam, B. H., eds.,* 1983, pp. 329–49.

Liviatan, Nissan. Inflation and the Composition of Deficit Finance. **In** *[Klein, L. R.],* 1983, pp. 84–100.

Looney, Robert E. and Frederiksen, P. C. The Feasibility of Alternative IMF-Type Stabilization Programs in Mexico, 1983–87. *J. Policy Modeling,* November 1983, *5*(3), pp. 461–70. **[G: Mexico]**

Lopes, Francisco L. and Bacha, Edmar L. Inflation, Growth and Wage Policy: A Brazilian Perspective. *J. Devel. Econ.,* Aug.–Oct. 1983, *13*(1–2), pp. 1–20. **[G: Brazil]**

López, Julio. The Mexican Economy: Present Situation, Perspectives and Alternatives. *World Devel.,* May 1983, *11*(5), pp. 455–65. **[G: Mexico]**

Lucas, Robert E., Jr. Econometric Policy Evaluation: A Critique. **In** *Brunner, K. and Meltzer, A. H., eds.,* 1983, *1976,* pp. 257–84.

Mackness, William. Fiscal Discipline and Rules for Controlling the Deficit: Some Unpleasant Keynesian Arithmetic: Comment. **In** *Conklin, D. W. and Courchene, T. J., eds.,* 1983, pp. 340–45.

Makinen, Gail E. Recent Developments in Macroeconomic Theory and Policy. *Atlantic Econ. J.,* December 1983, *11*(4), pp. 84–88.

Malinvaud, Edmond. Keynes and the Management of Real National Income and Expenditure: Comment. **In** *Worswick, D. and Trevithick, J., eds.,* 1983, pp. 157–62.

Mandel, Ernest. World Crisis and the Monetarist Answer. **In** *Jansen, K., ed.,* 1983, pp. 79–95. **[G: OECD]**

Mansfield, Charles Y. Multilevel Government: Some Consequences for Fiscal Stabilization Policy. *Bull. Int. Fiscal Doc.,* 1983, *37*(6), pp. 243–57. **[G: Selected MDCs; Selected LDCs]**

Marshall S., Jorge; Mardones S., José Luis and Marshall L., Isabel. IMF Conditionality: The Experiences of Argentina, Brazil, and Chile. **In** *Williamson, J., ed.,* 1983, pp. 275–321. **[G: Chile; Brazil; Argentina]**

Martellaro, Joseph A. Alcuni aspetti dell'economia

politica americana attuale: base storica, ragioni e metodi. (A Few Aspects of the Present American Economic Policy: Historical Grounds, Reasons and Methods. With English summary.) *Rivista Int. Sci. Econ. Com.*, September 1983, *30*(9), pp. 873–85. **[G: U.S.]**

Marzetti, Silva. Tasso ottimale di crescita e bilancio pubblico. (Optimum Growth Rate and Deficit Spending. With English summary.) *Rivista Int. Sci. Econ. Com.*, April-May 1983, *30*(4–5), pp. 339–54. **[G: OECD]**

Masera, Rainer S. Inflation, Stabilization and Economic Recovery in Italy after the War: Vera Lutz's Assessment. *Banca Naz. Lavoro Quart. Rev.*, March 1983, (144), pp. 29–50. **[G: Italy]**

Mathur, Vijay K. and Stein, Sheldon H. Regional Impact of Monetary and Fiscal Policy: A Reply. *J. Reg. Sci.*, May 1983, *23*(2), pp. 263–65. **[G: U.S.]**

Maynard, Geoffrey and Rose, Harold B. Wages and Employment: A Reply [Monetarism, Wages, and Employment Policy in the United Kingdom]. *J. Post Keynesian Econ.*, Fall 1983, *6*(1), pp. 97–100.

McCallum, John. Policy "Credibility" and Economic Behavior. *J. Post Keynesian Econ.*, Fall 1983, *6*(1), pp. 47–52. **[G: U.S.]**

McCallum, John. Stabilization Policy and Endogenous Wage Stickiness. *Amer. Econ. Rev.*, June 1983, *73*(3), pp. 414–19.

McDaniel, Bruce A. and Silvia, John E. Economic Stabilization, Supply Side Economics, and the Social Economist. *Rev. Soc. Econ.*, October 1983, *41*(2), pp. 109–23.

McKay, David. The Political Economy of Economic Policy. **In** *Jones, R. J. B., ed.*, 1983, pp. 93–117. **[G: U.K.]**

McLure, Charles E., Jr. Financing Private Business in an Inflationary Context: The Experience of Argentina between 1967 and 1980: Comment. **In** *Armella, P. A.; Dornbusch, R. and Obstfeld, M., eds.*, 1983, pp. 180–83. **[G: Argentina]**

Meade, James. A New Keynesian Approach to Full Employment. *Lloyds Bank Rev.*, October 1983, (150), pp. 1–18.

Meade, James. A New Keynesian Approach to Full Employment. *Nationaløkon. Tidsskr.*, 1983, *121*(3), pp. 299–316.

Mehrling, Perry. Has Mrs. Thatcher Exorcised the Demons? *Challenge*, January/February 1983, *25*(6), pp. 57–60. **[G: U.K.]**

Meinander, Nils. Huru angripa stagflationen? (How Should We Tackle Stagflation? With English Summary.) *Ekon. Samfundets Tidskr.*, 1983, *36*(1), pp. 9–14.

Melitz, Jacques. 'Inflation, Financial and Fiscal Structure, and the Monetary Mechanism' by L. Papademos and F. Modigliani: Comment. *Europ. Econ. Rev.*, March/April 1983, *21*(1/2), pp. 257–59.

Meltzer, Allan H. Present and Future in an Uncertain World. **In** *Sanford, T., ed.*, 1983, pp. 37–55. **[G: U.S.]**

Miller, G. William. Regrowing the American Economy: Introduction. **In** *Miller, G. W., ed.*, 1983, pp. 1–11. **[G: U.S.]**

Miller, Preston J. Budget Deficit Mythology. *Fed. Res. Bank Minn. Rev.*, Fall 1983, *7*(4), pp. 1–13. **[G: U.S.]**

Minsky, Hyman P. Pitfalls Due to Financial Fragility. **In** *Weintraub, S. and Goodstein, M., eds.*, 1983, pp. 104–19. **[G: U.S.]**

Moffitt, Michael. Floating Has Failed: A Response to Herb Stein. *Challenge*, November/December 1983, *26*(5), pp. 51–53. **[G: U.S.]**

Moriguchi, Chikashi. Japan's Macroeconomic Policies during the 1970s. **In** *[Klein, L. R.]*, 1983, pp. 282–95. **[G: Japan]**

Morris, Frank E. The Political Economy of Central Banking in the United States or Quis Custodiet Ipsos Custodes: Discussion. **In** *Hodgman, D. R., ed.*, 1983, pp. 141–44. **[G: U.S.]**

Mundell, Robert A. The Origins and Evolution of Monetarism. **In** *Jansen, K., ed.*, 1983, pp. 43–54.

Musgrave, Richard A. The Reagan Administration's Fiscal Policy: A Critique. **In** *Stubblebine, Wm. C. and Willett, T. D., eds.*, 1983, pp. 115–32. **[G: U.S.]**

Nguyen, Duc-Tho and Turnovsky, Stephen J. The Dynamic Effects of Fiscal and Monetary Policies under Bond Financing: A Theoretical Simulation Approach to Crowding Out. *J. Monet. Econ.*, January 1983, *11*(1), pp. 45–71.

Nielsen, Peter Erling. Behov og begrænsninger i 1980'ernes pengepolitik. (Recent Developments in Danish Monetary Policy. With English summary.) *Nationaløkon. Tidsskr.*, 1983, *121*(1), pp. 61–73. **[G: Denmark]**

Niskanen, William A. The Reagan Administration's Fiscal Policy: A Critique: Response: Reducing the Federal Share of National Output. **In** *Stubblebine, Wm. C. and Willett, T. D., eds.*, 1983, pp. 133–35. **[G: U.S.]**

Nordhaus, William D. Macroconfusion: The Dilemmas of Economic Policy. **In** *Tobin, J., ed.*, 1983, pp. 247–67. **[G: OECD]**

Oates, Wallace E. The Economics of the New Federalism: Response: Strengths and Weaknesses of the New Federalism. **In** *Stubblebine, Wm. C. and Willett, T. D., eds.*, 1983, pp. 153–57. **[G: U.S.]**

Obstfeld, Maurice. Exchange Rates, Inflation, and the Sterilization Problem: Germany, 1975–1981. *Europ. Econ. Rev.*, March/April 1983, *21*(1/2), pp. 161–89. **[G: W. Germany]**

Okun, Arthur M. Achieving Sustained Prosperity. **In** *Okun, A. M.*, 1983, *1970*, pp. 424–49. **[G: U.S.]**

Okun, Arthur M. Conflicting National Goals. **In** *Okun, A. M.*, 1983, *1976*, pp. 221–49. **[G: U.S.]**

Okun, Arthur M. Inflation: Its Mechanics and Welfare Costs. **In** *Okun, A. M.*, 1983, *1975*, pp. 79–118. **[G: U.S.; 8210]**

Okun, Arthur M. Inflation: The Problems and Prospects before Us. **In** *Okun, A. M.*, 1983, *1970*, pp. 3–34. **[G: U.S.]**

Okun, Arthur M. Monetary Policy, Debt Management and Interest Rates: A Quantitative Appraisal. **In** *Okun, A. M.*, 1983, *1963*, pp. 253–303. **[G: U.S.]**

Okun, Arthur M. Rules and Roles for Fiscal and Monetary Policy. **In** *Okun, A. M.*, 1983, *1971*, pp. 375–401. **[G: U.S.]**

Okun, Arthur M. The Great Stagflation Swamp. **In**

Okun, A. M., 1983, *1977*, pp. 49–62. **[G: U.S.]**

Okun, Arthur M. The Mirage of Steady Inflation. **In** *Okun, A. M.*, 1983, *1971*, pp. 35–48. **[G: U.S.; OECD]**

Okun, Arthur M. The Role of Aggregate Demand in Alleviating Unemployment. **In** *Okun, A. M.*, 1983, *1965*, pp. 159–70. **[G: U.S.]**

Onitiri, H. M. A. Economics and Development Policy. *Int. Soc. Sci. J.*, 1983, *35*(3), pp. 507–16.

Papademos, Lucas and Modigliani, Franco. Inflation, Financial and Fiscal Structure, and the Monetary Mechanism. *Europ. Econ. Rev.*, March/April 1983, *21*(1/2), pp. 203–50.

Parguez, A. La monnaie, la crise et l'épargne ou les conséquences économiques de l'austérité. (Money, Crisis and Saving: The Economic Consequences of Austerity. With English summary.) *Écon. Soc.*, September–October–November 1983, *17*(9–10–11), pp. 1421–50.

Parkin, Vincent. Economic Liberalism in Chile, 1973–82: A Model for Growth and Development or a Recipe for Stagnation and Impoverishment. *Cambridge J. Econ.*, June 1983, *7*(2), pp. 101–24. **[G: Chile]**

Pechman, Joseph A. and Carr, Julie A. Macro-economics Prices & Quantities. **In** *Tobin, J., ed.*, 1983, pp. 1–18.

Pen, Jan. Stagnation Explained? *De Economist*, 1983, *131*(4), pp. 457–73.

Penner, Rudolph G. Fiscal Management. **In** *Miller, G. W., ed.*, 1983, pp. 52–71. **[G: U.S.]**

Phelps, Edmund S. The Trouble with "Rational Expectations" and the Problem of Inflation Stabilization. **In** *Frydman, R. and Phelps, E. S., eds.*, 1983, pp. 31–41.

Please, Stanley. IMF Conditionality: Country Studies: Comments, Chapters 15–16. **In** *Williamson, J., ed.*, 1983, pp. 415–20.

Porter, Roger B. Economic Advice to the President: From Eisenhower to Reagan. *Polit. Sci. Quart.*, Fall 1983, *98*(3), pp. 403–26. **[G: U.S.]**

Posthumus, Godert. The Netherlands: Financial-Economic Adjustment Policies in the 1970s. **In** *de Cecco, M., ed.*, 1983, pp. 74–98. **[G: Netherlands]**

Prescott, Edward C. Should Control Theory Be Used for Economic Stabilization? **In** *Brunner, K. and Meltzer, A. H., eds.*, 1983, *1977*, pp. 285–310.

Prest, A. R. Taxation Policy. **In** *Seldon, A., et al.*, 1983, pp. 49–69. **[G: U.K.]**

Radke, Detlef and Taake, Hans-Helmut. Financial Crisis Management in Egypt and Turkey. *J. World Trade Law*, July–August 1983, *17*(4), pp. 325–36. **[G: Turkey; Egypt]**

Reinikainen, Veikko. Talouspolitiikan suunnan valinnan teoriaa. (Choosing the Nature and Direction of Economic Policy in the 1980s. With English summary.) *Kansant. Aikak.*, 1983, *79*(3), pp. 270–77. **[G: Finland]**

Richardson, H. W. Fiscal Policy in the 1930s. **In** *Feinstein, C., ed.*, 1983, *1967*, pp. 68–92. **[G: U.K.]**

Richmond, W. H. S. M. Bruce and Australian Economic Policy 1923–29. *Australian Econ. Hist. Rev.*, September 1983, *23*(2), pp. 238–57. **[G: Australia]**

Rivlin, Alice. The Reagan Administration's Fiscal Policy: A Critique: Response: The Deficit Dilemma. **In** *Stubblebine, Wm. C. and Willett, T. D., eds.*, 1983, pp. 135–37. **[G: U.S.]**

Robinson, Derek and Mayhew, Ken. Pay Policies for the Future: Conclusions. **In** *Robinson, D. and Mayhew, K., eds.*, 1983, pp. 127–39. **[G: U.K.]**

Rocard, Michel. Les Enjeux de la Décennie 80. (The Challenge of the Eighties. With English summary.) *Aussenwirtschaft*, March 1983, *38*(1), pp. 87–113. **[G: France]**

Rockwood, Charles E. The Dismal Science of Stagflation Control. **In** *Weintraub, S. and Goodstein, M., eds.*, 1983, pp. 139–50. **[G: U.S.]**

Rodriguez, Carlos Alfredo. Politicas de estabilizacion en la economia argentina, 1978–1982. (With English summary.) *Cuadernos Econ.*, April 1983, *20*(59), pp. 21–42. **[G: Argentina]**

Salant, Stephen W. The Vulnerability of Price Stabilization Schemes to Speculative Attack. *J. Polit. Econ.*, February 1983, *91*(1), pp. 1–38.

Sargent, Thomas J. Stopping Moderate Inflations: The Methods of Poincaré and Thatcher. **In** *Dornbusch, R. and Simonsen, M. H., eds.*, 1983, pp. 54–96. **[G: France; U.K.]**

Sauernheimer, Karlhans. Die aussenwirtschaftlichen Implikationen des "New Cambridge Approach." (The "New Cambridge" Approach and External Balance. With English summary.) *Konjunkturpolitik*, 1983, *29*(6), pp. 348–66.

Scandizzo, Pasquale L.; Hazell, Peter B. R. and Anderson, Jock R. Producers' Price Expectations and the Size of the Welfare Gains from Price Stabilisation. *Rev. Marketing Agr. Econ.*, August 1983, *51*(2), pp. 93–107.

Schröder, Jürgen. Exchange Rates, Real Economic Activity and the Balance of Payments: Evidence from the 1960s: Comment. **In** *Claassen, E. and Salin, P., eds.*, 1983, pp. 144–48. **[G: Selected Countries]**

Seidman, Laurence S. Keynesian Stimulus without Inflation. *J. Post Keynesian Econ.*, Fall 1983, *6*(1), pp. 39–46.

Sellekaerts, Willy. Coping with Stagflation. *Atlantic Econ. J.*, December 1983, *11*(4), pp. 14–19. **[G: U.S.]**

Şenses, Fikret. An Assessment of Turkey's Liberalization Attempts since 1980 against the Background of Her Stabilization Program. *METU*, 1983, *10*(3), pp. 271–321. **[G: Turkey]**

Sharefkin, Mark. Stabilization and Growth Policy with Uncertain Oil Prices: Some Rules of Thumb. **In** *Eliasson, G.; Sharefkin, M. and Ysander, B.-C., eds.*, 1983, pp. 327–74.

Sharpley, Jennifer. Economic Management and IMF Conditionality in Jamaica. **In** *Williamson, J., ed.*, 1983, pp. 233–62. **[G: Jamaica]**

Sheikh, M. A.; Grady, P. and Lapointe, P.-H. The Effectiveness of Fiscal Policy in a Keynesian–Monetarist Model of Canada. *Empirical Econ.*, 1983, *8*(3–4), pp. 139–68. **[G: Canada]**

Siebrand, Jan C. and van der Windt, Nico. Economic Crisis and Economic Policy in the Thirties and the Seventies. *De Economist*, 1983, *131*(4), pp. 517–47. **[G: Netherlands]**

Sinn, Hans-Werner. Pro und contra Crowding-Out: Zur Stichhaltigkeit dreier populärer Argumente.

(Pro and Contra Crowding Out: On the Soundness of Three Popular Arguments. With English summary.) *Kredit Kapital,* 1983, *16*(4), pp. 488–512. **[G: W. Germany]**

Sjaastad, Larry A. Macroconfusion: The Dilemmas of Economic Policy: Comment. **In** *Tobin, J., ed.,* 1983, pp. 276–79. **[G: Chile; Argentina]**

Smithin, John Nicholas. A Note on the Welfare Cost of Perfectly Anticipated Inflation. *Bull. Econ. Res.,* May 1983, *35*(1), pp. 65–69.

Solow, Robert M. Keynes and the Management of Real National Income and Expenditure: Comment. **In** *Worswick, D. and Trevithick, J., eds.,* 1983, pp. 162–68.

Solow, Robert M. Macroconfusion: The Dilemmas of Economic Policy: Comment. **In** *Tobin, J., ed.,* 1983, pp. 279–84. **[G: U.S.]**

Sommers, Albert T. The Evolution of Economic Policy: Preparing for Long-term Recovery. **In** *Miller, G. W., ed.,* 1983, pp. 12–35. **[G: U.S.]**

Soskice, David. Economic Theory and Unemployment: Progress and Regress since 1936? *Ind. Relat.,* Spring 1983, *22*(2), pp. 319–33.

Spaventa, Luigi. Two Letters of Intent: External Crises and Stabilization Policy, Italy, 1973–77. **In** *Williamson, J., ed.,* 1983, pp. 441–73. **[G: Italy]**

Sprinkel, Beryl W. Fighting Stagflation: Macroeconomics under Reagan: Response: Internal Consistency of the Reagan Program. **In** *Stubblebine, Wm. C. and Willett, T. D., eds.,* 1983, pp. 30–36. **[G: U.S.]**

Spronk, Jaap and Veeneklaas, Frank. Scenarios for Economic Development: A Feasibility Study by Means of Interactive Multiple Goal Programming. **In** *Hansen, P., ed.,* 1983, pp. 356–71. **[G: Netherlands]**

Stein, Herbert. Starting Over: A New Bipartisan Economic Policy. *Challenge,* March/April 1983, *26*(1), pp. 50–54. **[G: U.S.]**

Stein, Herbert. We Can Learn from the Past: Interview. *Challenge,* Sept.-Oct. 1983, *26*(4), pp. 25–33. **[G: U.S.]**

Stolper, Wolfgang F. Fiscal and Monetary Policy in the Context of Development: A Schumpeterian Approach. **In** *Biehl, D.; Roskamp, K. W. and Stolper, W. F., eds.,* 1983, pp. 127–47.

Stöppler, Siegmar and Stein, Jens-Peter. A Study of Adaptive Revision of Target Values in an Econometric Decision Model. **In** *Gruber, J., ed.,* 1983, pp. 221–41. **[G: W. Germany]**

Stubblebine, Wm. Craig. The Economics of the New Federalism. **In** *Stubblebine, Wm. C. and Willett, T. D., eds.,* 1983, pp. 143–51. **[G: U.S.]**

Tanzi, Vito. Taxation and Price Stabilization. **In** *[Goode, R.],* 1983, pp. 409–30.

Tedeschi, Jardena. La stabilizzazione del reddito reale come obiettivo di politica economica, con un'applicazione all'economia egiziana. (The Stabilization of Real Income as a Goal of Economic Policy with an Application to the Egyptian Economy. With English summary.) *Rivista Int. Sci. Econ. Com.,* December 1983, *30*(12), pp. 1161–70. **[G: Egypt]**

Thurow, Lester C. An International Keynesian Yank. *Challenge,* March/April 1983, *26*(1), pp. 36–39. **[G: MDCs]**

Thygesen, Niels. Praktisk relevans af keynesiansk teori i dag. (With English summary.) *Nationaløkon. Tidsskr.,* 1983, *121*(3), pp. 332–44.

Tilbery, Henry. Indexation in the Brazilian Taxation System. **In** *de Ulhôa Canto, G.; da Silva Martins, I. G. and van Hoorn, J., Jr., eds.,* 1983, pp. 47–98. **[G: Brazil]**

Tobin, James. Keynes' Policies in Theory and Practice. *Challenge,* November/December 1983, *26*(5), pp. 5–11.

Tobin, James. Macroeconomics and Fiscal Policy. **In** *Brown, E. C. and Solow, R. M., eds.,* 1983, pp. 189–201.

Tobin, James. Okun on Macroeconomic Policy: A Final Comment. **In** *Tobin, J., ed.,* 1983, pp. 297–300.

Tobin, James. The Conservative Counter-Revolution in Economic Policy. *J. Econ. Educ.,* Winter 1983, *14*(1), pp. 30–39. **[G: U.S.]**

Tobin, James. Unemployment, Interest and Money. **In** *Sanford, T., ed.,* 1983, pp. 1–25. **[G: U.S.]**

Tondini, Giovanni. Controllabilità e teoria della politica economica. (Controllability and the Theory of Economic Policy. With English summary.) *Giorn. Econ.,* May-June 1983, *42*(5–6), pp. 307–19.

Turnovsky, Stephen J. Wage Indexation and Exchange Market Interventions in a Small Open Economy. *Can. J. Econ.,* November 1983, *16*(4), pp. 574–92.

Tweeten, Luther. Impact of Federal Fiscal–Monetary Policy on Farm Structure. *Southern J. Agr. Econ.,* July 1983, *15*(1), pp. 61–68. **[G: U.S.]**

Ulmer, Melville J. Ideologies and Economic Science. *Atlantic Econ. J.,* March 1983, *11*(1), pp. 17–23.

Vaubel, Roland. Coordination or Competition among National Macro-economic Policies? **In** *[Giersch, H.],* 1983, pp. 3–28. **[G: OECD]**

Vaughan, Roger J. Inflation and Unemployment Surviving the 1980s. **In** *Barker, M., ed. (II),* 1983, pp. 93–247. **[G: U.S.]**

Vedel, Claude. Politique Monétaire et Politique Budgétaire dans un Modèle Dynamique Synthétique d'une Economie en Croissance. **In** *Biehl, D.; Roskamp, K. W. and Stolper, W. F., eds.,* 1983, pp. 101–26.

Volcker, Paul A. Statement to U.S. House Committee on Banking, Finance and Urban Affairs, July 20, 1983. *Fed. Res. Bull.,* August 1983, *69*(8), pp. 601–09. **[G: U.S.]**

Wahlroos, Björn. Hienosäätöpolitiikka ja taloutemme sopeutumiskyky. (Economic Adjustment and "Fine-Tuning" Policies in Finland. With English summary.) *Kansant. Aikak.,* 1983, *79*(3), pp. 284–90. **[G: Finland]**

Wallenius, Hannele and Wallenius, Jyrki. A Methodology for Solving the Multiple Criteria Macroeconomic Policy Problem. **In** *Gruber, J., ed.,* 1983, pp. 310–33. **[G: Finland]**

Walsh, Brendan M. Ireland in the European Monetary System: The Effects of a Change in Exchange Rate Regime. **In** *de Cecco, M., ed.,* 1983, pp. 160–88. **[G: Ireland]**

Wiedemann, Paul. Policy Modeling, Planning, and Flexibility. *Jahr. Nationalökon. Statist.,* March 1983, *198*(2), pp. 161–72.

Willett, Thomas D. Fighting Stagflation: Macroeconomics under Reagan. **In** *Stubblebine, Wm. C. and Willett, T. D., eds.*, 1983, pp. 11–26. **[G: U.S.]**

Willett, Thomas D. and Wolf, Matthias. The Vicious Circle Debate: Some Conceptual Distinctions. *Kyklos*, 1983, *36*(2), pp. 231–48.

Wohltmann, Hans-Werner. Die optimale Kombination "intuitiver" Stabilisierungspolitiken im Phillips-Modell. (The Optimal Combination of "Intuitive" Stabilization Policies in the Phillips Model. With English summary.) *Z. ges. Staatswiss.*, June 1983, *139*(2), pp. 245–58.

Wood, Geoffrey E. Inflation and the Labour Market. **In** *Seldon, A., et al.*, 1983, pp. 35–46. **[G: U.K.]**

Woolley, John T. Political Factors in Monetary Policy. **In** *Hodgman, D. R., ed.*, 1983, pp. 177–203. **[G: U.K.; France; W. Germany]**

Zoeteweij, Bert. Anti-Inflation Policies in the Industrialised Market Economy Countries (Part II). *Int. Lab. Rev.*, November–December 1983, *122*(6), pp. 691–707.

Zoeteweij, Bert. Anti-Inflation Policies in the Industrialised Market Economy Countries (Part 1). *Int. Lab. Rev.*, Sept.–Oct. 1983, *122*(5), pp. 563–77. **[G: MDCs]**

Zwick, Burton. Economic Projections. **In** *Shadow Open Market Committee.*, 1983, pp. 47–51. **[G: U.S.]**

1332 Price and Incomes Policy

Angelier, J.-P. Problématique pour un système de prix de l'énergie dans un pays en voie de développement: l'exemple du Nicaragua. (Questions about a Price System of Energy in a Developing Country: The Example of Nicaragua. With English summary.) *Écon. Soc.*, December 1983, *17*(12), pp. 2033–51. **[G: Nicaragua]**

Ashenfelter, Orley and Layard, Richard. Incomes Policy and Wage Differentials. *Economica*, May 1983, *50*(198), pp. 127–43. **[G: U.K.]**

Asselain, Jean-Charles. La répartition des revenus en Hongrie: Deuxième partie: les incertitudes des années 70. (With English summary.) *Écon. Soc.*, January 1983, *17*(1), pp. 43–88. **[G: Hungary]**

Blackaby, F. Post-mortem on British Economic Policy 1960–76. **In** *[Saunders, C. T.]*, 1983, pp. 259–70. **[G: U.K.]**

Blandy, Richard and Creigh, Stephen. The Australian Labour Market, June 1983. *Australian Bull. Lab.*, June 1983, *9*(3), pp. 159–89. **[G: Australia]**

Bosanquet, Nick. Tax-Based Incomes Policies. **In** *Robinson, D. and Mayhew, K., eds.*, 1983, pp. 33–49.

Bosanquet, Nick. Tax-based Incomes Policies. *Oxford Bull. Econ. Statist.*, February 1983, *45*(1), pp. 33–49.

Brittan, Samuel. Unemployment and Pay. **In** *Brittan, S.*, 1983, pp. 159–85. **[G: U.K.; OECD]**

Brown, William. Central Co-ordination. *Oxford Bull. Econ. Statist.*, February 1983, *45*(1), pp. 51–62. **[G: U.K.]**

Canterbery, E. Ray. Tax Reform and Incomes Policy: A VATIP Proposal. *J. Post Keynesian Econ.*, Spring 1983, *5*(3), pp. 430–39. **[G: U.S.]**

Chew, Soon-Beng. Some Observations on the Incomes Policy Hypotheses and the Level of Aggregation in Incomes Policy Studies. *Indian Econ. J.*, July–September 1983, *31*(1), pp. 35–42.

Christofides, L. N. and Wilton, D. A. Incomes Policy Reconsidered. *J. Macroecon.*, Winter 1983, *5*(1), pp. 119–34. **[G: Canada]**

Colombatto, Enrico. Aspetti dinamici dell'indennità di contingenza. (Dynamic Issues in the Wage-Indexation Mechanism. With English summary.) *Giorn. Econ.*, March-April 1983, *42*(3–4), pp. 239–54.

Cottle, Rex L. and Wallace, Myles S. Economic Effects of Non-Binding Price Constraints. *J. Ind. Econ.*, June 1983, *31*(4), pp. 469–74.

Coursey, Don L. and Smith, Vernon L. Price Controls in a Posted Offer Market. *Amer. Econ. Rev.*, March 1983, *73*(1), pp. 218–21.

Crouch, Colin. Corporative Industrial Relations and the Welfare State. **In** *Jones, R. J. B., ed.*, 1983, pp. 139–66. **[G: OECD]**

Davidson, Lawrence S. The Macroeconomic Impact of the Nixon Wage and Price Controls: A General Equilibrium Approach. *J. Macroecon.*, Fall 1983, *5*(4), pp. 399–420. **[G: U.S.]**

De Wolff, P. Income Policy Developments in the Netherlands. *Ind. Relat.*, Spring 1983, *22*(2), pp. 203–23. **[G: Netherlands]**

Eichner, Alfred S. Income Conflicts, Inflation, and Controls: A Response. *J. Post Keynesian Econ.*, Summer 1983, *5*(4), pp. 603–07. **[G: U.S.]**

Emerson, Michael. A View of Current European Indexation Experiences. **In** *Dornbusch, R. and Simonsen, M. H., eds.*, 1983, pp. 160–79. **[G: Europe]**

Ezhov, A. Improving the Mechanism of Planned Price Control. *Prob. Econ.*, May 1983, *26*(1), pp. 20–37. **[G: U.S.S.R.]**

Fischer, Stanley. Indexing and Inflation. *J. Monet. Econ.*, November 1983, *12*(4), pp. 519–41. **[G: Selected Countries]**

Hansson, Ingemar. Inflation and Price Controls in Sweden. *Scand. J. Econ.*, 1983, *85*(3), pp. 415–23. **[G: Sweden]**

Hunter, L. C. Arbitration. *Oxford Bull. Econ. Statist.*, February 1983, *45*(1), pp. 63–83. **[G: U.K.]**

Karni, Edi. On Optimal Wage Indexation. *J. Polit. Econ.*, April 1983, *91*(2), pp. 282–92.

Kymn, Kern O. and Cushing, Brian J. The Kennedy Wage–Price Guidelines: Revisited. *Atlantic Econ. J.*, December 1983, *11*(4), pp. 83. **[G: U.S.]**

Lerner, Abba P. Employment Theory and Employment Policy. **In** *Lerner, A. P.*, 1983, *1967*, pp. 375–92.

Lerner, Abba P. Phase Three. **In** *Lerner, A. P.*, 1983, *1972*, pp. 481–92.

Lerner, Abba P. Sellers' Inflation and Inflationary Depression. **In** *Lerner, A. P.*, 1983, *1961*, pp. 469–80.

Levi, Maurice and Dexter, Albert. Regulated Prices and Their Consequences. *Can. Public Policy*, March 1983, *9*(1), pp. 24–31. **[G: Canada]**

Levine, A. L. Price and Incomes Policy: A 'Sraffian' Perspective. *Math. Soc. Sci.*, November 1983, *6*(2), pp. 215–25.

Macedo, Roberto. Wage Indexation and Inflation:

The Recent Brazilian Experience. **In** *Dornbusch, R. and Simonsen, M. H., eds.*, 1983, pp. 133–59. **[G: Brazil]**

Mayhew, Ken. Traditional Incomes Policies. **In** *Robinson, D. and Mayhew, K., eds.*, 1983, pp. 15–32. **[G: U.K.]**

Mayhew, Ken. Traditional Incomes Policies. *Oxford Bull. Econ. Statist.*, February 1983, *45*(1), pp. 15–32. **[G: U.K.]**

McMenamin, J. Stuart and Russell, R. Robert. Measuring Labor Compensation in Controls Programs. **In** *Triplett, J. E., ed.*, 1983, pp. 423–48. **[G: U.S.]**

Newton, Keith. Labour Market Policies for Australian Stagflation: A Canadian Viewpoint. *Australian Bull. Lab.*, December 1983, *10*(1), pp. 24–35. **[G: Canada; Australia]**

Nichols, Donald A. Wage Measurement Questions Raised by an Incomes Policy. **In** *Triplett, J. E., ed.*, 1983, pp. 449–62. **[G: U.S.]**

Okun, Arthur M. A Reward TIP. **In** *Okun, A. M.*, 1983, *1979*, pp. 67–75. **[G: U.S.]**

Okun, Arthur M. Wage–Price: Guideposts—Yes. **In** *Okun, A. M.*, 1983, *1972*, pp. 63–66. **[G: U.S.]**

Pankert, Alfred. Government Influence on Wage Bargaining: The Limits Set by International Labour Standards. *Int. Lab. Rev.*, Sept.–Oct. 1983, *122*(5), pp. 579–91. **[G: ILO]**

Peaucelle, Irina; Petit, Pascal and Saillard, Yves. Dépenses publiques: structure et évolution par rapport au PIB. Les enseignements d'un modèle macroéconomique. *Revue Écon. Polit.*, January–February 1983, *93*(1), pp. 62–85. **[G: France; EEC]**

Rakowski, James J. Income Conflicts, Inflation, and Controls. *J. Post Keynesian Econ.*, Summer 1983, *5*(4), pp. 590–602. **[G: U.S.]**

Robinson, Derek. Indirect and Partial Measures. *Oxford Bull. Econ. Statist.*, February 1983, *45*(1), pp. 105–25. **[G: U.K.]**

Robinson, Derek and Mayhew, Ken. Pay Policies for the Future: Introduction. **In** *Robinson, D. and Mayhew, K., eds.*, 1983, pp. 3–13. **[G: U.K.]**

Robinson, Derek and Mayhew, Ken. Pay Policies for the Future: Introduction. *Oxford Bull. Econ. Statist.*, February 1983, *45*(1), pp. 3–13. **[G: U.K.]**

Robinson, Derek and Mayhew, Ken. Pay Policies for the Future: Conclusions. *Oxford Bull. Econ. Statist.*, February 1983, *45*(1), pp. 127–39. **[G: U.K.]**

Seidman, Laurence S. A "Third Way" for Feldstein: TIP. *Challenge*, Sept.–Oct. 1983, *26*(4), pp. 44–48. **[G: U.S.]**

Seidman, Laurence S. A TIP for the Stagflation Era (and Other Complementary Policies). **In** *Weintraub, S. and Goodstein, M., eds.*, 1983, pp. 125–38.

Seidman, Laurence S. Sidney Weintraub, the Man and His Ideas. *Challenge*, November/December 1983, *26*(5), pp. 22–28.

Seton, Francis. A "Phillipsoid" Wage–Push Flation: "In–," "Stag–," or "Slump–." *J. Post Keynesian Econ.*, Spring 1983, *5*(3), pp. 440–53.

Simonsen, Mario Henrique. Indexation: Current Theory and the Brazilian Experience. **In** *Dornbusch, R. and Simonsen, M. H., eds.*, 1983, pp. 99–132. **[G: Brazil]**

Tobin, James. Inflation: Monetary and Structural Causes and Cures. **In** *Schmukler, N. and Marcus, E., eds.*, 1983, pp. 3–16.

Tomlinson, Jim D. Regulating the Capitalist Enterprise: The Impossible Dream? *Scot. J. Polit. Econ.*, February 1983, *30*(1), pp. 54–68. **[G: U.K.]**

Vicarelli, Fausto. Incomes Policy and International Money: Comment [International Money and International Economic Relations]. **In** *Kregel, J. A., ed.*, 1983, pp. 182–85. **[G: Selected Countries]**

Viscusi, W. Kip. The Political Economy of Wage and Price Regulation: The Case of the Carter Pay-Price Standards. **In** *Zeckhauser, R. J. and Leebaert, D., eds.*, 1983, pp. 155–74. **[G: U.S.]**

Zoeteweij, Bert. Anti-Inflation Policies in the Industrialised Market Economy Countries (Part II). *Int. Lab. Rev.*, November–December 1983, *122*(6), pp. 691–707.

134 Inflation and Deflation

1340 General

Abbott, Walter F. and Leasure, J. W. Income Level and Inflation in the United States: 1947–1977. **In** *Schmukler, N. and Marcus, E., eds.*, 1983, pp. 804–19. **[G: U.S.]**

Afridi, Usman and Qadir, Asghar. Dual Sector Inflation in Pakistan. *Pakistan Devel. Rev.*, Autumn 1983, *22*(3), pp. 191–210. **[G: Pakistan]**

Alperovitz, Gar. Social Justice and the New Inflation. **In** *Skurski, R., ed.*, 1983, pp. 159–97. **[G: U.S.]**

Anderson, F. J.; Beaudreau, B. C. and Bonsor, N. C. Effective Corporate Tax Rates, Inflation, and Contestability. *Can. J. Econ.*, November 1983, *16*(4), pp. 686–703. **[G: Canada; U.S.]**

Appelbaum, Eileen. Women in the Stagflation Economy. **In** *Weintraub, S. and Goodstein, M., eds.*, 1983, pp. 34–47. **[G: U.S.]**

Auerbach, Alan J. Inflation and the Choice of Asset Life. **In** *Auerbach, A. J.*, 1983, *1979*, pp. 100–117.

Auerbach, Alan J. Inflation and the Tax Treatment of Firm Behavior. **In** *Auerbach, A. J.*, 1983, *1981*, pp. 95–99.

Balabkins, Nicholas W. Repressed Inflation and Uncertainty in Postwar Germany. **In** *Schmukler, N. and Marcus, E., eds.*, 1983, pp. 353–72. **[G: U.S.; Germany]**

Barros, Cassio Mesquita, Jr. Monetary Correction in Labor Legislation. **In** *de Ulhôa Canto, G.; da Silva Martins, I. G. and van Hoorn, J., Jr., eds.*, 1983, pp. 152–86. **[G: Brazil]**

Batavia, Bala and Lash, Nicholas A. Self-Perpetuating "Inflation": The Case of Turkey. *J. Econ. Devel.*, December 1983, *8*(2), pp. 149–66. **[G: Turkey]**

Bator, Francis M. America's Inflation. **In** *Weintraub, S. and Goodstein, M., eds.*, 1983, pp. 3–14. **[G: U.S.]**

Baumann, Johann H. A Disaggregate Short Run Phillips Curve for Austria: The Effects of Regional Unemployment Dispersion and Spatial Wage Transfer on the National Wage Rate. *Z. Nationalökon.*, 1983, *43*(2), pp. 189–211. **[G: Austria]**

Beckerman, Paul. Index-linked Financial Assets and

the Brazilian Inflation-Feedback Mechanism. **In** *Schmukler, N. and Marcus, E., eds.*, 1983, pp. 571–651. **[G: Brazil]**

Berch, Bettina. The Inflation of Housework. **In** *Schmukler, N. and Marcus, E., eds.*, 1983, pp. 860–66.

Bernholz, Peter. Inflation and Monetary Constitutions in Historical Perspective. *Kyklos*, 1983, *36*(3), pp. 397–419. **[G: Germany; France; U.K.; U.S.]**

Biffignandi, Silvia and Stefani, Silvana. On Testing the Impact of Inflation on Stock Market: An Approach through Alternative Methodologies. *Econ. Notes*, 1983, (1), pp. 173–90. **[G: Italy]**

Bladen-Hovell, R. C. and Richards, G. M. Inflation and Australian Savings Behaviour, 1959–1981. *Australian Econ. Pap.*, December 1983, *22*(41), pp. 290–301. **[G: Australia]**

Bomberger, William A. and Makinen, Gail E. Some Further Thoughts on the Hungarian Hyperinflation of 1945–46. *S. Afr. J. Econ.*, December 1983, *51*(4), pp. 564–66. **[G: Hungary]**

Branson, William H. Fighting Stagflation: Macroeconomics under Reagan: Responses: The Problem Is Not Credibility. **In** *Stubblebine, Wm. C. and Willett, T. D., eds.*, 1983, pp. 27–29. **[G: U.S.]**

Brenner, Menachem and Galai, Dan. The Effect of Inflation on the Rate of Return on Common Stocks in an Inflation Intensive Capital Market: The Israeli Case 1965–79. **In** *Schmukler, N. and Marcus, E., eds.*, 1983, pp. 616–24. **[G: Israel]**

Brenner, Menachem and Landskroner, Yoram. Inflation Uncertainties and Returns on Bonds. *Economica*, November 1983, *50*(200), pp. 463–68. **[G: U.S.]**

Brimmer, Andrew F. Monetary Policy and Economic Activity: Benefits and Costs of Monetarism. *Amer. Econ. Rev.*, May 1983, *73*(2), pp. 1–12. **[G: U.S.]**

Browne, Stephen B. Measuring the Current Rate of Inflation: Comment. **In** *Diewert, W. E. and Montmarquette, C., eds.*, 1983, pp. 894–99. **[G: Canada]**

Buckley, Robert M. Inflation, Homeownership Tax Subsidies, and Fiscal Illusion [The Interaction of Inflation and the U.S. Tax Subsidies of Housing]. *Nat. Tax J.*, December 1983, *36*(4), pp. 521–23. **[G: U.S.]**

Buiter, Willem H. and Miller, Marcus H. Changing the Rules: Economic Consequences of the Thatcher Regime. *Brookings Pap. Econ. Act.*, 1983, (2), pp. 305–79. **[G: U.K.]**

Butler, Donald T. Why Doesn't Business Float Indexed Bonds? *Bus. Econ.*, January 1983, *18*(1), pp. 57–58. **[G: U.S.]**

Cagan, Phillip and Fellner, William. Tentative Lessons from the Recent Disinflationary Effort. *Brookings Pap. Econ. Act.*, 1983, (2), pp. 603–08. **[G: U.S.]**

Cavallo, Domingo F. Comments on Indexation and Stability from an Observer of the Argentinean Economy. **In** *Dornbusch, R. and Simonsen, M. H., eds.*, 1983, pp. 318–20. **[G: Argentina]**

Chambers, Robert G. Impact of Federal Fiscal–Monetary Policy on Farm Structure: Discussion. *Southern J. Agr. Econ.*, July 1983, *15*(1), pp. 69–71. **[G: U.S.]**

Chappell, Henry W., Jr. Presidential Popularity and Macroeconomic Performance: Are Voters Really So Naive? *Rev. Econ. Statist.*, August 1983, *65*(3), pp. 385–92. **[G: U.S.]**

Chappell, Henry W., Jr. and Keech, William R. Welfare Consequences of the Six-Year Presidential Term Evaluated in the Context of a Model of the U.S. Economy. *Amer. Polit. Sci. Rev.*, March 1983, *77*(1), pp. 75–91. **[G: U.S.]**

Chauveau, Thierry. L'inflation et les entreprises. (About Firms and Inflation. With English summary.) *Revue Écon.*, September 1983, *34*(5), pp. 897–925. **[G: France]**

Chick, Victoria. A Question of Relevance: The *General Theory* in Keynes's Time and Ours. *S. Afr. J. Econ.*, September 1983, *51*(3), pp. 380–406. **[G: U.K.]**

Childers, Thomas. Inflation and Electoral Politics in Germany 1919–29. **In** *Schmukler, N. and Marcus, E., eds.*, 1983, pp. 373–85. **[G: Germany]**

Ciampi, Carlo Azeglio. Le scelte da compiere per una ripresa nella stabilità. (Choices for Achievement of Recovery with Stability. With English summary.) *Bancaria*, February 1983, *39*(2), pp. 115–30. **[G: Italy]**

Craine, Roger. The Baby Boom, the Housing Market and the Stock Market. *Fed. Res. Bank San Francisco Econ. Rev.*, Spring 1983, (2), pp. 6–11. **[G: U.S.]**

Craven, Barrie M. and Wright, Grahame A. The Thatcher Experiment. *J. Macroecon.*, Winter 1983, *5*(1), pp. 21–40. **[G: U.K.]**

Davis, Kevin. Inflation and the Financial System: Discussion. **In** *Pagan, A. R. and Trivedi, P. K., eds.*, 1983, pp. 221–23. **[G: Australia]**

De Grauwe, Paul. Symptoms of an Overvalued Currency: The Case of the Belgian Franc. **In** *de Cecco, M., ed.*, 1983, pp. 99–116. **[G: Belgium]**

Donner, Arthur. Perspective on Canada's Stagflation Economy. **In** *Weintraub, S. and Goodstein, M., eds.*, 1983, pp. 205–13. **[G: Canada]**

Dreyer, Jacob. Fighting Stagflation: Macroeconomics under Reagan: Response: Some International Aspects of U.S. Macroeconomic Policy. **In** *Stubblebine, Wm. C. and Willett, T. D., eds.*, 1983, pp. 36–40. **[G: U.S.]**

Eliasson, Gunnar; Sharefkin, Mark and Ysander, Bengt-Christer. Stability and Macroeconomic Policy: The Lesson of the 1970s. **In** *Eliasson, G.; Sharefkin, M. and Ysander, B.-C., eds.*, 1983, pp. 11–49. **[G: OECD]**

Elton, Edwin; Gruber, Martin and Rentzler, Joel. The Arbitrage Pricing Model and Returns on Assets under Uncertain Inflation. *J. Finance*, May 1983, *38*(2), pp. 525–37.

Englander, A. Steven and Los, Cornelis A. Recovery without Accelerating Inflation? *Fed. Res. Bank New York Quart. Rev.*, Summer 1983, *8*(2), pp. 19–28. **[G: U.S.]**

Feldman, Gerald D. The Historian and the German Inflation. **In** *Schmukler, N. and Marcus, E., eds.*, 1983, pp. 386–99. **[G: Germany]**

Feldstein, Martin S. Inflation, Tax Rules, and Capital Formation: An Introductory Overview. **In** *Feldstein, M. (II)*, 1983, pp. 1–14. **[G: U.S.]**

Feldstein, Martin S. and Slemrod, Joel. Inflation and the Excess Taxation of Capital Gains on Corporate Stock. **In** *Feldstein, M. (II)*, 1983, *1979*, pp.

101–15. [G: U.S.]

Feldstein, Martin S. and Summers, Lawrence H. Inflation and the Taxation of Capital Income in the Corporate Sector. **In** *Feldstein, M. (II),* 1983, *1979,* pp. 116–50. [G: U.S.]

Fischer, Stanley. Inflación y crecimiento. (With English summary.) *Cuadernos Econ.,* December 1983, *20*(61), pp. 267–78. [G: LDCs]

Fischer, Stanley. On the Nonexistence of Privately Issued Index Bonds in the U.S. Capital Market. **In** *Dornbusch, R. and Simonsen, M. H., eds.,* 1983, *1977,* pp. 247–66. [G: U.S.]

Fishburn, Geoffrey F. Normative Aspects of Indexation Schemes. *Public Finance,* 1983, *38*(1), pp. 27–37.

FitzGerald, E. V. K. Mexico–United States Economic Relations and the World Cycle: A European View. **In** *Reynolds, C. W. and Tello, C., eds.,* 1983, pp. 349–67. [G: U.S.; Mexico]

Fleming, M. C. and Nellis, Joseph G. A Regional Comparison of House Price Inflation Rates in Britain 1967—A Comment. *Urban Stud.,* February 1983, *20*(1), pp. 91–94. [G: U.K.]

Flynn, Dennis O. Sixteenth-Century Inflation from a Production Point of View. **In** *Schmukler, N. and Marcus, E., eds.,* 1983, pp. 157–69. [G: Europe; U.S.]

Garrison, Charles B. and Mayhew, Anne. The Alleged Vietnam War Origins of the Current Inflation: A Comment. *J. Econ. Issues,* March 1983, *17*(1), pp. 175–86. [G: U.S.]

Geske, Robert and Roll, Richard. The Fiscal and Monetary Linkage between Stock Returns and Inflation. *J. Finance,* March 1983, *38*(1), pp. 1–33. [G: U.S.]

Giroux, Gary; Shearon, Winston and Grossman, Steven. How Does Inflation Affect a BHC's Rate of Return? *J. Bank Res.,* Summer 1983, *14*(2), pp. 164–69. [G: U.S.]

Gordon, Myron J. The Impact of Real Factors and Inflation on the Performance of the U.S. Stock Market from 1960 to 1980. *J. Finance,* May 1983, *38*(2), pp. 553–63. [G: U.S.]

Goria, Giovanni. Rientro dall'inflazione, condizione per la ripresa dello sviluppo. (Reduction of Inflation, a Condition for the Return to Economic Growth in Italy. With English summary.) *Bancaria,* March 1983, *39*(3), pp. 237–41. [G: Italy]

Gray, M. R. Inflation and the Financial System: Discussion. **In** *Pagan, A. R. and Trivedi, P. K., eds.,* 1983, pp. 220. [G: Australia]

Grebler, Leo. Inflation: A Blessing or a Curse? *Ann. Amer. Acad. Polit. Soc. Sci.,* January 1983, *465,* pp. 21–34. [G: U.S.]

Greenfield, Robert L. and Yeager, Leland B. A Laissez-Faire Approach to Monetary Stability. *J. Money, Credit, Banking,* August 1983, *15*(3), pp. 302–15.

Grinover, Ada Pellegrini. Monetary Correction in the Law Courts. **In** *de Ulhôa Canto, G.; da Silva Martins, I. G. and van Hoorn, J., Jr., eds.,* 1983, pp. 187–91. [G: Brazil]

Gruen, Fred H. Australian Inflation and the Distribution of Income and Wealth—A Preliminary View. **In** *Pagan, A. R. and Trivedi, P. K., eds.,* 1983, pp. 225–60. [G: Australia]

Gultekin, N. Bulent. Stock Market Returns and Inflation: Evidence from Other Countries. *J. Finance,* March 1983, *38*(1), pp. 49–65. [G: Selected Countries]

Haines, Walter W. The Myth of Continuous Inflation: United States Experience, 1700–1980. **In** *Schmukler, N. and Marcus, E., eds.,* 1983, pp. 183–204. [G: U.S.]

Harris, Ralph. The Mould to Be Broken. **In** *Seldon, A., et al.,* 1983, pp. 15–31. [G: U.K.]

Harwood, Edwin. Toward a Sociology of Inflation. **In** *Schmukler, N. and Marcus, E., eds.,* 1983, pp. 792–803.

Hasbrouck, Joel. The Impact of Inflation upon Corporate Taxation. *Nat. Tax J.,* March, 1983, *36*(1), pp. 65–81. [G: U.S.]

Heller, Walter W. What's Right with Economics? **In** *Marr, W. L. and Raj, B., eds.,* 1983, pp. 337–74. [G: U.S.]

Hendricks, Wallace E. and Kahn, Lawrence M. Cost-of-Living Clauses in Union Contracts: Determinants and Effects. *Ind. Lab. Relat. Rev.,* April 1983, *36*(3), pp. 447–60. [G: U.S.]

Hirsch, Albert A. Macroeconomic Effects of Price Shocks: A Simulation Study. *Surv. Curr. Bus.,* February 1983, *63*(2), pp. 30–43. [G: U.S.]

Hoffmann, Lutz and Jarass, Lorenz. The Impact of Rising Oil Prices of Oil-Importing Developing Countries and the Scope for Adjustment. *Weltwirtsch. Arch.,* 1983, *119*(2), pp. 297–316. [G: India; Brazil; Kenya]

Holtfrerich, Carl-Ludwig. Political Factors of the German Inflation 1914–23. **In** *Schmukler, N. and Marcus, E., eds.,* 1983, pp. 400–416. [G: Germany]

Hotson, John H. What's Wrong with Mainstream Macroeconomics? *Eastern Econ. J.,* July–September 1983, *9*(3), pp. 246–57. [G: U.S.]

Irvine, F. Owen, Jr. The Real Rate of Interest, for Whom? *Appl. Econ.,* October 1983, *15*(5), pp. 635–48. [G: U.S.]

Irvine, Reed J. and Emery, Robert F. Interest Rates as an Anti-inflationary Instrument in Taiwan. **In** *Von Pischke, J. D.; Adams, D. W. and Donald, G., eds.,* 1983, pp. 393–97. [G: Taiwan]

Isarescu, Mugur. Inflation in Romania during the Post-World War I Period. **In** *Schmukler, N. and Marcus, E., eds.,* 1983, pp. 500–509. [G: Romania]

Josefsson, Märtha and Örtengren, Johan. Crises, Inflation and Relative Prices: Investigations into Price Structure Stability in Swedish Industry 1913–80. **In** *Eliasson, G.; Sharefkin, M. and Ysander, B.-C., eds.,* 1983, pp. 53–110. [G: Sweden]

Judd, John P. The Recent Decline in Velocity: Instability in Money Demand of Inflation? *Fed. Res. Bank San Francisco Econ. Rev.,* Spring 1983, (2), pp. 12–19. [G: U.S.]

Judd, John P. and McElhattan, Rose. The Behavior of Money and the Economy in 1982–83. *Fed. Res. Bank San Francisco Econ. Rev.,* Summer 1983, (3), pp. 46–51. [G: U.S.]

Katona, George. The Psychology of Inflation. **In** *Schmukler, N. and Marcus, E., eds.,* 1983, pp. 745–53.

Kau, James B. and Keenan, Donald C. Inflation, Taxes and Housing: A Theoretical Analysis. *J. Public Econ.,* June 1983, *21*(1), pp. 93–104.

Kaufmann, Hugo M. Two Decades of Inflation in Western Industrialized Countries under Fixed and Flexible Exchange Rates. **In** *Schmukler, N. and Marcus, E., eds.*, 1983, pp. 707–20. **[G: OECD]**

Kiefer, David. Inflation and Homeownership Tax Subsidies: A Correction. *Nat. Tax J.*, December 1983, *36*(4), pp. 525–27. **[G: U.S.]**

Kitching, Beverly. Don't Blame the Arabs: World Wide Inflation Built In before the Oil Crisis. *Rivista Int. Sci. Econ. Com.*, June 1983, *30*(6), pp. 561–65. **[G: U.S.]**

Klein, Lawrence R. Inflation: Its Causes and Possible Cures. **In** *Dutta, M.; Hartline, J. C. and Loeb, P. D., eds.*, 1983, pp. 26–32. **[G: U.S.]**

Kopits, George. Inflation, Income Taxation, and Economic Behavior. **In** *[Goode, R.]*, 1983, pp. 371–87. **[G: OECD]**

Landau, Zbigniew. Inflation in Poland after World War I. **In** *Schmukler, N. and Marcus, E., eds.*, 1983, pp. 510–23. **[G: Poland]**

Lerman, Zvi. The Structure of Interest Rates and Inflation. **In** *Levy, H., ed.*, 1983, pp. 183–215. **[G: U.S.]**

Lewis, W. Arthur. Inflation and Growth in Latin America: Closing Remarks. **In** *Lewis, W. A.*, 1983, *1964*, pp. 639–51.

Lusa, Erna. Inflazione e bilanci delle imprese. (Inflation and Businesses' Financial Statement. With English summary.) *Bancaria*, October 1983, *39*(10), pp. 968–85. **[G: Italy]**

Malamud, Bernard. John H. Williams on the German Inflation: The International Amplification of Monetary Disturbances. **In** *Schmukler, N. and Marcus, E., eds.*, 1983, pp. 417–34. **[G: Germany]**

Mancera, Miguel. Panel Discussion: The Capital Market under Conditions of High and Variable Inflation. **In** *Armella, P. A.; Dornbusch, R. and Obstfeld, M., eds.*, 1983, pp. 279–81.

Marcus, Edward. Inflation, the Terms of Trade, and National Income Estimates. **In** *Schmukler, N. and Marcus, E., eds.*, 1983, pp. 116–19.

Masera, Rainer S. Inflation, Stabilization and Economic Recovery in Italy after the War: Vera Lutz's Assessment. *Banca Naz. Lavoro Quart. Rev.*, March 1983, (144), pp. 29–50. **[G: Italy]**

McKinney, George W., Jr. The Need for Militant Moderatism. *Challenge*, March/April 1983, *26*(1), pp. 39–42.

Medio, Alfredo. Worldwide Inflation and Its Impact on Less Developed Countries: Part II. *Econ. Forum*, Winter 1983-84, *14*(2), pp. 59–95. **[G: LDCs]**

Medio, Alfredo. Worldwide Inflation and Its Impact on Less Developed Countries. *Econ. Forum*, Summer 1983, *14*(1), pp. 1–26. **[G: Global]**

Metwally, M. M. and Tamaschke, H. U. The Effect of Inflation and Technology on Factor Shares. *Appl. Econ.*, December 1983, *15*(6), pp. 777–91. **[G: Selected Countries]**

Milbourne, Ross D. Price Expectations and the Demand for Money: Resolution of a Paradox. *Rev. Econ. Statist.*, November 1983, *65*(4), pp. 633–38. **[G: Australia; U.S.]**

Miles, James A. Taxes and the Fisher Effect: A Clarifying Analysis. *J. Finance*, March 1983, *38*(1), pp. 67–77.

Modigliani, Franco. Government Deficits, Inflation, and Future Generations. **In** *Conklin, D. W. and Courchene, T. J., eds.*, 1983, pp. 55–77. **[G: OECD]**

Moore, Geoffrey H. Cyclical Fluctuations and Secular Inflation. **In** *Moore, G. H.*, 1983, pp. 237–44. **[G: U.S.]**

Moore, Geoffrey H. Employment, Unemployment, and the Inflation–Recession Dilemma. **In** *Moore, G. H.*, 1983, *1976*, pp. 211–32. **[G: U.S.]**

Moore, Geoffrey H. Five Little-known Facts about Inflation. **In** *Moore, G. H.*, 1983, *1977*, pp. 171–74. **[G: U.S.]**

Moore, Geoffrey H. Inflation and Profits. **In** *Moore, G. H.*, 1983, *1977*, pp. 281–85. **[G: U.S.]**

Moore, Geoffrey H. Inflation and Statistics. **In** *Moore, G. H.*, 1983, *1980*, pp. 287–311. **[G: U.S.]**

Moore, Geoffrey H. Inflation and Statistics—Again. **In** *Moore, G. H.*, 1983, *1981*, pp. 313–29. **[G: U.S.]**

Moore, Geoffrey H. Recession Slows Inflation. **In** *Moore, G. H.*, 1983, *1979*, pp. 233–36. **[G: Japan; U.K.; U.S.; W. Germany]**

de Moraes, Bernardo Ribeiro. The Monetary Correction of Tax Debts within the Framework of Brazilian Law. **In** *de Ulhôa Canto, G.; da Silva Martins, I. G. and van Hoorn, J., Jr., eds.*, 1983, pp. 99–135. **[G: Brazil]**

Morgan, James N. Effects of Inflation on Attitudes, Status, and Behavior. **In** *Duncan, G. J. and Morgan, J. N., eds.*, 1983, pp. 60–92. **[G: U.S.]**

Motley, Brian. Real Interest Rates, Money and Government Deficits. *Fed. Res. Bank San Francisco Econ. Rev.*, Summer 1983, (3), pp. 31–45. **[G: U.S.]**

Niemi, Beth T. and Lloyd, Cynthia B. Inflation and Female Labor Force Participation. **In** *Schmukler, N. and Marcus, E., eds.*, 1983, pp. 820–37. **[G: U.S.]**

Okun, Arthur M. A Reward TIP. **In** *Okun, A. M.*, 1983, *1979*, pp. 67–75. **[G: U.S.]**

Okun, Arthur M. Inflation: The Problems and Prospects before Us. **In** *Okun, A. M.*, 1983, *1970*, pp. 3–34. **[G: U.S.]**

Okun, Arthur M. The Great Stagflation Swamp. **In** *Okun, A. M.*, 1983, *1977*, pp. 49–62. **[G: U.S.]**

Okun, Arthur M. The Mirage of Steady Inflation. **In** *Okun, A. M.*, 1983, *1971*, pp. 35–48. **[G: U.S.; OECD]**

Okun, Arthur M. The National Accounts in an Inflationary World. **In** *Foss, M. F., ed.*, 1983, pp. 323–26. **[G: U.S.]**

Okun, Arthur M. Wage–Price: Guideposts—Yes. **In** *Okun, A. M.*, 1983, *1972*, pp. 63–66. **[G: U.S.]**

de Oliveira Campos, Roberto. Indexation—Causes and Consequences. **In** *de Ulhôa Canto, G.; da Silva Martins, I. G. and van Hoorn, J., Jr., eds.*, 1983, pp. 9–12. **[G: Brazil]**

Ott, Attiat F. The Effect of Inflation on the Balance Sheet of the State–Local Sector. **In** *Break, G. F., ed.*, 1983, pp. 11–28. **[G: U.S.]**

de Pablo, Juan Carlos. Panel Discussion: The Capital Market under Conditions of High and Variable Inflation. **In** *Armella, P. A.; Dornbusch, R. and*

Obstfeld, M., eds., 1983, pp. 277–79. **[G: Argentina]**

Pagan, A. R. and Gray, M. R. Inflation and Investment: An Historical Overview. **In** *Pagan, A. R. and Trivedi, P. K., eds.*, 1983, pp. 262–81. **[G: Australia]**

Paish, F. W. Inflation and the Balance of Payments in the United Kingdom 1952–1967. **In** *Feinstein, C., ed.*, 1983, *1968*, pp. 133–46. **[G: U.K.]**

Perry, George L. What Have We Learned about Disinflation? *Brookings Pap. Econ. Act.*, 1983, (2), pp. 587–602. **[G: U.S.]**

Pick, J. F. Erratum: Introduction of an Inflation-Adjusted Tax Base in Israel. *Bull. Int. Fiscal Doc.*, November 1983, *37*(11), pp. 496. **[G: Israel]**

Pick, J. F. Introduction of an Inflation-Adjusted Tax Base in Israel. *Bull. Int. Fiscal Doc.*, 1983, *37*(6), pp. 259–63. **[G: Israel]**

Ránki, György. Inflation in Hungary. **In** *Schmukler, N. and Marcus, E., eds.*, 1983, pp. 524–30. **[G: Hungary]**

Ránki, György. Inflation in Post-World War I East Central Europe. **In** *Schmukler, N. and Marcus, E., eds.*, 1983, pp. 475–87. **[G: E. Europe]**

Rao, P. Someshwar and Lodh, Bimal K. Anatomy of Canadian Inflation: An Analysis with CANDIDE Model 2.0. *Empirical Econ.*, 1983, *8*(1), pp. 15–45. **[G: Canada]**

Rhoades, D. and Elhawary-Rivet, N. Measuring the Current Rate of Inflation. **In** *Diewert, W. E. and Montmarquette, C., eds.*, 1983, pp. 877–93. **[G: Canada]**

Richardson, Sue. Inflation and the Dispersion of Pay. **In** *Blandy, R. and Covick, O., eds.*, 1983, pp. 37–60. **[G: Australia]**

Rockwood, Charles E. The Dismal Science of Stagflation Control. **In** *Weintraub, S. and Goodstein, M., eds.*, 1983, pp. 139–50. **[G: U.S.]**

Rutterford, Janette. Index-Linked Gilts. *Nat. Westminster Bank Quart. Rev.*, November 1983, pp. 2–17. **[G: U.K.]**

Sardy, Hyman. The Economic Impact of Inflation on Urban Areas. **In** *Schmukler, N. and Marcus, E., eds.*, 1983, pp. 312–25. **[G: U.S.]**

Sargent, Thomas J. Stopping Moderate Inflations: The Methods of Poincaré and Thatcher. **In** *Dornbusch, R. and Simonsen, M. H., eds.*, 1983, pp. 54–96. **[G: France; U.K.]**

Scherer, Joseph. Stop Blaming Bracket Creep. *Challenge*, November/December 1983, *26*(5), pp. 53–54. **[G: U.S.]**

Seidman, Laurence S. A "Third Way" for Feldstein: TIP. *Challenge*, Sept.–Oct. 1983, *26*(4), pp. 44–48. **[G: U.S.]**

Sellekaerts, Willy. Coping with Stagflation. *Atlantic Econ. J.*, December 1983, *11*(4), pp. 14–19. **[G: U.S.]**

Sheehan, Richard G. and Kelly, Neil. Oil Prices and World Inflation. *J. Econ. Bus.*, June 1983, *35*(2), pp. 235–38. **[G: U.S.]**

Shoesmith, Eddie and Millner, Geoffrey. Cost Inflation and the London Orchestras. **In** *Hendon, W. S. and Shanahan, J. L., eds.*, 1983, pp. 65–76. **[G: U.K.]**

da Silva Martins, Ives Gandra. Monetary Correction in the National Tax Code. **In** *de Ulhôa Canto, G.; da Silva Martins, I. G. and van Hoorn, J., Jr., eds.*, 1983, pp. 32–46. **[G: Brazil]**

Simonsen, Mario Henrique. Panel Discussion: The Capital Market under Conditions of High and Variable Inflation. **In** *Armella, P. A.; Dornbusch, R. and Obstfeld, M., eds.*, 1983, pp. 281–83.

Snyder, Donald C. and Schiller, Bradley R. The Effect of Inflation on the Elderly. **In** *Schmukler, N. and Marcus, E., eds.*, 1983, pp. 867–81. **[G: U.S.]**

Solnik, Bruno. The Relation between Stock Prices and Inflationary Expectations: The International Evidence. *J. Finance*, March 1983, *38*(1), pp. 35–48. **[G: Selected OECD]**

Sprinkel, Beryl W. Fighting Stagflation: Macroeconomics under Reagan: Response: Internal Consistency of the Reagan Program. **In** *Stubblebine, Wm. C. and Willett, T. D., eds.*, 1983, pp. 30–36. **[G: U.S.]**

Stammer, D. W. and Valentine, T. J. Inflation and the Financial System. **In** *Pagan, A. R. and Trivedi, P. K., eds.*, 1983, pp. 183–219. **[G: Australia]**

Sugrue, Diarmuid. Sectoral Inflation Rates. *Irish Banking Rev.*, June 1983, pp. 29–32. **[G: Ireland]**

Szabo Pelsoczi, Miklos. Inflation and the International Monetary Order. **In** *Schmukler, N. and Marcus, E., eds.*, 1983, pp. 340–49.

Teichova, Alice. A Comparative View of the Inflation of the 1920s in Austria and Czechoslovakia. **In** *Schmukler, N. and Marcus, E., eds.*, 1983, pp. 531–67. **[G: Austria; Czechoslovakia]**

Thoreson, Per E. Inflation Controlled by Energy Prices. *Energy Econ.*, July 1983, *5*(3), pp. 202–06. **[G: Global]**

Tilbery, Henry. Indexation in the Brazilian Taxation System. **In** *de Ulhôa Canto, G.; da Silva Martins, I. G. and van Hoorn, J., Jr., eds.*, 1983, pp. 47–98. **[G: Brazil]**

Tracy, Ronald L. and Trescott, Paul B. Monetary Policy and Inflation in the United States, 1912–1978: Evidence from Monthly Data. **In** *Schmukler, N. and Marcus, E., eds.*, 1983, pp. 205–25. **[G: U.S.]**

Triplett, Jack E. Escalation Measures: What Is the Answer? What Is the Question? **In** *Diewert, W. E. and Montmarquette, C., eds.*, 1983, pp. 457–82.

Trivedi, P. K. Investment—Inflation Linkages in the NIF-10 Model: Discussion. **In** *Pagan, A. R. and Trivedi, P. K., eds.*, 1983, pp. 311–17. **[G: Australia]**

Tuccillo, John A. Inflation, Housing Prices, and Investment: A U.S. Perspective. **In** *Gau, G. W. and Goldberg, M. A., eds.*, 1983, pp. 259–88. **[G: U.S.]**

Tweeten, Luther. Impact of Federal Fiscal–Monetary Policy on Farm Structure. *Southern J. Agr. Econ.*, July 1983, *15*(1), pp. 61–68. **[G: U.S.]**

Van Cauwenberghe, E. H. G. Inflation in the Southern Low Countries, from the Fourteenth to the Seventeenth Century: A Record of Some Significant Periods of High Prices. **In** *Schmukler, N. and Marcus, E., eds.*, 1983, pp. 147–56. **[G: U.K.; Low Countries]**

Van Cott, T. Norman and Wipf, Larry J. Tariff Reduction via Inflation: U.S. Specific Tariffs 1972–1979. *Weltwirtsch. Arch.*, 1983, *119*(4), pp. 724–33. **[G: U.S.]**

Van der Wee, Herman. A Contribution to the Study of Inflation in the Interwar Period. **In** *Schmukler, N. and Marcus, E., eds.*, 1983, pp. 677–85. **[G: Belgium]**

Vaughan, Roger J. Inflation and Unemployment Surviving the 1980s. **In** *Barker, M., ed. (II)*, 1983, pp. 93–247. **[G: U.S.]**

Vidich, Arthur J. Social and Political Consequences of Inflation and Declining Abundance. **In** *Schmukler, N. and Marcus, E., eds.*, 1983, pp. 771–91. **[G: U.S.]**

Virts, John R. and Wilson, George W. Inflation and the Behavior of Sectoral Prices. *Bus. Econ.*, May 1983, *18*(3), pp. 45–54. **[G: U.S.]**

Walker, John F. and Vatter, Harold G. Demonstrating the Undemonstrable: A Reply to Garrison and Mayhew [The Princess and the Pea; or, The Alleged Vietnam War Origins of the Current Inflation]. *J. Econ. Issues*, March 1983, *17*(1), pp. 186–96. **[G: U.S.]**

Wallich, Henry C. Statement to the U.S. House Subcommittee on Domestic Monetary Policy of the Committee on Banking, Finance and Urban Affairs, October 5, 1983. *Fed. Res. Bull.*, October 1983, *69*(10), pp. 776–81. **[G: U.S.]**

Watts, Nita. Inflation in the USSR and Eastern Europe. **In** *[Saunders, C. T.]*, 1983, pp. 127–55. **[G: E. Europe; U.S.S.R.]**

Webber, David J. The Nature and Components of a Political Theory of Inflation. **In** *Schmukler, N. and Marcus, E., eds.*, 1983, pp. 754–70.

Weller, Barry R. The Political Business Cycle: A Discriminating Analysis. *Soc. Sci. Quart.*, June 1983, *64*(2), pp. 398–403. **[G: U.S.]**

Wetzler, James W. Proposals to Index Capital Gains. **In** *Walker, C. E. and Bloomfield, M. E., eds.*, 1983, pp. 154–57. **[G: U.S.]**

Wilcox, James A. The Missing Fisher Effect on Nominal Interest Rates in the 1950s. *Rev. Econ. Statist.*, November 1983, *65*(4), pp. 644–47. **[G: U.S.]**

Willett, Thomas D. Fighting Stagflation: Macroeconomics under Reagan. **In** *Stubblebine, Wm. C. and Willett, T. D., eds.*, 1983, pp. 11–26. **[G: U.S.]**

Wilson, Thomas F. Institutional Change as a Source of Excessive Monetary Expansion. **In** *Schmukler, N. and Marcus, E., eds.*, 1983, pp. 79–93. **[G: U.S.]**

Woodruff, A. M. The Property Tax in Periods of Instable Prices. **In** *Harriss, C. L., ed.*, 1983, pp. 123–32. **[G: U.S.]**

Wyntjes, Sherrin Marshall. Raising Hell or Raising the Rent: The Gentry's Response to Inflation in Sixteenth-Century Holland and Utrecht. **In** *Schmukler, N. and Marcus, E., eds.*, 1983, pp. 170–82. **[G: Netherlands]**

1342 Inflation Theories; Studies Illustrating Inflation Theories

Abrams, Richard K.; Froyen, Richard T. and Waud, Roger N. The Variability of Output-Inflation Tradeoffs. *J. Econ. Dynam. Control*, May 1983, *5*(2/3), pp. 151–71. **[G: U.S.; Canada; U.K.]**

Addison, John T. and Burton, John. The Sociopolitical Analysis of Global Inflation: A Theoretical and Empirical Examination of an Influential Basic Explanation. *Amer. J. Econ. Soc.*, January 1983, *42*(1), pp. 13–28. **[G: OECD; Selected LDCs]**

Aizenman, Joshua. Government Size, Optimal Inflation Tax, and Tax Collection Costs. *Eastern Econ. J.*, April–June 1983, *9*(2), pp. 103–05.

Albin, Peter S. Policy Failure, Growth Failure, and Inflation. **In** *Schmukler, N. and Marcus, E., eds.*, 1983, pp. 278–90. **[G: U.S.]**

Alesina, Alberto. Inflazione, indicizzazione e stabilità macroeconimica. (Inflation, Indexation, and Macroeconomic Stability. With English summary.) *Giorn. Econ.*, January–February 1983, *42*(1–2), pp. 91–112.

Allsbrook, Ogden O., Jr. and Gilliam, Kenneth P. An Industrial Interpretation of Inflationary Unemployment. *Kredit Kapital*, 1983, *16*(4), pp. 479–87.

Angel, Michael G. and Nitsch, Thomas O. Inflation and the Rationality of Investing in Projects with Negative Net Present Values. *Amer. Econ.*, Fall 1983, *27*(2), pp. 58–66.

Anstie, Roslyn K.; Gray, M. R. and Pagan, A. R. Inflation and the Consumption Ratio. **In** *Pagan, A. R. and Trivedi, P. K., eds.*, 1983, pp. 322–49. **[G: Australia]**

Arnaudo, Aldo A. Posibilidades de una política monetaria monetarista en una economía inflacionaría: Argentina 1978–1981. (The Feasibility of a Monetarist Monetary Policy in an Inflationary Economy: Argentina, 1978–1981. With English summary.) *Económica*, January–April 1983, *29*(1), pp. 3–25. **[G: Argentina]**

Artus, Patrick. Formation conjointe des prix et des salaires dans cinq grands pays industriels: Peuton comprendre les écarts entre les taux d'inflation? (The Joint Determination of Prices and Wages in Five Large Industrial Countries: Can We Explain the Differentials in Inflation? With English summary.) *Ann. INSEE*, Jan.–Mar. 1983, (49), pp. 5–52. **[G: U.S.; France; Japan; W. Germany; U.K.]**

Atesoglu, H. Sonmez. Inflation and Unemployment Models. *Nebr. J. Econ. Bus.*, Summer 1983, *22*(3), pp. 53–65. **[G: U.S.]**

Auernheimer, Leonardo. Deficit, gasto publico y el impuesto inflacionario: dos modelos de "dinero pasivo." (With English summary.) *Cuadernos Econ.*, April 1983, *20*(59), pp. 75–84. **[G: Argentina]**

Auernheimer, Leonardo. The Revenue-Maximizing Inflation Rate and the Treatment of the Transition to Equilibrium. *J. Money, Credit, Banking*, August 1983, *15*(3), pp. 368–76.

Baldwin, Carliss Y. Administered Prices Fifty Years Later: A Comment of Gardiner C. Means: Corporate Power in the Marketplace. *J. Law Econ.*, June 1983, *26*(2), pp. 487–96. **[G: U.S.]**

Ball, R. J. and Burns, T. The Inflationary Mechanism in the U.K. Economy. **In** *Feinstein, C., ed.*, 1983, *1976*, pp. 258–79. **[G: U.K.]**

Banaian, King; Laney, Leroy O. and Willett, Thomas D. Central Bank Independence: An International

Comparison. *Fed. Res. Bank Dallas Econ. Rev.*, March 1983, pp. 1–13. **[G: OECD]**

Barro, Robert J. Inflation, Debt, and Indexation: Opening Remarks. **In** *Dornbusch, R. and Simonsen, M. H., eds.*, 1983, pp. 311–17.

Barro, Robert J. Inflationary Finance under Discretion and Rules. *Can. J. Econ.*, February 1983, *16*(1), pp. 1–16.

Baumgarten, Klaus. Adjustment to Variations in Prices of Imported Inputs: The Role of Economic Structure—A Comment. *Weltwirtsch. Arch.*, 1983, *119*(3), pp. 575–78.

Beckerman, Paul. Inflation and Inflation Feedback. **In** *Schmukler, N. and Marcus, E., eds.*, 1983, pp. 17–32.

Behrman, Jere R. and Taubman, Paul. Redistribution of Earnings by Unemployment and Inflation. **In** *[Klein, L. R.]*, 1983, pp. 262–81. **[G: U.S.]**

Benavie, Arthur. Achieving External and Internal Targets with Exchange-Rate and Interest-Rate Intervention. *J. Int. Money Finance*, April 1983, *2*(1), pp. 75–85.

Benedetti, Eugenio. Il divario tra il saggio di interesse naturale e monetario in regime di inflazione e in ipotesi diverse di indicizzazione. (The Difference between the Natural and the Money Rate of Interest in an Inflationary Economy under Different Hypotheses of Indexation of the Public Deficit. With English summary.) *Giorn. Econ.*, March-April 1983, *42*(3–4), pp. 179–92. **[G: Italy]**

Bhandari, Jagdeep S. Indexation, Deficit Finance and the Inflationary Process. *Southern Econ. J.*, April 1983, *49*(4), pp. 1077–93.

Blackley, Dixie and Follain, James R. Inflation, Tax Advantages to Homeownership and the Locational Choices of Households. *Reg. Sci. Urban Econ.*, November 1983, *13*(4), pp. 505–16. **[G: U.S.]**

Blanchard, Olivier J. Price Asynchronization and Price Level Inertia. **In** *Dornbusch, R. and Simonsen, M. H., eds.*, 1983, pp. 3–24. **[G: U.S.]**

Blejer, Mario I. On the Anatomy of Inflation: The Variability of Relative Commodity Prices in Argentina. *J. Money, Credit, Banking*, November 1983, *15*(4), pp. 469–82. **[G: Argentina]**

Bodie, Zvi. Commodity Futures as a Hedge against Inflation. *J. Portfol. Manage.*, Spring 1983, *9*(3), pp. 12–17. **[G: U.S.]**

Bodie, Zvi and Pesando, James E. Retirement Annuity Design in an Inflationary Climate. **In** *Bodie, Z. and Shoven, J. B., eds.*, 1983, pp. 291–316, 322–23. **[G: U.S.]**

Bohanon, Cecil E. The Tax-Price Implications of Bracket-Creep. *Nat. Tax J.*, December 1983, *36*(4), pp. 535–38.

Boltho, Andrea. Is Western Europe Caught in an 'Expectations Trap'? *Lloyds Bank Rev.*, April 1983, (148), pp. 1–13. **[G: W. Europe]**

Bomberger, William A. and Makinen, Gail E. The Hungarian Hyperinflation and Stabilization of 1945–1946. *J. Polit. Econ.*, October 1983, *91*(5), pp. 801–24. **[G: Hungary]**

Bomhoff, Edward J. Permanent and Transitory Changes in Monetary Policy: A Comment. *Carnegie-Rochester Conf. Ser. Public Policy*, Autumn 1983, *19*, pp. 211–23. **[G: Switzerland; U.S.; W. Germany]**

Bossons, John. Observations on the Indexation of Old Age Pensions: Comment. **In** *Bodie, Z. and Shoven, J. B., eds.*, 1983, pp. 252–57. **[G: U.S.]**

Bowers, Patricia F. A Theoretical Analysis of the Exchange Process and Inflation. **In** *Schmukler, N. and Marcus, E., eds.*, 1983, pp. 120–32.

Brandsma, Andries S. and Van Der Windt, Nico. Wage Bargaining and the Phillips Curve: A Macroeconomic View. *Appl. Econ.*, February 1983, *15*(1), pp. 61–71. **[G: Netherlands]**

Brazelton, W. Robert. Price Adjustments during Inflation in Non-Competitive Markets: A Micro-Macro Comment. *Jahr. Nationalökon. Statist.*, November 1983, *198*(6), pp. 557–61.

Brenner, Menachem and Venezia, Itzhak. The Effects of Inflation and Taxes on Growth Investments and Replacement Policies. *J. Finance*, December 1983, *38*(5), pp. 1519–28.

Brenner, Y. S. Sources of Inflation: Old and New. **In** *Schmukler, N. and Marcus, E., eds.*, 1983, pp. 94–115.

Brimmer, Andrew F. Monetary Policy and Inflationary Expectations. *Challenge*, March/April 1983, *26*(1), pp. 32–35. **[G: U.S.]**

Brittan, Samuel. Jobs, Output and Prices. **In** *Brittan, S.*, 1983, pp. 105–24. **[G: U.K.; U.S.]**

Brittan, Samuel. The Case for Money GDP. **In** *Brittan, S.*, 1983, pp. 125–42. **[G: U.K.; U.S.]**

Britton, A. J. C. Public Sector Borrowing. *Nat. Inst. Econ. Rev.*, February 1983, (103), pp. 50–55. **[G: U.K.]**

Brockway, George P. On Speculation: A Footnote to Keynes. *J. Post Keynesian Econ.*, Summer 1983, *5*(4), pp. 515–22.

Brown, A. J. The Demand-Side Economics of Inflation: Comment. **In** *Worswick, D. and Trevithick, J., eds.*, 1983, pp. 238–44.

Browne, Lynn E. Wages and Inflation. *New Eng. Econ. Rev.*, May/June 1983, pp. 63–66. **[G: U.S.]**

Brunner, Karl. The Politics of Myopia and Its Ideology. **In** *Shadow Open Market Committee.*, 1983, pp. 7–17. **[G: U.S.]**

Butler, Donald T. Why Doesn't Business Float Indexed Bonds? *Bus. Econ.*, January 1983, *18*(1), pp. 57–58. **[G: U.S.]**

Büttler, Hans-Jürg and Schiltknecht, Kurt. Transitory Changes in Monetary Policy and Their Implications in Money-Stock Control. *Carnegie-Rochester Conf. Ser. Public Policy*, Autumn 1983, *19*, pp. 171–209.

Cagan, Phillip. The Trouble with "Rational Expectations" and the Problem of Inflation Stabilization: Comment. **In** *Frydman, R. and Phelps, E. S., eds.*, 1983, pp. 41–45.

Calmfors, Lars. Output, Inflation and the Terms of Trade in a Small Open Economy. *Kyklos*, 1983, *36*(1), pp. 40–65.

Calvet, J. and Di Ruzza, R. Quelques hypothèses sur l'étude de l'inflation en période de crise. (Hypothesis on the Study of Inflation during a Crisis Period. With English summary.) *Écon. Soc.*, September-October-November 1983, *17*(9–10–11), pp. 1537–50. **[G: France]**

Calvo, Guillermo A. and Peel, David A. Growth and

Inflationary Finance: Variations on a Mundellian Theme. *J. Polit. Econ.*, October 1983, *91*(5), pp. 880–87.

Carmichael, Jeffrey and Stebbing, Peter W. Some Macroeconomic Implications of the Interaction between Inflation and Taxation. **In** *Pagan, A. R. and Trivedi, P. K., eds.*, 1983, pp. 102–36. **[G: Australia]**

Cassese, Anthony and Lothian, James R. The Timing of Monetary and Price Changes and the International Transmission of Inflation. **In** *Darby, M. P. and Lothian, J. R., et al.*, 1983, pp. 58–82. **[G: OECD]**

Cebula, Richard J. A Methodological Note on the Phillips Curve for the United States. *Rivista Int. Sci. Econ. Com.*, January 1983, *30*(1), pp. 91–95. **[G: U.S.]**

Cecchetti, Stephen G., et al. OPEC II and the Wage-Price Spiral. **In** *Zeckhauser, R. J. and Leebaert, D., eds.*, 1983, pp. 137–54. **[G: U.S.]**

de Cecco, Marcello. The Vicious/Virtuous Circle Debate in the Twenties and the Seventies. *Banca Naz. Lavoro Quart. Rev.*, September 1983, (146), pp. 285–303. **[G: Europe]**

Chang, Winston W.; Kemp, Murray C. and Long, Ngo Van. Money, Inflation, and Maximizing Behavior: The Case of Many Countries. *J. Macroecon.*, Summer 1983, *5*(3), pp. 251–63.

Chen, Chau-nan and Tsaur, Tien-wang. Currency Substitution and Foreign Inflation. *Quart. J. Econ.*, February 1983, *98*(1), pp. 177–84.

Cherry, Robert. A Marxist Critique of Natural Unemployment Rate Theories. **In** *Schmukler, N. and Marcus, E., eds.*, 1983, pp. 133–43.

Choudhri, Ehsan U. The Transmission of Inflation in a Small Economy: An Empirical Analysis of the Influence of U.S. Monetary Disturbances on Canadian Inflation, 1962–80. *J. Int. Money Finance*, August 1983, *2*(2), pp. 167–78. **[G: Canada]**

Chowdhury, Anisuzzaman. The Decentralized Labor Market and the Nonmarket Consideration of Wage Change. *J. Post Keynesian Econ.*, Summer 1983, *5*(4), pp. 648–63.

Christofides, L. N. and Wilton, D. A. The Determinants of Contract Length: An Empirical Analysis Based on Canadian Micro Data. *J. Monet. Econ.*, August 1983, *12*(2), pp. 309–19. **[G: Canada]**

Clements, Kenneth W. Perspectives on the Effects of Inflation in Australia. **In** *Pagan, A. R. and Trivedi, P. K., eds.*, 1983, pp. 363–69. **[G: Australia]**

Coe, David T. and Holtham, Gerald. Output Responsiveness and Inflation: An Aggregate Study. *OECD Econ. Stud.*, Autumn 1983, (1), pp. 93–145. **[G: OECD]**

Colander, David C. Towards a Real Theory of Inflation. **In** *Schmukler, N. and Marcus, E., eds.*, 1983, pp. 33–49.

Conklin, David and Sayeed, Adil. Overview of the Deficit Debate. **In** *Conklin, D. W. and Courchene, T. J., eds.*, 1983, pp. 12–54. **[G: Canada]**

Connolly, Michael B. Optimum Currency Pegs for Latin America. *J. Money, Credit, Banking*, February 1983, *15*(1), pp. 56–72. **[G: Latin America]**

Csikós-Nagy, Béla and Rácz, László. Rise of the Price Level and Its Factors in Hungary. *Acta Oecon.*, 1983, *30*(2), pp. 161–77. **[G: Hungary]**

Cukierman, Alex. Relative Price Variability and Inflation: A Survey and Further Results. *Carnegie-Rochester Conf. Ser. Public Policy*, Autumn 1983, *19*, pp. 103–57.

Cukierman, Alex. Relative Price Variability and Inflation: A Survey and Further Results: Reply. *Carnegie-Rochester Conf. Ser. Public Policy*, Autumn 1983, *19*, pp. 167–70.

Dabysing, S. and Jones, D. I. H. A Simplified Post-Keynesian Model of Inflation for Teaching Purposes. *Brit. Rev. Econ. Issues*, Autumn 1983, *5*(13), pp. 87–105.

Darby, Michael R. The Importance of Oil Price Changes in the 1970s World Inflation. **In** *Darby, M. P. and Lothian, J. R., et al.*, 1983, pp. 232–72. **[G: OECD]**

Darby, Michael R. The United States as an Exogenous Source of World Inflation under the Bretton Woods System. **In** *Darby, M. P. and Lothian, J. R., et al.*, 1983, pp. 478–90. **[G: U.S.]**

Darby, Michael R. and Lothian, James R. Conclusions on the International Transmission of Inflation. **In** *Darby, M. P. and Lothian, J. R., et al.*, 1983, pp. 493–523. **[G: OECD]**

Darby, Michael R. and Stockman, Alan C. The Mark III International Transmission Model: Estimates. **In** *Darby, M. P. and Lothian, J. R., et al.*, 1983, pp. 113–61. **[G: OECD]**

Darby, Michael R. and Stockman, Alan C. The Mark III International Transmission Model: Specification. **In** *Darby, M. P. and Lothian, J. R., et al.*, 1983, pp. 85–112. **[G: OECD]**

Davidson, Russell and MacKinnon, James G. Inflation and the Savings Rate. *Appl. Econ.*, December 1983, *15*(6), pp. 731–43. **[G: U.S.; Canada]**

Dewald, William G. Fast and Gradual Anti-inflation Policies: Evidence for Germany, Italy, and the United States. **In** *Schmukler, N. and Marcus, E., eds.*, 1983, pp. 689–706. **[G: W. Germany; Italy; France]**

Dieckheuer, Gustav. Staatliches budgetdefizit, Wachstum des Produktionspotentials und gesamtwirtschaftliche Inflationsrate. (Budget Deficits, Production Growth and Inflation. With English summary.) *Z. ges. Staatswiss.*, March 1983, *139*(1), pp. 80–99.

Dietrich, J. Kimball and Joines, Douglas H. Rational Expectations, Informational Efficiency, and Tests Using Survey Data: A Comment [The Formation of Inflationary Expectations]. *Rev. Econ. Statist.*, August 1983, *65*(3), pp. 525–29. **[G: U.S.]**

Douglas, Allen. Georges Valois and the Franc—Or: A Right-Wing Reaction to Inflation. **In** *Schmukler, N. and Marcus, E., eds.*, 1983, pp. 226–45.

Driffill, E. John. Shock Treatment for Inflation: A Note on Optimal Policy in a Buiter/Miller Model. *Europ. Econ. Rev.*, December 1983, *23*(3), pp. 291–97.

Ebrill, Liam P. and Possen, Uri M. Taxation, Inflation, and the Terms of Trade. *J. Public Econ.*, December 1983, *22*(3), pp. 375–86.

Edwards, Sebastian. The Short-Run Relation between Growth and Inflation in Latin America: Comment. *Amer. Econ. Rev.*, June 1983, *73*(3), pp. 477–82. [G: Latin America]

Eichner, Alfred S. Income Conflicts, Inflation, and Controls: A Response. *J. Post Keynesian Econ.*, Summer 1983, *5*(4), pp. 603–07. [G: U.S.]

Eltis, Walter. The Interconnection between Public Expenditure and Inflation in Britain. *Amer. Econ. Rev.*, May 1983, *73*(2), pp. 291–96. [G: U.K.]

Emerson, Michael. A View of Current European Indexation Experiences. **In** *Dornbusch, R. and Simonsen, M. H., eds.*, 1983, pp. 160–79. [G: Europe]

Engle, Robert F. Estimates of the Variance of U.S. Inflation Based upon the ARCH Model. *J. Money, Credit, Banking*, August 1983, *15*(3), pp. 286–301. [G: U.S.]

Evans, J. L. Erratum: The Dynamic Behaiour of Alternative Price Adjustment Mechanisms. *Manchester Sch. Econ. Soc. Stud.*, December 1983, *51*(4), pp. 399–400.

Evans, J. L. The Dynamic Behaviour of Alternative Price Adjustment Mechanisms. *Manchester Sch. Econ. Soc. Stud.*, March 1983, *51*(1), pp. 33–44.

Evans, Paul. Price-Level Instability and Output in the U.S. *Econ. Inquiry*, April 1983, *21*(2), pp. 172–87.

Fama, Eugene F. Stock Returns, Real Activity, Inflation, and Money: Reply. *Amer. Econ. Rev.*, June 1983, *73*(3), pp. 471–72. [G: U.S.]

Fand, David I. Monetary-Fiscal Policy for Promoting Growth: The Merits and Shortcomings of the Keynesian Approach. **In** *Biehl, D.; Roskamp, K. W. and Stolper, W. F., eds.*, 1983, pp. 89–100. [G: U.S.]

Faxén, Karl-Olof. Stability in Economic Growth under Uncertainty—Growth of Knowledge, Decision Processes and Contingency Contracts. **In** *Eliasson, G.; Sharefkin, M. and Ysander, B.-C., eds.*, 1983, pp. 375–417. [G: OECD]

Feldstein, Martin S. Fiscal Policies, Inflation, and Capital Formation. **In** *Feldstein, M. (II)*, 1983, *1980*, pp. 61–80.

Feldstein, Martin S. Inflation and the Stock Market. **In** *Feldstein, M. (II)*, 1983, *1980*, pp. 186–98. [G: U.S.]

Feldstein, Martin S. Inflation, Income Taxes, and the Rate of Interest: A Theoretical Analysis. **In** *Feldstein, M. (I)*, 1983, *1976*, pp. 448–64.

Feldstein, Martin S. Inflation, Income Taxes, and the Rate of Interest: A Theoretical Analysis. **In** *Feldstein, M. (II)*, 1983, *1976*, pp. 28–43.

Feldstein, Martin S. Inflation, Portfolio Choice, and the Prices of Land and Corporate Stock. **In** *Feldstein, M. (II)*, 1983, *1980*, pp. 229–40.

Feldstein, Martin S. Inflation, Tax Rules, and Capital Formation: A Summary of the Theoretical Models. **In** *Feldstein, M. (II)*, 1983, pp. 17–27.

Feldstein, Martin S. Inflation, Tax Rules, and the Prices of Land and Gold. **In** *Feldstein, M. (II)*, 1983, *1980*, pp. 221–28.

Feldstein, Martin S. Inflation, Tax Rules, and the Accumulation of Residential and Nonresidential Capital. **In** *Feldstein, M. (II)*, 1983, *1982*, pp. 81–98. [G: U.S.]

Feldstein, Martin S. Inflation, Tax Rules, and the Stock Market. **In** *Feldstein, M. (II)*, 1983, *1980*, pp. 199–220. [G: U.S.]

Feldstein, Martin S. Should Private Pensions Be Indexed? **In** *Bodie, Z. and Shoven, J. B., eds.*, 1983, pp. 211–30.

Feldstein, Martin S.; Green, Jerry R. and Sheshinski, Eytan. Inflation and Taxes in a Growing Economy with Debt and Equity Finance. **In** *Feldstein, M. (II)*, 1983, *1978*, pp. 44–60. [G: U.S.]

Feldstein, Martin S. and Summers, Lawrence. Inflation, Tax Rules, and the Long-term Interest Rate. **In** *Feldstein, M. (II)*, 1983, *1978*, pp. 153–85. [G: U.S.]

Figlewski, Stephen and Wachtel, Paul. Rational Expectations, Informational Efficiency, and Tests Using Survey Data: A Reply [The Formation of Inflationary Expectations]. *Rev. Econ. Statist.*, August 1983, *65*(3), pp. 529–31. [G: U.S.]

Fischer, Stanley. Indexing and Inflation. *J. Monet. Econ.*, November 1983, *12*(4), pp. 519–41. [G: Selected Countries]

Fischer, Stanley. Seigniorage and Fixed Exchange Rates: An Optimal Inflation Tax Analysis. **In** *Armella, P. A.; Dornbusch, R. and Obstfeld, M., eds.*, 1983, pp. 59–69.

Fischer, Stanley. Towards an Understanding of the Costs of Inflation: II. **In** *Brunner, K. and Meltzer, A. H., eds.*, 1983, *1981*, pp. 311–47. [G: U.S.]

Fischer, Stanley. Welfare Aspects of Government Issue of Indexed Bonds. **In** *Dornbusch, R. and Simonsen, M. H., eds.*, 1983, pp. 223–46.

Fitzgerald, M. Desmond and Pollio, Gerald. Money, Activity and Prices: Some Inter-Country Evidence. *Europ. Econ. Rev.*, December 1983, *23*(3), pp. 299–314. [G: Selected OECD]

Fleming, J. The Demand-Side Economics of Inflation: Comment. **In** *Worswick, D. and Trevithick, J., eds.*, 1983, pp. 244–47.

Flood, Robert P. and Garber, Peter M. Process Consistency and Monetary Reform: Some Further Evidence. *J. Monet. Econ.*, August 1983, *12*(2), pp. 279–95. [G: Europe]

Fortune, J. N. Expectations, Capital Formation, Sales and Capacity Utilization. *Empirical Econ.*, 1983, *8*(3–4), pp. 177–86.

Fosu, Augustin Kwasi and Strobel, Frederick R. International Impacts on U.S. Inflation in the 1970s. *Eastern Econ. J.*, October–December 1983, *9*(4), pp. 323–31. [G: U.S.]

Franco, Giampiero and Mengarelli, Gianluigi. Ancora a proposito dei mezzi di finanziamento del deficit pubblico: una risposta allargata. (The Means for Financing the Public Deficit: An Extended Reply. With English summary.) *Bancaria*, January 1983, *39*(1), pp. 34–38. [G: Italy]

Fried, Joel and Howitt, Peter. The Effects of Inflation on Real Interest Rates. *Amer. Econ. Rev.*, December 1983, *73*(5), pp. 968–80.

Gahlen, Bernhard. Preise und Mengen in kurz-und langfristiger Analyse: II. (Prices and Quantities in Short- and Long-Run Analysis: II. With English summary.) *Kyklos*, 1983, *36*(4), pp. 548–74.

Galli, Giampaolo and Masera, Rainer S. Real Rates of Interest and Public Sector Deficits: An Empirical Investigation. *Econ. Notes*, 1983, (3), pp. 5–41. [G: N. America; Italy; Germany; France; U.K.]

Gandolfi, Arthur E. and Lothian, James R. International Price Behavior and the Demand for

Money. *Econ. Inquiry,* July 1983, *21* (3), pp. 295–311. **[G: OECD]**

Gandolfi, Arthur E. and Lothian, James R. International Price Behavior and the Demand for Money. In *Darby, M. P. and Lothian, J. R., et al.,* 1983, pp. 421–61. **[G: OECD]**

Gardner, Bernard and Marlow, Peter. An International Comparison of the Fiscal Treatment of Shipping. *J. Ind. Econ.,* June 1983, *31* (4), pp. 397–415. **[G: EEC; Japan; U.S.; Liberia]**

Genberg, Hans. Overshooting and Asymmetries in the Transmission of Foreign Price Shocks to the Swedish Economy. In *Eliasson, G.; Sharefkin, M. and Ysander, B.-C., eds.,* 1983, pp. 199–222. **[G: Sweden]**

Goodhart, Charles A. E. 'Inflation, Financial and Fiscal Structure, and the Monetary Mechanism' by L. Papademos and F. Modigliani: Comment. *Europ. Econ. Rev.,* March/April 1983, *21* (1/2), pp. 251–56.

Goodwin, R. M. A Note on the Theory of the Inflationary Process. In *Goodwin, R. M.,* 1983, *1952,* pp. 57–74.

Goodwin, R. M. The World Matrix Multiplier. In *Goodwin, R. M.,* 1983, pp. 30–56.

Gourlaouen, Jean-Pierre. Une analyse économétrique des liens entre l'inflation, le chomage et la nature des anticipations. (An Econometric Analysis of Inflation, Unemployment and the Nature of Expectations. With English summary.) *Revue Écon.,* September 1983, *34* (5), pp. 971–86. **[G: France]**

Gowland, D. H. Consumption, Saving and Inflation. In *Gowland, D. H., ed.,* 1983, pp. 119–39. **[G: U.K.]**

Gowland, D. H. Inflation: Some New Perspectives. In *Gowland, D. H., ed.,* 1983, pp. 89–118.

Gramlich, Edward M. Models of Inflation Expectations Formation: A Comparison of Household and Economist Forecasts. *J. Money, Credit, Banking,* May 1983, *15* (2), pp. 155–73. **[G: U.S.]**

Gray, Jo Anna. Wage Indexation, Incomplete Information, and the Aggregate Supply Curve. In *Dornbusch, R. and Simonsen, M. H., eds.,* 1983, pp. 25–45.

Gultekin, N. Bulent. Stock Market Returns and Inflation Forecasts. *J. Finance,* June 1983, *38* (3), pp. 663–73. **[G: U.S.]**

Gutierrez-Camara, José L. and Huss, Hans-Joachim. The Interaction between Floating Exchange Rates, Money, and Prices—An Empirical Analysis. *Weltwirtsch. Arch.,* 1983, *119* (3), pp. 401–28. **[G: U.S.; Japan; Canada; W. Europe]**

Hafer, R. W. Inflation: Assessing Its Recent Behavior and Future Prospects. *Fed. Res. Bank St. Louis Rev.,* August/September 1983, *65* (7), pp. 36–41.

Hahn, F. H. Inflation, Debt, and Indexation: Panel Comments. In *Dornbusch, R. and Simonsen, M. H., eds.,* 1983, pp. 321–23.

Hahn, F. H. Keynesianism, Monetarism, and Rational Expectations: Some Reflections and Conjectures: Comment. In *Frydman, R. and Phelps, E. S., eds.,* 1983, pp. 223–30.

Hansen, Lars Peter and Sargent, Thomas J. Aggregation over Time and the Inverse Optimal Predictor Problem for Adaptive Expectations in Conginuous Time. *Int. Econ. Rev.,* February 1983, *24* (1), pp. 1–20. **[G: U.S.]**

Hanson, James A. The Short-Run Relation between Growth and Inflation in Latin America: Reply. *Amer. Econ. Rev.,* June 1983, *73* (3), pp. 483–85. **[G: Latin America]**

Hansson, Ingemar. Inflation and Price Controls in Sweden. *Scand. J. Econ.,* 1983, *85* (3), pp. 415–23. **[G: Sweden]**

Hart, Robert A. The Phillips Curve and Cyclical Manhour Variation. *Oxford Econ. Pap.,* July 1983, *35* (2), pp. 186–201. **[G: U.K.]**

Hausmann, Ricardo and Lipietz, Alain. Marx et la divergence entre production en valeur et revenus nominaux. (With English summary.) *Revue Écon. Polit.,* March–April 1983, *93* (2), pp. 270–300.

Hercowitz, Zvi. Anticipated Inflation, the Frequency of Transactions, and the Slope of the Phillips Curve. *J. Money, Credit, Banking,* May 1983, *15* (2), pp. 139–54.

Hesselman, Linda. The Macroeconomic Role of Relative Price Variability in the USA and the UK. *Appl. Econ.,* April 1983, *15* (2), pp. 225–33. **[G: U.K.; U.S.]**

Hochman, Shalom J. and Palmon, Oded. The Irrelevance of Capital Structure for the Impact of Inflation on Investment. *J. Finance,* June 1983, *38* (3), pp. 785–94.

Hojman, David E. Wages, Unemployment and Expectations in Developing Countries: The Labour Market and the Augmented Phillips Curve for Chile. *J. Econ. Stud.,* 1983, *10* (1), pp. 3–16. **[G: Chile]**

Horne, Jocelyn. Rational Expectations and the Defris–Williams Inflationary Expectations Series: A Reply. *Econ. Rec.,* September 1983, *59* (166), pp. 293–94. **[G: Australia]**

Horvath, Janos. A Theory of Institutional Inflation. In *Schmukler, N. and Marcus, E., eds.,* 1983, pp. 50–78.

Hosek, William R. Stochastic Properties of the Real Interest Rate. *Appl. Econ.,* December 1983, *15* (6), pp. 793–805. **[G: U.S.]**

Howard, Michael. Control of Inflation in a Small, Open Economy: A Comment. *Amer. Econ.,* Fall 1983, *27* (2), pp. 83–85.

Huber, Paul B. Pensions and Inflation: A Comment [Inflation and the Standard of Living of Pensioners: A Case Study]. *Can. Public Policy,* June 1983, *9* (2), pp. 250–55. **[G: Canada]**

Ioannidis, Christos and Peel, David A. Involuntary Saving through Unanticipated Inflation: Some Further Empirical Evidence. *Empirical Econ.,* 1983, *8* (2), pp. 87–92. **[G: Canada; Japan; U.K.; U.S.]**

Jha, Raghbendra and Lächler, Ulrich. Inflation and Economic Growth in a Competitive Economy with Exhaustible Resources. *J. Econ. Behav. Organ.,* June–September 1983, *4* (2–3), pp. 113–29.

Jonas, Paul. Problems of Current Inflation in the United States. In *Schmukler, N. and Marcus, E., eds.,* 1983, pp. 291–300. **[G: U.S.]**

Kane, Alex; Rosenthal, Leonard and Ljung, Greta. Tests of the Fisher Hypothesis with International

Data: Theory and Evidence. *J. Finance,* May 1983, *38*(2), pp. 539–51. **[G: W. Europe; U.S.]**

Kanniainen, Vesa and Tornberg, Pertti. Inflation in an Open Economy: Tests with Finnish Data 1960(I)–1981(IV). *Weltwirtsch. Arch.,* 1983, *119*(2), pp. 317–28. **[G: Finland]**

Katseli, Louka T. and Marion, Nancy P. Adjustment to Variations in Prices of Imported Inputs: The Role of Economic Structure—A Reply. *Weltwirtsch. Arch.,* 1983, *119*(3), pp. 579–80.

Katz, Eliakim and Rosenberg, Jacob. Inflation Variability, Real-Wage Variability and Production Inefficiency. *Economica,* November 1983, *50*(200), pp. 469–75.

Korteweg, Pieter. The Economics of Inflation and Output Fluctuations in the Netherlands, 1954–1975: A Test of Some Implications of the Dominant Impulse-cum-Rational Expectations Hypothesis. **In** *Brunner, K. and Meltzer, A. H., eds.,* 1983, *1978,* pp. 25–79. **[G: Netherlands]**

Koutsoyiannis, A. A Short-Run Pricing Model for a Speculative Asset, Tested with Data from the Gold Bullion Market. *Appl. Econ.,* October 1983, *15*(5), pp. 563–81.

Kröger, Jürgen. Devisenkurse, Leistungsbilanz und interne Anpassungsprozesse. (Exchange Rates, the Current Account Balance, and Internal Adjustment Processes. With English summary.) *Konjunkturpolitik,* 1983, *29*(1), pp. 1–20. **[G: W. Germany]**

Kubin, Ingrid. Zur Bedeutung der Phillips-Phänomene. (On the Interpretation of the Phillips Phenomena. With English summary.) *Jahr. Nationalökon. Statist.,* July 1983, *198*(4), pp. 318–33.

Lächler, Ulrich. A Macrotheoretic Analysis of Inflation, Taxes, and the Price of Equity. *J. Macroecon.,* Summer 1983, *5*(3), pp. 281–301.

Laidler, David and Bentley, Brian. A Small Macro-Model of the Post-War United States. *Manchester Sch. Econ. Soc. Stud.,* December 1983, *51*(4), pp. 317–40. **[G: U.S.]**

Laterza, Edoardo Lecaldano Sasso and Quintieri, Beniamino. È il debito pubblico più inflazionistico della base monetaria? (Is Public Debt More Inflationary than the Monetary Base? With English summary.) *Bancaria,* January 1983, *39*(1), pp. 27–33. **[G: Italy]**

Lawrence, Colin. Rational Expectations, Supply Shocks and the Stability of the Inflation–Output Tradeoff: Some Time Series Evidence for the United Kingdom, 1957–1977. *J. Monet. Econ.,* March 1983, *11*(2), pp. 225–45. **[G: U.K.]**

Leach, John. Inflation as a Commodity Tax. *Can. J. Econ.,* August 1983, *16*(3), pp. 508–16.

Leibenstein, Harvey. Notes on the X-efficiency Approach to Inflation, Productivity and Unemployment. **In** *Weisbrod, B. and Hughes, H., eds.,* 1983, pp. 84–96.

Leijonhufvud, Axel. Keynesianism, Monetarism, and Rational Expectations: Some Reflections and Conjectures. **In** *Frydman, R. and Phelps, E. S., eds.,* 1983, pp. 203–23.

Lerner, Abba P. Employment Theory and Employment Policy. **In** *Lerner, A. P.,* 1983, *1967,* pp. 375–92.

Lerner, Abba P. From Pre-Keynes to Post-Keynes. **In** *Lerner, A. P.,* 1983, *1977,* pp. 399–427.

Lerner, Abba P. On Keynes, Policy, and Theory—A Grumble. **In** *Lerner, A. P.,* 1983, pp. 441–51.

Lerner, Abba P. Phase Three. **In** *Lerner, A. P.,* 1983, *1972,* pp. 481–92.

Lerner, Abba P. Sellers' Inflation and Inflationary Depression. **In** *Lerner, A. P.,* 1983, *1961,* pp. 469–80.

Lerner, Abba P. The Inflationary Process. **In** *Lerner, A. P.,* 1983, *1949,* pp. 461–68.

Lerner, Abba P. and Colander, David C. MAP: A Cure for Inflation. **In** *Lerner, A. P.,* 1983, *1979,* pp. 493–503.

Levhari, David. The Effects of Government Intermediation in the Indexed Bonds Market on Consumer Behavior. **In** *Dornbusch, R. and Simonsen, M. H., eds.,* 1983, pp. 281–307.

Levi, Maurice and Dexter, Albert. Regulated Prices and Their Consequences. *Can. Public Policy,* March 1983, *9*(1), pp. 24–31. **[G: Canada]**

Lindbeck, Assar. Budget Expansion and Cost Inflation. *Amer. Econ. Rev.,* May 1983, *73*(2), pp. 285–90.

Liviatan, Nissan. Inflation and the Composition of Deficit Finance. **In** *[Klein, L. R.],* 1983, pp. 84–100.

Liviatan, Nissan. On the Interaction between Wage and Asset Indexation. **In** *Dornbusch, R. and Simonsen, M. H., eds.,* 1983, pp. 267–80.

Lloyd, Peter J. The Microeconomic Effects of Tax-inflation Interactions: General Equilibrium Estimates for Australia: Discussion. **In** *Pagan, A. R. and Trivedi, P. K., eds.,* 1983, pp. 178–82. **[G: Australia]**

Lombra, Raymond E. and Mehra, Yash P. Aggregate Demand, Food Prices, and the Underlying Rate of Inflation. *J. Macroecon.,* Fall 1983, *5*(4), pp. 383–98.

Lopes, Francisco L. and Bacha, Edmar L. Inflation, Growth and Wage Policy: A Brazilian Perspective. *J. Devel. Econ.,* Aug.–Oct. 1983, *13*(1–2), pp. 1–20. **[G: Brazil]**

Lui, Francis T. Cagan's Hypothesis and the First Nationwide Inflation of Paper Money in World History. *J. Polit. Econ.,* December 1983, *91*(6), pp. 1067–74. **[G: China]**

Macedo, Roberto. Wage Indexation and Inflation: The Recent Brazilian Experience. **In** *Dornbusch, R. and Simonsen, M. H., eds.,* 1983, pp. 133–59. **[G: Brazil]**

Machlup, Fritz. The Political Economy of Inflation. *Cato J.,* Spring 1983, *3*(1), pp. 15–21. **[G: U.S.; Austria; Germany]**

Makin, John H. Real Interest, Money Surprises, Anticipated Inflation and Fiscal Deficits. *Rev. Econ. Statist.,* August 1983, *65*(3), pp. 374–84. **[G: U.S.]**

Malliaris, A. G. and Pournakis, M. An Eclectic Approach to the Problem of the International Transmission of Inflation. *Econ. Int.,* May–August–November 1983, *36*(2–3–4), pp. 180–91. **[G: Global]**

Marquez, Jaime R. A Proposition on Short-Run Departures from the Law-of-One-Price: An Extension. *Europ. Econ. Rev.,* September 1983, *23*(1),

pp. 99–101.

Mayhew, Ken. Traditional Incomes Policies. *Oxford Bull. Econ. Statist.*, February 1983, *45*(1), pp. 15–32. **[G: U.K.]**

McCallum, John. Inflation and Social Consensus in the Seventies. *Econ. J.*, December 1983, *93*(372), pp. 784–805. **[G: Selected OECD]**

McDermott, John. Exchange-Rate Indexation in a Monetary Model: Theory and Evidence. *J. Int. Money Finance*, August 1983, *2*(2), pp. 197–213. **[G: Brazil]**

McGee, Robert T. Some Implications of the Natural Rate Hypotheses. *J. Macroecon.*, Summer 1983, *5*(3), pp. 303–16.

McGuire, Timothy W. Price Change Expectations and the Phillips Curve. **In** *Brunner, K. and Meltzer, A. H., eds.*, 1983, *1976*, pp. 81–127. **[G: U.S.]**

Means, Gardiner C. Corporate Power in the Marketplace. *J. Law Econ.*, June 1983, *26*(2), pp. 467–85. **[G: U.S.]**

Melitz, Jacques. 'Inflation, Financial and Fiscal Structure, and the Monetary Mechanism' by L. Papademos and F. Modigliani: Comment. *Europ. Econ. Rev.*, March/April 1983, *21*(1/2), pp. 257–59.

Merton, Robert C. On Consumption Indexed Public Pension Plans. **In** *Bodie, Z. and Shoven, J. B., eds.*, 1983, pp. 259–76, 287–89. **[G: U.S.]**

Miller, Preston J. Higher Deficit Policies Lead to Higher Inflation. *Fed. Res. Bank Minn. Rev.*, Winter 1983, *7*(1), pp. 8–19. **[G: U.S.]**

Minsky, Hyman P. Institutional Roots of American Inflation. **In** *Schmukler, N. and Marcus, E., eds.*, 1983, pp. 265–77. **[G: U.S.]**

Modigliani, Franco. Debt, Dividend Policy, Taxes, Inflation, and Market Valuation: Erratum. *J. Finance*, June 1983, *38*(3), pp. 1041–42.

Modigliani, Franco. Retirement Annuity Design in an Inflationary Climate: Comment. **In** *Bodie, Z. and Shoven, J. B., eds.*, 1983, pp. 316–22. **[G: U.S.]**

Modigliani, Franco. The Nonadjustment of Nominal Interest Rates: A Study of the Fisher Effect: Comment. **In** *Tobin, J., ed.*, 1983, pp. 241–44. **[G: U.S.]**

Monke, Eric. Traded and Non-Traded Goods: An Empirical Test with Nigerian Data. *J. Devel. Econ.*, December 1983, *13*(3), pp. 349–60. **[G: Nigeria]**

Montesano, Aldo. Debito pubblico o base monetaria? Una risposta. (Public Debt or Monetary Base? A Reply. With English summary.) *Bancaria*, January 1983, *39*(1), pp. 39–41.

Moosa, Suleman A. The Double Whammy of Stagflation and Uncertainty. *Kredit Kapital*, 1983, *16*(3), pp. 297–315. **[G: U.S.]**

Moosa, Suleman A. The Treatment of Uncertainty in the Application of Rational Expectations to the Analysis of Economic Policy. *Appl. Econ.*, August 1983, *15*(4), pp. 451–58.

Moriguchi, Chikashi. Japan's Macroeconomic Policies during the 1970s. **In** *[Klein, L. R.]*, 1983, pp. 282–95. **[G: Japan]**

Mutambuka, Pierre. "Inflationary Expectations and Monetary Adjustment in Nigeria: 1960–1978": Some Comments. *Pakistan Devel. Rev.*, Winter 1983, *22*(4), pp. 301–05. **[G: Nigeria]**

Myerson, Roger B. A Dynamic Microeconomic Model with Durable Goods and Adaptive Expectations. *J. Econ. Behav. Organ.*, December 1983, *4*(4), pp. 309–51.

Nakamura, Jiro. The Role of the Labor Market for Solving the Problem of Stagflation. *Econ. Stud. Quart.*, August 1983, *34*(2), pp. 147–55. **[G: Japan]**

Navarro, Alfredo M. and Rayó, Antonio R. Precios, Causalidad y Dinero en Argentina. (Prices, Causality and Money in Argentina. With English summary.) *Económica*, May–December 1983, *29*(2–3), pp. 267–84. **[G: Argentina]**

Nevile, J. W. Inflation and the Consumption Ratio: Discussion. **In** *Pagan, A. R. and Trivedi, P. K., eds.*, 1983, pp. 356–61. **[G: Australia]**

Nichols, Donald A. Macroeconomic Determinants of Wage Adjustments in White-Collar Occupations. *Rev. Econ. Statist.*, May 1983, *65*(2), pp. 203–13. **[G: U.S.]**

Obstfeld, Maurice and Rogoff, Kenneth S. Speculative Hyperinflations in Maximizing Models: Can We Rule Them Out? *J. Polit. Econ.*, August 1983, *91*(4), pp. 675–87.

Okun, Arthur M. Inflation: Its Mechanics and Welfare Costs. **In** *Okun, A. M.*, 1983, *1975*, pp. 79–118. **[G: U.S.; 8210]**

Okun, Arthur M. The Invisible Handshake and the Inflationary Process. **In** *Okun, A. M.*, 1983, *1980*, pp. 119–30.

Ormerod, Paul. Alternative Models of Inflation in the United Kingdom under the Assumption of Rational Expectations. **In** *Schmukler, N. and Marcus, E., eds.*, 1983, pp. 643–58. **[G: U.K.]**

Oulton, Nicholas. Persistence of Wages, Prices and Output under Rational Expectations When the Labour Market Is Dominated by Workplace Bargaining. *Manchester Sch. Econ. Soc. Stud.*, June 1983, *51*(2), pp. 111–28. **[G: U.K.]**

Pagan, A. R.; Hall, A. D. and Trivedi, P. K. Assessing the Variability of Inflation. *Rev. Econ. Stud.*, October 1983, *50*(4), pp. 585–96. **[G: Australia]**

Pagan, A. R. and Trivedi, P. K. The Effects of Inflation: A Review with Special Reference to Australia. **In** *Pagan, A. R. and Trivedi, P. K., eds.*, 1983, pp. 11–100. **[G: Australia]**

Panayotopoulos, Dimitris. The "Vicious Circle" Hypothesis: The Greek Case. *Kredit Kapital*, 1983, *16*(3), pp. 394–404. **[G: Greece]**

Papademos, Lucas and Modigliani, Franco. Inflation, Financial and Fiscal Structure, and the Monetary Mechanism. *Europ. Econ. Rev.*, March/April 1983, *21*(1/2), pp. 203–50.

Papadia, F. Rationality of Inflationary Expectations in the European Economic Communties Countries. *Empirical Econ.*, 1983, *8*(3–4), pp. 187–202. **[G: EEC]**

Parkin, Michael. What Can Macroeconomic Theory Tell Us about the Way Deficits Should Be Measured? **In** *Conklin, D. W. and Courchene, T. J., eds.*, 1983, pp. 150–77.

Parks, Richard W. and Cutler, Harvey. Relative Price Variability and Inflation: A Survey and Further Results: A Comment. *Carnegie-Rochester Conf.*

Ser. Public Policy, Autumn 1983, *19,* pp. 159–66.

Pearce, Douglas K. The Transmission of Inflation between the United States and Canada: An Empirical Analysis. *J. Macroecon.,* Summer 1983, *5*(3), pp. 265–79. **[G: Canada; U.S.]**

Pechman, Joseph A. and Carr, Julie A. Macro-economics Prices & Quantities. **In** *Tobin, J., ed.,* 1983, pp. 1–18.

Pedersen, Peder J. Inflationary Effects of Unemployment Insurance—An International Survey. **In** *Söderström, L., ed.,* 1983, pp. 225–49. **[G: OECD]**

Pedersen, Peder J. Lønudviklingen i Danmark 1911–1976—stabilitet og specifikation. (Phillips Curves Investigations of Danish Data Covering the Period 1911 to 1976. With English summary.) *Nationaløkon. Tidsskr.,* 1983, *121*(1), pp. 102–29. **[G: Denmark]**

Peebles, Gavin. Inflation, Money and Banking in China: In Support of the Purchasing Power Approach. *ACES Bull. (See Comp. Econ. Stud. after 8/85),* Summer 1983, *25*(2), pp. 81–103. **[G: China]**

Peek, Joe and Wilcox, James A. The Postwar Stability of the Fisher Effect. *J. Finance,* September 1983, *38*(4), pp. 1111–24. **[G: U.S.]**

Peel, David A. On Inflation and Economic Growth. *Singapore Econ. Rev.,* April 1983, *28*(1), pp. 53–58. **[G: LDCs]**

Pemberton, James. A New Model of Inflation Expectations in a Simple Macroeconomic Model. *Economica,* August 1983, *50*(199), pp. 281–89.

Perazzelli, P. A. and Perrin, J. R. Investment—Inflation Linkages in the NIF-10 Model. **In** *Pagan, A. R. and Trivedi, P. K., eds.,* 1983, pp. 283–310. **[G: Australia]**

Pfister, Jürgen. Die neuere Ursachenkontroverse in der Inflationstheorie. (The Recent Controversy on Causes in Inflation Theory. With English summary.) *Kredit Kapital,* 1983, *16*(1), pp. 62–80.

Phelps, Edmund S. The Trouble with "Rational Expectations" and the Problem of Inflation Stabilization. **In** *Frydman, R. and Phelps, E. S., eds.,* 1983, pp. 31–41.

Picard, Pierre. Inflation and Growth in a Disequilibrium Macroeconomic Model. *J. Econ. Theory,* August 1983, *30*(2), pp. 266–95.

Piggott, John. The Microeconomic Effects of Tax-inflation Interactions: General Equilibrium Estimates for Australia. **In** *Pagan, A. R. and Trivedi, P. K., eds.,* 1983, pp. 138–77. **[G: Australia]**

van der Ploeg, Frederick. Economic Growth and Conflict over the Distribution of Income. *J. Econ. Dynam. Control,* November 1983, *6*(3), pp. 253–79.

Pohl, Rüdiger. Nicht-neutrale Inflation. (Non-neutral Inflation. With English summary.) *Kredit Kapital,* 1983, *16*(4), pp. 458–78.

Praet, Peter. Inflation–Induced Wealth Tax in Belgium. *Rev. Income Wealth,* June 1983, *29*(2), pp. 209–14. **[G: Belgium]**

Protopapadakis, Aris. The Endogeneity of Money during the German Hyperinflation: A Reappraisal. *Econ. Inquiry,* January 1983, *21*(1), pp. 72–92. **[G: Germany]**

Rabeau, Yves. Les services et l'inflation: Le cas Canadien. (With English summary.) *Revue Écon. Polit.,* May–June 1983, *93*(3), pp. 421–36. **[G: Canada]**

Rakowski, James J. Income Conflicts, Inflation, and Controls. *J. Post Keynesian Econ.,* Summer 1983, *5*(4), pp. 590–602. **[G: U.S.]**

Ram, Rati and Spencer, David E. Stock Returns, Real Activity, Inflation, and Money: Comment. *Amer. Econ. Rev.,* June 1983, *73*(3), pp. 463–70. **[G: U.S.]**

Ramb, Bernd-Thomas. Die horizontale Phillips-Kurve: Die Quasineutralität der Arbeitslosenquote bezüglich der Inflationsrate. (The Horizontal Phillips-Curve. The Quasi-Neutrality of the Unemployment Rate in Reference to the Inflation Rate. With English summary.) *Z. Wirtschaft. Sozialwissen.,* 1983, *103*(5), pp. 419–36. **[G: W. Germany]**

Rea, John D. The Explanatory Power of Alternative Theories of Inflation and Unemployment, 1895–1979. *Rev. Econ. Statist.,* May 1983, *65*(2), pp. 183–95. **[G: U.S.]**

Rice, G. Randolph. The Variance of Expected Inflation and the Rate of Inflation: Implications from Inter-Industry Wage Equations. *Appl. Econ.,* August 1983, *15*(4), pp. 553–61. **[G: U.K.]**

Riddell, W. Craig. The Responsiveness of Wage Settlements in Canada and Economic Policy. *Can. Public Policy,* March 1983, *9*(1), pp. 9–23. **[G: Canada; U.S.]**

Robinson, Derek and Mayhew, Ken. Pay Policies for the Future: Introduction. *Oxford Bull. Econ. Statist.,* February 1983, *45*(1), pp. 3–13. **[G: U.K.]**

Robinson, Derek and Mayhew, Ken. Pay Policies for the Future: Conclusions. *Oxford Bull. Econ. Statist.,* February 1983, *45*(1), pp. 127–39. **[G: U.K.]**

Rosefielde, Steven. Disguised Inflation in Soviet Industry: A Reply to James Steiner. *J. Compar. Econ.,* March 1983, *7*(1), pp. 71–76. **[G: U.S.S.R.]**

Rosser, J. Barkley, Jr. Infrastructure Investment and Inflation in Saudi Arabia. *Econ. Forum,* Summer 1983, *14*(1), pp. 143–47. **[G: Saudi Arabia]**

Rotemberg, Julio J. Aggregate Consequences of Fixed Costs of Price Adjustment [Sticky Prices and Disequilibrium Adjustment in a Rational Model of the Inflationary Process]. *Amer. Econ. Rev.,* June 1983, *73*(3), pp. 433–36.

Rousseau, Henri-Paul. The Dome Syndrome: The Debt Overhanging Canadian Government and Business. *Can. Public Policy,* March 1983, *9*(1), pp. 37–52. **[G: Canada]**

Rowley, Charles K. and Wiseman, Jack. Inflation versus Unemployment: Is the Government Impotent? *Nat. Westminster Bank Quart. Rev.,* February 1983, pp. 2–12.

Samuelson, Paul A. On Consumption Indexed Public Pension Plans: Comment. **In** *Bodie, Z. and Shoven, J. B., eds.,* 1983, pp. 276–87. **[G: U.S.]**

Saunders, Peter. A Disaggregate Study of the Rationality of Australian Producers' Price Expectations. *Manchester Sch. Econ. Soc. Stud.,* December 1983, *51*(4), pp. 380–98. **[G: Australia]**

Saunders, Peter. Rational Expectations and the De-fris–Williams Inflationary Expectations Series: A Comment. *Econ. Rec.,* September 1983, *59*(166), pp. 290–92. **[G: Australia]**

Schaafsma, Joseph. A Response [Inflation and the Standard of Living of Pensioners: A Case Study]. *Can. Public Policy,* June 1983, *9*(2), pp. 255–56. **[G: Canada]**

Schilirò, Daniele. On Some Aspects of Inflationary Process in Post-Keynesian Macro-Theory. *Econ. Notes,* 1983, (3), pp. 152–60.

Schulz, James H. Private Pensions, Inflation, and Employment. **In** *Parnes, H. S., ed.,* 1983, pp. 241–64. **[G: U.S.]**

Scitovsky, Tibor. The Demand-Side Economics of Inflation. **In** *Worswick, D. and Trevithick, J., eds.,* 1983, pp. 223–38.

Seccareccia, Mario S. A Reconsideration of the Underlying Structuralist Explanation of Price Movements in Keynes' 'Treatise on Money.' *Eastern Econ. J.,* July–September 1983, *9*(3), pp. 272–83. **[G: Canada]**

Seers, Dudley. Structuralism vs Monetarism in Latin America: A Reappraisal of a Great Debate, with Lessons for Europe in the 1980s. **In** *Jansen, K., ed.,* 1983, pp. 110–26. **[G: Latin America]**

Seidman, Laurence S. A TIP for the Stagflation Era (and Other Complementary Policies). **In** *Weintraub, S. and Goodstein, M., eds.,* 1983, pp. 125–38.

Seidman, Laurence S. Keynesian Stimulus without Inflation. *J. Post Keynesian Econ.,* Fall 1983, *6*(1), pp. 39–46.

Seidman, Laurence S. Sidney Weintraub, the Man and His Ideas. *Challenge,* November/December 1983, *26*(5), pp. 22–28.

Selden, Richard T. The Inflationary Seventies: Comparisons among Selected High-income Countries. **In** *Schmukler, N. and Marcus, E., eds.,* 1983, pp. 721–41. **[G: OECD]**

Seton, Francis. A "Phillipsoid" Wage–Push Flation: "In–," "Stag–," or "Slump–." *J. Post Keynesian Econ.,* Spring 1983, *5*(3), pp. 440–53.

Severn, Alan K. Formation of Inflation Expectations in the U.K.: Pitfalls in the Use of the Error-Learning Model. *Europ. Econ. Rev.,* January 1983, *20*(1–3), pp. 349–63. **[G: U.K.]**

Shepherd, A. Ross. A Backward Bending Supply of Labor Schedule and the Short Run Phillips Curve: Comment. *Southern Econ. J.,* January 1983, *49*(3), pp. 867–70.

Simonsen, Mario Henrique. Indexation: Current Theory and the Brazilian Experience. **In** *Dornbusch, R. and Simonsen, M. H., eds.,* 1983, pp. 99–132. **[G: Brazil]**

Simos, Evangelos O. and Triantis, John E. Do Energy Prices and Productivity Developments Affect Inflation Expectations? *Rivista Int. Sci. Econ. Com.,* October–November 1983, *30*(10–11), pp. 923–34. **[G: U.S.]**

Singleton, Kenneth J. Real and Nominal Factors in the Cyclical Behavior of Interest Rates, Output, and Money. *J. Econ. Dynam. Control,* May 1983, *5*(2/3), pp. 289–309. **[G: U.S.]**

Smithin, John Nicholas. A Note on the Welfare Cost of Perfectly Anticipated Inflation. *Bull. Econ. Res.,* May 1983, *35*(1), pp. 65–69.

Smyth, David J. Taxes and Inflation. **In** *Schmukler, N. and Marcus, E., eds.,* 1983, pp. 326–39.

Spaventa, Luigi. Feedbacks between Exchange-Rate Movements and Domestic Inflation: Vicious and Not So Virtuous Cycles, Old and New. *Int. Soc. Sci. J.,* 1983, *35*(3), pp. 517–34. **[G: Europe]**

Steigmann, A. John. What Price Disinflation. *Bus. Econ.,* January 1983, *18*(1), pp. 59–61. **[G: U.S.]**

Steiner, James E. Disguised Inflation in Soviet Industry: A Final Reply to Steven Rosefielde. *J. Compar. Econ.,* December 1983, *7*(4), pp. 449–51. **[G: U.S.S.R.]**

Stiglitz, Joseph E. On the Relevance or Irrelevance of Public Financial Policy: Indexation, Price Rigidities, and Optimal Monetary Policies. **In** *Dornbusch, R. and Simonsen, M. H., eds.,* 1983, pp. 183–222.

Strebel, Paul J. Contract Revision and Price Quantity Adjustment: A Catastrophe Model. *Atlantic Econ. J.,* March 1983, *11*(1), pp. 24–35.

Summers, Lawrence H. Observations on the Indexation of Old Age Pensions. **In** *Bodie, Z. and Shoven, J. B., eds.,* 1983, pp. 231–51, 257–58. **[G: U.S.]**

Summers, Lawrence H. The Nonadjustment of Nominal Interest Rates: A Study of the Fisher Effect. **In** *Tobin, J., ed.,* 1983, pp. 204–41. **[G: U.S.]**

Sumner, M. T. and Ward, R. The Reappearing Phillips Curve. *Oxford Econ. Pap.,* Supplement November 1983, *35,* pp. 306–20. **[G: U.K.]**

Tang, De-piao and Hu, Teh-wei. Money, Prices, and Causality: The Chinese Hyperinflation, 1945–49. *J. Macroecon.,* Fall 1983, *5*(4), pp. 503–10. **[G: China]**

Tanzi, Vito. Taxation and Price Stabilization. **In** *[Goode, R.],* 1983, pp. 409–30.

Tarantelli, Ezio. Foundations of a Likelihood Theory of Employment and Inflation. **In** *Fitoussi, J.-P., ed.,* 1983, pp. 185–203.

Tarantelli, Ezio. The Regulation of Inflation in Western Countries and the Degree of Neocorporatism. *Economia,* May 1983, *7*(2), pp. 199–238. **[G: OECD]**

Tavlas, George S. A Model of the Inflationary Process in Six Major O.E.C.D. Economies: Empirical Results and Policy Implications. *J. Policy Modeling,* March 1983, *5*(1), pp. 19–35. **[G: N. America; France; Germany; Japan; U.K.]**

Taylor, John B. Union Wage Settlements during a Disinflation. *Amer. Econ. Rev.,* December 1983, *73*(5), pp. 981–93. **[G: U.S.]**

Tobin, James. Inflation: Monetary and Structural Causes and Cures. **In** *Schmukler, N. and Marcus, E., eds.,* 1983, pp. 3–16.

Tompkinson, Paul and Common, Michael S. Evidence on the Rationality of Expectations in the British Manufacturing Sector. *Appl. Econ.,* August 1983, *15*(4), pp. 425–36. **[G: U.K.]**

Valentine, T. J. Investment—Inflation Linkages in the NIF-10 Model: Discussion. **In** *Pagan, A. R. and Trivedi, P. K., eds.,* 1983, pp. 318–20. **[G: Australia]**

Vizeu, M. Clementina. A Note on Demand and Cost Inflation and the Phillips Curve. *Economia,* May 1983, *7*(2), pp. 395–405.

Wagner, Adolf. Wirkungen einer Sozialabgabenbemessung nach Wertschöpfungsgrössen statt nach Arbeitskosten. (Effects of Employers' Social

Security Contributions if Based Not on Labour Cost but on Value Added. With English summary.) *Ifo-Studien*, 1983, *29*(4), pp. 255–71. **[G: W. Germany]**

Wallace, Myles S. A Backward Bending Supply of Labor Schedule and the Short Run Phillips Curve: Reply. *Southern Econ. J.*, January 1983, *49*(3), pp. 871–73.

Wallich, Henry C. Changes in Monetary Policy and the Fight against Inflation. *Cato J.*, Spring 1983, *3*(1), pp. 147–54. **[G: U.S.]**

Watanabe, Ken-ichi. An Adaptation of Weintraub's Model. *J. Post Keynesian Econ.*, Winter 1982–83, *5*(2), pp. 228–44.

Webb, Steven B. Money Demand and Expectations in the German Hyperinflation: A Survey of the Models. **In** *Schmukler, N. and Marcus, E., eds.*, 1983, pp. 435–49.

Willett, Thomas D. and Wolf, Matthias. The Vicious Circle Debate: Some Conceptual Distinctions. *Kyklos*, 1983, *36*(2), pp. 231–48.

Williams, Ross A. and Ouliaris, Sam. Inflation and the Consumption Ratio: Comments. **In** *Pagan, A. R. and Trivedi, P. K., eds.*, 1983, pp. 350–55. **[G: Australia]**

Wood, Geoffrey E. Inflation and the Labour Market. **In** *Seldon, A., et al.*, 1983, pp. 35–46. **[G: U.K.]**

Wood, John H. Interest Rates and Inflation: An Old and Unexplained Relationship. *Fed. Res. Bank Dallas Econ. Rev.*, January 1983, pp. 11–23. **[G: U.S.]**

Wörgötter, Andreas. A Note on the Stable Phillips Curve in Austria. *Empirica*, 1983, (1), pp. 29–40. **[G: Austria]**

Zoeteweij, Bert. Anti-Inflation Policies in the Industrialised Market Economy Countries (Part II). *Int. Lab. Rev.*, November–December 1983, *122*(6), pp. 691–707.

Zoeteweij, Bert. Anti-Inflation Policies in the Industrialised Market Economy Countries (Part 1). *Int. Lab. Rev.*, Sept.–Oct. 1983, *122*(5), pp. 563–77. **[G: MDCs]**

200 Quantitative Economic Methods and Data

210 Econometric, Statistical, and Mathematical Methods and Models

211 Econometric and Statistical Methods and Models

2110 General

Abel, Andrew B. and Mishkin, Frederic S. On the Econometric Testing of Rationality-Market Efficiency. *Rev. Econ. Statist.*, May 1983, *65*(2), pp. 318–23. **[G: U.S.]**

Agresti, Alan. A Survey of Strategies for Modeling Cross-Classifications Having Ordinal Variables. *J. Amer. Statist. Assoc.*, March 1983, *78*(381), pp. 184–98.

Aivazian, S. A. Applied Statistics and Probabilistic Modeling in Economics. *Matekon*, Fall 1983, *20*(1), pp. 29–56. **[G: U.S.S.R.]**

Allais, Maurice. Frequency, Probability and Chance. **In** *Stigum, B. P. and Wenstøp, F., eds.*, 1983, pp. 35–86.

Amato, Vittorio. Metrica dello spazio statistico. (Metric of the Statistical Space. With English summary.) *Statistica*, April–June 1983, *43*(2), pp. 219–29.

Anderson, T. W. On the Relevance of Finite Sample Distribution Theory: Comments. *Econometric Rev.*, 1983, *2*(1), pp. 41–47.

Atkinson, Anthony B. On the Measurement of Inequality. **In** *Atkinson, A. B.*, 1983, *1970*, pp. 15–36. **[G: MDCs; LDCs]**

Atkinson, Anthony B. The Measurement of Economic Mobility. **In** *Atkinson, A. B.*, 1983, *1981*, pp. 61–75.

Barbu, G. On Computer Generation of Random Variables as Ratio of Uniform Random Variables. *Econ. Computat. Cybern. Stud. Res.*, 1983, *18*(4), pp. 33–50.

Basmann, R. L. On the Relevance of Finite Sample Distribution Theory: Comment. *Econometric Rev.*, 1983, *2*(1), pp. 49–53.

Beach, Charles M. and Davidson, Russell. Distribution-Free Statistical Inference with Lorenz Curves and Income Shares. *Rev. Econ. Stud.*, October 1983, *50*(4), pp. 723–35.

Benjamini, Yoav. Is the *t* Test Really Conservative When the Parent Distribution Is Long-Tailed? *J. Amer. Statist. Assoc.*, September 1983, *78*(383), pp. 645–54.

Berk, Richard A. and Rauma, David. Capitalizing on Nonrandom Assignment to Treatments: A Regression-Discontinuity Evaluation of a Crime-Control Program. *J. Amer. Statist. Assoc.*, March 1983, *78*(381), pp. 21–27. **[G: U.S.]**

Berrebi, Z. M. and Silber, Jacques. On an Absolute Measure of Distributional Change. *Europ. Econ. Rev.*, July 1983, *22*(2), pp. 139–46.

Blyth, Colin R. and Still, Harold A. Binomial Confidence Intervals. *J. Amer. Statist. Assoc.*, March 1983, *78*(381), pp. 108–16.

Bologna, Salvatore. Alcune famiglie di distribuzioni su intervalli limitati. (Some Families of Distributions for Finite Ranges. With English summary.) *Statistica*, April–June 1983, *43*(2), pp. 301–17.

Brockett, Patrick L. On the Misuse of the Central Limit Theorem in Some Risk Calculations. *J. Risk Ins.*, December 1983, *50*(4), pp. 727–31.

Brunazzo, Antonio. Sulla distribuzione campionaria asintotica dell'indice di etorogeneita' di Leti. (On the Asymptotic Sampling Distribution of the Leti's Heterogeneity Index. With English summary.) *Statistica*, July–September 1983, *43*(3), pp. 433–44.

Cenuşă, G. and Burlacu, V. Random Functions *N*—Almost Periodic. *Econ. Computat. Cybern. Stud. Res.*, 1983, *18*(4), pp. 59–65.

Colombi, Roberto. Sull'impiego di alcune funzioni di distanza nella costruzione di indici di concentrazione, di eterogeneità, di dissomiglianza per serie sconnesse e di diversità di ripartizione. (About the Use of Some Distance Functions. With English summary.) *Statistica*, April–June 1983, *43*(2), pp. 319–31.

Dastoor, Naorayex, K. Some Aspects of Testing Non-Nested Hypotheses. *J. Econometrics,* February 1983, *21*(2), pp. 213–28.

De Jong, Piet and Boyle, Phelim P. Monitoring Mortality: A State-Space Approach. *J. Econometrics,* September 1983, *23*(1), pp. 131–46.

De Vylder, F. Practical Models in Credibility Theory, Including Parameter Estimation. *J. Econometrics,* September 1983, *23*(1), pp. 147–64.

DeRiggi, Dennis F. Unimodality of Likelihood Functions for the Binomial Distribution. *J. Amer. Statist. Assoc.,* March 1983, *78*(381), pp. 181–83.

Drèze, Jacques H. Nonspecialist Teaching of Econometrics: A Personal Comment and Personalistic Lament [University Teaching of Econometrics: A Personal View]. *Econometric Rev.,* 1983, *2*(2), pp. 291–99.

Dykstra, Richard L. and Robertson, Tim. On Testing Monotone Tendencies. *J. Amer. Statist. Assoc.,* June 1983, *78*(382), pp. 342–50.

Efron, Bradley. Estimating the Error Rate of a Prediction Rule Improvement on Cross-Validation. *J. Amer. Statist. Assoc.,* June 1983, *78*(382), pp. 316–31.

Engle, Robert F.; Hendry, David F. and Richard, Jean-François. Exogeneity. *Econometrica,* March 1983, *51*(2), pp. 277–304.

Fatti, L. P. The Random-Effects Model in Discriminant Analysis. *J. Amer. Statist. Assoc.,* September 1983, *78*(383), pp. 679–87.

Fielitz, Bruce D. and Rozelle, James P. Stable Distributions and the Mixtures of Distributions Hypotheses for Common Stock Returns. *J. Amer. Statist. Assoc.,* March 1983, *78*(381), pp. 28–36. [G: U.S.]

Fowlkes, E. B. and Mallows, C. L. A Method for Comparing Two Hierarchical Clusterings: Rejoinder. *J. Amer. Statist. Assoc.,* September 1983, *78*(383), pp. 584.

Fowlkes, E. B. and Mallows, C. L. A Method for Comparing Two Hierarchical Clusterings. *J. Amer. Statist. Assoc.,* September 1983, *78*(383), pp. 553–69.

Freedman, David and Lane, David. A Nonstochastic Interpretation of Reported Significance Levels. *J. Bus. Econ. Statist.,* October 1983, *1*(4), pp. 292–98. [G: U.S.]

Garrelfs, Horst. Die Wilcoxon-Verteilung bei Vorliegen von Bindungen in kleinen Stichproben. (Small Sample Distribution of the Wilcoxon Statistic under Ties. With English summary.) *Jahr. Nationalökon. Statist.,* January 1983, *198*(1), pp. 49–75.

Geary, R. C. R. A. Fisher: A Memoir. *Econ. Soc. Rev.,* April 1983, *14*(3), pp. 167–71.

Gilula, Zvi and Krieger, Abba M. The Decomposability and Monotonicity of Pearson's Chi-Square for Collapsed Contingency Tables with Applications. *J. Amer. Statist. Assoc.,* March 1983, *78*(381), pp. 176–80.

Goldstein, Michael. The Prevision of a Prevision. *J. Amer. Statist. Assoc.,* December 1983, *78*(384), pp. 817–19.

Goovaerts, M. J. and De Vylder, F. Upper and Lower Bounds on Infinite Time Ruin Probabilities in Case of Constraints on Claim Size Distributions. *J. Econometrics,* September 1983, *23*(1), pp. 77–90.

Hogg, Robert V. and Klugman, Stuart A. On the Estimation of Long Tailed Skewed Distributions with Actuarial Applications. *J. Econometrics,* September 1983, *23*(1), pp. 91–102. [G: U.S.]

Iritani, Jun and Kuga, Kiyoshi. Duality between the Lorenz Curves and the Income Distribution Functions. *Econ. Stud. Quart.,* April 1983, *34*(1), pp. 9–21.

Isaki, Cary T. Variance Estimation Using Auxiliary Information. *J. Amer. Statist. Assoc.,* March 1983, *78*(381), pp. 117–23.

Jolliffe, Ian T. and Morgan, Byron J. T. A Method for Comparing Two Hierarchical Clusterings: Comment. *J. Amer. Statist. Assoc.,* September 1983, *78*(383), pp. 580–81.

Kempthorne, Oscar. A Review of R. A. Fisher: An Appreciation. *J. Amer. Statist. Assoc.,* June 1983, *78*(382), pp. 482–90.

Kmenta, Jan. Some Notes on the Relevance of Finite Sample Distribution Theory. *Econometric Rev.,* 1983, *2*(1), pp. 55–60.

Lad, Frank. The Construction of Probability Theory: A Marxist Discussion. *Sci. Soc.,* Fall 1983, *47*(3), pp. 285–99.

Largeault, J. Probabilités et déterminisme. (Probabilities and Determinatism. With English summary.) *Écon. Soc.,* June 1983, *17*(6), pp. 951–58.

Leamer, Edward E. Let's Take the Con Out of Econometrics. *Amer. Econ. Rev.,* March 1983, *73*(1), pp. 31–43. [G: U.S.]

de Leeuw, Jan; Keller, Wouter J. and Wansbeek, Tom. Interfaces between Econometrics and Psychometrics: Editors' Introduction. *J. Econometrics,* May/June 1983, *22*(1/2), pp. 1–12.

Lingappaiah, Giri S. Prediction in Samples from the Inverse Gaussian Distribution. *Statistica,* April–June 1983, *43*(2), pp. 259–65.

Lovell, C. A. Knox and Sickles, Robin C. Testing Efficiency Hypotheses in Joint Production: A Parametric Approach. *Rev. Econ. Statist.,* February 1983, *65*(1), pp. 51–58. [G: U.S.]

Maasoumi, Esfandiar. On the Relevance of Finite Sample Distribution Theory? *Econometric Rev.,* 1983, *2*(1), pp. 61–69.

Mărgăritescu, E. and Nicolae, T. Some Contributions to the Study of Variation Coefficient. *Econ. Computat. Cybern. Stud. Res.,* 1983, *18*(1), pp. 51–61.

Mariano, Roberto S. On the Relevance of Finite Sample Distribution Theory: Comment. *Econometric Rev.,* 1983, *2*(1), pp. 71–74.

Mazodier, Pascal. University Teaching of Econometrics: A Personal View: Comment. *Econometric Rev.,* 1983, *2*(2), pp. 301–06.

Missiakoulis, Spyros. Sargan Densities: Which One? *J. Econometrics,* October 1983, *23*(2), pp. 223–33.

Morimune, Kimio. On the Relevance of Finite Sample Distribution Theory: Comment. *Econometric Rev.,* 1983, *2*(1), pp. 75–80.

Panjer, Harry H. and Willmot, Gordon E. Compound Poisson Models in Actuarial Risk Theory. *J. Econometrics,* September 1983, *23*(1), pp. 63–76.

Phillips, P. C. B. Exact Small Sample Theory in the Simultaneous Equations Model. **In** *Griliches, Z. and Intriligator, M. D., eds.*, 1983, pp. 449–516.

Phillips, P. C. B. On University Education in Econometrics. *Econometric Rev.*, 1983, *2*(2), pp. 307–15.

Phillips, P. C. B. ERAs: A New Approach to Small Sample Theory. *Econometrica*, September 1983, *51*(5), pp. 1505–25.

Purcaru, I. and Sacuiu, I. On Classical Statistical Correlation. *Econ. Computat. Cybern. Stud. Res.*, 1983, *18*(2), pp. 61–63.

Sacuiu, I. and Moscovici, E. Methods of Constructing and Generating Correlated Random Variables. *Econ. Computat. Cybern. Stud. Res.*, 1983, *18*(1), pp. 23–29.

Sahlin, Nils-Eric. On Second Order Probabilities and the Notion of Epistemic Risk. **In** *Stigum, B. P. and Wenstøp, F., eds.*, 1983, pp. 95–104.

Sawa, Takamitsu. University Teaching of Econometrics: A Personal View: Comment. *Econometric Rev.*, 1983, *2*(2), pp. 317–22.

Sebenius, James K. and Geanakoplos, John. Don't Bet on It: Contingent Agreements with Asymmetric Information. *J. Amer. Statist. Assoc.*, June 1983, *78*(382), pp. 424–26.

Sowey, Eric R. The Teaching of Econometrics: Several Personal Views. *Econometric Rev.*, 1983, *2*(2), pp. 329–33.

Sowey, Eric R. University Teaching of Econometrics: A Personal View. *Econometric Rev.*, 1983, *2*(2), pp. 255–89.

Suzawa, Gilbert S. Note on Kakwani and Podder Method of Fitting Lorenz Curves. **In** *[Yamada, I.]*, 1983, pp. 122–26. **[G: Australia]**

Talwar, Prem P. Detecting a Shift in Location: Some Robust Tests. *J. Econometrics*, December 1983, *23*(3), pp. 353–67. **[G: U.S.]**

Taylor, William E. On the Relevance of Finite Sample Distribution Theory: Reply. *Econometric Rev.*, 1983, *2*(1), pp. 81–84.

Taylor, William E. On the Relevance of Finite Sample Distribution Theory. *Econometric Rev.*, 1983, *2*(1), pp. 1–39.

Theil, Henri. Linear Algebra and Matrix Methods in Econometrics. **In** *Griliches, Z. and Intriligator, M. D., eds.*, 1983, pp. 3–65.

Turner, D. W. A Method for Comparing Two Hierarchical Clusterings: Comment. *J. Amer. Statist. Assoc.*, September 1983, *78*(383), pp. 583.

Tweeten, Luther. Hypotheses Testing in Economic Science. *Amer. J. Agr. Econ.*, August 1983, *65*(3), pp. 548–52.

Van Ness, John W. A Method for Comparing Two Hierarchical Clusterings: Comment. *J. Amer. Statist. Assoc.*, September 1983, *78*(383), pp. 576–79.

Wallace, David L. A Method for Comparing Two Hierarchical Clusterings: Comment. *J. Amer. Statist. Assoc.*, September 1983, *78*(383), pp. 569–76.

White, Halbert. Corrigendum [Maximum Likelihood Estimation of Misspecified Models]. *Econometrica*, March 1983, *51*(2), pp. 513.

Wold, Herman. Utility Analysis from the Point of View of Model Building. **In** *Stigum, B. P. and Wenstøp, F., eds.*, 1983, pp. 87–93.

Wong, M. Anthony. A Method for Comparing Two Hierarchical Clusterings: Comment. *J. Amer. Statist. Assoc.*, September 1983, *78*(383), pp. 582–83.

Wright, George. Probabilistic Forecasts: Some Results and Speculations. **In** *Stigum, B. P. and Wenstøp, F., eds.*, 1983, pp. 217–32.

Wright, George and Whalley, Peter. The Supra-additivity of Subjective Probability. **In** *Stigum, B. P. and Wenstøp, F., eds.*, 1983, pp. 233–44.

Zagier, Don. Inequalities for the Gini Coefficient of Composite Populations. *J. Math. Econ.*, October 1983, *12*(2), pp. 103–18.

Zellner, Arnold. Statistical Theory and Econometrics. **In** *Griliches, Z. and Intriligator, M. D., eds.*, 1983, pp. 67–178.

Zellner, Arnold. University Teaching of Econometrics: A Personal View: Comment. *Econometric Rev.*, 1983, *2*(2), pp. 323–27.

Zieschang, Kimberly D. A Note on the Decomposition of Cost Efficiency into Technical and Allocative Components. *J. Econometrics*, December 1983, *23*(3), pp. 401–05.

2112 Inferential Problems in Simultaneous Equation Systems

Amemiya, Takeshi. A Comparison of the Amemiya GLS and the Lee–Maddala–Trost G2SLS in a Simultaneous-Equations Tobit Model. *J. Econometrics*, December 1983, *23*(3), pp. 295–300.

Amemiya, Takeshi. Non-linear Regression Models. **In** *Griliches, Z. and Intriligator, M. D., eds.*, 1983, pp. 333–389.

Anderson, T. W.; Kunitomo, Naoto and Sawa, Takamitsu. Comparison of the Densities of the TSLS and LIMLK Estimators for Simultaneous Equations. **In** *[Klein, L. R.]*, 1983, pp. 103–24.

Anderson, T. W.; Morimune, Kimio and Sawa, Takamitsu. The Numerical Values of Some Key Parameters in Econometric Models. *J. Econometrics*, February 1983, *21*(2), pp. 229–43.

Bagozzi, Richard P. Issues in the Application of Covariance Structure Analysis: A Further Comment. *J. Cons. Res.*, March 1983, *9*(4), pp. 449–50.

Bentler, P. M. Simultaneous Equation Systems as Moment Structure Models: With an Introduction to Latent Variable Models. *J. Econometrics*, May/June 1983, *22*(1/2), pp. 13–42.

Bhargava, Alok and Sargan, John Denis. Estimating Dynamic Random Effects Models from Panel Data Covering Short Time Periods. *Econometrica*, November 1983, *51*(6), pp. 1635–59.

Brown, Bryan W. The Identification Problem in Systems Nonlinear in the Variables. *Econometrica*, January 1983, *51*(1), pp. 175–96.

Cumby, Robert E.; Huizinga, John and Obstfeld, Maurice. Errata: Two-Step Two-Stage Least Squares Estimation in Models with Rational Expectations. *J. Econometrics*, December 1983, *23*(3), pp. 407. **[G: U.S.]**

Cumby, Robert E.; Huizinga, John and Obstfeld, Maurice. Two-Step Two-Stage Least Squares Estimation in Models with Rational Expectations. *J.*

Econometrics, April 1983, *21* (3), pp. 333–55. [G: U.S.]

Davidson, Russell and MacKinnon, James G. Testing the Specification of Multivariate Models in the Presence of Alternative Hypotheses. *J. Econometrics,* December 1983, *23*(3), pp. 301–13.

Deistler, Manfred. The Properties of the Parameterization of ARMAX Systems and Their Relevance for Structural Estimation and Dynamic Specification. *Econometrica,* July 1983, *51* (4), pp. 1187–207.

Dhrymes, Phoebus J. The Asymptotic Relative Inefficiency of Partially Restricted Reduced Forms. **In** *[Klein, L. R.],* 1983, pp. 125–39.

Dijkstra, Theo. Some Comments on Maximum Likelihood and Partial Least Squares Methods. *J. Econometrics,* May/June 1983, *22* (1/2), pp. 67–90.

Don, F. J. Henk. Corrigenda: Restrictions on Variables. *J. Econometrics,* October 1983, *23*(2), pp. 291–92. [G: Netherlands]

Drèze, Jacques H. and Richard, Jean-François. Bayesian Analysis of Simultaneous Equation Systems. **In** *Griliches, Z. and Intriligator, M. D., eds.,* 1983, pp. 517–98.

Ericsson, Neil R. Asymptotic Properties of Instrumental Variables Statistics for Testing Non-Nested Hypotheses. *Rev. Econ. Stud.,* April 1983, *50*(2), pp. 287–304.

Fair, Ray C. and Taylor, John B. Solution and Maximum Likelihood Estimation of Dynamic Nonlinear Rational Expectations Models. *Econometrica,* July 1983, *51* (4), pp. 1169–85.

Fornell, Claes. Issues in the Application of Covariance Structure Analysis: A Comment. *J. Cons. Res.,* March 1983, *9*(4), pp. 443–48.

Geraci, Vincent J. Errors in Variables and the Individual Structural Equation. *Int. Econ. Rev.,* February 1983, *24*(1), pp. 217–36.

Godfrey, Leslie G. Testing Non-Nested Models after Estimation by Instrumental Variables or Least Squares. *Econometrica,* March 1983, *51* (2), pp. 355–65.

Gourieroux, Christian and Monfort, Alain. Méthodes d'estimation pour les modèles avec prix planchers. (Estimation Methods for Models with Price Floors. With English summary.) *Ann. INSEE,* April–June 1983, (50), pp. 49–71.

Guttman, Irwin and Menzefricke, Ulrich. Bayesian Inference in Multivariate Regression with Missing Observations on the Response Variables. *J. Bus. Econ. Statist.,* July 1983, *1* (3), pp. 239–48. [G: Canada]

Hatanaka, Michio and Odaki, Mitsuhiro. Policy Analyses with and without a Priori Conditions. *Econ. Stud. Quart.,* December 1983, *34*(3), pp. 193–210.

Hausman, Jerry A. Specification and Estimation of Simultaneous Equation Models. **In** *Griliches, Z. and Intriligator, M. D., eds.,* 1983, pp. 391–448.

Hausman, Jerry A. and Taylor, William E. Identification in Linear Simultaneous Equations Models with Covariance Restrictions: An Instrumental Variables Interpretation. *Econometrica,* September 1983, *51* (5), pp. 1527–49.

Holly, Alberto. Une présentation unifiée des tests d'exogénéité dans les modèles à équations simultanées. (A Unified Presentation of Tests of Exogeneity in Simultaneous-Equation Models. With English summary.) *Ann. INSEE,* April–June 1983, (50), pp. 3–24.

Hsiao, Cheng. Identification. **In** *Griliches, Z. and Intriligator, M. D., eds.,* 1983, pp. 223–83.

Kariya, Takeaki. The Non-Unbiasedness of the Wu Test. *Econ. Stud. Quart.,* August 1983, *34*(2), pp. 179–84.

Kunitomo, Naoto; Morimune, Kimio and Tsukuda, Yoshihiko. Asymptotic Expansions of the Distributions of the Test Statistics for Overidentifying Restrictions in a System of Simultaneous Equations. *Int. Econ. Rev.,* February 1983, *24*(1), pp. 199–215.

Manski, Charles F. Closest Empirical Distribution Estimation. *Econometrica,* March 1983, *51* (2), pp. 305–19.

Mariano, Roberto S. and Brown, Bryan W. Asymptotic Behavior of Predictors in a Nonlinear Simultaneous System. *Int. Econ. Rev.,* October 1983, *24*(3), pp. 523–36.

Matsuyama, Keisuke and Tamura, Yasuhiro. On Calculation of Causal Orderings of Variables Appearing in Simultaneous Equations. *Econ. Computat. Cybern. Stud. Res.,* 1983, *18* (1), pp. 73–85.

McCarthy, Michael D. The Existence of Moments of FIML and Other Restricted Reduced-Form Estimates. **In** *[Klein, L. R.],* 1983, pp. 140–52.

Morimune, Kimio. Approximate Distributions of *k*-Class Estimators When the Degree of Overidentifiability Is Large Compared with the Sample Size. *Econometrica,* May, 1983, *51* (3), pp. 821–41.

Muthén, Bengt. Latent Variable Structural Equation Modeling with Categorical Data. *J. Econometrics,* May/June 1983, *22* (1/2), pp. 43–65.

Phillips, P. C. B. Exact Small Sample Theory in the Simultaneous Equations Model. **In** *Griliches, Z. and Intriligator, M. D., eds.,* 1983, pp. 449–516.

Pollock, D. S. G. Varieties of the LIML Estimator. *Australian Econ. Pap.,* December 1983, *22* (41), pp. 499–506.

Powell, James L. The Asymptotic Normality of Two-Stage Least Absolute Deviations Estimators. *Econometrica,* September 1983, *51* (5), pp. 1569–75.

Sargan, John Denis. Identification and Lack of Identification. *Econometrica,* November 1983, *51* (6), pp. 1605–33.

Sevestre, Patrick and Trognon, Alain. Propriétés de grands échantillons d'une classe d'estimateurs des modèles autorégressifs à erreurs composées. (Large-Sample Properties of a Class of Estimators of Autoregressive Error-Components Models. With English summary.) *Ann. INSEE,* April–June 1983, (50), pp. 25–48.

Srivastava, V. K. and Srivastava, A. K. A Note on Moments of *k*-Class Estimators for Negative *k*. *J. Econometrics,* February 1983, *21* (2), pp. 257–60.

Startz, Richard. Testing Rational Expectations by the Use of Overidentifying Restrictions. *J. Econometrics,* December 1983, *23*(3), pp. 343–51. [G: U.S.; W. Germany]

Swamy, Paravastu A. V. B. and Mehta, Jatinder S.

Further Results on Zellner's Minimum Expected Loss and Full Information Maximum Likelihood Estimators for Undersized Samples. *J. Bus. Econ. Statist.*, April 1983, *1* (2), pp. 154–62. [G: U.S.]

Szroeter, Jerzy. Generalized Wald Methods for Testing Nonlinear Implicit and Overidentifying Restrictions. *Econometrica*, March 1983, *51* (2), pp. 335–53.

Wegge, Leon L. and Feldman, Mark. Comment to the Editor [Identification and Rational Expectations Models]. *J. Econometrics*, February 1983, *21* (2), pp. 255–56.

Wegge, Leon L. and Feldman, Mark. Identifiability Criteria for Muth-Rational Expectations Models. *J. Econometrics*, February 1983, *21* (2), pp. 245–54.

Wu, De-Min. Tests of Causality, Predeterminedness and Exogeneity. *Int. Econ. Rev.*, October 1983, *24* (3), pp. 547–58.

2113 Distributed Lags and Correlated Disturbance Terms; Inferential Problems in Single Equation Models

Aguirre-Torres, Victor and Gallant, A. Ronald. The Null and Non-Null Asymptotic Distribution of the Cox Test for Multivariate Nonlinear Regression: Alternatives and a New Distribution-Free Cox Test. *J. Econometrics*, January 1983, *21* (1), pp. 5–33.

Amemiya, Takeshi. A Comparison of the Amemiya GLS and the Lee–Maddala–Trost G2SLS in a Simultaneous-Equations Tobit Model. *J. Econometrics*, December 1983, *23* (3), pp. 295–300.

Amemiya, Takeshi. Non-linear Regression Models. In *Griliches, Z. and Intriligator, M. D., eds.*, 1983, pp. 333–389.

Amemiya, Takeshi. Partially Generalized Least Squares and Two-Stage Least Squares Estimators. *J. Econometrics*, October 1983, *23* (2), pp. 275–83.

Antle, John M. Testing the Stochastic Structure of Production: A Flexible Moment-based Approach. *J. Bus. Econ. Statist.*, July 1983, *1* (3), pp. 192–201. [G: U.S.]

Attfield, Clifford L. F. Consistent Estimation of Certain Parameters in the Unobservable Variable Model When There Is Specification Error. *Rev. Econ. Statist.*, February 1983, *65* (1), pp. 164–67.

Avery, Robert B.; Hansen, Lars Peter and Hotz, V. Joseph. Multiperiod Probit Models and Orthogonality Condition Estimation. *Int. Econ. Rev.*, February 1983, *24* (1), pp. 21–35.

Baksalary, Jerzy K. An Invariance Property of Farebrother's Procedure for Estimation with Aggregated Data. *J. Econometrics*, August 1983, *22* (3), pp. 317–22.

Balestra, Pietro. A Note on Amemiya's Partially Generalized Least Squares. *J. Econometrics*, October 1983, *23* (2), pp. 285–90.

Ballatori, Enzo. Un metodo di transformazione delle stime nei modelli lineari generalizzati. (A Transformation Method of Estimates in the Generalized Linear Models. With English summary.) *Statistica*, April–June 1983, *43* (2), pp. 267–74.

Baltagi, Badi H. and Griffin, James M. Gasoline Demand in the OECD: An Application of Pooling and Testing Procedures. *Europ. Econ. Rev.*, July 1983, *22* (2), pp. 117–37. [G: OECD]

Behrman, Jere R.; Knight, John B. and Sabot, Richard H. A Simulation Alternative to the Comparative R^2 Approach to Decomposing Inequality. *Oxford Bull. Econ. Statist.*, August 1983, *45* (3), pp. 307–12.

Bera, Anil K. and McAleer, Michael. Some Exact Tests for Model Specification. *Rev. Econ. Statist.*, May 1983, *65* (2), pp. 351–54.

Bergstrom, Albert Rex. Gaussian Estimation of Structural Parameters in Higher Order Continuous Time Dynamic Models. *Econometrica*, January 1983, *51* (1), pp. 117–52.

Bewley, R. A. Tests of Restrictions in Large Demand Systems. *Europ. Econ. Rev.*, January 1983, *20* (1–3), pp. 257–69.

Bickel, Peter J. Minimax Aspects of Bounded-Influence Regression: Comment. *J. Amer. Statist. Assoc.*, March 1983, *78* (381), pp. 75–77.

Bierens, Herman J. Uniform Consistency of Kernel Estimators of a Regression Function under Generalized Conditions. *J. Amer. Statist. Assoc.*, September 1983, *78* (383), pp. 699–707.

Breiman, L. and Freedman, David. How Many Variables Should Be Entered in a Regression Equation? *J. Amer. Statist. Assoc.*, March 1983, *78* (381), pp. 131–36.

Byron, Ray P. and Bera, Anil K. Least Squares Approximations to Unknown Regression Functions: A Comment. *Int. Econ. Rev.*, February 1983, *24* (1), pp. 255–60.

Byron, Ray P. and Bera, Anil K. Linearized Estimation of Nonlinear Single Equation Functions. *Int. Econ. Rev.*, February 1983, *24* (1), pp. 237–48.

Carroll, Raymond J. Minimax Aspects of Bounded-Influence Regression: Comment. *J. Amer. Statist. Assoc.*, March 1983, *78* (381), pp. 78–79.

Chen, Chan-Fu. Score Tests for Regression Models. *J. Amer. Statist. Assoc.*, March 1983, *78* (381), pp. 158–61.

Colombino, Ugo. Variabili dipendenti limitate e selezione non casuale delle osservazioni: una applicazione alla stima della funzione di salario e di offerta di lavoro delle donne sposate in Italia. (Limited Dependent Variables and Non-Random Sample Selection: An Application to the Wage and Labour Supply Function of Married Women in Italy. With English summary.) *Giorn. Econ.*, May-June 1983, *42* (5–6), pp. 369–85. [G: Italy]

Conniffe, Denis. Comments on the Weighted Regression Approach to Missing Values. *Econ. Soc. Rev.*, July 1983, *14* (4), pp. 259–71.

Conniffe, Denis. Small-Sample Properties of Estimators of Regression Coefficients Given a Common Pattern of Missing Data. *Rev. Econ. Stud.*, January 1983, *50* (1), pp. 111–20.

Cook, R. Dennis and Weisberg, Sanford. Minimax Aspects of Bounded-Influence Regression: Comment. *J. Amer. Statist. Assoc.*, March 1983, *78* (381), pp. 74–75.

Cosslett, Stephen R. Distribution–Free Maximum Likelihood Estimator of the Binary Choice Model. *Econometrica*, May, 1983, *51* (3), pp. 765–82.

Coursey, Don and Nyquist, Hans. On Least Absolute Error Estimation of Linear Regression Models with Dependent Stable Residuals. *Rev. Econ. Statist.*, November 1983, *65* (4), pp. 687–92.

Cragg, John G. More Efficient Estimation in the Presence of Heteroscedasticity of Unknown Form. *Econometrica,* May, 1983, *51* (3), pp. 751–63.

Dastoor, Naorayex, K. Some Aspects of Testing Non-Nested Hypotheses. *J. Econometrics,* February 1983, *21* (2), pp. 213–28.

Davidson, Russell and MacKinnon, James G. Testing the Specification of Multivariate Models in the Presence of Alternative Hypotheses. *J. Econometrics,* December 1983, *23* (3), pp. 301–13.

Dijkstra, Theo. Some Comments on Maximum Likelihood and Partial Least Squares Methods. *J. Econometrics,* May/June 1983, *22* (1/2), pp. 67–90.

Doksum, Kjell A. and Wong, Chi-Wing. Statistical Tests Based on Transformed Data. *J. Amer. Statist. Assoc.*, June 1983, *78* (382), pp. 411–17.

Domowitz, Ian. Diagnostic Tests as Residual Analysis: Comment. *Econometric Rev.*, 1983, *2* (2), pp. 219–22.

Doran, Howard E. and Griffiths, William E. On the Relative Efficiency of Estimators Which Include the Initial Observations in the Estimation of Seemingly Unrelated Regressions with First-Order Autoregressive Disturbances. *J. Econometrics,* October 1983, *23* (2), pp. 165–91.

Duan, Naihua. Smearing Estimate: A Nonparametric Retransformation Method. *J. Amer. Statist. Assoc.*, September 1983, *78* (383), pp. 605–10.

Dufour, J.-M.; Gaudry, M. J. I. and Hafer, R. W. A Warning on the Use of the Cochrane–Orcutt Procedure Based on a Money Demand Equation. *Empirical Econ.*, 1983, *8* (2), pp. 111–17. **[G: U.S.]**

DuMouchel, William H. and Duncan, Greg J. Using Sample Survey Weights in Multiple Regression Analyses of Stratified Samples. *J. Amer. Statist. Assoc.*, September 1983, *78* (383), pp. 535–43.

Duncan, Gregory M. Estimation and Inference for Heteroscedastic Systems of Equations. *Int. Econ. Rev.*, October 1983, *24* (3), pp. 559–66.

Duncan, Gregory M. Sample Selectivity as a Proxy Variable Problem: On the Use and Misuse of Gaussian Selectivity Corrections. In *Reid, J. D., Jr., ed.*, 1983, pp. 333–45.

Dykstra, Richard L. An Algorithm for Restricted Least Squares Regression. *J. Amer. Statist. Assoc.*, December 1983, *78* (384), pp. 837–42.

Engle, Robert F. Diagnostic Tests as Residual Analysis: Comment. *Econometric Rev.*, 1983, *2* (2), pp. 223–28.

Ericsson, Neil R. Asymptotic Properties of Instrumental Variables Statistics for Testing Non-Nested Hypotheses. *Rev. Econ. Stud.*, April 1983, *50* (2), pp. 287–304.

Finster, Mark. A Frequentistic Approach to Sequential Estimation in the General Linear Model. *J. Amer. Statist. Assoc.*, June 1983, *78* (382), pp. 403–07.

Fisher, Gordon R. Tests for Two Separate Regressions. *J. Econometrics,* January 1983, *21* (1), pp. 117–32.

Fomby, Thomas B. and Guilkey, David K. An Examination of Two-Step Estimators for Models with Lagged Dependent Variables and Autocorrelated Errors. *J. Econometrics,* August 1983, *22* (3), pp. 291–300.

Ghosh, S.; Gilbert, C. L. and Hallett, A. J. Hughes. Tests of Functional Form in Dynamic Econometric Models: Some Empirical Experience. *Empirical Econ.*, 1983, *8* (2), pp. 63–69.

Gilstein, C. Zachary and Leamer, Edward E. Robust Sets of Regression Estimates. *Econometrica,* March 1983, *51* (2), pp. 321–33.

Gilstein, C. Zachary and Leamer, Edward E. The Set of Weighted Regression Estimates. *J. Amer. Statist. Assoc.*, December 1983, *78* (384), pp. 942–48.

Godfrey, Leslie G. Diagnostic Tests as Residual Analysis: Comment. *Econometric Rev.*, 1983, *2* (2), pp. 229–33.

Godfrey, Leslie G. Testing Non-Nested Models after Estimation by Instrumental Variables or Least Squares. *Econometrica,* March 1983, *51* (2), pp. 355–65.

Godfrey, Leslie G. and Pesaran, M. H. Tests of Non-Nested Regression Models: Small Sample Adjustments and Monte Carlo Evidence. *J. Econometrics,* January 1983, *21* (1), pp. 133–54.

Gourieroux, Christian; Monfort, Alain and Trognon, Alain. Testing Nested or Non-Nested Hypotheses. *J. Econometrics,* January 1983, *21* (1), pp. 83–115.

Greene, William H. Estimation of Limited Dependent Variable Models by Ordinary Least Squares and the Method of Moments. *J. Econometrics,* February 1983, *21* (2), pp. 195–212. **[G: U.S.]**

Greenwald, Bruce C. A General Analysis of Bias in the Estimated Standard Errors of Least Squares Coefficients. *J. Econometrics,* August 1983, *22* (3), pp. 323–38.

Gregory, Allan W. and McAleer, Michael. Testing Non-Nested Specifications of Money Demand for Canada. *Can. J. Econ.*, November 1983, *16* (4), pp. 593–602. **[G: Canada]**

Guilkey, David K.; Lovell, C. A. Knox and Sickles, Robin C. A Comparison of the Performance of Three Flexible Functional Forms. *Int. Econ. Rev.*, October 1983, *24* (3), pp. 591–616.

Haggstrom, Gus W. Logistic Regression and Discriminant Analysis by Ordinary Least Squares. *J. Bus. Econ. Statist.*, July 1983, *1* (3), pp. 229–38. **[G: U.S.]**

Hall, A. D. Confidence Contours for Two Test Statistics for Non-Nested Regression Models. *J. Econometrics,* January 1983, *21* (1), pp. 155–60.

Hanssens, Dominique M. and Liu, Lon-Mu. Lag Specification in Rational Distributed Lag Structural Models. *J. Bus. Econ. Statist.*, October 1983, *1* (4), pp. 316–25. **[G: U.S.]**

Hayashi, Fumio and Sims, Christopher A. Nearly Efficient Estimation of Time Series Models with Predetermined, but Not Exogenous, Instruments. *Econometrica,* May, 1983, *51* (3), pp. 783–98.

Heiberger, Richard M.; Velleman, Paul F. and Ypelaar, M. Agelia. Generating Test Data with Independently Controllable Features for Multivariate General Linear Forms. *J. Amer. Statist. Assoc.*, September 1983, *78*(383), pp. 585–95.

Hendry, David F. Model Specification Tests against Non-Nested Alternatives: Comment. *Econometric Rev.*, 1983, *2*(1), pp. 111–14.

Hendry, David F. and Marshall, Robert C. On High and Low R^2 Contributions. *Oxford Bull. Econ. Statist.*, August 1983, *45*(3), pp. 313–16.

Hettmansperger, Thomas P. and McKean, Joseph W. A Geometric Interpretation of Inferences Based on Ranks in the Linear Model. *J. Amer. Statist. Assoc.*, December 1983, *78*(384), pp. 885–93.

Hsieh, David A. A Heteroscedasticity-Consistent Covariance Matrix Estimator for Time Series Regressions. *J. Econometrics*, August 1983, *22*(3), pp. 281–90.

Huber, Peter J. Minimax Aspects of Bounded-Influence Regression: Rejoinder. *J. Amer. Statist. Assoc.*, March 1983, *78*(381), pp. 80.

Huber, Peter J. Minimax Aspects of Bounded-Influence Regression. *J. Amer. Statist. Assoc.*, March 1983, *78*(381), pp. 66–72.

Hussain, S. S. and Sprent, P. Non-Parametric Regression. *J. Roy. Statist. Soc.*, 1983, *146*(2), pp. 182–91.

Johnson, Wesley and Geisser, Seymour. A Predictive View of the Detection and Characterization of Influential Observations in Regression Analysis. *J. Amer. Statist. Assoc.*, March 1983, *78*(381), pp. 137–44.

Judge, G. G. and Bock, M. E. Biased Estimation. In *Griliches, Z. and Intriligator, M. D., eds.*, 1983, pp. 599–649.

Kaplan, Jack S. A Method for Calculating MINQUE Estimators of Variance Components. *J. Amer. Statist. Assoc.*, June 1983, *78*(382), pp. 476–77.

Kapteyn, Arie and Wansbeek, Tom. Identification in the Linear Errors in Variables Model. *Econometrica*, November 1983, *51*(6), pp. 1847–49.

Kelejian, Harry H. and Stephan, Scott W. Inference in Random Coefficient Panel Data Models: A Correction and Clarification of the Literature. *Int. Econ. Rev.*, February 1983, *24*(1), pp. 249–54.

Keller, Wouter J. and Wansbeek, Tom. Multivariate Methods for Quantitative and Qualitative Data. *J. Econometrics*, May/June 1983, *22*(1/2), pp. 91–111.

Kennedy, Peter E. Logarithmic Dependent Variables and Prediction Bias. *Oxford Bull. Econ. Statist.*, November 1983, *45*(4), pp. 389–92.

Kennedy, Peter E. On an Inappropriate Means of Reducing Multicollinearity. *Reg. Sci. Urban Econ.*, November 1983, *13*(4), pp. 579–81.

Kinal, Terrence and Lahiri, Kajal. Specification Error Analysis with Stochastic Regressors. *Econometrica*, July 1983, *51*(4), pp. 1209–19.

King, Maxwell L. Testing for Autoregressive against Moving Average Errors in the Linear Regression Model. *J. Econometrics*, January 1983, *21*(1), pp. 35–51.

King, Maxwell L. The Durbin-Watson Test for Serial Correlation: Bounds for Regressions Using Monthly Data. *J. Econometrics*, April 1983, *21*(3), pp. 357–66.

Klein, Roger W. Model Specification Tests against Non-Nested Alternatives: Comment. *Econometric Rev.*, 1983, *2*(1), pp. 115–19.

Kohn, Robert. Consistent Estimation of Minimal Subset Dimension. *Econometrica*, March 1983, *51*(2), pp. 367–76.

Krasker, William S.; Kuh, Edwin and Welsch, Roy E. Estimation for Dirty Data and Flawed Models. In *Griliches, Z. and Intriligator, M. D., eds.*, 1983, pp. 651–98.

Krasker, William S. and Welsch, Roy E. Minimax Aspects of Bounded-Influence Regression: Comment. *J. Amer. Statist. Assoc.*, March 1983, *78*(381), pp. 72–73.

Lancaster, Tony. Generalised Residuals and Heterogeneous Duration Models: The Exponential Case. *Bull. Econ. Res.*, November 1983, *35*(2), pp. 71–85.

Leamer, Edward E. Model Choice and Specification Analysis. In *Griliches, Z. and Intriligator, M. D., eds.*, 1983, pp. 285–330.

Leamer, Edward E. and Leonard, Herman B. Reporting the Fragility of Regression Estimates. *Rev. Econ. Statist.*, May 1983, *65*(2), pp. 306–17.

Lee, Lung-Fei. A Test for Distributional Assumptions for the Stochastic Frontier Functions. *J. Econometrics*, August 1983, *22*(3), pp. 245–67.

Lee, Lung-Fei. Generalized Econometric Models with Selectivity. *Econometrica*, March 1983, *51*(2), pp. 507–12.

Lee, Lung-Fei. On Maximum Likelihood Estimation of Stochastic Frontier Production Models. *J. Econometrics*, October 1983, *23*(2), pp. 269–74.

Levine, David K. A Remark on Serial Correlation in Maximum Likelihood. *J. Econometrics*, December 1983, *23*(3), pp. 337–42.

Lovell, Michael C. Data Mining. *Rev. Econ. Statist.*, February 1983, *65*(1), pp. 1–12.

Luscia, Fausta. Impiego di tecniche bayesiane non parametriche nel modello lineare genereale. (Nonparametric Bayesian Approach to the Linear Regression Model. With English summary.) *Giorn. Econ.*, January–February 1983, *42*(1–2), pp. 79–89.

MacKinnon, James G. Model Specification Tests against Non-Nested Alternatives. *Econometric Rev.*, 1983, *2*(1), pp. 85–110.

MacKinnon, James G. Model Specification Tests against Non-Nested Alternatives: Comment. *Econometric Rev.*, 1983, *2*(1), pp. 151–58.

MacKinnon, James G.; White, Halbert and Davidson, Russell. Tests for Model Specification in the Presence of Alternative Hypotheses: Some Further Results. *J. Econometrics*, January 1983, *21*(1), pp. 53–70.

Maekawa, Koichi. An Approximation to the Distribution of the Least Squares Estimator in an Autoregressive Model with Exogenous Variables. *Econometrica*, January 1983, *51*(1), pp. 229–38.

Malhotra, Naresh K. A Comparison of the Predictive Validity of Procedures for Analyzing Binary Data. *J. Bus. Econ. Statist.*, October 1983, *1*(4), pp. 326–36. **[G: U.S.]**

Mallows, C. L. Minimax Aspects of Bounded-Influence Regression: Comment. *J. Amer. Statist. Assoc.*, March 1983, *78*(381), pp. 77.

McAleer, Michael and Bera, Anil K. Model Specification Tests against Non-Nested Alternatives: Comment. *Econometric Rev.*, 1983, *2*(1), pp. 121–30.

McDonald, John and Darroch, John. Consistent Estimation of Equations with Composite Moving Average Disturbance Terms. *J. Econometrics,* October 1983, *23*(2), pp. 253–67.

McGowan, Ian. Choice of Functional Form in Economics. *Brit. Rev. Econ. Issues,* Spring 1983, *5*(12), pp. 32–45.

Menges, Günter. Unscharfe Konzepte in der Ökonometrie. (Concepts of Uncertainty in Econometrics. With English summary.) *Ifo-Studien,* 1983, *29*(3), pp. 163–73.

Mizon, Grayham E. and Richard, Jean-François. Model Specification Tests against Non-Nested Alternatives: Comment. *Econometric Rev.*, 1983, *2*(1), pp. 131–36.

Morimune, Kimio. Model Specification Tests against Non-Nested Alternatives: Comment. *Econometric Rev.*, 1983, *2*(1), pp. 137–43.

Muthén, Bengt. Latent Variable Structural Equation Modeling with Categorical Data. *J. Econometrics,* May/June 1983, *22*(1/2), pp. 43–65.

Naiman, Daniel Q. Comparing Scheffé-Type to Constant-Width Confidence Bounds in Regression. *J. Amer. Statist. Assoc.*, December 1983, *78*(384), pp. 906–12.

Nicholls, D. F. and Pagan, A. R. Heteroscedasticity in Models with Lagged Dependent Variables. *Econometrica,* July 1983, *51*(4), pp. 1233–42.

Nowak, Eugen. Identification of the Dynamic Shock-Error Model with Autocorrelated Errors. *J. Econometrics,* October 1983, *23*(2), pp. 211–21.

Nyblom, Jukka and Mäkeläinen, Timo. Comparisons of Tests for the Presence of Random Walk Coefficients in a Simple Linear Model. *J. Amer. Statist. Assoc.*, December 1983, *78*(384), pp. 856–64.

Pagan, A. R. and Hall, A. D. Diagnostic Tests as Residual Analysis. *Econometric Rev.*, 1983, *2*(2), pp. 159–218.

Pagan, A. R. and Hall, A. D. Diagnostic Tests as Residual Analysis: Reply. *Econometric Rev.*, 1983, *2*(2), pp. 249–54.

Pakes, Ariél. On Group Effects and Errors in Variables in Aggregation. *Rev. Econ. Statist.*, February 1983, *65*(1), pp. 168–73. **[G: U.S.]**

Passamani, Giuliana. Il problema della verifica della correlazione seriale degli errori in modelli di regressione con variabili endogene ritardate: il test asintotico *h* ed il suo comportamento nel caso di serie storiche limitate. (Testing the Serial Correlation of Errors in Regression Models with Lagged Endogenous Variables: The Asymptotic *h* Test and Its Behaviour in the Case of Limited Time Series. With Engli. *Statistica,* January–March 1983, *43*(1), pp. 67–81 .

Pesaran, M. H. Model Specification Tests against Non-Nested Alternatives: Comment. *Econometric Rev.*, 1983, *2*(1), pp. 145–49.

Poirier, Dale J. and Ruud, Paul A. Diagnostic Testing in Missing Data Models. *Int. Econ. Rev.*, October 1983, *24*(3), pp. 537–46.

Pregibon, Daryl. Diagnostic Tests as Residual Analysis: Comment. *Econometric Rev.*, 1983, *2*(2), pp. 235–39.

Pryor, Frederic L. An Econometric Shoal Warning for Comparative Economists. *ACES Bull. (See Comp. Econ. Stud. after 8/85),* Fall 1983, *25*(3), pp. 71–73.

Ramsey, James B. Diagnostic Tests as Residual Analysis: Perspective and Comment. *Econometric Rev.*, 1983, *2*(2), pp. 241–48.

del Rey, Eusebio Cleto. Problemas de cómputo de la corrección por sesgo en el caso lognormal. (Computational Problems of the Bias Corrections in the Lognormal Case. With English summary.) *Económica,* January–April 1983, *29*(1), pp. 27–43. **[G: Argentina]**

Ruud, Paul A. Sufficient Conditions for the Consistency of Maximum Likelihood Estimation Despite Misspecifications of Distribution in Multinsm KreDiscrete Choice Models. *Econometrica,* January 1983, *51*(1), pp. 225–28.

Sargan, John Denis and Bhargava, Alok. Maximum Likelihood Estimation of Regression Models with First Order Moving Average Errors When the Root Lies on the Unit Circle. *Econometrica,* May, 1983, *51*(3), pp. 799–820.

Sargan, John Denis and Bhargava, Alok. Testing Residuals from Least Squares Regression for Being Generated by the Gaussian Random Walk. *Econometrica,* January 1983, *51*(1), pp. 153–74.

Sargan, John Denis and Mehta, Fatemeh. A Generalization of the Durbin Significance Test and Its Application to Dynamic Specification. *Econometrica,* September 1983, *51*(5), pp. 1551–67.

Saxena, Ashok K. and Bhatnagar, Ravi K. Location Invariance of Mixed Regression Estimator(s). *Statistica,* July–September 1983, *43*(3), pp. 479–82.

Schmidt, Peter. A Note on a Fixed Effect Model with Arbitrary Interpersonal Covariance. *J. Econometrics,* August 1983, *22*(3), pp. 391–93.

Schwert, G. William. Tests of Causality: The Message in the Innovations. **In** *Brunner, K. and Meltzer, A. H., eds.*, 1983, *1979,* pp. 215–56.

Seaks, Terry G. and Layson, Stephen K. Box-Cox Estimation with Standard Econometric Problems. *Rev. Econ. Statist.*, February 1983, *65*(1), pp. 160–64.

Smith, Marlene A. and Maddala, G. S. Multiple Model Testing for Non-Nested Heteroskedastic Censored Regression Models. *J. Econometrics,* January 1983, *21*(1), pp. 71–81.

Spitzer, John J. and Baillie, Richard T. Small-Sample Properties of Predictions from the Regression Model with Autoregressive Errors. *J. Amer. Statist. Assoc.*, June 1983, *78*(382), pp. 258–63.

Stewart, Mark B. On Least Squares Estimation When the Dependent Variable Is Grouped. *Rev. Econ. Stud.*, October 1983, *50*(4), pp. 737–53.

Swamy, Paravastu A. V. B. and Mehta, Jatinder S. Ridge Regression Estimation of the Rotterdam Model. *J. Econometrics,* August 1983, *22*(3), pp. 365–90.

Tanaka, Katsuto. Non-Normality of the Lagrange Multiplier Statistic for Testing the Constancy of Regression Coefficients. *Econometrica,* September 1983, *51*(5), pp. 1577–82.

Tsurumi, Hiroki. A Bayesian and Maximum Likelihood Analysis of a Gradual Switching Regression Model with Sampling Experiments. *Econ. Stud. Quart.*, December 1983, *34*(3), pp. 237–48.

Tyrrell, Timothy J. The Use of Polynomials to Shift Coefficients in Linear Regression Models. *J. Bus. Econ. Statist.*, July 1983, *1*(3), pp. 249–52.

Ullah, Aman; Srivastava, V. K. and Chandra, Ram. Properties of Shrinkage Estimators in Linear Regression When Disturbances Are Not Normal. *J. Econometrics,* April 1983, *21*(3), pp. 389–402.

Uusipaikka, Esa. Exact Confidence Bands for Linear Regression over Intervals. *J. Amer. Statist. Assoc.*, September 1983, *78*(383), pp. 638–44.

Watson, Mark W. and Engle, Robert F. Alternative Algorithms for the Estimation of Dynamic Factor, MIMIC and Varying Coefficient Regression Models. *J. Econometrics,* December 1983, *23*(3), pp. 385–400. **[G: U.S.]**

Watson, P. K. Kalman Filtering as an Alternative to Ordinary Least Squares—Some Theoretical Considerations and Empirical Results. *Empirical Econ.*, 1983, *8*(2), pp. 71–85.

Wecker, William E. and Ansley, Craig F. The Signal Extraction Approach to Nonlinear Regression and Spline Smoothing. *J. Amer. Statist. Assoc.*, March 1983, *78*(381), pp. 81–89.

Wegman, Edward J. and Wright, Ian W. Splines in Statistics. *J. Amer. Statist. Assoc.*, June 1983, *78*(382), pp. 351–65.

Young, A. S. A Comparative Analysis of Prior Families for Distributed Lags. *Empirical Econ.*, 1983, *8*(3–4), pp. 215–27.

Zehnwirth, Ben. Hachemeister's Bayesian Regression Model Revisited. *J. Econometrics,* September 1983, *23*(1), pp. 119–29.

2114 Multivariate Analysis, Statistical Information Theory, and Other Special Inferential Problems; Queuing Theory; Markov Chains

Andersen, Erling B. Latent Trait Models. *J. Econometrics,* May/June 1983, *22*(1/2), pp. 215–27.

Bartholomew, D. J. Latent Variable Models for Ordered Categorical Data. *J. Econometrics,* May/June 1983, *22*(1/2), pp. 229–43.

Deville, J.-C. and Saporta, G. Correspondence Analysis, with an Extension towards Nominal Time Series. *J. Econometrics,* May/June 1983, *22*(1/2), pp. 169–89.

Dey, Dipak K. and Berger, James O. On Truncation of Shrinkage Estimators in Simultaneous Estimation of Normal Means. *J. Amer. Statist. Assoc.*, December 1983, *78*(384), pp. 865–69.

Fienberg, Stephen E. and Meyer, Michael M. Loglinear Models and Categorical Data Analysis with Psychometric and Econometric Applications. *J. Econometrics,* May/June 1983, *22*(1/2), pp. 191–214.

Guttman, Irwin and Menzefricke, Ulrich. Bayesian Inference in Multivariate Regression with Missing Observations on the Response Variables. *J. Bus. Econ. Statist.*, July 1983, *1*(3), pp. 239–48. **[G: Canada]**

Heiser, Willem J. and Meulman, Jacqueline. Analyzing Rectangular Tables by Joint and Constrained Multidimensional Scaling. *J. Econometrics,* May/June 1983, *22*(1/2), pp. 139–67.

Jewell, William S. Enriched Multinormal Priors Revisited. *J. Econometrics,* September 1983, *23*(1), pp. 5–35.

de Jong, Piet; Greig, Malcolm and Madan, Dilip. Testing for Random Pairing. *J. Amer. Statist. Assoc.,* June 1983, *78*(382), pp. 332–36.

Keller, Wouter J. and Wansbeek, Tom. Multivariate Methods for Quantitative and Qualitative Data. *J. Econometrics,* May/June 1983, *22*(1/2), pp. 91–111.

de Leeuw, Jan. Models and Methods for the Analysis of Correlation Coefficients. *J. Econometrics,* May/June 1983, *22*(1/2), pp. 113–37.

Maddala, G. S. Methods of Estimation for Models of Markets with Bounded Price Variation. *Int. Econ. Rev.*, June 1983, *24*(2), pp. 361–78.

Muliere, Pietro and Scarsini, Marco. Impostazione Bayesiana di un problema di analisi della varianza a due criteri. (A Bayesian Approach to a Two-Way Analysis of a Variance Problem. With English summary.) *Giorn. Econ.*, July–August 1983, *42*(7–8), pp. 519–26.

Schweitzer, Walter. Analyse und Prognose der Binnenwanderungen in der Bundesrepublik Deutschland mit Markov-Modellen. (Analysis and Forecast of Internal Migrations within the Federal Republic of Germany Using Markov Models. With English summary.) *Ifo-Studien,* 1983, *29*(3), pp. 217–41. **[G: W. Germany]**

Wright, Roger L. Finite Population Sampling with Multivariate Auxiliary Information. *J. Amer. Statist. Assoc.,* December 1983, *78*(384), pp. 879–84.

2115 Bayesian Statistics and Bayesian Econometrics

Arnold, Barry C. and Press, S. James. Bayesian Inference for Pareto Populations. *J. Econometrics,* April 1983, *21*(3), pp. 287–306. **[G: U.S.]**

Berger, James O. Parametric Empirical Bayes Inference: Theory and Applications: Comment. *J. Amer. Statist. Assoc.*, March 1983, *78*(381), pp. 55–57.

Dempster, A. P. Parametric Empirical Bayes Inference: Theory and Applications: Comment. *J. Amer. Statist. Assoc.*, March 1983, *78*(381), pp. 57–58.

Drèze, Jacques H. and Richard, Jean-François. Bayesian Analysis of Simultaneous Equation Systems. **In** *Griliches, Z. and Intriligator, M. D., eds.*, 1983, pp. 517–98.

Goel, Prem K. Information Measures and Bayesian Hierarchical Models. *J. Amer. Statist. Assoc.*, June 1983, *78*(382), pp. 408–10.

Goldstein, Michael. General Variance Modifications for Linear Bayes Estimators. *J. Amer. Statist. Assoc.,* September 1983, *78*(383), pp. 616–18.

Hsiao, Cheng. Identification. **In** *Griliches, Z. and Intriligator, M. D., eds.*, 1983, pp. 223–83.

Jewell, William S. Enriched Multinormal Priors Revisited. *J. Econometrics,* September 1983, *23*(1), pp. 5–35.

Krantz, David H. and Miyamoto, John. Priors and

Likelihood Ratios as Evidence. *J. Amer. Statist. Assoc.*, June 1983, *78*(382), pp. 418–23.

Leamer, Edward E. Model Choice and Specification Analysis. In *Griliches, Z. and Intriligator, M. D., eds.*, 1983, pp. 285–330.

Leonard, Tom. Parametric Empirical Bayes Inference: Theory and Applications: Comment. *J. Amer. Statist. Assoc.*, March 1983, *78*(381), pp. 59–60.

Lindley, Dennis V. Parametric Empirical Bayes Inference: Theory and Applications: Comment. *J. Amer. Statist. Assoc.*, March 1983, *78*(381), pp. 61–62.

Luscia, Fausta. Impiego di tecniche bayesiane non parametriche nel modello lineare genereale. (Nonparametric Bayesian Approach to the Linear Regression Model. With English summary.) *Giorn. Econ.*, January–February 1983, *42*(1–2), pp. 79–89.

Monahan, John F. Fully Bayesian Analysis of ARMA Time Series Models. *J. Econometrics*, April 1983, *21*(3), pp. 307–31.

Morris, Carl N. Parametric Empirical Bayes Inference: Theory and Applications: Rejoinder. *J. Amer. Statist. Assoc.*, March 1983, *78*(381), pp. 63–65.

Morris, Carl N. Parametric Empirical Bayes Inference: Theory and Applications. *J. Amer. Statist. Assoc.*, March 1983, *78*(381), pp. 47–55.

Shapiro, C. P. Sequential Allocation and Optional Stopping in Bayesian Simultaneous Estimation. *J. Amer. Statist. Assoc.*, June 1983, *78*(382), pp. 396–402.

Stigler, Stephen M. Parametric Empirical Bayes Inference: Theory and Applications: Comment. *J. Amer. Statist. Assoc.*, March 1983, *78*(381), pp. 62–63.

Tsurumi, Hiroki. A Bayesian and Maximum Likelihood Analysis of a Gradual Switching Regression Model with Sampling Experiments. *Econ. Stud. Quart.*, December 1983, *34*(3), pp. 237–48.

Vardeman, Stephen and Meeden, Glen. Calibration, Sufficiency, and Domination Considerations for Bayesian Probability Assessors. *J. Amer. Statist. Assoc.*, December 1983, *78*(384), pp. 808–16.

Zehnwirth, Ben. Hachemeister's Bayesian Regression Model Revisited. *J. Econometrics*, September 1983, *23*(1), pp. 119–29.

2116 Time Series and Spectral Analysis

Anderson, Richard G.; Johannes, James M. and Rasche, Robert H. A New Look at the Relationship between Time-Series and Structural Econometric Models. *J. Econometrics*, October 1983, *23*(2), pp. 234–51.

Ansley, Craig F. Forecasting Economic Time Series with Structural and Box–Jenkins Models: A Case Study: Comment. *J. Bus. Econ. Statist.*, October 1983, *1*(4), pp. 307–09. **[G: France; U.S.]**

Bell, W. R. and Hillmer, S. C. Modeling Time Series with Calendar Variations. *J. Amer. Statist. Assoc.*, September 1983, *78*(383), pp. 526–34.

Bergstrom, Albert Rex. Gaussian Estimation of Structural Parameters in Higher Order Continuous Time Dynamic Models. *Econometrica*, January 1983, *51*(1), pp. 117–52.

Bordignon, Silvano and Masarotto, Guido. Una classe di modelli non stazionari. (A Class of Non-Stationary Models. With English summary.) *Statistica*, January–March 1983, *43*(1), pp. 83–104.

Borsu-Bilande, A. Application des méthodes de Box et Jenkins à la construction d'un indice de conjoncture. (With English summary.) *Cah. Écon. Bruxelles*, 4th Trimester 1983, (100), pp. 594–620.

Byrne, Philip J. and Arnold, Steven F. Inference about Multivariate Means for a Nonstationary Autoregressive Model. *J. Amer. Statist. Assoc.*, December 1983, *78*(384), pp. 850–55.

Cholette, Pierre A. La désaisonnalisation pour le non-spécialiste. (Seasonal Adjustment for the Non-Specialist. With English summary.) *L'Actual. Econ.*, March 1983, *59*(1), pp. 144–52.

Deistler, Manfred. The Properties of the Parameterization of ARMAX Systems and Their Relevance for Structural Estimation and Dynamic Specification. *Econometrica*, July 1983, *51*(4), pp. 1187–207.

Edwards, Charles E. and Stansell, Stanley R. New Car Sales Data and Automobile Company Stock Prices: A Study of the Causal Relationships. *Bus. Econ.*, May 1983, *18*(3), pp. 27–35. **[G: U.S.]**

Erlat, Halûk. Nedensellik Sinamalari Üzerine. (On Tests of Causality. With English summary.) *METU*, 1983, *10*(1), pp. 65–96.

Evans, Lewis and Wells, Graeme. Pierce and Haugh on Characterizations of Causality: A Re-examination. *J. Econometrics*, December 1983, *23*(3), pp. 331–35.

Figlewski, Stephen. Optimal Price Forecasting Using Survey Data. *Rev. Econ. Statist.*, February 1983, *65*(1), pp. 13–21. **[G: U.S.]**

Findley, David F. Forecasting Economic Time Series with Structural and Box–Jenkins Models: A Case Study: Comment. *J. Bus. Econ. Statist.*, October 1983, *1*(4), pp. 309–11.

Fomby, Thomas B. and Guilkey, David K. An Examination of Two–Step Estimators for Models with Lagged Dependent Variables and Autocorrelated Errors. *J. Econometrics*, August 1983, *22*(3), pp. 291–300.

Gersch, Will and Kitagawa, Genshiro. The Prediction of Time Series with Trends and Seasonalities. *J. Bus. Econ. Statist.*, July 1983, *1*(3), pp. 253–64.

Geweke, John; Meese, Richard A. and Dent, Warren. Comparing Alternative Tests of Causality in Temporal Systems: Analytic Results and Experimental Evidence. *J. Econometrics*, February 1983, *21*(2), pp. 161–94.

Grillenzoni, Carlo. Construzione di un modello a serie storiche multivariato: un approccio disaggregato-simultaneo. (Building a Multivariate Time Series Model: A Simultaneous Disaggregated Approach. With English summary.) *Statistica*, January–March 1983, *43*(1), pp. 133–53.

Grillenzoni, Carlo. La distribuzione asintotica dei *gain* in funzioni di impulso–risposta non lineari. (The Asymptotic Distribution of Gains in Non Linear Impulse–Response Functions. With English summary.) *Statistica*, July–September 1983,

43(3), pp. 451–74.

Gutierrez-Camara, José L. and Huss, Hans-Joachim. The Interaction between Floating Exchange Rates, Money, and Prices—An Empirical Analysis. *Weltwirtsch. Arch.*, 1983, *119*(3), pp. 401–28. **[G: U.S.; Japan; Canada; W. Europe]**

Hansen, Lars Peter and Sargent, Thomas J. Aggregation over Time and the Inverse Optimal Predictor Problem for Adaptive Expectations in Conginuous Time. *Int. Econ. Rev.*, February 1983, *24*(1), pp. 1–20. **[G: U.S.]**

Hansen, Lars Peter and Sargent, Thomas J. The Dimensionality of the Aliasing Problem in Models with Rational Spectral Densities. *Econometrica*, March 1983, *51*(2), pp. 377–87.

Hanssens, Dominique M. and Liu, Lon-Mu. Lag Specification in Rational Distributed Lag Structural Models. *J. Bus. Econ. Statist.*, October 1983, *1*(4), pp. 316–25. **[G: U.S.]**

Harvey, A. C. and Todd, P. H. J. Forecasting Economic Time Series with Structural and Box-Jenkins Models: A Case Study. *J. Bus. Econ. Statist.*, October 1983, *1*(4), pp. 299–307. **[G: U.K.]**

Harvey, A. C. and Todd, P. H. J. Forecasting Economic Time Series with Structural and Box-Jenkins Models: A Case Study: Response. *J. Bus. Econ. Statist.*, October 1983, *1*(4), pp. 313–15. **[G: U.S.]**

Hatanaka, Michio. Confidence Judgment of the Extrapolation from a Dynamic Money Demand Function. *J. Econ. Dynam. Control*, September 1983, *6*(1/2), pp. 55–78. **[G: U.S.]**

Hatanaka, Michio and Odaki, Mitsuhiro. Policy Analyses with and without a Priori Conditions. *Econ. Stud. Quart.*, December 1983, *34*(3), pp. 193–210.

Hayashi, Fumio and Sims, Christopher A. Nearly Efficient Estimation of Time Series Models with Predetermined, but Not Exogenous, Instruments. *Econometrica*, May, 1983, *51*(3), pp. 783–98.

Haynes, Stephen E. The Subtle Danger of Symmetry Restrictions in Time Series Regressions, with Application to Fertility Models. *Southern Econ. J.*, October 1983, *50*(2), pp. 521–28. **[G: Finland]**

Hsiao, Cheng. Identification. **In** *Griliches, Z. and Intriligator, M. D., eds.*, 1983, pp. 223–83.

Hsieh, David A. A Heteroscedasticity-Consistent Covariance Matrix Estimator for Time Series Regressions. *J. Econometrics*, August 1983, *22*(3), pp. 281–90.

King, Maxwell L. Testing for Autoregressive against Moving Average Errors in the Linear Regression Model. *J. Econometrics*, January 1983, *21*(1), pp. 35–51.

de Leeuw, Frank and McKelvey, Michael J. A "True" Time Series and Its Indicators. *J. Amer. Statist. Assoc.*, March 1983, *78*(381), pp. 37–46.

Litterman, Robert B. A Random Walk, Markov Model for the Distribution of Time Series. *J. Bus. Econ. Statist.*, April 1983, *1*(2), pp. 169–73. **[G: U.S.]**

Machak, Joseph A.; Spivey, W. Allen and Wrobleski, William J. Analyzing Permanent and Transient Influences in Multiple Time Series Models. *J. Bus. Econ. Statist.*, January 1983, *1*(1), pp. 57–65. **[G: U.S.]**

Maekawa, Koichi. An Approximation to the Distribution of the Least Squares Estimator in an Autoregressive Model with Exogenous Variables. *Econometrica*, January 1983, *51*(1), pp. 229–38.

Maravall, Agustin. An Application of Nonlinear Time Series Forecasting. *J. Bus. Econ. Statist.*, January 1983, *1*(1), pp. 66–74. **[G: Spain]**

McDonald, John and Darroch, John. Consistent Estimation of Equations with Composite Moving Average Disturbance Terms. *J. Econometrics*, October 1983, *23*(2), pp. 253–67.

Monahan, John F. Fully Bayesian Analysis of ARMA Time Series Models. *J. Econometrics*, April 1983, *21*(3), pp. 307–31.

Newbold, Paul. Forecasting Economic Time Series with Structural and Box-Jenkins Models: A Case Study: Comment. *J. Bus. Econ. Statist.*, October 1983, *1*(4), pp. 311–12.

Noble, Nicholas R. and Fields, T. Windsor. Sunspots and Cycles: Comment. *Southern Econ. J.*, July 1983, *50*(1), pp. 251–54.

Nowak, Eugen. Identification of the Dynamic Shock-Error Model with Autocorrelated Errors. *J. Econometrics*, October 1983, *23*(2), pp. 211–21.

Park, Choon Y. and Heikes, Russell G. A Note on Balestra's (1980) Approximate Estimator for the First-Order Moving Average Process. *J. Econometrics*, April 1983, *21*(3), pp. 387–88.

Pierce, David A. Seasonal Adjustment of the Monetary Aggregates: Summary of the Federal Reserve's Committee Report. *J. Bus. Econ. Statist.*, January 1983, *1*(1), pp. 37–42. **[G: U.S.]**

Pierce, David A.; Grupe, Michael R. and Cleveland, William P. Seasonal Adjustment of the Weekly Monetary Aggregates: A Model-Based Approach. *Fed. Res. Bull.*, August 1983, *69*(8), pp. 592. **[G: U.S.]**

Salathe, Larry E.; Price, J. Michael and Gadson, Kenneth E. The Food and Agricultural Policy Simulator: An Addendum [On the Misuse of Theil's Inequality Coefficient]. *Agr. Econ. Res.*, July 1983, *35*(3), pp. 40–42.

Sargan, John Denis and Bhargava, Alok. Maximum Likelihood Estimation of Regression Models with First Order Moving Average Errors When the Root Lies on the Unit Circle. *Econometrica*, May, 1983, *51*(3), pp. 799–820.

Sargan, John Denis and Mehta, Fatemeh. A Generalization of the Durbin Significance Test and Its Application to Dynamic Specification. *Econometrica*, September 1983, *51*(5), pp. 1551–67.

Schlicht, Ekkehart and Pauly, Ralf. Descriptive Seasonal Adjustment by Minimizing Perturbations. *Empirica*, 1983, (1), pp. 15–28.

Schwert, G. William. Tests of Causality: The Message in the Innovations. In *Brunner, K. and Meltzer, A. H., eds.*, 1983, *1979*, pp. 215–56.

Sheehan, Richard G. and Grieves, Robin. Sunspots and Cycles: Reply. *Southern Econ. J.*, July 1983, *50*(1), pp. 255–56.

Spitzer, John J. and Baillie, Richard T. Small-Sample Properties of Predictions from the Regression Model with Autoregressive Errors. *J. Amer. Statist. Assoc.*, June 1983, *78*(382), pp. 258–63.

Spliid, Henrik. A Fast Estimation Method for the

Vector Autoregressive Moving Average Model with Exogenous Variables. *J. Amer. Statist. Assoc.*, December 1983, *78* (384), pp. 843–49. [G: U.K.]

Stroeker, Roelof J. Approximations of the Eigenvalues of the Covariance Matrix of a First-Order Autoregressive Process. *J. Econometrics*, August 1983, *22* (3), pp. 269–79.

Tanaka, Katsuto. Asymptotic Expansions Associated with the AR(1) Model with Unknown Mean. *Econometrica*, July 1983, *51* (4), pp. 1221–31.

Tanaka, Katsuto. Estimation for Transients in the Frequency Domain. *J. Amer. Statist. Assoc.*, September 1983, *78* (383), pp. 718–24.

Tiao, George C. and Tsay, Ruey S. Multiple Time Series Modeling and Extended Sample Cross-Correlations. *J. Bus. Econ. Statist.*, January 1983, *1* (1), pp. 43–56. [G: U.S.]

Townsend, Robert M. Forecasting the Forecasts of Others. *J. Polit. Econ.*, August 1983, *91* (4), pp. 546–88.

Weissenberger, Edgar and Thomas, J. J. The Causal Role of Money in West Germany. *Weltwirtsch. Arch.*, 1983, *119* (1), pp. 64–83. [G: W. Germany]

Wilcox, James A. Disaggregating Data Using Related Series. *J. Bus. Econ. Statist.*, July 1983, *1* (3), pp. 187–91. [G: U.S.]

Winkler, Robert L. and Makridakis, Spyros. The Combination of Forecasts. *J. Roy. Statist. Soc.*, 1983, *146* (2), pp. 150–57. [G: U.S.]

Wu, De-Min. Tests of Causality, Predeterminedness and Exogeneity. *Int. Econ. Rev.*, October 1983, *24* (3), pp. 547–58.

2117 Survey Methods; Sampling Methods

Calder, Bobby J.; Philips, Lynn W. and Tybout, Alice M. Beyond External Validity. *J. Cons. Res.*, June 1983, *10* (1), pp. 112–24.

Dalenius, Tore. An Evaluation of Model-Dependent and Probability-Sampling Inferences in Sample Surveys: Comment. *J. Amer. Statist. Assoc.*, December 1983, *78* (384), pp. 799–800.

Greenfield, C. C. On Estimators for Dual Record Systems. *J. Roy. Statist. Soc.*, 1983, *146* (3), pp. 273–80. [G: Indonesia]

Hansen, Morris H.; Madow, William G. and Tepping, Benjamin J. An Evaluation of Model-Dependent and Probability-Sampling Inferences in Sample Surveys: Comments. *J. Amer. Statist. Assoc.*, December 1983, *78* (384), pp. 805–07.

Hansen, Morris H.; Madow, William G. and Tepping, Benjamin J. An Evaluation of Model-Dependent and Probability-Sampling Inferences in Sample Surveys. *J. Amer. Statist. Assoc.*, December 1983, *78* (384), pp. 776–93.

Hauser, Robert M. and Massagli, Michael P. Some Models of Agreement and Disagreement in Repeated Measurements of Occupation. *Demography*, November 1983, *20* (4), pp. 449–60. [G: U.S.]

Hoem, Jan M. Distortions Caused by Nonobservation of Periods of Cohabitation before the Latest. *Demography*, November 1983, *20* (4), pp. 491–506. [G: U.S.]

Keating, Giles. The Effect of Answering Practices on the Relationship between CBI Survey Data and Official Data: Erratum. *Appl. Econ.*, June 1983, *15* (3), pp. 424. [G: U.K.]

Keating, Giles. The Effect of Answering Practices on the Relationship between CBI Survey Data and Official Data. *Appl. Econ.*, April 1983, *15* (2), pp. 213–24. [G: U.K.]

Liao, H. and Sedransk, J. Selection of Strata Sample Sizes for the Comparison of Domain Means. *J. Amer. Statist. Assoc.*, December 1983, *78* (384), pp. 870–78.

Little, Roderick J. A. An Evaluation of Model-Dependent and Probability-Sampling Inferences in Sample Surveys: Comment. *J. Amer. Statist. Assoc.*, December 1983, *78* (384), pp. 797–99.

Lynch, John G., Jr. The Role of External Validity in Theoretical Research. *J. Cons. Res.*, June 1983, *10* (1), pp. 109–11.

McGrath, Joseph E. and Brinberg, David. External Validity and the Research Process: A Comment on the Calder/Lynch Dialogue. *J. Cons. Res.*, June 1983, *10* (1), pp. 115–24.

Menzefricke, Ulrich. On Sampling Plan Selection with Dollar-Unit Sampling. *J. Acc. Res.*, Spring 1983, *21* (1), pp. 96–105.

Olsen, Robert A. Sample Size and Markowitz Diversification. *J. Portfol. Manage.*, Fall 1983, *10* (1), pp. 18–22. [G: U.S.]

Royall, Richard M. An Evaluation of Model-Dependent and Probability-Sampling Inferences in Sample Surveys: Comment. *J. Amer. Statist. Assoc.*, December 1983, *78* (384), pp. 794–96.

Rubin, Donald B. An Evaluation of Model-Dependent and Probability-Sampling Inferences in Sample Surveys: Comments. *J. Amer. Statist. Assoc.*, December 1983, *78* (384), pp. 803–05.

Smith, T. M. Fred. An Evaluation of Model-Dependent and Probability-Sampling Inferences in Sample Surveys: Comments. *J. Amer. Statist. Assoc.*, December 1983, *78* (384), pp. 801–02.

Smith, T. M. Fred. On the Validity of Inferences from Non-Random Samples. *J. Roy. Statist. Soc.*, 1983, *146* (4), pp. 394–403.

Wright, Roger L. Finite Population Sampling with Multivariate Auxiliary Information. *J. Amer. Statist. Assoc.*, December 1983, *78* (384), pp. 879–84.

2118 Theory of Index Numbers and Aggregation

Barnett, William A. New Indices of Money Supply and the Flexible Laurent Demand System. *J. Bus. Econ. Statist.*, January 1983, *1* (1), pp. 7–23. [G: U.S.]

Barnett, William A. Understanding the New Divisia Monetary Aggregates. *Rev. Public Data Use (See J. Econ. Soc. Meas. after 4/85)*, December 1983, *11* (4), pp. 349–55. [G: U.S.]

Berndt, Ernst R. Quality Adjustment, Hedonics, and Modern Empirical Demand Analysis. **In** *Diewert, W. E. and Montmarquette, C., eds.*, 1983, pp. 817–63.

Blackorby, Charles. Axiomatic Foundation of Price Indexes and Purchasing Power Parities: Comment. **In** *Diewert, W. E. and Montmarquette, C., eds.*, 1983, pp. 451–54.

Blackorby, Charles and Donaldson, David. Preference Diversity and Aggregate Economic Cost-of-Living Indexes. In *Diewert, W. E. and Montmarquette, C., eds.*, 1983, pp. 373–409.

Brown, Keith C. and Kadiyala, K. Rao. Construction of Economic Index Numbers with an Incomplete Set of Data. *Rev. Econ. Statist.*, August 1983, *65*(3), pp. 520–24. **[G: Selected MDCs]**

Brown, Murray and Greenberg, Richard. The Divisia Index of Technological Change, Path Independence and Endogenous Prices. *Scand. J. Econ.*, 1983, *85*(2), pp. 239–47.

Browne, Stephen B. Measuring the Current Rate of Inflation: Comment. In *Diewert, W. E. and Montmarquette, C., eds.*, 1983, pp. 894–99. **[G: Canada]**

Dagum, Estela Bee and Morry, Marietta. The Estimation of Seasonal Variations in Consumer Price Indexes. In *Diewert, W. E. and Montmarquette, C., eds.*, 1983, pp. 919–67. **[G: Canada]**

Denny, Michael G. S. and Fuss, Melvyn A. A General Approach to Intertemporal and Interspatial Productivity Comparisons. *J. Econometrics*, December 1983, *23*(3), pp. 315–30. **[G: Canada; U.S.; Japan]**

Denny, Michael G. S. and Fuss, Melvyn A. The Use of Discrete Variables in Superlative Index Number Comparisons. *Int. Econ. Rev.*, June 1983, *24*(2), pp. 419–21.

Diewert, W. Erwin. An Overview of the Papers on Price Level Measurement. In *Diewert, W. E. and Montmarquette, C., eds.*, 1983, pp. 59–70.

Diewert, W. Erwin. The Theory of the Cost-of-Living Index and the Measurement of Welfare Change. In *Diewert, W. E. and Montmarquette, C., eds.*, 1983, pp. 163–233.

Diewert, W. Erwin. The Theory of the Output Price Index and the Measurement of Real Output Change. In *Diewert, W. E. and Montmarquette, C., eds.*, 1983, pp. 1049–1113.

Diewert, W. Erwin. The Treatment of Seasonality in the Cost-of-Living Index. In *Diewert, W. E. and Montmarquette, C., eds.*, 1983, pp. 1019–45.

Donaldson, David and Weymark, John A. Ethically Flexible Gini Indices for Income Distributions in the Continuum. *J. Econ. Theory*, April 1983, *29*(2), pp. 353–58.

DuMouchel, William H. and Duncan, Greg J. Using Sample Survey Weights in Multiple Regression Analyses of Stratified Samples. *J. Amer. Statist. Assoc.*, September 1983, *78*(383), pp. 535–43.

Early, John F. and Sinclair, James H. Quality Adjustment in the Producer Price Indexes. In *Foss, M. F., ed.*, 1983, pp. 107–42. **[G: U.S.]**

Eichhorn, Wolfgang and Voeller, Joachim. Axiomatic Foundation of Price Indexes and Purchasing Power Parities. In *Diewert, W. E. and Montmarquette, C., eds.*, 1983, pp. 411–50.

Geroski, P. A. Some Reflections on the Theory and Application of Concentration Indices. *Int. J. Ind. Organ.*, 1983, *1*(1), pp. 79–94. **[G: U.S.]**

Gordon, Robert J. Energy Efficiency, User-Cost Change, and the Measurement of Durable Goods Prices. In *Foss, M. F., ed.*, 1983, pp. 205–53. **[G: U.S.]**

Gordon, Robert J. Energy Efficiency, User-Cost Change, and the Measurement of Durable Goods Prices: Reply. In *Foss, M. F., ed.*, 1983, pp. 265–68. **[G: U.S.]**

Griliches, Zvi. Quality Adjustment in the Producer Price Indexes: Comment. In *Foss, M. F., ed.*, 1983, pp. 142–45. **[G: U.S.]**

Jöhr, Walter Adolf and Jetzer, Jean-Pierre. Auf der Suche nach der besten Gleichungs-Sequenz für die Indexberechnung. Ein Beitrag zur Diskussion über den schweizerischen Index der Konsumentenpreise. (Searching for the Best Combination of the Optimal Equations for Calculating the Index. A Contribution to the Discussion on the Swiss Consumer Price Index. With English summary.) *Schweiz. Z. Volkswirtsch. Statist.*, December 1983, *119*(4), pp. 419–563. **[G: Switzerland]**

Jorgenson, Dale W. and Slesnick, Daniel T. Individual and Social Cost-of-Living Indexes. In *Diewert, W. E. and Montmarquette, C., eds.*, 1983, pp. 241–323. **[G: U.S.]**

Kneepkens, Huib H. Eine neue Deutung von alten ungewogenen Indexzahlen. (A New Interpretation of Old Unweighted Index Numbers. With English summary.) *Jahr. Nationalökon. Statist.*, July 1983, *198*(4), pp. 369–73.

Kundu, Amitabh and Smith, Tony E. An Impossibility Theorem on Poverty Indices. *Int. Econ. Rev.*, June 1983, *24*(2), pp. 423–34.

Pollak, Robert A. The Theory of the Cost-of-Living Index. In *Diewert, W. E. and Montmarquette, C., eds.*, 1983, pp. 87–161.

Pollak, Robert A. The Treatment of 'Quality' in the Cost of Living Index. *J. Public Econ.*, February 1983, *20*(1), pp. 25–53.

Rhoades, D. and Elhawary-Rivet, N. Measuring the Current Rate of Inflation. In *Diewert, W. E. and Montmarquette, C., eds.*, 1983, pp. 877–93. **[G: Canada]**

Russell, R. Robert. Individual and Social Cost-of-Living Indexes: Comments. In *Diewert, W. E. and Montmarquette, C., eds.*, 1983, pp. 324–36. **[G: U.S.]**

Russell, R. Robert. The Theory of the Cost-of-Living Index and the Measurement of Welfare Change: Comments. In *Diewert, W. E. and Montmarquette, C., eds.*, 1983, pp. 234–39.

Russell, Thomas. Notes on Exact Aggregation. In *[Yamada, I.]*, 1983, pp. 171–76.

Samuelson, Paul A. Rigorous Observational Positivism: Klein's Envelope Aggregation; Thermodynamics and Economic Isomorphisms. In *[Klein, L. R.]*, 1983, pp. 1–38.

Stahl, Dale O., II. Quasi-Homothetic Preferences, the Generalized Divisia Quantity Index, and Aggregation. *Economica*, February 1983, *50*(197), pp. 87–93.

Szulc, Bohdan J. Linking Price Index Numbers. In *Diewert, W. E. and Montmarquette, C., eds.*, 1983, pp. 537–66.

Triplett, Jack E. Concepts of Quality in Input and Output Price Measures: A Resolution of the User-Value Resource-Cost Debate. In *Foss, M. F., ed.*, 1983, pp. 269–311.

Triplett, Jack E. Energy Efficiency, User-Cost Change, and the Measurement of Durable Goods Prices: Comment. In *Foss, M. F., ed.*, 1983, pp. 253–65. **[G: U.S.]**

Triplett, Jack E. Quality Adjustment, Hedonics, and Modern Empirical Demand Analysis: Comment. **In** *Diewert, W. E. and Montmarquette, C., eds.,* 1983, pp. 864–75.

Weitzman, Martin L. On the Meaning of Comparative Factor Productivity. **In** *[Erlich, A.],* 1983, pp. 166–70.

2119 Experimental Design; Social Experiments

Ashenfelter, Orley. Determining Participation in Income-Tested Social Programs. *J. Amer. Statist. Assoc.,* September 1983, *78*(383), pp. 517–25. **[G: U.S.]**

Bendick, Marc, Jr. and Struyk, Raymond J. The Great Housing Experiment: Lessons for Future Social Experiments. **In** *Friedman, J. and Weinberg, D. H., eds.,* 1983, pp. 258–65. **[G: U.S.]**

Lowry, Ira S. The Great Housing Experiment: The Supply Experiment. **In** *Friedman, J. and Weinberg, D. H., eds.,* 1983, pp. 23–36. **[G: U.S.]**

212 Construction, Analysis, and Use of Econometric Models

2120 Construction, Analysis, and Use of Econometric Models

Aivazian, S. A. Applied Statistics and Probabilistic Modeling in Economics. *Matekon,* Fall 1983, *20*(1), pp. 29–56. **[G: U.S.S.R.]**

Anderson, Richard G.; Johannes, James M. and Rasche, Robert H. A New Look at the Relationship between Time-Series and Structural Econometric Models. *J. Econometrics,* October 1983, *23*(2), pp. 234–51.

Antle, John M. Testing the Stochastic Structure of Production: A Flexible Moment-based Approach. *J. Bus. Econ. Statist.,* July 1983, *1*(3), pp. 192–201. **[G: U.S.]**

Basu, Dipak R. and Lazaridis, Alexis. Stochastic Optimal Control by Pseudo-Inverse. *Rev. Econ. Statist.,* May 1983, *65*(2), pp. 347–50.

Baum, Christopher F. Evaluating Macroeconomic Policy: Optimal Control Solutions versus Suboptimal Alternatives. **In** *Gruber, J., ed.,* 1983, pp. 81–109. **[G: U.S.]**

Bhargava, Alok and Sargan, John Denis. Estimating Dynamic Random Effects Models from Panel Data Covering Short Time Periods. *Econometrica,* November 1983, *51*(6), pp. 1635–59.

Blanchard, Olivier J. Methods of Solution and Simulation for Dynamic Rational Expectations Models. *Écon. Appl.,* 1983, *36*(1), pp. 27–46.

Brandsma, Andries S.; Hughes Hallett, A. J. and van der Windt, Nico. Optimal Control of Large Nonlinear Models: An Efficient Method of Policy Search Applied to the Dutch Economy. *J. Policy Modeling,* June 1983, *5*(2), pp. 253–70. **[G: Netherlands]**

Buiter, Willem H. Expectations and Control Theory. *Écon. Appl.,* 1983, *36*(1), pp. 129–56.

Calzolari, Giorgio. Asymptotic Distribution of Power Spectra and Peak Frequencies in the Stochastic Response of Econometric Models. *J. Econ. Dynam. Control,* May 1983, *5*(2/3), pp. 235–47. **[G: U.S.]**

Campbell, Robert B. Cost Function Bias and Linear Quadratic Stabilisation. *Australian Econ. Pap.,* December 1983, *22*(41), pp. 495–98.

Condie, James M., et al. A Brief Description of the FRB Modeleasy/Fedeasy Econometric Language. *J. Econ. Dynam. Control,* February 1983, *5*(1), pp. 75–79.

Cooper, Russel J. and McLaren, Keith R. The ORANI-MACRO Interface: An Illustrative Exposition. *Econ. Rec.,* June 1983, *59*(165), pp. 166–79. **[G: Australia]**

Craine, Roger and Hardouvelis, Gikas A. Are Rational Expectations for Real? *Greek Econ. Rev.,* April 1983, *5*(1), pp. 5–32. **[G: U.S.]**

Cumby, Robert E.; Huizinga, John and Obstfeld, Maurice. Errata: Two-Step Two-Stage Least Squares Estimation in Models with Rational Expectations. *J. Econometrics,* December 1983, *23*(3), pp. 407. **[G: U.S.]**

Cumby, Robert E.; Huizinga, John and Obstfeld, Maurice. Two-Step Two-Stage Least Squares Estimation in Models with Rational Expectations. *J. Econometrics,* April 1983, *21*(3), pp. 333–55. **[G: U.S.]**

Deissenberg, Christophe. Interactive Solution of Multiple Objective, Dynamic, Macroeconomic Stabilization Problems: A Comparative Study. **In** *Gruber, J., ed.,* 1983, pp. 305–09.

Don, F. J. Henk. Corrigenda: Restrictions on Variables. *J. Econometrics,* October 1983, *23*(2), pp. 291–92. **[G: Netherlands]**

Don, F. J. Henk. Uncertainty and the Vigour of Policy: A Stronger Result [Uncertainty and the Vigour of Policy: Some Implications of Quadratic Preferences]. *J. Econ. Dynam. Control,* September 1983, *6*(1/2), pp. 187–91.

Dormont, Brigitte. Substitution et coûts des facteurs: une approche en termes de modèles à erreurs sur les variables. (On the Use of a Theoretical Constraint to Eliminate Error-in-Variables Biases. With English summary.) *Ann. INSEE,* April–June 1983, (50), pp. 73–92. **[G: France]**

Drud, Arne. A Survey of Model Representations and Simulation Algorithms in Some Existing Modeling Systems. *J. Econ. Dynam. Control,* February 1983, *5*(1), pp. 5–35.

Drud, Arne. Interfacing Modeling Systems and Solution Algorithms. *J. Econ. Dynam. Control,* February 1983, *5*(1), pp. 131–49.

Eliasson, Gunnar. On the Optimal Rate of Structural Adjustment. **In** *Eliasson, G.; Sharefkin, M. and Ysander, B.-C., eds.,* 1983, pp. 269–323. **[G: Sweden]**

Fair, Ray C. An Outline of a Multicountry Econometric Model. **In** *Hickman, B. G., ed.,* 1983, pp. 85–92. **[G: Global]**

Fair, Ray C. and Taylor, John B. Solution and Maximum Likelihood Estimation of Dynamic Nonlinear Rational Expectations Models. *Econometrica,* July 1983, *51*(4), pp. 1169–85.

Fischer, J. and Uebe, Götze. The "Optimal" Control of the RWI-Model. **In** *Gruber, J., ed.,* 1983, pp. 10–20. **[G: W. Germany]**

Friedmann, Ralph. The Asymptotic Distribution of Optimal Policy Feedback Coefficients. **In** *Gruber, J., ed.,* 1983, pp. 131–47. **[G: U.S.]**

Ghosh, S.; Gilbert, C. L. and Hallett, A. J. Hughes.

Tests of Functional Form in Dynamic Econometric Models: Some Empirical Experience. *Empirical Econ.*, 1983, *8*(2), pp. 63–69.

Gilli, Manfred; Ritschard, Gilbert and Royer, Daniel. Pour une approche structurale en économie. (Towards a Structural Approach in Economics. With English summary.) *Revue Écon.*, March 1983, *34*(2), pp. 277–304.

Gruber, Josef. Introduction: Towards Observed Preferences in Econometric Decision Models. In *Gruber, J., ed.*, 1983, pp. 1–9.

Gutierrez-Camara, José L. and Huss, Hans-Joachim. The Interaction between Floating Exchange Rates, Money, and Prices—An Empirical Analysis. *Weltwirtsch. Arch.*, 1983, *119*(3), pp. 401–28. [G: U.S.; Japan; Canada; W. Europe]

Haas, Hansjorg. Conflict, Cooperation and Social Preference Functions. In *Gruber, J., ed.*, 1983, pp. 148–69. [G: U.S.]

Hatanaka, Michio and Odaki, Mitsuhiro. Policy Analyses with and without a Priori Conditions. *Econ. Stud. Quart.*, December 1983, *34*(3), pp. 193–210.

Heady, Earl O. Models for Agricultural Policy: The CARD Example. *Europ. Rev. Agr. Econ.*, 1983, *10*(1), pp. 1–14. [G: U.S.]

Heady, Earl O.; Langley, James A. and Huang, Wenyuan. A Recursive Adaptive Hybrid Model for National and Interregional Analysis. In *Gruber, J., ed.*, 1983, pp. 183–220. [G: U.S.]

Heike, Hans-Dieter and Rossa, Harald. Optimal Stabilization with a Quarterly Model of the Federal Republic of Germany. In *Gruber, J., ed.*, 1983, pp. 21–47. [G: W. Germany]

Hendry, David F. Econometric Modelling: The "Consumption Function" in Retrospect. *Scot. J. Polit. Econ.*, November 1983, *30*(3), pp. 193–220. [G: U.K.]

Hendry, David F. Model Specification Tests against Non-Nested Alternatives: Comment. *Econometric Rev.*, 1983, *2*(1), pp. 111–14.

Hendry, David F. On Keynesian Model Building and the Rational Expectations Critique: A Question of Methodology. *Cambridge J. Econ.*, March 1983, *7*(1), pp. 69–75.

Hickman, Bert G. A Cross Section of Global International Economic Models. In *Hickman, B. G., ed.*, 1983, pp. 3–26.

Hoffman, Dennis L. and Schlagenhauf, Don E. Rationality, Specification Tests, and Macroeconomic Models. *J. Econometrics*, April 1983, *21*(3), pp. 367–86. [G: U.S.]

Hosouchi, Isamu. Computation of Feedback Control Methods with Time-Varying Parameters. *Econ. Stud. Quart.*, April 1983, *34*(1), pp. 22–37.

House, Robert. Optimizing Models: A Comparison of Optimizing Modeling Methodologies: Discussion. In *Baum, K. H. and Schertz, L. P., eds.*, 1983, pp. 351–57.

Intriligator, Michael D. Economic and Econometric Models. In *Griliches, Z. and Intriligator, M. D., eds.*, 1983, pp. 181–221.

Jorgenson, Dale W. Modeling Production for General Equilibrium Analysis. *Scand. J. Econ.*, 1983, *85*(2), pp. 101–12. [G: U.S.]

Kaufman, Roger T. and Woglom, Geoffrey. Estimating Models with Rational Expectations. *J. Money, Credit, Banking*, August 1983, *15*(3), pp. 275–85.

Keyzer, Michiel A. Policy Adjustment Rules in an Open Exchange Model with Money and Endogenous Balance of Trade Deficit. In *Kelley, A. C.; Sanderson, W. C. and Williamson, J. G., eds.*, 1983, pp. 57–70.

Kirchgässner, Gebhard. Ökonometrie: Datenanalyse oder Theorienüberprüfung? (Econometrics: Data Analysis or Statistical Testing of Economic Theories? With English summary.) *Jahr. Nationalökon. Statist.*, November 1983, *198*(6), pp. 511–38.

Kirchgässner, Gebhard. An Application of Optimal Control to a Small Model of Politico-economic Interaction. In *Gruber, J., ed.*, 1983, pp. 55–80. [G: W. Germany]

Klein, Roger W. Model Specification Tests against Non-Nested Alternatives: Comment. *Econometric Rev.*, 1983, *2*(1), pp. 115–19.

Krasker, William S.; Kuh, Edwin and Welsch, Roy E. Estimation for Dirty Data and Flawed Models. In *Griliches, Z. and Intriligator, M. D., eds.*, 1983, pp. 651–98.

Krelle, Wilhelm E. An Outline of a Multicountry Econometric Model: Comment. In *Hickman, B. G., ed.*, 1983, pp. 93–95. [G: Global]

Larson, Don. Summary Statistics and Forecasting Performance. *Agr. Econ. Res.*, July 1983, *35*(3), pp. 11–22. [G: U.S.]

Law, I. A. and Lewis, P. E. T. A Bayesian Approach to Expectations Formation. *Brit. Rev. Econ. Issues*, Spring 1983, *5*(12), pp. 46–56. [G: U.K.]

Lawson, Tony. Different Approaches to Economic Modelling [On Keynesian Model Building and the Rational Expectations Critique]. *Cambridge J. Econ.*, March 1983, *7*(1), pp. 77–84.

Leamer, Edward E. Model Choice and Specification Analysis. In *Griliches, Z. and Intriligator, M. D., eds.*, 1983, pp. 285–330.

Lee, Lung-Fei. A Test for Distributional Assumptions for the Stochastic Frontier Functions. *J. Econometrics*, August 1983, *22*(3), pp. 245–67.

Lee, Lung-Fei. Generalized Econometric Models with Selectivity. *Econometrica*, March 1983, *51*(2), pp. 507–12.

Leserer, Michael. A Fine-tuning Scheme for Economic Decision Rules. In *Gruber, J., ed.*, 1983, pp. 111–15.

MacKinnon, James G. Model Specification Tests against Non-Nested Alternatives. *Econometric Rev.*, 1983, *2*(1), pp. 85–110.

MacKinnon, James G. Model Specification Tests against Non-Nested Alternatives: Comment. *Econometric Rev.*, 1983, *2*(1), pp. 151–58.

Maddala, G. S. Methods of Estimation for Models of Markets with Bounded Price Variation. *Int. Econ. Rev.*, June 1983, *24*(2), pp. 361–78.

Mariano, Roberto S. and Brown, Bryan W. Asymptotic Behavior of Predictors in a Nonlinear Simultaneous System. *Int. Econ. Rev.*, October 1983, *24*(3), pp. 523–36.

Matsuyama, Keisuke and Tamura, Yasuhiro. On Calculation of Causal Orderings of Variables Appearing in Simultaneous Equations. *Econ. Computat. Cybern. Stud. Res.*, 1983, *18*(1), pp. 73–85.

McAleer, Michael and Bera, Anil K. Model Specification Tests against Non-Nested Alternatives: Comment. *Econometric Rev.*, 1983, *2*(1), pp. 121–30.

McClements, L. D. Some Aspects of Model Building. **In** *Marr, W. L. and Raj, B., eds.*, 1983, *1973*, pp. 203–27.

Meeraus, Alexander. An Algebraic Approach to Modeling. *J. Econ. Dynam. Control*, February 1983, *5*(1), pp. 81–108.

Merz, Joachim. FELES: The Functionalized Extended Linear Expenditure System: Theory, Estimation Procedures and Application to Individual Household Consumption Expenditures Involving Socioeconomic and Sociodemographic Characteristics. *Europ. Econ. Rev.*, December 1983, *23*(3), pp. 359–94. **[G: W. Germany]**

Micheli, Giuseppe A. Le trappole del controllo ottimo parametrico della popolazione. (The Pitfalls of the Optimal Control of Population. With English summary.) *Giorn. Econ.*, May-June 1983, *42*(5–6), pp. 321–46. **[G: Italy]**

Migliaro, A. The Five Economic Theories Underlying Econometric Models. **In** *Migliaro, A. and Jain, C. L., eds.*, 1983, pp. 10–14.

Mihailov, Boris. Modeling Alternative Socioeconomic Mechanisms. **In** *Kelley, A. C.; Sanderson, W. C. and Williamson, J. G., eds.*, 1983, pp. 141–65.

Mizon, Grayham E. and Richard, Jean-François. Model Specification Tests against Non-Nested Alternatives: Comment. *Econometric Rev.*, 1983, *2*(1), pp. 131–36.

Morimune, Kimio. Model Specification Tests against Non-Nested Alternatives: Comment. *Econometric Rev.*, 1983, *2*(1), pp. 137–43.

Nepomiastchy, Pierre and Rechenmann, François. The Equation Writing External Language of the Moduleco Software. *J. Econ. Dynam. Control*, February 1983, *5*(1), pp. 37–57.

Norman, Alfred L.; Lasdon, Leon S. and Hsin, Jun Kuan. A Comparison of Methods for Solving and Optimizing a Large Non-Linear Econometric Model. *J. Econ. Dynam. Control*, September 1983, *6*(1/2), pp. 3–24.

O'Brien, Mike J. Optimal Macroeconomic Policy with Constrained Instruments. *J. Econ. Dynam. Control*, September 1983, *6*(1/2), pp. 193–200.

Ohtani, Kazuhiro. A Bayesian Analysis of the Generalized Production Function with Heteroscedasticity. *Econ. Stud. Quart.*, August 1983, *34*(2), pp. 171–78. **[G: U.S.]**

Peach, James T. and Webb, James L. Randomly Specified Macroeconomic Models: Some Implications for Model Selection. *J. Econ. Issues*, September 1983, *17*(3), pp. 697–720. **[G: U.S.]**

Pesaran, M. H. Model Specification Tests against Non-Nested Alternatives: Comment. *Econometric Rev.*, 1983, *2*(1), pp. 145–49.

Peterson, William; Barker, Terry and van der Ploeg, Rick. Software Support for Multisectoral Dynamic Models of National Economies. *J. Econ. Dynam. Control*, February 1983, *5*(1), pp. 109–30.

Petkovski, Djordjija B. Decentralized Control Strategies for Large-Scale Discrete-Time Systems. **In** *Gruber, J., ed.*, 1983, pp. 170–82.

Prescott, Edward C. Should Control Theory Be Used for Economic Stabilization? **In** *Brunner, K. and Meltzer, A. H., eds.*, 1983, *1977*, pp. 285–310.

Quandt, Richard E. Switching between Equilibrium and Disequilibrium. *Rev. Econ. Statist.*, November 1983, *65*(4), pp. 684–87. **[G: U.S.]**

Raduchel, William and Eckstein, Otto. Economic Modeling Languages: The DRI Experience. *J. Econ. Dynam. Control*, February 1983, *5*(1), pp. 59–74.

Resek, Robert W. Comparative Performance of Multiple Reaction Function Equations Estimated by Canonical Methods. **In** *Hodgman, D. R., ed.*, 1983, pp. 336–52. **[G: W. Germany; U.K.; Italy; France]**

Riess, Hugo Christian. Some Experiences with the Control of a Macroeconometric Model with a Scalarvalued Objective Function from the Viewpoint of Applied Economic Research. **In** *Gruber, J., ed.*, 1983, pp. 48–54.

Ritschard, Gilbert. Computable Qualitative Comparative Static Techniques. *Econometrica*, July 1983, *51*(4), pp. 1145–68.

Salathe, Larry E.; Price, J. Michael and Gadson, Kenneth E. The Food and Agricultural Policy Simulator: An Addendum [On the Misuse of Theil's Inequality Coefficient]. *Agr. Econ. Res.*, July 1983, *35*(3), pp. 40–42.

Schleicher, Stefan. Forecasting Theory for Hierarchical Systems with Applications to Multicountry Models. **In** *[Klein, L. R.]*, 1983, pp. 153–71.

Schoonbeek, L. On the Number of Non-Zero Eigenvalues of a Dynamic Linear Econometric Model: A Note. *Empirical Econ.*, 1983, *8*(2), pp. 119–23. **[G: W. Germany]**

Selody, Jack G. and Lynch, Kevin G. Modeling Government Fiscal Behavior in Canada. *J. Policy Modeling*, June 1983, *5*(2), pp. 271–91. **[G: Canada]**

Sickles, Robin C. and Thurman, Stephan S. Consistent Price Determination of Income and Production: A Singular Equation System Applied to the MPS Model. *J. Policy Modeling*, March 1983, *5*(1), pp. 125–48. **[G: U.S.]**

Stöppler, Siegmar and Stein, Jens-Peter. A Study of Adaptive Revision of Target Values in an Econometric Decision Model. **In** *Gruber, J., ed.*, 1983, pp. 221–41. **[G: W. Germany]**

Streuff, Hartmut and Gruber, Josef. The Interactive Multiobjective Optimization Method by Elemer E. Rosinger: A Computer Program and Aspects of Applications. **In** *Gruber, J., ed.*, 1983, pp. 334–64. **[G: W. Germany]**

Sworder, D. D. Utilization of Repair Capability in a Stochastic Dynamic System. *J. Econ. Dynam. Control*, July 1983, *5*(4), pp. 371–85.

Theil, Henri. Linear Algebra and Matrix Methods in Econometrics. **In** *Griliches, Z. and Intriligator, M. D., eds.*, 1983, pp. 3–65.

Tondini, Giovanni. Controllabilità e teoria della politica economica. (Controllability and the Theory of Economic Policy. With English summary.) *Giorn. Econ.*, May-June 1983, *42*(5–6), pp. 307–19.

Uebe, Götze. A Nonlinear Difference Equation of Malgrange. *Ann. INSEE*, Jan.–Mar. 1983, (49), pp. 123–31.

Vallée, R. and Nicolau, Ed. Econometric Models and Generalized Laplace Transforms. *Econ. Compu-*

tat. Cybern. Stud. Res., 1983, *18*(4), pp. 79–82.

Visco, Ignazio. Comparative Performance of Multiple Reaction Function Equations Estimated by Canonical Methods: Discussion. **In** *Hodgman, D. R., ed.*, 1983, pp. 353–58.

Wallenius, Hannele and Wallenius, Jyrki. A Methodology for Solving the Multiple Criteria Macroeconomic Policy Problem. **In** *Gruber, J., ed.*, 1983, pp. 310–33. **[G: Finland]**

Wegge, Leon L. and Feldman, Mark. Identifiability Criteria for Muth-Rational Expectations Models. *J. Econometrics*, February 1983, *21*(2), pp. 245–54.

Wohltmann, Hans-Werner and Krömer, W. A Note on Buiter's Sufficient Condition for Perfect Output Controllability of a Rational Expectations Model. *J. Econ. Dynam. Control*, September 1983, *6*(1/2), pp. 201–05.

Young, A. S. A Comparative Analysis of Prior Families for Distributed Lags. *Empirical Econ.*, 1983, *8*(3–4), pp. 215–27.

213 Mathematical Methods and Models

2130 General

Albin, Peter S. and Gottinger, Hans W. Structure and Complexity in Economic and Social Systems. *Math. Soc. Sci.*, September 1983, *5*(3), pp. 253–68.

Arrow, Kenneth J. The Genesis of Dynamic Systems Governed by Metzler Matrices. **In** *Arrow, K. J., Vol. 2*, 1983, *1976*, pp. 245–64.

Bridges, Douglas S. Numerical Representation of Intransitive Preferences on a Countable Set. *J. Econ. Theory*, June 1983, *30*(1), pp. 213–17.

Chew, Soo Hong. A Generalization of the Quasilinear Mean with Applications to the Measurement of Income Inequality and Decision Theory Resolving the Allais Paradox. *Econometrica*, July 1983, *51*(4), pp. 1065–92.

Cooper, Russel J. and McLaren, Keith R. The ORANI-MACRO Interface: An Illustrative Exposition. *Econ. Rec.*, June 1983, *59*(165), pp. 166–79. **[G: Australia]**

Crouzeix, J.-P. Duality between Direct and Indirect Utility Functions: Differentiability Properties. *J. Math. Econ.*, October 1983, *12*(2), pp. 149–65.

Debreu, Gerard. Representation of a Preference Ordering by a Numerical Function. **In** *Debreu, G.*, 1983, *1954*, pp. 105–10.

Debreu, Gerard. Topological Methods in Cardinal Utility Theory. **In** *Debreu, G.*, 1983, *1960*, pp. 120–32.

Ikeda, Mineo. Differentiable Manifolds and Economic Structures. **In** *[Yamada, I.]*, 1983, pp. 143–55.

Ivanovic, Branislav. The Selections of Elements from a Given Set Relative to One Criterion. *Econ. Anal. Worker's Manage.*, 1983, *17*(4), pp. 341–60.

Kushman, John E. A Modified Minkowski Theorem and Applications. *Atlantic Econ. J.*, September 1983, *11*(3), pp. 114.

Lady, George M. The Structure of Qualitatively Determinate Relationships. *Econometrica*, January 1983, *51*(1), pp. 197–218.

Lady, George M. and Maybee, John S. Qualitatively Invertible Matrices. *Math. Soc. Sci.*, December 1983, *6*(3), pp. 397–407.

Otani, Kiyoshi. A Characterization of Quasi-Concave Functions. *J. Econ. Theory*, October 1983, *31*(1), pp. 194–96.

Ritschard, Gilbert. Computable Qualitative Comparative Static Techniques. *Econometrica*, July 1983, *51*(4), pp. 1145–68.

Segal, Uzi. A Theorem on the Additivity of the Quasi-Concave Closure of an Additive Convex Function. *J. Math. Econ.*, July 1983, *11*(3), pp. 261–66.

Suzumura, Kotaro. Perron–Frobenius Theorem on Non-Negative Square Matrices: An Elementary Proof. *Hitotsubashi J. Econ.*, December 1983, *24*(2), pp. 137–41.

Theil, Henri. Linear Algebra and Matrix Methods in Econometrics. **In** *Griliches, Z. and Intriligator, M. D., eds.*, 1983, pp. 3–65.

2132 Optimization Techniques

Araujo, A. and Scheinkman, José A. Maximum Principle and Transversality Condition for Concave Infinite Horizon Economic Models. *J. Econ. Theory*, June 1983, *30*(1), pp. 1–16.

Crama, Yves and Hansen, Pierre. An Introduction to the Electre Research Programme. **In** *Hansen, P., ed.*, 1983, pp. 31–42.

Donaldson, John B. and Mehra, Rajnish. Stochastic Growth with Correlated Production Shocks. *J. Econ. Theory*, April 1983, *29*(2), pp. 282–312.

Feinstein, C. D. and Oren, Shmuel S. Local Stability Properties of the Modified Hamiltonian Dynamic System. *J. Econ. Dynam. Control*, December 1983, *6*(4), pp. 387–97.

Gal, Tomas. On Efficient Sets in Vector Maximum Problems—A Brief Survey. **In** *Hansen, P., ed.*, 1983, pp. 94–114.

Gol'shtein, E. G. and Tretiakov, N. V. Modified Lagrange Functions and Their Applications. *Matekon*, Winter 1983–84, *20*(2), pp. 74–107.

Habenicht, W. Quad Trees, a Datastructure for Discrete Vector Optimization Problems. **In** *Hansen, P., ed.*, 1983, pp. 136–45.

Hartl, Richard. Optimal Maintenance and Production Rates for a Machine: A Nonlinear Economic Control Problem. *J. Econ. Dynam. Control*, November 1983, *6*(3), pp. 281–306.

Hogan, William W. and Weyant, John P. Methods and Algorithms for Energy Model Composition: Optimization in a Network of Process Models. **In** *Lev, B., ed.*, 1983, pp. 3–43.

Kydes, Andy S. An Energy Case Study Using the Brookhaven National Laboratory Time-stepped Energy System Optimization Model (TESOM) **In** *Lev, B., ed.*, 1983, pp. 425–43. **[G: U.S.]**

Martynov, G. V. Two-Stage Optimization of a Multibranch Complex Using the "Branch-Complex" Framework. *Matekon*, Spring 1983, *19*(3), pp. 74–97.

Martynov, G. V. and Pitelin, A. K. A Two-Stage System for Optimizing the Development and Location of a Multibranch Complex Which Uses

Variants for the Branch Models. *Matekon,* Winter 1983–84, *20*(2), pp. 55–73.

Quandt, Richard E. Computational Problems and Methods. **In** *Griliches, Z. and Intriligator, M. D., eds.,* 1983, pp. 699–764.

Serafini, Paolo. Convergence of Dual Variables in Interactive Vector Optimization. **In** *Hansen, P., ed.,* 1983, pp. 347–55.

Streuff, Hartmut and Gruber, Josef. The Interactive Multiobjective Optimization Method by Elemer E. Rosinger: A Computer Program and Aspects of Applications. **In** *Gruber, J., ed.,* 1983, pp. 334–64. **[G: W. Germany]**

Wendell, Richard E. Efficiency and Solution Approaches to Bi-objective Mathematical Programs. **In** *Hansen, P., ed.,* 1983, pp. 389–99.

Werbos, Paul J. Solving and Optimizing Complex Systems: Lessons from the EIA Long-term Energy Model. **In** *Lev, B., ed.,* 1983, pp. 163–80.

White, D. J. The Foundations of Multi-objective Interactive Programming—Some Questions. **In** *Hansen, P., ed.,* 1983, pp. 406–15.

Yakin, M. Zafer. Optimal Operations of Power Systems: A Survey. **In** *Lev, B., ed.,* 1983, pp. 563–84.

2133 Existence and Stability Conditions of Equilibrium

Braulke, Michael. Price Responsiveness and Market Conditions. *Econometrica,* July 1983, *51*(4), pp. 971–80.

Debreu, Gerard. A Social Equilibrium Existence Theorem. **In** *Debreu, G.,* 1983, *1952,* pp. 50–58.

Debreu, Gerard. New Concepts and Techniques for Equilibrium Analysis. **In** *Debreu, G.,* 1983, *1962,* pp. 133–50.

Debreu, Gerard. The Application to Economics of Differential Topology and Global Analysis: Regular Differentiable Economies. **In** *Debreu, G.,* 1983, *1976,* pp. 232–41.

Hands, Douglas W. Stability in a Discrete Time Model of the Walrasian Tâtonnement. *J. Econ. Dynam. Control,* December 1983, *6*(4), pp. 399–411.

Honkapohja, Seppo and Ito, Takatoshi. Stability and Regime Switching. *J. Econ. Theory,* February 1983, *29*(1), pp. 22–48.

Nishimura, Kiyohiko G. A New Concept of Stability and Dynamical Economic Systems. *J. Econ. Dynam. Control,* September 1983, *6*(1/2), pp. 25–40.

2134 Computational Techniques

Achary, K. K. A Branch and Bound Algorithm for Determining Efficient Solution Pairs in a Special Type of Transportation Problem. *Econ. Computat. Cybern. Stud. Res.,* 1983, *18*(4), pp. 83–92.

Dumitrescu, T. On the Numerical Solution of a Class of Nonlinear Complementarity Problems. *Econ. Computat. Cybern. Stud. Res.,* 1983, *18*(4), pp. 25–31.

Dykstra, Richard L. An Algorithm for Restricted Least Squares Regression. *J. Amer. Statist. Assoc.,* December 1983, *78*(384), pp. 837–42.

Gershon, Mark and Duckstein, Lucien. An Algorithm for Choosing a Multiobjective Technique. **In** *Hansen, P., ed.,* 1983, pp. 53–62.

Ginsburgh, Victor and Waelbroeck, Jean. Generalized Tâtonnement and the Solution of Economic Models. *Econ. Rec.,* June 1983, *59*(165), pp. 111–17.

Greis, Noel P.; Wood, Eric F. and Steuer, Ralph E. Multicriteria Analysis of Water Allocation in a River Basin: The Tchebycheff Approach. *Water Resources Res.,* August 1983, *19*(4), pp. 865–75. **[G: U.S.]**

Hicks, John. Linear Theory. **In** *Hicks, J.,* 1983, *1960,* pp. 246–91.

Matsuyama, Keisuke and Tamura, Yasuhiro. On Calculation of Causal Orderings of Variables Appearing in Simultaneous Equations. *Econ. Computat. Cybern. Stud. Res.,* 1983, *18*(1), pp. 73–85.

Maybee, John S. and Maybee, Stuart J. An Algorithm for Identifying Morishima and Anti-Morishima Matrices and Balanced Digraphs. *Math. Soc. Sci.,* October 1983, *6*(1), pp. 99–103.

Wallin, Jan. En datormodell för planering av interna kontrollsystem. (Computer-Assisted Internal Control Design: A Multicriteria Approach. With English summary.) *Liiketaloudellinen Aikak.,* 1983, *32*(2), pp. 175–92.

2135 Construction, Analysis, and Use of Mathematical Programming Models

Anderson, E. J. and Philpott, A. B. An Algorithm for a Continuous Version of the Assignment Problem. **In** *Fiacco, A. V. and Kortanek, K. O., eds.,* 1983, pp. 108–17.

Boneh, Arnon. PREDUCE—A Probabilistic Algorithm Identifying Redundancy by a Random Feasible Point Generator (RFPG). **In** *Karwan, M. H., et al.,* 1983, pp. 108–34.

Borwein, Jonathan M. Semi-infinite Programming Duality: How Special Is It? **In** *Fiacco, A. V. and Kortanek, K. O., eds.,* 1983, pp. 10–36.

Bos, Henk C. Some Simple Thoughts on Model Building for Developing Countries. *Pakistan Devel. Rev.,* Summer 1983, *22*(2), pp. 63–71.

Bradley, Gordon H.; Brown, Gerald G. and Graves, Glenn W. Structural Redundancy in Large-Scale Optimization Models. **In** *Karwan, M. H., et al.,* 1983, pp. 145–69.

Dembo, Ron and Zipkin, Paul. Construction and Evaluation of Compact Refinery Models. **In** *Lev, B., ed.,* 1983, pp. 525–40.

Duesing, Erick C. Multiple Objective Linear Programming and the Theory of the Firm: I. Substitution and Sensitivity Analysis. **In** *Hansen, P., ed.,* 1983, pp. 43–52.

Duffin, R. J.; Jeroslow, Robert G. and Karlovitz, Les A. Duality in Semi-infinite Linear Programming. **In** *Fiacco, A. V. and Kortanek, K. O., eds.,* 1983, pp. 50–62.

Fabian, Cs. Interactive Integer Programming. *Econ. Computat. Cybern. Stud. Res.,* 1983, *18*(2), pp. 65–72.

Gal, Tomas. A Method for Determining Redundant Constraints. **In** *Karwan, M. H., et al.,* 1983, pp. 36–52.

Grauer, M. Reference Point Optimization—The

Nonlinear Case. In *Hansen, P., ed.*, 1983, pp. 126–35.

Hafkamp, Wim and Nijkamp, Peter. Conflict Analysis and Compromise Strategies in Integrated Spatial Systems. *Reg. Sci. Urban Econ.*, February 1983, *13*(1), pp. 115–40.

Hinloopen, Edwin; Nijkamp, Peter and Rietveld, Piet. Qualitative Discrete Multiple Criteria Choice Models in Regional Planning. *Reg. Sci. Urban Econ.*, February 1983, *13*(1), pp. 77–102. **[G: Belgium; Netherlands]**

Ho, James K. Multiple Criteria Optimization Using Analytic Hierarchies and Holistic Preferences. **In** *Hansen, P., ed.*, 1983, pp. 156–66.

Holin, S. and Prevot, M. An Application of the Multiobjective Programming to the French Industry. **In** *Hansen, P., ed.*, 1983, pp. 167–76. **[G: France]**

Kemperman, J. H. B. On the Role of Duality in the Theory of Moments. **In** *Fiacco, A. V. and Kortanek, K. O., eds.*, 1983, pp. 63–92.

Klein, Dieter and Holm, Soren J. Some Reduction of Linear Programs Using Bounds on Problem Variables. **In** *Karwan, M. H., et al.*, 1983, pp. 80–86.

Kornbluth, J. S. H. Max–Min Programming with Linear Fractional Functions; Algorithms and Examples. **In** *Hansen, P., ed.*, 1983, pp. 204–13.

Mattheiss, Theodore H. A Method for Finding Redundant Constraints of a System of Linear Inequalities. **In** *Karwan, M. H., et al.*, 1983, pp. 68–79.

McCarl, Bruce A. and Nelson, Carl H. Multiple Optimal Solutions in Linear Programming Models: Comment. *Amer. J. Agr. Econ.*, February 1983, *65*(1), pp. 181–83.

Michałowski, W. and Żółkiewski, Zbigniew. An Interactive Approach to the Solution of a Linear Production Planning Problem with Multiple Objectives. **In** *Hansen, P., ed.*, 1983, pp. 260–68.

Narula, Subhash C. and Nwosu, Adiele D. Two-Level Hierarchical Programming Problem. **In** *Hansen, P., ed.*, 1983, pp. 290–99.

Nijkamp, Peter and Rietveld, Piet. Multiobjective Decision Analysis in a Regional Context: Introduction. *Reg. Sci. Urban Econ.*, February 1983, *13*(1), pp. 1–3.

Nykowski, Ireneusz and Zólkiewski, Zbigniew. On Some Connections between Bicriteria and Fractional Programming Problems. **In** *Hansen, P., ed.*, 1983, pp. 300–309.

Paris, Quirino. Multiple Optimal Solutions in Linear Programming Models: Reply. *Amer. J. Agr. Econ.*, February 1983, *65*(1), pp. 184–86.

Parks, Melvin Lee, Jr. and Soyster, Allen L. Semi-infinite and Fuzzy Set Programming. **In** *Fiacco, A. V. and Kortanek, K. O., eds.*, 1983, pp. 219–35.

Plato, Gerald and Gordon, Douglas. Dynamic Programming and the Economics of Optimal Grain Storage. *Agr. Econ. Res.*, January 1983, *35*(1), pp. 10–22.

Prescott, Edward C. Should Control Theory Be Used for Economic Stabilization? **In** *Brunner, K. and Meltzer, A. H., eds.*, 1983, *1977*, pp. 285–310.

Reeves, Gary R. and Franz, Lori S. A Simplified Approach to Interactive MOLP. **In** *Hansen, P., ed.*, 1983, pp. 310–16.

Rubin, David S. Finding Redundant Constraints in Sets of Linear Inequalities. **In** *Karwan, M. H., et al.*, 1983, pp. 60–67.

Sethi, Awanti P. and Thompson, Gerald L. The Noncandidate Constraint Method. **In** *Karwan, M. H., et al.*, 1983, pp. 135–44.

Spronk, Jaap and Veeneklaas, Frank. A Feasibility Study of Economic and Environmental Scenarios by Means of Interactive Multiple Goal Programming. *Reg. Sci. Urban Econ.*, February 1983, *13*(1), pp. 141–60. **[G: Netherlands]**

Ştefănescu, Viorica. Nondominated Solutions and Optimization Methods for the Multi-Objective Programming Problem. *Econ. Computat. Cybern. Stud. Res.*, 1983, *18*(3), pp. 77–83.

Sworder, D. D. Utilization of Repair Capability in a Stochastic Dynamic System. *J. Econ. Dynam. Control*, July 1983, *5*(4), pp. 371–85.

Takayama, T. and Uri, Noel D. A Note on Spatial and Temporal Price and Allocation Modeling: Quadratic Programming or Linear Complementarity Programming? *Reg. Sci. Urban Econ.*, November 1983, *13*(4), pp. 455–70.

Tauer, Loren W. Target MOTAD. *Amer. J. Agr. Econ.*, August 1983, *65*(3), pp. 606–10.

Telgen, Jan. Identifying Redundancy in Systems of Linear Constraints. **In** *Karwan, M. H., et al.*, 1983, pp. 53–59.

Werczberger, Elia. Multiperson Multitarget Decision Making, Using the Versatility Criterion. *Reg. Sci. Urban Econ.*, February 1983, *13*(1), pp. 103–13.

Wierzbicki, Andrzej P. Critical Essay on the Methodology of Multiobjective Analysis. *Reg. Sci. Urban Econ.*, February 1983, *13*(1), pp. 5–29.

Williams, H. Paul. A Reduction Procedure for Linear and Integer Programming Models. **In** *Karwan, M. H., et al.*, 1983, pp. 87–107.

Wolsey, L. A. Fundamental Properties of Certain Discrete Location Problems. **In** *Thisse, J.-F. and Zoller, H. G., eds.*, 1983, pp. 331–55.

Wright, Jeffrey; ReVelle, Charles and Cohon, Jared. A Multiobjective Integer Programming Model for the Land Acquisition Problem. *Reg. Sci. Urban Econ.*, February 1983, *13*(1), pp. 31–53.

Zalai, Ernö. Adaptability of Nonlinear Equilibrium Models to Central Planning. *Acta Oecon.*, 1983, *30*(3–4), pp. 433–45.

Zionts, Stanley. A Report on a Project on Multiple Criteria Decision Making, 1982. **In** *Hansen, P., ed.*, 1983, pp. 416–30.

Zionts, Stanley and Wallenius, Jyrki. A Method for Identifying Redundant Constraints and Extraneous Variables in Linear Programming. **In** *Karwan, M. H., et al.*, 1983, pp. 28–35.

214 Computer Programs

2140 Computer Programs

Barbu, G. On Computer Generation of Random Variables as Ratio of Uniform Random Variables. *Econ. Computat. Cybern. Stud. Res.*, 1983, *18*(4), pp. 33–50.

Cohen, Steven B. Present Limitations in the Availability of Statistical Software for the Analysis of Complex Survey Data. *Rev. Public Data Use (See J. Econ. Soc. Meas. after 4/85)*, December 1983, *11*(4), pp. 338–44.

Condie, James M., et al. A Brief Description of the FRB Modeleasy/Fedeasy Econometric Language. *J. Econ. Dynam. Control*, February 1983, *5*(1), pp. 75–79.

Drud, Arne. A Survey of Model Representations and Simulation Algorithms in Some Existing Modeling Systems. *J. Econ. Dynam. Control*, February 1983, *5*(1), pp. 5–35.

Drud, Arne. Interfacing Modeling Systems and Solution Algorithms. *J. Econ. Dynam. Control*, February 1983, *5*(1), pp. 131–49.

Guazzo, Mauro and Tempo, Maurizio. L'applicazione di un "query language" al sistema bancario italiano. (The Application of a "Query Language" to the Italian Banking system. With English summary.) *Bancaria*, March 1983, *39*(3), pp. 284–89. **[G: Italy]**

Jones, Jack William. Applying a Computer-based Enhanced Oil Recovery Simulation Model to Reservoir Economic Analysis. **In** *Lev, B., ed.*, 1983, pp. 255–70. **[G: U.S.]**

Meeraus, Alexander. An Algebraic Approach to Modeling. *J. Econ. Dynam. Control*, February 1983, *5*(1), pp. 81–108.

Nepomiastchy, Pierre and Rechenmann, François. The Equation Writing External Language of the Moduleco Software. *J. Econ. Dynam. Control*, February 1983, *5*(1), pp. 37–57.

Peterson, William; Barker, Terry and van der Ploeg, Rick. Software Support for Multisectoral Dynamic Models of National Economies. *J. Econ. Dynam. Control*, February 1983, *5*(1), pp. 109–30.

Quandt, Richard E. Computational Problems and Methods. **In** *Griliches, Z. and Intriligator, M. D., eds.*, 1983, pp. 699–764.

Raduchel, William and Eckstein, Otto. Economic Modeling Languages: The DRI Experience. *J. Econ. Dynam. Control*, February 1983, *5*(1), pp. 59–74.

215 Experimental Economic Methods

2150 Experimental Economic Methods

Albers, Wulf and Albers, Gisela. Prominence and Aspiration Adjustment in Location Games. **In** *Tietz, R., ed.*, 1983, pp. 243–58.

Bartos, Otomar J.; Tietz, Reinhard and McLean, Carolyn. Toughness and Fairness in Negotiation. **In** *Tietz, R., ed.*, 1983, pp. 35–51.

Bazerman, Max H. and Samuelson, William F. The Winner's Curse: An Empirical Investigation. **In** *Tietz, R., ed.*, 1983, pp. 186–200.

Bendick, Marc, Jr. and Struyk, Raymond J. The Great Housing Experiment: Lessons for Future Social Experiments. **In** *Friedman, J. and Weinberg, D. H., eds.*, 1983, pp. 258–65. **[G: U.S.]**

Bigoness, William J. and Grigsby, David W. The Effects of Need for Achievement and Alternative Forms of Arbitration upon Bargaining Behavior. **In** *Tietz, R., ed.*, 1983, pp. 122–35.

Brandstätter, Hermann; Kette, Gerhard and Sageder, Josef. Expectations, Attributions, and Behavior in Bargaining with Liked and Disliked Partners. **In** *Tietz, R., ed.*, 1983, pp. 136–52.

Carter, Grace M.; Coleman, Sinclair B. and Wendt, James C. The Great Housing Experiment: Participation under Open Enrollment. **In** *Friedman, J. and Weinberg, D. H., eds.*, 1983, pp. 73–90. **[G: U.S.]**

Cole, Steven G. and Nail, Paul. Social Learning vs. Direct Experience as Determinants of Aspiration Level and Bargaining Behavior. **In** *Tietz, R., ed.*, 1983, pp. 231–42.

Crössmann, H. Jürgen and Tietz, Reinhard. Market Behavior Based on Aspiration Levels. **In** *Tietz, R., ed.*, 1983, pp. 170–85.

Crott, Helmut W.; Luhr, Rudolf and Rombach, Cornelia. The Effects of the Level of Aspiration and Experience in Three-person Bargaining Games. **In** *Tietz, R., ed.*, 1983, pp. 276–90.

Druckman, Daniel; Karis, Demetrios and Donchin, Emanuel. Information-processing in Bargaining: Reactions to an Opponent's Shift in Concession Strategy. **In** *Tietz, R., ed.*, 1983, pp. 153–69.

Forman, Robin and Laing, James D. Game-Theoretic Expectations, Interest Groups, and Salient Majorities in Committees. **In** *Tietz, R., ed.*, 1983, pp. 321–36.

Friedman, Joseph and Weinberg, Daniel H. The Great Housing Experiment: History and Overview. **In** *Friedman, J. and Weinberg, D. H., eds.*, 1983, pp. 11–22. **[G: U.S.]**

Güth, Werner and Schwarze, Bernd. Auctioning Strategic Roles to Observe Aspiration Levels for Conflict Situations. **In** *Tietz, R., ed.*, 1983, pp. 217–30.

Hamilton, William L. The Great Housing Experiment: Economic and Racial/Ethnic Concentration. **In** *Friedman, J. and Weinberg, D. H., eds.*, 1983, pp. 210–19. **[G: U.S.]**

Hamilton, William L. The Great Housing Experiment: The Administrative Agency Experiment. **In** *Friedman, J. and Weinberg, D. H., eds.*, 1983, pp. 56–69. **[G: U.S.]**

Harnett, Donald L. and Wall, James A., Jr. Aspiration/Competitive Effects on the Mediation of Bargaining. **In** *Tietz, R., ed.*, 1983, pp. 8–21.

Hillestad, Carol E. and McDowell, James L. The Great Housing Experiment: Neighborhood Change. **In** *Friedman, J. and Weinberg, D. H., eds.*, 1983, pp. 220–31. **[G: U.S.]**

Holshouser, William L., Jr. The Great Housing Experiment: The Role of Supportive Services. **In** *Friedman, J. and Weinberg, D. H., eds.*, 1983, pp. 112–24. **[G: U.S.]**

Kennedy, Stephen D. The Great Housing Experiment: The Demand Experiment. **In** *Friedman, J. and Weinberg, D. H., eds.*, 1983, pp. 37–55. **[G: U.S.]**

Kennedy, Stephen D. and MacMillan, Jean E. The Great Housing Experiment: Participation under Random Assignment. **In** *Friedman, J. and Weinberg, D. H., eds.*, 1983, pp. 91–111. **[G: U.S.]**

Komorita, Samuel; Lange, Rense and Hamilton, Thomas. The Effects of Level of Aspiration in Coalition Bargaining. **In** *Tietz, R., ed.*, 1983, pp. 291–305.

Kravitz, David A. and Dobson, Mickie. Motivations

and Cognitions in Coalition Formation. In *Tietz, R., ed.*, 1983, pp. 306–20.

Mayo, Stephen K. Benefits from Subsidized Housing. In *Friedman, J. and Weinberg, D. H., eds.*, 1983, pp. 235–57. **[G: U.S.]**

McCarthy, Kevin F. Housing Search and Residential Mobility. In *Friedman, J. and Weinberg, D. H., eds.*, 1983, pp. 191–209. **[G: U.S.]**

Mueller, Guenter F. and Galinat, Withold H. Bargaining Efficiency in Real-Life Buyer–Seller-Interaction: A Fieldexperiment. In *Tietz, R., ed.*, 1983, pp. 80–90.

Mulford, John E. The Great Housing Experiment: Earmarked Income Supplements. In *Friedman, J. and Weinberg, D. H., eds.*, 1983, pp. 163–74. **[G: U.S.]**

Olsen, Edgar O. The Great Housing Experiment: Implications for Housing Policy. In *Friedman, J. and Weinberg, D. H., eds.*, 1983, pp. 266–75. **[G: U.S.]**

Plott, Charles R. and Agha, Gul. Intertemporal Speculation with a Random Demand in an Experimental Market. In *Tietz, R., ed.*, 1983, pp. 201–16.

Pruitt, Dean G., et al. Incentives for Cooperation in Integrative Bargaining. In *Tietz, R., ed.*, 1983, pp. 22–34.

Rapoport, Amnon and Kahan, James P. Standards of Fairness in 3-quota, 4-person Games. In *Tietz, R., ed.*, 1983, pp. 337–51.

Roth, Alvin E. and Murnighan, J. Keith. Information and Aspirations in Two-person Bargaining. In *Tietz, R., ed.*, 1983, pp. 91–103.

Rydell, C. Peter and Barnett, C. Lance. Price Effects of Housing Allowances. In *Friedman, J. and Weinberg, D. H., eds.*, 1983, pp. 175–88. **[G: U.S.]**

Scholz, Roland W.; Fleischer, Andreas and Bentrup, Andreas. Aspiration Forming and Predictions Based on Aspiration Levels Compared between Professional and Nonprofessional Bargainers. In *Tietz, R., ed.*, 1983, pp. 104–21.

Selten, Reinhard. Equal Division Payoff Bounds for 3-Person Characteristic Function Experiments. In *Tietz, R., ed.*, 1983, pp. 265–75.

Selten, Reinhard and Krischker, Wilhelm. Comparison of Two Theories for Characteristic Function Experiments. In *Tietz, R., ed.*, 1983, pp. 259–64.

Tietz, Reinhard. Aspiration-oriented Decision Making—In Memoriam Heinz Sauermann. In *Tietz, R., ed.*, 1983, pp. 1–7.

Tietz, Reinhard and Bartos, Otomar J. Balancing of Aspiration Levels as Fairness Principle in Negotiations. In *Tietz, R., ed.*, 1983, pp. 52–66.

Werner, Thomas and Tietz, Reinhard. The Search Process in Bilateral Negotiations. In *Tietz, R., ed.*, 1983, pp. 67–79.

220 Economic and Social Statistical Data and Analysis

2200 General

Aivazian, S. A. Applied Statistics and Probabilistic Modeling in Economics. *Matekon,* Fall 1983, *20*(1), pp. 29–56. **[G: U.S.S.R.]**

Armbruster, Walter J.; Helmuth, John W. and Manley, William T. Data Systems in the Food and Fiber Sector. In *Farris, P. L., ed.*, 1983, pp. 163–83. **[G: U.S.]**

Atkinson, Anthony B. and Micklewright, J. On the Reliability of Income Data in the Family Expenditure Survey 1970–1977. *J. Roy. Statist. Soc.*, 1983, *146*(1), pp. 33–53. **[G: U.K.]**

Barkenbus, Jack N. Southern State Energy Data Needs. *Rev. Public Data Use (See J. Econ. Soc. Meas. after 4/85),* March 1983, *11*(1), pp. 49–55. **[G: U.S.]**

Bell, Carolyn Shaw. The Erosion of Federal Statistics. *Challenge,* March/April 1983, *26*(1), pp. 48–50. **[G: U.S.]**

Bergesen, Albert. Modeling Long Waves of Crisis in the World-System. In *Bergesen, A., ed.*, 1983, pp. 73–92.

Bilsborrow, Richard E. and Akin, John S. U.S. and Canadian Migration Data: Reply to Robert Nakosteen. *Rev. Public Data Use (See J. Econ. Soc. Meas. after 4/85),* March 1983, *11*(1), pp. 73–74. **[G: U.S.; Canada]**

Bonnen, James T. The Dilemma of Agricultural Economists: Discussion. *Amer. J. Agr. Econ.*, December 1983, *65*(5), pp. 889–90. **[G: U.S.]**

Brown, Charles. Estimating Wage-fringe Trade-offs: Some Data Problems: Comment. In *Triplett, J. E., ed.*, 1983, pp. 367–69. **[G: U.S.]**

Cartwright, David W. Establishment Reporting in Major Administrative Record Systems. *Rev. Public Data Use (See J. Econ. Soc. Meas. after 4/85),* March 1983, *11*(1), pp. 1–10. **[G: U.S.]**

Celestin, Jean-Bernard. Manpower Planning and Labour Market Information in French-Speaking Africa. *Int. Lab. Rev.*, July–August 1983, *122*(4), pp. 507–22. **[G: LDCs]**

Cochrane, Willard W. The Economic Research Service: 22 Years Later. *Agr. Econ. Res.*, April 1983, *35*(2), pp. 29–38. **[G: U.S.]**

Daniel, Raymond. The Dilemma of Agricultural Economists: Discussion. *Amer. J. Agr. Econ.*, December 1983, *65*(5), pp. 891–92. **[G: U.S.]**

Daymont, Thomas N. and Andrisani, Paul J. The Research Uses of the National Longitudinal Surveys: An Update. *Rev. Public Data Use (See J. Econ. Soc. Meas. after 4/85),* October 1983, *11*(3), pp. 203–310. **[G: U.S.]**

Deville, J.-C. and Malinvaud, Edmond. Data Analysis in Official Socio-Economic Statistics. *J. Roy. Statist. Soc.*, 1983, *146*(4), pp. 335–52.

Donovan, Donal. Measuring Macroeconomic Performance. *Finance Develop.*, June 1983, *20*(2), pp. 2–5.

Elton, C. J. The Impact of the Rayner Review on Unemployment and Employment Statistics. *Reg. Stud.*, April 1983, *17*(2), pp. 143–46. **[G: U.K.]**

Gardner, Bruce L. Fact and Fiction in the Public Data Budget Crunch. *Amer. J. Agr. Econ.*, December 1983, *65*(5), pp. 882–88. **[G: U.S.]**

Ghosh, Ranen. Analytical Implications of Time Series Economic Variable Data: Re—Economic Development. *Econ. Aff.*, April–June 1983, *28*(2), pp. 664–74, 681. **[G: Nigeria; LDCs]**

Grootaert, Christiaan. The Conceptual Basis of Measures of Household Welfare and Their Implied

Survey Data Requirements. *Rev. Income Wealth,* March 1983, *29*(1), pp. 1–21.

Holub, Hans Werner. Some Critical Reflections on Measures of Net Economic Welfare [A Theoretical Framework for the Measurement of Well-Being]. *Rev. Income Wealth,* September 1983, *29*(3), pp. 317–21.

Jensen, Poul. Towards a Register-Based Statistical System—Some Danish Experience. *Statist. J.,* March 1983, *1*(3), pp. 341–65. **[G: Denmark]**

Just, Richard E. The Impact of Less Data on the Agricultural Economy and Society. *Amer. J. Agr. Econ.,* December 1983, *65*(5), pp. 872–81. **[G: U.S.]**

Kay, Linda B. A Survey of New Zealand Labour Market Data. **In** *Easton, B., ed.,* 1983, pp. 171–202. **[G: New Zealand]**

Kumar, Pradeep. The Current Industrial Relations Scene in Canada, 1983: Technical Notes. **In** *Wood, W. D. and Kumar, P., eds.,* 1983, pp. 479–92. **[G: Canada]**

Leontief, Wassily W. An Information System for Policy Decisions in a Modern Economy. **In** *Dutta, M.; Hartline, J. C. and Loeb, P. D., eds.,* 1983, *1979,* pp. 17–25. **[G: U.S.]**

Lothian, James R. The International Data Base: An Introductory Overview. **In** *Darby, M. P. and Lothian, J. R., et al.,* 1983, pp. 46–57. **[G: OECD]**

Malinvaud, Edmond. From Statistics to Data Management—The French Difficulties. *Statist. J.,* March 1983, *1*(3), pp. 285–96. **[G: France]**

Moore, Geoffrey H. The Forty-second Anniversary of the Leading Indicators. **In** *Moore, G. H.,* 1983, *1979,* pp. 369–400. **[G: U.S.]**

Moore, Geoffrey H. When Lagging Indicators Lead: The History of an Idea. **In** *Moore, G. H.,* 1983, *1978,* pp. 361–67. **[G: U.S.]**

Moore, Geoffrey H. Why the Leading Indicators Really Do Lead. **In** *Moore, G. H.,* 1983, *1978,* pp. 339–51. **[G: U.S.]**

Moore, Geoffrey H. and Moore, Melita H. An Introduction to International Economic Indicators. **In** *Moore, G. H.,* 1983, pp. 65–91. **[G: OECD]**

Morrill, Richard L. Migration Data: A Comment [Data Availability versus Data Needs for Analyzing the Determinants and Consequences of Internal Migration: An Evaluation of U.S. Survey Data] [Internal Migration in the United States: An Evaluation of Federal Data]. *Rev. Public Data Use (See J. Econ. Soc. Meas. after 4/85),* December 1983, *11*(4), pp. 345–47. **[G: U.S.]**

Mullner, Ross M. and Byre, Calvin S. Toward an Inventory of U.S. Health Care Data Bases. *Rev. Public Data Use (See J. Econ. Soc. Meas. after 4/85),* March 1983, *11*(1), pp. 57–65. **[G: U.S.]**

Mullner, Ross M.; Byre, Calvin S. and Killingsworth, Cleve L. An Inventory of U.S. Health Care Data Bases. *Rev. Public Data Use (See J. Econ. Soc. Meas. after 4/85),* June 1983, *11*(2), pp. 85–192. **[G: U.S.]**

Nakosteen, Robert A. U.S. and Canadian Migration Data: A Comment. *Rev. Public Data Use (See J. Econ. Soc. Meas. after 4/85),* March 1983, *11*(1), pp. 69–71. **[G: U.S.; Canada]**

Rawski, Thomas G. New Sources for Studying China's Economy. *J. Econ. Hist.,* December 1983, *43*(4), pp. 997–1002. **[G: China]**

Regis, Giuseppe. Il primo annuario statistico della Cina Popolare. (The First Statistical Yearbook of the People's Republic of China. With English summary.) *Rivista Int. Sci. Econ. Com.,* February 1983, *30*(2), pp. 176–86. **[G: China]**

Rice, Dorothy P. Health Care Data in the United States. *Rev. Public Data Use (See J. Econ. Soc. Meas. after 4/85),* June 1983, *11*(2), pp. 79–84. **[G: U.S.]**

Rossi, Fiorenzo. Il controllo dei dati nel censimento della popolazione del 1981 in Italia. (The Post-Enumeration Surveys of the 1981 Population Census of Italy. With English summary.) *Statistica,* October–December 1983, *43*(4), pp. 661–72. **[G: Italy]**

Rubin, Donald B. Imputing Income in the CPS: Comments on "Measures of Aggregate Labor Cost in the United States." **In** *Triplett, J. E., ed.,* 1983, pp. 333–43. **[G: U.S.]**

Sakakibara, Eisuke and Feldman, Robert A. The Japanese Financial System in Comparative Perspective. *J. Compar. Econ.,* March 1983, *7*(1), pp. 1–24. **[G: U.S.; Japan]**

Smith, Robert S. and Ehrenberg, Ronald G. Estimating Wage-fringe Trade-offs: Some Data Problems. **In** *Triplett, J. E., ed.,* 1983, pp. 347–67. **[G: U.S.]**

de Vries, W. F. M. Co-ordination as an Instrument to Improve the Quality of Statistics. *Statist. J.,* March 1983, *1*(3), pp. 311–19.

Weber, J.-L. The French Natural Patrimony Accounts. *Statist. J.,* October 1983, *1*(4), pp. 419–44. **[G: France]**

221 National Income Accounting

2210 National Income Accounting Theory and Procedures

Anson-Mayer, Monique. Le mythe de la comptabilité nationale en Afrique. *Revue Écon. Polit.,* January–February 1983, *93*(1), pp. 86–112. **[G: Africa]**

Babeau, André. The Macro-Economic Wealth–Income Ratio of Households. *Rev. Income Wealth,* December 1983, *29*(4), pp. 347–70. **[G: France; U.S.]**

Berger, S. Dividing Government Product between Intermediate and Final Uses: A Comment. *Rev. Income Wealth,* September 1983, *29*(3), pp. 333–34.

Buiter, Willem H. Measurement of the Public Sector Deficit and Its Implications for Policy Evaluation and Design. *Int. Monet. Fund Staff Pap.,* June 1983, *30*(2), pp. 306–49.

Charmes, Jacques. Comment mesurer la contribution du secteur non structuré à la production nationale dans les pays du tiers monde? (With English summary.) *Rev. Income Wealth,* December 1983, *29*(4), pp. 429–44. **[G: Tunisia; Nigeria]**

Cohen, Morris. The GNP Data Improvement Project (The Creamer Report): Overview and Business Cycle Perspective. **In** *Foss, M. F., ed.,* 1983, pp. 384–97. **[G: U.S.]**

Cole, Rosanne. The GNP Data Improvement Project

(The Creamer Report): Overview and Business Cycle Perspective: Comment. **In** *Foss, M. F., ed.*, 1983, pp. 397–402. **[G: U.S.]**

la Cour, Aage. Realøkonomiske sammenligninger mellem forskellige lande. (International Comparisons of Real GNP. With English summary.) *Nationaløkon. Tidsskr.*, 1983, *121* (2), pp. 245–58. **[G: EEC; U.S.; Japan]**

Creamer, Daniel. The GNP Data Improvement Project (The Creamer Report): Overview and Business Cycle Perspective: Some Comments on Papers on the Creamer Report. **In** *Foss, M. F., ed.*, 1983, pp. 421–24. **[G: U.S.]**

Cuyvers, Ludo. Keynes's Collaboration with Erwin Rothbarth. *Econ. J.*, September 1983, *93* (371), pp. 629–36.

Denison, Edward F. Round Table of GNP Users: Introductory Statement. **In** *Foss, M. F., ed.*, 1983, pp. 313–15. **[G: U.S.]**

Eckstein, Otto. The NIPA Accounts: A User's View. **In** *Foss, M. F., ed.*, 1983, pp. 315–17. **[G: U.S.]**

Fell, H. A. and Greenfield, C. C. Measuring Economic Growth. *Rev. Income Wealth*, June 1983, *29* (2), pp. 205–08.

Gorman, John A. Data Needs in Flow of Funds. **In** *Foss, M. F., ed.*, 1983, pp. 409–15. **[G: U.S.]**

Greenspan, Alan. Weekly GNP. **In** *Foss, M. F., ed.*, 1983, pp. 317–19. **[G: U.S.]**

Grimm, Bruce T. and Hirsch, Albert A. The Impact of the 1976 NIPA Benchmark Revision on the Structure and Predictive Accuracy of the BEA Quarterly Econometric Model. **In** *Foss, M. F., ed.*, 1983, pp. 333–80. **[G: U.S.]**

Hicks, John. The Social Accounting of Classical Models. **In** *Hicks, J.*, 1983, pp. 17–31.

Hymans, Saul H. The Impact of the 1976 NIPA Benchmark Revision on the Structure and Predictive Accuracy of the BEA Quarterly Econometric Model: Comment. **In** *Foss, M. F., ed.*, 1983, pp. 380–82. **[G: U.S.]**

Jorgenson, Dale W. and Pachon, Alvaro. The Accumulation of Human and Non-human Capital. **In** *Modigliani, F. and Hemming, R., eds.*, 1983, pp. 302–50. **[G: U.S.]**

Katz, Arnold J. Valuing the Services of Consumer Durables. *Rev. Income Wealth*, December 1983, *29* (4), pp. 405–27. **[G: U.S.]**

Kendrick, John W. The GNP Data Improvement Report from the Perspective of Its Use to Measure Economic Growth: Comment. **In** *Foss, M. F., ed.*, 1983, pp. 407–08. **[G: U.S.]**

Klein, Lawrence R. NIPA Statistics: A User's View. **In** *Foss, M. F., ed.*, 1983, pp. 319–23. **[G: U.S.]**

Krantz, Olle. Historical National Accounts—Some Methodological Notes. *Scand. Econ. Hist. Rev.*, 1983, *31* (2), pp. 109–31. **[G: Europe]**

Kutscher, Ronald E. The GNP Data Improvement Report from the Perspective of Its Use to Measure Economic Growth. **In** *Foss, M. F., ed.*, 1983, pp. 403–07. **[G: U.S.]**

Lenti, Libero. Produzione-distribuzione "versus" trasferimento dei redditi. (Production-Distribution "versus" Income Transfer. With English summary.) *Giorn. Econ.*, May-June 1983, *42* (5–6), pp. 277–88. **[G: Italy]**

Maddison, Angus. A Comparison of Levels of GDP Per Capita in Developed and Developing Countries, 1700–1980. *J. Econ. Hist.*, March 1983, *43* (1), pp. 27–41. **[G: MDCs; LDCs]**

Marcus, Edward. Inflation, the Terms of Trade, and National Income Estimates. **In** *Schmukler, N. and Marcus, E., eds.*, 1983, pp. 116–19.

Okun, Arthur M. Potential GNP: Its Measurement and Significance. **In** *Okun, A. M.*, 1983, *1962*, pp. 145–58. **[G: U.S.]**

Okun, Arthur M. The National Accounts in an Inflationary World. **In** *Foss, M. F., ed.*, 1983, pp. 323–26. **[G: U.S.]**

Parker, Robert P. The GNP Data Improvement Project (The Creamer Report): Overview and Business Cycle Perspective: A Bureau of Economic Analysis Perspective. **In** *Foss, M. F., ed.*, 1983, pp. 424–27. **[G: U.S.]**

Rabin, Alan and Keilany, Ziad. The Role of "Interest" in the National Income Accounts. *Atlantic Econ. J.*, July 1983, *11* (2), pp. 98.

Reich, U.-P. Reply [Dividing Government Product between Intermediate and Final Uses]. *Rev. Income Wealth*, September 1983, *29* (3), pp. 334–35.

Ruggles, Nancy D. and Ruggles, Richard. The Treatment of Pensions and Insurance in National Accounts. *Rev. Income Wealth*, December 1983, *29* (4), pp. 371–404. **[G: U.S.]**

Ruggles, Richard. The United States National Income Accounts, 1947–1977: Their Conceptual Basis and Evolution. **In** *Foss, M. F., ed.*, 1983, pp. 15–96. **[G: U.S.]**

Sanz, Ricardo. Desagregacion temporal de series economicas. (With English summary.) *Cuadernos Econ.*, April 1983, *20* (59), pp. 85–100. **[G: Spain]**

Sarma, I. R. K. Capital Formation and Saving in India, 1950–51 to 1979–80, Report of the Working Group on Savings, Some Observations. *Margin*, July 1983, *15* (4), pp. 29–33. **[G: India]**

Schimmler, Harry. Some Conceptual Dilemmas in the Use of Present National Accounts. *Rev. Income Wealth*, September 1983, *29* (3), pp. 323–32.

St.-Hilaire, France and Whalley, John. A Microconsistent Equilibrium Data Set for Canada for Use in Tax Policy Analysis. *Rev. Income Wealth*, June 1983, *29* (2), pp. 175–204. **[G: Canada]**

Stein, Bruno and Wenig, Alois. The Economics of the Shadow Economy: A Conference Report. *Z. ges. Staatswiss.*, December 1983, *139* (4), pp. 690–707.

Thornton, Judith. Twenty-Five Years of Soviet National Income Accounting: From Adjusted Factor Cost to Ultra-Adjusted Factor Cost. *ACES Bull. (See Comp. Econ. Stud. after 8/85)*, Fall 1983, *25* (3), pp. 53–67. **[G: U.S.S.R.]**

Tice, Helen Stone. The United States National Income Accounts, 1947–1977: Their Conceptual Basis and Evolution: Comment. **In** *Foss, M. F., ed.*, 1983, pp. 96–104. **[G: U.S.]**

2212 National Income Accounts

Abedian, I. A Quantitative Review of the Economy of Transkei. *S. Afr. J. Econ.*, June 1983, *51* (2), pp. 252–69. [G: S. Africa]

Aron, Paul H. and Aron, Laurie J. Japan: Equity Markets. In *George, A. M. and Giddy, I. H., eds., Vol. 2,* 1983, pp. 6.7:1–40. [G: Japan]

Aron, Paul H. and Aron, Laurie J. The Asian Equities Markets. In *George, A. M. and Giddy, I. H., eds., Vol. 2,* 1983, pp. 6.9:1–54. [G: Australia; Singapore; Malaysia; Hong Kong]

Asimakopulos, A. A Kaleckian Profits Equation and the United States Economy, 1950–82. *Metroecon.,* February–June 1983, *35*(1–2), pp. 1–27. [G: U.S.]

Asimakopulos, A. Profit and Paper Profit: Some Kaleckian Evolution: A Comment. *J. Post Keynesian Econ.,* Fall 1983, *6*(1), pp. 125–32.

Auerbach, Alan J. and Kotlikoff, Laurence J. National Savings, Economic Welfare, and the Structure of Taxation. In *Feldstein, M., ed.,* 1983, pp. 459–93. [G: U.S.]

Bach, Christopher L. U.S. International Transactions, Fourth Quarter and Year 1982. *Surv. Curr. Bus.,* March 1983, *63*(3), pp. 42–69. [G: U.S.]

Bono Martínez, E.; Jordán Galduf, J. M. and Tomás Carpi, J.-A. Notas sobre crisis de legitimación, déficit público y transición política en España. (Notes on the Crisis of Legitimacy, the Public Deficit and Transitional Politics in Spain. With English summary.) *Écon. Soc.,* September–October–November 1983, *17*(9–10–11), pp. 1741–61. [G: Spain]

Carson, Carol S. Net Exports of Goods and Services, 1980–82. *Surv. Curr. Bus.,* March 1983, *63*(3), pp. 31–41. [G: U.S.]

Chung, William K. and Fouch, Gregory G. Foreign Direct Investment in the United States in 1982. *Surv. Curr. Bus.,* August 1983, *63*(8), pp. 31–41. [G: U.S.]

Crafts, N. F. R. Gross National Product in Europe 1870–1910: Some New Estimates. *Exploration Econ. Hist.,* October 1983, *20*(4), pp. 387–401. [G: Europe]

Datt, Ruddar. The Parallel Economy in India. *Indian Econ. J.,* April-June 1983, *30*(4), pp. 19–54. [G: India]

Denison, Edward F. The Interruption of Productivity Growth in the United States. *Econ. J.,* March 1983, *93*(369), pp. 56–77. [G: U.S.]

DiLullo, Anthony J. U.S. International Transactions, Second Quarter 1983. *Surv. Curr. Bus.,* September 1983, *63*(9), pp. 34–56. [G: U.S.]

Durgin, Frank A., Jr. The Relationship of the Death of Stalin to the Economic Change of the Post-Stalin Era or Was Stalin's Departure Really Necessary? In *Stuart, R. C., ed.,* 1983, pp. 118–42. [G: U.S.S.R.]

Erdös, Peter and Molnár, Ferenc. An Answer to Asimakopulos's Comment [Profit and Paper Profit: Some Kaleckian Evolution]. *J. Post Keynesian Econ.,* Fall 1983, *6*(1), pp. 133–39.

Feldstein, Martin S. Has the Rate of Investment Fallen? *Rev. Econ. Statist.,* February 1983, *65*(1), pp. 144–49. [G: U.S.]

FitzGerald, E. V. K. State Capitalism in Peru: A Model of Economic Development and Its Limitations. In *McClintock, C. and Lowenthal, A. F., eds.,* 1983, pp. 65–93. [G: Peru]

Frey, Bruno S. and Weck, Hannelore. Estimating the Shadow Economy: A 'Naive' Approach. *Oxford Econ. Pap.,* March 1983, *35*(1), pp. 23–44. [G: OECD]

Frey, Bruno S. and Weck, Hannelore. What Produces a Hidden Economy? An International Cross Section Analysis. *Southern Econ. J.,* January 1983, *49*(3), pp. 822–32.

Gottheil, Fred M. Establishing the Preconditions to Long-run Development: Egypt after the Treaty. In *Starr, J. R., ed.,* 1983, pp. 35–45. [G: Egypt]

Gould, Frank. Public Expenditure in Japan: A Comparative View. *Hitotsubashi J. Econ.,* February 1983, *23*(2), pp. 57–67. [G: OECD]

Halan, Yogesh C. Inflation, Poverty and the Third World: India's Experience. In *Schmukler, N. and Marcus, E., eds.,* 1983, pp. 625–42. [G: India]

Heston, Alan W. National Income. In *Kumar, D., ed.,* 1983, pp. 376–462. [G: India]

Heston, Alan W. A Different Perspective of Pakistan's Economy: The Structure of Expenditures and Prices, 1975–81. *Pakistan Devel. Rev.,* Autumn 1983, *22*(3), pp. 163–77. [G: Pakistan; LDCs; MDCs]

Howenstine, Ned G. Gross Product of U.S. Multinational Companies, 1977. *Surv. Curr. Bus.,* February 1983, *63*(2), pp. 24–29. [G: U.S.]

Iglesias, Enrique V. Reflections on the Latin American Economy in 1982. *Cepal Rev.,* April 1983, (19), pp. 7–49. [G: Latin America]

Iliev, Ivan and Naoumov, Nicolas. Human Resources and Employment in the Peoples' Republic of Bulgaria. In *Weisbrod, B. and Hughes, H., eds.,* 1983, pp. 48–54. [G: Bulgaria]

Jalla, Ermanno. Le variazioni annuali di alcune grandezze economiche. (The Yearly Variations of Some Economic Data. With English summary.) *Statistica,* July–September 1983, *43*(3), pp. 489–506. [G: Italy]

Jamal, Vali. Nomads and Farmers: Incomes and Poverty in Rural Somalia. In *Ghai, D. and Radwan, S., eds.,* 1983, pp. 281–311. [G: Somalia]

Jorge, Antonio and Salazar-Carrillo, Jorge. External Debt and Development in Latin America: A Background Paper. In *Jorge, A.; Salazar-Carillo, J. and Higonnet, R. P., eds.,* 1983, pp. 1–35. [G: Latin America]

Keller, Wouter J. and Wansbeek, Tom. Private Consumption Expenditures and Price Index Numbers for the Netherlands 1951–1977. *Rev. Public Data Use (See J. Econ. Soc. Meas. after 4/85),* December 1983, *11*(4), pp. 311–13. [G: Netherlands]

Kirchgässner, Gebhard. Size and Development of the West German Shadow Economy, 1955–1980. *Z. ges. Staatswiss.,* June 1983, *139*(2), pp. 197–214. [G: W. Germany]

Kozlow, Ralph. Capital Expenditures by Majority–Owned Foreign Affiliates of U.S. Companies, 1983. *Surv. Curr. Bus.,* March 1983, *63*(3), pp. 25–30. [G: U.S.]

Kozlow, Ralph. Capital Expenditures by Majority-Owned Foreign Affiliates of U.S. Companies, 1983 and 1984. *Surv. Curr. Bus.,* September 1983, *63*(9), pp. 27–33. [G: U.S.]

Kravis, Irving B.; Heston, Alan W. and Summers, Robert. The Share of Services in Economic

Growth. **In** *[Klein, L. R.]*, 1983, pp. 188–218. **[G: U.S.; U.K.; France]**

Krueger, Russell C. U.S. International Transactions, First Quarter 1983. *Surv. Curr. Bus.*, June 1983, *63*(6), pp. 33–67. **[G: U.S.]**

Landefeld, J. Steven and Seskin, Eugene P. Plant and Equipment Expenditures, the Four Quarters of 1983. *Surv. Curr. Bus.*, June 1983, *63*(6), pp. 19–23. **[G: U.S.]**

Landefeld, J. Steven and Seskin, Eugene P. Plant and Equipment Expenditures, Quarters of 1983 and First and Second Quarters of 1984. *Surv. Curr. Bus.*, December 1983, *63*(12), pp. 19–24. **[G: U.S.]**

Levin, David J. Receipts and Expenditures of State Governments and of Local Governments, 1968–81. *Surv. Curr. Bus.*, May 1983, *63*(5), pp. 25–38. **[G: U.S.]**

Levin, David J. State and Local Government Fiscal Position in 1982. *Surv. Curr. Bus.*, January 1983, *63*(1), pp. 19–22. **[G: U.S.]**

Lewis, W. Arthur. Patterns of Public Revenue and Expenditure. **In** *Lewis, W. A.*, 1983, *1956*, pp. 573–614. **[G: LDCs; MDCs]**

Liang, Ming-Yih. Savings in Taiwan: An Empirical Investigation. *J. Econ. Devel.*, July 1983, *8*(1), pp. 109–29. **[G: Taiwan]**

Lim, Chong Yah. Singapore's Economic Development: Retrospect and Prospect. **In** *Chen, P. S. J., ed.*, 1983, pp. 89–104. **[G: Singapore]**

Linz, Susan J. Measuring the Carryover Cost of WWII to the Soviet People: 1945–1953. *Exploration Econ. Hist.*, October 1983, *20*(4), pp. 375–86. **[G: U.S.S.R.]**

McCormick, William. Military Transactions in the U.S. International Accounts, 1976–82. *Surv. Curr. Bus.*, May 1983, *63*(5), pp. 18–24. **[G: U.S.]**

Moore, Geoffrey H. Inflation and Statistics—Again. **In** *Moore, G. H.*, 1983, *1981*, pp. 313–29. **[G: U.S.]**

Nasilowski, Mieczyslaw. Accumulation in a Socialist Economy: The Case of Poland. **In** *Modigliani, F. and Hemming, R., eds.*, 1983, pp. 235–54. **[G: Poland]**

Okun, Arthur M. A Postmortem of the 1974 Recession. **In** *Okun, A. M.*, 1983, *1975*, pp. 482–95. **[G: U.S.]**

Okun, Arthur M. A Review of Some Economic Forecasts for 1955–57. **In** *Okun, A. M.*, 1983, *1959*, pp. 507–24. **[G: U.S.]**

Okun, Arthur M. Measuring the Impact of the 1964 Tax Reduction. **In** *Okun, A. M.*, 1983, *1968*, pp. 405–23. **[G: U.S.]**

Park, Thae S. Federal Personal Income Taxes: Liabilities and Payments, 1977–81. *Surv. Curr. Bus.*, January 1983, *63*(1), pp. 27–30. **[G: U.S.]**

Park, Thae S. Personal Income and Adjusted Gross Income, 1977–81. *Surv. Curr. Bus.*, April 1983, *63*(4), pp. 28–33. **[G: U.S.]**

Peterson, J. C. and Jones, D. I. H. Government Expenditure and Resource Crowding Out: A Brief Examination of Some Aspects of the Bacon and Eltis Hypothesis. *Rivista Int. Sci. Econ. Com.*, December 1983, *30*(12), pp. 1100–114. **[G: U.K.; W. Germany]**

Právo, Rude. Accelerating Rate of Development: Report on the Development of the National Economy and Fulfilment of the Plan in Czechoslovakia in the First Six Months of 1983. *Czech. Econ. Digest.*, November 1983, (7), pp. 3–21. **[G: Czechoslovakia]**

Quiñones, Fernando Gonzáles. Employment and Development in Latin America. **In** *Urquidi, V. L. and Reyes, S. T., eds.*, 1983, pp. 406–23. **[G: Latin America]**

Reddaway, Brian. Macroeconomic Performance in Perspective. **In** *Shepherd, D.; Turk, J. and Silberston, A., eds.*, 1983, pp. 200–226. **[G: U.K.; OECD]**

Ruggeri, G. C. A Note on the Energy–GNP Relationship in Canada, 1961–1980. *J. Energy Devel.*, Spring 1983, *8*(2), pp. 341–46. **[G: Canada]**

Russo, William J., Jr. and Rutledge, Gary L. Plant and Equipment Expenditures by Business for Pollution Abatement, 1982 and Planned 1983. *Surv. Curr. Bus.*, June 1983, *63*(6), pp. 24–26. **[G: U.S.]**

Rutledge, Gary L. and Lease-Trevathan, Susan. Pollution Abatement and Control Expenditures, 1972–81. *Surv. Curr. Bus.*, February 1983, *63*(2), pp. 15–23. **[G: U.S.]**

Sachs, Abner and Ziemer, Richard C. Implicit Price Deflators for Military Construction. *Surv. Curr. Bus.*, November 1983, *63*(11), pp. 14–18. **[G: U.S.]**

Saito, Mitsuo. Finance and Economic Growth: The Japanese Experience. **In** *[Klein, L. R.]*, 1983, pp. 296–313. **[G: Japan]**

Salazar-Carrillo, Jorge. Real Product and Price Comparisons for Latin America and Other World Countries. *Econ. Develop. Cult. Change*, July 1983, *31*(4), pp. 757–73. **[G: Latin America; Selected LDCs; Selected MDCs]**

Salib, Anis B. Energy, GDP, and the Structure of Demand: An International Comparison Using Input-Output Techniques. *J. Energy Devel.*, Autumn 1983, *9*(1), pp. 55–61. **[G: U.S.; U.K.; Japan; France; Italy]**

Sargent, Thomas J. Stopping Moderate Inflations: The Methods of Poincaré and Thatcher. **In** *Dornbusch, R. and Simonsen, M. H., eds.*, 1983, pp. 54–96. **[G: France; U.K.]**

Schinasi, Garry J. Business Fixed Investment: Recent Developments and Outlook. *Fed. Res. Bull.*, January 1983, *69*(1), pp. 1–10. **[G: U.S.]**

Scholl, Russell B. The International Investment Position of the United States in 1982. *Surv. Curr. Bus.*, August 1983, *63*(8), pp. 42–48. **[G: U.S.]**

Schydlowsky, Daniel M. and Wicht, Juan J. The Anatomy of an Economic Failure. **In** *McClintock, C. and Lowenthal, A. F., eds.*, 1983, pp. 94–143. **[G: Peru]**

Seskin, Eugene P. and Landefeld, J. Steven. Plant and Equipment Expenditures, First and Second Quarters and Second Half of 1983. *Surv. Curr. Bus.*, March 1983, *63*(3), pp. 19–24. **[G: U.S.]**

Seskin, Eugene P. and Landefeld, J. Steven. Plant and Equipment Expenditures, the Four Quarters of 1983. *Surv. Curr. Bus.*, September 1983, *63*(9), pp. 19–26. **[G: U.S.]**

Singh, A. J. and Singh, Tirath. Black Money—Genesis, Estimation, Causes and Remedies. *Econ. Aff.*,

January–March 1983, *28*(1), pp. 632–43. [G: India]

Starzec, Krzysztof. L'économie polonaise vue à travers des circuits parallèles. (Polish "Official" and "Unofficial" Economy: An Empirical Approach. With English summary.) *Consommation*, October–December 1983, *30*(4), pp. 55–94. [G: Poland]

Tanzi, Vito. The Underground Economy. *Finance Develop.*, December 1983, *20*(4), pp. 10–13. [G: Selected Countries]

Tanzi, Vito. The Underground Economy in the United States: Annual Estimates, 1930–80. *Int. Monet. Fund Staff Pap.*, June 1983, *30*(2), pp. 283–305. [G: U.S.]

Teckenberg, Wolfgang. Economic Well-being in the Soviet Union Inflation and the Distribution of Resources. In *Schmukler, N. and Marcus, E., eds.*, 1983, pp. 659–76. [G: U.S.S.R.]

Theil, Henri. World Product and Income: A Review Article. *J. Polit. Econ.*, June 1983, *91*(3), pp. 505–17.

Thorp, Rosemary. The Evolution of Peru's Economy. In *McClintock, C. and Lowenthal, A. F., eds.*, 1983, pp. 39–61. [G: Peru]

Thrall, Grant Ian and Erol, Cengiz. A Dynamic Equilibrium Model of Regional Capital Investment with Supporting Evidence from Canada and the United States. *Econ. Geogr.*, July 1983, *59*(3), pp. 272–81. [G: Canada; U.S.]

Waite, Charles A. and Wakefield, Joseph C. Federal Fiscal Programs. *Surv. Curr. Bus.*, February 1983, *63*(2), pp. 8–14. [G: U.S.]

Wakefield, Joseph C. Federal Budget Developments. *Surv. Curr. Bus.*, April 1983, *63*(4), pp. 24–27. [G: U.S.]

Whichard, Obie G. U.S. Direct Investment Abroad in 1982. *Surv. Curr. Bus.*, August 1983, *63*(8), pp. 14–30. [G: U.S.]

Wilcox, James A. Disaggregating Data Using Related Series. *J. Bus. Econ. Statist.*, July 1983, *1*(3), pp. 187–91. [G: U.S.]

Woodward, John T.; Seskin, Eugene P. and Landefeld, J. Steven. Plant and Equipment Expenditures, 1983. *Surv. Curr. Bus.*, January 1983, *63*(1), pp. 31–33. [G: U.S.]

2213 Income Distribution

Altimir, Oscar. Poverty in Latin America: An Examination of the Evidence. **In** *Urquidi, V. L. and Reyes, S. T., eds.*, 1983, pp. 279–98. [G: Latin America]

Amos, Orley M., Jr. The Relationship between Regional Income Inequality, Personal Income Inequality, and Development. *Reg. Sci. Persp.*, 1983, *13*(1), pp. 3–14. [G: U.S.]

Arnold, Barry C. and Press, S. James. Bayesian Inference for Pareto Populations. *J. Econometrics*, April 1983, *21*(3), pp. 287–306. [G: U.S.]

Atkinson, Anthony B.; Maynard, Alan K. and Trinder, C. G. Evidence on Intergenerational Income Mobility in Britain: Some Further Preliminary Results. **In** *Weisbrod, B. and Hughes, H., eds.*, 1983, pp. 290–308. [G: U.K.]

Atkinson, Anthony B. Income Distribution and Inequality of Opportunity. **In** *Atkinson, A. B.*, 1983, *1980*, pp. 77–92.

Atkinson, Anthony B. Introduction to Part I: Inequality and Mobility. **In** *Atkinson, A. B.*, 1983, pp. 3–13.

Atkinson, Anthony B. On the Measurement of Inequality. **In** *Atkinson, A. B.*, 1983, *1970*, pp. 15–36. [G: MDCs; LDCs]

Atkinson, Anthony B. and Bourguignon, François. The Comparison of Multi-dimensioned Distributions of Economic Status. **In** *Atkinson, A. B.*, 1983, pp. 37–59.

Balcer, Yves, et al. Income Redistribution and the Structure of Indirect Taxation. **In** *Helpman, E.; Razin, A. and Sadka, E., eds.*, 1983, pp. 279–97. [G: U.S.]

Bates, Timothy. The Declining Relative Incomes of Urban Black Households. *Challenge*, May/June 1983, *26*(2), pp. 48–49. [G: U.S.]

Beach, Charles M. and Davidson, Russell. Distribution-Free Statistical Inference with Lorenz Curves and Income Shares. *Rev. Econ. Stud.*, October 1983, *50*(4), pp. 723–35.

Behrman, Jere R. and Taubman, Paul. Redistribution of Earnings by Unemployment and Inflation. **In** *[Klein, L. R.]*, 1983, pp. 262–81. [G: U.S.]

Bequele, Assefa. Stagnation and Inequality in Ghana. **In** *Ghai, D. and Radwan, S., eds.*, 1983, pp. 219–47. [G: Ghana]

Berrebi, Z. M. and Silber, Jacques. On an Absolute Measure of Distributional Change. *Europ. Econ. Rev.*, July 1983, *22*(2), pp. 139–46.

Berry, Albert. Agrarian Structure, Rural Labour Markets and Trends in Rural Incomes in Latin America. **In** *Urquidi, V. L. and Reyes, S. T., eds.*, 1983, pp. 174–94. [G: Brazil; Colombia; Mexico]

Berry, Albert. Predicting Income Distribution in Latin America during the 1980s. **In** *Ritter, A. R. M. and Pollock, D. H., eds.*, 1983, pp. 57–84. [G: Latin America]

Berry, Albert; Bourguignon, François and Morrisson, Christian. Changes in the World Distribution of Income between 1950 and 1977. *Econ. J.*, June 1983, *93*(370), pp. 331–50.

Berry, Albert; Bourguignon, François and Morrisson, Christian. The Level of World Inequality: How Much Can One Say? *Rev. Income Wealth*, September 1983, *29*(3), pp. 217–41. [G: Global]

Bienen, Henry S. Income Distribution and Politics in Nigeria. **In** *Zartman, I. W., ed.*, 1983, pp. 85–104. [G: Nigeria]

Blyn, George. Income Distribution among Haryana and Punjab Cultivators, 1968/69–1975/76. *Indian Econ. Rev.*, July–December 1983, *18*(2), pp. 199–224. [G: India]

Bornschier, Volker. World Economy, Level Development and Income Distribution: An Integration of Different Approaches to the Explanation of Income Inequality. *World Devel.*, January 1983, *11*(1), pp. 11–20. [G: Global; LDCs]

Boulding, Kenneth E. The Stability of Inequality. **In** *Letwin, W., ed.*, 1983, *1975*, pp. 261–75. [G: U.S.]

Bourguignon, Francois; Michel, G. and Miqueu, D. Short-Run Rigidities and Long-Run Adjustments in a Computable General Equilibrium Model of

Income Distribution and Development. *J. Devel. Econ.*, Aug.–Oct. 1983, *13*(1–2), pp. 21–43. [G: Venezuela]

Braulke, Michael. A Note on Kuznets' U. *Rev. Econ. Statist.*, February 1983, *65*(1), pp. 135–39.

Braulke, Michael. An Approximation to the Gini Coefficient for a Population Based on Sparse Information for Sub-Groups. *J. Devel. Econ.*, February/April 1983, *12*(1/2), pp. 75–81. [G: LDCs]

Cain, Louis P. Incomes in the Twentieth Century United States: Discussion. *J. Econ. Hist.*, March 1983, *43*(1), pp. 241–42. [G: U.S.]

Chakrabarty, Gurupada. Sen's Welfare Measure and Sources of Income. *Margin*, April 1983, *15*(3), pp. 73–78.

Chakrabarty, Gurupada. Studies on Size Distribution of Income and Consumption—A Review. *Margin*, October 1983, *16*(1), pp. 57–83. [G: India]

Chaudhry, M. Ghaffar. Green Revolution and Redistribution of Rural Incomes: Pakistan's Experience—A Reply. *Pakistan Devel. Rev.*, Summer 1983, *22*(2), pp. 117–23.

Colclough, Christopher and Fallon, Peter. Rural Poverty in Botswana: Dimensions, Causes and Constraints. **In** *Ghai, D. and Radwan, S., eds.*, 1983, pp. 129–53. [G: Botswana]

Coleman, James S. Equality of Opportunity and Equality of Results. **In** *Letwin, W., ed.*, 1983, *1973*, pp. 189–98. [G: U.S.]

Collier, Paul. Oil and Inequality in Rural Nigeria. **In** *Ghai, D. and Radwan, S., eds.*, 1983, pp. 191–217. [G: Nigeria]

Cortázar, René. Chile: Resultados distributivos 1973–82. (With English summary.) *Desarrollo Econ.*, October-December 1983, *23*(91), pp. 369–94. [G: Chile]

DaVanzo, Julie and Kusnic, Michael W. Ethnic Differences in Income in Peninsular Malaysia: Their Sensitivity to the Definition and Measurement of Income. *Singapore Econ. Rev.*, October 1983, *28*(2), pp. 22–45. [G: Malaysia]

De Janvry, Alain and Sadoulet, Elisabeth. Social Articulation as a Condition for Equitable Growth. *J. Devel. Econ.*, December 1983, *13*(3), pp. 275–303. [G: Brazil; Mexico; LDCs]

Deichert, Jerome A. and Dobitz, Clifford P. Inequality in the Distribution of Income: United States, March 1979. *Nebr. J. Econ. Bus.*, Spring 1983, *22*(2), pp. 22–32. [G: U.S.]

Donaldson, David and Weymark, John A. Ethically Flexible Gini Indices for Income Distributions in the Continuum. *J. Econ. Theory*, April 1983, *29*(2), pp. 353–58.

Drobny, Andres and Wells, John. Wages, Minimum Wages, and Income Distribution in Brazil: Results from the Construction Industry. *J. Devel. Econ.*, December 1983, *13*(3), pp. 305–30. [G: Brazil]

Eckstein, Susan. Revolution and Redistribution in Latin America. **In** *McClintock, C. and Lowenthal, A. F., eds.*, 1983, pp. 347–86. [G: Latin America]

Erdilek, Asim. Inequity Based on Inefficiency: The Turkish Case [A Review Article]. *Weltwirtsch. Arch.*, 1983, *119*(4), pp. 754–62. [G: Turkey]

Espinguet, Patrice and Terraza, Michel. Essai d'extrapolation des distributions de salaires français. (An Attempt to Extrapolate the Distribution of French Wages. With English summary.) *Écon. Appl.*, 1983, *36*(2–3), pp. 535–61. [G: France]

Euler, Manfred. Die Einkommensverteilung und-entwicklung in der Bundesrepublik Deutschland 1962–1978 nach Ergebnissen der Einkommens- und Verbrauchsstichproben (Income Distribution and Development in the Federal Republic of Germany 1962–1978 Based on Results of Income and Expenditure Surveys. With English summary.) *Konjunkturpolitik*, 1983, *29*(4), pp. 199–228. [G: W. Germany]

Feenberg, Daniel R. The Economic Status of the Elderly: Comment. **In** *Bodie, Z. and Shoven, J. B., eds.*, 1983, pp. 393–96. [G: U.S.]

Field, Frank. Breaking the Mould: The Thatcher Government's Fiscal Policies. **In** *Field, F., ed.*, 1983, pp. 56–68. [G: U.K.]

Foster, James E. An Axiomatic Characterization of the Theil Measure of Income Inequality. *J. Econ. Theory*, October 1983, *31*(1), pp. 105–21.

Fox, M. Louise. Income Distribution in Post-1964 Brazil: New Results. *J. Econ. Hist.*, March 1983, *43*(1), pp. 261–71. [G: Brazil]

Friesen, Peter H. and Miller, Danny. Annual Inequality and Lifetime Inequality. *Quart. J. Econ.*, February 1983, *98*(1), pp. 139–55. [G: U.S.]

Ghai, Dharam and Radwan, Samir. Agrarian Change, Differentiation and Rural Poverty in Africa: A General Survey. **In** *Ghai, D. and Radwan, S., eds.*, 1983, pp. 1–29. [G: Sub-Saharan Africa]

Ghai, Dharam and Radwan, Samir. Growth and Inequality: Rural Development in Malawi, 1964–78. **In** *Ghai, D. and Radwan, S., eds.*, 1983, pp. 71–97. [G: Malawi]

Gooneratne, W. and Gunawardena, P. J. Poverty and Inequality in Rural Sri Lanka. **In** *Khan, A. R. and Lee, E., eds.*, 1983, pp. 247–71. [G: Sri Lanka]

Griffin, Keith and Griffin, Kimberley. Institutional Change and Income Distribution in the Chinese Countryside. *Oxford Bull. Econ. Statist.*, August 1983, *45*(3), pp. 223–48. [G: China]

Gruen, Fred H. Australian Inflation and the Distribution of Income and Wealth—A Preliminary View. **In** *Pagan, A. R. and Trivedi, P. K., eds.*, 1983, pp. 225–60. [G: Australia]

Gupta, Kanhaya L. and Islam, M. Anisul. Income Distribution and Economic Growth: Some Empirical Evidence. *J. Econ. Devel.*, July 1983, *8*(1), pp. 25–44. [G: Selected Countries]

Hancock, Karen. Understanding the Scottish Economy: 'Rich Man, Poor Man . . .' (Distribution of Income). **In** *Ingham, K. P. D. and Love, J., eds.*, 1983, pp. 151–60. [G: U.K.]

Hart, Peter E. The Size Mobility of Earnings. *Oxford Bull. Econ. Statist.*, May 1983, *45*(2), pp. 181–93. [G: U.K.]

Hartog, Joop. Inequality Reduction by Income Taxes: Just How Much? An Investigation for the Netherlands, 1914–1973. *Empirical Econ.*, 1983, *8*(1), pp. 9–13. [G: Netherlands]

Heyzer, Noeleen. International Production and Social Change: An Analysis of the State, Employment, and Trade Unions in Singapore. **In** *Chen, P. S. J., ed.*, 1983, pp. 105–28. [G: Singapore]

Hurd, Michael D. and Shoven, John B. The Economic Status of the Elderly. **In** *Bodie, Z. and Shoven, J. B., eds.*, 1983, pp. 359–93, 396–97. **[G: U.S.]**

Iritani, Jun and Kuga, Kiyoshi. Duality between the Lorenz Curves and the Income Distribution Functions. *Econ. Stud. Quart.*, April 1983, *34*(1), pp. 9–21.

Islam, Rizwanul. Poverty and Income Distribution in Rural Nepal. **In** *Khan, A. R. and Lee, E., eds.*, 1983, pp. 165–83. **[G: Nepal]**

Jüttner, D. Johannes and Murray, John H. Notes and Numbers on Marx's Falling Rate of Profit. *Econ. Rec.*, December 1983, *59*(167), pp. 375–83. **[G: Australia]**

Katz, Claudio J.; Mahler, Vincent A. and Franz, Michael G. The Impact of Taxes on Growth and Distribution in Developed Capitalist Countries: A Cross-National Study. *Amer. Polit. Sci. Rev.*, December 1983, *77*(4), pp. 871–86. **[G: Selected OECD]**

Kearl, J. R. and Pope, Clayne L. The Life Cycle in Economic History. *J. Econ. Hist.*, March 1983, *43*(1), pp. 149–58. **[G: U.S.]**

Khan, Mahmood Hasan. "Green Revolution and Redistribution of Rural Incomes: Pakistan's Experience"—A Comment. *Pakistan Devel. Rev.*, Spring 1983, *22*(1), pp. 47–56. **[G: Pakistan]**

Knight, John B. and Sabot, Richard H. Educational Expansion and the Kuznets Effect. *Amer. Econ. Rev.*, December 1983, *73*(5), pp. 1132–36. **[G: Kenya; Tanzania]**

Koo, Anthony Y. C.; Quan, Nguyen and Rasche, Robert H. Identification of the Lorenz Curve by Lorenz Coefficient: A Reply. *Weltwirtsch. Arch.*, 1983, *119*(2), pp. 368–69. **[G: Selected Countries]**

Kristol, Irving. Some Personal Reflections on Economic Well-being and Income Distribution. **In** *Kristol, I.*, 1983, *1980*, pp. 194–201.

Lee, Eddy. Export-led Rural Development: The Ivory Coast. **In** *Ghai, D. and Radwan, S., eds.*, 1983, pp. 99–127. **[G: Ivory Coast]**

Lehrer, Evelyn and Nerlove, Marc. The Impact of Female Life-cycle Time-allocation Decisions on Income Distribution among Families. **In** *Weisbrod, B. and Hughes, H., eds.*, 1983, pp. 274–89. **[G: U.S.]**

Letwin, William. The Case Against Equality. **In** *Letwin, W., ed.*, 1983, pp. 1–70. **[G: U.K.]**

Lindbeck, Assar. Interpreting Income Distributions in a Welfare State: The Case of Sweden. *Europ. Econ. Rev.*, July 1983, *22*(2), pp. 227–56. **[G: Sweden]**

Lindert, Peter H. and Williamson, Jeffrey G. Erratum [Revising England's Social Tables, 1688–1812] [Reinterpreting Britain's Social Tables, 1688–1913]. *Exploration Econ. Hist.*, July 1983, *20*(3), pp. 329–30. **[G: U.K.]**

Lindert, Peter H. and Williamson, Jeffrey G. Reinterpreting Britain's Social Tables, 1688–1913. *Exploration Econ. Hist.*, January 1983, *20*(1), pp. 94–109. **[G: U.K.]**

Lustig, Nora. Distribution of Income and Patterns of Consumption in Mexico: Empirical Testing of Some Latin American Structuralist Hypotheses. **In** *Urquidi, V. L. and Reyes, S. T., eds.*, 1983, pp. 236–51. **[G: Mexico]**

Mathur, Ashok. Regional Development and Income Disparities in India: A Sectoral Analysis. *Econ. Develop. Cult. Change*, April 1983, *31*(3), pp. 475–505. **[G: India]**

Mayer, Francine. Les modèles de répartition des revenus de type intégré: quelques éléments de comparaison. (Integrated Income Distribution Models: Some Comparisons. With English summary.) *L'Actual. Econ.*, March 1983, *59*(1), pp. 121–34.

Menchik, Paul L. and David, Martin H. Income Distribution, Lifetime Savings, and Bequests. *Amer. Econ. Rev.*, September 1983, *73*(4), pp. 672–90. **[G: U.S.]**

Metwally, M. M. and Tamaschke, H. U. The Effect of Inflation and Technology on Factor Shares. *Appl. Econ.*, December 1983, *15*(6), pp. 777–91. **[G: Selected Countries]**

Nord, Stephen. An Interstate Analysis of Changes in Nonwhite and White Family Incomes 1960 to 1970. *Eastern Econ. J.*, January–March 1983, *9*(1), pp. 13–21. **[G: U.S.]**

Normand, Denis; Hawley, Gilbert and Gillespie, W. Irwin. In Search of the Changing Distribution of Income during the Post-War Period in Canada and the United States. *Public Finance*, 1983, *38*(2), pp. 267–81. **[G: U.S.; Canada]**

North, Liisa L. Problems of Democratization in Peru and Ecuador. **In** *Ritter, A. R. M. and Pollock, D. H., eds.*, 1983, pp. 214–39. **[G: Peru; Ecuador]**

Nugent, Jeffrey B. and Tarawneh, Fayez A. The Anatomy of Changes in Income Distribution and Poverty among Mexico's Economically Active Population between 1950 and 1970. *J. Devel. Areas*, January 1983, *17*(2), pp. 197–226. **[G: Mexico]**

Okner, Benjamin A. and Bawden, D. Lee. Recent Changes in Federal Income Redistribution Policy. *Nat. Tax J.*, September 1983, *36*(3), pp. 347–60. **[G: U.S.]**

Orsatti, Alvaro. La nueva distribución funcional del ingreso en la Argentina. (With English summary.) *Desarrollo Econ.*, October-December 1983, *23*(91), pp. 315–37. **[G: Argentina]**

Pang, Eng Fong. Race, Income Distribution, and Development in Malaysia and Singapore. **In** *Lim, L. Y. C. and Gosling, L. A. P., eds.*, 1983, pp. 316–35. **[G: Malaysia; Singapore]**

Panning, William H. Inequality, Social Comparison, and Relative Deprivation. *Amer. Polit. Sci. Rev.*, June 1983, *77*(2), pp. 323–29.

Parikh, Ashok and Das, Tarun. Inequality Index with Differences in Inequality Aversion for Income and Population Groups. *Rivista Int. Sci. Econ. Com.*, April-May 1983, *30*(4–5), pp. 362–74. **[G: U.S.]**

Pfeffermann, Guy and Webb, Richard. Poverty and Income Distribution in Brazil. *Rev. Income Wealth*, June 1983, *29*(2), pp. 101–24. **[G: Brazil]**

Phelps, Brown Henry. Egalitarianism and the Distribution of Wealth and Income in the U.K. *Ind. Relat.*, Spring 1983, *22*(2), pp. 186–202. **[G: U.K.]**

Playford, Clive and Pond, Chris. The Right to Be Unequal: Inequality in Incomes. **In** *Field, F., ed.,* 1983, pp. 34–55. **[G: U.K.]**

Podgursky, Michael. Unions and Family Income Inequality. *J. Human Res.,* Fall 1983, *18* (4), pp. 574–91. **[G: U.S.]**

van Praag, Bernard M. S.; Hagenaars, Aldi J. M. and van Eck, Wim. The Influence of Classification and Observation Errors on the Measurement of Income Inequality. *Econometrica,* July 1983, *51* (4), pp. 1093–108. **[G: Netherlands]**

Prahladachar, M. Income Distribution Effects on the Green Revolution in India: A Review of Empirical Evidence. *World Devel.,* November 1983, *11* (11), pp. 927–44. **[G: India]**

Radner, Daniel B. Adjusted Estimates of the Size Distribution of Family Money Income. *J. Bus. Econ. Statist.,* April 1983, *1* (2), pp. 136–46. **[G: U.S.]**

Ram, Rati. Comparison of the Actual and Projected Cross-Country Inequality in the Mid-1970's. *Atlantic Econ. J.,* December 1983, *11* (4), pp. 79. **[G: Global]**

Ranis, Gustav. Alternative Patterns of Distribution and Growth in the Mixed Economy: The Philippines and Taiwan. **In** *Stewart, F., ed.,* 1983, pp. 83–107. **[G: Philippines; Taiwan]**

Ranis, Gustav. Employment and Income Distribution Constraints in Latin America. **In** *Urquidi, V. L. and Reyes, S. T., eds.,* 1983, pp. 131–50. **[G: Taiwan; Colombia; Mexico]**

Ransom, Michael R. and Cramer, Jan S. Income Distribution Functions with Disturbances. *Europ. Econ. Rev.,* August 1983, *22* (3), pp. 363–72. **[G: U.S.]**

Rice, G. Randolph and Lozada, Gabriel A. The Effects of Unemployment and Inflation on the Income Distribution: A Regional View. *Atlantic Econ. J.,* July 1983, *11* (2), pp. 12–21. **[G: U.S.]**

Rodgers, Gerry. Population Growth, Inequality and Poverty. *Int. Lab. Rev.,* July–August 1983, *122* (4), pp. 443–60. **[G: LDCs]**

Saith, Ashwani. Development and Distribution: A Critique of the Cross-Country U-Hypothesis. *J. Devel. Econ.,* December 1983, *13* (3), pp. 367–82. **[G: LDCs]**

Schmittlein, David C. Some Sampling Properties of a Model for Income Distribution. *J. Bus. Econ. Statist.,* April 1983, *1* (2), pp. 147–53. **[G: U.S.]**

Schmitz, Mark and Fishback, Price V. The Distribution of Income in the Great Depression: Preliminary State Estimates. *J. Econ. Hist.,* March 1983, *43* (1), pp. 217–30. **[G: U.S.]**

Sheshinski, Eytan. Wage Policy in the Public Sector and Income Distribution. **In** *Helpman, E.; Razin, A. and Sadka, E., eds.,* 1983, pp. 299–309.

Shorrocks, Anthony F. Ranking Income Distributions. *Economica,* February 1983, *50* (197), pp. 3–17.

Shorrocks, Anthony F. The Impact of Income Components on the Distribution of Family Incomes. *Quart. J. Econ.,* May 1983, *98* (2), pp. 311–26. **[G: U.S.]**

Silber, Jacques. ELL (The Equivalent Length of Life) or Another Attempt at Measuring Development. *World Devel.,* January 1983, *11* (1), pp. 21–29. **[G: Global]**

Smiley, Gene. Did Incomes for Most of the Population Fall from 1923 through 1929? *J. Econ. Hist.,* March 1983, *43* (1), pp. 209–16. **[G: U.S.]**

Southwick, Lawrence, Jr. and Cadigan, John F., Jr. The Medical Expense Deduction and Income Levels: Progressive or Regressive? *J. Econ. Bus.,* 1983, *35* (1), pp. 61–70. **[G: U.S.]**

Stewart, Frances. Inequality, Technology and Payments Systems. **In** *Stewart, F., ed.,* 1983, pp. 1–31. **[G: Selected LDCs; Selected MDCs]**

Stewart, Frances. Payments Systems and Third World Development: Some Conclusions. **In** *Stewart, F., ed.,* 1983, pp. 306–23.

Sturm, Peter H. Determinants of Saving: Theory and Evidence. *OECD Econ. Stud.,* Autumn 1983, (1), pp. 147–96. **[G: OECD]**

Suzawa, Gilbert S. Note on Kakwani and Podder Method of Fitting Lorenz Curves. **In** *[Yamada, I.],* 1983, pp. 122–26. **[G: Australia]**

Swidinsky, Robert. Working Wives, Income Distribution and Poverty. *Can. Public Policy,* March 1983, *9* (1), pp. 71–80. **[G: Canada]**

Tendulkar, Suresh D. Economic Inequality in an Indian Perspective. **In** *Béteille, A., ed.,* 1983, pp. 71–128. **[G: India]**

Thon, Dominique. Lorenz Curves and Lorenz Coefficients: A Sceptical Note. *Weltwirtsch. Arch.,* 1983, *119* (2), pp. 364–67. **[G: Selected Countries]**

Thoris, Gérard. Les limites de la redistribution des revenus: perspective macroéconomique. (With English summary.) *Revue Écon. Polit.,* September–October 1983, *93* (5), pp. 682–92. **[G: France]**

Tokman, Victor E. The Influence of the Urban Informal Sector on Economic Inequality. **In** *Stewart, F., ed.,* 1983, pp. 108–37. **[G: Mexico; Chile]**

Wedderburn, Dorothy. Policy Issues in the Distribution of Income and Wealth: Some Lessons from the Diamond Commission. **In** *Field, F., ed.,* 1983, pp. 69–87. **[G: U.K.]**

Weeks, John. The State and Income Redistribution in Peru, 1968–76, with Special Reference to Manufacturing. **In** *Stewart, F., ed.,* 1983, pp. 62–82. **[G: Peru]**

Yoshida, Tateo. The Lorenz Partial Ordering and Lerner's Probabilistic Egalitarianism. *Econ. Stud. Quart.,* December 1983, *34* (3), pp. 225–36.

Zagier, Don. Inequalities for the Gini Coefficient of Composite Populations. *J. Math. Econ.,* October 1983, *12* (2), pp. 103–18.

222 Input-Output

2220 Input-Output

Algera, S. B.; Mantelaers, P. A. H. M. and van Tuinen, H. K. Problems in the Compilation of Input–Output Tables in the Netherlands. *Rev. Income Wealth,* March 1983, *29* (1), pp. 67–87. **[G: Netherlands]**

Anderson, A. W. and Manning, T. W. The Use of Input–Output Analysis in Evaluating Water Resource Development. *Can. J. Agr. Econ.,* March

1983, *31* (1), pp. 15–26. **[G: Canada]**

Anderson, Donald W. Development of Product-Specific Output Projections Using an Input–Output Model. *Empirical Econ.*, 1983, *8* (1), pp. 1–8. **[G: U.S.]**

Arrow, Kenneth J. Import Substitution in Leontief Models. **In** *Arrow, K. J., Vol. 2,* 1983, *1954,* pp. 92–106.

Bonnici, Josef. The Relevance of Input Substitution in the Inter-Industry Model. *Europ. Econ. Rev.*, August 1983, *22* (3), pp. 277–96. **[G: Malta]**

Butcher, Geoff. Employment Multipliers from Input/Output Tables. **In** *Easton, B., ed.*, 1983, pp. 141–57. **[G: New Zealand]**

Caselli, Gian Paolo and Pastrello, Gabriele. L'approccio strutturale: teoria dei grafi e analisi input-output. Un'applicazione a tre economie europee: Italia, Francia e Germania. (The Structural Approach: Graph Theory and Input–Output Analysis: An Application to Three European Economies: Italy, France and Germany. With English summary.) *Statistica,* July–September 1983, *43* (3), pp. 507–32. **[G: Italy; France; W. Germany]**

de Castro, Steve. Comparison of Turnpikes with Consumption Maximising Sectoral Growth Paths for Jamaica, 1957–1971. *J. Devel. Econ.*, Aug.–Oct. 1983, *13* (1–2), pp. 175–95. **[G: Jamaica]**

Craven, John. Input–Output Analysis and Technical Change. *Econometrica,* May, 1983, *51* (3), pp. 585–98.

Dadaian, V. S. and Shevtsova, V. E. The Potential Uses for Forecasting and Analysis of a Balance of the Flows of Gross World Output between Regions. *Matekon,* Winter 1983–84, *20* (2), pp. 3–23. **[G: Selected Countries]**

Duchin, Faye. The World Model: An Interregional Input–Output Model of the World Economy. **In** *Hickman, B. G., ed.*, 1983, pp. 167–80. **[G: Global]**

Filippini, Luigi. Price and Quantity Adjustment in a Dynamic Closed Model: The Dual Stability Theorem. *J. Macroecon.*, Spring 1983, *5* (2), pp. 185–96.

Hall, P. H. Strikes and Their Repercussions. *Greek Econ. Rev.*, August 1983, *5* (2), pp. 182–92.

Henry, Mark S. A Cost Effective Approach to Primary Input–Output Data Collection: Reply. *Rev. Public Data Use (See J. Econ. Soc. Meas. after 4/85),* October 1983, *11* (3), pp. 193–95.

Henry, Mark S. The Impact of Natural Gas Price Deregulation on the South Carolina Food-Processing Sectors. *Southern J. Agr. Econ.*, December 1983, *15* (2), pp. 41–48. **[G: U.S.]**

Hewings, Geoffrey J. D. A Cost Effective Approach to Primary Input–Output Data Collection: Some Comments. *Rev. Public Data Use (See J. Econ. Soc. Meas. after 4/85),* October 1983, *11* (3), pp. 197–99.

Iaramenko, Iu. V., et al. An Input–Output Model in Physical and Value Terms. *Matekon,* Summer 1983, *19* (4), pp. 45–61.

Ichimura, Shinichi. Project FUGI and the Future of ESCAP Developing Countries: Comment. **In** *Hickman, B. G., ed.*, 1983, pp. 254–57. **[G: Global]**

Kaya, Yoichi; Onishi, Akira and Suzuki, Yutaka. Project FUGI and the Future of ESCAP Developing Countries. **In** *Hickman, B. G., ed.*, 1983, pp. 237–54. **[G: Global]**

Klein, Lawrence R. NIPA Statistics: A User's View. **In** *Foss, M. F., ed.*, 1983, pp. 319–23. **[G: U.S.]**

Kuboniwa, Masaaki. A Comparison of Convergence Speed of Old and New Iterative Processes for an Input–Output System. *Hitotsubashi J. Econ.*, December 1983, *24* (2), pp. 143–48.

Lahiri, Sajal. Capacity Constraints, Alternative Technologies and Input–Output Analysis. *Europ. Econ. Rev.*, July 1983, *22* (2), pp. 219–26.

Lorenzen, Gunter. Input-Output-Analysen mit unvollständigen Input-Output-Tabellen. (Input-Output Analysis with Incomplete Input-Output Tables. With English summary.) *Z. Wirtschaft. Sozialwissen.*, 1983, *103* (1), pp. 43–55.

Maresi, Emanuela. Alcune considerazioni sui metodi di aggiornamento e proiezione di tavole intersettoriali. (An Evaluation of Methods of Revising, Adjusting and Projecting Input–Output Matrices. With English summary.) *Statistica,* October–December 1983, *43* (4), pp. 681–96.

Mules, T. J. Input–Output Analysis in Australia: An Agricultural Perspective. *Rev. Marketing Agr. Econ.*, April 1983, *51* (1), pp. 9–30. **[G: Australia]**

Nyhus, Douglas E. and Almon, Clopper. Linked Input–Output Models for France, the Federal Republic of Germany, and Belgium. **In** *Hickman, B. G., ed.*, 1983, pp. 183–99. **[G: Belgium; France; W. Germany]**

O'Hagan, John and Mooney, David. Input–Output Multipliers in a Small Open Economy: An Application to Tourism. *Econ. Soc. Rev.*, July 1983, *14* (4), pp. 273–79. **[G: Ireland]**

Rogovskii, E. A. Problems in Developing Dynamic Models to Forecast the Input–Output Structure of the Economy. *Matekon,* Spring 1983, *19* (3), pp. 52–73.

Salib, Anis B. Energy, GDP, and the Structure of Demand: An International Comparison Using Input–Output Techniques. *J. Energy Devel.*, Autumn 1983, *9* (1), pp. 55–61. **[G: U.S.; U.K.; Japan; France; Italy]**

Spronk, Jaap and Veeneklaas, Frank. A Feasibility Study of Economic and Environmental Scenarios by Means of Interactive Multiple Goal Programming. *Reg. Sci. Urban Econ.*, February 1983, *13* (1), pp. 141–60. **[G: Netherlands]**

Todorov, Wassil. An Alternative Input–Output Method for Calculating the Amount of Labour Contained in Production. *Konjunkturpolitik,* 1983, *29* (4), pp. 248–60.

223 Financial Accounts

2230 Financial Accounts; Financial Statistics; Empirical Analyses of Capital Adequacy

Abel, Andrew B. Financing Private Business in an Inflationary Context: The Experience of Argentina between 1967 and 1980: Comment. **In** *Armella, P. A.; Dornbusch, R. and Obstfeld, M., eds.*, 1983, pp. 183–85. **[G: Argentina]**

Balderston, T. The Beginning of the Depression in

Germany, 1927–30: Investment and the Capital Market. *Econ. Hist. Rev., 2nd Ser.*, August 1983, *36*(3), pp. 395–415. **[G: Germany]**

Beckerman, Paul. Index-linked Financial Assets and the Brazilian Inflation-Feedback Mechanism. **In** *Schmukler, N. and Marcus, E., eds.*, 1983, pp. 571–651. **[G: Brazil]**

Butkiewicz, James L. The Market Value of Outstanding Government Debt: Comment. *J. Monet. Econ.*, May 1983, *11*(3), pp. 373–79. **[G: U.S.]**

Cagan, Phillip. The Roles of Money and Credit in Macroeconomic Analysis: Comment. **In** *Tobin, J., ed.*, 1983, pp. 189–93. **[G: U.S.]**

Camaiti, Romolo. Le statistiche bancaria nel quadro della statistica del credito e monetaria. (Banking Statistics in Italy in the Framework of Credit and Monetary Statistics. With English summary.) *Bancaria,* May–June 1983, *39*(5–6), pp. 498–516. **[G: Italy]**

Cavallo, Domingo F. and Petrei, A. Humberto. Financing Private Business in an Inflationary Context: The Experience of Argentina between 1967 and 1980. **In** *Armella, P. A.; Dornbusch, R. and Obstfeld, M., eds.*, 1983, pp. 153–80. **[G: Argentina]**

Cotta, Alain. Investissement industriel et croissance de l'économie française. (Industrial Investment and French Economic Growth. With English summary.) *Revue Écon.*, July 1983, *34*(4), pp. 691–731. **[G: France]**

Cotula, Anna Maria Biscaini. Le statistiche bancarie in Italia: origini e connotati. (Banking Statistics in Italy: Origins and Characteristics. With English summary.) *Bancaria,* July 1983, *39*(7), pp. 605–21. **[G: Italy]**

Cox, W. Michael and Hirschhorn, Eric. The Market Value of U.S. Government Debt; Monthly, 1942–1980. *J. Monet. Econ.*, March 1983, *11*(2), pp. 261–72. **[G: U.S.]**

Friedman, Benjamin M. Implications of the Government Deficit for U.S. Capital Formation. **In** *Federal Reserve Bank of Boston,* 1983, pp. 73–95. **[G: U.S.]**

Friedman, Benjamin M. The Roles of Money and Credit in Macroeconomic Analysis. **In** *Tobin, J., ed.*, 1983, pp. 161–89. **[G: U.S.]**

Gorman, John A. Data Needs in Flow of Funds. **In** *Foss, M. F., ed.*, 1983, pp. 409–15. **[G: U.S.]**

Henry, S. G. B. and Wren-Lewis, S. Investment and Stockbuilding. **In** *Britton, A., ed.*, 1983, pp. 28–39. **[G: U.K.]**

Klein, Lawrence R. NIPA Statistics: A User's View. **In** *Foss, M. F., ed.*, 1983, pp. 319–23. **[G: U.S.]**

Kopcke, Richard W. Will Big Deficits Spoil the Recovery? **In** *Federal Reserve Bank of Boston,* 1983, pp. 141–68. **[G: U.S.]**

McLure, Charles E., Jr. Financing Private Business in an Inflationary Context: The Experience of Argentina between 1967 and 1980: Comment. **In** *Armella, P. A.; Dornbusch, R. and Obstfeld, M., eds.*, 1983, pp. 180–83. **[G: Argentina]**

Miller, Preston J. Will Big Deficits Spoil the Recovery? Discussion. **In** *Federal Reserve Bank of Boston,* 1983, pp. 169–73. **[G: U.S.]**

Monti, Mario. Financial Structure and Capital Accumulation: A Comparative Note on Japan and Italy. **In** *Fodella, G., ed.*, 1983, pp. 107–12. **[G: Japan; Italy]**

Osborne, Dale K. Is the Southwest Short of Capital? *Fed. Res. Bank Dallas Econ. Rev.*, January 1983, pp. 1–10. **[G: U.S.]**

Pagan, A. R. and Gray, M. R. Inflation and Investment: An Historical Overview. **In** *Pagan, A. R. and Trivedi, P. K., eds.*, 1983, pp. 262–81. **[G: Australia]**

Papanek, Gustav F. Aid, Growth and Equity in Southern Asia. **In** *Parkinson, J. R., ed.*, 1983, pp. 169–82. **[G: S. Asia]**

Qureshi, Zia M. Determinants of Corporate Saving in Pakistan: A Macro-econometric Analysis. *Pakistan Devel. Rev.*, Summer 1983, *22*(2), pp. 73–96. **[G: Pakistan]**

Samouilidis, J-Emmanuel and Mitropoulos, Costas S. Energy Investment and Economic Growth: A Simplified Approach. *Energy Econ.*, October 1983, *5*(4), pp. 237–46. **[G: U.K.]**

Shiller, Robert J. The Roles of Money and Credit in Macroeconomic Analysis: Comment. **In** *Tobin, J., ed.*, 1983, pp. 193–99. **[G: U.S.]**

Solow, Robert M. Implications of the Government Deficit for U.S. Capital Formation: Discussion. **In** *Federal Reserve Bank of Boston,* 1983, pp. 96–98. **[G: U.S.]**

Sturm, Peter H. Determinants of Saving: Theory and Evidence. *OECD Econ. Stud.*, Autumn 1983, (1), pp. 147–96. **[G: OECD]**

Tannenwald, Robert. The Outlook for Business Fixed Investment. *New Eng. Econ. Rev.*, July–August 1983, pp. 31–35. **[G: U.S.]**

Wojnilower, Albert M. Implications of the Government Deficit for U.S. Capital Formation: Discussion. **In** *Federal Reserve Bank of Boston,* 1983, pp. 99–111. **[G: U.S.]**

224 National Wealth and Balance Sheets

2240 National Wealth and Balance Sheets

Atkinson, Anthony B. Inheritance and the Redistribution of Wealth. **In** *Atkinson, A. B.*, 1983, pp. 171–96.

Atkinson, Anthony B. Introduction to Part II: Wealth and Redistribution. **In** *Atkinson, A. B.*, 1983, pp. 109–14. **[G: U.K.]**

Atkinson, Anthony B. The Distribution of Wealth and the Individual Life-Cycle. **In** *Atkinson, A. B.*, 1983, *1971,* pp. 131–45. **[G: U.K.]**

Atkinson, Anthony B. and Harrison, A. J. The Analysis of Trends over Time in the Distribution of Personal Wealth in Britain. **In** *Atkinson, A. B.*, 1983, *1979,* pp. 115–30. **[G: U.K.]**

Babeau, André. Le rapport macro-économique du patrimoine au revenu des ménages. (The Macro-Economic Wealth-Income Ration of Households. With English summary.) *Revue Écon.*, January 1983, *34*(1), pp. 64–123. **[G: France; U.S.]**

Babeau, André. The Macro-Economic Wealth–Income Ratio of Households. *Rev. Income Wealth,* December 1983, *29*(4), pp. 347–70. **[G: France; U.S.]**

Berend, Iván T. The Renewal Cycle of Fixed Assets under the Conditions of the 1980s in Hungary.

Acta Oecon., 1983, *30*(3–4), pp. 401–11. **[G: Hungary]**

Bernstein, Peter L. Capital Stock and Management Decisions. *J. Post Keynesian Econ.*, Fall 1983, *6*(1), pp. 20–38. **[G: U.S.]**

Blinder, Alan S.; Gordon, Roger H. and Wise, Donald E. Social Security, Bequests and the Life Cycle Theory of Saving: Cross-sectional Tests. **In** *Modigliani, F. and Hemming, R., eds.*, 1983, pp. 89–122. **[G: U.S.]**

Chinloy, Peter. Housing Repair and Housing Stocks. **In** *Gau, G. W. and Goldberg, M. A., eds.*, 1983, pp. 139–58. **[G: Canada]**

Dunn, A. T. and Hoffman, P. D. R. B. Distribution of Wealth in the United Kingdom: Effect of Including Pension Rights and Analysis by Age-Group. *Rev. Income Wealth*, September 1983, *29*(3), pp. 243–82. **[G: U.K.]**

Feenberg, Daniel R. The Economic Status of the Elderly: Comment. **In** *Bodie, Z. and Shoven, J. B., eds.*, 1983, pp. 393–96. **[G: U.S.]**

Feldstein, Martin S. Inflation, Tax Rules, and the Accumulation of Residential and Nonresidential Capital. **In** *Feldstein, M. (II)*, 1983, *1982*, pp. 81–98. **[G: U.S.]**

Feldstein, Martin S. Social Security Benefits and the Accumulation of Pre-retirement Wealth. **In** *Modigliani, F. and Hemming, R., eds.*, 1983, pp. 3–23. **[G: U.S.]**

Goldsmith, Raymond W. Saving and Changes in National and Sectoral Balance Sheets. **In** *Modigliani, F. and Hemming, R., eds.*, 1983, pp. 289–301. **[G: Selected Countries]**

Greenwood, Daphne. An Estimation of U.S. Family Wealth and Its Distribution from Microdata, 1973. *Rev. Income Wealth*, March 1983, *29*(1), pp. 23–44. **[G: U.S.]**

Hurd, Michael D. and Shoven, John B. The Economic Status of the Elderly. **In** *Bodie, Z. and Shoven, J. B., eds.*, 1983, pp. 359–93, 396–97. **[G: U.S.]**

Jorgenson, Dale W. and Pachon, Alvaro. The Accumulation of Human and Non-human Capital. **In** *Modigliani, F. and Hemming, R., eds.*, 1983, pp. 302–50. **[G: U.S.]**

Kearl, J. R. and Pope, Clayne L. The Life Cycle in Economic History. *J. Econ. Hist.*, March 1983, *43*(1), pp. 149–58. **[G: U.S.]**

Lantzke, Ulf. Investment and Energy. **In** *Heertje, A., ed.*, 1983, pp. 117–51. **[G: W. Europe]**

Lim, David. The Political Economy of the New Economic Policy in Malaysia. **In** *Lim, D., ed.*, 1983, pp. 3–22. **[G: Malaysia]**

Miller, Edward M. A Problem in the Measurement of Capital Embodied Productivity Change. *Eastern Econ. J.*, January–March 1983, *9*(1), pp. 29–36.

Miller, Edward M. Capital Aggregation in the Presence of Obsolescence-Inducing Technical Change. *Rev. Income Wealth*, September 1983, *29*(3), pp. 283–96.

Modigliani, Franco and Sterling, Arlie. Determinants of Private Saving with Special Reference to the Role of Social Security—Cross-country Tests. **In** *Modigliani, F. and Hemming, R., eds.*, 1983, pp. 24–55. **[G: Selected OECD]**

Oja, Gail. The Distribution of Wealth in Canada. *Rev. Income Wealth*, June 1983, *29*(2), pp. 161–73. **[G: Canada]**

Papp, F. J. A Note on the Functional Equations Satisfied by Russell's Function for Wage Income and Optimal Consumption Plan [The Share of Top Wealth Holders: The Life Cycle, Inheritance and Efficient Markets]. *Ann. INSEE*, Jan.–Mar. 1983, (49), pp. 133–39.

Peterson, George E. Rebuilding Public Infrastructure: The Institutional Choices. **In** *Lefcoe, G., ed.*, 1983, pp. 109–23. **[G: U.S.]**

Polanyi, George and Wood, John B. How Unevenly Is Wealth Spread Today? **In** *Letwin, W., ed.*, 1983, *1974*, pp. 229–60. **[G: U.K.]**

Pond, Chris. Wealth and the Two Nations. **In** *Field, F., ed.*, 1983, pp. 9–33. **[G: U.K.]**

Reddin, Mike. Pensions, Wealth and the Extension of Inequality. **In** *Field, F., ed.*, 1983, pp. 138–58. **[G: U.K.]**

Schwarz, L. D. and Jones, L. J. Wealth, Occupations, and Insurance in the Late Eighteenth Century: The Policy Registers of the Sun Fire Office. *Econ. Hist. Rev., 2nd Ser.*, August 1983, *36*(3), pp. 365–73. **[G: U.K.]**

Soltow, Lee. Kentucky Wealth at the End of the Eighteenth Century. *J. Econ. Hist.*, September 1983, *43*(3), pp. 617–33. **[G: U.S.]**

Soltow, Lee. Land Fragmentation as an Index of History in the Virginia Military District of Ohio. *Exploration Econ. Hist.*, July 1983, *20*(3), pp. 263–73. **[G: U.S.]**

Soltow, Lee. Long-Run Wealth Inequality in Malaysia. *Singapore Econ. Rev.*, October 1983, *28*(2), pp. 79–97. **[G: Malaysia]**

Sutherland, Alister. The Taxation of Agricultural Wealth: Northfield and After. **In** *Field, F., ed.*, 1983, pp. 88–117. **[G: U.K.]**

Varaiya, Pravin and Wiseman, Michael. Reindustrialization and the Outlook for Declining Areas. **In** *Henderson, J. V., ed.*, 1983, pp. 167–90. **[G: U.S.]**

Wedderburn, Dorothy. Policy Issues in the Distribution of Income and Wealth: Some Lessons from the Diamond Commission. **In** *Field, F., ed.*, 1983, pp. 69–87. **[G: U.K.]**

Williams, Ross A. Ownership of Dwellings and Personal Wealth in Australia. *Australian Econ. Rev.*, 2nd Quarter 1983, (62), pp. 55–62. **[G: Australia]**

Wolff, Edward N. The Size Distribution of Household Disposable Wealth in the United States. *Rev. Income Wealth*, June 1983, *29*(2), pp. 125–46. **[G: U.S.]**

225 Social Indicators: Data and Analysis

2250 Social Indicators: Data and Analysis

Adelman, Irma and Hihn, Jairus M. The Political Economy of Investment in Human Capital. **In** *Streeten, P. and Maier, H., eds.*, 1983, pp. 117–46. **[G: LDCs]**

Andréani, Edgard. Quantification sociale et évaluation des politiques sociales. (With English summary.) *Revue Écon. Polit.*, May–June 1983, *93*(3), pp. 362–76. [G: France]

Bentham, C. G. Urban Problems and Public Dissatisfaction in the Metropolitan Areas of England. *Reg. Stud.*, October 1983, *17*(5), pp. 339–46. [G: U.K.]

Bertrand, René. Possible Social Policy Developments and Corresponding Statistical Requirements. *Rev. Income Wealth,* March 1983, *29*(1), pp. 89–93.

Clemmer, Richard B. and Simonson, John C. Trends in Substandard Housing, 1940–1980. *Amer. Real Estate Urban Econ. Assoc. J.*, Winter 1983, *10*(4), pp. 442–64. [G: U.S.]

Cobas, José A. Estimating the Urban Family Budget with a Pooled Cross-Section/Times-Series Model: A Reply to Hogan [A Method to Estimate the Bureau of Labor Statistics Family Budgets for All Standard Metropolitan Statistical Areas]. *Soc. Sci. Quart.*, June 1983, *64*(2), pp. 416–17. [G: U.S.]

Dahmann, Donald C. Subjective Assessments of Neighborhood Quality by Size of Place. *Urban Stud.*, February 1983, *20*(1), pp. 31–45. [G: U.S.]

Darbon, Sébastien. Assurance maladie et redistribution du revenu: Une question de méthodes. (With English summary.) *Revue Écon. Polit.*, May–June 1983, *93*(3), pp. 397–420. [G: France]

Dellaportas, George. Classification of Nations as Developed and Less Developed: An Arrangement by Discriminant Analysis of Socioeconomic Data. *Amer. J. Econ. Soc.*, April 1983, *42*(2), pp. 153–66. [G: Global; LDCs; MDCs]

Ghali, Moheb, et al. Economic Factors and the Composition of Juvenile Property Crimes. *Appl. Econ.*, April 1983, *15*(2), pp. 267–81. [G: U.S.]

Grigsby, William G. and Corl, Thomas C. Declining Neighborhoods: Problem or Opportunity? *Ann. Amer. Acad. Polit. Soc. Sci.*, January 1983, *465*, pp. 86–97. [G: U.S.]

Hayden, F. Gregory. Integration of Social Indicators into Holistic Geobased Models. *J. Econ. Issues*, June 1983, *17*(2), pp. 325–34.

Hogan, Timothy D. Estimating the Urban Family Budget with a Pooled Cross-Section/Time-Series Model [A Method to Estimate the Bureau of Labor Statistics Family Budgets for All Standard Metropolitan Statistical Areas]. *Soc. Sci. Quart.*, June 1983, *64*(2), pp. 413–16. [G: U.S.]

Horn, Robert V. Cultural Statistics and Indicators. *J. Cult. Econ.*, December 1983, *7*(2), pp. 25–40.

Kwon, Jene K. Toward Incentive Transfers, Global Tax and Welfare Indices. *J. Econ. Devel.*, December 1983, *8*(2), pp. 71–87. [G: LDCs; MDCs]

Lévy, Emile. La mesure de l'efficacité dans l'évaluation des politiques sociales: L'exemple de la santé. (With English summary.) *Revue Écon. Polit.*, May–June 1983, *93*(3), pp. 377–87. [G: France]

Lewis, W. Arthur. Patterns of Public Revenue and Expenditure. **In** *Lewis, W. A.*, 1983, *1956*, pp. 573–614. [G: LDCs; MDCs]

Liu, Ben-chieh. Variations in Economic Quality of Life Indicators in the U.S.A.: An Interstate Observation over Time. *Math. Soc. Sci.*, August 1983, *5*(1), pp. 107–20. [G: U.S.]

Mushkat, Miron. The Societal Accounting Movement: A Critical Appraisal. *METU,* 1983, *10*(2), pp. 199–216.

Roneck, Dennis W. and Lobosco, Antoinette. The Effect of High Schools on Crime in Their Neighborhoods. *Soc. Sci. Quart.*, September 1983, *64*(3), pp. 598–613. [G: U.S.]

Weatherby, Norman L.; Nam, Charles B. and Isaac, Larry W. Development, Inequality, Health Care, and Mortality at the Older Ages: A Cross-National Analysis. *Demography,* February 1983, *20*(1), pp. 27–43. [G: Selected MDCs; Selected LDCs]

Weiss, Thomas G. and Jennings, Anthony. What Are the Least Developed Countries and What Benefits May Result from the Paris Conference? *World Devel.*, April 1983, *11*(4), pp. 337–57. [G: MDCs; LDCs]

226 Productivity and Growth: Theory and Data

2260 Productivity and Growth: Theory and Data

Abramovitz, Moses. Notes on International Differences in Productivity Growth Rates. **In** *Mueller, D. C., ed.*, 1983, pp. 79–89. [G: OECD]

Adams, F. Gerard and Klein, Lawrence R. Economic Evaluation of Industrial Policies for Growth and Competitiveness: Overview. **In** *Adams, F. G. and Klein, L. R., eds.*, 1983, pp. 3–11. [G: U.S.]

Albert, Michel. Growth, Investment and Employment in Europe in the 1980s. **In** *Heertje, A., ed.*, 1983, pp. 41–55. [G: EEC]

Andreassen, Arthur J.; Saunders, Norman C. and Su, Betty W. Economic Outlook for the 1990's: Three Scenarios for Economic Growth. *Mon. Lab. Rev.*, November 1983, *106*(11), pp. 11–23. [G: U.S.]

Antos, Joseph R. Current and Historical Availability of BLS Wage, Price, and Productivity Series by SIC Industries. **In** *Triplett, J. E., ed.*, 1983, pp. 465–502. [G: U.S.]

Asimakopulos, A. A Kaleckian Profits Equation and the United States Economy, 1950–82. *Metroecon.*, February–June 1983, *35*(1–2), pp. 1–27. [G: U.S.]

Asselain, Jean-Charles and Morrisson, Christian. Economic Growth and Interest Groups: The French Experience. **In** *Mueller, D. C., ed.*, 1983, pp. 157–75. [G: France]

Baily, Martin Neil. 'Comparing Productivity Growth: An Exploration of French and U.S. Industrial and Firm Data' by Z. Griliches and J. Mairesse: Comment. *Europ. Econ. Rev.*, March/April 1983, *21*(1/2), pp. 121–23. [G: U.S.; France]

Baily, Martin Neil. Productivity Trends: Comment. **In** *Schurr, S. H.; Sonenblum, S. and Wood, D. O., eds.*, 1983, pp. 121–26. [G: OECD; U.S.]

Beckerman, Wilfred. The Case for Economic Growth. **In** *Snoeyenbos, M.; Almeder, R. and Humber, J., eds.*, 1983, *1974*, pp. 453–60.

Beebe, Jack H. and Haltmaier, Jane. Disaggregation and the Labor Productivity Index. *Rev. Econ. Statist.*, August 1983, *65*(3), pp. 487–91.

Bergson, Abram. Technological Progress. **In** *Bergson, A. and Levine, H. S., eds.*, 1983, pp. 34–78. [G: U.S.S.R.]

Bernanke, Ben S. On the Sources of Labor Productivity Variation in U.S. Manufacturing, 1947–1980. *Rev. Econ. Statist.*, May 1983, *65*(2), pp. 214–24.

Berndt, Ernst R. The Energy Connection to Recent Productivity Behavior: Comment. **In** *Schurr, S. H.; Sonenblum, S. and Wood, D. O., eds.*, 1983, pp. 179–83. **[G: U.S.]**

Bhagwati, Jagdish N. and Hansen, Bent. Should Growth Rates Be Evaluated at International Prices? **In** *Bhagwati, J. N., Vol. 1*, 1983, *1973*, pp. 598–613.

Blakemore, Arthur E. and Schlagenhauf, Don E. Estimation of the Trend Rate of Growth of Productivity. *Appl. Econ.*, December 1983, *15*(6), pp. 807–14. **[G: U.S.]**

Blandy, Richard and Harrison, David. The Australian Labour Market, March 1983. *Australian Bull. Lab.*, March 1983, *9*(2), pp. 75–92. **[G: Australia]**

Böhm, Bernhard and Clemenz, Gerhard. The Development of Factor Productivity in an International Comparison. *Empirica*, 1983, (1), pp. 41–66. **[G: Selected OECD]**

Boltho, Andrea. Italian and Japanese Postwar Growth: Some Similarities and Differences. **In** *Fodella, G., ed.*, 1983, pp. 48–63. **[G: Japan]**

Boskin, Michael J. Saving Incentives: The Role of Tax Policy. **In** *Walker, C. E. and Bloomfield, M. E., eds.*, 1983, pp. 93–111. **[G: U.S.]**

Bowles, Samuel and Eatwell, John. Between Two Worlds: Interest Groups, Class Structure, and Capitalist Growth. **In** *Mueller, D. C., ed.*, 1983, pp. 217–30.

Bruno, Michael. 'Comparing Productivity Growth: An Exploration of French and U.S. Industrial and Firm Data' by Z. Griliches and J. Mairesse: Comment. *Europ. Econ. Rev.*, March/April 1983, *21*(1/2), pp. 125–27. **[G: U.S.; France]**

Buiter, Willem H. and Miller, Marcus H. Changing the Rules: Economic Consequences of the Thatcher Regime. *Brookings Pap. Econ. Act.*, 1983, (2), pp. 305–79. **[G: U.K.]**

Capie, Forrest. Tariff Protection and Economic Performance in the Nineteenth Century. **In** *Black, J. and Winters, L. A., eds.*, 1983, pp. 1–24. **[G: Europe; U.S.]**

Cappellin, Riccardo. Productivity Growth and Technological Change in a Regional Perspective. *Giorn. Econ.*, July–August 1983, *42*(7–8), pp. 459–82. **[G: Italy; France]**

Chan, M. W. Luke and Mountain, Dean C. Economies of Scale and the Tornqvist Discrete Measure of Productivity Growth. *Rev. Econ. Statist.*, November 1983, *65*(4), pp. 663–67. **[G: Canada]**

Choi, Kwang. A Statistical Test of Olson's Model. **In** *Mueller, D. C., ed.*, 1983, pp. 57–78. **[G: OECD]**

Cohen, Edwin S. Expanding Saving Incentives: Practical and Political Problems. **In** *Walker, C. E. and Bloomfield, M. E., eds.*, 1983, pp. 112–15. **[G: U.S.]**

Coleman, D. C. Proto-Industrialization: A Concept Too Many. *Econ. Hist. Rev., 2nd Ser.*, August 1983, *36*(3), pp. 435–48.

Cooper, Richard N. Is Trade Deindustrializing America? A Medium-Term Perspective: Comments and Discussion. *Brookings Pap. Econ. Act.*, 1983, (1), pp. 162–71. **[G: U.S.]**

Council on Environ. Quality and the Dept. of State. The Global 2000 Report to the President: Entering the 21st Century. **In** *Glassner, M. I., ed.*, 1983, *1980*, pp. 647–75. **[G: Global]**

Crafts, N. F. R. British Economic Growth, 1700–1831: A Review of the Evidence. *Econ. Hist. Rev., 2nd Ser.*, May 1983, *36*(2), pp. 177–99. **[G: U.K.]**

Cripps, Francis and Ward, Terry. Government Policies, European Recession and Problems of Recovery. *Cambridge J. Econ.*, March 1983, *7*(1), pp. 85–99. **[G: W. Europe]**

Dean, James W. Polyarchy and Economic Growth. **In** *Mueller, D. C., ed.*, 1983, pp. 231–57. **[G: U.S.]**

Denison, Edward F. The Interruption of Productivity Growth in the United States. *Econ. J.*, March 1983, *93*(369), pp. 56–77. **[G: U.S.]**

Denny, Michael G. S. and Fuss, Melvyn A. A General Approach to Intertemporal and Interspatial Productivity Comparisons. *J. Econometrics*, December 1983, *23*(3), pp. 315–30. **[G: Canada; U.S.; Japan]**

Destanne de Bernis, Gérard. De l'existence de points de passage obligatoires pour une politique de développement. (On the Existence of Obligatory Passage Points for Development Policy. With English summary.) *Écon. Soc.*, February 1983, *17*(2), pp. 213–59.

Diewert, W. Erwin. The Theory of the Output Price Index and the Measurement of Real Output Change. **In** *Diewert, W. E. and Montmarquette, C., eds.*, 1983, pp. 1049–1113.

Dirksen, Erik. Chinese Industrial Productivity in an International Context. *World Devel.*, April 1983, *11*(4), pp. 381–87. **[G: China]**

Durgin, Frank A., Jr. More on the New Model of Soviet Growth. *ACES Bull. (See Comp. Econ. Stud. after 8/85)*, Spring 1983, *25*(1), pp. 35–46. **[G: U.S.S.R.]**

Ellis, Michael. Supply-Side Linkage of Capacity Utilization and Labor Productivity: U.S. Manufacturing, 1954–1980. *Bus. Econ.*, May 1983, *18*(3), pp. 62–69. **[G: U.S.]**

English, Jon and Marchione, Anthony R. Productivity: A New Perspective. *Calif. Manage. Rev.*, January 1983, *25*(2), pp. 57–66. **[G: U.S.]**

Fabricant, Solomon. The Productivity-Growth Slowdown—A Review of the "Facts." **In** *Schurr, S. H.; Sonenblum, S. and Wood, D. O., eds.*, 1983, pp. 47–70. **[G: U.S.]**

Feder, Gershon. On Exports and Economic Growth. *J. Devel. Econ.*, February/April 1983, *12*(1/2), pp. 59–73.

Fellner, William. The Effect of Government Absorption of Savings on Capital Formation. **In** *Walker, C. E. and Bloomfield, M. E., eds.*, 1983, pp. 116–18. **[G: U.S.]**

Fischer, Stanley. Macroconfusion: The Dilemmas of Economic Policy: Comment. **In** *Tobin, J., ed.*, 1983, pp. 267–76.

Fluet, Claude and Lefebvre, Pierre. Gains de productivité globale, prix relatifs et rémunération des facteurs dans les industries manufacturières au Québec. (Total Factor Productivity Growth,

Relative Prices and Earnings in Quebec Manufacturing Industries. With English summary.) *L'Actual. Econ.*, December 1983, *59*(4), pp. 651–68. **[G: Canada]**

Foreign Policy Association. Protecting World Resources: Is Time Running Out? **In** *Glassner, M. I., ed.*, 1983, *1982*, pp. 53–71.

Fuà, Giorgio. Problems of Lagged Development in OECD Europe: A Study of Six Countries. *Rivista Int. Sci. Econ. Com.*, March 1983, *30*(3), pp. 228–43. **[G: Selected European]**

Fulco, Lawrence J. Recent Productivity Measures Depict Growth Patterns since 1980. *Mon. Lab. Rev.*, December 1983, *106*(12), pp. 45–48. **[G: U.S.]**

Gavrilov, R. Rates, Factors, and New Indicators of the Growth of Labor Productivity. *Prob. Econ.*, March 1983, *25*(11), pp. 3–18. **[G: U.S.S.R.]**

Giersch, Herbert. Socialist Elements as Limits to Economic Growth. **In** *Lenel, H. O.; Willgerodt, H. and Molsberger, J.*, 1983, pp. 3–12. **[G: OECD]**

Giersch, Herbert and Wolter, Frank. Towards an Explanation of the Productivity Slowdown: An Acceleration-Deceleration Hypothesis. *Econ. J.*, March 1983, *93*(369), pp. 35–55. **[G: OECD]**

Glastetter, Werner. Einige Überlegungen zum Wachstumspfad der Bundesrepublik Deutschland. (Some Reflections on the Path of Real Growth in the Federal Republic of Germany. With English summary.) *Kredit Kapital*, 1983, *16*(3), pp. 316–30. **[G: W. Germany]**

Grabowski, Richard. A Note on Japanese Development. *Econ. Forum*, Summer 1983, *14*(1), pp. 127–30. **[G: Japan]**

Griliches, Zvi. Productivity Trends: Comment. **In** *Schurr, S. H.; Sonenblum, S. and Wood, D. O., eds.*, 1983, pp. 127–30. **[G: OECD; U.S.]**

Griliches, Zvi and Mairesse, Jacques. Comparing Productivity Growth: An Exploration of French and U.S. Industrial and Firm Data. *Europ. Econ. Rev.*, March/April 1983, *21*(1/2), pp. 89–119. **[G: U.S.; France]**

Haig, Bryan D. and Cain, Neville G. Industrialization and Productivity: Australian Manufacturing in the 1920s and 1950s. *Exploration Econ. Hist.*, April 1983, *20*(2), pp. 183–98. **[G: Australia]**

Hennart, Jean-François. The Political Economy of Comparative Growth Rates: The Case of France. **In** *Mueller, D. C., ed.*, 1983, pp. 176–202. **[G: France]**

Hertford, Reed. Issues in International Agricultural Development: Discussion. *Amer. J. Agr. Econ.*, May 1983, *65*(2), pp. 455–57.

Hicks, John. Structural Unemployment and Economic Growth: A "Labor Theory of Value" Model. **In** *Mueller, D. C., ed.*, 1983, pp. 53–56.

Hicks, Ursula K. Divergent Growth Rates: Some Experiences of the United Kingdom and Italy. **In** *Mueller, D. C., ed.*, 1983, pp. 132–56. **[G: Italy; U.K.]**

Hildred, William M. Some Methodological and Political Issues Surrounding Productivity. *J. Econ. Issues*, December 1983, *17*(4), pp. 1075–86.

Hsaio, Frank S. T. and Hsaio, Mei-Chu Wang. Some Development Indicators of Taiwan: A Comparative Study. *J. Econ. Devel.*, July 1983, *8*(1), pp. 45–58. **[G: Taiwan]**

Inkster, Ian. Technology as the Cause of the Industrial Revolution: Some Comments. *J. Europ. Econ. Hist.*, Winter 1983, *12*(3), pp. 651–57. **[G: U.K.]**

Jones, R. A. Mechanization, Learning Periods, and Productivity Change in the South African Coal Mining Industry: 1950–80. *S. Afr. J. Econ.*, December 1983, *51*(4), pp. 507–22. **[G: S. Africa]**

Jonscher, Charles. Information Resources and Economic Productivity. *Info. Econ. Policy*, 1983, *1*(1), pp. 13–35. **[G: U.S.]**

Jorgenson, Dale W. Energy Prices and Productivity Growth. **In** *Schurr, S. H.; Sonenblum, S. and Wood, D. O., eds.*, 1983, pp. 133–53. **[G: U.S.]**

Katz, Claudio J.; Mahler, Vincent A. and Franz, Michael G. The Impact of Taxes on Growth and Distribution in Developed Capitalist Countries: A Cross-National Study. *Amer. Polit. Sci. Rev.*, December 1983, *77*(4), pp. 871–86. **[G: Selected OECD]**

Kendrick, John W. Entrepreneurship, Productivity, and Economic Growth. **In** *Backman, J., ed.*, 1983, pp. 111–48. **[G: OECD]**

Kendrick, John W. International Comparisons of Recent Productivity Trends. **In** *Schurr, S. H.; Sonenblum, S. and Wood, D. O., eds.*, 1983, pp. 71–120. **[G: OECD]**

Kendrick, John W. The GNP Data Improvement Report from the Perspective of Its Use to Measure Economic Growth: Comment. **In** *Foss, M. F., ed.*, 1983, pp. 407–08. **[G: U.S.]**

Keohane, Robert O. Associative American Development, 1776–1860: Economic Growth and Political Disintegration. **In** *Ruggie, J. G., ed.*, 1983, pp. 43–90. **[G: U.S.]**

Keyserling, Leon H. U.S. Economy, Performance and Prospects, and Needed Corrective Policies. *Atlantic Econ. J.*, September 1983, *11*(3), pp. 9–43. **[G: U.S.]**

King, Richard A. Relation to Global Modeling to Development Planning. *Amer. J. Agr. Econ.*, May 1983, *65*(2), pp. 438–44.

Kravis, Irving B.; Heston, Alan W. and Summers, Robert. The Share of Services in Economic Growth. **In** *[Klein, L. R.]*, 1983, pp. 188–218. **[G: U.S.; U.K.; France]**

Krueger, Anne O. The Effects of Trade Strategies on Growth. *Finance Develop.*, June 1983, *20*(2), pp. 6–8. **[G: Selected LDCs]**

Kutscher, Ronald E. The GNP Data Improvement Report from the Perspective of Its Use to Measure Economic Growth. **In** *Foss, M. F., ed.*, 1983, pp. 403–07. **[G: U.S.]**

Kutscher, Ronald E. and Mark, Jerome A. The Service-Producing Sector: Some Common Perceptions Reviewed. *Mon. Lab. Rev.*, April 1983, *106*(4), pp. 21–24. **[G: U.S.]**

Landau, Daniel L. Government Expenditure and Economic Growth: A Cross-Country Study. *Southern Econ. J.*, January 1983, *49*(3), pp. 783–92.

Langham, Max R. and Ahmad, Ismet. Measuring Productivity in Economic Growth. *Amer. J. Agr. Econ.*, May 1983, *65*(2), pp. 445–51. **[G: Indonesia]**

Lawrence, Robert Z. Is Trade Deindustrializing

America? A Medium-Term Perspective. *Brookings Pap. Econ. Act.*, 1983, (1), pp. 129–61. [G: U.S.]

Ledebur, Larry C. and Moomaw, Ronald L. A Shift-Share Analysis of Regional Labor Productivity in Manufacturing. *Growth Change,* January 1983, *14*(1), pp. 2–9. [G: U.S.]

Lehner, Franz. Pressure Politics and Economic Growth: Olson's Theory and the Swiss Experience. In *Mueller, D. C., ed.*, 1983, pp. 203–14. [G: Switzerland]

Leiken, Alan M.; Stern, Eve and Baines, Ruth E. The Effect of Clinical Education Programs on Hospital Production. *Inquiry,* Spring 1983, *20*(1), pp. 88–92. [G: U.S.]

van Lennep, Emile. The Outlook for Europe's Economic Development. In *Heertje, A., ed.*, 1983, pp. 1–40.

Leray, Catherine. L'appréhension de l'efficacité dans les entreprises publiques industrielles et commerciales. (An Efficiency Assessment of Industrial and Commercial Enterprise both Public and Private. With English summary.) *Revue Écon.*, May 1983, *34*(3), pp. 612–54. [G: France]

Levitt, Arthur, Jr. Why Growth Is Important. In *Federal Reserve Bank of Atlanta,* 1983, pp. 15–21. [G: U.S.]

Lewis, W. Arthur. Socialism and Economic Growth. In *Lewis, W. A.*, 1983, *1971,* pp. 669–82.

Lindbeck, Assar. The Recent Slowdowns of Productivity Growth. *Econ. J.*, March 1983, *93*(369), pp. 13–34. [G: OECD]

Lundahl, Mats. Teknologiska förändringar och ekonomisk tillväxt i u-länder. (Technological Change and Economic Growth in the Developing Countries. With English summary.) *Ekon. Samfundets Tidskr.*, 1983, *36*(3), pp. 91–106. [G: LDCs; MDCs]

Maddison, Angus. A Comparison of Levels of GDP Per Capita in Developed and Developing Countries, 1700–1980. *J. Econ. Hist.*, March 1983, *43*(1), pp. 27–41. [G: MDCs; LDCs]

Maddison, Angus. Economic Stagnation since 1973, Its Nature and Causes: A Six Country Survey. *De Economist,* 1983, *131* (4), pp. 585–608. [G: Selected OECD]

Major, Iván. The Years 1978–1981 and the "Long Stages" in the Development of the Hungarian Economy. *Acta Oecon.*, 1983, *30*(3–4), pp. 381–99. [G: Hungary]

Maki, Dennis R. The Effects of Unions and Strikes on the Rate of Growth of Total Factor Productivity in Canada. *Appl. Econ.*, February 1983, *15*(1), pp. 29–41. [G: Canada]

Mark, Jerome A. and Waldorf, William H. Multifactor Productivity: A New BLS Measure. *Mon. Lab. Rev.*, December 1983, *106*(12), pp. 3–15. [G: U.S.]

Marsden, Keith. Taxes and Growth. *Finance Develop.*, September 1983, *20*(3), pp. 40–43. [G: Selected Countries]

Mathias, Peter. The Machine: Icon of Economic Growth. In *Macdonald, S.; Lamberton, D. M. and Mandeville, T., eds.*, 1983, pp. 11–25. [G: U.K.]

Mattei, Franco. Innovazione e capitale. (Innovation and Capital. With English summary.) *Bancaria,* September 1983, *39*(9), pp. 816–18.

McCombie, John S. L. and de Ridder, John R. Increasing Returns, Productivity, and Output Growth: The Case of the United States. *J. Post Keynesian Econ.*, Spring 1983, *5*(3), pp. 373–87. [G: U.S.]

Mestmäcker, Ernst-Joachim. Socialist Elements as Limits to Economic Growth: Comment. In *Lenel, H. O.; Willgerodt, H. and Molsberger, J.*, 1983, pp. 13–15. [G: OECD]

Mihaljek, Dubravko. Osvrt na kretanje privrednog rasta u zemljama južne Evrope i nekim vanevropskim zemljama u razdoblju 1952–1981. (A Review on the Course of Economic Growth in South European and Some Non-European Countries 1952–1981. With English summary.) *Econ. Anal. Worker's Manage.*, 1983, *17*(3), pp. 279–308. [G: Selected Countries]

Miller, Edward M. A Difficulty in Measuring Productivity with a Perpetual Inventory Capital Stock Measure. *Oxford Bull. Econ. Statist.*, August 1983, *45*(3), pp. 297–306.

Miller, Edward M. A Problem in the Measurement of Capital Embodied Productivity Change. *Eastern Econ. J.*, January–March 1983, *9*(1), pp. 29–36.

Montanari, Silvano. La produttività nelle regioni comunitarie europee per branca di attività nel 1970 e nel 1973. (Productivity in European Community Regions for Branches of Activity in 1970 and 1973. With English summary.) *Rivista Int. Sci. Econ. Com.*, July 1983, *30*(7), pp. 654–66. [G: EEC]

Moomaw, Ronald L. Spatial Productivity Variations in Manufacturing: A Critical Survey of Cross-Sectional Analyses. *Int. Reg. Sci. Rev.*, June 1983, *8*(1), pp. 1–22. [G: U.S.]

Moore, Geoffrey H. Growth Cycles: A New–Old Concept. In *Moore, G. H.*, 1983, *1979,* pp. 61–64. [G: U.S.]

Moore, Geoffrey H. and Cullity, John P. Trends and Cycles in Productivity, Unit Costs, and Prices: An International Perspective. In *Moore, G. H.*, 1983, *1982,* pp. 245–80. [G: Japan; U.K.; U.S.; W. Germany]

Moore, Geoffrey H. and Moore, Melita H. An Introduction to International Economic Indicators. In *Moore, G. H.*, 1983, pp. 65–91. [G: OECD]

Moore, W. Henson. The Congressional Outlook for Increased Saving Incentives. In *Walker, C. E. and Bloomfield, M. E., eds.*, 1983, pp. 119–20. [G: U.S.]

Moran, Cristián. Export Fluctuations and Economic Growth: An Empirical Analysis. *J. Devel. Econ.*, February/April 1983, *12*(1/2), pp. 195–218. [G: LDCs]

Morris, Derek J. Comment on the Paper by Professor Lindbeck [The Recent Slowdowns of Productivity Growth]. *Econ. J.*, March 1983, *93*(369), pp. 78–83. [G: OECD]

Mueller, Dennis C. The Political Economy of Growth: Introduction. In *Mueller, D. C., ed.*, 1983, pp. 1–3. [G: OECD]

Mueller, Dennis C. The Political Economy of Growth and Redistribution. In *Mueller, D. C., ed.*, 1983, pp. 261–76. [G: OECD]

Murrell, Peter. The Comparative Structure of the Growth of the West German and British Manufacturing Industries. In *Mueller, D. C., ed.*, 1983, pp. 109–31. **[G: W. Germany; U.K.]**

Nichols, Donald A. The Prospects for Economic Growth in the United States, 1980–2000. In *Reynolds, C. W. and Tello, C., eds.*, 1983, pp. 109–32. **[G: U.S.]**

Niemi, Albert W., Jr. Gross State Product and Productivity in the Southeast, 1950–80. *Growth Change*, April 1983, *14*(2), pp. 3–8. **[G: U.S.]**

Nordhaus, William D. Energy Productivity and Total Productivity: Comment. In *Schurr, S. H.; Sonenblum, S. and Wood, D. O., eds.*, 1983, pp. 215–19. **[G: U.S.]**

Nordhaus, William D. Macroconfusion: The Dilemmas of Economic Policy. In *Tobin, J., ed.*, 1983, pp. 247–67. **[G: OECD]**

Nordhaus, William D. Reflections on Monetarism, Stagnation and Other North American Exports. *Int. Soc. Sci. J.*, 1983, *35*(3), pp. 493–506. **[G: U.S.]**

Norsworthy, J. R. Energy Prices, Technical Change, and Productivity Growth. In *Schurr, S. H.; Sonenblum, S. and Wood, D. O., eds.*, 1983, pp. 155–77. **[G: U.S.]**

Norsworthy, J. R. and Malmquist, David H. Input Measurement and Productivity Growth in Japanese and U.S. Manufacturing. *Amer. Econ. Rev.*, December 1983, *73*(5), pp. 947–67. **[G: Japan; U.S.]**

Okun, Arthur M. Postwar Macroeconomics: The Evolution of Events and Ideas. In *Okun, A. M.*, 1983, *1981*, pp. 496–504. **[G: U.S.]**

Olson, Mancur. Public Choice and Growth: Barriers to Trade, Factor Mobility, and Growth. In *Biehl, D.; Roskamp, K. W. and Stolper, W. F., eds.*, 1983, pp. 15–40. **[G: OECD]**

Olson, Mancur. The Ideal Environment for Nuturing Growth. In *Federal Reserve Bank of Atlanta*, 1983, pp. 3–13. **[G: U.S.]**

Olson, Mancur. The Political Economy of Comparative Growth Rates. In *Mueller, D. C., ed.*, 1983, pp. 7–52. **[G: U.S.]**

Opie, Roger. Economic Planning and Growth. In *Feinstein, C., ed.*, 1983, *1972*, pp. 147–68. **[G: U.K.]**

Oppenländer, Karl Heinrich. Auswirkungen des technischen Wandels auf Beschäftigtenzahl und Beschäftigtenstruktur. (The Effects of Technical Change on Number Employed and on the Structure of Employment. With English summary.) *Ifo-Studien*, 1983, *29*(2), pp. 77–99. **[G: W. Germany]**

Oshima, Harry T. The Industrial and Demographic Transitions in East Asia. *Population Devel. Rev.*, December 1983, *9*(4), pp. 583–607. **[G: E. Asia]**

Peterson, J. C. and Jones, D. I. H. Government Expenditure and Resource Crowding Out: A Brief Examination of Some Aspects of the Bacon and Eltis Hypothesis. *Rivista Int. Sci. Econ. Com.*, December 1983, *30*(12), pp. 1100–114. **[G: U.K.; W. Germany]**

Pick, Miloš. Criteria of Effectiveness of Structural Changes of Production. *Czech. Econ. Pap.*, 1983, (21), pp. 55–69. **[G: Czechoslovakia]**

Pindyck, Robert S. The Energy Connection to Recent Productivity Behavior: Comment. In *Schurr, S. H.; Sonenblum, S. and Wood, D. O., eds.*, 1983, pp. 183–85. **[G: U.S.]**

Pittman, Russell W. Multilateral Productivity Comparisons with Undesirable Outputs. *Econ. J.*, December 1983, *93*(372), pp. 883–91. **[G: U.S.]**

Prais, S. J. Comment on the Paper by Professor Giersch and Dr. Wolter [Towards an Explanation of the Productivity Slowdown: An Acceleration-Deceleration Hypothesis]. *Econ. J.*, March 1983, *93*(369), pp. 84–88.

Pryor, Frederic L. A Quasi-test of Olson's Hypotheses. In *Mueller, D. C., ed.*, 1983, pp. 90–105. **[G: Selected Countries]**

Raisian, John. Union Dues and Wage Premiums. *J. Lab. Res.*, Winter 1983, *4*(1), pp. 1–18. **[G: U.S.]**

Reddaway, Brian. Macroeconomic Performance in Perspective. In *Shepherd, D.; Turk, J. and Silberston, A., eds.*, 1983, pp. 200–226. **[G: U.K.; OECD]**

Rymes, T. K. More on the Measurement of Total Factor Productivity. *Rev. Income Wealth*, September 1983, *29*(3), pp. 297–316.

Schurr, Sam H. Energy Efficiency and Economic Efficiency: An Historical Perspective. In *Schurr, S. H.; Sonenblum, S. and Wood, D. O., eds.*, 1983, pp. 203–14. **[G: U.S.]**

Scitovsky, Tibor. The Prospects for Economic Growth in the United States, 1980–2000: Comments. In *Reynolds, C. W. and Tello, C., eds.*, 1983, pp. 133–35. **[G: U.S.]**

Singer, Hans W. North–South Multipliers. *World Devel.*, May 1983, *11*(5), pp. 451–54. **[G: LDCs]**

Singh, Inderjit. Issues in International Agricultural Development: Discussion. *Amer. J. Agr. Econ.*, May 1983, *65*(2), pp. 452–54.

Sjaastad, Larry A. Macroconfusion: The Dilemmas of Economic Policy: Comment. In *Tobin, J., ed.*, 1983, pp. 276–79. **[G: Chile; Argentina]**

Smith, A. D. and Hitchens, D. M. W. N. Comparative British and American Productivity in Retailing. *Nat. Inst. Econ. Rev.*, May 1983, (104), pp. 45–60. **[G: U.S.; U.K.]**

Solow, Robert M. Macroconfusion: The Dilemmas of Economic Policy: Comment. In *Tobin, J., ed.*, 1983, pp. 279–84. **[G: U.S.]**

Sonenblum, Sidney. Energy Productivity and Total Productivity: Comment. In *Schurr, S. H.; Sonenblum, S. and Wood, D. O., eds.*, 1983, pp. 219–45. **[G: U.S.]**

Sonenblum, Sidney. Energy, Productivity, and Economic Growth: Overview and Commentary. In *Schurr, S. H.; Sonenblum, S. and Wood, D. O., eds.*, 1983, pp. 3–43. **[G: U.S.; Selected Countries]**

Spronk, Jaap and Veeneklaas, Frank. Scenarios for Economic Development: A Feasibility Study by Means of Interactive Multiple Goal Programming. In *Hansen, P., ed.*, 1983, pp. 356–71. **[G: Netherlands]**

Ståhl, Ingemar. Sweden at the End of the Middle Way. In *Pejovich, S., ed.*, 1983, pp. 119–39. **[G: Sweden; OECD]**

Steedman, Ian. On the Measurement and Aggregation of Productivity Increase. *Metroecon.*, October 1983, *35*(3), pp. 223–33.

Sullivan, Sherman R. Implications of Production Functions: Yugoslav Economic Growth—1952–1974. *Amer. Econ.*, Fall 1983, *27*(2), pp. 67–73.

Thurow, Lester C. America in a Competitive Economic World. **In** *Miller, G. W., ed.*, 1983, pp. 36–51. **[G: U.S.]**

Tikidzhiev, R. Balance in the Reproduction of Fixed Capital and Labor Resources. *Prob. Econ.*, March 1983, *25*(11), pp. 19–35. **[G: U.S.S.R.]**

Toffler, Alvin. Toward a Third Wave Economy. **In** *Federal Reserve Bank of Atlanta*, 1983, pp. 139–42. **[G: U.S.]**

Uri, Noel D. Embodied and Disembodied Technical Change Revisited. *Econ. Int.*, May–August–November 1983, *36*(2–3–4), pp. 278–94. **[G: U.S.]**

Val'tukh, K. K. The Investment Complex and the Intensification of Production. *Prob. Econ.*, April 1983, *25*(12), pp. 3–29. **[G: U.S.S.R.]**

Vatter, Harold G. and Walker, John F. Can the Good Performance of the 1960s Be Repeated in the 1980s? *J. Econ. Issues*, June 1983, *17*(2), pp. 369–78. **[G: U.S.]**

Wabe, J. Stuart and Gutierrez-Camara, José L. Capital Utilisation, Capital Intensity and Factor Productivity: A Comparison of Factories in Developing and Industrialised Countries. *J. Econ. Stud.*, 1983, *10*(3), pp. 3–11. **[G: Selected Countries]**

Waverman, Leonard. The Energy Connection to Recent Productivity Behavior: Comment. **In** *Schurr, S. H.; Sonenblum, S. and Wood, D. O., eds.*, 1983, pp. 185–88. **[G: U.S.]**

Weede, Erich. The Impact of Democracy on Economic Growth: Some Evidence from Cross–National Analysis. *Kyklos*, 1983, *36*(1), pp. 21–39.

Wegner, Manfred. Erklärungen für das Arbeitsplatzwunder in den USA und für die stagnierende Beschäftigung in der EG. (Employment Creation in the U.S.A. and the European Community. With English summary.) *Ifo-Studien*, 1983, *29*(2), pp. 101–37. **[G: U.S.; EEC]**

Weisskopf, Thomas E.; Bowles, Samuel and Gordon, David M. Hearts and Minds: A Social Model of U.S. Productivity Growth. *Brookings Pap. Econ. Act.*, 1983, (2), pp. 381–450. **[G: U.S.]**

Weitzman, Martin L. On the Meaning of Comparative Factor Productivity. **In** *[Erlich, A.]*, 1983, pp. 166–70.

Woods, Thomas J. Energy Productivity and Total Productivity: Comment. **In** *Schurr, S. H.; Sonenblum, S. and Wood, D. O., eds.*, 1983, pp. 253–57. **[G: U.S.]**

Zoeteweij, Bert. Anti-Inflation Policies in the Industrialised Market Economy Countries (Part II). *Int. Lab. Rev.*, November–December 1983, *122*(6), pp. 691–707.

Zoeteweij, Bert. Anti-Inflation Policies in the Industrialised Market Economy Countries (Part 1). *Int. Lab. Rev.*, Sept.–Oct. 1983, *122*(5), pp. 563–77. **[G: MDCs]**

227 Prices

2270 Prices

Abbott, Walter F. and Leasure, J. W. Income Level and Inflation in the United States: 1947–1977. **In** *Schmukler, N. and Marcus, E., eds.*, 1983, pp. 804–19. **[G: U.S.]**

Afridi, Usman and Qadir, Asghar. Dual Sector Inflation in Pakistan. *Pakistan Devel. Rev.*, Autumn 1983, *22*(3), pp. 191–210. **[G: Pakistan]**

Alogoskoufis, George S. and Pissarides, Christopher A. A Test of Price Sluggishness in the Simple Rational Expectations Model: U.K. 1950–1980. *Econ. J.*, September 1983, *93*(371), pp. 616–28. **[G: U.K.]**

Ariovich, G. The Impact of Political Tension on the Price of Gold. *J. Stud. Econ. Econometrics*, July 1983, (16), pp. 17–37.

Bánhidi, Ferenc and Gábor, László. The Price Model. *Matekon*, Spring 1983, *19*(3), pp. 18–35. **[G: Hungary]**

Barer, Morris L. and Evans, Robert G. Prices, Proxies and Productivity: An Historical Analysis of Hospital and Medical Care in Canada. **In** *Diewert, W. E. and Montmarquette, C., eds.*, 1983, pp. 705–77. **[G: Canada]**

Barnett, Richard C.; Bessler, David A. and Thompson, Robert L. The Money Supply and Nominal Agricultural Prices. *Amer. J. Agr. Econ.*, May 1983, *65*(2), pp. 303–07. **[G: U.S.]**

Baumgarten, Cynthia and Hodgins, Cyril D. Price Measurement Review Program: Consultations Feedback Report. **In** *Diewert, W. E. and Montmarquette, C., eds.*, 1983, pp. 19–37. **[G: Canada]**

Belongia, Michael T. and King, Richard A. A Monetary Analysis of Food Price Determination. *Amer. J. Agr. Econ.*, February 1983, *65*(1), pp. 131–35. **[G: U.S.]**

Belongia, Michael T. Why Do Food Prices Increase? *Fed. Res. Bank St. Louis Rev.*, April 1983, *65*(4), pp. 5–12. **[G: U.S.]**

Berndt, Ernst R. Quality Adjustment, Hedonics, and Modern Empirical Demand Analysis. **In** *Diewert, W. E. and Montmarquette, C., eds.*, 1983, pp. 817–63.

Bird, Peter J. W. N. Tests for a Threshold Effect in the Price–Cost Relationship. *Cambridge J. Econ.*, March 1983, *7*(1), pp. 37–53. **[G: U.K.]**

Blackorby, Charles. Axiomatic Foundation of Price Indexes and Purchasing Power Parities: Comment. **In** *Diewert, W. E. and Montmarquette, C., eds.*, 1983, pp. 451–54.

Blackorby, Charles and Donaldson, David. Preference Diversity and Aggregate Economic Cost-of-Living Indexes. **In** *Diewert, W. E. and Montmarquette, C., eds.*, 1983, pp. 373–409.

Blanchard, Olivier J. Price Asynchronization and Price Level Inertia. **In** *Dornbusch, R. and Simonsen, M. H., eds.*, 1983, pp. 3–24. **[G: U.S.]**

Bossons, John. Leisure Time and the Measurement of Economic Welfare: Comment. **In** *Diewert, W. E. and Montmarquette, C., eds.*, 1983, pp. 368–72. **[G: Canada]**

Bosworth, Barry P. A Century of Evidence on Wage and Price Stickiness in the United States, the United Kingdom and Japan: Comment. **In** *Tobin, J., ed.*, 1983, pp. 121–24. **[G: U.S.; U.K.; Japan]**

Bouis, Howarth E. Seasonal Rice Price Variation in the Philippines: Measuring the Effects of Government Intervention. *Food Res. Inst. Stud.*, 1983, *19*(1), pp. 81–92. **[G: Philippines]**

Boynton, Robert D.; Blake, Brian F. and Uhl, Joseph N. Retail Price Reporting Effects in Local Food Markets. *Amer. J. Agr. Econ.*, February 1983, *65*(1), pp. 20–29. **[G: U.S.]**

Brown, Mark and Johnson, Stanley R. Food Stamps: Program Parameters and Standards of Living for Low-Income Households. *Southern J. Agr. Econ.*, July 1983, *15*(1), pp. 43–49. **[G: U.S.]**

Browne, Stephen B. Measuring the Current Rate of Inflation: Comment. **In** *Diewert, W. E. and Montmarquette, C., eds.*, 1983, pp. 894–99. **[G: Canada]**

Bunn, Julie A. and Triplett, Jack E. Reconciling the CPI-U and the PCE Deflator: 3rd Quarter. *Mon. Lab. Rev.*, February 1983, *106*(2), pp. 37–38. **[G: U.S.]**

Buzelay, A. Variation des taux de change, structure des prix relatifs et balance commerciale. (Variations in Exchange Rates, the Structure of Relative Prices and the Trade Balance. With English summary.) *Écon. Soc.*, July-August 1983, *17*(7–8), pp. 1233–57. **[G: W. Germany; U.K.; France]**

Cagan, Phillip and Moore, Geoffrey H. How to Fix the CPI. **In** *Moore, G. H.*, 1983, *1981*, pp. 331–36. **[G: U.S.]**

Callahan, David; Robertson, Douglass and Scheibel, Lorie. Inflation Patterns in the Initial Stages of Recovery. *Mon. Lab. Rev.*, September 1983, *106*(9), pp. 22–26. **[G: U.S.]**

Calvet, J. and Di Ruzza, R. Quelques hypothèses sur l'étude de l'inflation en période de crise. (Hypothesis on the Study of Inflation during a Crisis Period. With English summary.) *Écon. Soc.*, September–October–November 1983, *17*(9–10–11), pp. 1537–50. **[G: France]**

Carlton, Dennis W. Equilibrium Fluctuations When Price and Delivery Lag Clear the Market. *Bell J. Econ. (See Rand J. Econ. after 4/85)*, Autumn 1983, *14*(2), pp. 562–72. **[G: U.S.]**

Cassese, Anthony and Lothian, James R. The Timing of Monetary and Price Changes and the International Transmission of Inflation. **In** *Darby, M. P. and Lothian, J. R., et al.*, 1983, pp. 58–82. **[G: OECD]**

Cebula, Richard J. Right-to-Work Laws and Geographic Differences in Living Costs: An Analysis of Effects of the 'Union Shop' Ban for the Years 1974, 1976, and 1978. *Amer. J. Econ. Soc.*, July 1983, *42*(3), pp. 329–40. **[G: U.S.]**

Chambers, Edward J. Recent Comparative Trends in the Canadian and U.S. CPIS: The Treatment of Homeownership. *Can. Public Policy*, June 1983, *9*(2), pp. 236–44. **[G: U.S.; Canada]**

Chau, L. C. Imports of Consumer Goods from China and the Economic Growth of Hong Kong. **In** *Youngson, A. J., ed.*, 1983, pp. 184–225. **[G: China; Hong Kong]**

Coda, Michael J. and Jankowski, John E., Jr. The Real Price of Imported Oil Revisited. *Energy J.*, October 1983, *4*(4), pp. 87–90. **[G: Global]**

Criqui, P. Prix du pétrole, prix des énergies finales et consommations d'énergie dans les cinq grandes économies de l'O.C.D.E. (Petroleum Price, Final Energies Prices and Energy Consumption in the Five Bigger Economies of O.E.C.D. With English summary.) *Écon. Soc.*, December 1983, *17*(12), pp. 1927–947. **[G: U.S.; Japan; France; U.K.; Germany]**

Csikós-Nagy, Béla and Rácz, László. Rise of the Price Level and Its Factors in Hungary. *Acta Oecon.*, 1983, *30*(2), pp. 161–77. **[G: Hungary]**

Curzio, Alberto Quadrio. Un futuro tranquillo per oro e materie prime (A Calm Future for Gold and Raw Materials. With English summary.) *L'Impresa*, 1983, *25*(6), pp. 51–57.

Dagum, Estela Bee and Morry, Marietta. The Estimation of Seasonal Variations in Consumer Price Indexes. **In** *Diewert, W. E. and Montmarquette, C., eds.*, 1983, pp. 919–67. **[G: Canada]**

Darby, Michael R. Movements in Purchasing Power Parity: The Short and Long Runs. **In** *Darby, M. P. and Lothian, J. R., et al.*, 1983, pp. 462–77. **[G: OECD]**

Darrough, Masako N. The Treatment of Housing in a Cost-of-Living Index: Rental Equivalence and User Cost. **In** *Diewert, W. E. and Montmarquette, C., eds.*, 1983, pp. 599–618. **[G: Canada]**

De Wolff, P. Income Policy Developments in the Netherlands. *Ind. Relat.*, Spring 1983, *22*(2), pp. 203–23. **[G: Netherlands]**

Denny, Michael G. S. and Fuss, Melvyn A. Regional Price Indexes: The Canadian Practice and Some Potential Extensions. **In** *Diewert, W. E. and Montmarquette, C., eds.*, 1983, pp. 783–816. **[G: Canada]**

Diewert, W. Erwin. An Overview of the Papers on Price Level Measurement. **In** *Diewert, W. E. and Montmarquette, C., eds.*, 1983, pp. 59–70.

Diewert, W. Erwin. The Theory of the Cost-of-Living Index and the Measurement of Welfare Change. **In** *Diewert, W. E. and Montmarquette, C., eds.*, 1983, pp. 163–233.

Diewert, W. Erwin. The Theory of the Output Price Index and the Measurement of Real Output Change. **In** *Diewert, W. E. and Montmarquette, C., eds.*, 1983, pp. 1049–1113.

Diewert, W. Erwin. The Treatment of Seasonality in the Cost-of-Living Index. **In** *Diewert, W. E. and Montmarquette, C., eds.*, 1983, pp. 1019–45.

van Dijk, G. and Mackel, C. Fundamental Changes in Price Relationships: An Investigation of the UK Feed Grain Market, 1971/72 to 1978/79, Using Spectral Analysis. *Europ. Rev. Agr. Econ.*, 1983, *10*(1), pp. 15–31. **[G: U.K.]**

Early, John F. and Sinclair, James H. Quality Adjustment in the Producer Price Indexes. **In** *Foss, M. F., ed.*, 1983, pp. 107–42. **[G: U.S.]**

Eichhorn, Wolfgang and Voeller, Joachim. Axiomatic Foundation of Price Indexes and Purchasing Power Parities. **In** *Diewert, W. E. and Montmarquette, C., eds.*, 1983, pp. 411–50.

Evans, Paul. Price-Level Instability and Output in the U.S. *Econ. Inquiry*, April 1983, *21*(2), pp. 172–87.

Felmingham, B. S. The Market Integration of Large and Small Economies: Australia, the U.S., and Japan. *J. Macroecon.*, Summer 1983, *5*(3), pp. 335–51. **[G: Australia; Japan; U.S.]**

Genereux, Pierre A. Impact of the Choice of Formulae on the Canadian Consumer Price Index. **In** *Diewert, W. E. and Montmarquette, C., eds.*, 1983, pp. 489–511. [G: Canada]

Gillingham, Robert. Measuring the Cost of Shelter for Homeowners: Theoretical and Empirical Considerations. *Rev. Econ. Statist.*, May 1983, *65*(2), pp. 254–65. [G: U.S.]

Gillingham, Robert and Greenlees, John S. The Incorporation of Direct Taxes into a Consumer Price Index. **In** *Diewert, W. E. and Montmarquette, C., eds.*, 1983, pp. 619–54. [G: U.S.]

Glushkov, N. T. Price Formation and the Economic Mechanism. *Prob. Econ.*, August 1983, *26*(4), pp. 24–56. [G: U.S.S.R.]

Gordon, Robert J. A Century of Evidence on Wage and Price Stickiness in the United States, the United Kingdom, and Japan. **In** *Tobin, J., ed.*, 1983, pp. 85–121. [G: U.S.; Japan; U.K.]

Gordon, Robert J. Energy Efficiency, User-Cost Change, and the Measurement of Durable Goods Prices: Reply. **In** *Foss, M. F., ed.*, 1983, pp. 265–68. [G: U.S.]

Gordon, Robert J. Energy Efficiency, User-Cost Change, and the Measurement of Durable Goods Prices. **In** *Foss, M. F., ed.*, 1983, pp. 205–53. [G: U.S.]

Gramlich, Edward M. Models of Inflation Expectations Formation: A Comparison of Household and Economist Forecasts. *J. Money, Credit, Banking*, May 1983, *15*(2), pp. 155–73. [G: U.S.]

Grant, Warren R., et al. Grain Price Interrelationships. *Agr. Econ. Res.*, January 1983, *35*(1), pp. 1–9. [G: U.S.]

Greenlees, John S. and Manser, Marilyn E. Prices, Proxies and Productivity: An Historical Analysis of Hospital and Medical Care in Canada: Comment. **In** *Diewert, W. E. and Montmarquette, C., eds.*, 1983, pp. 778–81. [G: Canada]

Griliches, Zvi. Quality Adjustment in the Producer Price Indexes: Comment. **In** *Foss, M. F., ed.*, 1983, pp. 142–45. [G: U.S.]

Grilli, Enzo R. and Yang, Maw-cheng. Real and Monetary Determinants of Non-oil Primary Commodity Price Movements. **In** *Kregel, J. A., ed.*, 1983, pp. 115–41. [G: OECD]

Hafer, R. W. Monetary Policy and the Price Rule: The Newest Odd Couple. *Fed. Res. Bank St. Louis Rev.*, February 1983, *65*(2), pp. 5–13. [G: U.S.]

Haines, Walter W. The Myth of Continuous Inflation: United States Experience, 1700–1980. **In** *Schmukler, N. and Marcus, E., eds.*, 1983, pp. 183–204. [G: U.S.]

Halan, Yogesh C. Inflation, Poverty and the Third World: India's Experience. **In** *Schmukler, N. and Marcus, E., eds.*, 1983, pp. 625–42. [G: India]

Hall, S. G. F.; Henry, S. G. B. and Trinder, Chris. Wages and Prices. **In** *Britton, A., ed.*, 1983, pp. 65–78. [G: U.K.]

Henderson, Dennis R.; Schrader, Lee F. and Rhodes, V. James. Public Price Reporting. **In** *Armbruster, W. J.; Henderson, D. R. and Knutson, Ronald D., eds.*, 1983, pp. 21–57. [G: U.S.]

Hendricks, Wallace E. and Kahn, Lawrence M. Cost-of-Living Clauses in Union Contracts: Determinants and Effects. *Ind. Lab. Relat. Rev.*, April 1983, *36*(3), pp. 447–60. [G: U.S.]

Hesselman, Linda. The Macroeconomic Role of Relative Price Variability in the USA and the UK. *Appl. Econ.*, April 1983, *15*(2), pp. 225–33. [G: U.K.; U.S.]

Heston, Alan W. A Different Perspective of Pakistan's Economy: The Structure of Expenditures and Prices, 1975–81. *Pakistan Devel. Rev.*, Autumn 1983, *22*(3), pp. 163–77. [G: Pakistan; LDCs; MDCs]

Hiemstra, Stephen J. Food Stamps, Program Parameters and Standards of Living for Low-Income Households: Discussion. *Southern J. Agr. Econ.*, July 1983, *15*(1), pp. 51–52. [G: U.S.]

Hirsch, Albert A. Macroeconomic Effects of Price Shocks: A Simulation Study. *Surv. Curr. Bus.*, February 1983, *63*(2), pp. 30–43. [G: U.S.]

Horne, Jocelyn. Rational Expectations and the Defris–Williams Inflationary Expectations Series: A Reply. *Econ. Rec.*, September 1983, *59*(166), pp. 293–94. [G: Australia]

Horsley, A. and Swann, G. M. P. A Time Series of Computer Price Functions. *Oxford Bull. Econ. Statist.*, November 1983, *45*(4), pp. 339–56.

Johnson, Mark J. Import Prices Decline, Export Indexes Mixed in the First 6 Months of 1983. *Mon. Lab. Rev.*, November 1983, *106*(11), pp. 59–70. [G: U.S.]

Johnson, Mark J. U.S. Foreign Trade Prices in 1982: Import Index Falls, Export Indexes Mixed. *Mon. Lab. Rev.*, May 1983, *106*(5), pp. 20–29. [G: U.S.]

Johnson, Mark J. U.S. Import and Export Price Indexes Show Declines during the First Half. *Mon. Lab. Rev.*, January 1983, *106*(1), pp. 17–23. [G: U.S.]

Jöhr, Walter Adolf and Jetzer, Jean-Pierre. Auf der Suche nach der besten Gleichungs-Sequenz für die Indexberechnung. Ein Beitrag zur Diskussion über den schweizerischen Index der Konsumentenpreise. (Searching for the Best Combination of the Optimal Equations for Calculating the Index. A Contribution to the Discussion on the Swiss Consumer Price Index. With English summary.) *Schweiz. Z. Volkswirtsch. Statist.*, December 1983, *119*(4), pp. 419–563. [G: Switzerland]

Jorgenson, Dale W. and Slesnick, Daniel T. Individual and Social Cost-of-Living Indexes. **In** *Diewert, W. E. and Montmarquette, C., eds.*, 1983, pp. 241–323. [G: U.S.]

Josefsson, Märtha and Örtengren, Johan. Crises, Inflation and Relative Prices: Investigations into Price Structure Stability in Swedish Industry 1913–80. **In** *Eliasson, G.; Sharefkin, M. and Ysander, B.-C., eds.*, 1983, pp. 53–110. [G: Sweden]

Keller, Wouter J. and Wansbeek, Tom. Private Consumption Expenditures and Price Index Numbers for the Netherlands 1951–1977. *Rev. Public Data Use (See J. Econ. Soc. Meas. after 4/85)*, December 1983, *11*(4), pp. 311–13. [G: Netherlands]

Laidler, David. The Consumer Price Index and Signals of Recession and Recovery: Comment. **In** *Diewert, W. E. and Montmarquette, C., eds.*, 1983, pp. 1133–35. [G: U.S.]

Leser, C. E. V. Short-Run and Long-Run Relative Price Changes. *J. Roy. Statist. Soc.*, 1983, *146*(2), pp. 172–81. [G: U.K.]

Lesser, William H. and Hall, L. L. Reporting Food Price Dispersions: Some Preliminary Findings.

Can. J. Agr. Econ., March 1983, *31*(1), pp. 95–104. **[G: U.S.]**

Lewis, W. Arthur. World Production, Prices and Trade, 1870–1960. **In** *Lewis, W. A.*, 1983, *1954*, pp. 175–208.

Lombra, Raymond E. and Mehra, Yash P. Aggregate Demand, Food Prices, and the Underlying Rate of Inflation. *J. Macroecon.*, Fall 1983, *5*(4), pp. 383–98.

Maciejewski, Edouard B. "Real" Effective Exchange Rate Indices: A Re-Examination of the Major Conceptual and Methodological Issues. *Int. Monet. Fund Staff Pap.*, September 1983, *30*(3), pp. 491–541.

Manser, Marilyn E. Deflation of Defense Purchases: Comment. **In** *Foss, M. F., ed.*, 1983, pp. 199–203. **[G: U.S.]**

Marquez, Jaime R. A Proposition on Short-Run Departures from the Law-of-One-Price: An Extension. *Europ. Econ. Rev.*, September 1983, *23*(1), pp. 99–101.

McAlpin, Michelle B. Price Movements and Fluctuations in Economic Activity (1860–1947). **In** *Kumar, D., ed.*, 1983, pp. 878–904. **[G: India]**

McElroy, Katherine Maddox; Siegfried, John J. and Sweeney, George H. The Incidence of Price Changes in the U.S. Economy. **In** *Craven, J. V., ed.*, 1983, *1982*, pp. 243–66.

Medio, Alfredo. Worldwide Inflation and Its Impact on Less Developed Countries. *Econ. Forum*, Summer 1983, *14*(1), pp. 1–26. **[G: Global]**

Medio, Alfredo. Worldwide Inflation and Its Impact on Less Developed Countries: Part II. *Econ. Forum*, Winter 1983-84, *14*(2), pp. 59–95. **[G: LDCs]**

Meinlschmidt, G. and Wohlfart, E. Zur Preisniveaumessung der Europäischen Gemeinschaft. Einige Methodenvorschläge zur Messung des Preisniveaus des Privaten Konsums der Europäischen Gemeinschaft für den Zeitraum 1975–1980. (On the Measurement of the Price Level in the European Community. With English summary.) *Schweiz. Z. Volkswirtsch. Statist.*, December 1983, *119*(4), pp. 565–74. **[G: EC]**

Montmarquette, Claude. Public Goods and Price Indexes. **In** *Diewert, W. E. and Montmarquette, C., eds.*, 1983, pp. 655–78. **[G: Canada]**

Moore, Geoffrey H. Inflation and Profits. **In** *Moore, G. H.*, 1983, *1977*, pp. 281–85. **[G: U.S.]**

Moore, Geoffrey H. Inflation and Statistics. **In** *Moore, G. H.*, 1983, *1980*, pp. 287–311. **[G: U.S.]**

Moore, Geoffrey H. Inflation and Statistics—Again. **In** *Moore, G. H.*, 1983, *1981*, pp. 313–29. **[G: U.S.]**

Moore, Geoffrey H. The Consumer Price Index and Signals of Recession and Recovery. **In** *Diewert, W. E. and Montmarquette, C., eds.*, 1983, pp. 1117–32. **[G: U.S.]**

Moore, Geoffrey H. The Cyclical Behavior of Prices. **In** *Moore, G. H.*, 1983, *1971*, pp. 175–210. **[G: U.S.]**

Moore, Geoffrey H. and Cullity, John P. Trends and Cycles in Productivity, Unit Costs, and Prices: An International Perspective. **In** *Moore, G. H.*, 1983, *1982*, pp. 245–80. **[G: Japan; U.K.; U.S.; W. Germany]**

Morandé, Felipe. Precios internos de bienes transables en Chile y la "ley de un solo precio." (With English summary.) *Cuadernos Econ.*, December 1983, *20*(61), pp. 295–311. **[G: Chile]**

Moschos, D. Aggregate Price Responses to Wage and Productivity Changes: Evidence from the U.S. *Empirical Econ.*, 1983, *8*(3–4), pp. 169–75. **[G: U.S.]**

Murray, Michael P. Mythical Demands and Mythical Supplies for Proper Estimation of Rosen's Hedonic Price Model. *J. Urban Econ.*, November 1983, *14*(3), pp. 326–37.

Nambiar, R. G. Comparative Prices in a Developing Economy: The Case of India. *J. Devel. Econ.*, February/April 1983, *12*(1/2), pp. 19–25. **[G: India]**

Okun, Arthur M. Inflation: Its Mechanics and Welfare Costs. **In** *Okun, A. M.*, 1983, *1975*, pp. 79–118. **[G: U.S.; 8210]**

Papadia, F. Rationality of Inflationary Expectations in the European Economic Communties Countries. *Empirical Econ.*, 1983, *8*(3–4), pp. 187–202. **[G: EEC]**

Piriou, Jean-Paul. L'indice des prix de la C.G.T.: Une analyse critique. (The Price Index of the C.G.T.: A Critical Analysis. With English summary.) *Consommation*, April–June 1983, *30*(2), pp. 35–68. **[G: France]**

Pollak, Robert A. The Theory of the Cost-of-Living Index. **In** *Diewert, W. E. and Montmarquette, C., eds.*, 1983, pp. 87–161.

Pollak, Robert A. The Treatment of 'Quality' in the Cost of Living Index. *J. Public Econ.*, February 1983, *20*(1), pp. 25–53.

Popkin, Joel. Longrun Effects of Cutbacks in Federal Statistical Programs: A Case Study of Price Statistics. *Rev. Public Data Use (See J. Econ. Soc. Meas. after 4/85)*, December 1983, *11*(4), pp. 331–37. **[G: U.S.]**

Quadrio-Curzio, Alberto. Alternative Explanations: [Real and Monetary Determinants of Non-oil Primary Commodity Price Movements]. **In** *Kregel, J. A., ed.*, 1983, pp. 142–52. **[G: OECD]**

Rafati, M. Reza. Price Determination in Monopolistic Markets with Inventory Adjustments: The Case of Nickel. *Weltwirtsch. Arch.*, 1983, *119*(1), pp. 152–68.

Ramsaran, Ramesh F. The Retail Price Index of Trinidad and Tobago and Its Relevance as a Measure of Changes in the Cost of Living. *Soc. Econ. Stud.*, December 1983, *32*(4), pp. 73–106. **[G: Trinidad and Tobago]**

Rees, Albert. The Improvement of Price Data. **In** *Foss, M. F., ed.*, 1983, pp. 417–21. **[G: U.S.]**

Rhoades, D. and Elhawary-Rivet, N. Measuring the Current Rate of Inflation. **In** *Diewert, W. E. and Montmarquette, C., eds.*, 1983, pp. 877–93. **[G: Canada]**

Rice, G. Randolph. The Variance of Expected Inflation and the Rate of Inflation: Implications from Inter-Industry Wage Equations. *Appl. Econ.*, August 1983, *15*(4), pp. 553–61. **[G: U.K.]**

Riddell, W. Craig. Leisure Time and the Measurement of Economic Welfare. **In** *Diewert, W. E. and Montmarquette, C., eds.*, 1983, pp. 337–67. **[G: Canada]**

Rosefielde, Steven. Disguised Inflation in Soviet Industry: A Reply to James Steiner. *J. Compar. Econ.*, March 1983, *7*(1), pp. 71–76. **[G: U.S.S.R.]**

Russell, R. Robert. Individual and Social Cost-of-Living Indexes: Comments. **In** *Diewert, W. E. and Montmarquette, C., eds.*, 1983, pp. 324–36. **[G: U.S.]**

Russell, R. Robert. The Theory of the Cost-of-Living Index and the Measurement of Welfare Change: Comments. **In** *Diewert, W. E. and Montmarquette, C., eds.*, 1983, pp. 234–39.

Sachs, Abner and Ziemer, Richard C. Implicit Price Deflators for Military Construction. *Surv. Curr. Bus.*, November 1983, *63*(11), pp. 14–18. **[G: U.S.]**

Salop, Steven C. A Century of Evidence on Wage and Price Stickiness in the United States, the United Kingdom, and Japan: Comment. **In** *Tobin, J., ed.*, 1983, pp. 124–33. **[G: U.S.; U.K.; Japan]**

Sardy, Hyman. The Economic Impact of Inflation on Urban Areas. **In** *Schmukler, N. and Marcus, E., eds.*, 1983, pp. 312–25. **[G: U.S.]**

Saunders, Peter. A Disaggregate Study of the Rationality of Australian Producers' Price Expectations. *Manchester Sch. Econ. Soc. Stud.*, December 1983, *51*(4), pp. 380–98. **[G: Australia]**

Saunders, Peter. Rational Expectations and the Defris–Williams Inflationary Expectations Series: A Comment. *Econ. Rec.*, September 1983, *59*(166), pp. 290–92. **[G: Australia]**

Schaefer, Gordon. Escalation Measures: What Is the Answer? What Is the Question? Comment. **In** *Diewert, W. E. and Montmarquette, C., eds.*, 1983, pp. 483–87.

Schapper, Paul R. Hospital Cost Inflation: The Case of Australia. *Inquiry*, Fall 1983, *20*(3), pp. 276–81. **[G: Australia]**

Severn, Alan K. Formation of Inflation Expectations in the U.K.: Pitfalls in the Use of the Error-Learning Model. *Europ. Econ. Rev.*, January 1983, *20*(1–3), pp. 349–63. **[G: U.K.]**

Steiner, James E. Disguised Inflation in Soviet Industry: A Final Reply to Steven Rosefielde. *J. Compar. Econ.*, December 1983, *7*(4), pp. 449–51. **[G: U.S.S.R.]**

Sugrue, Diarmuid. Sectoral Inflation Rates. *Irish Banking Rev.*, June 1983, pp. 29–32. **[G: Ireland]**

Sukhatme, Vasant. Farm Prices in India and Abroad: Implications for Production. *Econ. Develop. Cult. Change*, October 1983, *32*(1), pp. 169–82. **[G: India]**

Sylos Labini, Paolo. Princes, Costs and Profits in the Manufacturing Industry: Italy and Japan. **In** *Fodella, G., ed.*, 1983, pp. 64–89. **[G: Italy; Japan]**

Sylos Labini, Paolo. Secular Movements in Primary and Manufactured Goods' Prices: Comment [Real and Monetary Determinants of Non-oil Primary Commodity Price Movements]. **In** *Kregel, J. A., ed.*, 1983, pp. 153–55.

Szulc, Bohdan J. Linking Price Index Numbers. **In** *Diewert, W. E. and Montmarquette, C., eds.*, 1983, pp. 537–66.

Taylor, Stephen J. Price Trends in Wool Prices when Sydney Futures Are Actively Traded. *Australian Econ. Pap.*, June 1983, *22*(40), pp. 99–105. **[G: Australia]**

Triplett, Jack E. Concepts of Quality in Input and Output Price Measures: A Resolution of the User-Value Resource-Cost Debate. **In** *Foss, M. F., ed.*, 1983, pp. 269–311.

Triplett, Jack E. Energy Efficiency, User-Cost Change, and the Measurement of Durable Goods Prices: Comment. **In** *Foss, M. F., ed.*, 1983, pp. 253–65. **[G: U.S.]**

Triplett, Jack E. Escalation Measures: What Is the Answer? What Is the Question? **In** *Diewert, W. E. and Montmarquette, C., eds.*, 1983, pp. 457–82.

Triplett, Jack E. Quality Adjustment, Hedonics, and Modern Empirical Demand Analysis: Comment. **In** *Diewert, W. E. and Montmarquette, C., eds.*, 1983, pp. 864–75.

Turner, Charlie G. Voluntary Export Restraints on Trade Going to the United States. *Southern Econ. J.*, January 1983, *49*(3), pp. 793–803. **[G: U.S.; Japan]**

Ziemer, Richard C. and Galbraith, Karl D. Deflation of Defense Purchases. **In** *Foss, M. F., ed.*, 1983, pp. 147–99. **[G: U.S.]**

228 Regional Statistics

2280 Regional Statistics

Bell, David. Understanding the Scottish Economy: What do Indicators Indicate? **In** *Ingham, K. P. D. and Love, J., eds.*, 1983, pp. 273–83. **[G: U.K.]**

Bretzfelder, Robert and Friedenberg, Howard. Regional and State Nonfarm Wages and Salaries Thus Far in the 1980's. *Surv. Curr. Bus.*, January 1983, *63*(1), pp. 23–26. **[G: U.S.]**

Garnick, Daniel H. Shifting Patterns in the Growth of Metropolitan and Nonmetropolitan Areas. *Surv. Curr. Bus.*, May 1983, *63*(5), pp. 39–44. **[G: U.S.]**

Harris, R. I. D. The Measurement of Capital Services in Production for UK Regions, 1968-78. *Reg. Stud.*, June 1983, *17*(3), pp. 169–80. **[G: U.K.]**

Johnson, Kenneth; Friedenberg, Howard and Downey, George. Tracking the BEA Regional and State Economic Projections. *Surv. Curr. Bus.*, May 1983, *63*(5), pp. 45–52. **[G: U.S.]**

Klein, Lawrence R. NIPA Statistics: A User's View. **In** *Foss, M. F., ed.*, 1983, pp. 319–23. **[G: U.S.]**

L'Esperance, Wilford L. and Shumay, Alexander J. Alternative Procedures for Estimating Gross State Product. **In** *Dutta, M.; Hartline, J. C. and Loeb, P. D., eds.*, 1983, pp. 65–79. **[G: U.S.]**

Nakosteen, Robert A. U.S. and Canadian Migration Data: A Comment. *Rev. Public Data Use (See J. Econ. Soc. Meas. after 4/85)*, March 1983, *11*(1), pp. 69–71. **[G: U.S.; Canada]**

Norris, Douglas. New Sources of Canadian Small Area Migration Data. *Rev. Public Data Use (See J. Econ. Soc. Meas. after 4/85)*, March 1983, *11*(1), pp. 11–25. **[G: Canada]**

O'Neill Adams, Margaret and Ross, Frances E. The Energy Data Base within the Kentucky Economic Information System. *Rev. Public Data Use (See J. Econ. Soc. Meas. after 4/85)*, March 1983, *11*(1), pp. 75–78. **[G: U.S.]**

Rapport, D. J. The Stress-Response Environmental

Statistical System and Its Applicability to the Laurentian Lower Great Lakes. *Statist. J.*, October 1983, *1*(4), pp. 377–405. [G: Canada]

Soltow, Lee. Kentucky Wealth at the End of the Eighteenth Century. *J. Econ. Hist.*, September 1983, *43*(3), pp. 617–33. [G: U.S.]

229 Microdata and Database Analysis

2290 Microdata and Database Analysis

Duncan, Joseph W. Private Sector Data on Business Failures. *Rev. Public Data Use (See J. Econ. Soc. Meas. after 4/85)*, March 1983, *11*(1), pp. 29–35. [G: U.S.]

300 Domestic Monetary and Fiscal Theory and Institutions

310 Domestic Monetary and Financial Theory and Institutions

3100 General

Adams, John. Financial Subinfeudation and the Penchant for Real Investment. *J. Econ. Issues*, June 1983, *17*(2), pp. 485–94. [G: India]

Bácskai, Tamás and Várhegyi, Éva. Monetization of the Hungarian Economy. *Acta Oecon.*, 1983, *31*(1–2), pp. 13–22. [G: Hungary]

Barro, Robert J. and Plosser, Charles I. Alternative Monetary Standards: Introduction. *J. Monet. Econ.*, July 1983, *12*(1), pp. 1–5.

Bernholz, Peter. Inflation and Monetary Constitutions in Historical Perspective. *Kyklos*, 1983, *36*(3), pp. 397–419. [G: Germany; France; U.K.; U.S.]

Bhatt, V. V. A Note on Financial Innovations and Development. *Rivista Int. Sci. Econ. Com.*, October–November 1983, *30*(10–11), pp. 1064–72.

Brunner, Karl and Meltzer, Allan H. Money, Monetary Policy, and Financial Institutions. *Carnegie-Rochester Conf. Ser. Public Policy*, Spring 1983, *18*, pp. 1–7. [G: U.S.; U.K.]

Carli, Guido. Per un sistema finanziario più moderno. (Towards a More Modern Financial System. With English summary.) *L'Impresa*, 1983, *25*(6), pp. 31–35. [G: Italy]

Christin, Ivan. Financial Systems: A Few Theoretical and Algebraic Considerations for Their Modeling. *Math. Soc. Sci.*, November 1983, *6*(2), pp. 171–93.

Fernández, Roque B. La crisis financiera Argentina: 1980–1982. (With English summary.) *Desarrollo Econ.*, April–June 1983, *23*(89), pp. 79–97. [G: Argentina]

Fisher, Peter S. The Role of the Public Sector in Local Development Finance: Evaluating Alternative Institutional Arrangements. *J. Econ. Issues*, March 1983, *17*(1), pp. 133–53.

Freedman, C. Financial Innovation in Canada: Causes and Consequences. *Amer. Econ. Rev.*, May 1983, *73*(2), pp. 101–06. [G: Canada]

Greenbaum, Stuart I. and Higgins, Bryon. Financial Innovation. In *Benston, G. J., ed.*, 1983, pp. 213–34. [G: U.S.]

Kane, Edward J. Policy Implications of Structural Changes in Financial Markets. *Amer. Econ. Rev.*, May 1983, *73*(2), pp. 96–100.

Lavoie, Marc. Loi de Minsky et loi d'entropie. (Minsky Law and Entropy Law. With English summary.) *Écon. Appl.*, 1983, *36*(2–3), pp. 287–331.

Mayhew, Anne. Ideology and the Great Depression: Monetary History Rewritten. *J. Econ. Issues*, June 1983, *17*(2), pp. 353–60. [G: U.S.]

Paquet, Gilles and Wallot, Jean-Pierre. Le système financier bas-canadien au tournant du XIXe siècle. (The Lower Canadian Financial System at the Turn of the 19th Century. With English summary.) *L'Actual. Econ.*, September 1983, *59*(3), pp. 456–513. [G: Canada]

Pigott, Charles. Financial Reform in Japan. *Fed. Res. Bank San Francisco Econ. Rev.*, Winter 1983, (1), pp. 25–46. [G: Japan; U.S.]

Revell, Jack. Efficiency in the Financial Sector. In *Shepherd, D.; Turk, J. and Silberston, A., eds.*, 1983, pp. 137–70. [G: U.K.]

Sakakibara, Eisuke and Feldman, Robert A. The Japanese Financial System in Comparative Perspective. *J. Compar. Econ.*, March 1983, *7*(1), pp. 1–24. [G: U.S.; Japan]

Silber, William L. The Process of Financial Innovation. *Amer. Econ. Rev.*, May 1983, *73*(2), pp. 89–95. [G: U.S.]

Travaglini, Guido. Un commento al Rapporto Campbell. (A Note on the Campbell Report. With English summary.) *Bancaria*, February 1983, *39*(2), pp. 174–77. [G: Australia]

Volcker, Paul A. Statement to the U.S. Senate Committee on Banking, Housing, and Urban Affairs, April 26, 1983. *Fed. Res. Bull.*, May 1983, *69*(5), pp. 356–64. [G: U.S.]

311 Domestic Monetary and Financial Theory and Policy

3110 Monetary Theory and Policy

Ahmed, Ziauddin; Iqbal, Munawar and Khan, M. Fahim. Money and Banking in Islam: Introduction. In *Ahmed, Z.; Iqbal, M. and Khan, M. F., eds.*, 1983, pp. 1–25.

Al-Jarhi, Ma'bid Ali. A Monetary and Financial Structure for an Interest-Free Economy: Institutions, Mechanism and Policy. In *Ahmed, Z.; Iqbal, M. and Khan, M. F., eds.*, 1983, pp. 69–87.

Arcelli, Mario. Is "Total Domestic Credit" Still a Valid Intermediate Monetary Policy Objective? *Rev. Econ. Cond. Italy*, October 1983, (3), pp. 413–28. [G: Italy]

Ariff, Mohamed. Monetary Policy in an Islamic Economy: Comment. In *Ahmed, Z.; Iqbal, M. and Khan, M. F., eds.*, 1983, pp. 47–52.

Axilrod, Stephen H. Strategies and Tactics for Monetary Control: A Comment on Brunner and Meltzer. *Carnegie-Rochester Conf. Ser. Public Policy*, Spring 1983, *18*, pp. 105–12. [G: U.S.]

Bandeen, Robert A. International Effects of High Interest Rates. In *Sanford, T., ed.*, 1983, pp. 157–66. [G: U.S.; Canada]

Barnett, William A. Understanding the New Divisia Monetary Aggregates. *Rev. Public Data Use (See J. Econ. Soc. Meas. after 4/85)*, December 1983,

11(4), pp. 349–55. **[G: U.S.]**

Batten, Dallas S. and Hafer, R. W. The Relative Impact of Monetary and Fiscal Actions on Economic Activity: A Cross-Country Comparison. *Fed. Res. Bank St. Louis Rev.*, January 1983, *65*(1), pp. 5–12.

Batten, Dallas S. and Stone, Courtenay C. Are Monetarists an Endangered Species? *Fed. Res. Bank St. Louis Rev.*, May 1983, *65*(5), pp. 5–16. **[G: U.S.]**

Baum, Thomas M. Empirische Analysen der Bundesbankautonomie. (Empirical Analyses on the Autonomy of the Deutsche Bundesbank. With English summary.) *Konjunkturpolitik*, 1983, *29*(3), pp. 163–86.

Bernanke, Ben S. Nonmonetary Effects of the Financial Crisis in Propagation of the Great Depression. *Amer. Econ. Rev.*, June 1983, *73*(3), pp. 257–76. **[G: U.S.]**

Block, Walter. Who Speaks for the Free Market: Monetarists or Supply-Siders? [What's Wrong with Supply-Side Economics] [The Trouble with Monetarism]. *Policy Rev.*, Spring 1983, (24), pp. 9–12. **[G: U.S.]**

Blomqvist, H. C. Finland's Monetary Autonomy. *Appl. Econ.*, June 1983, *15*(3), pp. 409–15.

Bomhoff, Edward J. Permanent and Transitory Changes in Monetary Policy: A Comment. *Carnegie-Rochester Conf. Ser. Public Policy*, Autumn 1983, *19*, pp. 211–23. **[G: Switzerland; U.S.; W. Germany]**

Brimmer, Andrew F. Monetary Policy and Economic Activity: Benefits and Costs of Monetarism. *Amer. Econ. Rev.*, May 1983, *73*(2), pp. 1–12. **[G: U.S.]**

Brothwell, John F. Wages and Employment: A Reply to Maynard and Rose [Monetarism, Wages, and Employment Policy in the United Kingdom]. *J. Post Keynesian Econ.*, Fall 1983, *6*(1), pp. 101–04.

Brunner, Karl and Meltzer, Allan H. Reply to Stephen Axilrod's Comments [Strategies and Tactics for Monetary Control]. *Carnegie-Rochester Conf. Ser. Public Policy*, Spring 1983, *18*, pp. 113–16. **[G: U.S.]**

Brunner, Karl and Meltzer, Allan H. Strategies and Tactics for Monetary Control. *Carnegie-Rochester Conf. Ser. Public Policy*, Spring 1983, *18*, pp. 59–103. **[G: U.S.]**

Burton, David. Flexible Exchange Rates and Perfect Foresight: The Implications of Domestic Monetary Policy for Foreign Prices and Stabilization Policy. *Weltwirtsch. Arch.*, 1983, *119*(2), pp. 201–13.

den Butter, Frank A. G. Choice of Monetary Policy Instruments in a Stochastic IS–LM Model: Some Empirical Remarks for the Netherlands. *De Economist*, 1983, *131*(1), pp. 46–54. **[G: Netherlands]**

Caranza, Cesare and Fazio, Antonio. L'evoluzione dei metodi di controllo monetario in Italia: 1974–1983. (Changes in Methods of Monetary Control in Italy, 1974–1983. With English summary.) *Bancaria*, September 1983, *39*(9), pp. 819–33. **[G: Italy]**

Chapra, M. Umer. Monetary Policy in an Islamic Economy. **In** *Ahmed, Z.; Iqbal, M. and Khan, M. F., eds.*, 1983, pp. 27–46.

Ciampi, Carlo Azeglio. Canoni e prassi nell'attività di banca centrale. (Principles and Practice in Central Banking. With English summary.) *Bancaria*, January 1983, *39*(1), pp. 12–18. **[G: Italy]**

Collins, Michael. Long-term Growth of the English Banking Sector and Money Stock, 1844–80. *Econ. Hist. Rev., 2nd Ser.*, August 1983, *36*(3), pp. 374–94. **[G: U.K.]**

Cooper, Kathleen M. Re-Thinking the Fundamentals of Interest Rate Determination. *Bus. Econ.*, January 1983, *18*(1), pp. 25–30. **[G: U.S.]**

Cornell, Bradford. Monetary Policy and the Daily Behavior of Interest Rates. *J. Econ. Bus.*, June 1983, *35*(2), pp. 189–203. **[G: U.S.]**

Cripps, Francis. What Is Wrong with Monetarism? **In** *Jansen, K., ed.*, 1983, pp. 55–68.

Darby, Michael R. The United States as an Exogenous Source of World Inflation under the Bretton Woods System. **In** *Darby, M. P. and Lothian, J. R., et al.*, 1983, pp. 478–90. **[G: U.S.]**

Darby, Michael R. and Lothian, James R. Conclusions on the International Transmission of Inflation. **In** *Darby, M. P. and Lothian, J. R., et al.*, 1983, pp. 493–523. **[G: OECD]**

Davidson, Lawrence S. and Hafer, R. W. Some Evidence on Selecting an Intermediate Target for Monetary Policy. *Southern Econ. J.*, October 1983, *50*(2), pp. 406–21. **[G: U.S.]**

Davis, Richard G. and Meek, Paul. Monetary Targeting—Variations on a Common Theme. **In** *Meek, P., ed.*, 1983, pp. 1–5. **[G: OECD]**

Dorn, James A. Introduction: A Historical Perspective on the Importance of Stable Money. *Cato J.*, Spring 1983, *3*(1), pp. 1–8. **[G: U.S.]**

Driscoll, Michael J.; du Plessis, J. J. A. and Ford, J. L. Monetary Aggregates and Economic Activity: Rejoinder. *S. Afr. J. Econ.*, June 1983, *51*(2), pp. 329–33. **[G: S. Africa]**

Driscoll, Michael J.; du Plessis, J. J. A. and Ford, J. L. Monetary Aggregates and Economic Activity: Reply. *S. Afr. J. Econ.*, June 1983, *51*(2), pp. 318–25. **[G: S. Africa]**

Dumas, Lloyd J. Resource Diversion and the Failure of Conventional Macrotheory. *J. Econ. Issues*, June 1983, *17*(2), pp. 555–64.

Ellman, Michael. Monetarism and the State Socialist World. **In** *Jansen, K., ed.*, 1983, pp. 96–109. **[G: CMEA]**

Feldstein, Martin S. The Fiscal Framework of Monetary Economics. *Econ. Inquiry*, January 1983, *21*(1), pp. 11–23. **[G: U.S.]**

Filc, Wolfgang. Internationale Wirschaft- und Währungsprobleme: Floating, Arbeitslosigkeit und Geldpolitik. (International Economic and Monetary Problems: Floating, Unemployment and Monetary Policy. With English summary.) *Kredit Kapital*, 1983, *16*(1), pp. 81–97. **[G: W. Germany]**

Franzsen, D. G. Monetary Policy in South Africa, 1932–82. *S. Afr. J. Econ.*, March 1983, *51*(1), pp. 88–133. **[G: S. Africa]**

Frazer, William J., Jr. Monetary Trends in the U.S. and the U.K.: Review Article. *Southern Econ. J.*, January 1983, *49*(3), pp. 833–46. **[G: U.S.; U.K.]**

Frey, Bruno S.; Pommerehne, Werner W. and Schneider, Friedrich. Are We All Monetarists

Now? An Empirical Inquiry. *J. Post Keynesian Econ.*, Fall 1983, *6*(1), pp. 89–96.

von Furstenberg, George M. Internationally Managed Moneys. *Amer. Econ. Rev.*, May 1983, *73*(2), pp. 54–58.

Garrison, Roger W. Gold: A Standard and an Institution [Why Gold?]. *Cato J.*, Spring 1983, *3*(1), pp. 233–38. [G: U.S.; U.K.]

Gerbier, B. Le thatcherisme: vers une économie mondiale anglo-américaine? (Thatcherism: Towards an Anglo-Saxon World Economy. With English summary.) *Écon. Soc.*, September–October–November 1983, *17*(9–10–11), pp. 1763–95. [G: U.K.]

Ghatak, Subrata. On Interregional Variations in Rural Interest Rates in India. *J. Devel. Areas*, October 1983, *18*(1), pp. 21–34. [G: India]

Gilbert, R. Alton. Two Measures of Reserves: Why Are They Different? *Fed. Res. Bank St. Louis Rev.*, June/July 1983, *65*(6), pp. 16–25. [G: U.S.]

Gonzalez-Vega, Claudio. Arguments for Interest Rate Reform. **In** *Von Pischke, J. D.; Adams, D. W. and Donald, G., eds.*, 1983, pp. 365–72.

Gotur, Padma. Interest Rates and the Developing World. *Finance Develop.*, December 1983, *20*(4), pp. 33–36. [G: LDCs]

Green, Jerry R. and Honkapohja, Seppo. Variance-Minimizing Monetary Policies with Lagged Price Adjustment and Rational Expectations. *Europ. Econ. Rev.*, January 1983, *20*(1–3), pp. 123–41.

Greenbaum, Stuart I. Legal Reserve Requirements: A Case Study in Bank Regulation. *J. Bank Res.*, Spring 1983, *14*(1), pp. 59–69. [G: U.S.]

Grieves, Robin. The Demand for Consumer Durables. *J. Money, Credit, Banking,* August 1983, *15*(3), pp. 316–26. [G: U.S.]

Hafer, R. W.; Hein, Scott E. and Koofere, Clemens J. M. Forecasting the Money Multiplier: Implications for Money Stock Control and Economic Activity. *Fed. Res. Bank St. Louis Rev.*, October 1983, *65*(8), pp. 22–33. [G: U.S.]

Hansen, Bent. Interest Rates and Foreign Capital in Egypt under British Occupation. *J. Econ. Hist.*, December 1983, *43*(4), pp. 867–84. [G: Egypt]

Harrington, R. L. Monetarisms: Real and Imaginary: A Review Article. *Manchester Sch. Econ. Soc. Stud.*, March 1983, *51*(1), pp. 63–71.

Heertje, Arnold. Monetarism: Is the Debate Closed? **In** *Jansen, K., ed.*, 1983, pp. 69–78.

Hein, Scott E. and Ott, Mack. Seasonally Adjusting Money: Procedures, Problems, Proposals. *Fed. Res. Bank St. Louis Rev.*, November 1983, *65*(9), pp. 16–25. [G: U.S.]

Heinsohn, Gunnar and Steiger, Otto. Private Property, Debts and Interest or: The Origin of Money and the Rise and Fall of Monetary Economies. *Stud. Econ.*, 1983, *38*(21), pp. 3–56.

Hodges, Richard and Cherry, John F. Cost-Control and Coinage: An Archaeological Approach to Economic Change in Anglo-Saxon England. **In** *Dalton, G., ed.*, 1983, pp. 131–83. [G: U.K.]

Horne, Jocelyn. The Money Formation Table Approach to Forecasting: An Evaluation of the Institute of Money Supply Forecasts. *Australian Econ. Rev.*, 1983, (64), pp. 69–77. [G: Australia]

Horvitz, Paul M. Legal Reserve Requirements: A Case Study in Bank Regulation: Discussant's Comments. *J. Bank Res.*, Spring 1983, *14*(1), pp. 69–72. [G: U.S.]

Hull, Everson. Money Growth and the Employment Aspirations of Black Americans. *Rev. Black Polit. Econ.*, Spring 1983, *12*(3), pp. 63–74. [G: U.S.]

Hüttl, Antónia; Losonczy, I. and Örszigety, G. The Financial Regulator Model. *Matekon*, Summer 1983, *19*(4), pp. 3–20. [G: Hungary]

Iqbal, Munawar. Monetary Policy in an Islamic Economy: Comment. **In** *Ahmed, Z.; Iqbal, M. and Khan, M. F., eds.*, 1983, pp. 52–57.

Jasinowski, Jerry. An Eclectic Economic View. **In** *Sanford, T., ed.*, 1983, pp. 167–77.

Johnson, Karen H. Foreign Experience with Targets for Money Growth. *Fed. Res. Bull.*, October 1983, *69*(10), pp. 745–54. [G: Selected OECD]

Judd, John P. Deregulated Deposit Rates and Monetary Policy. *Fed. Res. Bank San Francisco Econ. Rev.*, Fall 1983, (4), pp. 27–44. [G: U.S.]

Jüttner, D. Johannes. Rates of Return, Investment Behaviour and Monetary Policy. *Kredit Kapital,* 1983, *16*(1), pp. 16–35.

Kang, Heejoon. The Effect of Monetary Changes on Interest Rates: A Comment. *Rev. Econ. Statist.*, May 1983, *65*(2), pp. 360–62. [G: U.S.]

Kapur, Basant K. Optimal Financial and Foreign-Exchange Liberalization of Less Developed Economies. *Quart. J. Econ.*, February 1983, *98*(1), pp. 41–62.

Kearney, Colm. Money and Monetarism: The British Experience. *Irish Banking Rev.*, December 1983, pp. 27–35. [G: U.K.]

King, Robert G. On the Economics of Private Money. *J. Monet. Econ.*, July 1983, *12*(1), pp. 127–58. [G: U.S.]

Klein, Lawrence R.; Friedman, Edward and Able, Stephen. Money in the Wharton Quarterly Model. *J. Money, Credit, Banking,* May 1983, *15*(2), pp. 237–59. [G: U.S.]

Kopcke, Richard W. Must the Ideal "Money Stock" Be Controllable? *New Eng. Econ. Rev.*, March/April 1983, pp. 10–23. [G: U.S.]

Kopecky, Kenneth J.; Parke, Darrel W. and Porter, Richard D. A Framework for Analyzing Money Stock Control under the Monetary Control Act. *J. Econ. Bus.*, June 1983, *35*(2), pp. 139–57. [G: U.S.]

Langfeldt, Enno. Kann eine monetäre Schätzgleichung zur Verbessrung der Konjunkturprognosen beitragen? (Can a Monetary Estimating Equation Contribute to Improvement of Trade Cycle Forecasts? With English summary.) *Kredit Kapital,* 1983, *16*(2), pp. 205–19. [G: W. Germany]

Larkins, Daniel J. The Monetary Aggregates: An Introduction to Definitional Issues. *Surv. Curr. Bus.*, January 1983, *63*(1), pp. 34–46. [G: U.S.]

Layton, Allan P. Is U.S. Monetary Growth a Leading Indicator of Australian Monetary Growth? *Econ. Rec.*, June 1983, *59*(165), pp. 180–85. [G: U.S.; Australia]

Lomax, David F. *Competition and Credit Control* [and] *Monetary Control in the United Kingdom:* A Review Essay. *J. Money, Credit, Banking,* November 1983, *15*(4), pp. 527–32.

Magnifico, Giovanni. Problems of the World Economy Today. *Econ. Notes,* 1983, (2), pp. 49–64. **[G: Global]**

Magnifico, Giovanni. Recent Aspects of Monetary Policy and Models of Monetary Analysis. *Rev. Econ. Cond. Italy,* February 1983, (1), pp. 9–32.

Maravall, Agustin. An Application of Nonlinear Time Series Forecasting. *J. Bus. Econ. Statist.,* January 1983, *1* (1), pp. 66–74. **[G: Spain]**

Maynard, Geoffrey and Rose, Harold B. Wages and Employment: A Reply [Monetarism, Wages, and Employment Policy in the United Kingdom]. *J. Post Keynesian Econ.,* Fall 1983, *6* (1), pp. 97–100.

McGillicuddy, John F. Interest Rates: Medicine or Symptoms. In *Sanford, T., ed.,* 1983, pp. 103–15. **[G: U.S.]**

McIvor, R. Craig. A Note on the University of Chicago's "Academic Scribblers." *J. Polit. Econ.,* October 1983, *91* (5), pp. 888–93.

McKinney, George W., Jr. Legal Reserve Requirements: A Case Study in Bank Regulation: Discussant's Comments. *J. Bank Res.,* Spring 1983, *14* (1), pp. 72–74. **[G: U.S.]**

McKinnon, Ronald I. and Tan, Kong-Yam. Currency Substitution and Instability in the World Dollar Standard: Reply. *Amer. Econ. Rev.,* June 1983, *73* (3), pp. 474–76. **[G: U.S.]**

Melkov, A. The Effectiveness of Bank Credit. *Prob. Econ.,* January 1983, *25* (9), pp. 71–87. **[G: U.S.S.R.]**

Meltzer, Allan H. Present and Future in an Uncertain World. In *Sanford, T., ed.,* 1983, pp. 37–55. **[G: U.S.]**

Mills, Terence C. The Information Content of the UK Monetary Components and Aggregates. *Bull. Econ. Res.,* May 1983, *35* (1), pp. 25–46. **[G: U.K.]**

Moore, Basil J. A Monument to Monetarism. *J. Post Keynesian Econ.,* Fall 1983, *6* (1), pp. 118–21. **[G: U.S.; U.K.]**

Moyer, R. Charles and Simonson, Donald G. Federal Financing Pressure: The Incidence of Crowding Out. *Rev. Bus. Econ. Res.,* Winter, 1983, *18* (2), pp. 25–39. **[G: U.S.]**

Mundell, Robert A. The Origins and Evolution of Monetarism. In *Jansen, K., ed.,* 1983, pp. 43–54.

Mutambuka, Pierre. "Inflationary Expectations and Monetary Adjustment in Nigeria: 1960–1978": Some Comments. *Pakistan Devel. Rev.,* Winter 1983, *22* (4), pp. 301–05. **[G: Nigeria]**

Nadri, M. Ishaq. A Monetary and Financial Structure for an Interest-Free Economy: Institutions, Mechanism and Policy: Comment. In *Ahmed, Z.; Iqbal, M. and Khan, M. F., eds.,* 1983, pp. 88–90.

Neumann, Manfred J. M. The Indicator Properties of the St. Louis Monetary Base. *J. Monet. Econ.,* November 1983, *12* (4), pp. 595–603.

Niehans, Jürg. Financial Innovation, Multinational Banking, and Monetary Policy. *J. Banking Finance,* 1983, *7* (4), pp. 537–51.

Nordhaus, William D. Reflections on Monetarism, Stagnation and Other North American Exports. *Int. Soc. Sci. J.,* 1983, *35* (3), pp. 493–506. **[G: U.S.]**

Polak, Jacques J. Monetarist Policies on a World Scale. In *Jansen, K., ed.,* 1983, pp. 175–88.

Protopapadakis, Aris. The Endogeneity of Money during the German Hyperinflation: A Reappraisal. *Econ. Inquiry,* January 1983, *21* (1), pp. 72–92. **[G: Germany]**

Raboy, David G. Who Speaks for the Free Market: Monetarists or Supply-Siders? [What's Wrong with Supply-Side Economics] [The Trouble with Monetarism]. *Policy Rev.,* Spring 1983, (24), pp. 13–16. **[G: U.S.]**

Rangel, Charles B. Interest Rates: Impact on the Budget. In *Sanford, T., ed.,* 1983, pp. 91–102. **[G: U.S.]**

Redish, Angela. The Economic Crisis of 1837–1839 in Upper Canada: Case Study of a Temporary Suspension of Specie Payments. *Exploration Econ. Hist.,* October 1983, *20* (4), pp. 402–17. **[G: U.S.; Canada]**

Reynolds, Alan. Who Speaks for the Free Market: Monetarists or Supply-Siders? [The Trouble with Monetarism]. *Policy Rev.,* Spring 1983, (24), pp. 16–18. **[G: U.S.]**

Reynolds, Alan. Why Gold? *Cato J.,* Spring 1983, *3* (1), pp. 211–32. **[G: U.S.; U.K.]**

Ricart I Costa, Joan E. and Greenbaum, Stuart I. Bank Forward Lending: A Note. *J. Finance,* September 1983, *38* (4), pp. 1315–22.

Roberts, Charles C. Kann eine monetäre Schätzgleichung zuar Verbesserung der Geldpolitik beitragen?—Kommentar zum Beitrag von Enno Langfeldt. (Can a Monetary Estimating Equation Contribute to Improvement of Monetary Policy? Comment on the Article by E. Langfeldt. With English summary.) *Kredit Kapital,* 1983, *16* (2), pp. 220–30. **[G: W. Germany]**

Rogers, Colin. Monetary Aggregates and Economic Activity: Further Comment. *S. Afr. J. Econ.,* June 1983, *51* (2), pp. 326–28. **[G: S. Africa]**

Rogers, Colin. Monetary Aggregates and Economic Activity: Comment. *S. Afr. J. Econ.,* June 1983, *51* (2), pp. 310–17. **[G: S. Africa]**

Ross, Myron H. Currency Substitution and Instability in the World Dollar Standard: Comment. *Amer. Econ. Rev.,* June 1983, *73* (3), pp. 473. **[G: U.S.]**

Santomero, Anthony M. Controlling Monetary Aggregates: The Discount Window. *J. Finance,* June 1983, *38* (3), pp. 827–43. **[G: U.S.]**

Shiller, Robert J.; Campbell, John Y. and Schoenholtz, Kermit L. Forward Rates and Future Policy: Interpreting the Term Structure of Interest Rates. *Brookings Pap. Econ. Act.,* 1983, (1), pp. 173–217. **[G: U.S.]**

Shubik, Martin. Interest Rates, Policy, Business and Theory. In *Sanford, T., ed.,* 1983, pp. 116–56.

Smith, Timothy J. Wampum as Primitive Valuables. In *Dalton, G., ed.,* 1983, pp. 225–46. **[G: U.S.]**

Spinelli, Franco. Currency Substitution, Flexible Exchange Rates, and the Case for International Monetary Cooperation: Discussion of a Recent Proposal. *Int. Monet. Fund Staff Pap.,* December 1983, *30* (4), pp. 755–83.

Steindl, Josef. The Control of the Economy. *Banca Naz. Lavoro Quart. Rev.,* September 1983, (146), pp. 235–48.

Stokes, Houston H. and Neuburger, Hugh. The Effect of Monetary Changes on Interest Rates: A Reply. *Rev. Econ. Statist.*, May 1983, *65*(2), pp. 362. **[G: U.S.]**

Summers, Lawrence H. On the Economics of Private Money: Comments. *J. Monet. Econ.*, July 1983, *12*(1), pp. 159–62. **[G: U.S.]**

Talamona, Mario. Sviluppo, moneta e credito: la "visione" di Schumpeter e il caso italiano. (Schumpeter's View on Growth, Money and Credit, and the "Italian Case." With English summary.) *Giorn. Econ.*, July–August 1983, *42*(7–8), pp. 405–29. **[G: Italy]**

Tatom, John A. Money Market Deposit Accounts, Super-NOWs and Monetary Policy. *Fed. Res. Bank St. Louis Rev.*, March 1983, *65*(3), pp. 5–16. **[G: U.S.]**

Thornton, Daniel L. Why Does Velocity Matter? *Fed. Res. Bank St. Louis Rev.*, December 1983, *65*(10), pp. 5–13. **[G: U.S.]**

Tindall, Michael L. and Atkins, Joseph C. Monetarism: The St. Louis Model and a Recent Monetarist Forecasting Model: A Reply. *Bus. Econ.*, January 1983, *18*(1), pp. 46–47. **[G: U.S.]**

Tobin, James. Financial Structure and Monetary Rules. *Kredit Kapital*, 1983, *16*(2), pp. 155–71. **[G: U.S.]**

Weiss, Laurence. Forward Rates and Future Policy: Interpreting the Term Structure of Interest Rates: Comments and Discussion. *Brookings Pap. Econ. Act.*, 1983, (1), pp. 218–23. **[G: U.S.]**

Willett, Thomas D. U.S. Monetary Policy and World Liquidity. *Amer. Econ. Rev.*, May 1983, *73*(2), pp. 43–47. **[G: U.S.]**

Williams, Edward G. Analyzing the World's Money. *J. Post Keynesian Econ.*, Summer 1983, *5*(4), pp. 625–34.

Wren-Lewis, Simon. Labour Supply and Wealth: Some Macroeconomic Policy Implications. *Manchester Sch. Econ. Soc. Stud.*, March 1983, *51*(1), pp. 1–15. **[G: U.K.]**

3112 Monetary Theory; Empirical Studies Illustrating Theory

Abel, Andrew B. and Mishkin, Frederic S. An Integrated View of Tests of Rationality, Market Efficiency and the Short-Run Neutrality of Monetary Policy. *J. Monet. Econ.*, January 1983, *11*(1), pp. 3–24.

Aftalion, Florin. The Political Economy of French Monetary Policy. In *Hodgman, D. R., ed.*, 1983, pp. 7–25. **[G: France]**

Akhtar, M. A. Effects of Interest Rates and Inflation on Aggregate Inventory Investment in the United States. *Amer. Econ. Rev.*, June 1983, *73*(3), pp. 319–28. **[G: U.S.]**

Aliber, Robert Z. Exchange-Rate Intervention: Arbitrage and Market Efficiency. In *[Giersch, H.]*, 1983, pp. 171–87. **[G: U.S.]**

Allen, Stuart D. A Note on the Implicit Interest Rate on Demand Deposits. *J. Macroecon.*, Spring 1983, *5*(2), pp. 233–39. **[G: U.S.]**

Allen, Stuart D. Did the Swiss Demand for Money Function Shift? *J. Econ. Bus.*, June 1983, *35*(2), pp. 239–44. **[G: Switzerland]**

Allen, Stuart D. and Hafer, R. W. Money Demand and the Term Structure of Interest Rates: Some Consistent Estimates. *J. Monet. Econ.*, January 1983, *11*(1), pp. 129–32. **[G: U.S.]**

Alogoskoufis, George S. and Pissarides, Christopher A. A Test of Price Sluggishness in the Simple Rational Expectations Model: U.K. 1950–1980. *Econ. J.*, September 1983, *93*(371), pp. 616–28. **[G: U.K.]**

Apostolakis, Bobby. Money Balances as Factor Inputs: An Empirical Evidence Based on Translog Specification. *Europ. Econ. Rev.*, November 1983, *23*(2), pp. 149–60. **[G: Greece]**

Arak, Marcelle; Englander, A. Steven and Tang, Eric M. P. Credit Cycles and the Pricing of the Prime Rate. *Fed. Res. Bank New York Quart. Rev.*, Summer 1983, *8*(2), pp. 12–18. **[G: U.S.]**

Arestis, P.; Karakitsos, Elias and Sarantis, N. Real Money Balances as a Factor of Production in the United Kingdom. *Rivista Int. Sci. Econ. Com.*, December 1983, *30*(12), pp. 1171–86. **[G: U.K.]**

Argy, Victor. Choice of Intermediate Money Target in a Deregulated and an Integrated Economy with Flexible Exchange Rates. *Int. Monet. Fund Staff Pap.*, December 1983, *30*(4), pp. 727–54.

Argy, Victor and Salop, Joanne. Price and Output Effects of Monetary and Fiscal Expansion in a Two-Country World under Flexible Exchange Rates. *Oxford Econ. Pap.*, July 1983, *35*(2), pp. 228–46.

Asako, Kazumi. The Utility Function and the Superneutrality of Money on the Transition Path [Capital Accumulation on the Transition Path in a Monetary Optimizing Model]. *Econometrica*, September 1983, *51*(5), pp. 1593–96.

Atkinson, P. E.; Blundell-Wignall, A. and Chouraqui, J.-C. Budget Financing and Monetary Targets, with Special Reference to the Seven Major OECD Countries. *Écon. Soc.*, July-August 1983, *17*(7–8), pp. 1057–96. **[G: OECD]**

Attfield, Clifford L. F. An Analysis of the Implications of Omitting Variables from the Monetary Growth Equation in a Model of Real Output and Unanticipated Money Growth. *Europ. Econ. Rev.*, December 1983, *23*(3), pp. 281–90.

Attfield, Clifford L. F. and Duck, Nigel W. The Influence of Unanticipated Money Growth on Real Output: Some Cross-Country Estimates. *J. Money, Credit, Banking*, November 1983, *15*(4), pp. 442–54. **[G: Selected Countries]**

Auernheimer, Leonardo. Deficit, gasto publico y el impuesto inflacionario: dos modelos de "dinero pasivo." (With English summary.) *Cuadernos Econ.*, April 1983, *20*(59), pp. 75–84. **[G: Argentina]**

Auernheimer, Leonardo. The Revenue-Maximizing Inflation Rate and the Treatment of the Transition to Equilibrium. *J. Money, Credit, Banking*, August 1983, *15*(3), pp. 368–76.

Ayanian, Robert. Expectations, Taxes, and Interest: The Search for the Darby Effect. *Amer. Econ. Rev.*, September 1983, *73*(4), pp. 762–65. **[G: U.S.]**

Azam, J. P. Money, Growth and Disequilibrium. *Economica*, August 1983, *50*(199), pp. 325–35.

Barnett, Richard C.; Bessler, David A. and Thompson, Robert L. The Money Supply and Nominal

Agricultural Prices. *Amer. J. Agr. Econ.*, May 1983, *65*(2), pp. 303–07. **[G: U.S.]**

Barnett, William A. New Indices of Money Supply and the Flexible Laurent Demand System. *J. Bus. Econ. Statist.*, January 1983, *1*(1), pp. 7–23. **[G: U.S.]**

Barro, Robert J. Inflationary Finance under Discretion and Rules. *Can. J. Econ.*, February 1983, *16*(1), pp. 1–16.

Barro, Robert J. and Gordon, David B. A Positive Theory of Monetary Policy in a Natural Rate Model. *J. Polit. Econ.*, August 1983, *91*(4), pp. 589–610.

Barro, Robert J. and Gordon, David B. Rules, Discretion and Reputation in a Model of Monetary Policy. *J. Monet. Econ.*, July 1983, *12*(1), pp. 101–21.

Barro, Robert J. and Gordon, David B. Una teoría positiva de política monetaria en un modelo de tasa natural. (With English summary.) *Cuadernos Econ.*, August 1983, *20*(60), pp. 211–28.

Basu, Kaushik. Transactions Demand for Money and Portfolio Diversification. *Indian Econ. J.*, July–September 1983, *31*(1), pp. 25–34.

Batten, Dallas S. and Thornton, Daniel L. Polynomial Distributed Lags and the Estimation of the St. Louis Equation. *Fed. Res. Bank St. Louis Rev.*, April 1983, *65*(4), pp. 13–25. **[G: U.S.]**

Bean, Charles R. Targeting Nominal Income: An Appraisal. *Econ. J.*, December 1983, *93*(372), pp. 806–19.

Beckerman, Paul. Non-positive Market-Clearing Real Rates of Interest. *J. Post Keynesian Econ.*, Fall 1983, *6*(1), pp. 53–64.

Beenstock, Michael. Rational Expectations and the Effect of Exchange-Rate Intervention on the Exchange Rate. *J. Int. Money Finance*, December 1983, *2*(3), pp. 319–31.

Beenstock, Michael and Dicks, G. R. An Aggregate Monetary Model of the World Economy. *Europ. Econ. Rev.*, May 1983, *21*(3), pp. 261–85.

Benavie, Arthur. Achieving External and Internal Targets with Exchange-Rate and Interest-Rate Intervention. *J. Int. Money Finance*, April 1983, *2*(1), pp. 75–85.

Benavie, Arthur. Optimal Monetary Policy under Rational Expectations with a Micro-Based Supply Function. *J. Macroecon.*, Spring 1983, *5*(2), pp. 149–66.

Benavie, Arthur and Froyen, Richard T. Combination Monetary Policies to Stabilize Price and Output under Rational Expectations. *J. Money, Credit, Banking*, May 1983, *15*(2), pp. 186–98.

Benedetti, Eugenio. Il divario tra il saggio di interesse naturale e monetario in regime di inflazione e in ipotesi diverse di indicizzazione. (The Difference between the Natural and the Money Rate of Interest in an Inflationary Economy under Different Hypotheses of Indexation of the Public Deficit. With English summary.) *Giorn. Econ.*, March-April 1983, *42*(3–4), pp. 179–92. **[G: Italy]**

Benhabib, Jess and Bull, Clive. The Optimal Quantity of Money: A Formal Treatment. *Int. Econ. Rev.*, February 1983, *24*(1), pp. 101–11.

Benninga, Simon and Protopapadakis, Aris. Real and Nominal Interest Rates under Uncertainty: The Fisher Theorem and the Term Structure. *J. Polit. Econ.*, October 1983, *91*(5), pp. 856–67.

Bernstein, Jeffrey I. and Fisher, Douglas. The Term Structure of Interest Rates and the Demand for Money: British Results from a Portfolio Model. *Southern Econ. J.*, July 1983, *50*(1), pp. 71–82. **[G: U.K.]**

Bewley, Truman. A Difficulty with the Optimum Quantity of Money. *Econometrica*, September 1983, *51*(5), pp. 1485–504.

Bigman, David and Lee, Chee Sung. Variability of Exchange and Interest Rates: The Floating Experience. **In** *Bigman, D. and Taya, T., eds.*, 1983, pp. 29–41. **[G: U.K.; W. Germany; Switzerland]**

Bini Smaghi, Lorenzo and Tardini, Pietro. The Effectiveness of Monetary Policy: An Empirical Investigation for Italy (1966–1981). *Giorn. Econ.*, September–October 1983, *42*(9–10), pp. 679–90. **[G: Italy]**

Bisignano, Joseph. Monetary Policy Regimes and International Term Structures of Interest Rates. *Fed. Res. Bank San Francisco Econ. Rev.*, Fall 1983, (4), pp. 7–26. **[G: U.S.; Canada; W. Germany]**

Black, Stanley W. The Use of Monetary Policy for Internal and External Balance in Ten Industrial Countries. **In** *Frenkel, J. A., ed.*, 1983, pp. 189–225. **[G: OECD]**

Blanchard, Olivier J. Price Asynchronization and Price Level Inertia. **In** *Dornbusch, R. and Simonsen, M. H., eds.*, 1983, pp. 3–24. **[G: U.S.]**

Blinder, Alan S. and Stiglitz, Joseph E. Money, Credit Constraints, and Economic Activity. *Amer. Econ. Rev.*, May 1983, *73*(2), pp. 297–302.

Bomhoff, Edward J. and Veugelers, Paul T. W. M. Money Creation and Economic Activity, 1967–1982. *De Economist*, 1983, *131*(4), pp. 498–516. **[G: Netherlands]**

Bonomo, Vittorio and Tanner, J. Ernest. Expected Monetary Changes and Relative Prices: A Look at Evidence from the Stock Market. *Southern Econ. J.*, October 1983, *50*(2), pp. 334–45. **[G: U.S.]**

Bordo, Michael David. Some Aspects of the Monetary Economics of Richard Cantillon. *J. Monet. Econ.*, August 1983, *12*(2), pp. 235–58.

Bordo, Michael David and Schwartz, Anna J. The Importance of Stable Money: Theory and Evidence. *Cato J.*, Spring 1983, *3*(1), pp. 63–82. **[G: U.S.]**

Boschen, John and Grossman, Herschel I. Monetary Information and Macroeconomic Fluctuations. **In** *Fitoussi, J.-P., ed.*, 1983, pp. 173–84.

Boskin, Michael J. and Sheshinski, Eytan. Optimal Tax Treatment of the Family: Married Couples. *J. Public Econ.*, April 1983, *20*(3), pp. 281–97. **[G: U.S.]**

Boughton, James M. Conditions for an Active Exchange Rate Policy with a Predetermined Monetary Target. *Int. Monet. Fund Staff Pap.*, September 1983, *30*(3), pp. 461–90.

Bowers, Patricia F. A Theoretical Analysis of the Exchange Process and Inflation. **In** *Schmukler, N. and Marcus, E., eds.*, 1983, pp. 120–32.

Branson, William H. Macroeconomic Determinants of Real Exchange Risk. **In** *Herring, R. J., ed.*, 1983, pp. 33–74. **[G: Japan; U.K.; U.S.; W. Germany]**

Branson, William H. and Buiter, Willem H. Monetary and Fiscal Policy with Flexible Exchange Rates. **In** *Bhandari, J. S. and Putnam, B. H., eds.*, 1983, pp. 251–85.

Bricall, Josep M. Algunos aspectos monetarios y financieros de la crisis. (Some Monetary and Financial Aspects of the Crisis. With English summary.) *Écon. Soc.*, September–October–November 1983, *17*(9–10–11), pp. 1611–30.

Brissimis, Sophocles N. and Leventakis, John A. Inflationary Expectations and the Demand for Money: The Greek Experience: A Comment and Some Different Results—A Reply. *Kredit Kapital*, 1983, *16*(2), pp. 265–66. **[G: Greece]**

Brittan, Samuel. Money in Longer Perspective. **In** *Brittan, S.*, 1983, pp. 143–55. **[G: U.S.]**

Brown, W. W. and Santoni, G. J. Monetary Growth and the Timing of Interest Rate Movements. *Fed. Res. Bank St. Louis Rev.*, August/September 1983, *65*(7), pp. 16–25. **[G: U.S.]**

Brox, James A. The Yield-Liquidity Trade-Off in Canadian Portfolios. *Quart. Rev. Econ. Bus.*, Autumn 1983, *23*(3), pp. 70–80. **[G: Canada]**

Brunner, Karl. Has Monetarism Failed? *Cato J.*, Spring 1983, *3*(1), pp. 23–62. **[G: U.S.]**

Brunner, Karl. The Politics of Myopia and Its Ideology. **In** *Shadow Open Market Committee.*, 1983, pp. 7–17. **[G: U.S.]**

Brunner, Karl; Cukierman, Alex and Meltzer, Allan H. Money and Economic Activity, Inventories and Business Cycles. *J. Monet. Econ.*, May 1983, *11*(3), pp. 281–319.

Bryant, John. The Role of Overlapping-Generations Models in Monetary Economics: A Comment. *Carnegie-Rochester Conf. Ser. Public Policy*, Spring 1983, *18*, pp. 45–50.

Buchanan, James M. Monetary Research, Monetary Rules, and Monetary Regimes [Rules vs. Discretion in Monetary Policy]. *Cato J.*, Spring 1983, *3*(1), pp. 143–46. **[G: U.S.]**

Buiter, Willem H. Real Effects of Anticipated and Unanticipated Money: Some Problems of Estimation and Hypothesis Testing. *J. Monet. Econ.*, March 1983, *11*(2), pp. 207–24.

Buiter, Willem H. and Miller, Marcus H. Real Exchange Rate Overshooting and the Output Cost of Bringing Down Inflation: Some Further Results. **In** *Frenkel, J. A., ed.*, 1983, pp. 317–58.

Bulgaru, M. Cybernetic Systems and Monetary Balance. *Econ. Computat. Cybern. Stud. Res.*, 1983, *18*(2), pp. 5–17.

Bull, Clive. Expectations of Others' Expectations and the Transitional Nonneutrality of Fully Believed Systematic Monetary Policy: Comment. **In** *Frydman, R. and Phelps, E. S., eds.*, 1983, pp. 66–68.

Bulow, Jeremy and Polemarchakis, Heraklis M. Retroactive Money. *Economica*, August 1983, *50*(199), pp. 301–10.

Burmeister, Edwin; Flood, Robert P. and Garber, Peter M. On the Equivalence of Solutions in Rational Expectations Models. *J. Econ. Dynam. Control*, May 1983, *5*(2/3), pp. 311–21.

Büttler, Hans-Jürg and Schiltknecht, Kurt. Transitory Changes in Monetary Policy and Their Implications in Money-Stock Control. *Carnegie-Rochester Conf. Ser. Public Policy*, Autumn 1983, *19*, pp. 171–209.

Cacciafesta, Remo. Condizione di equilibrio della gestione bancaria ed equazione ricorrente della raccolta. (Conditions for Equilibrium of the Banking-Management and Recurrent-Deposits Equations. With English summary.) *Bancaria*, May–June 1983, *39*(5–6), pp. 517–18.

Cachin, Antoine. Change et intérêt en flexibilité. (Exchange and Interest in Flexibility. With English summary.) *Écon. Soc.*, July-August 1983, *17*(7–8), pp. 1213–31.

Cagan, Phillip. Alcuni aspetti della politica economica degli Stati Uniti. (Current Issues in United States Macro Policy. With English summary.) *Bancaria*, February 1983, *39*(2), pp. 131–38. **[G: U.S.]**

Cagan, Phillip. The Roles of Money and Credit in Macroeconomic Analysis: Comment. **In** *Tobin, J., ed.*, 1983, pp. 189–93. **[G: U.S.]**

Callier, Philippe. Eurobanks and Liquidity Creation: A Broader Perspective. *Weltwirtsch. Arch.*, 1983, *119*(2), pp. 214–25.

Calvo, Guillermo A. Staggered Prices in a Utility-Maximizing Framework. *J. Monet. Econ.*, September 1983, *12*(3), pp. 383–98.

Calvo, Guillermo A. and Peel, David A. Growth and Inflationary Finance: Variations on a Mundellian Theme. *J. Polit. Econ.*, October 1983, *91*(5), pp. 880–87.

Canarella, Giorgio and Garston, Neil. Structural Neutrality and the Determination of Nominal Interest Rates. *Rivista Int. Sci. Econ. Com.*, October–November 1983, *30*(10–11), pp. 908–22. **[G: U.S.]**

Canzoneri, Matthew B.; Henderson, Dale W. and Rogoff, Kenneth S. The Information Content of the Interest Rate and Optimal Monetary Policy. *Quart. J. Econ.*, November 1983, *98*(4), pp. 545–66.

Caranza, Cesare and Fazio, Antonio. Methods of Monetary Control in Italy: 1974–1983. **In** *Hodgman, D. R., ed.*, 1983, pp. 65–88. **[G: Italy]**

Cardoso, Eliana A. A Money Demand Equation for Brazil. *J. Devel. Econ.*, February/April 1983, *12*(1/2), pp. 183–93. **[G: Brazil]**

Cargill, Thomas F. and Meyer, Robert A. Forecasting the Term Structure of Interest Rates and Portfolio Planning Models. *J. Econ. Bus.*, August 1983, *35*(3/4), pp. 399–411. **[G: U.S.]**

Carmichael, Jeffrey and Stebbing, Peter W. Fisher's Paradox and the Theory of Interest. *Amer. Econ. Rev.*, September 1983, *73*(4), pp. 619–30. **[G: Australia; U.S.]**

Carns, Frederick and Lombra, Raymond E. Rational Expectations and Short-Run Neutrality: A Reexamination of the Role of Anticipated Money Growth. *Rev. Econ. Statist.*, November 1983, *65*(4), pp. 639–43. **[G: U.S.]**

Carraro, Carlo. Ottimalità della politica economica nei modelli con aspettative razionali. (The Optimality of Economic Policy in the Rational Expectations Models. With English summary.) *Giorn.*

Econ., September–October 1983, *42*(9–10), pp. 643–65.

Casale, Giuseppe. Capitale, interesse, profitto ed equa tassazione. (Capital, Interest and Fiscal Equity. With English summary.) *Giorn. Econ.*, March-April 1983, *42*(3–4), pp. 153–78.

Cassese, Anthony and Lothian, James R. The Timing of Monetary and Price Changes and the International Transmission of Inflation. **In** *Darby, M. P. and Lothian, J. R., et al.*, 1983, pp. 58–82. **[G: OECD]**

Cesarano, Filippo. The Rational Expectations Hypothesis in Retrospect. *Amer. Econ. Rev.*, March 1983, *73*(1), pp. 198–203.

Chan, Louis Kuo Chi. Uncertainty and the Neutrality of Government Financing Policy. *J. Monet. Econ.*, May 1983, *11*(3), pp. 351–72.

Chang, Winston W.; Hamberg, Daniel and Hirata, Junichi. Liquidity Preference as Behavior toward Risk Is a Demand for Short-Term Securities—Not Money. *Amer. Econ. Rev.*, June 1983, *73*(3), pp. 420–27.

Chang, Winston W.; Kemp, Murray C. and Long, Ngo Van. Money, Inflation, and Maximizing Behavior: The Case of Many Countries. *J. Macroecon.*, Summer 1983, *5*(3), pp. 251–63.

Chauveau, Thierry and Frochen, Patrick. Étude du comportement de l'épargnant français vis-à-vis des liquidités 1971–1981. (French Households and Liquid Assets (1971–1981). With English summary.) *Revue Écon.*, January 1983, *34*(1), pp. 152–81. **[G: France]**

Chen, Chau-nan and Tsaur, Tien-wang. Currency Denominations, Currency Substitutions, and the Price Level. *J. Macroecon.*, Fall 1983, *5*(4), pp. 511–13.

Chetty, V. K. and Lahiri, Ashok K. On the Effectiveness of Monetary and Fiscal Policies in a Keynesian Model. *Europ. Econ. Rev.*, September 1983, *23*(1), pp. 33–54.

Christ, Carl F. Rules vs. Discretion in Monetary Policy. *Cato J.*, Spring 1983, *3*(1), pp. 121–41. **[G: U.S.]**

Claassen, Emil-Maria. Aspects of the Optimal Management of Exchange Rates. **In** *Claassen, E. and Salin, P., eds.*, 1983, pp. 226–30.

Claassen, Emil-Maria. The Keynesian and Classical Determination of the Exchange Rate. *Weltwirtsch. Arch.*, 1983, *119*(1), pp. 19–35.

Claassen, Emil-Maria. The Nominal and Real Exchange Rate in a Quantity-Theoretical Two-Country Model. **In** *Claassen, E. and Salin, P., eds.*, 1983, pp. 57–68.

Claassen, Emil-Maria. What Are the Scope and Limits of Fruitful International Monetary Cooperation in the 1980s? Comment. **In** *von Furstenberg, G. M., ed.*, 1983, pp. 409–19.

Clarida, Richard H. and Friedman, Benjamin M. Why Have Short-Term Interest Rates Been So High? *Brookings Pap. Econ. Act.*, 1983, (2), pp. 553–78. **[G: U.S.]**

Clifton, Eric V. The Effects of Increased Interest-Rate Volatility on LDCs. *J. Int. Money Finance*, April 1983, *2*(1), pp. 67–74.

Cobham, David. Reverse Causation in the Monetary Approach: An Econometric Test for the U.K. *Manchester Sch. Econ. Soc. Stud.*, December 1983, *51*(4), pp. 360–79. **[G: U.K.]**

Collyns, Charles. On the Monetary Analysis of an Open Economy. *Int. Monet. Fund Staff Pap.*, June 1983, *30*(2), pp. 421–44.

Conti, Giuliano. Changes in Foreign Interest Rates and Domestic Stability: A Static and Dynamic Analysis. *Rivista Polit. Econ.*, Supplement Dec. 1983, *73*(12), pp. 23–67.

Cornell, Bradford. Money Supply Announcements and Interest Rates: Another View. *J. Bus.*, January 1983, *56*(1), pp. 1–23. **[G: U.S.]**

Cornell, Bradford. The Money Supply Announcements Puzzle: Review and Interpretation. *Amer. Econ. Rev.*, September 1983, *73*(4), pp. 644–57. **[G: U.S.]**

Cox, W. Michael. Government Revenue from Deficit Finance. *Can. J. Econ.*, May 1983, *16*(2), pp. 264–74.

Craine, Roger and Hardouvelis, Gikas A. Are Rational Expectations for Real? *Greek Econ. Rev.*, April 1983, *5*(1), pp. 5–32. **[G: U.S.]**

Cuddington, John T. Currency Substitution, Capital Mobility and Money Demand. *J. Int. Money Finance*, August 1983, *2*(2), pp. 111–33. **[G: Canada; W. Germany; U.K.; U.S.]**

Cumby, Robert E.; Huizinga, John and Obstfeld, Maurice. Errata: Two-Step Two-Stage Least Squares Estimation in Models with Rational Expectations. *J. Econometrics*, December 1983, *23*(3), pp. 407. **[G: U.S.]**

Cumby, Robert E. and Obstfeld, Maurice. Capital Mobility and the Scope for Sterilization: Mexico in the 1970s. **In** *Armella, P. A.; Dornbusch, R. and Obstfeld, M., eds.*, 1983, pp. 245–69. **[G: Mexico]**

Cuthbertson, K. The Monetary Sector. **In** *Britton, A., ed.*, 1983, pp. 98–110. **[G: U.K.]**

Daniel, Betty C. and Fried, Harold O. Currency Substitution, Postal Strikes, and Canadian Money Demand. *Can. J. Econ.*, November 1983, *16*(4), pp. 612–24. **[G: Canada]**

Darby, Michael R. Actual versus Unanticipated Changes in Aggregate Demand Variables: A Sensitivity Analysis of the Real-Income Equation. **In** *Darby, M. P. and Lothian, J. R., et al.*, 1983, pp. 273–88. **[G: OECD]**

Darby, Michael R. International Transmission of Monetary and Fiscal Shocks under Pegged and Floating Exchange Rates: Simulation Experiments. **In** *Darby, M. P. and Lothian, J. R., et al.*, 1983, pp. 162–231. **[G: OECD]**

Darby, Michael R. International Transmission under Pegged and Floating Exchange Rates: An Empirical Comparison. **In** *Bhandari, J. S. and Putnam, B. H., eds.*, 1983, pp. 427–71. **[G: OECD]**

Darby, Michael R. Sterilization and Monetary Control: Concepts, Issues, and a Reduced-Form Test. **In** *Darby, M. P. and Lothian, J. R., et al.*, 1983, pp. 291–313. **[G: OECD]**

Darrat, Ali F. Patinkin's Neutral Shift in Liquidity Preference: A Note. *Indian Econ. J.*, July–September 1983, *31*(1), pp. 107–09. **[G: Patinkin]**

Davidson, Paul. Monetarism and Reaganomics. **In** *Weintraub, S. and Goodstein, M., eds.*, 1983, pp. 92–103. **[G: U.S.]**

Davis, Kevin. Inflation and the Financial System: Discussion. **In** *Pagan, A. R. and Trivedi, P. K., eds.,* 1983, pp. 221–23. **[G: Australia]**

De Grauwe, Paul. What Are the Scope and Limits of Fruitful International Monetary Cooperation in the 1980s? **In** *von Furstenberg, G. M., ed.,* 1983, pp. 375–408. **[G: OECD]**

DeAntoni, Elisabetta. Andamento dei depositi ed emissioni di titoli: Alcume riflessioni in tema di disintermediazione bancaria e concorrenza del Tesoro. (The Trend of Deposits and Issuance of Securities: On Banking Disintermediation and Treasury Competition. With English summary.) *Bancaria,* April 1983, *39*(4), pp. 389–401. **[G: Italy]**

Dewald, William G. Fast and Gradual Anti-inflation Policies: Evidence for Germany, Italy, and the United States. **In** *Schmukler, N. and Marcus, E., eds.,* 1983, pp. 689–706. **[G: W. Germany; Italy; France]**

Di Tata, Juan Carlos. Expectations of Others' Expectations and the Transitional Nonneutrality of Fully Believed Systematic Monetary Policy. **In** *Frydman, R. and Phelps, E. S., eds.,* 1983, pp. 47–66.

Diamond, Douglas W. and Dybvig, Philip H. Bank Runs, Deposit Insurance, and Liquidity. *J. Polit. Econ.,* June 1983, *91* (3), pp. 401–19.

Djajić, Slobodan. Monetary and Commercial Policy in a Two-Country Flexible Exchange Rate Model with Perfect Capital Mobility. *J. Monet. Econ.,* September 1983, *12*(3), pp. 399–416.

Dotsey, Michael and King, Robert G. Monetary Instruments and Policy Rules in a Rational Expectations Environment. *J. Monet. Econ.,* September 1983, *12*(3), pp. 357–82.

Drabicki, John Z. and Takayama, Akira. An Optimal Monetary Policy in an Aggregate Neoclassical Model of Economic Growth. *J. Macroecon.,* Winter 1983, *5*(1), pp. 53–74.

Driffill, E. John. Shock Treatment for Inflation: A Note on Optimal Policy in a Buiter/Miller Model. *Europ. Econ. Rev.,* December 1983, *23*(3), pp. 291–97.

Driscoll, Michael J. and Lahiri, Ashok K. Income-Velocity of Money in Agricultural Developing Economies. *Rev. Econ. Statist.,* August 1983, *65*(3), pp. 393–401. **[G: Selected LDCs]**

Driscoll, Michael J., et al. Money, Output, Rational Expectations and Neutrality: Some Econometric Results for the UK. *Economica,* August 1983, *50*(199), pp. 259–68. **[G: U.K.]**

Driscoll, Michael J., et al. Testing of the Rational Expectations and Structural Neutrality Hypotheses. *J. Macroecon.,* Summer 1983, *5*(3), pp. 353–60. **[G: U.S.]**

Driscoll, Michael J., et al. Testing the Rational Expectations and Structural Neutrality Hypotheses: Some Econometric Results for Austria 1965(1)–1979(4). *Empirica,* 1983, (1), pp. 3–13. **[G: Austria]**

Duck, Nigel W. The Effects of Uncertainty about the Money Supply Process in a Rational Expectations Macroeconomic Model. *Scot. J. Polit. Econ.,* June 1983, *30*(2), pp. 142–52.

Dudler, Hermann-Josef. The Monetary Policy Decision Process in the Federal Republic of Germany: Discussion. **In** *Hodgman, D. R., ed.,* 1983, pp. 59–64. **[G: W. Germany]**

Dufour, J.-M.; Gaudry, M. J. I. and Hafer, R. W. A Warning on the Use of the Cochrane–Orcutt Procedure Based on a Money Demand Equation. *Empirical Econ.,* 1983, *8*(2), pp. 111–17. **[G: U.S.]**

Dumas, Bernard and Poncet, Patrice. La demande de dollars des agents économiques ne résidant pas aux U.S.A. (The Dollar Demand of Non-Resident Economic Agents in the U.S.A. With English summary.) *Écon. Soc.,* July-August 1983, *17*(7–8), pp. 1185–1212.

Eaton, Jonathan and Turnovsky, Stephen J. Covered Interest Parity, Uncovered Interest Parity and Exchange Rate Dynamics. *Econ. J.,* September 1983, *93*(371), pp. 555–75.

Eatwell, John. The Analytical Foundations of Monetarism. **In** *Eatwell, J. and Milgate, M., eds.,* 1983, pp. 203–13.

Eden, Benjamin. Competitive Price Setting, Price Flexibility, and Linkage to the Money Supply. *Carnegie-Rochester Conf. Ser. Public Policy,* Autumn 1983, *19*, pp. 253–99.

Eden, Benjamin. Competitive Price Setting, Price Flexibility, and Linkage to the Money Supply: Reply. *Carnegie-Rochester Conf. Ser. Public Policy,* Autumn 1983, *19*, pp. 313–16.

Eden, Benjamin. On the Unit of Account Function of Money: The Use of Local Currency When Less Inflationary Currencies are Available. *Econ. Inquiry,* July 1983, *21* (3), pp. 361–73.

Edwards, Sebastian. La relacion entre las tasas de interes y el tipo de cambio bajo un sistema de cambio flotante. (With English summary.) *Cuadernos Econ.,* April 1983, *20*(59), pp. 65–74.

Elyasiani, Elyas. The Two Product Banking Firm under Uncertainty. *Southern Econ. J.,* April 1983, *49*(4), pp. 1002–17.

Evans, J. L. Erratum: The Dynamic Behaiour of Alternative Price Adjustment Mechanisms. *Manchester Sch. Econ. Soc. Stud.,* December 1983, *51* (4), pp. 399–400.

Evans, J. L. The Dynamic Behaviour of Alternative Price Adjustment Mechanisms. *Manchester Sch. Econ. Soc. Stud.,* March 1983, *51* (1), pp. 33–44.

Fackler, James S. and McMillin, W. Douglas. Specification and Stability of the Goldfeld Money Demand Function. *J. Macroecon.,* Fall 1983, *5*(4), pp. 437–59.

Fama, Eugene F. Financial Intermediation and Price Level Control. *J. Monet. Econ.,* July 1983, *12*(1), pp. 7–28. **[G: U.S.]**

Fama, Eugene F. Stock Returns, Real Activity, Inflation, and Money: Reply. *Amer. Econ. Rev.,* June 1983, *73*(3), pp. 471–72. **[G: U.S.]**

Fase, M. M. G. The 1930 Correspondence between Koopmans, Robertson and Gregory. *De Economist,* 1983, *131* (3), pp. 305–43.

Feldstein, Martin S. Fiscal Policies, Inflation, and Capital Formation. **In** *Feldstein, M. (II),* 1983, *1980,* pp. 61–80.

Feldstein, Martin S. and Summers, Lawrence. Inflation, Tax Rules, and the Long-term Interest Rate.

In *Feldstein, M. (II)*, 1983, *1978*, pp. 153–85. **[G: U.S.]**

Ferguson, J. David and Hart, William R. Income Determination in Market Disequilibrium: The Implications of Spillover for the Design of Monetary Policy. *J. Macroecon.*, Summer 1983, *5*(3), pp. 317–33.

Fischer, Otfrid. Die Kapitalkostensätze einlagenfinanzierter Kredite bei unterschiedlichem Marktzinsniveau. (On Capital Cost Rates of Deposit-Financed Loans at Different Interest Levels. With English summary.) *Kredit Kapital*, 1983, *16*(3), pp. 405–29. **[G: W. Germany]**

Fischer, Stanley. A Framework for Monetary and Banking Analysis. *Econ. J.*, Supplement March 1983, pp. 1–16.

Fischer, Stanley. Indexing and Inflation. *J. Monet. Econ.*, November 1983, *12*(4), pp. 519–41. **[G: Selected Countries]**

Fischer, Stanley. Optimal Fiscal and Monetary Policy in an Economy without Capital: Comments. *J. Monet. Econ.*, July 1983, *12*(1), pp. 95–99.

Fischer, Stanley. Optimal Stabilization and the Proper Exercise of the Monetary-Policy Instruments under Flexible Exchange Rates: Comment. **In** *Claassen, E. and Salin, P., eds.*, 1983, pp. 256–59.

Fischer, Stanley. Towards an Understanding of the Costs of Inflation: II. **In** *Brunner, K. and Meltzer, A. H., eds.*, 1983, *1981*, pp. 311–47. **[G: U.S.]**

Fischer, Stanley. Welfare Aspects of Government Issue of Indexed Bonds. **In** *Dornbusch, R. and Simonsen, M. H., eds.*, 1983, pp. 223–46.

Fitzgerald, M. Desmond and Pollio, Gerald. Money, Activity and Prices: Some Inter-Country Evidence. *Europ. Econ. Rev.*, December 1983, *23*(3), pp. 299–314. **[G: Selected OECD]**

Flood, Robert P. Real Exchange Rate Overshooting and the Output Cost of Bringing Down Inflation: Some Further Results: Comment. **In** *Frenkel, J. A., ed.*, 1983, pp. 359–65.

Flood, Robert P. and Garber, Peter M. A Model of Stochastic Process Switching. *Econometrica*, May, 1983, *51*(3), pp. 537–51.

Flood, Robert P. and Garber, Peter M. Process Consistency and Monetary Reform: Some Further Evidence. *J. Monet. Econ.*, August 1983, *12*(2), pp. 279–95. **[G: Europe]**

Foley, Duncan K. Money and Effective Demand in Marx's Scheme of Expanded Reproduction. **In** *[Erlich, A.]*, 1983, pp. 19–33.

Franco, Giampiero and Mengarelli, Gianluigi. Ancora a proposito dei mezzi di finanziamento del deficit pubblico: una risposta allargata. (The Means for Financing the Public Deficit: An Extended Reply. With English summary.) *Bancaria*, January 1983, *39*(1), pp. 34–38. **[G: Italy]**

Frankel, Jeffrey A. Monetary and Portfolio-Balance Models of Exchange Rate Determination. **In** *Bhandari, J. S. and Putnam, B. H., eds.*, 1983, pp. 84–115. **[G: U.S.; W. Germany]**

Frenkel, Jacob A. Capital Mobility and the Scope for Sterilization: Mexico in the 1970s: Comment. **In** *Armella, P. A.; Dornbusch, R. and Obstfeld, M., eds.*, 1983, pp. 269–76. **[G: Mexico]**

Frenkel, Jacob A. International Liquidity and Monetary Control. **In** *von Furstenberg, G. M., ed.*, 1983, pp. 65–109. **[G: Selected Countries]**

Frenkel, Jacob A. Monetary Policy: Domestic Targets and International Constraints. *Amer. Econ. Rev.*, May 1983, *73*(2), pp. 48–53.

Frenkel, Jacob A. and Aizenman, Joshua. Aspects of the Optimal Management of Exchange Rates. **In** *Claassen, E. and Salin, P., eds.*, 1983, pp. 201–25.

Fried, Joel and Howitt, Peter. The Effects of Inflation on Real Interest Rates. *Amer. Econ. Rev.*, December 1983, *73*(5), pp. 968–80.

Friedman, Benjamin M. Monetary Policy with a Credit Aggregate Target. *Carnegie-Rochester Conf. Ser. Public Policy*, Spring 1983, *18*, pp. 117–47. **[G: U.S.]**

Friedman, Benjamin M. Monetary Policy Management. **In** *Miller, G. W., ed.*, 1983, pp. 72–99. **[G: U.S.]**

Friedman, Benjamin M. The Roles of Money and Credit in Macroeconomic Analysis. **In** *Tobin, J., ed.*, 1983, pp. 161–89. **[G: U.S.]**

Friedman, Milton. A Monetarist View. *J. Econ. Educ.*, Fall 1983, *14*(4), pp. 44–55. **[G: U.S.; U.K.; Japan]**

Froyen, Richard T. and Kopecky, Kenneth J. A Note on Reserve Requirements and Monetary Control with a Flexible Deposit Rate. *J. Banking Finance*, March 1983, *7*(1), pp. 101–09. **[G: U.S.]**

von Furstenberg, George M. Changes in U.S. Interest Rates and Their Effects on European Interest and Exchange Rates. **In** *Bigman, D. and Taya, T., eds.*, 1983, pp. 257–82. **[G: U.S.; U.K.; W. Germany; France]**

von Furstenberg, George M. The Uncertain Effects of Inflationary Finance on Growth in Developing Countries. *Public Finance*, 1983, *38*(2), pp. 232–66. **[G: U.S.]**

Galli, Giampaolo. Monetary and Credit Targets in an Open Economy: Discussion. **In** *Hodgman, D. R., ed.*, 1983, pp. 307–12.

Galli, Giampaolo and Masera, Rainer S. Real Rates of Interest and Public Sector Deficits: An Empirical Investigation. *Econ. Notes*, 1983, (3), pp. 5–41. **[G: N. America; Italy; Germany; France; U.K.]**

Gandolfi, Arthur E. and Lothian, James R. International Price Behavior and the Demand for Money. **In** *Darby, M. P. and Lothian, J. R., et al.*, 1983, pp. 421–61. **[G: OECD]**

Gandolfi, Arthur E. and Lothian, James R. International Price Behavior and the Demand for Money. *Econ. Inquiry*, July 1983, *21*(3), pp. 295–311. **[G: OECD]**

Gardner, Grant W. The Choice of Monetary Policy Instruments in an Open Economy. *J. Int. Money Finance*, December 1983, *2*(3), pp. 347–54.

Garegnani, Pierangelo. Notes on Consumption, Investment and Effective Demand: Reply. **In** *Eatwell, J. and Milgate, M., eds.*, 1983, *1979*, pp. 72–78.

Garegnani, Pierangelo. Notes on Consumption, Investment and Effective Demand. **In** *Eatwell, J. and Milgate, M., eds.*, 1983, *1978*, pp. 21–69.

Gärtner, Manfred. Asset Market Models of the Small Open Economy with Endogenous Money Supply Expectations. *Z. ges. Staatswiss.*, December 1983,

139(4), pp. 643–59.

Geske, Robert and Roll, Richard. The Fiscal and Monetary Linkage between Stock Returns and Inflation. *J. Finance,* March 1983, *38*(1), pp. 1–33. **[G: U.S.]**

Gillard, Etienne. Le revenu des Banques centrales: Un schéma simple sur sa formation et son affectation. (Central Bank Review: A Simple Framework or Where Does It Come from and Where Does It Go To. With English summary.) *Revue Écon.,* November 1983, *34*(6), pp. 1164–87. **[G: France; U.S.]**

Giovannini, Alberto. The Interest Elasticity of Savings in Developing Countries: The Existing Evidence. *World Devel.,* July 1983, *11*(7), pp. 601–07. **[G: Selected LDCs]**

Girão, José António. Aspectos da política económica em países em desenvolvimento: o caso de Portugal. (With English summary.) *Economia,* January 1983, *7*(1), pp. 51–69. **[G: Portugal]**

Godley, Wynne. Keynes and the Management of Real National Income and Expenditure. **In** *Worswick, D. and Trevithick, J., eds.,* 1983, pp. 135–57.

Goodfriend, Marvin. Discount Window Borrowing, Monetary Policy, and the Post-October 6, 1979 Federal Reserve Operating Procedure. *J. Monet. Econ.,* September 1983, *12*(3), pp. 343–56. **[G: U.S.]**

Goodhart, Charles A. E. 'Inflation, Financial and Fiscal Structure, and the Monetary Mechanism' by L. Papademos and F. Modigliani: Comment. *Europ. Econ. Rev.,* March/April 1983, *21*(1/2), pp. 251–56.

Goodhart, Charles A. E. Monetary Policy, Money Supply, and the Federal Reserve's Operating Procedures: Implementation of Federal Reserve Open Market Operations: Comment. **In** *Meek, P., ed.,* 1983, pp. 46–50. **[G: U.K.; U.S.; Canada]**

Goodhart, Charles A. E. On Keynes and Monetarism: Comment. **In** *Worswick, D. and Trevithick, J., eds.,* 1983, pp. 75–81.

Gordon, Roger H. An Optimal Taxation Approach to Fiscal Federalism. *Quart. J. Econ.,* November 1983, *98*(4), pp. 567–86.

Gough, Robert A., Jr. The Future Constraints on Interest Rates. **In** *Sanford, T., ed.,* 1983, pp. 56–78. **[G: U.S.]**

Gowland, D. H. Interest Rates. **In** *Gowland, D. H., ed.,* 1983, pp. 35–56.

Gowland, D. H. Issues in Macroeconomics. **In** *Gowland, D. H., ed.,* 1983, pp. 57–87.

Gowland, D. H. Techniques of Monetary Control. **In** *Gowland, D. H., ed.,* 1983, pp. 1–33. **[G: U.K.]**

Grant, John. Deficits and Capital Markets. **In** *Conklin, D. W. and Courchene, T. J., eds.,* 1983, pp. 261–83. **[G: Canada]**

Granziol, Markus and Schelbert, Heidi. Ex ante Real-Zinssätze am Euromarkt. (Ex ante Real Euro Interest Rates. With English summary.) *Z. Wirtschaft. Sozialwissen.,* 1983, *103*(5), pp. 437–59. **[G: Selected OECD]**

Gray, Jo Anna. Wage Indexation, Incomplete Information, and the Aggregate Supply Curve. **In** *Dornbusch, R. and Simonsen, M. H., eds.,* 1983, pp. 25–45.

Gray, M. R. Inflation and the Financial System: Discussion. **In** *Pagan, A. R. and Trivedi, P. K., eds.,* 1983, pp. 220. **[G: Australia]**

Greenfield, Robert L. and Yeager, Leland B. A Laissez-Faire Approach to Monetary Stability. *J. Money, Credit, Banking,* August 1983, *15*(3), pp. 302–15.

Greenwood, Jeremy. Expectations, the Exchange Rate, and the Current Account. *J. Monet. Econ.,* November 1983, *12*(4), pp. 543–69.

Gregory, Allan W. and McAleer, Michael. Testing Non-Nested Specifications of Money Demand for Canada. *Can. J. Econ.,* November 1983, *16*(4), pp. 593–602. **[G: Canada]**

Grossman, Herschel I. The Natural-Rate Hypothesis, the Rational-Expectations Hypothesis, and the Remarkable Survival of Non-Market-Clearing Assumptions. *Carnegie-Rochester Conf. Ser. Public Policy,* Autumn 1983, *19,* pp. 225–45.

Grossman, Sanford J. and Weiss, Laurence. A Transactions-Based Model of the Monetary Transmission Mechanism. *Amer. Econ. Rev.,* December 1983, *73*(5), pp. 871–80.

Gruben, William C. and Lawler, Patrick J. Currency Substitution: The Use of Dollar Coin and Currency in the Texas Border Area of Mexico. *Fed. Res. Bank Dallas Econ. Rev.,* July 1983, pp. 10–20. **[G: Mexico; U.S.]**

Gultekin, N. Bulent. Stock Market Returns and Inflation Forecasts. *J. Finance,* June 1983, *38*(3), pp. 663–73. **[G: U.S.]**

Gupta, G. S. and Laumas, G. S. Some Properties of Fiscal and Monetary Policy Multipliers. *Southern Econ. J.,* April 1983, *49*(4), pp. 1137–40.

Gutierrez-Camara, José L. and Huss, Hans-Joachim. The Interaction between Floating Exchange Rates, Money, and Prices—An Empirical Analysis. *Weltwirtsch. Arch.,* 1983, *119*(3), pp. 401–28. **[G: U.S.; Japan; Canada; W. Europe]**

Habeler, Gottfried. A Comment on "The Importance of Stable Money." *Cato J.,* Spring 1983, *3*(1), pp. 83–91. **[G: U.S.; U.K.; Austria; Germany]**

Hafer, R. W. Inflation: Assessing Its Recent Behavior and Future Prospects. *Fed. Res. Bank St. Louis Rev.,* August/September 1983, *65*(7), pp. 36–41.

Hafer, R. W. Weekly Money Supply Forecasts: Effects of the October 1979 Change in Monetary Control Procedures. *Fed. Res. Bank St. Louis Rev.,* April 1983, *65*(4), pp. 26–32. **[G: U.S.]**

Hahn, F. H. On Keynes and Monetarism: Comment. **In** *Worswick, D. and Trevithick, J., eds.,* 1983, pp. 72–75.

Hahn, Frank. Keynesianism, Monetarism, and Rational Expectations: Some Reflections and Conjectures: Comment. **In** *Frydman, R. and Phelps, E. S., eds.,* 1983, pp. 223–30.

Hall, Robert E. Optimal Fiduciary Monetary Systems. *J. Monet. Econ.,* July 1983, *12*(1), pp. 33–50.

Hall, S. G. F. Money and the Walrasian Utility Function. *Oxford Econ. Pap.,* July 1983, *35*(2), pp. 247–53.

Hansen, Lars Peter and Sargent, Thomas J. Aggregation over Time and the Inverse Optimal Predictor Problem for Adaptive Expectations in

Conginuous Time. *Int. Econ. Rev.*, February 1983, *24*(1), pp. 1–20. **[G: U.S.]**

Hansen, Robert S. and Thatcher, John G. On the Nature of Credit Demand and Credit Rationing in Competitive Credit Markets. *J. Banking Finance,* June 1983, *7*(2), pp. 273–84.

Haraf, William S. Tests of a Rational Expectations-Structural Neutrality Model with Persistent Effects of Monetary Disturbances. *J. Monet. Econ.*, January 1983, *11*(1), pp. 103–16.

Hatanaka, Michio. Confidence Judgment of the Extrapolation from a Dynamic Money Demand Function. *J. Econ. Dynam. Control,* September 1983, *6*(1/2), pp. 55–78. **[G: U.S.]**

Hawawini, Gabriel A. The Theory of Risk Aversion and Liquidity Preference: A Geometric Exposition. *Amer. Econ.*, Fall 1983, *27*(2), pp. 42–49.

Hayakawa, Hiroaki. Rationality of Liquidity Preferences and the Neoclassical Monetary Growth Model. *J. Macroecon.*, Fall 1983, *5*(4), pp. 495–501.

Hazari, Bharat R. The IS-LM Curves Revisited with the Aid of Geometry of International Trade. *Indian Econ. J.*, January-March 1983, *30*(3), pp. 17–24.

Hein, Scott E. and Veugelers, Paul T. W. M. Predicting Velocity Growth: A Time Series Perspective. *Fed. Res. Bank St. Louis Rev.*, October 1983, *65*(8), pp. 34–43. **[G: U.S.]**

Helpman, Elhanan. Financial Intermediation and Price Level Control: Comment. *J. Monet. Econ.*, July 1983, *12*(1), pp. 29–31.

Henderson, Dale W. Monetary, Fiscal and Exchange Rate Policy in a Two-Country, Short-Run, Macro Economic Model. *Écon. Soc.*, July-August 1983, *17*(7–8), pp. 1149–83.

Henderson, Dale W. and Waldo, Douglas G. Reserve Requirements on Eurocurrency Deposits: Implications for the Stabilization of Real Outputs. **In** *Bhandari, J. S. and Putnam, B. H., eds.*, 1983, pp. 350–83.

Hercowitz, Zvi. Anticipated Inflation, the Frequency of Transactions, and the Slope of the Phillips Curve. *J. Money, Credit, Banking,* May 1983, *15*(2), pp. 139–54.

Hicks, John. Is Interest the Price of a Factor of Production? **In** *Hicks, J.*, 1983, *1979*, pp. 113–28.

Himarios, Daniel. Inflationary Expectations and the Demand for Money: The Greek Experience: A Comment and Some Different Results. *Kredit Kapital,* 1983, *16*(2), pp. 253–64. **[G: Greece]**

Hirayama, Asazi. Quality Uncertainty, Commerce and Money. *Econ. Stud. Quart.*, December 1983, *34*(3), pp. 249–58.

Hodgman, Donald R. and Resek, Robert W. Determinants of Monetary Policy in France, The Federal Republic of Germany, Italy and the United Kingdom: A Comparative Analysis. **In** *Hodgman, D. R., ed.*, 1983, pp. 147–70. **[G: U.K.; W. Germany; France; Italy]**

Hoelscher, Gregory P. Federal Borrowing and Short Term Interest Rates. *Southern Econ. J.*, October 1983, *50*(2), pp. 319–33. **[G: U.S.]**

Hoffman, Dennis L. and Schlagenhauf, Don E. Rational Expectations and Monetary Models of Exchange Rate Determination: An Empirical Examination. *J. Monet. Econ.*, March 1983, *11*(2), pp. 247–60. **[G: W. Germany; U.S.; U.K.; France]**

Horne, Jocelyn. The Asset Market Model of the Balance of Payments and the Exchange Rate: A Survey of Empirical Evidence. *J. Int. Money Finance,* August 1983, *2*(2), pp. 89–109. **[G: Italy; Australia; Netherlands; W. Germany; U.K.]**

Hosek, William R. Stochastic Properties of the Real Interest Rate. *Appl. Econ.*, December 1983, *15*(6), pp. 793–805. **[G: U.S.]**

Howard, David H. and Johnson, Karen H. The Behavior of Monetary Aggregates in Major Industrialized Countries. *J. Money, Credit, Banking,* November 1983, *15*(4), pp. 455–68. **[G: U.K.; Switzerland]**

Howard, Michael. The Demand for Money in a Developing Money Market: The Evidence from Trinidad and Tobago. *Amer. Econ.*, Spring 1983, *27*(1), pp. 40–46. **[G: Trinidad; Tobago]**

Irvine, F. Owen, Jr. The Real Rate of Interest, for Whom? *Appl. Econ.*, October 1983, *15*(5), pp. 635–48. **[G: U.S.]**

Irvine, Reed J. and Emery, Robert F. Interest Rates as an Anti-inflationary Instrument in Taiwan. **In** *Von Pischke, J. D.; Adams, D. W. and Donald, G., eds.*, 1983, pp. 393–97. **[G: Taiwan]**

Izenson, Mark Steven. A Brief Note on the Relationship between Investment and the Interest Rate in the United States, 1970–1979. *Econ. Notes,* 1983, (1), pp. 135–39. **[G: U.S.]**

Jaeger, Franz. Die Geldpolitik der Schweizerischen Nationalbank: Theoretische Fundierung und konkrete Ausgestaltung. (Swiss Monetary Policy. With English summary.) *Aussenwirtschaft,* September 1983, *38*(3), pp. 285–335. **[G: Switzerland]**

Jansen, Karel. Monetarism: Economic Crisis and the Third World: An Introduction. **In** *Jansen, K., ed.*, 1983, pp. 1–42.

Johannes, James M. and Rasche, Robert H. Analysis and Forecasts of Money Multiplier Behavior 1982–4. **In** *Shadow Open Market Committee.*, 1983, pp. 35–39. **[G: U.S.]**

Jones, David S. and Roley, V. Vance. Rational Expectations and the Expectations Model of the Term Structure: A Test Using Weekly Data. *J. Monet. Econ.*, September 1983, *12*(3), pp. 453–65.

Jonung, Lars. Monetization and the Behavior of Velocity in Sweden, 1871–1913. *Exploration Econ. Hist.*, October 1983, *20*(4), pp. 418–39. **[G: Sweden]**

Jonung, Lars. Money and Prices in Sweden, 1871–1970: A Comment. *Scand. J. Econ.*, 1983, *85*(3), pp. 433–36.

Jordan, Jerry L. Monetary Policy Options and the Economic Outlook. **In** *Shadow Open Market Committee.*, 1983, pp. 29–34. **[G: U.S.]**

Jordan, Jerry L. Oops, Another Money Demand Shift. **In** *Shadow Open Market Committee.*, 1983, pp. 25–27. **[G: U.S.]**

Judd, John P. The Recent Decline in Velocity: Instability in Money Demand of Inflation? *Fed. Res. Bank San Francisco Econ. Rev.*, Spring 1983, (2), pp. 12–19. **[G: U.S.]**

Judd, John P. and McElhattan, Rose. The Behavior of Money and the Economy in 1982–83. *Fed. Res.*

Bank San Francisco Econ. Rev., Summer 1983, (3), pp. 46–51. **[G: U.S.]**

Judge, Guy. The Stability of Behavioural Relationships and Their Empirical Estimates: Some Issues of Terminology and Methodology, with Special Reference to the Demand for Money Function. *Brit. Rev. Econ. Issues,* Spring 1983, *5*(12), pp. 1–14.

Kaen, Fred R. and Hachey, George A. Eurocurrency and National Money Market Interest Rates: An Empirical Investigation of Causality. *J. Money, Credit, Banking,* August 1983, *15*(3), pp. 327–38. **[G: U.K.; U.S.]**

Kaen, Fred R.; Helms, Billy P. and Booth, G. Geoffrey. The Integration of Eurodollar and U.S. Money Market Interest Rates in the Futures Market. *Weltwirtsch. Arch.*, 1983, *119*(4), pp. 601–15. **[G: U.S.; W. Europe]**

Kamaiah, Bandi; Abraham, Joseph and Naidu, C. Gajendra. Functional Forms and Temporal Changes in Money Demand Elasticities: Some Evidence for India. *Margin,* April 1983, *15*(3), pp. 59–72. **[G: India]**

Kane, Alex; Rosenthal, Leonard and Ljung, Greta. Tests of the Fisher Hypothesis with International Data: Theory and Evidence. *J. Finance,* May 1983, *38*(2), pp. 539–51. **[G: W. Europe; U.S.]**

Kane, Edward J. Nested Tests of Alternative Term-Structure Theories. *Rev. Econ. Statist.*, February 1983, *65*(1), pp. 115–23. **[G: U.S.]**

Kharadia, V. C. The Behaviour of the Currency–Demand Deposits Ratio in India, Its Effects on Money Supply and Implications for Monetary Policy. *Indian Econ. J.*, July–September 1983, *31*(1), pp. 89–106. **[G: India]**

Kim, Dae Sik. Monetary Accommodations under External Supply Shocks in Korea: Some Empirical Results. *J. Econ. Devel.*, July 1983, *8*(1), pp. 161–80. **[G: S. Korea]**

Kimbrough, Kent P. Exchange-Rate Policy and Monetary Information. *J. Int. Money Finance*, December 1983, *2*(3), pp. 333–46.

King, Robert G. Interest Rates, Aggregate Information, and Monetary Policy. *J. Monet. Econ.*, August 1983, *12*(2), pp. 199–234.

Klamer, Arjo. Conversations with Economists: New Classical Economists and Opponents Speak Out on the Current Controversy in Macroeconomics: A Background for the Conversations. **In** *Klamer, A.*, 1983, pp. 1–25.

Klovland, Jan Tore. The Demand for Money in Secular Perspective: The Case of Norway, 1867–1980. *Europ. Econ. Rev.*, July 1983, *22*(2), pp. 193–218. **[G: Norway]**

Knight, Malcolm D. and Mathieson, Donald J. Economic Change and Policy Response in Canada under Fixed and Flexible Exchange Rates. **In** *Bhandari, J. S. and Putnam, B. H., eds.*, 1983, pp. 500–529. **[G: Canada]**

Komiya, Ryutaro. International Liquidity and Monetary Control: Comment. **In** *von Furstenberg, G. M., ed.*, 1983, pp. 110–15.

Koskela, Erkki. Credit Rationing and Non-price Loan Terms: A Re-examination. *J. Banking Finance,* September 1983, *7*(3), pp. 405–16.

Kouri, Pentti J. K. Macroeconomic Adjustment to Interest Rate Disturbances: Real and Monetary Aspects. **In** *Claassen, E. and Salin, P., eds.*, 1983, pp. 73–97.

Kumar, Ramesh C. Money in Development: A Monetary Growth Model à la McKinnon. *Southern Econ. J.*, July 1983, *50*(1), pp. 18–36.

Labia, J. F. Keynes's Impact on Monetary Economics (Review Article). *S. Afr. J. Econ.*, September 1983, *51*(3), pp. 446–56.

Laidler, David and Bentley, Brian. A Small Macro-Model of the Post-War United States. *Manchester Sch. Econ. Soc. Stud.*, December 1983, *51*(4), pp. 317–40. **[G: U.S.]**

Lanyi, Anthony and Saracoglu, Rüşdü. The Importance of Interest Rates in Developing Economies. *Finance Develop.*, June 1983, *20*(2), pp. 20–23. **[G: Selected LDCs]**

Laskar, Daniel M. Short-run Independence of Monetary Policy under a Pegged Exchange-Rates System: An Econometric Approach. **In** *Darby, M. P. and Lothian, J. R., et al.*, 1983, pp. 314–48. **[G: OECD]**

Laterza, Edoardo Lecaldano Sasso and Quintieri, Beniamino. È il debito pubblico più inflazionistico della base monetaria? (Is Public Debt More Inflationary than the Monetary Base? With English summary.) *Bancaria,* January 1983, *39*(1), pp. 27–33. **[G: Italy]**

Laumas, G. S. The Demand for Money in the Recent Period. *Eastern Econ. J.*, January–March 1983, *9*(1), pp. 1–5. **[G: U.S.]**

Laumas, Prem S. and Williams, Martin. Household Demand for Money in an Underdeveloped Economy: A Case Study of India. *Pakistan Devel. Rev.*, Spring 1983, *22*(1), pp. 37–46. **[G: India]**

Lavoie, Don C. Economic Calculation and Monetary Stability. *Cato J.*, Spring 1983, *3*(1), pp. 163–70.

Lavoie, Don C. Some Strengths in Marx's Disequilibrium Theory of Money. *Cambridge J. Econ.*, March 1983, *7*(1), pp. 55–68.

Law, I. A. and Lewis, P. E. T. A Bayesian Approach to Expectations Formation. *Brit. Rev. Econ. Issues,* Spring 1983, *5*(12), pp. 46–56. **[G: U.K.]**

Lawrence, Colin. Rational Expectations, Supply Shocks and the Stability of the Inflation–Output Tradeoff: Some Time Series Evidence for the United Kingdom, 1957–1977. *J. Monet. Econ.*, March 1983, *11*(2), pp. 225–45. **[G: U.K.]**

Leach, John. A Comment on the Foundations of the Precautionary Demand for Money. *J. Monet. Econ.*, March 1983, *11*(2), pp. 273–80.

Lee, Dan. Effects of Open Market Operations and Foreign Exchange Market Operations under Flexible Exchange Rates. **In** *Darby, M. P. and Lothian, J. R., et al.*, 1983, pp. 349–79.

Lee, S. Y. and Li, W. K. Money, Income and Prices and Their Lead-Lag Relationships in Singapore. *Singapore Econ. Rev.*, April 1983, *28*(1), pp. 73–87. **[G: Singapore]**

Leiderman, Leonardo. The Response of Real Wages to Unanticipated Money Growth. *J. Monet. Econ.*, January 1983, *11*(1), pp. 73–88. **[G: U.S.]**

Leiderman, Leonardo. The Use of Monetary Policy for Internal and External Balance in Ten Industrial Countries: Comment. **In** *Frenkel, J. A., ed.*, 1983, pp. 226–29. **[G: OECD]**

Leijonhufvud, Axel. Keynesianism, Monetarism, and Rational Expectations: Some Reflections and Conjectures. **In** *Frydman, R. and Phelps, E. S., eds.*, 1983, pp. 203–23.

Lerman, Zvi. The Structure of Interest Rates and Inflation. **In** *Levy, H., ed.*, 1983, pp. 183–215. **[G: U.S.]**

Lerner, Abba P. A Note on the Rate of Interest and the Value of Assets. **In** *Lerner, A. P.*, 1983, *1961*, pp. 545–49.

Lerner, Abba P. Alternative Formulations of the Theory of Interest. **In** *Lerner, A. P.*, 1983, *1938*, pp. 507–26.

Lerner, Abba P. Interest Theory—Supply and Demand for Loans or Supply and Demand for Cash. **In** *Lerner, A. P.*, 1983, *1944*, pp. 527–30.

Lerner, Abba P. Money as a Creature of the State. **In** *Lerner, A. P.*, 1983, *1947*, pp. 455–60.

Lerner, Abba P. Some Swedish Stepping Stones in Economic Theory: Review Article. **In** *Lerner, A. P.*, 1983, *1940*, pp. 333–50.

Lewin, Peter. Competitive Money: A Comment. *Cato J.*, Spring 1983, *3*(1), pp. 301–04.

Lizondo, José Saúl. Interest Differential and Covered Arbitrage. **In** *Armella, P. A.; Dornbusch, R. and Obstfeld, M., eds.*, 1983, pp. 221–40. **[G: Mexico; U.S.]**

Long, John B., Jr. Theories of Intermediated Structures: A Comment. *Carnegie-Rochester Conf. Ser. Public Policy*, Spring 1983, *18*, pp. 273–78.

Lucas, Robert E., Jr. Expectations and the Neutrality of Money. *J. Econ. Theory*, October 1983, *31*(1), pp. 197–99.

Lucas, Robert E., Jr. and Stokey, Nancy L. Optimal Fiscal and Monetary Policy in an Economy without Capital. *J. Monet. Econ.*, July 1983, *12*(1), pp. 55–93.

Machak, Joseph A.; Spivey, W. Allen and Wrobleski, William J. Analyzing Permanent and Transient Influences in Multiple Time Series Models. *J. Bus. Econ. Statist.*, January 1983, *1*(1), pp. 57–65. **[G: U.S.]**

Machlup, Fritz. The Rationality of 'Rational Expectations.' *Kredit Kapital*, 1983, *16*(2), pp. 172–83.

Magnifico, Giovanni. L'economia mondiale ad una svolta: qualche proposta. (The World Economy at a Turning-Point: Some Proposals. With English summary.) *Bancaria*, March 1983, *39*(3), pp. 242–48.

Makin, John H. Real Interest, Money Surprises, Anticipated Inflation and Fiscal Deficits. *Rev. Econ. Statist.*, August 1983, *65*(3), pp. 374–84. **[G: U.S.]**

Malinvaud, Edmond. Keynes and the Management of Real National Income and Expenditure: Comment. **In** *Worswick, D. and Trevithick, J., eds.*, 1983, pp. 157–62.

Mandel, Ernest. World Crisis and the Monetarist Answer. **In** *Jansen, K., ed.*, 1983, pp. 79–95. **[G: OECD]**

Maravall, Agustin and Pierce, David A. Preliminary-Data Error and Monetary Aggregate Targeting. *J. Bus. Econ. Statist.*, July 1983, *1*(3), pp. 179–86. **[G: U.S.]**

Marino, Loretta. Integrazione dei mercati dei capitali, politica monetaria e cambi flessibili. (Domestic Monetary Policy and Financial Integration under Flexible Rates. With English summary.) *Giorn. Econ.*, March-April 1983, *42*(3–4), pp. 193–214.

Martin, John P. Nominal and Real Exchange Rates: Issues and Some Evidence: Comment. **In** *Claassen, E. and Salin, P., eds.*, 1983, pp. 28–31. **[G: Selected OECD]**

Marty, Alvin L. Indexing to the Money Supply: Pros and Cons: A Comment [Competitive Price Setting, Price Flexibility, and Linkage to the Money Supply]. *Carnegie-Rochester Conf. Ser. Public Policy*, Autumn 1983, *19*, pp. 301–11.

Mascaro, Angelo and Meltzer, Allan H. Long- and Short-Term Interest Rates in a Risky World. *J. Monet. Econ.*, November 1983, *12*(4), pp. 485–518. **[G: U.S.]**

Masera, Rainer S. International Liquidity and Monetary Control: Comment. **In** *von Furstenberg, G. M., ed.*, 1983, pp. 123–28.

McCallum, Bennett T. A Model of Commodity Money: Comments. *J. Monet. Econ.*, July 1983, *12*(1), pp. 189–96.

McCallum, Bennett T. On Non-Uniqueness in Rational Expectations Models: An Attempt at Perspective. *J. Monet. Econ.*, March 1983, *11*(2), pp. 139–68.

McCallum, Bennett T. Reply to Bryant and Wallace [The Role of Overlapping-Generations Models in Monetary Economics]. *Carnegie-Rochester Conf. Ser. Public Policy*, Spring 1983, *18*, pp. 57–58.

McCallum, Bennett T. The Role of Overlapping-Generations Models in Monetary Economics. *Carnegie-Rochester Conf. Ser. Public Policy*, Spring 1983, *18*, pp. 9–44.

McCallum, Bennett T. The Role of Overlapping-Generations Models in Monetary Economics. **In** *Brunner, K. and Meltzer, A. H., eds.*, 1983, *1983*, pp. 129–64.

McCallum, Bennett T. and Hoehn, James G. Instrument Choice for Money Stock Control with Contemporaneous and Lagged Reserve Requirements: A Note. *J. Money, Credit, Banking*, February 1983, *15*(1), pp. 96–101.

McCallum, John. Stabilization Policy and Endogenous Wage Stickiness. *Amer. Econ. Rev.*, June 1983, *73*(3), pp. 414–19.

McGee, Robert T. Some Implications of the Natural Rate Hypotheses. *J. Macroecon.*, Summer 1983, *5*(3), pp. 303–16.

McGuire, Timothy W. Price Change Expectations and the Phillips Curve. **In** *Brunner, K. and Meltzer, A. H., eds.*, 1983, *1976*, pp. 81–127. **[G: U.S.]**

McKenzie, George and Thomas, Stephen. Liquidity, Credit Creation and International Banking: An Econometric Investigation. *J. Banking Finance*, 1983, *7*(4), pp. 467–80. **[G: U.K.]**

Mehta, Granshyam. Comments on Professor Minoguchi's Interpretation of the *Treatise* and the *General Theory*. *Hitotsubashi J. Econ.*, December 1983, *24*(2), pp. 153–58.

Meiselman, David I. Is Gold the Question? [Gold Standards: True and False]. *Cato J.*, Spring 1983, *3*(1), pp. 269–75. **[G: U.S.]**

Melitz, Jacques. 'Inflation, Financial and Fiscal

Structure, and the Monetary Mechanism' by L. Papademos and F. Modigliani: Comment. *Europ. Econ. Rev.*, March/April 1983, *21* (1/2), pp. 257–59.

Melitz, Jacques. Optimal Stabilization and the Proper Exercise of the Monetary-Policy Instruments under Flexible Exchange Rates. **In** *Claassen, E. and Salin, P., eds.*, 1983, pp. 231–55.

Meltzer, Allan H. Monetary Reform in an Uncertain Environment. *Cato J.*, Spring 1983, *3* (1), pp. 93–112. **[G: U.S.]**

Meltzer, Allan H. On Keynes and Monetarism. **In** *Worswick, D. and Trevithick, J., eds.*, 1983, pp. 49–72.

Meltzer, Allan H. Recent Behavior of Base Velocity. **In** *Shadow Open Market Committee.*, 1983, pp. 19–24.

Melvin, Michael. Expected Inflation and Interest Rates: Reply. *Amer. Econ. Rev.*, June 1983, *73* (3), pp. 503–06.

Melvin, Michael. The Vanishing Liquidity Effect of Money on Interest: Analysis and Implications for Policy. *Econ. Inquiry*, April 1983, *21* (2), pp. 188–202. **[G: U.S.]**

Merrick, John J., Jr. Financial Market Efficiency, the Decomposition of "Anticipated" versus "Unanticipated" Money Growth, and Further Tests of the Relation between Money and Real Output: A Note. *J. Money, Credit, Banking*, May 1983, *15* (2), pp. 222–32. **[G: U.S.]**

Meyer, Paul A. Money Multipliers and the Slopes of IS-LM. *Southern Econ. J.*, July 1983, *50* (1), pp. 226–29.

Milbourne, Ross D. Credit Flows and the Money Supply. *Australian Econ. Pap.*, December 1983, *22* (41), pp. 418–30.

Milbourne, Ross D. Optimal Money Holding under Uncertainty. *Int. Econ. Rev.*, October 1983, *24* (3), pp. 685–98.

Milbourne, Ross D. Price Expectations and the Demand for Money: Resolution of a Paradox. *Rev. Econ. Statist.*, November 1983, *65* (4), pp. 633–38. **[G: Australia; U.S.]**

Milbourne, Ross D.; Buckholtz, P. and Wasan, M. T. A Thoretical Derivation of the Functional Form of Short Run Money Holdings. *Rev. Econ. Stud.*, July 1983, *50* (3), pp. 531–41.

Milgate, Murray. Keynes on the 'Classical' Theory of Interest. **In** *Eatwell, J. and Milgate, M., eds.*, 1983, *1977*, pp. 79–92.

Minford, A. P. L. and Peel, David A. Some Implications of Partial Current Information Sets in Macroeconomic Models Embodying Rational Expectations. *Manchester Sch. Econ. Soc. Stud.*, September 1983, *51* (3), pp. 235–49.

Minford, Patrick. Equilibrium Price-Output and the (Non)Insulating Properties of Fixed Exchange Rates: A Comment. *J. Int. Money Finance*, December 1983, *2* (3), pp. 355–56.

Minoguchi, Takeo. Reply [The Process of Writing the *General Theory* as a 'Monetary Theory of Production'] [Some Questions about IS-LM Interpretation of the *General Theory*]. *Hitotsubashi J. Econ.*, December 1983, *24* (2), pp. 159.

Mishkin, Frederic S. The Remarkable Survival of Non-Market-Clearing Assumptions: A Comment. *Carnegie-Rochester Conf. Ser. Public Policy*, Autumn 1983, *19*, pp. 247–51.

Mitchell, Douglas W. A Note on Two-Stage Monetary Policy under Multiplier Uncertainty. *Eastern Econ. J.*, April–June 1983, *9* (2), pp. 107–09.

Modigliani, Franco. The Nonadjustment of Nominal Interest Rates: A Study of the Fisher Effect: Comment. **In** *Tobin, J., ed.*, 1983, pp. 241–44. **[G: U.S.]**

Molho, Lazaros E. On Testing the Efficacy of Selective Credit Controls. *J. Money, Credit, Banking*, February 1983, *15* (1), pp. 120–22. **[G: U.S.]**

Montesano, Aldo. Debito pubblico o base monetaria? Una risposta. (Public Debt or Monetary Base? A Reply. With English summary.) *Bancaria*, January 1983, *39* (1), pp. 39–41.

Moore, Basil J. Unpacking the Post Keynesian Black Box: Bank Lending and the Money Supply. *J. Post Keynesian Econ.*, Summer 1983, *5* (4), pp. 537–56. **[G: U.S.]**

Moosa, Suleman A. The Double Whammy of Stagflation and Uncertainty. *Kredit Kapital*, 1983, *16* (3), pp. 297–315. **[G: U.S.]**

Moosa, Suleman A. The Treatment of Uncertainty in the Application of Rational Expectations to the Analysis of Economic Policy. *Appl. Econ.*, August 1983, *15* (4), pp. 451–58.

Moriguchi, Chikashi. Japan's Macroeconomic Policies during the 1970s. **In** *[Klein, L. R.]*, 1983, pp. 282–95. **[G: Japan]**

Morris, Frank E. Monetarism without Money. **In** *Sanford, T., ed.*, 1983, pp. 26–36. **[G: U.S.]**

Motley, Brian. Real Interest Rates, Money and Government Deficits. *Fed. Res. Bank San Francisco Econ. Rev.*, Summer 1983, (3), pp. 31–45. **[G: U.S.]**

Mundell, Robert A. International Monetary Options. *Cato J.*, Spring 1983, *3* (1), pp. 189–210. **[G: Global]**

Navarro, Alfredo M. and Rayó, Antonio R. Precios, Causalidad y Dinero en Argentina. (Prices, Causality and Money in Argentina. With English summary.) *Económica*, May–December 1983, *29* (2–3), pp. 267–84. **[G: Argentina]**

Neldner, Manfred. Portfoliostruktur der Geschäfsbanken und Geldumlaufgeschwindigkeit. Der empirische Befund für die Bundesrepublik Deutschland. (Portfolio Structures of Commercial Banks and the Velocity of the Circulation of Money: The Empirical Findings for the Federal Republic of Germany. With English summary.) *Kredit Kapital*, 1983, *16* (4), pp. 568–86. **[G: W. Germany]**

Nell, Edward J. On Monetary Circulation and the Rate of Exploitation. *Econ. Forum*, Spring 1983 Supplement, *13*, pp. 1–38.

Nguyen, Duc-Tho and Turnovsky, Stephen J. The Dynamic Effects of Fiscal and Monetary Policies under Bond Financing: A Theoretical Simulation Approach to Crowding Out. *J. Monet. Econ.*, January 1983, *11* (1), pp. 45–71.

Nichols, Donald A.; Small, David H. and Webster, Charles E., Jr. Why Interest Rates Rise When an Unexpectedly Large Money Stock Is Announced. *Amer. Econ. Rev.*, June 1983, *73* (3), pp. 383–88.

Niehans, Jürg. Real Exchange Rate Overshooting and the Output Cost of Bringing Down Inflation: Some Further Results: Comment. **In** *Frenkel, J. A., ed.*, 1983, pp. 365–68.

Nisar, Shaheena and Aslam, Naheed. The Demand for Money and the Term Structure of Interest Rates in Pakistan. *Pakistan Devel. Rev.*, Summer 1983, *22*(2), pp. 97–116. **[G: Pakistan]**

O'Connell, Joan. Exchange Rate Expectations and the Short-Run Effectiveness of Monetary Policy. *J. Econ. Stud.*, 1983, *10*(2), pp. 21–28.

O'Driscoll, Gerald P., Jr. A Free-Market Money: Comment [Stable Money and Free-Market Currencies]. *Cato J.*, Spring 1983, *3*(1), pp. 327–33.

Obeng, Kofi. Fare Subsidies to Achieve Pareto Optimality—A Benefit Cost Approach. *Logist. Transp. Rev.*, December 1983, *19*(4), pp. 367–84. **[G: U.S.]**

Oberhauser, Alois. Die Bedeutung der Verteilungszusammenhänge für Geldtheorie und Geldpolitik. Dargestellt am Beispiel der Staatsverschuldung. (The Implications of the Distribution Mechanism for Monetary Theory and Policy: Exemplified by Public Debt. With English summary.) *Jahr. Nationalökon. Statist.*, January 1983, *198*(1), pp. 3–19.

Obstfeld, Maurice and Rogoff, Kenneth S. Speculative Hyperinflations in Maximizing Models: Can We Rule Them Out? *J. Polit. Econ.*, August 1983, *91*(4), pp. 675–87.

Ochs, Jack and Rush, Mark. The Persistence of Interest-Rate Effects on the Demand for Currency. *J. Money, Credit, Banking*, November 1983, *15*(4), pp. 499–505. **[G: U.S.]**

Okun, Arthur M. Monetary Policy, Debt Management and Interest Rates: A Quantitative Appraisal. **In** *Okun, A. M.*, 1983, *1963*, pp. 253–303. **[G: U.S.]**

Olivera, Julio H. G. Dinero pasivo internacional y hegemonia monetaria. (With English summary.) *Desarrollo Econ.*, April–June 1983, *23*(89), pp. 3–9.

Olsen, Leif H. Monetary Rules, Discretion, and the Constitution [What Type of Monetary Rule?]. *Cato J.*, Spring 1983, *3*(1), pp. 185–88. **[G: U.S.]**

Orléan, André. Régulation monétaire et anticipations rationnelles. (Monetary Regulation and Rational Expectations. With English summary.) *Écon. Appl.*, 1983, *36*(1), pp. 207–28.

Ortiz, Guillermo. Currency Substitution in Mexico: The Dollarization Problem. *J. Money, Credit, Banking*, May 1983, *15*(2), pp. 174–85. **[G: Mexico]**

Ortiz, Guillermo. Dollarization in Mexico: Causes and Consequences. **In** *Armella, P. A.; Dornbusch, R. and Obstfeld, M., eds.*, 1983, pp. 71–95. **[G: Mexico]**

Oxley, Leslie T. Functional and Structural Breaks in the UK Demand for Money Function: 1963–1979. *J. Econ. Stud.*, 1983, *10*(3), pp. 22–41. **[G: U.K.]**

Oxley, Leslie T. The Functional Form of the U.K. Demand for "Broad" Money, 1963–1979. *Scot. J. Polit. Econ.*, February 1983, *30*(1), pp. 69–74. **[G: U.K.]**

Padoa-Schioppa, Tommaso. Determinants of Monetary Policy in France, The Federal Republic of Germany, Italy and the United Kingdom: A Comparative Analysis: Discussion. **In** *Hodgman, D. R., ed.*, 1983, pp. 171–76. **[G: U.K.; W. Germany; France; Italy]**

Pala, Gianfranco. Money, Course of Exchanges and Rate of Exploitation. An Introductory Marxian Reading. *Econ. Notes*, 1983, (3), pp. 122–51. **[G: OECD]**

Papademos, Lucas and Modigliani, Franco. Inflation, Financial and Fiscal Structure, and the Monetary Mechanism. *Europ. Econ. Rev.*, March/April 1983, *21*(1/2), pp. 203–50.

Papademos, Lucas and Rozwadowski, Franek. Monetary and Credit Targets in an Open Economy. **In** *Hodgman, D. R., ed.*, 1983, pp. 275–306.

Parguez, A. La monnaie, la crise et l'épargne ou les conséquences économiques de l'austérité. (Money, Crisis and Saving: The Economic Consequences of Austerity. With English summary.) *Écon. Soc.*, September–October–November 1983, *17*(9–10–11), pp. 1421–50.

Patinkin, Don. Monetary Economics. **In** *Brown, E. C. and Solow, R. M., eds.*, 1983, pp. 157–67.

Pearce, Douglas K. and Roley, V. Vance. The Reaction of Stock Prices to Unanticipated Changes in Money: A Note. *J. Finance*, September 1983, *38*(4), pp. 1323–33. **[G: U.S.]**

Pechman, Joseph A. and Carr, Julie A. Macro-economics Prices & Quantities. **In** *Tobin, J., ed.*, 1983, pp. 1–18.

Peebles, Gavin. Inflation, Money and Banking in China: In Support of the Purchasing Power Approach. *ACES Bull. (See Comp. Econ. Stud. after 8/85)*, Summer 1983, *25*(2), pp. 81–103. **[G: China]**

Peek, Joe and Wilcox, James A. The Postwar Stability of the Fisher Effect. *J. Finance*, September 1983, *38*(4), pp. 1111–24. **[G: U.S.]**

Pesando, James E. On Expectations, Term Premiums and the Volatility of Long-Term Interest Rates. *J. Monet. Econ.*, September 1983, *12*(3), pp. 467–74. **[G: Canada]**

Pierce, David A. Seasonal Adjustment of the Monetary Aggregates: Summary of the Federal Reserve's Committee Report. *J. Bus. Econ. Statist.*, January 1983, *1*(1), pp. 37–42. **[G: U.S.]**

Pindyck, Robert S. Liquidity, Credit Creation and International Banking: An Econometric Investigation: Comment. *J. Banking Finance*, 1983, *7*(4), pp. 481–82. **[G: U.K.]**

Pohl, Rüdiger. Nicht-neutrale Inflation. (Non-neutral Inflation. With English summary.) *Kredit Kapital*, 1983, *16*(4), pp. 458–78.

Polasek, Wolfgang. Multivariate Time Series Models for Austrian Interest Rates. *Empirica*, 1983, (2), pp. 129–57. **[G: Austria]**

Portes, Richard. Central Planning and Monetarism: Fellow Travelers? **In** *[Erlich, A.]*, 1983, pp. 149–65.

Protopapadakis, Aris. Expectations, Exchange Rates and Monetary Theory: The Case of the German Hyperinflation. *J. Int. Money Finance*, April 1983, *2*(1), pp. 47–65. **[G: W. Germany]**

Purvis, Douglas D. International Liquidity and Monetary Control: Comment. **In** *von Furstenberg,*

G. M., ed., 1983, pp. 115–23.

Radecki, Lawrence J. and Wenninger, John. Shifts in Money Demand: Consumers versus Business. *Fed. Res. Bank New York Quart. Rev.*, Summer 1983, *8*(2), pp. 1–11. **[G: U.S.]**

Ram, Rati and Biswas, Basudeb. Stability of Demand for Money in India: Some Further Evidence. *Indian Econ. J.*, July–September 1983, *31*(1), pp. 77–88. **[G: India]**

Ram, Rati and Spencer, David E. Stock Returns, Real Activity, Inflation, and Money: Comment. *Amer. Econ. Rev.*, June 1983, *73*(3), pp. 463–70. **[G: U.S.]**

Ramachandra, V. S. Direction of Causality between Monetary and Real Variables in India—An Empirical Result. *Indian Econ. J.*, July–September 1983, *31*(1), pp. 65–76. **[G: India]**

Rasche, Robert H. Monetary Policy with a Credit Aggregate Target: Comment on the Friedman Paper. *Carnegie-Rochester Conf. Ser. Public Policy*, Spring 1983, *18*, pp. 149–55. **[G: U.S.]**

Ratner, Jonathan B. A Doubtful Post Keynesian Unemployment Model. *J. Post Keynesian Econ.*, Spring 1983, *5*(3), pp. 474–82.

Raymond, Robert. The Political Economy of French Monetary Policy: Discussion. **In** *Hodgman, D. R., ed.*, 1983, pp. 26–33. **[G: France]**

Redslob, Alain. Rationalité des anticipations et théorie de la politique monétaire: une note critique. (Rational Expectations Hypothesis and the Theory of Monetary Policy: A Critical Note. With English summary.) *Écon. Soc.*, July-August 1983, *17*(7–8), pp. 1259–75.

Riley, James C. and McCusker, John J. Money Supply, Economic Growth, and the Quantity Theory of Money: France, 1650–1788. *Exploration Econ. Hist.*, July 1983, *20*(3), pp. 274–93. **[G: France]**

Robinson, Joan. Notes on Consumption, Investment and Effective Demand: Comment. **In** *Eatwell, J. and Milgate, M., eds.*, 1983, *1979*, pp. 70–71.

Rogoff, Kenneth S. Interest Differential and Covered Arbitrage: Comment. **In** *Armella, P. A.; Dornbusch, R. and Obstfeld, M., eds.*, 1983, pp. 241–43. **[G: Mexico; U.S.]**

Roley, V. Vance. Symmetry Restrictions in a System of Financial Asset Demands: Theoretical and Empirical Results. *Rev. Econ. Statist.*, February 1983, *65*(1), pp. 124–30. **[G: U.S.]**

Roley, V. Vance. The Response of Short-Term Interest Rates to Weekly Money Announcements. *J. Money, Credit, Banking*, August 1983, *15*(3), pp. 344–54. **[G: U.S.]**

Rotemberg, Julio J. Monetary Policy and Costs of Price Adjustment. *J. Econ. Dynam. Control*, May 1983, *5*(2/3), pp. 267–88.

Rotemberg, Julio J. Supply Shocks, Sticky Prices, and Monetary Policy. *J. Money, Credit, Banking*, November 1983, *15*(4), pp. 489–98.

Roth, Jean-Pierre. The Setting of Monetary Objectives in Germany: The Implementation of Monetary Objectives in Germany—Open Market Operations and Credit Facilities: Comment. **In** *Meek, P., ed.*, 1983, pp. 30–31. **[G: W. Germany; Switzerland]**

Rugina, Anghel N. What Is the Alternative for the East? Neither Orthodox Marxism nor Capitalism but "Liberal Socialism." *Int. J. Soc. Econ.*, 1983, *10*(4), pp. 3–67.

Saïdi, Nasser and Swoboda, Alexander. Nominal and Real Exchange Rates: Issues and Some Evidence. **In** *Claassen, E. and Salin, P., eds.*, 1983, pp. 3–27. **[G: Selected OECD]**

Saint-Etienne, Christian. L'offre et la demande de monnaie dans la France de l'entre-deux-guerres (1920–1939). (Supply and Demand of Money in France in the Interwar Period (1920–1939). With English summary.) *Revue Écon.*, March 1983, *34*(2), pp. 344–67. **[G: France]**

Salerno, Joseph T. Gold Standards: True and False. *Cato J.*, Spring 1983, *3*(1), pp. 239–67. **[G: U.S.]**

Salvas-Bronsard, Lise. Grandmont et la théorie de la valeur. (Grandmont and the Theory of Value: A Review Article. With English summary.) *L'Actual. Econ.*, March 1983, *59*(1), pp. 108–20.

Sargent, Thomas J. Dollarization in Mexico: Causes and Consequences: Comment. **In** *Armella, P. A.; Dornbusch, R. and Obstfeld, M., eds.*, 1983, pp. 95–106.

Sargent, Thomas J. and Wallace, Neil. A Model of Commodity Money. *J. Monet. Econ.*, July 1983, *12*(1), pp. 163–87.

Schiltknecht, Kurt. Switzerland: The Pursuit of Monetary Objectives. **In** *Meek, P., ed.*, 1983, pp. 72–79. **[G: Switzerland]**

Schnitzel, Paul. Testing for the Direction of Causation between the Domestic Monetary Base and the Eurodollar System. *Weltwirtsch. Arch.*, 1983, *119*(4), pp. 616–29.

Seccareccia, Mario S. A Reconsideration of the Underlying Structuralist Explanation of Price Movements in Keynes' 'Treatise on Money.' *Eastern Econ. J.*, July–September 1983, *9*(3), pp. 272–83. **[G: Canada]**

Seers, Dudley. Structuralism vs Monetarism in Latin America: A Reappraisal of a Great Debate, with Lessons for Europe in the 1980s. **In** *Jansen, K., ed.*, 1983, pp. 110–26. **[G: Latin America]**

Selden, Richard T. The Inflationary Seventies: Comparisons among Selected High-income Countries. **In** *Schmukler, N. and Marcus, E., eds.*, 1983, pp. 721–41. **[G: OECD]**

Shackle, George L. S. Levels of Simplicity in Keynes's Theory of Money and Employment. *S. Afr. J. Econ.*, September 1983, *51*(3), pp. 357–67.

Shafer, Jeffrey R. Why Have Short-Term Interest Rates Been So High? Comments and Discussion. *Brookings Pap. Econ. Act.*, 1983, (2), pp. 579–85. **[G: U.S.]**

Shaller, Douglas R. Working Capital Finance Considerations in a National Income Theory. *Amer. Econ. Rev.*, March 1983, *73*(1), pp. 156–65.

Sheehan, Richard G. Money–Income Causality: Results for Six Countries. *J. Macroecon.*, Fall 1983, *5*(4), pp. 473–94. **[G: OECD]**

Sheikh, M. A.; Grady, P. and Lapointe, P.-H. The Effectiveness of Fiscal Policy in a Keynesian–Monetarist Model of Canada. *Empirical Econ.*, 1983, *8*(3–4), pp. 139–68. **[G: Canada]**

Shiller, Robert J. The Roles of Money and Credit in Macroeconomic Analysis: Comment. **In** *Tobin, J., ed.*, 1983, pp. 193–99. **[G: U.S.]**

Shimamoto, Reiichi. Monetary Control in Japan. **In**

Meek, P., ed., 1983, pp. 80–85. **[G: Japan]**

Shoshan, Boaz. Money Supply and Grain Prices in Fifteenth-Century Egypt. *Econ. Hist. Rev., 2nd Ser.*, February 1983, *36*(1), pp. 47–67. **[G: Egypt]**

Siddiqi, Muhammad Nejatullah. Economics of Profit-sharing. **In** *Siddiqi, M. N.*, 1983, pp. 97–123.

Siddiqi, Muhammad Nejatullah. Islamic Approaches to Money, Banking and Monetary Policy. **In** *Siddiqi, M. N.*, 1983, pp. 15–50.

Siddiqi, Muhammad Nejatullah. Monetary Theory of Islamic Economics. **In** *Siddiqi, M. N.*, 1983, pp. 125–31.

Siegel, Jeremy J. Operational Interest Rate Rules. *Amer. Econ. Rev.*, December 1983, *73*(5), pp. 1102–09.

Siegel, Jeremy J. Technological Change and the Superneutrality of Money. *J. Money, Credit, Banking*, August 1983, *15*(3), pp. 363–67.

Sievert, Olaf. Disillusionment in the Conduct of Exchange-Rate Policies. **In** *[Giersch, H.]*, 1983, pp. 188–208. **[G: OECD; W. Germany]**

Sijben, Jacques J. A Fixed Monetary-Growth Rule: Theoretical Foundations and Recent Experiences. *De Economist*, 1983, *131*(2), pp. 217–55. **[G: W. Germany; Switzerland; U.K.; U.S.]**

Simos, Evangelos O. and Triantis, John E. Human Wealth and Price Variability in the Demand for Money: U.S. Post-War Evidence. *Econ. Notes*, 1983, (2), pp. 161–74. **[G: U.S.]**

Sims, Christopher A. Is There a Monetary Business Cycle? *Amer. Econ. Rev.*, May 1983, *73*(2), pp. 228–33.

Singleton, Kenneth J. Real and Nominal Factors in the Cyclical Behavior of Interest Rates, Output, and Money. *J. Econ. Dynam. Control*, May 1983, *5*(2/3), pp. 289–309. **[G: U.S.]**

Sinha, Narain. Determination of Money Supply and Interest Rates in the Indian Economy. *Indian Econ. J.*, July–September 1983, *31*(1), pp. 51–64. **[G: India]**

Sinn, Hans-Werner. International Capital Movements, Flexible Exchange Rates, and the IS-LM Model: A Comparison between the Portfolio-Balance and the Flow Hypotheses. *Weltwirtsch. Arch.*, 1983, *119*(1), pp. 36–63.

Slovin, Myron B. and Sushka, Marie Elizabeth. Money, Interest Rates, and Risk. *J. Monet. Econ.*, September 1983, *12*(3), pp. 475–82. **[G: U.S.]**

Slovin, Myron B. and Sushka, Marie Elizabeth. The Stability of the Demand for Money: The Case of the Corporate Sector. *J. Macroecon.*, Summer 1983, *5*(3), pp. 361–72. **[G: U.S.]**

Smith, Bruce D. Limited Information, Credit Rationing, and Optimal Government Lending Policy. *Amer. Econ. Rev.*, June 1983, *73*(3), pp. 305–18.

Smithin, John Nicholas. A Note on the Welfare Cost of Perfectly Anticipated Inflation. *Bull. Econ. Res.*, May 1983, *35*(1), pp. 65–69.

Smyth, David J. The Effect of an Autonomous Expenditure Increase on the Excess Demand for Money. *Atlantic Econ. J.*, March 1983, *11*(1), pp. 64–67.

Solow, Robert M. Keynes and the Management of Real National Income and Expenditure: Comment. **In** *Worswick, D. and Trevithick, J., eds.*, 1983, pp. 162–68.

Spinelli, Franco. Fixed Exchange Rates and Adaptive Expectations Monetarism: The Italian Case. *Rev. Econ. Cond. Italy*, February 1983, (1), pp. 97–124. **[G: Italy]**

Sprinkel, Beryl W. Can the Fed Control Money? *Cato J.*, Spring 1983, *3*(1), pp. 155–62. **[G: U.S.]**

Stammer, D. W. and Valentine, T. J. Inflation and the Financial System. **In** *Pagan, A. R. and Trivedi, P. K., eds.*, 1983, pp. 183–219. **[G: Australia]**

Stanhouse, Bryan E. Stochastic Reserve Losses, Bank Credit Expansion and Bayesian Information. *J. Monet. Econ.*, August 1983, *12*(2), pp. 321–30.

Startz, Richard. Competition and Interest Rate Ceilings in Commercial Banking. *Quart. J. Econ.*, May 1983, *98*(2), pp. 255–65.

Steigmann, A. John. What Price Disinflation. *Bus. Econ.*, January 1983, *18*(1), pp. 59–61. **[G: U.S.]**

Stephens, J. Kirker. Money and Output: Some Surprising Results. *Atlantic Econ. J.*, December 1983, *11*(4), pp. 78.

Stiglitz, Joseph E. On the Relevance or Irrelevance of Public Financial Policy: Indexation, Price Rigidities, and Optimal Monetary Policies. **In** *Dornbusch, R. and Simonsen, M. H., eds.*, 1983, pp. 183–222.

Stockman, Alan C. Optimal Fiduciary Monetary Systems: Comments. *J. Monet. Econ.*, July 1983, *12*(1), pp. 51–54.

Stockman, Alan C. Real Exchange Rates under Alternative Nominal Exchange-Rate Systems. *J. Int. Money Finance*, August 1983, *2*(2), pp. 147–66. **[G: Global]**

Stockman, Alan C. The Use of Monetary Policy for Internal and External Balance in Ten Industrial Countries: Comment. **In** *Frenkel, J. A., ed.*, 1983, pp. 229–33. **[G: OECD]**

Suddards, C. G. The Behaviour of Building Societies and the Variability of the Mortgage Rate. *S. Afr. J. Econ.*, December 1983, *51*(4), pp. 530–43. **[G: U.K.; S. Africa]**

Summers, Lawrence H. The Nonadjustment of Nominal Interest Rates: A Study of the Fisher Effect. **In** *Tobin, J., ed.*, 1983, pp. 204–41. **[G: U.S.]**

Sundaresan, Mahadevan. Constant Absolute Risk Aversion Preferences and Constant Equilibrium Interest Rates. *J. Finance*, March 1983, *38*(1), pp. 205–12.

Sundell, Paul A. The Adjustment of Nominal Interest Rates to Inflation: A Review of Recent Literature. *Agr. Econ. Res.*, October 1983, *35*(4), pp. 15–26. **[G: U.S.]**

Symons, J. S. V. Money and the Real Interest Rate in the U.K. *Manchester Sch. Econ. Soc. Stud.*, September 1983, *51*(3), pp. 250–65. **[G: U.K.]**

Tang, De-piao and Hu, Teh-wei. Money, Prices, and Causality: The Chinese Hyperinflation, 1945–49. *J. Macroecon.*, Fall 1983, *5*(4), pp. 503–10. **[G: China]**

Tanzi, Vito. Expected Inflation and Interest Rates: Comment. *Amer. Econ. Rev.*, June 1983, *73*(3), pp. 501–02.

Taslim, Mohammad Ali. Aid-Elasticity of Demand for Money in Bangladesh. *Indian Econ. Rev.*,

July–December 1983, *18*(2), pp. 285–91. **[G: Bangladesh]**

Tatom, John A. Was the 1982 Velocity Decline Unusual? *Fed. Res. Bank St. Louis Rev.*, August/September 1983, *65*(7), pp. 5–15. **[G: U.S.]**

Taylor, John B. Rules, Discretion and Reputation in a Model of Monetary Policy: Comments. *J. Monet. Econ.*, July 1983, *12*(1), pp. 123–25.

Temin, Peter. Monetary Trends and Other Phenomena. *J. Econ. Hist.*, September 1983, *43*(3), pp. 729–39. **[G: U.S.]**

Thornton, Daniel L. Bank Money, Net Wealth, and the Real-Balance Effect. *J. Macroecon.*, Winter 1983, *5*(1), pp. 105–17.

Thornton, Daniel L. Lagged and Contemporaneous Reserve Accounting: An Alternative View. *Fed. Res. Bank St. Louis Rev.*, November 1983, *65*(9), pp. 26–33. **[G: U.S.]**

Thygesen, Niels. What Are the Scope and Limits of Fruitful International Monetary Cooperation in the 1980s? Comment. **In** *von Furstenberg, G. M., ed.*, 1983, pp. 419–28.

Tillmann, Georg. Existence of a Temporary Equilibrium in a Three-Commodity Model. *Rev. Econ. Stud.*, July 1983, *50*(3), pp. 573–79.

Timberlake, Richard H., Jr. Methodological Considerations in Demand-for-Money Construction. *Kredit Kapital*, 1983, *16*(3), pp. 381–93.

Tobin, James. Liquidity Preference as Behaviour towards Risk. **In** *Archer, S. H. and D'Ambrosia, C. A.*, 1983, *1958*, pp. 101–25.

Tobin, James. Monetary Policy: Rules, Targets, and Shocks. *J. Money, Credit, Banking*, November 1983, *15*(4), pp. 506–18.

Tobin, James. Unemployment, Interest and Money. **In** *Sanford, T., ed.*, 1983, pp. 1–25. **[G: U.S.]**

Tonveronachi, Mario. Friedman and Schwartz on Monetary Trends in the USA and the UK from 1867 to 1975: A First Assessment. *Banca Naz. Lavoro Quart. Rev.*, June 1983, (145), pp. 117–42. **[G: U.S.; U.K.]**

Townsend, Robert M. Financial Structure and Economic Activity. *Amer. Econ. Rev.*, December 1983, *73*(5), pp. 895–911.

Townsend, Robert M. Reply to John Long's Comments [Theories of Intermediated Structures]. *Carnegie-Rochester Conf. Ser. Public Policy*, Spring 1983, *18*, pp. 279–80.

Townsend, Robert M. Theories of Intermediated Structures. *Carnegie-Rochester Conf. Ser. Public Policy*, Spring 1983, *18*, pp. 221–72.

Tracy, Ronald L. and Trescott, Paul B. Monetary Policy and Inflation in the United States, 1912–1978: Evidence from Monthly Data. **In** *Schmukler, N. and Marcus, E., eds.*, 1983, pp. 205–25. **[G: U.S.]**

Vaciago, Giacomo. Methods of Monetary Control in Italy: 1974–1983: Discussion. **In** *Hodgman, D. R., ed.*, 1983, pp. 89–92. **[G: Italy]**

Vanderhoff, James. Support for Rational Expectations Models with U.S. Data. *J. Monet. Econ.*, August 1983, *12*(2), pp. 297–308. **[G: U.S.]**

VanHoose, David D. Monetary Policy under Alternative Bank: Market Structures. *J. Banking Finance*, September 1983, *7*(3), pp. 383–404. **[G: U.S.]**

Vogel, Robert C. Implementing Interest Rate Reform. **In** *Von Pischke, J. D.; Adams, D. W. and Donald, G., eds.*, 1983, pp. 387–92.

Wallace, Neil. A Comment on McCallum [The Role of Overlapping-Generations Models in Monetary Economics]. *Carnegie-Rochester Conf. Ser. Public Policy*, Spring 1983, *18*, pp. 51–56.

Wallace, Neil. A Legal Restrictions Theory of the Demand for "Money" and the Role of Monetary Policy. *Fed. Res. Bank Minn. Rev.*, Winter 1983, *7*(1), pp. 1–7. **[G: U.S.]**

Wallich, Henry C. Statement to the U.S. House Subcommittee on Domestic Monetary Policy of the Committee on Banking, Finance and Urban Affairs, October 5, 1983. *Fed. Res. Bull.*, October 1983, *69*(10), pp. 776–81. **[G: U.S.]**

Watson, Mark W. Imperfect Information and Wage Inertia in the Business Cycle: A Comment. *J. Polit. Econ.*, October 1983, *91*(5), pp. 876–79.

Webb, Steven B. Money Demand and Expectations in the German Hyperinflation: A Survey of the Models. **In** *Schmukler, N. and Marcus, E., eds.*, 1983, pp. 435–49.

Weintraub, Robert E. What Type of Monetary Rule? *Cato J.*, Spring 1983, *3*(1), pp. 171–83. **[G: U.S.]**

Weissenberger, Edgar and Thomas, J. J. The Causal Role of Money in West Germany. *Weltwirtsch. Arch.*, 1983, *119*(1), pp. 64–83. **[G: W. Germany]**

Wells, Curt. A Reconsideration of the Causal Relationship between Money and Prices in Sweden, 1871–1970. *Scand. J. Econ.*, 1983, *85*(3), pp. 425–32. **[G: Sweden]**

Wells, Paul. A Post Keynesian View of Liquidity Preference and the Demand for Money. *J. Post Keynesian Econ.*, Summer 1983, *5*(4), pp. 523–36.

Wette, Hildegard C. Collateral in Credit Rationing in Markets with Imperfect Information: Note. *Amer. Econ. Rev.*, June 1983, *73*(3), pp. 442–45.

White, Lawrence H. Competitive Money, Inside and Out. *Cato J.*, Spring 1983, *3*(1), pp. 281–99.

van Wijnbergen, Sweder. Credit Policy, Inflation and Growth in a Financially Repressed Economy. *J. Devel. Econ.*, Aug.–Oct. 1983, *13*(1–2), pp. 45–65.

van Wijnbergen, Sweder. Interest Rate Management in LDCs. *J. Monet. Econ.*, September 1983, *12*(3), pp. 433–52. **[G: LDCs]**

Wilcox, James A. The Missing Fisher Effect on Nominal Interest Rates in the 1950s. *Rev. Econ. Statist.*, November 1983, *65*(4), pp. 644–47. **[G: U.S.]**

Wilcox, James A. Why Real Interest Rates Were So Low in the 1970's. *Amer. Econ. Rev.*, March 1983, *73*(1), pp. 44–53. **[G: U.S.]**

Willms, Manfred. The Monetary Policy Decision Process in the Federal Republic of Germany. **In** *Hodgman, D. R., ed.*, 1983, pp. 34–58. **[G: W. Germany]**

Wood, John H. Interest Rates and Inflation: An Old and Unexplained Relationship. *Fed. Res. Bank Dallas Econ. Rev.*, January 1983, pp. 11–23. **[G: U.S.]**

Woodward, Susan E. The Liquidity Premium and the Solidity Premium. *Amer. Econ. Rev.*, June 1983, *73*(3), pp. 348–61.

Yeager, Leland B. Stable Money and Free-Market

Currencies. *Cato J.*, Spring 1983, *3*(1), pp. 305–26.

Yoo, Jang H. and Kim, In Kie. Aggregate Supply and the Productivity of Money—A Transaction Cost Approach. *J. Econ. Devel.*, December 1983, *8*(2), pp. 25–44.

Zinn, Karl Georg. Zyklus, Stabilität und Geldneutralität. Ein lehrgeschichtliche Ergänzung zum Problem der potentialorientierten Geldpolitik auf der Grundlage von Schumpeters Entwicklungstheorie. (Business Cycle, Stability, and Neutral Money. With English summary.) *Konjunkturpolitik*, 1983, *29*(6), pp. 329–47.

3116 Monetary Policy, Including All Central Banking Topics

Aftalion, Florin. The Political Economy of French Monetary Policy. In *Hodgman, D. R., ed.*, 1983, pp. 7–25. **[G: France]**

Allen, Stuart D. and Smith, Michael D. Government Borrowing and Monetary Accommodation. *J. Monet. Econ.*, November 1983, *12*(4), pp. 605–16. **[G: U.S.]**

Androsch, Hannes. Sul ruolo della banca nell'ambito della politica economica. (The Role of Banking in Economic Policy. With English summary.) *Bancaria*, August 1983, *39*(8), pp. 695–701.

Argy, Victor. France's Experience with Monetary and Exchange Rate Management: March 1973 to End-1981. *Banca Naz. Lavoro Quart. Rev.*, December 1983, (147), pp. 387–411. **[G: France]**

Arnaudo, Aldo A. Posibilidades de una política monetaria monetarista en una economía inflacionaría: Argentina 1978–1981. (The Feasibility of a Monetarist Monetary Policy in an Inflationary Economy: Argentina, 1978–1981. With English summary.) *Económica*, January–April 1983, *29*(1), pp. 3–25. **[G: Argentina]**

Artus, Jacques R. Toward a More Orderly Exchange Rate System. *Finance Develop.*, March 1983, *20*(1), pp. 10–13. **[G: U.K.; U.S.; France; Japan; W. Germany]**

Atkinson, P. E.; Blundell-Wignall, A. and Chouraqui, J.-C. Budget Financing and Monetary Targets, with Special Reference to the Seven Major OECD Countries. *Écon. Soc.*, July-August 1983, *17*(7–8), pp. 1057–96. **[G: OECD]**

Axilrod, Stephen H. Monetary Policy, Money Supply, and the Federal Reserve's Operating Procedures. In *Meek, P., ed.*, 1983, pp. 32–41. **[G: U.S.]**

Bacha, Edmar L. A Critique of Southern Cone Monetarism. *Int. Soc. Sci. J.*, 1983, *35*(3), pp. 413–23. **[G: Argentina; Chile; Uruguay]**

Banaian, King; Laney, Leroy O. and Willett, Thomas D. Central Bank Independence: An International Comparison. *Fed. Res. Bank Dallas Econ. Rev.*, March 1983, pp. 1–13. **[G: OECD]**

Basevi, Giorgio and Calzolari, Michele. Monetary Authorities' Reaction Functions in a Model of Exchange-Rate Determination for the European Monetary System. In *De Grauwe, P. and Peeters, T., eds.*, 1983, pp. 267–82. **[G: EEC]**

Basevi, Giorgio; Calzolari, Michele and Colombo, Caterina. Monetary Authorities' Reaction Functions and the European Monetary System. In *Hodgman, D. R., ed.*, 1983, pp. 228–44. **[G: France; Netherlands; W. Germany; Italy; Belgium]**

Batavia, Bala and Lash, Nicholas A. Self-Perpetuating "Inflation": The Case of Turkey. *J. Econ. Devel.*, December 1983, *8*(2), pp. 149–66. **[G: Turkey]**

Batchelor, R. A. British Economic Policy under Margaret Thatcher: A Mid Term Examination: A Comment on Darby and Lothian. *Carnegie-Rochester Conf. Ser. Public Policy*, Spring 1983, *18*, pp. 209–19. **[G: U.K.]**

Batten, Dallas S. and Thornton, Daniel L. M1 or M2: Which Is the Better Monetary Target? *Fed. Res. Bank St. Louis Rev.*, June/July 1983, *65*(6), pp. 36–42. **[G: U.S.]**

Beebe, Jack H. Bank Capital Risk in the Post-1979 Monetary and Deregulatory Environment. *Fed. Res. Bank San Francisco Econ. Rev.*, Summer 1983, (3), pp. 7–18. **[G: U.S.]**

Beers, David T.; Sargent, Thomas J. and Wallace, Neil. Speculations about the Speculation against the Hong Kong Dollar. *Fed. Res. Bank Minn. Rev.*, Fall 1983, *7*(4), pp. 14–22. **[G: Hong Kong]**

Béguelin, Jean-Pierre; Büttler, Hans-Jürg and Schiltknecht, Kurt. A First Look at Entropy, Monetary Policy, and Expected Inflation Rates in the Determination of Exchange Rates. *Z. Nationalökon.*, Supplement 3, 1983, *43*, pp. 205–20. **[G: Switzerland; Germany; U.S.]**

Bennett, Paul. Reactions to Discount Rate Cuts. *Fed. Res. Bank New York Quart. Rev.*, Autumn 1983, *8*(3), pp. 25–26. **[G: U.S.]**

Benston, George J. Federal Regulation of Banking: Analysis and Policy Recommendations. *J. Bank Res.*, Winter 1983, *13*(4), pp. 216–44. **[G: U.S.]**

Berti, Gian Luigi. Il sistema monetario e la moneta d'oro di San Marino. (The Monetary System and the Gold Coin of San Marino. With English summary.) *Bancaria*, March 1983, *39*(3), pp. 259–78. **[G: Italy; San Marino]**

Bisignano, Joseph. Monetary Policy Regimes and International Term Structures of Interest Rates. *Fed. Res. Bank San Francisco Econ. Rev.*, Fall 1983, (4), pp. 7–26. **[G: U.S.; Canada; W. Germany]**

Bomhoff, Edward J. and Korteweg, Pieter. Exchange Rate Variability and Monetary Policy under Rational Expectations: Some Euro-American Experience, 1973–1979. *J. Monet. Econ.*, March 1983, *11*(2), pp. 169–206. **[G: U.S.; EEC]**

Boughton, James M. Alternatives to Intervention: Domestic Instruments and External Objectives. In *Hodgman, D. R., ed.*, 1983, pp. 313–30.

Bradfield, Michael. Statement to U.S. House Subcommittee on Commerce, Consumer, and Monetary Affairs of the Committee on Government Operations, July 21, 1983. *Fed. Res. Bull.*, August 1983, *69*(8), pp. 609–17. **[G: U.S.]**

Brimmer, Andrew F. Monetary Policy and Inflationary Expectations. *Challenge*, March/April 1983, *26*(1), pp. 32–35. **[G: U.S.]**

Brittan, Samuel. Breaking the Mould. In *Brittan, S.*, 1983, pp. 239–63. **[G: U.K.]**

Brown, Donald M. Bank Holding Company Performance Studies and the Public Interest: Normative Uses for Positive Analysis? *Fed. Res. Bank St. Louis Rev.*, March 1983, *65*(3), pp. 26–34. **[G: U.S.]**

Bryant, Ralph C. Eurocurrency Banking: Alarmist Concerns and Genuine Issues. *OECD Econ. Stud.*, Autumn 1983, (1), pp. 7–41. **[G: W. Europe]**

Butlin, S. J. Australian Central Banking, 1945–59. *Australian Econ. Hist. Rev.*, September 1983, *23*(2), pp. 95–192. **[G: Australia]**

Cachin, Antoine. La politique française de déconnexion des taux d'intérêt. (With English summary.) *Revue Écon. Polit.*, September–October 1983, *93*(5), pp. 732–39. **[G: France]**

de Camargo Vidigal, Geraldo. Monetary Correction in Bank Contracts. **In** *de Ulhôa Canto, G.; da Silva Martins, I. G. and van Hoorn, J., Jr., eds.*, 1983, pp. 136–51. **[G: Brazil]**

Capra, James R. Federal Deficits and Private Credit Demands: Economic Impact Analysis. *Fed. Res. Bank New York Quart. Rev.*, Summer 1983, *8*(2), pp. 29–44. **[G: U.S.]**

Caranza, Cesare and Fazio, Antonio. Methods of Monetary Control in Italy: 1974–1983. **In** *Hodgman, D. R., ed.*, 1983, pp. 65–88. **[G: Italy]**

Carlson, Keith M. and Hein, Scott E. Four Econometric Models and Monetary Policy: The Longer-Run View. *Fed. Res. Bank St. Louis Rev.*, January 1983, *65*(1), pp. 13–24. **[G: U.S.]**

de Cecco, Marcello. Political Factors in Monetary Policy: Discussion. **In** *Hodgman, D. R., ed.*, 1983, pp. 204–05. **[G: U.K.; France; W. Germany]**

Chapra, M. Umer. Elimination of Interest from the Economy: Report: Comment. **In** *Ahmed, Z.; Iqbal, M. and Khan, M. F., eds.*, 1983, pp. 212–23. **[G: Pakistan]**

Cheng, Hang-Sheng. Financial Reform in Australia and New Zealand. *Fed. Res. Bank San Francisco Econ. Rev.*, Winter 1983, (1), pp. 9–24. **[G: Australia; New Zealand]**

Chisholm, Derek. La Banque du Canada était-elle nécessaire? (Was the Bank of Canada Really Necessary? With English summary.) *L'Actual. Econ.*, September 1983, *59*(3), pp. 551–74.

Ciampi, Carlo Azeglio. Coordinamento internazionale della vigilanza ed efficienza del sistema bancario. (International Coordination of the Supervision, and Efficiency of the Banking System. With English summary.) *Bancaria*, March 1983, *39*(3), pp. 233–36. **[G: Italy]**

Ciampi, Carlo Azeglio. Le scelte da compiere per una ripresa nella stabilità. (Choices for Achievement of Recovery with Stability. With English summary.) *Bancaria*, February 1983, *39*(2), pp. 115–30. **[G: Italy]**

Cingano, Francesco. L'intermediazione bancaria: limiti operativi attuali e prospettive di ampliamento funzionale (Banking Intermediation: Present Operational Limits and Prospects for Enlargement of Role. With English summary.) *Bancaria*, February 1983, *39*(2), pp. 147–53. **[G: Italy]**

Coes, Donald V. Exchange Market Intervention in Four European Countries. **In** *Hodgman, D. R., ed.*, 1983, pp. 206–22. **[G: France; W. Germany; U.K.; Italy]**

Coleby, A. L. The Bank of England's Operational Procedures for Meeting Monetary Objectives. **In** *Meek, P., ed.*, 1983, pp. 60–67. **[G: U.K.]**

Cooper, Richard N. International Aspects of U.S. Monetary and Fiscal Policy: Discussion. **In** *Federal Reserve Bank of Boston*, 1983, pp. 134–37. **[G: U.S.; OECD]**

Corrigan, E. Gerald. Statement to U.S. House Subcommittee on Domestic Monetary Policy of the Committee on Banking, Finance and Urban Affairs and the Subcommittee on Commerce, Consumer, and Monetary Affairs of the Committee on Government Operations, June 16, 1983. *Fed. Res. Bull.*, July 1983, *69*(7), pp. 524–31. **[G: U.S.]**

Costi, Renzo. Riflessioni in tema di enti creditizi pubblici. (Public Credit Institutions. With English summary.) *Bancaria*, July 1983, *39*(7), pp. 581–92. **[G: Italy]**

Craven, Barrie M. and Wright, Grahame A. The Thatcher Experiment. *J. Macroecon.*, Winter 1983, *5*(1), pp. 21–40. **[G: U.K.]**

Cross, Sam Y. Treasury and Federal Reserve Foreign Exchange Operations. *Fed. Res. Bank New York Quart. Rev.*, Summer 1983, *8*(2), pp. 45–49. **[G: U.S.]**

Cross, Sam Y. Treasury and Federal Reserve Foreign Exchange Operations. *Fed. Res. Bank New York Quart. Rev.*, Spring 1983, *8*(1), pp. 55–78. **[G: U.S.]**

Cross, Sam Y. Treasury and Federal Reserve Foreign Exchange Operations. *Fed. Res. Bank New York Quart. Rev.*, Autumn 1983, *8*(3), pp. 48–68. **[G: U.S.]**

Cross, Sam Y. Treasury and Federal Reserve Foreign Exchange Operations. *Fed. Res. Bank New York Quart. Rev.*, Winter 1983-84, *8*(4), pp. 71–74. **[G: U.S.]**

Cross, Sam Y. Treasury and Federal Reserve Foreign Exchange Operations. *Fed. Res. Bull.*, March 1983, *69*(3), pp. 141–63. **[G: U.S.]**

Cross, Sam Y. Treasury and Federal Reserve Foreign Exchange Operations. *Fed. Res. Bull.*, September 1983, *69*(9), pp. 672–92. **[G: U.S.]**

Cross, Sam Y. Treasury and Federal Reserve Foreign Exchange Operations: Interim Report. *Fed. Res. Bull.*, December 1983, *69*(12), pp. 893–95. **[G: U.S.]**

Cross, Sam Y. Treasury and Federal Reserve Foreign Exchange Operations: Interim Report. *Fed. Res. Bull.*, June 1983, *69*(6), pp. 404–08. **[G: U.S.]**

Cumby, Robert E. and Obstfeld, Maurice. Capital Mobility and the Scope for Sterilization: Mexico in the 1970s. **In** *Armella, P. A.; Dornbusch, R. and Obstfeld, M., eds.*, 1983, pp. 245–69. **[G: Mexico]**

Darby, Michael R. and Lothian, James R. British Economic Policy under Margaret Thatcher: A Midterm Examination. *Carnegie-Rochester Conf. Ser. Public Policy*, Spring 1983, *18*, pp. 157–207. **[G: U.K.]**

Davis, Richard G. The United Kingdom—Setting Monetary Objectives: The Bank of England's Operational Procedures for Meeting Monetary Objectives: Comment. **In** *Meek, P., ed.*, 1983, pp. 68–69. **[G: U.K.]**

Davis, Richard G. and Meek, Paul. Monetary Targeting—Variations on a Common Theme. In *Meek, P., ed.*, 1983, pp. 1–5. [G: OECD]

De Grauwe, Paul and Frattianni, Michele. U.S. Economic Policies: Are They a Burden on the Rest of the World? *Econ. Notes*, 1983, (3), pp. 69–85. [G: OECD]

DeAntoni, Elisabetta. Andamento dei depositi ed emissioni di titoli: Alcume riflessioni in tema di disintermediazione bancaria e concorrenza del Tesoro. (The Trend of Deposits and Issuance of Securities: On Banking Disintermediation and Treasury Competition. With English summary.) *Bancaria*, April 1983, *39*(4), pp. 389–401. [G: Italy]

Dickman, A. B. Market-Orientated Policies and Financial Markets. *S. Afr. J. Econ.*, December 1983, *51*(4), pp. 467–85. [G: S. Africa]

Dini, Lamberto. Il trattamento delle crisi bancarie in Italia. (Handling of Bank Crisis in Italy. With English summary.) *Bancaria*, May–June 1983, *39*(5–6), pp. 471–76. [G: Italy]

Dudler, Hermann-Josef. The Implementation of Monetary Objectives in Germany—Open Market Operations and Credit Facilities. In *Meek, P., ed.*, 1983, pp. 18–29. [G: W. Germany]

Dudler, Hermann-Josef. The Monetary Policy Decision Process in the Federal Republic of Germany: Discussion. In *Hodgman, D. R., ed.*, 1983, pp. 59–64. [G: W. Germany]

Duesenberry, James S. The Political Economy of Central Banking in the United States or Quis Custodiet Ipsos Custodes. In *Hodgman, D. R., ed.*, 1983, pp. 123–40. [G: U.S.]

Eckstein, Otto. International Aspects of U.S. Monetary and Fiscal Policy: Discussion. In *Federal Reserve Bank of Boston*, 1983, pp. 138–40. [G: U.S.; OECD]

Eisenmenger, Robert W. Alternatives to Intervention: Domestic Instruments and External Objectives: Discussion. In *Hodgman, D. R., ed.*, 1983, pp. 331–35.

Fforde, John. The United Kingdom—Setting Monetary Objectives. In *Meek, P., ed.*, 1983, pp. 51–59. [G: U.K.]

Ffrench-Davis, Ricardo. The Monetarist Experiment in Chile: A Critical Survey. *World Devel.*, November 1983, *11*(11), pp. 905–26. [G: Chile]

Fieleke, Norman S. Exchange Market Intervention in Four European Countries: Discussion. In *Hodgman, D. R., ed.*, 1983, pp. 223–27. [G: France; U.K.; W. Germany; Italy]

Figlewski, Stephen and Urich, Thomas. Optimal Aggregation of Money Supply Forecasts: Accuracy, Profitability and Market Efficiency. *J. Finance*, June 1983, *38*(3), pp. 695–710. [G: U.S.]

Frenkel, Jacob A. Capital Mobility and the Scope for Sterilization: Mexico in the 1970s: Comment. In *Armella, P. A.; Dornbusch, R. and Obstfeld, M., eds.*, 1983, pp. 269–76. [G: Mexico]

Frenkel, Jacob A. International Liquidity and Monetary Control. In *Kaushik, S. K., ed.*, 1983, pp. 31–72. [G: LDCs; MDCs]

Friedman, Milton. Monetary Variability: United States and Japan. *J. Money, Credit, Banking*, August 1983, *15*(3), pp. 339–43. [G: U.S.; Japan]

Furukawa, Akira. The Effectiveness of Lending Window Guidance and Well-Developed Open Money Market. (In Japanese. With English summary.) *Osaka Econ. Pap.*, March 1983, *32*(4), pp. 11–20. [G: Japan]

Gardner, Bruce L. Discussion [Governments and Agricultural Markets in Africa] [Why Do Governments Do What They Do? The Case of Food Price Policy]. In *Johnson, D. G. and Schuh, G. E., eds.*, 1983, pp. 219–26.

Garn, Jake. A View of the new Financial Environment. In *Sanford, T., ed.*, 1983, pp. 79–90. [G: U.S.]

Giles, R. Philip. United States: Banking, Money, and Bond Markets. In *George, A. M. and Giddy, I. H., eds., Vol. 1*, 1983, pp. 4.2:1–27. [G: U.S.]

Gillard, Etienne. Le revenu des Banques centrales: Un schéma simple sur sa formation et son affectation. (Central Bank Review: A Simple Framework or Where Does It Come from and Where Does It Go To. With English summary.) *Revue Écon.*, November 1983, *34*(6), pp. 1164–87. [G: France; U.S.]

Goldschmidt, Amnon. U.S. Banking Regulation and Foreign Banks' Entry into the United States: Comment. *J. Banking Finance*, 1983, *7*(4), pp. 581–82. [G: U.S.]

Goodhart, Charles A. E. Monetary Policy, Money Supply, and the Federal Reserve's Operating Procedures: Implementation of Federal Reserve Open Market Operations: Comment. In *Meek, P., ed.*, 1983, pp. 46–50. [G: U.K.; U.S.; Canada]

Goodhart, Charles A. E. The Monetary Policy Decision Process in the United Kingdom: Discussion. In *Hodgman, D. R., ed.*, 1983, pp. 114–22. [G: U.K.]

Goria, Giovanni. Rientro dall'inflazione, condizione per la ripresa dello sviluppo. (Reduction of Inflation, a Condition for the Return to Economic Growth in Italy. With English summary.) *Bancaria*, March 1983, *39*(3), pp. 237–41. [G: Italy]

Gorinson, Stanley M. Depository Institution Regulatory Reform in the 1980s: The Issue of Geographic Restrictions. *Antitrust Bull.*, Spring 1983, *28*(1), pp. 227–54. [G: U.S.]

Gowland, D. H. Techniques of Monetary Control. In *Gowland, D. H., ed.*, 1983, pp. 1–33. [G: U.K.]

Greenfield, Robert L. The Fed's Fallacious Account of Its Own Activities [Monetary Reform in an Uncertain Environment]. *Cato J.*, Spring 1983, *3*(1), pp. 113–20. [G: U.S.]

Grissa, Abdessatar. The French Monetary and Exchange Rate Experience in the 1920s. In *Claassen, E. and Salin, P., eds.*, 1983, pp. 261–80. [G: France]

Grubel, Herbert G. Interest Payments on Commercial Bank Reserves to Curb Euro-money Markets. In *[Giersch, H.]*, 1983, pp. 117–35. [G: OECD]

Hafer, R. W. Monetary Policy and the Price Rule: The Newest Odd Couple. *Fed. Res. Bank St. Louis Rev.*, February 1983, *65*(2), pp. 5–13. [G: U.S.]

Hafer, R. W. and Hein, Scott E. The Wayward Money Supply: A Post-Mortem of 1982. *Fed. Res. Bank St. Louis Rev.*, March 1983, *65*(3), pp. 17–25. [G: U.S.]

Halttunen, Hannu and Korkman, Sixten. External

Shocks and Adjustment Policies in Finland, 1973–80. In *de Cecco, M., ed.*, 1983, pp. 7–33. **[G: Finland]**

Hamberg, Daniel. Federal Reserve Policy Since 1979. *Banca Naz. Lavoro Quart. Rev.*, December 1983, (147), pp. 413–23. **[G: U.S.]**

Heymann, H. G. and Venkataraman, V. K. An Empirical Study of the Marginal Reserve Requirements and the Exchange Value of the Dollar. *Bus. Econ.*, May 1983, *18*(3), pp. 55–61. **[G: U.S.]**

Hixon, William F. A New Perspective on the Economic Crisis. *Eastern Econ. J.*, July–September 1983, *9*(3), pp. 221–31. **[G: U.S.]**

Hodgman, Donald R. and Resek, Robert W. Determinants of Monetary Policy in France, The Federal Republic of Germany, Italy and the United Kingdom: A Comparative Analysis. In *Hodgman, D. R., ed.*, 1983, pp. 147–70. **[G: U.K.; W. Germany; France; Italy]**

Hoehn, James G. Recent Monetary Control Procedures and the Response of Interest Rates to Fluctuations in Money Growth. *Fed. Res. Bank Dallas Econ. Rev.*, September 1983, pp. 1–10. **[G: U.S.]**

Hoffman, Dennis L.; Low, Stuart A. and Reineberg, Hubert H. Recent Evidence on the Relationship between Money Growth and Budget Deficits. *J. Macroecon.*, Spring 1983, *5*(2), pp. 223–31. **[G: U.S.]**

Holzmann, Robert and Winckler, Georg. Austrian Economic Policy: Some Theoretical and Critical Remarks on "Austro-Keynesianism." *Empirica*, 1983, (2), pp. 183–203. **[G: Austria]**

Horvitz, Paul M. Payments System Developments and Public Policy. In *Benston, G. J., ed.*, 1983, pp. 64–93. **[G: U.S.]**

Horvitz, Paul M. Reorganization of the Financial Regulatory Agencies. *J. Bank Res.*, Winter 1983, *13*(4), pp. 245–63. **[G: U.S.]**

Hotson, John H. What's Wrong with Mainstream Macroeconomics? *Eastern Econ. J.*, July–September 1983, *9*(3), pp. 246–57. **[G: U.S.]**

Hubbard, Carl M. Money Market Funds, Money Supply, and Monetary Control: A Note. *J. Finance*, September 1983, *38*(4), pp. 1305–10. **[G: U.S.]**

Irvine, Reed J. and Emery, Robert F. Interest Rates as an Anti-inflationary Instrument in Taiwan. In *Von Pischke, J. D.; Adams, D. W. and Donald, G., eds.*, 1983, pp. 393–97. **[G: Taiwan]**

Jaeger, Franz. Die Geldpolitik der Schweizerischen Nationalbank: Theoretische Fundierung und konkrete Ausgestaltung. (Swiss Monetary Policy. With English summary.) *Aussenwirtschaft*, September 1983, *38*(3), pp. 285–335. **[G: Switzerland]**

de Janvry, Alain. Why Do Governments Do What They Do? The Case of Food Price Policy. In *Johnson, D. G. and Schuh, G. E., eds.*, 1983, pp. 185–212. **[G: U.S.; India; Colombia; Egypt]**

Johannes, James M. and Rasche, Robert H. Analysis and Forecasts of Money Multiplier Behavior 1982–4. In *Shadow Open Market Committee.*, 1983, pp. 35–39. **[G: U.S.]**

Jordan, Jerry L. Monetary Policy Options and the Economic Outlook. In *Shadow Open Market Committee.*, 1983, pp. 29–34. **[G: U.S.]**

Karjalainen, Ahti. Keskuspankkipolitiikan mahdollisuudet ja rajoitukset. (The Scope for and Limits to Central Bank Policy. With English summary.) *Kansant. Aikak.*, 1983, *79*(2), pp. 149–54. **[G: Finland]**

Kaufman, Henry. Financial Institutions in Ferment. *Challenge*, May/June 1983, *26*(2), pp. 20–25. **[G: U.S.]**

Keating, Maryann O'Hagan and Keating, Barry P. A Test of the Federal Reserve's Degree of Domestic Money Stock Control, Given International Capital Flows and Fixed Exchange Rates. *Quart. Rev. Econ. Bus.*, Spring 1983, *23*(1), pp. 46–57. **[G: U.S.]**

Kincaid, G. Russell. What Are Credit Ceilings? *Finance Develop.*, March 1983, *20*(1), pp. 28–29.

Komlos, John H. The Diffusion of Financial Technology into the Austro-Hungarian Monarchy toward the End of the Nineteenth Century. In *Komlos, J., ed.*, 1983, pp. 137–63. **[G: Austria; Hungary]**

Krugman, Paul R. International Aspects of U.S. Monetary and Fiscal Policy. In *Federal Reserve Bank of Boston*, 1983, pp. 112–33. **[G: U.S.; OECD]**

Lamfalussy, Alexandre. Implications of Monetary Targeting for Exchange-rate Policy: Exchange-rate Management and the Conduct of Monetary Policy: Comment. In *Meek, P., ed.*, 1983, pp. 132–33. **[G: W. Germany; Japan]**

Laney, Leroy O. and Willett, Thomas D. Presidential Politics, Budget Deficits, and Monetary Policy in the United States; 1960–1976. *Public Choice*, 1983, *40*(1), pp. 53–69. **[G: U.S.]**

Langoni, Carlos Geraldo and Haddad, Claudio Luiz da Silva. The Implementation of Monetary Policy in Brazil in 1981. In *Meek, P., ed.*, 1983, pp. 86–99. **[G: Brazil]**

Lindblom, Seppo. Havaintoja maamme korkokeskustelusta ja korkoproblematiikasta. (The Discussion of the Interest Rate In Finland. With English summary.) *Kansant. Aikak.*, 1983, *79*(1), pp. 26–37. **[G: Finland]**

Lombra, Raymond E. and Moran, Michael. Policy Advice and Policymaking at the Federal Reserve. In *Brunner, K. and Meltzer, A. H., eds.*, 1983, *1980*, pp. 385–444. **[G: U.S.]**

Lopez Roa, A. L. Efectos de la crisis económica sobre el sistema financiero: el caso de España. (The Impact of Economic Crisis on the Financial System: The Spanish Case. With English summary.) *Écon. Soc.*, September–October–November 1983, *17*(9–10–11), pp. 1631–45. **[G: Spain]**

Lucia, Joseph L. Allan Sproul and the Treasury–Federal Reserve Accord, 1951. *Hist. Polit. Econ.*, Spring 1983, *15*(1), pp. 106–21.

Maier, Steven F. The Conflicting Roles of the Fed as a Regulator and a Competitor: Discussant's Comments. *J. Bank Res.*, Spring 1983, *14*(1), pp. 90–92. **[G: U.S.]**

Marsh, Terry A. and Rosenfeld, Eric R. Stochastic Processes for Interest Rates and Equilibrium Bond Prices. *J. Finance*, May 1983, *38*(2), pp. 635–46. **[G: U.S.]**

Martin, Preston. Statement to U.S. House Subcommittee on Administrative Law and Governmental Relations of the Committee on the Judiciary, July 14, 1983. *Fed. Res. Bull.*, August 1983, *69*(8), pp. 595–99. **[G: U.S.]**

März, Eduard and Weber, Fritz. The Reconstruction of the Credit-Anstalt: Commentary. **In** *Teichova, A. and Cottrell, P. L., eds.*, 1983, pp. 430–36. **[G: Austria]**

Mayhew, Anne. Ideology and the Great Depression: Monetary History Rewritten. *J. Econ. Issues,* June 1983, *17*(2), pp. 353–60. **[G: U.S.]**

McKinnon, Ronald I. Dollar Overvaluation against the Yen and Mark in 1983: How to Coordinate Central Bank Policies. *Aussenwirtschaft,* December 1983, *38*(4), pp. 357–72. **[G: Selected OECD; U.S.; Japan]**

Meek, Paul. The United Kingdom—Setting Monetary Objectives: The Bank of England's Operational Procedures for Meeting Monetary Objectives: Comment. **In** *Meek, P., ed.*, 1983, pp. 70–71. **[G: U.K.]**

Mehrling, Perry. Has Mrs. Thatcher Exorcised the Demons? *Challenge,* January/February 1983, *25*(6), pp. 57–60. **[G: U.K.]**

Meltzer, Allan H. Recent Behavior of Base Velocity. **In** *Shadow Open Market Committee.*, 1983, pp. 19–24.

Morris, Frank E. Monetarism without Money. *New Eng. Econ. Rev.*, March/April 1983, pp. 5–9. **[G: U.S.]**

Morris, Frank E. The Political Economy of Central Banking in the United States or Quis Custodiet Ipsos Custodes: Discussion. **In** *Hodgman, D. R., ed.*, 1983, pp. 141–44. **[G: U.S.]**

O'Brien of Lothbury [Lord]. Il problema dell'autonomia della banca centrale. (The Independence of Central Banks. With English summary.) *Bancaria,* January 1983, *39*(1), pp. 19–26. **[G: U.S.; U.K.; W. Germany]**

Ohta, Takeshi. Exchange-rate Management and the Conduct of Monetary Policy. **In** *Meek, P., ed.*, 1983, pp. 126–31. **[G: Japan]**

Okun, Arthur M. Monetary Policy, Debt Management and Interest Rates: A Quantitative Appraisal. **In** *Okun, A. M.*, 1983, *1963,* pp. 253–303. **[G: U.S.]**

Okun, Arthur M. The Conduct of Monetary Policy. **In** *Okun, A. M.*, 1983, *1975,* pp. 471–81. **[G: U.S.]**

Olsen, Leif H. Monetary Rules, Discretion, and the Constitution [What Type of Monetary Rule?]. *Cato J.*, Spring 1983, *3*(1), pp. 185–88. **[G: U.S.]**

Ortiz, Guillermo. Dollarization in Mexico: Causes and Consequences. **In** *Armella, P. A.; Dornbusch, R. and Obstfeld, M., eds.*, 1983, pp. 71–95. **[G: Mexico]**

Ortiz, Guillermo. The Implementation of Monetary Policy in Brazil in 1981: The Canadian Experience with Monetary Targeting: The Formulation and Implementation of Monetary Policy in France: Comment: **In** *Meek, P., ed.*, 1983, pp. 115–17. **[G: Mexico; Brazil; Canada; France]**

Paarlberg, Robert L. Discussion [Governments and Agricultural Markets in Africa] [Why Do Governments Do What They Do? The Case of Food Price Policy]. **In** *Johnson, D. G. and Schuh, G. E., eds.*, 1983, pp. 213–18. **[G: India; U.S.]**

Padoa-Schioppa, Tommaso. Determinants of Monetary Policy in France, The Federal Republic of Germany, Italy and the United Kingdom: A Comparative Analysis: Discussion. **In** *Hodgman, D. R., ed.*, 1983, pp. 171–76. **[G: U.K.; W. Germany; France; Italy]**

Pakistan Council of Islamic Ideology. Elimination of Interest from the Economy: Report. **In** *Ahmed, Z.; Iqbal, M. and Khan, M. F., eds.*, 1983, pp. 103–211. **[G: Pakistan]**

Partee, J. Charles. Statement to the Subcommittee on Domestic Monetary Policy, U.S. House Committee on Banking, Finance, and Urban Affairs, March 10, 1983. *Fed. Res. Bull.*, March 1983, *69*(3), pp. 193–96. **[G: U.S.]**

Partee, J. Charles. Statement to the U.S. Senate Committee on Banking, Housing, and Urban Affairs, April 12, 1983. *Fed. Res. Bull.*, May 1983, *69*(5), pp. 340–41. **[G: U.S.]**

Pierce, David A.; Grupe, Michael R. and Cleveland, William P. Seasonal Adjustment of the Weekly Monetary Aggregates: A Model-Based Approach. *Fed. Res. Bull.*, August 1983, *69*(8), pp. 592. **[G: U.S.]**

Pigott, Charles. Financial Reform in Japan. *Fed. Res. Bank San Francisco Econ. Rev.*, Winter 1983, (1), pp. 25–46. **[G: Japan; U.S.]**

Pitchford, J. D. Unemployment, Real Wages and the Money Supply in Australia. *Econ. Rec.*, June 1983, *59*(165), pp. 118–31. **[G: Australia]**

Rashid, Salim. Edward Copleston, Robert Peel, and Cash Payments. *Hist. Polit. Econ.*, Summer 1983, *15*(2), pp. 249–59. **[G: U.K.]**

Raymond, Robert. The Formulation and Implementation of Monetary Policy in France. **In** *Meek, P., ed.*, 1983, pp. 105–14. **[G: France]**

Raymond, Robert. The Political Economy of French Monetary Policy: Discussion. **In** *Hodgman, D. R., ed.*, 1983, pp. 26–33. **[G: France]**

Reuss, Henry S. The Once and Future Fed. *Challenge,* March/April 1983, *26*(1), pp. 26–32. **[G: U.S.]**

Rosenberg, Michael R. Foreign Exchange Controls: An International Comparison. **In** *George, A. M. and Giddy, I. H., eds., Vol. 1,* 1983, pp. 2.2:1–66.

Rosenblum, Harvey. The Conflicting Roles of the Fed as a Regulator and a Competitor: Discussant's Comments. *J. Bank Res.*, Spring 1983, *14*(1), pp. 92–95. **[G: U.S.]**

Roth, Jean-Pierre. The Setting of Monetary Objectives in Germany: The Implementation of Monetary Objectives in Germany—Open Market Operations and Credit Facilities: Comment. **In** *Meek, P., ed.*, 1983, pp. 30–31. **[G: W. Germany; Switzerland]**

Salvemini, Maria Teresa. The Treasury and the Money Market: The New Responsibilities after the Divorce. *Rev. Econ. Cond. Italy,* February 1983, (1), pp. 33–54. **[G: Italy]**

Sassoon, David M. U.S. Financial Deregulation: Upheaval and Promise: Comment. *J. Banking Finance,* 1983, *7*(4), pp. 567–68. **[G: U.S.]**

Saunders, Anthony. Depositors' Risk Perceptions and Bank Failure in a System with Co-operative Loan Support. *Weltwirtsch. Arch.*, 1983, *119*(3), pp. 543–53. **[G: U.K.]**

Sayad, João. The Impact of Rural Credit on Production and Income Distribution in Brazil. **In** *Von*

Pischke, J. D.; Adams, D. W. and Donald, G., eds., 1983, pp. 379–86. **[G: Brazil]**

Schiltknecht, Kurt. Switzerland: The Pursuit of Monetary Objectives. **In** *Meek, P., ed.*, 1983, pp. 72–79. **[G: Switzerland]**

Schlesinger, Helmut. The Setting of Monetary Objectives in Germany. **In** *Meek, P., ed.*, 1983, pp. 6–17. **[G: W. Germany]**

Scholl, Franz. Implications of Monetary Targeting for Exchange-rate Policy. **In** *Meek, P., ed.*, 1983, pp. 118–25. **[G: W. Germany]**

Schwartz, Anna J. The Postwar Institutional Evolution of the International Monetary System. **In** *Darby, M. P. and Lothian, J. R., et al.*, 1983, pp. 14–45. **[G: OECD]**

Shadow Open Market Committee. Policy Statement. **In** *Shadow Open Market Committee.*, 1983, pp. 1–5. **[G: U.S.]**

Shimamoto, Reiichi. Monetary Control in Japan. **In** *Meek, P., ed.*, 1983, pp. 80–85. **[G: Japan]**

Short, Eugenie D. and O'Driscoll, Gerald P., Jr. Deregulation and Deposit Insurance. *Fed. Res. Bank Dallas Econ. Rev.*, September 1983, pp. 11–23. **[G: U.S.]**

Shughart, William F., II and Tollison, Robert D. Preliminary Evidence on the Use of Inputs by the Federal Reserve System. *Amer. Econ. Rev.*, June 1983, *73*(3), pp. 291–304.

Sicat, Gerardo P. Toward a Flexible Interest Rate Policy, or Losing Interest in the Usury Law. **In** *Von Pischke, J. D.; Adams, D. W. and Donald, G., eds.*, 1983, pp. 373–78. **[G: Philippines]**

Siddiqi, Nejatullah. Elimination of Interest from the Economy: Report: Comment. **In** *Ahmed, Z.; Iqbal, M. and Khan, M. F., eds.*, 1983, pp. 223–32. **[G: Pakistan]**

Sitzia, Bruno. Monetary Authorities' Reaction Functions and the European Monetary System: Discussion. **In** *Hodgman, D. R., ed.*, 1983, pp. 245.

Skaggs, Neil T. The Federal Reserve System and Congressional Demands for Information. *Soc. Sci. Quart.*, September 1983, *64*(3), pp. 566–81. **[G: U.S.]**

Skaggs, Neil T. and Wasserkrug, Cheryl L. Banking Sector Influence on the Relationship of Congress to the Federal Reserve System. *Public Choice*, 1983, *41*(2), pp. 295–306. **[G: U.S.]**

Sørensen, Peter Birch. Devaluering og finanspolitik under alternative pengepolitiske regimer. (Fiscal and Exchange Rate Policies under Different Monetary Policies Regimes. With English summary.) *Nationaløkon. Tidsskr.*, 1983, *121*(1), pp. 83–101. **[G: Denmark]**

Sprinkel, Beryl W. Can the Fed Control Money? *Cato J.*, Spring 1983, *3*(1), pp. 155–62. **[G: U.S.]**

Steedman, Ian and Metcalfe, J. S. Britain's Falling Money Supply: A Statistical Note. *Appl. Econ.*, February 1983, *15*(1), pp. 23–28. **[G: U.K.]**

Sternlight, Peter D. Implementation of Federal Reserve Open Market Operations. **In** *Meek, P., ed.*, 1983, pp. 42–45. **[G: U.S.]**

Stiefel, Dieter. The Reconstruction of the Credit-Anstalt. **In** *Teichova, A. and Cottrell, P. L., eds.*, 1983, pp. 415–30. **[G: Austria]**

Taya, Teizo. Effectiveness of Exchange Market Intervention in Moderating the Speed of Exchange Rate Movements: An Empirical Study of the Case of Japan. **In** *Bigman, D. and Taya, T., eds.*, 1983, pp. 217–55. **[G: Japan]**

Teck, Alan and Johns, William B. Portfolio Decisions of Central Banks. **In** *George, A. M. and Giddy, I. H., eds., Vol. 2*, 1983, pp. 8.4:1–16.

Thiessen, Gordon G. The Canadian Experience with Monetary Targeting. **In** *Meek, P., ed.*, 1983, pp. 100–104. **[G: Canada]**

Thornton, Daniel L. The FOMC in 1982: De-emphasizing M1. *Fed. Res. Bank St. Louis Rev.*, June/July 1983, *65*(6), pp. 26–35. **[G: U.S.]**

Thys-Clement, Françoise. Monetary Authorities' Reaction Functions in a Model of Exchange-Rate Determination for the European Monetary System: Comment. **In** *De Grauwe, P. and Peeters, T., eds.*, 1983, pp. 283–84. **[G: EEC]**

Torell, John R., III. U.S. Financial Deregulation: Upheaval and Promise. *J. Banking Finance*, 1983, *7*(4), pp. 561–65. **[G: U.S.]**

de Ulhôa Canto, Gilberto. Monetary Correction and the Legal Tender of the Cruzeiro. **In** *de Ulhôa Canto, G.; da Silva Martins, I. G. and van Hoorn, J., Jr., eds.*, 1983, pp. 13–16. **[G: Brazil]**

Vaciago, Giacomo. Methods of Monetary Control in Italy: 1974–1983: Discussion. **In** *Hodgman, D. R., ed.*, 1983, pp. 89–92. **[G: Italy]**

Volcker, Paul A. Monetary Policy for the 1980s. **In** *Walker, C. E. and Bloomfield, M. E., eds.*, 1983, pp. 35–43. **[G: U.S.]**

Volcker, Paul A. Statement to the U.S. House Committee on Banking, Finance and Urban Affairs, April 12, 1983. *Fed. Res. Bull.*, May 1983, *69*(5), pp. 337–40. **[G: U.S.]**

Volcker, Paul A. Statement to the U.S. House Committee on the Budget, March 8, 1983. *Fed. Res. Bull.*, March 1983, *69*(3), pp. 187–93. **[G: U.S.]**

Volcker, Paul A. Statement to the U.S. House Subcommittee on Domestic Monetary Policy of the Committee on Banking, Finance and Urban Affairs, October 18, 1983. *Fed. Res. Bull.*, November 1983, *69*(11), pp. 839–42. **[G: U.S.]**

Volcker, Paul A. Statement to the U.S. Senate Committee on Banking, Housing, and Urban Affairs, February 16, 1983. *Fed. Res. Bull.*, March 1983, *69*(3), pp. 167–74. **[G: U.S.]**

Volcker, Paul A. Statement to the U.S. Senate Committee on Banking, Housing, and Urban Affairs, September 13, 1983. *Fed. Res. Bull.*, October 1983, *69*(10), pp. 757–69. **[G: U.S.]**

Volcker, Paul A. Statement to the U.S. Senate Committee on the Budget, February 24, 1983. *Fed. Res. Bull.*, March 1983, *69*(3), pp. 181–86. **[G: U.S.]**

Volcker, Paul A. Statement to U.S. House Committee on Banking, Finance and Urban Affairs, July 20, 1983. *Fed. Res. Bull.*, August 1983, *69*(8), pp. 601–09. **[G: U.S.]**

Volcker, Paul A. Statement to U.S. House Subcommittee on Domestic Monetary Policy of the Committee on Banking, Finance and Urban Affairs, August 3, 1983. *Fed. Res. Bull.*, August 1983, *69*(8), pp. 617–21. **[G: U.S.]**

Walker, David A. U.S. Banking Regulation and Foreign Banks' Entry into the United States. *J. Banking Finance*, 1983, *7*(4), pp. 569–80. **[G: U.S.]**

Wallace, Myles S. and Warner, John T. A Note: Presidential Elections and Federal Reserve Policy. *J. Post Keynesian Econ.*, Spring 1983, *5*(3), pp. 489–92.

Wallich, Henry C. Changes in Monetary Policy and the Fight against Inflation. *Cato J.*, Spring 1983, *3*(1), pp. 147–54. **[G: U.S.]**

Weintraub, Robert E. What Type of Monetary Rule? *Cato J.*, Spring 1983, *3*(1), pp. 171–83. **[G: U.S.]**

Weiss, Jakob. The Effects of the Current Turbulent Times on American Multinational Banking: An Overview: Comment. *J. Banking Finance*, 1983, *7*(4), pp. 639. **[G: U.S.; LDCs]**

West, Robert Craig. The Evolution and Devolution of Bank Regulations in the United States. *J. Econ. Issues*, June 1983, *17*(2), pp. 361–67. **[G: U.S.]**

White, George C. The Conflicting Roles of the Fed as a Regulator and a Competitor. *J. Bank Res.*, Spring 1983, *14*(1), pp. 75–90. **[G: U.S.]**

Willms, Manfred. The Monetary Policy Decision Process in the Federal Republic of Germany. **In** *Hodgman, D. R., ed.*, 1983, pp. 34–58. **[G: W. Germany]**

Wilson, J. S. G. Recent Changes in London's Money Market Arrangements. *Banca Naz. Lavoro Quart. Rev.*, March 1983, (144), pp. 81–102. **[G: U.K.]**

Wilson, Thomas F. Institutional Change as a Source of Excessive Monetary Expansion. **In** *Schmukler, N. and Marcus, E., eds.*, 1983, pp. 79–93. **[G: U.S.]**

Wood, Geoffrey E. The Monetary Policy Decision Process in the United Kingdom. **In** *Hodgman, D. R., ed.*, 1983, pp. 93–113. **[G: U.K.]**

Woolley, John T. Political Factors in Monetary Policy. **In** *Hodgman, D. R., ed.*, 1983, pp. 177–203. **[G: U.K.; France; W. Germany]**

Zecher, J. Richard. The Effects of the Current Turbulent Times on American Multinational Banking: An Overview. *J. Banking Finance*, 1983, *7*(4), pp. 625–37. **[G: U.S.; LDCs]**

312 Commercial Banking

3120 Commercial Banking

Adler, Paul. Trente ans d'automatisation et couts opératoires dans les banques françaises. (Thirty Years of Automation and Operating Costs in French Banks. With English summary.) *Revue Écon.*, September 1983, *34*(5), pp. 987–1020. **[G: France]**

Aftalion, Florin and Bompaire, Frédéric. France: Banking, Money, and Bond Markets. **In** *George, A. M. and Giddy, I. H., eds., Vol. 1*, 1983, pp. 4.5:1–26. **[G: France]**

Agabani, Fuoad. Islamic Banking as Practised Now in the World: Comment. **In** *Ahmed, Z.; Iqbal, M. and Khan, M. F., eds.*, 1983, pp. 277–84. **[G: Sudan]**

Aharony, Joseph and Swary, Itzhak. Contagion Effects of Bank Failures: Evidence from Capital Markets. *J. Bus.*, July 1983, *56*(3), pp. 305–22. **[G: U.S.]**

Ahmad, Ziauddin. Profitability of Islamic PLS Banks Competing with Interest Banks: Problems and Prospects: Comment. *J. Res. Islamic Econ.*, Summer 1983, *1*(1), pp. 66–68.

Al-Jarhi, Ma'bid Ali. A Monetary and Financial Structure for an Interest-Free Economy: Institutions, Mechanism and Policy. **In** *Ahmed, Z.; Iqbal, M. and Khan, M. F., eds.*, 1983, pp. 69–87.

Allen, Deborah L. Japan: Banking, Money, and Bond Markets. **In** *George, A. M. and Giddy, I. H., eds., Vol. 1*, 1983, pp. 4.7:1–33. **[G: Japan]**

Alonzi, Loreto P. and Hutchinson, Peter M. Risk Aversion's Impact on Bank Mortgage Lending: Evidence from the USA. *Rivista Int. Sci. Econ. Com.*, October–November 1983, *30*(10–11), pp. 1039–56. **[G: U.S.]**

Andersson, Bertil. Early History of Banking in Gothenburg Discount House Operations, 1783–1818. *Scand. Econ. Hist. Rev.*, 1983, *31*(1), pp. 50–67. **[G: Sweden]**

Androsch, Hannes. Sul ruolo della banca nell'ambito della politica economica. (The Role of Banking in Economic Policy. With English summary.) *Bancaria*, August 1983, *39*(8), pp. 695–701.

Bain, Andrew D. Understanding the Scottish Economy: Markets for Finance. **In** *Ingham, K. P. D. and Love, J., eds.*, 1983, pp. 55–64. **[G: U.K.]**

Basch, Donald L. Regulatory Transition and Depositor Inertia: The Response of Massachusetts Commercial Banks to NOW Accounts. *J. Bank Res.*, Winter 1983, *13*(4), pp. 264–73. **[G: U.S.]**

Bashir, B. A. Portfolio Management of Islamic Banks: 'Certainty Model' *J. Banking Finance*, September 1983, *7*(3), pp. 339–54.

Baxter, William F. Bank Interchange of Transactional Paper: Legal and Economic Perspectives. *J. Law Econ.*, October 1983, *26*(3), pp. 541–88.

Beebe, Jack H. Bank Capital Risk in the Post-1979 Monetary and Deregulatory Environment. *Fed. Res. Bank San Francisco Econ. Rev.*, Summer 1983, (3), pp. 7–18. **[G: U.S.]**

Benson, Bruce L. The Economic Theory of Regulation as an Explanation of Policies toward Bank Mergers and Holding Company Acquisitions. *Antitrust Bull.*, Winter 1983, *28*(4), pp. 839–62. **[G: U.S.]**

Benston, George J. Federal Regulation of Banking: Analysis and Policy Recommendations. *J. Bank Res.*, Winter 1983, *13*(4), pp. 216–44. **[G: U.S.]**

Benston, George J. The Regulation of Financial Services. **In** *Benston, G. J., ed.*, 1983, pp. 28–63. **[G: U.S.]**

Berti, Gian Luigi. Su alcune questioni inerenti ai rapporti valutari fra San Marino e Italia. (Topics Inherent in the Foreign-Exchange Agreements between San Marino and Italy. With English summary.) *Bancaria*, March 1983, *39*(3), pp. 279–83. **[G: San Marino; Italy]**

Bianchi, Tancredi. Elementi economico-aziendali per un'analisi del grado di efficienza delle banche. (Operating Factors for the Analysis of the Degree of Banks' Efficiency. With English summary.) *Bancaria*, November 1983, *39*(11), pp. 1043–050. **[G: Italy]**

Black, Harold A. Deregulation and Locational Rents in Banking: Discussant's Comments. *J. Bank Res.*, Spring 1983, *14*(1), pp. 107–08. **[G: U.S.]**

Bomhoff, Edward J. Permanent and Transitory

Changes in Monetary Policy: A Comment. *Carnegie-Rochester Conf. Ser. Public Policy,* Autumn 1983, *19,* pp. 211–23. **[G: Switzerland; U.S.; W. Germany]**

Booth, James R. NOW Accounts: The Competitive Battle in the Western States. *J. Bank Res.,* Winter 1983, *13*(4), pp. 317–20. **[G: U.S.]**

Bradfield, Michael. Statement to U.S. House Subcommittee on Commerce, Consumer, and Monetary Affairs of the Committee on Government Operations, July 21, 1983. *Fed. Res. Bull.,* August 1983, *69*(8), pp. 609–17. **[G: U.S.]**

Brealey, Richard A.; Hodges, Stewart D. and Selby, Michael J. P. The Risk of Bank-Loan Portfolios. **In** *Brenner, M., ed.,* 1983, pp. 153–82. **[G: U.S.]**

Brown, Donald M. Bank Holding Company Performance Studies and the Public Interest: Normative Uses for Positive Analysis? *Fed. Res. Bank St. Louis Rev.,* March 1983, *65*(3), pp. 26–34. **[G: U.S.]**

Brown, Donald M. The Effect of State Banking Laws on Holding Company Banks. *Fed. Res. Bank St. Louis Rev.,* August/September 1983, *65*(7), pp. 26–35. **[G: U.S.]**

Bruni, Franco. Interest and Exchange Rate Volatility: Implications for Bank Management. *Giorn. Econ.,* July–August 1983, *42*(7–8), pp. 431–58. **[G: OECD]**

Bryant, Ralph C. Eurocurrency Banking: Alarmist Concerns and Genuine Issues. *OECD Econ. Stud.,* Autumn 1983, (1), pp. 7–41. **[G: W. Europe]**

Buchanan, Donald D. Implications of Deregulation for Product Lines and Geographical Markets of Financial Institutions: Discussant's Comments. *J. Bank Res.,* Spring 1983, *14*(1), pp. 21–23. **[G: U.S.]**

Büttler, Hans-Jürg and Schiltknecht, Kurt. Transitory Changes in Monetary Policy and Their Implications in Money-Stock Control. *Carnegie-Rochester Conf. Ser. Public Policy,* Autumn 1983, *19,* pp. 171–209.

Byler, Ezra U. and Baker, James C. S.W.I.F.T.: A Fast Method to Facilitate International Financial Transactions. *J. World Trade Law,* September–October 1983, *17*(5), pp. 458–65.

Calabresi, Gian Franco. Concorrenza, stabilità ed efficienza nell'ambito delle casse di risparmio. (Competitivity, Stability and Efficiency of Savings Banks. With English summary.) *Bancaria,* December 1983, *39*(12), pp. 1266–75. **[G: Italy]**

Callier, Philippe. Eurobanks and Liquidity Creation: A Broader Perspective. *Weltwirtsch. Arch.,* 1983, *119*(2), pp. 214–25.

Caloia, Angelo. Il rapporto banca/impresa nel processo di internazionalizzazione. (Banks and Businesses in the Internationalisation Process. With English summary.) *L'Impresa,* 1983, *25*(1), pp. 43–48. **[G: Italy]**

de Camargo Vidigal, Geraldo. Monetary Correction in Bank Contracts. **In** *de Ulhôa Canto, G.; da Silva Martins, I. G. and van Hoorn, J., Jr., eds.,* 1983, pp. 136–51. **[G: Brazil]**

Campfield, Thomas M. and O'Brien, John G. Foreign Exchange Trading Practices: The Interbank Market. **In** *George, A. M. and Giddy, I. H., eds., Vol. 1,* 1983, pp. 2.4:1–25. **[G: Selected Countries]**

Capriglione, Francesco. Segreto della banca, segreto delle banche, segreto bancario. (Banking Confidentiality. With English summary.) *Bancaria,* March 1983, *39*(3), pp. 249–58. **[G: Italy]**

Carron, Andrew S. The Political Economy of Financial Regulation. **In** *Noll, R. G. and Owen, B. M.,* 1983, pp. 69–83. **[G: U.S.]**

Caselli, Clara. L'attività di ricerca nella banca: verso nuovi modelli. (New Trends in Research by Italian Banks. With English summary.) *Bancaria,* September 1983, *39*(9), pp. 834–48. **[G: Italy]**

Casey, Cornelius J. Prior Probability Disclosure and Loan Officers' Judgments: Some Evidence of the Impact. *J. Acc. Res.,* Spring 1983, *21*(1), pp. 300–307.

Cassese, Sabino. The "Division of Labour in Banking." The Functional and Geographical Distribution of Credit from 1936 to Today. *Rev. Econ. Cond. Italy,* October 1983, (3), pp. 381–411. **[G: Italy]**

Chandavarkar, A. G. Money and Credit (1858–1947). **In** *Kumar, D., ed.,* 1983, pp. 762–803. **[G: India]**

Cheng, Hang-Sheng. Financial Reform in Australia and New Zealand. *Fed. Res. Bank San Francisco Econ. Rev.,* Winter 1983, (1), pp. 9–24. **[G: Australia; New Zealand]**

Ciampi, Carlo Azeglio. Coordinamento internazionale della vigilanza ed efficienza del sistema bancario. (International Coordination of the Supervision, and Efficiency of the Banking System. With English summary.) *Bancaria,* March 1983, *39*(3), pp. 233–36. **[G: Italy]**

Cingano, Francesco. L'intermediazione bancaria: limiti operativi attuali e prospettive di ampliamento funzionale (Banking Intermediation: Present Operational Limits and Prospects for Enlargement of Role. With English summary.) *Bancaria,* February 1983, *39*(2), pp. 147–53. **[G: Italy]**

Cohen, Kalman J. The Reform of Banking Regulation: An Overview. *J. Bank Res.,* Spring 1983, *14*(1), pp. 3–7. **[G: U.S.]**

Collins, Michael. Long-term Growth of the English Banking Sector and Money Stock, 1844–80. *Econ. Hist. Rev., 2nd Ser.,* August 1983, *36*(3), pp. 374–94. **[G: U.K.]**

Conigliani, Claudio. Dimensioni aziendali, costi ed efficienza nel sistema bancario italiano. (Operating Dimensions, Costs and Efficiency in the Italian Banking System. With English summary.) *Bancaria,* December 1983, *39*(12), pp. 1206–220. **[G: Italy]**

Corbellini, Marco. Efficienza e costo dell'attività di intermediazione bancaria in un regime vincolistico. Alcune evidenze empiriche da un decennio di controlli diretti. (Banking-Intermediation Efficiency and Costs in the Regulatory System. Empirical Conclusions Based on a Decade of Direct Controls. With English summary.) *Bancaria,* November 1983, *39*(11), pp. 1092–1108. **[G: Italy]**

Cornyn, Anthony G. Financial Developments of Bank Holding Companies in 1982. *Fed. Res. Bull.,* July 1983, *69*(7), pp. 508–14. **[G: U.S.]**

Corrigan, E. Gerald. Statement to the Subcommittee on Telecommunications, Consumer Protection, and Finance of the U.S. House Committee on

Energy and Commerce, June 28, 1983. *Fed. Res. Bull.*, July 1983, *69*(7), pp. 532–35. **[G: U.S.]**

Corti, Mario A. Switzerland: Banking, Money, and Bond Markets. **In** *George, A. M. and Giddy, I. H., eds., Vol. 1*, 1983, pp. 4.6:1–50. **[G: Switzerland]**

Costi, Renzo. Riflessioni in tema di enti creditizi pubblici. (Public Credit Institutions. With English summary.) *Bancaria*, July 1983, *39*(7), pp. 581–92. **[G: Italy]**

Cottrell, P. L. Aspects of Western Equity Investment in the Banking Systems of East Central Europe. **In** *Teichova, A. and Cottrell, P. L., eds.*, 1983, pp. 309–47. **[G: Austria; Czechoslovakia; Hungary]**

Cotula, Anna Maria Biscaini. Le statistiche bancarie in Italia: origini e connotati. (Banking Statistics in Italy: Origins and Characteristics. With English summary.) *Bancaria*, July 1983, *39*(7), pp. 605–21. **[G: Italy]**

Crane, Dwight B. and Hayes, Samuel L., III. The Evolution of International Banking Competition and Its Implications for Regulation. *J. Bank Res.*, Spring 1983, *14*(1), pp. 39–53. **[G: U.S.; OECD; Selected LDCs]**

Creutzberg, Alexander F. An Empirical Evaluation of Bank Objective Functions. *Kansant. Aikak.*, 1983, *79*(2), pp. 203–14. **[G: Finland]**

Cucinotta, Giovanni. Bank Corporate Lending in Italy, Germany, United Kingdom during the Decade 1968–1978: A Comparative Study. *Econ. Notes*, 1983, (1), pp. 153–72. **[G: Italy; Germany; U.K.]**

Curry, Timothy J. and Rose, John T. Multibank Holding Companies: Recent Evidence on Competition and Performance in Banking Markets. *J. Bank Res.*, Autumn 1983, *14*(3), pp. 212–20. **[G: U.S.]**

Dale, Richard S. International Banking Is Out of Control. *Challenge*, January/February 1983, *25*(6), pp. 14–19.

Dalton, Dan R.; Krackhardt, David M. and Porter, Lyman W. The Impact of Teller Turnover in Banking: First Appearances Are Deceiving. *J. Bank Res.*, Autumn 1983, *14*(3), pp. 184–92. **[G: U.S.]**

Davis, Samuel G. and Reutzel, Edward T. EXPRESSEND: A Check Clearing Decision Support System for Endpoint Selection. *J. Bank Res.*, Autumn 1983, *14*(3), pp. 203–11. **[G: U.S.]**

DeMagistris, Robin C. and Esaki, Howard. MMDA Rates and Flows. *Fed. Res. Bank New York Quart. Rev.*, Autumn 1983, *8*(3), pp. 26–27. **[G: U.S.]**

Deshmukh, Sudhakar D.; Greenbaum, Stuart I. and Kanatas, George. Interest Rate Uncertainty and the Financial Intermediary's Choice of Exposure. *J. Finance*, March 1983, *38*(1), pp. 141–47.

Deshmukh, Sudhakar D.; Greenbaum, Stuart I. and Kanatas, George. Lending Policies of Financial Intermediaries Facing Credit and Funding Risk. *J. Finance*, June 1983, *38*(3), pp. 873–86.

Devlin, Robert T. Renegotiation of Latin America's Debt: An Analysis of the Monopoly Power of Private Banks. *Cepal Rev.*, August 1983, (20), pp. 101–12. **[G: Latin America]**

Diamond, Douglas W. and Dybvig, Philip H. Bank Runs, Deposit Insurance, and Liquidity. *J. Polit. Econ.*, June 1983, *91*(3), pp. 401–19.

DiBlasi, Paolo. Prifili giuridici delle tecniche di valutazione dei crediti nei bilanci bancari. (Legal Aspects of Loans Valuation in the Banks' Balance-Sheets. With English summary.) *Bancaria*, April 1983, *39*(4), pp. 402–09. **[G: Italy]**

Dietrich, J. Kimball and James, Christopher M. Regulation and the Determination of Bank Capital Changes: A Note [Regulatory Influence on Bank Capital Investment] [Capital Investment in Commercial Banking and Its Relation to Portfolio Regulation]. *J. Finance*, December 1983, *38*(5), pp. 1651–58. **[G: U.S.]**

Dini, Lamberto. Il trattamento delle crisi bancarie in Italia. (Handling of Bank Crisis in Italy. With English summary.) *Bancaria*, May–June 1983, *39*(5–6), pp. 471–76. **[G: Italy]**

Dini, Lamberto. Strategia e organizzazione nelle aziende di credito. (Commercial Banks' Strategy and Organization. With English summary.) *Bancaria*, October 1983, *39*(10), pp. 926–28. **[G: Italy]**

Dufey, Gunter and Krishnan, E. West Germany: Banking, Money, and Bond Markets. **In** *George, A. M. and Giddy, I. H., eds., Vol. 1*, 1983, pp. 4.4:1–26. **[G: W. Germany]**

Dunham, Constance. Unraveling the Complexity of NOW Account Pricing. *New Eng. Econ. Rev.*, May/June 1983, pp. 30–45. **[G: U.S.]**

Egge, Åsmund. Transformation of Bank Structures in the Industrial Period: The Case of Norway 1830–1914. *J. Europ. Econ. Hist.*, Fall 1983, *12*(2), pp. 271–94. **[G: Norway]**

Eisenbeis, Robert A. Bank Holding Companies and Public Policy. **In** *Benston, G. J., ed.*, 1983, pp. 127–55. **[G: U.S.]**

Eisenbeis, Robert A. What Is the Role of Government in a Major Restructuring of Financial Institutions in the 80s?: Discussant's Comments. *J. Bank Res.*, Spring 1983, *14*(1), pp. 33–36. **[G: U.S.]**

Eizenga, Weitze. Le banche e l'andamento dei tassi d'interesse. (Banks and Interest Rate Developments. With English summary.) *Bancaria*, February 1983, *39*(2), pp. 154–60. **[G: U.S.; Netherlands]**

Elliott, James V. What Is the Role of Government in a Major Restructuring of Financial Institutions in 1980s? *J. Bank Res.*, Spring 1983, *14*(1), pp. 25–32. **[G: U.S.]**

Elyasiani, Elyas. The Two Product Banking Firm under Uncertainty. *Southern Econ. J.*, April 1983, *49*(4), pp. 1002–17.

Eng, Maximo and Lees, Francis A. Eurocurrency Centers. **In** *George, A. M. and Giddy, I. H., eds., Vol. 1*, 1983, pp. 3.6:1–29. **[G: Selected Countries]**

Feuer, K. Le calcul de rentabilité des enterprises de financement. (How to Calculate the Probability of Financial Companies. With English summary.) *Ann. Sci. Écon. Appl.*, 1983, *39*(2), pp. 95–112.

Fischer, Otfrid. Die Kapitalkostensätze einlagenfinanzierter Kredite bei unterschiedlichem Marktzinsniveau. (On Capital Cost Rates of Deposit-Financed Loans at Different Interest Levels. With English summary.) *Kredit Kapital*, 1983,

16(3), pp. 405–29. [G: W. Germany]

Fischer, Stanley. A Framework for Monetary and Banking Analysis. *Econ. J.,* Supplement March 1983, pp. 1–16.

Flanders, M. June. The Effects of Political Economic and Institutional Developments on International Banks: Comment. *J. Banking Finance,* 1983, *7*(4), pp. 623–24. [G: LDCs]

Flannery, Mark J. Can State Bank Examination Data Replace FDIC Examination Visits? *J. Bank Res.,* Winter 1983, *13*(4), pp. 312–16. [G: U.S.]

Flannery, Mark J. Correspondent Services and Cost Economies in Commercial Banking. *J. Banking Finance,* March 1983, *7*(1), pp. 83–99. [G: U.S.]

Flannery, Mark J. Interest Rates and Bank Profitability: Additional Evidence. *J. Money, Credit, Banking,* August 1983, *15*(3), pp. 355–62. [G: U.S.]

Forestieri, Giancarlo. Efficienza e stabilità delle istituzioni creditizie: implicazioni organizzative e gestionali. (Efficiency and Stability of Credit Institutions: Organizational and Management Implications. With English summary.) *Bancaria,* November 1983, *39*(11), pp. 1051–065. [G: Italy]

Franco, Daniele. I conti economici e le situazioni patrimoniali degli istituti di credito speciale: 1975–1982. (Profit and Loss Accounts and Balance Sheets of Special Credit Institutions: 1975–1982. With English summary.) *Bancaria,* December 1983, *39*(12), pp. 1231–265. [G: Italy]

Frieder, Larry A. and Apilado, Vincent P. Bank Holding Company Expansion: A Refocus on Its Financial Rationale. *J. Finan. Res.,* Spring 1983, *6*(1), pp. 67–81. [G: U.S.]

Friedli, Georg. Statements on International Legal Assistance from the Viewpoint of One of the Large Swiss Banks. *Wirtsch. Recht,* 1983, *35*(2/3), pp. 245–47. [G: Switzerland]

Friedman, Richard M. and Roberts, William W. The Carry-Forward Provision and Management of Bank Reserves. *J. Finance,* June 1983, *38*(3), pp. 845–55. [G: U.S.]

Fuhrmann, Wilfried. Zum Kapitalverkehr zwischen deutschen und ausländischen Kreditinstituten. (Capital Movements between German and Foreign Banks. With English summary.) *Kredit Kapital,* 1983, *16*(2), pp. 267–83. [G: W. Germany]

Furlong, Frederick T. New Deposit Instruments. *Fed. Res. Bull.,* May 1983, *69*(5), pp. 319–26. [G: U.S.]

Furukawa, Akira. The Effectiveness of Lending Window Guidance and Well-Developed Open Money Market. (In Japanese. With English summary.) *Osaka Econ. Pap.,* March 1983, *32*(4), pp. 11–20. [G: Japan]

Gagnon, Joseph. What Is a Commercial Loan? *New Eng. Econ. Rev.,* July–August 1983, pp. 37–41. [G: U.S.]

Galitz, Lawrence C. InterBank: A Bank Management Simulation Exercise. *J. Banking Finance,* September 1983, *7*(3), pp. 355–82. [G: U.K.]

Gendreau, Brian C. The Implicit Return on Bankers' Balances. *J. Money, Credit, Banking,* November 1983, *15*(4), pp. 411–24. [G: U.S.]

George, Abraham M. Survey of Worldwide Banking Practices and Institutions. **In** *George, A. M. and Giddy, I. H., eds., Vol. 1,* 1983, pp. 4.1:1–28. [G: Selected Countries]

Giddy, Ian H. Interbank Arbitrage in the European Market. **In** *Kaushik, S. K., ed.,* 1983, pp. 131–45. [G: Global]

Giddy, Ian H. The Theory and Industrial Organization of International Banking. **In** *Hawkins, R. G.; Levich, R. M. and Wihlborg, C. G., eds.,* 1983, pp. 195–243. [G: U.S.]

Gilbert, R. Alton. Economies of Scale in Correspondent Banking. *J. Money, Credit, Banking,* November 1983, *15*(4), pp. 483–88. [G: U.S.]

Gilbert, R. Alton. Two Measures of Reserves: Why Are They Different? *Fed. Res. Bank St. Louis Rev.,* June/July 1983, *65*(6), pp. 16–25. [G: U.S.]

Giles, R. Philip. United States: Banking, Money, and Bond Markets. **In** *George, A. M. and Giddy, I. H., eds., Vol. 1,* 1983, pp. 4.2:1–27. [G: U.S.]

Giroux, Gary; Shearon, Winston and Grossman, Steven. How Does Inflation Affect a BHC's Rate of Return? *J. Bank Res.,* Summer 1983, *14*(2), pp. 164–69. [G: U.S.]

Giurleo, Diego S. Canada: Banking, Money, and Bond Markets. **In** *George, A. M. and Giddy, I. H., eds., Vol. 1,* 1983, pp. 4.8:1–35. [G: Canada]

Godano, Giuseppe. L'internazionalizzazione del mercato finanziario giapponese. (The Internationalization of the Japanese Financial Market. With English summary.) *Bancaria,* October 1983, *39*(10), pp. 986–94. [G: Japan]

Goldschmidt, Amnon. The Cost–Output Relationship of Banks Revisited. *Europ. Econ. Rev.,* July 1983, *22*(2), pp. 177–91. [G: Israel]

Goldschmidt, Amnon. U.S. Banking Regulation and Foreign Banks' Entry into the United States: Comment. *J. Banking Finance,* 1983, *7*(4), pp. 581–82. [G: U.S.]

Golzio, Silvio. Il costo del denaro e le sue determinanti. (Cost of Money and Its Components. With English summary.) *Bancaria,* March 1983, *39*(3), pp. 227–32. [G: Italy]

González, Altina and López Veraza, Joachín. La Nacionalizacion de los Sistemas Bancarios. *Economia,* January 1983, *7*(1), pp. 135–61. [G: E. Europe; France; Italy; Portugal]

Goodfriend, Marvin. Discount Window Borrowing, Monetary Policy, and the Post–October 6, 1979 Federal Reserve Operating Procedure. *J. Monet. Econ.,* September 1983, *12*(3), pp. 343–56. [G: U.S.]

Goodman, Laurie S. The Effects of the Repeal of the McFadden Act on Resource Allocation within the International Bank. *Atlantic Econ. J.,* July 1983, *11*(2), pp. 63–71. [G: U.S.]

Goodman, Laurie S. and Langer, Martha J. Accounting for Interest Rate Futures in Bank Asset–Liability Management. *J. Futures Markets,* Winter 1983, *3*(4), pp. 415–27. [G: U.S.]

Goria, Giovanni. Rientro dall'inflazione, condizione per la ripresa dello sviluppo. (Reduction of Inflation, a Condition for the Return to Economic Growth in Italy. With English summary.) *Bancaria,* March 1983, *39*(3), pp. 237–41. [G: Italy]

Gorinson, Stanley M. Depository Institution Regulatory Reform in the 1980s: The Issue of Geographic Restrictions. *Antitrust Bull.,* Spring 1983,

28(1), pp. 227–54. **[G: U.S.]**

Greenbaum, Stuart I. Legal Reserve Requirements: A Case Study in Bank Regulation. *J. Bank Res.*, Spring 1983, *14*(1), pp. 59–69. **[G: U.S.]**

Greenbaum, Stuart I. and Higgins, Bryon. Financial Innovation. **In** *Benston, G. J., ed.*, 1983, pp. 213–34. **[G: U.S.]**

Grubel, Herbert G. Interest Payments on Commercial Bank Reserves to Curb Euro-money Markets. **In** *[Giersch, H.]*, 1983, pp. 117–35. **[G: OECD]**

Grubel, Herbert G. The New International Banking. *Banca Naz. Lavoro Quart. Rev.*, September 1983, (146), pp. 263–84. **[G: Canada]**

Guazzo, Mauro and Tempo, Maurizio. L'applicazione di un "query language" al sistema bancario italiano. (The Application of a "Query Language" to the Italian Banking system. With English summary.) *Bancaria*, March 1983, *39*(3), pp. 284–89. **[G: Italy]**

Hafer, R. W. The Prime Rate and the Cost of Funds: Is the Prime Too High? *Fed. Res. Bank St. Louis Rev.*, May 1983, *65*(5), pp. 17–21. **[G: U.S.]**

Hannan, Timothy H. Bank Profitability and the Threat of Entry. *J. Bank Res.*, Summer 1983, *14*(2), pp. 157–63. **[G: U.S.]**

Hannan, Timothy H. Prices, Capacity, and the Entry Decision: A Conditional Logit Analysis. *Southern Econ. J.*, October 1983, *50*(2), pp. 539–50. **[G: U.S.]**

Hansen, Derek. Banking and Small Business. **In** *Barker, M., ed. (I)*, 1983, pp. 359–473.

Heimann, John G. The Effects of Political, Economic and Institutional Development on International Banks. *J. Banking Finance*, 1983, *7*(4), pp. 615–21. **[G: LDCs]**

Hesberg, Dieter. Risikovorsorge durch Kreditausfallund Zinsänderungsrückstellungen im Jahresabschluss von Banken. (Risk Safeguards by Way of Reserve for Credit Losses and Interest Rate Changes. With English summary.) *Kredit Kapital*, 1983, *16*(4), pp. 531–67. **[G: EEC]**

Hester, Donald D. Deregulation and Locational Rents in Banking. *J. Bank Res.*, Spring 1983, *14*(1), pp. 96–107. **[G: U.S.]**

Heth, Meir. Protectionism and International Banking: Sectorial Efficiency, Competitive Structure and National Policy: Comment. *J. Banking Finance*, 1983, *7*(4), pp. 611–14. **[G: Selected Countries]**

Hicks, Sydney Smith. Aggregate Bank Portfolio Statistics: Do They Tell Us Anything? *J. Bank Res.*, Autumn 1983, *14*(3), pp. 221–26. **[G: U.S.]**

Hisrich, Robert D.; Krasnakevich, John and Peters, Michael P. Effectively Managing Consumer Credit through Computer Graphics. *J. Bank Res.*, Winter 1983, *13*(4), pp. 304–08. **[G: U.S.]**

Ho, Thomas S. Y. and Saunders, Anthony. Fixed Rate Loan Commitments, Take-Down Risk, and the Dynamics of Hedging with Futures. *J. Finan. Quant. Anal.*, December 1983, *18*(4), pp. 499–516.

Horvitz, Paul M. Legal Reserve Requirements: A Case Study in Bank Regulation: Discussant's Comments. *J. Bank Res.*, Spring 1983, *14*(1), pp. 69–72. **[G: U.S.]**

Horvitz, Paul M. Payments System Developments and Public Policy. **In** *Benston, G. J., ed.*, 1983, pp. 64–93. **[G: U.S.]**

Horvitz, Paul M. Reorganization of the Financial Regulatory Agencies. *J. Bank Res.*, Winter 1983, *13*(4), pp. 245–63. **[G: U.S.]**

Houpt, James V. Foreign Ownership of U.S. Banks: Trends and Effects. *J. Bank Res.*, Summer 1983, *14*(2), pp. 144–56. **[G: U.S.]**

Hubbard, Carl M. Money Market Funds, Money Supply, and Monetary Control: A Note. *J. Finance*, September 1983, *38*(4), pp. 1305–10. **[G: U.S.]**

Huertas, Thomas F. The Regulation of Financial Institutions: A Historical Perspective on Current Issues. **In** *Benston, G. J., ed.*, 1983, pp. 6–27. **[G: U.S.]**

Hull, Webster. Implications of Deregulation for Product Lines and Geographical Markets of Financial Institutions: Discussant's Comments. *J. Bank Res.*, Spring 1983, *14*(1), pp. 23–24. **[G: U.S.]**

Hultman, Charles W. Foreign Banking in the U.S.: A Review of Recent Developments. *Rivista Int. Sci. Econ. Com.*, October–November 1983, *30*(10–11), pp. 1022–38. **[G: U.S.]**

Jacobs, Rodney L. Fixed-Rate Lending and Interest Rate Futures Hedging. *J. Bank Res.*, Autumn 1983, *14*(3), pp. 193–202. **[G: U.S.]**

James, Christopher M. An Analysis of Intra-Industry Differences in the Effect of Regulation: The Case of Deposit Rate Ceilings. *J. Monet. Econ.*, September 1983, *12*(3), pp. 417–32. **[G: U.S.]**

James, Christopher M. Pricing Alternatives for Loan Commitments: A Note. *J. Bank Res.*, Winter 1983, *13*(4), pp. 300–303. **[G: U.S.]**

Johnson, G. G. Aspects of the Safety Net for International Banking. *Finance Develop.*, September 1983, *20*(3), pp. 30–33.

Kareken, John H. Deposit Insurance Reform or Deregulation Is the Cart, Not the Horse. *Fed. Res. Bank Minn. Rev.*, Spring 1983, *7*(2), pp. 1–9. **[G: U.S.]**

Kareken, John H. The First Step in Bank Deregulation: What about the FDIC? *Amer. Econ. Rev.*, May 1983, *73*(2), pp. 198–203. **[G: U.S.]**

Karna, Adi S. and Graddy, Duane B. Bank Holding Company Leverage, Risk Perception, and Cost of Capital. *Rev. Bus. Econ. Res.*, Fall 1983, *19*(1), pp. 99–109. **[G: U.S.]**

Kaufman, George G.; Mote, Larry R. and Rosenblum, Harvey. Implications of Deregulation for Product Lines and Geographical Markets of Financial Institutions. *J. Bank Res.*, Spring 1983, *14*(1), pp. 8–21. **[G: U.S.]**

Kaufman, George G.; Mote, Larry R. and Rosenblum, Harvey. The Future of Commercial Banks in the Financial Services Industry. **In** *Benston, G. J., ed.*, 1983, pp. 94–126. **[G: U.S.]**

Kaufman, Henry. Financial Institutions in Ferment. *Challenge*, May/June 1983, *26*(2), pp. 20–25. **[G: U.S.]**

Keen, Howard, Jr. The Impact of a Dividend Cut Announcement of Bank Share Prices. *J. Bank Res.*, Winter 1983, *13*(4), pp. 274–81. **[G: U.S.]**

Kennedy, William F. and Scott, David F., Jr. Some Observations on the Dividend Policies of Large Commercial Banks. *J. Bank Res.*, Winter 1983,

13(4), pp. 292–96. [G: U.S.]

Khan, M. Fahim. Islamic Banking as Practised Now in the World. **In** *Ahmed, Z.; Iqbal, M. and Khan, M. F., eds.*, 1983, pp. 259–76. [G: Islamic Countries]

Khoury, Sarkis J. and Pirog, Robert. An Economic Analysis of the Demand for Trade Loans from Multinational Banks. *Bus. Econ.*, September 1983, *18*(4), pp. 40–45. [G: U.S.]

Kindleberger, Charles P. International Banks as Leaders or Followers of International Business: An Historical Perspective. *J. Banking Finance,* 1983, *7*(4), pp. 583–95. [G: Europe; U.S.; Latin America]

King, Robert G. On the Economics of Private Money. *J. Monet. Econ.*, July 1983, *12*(1), pp. 127–58. [G: U.S.]

Komlos, John H. The Diffusion of Financial Technology into the Austro-Hungarian Monarchy toward the End of the Nineteenth Century. **In** *Komlos, J., ed.*, 1983, pp. 137–63. [G: Austria; Hungary]

Koppenhaver, G. D. A T-Bill Futures Hedging Strategy for Bank. *Fed. Res. Bank Dallas Econ. Rev.*, March 1983, pp. 15–28. [G: U.S.]

Koskela, Erkki. Credit Rationing and Non-price Loan Terms: A Re-examination. *J. Banking Finance,* September 1983, *7*(3), pp. 405–16.

Kwast, Myron L. and Black, Harold A. An Analysis of the Behavior of Mature Black-Owned Commercial Banks. *J. Econ. Bus.*, 1983, *35*(1), pp. 41–54. [G: U.S.]

Lafrance, Robert. Évaluation de l'hypothèse de la moyenne-variance: une application au portefeuille des banques canadiennes. (An Evolution of the Mean-Variance Hypothesis: The Case of Portfolios of Canadian Banks. With English summary.) *L'Actual. Econ.*, March 1983, *59*(1), pp. 20–37. [G: Canada]

Lam, Chun H. and Boudreaux, Kenneth J. Compensating Balances, Deficiency Fees, and Lines of Credit. *J. Banking Finance,* September 1983, *7*(3), pp. 307–22.

Lanciotti, Giulio. Obiettivi e strumenti della vigilanza strutturale. Schemi di riferimento e regole ottimali per l'autorizzazione all'apertura di dipendenze bancarie. (Structural Supervisory Objectives and Tools: Reference Schemes and Optimal Rules for Authorization of the Opening of New Bank Branches. With English summary.) *Bancaria,* December 1983, *39*(12), pp. 1221–230. [G: Italy]

Lassila, Jaakko. Uusien rahamarkkinatekijöiden vaikutus pankkien hinnoitteluun. (The Effect of New Money Market Trends on the Pricing of Banking Services in Finland. With English summary.) *Kansant. Aikak.*, 1983, *79*(3), pp. 291–99. [G: Finland]

Laub, P. Michael and Hoffman, Charles F. The Structure of the Financial Services Industry. *Contemp. Policy Issue,* January 1983, (2), pp. 1–17.

Lessard, Donald R. North–South: The Implications for Multinational Banking. *J. Banking Finance,* 1983, *7*(4), pp. 521–36. [G: Global]

Lévy-Leboyer, M. Aspects of Western Equity Investment in the Banking Systems of East Central Europe: Commentary. **In** *Teichova, A. and Cottrell, P. L., eds.*, 1983, pp. 347–49. [G: Austria; Czechoslovakia; Hungary]

Lewis, Carole I. Explicit Pricing of Correspondent Services. **In** *Kaushik, S. K., ed.*, 1983, pp. 167–71. [G: U.S.]

Little, Jane Sneddon. Eurobank Maturity Transformation and LDC Debts. *New Eng. Econ. Rev.*, September/October 1983, pp. 15–19. [G: LDCs; MDCs]

Logue, Dennis E. and Senbet, Lemma W. External Currency Market Equilibrium and Its Implications for Regulation of the Eurocurrency Market. *J. Finance,* May 1983, *38*(2), pp. 435–47.

Lopez Roa, A. L. Efectos de la crisis económica sobre el sistema financiero: el caso de España. (The Impact of Economic Crisis on the Financial System: The Spanish Case. With English summary.) *Écon. Soc.*, September–October–November 1983, *17*(9–10–11), pp. 1631–45. [G: Spain]

Maccarone, Michele. Revisione e certificazione dei bilanci: profili generali e problematiche relative ai bilanci bancari. (Auditing and Certification of Financial Statements: Considerations Relating to Banks' Financial Statements. With English summary.) *Bancaria,* August 1983, *39*(8), pp. 710–27. [G: Italy]

Maier, Steven F. The Conflicting Roles of the Fed as a Regulator and a Competitor: Discussant's Comments. *J. Bank Res.*, Spring 1983, *14*(1), pp. 90–92. [G: U.S.]

Maier, Steven F. and Vander Weide, James H. What Lockbox and Disbursement Models Really Do. *J. Finance,* May 1983, *38*(2), pp. 361–71.

Mallinson, Eugenie. Profitability of Insured Commercial Banks in the First Half of 1983. *Fed. Res. Bull.*, December 1983, *69*(12), pp. 885–92. [G: U.S.]

Marcus, Alan J. The Bank Capital Decision: A Time Series-Cross Section Analysis. *J. Finance,* September 1983, *38*(4), pp. 1217–32. [G: U.S.]

Marlow, Michael L. Entry and Performance in Financial Markets. *J. Bank Res.*, Autumn 1983, *14*(3), pp. 227–30. [G: U.S.]

Martell, Terrence F. The Accuracy of Deposit Forecasts Generated by the Bank Chartering Process. *J. Bank Res.*, Winter 1983, *13*(4), pp. 309–11. [G: U.S.]

Martin, Preston. Statement to the U.S. Senate Subcommittee on Consumer Affairs of the Committee on Banking, Housing, and Urban Affairs, September 28, 1983. *Fed. Res. Bull.*, October 1983, *69*(10), pp. 773–76. [G: U.S.]

Martin, Preston. Statement to U.S. House Subcommittee on Administrative Law and Governmental Relations of the Committee on the Judiciary, July 14, 1983. *Fed. Res. Bull.*, August 1983, *69*(8), pp. 595–99. [G: U.S.]

März, Eduard and Weber, Fritz. The Antecedents of the Austrian Financial Crash of 1931. *Z. Wirtschaft. Sozialwissen.*, 1983, *103*(5), pp. 497–519. [G: Austria]

März, Eduard and Weber, Fritz. The Reconstruction of the Credit-Anstalt: Commentary. **In** *Teichova, A. and Cottrell, P. L., eds.*, 1983, pp. 430–36. [G: Austria]

März, Eduard. The Austrian Credit Mobilier in a

Time of Transition. In *Komlos, J., ed.*, 1983, pp. 117–35. **[G: Austria]**

Marzano, Ferruccio, et al. The Southern Banking System, the Development of the Mezzogiorno and the Entry of Foreign Banks into Italy. *Rev. Econ. Cond. Italy*, February 1983, (1), pp. 55–96. **[G: Italy]**

Mathieson, Donald J. Estimating Models of Financial Market Behavior during Periods of Extensive Structural Reform: The Experience of Chile. *Int. Monet. Fund Staff Pap.*, June 1983, *30*(2), pp. 350–93. **[G: Chile]**

McKinney, George W., Jr. Legal Reserve Requirements: A Case Study in Bank Regulation: Discussant's Comments. *J. Bank Res.*, Spring 1983, *14*(1), pp. 72–74. **[G: U.S.]**

Meeker, Larry G.; Joy, O. Maurice and Cogger, Kenneth O. Valuation of Controlling Shares in Closely Held Banks. *J. Banking Finance*, June 1983, *7*(2), pp. 175–88. **[G: U.S.]**

Mees, Philip. International Cash Management. In *George, A. M. and Giddy, I. H., eds., Vol. 2*, 1983, pp. 8.11B:1–25.

Melnik, Arie. The Role of Banks in the International Financial System: Comment. *J. Banking Finance*, 1983, *7*(4), pp. 465–66. **[G: OECD; LDCs]**

Michel, B. Aspects of Western Equity Investment in the Banking Systems of East Central Europe: Commentary. In *Teichova, A. and Cottrell, P. L., eds.*, 1983, pp. 350–53. **[G: Austria; Czechoslovakia; Hungary]**

Molho, Lazaros E. The Determinants of Commercial Bank Loan Supply in Greece: An Empirical Investigation. *Greek Econ. Rev.*, April 1983, *5*(1), pp. 65–88. **[G: Greece]**

Moriarty, Rowland T.; Kimball, Ralph C. and Gay, John H. The Management of Corporate Banking Relationships. *Sloan Manage. Rev.*, Spring 1983, *24*(3), pp. 3–15. **[G: U.S.]**

Morse, Joel N. Banking in a Volatile World: Setting Country Lending Limits. In *Hansen, P., ed.*, 1983, pp. 269–79.

Munn, Charles W. The Coming of Joint-Stock Banking in Scotland and Ireland, c. 1820–1845. In *Devine, T. M. and Dickson, D., eds.*, 1983, pp. 204–18. **[G: U.K.; Ireland]**

Murphy, Neil B. Determinants of ATM Activity: The Impact of Card Base, Location, Time in Place and System. *J. Bank Res.*, Autumn 1983, *14*(3), pp. 231–33. **[G: U.S.]**

Nadri, M. Ishaq. A Monetary and Financial Structure for an Interest-Free Economy: Institutions, Mechanism and Policy: Comment. In *Ahmed, Z.; Iqbal, M. and Khan, M. F., eds.*, 1983, pp. 88–90.

Neldner, Manfred. Portfoliostruktur der Geschäfsbanken und Geldumlaufgeschwindigkeit. Der empirische Befund für die Bundesrepublik Deutschland. (Portfolio Structures of Commercial Banks and the Velocity of the Circulation of Money: The Empirical Findings for the Federal Republic of Germany. With English summary.) *Kredit Kapital*, 1983, *16*(4), pp. 568–86. **[G: W. Germany]**

Nelson, Paul Gunnar. What Is the Role of Government in a Major Restructuring of Financial Institutions in the 80s?: Discussant's Comments. *J. Bank Res.*, Spring 1983, *14*(1), pp. 36–38. **[G: U.S.]**

Nienhaus, Volker. Profitability of Islamic PLS Banks Competing with Interest Banks: Problems and Prospects. *J. Res. Islamic Econ.*, Summer 1983, *1*(1), pp. 37–47.

Nygren, Ingemar. Transformation of Bank Structures in the Industrial Period. The Case of Sweden 1820–1913. *J. Europ. Econ. Hist.*, Spring 1983, *12*(1), pp. 29–68. **[G: Sweden]**

O'Hara, Maureen. A Dynamic Theory of the Banking Firm. *J. Finance*, March 1983, *38*(1), pp. 127–40.

Opper, Barbara Negri. Profitability of Insured Commercial Banks in 1982. *Fed. Res. Bull.*, July 1983, *69*(7), pp. 489–507. **[G: U.S.]**

Orgler, Yair E. and Taggart, Robert A., Jr. Implications of Corporate Capital Structure Theory for Banking Institutions: A Note. *J. Money, Credit, Banking*, May 1983, *15*(2), pp. 212–21.

Park, Yoon S. Asian Money Markets. In *George, A. M. and Giddy, I. H., eds., Vol. 1*, 1983, pp. 4.10:1–20. **[G: Singapore; Hong Kong; Malaysia; Australia; S. Korea]**

Parravicini, Giannino. La banca oggi e domani. Riflessioni e previsioni. (Banking Today and Tomorrow: Remarks and Forecasts. With English summary.) *Bancaria*, December 1983, *39*(12), pp. 1171–77. **[G: Italy]**

Partee, J. Charles. Statement to the U.S. House Subcommittee on Financial Institutions Supervision, Regulation and Insurance of the Committee on Banking, Finance and Urban Affairs, October 27, 1983. *Fed. Res. Bull.*, November 1983, *69*(11), pp. 846–52. **[G: U.S.]**

Passacantando, Franco. Costi e margini del sistema bancario italiano: un'analisi comparata. (Cost and Margins in the Italian Banking System: A Comparative Analysis. With English summary.) *Bancaria*, November 1983, *39*(11), pp. 1066–079. **[G: U.S.; W. Europe]**

Patarnello, Arturo. Struttura, operatori ed evoluzione technica del mercato dei fondi interbancari in Italia (1979–1982). (Structure, Operators and Technical Evolution of the Interbank Market in Italy (1979–1982). With English summary.) *Bancaria*, August 1983, *39*(8), pp. 728–40. **[G: Italy]**

Patrick, Thomas and Johnson, James. Improving Commercial Loan Profitability. *Rivista Int. Sci. Econ. Com.*, October–November 1983, *30*(10–11), pp. 1057–63. **[G: U.S.]**

Peebles, Gavin. Inflation, Money and Banking in China: In Support of the Purchasing Power Approach. *ACES Bull. (See Comp. Econ. Stud. after 8/85)*, Summer 1983, *25*(2), pp. 81–103. **[G: China]**

Pepe, Federico. Le moderne funzioni gestionali nella banca per un incremento di efficienza e di produttività. (Modern Banking-Management Functions for Greater Efficiency and Productivity. With English summary.) *Bancaria*, April 1983, *39*(4), pp. 357–70. **[G: Italy]**

Phillips, Almarin and Jacobs, Donald P. Reflections on the Hunt Commission. In *Benston, G. J., ed.*, 1983, pp. 235–65. **[G: U.S.]**

Pierce, James L. Some Public Policy Issues Raised

by the Deregulation of Financial Institutions. *Contemp. Policy Issue*, January 1983, (2), pp. 33–48.

Porta, Angelo. La fiscalità implicita nei controlli sul sistema bancario italiano e i tassi di interesse: alcune quantificazioni preliminari. (The Regulation of the Italian Banking System as a Form of "Disguised Taxation": Some Preliminary Evidence on Its Impact on Interest Rates. With English summary.) *Giorn. Econ.*, November–December 1983, *42*(11–12), pp. 725–47. **[G: Italy]**

Pozdena, Randall J. and Iben, Ben. Pricing Debt Instruments: The Options Approach. *Fed. Res. Bank San Francisco Econ. Rev.*, Summer 1983, (3), pp. 19–30. **[G: U.S.]**

Proctor, Allen J. and Donahoo, Kathleene K. Commercial Bank Investment in Municipal Securities. *Fed. Res. Bank New York Quart. Rev.*, Winter 1983-84, *8*(4), pp. 26–37. **[G: U.S.]**

Redish, Angela. The Economic Crisis of 1837–1839 in Upper Canada: Case Study of a Temporary Suspension of Specie Payments. *Exploration Econ. Hist.*, October 1983, *20*(4), pp. 402–17. **[G: U.S.; Canada]**

Redslob, Alain. Considérations sur les nouvelles structures bancaires. (With English summary.) *Revue Écon. Polit.*, September–October 1983, *93*(5), pp. 720–31. **[G: France]**

Reeve, James M. Loan Evaluations under Accounting Disclosure Alternatives. *J. Bank Res.*, Autumn 1983, *14*(3), pp. 234–36.

Revell, Jack R. S. Adeguatezza del capitale, riserve occulte ed accantonamenti nelle aziende di credito. (Capital Adequacy, Hidden Reserves and Provisions. With English summary.) *Bancaria*, April 1983, *39*(4), pp. 346–56. **[G: Europe; U.S.]**

Rhoades, Stephen A. A Note on the Resource-Allocation Efficiency of MBHCs versus Independent Banks. *Quart. Rev. Econ. Bus.*, Summer 1983, *23*(2), pp. 112–17. **[G: U.S.]**

Rhoades, Stephen A. Concentration of World Banking and the role of U.S. Banks among the 100 Largest, 1956–1980. *J. Banking Finance*, September 1983, *7*(3), pp. 427–37. **[G: Selected Countries; U.S.]**

Rhoades, Stephen A. and Rutz, Roger D. Economic Power and Political Influence: An Empirical Analysis of Bank Regulatory Decisions. *Atlantic Econ. J.*, July 1983, *11*(2), pp. 79–86. **[G: U.S.]**

Ricart I Costa, Joan E. and Greenbaum, Stuart I. Bank Forward Lending: A Note. *J. Finance*, September 1983, *38*(4), pp. 1315–22.

Rolnick, Arthur J. and Weber, Warren E. New Evidence on the Free Banking Era. *Amer. Econ. Rev.*, December 1983, *73*(5), pp. 1080–91. **[G: U.S.]**

Rondelli, Lucio. Le tendenze all'innovazione nel sistema finanziario: prospettive e problemi per le banche italiane. (Innovation in the Financial System: Prospects and Challenges for Italian Banks. With English summary.) *Bancaria*, December 1983, *39*(12), pp. 1178–185. **[G: Italy]**

Rose, John T. Branch Banking and the State/National Charter Decision. *J. Bank Res.*, Summer 1983, *14*(2), pp. 170–72. **[G: U.S.]**

Rose, John T. and Savage, Donald T. Bank Holding Company *De Novo* Entry, Bank Performance, and Holding Company Size. *Quart. Rev. Econ. Bus.*, Winter 1983, *23*(4), pp. 54–62. **[G: U.S.]**

Rose, John T. and Talley, Samuel H. Financial Transactions within Bank Holding Companies. *Fed. Res. Bull.*, May 1983, *69*(5), pp. 333–34. **[G: U.S.]**

Rosen, Kenneth T. and Katz, Larry. Money Market Mutual Funds: An Experiment in Ad Hoc Deregulation: A Note. *J. Finance*, June 1983, *38*(3), pp. 1011–17. **[G: U.S.]**

Rosenblum, Harvey. The Conflicting Roles of the Fed as a Regulator and a Competitor: Discussant's Comments. *J. Bank Res.*, Spring 1983, *14*(1), pp. 92–95. **[G: U.S.]**

Ruozi, Roberto. Personnel-Management in Banking. *Bancaria*, April 1983, *39*(4), pp. 377–88. **[G: Italy]**

Ryan, John E. Statement to U.S. House Commerce, Consumer, and Monetary Affairs Subcommittee of the Committee on Government Operations, June 28, 1983. *Fed. Res. Bull.*, July 1983, *69*(7), pp. 535–37. **[G: U.S.]**

Sannucci, Valeria. L'andamento dei profitti bancari rispetto al ciclo economico. (The Trend of Banking Profits Relative to the Business Cycle. With English summary.) *Bancaria*, November 1983, *39*(11), pp. 1080–091. **[G: U.S.; Italy]**

Santomero, Anthony M. Fixed versus Variable Rate Loans. *J. Finance*, December 1983, *38*(5), pp. 1363–80.

Sassoon, David M. U.S. Financial Deregulation: Upheaval and Promise: Comment. *J. Banking Finance*, 1983, *7*(4), pp. 567–68. **[G: U.S.]**

Saunders, Anthony. Depositors' Risk Perceptions and Bank Failure in a System with Co-operative Loan Support. *Weltwirtsch. Arch.*, 1983, *119*(3), pp. 543–53. **[G: U.K.]**

Schroeder, Frederick J. Developments in Consumer Electronic Fund Transfers. *Fed. Res. Bull.*, June 1983, *69*(6), pp. 395–403. **[G: U.S.]**

Sealey, C. W., Jr. Valuation, Capital Structure, and Shareholder Unanimity for Depository Financial Intermediaries. *J. Finance*, June 1983, *38*(3), pp. 857–71.

Seaver, William L. and Fraser, Donald R. Branch Banking and the Availability of Banking Offices in Nonmetropolitan Areas. *Atlantic Econ. J.*, July 1983, *11*(2), pp. 72–78. **[G: U.S.]**

Sheffer, Eliezer. The Role of International Banking in the 'Oil Surplus' Adjustment Process: Comment. *J. Banking Finance*, 1983, *7*(4), pp. 519–20. **[G: Global]**

Short, Eugenie D. and O'Driscoll, Gerald P., Jr. Deregulation and Deposit Insurance. *Fed. Res. Bank Dallas Econ. Rev.*, September 1983, pp. 11–23. **[G: U.S.]**

Shull, Bernard. The Separation of Banking and Commerce: Origin, Development, and Implications for Antitrust. *Antitrust Bull.*, Spring 1983, *28*(1), pp. 255–79. **[G: U.S.]**

Siddiqi, Muhammad Nejatullah. Banking in an Islamic Framework. **In** *Siddiqi, M. N.*, 1983, pp. 51–65.

Siddiqi, Muhammad Nejatullah. Islamic Approaches to Money, Banking and Monetary Policy. **In** *Sid-*

diqi, M. N., 1983, pp. 15–50.

Siddiqi, Muhammad Nejatullah. Issues in Islamisation of Banking. **In** *Siddiqi, M. N.,* 1983, pp. 133–45. **[G: Pakistan]**

Siddiqi, Muhammad Nejatullah. Profitability of Islamic PLS Banks Comparing with Interest Banks: Problems and Prospects: Comment. *J. Res. Islamic Econ.,* Summer 1983, *1*(1), pp. 63–65.

Siddiqi, Muhammad Nejatullah. Rationale of Islamic Banking. **In** *Siddiqi, M. N.,* 1983, pp. 67–96.

Simonson, Donald G.; Stowe, John D. and Watson, Collin J. A Canonical Correlation Analysis of Commercial Bank Asset/Liability Structures. *J. Finan. Quant. Anal.,* March 1983, *18*(1), pp. 125–40. **[G: U.S.]**

Sinkey, Joseph F., Jr. The Performance of First Pennsylvania Bank Prior to Its Bail Out. *J. Bank Res.,* Summer 1983, *14*(2), pp. 119–33. **[G: U.S.]**

Skelton, Jeffrey L. Banks, Firms and the Relative Pricing of Tax-Exempt and Taxable Bonds. *J. Finan. Econ.,* November 1983, *12*(3), pp. 343–55. **[G: U.S.]**

Slovin, Myron B. and Sushka, Marie Elizabeth. A Model of the Commercial Loan Rate. *J. Finance,* December 1983, *38*(5), pp. 1583–96. **[G: U.S.]**

Smirlock, Michael L. and Marshall, William J. Monopoly Power and Expense-Preference Behavior: Theory and Evidence to the Contrary. *Bell J. Econ. (See Rand J. Econ. after 4/85),* Spring 1983, *14*(1), pp. 166–78. **[G: U.S.]**

Spedale, Domenico. La programmazione operativa nelle aziende di credito. (Commercial Banks' Operational Planning. With English summary.) *Bancaria,* July 1983, *39*(7), pp. 622–28.

Stanhouse, Bryan E. Stochastic Reserve Losses, Bank Credit Expansion and Bayesian Information. *J. Monet. Econ.,* August 1983, *12*(2), pp. 321–30.

Startz, Richard. Competition and Interest Rate Ceilings in Commercial Banking. *Quart. J. Econ.,* May 1983, *98*(2), pp. 255–65.

Steindl, Frank G. and Weinrobe, Maurice D. Natural Hazards and Deposit Behavior at Financial Institutions: A Note. *J. Banking Finance,* March 1983, *7*(1), pp. 111–18. **[G: U.S.]**

Stevens, Jerry L. Bank Market Concentration and Costs: Is There X-Inefficiency in Banking? *Bus. Econ.,* May 1983, *18*(3), pp. 36–44. **[G: U.S.]**

Stiefel, Dieter. The Reconstruction of the Credit-Anstalt. **In** *Teichova, A. and Cottrell, P. L., eds.,* 1983, pp. 415–30. **[G: Austria]**

Stone, Bernell K. The Design of a Company's Banking System. *J. Finance,* May 1983, *38*(2), pp. 373–85.

Struck, Peter L. and Mandell, Lewis. The Effect of Bank Deregulation on Small Business: A Note. *J. Finance,* June 1983, *38*(3), pp. 1025–31. **[G: U.S.]**

Summers, Lawrence H. On the Economics of Private Money: Comments. *J. Monet. Econ.,* July 1983, *12*(1), pp. 159–62. **[G: U.S.]**

Swanson, Peggy E. Compensating Balances and Foreigners' Dollar Deposits in United States Banks. *J. Finan. Res.,* Fall 1983, *6*(3), pp. 257–63. **[G: U.S.]**

Swary, Itzhak. Bank Acquisition of Non-bank Firms: An Empirical Analysis of Administrative Decisions. *J. Banking Finance,* June 1983, *7*(2), pp. 213–30. **[G: U.S.]**

Szegö, Giorgio P. The role of International Banking in the 'Oil Surplus' Adjustment Process. *J. Banking Finance,* 1983, *7*(4), pp. 497–518. **[G: Global]**

Talamona, Mario. In tema di esperienze e prospettive del "marketing" bancario: Uno strumento per migliorare l'efficienza produttiva e allocativa del sistema creditizio. (Experience and Prospects of Marketing in Banking: A Tool for Improving Productivity and Efficiency of Resources-Allocation in the Banking System. With English summary.) *Bancaria,* April 1983, *39*(4), pp. 371–76. **[G: Italy]**

Talley, Samuel H. Bank Capital Trends and Financing. *Fed. Res. Bull.,* February 1983, *69*(2), pp. 71–72. **[G: U.S.]**

Tarhan, Vefa and Spindt, Paul A. Bank Earning Asset Behavior and Causality between Reserves and Money: Lagged versus Contemporaneous Reserve Accounting. *J. Monet. Econ.,* August 1983, *12*(2), pp. 331–41. **[G: U.S.]**

Teeters, Nancy H. The Role of Banks in the International Financial System. *J. Banking Finance,* 1983, *7*(4), pp. 453–63. **[G: OECD; LDCs]**

Teeters, Nancy H. and Terrell, Henry S. The Role of Banks in the International Financial System. *Fed. Res. Bull.,* September 1983, *69*(9), pp. 663–71. **[G: OECD; Non-OPEC LDCs]**

Telgen, Jan. An MCDM Problem in Banking. **In** *Hansen, P., ed.,* 1983, pp. 372–78. **[G: Netherlands]**

Terrell, Henry S. and Mills, Rodney H. International Banking Facilities and the Eurodollar Market. *Fed. Res. Bull.,* August 1983, *69*(8), pp. 591. **[G: U.S.]**

Tese, Vincent. Deregulation in the Banking Industry. **In** *Kaushik, S. K., ed.,* 1983, pp. 9–15. **[G: U.S.]**

Thakor, Anjan V. and Callaway, Richard. Costly Information Production Equilibria in the Bank Credit Market with Applications to Credit Rationing. *J. Finan. Quant. Anal.,* June 1983, *18*(2), pp. 229–56.

Toevs, Alden L. Gap Management: Managing Interest Rate Risk in Banks and Thrifts. *Fed. Res. Bank San Francisco Econ. Rev.,* Spring 1983, (2), pp. 20–35. **[G: U.S.]**

Torell, John R., III. U.S. Financial Deregulation: Upheaval and Promise. *J. Banking Finance,* 1983, *7*(4), pp. 561–65. **[G: U.S.]**

Tschoegl, Adrian E. Size, Growth, and Transnationality among the World's Largest Banks. *J. Bus.,* April 1983, *56*(2), pp. 187–201.

Vander Weide, James H. Deregulation and Locational Rents in Banking: Discussant's Comments. *J. Bank Res.,* Spring 1983, *14*(1), pp. 108–09. **[G: U.S.]**

Vastrup, Claus. Economic Motives for Foreign Banking: The Danish Case. *Kredit Kapital,* 1983, *16*(1), pp. 117–25. **[G: Denmark]**

Veit, E. Theodore and Reiff, Wallace W. Commercial Banks and Interest Rate Futures: A Hedging Survey. *J. Futures Markets,* Fall 1983, *3*(3), pp. 283–93. **[G: U.S.]**

Verde, Antimo. Some Considerations about Italy's

Foreign Debts (1977–1982). *Rivista Polit. Econ.*, Supplement Dec. 1983, *73*(12), pp. 147–87. [G: Italy]

Volcker, Paul A. Statement to the U.S. Senate Committee on Banking, Housing, and Urban Affairs, September 13, 1983. *Fed. Res. Bull.*, October 1983, *69*(10), pp. 757–69. [G: U.S.]

Volker, Paul A. A Note on Factors Influencing the Utilization of Bankcard. *Econ. Rec.*, September 1983, *59*(166), pp. 281–89. [G: Australia]

Walker, David A. U.S. Banking Regulation and Foreign Banks' Entry into the United States. *J. Banking Finance*, 1983, *7*(4), pp. 569–80. [G: U.S.]

Walsh, Carl E. Taxation of Interest Income, Deregulation and the Banking Industry. *J. Finance*, December 1983, *38*(5), pp. 1529–42. [G: U.S.]

Walter, Ingo. The Evolution of International Banking Competition and Its Implications for Regulation: Discussant's Comments. *J. Bank Res.*, Spring 1983, *14*(1), pp. 53–54. [G: U.S.; OECD; Selected LDCs]

Walter, Ingo and Gray, H. Peter. Protectionism and International Banking: Sectorial Efficiency, Competitive Structure and National Policy. *J. Banking Finance*, 1983, *7*(4), pp. 597–609. [G: Selected Countries]

Walter, Judith A. The Evolution of International Banking Competition and Its Implications for Regulation: Discussant's Comments. *J. Bank Res.*, Spring 1983, *14*(1), pp. 55–58. [G: U.S.; OECD; Selected LDCs]

Weiss, Jakob. The Effects of the Current Turbulent Times on American Multinational Banking: An Overview: Comment. *J. Banking Finance*, 1983, *7*(4), pp. 639. [G: U.S.; LDCs]

Welch, Patrick J. Concentration in Local Commercial Banking Markets: A Study of the Eighth Federal Reserve District. *Fed. Res. Bank St. Louis Rev.*, October 1983, *65*(8), pp. 15–21. [G: U.S.]

West, Robert Craig. The Evolution and Devolution of Bank Regulations in the United States. *J. Econ. Issues*, June 1983, *17*(2), pp. 361–67. [G: U.S.]

Wette, Hildegard C. Collateral in Credit Rationing in Markets with Imperfect Information: Note. *Amer. Econ. Rev.*, June 1983, *73*(3), pp. 442–45.

White, George C. The Conflicting Roles of the Fed as a Regulator and a Competitor. *J. Bank Res.*, Spring 1983, *14*(1), pp. 75–90. [G: U.S.]

Wollmar, Stellan. Conducting Correspondent Banking with the Developing World. **In** *Kaushik, S. K., ed.*, 1983, pp. 173–81. [G: U.S.; LDCs]

Wood, John H. Familiar Developments in Bank Loan Markets. *Fed. Res. Bank Dallas Econ. Rev.*, November 1983, pp. 1–13. [G: U.S.]

Yannopoulos, George N. The Growth of Transnational Banking. **In** *Casson, M., ed.*, 1983, pp. 236–57. [G: LDCs; OECD]

Zakharov, V. Credit and Banks in the Economic Management System. *Prob. Econ.*, May 1983, *26*(1), pp. 3–19. [G: U.S.S.R.]

Zecher, J. Richard. The Effects of the Current Turbulent Times on American Multinational Banking: An Overview. *J. Banking Finance*, 1983, *7*(4), pp. 625–37. [G: U.S.; LDCs]

Zoltners, Andris A. A Manpower Sizing and Resource Allocation Model for Commercial Lending. *J. Bank Res.*, Summer 1983, *14*(2), pp. 134–43. [G: U.S.]

313 Capital Markets

3130 General

Abel, Andrew B. and Mishkin, Frederic S. On the Econometric Testing of Rationality-Market Efficiency. *Rev. Econ. Statist.*, May 1983, *65*(2), pp. 318–23. [G: U.S.]

van Agtmael, Antoine W. Securities Markets in Developing Countries. **In** *George, A. M. and Giddy, I. H., eds., Vol. 2*, 1983, pp. 6.10:1–12.

Arnott, Robert D. What Hath MPT Wrought: Which Risks Reap Rewards? *J. Portfol. Manage.*, Fall 1983, *10*(1), pp. 5–11. [G: U.S.]

Ball, Clifford A. and Torous, Walter N. A Simplified Jump Process for Common Stock Returns. *J. Finan. Quant. Anal.*, March 1983, *18*(1), pp. 53–65. [G: U.S.]

Bhatt, V. V. Financial Innovations and Development. **In** *Von Pischke, J. D.; Adams, D. W. and Donald, G., eds.*, 1983, pp. 43–49.

Bliss, Christopher. Consistent Temporary Equilibrium. **In** *Fitoussi, J.-P., ed.*, 1983, pp. 141–52.

Cargill, Thomas F. and Meyer, Robert A. Forecasting the Term Structure of Interest Rates and Portfolio Planning Models. *J. Econ. Bus.*, August 1983, *35*(3/4), pp. 399–411. [G: U.S.]

Chan, Yuk-Shee. On the Positive Role of Financial Intermediation in Allocation of Venture Capital in a Market with Imperfect Information. *J. Finance*, December 1983, *38*(5), pp. 1543–68.

Copeland, Basil L., Jr. Do Stock Prices Move Too Much to Be Justified by Subsequent Changes in Dividends?: Comment. *Amer. Econ. Rev.*, March 1983, *73*(1), pp. 234–35.

Dickman, A. B. Market-Orientated Policies and Financial Markets. *S. Afr. J. Econ.*, December 1983, *51*(4), pp. 467–85. [G: S. Africa]

Doherty, Neil A. The Measurement of Firm and Market Capacity. *J. Risk Ins.*, June 1983, *50*(2), pp. 224–34. [G: Canada]

Edmister, Robert O. and James, Christopher M. Is Illiquidity a Bar to Buying Small Cap Stocks? *J. Portfol. Manage.*, Summer 1983, *9*(4), pp. 14–19. [G: U.S.]

Fowler, David J. and Rorke, C. Harvey. Risk Measurement When Shares Are Subject to Infrequent Trading: Comment [Risk Measurement When Shares Are Subject to Infrequent Trading] [Estimating Betas from Non-Synchronous Data]. *J. Finan. Econ.*, August 1983, *12*(2), pp. 279–83.

Goss, Barry A. The Semi-Strong Form Efficiency of the London Metal Exchange. *Appl. Econ.*, October 1983, *15*(5), pp. 681–98. [G: U.K.]

Hasbrouck, Joel. On Estimates of Long-Run Rates of Return: A Note. *J. Finan. Quant. Anal.*, December 1983, *18*(4), pp. 455–61.

Hawawini, Gabriel A. and Vora, Ashok. Is Adjusting Beta Estimates an Illusion? *J. Portfol. Manage.*, Fall 1983, *10*(1), pp. 23–26. [G: U.S.]

Helmers, Glenn A. Risk Management in Models of the Farm: Modeling Farm Decisionmaking to Account for Risk: Discussion. In *Baum, K. H. and Schertz, L. P., eds.*, 1983, pp. 195–99.

Jobson, J. D. and Korkie, Bob. Statistical Inference in Two-Parameter Portfolio Theory with Multiple Regression Software. *J. Finan. Quant. Anal.*, June 1983, *18*(2), pp. 189–97.

Levy, Haim. The Capital Asset Pricing Model: Theory and Empiricism. *Econ. J.*, March 1983, *93*(369), pp. 145–65. [G: U.S.]

MacFarlane, A. J. E. The Role of Traded Options in Portfolio Management. In *Corner, D. and Mayes, D. G., eds.*, 1983, pp. 108–33. [G: U.K.]

Mancera, Miguel. Panel Discussion: The Capital Market under Conditions of High and Variable Inflation. In *Armella, P. A.; Dornbusch, R. and Obstfeld, M., eds.*, 1983, pp. 279–81.

Mieszkowski, Peter. A General Equilibrium Model of Taxation with Endogenous Financial Behavior: Comment. In *Feldstein, M., ed.*, 1983, pp. 455–58. [G: U.S.]

de Pablo, Juan Carlos. Panel Discussion: The Capital Market under Conditions of High and Variable Inflation. In *Armella, P. A.; Dornbusch, R. and Obstfeld, M., eds.*, 1983, pp. 277–79. [G: Argentina]

Perry, Philip R. More Evidence on the Nature of the Distribution of Security Returns. *J. Finan. Quant. Anal.*, June 1983, *18*(2), pp. 211–21. [G: U.S.]

Purcell, Wayne D. Hedging Procedures and Other Marketing Considerations. In *Baum, K. H. and Schertz, L. P., eds.*, 1983, pp. 181–94.

Reed, Howard Curtis. Appraising Corporate Investment Policy: A Financial Center Theory of Foreign Direct Investment. In *Kindleberger, C. P. and Audretsch, D. B., eds.*, 1983, pp. 219–44. [G: Global]

Salant, Stephen W. The Vulnerability of Price Stabilization Schemes to Speculative Attack. *J. Polit. Econ.*, February 1983, *91*(1), pp. 1–38.

Schwert, G. William. Size and Stock Returns, and Other Empirical Regularities. *J. Finan. Econ.*, June 1983, *12*(1), pp. 3–12. [G: U.S.]

Sharpe, William F. Erratum: Factors in NYSE Security Returns, 1931–1979. *J. Portfol. Manage.*, Winter 1983, *9*(2), pp. 79. [G: U.S.]

Shiller, Robert J. Do Stock Prices Move Too Much to Be Justified by Subsequent Changes in Dividends?: Reply. *Amer. Econ. Rev.*, March 1983, *73*(1), pp. 236–37.

Shiller, Robert J. Tax Reform and Corporate Investment: A Microeconometric Simulation Study: Comment. In *Feldstein, M., ed.*, 1983, pp. 281–87. [G: U.S.]

Shiller, Robert J.; Campbell, John Y. and Schoenholtz, Kermit L. Forward Rates and Future Policy: Interpreting the Term Structure of Interest Rates. *Brookings Pap. Econ. Act.*, 1983, (1), pp. 173–217. [G: U.S.]

Simonsen, Mario Henrique. Panel Discussion: The Capital Market under Conditions of High and Variable Inflation. In *Armella, P. A.; Dornbusch, R. and Obstfeld, M., eds.*, 1983, pp. 281–83.

Slemrod, Joel. A General Equilibrium Model of Taxation with Endogenous Financial Behavior. In *Feldstein, M., ed.*, 1983, pp. 427–54. [G: U.S.]

Sonka, Steven T. Risk Management in Models of the Farm: Thoughts on Modeling Risk Management on the Farm: Discussion. In *Baum, K. H. and Schertz, L. P., eds.*, 1983, pp. 200–203.

Theobald, Michael. The Analytic Relationship between Intervaling and Nontrading Effects in Continuous Time. *J. Finan. Quant. Anal.*, June 1983, *18*(2), pp. 199–209.

Trapp, James N. Risk Management in Models of the Farm: The Need for Prescriptive Risk-Management Models: A Suggested Methodological Approach: Discussion. In *Baum, K. H. and Schertz, L. P., eds.*, 1983, pp. 204–09.

Wallace, Neil. A Legal Restrictions Theory of the Demand for "Money" and the Role of Monetary Policy. *Fed. Res. Bank Minn. Rev.*, Winter 1983, *7*(1), pp. 1–7. [G: U.S.]

Weiss, Laurence. Forward Rates and Future Policy: Interpreting the Term Structure of Interest Rates: Comments and Discussion. *Brookings Pap. Econ. Act.*, 1983, (1), pp. 218–23. [G: U.S.]

West, Richard R. Innovations in Bond Portfolio Management: Summary. In *Kaufman, G. G.; Bierwag, G. O. and Toevs, A., eds.*, 1983, pp. 299–303.

3131 Capital Markets: Theory, Including Portfolio Selection, and Empirical Studies Illustrating Theory

Abel, Andrew B. and Mishkin, Frederic S. An Integrated View of Tests of Rationality, Market Efficiency and the Short-Run Neutrality of Monetary Policy. *J. Monet. Econ.*, January 1983, *11*(1), pp. 3–24.

Adler, Michael. Designing Spreads in Forward Exchange Contracts and Foreign Exchange Futures. *J. Futures Markets*, Winter 1983, *3*(4), pp. 355–68.

Adler, Michael and Dumas, Bernard. International Portfolio Choice and Corporation Finance: A Synthesis. *J. Finance*, June 1983, *38*(3), pp. 925–84.

Aldersley, J. The Role of Risk in Industry Analysis. In *Corner, D. and Mayes, D. G., eds.*, 1983, pp. 95–106.

Aliber, Robert Z. Money, Multinationals, and Sovereigns. In *Kindleberger, C. P. and Audretsch, D. B., eds.*, 1983, pp. 245–59. [G: OECD]

Allen, Beth. Expectations Equilibria with Dispersed Information: Existence with Approximate Rationality in a Model with a Continuum of Agents and Finitely Many States of the World. *Rev. Econ. Stud.*, April 1983, *50*(2), pp. 267–85.

Andersen, Torben M. Price and Quantity Signals in Financial Markets. *Z. Nationalökon.*, 1983, *43*(2), pp. 109–29.

Anderson, Ronald W. and Danthine, Jean-Pierre. Hedger Diversity in Futures Markets. *Econ. J.*, June 1983, *93*(370), pp. 370–89.

Anderson, Ronald W. and Danthine, Jean-Pierre. The Time Pattern of Hedging and the Volatility of Futures Prices. *Rev. Econ. Stud.*, April 1983, *50*(2), pp. 249–66.

Arrow, Kenneth J. The Role of Securities in the Optimal Allocation of Risk Bearing. In *Arrow, K. J., Vol. 2*, 1983, *1963*, pp. 46–57.

Arzac, Enrique R. A Mechanism for the Allocation

of Corporate Investment. *J. Finan. Quant. Anal.*, June 1983, *18*(2), pp. 175–88.

Auerbach, Alan J. Stockholder Tax Rates and Firm Attributes. *J. Public Econ.*, July 1983, *21*(2), pp. 107–27. [G: U.S.]

Auerbach, Alan J. and King, Mervyn A. Taxation, Portfolio Choice, and Debt-Equity Ratios: A General Equilibrium Model. *Quart. J. Econ.*, November 1983, *98*(4), pp. 587–609.

Babbel, David F. Duration and the Term Structure of Interest Rate Volatility. **In** *Kaufman, G. G.; Bierwag, G. O. and Toevs, A., eds.*, 1983, pp. 239–65. [G: U.S.]

Ball, Clifford A. and Torous, Walter N. Bond Price Dynamics and Options. *J. Finan. Quant. Anal.*, December 1983, *18*(4), pp. 517–31.

Bashir, B. A. Portfolio Management of Islamic Banks: 'Certainty Model' *J. Banking Finance*, September 1983, *7*(3), pp. 339–54.

Basu, Kaushik. Transactions Demand for Money and Portfolio Diversification. *Indian Econ. J.*, July–September 1983, *31*(1), pp. 25–34.

Batlin, Carl Alan. Interest Rate Risk, Prepayment Risk, and the Futures Market Hedging Strategies of Financial Intermediaries. *J. Futures Markets*, Summer 1983, *3*(2), pp. 177–84.

Batlin, Carl Alan. Production under Price Uncertainty with Imperfect Time Hedging Opportunities in Futures Markets. *Southern Econ. J.*, January 1983, *49*(3), pp. 681–92.

Bawa, Vijay S. and Goroff, Daniel L. Stochastic Dominance, Efficiency and Separation in Financial Markets. *J. Econ. Theory*, August 1983, *30*(2), pp. 410–14.

Benninga, Simon. Nonlinear Pricing Systems in Finance. **In** *Levy, H., ed.*, 1983, pp. 21–42.

Bernstein, Jeffrey I. and Fisher, Douglas. The Term Structure of Interest Rates and the Demand for Money: British Results from a Portfolio Model. *Southern Econ. J.*, July 1983, *50*(1), pp. 71–82. [G: U.K.]

Bethke, William M. and Boyd, Susan E. Should Dividend Discount Models Be Yield Tilted? *J. Portfol. Manage.*, Spring 1983, *9*(3), pp. 23–27.

Bierwag, G. O.; Kaufman, George G. and Toevs, Alden L. Bond Portfolio Immunization and Stochastic Process Risk. *J. Bank Res.*, Winter 1983, *13*(4), pp. 282–91. [G: U.S.]

Bierwag, G. O.; Kaufman, George G. and Toevs, Alden L. Immunization Strategies for Funding Multiple Liabilities. *J. Finan. Quant. Anal.*, March 1983, *18*(1), pp. 113–23.

Bierwag, G. O.; Kaufman, George G. and Toevs, Alden L. Recent Developments in Bond Portfolio Immunization Strategies. **In** *Kaufman, G. G.; Bierwag, G. O. and Toevs, A., eds.*, 1983, pp. 105–57. [G: U.S.]

Bierwag, G. O.; Kaufman, George G. and Toevs, Alden L. Single-Factor Duration Models in a Discrete General Equilibrium Framework. **In** *Kaufman, G. G.; Bierwag, G. O. and Toevs, A., eds.*, 1983, pp. 307–23.

Bierwag, G. O., et al. The Art of Risk Management in Bond Portfolios. **In** *Kaufman, G. G.; Bierwag, G. O. and Toevs, A., eds.*, 1983, pp. 325–45. [G: U.S.]

Bigman, David; Goldfarb, David and Schechtman, Edna. Futures Market Efficiency and the Time Content of the Information Sets. *J. Futures Markets*, Fall 1983, *3*(3), pp. 321–34. [G: U.S.]

Black, Fischer. Investing for the Short and the Long Term: Comment. **In** *Bodie, Z. and Shoven, J. B., eds.*, 1983, pp. 174–75. [G: U.S.]

Black, Fischer and Scholes, Myron S. The Pricing Options and Corporate Liabilities. **In** *Archer, S. H. and D'Ambrosia, C. A.*, 1983, *1973*, pp. 276–92.

Blomeyer, Edward C. and Klemkosky, Robert C. Tests of Market Efficiency for American Call Options. **In** *Brenner, M., ed.*, 1983, pp. 101–21. [G: U.S.]

Blume, Marshall E. The Pricing of Capital Assets in a Multiperiod World. *J. Banking Finance*, March 1983, *7*(1), pp. 31–44.

Bodily, Samuel E. and White, Chelsea C., III. Optimal Consumption and Portfolio Strategies in a Continuous-Time Model with Summary-Dependent Preferences. **In** *Hansen, P., ed.*, 1983, pp. 1–7.

Bookstaber, Richard M. Futures Market Participation with Differential Information. **In** *Levy, H., ed.*, 1983, pp. 165–81.

Booth, Laurence D. Optimal Portfolio Composition and the CAPM. *J. Econ. Bus.*, June 1983, *35*(2), pp. 205–11.

Bosch, Jean-Claude. Speculation and the Market for Recommendations. *J. Finan. Res.*, Summer 1983, *6*(2), pp. 103–13.

Bosshardt, Donald I. Spanning, Pareto Optimality, and the Mean-Variance Model. *Int. Econ. Rev.*, October 1983, *24*(3), pp. 649–69.

Brealey, Richard A.; Hodges, Stewart D. and Selby, Michael J. P. The Risk of Bank-Loan Portfolios. **In** *Brenner, M., ed.*, 1983, pp. 153–82. [G: U.S.]

Brennan, Michael J. and Schwartz, Eduardo S. An Equilibrium Model of Bond Pricing and a Test of Market Efficiency. **In** *Brenner, M., ed.*, 1983, *1982*, pp. 125–51.

Brennan, Michael J. and Schwartz, Eduardo S. Duration, Bond Pricing, and Portfolio Management. **In** *Kaufman, G. G.; Bierwag, G. O. and Toevs, A., eds.*, 1983, pp. 3–36. [G: U.S.]

Brenner, Menachem and Landskroner, Yoram. Inflation Uncertainties and Returns on Bonds. *Economica*, November 1983, *50*(200), pp. 463–68. [G: U.S.]

Brewer, Thomas L. Political Sources of Risk in the International Money Markets: Conceptual, Methodological, and Interpretive Refinements. *J. Int. Bus. Stud.*, Spring/Summer 1983, *14*(1), pp. 161–64.

Brief, Richard P. Yield Approximations: A Historical Perspective: A Correction. *J. Finance*, June 1983, *38*(3), pp. 1039.

Brooks, LeRoy D.; Ingram, Robert W. and Copeland, Ronald M. Credit Risk, Beta, and Bond Ratings. *Nebr. J. Econ. Bus.*, Winter, 1983, *22*(1), pp. 3–14. [G: U.S.]

Brown, David and Huang, Chi-fu. Option Pricing in a Lognormal Securities Market with Discrete Trading: A Comment. *J. Finan. Econ.*, August 1983, *12*(2), pp. 285–86.

Brown, Stephen J. and Weinstein, Mark I. A New Approach to Testing Asset Pricing Models: The Bilinear Paradigm. *J. Finance,* June 1983, *38*(3), pp. 711–43. **[G: U.S.]**

Buiter, Willem H. Implications for the Adjustment Process of International Asset Risks: Exchange Controls, Intervention and Policy Risk, and Sovereign Risk. **In** *Hawkins, R. G.; Levich, R. M. and Wihlborg, C. G., eds.,* 1983, pp. 69–102.

Burton, Edwin T. Observations on the Theory of Option Pricing on Debt Instruments. **In** *Brenner, M., ed.,* 1983, pp. 35–44.

Canto, Victor A.; Findlay, M. Chapman, III and Reinganum, Marc R. The Monetary Approach to Stock Returns and Inflation. *Southern Econ. J.,* October 1983, *50*(2), pp. 396–405.

Cargill, Thomas F. and Meyer, Robert A. Estimating the Value of Risk Information. **In** *Levy, H., ed.,* 1983, pp. 43–61.

Carmichael, Jeffrey and Stebbing, Peter W. Fisher's Paradox and the Theory of Interest. *Amer. Econ. Rev.,* September 1983, *73*(4), pp. 619–30. **[G: Australia; U.S.]**

Carter, Colin A.; Rausser, Gordon C. and Schmitz, Andrew. Efficient Asset Portfolios and the Theory of Normal Backwardation. *J. Polit. Econ.,* April 1983, *91*(2), pp. 319–31. **[G: U.S.]**

Chamberlain, Gary. A Characterization of the Distributions That Imply Mean-Variance Utility Functions. *J. Econ. Theory,* February 1983, *29*(1), pp. 185–201.

Chamberlain, Gary. Funds, Factors, and Diversification in Arbitrage Pricing Models. *Econometrica,* September 1983, *51*(5), pp. 1305–23.

Chamberlain, Gary and Rothschild, Michael. Arbitrage, Factor Structure, and Mean-Variance Analysis on Large Asset Markets. *Econometrica,* September 1983, *51*(5), pp. 1281–304.

Chance, Don M. Floating Rate Notes and Immunization. *J. Finan. Quant. Anal.,* September 1983, *18*(3), pp. 365–80.

Chen, Nai-fu. Some Empirical Tests of the Theory of Arbitrage Pricing. *J. Finance,* December 1983, *38*(5), pp. 1393–1414. **[G: U.S.]**

Chen, Nai-fu and Ingersoll, Jonathan E., Jr. Exact Pricing in Linear Factor Models with Finitely Many Assets: A Note. *J. Finance,* June 1983, *38*(3), pp. 985–88.

Chen, Son-Nan and Brown, Stephen J. Estimation Risk and Simple Rules for Optimal Portfolio Selection. *J. Finance,* September 1983, *38*(4), pp. 1087–93. **[G: U.S.]**

Chiang, Raymond and Pettway, Richard H. A Note on the Components and Segmentation of Bond Default Risk. *Southern Econ. J.,* April 1983, *49*(4), pp. 1155–61.

Christofi, Andreas. How to Maximize Stationarity of Beta: A Comment. *J. Portfol. Manage.,* Summer 1983, *9*(4), pp. 67. **[G: U.S.]**

Cochrane, W. G. and Lyall, K. J. Portfolio Theory and the Management of Investment Trust Companies. **In** *Corner, D. and Mayes, D. G., eds.,* 1983, pp. 75–94.

Cohen, Kalman J., et al. Friction in the Trading Process and the Estimation of Systematic Risk. *J. Finan. Econ.,* August 1983, *12*(2), pp. 263–78.

Conine, Thomas E., Jr. A Note on the Riskless Option Hedge. *Quart. Rev. Econ. Bus.,* Summer 1983, *23*(2), pp. 108–11.

Constantinides, George M. Capital Market Equilibrium with Personal Tax. *Econometrica,* May, 1983, *51*(3), pp. 611–36.

Copeland, Thomas E. and Galai, Dan. Information Effects on the Bid-Ask Spread. *J. Finance,* December 1983, *38*(5), pp. 1457–69.

Cornell, Bradford. The Money Supply Announcements Puzzle: Review and Interpretation. *Amer. Econ. Rev.,* September 1983, *73*(4), pp. 644–57. **[G: U.S.]**

Corner, Desmond; Mayes, David G. and Woodward, R. Modern Portfolio Theory and Investment Management. **In** *Corner, D. and Mayes, D. G., eds.,* 1983, pp. 1–20.

Cox, John C. and Rubinstein, Mark. A Survey of Alternative Option-pricing Models. **In** *Brenner, M., ed.,* 1983, pp. 3–33. **[G: U.S.]**

Dalal, Ardeshir J. Comparative Statics and Asset Substitutability/Complementarity in a Portfolio Model: A Dual Approach. *Rev. Econ. Stud.,* April 1983, *50*(2), pp. 355–67.

Dalal, Ardeshir J. On the Use of a Covariance Function in a Portfolio Model. *J. Finan. Quant. Anal.,* June 1983, *18*(2), pp. 223–27.

Divecha, Arjun and Morse, Dale. Market Responses to Dividend Increases and Changes in Payout Ratios. *J. Finan. Quant. Anal.,* June 1983, *18*(2), pp. 163–73. **[G: U.S.]**

Dooley, Michael P. and Isard, Peter. The Portfolio-Balance Model of Exchange Rates and Some Structural Estimates of the Risk Premium. *Int. Monet. Fund Staff Pap.,* December 1983, *30*(4), pp. 683–702. **[G: U.S.; W. Germany]**

Dornbusch, Rudiger. Exchange Rate Risk and the Macroeconomics of Exchange Rate Determination. **In** *Hawkins, R. G.; Levich, R. M. and Wihlborg, C. G., eds.,* 1983, pp. 3–27.

Dybvig, Philip H. An Explicit Bound on Individual Assets' Deviations from Apt Pricing in a Finite Economy. *J. Finan. Econ.,* December 1983, *12*(4), pp. 483–96.

Dyl, Edward A. and Martin, Stanley A., Jr. Rules of Thumb for the Analysis of Tax Swaps. *J. Portfol. Manage.,* Fall 1983, *10*(1), pp. 71–74.

Easley, David and Jarrow, Robert A. Consensus Beliefs Equilibrium and Market Efficiency. *J. Finance,* June 1983, *38*(3), pp. 903–11.

Eckardt, Walter L., Jr. and Begamery, Bruce D. Short Selling: The Mutual Fund Alternative. *J. Finan. Res.,* Fall 1983, *6*(3), pp. 231–38.

Edwards, Sebastian. Floating Exchange Rates, Expectations and New Information. *J. Monet. Econ.,* May 1983, *11*(3), pp. 321–36.

Einzig, Robert S. Comments on "Techniques and Success in Forecasting Exchange Rates: Should It Be Done? Does It Matter? The Long and the Short of It." **In** *Hawkins, R. G.; Levich, R. M. and Wihlborg, C. G., eds.,* 1983, pp. 187–91.

Elton, Edwin; Gruber, Martin and Rentzler, Joel. The Arbitrage Pricing Model and Returns on Assets under Uncertain Inflation. *J. Finance,* May 1983, *38*(2), pp. 525–37.

Emanuel, David C. A Theoretical Model for Valuing

Preferred Stock. *J. Finance,* September 1983, *38*(4), pp. 1133–55.

Enders, Walter and Lapan, Harvey E. On the Relationship between the Exchange Regime and the Portfolio Rules of Optimizing Agents. *J. Int. Econ.,* November 1983, *15*(3/4), pp. 199–224.

Fama, Eugene F. Efficient Capital Markets: A Review of Theory and Empirical Work. **In** *Archer, S. H. and D'Ambrosia, C. A.,* 1983, *1970,* pp. 183–222.

Fama, Eugene F. Stock Returns, Real Activity, Inflation, and Money: Reply. *Amer. Econ. Rev.,* June 1983, *73*(3), pp. 471–72. **[G: U.S.]**

Feldstein, Martin S. Inflation and the Stock Market. **In** *Feldstein, M. (II),* 1983, *1980,* pp. 186–98. **[G: U.S.]**

Feldstein, Martin S. Inflation, Portfolio Choice, and the Prices of Land and Corporate Stock. **In** *Feldstein, M. (II),* 1983, *1980,* pp. 229–40.

Feldstein, Martin S. Inflation, Tax Rules, and the Stock Market. **In** *Feldstein, M. (II),* 1983, *1980,* pp. 199–220. **[G: U.S.]**

Feldstein, Martin S. Personal Taxation and Portfolio Composition: An Econometric Analysis. **In** *Feldstein, M. (I),* 1983, *1976,* pp. 194–215. **[G: U.S.]**

Feldstein, Martin S. The Effects of Taxation on Risk Taking. **In** *Feldstein, M. (I),* 1983, *1969,* pp. 183–93.

Feldstein, Martin S. and Mørck, Randall. Pension Funding Decisions, Interest Rate Assumptions, and Share Prices. **In** *Bodie, Z. and Shoven, J. B., eds.,* 1983, pp. 177–207, 209–10. **[G: U.S.]**

Feldstein, Martin S. and Slemrod, Joel. Personal Taxation, Portfolio Choice, and the Effect of the Corporation Income Tax. **In** *Feldstein, M. (I),* 1983, *1980,* pp. 255–66. **[G: U.S.]**

Ferguson, Robert. An Efficient Stock Market? Ridiculous! *J. Portfol. Manage.,* Summer 1983, *9*(4), pp. 31–38.

Ferson, Wayne E. Expectations of Real Interest Rates and Aggregate Consumption: Empirical Tests. *J. Finan. Quant. Anal.,* December 1983, *18*(4), pp. 477–97. **[G: U.S.]**

Fischer, Stanley. Investing for the Short and the Long Term. **In** *Bodie, Z. and Shoven, J. B., eds.,* 1983, pp. 153–76. **[G: U.S.]**

Fisher, Lawrence and Leibowitz, Martin L. Effects of Alternative Anticipations of Yield-Curve Behavior on the Composition of Immunized Portfolios and on Their Target Returns. **In** *Kaufman, G. G.; Bierwag, G. O. and Toevs, A., eds.,* 1983, pp. 185–226. **[G: U.S.]**

Flavin, Marjorie A. Excess Volatility in the Financial Markets: A Reassessment of the Empirical Evidence. *J. Polit. Econ.,* December 1983, *91*(6), pp. 929–56. **[G: U.S.]**

Fong, H. Gifford and Vasicek, Oldrich. Return Maximization for Immunized Portfolios. **In** *Kaufman, G. G.; Bierwag, G. O. and Toevs, A., eds.,* 1983, pp. 227–38.

Francis, Jack Clark and Lee, Cheng Few. Investment Horizon, Risk Proxies, Skewness, and Mutual Fund Performance: A Theoretical Analysis and Empirical Investigation. **In** *Levy, H., ed.,* 1983, pp. 1–19. **[G: U.S.]**

Frankel, Jeffrey A. Estimation of Portfolio-Balanced Functions That Are Mean-Variance Optimizing: The Mark and the Dollar. *Europ. Econ. Rev.,* December 1983, *23*(3), pp. 315–27. **[G: U.S.; W. Germany]**

Frankel, Jeffrey A. Monetary and Portfolio-Balance Models of Exchange Rate Determination. **In** *Bhandari, J. S. and Putnam, B. H., eds.,* 1983, pp. 84–115. **[G: U.S.; W. Germany]**

French, Kenneth R.; Ruback, Richard S. and Schwert, G. William. Effects of Nominal Contracting on Stock Returns. *J. Polit. Econ.,* February 1983, *91*(1), pp. 70–96.

Frenkel, Jacob A. Comments on "Exchange Rate Risk and the Macroeconomics of Exchange Rate Determination." **In** *Hawkins, R. G.; Levich, R. M. and Wihlborg, C. G., eds.,* 1983, pp. 29–34.

Frenkel, Jacob A. Flexible Exchange Rates, Prices, and the Role of "News": Lessons from the 1970s. **In** *Bhandari, J. S. and Putnam, B. H., eds.,* 1983, pp. 3–41. **[G: U.S.]**

Galai, Dan. A Survey of Empirical Tests of Option-pricing Models. **In** *Brenner, M., ed.,* 1983, pp. 45–80.

Galai, Dan. The Components of the Return from Hedging Options against Stocks. *J. Bus.,* January 1983, *56*(1), pp. 45–54.

Garbade, Kenneth D. and Silber, William L. Cash Settlement of Futures Contracts: An Economic Analysis. *J. Futures Markets,* Winter 1983, *3*(4), pp. 451–72.

Garbade, Kenneth D. and Silber, William L. Futures Contracts on Commodities with Multiple Varieties: An Analysis of Premiums and Discounts. *J. Bus.,* July 1983, *56*(3), pp. 249–72. **[G: U.S.]**

Garman, Mark B. and Kohlhagen, Steven W. Foreign Currency Option Values. *J. Int. Money Finance,* December 1983, *2*(3), pp. 231–37.

Gatti, James F. Risk and Return on Corporate Bonds: A Synthesis. *Quart. Rev. Econ. Bus.,* Summer 1983, *23*(2), pp. 53–70. **[G: U.S.]**

Gavish, Bezalel and Kalay, Avner. On the Asset Substitution Problem. *J. Finan. Quant. Anal.,* March 1983, *18*(1), pp. 21–30.

Gay, Gerald D. and Kolb, Robert W. Interest Rate Futures as a Tool for Immunization. *J. Portfol. Manage.,* Fall 1983, *10*(1), pp. 65–70. **[G: U.S.]**

Gay, Gerald D. and Kolb, Robert W. The Management of Interest Rate Risk. *J. Portfol. Manage.,* Winter 1983, *9*(2), pp. 65–70.

Geske, Robert and Roll, Richard. The Fiscal and Monetary Linkage between Stock Returns and Inflation. *J. Finance,* March 1983, *38*(1), pp. 1–33. **[G: U.S.]**

Gidday, Ian H. Foreign Exchange Options. *J. Futures Markets,* Summer 1983, *3*(2), pp. 143–66.

Gilster, John E., Jr. Capital Market Equilibrium with Divergent Investment Horizon Length Assumptions. *J. Finan. Quant. Anal.,* June 1983, *18*(2), pp. 257–68.

Goldenberg, David H. Usefulness of Treasury Bill Futures as Hedging Instruments: Comment. *J. Futures Markets,* Summer 1983, *3*(2), pp. 225–26. **[G: U.S.]**

Gowland, D. H. Interest Rates. **In** *Gowland, D. H., ed.,* 1983, pp. 35–56.

Grabbe, J. Orlin. The Pricing of Call and Put Options on Foreign Exchange. *J. Int. Money Finance,* December 1983, *2*(3), pp. 239–53.

Green, Jerry R. and Shoven, John B. The Effects of Financing Opportunities and Bankruptcy on Entrepreneurial Risk Bearing. **In** *Ronen, J., ed.,* 1983, pp. 49–74.

Greenberg, Edward; Marshall, William J. and Yawitz, Jess B. Firm Behavior under Conditions of Uncertainty and the Theory of Finance. *Quart. Rev. Econ. Bus.,* Summer 1983, *23*(2), pp. 6–22.

Gregory, N. A. Testing an Aggressive Investment Strategy Using Value Line Ranks: A Comment. *J. Finance,* March 1983, *38*(1), pp. 257. **[G: U.S.]**

Grinblatt, Mark and Titman, Sheridan. Factor Pricing in a Finite Economy. *J. Finan. Econ.,* December 1983, *12*(4), pp. 497–507.

Gultekin, N. Bulent. Stock Market Returns and Inflation: Evidence from Other Countries. *J. Finance,* March 1983, *38*(1), pp. 49–65. **[G: Selected Countries]**

Guy, James R. F. Comments on "A Simple Approach to the Pricing of Risky Assets with Uncertain Exchange Rates." **In** *Hawkins, R. G.; Levich, R. M. and Wihlborg, C. G., eds.,* 1983, pp. 61–67.

Haley, Charles W. The Dynamics of the Term Structure and Alternative Portfolio Immunization Strategies: Comments. **In** *Kaufman, G. G.; Bierwag, G. O. and Toevs, A., eds.,* 1983, pp. 103–04. **[G: U.S.]**

Hamada, Robert S. Portfolio Analysis, Market Equilibrium and Corporation Finance. **In** *Archer, S. H. and D'Ambrosia, C. A.,* 1983, *1969,* pp. 441–61.

Hanna, Mark. Testing an Aggressive Investment Strategy Using Value Line Ranks: A Comment. *J. Finance,* March 1983, *38*(1), pp. 259–62. **[G: U.S.]**

Hansen, Lars Peter and Singleton, Kenneth J. Stochastic Consumption, Risk Aversion, and the Temporal Behavior of Asset Returns. *J. Polit. Econ.,* April 1983, *91*(2), pp. 249–65. **[G: U.S.]**

Hawawini, Gabriel A. The Theory of Risk Aversion and Liquidity Preference: A Geometric Exposition. *Amer. Econ.,* Fall 1983, *27*(2), pp. 42–49.

Hess, Patrick J. Test for Tax Effects in the Pricing of Financial Assets. *J. Bus.,* October 1983, *56*(4), pp. 537–54. **[G: U.S.]**

Hessel, Christopher A. and Huffman, Lucy T. Incorporation of Tax Considerations into the Computation of Duration. *J. Finan. Res.,* Fall 1983, *6*(3), pp. 213–15.

Ho, Thomas S. Y. and Stoll, Hans R. The Dynamics of Dealer Markets under Competition. *J. Finance,* September 1983, *38*(4), pp. 1053–74.

Hochman, Shalom J. The Beta Coefficient: An Instrumental Variables Approach. **In** *Levy, H., ed.,* 1983, pp. 123–51. **[G: U.S.]**

Holloway, Clark. Testing an Aggressive Investment Strategy Using Value Line Ranks: A Reply. *J. Finance,* March 1983, *38*(1), pp. 263–70. **[G: U.S.]**

Hsia, Chi-Cheng. On Binomial Option Pricing. *J. Finan. Res.,* Spring 1983, *6*(1), pp. 41–46.

Huberman, Gur and Ross, Stephen A. Portfolio Turnpike Theorems, Risk Aversion, and Regularly Varying Utility Functions. *Econometrica,* September 1983, *51*(5), pp. 1345–61.

Ingersoll, Jonathan E., Jr. Is Immunization Feasible? Evidence from the CRSP Data. **In** *Kaufman, G. G.; Bierwag, G. O. and Toevs, A., eds.,* 1983, pp. 163–82. **[G: U.S.]**

James, Christopher M. and Edmister, Robert O. The Relation between Common Stock Returns Trading Activity and Market Value. *J. Finance,* September 1983, *38*(4), pp. 1075–86. **[G: U.S.]**

Jarrow, Robert A. and Rudd, Andrew. A Comparison of the APT and CAPM: A Note. *J. Banking Finance,* June 1983, *7*(2), pp. 295–303.

Jarrow, Robert A. and Rudd, Andrew. Tests of an Approximate Option-Valuation Formula. **In** *Brenner, M., ed.,* 1983, pp. 81–100. **[G: U.S.]**

Jennings, Robert H. and Barry, Christopher B. Information Dissemination and Portfolio Choice. *J. Finan. Quant. Anal.,* March 1983, *18*(1), pp. 1–19.

John, Kose. Collective Fineness of Stock Prices and Efficiency of Financial Markets. *Europ. Econ. Rev.,* November 1983, *23*(2), pp. 223–30.

John, Kose and Majthay, Antal. Structural Stability of Market Models. *Math. Soc. Sci.,* August 1983, *5*(1), pp. 89–95.

Johnson, H. E. An Analytic Approximation for the American Put Price. *J. Finan. Quant. Anal.,* March 1983, *18*(1), pp. 141–48.

Jones, David S. and Roley, V. Vance. Rational Expectations and the Expectations Model of the Term Structure: A Test Using Weekly Data. *J. Monet. Econ.,* September 1983, *12*(3), pp. 453–65.

Jordan, J. S. On the Efficient Markets Hypothesis. *Econometrica,* September 1983, *51*(5), pp. 1325–43.

Kahl, Kandice H. Determination of the Recommended Hedging Ratio. *Amer. J. Agr. Econ.,* August 1983, *65*(3), pp. 603–05.

Kane, Edward J. Nested Tests of Alternative Term-Structure Theories. *Rev. Econ. Statist.,* February 1983, *65*(1), pp. 115–23. **[G: U.S.]**

Karlik, John R. Comments on "Exchange Rate Risk and the Macroeconomics of Exchange Rate Determination." **In** *Hawkins, R. G.; Levich, R. M. and Wihlborg, C. G., eds.,* 1983, pp. 35–37.

Kawai, Masahiro. Price Volatility of Storable Commodities under Rational Expectations in Spot and Futures Markets. *Int. Econ. Rev.,* June 1983, *24*(2), pp. 435–59.

Kawai, Masahiro. Spot and Futures Prices of Nonsotrable Commodities under Rational Expectations. *Quart. J. Econ.,* May 1983, *98*(2), pp. 235–54.

Khang, Chulsoon. A Dynamic Global Portfolio Immunization Strategy in the World of Multiple Interest Rate Changes: A Dynamic Immunization and Minimax Theorem. *J. Finan. Quant. Anal.,* September 1983, *18*(3), pp. 355–63.

Kihlstrom, Richard E. and Laffont, Jean-Jacques. Taxation and Risk Taking in General Equilibrium Models with Free Entry. *J. Public Econ.,* July 1983, *21*(2), pp. 159–81.

Kochman, Ladd and Daniel, Ross. Testing the Black–Scholes Option Pricing Model: A Shortcut. *Atlantic Econ. J.,* July 1983, *11*(2), pp. 101. **[G: U.S.]**

Korkie, Bob. External vs. Internal Performance Evaluation. *J. Portfol. Manage.,* Spring 1983, *9*(3),

pp. 36–42.

Kouri, Pentti J. K. Macroeconomic Adjustment to Interest Rate Disturbances: Real and Monetary Aspects. **In** *Claassen, E. and Salin, P., eds.*, 1983, pp. 73–97.

Koutsoyiannis, A. A Short-Run Pricing Model for a Speculative Asset, Tested with Data from the Gold Bullion Market. *Appl. Econ.*, October 1983, *15*(5), pp. 563–81.

Kraus, Alan and Litzenberger, Robert H. On the Distributional Conditions for a Consumption-Oriented Three Moment CAPM. *J. Finance*, December 1983, *38*(5), pp. 1381–91.

Kryzanowski, Lawrence and To, Minh Chau. General Factor Models and the Structure of Security Returns. *J. Finan. Quant. Anal.*, March 1983, *18*(1), pp. 31–52. **[G: U.S.]**

Kuberek, Robert C. and Pefley, Norman G. Hedging Corporate Debt with U.S. Treasury Bond Futures. *J. Futures Markets*, Winter 1983, *3*(4), pp. 345–53. **[G: U.S.]**

Kwon, Young K. On Negligibility of Asset-Specific Risks at the Capital Market Equilibrium. *Australian Econ. Pap.*, December 1983, *22*(41), pp. 476–86.

Lächler, Ulrich. A Macrotheoretic Analysis of Inflation, Taxes, and the Price of Equity. *J. Macroecon.*, Summer 1983, *5*(3), pp. 281–301.

Lafrance, Robert. Évaluation de l'hypothèse de la moyenne-variance: une application au portefeuille des banques canadiennes. (An Evolution of the Mean-Variance Hypothesis: The Case of Portfolios of Canadian Banks. With English summary.) *L'Actual. Econ.*, March 1983, *59*(1), pp. 20–37. **[G: Canada]**

Lakonishok, Josef and Vermaelen, Theo. Tax Reform and Ex-Dividend Day Behavior. *J. Finance*, September 1983, *38*(4), pp. 1157–79. **[G: Canada]**

Langetieg, Terence C. Duration, Bond Pricing, and Portfolio Management: Comments. **In** *Kaufman, G. G.; Bierwag, G. O. and Toevs, A., eds.*, 1983, pp. 37–41. **[G: U.S.]**

Lee, Cheng Few and Chen, Son-Nan. Random Coefficient Models of Security Returns: A Comment [A Random Coefficient Model for Reexamining Risk Decomposition Method and Risk-Return Relationship Test]. *Quart. Rev. Econ. Bus.*, Spring 1983, *23*(1), pp. 99–109. **[G: U.S.]**

Lee, Wayne L.; Thakor, Anjan V. and Vora, Gautam. Screening, Market Signalling, and Capital Structure Theory. *J. Finance*, December 1983, *38*(5), pp. 1507–18.

Lerman, Zvi. The Structure of Interest Rates and Inflation. **In** *Levy, H., ed.*, 1983, pp. 183–215. **[G: U.S.]**

Lerner, Abba P. A Note on the Rate of Interest and the Value of Assets. **In** *Lerner, A. P.*, 1983, *1961*, pp. 545–49.

Lessard, Donald R. Comments on "Implications for the Adjustment Process of International Asset Risks: Exchange Controls, Intervention and Policy Risk, and Sovereign Risk." **In** *Hawkins, R. G.; Levich, R. M. and Wihlborg, C. G., eds.*, 1983, pp. 107–10.

Lessard, Donald R. Principles of International Portfolio Selection. **In** *George, A. M. and Giddy, I. H., eds., Vol. 2*, 1983, pp. 8.2:1–19. **[G: Selected Countries]**

Levhari, David. The Effects of Government Intermediation in the Indexed Bonds Market on Consumer Behavior. **In** *Dornbusch, R. and Simonsen, M. H., eds.*, 1983, pp. 281–307.

Levich, Richard M. Comments on "Techniques and Success in Forecasting Exchange Rates: Should It Be Done? Does It Matter? The Long and the Short of It." **In** *Hawkins, R. G.; Levich, R. M. and Wihlborg, C. G., eds.*, 1983, pp. 181–86.

Litzenberger, Robert H. and Ramaswamy, Krishna. The Effect of Personal Taxes and Dividends on Capital Asset Prices: Theory and Empirical Evidence. **In** *Archer, S. H. and D'Ambrosia, C. A.*, 1983, *1979*, pp. 690–722. **[G: U.S.]**

Liviatan, Nissan. On the Interaction between Wage and Asset Indexation. **In** *Dornbusch, R. and Simonsen, M. H., eds.*, 1983, pp. 267–80.

Liviatan, Nissan. On Equilibrium Wage Indexation and Neutrality of Indexation Policy. **In** *Armella, P. A.; Dornbusch, R. and Obstfeld, M., eds.*, 1983, pp. 107–24.

Lloyd, William P. and Modani, Naval K. Stocks, Bonds, Bills, and Time Diversification. *J. Portfol. Manage.*, Spring 1983, *9*(3), pp. 7–11. **[G: U.S.]**

MacBeth, James D. and Merville, Larry J. An Empirical Examination of the Black–Scholes Call Option Pricing Model. **In** *Archer, S. H. and D'Ambrosia, C. A.*, 1983, *1979*, pp. 293–306. **[G: U.S.]**

de Macedo, Jorge Braga. Optimal Currency Diversification for a Class of Risk-Averse International Investors. *J. Econ. Dynam. Control*, May 1983, *5*(2/3), pp. 173–85.

MacQueen, Jason. Two Applications of Modern Portfolio Theory to Portfolio Risk Analysis. **In** *Corner, D. and Mayes, D. G., eds.*, 1983, pp. 21–53. **[G: U.K.]**

Makin, John H. Techniques and Success in Forecasting Exchange Rates: Should It Be Done? Does It Matter? The Long and the Short of It. **In** *Hawkins, R. G.; Levich, R. M. and Wihlborg, C. G., eds.*, 1983, pp. 149–80.

Makowski, Louis. Competition and Unanimity Revisited. *Amer. Econ. Rev.*, June 1983, *73*(3), pp. 329–39.

Makowski, Louis. Competitive Stock Markets. *Rev. Econ. Stud.*, April 1983, *50*(2), pp. 305–30.

Markowitz, Harry M. Nonnegative or Not Nonnegative: A Question about CAPMs. *J. Finance*, May 1983, *38*(2), pp. 283–95.

Markowitz, Harry M. Portfolio Selection. **In** *Archer, S. H. and D'Ambrosia, C. A.*, 1983, *1952*, pp. 88–101.

Mascaro, Angelo and Meltzer, Allan H. Long- and Short-Term Interest Rates in a Risky World. *J. Monet. Econ.*, November 1983, *12*(4), pp. 485–518. **[G: U.S.]**

Mayers, David and Smith, Clifford W., Jr. The Interdependence of Individual Portfolio Decisions and the Demand for Insurance. *J. Polit. Econ.*, April 1983, *91*(2), pp. 304–11.

Mayes, David G. and Savage, David. The Contrast between Portfolio Theory and Econometric Models of the U.K. Monetary Sector. **In** *Corner, D.*

and Mayes, D. G., eds., 1983, pp. 211–44. [G: U.K.]

Mayshar, Joram. On Divergence of Opinion and Imperfections in Capital Markets. *Amer. Econ. Rev.*, March 1983, *73*(1), pp. 114–28.

McDaniel, William R. Convertible Bonds in Perfect and Imperfect Markets. *J. Finan. Res.*, Spring 1983, *6*(1), pp. 51–65.

McDonald, Bill. An Empirical Examination of the Preference Structure for the Distribution of Earnings. *J. Econ. Bus.*, August 1983, *35*(3/4), pp. 441–51. [G: U.S.]

McDonald, Bill. Functional Forms and the Capital Asset Pricing Model. *J. Finan. Quant. Anal.*, September 1983, *18*(3), pp. 319–29. [G: U.S.]

McDonald, Robert L. and Siegel, Daniel. A Note On the Design of Commodity Options Contracts: A Comment. *J. Futures Markets*, Spring 1983, *3*(1), pp. 43–46.

McKinnon, Ronald I. The J-Curve, Stabilizing Speculation, and Capital Constraints on Foreign Exchange Dealers. **In** *Bigman, D. and Taya, T., eds.*, 1983, pp. 103–27.

Melvin, Michael. An Alternative Approach to International Capital Flows. **In** *Darby, M. P. and Lothian, J. R., et al.*, 1983, pp. 380–417. [G: Canada; Italy; U.K.; U.S.; W. Germany]

Merton, Robert C. Financial Economics. **In** *Brown, E. C. and Solow, R. M., eds.*, 1983, pp. 105–40.

Mildenstein, Eckart and Schleef, Harold J. The Optimal Pricing Policy of a Monopolistic Marketmaker in the Equity Market. *J. Finance*, March 1983, *38*(1), pp. 218–31.

Miles, James A. and Rosenfeld, James D. The Effect of Voluntary Spin-Off Announcements on Shareholder Wealth. *J. Finance*, December 1983, *38*(5), pp. 1597–1606. [G: U.S.]

Milgrom, Paul R. Private Information in an Auction-like Securities Market. **In** *Engelbrecht-Wiggans, R.; Shubik, M. and Stark, R. M., eds.*, 1983, pp. 137–47.

Miller, Merton H. Debt and Taxes. **In** *Archer, S. H. and D'Ambrosia, C. A.*, 1983, *1977*, pp. 462–78.

Miller, Merton H. and Modigliani, Franco. Dividend Policy, Growth, and the Valuation of Shares. **In** *Archer, S. H. and D'Ambrosia, C. A.*, 1983, *1961*, pp. 630–57.

Miller, Merton H. and Scholes, Myron S. Dividends and Taxes. **In** *Archer, S. H. and D'Ambrosia, C. A.*, 1983, *1978*, pp. 658–89.

Milne, Frank and Shefrin, H. M. Welfare Losses Arising from Increased Public Information, and/or the Opening of New Securities Markets: Examples of the General Theory of the Second Best. **In** *Stigum, B. P. and Wenstøp, F., eds.*, 1983, pp. 385–95.

Modigliani, Franco. Debt, Dividend Policy, Taxes, Inflation, and Market Valuation: Erratum. *J. Finance*, June 1983, *38*(3), pp. 1041–42.

Monroe, Margaret A. On the Estimation of Supply and Demand Functions: The Case of Interest Rate Futures Markets. **In** *Levy, H., ed.*, 1983, pp. 91–122. [G: U.S.]

Morin, Roger A. and Fernandez Suarez, Antonio. Risk Aversion Revisited. *J. Finance*, September 1983, *38*(4), pp. 1201–16. [G: Canada]

Mossin, Jan. Equilibrium in a Capital Asset Market. **In** *Archer, S. H. and D'Ambrosia, C. A.*, 1983, *1966*, pp. 144–59.

Myers, Stewart C. A Time-State-Preference Model of Security Valuation. **In** *Archer, S. H. and D'Ambrosia, C. A.*, 1983, *1968*, pp. 160–82.

Myers, Stewart C. Pension Funding Decisions, Interest Rate Assumptions, and Share Prices: Comment. **In** *Bodie, Z. and Shoven, J. B., eds.*, 1983, pp. 207–09. [G: U.S.]

Nakayama, H.; Takeguchi, T. and Sano, M. Interactive Graphics for Portfolio Selection. **In** *Hansen, P., ed.*, 1983, pp. 280–89. [G: Japan]

Nelson, Jeffrey and Schaefer, Stephen. The Dynamics of the Term Structure and Alternative Portfolio Immunization Strategies. **In** *Kaufman, G. G.; Bierwag, G. O. and Toevs, A., eds.*, 1983, pp. 61–101. [G: U.S.]

Olsen, Robert A. Sample Size and Markowitz Diversification. *J. Portfol. Manage.*, Fall 1983, *10*(1), pp. 18–22. [G: U.S.]

Owen, Joel and Rabinovitch, Ramon. On the Class of Elliptical Distributions and Their Applications to the Theory of Portfolio Choice. *J. Finance*, June 1983, *38*(3), pp. 745–52.

Pearce, Douglas K. and Roley, V. Vance. The Reaction of Stock Prices to Unanticipated Changes in Money: A Note. *J. Finance*, September 1983, *38*(4), pp. 1323–33. [G: U.S.]

Peavy, John W., III and Goodman, David A. The Significance of P/Es for Portfolio Returns. *J. Portfol. Manage.*, Winter 1983, *9*(2), pp. 43–47. [G: U.S.]

Pesando, James E. On Expectations, Term Premiums and the Volatility of Long-Term Interest Rates. *J. Monet. Econ.*, September 1983, *12*(3), pp. 467–74. [G: Canada]

Pitts, C. G. C. and Selby, Michael J. P. The Pricing of Corporate Debt: A Further Note. *J. Finance*, September 1983, *38*(4), pp. 1311–13.

Polemarchakis, Heraklis M. Observable Probabilistic Beliefs. *J. Math. Econ.*, January 1983, *11*(1), pp. 65–75.

Poncet, Patrice. Optimum Consumption and Portfolio Rules with Money as an Asset. *J. Banking Finance*, June 1983, *7*(2), pp. 231–52.

Poterba, James M. and Summers, Lawrence H. Dividend Taxes, Corporate Investment, and 'Q.'. *J. Public Econ.*, November 1983, *22*(2), pp. 135–67. [G: U.K.]

Ram, Rati and Spencer, David E. Stock Returns, Real Activity, Inflation, and Money: Comment. *Amer. Econ. Rev.*, June 1983, *73*(3), pp. 463–70. [G: U.S.]

Ríos-García, S. and Ríos-Insua, S. The Portfolio Selection Problem with Multiattributes and Multiple Criteria. **In** *Hansen, P., ed.*, 1983, pp. 317–25.

Roley, V. Vance. Symmetry Restrictions in a System of Financial Asset Demands: Theoretical and Empirical Results. *Rev. Econ. Statist.*, February 1983, *65*(1), pp. 124–30. [G: U.S.]

Roll, Richard. Ambiguity When Performance Is Measured by the Securities Market Line. **In** *Archer, S. H. and D'Ambrosia, C. A.*, 1983, *1978*, pp. 222–43.

Roll, Richard and Ross, Stephen A. An Empirical

Investigation of the Arbitrage Pricing Theory. **In** *Archer, S. H. and D'Ambrosia, C. A.*, 1983, *1980*, pp. 244–74.

Ross, Stephen A. and Walsh, Michael M. A Simple Approach to the Pricing of Risky Assets with Uncertain Exchange Rates. **In** *Hawkins, R. G.; Levich, R. M. and Wihlborg, C. G., eds.*, 1983, pp. 39–54.

Rothenberg, Jerome. Housing Investment, Housing Consumption, and Tenure Choice. **In** *Grieson, R. E., ed.*, 1983, pp. 29–55.

Roy, S. Paul. Analyst Forecasts and Dividend Information. *J. Econ. Stud.*, 1983, *10*(2), pp. 3–20. **[G: U.S.]**

Rubinstein, Mark. Displaced Diffusion Option Pricing. *J. Finance*, March 1983, *38*(1), pp. 213–17. **[G: Europe]**

Santomero, Anthony M. Fixed versus Variable Rate Loans. *J. Finance*, December 1983, *38*(5), pp. 1363–80.

Sears, R. Stephen and Trennepohl, Gary L. Diversification and Skewness in Option Portfolios. *J. Finan. Res.*, Fall 1983, *6*(3), pp. 199–212. **[G: U.S.]**

Seiders, David F. Managing Mortgage Interest-Rate Risks in Forward, Futures, and Options Markets. *Amer. Real Estate Urban Econ. Assoc. J.*, Summer 1983, *11*(2), pp. 237–63. **[G: U.S.]**

Sharpe, William F. Capital Asset Prices: A Theory of Market Equilibrium under Conditions of Risk. **In** *Archer, S. H. and D'Ambrosia, C. A.*, 1983, *1964*, pp. 126–43.

Sharpe, William F. Recent Developments in Bond Portfolio Immunization Strategies: Comments. **In** *Kaufman, G. G.; Bierwag, G. O. and Toevs, A., eds.*, 1983, pp. 159–62. **[G: U.S.]**

Simonsen, Mario Henrique. On Equilibrium Wage Indexation and Neutrality of Indexation Policy: Comment. **In** *Armella, P. A.; Dornbusch, R. and Obstfeld, M., eds.*, 1983, pp. 124–30.

Skelton, Jeffrey L. Banks, Firms and the Relative Pricing of Tax-Exempt and Taxable Bonds. *J. Finan. Econ.*, November 1983, *12*(3), pp. 343–55. **[G: U.S.]**

Smith, David B. A Framework for Analyzing Nonconvertible Preferred Stock Risk. *J. Finan. Res.*, Summer 1983, *6*(2), pp. 127–39.

Smith, Vernon L. and Williams, Arlington W. An Experimental Comparison of Alternative Rules for Competitive Market Exchange. **In** *Engelbrecht-Wiggans, R.; Shubik, M. and Stark, R. M., eds.*, 1983, pp. 307–34.

Solnik, Bruno. International Arbitrage Pricing Theory. *J. Finance*, May 1983, *38*(2), pp. 449–57.

Solnik, Bruno. The Relation between Stock Prices and Inflationary Expectations: The International Evidence. *J. Finance*, March 1983, *38*(1), pp. 35–48. **[G: Selected OECD]**

Sorensen, Roy A. An "Essential Reservation" about the EMH. *J. Portfol. Manage.*, Summer 1983, *9*(4), pp. 29–30.

Sprecher, C. Ronald and Pertl, Mars A. Large Losses, Risk Management and Stock Prices. *J. Risk Ins.*, March 1983, *50*(1), pp. 107–17.

Stambaugh, Robert F. Arbitrage Pricing with Information. *J. Finan. Econ.*, November 1983, *12*(3), pp. 357–69.

Stambaugh, Robert F. Testing the CAPM with Broader Market Indexes: A Problem of Mean-Deficiency. *J. Banking Finance*, March 1983, *7*(1), pp. 5–16. **[G: U.S.]**

Stapleton, R. C. and Subrahmanyam, Marti G. The Market Model and Capital Asset Pricing Theory: A Note. *J. Finance*, December 1983, *38*(5), pp. 1637–42.

Stein, William; Pfaffenberger, Roger and Kumar, P. C. On the Estimation Risk in First-Order Stochastic Dominance: A Note. *J. Finan. Quant. Anal.*, December 1983, *18*(4), pp. 471–76.

Sterk, William E. Comparative Performance of the Black-Scholes and Roll-Geske-Whaley Option Pricing Models. *J. Finan. Quant. Anal.*, September 1983, *18*(3), pp. 345–54. **[G: U.S.]**

Stern, Robert M. Comments on "Implications for the Adjustment Process of International Asset Risks: Exchange Controls, Intervention and Policy Risk, and Sovereign Risk." **In** *Hawkins, R. G.; Levich, R. M. and Wihlborg, C. G., eds.*, 1983, pp. 103–06.

Stokie, Michael D. Parameter Stationarity in the Distribution of Stock Market Returns. *Australian J. Manage.*, June 1983, *8*(1), pp. 83–90. **[G: Australia]**

Strahm, Norman D. Preference Space Evaluation of Trading System Performance. *J. Futures Markets*, Fall 1983, *3*(3), pp. 259–81.

Streit, M. E. Heterogene Erwartungen, Preisbildung und Informationseffizienz auf spekulativen Märkten. (Heterogenous Expectations, Price Formation, and Informational Efficiency in Speculative Markets. With English summary.) *Z. ges. Staatswiss.*, March 1983, *139*(1), pp. 67–79.

Stulz, René M. The Demand for Foreign Bonds. *J. Int. Econ.*, November 1983, *15*(3/4), pp. 225–38.

Subrahmanyam, Marti G. Comments on "A Simple Approach to the Pricing of Risky Assets with Uncertain Exchange Rates." **In** *Hawkins, R. G.; Levich, R. M. and Wihlborg, C. G., eds.*, 1983, pp. 55–59.

Sundaresan, Mahadevan. Constant Absolute Risk Aversion Preferences and Constant Equilibrium Interest Rates. *J. Finance*, March 1983, *38*(1), pp. 205–12.

Swidler, Steve and Vanderheiden, Paul. Another Opinion Regarding Divergence of Opinion and Return. *J. Finan. Res.*, Spring 1983, *6*(1), pp. 47–50.

Tauchen, George E. and Pitts, Mark. The Price Variability-Volume Relationship on Speculative Markets. *Econometrica*, March 1983, *51*(2), pp. 485–505. **[G: U.S.]**

Tobin, James. Liquidity Preference as Behaviour towards Risk. **In** *Archer, S. H. and D'Ambrosia, C. A.*, 1983, *1958*, pp. 101–25.

Tole, Thomas M. How to Maximize Stationarity of Beta: Reply. *J. Portfol. Manage.*, Summer 1983, *9*(4), pp. 68. **[G: U.S.]**

Trueman, Brett. Optimality of the Disclosure of Private Information in a Production-Exchange Economy. *J. Finance*, June 1983, *38*(3), pp. 913–24.

Turnovsky, Stephen J. The Determination of Spot and Futures Prices with Storable Commodities.

Econometrica, September 1983, *51*(5), pp. 1363–87.

Turnovsky, Stephen J. and Ball, Katrina M. Covered Interest Parity and Speculative Efficiency: Some Empirical Evidence for Australia. *Econ. Rec.,* September 1983, *59*(166), pp. 271–80. **[G: Australia]**

Van Auken, Howard E. Tender Offers in a Contingent Claims Framework. *Rev. Bus. Econ. Res.,* Fall 1983, *19*(1), pp. 45–55.

Vanderhoof, Irwin T. The Use of Duration in the Dynamic Programming of Investments. **In** *Kaufman, G. G.; Bierwag, G. O. and Toevs, A., eds.,* 1983, pp. 43–57.

Varian, Hal R. Nonparametric Tests of Models of Investor Behavior. *J. Finan. Quant. Anal.,* September 1983, *18*(3), pp. 269–78.

Verrecchia, Robert E. Discretionary Disclosure. *J. Acc. Econ.,* December 1983, *5*(3), pp. 179–94.

Walsh, Carl E. Asset Prices, Asset Stocks and Rational Expectations. *J. Monet. Econ.,* May 1983, *11*(3), pp. 337–49.

Ward, Ronald W. and Behr, Robert M. Futures Trading Liquidity: An Application of a Futures Trading Model. *J. Futures Markets,* Summer 1983, *3*(2), pp. 207–24. **[G: U.S.]**

Webb, David C. Contingent Claims, Personal Loans and the Irrelevance of Corporate Financial Structure. *Econ. J.,* December 1983, *93*(372), pp. 832–46.

Woodward, Susan E. The Liquidity Premium and the Solidity Premium. *Amer. Econ. Rev.,* June 1983, *73*(3), pp. 348–61.

Wyplosz, Charles A. The Exchange and Interest Rate Term Structure under Risk Aversion and Rational Expectations. *J. Int. Econ.,* February 1983, *14*(1/2), pp. 123–39.

Yawitz, Jess B.; Maloney, Kevin J. and Marshall, William J. The Term Structure and Callable Bond Yield Spreads. *J. Portfol. Manage.,* Winter 1983, *9*(2), pp. 57–63.

Yilmaz, Mustafa R. The Use of Risk and Return Models for Multiattribute Decisions with Decomposable Utilities. *J. Finan. Quant. Anal.,* September 1983, *18*(3), pp. 279–85.

3132 Capital Markets: Empirical Studies, Including Regulation

Aftalion, Florin and Bompaire, Frédéric. France: Banking, Money, and Bond Markets. **In** *George, A. M. and Giddy, I. H., eds., Vol. 1,* 1983, pp. 4.5:1–26. **[G: France]**

Agmon, Tamir and Arad, Ruth. Currency-Related Risk and Risk Premium in the World's Currency Market. *Europ. Econ. Rev.,* August 1983, *22*(3), pp. 257–64.

van Agtmael, Antoine W. Issuance of Eurobonds: Syndication and Underwriting Techniques and Costs. **In** *George, A. M. and Giddy, I. H., eds., Vol. 1,* 1983, pp. 5.2:1–24. **[G: OECD]**

Aivazian, Varouj A., et al. Mean-Variance Utility Functions and the Demand for Risky Assets: An Empirical Analysis Using Flexible Functional Forms. *J. Finan. Quant. Anal.,* December 1983, *18*(4), pp. 411–24. **[G: U.K.]**

Aldersley, J. The Role of Risk in Industry Analysis. **In** *Corner, D. and Mayes, D. G., eds.,* 1983, pp. 95–106.

Allen, Deborah L. Japan: Banking, Money, and Bond Markets. **In** *George, A. M. and Giddy, I. H., eds., Vol. 1,* 1983, pp. 4.7:1–33. **[G: Japan]**

Amoako-Adu, Ben. The Canadian Tax Reform and Its Effect on Stock Prices: A Note. *J. Finance,* December 1983, *38*(5), pp. 1669–75. **[G: Canada]**

Andersen, Peter. Fiscal Policy 'Crowding-Out' of Private Investment in an Open Economy: The Case of Canada: Comment. **In** *Conklin, D. W. and Courchene, T. J., eds.,* 1983, pp. 249–53. **[G: U.S.; Canada]**

Anderson, James A. and St. Pierre, Kent E. Market Efficiency and Legal Liability: A Reply [The Potential Impact of Knowledge of Market Efficiency on the Legal Liability of Auditors]. *Accounting Rev.,* October 1983, *58*(4), pp. 833–36. **[G: U.S.]**

Arak, Marcelle. The Effect of the Tax Treatment of Treasury-Bill Futures on Their Rates. *J. Futures Markets,* Spring 1983, *3*(1), pp. 65–73. **[G: U.S.]**

Arak, Marcelle and Guentner, K. The Market for Tax-Exempt Issues: Why Are the Yields So High? *Nat. Tax J.,* June 1983, *36*(2), pp. 145–61. **[G: U.S.]**

Arbel, Avner and Strebel, Paul J. Pay Attention to Neglected Firms! *J. Portfol. Manage.,* Winter 1983, *9*(2), pp. 37–42. **[G: U.S.]**

Ariovich, G. The Impact of Political Tension on the Price of Gold. *J. Stud. Econ. Econometrics,* July 1983, (16), pp. 17–37.

Aron, Paul H. and Aron, Laurie J. Japan: Equity Markets. **In** *George, A. M. and Giddy, I. H., eds., Vol. 2,* 1983, pp. 6.7:1–40. **[G: Japan]**

Aron, Paul H. and Aron, Laurie J. The Asian Equities Markets. **In** *George, A. M. and Giddy, I. H., eds., Vol. 2,* 1983, pp. 6.9:1–54. **[G: Australia; Singapore; Malaysia; Hong Kong]**

Asay, Michael R. A Note on the Design of Commodity Option Contracts: Reply. *J. Futures Markets,* Fall 1983, *3*(3), pp. 335–38.

Asquith, K. Paul. Merger Bids, Uncertainty, and Stockholder Returns. *J. Finan. Econ.,* April 1983, *11*(1–4), pp. 51–83. **[G: U.S.]**

Asquith, K. Paul; Bruner, Robert F. and Mullins, David W., Jr. The Gains to Bidding Firms from Merger. *J. Finan. Econ.,* April 1983, *11*(1–4), pp. 121–39. **[G: U.S.]**

Asquith, K. Paul and Mullins, David W., Jr. The Impact of Initiating Dividend Payments on Shareholders' Wealth. *J. Bus.* Janurary 1983, *56*(1), pp. 77–96.

Baesel, Jerome B.; Shows, George and Thorp, Edward. The Cost of Liquidity Services in Listed Options: A Note. *J. Finance,* June 1983, *38*(3), pp. 989–95. **[G: U.S.]**

Baillie, Richard T.; Lippens, Robert E. and McMahon, Patrick C. Testing Rational Expectations and Efficiency in the Foreign Exchange Market. *Econometrica,* May, 1983, *51*(3), pp. 553–63. **[G: U.S.]**

Baldwin, Carliss Y. and Mason, Scott P. The Resolution of Claims in Financial Distress: The Case of Massey Ferguson. *J. Finance,* May 1983, *38*(2),

pp. 505–16. [G: U.S.]

Barone-Adesi, Giovanni and Talwar, Prem P. Market Models and Heteroscedasticity of Residual Security Returns. *J. Bus. Econ. Statist.*, April 1983, *1*(2), pp. 163–68. [G: U.S.]

Basu, Sanjoy. The Relationship between Earnings' Yield, Market Value and Return for NYSE Common Stocks: Further Evidence. *J. Finan. Econ.*, June 1983, *12*(1), pp. 129–56. [G: U.S.]

Beckers, Stan. Variances of Security Price Returns Based on High, Low, and Closing Prices. *J. Bus.*, January 1983, *56*(1), pp. 97–112.

Beckers, Stan and Soenen, Luc A. Gold Options, an Attractive Investment Instrument for the Non–U.S. Investor—The Case of the Belgian and Dutch Investor. *De Economist*, 1983, *131*(1), pp. 80–87. [G: Belgium; Netherlands]

Bell, Timothy Barnes. Market Reaction to Reserve Recognition Accounting. *J. Acc. Res.*, Spring 1983, *21*(1), pp. 1–17. [G: U.S.]

Belongia, Michael T. Commodity Options: A New Risk Management Tool for Agricultural Markets. *Fed. Res. Bank St. Louis Rev.*, June/July 1983, *65*(6), pp. 5–15. [G: U.S.]

Berglund, Tom; Wahlroos, Björn and Grandell, Lars. KOP:s och UNITAS generalindex för Hesingfors fondbörs i ljuset av ett nytt värdevägt index. (The KOP and the UNITAS indeces for the Helsinki Stock Exchange in Light of a New Value Weighted Index. With English summary.) *Liiketaloudellinen Aikak.*, 1983, *32*(1), pp. 30–41. [G: Finland]

Berglund, Tom; Wahlroos, Björn and Örnmark, Anders. The Weak-Form Efficiency of the Finnish and Scandinavian Stock Exchanges: A Comparative Note on Thin Trading. *Scand. J. Econ.*, 1983, *85*(4), pp. 521–30. [G: Scandinavia]

Bernard, Victor L. and Frecka, Thomas J. Evidence on the Existence of Common Stock Inflation Hedges. *J. Finan. Res.*, Winter 1983, *6*(4), pp. 301–12. [G: U.S.]

Bernstein, Peter L. Where Are the Maws with So Many Gulls to Feed Them? *J. Portfol. Manage.*, Fall 1983, *10*(1), pp. 4.

Bey, Roger P. Market Model Stationarity of Individual Public Utilities. *J. Finan. Quant. Anal.*, March 1983, *18*(1), pp. 67–85. [G: U.S.]

Bey, Roger P. The Market Model as an Appropriate Description of the Stochastic Process Generating Security Returns. *J. Finan. Res.*, Winter 1983, *6*(4), pp. 257–88. [G: U.S.]

Bhagat, Sanjai. The Effect of Pre-Emptive Right Amendments on Shareholder Wealth. *J. Finan. Econ.*, November 1983, *12*(3), pp. 289–310. [G: U.S.]

Bhattacharya, Mihir. Transactions Data Tests of Efficiency of the Chicago Board Options Exchange. *J. Finan. Econ.*, August 1983, *12*(2), pp. 161–85. [G: U.S.]

Bierman, Harold, Jr. A Comment of Optimizing Municipal Bond Bids. *J. Bank Res.*, Summer 1983, *14*(2), pp. 173–74. [G: U.S.]

Bierwag, G. O.; Kaufman, George G. and Toevs, Alden L. Recent Developments in Bond Portfolio Immunization Strategies. **In** *Kaufman, G. G.; Bierwag, G. O. and Toevs, A., eds.*, 1983, pp. 105–57. [G: U.S.]

Biffignandi, Silvia and Stefani, Silvana. On Testing the Impact of Inflation on Stock Market: An Approach through Alternative Methodologies. *Econ. Notes*, 1983, (1), pp. 173–90. [G: Italy]

Bilson, John F. O. The Evaluation and Use of Foreign Exchange Rate Forecasting Services. **In** *Herring, R. J., ed.*, 1983, pp. 149–79. [G: OECD]

Bird, Ron; Chin, Helen and McCrae, Michael. The Performance of Australian Superannuation Funds. *Australian J. Manage.*, June 1983, *8*(1), pp. 49–69. [G: Australia]

Bjerring, James H.; Lakonishok, Josef and Vermaelen, Theo. Stock Prices and Financial Analysts' Recommendations. *J. Finance*, March 1983, *38*(1), pp. 187–204. [G: Canada]

Blejer, Mario I. and Khan, Mohsin S. The Foreign Exchange Market in a Highly-Open Developing Economy: The Case of Singapore. *J. Devel. Econ.*, February/April 1983, *12*(1/2), pp. 237–49. [G: Singapore]

Bletsas, Apostolos C. and Tebbutt, S. G. Thin Capital Markets: A Case Study of the Kuwaiti Stock Markets: A Note. *Appl. Econ.*, February 1983, *15*(1), pp. 121–22. [G: Kuwait]

Bloch, Howard and Pupp, Roger. The January Barometer Revisited and Rejected. *J. Portfol. Manage.*, Winter 1983, *9*(2), pp. 48–50. [G: U.S.]

Blum, Gerald A. and Lewellen, Wilbur G. Negotiated Brokerage Commissions and the Individual Investor. *J. Finan. Quant. Anal.*, September 1983, *18*(3), pp. 331–43. [G: U.S.]

Blume, Marshall E. and Stambaugh, Robert F. Biases in Computed Returns: An Application to the Size Effect. *J. Finan. Econ.*, November 1983, *12*(3), pp. 387–404. [G: U.S.]

Bodie, Zvi. Commodity Futures as a Hedge against Inflation. *J. Portfol. Manage.*, Spring 1983, *9*(3), pp. 12–17. [G: U.S.]

Bonomo, Vittorio and Tanner, J. Ernest. Expected Monetary Changes and Relative Prices: A Look at Evidence from the Stock Market. *Southern Econ. J.*, October 1983, *50*(2), pp. 334–45. [G: U.S.]

Boothe, Paul M. Speculative Profit Opportunities in the Canadaian Foreign Exchange Market, 1974–78. *Can. J. Econ.*, November 1983, *16*(4), pp. 603–11. [G: Canada; U.S.]

Bowen, Robert M.; Castanias, Richard P. and Daley, Lane A. Intra-Industry Effects of the Accident at Three Mile Island. *J. Finan. Quant. Anal.*, March 1983, *18*(1), pp. 87–111. [G: U.S.]

Bowlin, Oswald D. and Dukes, William P. The Dual Nature of Beta Responsiveness. *J. Portfol. Manage.*, Winter 1983, *9*(2), pp. 51–56. [G: U.S.]

Bradley, Michael; Desai, Anand and Kim, E. Han. The Rationale behind Interfirm Tender Offers: Information or Synergy? *J. Finan. Econ.*, April 1983, *11*(1–4), pp. 183–206. [G: U.S.]

Bradley, Michael and Wakeman, L. Macdonald. The Wealth Effects of Targeted Share Repurchases. *J. Finan. Econ.*, April 1983, *11*(1–4), pp. 301–28. [G: U.S.]

Branch, Ben; Gleit, Alan and Tamule, Harold B. On the Instability of Alphas. *Rev. Bus. Econ. Res.*, Winter, 1983, *18*(2), pp. 78–81. [G: U.S.]

Braswell, Ronald C.; Nosari, E. Joe and Sumners, Dewitt L. A Comparison of the True Interest Costs of Competitive and Negotiated Underwritings in the Municipal Bond Market: A Note. *J. Money, Credit, Banking,* February 1983, *15*(1), pp. 102–06. **[G: U.S.]**

Braswell, Ronald C.; Sumners, Dewitt L. and Reinhart, Walter J. The Effect of the Tax Act of 1982 on the Appropriate Coupon Rate Strategy for Issuing Corporate Bonds. *Nat. Tax J.,* June 1983, *36*(2), pp. 255–56. **[G: U.S.]**

Brenner, Menachem and Galai, Dan. The Effect of Inflation on the Rate of Return on Common Stocks in an Inflation Intensive Capital Market: The Israeli Case 1965–79. **In** *Schmukler, N. and Marcus, E., eds.,* 1983, pp. 616–24. **[G: Israel]**

Breuer, Rolf E. Frankfurt: Equity Markets. **In** *George, A. M. and Giddy, I. H., eds., Vol. 2,* 1983, pp. 6.4:1–32. **[G: W. Germany]**

Brickley, James A. Shareholder Wealth, Information Signaling and the Specially Designated Dividend: An Empirical Study. *J. Finan. Econ.,* August 1983, *12*(2), pp. 187–209. **[G: U.S.]**

Briones, Rodrigo. Latin American Money Markets. **In** *George, A. M. and Giddy, I. H., eds., Vol. 1,* 1983, pp. 4.9:1–14. **[G: Latin America]**

Brooks, LeRoy D.; Ingram, Robert W. and Copeland, Ronald M. Credit Risk, Beta, and Bond Ratings. *Nebr. J. Econ. Bus.,* Winter, 1983, *22*(1), pp. 3–14. **[G: U.S.]**

Brown, Philip; Kleidon, Allan W. and Marsh, Terry A. New Evidence on the Nature of Size-Related Anomalies in Stock Prices. *J. Finan. Econ.,* June 1983, *12*(1), pp. 33–56.

Brown, Philip, et al. Stock Return Seasonalities and the Tax-Loss Selling Hypothesis: Analysis of the Arguments and Australian Evidence. *J. Finan. Econ.,* June 1983, *12*(1), pp. 105–27. **[G: U.S.]**

Brown, R. L. and Shevlin, T. J. Modelling Option Prices in Australia Using the Black–Scholes Model. *Australian J. Manage.,* June 1983, *8*(1), pp. 1–20. **[G: Australia]**

Brox, James A. The Yield-Liquidity Trade-Off in Canadian Portfolios. *Quart. Rev. Econ. Bus.,* Autumn 1983, *23*(3), pp. 70–80. **[G: Canada]**

Brush, John S. and Boles, Keith E. The Predictive Power in Relative Strength & CAPM. *J. Portfol. Manage.,* Summer 1983, *9*(4), pp. 20–23. **[G: U.S.]**

Bryant, Ralph C. Floating Exchange Rates after Ten Years: Comments and Discussion. *Brookings Pap. Econ. Act.,* 1983, (1), pp. 71–79. **[G: U.S.; U.K.; Japan; W. Germany]**

Burns, Malcolm R. An Empirical Analysis of Stockholder Injury under § 2 of the Sherman Act. *J. Ind. Econ.,* June 1983, *31*(4), pp. 333–62. **[G: U.S.]**

de Capitani, Werner. The Swiss Banks and the United States Securities Laws. *Wirtsch. Recht,* 1983, *35*(2/3), pp. 182–93. **[G: U.S.; Switzerland]**

Carleton, Willard T.; Chambers, Donald R. and Lakonishok, Josef. Inflation Risk and Regulatory Lag. *J. Finance,* May 1983, *38*(2), pp. 419–31. **[G: U.S.]**

Carlton, Dennis W. Futures Trading, Market Interrelationships, and Industry Structure. *Amer. J. Agr. Econ.,* May 1983, *65*(2), pp. 380–87. **[G: U.S.]**

Carpenter, Michael D. and Chew, I. Keong. The Effects of Default Risk on the Market Model. *J. Finan. Res.,* Fall 1983, *6*(3), pp. 223–29. **[G: U.S.]**

Chandy, P. R. and Cherry, Richard. The Realized Yield Behavior of Junk Bonds. *Rev. Bus. Econ. Res.,* Winter, 1983, *18*(2), pp. 40–50. **[G: U.S.]**

Chang, Lucia S.; Most, Kenneth S. and Brain, Carlos W. The Utility of Annual Reports: An International Study. *J. Int. Bus. Stud.,* Spring/Summer 1983, *14*(1), pp. 63–84. **[G: New Zealand; U.S.; U.K.]**

Cheney, John M. Rating Classification and Bond Yield Volatility. *J. Portfol. Manage.,* Spring 1983, *9*(3), pp. 51–57. **[G: U.S.]**

Choi, Dosoung and Philippatos, George C. An Examination of Merger Synergism. *J. Finan. Res.,* Fall 1983, *6*(3), pp. 239–56.

Choi, Dosoung and Strong, Robert A. The Pricing of When-Issued Common Stock: A Note. *J. Finance,* September 1983, *38*(4), pp. 1293–98. **[G: U.S.]**

Chow, Chee W. The Impacts of Accounting Regulation on Bondholder and Shareholder Wealth: The Case of the Securities Acts. *Accounting Rev.,* July 1983, *58*(3), pp. 485–520. **[G: U.S.]**

Christensen, Peter E. Immunization at Smith Barney. **In** *Kaufman, G. G.; Bierwag, G. O. and Toevs, A., eds.,* 1983, pp. 269–73. **[G: U.S.]**

Chua, Jess H. and Woodward, Richard S. J. M. Keynes's Investment Performance: A Note. *J. Finance,* March 1983, *38*(1), pp. 232–35. **[G: U.K.]**

Clark, Truman A. and Weinstein, Mark I. The Behavior of the Common Stock of Bankrupt Firms. *J. Finance,* May 1983, *38*(2), pp. 489–504. **[G: U.S.]**

Conroy, Robert M. and Rendleman, Richard J., Jr. Pricing Commodities When Both Price and Output Are Uncertain. *J. Futures Markets,* Winter 1983, *3*(4), pp. 439–50.

Contoni, Renato. Le Borse estere nel 1982. (Foreign Stock Markets in 1982. With English summary.) *Bancaria,* January 1983, *39*(1), pp. 42–52. **[G: U.S.; EEC; Japan; Australia; Hong Kong]**

Cornell, Bradford. Money Supply Announcements and Interest Rates: Another View. *J. Bus.,* January 1983, *56*(1), pp. 1–23. **[G: U.S.]**

Cornell, Bradford and French, Kenneth R. Taxes and the Pricing of Stock Index Futures. *J. Finance,* June 1983, *38*(3), pp. 675–94.

Cornell, Bradford and French, Kenneth R. The Pricing of Stock Index Futures. *J. Futures Markets,* Spring 1983, *3*(1), pp. 1–14. **[G: U.S.]**

Corner, Desmond and Matatko, J. Risk and Rates of Return in British Unit Trusts: Bull and Bear Market Movements, 1973–8. **In** *Corner, D. and Mayes, D. G., eds.,* 1983, pp. 54–72. **[G: U.K.]**

Corti, Mario A. Switzerland: Banking, Money, and Bond Markets. **In** *George, A. M. and Giddy, I. H., eds., Vol. 1,* 1983, pp. 4.6:1–50. **[G: Switzerland]**

Craine, Roger. The Baby Boom, the Housing Market and the Stock Market. *Fed. Res. Bank San Fran-*

cisco Econ. Rev., Spring 1983, (2), pp. 6–11. [G: U.S.]

Dann, Larry Y. and DeAngelo, Harry. Standstill Agreements, Privately Negotiated Stock Repurchases, and the Market for Corporate Control. *J. Finan. Econ.*, April 1983, *11* (1–4), pp. 275–300. [G: U.S.]

Davis, Kevin. Inflation and the Financial System: Discussion. **In** *Pagan, A. R. and Trivedi, P. K., eds.*, 1983, pp. 221–23. [G: Australia]

De Marchi, Gianluigi. La polizza di credito commerciale, versione italiana del commercial paper. (Commercial Credit Policies, the Italian Version of Commercial Paper. With English summary.) *L'Impresa*, 1983, *25*(2), pp. 65–68. [G: Italy]

DeAngelo, Harry and Rice, Edward M. Antitakeover Charter Amendments and Stockholder Wealth. *J. Finan. Econ.*, April 1983, *11* (1–4), pp. 329–59. [G: U.S.]

Dietrich, J. Kimball and Heckerman, D. G. Determinants of the Systematic Risk of Electric Utilities: Theory and Estimation. *Appl. Econ.*, October 1983, *15*(5), pp. 619–33. [G: U.S.]

Dimson, E. and Marsh, P. R. The Stability of UK Risk Measures and the Problem of Thin Trading. *J. Finance*, June 1983, *38*(3), pp. 753–83. [G: U.K.]

Dodd, Peter and Warner, Jerold B. On Corporate Governance: A Study of Proxy Contests. *J. Finan. Econ.*, April 1983, *11* (1–4), pp. 401–38. [G: U.S.]

Dornbusch, Rudiger. Floating Exchange Rates after Ten Years: Comments and Discussion. *Brookings Pap. Econ. Act.*, 1983, (1), pp. 79–86. [G: U.S.; U.K.; Japan; W. Germany]

Dufey, Gunter and Krishnan, E. West Germany: Banking, Money, and Bond Markets. **In** *George, A. M. and Giddy, I. H., eds., Vol. 1*, 1983, pp. 4.4:1–26. [G: W. Germany]

Dullum, Kåre B. and Stonehill, Arthur. Towards an International Cost of Capital. *Nationaløkon. Tidsskr.*, 1983, *121* (1), pp. 43–60. [G: Denmark]

Dunn, Kenneth B. and Singleton, Kenneth J. An Empirical Analysis of the Pricing of Mortgage-Backed Securities. *J. Finance*, May 1983, *38*(2), pp. 612–23. [G: U.S.]

Dunn, Patricia C. and Theisen, Rolf D. How Consistently Do Active Managers Win? *J. Portfol. Manage.*, Summer 1983, *9*(4), pp. 47–50. [G: U.S.]

Eckbo, B. Espen. Horizontal Mergers, Collusion, and Stockholder Wealth. *J. Finan. Econ.*, April 1983, *11* (1–4), pp. 241–73. [G: U.S.]

Edelman, Richard B. Telecommunications Betas: Are They Stable and Unique? *J. Portfol. Manage.*, Fall 1983, *10*(1), pp. 46–52. [G: U.S.]

Edwards, Charles E. and Stansell, Stanley R. New Car Sales Data and Automobile Company Stock Prices: A Study of the Causal Relationships. *Bus. Econ.*, May 1983, *18*(3), pp. 27–35. [G: U.S.]

Edwards, Franklin R. Futures Markets in Transition: The Uneasy Balance between Government and Self-regulation. *J. Futures Markets*, Summer 1983, *3*(2), pp. 191–206.

Edwards, Franklin R. The Clearing Association in Futures Markets: Guarantor and Regulator. *J. Futures Markets*, Winter 1983, *3*(4), pp. 369–92. [G: U.S.]

Eger, Carol Ellen. An Empirical Test of the Redistribution Effect in Pure Exchange Mergers. *J. Finan. Quant. Anal.*, December 1983, *18*(4), pp. 547–72. [G: U.S.]

Ehrlich, Edna E. Foreign Pension Fund Investments in the United States. *Fed. Res. Bank New York Quart. Rev.*, Spring 1983, *8*(1), pp. 1–12. [G: Canada; Netherlands; Japan; U.K.; U.S.]

Elton, Edwin; Gruber, Martin and Rentzler, Joel. A Simple Examination of the Empirical Relationship between Dividend Yields and Deviations from the CAPM. *J. Banking Finance*, March 1983, *7*(1), pp. 135–46. [G: U.S.]

Estep, Tony; Hanson, Nick and Johnson, Cal. Errata [Sources of Value and Risk in Common Stocks]. *J. Portfol. Manage.*, Fall 1983, *10*(1), pp. 17. [G: U.S.]

Estep, Tony; Hanson, Nick and Johnson, Cal. Sources of Value and Risk in Common Stocks. *J. Portfol. Manage.*, Summer 1983, *9*(4), pp. 5–13. [G: U.S.]

Feldstein, Martin S. and Slemrod, Joel. The Lock-in Effect of the Capital Gains Tax: Some Time-Series Evidence. **In** *Feldstein, M. (I)*, 1983, *1978*, pp. 251–54. [G: U.S.]

Feldstein, Martin S.; Slemrod, Joel and Yitzhaki, Shlomo. The Effects of Taxation on the Selling of Corporate Stock and the Realization of Capital Gains. **In** *Feldstein, M. (I)*, 1983, *1980*, pp. 237–50. [G: U.S.]

Feldstein, Martin S. and Yitzhaki, Shlomo. The Effects of the Capital Gains Tax on the Selling and Switching of Common Stock. **In** *Feldstein, M. (I)*, 1983, *1978*, pp. 216–36. [G: U.S.]

Fielitz, Bruce D. Calculating the Bond Equivalent Yield for T-Bills. *J. Portfol. Manage.*, Spring 1983, *9*(3), pp. 58–60. [G: U.S.]

Fielitz, Bruce D. and Rozelle, James P. Stable Distributions and the Mixtures of Distributions Hypotheses for Common Stock Returns. *J. Amer. Statist. Assoc.*, March 1983, *78*(381), pp. 28–36. [G: U.S.]

Figlewski, Stephen and Fitzgerald, M. Desmond. Options on Commodity Futures: Recent Experience in the London Market. **In** *Brenner, M., ed.*, 1983, pp. 223–35. [G: U.K.]

Fischer, P. J. Note, Advance Refunding and Municipal Bond Market Efficiency. *J. Econ. Bus.*, 1983, *35*(1), pp. 11–20. [G: U.S.]

Fischer, Stanley. On the Nonexistence of Privately Issued Index Bonds in the U.S. Capital Market. **In** *Dornbusch, R. and Simonsen, M. H., eds.*, 1983, *1977*, pp. 247–66. [G: U.S.]

Fong, H. Gifford. Immunization in Practice: Comments. **In** *Kaufman, G. G.; Bierwag, G. O. and Toevs, A., eds.*, 1983, pp. 275–77.

Fong, H. Gifford; Pearson, Charles and Vasicek, Oldrich. Bond Performance: Analyzing Sources of Return. *J. Portfol. Manage.*, Spring 1983, *9*(3), pp. 46–50. [G: U.S.]

Forker, J. J. Managerial Quality, Financial Structure and Signalling: A Test of Pricing Efficiency in the UK Equity Securities Market. *Managerial Dec. Econ.*, December 1983, *4*(4), pp. 266–77. [G: U.K.]

Fraser, Donald R. and Stern, Jerrold J. Flower Bonds,

Tax Changes, and the Efficiency of the Bond Market. *Rev. Bus. Econ. Res.*, Winter, 1983, *18*(2), pp. 13–24. [G: U.S.]

French, Dan W.; Groth, John C. and Kolari, James W. Current Investor Expectations and Better Betas. *J. Portfol. Manage.*, Fall 1983, *10*(1), pp. 12–17. [G: U.S.]

French, Dan W. and Henderson, Glenn V., Jr. Risk and Return of Long and Short Option Portfolios Using the Black-Scholes Model. *Rev. Bus. Econ. Res.*, Fall 1983, *19*(1), pp. 56–66. [G: U.S.]

French, Kenneth R. A Comparison of Futures and Forward Prices. *J. Finan. Econ.*, November 1983, *12*(3), pp. 311–42. [G: U.K.; U.S.]

Galai, Dan. Pricing of Optional Bonds. *J. Banking Finance*, September 1983, *7*(3), pp. 323–37. [G: Israel]

Galli, Alexander. Switzerland: Equity Markets. **In** *George, A. M. and Giddy, I. H., eds., Vol. 2*, 1983, pp. 6.6:1–26. [G: Switzerland]

Gandhi, Devinder K.; Saunders, Anthony and Woodward, Richard S. Thin Capital Markets: A Case Study of the Kuwaiti Stock Market: A Reply. *Appl. Econ.*, February 1983, *15*(1), pp. 123–24. [G: Kuwait]

Garbade, Kenneth D. and Silber, William L. Price Movements and Price Discovery in Futures and Cash Markets. *Rev. Econ. Statist.*, May 1983, *65*(2), pp. 289–97. [G: U.S.]

Gau, George W. and Goldberg, Michael A. Interest Rate Risk, Residential Mortgages and Financial Futures Markets. *Amer. Real Estate Urban Econ. Assoc. J.*, Winter 1983, *11*(4), pp. 445–61. [G: U.S.]

Gay, Gerald D.; Kolb, Robert W. and Chiang, Raymond. Interest Rate Hedging: An Empirical Test of Alternative Strategies. *J. Finan. Res.*, Fall 1983, *6*(3), pp. 187–97. [G: U.S.]

George, Abraham M. Currency Exposure Management. **In** *George, A. M. and Giddy, I. H., eds., Vol. 2*, 1983, pp. 8.8:1–33.

George, Abraham M. The United States Equity Markets. **In** *George, A. M. and Giddy, I. H., eds., Vol. 1*, 1983, pp. 6.1:1–40. [G: U.S.]

George, Abraham M. and Ittoop, Vinita M. International Portfolio Diversification: Risks and Returns. **In** *George, A. M. and Giddy, I. H., eds., Vol. 2*, 1983, pp. 8.3:1–53. [G: U.S.; U.K.; Japan; W. Germany]

Geske, Robert; Roll, Richard and Shastri, Kuldeep. Over-the-Counter Option Market Dividend Protection and "Biases" in the Black-Scholes Model: A Note. *J. Finance*, September 1983, *38*(4), pp. 1271–77. [G: U.S.]

Gidlow, R. M. Hedging Policies of the South African Gold Mining Industry. *S. Afr. J. Econ.*, June 1983, *51*(2), pp. 270–82. [G: S. Africa]

Giles, R. Philip. United States: Banking, Money, and Bond Markets. **In** *George, A. M. and Giddy, I. H., eds., Vol. 1*, 1983, pp. 4.2:1–27. [G: U.S.]

Giurleo, Diego S. Canada: Banking, Money, and Bond Markets. **In** *George, A. M. and Giddy, I. H., eds., Vol. 1*, 1983, pp. 4.8:1–35. [G: Canada]

Givoly, Dan and Ovadia, Arie. Year-End Tax-Induced Sales and Stock Market Seasonality. *J. Finance*, March 1983, *38*(1), pp. 171–85. [G: U.S.]

Glickstein, David A. and Wubbels, Rolf E. Dow Theory Is Alive and Well! *J. Portfol. Manage.*, Spring 1983, *9*(3), pp. 28–32. [G: U.S.]

Gnes, Paolo. The Financial Structure and Financing of Firms: Developments and Prospects. *Rev. Econ. Cond. Italy*, June 1983, (2), pp. 301–23. [G: Italy]

Goodman, Laurie S. New Options Markets. *Fed. Res. Bank New York Quart. Rev.*, Autumn 1983, *8*(3), pp. 35–47. [G: U.S.]

Gordon, Myron J. The Impact of Real Factors and Inflation on the Performance of the U.S. Stock Market from 1960 to 1980. *J. Finance*, May 1983, *38*(2), pp. 553–63. [G: U.S.]

Gordon, Roger H. and Slemrod, Joel. A General Equilibrium Simulation Study of Subsidies to Municipal Expenditures. *J. Finance*, May 1983, *38*(2), pp. 585–94. [G: U.S.]

Gouldey, Bruce K. and Gray, Gary J. Implementing Mean-Variance Theory in the Selection of U.S. Government Bond Portfolios: Reply. *J. Bank Res.*, Autumn 1983, *14*(3), pp. 237–38. [G: U.S.]

Grammatikos, Theoharry and Saunders, Anthony. Stability and the Hedging Performance of Foreign Currency Futures. *J. Futures Markets*, Fall 1983, *3*(3), pp. 295–305. [G: Canada; U.K.; Japan; W. Germany; Switzerland]

Grant, John. Deficits and Capital Markets. **In** *Conklin, D. W. and Courchene, T. J., eds.*, 1983, pp. 261–83. [G: Canada]

Gray, M. R. Inflation and the Financial System: Discussion. **In** *Pagan, A. R. and Trivedi, P. K., eds.*, 1983, pp. 220. [G: Australia]

Gultekin, Mustafa N. and Gultekin, N. Bulent. Stock Market Seasonality: International Evidence. *J. Finan. Econ.*, December 1983, *12*(4), pp. 469–81. [G: OECD]

Gultekin, N. Bulent. Stock Market Returns and Inflation Forecasts. *J. Finance*, June 1983, *38*(3), pp. 663–73. [G: U.S.]

Gurwitz, Aaron S. Twelve Improvements in the Municipal Credit System. *Fed. Res. Bank New York Quart. Rev.*, Winter 1983-84, *8*(4), pp. 14–25. [G: U.S.]

Halpern, Paul. Corporate Acquisitions: A Theory of Special Cases? A Review of Event Studies Applied to Acquisitions. *J. Finance*, May 1983, *38*(2), pp. 297–317.

Hammond, Peter J. Overlapping Expectations and Hart's Conditions for Equilibrium in a Securities Model. *J. Econ. Theory*, October 1983, *31*(1), pp. 170–75.

Harrington, Scott E. The Relationship between Risk and Return: Evidence for Life Insurance Stocks. *J. Risk Ins.*, December 1983, *50*(4), pp. 587–610. [G: U.S.]

Harris, John M., Jr.; Roenfeldt, Rodney L. and Cooley, Philip L. Evidence of Financial Leverage Clienteles. *J. Finance*, September 1983, *38*(4), pp. 1125–32. [G: U.S.]

Harris, William G. Inflation Risk as Determinant of the Discount Rate in Tort Settlements. *J. Risk Ins.*, June 1983, *50*(2), pp. 265–80. [G: U.S.]

Harrison, Walter T., Jr.; Tomassini, Lawrence A. and Dietrich, J. Richard. The Use of Control Groups in Capital Market Research. *J. Acc. Res.*, Spring 1983, *21* (1), pp. 65–77. [G: U.S.]

Hendershott, Patric H.; Shilling, James D. and Villani, Kevin E. Measurement of the Spreads between Yields on Various Mortgage Contracts and Treasury Securities. *Amer. Real Estate Urban Econ. Assoc. J.*, Winter 1983, *11* (4), pp. 476–90. [G: U.S.]

Hetherington, Norriss S. Taking the Risk Out of Risk Arbitrage. *J. Portfol. Manage.*, Summer 1983, *9* (4), pp. 24–25. [G: U.S.]

Hill, Joanne; Liro, Joseph and Schneeweis, Thomas. Hedging Performance of GNMA Futures under Rising and Falling Interest Rates. *J. Futures Markets,* Winter 1983, *3* (4), pp. 403–13. [G: U.S.]

Hill, Joanne and Schneeweis, Thomas. International Diversification of Equities and Fixed-Income Securities. *J. Finan. Res.*, Winter 1983, *6* (4), pp. 333–43. [G: W. Europe; U.S.; Japan]

Hill, Joanne and Schneeweis, Thomas. The Effect of Three Mile Island on Electric Utility Stock Prices: A Note. *J. Finance,* September 1983, *38* (4), pp. 1285–92. [G: U.S.]

Hirschfeld, David J. A Fundamental Overview of the Energy Futures Market. *J. Futures Markets,* Spring 1983, *3* (1), pp. 75–100. [G: U.S.]

Hite, Gailen L. and Owers, James E. Security Price Reactions around Corporate Spin-Off Announcements. *J. Finan. Econ.*, December 1983, *12* (4), pp. 409–36. [G: U.S.]

Hoag, James W. The Valuation of Commodity Options. **In** *Brenner, M., ed.*, 1983, pp. 183–221. [G: U.K.]

Hubley, Roger. Canada: Equity Markets. **In** *George, A. M. and Giddy, I. H., eds., Vol. 2,* 1983, pp. 6.8:1–24. [G: Canada]

Hughes, M. The Consequences of the Removal of Exchange Controls on Portfolios and the Flow of Funds in the U.K. **In** *Corner, D. and Mayes, D. G., eds.*, 1983, pp. 181–206. [G: U.K.]

Ibbotson, Roger G. and Siegel, Laurence B. The World Market Wealth Portfolio. *J. Portfol. Manage.*, Winter 1983, *9* (2), pp. 5–17. [G: OECD; Hong Kong; Singapore]

Ingersoll, Jonathan E., Jr. Is Immunization Feasible? Evidence from the CRSP Data. **In** *Kaufman, G. G.; Bierwag, G. O. and Toevs, A., eds.*, 1983, pp. 163–82. [G: U.S.]

Ingram, Robert W.; Brooks, LeRoy D. and Copeland, Ronald M. The Information Content of Municipal Bond Rating Changes: A Note. *J. Finance,* June 1983, *38* (3), pp. 997–1003. [G: U.S.]

Ingram, Robert W. and Chewning, Eugene G. The Effect of Financial Disclosure Regulation on Security Market Behavior. *Accounting Rev.*, July 1983, *58* (3), pp. 562–80. [G: U.S.]

Jacquillat, Bertrand. Paris: Equity Markets. **In** *George, A. M. and Giddy, I. H., eds., Vol. 2,* 1983, pp. 6.5:1–26. [G: France]

Jain, Prem C. The Impact of Accounting Regulation on the Stock Market: The Case of Oil and Gas Companies—Some Additional Results. *Accounting Rev.*, July 1983, *58* (3), pp. 633–38. [G: U.S.]

Jean, William H. and Helms, Billy P. Geometric Mean Approximations. *J. Finan. Quant. Anal.*, September 1983, *18* (3), pp. 287–93. [G: U.S.]

Jensen, Michael C. and Ruback, Richard S. The Market for Corporate Control: The Scientific Evidence. *J. Finan. Econ.*, April 1983, *11* (1–4), pp. 5–50. [G: U.S.]

Kaen, Fred R.; Helms, Billy P. and Booth, G. Geoffrey. The Integration of Eurodollar and U.S. Money Market Interest Rates in the Futures Market. *Weltwirtsch. Arch.*, 1983, *119* (4), pp. 601–15. [G: U.S.; W. Europe]

Karathanassis, G. and Tolias, T. Factors Affecting Share Prices: A Statistical Analysis of Prices on the Greek Stock Exchange. *Rivista Int. Sci. Econ. Com.*, December 1983, *30* (12), pp. 1150–60. [G: Greece]

Keen, Howard, Jr. The Impact of a Dividend Cut Announcement of Bank Share Prices. *J. Bank Res.*, Winter 1983, *13* (4), pp. 274–81. [G: U.S.]

Keim, Donald B. Size-Related Anomalies and Stock Return Seasonality: Further Empirical Evidence. *J. Finan. Econ.*, June 1983, *12* (1), pp. 13–32. [G: U.S.]

Kidwell, David S. and Koch, Timothy W. Market Segmentation and the Term Structure of Municipal Yields. *J. Money, Credit, Banking,* February 1983, *15* (1), pp. 40–55. [G: U.S.]

Kidwell, David S. and Trzcinka, Charles A. The Impact of the New York City Fiscal Crisis on the Interest Cost of New Issue Municipal Bonds. *J. Finan. Quant. Anal.*, September 1983, *18* (3), pp. 381–99. [G: U.S.]

Kindleberger, Charles P. Key Currencies and Financial Centres. **In** *[Giersch, H.],* 1983, pp. 75–90. [G: OECD]

Klein, Barry L. and Rubin, Robert M. The Gold Market. **In** *George, A. M. and Giddy, I. H., eds., Vol. 1,* 1983, pp. 2.6:1–20.

Klein Haneveld, Henk A. Perspective: International Portfolio Diversification: A Practitioner's Point of View. **In** *Herring, R. J., ed.*, 1983, pp. 143–47. [G: OECD]

Klein, Martin. Ist die Theorie effizienter Märkte empirisch widerlegt? (Is the Theory of Efficient Markets Empirically Refuted? With English summary.) *Kredit Kapital,* 1983, *16* (1), pp. 126–40.

Kohlhagen, Steven W. Overlapping National Investment Portfolios: Evidence and Implications of International Integration of Secondary Markets for Financial Assets. **In** *Hawkins, R. G.; Levich, R. M. and Wihlborg, C. G., eds.*, 1983, pp. 113–37. [G: OECD]

Kolb, Robert W. and Gay, Gerald D. The Performance of Live Cattle Futures as Predictors of Subsequent Spot Prices. *J. Futures Markets,* Spring 1983, *3* (1), pp. 55–63. [G: U.S.]

Kolb, Robert W.; Morin, Roger A. and Gay, Gerald D. Regulation, Regulatory Lag, and the Use of Futures Markets. *J. Finance,* May 1983, *38* (2), pp. 405–18. [G: U.S.]

Kon, Stanley J. The Market-Timing Performance of Mutual Fund Managers. *J. Bus.*, July 1983, *56* (3), pp. 323–47. [G: U.S.]

Koppenhaver, G. D. A T-Bill Futures Hedging Strategy for Bank. *Fed. Res. Bank Dallas Econ. Rev.*, March 1983, pp. 15–28. [G: U.S.]

Koppenhaver, G. D. The Forward Pricing Efficiency

of the Live Cattle Futures Market. *J. Futures Markets,* Fall 1983, *3*(3), pp. 307–19. **[G: U.S.]**

Koutsoyiannis, A. A Short-Run Pricing Model for a Speculative Asset, Tested with Data from the Gold Bullion Market. *Appl. Econ.,* October 1983, *15*(5), pp. 563–81.

Kritzman, Mark. Can Bond Managers Perform Consistently? *J. Portfol. Manage.,* Summer 1983, *9*(4), pp. 54–56. **[G: U.S.]**

Kudla, Ronald J. and McInish, Thomas H. Valuation Consequences of Corporate Spin-Offs. *Rev. Bus. Econ. Res.,* Winter, 1983, *18*(2), pp. 71–77. **[G: U.S.]**

Larcker, David F. The Association between Performance Plan Adoption and Corporate Capital Investment. *J. Acc. Econ.,* April 1983, *5*(1), pp. 3–30. **[G: U.S.]**

Larcker, David F. and Revsine, Lawrence. The Oil and Gas Accounting Controversy: An Analysis of Economic Consequences. *Accounting Rev.,* October 1983, *58*(4), pp. 706–32. **[G: U.S.]**

Largay, James A., III and Paul, Jack W. Market Efficiency and the Legal Liability of Auditors: Comment. *Accounting Rev.,* October 1983, *58*(4), pp. 820–32. **[G: U.S.]**

Lasserre, Pierre. L'aide aux mines d'or ou Les silences du fantôme de Bretton Woods. (With English summary.) *Can. Public Policy,* December 1983, *9*(4), pp. 446–57. **[G: Canada]**

Lease, Ronald C.; McConnell, John J. and Mikkelson, Wayne H. The Market Value of Control in Publicly-Traded Corporations. *J. Finan. Econ.,* April 1983, *11*(1–4), pp. 439–71. **[G: U.S.]**

Lee, Cheng-Few and Leuthold, Raymond M. Investment Horizon, Risk, and Return in Commodity Futures Markets: An Empirical Analysis with Daily Data. *Quart. Rev. Econ. Bus.,* Autumn 1983, *23*(3), pp. 6–18. **[G: U.S.]**

Leonard, Paul A. Some Factors Determining Municipal Revenue Bond Interest Costs. *J. Econ. Bus.,* 1983, *35*(1), pp. 71–82. **[G: U.S.]**

Lerner, Eugene M. and Theerathorn, Pochara. The Returns of Different Investment Strategies. *J. Portfol. Manage.,* Summer 1983, *9*(4), pp. 26–28. **[G: U.S.]**

Leuthold, Raymond M. Commercial Use and Speculative Measures of the Livestock Commodity Futures Markets. *J. Futures Markets,* Summer 1983, *3*(2), pp. 113–35. **[G: U.S.]**

Levy, Haim. Economic Evaluation of Voting Power of Common Stock. *J. Finance,* March 1983, *38*(1), pp. 79–93. **[G: U.S.]**

Levy, Haim and Sarnat, Marshall. International Portfolio Diversification. **In** *Herring, R. J., ed.,* 1983, pp. 115–42. **[G: OECD]**

Linn, Scott C. and McConnell, John J. An Empirical Investigation of the Impact of 'Antitakeover' Amendments on Common Stock Prices. *J. Finan. Econ.,* April 1983, *11*(1–4), pp. 361–99. **[G: U.S.]**

Lipartito, Kenneth J. The New York Cotton Exchange and the Development of the Cotton Futures Market. *Bus. Hist. Rev.,* Spring 1983, *57*(1), pp. 50–72. **[G: U.S.]**

Litvak, Lawrence. Pension Funds and Economic Renewal. **In** *Barker, M., ed. (I),* 1983, pp. 159–301. **[G: U.S.]**

Litvak, Lawrence and Daniels, Belden. Innovations in Development Finance. **In** *Barker, M., ed. (I),* 1983, pp. 1–158. **[G: U.S.]**

Lizondo, Jose Saul. Foreign Exchange Futures Prices under Fixed Exchange Rates. *J. Int. Econ.,* February 1983, *14*(1/2), pp. 69–84. **[G: Mexico]**

Lofthouse, Stephen. The Efficient Market Theory: A Case Study. *Rivista Int. Sci. Econ. Com.,* October–November 1983, *30*(10–11), pp. 1073–91. **[G: U.K.]**

Longstreth, Bevis. Toward Neutral Principles of International Securities Regulation. *Wirtsch. Recht,* 1983, *35*(2/3), pp. 164–81.

Maccarone, Michele. Vendita a domicilio di valori mobiliari. (Door-to-Door Selling of Securities. With English summary.) *Bancaria,* May–June 1983, *39*(5–6), pp. 523–25. **[G: Italy]**

Madura, Jeff. Empirical Measurement of Exchange Rate Betas. *J. Portfol. Manage.,* Summer 1983, *9*(4), pp. 43–46. **[G: Switzerland; EEC; U.S.; Canada; Japan]**

Madura, Jeff and Nosari, E. Joe. Speculation in International Money Markets. *Atlantic Econ. J.,* July 1983, *11*(2), pp. 87–90.

Magraw, Daniel. Legal Aspects of International Bonds. **In** *George, A. M. and Giddy, I. H., eds., Vol. 1,* 1983, pp. 5.3:1–30. **[G: EEC; U.S.]**

Maimera, Fabrizio. Sulla tipizzazione dei titoli atipici. (Regulation of Atypical Securities. With English summary.) *Bancaria,* May–June 1983, *39*(5–6), pp. 519–22. **[G: Italy]**

Marsh, Terry A. and Rosenfeld, Eric R. Stochastic Processes for Interest Rates and Equilibrium Bond Prices. *J. Finance,* May 1983, *38*(2), pp. 635–46. **[G: U.S.]**

Marston, Richard C. Comments on "Overlapping National Investment Portfolios: Evidence and Implications of International Integration of Secondary Markets for Financial Assets." **In** *Hawkins, R. G.; Levich, R. M. and Wihlborg, C. G., eds.,* 1983, pp. 139–43. **[G: OECD]**

Martin, John D. and Petty, J. William. An Analysis of the Performance of Publicly Traded Venture Capital Companies. *J. Finan. Quant. Anal.,* September 1983, *18*(3), pp. 401–10. **[G: U.S.]**

Martin, Linda J. and Henderson, Glenn V., Jr. On Bond Ratings and Pension Obligations: A Note. *J. Finan. Quant. Anal.,* December 1983, *18*(4), pp. 463–70. **[G: U.S.]**

Masulis, Ronald W. The Impact of Capital Structure Change on Firm Value: Some Estimates. *J. Finance,* March 1983, *38*(1), pp. 107–26. **[G: U.S.]**

Mathur, Ike and Hanagan, Kyran. Are Multinational Corporations Superior Investment Vehicles for Achieving International Diversification? *J. Int. Bus. Stud.,* Winter 1983, *14*(3), pp. 135–46.

Maycock, James E. The United Kingdom: Money and Bond Markets. **In** *George, A. M. and Giddy, I. H., eds., Vol. 1,* 1983, pp. 4.3:1–21. **[G: U.K.]**

McCallum, John S. A Comment on Implementing Mean-Variance Theory in the Selection of U.S. Government Bond Portfolios. *J. Bank Res.,* Summer 1983, *14*(2), pp. 175–76. **[G: U.S.]**

McDonald, Bill. An Empirical Examination of the Preference Structure for the Distribution of Earnings. *J. Econ. Bus.,* August 1983, *35*(3/4), pp.

441–51. [G: U.S.]

McDonald, Bill. Beta Nonstationarity and the Use of the Chen and Lee Estimator: A Note. *J. Finance,* June 1983, *38*(3), pp. 1005–09. [G: U.S.]

McDonald, Bill and Morris, Michael H. The Existence of Heteroschedasticity and Its Effect on Estimates of the Market Model Parameters. *J. Finan. Res.,* Summer 1983, *6*(2), pp. 115–26.

McNichols, Maureen and Manegold, James G. The Effect of the Information Environment on the Relationship between Financial Disclosure and Security Price Variability. *J. Acc. Econ.,* April 1983, *5*(1), pp. 49–74. [G: U.S.]

Meek, Gary K. U.S. Securities Market Responses to Alternate Earnings Disclosures of Non-U.S. Multinational Corporations. *Accounting Rev.,* April 1983, *58*(2), pp. 394–402. [G: U.S.]

Meeker, Larry G.; Joy, O. Maurice and Cogger, Kenneth O. Valuation of Controlling Shares in Closely Held Banks. *J. Banking Finance,* June 1983, *7*(2), pp. 175–88. [G: U.S.]

Meese, Richard A. and Rogoff, Kenneth S. Empirical Exchange Rate Models of the Seventies: Do They Fit Out of Sample? *J. Int. Econ.,* February 1983, *14*(1/2), pp. 3–24. [G: U.S.]

Mendelson, Morris. The Eurobond and Foreign Bond Markets. **In** *George, A. M. and Giddy, I. H., eds., Vol. 1,* 1983, pp. 5.1:1–31. [G: OECD]

Merrett, A. J. and Newbould, Gerald D. Integrating Financial Performance & Stock Valuation. *J. Portfol. Manage.,* Fall 1983, *10*(1), pp. 27–32. [G: U.S.]

Miller, Paul F., Jr. Managing Investment Portfolios: A Review Article. *J. Portfol. Manage.,* Summer 1983, *9*(4), pp. 57.

Modani, Naval K.; Cooley, Philip L. and Roenfeldt, Rodney L. Stability of Market Risk Surrogates. *J. Finan. Res.,* Spring 1983, *6*(1), pp. 33–40. [G: U.S.]

Modest, David M. and Sundaresan, Mahadevan. The Relationship between Spot and Futures Prices in Stock Index Futures Markets: Some Preliminary Evidence. *J. Futures Markets,* Spring 1983, *3*(1), pp. 15–41. [G: U.S.]

Moore, Geoffrey H. Security Markets and Business Cycles. **In** *Moore, G. H.,* 1983, *1975,* pp. 139–60. [G: U.S.]

Morse, Dale and Ushman, Neal. The Effect of Information Announcements on the Market Microstructure. *Accounting Rev.,* April 1983, *58*(2), pp. 247–58. [G: U.S.]

Moyer, R. Charles and Chatfield, Robert. Market Power and Systematic Risk. *J. Econ. Bus.,* 1983, *35*(1), pp. 123–30. [G: U.S.]

Moyer, R. Charles and Simonson, Donald G. Federal Financing Pressure: The Incidence of Crowding Out. *Rev. Bus. Econ. Res.,* Winter, 1983, *18*(2), pp. 25–39. [G: U.S.]

Muller, Frederick L.; Fielitz, Bruce D. and Greene, Myron T. Errata [S&P Quality Group Rankings: Risk and Return]. *J. Portfol. Manage.,* Fall 1983, *10*(1), pp. 17. [G: U.S.]

Muller, Frederick L.; Fielitz, Bruce D. and Greene, Myron T. S&P Quality Group Rankings: Risk and Return. *J. Portfol. Manage.,* Summer 1983, *9*(4), pp. 39–42. [G: U.S.]

Murray, Dennis. The Effect of Certain Research Design Choices on the Assessment of the Market's Reaction to LIFO Changes: A Methodological Study. *J. Acc. Res.,* Spring 1983, *21*(1), pp. 128–40. [G: U.S.]

Nauss, Robert M. and Keeler, Bradford R. Optimizing Municipal Bond Bids: Reply. *J. Bank Res.,* Autumn 1983, *14*(3), pp. 239–40. [G: U.S.]

Nunn, Kenneth P., Jr.; Madden, Gerald P. and Gombola, Michael J. Are Some Insiders More "Inside" than Others? *J. Portfol. Manage.,* Spring 1983, *9*(3), pp. 18–22. [G: U.S.]

Olsen, Robert A. The Impact of Inflation on Human Capital as a Diversifiable Asset. *Rev. Bus. Econ. Res.,* Fall 1983, *19*(1), pp. 13–25. [G: U.S.]

Oppenheimer, Henry R. and Schlarbaum, Gary G. Investment Policies of Property–Liability Insurers and Pension Plans: A Lesson from Ben Graham. *J. Risk Ins.,* December 1983, *50*(4), pp. 611–30. [G: U.S.]

Osbon, Anthony D. The Market Environment for Utility Securities. **In** *[Bonbright, J. C.],* 1983, pp. 235–47. [G: U.S.]

Palmon, Dan and Yaari, Uzi. Taxation of Capital Gains and the Behavior of Stock Prices over the Dividend Cycle. *Amer. Econ.,* Spring 1983, *27*(1), pp. 13–22.

Paltschik, Mikael and Strandvik, Tore. Konsumentperspektiv på aktiesparandet. (A Consumer Perspective on Company Shares as a Form of Savings. With English summary.) *Ekon. Samfundets Tidskr.,* 1983, *36*(1), pp. 25–36. [G: Finland]

Park, Yoon S. Asian Money Markets. **In** *George, A. M. and Giddy, I. H., eds., Vol. 1,* 1983, pp. 4.10:1–20. [G: Singapore; Hong Kong; Malaysia; Australia; S. Korea]

Parry, Robert W., Jr. Moody's Analytical Overview of 25 Leading U.S. Cities—Revisited. *Public Finance Quart.,* January 1983, *11*(1), pp. 79–93. [G: U.S.]

Peavy, John W., III and Edgar, S. Michael. A Multiple Discriminant Analysis of BHC Commercial Paper Ratings. *J. Banking Finance,* June 1983, *7*(2), pp. 161–73. [G: U.S.]

Penman, Stephen H. The Predictive Content of Earnings Forecasts and Dividends. *J. Finance,* September 1983, *38*(4), pp. 1181–99. [G: U.S.]

Pincus, Morton. Information Characteristics of Earnings Announcements and Stock Market Behavior. *J. Acc. Res.,* Spring 1983, *21*(1), pp. 155–83. [G: U.S.]

Pozdena, Randall J. and Iben, Ben. Pricing Debt Instruments: The Options Approach. *Fed. Res. Bank San Francisco Econ. Rev.,* Summer 1983, (3), pp. 19–30. [G: U.S.]

Protopapadakis, Aris. Some Indirect Evidence on Effective Capital Gains Tax Rates. *J. Bus.,* April 1983, *56*(2), pp. 127–38. [G: U.S.]

Protopapadakis, Aris and Stoll, Hans R. Spot and Futures Prices and the Law of One Price. *J. Finance,* December 1983, *38*(5), pp. 1431–55. [G: U.S.; U.K.]

Puchon, Gilles. Defining and Measuring Currency Exposure. **In** *George, A. M. and Giddy, I. H., eds.,*

Vol. 2, 1983, pp. 8.7:1–18.

Puglisi, Donald J. and Vignola, Anthony J., Jr. An Examination of Federal Agency Debt Pricing Practices. *J. Finan. Res.,* Summer 1983, *6*(2), pp. 83–92. [G: U.S.]

Putnam, Bluford H. Comments on "Overlapping National Investment Portfolios: Evidence and Implications of International Integration of Secondary Markets of Financial Assets." **In** *Hawkins, R. G.; Levich, R. M. and Wihlborg, C. G., eds.,* 1983, pp. 145–48. [G: OECD]

Quinn, Brian Scott and Aldred, Peregrine. The Eurobond Secondary Market. **In** *George, A. M. and Giddy, I. H., eds., Vol. 1,* 1983, pp. 5.4:1–17.

Rausser, Gordon C. and Carter, Colin A. Futures Market Efficiency in the Soybean Complex. *Rev. Econ. Statist.,* August 1983, *65*(3), pp. 469–78. [G: U.S.]

Reilly, Frank K.; Griggs, Frank T. and Wong, Wenchi. Determinants of the Aggregate Stock Market Earnings Multiple. *J. Portfol. Manage.,* Fall 1983, *10*(1), pp. 36–45. [G: U.S.]

Reinganum, Marc R. Portfolio Strategies Based on Market Capitalization. *J. Portfol. Manage.,* Winter 1983, *9*(2), pp. 29–36. [G: U.S.]

Reinganum, Marc R. The Anomalous Stock Market Behavior of Small Firms in January: Empirical Tests for Tax-Loss Selling Effects. *J. Finan. Econ.,* June 1983, *12*(1), pp. 89–104. [G: U.S.]

Reinganum, Marc R. and Smith, Janet Kiholm. Investor Preference for Large Firms: New Evidence on Economies of Size. *J. Ind. Econ.,* December 1983, *32*(2), pp. 213–27. [G: U.S.]

Renshaw, Edward F. The Anatomy of Stock Market Cycles. *J. Portfol. Manage.,* Fall 1983, *10*(1), pp. 53–57. [G: U.S.]

Ritchken, Peter H. and Salkin, Harvey M. Safety First Selection Techniques for Option Spreads. *J. Portfol. Manage.,* Spring 1983, *9*(3), pp. 61–67.

Roll, Eric. Financing Investment. **In** *Heertje, A., ed.,* 1983, pp. 188–218. [G: W. Europe]

Roll, Richard. On Computing Mean Returns and the Small Firm Premium. *J. Finan. Econ.,* November 1983, *12*(3), pp. 371–86. [G: U.S.]

Roll, Richard. Vas ist das? *J. Portfol. Manage.,* Winter 1983, *9*(2), pp. 18–28. [G: U.S.]

Rosen, Jeffrey S. The Impact of the Futures Trading Act of 1982 upon Commodity Regulation. *J. Futures Markets,* Fall 1983, *3*(3), pp. 235–58. [G: U.S.]

Rosen, Kenneth T. and Katz, Larry. Money Market Mutual Funds: An Experiment in Ad Hoc Deregulation: A Note. *J. Finance,* June 1983, *38*(3), pp. 1011–17. [G: U.S.]

Rosenfeld, James D. The Effect of Common-Stock Dividend Reductions on the Returns of Nonconvertible Preferred Stocks: A Note. *J. Finance,* June 1983, *38*(3), pp. 1019–24. [G: U.S.]

Rosenthal, Leonard. An Empirical Test of the Efficiency of the ADR Market. *J. Banking Finance,* March 1983, *7*(1), pp. 17–29. [G: U.S.]

Rotberg, Eugene H. Perspective: Some Informal Remarks on Debt Management and Liquidity. **In** *Herring, R. J., ed.,* 1983, pp. 212–19.

Ruback, Richard S. Assessing Competition in the Market for Corporate Acquisitions. *J. Finan. Econ.,* April 1983, *11*(1–4), pp. 141–53. [G: U.S.]

Ruback, Richard S. The Cities Service Takeover: A Case Study. *J. Finance,* May 1983, *38*(2), pp. 319–30. [G: U.S.]

Rushinek, Avi, et al. The Construction of an International Investor's Perception Model for Corporate Published Forecasted Financial Reports for the USA, the UK and New Zealand. *Managerial Dec. Econ.,* December 1983, *4*(4), pp. 258–65. [G: New Zealand; U.K.; U.S.]

Rutterford, Janette. Index-Linked Gilts. *Nat. Westminster Bank Quart. Rev.,* November 1983, pp. 2–17. [G: U.K.]

Saint-Pierre, Jacques. Les taux de commission sur les transactions boursières au Canada: Acte II. (Commission Rates on Stock Exchange Transactions in Canada: Act II. With English summary.) *L'Actual. Econ.,* June 1983, *59*(2), pp. 350–72. [G: Canada]

Salinger, Michael A. and Summers, Lawrence H. Tax Reform and Corporate Investment: A Microeconometric Simulation Study. **In** *Feldstein, M., ed.,* 1983, pp. 247–81. [G: U.S.]

Salvemini, Maria Teresa. The Treasury and the Money Market: The New Responsibilities after the Divorce. *Rev. Econ. Cond. Italy,* February 1983, (1), pp. 33–54. [G: Italy]

Scherr, Bruce A. and Madsen, Howard C. Observations on the Relationship between Agricultural Commodity Prices and Real Interest Rates. *J. Futures Markets,* Spring 1983, *3*(1), pp. 47–54. [G: U.S.]

Schipper, Katherine and Smith, Abbie. Effects of Recontracting on Shareholder Wealth: The Case of Voluntary Spin-Offs. *J. Finan. Econ.,* December 1983, *12*(4), pp. 437–67. [G: U.S.]

Schipper, Katherine and Thompson, Rex. Evidence on the Capitalized Value of Merger Activity for Acquiring Firms. *J. Finan. Econ.,* April 1983, *11*(1–4), pp. 85–119. [G: U.S.]

Schipper, Katherine and Thompson, Rex. The Impact of Merger-Related Regulations on the Shareholders of Acquiring Firms. *J. Acc. Res.,* Spring 1983, *21*(1), pp. 184–221. [G: U.S.]

Schmidt, Hartmut. Marktorganisationsbestimmte Kosten und Transaktionskosten als börsenpolitische Kategorien—Grundsätzliche Überlegungen zur Weiterentwicklung des Anlegerschutzes aus ökonomischer Sicht. (Costs and Transaction Costs Determined by Market Organization as Categories in Stock Exchange Policy. With English summary.) *Kredit Kapital,* 1983, *16*(2), pp. 184–204.

Schultz, Paul. Transaction Costs and the Small Firm Effect: A Comment. *J. Finan. Econ.,* June 1983, *12*(1), pp. 81–88. [G: U.S.]

Sears, R. Stephen and Trennepohl, Gary L. Diversification and Skewness in Option Portfolios. *J. Finan. Res.,* Fall 1983, *6*(3), pp. 199–212. [G: U.S.]

Senchack, Andrew J., Jr. and Easterwood, John C. Cross Hedging CDs with Treasury Bill Futures. *J. Futures Markets,* Winter 1983, *3*(4), pp. 429–38. [G: U.S.]

Shafer, Jeffrey R. and Loopesko, Bonnie E. Floating Exchange Rates after Ten Years. *Brookings Pap. Econ. Act.,* 1983, (1), pp. 1–70. [G: U.S.; U.K.; Japan; W. Germany]

Shane, Philip B. and Spicer, Barry H. Market Response to Environmental Information Produced Outside the Firm. *Accounting Rev.*, July 1983, *58*(3), pp. 521–38. **[G: U.S.]**

Sharma, Jandhyala L. Efficient Capital Markets and Random Character of Stock Price Behavior in a Developing Economy. *Indian Econ. J.*, October–December 1983, *31*(2), pp. 53–70. **[G: India]**

Sharpe, I. G. New Information and Australian Equity Returns: A Multivariate Analysis. *Australian J. Manage.*, June 1983, *8*(1), pp. 21–34. **[G: Australia]**

Sharpe, William F. Recent Developments in Bond Portfolio Immunization Strategies: Comments. **In** *Kaufman, G. G.; Bierwag, G. O. and Toevs, A., eds.*, 1983, pp. 159–62. **[G: U.S.]**

Shawky, Hany; Forbes, Ronald and Frankle, Alan. Liquidity Services and Capital Market Equilibrium: The Case for Money Market Mutual Funds. *J. Finan. Res.*, Summer 1983, *6*(2), pp. 141–52. **[G: U.S.]**

Sherman, Eugene J. A Gold Pricing Model. *J. Portfol. Manage.*, Spring 1983, *9*(3), pp. 68–70.

Singleton, J. Clay; Gronewoller, Paul L. and Hennessey, Harry W. The Time Invariance Properties of Important Bond Rating Standards. *Rev. Bus. Econ. Res.*, Fall 1983, *19*(1), pp. 75–86. **[G: U.S.]**

Skelton, Jeffrey L. Relative Risk in Municipal and Corporate Debt. *J. Finance,* May 1983, *38*(2), pp. 625–34. **[G: U.S.]**

Skony, Marilyn P. The Foreign Exchange Futures Market. **In** *George, A. M. and Giddy, I. H., eds., Vol. 1,* 1983, pp. 2.5:1–21.

Smith, David B. A Framework for Analyzing Nonconvertible Preferred Stock Risk. *J. Finan. Res.*, Summer 1983, *6*(2), pp. 127–39.

Solomon, Anthony M. Statement to the Subcommittee on Domestic Monetary Policy of the U.S. House Committee on Banking, Finance, and Urban Affairs, April 25, 1983. *Fed. Res. Bull.*, May 1983, *69*(5), pp. 346–56. **[G: U.S.]**

Sorensen, Eric H. Who Puts The Slope in the Municipal Yield Curve? *J. Portfol. Manage.*, Summer 1983, *9*(4), pp. 61–65. **[G: U.S.]**

Speakes, Jeffrey K. The Phased-In Money Market Certificate Hedge. *J. Futures Markets,* Summer 1983, *3*(2), pp. 185–90.

Spiceland, J. David and Trapnell, Jerry E. The Effect of Market Conditions and Risk Classifications on Market Model Parameters. *J. Finan. Res.*, Fall 1983, *6*(3), pp. 217–22. **[G: U.S.]**

Spilka, Walter, Jr. An Overview of the USDA Crop and Livestock Information System. *J. Futures Markets,* Summer 1983, *3*(2), pp. 167–76. **[G: U.S.]**

Stambaugh, Robert F. Testing the CAPM with Broader Market Indexes: A Problem of Mean-Deficiency. *J. Banking Finance,* March 1983, *7*(1), pp. 5–16. **[G: U.S.]**

Stammer, D. W. and Valentine, T. J. Inflation and the Financial System. **In** *Pagan, A. R. and Trivedi, P. K., eds.*, 1983, pp. 183–219. **[G: Australia]**

Stansell, Stanley R. A Study of the Causal Relationships between Treasury Bill Futures Prices and the Volume of Futures Traded. *Quarterly Journal of Business and Economics,* Autumn 1983, *22*(4), pp. 3–24. **[G: U.S.]**

Steffanci, Thomas J. Bond Immunization in Practice. **In** *Kaufman, G. G.; Bierwag, G. O. and Toevs, A., eds.*, 1983, pp. 281–85. **[G: U.S.]**

Stenius, Marianne. Testing the Efficiency of the Finnish Bond Market. *Liiketaloudellinen Aikak.*, 1983, *32*(1), pp. 19–29. **[G: Finland]**

Stennis, Earl A.; Pinar, Musa and Allen, Albert J. The Futures Market and Price Discovery in the Textile Industry. *Amer. J. Agr. Econ.*, May 1983, *65*(2), pp. 308–10. **[G: U.S.]**

Stillman, Robert. Examining Antitrust Policy towards Horizontal Mergers. *J. Finan. Econ.*, April 1983, *11*(1–4), pp. 225–40. **[G: U.S.]**

Stoll, Hans R. and Whaley, Robert E. Transaction Costs and the Small Firm Effect. *J. Finan. Econ.*, June 1983, *12*(1), pp. 57–79. **[G: U.S.]**

Stover, Roger D. The Interaction between Pricing and Underwriting Spread in the New Issue Convertible Debt Market. *J. Finan. Res.*, Winter 1983, *6*(4), pp. 323–32. **[G: U.S.]**

Strong, Robert A. Do Share Price and Stock Splits Matter? *J. Portfol. Manage.*, Fall 1983, *10*(1), pp. 58–64. **[G: U.S.]**

Swanson, Peggy E. Compensating Balances and Foreigners' Dollar Deposits in United States Banks. *J. Finan. Res.*, Fall 1983, *6*(3), pp. 257–63. **[G: U.S.]**

Swary, Itzhak. Bank Acquisition of Non-bank Firms: An Empirical Analysis of Administrative Decisions. *J. Banking Finance,* June 1983, *7*(2), pp. 213–30. **[G: U.S.]**

Talwar, Prem P. Detecting a Shift in Location: Some Robust Tests. *J. Econometrics,* December 1983, *23*(3), pp. 353–67. **[G: U.S.]**

Taylor, John C. and Clements, Kenneth W. A Simple Portfolio Allocation Model of Financial Wealth. *Europ. Econ. Rev.*, November 1983, *23*(2), pp. 241–51. **[G: Australia]**

Taylor, Michael and Thrift, Nigel. The Role of Finance in the Evolution and Functioning of Industrial Systems. **In** *Hamilton, F. E. I. and Linge, G. J. R., eds.*, 1983, pp. 359–85. **[G: U.K.; U.S.]**

Taylor, Stephen J. Price Trends in Wool Prices when Sydney Futures Are Actively Traded. *Australian Econ. Pap.*, June 1983, *22*(40), pp. 99–105. **[G: Australia]**

Taylor, William M. The Estimation of Quality-Adjusted Rates of Return in Stamp Auctions. *J. Finance,* September 1983, *38*(4), pp. 1095–110. **[G: U.S.]**

Thompson, R. S. Diversifying Mergers and Risk: Some Empirical Tests. *J. Econ. Stud.*, 1983, *10*(3), pp. 12–21. **[G: U.K.]**

Tronzano, Marco. Testing the Efficiency of the Spot Foreign-Exchange Market: Some Preliminary Results for the Italian Lira. *Econ. Int.*, May–August–November 1983, *36*(2–3–4), pp. 262–77. **[G: Italy]**

Vagts, Detlev F. The Scope of Application and Enforcement of U.S. Laws. *Wirtsch. Recht,* 1983, *35*(2/3), pp. 72–97. **[G: U.S.]**

Valentine, Stuart. The U.K. Equity Markets. **In** *George, A. M. and Giddy, I. H., eds., Vol. 2,* 1983, pp. 6.3:1–44. **[G: U.K.]**

Van Horne, James C. and Heaton, Hal B. Government Security Dealers' Positions, Information and Interest-Rate Expectations: A Note. *J. Fi-*

nance, December 1983, *38*(5), pp. 1643–49. [G: U.S.]

Van Horne, James C. and Heaton, Hal B. Securities Inventories and Excess Returns. *J. Finan. Res.,* Summer 1983, *6*(2), pp. 93–102. [G: U.S.]

Vessilier, Elisabeth. Aspects financiers des nationalisations. (Financial Aspects of Nationalisations. With English summary.) *Revue Écon.,* May 1983, *34*(3), pp. 466–95. [G: France]

Visser, F. and Affleck-Graves, J. F. An Analysis of the Comovement of Shares Listed on the Johannesburg Stock Exchange. *J. Stud. Econ. Econometrics,* July 1983, (17), pp. 28–49. [G: S. Africa]

Walker, Townsend. The Mechanics of Covering Foreign Exchange Exposures. In *George, A. M. and Giddy, I. H., eds., Vol. 2,* 1983, pp. 8.9:1–58.

Wansley, James W.; Roenfeldt, Rodney L. and Cooley, Philip L. Abnormal Returns from Merger Profiles. *J. Finan. Quant. Anal.,* June 1983, *18*(2), pp. 149–62. [G: U.S.]

Ward, C. W. R. Methods of Incorporating Risk in the Analysis of Commercial Property Investment: Multi-period Asset Pricing Approach. In *Corner, D. and Mayes, D. G., eds.,* 1983, pp. 135–61. [G: U.K.]

Ward, James S. Immunization in Practice: Comments. In *Kaufman, G. G.; Bierwag, G. O. and Toevs, A., eds.,* 1983, pp. 287–91. [G: U.S.]

Ward, Ronald W. and Behr, Robert M. Allocating Nonreported Futures Commitments. *J. Futures Markets,* Winter 1983, *3*(4), pp. 393–401. [G: U.S.]

Waymire, Gregory and Pownall, Grace. Some Evidence on Potential Effects of Contemporaneous Earnings Disclosures in Tests of Capital Market Effects Associated with FASB Exposure Draft No. 19. *J. Acc. Res.,* Autumn 1983, *21*(2), pp. 629–43. [G: U.S.]

Weinstein, Mark I. Bond Systematic Risk and the Option Pricing Model. *J. Finance,* December 1983, *38*(5), pp. 1415–29. [G: U.S.]

Whiteside, Mary M.; Dukes, William P. and Dunne, Patrick M. Short Term Impact of Option Trading on Underlying Securities. *J. Finan. Res.,* Winter 1983, *6*(4), pp. 313–21. [G: U.S.]

Wier, Peggy. The Costs of Antimerger Lawsuits: Evidence from the Stock Market. *J. Finan. Econ.,* April 1983, *11*(1–4), pp. 207–24. [G: U.S.]

Wirick, R. G. Fiscal Policy 'Crowding-Out' of Private Investment in an Open Economy: The Case of Canada. In *Conklin, D. W. and Courchene, T. J., eds.,* 1983, pp. 215–49. [G: U.S.; Canada]

Wolf, Charles and Pohlman, Larry. The Recovery of Risk Preferences from Actual Choices. *Econometrica,* May, 1983, *51*(3), pp. 843–50. [G: U.S.]

Wood, John H. Familiar Developments in Bank Loan Markets. *Fed. Res. Bank Dallas Econ. Rev.,* November 1983, pp. 1–13. [G: U.S.]

Woodward, Richard S. The Performance of U.K. Investment Trusts as Internationally Diversified Portfolios over the Period 1968 to 1977. *J. Banking Finance,* September 1983, *7*(3), pp. 417–26. [G: U.K.]

Woolridge, J. Randall. Dividend Changes and Security Prices. *J. Finance,* December 1983, *38*(5), pp. 1607–15. [G: U.S.]

Woolridge, J. Randall. Ex-Date Stock Price Adjustment to Stock Dividends: A Note. *J. Finance,* March 1983, *38*(1), pp. 247–55. [G: U.S.]

Woolridge, J. Randall. Stock Dividends as Signals. *J. Finan. Res.,* Spring 1983, *6*(1), pp. 1–12. [G: U.S.]

Wymeersch, Eddy. Securities Market Regulation in Europe. In *George, A. M. and Giddy, I. H., eds., Vol. 1,* 1983, pp. 6.2:1–51. [G: EEC]

Yalawar, Yalaguresh B. Determinants of Callable Convertible Bond Prices. *J. Econ. Bus.,* June 1983, *35*(2), pp. 169–87. [G: U.S.]

Zemon, Ray B. The Role of Immunization in Bond Management. In *Kaufman, G. G.; Bierwag, G. O. and Toevs, A., eds.,* 1983, pp. 293–96. [G: U.S.]

314 Financial Intermediaries

3140 Financial Intermediaries

Aftalion, Florin and Bompaire, Frédéric. France: Banking, Money, and Bond Markets. In *George, A. M. and Giddy, I. H., eds., Vol. 1,* 1983, pp. 4.5:1–26. [G: France]

Allen, Deborah L. Japan: Banking, Money, and Bond Markets. In *George, A. M. and Giddy, I. H., eds., Vol. 1,* 1983, pp. 4.7:1–33. [G: Japan]

Baer, Herbert. Thrift Dominance and Specialization in Housing Finance: The Role of Taxation. *Housing Finance Rev.,* Oct 1983, *2*(4), pp. 353–67. [G: U.S.]

Bain, Andrew D. Understanding the Scottish Economy: Markets for Finance. In *Ingham, K. P. D. and Love, J., eds.,* 1983, pp. 55–64. [G: U.K.]

Barker, Michael. Financing State and Local Economic Development: Introduction. In *Barker, M., ed. (I),* 1983, pp. xv–xxvii. [G: U.S.]

Barth, James R.; Cordes, Joseph J. and Yezer, Anthony M. J. An Analysis of Informational Restrictions on the Lending Decisions of Financial Institutions. *Econ. Inquiry,* July 1983, *21*(3), pp. 349–60. [G: U.S.]

Batlin, Carl Alan. Interest Rate Risk, Prepayment Risk, and the Futures Market Hedging Strategies of Financial Intermediaries. *J. Futures Markets,* Summer 1983, *3*(2), pp. 177–84.

Baxter, William F. Bank Interchange of Transactional Paper: Legal and Economic Perspectives. *J. Law Econ.,* October 1983, *26*(3), pp. 541–88.

Benston, George J. The Regulation of Financial Services. In *Benston, G. J., ed.,* 1983, pp. 28–63. [G: U.S.]

Boggs, H. Glenn, II and Lilly, Claude C., III. FSLIC: A Financial Buffer? *Calif. Manage. Rev.,* January 1983, *25*(2), pp. 96–106. [G: U.S.]

Booth, James R. NOW Accounts: The Competitive Battle in the Western States. *J. Bank Res.,* Winter 1983, *13*(4), pp. 317–20. [G: U.S.]

Bradfield, Michael. Statement to U.S. House Subcommittee on Commerce, Consumer, and Monetary Affairs of the Committee on Government Operations, July 21, 1983. *Fed. Res. Bull.,* August 1983, *69*(8), pp. 609–17. [G: U.S.]

Bussière, Eric. The Interests of the Banque de l'Union Parisienne in Czechoslovakia, Hungary and the Balkans, 1919–30. **In** *Teichova, A. and Cottrell, P. L., eds.,* 1983, pp. 399–410. **[G: France; Central Europe]**

Calabresi, Gian Franco. Concorrenza, stabilità ed efficienza nell'ambito delle casse di risparmio. (Competitivity, Stability and Efficiency of Savings Banks. With English summary.) *Bancaria,* December 1983, *39*(12), pp. 1266–75. **[G: Italy]**

Carron, Andrew S. The Political Economy of Financial Regulation. **In** *Noll, R. G. and Owen, B. M.,* 1983, pp. 69–83. **[G: U.S.]**

Chan, Yuk-Shee. On the Positive Role of Financial Intermediation in Allocation of Venture Capital in a Market with Imperfect Information. *J. Finance,* December 1983, *38*(5), pp. 1543–68.

Chandavarkar, A. G. Money and Credit (1858–1947). **In** *Kumar, D., ed.,* 1983, pp. 762–803. **[G: India]**

Chateau, John-Peter D. The Demand for and Supply of Deposits by Credit Unions: The Caisses Populaires' Case—Reply and Comments. *J. Banking Finance,* June 1983, *7*(2), pp. 289–93.

Cheng, Hang-Sheng. Financial Reform in Australia and New Zealand. *Fed. Res. Bank San Francisco Econ. Rev.,* Winter 1983, (1), pp. 9–24. **[G: Australia; New Zealand]**

Christensen, Peter E. Immunization at Smith Barney. **In** *Kaufman, G. G.; Bierwag, G. O. and Toevs, A., eds.,* 1983, pp. 269–73. **[G: U.S.]**

Cingano, Francesco. L'intermediazione bancaria: limiti operativi attuali e prospettive di ampliamento funzionale (Banking Intermediation: Present Operational Limits and Prospects for Enlargement of Role. With English summary.) *Bancaria,* February 1983, *39*(2), pp. 147–53. **[G: Italy]**

Cochrane, W. G. and Lyall, K. J. Portfolio Theory and the Management of Investment Trust Companies. **In** *Corner, D. and Mayes, D. G., eds.,* 1983, pp. 75–94.

Corti, Mario A. Switzerland: Banking, Money, and Bond Markets. **In** *George, A. M. and Giddy, I. H., eds., Vol. 1,* 1983, pp. 4.6:1–50. **[G: Switzerland]**

Costi, Renzo. Riflessioni in tema di enti creditizi pubblici. (Public Credit Institutions. With English summary.) *Bancaria,* July 1983, *39*(7), pp. 581–92. **[G: Italy]**

Cottrell, P. L. The Hungarian General Credit Bank in the 1920s: Commentary. **In** *Teichova, A. and Cottrell, P. L., eds.,* 1983, pp. 374. **[G: Hungary]**

Crapp, Harvey R. Scale Economies in the N.S.W. Credit Union Industry. *Australian J. Manage.,* June 1983, *8*(1), pp. 35–48. **[G: Australia]**

DeMagistris, Robin C. and Esaki, Howard. MMDA Rates and Flows. *Fed. Res. Bank New York Quart. Rev.,* Autumn 1983, *8*(3), pp. 26–27. **[G: U.S.]**

Deshmukh, Sudhakar D.; Greenbaum, Stuart I. and Kanatas, George. Interest Rate Uncertainty and the Financial Intermediary's Choice of Exposure. *J. Finance,* March 1983, *38*(1), pp. 141–47.

Deshmukh, Sudhakar D.; Greenbaum, Stuart I. and Kanatas, George. Lending Policies of Financial Intermediaries Facing Credit and Funding Risk. *J. Finance,* June 1983, *38*(3), pp. 873–86.

Dufey, Gunter and Krishnan, E. West Germany: Banking, Money, and Bond Markets. **In** *George, A. M. and Giddy, I. H., eds., Vol. 1,* 1983, pp. 4.4:1–26. **[G: W. Germany]**

Dunham, Constance. Unraveling the Complexity of NOW Account Pricing. *New Eng. Econ. Rev.,* May/June 1983, pp. 30–45. **[G: U.S.]**

Dunham, Constance and Guerin-Calvert, Margaret. How Quickly Can Thrifts Move into Commercial Lending? *New Eng. Econ. Rev.,* November/December 1983, pp. 42–54. **[G: U.S.]**

Eisenbeis, Robert A. What Is the Role of Government in a Major Restructuring of Financial Institutions in the 80s?: Discussant's Comments. *J. Bank Res.,* Spring 1983, *14*(1), pp. 33–36. **[G: U.S.]**

Eizenga, Weitze. Le banche e l'andamento dei tassi d'interesse. (Banks and Interest Rate Developments. With English summary.) *Bancaria,* February 1983, *39*(2), pp. 154–60. **[G: U.S.; Netherlands]**

Elliott, James V. What Is the Role of Government in a Major Restructuring of Financial Institutions in 1980s? *J. Bank Res.,* Spring 1983, *14*(1), pp. 25–32. **[G: U.S.]**

Feuer, K. Le calcul de rentabilité des enterprises de financement. (How to Calculate the Probability of Financial Companies. With English summary.) *Ann. Sci. Écon. Appl.,* 1983, *39*(2), pp. 95–112.

Friedman, Benjamin M. Pension Funding, Pension Asset Allocation, and Corporate Finance: Evidence from Individual Company Data. **In** *Bodie, Z. and Shoven, J. B., eds.,* 1983, pp. 107–47, 152. **[G: U.S.]**

Furlong, Frederick T. New Deposit Instruments. *Fed. Res. Bull.,* May 1983, *69*(5), pp. 319–26. **[G: U.S.]**

Gagnon, Joseph. What Is a Commercial Loan? *New Eng. Econ. Rev.,* July–August 1983, pp. 37–41. **[G: U.S.]**

Gagnon, Joseph and Yokas, Steve. Recent Developments in Federal and New England Banking Laws. *New Eng. Econ. Rev.,* January/February 1983, pp. 18–27. **[G: U.S.]**

Giles, R. Philip. United States: Banking, Money, and Bond Markets. **In** *George, A. M. and Giddy, I. H., eds., Vol. 1,* 1983, pp. 4.2:1–27. **[G: U.S.]**

Giurleo, Diego S. Canada: Banking, Money, and Bond Markets. **In** *George, A. M. and Giddy, I. H., eds., Vol. 1,* 1983, pp. 4.8:1–35. **[G: Canada]**

Gorinson, Stanley M. Depository Institution Regulatory Reform in the 1980s: The Issue of Geographic Restrictions. *Antitrust Bull.,* Spring 1983, *28*(1), pp. 227–54. **[G: U.S.]**

Greenbaum, Stuart I. and Higgins, Bryon. Financial Innovation. **In** *Benston, G. J., ed.,* 1983, pp. 213–34. **[G: U.S.]**

Guttentag, Jack M. A Note on Hedging and Solvency: The Case of a Phoenix. *J. Futures Markets,* Summer 1983, *3*(2), pp. 137–41.

Horvitz, Paul M. Payments System Developments and Public Policy. **In** *Benston, G. J., ed.,* 1983, pp. 64–93. **[G: U.S.]**

Horvitz, Paul M. Reorganization of the Financial Regulatory Agencies. *J. Bank Res.,* Winter 1983, *13*(4), pp. 245–63. **[G: U.S.]**

Hubbard, Carl M. Money Market Funds, Money Supply, and Monetary Control: A Note. *J. Finance,* September 1983, *38*(4), pp. 1305–10. **[G: U.S.]**

Huertas, Thomas F. The Regulation of Financial Institutions: A Historical Perspective on Current Issues. **In** *Benston, G. J., ed.,* 1983, pp. 6–27. **[G: U.S.]**

Hull, Webster. Implications of Deregulation for Product Lines and Geographical Markets of Financial Institutions: Discussant's Comments. *J. Bank Res.,* Spring 1983, *14*(1), pp. 23–24. **[G: U.S.]**

Kane, Edward J. The Role of Government in the Thrift Industry's Net-worth Crisis. **In** *Benston, G. J., ed.,* 1983, pp. 156–84. **[G: U.S.]**

Kaufman, George G.; Mote, Larry R. and Rosenblum, Harvey. Implications of Deregulation for Product Lines and Geographical Markets of Financial Institutions. *J. Bank Res.,* Spring 1983, *14*(1), pp. 8–21. **[G: U.S.]**

Kaufman, George G.; Mote, Larry R. and Rosenblum, Harvey. The Future of Commercial Banks in the Financial Services Industry. **In** *Benston, G. J., ed.,* 1983, pp. 94–126. **[G: U.S.]**

Kaufman, Henry. Financial Institutions in Ferment. *Challenge,* May/June 1983, *26*(2), pp. 20–25. **[G: U.S.]**

Lahikainen, Pekka. Rahoitusjärjestelmämme kehittäminen vakuutusyhtiöiden näkökulmasta. (Developing the Finnish Financial System—The View of Insurance Companies. With English summary.) *Kansant. Aikak.,* 1983, *79*(2), pp. 160–73. **[G: Finland]**

Laub, P. Michael and Hoffman, Charles F. The Structure of the Financial Services Industry. *Contemp. Policy Issue,* January 1983, (2), pp. 1–17.

Light, Jay O. Pension Funding, Pension Asset Allocation, and Corporate Finance: Evidence from Individual Company Data: Comment. **In** *Bodie, Z. and Shoven, J. B., eds.,* 1983, pp. 147–51. **[G: U.S.]**

Litvak, Lawrence. Pension Funds and Economic Renewal. **In** *Barker, M., ed. (I),* 1983, pp. 159–301. **[G: U.S.]**

Litvak, Lawrence and Daniels, Belden. Innovations in Development Finance. **In** *Barker, M., ed. (I),* 1983, pp. 1–158. **[G: U.S.]**

Long, John B., Jr. Theories of Intermediated Structures: A Comment. *Carnegie-Rochester Conf. Ser. Public Policy,* Spring 1983, *18,* pp. 273–78.

Lopez Roa, A. L. Efectos de la crisis económica sobre el sistema financiero: el caso de España. (The Impact of Economic Crisis on the Financial System: The Spanish Case. With English summary.) *Écon. Soc.,* September–October–November 1983, *17*(9–10–11), pp. 1631–45. **[G: Spain]**

Marlow, Michael L. A Canonical Correlation Analysis of Savings and Loan Association Performance. *Appl. Econ.,* December 1983, *15*(6), pp. 815–20. **[G: U.S.]**

Maycock, James E. The United Kingdom: Money and Bond Markets. **In** *George, A. M. and Giddy, I. H., eds., Vol. 1,* 1983, pp. 4.3:1–21. **[G: U.K.]**

Mayer, Thomas and Nathan, Harold. Mortgage Rates and Regulation Q: A Note. *J. Money, Credit, Banking,* February 1983, *15*(1), pp. 107–15. **[G: U.S.]**

Moscovitch, Allan. Les sociétés de construction au Canada avant 1867: préliminaries à une analyse. (Building Societies in Canada before 1867: Prolegomena to the Analysis. With English summary.) *L'Actual. Econ.,* September 1983, *59*(3), pp. 514–30. **[G: Canada]**

Munnell, Alicia H. The Pitfalls of Social Investing: The Case of Public Pensions and Housing. *New Eng. Econ. Rev.,* September/October 1983, pp. 20–41. **[G: U.S.]**

Murray, John D. and White, Robert W. Economies of Scale and Economies of Scope in Multiproduct Financial Institutions: A Study of British Columbia Credit Unions. *J. Finance,* June 1983, *38*(3), pp. 887–902. **[G: Canada]**

Nelson, Paul Gunnar. What Is the Role of Government in a Major Restructuring of Financial Institutions in the 80s?: Discussant's Comments. *J. Bank Res.,* Spring 1983, *14*(1), pp. 36–38. **[G: U.S.]**

Oppenheimer, Henry R. and Schlarbaum, Gary G. Investment Policies of Property–Liability Insurers and Pension Plans: A Lesson from Ben Graham. *J. Risk Ins.,* December 1983, *50*(4), pp. 611–30. **[G: U.S.]**

Park, Yoon S. Asian Money Markets. **In** *George, A. M. and Giddy, I. H., eds., Vol. 1,* 1983, pp. 4.10:1–20. **[G: Singapore; Hong Kong; Malaysia; Australia; S. Korea]**

Paternello, Arturo. Struttura, operatori ed evoluzione tecnica del mercato dei fondi interbancari in Italia (1979–1982). (Structure, Operators, and Technical Evolution of the Interbank Market in Italy (1979–1982). With English summary.) *Bancaria,* September 1983, *39*(9), pp. 849–59. **[G: Italy]**

Peterson, Richard L. and Kidwell, David S. Credit Union Participation in the Mortgage Markets. *Nebr. J. Econ. Bus.,* Winter, 1983, *22*(1), pp. 45–57. **[G: U.S.]**

Phillips, Almarin and Jacobs, Donald P. Reflections on the Hunt Commission. **In** *Benston, G. J., ed.,* 1983, pp. 235–65. **[G: U.S.]**

Pierce, James L. Some Public Policy Issues Raised by the Deregulation of Financial Institutions. *Contemp. Policy Issue,* January 1983, (2), pp. 33–48.

Ránki, György. The Hungarian General Credit Bank in the 1920s. **In** *Teichova, A. and Cottrell, P. L., eds.,* 1983, pp. 355–73. **[G: Hungary]**

Rosen, Kenneth T. and Katz, Larry. Money Market Mutual Funds: An Experiment in Ad Hoc Deregulation: A Note. *J. Finance,* June 1983, *38*(3), pp. 1011–17. **[G: U.S.]**

Ryan, Pat. The Financial Role of Pension Funds in Ireland. *Irish Banking Rev.,* March 1983, pp. 6–14. **[G: Ireland]**

Santomero, Anthony M. Fixed versus Variable Rate Loans. *J. Finance,* December 1983, *38*(5), pp. 1363–80.

Seah, Linda. Public Enterprise and Economic Development. **In** *Chen, P. S. J., ed.,* 1983, pp. 129–59. **[G: Singapore]**

Sealey, C. W., Jr. Valuation, Capital Structure, and Shareholder Unanimity for Depository Financial Intermediaries. *J. Finance,* June 1983, *38*(3), pp. 857–71.

Shome, Parthasarathi and Saito, Katrine W. The

Impact of Contractual Savings on Resource Mobilization and Allocation: The Experience of Malaysia. **In** *Lim, D., ed.*, 1983, *1978*, pp. 288–302. **[G: Malaysia]**

Short, Eugenie D. and O'Driscoll, Gerald P., Jr. Deregulation and Deposit Insurance. *Fed. Res. Bank Dallas Econ. Rev.*, September 1983, pp. 11–23. **[G: U.S.]**

Sicat, Gerardo P. Toward a Flexible Interest Rate Policy, or Losing Interest in the Usury Law. **In** *Von Pischke, J. D.; Adams, D. W. and Donald, G., eds.*, 1983, pp. 373–78. **[G: Philippines]**

Smith, Donald J. The Demand for and Supply of Deposits by Credit Unions: The Caisses Populaires' Case—Correction and Comment. *J. Banking Finance*, June 1983, *7*(2), pp. 285–87.

Smith, Wallace F. The Trouble with Money: Is It Time to Socialize Residential Finance? **In** *Lefcoe, G., ed.*, 1983, pp. 163–80. **[G: U.S.]**

Speakes, Jeffrey K. The Phased-In Money Market Certificate Hedge. *J. Futures Markets*, Summer 1983, *3*(2), pp. 185–90.

Steffanci, Thomas J. Bond Immunization in Practice. **In** *Kaufman, G. G.; Bierwag, G. O. and Toevs, A., eds.*, 1983, pp. 281–85. **[G: U.S.]**

Steindl, Frank G. and Weinrobe, Maurice D. Natural Hazards and Deposit Behavior at Financial Institutions: A Note. *J. Banking Finance*, March 1983, *7*(1), pp. 111–18. **[G: U.S.]**

Suddards, C. G. The Behaviour of Building Societies and the Variability of the Mortgage Rate. *S. Afr. J. Econ.*, December 1983, *51*(4), pp. 530–43. **[G: U.K.; S. Africa]**

Taylor, Michael and Thrift, Nigel. The Role of Finance in the Evolution and Functioning of Industrial Systems. **In** *Hamilton, F. E. I. and Linge, G. J. R., eds.*, 1983, pp. 359–85. **[G: U.K.; U.S.]**

Taylor, Ryland A. The Credit Union as a Co-operative Institution. **In** *Kennedy, L., ed.*, 1983, *1971*, pp. 61–75. **[G: U.S.]**

Tese, Vincent. Deregulation in the Banking Industry. **In** *Kaushik, S. K., ed.*, 1983, pp. 9–15. **[G: U.S.]**

Thygerson, Kenneth J. Financial Restructuring: Impact on Housing. *Contemp. Policy Issue*, January 1983, (2), pp. 18–32. **[G: U.S.]**

Toevs, Alden L. Gap Management: Managing Interest Rate Risk in Banks and Thrifts. *Fed. Res. Bank San Francisco Econ. Rev.*, Spring 1983, (2), pp. 20–35. **[G: U.S.]**

Townsend, Robert M. Reply to John Long's Comments [Theories of Intermediated Structures]. *Carnegie-Rochester Conf. Ser. Public Policy*, Spring 1983, *18*, pp. 279–80.

Townsend, Robert M. Theories of Intermediated Structures. *Carnegie-Rochester Conf. Ser. Public Policy*, Spring 1983, *18*, pp. 221–72.

Vanderhoof, Irwin T. The Use of Duration in the Dynamic Programming of Investments. **In** *Kaufman, G. G.; Bierwag, G. O. and Toevs, A., eds.*, 1983, pp. 43–57.

Volcker, Paul A. Statement to the U.S. Senate Committee on Banking, Housing, and Urban Affairs, September 13, 1983. *Fed. Res. Bull.*, October 1983, *69*(10), pp. 757–69. **[G: U.S.]**

Ward, James S. Immunization in Practice: Comments. **In** *Kaufman, G. G.; Bierwag, G. O. and Toevs, A., eds.*, 1983, pp. 287–91. **[G: U.S.]**

Wilson, J. S. G. Recent Changes in London's Money Market Arrangements. *Banca Naz. Lavoro Quart. Rev.*, March 1983, (144), pp. 81–102. **[G: U.K.]**

315 Credit to Business, Consumer, etc. (including mortgages)

3150 General

Cagan, Phillip. The Roles of Money and Credit in Macroeconomic Analysis: Comment. **In** *Tobin, J., ed.*, 1983, pp. 189–93. **[G: U.S.]**

Capra, James R. Federal Deficits and Private Credit Demands: Economic Impact Analysis. *Fed. Res. Bank New York Quart. Rev.*, Summer 1983, *8*(2), pp. 29–44. **[G: U.S.]**

Chateau, John-Peter D. Credit Rationing as a (Temporary) Suboptimal Equilibrium with Imperfect Information. *Europ. Econ. Rev.*, November 1983, *23*(2), pp. 195–201.

Friedman, Benjamin M. The Roles of Money and Credit in Macroeconomic Analysis. **In** *Tobin, J., ed.*, 1983, pp. 161–89. **[G: U.S.]**

Garn, Jake. A View of the new Financial Environment. **In** *Sanford, T., ed.*, 1983, pp. 79–90. **[G: U.S.]**

Gough, Robert A., Jr. The Future Constraints on Interest Rates. **In** *Sanford, T., ed.*, 1983, pp. 56–78. **[G: U.S.]**

Jacobs, Rodney L. Fixed-Rate Lending and Interest Rate Futures Hedging. *J. Bank Res.*, Autumn 1983, *14*(3), pp. 193–202. **[G: U.S.]**

Partee, J. Charles. Statement to the U.S. Senate Committee on Banking, Housing, and Urban Affairs, April 12, 1983. *Fed. Res. Bull.*, May 1983, *69*(5), pp. 340–41. **[G: U.S.]**

Reichert, Alan K.; Cho, Chien-Ching and Wagner, George M. An Examination of the Conceptual Issues Involved in Developing Credit-scoring Models. *J. Bus. Econ. Statist.*, April 1983, *1*(2), pp. 101–14. **[G: U.S.]**

Rhyne, Elisabeth H. Federal Credit Activities. **In** *Pechman, J. A., ed.*, 1983, pp. 231–42. **[G: U.S.]**

Shiller, Robert J. The Roles of Money and Credit in Macroeconomic Analysis: Comment. **In** *Tobin, J., ed.*, 1983, pp. 193–99. **[G: U.S.]**

Stiglitz, Joseph E. and Weiss, Andrew. Incentive Effects of Terminations: Applications to the Credit and Labor Markets. *Amer. Econ. Rev.*, December 1983, *73*(5), pp. 912–27.

Teeters, Nancy H. Statement to the Subcommittee on Consumer Affairs and Coinage, U.S. House Committee on Banking, Finance, and Urban Affairs, March 10, 1983. *Fed. Res. Bull.*, March 1983, *69*(3), pp. 197–98. **[G: U.S.]**

Thakor, Anjan V. and Callaway, Richard. Costly Information Production Equilibria in the Bank Credit Market with Applications to Credit Rationing. *J. Finan. Quant. Anal.*, June 1983, *18*(2), pp. 229–56.

Tybout, James R. Credit Rationing and Investment Behavior in a Developing Country. *Rev. Econ. Statist.*, November 1983, *65*(4), pp. 598–607. **[G: Colombia]**

Wette, Hildegard C. Collateral in Credit Rationing in Markets with Imperfect Information: Note. *Amer. Econ. Rev.*, June 1983, *73*(3), pp. 442–45.

315 Credit to Business, Consumer, etc. (including mortgages)

Wood, John H. Familiar Developments in Bank Loan Markets. *Fed. Res. Bank Dallas Econ. Rev.*, November 1983, pp. 1–13. [G: U.S.]

Zuberi, Habib A. Institutional Credit and Balanced Growth: A Case Study of Pakistan. *J. Econ. Devel.*, December 1983, *8*(2), pp. 167–84. [G: Pakistan]

3151 Consumer Finance

Barth, James R.; Cordes, Joseph J. and Yezer, Anthony M. J. An Analysis of Informational Restrictions on the Lending Decisions of Financial Institutions. *Econ. Inquiry*, July 1983, *21*(3), pp. 349–60. [G: U.S.]

Barth, James R., et al. The Effect of Government Regulations on Personal Loan Markets: A Tobit Estimation of a Microeconomic Model. *J. Finance*, September 1983, *38*(4), pp. 1233–51. [G: U.S.]

Hisrich, Robert D.; Krasnakevich, John and Peters, Michael P. Effectively Managing Consumer Credit through Computer Graphics. *J. Bank Res.*, Winter 1983, *13*(4), pp. 304–08. [G: U.S.]

Manage, Neela D. Further Evidence on Estimating Regulated Personal Loan Market Relationships. *Quart. Rev. Econ. Bus.*, Winter 1983, *23*(4), pp. 63–80. [G: U.S.]

Martin, Preston. Statement to the Subcommittee on Consumer Affairs, U.S. Senate Committee on Banking, Housing, and Urban Affairs, March 17, 1983. *Fed. Res. Bull.*, April 1983, *69*(4), pp. 263–66. [G: U.S.]

Molho, Lazaros E. On Testing the Efficacy of Selective Credit Controls. *J. Money, Credit, Banking*, February 1983, *15*(1), pp. 120–22. [G: U.S.]

Mouillart, Michel. Endettement des ménages et rationnement du crédit. (Households Indebtedness and Credit Rationing. With English summary.) *Consommation*, July–Sept. 1983, *30*(3), pp. 23–59. [G: France]

Nellis, Joseph G. and Thom, Rodney D. The Demand for Mortgage Finance in the United Kingdom. *Appl. Econ.*, August 1983, *15*(4), pp. 521–29. [G: U.K.]

Peterson, Richard L. Consumer Finance. **In** *Benston, G. J., ed.*, 1983, pp. 185–212. [G: U.S.]

Peterson, Richard L. Usury Laws and Consumer Credit: A Note. *J. Finance*, September 1983, *38*(4), pp. 1299–1304. [G: U.S.]

Schwartz, Alan. The Enforceability of Security Interests in Consumer Goods. *J. Law Econ.*, April 1983, *26*(1), pp. 117–62. [G: U.S.]

Silver, Rugenia. Federal and State Laws on Consumer Financial Services: The Doctrine of Preemption. *Fed. Res. Bull.*, November 1983, *69*(11), pp. 823–29. [G: U.S.]

Volker, Paul A. A Note on Factors Influencing the Utilization of Bankcard. *Econ. Rec.*, September 1983, *59*(166), pp. 281–89. [G: Australia]

3152 Mortgage Market

Agarwal, Vinod B. and Phillips, Richard A. The Effect of Mortgage Rate Buydowns on Housing Prices: Recent Evidence from FHA-VA Transactions. *Amer. Real Estate Urban Econ. Assoc. J.*, Winter 1983, *11*(4), pp. 491–503. [G: U.S.]

Alonzi, Loreto P. and Hutchinson, Peter M. Risk Aversion's Impact on Bank Mortgage Lending: Evidence from the USA. *Rivista Int. Sci. Econ. Com.*, October–November 1983, *30*(10–11), pp. 1039–56. [G: U.S.]

Anstie, Roslyn K.; Findlay, Christopher C. and Harper, Ian. The Impact of Inflation and Taxation on Tenure Choice and the Redistributive Effects of Home-Mortgage Interest Rate Regulation. *Econ. Rec.*, June 1983, *59*(165), pp. 105–10. [G: Australia]

Baer, Herbert. Thrift Dominance and Specialization in Housing Finance: The Role of Taxation. *Housing Finance Rev.*, Oct 1983, *2*(4), pp. 353–67. [G: U.S.]

Barth, James R.; Cordes, Joseph J. and Yezer, Anthony M. J. An Analysis of Informational Restrictions on the Lending Decisions of Financial Institutions. *Econ. Inquiry*, July 1983, *21*(3), pp. 349–60. [G: U.S.]

Barth, James R. and Yezer, Anthony M. J. Default Risk on Home Mortgages: A Further Test of Competing Hypotheses. *J. Risk Ins.*, September 1983, *50*(3), pp. 500–505.

Bloom, David E.; Preiss, Beth and Trussell, James. Mortgage Lending Discrimination and the Decision to Apply: A Methodological Note. *Amer. Real Estate Urban Econ. Assoc. J.*, Spring 1983, *11*(1), pp. 97–103. [G: U.S.]

Boehm, Thomas P. and McKenzie, Joseph A. The Affordability of Alternative Mortgage Instruments: A Household Analysis. *Housing Finance Rev.*, Oct 1983, *2*(4), pp. 287–94. [G: U.S.]

Buckley, Robert M. and Van Order, Robert A. Housing and the Economy: Popular Myths. *Amer. Real Estate Urban Econ. Assoc. J.*, Winter 1983, *10*(4), pp. 421–41. [G: U.S.]

Campbell, Tim S. and Dietrich, J. Kimball. The Determinants of Default on Insured Conventional Residential Mortgage Loans. *J. Finance*, December 1983, *38*(5), pp. 1569–81. [G: U.S.]

Capozza, Dennis R. and Gau, George W. Optimal Mortgage Instrument Designs. **In** *Gau, G. W. and Goldberg, M. A., eds.*, 1983, pp. 233–58. [G: U.S.; Canada]

Carr, Jack L. and Smith, Lawrence B. Inflation, Uncertainty and Future Mortgage Instruments. **In** *Gau, G. W. and Goldberg, M. A., eds.*, 1983, pp. 203–31. [G: Canada]

Chen, Alexander. Alternative Reverse Mortgages: A Simulation Analysis of Initial Benefits in Baltimore. *Housing Finance Rev.*, Oct 1983, *2*(4), pp. 295–308. [G: U.S.]

Clauretie, Terrence M. A Note on the Bias in House Price Capitalization Models. *Amer. Real Estate Urban Econ. Assoc. J.*, Winter 1983, *11*(4), pp. 521–24.

Colton, Kent W. The Report of the President's Commission on Housing: The Nation's System of Housing Finance. *Amer. Real Estate Urban Econ. Assoc. J.*, Summer 1983, *11*(2), pp. 133–65. [G: U.S.]

Crawford, Peggy J. and Harper, Charles P. The Effect of the AML Index on the Borrower. *Housing Finance Rev.*, Oct 1983, *2*(4), pp. 309–20. [G: U.S.]

Daly, Michael J. and Macnaughton, Alan. Reverse Annuity Mortgages and Recent Tax Changes. *Can. Public Policy,* September 1983, *9*(3), pp. 398. **[G: Canada]**

Dhrymes, Phoebus J. On the Determinants of the Probability of First-Home Acquisition and Its Relation to Credit Stringency. **In** *Grieson, R. E., ed.,* 1983, pp. 59–103. **[G: U.S.]**

Gau, George W. and Goldberg, Michael A. Interest Rate Risk, Residential Mortgages and Financial Futures Markets. *Amer. Real Estate Urban Econ. Assoc. J.,* Winter 1983, *11*(4), pp. 445–61. **[G: U.S.]**

Gehr, Adam K., Jr. and Berry, Thomas. FNMA Auction Results as a Forecaster of Residential Mortgage Yields: A Comment. *J. Money, Credit, Banking,* February 1983, *15*(1), pp. 116–19. **[G: U.S.]**

Goldberg, Michael A. and Gau, George W. North American Housing Markets into the Twenty-First Century: Introduction. **In** *Gau, G. W. and Goldberg, M. A., eds.,* 1983, pp. xv–xxv. **[G: Canada; U.S.]**

Grebler, Leo. The Commission's Recommendations on Housing Finance. *Amer. Real Estate Urban Econ. Assoc. J.,* Summer 1983, *11*(2), pp. 166–81. **[G: U.S.]**

Harris, John M., Jr. Alternative Mortgage Instruments: Comparisons and a Proposal. *J. Finan. Res.,* Summer 1983, *6*(2), pp. 153–62.

Hendershott, Patric H.; Shilling, James D. and Villani, Kevin E. Measurement of the Spreads between Yields on Various Mortgage Contracts and Treasury Securities. *Amer. Real Estate Urban Econ. Assoc. J.,* Winter 1983, *11*(4), pp. 476–90. **[G: U.S.]**

Hendershott, Patric H. and Villani, Kevin E. Housing Finance in America in the Year 2001. **In** *Gau, G. W. and Goldberg, M. A., eds.,* 1983, pp. 181–202. **[G: U.S.]**

Kunkel, Lawrence R. The Effect of Illinois and Wisconsin Usury Laws on the Supply and Quality of Mortgage Credit Offered. *Housing Finance Rev.,* Oct 1983, *2*(4), pp. 321–41. **[G: U.S.]**

Litvak, Lawrence. Pension Funds and Economic Renewal. **In** *Barker, M., ed. (I),* 1983, pp. 159–301. **[G: U.S.]**

Marlow, Michael L. Entry and Performance in Financial Markets. *J. Bank Res.,* Autumn 1983, *14*(3), pp. 227–30. **[G: U.S.]**

Martin, Preston. Statement to the Subcommittee on Financial Institutions Supervision, Regulation and Insurance, U.S. House Committee on Banking, Finance, and Urban Affairs, February 24, 1983. *Fed. Res. Bull.,* March 1983, *69*(3), pp. 177–81. **[G: U.S.]**

Martin, Preston. Statement to the U.S. Senate Subcommittee on Housing and Urban Affairs of the Committee on Banking, Housing, and Urban Affairs, September 22, 1983. *Fed. Res. Bull.,* October 1983, *69*(10), pp. 769–73. **[G: U.S.]**

Mayer, Thomas and Nathan, Harold. Mortgage Rates and Regulation Q: A Note. *J. Money, Credit, Banking,* February 1983, *15*(1), pp. 107–15. **[G: U.S.]**

McFarlane, Larry A. British Investment and the Land: Nebraska, 1877–1946. *Bus. Hist. Rev.,* Summer 1983, *57*(2), pp. 258–72. **[G: U.K.; U.S.]**

Meador, Mark. The Effects on Mortgage Repayments of Restrictions of the Enforcement of Due-on-Sale Clauses: The California Experience. *Amer. Real Estate Urban Econ. Assoc. J.,* Winter 1983, *10*(4), pp. 465–74. **[G: U.S.]**

Morrell, Stephen O. and Saba, Richard P. The Effects of Federal Home Loan Mortgage Corporation Secondary Market on Regional Mortgage Yield Differentials. *Quart. Rev. Econ. Bus.,* Spring 1983, *23*(1), pp. 85–97. **[G: U.S.]**

Mouillart, Michel. Endettement des ménages et rationnement du crédit. (Households Indebtedness and Credit Rationing. With English summary.) *Consommation,* July–Sept. 1983, *30*(3), pp. 23–59. **[G: France]**

Peterson, Richard L. Consumer Finance. **In** *Benston, G. J., ed.,* 1983, pp. 185–212. **[G: U.S.]**

Peterson, Richard L. and Kidwell, David S. Credit Union Participation in the Mortgage Markets. *Nebr. J. Econ. Bus.,* Winter, 1983, *22*(1), pp. 45–57. **[G: U.S.]**

Preiss, Beth. The Garn–St Germain Act and Due-on-sale-clause Enforcement. *Housing Finance Rev.,* Oct 1983, *2*(4), pp. 369–77. **[G: U.S.]**

Riedy, Mark J. Where Will the Money Come From? *Ann. Amer. Acad. Polit. Soc. Sci.,* January 1983, *465,* pp. 14–20. **[G: U.S.]**

Sagalyn, Lynne Beyer. Mortgage Lending in Older Urban Neighborhoods: Lessons from Past Experience. *Ann. Amer. Acad. Polit. Soc. Sci.,* January 1983, *465,* pp. 98–108. **[G: U.S.]**

Sandilands, Roger J. Understanding the Scottish Economy: Housing Schemes and Schemes for Housing. **In** *Ingham, K. P. D. and Love, J., eds.,* 1983, pp. 127–38. **[G: U.K.]**

Seiders, David F. Managing Mortgage Interest-Rate Risks in Forward, Futures, and Options Markets. *Amer. Real Estate Urban Econ. Assoc. J.,* Summer 1983, *11*(2), pp. 237–63. **[G: U.S.]**

Seiders, David F. Mortgage Pass-Through Securities: Progress and Prospects. *Amer. Real Estate Urban Econ. Assoc. J.,* Summer 1983, *11*(2), pp. 264–87. **[G: U.S.]**

Shear, William B. and Yezer, Anthony M. J. An Indirect Test for Differential Treatment of Borrowers in Mortgage Markets. *Amer. Real Estate Urban Econ. Assoc. J.,* Winter 1983, *10*(4), pp. 405–20. **[G: U.S.]**

Sirmans, G. Stacy; Smith, Stanley D. and Sirmans, C. F. Assumption Financing and Selling Price of Single-Family Homes. *J. Finan. Quant. Anal.,* September 1983, *18*(3), pp. 307–17. **[G: U.S.]**

Smith, Wallace F. The Trouble with Money: Is It Time to Socialize Residential Finance? **In** *Lefcoe, G., ed.,* 1983, pp. 163–80. **[G: U.S.]**

Suddards, C. G. The Behaviour of Building Societies and the Variability of the Mortgage Rate. *S. Afr. J. Econ.,* December 1983, *51*(4), pp. 530–43. **[G: U.K.; S. Africa]**

Thom, D. Rodney. House Prices, Inflation and the Mortgage Market. *Econ. Soc. Rev.,* October 1983, *15*(1), pp. 57–68. **[G: Ireland]**

Thygerson, Kenneth J. Financial Restructuring: Impact on Housing. *Contemp. Policy Issue,* January

1983, (2), pp. 18–32. [G: U.S.]

Tuccillo, John A. The Tax Treatment of Mortgage Investment. *Amer. Real Estate Urban Econ. Assoc. J.*, Summer 1983, *11*(2), pp. 288–99. [G: U.S.]

Van Lierop, Johannes and Kalish, Lionel. An Economic Analysis of the Mortgage Servicing Contract. *Housing Finance Rev.*, Oct 1983, *2*(4), pp. 343–50.

Weinrobe, Maurice D. Home Equity Conversion Instruments with Fixed Term to Maturity: Alternatives to End of Term Pay-Off. *Amer. Real Estate Urban Econ. Assoc. J.*, Spring 1983, *11*(1), pp. 83–96. [G: U.S.]

Werthan, Susan M. Alternative Mortgages and Truth in Lending. *Fed. Res. Bull.*, May 1983, *69*(5), pp. 327–32. [G: U.S.]

Wetzel, William E., Jr. Angels and Informal Risk Capital. *Sloan Manage. Rev.*, Summer 1983, *24*(4), pp. 23–34. [G: U.S.]

3153 Business Credit

Allen, Franklin. Credit Rationing and Payment Incentives. *Rev. Econ. Stud.*, October 1983, *50*(4), pp. 639–46.

Arak, Marcelle; Englander, A. Steven and Tang, Eric M. P. Credit Cycles and the Pricing of the Prime Rate. *Fed. Res. Bank New York Quart. Rev.*, Summer 1983, *8*(2), pp. 12–18. [G: U.S.]

Arcuti, Luigi. Gli istituti di credito mobiliare tra crisi e innovazione. (Industrial Credit Institutions: From the Crisis to Innovation. With English summary.) *Bancaria*, December 1983, *39*(12), pp. 1186–1205. [G: Italy]

Barker, Michael. Financing State and Local Economic Development: Introduction. **In** *Barker, M., ed. (I)*, 1983, pp. xv–xxvii. [G: U.S.]

Bolnick, Bruce R. Concessional Credit for Small Scale Enterprise: A Reply. *Bull. Indonesian Econ. Stud.*, April 1983, *19*(1), pp. 90–96. [G: Indonesia]

Bruch, Mathias. Sources of Financing of Small-Scale Manufacturers: A Micro-Analysis for Malaysia. *Singapore Econ. Rev.*, April 1983, *28*(1), pp. 21–33. [G: Malaysia]

Cingano, Francesco. L'intermediazione bancaria: limiti operativi attuali e prospettive di ampliamento funzionale (Banking Intermediation: Present Operational Limits and Prospects for Enlargement of Role. With English summary.) *Bancaria*, February 1983, *39*(2), pp. 147–53. [G: Italy]

Ciocca, Pierluigi. La valutazione dell'affidabilità della clientela de parte delle banche: criteri e prassi operative. (Banks' Evolution of Client Creditworthiness: Operational Criteria and Practice. With English summary.) *Bancaria*, October 1983, *39*(10), pp. 929–44. [G: Italy]

Cucinotta, Giovanni. Bank Corporate Lending in Italy, Germany, United Kingdom during the Decade 1968–1978: A Comparative Study. *Econ. Notes*, 1983, (1), pp. 153–72. [G: Italy; Germany; U.K.]

Fried, Joel. Government Loan and Guarantee Programs. *Fed. Res. Bank St. Louis Rev.*, December 1983, *65*(10), pp. 22–30. [G: U.S.]

Giannoni, Anna Maria. L'andamento del grado di rischio nell'attività bancaria. (The Risk-Degree in Italian Banking. With English summary.) *Bancaria*, October 1983, *39*(10), pp. 953–67. [G: Italy]

Giddy, Ian H. and Ismael, Mona A. International Trade Financing Techniques. **In** *George, A. M. and Giddy, I. H., eds., Vol. 2*, 1983, pp. 7.1:1–30.

Gui, Benedetto. Struttura finanziaria e "Moral Risk" in imprese non quotate nel mercato azionario. (Financial Structure and Moral Risk When Firms' Shares Are Not Traded. With English summary.) *Rivista Int. Sci. Econ. Com.*, February 1983, *30*(2), pp. 125–42.

Hansen, Derek. Banking and Small Business. **In** *Barker, M., ed. (I)*, 1983, pp. 359–473.

Hansen, Robert S. and Thatcher, John G. On the Nature of Credit Demand and Credit Rationing in Competitive Credit Markets. *J. Banking Finance*, June 1983, *7*(2), pp. 273–84.

Hatch, James; Wynant, Larry and Grant, Mary Jane. Federal Lending Programs for Small Business: No Longer Needed? *Can. Public Policy*, September 1983, *9*(3), pp. 362–73. [G: Canada]

Ho, Thomas S. Y. and Saunders, Anthony. Fixed Rate Loan Commitments, Take-Down Risk, and the Dynamics of Hedging with Futures. *J. Finan. Quant. Anal.*, December 1983, *18*(4), pp. 499–516.

James, Christopher M. Pricing Alternatives for Loan Commitments: A Note. *J. Bank Res.*, Winter 1983, *13*(4), pp. 300–303. [G: U.S.]

Koskela, Erkki. Credit Rationing and Non-price Loan Terms: A Re-examination. *J. Banking Finance*, September 1983, *7*(3), pp. 405–16.

Lam, Chun H. and Boudreaux, Kenneth J. Compensating Balances, Deficiency Fees, and Lines of Credit. *J. Banking Finance*, September 1983, *7*(3), pp. 307–22.

Lemle, J. Stuart. Sources of International Trade Financing. **In** *George, A. M. and Giddy, I. H., eds., Vol. 2*, 1983, pp. 7.2:1–30. [G: U.K.; W. Germany; France; Japan]

Litvak, Lawrence and Daniels, Belden. Innovations in Development Finance. **In** *Barker, M., ed. (I)*, 1983, pp. 1–158. [G: U.S.]

März, Eduard. The Austrian Credit Mobilier in a Time of Transition. **In** *Komlos, J., ed.*, 1983, pp. 117–35. [G: Austria]

McLeod, R. H. Concessional Credit for Small Scale Enterprise: A Comment. *Bull. Indonesian Econ. Stud.*, April 1983, *19*(1), pp. 83–89. [G: Indonesia]

Milbourne, Ross D. Credit Flows and the Money Supply. *Australian Econ. Pap.*, December 1983, *22*(41), pp. 418–30.

Nanni, Carla. Il rapporto di fido bancario nell'opinione delle imprese finanziate: sintesi dei risultati di un'indagine campionaria. (The Business View of Bank–Borrower Relations: Synthesis of the Results of a Sample Survey. With English summary.) *Bancaria*, October 1983, *39*(10), pp. 945–52. [G: Italy]

Schepanski, Albert. Tests of Theories of Information Processing Behavior in Credit Judgment. *Ac-*

counting Rev., July 1983, *58*(3), pp. 581–99.

Seah, Linda. Public Enterprise and Economic Development. **In** *Chen, P. S. J., ed.*, 1983, pp. 129–59. **[G: Singapore]**

Struck, Peter L. and Mandell, Lewis. The Effect of Bank Deregulation on Small Business: A Note. *J. Finance,* June 1983, *38*(3), pp. 1025–31. **[G: U.S.]**

Zaitsev, A. P. The State Bank and the Enterprise: Is the Influence of Bank Credit Effective? *Prob. Econ.*, September 1983, *26*(5), pp. 43–56. **[G: U.S.S.R.]**

Zakharov, V. Credit and Banks in the Economic Management System. *Prob. Econ.*, May 1983, *26*(1), pp. 3–19. **[G: U.S.S.R.]**

Zotov, M. Financial Problems in Managing the Investment Process. *Prob. Econ.*, September 1983, *26*(5), pp. 25–42. **[G: U.S.S.R.]**

320 Fiscal Theory and Policy; Public Finance

3200 General

Afxentiou, Panayiotis C. Economic Development and Government Revenue and Expenditure Theorizing: A Critical Appraisal. *Econ. Notes,* 1983, (1), pp. 98–111.

Aitkin, D. A. Where Does Australia Stand? **In** *Withers, G., ed.*, 1983, pp. 13–31. **[G: OECD; Australia]**

Bénard, Jean. Colloque de Paris, juin 1981: les progrès récents de l'analyse économique des dépenses publiques. (With English summary.) *Revue Écon. Polit.*, July–August 1983, *93*(4), pp. 509–50.

Bennett, James T. and DiLorenzo, Thomas J. The Ricardian Equivalence Theorem: Evidence from the Off-Budget Public Sector. *Public Finance,* 1983, *38*(2), pp. 309–16. **[G: U.S.]**

Bjelke-Petersen, Joh. Australian Federalism: A Queensland View. **In** *Patience, A. and Scott, J., eds.*, 1983, pp. 63–74. **[G: Australia]**

Brennan, Geoffrey and Pincus, Jonathan J. Government Expenditure Growth and Resource Allocation: The Nebulous Connection. *Oxford Econ. Pap.*, November 1983, *35*(3), pp. 351–65.

Brittan, Samuel. The Wenceslas Myth. **In** *Brittan, S.*, 1983, *1981,* pp. 3–21.

Frey, Bruno S. and Weck, Hannelore. What Produces a Hidden Economy? An International Cross Section Analysis. *Southern Econ. J.*, January 1983, *49*(3), pp. 822–32.

Gemmell, Norman. International Comparisons of the Effects of Nonmarket-Sector Growth. *J. Compar. Econ.*, December 1983, *7*(4), pp. 368–81. **[G: Selected MDCs; Selected LDCs]**

Gorton, John. Australian Federalism: A View from Canberra. **In** *Patience, A. and Scott, J., eds.*, 1983, pp. 12–27. **[G: Australia]**

Gould, Frank. The Development of Public Expenditures in Western, Industrialised Countries: A Comparative Analysis. *Public Finance,* 1983, *38*(1), pp. 38–69. **[G: OECD]**

Hamer, R. J. Australian Federalism: A View from Victoria. **In** *Patience, A. and Scott, J., eds.*, 1983, pp. 49–62. **[G: Australia]**

Head, Brian W. The Political Crisis of Australian Federalism. **In** *Patience, A. and Scott, J., eds.*, 1983, pp. 75–93. **[G: Australia]**

Herber, Bernard P. and Pawlik, Paul U. Measuring Government's Role in the Mixed Economy: A New Approach. *Nat. Tax J.*, March, 1983, *36*(1), pp. 45–56. **[G: U.S.]**

Hyde, John. Small Government and Social Equity: Discussion. **In** *Withers, G., ed.*, 1983, pp. 74–81. **[G: Australia]**

Ingberg, Mikael. Den offentliga sektorns roll i inkomstfördelnings- och finanspolitiken. (The Role of the Public Sector in Income Distribution and Fiscal Policies. With English summary.) *Ekon. Samfundets Tidskr.*, 1983, *36*(4), pp. 163–75. **[G: Finland]**

Jessen, Franz. Addictive Goods and the Growth of Government. *Public Choice,* 1983, *40*(1), pp. 101–03.

Kelman, Steven. Limited Government: An Incoherent Concept. *J. Policy Anal. Manage.*, Fall 1983, *3*(1), pp. 31–44.

Klein, Philip A. Reagan's Economic Policies: An Institutional Assessment. *J. Econ. Issues,* June 1983, *17*(2), pp. 463–74. **[G: U.S.]**

Kumar, Dharma. The Fiscal System. **In** *Kumar, D., ed.*, 1983, pp. 905–44. **[G: India]**

Le Pen, Claude. L'élasticité-revenu des dépenses publiques: Les problèmes théoretiques et empiriques de son évaluation. (The Income Elasticity of Public Spending: The Theoretical and Empirical Problems of Its Evaluation. With English summary.) *Consommation,* April–June 1983, *30*(2), pp. 75–115. **[G: France; OECD]**

Lerner, Abba P. Economics, Poliltics, and Administration. **In** *Lerner, A. P.*, 1983, *1951,* pp. 315–30.

Lowery, David. The Hidden Impact of Fiscal Caps: Implications of the Beck Phenomenon. *Public Budg. Finance,* Autumn 1983, *3*(3), pp. 19–32. **[G: U.S.]**

Meltzer, Allan H. and Richard, Scott F. Further Tests of a Rational Theory of the Size of Government: Rejoinder. *Public Choice,* 1983, *41*(3), pp. 423–26. **[G: U.S.]**

Meltzer, Allan H. and Richard, Scott F. Tests of a Rational Theory of the Size of Government. *Public Choice,* 1983, *41*(3), pp. 403–18. **[G: U.S.]**

Murnane, Richard J. How Clients' Characteristics Affect Organization Performance: Lessons from Education. *J. Policy Anal. Manage.*, Spring 1983, *2*(3), pp. 403–17. **[G: U.S.]**

Niskanen, William A. The Growth of Government and the Growth of the Economy. **In** *Biehl, D.; Roskamp, K. W. and Stolper, W. F., eds.*, 1983, pp. 1–14. **[G: U.S.]**

Okun, Arthur M. Our Blend of Democracy and Capitalism: It Works, but Is in Danger. **In** *Okun, A. M.*, 1983, *1979,* pp. 632–44. **[G: U.S.]**

Parish, R. M. Government and Economic Management. **In** *Withers, G., ed.*, 1983, pp. 83–94.

Passmore, J. A. Bigger or Smaller Government? Review and Major Conclusions. **In** *Withers, G., ed.*, 1983, pp. 107–13.

Passmore, J. A. Small Government: Some Issues. **In**

Withers, G., ed., 1983, pp. 1–11.

Peaucelle, Irina; Petit, Pascal and Saillard, Yves. Dépenses publiques: structure et évolution par rapport au PIB. Les enseignements d'un modèle macroéconomique. *Revue Écon. Polit.*, January–February 1983, *93*(1), pp. 62–85. **[G: France; EEC]**

Rowley, Charles K. The Failure of Government to Perform Its Proper Task. **In** *Lenel, H. O.; Willgerodt, H. and Molsberger, J.*, 1983, pp. 39–58. **[G: OECD]**

Sahni, Balbir S. Public Sectors in Less Developed Countries: Development Goals and Efficiency. *Ann. Pub. Co-op. Econ.*, July–September 1983, *54*(3), pp. 325–35. **[G: LDCs]**

Sandler, Todd; Cauley, Jon and Tschirhart, John. Toward a Unified Theory of Nonmarket Institutional Structures. *Australian Econ. Pap.*, June 1983, *22*(40), pp. 233–54.

Schneider, Friedrich and Pommerehne, Werner W. Macroeconomia della crescita in disequilibrio e settore pubblico in espansione: il peso delle differenze istituzionali. (The Macroeconomics of Unbalanced Growth and the Expanding Public Sector: The Influence of Institutional Differences. With English summary.) *Rivista Int. Sci. Econ. Com.*, April-May 1983, *30*(4–5), pp. 306–19. **[G: Switzerland]**

Scott, Jeffrey. Australian Federalism Renewed. **In** *Patience, A. and Scott, J., eds.*, 1983, pp. 1–11. **[G: Australia]**

Sharman, Campbell. Fraser, the States and Federalism. **In** *Patience, A. and Scott, J., eds.*, 1983, pp. 188–200. **[G: Australia]**

Sinn, Hans-Werner. Pro und contra Crowding-Out: Zur Stichhaltigkeit dreier populärer Argumente. (Pro and Contra Crowding Out: On the Soundness of Three Popular Arguments. With English summary.) *Kredit Kapital*, 1983, *16*(4), pp. 488–512. **[G: W. Germany]**

Stretton, Hugh. Where Does Australia Stand? Discussion. **In** *Withers, G., ed.*, 1983, pp. 32–36.

Tullock, Gordon. Further Tests of a Rational Theory of the Size of Government. *Public Choice*, 1983, *41*(3), pp. 419–21. **[G: U.S.]**

Whitlam, E. G. The Cost of Federalism. **In** *Patience, A. and Scott, J., eds.*, 1983, pp. 28–48. **[G: Australia]**

Wilenski, P. S. Small Government and Social Equity. **In** *Withers, G., ed.*, 1983, pp. 37–73. **[G: Australia]**

Withers, Glenn A. Government and Economic Management: Discussion. **In** *Withers, G., ed.*, 1983, pp. 95–105.

Young, Ken. Beyond Centralism. **In** *Young, K., ed.*, 1983, pp. 1–10.

321 Fiscal Theory and Policy

3210 Fiscal Theory and Policy

Abrams, Richard K.; Froyen, Richard T. and Waud, Roger N. The State of the Federal Budget and the State of the Economy. *Econ. Inquiry*, October 1983, *21*(4), pp. 485–503. **[G: U.S.]**

Aizenman, Joshua. Government Size, Optimal Inflation Tax, and Tax Collection Costs. *Eastern Econ. J.*, April–June 1983, *9*(2), pp. 103–05.

Alkin, Marvin C. and Solmon, Lewis C. Conducting Benefit–Cost Analysis of Program Evaluation. **In** *Alkin, M. C. and Solmon, L. C., eds.*, 1983, pp. 137–47.

Alkin, Marvin C. and Solmon, Lewis C. The Costs of Evaluation: Editors' Postnote. **In** *Alkin, M. C. and Solmon, L. C., eds.*, 1983, pp. 189–95.

Anandalingam, G. Project Impact Analysis as an Optimal Control Problem. *J. Econ. Dynam. Control*, November 1983, *6*(3), pp. 207–37. **[G: Sri Lanka]**

Arrow, Kenneth J. A Utilitarian Approach to the Concept of Equality in Public Expenditures. **In** *Arrow, K. J., Vol. 1*, 1983, *1971*, pp. 88–95.

Atkinson, Anthony B. Smoking and the Economics of Government Intervention. **In** *Atkinson, A. B.*, 1983, *1974*, pp. 371–82. **[G: U.K.; U.S.]**

Batten, Dallas S. and Hafer, R. W. The Relative Impact of Monetary and Fiscal Actions on Economic Activity: A Cross-Country Comparison. *Fed. Res. Bank St. Louis Rev.*, January 1983, *65*(1), pp. 5–12.

Bell, Clive and Devarajan, Shantayanan. Shadow Prices for Project Evaluation under Alternative Macroeconomic Specifications. *Quart. J. Econ.*, August 1983, *98*(3), pp. 457–77.

Bhagwati, Jagdish N. and Srinivasan, T. N. Domestic Resource Costs, Effective Rates of Protection, and Project Analysis in Tariff-distorted Economies. **In** *Bhagwati, J. N., Vol. 1*, 1983, *1980*, pp. 571–76.

Bhagwati, Jagdish N. and Srinivasan, T. N. On Inferring Resource-allocational Implications from DRC Calculations in Trade-distorted Small Open Economies. **In** *Bhagwati, J. N., Vol. 1*, 1983, *1979*, pp. 582–97.

Bhagwati, Jagdish N. and Srinivasan, T. N. The Evaluation of Projects at World Prices under Trade Distortions: Quantitative Restrictions, Monopoly Power in Trade and Nontraded Goods. **In** *Bhagwati, J. N., Vol. 1*, 1983, *1981*, pp. 543–57.

Bhagwati, Jagdish N.; Srinivasan, T. N. and Wan, Henry, Jr. Value Subtracted, Negative Shadow Prices of Factors in Project Evaluation, and Immiserising Growth: Three Paradoxes in the Presence of Trade Distortions. **In** *Bhagwati, J. N., Vol. 1*, 1983, *1978*, pp. 577–81.

Bhagwati, Jagdish N. and Wan, Henry, Jr. The "Stationarity" of Shadow Prices of Factors in Project Evaluation, with and without Distortions. **In** *Bhagwati, J. N., Vol. 1*, 1983, *1979*, pp. 558–70.

Bhattacharyya, Kalyan and Mukhopadhyay, Arunendu. Financial Analysis of Alternative Lift Irrigation Projects—A Case Study in Nadia District of West Bengal. *Econ. Aff.*, January–March 1983, *28*(1), pp. 614–23. **[G: India]**

Block, Walter. Who Speaks for the Free Market: Monetarists or Supply-Siders? [What's Wrong with Supply-Side Economics] [The Trouble with Monetarism]. *Policy Rev.*, Spring 1983, (24), pp. 9–12. **[G: U.S.]**

Bresson, Yoland and Sinsou, J. Paul. L'intégration de la répartition des revenus dans l'analyse des projets d'investissements: une mesure des avantages collectifs à partir du seuil de pauvreté. (A Renewal of Investment Project Appraisal by Integration of Income Distribution and Evaluation of a "Poverty Threshold." With English summary.) *Écon. Appl.*, 1983, *36* (2–3), pp. 509–33.

Brubaker, Earl R. On the Margolis 'Thought Experiment,' and the Applicability of Demand-Revealing Mechanisms to Large-Group Decisions [A Thought Experiment on Demand-Revealing Mechanisms]. *Public Choice*, 1983, *41* (2), pp. 315–19.

Burgess, David F. The Impact of Foreign Trade Distortions on the Social Discount Rate. *Can. J. Econ.*, August 1983, *16* (3), pp. 486–507. **[G: Canada]**

Canarella, Giorgio and Garston, Neil. Monetary and Public Debt Shocks: Tests and Efficient Estimates. *J. Money, Credit, Banking*, May 1983, *15* (2), pp. 199–211. **[G: U.S.]**

Chelimsky, Eleanor. Improving the Cost Effectiveness of Evaluation. In *Alkin, M. C. and Solmon, L. C., eds.*, 1983, pp. 149–70. **[G: U.S.]**

Choudhury, Masudul Alam. Towards an Evaluative Study of Joint Venture Projects with Socio-economic Indicators. *Singapore Econ. Rev.*, October 1983, *28* (2), pp. 59–78. **[G: Mauritania]**

Congdon, Tim. Who Speaks for the Free Market: Monetarists or Supply-Siders? [What's Wrong with Supply-Side Economics]. *Policy Rev.*, Spring 1983, (24), pp. 16. **[G: U.S.]**

Copeland, Laurence S. Public Sector Prices and the Real Exchange-Rate in the UK Recession. *Bull. Econ. Res.*, November 1983, *35* (2), pp. 97–121. **[G: U.K.]**

Diewert, W. Erwin. Cost–Benefit Analysis and Project Evaluation: A Comparison of Alternative Approaches. *J. Public Econ.*, December 1983, *22* (3), pp. 265–302.

Dominique, C-René. Labor-Surplus Project Appraisal Methods: Didactic and Operational Differences, and Value Judgements between OECD and UNIDO. *J. Econ. Devel.*, July 1983, *8* (1), pp. 59–88.

Feldstein, Martin S. The Fiscal Framework of Monetary Economics. *Econ. Inquiry*, January 1983, *21* (1), pp. 11–23. **[G: U.S.]**

Fölscher, G. C. K. A Note on the Social Discount Rate—(SDR). *J. Stud. Econ. Econometrics*, July 1983, (16), pp. 50–62.

Green, Edward J. Equilibrium and Efficiency under Pure Entitlement Systems: Errata. *Public Choice*, 1983, *41* (1), pp. 237–38.

Hamilton, Bruce W. The Flypaper Effect and Other Anomalies. *J. Public Econ.*, December 1983, *22* (3), pp. 347–61.

Harrod, R. F. Keynes and the Macmillan Committee: Proposals for Public Works and Protection. In *Feinstein, C., ed.*, 1983, *1951*, pp. 31–46. **[G: U.K.]**

Heller, Walter W. What's Right with Economics? In *Marr, W. L. and Raj, B., eds.*, 1983, pp. 337–74. **[G: U.S.]**

Jennings, Anthony. The Recurrent Cost Problem in the Least Developed Countries. *J. Devel. Stud.*, July 1983, *19* (4), pp. 504–21. **[G: LDCs; OECD]**

Johnson, Ronald. Supply-Side Economics: The Rise to Prominence. *Rev. Black Polit. Econ.*, Winter 1983, *12* (2), pp. 189–202. **[G: U.S.]**

Kehoe, Timothy J. and Serra-Puche, Jaime. A Computational General Equilibrium Model with Endogenous Unemployment: An Analysis of the 1980 Fiscal Reform in Mexico. *J. Public Econ.*, October 1983, *22* (1), pp. 1–26. **[G: Mexico]**

Kiefer, Donald W. Measurement of the Progressivity of Public Expenditures and Net Fiscal Incidence: Comment. *Southern Econ. J.*, October 1983, *50* (2), pp. 578–86.

Kienzle, Edward C. Measurement of the Progressivity of Public Expenditures and Net Fiscal Incidence: Reply. *Southern Econ. J.*, October 1983, *50* (2), pp. 587–88.

Knoester, Anthonie. Stagnation and the Inverted Haavelmo Effect: Some International Evidence. *De Economist*, 1983, *131* (4), pp. 548–84. **[G: U.S.; U.K.; Netherlands; W. Germany]**

Kremers, J. J. M. Public Debt Creation in the Netherlands, 1953–1980. *De Economist*, 1983, *131* (2), pp. 196–216. **[G: Netherlands]**

Mansfield, Charles Y. Multilevel Government: Some Consequences for Fiscal Stabilization Policy. *Bull. Int. Fiscal Doc.*, 1983, *37* (6), pp. 243–57. **[G: Selected MDCs; Selected LDCs]**

Margolis, Howard. Reply to Brubaker and Tullock [A Thought Experiment on Demand-Revealing Mechanisms]. *Public Choice*, 1983, *41* (2), pp. 321–25.

Marzetti, Silva. Tasso ottimale di crescita e bilancio pubblico. (Optimum Growth Rate and Deficit Spending. With English summary.) *Rivista Int. Sci. Econ. Com.*, April-May 1983, *30* (4–5), pp. 339–54. **[G: OECD]**

Mendelsohn, Robert. The Choice of Discount Rates for Public Projects: Reply. *Amer. Econ. Rev.*, June 1983, *73* (3), pp. 499–500.

Mitsui, Toshihide. Asymptotic Efficiency of the Pivotal Mechanism with General Project Space. *J. Econ. Theory*, December 1983, *31* (2), pp. 318–31.

Nagao, Yoshimi; Kuroda, Katsuhiko and Wakai, Ikujiro. Decisionmaking under Conflict in Project Evaluation. In *Isard, W. and Nagao, Y., eds.*, 1983, pp. 73–90.

Nevile, J. W. The Role of Fiscal Policy in the Eighties. *Econ. Rec.*, March 1983, *59* (164), pp. 1–15.

Normand, Denis; Hawley, Gilbert and Gillespie, W. Irwin. In Search of the Changing Distribution of Income during the Post-War Period in Canada and the United States. *Public Finance*, 1983, *38* (2), pp. 267–81. **[G: U.S.; Canada]**

Okamura, Makoto. Public Goods Supply and Incentive Compatibility: A Survey. (In Japanese. With English summary.) *Osaka Econ. Pap.*, March 1983, *32* (4), pp. 61–78.

Pasour, E. C., Jr. A Limited Defense of Pareto Optimal Redistribution: Comment. *Public Choice*, 1983, *41* (3), pp. 451–54.

Raboy, David G. Who Speaks for the Free Market: Monetarists or Supply-Siders? [What's Wrong with Supply-Side Economics] [The Trouble with Monetarism]. *Policy Rev.*, Spring 1983, (24), pp. 13–16. **[G: U.S.]**

Rath, B. Estimation of SWR: An Empirical Verification from a Multi-Purpose Project in Orissa. *Indian Econ. J.*, April-June 1983, *30*(4), pp. 97–102. **[G: India]**

Rein, Martin. Comprehensive Program Evaluation. **In** *Rein, M.*, 1983, *1981*, pp. 158–73. **[G: U.S.]**

Rein, Martin and White, Sheldon. Policy Research: Belief and Doubt. **In** *Rein, M.*, 1983, *1977*, pp. 195–220. **[G: U.S.]**

Rowley, Charles K. The Post-war Economic Failure of British Government: A Public Choice Perspective. **In** *Seldon, A., et al.*, 1983, pp. 131–48. **[G: U.K.]**

Sandmo, Agnar. Leif Johansen's Contribution to Public Economics. *J. Public Econ.*, August 1983, *21*(3), pp. 317–24.

Selody, Jack G. and Lynch, Kevin G. Modeling Government Fiscal Behavior in Canada. *J. Policy Modeling*, June 1983, *5*(2), pp. 271–91. **[G: Canada]**

Sharma, Jandhyala L. The Choice of Discount Rates for Public Projects: Comment. *Amer. Econ. Rev.*, June 1983, *73*(3), pp. 497–98.

Srinivasan, T. N. and Bhagwati, Jagdish N. Shadow Prices for Project Selection in the Presence of Distortions: Effective Rates of Protection and Domestic Resource Costs. **In** *Bhagwati, J. N., Vol. 1*, 1983, *1978*, pp. 523–42.

Steindl, Josef. The Control of the Economy. *Banca Naz. Lavoro Quart. Rev.*, September 1983, (146), pp. 235–48.

Swan, Peter L. The Marginal Cost of Base-Load Power: An Application to Alcoa's Portland Smelter. *Econ. Rec.*, December 1983, *59*(167), pp. 332–44. **[G: Australia]**

Thillainathan, R. Discriminatory Allocation of Public Expenditure Benefits for Reducing Inter-racial Inequality in Malaysia—An Evaluation. **In** *Lim, D., ed.*, 1983, *1980*, pp. 23–40. **[G: Malaysia]**

Tisdell, Clem A. Allocation of Public Funds to Projects Reducing Risk with Special Reference to Medical Research. *Rivista Int. Sci. Econ. Com.*, June 1983, *30*(6), pp. 555–60.

Ward, William A. On Estimating Shadow Wage Rates for Portugal. *Economia*, October 1983, *7*(3), pp. 543–54. **[G: Portugal]**

Warr, Peter G. Domestic Resource Cost as an Investment Criterion. *Oxford Econ. Pap.*, July 1983, *35*(2), pp. 302–06.

Warr, Peter G. Private Benevolence and Distributional Weights for Benefit-Cost Analysis. *Public Finance*, 1983, *38*(2), pp. 293–308.

Wren-Lewis, Simon. Labour Supply and Wealth: Some Macroeconomic Policy Implications. *Manchester Sch. Econ. Soc. Stud.*, March 1983, *51*(1), pp. 1–15. **[G: U.K.]**

3212 Fiscal Theory; Empirical Studies Illustrating Fiscal Theory

Aaron, Henry J. Modeling Alternative Solutions to the Long-run Social Security Funding Problem: Comment. **In** *Feldstein, M., ed.*, 1983, pp. 237–46. **[G: U.S.]**

Aaron, Henry J. The Value Added Tax: A Triumph of Form over Substance. **In** *Walker, C. E. and Bloomfield, M. E., eds.*, 1983, pp. 214–17.

Abel, Andrew B. Tax Neutrality in the Presence of Adjustment Costs. *Quart. J. Econ.*, November 1983, *98*(4), pp. 705–12.

Ahsan, Syed M. Professor Baumol and the Social Rate of Discount—A Comment. *Public Finance*, 1983, *38*(3), pp. 459–64.

Alm, James. Intergovernmental Grants and Social Welfare. *Public Finance*, 1983, *38*(3), pp. 376–97.

Anderson, Jock R. On Risk Deductions in Public Project Appraisal. *Australian J. Agr. Econ.*, December 1983, *27*(3), pp. 231–39.

Ansari, M. M. Tax Ratio and Tax Effort Analysis: A Critical Evaluation. *Bull. Int. Fiscal Doc.*, August 1983, *37*(8), pp. 345–53. **[G: LDCs]**

Argy, Victor and Salop, Joanne. Price and Output Effects of Monetary and Fiscal Expansion in a Two-Country World under Flexible Exchange Rates. *Oxford Econ. Pap.*, July 1983, *35*(2), pp. 228–46.

Atkinson, Anthony B. Capital Taxes, the Redistribution of Wealth and Individual Savings. **In** *Atkinson, A. B.*, 1983, *1971*, pp. 147–69.

Atkinson, Anthony B. Horizontal Equity and the Distribution of the Tax Burden. **In** *Atkinson, A. B.*, 1983, *1980*, pp. 93–105.

Atkinson, Anthony B. How Progressive Should Income Tax Be? **In** *Atkinson, A. B.*, 1983, *1973*, pp. 295–314.

Atkinson, Anthony B. Introduction to Part III: Design of Taxation. **In** *Atkinson, A. B.*, 1983, pp. 199–203.

Atkinson, Anthony B. Optimal Taxation and the Direct versus Indirect Tax Controversy. **In** *Atkinson, A. B.*, 1983, *1977*, pp. 243–58.

Atkinson, Anthony B. and Sandmo, Agnar. Welfare Implications of the Taxation of Savings. **In** *Atkinson, A. B.*, 1983, *1980*, pp. 271–93.

Atkinson, Anthony B. and Stern, Nicholas H. Pigou, Taxation and Public Goods. **In** *Atkinson, A. B.*, 1983, pp. 259–70.

Atkinson, Anthony B. and Stiglitz, Joseph E. The Design of Tax Structure: Direct versus Indirect Taxation. **In** *Atkinson, A. B.*, 1983, *1976*, pp. 223–42.

Atkinson, Anthony B. and Stiglitz, Joseph E. The Structure of Indirect Taxation and Economic Efficiency. **In** *Atkinson, A. B.*, 1983, *1972*, pp. 205–21. **[G: Sweden; Canada; U.K.; OEEC]**

Auerbach, Alan J. Efficient Design of Investment Incentives. **In** *Auerbach, A. J.*, 1983, *1981*, pp. 51–57.

Auerbach, Alan J. Tax Neutrality and the Social Discount Rate. **In** *Auerbach, A. J.*, 1983, *1982*, pp. 33–50.

Auerbach, Alan J. Taxation, Corporate Financial Policy and the Cost of Capital. *J. Econ. Lit.*, September 1983, *21*(3), pp. 905–40.

Auerbach, Alan J. The Optimal Taxation of Heterogeneous Capital. **In** *Auerbach, A. J.*, 1983, *1979*, pp. 9–32.

Auerbach, Alan J. and Kotlikoff, Laurence J. National Savings, Economic Welfare, and the Structure of Taxation. **In** *Feldstein, M., ed.*, 1983, pp. 459–93. **[G: U.S.]**

Auerbach, Alan J.; Kotlikoff, Laurence J. and Skin-

ner, Jonathan. The Efficiency Gains from Dynamic Tax Reform. *Int. Econ. Rev.*, February 1983, *24*(1), pp. 81–100.

Baker, Samuel H. The Determinants of Median Voter Tax Liability: An Empirical Test of the Fiscal Illusion Hypothesis. *Public Finance Quart.*, January 1983, *11*(1), pp. 95–108. **[G: U.S.]**

Balcer, Yves. The Taxation of Capital Gains: Samuelson's Fundamental Principle. *Public Finance*, 1983, *38*(1), pp. 1–15.

Balcer, Yves and Sadka, Efraim. Horizontal Equity in Models of Self-selection with Applications to Income Tax and Signaling Cases. **In** *Helpman, E.; Razin, A. and Sadka, E., eds.*, 1983, pp. 235–53.

Balcer, Yves, et al. Income Redistribution and the Structure of Indirect Taxation. **In** *Helpman, E.; Razin, A. and Sadka, E., eds.*, 1983, pp. 279–97. **[G: U.S.]**

Ballard, Charles L. and Shoven, John B. Taxes and Capital Formation. **In** *[Goode, R.]*, 1983, pp. 389–407. **[G: U.S.]**

Baumol, William J. Professor Ahsan and the Social Rate of Discount—A Reply. *Public Finance*, 1983, *38*(3), pp. 465–67.

Beck, John H. Tax Competition, Uniform Assessment, and the Benefit Principle. *J. Urban Econ.*, March 1983, *13*(2), pp. 127–46.

Beenstock, Michael. Social Policy for Social Democracy. **In** *Seldon, A., et al.*, 1983, pp. 73–86. **[G: U.K.]**

Bell, Edward B.; Bodenhorn, Diran and Taub, Allan J. Ranking Alternative Taxable Income Streams. *Nat. Tax J.*, June 1983, *36*(2), pp. 225–31.

Bennett, James T. The Impact of the Composition of Government Spending on Private Consumption and Investment: Some Empirical Evidence. *J. Econ. Bus.*, June 1983, *35*(2), pp. 213–20. **[G: U.S.]**

Bhagwati, Jagdish N. and Hamada, Koichi. Tax Policy in the Presence of Emigration. **In** *Bhagwati, J. N., Vol. 2*, 1983, *1982*, pp. 169–95.

Bhagwati, Jagdish N. and Ramaswami, V. K. Domestic Distortions, Tariffs and the Theory of Optimum Subsidy. **In** *Bhagwati, J. N., Vol. 1*, 1983, *1963*, pp. 238–44.

Bhagwati, Jagdish N.; Ramaswami, V. K. and Srinivasan, T. N. Domestic Distortions, Tariffs, and the Theory of Optimum Subsidy: Some Further Results. **In** *Bhagwati, J. N., Vol. 1*, 1983, *1969*, pp. 245–50.

Bhandari, Jagdeep S. Indexation, Deficit Finance and the Inflationary Process. *Southern Econ. J.*, April 1983, *49*(4), pp. 1077–93.

Bhatia, Kul B. Tax Effects, Relative Prices, and Economic Growth. **In** *Biehl, D.; Roskamp, K. W. and Stolper, W. F., eds.*, 1983, pp. 349–65. **[G: U.S.]**

Blewett, Robert A. Fiscal Externalities and Residential Growth Controls: A Theory-of-Clubs Perspective. *Public Finance Quart.*, January 1983, *11*(1), pp. 3–20.

Boadway, Robin W.; Bruce, Neil and Mintz, Jack M. On the Neutrality of Flow-of-Funds Corporate Taxation. *Economica*, February 1983, *50*(197), pp. 49–61.

Boadway, Robin W. and Oswald, Andrew J. Unemployment Insurance and Redistributive Taxation. *J. Public Econ.*, March 1983, *20*(2), pp. 193–210.

Bohanon, Cecil E. McCaleb on Lindahl: A Comment [A Reconsideration of the Lindahl Model]. *Public Finance*, 1983, *38*(2), pp. 326–31.

Bohanon, Cecil E. The Tax-Price Implications of Bracket-Creep. *Nat. Tax J.*, December 1983, *36*(4), pp. 535–38.

Boren, David L. Policies, Problems, and Politics of the Consumption Based Tax. **In** *Walker, C. E. and Bloomfield, M. E., eds.*, 1983, pp. 253–56.

Bös, Dieter. An Optimal Taxation Approach to Fiscal Federalism: Comment. **In** *McLure, C. E., Jr., ed.*, 1983, pp. 43–47.

Boskin, Michael J.; Avrin, Marcy and Cone, Kenneth. Modeling Alternative Solutions to the Long-run Social Security Funding Problem. **In** *Feldstein, M., ed.*, 1983, pp. 211–37. **[G: U.S.]**

Bossons, John. Rapporteur's Remarks: Discussion. **In** *Conklin, D. W. and Courchene, T. J., eds.*, 1983, pp. 358–60.

Bossons, John. What Can Macroeconomic Theory Tell Us about the Way Deficits Should Be Measured? Comment. **In** *Conklin, D. W. and Courchene, T. J., eds.*, 1983, pp. 181–86.

Bradford, David F. The Choice Between Income and Consumption Taxes. **In** *Walker, C. E. and Bloomfield, M. E., eds.*, 1983, pp. 229–52.

Branson, William H. and Buiter, Willem H. Monetary and Fiscal Policy with Flexible Exchange Rates. **In** *Bhandari, J. S. and Putnam, B. H., eds.*, 1983, pp. 251–85.

Brennan, Geoffrey. Estate Gift Duty and the Family: Prolegomena to a Theory of the Family Unit. **In** *Penner, R. G., ed.*, 1983, pp. 109–26.

Brennan, Geoffrey. Tax Effectiveness and Tax Equity in Federal Countries: Comment. **In** *McLure, C. E., Jr., ed.*, 1983, pp. 87–93. **[G: MDCs]**

Brennan, Geoffrey. Who Should Tax, Where and What? Comment. **In** *McLure, C. E., Jr., ed.*, 1983, pp. 20–23.

Brennan, Geoffrey and Buchanan, James M. Normative Tax Theory for a Federal Polity: Some Public Choice Preliminaries. **In** *McLure, C. E., Jr., ed.*, 1983, pp. 52–65.

Brennan, Geoffrey and Buchanan, James M. The Tax System as Social Overhead Capital: A Constitutional Perspective on Fiscal Norms. **In** *Biehl, D.; Roskamp, K. W. and Stolper, W. F., eds.*, 1983, pp. 41–54.

Brennan, Geoffrey; Lee, Dwight R. and Walsh, Cliff. Monopoly Markets in Public Goods: The Case of the Uniform All-or-None Price. *Public Finance Quart.*, October 1983, *11*(4), pp. 465–90.

Brennan, Geoffrey and Pincus, Jonathan J. Government Expenditure Growth and Resource Allocation: The Nebulous Connection. *Oxford Econ. Pap.*, November 1983, *35*(3), pp. 351–65.

Britton, A. J. C. Public Sector Borrowing. *Nat. Inst. Econ. Rev.*, February 1983, (103), pp. 50–55. **[G: U.K.]**

Brown, Eleanor. Comment: Bequests and Horizontal Equity under a Consumption Tax [The Incidence of a Lifetime Consumption Tax]. *Nat. Tax J.*, December 1983, *36*(4), pp. 511–13. **[G: U.S.]**

Bruce, Neil and Purvis, Douglas D. Fiscal Discipline

and Rules for Controlling the Deficit: Some Unpleasant Keynesian Arithmetic. **In** *Conklin, D. W. and Courchene, T. J., eds.*, 1983, pp. 323–40.

Brueckner, Jan K. Central-City Income Redistribution and the Flight to the Suburbs: A Stylized Model. *Reg. Sci. Urban Econ.*, May 1983, *13*(2), pp. 177–93.

Bryant, John. Government Irrelevance Results: A Simple Exposition. *Amer. Econ. Rev.*, September 1983, *73*(4), pp. 758–61.

Buchanan, James M. 'La Scienza delle Finanze': The Italian Tradition in Fiscal Theory. **In** *Groenewegen, P. and Halevi, J., eds.*, 1983, pp. 79–115.

Buiter, Willem H. The Theory of Optimum Deficits and Debt. **In** *Federal Reserve Bank of Boston*, 1983, pp. 46–69. **[G: U.K.]**

Burbridge, John B. Government Debt in an Overlapping-Generations Model with Bequests and Gifts. *Amer. Econ. Rev.*, March 1983, *73*(1), pp. 222–27. **[G: U.S.]**

Burbridge, John B. Social Security and Savings Plans in Overlapping-Generations Models. *J. Public Econ.*, June 1983, *21*(1), pp. 79–92. **[G: U.S.]**

Cansier, Dieter. Einperioden-Multiplikatoren gegebener Haushaltsdefizite nach dem Blinder–Solow-Modell: Erwiderung. (Single-Period Multipliers of Given Budget Deficits in Accordance with the Blinder–Solow Model: Reply. With English summary.) *Kredit Kapital*, 1983, *16*(1), pp. 54–61.

Canto, Victor A. and Joines, Douglas H. Taxation, Revenue, and Welfare. *Econ. Inquiry*, July 1983, *21*(3), pp. 431–38.

Carlberg, Michael. Is Deficit Spending Feasible in the Long Run? *Z. Wirtschaft. Sozialwissen.*, 1983, *103*(5), pp. 409–18.

Carmichael, Jeffrey and Stebbing, Peter W. Some Macroeconomic Implications of the Interaction between Inflation and Taxation. **In** *Pagan, A. R. and Trivedi, P. K., eds.*, 1983, pp. 102–36. **[G: Australia]**

Casale, Giuseppe. Capitale, interesse, profitto ed equa tassazione. (Capital, Interest and Fiscal Equity. With English summary.) *Giorn. Econ.*, March-April 1983, *42*(3–4), pp. 153–78.

Chan, Louis Kuo Chi. Uncertainty and the Neutrality of Government Financing Policy. *J. Monet. Econ.*, May 1983, *11*(3), pp. 351–72.

Chetty, V. K. and Lahiri, Ashok K. On the Effectiveness of Monetary and Fiscal Policies in a Keynesian Model. *Europ. Econ. Rev.*, September 1983, *23*(1), pp. 33–54.

Christainsen, Gregory B. Using Donor Preferences in Evaluating Public Expenditures: A Suggested Procedure. *Public Finance Quart.*, July 1983, *11*(3), pp. 283–98. **[G: U.S.]**

Conklin, David and Sayeed, Adil. Overview of the Deficit Debate. **In** *Conklin, D. W. and Courchene, T. J., eds.*, 1983, pp. 12–54. **[G: Canada]**

Conn, David. The Scope of Satisfactory Mechanisms for the Provision of Public Goods. *J. Public Econ.*, March 1983, *20*(2), pp. 249–63.

Cox, W. Michael. Government Revenue from Deficit Finance. *Can. J. Econ.*, May 1983, *16*(2), pp. 264–74.

Crane, Steven E. Interpreting the Distribution of Government Expenditures in Budget Incidence Studies. *Nat. Tax J.*, June 1983, *36*(2), pp. 243–47.

Cullis, John G. and Jones, Philip R. The Welfare State and Private Alternatives: Towards an Existence Proof. *Scot. J. Polit. Econ.*, June 1983, *30*(2), pp. 97–113.

Currie, David and Gazioglou, Shaziye. Wealth Effects, Treasury Bill Financing, and Stability. *J. Public Econ.*, August 1983, *21*(3), pp. 397–403.

Darby, Michael R. Actual versus Unanticipated Changes in Aggregate Demand Variables: A Sensitivity Analysis of the Real-Income Equation. **In** *Darby, M. P. and Lothian, J. R., et al.*, 1983, pp. 273–88. **[G: OECD]**

Darby, Michael R. International Transmission of Monetary and Fiscal Shocks under Pegged and Floating Exchange Rates: Simulation Experiments. **In** *Darby, M. P. and Lothian, J. R., et al.*, 1983, pp. 162–231. **[G: OECD]**

Dean, James M. Public Good Benefits and Interdependence. *Econ. Notes*, 1983, (1), pp. 130–34.

Deaton, Angus. An Explicit Solution to an Optimal Tax Problem. *J. Public Econ.*, April 1983, *20*(3), pp. 333–46. **[G: U.S.; U.K.]**

Debreu, Gerard. A Classical Tax-Subsidy Problem. **In** *Debreu, G.*, 1983, *1954*, pp. 59–67.

Demopoulos, George D.; Katsimbris, George M. and Miller, Stephen M. Do Macroeconomic Policy Decisions Affect the Private Sector Ex Ante?—The EEC Experience with Crowding Out. **In** *Hodgman, D. R., ed.*, 1983, pp. 246–67. **[G: EEC]**

Dieckheuer, Gustav. Staatliches budgetdefizit, Wachstum des Produktionspotentials und gesamtwirtschaftliche Inflationsrate. (Budget Deficits, Production Growth and Inflation. With English summary.) *Z. ges. Staatswiss.*, March 1983, *139*(1), pp. 80–99.

Diewert, W. Erwin. The Measurement of Waste within the Production Sector of an Open Economy. *Scand. J. Econ.*, 1983, *85*(2), pp. 159–79.

Dodgson, John S. On the Accuracy and Appropriateness of Alternative Measures of Excess Burden. *Econ. J.*, Supplement March 1983, pp. 106–14. **[G: U.K.]**

Driffill, E. John and Rosen, Harvey S. Taxation and Excess Burden: A Life Cycle Perspective. *Int. Econ. Rev.*, October 1983, *24*(3), pp. 671–83.

Dybvig, Philip H. and Spatt, Chester S. Adoption Externalities as Public Goods. *J. Public Econ.*, March 1983, *20*(2), pp. 231–47.

Eagly, Robert V. Tax Incidence in Ricardian Analysis. *Public Finance*, 1983, *38*(2), pp. 217–31.

Ebrill, Liam P. and Hartman, David G. The Corporate Income Tax, Entrepreneurship, and the Noncorporate Sector. *Public Finance Quart.*, October 1983, *11*(4), pp. 419–36.

Eckart, Wolfgang. The Neutrality of Land Taxation in an Uncertain World. *Nat. Tax J.*, June 1983, *36*(2), pp. 237–41.

Eisner, Robert. Tax Policy and Investment. **In** *Biehl, D.; Roskamp, K. W. and Stolper, W. F., eds.*, 1983, pp. 167–80.

Epple, Dennis; Filimon, Radu and Romer, Thomas.

Housing, Voting, and Moving: Equilibrium in a Model of Local Public Goods with Multiple Jurisdictions. **In** *Henderson, J. V., ed.*, 1983, pp. 59–90.

Evans, Owen J. Tax Policy, the Interest Elasticity of Saving, and Capital Accumulation: Numerical Analysis of Theoretical Models. *Amer. Econ. Rev.*, June 1983, *73*(3), pp. 398–410. **[G: U.S.]**

Fane, G. and Sieper, E. Preference Revelation and Monopsony. *J. Public Econ.*, April 1983, *20*(3), pp. 357–72.

Faridi, F. R. Theory of Fiscal Policy in an Islamic State. *J. Res. Islamic Econ.*, Summer 1983, *1*(1), pp. 17–35.

Feenberg, Daniel R. and Rosen, Harvey S. Alternative Tax Treatments of the Family: Simulation Methodology and Results. **In** *Feldstein, M., ed.*, 1983, pp. 7–41. **[G: U.S.]**

Feige, Edgar L. and McGee, Robert T. Sweden's Laffer Curve: Taxation and the Unobserved Economy. *Scand. J. Econ.*, 1983, *85*(4), pp. 499–519. **[G: Sweden]**

Feldstein, Martin S. Fiscal Policies, Inflation, and Capital Formation. **In** *Feldstein, M. (II)*, 1983, *1980*, pp. 61–80.

Feldstein, Martin S. Incidence of a Capital Income Tax in a Growing Economy with Variable Savings Rates. **In** *Feldstein, M. (I)*, 1983, *1974*, pp. 400–413.

Feldstein, Martin S. Inflation, Income Taxes, and the Rate of Interest: A Theoretical Analysis. **In** *Feldstein, M. (I)*, 1983, *1976*, pp. 448–64.

Feldstein, Martin S. Tax Incidence in a Growing Economy with Variable Factor Supply. **In** *Feldstein, M. (I)*, 1983, *1974*, pp. 377–99.

Feldstein, Martin S. The Effects of Taxation on Risk Taking. **In** *Feldstein, M. (I)*, 1983, *1969*, pp. 183–93.

Feldstein, Martin S. The Rate of Return, Taxation, and Personal Savings. **In** *Feldstein, M. (I)*, 1983, *1978*, pp. 29–35.

Feldstein, Martin S. The Surprising Incidence of a Tax on Pure Rent: A New Answer to an Old Question. **In** *Feldstein, M. (I)*, 1983, *1977*, pp. 414–26.

Feldstein, Martin S.; Green, Jerry R. and Sheshinski, Eytan. Corporate Financial Policy and Taxation in a Growing Economy. **In** *Feldstein, M. (I)*, 1983, *1979*, pp. 427–47. **[G: U.S.]**

Feldstein, Martin S. and Slemrod, Joel. Personal Taxation, Portfolio Choice, and the Effect of the Corporation Income Tax. **In** *Feldstein, M. (I)*, 1983, *1980*, pp. 255–66. **[G: U.S.]**

Feldstein, Martin S. and Summers, Lawrence H. Inflation, Tax Rules, and the Long-term Interest Rate. **In** *Feldstein, M. (II)*, 1983, *1978*, pp. 153–85. **[G: U.S.]**

Fischer, Stanley. Optimal Fiscal and Monetary Policy in an Economy without Capital: Comments. *J. Monet. Econ.*, July 1983, *12*(1), pp. 95–99.

Fischer, Stanley. Seigniorage and Fixed Exchange Rates: An Optimal Inflation Tax Analysis. **In** *Armella, P. A.; Dornbusch, R. and Obstfeld, M., eds.*, 1983, pp. 59–69.

Fischer, Stanley. Welfare Aspects of Government Issue of Indexed Bonds. **In** *Dornbusch, R. and Simonsen, M. H., eds.*, 1983, pp. 223–46.

Fishburn, Geoffrey F. Normative Aspects of Indexation Schemes. *Public Finance*, 1983, *38*(1), pp. 27–37.

Flam, Harry; Persson, Torsten and Svensson, Lars E. O. Optimal Subsidies to Declining Industries: Efficiency and Equity Considerations. *J. Public Econ.*, December 1983, *22*(3), pp. 327–45.

Forster, Bruce A. and Rees, Ray. The Optimal Rate of Decline of an Inefficient Industry. *J. Public Econ.*, November 1983, *22*(2), pp. 227–42.

Foulon, A. Les différents aspects de l'efficacité redistributive des politiques sociales. (With English summary.) *Revue Écon. Polit.*, May–June 1983, *93*(3), pp. 316–27.

Frowen, S. F. and Arestis, P. Impacts of Fiscal Actions on Aggregate Income and the Monetarist Controversy: An Empirical Investigation. **In** *[Saunders, C. T.]*, 1983, pp. 271–89. **[G: U.K.]**

Fuchs, Gérard and Guesnerie, Roger. Structure of Tax Equilibria. *Econometrica*, March 1983, *51*(2), pp. 403–34.

Fullerton, Don. Transition Losses of Partially Mobile Industry-Specific Capital. *Quart. J. Econ.*, February 1983, *98*(1), pp. 107–25. **[G: U.S.]**

Fullerton, Don and Gordon, Roger H. A Reexamination of Tax Distortions in General Equilibrium Models. **In** *Feldstein, M., ed.*, 1983, pp. 369–420. **[G: U.S.]**

Gehrels, Franz. Optimal Private and Collective Consumption in a Growing Economy. *Public Finance*, 1983, *38*(2), pp. 202–16.

Goldsmith, Art. Short-Run Macroeconomic Consequences of Government-Financed Human Capital Expenditures. *Quart. Rev. Econ. Bus.*, Summer 1983, *23*(2), pp. 89–107. **[G: U.S.]**

Goodman, Allen C. Capitalization of Property Tax Differentials within and among Municipalities. *Land Econ.*, May 1983, *59*(2), pp. 211–19. **[G: U.S.]**

Gordon, Roger H. An Optimal Taxation Approach to Fiscal Federalism. **In** *McLure, C. E., Jr., ed.*, 1983, pp. 26–42.

Goulder, Lawrence H.; Shoven, John B. and Whalley, John. Domestic Tax Policy and the Foreign Sector: The Importance of Alternative Foreign Sector Formulations to Results from a General Equilibrium Tax Analysis Model. **In** *Feldstein, M., ed.*, 1983, pp. 333–64. **[G: U.S.]**

Gowland, D. H. Issues in Macroeconomics. **In** *Gowland, D. H., ed.*, 1983, pp. 57–87.

Grewal, Bhajan S. An Optimal Taxation Approach to Fiscal Federalism: Comment. **In** *McLure, C. E., Jr., ed.*, 1983, pp. 48–51.

Grout, Paul. Imperfect Information, Markets and Public Provision of Education. *J. Public Econ.*, October 1983, *22*(1), pp. 113–21.

Guesnerie, Roger. La théorie de la fiscalité sur les transactions entre les ménages et les entreprises: Une présentation synthétique de travaux récents. (Taxing Transactions between Households and Firms: A Synthetical Presentation of Recent Theoretical Work. With English summary.) *Ann. INSEE*, July–September 1983, (51), pp. 7–38.

Gustafson, Charles. Estate Gift Duty and the Family: Prolegomena to a Theory of the Family Unit:

Commentary. **In** *Penner, R. G., ed.*, 1983, pp. 133–36.

Hagen, Kåre P. Optimal Shadow Prices and Discount Rates for Budget-Constrained Public Firms. *J. Public Econ.*, October 1983, *22* (1), pp. 27–48.

Hansson, Ingemar and Stuart, Charles. Taxation, Government Spending, and Labor Supply: A Diagrammatic Exposition. *Econ. Inquiry*, October 1983, *21* (4), pp. 584–87.

Hartman, David G. Domestic Tax Policy and the Foreign Sector: The Importance of Alternative Foreign Sector Formulations to Results from a General Equilibrium Tax Analysis Model: Comment. **In** *Feldstein, M., ed.*, 1983, pp. 364–67. **[G: U.S.]**

Hausman, Jerry A. Stochastic Problems in the Simulation of Labor Supply. **In** *Feldstein, M., ed.*, 1983, pp. 47–69. **[G: U.S.]**

Heckman, James J. Stochastic Problems in the Simulation of Labor Supply: Comment. **In** *Feldstein, M., ed.*, 1983, pp. 70–82. **[G: U.S.]**

Henderson, Dale W. Monetary, Fiscal and Exchange Rate Policy in a Two-Country, Short-Run, Macro Economic Model. *Écon. Soc.*, July-August 1983, *17* (7–8), pp. 1149–83.

van Herwaarden, F. G. and de Kam, C. A. An Operational Concept of the Ability to Pay Principle (with an Application for the Netherlands, 1973). *De Economist*, 1983, *131* (1), pp. 55–64. **[G: Netherlands]**

Hettich, Walter. Reforms of the Tax Base and Horizontal Equity. *Nat. Tax J.*, December 1983, *36* (4), pp. 417–27. **[G: U.S.]**

Hicks, John. The Concept of Business Income. **In** *Hicks, J.*, 1983, *1979*, pp. 189–203.

Hockley, G. C. and Harbour, G. Revealed Preferences between Public Expenditures and Taxation Cuts: Public Sector Choice [A New Approach to the Demand for Public Goods]. *J. Public Econ.*, December 1983, *22* (3), pp. 387–99. **[G: U.K.]**

Holcombe, Randall G. and Zardkoohi, Asghar. The Effect of Macroeconomic Variables on State and Local Government Expenditures. *Atlantic Econ. J.*, December 1983, *11* (4), pp. 34–41. **[G: U.S.]**

Hutton, John P. and Lambert, Peter J. Inequality and Revenue Elasticity in Tax Reform. *Scot. J. Polit. Econ.*, November 1983, *30* (3), pp. 221–34. **[G: U.K.; U.S.]**

Ihori, Toshihiro. Welfare Criteria for Tax Reforms: An Extension. *J. Public Econ.*, April 1983, *20* (3), pp. 387–89.

Ioannides, Yannis M. and Sato, Ryuzo. Taxation and the Distribution of Income and Wealth. **In** *Biehl, D.; Roskamp, K. W. and Stolper, W. F., eds.*, 1983, pp. 367–86.

Izenson, Mark Steven. A Brief Note on the Relationship between Investment and the Interest Rate in the United States, 1970–1979. *Econ. Notes*, 1983, (1), pp. 135–39. **[G: U.S.]**

Kanbur, S. M. Ravi. Labour Supply under Uncertainty with Piecewise Linear Tax Regimes. *Economica*, November 1983, *50* (200), pp. 379–94.

Kay, J. A. and Keen, Michael J. How Should Commodities Be Taxed? Market Structure, Product Heterogeneity and the Optimal Structure of Commodity Taxes. *Europ. Econ. Rev.*, December 1983, *23* (3), pp. 339–58.

Khan, M. Ali. Public Inputs and the Pure Theory of Trade. *Z. Nationalökon.*, 1983, *43* (2), pp. 131–56.

Kihlstrom, Richard E. and Laffont, Jean-Jacques. Taxation and Risk Taking in General Equilibrium Models with Free Entry. *J. Public Econ.*, July 1983, *21* (2), pp. 159–81.

Kim, Il-Chung. Financing the Environmental Capacity through Income Tax. *Reg. Sci. Persp.*, 1983, *13* (2), pp. 26–38.

Kogels, H. A. Unitary Taxation: An International Approach. *Bull. Int. Fiscal Doc.*, February 1983, *37* (2), pp. 65–68. **[G: U.S.]**

Kolstad, Charles D. and Wolak, Frank A., Jr. Competition in Interregional Taxation: The Case of Western Coal. *J. Polit. Econ.*, June 1983, *91* (3), pp. 443–60. **[G: U.S.]**

Kopcke, Richard W. Do Macroeconomic Policy Decisions Affect the Private Sector Ex Ante?—The EEC Experience with Crowding Out: Discussion. **In** *Hodgman, D. R., ed.*, 1983, pp. 268–72. **[G: EEC]**

Kopits, George. Inflation, Income Taxation, and Economic Behavior. **In** *[Goode, R.]*, 1983, pp. 371–87. **[G: OECD]**

Kormendi, Roger C. Government Debt, Government Spending, and Private Sector Behavior. *Amer. Econ. Rev.*, December 1983, *73* (5), pp. 994–1010. **[G: U.S.]**

Koskela, Erkki and Virén, Matti. National Debt Neutrality: Some International Evidence. *Kyklos*, 1983, *36* (4), pp. 575–88. **[G: Selected OECD]**

Kovenock, Daniel J. and Rothschild, Michael. Capital Gains Taxation in an Economy with an 'Austrian Sector.' *J. Public Econ.*, July 1983, *21* (2), pp. 215–56. **[G: U.S.]**

Krzyzaniak, Marian. The Dynamic Incidence of the Levy on Income, Government Expenditures Wasteful. *Public Finance*, 1983, *38* (3), pp. 339–61.

Kwon, O. Yul. The Neutral, Pure Profit, and Rate-of-Return Taxes: Their Equivalence and Differences. *Public Finance*, 1983, *38* (1), pp. 81–97.

Lächler, Ulrich. A Macrotheoretic Analysis of Inflation, Taxes, and the Price of Equity. *J. Macroecon.*, Summer 1983, *5* (3), pp. 281–301.

Laffont, Jean-Jacques and Maskin, Eric S. A Characterization of Strongly Locally Incentive Compatible Planning Procedures with Public Goods. *Rev. Econ. Stud.*, January 1983, *50* (1), pp. 171–86.

Laidler, David. Rapporteur's Remarks. **In** *Conklin, D. W. and Courchene, T. J., eds.*, 1983, pp. 346–58.

Leach, John. Inflation as a Commodity Tax. *Can. J. Econ.*, August 1983, *16* (3), pp. 508–16.

Lee, Dwight R. The Effectiveness of Supply-Side Tax Cuts under Alternative Political Models. *Atlantic Econ. J.*, September 1983, *11* (3), pp. 49–55.

Leibinger, Hans-Bodo and Rohwer, Bernd. Was kann die Fiskalpolitik noch leisten? (What Can Fiscal Policy Still Accomplish? With English summary.) *Konjunkturpolitik*, 1983, *29* (3), pp. 141–62.

Lerner, Abba P. Functional Finance and the Federal Debt. **In** *Lerner, A. P.*, 1983, *1943*, pp. 297–310.

Lerner, Abba P. High Full Employment and Low Full Employment. **In** *Lerner, A. P.,* 1983, *1951,* pp. 279–96.

Lerner, Abba P. On Optimal Taxes with an Untaxable Sector. **In** *Lerner, A. P.,* 1983, *1970,* pp. 193–203.

Lerner, Abba P. The Burden of Debt. **In** *Lerner, A. P.,* 1983, *1961,* pp. 311–13.

Lerner, Abba P. The Economic Steering Wheel: The Story of the People's New Clothes. **In** *Lerner, A. P.,* 1983, *1941,* pp. 271–77.

Lindbeck, Assar. Budget Expansion and Cost Inflation. *Amer. Econ. Rev.,* May 1983, *73*(2), pp. 285–90.

Lindsey, Lawrence B. Alternatives to the Current Maximum Tax on Earned Income. **In** *Feldstein, M., ed.,* 1983, pp. 83–102. **[G: U.S.]**

Lipnowski, Irwin and Maital, Shlomo. Voluntary Provision of a Pure Public Good as the Game of 'Chicken.' *J. Public Econ.,* April 1983, *20*(3), pp. 381–86.

Litzenberger, Robert H. and Ramaswamy, Krishna. The Effect of Personal Taxes and Dividends on Capital Asset Prices: Theory and Empirical Evidence. **In** *Archer, S. H. and D'Ambrosia, C. A.,* 1983, *1979,* pp. 690–722. **[G: U.S.]**

Liviatan, Nissan. Inflation and the Composition of Deficit Finance. **In** *[Klein, L. R.],* 1983, pp. 84–100.

Lloyd, Peter J. The Microeconomic Effects of Tax-inflation Interactions: General Equilibrium Estimates for Australia: Discussion. **In** *Pagan, A. R. and Trivedi, P. K., eds.,* 1983, pp. 178–82. **[G: Australia]**

Lollivier, Stefan and Rochet, Jean-Charles. Bunching and Second-Order Conditions: A Note on Optimal Tax Theory. *J. Econ. Theory,* December 1983, *31*(2), pp. 392–400.

Løtz, Jorgen R. The Role of Local Government Taxation: The Tiebout Effect and Equalization. **In** *[Goode, R.],* 1983, pp. 279–93.

Lucas, Robert E., Jr. and Stokey, Nancy L. Optimal Fiscal and Monetary Policy in an Economy without Capital. *J. Monet. Econ.,* July 1983, *12*(1), pp. 55–93.

Lyon, Kenneth S. Intertemporal Consumption Theory and the Balanced Budget Multiplier. *Southern Econ. J.,* July 1983, *50*(1), pp. 206–12.

Mackness, William. Fiscal Discipline and Rules for Controlling the Deficit: Some Unpleasant Keynesian Arithmetic: Comment. **In** *Conklin, D. W. and Courchene, T. J., eds.,* 1983, pp. 340–45.

Madre, Jean-Loup. Construction d'indicateurs de redistribution. (The Construction of Redistribution Indicators. With English summary.) *Consommation,* July–Sept. 1983, *30*(3), pp. 3–22. **[G: France]**

Makin, John H. Real Interest, Money Surprises, Anticipated Inflation and Fiscal Deficits. *Rev. Econ. Statist.,* August 1983, *65*(3), pp. 374–84. **[G: U.S.]**

Mantel, Rolf R. Equilibrio General y Tributación óptima. (General Equilibrum and Optimum Taxation. With English summary.) *Económica,* May–December 1983, *29*(2–3), pp. 135–51.

Margolis, Howard. A Note on Demand-Revealing. *Public Choice,* 1983, *40*(2), pp. 217–25.

Marrelli, Massimo and Salvadori, Neri. Tax Incidence and Growth Models. *Public Finance,* 1983, *38*(3), pp. 409–18.

Masson, Paul R. Les effets à long terme de différentes règles de financement du gouvernement. (Long Term Effects of Different Financing Methods of Government. With English summary.) *L'Actual. Econ.,* June 1983, *59*(2), pp. 266–82. **[G: Canada]**

Mathews, Russell. Tax Effectiveness and Tax Equity in Federal Countries: Reply. **In** *McLure, C. E., Jr., ed.,* 1983, pp. 98–99. **[G: MDCs]**

Mathews, Russell. Tax Effectiveness and Tax Equity in Federal Countries. **In** *McLure, C. E., Jr., ed.,* 1983, pp. 70–86. **[G: MDCs]**

Mathieson, Donald J. Estimating Models of Financial Market Behavior during Periods of Extensive Structural Reform: The Experience of Chile. *Int. Monet. Fund Staff Pap.,* June 1983, *30*(2), pp. 350–93. **[G: Chile]**

McCaleb, Thomas S. Economic Paradigms of Government and the Market: A Further Look at the Lindahl Model. *Public Finance,* 1983, *38*(2), pp. 332–37.

McDonald, Robert L. Government Debt and Private Leverage: An Extension of the Miller Theorem. *J. Public Econ.,* December 1983, *22*(3), pp. 303–25. **[G: U.S.]**

McElroy, F. W. A Simple Supply-Side Model. *Econ. Int.,* May–August–November 1983, *36*(2–3–4), pp. 192–98.

McLure, Charles E., Jr. A Reexamination of Tax Distortions in General Equilibrium Models: Comment. **In** *Feldstein, M., ed.,* 1983, pp. 421–26. **[G: U.S.]**

McLure, Charles E., Jr. Assignment of Corporate Income Taxes in a Federal System. **In** *McLure, C. E., Jr., ed.,* 1983, pp. 101–24. **[G: Selected OECD; U.S.]**

McLure, Charles E., Jr. Fiscal Federalism and the Taxation of Economic Rents. **In** *Break, G. F., ed.,* 1983, pp. 133–60.

McLure, Charles E., Jr. Value Added Tax: Has the Time Come? **In** *Walker, C. E. and Bloomfield, M. E., eds.,* 1983, pp. 185–213.

McMillan, Melville L. A Further Consideration of Coalitions under the Demand-Revealing Process. *Public Choice,* 1983, *40*(2), pp. 227–30.

Melvin, J. R. Political Structure and the Pursuit of Economic Objectives. **In** *Trebilcock, M. J., et al., eds.,* 1983, pp. 111–58. **[G: Canada]**

Menchik, Paul L. and David, Martin H. Reply and Comment [The Incidence of a Lifetime Consumption Tax]. *Nat. Tax J.,* December 1983, *36*(4), pp. 515–20. **[G: U.S.]**

Merton, Robert C. On the Role of Social Security as a Means for Efficient Risk Sharing in an Economy Where Human Capital Is Not Tradable. **In** *Bodie, Z. and Shoven, J. B., eds.,* 1983, pp. 325–58. **[G: U.S.]**

Mieszkowski, Peter. A General Equilibrium Model of Taxation with Endogenous Financial Behavior: Comment. **In** *Feldstein, M., ed.,* 1983, pp. 455–58. **[G: U.S.]**

Miles, James A. Taxes and the Fisher Effect: A Clarifying Analysis. *J. Finance,* March 1983, *38*(1), pp. 67–77.

Miller, Merton H. and Scholes, Myron S. Dividends and Taxes. **In** *Archer, S. H. and D'Ambrosia, C. A.,* 1983, *1978,* pp. 658–89.

Miller, Preston J. Higher Deficit Policies Lead to Higher Inflation. *Fed. Res. Bank Minn. Rev.,* Winter 1983, *7*(1), pp. 8–19. **[G: U.S.]**

Minarik, Joseph J. Alternatives to the Current Maximum Tax on Earned Income: Comment. **In** *Feldstein, M., ed.,* 1983, pp. 103–08. **[G: U.S.]**

Modigliani, Franco. Government Deficits, Inflation, and Future Generations. **In** *Conklin, D. W. and Courchene, T. J., eds.,* 1983, pp. 55–77. **[G: OECD]**

Moreh, J. Optimal Taxation and Public Goods. *Public Finance Quart.,* April 1983, *11*(2), pp. 181–201.

Morrison, Clarence C. and Pfouts, Ralph W. Hotelling's Proof of the Marginal Cost Pricing Theorem: A Correction. *Atlantic Econ. J.,* March 1983, *11*(1), pp. 113.

Muench, Thomas and Walker, Mark. Are Groves–Ledyard Equilibria Attainable? [Optimal Allocation of Public Goods: A Solution to the "Free Rider" Problem]. *Rev. Econ. Stud.,* April 1983, *50*(2), pp. 393–96.

Musgrave, Peggy B. Assignment of Corporate Income Taxes in a Federal System: Comment. **In** *McLure, C. E., Jr., ed.,* 1983, pp. 127–28. **[G: Selected OECD; U.S.]**

Musgrave, Richard A. Public Goods. **In** *Brown, E. C. and Solow, R. M., eds.,* 1983, pp. 141–56.

Musgrave, Richard A. Who Should Tax, Where, and What? **In** *McLure, C. E., Jr., ed.,* 1983, pp. 2–19.

Ng, Yew-Kwang and McGregor, L. Macroeconomics with Non-Perfect Competition: Tax Cuts and Wage Increases. *Australian Econ. Pap.,* December 1983, *22*(41), pp. 431–47.

Nguyen, Duc-Tho and Turnovsky, Stephen J. The Dynamic Effects of Fiscal and Monetary Policies under Bond Financing: A Theoretical Simulation Approach to Crowding Out. *J. Monet. Econ.,* January 1983, *11*(1), pp. 45–71.

Nowotny, Ewald. Who Should Tax, Where and What? Comment. **In** *McLure, C. E., Jr., ed.,* 1983, pp. 24–25.

O'Hare, Michael and Mundel, David S. When to Pay for Sunk Benefits. **In** *Zeckhauser, R. J. and Leebaert, D., eds.,* 1983, pp. 255–61.

Oakland, William H. Income Redistribution in a Federal System. **In** *Zodrow, G. R., ed.,* 1983, pp. 131–43.

Oates, Wallace E. Tax Effectiveness and Tax Equity in Federal Countries: Comment. **In** *McLure, C. E., Jr., ed.,* 1983, pp. 94–97. **[G: MDCs]**

Oates, Wallace E. The Regulation of Externalities: Efficient Behavior by Sources and Victims. *Public Finance,* 1983, *38*(3), pp. 362–75.

Okamura, Makoto and Kamiya, Kazuya. A Generalization of Tax Incidence Analysis. *Osaka Econ. Pap.,* September 1983, *33*(1–2), pp. 71–83.

Okuno, Nobuhiro and Yakita, Akira. An Optimal Rule on the Supply of Public Goods in a Dynamic Setting. *Public Finance,* 1983, *38*(3), pp. 419–28.

Oswald, Andrew J. Altruism, Jealousy and the Theory of Optimal Non-Linear Taxation. *J. Public Econ.,* February 1983, *20*(1), pp. 77–87.

Padoa Schioppa, Fiorella. Crowding Out in an Inflationary Open Economy: The Italian Case. *Europ. Econ. Rev.,* September 1983, *23*(1), pp. 117–39. **[G: Italy]**

Palmon, Dan and Yaari, Uzi. Taxation of Capital Gains and the Behavior of Stock Prices over the Dividend Cycle. *Amer. Econ.,* Spring 1983, *27*(1), pp. 13–22.

Parkin, Michael. What Can Macroeconomic Theory Tell Us about the Way Deficits Should Be Measured? **In** *Conklin, D. W. and Courchene, T. J., eds.,* 1983, pp. 150–77.

Parkin, Michael. What Can Macroeconomic Theory Tell Us about the Way Deficits Should be Measured? Reply. **In** *Conklin, D. W. and Courchene, T. J., eds.,* 1983, pp. 186–88.

Peacock, Alan. Welfare Economics, Public Finance and Selective Aid Policies. **In** *[Giersch, H.],* 1983, pp. 238–53. **[G: U.K.]**

Penati, Alessandro. Expansionary Fiscal Policy and the Exchange Rate: A Review. *Int. Monet. Fund Staff Pap.,* September 1983, *30*(3), pp. 542–69.

Penner, Rudolph G. The Theory of Optimum Deficits and Debt: Discussion. **In** *Federal Reserve Bank of Boston,* 1983, pp. 70–72. **[G: U.K.]**

Penner, Rudolph G. Public Policy and Aggregate Saving. *Bus. Econ.,* March 1983, *18*(2), pp. 1–10. **[G: U.S.]**

Pentecost, Eric J. Government Financing Constraint, Wealth Effects and External Balances: Comment. *Southern Econ. J.,* April 1983, *49*(4), pp. 1174–81.

Perelman, Sergio and Pestieau, Pierre. Déficit budgétaire et épargne nationale. (With English summary.) *Cah. Écon. Bruxelles,* 1983, *98*(2), pp. 194–207. **[G: Belgium]**

Persson, Mats. The Distribution of Abilities and the Progressive Income Tax. *J. Public Econ.,* October 1983, *22*(1), pp. 73–88.

Pestieau, Pierre. Fiscal Mobility and Local Public Goods: A Survey of the Empirical and Theoretical Studies of the Tiebout Model. **In** *Thisse, J.-F. and Zoller, H. G., eds.,* 1983, pp. 11–41.

Piffano, Horacio L. P. La Incidencia de la Imposición Indirecta en un Enfoque de Equilibrio Parcial. (The Incidence of Indirect Taxation in a Partial Equilibrium Approach. With English summary.) *Económica,* May–December 1983, *29*(2–3), pp. 153–216.

Piggott, John. The Microeconomic Effects of Tax-inflation Interactions: General Equilibrium Estimates for Australia. **In** *Pagan, A. R. and Trivedi, P. K., eds.,* 1983, pp. 138–77. **[G: Australia]**

Pissarides, Christopher A. Efficiency Aspects of the Financing of Unemployment Insurance and Other Government Expenditure. *Rev. Econ. Stud.,* January 1983, *50*(1), pp. 57–69.

Pohjola, Matti. Workers' Investment Funds and the Dynamic Inefficiency of Capitalism. *J. Public Econ.,* March 1983, *20*(2), pp. 271–79.

Quick, Perry D. The Consumption Based Tax: Prospects for Reform. **In** *Walker, C. E. and Bloomfield, M. E., eds.,* 1983, pp. 261–64.

Rao, T. V. S. Ramamohan. Public Goods and Disequilibrium Growth. *Rivista Int. Sci. Econ. Com.*, April-May 1983, *30*(4–5), pp. 321–38.

Razin, Assaf and Svensson, Lars E. O. The Current Account and the Optimal Government Debt. *J. Int. Money Finance*, August 1983, *2*(2), pp. 215–24.

Rezk, Ernesto. Flexibilidad automática en la Argentina: un ejercicio macroestático. (With English summary.) *Desarrollo Econ.*, July–September 1983, *23*(90), pp. 233–54. **[G: Argentina]**

Richter, Wolfram F. From Ability to Pay to Concepts of Equal Sacrifice. *J. Public Econ.*, March 1983, *20*(2), pp. 211–29.

Roskamp, Karl W. and Neumann, Manfred. Human Capital Formation and Public Finance: A Dynamic Model. **In** *Biehl, D.; Roskamp, K. W. and Stolper, W. F., eds.*, 1983, pp. 207–16.

Rubinfeld, Daniel L. Normative Tax Theory for a Federal Polity: Some Public Choice Preliminaries: Comment. **In** *McLure, C. E., Jr., ed.*, 1983, pp. 67–69.

Sah, Raaj Kumar. How Much Redistribution Is Possible through Commodity Taxes? *J. Public Econ.*, February 1983, *20*(1), pp. 89–101.

Salinger, Michael A. and Summers, Lawrence H. Tax Reform and Corporate Investment: A Microeconometric Simulation Study. **In** *Feldstein, M., ed.*, 1983, pp. 247–81. **[G: U.S.]**

Sandmo, Agnar. Ex Post Welfare Economics and the Theory of Merit Goods. *Economica*, February 1983, *50*(197), pp. 19–33.

Sandmo, Agnar. Progressive Taxation, Redistribution, and Labor Supply. *Scand. J. Econ.*, 1983, *85*(3), pp. 311–23.

Scarfe, Brian L. What Can Macroeconomic Theory Tell Us about the Way Deficits Should Be Measured? Comment. **In** *Conklin, D. W. and Courchene, T. J., eds.*, 1983, pp. 177–81.

Scarth, William M. Tax-Related Incomes Policies and Macroeconomic Stability. *J. Macroecon.*, Winter 1983, *5*(1), pp. 91–103.

Scheele, Erwin. Vermögensrestriktion, Budgetrestriktionen, Wirkungen der Staatsverschuldung und die Budget-Multiplikatoren von Dieter Cansier. (Wealth Restriction, Budget Restriction, Effects of Public Debt and D. Cansier's Budget Multipliers. With English summary.) *Kredit Kapital*, 1983, *16*(1), pp. 36–53.

Schweizer, Urs. Efficient Exchange with a Variable Number of Consumers. *Econometrica*, May, 1983, *51*(3), pp. 575–84.

Schweizer, Urs. Grundsätzliche Überlegungen zur Projektbewertung am Beispiel des Strassenbaus. (Some Thoughts on Expenditure Evaluation: The Case of Highway Construction. With English summary.) *Z. Wirtschaft. Sozialwissen.*, 1983, *103*(4), pp. 369–88.

Seibert, Donald V. A Retailer's Perspective on the Value Added Tax. **In** *Walker, C. E. and Bloomfield, M. E., eds.*, 1983, pp. 218–22.

Seidman, Laurence S. Taxes in a Life Cycle Growth Model with Bequests and Inheritances. *Amer. Econ. Rev.*, June 1983, *73*(3), pp. 437–41.

Semmler, Willi. On the Classical Theory of Taxation. An Analysis of Tax Incidence in a Linear Production Model. *Metroecon.*, February–June 1983, *35*(1–2), pp. 129–46.

Shah, Anup R. K. The Size of the Lifetime Excess Burden of a Tax. *Europ. Econ. Rev.*, January 1983, *20*(1–3), pp. 1–11.

Shaller, Douglas R. The Tax-Cut-But-Revenue-Will-Not-Decline Hypothesis and the Classical Macromodel. *Southern Econ. J.*, April 1983, *49*(4), pp. 1147–54. **[G: U.S.]**

Shaller, Douglas R. Working Capital Finance Considerations in a National Income Theory. *Amer. Econ. Rev.*, March 1983, *73*(1), pp. 156–65.

Shannon, James M. Why Congress Will Not Accept the Value Added Tax. **In** *Walker, C. E. and Bloomfield, M. E., eds.*, 1983, pp. 222–25.

Shapiro, Edward. Leisure–Income Indifference Curves and the Laffer Curve. *Amer. Econ.*, Spring 1983, *27*(1), pp. 37–39.

Sheikh, M. A.; Grady, P. and Lapointe, P.-H. The Effectiveness of Fiscal Policy in a Keynesian–Monetarist Model of Canada. *Empirical Econ.*, 1983, *8*(3–4), pp. 139–68. **[G: Canada]**

Shiller, Robert J. Tax Reform and Corporate Investment: A Microeconometric Simulation Study: Comment. **In** *Feldstein, M., ed.*, 1983, pp. 281–87. **[G: U.S.]**

Shilony, Yuval. More Methodological Notes on Welfare Calculus. *J. Transp. Econ. Policy*, January 1983, *17*(1), pp. 95–98.

Slemrod, Joel. A General Equilibrium Model of Taxation with Endogenous Financial Behavior. **In** *Feldstein, M., ed.*, 1983, pp. 427–54. **[G: U.S.]**

Slemrod, Joel. Do We Know How Progressive the Income Tax System Should Be? *Nat. Tax J.*, September 1983, *36*(3), pp. 361–69. **[G: U.S.]**

Slemrod, Joel and Yitzhaki, Shlomo. On Choosing a Flat-Rate Income Tax System. *Nat. Tax J.*, March, 1983, *36*(1), pp. 31–44. **[G: U.S.]**

Slivinski, Alan D. Income Distribution Evaluation and the Law of One Price. *J. Public Econ.*, February 1983, *20*(1), pp. 103–12.

Smith, Alasdair. Tax Reform and Temporary Inefficiency. *J. Public Econ.*, March 1983, *20*(2), pp. 265–70.

Smyth, David J. Taxes and Inflation. **In** *Schmukler, N. and Marcus, E., eds.*, 1983, pp. 326–39.

Snower, Dennis J. Imperfect Competition, Underemployment and Crowding-Out. *Oxford Econ. Pap.*, Supplement November 1983, *35*, pp. 245–70.

Stahl, Konrad and Varaiya, Pravin. Local Collective Goods: A Critical Re-examination of the Tiebout Model. **In** *Thisse, J.-F. and Zoller, H. G., eds.*, 1983, pp. 43–53.

Starrett, David A. Welfare Measures Based on Capitalization: A Unified General Treatment. **In** *Henderson, J. V., ed.*, 1983, pp. 117–35.

Stern, Nicholas. Tax Reform: Income Distribution, Government Revenue and Planning. *Indian Econ. Rev.*, January–June 1983, *18*(1), pp. 17–33. **[G: India]**

Stern, Nicholas. Taxation for Efficiency. **In** *Shepherd, D.; Turk, J. and Silberston, A., eds.*, 1983, pp. 77–107. **[G: OECD]**

Stiglitz, Joseph E. National Savings, Economic Welfare, and the Structure of Taxation: Comment. **In** *Feldstein, M., ed.*, 1983, pp. 493–98. **[G: U.S.]**

Stiglitz, Joseph E. On the Relevance or Irrelevance of Public Financial Policy: Indexation, Price Rigidities, and Optimal Monetary Policies. **In** *Dornbusch, R. and Simonsen, M. H., eds.*, 1983, pp. 183–222.

Stiglitz, Joseph E. Public Goods in Open Economics with Heterogeneous Individuals. **In** *Thisse, J.-F. and Zoller, H. G., eds.*, 1983, pp. 55–78.

Stiglitz, Joseph E. Some Aspects of the Taxation of Capital Gains. *J. Public Econ.*, July 1983, *21* (2), pp. 257–94.

Stiglitz, Joseph E. The Theory of Local Public Goods Twenty-Five Years after Tiebout: A Perspective. **In** *Zodrow, G. R., ed.*, 1983, pp. 17–53.

Stournaras, Yannis A. Optimal Tariffs to Raise Revenue in the Presence of Unemployment. *Greek Econ. Rev.*, April 1983, *5* (1), pp. 33–44.

Straszheim, Mahlon R. Public Sector Capitalization Models with Heterogeneous Housing Stocks. **In** *Henderson, J. V., ed.*, 1983, pp. 137–63.

Summers, Lawrence H. An Equity Case for Consumption Taxation. **In** *Walker, C. E. and Bloomfield, M. E., eds.*, 1983, pp. 257–60.

Tanzi, Vito. Taxation and Price Stabilization. **In** *[Goode, R.]*, 1983, pp. 409–30.

Terny, Guy. Finances Publiques et Formation du Capital Humain: Elements d'une Strategie alternative de Financement de l'Enseignement superieur. **In** *Biehl, D.; Roskamp, K. W. and Stolper, W. F., eds.*, 1983, pp. 217–50.

Thygesen, Niels. Praktisk relevans af keynesiansk teori i dag. (With English summary.) *Nationaløkon. Tidsskr.*, 1983, *121* (3), pp. 332–44.

Tisdell, Clem A. Public Finance and the Appropriation of Gains from International Tourists: Some Theory with ASEAN and Australian Illustrations. *Singapore Econ. Rev.*, April 1983, *28* (1), pp. 3–20. **[G: Australia; S. E. Asia]**

Tobin, James. Unemployment, Interest and Money. **In** *Sanford, T., ed.*, 1983, pp. 1–25. **[G: U.S.]**

Ueda, Kazuo and Hamada, Koichi. Migration, Alternative Tax Regimes and Capital Accumulation. **In** *Weisbrod, B. and Hughes, H., eds.*, 1983, pp. 368–84.

Ullman, Al. The Potential of the Value Added Tax. **In** *Walker, C. E. and Bloomfield, M. E., eds.*, 1983, pp. 225–27.

Wagner, Richard E. Estate Gift Duty and the Family: Prolegomena to a Theory of the Family Unit: Commentary. **In** *Penner, R. G., ed.*, 1983, pp. 127–33.

Wickström, Bengt-Arne. Income Redistribution and the Demand for Social Insurance. **In** *Söderström, L., ed.*, 1983, pp. 21–33.

Wildasin, David E. The Welfare Effects of Intergovernmental Grants in an Economy with Independent Jurisdictions. *J. Urban Econ.*, March 1983, *13* (2), pp. 147–64.

Willig, Robert D. Sector Differentiated Capital Taxation with Imperfect Competition and Inter-Industry Flows. *J. Public Econ.*, July 1983, *21* (2), pp. 295–316.

Winer, Stanley L. Some Evidence on the Effect of the Separation of Spending and Taxing Decisions. *J. Polit. Econ.*, February 1983, *91* (1), pp. 126–40. **[G: Canada]**

Wise, David A. Alternative Tax Treatments of the Family: Simulation Methodology and Results: Comment. **In** *Feldstein, M., ed.*, 1983, pp. 41–46. **[G: U.S.]**

Wren-Lewis, Simon. On the Validation of Cost Push: A Comment. *J. Public Econ.*, October 1983, *22* (1), pp. 123–25.

Xu, Riqing. A Preliminary Discussion of Comprehensive Public Finance. *Chinese Econ. Stud.*, Winter 1982/83, *16* (2), pp. 20–28. **[G: China]**

Yamada, Masatoshi. A Reconciliation between Equity and Efficiency in Public Goods Economy. *Z. Nationalökon.*, 1983, *43* (1), pp. 71–79.

Yu, Eden S. H. and Wang, Leonard F. S. Government Financing Constraint, Wealth Effects and External Balances: Reply. *Southern Econ. J.*, April 1983, *49* (4), pp. 1182–85.

Zee, Howell H. Tax Incidence in a Two-Sector Model with Variable Labor Supply. *Southern Econ. J.*, July 1983, *50* (1), pp. 240–50.

Zodrow, George R. and Mieszkowski, Peter. The Incidence of the Property Tax: The Benefit View versus the New View. **In** *Zodrow, G. R., ed.*, 1983, pp. 109–29.

Zwiener, Rudolf. "Crowding-out" durch öffentliche Investitionen? Eine Diskussion der Modellergebnisse der Deutschen Bundesbank und eine Gegenüberstellung mit den Ergebnissen der DIW-Version des ökonometrischen Konjunkturmodells der Wirtschaftsforschungsinstitute. ("Crowding-Out" through Public Investment. With English summary.) *Konjunkturpolitik*, 1983, *29* (3), pp. 121–40. **[G: W. Germany]**

3216 Fiscal Policy

Allen, Stuart D. and Smith, Michael D. Government Borrowing and Monetary Accommodation. *J. Monet. Econ.*, November 1983, *12* (4), pp. 605–16. **[G: U.S.]**

Andel, Norbert. Directions of Tax Harmonisation in the EEC. **In** *[Goode, R.]*, 1983, pp. 295–316. **[G: EEC]**

Andersen, Peter. Fiscal Policy 'Crowding-Out' of Private Investment in an Open Economy: The Case of Canada: Comment. **In** *Conklin, D. W. and Courchene, T. J., eds.*, 1983, pp. 249–53. **[G: U.S.; Canada]**

Autenne, M. Jacques and Scholsem, M. Jean-Claude. Problèmes internationaux du domaine des taxes sur le chiffre d'affaires: Belgique. (With English summary.) **In** *International Fiscal Association (I)*, 1983, pp. 289–317. **[G: Belgium]**

Baguley, Robert W. Government Deficits: Historical Analysis and Present Policy Alternatives: Comment. **In** *Conklin, D. W. and Courchene, T. J., eds.*, 1983, pp. 317–19. **[G: Canada]**

Batavia, Bala and Lash, Nicholas A. Self-Perpetuating "Inflation": The Case of Turkey. *J. Econ. Devel.*, December 1983, *8* (2), pp. 149–66. **[G: Turkey]**

Batchelor, R. A. British Economic Policy under Margaret Thatcher: A Mid Term Examination: A Comment on Darby and Lothian. *Carnegie-Rochester Conf. Ser. Public Policy*, Spring 1983, *18*, pp. 209–19. **[G: U.K.]**

Berson, David. The Reagan Administration's Fiscal Policy: A Critique: Response: Will Tax Incentives Increase Investment? **In** *Stubblebine, Wm. C. and Willett, T. D., eds.*, 1983, pp. 137–39. **[G: U.S.]**

Boadway, Robin and Flatters, Frank. Efficiency, Equity, and the Allocation of Resource Rents. **In** *McLure, C. E., Jr. and Mieszkowski, P., eds.*, 1983, pp. 99–123. **[G: Canada]**

Bono Martínez, E.; Jordán Galduf, J. M. and Tomás Carpi, J.-A. Notas sobre crisis de legitimación, déficit público y transición política en España. (Notes on the Crisis of Legitimacy, the Public Deficit and Transitional Politics in Spain. With English summary.) *Écon. Soc.*, September–October–November 1983, *17*(9–10–11), pp. 1741–61. **[G: Spain]**

Borchert, Manfred. Einige aussenwirtschaftliche Aspekte staatlicher Verschuldung. (Some International Economic Aspects of Public Debt. With English summary.) *Kredit Kapital*, 1983, *16*(4), pp. 513–27. **[G: W. Germany]**

Breneman, David W. Where Would Tuition Tax Credits Take Us? Should We Agree to Go? **In** *James, T. and Levin, H. M., eds.*, 1983, pp. 101–14. **[G: U.S.]**

Brooks, Simon J.; Henry, Brian and Karakitsos, Elias. Policy Trade-Offs in the NIESR Model: Exercises Using Optimal Control. *Nat. Inst. Econ. Rev.*, August 1983, (105), pp. 36–45. **[G: U.K.]**

Browne, G. W. G. Fifty Years of Public Finance. *S. Afr. J. Econ.*, March 1983, *51*(1), pp. 134–73. **[G: S. Africa]**

Bruce, Neil and Purvis, Douglas D. Fiscal Policy and Recovery from the Great Recession. *Can. Public Policy*, March 1983, *9*(1), pp. 53–67. **[G: Canada]**

Carlson, Keith M. The Critical Role of Economic Assumptions in the Evaluation of Federal Budget Programs. *Fed. Res. Bank St. Louis Rev.*, October 1983, *65*(8), pp. 5–14. **[G: U.S.]**

Catterall, James S. Tuition Tax Credits: Issues of Equity. **In** *James, T. and Levin, H. M., eds.*, 1983, pp. 130–50. **[G: U.S.]**

Conklin, David and Sayeed, Adil. Overview of the Deficit Debate. **In** *Conklin, D. W. and Courchene, T. J., eds.*, 1983, pp. 12–54. **[G: Canada]**

Cooper, Richard N. International Aspects of U.S. Monetary and Fiscal Policy: Discussion. **In** *Federal Reserve Bank of Boston*, 1983, pp. 134–37. **[G: U.S.; OECD]**

Cortizo, J. Soto. International Problems in the Field of General Taxes on Sales of Goods and Services: Mexico. **In** *International Fiscal Association (I)*, 1983, pp. 497–510. **[G: Mexico]**

Courchene, Thomas J. Canada's New Equalization Program: Description and Evaluation. *Can. Public Policy*, December 1983, *9*(4), pp. 458–75. **[G: Canada]**

Courchene, Thomas J. Efficiency, Equity, and the Allocation of Resource Rents: Comments. **In** *McLure, C. E., Jr. and Mieszkowski, P., eds.*, 1983, pp. 125–33. **[G: Canada]**

Darby, Michael R. and Lothian, James R. British Economic Policy under Margaret Thatcher: A Midterm Examination. *Carnegie-Rochester Conf. Ser. Public Policy*, Spring 1983, *18*, pp. 157–207. **[G: U.K.]**

De Grauwe, Paul. Symptoms of an Overvalued Currency: The Case of the Belgian Franc. **In** *de Cecco, M., ed.*, 1983, pp. 99–116. **[G: Belgium]**

De Grauwe, Paul and Frattianni, Michele. U.S. Economic Policies: Are They a Burden on the Rest of the World? *Econ. Notes*, 1983, (3), pp. 69–85. **[G: OECD]**

De Wulf, Luc. Taxation and Income Distribution. **In** *[Goode, R.]*, 1983, pp. 345–70. **[G: LDCs]**

Doyle, Maurice F. Management of the Public Finances in Ireland since 1961. *Public Budg. Finance*, Summer 1983, *3*(2), pp. 64–78. **[G: Ireland]**

Duncan, Tim. La política fiscal durante el gobierno de Juárez Celman, 1886–1890: Una audaz estrategia financiera internacional. (With English summary.) *Desarrollo Econ.*, April–June 1983, *23*(89), pp. 11–34. **[G: Argentina]**

Eckstein, Otto. International Aspects of U.S. Monetary and Fiscal Policy: Discussion. **In** *Federal Reserve Bank of Boston*, 1983, pp. 138–40. **[G: U.S.; OECD]**

El-Agraa, Ali M. EC Fiscal Policy. **In** *El-Agraa, A. M., ed.*, 1983, pp. 237–50. **[G: EEC]**

Ellwood, John W. Budget Control in a Redistributive Environment. **In** *Schick, A., ed.*, 1983, pp. 69–99. **[G: U.S.]**

Emminger, Otmar. Investment and Government Policy. **In** *Heertje, A., ed.*, 1983, pp. 72–99. **[G: OECD]**

Feder, Arthur A.; Levin, Leonard D. and Thayer, Kathe I. International Problems in the Field of General Taxes on Sales of Goods and Services: United States. **In** *International Fiscal Association (I)*, 1983, pp. 363–79. **[G: U.S.]**

Feldstein, Martin S. and Flemming, John. Tax Policy, Corporate Saving, and Investment Behavior in Britain. **In** *Feldstein, M. (I)*, 1983, *1971*, pp. 269–94. **[G: U.K.]**

Field, Frank. Breaking the Mould: The Thatcher Government's Fiscal Policies. **In** *Field, F., ed.*, 1983, pp. 56–68. **[G: U.K.]**

Field, Frank. Introduction: The Politics of Wealth. **In** *Field, F., ed.*, 1983, pp. 1–8. **[G: U.K.]**

Filippi, Piera. Problèmes internationaux du domaine des taxes sur le chiffre d'affaires: Italie. (With English summary.) **In** *International Fiscal Association (I)*, 1983, pp. 443–62. **[G: Italy]**

Fink, Hans. International Problems in the Field of General Taxes on Sales of Goods and Services: Sweden. **In** *International Fiscal Association (I)*, 1983, pp. 573–92. **[G: Sweden]**

Forte, Francesco. Tax Policy in Italy. *Bull. Int. Fiscal Doc.*, Sept.–Oct. 1983, *37*(9–10), pp. 393–98. **[G: Italy]**

Friedman, Benjamin M. Implications of the Government Deficit for U.S. Capital Formation. **In** *Federal Reserve Bank of Boston*, 1983, pp. 73–95. **[G: U.S.]**

Frint, W. Internationale Probleme auf dem Gebiet der Umsatzbesteuerung: Österreich. (With English summary.) **In** *International Fiscal Association (I)*, 1983, pp. 265–88. **[G: Austria]**

von Furstenberg, George M. Fiscal Deficits: From

Business as Usual to a Breach of the Policy Rules? *Nat. Tax J.*, December 1983, *36*(4), pp. 443–57. **[G: U.S.]**

Galper, Harvey. Tax Policy. In *Pechman, J. A., ed.*, 1983, pp. 173–200. **[G: U.S.]**

Garrison, Charles B. The 1964 Tax Cut: Supply-Side Economics or Demand Stimulus? *J. Econ. Issues*, September 1983, *17*(3), pp. 681–96. **[G: U.S.]**

Gerbes, R. Problèmes internationaux du domaine des taxes sur le chiffre d'affaires: Luxembourg. (With English summary.) In *International Fiscal Association (I)*, 1983, pp. 471–95. **[G: Luxembourg]**

Graça de Lemos, Maria Teresa. Problèmes internationaux du domaine des taxes sur le chiffre d'affaires: Portugal. (With English summary.) In *International Fiscal Association (I)*, 1983, pp. 545–60. **[G: Portugal]**

Grant, John and Ip, Irene. The Federal Budget and Medium-Term Economic Strategy. *Can. Public Policy*, September 1983, *9*(3), pp. 383–89. **[G: Canada]**

Grilli, Enzo R. Il deficit pubblico spiazza le imprese. (The Public Spending Deficit Wrong Foots Companies. With English summary.) *L'Impresa*, 1983, *25*(6), pp. 25–28. **[G: Italy]**

Groenewegen, Peter D. The Political Economy of Federalism, 1901–81. In *Head, B. W., ed.*, 1983, pp. 169–95. **[G: Australia]**

Harris, D. W. and Oser, R. A. International Problems in the Field of General Taxes on Sales of Goods and Services: Australia. In *International Fiscal Association (I)*, 1983, pp. 247–63. **[G: Australia]**

Head, John G. and Bird, Richard M. Tax Policy Options in the 1980s. In *[Goode, R.]*, 1983, pp. 3–29. **[G: Australia; Canada; U.K.; U.S.]**

Herschtel, Marie-Luise. Les finances publiques françaises: résultats 1982 et perspectives 1983. (With English summary.) *Revue Écon. Polit.*, September–October 1983, *93*(5), pp. 693–703. **[G: France]**

Hinchliffe, Keith and Allan, Bill. Public Expenditure Planning in Papua New Guinea: An Evaluation of Innovation. *World Devel.*, November 1983, *11*(11), pp. 957–69. **[G: Papua New Guinea]**

Hoelscher, Gregory P. Federal Borrowing and Short Term Interest Rates. *Southern Econ. J.*, October 1983, *50*(2), pp. 319–33. **[G: U.S.]**

Holzmann, Robert and Winckler, Georg. Austrian Economic Policy: Some Theoretical and Critical Remarks on "Austro-Keynesianism." *Empirica*, 1983, (2), pp. 183–203. **[G: Austria]**

Ingberg, Mikael. Den offentliga sektorns roll i inkomstfördelnings- och finanspolitiken. (The Role of the Public Sector in Income Distribution and Fiscal Policies. With English summary.) *Ekon. Samfundets Tidskr.*, 1983, *36*(4), pp. 163–75. **[G: Finland]**

James, Thomas and Levin, Henry M. Public Dollars for Private Schools: Introduction. In *James, T. and Levin, H. M., eds.*, 1983, pp. 3–13. **[G: U.S.]**

Jensen, Donald N. Constitutional and Legal Implications of Tuition Tax Credits. In *James, T. and Levin, H. M., eds.*, 1983, pp. 151–72. **[G: U.S.]**

Jonung, Lars. Lessons from Swedish Stabilization Policy in the 1970s. *Nat. Westminster Bank Quart. Rev.*, February 1983, pp. 21–34. **[G: Sweden]**

Kelly, Margaret. Fiscal Deficits and Fund-Supported Programs. *Finance Develop.*, September 1983, *20*(3), pp. 37–39.

Kloten, Norbert and Ketterer, K. H. Fiscal Policy in West Germany: Anticyclical versus Expenditure-reducing Policies. In *[Saunders, C. T.]*, 1983, pp. 291–307. **[G: W. Germany]**

Krugman, Paul R. International Aspects of U.S. Monetary and Fiscal Policy. In *Federal Reserve Bank of Boston*, 1983, pp. 112–33. **[G: U.S.; OECD]**

Laney, Leroy O. and Willett, Thomas D. Presidential Politics, Budget Deficits, and Monetary Policy in the United States; 1960–1976. *Public Choice*, 1983, *40*(1), pp. 53–69. **[G: U.S.]**

Longanecker, David A. The Public Cost of Tuition Tax Credits. In *James, T. and Levin, H. M., eds.*, 1983, pp. 115–29. **[G: U.S.]**

Longo, Carlos A. Deficiencies of Current Taxation of Capital Income. *Bull. Int. Fiscal Doc.*, 1983, *37*(7), pp. 291–301. **[G: Brazil]**

McCallum, John. Government Deficits: Historical Analysis and Present Policy Alternatives. In *Conklin, D. W. and Courchene, T. J., eds.*, 1983, pp. 284–317. **[G: Canada]**

Musgrave, Richard A. The Reagan Administration's Fiscal Policy: A Critique. In *Stubblebine, Wm. C. and Willett, T. D., eds.*, 1983, pp. 115–32. **[G: U.S.]**

Mutén, Leif. Some Topical Issues Concerning International Double Taxation. In *[Goode, R.]*, 1983, pp. 317–42.

Niskanen, William A. The Reagan Administration's Fiscal Policy: A Critique: Response: Reducing the Federal Share of National Output. In *Stubblebine, Wm. C. and Willett, T. D., eds.*, 1983, pp. 133–35. **[G: U.S.]**

Noemie, Michel. Problèmes Internationaux du domaine des taxes sur le chiffre d'affaires: France. (With English summary.) In *International Fiscal Association (I)*, 1983, pp. 393–412. **[G: France]**

Okun, Arthur M. Measuring the Impact of the 1964 Tax Reduction. In *Okun, A. M.*, 1983, *1968*, pp. 405–23. **[G: U.S.]**

Okun, Arthur M. The Personal Tax Surcharge and Consumer Demand, 1968–70. In *Okun, A. M.*, 1983, *1971*, pp. 338–74. **[G: U.S.]**

Penner, Rudolph G. Fiscal Management. In *Miller, G. W., ed.*, 1983, pp. 52–71. **[G: U.S.]**

Prest, A. R. Taxation Policy. In *Seldon, A., et al.*, 1983, pp. 49–69. **[G: U.K.]**

Quaden, Guy. L'expérience belge des déficits publics. (Belgian Experience with Public Deficits. With English summary.) *Ann. Pub. Co-op. Econ.*, July–September 1983, *54*(3), pp. 313–24.

Rau, Günter. Internationale Probleme auf dem Gebiet der Umsatzbesteuerung: Deutschland. (With English summary.) In *International Fiscal Association (I)*, 1983, pp. 197–217. **[G: W. Germany]**

Ray, John. An Empirical Study of the Political Business Cycle: Government Fiscal Policy and the Business Cycle in the United States. *Econ. Forum*, Winter 1983-84, *14*(2), pp. 19–40. **[G: U.S.]**

Razavi, Hossein. An Analysis of Iran's Oil Production Policy: A Welfare Maximization Approach. *Appl.*

Econ., April 1983, *15*(2), pp. 243–54. **[G: Iran]**

Richardson, H. W. Fiscal Policy in the 1930s. **In** *Feinstein, C., ed.*, 1983, *1967*, pp. 68–92. **[G: U.K.]**

Rivlin, Alice. The Reagan Administration's Fiscal Policy: A Critique: Response: The Deficit Dilemma. **In** *Stubblebine, Wm. C. and Willett, T. D., eds.*, 1983, pp. 135–37. **[G: U.S.]**

Rousseau, Henri-Paul. The Dome Syndrome: The Debt Overhanging Canadian Government and Business. *Can. Public Policy,* March 1983, *9*(1), pp. 37–52. **[G: Canada]**

Ruibal, Rubén R. International Problems in the Field of General Taxes on Sales of Goods and Services: Argentina. **In** *International Fiscal Association (I),* 1983, pp. 219–45. **[G: Argentina]**

Ruppe, Hans Georg. International Problems in the Field of General Taxes on Sales of Goods and Services: General Report. **In** *International Fiscal Association (I),* 1983, pp. 109–48. **[G: Global]**

Salonen, Pekka. Internationale Probleme auf dem Gebiet der Umsatzbesteuerung: Finnland. (With English summary.) **In** *International Fiscal Association (I),* 1983, pp. 381-91. **[G: Finland]**

Sato, Mitsuo. International Problems in the Field of General Taxes on Sales of Goods and Services: Japan. **In** *International Fiscal Association (I),* 1983, pp. 463–70. **[G: Japan]**

Schneider, Anna and Rosenberg, Rivka. International Problems in the Field of General Taxes on Sales of Goods and Services: Israel. **In** *International Fiscal Association (I),* 1983, pp. 425–41. **[G: Israel]**

Shoup, Carl S. The Property Tax versus Sales and Income Taxes. **In** *Harriss, C. L., ed.*, 1983, pp. 31–41.

Simons, A. L. C. International Problems in the Field of General Taxes on Sales of Goods and Services: Netherlands. **In** *International Fiscal Association (I),* 1983, pp. 529–44. **[G: Netherlands]**

Skjonsberg, Anne. International Problems in the Field of General Taxes on Sales of Goods and Services: Norway. **In** *International Fiscal Association (I),* 1983, pp. 511-27. **[G: Norway]**

Solow, Robert M. Implications of the Government Deficit for U.S. Capital Formation: Discussion. **In** *Federal Reserve Bank of Boston,* 1983, pp. 96–98. **[G: U.S.]**

de Souza, Hamilton Dias. International Problems in the Field of General Taxes on Sales of Goods and Services: Brazil. **In** *International Fiscal Association (I),* 1983, pp. 319–34. **[G: Brazil]**

St. Amand, Stephen W.; Herndon, John Thomas and Cole, James Nathan. New Federalism: A Question of Finances and Timing. *Public Budg. Finance,* Spring 1983, *3*(1), pp. 57–65. **[G: U.S.]**

St.-Hilaire, France and Whalley, John. A Microconsistent Equilibrium Data Set for Canada for Use in Tax Policy Analysis. *Rev. Income Wealth,* June 1983, *29*(2), pp. 175–204. **[G: Canada]**

Stein, Herbert. Starting Over: A New Bipartisan Economic Policy. *Challenge,* March/April 1983, *26*(1), pp. 50–54. **[G: U.S.]**

Tsingris, Demetrius. International Problems in the Field of General Taxes on Sales of Goods and Services: Greece. **In** *International Fiscal Association (I),* 1983, pp. 413–24. **[G: Greece]**

Vaughan, Roger J. Inflation and Unemployment Surviving the 1980s. **In** *Barker, M., ed. (II),* 1983, pp. 93–247. **[G: U.S.]**

de Voil, Paul. International Problems in the Field of General Taxes on Sales of Goods and Services: United Kingdom. **In** *International Fiscal Association (I),* 1983, pp. 561–71. **[G: U.K.]**

Wilson, T. A. and Dungan, D. P. Medium-Term Fiscal Planning for Recovery. *Can. Public Policy,* September 1983, *9*(3), pp. 390–97. **[G: Canada]**

Wirick, R. G. Fiscal Policy 'Crowding-Out' of Private Investment in an Open Economy: The Case of Canada. **In** *Conklin, D. W. and Courchene, T. J., eds.*, 1983, pp. 215–49. **[G: U.S.; Canada]**

Wojnilower, Albert M. Implications of the Government Deficit for U.S. Capital Formation: Discussion. **In** *Federal Reserve Bank of Boston,* 1983, pp. 99–111. **[G: U.S.]**

322 National Government Expenditures and Budgeting

3220 General

Aaron, Henry J. Tax Prospects: Implications of Budget Problems. *Nat. Tax J.*, September 1983, *36*(3), pp. 265–73. **[G: U.S.]**

Browne, G. W. G. Fifty Years of Public Finance. *S. Afr. J. Econ.*, March 1983, *51*(1), pp. 134–73. **[G: S. Africa]**

Canarella, Giorgio and Garston, Neil. Monetary and Public Debt Shocks: Tests and Efficient Estimates. *J. Money, Credit, Banking,* May 1983, *15*(2), pp. 199–211. **[G: U.S.]**

Davie, Bruce F. Tax Prospects: Implications of Budget Problems: Comments on Henry Aaron's Paper. *Nat. Tax J.*, September 1983, *36*(3), pp. 281–83. **[G: U.S.]**

Dildine, Larry L. Tax Prospects: Implications of Budget Problems: Remarks. *Nat. Tax J.*, September 1983, *36*(3), pp. 279. **[G: U.S.]**

Frey, René L. and Leu, Robert E. Umverteilung über den Staatshaushalt: Die personnel Budgetinzidenz der Schweiz 1977. (Redistribution through the Public Sector: Personal Budget Incidence in Switzerland, 1977. With English summary.) *Schweiz. Z. Volkswirtsch. Statist.*, March 1983, *119*(1), pp. 1–21. **[G: Switzerland]**

Gephardt, Richard. Reflections on Revenue Legislation. *Nat. Tax J.*, September 1983, *36*(3), pp. 293–95. **[G: U.S.]**

Harberger, Arnold C. The State of the Corporate Income Tax: Who Pays It? Should It Be Repealed? **In** *Walker, C. E. and Bloomfield, M. E., eds.*, 1983, pp. 161–70.

Herschtel, Marie-Luise. Les finances publiques françaises: résultats 1982 et perspectives 1983. (With English summary.) *Revue Écon. Polit.*, September–October 1983, *93*(5), pp. 693–703. **[G: France]**

Lim, David. Instability of Government Revenue and Expenditure in Less Developed Countries. *World Devel.*, May 1983, *11*(5), pp. 447–50. **[G: LDCs]**

Mackay, Robert J. and Weaver, Carolyn L. Commodity Bundling and Agenda Control in the Public Sector. *Quart. J. Econ.*, November 1983, *98*(4),

pp. 611–35.

McLure, Charles E., Jr. Value Added Tax: Has the Time Come? **In** *Walker, C. E. and Bloomfield, M. E., eds.*, 1983, pp. 185–213.

Nellor, David C. L. The Size of Government, Capital Accumulation, and the Tax Base. *Public Finance Quart.*, July 1983, *11*(3), pp. 321–45. **[G: U.S.]**

Nolan, John S. Tax Prospects: Implications of Budget Problems: Remarks. *Nat. Tax J.*, September 1983, *36*(3), pp. 285–88. **[G: U.S.]**

Okun, Arthur M. The Full Employment Surplus Revisited. **In** *Okun, A. M.*, 1983, *1970*, pp. 304–37. **[G: U.S.]**

Ruggeri, Giovanni. Public Finances: What Cure? *Rev. Econ. Cond. Italy*, February 1983, (1), pp. 141–49. **[G: Italy]**

Sherman, Howard J. Cyclical Behavior of Government Fiscal Policy. *J. Econ. Issues*, June 1983, *17*(2), pp. 379–88. **[G: U.S.]**

Vessilier, Elisabeth. Aspects financiers des nationalisations. (Financial Aspects of Nationalisations. With English summary.) *Revue Écon.*, May 1983, *34*(3), pp. 466–95. **[G: France]**

Walker, Charls E. Tax Prospects: Implications of Budget Problems: Comments. *Nat. Tax J.*, September 1983, *36*(3), pp. 289–91. **[G: U.S.]**

3221 National Government Expenditures

Aaron, Henry J. Setting National Priorities: The 1984 Budget: The Choices Ahead. **In** *Pechman, J. A., ed.*, 1983, pp. 201–24. **[G: U.S.]**

Aitkin, D. A. Where Does Australia Stand? **In** *Withers, G., ed.*, 1983, pp. 13–31. **[G: OECD; Australia]**

Anton, Thomas J. The Regional Distribution of Federal Expenditures, 1971–1980. *Nat. Tax J.*, December 1983, *36*(4), pp. 429–42. **[G: U.S.]**

Ball, Nicole. Military Expenditure and Socio-Economic Development. *Int. Soc. Sci. J.*, 1983, *35*(1), pp. 81–97. **[G: LDCs]**

Ball, Nicole. The Structure of the Defense Industry: Appendix 1: The United Kingdom. **In** *Ball, N. and Leitenberg, M., eds.*, 1983, pp. 344–60. **[G: U.K.]**

Bixby, Ann Kallman. Social Welfare Expenditures, Fiscal Year 1980. *Soc. Sec. Bull.*, August 1983, *46*(8), pp. 9–17. **[G: U.S.]**

Blöndal, Gisli. Balancing the Budget: Budgeting Practices and Fiscal Policy Issues in Iceland. *Public Budg. Finance*, Summer 1983, *3*(2), pp. 47–63. **[G: Iceland]**

Bonnen, James T. The Dilemma of Agricultural Economists: Discussion. *Amer. J. Agr. Econ.*, December 1983, *65*(5), pp. 889–90. **[G: U.S.]**

Buglione, Enrico and France, George. Skewed Fiscal Federalism in Italy: Implications for Public Expenditure Control. *Public Budg. Finance*, Autumn 1983, *3*(3), pp. 43–63. **[G: Italy]**

Burke, Gerald. Public Educational Expenditure in the 1970s and 1980s. *Australian Econ. Rev.*, 3rd Quarter 1983, (63), pp. 34–45. **[G: Australia]**

Crane, Steven E. Interpreting the Distribution of Government Expenditures in Budget Incidence Studies. *Nat. Tax J.*, June 1983, *36*(2), pp. 243–47.

Daniel, Raymond. The Dilemma of Agricultural Economists: Discussion. *Amer. J. Agr. Econ.*, December 1983, *65*(5), pp. 891–92. **[G: U.S.]**

Domke, William K.; Eichenberg, Richard C. and Kelleher, Catherine M. The Illusion of Choice: Defense and Welfare in Advanced Industrial Democracies, 1948–1978. *Amer. Polit. Sci. Rev.*, March 1983, *77*(1), pp. 19–35. **[G: U.S.; U.K.; W. Germany; France]**

Doyle, Maurice F. Management of the Public Finances in Ireland since 1961. *Public Budg. Finance*, Summer 1983, *3*(2), pp. 64–78. **[G: Ireland]**

Dunne, J. P. and Smith, R. P. The Allocative Efficiency of Government Expenditure: Some Comparative Tests. *Europ. Econ. Rev.*, January 1983, *20*(1–3), pp. 381–94. **[G: Australia; Sweden; U.K.; Portugal]**

Elliott, Ralph D. and Hawkins, Benjamin M. The Impact of Government Spending on the Level of Private Sector Strike Activity. *Atlantic Econ. J.*, July 1983, *11*(2), pp. 22–28. **[G: U.S.]**

Elliott, Ralph D.; Hawkins, Benjamin M. and Hughes, Woodrow W., Jr. Does Government Spending Affect Industrial Concentration? *Nebr. J. Econ. Bus.*, Summer 1983, *22*(3), pp. 44–52. **[G: U.S.]**

Eltis, Walter. The Interconnection between Public Expenditure and Inflation in Britain. *Amer. Econ. Rev.*, May 1983, *73*(2), pp. 291–96. **[G: U.K.]**

Fellner, William. Reducing Government Expenditure Growth: A British View: Comment. **In** *Giersch, H., ed.*, 1983, pp. 25–30. **[G: U.K.]**

Fels, Gerhard. How to Reduce Government Growth: An American View: Comment. **In** *Giersch, H., ed.*, 1983, pp. 48–52. **[G: U.S.]**

Frank, Max. Dépenses fiscales: problèmes controversés et d'actualité. (With English summary.) *Cah. Écon. Bruxelles*, Third Trimestre 1983, (99), pp. 387–416. **[G: Canada; W. Germany; U.S.; France]**

Gardner, Bruce L. Fact and Fiction in the Public Data Budget Crunch. *Amer. J. Agr. Econ.*, December 1983, *65*(5), pp. 882–88. **[G: U.S.]**

Gould, Frank. Public Expenditure in Japan: A Comparative View. *Hitotsubashi J. Econ.*, February 1983, *23*(2), pp. 57–67. **[G: OECD]**

Gould, Frank. The Development of Public Expenditures in Western, Industrialised Countries: A Comparative Analysis. *Public Finance*, 1983, *38*(1), pp. 38–69. **[G: OECD]**

Graham, W. C. Government Procurement Policies: GATT, the EEC, and the United States. **In** *Trebilcock, M. J., et al., eds.*, 1983, pp. 355–93. **[G: U.S.; EEC]**

Hartley, Keith and Lynk, Edward L. Budget Cuts and Public Sector Employment: The Case of Defence. *Appl. Econ.*, August 1983, *15*(4), pp. 531–40. **[G: U.K.]**

Herber, Bernard P. and Pawlik, Paul U. Measuring Government's Role in the Mixed Economy: A New Approach. *Nat. Tax J.*, March, 1983, *36*(1), pp. 45–56. **[G: U.S.]**

Holcombe, Randall G. and Zardkoohi, Asghar. On the Distribution of Federal Taxes and Expenditures, and the New War between the States. *Pub-*

lic Choice, 1983, *40*(2), pp. 165–74. [G: U.S.]

Hyde, John. Small Government and Social Equity: Discussion. In *Withers, G., ed.*, 1983, pp. 74–81. [G: Australia]

Just, Richard E. The Impact of Less Data on the Agricultural Economy and Society. *Amer. J. Agr. Econ.*, December 1983, *65*(5), pp. 872–81. [G: U.S.]

Kaufmann, William W. The Defense Budget. In *Pechman, J. A., ed.*, 1983, pp. 39–79. [G: U.S.]

Kim, Dong-Kun and Kang, In-Jae. The Budget System and Structure in Korea. *Public Budg. Finance*, Winter 1983, *3*(4), pp. 85–96. [G: Korea]

Kim, Wan-Soon and Abbott, Graham. Budget Procedures and Policies in the ASEAN Countries. *Public Budg. Finance*, Winter 1983, *3*(4), pp. 71–84. [G: ASEAN]

Kolodziej, Edward A. The Structure of the Defense Industry: France. In *Ball, N. and Leitenberg, M., eds.*, 1983, pp. 81–110. [G: France]

Landau, Daniel L. Government Expenditure and Economic Growth: A Cross-Country Study. *Southern Econ. J.*, January 1983, *49*(3), pp. 783–92.

Levy, David M. and Terleckyj, Nestor E. Effects of Government R&D on Private R&D Investment and Productivity: A Macroeconomic Analysis. *Bell J. Econ. (See Rand J. Econ. after 4/85)*, Autumn 1983, *14*(2), pp. 551–61. [G: U.S.]

Lewis, W. Arthur. Patterns of Public Revenue and Expenditure. In *Lewis, W. A.*, 1983, *1956*, pp. 573–614. [G: LDCs; MDCs]

Meerman, Jacob. Minimizing the Burden of Recurrent Costs. *Finance Develop.*, December 1983, *20*(4), pp. 41–43. [G: Africa]

Meier, Kenneth J. and Copeland, Gary W. Interest Groups and Public Policy. *Soc. Sci. Quart.*, September 1983, *64*(3), pp. 641–46. [G: U.S.]

Minsky, Hyman P. Pitfalls Due to Financial Fragility. In *Weintraub, S. and Goodstein, M., eds.*, 1983, pp. 104–19. [G: U.S.]

Mountfield, Peter. Recent Developments in the Control of Public Expenditure in the United Kingdom. *Public Budg. Finance*, Autumn 1983, *3*(3), pp. 81–102. [G: U.K.]

Munnell, Alicia H. Wars Are Expensive: Veterans and the Budget. *New Eng. Econ. Rev.*, March/April 1983, pp. 46–64. [G: U.S.]

Murthy, N. R. Vasudeva. Endogenous Government Consumption Expenditure: Some Econometric Evidence for the Indian Economy. *Indian Econ. J.*, July–September 1983, *31*(1), pp. 43–50. [G: India]

Musgrave, Peggy B. Controlling Government Spending: Response: The Need for Precision. In *Stubblebine, Wm. C. and Willett, T. D., eds.*, 1983, pp. 109–13. [G: U.S.]

Nagarajan, P. 'Displacement Effect' in Government Spending in Sweden: A Reexamination. *Public Finance*, 1983, *38*(1), pp. 156–62. [G: Sweden]

Ott, Attiat F. Controlling Government Spending. In *Stubblebine, Wm. C. and Willett, T. D., eds.*, 1983, pp. 79–107. [G: U.S.]

Peacock, Alan. Reducing Government Expenditure Growth: A British View. In *Giersch, H., ed.*, 1983, pp. 1–24. [G: U.K.]

Peaucelle, Irina; Petit, Pascal and Saillard, Yves. Dépenses publiques: structure et évolution par rapport au PIB. Les enseignements d'un modèle macroéconomique. *Revue Écon. Polit.*, January–February 1983, *93*(1), pp. 62–85. [G: France; EEC]

Pechman, Joseph A. The Budget and the Economy. In *Pechman, J. A., ed.*, 1983, pp. 15–37. [G: U.S.]

Penner, Rudolph G. Fiscal Management. In *Miller, G. W., ed.*, 1983, pp. 52–71. [G: U.S.]

Penner, Rudolph G. How to Reduce Government Growth: An American View. In *Giersch, H., ed.*, 1983, pp. 31–47. [G: U.S.]

Peterson, J. C. and Jones, D. I. H. Government Expenditure and Resource Crowding Out: A Brief Examination of Some Aspects of the Bacon and Eltis Hypothesis. *Rivista Int. Sci. Econ. Com.*, December 1983, *30*(12), pp. 1100–114. [G: U.K.; W. Germany]

Rhyne, Elisabeth H. Federal Credit Activities. In *Pechman, J. A., ed.*, 1983, pp. 231–42. [G: U.S.]

Rowley, Charles K. The Post-war Economic Failure of British Government: A Public Choice Perspective. In *Seldon, A., et al.*, 1983, pp. 131–48. [G: U.K.]

Shepherd, David. The Impact of Public Expenditure. In *Shepherd, D.; Turk, J. and Silberston, A., eds.*, 1983, pp. 108–36. [G: U.K.]

Solano, Paul L. Institutional Explanations of Public Expenditures among High Income Democracies. *Public Finance*, 1983, *38*(3), pp. 440–58. [G: OECD]

Stretton, Hugh. Where Does Australia Stand? Discussion. In *Withers, G., ed.*, 1983, pp. 32–36.

Verner, Joel G. Budgetary Trade-Offs between Education and Defense in Latin America: A Research Note. *J. Devel. Areas*, October 1983, *18*(1), pp. 77–91. [G: Latin America]

Wilenski, P. S. Small Government and Social Equity. In *Withers, G., ed.*, 1983, pp. 37–73. [G: Australia]

Wolfe, C. Stephen and Burkhead, Jesse. Fiscal Trends in Selected Industrialized Countries. *Public Budg. Finance*, Winter 1983, *3*(4), pp. 97–102. [G: OECD]

3226 National Government Budgeting and Deficits

Aaron, Henry J. Setting National Priorities: The 1984 Budget: The Choices Ahead. In *Pechman, J. A., ed.*, 1983, pp. 201–24. [G: U.S.]

Abrams, Richard K.; Froyen, Richard T. and Waud, Roger N. The State of the Federal Budget and the State of the Economy. *Econ. Inquiry*, October 1983, *21*(4), pp. 485–503. [G: U.S.]

Atkinson, P. E.; Blundell-Wignall, A. and Chouraqui, J.-C. Budget Financing and Monetary Targets, with Special Reference to the Seven Major OECD Countries. *Écon. Soc.*, July-August 1983, *17*(7–8), pp. 1057–96. [G: OECD]

Baguley, Robert W. Government Deficits: Historical Analysis and Present Policy Alternatives: Comment. In *Conklin, D. W. and Courchene, T. J., eds.*, 1983, pp. 317–19. [G: Canada]

Baldwin, Carliss Y.; Lessard, Donald R. and Mason,

Scott P. Budgetary Time Bombs: Controlling Government Loan Guarantees. *Can. Public Policy,* September 1983, *9*(3), pp. 338–46. **[G: Canada]**

Benson, Bruce L. Logrolling and High Demand Committee Review. *Public Choice,* 1983, *41*(3), pp. 427–34.

de Bever, Leo. Deficits and the Economy to 1990: Projections and Alternatives: Comment. **In** *Conklin, D. W. and Courchene, T. J., eds.,* 1983, pp. 148–49. **[G: Canada]**

Blöndal, Gisli. Balancing the Budget: Budgeting Practices and Fiscal Policy Issues in Iceland. *Public Budg. Finance,* Summer 1983, *3*(2), pp. 47–63. **[G: Iceland]**

Bossons, John. Rapporteur's Remarks: Discussion. **In** *Conklin, D. W. and Courchene, T. J., eds.,* 1983, pp. 358–60.

Bossons, John. What Can Macroeconomic Theory Tell Us about the Way Deficits Should Be Measured? Comment. **In** *Conklin, D. W. and Courchene, T. J., eds.,* 1983, pp. 181–86.

Bosworth, Barry P. Measuring and Analyzing the Cyclically Adjusted Budget: Discussion. **In** *Federal Reserve Bank of Boston,* 1983, pp. 43–45. **[G: U.S.]**

Bowsher, Charles A. Reforming the Federal Budget Process. *Public Budg. Finance,* Spring 1983, *3*(1), pp. 113–15. **[G: U.S.]**

Bruce, Neil and Purvis, Douglas D. Fiscal Discipline and Rules for Controlling the Deficit: Some Unpleasant Keynesian Arithmetic. **In** *Conklin, D. W. and Courchene, T. J., eds.,* 1983, pp. 323–40.

Caiden, Naomi. Guidelines to Federal Budget Reform. *Public Budg. Finance,* Winter 1983, *3*(4), pp. 4–22. **[G: U.S.]**

Caiden, Naomi. The Politics of Subtraction. **In** *Schick, A., ed.,* 1983, pp. 100–130. **[G: U.S.]**

Capra, James R. Federal Deficits and Private Credit Demands: Economic Impact Analysis. *Fed. Res. Bank New York Quart. Rev.,* Summer 1983, *8*(2), pp. 29–44. **[G: U.S.]**

Carlson, Keith M. The Critical Role of Economic Assumptions in the Evaluation of Federal Budget Programs. *Fed. Res. Bank St. Louis Rev.,* October 1983, *65*(8), pp. 5–14. **[G: U.S.]**

Conklin, David and Sayeed, Adil. Overview of the Deficit Debate. **In** *Conklin, D. W. and Courchene, T. J., eds.,* 1983, pp. 12–54. **[G: Canada]**

Cutt, James. The Evolution of Expenditure Budgeting in Australia. *Public Budg. Finance,* Summer 1983, *3*(2), pp. 7–27. **[G: Australia]**

Davis, Russell; Wilen, James E. and Jergovic, Rosemarie. Oil and Gas Royalty Recovery Policy on Federal and Indian Lands. *Natural Res. J.,* April 1983, *23*(2), pp. 391–416. **[G: U.S.]**

Davis, Russell; Wilen, James E. and Jergovic, Rosemarie. Royalty Management in the New Minerals Management Service: A Reply to Sant, Haspel, and Boldt. *Natural Res. J.,* April 1983, *23*(2), pp. 435–39. **[G: U.S.]**

Doern, G. Bruce. Canada's Budgetary Dilemmas: Tax and Expenditure Reform. *Public Budg. Finance,* Summer 1983, *3*(2), pp. 28–46. **[G: Canada]**

Dungan, D. P. and Wilson, T. A. Deficits and the Economy to 1990: Projections and Alternatives. **In** *Conklin, D. W. and Courchene, T. J., eds.,* 1983, pp. 116–48. **[G: Canada]**

Ellwood, John W. Budget Control in a Redistributive Environment. **In** *Schick, A., ed.,* 1983, pp. 69–99. **[G: U.S.]**

Emmanuel, A. B. C. Zambia's 1983 Budget. *Bull. Int. Fiscal Doc.,* November 1983, *37*(11), pp. 491–92. **[G: Zambia]**

Eriksson, Björn. Sweden's Budget System in a Changing World. *Public Budg. Finance,* Autumn 1983, *3*(3), pp. 64–80. **[G: Sweden]**

Feldstein, Martin S. Budget Deficits and Political Choices. *Challenge,* January/February 1983, *25*(6), pp. 53–56. **[G: U.S.]**

Fisher, Louis. Annual Authorizations: Durable Roadblocks to Biennial Budgeting. *Public Budg. Finance,* Spring 1983, *3*(1), pp. 23–40. **[G: U.S.]**

Fisher, Louis. Chadha's Impact on the Budget Process. *Public Budg. Finance,* Winter 1983, *3*(4), pp. 103–07. **[G: U.S.]**

Franco, Giampiero and Mengarelli, Gianluigi. Ancora a proposito dei mezzi di finanziamento del deficit pubblico: una risposta allargata. (The Means for Financing the Public Deficit: An Extended Reply. With English summary.) *Bancaria,* January 1983, *39*(1), pp. 34–38. **[G: Italy]**

Ge, Zhida. On the Issue of Balancing the State Budget. *Chinese Econ. Stud.,* Winter 1982/83, *16*(2), pp. 107–23. **[G: China]**

Glynn, Dermot. Is Government Borrowing Now Too Low? *Lloyds Bank Rev.,* January 1983, (147), pp. 21–41. **[G: U.K.]**

Goodisman, Leonard D. Budgeting and Field Discretion in Disaster Relief. *Public Budg. Finance,* Spring 1983, *3*(1), pp. 89–102. **[G: U.S.]**

Gough, Robert A., Jr. The Future Constraints on Interest Rates. **In** *Sanford, T., ed.,* 1983, pp. 56–78. **[G: U.S.]**

Grant, John. Deficits and Capital Markets. **In** *Conklin, D. W. and Courchene, T. J., eds.,* 1983, pp. 261–83. **[G: Canada]**

Grant, John and Ip, Irene. The Federal Budget and Medium-Term Economic Strategy. *Can. Public Policy,* September 1983, *9*(3), pp. 383–89. **[G: Canada]**

Gray, Barry and Derody, Beatrice. Some Aspects of the 1983–84 Budget. *Australian Econ. Rev.,* 3rd Quarter 1983, (63), pp. 3–18. **[G: Australia]**

Grilli, Enzo R. Il deficit pubblico spiazza le imprese. (The Public Spending Deficit Wrong Foots Companies. With English summary.) *L'Impresa,* 1983, *25*(6), pp. 25–28. **[G: Italy]**

Havens, Harry S. A Public Accounting: Integrating Evaluation and Budgeting. *Public Budg. Finance,* Summer 1983, *3*(2), pp. 102–13.

Jao, Y. C. Hong Kong 1983–84 Budget: Tax Proposals. *Bull. Int. Fiscal Doc.,* 1983, *37*(6), pp. 265–67. **[G: Hong Kong]**

Kershaw, Robert. Congressional Budget Reform Developments. *Public Budg. Finance,* Autumn 1983, *3*(3), pp. 118–22. **[G: U.S.]**

Kim, Dong-Kun and Kang, In-Jae. The Budget System and Structure in Korea. *Public Budg. Finance,* Winter 1983, *3*(4), pp. 85–96. **[G: Korea]**

Kim, Wan-Soon and Abbott, Graham. Budget Procedures and Policies in the ASEAN Countries. *Public Budg. Finance,* Winter 1983, *3*(4), pp. 71–84. **[G: ASEAN]**

Kloten, Norbert and Ketterer, K. H. Fiscal Policy in West Germany: Anticyclical versus Expenditure-reducing Policies. **In** *[Saunders, C. T.],* 1983, pp. 291–307. **[G: W. Germany]**

Korff, Hans Clausen. Planning and Budgeting in the Federal Republic of Germany. *Public Budg. Finance,* Winter 1983, *3*(4), pp. 57–70. **[G: W. Germany]**

Kuespert, Edward F. Limitations on Moving Ahead, While Cutting Back. *Public Budg. Finance,* Summer 1983, *3*(2), pp. 79–82. **[G: U.S.]**

Laband, David N. Federal Budget Cuts: Bureaucrats Trim the Meat, Not the Fat. *Public Choice,* 1983, *41*(2), pp. 311–14. **[G: U.S.]**

Laidler, David. Rapporteur's Remarks. **In** *Conklin, D. W. and Courchene, T. J., eds.,* 1983, pp. 346–58.

Laterza, Edoardo Lecaldano Sasso and Quintieri, Beniamino. È il debito pubblico più inflazionistico della base monetaria? (Is Public Debt More Inflationary than the Monetary Base? With English summary.) *Bancaria,* January 1983, *39*(1), pp. 27–33. **[G: Italy]**

Leeuw, Frank and de Holloway, Thomas M. Cyclical Adjustment of the Federal Budget and Federal Debt. *Surv. Curr. Bus.,* December 1983, *63*(12), pp. 25–40. **[G: U.S.]**

de Leeuw, Frank and Holloway, Thomas M. Measuring and Analyzing the Cyclically Adjusted Budget. **In** *Federal Reserve Bank of Boston,* 1983, pp. 1–42. **[G: U.S.]**

Levy, Michael E. "Staying the Course" Won't Help the Budget. *Challenge,* May/June 1983, *26*(2), pp. 34–39. **[G: U.S.]**

Levy, Mickey D. Federal Budget Outlook—A Report to the SOMC. **In** *Shadow Open Market Committee.,* 1983, pp. 41–45. **[G: U.S.]**

Lim, David. Government Recurrent Expenditure and Economic Growth in Less Developed Countries. *World Devel.,* April 1983, *11*(4), pp. 377–80. **[G: LDCs]**

Lindbeck, Assar. Budget Expansion and Cost Inflation. *Amer. Econ. Rev.,* May 1983, *73*(2), pp. 285–90.

Loose, Verne W. Letter [Budget Deficits and Political Choices]. *Challenge,* May/June 1983, *26*(2), pp. 63–64. **[G: U.S.]**

Lowery, David. The Hidden Impact of Fiscal Caps: Implications of the Beck Phenomenon. *Public Budg. Finance,* Autumn 1983, *3*(3), pp. 19–32. **[G: U.S.]**

Machiraju, H. R. The Central Budget for 1983–84—An Assessment. *Margin,* April 1983, *15*(3), pp. 30–44. **[G: India]**

Mackness, William. Fiscal Discipline and Rules for Controlling the Deficit: Some Unpleasant Keynesian Arithmetic: Comment. **In** *Conklin, D. W. and Courchene, T. J., eds.,* 1983, pp. 340–45.

Martino, Antonio. Invisible Taxation: The Growth of Italy's Leviathan. *Policy Rev.,* Summer 1983, (25), pp. 46–51. **[G: Italy]**

Mathiasen, David G. Recent Developments in the Composition and the Formulation of the United States Federal Budget. *Public Budg. Finance,* Autumn 1983, *3*(3), pp. 103–15. **[G: U.S.]**

McCallum, John. Government Deficits: Historical Analysis and Present Policy Alternatives. **In** *Conklin, D. W. and Courchene, T. J., eds.,* 1983, pp. 284–317. **[G: Canada]**

McKinnon, Ian. What Does the Public Think about Deficits? What Does Bay Street Think about Deficits? **In** *Conklin, D. W. and Courchene, T. J., eds.,* 1983, pp. 189–214. **[G: Canada]**

Miller, Preston J. Budget Deficit Mythology. *Fed. Res. Bank Minn. Rev.,* Fall 1983, *7*(4), pp. 1–13. **[G: U.S.]**

Modigliani, Franco. Government Deficits, Inflation, and Future Generations. **In** *Conklin, D. W. and Courchene, T. J., eds.,* 1983, pp. 55–77. **[G: OECD]**

Montesano, Aldo. Debito pubblico o base monetaria? Una risposta. (Public Debt or Monetary Base? A Reply. With English summary.) *Bancaria,* January 1983, *39*(1), pp. 39–41.

Moore, Geoffrey H. The Federal Deficit as a Business Cycle Stabilizer. **In** *Moore, G. H.,* 1983, *1976,* pp. 127–37. **[G: U.S.]**

Morris, Frank E. Monetarism without Money. **In** *Sanford, T., ed.,* 1983, pp. 26–36. **[G: U.S.]**

Motley, Brian. Real Interest Rates, Money and Government Deficits. *Fed. Res. Bank San Francisco Econ. Rev.,* Summer 1983, (3), pp. 31–45. **[G: U.S.]**

Mountfield, Peter. Recent Developments in the Control of Public Expenditure in the United Kingdom. *Public Budg. Finance,* Autumn 1983, *3*(3), pp. 81–102. **[G: U.K.]**

Parkin, Michael. What Can Macroeconomic Theory Tell Us about the Way Deficits Should be Measured? Reply. **In** *Conklin, D. W. and Courchene, T. J., eds.,* 1983, pp. 186–88.

Parkin, Michael. What Can Macroeconomic Theory Tell Us about the Way Deficits Should Be Measured? **In** *Conklin, D. W. and Courchene, T. J., eds.,* 1983, pp. 150–77.

Pechman, Joseph A. Estimates of the Structural Deficit. **In** *Pechman, J. A., ed.,* 1983, pp. 225–30. **[G: U.S.]**

Pechman, Joseph A. Setting National Priorities: The 1984 Budget: Introduction and Summary. **In** *Pechman, J. A., ed.,* 1983, pp. 1–14. **[G: U.S.]**

Pechman, Joseph A. The Budget and the Economy. **In** *Pechman, J. A., ed.,* 1983, pp. 15–37. **[G: U.S.]**

Pitsvada, Bernard T. Flexibility in Federal Budget Execution. *Public Budg. Finance,* Summer 1983, *3*(2), pp. 83–101. **[G: U.S.]**

Premchand, A. Government and Public Enterprise: The Budget Link. **In** *[Ramanadham, V. V.],* 1983, pp. 24–47.

Premchand, A. Governmental Budgeting: State of the Arts. *Public Budg. Finance,* Summer 1983, *3*(2), pp. 4–6.

Reischauer, Robert D. Getting, Using, and Misusing Economic Information. **In** *Schick, A., ed.,* 1983, pp. 38–68. **[G: U.S.]**

Rohwer, Bernd. Strukturelles Defizit und Konsolidierungsbedarf. (Structural Budget Deficits and Requirements for Consolidation. With English summary.) *Ifo-Studien,* 1983, *29*(4), pp. 299–318. **[G: W. Germany]**

Salvemini, Maria Teresa. Reflections on the Olivetti Papers. *Public Budg. Finance,* Spring 1983, *3*(1), pp. 83–88. **[G: Italy]**

Sant, Donald T.; Haspel, Abraham E. and Boldt, Robert E. Oil and Gas Royalty Recovery Policy on Federal and Indian Lands: A Response. *Natural Res. J.,* April 1983, *23*(2), pp. 417–33. **[G: U.S.]**

Saulnier, Raymond J. The President's Economic Report: A Critique. *J. Portfol. Manage.,* Summer 1983, *9*(4), pp. 58–59. **[G: U.S.]**

Sayers, R. S. 1941—The First Keynesian Budget. **In** *Feinstein, C., ed.,* 1983, *1956,* pp. 107–17. **[G: U.K.]**

Scarfe, Brian L. What Can Macroeconomic Theory Tell Us about the Way Deficits Should Be Measured? Comment. **In** *Conklin, D. W. and Courchene, T. J., eds.,* 1983, pp. 177–81.

St. Amand, Stephen W.; Herndon, John Thomas and Cole, James Nathan. New Federalism: A Question of Finances and Timing. *Public Budg. Finance,* Spring 1983, *3*(1), pp. 57–65. **[G: U.S.]**

Tobin, James. Unemployment, Interest and Money. **In** *Sanford, T., ed.,* 1983, pp. 1–25. **[G: U.S.]**

Waite, Charles A. and Wakefield, Joseph C. Federal Fiscal Programs. *Surv. Curr. Bus.,* February 1983, *63*(2), pp. 8–14. **[G: U.S.]**

Wakefield, Joseph C. Federal Budget Developments. *Surv. Curr. Bus.,* April 1983, *63*(4), pp. 24–27. **[G: U.S.]**

Wakefield, Joseph C. Federal Budget Developments. *Surv. Curr. Bus.,* August 1983, *63*(8), pp. 11–13. **[G: U.S.]**

Wilson, T. A. and Dungan, D. P. Medium-Term Fiscal Planning for Recovery. *Can. Public Policy,* September 1983, *9*(3), pp. 390–97. **[G: Canada]**

Wolfe, C. Stephen and Burkhead, Jesse. Fiscal Trends in Selected Industrialized Countries. *Public Budg. Finance,* Winter 1983, *3*(4), pp. 97–102. **[G: OECD]**

Young, Robert A. Business and Budgeting: Recent Proposals for Reforming the Revenue Budgetary Process. *Can. Public Policy,* September 1983, *9*(3), pp. 347–61. **[G: Canada]**

3228 National Government Debt Management

Britton, A. J. C. Public Sector Borrowing. *Nat. Inst. Econ. Rev.,* February 1983, (103), pp. 50–55. **[G: U.K.]**

Buiter, Willem H. Measurement of the Public Sector Deficit and Its Implications for Policy Evaluation and Design. *Int. Monet. Fund Staff Pap.,* June 1983, *30*(2), pp. 306–49.

Butkiewicz, James L. The Market Value of Outstanding Government Debt: Comment. *J. Monet. Econ.,* May 1983, *11*(3), pp. 373–79. **[G: U.S.]**

Cox, W. Michael and Hirschhorn, Eric. The Market Value of U.S. Government Debt; Monthly, 1942–1980. *J. Monet. Econ.,* March 1983, *11*(2), pp. 261–72. **[G: U.S.]**

Friedman, Benjamin M. Implications of the Government Deficit for U.S. Capital Formation. **In** *Federal Reserve Bank of Boston,* 1983, pp. 73–95. **[G: U.S.]**

von Furstenberg, George M. Fiscal Deficits: From Business as Usual to a Breach of the Policy Rules? *Nat. Tax J.,* December 1983, *36*(4), pp. 443–57. **[G: U.S.]**

Galli, Giampaolo and Masera, Rainer S. Real Rates of Interest and Public Sector Deficits: An Empirical Investigation. *Econ. Notes,* 1983, (3), pp. 5–41. **[G: N. America; Italy; Germany; France; U.K.]**

Grant, John. Deficits and Capital Markets. **In** *Conklin, D. W. and Courchene, T. J., eds.,* 1983, pp. 261–83. **[G: Canada]**

Harriss, C. Lowell. Management of the Federal Debt: Lengthening the Average Maturity by Funding More into Long Term Issues Would Be Realistic. *Amer. J. Econ. Soc.,* January 1983, *42*(1), pp. 113–15. **[G: U.S.]**

Hoffman, Dennis L.; Low, Stuart A. and Reineberg, Hubert H. Recent Evidence on the Relationship between Money Growth and Budget Deficits. *J. Macroecon.,* Spring 1983, *5*(2), pp. 223–31. **[G: U.S.]**

Hymans, Saul H. The Deficit and the Fiscal and Monetary Policy Mix: Discussion. **In** *Federal Reserve Bank of Boston,* 1983, pp. 195–98. **[G: U.S.]**

Klein, Lawrence R. The Deficit and the Fiscal and Monetary Policy Mix. **In** *Federal Reserve Bank of Boston,* 1983, pp. 174–94. **[G: U.S.]**

Kopcke, Richard W. Will Big Deficits Spoil the Recovery? **In** *Federal Reserve Bank of Boston,* 1983, pp. 141–68. **[G: U.S.]**

Kremers, J. J. M. Public Debt Creation in the Netherlands, 1953–1980. *De Economist,* 1983, *131*(2), pp. 196–216. **[G: Netherlands]**

Leeuw, Frank and de Holloway, Thomas M. Cyclical Adjustment of the Federal Budget and Federal Debt. *Surv. Curr. Bus.,* December 1983, *63*(12), pp. 25–40. **[G: U.S.]**

Miller, Preston J. Will Big Deficits Spoil the Recovery? Discussion. **In** *Federal Reserve Bank of Boston,* 1983, pp. 169–73. **[G: U.S.]**

Moyer, R. Charles and Simonson, Donald G. Federal Financing Pressure: The Incidence of Crowding Out. *Rev. Bus. Econ. Res.,* Winter, 1983, *18*(2), pp. 25–39. **[G: U.S.]**

Musgrave, Peggy B. Controlling Government Spending: Response: The Need for Precision. **In** *Stubblebine, Wm. C. and Willett, T. D., eds.,* 1983, pp. 109–13. **[G: U.S.]**

Ott, Attiat F. Controlling Government Spending. **In** *Stubblebine, Wm. C. and Willett, T. D., eds.,* 1983, pp. 79–107. **[G: U.S.]**

Puglisi, Donald J. and Vignola, Anthony J., Jr. An Examination of Federal Agency Debt Pricing Practices. *J. Finan. Res.,* Summer 1983, *6*(2), pp. 83–92. **[G: U.S.]**

Quaden, Guy. L'expérience belge des déficits publics. (Belgian Experience with Public Deficits. With English summary.) *Ann. Pub. Co-op. Econ.,* July–September 1983, *54*(3), pp. 313–24.

Rousseau, Henri-Paul. The Dome Syndrome: The Debt Overhanging Canadian Government and Business. *Can. Public Policy,* March 1983, *9*(1), pp. 37–52. **[G: Canada]**

Rowley, Charles K. The Political Economy of the Public Sector. **In** *Jones, R. J. B., ed.*, 1983, pp. 17–63. **[G: U.K.]**

Rutterford, Janette. Index-Linked Gilts. *Nat. Westminster Bank Quart. Rev.*, November 1983, pp. 2–17. **[G: U.K.]**

Shepherd, David. The Impact of Public Expenditure. **In** *Shepherd, D.; Turk, J. and Silberston, A., eds.*, 1983, pp. 108–36. **[G: U.K.]**

Solow, Robert M. Implications of the Government Deficit for U.S. Capital Formation: Discussion. **In** *Federal Reserve Bank of Boston*, 1983, pp. 96–98. **[G: U.S.]**

Wojnilower, Albert M. Implications of the Government Deficit for U.S. Capital Formation: Discussion. **In** *Federal Reserve Bank of Boston*, 1983, pp. 99–111. **[G: U.S.]**

323 National Taxation, Revenue, and Subsidies

3230 National Taxation, Revenue, and Subsidies

Aaron, Henry J. Cutting Back the Social Welfare State. **In** *[Goode, R.]*, 1983, pp. 199–213. **[G: U.S.]**

Aaron, Henry J. Distributional Effects of the Reagan Program: Response: Raising Some Doubts. **In** *Stubblebine, Wm. C. and Willett, T. D., eds.*, 1983, pp. 199–202. **[G: U.S.]**

Aaron, Henry J. Setting National Priorities: The 1984 Budget: The Choices Ahead. **In** *Pechman, J. A., ed.*, 1983, pp. 201–24. **[G: U.S.]**

Aaron, Henry J. Tax Prospects: Implications of Budget Problems. *Nat. Tax J.*, September 1983, *36* (3), pp. 265–73. **[G: U.S.]**

Aaron, Henry J. The Value Added Tax: A Triumph of Form over Substance. **In** *Walker, C. E. and Bloomfield, M. E., eds.*, 1983, pp. 214–17.

Adar, Zvi and Agmon, Tamir. Financing Synthetic Fuels Investments in the United States: Public Support and Private Investment. **In** *Aronson, J. D. and Cowhey, P. F., eds.*, 1983, pp. 157–78. **[G: U.S.]**

Agell, Jonas. Subsidy to Capital through Tax Incentives in the ASEAN Countries: An Application of the Cost of Capital Approach under Inflationary Situations. *Singapore Econ. Rev.*, October 1983, *28* (2), pp. 98–128. **[G: ASEAN]**

Aitkin, D. A. Where Does Australia Stand? **In** *Withers, G., ed.*, 1983, pp. 13–31. **[G: OECD; Australia]**

Alam, Kazi Firoz. The Dividend Behavior of Companies in the U.K. Manufacturing Industry. *METU*, 1983, *10* (2), pp. 155–77. **[G: U.K.]**

Alchin, Terry Maxwell. Intertemporal Comparisons of Income Tax Progressivity: 1950–51 to 1979–80. *Australian Econ. Pap.*, June 1983, *22* (40), pp. 90–98. **[G: Australia; U.S.]**

Allie, Émile and Lefebvre, Pierre. L'aide sociale et le supplément au revenu de travail: une simulation économique des revenus (salaires) de réserve. (A Simulation of the Impact of the Quebec Minimum Income System on Reservation Wages (Income). With English summary.) *L'Actual. Econ.*, June 1983, *59* (2), pp. 190–207. **[G: Canada]**

Alt, James E. The Evolution of Tax Structures. *Public Choice*, 1983, *41* (1), pp. 181–222.

Amoako-Adu, Ben. The Canadian Tax Reform and Its Effect on Stock Prices: A Note. *J. Finance*, December 1983, *38* (5), pp. 1669–75. **[G: Canada]**

Andel, Norbert. Directions of Tax Harmonisation in the EEC. **In** *[Goode, R.]*, 1983, pp. 295–316. **[G: EEC]**

Anderson, F. J.; Beaudreau, B. C. and Bonsor, N. C. Effective Corporate Tax Rates, Inflation, and Contestability. *Can. J. Econ.*, November 1983, *16* (4), pp. 686–703. **[G: Canada; U.S.]**

Andersson, Edward. Corporate Tax Laws as Instruments of Economic Policy: Some Finnish Experiences. *Bull. Int. Fiscal Doc.*, January 1983, *37* (1), pp. 35–39. **[G: Finland]**

Andrews, William D. The Achilles' Heel of the Comprehensive Income Tax. **In** *Walker, C. E. and Bloomfield, M. E., eds.*, 1983, pp. 278–85.

Ansari, M. M. Tax Ratio and Tax Effort Analysis: A Critical Evaluation. *Bull. Int. Fiscal Doc.*, August 1983, *37* (8), pp. 345–53. **[G: LDCs]**

Anstie, Roslyn K.; Findlay, Christopher C. and Harper, Ian. The Impact of Inflation and Taxation on Tenure Choice and the Redistributive Effects of Home-Mortgage Interest Rate Regulation. *Econ. Rec.*, June 1983, *59* (165), pp. 105–10. **[G: Australia]**

Arak, Marcelle. The Effect of the Tax Treatment of Treasury-Bill Futures on Their Rates. *J. Futures Markets*, Spring 1983, *3* (1), pp. 65–73. **[G: U.S.]**

Ashenfelter, Orley. Determining Participation in Income-Tested Social Programs. *J. Amer. Statist. Assoc.*, September 1983, *78* (383), pp. 517–25. **[G: U.S.]**

Atkinson, Anthony B. Horizontal Equity and the Distribution of the Tax Burden. **In** *Atkinson, A. B.*, 1983, *1980*, pp. 93–105.

Atkinson, Anthony B. Housing Allowances, Income Maintenance and Income Taxation. **In** *Atkinson, A. B.*, 1983, *1977*, pp. 323–35.

Atkinson, Anthony B. Introduction to Part III: Design of Taxation. **In** *Atkinson, A. B.*, 1983, pp. 199–203.

Atkinson, Anthony B. Introduction to Part IV: Issues of Public Policy. **In** *Atkinson, A. B.*, 1983, pp. 317–22.

Atkinson, Anthony B. Optimal Taxation and the Direct versus Indirect Tax Controversy. **In** *Atkinson, A. B.*, 1983, *1977*, pp. 243–58.

Atkinson, Anthony B. The Income Tax Treatment of Charitable Contributions. **In** *Atkinson, A. B.*, 1983, *1976*, pp. 357–70.

Atkinson, Anthony B. and King, Mervyn A. Housing Policy, Taxation and Reform. **In** *Atkinson, A. B.*, 1983, *1980*, pp. 337–56. **[G: U.K.]**

Atkinson, Anthony B.; King, Mervyn A. and Sutherland, H. The Analysis of Personal Taxation and Social Security. *Nat. Inst. Econ. Rev.*, November 1983, (106), pp. 63–74. **[G: U.K.]**

Atkinson, Anthony B. and Sandmo, Agnar. Welfare Implications of the Taxation of Savings. **In** *Atkinson, A. B.*, 1983, *1980*, pp. 271–93.

Atkinson, Anthony B. and Stiglitz, Joseph E. The Design of Tax Structure: Direct versus Indirect

Taxation. In *Atkinson, A. B.*, 1983, *1976*, pp. 223–42.

Atkinson, Anthony B. and Stiglitz, Joseph E. The Structure of Indirect Taxation and Economic Efficiency. In *Atkinson, A. B.*, 1983, *1972*, pp. 205–21. **[G: Sweden; Canada; U.K.; OEEC]**

Auerbach, Alan J. Corporate Taxation in the United States. *Brookings Pap. Econ. Act.*, 1983, (2), pp. 451–513. **[G: U.S.]**

Auerbach, Alan J. Does ACRS Foster Efficient Capital Allocation? In *Walker, C. E. and Bloomfield, M. E., eds.*, 1983, pp. 77–78. **[G: U.S.]**

Auerbach, Alan J. Inflation and the Tax Treatment of Firm Behavior. In *Auerbach, A. J.*, 1983, *1981*, pp. 95–99.

Auerbach, Alan J. Share Valuation and Corporate Equity Policy. In *Auerbach, A. J.*, 1983, *1979*, pp. 63–77.

Auerbach, Alan J. Stockholder Tax Rates and Firm Attributes. *J. Public Econ.*, July 1983, *21* (2), pp. 107–27. **[G: U.S.]**

Auerbach, Alan J. Tax Neutrality and the Social Discount Rate. In *Auerbach, A. J.*, 1983, *1982*, pp. 33–50.

Auerbach, Alan J. The Optimal Taxation of Heterogeneous Capital. In *Auerbach, A. J.*, 1983, *1979*, pp. 9–32.

Auerbach, Alan J. Wealth Maximization and the Cost of Capital. In *Auerbach, A. J.*, 1983, *1979*, pp. 78–91.

Auerbach, Alan J. Welfare Aspects of Current U.S. Corporate Taxation. *Amer. Econ. Rev.*, May 1983, *73* (2), pp. 76–81. **[G: U.S.]**

Auerbach, Alan J. and King, Mervyn A. Taxation, Portfolio Choice, and Debt-Equity Ratios: A General Equilibrium Model. *Quart. J. Econ.*, November 1983, *98* (4), pp. 587–609.

Auerbach, Alan J. and Kotlikoff, Laurence J. National Savings, Economic Welfare, and the Structure of Taxation. In *Feldstein, M., ed.*, 1983, pp. 459–93. **[G: U.S.]**

Auerbach, Alan J.; Kotlikoff, Laurence J. and Skinner, Jonathan. The Efficiency Gains from Dynamic Tax Reform. *Int. Econ. Rev.*, February 1983, *24* (1), pp. 81–100.

Auten, Gerald E. Capital Gains: An Evaluation of the 1978 and 1981 Tax Cuts. In *Walker, C. E. and Bloomfield, M. E., eds.*, 1983, pp. 121–48. **[G: U.S.]**

Autenne, M. Jacques and Scholsem, M. Jean-Claude. Problèmes internationaux du domaine des taxes sur le chiffre d'affaires: Belgique. (With English summary.) In *International Fiscal Association (I)*, 1983, pp. 289–317. **[G: Belgium]**

Ayanian, Robert. Expectations, Taxes, and Interest: The Search for the Darby Effect. *Amer. Econ. Rev.*, September 1983, *73* (4), pp. 762–65. **[G: U.S.]**

Babbel, David F. and Staking, Kim B. An Engel Curve Analysis of Gambling and Insurance in Brazil. *J. Risk Ins.*, December 1983, *50* (4), pp. 688–96. **[G: Brazil]**

Baer, Herbert. Thrift Dominance and Specialization in Housing Finance: The Role of Taxation. *Housing Finance Rev.*, Oct 1983, *2* (4), pp. 353–67. **[G: U.S.]**

Bailey, Martin J. Alternative Tax Rules and Personal Saving Incentives: Microeconomic Data and Behavioral Simulations: Comment. In *Feldstein, M., ed.*, 1983, pp. 209–10. **[G: U.S.]**

Baker, Samuel H. The Determinants of Median Voter Tax Liability: An Empirical Test of the Fiscal Illusion Hypothesis. *Public Finance Quart.*, January 1983, *11* (1), pp. 95–108. **[G: U.S.]**

Balcer, Yves. The Taxation of Capital Gains: Samuelson's Fundamental Principle. *Public Finance*, 1983, *38* (1), pp. 1–15.

Balcer, Yves and Sadka, Efraim. Horizontal Equity in Models of Self-selection with Applications to Income Tax and Signaling Cases. In *Helpman, E.; Razin, A. and Sadka, E., eds.*, 1983, pp. 235–53.

Balcer, Yves, et al. Income Redistribution and the Structure of Indirect Taxation. In *Helpman, E.; Razin, A. and Sadka, E., eds.*, 1983, pp. 279–97. **[G: U.S.]**

Baldwin, Carliss Y.; Lessard, Donald R. and Mason, Scott P. Budgetary Time Bombs: Controlling Government Loan Guarantees. *Can. Public Policy*, September 1983, *9* (3), pp. 338–46. **[G: Canada]**

Ballard, Charles L. and Shoven, John B. Taxes and Capital Formation. In *[Goode, R.]*, 1983, pp. 389–407. **[G: U.S.]**

Ballentine, J. Gregory. A Framework for Evaluating a Flat Rate Tax. In *Walker, C. E. and Bloomfield, M. E., eds.*, 1983, pp. 311–14. **[G: U.S.]**

Ballentine, J. Gregory. Tax Prospects: Implications of Budget Problems: Remarks. *Nat. Tax J.*, September 1983, *36* (3), pp. 275–77. **[G: U.S.]**

Barman, Kiran and Bisonoi, Usha. Value Added Tax as an Alternative to Corporation Tax. *Econ. Aff.*, October–December 1983, *28* (4), pp. 860–65. **[G: India]**

Barro, Robert J. and Sahasakul, Chaipat. Measuring the Average Marginal Tax Rate from the Individual Income Tax. *J. Bus.*, October 1983, *56* (4), pp. 419–52. **[G: U.S.]**

Bates, Robert H. Governments and Agricultural Markets in Africa. In *Johnson, D. G. and Schuh, G. E., eds.*, 1983, pp. 153–83. **[G: Africa]**

Baumgarten, Klaus. Auswirkungen der Besteuerung importierter Zwischenprodukte. (Consequences of Taxation of Imported Intermediate Goods. With English summary.) *Jahr. Nationalökon. Statist.*, May 1983, *198* (3), pp. 251–68.

Baumol, William J. Toward Operational Models of Entrepreneurship. In *Ronen, J., ed.*, 1983, pp. 29–48.

Bawly, Dan and Lapidoth, Arye. Tax Avoidance/Tax Evasion: Israel. In *International Fiscal Association (II)*, 1983, pp. 431–47. **[G: Israel]**

Beach, Charles M. and Balfour, Frederick S. Estimated Payroll Tax Incidence and Aggregate Demand for Labour in the United Kingdom. *Economica*, February 1983, *50* (197), pp. 35–48. **[G: U.K.]**

Beck, John H. Tax Competition, Uniform Assessment, and the Benefit Principle. *J. Urban Econ.*, March 1983, *13* (2), pp. 127–46.

Becker, Irene. Umverteilungswirkungen monetärer Transfers—Eine empirische Analyse von Steuern, Sozialabgaben und Sozialleistungen. (Redistributive Effects of Monetary Transfers—An Empirical Analysis of Taxes, Payroll Taxes and Social Transfers in the Federal Republic of Germany. With English summary.) *Ifo-Studien*, 1983, *29*(4), pp. 273–98. **[G: W. Germany]**

Bellemare, D. and Poulin Simon, L. La tendance à la sélectivité ou les tensions difficiles entre les stratégies d'assurance et d'assistance. (Tendencies towards Selectivity or Tensions between Insurance and Assistance Strategies. With English summary.) *Écon. Soc.*, March–April 1983, *17*(3–4), pp. 655–89. **[G: Canada]**

Benzoni, L. and Leveau, C. La formation des prix de l'énergie: Essai sur la dynamique du système énergétique (France 1973–1983). (Formation of the Energy Prices: An Essay on the Dynamics of the Energy System. With English summary.) *Écon. Soc.*, December 1983, *17*(12), pp. 1869–1926. **[G: France]**

Berger, Curtis J. Controlling Urban Growth via Tax Policy. **In** *Carr, J. H. and Duensing, E. E., eds.*, 1983, *1979*, pp. 254–74. **[G: U.S.]**

Bergeron, Michel. Some Misunderstandings about Tax Expenditures. *Can. Public Policy*, March 1983, *9*(1), pp. 140–43. **[G: Canada]**

Berglas, Eitan, et al. A Threshold Fund. **In** *Helpman, E.; Razin, A. and Sadka, E., eds.*, 1983, pp. 181–205. **[G: Israel]**

Bergström, Sture. Tax Avoidance/Tax Evasion: Sweden. **In** *International Fiscal Association (II)*, 1983, pp. 601–16. **[G: Sweden]**

Berliant, Marcus C. and Strauss, Robert P. Measuring the Distribution of Personal Taxes. **In** *Zeckhauser, R. J. and Leebaert, D., eds.*, 1983, pp. 97–115. **[G: U.S.]**

Berson, David. The Reagan Administration's Fiscal Policy: A Critique: Response: Will Tax Incentives Increase Investment? **In** *Stubblebine, Wm. C. and Willett, T. D., eds.*, 1983, pp. 137–39. **[G: U.S.]**

Bethke, William M. and Boyd, Susan E. Should Dividend Discount Models Be Yield Tilted? *J. Portfol. Manage.*, Spring 1983, *9*(3), pp. 23–27.

Betson, David M. Complementary Strategies for Policy Analysis: Combining Microeconomic and Regional Simulation Models. *Reg. Sci. Urban Econ.*, May 1983, *13*(2), pp. 213–29. **[G: U.S.]**

Bhagwati, Jagdish N. International Migration of the Highly Skilled: Economics, Ethics and Taxes. **In** *Bhagwati, J. N., Vol. 2*, 1983, *1979*, pp. 57–71.

Bhagwati, Jagdish N. and Hamada, Koichi. Tax Policy in the Presence of Emigration. **In** *Bhagwati, J. N., Vol. 2*, 1983, *1982*, pp. 169–95.

Bhatia, Kul B. Tax Effects, Relative Prices, and Economic Growth. **In** *Biehl, D.; Roskamp, K. W. and Stolper, W. F., eds.*, 1983, pp. 349–65. **[G: U.S.]**

Bird, Richard M. Income Tax Reform in Developing Countries: The Administrative Dimension. *Bull. Int. Fiscal Doc.*, January 1983, *37*(1), pp. 3–14. **[G: LDCs]**

Bischel, Jon E.; Gann, Pamela B. and Klein, Susan F. Tax Avoidance/Tax Evasion: United States. **In** *International Fiscal Association (II)*, 1983, pp. 333–55. **[G: U.S.]**

Blackley, Dixie and Follain, James R. Inflation, Tax Advantages to Homeownership and the Locational Choices of Households. *Reg. Sci. Urban Econ.*, November 1983, *13*(4), pp. 505–16. **[G: U.S.]**

Blaug, Mark. Declining Subsidies to Higher Education: An Economic Analysis. **In** *Giersch, H., ed.*, 1983, pp. 125–43. **[G: OECD]**

Blaug, Mark. Justifications for Subsidies to the Arts: A Reply to F. F. Ridley, "Cultural Economics and the Culture of Economists." *J. Cult. Econ.*, June 1983, *7*(1), pp. 19–22.

Blomquist, N. Sören. The Effect of Income Taxation on the Labor Supply of Married Men in Sweden. *J. Public Econ.*, November 1983, *22*(2), pp. 169–97. **[G: Sweden]**

Bloom, David H. and Sweeney, Charles A. Tax Avoidance/Tax Evasion: Australia. **In** *International Fiscal Association (II)*, 1983, pp. 227–44. **[G: Australia]**

Boadway, Robin W.; Bruce, Neil and Mintz, Jack M. On the Neutrality of Flow-of-Funds Corporate Taxation. *Economica*, February 1983, *50*(197), pp. 49–61.

Bohanon, Cecil E. The Tax-Price Implications of Bracket-Creep. *Nat. Tax J.*, December 1983, *36*(4), pp. 535–38.

Bohanon, Cecil E. and Van Cott, T. Norman. A Note on the Political Economy of Indexation. *Public Finance Quart.*, January 1983, *11*(1), pp. 121–27. **[G: U.S.]**

Boidman, Nathan. Tax Evasion: The Present State of Non-Compliance. *Bull. Int. Fiscal Doc.*, Sept.–Oct. 1983, *37*(9–10), pp. 451–79. **[G: Selected Countries]**

Boren, David L. Policies, Problems, and Politics of the Consumption Based Tax. **In** *Walker, C. E. and Bloomfield, M. E., eds.*, 1983, pp. 253–56.

Bös, Dieter. Tax Assignment and Revenue Sharing in the Federal Republic of Germany and Switzerland: Comment. **In** *McLure, C. E., Jr., ed.*, 1983, pp. 289–92. **[G: Switzerland; W. Germany]**

Bosanquet, Nick. Tax-Based Incomes Policies. *Oxford Bull. Econ. Statist.*, February 1983, *45*(1), pp. 33–49.

Boskin, Michael J. Distributional Effects of the Reagan Program. **In** *Stubblebine, Wm. C. and Willett, T. D., eds.*, 1983, pp. 179–98. **[G: U.S.]**

Boskin, Michael J. Saving Incentives: The Role of Tax Policy. **In** *Walker, C. E. and Bloomfield, M. E., eds.*, 1983, pp. 93–111. **[G: U.S.]**

Boskin, Michael J. and Sheshinski, Eytan. Optimal Tax Treatment of the Family: Married Couples. *J. Public Econ.*, April 1983, *20*(3), pp. 281–97. **[G: U.S.]**

Bradford, David F. The Choice Between Income and Consumption Taxes. **In** *Walker, C. E. and Bloomfield, M. E., eds.*, 1983, pp. 229–52.

Brannon, Gerard. The Tax Treatment of Households of Different Size: Commentary. **In** *Penner, R. G., ed.*, 1983, pp. 104–06.

Braswell, Ronald C.; Sumners, Dewitt L. and Reinhart, Walter J. The Effect of the Tax Act of 1982 on the Appropriate Coupon Rate Strategy for Issuing Corporate Bonds. *Nat. Tax J.*, June 1983, *36*(2), pp. 255–56. **[G: U.S.]**

Breneman, David W. Where Would Tuition Tax

Credits Take Us? Should We Agree to Go? **In** *James, T. and Levin, H. M., eds.*, 1983, pp. 101–14. **[G: U.S.]**

Brennan, Geoffrey. Estate Gift Duty and the Family: Prolegomena to a Theory of the Family Unit. **In** *Penner, R. G., ed.*, 1983, pp. 109–26.

Brennan, Geoffrey. Tax Effectiveness and Tax Equity in Federal Countries: Comment. **In** *McLure, C. E., Jr., ed.*, 1983, pp. 87–93. **[G: MDCs]**

Brennan, Geoffrey and Buchanan, James M. The Tax System as Social Overhead Capital: A Constitutional Perspective on Fiscal Norms. **In** *Biehl, D.; Roskamp, K. W. and Stolper, W. F., eds.*, 1983, pp. 41–54.

Brock, William E. The Outlook for International Trade. **In** *Walker, C. E. and Bloomfield, M. E., eds.*, 1983, pp. 344–46.

Brown, Eleanor. Comment: Bequests and Horizontal Equity under a Consumption Tax [The Incidence of a Lifetime Consumption Tax]. *Nat. Tax J.*, December 1983, *36*(4), pp. 511–13. **[G: U.S.]**

Brown, Malcolm C. Tax Assignment and Revenue Sharing in Canada: Comment. **In** *McLure, C. E., Jr., ed.*, 1983, pp. 251–56. **[G: Canada]**

Brown, Philip, et al. Stock Return Seasonalities and the Tax-Loss Selling Hypothesis: Analysis of the Arguments and Australian Evidence. *J. Finan. Econ.*, June 1983, *12*(1), pp. 105–27. **[G: U.S.]**

Buchanan, James M. The Flat Rate Tax and the Fiscal Appetite. **In** *Walker, C. E. and Bloomfield, M. E., eds.*, 1983, pp. 314–16.

Buckley, Robert M. Inflation, Homeownership Tax Subsidies, and Fiscal Illusion [The Interaction of Inflation and the U.S. Tax Subsidies of Housing]. *Nat. Tax J.*, December 1983, *36*(4), pp. 521–23. **[G: U.S.]**

de Buitléir, Donal. The Report of the Commission on Taxation—One Year After. *Irish Banking Rev.*, September 1983, pp. 21–32. **[G: Ireland]**

Burtless, Gary T. and Greenberg, David. Measuring the Impact of NIT Experiments on Work Effort. *Ind. Lab. Relat. Rev.*, July 1983, *36*(4), pp. 592–605. **[G: U.S.]**

Busby, Horace W. The Political Environment. **In** *Walker, C. E. and Bloomfield, M. E., eds.*, 1983, pp. 3–11. **[G: U.S.]**

Buser, Stephen A. and Sanders, Anthony B. Tenure Decisions under a Progressive Tax Structure. *Amer. Real Estate Urban Econ. Assoc. J.*, Fall 1983, *11*(3), pp. 371–81.

Byrne, William J. The Elasticity of the Tax System of Zambia, 1966–1977. *World Devel.*, February 1983, *11*(2), pp. 153–62. **[G: Zambia]**

Caballero, M. A. Garcia. Colombia: Revision of Government Decrees. *Bull. Int. Fiscal Doc.*, December 1983, *37*(12), pp. 546–50. **[G: Columbia]**

Canterbery, E. Ray. Tax Reform and Incomes Policy: A VATIP Proposal. *J. Post Keynesian Econ.*, Spring 1983, *5*(3), pp. 430–39. **[G: U.S.]**

Carlsson, Bo A. W. Industrial Subsidies in Sweden: Macro-Economic Effects and an International Comparison. *J. Ind. Econ.*, September 1983, *32*(1), pp. 1–23. **[G: Sweden; W. Germany; U.K.; Norway; Italy]**

Carmichael, Jeffrey and Stebbing, Peter W. Some Macroeconomic Implications of the Interaction between Inflation and Taxation. **In** *Pagan, A. R. and Trivedi, P. K., eds.*, 1983, pp. 102–36. **[G: Australia]**

Caspar, Pierre. French Law on Continuing Vocational Training. **In** *Levin, H. M. and Schütze, H. G., eds.*, 1983, pp. 257–72. **[G: France]**

Catterall, James S. Tuition Tax Credits: Issues of Equity. **In** *James, T. and Levin, H. M., eds.*, 1983, pp. 130–50. **[G: U.S.]**

Checkoway, Barry. Large Builders, Federal Housing Programmes, and Postwar Suburbanization. **In** *Lake, R. W., ed.*, 1983, *1980*, pp. 173–96. **[G: U.S.]**

Chirinko, Robert S. and Eisner, Robert. Tax Policy and Investment in Major U.S. Macroeconomic Econometric Models. *J. Public Econ.*, March 1983, *20*(2), pp. 139–66. **[G: U.S.]**

Christainsen, Gregory B. Using Donor Preferences in Evaluating Public Expenditures: A Suggested Procedure. *Public Finance Quart.*, July 1983, *11*(3), pp. 283–98. **[G: U.S.]**

Christoffel, Pamela H. An Opportunity Deferred: Lifelong Learning in the United States. **In** *Levin, H. M. and Schütze, H. G., eds.*, 1983, pp. 225–34. **[G: U.S.]**

Church, Albert M. Taxation of Energy Resources: Comments. **In** *McLure, C. E., Jr. and Mieszkowski, P., eds.*, 1983, pp. 93–98. **[G: U.S.]**

Clotfelter, Charles T. Tax Evasion and Tax Rates: An Analysis of Individual Returns. *Rev. Econ. Statist.*, August 1983, *65*(3), pp. 363–73. **[G: U.S.]**

Clotfelter, Charles T. Tax-Induced Distortions and the Business–Pleasure Borderline: The Case of Travel and Entertainment. *Amer. Econ. Rev.*, December 1983, *73*(5), pp. 1053–65. **[G: U.S.]**

Cnossen, Sijbren. Harmonization of Indirect Taxes in the EEC. **In** *McLure, C. E., Jr., ed.*, 1983, pp. 150–68. **[G: EEC]**

Cnossen, Sijbren. Sales Taxation in OECD Member Countries. *Bull. Int. Fiscal Doc.*, April 1983, *37*(4), pp. 147–60. **[G: OECD]**

Cnossen, Sijbren. The Imputation System in the EEC. **In** *[Goode, R.]*, 1983, pp. 85–106. **[G: EEC]**

Cogan, John F. Labor Supply and Negative Income Taxation: New Evidence from the New Jersey–Pennsylvania Experiment. *Econ. Inquiry*, October 1983, *21*(4), pp. 465–84. **[G: U.S.]**

Cohen, Edwin S. Expanding Saving Incentives: Practical and Political Problems. **In** *Walker, C. E. and Bloomfield, M. E., eds.*, 1983, pp. 112–15. **[G: U.S.]**

Cohen, Edwin S. Family Issues in Taxation: Commentary. **In** *Penner, R. G., ed.*, 1983, pp. 27–30. **[G: U.S.]**

Collins, Eileen L. R & D and Labor Productivity: Can Tax Incentives Help? **In** *Weintraub, S. and Goodstein, M., eds.*, 1983, pp. 48–58. **[G: U.S.]**

Conable, Barber B., Jr. The Political Problems of Implementing a Comprehensive Income Tax. **In** *Walker, C. E. and Bloomfield, M. E., eds.*, 1983, pp. 285–88.

Connally, John B. The Challenge for Tax Reform. **In** *Walker, C. E. and Bloomfield, M. E., eds.*, 1983, pp. 13–21. **[G: U.S.]**

Constantinides, George M. Capital Market Equilibrium with Personal Tax. *Econometrica,* May, 1983, *51* (3), pp. 611–36.

Cook, Philip J. The Effect of Liquor Taxes on Drinking, Cirrhosis, and Auto Fatalities. **In** *Zeckhauser, R. J. and Leebaert, D., eds.,* 1983, pp. 203–20. **[G: U.S.]**

Cooper, Ian and Franks, Julian R. The Interaction of Financing and Investment Decisions When the Firm Has Unused Tax Credits. *J. Finance,* May 1983, *38* (2), pp. 571–83.

Cordes, Joseph J.; Goldfarb, Robert S. and Barth, James R. Compensating When the Government Harms. **In** *Zeckhauser, R. J. and Leebaert, D., eds.,* 1983, pp. 295–309.

Cordes, Joseph J. and Sheffrin, Steven M. Estimating the Tax Advantage of Corporate Debt. *J. Finance,* March 1983, *38* (1), pp. 95–105. **[G: U.S.]**

Cornell, Bradford and French, Kenneth R. Taxes and the Pricing of Stock Index Futures. *J. Finance,* June 1983, *38* (3), pp. 675–94.

Cortizo, J. Soto. International Problems in the Field of General Taxes on Sales of Goods and Services: Mexico. **In** *International Fiscal Association (I),* 1983, pp. 497–510. **[G: Mexico]**

Courant, Paul N. On the Effects of Federal Capital Taxation on Growing and Declining Areas. *J. Urban Econ.,* September 1983, *14* (2), pp. 242–61. **[G: U.S.]**

Cranston, Alan. The Option of a Tax Deferred Rollover on Capital Gains. **In** *Walker, C. E. and Bloomfield, M. E., eds.,* 1983, pp. 149–50. **[G: U.S.]**

Craven, Barrie M. and Wright, Grahame A. The Thatcher Experiment. *J. Macroecon.,* Winter 1983, *5* (1), pp. 21–40. **[G: U.K.]**

Cronin, Francis J. Federal Tax Regulations and the Housing Demands of Owner Occupants. *Land Econ.,* August 1983, *59* (3), pp. 305–14. **[G: U.S.]**

Dajani, Mazen K. Taxation and Investment in Jordan. *Bull. Int. Fiscal Doc.,* January 1983, *37* (1), pp. 31–34. **[G: Jordan]**

Daly, Michael J. Some Microeconometric Evidence Concerning the Effect of the Canada Pension Plan on Personal Saving. *Economica,* February 1983, *50* (197), pp. 63–69. **[G: Canada]**

Datt, Ruddar. The Parallel Economy in India. *Indian Econ. J.,* April-June 1983, *30* (4), pp. 19–54. **[G: India]**

David, Jane L. School Improvement and Programs for Special Populations: Finance and Governance Linkages. **In** *Odden, A. and Webb, L. D., eds.,* 1983, pp. 109–25. **[G: U.S.]**

Davie, Bruce F. Tax Prospects: Implications of Budget Problems: Comments on Henry Aaron's Paper. *Nat. Tax J.,* September 1983, *36* (3), pp. 281–83. **[G: U.S.]**

De Wulf, Luc. Taxation and Income Distribution. **In** *[Goode, R.],* 1983, pp. 345–70. **[G: LDCs]**

Deardorff, Alan V. and Stern, Robert M. The Effects of Domestic Tax/Subsidies and Import Tariffs on the Structures of Protection in the United States, United Kingdom and Japan. **In** *Black, J. and Winters, L. A., eds.,* 1983, pp. 43–64. **[G: U.K.; U.S.; Japan]**

Deaton, Angus. An Explicit Solution to an Optimal Tax Problem. *J. Public Econ.,* April 1983, *20* (3), pp. 333–46. **[G: U.S.; U.K.]**

Dee, Robert F. Is Repeal of the Corporate Income Tax Possible? **In** *Walker, C. E. and Bloomfield, M. E., eds.,* 1983, pp. 171–72.

Devaney, Barbara. Total Work Effort under a Negative Income Tax. *J. Policy Anal. Manage.,* Summer 1983, *2* (4), pp. 625–27. **[G: U.S.]**

Dewees, Donald N.; Mathewson, G. Frank and Trebilcock, Michael J. Policy Alternatives in Quality Regulation. **In** *Dewees, D. N., ed.,* 1983, pp. 27–51.

Dezza, Marcello Cogliati. Tax Avoidance/Tax Evasion: Italy. **In** *International Fiscal Association (II),* 1983, pp. 449–68. **[G: Italy]**

Dichtl, Erwin; Raffée, Hans and Wellenreuther, Hans. Public Policy towards Small and Medium-Sized Retail Businesses in the Federal Republic of Germany. *Rivista Int. Sci. Econ. Com.,* April-May 1983, *30* (4–5), pp. 424–39. **[G: W. Germany]**

Dodgson, John S. Expenditure Function Estimates of the Efficiency and Distributive Impact of Indirect Taxes in the United Kingdom. *Europ. Econ. Rev.,* January 1983, *20* (1–3), pp. 59–78. **[G: U.K.]**

Dodgson, John S. On the Accuracy and Appropriateness of Alternative Measures of Excess Burden. *Econ. J.,* Supplement March 1983, pp. 106–14. **[G: U.K.]**

Doern, G. Bruce. Canada's Budgetary Dilemmas: Tax and Expenditure Reform. *Public Budg. Finance,* Summer 1983, *3* (2), pp. 28–46. **[G: Canada]**

Dolton, Peter J. and Makepeace, G. H. A Regression Analysis of the UGC's Financial Recommendations for Universities. *Appl. Econ.,* February 1983, *15* (1), pp. 107–19. **[G: U.K.]**

Downs, Anthony. The Coming Crunch in Rental Housing. *Ann. Amer. Acad. Polit. Soc. Sci.,* January 1983, *465,* pp. 76–85. **[G: U.S.]**

Due, John F. The Experience of Zimbabwe with a Retail Sales Tax. *Bull. Int. Fiscal Doc.,* February 1983, *37* (2), pp. 51–58. **[G: Zimbabwe]**

Duffy, M. The Demand for Alcoholic Drink in the United Kingdom, 1963–78. *Appl. Econ.,* February 1983, *15* (1), pp. 125–40. **[G: U.K.]**

Dupuis, Xavier. La surqualité: le spectacle subventionné malade de la bureaucratie? (The Subsidized Performing Arts: Overquality, a Bureaucratic Disease. With English Summary.) *Revue Écon.,* November 1983, *34* (6), pp. 1089–115. **[G: France]**

Dworin, Lowell and Deakin, Edward B. The Profitability of Outer Continental Shelf Drilling Ventures: An Alternative Approach. *Nat. Tax J.,* March, 1983, *36* (1), pp. 57–63. **[G: U.S.]**

Dyl, Edward A. and Spahr, Ronald W. Taxes and the Refunding of Discount Bonds. *J. Finan. Res.,* Winter 1983, *6* (4), pp. 265–73. **[G: U.S.]**

Eagly, Robert V. Tax Incidence in Ricardian Analysis. *Public Finance,* 1983, *38* (2), pp. 217–31.

Ebrill, Liam P. and Hartman, David G. The Corporate Income Tax, Entrepreneurship, and the Noncorporate Sector. *Public Finance Quart.,* October 1983, *11* (4), pp. 419–36.

Ebrill, Liam P. and Possen, Uri M. Taxation, Inflation, and the Terms of Trade. *J. Public Econ.*, December 1983, *22*(3), pp. 375–86.

Eck, Theodore R. Energy Economics and Taxation. *J. Energy Devel.*, Spring 1983, *8*(2), pp. 293–304. **[G: U.S.]**

Eekhoff, Johann. The Role of Government in the Housing Sector: Comment. **In** *Giersch, H., ed.*, 1983, pp. 225–31. **[G: U.S.]**

Egger, Roscoe L., Jr. United States: Offshore Tax Havens and Tax Treaty Countries. *Bull. Int. Fiscal Doc.*, December 1983, *37*(12), pp. 557–60. **[G: U.S.]**

Eisner, Robert. Government Policy, Saving and Investment. *J. Econ. Educ.*, Spring 1983, *14*(2), pp. 38–49. **[G: U.S.]**

Eisner, Robert. Tax Policy and Investment. **In** *Biehl, D.; Roskamp, K. W. and Stolper, W. F., eds.*, 1983, pp. 167–80.

Elvinger, André and Kremer, Claude. Evasion fiscale/Fraude fiscale: Luxembourg. (With English summary.) **In** *International Fiscal Association (II)*, 1983, pp. 491–510. **[G: Luxembourg]**

Encarnation, Dennis J. Public Finance and Regulation of Nonpublic Education: Retrospect and Prospect. **In** *James, T. and Levin, H. M., eds.*, 1983, pp. 175–95. **[G: U.S.]**

Evans, Alan W. Errata [The Determination of the Price of Land]. *Urban Stud.*, November 1983, *20*(4), pp. 391.

Evans, Alan W. The Determination of the Price of Land. *Urban Stud.*, May 1983, *20*(2), pp. 119–29.

Evans, Owen J. Tax Policy, the Interest Elasticity of Saving, and Capital Accumulation: Numerical Analysis of Theoretical Models. *Amer. Econ. Rev.*, June 1983, *73*(3), pp. 398–410. **[G: U.S.]**

Fabozzi, Frank J. and Yaari, Uzi. Valuation of Safe Harbor Tax Benefit Transfer Leases. *J. Finance*, May 1983, *38*(2), pp. 595–606. **[G: U.S.]**

Farber, Andrè. A qui profitent les mesures d'encouragement du capital à risque? (With English summary.) *Cah. Écon. Bruxelles*, 1983, *97*(1), pp. 3–13. **[G: Belgium]**

Feder, Arthur A.; Levin, Leonard D. and Thayer, Kathe I. International Problems in the Field of General Taxes on Sales of Goods and Services: United States. **In** *International Fiscal Association (I)*, 1983, pp. 363–79. **[G: U.S.]**

Feenberg, Daniel R. The Tax Treatment of Married Couples and the 1981 Tax Law. **In** *Penner, R. G., ed.*, 1983, pp. 32–63. **[G: U.S.]**

Feenberg, Daniel R. and Rosen, Harvey S. Alternative Tax Treatments of the Family: Simulation Methodology and Results. **In** *Feldstein, M., ed.*, 1983, pp. 7–41. **[G: U.S.]**

Feige, Edgar L. and McGee, Robert T. Sweden's Laffer Curve: Taxation and the Unobserved Economy. *Scand. J. Econ.*, 1983, *85*(4), pp. 499–519. **[G: Sweden]**

Feldstein, Martin S. Corporate Taxation and Dividend Behavior. **In** *Feldstein, M. (I)*, 1983, *1970*, pp. 90–113.

Feldstein, Martin S. Corporate Taxation and Dividend Behavior: A Reply and Extension. **In** *Feldstein, M. (I)*, 1983, *1972*, pp. 114–22.

Feldstein, Martin S. Fiscal Policy for the 1980s. **In** *Walker, C. E. and Bloomfield, M. E., eds.*, 1983, pp. 23–34. **[G: U.S.]**

Feldstein, Martin S. Inflation and the Stock Market. **In** *Feldstein, M. (II)*, 1983, *1980*, pp. 186–98. **[G: U.S.]**

Feldstein, Martin S. Inflation, Income Taxes, and the Rate of Interest: A Theoretical Analysis. **In** *Feldstein, M. (I)*, 1983, *1976*, pp. 448–64.

Feldstein, Martin S. Inflation, Income Taxes, and the Rate of Interest: A Theoretical Analysis. **In** *Feldstein, M. (II)*, 1983, *1976*, pp. 28–43.

Feldstein, Martin S. Inflation, Portfolio Choice, and the Prices of Land and Corporate Stock. **In** *Feldstein, M. (II)*, 1983, *1980*, pp. 229–40.

Feldstein, Martin S. Inflation, Tax Rules, and the Prices of Land and Gold. **In** *Feldstein, M. (II)*, 1983, *1980*, pp. 221–28.

Feldstein, Martin S. Inflation, Tax Rules, and Investment: Some Econometric Evidence. **In** *Feldstein, M. (II)*, 1983, *1982*, pp. 243–85. **[G: U.S.]**

Feldstein, Martin S. Inflation, Tax Rules, and the Stock Market. **In** *Feldstein, M. (II)*, 1983, *1980*, pp. 199–220. **[G: U.S.]**

Feldstein, Martin S. Inflation, Tax Rules, and Capital Formation: A Summary of the Theoretical Models. **In** *Feldstein, M. (II)*, 1983, pp. 17–27.

Feldstein, Martin S. Inflation, Tax Rules, and the Accumulation of Residential and Nonresidential Capital. **In** *Feldstein, M. (II)*, 1983, *1982*, pp. 81–98. **[G: U.S.]**

Feldstein, Martin S. Inflation, Tax Rules, and Capital Formation: An Introductory Overview. **In** *Feldstein, M. (II)*, 1983, pp. 1–14. **[G: U.S.]**

Feldstein, Martin S. Inflation, Tax Rules, and Investment: Some Econometric Evidence. **In** *Feldstein, M. (I)*, 1983, *1982*, pp. 331–73. **[G: U.S.]**

Feldstein, Martin S. Personal Taxation and Portfolio Composition: An Econometric Analysis. **In** *Feldstein, M. (I)*, 1983, *1976*, pp. 194–215. **[G: U.S.]**

Feldstein, Martin S. Tax Incentives, Corporate Saving, and Capital Accumulation in the United States. **In** *Feldstein, M. (I)*, 1983, *1973*, pp. 123–34. **[G: U.S.]**

Feldstein, Martin S. Tax Incidence in a Growing Economy with Variable Factor Supply. **In** *Feldstein, M. (I)*, 1983, *1974*, pp. 377–99.

Feldstein, Martin S. The Effects of Taxation on Risk Taking. **In** *Feldstein, M. (I)*, 1983, *1969*, pp. 183–93.

Feldstein, Martin S. The Surprising Incidence of a Tax on Pure Rent: A New Answer to an Old Question. **In** *Feldstein, M. (I)*, 1983, *1977*, pp. 414–26.

Feldstein, Martin S.; Dicks-Mireaux, Louis-David L. and Poterba, James M. The Effective Tax Rate and the Pretax Rate of Return. *J. Public Econ.*, July 1983, *21*(2), pp. 129–58. **[G: U.S.]**

Feldstein, Martin S. and Fane, George. Taxes, Corporate Dividend Policy, and Personal Savings: The British Postwar Experience. **In** *Feldstein, M. (I)*, 1983, *1973*, pp. 135–55. **[G: U.K.]**

Feldstein, Martin S. and Feenberg, Daniel R. Alternative Tax Rules and Personal Saving Incentives: Microeconomic Data and Behavioral Simulations. **In** *Feldstein, M., ed.*, 1983, pp. 173–209. **[G: U.S.]**

Feldstein, Martin S. and Frisch, Daniel J. Corporate Tax Integration: The Estimated Effects on Capital Accumulation and Tax Distribution of Two Integration Proposals. **In** *Feldstein, M. (I),* 1983, *1977,* pp. 156–79. **[G: U.S.]**

Feldstein, Martin S. and Green, Jerry R. Why Do Companies Pay Dividends? **In** *Feldstein, M. (I),* 1983, *1983,* pp. 69–89.

Feldstein, Martin S. and Green, Jerry R. Why Do Companies Pay Dividends? *Amer. Econ. Rev.,* March 1983, *73*(1), pp. 17–30.

Feldstein, Martin S.; Green, Jerry R. and Sheshinski, Eytan. Corporate Financial Policy and Taxation in a Growing Economy. **In** *Feldstein, M. (I),* 1983, *1979,* pp. 427–47. **[G: U.S.]**

Feldstein, Martin S.; Green, Jerry R. and Sheshinski, Eytan. Inflation and Taxes in a Growing Economy with Debt and Equity Finance. **In** *Feldstein, M. (II),* 1983, *1978,* pp. 44–60. **[G: U.S.]**

Feldstein, Martin S. and Lindsey, Lawrence B. Simulating Nonlinear Tax Rules and Nonstandard Behavior: An Application to the Tax Treatment of Charitable Contributions. **In** *Feldstein, M., ed.,* 1983, pp. 139–67. **[G: U.S.]**

Feldstein, Martin S.; Poterba, James M. and Dicks-Mireaux, Louis-David L. The Effective Tax Rate and the Pretax Rate of Return. **In** *Feldstein, M. (I),* 1983, *1982,* pp. 36–68. **[G: U.S.]**

Feldstein, Martin S. and Slemrod, Joel. Inflation and the Excess Taxation of Capital Gains on Corporate Stock. **In** *Feldstein, M. (II),* 1983, *1979,* pp. 101–15. **[G: U.S.]**

Feldstein, Martin S. and Slemrod, Joel. Personal Taxation, Portfolio Choice, and the Effect of the Corporation Income Tax. **In** *Feldstein, M. (I),* 1983, *1980,* pp. 255–66. **[G: U.S.]**

Feldstein, Martin S. and Slemrod, Joel. The Lock-in Effect of the Capital Gains Tax: Some Time-Series Evidence. **In** *Feldstein, M. (I),* 1983, *1978,* pp. 251–54. **[G: U.S.]**

Feldstein, Martin S.; Slemrod, Joel and Yitzhaki, Shlomo. The Effects of Taxation on the Selling of Corporate Stock and the Realization of Capital Gains. **In** *Feldstein, M. (I),* 1983, *1980,* pp. 237–50. **[G: U.S.]**

Feldstein, Martin S. and Summers, Lawrence H. Inflation and the Taxation of Capital Income in the Corporate Sector. **In** *Feldstein, M. (II),* 1983, *1979,* pp. 116–50. **[G: U.S.]**

Feldstein, Martin S. and Summers, Lawrence H. Inflation, Tax Rules, and the Long-term Interest Rate. **In** *Feldstein, M. (II),* 1983, *1978,* pp. 153–85. **[G: U.S.]**

Feldstein, Martin S. and Yitzhaki, Shlomo. The Effects of the Capital Gains Tax on the Selling and Switching of Common Stock. **In** *Feldstein, M. (I),* 1983, *1978,* pp. 216–36. **[G: U.S.]**

Fellner, William. The Effect of Government Absorption of Savings on Capital Formation. **In** *Walker, C. E. and Bloomfield, M. E., eds.,* 1983, pp. 116–18. **[G: U.S.]**

Field, Anthony. Experiment and Public Accountability. **In** *Hendon, W. S. and Shanahan, J. L., eds.,* 1983, pp. 31–37. **[G: U.K.]**

Field, Frank. Breaking the Mould: The Thatcher Government's Fiscal Policies. **In** *Field, F., ed.,* 1983, pp. 56–68. **[G: U.K.]**

Filho, Olimpio Guernieri. Tax Avoidance/Tax Evasion: Brazil. **In** *International Fiscal Association (II),* 1983, pp. 285–93. **[G: Brazil]**

Filippi, Piera. Problèmes internationaux du domaine des taxes sur le chiffre d'affaires: Italie. (With English summary.) **In** *International Fiscal Association (I),* 1983, pp. 443–62. **[G: Italy]**

Fink, Hans. International Problems in the Field of General Taxes on Sales of Goods and Services: Sweden. **In** *International Fiscal Association (I),* 1983, pp. 573–92. **[G: Sweden]**

Fishburn, Geoffrey F. Normative Aspects of Indexation Schemes. *Public Finance,* 1983, *38*(1), pp. 27–37.

Flam, Harry; Persson, Torsten and Svensson, Lars E. O. Optimal Subsidies to Declining Industries: Efficiency and Equity Considerations. *J. Public Econ.,* December 1983, *22*(3), pp. 327–45.

Ford, Ramona L. Revitalizing the Distressed Community: GSOC and ESOP Alternatives to Enterprise Zones. *Growth Change,* October 1983, *14*(4), pp. 22–31. **[G: U.S.]**

Forte, Francesco. Tax Policy in Italy. *Bull. Int. Fiscal Doc.,* Sept.–Oct. 1983, *37*(9–10), pp. 393–98. **[G: Italy]**

Frank, Max. Towards the Adoption of a Progressive Personal Expenditure Tax? A General Outlook. *Public Finance,* 1983, *38*(2), pp. 185–201. **[G: U.S.; Sweden]**

Fraser, Donald R. and Stern, Jerrold J. Flower Bonds, Tax Changes, and the Efficiency of the Bond Market. *Rev. Bus. Econ. Res.,* Winter, 1983, *18*(2), pp. 13–24. **[G: U.S.]**

Freeman, Robert N. Alternative Measures of Profit Margin: An Empirical Study of the Potential Information Content of Current Cost Accounting. *J. Acc. Res.,* Spring 1983, *21*(1), pp. 42–64. **[G: U.S.]**

Frey, René L. and Leu, Robert E. Umverteilung über den Staatshaushalt: Die personnel Budgetinzidenz der Schweiz 1977. (Redistribution through the Public Sector: Personal Budget Incidence in Switzerland, 1977. With English summary.) *Schweiz. Z. Volkswirtsch. Statist.,* March 1983, *119*(1), pp. 1–21. **[G: Switzerland]**

Friend, Irwin and Hasbrouck, Joel. Saving and After-Tax Rates of Return. *Rev. Econ. Statist.,* November 1983, *65*(4), pp. 537–43. **[G: U.S.]**

Frint, W. Internationale Probleme auf dem Gebiet der Umsatzbesteuerung: Österreich. (With English summary.) **In** *International Fiscal Association (I),* 1983, pp. 265–88. **[G: Austria]**

Frisch, Daniel J. Issues in the Taxation of Foreign Source Income. **In** *Feldstein, M., ed.,* 1983, pp. 289–330. **[G: U.S.]**

Froomkin, Joseph. Financing Graduate Students. **In** *Froomkin, J., ed.,* 1983, pp. 97–107. **[G: U.S.]**

Fuller, Winship C.; Manski, Charles F. and Wise, David A. The Impact of the Basic Educational Opportunity Grant Program on College Enrollments. **In** *Helpman, E.; Razin, A. and Sadka, E., eds.,* 1983, pp. 123–42. **[G: U.S.]**

Fullerton, Don. Transition Losses of Partially Mobile Industry-Specific Capital. *Quart. J. Econ.,* February 1983, *98*(1), pp. 107–25. **[G: U.S.]**

Fullerton, Don and Gordon, Roger H. A Reexamination of Tax Distortions in General Equilibrium Models. **In** *Feldstein, M., ed.,* 1983, pp. 369–420. **[G: U.S.]**

Fullerton, Don and Hamdan, Lawrence A. The Aborted Phase-In of Marginal Effective Corporate Tax Rates. *Public Finance Quart.,* October 1983, *11*(4), pp. 437–64. **[G: U.S.]**

Fullerton, Don; Shoven, John B. and Whalley, John. Replacing the U.S. Income Tax with a Progressive Consumption Tax: A Sequenced General Equilibrium Approach. *J. Public Econ.,* February 1983, *20*(1), pp. 3–23. **[G: U.S.]**

Gahin, Fikry S. The Financial Feasibility of Tax-Sheltered Individual Retirement Plans. *J. Risk Ins.,* March 1983, *50*(1), pp. 84–106. **[G: U.S.]**

Gallagher, James R. Advance Corporation Tax (ACT)—Finance Act 1983. *Irish Banking Rev.,* June 1983, pp. 9–19. **[G: Ireland]**

Galper, Harvey. Simulating Nonlinear Tax Rules and Nonstandard Behavior: An Application to the Tax Treatment of Charitable Contributions: Comment. **In** *Feldstein, M., ed.,* 1983, pp. 167–72. **[G: U.S.]**

Galper, Harvey. Tax Policy. **In** *Pechman, J. A., ed.,* 1983, pp. 173–200. **[G: U.S.]**

Galper, Harvey and Toder, Eric. Owning or Leasing: Bennington College, and the U.S. Tax System. *Nat. Tax J.,* June 1983, *36*(2), pp. 257–61. **[G: U.S.]**

Gandhi, Ved P. Tax Assignment and Revenue Sharing in Brazil, India, Malaysia, and Nigeria. **In** *McLure, C. E., Jr., ed.,* 1983, pp. 328–59. **[G: Brazil; India; Malaysia; Nigeria]**

Garbacz, Christopher and Thayer, Mark A. An Experiment in Valuing Senior Companion Program Services. *J. Human Res.,* Winter 1983, *18*(1), pp. 147–53. **[G: U.S.]**

Gardner, Bernard and Marlow, Peter. An International Comparison of the Fiscal Treatment of Shipping. *J. Ind. Econ.,* June 1983, *31*(4), pp. 397–415. **[G: EEC; Japan; U.S.; Liberia]**

Gardner, Bruce L. Discussion [Governments and Agricultural Markets in Africa] [Why Do Governments Do What They Do? The Case of Food Price Policy]. **In** *Johnson, D. G. and Schuh, G. E., eds.,* 1983, pp. 219–26.

Garnaut, Ross. Energy Policy, Taxation of Natural Resources and Fiscal Federalism: Comment. **In** *McLure, C. E., Jr., ed.,* 1983, pp. 146–47.

Garrison, Charles B. The 1964 Tax Cut: Supply-Side Economics or Demand Stimulus? *J. Econ. Issues,* September 1983, *17*(3), pp. 681–96. **[G: U.S.]**

Gassner, Wolfgang. Steuervermeidung/Steuerhinterziehung: Osterreich. (With English summary.) **In** *International Fiscal Association (II),* 1983, pp. 245–63. **[G: Austria]**

Gemello, John M. and Osman, Jack W. The Choice for Public and Private Education: An Economist's View. **In** *James, T. and Levin, H. M., eds.,* 1983, pp. 196–209. **[G: U.S.]**

Genser, Bernd. Household Outlay Index: A Measure of Real Purchasing Power and Tax Progressivity. *Empirica,* 1983, (2), pp. 205–14. **[G: Austria]**

Genser, Bernd and Holzmann, Robert. Zur Operationalisierung von steuerstatistischem Datenmaterial. (Remodelling Tax Return Data for User Purposes. With English summary.) *Jahr. Nationalökon. Statist.,* July 1983, *198*(4), pp. 341–61.

Gephardt, Richard. Reflections on Revenue Legislation. *Nat. Tax J.,* September 1983, *36*(3), pp. 293–95. **[G: U.S.]**

Gerbes, R. Problèmes internationaux du domaine des taxes sur le chiffre d'affaires: Luxembourg. (With English summary.) **In** *International Fiscal Association (I),* 1983, pp. 471–95. **[G: Luxembourg]**

Gillingham, Robert and Greenlees, John S. The Incorporation of Direct Taxes into a Consumer Price Index. **In** *Diewert, W. E. and Montmarquette, C., eds.,* 1983, pp. 619–54. **[G: U.S.]**

Givoly, Dan and Ovadia, Arie. Year-End Tax-Induced Sales and Stock Market Seasonality. *J. Finance,* March 1983, *38*(1), pp. 171–85. **[G: U.S.]**

Gjesti, Per O. Tax Avoidance/Tax Evasion: Norway. **In** *International Fiscal Association (II),* 1983, pp. 525–32. **[G: Norway]**

Gladieux, Lawrence E. The Issue of Equity in College Finance. **In** *Froomkin, J., ed.,* 1983, pp. 72–83. **[G: U.S.]**

Glazer, Nathan. The Future under Tuition Tax Credits. **In** *James, T. and Levin, H. M., eds.,* 1983, pp. 87–100. **[G: U.S.]**

Gleeson, Michael E. Rental Vouchers and Homeownership Subsidies: A Dynamic Duo. *J. Policy Anal. Manage.,* Summer 1983, *2*(4), pp. 621–25. **[G: U.S.]**

Gofran, K. A. Bangladesh: New Developments. *Bull. Int. Fiscal Doc.,* November 1983, *37*(11), pp. 509–11. **[G: Bangladesh]**

González de Rechter, Beatriz S. Tax Avoidance/Tax Evasion: Argentina. **In** *International Fiscal Association (II),* 1983, pp. 211–25. **[G: Argentina]**

Goode, Richard. The Comprehensive Income Tax: Advantages and Disadvantages. **In** *Walker, C. E. and Bloomfield, M. E., eds.,* 1983, pp. 265–77. **[G: OECD]**

Goodisman, Leonard D. Budgeting and Field Discretion in Disaster Relief. *Public Budg. Finance,* Spring 1983, *3*(1), pp. 89–102. **[G: U.S.]**

Gordon, Roger H. Social Security and Labor Supply Incentives. *Contemp. Policy Issue,* April 1983, (3), pp. 16–22. **[G: U.S.]**

Gordon, Roger H. and Slemrod, Joel. A General Equilibrium Simulation Study of Subsidies to Municipal Expenditures. *J. Finance,* May 1983, *38*(2), pp. 585–94. **[G: U.S.]**

Goulder, Lawrence H.; Shoven, John B. and Whalley, John. Domestic Tax Policy and the Foreign Sector: The Importance of Alternative Foreign Sector Formulations to Results from a General Equilibrium Tax Analysis Model. **In** *Feldstein, M., ed.,* 1983, pp. 333–64. **[G: U.S.]**

Graça de Lemos, Maria Teresa. Problèmes internationaux du domaine des taxes sur le chiffre d'affaires: Portugal. (With English summary.) **In** *International Fiscal Association (I),* 1983, pp. 545–60. **[G: Portugal]**

Graetz, Michael J. To Praise the Estate Tax, Not to Bury It. *Yale Law J.,* December 1983, *93*(2), pp. 259–86. **[G: U.S.]**

Gravelle, Jane G. Capital Income Taxation and Efficiency in the Allocation of Investment. *Nat. Tax J.*, September 1983, *36*(3), pp. 297–306. **[G: U.S.]**

Greaves, Cameron G. Hong Kong: Tax Treatment of Patent Rights, Etc. *Bull. Int. Fiscal Doc.*, December 1983, *37*(12), pp. 551. **[G: Hong Kong]**

Greenberg, David and Halsey, Harlan. Systematic Misreporting and Effects of Income Maintenance Experiments on Work Effort: Evidence from the Seattle–Denver Experiment. *J. Lab. Econ.*, October 1983, *1*(4), pp. 380–407. **[G: U.S.]**

Grewal, Bhajan S. Tax Assignment and Revenue Sharing in Brazil, India, Malaysia, and Nigeria: Comment. **In** *McLure, C. E., Jr., ed.*, 1983, pp. 362–63. **[G: Brazil; India; Malaysia; Nigeria]**

Grier, Paul and Strebel, Paul J. An Implicit Clientele Test of the Relationship between Taxation and Capital Structure. *J. Finan. Res.*, Summer 1983, *6*(2), pp. 163–74. **[G: U.S.]**

Groenewegen, Peter D. Tax Assignment and Revenue Sharing in Australia: Reply. **In** *McLure, C. E., Jr., ed.*, 1983, pp. 327. **[G: Australia]**

Groenewegen, Peter D. Tax Assignment and Revenue Sharing in Australia. **In** *McLure, C. E., Jr., ed.*, 1983, pp. 293–318. **[G: Australia]**

Gruen, Fred H. Australian Inflation and the Distribution of Income and Wealth—A Preliminary View. **In** *Pagan, A. R. and Trivedi, P. K., eds.*, 1983, pp. 225–60. **[G: Australia]**

Guesnerie, Roger. La théorie de la fiscalité sur les transactions entre les ménages et les entreprises: Une présentation synthétique de travaux récents. (Taxing Transactions between Households and Firms: A Synthetical Presentation of Recent Theoretical Work. With English summary.) *Ann. INSEE*, July–September 1983, (51), pp. 7–38.

Gustafson, Charles. Estate Gift Duty and the Family: Prolegomena to a Theory of the Family Unit: Commentary. **In** *Penner, R. G., ed.*, 1983, pp. 133–36.

Gwartney, James and Stroup, Richard. Labor Supply and Tax Rates: A Correction of the Record. *Amer. Econ. Rev.*, June 1983, *73*(3), pp. 446–51.

Hadwin, J. F. The Medieval Lay Subsidies and Economic History. *Econ. Hist. Rev., 2nd Ser.*, May 1983, *36*(2), pp. 200–217. **[G: U.K.]**

Hall, Robert E. and Rabushka, Alvin. The Flat Rate Tax: A Proposal for Tax Simplification. **In** *Walker, C. E. and Bloomfield, M. E., eds.*, 1983, pp. 297–310. **[G: U.S.]**

Hall, S. G. F. North Sea Oil. **In** *Britton, A., ed.*, 1983, pp. 91–97. **[G: U.K.]**

Hansen, Derek. Banking and Small Business. **In** *Barker, M., ed. (I)*, 1983, pp. 359–473.

Hansen, W. Lee. Impact of Student Financial Aid on Access. **In** *Froomkin, J., ed.*, 1983, pp. 84–96. **[G: U.S.]**

Harber, Richard Paul, Jr. Brazil's Fiscal Incentive System and the Northeast: An Econometric Analysis. *J. Econ. Devel.*, July 1983, *8*(1), pp. 131–59. **[G: Brazil]**

Harris, D. W. and Oser, R. A. International Problems in the Field of General Taxes on Sales of Goods and Services: Australia. **In** *International Fiscal Association (I)*, 1983, pp. 247–63. **[G: Australia]**

Harris, I. W. Tax Avoidance/Tax Evasion: Hong Kong. **In** *International Fiscal Association (II)*, 1983, pp. 419–29. **[G: Hong Kong]**

Harris, Robert S. and Pringle, John J. Implications of Miller's Argument for Capital Budgeting. *J. Finan. Res.*, Spring 1983, *6*(1), pp. 13–23.

Harrison, J. Michael and Sharpe, William F. Optimal Funding and Asset Allocation Rules for Defined-Benefit Pension Plans. **In** *Bodie, Z. and Shoven, J. B., eds.*, 1983, pp. 91–103, 105. **[G: U.S.]**

Hartman, David G. Domestic Tax Policy and the Foreign Sector: The Importance of Alternative Foreign Sector Formulations to Results from a General Equilibrium Tax Analysis Model: Comment. **In** *Feldstein, M., ed.*, 1983, pp. 364–67. **[G: U.S.]**

Hartog, Joop. Inequality Reduction by Income Taxes: Just How Much? An Investigation for the Netherlands, 1914–1973. *Empirical Econ.*, 1983, *8*(1), pp. 9–13. **[G: Netherlands]**

Hasbrouck, Joel. The Impact of Inflation upon Corporate Taxation. *Nat. Tax J.*, March, 1983, *36*(1), pp. 65–81. **[G: U.S.]**

Hatch, James; Wynant, Larry and Grant, Mary Jane. Federal Lending Programs for Small Business: No Longer Needed? *Can. Public Policy*, September 1983, *9*(3), pp. 362–73. **[G: Canada]**

Hatchuel, Georges. Les ressources des familles et l'impact des prestations familiales. (Families' Income and the Impact of Social Benefits. With English summary.) *Consommation*, January/March 1983, *30*(1), pp. 53–92. **[G: France]**

Hatsopoulos, George N. The Effects of ERTA and TEFRA on the Cost of Capital. **In** *Walker, C. E. and Bloomfield, M. E., eds.*, 1983, pp. 79–88. **[G: U.S.]**

Hausman, Jerry A. Stochastic Problems in the Simulation of Labor Supply. **In** *Feldstein, M., ed.*, 1983, pp. 47–69. **[G: U.S.]**

Head, John G. Tax Assignment and Revenue Sharing in Canada: Comment. **In** *McLure, C. E., Jr., ed.*, 1983, pp. 257–59. **[G: Canada]**

Head, John G. Tax Assignment and Revenue Sharing in Australia: Comment. **In** *McLure, C. E., Jr., ed.*, 1983, pp. 319–22. **[G: Australia]**

Head, John G. and Bird, Richard M. Tax Policy Options in the 1980s. **In** *[Goode, R.]*, 1983, pp. 3–29. **[G: Australia; Canada; U.K.; U.S.]**

Heckman, James J. Stochastic Problems in the Simulation of Labor Supply: Comment. **In** *Feldstein, M., ed.*, 1983, pp. 70–82. **[G: U.S.]**

Helliwell, John F.; MacGregor, Mary E. and Plourde, Andre. The National Energy Program Meets Falling World Oil Prices. *Can. Public Policy*, September 1983, *9*(3), pp. 284–96. **[G: Canada]**

Hemming, Richard and Keen, Michael J. Single-Crossing Conditions in Comparisons of Tax Progressivity. *J. Public Econ.*, April 1983, *20*(3), pp. 373–80.

Hendershott, Patric H. The Distribution of Gains and Losses from Changes in the Tax Treatment of Housing: Comment. **In** *Feldstein, M., ed.*, 1983, pp. 133–37. **[G: U.K.]**

Hendershott, Patric H. and Slemrod, Joel. Taxes and the User Cost of Capital for Owner-Occupied Housing. *Amer. Real Estate Urban Econ. Assoc.*

J., Winter 1983, *10*(4), pp. 375–93. **[G: U.S.]**

van Herwaarden, F. G. and de Kam, C. A. An Operational Concept of the Ability to Pay Principle (with an Application for the Netherlands, 1973). *De Economist,* 1983, *131*(1), pp. 55–64. **[G: Netherlands]**

Hess, Patrick J. Test for Tax Effects in the Pricing of Financial Assets. *J. Bus.*, October 1983, *56*(4), pp. 537–54. **[G: U.S.]**

Hessel, Christopher A. and Huffman, Lucy T. Incorporation of Tax Considerations into the Computation of Duration. *J. Finan. Res.*, Fall 1983, *6*(3), pp. 213–15.

Hettich, Walter. Reforms of the Tax Base and Horizontal Equity. *Nat. Tax J.*, December 1983, *36*(4), pp. 417–27. **[G: U.S.]**

Hickman, Frederic W. Changes in Capital Cost Recovery Policies: Costs and Benefits. **In** *Walker, C. E. and Bloomfield, M. E., eds.*, 1983, pp. 89–91. **[G: U.S.]**

Holcombe, Randall G. and Zardkoohi, Asghar. On the Distribution of Federal Taxes and Expenditures, and the New War between the States. *Public Choice,* 1983, *40*(2), pp. 165–74. **[G: U.S.]**

Holcombe, Randall G. and Zardkoohi, Asghar. The Determinants of Federal Grants: Reply. *Southern Econ. J.*, July 1983, *50*(1), pp. 275–76. **[G: U.S.]**

Holmlund, Bertil. Payroll Taxes and Wage Inflation: The Swedish Experience. *Scand. J. Econ.*, 1983, *85*(1), pp. 1–15. **[G: Sweden]**

Horst, Thomas. Issues in the Taxation of Foreign Source Income: Comment. **In** *Feldstein, M., ed.*, 1983, pp. 331–32. **[G: U.S.]**

Horst, Thomas and Hufbauer, Gary Clyde. International Tax Issues: Aspects of Basic Income Tax Reform. **In** *Walker, C. E. and Bloomfield, M. E., eds.*, 1983, pp. 325–43.

Hu, Sheng Cheng. Value-Added Tax as a Source of Social Security Financing. *Public Finance Quart.*, April 1983, *11*(2), pp. 154–80. **[G: U.S.]**

Hunter, William J. Tax Structure and Bureaucratic Bargaining. *Public Finance Quart.*, July 1983, *11*(3), pp. 347–64.

Hussey, C. E., II and Berkson, Stuart M. Tax Policy and International Capital Flows. **In** *Walker, C. E. and Bloomfield, M. E., eds.*, 1983, pp. 346–53. **[G: U.S.]**

Hutton, John P. and Lambert, Peter J. Inequality and Revenue Elasticity in Tax Reform. *Scot. J. Polit. Econ.*, November 1983, *30*(3), pp. 221–34. **[G: U.K.; U.S.]**

Ihori, Toshihiro. Welfare Criteria for Tax Reforms: An Extension. *J. Public Econ.*, April 1983, *20*(3), pp. 387–89.

Ilzkovitz, Fabienne. L'information des consommateurs . . . Une condition de l'efficacité des primes à l'isolation? (With English summary.) *Cah. Écon. Bruxelles,* 4th Trimester 1983, (100), pp. 534–60. **[G: Belgium]**

Ippolito, Richard A. Public Policy towards Private Pensions. *Contemp. Policy Issue,* April 1983, (3), pp. 53–76. **[G: U.S.]**

Ishi, Hiromitsu. An overview of Postwar Tax Policies in Japan. *Hitotsubashi J. Econ.*, February 1983, *23*(2), pp. 21–39. **[G: Japan]**

Ishi, Hiromitsu. Tax Avoidance/Tax Evasion: Japan. **In** *International Fiscal Association (II),* 1983, pp. 477–89. **[G: Japan]**

Izraeli, Oded. Federal Individual Income Tax and Allocation of Labor between SMSA's. *J. Reg. Sci.*, February 1983, *23*(1), pp. 105–13. **[G: U.S.]**

Jain, Anil Kumar and Jain, Inu. A Brief Review of the Indian Tax System. *Bull. Int. Fiscal Doc.*, May 1983, *37*(5), pp. 215–21. **[G: India]**

James, Thomas. Questions about Educational Choice: An Argument from History. **In** *James, T. and Levin, H. M., eds.*, 1983, pp. 55–70. **[G: U.S.]**

James, Thomas and Levin, Henry M. Public Dollars for Private Schools: Introduction. **In** *James, T. and Levin, H. M., eds.*, 1983, pp. 3–13. **[G: U.S.]**

de Janvry, Alain. Why Do Governments Do What They Do? The Case of Food Price Policy. **In** *Johnson, D. G. and Schuh, G. E., eds.*, 1983, pp. 185–212. **[G: U.S.; India; Colombia; Egypt]**

Jehle, Eugen. The Tax System of the Kingdom of Tonga: A Brief Survey. *Bull. Int. Fiscal Doc.*, December 1983, *37*(12), pp. 553–56. **[G: Tonga]**

Jehle, Eugen. The Tax System of Tahiti (French Polynesia): A Brief Survey. *Bull. Int. Fiscal Doc.*, August 1983, *37*(8), pp. 358–60. **[G: Tahiti]**

Jenkin, Peter J. H. Tax Avoidance/Tax Evasion: New Zealand. **In** *International Fiscal Association (II),* 1983, pp. 533–44. **[G: New Zealand]**

Jensen, Donald N. Constitutional and Legal Implications of Tuition Tax Credits. **In** *James, T. and Levin, H. M., eds.*, 1983, pp. 151–72. **[G: U.S.]**

Johnson, James D. and Short, Sara D. Commodity Programs: Who Has Received the Benefits? *Amer. J. Agr. Econ.*, December 1983, *65*(5), pp. 912–21. **[G: U.S.]**

Jones, James R. Prospects for Enactment of a Flat Rate Tax. **In** *Walker, C. E. and Bloomfield, M. E., eds.*, 1983, pp. 316–19.

Jones, Philip R. Aid to Charities. *Int. J. Soc. Econ.*, 1983, *10*(2), pp. 3–11. **[G: U.K.]**

Jüttemeier, Karl Heinz and Schatz, Klaus-Werner. West Germany: Managing without a State Investment Company. **In** *Hindley, B., ed.*, 1983, pp. 227–62. **[G: W. Germany]**

Kain, John F. America's Persistent Housing Crises: Errors in Analysis and Policy. *Ann. Amer. Acad. Polit. Soc. Sci.*, January 1983, *465*, pp. 136–48. **[G: U.S.]**

Kakwani, Nanak. Progressivity Index of Sales Tax on Individual Expenditure Items in Australia. *Econ. Rec.*, March 1983, *59*(164), pp. 61–79. **[G: Australia]**

Kanbur, S. M. Ravi. Labour Supply under Uncertainty with Piecewise Linear Tax Regimes. *Economica,* November 1983, *50*(200), pp. 379–94.

Katz, Claudio J.; Mahler, Vincent A. and Franz, Michael G. The Impact of Taxes on Growth and Distribution in Developed Capitalist Countries: A Cross-National Study. *Amer. Polit. Sci. Rev.*, December 1983, *77*(4), pp. 871–86. **[G: Selected OECD]**

Katz, Eliakim. Relative Risk Aversion in Comparative Statics. *Amer. Econ. Rev.*, June 1983, *73*(3), pp. 452–53.

Kau, James B. and Keenan, Donald C. Inflation, Taxes and Housing: A Theoretical Analysis. *J. Public Econ.*, June 1983, *21* (1), pp. 93–104.

Keene, Karlyn. What Do We Know about the Public's Attitude on Progressivity? *Nat. Tax J.*, September 1983, *36*(3), pp. 371–76. **[G: U.S.]**

Kiefer, David. Inflation and Homeownership Tax Subsidies: A Correction. *Nat. Tax J.*, December 1983, *36*(4), pp. 525–27. **[G: U.S.]**

Kiefer, Donald W. Measurement of the Progressivity of Public Expenditures and Net Fiscal Incidence: Comment. *Southern Econ. J.*, October 1983, *50*(2), pp. 578–86.

Kienzle, Edward C. Measurement of the Progressivity of Public Expenditures and Net Fiscal Incidence: Reply. *Southern Econ. J.*, October 1983, *50*(2), pp. 587–88.

Kim, Dong-Kun and Kang, In-Jae. The Budget System and Structure in Korea. *Public Budg. Finance,* Winter 1983, *3*(4), pp. 85–96. **[G: Korea]**

Kim, Wan-Soon and Abbott, Graham. Budget Procedures and Policies in the ASEAN Countries. *Public Budg. Finance,* Winter 1983, *3*(4), pp. 71–84. **[G: ASEAN]**

King, Mervyn A. The Distribution of Gains and Losses from Changes in the Tax Treatment of Housing. **In** *Feldstein, M., ed.*, 1983, pp. 109–32. **[G: U.K.]**

King, Mervyn A. Welfare Analysis of Tax Reforms Using Household Data. *J. Public Econ.*, July 1983, *21* (2), pp. 183–214. **[G: U.K.]**

Klein, Lawrence R. Inflation: Its Causes and Possible Cures. **In** *Dutta, M.; Hartline, J. C. and Loeb, P. D., eds.*, 1983, pp. 26–32. **[G: U.S.]**

Knight, Ester. Women and the UK Tax System: The Case for Reform? *Cambridge J. Econ.*, June 1983, *7*(2), pp. 151–65. **[G: U.K.]**

Knoester, Anthonie. Stagnation and the Inverted Haavelmo Effect: Some International Evidence. *De Economist,* 1983, *131* (4), pp. 548–84. **[G: U.S.; U.K.; Netherlands; W. Germany]**

Koch-Nielsen, Robert and Schmith, Esther. Tax Avoidance/Tax Evasion: Denmark. **In** *International Fiscal Association (II),* 1983, pp. 317–31. **[G: Denmark]**

Kogels, H. A. Unitary Taxation: An International Approach. *Bull. Int. Fiscal Doc.*, February 1983, *37*(2), pp. 65–68. **[G: U.S.]**

Kolstad, Charles D. and Wolak, Frank A., Jr. Competition in Interregional Taxation: The Case of Western Coal. *J. Polit. Econ.*, June 1983, *91* (3), pp. 443–60. **[G: U.S.]**

Koo, Anthony Y. C. and Fisher, Ronald C. Natural Gas Price Deregulation and Windfall Profits Taxation. *Southern Econ. J.*, October 1983, *50*(2), pp. 529–38. **[G: U.S.]**

Kooiman, K. Article 16: The U.S. Attitude to Treaty Shopping. *Bull. Int. Fiscal Doc.*, May 1983, *37*(5), pp. 195–200. **[G: U.S.; Australia; Argentina; Jamaica; New Zealand]**

Kopits, George. Inflation, Income Taxation, and Economic Behavior. **In** *[Goode, R.],* 1983, pp. 371–87. **[G: OECD]**

Koskela, Erkki. A Note on Progression, Penalty Schemes and Tax Evasion. *J. Public Econ.*, October 1983, *22*(1), pp. 127–33.

Koskela, Erkki. On the Shape of Tax Schedule, the Probability of Detection, and the Penalty Schemes as Deterrents to Tax Evasion. *Public Finance,* 1983, *38*(1), pp. 70–80.

Kotlikoff, Laurence J. National Savings and Economic Policy: The Efficacy of Investment vs. Savings Incentives. *Amer. Econ. Rev.*, May 1983, *73*(2), pp. 82–87. **[G: U.S.]**

Kovenock, Daniel J. and Rothschild, Michael. Capital Gains Taxation in an Economy with an 'Austrian Sector.' *J. Public Econ.*, July 1983, *21* (2), pp. 215–56. **[G: U.S.]**

Kramer, Gerald H. Is There a Demand for Progressivity?: A Comment. *Public Choice,* 1983, *41* (1), pp. 223–28.

Kramer, Martin. A Decade of Growth in Student Assistance. **In** *Froomkin, J., ed.*, 1983, pp. 61–71. **[G: U.S.]**

Kramer, R. D. Attempts to Curb Treaty Shopping in U.S.–Dutch Treaty Negotiations. *Bull. Int. Fiscal Doc.*, March 1983, *37*(3), pp. 107–09. **[G: U.S.; Netherlands]**

Krzyzaniak, Marian. The Dynamic Incidence of the Levy on Income, Government Expenditures Wasteful. *Public Finance,* 1983, *38*(3), pp. 339–61.

Kwako, Thomas L. International Trade Law Implications of Latin American Tax Practices. **In** *Czinkota, M. R., ed. (II),* 1983, pp. 85–106. **[G: Latin America; OECD]**

Kwon, Jene K. Toward Incentive Transfers, Global Tax and Welfare Indices. *J. Econ. Devel.*, December 1983, *8*(2), pp. 71–87. **[G: LDCs; MDCs]**

Kwon, O. Yul. The Neutral, Pure Profit, and Rate-of-Return Taxes: Their Equivalence and Differences. *Public Finance,* 1983, *38*(1), pp. 81–97.

Kydland, Finn E. Implications of Dynamic Optimal Taxation for the Evolution of Tax Structures: A Comment. *Public Choice,* 1983, *41* (1), pp. 229–35.

Laffer, Arthur B. Supply-Side Economics and the Reagan Program: Response: Not Enough Incentives. **In** *Stubblebine, Wm. C. and Willett, T. D., eds.*, 1983, pp. 71–76. **[G: U.S.]**

Lakonishok, Josef and Vermaelen, Theo. Tax Reform and Ex-Dividend Day Behavior. *J. Finance,* September 1983, *38*(4), pp. 1157–79. **[G: Canada]**

Lane, W. R. Harmonization of Taxes in Australia. **In** *McLure, C. E., Jr., ed.*, 1983, pp. 172–76. **[G: Australia]**

Lanthier, Allan R. Canada: The 1982 Changes to the Taxation of International Income. *Bull. Int. Fiscal Doc.*, April 1983, *37*(4), pp. 171–79. **[G: Canada]**

Lasserre, Pierre. L'aide aux mines d'or ou Les silences du fantôme de Bretton Woods. (With English summary.) *Can. Public Policy,* December 1983, *9*(4), pp. 446–57. **[G: Canada]**

Layard, Richard and Nickell, S. J. Marginal Employment Subsidies Again: A Brief Response to Whitely and Wilson. *Econ. J.*, December 1983, *93*(372), pp. 881–82.

Lehner, Moris. Steuervermeidung/Steuerhinterziehung: Deutschland. (With English summary.) **In**

International Fiscal Association (II), 1983, pp. 193–210. **[G: W. Germany]**

Lerner, Abba P. On Optimal Taxes with an Untaxable Sector. **In** *Lerner, A. P.*, 1983, *1970*, pp. 193–203.

Levin, Henry M. Comprehensive Models for Financing Recurrent Education: Individual Entitlements. **In** *Levin, H. M. and Schütze, H. G., eds.*, 1983, pp. 39–66. **[G: OECD]**

Lewis, Gordon H. The Day Care Tangle: Unexpected Outcomes When Programs Interact. *J. Policy Anal. Manage.*, Summer 1983, *2*(4), pp. 531–47. **[G: U.S.]**

Lewis, W. Arthur. Patterns of Public Revenue and Expenditure. **In** *Lewis, W. A.*, 1983, *1956*, pp. 573–614. **[G: LDCs; MDCs]**

Lieberman, Edward H. A Foreign Tax under New Proposed Foreign Tax Credit Regulations. *Bull. Int. Fiscal Doc.*, 1983, *37*(7), pp. 323–24. **[G: U.S.]**

Lim, David. Fiscal Incentives and Direct Foreign Investment in Less Developed Countries. *J. Devel. Stud.*, January 1983, *19*(2), pp. 207–12. **[G: LDCs]**

Lim, David. Tax Incentives and Resource Utilization in Peninsular Malaysian Manufacturing. **In** *Lim, D., ed.*, 1983, *1981*, pp. 277–87. **[G: Malaysia]**

Lindsey, Lawrence B. Alternatives to the Current Maximum Tax on Earned Income. **In** *Feldstein, M., ed.*, 1983, pp. 83–102. **[G: U.S.]**

Linn, Johannes F. Tax Assignment and Revenue Sharing in Brazil, India, Malaysia, and Nigeria: Comment. **In** *McLure, C. E., Jr., ed.*, 1983, pp. 360–61. **[G: Brazil; India; Malaysia; Nigeria]**

Litzenberger, Robert H. and Ramaswamy, Krishna. The Effect of Personal Taxes and Dividends on Capital Asset Prices: Theory and Empirical Evidence. **In** *Archer, S. H. and D'Ambrosia, C. A.*, 1983, *1979*, pp. 690–722. **[G: U.S.]**

Lloyd, Peter J. The Microeconomic Effects of Tax-inflation Interactions: General Equilibrium Estimates for Australia: Discussion. **In** *Pagan, A. R. and Trivedi, P. K., eds.*, 1983, pp. 178–82. **[G: Australia]**

Lodin, Sven-Olof. Income and Expenditure Taxes in Practice. **In** *[Goode, R.]*, 1983, pp. 109–38. **[G: Sweden]**

Longanecker, David A. The Public Cost of Tuition Tax Credits. **In** *James, T. and Levin, H. M., eds.*, 1983, pp. 115–29. **[G: U.S.]**

Longo, Carlos A. Deficiencies of Current Taxation of Capital Income. *Bull. Int. Fiscal Doc.*, 1983, *37*(7), pp. 291–301. **[G: Brazil]**

Looney, J. W. Tax and Other Legal Considerations in the Organization of the Farm Firm. **In** *Baum, K. H. and Schertz, L. P., eds.*, 1983, pp. 135–45. **[G: U.S.]**

Loughran, Mary. The Abolition of Turnover Tax Borders in the EEC: A Step in Two Different Directions—Commission Proposals on Travellers' Tax-Free Allowances and Duty-Free Shops. *Bull. Int. Fiscal Doc.*, 1983, *37*(7), pp. 311–19. **[G: EEC]**

Luksetich, William A. The Determinants of Federal Grants: Comment. *Southern Econ. J.*, July 1983, *50*(1), pp. 270–74. **[G: U.S.]**

Madre, Jean-Loup. Construction d'indicateurs de redistribution. (The Construction of Redistribution Indicators. With English summary.) *Consommation*, July–Sept. 1983, *30*(3), pp. 3–22. **[G: France]**

Maher, Michael W. and Nantell, Timothy J. The Tax Effects of Inflation: Depreciation, Debt, and Miller's Equilibrium Tax Rates. *J. Acc. Res.*, Spring 1983, *21*(1), pp. 329–40.

Main, Brian G. M. Corporate Insurance Purchases and Taxes. *J. Risk Ins.*, June 1983, *50*(2), pp. 197–223. **[G: U.S.]**

Mancera, Miguel. Panel Discussion: The Capital Market under Conditions of High and Variable Inflation. **In** *Armella, P. A.; Dornbusch, R. and Obstfeld, M., eds.*, 1983, pp. 279–81.

Manning, Ian. The 1983–84 Budget and Tax Reform. *Australian Econ. Rev.*, 3rd Quarter 1983, (63), pp. 19–25. **[G: Australia]**

Mantel, Rolf R. Equilibrio General y Tributación óptima. (General Equilibrum and Optimum Taxation. With English summary.) *Económica*, May–December 1983, *29*(2–3), pp. 135–51.

Marsden, Keith. Taxes and Growth. *Finance Develop.*, September 1983, *20*(3), pp. 40–43. **[G: Selected Countries]**

Martin, John P. and Page, John M., Jr. The Impact of Subsidies on X-Efficiency in LDC Industry: Theory and an Empirical Test. *Rev. Econ. Statist.*, November 1983, *65*(4), pp. 608–17. **[G: Ghana]**

Martino, Antonio. Invisible Taxation: The Growth of Italy's Leviathan. *Policy Rev.*, Summer 1983, (25), pp. 46–51. **[G: Italy]**

Masson, Paul R. Les effets à long terme de différentes règles de financement du gouvernement. (Long Term Effects of Different Financing Methods of Government. With English summary.) *L'Actual. Econ.*, June 1983, *59*(2), pp. 266–82. **[G: Canada]**

Mathews, Russell. Tax Effectiveness and Tax Equity in Federal Countries. **In** *McLure, C. E., Jr., ed.*, 1983, pp. 70–86. **[G: MDCs]**

Mathews, Russell. Tax Effectiveness and Tax Equity in Federal Countries: Reply. **In** *McLure, C. E., Jr., ed.*, 1983, pp. 98–99. **[G: MDCs]**

McClure, J. Harold and Willett, Thomas D. Understanding the Supply-Siders. **In** *Stubblebine, Wm. C. and Willett, T. D., eds.*, 1983, pp. 59–69. **[G: U.S.]**

McDonald, Robert L. Government Debt and Private Leverage: An Extension of the Miller Theorem. *J. Public Econ.*, December 1983, *22*(3), pp. 303–25. **[G: U.S.]**

McGreevy, T. E. and Thomson, A. W. J. Regional Policy and Company Investment Behaviour. *Reg. Stud.*, October 1983, *17*(5), pp. 347–57. **[G: U.K.]**

McGuigan, Jim. The Death of the Grants to Writers Program in England. *J. Cult. Econ.*, June 1983, *7*(1), pp. 33–41. **[G: U.K.]**

McIntyre, Michael J. The Tax Treatment of Households of Different Size: Commentary. **In** *Penner, R. G., ed.*, 1983, pp. 98–103. **[G: U.S.]**

McLure, Charles E., Jr. A Reexamination of Tax Distortions in General Equilibrium Models: Comment. **In** *Feldstein, M., ed.*, 1983, pp. 421–26. **[G: U.S.]**

McLure, Charles E., Jr. Assignment of Corporate Income Taxes in a Federal System. **In** *McLure, C. E., Jr., ed.*, 1983, pp. 101–24. **[G: Selected OECD; U.S.]**

McLure, Charles E., Jr. and Mieszkowski, Peter. Taxation of Mineral Wealth and Interregional Conflicts. **In** *McLure, C. E., Jr. and Mieszkowski, P., eds.*, 1983, pp. 1–10. **[G: U.S.; Canada]**

Meloe, Tor. The Energy Industry and Federal Tax Policy. **In** *Walker, C. E. and Bloomfield, M. E., eds.*, 1983, pp. 172–76. **[G: U.S.]**

Melvin, Michael. Expected Inflation and Interest Rates: Reply. *Amer. Econ. Rev.*, June 1983, *73*(3), pp. 503–06.

Menchik, Paul L. and David, Martin H. Reply and Comment [The Incidence of a Lifetime Consumption Tax]. *Nat. Tax J.*, December 1983, *36*(4), pp. 515–20. **[G: U.S.]**

Messere, Ken. Trends in OECD Tax Revenues. **In** *[Goode, R.]*, 1983, pp. 31–57. **[G: OECD]**

Meulders, Danièle and Six, Jean-Louis. Budget des dépenses fiscales relatives à l'impôt des personnes physiques (exercice d'imposition 1981). (With English summary.) *Cah. Écon. Bruxelles*, 1983, *98*(2), pp. 274–96. **[G: Belgium]**

Meyer, John R. and Tye, William B. Rational Policies for Development of International Air Transportation. **In** *Khachaturov, T. S. and Goodwin, P. B., eds.*, 1983, pp. 245–64. **[G: Global; U.S.]**

Mieszkowski, Peter. A General Equilibrium Model of Taxation with Endogenous Financial Behavior: Comment. **In** *Feldstein, M., ed.*, 1983, pp. 455–58. **[G: U.S.]**

Mieszkowski, Peter. Energy Policy, Taxation of Natural Resources, and Fiscal Federalism. **In** *McLure, C. E., Jr., ed.*, 1983, pp. 128–45. **[G: U.S.]**

Mieszkowski, Peter. The Tax Treatment of Married Couples and the 1981 Tax Law: Commentary. **In** *Penner, R. G., ed.*, 1983, pp. 69–70. **[G: U.S.]**

Mieszkowski, Peter and Toder, Eric. Taxation of Energy Resources. **In** *McLure, C. E., Jr. and Mieszkowski, P., eds.*, 1983, pp. 65–91. **[G: U.S.]**

Miller, Merton H. Debt and Taxes. **In** *Archer, S. H. and D'Ambrosia, C. A.*, 1983, *1977*, pp. 462–78.

Miller, Merton H. and Scholes, Myron S. Dividends and Taxes. **In** *Archer, S. H. and D'Ambrosia, C. A.*, 1983, *1978*, pp. 658–89.

Minarik, Joseph J. Alternatives to the Current Maximum Tax on Earned Income: Comment. **In** *Feldstein, M., ed.*, 1983, pp. 103–08. **[G: U.S.]**

Minarik, Joseph J. Family Issues in Taxation: Commentary. **In** *Penner, R. G., ed.*, 1983, pp. 23–27. **[G: U.S.]**

Mirowski, Philip and Schwartz, Arthur R. The Falling Share of Corporate Taxation. *J. Post Keynesian Econ.*, Winter 1982–83, *5*(2), pp. 245–56.

Monke, Eric. Tariffs, Implementation Costs, and Optimal Policy Choice. *Weltwirtsch. Arch.*, 1983, *119*(2), pp. 281–96. **[G: Ivory Coast; Senegal; Liberia]**

Montmarquette, Claude. Public Goods and Price Indexes. **In** *Diewert, W. E. and Montmarquette, C., eds.*, 1983, pp. 655–78. **[G: Canada]**

Moore, Robert L. Self-Employment and the Incidence of the Payroll Tax. *Nat. Tax J.*, December 1983, *36*(4), pp. 491–501. **[G: U.S.]**

Moore, W. Henson. The Congressional Outlook for Increased Saving Incentives. **In** *Walker, C. E. and Bloomfield, M. E., eds.*, 1983, pp. 119–20. **[G: U.S.]**

de Moraes, Bernardo Ribeiro. The Monetary Correction of Tax Debts within the Framework of Brazilian Law. **In** *de Ulhôa Canto, G.; da Silva Martins, I. G. and van Hoorn, J., Jr., eds.*, 1983, pp. 99–135. **[G: Brazil]**

Moreh, J. Optimal Taxation and Public Goods. *Public Finance Quart.*, April 1983, *11*(2), pp. 181–201.

Moreira, Raul. Tax Avoidance/Tax Evasion: Mexico. **In** *International Fiscal Association (II)*, 1983, pp. 511–23. **[G: Mexico]**

Morse, Dale and Richardson, Gordon. The LIFO/FIFO Decision. *J. Acc. Res.*, Spring 1983, *21*(1), pp. 106–27. **[G: U.S.]**

Moynihan, Daniel Patrick. Political and Economic Complexity in International Tax Issues. **In** *Walker, C. E. and Bloomfield, M. E., eds.*, 1983, pp. 353–57.

Muller, Carol Blue. The Social and Political Consequences of Increased Public Support for Private Schools. **In** *James, T. and Levin, H. M., eds.*, 1983, pp. 39–54. **[G: U.S.]**

Mumy, Gene E. and Manson, William D. Payroll Taxes, Social Security, and the Unique Tax Advantage of Company Pensions. *J. Risk Ins.*, March 1983, *50*(1), pp. 161–65.

Murnane, Richard J. The Uncertain Consequences of Tuition Tax Credits: An Analysis of Student Achievement and Economic Incentives. **In** *James, T. and Levin, H. M., eds.*, 1983, pp. 210–22. **[G: U.S.]**

Murphy, D. G. Zimbabwe: A Survey of Its Tax System. *Bull. Int. Fiscal Doc.*, January 1983, *37*(1), pp. 27–29. **[G: Zimbabwe]**

Murray, Michael P. Subsidized and Unsubsidized Housing Starts: 1961–1977. *Rev. Econ. Statist.*, November 1983, *65*(4), pp. 590–97. **[G: U.S.]**

Musgrave, Peggy B. Assignment of Corporate Income Taxes in a Federal System: Comment. **In** *McLure, C. E., Jr., ed.*, 1983, pp. 127–28. **[G: Selected OECD; U.S.]**

Musgrave, Peggy B. Tax Assignment and Revenue Sharing in Australia: Comment. **In** *McLure, C. E., Jr., ed.*, 1983, pp. 323–26. **[G: Australia; Canada; U.S.; W. Germany]**

Musgrave, Richard A. Tax Assignment and Revenue Sharing in the Federal Republic of Germany and Switzerland: Comment. **In** *McLure, C. E., Jr., ed.*, 1983, pp. 287–88. **[G: W. Germany; Switzerland]**

Mutén, Leif. Some Topical Issues Concerning International Double Taxation. **In** *[Goode, R.]*, 1983, pp. 317–42.

Muth, Richard F. Effects of the U.S. Tax System on Housing Prices and Consumption. **In** *Grieson, R. E., ed.*, 1983, pp. 11–27. **[G: U.S.]**

Naunton, Stewart. Papua New Guinea: 1983 Budget Income Tax Amendments. *Bull. Int. Fiscal Doc.*, 1983, *37*(7), pp. 303–10. **[G: Papua New Guinea]**

Nellor, David C. L. The Size of Government, Capital Accumulation, and the Tax Base. *Public Finance Quart.*, July 1983, *11*(3), pp. 321–45. **[G: U.S.]**

Nelson, James C. Policy Issues and Economic Effects

of Public Aids to Domestic Transport. **In** *Nelson, J. C.*, 1983, *1959*, pp. 353–70.

Nelson, Richard R. Government Support of Technical Progress: Lessons from History. *J. Policy Anal. Manage.*, Summer 1983, *2*(4), pp. 499–514. **[G: U.S.]**

Neubeck, Kenneth J. Income Maintenance Experimentation: Cui Bono. **In** *Goldstein, R. and Sachs, S. M., eds.*, 1983, pp. 253–59. **[G: U.S.]**

Noemie, Michel. Problèmes Internationaux du domaine des taxes sur le chiffre d'affaires: France. (With English summary.) **In** *International Fiscal Association (I)*, 1983, pp. 393–412. **[G: France]**

Nolan, John S. Costs and Benefits of Adopting a Flat Rate Tax. **In** *Walker, C. E. and Bloomfield, M. E., eds.*, 1983, pp. 319–22.

Nolan, John S. Tax Prospects: Implications of Budget Problems: Remarks. *Nat. Tax J.*, September 1983, *36*(3), pp. 285–88. **[G: U.S.]**

Nooteboom, A. Tax Avoidance/Tax Evasion: Netherlands. **In** *International Fiscal Association (II)*, 1983, pp. 545–66. **[G: Netherlands]**

Nowotny, Ewald. Tax Assignment and Revenue Sharing in the Federal Republic of Germany and Switzerland. **In** *McLure, C. E., Jr., ed.*, 1983, pp. 260–86. **[G: Switzerland; W. Germany]**

O'Hara, Maureen. Tax-Exempt Financing: Some Lessons from History. *J. Money, Credit, Banking*, November 1983, *15*(4), pp. 425–41. **[G: U.S.]**

O'Hare, Michael and Mundel, David S. When to Pay for Sunk Benefits. **In** *Zeckhauser, R. J. and Leebaert, D., eds.*, 1983, pp. 255–61.

O'Neill, June. Family Issues in Taxation. **In** *Penner, R. G., ed.*, 1983, pp. 1–22. **[G: U.S.]**

Oates, Wallace E. Tax Assignment and Revenue Sharing in the United States: Comment. **In** *McLure, C. E., Jr., ed.*, 1983, pp. 228–30. **[G: U.S.]**

Oates, Wallace E. Tax Effectiveness and Tax Equity in Federal Countries: Comment. **In** *McLure, C. E., Jr., ed.*, 1983, pp. 94–97. **[G: MDCs]**

Okamura, Makoto and Kamiya, Kazuya. A Generalization of Tax Incidence Analysis. *Osaka Econ. Pap.*, September 1983, *33*(1–2), pp. 71–83.

Okner, Benjamin A. and Bawden, D. Lee. Recent Changes in Federal Income Redistribution Policy. *Nat. Tax J.*, September 1983, *36*(3), pp. 347–60. **[G: U.S.]**

Okun, Arthur M. A Reward TIP. **In** *Okun, A. M.*, 1983, *1979*, pp. 67–75. **[G: U.S.]**

Okun, Arthur M. Measuring the Impact of the 1964 Tax Reduction. **In** *Okun, A. M.*, 1983, *1968*, pp. 405–23. **[G: U.S.]**

Okun, Arthur M. The Full Employment Surplus Revisited. **In** *Okun, A. M.*, 1983, *1970*, pp. 304–37. **[G: U.S.]**

Okun, Arthur M. The Personal Tax Surcharge and Consumer Demand, 1968–70. **In** *Okun, A. M.*, 1983, *1971*, pp. 338–74. **[G: U.S.]**

Olsen, Edgar O. The Great Housing Experiment: Implications for Housing Policy. **In** *Friedman, J. and Weinberg, D. H., eds.*, 1983, pp. 266–75. **[G: U.S.]**

Olsen, Edgar O. The Role of Government in the Housing Sector. **In** *Giersch, H., ed.*, 1983, pp. 199–224. **[G: U.S.]**

Olsen, Edgar O. and Reeder, William J. Misdirected Rental Subsidies. *J. Policy Anal. Manage.*, Summer 1983, *2*(4), pp. 614–20. **[G: U.S.]**

Oswald, Andrew J. Altruism, Jealousy and the Theory of Optimal Non-Linear Taxation. *J. Public Econ.*, February 1983, *20*(1), pp. 77–87.

Owens, Jeffery P. Tax Expenditures and Direct Expenditures as Instruments of Social Policy. **In** *[Goode, R.]*, 1983, pp. 171–97. **[G: OECD]**

Paarlberg, Robert L. Discussion [Governments and Agricultural Markets in Africa] [Why Do Governments Do What They Do? The Case of Food Price Policy]. **In** *Johnson, D. G. and Schuh, G. E., eds.*, 1983, pp. 213–18. **[G: India; U.S.]**

Packwood, Bob. An Opportunity for Tax Reform. **In** *Walker, C. E. and Bloomfield, M. E., eds.*, 1983, pp. 323–25.

Palmon, Dan and Yaari, Uzi. Taxation of Capital Gains and the Behavior of Stock Prices over the Dividend Cycle. *Amer. Econ.*, Spring 1983, *27*(1), pp. 13–22.

Park, Thae S. Federal Personal Income Taxes: Liabilities and Payments, 1977–81. *Surv. Curr. Bus.*, January 1983, *63*(1), pp. 27–30. **[G: U.S.]**

Patrick, Robert J., Jr. Tax Treaty Shopping. *Bull. Int. Fiscal Doc.*, March 1983, *37*(3), pp. 105–06. **[G: U.S.; OECD]**

Peacock, Alan. The Disaffection of the Taxpayer. *Atlantic Econ. J.*, March 1983, *11*(1), pp. 7–15.

Pechman, Joseph A. Anatomy of the U.S. Individual Income Tax. **In** *[Goode, R.]*, 1983, pp. 61–84. **[G: U.S.]**

Pechman, Joseph A. Another View of the Corporate Income Tax. **In** *Walker, C. E. and Bloomfield, M. E., eds.*, 1983, pp. 177–80.

Pen, Jan. A Very Cultural Economist's Ideas about the Locus of Decision-making. **In** *Hendon, W. S. and Shanahan, J. L., eds.*, 1983, pp. 16–30.

Pepper, H. W. T. Tax Changes in a Low Tax Country: The 1983–84 Budget in Bermuda. *Bull. Int. Fiscal Doc.*, August 1983, *37*(8), pp. 364. **[G: Bermuda]**

Pepper, H. W. T. Tax Changes in Jamaica: The 1983–84 Budget. *Bull. Int. Fiscal Doc.*, November 1983, *37*(11), pp. 487. **[G: Jamaica]**

Pepper, H. W. T. The MIRAS Touch: Private Sector Involvement in Tax Administration. *Bull. Int. Fiscal Doc.*, 1983, *37*(7), pp. 325–26. **[G: U.K.]**

Persson, Mats. The Distribution of Abilities and the Progressive Income Tax. *J. Public Econ.*, October 1983, *22*(1), pp. 73–88.

Pfähler, Wilhelm. Measuring Redistributional Effects of Tax Progressivity by Lorenz Curves. *Jahr. Nationalökon. Statist.*, May 1983, *198*(3), pp. 237–49.

Phelps, Charles E. Tax Policy, Health Insurance and Health Care. **In** *Meyer, J. A., ed.*, 1983, pp. 198–224. **[G: U.S.]**

Phelps Brown, Henry. Egalitarianism and the Distribution of Wealth and Income in the U.K. *Ind. Relat.*, Spring 1983, *22*(2), pp. 186–202. **[G: U.K.]**

Phelps Brown, Henry. What Is the British Predicament? **In** *Feinstein, C., ed.*, 1983, *1977*, pp. 207–25. **[G: U.K.]**

Pick, J. F. Erratum: Introduction of an Inflation-Adjusted Tax Base in Israel. *Bull. Int. Fiscal Doc.*, November 1983, *37*(11), pp. 496. **[G: Israel]**

Pick, J. F. Introduction of an Inflation-Adjusted Tax Base in Israel. *Bull. Int. Fiscal Doc.*, 1983, *37*(6), pp. 259–63. **[G: Israel]**

Piffano, Horacio L. P. La Incidencia de la Imposición Indirecta en un Enfoque de Equilibrio Parcial. (The Incidence of Indirect Taxation in a Partial Equilibrium Approach. With English summary.) *Económica*, May–December 1983, *29*(2–3), pp. 153–216.

Piggott, John. The Microeconomic Effects of Tax-inflation Interactions: General Equilibrium Estimates for Australia. **In** *Pagan, A. R. and Trivedi, P. K., eds.*, 1983, pp. 138–77. **[G: Australia]**

Plasschaert, Sylvain R. F. The Comparatively Limited Role of Income Taxation in Developing Countries. *Bull. Int. Fiscal Doc.*, April 1983, *37*(4), pp. 161–67. **[G: LDCs; OECD]**

Playford, Clive and Pond, Chris. The Right to Be Unequal: Inequality in Incomes. **In** *Field, F., ed.*, 1983, pp. 34–55. **[G: U.K.]**

Pohmer, Dieter. Value-added Tax after Ten Years: The European Experience. **In** *[Goode, R.]*, 1983, pp. 243–55. **[G: W. Europe]**

Pommerehne, Werner W. Steuerhinterziehung und Schwarzarbeit als Grenzen der Staatstätigkeit. (Tax Evasion and Underground Activities as Limits of Government's Growth. With English summary.) *Schweiz. Z. Volkswirtsch. Statist.*, September 1983, *119*(3), pp. 261–84. **[G: Switzerland]**

Pond, Chris. Wealth and the Two Nations. **In** *Field, F., ed.*, 1983, pp. 9–33. **[G: U.K.]**

Posner, Richard A. Economic Justice and the Economist. **In** *Letwin, W., ed.*, 1983, *1973*, pp. 345–59. **[G: U.S.]**

Poterba, James M. and Summers, Lawrence H. Dividend Taxes, Corporate Investment, and '*Q*.'. *J. Public Econ.*, November 1983, *22*(2), pp. 135–67. **[G: U.K.]**

Praet, Peter. Inflation-Induced Wealth Tax in Belgium. *Rev. Income Wealth*, June 1983, *29*(2), pp. 209–14. **[G: Belgium]**

Prest, A. R. Taxation Policy. **In** *Seldon, A., et al.*, 1983, pp. 49–69. **[G: U.K.]**

Prest, Wilfred. Tax Assignment and Revenue Sharing in the United States: Comment. **In** *McLure, C. E., Jr., ed.*, 1983, pp. 231–33. **[G: Australia; U.S.]**

Prot, B. and Rolland, P. La fiscalité comme outil de la politique de la demande. (The Tax System as a Tool of the Demand Policy. With English summary.) *Écon. Soc.*, December 1983, *17*(12), pp. 2077–88.

Protopapadakis, Aris. Some Indirect Evidence on Effective Capital Gains Tax Rates. *J. Bus.*, April 1983, *56*(2), pp. 127–38. **[G: U.S.]**

Pucher, John; Markstedt, Anders and Hirschman, Ira. Impacts of Subsidies on the Costs of Urban Public Transport. *J. Transp. Econ. Policy*, May 1983, *17*(2), pp. 155–76. **[G: U.S.]**

Quick, Perry D. The Consumption Based Tax: Prospects for Reform. **In** *Walker, C. E. and Bloomfield, M. E., eds.*, 1983, pp. 261–64.

Quinn, Brian Scott and Aldred, Peregrine. The Eurobond Secondary Market. **In** *George, A. M. and Giddy, I. H., eds., Vol. 1*, 1983, pp. 5.4:1–17.

Raboy, David G. Capital Composition Changes: Effects of Changing Haig–Simons Income Tax Rates. *Public Finance Quart.*, January 1983, *11*(1), pp. 67–78.

Rahn, Richard W. Supply-Side Economics: The U.S. Experience. **In** *Stubblebine, Wm. C. and Willett, T. D., eds.*, 1983, pp. 43–57. **[G: U.S.]**

Rau, Günter. Internationale Probleme auf dem Gebiet der Umsatzbesteuerung: Deutschland. (With English summary.) **In** *International Fiscal Association (I)*, 1983, pp. 197–217. **[G: W. Germany]**

Reiners, Gernot H. Leasing in an International Context. **In** *George, A. M. and Giddy, I. H., eds., Vol. 2*, 1983, pp. 7.4:1–28. **[G: OECD]**

Reinganum, Marc R. The Anomalous Stock Market Behavior of Small Firms in January: Empirical Tests for Tax-Loss Selling Effects. *J. Finan. Econ.*, June 1983, *12*(1), pp. 89–104. **[G: U.S.]**

Resnick, Steven R. Lower Capital Gains Tax Rates and the Stock Market. **In** *Walker, C. E. and Bloomfield, M. E., eds.*, 1983, pp. 150–53. **[G: U.S.]**

Reynolds, B. J. Tax Avoidance/Tax Evasion: United Kingdom. **In** *International Fiscal Association (II)*, 1983, pp. 581–99. **[G: U.K.]**

Rezk, Ernesto. Flexibilidad automática en la Argentina: un ejercicio macroestático. (With English summary.) *Desarrollo Econ.*, July–September 1983, *23*(90), pp. 233–54. **[G: Argentina]**

Rhyne, Elisabeth H. Federal Credit Activities. **In** *Pechman, J. A., ed.*, 1983, pp. 231–42. **[G: U.S.]**

Richter, Wolfram F. From Ability to Pay to Concepts of Equal Sacrifice. *J. Public Econ.*, March 1983, *20*(2), pp. 211–29.

Robins, Philip K.; West, Richard W. and Stieger, Gary L. Labor Supply Response to a Negative Income Tax. **In** *Zeckhauser, R. J. and Leebaert, D., eds.*, 1983, pp. 78–96. **[G: U.S.]**

Robinson, Warren C. Educational Disinvestment: Who Benefits from Subsidies? Does Anyone? *Policy Rev.*, Fall 1983, (26), pp. 59–64. **[G: U.S.]**

Rock, Steven M. Measurement of Tax Progressivity: Application. *Public Finance Quart.*, January 1983, *11*(1), pp. 109–20. **[G: U.S.]**

Rodrigues Pardal, Francisco. Evasion fiscale/Fraude fiscale: Portugal. (With English summary.) **In** *International Fiscal Association (II)*, 1983, pp. 567–79. **[G: Portugal]**

Rosenberg, Sam. Reagan Social Policy and Labour Force Restructuring. *Cambridge J. Econ.*, June 1983, *7*(2), pp. 179–96. **[G: U.S.]**

Rosenblum, Jay. The Swank Decision: Economic Interest in Coal Not Dependent on Lease Terminability. *Natural Res. J.*, January 1983, *23*(1), pp. 247–54. **[G: U.S.]**

Rothschild, Leonard W., Jr. and Beattie, John R. U.S. Expected to Replace DISC with New Foreign Sales Corporation. *Bull. Int. Fiscal Doc.*, August 1983, *37*(8), pp. 339–43. **[G: U.S.]**

Rousslang, Don and Pelzman, Joseph. The Benefits and Costs of the Deferral of U.S. Taxes on Retained Earnings of Controlled Foreign Corporations. *Europ. Econ. Rev.*, January 1983, *20*(1–3), pp. 79–94. **[G: U.S.]**

Ruane, Frances P. Government Financial and Tax Incentives and Industrial Employment. *Irish Banking Rev.*, June 1983, pp. 20–28. **[G: Ireland]**

Rubenson, Kjell. Financing Paid Educational Leave: The Swedish Model. **In** *Levin, H. M. and Schütze, H. G., eds.*, 1983, pp. 237–55. **[G: Sweden]**

Rubinfeld, Daniel L. Tax Assignment and Revenue Sharing in the United States. **In** *McLure, C. E., Jr., ed.*, 1983, pp. 205–27. **[G: U.S.]**

Rudder, Catherine E. Tax Policy: Structure and Choice. **In** *Schick, A., ed.*, 1983, pp. 196–220. **[G: U.S.]**

Ruibal, Rubén R. International Problems in the Field of General Taxes on Sales of Goods and Services: Argentina. **In** *International Fiscal Association (I)*, 1983, pp. 219–45. **[G: Argentina]**

Ruppe, Hans Georg. International Problems in the Field of General Taxes on Sales of Goods and Services: General Report. **In** *International Fiscal Association (I)*, 1983, pp. 109–48. **[G: Global]**

Rusin, Michael. Problems in Modeling Crude Oil Price Decontrol and Windfall Profits Tax Proposals: A Case Study. **In** *Thrall, R. M.; Thompson, R. G. and Holloway, M. L., eds.*, 1983, pp. 29–50. **[G: U.S.]**

Rutgaizer, V. The Working Person in the Distribution and Consumption Sphere. *Prob. Econ.*, January 1983, *25*(9), pp. 16–35. **[G: U.S.S.R.]**

Saffran, Bernard. The Tax Treatment of Married Couples and the 1981 Tax Law: Commentary. **In** *Penner, R. G., ed.*, 1983, pp. 64–68. **[G: U.S.]**

Sah, Raaj Kumar. How Much Redistribution Is Possible through Commodity Taxes? *J. Public Econ.*, February 1983, *20*(1), pp. 89–101.

Salonen, Pekka. Internationale Probleme auf dem Gebiet der Umsatzbesteuerung: Finnland. (With English summary.) **In** *International Fiscal Association (I)*, 1983, pp. 381–91. **[G: Finland]**

Sandford, Cedric. Capital Taxes—Past, Present and Future. *Lloyds Bank Rev.*, October 1983, (150), pp. 34–49. **[G: U.K.]**

Sato, Mitsuo. International Problems in the Field of General Taxes on Sales of Goods and Services: Japan. **In** *International Fiscal Association (I)*, 1983, pp. 463–70. **[G: Japan]**

Saunders, Charles B., Jr. Reshaping Federal Aid to Higher Education. **In** *Froomkin, J., ed.*, 1983, pp. 119–34. **[G: U.S.]**

Scherer, Joseph. Stop Blaming Bracket Creep. *Challenge*, November/December 1983, *26*(5), pp. 53–54. **[G: U.S.]**

Schneider, Anna and Rosenberg, Rivka. International Problems in the Field of General Taxes on Sales of Goods and Services: Israel. **In** *International Fiscal Association (I)*, 1983, pp. 425–41. **[G: Israel]**

Schneider, Friedrich and Pommerehne, Werner W. Private Demand for Public Subsidies to the Arts: A Study in Voting and Expenditure Theory. **In** *Hendon, W. S. and Shanahan, J. L., eds.*, 1983, pp. 192–206. **[G: Switzerland]**

Scholz, John Karl. Tax Expenditures. **In** *Pechman, J. A., ed.*, 1983, pp. 243–48. **[G: U.S.]**

Schueler, Manfred and Terry, Chris. Comparisons of the Structural Progressivity of the Personal Income Tax. *Australian Econ. Pap.*, June 1983, *22*(40), pp. 83–89. **[G: Australia]**

Schwab, Robert M. Expected Inflation and Housing: Tax and Cash Flow Considerations. *Southern Econ. J.*, April 1983, *49*(4), pp. 1162–68.

Scitovsky, Tibor. Subsidies for the Arts: The Economic Argument. **In** *Hendon, W. S. and Shanahan, J. L., eds.*, 1983, pp. 6–15.

Seibert, Donald V. A Retailer's Perspective on the Value Added Tax. **In** *Walker, C. E. and Bloomfield, M. E., eds.*, 1983, pp. 218–22.

Seidman, Laurence S. Taxes in a Life Cycle Growth Model with Bequests and Inheritances. *Amer. Econ. Rev.*, June 1983, *73*(3), pp. 437–41.

Semmler, Willi. On the Classical Theory of Taxation. An Analysis of Tax Incidence in a Linear Production Model. *Metroecon.*, February–June 1983, *35*(1–2), pp. 129–46.

Shafer, Joel and Solursh, John M. Tax Avoidance/Tax Evasion: Canada. **In** *International Fiscal Association (II)*, 1983, pp. 295–315. **[G: Canada]**

Shah, Anup R. K. The Size of the Lifetime Excess Burden of a Tax. *Europ. Econ. Rev.*, January 1983, *20*(1–3), pp. 1–11.

Shannon, James M. Why Congress Will Not Accept the Value Added Tax. **In** *Walker, C. E. and Bloomfield, M. E., eds.*, 1983, pp. 222–25.

Sherman, Joel D. Public Finance of Private Schools: Observations from Abroad. **In** *James, T. and Levin, H. M., eds.*, 1983, pp. 71–83. **[G: Canada; Australia]**

Shibata, Hirofumi. Fiscal Measures against Pollution: Are Effluent Taxes and Abatement Subsidies Equivalent? **In** *Biehl, D.; Roskamp, K. W. and Stolper, W. F., eds.*, 1983, pp. 399–418.

Shih, Anne and Au-Yeung, P. K. Revenue Law and Practice in the People's Republic of China. *Bull. Int. Fiscal Doc.*, March 1983, *37*(3), pp. 99–104. **[G: China]**

Shoup, Carl S. Current Trends in Excise Taxation. **In** *[Goode, R.]*, 1983, pp. 257–75. **[G: OECD]**

Shoup, Carl S. Harmonization of Indirect Taxes in the EEC: Comment. **In** *McLure, C. E., Jr., ed.*, 1983, pp. 169–71. **[G: EEC]**

Shoup, Carl S. The Property Tax versus Sales and Income Taxes. **In** *Harriss, C. L., ed.*, 1983, pp. 31–41.

Shoven, John B. Applied General-Equilibrium Tax Modeling. *Int. Monet. Fund Staff Pap.*, June 1983, *30*(2), pp. 394–420. **[G: U.S.]**

Siembos, Tryfon. Tax Avoidance/Tax Evasion: Greece. **In** *International Fiscal Association (II)*, 1983, pp. 401–18. **[G: Greece]**

da Silva Martins, Ives Gandra. Brazil: The Supplementary Income Tax on the Remittance of Dividends Abroad Revisited. *Bull. Int. Fiscal Doc.*, January 1983, *37*(1), pp. 30. **[G: Brazil]**

da Silva Martins, Ives Gandra. Monetary Correction in the National Tax Code. **In** *de Ulhôa Canto, G.; da Silva Martins, I. G. and van Hoorn, J., Jr., eds.*, 1983, pp. 32–46. **[G: Brazil]**

Simons, A. L. C. International Problems in the Field of General Taxes on Sales of Goods and Services:

Netherlands. **In** *International Fiscal Association (I),* 1983, pp. 529–44. **[G: Netherlands]**

Sinai, Allen and Eckstein, Otto. Tax Policy and Business Fixed Investment Revisited. *J. Econ. Behav. Organ.,* June–September 1983, *4*(2–3), pp. 131–62. **[G: U.S.]**

Sinai, Allen; Lin, Andrew and Robins, Russell. Taxes, Saving, and Investment: Some Empirical Evidence. *Nat. Tax J.,* September 1983, *36*(3), pp. 321–45. **[G: U.S.]**

Singh, A. J. and Singh, Tirath. Black Money—Genesis, Estimation, Causes and Remedies. *Econ. Aff.,* January–March 1983, *28*(1), pp. 632–43. **[G: India]**

Sirén, Pekka. Terveydenhuollon menot, rakenne ja rahoitus. (Health Care Expenditure, Structure and Financing in Finland. With English summary.) *Kansant. Aikak.,* 1983, *79*(4), pp. 418–35. **[G: Finland]**

Skelton, Jeffrey L. Banks, Firms and the Relative Pricing of Tax-Exempt and Taxable Bonds. *J. Finan. Econ.,* November 1983, *12*(3), pp. 343–55. **[G: U.S.]**

Skjonsberg, Anne. International Problems in the Field of General Taxes on Sales of Goods and Services: Norway. **In** *International Fiscal Association (I),* 1983, pp. 511–27. **[G: Norway]**

Slemrod, Joel. A General Equilibrium Model of Taxation with Endogenous Financial Behavior. **In** *Feldstein, M., ed.,* 1983, pp. 427–54. **[G: U.S.]**

Slemrod, Joel. Do We Know How Progressive the Income Tax System Should Be? *Nat. Tax J.,* September 1983, *36*(3), pp. 361–69. **[G: U.S.]**

Slemrod, Joel and Yitzhaki, Shlomo. On Choosing a Flat-Rate Income Tax System. *Nat. Tax J.,* March, 1983, *36*(1), pp. 31–44. **[G: U.S.]**

Smith, Alasdair. Tax Reform and Temporary Inefficiency. *J. Public Econ.,* March 1983, *20*(2), pp. 265–70.

Smith, Lawrence B. The Crisis in Rental Housing: A Canadian Perspective. *Ann. Amer. Acad. Polit. Soc. Sci.,* January 1983, *465,* pp. 58–75. **[G: Canada]**

Soos, Piroska E. United States: Controlled Foreign Corporations—A Victory for Taxpayers. *Bull. Int. Fiscal Doc.,* May 1983, *37*(5), pp. 201–06. **[G: U.S.]**

Southwick, Lawrence, Jr. and Cadigan, John F., Jr. The Medical Expense Deduction and Income Levels: Progressive or Regressive? *J. Econ. Bus.,* 1983, *35*(1), pp. 61–70. **[G: U.S.]**

de Souza, Hamilton Dias. International Problems in the Field of General Taxes on Sales of Goods and Services: Brazil. **In** *International Fiscal Association (I),* 1983, pp. 319–34. **[G: Brazil]**

Spiro, Erwin. The 1983 Income Tax Changes in the Republic of South Africa. *Bull. Int. Fiscal Doc.,* 1983, *37*(6), pp. 275–77. **[G: S. Africa]**

St.-Hilaire, France and Whalley, John. A Microconsistent Equilibrium Data Set for Canada for Use in Tax Policy Analysis. *Rev. Income Wealth,* June 1983, *29*(2), pp. 175–204. **[G: Canada]**

Ståhl, Ingemar. Sweden at the End of the Middle Way. **In** *Pejovich, S., ed.,* 1983, pp. 119–39. **[G: Sweden; OECD]**

Stern, Joel M. Optimality and Property Taxation: An Alternative Approach. **In** *Harriss, C. L., ed.,* 1983, pp. 204–07.

Stern, Nicholas. Tax Reform: Income Distribution, Government Revenue and Planning. *Indian Econ. Rev.,* January–June 1983, *18*(1), pp. 17–33. **[G: India]**

Stern, Nicholas. Taxation for Efficiency. **In** *Shepherd, D.; Turk, J. and Silberston, A., eds.,* 1983, pp. 77–107. **[G: OECD]**

Steuerle, Eugene. Building New Wealth by Preserving Old Wealth: Savings and Investment Tax Incentives in the Postwar Era. *Nat. Tax J.,* September 1983, *36*(3), pp. 307–19. **[G: U.S.]**

Steuerle, Eugene. The Tax Treatment of Households of Different Size. **In** *Penner, R. G., ed.,* 1983, pp. 73–97. **[G: U.S.]**

Stickney, Clyde P.; Weil, Roman L. and Wolfson, Mark A. Income Taxes and Tax-Transfer Leases: General Electric's Accounting for a Molotov Cocktail. *Accounting Rev.,* April 1983, *58*(2), pp. 439–59.

Stiegler, Harald. Assessment of the Expedience of Subsidies for the Restoration of Financial Soundness under Operational Analysis Aspects. *Rivista Int. Sci. Econ. Com.,* June 1983, *30*(6), pp. 531–39.

Stiglitz, Joseph E. National Savings, Economic Welfare, and the Structure of Taxation: Comment. **In** *Feldstein, M., ed.,* 1983, pp. 493–98. **[G: U.S.]**

Stiglitz, Joseph E. Some Aspects of the Taxation of Capital Gains. *J. Public Econ.,* July 1983, *21*(2), pp. 257–94.

Stretton, Hugh. Where Does Australia Stand? Discussion. **In** *Withers, G., ed.,* 1983, pp. 32–36.

Subrahmanyam, Ganti. Some Implications of the Popular Approach to Tax Elasticity Estimation. *Margin,* October 1983, *16*(1), pp. 30–36.

Subrahmanyam, Ganti and Kamaiah, Bandi. Administrative Costs and Tax Substitution: Some Econometric Evidence. *Public Finance,* 1983, *38*(2), pp. 282–92. **[G: India]**

Sukarya, Sutadi and Sutomo. Tax Avoidance/Tax Evasion: Indonesia. **In** *International Fiscal Association (II),* 1983, pp. 469–75. **[G: Indonesia]**

Sullivan, Sean and Gibson, Rosemary. Tax-related Issues in Health Care Market Reform. **In** *Meyer, J. A., ed.,* 1983, pp. 185–97. **[G: U.S.]**

Summers, Lawrence H. An Equity Case for Consumption Taxation. **In** *Walker, C. E. and Bloomfield, M. E., eds.,* 1983, pp. 257–60.

Sunley, Emil M. A Note on the Proposed Higher Education Tax Incentive. *Nat. Tax J.,* March, 1983, *36*(1), pp. 123–24. **[G: U.S.]**

Sunley, Emil M. Broadening the Tax Base through a Comprehensive Income Tax. **In** *Walker, C. E. and Bloomfield, M. E., eds.,* 1983, pp. 289–95. **[G: U.S.]**

Sutherland, Alister. The Taxation of Agricultural Wealth: Northfield and After. **In** *Field, F., ed.,* 1983, pp. 88–117. **[G: U.K.]**

Symms, Steven D. Political Reality and the Corporate Income Tax. **In** *Walker, C. E. and Bloomfield, M. E., eds.,* 1983, pp. 180–81.

Tait, Alan A. Net Wealth, Gift, and Transfer Taxes.

In *[Goode, R.]*, 1983, pp. 139–68. **[G: OECD]**

Tannenwald, Robert. Redistribution of Wealth in Conversion to a Flat Rate Tax. *New Eng. Econ. Rev.*, January/February 1983, pp. 5–17. **[G: U.S.]**

Tanzi, Vito. Expected Inflation and Interest Rates: Comment. *Amer. Econ. Rev.*, June 1983, *73*(3), pp. 501–02.

Tarullo, Daniel K. The MTN Subsidies Code: Agreement without Consensus. **In** *Rubin, S. J. and Hufbauer, G. C., eds.*, 1983, pp. 63–99. **[G: Global]**

Taylor, Amy K. and Wilensky, Gail R. The Effect of Tax Policies on Expenditures for Private Health Insurance. **In** *Meyer, J. A., ed.*, 1983, pp. 163–84. **[G: U.S.]**

Tepper, Irwin. Optimal Funding and Asset Allocation Rules for Defined-Benefit Pension Plans: Comment. **In** *Bodie, Z. and Shoven, J. B., eds.*, 1983, pp. 104–05. **[G: U.S.]**

Thillainathan, R. Discriminatory Allocation of Public Expenditure Benefits for Reducing Inter-racial Inequality in Malaysia—An Evaluation. **In** *Lim, D., ed.*, 1983, *1980*, pp. 23–40. **[G: Malaysia]**

Thirsk, Wayne R. Energy Policy, Taxation of Natural Resources and Fiscal Federalism: Comment. **In** *McLure, C. E., Jr., ed.*, 1983, pp. 148–49. **[G: U.S.]**

Thirsk, Wayne R. Fiscal Harmonization in the United States, Australia, West Germany, Switzerland, and the EEC. **In** *Trebilcock, M. J., et al., eds.*, 1983, pp. 424–55. **[G: OECD]**

Thirsk, Wayne R. Tax Assignment and Revenue Sharing in Canada. **In** *McLure, C. E., Jr., ed.*, 1983, pp. 234–50. **[G: Canada]**

Thirsk, Wayne R. Tax Harmonization in Canada. **In** *Break, G. F., ed.*, 1983, pp. 53–74. **[G: Canada]**

Tikka, Kari S. Tax Avoidance/Tax Evasion: Finland. **In** *International Fiscal Association (II)*, 1983, pp. 357–71. **[G: Finland]**

Tilbery, Henry. Indexation in the Brazilian Taxation System. **In** *de Ulhôa Canto, G.; da Silva Martins, I. G. and van Hoorn, J., Jr., eds.*, 1983, pp. 47–98. **[G: Brazil]**

Tisdell, Clem A. Public Finance and the Appropriation of Gains from International Tourists: Some Theory with ASEAN and Australian Illustrations. *Singapore Econ. Rev.*, April 1983, *28*(1), pp. 3–20. **[G: Australia; S. E. Asia]**

Titus, Varkey K. India: Revenue Performance of Agricultural Taxes during the Plan Periods. *Bull. Int. Fiscal Doc.*, December 1983, *37*(12), pp. 541–45. **[G: India]**

Tsingris, Demetrius. International Problems in the Field of General Taxes on Sales of Goods and Services: Greece. **In** *International Fiscal Association (I)*, 1983, pp. 413–24. **[G: Greece]**

Tsolakis, D. Taxation and Consumption of Wine. *Rev. Marketing Agr. Econ.*, August 1983, *51*(2), pp. 155–65. **[G: Australia]**

Tuccillo, John A. The Tax Treatment of Mortgage Investment. *Amer. Real Estate Urban Econ. Assoc. J.*, Summer 1983, *11*(2), pp. 288–99. **[G: U.S.]**

Tucker, S. N. An Analysis of Housing Subsidy Schemes in Australia. *Urban Stud.*, November 1983, *20*(4), pp. 439–53. **[G: Australia]**

Ture, Norman B. The Accelerated Cost Recovery System: An Evaluation of the 1981 and 1982 Cost Recovery Provisions. **In** *Walker, C. E. and Bloomfield, M. E., eds.*, 1983, pp. 47–76. **[G: U.S.]**

Uckmar, V. Tax Avoidance/Tax Evasion: General Report. **In** *International Fiscal Association (II)*, 1983, pp. 15–53. **[G: OECD]**

Ullman, Al. The Potential of the Value Added Tax. **In** *Walker, C. E. and Bloomfield, M. E., eds.*, 1983, pp. 225–27.

Van Regemorter, Denise. Les effectifs et les revenus de la catégorie des invalides en Belgique. (With English summary.) *Cah. Écon. Bruxelles*, 1983, *97*(1), pp. 104–14. **[G: Belgium]**

de Voil, Paul. International Problems in the Field of General Taxes on Sales of Goods and Services: United Kingdom. **In** *International Fiscal Association (I)*, 1983, pp. 561–71. **[G: U.K.]**

Wagner, Richard E. Estate Gift Duty and the Family: Prolegomena to a Theory of the Family Unit: Commentary. **In** *Penner, R. G., ed.*, 1983, pp. 127–33.

Wagner, Richard E. The Egalitarian Imperative. **In** *Letwin, W., ed.*, 1983, *1977*, pp. 297–312.

Wah, Leong Khai. Malaysia: Foreign Contractors: Section 107A of the Income Tax Act 1967. *Bull. Int. Fiscal Doc.*, December 1983, *37*(12), pp. 535–39. **[G: Malaysia]**

Wahby, Mandy J. Petroleum Taxation and Efficiency: The Canadian System in Question. *J. Energy Devel.*, Autumn 1983, *9*(1), pp. 111–27. **[G: Canada]**

Walker, Charls E. Tax Prospects: Implications of Budget Problems: Comments. *Nat. Tax J.*, September 1983, *36*(3), pp. 289–91. **[G: U.S.]**

Walsh, Carl E. Taxation of Interest Income, Deregulation and the Banking Industry. *J. Finance*, December 1983, *38*(5), pp. 1529–42. **[G: U.S.]**

Weicher, John C. Re-Evaluating Housing Policy Alternatives: What Do We Really Know? *Amer. Real Estate Urban Econ. Assoc. J.*, Spring 1983, *11*(1), pp. 1–10. **[G: U.S.]**

Weidenbaum, Murray L. Energy Development and U.S. Government Policy: Some Recommendations for Using Market Forces to Achieve Optimum National Goals. *Amer. J. Econ. Soc.*, July 1983, *42*(3), pp. 257–74. **[G: U.S.]**

Wetzler, James W. Proposals to Index Capital Gains. **In** *Walker, C. E. and Bloomfield, M. E., eds.*, 1983, pp. 154–57. **[G: U.S.]**

Whalley, John. The Impact of Federal Policies on Interprovincial Activity. **In** *Trebilcock, M. J., et al., eds.*, 1983, pp. 201–42. **[G: Canada]**

White, Richard A. Employee Preferences for Nontaxable Compensation Offered in a Cafeteria Compensation Plan: An Empirical Study. *Accounting Rev.*, July 1983, *58*(3), pp. 539–61. **[G: U.S.]**

Whiteman, Peter G. Consultation, Enactment and Interpretation of Legislation: The United Kingdom Approach. *Bull. Int. Fiscal Doc.*, December 1983, *37*(12), pp. 531–34. **[G: U.K.]**

Whitley, J. D. and Wilson, Robert A. The Macroeconomic Merits of a Marginal Employment Subsidy. *Econ. J.*, December 1983, *93*(372), pp. 862–80.

Wiegard, Wolfgang. Environmental Externalities

and Corrective Input and Output Taxes. *Atlantic Econ. J.*, March 1983, *11* (1), pp. 36–41.

Wilkins, John G. Priorities for the Reform of International Tax Policy. **In** *Walker, C. E. and Bloomfield, M. E., eds.*, 1983, pp. 357–59. **[G: U.S.]**

Willig, Robert D. Sector Differentiated Capital Taxation with Imperfect Competition and Inter-Industry Flows. *J. Public Econ.*, July 1983, *21* (2), pp. 295–316.

Willms, J. Douglas. Do Private Schools Produce Higher Levels of Academic Achievement? New Evidence for the Tuition Tax Credit Debate. **In** *James, T. and Levin, H. M., eds.*, 1983, pp. 223–31. **[G: U.S.]**

Wise, David A. Alternative Tax Treatments of the Family: Simulation Methodology and Results: Comment. **In** *Feldstein, M., ed.*, 1983, pp. 41–46. **[G: U.S.]**

Witt, Peter-Christian. Tax Policies, Tax Assessment and Inflation; Toward a Sociology of Public Finances in the German Inflation 1914–23. **In** *Schmukler, N. and Marcus, E., eds.*, 1983, pp. 450–72. **[G: Germany]**

Wright, L. Hart. Personal, Living or Family Matters and the Value Added Tax. *Mich. Law Rev.*, December 1983, *82* (3), pp. 419–30. **[G: U.S.]**

Yitzhaki, Shlomo. On Two Proposals to Promote Saving. *Public Finance Quart.*, July 1983, *11* (3), pp. 299–319. **[G: U.S.]**

Young, Robert A. Business and Budgeting: Recent Proposals for Reforming the Revenue Budgetary Process. *Can. Public Policy*, September 1983, *9*(3), pp. 347–61. **[G: Canada]**

Ysander, Bengt-Christer. Oil Prices and Economic Stability: The Macroeconomic Impact of Oil Price Shocks on the Swedish Economy. **In** *Eliasson, G.; Sharefkin, M. and Ysander, B.-C., eds.*, 1983, pp. 225–44. **[G: Sweden]**

Zimmerman, Jerold L. Taxes and Firm Size. *J. Acc. Econ.*, August 1983, *5*(2), pp. 119–49. **[G: U.S.]**

Zschau, Ed. Was the 1978 Capital Gains Tax Cut Successful? **In** *Walker, C. E. and Bloomfield, M. E., eds.*, 1983, pp. 157–59. **[G: U.S.]**

324 State and Local Government Finance

3240 General

Askew, Ian. The Location of Service Facilities in Rural Areas: A Model for Generating and Evaluating Alternative Solutions. *Reg. Stud.*, October 1983, *17*(5), pp. 305–13. **[G: U.K.]**

Baber, William R. Toward Understanding the Role of Auditing in the Public Sector. *J. Acc. Econ.*, December 1983, *5*(3), pp. 213–27. **[G: U.S.]**

Bahl, Roy. Strengthening the Fiscal Performance of Philippine Local Governments. **In** *Bahl, R. and Miller, B. D., eds.*, 1983, pp. 228–55. **[G: Philippines]**

Bahl, Roy and Schroeder, Larry. Intergovernmental Fiscal Relations. **In** *Bahl, R. and Miller, B. D., eds.*, 1983, pp. 100–139. **[G: Philippines]**

Bahl, Roy W. and Linn, Johannes F. The Assignment of Local Government Revenues in Developing Countries. **In** *McLure, C. E., Jr., ed.*, 1983, pp. 177–99. **[G: Selected LDCs]**

Bennett, R. J. A Model of Local Authority Fiscal Behavior: A Comment on the Paper by Cuthbertson, Foreman-Peck, and Gripaios. *Public Finance*, 1983, *38*(2), pp. 317–21. **[G: U.K.]**

Blewett, Robert A. Fiscal Externalities and Residential Growth Controls: A Theory-of-Clubs Perspective. *Public Finance Quart.*, January 1983, *11* (1), pp. 3–20.

Boadway, Robin and Flatters, Frank. Efficiency, Equity, and the Allocation of Resource Rents. **In** *McLure, C. E., Jr. and Mieszkowski, P., eds.*, 1983, pp. 99–123. **[G: Canada]**

Bös, Dieter. An Optimal Taxation Approach to Fiscal Federalism: Comment. **In** *McLure, C. E., Jr., ed.*, 1983, pp. 43–47.

Bradbury, Katharine L. Revenues and Expenditures in New England's Largest Cities and Towns. *New Eng. Econ. Rev.*, July–August 1983, pp. 42–53. **[G: U.S.]**

Bradbury, Katharine L. Structural Fiscal Distress in Cities—Causes and Consequences. *New Eng. Econ. Rev.*, January/February 1983, pp. 32–43. **[G: U.S.]**

Break, George F. State and Local Finance: The Pressure of the 1980s: Introduction. **In** *Break, G. F., ed.*, 1983, pp. 3–8. **[G: U.S.]**

Brecher, Charles and Horton, Raymond D. Setting Municipal Priorities, 1984: Introduction. **In** *Brecher, C. and Horton, R. D., eds.*, 1983, pp. 1–16. **[G: U.S.]**

Brennan, Geoffrey. Who Should Tax, Where and What? Comment. **In** *McLure, C. E., Jr., ed.*, 1983, pp. 20–23.

Brueckner, Jan K. Property Value Maximization and Public Sector Efficiency. *J. Urban Econ.*, July 1983, *14*(1), pp. 1–15.

Cason, Forrest M. Land-Use Concomitants of Urban Fiscal Squeeze. **In** *Carr, J. H. and Duensing, E. E., eds.*, 1983, *1981*, pp. 67–81. **[G: U.S.]**

Cebula, Richard J. and Avery, K. Leslie. The Tiebout Hypothesis in the United States: An Analysis of Black Consumer-Voters, 1970–75. *Public Choice*, 1983, *41* (2), pp. 307–10. **[G: U.S.]**

Cebula, Richard J. and Chevlin, Linda. Reply [Proposition 4, Tax Reduction Mirage: An Exploratory Note on Its Potential Spending and Tax Impacts]. *Amer. J. Econ. Soc.*, January 1983, *42* (1), pp. 122–24. **[G: U.S.]**

Courchene, Thomas J. Canada's New Equalization Program: Description and Evaluation. *Can. Public Policy*, December 1983, *9* (4), pp. 458–75. **[G: Canada]**

Courchene, Thomas J. Efficiency, Equity, and the Allocation of Resource Rents: Comments. **In** *McLure, C. E., Jr. and Mieszkowski, P., eds.*, 1983, pp. 125–33. **[G: Canada]**

Cushing, Brian J. and Straszheim, Mahlon R. Agglomeration Economies in the Public and Private Sector: Urban Spatial and Fiscal Structure. **In** *Quigley, J. M., ed.*, 1983, pp. 223–42. **[G: U.S.]**

Cuthbertson, K.; Foreman-Peck, J. and Gripaios, P. A Model of Local Authority Fiscal Behaviour: A Reply. *Public Finance*, 1983, *38* (2), pp. 322–25. **[G: U.K.]**

Dearborn, Philip M. The Growing State–Local Deficit Threat: Remarks. *Nat. Tax J.*, September 1983,

36(3), pp. 407–09. **[G: U.S.]**

Deaton, Brady J. New Institutional Arrangements for Supplying Local Public Services under New Federalism with Special Reference to Education. *Amer. J. Agr. Econ.*, December 1983, *65*(5), pp. 1124–30. **[G: U.S.]**

Fisher, Peter S. The Role of the Public Sector in Local Development Finance: Evaluating Alternative Institutional Arrangements. *J. Econ. Issues,* March 1983, *17*(1), pp. 133–53.

Fortune, Peter. A Test of the Cobb-Douglas Assumption for Local Governments. *Nat. Tax J.*, June 1983, *36*(2), pp. 233–36.

Frey, René L. and Leu, Robert E. Umverteilung über den Staatshaushalt: Die personnel Budgetinzidenz der Schweiz 1977. (Redistribution through the Public Sector: Personal Budget Incidence in Switzerland, 1977. With English summary.) *Schweiz. Z. Volkswirtsch. Statist.*, March 1983, *119*(1), pp. 1–21. **[G: Switzerland]**

Gandhi, Ved P. The Assignment of Local Government Revenues in Developing Countries: Comment. **In** *McLure, C. E., Jr., ed.*, 1983, pp. 200–202. **[G: Selected LDCs]**

Gold, Steven D. Recent Developments in State Finances. *Nat. Tax J.*, March, 1983, *36*(1), pp. 1–29. **[G: U.S.]**

Gordon, Roger H. An Optimal Taxation Approach to Fiscal Federalism. **In** *McLure, C. E., Jr., ed.*, 1983, pp. 26–42.

Greenberg, Joseph. Local Public Goods with Mobility: Existence and Optimality of a General Equilibrium. *J. Econ. Theory,* June 1983, *30*(1), pp. 17–33.

Grewal, Bhajan S. An Optimal Taxation Approach to Fiscal Federalism: Comment. **In** *McLure, C. E., Jr., ed.*, 1983, pp. 48–51.

Groenewegen, Peter D. The Fiscal Crisis of Australian Federalism. **In** *Patience, A. and Scott, J., eds.*, 1983, pp. 123–58. **[G: Australia]**

Hall, Arden R. and Smith, William D. The Financial Condition of Public Employee Pension Plans. **In** *Hirsch, W. Z., ed.*, 1983, pp. 247–73. **[G: U.S.]**

Hamilton, Bruce W. A Review: Is the Property Tax a Benefit Tax? **In** *Zodrow, G. R., ed.*, 1983, pp. 85–107.

Hamilton, Bruce W. The Flypaper Effect and Other Anomalies. *J. Public Econ.*, December 1983, *22*(3), pp. 347–61.

Hilley, John L. The Distributive Impact of Education Finance Reform. *Nat. Tax J.*, December 1983, *36*(4), pp. 503–09. **[G: U.S.]**

Hirsch, Werner Z. and Rufolo, Anthony M. Shirking, Monitoring Costs, and Municipal Labor Productivity. **In** *Hirsch, W. Z., ed.*, 1983, pp. 277–310.

Hoachlander, E. Gareth. Financing Public Education in the Wake of Federal and State Spending Cuts: Crisis and Opportunities. **In** *Lefcoe, G., ed.*, 1983, pp. 125–45. **[G: U.S.]**

Hochman, Harold M. and Nitzan, Shmuel. Tiebout and Sympathy. *Math. Soc. Sci.*, November 1983, *6*(2), pp. 195–214.

Hoffman, Joan. Urban Squeeze Plays: New York City Crises of the 1930s and 1970s. *Rev. Radical Polit. Econ.*, Summer 1983, *15*(2), pp. 29–57. **[G: U.S.]**

Holcombe, Randall G. and Zardkoohi, Asghar. On the Distribution of Federal Taxes and Expenditures, and the New War between the States. *Public Choice,* 1983, *40*(2), pp. 165–74. **[G: U.S.]**

Hulten, Charles R. and Robertson, James W. Labor Productivity in the Local Public Sector. **In** *Hirsch, W. Z., ed.*, 1983, pp. 342–88. **[G: U.S.]**

Hyde, John. Small Government and Social Equity: Discussion. **In** *Withers, G., ed.*, 1983, pp. 74–81. **[G: Australia]**

Jackson, Peter M. Urban Fiscal Stress in U.K. Cities. **In** *Biehl, D.; Roskamp, K. W. and Stolper, W. F., eds.*, 1983, pp. 329–47. **[G: U.K.]**

Jud, G. Donald. School Quality and Intra-Metropolitan Mobility: A Further Test of the Tiebout Hypothesis. *J. Behav. Econ.*, Winter 1983, *12*(2), pp. 37–55. **[G: U.S.]**

Jurion, Bernard J. A Theory of Public Services with Distance-Sensitive Utility. **In** *Thisse, J.-F. and Zoller, H. G., eds.*, 1983, pp. 95–116.

Kakabadse, Andrew. Bureaucracy and the Social Services: A Comparative Study of English Social Service Departments. *Int. J. Soc. Econ.*, 1983, *10*(5), pp. 3–13. **[G: U.K.]**

Kimbell, Larry J. and Shulman, David. Reaganomics: Implications for California Governments. **In** *Lefcoe, G., ed.*, 1983, pp. 3–14. **[G: U.S.]**

Kirkland, Kenneth J. "Creative Accounting" and Short-Term Debt: State Responses to the Deficit Threat. *Nat. Tax J.*, September 1983, *36*(3), pp. 395–99. **[G: U.S.]**

Kristensen, Ole P. Public versus Private Provision of Governmental Services: The Case of Danish Fire Protection Services. *Urban Stud.*, February 1983, *20*(1), pp. 1–9. **[G: Denmark]**

Ladd, Helen F. and Wilson, Julie Boatright. Who Supports Tax Limitations: Evidence from Massachusetts' Proposition 2½ *J. Policy Anal. Manage.*, Winter 1983, *2*(2), pp. 256–79. **[G: U.S.]**

Levin, David J. Receipts and Expenditures of State Governments and of Local Governments, 1968–81. *Surv. Curr. Bus.*, May 1983, *63*(5), pp. 25–38. **[G: U.S.]**

Levin, David J. State and Local Government Fiscal Position in 1982. *Surv. Curr. Bus.*, January 1983, *63*(1), pp. 19–22. **[G: U.S.]**

Levine, Charles H.; Rubin, Irene S. and Wolohojian, George C. Fiscal Stress and Local Government Adaptations: Toward a Multi-stage Theory of Retrenchment. **In** *Henderson, J. V., ed.*, 1983, pp. 253–303. **[G: U.S.]**

Lewis, W. Arthur. Patterns of Public Revenue and Expenditure. **In** *Lewis, W. A.*, 1983, *1956,* pp. 573–614. **[G: LDCs; MDCs]**

Litvak, Lawrence and Daniels, Belden. Innovations in Development Finance. **In** *Barker, M., ed. (I),* 1983, pp. 1–158. **[G: U.S.]**

Løtz, Jorgen R. The Role of Local Government Taxation: The Tiebout Effect and Equalization. **In** *[Goode, R.],* 1983, pp. 279–93.

McDowell, George R. Local Services in the New Federalism: Discussion. *Amer. J. Agr. Econ.*, December 1983, *65*(5), pp. 1133–35. **[G: U.S.]**

McGuire, Therese. Firm Location in a Tiebout World. *J. Reg. Sci.*, May 1983, *23*(2), pp. 211–22.

Miller, Gerald H. The Growing State–Local Deficit

Threat: Remarks. *Nat. Tax J.*, September 1983, *36*(3), pp. 383–93. **[G: U.S.]**

Montgomery, John D. When Local Participation Helps. *J. Policy Anal. Manage.*, Fall 1983, *3*(1), pp. 90–105. **[G: Selected LDCs]**

Munnell, Alicia H. The Pitfalls of Social Investing: The Case of Public Pensions and Housing. *New Eng. Econ. Rev.*, September/October 1983, pp. 20–41. **[G: U.S.]**

Musgrave, Richard A. Who Should Tax, Where, and What? **In** *McLure, C. E., Jr., ed.*, 1983, pp. 2–19.

Nice, David C. Representation in the States: Policymaking and Ideology. *Soc. Sci. Quart.*, June 1983, *64*(2), pp. 404–11. **[G: U.S.]**

Nowotny, Ewald. Who Should Tax, Where and What? Comment. **In** *McLure, C. E., Jr., ed.*, 1983, pp. 24–25.

Oakland, William H. Income Redistribution in a Federal System. **In** *Zodrow, G. R., ed.*, 1983, pp. 131–43.

Ostrosky, Anthony L. and Renas, Stephen M. Proposition 4, Tax Reduction Mirage: A Comment on the Cebular–Chevlin Attempt to Estimate Its Potential Impacts. *Amer. J. Econ. Soc.*, January 1983, *42*(1), pp. 121–22. **[G: U.S.]**

Palumbo, George. City Government Expenditures and City Government Reality: A Comment on Sjoquist. *Nat. Tax J.*, June 1983, *36*(2), pp. 249–51. **[G: U.S.]**

Pestieau, Pierre. Fiscal Mobility and Local Public Goods: A Survey of the Empirical and Theoretical Studies of the Tiebout Model. **In** *Thisse, J.-F. and Zoller, H. G., eds.*, 1983, pp. 11–41.

Petersen, John. The Growing State–Local Deficit Threat. *Nat. Tax J.*, September 1983, *36*(3), pp. 411–14. **[G: U.S.]**

Plaut, Thomas R. and Pluta, Joseph E. Business Climate, Taxes and Expenditures, and State Industrial Growth in the United States. *Southern Econ. J.*, July 1983, *50*(1), pp. 99–119. **[G: U.S.]**

Poole, Robert W., Jr. Objections to Privatization. *Policy Rev.*, Spring 1983, (24), pp. 105–19. **[G: U.S.]**

Raffa, Frederick A. and Haulman, Clyde A. The Impact of a PSE Program on Employment and Participants. *Growth Change*, October 1983, *14*(4), pp. 14–21. **[G: U.S.]**

Rose-Ackerman, Susan. Beyond Tiebout: Modeling the Political Economy of Local Government. **In** *Zodrow, G. R., ed.*, 1983, pp. 55–83.

Rose-Ackerman, Susan. Tiebout Models and the Competitive Ideal: An Essay on the Political Economy of Local Government. **In** *Quigley, J. M., ed.*, 1983, pp. 23–46.

Sardy, Hyman. The Economic Impact of Inflation on Urban Areas. **In** *Schmukler, N. and Marcus, E., eds.*, 1983, pp. 312–25. **[G: U.S.]**

Schweizer, Urs. Edgeworth and the Henry George Theorem: How to Finance Local Public Projects. **In** *Thisse, J.-F. and Zoller, H. G., eds.*, 1983, pp. 79–93.

Shannon, John. Austerity Federalism—The State–Local Response. *Nat. Tax J.*, September 1983, *36*(3), pp. 377–82. **[G: U.S.]**

Sjoquist, David L. Reply and Comment on Palumbo [The Effect of the Number of Local Governments on Central City Expenditures]. *Nat. Tax J.*, June 1983, *36*(2), pp. 253–54. **[G: U.S.]**

Skaperdas, Peter D. State and Local Governments: An Assessment of Their Financial Position and Fiscal Policies. *Fed. Res. Bank New York Quart. Rev.*, Winter 1983-84, *8*(4), pp. 1–13. **[G: U.S.]**

Slack, N. Enid and Bird, Richard M. Local Response to Intergovernmental Fiscal Transfers: The Case of Colombia. *Public Finance*, 1983, *38*(3), pp. 429–39. **[G: Colombia]**

Smith, Robert S. Salaries and Pension Funding: Are Public Safety Officers Given Preference over Taxpayers? **In** *Hirsch, W. Z., ed.*, 1983, pp. 188–211. **[G: U.S.]**

Sonstelie, Jon C. The Public Finance of Education: Subsidy versus Supply. **In** *Break, G. F., ed.*, 1983, pp. 161–82. **[G: U.S.]**

Stahl, Konrad and Varaiya, Pravin. Local Collective Goods: A Critical Re-examination of the Tiebout Model. **In** *Thisse, J.-F. and Zoller, H. G., eds.*, 1983, pp. 43–53.

Starrett, David A. Welfare Measures Based on Capitalization: A Unified General Treatment. **In** *Henderson, J. V., ed.*, 1983, pp. 117–35.

Stiglitz, Joseph E. The Theory of Local Public Goods Twenty-Five Years after Tiebout: A Perspective. **In** *Zodrow, G. R., ed.*, 1983, pp. 17–53.

Straszheim, Mahlon R. Public Sector Capitalization Models with Heterogeneous Housing Stocks. **In** *Henderson, J. V., ed.*, 1983, pp. 137–63.

Swales, J. K. Understanding the Scottish Economy: Government Expenditure and Revenues. **In** *Ingham, K. P. D. and Love, J., eds.*, 1983, pp. 163–72. **[G: U.K.]**

Trebilcock, Michael J., et al. Provincially Induced Barriers to Trade in Canada: A Survey. **In** *Trebilcock, M. J., et al., eds.*, 1983, pp. 243–351. **[G: Canada]**

Vaughan, Roger J. Economists, Economics, and State Economic Policy. *Amer. Econ. Rev.*, May 1983, *73*(2), pp. 169–71. **[G: U.S.]**

Vaughan, Roger J. Inflation and Unemployment Surviving the 1980s. **In** *Barker, M., ed. (II)*, 1983, pp. 93–247. **[G: U.S.]**

Wildasin, David E. The Welfare Effects of Intergovernmental Grants in an Economy with Independent Jurisdictions. *J. Urban Econ.*, March 1983, *13*(2), pp. 147–64.

Wilenski, P. S. Small Government and Social Equity. **In** *Withers, G., ed.*, 1983, pp. 37–73. **[G: Australia]**

Zimmerman, Dennis. Resource Misallocation from Interstate Tax Exportation: Estimates of Excess Spending and Welfare Loss in a Median Voter Framework. *Nat. Tax J.*, June 1983, *36*(2), pp. 183–201. **[G: U.S.]**

Zodrow, George R. The Tiebout Model after Twenty-five Years: An Overview. **In** *Zodrow, G. R., ed.*, 1983, pp. 1–15.

3241 State and Local Government Expenditures and Budgeting

Amberg, Stephen. Springfield: Cut First, Restore Later. **In** *Susskind, L. E. and Serio, J. F., eds.*,

1983, pp. 239–51. [G: U.S.]

Ansari, M. M. Variations in Plan Expenditure and Physical Achievement among the Indian States: An Empirical Analysis. *Margin,* April 1983, *15*(3), pp. 49–58. [G: India]

Auld, D. A. L. The Ontario Budget Deficit: A Cause for Concern? **In** *Conklin, D. W. and Courchene, T. J., eds.,* 1983, pp. 78–106. [G: Canada]

Bahl, Roy and Schroeder, Larry. Local Government Structure, Financial Management, and Fiscal Conditions. **In** *Bahl, R. and Miller, B. D., eds.,* 1983, pp. 1–45. [G: Philippines]

Botner, Stanley B. Revenue Limitation—Missouri Style. *Public Budg. Finance,* Winter 1983, *3*(4), pp. 23–27. [G: U.S.]

Bradbury, Katharine L.; Ladd, Helen F. and Christopherson, Claire. The Initial Impacts on State and Local Finances. **In** *Susskind, L. E. and Serio, J. F., eds.,* 1983, pp. 293–324. [G: U.S.]

Brecher, Charles and Horton, Raymond D. Expenditures. **In** *Brecher, C. and Horton, R. D., eds.,* 1983, pp. 68–96. [G: U.S.]

Brown, Byron W. and Saks, Daniel H. Spending for Local Public Education: Income Distribution and the Aggregation of Private Demands. *Public Finance Quart.,* January 1983, *11*(1), pp. 21–45. [G: U.S.]

Buglione, Enrico and France, George. Skewed Fiscal Federalism in Italy: Implications for Public Expenditure Control. *Public Budg. Finance,* Autumn 1983, *3*(3), pp. 43–63. [G: Italy]

Campbell, Thomas. Arlington: Setting Budget Priorities. **In** *Susskind, L. E. and Serio, J. F., eds.,* 1983, pp. 113–27. [G: U.S.]

Colon, Melvyn. Amesbury: Linking Salaries to State Aid. **In** *Susskind, L. E. and Serio, J. F., eds.,* 1983, pp. 107–12. [G: U.S.]

Colon, Melvyn. Bridgewater: Drawing the Lines for a Budget Battle. **In** *Susskind, L. E. and Serio, J. F., eds.,* 1983, pp. 129–40. [G: U.S.]

Cutt, James. The Evolution of Expenditure Budgeting in Australia. *Public Budg. Finance,* Summer 1983, *3*(2), pp. 7–27. [G: Australia]

Dean, James M. Public Good Benefits and Interdependence. *Econ. Notes,* 1983, (1), pp. 130–34.

Dowall, David E. The Effects of Tax and Expenditure Limitations on Local Land Use Policies. **In** *Quigley, J. M., ed.,* 1983, pp. 69–87. [G: U.S.]

Edwards, A. R. Decentralization of Arts Subsidy for Orchestra and Theater in the Netherlands. *J. Cult. Econ.,* June 1983, *7*(1), pp. 83–94. [G: Netherlands]

Flatt, William P. Financing Agricultural Research and Education in a Period of Tight Budgets. *Southern J. Agr. Econ.,* July 1983, *15*(1), pp. 11–17. [G: U.S.]

Giertz, J. Fred. State–Local Centralization and Income: A Theoretical Framework and Further Empirical Results. *Public Finance,* 1983, *38*(3), pp. 398–408. [G: U.S.]

Gold, Steven D. Results of Local Spending and Revenue Limitations: A Survey. **In** *Quigley, J. M., ed.,* 1983, pp. 109–47. [G: U.S.]

Gordon, Roger H. and Slemrod, Joel. A General Equilibrium Simulation Study of Subsidies to Municipal Expenditures. *J. Finance,* May 1983, *38*(2), pp. 585–94. [G: U.S.]

Gould, Frank. The Development of Public Expenditures in Western, Industrialised Countries: A Comparative Analysis. *Public Finance,* 1983, *38*(1), pp. 38–69. [G: OECD]

Green, Cynthia B. and Sanger, Mary Bryna. Aiding the Poor. **In** *Brecher, C. and Horton, R. D., eds.,* 1983, pp. 99–130. [G: U.S.]

Greiner, John M. and Hatry, Harry P. Coping with Cutbacks: Responses in 17 Local Governments. **In** *Susskind, L. E. and Serio, J. F., eds.,* 1983, pp. 373–475. [G: U.S.]

Greytak, David and Diokno, Benjamin. Local Government Public Enterprises. **In** *Bahl, R. and Miller, B. D., eds.,* 1983, pp. 140–87. [G: Philippines]

Grosskopf, Shawna P. and Hayes, Kathy. Do Local Governments Maximize Anything? *Public Finance Quart.,* April 1983, *11*(2), pp. 202–16. [G: U.S.]

Grosskopf, Shawna P.; Hayes, Kathy and Sivan, David. Municipal Pensions, Funding and Wage Capitalization. *Nat. Tax J.,* March, 1983, *36*(1), pp. 115–21. [G: U.S.]

Hansen, Derek. Banking and Small Business. **In** *Barker, M., ed. (I),* 1983, pp. 359–473.

Hawkins, Sue C. SSI: Trends in State Supplementation, 1979–81. *Soc. Sec. Bull.,* June 1983, *46*(6), pp. 3–8. [G: U.S.]

Hirsch, Werner Z. California's Revenue Limitation Measure and Its Side Effects. **In** *Quigley, J. M., ed.,* 1983, pp. 49–67. [G: U.S.]

Hoggan, Daniel H.; Bagley, Jay M. and Kimball, Kirk R. Inadvertent Income Redistribution Effects of State Water Development Financing. *Growth Change,* October 1983, *14*(4), pp. 32–36. [G: U.S.]

Holcombe, Randall G. and Zardkoohi, Asghar. The Effect of Macroeconomic Variables on State and Local Government Expenditures. *Atlantic Econ. J.,* December 1983, *11*(4), pp. 34–41. [G: U.S.]

Irvine, Ian J. and Smith, J. Barry. The Estimation of Local Government Expenditure Responses to Inter-Governmental Transfers. *Rev. Econ. Statist.,* August 1983, *65*(3), pp. 534–36. [G: U.S.]

Kelley, Joseph T. NCGA's Budgetary Reporting in State and Local Governments. *Public Budg. Finance,* Spring 1983, *3*(1), pp. 116–18. [G: U.S.]

Kim, Karl E. Impacts on Municipal Appropriation Levels. **In** *Susskind, L. E. and Serio, J. F., eds.,* 1983, pp. 357–71. [G: U.S.]

Kloten, Norbert and Ketterer, K. H. Fiscal Policy in West Germany: Anticyclical versus Expenditure-reducing Policies. **In** *[Saunders, C. T.],* 1983, pp. 291–307. [G: W. Germany]

Laing, Andrew. Burlington: A Worst Case Scenario. **In** *Susskind, L. E. and Serio, J. F., eds.,* 1983, pp. 141–48. [G: U.S.]

Laing, Andrew. Marshfield: Budget Cutting, a Joint Effort. **In** *Susskind, L. E. and Serio, J. F., eds.,* 1983, pp. 193–202. [G: U.S.]

Laing, Andrew. Wayland: Dealing with Uncertainty. **In** *Susskind, L. E. and Serio, J. F., eds.,* 1983, pp. 253–60. [G: U.S.]

Lowery, David. The Hidden Impact of Fiscal Caps: Implications of the Beck Phenomenon. *Public*

Budg. Finance, Autumn 1983, *3*(3), pp. 19–32. [G: U.S.]

Martinez-Vazquez, Jorge. Renters' Illusion or Savvy? *Public Finance Quart.,* April 1983, *11*(2), pp. 237–47. [G: U.S.]

Megdal, Sharon Bernstein. The Determination of Local Public Expenditures and the Principal and Agent Relation: A Case Study. *Public Choice,* 1983, *40*(1), pp. 71–87. [G: U.S.]

Mieszkowski, Peter and Stein, Robert M. Trends and Prospects in State and Local Finance. *J. Urban Econ.,* September 1983, *14*(2), pp. 224–41. [G: U.S.]

Mollenkopf, John. Economic Development. **In** *Brecher, C. and Horton, R. D., eds.,* 1983, pp. 131–57. [G: U.S.]

Netzer, Dick. Privatization. **In** *Brecher, C. and Horton, R. D., eds.,* 1983, pp. 158–87. [G: U.S.]

Nord, Stephen. On the Determinants of Public Education Expenditures. *Amer. Econ.,* Fall 1983, *27*(2), pp. 21–28. [G: U.S.]

Ott, Attiat F. The Effect of Inflation on the Balance Sheet of the State–Local Sector. **In** *Break, G. F., ed.,* 1983, pp. 11–28. [G: U.S.]

Perles, Susan P. Impact of CETA-PSE on Local Public Sector Employment Expenditures. **In** *Hirsch, W. Z., ed.,* 1983, pp. 122–57. [G: U.S.]

Peterson, George E. Rebuilding Public Infrastructure: The Institutional Choices. **In** *Lefcoe, G., ed.,* 1983, pp. 109–23. [G: U.S.]

Raimondo, Henry J. State Limitations on Local Taxing and Spending: Theory and Practice. *Public Budg. Finance,* Autumn 1983, *3*(3), pp. 33–42. [G: U.S.]

Romer, Thomas and Rosenthal, Howard. Voting and Spending: Some Empirical Relationships in the Political Economy of Local Public Finance. **In** *Zodrow, G. R., ed.,* 1983, pp. 165–83. [G: U.S.]

Rubin, Jerome. Quincy: Schools Take a Big Cut. **In** *Susskind, L. E. and Serio, J. F., eds.,* 1983, pp. 203–15. [G: U.S.]

Rubin, Jerome. Salem: Controversy over Cuts. **In** *Susskind, L. E. and Serio, J. F., eds.,* 1983, pp. 217–30. [G: U.S.]

Rubin, Jerome and Campbell, Thomas. Chelsea: A Mayor Proposes. **In** *Susskind, L. E. and Serio, J. F., eds.,* 1983, pp. 171–80. [G: U.S.]

Schneider, Friedrich and Pommerehne, Werner W. Macroeconomia della crescita in disequilibrio e settore pubblico in espansione: il peso delle differenze istituzionali. (The Macroeconomics of Unbalanced Growth and the Expanding Public Sector: The Influence of Institutional Differences. With English summary.) *Rivista Int. Sci. Econ. Com.,* April-May 1983, *30*(4–5), pp. 306–19. [G: Switzerland]

Sonstelie, Jon C. The Public Finance of Education: Subsidy versus Supply. **In** *Break, G. F., ed.,* 1983, pp. 161–82. [G: U.S.]

Stinson, Thomas F. and Larson, Ronald B. A Poverty of Government Services: Estimates 1962, 1972, 1977. **In** *Goldstein, R. and Sachs, S. M., eds.,* 1983, pp. 102–14. [G: U.S.]

Stoevener, Herbert H. Financing Agricultural Research and Education in a Period of Tight Budgets: Discussion. *Southern J. Agr. Econ.,* July 1983, *15*(1), pp. 19–20. [G: U.S.]

Street, Andrew. Local Authority Capital Spending on Roads and Its Financing. *Nat. Westminster Bank Quart. Rev.,* November 1983, pp. 48–57. [G: U.K.]

Susskind, Lawrence and Horan, Cynthia. Understanding How and Why the Most Drastic Cuts Were Avoided. **In** *Susskind, L. E. and Serio, J. F., eds.,* 1983, pp. 263–91. [G: U.S.]

Tummala, Krishna K. and Wessel, Marilyn F. Budgeting by the Ballot: Initiatives in the State of Montana. *Public Budg. Finance,* Spring 1983, *3*(1), pp. 66–82. [G: U.S.]

Van Horn, Carl E. and Raimondo, Henry J. Living with Less: New Jersey Copes with Federal Aid Cutbacks. *Public Budg. Finance,* Spring 1983, *3*(1), pp. 41–56. [G: U.S.]

White, W. R. The Ontario Budget Deficit: A Cause for Concern? Comment. **In** *Conklin, D. W. and Courchene, T. J., eds.,* 1983, pp. 107–13. [G: Canada]

Wilson, Earl R. Fiscal Performance and Municipal Bond Borrowing Costs. *Public Budg. Finance,* Winter 1983, *3*(4), pp. 28–41. [G: U.S.]

3242 State and Local Government Taxation, Subsidies, and Revenue

Acheson, Keith. The Pricing Practices of the Liquor Control Board of Ontario: Reconsidered. *Can. J. Econ.,* February 1983, *16*(1), pp. 161–66. [G: Canada]

Alt, Christopher B.; Baumann, Michael G. and Zimmerman, Martin B. The Economics of Western Coal Severance Taxes. *J. Bus.,* October 1983, *56*(4), pp. 519–36. [G: U.S.]

Althaus, Paul G. and Schachter, Joseph. Interstate Migration and the New Federalism. *Soc. Sci. Quart.,* March 1983, *64*(1), pp. 35–45. [G: U.S.]

Bahl, Roy and Schroeder, Larry. Local Government Structure, Financial Management, and Fiscal Conditions. **In** *Bahl, R. and Miller, B. D., eds.,* 1983, pp. 1–45. [G: Philippines]

Bahl, Roy and Schroeder, Larry. The Business License Tax. **In** *Bahl, R. and Miller, B. D., eds.,* 1983, pp. 82–99. [G: Philippines]

Bahl, Roy and Schroeder, Larry. The Real Property Tax. **In** *Bahl, R. and Miller, B. D., eds.,* 1983, pp. 46–81. [G: Philippines; Selected LDCs]

Bahl, Roy W. State Energy Revenues: Comments. **In** *McLure, C. E., Jr. and Mieszkowski, P., eds.,* 1983, pp. 61–63. [G: U.S.]

Barnett, Richard R. The Effect of Matching Grants on Local Authority User Charges: A Critique of the Gibson Model. *Public Finance,* 1983, *38*(1), pp. 163–69. [G: U.K.]

Behrens, John O. The General Nature of "the" Property Tax Today. **In** *Harriss, C. L., ed.,* 1983, pp. 14–30. [G: U.S.]

Bennett, R. J. Alternative Local Government Taxes in Britain. *Reg. Stud.,* December 1983, *17*(6), pp. 478–81. [G: U.K.]

Berger, Curtis J. Controlling Urban Growth via Tax Policy. **In** *Carr, J. H. and Duensing, E. E., eds.,* 1983, *1979*, pp. 254–74. [G: U.S.]

Bird, Richard M. and Slack, N. Enid. Urban Finance

and User Charges. In *Break, G. F., ed.*, 1983, pp. 211–37. [G: U.S.; Canada]

Bloom, Howard S.; Ladd, Helen F. and Yinger, John. Are Property Taxes Capitalized into House Values? In *Zodrow, G. R., ed.*, 1983, pp. 145–63. [G: U.S.]

Bös, Dieter. Tax Assignment and Revenue Sharing in the Federal Republic of Germany and Switzerland: Comment. In *McLure, C. E., Jr., ed.*, 1983, pp. 289–92. [G: Switzerland; W. Germany]

Bowman, John H. and Mikesell, John L. Recent Changes in State Gasoline Taxation: An Analysis of Structure and Rates. *Nat. Tax J.*, June 1983, *36*(2), pp. 163–82. [G: U.S.]

Bradbury, Katharine L.; Ladd, Helen F. and Christopherson, Claire. The Initial Impacts on State and Local Finances. In *Susskind, L. E. and Serio, J. F., eds.*, 1983, pp. 293–324. [G: U.S.]

Brennan, Geoffrey. Tax Effectiveness and Tax Equity in Federal Countries: Comment. In *McLure, C. E., Jr., ed.*, 1983, pp. 87–93. [G: MDCs]

Brown, Malcolm C. Tax Assignment and Revenue Sharing in Canada: Comment. In *McLure, C. E., Jr., ed.*, 1983, pp. 251–56. [G: Canada]

Brueckner, Jan K. Central-City Income Redistribution and the Flight to the Suburbs: A Stylized Model. *Reg. Sci. Urban Econ.*, May 1983, *13*(2), pp. 177–93.

Campbell, Thomas. Framingham: Gambling on Revaluation. In *Susskind, L. E. and Serio, J. F., eds.*, 1983, pp. 181–91. [G: U.S.]

Charney, Alberta H. Intraurban Manufacturing Location Decisions and Local Tax Differentials. *J. Urban Econ.*, September 1983, *14*(2), pp. 184–205. [G: U.S.]

Chernick, Howard and Reschovsky, Andrew. Tax Policies for Managing Urban Decline: A Microsimulation Approach. In *Henderson, J. V., ed.*, 1983, pp. 217–51. [G: U.S.]

Chernick, Howard and Reschovsky, Andrew. The Consequences of Limitations on Growth in the Property Tax Base. In *Quigley, J. M., ed.*, 1983, pp. 89–107. [G: U.S.]

Christopher, Anthony. Rates and the Distribution of Income: Fact and Fantasy. In *Field, F., ed.*, 1983, pp. 118–37. [G: U.K.]

Church, Albert M. Taxation of Energy Resources: Comments. In *McLure, C. E., Jr. and Mieszkowski, P., eds.*, 1983, pp. 93–98. [G: U.S.]

Cline, Robert J. and Shannon, John. The Property Tax in a Model State–Local Revenue System. In *Harriss, C. L., ed.*, 1983, pp. 42–56. [G: U.S.]

Cnossen, Sijbren. Harmonization of Indirect Taxes in the EEC. In *McLure, C. E., Jr., ed.*, 1983, pp. 150–68. [G: EEC]

Coffin, Donald A. and Nelson, Michael A. An Empirical Test: The Economic Effects of Land Value Taxation—Comment. *Growth Change*, July 1983, *14*(3), pp. 44–46. [G: U.S.]

Colon, Melvyn. Sandwich: Selectmen Take the Lead. In *Susskind, L. E. and Serio, J. F., eds.*, 1983, pp. 231–38. [G: U.S.]

Conard, Rebecca. Suburban Encroachment on the Old North 40: The Search for Effective Measures to Preserve Agricultural Land. *Amer. J. Econ. Soc.*, April 1983, *42*(2), pp. 193–208. [G: U.S.]

Cord, Steven B. Taxing Land More Than Buildings: The Record in Pennsylvania. In *Harriss, C. L., ed.*, 1983, pp. 172–79. [G: U.S.]

Corusy, Paul V. Improving the Administration of the Property Tax. In *Harriss, C. L., ed.*, 1983, pp. 86–94. [G: U.S.]

Coughlan, Patrick C. Financing Alternatives Available to Local Governments. In *Lefcoe, G., ed.*, 1983, pp. 147–57. [G: U.S.]

Cuciti, Peggy; Galper, Harvey and Lucke, Robert. State Energy Revenues. In *McLure, C. E., Jr. and Mieszkowski, P., eds.*, 1983, pp. 11–60. [G: U.S.]

Cwi, David. Arts Councils as Public Agencies: The Policy Impact of Mission, Role and Operations. In *Hendon, W. S. and Shanahan, J. L., eds.*, 1983, pp. 38–46. [G: U.S.]

Davis, Russell; Wilen, James E. and Jergovic, Rosemarie. Oil and Gas Royalty Recovery Policy on Federal and Indian Lands. *Natural Res. J.*, April 1983, *23*(2), pp. 391–416. [G: U.S.]

Davis, Russell; Wilen, James E. and Jergovic, Rosemarie. Royalty Management in the New Minerals Management Service: A Reply to Sant, Haspel, and Boldt. *Natural Res. J.*, April 1983, *23*(2), pp. 435–39. [G: U.S.]

Davis, Sherry Tvedt. A Brief History of Proposition 2½ In *Susskind, L. E. and Serio, J. F., eds.*, 1983, pp. 3–9. [G: U.S.]

Dowall, David E. The Effects of Tax and Expenditure Limitations on Local Land Use Policies. In *Quigley, J. M., ed.*, 1983, pp. 69–87. [G: U.S.]

Downing, Paul B. and Frank, James E. Recreational Impact Fees: Characteristics and Current Usage. *Nat. Tax J.*, December 1983, *36*(4), pp. 477–90. [G: U.S.]

Drennan, Matthew. The Local Economy and Local Revenues. In *Brecher, C. and Horton, R. D., eds.*, 1983, pp. 19–44. [G: U.S.]

Due, John F. The Retail Sales Tax: The United States Experience. In *[Goode, R.]*, 1983, pp. 217–41. [G: Canada; U.S.]

Eckart, Wolfgang. The Neutrality of Land Taxation in an Uncertain World. *Nat. Tax J.*, June 1983, *36*(2), pp. 237–41.

Eisinger, Peter K. Municipal Residency Requirements and the Local Economy. *Soc. Sci. Quart.*, March 1983, *64*(1), pp. 85–96. [G: U.S.]

Ellis, Larry V.; Combs, J. Paul and Weber, William. Administrative Inequity in the Property Tax: Further Evidence. *Public Finance Quart.*, October 1983, *11*(4), pp. 491–506. [G: U.S.]

Emerson, Craig and Lloyd, Peter J. Improving Mineral Taxation Policy in Australia. *Econ. Rec.*, September 1983, *59*(166), pp. 232–44. [G: Australia]

Frankena, Mark W. The Efficiency of Public Transport Objectives and Subsidy Formulas. *J. Transp. Econ. Policy*, January 1983, *17*(1), pp. 67–76.

Gaffney, Mason. Tax Exporting and the Commerce Clause: Comments. In *McLure, C. E., Jr. and Mieszkowski, P., eds.*, 1983, pp. 199–203. [G: U.S.]

Gandhi, Ved P. Tax Assignment and Revenue Sharing in Brazil, India, Malaysia, and Nigeria. In *McLure, C. E., Jr., ed.*, 1983, pp. 328–59. [G: Brazil; India; Malaysia; Nigeria]

Garnaut, Ross. Energy Policy, Taxation of Natural Resources and Fiscal Federalism: Comment. **In** *McLure, C. E., Jr., ed.*, 1983, pp. 146–47.

Geiogue, Harold E. Tax Limitation Measures: Their Impact in California. **In** *Levin, H. M. and Schütze, H. G., eds.*, 1983, pp. 203–24. **[G: U.S.]**

Gibson, J. G. The Effect of Matching Grants on Local Authority User Charges: Some Further Results. *Public Finance*, 1983, *38*(1), pp. 170–75. **[G: U.K.]**

Gold, Steven D. Circuit-breakers and Other Relief Measures. **In** *Harriss, C. L., ed.*, 1983, pp. 148–57. **[G: U.S.]**

Gold, Steven D. Results of Local Spending and Revenue Limitations: A Survey. **In** *Quigley, J. M., ed.*, 1983, pp. 109–47. **[G: U.S.]**

Goodman, Allen C. Capitalization of Property Tax Differentials within and among Municipalities. *Land Econ.*, May 1983, *59*(2), pp. 211–19. **[G: U.S.]**

Gordon, Roger H. and Slemrod, Joel. A General Equilibrium Simulation Study of Subsidies to Municipal Expenditures. *J. Finance*, May 1983, *38*(2), pp. 585–94. **[G: U.S.]**

Grewal, Bhajan S. Tax Assignment and Revenue Sharing in Brazil, India, Malaysia, and Nigeria: Comment. **In** *McLure, C. E., Jr., ed.*, 1983, pp. 362–63. **[G: Brazil; India; Malaysia; Nigeria]**

Groenewegen, Peter D. Tax Assignment and Revenue Sharing in Australia. **In** *McLure, C. E., Jr., ed.*, 1983, pp. 293–318. **[G: Australia]**

Groenewegen, Peter D. Tax Assignment and Revenue Sharing in Australia: Reply. **In** *McLure, C. E., Jr., ed.*, 1983, pp. 327. **[G: Australia]**

Hamilton, Bruce W. A Review: Is the Property Tax a Benefit Tax? **In** *Zodrow, G. R., ed.*, 1983, pp. 85–107.

Harris, William T. Property Tax Circuit-Breakers: Good Causes but Bad Economics. *Amer. J. Econ. Soc.*, April 1983, *42*(2), pp. 209–16. **[G: U.S.]**

Harriss, C. Lowell. Taxation and the Economic Health of Regulated Utilities in a World of Inflation: Selected Elements. **In** *[Bonbright, J. C.]*, 1983, pp. 227–33.

Hayton, K. Community Business in Scotland. *Reg. Stud.*, June 1983, *17*(3), pp. 204–08. **[G: U.K.]**

Head, John G. Tax Assignment and Revenue Sharing in Canada: Comment. **In** *McLure, C. E., Jr., ed.*, 1983, pp. 257–59. **[G: Canada]**

Head, John G. Tax Assignment and Revenue Sharing in Australia: Comment. **In** *McLure, C. E., Jr., ed.*, 1983, pp. 319–22. **[G: Australia]**

Head, John G. and Bird, Richard M. Tax Policy Options in the 1980s. **In** *[Goode, R.]*, 1983, pp. 3–29. **[G: Australia; Canada; U.K.; U.S.]**

Heavey, Jerome F. Patterns of Property Tax Exploitation Produced by Infrequent Assessments. *Amer. J. Econ. Soc.*, October 1983, *42*(4), pp. 441–49. **[G: U.S.]**

Heilbrun, James. Who Bears the Burden of the Property Tax? **In** *Harriss, C. L., ed.*, 1983, pp. 57–71. **[G: U.S.]**

Hellerstein, Walter. Legal Constraints on State Taxation of Natural Resources. **In** *McLure, C. E., Jr. and Mieszkowski, P., eds.*, 1983, pp. 135–66. **[G: U.S.]**

Helliwell, John F.; MacGregor, Mary E. and Plourde, Andre. The National Energy Program Meets Falling World Oil Prices. *Can. Public Policy*, September 1983, *9*(3), pp. 284–96. **[G: Canada]**

Hendon, William S. Admission Income and Historic Houses: Higher Revenue Is Associated with Price Policy, More Services and Less Education. *Amer. J. Econ. Soc.*, October 1983, *42*(4), pp. 473–82. **[G: U.K.]**

Henke, Klaus-Dirk. Restructuring Fiscal Federalism: Comment. **In** *Giersch, H., ed.*, 1983, pp. 70–81. **[G: U.S.]**

Hewett, Roger S. and Stephenson, Susan C. State Tax Revenues under Competition. *Nat. Tax J.*, March, 1983, *36*(1), pp. 95–101. **[G: U.S.]**

Hicks, Donald A. The Property Tax in a New Industrial Era. **In** *Harriss, C. L., ed.*, 1983, pp. 208–21. **[G: U.S.]**

Hirsch, Werner Z. California's Revenue Limitation Measure and Its Side Effects. **In** *Quigley, J. M., ed.*, 1983, pp. 49–67. **[G: U.S.]**

Holland, Daniel M. and McCarney, Patricia L. User Fees and Charges. **In** *Susskind, L. E. and Serio, J. F., eds.*, 1983, pp. 81–103. **[G: U.S.]**

Hushak, Leroy J. Advantages and Limitations of Using Traditional Methods to Provide Local Public Services in a New Federalism Era. *Amer. J. Agr. Econ.*, December 1983, *65*(5), pp. 1118–23. **[G: U.S.]**

Ihlanfeldt, Keith R. and Boehm, Thomas P. Property Taxation and the Demand for Homeownership. *Public Finance Quart.*, January 1983, *11*(1), pp. 47–66. **[G: U.S.]**

Jacobs, David and Waldman, Don E. Toward a Fiscal Sociology: Determinants of Tax Regressivity in the American States. *Soc. Sci. Quart.*, September 1983, *64*(3), pp. 550–65. **[G: U.S.]**

Jennings, Karen L. Supreme Court Opens Door to More State Revenues from Mined Resources. *Natural Res. J.*, January 1983, *23*(1), pp. 213–18. **[G: U.S.]**

Kindahl, James K. Tax Limits and Property Values. *Land Econ.*, August 1983, *59*(3), pp. 315–23. **[G: U.S.]**

Klutznick, Philip M. The Effects of Property Taxation on Investment Decisions. **In** *Harriss, C. L., ed.*, 1983, pp. 72–85. **[G: U.S.]**

Kwon, O. Yul. Neutral Taxation and Provincial Mineral Royalties: The Manitoba Metallic Minerals and Saskatchewan Uranium Royalties. *Can. Public Policy*, June 1983, *9*(2), pp. 189–99. **[G: Canada]**

Lane, W. R. Harmonization of Taxes in Australia. **In** *McLure, C. E., Jr., ed.*, 1983, pp. 172–76. **[G: Australia]**

Lawrence, Jan. Cambridge: A Search for New Revenues. **In** *Susskind, L. E. and Serio, J. F., eds.*, 1983, pp. 149–70. **[G: U.S.]**

Liebowitz, S. J. and Bridgeman, Guy A. The Pricing Practices of the Liquor Control Board of Ontario: Revisited. *Can. J. Econ.*, February 1983, *16*(1), pp. 154–61. **[G: Canada]**

Lindsey, N. Fostering New Enterprises: Enterprise Workshops in Birmingham. *Reg. Stud.*, June 1983, *17*(3), pp. 208–10. **[G: U.K.]**

Linn, Johannes F. Tax Assignment and Revenue Sharing in Brazil, India, Malaysia, and Nigeria: Comment. In *McLure, C. E., Jr., ed.*, 1983, pp. 360–61. **[G: Brazil; India; Malaysia; Nigeria]**

Litterman, Robert B. and Supel, Thomas M. Using Vector Autoregressions to Measure the Uncertainty in Minnesota's Revenue Forecasts. *Fed. Res. Bank Minn. Rev.*, Spring 1983, *7*(2), pp. 10–22. **[G: U.S.]**

Lowery, David. Limitations on Taxing and Spending Powers: An Assessment of Their Effectiveness. *Soc. Sci. Quart.*, June 1983, *64*(2), pp. 247–63. **[G: U.S.]**

Lynn, Arthur D., Jr. The Property Tax in the 1980s: Evolution or Devolution? In *Break, G. F., ed.*, 1983, pp. 201–09. **[G: U.S.]**

Martin, Dolores Tremewan and Schmidt, James R. Expenditure Effects of Metropolitan Tax Base Sharing: A Public Choice Analysis. *Public Choice*, 1983, *40*(2), pp. 175–86.

Mathews, Russell. Tax Effectiveness and Tax Equity in Federal Countries: Reply. In *McLure, C. E., Jr., ed.*, 1983, pp. 98–99. **[G: MDCs]**

Mathews, Russell. Tax Effectiveness and Tax Equity in Federal Countries. In *McLure, C. E., Jr., ed.*, 1983, pp. 70–86. **[G: MDCs]**

Mathis, Edward J. and Zech, Charles E. An Empirical Test: The Economic Effects of Land Value Taxation—Reply. *Growth Change*, July 1983, *14*(3), pp. 47–48. **[G: U.S.]**

McCarney, Patricia L. Increasing Reliance on User Fees and Charges. In *Susskind, L. E. and Serio, J. F., eds.*, 1983, pp. 351–55. **[G: U.S.]**

McDonald, John F. An Economic Analysis of Local Inducements for Business. *J. Urban Econ.*, May 1983, *13*(3), pp. 322–36. **[G: U.S.]**

McKenzie, Richard B. Restructuring Fiscal Federalism. In *Giersch, H., ed.*, 1983, pp. 53–69. **[G: U.S.]**

McLure, Charles E., Jr. Assignment of Corporate Income Taxes in a Federal System. In *McLure, C. E., Jr., ed.*, 1983, pp. 101–24. **[G: Selected OECD; U.S.]**

McLure, Charles E., Jr. Fiscal Federalism and the Taxation of Economic Rents. In *Break, G. F., ed.*, 1983, pp. 133–60.

McLure, Charles E., Jr. State Corporate Income Taxes. In *Break, G. F., ed.*, 1983, pp. 29–52. **[G: U.S.]**

McLure, Charles E., Jr. Tax Exporting and the Commerce Clause. In *McLure, C. E., Jr. and Mieszkowski, P., eds.*, 1983, pp. 169–92. **[G: U.S.]**

Megdal, Sharon Bernstein. Equalization of Expenditures and the Demand for Local Public Education: The Case of New Jersey. *Public Finance Quart.*, July 1983, *11*(3), pp. 365–76. **[G: U.S.]**

Mercer, Lloyd J. and Morgan, W. Douglas. The Relative Efficiency and Revenue Potential of Local User Charges: The California Case. *Nat. Tax J.*, June 1983, *36*(2), pp. 203–12. **[G: U.S.]**

Messere, Ken. Trends in OECD Tax Revenues. In *[Goode, R.]*, 1983, pp. 31–57. **[G: OECD]**

Mieszkowski, Peter. Energy Policy, Taxation of Natural Resources, and Fiscal Federalism. In *McLure, C. E., Jr., ed.*, 1983, pp. 128–45. **[G: U.S.]**

Mieszkowski, Peter and Toder, Eric. Taxation of Energy Resources. In *McLure, C. E., Jr. and Mieszkowski, P., eds.*, 1983, pp. 65–91. **[G: U.S.]**

Mills, David E. Real Estate Speculation and Antispeculation Taxes. *Growth Change*, July 1983, *14*(3), pp. 12–22. **[G: U.S.]**

Mumy, Gene E. Pension Underfunding, Municipal Debt, and the Compensation of Municipal Employees. In *Hirsch, W. Z., ed.*, 1983, pp. 161–87.

Musgrave, Peggy B. Assignment of Corporate Income Taxes in a Federal System: Comment. In *McLure, C. E., Jr., ed.*, 1983, pp. 127–28. **[G: Selected OECD; U.S.]**

Musgrave, Peggy B. Tax Assignment and Revenue Sharing in Australia: Comment. In *McLure, C. E., Jr., ed.*, 1983, pp. 323–26. **[G: Australia; Canada; U.S.; W. Germany]**

Musgrave, Richard A. Tax Assignment and Revenue Sharing in the Federal Republic of Germany and Switzerland: Comment. In *McLure, C. E., Jr., ed.*, 1983, pp. 287–88. **[G: W. Germany; Switzerland]**

Mutti, John H. and Morgan, William E. The Exportation of State and Local Taxes in a Multilateral Framework: The Case of Household Type Taxes. *Nat. Tax J.*, December 1983, *36*(4), pp. 459–75. **[G: U.S.]**

Nathan, Richard P. State and Local Governments under Federal Grants: Toward a Predictive Theory. *Polit. Sci. Quart.*, Spring 1983, *98*(1), pp. 47–57. **[G: U.S.]**

Netzer, Dick. Does the Property Tax Have a Future? In *Harriss, C. L., ed.*, 1983, pp. 222–36. **[G: U.S.]**

Newman, Robert J. Industry Migration and Growth in the South. *Rev. Econ. Statist.*, February 1983, *65*(1), pp. 76–86. **[G: U.S.]**

Nowotny, Ewald. Tax Assignment and Revenue Sharing in the Federal Republic of Germany and Switzerland. In *McLure, C. E., Jr., ed.*, 1983, pp. 260–86. **[G: Switzerland; W. Germany]**

Oates, Wallace E. Tax Assignment and Revenue Sharing in the United States: Comment. In *McLure, C. E., Jr., ed.*, 1983, pp. 228–30. **[G: U.S.]**

Oates, Wallace E. Tax Effectiveness and Tax Equity in Federal Countries: Comment. In *McLure, C. E., Jr., ed.*, 1983, pp. 94–97. **[G: MDCs]**

Ott, Attiat F. The Effect of Inflation on the Balance Sheet of the State–Local Sector. In *Break, G. F., ed.*, 1983, pp. 11–28. **[G: U.S.]**

Otto, Daniel. Local Services in the New Federalism: Discussion. *Amer. J. Agr. Econ.*, December 1983, *65*(5), pp. 1131–32. **[G: U.S.]**

Papke, James A. The Response of State–Local Government Taxation to Fiscal Crisis. *Nat. Tax J.*, September 1983, *36*(3), pp. 401–05. **[G: U.S.]**

Pogue, Thomas F. The Incidence of Property Tax Relief via State Aid to Local Governments. *Land Econ.*, November 1983, *59*(4), pp. 420–31. **[G: U.S.]**

Prest, Wilfred. Tax Assignment and Revenue Sharing in the United States: Comment. In *McLure, C. E., Jr., ed.*, 1983, pp. 231–33. **[G: Australia; U.S.]**

Raimondo, Henry J. State Limitations on Local Taxing and Spending: Theory and Practice. *Public Budg. Finance*, Autumn 1983, *3*(3), pp. 33–42. **[G: U.S.]**

Rasmussen, David W. and Struyk, Raymond J. A

Housing Strategy for the City of Detroit: Policy Perspectives Based on Economic Analysis. **In** *Quigley, J. M., ed.*, 1983, pp. 151–93. **[G: U.S.]**

Reeves, H. Clyde. Leadership for Change. **In** *Harriss, C. L., ed.*, 1983, pp. 1–13. **[G: U.S.]**

Richardson, James A. and Scott, Loren C. Resource Location Patterns and State Severance Taxes: Some Empirical Evidence. *Natural Res. J.*, April 1983, *23*(2), pp. 351–64. **[G: U.S.]**

Riew, John. Property Taxation and Economic Development: With Focus on Korea. *J. Econ. Devel.*, December 1983, *8*(2), pp. 7–24. **[G: S. Korea]**

Rock, Steven M. The Incidence of Household-Based Taxes: Evidence from the Consumer Expenditure Survey. *Amer. Econ.*, Fall 1983, *27*(2), pp. 37–41. **[G: U.S.]**

Roemer, Arthur C. Classification of Property. **In** *Harriss, C. L., ed.*, 1983, pp. 108–22. **[G: U.S.]**

Rothenberg, Jerome and Smoke, Paul. The Pattern of Differential Impacts. **In** *Susskind, L. E. and Serio, J. F., eds.*, 1983, pp. 477–503. **[G: U.S.]**

Rubin, Jerome. Quincy: Schools Take a Big Cut. **In** *Susskind, L. E. and Serio, J. F., eds.*, 1983, pp. 203–15. **[G: U.S.]**

Rubin, Jerome and Campbell, Thomas. Chelsea: A Mayor Proposes. **In** *Susskind, L. E. and Serio, J. F., eds.*, 1983, pp. 171–80. **[G: U.S.]**

Rubinfeld, Daniel L. Tax Assignment and Revenue Sharing in the United States. **In** *McLure, C. E., Jr., ed.*, 1983, pp. 205–27. **[G: U.S.]**

Rubinfeld, Daniel L. and Wolkoff, Michael J. The Distributional Impact of Statewide Property Tax Relief: The Michigan Case. *Public Finance Quart.*, April 1983, *11*(2), pp. 131–53. **[G: U.S.]**

Rybeck, Walter. The Property Tax as a Super User Charge. **In** *Harriss, C. L., ed.*, 1983, pp. 133–47. **[G: U.S.]**

Sandrey, Ronald A.; Buccola, Steven T. and Brown, William G. Pricing Policies for Antlerless Elk Hunting Permits. *Land Econ.*, November 1983, *59*(4), pp. 432–43. **[G: U.S.]**

Sant, Donald T.; Haspel, Abraham E. and Boldt, Robert E. Oil and Gas Royalty Recovery Policy on Federal and Indian Lands: A Response. *Natural Res. J.*, April 1983, *23*(2), pp. 417–33. **[G: U.S.]**

Sheehan, Michael F. Land Speculation in Southern California: Energy Monopoly, Fiscal Crisis and the Future. *Amer. J. Econ. Soc.*, January 1983, *42*(1), pp. 67–74. **[G: U.S.]**

Shoup, Carl S. Harmonization of Indirect Taxes in the EEC: Comment. **In** *McLure, C. E., Jr., ed.*, 1983, pp. 169–71. **[G: EEC]**

Shoup, Carl S. The Property Tax versus Sales and Income Taxes. **In** *Harriss, C. L., ed.*, 1983, pp. 31–41.

Shoup, Donald C. Intervention through Property Taxation and Public Ownership. **In** *Dunkerley, H. B., ed.*, 1983, pp. 132–52.

Stein, Robert M.; Hamm, Keith E. and Freeman, Patricia K. An Analysis of Support for Tax Limitation Referenda. *Public Choice*, 1983, *40*(2), pp. 187–94. **[G: U.S.]**

Stern, Joel M. Optimality and Property Taxation: An Alternative Approach. **In** *Harriss, C. L., ed.*, 1983, pp. 204–07.

Strudler, Michael and Strand, Ivar E., Jr. Pricing as a Policy to Reduce Sewage Costs. *Water Resources Res.*, February 1983, *19*(1), pp. 53–56. **[G: U.S.]**

Subrahmanyam, Ganti. On the Possibility of Conflict in Inter-State Tax Efforts: A General Note. *Margin*, April 1983, *15*(3), pp. 45–48. **[G: India]**

Susskind, Lawrence and Horan, Cynthia. Proposition 2½: The Response to Tax Restrictions in Massachusetts. **In** *Harriss, C. L., ed.*, 1983, pp. 158–71. **[G: U.S.]**

Susskind, Lawrence and Horan, Cynthia. Understanding How and Why the Most Drastic Cuts Were Avoided. **In** *Susskind, L. E. and Serio, J. F., eds.*, 1983, pp. 263–91. **[G: U.S.]**

Thimmaiah, G. Sales Tax Controversy in India: An Evaluation. *Bull. Int. Fiscal Doc.*, March 1983, *37*(3), pp. 111–27. **[G: India]**

Thirsk, Wayne R. Energy Policy, Taxation of Natural Resources and Fiscal Federalism: Comment. **In** *McLure, C. E., Jr., ed.*, 1983, pp. 148–49. **[G: U.S.]**

Thirsk, Wayne R. Fiscal Harmonization in the United States, Australia, West Germany, Switzerland, and the EEC. **In** *Trebilcock, M. J., et al., eds.*, 1983, pp. 424–55. **[G: OECD]**

Thirsk, Wayne R. Tax Assignment and Revenue Sharing in Canada. **In** *McLure, C. E., Jr., ed.*, 1983, pp. 234–50. **[G: Canada]**

Thirsk, Wayne R. Tax Harmonization in Canada. **In** *Break, G. F., ed.*, 1983, pp. 53–74. **[G: Canada]**

Tosti, Alan. Proposition 2½ Amended: What Communities Can and Cannot Do. **In** *Susskind, L. E. and Serio, J. F., eds.*, 1983, pp. 11–20. **[G: U.S.]**

Warren, D. M. and Issachar, Joe D. Strategies for Understanding and Changing Local Revenue Policies and Practices in Ghana's Decentralization Programme. *World Devel.*, September 1983, *11*(9), pp. 835–44. **[G: Ghana]**

Watters, Elsie M. Recent Developments in State Finances: A Clarification [Homeowner Property Taxes, Inflation and Property Tax Relief]. *Nat. Tax J.*, December 1983, *36*(4), pp. 541–42. **[G: U.S.]**

Wheaton, William C. Interstate Differences in the Level of Business Taxation. *Nat. Tax J.*, March, 1983, *36*(1), pp. 83–94. **[G: U.S.]**

Wheaton, William C. Interstate Differences in the Level of Business Taxation: A Correction. *Nat. Tax J.*, December 1983, *36*(4), pp. 543. **[G: U.S.]**

White, Fred C. Trade-Off in Growth and Stability in State Taxes. *Nat. Tax J.*, March, 1983, *36*(1), pp. 103–14. **[G: U.S.]**

Woodruff, A. M. The Property Tax in Periods of Instable Prices. **In** *Harriss, C. L., ed.*, 1983, pp. 123–32. **[G: U.S.]**

Woolery, Arlo. Alternative Methods of Taxing Property. **In** *Harriss, C. L., ed.*, 1983, pp. 180–88. **[G: U.S.]**

Zimmerman, Martin B. Tax Exporting and the Commerce Clause: Comments. **In** *McLure, C. E., Jr. and Mieszkowski, P., eds.*, 1983, pp. 193–95. **[G: U.S.]**

Zodrow, George R. and Mieszkowski, Peter. The Incidence of the Property Tax: The Benefit View versus the New View. **In** *Zodrow, G. R., ed.*, 1983, pp. 109–29.

3243 State and Local Government Borrowing

Glynn, Dermot. Is Government Borrowing Now Too Low? *Lloyds Bank Rev.*, January 1983, (147), pp. 21–41. **[G: U.K.]**

Gurwitz, Aaron S. Twelve Improvements in the Municipal Credit System. *Fed. Res. Bank New York Quart. Rev.*, Winter 1983-84, *8*(4), pp. 14–25. **[G: U.S.]**

Hubbell, L. Kenneth. Local Government Credit Financing. **In** *Bahl, R. and Miller, B. D., eds.*, 1983, pp. 188–227. **[G: Philippines]**

Hushak, Leroy J. Advantages and Limitations of Using Traditional Methods to Provide Local Public Services in a New Federalism Era. *Amer. J. Agr. Econ.*, December 1983, *65*(5), pp. 1118–23. **[G: U.S.]**

Kidwell, David S. and Trzcinka, Charles A. The Impact of the New York City Fiscal Crisis on the Interest Cost of New Issue Municipal Bonds. *J. Finan. Quant. Anal.*, September 1983, *18*(3), pp. 381–99. **[G: U.S.]**

Leonard, Paul A. Some Factors Determining Municipal Revenue Bond Interest Costs. *J. Econ. Bus.*, 1983, *35*(1), pp. 71–82. **[G: U.S.]**

Otto, Daniel. Local Services in the New Federalism: Discussion. *Amer. J. Agr. Econ.*, December 1983, *65*(5), pp. 1131–32. **[G: U.S.]**

Proctor, Allen J. and Donahoo, Kathleene K. Commercial Bank Investment in Municipal Securities. *Fed. Res. Bank New York Quart. Rev.*, Winter 1983-84, *8*(4), pp. 26–37. **[G: U.S.]**

Sorensen, Eric H. Who Puts The Slope in the Municipal Yield Curve? *J. Portfol. Manage.*, Summer 1983, *9*(4), pp. 61–65. **[G: U.S.]**

Taylor, W. B. Borrowing by Local Authorities in the United Kingdom. *Nat. Westminster Bank Quart. Rev.*, August 1983, pp. 60–69. **[G: U.K.]**

Vasché, Jon David. State and Local Government Options for Reducing Borrowing Costs. *Public Budg. Finance*, Winter 1983, *3*(4), pp. 42–56. **[G: U.S.]**

Wilson, Earl R. Fiscal Performance and Municipal Bond Borrowing Costs. *Public Budg. Finance*, Winter 1983, *3*(4), pp. 28–41. **[G: U.S.]**

325 Intergovernmental Financial Relationships

3250 Intergovernmental Financial Relationships

Alm, James. Intergovernmental Grants and Social Welfare. *Public Finance*, 1983, *38*(3), pp. 376–97.

Alm, James. The Optimal Structure of Intergovernmental Grants. *Public Finance Quart.*, October 1983, *11*(4), pp. 387–417. **[G: U.S.]**

Anton, Thomas J. The Regional Distribution of Federal Expenditures, 1971–1980. *Nat. Tax J.*, December 1983, *36*(4), pp. 429–42. **[G: U.S.]**

Bahl, Roy and Schroeder, Larry. Intergovernmental Fiscal Relations. **In** *Bahl, R. and Miller, B. D., eds.*, 1983, pp. 100–139. **[G: Philippines]**

Bahl, Roy and Schroeder, Larry. Local Government Structure, Financial Management, and Fiscal Conditions. **In** *Bahl, R. and Miller, B. D., eds.*, 1983, pp. 1–45. **[G: Philippines]**

Bahl, Roy W. and Linn, Johannes F. The Assignment of Local Government Revenues in Developing Countries. **In** *McLure, C. E., Jr., ed.*, 1983, pp. 177–99. **[G: Selected LDCs]**

Barnett, Richard R. The Effect of Matching Grants on Local Authority User Charges: A Critique of the Gibson Model. *Public Finance*, 1983, *38*(1), pp. 163–69. **[G: U.K.]**

Boadway, Robin; Flatters, F. and Leblanc, A. Revenue Sharing and the Equlization of Natural Resource Revenues. *Can. Public Policy*, June 1983, *9*(2), pp. 174–80. **[G: Canada]**

Boadway, Robin and Flatters, Frank. Efficiency, Equity, and the Allocation of Resource Rents. **In** *McLure, C. E., Jr. and Mieszkowski, P., eds.*, 1983, pp. 99–123. **[G: Canada]**

Bös, Dieter. Tax Assignment and Revenue Sharing in the Federal Republic of Germany and Switzerland: Comment. **In** *McLure, C. E., Jr., ed.*, 1983, pp. 289–92. **[G: Switzerland; W. Germany]**

Bradbury, Katharine L.; Ladd, Helen F. and Christopherson, Claire. The Initial Impacts on State and Local Finances. **In** *Susskind, L. E. and Serio, J. F., eds.*, 1983, pp. 293–324. **[G: U.S.]**

Brennan, Geoffrey. Who Should Tax, Where and What? Comment. **In** *McLure, C. E., Jr., ed.*, 1983, pp. 20–23.

Brennan, Geoffrey and Buchanan, James M. Normative Tax Theory for a Federal Polity: Some Public Choice Preliminaries. **In** *McLure, C. E., Jr., ed.*, 1983, pp. 52–65.

Breton, Albert. Federalism versus Centralism in Regional Growth. **In** *Biehl, D.; Roskamp, K. W. and Stolper, W. F., eds.*, 1983, pp. 251–63.

Brown, Malcolm C. Tax Assignment and Revenue Sharing in Canada: Comment. **In** *McLure, C. E., Jr., ed.*, 1983, pp. 251–56. **[G: Canada]**

Chen, Yun. Problems We Must Pay Attention to after the Reform of the System. **In** *Ch'en, Y.*, 1983, *1957*, pp. 73–75. **[G: China]**

Cloutier, Norman R. Growth Centers and the Spatial Distribution of Development Funds: The Case of West Virginia. *Reg. Sci. Persp.*, 1983, *13*(1), pp. 15–24. **[G: U.S.]**

Colon, Melvyn. Amesbury: Linking Salaries to State Aid. **In** *Susskind, L. E. and Serio, J. F., eds.*, 1983, pp. 107–12. **[G: U.S.]**

Colon, Melvyn. Bridgewater: Drawing the Lines for a Budget Battle. **In** *Susskind, L. E. and Serio, J. F., eds.*, 1983, pp. 129–40. **[G: U.S.]**

Courchene, Thomas J. A Constitutional Perspective on Federal–Provincial Sharing of Revenues from Natural Resources: Comments. **In** *McLure, C. E., Jr. and Mieszkowski, P., eds.*, 1983, pp. 237–43. **[G: Canada]**

Courchene, Thomas J. Analytical Perspectives on the Canadian Economic Union. **In** *Trebilcock, M. J., et al., eds.*, 1983, pp. 51–110. **[G: Canada]**

Courchene, Thomas J. Canada's New Equalization Program: Description and Evaluation. *Can. Public Policy*, December 1983, *9*(4), pp. 458–75. **[G: Canada]**

Courchene, Thomas J. Efficiency, Equity, and the Allocation of Resource Rents: Comments. **In** *McLure, C. E., Jr. and Mieszkowski, P., eds.*, 1983, pp. 125–33. [G: Canada]

Dales, John H. Distortions and Dissipations. *Can. Public Policy,* June 1983, *9*(2), pp. 257–63. [G: Canada]

Dawson, Diane A. Financial Incentives for Change. **In** *Young, K., ed.,* 1983, pp. 11–31. [G: U.K.]

Deaton, Brady J. New Institutional Arrangements for Supplying Local Public Services under New Federalism with Special Reference to Education. *Amer. J. Agr. Econ.,* December 1983, *65*(5), pp. 1124–30. [G: U.S.]

Doolittle, Frederick C. Federal Grants for Urban Economic Development. **In** *Break, G. F., ed.,* 1983, pp. 75–91. [G: U.S.]

Gandhi, Ved P. Tax Assignment and Revenue Sharing in Brazil, India, Malaysia, and Nigeria. **In** *McLure, C. E., Jr., ed.,* 1983, pp. 328–59. [G: Brazil; India; Malaysia; Nigeria]

Gandhi, Ved P. The Assignment of Local Government Revenues in Developing Countries: Comment. **In** *McLure, C. E., Jr., ed.,* 1983, pp. 200–202. [G: Selected LDCs]

Gibson, J. G. The Effect of Matching Grants on Local Authority User Charges: Some Further Results. *Public Finance,* 1983, *38*(1), pp. 170–75. [G: U.K.]

Gold, Steven D. Recent Developments in State Finances. *Nat. Tax J.,* March, 1983, *36*(1), pp. 1–29. [G: U.S.]

Goldsmith, Mike. The Role of Central Government in Local Economic Development: Comment. **In** *Young, K., ed.,* 1983, pp. 129–32. [G: U.K.]

Gordon, Roger H. An Optimal Taxation Approach to Fiscal Federalism. *Quart. J. Econ.,* November 1983, *98*(4), pp. 567–86.

Gorton, John. Australian Federalism: A View from Canberra. **In** *Patience, A. and Scott, J., eds.,* 1983, pp. 12–27. [G: Australia]

Grewal, Bhajan S. Tax Assignment and Revenue Sharing in Brazil, India, Malaysia, and Nigeria: Comment. **In** *McLure, C. E., Jr., ed.,* 1983, pp. 362–63. [G: Brazil; India; Malaysia; Nigeria]

Groenewegen, Peter D. Tax Assignment and Revenue Sharing in Australia. **In** *McLure, C. E., Jr., ed.,* 1983, pp. 293–318. [G: Australia]

Groenewegen, Peter D. Tax Assignment and Revenue Sharing in Australia: Reply. **In** *McLure, C. E., Jr., ed.,* 1983, pp. 327. [G: Australia]

Groenewegen, Peter D. The Fiscal Crisis of Australian Federalism. **In** *Patience, A. and Scott, J., eds.,* 1983, pp. 123–58. [G: Australia]

Grossman, David A. Intergovernmental Aid. **In** *Brecher, C. and Horton, R. D., eds.,* 1983, pp. 45–67. [G: U.S.]

Hall, Peter. Housing, Planning, Land, and Local Finance: The British Experience. **In** *Lefcoe, G., ed.,* 1983, pp. 47–58. [G: U.K.]

Hamer, R. J. Australian Federalism: A View from Victoria. **In** *Patience, A. and Scott, J., eds.,* 1983, pp. 49–62. [G: Australia]

Hansell, David A. and Warring, Wendy. Making the Old Federalism Work: Section 1983 and the Rights of Grant-in-Aid Beneficiaries. *Yale Law J.,* May 1983, *92*(6), pp. 1001–21.

Head, Brian W. The Political Crisis of Australian Federalism. **In** *Patience, A. and Scott, J., eds.,* 1983, pp. 75–93. [G: Australia]

Head, John G. Tax Assignment and Revenue Sharing in Canada: Comment. **In** *McLure, C. E., Jr., ed.,* 1983, pp. 257–59. [G: Canada]

Head, John G. Tax Assignment and Revenue Sharing in Australia: Comment. **In** *McLure, C. E., Jr., ed.,* 1983, pp. 319–22. [G: Australia]

Helliwell, John F.; MacGregor, Mary E. and Plourde, Andre. The National Energy Program Meets Falling World Oil Prices. *Can. Public Policy,* September 1983, *9*(3), pp. 284–96. [G: Canada]

Henke, Klaus-Dirk. Restructuring Fiscal Federalism: Comment. **In** *Giersch, H., ed.,* 1983, pp. 70–81. [G: U.S.]

Hirsch, Werner Z. California's Revenue Limitation Measure and Its Side Effects. **In** *Quigley, J. M., ed.,* 1983, pp. 49–67. [G: U.S.]

Holcombe, Randall G. and Zardkoohi, Asghar. The Determinants of Federal Grants: Reply. *Southern Econ. J.,* July 1983, *50*(1), pp. 275–76. [G: U.S.]

Holcombe, Randall G. and Zardkoohi, Asghar. The Effect of Macroeconomic Variables on State and Local Government Expenditures. *Atlantic Econ. J.,* December 1983, *11*(4), pp. 34–41. [G: U.S.]

Horowitz, Irving Louis. From the New Deal to the New Federalism: Presidential Ideology in the U.S. from 1932 to 1982. *Amer. J. Econ. Soc.,* April 1983, *42*(2), pp. 129–48. [G: U.S.]

Hushak, Leroy J. Advantages and Limitations of Using Traditional Methods to Provide Local Public Services in a New Federalism Era. *Amer. J. Agr. Econ.,* December 1983, *65*(5), pp. 1118–23. [G: U.S.]

Irvine, Ian J. and Smith, J. Barry. The Estimation of Local Government Expenditure Responses to Inter-Governmental Transfers. *Rev. Econ. Statist.,* August 1983, *65*(3), pp. 534–36. [G: U.S.]

Jackman, Richard. Financial Incentives for Change: Comment. **In** *Young, K., ed.,* 1983, pp. 31–34. [G: U.K.]

Kiel, Lisa J. and McKenzie, Richard B. The Impact of Tenure on the Flow of Federal Benefits to SMSA's. *Public Choice,* 1983, *41*(2), pp. 285–93. [G: U.S.]

Linn, Johannes F. Tax Assignment and Revenue Sharing in Brazil, India, Malaysia, and Nigeria: Comment. **In** *McLure, C. E., Jr., ed.,* 1983, pp. 360–61. [G: Brazil; India; Malaysia; Nigeria]

Lovell, Catherine H. and Egan, Hanria R. Fiscal Notes and Mandate Reimbursement in the Fifty States. *Public Budg. Finance,* Autumn 1983, *3*(3), pp. 3–18. [G: U.S.]

Luksetich, William A. The Determinants of Federal Grants: Comment. *Southern Econ. J.,* July 1983, *50*(1), pp. 270–74. [G: U.S.]

Madden, J. R.; Challen, D. W. and Hagger, A. J. The Grants Commission's Relativities Proposals: Effects on the State Economies. *Australian Econ. Pap.,* December 1983, *22*(41), pp. 302–21. [G: Australia]

Mathews, Russell. Intergovernmental Fiscal Relations and Regional Growth in a Federal Context. **In** *Biehl, D.; Roskamp, K. W. and Stolper, W. F., eds.,* 1983, pp. 265–96. [G: Australia]

McDowell, George R. Local Services in the New

Federalism: Discussion. *Amer. J. Agr. Econ.*, December 1983, *65*(5), pp. 1133–35. [G: U.S.]

McKenzie, Richard B. Restructuring Fiscal Federalism. In *Giersch, H., ed.*, 1983, pp. 53–69. [G: U.S.]

McLure, Charles E., Jr. and Mieszkowski, Peter. Taxation of Mineral Wealth and Interregional Conflicts. In *McLure, C. E., Jr. and Mieszkowski, P., eds.*, 1983, pp. 1–10. [G: U.S.; Canada]

Melvin, J. R. Political Structure and the Pursuit of Economic Objectives. In *Trebilcock, M. J., et al., eds.*, 1983, pp. 111–58. [G: Canada]

Meyers, Roy and Curtin, Mary Ann. State and Local Cost Estimates. *Public Budg. Finance*, Autumn 1983, *3*(3), pp. 116–18. [G: U.S.]

Mieszkowski, Peter and Stein, Robert M. Trends and Prospects in State and Local Finance. *J. Urban Econ.*, September 1983, *14*(2), pp. 224–41. [G: U.S.]

Miller, Gerald H. The Growing State–Local Deficit Threat: Remarks. *Nat. Tax J.*, September 1983, *36*(3), pp. 383–93. [G: U.S.]

Musgrave, Peggy B. Tax Assignment and Revenue Sharing in Australia: Comment. In *McLure, C. E., Jr., ed.*, 1983, pp. 323–26. [G: Australia; Canada; U.S.; W. Germany]

Musgrave, Richard A. Tax Assignment and Revenue Sharing in the Federal Republic of Germany and Switzerland: Comment. In *McLure, C. E., Jr., ed.*, 1983, pp. 287–88. [G: W. Germany; Switzerland]

Musgrave, Richard A. Who Should Tax, Where, and What? In *McLure, C. E., Jr., ed.*, 1983, pp. 2–19.

Nathan, Richard P. Research Issues in the Evaluation of Broad-gauged and Multipurpose Grants-in-Aid. In *Break, G. F., ed.*, 1983, pp. 93–105. [G: U.S.]

Nathan, Richard P. State and Local Governments under Federal Grants: Toward a Predictive Theory. *Polit. Sci. Quart.*, Spring 1983, *98*(1), pp. 47–57. [G: U.S.]

Nowotny, Ewald. Tax Assignment and Revenue Sharing in the Federal Republic of Germany and Switzerland. In *McLure, C. E., Jr., ed.*, 1983, pp. 260–86. [G: Switzerland; W. Germany]

Nowotny, Ewald. Who Should Tax, Where and What? Comment. In *McLure, C. E., Jr., ed.*, 1983, pp. 24–25.

Oates, Wallace E. Tax Assignment and Revenue Sharing in the United States: Comment. In *McLure, C. E., Jr., ed.*, 1983, pp. 228–30. [G: U.S.]

Oates, Wallace E. The Economics of the New Federalism: Response: Strengths and Weaknesses of the New Federalism. In *Stubblebine, Wm. C. and Willett, T. D., eds.*, 1983, pp. 153–57. [G: U.S.]

Otto, Daniel. Local Services in the New Federalism: Discussion. *Amer. J. Agr. Econ.*, December 1983, *65*(5), pp. 1131–32. [G: U.S.]

Pogue, Thomas F. The Incidence of Property Tax Relief via State Aid to Local Governments. *Land Econ.*, November 1983, *59*(4), pp. 420–31. [G: U.S.]

Prest, Wilfred. Tax Assignment and Revenue Sharing in the United States: Comment. In *McLure, C. E., Jr., ed.*, 1983, pp. 231–33. [G: Australia; U.S.]

Prichard, J. Robert S. and Benedickson, Jamie. Securing the Canadian Economic Union: Federalism and Internal Barriers to Trade. In *Trebilcock, M. J., et al., eds.*, 1983, pp. 3–50. [G: Canada]

Raimondo, Henry J. Municipal Hardship in New Jersey and the Distribution of Intergovernmental Grants, 1961–1977. In *Dutta, M.; Hartline, J. C. and Loeb, P. D., eds.*, 1983, pp. 173–89. [G: U.S.]

Raimondo, Henry J. The Political Economy of State Intergovernmental Grants. *Growth Change*, April 1983, *14*(2), pp. 17–23. [G: U.S.]

Ranjana. Inter-Governmental Fiscal Transfers: A New Disaggregative Approach (A Case Study of India, 1952–77). *Margin*, July 1983, *15*(4), pp. 78–91. [G: India]

Regens, James L. and Rycroft, Robert W. Intergovernmental Issues in Managing Sunbelt Growth. In *Ballard, S. C. and James, T. E., eds.*, 1983, pp. 162–79. [G: U.S.]

Rose-Ackerman, Susan. Cooperative Federalism and Co-Optation. *Yale Law J.*, June 1983, *92*(7), pp. 1344–48.

Rubinfeld, Daniel L. Normative Tax Theory for a Federal Polity: Some Public Choice Preliminaries: Comment. In *McLure, C. E., Jr., ed.*, 1983, pp. 67–69.

Rubinfeld, Daniel L. Tax Assignment and Revenue Sharing in the United States. In *McLure, C. E., Jr., ed.*, 1983, pp. 205–27. [G: U.S.]

Scott, Jeffrey. Australian Federalism Renewed. In *Patience, A. and Scott, J., eds.*, 1983, pp. 1–11. [G: Australia]

Shannon, John. Austerity Federalism—The State–Local Response. *Nat. Tax J.*, September 1983, *36*(3), pp. 377–82. [G: U.S.]

Silkman, Richard H. and Young, Dennis R. X-Efficiency, State Formula Grants, and Public Library Systems. In *Quigley, J. M., ed.*, 1983, pp. 195–222. [G: U.S.]

Slack, N. Enid and Bird, Richard M. Local Response to Intergovernmental Fiscal Transfers: The Case of Colombia. *Public Finance*, 1983, *38*(3), pp. 429–39. [G: Colombia]

St. Amand, Stephen W.; Herndon, John Thomas and Cole, James Nathan. New Federalism: A Question of Finances and Timing. *Public Budg. Finance*, Spring 1983, *3*(1), pp. 57–65. [G: U.S.]

Stewart, Murray. The Role of Central Government in Local Economic Development. In *Young, K., ed.*, 1983, pp. 105–29. [G: U.K.]

Stubblebine, Wm. Craig. The Economics of the New Federalism. In *Stubblebine, Wm. C. and Willett, T. D., eds.*, 1983, pp. 143–51. [G: U.S.]

Susskind, Lawrence and Horan, Cynthia. Understanding How and Why the Most Drastic Cuts Were Avoided. In *Susskind, L. E. and Serio, J. F., eds.*, 1983, pp. 263–91. [G: U.S.]

Thirsk, Wayne R. Fiscal Harmonization in the United States, Australia, West Germany, Switzerland, and the EEC. In *Trebilcock, Michael J., et al., eds.*, 1983, pp. 424–55. [G: OECD]

Thirsk, Wayne R. Tax Assignment and Revenue Sharing in Canada. In *McLure, C. E., Jr., ed.*, 1983, pp. 234–50. [G: Canada]

Thirsk, Wayne R. Tax Harmonization in Canada. In *Break, G. F., ed.*, 1983, pp. 53–74. [G: Canada]

Tolley, George S.; Krumm, Ronald J. and Sanders, Jeffrey. On the Effects of Federal Aid. *Amer. Econ. Rev.*, May 1983, *73*(2), pp. 159–63. [G: U.S.]

Trebilcock, Michael J., et al. Federalism and the Canadian Economic Union: Summary and Implications. **In** *Trebilcock, M. J., et al., eds.*, 1983, pp. 542–60. [G: Canada]

Van Horn, Carl E. and Raimondo, Henry J. Living with Less: New Jersey Copes with Federal Aid Cutbacks. *Public Budg. Finance*, Spring 1983, *3*(1), pp. 41–56. [G: U.S.]

Watters, Elsie M. Outlook for State–Local Government Finances. **In** *Harriss, C. L., ed.*, 1983, pp. 189–203. [G: U.S.]

West, Katherine. Federalism and Resources Development: The Politics of State Inequality. **In** *Patience, A. and Scott, J., eds.*, 1983, pp. 107–22. [G: Australia]

Whalley, John. Induced Distortions of Interprovincial Activity: An Overview of Issues. **In** *Trebilcock, M. J., et al., eds.*, 1983, pp. 161–200. [G: Canada]

Whalley, John. The Impact of Federal Policies on Interprovincial Activity. **In** *Trebilcock, M. J., et al., eds.*, 1983, pp. 201–42. [G: Canada]

Whyte, John D. A Constitutional Perspective on Federal–Provincial Sharing of Revenues from Natural Resources. **In** *McLure, C. E., Jr. and Mieszkowski, P., eds.*, 1983, pp. 205–35. [G: Canada]

Wildasin, David E. The Welfare Effects of Intergovernmental Grants in an Economy with Independent Jurisdictions. *J. Urban Econ.*, March 1983, *13*(2), pp. 147–64.

Young, Ken. Beyond Centralism. **In** *Young, K., ed.*, 1983, pp. 1–10.

Zimmermann, Horst. Grants to Communities in Their Relation to National Growth. **In** *Biehl, D.; Roskamp, K. W. and Stolper, W. F., eds.*, 1983, pp. 297–313. [G: W. Germany]

400 International Economics

4000 General

Bergsten, C. Fred. Can We Prevent a World Economic Crisis? *Challenge*, January/February 1983, *25*(6), pp. 4–13. [G: U.S.]

Bergsten, C. Fred. Failure at Versailles. **In** *Bergsten, C. F.*, 1983, *1982*, pp. 103–09.

Bergsten, C. Fred. Preventing a Global Economic Crisis. **In** *Bergsten, C. F.*, 1983, *1982*, pp. 57–70.

Bergsten, C. Fred. The Institute for International Economics. **In** *Bergsten, C. F.*, 1983, *1982*, pp. 233–37.

Bergsten, C. Fred. The Pragmatic Approach to North–South Relations. **In** *Bergsten, C. F.*, 1983, *1981*, pp. 209–18.

Bergsten, C. Fred. The United States and the World Economy. **In** *Bergsten, C. F.*, 1983, *1982*, pp. 3–12. [G: U.S.]

Bergsten, C. Fred. The Versailles Summit: A Proposed Package. **In** *Bergsten, C. F.*, 1983, pp. 93–101.

Bissell, Richard E. Political Origins of the New International Economic Order. **In** *Thompson, W. S., ed.*, 1983, pp. 223–37.

Bognár, József. Is It Possible to Recover from the World Economic Crisis? (Economic Dependence in an Age of Interdependence). *Acta Oecon.*, 1983, *30*(1), pp. 1–12. [G: Global]

Bressand, Albert. Mastering the "Worldeconomy." *Foreign Aff.*, Spring 1983, *61*(4), pp. 745–72.

Burki, Shahid Javed. UNCTAD VI: For Better or for Worse? *Finance Develop.*, December 1983, *20*(4), pp. 16–19.

Caron, David D. Reconciling Domestic Principles and International Cooperation. **In** *Oxman, B. H.; Caron, D. D. and Buderi, C. L. O., eds.*, 1983, pp. 3–10. [G: U.S.]

Chase-Dunn, Christopher. Inequality, Structural Mobility, and Dependency Reversal in the Capitalist World Economy. **In** *Doran, C. F.; Modelski, G. and Clark, C., eds.*, 1983, pp. 73–95. [G: Selected Countries]

Chen, Xiu-Ying. North–South Negotiations and the New International Economic Order. **In** *Gauhar, A., ed. (I)*, 1983, pp. 69–79.

Clark, Cal; Doran, Charles F. and Modelski, George. North/South Relations: Studies of Dependency Reversal: Introduction. **In** *Doran, C. F.; Modelski, G. and Clark, C., eds.*, 1983, pp. ix–xx.

Cohen, Lewis I. International Cooperation on Seabed Mining. **In** *Oxman, B. H.; Caron, D. D. and Buderi, C. L. O., eds.*, 1983, pp. 101–09. [G: OECD]

Doran, Charles F. Structuring the Concept of Dependency Reversal. **In** *Doran, C. F.; Modelski, G. and Clark, C., eds.*, 1983, pp. 1–27.

Driehuis, Wim and Klant, Jan J. The Nature and Causes of the World Depression. *De Economist*, 1983, *131*(4), pp. 474–97.

Ewing, A. F. Brandt Mark II. *J. World Trade Law*, May–June 1983, *17*(3), pp. 259–66.

Gauhar, Altaf. Third World Strategy: Foreword. **In** *Gauhar, A., ed. (II)*, 1983, pp. vii–xvi.

Giscard d'Estaing, Valéry. New Opportunities and New Challenges. *Foreign Aff.*, Fall 1983, *62*(1), pp. 176–99. [G: Global]

Goldwin, Robert A. Common Sense vs. "The Common Heritage." **In** *Oxman, B. H.; Caron, D. D. and Buderi, C. L. O., eds.*, 1983, pp. 59–75. [G: U.S.]

Goodman, Allan E. Myth versus Reality in "North–South" Negotiations. **In** *Thompson, W. S., ed.*, 1983, pp. 35–52.

Goulet, Denis. Overcoming Injustice: Possibilities and Limits. **In** *Skurski, R., ed.*, 1983, pp. 113–58.

Haas, Ernst B. Words Can Hurt You; or, Who Said What to Whom about Regimes. **In** *Krasner, S. D., ed.*, 1983, *1982*, pp. 23–59.

Hague, Douglas. Discussion and Conclusion: A Global Perspective on the World Economy. *Int. Soc. Sci. J.*, 1983, *35*(3), pp. 535–47. [G: Global]

ul Haq, Mahbub. A View from the South: The Second Phase of the North–South Dialogue. **In** *To-*

daro, M. P., ed., 1983, 1979, pp. 384–91.

Hope, Kempe R. Basic Needs and Technology Transfer Issues in the 'New International Economic Order.' *Amer. J. Econ. Soc.*, October 1983, *42*(4), pp. 393–404. **[G: LDCs]**

Horvat, Branko. The World Economy from the Socialist Viewpoint. *Int. Soc. Sci. J.*, 1983, *35*(3), pp. 469–92. **[G: Global]**

Horvat, Branko. The World Economy from the Socialist Viewpoint. *Econ. Anal. Worker's Manage.*, 1983, *17*(1), pp. 1–25.

Independent Comm. on Int. Development Issues. North–South: The Setting. **In** *Glassner, M. I., ed.*, 1983, *1980*, pp. 80–96. **[G: LDCs; MDCs]**

Jamal, Amir M. Man at the Centre of Economic Purpose. **In** *Gauhar, A., ed. (II)*, 1983, pp. 24–29.

Jamal, Amir M. South–South. **In** *Gauhar, A., ed. (I)*, 1983, pp. 231–34.

Jones, R. J. Barry. Perspectives on International Political Economy. **In** *Jones, R. J. B., ed.*, 1983, pp. 169–208.

Kahler, Miles. Europe and Its "Privileged Partners" in Africa and the Middle East. **In** *Tsoukalis, L., ed.*, 1983, pp. 199–218. **[G: EEC]**

Keohane, Robert O. The Demand for International Regimes. **In** *Krasner, S. D., ed.*, 1983, *1982*, pp. 141–71.

Krasner, Stephen D. Regimes and the Limits of Realism: Regimes as Autonomous Variables. **In** *Krasner, S. D., ed.*, 1983, *1982*, pp. 355–68.

Krasner, Stephen D. Structural Causes and Regime Consequences: Regimes as Intervening Variables. **In** *Krasner, S. D., ed.*, 1983, *1982*, pp. 1–21.

Leff, Nathaniel H. Beyond the New International Economic Order. **In** *Thompson, W. S., ed.*, 1983, pp. 239–65.

Lerner, Abba P. Projecting the New Economic World Order. **In** *Lerner, A. P.*, 1983, *1978*, pp. 685–95.

Lewis, W. Arthur. The Slowing Down of the Engine of Growth. **In** *Lewis, W. A.*, 1983, *1980*, pp. 283–92.

Magnifico, Giovanni. Problems of the World Economy Today. *Econ. Notes*, 1983, (2), pp. 49–64. **[G: Global]**

Mazrui, Ali A. Exit Visa from the World System: Dilemmas of Cultural and Economic Disengagement. **In** *Gauhar, A., ed. (II)*, 1983, pp. 134–48.

Modelski, George. Dependency Reversal in the Modern State System: A Long Cycle Perspective. **In** *Doran, C. F.; Modelski, G. and Clark, C., eds.*, 1983, pp. 49–72.

Modelski, George; Clark, Cal and Doran, Charles F. North/South Relations: Studies of Dependency Reversal: Conclusion. **In** *Doran, C. F.; Modelski, G. and Clark, C., eds.*, 1983, pp. 239–48.

Nijkamp, Peter. International Conflict Analysis. **In** *Isard, W. and Nagao, Y., eds.*, 1983, pp. 117–37. **[G: Global]**

Norbye, O. D. Koht. Mass Poverty and International Income Transfers. **In** *Parkinson, J. R., ed.*, 1983, pp. 15–39.

Nyerere, Julius K. South–South Option. **In** *Gauhar, A., ed. (II)*, 1983, pp. 9–16.

Nyerere, Julius K. The Poor Speak Out. **In** *Glassner, M. I., ed.*, 1983, *1978*, pp. 118–21. **[G: LDCs]**

O'Brien, Rita Cruise and Helleiner, Gerald K. The Political Economy of Information in a Changing International Economic Order. **In** *O'Brien, R. C., ed.*, 1983, pp. 1–27.

Oxman, Bernard H. Law of the Sea and the Future of the International Order: The Two Conferences. **In** *Oxman, B. H.; Caron, D. D. and Buderi, C. L. O., eds.*, 1983, pp. 127–44.

Oxman, Bernard H. Summary of the Law of the Sea Convention. **In** *Oxman, B. H.; Caron, D. D. and Buderi, C. L. O., eds.*, 1983, pp. 147–61.

Paavonen, Tapani. Reformist Programmes in the Planning for Post-War Economic Policy during World War II. *Scand. Econ. Hist. Rev.*, 1983, *31*(3), pp. 178–200. **[G: OECD]**

Pinto, M. C. W. The Developing Countries and the Exploitation of the Deep Seabed. **In** *Glassner, M. I., ed.*, 1983, *1980*, pp. 600–614. **[G: Global]**

Ramphal, Shridath S. South–South: Parameters and Pre-conditions. **In** *Gauhar, A., ed. (II)*, 1983, pp. 17–23.

Ruggie, John Gerard. International Interdependence and National Welfare. **In** *Ruggie, J. G., ed.*, 1983, pp. 1–39. **[G: LDCs; MDCs]**

Ruggie, John Gerard. Political Structure and Change in the International Economic Order: The North–South Dimension. **In** *Ruggie, J. G., ed.*, 1983, pp. 423–87. **[G: LDCs; MDCs]**

Schatz, Sayre P. Socializing Adaptation: A Perspective on World Capitalism. *World Devel.*, January 1983, *11*(1), pp. 1–10. **[G: Global]**

Simai, M. Stages of Internationalization (A Contribution to the Establishment of a Theoretical Framework). *Acta Oecon.*, 1983, *30*(1), pp. 13–30. **[G: Global]**

Smith, Tony. The Case of Dependency Theory. **In** *Thompson, W. S., ed.*, 1983, pp. 203–22.

Stein, Arthur A. Coordination and Collaboration: Regimes in an Anarchic World. **In** *Krasner, S. D., ed.*, 1983, *1982*, pp. 115–40.

Strange, Susan. *Cave! hic dragones:* A Critique of Regime Analysis. **In** *Krasner, S. D., ed.*, 1983, *1982*, pp. 337–54.

Strange, Susan. Structures, Values and Risk in the Study of the International Political Economy. **In** *Jones, R. J. B., ed.*, 1983, pp. 209–30.

Streeten, Paul. Development Dichotomies. *World Devel.*, October 1983, *11*(10), pp. 875–89.

Tooze, Roger. 'Sectoral Analysis' and the International Political Economy. **In** *Jones, R. J. B., ed.*, 1983, pp. 231–41.

van Veen, P. Trends in World Trade. *S. Afr. J. Econ.*, December 1983, *51*(4), pp. 486–506. **[G: Global]**

Wionczek, Miguel S. Some Reflections on Economic Information Gathering and Processing within the Framework of the North–South Conflict. **In** *O'Brien, R. C., ed.*, 1983, pp. 148–53.

Worsley, Peter. One World or Three? A Critique of the World-System Theory of Immanuel Wallerstein. **In** *Held, D., et al., eds.*, 1983, *1980*, pp. 504–25.

Young, Oran R. Regime Dynamics: The Rise and Fall of International Regimes. **In** *Krasner, S. D., ed.*, 1983, *1982*, pp. 93–113.

410 International Trade Theory

411 International Trade Theory

4110 General

Bell, Clive and Devarajan, Shantayanan. Shadow Prices for Project Evaluation under Alternative Macroeconomic Specifications. *Quart. J. Econ.*, August 1983, *98*(3), pp. 457–77.

Bhagwati, Jagdish N. Directly Unproductive, Profit-seeking (DUP) Activities. **In** *Bhagwati, J. N., Vol. 1,* 1983, *1982,* pp. 259–73.

Bhagwati, Jagdish N. and Hansen, Bent. A Theoretical Analysis of Smuggling. **In** *Bhagwati, J. N., Vol. 1,* 1983, *1973,* pp. 286–301.

Blankmeyer, Eric. A Welfare Gain from a Stable Exchange Rate. *Atlantic Econ. J.*, December 1983, *11*(4), pp. 74–75.

Dutta, Manoranjan. Non-Market Information and International Trade Theory. *J. Econ. Devel.*, July 1983, *8*(1), pp. 7–23.

Fried, Harold O. Immiserizing Growth and Inferior Goods. *Atlantic Econ. J.*, March 1983, *11*(1), pp. 73–74.

Rivera-Batiz, Francisco L. Trade Theory, Distribution of Income, and Immigration. *Amer. Econ. Rev.*, May 1983, *73*(2), pp. 183–87.

Roosa, Robert V. The Gap between Trade Theory and Capital Flows. *Challenge,* March/April 1983, *26*(1), pp. 54–57.

4112 Theory of International Trade

Ali, Ifzal. Product Differentiation, Non-Economic Objectives and Trade Policy. *Indian Econ. Rev.*, January–June 1983, *18*(1), pp. 61–71.

Amsden, Alice H. 'De-Skilling,' Skilled Commodities, and the NICs' Emerging Competitive Advantage. *Amer. Econ. Rev.*, May 1983, *73*(2), pp. 333–37.

Aw, Bee-Yan. The Interpretation of Cross-Section Regression Tests of the Heckscher–Ohlin Theorem with Many Goods and Factors. *J. Int. Econ.*, February 1983, *14*(1/2), pp. 163–67.

Aw, Bee-Yan. Trade Imbalance and the Leontief Paradox. *Weltwirtsch. Arch.*, 1983, *119*(4), pp. 734–38.

Bergstrand, Jeffrey H. Measurement and Determinants of Intra-industry International Trade. **In** *Tharakan, P. K. M., ed.*, 1983, pp. 201–53. **[G: OECD]**

Bhagwati, Jagdish N. Alternative Theories of Illegal Trade: Economic Consequences and Statistical Detection. **In** *Bhagwati, J. N., Vol. 1,* 1983, *1981,* pp. 325–42.

Bhagwati, Jagdish N. Distortions and Immiserising Growth: A Generalization. **In** *Bhagwati, J. N., Vol. 1,* 1983, *1968,* pp. 116–20.

Bhagwati, Jagdish N. Immiserising Growth: A Geometrical Note. **In** *Bhagwati, J. N., Vol. 1,* 1983, *1958,* pp. 110–15.

Bhagwati, Jagdish N. International Factor Movements and National Advantage. **In** *Bhagwati, J. N., Vol. 2,* 1983, *1979,* pp. 3–30.

Bhagwati, Jagdish N. International Trade and Economic Expansion. **In** *Bhagwati, J. N., Vol. 1,* 1983, *1958,* pp. 97–109.

Bhagwati, Jagdish N. Optimal Policies and Immiserising Growth. **In** *Bhagwati, J. N., Vol. 1,* 1983, *1969,* pp. 130–33.

Bhagwati, Jagdish N. Protection, Real Wages and Real Incomes. **In** *Bhagwati, J. N., Vol. 1,* 1983, *1959,* pp. 151–66.

Bhagwati, Jagdish N. The Heckscher–Ohlin Theorem in the Multi-commodity Case. **In** *Bhagwati, J. N., Vol. 2,* 1983, *1972,* pp. 462–65.

Bhagwati, Jagdish N. The Proofs of the Theorems on Comparative Advantage. **In** *Bhagwati, J. N., Vol. 2,* 1983, *1967,* pp. 453–61.

Bhagwati, Jagdish N. The Pure Theory of International Trade: A Survey. **In** *Bhagwati, J. N., Vol. 2,* 1983, *1969,* pp. 313–432.

Bhagwati, Jagdish N. The Theory and Practice of Commercial Policy: Departures from Unified Exchange Rates. **In** *Bhagwati, J. N., Vol. 1,* 1983, *1968,* pp. 3–72.

Bhagwati, Jagdish N. The Theory of Immiserising Growth: Further Applications. **In** *Bhagwati, J. N., Vol. 1,* 1983, *1973,* pp. 121–29.

Bhagwati, Jagdish N. and Brecher, Richard A. National Welfare in an Open Economy in the Presence of Foreign-owned Factors of Production. **In** *Bhagwati, J. N., Vol. 2,* 1983, *1980,* pp. 212–25.

Bhagwati, Jagdish N.; Brecher, Richard A. and Hatta, Tatsuo. The Generalized Theory of Transfers and Welfare: Bilateral Transfers in a Multilateral World. *Amer. Econ. Rev.*, September 1983, *73*(4), pp. 606–18.

Bhagwati, Jagdish N. and Hamada, Koichi. The Brain Drain, International Integration of Markets for Professionals and Unemployment: A Theoretical Analysis. **In** *Bhagwati, J. N., Vol. 2,* 1983, *1974,* pp. 103–26.

Bhagwati, Jagdish N. and Johnson, Harry G. A Generalized Theory of the Effects of Tariffs on the Terms of Trade. **In** *Bhagwati, J. N., Vol. 1,* 1983, *1961,* pp. 167–95.

Bhagwati, Jagdish N. and Johnson, Harry G. Notes on Some Controversies in the Theory of International Trade. **In** *Bhagwati, J. N., Vol. 2,* 1983, *1960,* pp. 433–52.

Bhagwati, Jagdish N. and Rodriguez, Carlos. Welfare-Theoretical Analyses of the Brain Drain. **In** *Bhagwati, J. N., Vol. 2,* 1983, *1975,* pp. 75–102.

Bhagwati, Jagdish N. and Srinivasan, T. N. On the Choice between Capital and Labour Mobility. **In** *Bhagwati, J. N., Vol. 2,* 1983, pp. 31–43.

Bhagwati, Jagdish N. and Srinivasan, T. N. On the Choice between Capital and Labour Mobility. *J. Int. Econ.*, May 1983, *14*(3/4), pp. 209–21.

Bhagwati, Jagdish N. and Srinivasan, T. N. On Inferring Resource-allocational Implications from DRC Calculations in Trade-distorted Small Open Economies. **In** *Bhagwati, J. N., Vol. 1,* 1983, *1979,* pp. 582–97.

Bhagwati, Jagdish N. and Srinivasan, T. N. The Theory of Wage Differentials: Production Response and Factor Price Equalisation. **In** *Bhagwati, J. N., Vol. 1,* 1983, *1971,* pp. 481–97.

Boon, Gerard K. Theory and Reality in North–South Trade: Some Explanations. *De Economist,* 1983, *131*(2), pp. 256–72.

Borkakoti, Jitendralal. Economic Methodology,

Trade Theory and Policy. **In** *Black, J. and Winters, L. A., eds.*, 1983, pp. 170–99.

Bowden, Roger J. The Conceptual Basis of Empirical Studies of Trade in Manufactured Commodities: A Constructive Critique. *Manchester Sch. Econ. Soc. Stud.*, September 1983, *51*(3), pp. 209–34.

Bowen, Harry P. Changes in the International Distribution of Resources and Their Impact on U.S. Comparative Advantage. *Rev. Econ. Statist.*, August 1983, *65*(3), pp. 402–14.

Bowen, Harry P. On the Theoretical Interpretation of Indices of Trade Intensity and Revealed Comparative Advantage. *Weltwirtsch. Arch.*, 1983, *119*(3), pp. 464–72.

Brander, James A. and Djajić, Slobodan. Rent-Extracting Tariffs and the Management of Exhaustible Resources. *Can. J. Econ.*, May 1983, *16*(2), pp. 288–98.

Brander, James A. and Krugman, Paul R. A 'Reciprocal Dumping' Model of International Trade. *J. Int. Econ.*, November 1983, *15*(3/4), pp. 313–21.

Brecher, Richard A. and Bhagwati, Jagdish N. Foreign Ownership and the Theory of Trade and Welfare. **In** *Bhagwati, J. N., Vol. 2,* 1983, *1981,* pp. 226–40.

Britto, Ronald. A Basic Approach to the Choice of Numeraire in Models of Trade with Price Risk. *Oxford Econ. Pap.*, March 1983, *35*(1), pp. 81–88.

Browne, F. X. Price Setting Behaviour for Traded Goods—The Irish Case. *Appl. Econ.*, April 1983, *15*(2), pp. 153–63. **[G: Ireland]**

Calvo, Guillermo A. and Wellisz, Stanislaw. International Factor Mobility and National Advantage. *J. Int. Econ.*, February 1983, *14*(1/2), pp. 103–14.

Casas, F. R. International Trade with Produced Transport Services. *Oxford Econ. Pap.*, March 1983, *35*(1), pp. 89–109.

Cheng, Leonard. Ex ante Plant Design, Portfolio Theory, and Uncertain Terms of Trade. *J. Int. Econ.*, February 1983, *14*(1/2), pp. 25–51.

Chichilnisky, Graciela. The Transfer Problem with Three Agents Once Again: Characterization, Uniqueness and Stability [Basic Goods, the Effects of Commodity Transfers and the International Economic Order]. *J. Devel. Econ.*, Aug.–Oct. 1983, *13*(1–2), pp. 237–47.

Clements, Kenneth W. and Semudram, Muthi. An International Comparison of the Price of Nontraded Goods. *Weltwirtsch. Arch.*, 1983, *119*(2), pp. 356–63. **[G: Selected LDCs; Selected MDCs]**

Djajić, Slobodan. Intermediate Inputs and International Trade: An Analysis of the Real and Monetary Aspects of a Change in the Price of Oil. *J. Int. Money Finance,* August 1983, *2*(2), pp. 179–95.

Dompierre, Michael B. The Heckscher–Ohlin Model with Three Factors and Two Goods: A Comment. *Econ. Rec.*, March 1983, *59*(164), pp. 88–90.

Dosi, Giovanni and Soete, L. Technology Gaps and Cost-based Adjustment: Some Explorations on the Determinants of International Competitiveness. *Metroecon.*, October 1983, *35*(3), pp. 197–222. **[G: OECD]**

Drabicki, John Z. and Takayama, Akira. The Theory of Comparative Advantage in a Monetary World. *Southern Econ. J.*, July 1983, *50*(1), pp. 1–17.

Dudley, Leonard and Trépanier, Carole. Les anticipations et la réponse des importations aux variations dans les prix et les taux de change. (Expectations and the Response of Imports to Price and Exchange-Rate Changes. With English summary.) *Revue Écon.*, November 1983, *34*(6), pp. 1145–63. **[G: W. Germany; France; Canada; U.S.]**

Ebrill, Liam P. and Possen, Uri M. Taxation, Inflation, and the Terms of Trade. *J. Public Econ.*, December 1983, *22*(3), pp. 375–86.

Ellis, C. Michael. An Alternative Interpretation and Empirical Test of the Linder Hypothesis. *Quarterly Journal of Business and Economics,* Autumn 1983, *22*(4), pp. 53–62. **[G: MDCs]**

Fase, M. M. G. On Professor Glejser's Technical Possibility of Testing Intra-industry and Inter-industry Specialization: A Comment. **In** *Tharakan, P. K. M., ed.*, 1983, pp. 45–46. **[G: EEC]**

Findlay, Ronald and Kierzkowski, Henryk. International Trade and Human Capital: A Simple General Equilibrium Model. *J. Polit. Econ.*, December 1983, *91*(6), pp. 957–78.

Fries, Timothy. The Possibility of an Immiserizing Transfer under Uncertainty. *J. Int. Econ.*, November 1983, *15*(3/4), pp. 297–311.

Fröhlich, Gerhard. A Theoretical Problem of Foreign Trade Effectiveness. *Soviet E. Europ. Foreign Trade,* Fall 1983, *19*(3), pp. 3–31. **[G: CMEA; OECD]**

Gavelin, Lars and Lundberg, L. Determinants of Intra-industry Trade: Testing Some Hypotheses on Swedish Trade Data. **In** *Tharakan, P. K. M., ed.*, 1983, pp. 161–200. **[G: Sweden; OECD]**

Geanakoplos, John and Heal, Geoffrey M. A Geometric Explanation of the Transfer Paradox in a Stable Economy [Basic Goods, the Effects of Commodity Transfers and the International Economic Order]. *J. Devel. Econ.*, Aug.–Oct. 1983, *13*(1–2), pp. 223–36.

Gerking, Shelby D. and Mutti, John H. Factor Rewards and the International Migration of Unskilled Labor: A Model with Capital Mobility. *J. Int. Econ.*, May 1983, *14*(3/4), pp. 367–80.

Glejser, H. Intra-industry and Inter-industry Trade Specialization: Trend and Cycle in the E.E.C. (1973–1979). **In** *Tharakan, P. K. M., ed.*, 1983, pp. 35–43. **[G: EEC]**

Grossman, Gene M. Partially Mobile Capital: A General Approach to Two-Sector Trade Theory. *J. Int. Econ.*, August 1983, *15*(1/2), pp. 1–17.

Gunning, Jan Willem. Basic Goods, the Effects of Commodity Transfers and the International Economic Order: Comment. *J. Devel. Econ.*, Aug.–Oct. 1983, *13*(1–2), pp. 197–203.

Gunning, Jan Willem. The Transfer Problem: A Rejoinder [Basic Goods, the Effects of Commodity Transfers and the International Economic Order]. *J. Devel. Econ.*, Aug.–Oct. 1983, *13*(1–2), pp. 249–50.

Hamada, Koichi and Bhagwati, Jagdish N. Domestic Distortions, Imperfect Information and the Brain Drain. **In** *Bhagwati, J. N., Vol. 2,* 1983, *1976,* pp. 127–41.

Hamilton, Carl and Svensson, Lars E. O. Should Direct or Total Factor Intensities Be Used in Tests of the Factor Proportions Hypothesis? *Weltwirtsch. Arch.*, 1983, *119*(3), pp. 453–63.

Hansson, Göte and Lundahl, Mats. The Rybczynski Theorem under Decreasing Returns to Scale. *Scand. J. Econ.*, 1983, *85*(4), pp. 531–40.

Harkness, Jon P. The Factor-Proportions Model with Many Nations, Goods and Factors: Theory and Evidence. *Rev. Econ. Statist.*, May 1983, *65*(2), pp. 298–305. **[G: Canada; U.S.]**

Haynes, Stephen E. and Stone, Joe A. Secular and Cyclical Responses of U.S. Trade to Income: An Evaluation of Traditional Models. *Rev. Econ. Statist.*, February 1983, *65*(1), pp. 87–95. **[G: U.S.]**

Helpman, Elhanan and Razin, Assaf. Increasing Returns, Monopolistic Competition, and Factor Movements: A Welfare Analysis. *J. Int. Econ.*, May 1983, *14*(3/4), pp. 263–76.

Hicks, John. Productivity and Trade. **In** *Hicks, J.*, 1983, *1953*, pp. 207–16.

Hicks, John. Productivity and Trade: Import Bias: A Reply to Critics. **In** *Hicks, J.*, 1983, *1959*, pp. 217–23.

Hicks, John. The Factor Price Equalisation Theorem. **In** *Hicks, J.*, 1983, *1959*, pp. 224–33.

Hill, John K. and Méndez, José A. Factor Mobility and the General Equilibrium Model of Production. *J. Int. Econ.*, August 1983, *15*(1/2), pp. 19–26.

Holden, Merle. Empirical Tests of the Heckscher-Ohlin Model for South Africa—A Reappraisal of the Methodology. *S. Afr. J. Econ.*, June 1983, *51*(2), pp. 243–51. **[G: S. Africa]**

Horn, Henrik E. O. Some Implications of Non-Homotheticity in Production in a Two-Sector General Equilibrium Model with Monopolistic Competition. *J. Int. Econ.*, February 1983, *14*(1/2), pp. 85–101.

Jones, Ronald W. International Trade Theory. **In** *Brown, E. C. and Solow, R. M., eds.*, 1983, pp. 69–103.

Jones, Ronald W. and Dei, Fumio. International Trade and Foreign Investment: A Simple Model. *Econ. Inquiry*, October 1983, *21*(4), pp. 449–64.

Jones, Ronald W. and Easton, Stephen T. Factor Intensities and Factor Substitution in General Equilibrium. *J. Int. Econ.*, August 1983, *15*(1/2), pp. 65–99.

Jones, Ronald W.; Neary, J. Peter and Ruane, Frances P. Two-Way Capital Flows: Cross-Hauling in a Model of Foreign Investment. *J. Int. Econ.*, May 1983, *14*(3/4), pp. 357–66.

Kellman, Mitchell H. Relative Prices and International Competitiveness: An Empirical Investigation. *Empirical Econ.*, 1983, *8*(3–4), pp. 125–38. **[G: Japan; Korea; India]**

Kennedy, Thomas E. and McHugh, Richard. Taste Similarity and Trade Intensity: A Test of the Linder Hypothesis for United States Exports. *Weltwirtsch. Arch.*, 1983, *119*(1), pp. 84–96. **[G: U.S.]**

Khan, M. Ali. Public Inputs and the Pure Theory of Trade. *Z. Nationalökon.*, 1983, *43*(2), pp. 131–56.

Khan, M. Ali and Naqvi, Syed Nawab Haider. Capital Markets and Urban Unemployment. *J. Int. Econ.*, November 1983, *15*(3/4), pp. 367–85.

Kohli, Ulrich R. Production in the Heckscher-Ohlin-Samuelson Model of International Trade Theory: A Simple Mathematical Treatment. *J. Econ. Stud.*, 1983, *10*(2), pp. 42–49.

Kohli, Ulrich R. Technology and the Demand for Imports. *Southern Econ. J.*, July 1983, *50*(1), pp. 137–50.

Kol, J. and Mennes, L. B. M. Two-way Trade and Intra-industry Trade with an Application to the Netherlands. **In** *Tharakan, P. K. M., ed.*, 1983, pp. 47–85. **[G: Netherlands]**

Krueger, Anne O. Alternative Trade Strategies and Employment. **In** *Weisbrod, B. and Hughes, H., eds.*, 1983, pp. 387–404. **[G: LDCs]**

Krugman, Paul R. New Theories of Trade among Industrial Countries. *Amer. Econ. Rev.*, May 1983, *73*(2), pp. 343–47.

Krugman, Paul R. The "New Theories" of International Trade and the Multinational Enterprise. **In** *Kindleberger, C. P. and Audretsch, D. B., eds.*, 1983, pp. 57–73.

Lawrence, Colin and Spiller, Pablo T. Product Diversity, Economies of Scale, and International Trade. *Quart. J. Econ.*, February 1983, *98*(1), pp. 63–83.

Lechuga, Alain. Un modèle généralisé de détermination de l'équivalent-travail de la production en économie ouverte. (With English summary.) *Revue Écon. Polit.*, May–June 1983, *93*(3), pp. 445–61. **[G: France]**

Lee, Tom K. Bilateral Trade, Dynamic Bargaining and Nonrenewable Resources. *J. Int. Econ.*, February 1983, *14*(1/2), pp. 169–78.

Léonard, Daniel and Manning, Richard. Advantageous Reallocations: A Constructive Example. *J. Int. Econ.*, November 1983, *15*(3/4), pp. 291–95.

Lerner, Abba P. Factor Prices and International Trade. **In** *Lerner, A. P.*, 1983, *1952*, pp. 95–109.

Lerner, Abba P. The Diagrammatical Representation of Demand Conditions in International Trade. **In** *Lerner, A. P.*, 1983, *1934*, pp. 71–86.

Lerner, Abba P. The Diagrammatical Representation of Cost Conditions in International Trade. **In** *Lerner, A. P.*, 1983, *1932*, pp. 59–69.

Lewis, W. Arthur. Economic Development with Unlimited Supplies of Labour. **In** *Lewis, W. A.*, 1983, *1954*, pp. 311–63.

Lipton, David and Sachs, Jeffrey D. Accumulation and Growth in a Two-Country Model: A Simulation Approach. *J. Int. Econ.*, August 1983, *15*(1/2), pp. 135–59.

Long, Ngo Van. The Effects of a Booming Export Industry on the Rest of the Economy. *Econ. Rec.*, March 1983, *59*(164), pp. 57–60.

Lyons, Bruce. What's So Special about International Trade? The Advantages and Problems of Foreign Competition. **In** *Shepherd, D.; Turk, J. and Silberston, A., eds.*, 1983, pp. 171–99.

Magee, Stephen P. and Brock, William A. A Model of Politics, Tariffs and Rentseeking in General Equilibrium. **In** *Weisbrod, B. and Hughes, H., eds.*, 1983, pp. 497–523.

Mai, Chao-cheng and Chiang, Jeong-wen. Transport Costs in International Trade Theory: A Comparison with the Analysis of Nontraded Goods—A Note. *Quart. J. Econ.*, May 1983, *98*(2), pp. 349–51.

Maneschi, Andrea. Dynamic Aspects of Ricardo's International Trade Theory. *Oxford Econ. Pap.*, March 1983, *35*(1), pp. 67–80.

Markusen, James R. Factor Movements and Commodity Trade as Complements. *J. Int. Econ.*, May 1983, *14*(3/4), pp. 341–56.

Maskus, Keith E. Evidence on Shifts in the Determinants of the Structure of U.S. Manufacturing Foreign Trade, 1958–76. *Rev. Econ. Statist.*, August 1983, *65*(3), pp. 415–22.

Mullor-Sebastián, Alicia. The Product Life Cycle Theory: Empirical Evidence. *J. Int. Bus. Stud.*, Winter 1983, *14*(3), pp. 95–105. **[G: U.S.]**

Musalem, Alberto Roque. Déficit operational en la producción de bienes no-comerciables en un modelo de equilibrio general: el caso argentino. (With English summary.) *Cuadernos Econ.*, August 1983, *20*(60), pp. 133–48. **[G: Argentina]**

Mutti, John H. and Gerking, Shelby D. Multinational Corporations and Discriminatory Investment Controls. *Weltwirtsch. Arch.*, 1983, *119*(4), pp. 649–62.

Nakamura, Toru and Nakamura, Yoichi. Structural Analysis of Global Trade. *Econ. Stud. Quart.*, December 1983, *34*(3), pp. 259–75. **[G: Global]**

Nobel, Klaus. Intra- vs. Inter-Industry Trade: The Case of Many Countries and Industries. *Z. Wirtschaft. Sozialwissen.*, 1983, *103*(4), pp. 341–49.

Panagariya, Arvind. Variable Returns to Scale and the Heckscher–Ohlin and Factor–Price–Equalization Theorems. *Weltwirtsch. Arch.*, 1983, *119*(2), pp. 259–80.

Polemarchakis, Heraklis M. On the Transer Paradox. *Int. Econ. Rev.*, October 1983, *24*(3), pp. 749–60.

Pomery, John. Restricted Stock Markets in Simple General Equilibrium Models with Production Uncertainty. *J. Int. Econ.*, November 1983, *15*(3/4), pp. 253–76.

Ravallion, Martin. Commodity Transfers and the International Economic Order: A Comment [Basic Goods, the Effects of Commodity Transfers and the International Economic Order]. *J. Devel. Econ.*, Aug.–Oct. 1983, *13*(1–2), pp. 205–12.

Rayment, P. B. W. Intra-'Industry' Specialisation and the Foreign Trade of Industrial Countries. **In** *[Saunders, C. T.]*, 1983, pp. 1–28. **[G: OECD]**

Reinikainen, Veikko and Kivikari, Urpo. On the Theory of East–West Economic Relations. **In** *Möttölä, K.; Bykov, O. N. and Korolev, I. S., eds.*, 1983, pp. 3–20. **[G: Selected Countries]**

Roemer, John E. Unequal Exchange, Labor Migration, and International Capital Flows: A Theoretical Synthesis. **In** *[Erlich, A.]*, 1983, pp. 34–60.

Roque, Fatima Moura. Trade Theory and the Portuguese Pattern of Trade. *Economia*, October 1983, *7*(3), pp. 455–69. **[G: Portugal]**

Saavedra-Rivano, Neantro and Wooton, Ian. The Choice between International Labour and Capital Mobility in a Dynamic Model of North–South Trade. *J. Int. Econ.*, May 1983, *14*(3/4), pp. 251–61.

Saghafi, Massoud Mokhtari and Nugent, Jeffrey B. Foreign Aid in the Form of Commodity Transfers That Increase the Income Gap between Rich and Poor Countries: The Chichilnisky Theorems Revisited. *J. Devel. Econ.*, Aug.–Oct. 1983, *13*(1–2), pp. 213–16.

Sanyal, Kalyan K. Vertical Specialization in a Ricardian Model with a Continuum of Stages of Production. *Economica*, February 1983, *50*(197), pp. 71–78.

Sapir, André. Foreign Competition, Immigration and Structural Adjustment. *J. Int. Econ.*, May 1983, *14*(3/4), pp. 381–94.

Schittko, Ulrich K. and Eckwert, B. A Two-Country Temporary Equilibrium Model with Quantity Rationing—On the Structure of Two-Country Disequilibria. *Jahr. Nationalökon. Statist.*, March 1983, *198*(2), pp. 97–121.

Schittko, Ulrich K. and Eckwert, B. The Role of Uncertainty in a Simple Temporary Equilibrium Model of International Trade with Quantity Rationing under Fixed Exchange Rates. *Z. Wirtschaft. Sozialwissen.*, 1983, *103*(5), pp. 461–83.

Sgro, Pasquale M. A Selective Review of Developments in International Trade Theory: Commercial Policy and Free Trade. *Rev. Marketing Agr. Econ.*, April 1983, *51*(1), pp. 31–50.

Srinivasan, T. N. International Factor Movements, Commodity Trade and Commercial Policy in a Specific Factor Model. *J. Int. Econ.*, May 1983, *14*(3/4), pp. 289–312.

Srinivasan, T. N. and Bhagwati, Jagdish N. Postscript [Basic Goods, the Effects of Commodity Transfers and the International Economic Order]. *J. Devel. Econ.*, Aug.–Oct. 1983, *13*(1–2), pp. 251–52.

Srinivasan, T. N. and Bhagwati, Jagdish N. On Transfer Paradoxes and Immiserizing Growth: Part 1: Comment [Basic Goods, the Effects of Commodity Transfers and the International Economic Order]. *J. Devel. Econ.*, Aug.–Oct. 1983, *13*(1–2), pp. 217–22.

Stegemann, Klaus. Wasteful Imports Due to Domestic Monopoly in a Spatially Differentiated Market. *Southern Econ. J.*, January 1983, *49*(3), pp. 734–42.

Stein, Leslie. Emmanuel's Unequal Exchange Thesis: A Critique. *Econ. Int.*, February 1983, *36*(1), pp. 70–88.

Stout, D. K. Technical Advance and Trade Advantage. **In** *Macdonald, S.; Lamberton, D. M. and Mandeville, T., eds.*, 1983, pp. 122–33.

Suzuki, Katsuhiko. A Synthesis of the Heckscher–Ohlin and the Neoclassical Models of International Trade: A Comment. *J. Int. Econ.*, February 1983, *14*(1/2), pp. 141–44.

Svensson, Lars E. O. and Razin, Assaf. The Terms of Trade and the Current Account: The Harberger–Laursen–Metzler Effect. *J. Polit. Econ.*, February 1983, *91*(1), pp. 97–125.

Tawada, Makoto and Okamoto, Hisayuki. International Trade with a Public Intermediate Good. *J. Int. Econ.*, August 1983, *15*(1/2), pp. 101–15.

Tharakan, P. K. M. Areas for Further Research. **In** *Tharakan, P. K. M., ed.*, 1983, pp. 255–62.

Tharakan, P. K. M. The Economics of Intra-industry Trade: A Survey. **In** *Tharakan, P. K. M., ed.*, 1983, pp. 1–34. **[G: OECD]**

Thompson, Henry. Trade and International Factor Mobility. *Atlantic Econ. J.*, December 1983, *11*(4), pp. 45–48.

Tironi, Ernesto. Distribution of Benefits from Regional Trade Liberalisation among Country Partners in the Presence of Transnational Corporations. **In** *Weisbrod, B. and Hughes, H., eds.*, 1983, pp. 547–62.

de Vries, C. G. International Growth with Free Trade in Equities and Goods: A Comment. *Int. Econ. Rev.*, October 1983, *24*(3), pp. 761–69.

Waelbroeck, Jean. Politique commerciale commune et théorie du commerce extérieur. (The Common Commercial Policy and the Theory of International Trade. With English summary.) *Écon. Appl.*, 1983, *36*(2–3), pp. 349–88. **[G: EEC]**

Wang, Linsheng. On the Role of Foreign Trade under Socialism. *Chinese Econ. Stud.*, Spring 1983, *16*(3), pp. 48–65. **[G: U.S.S.R.; China]**

Weintraub, E. Roy. On the Existence of a Competitive Equilibrium: 1930–1954. *J. Econ. Lit.*, March 1983, *21*(1), pp. 1–39.

Wong, Kar-Yiu. On Choosing among Trade in Goods and International Capital and Labor Mobility: A Theoretical Analysis. *J. Int. Econ.*, May 1983, *14*(3/4), pp. 223–50.

Woodland, Alan D. Stability, Capital Mobility and Trade. *Int. Econ. Rev.*, June 1983, *24*(2), pp. 475–83.

Yano, Makoto. Welfare Aspects of the Transfer Problem. *J. Int. Econ.*, November 1983, *15*(3/4), pp. 277–89.

Zakharov, S. N. and Shagalov, G. L. Methods for Determining the Efficiency of Foreign Economic Relations. *Matekon*, Fall 1983, *20*(1), pp. 57–77.

Zhao, Yushen. On Estimation of the Gain and Loss of Foreign Trade. *Chinese Econ. Stud.*, Spring 1983, *16*(3), pp. 76–84.

4113 Theory of Protection

Aizenman, Joshua. Dynamics of Trade Liberalization Policy. *J. Devel. Econ.*, Aug.–Oct. 1983, *13*(1–2), pp. 133–42.

Anderson, Richard K. and Takayama, Akira. Tariffs, Balance of Payments, and the Lerner Symmetry Relation in a Monetary Economy. *Z. ges. Staatswiss.*, March 1983, *139*(1), pp. 1–18.

Benson, Bruce L. and Hartigan, James C. Tariffs Which Lower Price in the Restricting Country: An Analysis of Spatial Markets. *J. Int. Econ.*, August 1983, *15*(1/2), pp. 117–33.

Berglas, Eitan. The Case for Unilateral Tariff Reductions: Foreign Tariffs Rediscovered [Is Unilateral Tariff Reduction Preferable to a Customs Union? The Curious Case of the Missing Foreign Tariff]. *Amer. Econ. Rev.*, December 1983, *73*(5), pp. 1141–42.

Bhagwati, Jagdish N. Distortions and Immiserising Growth: A Generalization. **In** *Bhagwati, J. N., Vol. 1*, 1983, *1968*, pp. 116–20.

Bhagwati, Jagdish N. Lobbying and Welfare. **In** *Bhagwati, J. N., Vol. 1*, 1983, *1980*, pp. 365–73.

Bhagwati, Jagdish N. Lobbying, DUP Activities and Welfare: A Response. **In** *Bhagwati, J. N., Vol. 1*, 1983, *1982*, pp. 374–80.

Bhagwati, Jagdish N. On the Equivalence of Tariffs and Quotas. **In** *Bhagwati, J. N., Vol. 1*, 1983, *1969*, pp. 196–214.

Bhagwati, Jagdish N. Optimal Policies and Immiserising Growth. **In** *Bhagwati, J. N., Vol. 1*, 1983, *1969*, pp. 130–33.

Bhagwati, Jagdish N. Protection, Real Wages and Real Incomes. **In** *Bhagwati, J. N., Vol. 1*, 1983, *1959*, pp. 151–66.

Bhagwati, Jagdish N. Shifting Comparative Advantage, Protectionist Demands, and Policy Response. **In** *Bhagwati, J. N., Vol. 2*, 1983, *1982*, pp. 253–84.

Bhagwati, Jagdish N. The Generalized Theory of Distortions and Welfare. **In** *Bhagwati, J. N., Vol. 1*, 1983, *1971*, pp. 73–94.

Bhagwati, Jagdish N. The Theory and Practice of Commercial Policy: Departures from Unified Exchange Rates. **In** *Bhagwati, J. N., Vol. 1*, 1983, *1968*, pp. 3–72.

Bhagwati, Jagdish N. The Theory of Immiserising Growth: Further Applications. **In** *Bhagwati, J. N., Vol. 1*, 1983, *1973*, pp. 121–29.

Bhagwati, Jagdish N. Trade Liberalization among LDCs, Trade Theory, and GATT Rules. **In** *Bhagwati, J. N., Vol. 1*, 1983, *1968*, pp. 411–33.

Bhagwati, Jagdish N. Trade-diverting Customs Unions and Welfare-Improvement: A Reply. **In** *Bhagwati, J. N., Vol. 2*, 1983, *1973*, pp. 474–76.

Bhagwati, Jagdish N. Trade-diverting Customs Unions and Welfare-Improvement: A Clarification. **In** *Bhagwati, J. N., Vol. 2*, 1983, *1971*, pp. 466–73.

Bhagwati, Jagdish N. and Brecher, Richard A. National Welfare in an Open Economy in the Presence of Foreign-owned Factors of Production. **In** *Bhagwati, J. N., Vol. 2*, 1983, *1980*, pp. 212–25.

Bhagwati, Jagdish N. and Johnson, Harry G. A Generalized Theory of the Effects of Tariffs on the Terms of Trade. **In** *Bhagwati, J. N., Vol. 1*, 1983, *1961*, pp. 167–95.

Bhagwati, Jagdish N. and Kemp, Murray C. Ranking of Tariffs under Monopoly Power in Trade. **In** *Bhagwati, J. N., Vol. 1*, 1983, *1969*, pp. 251–56.

Bhagwati, Jagdish N. and Ramaswami, V. K. Domestic Distortions, Tariffs and the Theory of Optimum Subsidy. **In** *Bhagwati, J. N., Vol. 1*, 1983, *1963*, pp. 238–44.

Bhagwati, Jagdish N.; Ramaswami, V. K. and Srinivasan, T. N. Domestic Distortions, Tariffs, and the Theory of Optimum Subsidy: Some Further Results. **In** *Bhagwati, J. N., Vol. 1*, 1983, *1969*, pp. 245–50.

Bhagwati, Jagdish N. and Srinivasan, T. N. Domestic Resource Costs, Effective Rates of Protection, and Project Analysis in Tariff-distorted Economies. **In** *Bhagwati, J. N., Vol. 1*, 1983, *1980*, pp. 571–76.

Bhagwati, Jagdish N. and Srinivasan, T. N. Optimal Intervention to Achieve Non-economic Objectives. **In** *Bhagwati, J. N., Vol. 1*, 1983, *1969*, pp. 399–410.

Bhagwati, Jagdish N. and Srinivasan, T. N. Optimal Trade Policy and Compensation under Endogenous Uncertainty: The Phenomenon of Market Disruption. **In** *Bhagwati, J. N., Vol. 1*, 1983, *1976*, pp. 434–54.

Bhagwati, Jagdish N. and Srinivasan, T. N. Revenue Seeking: A Generalization of the Theory of Tariffs. **In** *Bhagwati, J. N., Vol. 1,* 1983, *1980,* pp. 343–61.

Bhagwati, Jagdish N. and Srinivasan, T. N. Revenue Seeking: A Generalization of the Theory of Tariffs—A Correction. **In** *Bhagwati, J. N., Vol. 1,* 1983, *1982,* pp. 362–64.

Bhagwati, Jagdish N. and Srinivasan, T. N. Smuggling and Trade Policy. **In** *Bhagwati, J. N., Vol. 1,* 1983, *1973,* pp. 302–14.

Bhagwati, Jagdish N. and Srinivasan, T. N. The Evaluation of Projects at World Prices under Trade Distortions: Quantitative Restrictions, Monopoly Power in Trade and Nontraded Goods. **In** *Bhagwati, J. N., Vol. 1,* 1983, *1981,* pp. 543–57.

Bhagwati, Jagdish N. and Srinivasan, T. N. The General Equilibrium Theory of Effective Protection and Resource Allocation. **In** *Bhagwati, J. N., Vol. 1,* 1983, *1973,* pp. 215–37.

Bhagwati, Jagdish N. and Srinivasan, T. N. The Welfare Consequences of Directly-Unproductive Profit-seeking (DUP) Lobbying Activities. **In** *Bhagwati, J. N., Vol. 1,* 1983, *1982,* pp. 274–85.

Bhagwati, Jagdish N.; Srinivasan, T. N. and Wan, Henry, Jr. Value Subtracted, Negative Shadow Prices of Factors in Project Evaluation, and Immiserising Growth: Three Paradoxes in the Presence of Trade Distortions. **In** *Bhagwati, J. N., Vol. 1,* 1983, *1978,* pp. 577–81.

Bhagwati, Jagdish N. and Tironi, Ernesto. Tariff Change, Foreign Capital and Immiserization. **In** *Bhagwati, J. N., Vol. 2,* 1983, *1980,* pp. 199–211.

Brecher, Richard A. Second-Best Policy for International Trade and Investment. *J. Int. Econ.,* May 1983, *14*(3/4), pp. 313–20.

Brecher, Richard A. and Bhagwati, Jagdish N. Foreign Ownership and the Theory of Trade and Welfare. **In** *Bhagwati, J. N., Vol. 2,* 1983, *1981,* pp. 226–40.

Brecher, Richard A. and Bhagwati, Jagdish N. Immiserizing Transfers from Abroad. **In** *Bhagwati, J. N., Vol. 2,* 1983, *1982,* pp. 505–16.

Brecher, Richard A. and Feenstra, Robert C. International Trade and Capital Mobility between Diversified Economies. *J. Int. Econ.,* May 1983, *14*(3/4), pp. 321–39.

Brecher, Richard A. and Findlay, Ronald. Tariffs, Foreign Capital and National Welfare with Sector-Specific Factors. *J. Int. Econ.,* May 1983, *14*(3/4), pp. 277–88.

Burgess, David F. Protection, Real Wages, Real Incomes, and Foreign Ownership: A Reply. *Can. J. Econ.,* May 1983, *16*(2), pp. 356–61. **[G: Canada]**

Burgess, David F. The Impact of Foreign Trade Distortions on the Social Discount Rate. *Can. J. Econ.,* August 1983, *16*(3), pp. 486–507. **[G: Canada]**

Butlin, M. W. Protection, Real Wages, Real Incomes, and Foreign Ownership: A Comment. *Can. J. Econ.,* May 1983, *16*(2), pp. 350–56. **[G: Australia]**

Calvo, Guillermo A. and Wellisz, Stanislaw. International Factor Mobility and National Advantage. *J. Int. Econ.,* February 1983, *14*(1/2), pp. 103–14.

Cassing, James H. A Note on Growth in the Presence of Tariffs. *J. Int. Econ.,* February 1983, *14*(1/2), pp. 115–21.

Cheng, Leonard. Ex ante Plant Design, Portfolio Theory, and Uncertain Terms of Trade. *J. Int. Econ.,* February 1983, *14*(1/2), pp. 25–51.

Corden, Warner Max. The Economic Effects of a Booming Sector. *Int. Soc. Sci. J.,* 1983, *35*(3), pp. 441–54.

Curtis, Douglas C. A. Trade Policy to Promote Entry with Scale Economies, Product Variety, and Export Potential. *Can. J. Econ.,* February 1983, *16*(1), pp. 109–21.

Das, Satya P. Optimum Tariffs on Final and Intermediate Goods. *Int. Econ. Rev.,* June 1983, *24*(2), pp. 493–508.

Dervis, Kemal. Foreign Protectionism and Resource Allocation in a Developing Economy: A General Equilibrium Analysis. **In** *Kelley, A. C.; Sanderson, W. C. and Williamson, J. G., eds.,* 1983, pp. 43–56.

Diewert, W. Erwin. The Measurement of Waste within the Production Sector of an Open Economy. *Scand. J. Econ.,* 1983, *85*(2), pp. 159–79.

Dinopoulos, Elias. Import Competition, International Factor Mobility and Lobbying Responses: The Schumpeterian Industry Case. *J. Int. Econ.,* May 1983, *14*(3/4), pp. 395–410.

Donnenfeld, Shabtai and Strebel, Paul J. Industry Structure and Trade Policy under Fluctuating Import Prices. *Europ. Econ. Rev.,* November 1983, *23*(2), pp. 203–15.

Driscoll, Michael J. and Ford, J. L. Protection and Optimal Trade-Restricting Policies under Uncertainty. *Manchester Sch. Econ. Soc. Stud.,* March 1983, *51*(1), pp. 21–32.

Easton, Stephen T. and Grubel, Herbert G. The Costs and Benefits of Protection in a Growing World. *Kyklos,* 1983, *36*(2), pp. 213–30. **[G: U.S.]**

Eaton, Jonathan, et al. The Impact of Monopoly Pricing on the Lerner Symmetry Theorem: A Comment. *Quart. J. Econ.,* August 1983, *98*(3), pp. 529–33.

Eichengreen, Barry J. Effective Projection and Exchange-Rate Determination. *J. Int. Money Finance,* April 1983, *2*(1), pp. 1–15.

Falvey, Rodney E. Protection and Import-Competing Product Selection in a Multi-Product Industry. *Int. Econ. Rev.,* October 1983, *24*(3), pp. 735–47.

Feenstra, Robert C. Shifting Comparative Advantage, Protectionist Demands, and Policy Response: Appendix: Product Creation and Trade Patterns: A Theoretical Note on the "Biological" Model of Trade in Similar Products. **In** *Bhagwati, J. N., Vol. 2,* 1983, *1982,* pp. 284–95.

Feenstra, Robert C. and Bhagwati, Jagdish N. Tariff Seeking and the Efficient Tariff. **In** *Bhagwati, J. N., Vol. 1,* 1983, *1982,* pp. 381–95.

Feltenstein, Andrew. A Computational General Equilibrium Approach to the Shadow Pricing of Trade Restrictions and the Adjustment of the Exchange Rate, with an Application to Argentina. *J. Policy Modeling,* November 1983, *5*(3), pp.

333–61. [G: Argentina]

Findlay, Ronald and Wellisz, Stanislaw. Some Aspects of the Political Economy of Trade Restrictions. *Kyklos,* 1983, *36*(3), pp. 469–81.

Flam, Harry; Persson, Torsten and Svensson, Lars E. O. Optimal Subsidies to Declining Industries: Efficiency and Equity Considerations. *J. Public Econ.,* December 1983, *22*(3), pp. 327–45.

Forster, Bruce A. and Rees, Ray. The Optimal Rate of Decline of an Inefficient Industry. *J. Public Econ.,* November 1983, *22*(2), pp. 227–42.

Hamilton, Bob and Whalley, John. Optimal Tariff Calculations in Alternative Trade Models and Some Possible Implications for Current World Trading Arrangements. *J. Int. Econ.,* November 1983, *15*(3/4), pp. 323–48.

Hatiboglu, Z. An Unconventional Approach to the Analysis of Growth in Developing Countries and Its Application in Turkey. *S. Afr. J. Econ.,* June 1983, *51*(2), pp. 297–309. [G: Turkey]

Hindley, Brian. Trade Policy, Economic Performance, and Britain's Economic Problems. **In** *Black, J. and Winters, L. A., eds.,* 1983, pp. 25–42. [G: U.K.]

Itagaki, Takao. Multinational Firms and the Theory of Effective Protection. *Oxford Econ. Pap.,* November 1983, *35*(3), pp. 447–62.

Krauss, Melvyn. Protectionism, the Welfare State, and the Third World. *Cato J.,* Winter 1983/84, *3*(3), pp. 673–78. [G: LDCs; U.S.; Europe]

Krieger, Ronald A. Economics and Protectionist Premises [Realism and Free-Trade Policy]. *Cato J.,* Winter 1983/84, *3*(3), pp. 667–72.

Krueger, Anne O. The Effects of Trade Strategies on Growth. *Finance Develop.,* June 1983, *20*(2), pp. 6–8. [G: Selected LDCs]

Leitzinger, Jeffrey J. and Tamor, Kenneth. Foreign Competition in Antitrust Law. *J. Law Econ.,* April 1983, *26*(1), pp. 87–102.

Lerner, Abba P. Foreign Trade III (In a Capitalist Economy.) **In** *Lerner, A. P.,* 1983, *1970,* pp. 111–23.

Lerner, Abba P. The Symmetry between Import and Export Taxes. **In** *Lerner, A. P.,* 1983, *1936,* pp. 87–94.

Magee, Stephen P. and Brock, William A. A Model of Politics, Tariffs and Rentseeking in General Equilibrium. **In** *Weisbrod, B. and Hughes, H., eds.,* 1983, pp. 497–523.

Marrese, Michael and Vaňous, Jan. Unconventional Gains from Trade. *J. Compar. Econ.,* December 1983, *7*(4), pp. 382–99. [G: CMEA]

Martin, Randolph C. and Pelzman, Joseph. The Regional Welfare Effects of Tariff Reductions on Textile Products. *J. Reg. Sci.,* August 1983, *23*(3), pp. 323–36. [G: U.S.]

Monke, Eric. Tariffs, Implementation Costs, and Optimal Policy Choice. *Weltwirtsch. Arch.,* 1983, *119*(2), pp. 281–96. [G: Ivory Coast; Senegal; Liberia]

Murray, Tracy; Schmidt, Wilson E. and Walter, Ingo. On the Equivalence of Import Quotas and Voluntary Export Restraint. *J. Int. Econ.,* February 1983, *14*(1/2), pp. 191–94.

Olson, Mancur. Public Choice and Growth: Barriers to Trade, Factor Mobility, and Growth. **In** *Biehl, D.; Roskamp, K. W. and Stolper, W. F., eds.,* 1983, pp. 15–40. [G: OECD]

Panagariya, Arvind. Import Objective, Distortions, and Optimal Tax Structure: A Generalization. *Quart. J. Econ.,* August 1983, *98*(3), pp. 515–24.

Ray, Edward John. The Impact of Monopoly Pricing on the Lerner Symmetry Theorem: Reply. *Quart. J. Econ.,* August 1983, *98*(3), pp. 535–37.

Sakashita, Noboru. Resolution of Mutual Loss Conflict Induced by the Embargo Threat. **In** *Isard, W. and Nagao, Y., eds.,* 1983, pp. 139–46.

Sapir, André. Foreign Competition, Immigration and Structural Adjustment. *J. Int. Econ.,* May 1983, *14*(3/4), pp. 381–94.

Sheer, Alain. The Deadweight Loss from an Optimum Tariff. *Weltwirtsch. Arch.,* 1983, *119*(3), pp. 569–74.

Srinivasan, T. N. and Bhagwati, Jagdish N. Alternative Policy Rankings in a Large, Open Economy with Sector-specific, Minimum Wages. **In** *Bhagwati, J. N., Vol. 1,* 1983, *1975,* pp. 505–20.

Srinivasan, T. N. and Bhagwati, Jagdish N. Shadow Prices for Project Selection in the Presence of Distortions: Effective Rates of Protection and Domestic Resource Costs. **In** *Bhagwati, J. N., Vol. 1,* 1983, *1978,* pp. 523–42.

Stournaras, Yannis A. Optimal Tariffs to Raise Revenue in the Presence of Unemployment. *Greek Econ. Rev.,* April 1983, *5*(1), pp. 33–44.

Thursby, Marie and Jensen, Richard. A Conjectural Variation Approach to Strategic Tariff Equilibria. *J. Int. Econ.,* February 1983, *14*(1/2), pp. 145–61.

Tower, Edward. On the Best Use of Trade Controls in the Presence of Foreign Market Power. *J. Int. Econ.,* November 1983, *15*(3/4), pp. 349–65.

Waelbroeck, Jean. Protection, Employment and Welfare in a 'Stagflating' Economy. **In** *Weisbrod, B. and Hughes, H., eds.,* 1983, pp. 475–96.

Wang, Leonard F. S. Specific Factor and Optimal Intervention to Achieve Non-Economic Objectives. *J. Econ. Stud.,* 1983, *10*(2), pp. 50–54.

Wang, Leonard F. S. and Kumar, Rishi. Optimal Intervention to Achieve Non-economic Objectives in the Presence of Foreign-Owned Factors of Production. *Greek Econ. Rev.,* April 1983, *5*(1), pp. 45–54.

Yeager, Leland B. and Tuerck, David G. Realism and Free-Trade Policy. *Cato J.,* Winter 1983/84, *3*(3), pp. 645–66. [G: U.S.]

Yeh, Yeong-Her. On the Distribution of Tariff and Import Quota Revenues. *Atlantic Econ. J.,* December 1983, *11*(4), pp. 42–44.

4114 Theory of International Trade and Economic Development

Ali, Ifzal. Product Differentiation, Non-Economic Objectives and Trade Policy. *Indian Econ. Rev.,* January–June 1983, *18*(1), pp. 61–71.

Bhagwati, Jagdish N. Immiserising Growth and Negative Shadow Factor Prices: A Comment. **In** *Bhagwati, J. N., Vol. 1,* 1983, pp. 134–35.

Bhagwati, Jagdish N. International Trade and Economic Expansion. **In** *Bhagwati, J. N., Vol. 1,* 1983, *1958,* pp. 97–109.

Bhagwati, Jagdish N. and Srinivasan, T. N. On Inferring Resource-allocational Implications from DRC Calculations in Trade-distorted Small Open Economies. **In** *Bhagwati, J. N., Vol. 1,* 1983, *1979,* pp. 582–97.

Bharat-Ram, Vinay. Import Substitution, Exchange Rates and Growth in the Context of a Developing Economy. *Greek Econ. Rev.,* August 1983, *5*(2), pp. 147–57. **[G: LDCs; India]**

Casar, José I. and Ros, Jaime. Trade and Capital Accumulation in a Process of Import Substitution. *Cambridge J. Econ.,* September/December 1983, *7*(3/4), pp. 257–67. **[G: Mexico]**

Cella, Guido. Politica di sostituzione delle importazioni industriali e competitività dell'economia italiana. (Import Substitution Policy and Competitiveness of the Italian Economy. With English summary.) *Giorn. Econ.,* March-April 1983, *42*(3–4), pp. 215–38. **[G: Italy]**

Chakravarty, Sukhamoy. Trade and Development: Some Basic Issues. *Int. Soc. Sci. J.,* 1983, *35*(3), pp. 424–40. **[G: Global]**

Dervis, Kemal. Foreign Protectionism and Resource Allocation in a Developing Economy: A General Equilibrium Analysis. **In** *Kelley, A. C.; Sanderson, W. C. and Williamson, J. G., eds.,* 1983, pp. 43–56.

Donges, Juergen B. Re-appraisal of Foreign Trade Strategies for Industrial Development. **In** *[Giersch, H.],* 1983, pp. 279–301. **[G: LDCs]**

Dos Santos, Theotonio. The Structure of Dependence. **In** *Todaro, M. P., ed.,* 1983, *1970,* pp. 68–75.

Engberg, Holger. Suggestions for Research Themes and Publications: International Trade and Development. *J. Int. Bus. Stud.,* Spring/Summer 1983, *14*(1), pp. 10–13.

Feder, Gershon. On Exports and Economic Growth. *J. Devel. Econ.,* February/April 1983, *12*(1/2), pp. 59–73.

Glezakos, Constantine. Instability and the Growth of Exports: A Misinterpretation of the Evidence from the Western Pacific Countries. *J. Devel. Econ.,* February/April 1983, *12*(1/2), pp. 229–36. **[G: E. Asia; S. Asia]**

Godfrey, Martin. Surplus Labour as a Source of Foreign Exchange? *World Devel.,* November 1983, *11*(11), pp. 945–56. **[G: LDCs]**

Gouri, Getta. Skill-Formation in Export-Led Industrial Strategy. *Indian Econ. J.,* January-March 1983, *30*(3), pp. 87–102. **[G: Korea]**

Havrylyshyn, Oli and Civan, E. Intra-industry Trade and the Stage of Development: A Regression Analysis of Industrial and Developing Countries. **In** *Tharakan, P. K. M., ed.,* 1983, pp. 111–40. **[G: MDCs; LDCs]**

He, Xinhoa. Exploit the Role of Foreign Trade and Accelerate the Rate of China's Economic Development. *Chinese Econ. Stud.,* Summer 1983, *16*(4), pp. 37–50. **[G: China]**

Jussawalla, Meheroo. Trade, Technology Transfer, and Development. **In** *Macdonald, S.; Lamberton, D. M. and Mandeville, T., eds.,* 1983, pp. 134–54. **[G: LDCs; MDCs]**

Keesing, Donald B. Trade Policy for Developing Countries. **In** *Todaro, M. P., ed.,* 1983, pp. 316–26.

Knudsen, Odin K. and Harbert, Lloyd S. The Causes of Export Instability: Comparing the Experiences of Two Decades. **In** *Bigman, D. and Taya, T., eds.,* 1983, pp. 149–66.

Krueger, Anne O. The Effects of Trade Strategies on Growth. *Finance Develop.,* June 1983, *20*(2), pp. 6–8. **[G: Selected LDCs]**

Kubo, Yuji, et al. Modelos de equilibrio general para el análisis de estrategias alternativas de comercio exterior: una aplicación a Corea. (With English summary.) *Cuadernos Econ.,* December 1983, *20*(61), pp. 313–43. **[G: S. Korea]**

Maneschi, Andrea. The Prebisch-Singer Thesis and the 'Widening Gap' between Developed and Developing Countries. *Can. J. Econ.,* February 1983, *16*(1), pp. 104–08.

Roemer, John E. Unequal Exchange, Labor Migration, and International Capital Flows: A Theoretical Synthesis. **In** *[Erlich, A.],* 1983, pp. 34–60.

Ruane, Frances P. Trade Policies and the Spatial Distribution of Development: A Two-Sector Analysis. *Int. Reg. Sci. Rev.,* June 1983, *8*(1), pp. 47–58. **[G: LDCs]**

Salvatore, Dominick. A Simultaneous Equations Model of Trade and Development with Dynamic Policy Simulations. *Kyklos,* 1983, *36*(1), pp. 66–90.

Sau, Ranjit. Trade and Growth in a Neo-Ricardian Model with Basic and Non-Basic Goods. *Econ. Int.,* May–August–November 1983, *36*(2–3–4), pp. 255–61.

Smith, Sheila and Toye, John. Trade Theory, Industrialization and Commercial Policies. **In** *Todaro, M. P., ed.,* 1983, *1979,* pp. 289–300.

Srinivasan, T. N. and Bhagwati, Jagdish N. Trade and Welfare in a Steady State. **In** *Bhagwati, J. N., Vol. 1,* 1983, *1980,* pp. 136–48.

Tan, Gerald. Export Instability, Export Growth and GDP Growth. *J. Devel. Econ.,* February/April 1983, *12*(1/2), pp. 219–27. **[G: OECD; E. Asia; S. Asia]**

Thirlwall, Anthony P. Confusion over Measuring the Relative Worth of Trade and Aid. *World Devel.,* January 1983, *11*(1), pp. 71–72. **[G: Sudan]**

Thirlwall, Anthony P. Foreign Trade Elasticities in Centre-Periphery Models of Growth and Development. *Banca Naz. Lavoro Quart. Rev.,* September 1983, (146), pp. 249–61.

Yuan, Wenqi and Wang, Jianmin. We Must Review and Reevaluate the Role of Foreign Trade in the Development of the National Economy. *Chinese Econ. Stud.,* Spring 1983, *16*(3), pp. 24–39. **[G: China]**

420 Trade Relations; Commercial Policy; International Economic Integration

4200 General

Adams, F. Gerard and Marquez, Jaime R. A Global Model of Oil-Price Impacts. **In** *[Klein, L. R.],* 1983, pp. 317–39. **[G: Global]**

Al-Sudeary, Abdelmuhsin. South–South Cooperation for Food Security. **In** *Gauhar, A., ed. (I),* 1983, pp. 227–30.

Alzamora, Carlos and Iglesias, Enrique V. Bases for a Latin American Response to the International Economic Crisis. *Cepal Rev.*, August 1983, (20), pp. 17–46. **[G: Latin America]**

Bhagwati, Jagdish N. Whither the Global Negotiations? *Finance Develop.*, September 1983, *20*(3), pp. 34–36. **[G: Global]**

Bienen, Henry S. Broadening Our Foreign Policy Goals: The United States and Sub-Saharan Africa. **In** *Lewis, J. P. and Kallab, V., eds.*, 1983, pp. 66–85. **[G: Sub-Saharan Africa; U.S.]**

Bornschier, Volker. Dependent Reproduction in the World System: A Study on the Incidence of Dependency Reversal. **In** *Doran, C. F.; Modelski, G. and Clark, C., eds.*, 1983, pp. 97–116.

Brundell, Peter; Horn, Henrik E. and Svedberg, Peter. More on the Causes of Instability in Export Earnings: Reply. *Oxford Bull. Econ. Statist.*, November 1983, *45*(4), pp. 385–88.

Csaba, László. Adjustment to the World Economy in Eastern Europe. *Acta Oecon.*, 1983, *30*(1), pp. 53–75. **[G: E. Europe]**

Csikós-Nagy, Béla. Hungary's Adjustment to the New World Market Relations. *Acta Oecon.*, 1983, *30*(1), pp. 77–88. **[G: Hungary]**

Deardorff, Alan V. and Stern, Robert M. Economic Effects of the Tokyo Round. *Southern Econ. J.*, January 1983, *49*(3), pp. 605–24.

Dell, Sidney. Keynes and the International Economic Order: Comment. **In** *Worswick, D. and Trevithick, J., eds.*, 1983, pp. 119–27.

Dornbusch, Rudiger. Keynes and the International Economic Order: Comment. **In** *Worswick, D. and Trevithick, J., eds.*, 1983, pp. 113–19.

Elmandjra, Mahdi. Europe and Its "Privileged Partners" in Africa and the Middle East: Comment. **In** *Tsoukalis, L., ed.*, 1983, pp. 223–26. **[G: EEC]**

Fureng, Dong. Some Problems Concerning China's Strategy in Foreign Economic Relations. *Int. Soc. Sci. J.*, 1983, *35*(3), pp. 455–67. **[G: China]**

Glezakos, Constantine and Nugent, Jeffrey B. More on the Causes of Instability in Export Earnings. *Oxford Bull. Econ. Statist.*, November 1983, *45*(4), pp. 379–83.

Goulder, Lawrence H.; Shoven, John B. and Whalley, John. Domestic Tax Policy and the Foreign Sector: The Importance of Alternative Foreign Sector Formulations to Results from a General Equilibrium Tax Analysis Model. **In** *Feldstein, M., ed.*, 1983, pp. 333–64. **[G: U.S.]**

Hartman, David G. Domestic Tax Policy and the Foreign Sector: The Importance of Alternative Foreign Sector Formulations to Results from a General Equilibrium Tax Analysis Model: Comment. **In** *Feldstein, M., ed.*, 1983, pp. 364–67. **[G: U.S.]**

Huan, Xiang. North–South Relations: Current Situation, Crux of the Problems and Perspectives. **In** *Gauhar, A., ed. (I)*, 1983, pp. 57–67.

Jayawardena, Lal. International Keynesianism—A Solution to the World Crisis? **In** *Jansen, K., ed.*, 1983, pp. 149–74.

Joffe, Josef. Mixing Money and Politics: Dollars and Détente. **In** *Becker, A. S., ed.*, 1983, pp. 15–20. **[G: CMEA; OECD]**

Katzenstein, Peter J. The Small European States in the International Economy: Economic Dependence and Corporatist Politics. **In** *Ruggie, J. G., ed.*, 1983, pp. 91–130. **[G: W. Europe]**

Knirsch, Peter. Political and Economic Determinants of East–West Economic Relations. *Acta Oecon.*, 1983, *31*(1–2), pp. 105–24. **[G: CMEA; OECD]**

Lewis, John P. The United States and the Third World, 1983: Can We Escape the Path of Mutual Injury? **In** *Lewis, J. P. and Kallab, V., eds.*, 1983, pp. 7–48. **[G: LDCs; OECD; U.S.]**

Lewis, W. Arthur. World Production, Prices and Trade, 1870–1960. **In** *Lewis, W. A.*, 1983, *1954*, pp. 175–208.

Littler, Craig R. Japan and China. **In** *Feuchtwang, S. and Hussain, A., eds.*, 1983, pp. 121–47. **[G: China; Japan]**

Lowenthal, Abraham F. Latin America and the Caribbean: Toward a New U.S. Policy. **In** *Lewis, J. P. and Kallab, V., eds.*, 1983, pp. 51–65. **[G: U.S.; Latin America]**

Madaiah, Madappa and Zuberi, Habib A. Towards a New International Economic Order: North–South Dialogue. *Indian Econ. J.*, January-March 1983, *30*(3), pp. 1–16.

Maldonado, Guillermo; Gana, Eduardo and Di Filippo, Armando. Latin America: Crisis, Co-operation and Development. *Cepal Rev.*, August 1983, (20), pp. 75–100. **[G: Latin America]**

Manzhulo, A. N. and Piskulov, Yu. V. Fundamentals and Principles of Soviet–Finnish Economic Cooperation. **In** *Möttölä, K.; Bykov, O. N. and Korolev, I. S., eds.*, 1983, pp. 32–40. **[G: Finland; U.S.S.R.]**

Muldoon, Robert D. Rethinking the Ground Rules for an Open World Economy: An Opportunity for American Political Leadership. *Foreign Aff.*, Summer 1983, *61*(5), pp. 1078–98. **[G: New Zealand; U.S.]**

Newfarmer, Richard S. A Look at Reagan's Revolution in Development Policy. *Challenge*, Sept.–Oct. 1983, *26*(4), pp. 34–43. **[G: U.S.; LDCs]**

Papadantonakis, Kostis. Mercantilism Inverted: World-Economic Crisis and Social Rectification in the United States in the 1980s. **In** *Bergesen, A., ed.*, 1983, pp. 193–202. **[G: U.S.]**

Parkinson, J. R. Poverty and Aid: Introduction: A Window on the World. **In** *Parkinson, J. R., ed.*, 1983, pp. 1–11.

Prebisch, Raúl. The Crisis of Capitalism and International Trade. *Cepal Rev.*, August 1983, (20), pp. 51–74. **[G: Latin America]**

Ramphal, Shridath S. North–South Cooperation: Why and How the South Must Persist. **In** *Gauhar, A., ed. (I)*, 1983, pp. 101–38. **[G: LDCs; MDCs]**

Rudolph, Lloyd I. and Rudolph, Susanne Hoeber. Broadening Our Foreign Policy Goals: The United States, India, and South Asia. **In** *Lewis, J. P. and Kallab, V., eds.*, 1983, pp. 86–113. **[G: India; S. Asia; U.S.]**

Ruggie, John Gerard. International Regimes, Transactions, and Change: Embedded Liberalism in the Postwar Economic Order. **In** *Krasner, S. D., ed.*, 1983, *1982*, pp. 195–231. **[G: Global]**

Ruggie, John Gerard. Political Structure and Change in the International Economic Order: The North–South Dimension. **In** *Ruggie, J. G., ed.*, 1983, pp. 423–87. **[G: LDCs; MDCs]**

Schott, Jeffrey J. The GATT Ministerial: A Postmortem. *Challenge*, May/June 1983, *26*(2), pp. 40–45. **[G: U.S.; EEC; LDCs]**

de la Serre, Françoise. Europe and Its "Privileged Partners" in Africa and the Middle East: Comment. In *Tsoukalis, L., ed.*, 1983, pp. 218–23. **[G: EEC]**

Shihata, Ibrahim F. I. The North–South Dialogue Revisited: Some Personal Reflections. In *Gauhar, A., ed. (I)*, 1983, pp. 81–100.

Shihata, Ibrahim F. I. The OPEC Fund and the North–South Dialogue—Some Personal Reflections. In *Shihata, I. F. I., et al.*, 1983, pp. 138–64. **[G: OPEC]**

Sideri, Sandro. Crisi mondiale, crisi dei modelli di sviluppo latino-americani e ralazioni economiche della Comunità Europea con l'America Latina. (The World Crisis, the Crisis of Latin American Development Models and the Economic Relations of the European Community with Latin America. With English summary.) *Giorn. Econ.*, September–October 1983, *42*(9–10), pp. 601–16. **[G: EEC; Latin America]**

Spencer, Barbara J. and Brander, James A. International R & D Rivalry and Industrial Strategy. *Rev. Econ. Stud.*, October 1983, *50*(4), pp. 707–22.

Tokman, Victor E. Wages and Employment in International Recessions: Recent Latin American Experience. *Cepal Rev.*, August 1983, (20), pp. 113–26. **[G: Latin America]**

Tumlir, Jan. International Economic Order and Democratic Constitutionalism. In *Lenel, H. O.; Willgerodt, H. and Molsberger, J.*, 1983, pp. 71–83.

Wang, Kaike. Tie Industry with Trade: An Important Way to Develop Foreign Trade. *Chinese Econ. Stud.*, Summer 1983, *16*(4), pp. 70–77. **[G: China]**

Williamson, John. Keynes and the International Economic Order. In *Worswick, D. and Trevithick, J., eds.*, 1983, pp. 87–113.

Zhang, Peiji and Cheng, Yugui. On the Promotion of South–South Cooperation and Its Measures. In *Gauhar, A., ed. (I)*, 1983, pp. 141–57.

Zhao, Yushen. On Export–Import Procedure. *Chinese Econ. Stud.*, Spring 1983, *16*(3), pp. 66–75.

421 Trade Relations

4210 Trade Relations

Abele, Hanns. A Model of Trade and Exchange Rates: Comment. In *Hickman, B. G., ed.*, 1983, pp. 311–13. **[G: OECD; Global]**

Adams, Richard H., Jr. The Role of Research in Policy Development: The Creation of the IMF Cereal Import Facility. *World Devel.*, July 1983, *11*(7), pp. 549–63. **[G: LDCs]**

Aggarwal, Mangat Ram. Trade: An Engine of Economic Development in ASEAN Countries. *Rivista Int. Sci. Econ. Com.*, September 1983, *30*(9), pp. 861–72. **[G: S.E. Asia]**

Aghevli, Bijan B. Economic Structure and Policy for External Balance: Comment. *Int. Monet. Fund Staff Pap.*, March 1983, *30*(1), pp. 67–70. **[G: U.S.; W. Europe]**

Aglietta, Michel. Policy Interdependence from a Latin American Perspective: Comment. *Int. Monet. Fund Staff Pap.*, March 1983, *30*(1), pp. 159–63. **[G: Latin America]**

Ahmad, Zakaria Haji and Cheong, K. C. Malaysia–Japan Trade: Issues and Prospects for the 1980s. In *Akrasanee, N., ed.*, 1983, pp. 57–78.

Aizenman, Joshua. Dynamics of Trade Liberalization Policy. *J. Devel. Econ.*, Aug.–Oct. 1983, *13*(1–2), pp. 133–42.

Akao, Nobutoshi. Japan's Economic Security: Introduction. In *Akao, N., ed.*, 1983, pp. 1–13. **[G: Japan]**

Akao, Nobutoshi. Japan's Search for Economic Security. In *Akao, N., ed.*, 1983, pp. 245–72. **[G: U.S.; Selected Countries]**

Akiyama, T. and Duncan, Ronald C. Coffee and Cocoa Trends: An Unfavorable Outlook for Developing Countries. *Finance Develop.*, March 1983, *20*(1), pp. 30–33. **[G: LDCs]**

Akrasanee, Narongchai. ASEAN–Japan Trade and Development: A Synthesis. In *Akrasanee, N., ed.*, 1983, pp. 1–35. **[G: ASEAN; Japan]**

Akrasanee, Narongchai and Dhiravegin, Likhit. Trade and Development in Thai–Japanese Relations. In *Akrasanee, N., ed.*, 1983, pp. 141–61. **[G: Japan; Thailand]**

Alessandrini, Sergio. Consorzi e trading companies per superare gli ostacoli. (The Use of Consortia and Trading Companies to Solve Problems. With English summary.) *L'Impresa*, 1983, *25*(1), pp. 37–41. **[G: Italy]**

Amsden, Alice H. 'De-Skilling,' Skilled Commodities, and the NICs' Emerging Competitive Advantage. *Amer. Econ. Rev.*, May 1983, *73*(2), pp. 333–37.

Amuzegar, Jahangir. Managing Oil Wealth. *Finance Develop.*, September 1983, *20*(3), pp. 19–22. **[G: OPEC; U.K.; Norway]**

Anastasopoulos, Anastasios and Sims, William A. The Regional Impact of the Disintegration of the Canadian Common Market: The Case of Quebec. *Southern Econ. J.*, January 1983, *49*(3), pp. 743–63. **[G: Canada]**

Anderson, Kym. Economic Growth, Comparative Advantage and Agricultural Trade of Pacific Rim Countries. *Rev. Marketing Agr. Econ.*, December 1983, *51*(3), pp. 231–48. **[G: OECD; LDCs]**

Antal, László. Conflicts of Financial Planning and Regulation in Hungary (The "Nature" of Restrictions). *Acta Oecon.*, 1983, *30*(3–4), pp. 341–67. **[G: Hungary]**

Apostolakis, Bobby. Une fonction translog de demande d'importation: le cas de la France. (A Translog Import Demand Function: The French Case. With English summary.) *L'Actual. Econ.*, March 1983, *59*(1), pp. 8–19. **[G: France]**

Aronson, Jonathan David and Cragg, Christopher. The Natural Gas Trade in the 1980s. In *Aronson, J. D. and Cowhey, P. F., eds.*, 1983, pp. 53–82. **[G: Japan; U.S.; W. Europe]**

Arriazu, Ricardo H. Policy Interdependence from a Latin American Perspective. *Int. Monet. Fund Staff Pap.*, March 1983, *30*(1), pp. 113–52. **[G: Latin America]**

Artus, Jacques R. Exchange Rate Regimes and European–U.S. Policy Interdependence: Comment. *Int. Monet. Fund Staff Pap.*, March 1983, *30*(1), pp. 103–08.

Avery, William P. The Politics of Crisis and Cooperation in the Andean Group. *J. Devel. Areas*, January 1983, *17*(2), pp. 155–83. **[G: Latin America]**

Aw, Bee-Yan. The Interpretation of Cross-Section Regression Tests of the Heckscher–Ohlin Theorem with Many Goods and Factors. *J. Int. Econ.*, February 1983, *14*(1/2), pp. 163–67.

Bach, Christopher L. U.S. International Transactions, Fourth Quarter and Year 1982. *Surv. Curr. Bus.*, March 1983, *63*(3), pp. 42–69. **[G: U.S.]**

Balassa, Bela. Industrial Prospects and Policies in the Developed Countries. **In** *[Giersch, H.]*, 1983, pp. 257–78. **[G: OECD; LDCs]**

Balassa, Bela. Policy Responses to External Shocks in Sub-Saharan African Countries. *J. Policy Modeling*, March 1983, *5*(1), pp. 75–105. **[G: Africa]**

Balassa, Bela. Trade Policy in the 1980s: New Issues in the 1980s: Comment. **In** *Cline W. R., ed.*, 1983, pp. 711–22.

Banks, Ferdinand E. European Reliance on Soviet Gas Exports. *Energy J.*, July 1983, *4*(3), pp. 95–96. **[G: Europe]**

Banks, Ferdinand E. Why Europe Needs Siberian Gas. **In** *Tempest, P., ed.*, 1983, pp. 191–96. **[G: W. Europe; U.S.S.R.]**

Barker, K. M. World Economy Forecast Post-Mortems: 1978–82. *Nat. Inst. Econ. Rev.*, May 1983, (104), pp. 32–37. **[G: OECD; Global]**

Barry, Mary. Latin American Exports of Textiles and Apparel—Background Report. **In** *Czinkota, M. R., ed. (II)*, 1983, pp. 126–40. **[G: Latin America; E. Asia]**

Batten, David F. International Conflict Management via Adaptive Learning and Multistage Compromises. *Conflict Manage. Peace Sci.*, Fall 1983, *7*(1), pp. 1–24.

Baumgarten, Klaus. Auswirkungen der Besteuerung importierter Zwischenprodukte. (Consequences of Taxation of Imported Intermediate Goods. With English summary.) *Jahr. Nationalökon. Statist.*, May 1983, *198*(3), pp. 251–68.

Bautista, Romeo M. Philippine–Japanese Trade Relations. *Philippine Econ. J.*, 198, *22*(1), pp. 1–28. **[G: Philippine; Japan]**

Bautista, Romeo M. and Villacorta, Wilfrido V. Economic and Political Factors Affecting Philippine–Japan Trade. **In** *Akrasanee, N., ed.*, 1983, pp. 79–115. **[G: Philippines; Japan]**

Bauwens, Luc and d'Alcantara, Gonzague. An Export Model for the Belgian Industry. *Europ. Econ. Rev.*, August 1983, *22*(3), pp. 265–76. **[G: Belgium]**

Beenstock, Michael and Warburton, Peter. Long-Term Trends in Economic Openness in the United Kingdom and the United States [Long Term Trends in Openness of National Economies]. *Oxford Econ. Pap.*, March 1983, *35*(1), pp. 130–35. **[G: U.K.; U.S.]**

Befus, David. Foreign-Trade Zones: The U.S. Case. **In** *Czinkota, M. R., ed. (II)*, 1983, pp. 279–89. **[G: U.S.]**

Bergsten, C. Fred. Interest Rates and the Trade Balance. **In** *Bergsten, C. F.*, 1983, pp. 173–75. **[G: U.S.]**

Bergsten, C. Fred. The Dollar, the Yen, and U.S. Trade. **In** *Bergsten, C. F.*, 1983, pp. 161–70. **[G: Japan; U.S.]**

Bergsten, C. Fred. The International Dimension. **In** *Miller, G. W., ed.*, 1983, pp. 151–68. **[G: U.S.]**

Bergsten, C. Fred. U.S. International Economic Policy in the 1980s. **In** *Bergsten, C. F.*, 1983, pp. 27–35. **[G: U.S.]**

Bergsten, C. Fred and Cline, William R. Trade Policy in the 1980s: An Overview. **In** *Cline W. R., ed.*, 1983, pp. 59–98. **[G: OECD]**

Bergstrand, Jeffrey H. Measurement and Determinants of Intra-industry International Trade. **In** *Tharakan, P. K. M., ed.*, 1983, pp. 201–53. **[G: OECD]**

Bhagwati, Jagdish N. On the Underinvoicing of Imports. **In** *Bhagwati, J. N., Vol. 1*, 1983, *1974*, pp. 315–24. **[G: OECD; Turkey]**

Bharat-Ram, Vinay. Import Substitution, Exchange Rates and Growth in the Context of a Developing Economy. *Greek Econ. Rev.*, August 1983, *5*(2), pp. 147–57. **[G: LDCs; India]**

Bilson, John F. O. and Hooke, A. W. Conference on Exchange Rate Regimes and Policy Interdependence: Overview. *Int. Monet. Fund Staff Pap.*, March 1983, *30*(1), pp. 185–207.

Binkley, James K. Marketing Costs and Instability in the International Grain Trade. *Amer. J. Agr. Econ.*, February 1983, *65*(1), pp. 57–64.

Bird, Graham. Low-Income Countries and International Financial Reform. *J. Devel. Areas*, October 1983, *18*(1), pp. 53–75. **[G: LDCs]**

Biswas, Basudeb. Declining Share of India in World Exports, 1950–1970. *Indian Econ. J.*, January–March 1983, *30*(3), pp. 75–86. **[G: India; Selected Countries]**

Black, Jeremy. Grain Exports and Neutrality. A Speculative Note on British Neutrality in the War of the Polish Succession. *J. Europ. Econ. Hist.*, Winter 1983, *12*(3), pp. 593–600. **[G: U.K.; Poland]**

Blair, Andrew R. The Relationship of MNC Direct Investment to Host Country Trade and Trade Policy: Some Preliminary Evidence. **In** *Goldberg, W. H., ed.*, 1983, pp. 270–301. **[G: Latin America]**

Boon, Gerard K. Theory and Reality in North–South Trade: Some Explanations. *De Economist*, 1983, *131*(2), pp. 256–72.

Borrus, Michael, et al. Trade and Development in the Semiconductor Industry: Japanese Challenge and American Response. **In** *Zysman, J. and Tyson, L., eds.*, 1983, pp. 142–248. **[G: Japan; U.S.]**

Bowen, Harry P. Changes in the International Distribution of Resources and Their Impact on U.S. Comparative Advantage. *Rev. Econ. Statist.*, August 1983, *65*(3), pp. 402–14.

Brada, Josef C. The Soviet–American Grain Agreement and the National Interest. *Amer. J. Agr. Econ.*, November 1983, *65*(4), pp. 651–56. **[G: U.S.; U.S.S.R.]**

Brada, Josef C. and Méndez, José A. Regional Economic Integration and the Volume of Intra-Regional Trade: A Comparison of Developed and Developing Country Experience. *Kyklos*, 1983, *36*(4), pp. 589–603. **[G: Selected Countries]**

Branson, William H. Economic Structure and Policy for External Balance. *Int. Monet. Fund Staff Pap.,* March 1983, *30*(1), pp. 39–66. **[G: U.S.; W. Europe]**

Bredahl, Maury E. and Green, Leonard. Residual Supplier Model of Coarse Grains Trade. *Amer. J. Agr. Econ.,* November 1983, *65*(4), pp. 785–90. **[G: Selected Countries]**

Brodsky, David A. Exchange Rate Changes and the Measurement of Export Instability. *Oxford Bull. Econ. Statist.,* August 1983, *45*(3), pp. 289–96.

Brodsky, David A. and Sampson, Gary P. Exchange Rate Variations Facing Individual Industries in Developing Countries. *J. Devel. Stud.,* April 1983, *19*(3), pp. 349–67. **[G: India; S. Korea; Ivory Coast; Tunisia]**

Brooks, S. Exports and Imports. **In** *Britton, A., ed.,* 1983, pp. 40–51. **[G: U.K.]**

Brosnan, Peter. The Wage Share in an Open Economy. *J. Post Keynesian Econ.,* Fall 1983, *6*(1), pp. 65–72.

Brown, Lester R. The U.S.–Soviet Food Connection. *Challenge,* January/February 1983, *25*(6), pp. 40–49. **[G: U.S.; U.S.S.R.]**

Browne, F. X. Price Setting Behaviour for Traded Goods—The Irish Case. *Appl. Econ.,* April 1983, *15*(2), pp. 153–63. **[G: Ireland]**

Bruce, Harry J.; Horwitch, Mel and Nueno, Pedro. The Evolution of the International Coal Trade: A Strategic and Decision-Making Perspective. *J. Int. Bus. Stud.,* Spring/Summer 1983, *14*(1), pp. 85–101. **[G: Hong Kong; OECD; S. Korea; Taiwan]**

Buiter, Willem H. Flexible Exchange Rates and Interdependence: Comment. *Int. Monet. Fund Staff Pap.,* March 1983, *30*(1), pp. 35–38. **[G: U.S.]**

Butler, Nicholas. The Ploughshares War between Europe and America. *Foreign Aff.,* Fall 1983, *62*(1), pp. 105–22. **[G: Europe; America]**

Cai, Tianzhang. Conventional Practice in Setting Export–Import Prices. *Chinese Econ. Stud.,* Spring 1983, *16*(3), pp. 85–92.

Cairncross, Alec. Long-term Trends in the Trade between Developing and Industrial Countries. **In** *Parkinson, J. R., ed.,* 1983, pp. 183–206. **[G: LDCs; MDCs]**

Caloia, Angelo. Il rapporto banca/impresa nel processo di internazionalizzazione. (Banks and Businesses in the Internationalisation Process. With English summary.) *L'Impresa,* 1983, *25*(1), pp. 43–48. **[G: Italy]**

Cannon, Terry. Foreign Investment and Trade; Origins of the Modernization Policy. **In** *Feuchtwang, S. and Hussain, A., eds.,* 1983, pp. 288–324. **[G: China]**

Capó, Luis R. International Drug Procurement and Market Intelligence: Cuba. *World Devel.,* March 1983, *11*(3), pp. 217–22. **[G: Cuba]**

Carson, Carol S. Net Exports of Goods and Services, 1980–82. *Surv. Curr. Bus.,* March 1983, *63*(3), pp. 31–41. **[G: U.S.]**

de Cecco, Marcello. International Economic Adjustment: Small Countries and the European Monetary System: Introduction. **In** *de Cecco, M., ed.,* 1983, pp. 1–6. **[G: W. Europe]**

Chakravarty, Sukhamoy. Trade and Development: Some Basic Issues. *Int. Soc. Sci. J.,* 1983, *35*(3), pp. 424–40. **[G: Global]**

Chau, L. C. Imports of Consumer Goods from China and the Economic Growth of Hong Kong. **In** *Youngson, A. J., ed.,* 1983, pp. 184–225. **[G: China; Hong Kong]**

Chaudhuri, K. N. Foreign Trade and Balance of Payments (1757–1947). **In** *Kumar, D., ed.,* 1983, pp. 804–77. **[G: India]**

Chia, Siow Yue. Singapore—EEC Economic Relations. **In** *Chen, P. S. J., ed.,* 1983, pp. 301–34. **[G: Singapore; EEC]**

Chu, Ke-young; Hwa, E. C. and Krishnamurty, K. Export Instability and Adjustments of Imports, Capital Inflows, and External Reserves: A Short-run Dynamic Model. **In** *Bigman, D. and Taya, T., eds.,* 1983, pp. 195–214. **[G: Sri Lanka; Finland]**

Čičin-Šain, Ante. The Effects of Economic Integration in East and West Europe on Non-member Countries: The Case of Yugoslavia. **In** *Saunders, C. T., ed.,* 1983, pp. 103–18. **[G: Yugoslavia; CMEA; EEC]**

Cieślak, Edmund. Aspects of Baltic Sea-Borne Trade in the Eighteenth Century: The Trade Relations between Sweden, Poland, Russia and Prussia. *J. Europ. Econ. Hist.,* Fall 1983, *12*(2), pp. 239–70. **[G: Germany; Poland; Sweden; U.S.S.R.]**

Cline, William R. "Reciprocity": A New Approach to World Trade Policy? **In** *Cline W. R., ed.,* 1983, *1982,* pp. 121–58. **[G: U.S.]**

Cline, William R. Trade Policy in the 1980s: Introduction and Summary. **In** *Cline W. R., ed.,* 1983, pp. 1–54.

Clunies Ross, Anthony. Scotland and the Third World. **In** *Ingham, K. P. D. and Love, J., eds.,* 1983, pp. 255–70. **[G: U.K.]**

Cochran, Laura E. Scottish–Irish Trade in the Eighteenth Century. **In** *Devine, T. M. and Dickson, D., eds.,* 1983, pp. 151–59. **[G: U.K.; Ireland]**

Coda, Michael J. and Jankowski, John E., Jr. The Real Price of Imported Oil Revisited. *Energy J.,* October 1983, *4*(4), pp. 87–90. **[G: Global]**

Cohen, Robert B. The Prospects for Trade and Protectionism in the Auto Industry. **In** *Cline W. R., ed.,* 1983, pp. 527–63. **[G: Selected Countries]**

Colayco, Rufo. Opportunities for new Directions in Philippine–Japanese Trade. *Philippine Econ. J.,* 198, *22*(1), pp. 46–52. **[G: U.S.; W. Germany]**

Colombatto, Enrico. L'economia della compensazione e della cooperazione nell'ambito del commercio Est–Ovest. (The Economics of Countertrade and Cooperation in East–West Trade. With English summary.) *Econ. Int.,* February 1983, *36*(1), pp. 1–19. **[G: CMEA; OECD]**

Conant, Melvin A. An Opportunity for Gulf Gas. **In** *Tempest, P., ed.,* 1983, pp. 197–201. **[G: W. Europe; Middle East]**

Cooper, Richard N. Is Trade Deindustrializing America? A Medium-Term Perspective: Comments and Discussion. *Brookings Pap. Econ. Act.,* 1983, (1), pp. 162–71. **[G: U.S.]**

Cooper, Richard N. Some Aspects of the 1982–83 Brazilian Payments Crisis: Comments and Discussion. *Brookings Pap. Econ. Act.*, 1983, (2), pp. 543–47. **[G: Brazil]**

Corredor, Jaime. The Economic Significance of Mexican Petroleum from the Perspective of Mexico–United States Relations. **In** *Reynolds, C. W. and Tello, C., eds.*, 1983, pp. 137–65. **[G: Mexico; U.S.]**

Costa, Antonio Maria. DYNAMICO: A Multilevel Programming Model of World Trade and Development. **In** *Hickman, B. G., ed.*, 1983, pp. 259–76. **[G: Global]**

Costa, G. C. and da Trivedi, Pushpa. India's Terms of Trade: An Alternative Method. *Indian Econ. J.*, January-March 1983, *30*(3), pp. 119–30. **[G: India]**

Crowson, Phillip. Non-fuel Mineral Procurement Policies. **In** *Akao, N., ed.*, 1983, pp. 145–67. **[G: Japan; Selected Countries]**

Csikós-Nagy, Béla. Liquidity Troubles and Economic Consolidation in Hungary. *Acta Oecon.*, 1983, *31*(1–2), pp. 1–11. **[G: Hungary]**

Cullen, Andrew. Structural Economic Domination and World Trade with Reference to Latin America: A Marxist Approach. *Soc. Econ. Stud.*, September 1983, *32*(3), pp. 35–81. **[G: Latin America]**

Curzio, Alberto Quadrio. Un futuro tranquillo per oro e materie prime (A Calm Future for Gold and Raw Materials. With English summary.) *L'Impresa*, 1983, *25*(6), pp. 51–57.

Cushman, David O. The Effects of Real Exchange Rate Risk on International Trade. *J. Int. Econ.*, August 1983, *15*(1/2), pp. 45–63. **[G: N. America; Japan; U.K.; France; W. Germany]**

Czinkota, Michael R. Services Trade: The Negotiation Agenda. **In** *Czinkota, M. R., ed. (I)*, 1983, pp. 285–302. **[G: U.S.]**

Czinkota, Michael R. and Johnston, Wesley J. Exporting: Does Sales Volume Make a Difference? *J. Int. Bus. Stud.*, Spring/Summer 1983, *14*(1), pp. 147–53. **[G: U.S.]**

Czinkota, Michael R. and LaLonde, Bernard J. An Analysis of Service Delivery in the Latin American Export Activities of U.S. Manufacturers. **In** *Czinkota, M. R., ed. (II)*, 1983, pp. 172–82. **[G: Latin America; U.S.]**

Dadaian, V. S. and Shevtsova, V. E. The Potential Uses for Forecasting and Analysis of a Balance of the Flows of Gross World Output between Regions. *Matekon*, Winter 1983–84, *20*(2), pp. 3–23. **[G: Selected Countries]**

Davies, Mel. Copper and Credit: Commission Agents and the South Australian Mining Association 1845–77. *Australian Econ. Hist. Rev.*, March 1983, *23*(1), pp. 58–77. **[G: Australia]**

Davies, Timothy. Changes in the Structure of the Wheat Trade in Seventeenth-Century Sicily and the Building of New Villages. *J. Europ. Econ. Hist.*, Fall 1983, *12*(2), pp. 371–405. **[G: Italy]**

Davis, Jeffrey M. The Economic Effects of Windfall Gains in Export Earnings, 1975–1978. *World Devel.*, February 1983, *11*(2), pp. 119–39. **[G: Latin American LDCs; African LDCs]**

De Angeli, Sergio. Nuove tecniche di finanziamento per lo sviluppo dell'esportazione. (New Financing Techniques to Stimulate Exports. With English summary.) *L'Impresa*, 1983, *25*(1), pp. 49–53. **[G: Italy]**

De Grauwe, Paul and Frattianni, Michele. U.S. Economic Policies: Are They a Burden on the Rest of the World? *Econ. Notes*, 1983, (3), pp. 69–85. **[G: OECD]**

Deardorff, Alan V. and Stern, Robert M. Changes in Trade and Employment in the Major Industrial Countries, 1970–76. **In** *Weisbrod, B. and Hughes, H., eds.*, 1983, pp. 447–74. **[G: MDCs; LDCs]**

Deardorff, Alan V. and Stern, Robert M. The Economic Effects of Complete Elimination of Post-Tokyo Round Tariffs: Reply. **In** *Cline W. R., ed.*, 1983, pp. 724. **[G: Selected Countries]**

Deardorff, Alan V. and Stern, Robert M. The Economic Effects of Complete Elimination of Post-Tokyo Round Tariffs. **In** *Cline W. R., ed.*, 1983, pp. 673–710. **[G: Selected Countries]**

Deese, David A. The Vulnerability of Modern Nations: Economic Diplomacy in East-West Relations. **In** *Nincic, M. and Wallensteen, P., eds.*, 1983, pp. 155–81. **[G: OECD; CMEA]**

Dhar, Sanjay. U.S. Trade with Latin America: Consequences of Financing Constraints. *Fed. Res. Bank New York Quart. Rev.*, Autumn 1983, *8*(3), pp. 14–18. **[G: U.S.; Latin America]**

Diaz-Alejandro, Carlos F. Some Aspects of the 1982–83 Brazilian Payments Crisis. *Brookings Pap. Econ. Act.*, 1983, (2), pp. 515–42. **[G: Brazil]**

Dick, Hermann, et al. The Short-Run Impact of Fluctuating Primary Commodity Prices on Three Developing Economies: Colombia, Ivory Coast and Kenya. *World Devel.*, May 1983, *11*(5), pp. 405–16. **[G: Colombia; Ivory Coast; Kenya]**

Diebold, John. The Information Technology Industries: A Case Study of High Technology Trade. **In** *Cline W. R., ed.*, 1983, pp. 639–71. **[G: U.S.; U.K.; France; W. Germany; Japan]**

DiLullo, Anthony J. U.S. International Transactions, Second Quarter 1983. *Surv. Curr. Bus.*, September 1983, *63*(9), pp. 34–56. **[G: U.S.]**

DiLullo, Anthony J. U.S. International Transactions, Third Quarter 1983. *Surv. Curr. Bus.*, December 1983, *63*(12), pp. 41–63. **[G: U.S.]**

Doerflinger, Thomas M. Commercial Specialization in Philadelphia's Merchant Community, 1750–1791. *Bus. Hist. Rev.*, Spring 1983, *57*(1), pp. 20–49. **[G: U.S.]**

Donges, Juergen B. Internationalization of Capital, International Division of Labour and the Role of the European Community: Comment. **In** *Tsoukalis, L., ed.*, 1983, pp. 140–43. **[G: EEC]**

Donges, Juergen B. Trade Policy in the 1980s: Discussion, Session 3: Comment. **In** *Cline W. R., ed.*, 1983, pp. 565–67.

Dornbusch, Rudiger. Flexible Exchange Rates and Interdependence. *Int. Monet. Fund Staff Pap.*, March 1983, *30*(1), pp. 3–30. **[G: U.S.]**

Dornbusch, Rudiger. Some Aspects of the 1982–83 Brazilian Payments Crisis: Comments and Discussion. *Brookings Pap. Econ. Act.*, 1983, (2), pp. 547–52. **[G: Brazil]**

Dosi, Giovanni and Soete, L. Technology Gaps and Cost-based Adjustment: Some Explorations on the Determinants of International Competitiveness. *Metroecon.*, October 1983, *35*(3), pp. 197–222. **[G: OECD]**

Drabek, Zdenek. Changes in Relative World Prices and Their Transmission into Economies Protected by Foreign Trade Monopoly. *Econ. Int.*, February 1983, *36*(1), pp. 20–34. **[G: CMEA]**

Drabek, Zdenek. External Disturbances and the Balance of Payments Adjustment in the Soviet Union. *Aussenwirtschaft,* June 1983, *38*(2), pp. 173–94. **[G: U.S.S.R.]**

Drabek, Zdenek. The Impact of Technological Differences on East–West Trade. *Weltwirtsch. Arch.*, 1983, *119*(4), pp. 630–48. **[G: CMEA; OECD]**

Driver, Ciaran. Import Substitution and the Work of the Sector Working Parties. *Appl. Econ.*, April 1983, *15*(2), pp. 165–76. **[G: U.K.]**

Dudley, Leonard. A Non-Linear Model of Import Demand under Price Uncertainty and Adjustment Costs. *Can. J. Econ.*, November 1983, *16*(4), pp. 625–40. **[G: OECD]**

Dudley, Leonard and Trépanier, Carole. Les anticipations et la réponse des importations aux variations dans les prix et les taux de change. (Expectations and the Response of Imports to Price and Exchange-Rate Changes. With English summary.) *Revue Écon.*, November 1983, *34*(6), pp. 1145–63. **[G: W. Germany; France; Canada; U.S.]**

Duncan, Ronald C. and Lutz, Ernst. Penetration of Industrial Country Markets by Agricultural Products from Developing Countries. *World Devel.*, September 1983, *11*(9), pp. 771–86. **[G: LDCs; MDCs]**

Ecevit, Zafer H. Labour Imports/Exports for Economic Development: The Middle East Experience. **In** *Weisbrod, B. and Hughes, H., eds.*, 1983, pp. 331–45. **[G: Middle East]**

Enders, Klaus and Herberg, Horst. The Dutch Disease: Causes, Consequences, Cures and Calmatives. *Weltwirtsch. Arch.*, 1983, *119*(3), pp. 473–97.

Ewing, A. F. OECD: Trade Unions and International Trade. *J. World Trade Law,* January–February 1983, *17*(1), pp. 87–89.

Falcon, Walter P. The World Food Economy: Recent Lessons for the United States and Mexico. **In** *Reynolds, C. W. and Tello, C., eds.*, 1983, pp. 251–58. **[G: U.S.; Mexico]**

Fase, M. M. G. On Professor Glejser's Technical Possibility of Testing Intra-industry and Inter-industry Specialization: A Comment. **In** *Tharakan, P. K. M., ed.*, 1983, pp. 45–46. **[G: EEC]**

Feldman, Robert A. and Proctor, Allen J. U.S. International Trade in Services. *Fed. Res. Bank New York Quart. Rev.*, Spring 1983, *8*(1), pp. 30–36. **[G: U.S.]**

Felmingham, B. S. The Market Integration of Large and Small Economies: Australia, the U.S., and Japan. *J. Macroecon.*, Summer 1983, *5*(3), pp. 335–51. **[G: Australia; Japan; U.S.]**

Fendt, Roberto, Jr. Promotion of Trade in Technical Services: The Brazilian Case. **In** *Czinkota, M. R., ed. (I)*, 1983, pp. 303–18. **[G: Brazil]**

Fesharaki, Fereidun and Isaak, David T. The Impact of Hydrocarbon Processing in OPEC Countries. **In** *Tempest, P., ed.*, 1983, pp. 205–13. **[G: OPEC]**

Fieleke, Norman S. Barter in the Space Age. *New Eng. Econ. Rev.*, November/December 1983, pp. 34–41. **[G: Global]**

Fieleke, Norman S. New England's Exports and U.S. Trade Policy. *New Eng. Econ. Rev.*, March/April 1983, pp. 24–27. **[G: U.S.]**

Fosu, Augustin Kwasi and Strobel, Frederick R. International Impacts on U.S. Inflation in the 1970s. *Eastern Econ. J.*, October–December 1983, *9*(4), pp. 323–31. **[G: U.S.]**

Fournelle, Frank; Muet, Pierre-Alain and Villa, Pierre. Le Commerce extérieur en France depuis 1950: Une étude économétrique des fonctions agrégées. (Foreign Trade in France since 1950: An Econometric Study of Aggregate Functions. With English summary.) *Ann. INSEE,* Jan.–Mar. 1983, (49), pp. 53–88. **[G: France]**

Fox, Douglas R. Motor Vehicles, Model Year 1983. *Surv. Curr. Bus.*, October 1983, *63*(10), pp. 20–24. **[G: U.S.]**

Frank, Isaiah. Trade Policy in the 1980s: The Setting: Comment. **In** *Cline W. R., ed.*, 1983, pp. 210–15.

Frenkel, Jacob A. Exchange Rate Regimes and European–U.S. Policy Interdependence: Comment. *Int. Monet. Fund Staff Pap.*, March 1983, *30*(1), pp. 108–12. **[G: U.S.; W. Europe]**

Fu, Zhengluo and An, Baojun. Strengthen Our Economic and Trade Relations with Oil-Producing Countries in the Middle East. *Chinese Econ. Stud.*, Summer 1983, *16*(4), pp. 27–36. **[G: China; OPEC]**

von Furstenberg, George M. Domestic Determinants of the Current Account Balance of the United States. *Quart. J. Econ.*, August 1983, *98*(3), pp. 401–25. **[G: U.S.]**

Gaffen, Michael. The World Coal Trade in the 1980s: The Rebirth of a Market. **In** *Aronson, J. D. and Cowhey, P. F., eds.*, 1983, pp. 83–104. **[G: Global]**

Galenson, Walter. Capitalists and Commissars. *Policy Rev.*, Spring 1983, (24), pp. 9. **[G: E. Europe; W. Europe; U.S.]**

Gallini, Nancy T.; Lewis, Tracy R. and Ware, Roger. Strategic Timing and Pricing of a Substitute in a Cartelized Resource Market. *Can. J. Econ.*, August 1983, *16*(3), pp. 429–46.

Gandolfi, Arthur E. and Lothian, James R. International Price Behavior and the Demand for Money. **In** *Darby, M. P. and Lothian, J. R., et al.*, 1983, pp. 421–61. **[G: OECD]**

Gandolfi, Arthur E. and Lothian, James R. International Price Behavior and the Demand for Money. *Econ. Inquiry,* July 1983, *21*(3), pp. 295–311. **[G: OECD]**

Gasparetto, Marialuisa Manfredini. Turchia: l'attività economica e l'interscambio. (Turkey: Economic Activity and Interexchange. With English summary.) *Rivista Int. Sci. Econ. Com.*, June 1983, *30*(6), pp. 566–88. **[G: Turkey]**

Gately, Dermot. OPEC: Retrospective and Prospects, 1973–1990. *Europ. Econ. Rev.*, May 1983, *21*(3), pp. 313–31. **[G: OPEC]**

Gattiker, Heinrich. Foreign Policy Objectives and the Extraterritorial Application of Law. *Wirtsch.*

Recht, 1983, *35*(2/3), pp. 154–61. [G: U.S.; Switzerland]

Gavelin, Lars. Determinants of the Structure of Swedish Foreign Trade in Manufactures, 1968–1979. *Scand. J. Econ.*, 1983, *85*(4), pp. 485–98. [G: Sweden]

Gavelin, Lars and Lundberg, L. Determinants of Intra-industry Trade: Testing Some Hypotheses on Swedish Trade Data. **In** *Tharakan, P. K. M., ed.*, 1983, pp. 161–200. [G: Sweden; OECD]

Gibbs, David C. The Effect of International and National Developments on the Clothing Industry of the Manchester Conurbation. **In** *Hamilton, F. E. I. and Linge, G. J. R., eds.*, 1983, pp. 233–54. [G: U.K.; Selected Countries]

Giddy, Ian H. and Ismael, Mona A. International Trade Financing Techniques. **In** *George, A. M. and Giddy, I. H., eds., Vol. 2*, 1983, pp. 7.1:1–30.

Glaessner, Thomas C. U.S. International Transactions in 1982. *Fed. Res. Bull.*, April 1983, *69*(4), pp. 251–60. [G: U.S.]

Glejser, H. Intra-industry and Inter-industry Trade Specialization: Trend and Cycle in the E.E.C. (1973–1979). **In** *Tharakan, P. K. M., ed.*, 1983, pp. 35–43. [G: EEC]

Glezakos, Constantine. Instability and the Growth of Exports: A Misinterpretation of the Evidence from the Western Pacific Countries. *J. Devel. Econ.*, February/April 1983, *12*(1/2), pp. 229–36. [G: E. Asia; S. Asia]

Gøbel, Erik. Danish Trade to the West Indies and Guinea, 1671–1754. *Scand. Econ. Hist. Rev.*, 1983, *31*(1), pp. 21–49. [G: Denmark; West Indies; Guinea]

Goldman, Marshall I. The Evolution and Possible Direction of U.S. Policy in East–West Trade. **In** *Becker, A. S., ed.*, 1983, pp. 155–76. [G: U.S.S.R.; U.S.]

Goldstein, Walter. Economic Nationalism and the Disruption of World Trade: The Impact of the Third Oil Shock. **In** *Lieber, R. J., ed.*, 1983, pp. 169–92. [G: LDCs; OECD; OPEC]

Goodwin, R. M. The World Matrix Multiplier. **In** *Goodwin, R. M.*, 1983, pp. 30–56.

Gould, Peter and Straussfogel, Debra. Revolution and Structural Disconnection: A Note on Portugal's International Trade. *Economia*, October 1983, *7*(3), pp. 435–53. [G: Portugal]

Gouri, Getta. Skill-Formation in Export-Led Industrial Strategy. *Indian Econ. J.*, January-March 1983, *30*(3), pp. 87–102. [G: Korea]

Grassman, Sven. Reply to Beenstock–Warburton and Kar [Long Term Trends in Openness of National Economies]. *Oxford Econ. Pap.*, March 1983, *35*(1), pp. 141–42. [G: U.K.; Brazil]

Grassman, Sven and Olsson, Hans. The Productivity Link between Exports and Domestic Demand: Sweden. **In** *de Cecco, M., ed.*, 1983, pp. 34–48. [G: Sweden]

Gray, H. Peter. A Negotiating Strategy for Trade in Services. *J. World Trade Law*, September–October 1983, *17*(5), pp. 377–88.

Green, Robert T. Import/Export Patterns in Manufactured Goods of Four Latin American Nations, 1963–78. **In** *Czinkota, M. R., ed. (II)*, 1983, pp. 26–47. [G: Argentina; Brazil; Colombia; Venezuela; U.S.]

Greenaway, David. Patterns of Intra-industry Trade in the United Kingdom. **In** *Tharakan, P. K. M., ed.*, 1983, pp. 141–60. [G: U.K.]

Greenaway, David and Milner, Chris R. On the Measurement of Intra-Industry Trade. *Econ. J.*, December 1983, *93*(372), pp. 900–908. [G: U.K.]

Griffin, Joseph P. Antitrust Law Issues in Countertrade. *J. World Trade Law*, May–June 1983, *17*(3), pp. 236–48. [G: U.S.]

Grjebine, André. Internationalization of Capital, International Division of Labour and the Role of the European Community: Comment. **In** *Tsoukalis, L., ed.*, 1983, pp. 143–46. [G: EEC]

Guillaume, Jean-Marie. A European View of East–West Trade in the 1980s. **In** *Becker, A. S., ed.*, 1983, pp. 135–54. [G: CMEA; U.S.; W. Europe]

Gupta, Sanjeev. India and the Second OPEC Oil Price Shock—An Economy-Wide Analysis. *Weltwirtsch. Arch.*, 1983, *119*(1), pp. 122–37. [G: India]

Haberler, Gottfried. Trade Policy in the 1980s: The Setting: Comment. **In** *Cline W. R., ed.*, 1983, pp. 203–09.

Halaga, Ondrej R. A Mercantilist Initiative to Compete with Venice: Kaschau's Fustian Monopoly (1411). *J. Europ. Econ. Hist.*, Fall 1983, *12*(2), pp. 407–35. [G: Czechoslovakia]

Hamilton, Carl and Svensson, Lars E. O. On the Choice between Capital Import and Labor Export. *Europ. Econ. Rev.*, January 1983, *20*(1–3), pp. 167–92.

Hanke, Steve H. U.S.-Japanese Trade: Myths and Realities. *Cato J.*, Winter 1983/84, *3*(3), pp. 757–69. [G: U.S.; Japan]

Hanson, John R., II. Export Earnings Instability before World War II: Price, Quantity, Supply, Demand? *Econ. Develop. Cult. Change*, April 1983, *31*(3), pp. 621–37.

Hanson, Philip. The Role of Trade and Technology Transfer in the Soviet Economy. **In** *Becker, A. S., ed.*, 1983, pp. 23–48. [G: OECD; U.S.S.R.]

Hardt, John P. and Tomlinson, Kate S. The Potential Role of Western Policy toward Eastern Europe in East–West Trade. **In** *Becker, A. S., ed.*, 1983, pp. 79–133.

Harkness, Jon P. The Factor-Proportions Model with Many Nations, Goods and Factors: Theory and Evidence. *Rev. Econ. Statist.*, May 1983, *65*(2), pp. 298–305. [G: Canada; U.S.]

Haudeville, Bernard. Echanges extérieurs, emploi et redéploiement industriel en France de 1974 à 1979. (With English summary.) *Rev. Econ. Ind.*, 3rd Trimester 1983, (25), pp. 21–37. [G: France]

Havrylyshyn, Oli and Alikhani, Iradj. Is There Cause for Export Optimism? *Finance Develop.*, June 1983, *20*(2), pp. 9–12. [G: Selected LDCs]

Havrylyshyn, Oli and Civan, E. Intra-industry Trade and the Stage of Development: A Regression Analysis of Industrial and Developing Countries. **In** *Tharakan, P. K. M., ed.*, 1983, pp. 111–40. [G: MDCs; LDCs]

Havrylyshyn, Oli and Wolf, Martin. Recent Trends in Trade among Developing Countries. *Europ.*

Econ. Rev., May 1983, 21(3), pp. 333–62. [G: LDCs]

Haynes, Stephen E. and Stone, Joe A. Secular and Cyclical Responses of U.S. Trade to Income: An Evaluation of Traditional Models. *Rev. Econ. Statist.*, February 1983, *65*(1), pp. 87–95. [G: U.S.]

Haynes, Stephen E. and Stone, Joe A. Specification of Supply Behavior in International Trade. *Rev. Econ. Statist.*, November 1983, *65*(4), pp. 626–32. [G: U.S.]

He, Xinhoa. Exploit the Role of Foreign Trade and Accelerate the Rate of China's Economic Development. *Chinese Econ. Stud.*, Summer 1983, *16*(4), pp. 37–50. [G: China]

Helleiner, Gerald K. Uncertainty, Information and the Economic Interests of the Developing Countries. In *O'Brien, R. C., ed.*, 1983, pp. 28–42.

Hemmilä, Pekka. Realization of Finnish–Soviet Five-Year Trade Agreements and Variations in Trade. In *Möttölä, K.; Bykov, O. N. and Korolev, I. S., eds.*, 1983, pp. 65–75. [G: U.S.S.R.; Finland]

Hentilä, Kalervo. Energy within the Trade between Finland and the Soviet Union. In *Möttölä, K.; Bykov, O. N. and Korolev, I. S., eds.*, 1983, pp. 93–99. [G: U.S.S.R.; Finland]

Henze, Arno. Nutzen-kosten-theoretische Überlegungen zur Sicherstellung der Versorgung für Krisenzeiten. (Theoretical Cost-Benefit-Considerations on Supply Security for Times of Crisis. With English summary.) *Z. Wirtschaft. Sozialwissen.*, 1983, *103*(2), pp. 129–42.

Herlihy, P. and Cowan, C. Trade in Live Pigs between Northern Ireland and the Republic of Ireland. *Irish J. Agr. Econ. Rural Soc.*, 1983, *9*(2), pp. 173–92. [G: Ireland; U.K.]

Hernández-Catá, Ernesto. Flexible Exchange Rates and Interdependence: Comment. *Int. Monet. Fund Staff Pap.*, March 1983, *30*(1), pp. 31–35. [G: U.S.]

Hewett, Edward. A. Foreign Economic Relations. In *Bergson, A. and Levine, H. S., eds.*, 1983, pp. 269–310. [G: U.S.S.R.]

Hewett, Edward A. Soviet Energy Prospects and Their Implications for East–West Trade. In *Becker, A. S., ed.*, 1983, pp. 49–75. [G: OECD; U.S.S.R.]

Hewitt, Adrian. Stabex: An Evaluation of the Economic Impact over the First Five Years. *World Devel.*, December 1983, *11*(12), pp. 1005–27. [G: LDCs; EEC]

Heyne, Paul. Do Trade Deficits Matter? *Cato J.*, Winter 1983/84, *3*(3), pp. 705–16. [G: U.S.]

Hiemenz, Ulrich. Export Growth in Developing Asian Countries: Past Trends and Policy Issues. *Weltwirtsch. Arch.*, 1983, *119*(4), pp. 686–708. [G: Hong Kong; S. Korea; Taiwan; S.E. Asia]

Hillman, Arye L. and Long, Ngo Van. Pricing and Depletion of an Exhaustible Resource When There Is Anticipation of Trade Disruption. *Quart. J. Econ.*, May 1983, *98*(2), pp. 215–33.

Holden, Merle. Empirical Tests of the Heckscher–Ohlin Model for South Africa—A Reappraisal of the Methodology. *S. Afr. J. Econ.*, June 1983, *51*(2), pp. 243–51. [G: S. Africa]

Holloway, David. The Structure of the Defense Industry: The Soviet Union. In *Ball, N. and Leitenberg, M., eds.*, 1983, pp. 50–80. [G: U.S.S.R.]

Holopainen, Kari. The System of Payment between Finland and the Soviet Union. In *Möttölä, K.; Bykov, O. N. and Korolev, I. S., eds.*, 1983, pp. 173–80. [G: U.S.S.R.; Finland]

Horwitz, Eva Christina. Price Elasticities in Swedish Foreign Trade. In *Eliasson, G.; Sharefkin, M. and Ysander, B.-C., eds.*, 1983, pp. 169–97. [G: Sweden; Selected Countries]

Hošková, Adéla. Uniform Principles for Evaluating the Economic Effect of International Specialization and Cooperation in Industry. *Soviet E. Europ. Foreign Trade*, Winter 1983–84, *19*(4), pp. 62–72.

Hsu, John C. Hong Kong in China's Foreign Trade: A Changing Role. In *Youngson, A. J., ed.*, 1983, pp. 156–83. [G: Hong Kong; China]

Hufbauer, Gary Clyde. Subsidy Issues after the Tokyo Round. In *Cline W. R., ed.*, 1983, *3*(3), pp. 327–61. [G: OECD]

Hufbauer, Gary Clyde. "U.S.–Japanese Trade": A Comment. *Cato J.*, Winter 1983/84, *3*(3), pp. 771–75. [G: U.S.; Japan]

Hughes, Helen. Inter-developing-country Trade and Employment. In *Weisbrod, B. and Hughes, H., eds.*, 1983, pp. 429–46. [G: LDCs]

Huh, Kyung Mo. Countertrade: Trade without Cash? *Finance Develop.*, December 1983, *20*(4), pp. 14–16.

Ihamuotila, Jaakko. Energia ja ulkomaankuppa. (Energy and Foreign Trade in Finland. With English summary.) *Kansant. Aikak.*, 1983, *79*(1), pp. 54–67. [G: OECD; Finland]

Inotai, András. Changes in the Commodity Pattern of Intraregional Trade in the European Economic Community. *Acta Oecon.*, 1983, *31*(3–4), pp. 261–86. [G: EEC]

Inotai, András. CMEA Integration and National Economic Policies: Adjustment to the Changed World Economic Environment. In *Saunders, C. T., ed.*, 1983, pp. 81–95. [G: CMEA]

Islam, Nurul. Economic Interdependence between Rich and Poor Nations. In *Gauhar, A., ed. (II)*, 1983, pp. 173–93. [G: LDCs; MDCs]

Izik-Hedri, Gabriella. A Hungarian–Austrian Industrial Free Trade Agreement. *Soviet E. Europ. Foreign Trade*, Winter 1983–84, *19*(4), pp. 73–89. [G: Finland; Hungary; Austria]

Jakubec, Jaroslav. Problems of East–West Trade. *Czech. Econ. Digest.*, September 1983, (6), pp. 58–67. [G: Global]

Jalla, Ermanno. Le variazioni annuali di alcune grandezze economiche. (The Yearly Variations of Some Economic Data. With English summary.) *Statistica*, July–September 1983, *43*(3), pp. 489–506. [G: Italy]

Jao, Y. C. Hong Kong's Role in Financing China's Modernization. In *Youngson, A. J., ed.*, 1983, pp. 12–76. [G: Hong Kong; China]

Jayawardena, D. L. U. Free Trade Zones. *J. World Trade Law*, September–October 1983, *17*(5), pp. 427–44. [G: Selected LDCs]

Jentleson, Bruce W. Khrushchev's Oil and Brezhnev's Natural Gas Pipelines. In *Lieber, R. J., ed.*, 1983, pp. 33–69. [G: U.S.S.R.; U.S.; W. Europe]

Johnson, Mark J. Import Prices Decline, Export Indexes Mixed in the First 6 Months of 1983. *Mon. Lab. Rev.*, November 1983, *106*(11), pp. 59–70. **[G: U.S.]**

Johnson, Mark J. U.S. Foreign Trade Prices in 1982: Import Index Falls, Export Indexes Mixed. *Mon. Lab. Rev.*, May 1983, *106*(5), pp. 20–29. **[G: U.S.]**

Johnson, Mark J. U.S. Import and Export Price Indexes Show Declines during the First Half. *Mon. Lab. Rev.*, January 1983, *106*(1), pp. 17–23. **[G: U.S.]**

Jones, Daniel T. Machine Tools: Technical Change and a Japanese Challenge. **In** *Shepherd, G.; Duchêne, F. and Saunders, C., eds.*, 1983, pp. 186–208. **[G: OECD]**

Jorge, Antonio and Salazar-Carrillo, Jorge. External Debt and Development in Latin America: A Background Paper. **In** *Jorge, A.; Salazar-Carillo, J. and Higonnet, R. P., eds.*, 1983, pp. 1–35. **[G: Latin America]**

Kádár, Béla. Changes in the World Economic Environment and Hungarian Industry. *Acta Oecon.*, 1983, *30*(1), pp. 111–27.

Kádár, Béla. World Economic Situation of the 1980s and Conclusions on the Development of the Hungarian Economy. *Acta Oecon.*, 1983, *30*(3–4), pp. 291–312. **[G: Hungary; OECD; CMEA]**

Kalirajan, K. P. South–South Co-operation: Trade Relations between Indonesia and South Asia. *Pakistan Devel. Rev.*, Winter 1983, *22*(4), pp. 261–82. **[G: Indonesia; S. Asia]**

Kanemitsu, Hideo. Trade Policy in the 1980s: The Players: Comment. **In** *Cline W. R., ed.*, 1983, pp. 313–18.

Kar, Dev Kumar. Long-Term Trends in Openness of National Economies: Comment. *Oxford Econ. Pap.*, March 1983, *35*(1), pp. 136–40. **[G: Selected OECD; Brazil]**

Karp, Larry S. and McCalla, Alex F. Dynamic Games and International Trade: An Application to the World Corn Market. *Amer. J. Agr. Econ.*, November 1983, *65*(4), pp. 641–50.

Katrak, Homi. Global Profit Maximization and the Export Performance of Foreign Subsidiaries in India. *Oxford Bull. Econ. Statist.*, May 1983, *45*(2), pp. 205–22. **[G: India]**

Katseli, Louka T. Macroeconomic Adjustment and Exchange-Rate Policy in Middle-Income Countries: Greece, Portugal and Spain in the 1970s. **In** *de Cecco, M., ed.*, 1983, pp. 189–211. **[G: Greece; Portugal; Spain]**

Kealy, Walter G., Jr. and Bolyard, Joan E. International Travel and Passenger Fares, 1982. *Surv. Curr. Bus.*, May 1983, *63*(5), pp. 12–17. **[G: U.S.]**

Keesing, Donald B. Linking Up to Distant Markets: South to North Exports of Manufactured Consumer Goods. *Amer. Econ. Rev.*, May 1983, *73*(2), pp. 338–42.

Kellman, Mitchell H. Relative Prices and International Competitiveness: An Empirical Investigation. *Empirical Econ.*, 1983, *8*(3–4), pp. 125–38. **[G: Japan; Korea; India]**

Kellman, Mitchell H. and Schroder, Tim. The Export Similarity Index: Some Structural Tests. *Econ. J.*, March 1983, *93*(369), pp. 193–98. **[G: EEC]**

Kellman, Mitchell H. and Yun, Yuosang. Korea: Tomorrow's Japan? *J. Econ. Devel.*, December 1983, *8*(2), pp. 89–123. **[G: Japan; S. Korea]**

Kennedy, Charles and Thirlwall, Anthony P. Import and Export Ratios and the Dynamic Harrod Trade Multiplier: A Reply to McGregor and Swales [Import Penetration, Export Performance and Harrod's Trade Multiplier]. *Oxford Econ. Pap.*, March 1983, *35*(1), pp. 125–29.

Kennedy, Thomas E. and McHugh, Richard. Taste Similarity and Trade Intensity: A Test of the Linder Hypothesis for United States Exports. *Weltwirtsch. Arch.*, 1983, *119*(1), pp. 84–96. **[G: U.S.]**

Khan, Mohsin S. Policy Interdependence from a Latin American Perspective: Comment. *Int. Monet. Fund Staff Pap.*, March 1983, *30*(1), pp. 153–59.

Khan, Mohsin S. and Knight, Malcolm D. Determinants of Current Account Balances of Non-Oil Developing Countries in the 1970s. *Int. Monet. Fund Staff Pap.*, December 1983, *30*(4), pp. 819–42. **[G: Non-Oil LDCs]**

Khan, Mohsin S. and Zahler, Roberto. The Macroeconomic Effects of Changes in Barriers to Trade and Capital Flows: A Simulation Analysis. *Int. Monet. Fund Staff Pap.*, June 1983, *30*(2), pp. 223–82.

Khoury, Sarkis J. and Pirog, Robert. An Economic Analysis of the Demand for Trade Loans from Multinational Banks. *Bus. Econ.*, September 1983, *18*(4), pp. 40–45. **[G: U.S.]**

Kim, Inchul. Energy and Growth in an Open Economy: The Korean Case. *J. Energy Devel.*, Autumn 1983, *9*(1), pp. 69–92. **[G: Korea]**

Kindleberger, Charles P. International Trade and National Prosperity. *Cato J.*, Winter 1983/84, *3*(3), pp. 623–37. **[G: MDCs]**

Knapman, Bruce and Schiavo-Campo, Salvatore. Growth and Fluctuations of Fiji's Exports, 1875–1978. *Econ. Develop. Cult. Change*, October 1983, *32*(1), pp. 97–119. **[G: Fiji]**

Knudsen, Odin K. and Harbert, Lloyd S. The Causes of Export Instability: Comparing the Experiences of Two Decades. **In** *Bigman, D. and Taya, T., eds.*, 1983, pp. 149–66.

Kohler, W. and McMahon, P. C. The Austrian Import Demand Equation: Testing for Dynamic Specification. *Z. ges. Staatswiss.*, December 1983, *139*(4), pp. 678–89. **[G: Austria]**

Kohli, Ulrich R. The Le Châtelier Principle and the Demand for Imports in the Short Run and the Medium Run: Australia, 1959–60—1978–79. *Econ. Rec.*, June 1983, *59*(165), pp. 149–65. **[G: Australia]**

Kohlmey, G. Structures économiques et division internationale du travail dans la région européenne du C.A.E.M. (With English summary.) *Écon. Soc.*, January 1983, *17*(1), pp. 89–113. **[G: E. Germany; CMEA]**

Kol, J. and Mennes, L. B. M. Two-way Trade and Intra-industry Trade with an Application to the Netherlands. **In** *Tharakan, P. K. M., ed.*, 1983, pp. 47–85. **[G: Netherlands]**

Kolodziej, Edward A. The Structure of the Defense

Industry: France. In *Ball, N. and Leitenberg, M., eds.*, 1983, pp. 81–110. **[G: France]**

Komiya, Ryutaro. Economic Structure and Policy for External Balance: Comment. *Int. Monet. Fund Staff Pap.*, March 1983, *30*(1), pp. 70–74. **[G: U.S.; W. Europe]**

Korth, Christopher M. The Promotion of Exports with Barter. In *Czinkota, M. R., ed. (I)*, 1983, pp. 37–50. **[G: Selected Countries]**

Köves, András and Oblath, G. Hungarian Foreign Trade in the 1970's. *Acta Oecon.*, 1983, *30*(1), pp. 89–109. **[G: Hungary]**

Kregel, J. A. The Interaction of United States and European Policies. In *Weintraub, S. and Goodstein, M., eds.*, 1983, pp. 192–204. **[G: U.S.; EEC]**

Krinsky, Itzhak. The Small Country Assumption: A Note on Canadian Exports. *Appl. Econ.*, February 1983, *15*(1), pp. 73–79. **[G: Canada]**

Krueger, Anne O. Protectionism, Exchange Rate Distortions, and Agricultural Trading Patterns. *Amer. J. Agr. Econ.*, December 1983, *65*(5), pp. 864–71. **[G: Global]**

Krueger, Russell C. U.S. International Transactions, First Quarter 1983. *Surv. Curr. Bus.*, June 1983, *63*(6), pp. 33–67. **[G: U.S.]**

Kumar, Ramesh C. and Akbar, S. The Generalised System of Preferences and Canadian Imports of Manufactured and Semi-Manufactured Products from Developing Countries. *J. Econ. Stud.*, 1983, *10*(1), pp. 17–30. **[G: Canada; non-OPEC LDCs]**

Kuntjoro-Jakti, Dorodjatun and Tjiptoherijanto, Prijono. Indonesia–Japan Trade Relations. In *Akrasanee, N., ed.*, 1983, pp. 37–55. **[G: Indonesia; Japan]**

Kyröläinen, Hannu. The Development of Finnish–Soviet Economic Relations since 1918. In *Möttölä, K.; Bykov, O. N. and Korolev, I. S., eds.*, 1983, pp. 220–32. **[G: U.S.S.R.; Finland]**

Lall, Sanjaya and Mohammad, Sharif. Foreign Ownership and Export Performance in the Large Corporate Sector of India. *J. Devel. Stud.*, October 1983, *20*(1), pp. 56–67. **[G: India]**

Lande, Eric. Les exportations canadiennes de marchandises: analyse préliminaire des mécanismes de survie. (Canadian Commodity Exports: A Preliminary Study in Survival. With English summary.) *L'Actual. Econ.*, September 1983, *59*(3), pp. 620–35. **[G: Canada]**

Langhammer, Rolf J. Sectoral Profiles of Import Licencing in Selected Developing Countries and Their Impact on North-South and South-South Trade Flows. *Konjunkturpolitik*, 1983, *29*(1), pp. 21–32. **[G: Selected LDCs]**

Langhammer, Rolf J. The Importance of 'Natural' Barriers to Trade among Developing Countries: Some Evidence from the Transport Cost Content in Brasilian Imports. *World Devel.*, May 1983, *11*(5), pp. 417–25. **[G: Brazil; LDCs]**

Lányi, Kamilla. Enterprise Identity—Interenterprise Relationships: A State Monopoly in a Competitive Position. *Eastern Europ. Econ.*, Spring–Summer 1983, *21*(3–4), pp. 26–48. **[G: Hungary]**

Larsen, Flemming; Llewellyn, John and Potter, Stephen. International Economic Linkages. *OECD Econ. Stud.*, Autumn 1983, (1), pp. 43–91. **[G: OECD]**

Latham, A. J. H. and Neal, Larry. The International Market in Rice and Wheat, 1868–1914. *Econ. Hist. Rev., 2nd Ser.*, May 1983, *36*(2), pp. 260–80. **[G: Selected LDCs; Selected MDCs]**

Lawrence, Robert Z. Is Trade Deindustrializing America? A Medium-Term Perspective. *Brookings Pap. Econ. Act.*, 1983, (1), pp. 129–61. **[G: U.S.]**

Le Van, Cuong. Étude de la stabilité du sentier d'équilibre d'une maquette dynamique d'économie ouverte. (A Study of the Stability of the Equilibrium Path of a Dynamic Maquette of an Open Economy. With English summary.) *Ann. INSEE*, April–June 1983, (50), pp. 93–111. **[G: France]**

Lechuga, Alain. Un modèle généralisé de détermination de l'équivalent-travail de la production en économie ouverte. (With English summary.) *Revue Écon. Polit.*, May–June 1983, *93*(3), pp. 445–61. **[G: France]**

Lee, Jong-Ying and Tilley, Daniel S. Irreversible Import Shares for Frozen Concentrated Orange Juice in Canada. *Southern J. Agr. Econ.*, December 1983, *15*(2), pp. 99–104. **[G: Brazil; Canada; U.S.]**

Lee, Lai To. Singapore and East Asia. In *Chen, P. S. J., ed.*, 1983, pp. 335–59. **[G: Singapore; E. Asia]**

Lemle, J. Stuart. Sources of International Trade Financing. In *George, A. M. and Giddy, I. H., eds., Vol. 2*, 1983, pp. 7.2:1–30. **[G: U.K.; W. Germany; France; Japan]**

Leontief, Wassily W.; Mariscal, Jorge and Sohn, Ira. Prospects for the Soviet Economy to the Year 2000. *J. Policy Modeling*, March 1983, *5*(1), pp. 1–18. **[G: U.S.S.R.]**

Lewis, W. Arthur. Aspects of Tropical Trade. In *Lewis, W. A.*, 1983, *1969*, pp. 235–81. **[G: OECD; LDCs]**

Lewis, W. Arthur. International Economics: International Competition in Manufactures. In *Lewis, W. A.*, 1983, *1969*, pp. 225–34. **[G: U.K.]**

Lewis, W. Arthur. The Rate of Growth of World Trade, 1830–1973. In *Lewis, W. A.*, 1983, *1981*, pp. 293–308.

Lewis, W. Arthur. Trade Drives. In *Lewis, W. A.*, 1983, *1957*, pp. 209–23. **[G: U.K.; Germany; U.S.; Japan]**

Lin, Liande. Thirty Years of Sino-Japanese Trade. *Chinese Econ. Stud.*, Summer 1983, *16*(4), pp. 51–62. **[G: China; Japan]**

Llewellyn, John. Resource Prices and Macroeconomic Policies: Lessons from Two Oil Price Shocks. *OECD Econ. Stud.*, Autumn 1983, (1), pp. 197–212. **[G: OECD]**

Lloyd, Peter J. and Procter, R. G. Commodity Decomposition of Export-Import Instability: New Zealand. *J. Devel. Econ.*, February/April 1983, *12*(1/2), pp. 41–57. **[G: New Zealand]**

Love, James. Concentration, Diversification and Earnings Instability: Some Evidence on Developing Countries' Exports of Manufactures and Primary Products. *World Devel.*, September 1983, *11*(9), pp. 787–93. **[G: Selected LDCs]**

Love, James and Stewart, William J. Scottish Trade.

In *Ingham, K. P. D. and Love, J., eds.*, 1983, pp. 28–37. **[G: U.K.]**

Lutz, James M. and Green, Robert T. The Product Life Cycle and the Export Position of the United States. *J. Int. Bus. Stud.*, Winter 1983, *14*(3), pp. 77–93. **[G: Japan; U.S.; U.K.; W. Germany]**

Lyman, Robert. Economic and Political Issues in International Natural Gas Trade: A Canadian View. *J. Energy Devel.*, Autumn 1983, *9*(1), pp. 49–54. **[G: Canada]**

Ma, Junlei. Current Status and Prospects of Sino-Japanese Economic and Trade Relations. *Chinese Econ. Stud.*, Summer 1983, *16*(4), pp. 63–69. **[G: China; Japan]**

Maizels, A. The Industrialisation of the Developing Countries. **In** *[Saunders, C. T.]*, 1983, pp. 29–50. **[G: LDCs]**

Maksimova, M. M. Economic Relations between the Socialist and the Capitalist Countries: Results, Problems, Prospects. **In** *Möttölä, K.; Bykov, O. N. and Korolev, I. S., eds.*, 1983, pp. 21–31. **[G: CMEA; OECD]**

Malmgren, Harald B. Threats to the Multilateral System. **In** *Cline W. R., ed.*, 1983, pp. 189–201.

Manne, Alan S. A Three-Region Model of Energy, International Trade, and Economic Growth. **In** *Hickman, B. G., ed.*, 1983, pp. 141–62. **[G: LDCs; OECD; OPEC]**

Marsden, John S. and Hollander, G. Floating Exchange Rates, Inflation and Selective Protectionism: Their Effects on the Competitiveness of Australian Industry. **In** *Black, J. and Winters, L. A., eds.*, 1983, pp. 92–129. **[G: Australia]**

Marvel, Howard P. and Ray, Edward John. The Kennedy Round: Evidence on the Regulation of International Trade in the United States. *Amer. Econ. Rev.*, March 1983, *73*(1), pp. 190–97. **[G: U.S.]**

Maskus, Keith E. Evidence on Shifts in the Determinants of the Structure of U.S. Manufacturing Foreign Trade, 1958–76. *Rev. Econ. Statist.*, August 1983, *65*(3), pp. 415–22.

Mayer, Thomas. Effects of Export Diversification in a Primary Commodity Export Country: Colombia. *J. Policy Modeling*, June 1983, *5*(2), pp. 233–52. **[G: Colombia]**

Mayes, David G. EC Trade Effects and Factor Mobility. **In** *El-Agraa, A. M., ed.*, 1983, pp. 88–121. **[G: EEC; U.K.]**

McAleese, Dermot. Competitiveness and Economic Performance: The Irish Experience. **In** *Black, J. and Winters, L. A., eds.*, 1983, pp. 65–91. **[G: Ireland; OECD]**

McColl, G. D. and Gallagher, D. R. Market Price and Resource Cost in Australia. **In** *Tempest, P., ed.*, 1983, pp. 179–87. **[G: Australia]**

McGregor, Peter G. and Swales, J. K. Import and Export Ratios and the Dynamic Harrod Trade Multiplier [Import Penetration, Export Performance and Harrod's Trade Multiplier]. *Oxford Econ. Pap.*, March 1983, *35*(1), pp. 110–24.

McMahon, L. A. and Harris, Stuart. Coal Development: Issues for Japan and Australia. **In** *Akao, N., ed.*, 1983, pp. 71–95. **[G: Japan; Australia]**

McMillan, Carl. Relations with Non-members: Comment. **In** *Saunders, C. T., ed.*, 1983, pp. 144–45. **[G: Austria; Finland; Yugoslavia; CMEA; EEC]**

McQueen, Matthew. Lomé and Industrial Co-operation: The Need for Reform. *J. World Trade Law*, November–December 1983, *17*(6), pp. 524–32. **[G: EEC; Selected LDCs]**

Mees, Philip. International Cash Management. **In** *George, A. M. and Giddy, I. H., eds., Vol. 2*, 1983, pp. 8.11B:1–25.

Mendl, Wolf. Japan–China: The Economic Nexus. **In** *Akao, N., ed.*, 1983, pp. 217–44. **[G: Japan; China]**

Mérey, Ildikó. Hungarian Export Problems and the Economic Environment. *Acta Oecon.*, 1983, *30*(2), pp. 179–91. **[G: Hungary]**

Michaely, Michael. Trade in a Changed World Economy. *World Devel.*, May 1983, *11*(5), pp. 397–403. **[G: OECD]**

Mitsos, Achilles G. J. The Industrial Sector. **In** *Sampedro, J. L. and Payno, J. A., eds.*, 1983, pp. 105–27. **[G: Greece; EEC]**

Modiano, Pietro and Onida, Fabrizio. Un'analisi disaggregata delle funzioni di domanda di esportazione dell'Italia e dei principali paesi industriali. (Export Functions for Italy and Main Industrial Countries: A Sectorially Disaggregated Analysis. With English summary.) *Giorn. Econ.*, January–February 1983, *42*(1–2), pp. 3–26. **[G: Italy; W. Europe; Japan; U.S.]**

Mohabbat, Khan A. and Dalal, Ardeshir J. Factor Substitution and Import Demand for South Korea: A Translog Analysis. *Weltwirtsch. Arch.*, 1983, *119*(4), pp. 709–23. **[G: S. Korea]**

Moore, Geoffrey H. Inflation and Statistics—Again. **In** *Moore, G. H.*, 1983, *1981*, pp. 313–29. **[G: U.S.]**

Moran, Cristián. Export Fluctuations and Economic Growth: An Empirical Analysis. *J. Devel. Econ.*, February/April 1983, *12*(1/2), pp. 195–218. **[G: LDCs]**

Morandé, Felipe. Precios internos de bienes transables en Chile y la "ley de un solo precio." (With English summary.) *Cuadernos Econ.*, December 1983, *20*(61), pp. 295–311. **[G: Chile]**

Mosóczy, Róbert. Possibilities of and Trends in the Development of International Economic Cooperation in the 1980s. *Acta Oecon.*, 1983, *30*(3–4), pp. 313–24. **[G: Hungary; CMEA]**

Mukherjee, Amitabha. Effects of Terms of Trade on Trade Balance with Emphasis on Devaluation: General & Sectoral Cases. *Indian Econ. J.*, January–March 1983, *30*(3), pp. 25–38. **[G: India]**

Müller, Ernst. The Common Market for Agricultural Products. **In** *Saunders, C. T., ed.*, 1983, pp. 183–91. **[G: CMEA; EEC]**

Mullor-Sebastián, Alicia. The Product Life Cycle Theory: Empirical Evidence. *J. Int. Bus. Stud.*, Winter 1983, *14*(3), pp. 95–105. **[G: U.S.]**

Mwase, Ngila. The Supply of Road Vehicles in Tanzania: The Problem of Suppressed Demand. *J. Transp. Econ. Policy*, January 1983, *17*(1), pp. 77–89. **[G: Tanzania]**

Mytelka, Lynn Krieger. The Limits of Export-led Development: The Ivory Coast's Experience with Manufactures. **In** *Ruggie, J. G., ed.*, 1983, pp. 239–70. **[G: Ivory Coast; Sub-Saharan Africa]**

Nagy, András. Structural Changes and Development

Alternatives in International Trade. **In** *Hickman, B. G., ed.*, 1983, pp. 283–95. **[G: Global]**

Nakagawa, Yukitsugu. What Should Be the Future Role of Japan in Today's International Scene? *Ann. Sci. Écon. Appl.*, 1983, *39*(3), pp. 187–96. **[G: Japan]**

Nakamura, Toru and Nakamura, Yoichi. Structural Analysis of Global Trade. *Econ. Stud. Quart.*, December 1983, *34*(3), pp. 259–75. **[G: Global]**

Nambiar, R. G. Comparative Prices in a Developing Economy: The Case of India. *J. Devel. Econ.*, February/April 1983, *12*(1/2), pp. 19–25. **[G: India]**

Nelson, Gerald C. Time for Tapioca, 1970 to 1980: European Demand and World Supply of Dried Cassava. *Food Res. Inst. Stud.*, 1983, *19*(1), pp. 25–49. **[G: EC]**

Nenonen, Tuomo and Linnainmaa, Hannu T. Regional Effects of the Eastern Trade: An Example from Northern Finland. **In** *Möttölä, K.; Bykov, O. N. and Korolev, I. S., eds.*, 1983, pp. 213–19. **[G: U.S.S.R.; Finland]**

Neumann, Manfred; Böbel, Ingo and Haid, Alfred. Business Cycle and Industrial Market Power: An Empirical Investigation for West German Industries, 1965–1977. *J. Ind. Econ.*, December 1983, *32*(2), pp. 187–96. **[G: W. Germany]**

Niall, D. Jane and Smith, Rhonda L. Development of High Fructose Syrup in the U.S. and Its Implications for Australia. *Rev. Marketing Agr. Econ.*, April 1983, *51*(1), pp. 51–70. **[G: U.S.; Australia]**

Nironen, Erkki. Transfer of Technology between Finland and the Soviet Union. **In** *Möttölä, K.; Bykov, O. N. and Korolev, I. S., eds.*, 1983, pp. 161–70. **[G: Finland; U.S.S.R.]**

Nobel, Klaus. Intra- vs. Inter-Industry Trade: The Case of Many Countries and Industries. *Z. Wirtschaft. Sozialwissen.*, 1983, *103*(4), pp. 341–49.

Nobuhara, Naotake and Akao, Nobutoshi. The Politics of Siberian Development. **In** *Akao, N., ed.*, 1983, pp. 197–215. **[G: Japan; U.S.S.R.]**

Nogués, Julio J. Alternative Trade Strategies and Employment in the Argentine Manufacturing Sector. *World Devel.*, December 1983, *11*(12), pp. 1029–42. **[G: Argentina]**

Nukazawa, Kazuo. Japan–ASEAN Trade Relations. **In** *Akrasanee, N., ed.*, 1983, pp. 163–91. **[G: Japan; ASEAN]**

Nyers, Rezsö. Interrelations between Policy and the Economic Reform in Hungary. *J. Compar. Econ.*, September 1983, *7*(3), pp. 211–24. **[G: Hungary]**

Nyhus, Douglas E. and Almon, Clopper. Linked Input–Output Models for France, the Federal Republic of Germany, and Belgium. **In** *Hickman, B. G., ed.*, 1983, pp. 183–99. **[G: Belgium; France; W. Germany]**

Ojeda, Mario. The Future of Relations between Mexico and the United States. **In** *Reynolds, C. W. and Tello, C., eds.*, 1983, pp. 315–30. **[G: U.S.; Mexico]**

Ollila, Esko. Kvalitativa faktorer vid utveckling av vår konkurrenskraft. (Qualitative Factors in the Development of Our International Competitiveness. With English summary.) *Ekon. Samfundets Tidskr.*, 1983, *36*(2), pp. 55–60. **[G: Finland]**

Onida, Fabrizio. Japan and Italy: Old and Newly Emerging Roles in the International Division of Labour. **In** *Fodella, G., ed.*, 1983, pp. 125–57. **[G: Japan; Italy]**

Onida, Fabrizio and Perasso, Giancarlo. Oil Export and Economic Development: OPEC Strategies and Opportunities for Western Economic Cooperation. *Rivista Int. Sci. Econ. Com.*, March 1983, *30*(3), pp. 293–303. **[G: OPEC; OECD]**

Onishi, Akira. North–South Relations: Alternative Policy Simulations for the World Economy in the 1980s. *J. Policy Modeling*, March 1983, *5*(1), pp. 55–74. **[G: Global]**

Owen, Roberts B. Extraterritorial Application of U.S. Trade and Financial Controls: Freezings, Vestings, Embargoes, etc. *Wirtsch. Recht*, 1983, *35*(2/3), pp. 142–53. **[G: U.S.]**

Pachauri, Rajendra K. and Labys, Walter C. Changing Markets for Coal: Opportunities for the Developing Countries. **In** *Tempest, P., ed.*, 1983, pp. 35–41. **[G: LDCs]**

Paldam, Martin. The International Element of Economic Fluctuations of 20 OECD-Countries 1948–1975. *Reg. Sci. Urban Econ.*, August 1983, *13*(3), pp. 429–54. **[G: OECD]**

Panoutsopoulos, Vasilis. East Asian and Latin American Export Performance in Industrial Country Markets in the 1970s. **In** *Black, J. and Winters, L. A., eds.*, 1983, pp. 130–69. **[G: E. Asia; Latin America]**

Park, Se-Hark. The Plight of Oil-Importing Developing Countries and South–South Cooperation on Energy. *J. Energy Devel.*, Autumn 1983, *9*(1), pp. 93–110. **[G: LDCs]**

Parkkinen, Pekka. The Impact of the Trade with the Soviet Union on Finnish Economy. **In** *Möttölä, K.; Bykov, O. N. and Korolev, I. S., eds.*, 1983, pp. 191–97. **[G: U.S.S.R.; Finland]**

Parmenter, Brian R. The IMPACT Macro Package and Export Demand Elasticities. *Australian Econ. Pap.*, December 1983, *22*(41), pp. 411–17. **[G: Australia]**

Pérez-Sainz, J. P. Transmigration and Accumulation in Indonesia. **In** *Oberai, A. S., ed.*, 1983, pp. 183–250. **[G: Indonesia]**

Pineye, Daniel. The Bases of Soviet Power in the Third World. *World Devel.*, December 1983, *11*(12), pp. 1083–95. **[G: LDCs; U.S.S.R.]**

Plaut, Steven E. 'Trade Shocks' in Economies Importing Only Intermediate Goods. *Europ. Econ. Rev.*, May 1983, *21*(3), pp. 363–79. **[G: Netherlands; Norway; U.K.]**

Polak, Jacques J. Conference on Exchange Rate Regimes and Policy Interdependence: Concluding Remark. *Int. Monet. Fund Staff Pap.*, March 1983, *30*(1), pp. 208–11.

Prausello, Franco. L'economia eurpea alle soglie degli anni 2000: lineamenti di analisi prospettiva. (With English summary.) *Econ. Int.*, May–August–November 1983, *36*(2–3–4), pp. 199–254. **[G: Europe]**

Rabino, Samuel. Webb-Pomerene and the Construction Industry. *Calif. Manage. Rev.*, January 1983, *25*(2), pp. 21–33. **[G: U.S.]**

Radell, Willard W., Jr. Cuban–Soviet Sugar Trade, 1960–1976: How Great Was the Subsidy? *J. Devel. Areas*, April 1983, *17*(3), pp. 365–81. **[G: Cuba]**

Ragazzi, Giorgio. La crisi dei PVS colpisce l'export italiano. (The Crisis in the Developing Countries Hits Italian Ports. With English summary.) *L'Impresa,* 1983, *25*(6), pp. 47–50. **[G: Italy]**

Rayment, P. B. W. Intra-'Industry' Specialisation and the Foreign Trade of Industrial Countries. **In** *[Saunders, C. T.],* 1983, pp. 1–28. **[G: OECD]**

Reich, Robert B. Beyond Free Trade. *Foreign Aff.,* Spring 1983, *61*(4), pp. 773–804. **[G: U.S.]**

Rejtö, Gábor. A Debate in Hungary on the Possibilities of Cooperation with Western Firms (1982–83): Review Article. *Acta Oecon.,* 1983, *31*(3–4), pp. 327–39. **[G: Hungary]**

Reynolds, Bruce L. Economic Reforms and External Imbalance in China, 1978–81. *Amer. Econ. Rev.,* May 1983, *73*(2), pp. 325–28. **[G: China]**

Reynolds, Clark W. Mexican–U.S. Interdependence: Economic and Social Perspectives. **In** *Reynolds, C. W. and Tello, C., eds.,* 1983, pp. 21–45. **[G: Mexico; U.S.]**

Reynolds, Clark W. and Tello, Carlos. U.S.–Mexico Relations: Economic and Social Aspects: Introduction. **In** *Reynolds, C. W. and Tello, C., eds.,* 1983, pp. 1–20. **[G: Mexico; U.S.]**

Reza, Sadrel. Revealed Comparative Advantage in the South Asian Manufacturing Sector: Some Estimates. *Indian Econ. J.,* October–December 1983, *31*(2), pp. 96–106. **[G: Bangladesh; India; Nepal; Pakistan; Sri Lanka]**

Rivero, Nicolás and Díaz Franjúl, Manuel. Thoughts on Sugar Diversification: An Inter-American Fuel Alcohol Program. **In** *Czinkota, M. R., ed. (II),* 1983, pp. 107–25. **[G: Latin America; U.S.]**

Roehl, Thomas. A Transactions Cost Approach to International Trading Structures: The Case of the Japanese General Trading Companies. *Hitotsubashi J. Econ.,* December 1983, *24*(2), pp. 119–35. **[G: Japan]**

Roque, Fatima Moura. Trade Theory and the Portuguese Pattern of Trade. *Economia,* October 1983, *7*(3), pp. 455–69. **[G: Portugal]**

Sabolo, Yves. Trade between Developing Countries, Technology Transfers and Employment. *Int. Lab. Rev.,* Sept.–Oct. 1983, *122*(5), pp. 593–608. **[G: LDCs]**

Sapir, André. Alternative Estimates of India's Transportation Cost Profile: A Reply [On the Incidence of Transportation Costs on India's Exports]. *J. Devel. Stud.,* April 1983, *19*(3), pp. 390. **[G: India]**

Sapir, André. On the Incidence of Transportation Costs on India's Exports. *J. Devel. Stud.,* January 1983, *19*(2), pp. 244–49. **[G: India]**

Sapir, André and Baldwin, Robert E. India and the Tokyo Round. *World Devel.,* July 1983, *11*(7), pp. 565–74. **[G: India; EEC; Japan; U.S.]**

Sargent, D. Alec. The United States' Role in the International Thermal Coal Market. *Energy J.,* January 1983, *4*(1), pp. 79–96. **[G: U.S.; OECD]**

Sarris, Alexander H. and Freebairn, John W. Endogenous Price Policies and International Wheat Prices. *Amer. J. Agr. Econ.,* May 1983, *65*(2), pp. 214–24.

Saxonhouse, Gary R. The Micro- and Macroeconomics of Foreign Sales to Japan. **In** *Cline W. R., ed.,* 1983, pp. 259–304. **[G: OECD; Korea]**

Scanlan, A. F. G. Communist Bloc Energy Supply and Demand. **In** *Tempest, P., ed.,* 1983, pp. 149–59. **[G: CMEA]**

Schiavone, Giuseppe. Relations with Non-members: Comment. **In** *Saunders, C. T., ed.,* 1983, pp. 146–47. **[G: Austria; Finland; Yugoslavia; CMEA; EEC]**

Schuh, G. Edward. Changing Trends in World Food Production and Trade. *Amer. Econ. Rev.,* May 1983, *73*(2), pp. 235–38.

Schumacher, D. Intra-industry Trade between the Federal Republic of Germany and Developing Countries: Extent and Some Characteristics. **In** *Tharakan, P. K. M., ed.,* 1983, pp. 87–109. **[G: W. Germany; LDCs]**

Scott, Walter Giorgio. PMI e mercati internationali. (Small and Medium Sized Businesses and Foreign Markets. With English summary.) *L'Impresa,* 1983, *25*(1), pp. 21–28. **[G: Italy]**

Scouller, John. 'Made in Scotland' (Production). **In** *Ingham, K. P. D. and Love, J., eds.,* 1983, pp. 15–27. **[G: U.K.]**

Secchi, Carlo. Radiografia della PMI che opera con l'estero. (In-Depth Study of Small and Medium-Sized Businesses Operating Abroad. With English summary.) *L'Impresa,* 1983, *25*(1), pp. 29–36. **[G: Italy]**

Seidelmann, Reimund. Energy Trade Relations between the Federal Republic of Germany and the USSR. **In** *Lieber, R. J., ed.,* 1983, pp. 71–103. **[G: U.S.S.R.; W. Germany]**

Sen, Raj Kumar. An Analysis of Export of a Few Agricultural Products Entering into Mass Consumption. *Indian Econ. J.,* January-March 1983, *30*(3), pp. 103–10. **[G: India]**

Shaikh, A. Hafeez and Zaman, Asad. Forecasting without Theory: Pakistan's Export of Cotton and Rice. *Pakistan J. Appl. Econ.,* Summer 1983, *2*(1), pp. 65–84. **[G: Pakistan]**

Shepherd, Geoffrey and Duchêne, François. Industrial Change and Intervention in Western Europe. **In** *Shepherd, G.; Duchêne, F. and Saunders, C., eds.,* 1983, pp. 1–25. **[G: W. Europe]**

Sing, Lim Hua and Choo, Lee Chin. Singapore–Japan Relations: Trade and Development. **In** *Akrasanee, N., ed.,* 1983, pp. 117–39. **[G: Singapore; Japan]**

Singer, Hans W. North–South Multipliers. *World Devel.,* May 1983, *11*(5), pp. 451–54. **[G: LDCs]**

Singh, Deo Raj. Proxy Effects of Market in India's Exports. *Indian Econ. J.,* January-March 1983, *30*(3), pp. 111–18. **[G: India]**

Sláma, Jiři. Gravity Model and Its Estimations for International Flows of Engineering Products, Chemicals and Patent Applications. *Acta Oecon.,* 1983, *30*(2), pp. 241–53. **[G: Yugoslavia; Europe; CMEA]**

Snower, Dennis J. DYNAMICO: A Multilevel Programming Model of World Trade and Development: Comment. **In** *Hickman, B. G., ed.,* 1983, pp. 276–79. **[G: Global]**

Sobhan, Rehman. Enhancing Trade between OPEC and the Developing Countries of Asia. **In** *Gauhar, A., ed. (II),* 1983, *1982,* pp. 104–20. **[G: OPEC; LDCs]**

Sorenson, Vernon L. and Rossmiller, George E. Future Options for U.S. Agricultural Trade Policy. *Amer. J. Agr. Econ.*, December 1983, *65*(5), pp. 893–900. [G: U.S.]

Spencer, Edson W. Japan: Stimulus or Scapegoat? *Foreign Aff.*, Fall 1983, *62*(1), pp. 123–37. [G: Japan; U.S.]

Spencer, Grant H. Real Exchange Rate Adjustment to Exogenous Terms of Trade Shocks. *Int. Monet. Fund Staff Pap.*, September 1983, *30*(3), pp. 570–600. [G: Australia; Denmark; Finland; Ireland; New Zealand]

Stankovsky, Jan. The Cases of Finland and Austria. In *Saunders, C. T., ed.*, 1983, pp. 119–43. [G: Austria; Finland; CMEA; EEC]

Stecco, Maurizio. Come entrare nel mercato nordamericano. (How to Enter the North-American Market. With English summary.) *L'Impresa*, 1983, *25*(1), pp. 63–68. [G: France; U.S.; Canada]

Stein, Leslie. Multinational Corporations in World Trade. *Singapore Econ. Rev.*, April 1983, *28*(1), pp. 34–52. [G: Global]

Stein, Robert. The State of French Colonial Commerce on the Eve of the Revolution. *J. Europ. Econ. Hist.*, Spring 1983, *12*(1), pp. 105–17. [G: France]

Steinberg, Gerald. The Structure of the Defense Industry: Israel. In *Ball, N. and Leitenberg, M., eds.*, 1983, pp. 278–309. [G: Israel]

Stern, Jonathan P. Natural Gas: The Perfect Answer to Energy Diversification. In *Akao, N., ed.*, 1983, pp. 97–117. [G: Japan]

Stone, Carl. Patterns of Insertion into the World Economy: Historical Profile and Contemporary Options. *Soc. Econ. Stud.*, September 1983, *32*(3), pp. 1–34. [G: Caribbean]

Sveikauskas, Leo A. Science and Technology in United States Foreign Trade. *Econ. J.*, September 1983, *93*(371), pp. 542–54. [G: U.S.]

Swoba, Alexander K. Exchange Rate Regimes and European–U.S. Policy Interdependence. *Int. Monet. Fund Staff Pap.*, March 1983, *30*(1), pp. 75–102. [G: U.S.; W. Europe]

Sydow, Peter. Economic Growth, CMEA Integration and Economic Cooperation with Capitalist Countries. In *Saunders, C. T., ed.*, 1983, pp. 41–57. [G: E. Germany]

Tan, Gerald. Export Instability, Export Growth and *GDP* Growth. *J. Devel. Econ.*, February/April 1983, *12*(1/2), pp. 219–27. [G: OECD; E. Asia; S. Asia]

Tange, Toshiko. Trade Frictions and Productivity Performance—Technological, Price, and Cost Competitiveness of Japan and U.S. Exports. *J. Policy Modeling*, November 1983, *5*(3), pp. 313–31. [G: Japan; U.S.]

Terpstra, Vern. Suggestions for Research Themes and Publications: International Marketing. *J. Int. Bus. Stud.*, Spring/Summer 1983, *14*(1), pp. 9–10.

Tharakan, P. K. M. The Economics of Intra-industry Trade: A Survey. In *Tharakan, P. K. M., ed.*, 1983, pp. 1–34. [G: OECD]

Thirlwall, Anthony P. A Trade Strategy for the United Kingdom. *J. Common Market Stud.*, September 1983, *22*(1), pp. 1–16. [G: U.K.]

Thomson, Arthur R. Integrated Design and Production Systems for Strategic Production. In *Wilson, B.; Berg, C. C. and French, D., eds.*, 1983, pp. 293–303. [G: U.S.; U.S.S.R.]

Thoreson, Per E. Inflation Controlled by Energy Prices. *Energy Econ.*, July 1983, *5*(3), pp. 202–06. [G: Global]

Tisdell, Clem A. Public Finance and the Appropriation of Gains from International Tourists: Some Theory with ASEAN and Australian Illustrations. *Singapore Econ. Rev.*, April 1983, *28*(1), pp. 3–20. [G: Australia; S. E. Asia]

Tower, Edward. Some Empirical Results on Trade and National Prosperity [International Trade and National Prosperity]. *Cato J.*, Winter 1983/84, *3*(3), pp. 639–44. [G: LDCs; MDCs]

Troncoso, Carlos Morales, et al. Small- and Medium-sized Companies in the Exportation of Manufactured Goods: The Situation in Mexico. In *Czinkota, M. R., ed. (II)*, 1983, pp. 143–54. [G: Mexico]

Tsurumi, Hiroki and Tsurumi, Yoshi. U.S.-Japan Automobile Trade: A Bayesian Test of a Product Life Cycle. *J. Econometrics*, October 1983, *23*(2), pp. 193–210.

Turner, Charlie G. Voluntary Export Restraints on Trade Going to the United States. *Southern Econ. J.*, January 1983, *49*(3), pp. 793–803. [G: U.S.; Japan]

Ueda, Kazuo. Trade Balance Adjustment with Imported Intermediate Goods: The Japanese Case. *Rev. Econ. Statist.*, November 1983, *65*(4), pp. 618–25. [G: Japan]

Urata, Shujiro. Factor Inputs and Japanese Manufacturing Trade Structure. *Rev. Econ. Statist.*, November 1983, *65*(4), pp. 678–84. [G: Japan]

Vanous, Jan. The Impact of the Oil Price Decline on the Soviet Union and Eastern Europe. *Energy J.*, July 1983, *4*(3), pp. 11–19. [G: E. Europe; U.S.S.R.]

van Veen, P. Trends in World Trade. *S. Afr. J. Econ.*, December 1983, *51*(4), pp. 486–506. [G: Global]

Végvári, Jenö. The Role of the CMEA in Hungarian Foreign Trade. *Acta Oecon.*, 1983, *30*(2), pp. 203–19. [G: Hungary; CMEA]

Vellai, Györgyi and Veliczky, József. A Statistical Analysis of the "Openness" of Economic Processes. *Acta Oecon.*, 1983, *30*(3–4), pp. 447–62. [G: Hungary]

Vukmanic, Frank G. Performance Requirements: The General Debate and a Review of Latin American Practices. In *Czinkota, M. R., ed. (II)*, 1983, pp. 48–84. [G: Latin America]

Wahlroos, Björn. Avreglering och industripolitik [Kvalitativa faktorer vid utveckling av vår konkurrenskraft]. (Lifting Controls and Industrial Policy. With English summary.) *Ekon. Samfundets Tidskr.*, 1983, *36*(2), pp. 61–63. [G: Finland]

Wallensteen, Peter. Economic Sanctions: Ten Modern Cases and Three Important Lessons. In *Nincic, M. and Wallensteen, P., eds.*, 1983, pp. 87–129. [G: Selected Countries]

Walsh, James I. Countertrade: Not Just for East-West Any More. *J. World Trade Law*, January–February 1983, *17*(1), pp. 3–11. [G: Selected MDCs; Selected LDCs]

Walter, Ingo. Structural Adjustment and Trade Policy in the International Steel Industry. **In** *Cline W. R., ed.*, 1983, pp. 483–525. [G: Selected Countries]

Wang, George C. Issues in China's International Trade: Editor's Introduction. *Chinese Econ. Stud.*, Spring 1983, *16*(3), pp. 6–9. [G: China; U.S.]

Wangwe, Samuel M. Industrialization and Resource Allocation in a Developing Country: The Case of Recent Experiences in Tanzania. *World Devel.*, June 1983, *11*(6), pp. 483–92. [G: Tanzania]

Warner, Dennis L. A Model of Trade and Exchange Rates. **In** *Hickman, B. G., ed.*, 1983, pp. 297–311. [G: OECD; Global]

Warner, Dennis L. and Kreinin, Mordechai E. Determinants of International Trade Flows. *Rev. Econ. Statist.*, February 1983, *65*(1), pp. 96–104.

Warr, Peter G. and Lloyd, Peter J. Do Australian Trade Policies Discriminate against Less Developed Countries? *Econ. Rec.*, December 1983, *59*(167), pp. 351–64. [G: Australia]

Wassermann, Ursula. UNCTAD: Proposals on Commodity Issues. *J. World Trade Law*, May–June 1983, *17*(3), pp. 266–69. [G: LDCs; MDCs]

Weidenbaum, Murray L. The High Cost of Protectionism. *Cato J.*, Winter 1983/84, *3*(3), pp. 777–91. [G: U.S.; Japan; W. Europe]

Williams, Harold R. and Baliga, Gurudutt M. The U.S. Export Trading Company Act of 1982: Nature and Evaluation. *J. World Trade Law*, May–June 1983, *17*(3), pp. 224–35. [G: U.S.]

Witter, Michael. Exchange Rate Policy in Jamaica: A Critical Assessment. *Soc. Econ. Stud.*, December 1983, *32*(4), pp. 1–50. [G: Jamaica]

Wolf, Martin. Managed Trade in Practice: Implications of the Textile Arrangements. **In** *Cline W. R., ed.*, 1983, pp. 455–82. [G: Selected Countries]

Wolf, Thomas A. East–West Trade: Economic Interests, Systemic Interaction and Political Rivalry. *ACES Bull. (See Comp. Econ. Stud. after 8/85)*, Summer 1983, *25*(2), pp. 23–59. [G: CMEA; OECD]

Wonder, Edward F. Mexican Oil and the Western Alliance. **In** *Lieber, R. J., ed.*, 1983, pp. 135–67. [G: Mexico; Central America; OECD]

Wright, Claudia. Neutral or Neutralized? Iraq, Iran, and the Superpowers. **In** *Tahir-Kheli, S. and Ayubi, S., eds.*, 1983, pp. 172–92. [G: Iraq; Iran]

Xu, Shiwei. On the Development of China's Foreign Trade. *Chinese Econ. Stud.*, Summer 1983, *16*(4), pp. 3–16. [G: China]

Yeats, Alexander J. On the Effects of Aggregation Bias in Alternative Estimates of India's Transportation Cost Profile: A Comment on Sapir's Estimation Procedure. *J. Devel. Stud.*, January 1983, *19*(2), pp. 250–52.

Yeats, Alexander J. Reply to Sapir [On the Incidence of Transportation Costs on India's Exports]. *J. Devel. Stud.*, April 1983, *19*(3), pp. 391. [G: India]

Yorke, Valerie. Oil, the Middle East and Japan's Search for Security. **In** *Akao, N., ed.*, 1983, pp. 45–70. [G: Middle East; Japan]

Yudanov, Yu. I. Soviet–Finnish Economic Cooperation: Significance for the National Economy of Both Countries. **In** *Möttölä, K.; Bykov, O. N. and Korolev, I. S., eds.*, 1983, pp. 198–212. [G: U.S.S.R.; Finland]

Zakharov, S. N. and Shagalov, G. L. Methods for Determining the Efficiency of Foreign Economic Relations. *Matekon*, Fall 1983, *20*(1), pp. 57–77.

Zhang, Li. Reform Blazes a New Path for Foreign Trade. *Chinese Econ. Stud.*, Summer 1983, *16*(4), pp. 17–26. [G: China]

Ziebura, Gilbert. Internationalization of Capital, International Division of Labour and the Role of the European Community. **In** *Tsoukalis, L., ed.*, 1983, pp. 127–40. [G: EEC]

Zou, Siyi. The Problem of Export Strategy. *Chinese Econ. Stud.*, Spring 1983, *16*(3), pp. 10–23. [G: China]

Zysman, John and Cohen, Stephen S. Double or Nothing: Open Trade and Competitive Industry. *Foreign Aff.*, Summer 1983, *61*(5), pp. 1113–39. [G: U.S.]

422 Commercial Policy

4220 Commercial Policy and Trade Regulations; Empirical Studies

Acheson, Keith. The Pricing Practices of the Liquor Control Board of Ontario: Reconsidered. *Can. J. Econ.*, February 1983, *16*(1), pp. 161–66. [G: Canada]

Aggarwal, Mangat Ram. Trade: An Engine of Economic Development in ASEAN Countries. *Rivista Int. Sci. Econ. Com.*, September 1983, *30*(9), pp. 861–72. [G: S.E. Asia]

Aggarwal, Vinod K. and Haggard, Stephan. The Politics of Protection in the U.S. Textile and Apparel Industries. **In** *Zysman, J. and Tyson, L., eds.*, 1983, pp. 249–312. [G: U.S.]

Ahearn, Raymond J. An Overview of the International Trading Environment. **In** *Rubin, S. J. and Graham, T. R., eds.*, 1983, pp. 18–32.

Ahmad, Zakaria Haji and Cheong, K. C. Malaysia–Japan Trade: Issues and Prospects for the 1980s. **In** *Akrasanee, N., ed.*, 1983, pp. 57–78.

Aislabie, C. J. The Australian Tariff as a Selective Employment Policy Instrument: An Empirical Study. *Australian Econ. Pap.*, June 1983, *22*(40), pp. 119–31. [G: Australia]

Aizenman, Joshua. Dynamics of Trade Liberalization Policy. *J. Devel. Econ.*, Aug.–Oct. 1983, *13*(1–2), pp. 133–42.

Aizenman, Joshua. On the Optimal Combination of Commercial and Exchange Rate Policies. *Southern Econ. J.*, July 1983, *50*(1), pp. 185–94.

Akrasanee, Narongchai and Dhiravegin, Likhit. Trade and Development in Thai–Japanese Relations. **In** *Akrasanee, N., ed.*, 1983, pp. 141–61. [G: Japan; Thailand]

Allen, Roy; Dodge, Claudia and Schmitz, Andrew. Voluntary Export Restraints as Protection Policy: The U.S. Beef Case. *Amer. J. Agr. Econ.*, May 1983, *65*(2), pp. 291–96. [G: U.S.]

Anastasopoulos, Anastasios and Sims, William A. The

Regional Impact of the Disintegration of the Canadian Common Market: The Case of Quebec. *Southern Econ. J.*, January 1983, *49*(3), pp. 743–63. **[G: Canada]**

Anderson, Gary M. and Tollison, Robert D. Apologiae for Chartered Monopolies in Foreign Trade, 1600–1800. *Hist. Polit. Econ.*, Winter 1983, *15*(4), pp. 549–66. **[G: U.K.]**

Anderson, Kym. The Peculiar Rationality of Beef Import Quotas in Japan. *Amer. J. Agr. Econ.*, February 1983, *65*(1), pp. 108–12.

Andersson, Christian. Protektionismen i världshandeln. (Protectionism in World Trade. With English summary.) *Ekon. Samfundets Tidskr.*, 1983, *36*(3), pp. 107–14. **[G: Finland]**

Andreyev, Yu. V. The Structures of Soviet–Finnish Economic Relations. **In** *Möttölä, K.; Bykov, O. N. and Korolev, I. S., eds.*, 1983, pp. 53–64. **[G: Finland; U.S.S.R.]**

Anjaria, S. J. et al. Protectionism. *Finance Develop.*, March 1983, *20*(1), pp. 2–5. **[G: LDCs]**

Autenne, M. Jacques and Scholsem, M. Jean-Claude. Problèmes internationaux du domaine des taxes sur le chiffre d'affaires: Belgique. (With English summary.) **In** *International Fiscal Association (I)*, 1983, pp. 289–317. **[G: Belgium]**

Baack, Bennett D. and Ray, Edward John. The Political Economy of Tariff Policy: A Case Study of the United States. *Exploration Econ. Hist.*, January 1983, *20*(1), pp. 73–93. **[G: U.S.]**

Baer, Werner. Import Substitution and Industrialization in Latin America: Experiences and Interpretations. **In** *Todaro, M. P., ed.*, 1983, *1972*, pp. 301–15. **[G: Latin America]**

Balassa, Bela. Industrial Prospects and Policies in the Developed Countries. **In** *[Giersch, H.]*, 1983, pp. 257–78. **[G: OECD; LDCs]**

Balassa, Bela. The Adjustment Experience of Developing Economies after 1973. **In** *Williamson, J., ed.*, 1983, pp. 145–74. **[G: LDCs]**

Balassa, Bela. Trade Policy in the 1980s: New Issues in the 1980s: Comment. **In** *Cline W. R., ed.*, 1983, pp. 711–22.

Balassa, Bela. Trade Policy in Mexico. *World Devel.*, September 1983, *11*(9), pp. 795–811. **[G: Mexico]**

Baldwin, Robert E. Trade Policy in the 1980s: Problems from the Past: Comment. **In** *Cline W. R., ed.*, 1983, pp. 425–30.

Batten, David F. International Conflict Management via Adaptive Learning and Multistage Compromises. *Conflict Manage. Peace Sci.*, Fall 1983, *7*(1), pp. 1–24.

Baumgarten, Klaus. Auswirkungen der Besteuerung importierter Zwischenprodukte. (Consequences of Taxation of Imported Intermediate Goods. With English summary.) *Jahr. Nationalökon. Statist.*, May 1983, *198*(3), pp. 251–68.

Bautista, Romeo M. Philippine–Japanese Trade Relations. *Philippine Econ. J.*, 198, *22*(1), pp. 1–28. **[G: Philippine; Japan]**

Bautista, Romeo M. and Villacorta, Wilfrido V. Economic and Political Factors Affecting Philippine–Japan Trade. **In** *Akrasanee, N., ed.*, 1983, pp. 79–115. **[G: Philippines; Japan]**

Befus, David. Foreign-Trade Zones: The U.S. Case. **In** *Czinkota, M. R., ed. (II)*, 1983, pp. 279–89. **[G: U.S.]**

Berglas, Eitan. The Case for Unilateral Tariff Reductions: Foreign Tariffs Rediscovered [Is Unilateral Tariff Reduction Preferable to a Customs Union? The Curious Case of the Missing Foreign Tariff]. *Amer. Econ. Rev.*, December 1983, *73*(5), pp. 1141–42.

Bergman, Lars. General Equilibrium Modeling of Trade-Liberalization Issues among Major World Trade Blocs: Comment. **In** *Hickman, B. G., ed.*, 1983, pp. 137–38. **[G: OECD; Global]**

Bergsten, C. Fred. International Investment: The Need for a New U.S. Policy. **In** *Bergsten, C. F.*, 1983, pp. 187–97. **[G: U.S.]**

Bergsten, C. Fred. International Money and U.S. Trade Policy. **In** *Bergsten, C. F.*, 1983, pp. 177–83. **[G: U.S.]**

Bergsten, C. Fred. The International Dimension. **In** *Miller, G. W., ed.*, 1983, pp. 151–68. **[G: U.S.]**

Bergsten, C. Fred and Cline, William R. Trade Policy in the 1980s: Conclusion and Policy Implications. **In** *Cline W. R., ed.*, 1983, pp. 747–78.

Bergsten, C. Fred and Cline, William R. Trade Policy in the 1980s: An Overview. **In** *Cline W. R., ed.*, 1983, pp. 59–98. **[G: OECD]**

Bergsten, C. Fred and Williamson, John. Exchange Rates and Trade Policy. **In** *Cline W. R., ed.*, 1983, pp. 99–120. **[G: U.S.; EEC; Japan]**

Berthelot, Yves. Trade Policy in the 1980s: The Players: Comment. **In** *Cline W. R., ed.*, 1983, pp. 310–12.

Bhagwati, Jagdish N. Market Disruption, Export Market Disruption, Compensation, and GATT Reform. **In** *Bhagwati, J. N., Vol. 1*, 1983, *1977*, pp. 455–77. **[G: U.S.]**

Bhagwati, Jagdish N. On the Underinvoicing of Imports. **In** *Bhagwati, J. N., Vol. 1*, 1983, *1974*, pp. 315–24. **[G: OECD; Turkey]**

Bhagwati, Jagdish N. Optimal Policies and Immiserising Growth. **In** *Bhagwati, J. N., Vol. 1*, 1983, *1969*, pp. 130–33.

Bhagwati, Jagdish N. Shifting Comparative Advantage, Protectionist Demands, and Policy Response. **In** *Bhagwati, J. N., Vol. 2*, 1983, *1982*, pp. 253–84.

Bhagwati, Jagdish N. Toward a Policy Synthesis: Panel Discussion. **In** *Cline W. R., ed.*, 1983, pp. 729–35.

Bhagwati, Jagdish N. Trade Liberalization among LDCs, Trade Theory, and GATT Rules. **In** *Bhagwati, J. N., Vol. 1*, 1983, *1968*, pp. 411–33.

Bhagwati, Jagdish N. and Srinivasan, T. N. Optimal Trade Policy and Compensation under Endogenous Uncertainty: The Phenomenon of Market Disruption. **In** *Bhagwati, J. N., Vol. 1*, 1983, *1976*, pp. 434–54.

Bhagwati, Jagdish N. and Srinivasan, T. N. Revenue Seeking: A Generalization of the Theory of Tariffs—A Correction. **In** *Bhagwati, J. N., Vol. 1*, 1983, *1982*, pp. 362–64.

Bhagwati, Jagdish N. and Srinivasan, T. N. Revenue Seeking: A Generalization of the Theory of Tariffs. **In** *Bhagwati, J. N., Vol. 1*, 1983, *1980*, pp. 343–61.

Bhagwati, Jagdish N. and Srinivasan, T. N. The Welfare Consequences of Directly-Unproductive Profit-seeking (DUP) Lobbying Activities. **In** *Bhagwati, J. N., Vol. 1,* 1983, *1982,* pp. 274–85.

Birnbaum, Karl E. Little Europe, Wider Europe and Western Economic Cooperation: Comment. **In** *Tsoukalis, L., ed.,* 1983, pp. 195–97. **[G: EEC; OECD]**

Blair, Andrew R. The Relationship of MNC Direct Investment to Host Country Trade and Trade Policy: Some Preliminary Evidence. **In** *Goldberg, W. H., ed.,* 1983, pp. 270–301. **[G: Latin America]**

Borrus, Michael. The Politics of Competitive Erosion in the U.S. Steel Industry. **In** *Zysman, J. and Tyson, L., eds.,* 1983, pp. 60–105. **[G: U.S.]**

Brada, Josef C. The Soviet–American Grain Agreement and the National Interest. *Amer. J. Agr. Econ.,* November 1983, *65*(4), pp. 651–56. **[G: U.S.; U.S.S.R.]**

Brezzo, Roberto and Perkal, Isaac. The Role of Marketing Incentives in Export Promotion: The Uruguayan Case. **In** *Czinkota, M. R., ed. (I),* 1983, pp. 51–65. **[G: Uruguay]**

Brusick, Philippe. UN Control of Restrictive Business Practices: A Decisive First Step. *J. World Trade Law,* July–August 1983, *17*(4), pp. 337–51.

Buckley, Peter J. Government–Industry Relations in Exporting: Lessons from the United Kingdom. **In** *Czinkota, M. R., ed. (I),* 1983, pp. 89–109. **[G: U.K.]**

Bulbeck, Chilla. State and Capital in Tariff Policy. **In** *Head, B. W., ed.,* 1983, pp. 219–37. **[G: Australia]**

Burgess, David F. Protection, Real Wages, Real Incomes, and Foreign Ownership: A Reply. *Can. J. Econ.,* May 1983, *16*(2), pp. 356–61. **[G: Canada]**

Butler, Nicholas. The Ploughshares War between Europe and America. *Foreign Aff.,* Fall 1983, *62*(1), pp. 105–22. **[G: Europe; America]**

Butlin, M. W. Protection, Real Wages, Real Incomes, and Foreign Ownership: A Comment. *Can. J. Econ.,* May 1983, *16*(2), pp. 350–56. **[G: Australia]**

Butt Philip, Alan. Industrial and Competition Policies: A New Look. **In** *El-Agraa, A. M., ed.,* 1983, pp. 125–46. **[G: EEC; U.K.]**

Byington, Russell and Olin, Gary. An Econometric Analysis of Freight Rate Disparities in U.S. Liner Trades. *Appl. Econ.,* June 1983, *15*(3), pp. 403–07. **[G: U.S.]**

Bykov, O. N. and Voronkov, L. S. Process of Détente in Europe and Soviet–Finnish Economic Cooperation. **In** *Möttölä, K.; Bykov, O. N. and Korolev, I. S., eds.,* 1983, pp. 233–46. **[G: U.S.S.R.; Finland]**

Camps, Miriam. Little Europe, Wider Europe and Western Economic Cooperation: Comment. **In** *Tsoukalis, L., ed.,* 1983, pp. 190–95. **[G: EEC; OECD]**

Cannon, Terry. Foreign Investment and Trade; Origins of the Modernization Policy. **In** *Feuchtwang, S. and Hussain, A., eds.,* 1983, pp. 288–324. **[G: China]**

Canto, Victor A. U.S. Trade Policy: History and Evidence. *Cato J.,* Winter 1983/84, *3*(3), pp. 679–96. **[G: U.S.]**

Canto, Victor A. and Laffer, Arthur B. The Effectiveness of Orderly Marketing Agreements: The Color TV Case. *Bus. Econ.,* January 1983, *18*(1), pp. 38–45. **[G: Japan; U.S.]**

Capie, Forrest. Tariff Protection and Economic Performance in the Nineteenth Century. **In** *Black, J. and Winters, L. A., eds.,* 1983, pp. 1–24. **[G: Europe; U.S.]**

Capie, Forrest. The British Tariff and Industrial Protection in the 1930s. **In** *Feinstein, C., ed.,* 1983, *1978,* pp. 93–106. **[G: U.K.]**

Carbaugh, Robert. The Consequences of Local Content Protection. *Bus. Econ.,* September 1983, *18*(4), pp. 55–62. **[G: U.S.]**

Carlsson, Bo A. W. Industrial Subsidies in Sweden: Macro-Economic Effects and an International Comparison. *J. Ind. Econ.,* September 1983, *32*(1), pp. 1–23. **[G: Sweden; W. Germany; U.K.; Norway; Italy]**

Castle, Emery N. The Role of Markets and Governments in the World Food Economy: Discussion. **In** *Johnson, D. G. and Schuh, G. E., eds.,* 1983, pp. 302–06.

Chambers, Robert G. International Trade, Gross Substitutability and the Domestic Farm–Retail Price Margin. *Europ. Rev. Agr. Econ.,* 1983, *10*(1), pp. 33–53.

Chau, L. C. Imports of Consumer Goods from China and the Economic Growth of Hong Kong. **In** *Youngson, A. J., ed.,* 1983, pp. 184–225. **[G: China; Hong Kong]**

Chen, Edward K. Y. The Impact of China's Four Modernizations on Hong Kong's Economic Development. **In** *Youngson, A. J., ed.,* 1983, pp. 77–103. **[G: China; Hong Kong]**

Chen, Yun. Manage Foreign Trade Work Well. **In** *Ch'en, Y.,* 1983, *1961,* pp. 139–43. **[G: China]**

Cline, William R. "Reciprocity": A New Approach to World Trade Policy? **In** *Cline W. R., ed.,* 1983, *1982,* pp. 121–58. **[G: U.S.]**

Cline, William R. Trade Policy in the 1980s: Introduction and Summary. **In** *Cline W. R., ed.,* 1983, pp. 1–54.

Cnossen, Sijbren. Harmonization of Indirect Taxes in the EEC. **In** *McLure, C. E., Jr., ed.,* 1983, pp. 150–68. **[G: EEC]**

Coffield, Shirley A. International Services–Trade Issues and the GATT. **In** *Rubin, S. J. and Graham, T. R., eds.,* 1983, pp. 69–108. **[G: U.S.; LDCs; OECD]**

Cohen, Robert B. The Prospects for Trade and Protectionism in the Auto Industry. **In** *Cline W. R., ed.,* 1983, pp. 527–63. **[G: Selected Countries]**

Colaiácovo, Juan Luis. A Model of Export Negotiations and the Small- and Medium-sized Firm: The Latin American Case. **In** *Czinkota, M. R., ed. (II),* 1983, pp. 183–97. **[G: Latin America]**

Connidis, Lilla Arnet. The Effective Rate of Protection for Motor Vehicle Manufacturing in Canada. *Can. J. Econ.,* February 1983, *16*(1), pp. 98–103. **[G: Canada]**

Contractor, Farok J. Technology Importation Policies in Developing Countries: Some Implications of Recent Theoretical and Empirical Evidence.

J. Devel. Areas, July 1983, *17*(4), pp. 499–519. **[G: LDCs]**

Cooper, Richard N. Toward a Policy Synthesis: Panel Discussion. **In** *Cline W. R., ed.*, 1983, pp. 735–39.

Corden, Warner Max. Toward a Policy Synthesis: Panel Discussion. **In** *Cline W. R., ed.*, 1983, pp. 739–46.

Cravinho, João. Characteristics and Motives for Entry. **In** *Sampedro, J. L. and Payno, J. A., eds.*, 1983, pp. 131–48. **[G: Portugal; EEC]**

Crowley, P. T.; O'Mara, L. P. and Campbell, R. Inport Quotas, Resource Development and Intersectoral Adjustment. *Australian Econ. Pap.*, December 1983, *22*(41), pp. 384–410. **[G: Australia]**

Crutchfield, Stephen R. Estimation of Foreign Willingness to Pay for United States Fishery Resources: Japanese Demand for Alaska Pollock. *Land Econ.*, February 1983, *59*(1), pp. 16–23. **[G: Japan; U.S.]**

Czinkota, Michael R. Services Trade: The Negotiation Agenda. **In** *Czinkota, M. R., ed. (I)*, 1983, pp. 285–302. **[G: U.S.]**

Das, Bhagirath L. The GATT Multi-Fibre Arrangement. *J. World Trade Law*, March–April 1983, *17*(2), pp. 95–105. **[G: LDCs; MDCs]**

Deardorff, Alan V. and Stern, Robert M. Tariff and Exchange Rate Protection under Fixed and Flexible Exchange Rates in the Major Industrialized Countries. **In** *Bhandari, J. S. and Putnam, B. H., eds.*, 1983, pp. 472–99. **[G: OECD]**

Deardorff, Alan V. and Stern, Robert M. The Economic Effects of Complete Elimination of Post-Tokyo Round Tariffs: Reply. **In** *Cline W. R., ed.*, 1983, pp. 724. **[G: Selected Countries]**

Deardorff, Alan V. and Stern, Robert M. The Economic Effects of Complete Elimination of Post-Tokyo Round Tariffs. **In** *Cline W. R., ed.*, 1983, pp. 673–710. **[G: Selected Countries]**

Deardorff, Alan V. and Stern, Robert M. The Effects of Domestic Tax/Subsidies and Import Tariffs on the Structures of Protection in the United States, United Kingdom and Japan. **In** *Black, J. and Winters, L. A., eds.*, 1983, pp. 43–64. **[G: U.K.; U.S.; Japan]**

Diaz-Alejandro, Carlos F. Trade Policy in the 1980s: The Players: Comment. **In** *Cline W. R., ed.*, 1983, pp. 305–09.

Diebold, John. The Information Technology Industries: A Case Study of High Technology Trade. **In** *Cline W. R., ed.*, 1983, pp. 639–71. **[G: U.S.; U.K.; France; W. Germany; Japan]**

Diebold, William, Jr. and Stalson, Helena. Negotiating Issues in International Services Transactions. **In** *Cline W. R., ed.*, 1983, pp. 581–609.

DiLorenzo, Thomas J.; Sementilli, Vincent M. and Southwick, Lawrence, Jr. The Lome Sugar Protocol: Increased Dependency for Fiji and Other ACP States. *Rev. Soc. Econ.*, April 1983, *41*(1), pp. 25–38. **[G: Fiji; ACP; EEC]**

Dinopoulos, Elias. Import Competition, International Factor Mobility and Lobbying Responses: The Schumpeterian Industry Case. *J. Int. Econ.*, May 1983, *14*(3/4), pp. 395–410.

Donges, Juergen B. Re-appraisal of Foreign Trade Strategies for Industrial Development. **In** *[Giersch, H.]*, 1983, pp. 279–301. **[G: LDCs]**

Donges, Juergen B. Trade Policy in the 1980s: Discussion, Session 3: Comment. **In** *Cline W. R., ed.*, 1983, pp. 565–67.

Donnenfeld, Shabtai. Domestic Regulation and the Preservation of Monopoly Power in Foreign Markets. *Southern Econ. J.*, April 1983, *49*(4), pp. 954–65.

Dymock, Paul and Vogt, Donna. Protectionist Pressures in the U.S. Congress: A Review of the 97th Congress in 1982. *J. World Trade Law*, November–December 1983, *17*(6), pp. 496–512. **[G: U.S.]**

Dymsza, William A. A National Export Strategy for Latin American Countries. **In** *Czinkota, M. R., ed. (II)*, 1983, pp. 5–25. **[G: Latin America]**

Easter, Christopher D. and Paris, Quirino. Supply Response with Stochastic Technology and Prices in Australia's Rural Export Industries. *Australian J. Agr. Econ.*, April 1983, *27*(1), pp. 12–30. **[G: U.S.; Australia]**

Easton, Stephen T. and Grubel, Herbert G. The Costs and Benefits of Protection in a Growing World. *Kyklos*, 1983, *36*(2), pp. 213–30. **[G: U.S.]**

Echols, Marsha A. The GATT Ministerial and International Trade in Agricultural Products. **In** *Rubin, S. J. and Graham, T. R., eds.*, 1983, pp. 109–33. **[G: Japan; U.S.; EEC]**

Eden, Lorraine. Transfer Pricing Policies under Tariff Barriers. *Can. J. Econ.*, November 1983, *16*(4), pp. 669–85. **[G: Canada]**

Eichengreen, Barry J. Protection, Real Wage Resistance and Employment. *Weltwirtsch. Arch.*, 1983, *119*(3), pp. 429–52.

Elsener, Ferdinand. Extraterritorial Application of U.S. Antitrust Laws: The Viewpoint of a European Corporate Lawyer. *Wirtsch. Recht*, 1983, *35*(2/3), pp. 130–40. **[G: U.S.]**

Erma, Reino. Aspects of the Application and Development of the General Conditions for Trade in Goods (Finland–CMEA) from the Standpoint of Trade between Finland and the Soviet Union. **In** *Möttölä, K.; Bykov, O. N. and Korolev, I. S., eds.*, 1983, pp. 86–89. **[G: Finland; CMEA; U.S.S.R.]**

Evans, Richard D. An Exercise in OPEC Taxonomy. *Antitrust Bull.*, Fall 1983, *28*(3), pp. 653–67. **[G: OPEC; U.S.]**

Falvey, Rodney E. Protection and Import-Competing Product Selection in a Multi-Product Industry. *Int. Econ. Rev.*, October 1983, *24*(3), pp. 735–47.

Feenstra, Robert C. Shifting Comparative Advantage, Protectionist Demands, and Policy Response: Appendix: Product Creation and Trade Patterns: A Theoretical Note on the "Biological" Model of Trade in Similar Products. **In** *Bhagwati, J. N., Vol. 2*, 1983, *1982*, pp. 284–95.

Feltenstein, Andrew. A Computational General Equilibrium Approach to the Shadow Pricing of Trade Restrictions and the Adjustment of the Exchange Rate, with an Application to Argentina. *J. Policy Modeling*, November 1983, *5*(3), pp. 333–61. **[G: Argentina]**

Fendt, Roberto, Jr. Promotion of Trade in Technical

Services: The Brazilian Case. **In** *Czinkota, M. R., ed. (I),* 1983, pp. 303–18. **[G: Brazil]**

Fieleke, Norman S. New England's Exports and U.S. Trade Policy. *New Eng. Econ. Rev.*, March/April 1983, pp. 24–27. **[G: U.S.]**

Findlay, Ronald and Wellisz, Stanislaw. Some Aspects of the Political Economy of Trade Restrictions. *Kyklos,* 1983, *36*(3), pp. 469–81.

Finger, J. Michael. The Political Economy of Trade Policy. *Cato J.,* Winter 1983/84, *3*(3), pp. 743–50. **[G: U.S.; W. Europe]**

Fink, Hans. International Problems in the Field of General Taxes on Sales of Goods and Services: Sweden. **In** *International Fiscal Association (I),* 1983, pp. 573–92. **[G: Sweden]**

Finlayson, Jock A. and Zacher, Mark W. The GATT and the Regulation of Trade Barriers: Regime Dynamics and Functions. **In** *Krasner, S. D., ed.,* 1983, *1981,* pp. 273–314. **[G: Global]**

Foster, David. The MTN Codes in the GATT Ministerial. **In** *Rubin, S. J. and Graham, T. R., eds.,* 1983, pp. 50–68.

Frank, Isaiah. Trade Policy in the 1980s: The Setting: Comment. **In** *Cline W. R., ed.,* 1983, pp. 210–15.

Franzmeyer, Fritz. New Developments in EEC and CMEA: Comments. **In** *Saunders, C. T., ed.,* 1983, pp. 100–102. **[G: EEC]**

Furtan, W. Harley; Nagy, Joseph G. and Storey, Gary G. The Impact on the Canadian Rapeseed Industry from Changes in Transport and Tariff Rates: Reply. *Amer. J. Agr. Econ.,* August 1983, *65*(3), pp. 618–19. **[G: Canada]**

Gadbaw, R. Michael. The Outlook for GATT as an Institution. **In** *Rubin, S. J. and Graham, T. R., eds.,* 1983, pp. 33–49.

Gallini, Nancy T.; Lewis, Tracy R. and Ware, Roger. Strategic Timing and Pricing of a Substitute in a Cartelized Resource Market. *Can. J. Econ.,* August 1983, *16*(3), pp. 429–46.

Galtung, Johan. On the Effects of International Economic Sanctions. **In** *Nincic, M. and Wallensteen, P., eds.,* 1983, pp. 17–60. **[G: Rhodesia]**

Gately, Dermot. OPEC: Retrospective and Prospects, 1973–1990. *Europ. Econ. Rev.,* May 1983, *21*(3), pp. 313–31. **[G: OPEC]**

Georgakopoulos, Theodore A. and Paschos, Panagiotis G. The Costs and Benefits of the CAP: Greece's Experience in 1981. *Europ. Rev. Agr. Econ.,* 1983, *10*(4), pp. 377–88. **[G: Greece]**

Goldman, Marshall I. The Evolution and Possible Direction of U.S. Policy in East–West Trade. **In** *Becker, A. S., ed.,* 1983, pp. 155–76. **[G: U.S.S.R.; U.S.]**

Goldstein, Walter. Economic Nationalism and the Disruption of World Trade: The Impact of the Third Oil Shock. **In** *Lieber, R. J., ed.,* 1983, pp. 169–92. **[G: LDCs; OECD; OPEC]**

Gomez-Ibanez, Jose A.; Leone, Robert A. and O'Connell, Stephen A. Restraining Auto Imports: Does Anyone Win? *J. Policy Anal. Manage.,* Winter 1983, *2*(2), pp. 196–219. **[G: U.S.; Japan]**

Gordon, David F. The Politics of International Sanctions: A Case Study of South Africa. **In** *Nincic, M. and Wallensteen, P., eds.,* 1983, pp. 183–210. **[G: S. Africa]**

Graham, Thomas R. GATT's Wandering Ministerial. **In** *Rubin, S. J. and Graham, T. R., eds.,* 1983, pp. 7–17.

Graham, Thomas R. and Rubin, Seymour J. U.S. Trade Policy toward Developing Countries. **In** *Rubin, S. J. and Graham, T. R., eds.,* 1983, pp. 152–64. **[G: LDCs; U.S.]**

Graham, W. C. Government Procurement Policies: GATT, the EEC, and the United States. **In** *Trebilcock, M. J., et al., eds.,* 1983, pp. 355–93. **[G: U.S.; EEC]**

Green, Jerrold D. Strategies for Evading Economic Sanctions. **In** *Nincic, M. and Wallensteen, P., eds.,* 1983, pp. 61–85. **[G: U.S.; Rhodesia; Cuba]**

Grey, Rodney de C. A Note on U.S. Trade Policy. **In** *Cline W. R., ed.,* 1983, pp. 243–57. **[G: U.S.]**

Griffith, Garry R. and Meilke, Karl D. The Impact on the Canadian Rapeseed Industry of Removing EEC Import Tariffs. *J. Policy Modeling,* March 1983, *5*(1), pp. 37–54. **[G: Canada; EEC]**

Griffith, Garry R. and Meilke, Karl D. The Impact on the Canadian Rapeseed Industry from Changes in Transport and Tariff Rates: Comment. *Amer. J. Agr. Econ.,* August 1983, *65*(3), pp. 615–17. **[G: Canada]**

Grilli, Enzo R. and La Noce, Mauro. The Political Economy of Protection in Italy: Some Empirical Evidence. *Banca Naz. Lavoro Quart. Rev.,* June 1983, (145), pp. 143–61. **[G: Italy]**

Guillaume, Jean-Marie. A European View of East–West Trade in the 1980s. **In** *Becker, A. S., ed.,* 1983, pp. 135–54. **[G: CMEA; U.S.; W. Europe]**

Haberler, Gottfried. Trade Policy in the 1980s: The Setting: Comment. **In** *Cline W. R., ed.,* 1983, pp. 203–09.

Hager, Wolfgang. Little Europe, Wider Europe and Western Economic Cooperation. **In** *Tsoukalis, L., ed.,* 1983, pp. 171–90. **[G: EEC; OECD]**

Haggard, Stephan and Moon, Chung-in. The South Korean State in the International Economy: Liberal, Dependent, or Mercantile? **In** *Ruggie, J. G., ed.,* 1983, pp. 131–89. **[G: S. Korea]**

Hamilton, Bob and Whalley, John. Optimal Tariff Calculations in Alternative Trade Models and Some Possible Implications for Current World Trading Arrangements. *J. Int. Econ.,* November 1983, *15*(3/4), pp. 323–48.

Hanke, Steve H. U.S.–Japanese Trade: Myths and Realities. *Cato J.,* Winter 1983/84, *3*(3), pp. 757–69. **[G: U.S.; Japan]**

Hanson, Philip. The Role of Trade and Technology Transfer in the Soviet Economy. **In** *Becker, A. S., ed.,* 1983, pp. 23–48. **[G: OECD; U.S.S.R.]**

Hardt, John P. and Tomlinson, Kate S. The Potential Role of Western Policy toward Eastern Europe in East–West Trade. **In** *Becker, A. S., ed.,* 1983, pp. 79–133.

Hathaway, Dale E. Agricultural Trade Policy for the 1980s. **In** *Cline W. R., ed.,* 1983, pp. 435–53.

Herlihy, P. and Cowan, C. Trade in Live Pigs between Northern Ireland and the Republic of Ireland. *Irish J. Agr. Econ. Rural Soc.,* 1983, *9*(2), pp. 173–92. **[G: Ireland; U.K.]**

Heth, Meir. Protectionism and International Banking: Sectorial Efficiency, Competitive Structure and National Policy: Comment. *J. Banking Fi-*

nance, 1983, *7*(4), pp. 611–14. **[G: Selected Countries]**

Hindley, Brian. Trade Policy, Economic Performance, and Britain's Economic Problems. **In** *Black, J. and Winters, L. A., eds.,* 1983, pp. 25–42. **[G: U.K.]**

Holt, Stephen C. Membership of the EC and Its Alternatives. **In** *El-Agraa, A. M., ed.,* 1983, pp. 41–55. **[G: EEC; U.K.]**

Holzman, Franklyn D. Dumping by Centrally Planned Economies: The Polish Golf Cart Case. **In** *[Erlich, A.],* 1983, pp. 133–48. **[G: Poland; U.S.]**

Holzmann, Robert and Winckler, Georg. Austrian Economic Policy: Some Theoretical and Critical Remarks on "Austro-Keynesianism." *Empirica,* 1983, (2), pp. 183–203. **[G: Austria]**

Homem de Melo, Fernando. Trade Policy, Technology, and Food Prices in Brazil. *Quart. Rev. Econ. Bus.,* Spring 1983, *23*(1), pp. 58–78. **[G: Brazil]**

Hufbauer, Gary Clyde. Subsidy Issues after the Tokyo Round. **In** *Cline W. R., ed.,* 1983, pp. 327–61. **[G: OECD]**

Hufbauer, Gary Clyde. "U.S.–Japanese Trade": A Comment. *Cato J.,* Winter 1983/84, *3*(3), pp. 771–75. **[G: U.S.; Japan]**

Hughes Hallett, A. J. and Brandsma, Andries S. How Effective Could Sanctions against the Soviet Union Be? *Weltwirtsch. Arch.,* 1983, *119*(3), pp. 498–522. **[G: U.S.S.R.]**

Hughes, Helen. Inter-developing-country Trade and Employment. **In** *Weisbrod, B. and Hughes, H., eds.,* 1983, pp. 429–46. **[G: LDCs]**

Inotai, András. CMEA Integration and National Economic Policies: Adjustment to the Changed World Economic Environment. **In** *Saunders, C. T., ed.,* 1983, pp. 81–95. **[G: CMEA]**

Izik-Hedri, Gabriella. A Hungarian–Austrian Industrial Free Trade Agreement. *Soviet E. Europ. Foreign Trade,* Winter 1983–84, *19*(4), pp. 73–89. **[G: Finland; Hungary; Austria]**

Jackson, John H. GATT Machinery and the Tokyo Round Agreements. **In** *Cline W. R., ed.,* 1983, pp. 159–87.

Janiszewski, Hubert A. Restrictive Provisions in Licensing Agreements to Poland. *J. World Trade Law,* March–April 1983, *17*(2), pp. 154–58. **[G: Poland; Selected MDCs]**

Jayawardena, D. L. U. Free Trade Zones. *J. World Trade Law,* September–October 1983, *17*(5), pp. 427–44. **[G: Selected LDCs]**

Jentleson, Bruce W. Khrushchev's Oil and Brezhnev's Natural Gas Pipelines. **In** *Lieber, R. J., ed.,* 1983, pp. 33–69. **[G: U.S.S.R.; U.S.; W. Europe]**

Johnson, Frederick I. On the Stability of Commodity Cartels. *Amer. Econ.,* Fall 1983, *27*(2), pp. 34–36. **[G: LDCs]**

Johnson, Wallace H. and Quintin, Yves. U.S. Reliability for Grain Deliveries: The Treaty Option. *J. World Trade Law,* September–October 1983, *17*(5), pp. 397–406. **[G: U.S.]**

Jones, Sidney L. Protectionism and the U.S. Economy [U.S. Trade Policy: History and Evidence]. *Cato J.,* Winter 1983/84, *3*(3), pp. 697–703. **[G: U.S.]**

Junguito, Roberto and Pizano, Diego. The Role of Information in Commodity Negotiations: The Case of Coffee. **In** *O'Brien, R. C., ed.,* 1983, pp. 78–87. **[G: MDCs; LDCs]**

Kaje, Matti and Niitamo, Olavi E. Scientific and Technological Cooperation between a Small Capitalist Country and a Big Socialist Country. **In** *Möttölä, K.; Bykov, O. N. and Korolev, I. S., eds.,* 1983, pp. 139–51. **[G: U.S.S.R.; Finland]**

Kaldor, Nicholas. The Role of Commodity Prices in Economic Recovery. *Lloyds Bank Rev.,* July 1983, (149), pp. 21–34.

Kane, N. Stephan. Reassessing the Bureaucratic Dimension of Foreign Policy Making: A Case Study of the Cuban Sugar Quota Decision, 1954–56. *Soc. Sci. Quart.,* March 1983, *64*(1), pp. 46–65. **[G: U.S.]**

Kanemitsu, Hideo. Trade Policy in the 1980s: The Players: Comment. **In** *Cline W. R., ed.,* 1983, pp. 313–18.

Keesing, Donald B. Trade Policy for Developing Countries. **In** *Todaro, M. P., ed.,* 1983, pp. 316–26.

Keohane, Robert O. Associative American Development, 1776–1860: Economic Growth and Political Disintegration. **In** *Ruggie, J. G., ed.,* 1983, pp. 43–90. **[G: U.S.]**

Kindleberger, Charles P. International Trade and National Prosperity. *Cato J.,* Winter 1983/84, *3*(3), pp. 623–37. **[G: MDCs]**

Kirthisingha, P. N. International Commodity Agreements. *Int. J. Soc. Econ.,* 1983, *10*(3), pp. 40–65.

Kissinger, Henry A. Salvare l'economia del mondo. (Saving the World Economy. With English summary.) *Mondo Aperto,* September-October 1983, *37*(5), pp. 245–54. **[G: OECD]**

Kokole, Omari H. STABEX Anatomised. **In** *Gauhar, A., ed. (II),* 1983, pp. 194–212. **[G: LDCs]**

Kolsen, H. M. Effective Rates of Protection and Hidden Sectoral Transfers by Public Authorities. *Australian J. Agr. Econ.,* August 1983, *27*(2), pp. 104–15. **[G: Australia]**

Korolev, I. S. The Mechanism of the Multilateral Economic Cooperation between the CMEA and Finland. **In** *Möttölä, K.; Bykov, O. N. and Korolev, I. S., eds.,* 1983, pp. 79–85. **[G: CMEA; Finland]**

Korth, Christopher M. The Promotion of Exports with Barter. **In** *Czinkota, M. R., ed. (I),* 1983, pp. 37–50. **[G: Selected Countries]**

Kostecki, M. M. Trade Control Measures and Decision Making. *Econ. Int.,* February 1983, *36*(1), pp. 35–52.

Krauss, Melvyn. Protectionism, the Welfare State, and the Third World. *Cato J.,* Winter 1983/84, *3*(3), pp. 673–78. **[G: LDCs; U.S.; Europe]**

Krinsky, Itzhak. The Small Country Assumption: A Note on Canadian Exports. *Appl. Econ.,* February 1983, *15*(1), pp. 73–79. **[G: Canada]**

Krishnamurti, R. Multilateral Trade Negotiations and the Developing Countries. **In** *Gauhar, A., ed. (II),* 1983, pp. 154–72.

Krueger, Anne O. Protectionism, Exchange Rate Distortions, and Agricultural Trading Patterns. *Amer. J. Agr. Econ.,* December 1983, *65*(5), pp. 864–71. **[G: Global]**

Kubo, Yuji, et al. Modelos de equilibrio general para el análisis de estrategias alternativas de comercio exterior: una aplicación a Corea. (With English summary.) *Cuadernos Econ.*, December 1983, *20*(61), pp. 313–43. **[G: S. Korea]**

Kuenne, Robert E. Lessons and Conjectures on OPEC. **In** *Weintraub, S. and Goodstein, M., eds.*, 1983, pp. 164–74. **[G: OPEC]**

Kumar, Ramesh C. and Akbar, S. The Generalised System of Preferences and Canadian Imports of Manufactured and Semi-Manufactured Products from Developing Countries. *J. Econ. Stud.*, 1983, *10*(1), pp. 17–30. **[G: Canada; non-OPEC LDCs]**

Kuntjoro-Jakti, Dorodjatun and Tjiptoherijanto, Prijono. Indonesia–Japan Trade Relations. **In** *Akrasanee, N., ed.*, 1983, pp. 37–55. **[G: Indonesia; Japan]**

Kwako, Thomas L. International Trade Law Implications of Latin American Tax Practices. **In** *Czinkota, M. R., ed. (II)*, 1983, pp. 85–106. **[G: Latin America; OECD]**

Kyröläinen, Hannu. The Development of Finnish–Soviet Economic Relations since 1918. **In** *Möttölä, K.; Bykov, O. N. and Korolev, I. S., eds.*, 1983, pp. 220–32. **[G: U.S.S.R.; Finland]**

Lane, W. R. Harmonization of Taxes in Australia. **In** *McLure, C. E., Jr., ed.*, 1983, pp. 172–76. **[G: Australia]**

Langhammer, Rolf J. Sectoral Profiles of Import Licencing in Selected Developing Countries and Their Impact on North-South and South-South Trade Flows. *Konjunkturpolitik*, 1983, *29*(1), pp. 21–32. **[G: Selected LDCs]**

Langhammer, Rolf J. The Importance of 'Natural' Barriers to Trade among Developing Countries: Some Evidence from the Transport Cost Content in Brasilian Imports. *World Devel.*, May 1983, *11*(5), pp. 417–25. **[G: Brazil; LDCs]**

Lanthier, Allan R. Canada: The 1982 Changes to the Taxation of International Income. *Bull. Int. Fiscal Doc.*, April 1983, *37*(4), pp. 171–79. **[G: Canada]**

Lányi, Kamilla. Enterprise Identity—Interenterprise Relationships: A State Monopoly in a Competitive Position. *Eastern Europ. Econ.*, Spring–Summer 1983, *21*(3–4), pp. 26–48. **[G: Hungary]**

Larsen, Flemming; Llewellyn, John and Potter, Stephen. International Economic Linkages. *OECD Econ. Stud.*, Autumn 1983, (1), pp. 43–91. **[G: OECD]**

Lerner, Abba P. OPEC—A Plan—If You Can't Beat Them, Join Them. **In** *Lerner, A. P.*, 1983, *1980*, pp. 125–27.

Liebowitz, S. J. and Bridgeman, Guy A. The Pricing Practices of the Liquor Control Board of Ontario: Revisited. *Can. J. Econ.*, February 1983, *16*(1), pp. 154–61. **[G: Canada]**

Lipson, Charles. The Transformation of Trade: The Sources and Effects of Regime Change. **In** *Krasner, S. D., ed.*, 1983, *1982*, pp. 233–71. **[G: OECD]**

Lyman, Robert. Economic and Political Issues in International Natural Gas Trade: A Canadian View. *J. Energy Devel.*, Autumn 1983, *9*(1), pp. 49–54. **[G: Canada]**

MacBean, Alasdair. Britain's International Economic Policy. **In** *Seldon, A., et al.*, 1983, pp. 151–66. **[G: U.K.]**

Magee, Stephen P. and Young, Leslie. Multinationals, Tariffs, and Capital Flows with Endogenous Politicians. **In** *Kindleberger, C. P. and Audretsch, D. B., eds.*, 1983, pp. 21–37.

Maizels, A. The Industrialisation of the Developing Countries. **In** *[Saunders, C. T.]*, 1983, pp. 29–50. **[G: LDCs]**

Malmgren, Harald B. Threats to the Multilateral System. **In** *Cline W. R., ed.*, 1983, pp. 189–201.

Mansur, Ahsan H. Determining the Appropriate Levels of Exchange Rates for Developing Economies: Some Methods and Issues. *Int. Monet. Fund Staff Pap.*, December 1983, *30*(4), pp. 784–818. **[G: LDCs]**

Marrese, Michael and Vaňous, Jan. Unconventional Gains from Trade. *J. Compar. Econ.*, December 1983, *7*(4), pp. 382–99. **[G: CMEA]**

Marsden, John S. and Hollander, G. Floating Exchange Rates, Inflation and Selective Protectionism: Their Effects on the Competitiveness of Australian Industry. **In** *Black, J. and Winters, L. A., eds.*, 1983, pp. 92–129. **[G: Australia]**

Marvel, Howard P. and Ray, Edward John. The Kennedy Round: Evidence on the Regulation of International Trade in the United States. *Amer. Econ. Rev.*, March 1983, *73*(1), pp. 190–97. **[G: U.S.]**

Mattadeen, Al C. Reflections after a Decade of OPEC Pricing Policies. *Nat. Westminster Bank Quart. Rev.*, May 1983, pp. 15–23. **[G: OPEC; OECD]**

Mayer, Thomas. Effects of Export Diversification in a Primary Commodity Export Country: Colombia. *J. Policy Modeling*, June 1983, *5*(2), pp. 233–52. **[G: Colombia]**

McCulloch, Rachel and Owen, Robert F. Linking Negotiations on Trade and Foreign Direct Investment. **In** *Kindleberger, C. P. and Audretsch, D. B., eds.*, 1983, pp. 334–58. **[G: Canada]**

McMahon, C. W. Financial Aspects of the International Economic Situation. *Nationaløkon. Tidsskr.*, 1983, *121*(1), pp. 74–82. **[G: OECD]**

McQueen, Matthew. Lomé and Industrial Co-operation: The Need for Reform. *J. World Trade Law*, November–December 1983, *17*(6), pp. 524–32. **[G: EEC; Selected LDCs]**

Millstein, James E. Decline in an Expanding Industry: Japanese Competition in Color Television. **In** *Zysman, J. and Tyson, L., eds.*, 1983, pp. 106–41. **[G: U.S.; Japan]**

Mitsos, Achilles G. J. The Industrial Sector. **In** *Sampedro, J. L. and Payno, J. A., eds.*, 1983, pp. 105–27. **[G: Greece; EEC]**

Monke, Eric. Tariffs, Implementation Costs, and Optimal Policy Choice. *Weltwirtsch. Arch.*, 1983, *119*(2), pp. 281–96. **[G: Ivory Coast; Senegal; Liberia]**

Moore, John L., Jr. Export Credit Arrangements. **In** *Rubin, S. J. and Hufbauer, G. C., eds.*, 1983, pp. 139–73. **[G: Global]**

Müller, Ernst. The Common Market for Agricultural Products. **In** *Saunders, C. T., ed.*, 1983, pp. 183–91. **[G: CMEA; EEC]**

Mytelka, Lynn Krieger. The Limits of Export-led Development: The Ivory Coast's Experience with Manufactures. In *Ruggie, J. G., ed.*, 1983, pp. 239–70. [G: Ivory Coast; Sub-Saharan Africa]

Nehmer, Stanley. Trade Policy in the 1980s: Discussion, Session 3: Comment. In *Cline W. R., ed.*, 1983, pp. 568–73. [G: U.S.]

Newfarmer, Richard S. The Private Sector and Development. In *Lewis, J. P. and Kallab, V., eds.*, 1983, pp. 117–38. [G: LDCs; U.S.]

Nincic, Miroslav and Wallensteen, Peter. Economic Coercion and Foreign Policy. In *Nincic, M. and Wallensteen, P., eds.*, 1983, pp. 1–15.

Nogués, Julio J. Alternative Trade Strategies and Employment in the Argentine Manufacturing Sector. *World Devel.*, December 1983, *11* (12), pp. 1029–42. [G: Argentina]

Nukazawa, Kazuo. Japan–ASEAN Trade Relations. In *Akrasanee, N., ed.*, 1983, pp. 163–91. [G: Japan; ASEAN]

Nunnenkamp, Peter. Technische Handelshemmnisse—Formen, Effekte und Harmonisierungsbestrebungen. (Technical Barriers to Trade. Types, Consequences and Harmonization Efforts. With English summary.) *Aussenwirtschaft*, December 1983, *38* (4), pp. 373–97. [G: EEC]

O'Leary, John F. Price Reactive versus Price Active Energy Policy. In *Tempest, P., ed.*, 1983, pp. 163–75. [G: U.S.]

Obdeijn, Herman. The New Africa Trading Company and the Struggle for Import Duties in the Congo Free State, 1886–1894. *African Econ. Hist.*, 1983, (12), pp. 195–212. [G: Congo]

Owen, Roberts B. Extraterritorial Application of U.S. Trade and Financial Controls: Freezings, Vestings, Embargoes, etc. *Wirtsch. Recht*, 1983, *35* (2/3), pp. 142–53. [G: U.S.]

Paarlberg, Robert L. Shifting and Sharing Adjustment Burdens: The Role of the Industrial Food-importing Nations. In *Glassner, M. I., ed.*, 1983, *1978*, pp. 197–218. [G: EEC; Japan; U.S.S.R.; Global]

Paarlberg, Robert L. Using Food Power: Opportunities, Appearances, and Damage Control. In *Nincic, M. and Wallensteen, P., eds.*, 1983, *1982*, pp. 131–53. [G: U.S.]

Paddock, Brian. Estimation of Producer Losses Arising from the Partial Embargo of Grain Exports to the USSR. *Can. J. Agr. Econ.*, July 1983, *31* (2), pp. 233–44. [G: Canada]

Pastor, Robert. The Cry-and-Sigh Syndrome: Congress and Trade Policy. In *Schick, A., ed.*, 1983, pp. 158–95. [G: U.S.]

Patterson, Gardner. The European Community as a Threat to the System. In *Cline W. R., ed.*, 1983, pp. 223–42.

Pelzman, Joseph. Economic Costs of Tariffs and Quotas on Textile and Apparel Products Imported into the United States: A Survey of the Literature and Implications for Policies. *Weltwirtsch. Arch.*, 1983, *119* (3), pp. 523–42. [G: U.S.]

Plaut, Steven E. 'Trade Shocks' in Economies Importing Only Intermediate Goods. *Europ. Econ. Rev.*, May 1983, *21* (3), pp. 363–79. [G: Netherlands; Norway; U.K.]

v. Rabenau, K. Trade Policies and Industrialization in a Developing Country: The Case of West Malaysia. In *Lim, D., ed.*, 1983, *1976*, pp. 257–76. [G: Malaysia]

Radell, Willard W., Jr. Cuban–Soviet Sugar Trade, 1960–1976: How Great Was the Subsidy? *J. Devel. Areas*, April 1983, *17* (3), pp. 365–81. [G: Cuba]

Rantanen, Paavo. The Development of the System of Bilateral Agreements between Finland and the Soviet Union. In *Möttölä, K.; Bykov, O. N. and Korolev, I. S., eds.*, 1983, pp. 43–52. [G: U.S.S.R.; Finland]

Ravenal, Earl C. The Economic Claims of National Security [U.S. Trade Policy and National Security]. *Cato J.*, Winter 1983/84, *3* (3), pp. 729–41. [G: U.S.]

Razavi, Hossein. Effect of Uncertainty on Oil Extraction Decisions. *J. Econ. Dynam. Control*, July 1983, *5* (4), pp. 359–70. [G: Iran]

Reich, Robert B. Beyond Free Trade. *Foreign Aff.*, Spring 1983, *61* (4), pp. 773–804. [G: U.S.]

Reid, Stanley. Export Research in a Crisis. In *Czinkota, M. R., ed. (I)*, 1983, pp. 129–53.

Richardson, J. David. Worker Adjustment to U.S. International Trade: Programs and Prospects. In *Cline W. R., ed.*, 1983, pp. 393–424. [G: U.S.]

Rothschild, Leonard W., Jr. and Beattie, John R. U.S. Expected to Replace DISC with New Foreign Sales Corporation. *Bull. Int. Fiscal Doc.*, August 1983, *37* (8), pp. 339–43. [G: U.S.]

Roy, Subroto. "The Political Economy of Trade Policy": A Comment. *Cato J.*, Winter 1983/84, *3* (3), pp. 751–55. [G: U.S.]

Rubin, Seymour J. Emerging Standards of International Trade and Investment: A Preface to the Codes. In *Rubin, S. J. and Hufbauer, G. C., eds.*, 1983, pp. 5–15.

Rubin, Seymour J. and Hufbauer, Gary Clyde. Emerging Standards of International Trade and Investment: Lessons from the Codes. In *Rubin, S. J. and Hufbauer, G. C., eds.*, 1983, pp. 175–96. [G: Global]

Ruibal, Rubén R. International Problems in the Field of General Taxes on Sales of Goods and Services: Argentina. In *International Fiscal Association (I)*, 1983, pp. 219–45. [G: Argentina]

Ruppe, Hans Georg. International Problems in the Field of General Taxes on Sales of Goods and Services: General Report. In *International Fiscal Association (I)*, 1983, pp. 109–48. [G: Global]

Ryan, John P., Jr. The Export Trading Company Act of 1982: Antitrust Panacea, Placebo, or Pitfall? *Antitrust Bull.*, Fall 1983, *28* (3), pp. 501–69. [G: U.S.]

Safarian, A. E. Trade-related Investment Issues. In *Cline W. R., ed.*, 1983, pp. 611–37.

Sakashita, Noboru. Resolution of Mutual Loss Conflict Induced by the Embargo Threat. In *Isard, W. and Nagao, Y., eds.*, 1983, pp. 139–46.

Salita, Domingo C. and Juanico, Meliton B. Export Processing Zones: New Catalysts for Economic Development. In *Hamilton, F. E. I. and Linge, G. J. R., eds.*, 1983, pp. 441–61. [G: Selected LDCs]

Salonen, Pekka. Internationale Probleme auf dem Gebiet der Umsatzbesteuerung: Finnland. (With English summary.) In *International Fiscal Association (I)*, 1983, pp. 381–91. [G: Finland]

Samolis, Frank R. SOS for the CBI: Lessons of the Caribbean Basin Initiative. In *Rubin, S. J. and Graham, T. R., eds.*, 1983, pp. 134–51. **[G: Caribbean; U.S.]**

Sapir, André. Alternative Estimates of India's Transportation Cost Profile: A Reply [On the Incidence of Transportation Costs on India's Exports]. *J. Devel. Stud.*, April 1983, *19*(3), pp. 390. **[G: India]**

Sapir, André. On the Incidence of Transportation Costs on India's Exports. *J. Devel. Stud.*, January 1983, *19*(2), pp. 244–49. **[G: India]**

Sapir, André and Baldwin, Robert E. India and the Tokyo Round. *World Devel.*, July 1983, *11*(7), pp. 565–74. **[G: India; EEC; Japan; U.S.]**

Sato, Mitsuo. International Problems in the Field of General Taxes on Sales of Goods and Services: Japan. In *International Fiscal Association (I)*, 1983, pp. 463–70. **[G: Japan]**

Sauer, Richard J. The Role of Markets and Governments in the World Food Economy: Discussion. In *Johnson, D. G. and Schuh, G. E., eds.*, 1983, pp. 307–10.

Sauernheimer, Karlhans. Die aussenwirtschaftlichen Implikationen des "New Cambridge Approach." (The "New Cambridge" Approach and External Balance. With English summary.) *Konjunkturpolitik*, 1983, *29*(6), pp. 348–66.

Saxonhouse, Gary R. The Micro- and Macroeconomics of Foreign Sales to Japan. In *Cline W. R., ed.*, 1983, pp. 259–304. **[G: OECD; Korea]**

Schneider, Anna and Rosenberg, Rivka. International Problems in the Field of General Taxes on Sales of Goods and Services: Israel. In *International Fiscal Association (I)*, 1983, pp. 425–41. **[G: Israel]**

Schott, Jeffrey J. The GATT Ministerial: A Postmortem. *Challenge*, May/June 1983, *26*(2), pp. 40–45. **[G: U.S.; EEC; LDCs]**

Schug, Walter. Die Bedeutung von internationalen Rohstoffabkommen für die Verbracherländer von agrarischen und mineralischen Grundstoffen. In *Lenel, H. O.; Willgerodt, H. and Molsberger, J.*, 1983, pp. 169–91. **[G: LDCs; MDCs]**

Schuh, G. Edward. The Role of Markets and Governments in the World Food Economy. In *Johnson, D. G. and Schuh, G. E., eds.*, 1983, pp. 277–301.

Schwartz, Warren F. Regulation of Industrial Subsidies in the EEC, the United States, and GATT. In *Trebilcock, M. J., et al., eds.*, 1983, pp. 394–423. **[G: EEC; U.S.]**

Sedjo, Roger A. and Wiseman, A. Clark. The Effectiveness of an Export Restriction on Logs. *Amer. J. Agr. Econ.*, February 1983, *65*(1), pp. 113–16. **[G: U.S.]**

Seidelmann, Reimund. Energy Trade Relations between the Federal Republic of Germany and the USSR. In *Lieber, R. J., ed.*, 1983, pp. 71–103. **[G: U.S.S.R.; W. Germany]**

Şenses, Fikret. An Assessment of Turkey's Liberalization Attempts since 1980 against the Background of Her Stabilization Program. *METU*, 1983, *10*(3), pp. 271–321. **[G: Turkey]**

Senti, Richard. Subventionen und Gegenmassnahmen in der geltenden Welthandelsordnung. (Subsidies and Countervailing Duties. With English summary.) *Aussenwirtschaft*, March 1983, *38*(1), pp. 21–38.

Sgro, Pasquale M. A Selective Review of Developments in International Trade Theory: Commercial Policy and Free Trade. *Rev. Marketing Agr. Econ.*, April 1983, *51*(1), pp. 31–50.

Shenefield, John H. Extraterritorial Application of United States Antitrust Laws: Economic Imperialism or Correcting the Evil at the Source? *Wirtsch. Recht*, 1983, *35*(2/3), pp. 116–29. **[G: U.S.]**

Shepherd, Geoffrey and Duchêne, François. Industrial Change and Intervention in Western Europe. In *Shepherd, G.; Duchêne, F. and Saunders, C., eds.*, 1983, pp. 1–25. **[G: W. Europe]**

Shoup, Carl S. Harmonization of Indirect Taxes in the EEC: Comment. In *McLure, C. E., Jr., ed.*, 1983, pp. 169–71. **[G: EEC]**

Silver, Melinda. Nuclear Power Plant Licensing—Jurisdiction to Consider Foreign Impacts. *Natural Res. J.*, January 1983, *23*(1), pp. 225–37. **[G: U.S.; Philippines]**

Simons, A. L. C. International Problems in the Field of General Taxes on Sales of Goods and Services: Netherlands. In *International Fiscal Association (I)*, 1983, pp. 529–44. **[G: Netherlands]**

Sing, Lim Hua and Choo, Lee Chin. Singapore–Japan Relations: Trade and Development. In *Akrasanee, N., ed.*, 1983, pp. 117–39. **[G: Singapore; Japan]**

Singh, Ajit. U.K. Industry and the World Economy: A Case of De-industrialisation? In *Feinstein, C., ed.*, 1983, *1977*, pp. 226–57. **[G: U.K.]**

Singh, Naunihal. Communication and Competence in Private Sector Involvement in International Trade Policy. In *Czinkota, M. R., ed. (I)*, 1983, pp. 110–26. **[G: India]**

Smith, Ian. Prospects for a New International Sugar Agreement. *J. World Trade Law*, July–August 1983, *17*(4), pp. 308–24. **[G: Selected LDCs; Selected MDCs]**

Song, Dae Hee and Hallberg, M. C. An Analytic Model of the Imperfect World Trade Market: A Case Study of World Wheat Cartels. *Can. J. Agr. Econ.*, November 1983, *31*(3), pp. 389–400. **[G: Global]**

Sorenson, Vernon L. and Rossmiller, George E. Future Options for U.S. Agricultural Trade Policy. *Amer. J. Agr. Econ.*, December 1983, *65*(5), pp. 893–900. **[G: U.S.]**

de Souza, Hamilton Dias. International Problems in the Field of General Taxes on Sales of Goods and Services: Brazil. In *International Fiscal Association (I)*, 1983, pp. 319–34. **[G: Brazil]**

Stallings, Barbara. International Capitalism and the Peruvian Military Government. In *McClintock, C. and Lowenthal, A. F., eds.*, 1983, pp. 144–80. **[G: Peru]**

Stankovsky, Jan. A Hungarian–Austrian Industrial Free Trade Agreement: Reply. *Soviet E. Europ. Foreign Trade*, Winter 1983–84, *19*(4), pp. 90–95.

Stefani, Giorgio. Special Economic Zones and Economic Policy in China. *Ann. Pub. Co-op. Econ.*, July–September 1983, *54*(3), pp. 289–312. **[G: China]**

Stein, Leslie. General Measures to Assist Workers and Firms in Adjusting to Injury from Freer Trade: Issues Raised by Various European Approaches and Some ad hoc Industry Measures Adopted Elsewhere. *Amer. J. Econ. Soc.*, July 1983, *42*(3), pp. 315–27. **[G: W. Europe; Canada; U.S.; Australia]**

Sylvan, David J. Ideology and the Concept of Economic Security. **In** *Nincic, M. and Wallensteen, P., eds.*, 1983, pp. 211–41.

Tan, Siew Ee and Lai, Yew Wah. Protection and Employment in the West Malaysian Manufacturing Industries. *Weltwirtsch. Arch.*, 1983, *119*(2), pp. 329–44. **[G: Malaysia]**

Tarullo, Daniel K. The MTN Subsidies Code: Agreement without Consensus. **In** *Rubin, S. J. and Hufbauer, G. C., eds.*, 1983, pp. 63–99. **[G: Global]**

Tesar, George and Tarleton, Jesse S. Stimulation of Manufacturing Firms to Export as Part of National Export Policy. **In** *Czinkota, M. R., ed. (I)*, 1983, pp. 24–36. **[G: U.S.]**

Thirlwall, Anthony P. A Trade Strategy for the United Kingdom. *J. Common Market Stud.*, September 1983, *22*(1), pp. 1–16. **[G: U.K.]**

Thursby, Marie and Jensen, Richard. A Conjectural Variation Approach to Strategic Tariff Equilibria. *J. Int. Econ.*, February 1983, *14*(1/2), pp. 145–61.

Timmer, C. Peter and Reich, Michael R. Japan and the U.S.: Trading Shots over Beef and Oranges. *Challenge*, Sept.–Oct. 1983, *26*(4), pp. 18–24. **[G: U.S.; Japan]**

Togan, Sübidey. The Welfare Costs of the CAP for Developing Countries under Alternative Policy Regimes: The Case of Turkey. *Europ. Rev. Agr. Econ.*, 1983, *10*(2), pp. 123–39. **[G: EEC; Turkey]**

Tower, Edward. On the Best Use of Trade Controls in the Presence of Foreign Market Power. *J. Int. Econ.*, November 1983, *15*(3/4), pp. 349–65.

Tower, Edward. Some Empirical Results on Trade and National Prosperity [International Trade and National Prosperity]. *Cato J.*, Winter 1983/84, *3*(3), pp. 639–44. **[G: LDCs; MDCs]**

Trzeciakowski, W. General Equilibrium Modelling of Trade-Liberalization Issues among Major World Trade Blocs: Comment. **In** *Hickman, B. G., ed.*, 1983, pp. 138–40. **[G: OECD; Global]**

Tumlir, Jan. Statement on Protectionism to SOMC. **In** *Shadow Open Market Committee.*, 1983, pp. 53–60.

Turner, Charlie G. Voluntary Export Restraints on Trade Going to the United States. *Southern Econ. J.*, January 1983, *49*(3), pp. 793–803. **[G: U.S.; Japan]**

Tyler, William G. The Anti-Export Bias in Commercial Policies and Export Performance: Some Evidence from the Recent Brazilian Experience. *Weltwirtsch. Arch.*, 1983, *119*(1), pp. 97–108. **[G: Brazil]**

Tyson, Laura D'Andrea and Zysman, John. American Industry in International Competition: Conclusions: What to Do Now? **In** *Zysman, J. and Tyson, L., eds.*, 1983, pp. 422–27.

Tyson, Laura D'Andrea and Zysman, John. American Industry in International Competition. **In** *Zysman, J. and Tyson, L., eds.*, 1983, pp. 15–59. **[G: U.S.]**

Vagts, Detlev F. The Scope of Application and Enforcement of U.S. Laws. *Wirtsch. Recht*, 1983, *35*(2/3), pp. 72–97. **[G: U.S.]**

Van Cott, T. Norman and Wipf, Larry J. Tariff Reduction via Inflation: U.S. Specific Tariffs 1972–1979. *Weltwirtsch. Arch.*, 1983, *119*(4), pp. 724–33. **[G: U.S.]**

Vernon, Raymond. Trade and Investment in Mexico–United States Relations. **In** *Reynolds, C. W. and Tello, C., eds.*, 1983, pp. 167–79. **[G: Mexico; U.S.]**

Vischer, Frank. The United States Jurisdictional Concepts Viewed from Abroad. *Wirtsch. Recht*, 1983, *35*(2/3), pp. 98–113. **[G: U.S.; Switzerland]**

Vukmanic, Frank G. Performance Requirements: The General Debate and a Review of Latin American Practices. **In** *Czinkota, M. R., ed. (II)*, 1983, pp. 48–84. **[G: Latin America]**

Wallensteen, Peter. Economic Sanctions: Ten Modern Cases and Three Important Lessons. **In** *Nincic, M. and Wallensteen, P., eds.*, 1983, pp. 87–129. **[G: Selected Countries]**

Walsh, James I. Countertrade: Not Just for East-West Any More. *J. World Trade Law*, January–February 1983, *17*(1), pp. 3–11. **[G: Selected MDCs; Selected LDCs]**

Walter, Ingo. Structural Adjustment and Trade Policy in the International Steel Industry. **In** *Cline W. R., ed.*, 1983, pp. 483–525. **[G: Selected Countries]**

Walter, Ingo and Gray, H. Peter. Protectionism and International Banking: Sectorial Efficiency, Competitive Structure and National Policy. *J. Banking Finance*, 1983, *7*(4), pp. 597–609. **[G: Selected Countries]**

Warr, Peter G. The Jakarta Export Processing Zone: Benefits and Costs. *Bull. Indonesian Econ. Stud.*, December 1983, *19*(3), pp. 28–49. **[G: Indonesia]**

Warr, Peter G. and Lloyd, Peter J. Do Australian Trade Policies Discriminate against Less Developed Countries? *Econ. Rec.*, December 1983, *59*(167), pp. 351–64. **[G: Australia]**

Wassermann, Ursula. UNCTAD: International Jute Agreement. *J. World Trade Law*, January–February 1983, *17*(1), pp. 65–67.

Wassermann, Ursula. UNCTAD: Proposals on Commodity Issues. *J. World Trade Law*, May–June 1983, *17*(3), pp. 266–69. **[G: LDCs; MDCs]**

Weidenbaum, Murray L. The Drift to Protectionism. *Challenge*, March/April 1983, *26*(1), pp. 44–47. **[G: U.S.]**

Weidenbaum, Murray L. The High Cost of Protectionism. *Cato J.*, Winter 1983/84, *3*(3), pp. 777–91. **[G: U.S.; Japan; W. Europe]**

Weinberg, Carl B.; Nadiri, M. I. and Choi, J. An Evaluation of the Effects of Commodity-Price Indexation on Developed and Developing Economies: An Application of the Rempis Model. **In** *Hickman, B. G., ed.*, 1983, pp. 219–34. **[G: Global]**

Weiss, Leonard. Managing Trade Relations in the 1980s: Reciprocity. **In** *Rubin, S. J. and Graham, T. R., eds.*, 1983, pp. 165–231. **[G: U.S.]**

Wells, R. J. G. An Evaluation of Malaysian Agricultural Commodity Protection. *Singapore Econ. Rev.*, April 1983, *28*(1), pp. 59–72. **[G: Malaysia]**

Whalley, John. General Equilibrium Modeling of Trade-Liberalization Issues among Major World Trade Blocs. **In** *Hickman, B. G., ed.*, 1983, pp. 121–36. **[G: OECD; Global]**

Willett, Thomas D. and Jalalighajar, Mehrdad. U.S. Trade Policy and National Security. *Cato J.*, Winter 1983/84, *3*(3), pp. 717–27. **[G: U.S.]**

Williams, Harold R. and Baliga, Gurudutt M. The U.S. Export Trading Company Act of 1982: Nature and Evaluation. *J. World Trade Law*, May–June 1983, *17*(3), pp. 224–35. **[G: U.S.]**

Wolf, Martin. Managed Trade in Practice: Implications of the Textile Arrangements. **In** *Cline W. R., ed.*, 1983, pp. 455–82. **[G: Selected Countries]**

Wolf, Thomas A. East–West Trade: Economic Interests, Systemic Interaction and Political Rivalry. *ACES Bull. (See Comp. Econ. Stud. after 8/85)*, Summer 1983, *25*(2), pp. 23–59. **[G: CMEA; OECD]**

Wolff, Alan Wm. Need for New GATT Rules to Govern Safeguard Actions. **In** *Cline W. R., ed.*, 1983, pp. 363–91.

Yeager, Leland B. and Tuerck, David G. Realism and Free-Trade Policy. *Cato J.*, Winter 1983/84, *3*(3), pp. 645–66. **[G: U.S.]**

Yeats, Alexander J. On the Effects of Aggregation Bias in Alternative Estimates of India's Transportation Cost Profile: A Comment on Sapir's Estimation Procedure. *J. Devel. Stud.*, January 1983, *19*(2), pp. 250–52.

Yeats, Alexander J. Reply to Sapir [On the Incidence of Transportation Costs on India's Exports]. *J. Devel. Stud.*, April 1983, *19*(3), pp. 391. **[G: India]**

Yoffie, David B. Adjustment in the Footwear Industry: The Consequences of Orderly Marketing Agreements. **In** *Zysman, J. and Tyson, L., eds.*, 1983, pp. 313–49. **[G: U.S.]**

Zerby, J. A. and Conlon, R. M. Joint Costs and Intra-Tariff Cross-Subsidies: The Case of Liner Shipping. *J. Ind. Econ.*, June 1983, *31*(4), pp. 383–96. **[G: Australia]**

423 Economic Integration

4230 General

Brecher, Richard A. and Bhagwati, Jagdish N. Foreign Ownership and the Theory of Trade and Welfare. **In** *Bhagwati, J. N., Vol. 2*, 1983, *1981*, pp. 226–40.

Gasparetto, Marialuisa Manfredini. La politica globale mediterranea. (A Mediterranean Global Policy. With English summary.) *Rivista Int. Sci. Econ. Com.*, March 1983, *30*(3), pp. 201–27. **[G: W. Europe]**

Metghalchi, Massoud. European Monetary Union: Potential Costs and Benefits. *Rivista Int. Sci. Econ. Com.*, October–November 1983, *30*(10–11), pp. 1002–21. **[G: W. Europe]**

Simai, M. Stages of Internationalization (A Contribution to the Establishment of a Theoretical Framework). *Acta Oecon.*, 1983, *30*(1), pp. 13–30. **[G: Global]**

4232 Theory of Economic Integration

Allen, Polly Reynolds. Policies to Correct Cyclical Imbalance within a Monetary Union. *J. Common Market Stud.*, March 1983, *21*(3), pp. 313–27.

Berglas, Eitan. The Case for Unilateral Tariff Reductions: Foreign Tariffs Rediscovered [Is Unilateral Tariff Reduction Preferable to a Customs Union? The Curious Case of the Missing Foreign Tariff]. *Amer. Econ. Rev.*, December 1983, *73*(5), pp. 1141–42.

Bhagwati, Jagdish N. Trade-diverting Customs Unions and Welfare-Improvement: A Reply. **In** *Bhagwati, J. N., Vol. 2*, 1983, *1973*, pp. 474–76.

Bhagwati, Jagdish N. Trade-diverting Customs Unions and Welfare-Improvement: A Clarification. **In** *Bhagwati, J. N., Vol. 2*, 1983, *1971*, pp. 466–73.

Bhagwati, Jagdish N. and Brecher, Richard A. National Welfare in an Open Economy in the Presence of Foreign-owned Factors of Production. **In** *Bhagwati, J. N., Vol. 2*, 1983, *1980*, pp. 212–25.

El-Agraa, Ali M. The Theory of Economic Integration: The Customs Union Aspects. **In** *El-Agraa, A. M., ed.*, 1983, pp. 59–74.

Haack, W. G. C. M. The Selectivity of Economic Integration Theories: A Comparison of Some Traditional and Marxist Approaches. *J. Common Market Stud.*, June 1983, *21*(4), pp. 365–87. **[G: EEC]**

Jones, Anthony J. Withdrawal from a Customs Union: A Macroeconomic Analysis. **In** *El-Agraa, A. M., ed.*, 1983, pp. 75–87.

Katseli, Louka T. Exchange Rates and Food in the European Community. *Europ. Econ. Rev.*, January 1983, *20*(1–3), pp. 319–32. **[G: EEC]**

Mussa, Michael. Optimal Economic Integration. **In** *Armella, P. A.; Dornbusch, R. and Obstfeld, M., eds.*, 1983, pp. 41–58.

Pelkmans, Jacques and Gremmen, Hans. The Empirical Measurement of Static Customs Union Effects. *Rivista Int. Sci. Econ. Com.*, July 1983, *30*(7), pp. 612–24.

Tumlir, Jan. Strong and Weak Elements in the Concept of European Integration. **In** *[Giersch, H.]*, 1983, pp. 29–56. **[G: EEC]**

Waelbroeck, Jean. Politique commerciale commune et théorie du commerce extérieur. (The Common Commercial Policy and the Theory of International Trade. With English summary.) *Écon. Appl.*, 1983, *36*(2–3), pp. 349–88. **[G: EEC]**

4233 Economic Integration: Policy and Empirical Studies

Armstrong, Harvey W. The Assignment of Regional Policy Powers within the EC. **In** *El-Agraa, A. M., ed.*, 1983, pp. 271–98. **[G: EEC; U.K.]**

Artisien, Patrick F. R. and Buckley, Peter J. Investment Legislation in Greece, Portugal and Spain: The Background to Foreign Investment in Mediterranean Europe. *J. World Trade Law*, November–December 1983, *17*(6), pp. 513–23. **[G: Greece; Portugal; Spain; EEC]**

Ashoff, Guido. The Textile Policy of the European Community towards the Mediterranean Countries: Effects and Future Options. *J. Common*

Market Stud., September 1983, *22*(1), pp. 17–45. [G: EEC]

Avery, William P. The Politics of Crisis and Cooperation in the Andean Group. *J. Devel. Areas,* January 1983, *17*(2), pp. 155–83. [G: Latin America]

Beenstock, Michael and Warburton, Peter. Long-Term Trends in Economic Openness in the United Kingdom and the United States [Long Term Trends in Openness of National Economies]. *Oxford Econ. Pap.*, March 1983, *35*(1), pp. 130–35. [G: U.K.; U.S.]

Belovic, A. Coordination of Capital Investment among CMEA Member Nations. *Prob. Econ.*, November 1983, *26*(7), pp. 47–64. [G: CMEA]

Beltrán, Lucas. Spain and the EEC. **In** *Lenel, H. O.; Willgerodt, H. and Molsberger, J.*, 1983, pp. 157–68. [G: Spain; EEC]

Birnbaum, Karl E. Little Europe, Wider Europe and Western Economic Cooperation: Comment. **In** *Tsoukalis, L., ed.*, 1983, pp. 195–97. [G: EEC; OECD]

Bognár, József. EEC and CMEA, General Comparisons: Comment. **In** *Saunders, C. T., ed.*, 1983, pp. 57–59. [G: CMEA; EEC]

Bogomolov, Oleg. New Integration Strategies for the CMEA Countries. **In** *Saunders, C. T., ed.*, 1983, pp. 193–210. [G: CMEA]

Bonnieux, F. and Rainelli, P. Regional Disparities in Western European Agriculture. *Europ. Rev. Agr. Econ.*, 1983, *10*(3), pp. 295–301. [G: EEC]

Brada, Josef C. and Méndez, José A. Regional Economic Integration and the Volume of Intra-Regional Trade: A Comparison of Developed and Developing Country Experience. *Kyklos*, 1983, *36*(4), pp. 589–603. [G: Selected Countries]

Bulmer, Simon. Domestic Politics and European Community Policy-Making. *J. Common Market Stud.*, June 1983, *21*(4), pp. 349–63. [G: EEC]

Butt Philip, Alan. Industrial and Competition Policies: A New Look. **In** *El-Agraa, A. M., ed.*, 1983, pp. 125–46. [G: EEC; U.K.]

Cal, Vasco. The Industrial Sector. **In** *Sampedro, J. L. and Payno, J. A., eds.*, 1983, pp. 167–83. [G: Portugal; EEC]

Camps, Miriam. Little Europe, Wider Europe and Western Economic Cooperation: Comment. **In** *Tsoukalis, L., ed.*, 1983, pp. 190–95. [G: EEC; OECD]

Cherol, Rachelle L. and Nuñez del Arco, José. Andean Multinational Enterprises: A New Approach to Multinational Investment in the Andean Group. *J. Common Market Stud.*, June 1983, *21*(4), pp. 409–28. [G: Bolivia; Colombia; Ecuador; Peru; Venezuela]

Chia, Siow Yue. Singapore—EEC Economic Relations. **In** *Chen, P. S. J., ed.*, 1983, pp. 301–34. [G: Singapore; EEC]

Čičin-Šain, Ante. The Effects of Economic Integration in East and West Europe on Non-member Countries: The Case of Yugoslavia. **In** *Saunders, C. T., ed.*, 1983, pp. 103–18. [G: Yugoslavia; CMEA; EEC]

Clark, Cal and Bahry, Donna. Political Relationships as a Reversal Mechanism in the Soviet Bloc. **In** *Doran, C. F.; Modelski, G. and Clark, C., eds.*, 1983, pp. 205–21.

Colombatto, Enrico. CMEA, Money and Ruble Convertibility. *Appl. Econ.*, August 1983, *15*(4), pp. 479–506. [G: CMEA]

Constâncio, Maria-José. The Assignment of Public Functions in Economic Integration: Comment. **In** *Tsoukalis, L., ed.*, 1983, pp. 123–25. [G: EEC]

Cox, Thomas S. Northern Actors in a South–South Setting: External Aid and East African Integration. *J. Common Market Stud.*, March 1983, *21*(3), pp. 283–312. [G: E. Africa]

Cravinho, João. Characteristics and Motives for Entry. **In** *Sampedro, J. L. and Payno, J. A., eds.*, 1983, pp. 131–48. [G: Portugal; EEC]

Crossier, Luis Carlos. The Industrial Sector. **In** *Sampedro, J. L. and Payno, J. A., eds.*, 1983, pp. 224–41. [G: Spain; EEC]

Czepurko, Aleksander. New Developments in EEC and CMEA: Comment. **In** *Saunders, C. T., ed.*, 1983, pp. 95–97. [G: CMEA; EEC]

Dankert, Pieter. The European Community—Past, Present and Future. **In** *Tsoukalis, L., ed.*, 1983, pp. 3–18. [G: EEC]

Deese, David A. The Vulnerability of Modern Nations: Economic Diplomacy in East–West Relations. **In** *Nincic, M. and Wallensteen, P., eds.*, 1983, pp. 155–81. [G: OECD; CMEA]

Donges, Juergen B. Internationalization of Capital, International Division of Labour and the Role of the European Community: Comment. **In** *Tsoukalis, L., ed.*, 1983, pp. 140–43. [G: EEC]

Drechsler, László, et al. Production Cooperations among CMEA Countries: Aims and Realities. *Acta Oecon.*, 1983, *30*(2), pp. 193–202. [G: CMEA]

Efstratoglou-Todoulou, Sophia. The Impact of the Common Agricultural Policy. **In** *Sampedro, J. L. and Payno, J. A., eds.*, 1983, pp. 85–104. [G: Greece; EEC]

El-Agraa, Ali M. Britain within the European Community: General Introduction. **In** *El-Agraa, A. M., ed.*, 1983, pp. 1–18. [G: EEC]

El-Agraa, Ali M. EC Fiscal Policy. **In** *El-Agraa, A. M., ed.*, 1983, pp. 237–50. [G: EEC]

El-Agraa, Ali M. Has Membership of the EC Been a Disaster for Britain? **In** *El-Agraa, A. M., ed.*, 1983, pp. 319–33. [G: EEC; U.K.]

El-Agraa, Ali M. The True Cost of the CAP. **In** *El-Agraa, A. M., ed.*, 1983, pp. 147–66. [G: EEC; U.K.]

Elmandjra, Mahdi. Europe and Its "Privileged Partners" in Africa and the Middle East: Comment. **In** *Tsoukalis, L., ed.*, 1983, pp. 223–26. [G: EEC]

Emerson, Michael. The Assignment of Public Functions in Economic Integration: Comment. **In** *Tsoukalis, L., ed.*, 1983, pp. 121–23. [G: EEC]

Erma, Reino. Aspects of the Application and Development of the General Conditions for Trade in Goods (Finland–CMEA) from the Standpoint of Trade between Finland and the Soviet Union. **In** *Möttölä, K.; Bykov, O. N. and Korolev, I. S., eds.*, 1983, pp. 86–89. [G: Finland; CMEA; U.S.S.R.]

Eussner, Ansgar. Industrial Policy and Southward Enlargement of the European Community: The

Case of Shipbuilding and Repairs. *J. Common Market Stud.*, December 1983, *22*(2), pp. 147–72. **[G: EEC]**

Fallenbuchl, Zbigniew M. The Multinationals' Part in Integration: Comment. **In** *Saunders, C. T., ed.*, 1983, pp. 173–78. **[G: CMEA; EEC]**

Fortin, Carlos. Marketing, Technical and Legal Information for Copper Producing Countries: The Case of CIPEC. **In** *O'Brien, R. C., ed.*, 1983, pp. 88–101. **[G: Selected Countries]**

Franzmeyer, Fritz. Convergencies and Divergencies in Recent Economic Policies of EEC Member Countries: A New Understanding of Economic Integration? **In** *Saunders, C. T., ed.*, 1983, pp. 67–80. **[G: EEC]**

Fraser, Neil. Scotland in Europe. **In** *Ingham, K. P. D. and Love, J., eds.*, 1983, pp. 245–54. **[G: U.K.]**

Gasparetto, Marialuisa Manfredini. La turchia nell' economia mediterranea e della CEE. (Turkey as an Associate Member of the EEC within the Mediterranean Economy. With English summary.) *Rivista Int. Sci. Econ. Com.*, March 1983, *30*(3), pp. 268–92. **[G: Turkey]**

Georgakopoulos, Theodore A. and Paschos, Panagiotis G. The Costs and Benefits of the CAP: Greece's Experience in 1981. *Europ. Rev. Agr. Econ.*, 1983, *10*(4), pp. 377–88. **[G: Greece]**

Grassman, Sven. Reply to Beenstock–Warburton and Kar [Long Term Trends in Openness of National Economies]. *Oxford Econ. Pap.*, March 1983, *35*(1), pp. 141–42. **[G: U.K.; Brazil]**

Grinev, Vladimir Sergeevich. The Management of the USSR's Economic Relations with the CMEA Countries. *Soviet E. Europ. Foreign Trade*, Fall 1983, *19*(3), pp. 80–89. **[G: CMEA; U.S.S.R.]**

Grjebine, André. Internationalization of Capital, International Division of Labour and the Role of the European Community: Comment. **In** *Tsoukalis, L., ed.*, 1983, pp. 143–46. **[G: EEC]**

Guruswamy, L. D.; Papps, I. and Storey, D. J. The Development and Impact of an EEC Directive: The Control of Discharges of Mercury to the Aquatic Environment. *J. Common Market Stud.*, September 1983, *22*(1), pp. 71–100. **[G: EEC; U.K.]**

Gwilliam, Kenneth M. The Future of the Common Transport Policy. **In** *El-Agraa, A. M., ed.*, 1983, pp. 167–86. **[G: EEC]**

Hager, Wolfgang. Little Europe, Wider Europe and Western Economic Cooperation. **In** *Tsoukalis, L., ed.*, 1983, pp. 171–90. **[G: EEC; OECD]**

Hartley, Keith. EC Defence Policy. **In** *El-Agraa, A. M., ed.*, 1983, pp. 299–316. **[G: EEC; U.K.]**

Hennart, Jean-François. The Political Economy of Comparative Growth Rates: The Case of France. **In** *Mueller, D. C., ed.*, 1983, pp. 176–202. **[G: France]**

Henyš, Otta. More Intensive Coordination of Economic Development of the CMEA Member Countries. *Czech. Econ. Digest.*, June 1983, (4), pp. 53–68. **[G: Czechoslovakia; CMEA]**

Hirsch, Zeev. Egypt and Israel: Paths of Cooperation. **In** *Starr, J. R., ed.*, 1983, pp. 53–70. **[G: Egypt; Israel]**

Holt, Stephen C. Membership of the EC and Its Alternatives. **In** *El-Agraa, A. M., ed.*, 1983, pp. 41–55. **[G: EEC; U.K.]**

Inotai, András. Changes in the Commodity Pattern of Intraregional Trade in the European Economic Community. *Acta Oecon.*, 1983, *31* (3–4), pp. 261–86. **[G: EEC]**

Inotai, András. CMEA Integration and National Economic Policies: Adjustment to the Changed World Economic Environment. **In** *Saunders, C. T., ed.*, 1983, pp. 81–95. **[G: CMEA]**

Kádár, Béla. Changes in the World Economic Environment and Hungarian Industry. *Acta Oecon.*, 1983, *30*(1), pp. 111–27.

Kahler, Miles. Europe and Its "Privileged Partners" in Africa and the Middle East. **In** *Tsoukalis, L., ed.*, 1983, pp. 199–218. **[G: EEC]**

Kampffmeyer, Thomas. Entwicklungsperspektiven der türkischen Aussenwirtschaftsbeziehungen—Konsequenzen für die westlichen Partnerländer. (Development Prospects for Turkish Economic Relations—Implications for the Western Partner Countries. With English summary.) *Aussenwirtschaft*, March 1983, *38*(1), pp. 39–63. **[G: Turkey; EEC]**

Kar, Dev Kumar. Long-Term Trends in Openness of National Economies: Comment. *Oxford Econ. Pap.*, March 1983, *35*(1), pp. 136–40. **[G: Selected OECD; Brazil]**

Kirchner, Emil and Williams, Karen. The Legal, Political and Institutional Implications of the Isoglucose Judgments 1980. *J. Common Market Stud.*, December 1983, *22*(2), pp. 173–90. **[G: EEC]**

Kirschke, Dieter. Maximizing Welfare in Customs Unions: The Case of Agricultural Price Policy Within the EEC. *Amer. J. Agr. Econ.*, November 1983, *65*(4), pp. 791–95. **[G: EEC]**

Kohlmey, G. Structures économiques et division internationale du travail dans la région européenne du C.A.E.M. (With English summary.) *Écon. Soc.*, January 1983, *17*(1), pp. 89–113. **[G: E. Germany; CMEA]**

Konstantinov, Iu. The Transferable Ruble: The Currency of the Socialist Community. *Prob. Econ.*, October 1983, *26*(6), pp. 71–93. **[G: U.S.S.R.; CMEA]**

Korah, Valentine. Exclusive Licenses of Patent and Plant Breeders' Rights under EEC Law after *Maize Seed. Antitrust Bull.*, Fall 1983, *28*(3), pp. 699–755. **[G: EEC]**

Korolev, I. S. The Mechanism of the Multilateral Economic Cooperation between the CMEA and Finland. **In** *Möttölä, K.; Bykov, O. N. and Korolev, I. S., eds.*, 1983, pp. 79–85. **[G: CMEA; Finland]**

Kotouč, Václav. Coordination of National Economic Plans of the CMEA Countries. *Czech. Econ. Digest.*, March 1983, (2), pp. 43–60. **[G: CMEA]**

Köves, András. "Implicit Subsidies" and Some Issues of Economic Relations within the CMEA (Remarks on the Analyses Made by Michael Marrese and Jan Vaňous). *Acta Oecon.*, 1983, *31* (1–2), pp. 125–36. **[G: CMEA]**

Laffan, Brigid. Policy Implementation in the European Community: The European Social Fund as a Case Study. *J. Common Market Stud.*, June 1983, *21*(4), pp. 389–408. **[G: EEC]**

Lau, Teik Soon. Singapore and ASEAN. **In** *Chen,*

P. S. J., ed., 1983, pp. 285–300. **[G: Singapore; ASEAN]**

Lavigne, Marie. EEC and CMEA, General Comparisons: Comment. **In** *Saunders, C. T., ed.*, 1983, pp. 60–62. **[G: CMEA; EEC]**

Lewis, Vaughan. The Caribbean Experience of the 1970s: Some Lessons in Regional and International Relations. *Soc. Econ. Stud.*, December 1983, *32*(4), pp. 107–28. **[G: Caribbean]**

Llewellyn, David T. EC Monetary Arrangements: Britain's Strategy. **In** *El-Agraa, A. M., ed.*, 1983, pp. 251–70. **[G: EEC; U.K.]**

Loughran, Mary. The Abolition of Turnover Tax Borders in the EEC: A Step in Two Different Directions—Commission Proposals on Travellers' Tax-Free Allowances and Duty-Free Shops. *Bull. Int. Fiscal Doc.*, 1983, *37*(7), pp. 311–19. **[G: EEC]**

Lozada-Heller, Robert. French Socialist Policy and the European Community. **In** *Lenel, H. O.; Willgerodt, H. and Molsberger, J.*, 1983, pp. 141–55. **[G: EEC; France]**

Lukaszewicz, Aleksander. Specific Programmes of EEC and CMEA: Comment. **In** *Saunders, C. T., ed.*, 1983, pp. 212–14. **[G: CMEA]**

Maillet, Pierre and Rollet, Philippe. La spécialisation industrielle dans la communauté européenne: des faits observés aux politiques nécessaires. (Industrial Specialization within the European Economic Community: From Observed Facts to Necessary Policies. With English summary.) *Rivista Int. Sci. Econ. Com.*, March 1983, *30*(3), pp. 244–67. **[G: EEC]**

Maldonado, Guillermo; Gana, Eduardo and Di Filippo, Armando. Latin America: Crisis, Co-operation and Development. *Cepal Rev.*, August 1983, (20), pp. 75–100. **[G: Latin America]**

van Marion, M. F. The Multinational and Integration: The Human Side of Economics. **In** *Saunders, C. T., ed.*, 1983, pp. 151–60. **[G: EEC]**

Maximova, Margarita. Socialist and Capitalist Integration: A Comparative Analysis. **In** *Saunders, C. T., ed.*, 1983, pp. 27–39. **[G: CMEA; EEC]**

Mayes, David G. EC Trade Effects and Factor Mobility. **In** *El-Agraa, A. M., ed.*, 1983, pp. 88–121. **[G: EEC; U.K.]**

McMillan, Carl. Relations with Non-members: Comment. **In** *Saunders, C. T., ed.*, 1983, pp. 144–45. **[G: Austria; Finland; Yugoslavia; CMEA; EEC]**

Mitsos, Achilles G. J. The Industrial Sector. **In** *Sampedro, J. L. and Payno, J. A., eds.*, 1983, pp. 105–27. **[G: Greece; EEC]**

Møller, J. Ørstrøm. Danish EC Decision-Making: An Insider's View. *J. Common Market Stud.*, March 1983, *21*(3), pp. 245–60. **[G: EEC]**

Møller, J. Ørstrøm. Financing the European Economic Community. *Nat. Westminster Bank Quart. Rev.*, November 1983, pp. 29–38. **[G: EEC]**

Mosóczy, Róbert. Possibilities of and Trends in the Development of International Economic Cooperation in the 1980s. *Acta Oecon.*, 1983, *30*(3–4), pp. 313–24. **[G: Hungary; CMEA]**

Müller, Ernst. The Common Market for Agricultural Products. **In** *Saunders, C. T., ed.*, 1983, pp. 183–91. **[G: CMEA; EEC]**

Nême, Colette. La politique économique et monétaire de la communauté économique européenne. (With English summary.) *Revue Écon. Polit.*, September–October 1983, *93*(5), pp. 761–71. **[G: EEC]**

Nyers, Rezsö. Tendencies of Tradition and Reform in CMEA Cooperation. *Acta Oecon.*, 1983, *30*(1), pp. 31–51. **[G: CMEA]**

O'Cleireacain, Seamus C. M. Northern Ireland and Irish Integration: The Role of the European Communities. *J. Common Market Stud.*, December 1983, *22*(2), pp. 107–24. **[G: Ireland; EEC; U.K.]**

Ondrácek, Mojmír. The Attitudes of Economists in the Socialist Countries to the Question of a CMEA Collective Currency. *Soviet E. Europ. Foreign Trade*, Winter 1983–84, *19*(4), pp. 3–25. **[G: CMEA]**

Patterson, Gardner. The European Community as a Threat to the System. **In** *Cline W. R., ed.*, 1983, pp. 223–42.

Payno, Juan Antonio. Characteristics and Motives for Entry. **In** *Sampedro, J. L. and Payno, J. A., eds.*, 1983, pp. 187–209. **[G: Spain; EEC]**

Payno, Juan Antonio. The Second Enlargment from the Perspective of the New Members. **In** *Sampedro, J. L. and Payno, J. A., eds.*, 1983, pp. 1–37. **[G: Greece; Portugal; Spain; EEC]**

Pearce, David W. and Westoby, Richard. Energy and the EC. **In** *El-Agraa, A. M., ed.*, 1983, pp. 187–212. **[G: EEC]**

Pelkmans, Jacques. The Assignment of Public Functions in Economic Integration. **In** *Tsoukalis, L., ed.*, 1983, pp. 97–121. **[G: EEC]**

Pepelasis, Admantios. The Agricultural Sector: The Implications of the Accession. **In** *Sampedro, J. L. and Payno, J. A., eds.*, 1983, pp. 70–84. **[G: Greece; EEC]**

Pinder, John. History, Politics and Institutions of the EC. **In** *El-Agraa, A. M., ed.*, 1983, pp. 21–40. **[G: EEC]**

Plascasovitis, Ilias. A Critique on the 'Study of the Regional Impact of the CAP.' *Europ. Rev. Agr. Econ.*, 1983, *10*(2), pp. 141–50. **[G: EEC]**

Price, Victoria Curzon. The European Community—Friend or Foe of the Market Economy? **In** *Lenel, H. O.; Willgerodt, H. and Molsberger, J.*, 1983, pp. 85–95. **[G: EEC]**

Rambure, Dominique. L'utilizzazione privata dell'Ecu. (The Private Utilization of Ecu. With English summary.) *Mondo Aperto*, November–December 1983, *37*(6), pp. 355–68. **[G: EEC]**

Rodríguez, José J. Romero. The Agricultural Sector. **In** *Sampedro, J. L. and Payno, J. A., eds.*, 1983, pp. 210–23. **[G: Spain; EEC]**

Rosenthal, Gert. Central American Economic Integration. **In** *Ritter, A. R. M. and Pollock, D. H., eds.*, 1983, pp. 147–57. **[G: Central America]**

Rossen, Stein. Industrial Cooperation within Regional Groupings of Developing Countries. **In** *Parkinson, J. R., ed.*, 1983, pp. 207–28.

Rusmich, Ladislav. Value Aspects of the Development of Socialist Integration. *Acta Oecon.*, 1983, *31*(3–4), pp. 241–59. **[G: CMEA]**

Sarris, Alexander H. European Community Enlargement and World Trade in Fruits and Vegetables. *Amer. J. Agr. Econ.*, May 1983, *65*(2), pp. 235–46. **[G: EEC]**

Saunders, Christopher T. EEC and CMEA: Two Processes of International Integration. **In** *Saunders, C. T., ed.*, 1983, pp. 13–26. **[G: CMEA; EEC]**

Schiavone, Giuseppe. New Developments in EEC and CMEA: Comment. **In** *Saunders, C. T., ed.*, 1983, pp. 97–100. **[G: CMEA; EEC]**

Schiavone, Giuseppe. Relations with Non-members: Comment. **In** *Saunders, C. T., ed.*, 1983, pp. 146–47. **[G: Austria; Finland; Yugoslavia; CMEA; EEC]**

de la Serre, Françoise. Europe and Its "Privileged Partners" in Africa and the Middle East: Comment. **In** *Tsoukalis, L., ed.*, 1983, pp. 218–23. **[G: EEC]**

Shihata, Ibrahim. OPEC as a Donor Group. **In** *Gauhar, A., ed. (II)*, 1983, pp. 30–47. **[G: OPEC]**

Shiriaev, Iu. Commodity-monetary Instruments in Socialist Economic Integration. *Soviet E. Europ. Foreign Trade,* Winter 1983–84, *19*(4), pp. 26–44. **[G: CMEA]**

Shiriaev, P. Cooperation in Investments: A Factor in the Intensification of Production in CMEA Member Nations. *Prob. Econ.*, May 1983, *26*(1), pp. 74–89.

Siotis, Jean. Characteristics and Motives for Entry. **In** *Sampedro, J. L. and Payno, J. A., eds.*, 1983, pp. 57–69. **[G: Greece]**

Sobhan, Rehman. Enhancing Trade between OPEC and the Developing Countries of Asia. **In** *Gauhar, A., ed. (II)*, 1983, *1982*, pp. 104–20. **[G: OPEC; LDCs]**

Stadlmann, Heinz. Il futuro della CEE è irto di spine. (The Troubled Future of the European Economic Community. With English summary.) *Mondo Aperto,* June-August 1983, *37*(3–4), pp. 173–78. **[G: EEC]**

Stankovsky, Jan. The Cases of Finland and Austria. **In** *Saunders, C. T., ed.*, 1983, pp. 119–43. **[G: Austria; Finland; CMEA; EEC]**

Strauss, Robert. Economic Effects of Monetary Compensatory Amounts. *J. Common Market Stud.*, March 1983, *21*(3), pp. 261–81. **[G: EEC]**

Sydow, Peter. Economic Growth, CMEA Integration and Economic Cooperation with Capitalist Countries. **In** *Saunders, C. T., ed.*, 1983, pp. 41–57. **[G: E. Germany]**

Trigo de Abreu, Armando. The Agricultural Sector. **In** *Sampedro, J. L. and Payno, J. A., eds.*, 1983, pp. 149–66. **[G: Portugal; EEC]**

Tsoukalis, Loukas. Looking into the Crystal Ball. **In** *Tsoukalis, L., ed.*, 1983, pp. 229–44. **[G: EEC]**

Tumlir, Jan. Strong and Weak Elements in the Concept of European Integration. **In** *[Giersch, H.]*, 1983, pp. 29–56. **[G: EEC]**

Válek, Vratislav. Selected Questions Concerning the Effectiveness of Joint Investment Activity by CMEA Members. *Soviet E. Europ. Foreign Trade,* Winter 1983–84, *19*(4), pp. 45–61. **[G: CMEA]**

Válek, Vratislav. The Practical Use of Economic Advantages *(Joint Enterprises within the CMEA Community). Czech. Econ. Digest.*, August 1983, (5), pp. 68–76. **[G: CMEA]**

Végvári, Jenö. The Role of the CMEA in Hungarian Foreign Trade. *Acta Oecon.*, 1983, *30*(2), pp. 203–19. **[G: Hungary; CMEA]**

Vencovský, František. Improvement of the Monetary Mechanism in the Process of the International Socialist Economic Integration. *Czech. Econ. Digest.*, March 1983, (2), pp. 3–15. **[G: CMEA]**

Wabe, J. Stuart; Eversley, J. T. and Despicht, N. S. Community Regional Policy in Changing Economic Conditions. *Banca Naz. Lavoro Quart. Rev.*, June 1983, (145), pp. 185–209. **[G: EEC]**

Welch, Diana. From 'Euro Beer' to 'Newcastle Brown': A Review of European Community Action to Dismantle Divergent 'Food' Laws. *J. Common Market Stud.*, September 1983, *22*(1), pp. 47–70. **[G: EEC]**

Wilkinson, Christopher. European Industrial Policies in an International Context. *Ann. Sci. Écon. Appl.*, 1983, *39*(3), pp. 197–206. **[G: EEC]**

Willgerodt, Hans. Die Agrarpolitik der Europäischen Gemeinschaft in der Krise. **In** *Lenel, H. O.; Willgerodt, H. and Molsberger, J.*, 1983, pp. 97–139. **[G: EEC]**

Ziebura, Gilbert. Internationalization of Capital, International Division of Labour and the Role of the European Community. **In** *Tsoukalis, L., ed.*, 1983, pp. 127–40. **[G: EEC]**

Zurawicki, Leon. Multinationals in the European Integration Areas. **In** *Saunders, C. T., ed.*, 1983, pp. 161–72. **[G: CMEA; EEC]**

430 International Finance

4300 General

Alzamora, Carlos and Iglesias, Enrique V. Bases for a Latin American Response to the International Economic Crisis. *Cepal Rev.*, August 1983, (20), pp. 17–46. **[G: Latin America]**

Bergsten, C. Fred. The International Dimension of U.S. Economic Policy. **In** *Bergsten, C. F.*, 1983, *1983*, pp. 13–26. **[G: U.S.]**

Franzsen, D. G. Monetary Policy in South Africa, 1932–82. *S. Afr. J. Econ.*, March 1983, *51*(1), pp. 88–133. **[G: S. Africa]**

Leven, Ronald and Roberts, David L. Latin America's Prospects for Recovery. *Fed. Res. Bank New York Quart. Rev.*, Autumn 1983, *8*(3), pp. 6–13. **[G: Latin America]**

Lothian, James R. The International Data Base: An Introductory Overview. **In** *Darby, M. P. and Lothian, J. R., et al.*, 1983, pp. 46–57. **[G: OECD]**

Ruggie, John Gerard. International Regimes, Transactions, and Change: Embedded Liberalism in the Postwar Economic Order. **In** *Krasner, S. D., ed.*, 1983, *1982*, pp. 195–231. **[G: Global]**

431 Open Economy Macroeconomics; Exchange Rates

4310 General

Bergsten, C. Fred. The International Implications of Reaganomics. **In** *Bergsten, C. F.*, 1983, *1982*, pp. 47–55.

Bergstrand, Jeffrey H. Selected Views of Exchange Rate Determination after a Decade of "Floating." *New Eng. Econ. Rev.*, May/June 1983, pp. 14–29. **[G: U.S.; Japan; W. Germany; Switzerland; U.K.]**

Bird, Graham. Should Developing Countries Use Currency Depreciation as a Tool of Balance of Payments Adjustment? A Review of the Theory and Evidence, and a Guide for the Policy Maker. *J. Devel. Stud.*, July 1983, *19*(4), pp. 461–84. **[G: African LDCs]**

Bootle, Roger. A New Approach to the Balance of Payments [Comment]. *Lloyds Bank Rev.*, April 1983, (148), pp. 49–53.

Bryant, Ralph C. Floating Exchange Rates after Ten Years: Comments and Discussion. *Brookings Pap. Econ. Act.*, 1983, (1), pp. 71–79. **[G: U.S.; U.K.; Japan; W. Germany]**

Chang, Winston W.; Kemp, Murray C. and Long, Ngo Van. Money, Inflation, and Maximizing Behavior: The Case of Many Countries. *J. Macroecon.*, Summer 1983, *5*(3), pp. 251–63.

Christ, Carl F. An Evaluation of the Economic Policy Proposals of the Joint Economic Committee of the 92nd and 93rd Congresses. **In** *Brunner, K. and Meltzer, A. H., eds.*, 1983, *1977*, pp. 349–83. **[G: U.S.]**

Congdon, Tim. A New Approach to the Balance of Payments [Reply]. *Lloyds Bank Rev.*, April 1983, (148), pp. 54–61.

Cooper, Richard N. Use of the SDR to Supplement or Substitute for Other Means of Finance: Comment. **In** *von Furstenberg, G. M., ed.*, 1983, pp. 361–67.

Corden, Warner Max. Is There an Important Role for an International Reserve Asset Such as the SDR? **In** *von Furstenberg, G. M., ed.*, 1983, pp. 213–47.

Darby, Michael R. The United States as an Exogenous Source of World Inflation under the Bretton Woods System. **In** *Darby, M. P. and Lothian, J. R., et al.*, 1983, pp. 478–90. **[G: U.S.]**

Darby, Michael R. and Lothian, James R. Conclusions on the International Transmission of Inflation. **In** *Darby, M. P. and Lothian, J. R., et al.*, 1983, pp. 493–523. **[G: OECD]**

Dornbusch, Rudiger. Floating Exchange Rates after Ten Years: Comments and Discussion. *Brookings Pap. Econ. Act.*, 1983, (1), pp. 79–86. **[G: U.S.; U.K.; Japan; W. Germany]**

Dornbusch, Rudiger. Functioning of the Current International Financial System: Strengths, Weaknesses, and Criteria for Evaluation: Comment. **In** *von Furstenberg, G. M., ed.*, 1983, pp. 45–51. **[G: Japan; U.S.; W. Germany]**

Feldstein, Martin S. Domestic Saving and International Capital Movements in the Long Run and the Short Run. *Europ. Econ. Rev.*, March/April 1983, *21*(1/2), pp. 129–51. **[G: OECD]**

Frenkel, Jacob A. An Introduction to Exchange Rates and International Macroeconomics. **In** *Frenkel, J. A., ed.*, 1983, pp. 1–17.

Goulder, Lawrence H.; Shoven, John B. and Whalley, John. Domestic Tax Policy and the Foreign Sector: The Importance of Alternative Foreign Sector Formulations to Results from a General Equilibrium Tax Analysis Model. **In** *Feldstein, M., ed.*, 1983, pp. 333–64. **[G: U.S.]**

Grassman, Sven. Is There an Important Role for an International Reserve Asset Such as the SDR? Comment. **In** *von Furstenberg, G. M., ed.*, 1983, pp. 248–52.

Grubel, Herbert G. Is There an Important Role for an International Reserve Asset Such as the SDR? Comment. **In** *von Furstenberg, G. M., ed.*, 1983, pp. 252–59.

Han, Kexin. On Adjustment of Foreign Trade Deficits. *Chinese Econ. Stud.*, Summer 1983, *16*(4), pp. 78–96. **[G: China]**

Hartman, David G. Domestic Tax Policy and the Foreign Sector: The Importance of Alternative Foreign Sector Formulations to Results from a General Equilibrium Tax Analysis Model: Comment. **In** *Feldstein, M., ed.*, 1983, pp. 364–67. **[G: U.S.]**

Kenen, Peter B. Use of the SDR to Supplement or Substitute for Other Means of Finance. **In** *von Furstenberg, G. M., ed.*, 1983, pp. 327–60.

Kim, Inchul. Energy and Growth in an Open Economy: The Korean Case. *J. Energy Devel.*, Autumn 1983, *9*(1), pp. 69–92. **[G: Korea]**

Larsen, Flemming; Llewellyn, John and Potter, Stephen. International Economic Linkages. *OECD Econ. Stud.*, Autumn 1983, (1), pp. 43–91. **[G: OECD]**

Lewis, John P. The United States and the Third World, 1983: Can We Escape the Path of Mutual Injury? **In** *Lewis, J. P. and Kallab, V., eds.*, 1983, pp. 7–48. **[G: LDCs; OECD; U.S.]**

Meade, James. A New Approach to the Balance of Payments [Comment]. *Lloyds Bank Rev.*, April 1983, (148), pp. 42–47.

Medio, Alfredo. Worldwide Inflation and Its Impact on Less Developed Countries: Part II. *Econ. Forum,* Winter 1983-84, *14*(2), pp. 59–95. **[G: LDCs]**

Muldoon, Robert D. Rethinking the Ground Rules for an Open World Economy: An Opportunity for American Political Leadership. *Foreign Aff.*, Summer 1983, *61*(5), pp. 1078–98. **[G: New Zealand; U.S.]**

Nakagawa, Yukitsugu. What Should Be the Future Role of Japan in Today's International Scene? *Ann. Sci. Écon. Appl.*, 1983, *39*(3), pp. 187–96. **[G: Japan]**

Polak, Jacques J. Conference on Exchange Rate Regimes and Policy Interdependence: Concluding Remark. *Int. Monet. Fund Staff Pap.*, March 1983, *30*(1), pp. 208–11.

Roosa, Robert V. The Gap between Trade Theory and Capital Flows. *Challenge,* March/April 1983, *26*(1), pp. 54–57.

Rubli-Kaiser, Federico. Currency Substitution: A Case for a Counterintuitive Result. *Atlantic Econ. J.*, March 1983, *11*(1), pp. 116. **[G: Canada]**

Sarma, K. S. An Examination of the Impact of Changes in the Prices of Fuels and Primary Metals on Nordic Countries Using a World Econometric Model. **In** *Eliasson, G.; Sharefkin, M. and Ysander, B.-C., eds.*, 1983, pp. 245–68. **[G: Nordic Countries; OECD]**

Shafer, Jeffrey R. and Loopesko, Bonnie E. Floating Exchange Rates after Ten Years. *Brookings Pap. Econ. Act.*, 1983, (1), pp. 1–70. **[G: U.S.; U.K.; Japan; W. Germany]**

Sinn, Hans-Werner. International Capital Movements, Flexible Exchange Rates, and the IS-LM

Model: A Comparison between the Portfolio-Balance and the Flow Hypotheses. *Weltwirtsch. Arch.*, 1983, *119*(1), pp. 36–63.

Swoboda, Alexander K. Functioning of the Current International Financial System: Strengths, Weaknesses, and Criteria for Evaluation: Comment. **In** *von Furstenberg, G. M., ed.*, 1983, pp. 56–63.

Thirlwall, Anthony P. A New Approach to the Balance of Payments [Comment]. *Lloyds Bank Rev.*, April 1983, (148), pp. 47–49.

Tobin, James. 'Domestic Saving and International Capital Movements in the Long Run and the Short Run' by M. Feldstein: Comment. *Europ. Econ. Rev.*, March/April 1983, *21*(1/2), pp. 153–56. **[G: OECD]**

Westphal, Uwe. 'Domestic Saving and International Capital Movements in the Long Run and the Short Run' by M. Feldstein: Comment. *Europ. Econ. Rev.*, March/April 1983, *21*(1/2), pp. 157–59. **[G: OECD]**

Willett, Thomas D. Functioning of the Current International Financial System: Strengths, Weaknesses, and Criteria for Evaluation. **In** *von Furstenberg, G. M., ed.*, 1983, pp. 5–44.

Williamson, John. Use of the SDR to Supplement or Substitute for Other Means of Finance: Comment. **In** *von Furstenberg, G. M., ed.*, 1983, pp. 367–73.

4312 Open Economy Macroeconomic Theory: Balance of Payments and Adjustment Mechanisms

Adam, Marie-Christine. The Relation between the Current Account and the Exchange Rate: A Survey of the Recent Literature: Comment. **In** *De Grauwe, P. and Peeters, T., eds.*, 1983, pp. 100–102. **[G: OECD]**

Aghevli, Bijan B. Economic Structure and Policy for External Balance: Comment. *Int. Monet. Fund Staff Pap.*, March 1983, *30*(1), pp. 67–70. **[G: U.S.; W. Europe]**

Ahtiala, Pekka. A Note on the J-Curve. *Scand. J. Econ.*, 1983, *85*(4), pp. 541–42.

Aizenman, Joshua. A Theory of Current Account and Exchange Rate Determinations. *Europ. Econ. Rev.*, December 1983, *23*(3), pp. 261–80.

Aizenman, Joshua. On the Optimal Combination of Commercial and Exchange Rate Policies. *Southern Econ. J.*, July 1983, *50*(1), pp. 185–94.

Amano, Akihiro. A Structural Approach to Capital Flows and Exchange Rates. *Z. Nationalökon.*, Supplement 3, 1983, *43*, pp. 3–28. **[G: Selected OECD]**

Anderson, Richard K. and Takayama, Akira. Tariffs, Balance of Payments, and the Lerner Symmetry Relation in a Monetary Economy. *Z. ges. Staatswiss.*, March 1983, *139*(1), pp. 1–18.

Aoki, Masanao. A Dynamic Model of Trade Adjustment and the Marshall–Lerner Condition. *Weltwirtsch. Arch.*, 1983, *119*(2), pp. 246–58.

Argy, Victor. Choice of Intermediate Money Target in a Deregulated and an Integrated Economy with Flexible Exchange Rates. *Int. Monet. Fund Staff Pap.*, December 1983, *30*(4), pp. 727–54.

Argy, Victor and Salop, Joanne. Price and Output Effects of Monetary and Fiscal Expansion in a Two-Country World under Flexible Exchange Rates. *Oxford Econ. Pap.*, July 1983, *35*(2), pp. 228–46.

Arriazu, Ricardo H. International Balance of Payments Financing and Adjustment: Comment. **In** *von Furstenberg, G. M., ed.*, 1983, pp. 149–56.

Bacha, Edmar Lisboa. Crecimiento con Oferta Limitada de Divisas: Una Reevaluación del Modelo de dos Brechas. (Growth with Limited Supplies of Foreign Exchange: A Reappraisal of the Two-Gap Model. With English summary.) *Económica*, May–December 1983, *29*(2–3), pp. 241–66.

Basevi, Giorgio and Calzolari, Michele. Monetary Authorities' Reaction Functions in a Model of Exchange-Rate Determination for the European Monetary System. **In** *De Grauwe, P. and Peeters, T., eds.*, 1983, pp. 267–82. **[G: EEC]**

Batra, Raveendra N. and Das, Satya P. International Investment and the Theory of Devaluation. *J. Int. Econ.*, August 1983, *15*(1/2), pp. 161–75.

Baumgarten, Klaus. Adjustment to Variations in Prices of Imported Inputs: The Role of Economic Structure—A Comment. *Weltwirtsch. Arch.*, 1983, *119*(3), pp. 575–78.

Benavie, Arthur. Achieving External and Internal Targets with Exchange-Rate and Interest-Rate Intervention. *J. Int. Money Finance*, April 1983, *2*(1), pp. 75–85.

Bennett, John and Phelps, Michael. A Model of Employment Creation in an Open Developing Economy. *Oxford Econ. Pap.*, November 1983, *35*(3), pp. 373–98.

Bhagwati, Jagdish N. Devaluation in a Small Economy with Flexible and Rigid, Real and Nominal, Prices. **In** *Bhagwati, J. N., Vol. 2*, 1983, *1978*, pp. 517–35.

Bhandari, Jagdeep S. Aggregate Dynamics in an Open Economy. *Manchester Sch. Econ. Soc. Stud.*, June 1983, *51*(2), pp. 129–51.

Bhandari, Jagdeep S. An Alternative Theory of Exchange Rate Dynamics. *Quart. J. Econ.*, May 1983, *98*(2), pp. 337–48.

Bhandari, Jagdeep S. and Tracy, Ronald L. Exchange Rate and Price Level Determination in a Stochastic Equilibrium Model. *J. Macroecon.*, Spring 1983, *5*(2), pp. 167–84.

Bigman, David. Exchange Rate Determination: Some Old Myths and New Paradigms. **In** *Bigman, D. and Taya, T., eds.*, 1983, pp. 73–102.

Bilson, John F. O. and Hooke, A. W. Conference on Exchange Rate Regimes and Policy Interdependence: Overview. *Int. Monet. Fund Staff Pap.*, March 1983, *30*(1), pp. 185–207.

Black, Stanley W. The Use of Monetary Policy for Internal and External Balance in Ten Industrial Countries. **In** *Frenkel, J. A., ed.*, 1983, pp. 189–225. **[G: OECD]**

Blackhurst, Richard. The Relation between the Current Account and the Exchange Rate: A Survey of the Recent Literature. **In** *De Grauwe, P. and Peeters, T., eds.*, 1983, pp. 58–99. **[G: OECD]**

Blanchard, Olivier Jean. Debt and the Current Account Deficit in Brazil. **In** *Armella, P. A.; Dornbusch, R. and Obstfeld, M., eds.*, 1983, pp. 187–97. **[G: Brazil]**

Bockelmann, Horst. 'Exchange Rates, Inflation, and the Sterilization Problem: Germany, 1975–1981' by M. Obstfeld: Comment. *Europ. Econ. Rev.*, March/April 1983, *21* (1/2), pp. 191–95. **[G: W. Germany]**

Bogdanowicz-Bindert, Christine A. Portugal, Turkey and Peru: Three Successful Stabilization Programmes under the Auspices of the IMF. *World Devel.*, January 1983, *11* (1), pp. 65–70. **[G: Portugal; Turkey; Peru]**

Boughton, James M. Conditions for an Active Exchange Rate Policy with a Predetermined Monetary Target. *Int. Monet. Fund Staff Pap.*, September 1983, *30* (3), pp. 461–90.

Branson, William H. Economic Structure and Policy for External Balance. *Int. Monet. Fund Staff Pap.*, March 1983, *30* (1), pp. 39–66. **[G: U.S.; W. Europe]**

Branson, William H. Macroeconomic Determinants of Real Exchange Risk. **In** *Herring, R. J., ed.*, 1983, pp. 33–74. **[G: Japan; U.K.; U.S.; W. Germany]**

Branson, William H. and Buiter, Willem H. Monetary and Fiscal Policy with Flexible Exchange Rates. **In** *Bhandari, J. S. and Putnam, B. H., eds.*, 1983, pp. 251–85.

Brecher, Richard A. and Bhagwati, Jagdish N. Foreign Ownership and the Theory of Trade and Welfare. **In** *Bhagwati, J. N., Vol. 2*, 1983, *1981*, pp. 226–40.

Bruno, Michael. International Balance of Payments Financing and Adjustment: Comment. **In** *von Furstenberg, G. M., ed.*, 1983, pp. 157–66.

Bruno, Michael. Real versus Financial Openness under Alternative Exchange Rate Regimes. **In** *Armella, P. A.; Dornbusch, R. and Obstfeld, M., eds.*, 1983, pp. 131–49.

Buiter, Willem H. Flexible Exchange Rates and Interdependence: Comment. *Int. Monet. Fund Staff Pap.*, March 1983, *30* (1), pp. 35–38. **[G: U.S.]**

Buiter, Willem H. and Eaton, Jonathan. International Balance of Payments Financing and Adjustment. **In** *von Furstenberg, G. M., ed.*, 1983, pp. 129–48.

Buiter, Willem H. and Miller, Marcus H. Real Exchange Rate Overshooting and the Output Cost of Bringing Down Inflation: Some Further Results. **In** *Frenkel, J. A., ed.*, 1983, pp. 317–58.

Buiter, Willem H. and Purvis, Douglas D. Oil, Disinflation, and Export Competitiveness: A Model of the "Dutch Disease." **In** *Bhandari, J. S. and Putnam, B. H., eds.*, 1983, pp. 221–47.

Burton, David. Devaluation, Long-Term Contracts and Rational Expectations. *Europ. Econ. Rev.*, September 1983, *23* (1), pp. 19–32.

Calmfors, Lars. Output, Inflation and the Terms of Trade in a Small Open Economy. *Kyklos*, 1983, *36* (1), pp. 40–65.

Calvo, Guillermo A. Staggered Contracts and Exchange Rate Policy. **In** *Frenkel, J. A., ed.*, 1983, pp. 235–52.

Calvo, Guillermo A. Trying to Stabilize: Some Theoretical Reflections Based on the Case of Argentina. **In** *Armella, P. A.; Dornbusch, R. and Obstfeld, M., eds.*, 1983, pp. 199–216. **[G: Argentina]**

Canto, Victor A. and Miles, Marc A. Exchange Rates in a Global Monetary Model with Currency Substitution and Rational Expectations. **In** *Bhandari, J. S. and Putnam, B. H., eds.*, 1983, pp. 157–75.

Canzoneri, Matthew B. Rational Destabilizing Speculation and Exchange Intervention Policy. *J. Macroecon.*, Winter 1983, *5* (1), pp. 75–90.

Caselli, Paola. Exchange Rate and Current Account Dynamics with Imperfect Flexible Real Wages. *Stud. Econ.*, 1983, *38* (19), pp. 73–121.

Casprini, Flavio. Productivity Changes and Employment in Small Open Economies. *Econ. Notes*, 1983, (1), pp. 42–58.

Cassese, Anthony and Lothian, James R. The Timing of Monetary and Price Changes and the International Transmission of Inflation. **In** *Darby, M. P. and Lothian, J. R., et al.*, 1983, pp. 58–82. **[G: OECD]**

Chiang, Thomas C. Short-Term Interest Rates, Price Expectations, and Exchange Rate Movements. *Rev. Bus. Econ. Res.*, Fall 1983, *19* (1), pp. 26–37. **[G: Canada; W. Europe; U.S.]**

Chiang, Thomas C. The Short-Term Interest Rate Differential and the Exchange Rate. *Atlantic Econ. J.*, July 1983, *11* (2), pp. 99.

Chiesa, Gabriella. Disturbi di offerta, natura della disoccupazione ed interventi di riassorbimento in un'economia aperta. (Supply Shocks, the Nature of Unemployment and Policies for Internal and External Balance in an Open Economy. With English summary.) *Giorn. Econ.*, September–October 1983, *42* (9–10), pp. 617–41.

Chrystal, K. Alec; Wilson, Nigel D. and Quinn, Philip. Demand for International Money, 1962–1977. *Europ. Econ. Rev.*, May 1983, *21* (3), pp. 287–98.

Chu, Ke-young; Hwa, E. C. and Krishnamurty, K. Export Instability and Adjustments of Imports, Capital Inflows, and External Reserves: A Short-run Dynamic Model. **In** *Bigman, D. and Taya, T., eds.*, 1983, pp. 195–214. **[G: Sri Lanka; Finland]**

Claassen, Emil-Maria. Aspects of the Optimal Management of Exchange Rates. **In** *Claassen, E. and Salin, P., eds.*, 1983, pp. 226–30.

Claassen, Emil-Maria. The Nominal and Real Exchange Rate in a Quantity-Theoretical Two-Country Model. **In** *Claassen, E. and Salin, P., eds.*, 1983, pp. 57–68.

Clifton, Eric V. The Effects of Increased Interest-Rate Volatility on LDCs. *J. Int. Money Finance*, April 1983, *2* (1), pp. 67–74.

Cline, William R. Economic Stabilization in Developing Countries: Theory and Stylized Facts. **In** *Williamson, J., ed.*, 1983, *1981*, pp. 175–208.

Collyns, Charles. On the Monetary Analysis of an Open Economy. *Int. Monet. Fund Staff Pap.*, June 1983, *30* (2), pp. 421–44.

Conti, Giuliano. Changes in Foreign Interest Rates and Domestic Stability: A Static and Dynamic Analysis. *Rivista Polit. Econ.*, Supplement Dec. 1983, *73* (12), pp. 23–67.

Cooper, Richard N. International Aspects of U.S. Monetary and Fiscal Policy: Discussion. **In** *Federal Reserve Bank of Boston*, 1983, pp. 134–37. **[G: U.S.; OECD]**

Corbo, Vittorio. Un modelo de corto plazo para una economía pequeña y abierta. (With English summary.) *Cuadernos Econ.*, August 1983, *20*(60), pp. 177–89.

Corden, Warner Max and Turnovsky, Stephen J. Negative International Transmission of Economic Expansion. *Europ. Econ. Rev.*, January 1983, *20*(1–3), pp. 289–310.

Cumby, Robert E. and Obstfeld, Maurice. Capital Mobility and the Scope for Sterilization: Mexico in the 1970s. **In** *Armella, P. A.; Dornbusch, R. and Obstfeld, M., eds.*, 1983, pp. 245–69. **[G: Mexico]**

Darby, Michael R. International Transmission of Monetary and Fiscal Shocks under Pegged and Floating Exchange Rates: Simulation Experiments. **In** *Darby, M. P. and Lothian, J. R., et al.*, 1983, pp. 162–231. **[G: OECD]**

Darby, Michael R. International Transmission under Pegged and Floating Exchange Rates: An Empirical Comparison. **In** *Bhandari, J. S. and Putnam, B. H., eds.*, 1983, pp. 427–71. **[G: OECD]**

Darby, Michael R. Sterilization and Monetary Control: Concepts, Issues, and a Reduced-Form Test. **In** *Darby, M. P. and Lothian, J. R., et al.*, 1983, pp. 291–313. **[G: OECD]**

Darby, Michael R. The Importance of Oil Price Changes in the 1970s World Inflation. **In** *Darby, M. P. and Lothian, J. R., et al.*, 1983, pp. 232–72. **[G: OECD]**

Darby, Michael R. and Stockman, Alan C. The Mark III International Transmission Model: Estimates. **In** *Darby, M. P. and Lothian, J. R., et al.*, 1983, pp. 113–61. **[G: OECD]**

Darby, Michael R. and Stockman, Alan C. The Mark III International Transmission Model: Specification. **In** *Darby, M. P. and Lothian, J. R., et al.*, 1983, pp. 85–112. **[G: OECD]**

Desai, Padma and Bhagwati, Jagdish N. Three Alternative Concepts of Foreign Exchange Difficulties in Centrally Planned Economies. **In** *Bhagwati, J. N., Vol. 2*, 1983, *1979*, pp. 536–46.

Díaz-Alejandro, Carlos F. IMF Conditionality: Country Studies: Comments, Chapters 11–14. **In** *Williamson, J., ed.*, 1983, pp. 341–46.

Djajić, Slobodan. Intermediate Inputs and International Trade: An Analysis of the Real and Monetary Aspects of a Change in the Price of Oil. *J. Int. Money Finance*, August 1983, *2*(2), pp. 179–95.

Djajić, Slobodan. Monetary and Commercial Policy in a Two-Country Flexible Exchange Rate Model with Perfect Capital Mobility. *J. Monet. Econ.*, September 1983, *12*(3), pp. 399–416.

Dooley, Michael P. and Isard, Peter. The Portfolio-Balance Model of Exchange Rates and Some Structural Estimates of the Risk Premium. *Int. Monet. Fund Staff Pap.*, December 1983, *30*(4), pp. 683–702. **[G: U.S.; W. Germany]**

Dornbusch, Rudiger. Exchange Rate Economics: Where Do We Stand? **In** *Bhandari, J. S. and Putnam, B. H., eds.*, 1983, pp. 45–83.

Dornbusch, Rudiger. Flexible Exchange Rates and Interdependence. *Int. Monet. Fund Staff Pap.*, March 1983, *30*(1), pp. 3–30. **[G: U.S.]**

Dornbusch, Rudiger. Issues Related to Conditionality: Comments, Chapters 7–10. **In** *Williamson, J., ed.*, 1983, pp. 223–30.

Dornbusch, Rudiger. Real Interest Rates, Home Goods, and Optimal External Borrowing. *J. Polit. Econ.*, February 1983, *91*(1), pp. 141–53.

Drabek, Zdenek. Changes in Relative World Prices and Their Transmission into Economies Protected by Foreign Trade Monopoly. *Econ. Int.*, February 1983, *36*(1), pp. 20–34. **[G: CMEA]**

Drabicki, John Z. and Takayama, Akira. The Theory of Comparative Advantage in a Monetary World. *Southern Econ. J.*, July 1983, *50*(1), pp. 1–17.

Dramais, André. A Portfolio Approach to the Determination of Exchange Rates within a Multicountry Model: Comment. **In** *De Grauwe, P. and Peeters, T., eds.*, 1983, pp. 208–09.

Driffill, E. John. Shock Treatment for Inflation: A Note on Optimal Policy in a Buiter/Miller Model. *Europ. Econ. Rev.*, December 1983, *23*(3), pp. 291–97.

Eaton, Jonathan and Turnovsky, Stephen J. Covered Interest Parity, Uncovered Interest Parity and Exchange Rate Dynamics. *Econ. J.*, September 1983, *93*(371), pp. 555–75.

Eaton, Jonathan and Turnovsky, Stephen J. Exchange Risk, Political Risk, and Macroeconomic Equilibrium. *Amer. Econ. Rev.*, March 1983, *73*(1), pp. 183–89.

Eckstein, Otto. International Aspects of U.S. Monetary and Fiscal Policy: Discussion. **In** *Federal Reserve Bank of Boston*, 1983, pp. 138–40. **[G: U.S.; OECD]**

Enders, Klaus and Herberg, Horst. The Dutch Disease: Causes, Consequences, Cures and Calmatives. *Weltwirtsch. Arch.*, 1983, *119*(3), pp. 473–97.

Enders, Walter and Lapan, Harvey E. On the Relationship between the Exchange Regime and the Portfolio Rules of Optimizing Agents. *J. Int. Econ.*, November 1983, *15*(3/4), pp. 199–224.

Feltenstein, Andrew. A Computational General Equilibrium Approach to the Shadow Pricing of Trade Restrictions and the Adjustment of the Exchange Rate, with an Application to Argentina. *J. Policy Modeling*, November 1983, *5*(3), pp. 333–61. **[G: Argentina]**

Ffrench-Davis, Ricardo. Trying to Stabilize: Some Theoretical Reflections Based on the Case of Argentina: Comment. **In** *Armella, P. A.; Dornbusch, R. and Obstfeld, M., eds.*, 1983, pp. 217–20. **[G: Argentina]**

Fischer, Stanley. Optimal Stabilization and the Proper Exercise of the Monetary-Policy Instruments under Flexible Exchange Rates: Comment. **In** *Claassen, E. and Salin, P., eds.*, 1983, pp. 256–59.

Fischer, Stanley. Seigniorage and Fixed Exchange Rates: An Optimal Inflation Tax Analysis. **In** *Armella, P. A.; Dornbusch, R. and Obstfeld, M., eds.*, 1983, pp. 59–69.

Fischer, Stanley. The SDR and the IMF: Toward a World Central Bank? **In** *von Furstenberg, G. M., ed.*, 1983, pp. 179–99.

Flood, Robert P. Real Exchange Rate Overshooting and the Output Cost of Bringing Down Inflation: Some Further Results: Comment. **In** *Frenkel,*

J. A., ed., 1983, pp. 359–65.

Flood, Robert P. and Garber, Peter M. A Model of Stochastic Process Switching. *Econometrica*, May, 1983, *51* (3), pp. 537–51.

Frankel, Jeffrey A. Estimation of Portfolio-Balanced Functions That Are Mean-Variance Optimizing: The Mark and the Dollar. *Europ. Econ. Rev.*, December 1983, *23* (3), pp. 315–27. **[G: U.S.; W. Germany]**

Frankel, Jeffrey A. Monetary and Portfolio-Balance Models of Exchange Rate Determination. **In** *Bhandari, J. S. and Putnam, B. H., eds.*, 1983, pp. 84–115. **[G: U.S.; W. Germany]**

Frenkel, Jacob A. 'Exchange Rates, Inflation, and the Sterilization Problem: Germany, 1975–1982' by M. Obstfeld: Comment. *Europ. Econ. Rev.*, March/April 1983, *21* (1/2), pp. 197–202. **[G: W. Germany]**

Frenkel, Jacob A. Capital Mobility and the Scope for Sterilization: Mexico in the 1970s: Comment. **In** *Armella, P. A.; Dornbusch, R. and Obstfeld, M., eds.*, 1983, pp. 269–76. **[G: Mexico]**

Frenkel, Jacob A. International Liquidity and Monetary Control. **In** *Kaushik, S. K., ed.*, 1983, pp. 31–72. **[G: LDCs; MDCs]**

Frenkel, Jacob A. Monetary Policy: Domestic Targets and International Constraints. *Amer. Econ. Rev.*, May 1983, *73* (2), pp. 48–53.

Frenkel, Jacob A. and Aizenman, Joshua. Aspects of the Optimal Management of Exchange Rates. **In** *Claassen, E. and Salin, P., eds.*, 1983, pp. 201–25.

Galli, Giampaolo. Monetary and Credit Targets in an Open Economy: Discussion. **In** *Hodgman, D. R., ed.*, 1983, pp. 307–12.

Garber, Peter M. Real versus Financial Openness under Alternative Exchange Rate Regimes: Comment. **In** *Armella, P. A.; Dornbusch, R. and Obstfeld, M., eds.*, 1983, pp. 150–52.

Gärtner, Manfred. Asset Market Models of the Small Open Economy with Endogenous Money Supply Expectations. *Z. ges. Staatswiss.*, December 1983, *139* (4), pp. 643–59.

Genberg, Hans. Overshooting and Asymmetries in the Transmission of Foreign Price Shocks to the Swedish Economy. **In** *Eliasson, G.; Sharefkin, M. and Ysander, B.-C., eds.*, 1983, pp. 199–222. **[G: Sweden]**

Giovannini, Alberto. An Alternative Test of the Rational Expectations-Perfect Substitutability Hypothesis: Deutsche Mark and Pound Sterling. *Empirical Econ.*, 1983, *8* (1), pp. 59–62. **[G: U.S.; U.K.; W. Germany]**

Glassman, Debra. Rational Expectations and the Foreign Exchange Market: Comment. **In** *Frenkel, J. A., ed.*, 1983, pp. 177–80. **[G: U.K.; U.S.; W. Germany]**

Gowland, D. H. Issues in Macroeconomics. **In** *Gowland, D. H., ed.*, 1983, pp. 57–87.

Grassman, Sven and Olsson, Hans. The Productivity Link between Exports and Domestic Demand: Sweden. **In** *de Cecco, M., ed.*, 1983, pp. 34–48. **[G: Sweden]**

Green, Reginald Herbold. Political–Economic Adjustment and IMF Conditionality: Tanzania 1974–81. **In** *Williamson, J., ed.*, 1983, pp. 347–80.

Greenwood, Jeremy. Expectations, the Exchange Rate, and the Current Account. *J. Monet. Econ.*, November 1983, *12* (4), pp. 543–69.

Gunning, Jan Willem. Rationing in an Open Economy: Fix-Price Equilibrium and Two-Gap Models. *Europ. Econ. Rev.*, September 1983, *23* (1), pp. 71–98.

Gylfason, Thorvaldur and Helliwell, John F. A Synthesis of Keynesian, Monetary, and Portfolio Approaches to Flexible Exchange Rates. *Econ. J.*, December 1983, *93* (372), pp. 820–31.

Gylfason, Thorvaldur and Schmid, Michael. Does Devaluation Cause Stagflation? *Can. J. Econ.*, November 1983, *16* (4), pp. 641–54. **[G: Selected Countries]**

Hacche, Graham and Townend, John C. Some Problems in Exchange Rate Modelling: The Case of Sterling. *Z. Nationalökon.*, Supplement 3, 1983, *43*, pp. 127–62. **[G: U.S.; U.K.]**

Hanson, James A. Contractionary Devaluation, Substitution in Production and Consumption, and the Role of the Labor Market. *J. Int. Econ.*, February 1983, *14* (1/2), pp. 179–89.

Hartley, Peter R. Rational Expectations and the Foreign Exchange Market. **In** *Frenkel, J. A., ed.*, 1983, pp. 153–77. **[G: U.K.; U.S.; W. Germany]**

Helliwell, John F. and Boothe, Paul M. Macroeconomic Implications of Alternative Exchange-Rate Models. **In** *De Grauwe, P. and Peeters, T., eds.*, 1983, pp. 21–53. **[G: Canada]**

Henderson, Dale W. Monetary, Fiscal and Exchange Rate Policy in a Two-Country, Short-Run, Macro Economic Model. *Écon. Soc.*, July-August 1983, *17* (7–8), pp. 1149–83.

Henderson, Dale W. and Waldo, Douglas G. Reserve Requirements on Eurocurrency Deposits: Implications for the Stabilization of Real Outputs. **In** *Bhandari, J. S. and Putnam, B. H., eds.*, 1983, pp. 350–83.

Hernández-Catá, Ernesto. Flexible Exchange Rates and Interdependence: Comment. *Int. Monet. Fund Staff Pap.*, March 1983, *30* (1), pp. 31–35. **[G: U.S.]**

Heyne, Paul. Do Trade Deficits Matter? *Cato J.*, Winter 1983/84, *3* (3), pp. 705–16. **[G: U.S.]**

Hickman, Bert G. and Filatov, Victor. A Decomposition of International Income Multipliers. **In** *[Klein, L. R.]*, 1983, pp. 340–67. **[G: OECD]**

Hoffman, Dennis L. and Schlagenhauf, Don E. Rational Expectations and Monetary Models of Exchange Rate Determination: An Empirical Examination. *J. Monet. Econ.*, March 1983, *11* (2), pp. 247–60. **[G: W. Germany; U.S.; U.K.; France]**

Hool, Bryce and Richardson, J. David. International Trade, Indebtedness, and Welfare Repercussions among Supply-constrained Economies under Floating Exchange Rates. **In** *Bhandari, J. S. and Putnam, B. H., eds.*, 1983, pp. 402–24. **[G: U.S.]**

Hooper, Peter; Haas, Richard D. and Symansky, Steven A. Revision of Exchange-Rate Determination in the MCM. **In** *De Grauwe, P. and Peeters, T., eds.*, 1983, pp. 210–35. **[G: U.S.]**

Hooper, Peter, et al. Alternative Approaches to General Equilibrium Modeling of Exchange Rates and Capital Flows: The MCM Experience. *Z. Nationalökon.*, Supplement 3, 1983, *43*, pp. 29–60. **[G: N. America; Germany; Japan; U.K.; OPEC]**

Horne, Jocelyn. The Asset Market Model of the Balance of Payments and the Exchange Rate: A Survey of Empirical Evidence. *J. Int. Money Finance,* August 1983, *2*(2), pp. 89–109. **[G: Italy; Australia; Netherlands; W. Germany; U.K.]**

Hrnčíř, Miroslav. External Balance in Planned Economy. *Czech. Econ. Pap.,* 1983, (21), pp. 71–87. **[G: Czechoslovakia]**

Jones, Michael. International Liquidity: A Welfare Analysis. *Quart. J. Econ.,* February 1983, *98*(1), pp. 1–23.

Jones, Ronald W. and Purvis, Douglas D. International Differences in Response to Common External Shocks: The Role of Purchasing Power Parity. **In** *Claassen, E. and Salin, P., eds.,* 1983, pp. 33–55.

Kaldor, Nicholas. Devaluation and Adjustment in Developing Countries. *Finance Develop.,* June 1983, *20*(2), pp. 35–37.

Karacaoglu, Girol. "Partial" Approaches to Balance-of-Payments Adjustment Yield Consistent Predictions under Identical Assumptions. *Weltwirtsch. Arch.,* 1983, *119*(2), pp. 226–45.

Katseli, Louka T. and Marion, Nancy P. Adjustment to Variations in Prices of Imported Inputs: The Role of Economic Structure—A Reply. *Weltwirtsch. Arch.,* 1983, *119*(3), pp. 579–80.

Kawai, Masahiro. Exchange Rate Volatility and Balance-of-Payments Instability in a Rational Expectations Model of Forward Exchange. **In** *Bigman, D. and Taya, T., eds.,* 1983, pp. 167–94.

Kennally, Gerald F. Some consequences of Opening a Neo-Keynesian Model. *Econ. J.,* June 1983, *93*(370), pp. 390–410.

Keyzer, Michiel A. Policy Adjustment Rules in an Open Exchange Model with Money and Endogenous Balance of Trade Deficit. **In** *Kelley, A. C.; Sanderson, W. C. and Williamson, J. G., eds.,* 1983, pp. 57–70.

Kim, Inchul. A Partial Adjustment Theory of the Balance of Payments. *J. Int. Money Finance,* April 1983, *2*(1), pp. 17–26.

Kimbrough, Kent P. Asset Preferences, Trade in Assets, and Exchange Rate Behavior during the Adjustment Process. *Atlantic Econ. J.,* July 1983, *11*(2), pp. 52–62.

Kimbrough, Kent P. Exchange-Rate Policy and Monetary Information. *J. Int. Money Finance,* December 1983, *2*(3), pp. 333–46.

Kimbrough, Kent P. Price, Output, and Exchange Rate Movements in the Open Economy. *J. Monet. Econ.,* January 1983, *11*(1), pp. 25–44.

Kimbrough, Kent P. Real Adjustment and Exchange Rate Dynamics: Comment. **In** *Frenkel, J. A., ed.,* 1983, pp. 308–12.

Kincaid, G. Russell. What Are Credit Ceilings? *Finance Develop.,* March 1983, *20*(1), pp. 28–29.

Knight, Malcolm D. and Mathieson, Donald J. Economic Change and Policy Response in Canada under Fixed and Flexible Exchange Rates. **In** *Bhandari, J. S. and Putnam, B. H., eds.,* 1983, pp. 500–529. **[G: Canada]**

Komiya, Ryutaro. Economic Structure and Policy for External Balance: Comment. *Int. Monet. Fund Staff Pap.,* March 1983, *30*(1), pp. 70–74. **[G: U.S.; W. Europe]**

Kouri, Pentti J. K. Balance of Payments and the Foreign Exchange Market: A Dynamic Partial Equilibrium Model. **In** *Bhandari, J. S. and Putnam, B. H., eds.,* 1983, pp. 116–56.

Kouri, Pentti J. K. Macroeconomic Adjustment to Interest Rate Disturbances: Real and Monetary Aspects. **In** *Claassen, E. and Salin, P., eds.,* 1983, pp. 73–97.

Kouri, Pentti J. K. Oil Shocks and Exchange Rate Dynamics: Comment. **In** *Frenkel, J. A., ed.,* 1983, pp. 272–80.

Krelle, Wilhelm E. and Sarrazin, Hermann T. Capital Flows and the Exchange Rate in the Bonn Model 11. *Z. Nationalökon.,* Supplement 3, 1983, *43,* pp. 163–201. **[G: Germany]**

Krugman, Paul R. International Aspects of U.S. Monetary and Fiscal Policy. **In** *Federal Reserve Bank of Boston,* 1983, pp. 112–33. **[G: U.S.; OECD]**

Krugman, Paul R. Oil Shocks and Exchange Rate Dynamics. **In** *Frenkel, J. A., ed.,* 1983, pp. 259–71.

Laidler, David, et al. A Small Macroeconomic Model of an Open Economy: The Case of Canada. **In** *Claassen, E. and Salin, P., eds.,* 1983, pp. 149–71. **[G: Canada]**

Langohr, Herwig. A Small Macroeconomic Model of an Open Economy: The Case of Canada: Comment. **In** *Claassen, E. and Salin, P., eds.,* 1983, pp. 172–77. **[G: Canada]**

Lapan, Harvey E. and Enders, Walter. Rational Expectations, Endogenous Currency Substitution, and Exchange Rate Determination. *Quart. J. Econ.,* August 1983, *98*(3), pp. 427–39.

Laskar, Daniel M. Short-run Independence of Monetary Policy under a Pegged Exchange-Rates System: An Econometric Approach. **In** *Darby, M. P. and Lothian, J. R., et al.,* 1983, pp. 314–48. **[G: OECD]**

Laussel, Didier and Montet, Christian. Fixed-Price Equilibria in a Two-Country Model of Trade: Existence and Comparative Statics. *Europ. Econ. Rev.,* August 1983, *22*(3), pp. 305–29.

Lee, Dan. Effects of Open Market Operations and Foreign Exchange Market Operations under Flexible Exchange Rates. **In** *Darby, M. P. and Lothian, J. R., et al.,* 1983, pp. 349–79.

Leiderman, Leonardo. The Use of Monetary Policy for Internal and External Balance in Ten Industrial Countries: Comment. **In** *Frenkel, J. A., ed.,* 1983, pp. 226–29. **[G: OECD]**

Lerner, Abba P. Foreign Trade III (In a Capitalist Economy.) **In** *Lerner, A. P.,* 1983, *1970,* pp. 111–23.

Levin, Jay H. A Model of Stabilization Policy in a Jointly Floating Currency Area. **In** *Bhandari, J. S. and Putnam, B. H., eds.,* 1983, pp. 329–49.

Levin, Jay H. The J-Curve, Rational Expectations, and the Stability of the Flexible Exchange Rate System. *J. Int. Econ.,* November 1983, *15*(3/4), pp. 239–51.

Levy, Victor. Demand for International Reserves and Exchange-Rate Intervention Policy in an Adjustable-Peg Economy. *J. Monet. Econ.,* January 1983, *11*(1), pp. 89–101. **[G: Turkey]**

Lipton, David and Sachs, Jeffrey D. Accumulation and Growth in a Two-Country Model: A Simulation Approach. *J. Int. Econ.,* August 1983, *15*(1/2), pp. 135–59.

de Macedo, Jorge Braga. Optimal Currency Diversification for a Class of Risk-Averse International Investors. *J. Econ. Dynam. Control,* May 1983, *5*(2/3), pp. 173–85.

Machlup, Fritz. Autonomous and Induced Items in the Balance of Payments. **In** *[Giersch, H.],* 1983, pp. 139–70.

Makepeace, G. H. and Pikoulakis, E. A Saving-Investment Approach to the Current Account of the Balance of Payments: Some Preliminary Empirical Estimates for the U.K. (1960–1980). *Greek Econ. Rev.,* December 1983, *5*(3), pp. 223–47. **[G: U.K.]**

Malamud, Bernard. John H. Williams on the German Inflation: The International Amplification of Monetary Disturbances. **In** *Schmukler, N. and Marcus, E., eds.,* 1983, pp. 417–34. **[G: Germany]**

Malliaris, A. G. and Pournakis, M. An Eclectic Approach to the Problem of the International Transmission of Inflation. *Econ. Int.,* May–August–November 1983, *36*(2–3–4), pp. 180–91. **[G: Global]**

Mansur, Ahsan H. Determining the Appropriate Levels of Exchange Rates for Developing Economies: Some Methods and Issues. *Int. Monet. Fund Staff Pap.,* December 1983, *30*(4), pp. 784–818. **[G: LDCs]**

Marino, Loretta. Integrazione dei mercati dei capitali, politica monetaria e cambi flessibili. (Domestic Monetary Policy and Financial Integration under Flexible Rates. With English summary.) *Giorn. Econ.,* March-April 1983, *42*(3–4), pp. 193–214.

Martin, John P. Nominal and Real Exchange Rates: Issues and Some Evidence: Comment. **In** *Claassen, E. and Salin, P., eds.,* 1983, pp. 28–31. **[G: Selected OECD]**

Marwah, Kanta and Klein, Lawrence R. A Model of Foreign Exchange Markets: Endogenising Capital Flows and Exchange Rates. *Z. Nationalökon.,* Supplement 3, 1983, *43,* pp. 61–95. **[G: Canada; Germany; France; U.K.; U.S.]**

Mathieson, Donald J. Estimating Models of Financial Market Behavior during Periods of Extensive Structural Reform: The Experience of Chile. *Int. Monet. Fund Staff Pap.,* June 1983, *30*(2), pp. 350–93. **[G: Chile]**

Mawuli, Agogo. Balance of Payments Problem as a Consequence of Rapid Capital Accumulation in Developing Countries. *Indian Econ. J.,* January–March 1983, *30*(3), pp. 39–64. **[G: LDCs]**

McDermott, John. Exchange-Rate Indexation in a Monetary Model: Theory and Evidence. *J. Int. Money Finance,* August 1983, *2*(2), pp. 197–213. **[G: Brazil]**

McKinnon, Ronald I. and Tan, Kong-Yam. Currency Substitution and Instability in the World Dollar Standard: Reply. *Amer. Econ. Rev.,* June 1983, *73*(3), pp. 474–76. **[G: U.S.]**

Meese, Richard A. and Rogoff, Kenneth S. The Out-of-Sample Failure of Empirical Exchange Rate Models: Sampling Error or Misspecification? **In** *Frenkel, J. A., ed.,* 1983, pp. 67–105. **[G: Japan; U.K.; U.S.; W. Germany]**

Melitz, Jacques. How Much Simplification Is Wise in Modelling Exchange Rates? **In** *De Grauwe, P. and Peeters, T., eds.,* 1983, pp. 1–18.

Melitz, Jacques. Optimal Stabilization and the Proper Exercise of the Monetary-Policy Instruments under Flexible Exchange Rates. **In** *Claassen, E. and Salin, P., eds.,* 1983, pp. 231–55.

Melvin, Michael. An Alternative Approach to International Capital Flows. **In** *Darby, M. P. and Lothian, J. R., et al.,* 1983, pp. 380–417. **[G: Canada; Italy; U.K.; U.S.; W. Germany]**

de Meza, David. The Transfer Problem in a Many-Country World: Is It Better to Give than Receive? *Manchester Sch. Econ. Soc. Stud.,* September 1983, *51*(3), pp. 266–75.

Minford, Patrick; Ioannidis, Christos and Marwaha, Satwant. Rational Expectations in a Multilateral Macro-Model. **In** *De Grauwe, P. and Peeters, T., eds.,* 1983, pp. 239–66.

Monke, Eric. Traded and Non-Traded Goods: An Empirical Test with Nigerian Data. *J. Devel. Econ.,* December 1983, *13*(3), pp. 349–60. **[G: Nigeria]**

Mussa, Michael. Empirical Regularities in the Behavior of Exchange Rates and Theories of the Foreign Exchange Market. **In** *Brunner, K. and Meltzer, A. H., eds.,* 1983, *1979,* pp. 165–213.

Mussa, Michael. Staggered Contracts and Exchange Rate Policy: Comment. **In** *Frenkel, J. A., ed.,* 1983, pp. 255–58.

Nabli, Mustapha K. Revision of Exchange-Rate Determination in the MCM: Comment. **In** *De Grauwe, P. and Peeters, T., eds.,* 1983, pp. 236–38. **[G: U.S.]**

Nashashibi, Karim. Devaluation in Developing Countries: The Difficult Choices. *Finance Develop.,* March 1983, *20*(1), pp. 14–17. **[G: LDCs]**

Neary, J. Peter and Purvis, Douglas D. Real Adjustment and Exchange Rate Dynamics. **In** *Frenkel, J. A., ed.,* 1983, pp. 285–308.

Niehans, Jürg. Real Exchange Rate Overshooting and the Output Cost of Bringing Down Inflation: Some Further Results: Comment. **In** *Frenkel, J. A., ed.,* 1983, pp. 365–68.

Obstfeld, Maurice. Exchange Rates, Inflation, and the Sterilization Problem: Germany, 1975–1981. *Europ. Econ. Rev.,* March/April 1983, *21*(1/2), pp. 161–89. **[G: W. Germany]**

Obstfeld, Maurice. Intertemporal Price Speculation and the Optimal Current-Account Deficit. *J. Int. Money Finance,* August 1983, *2*(2), pp. 135–45.

Obstfeld, Maurice. Rational Expectations and the Foreign Exchange Market: Comment. **In** *Frenkel, J. A., ed.,* 1983, pp. 180–87. **[G: U.K.; U.S.; W. Germany]**

Olivera, Julio H. G. Dinero pasivo internacional y hegemonia monetaria. (With English summary.) *Desarrollo Econ.,* April–June 1983, *23*(89), pp. 3–9.

Ortiz, Guillermo. Dollarization in Mexico: Causes and Consequences. **In** *Armella, P. A.; Dornbusch, R. and Obstfeld, M., eds.,* 1983, pp. 71–95. **[G: Mexico]**

Owen, Robert F. How Much Simplification Is Wise in Modelling Exchange Rates? Comment. **In** *De Grauwe, P. and Peeters, T., eds.,* 1983, pp. 19–20.

Padoa Schioppa, Fiorella. Crowding Out in an Inflationary Open Economy: The Italian Case. *Europ. Econ. Rev.*, September 1983, *23*(1), pp. 117–39. **[G: Italy]**

Papademos, Lucas and Rozwadowski, Franek. Monetary and Credit Targets in an Open Economy. **In** *Hodgman, D. R., ed.*, 1983, pp. 275–306.

Parguez, A. La monnaie, la crise et l'épargne ou les conséquences économiques de l'austérité. (Money, Crisis and Saving: The Economic Consequences of Austerity. With English summary.) *Écon. Soc.*, September–October–November 1983, *17*(9–10–11), pp. 1421–50.

Parkin, Michael. The SDR and the IMF: Toward a World Central Bank? Comment. **In** *von Furstenberg, G. M., ed.*, 1983, pp. 200–208.

Penati, Alessandro. Expansionary Fiscal Policy and the Exchange Rate: A Review. *Int. Monet. Fund Staff Pap.*, September 1983, *30*(3), pp. 542–69.

Pentecost, Eric J. Government Financing Constraint, Wealth Effects and External Balances: Comment. *Southern Econ. J.*, April 1983, *49*(4), pp. 1174–81.

Persson, Torsten and Svensson, Lars E. O. Is Optimism Good in a Keynesian Economy? *Economica*, August 1983, *50*(199), pp. 291–300.

Ranuzzi, Paolo. A Balance of Payments Model for Exchange Rate Determination. *Rivista Int. Sci. Econ. Com.*, October–November 1983, *30*(10–11), pp. 971–91. **[G: France; Italy; U.K.; W. Germany]**

Ranuzzi, Paolo. A Portfolio Approach to the Determination of Exchange Rates within a Multicountry Model. **In** *De Grauwe, P. and Peeters, T., eds.*, 1983, pp. 175–207. **[G: U.K.; W. Germany; France; Italy]**

Razin, Assaf and Svensson, Lars E. O. The Current Account and the Optimal Government Debt. *J. Int. Money Finance*, August 1983, *2*(2), pp. 215–24.

Ritschard, Gilbert and Royer, Daniel. A Geometric Approach to Disequilibrium Exchange Rate Fluctuations: The Case of Switzerland. *Europ. Econ. Rev.*, August 1983, *22*(3), pp. 373–404. **[G: Switzerland]**

Roper, Don. The SDR and the IMF: Toward a World Central Bank? Comment. **In** *von Furstenberg, G. M., ed.*, 1983, pp. 208–12.

Ross, Myron H. Currency Substitution and Instability in the World Dollar Standard: Comment. *Amer. Econ. Rev.*, June 1983, *73*(3), pp. 473. **[G: U.S.]**

Rothschild, Kurt W. Geldmenge, Währungsreserven und Wechselkursänderungen. (Money, Foreign Exchange Reserves, and Exchange Rate Variations. With English summary.) *Jahr. Nationalökon. Statist.*, July 1983, *198*(4), pp. 311–17.

Roy, Raj and Rassuli, Ali. Flexible Exchange Regime and Sub-Account Instability in Balances of Payments. *Rivista Int. Sci. Econ. Com.*, October–November 1983, *30*(10–11), pp. 992–1001. **[G: Selected Countries]**

Ruiz, Maria L. Price Rigidities and the Effects of Revaluation [Effectiveness of Exchange Rate Policy for Trade Account Adjustments]. *Econ. Notes*, 1983, (1), pp. 191–95.

Sacerdoti, Emilio. Componenti attese ed inattese della variazione dei tassi di cambio: una rassegna di contributi empirici. (Expected and Unexpected Components of Exchange Rate Changes: A Review of Empirical Contribution. With English summary.) *Giorn. Econ.*, January–February 1983, *42*(1–2), pp. 27–54.

Sachs, Jeffrey D. Aspects of the Current Account Behavior of OECD Economies. **In** *Claassen, E. and Salin, P., eds.*, 1983, pp. 101–22. **[G: OECD]**

Sachs, Jeffrey D. Real Adjustment and Exchange Rate Dynamics: Comment. **In** *Frenkel, J. A., ed.*, 1983, pp. 313–16.

Saïdi, Nasser. The Out-of-Sample Failure of Empirical Exchange Rate Models: Sampling Error or Misspecification? Comment. **In** *Frenkel, J. A., ed.*, 1983, pp. 105–09. **[G: Japan; U.K.; U.S.; W. Germany]**

Saïdi, Nasser and Swoboda, Alexander. Nominal and Real Exchange Rates: Issues and Some Evidence. **In** *Claassen, E. and Salin, P., eds.*, 1983, pp. 3–27. **[G: Selected OECD]**

Salemi, Michael K. The Out-of-Sample Failure of Empirical Exchange Rate Models: Sampling Error or Misspecification? Comment. **In** *Frenkel, J. A., ed.*, 1983, pp. 110–12. **[G: Japan; U.K.; U.S.; W. Germany]**

Santacoloma, J.-F. Open Economy Macroeconomics: An Overview. *Écon. Soc.*, July-August 1983, *17*(7–8), pp. 1097–1148.

Sargent, Thomas J. Dollarization in Mexico: Causes and Consequences: Comment. **In** *Armella, P. A.; Dornbusch, R. and Obstfeld, M., eds.*, 1983, pp. 95–106.

Sauernheimer, Karlhans. Die aussenwirtschaftlichen Implikationen des "New Cambridge Approach." (The "New Cambridge" Approach and External Balance. With English summary.) *Konjunkturpolitik*, 1983, *29*(6), pp. 348–66.

Sawyer, J. A.; Dungan, D. P. and Jump, G. V. The Transmission of World Economic Expansion to an Open Economy: Some Experiments for Canada. **In** *[Klein, L. R.]*, 1983, pp. 368–92. **[G: Canada]**

Schittko, Ulrich K. and Eckwert, B. A Two-Country Temporary Equilibrium Model with Quantity Rationing—On the Structure of Two-Country Disequilibria. *Jahr. Nationalökon. Statist.*, March 1983, *198*(2), pp. 97–121.

Schittko, Ulrich K. and Eckwert, B. The Role of Uncertainty in a Simple Temporary Equilibrium Model of International Trade with Quantity Rationing under Fixed Exchange Rates. *Z. Wirtschaft. Sozialwissen.*, 1983, *103*(5), pp. 461–83.

Shepherd, A. Ross. A Backward Bending Supply of Labor Schedule and the Short Run Phillips Curve: Comment. *Southern Econ. J.*, January 1983, *49*(3), pp. 867–70.

Sihag, Balbir S. Precautionary Demand for International Reserves. *Indian Econ. J.*, January-March 1983, *30*(3), pp. 65–74. **[G: Selected Countries]**

Sinclair, P. J. N. How Does an Energy Price Shock Affect Aggregate Output and Employment? *Greek Econ. Rev.*, August 1983, *5*(2), pp. 123–46.

Spaventa, Luigi. Two Letters of Intent: External Crises and Stabilization Policy, Italy, 1973–77. **In** *Williamson, J., ed.*, 1983, pp. 441–73. **[G: Italy]**

Spencer, Grant H. Real Exchange Rate Adjustment to Exogenous Terms of Trade Shocks. *Int. Monet. Fund Staff Pap.*, September 1983, *30*(3), pp. 570–600. **[G: Australia; Denmark; Finland; Ireland; New Zealand]**

Spinelli, Franco. Currency Substitution, Flexible Exchange Rates, and the Case for International Monetary Cooperation: Discussion of a Recent Proposal. *Int. Monet. Fund Staff Pap.*, December 1983, *30*(4), pp. 755–83.

Stahl, Heinz-Michael. Brasiliens Finanzierungskrise: Ursachen—Anpassungsmassnahmen—Perspektiven. (Brazil's Current Financial Crisis—Causes and Perspectives. With English summary.) *Konjunkturpolitik*, 1983, *29*(3), pp. 187–98. **[G: Brazil]**

Stockman, Alan C. The Use of Monetary Policy for Internal and External Balance in Ten Industrial Countries: Comment. **In** *Frenkel, J. A., ed.*, 1983, pp. 229–33. **[G: OECD]**

Stulz, René M. The Demand for Foreign Bonds. *J. Int. Econ.*, November 1983, *15*(3/4), pp. 225–38.

Svensson, Lars E. O. and Razin, Assaf. The Terms of Trade and the Current Account: The Harberger–Laursen–Metzler Effect. *J. Polit. Econ.*, February 1983, *91*(1), pp. 97–125.

Tarkka, Juha and Pikkarainen, Pentti. Hinnat, palkat ja avoimen sektorin kasvu. (Prices, Wages and Open Sector Growth. With English summary.) *Kansant. Aikak.*, 1983, *79*(2), pp. 180–93. **[G: Finland]**

Taylor, John B. Staggered Contracts and Exchange Rate Policy: Comment. **In** *Frenkel, J. A., ed.*, 1983, pp. 252–55.

Thirlwall, Anthony P. Foreign Trade Elasticities in Centre-Periphery Models of Growth and Development. *Banca Naz. Lavoro Quart. Rev.*, September 1983, (146), pp. 249–61.

Thys-Clement, Françoise. Monetary Authorities' Reaction Functions in a Model of Exchange-Rate Determination for the European Monetary System: Comment. **In** *De Grauwe, P. and Peeters, T., eds.*, 1983, pp. 283–84. **[G: EEC]**

Togan, Sübidey. Effects of Alternative Policy Regimes on Foreign-Payments Imbalances. *Pakistan Devel. Rev.*, Winter 1983, *22*(4), pp. 239–60. **[G: Turkey]**

Tremblay, Rodrigue. L'endettement international et les problèmes d'adjustement: une perspective générale. (International Indebtedness and Adjustment Problems: A Review. With English summary.) *L'Actual. Econ.*, June 1983, *59*(2), pp. 283–324. **[G: LDCs]**

Tullio, Giuseppe. The Role of Savings and Investment in Current Account Determination: The Case of the Federal Republic of Germany (1973–1979). *Kredit Kapital*, 1983, *16*(3), pp. 351–70. **[G: W. Germany]**

Turnovsky, Stephen J. Exchange Market Intervention Policies in a Small Open Economy. **In** *Bhandari, J. S. and Putnam, B. H., eds.*, 1983, pp. 286–311.

Turnovsky, Stephen J. Expanding Exports and the Structure of the Domestic Economy: A Monetary Analysis. *Econ. Rec.*, September 1983, *59*(166), pp. 245–59.

Turnovsky, Stephen J. Wage Indexation and Exchange Market Interventions in a Small Open Economy. *Can. J. Econ.*, November 1983, *16*(4), pp. 574–92.

Ueda, Kazuo. Permanent and Temporary Changes in the Exchange Rate and Trade Balance Dynamics. *J. Int. Econ.*, August 1983, *15*(1/2), pp. 27–43.

Vander Kraats, Ronald H. and Booth, Laurence D. Empirical Tests of the Monetary Approach to Exchange-Rate Determination. *J. Int. Money Finance*, December 1983, *2*(3), pp. 255–78. **[G: W. Europe; Canada; Japan]**

Vaubel, Roland. Coordination or Competition among National Macro-economic Policies? **In** *[Giersch, H.]*, 1983, pp. 3–28. **[G: OECD]**

de Vries, Rimmer. International Balance of Payments Financing and Adjustment: Comment. **In** *von Furstenberg, G. M., ed.*, 1983, pp. 166–78.

Vuchelen, Jozef. Macroeconomic Implications of Alternative Exchange-Rate Models: Comment. **In** *De Grauwe, P. and Peeters, T., eds.*, 1983, pp. 54–57. **[G: Canada]**

Wallace, Myles S. A Backward Bending Supply of Labor Schedule and the Short Run Phillips Curve: Reply. *Southern Econ. J.*, January 1983, *49*(3), pp. 871–73.

Whitman, Marina v. N. Perspective: On Exchange Rate Analysis and Foreign Exchange Risk. **In** *Herring, R. J., ed.*, 1983, pp. 75–83.

Wilson, Charles. Oil Shocks and Exchange Rate Dynamics: Comment. **In** *Frenkel, J. A., ed.*, 1983, pp. 281–83.

Winder, Robert C. Currency Substitution and Exchange Rate Analysis: An Empirical Test. *Rev. Bus. Econ. Res.*, Fall 1983, *19*(1), pp. 38–44. **[G: U.S.; W. Germany]**

Witte, Willard E. Policy Interdependence under Flexible Exchange Rates: A Dynamic Analysis of Price Interactions. **In** *Bhandari, J. S. and Putnam, B. H., eds.*, 1983, pp. 312–28.

Wyplosz, Charles A. Aspects of the Current Account Behavior of OECD Economies: Comment. **In** *Claassen, E. and Salin, P., eds.*, 1983, pp. 123–28. **[G: OECD]**

Wyplosz, Charles A. The Exchange and Interest Rate Term Structure under Risk Aversion and Rational Expectations. *J. Int. Econ.*, February 1983, *14*(1/2), pp. 123–39.

Yu, Eden S. H. and Wang, Leonard F. S. Government Financing Constraint, Wealth Effects and External Balances: Reply. *Southern Econ. J.*, April 1983, *49*(4), pp. 1182–85.

4313 Open Economy Macroeconomic Studies: Balance of Payments and Adjustment Mechanisms

Aglietta, Michel. Policy Interdependence from a Latin American Perspective: Comment. *Int. Monet. Fund Staff Pap.*, March 1983, *30*(1), pp. 159–63. **[G: Latin America]**

Arriazu, Ricardo H. Policy Interdependence from

a Latin American Perspective. *Int. Monet. Fund Staff Pap.*, March 1983, *30*(1), pp. 113–52. **[G: Latin America]**

Artus, Jacques R. Exchange Rate Regimes and European–U.S. Policy Interdependence: Comment. *Int. Monet. Fund Staff Pap.*, March 1983, *30*(1), pp. 103–08.

Atkinson, F. J.; Brooks, Simon J. and Hall, S. G. F. The Economic Effects of North Sea Oil. *Nat. Inst. Econ. Rev.*, May 1983, (104), pp. 38–44. **[G: U.K.]**

Balassa, Bela. Policy Responses to External Shocks in Sub-Saharan African Countries. *J. Policy Modeling,* March 1983, *5*(1), pp. 75–105. **[G: Africa]**

Balassa, Bela. The Adjustment Experience of Developing Economies after 1973. **In** *Williamson, J., ed.*, 1983, pp. 145–74. **[G: LDCs]**

Balassa, Bela. Trade Policy in Mexico. *World Devel.*, September 1983, *11*(9), pp. 795–811. **[G: Mexico]**

Barr, G. D. I. and Kantor, B. S. A Rational Expectations Analysis of the South African Business Cycles. *J. Stud. Econ. Econometrics,* July 1983, (16), pp. 5–16. **[G: S. Africa]**

Bennett, Karl M. Exchange Rate Policy and External Imbalance: The Jamaican Experience, 1973–1982. *Soc. Econ. Stud.*, December 1983, *32*(4), pp. 51–72. **[G: Jamaica]**

Bergsten, C. Fred. The Dollar, the Yen, and U.S. Trade. **In** *Bergsten, C. F.*, 1983, pp. 161–70. **[G: Japan; U.S.]**

Bergsten, C. Fred. The Villain Is an Overvalued Dollar. **In** *Bergsten, C. F.*, 1983, *1982,* pp. 79–91. **[G: U.S.]**

Bergsten, C. Fred. What to Do about Japan. **In** *Bergsten, C. F.*, 1983, *1982,* pp. 145–59. **[G: U.S.; Japan]**

Bird, Graham. Low-Income Countries and International Financial Reform. *J. Devel. Areas,* October 1983, *18*(1), pp. 53–75. **[G: LDCs]**

Blomqvist, H. C. Finland's Monetary Autonomy. *Appl. Econ.*, June 1983, *15*(3), pp. 409–15.

Borchert, Manfred. Einige aussenwirtschaftliche Aspekte staatlicher Verschuldung. (Some International Economic Aspects of Public Debt. With English summary.) *Kredit Kapital,* 1983, *16*(4), pp. 513–27. **[G: W. Germany]**

de Capitani, Werner. The Swiss Banks and the United States Securities Laws. *Wirtsch. Recht,* 1983, *35*(2/3), pp. 182–93. **[G: U.S.; Switzerland]**

Caprio, Jerry and Clark, Peter B. Oil Price Shocks in a Portfolio-Balance Model. *J. Econ. Bus.*, June 1983, *35*(2), pp. 221–33. **[G: U.S.]**

de Cecco, Marcello. International Economic Adjustment: Small Countries and the European Monetary System: Introduction. **In** *de Cecco, M., ed.*, 1983, pp. 1–6. **[G: W. Europe]**

Cella, Guido. Politica di sostituzione delle importazioni industriali e competitività dell'economia italiana. (Import Substitution Policy and Competitiveness of the Italian Economy. With English summary.) *Giorn. Econ.*, March-April 1983, *42*(3–4), pp. 215–38. **[G: Italy]**

Chaudhuri, K. N. Foreign Trade and Balance of Payments (1757–1947). **In** *Kumar, D., ed.*, 1983, pp. 804–77. **[G: India]**

Ciampi, Carlo Azeglio. La via obbligata per il risanamento dell'economia. (The Obligatory Path for Rehabilitation of the Economy. With English summary.) *Bancaria,* August 1983, *39*(8), pp. 683–89. **[G: Italy]**

Cobham, David. Reverse Causation in the Monetary Approach: An Econometric Test for the U.K. *Manchester Sch. Econ. Soc. Stud.*, December 1983, *51*(4), pp. 360–79. **[G: U.K.]**

Connolly, Michael B. Exchange Rates, Real Economic Activity and the Balance of Payments: Evidence from the 1960s. **In** *Claassen, E. and Salin, P., eds.*, 1983, pp. 129–43. **[G: Selected Countries]**

Cooper, Richard N. Some Aspects of the 1982–83 Brazilian Payments Crisis: Comments and Discussion. *Brookings Pap. Econ. Act.*, 1983, (2), pp. 543–47. **[G: Brazil]**

Csikós-Nagy, Béla. Liquidity Troubles and Economic Consolidation in Hungary. *Acta Oecon.*, 1983, *31*(1–2), pp. 1–11. **[G: Hungary]**

Cumby, Robert E. Trade Credit, Exchange Controls, and Monetary Independence: Evidence from the United Kingdom. *J. Int. Econ.*, February 1983, *14*(1/2), pp. 53–67. **[G: U.K.]**

Dale, William B. Financing and Adjustment of Payments Imbalances. **In** *Williamson, J., ed.*, 1983, pp. 3–16.

De Grauwe, Paul. Symptoms of an Overvalued Currency: The Case of the Belgian Franc. **In** *de Cecco, M., ed.*, 1983, pp. 99–116. **[G: Belgium]**

De Grauwe, Paul and Frattianni, Michele. U.S. Economic Policies: Are They a Burden on the Rest of the World? *Econ. Notes,* 1983, (3), pp. 69–85. **[G: OECD]**

Díiaz-Alejandro, Carlos F. Some Aspects of the 1982–83 Brazilian Payments Crisis. *Brookings Pap. Econ. Act.*, 1983, (2), pp. 515–42. **[G: Brazil]**

Díaz-Alejandro, Carlos F. Stories of the 1930s for the 1980s. **In** *Armella, P. A.; Dornbusch, R. and Obstfeld, M., eds.*, 1983, pp. 5–35. **[G: Latin America]**

DiLullo, Anthony J. U.S. International Transactions, Third Quarter 1983. *Surv. Curr. Bus.*, December 1983, *63*(12), pp. 41–63. **[G: U.S.]**

Dornbusch, Rudiger. Some Aspects of the 1982–83 Brazilian Payments Crisis: Comments and Discussion. *Brookings Pap. Econ. Act.*, 1983, (2), pp. 547–52. **[G: Brazil]**

Drabek, Zdenek. External Disturbances and the Balance of Payments Adjustment in the Soviet Union. *Aussenwirtschaft,* June 1983, *38*(2), pp. 173–94. **[G: U.S.S.R.]**

Eckaus, Richard S. IMF Conditionality: Country Studies: Comments, Chapters 20–21. **In** *Williamson, J., ed.*, 1983, pp. 4320. **[G: Turkey; India]**

Edwards, Sebastian. The Demand for International Reserves and Exchange Rate Adjustments: The Case of LDCs, 1964–1972. *Economica,* August 1983, *50*(199), pp. 269–80. **[G: LDCs]**

Eisner, Robert. Which Way for France? *Challenge,* July/August 1983, *26*(3), pp. 34–41. **[G: France]**

Feldman, Robert A. and Proctor, Allan J. U.S. International Trade in Services. *Fed. Res. Bank New York Quart. Rev.*, Spring 1983, *8*(1), pp.

30–36. [G: U.S.]

Fendt, Robert, Jr. Growth and Debt: Issues and Prospects for the Brazilian Economy in the Eighties. **In** *Jorge, A.; Salazar-Carillo, J. and Higonnet, R. P., eds.*, 1983, pp. 125–37. **[G: Brazil]**

Fildes, Robert A. and Fitzgerald, M. Desmond. The Use of Information in Balance of Payments Forecasting. *Economica*, August 1983, *50*(199), pp. 249–58. **[G: U.K.]**

Flassbeck, Heiner. Das Leistungsbilanzrätsel. Eine kritische Betrachtung zum Stand der Wechselkurstheorie. (The Riddle of the German Balance of Payments—A Critical Assessment of the State of Exchange Rate Theory. With English summary.) *Konjunkturpolitik*, 1983, *29*(5), pp. 261–84. **[G: W. Germany]**

Frenkel, Jacob A. Exchange Rate Regimes and European–U.S. Policy Interdependence: Comment. *Int. Monet. Fund Staff Pap.*, March 1983, *30*(1), pp. 108–12. **[G: U.S.; W. Europe]**

Frenkel, Jacob A. International Liquidity and Monetary Control. **In** *von Furstenberg, G. M., ed.*, 1983, pp. 65–109. **[G: Selected Countries]**

Fuhrmann, Wilfried. Zum Kapitalverkehr zwischen deutschen und ausländischen Kreditinstituten. (Capital Movements between German and Foreign Banks. With English summary.) *Kredit Kapital*, 1983, *16*(2), pp. 267–83. **[G: W. Germany]**

Glaessner, Thomas C. U.S. International Transactions in 1982. *Fed. Res. Bull.*, April 1983, *69*(4), pp. 251–60. **[G: U.S.]**

Goodwin, R. M. The World Matrix Multiplier. **In** *Goodwin, R. M.*, 1983, pp. 30–56.

Gupta, Sanjeev. India and the Second OPEC Oil Price Shock—An Economy-Wide Analysis. *Weltwirtsch. Arch.*, 1983, *119*(1), pp. 122–37. **[G: India]**

Gwin, Catherine. Financing India's Structural Adjustment: The Role of the Fund. **In** *Williamson, J., ed.*, 1983, pp. 511–31. **[G: India]**

Halttunen, Hannu and Korkman, Sixten. External Shocks and Adjustment Policies in Finland, 1973–80. **In** *de Cecco, M., ed.*, 1983, pp. 7–33. **[G: Finland]**

Hankel, Wilhelm. The Global Financial Crisis—A Case Study in Modern Alchemy—Facts, Legends and Realities. **In** *Kaushik, S. K., ed.*, 1983, pp. 191–97. **[G: Global]**

Hewett, Edward A. Foreign Economic Relations. **In** *Bergson, A. and Levine, H. S., eds.*, 1983, pp. 269–310. **[G: U.S.S.R.]**

Heyne, Paul. Do Trade Deficits Matter? *Cato J.*, Winter 1983/84, *3*(3), pp. 705–16. **[G: U.S.]**

Hoffmann, Lutz and Jarass, Lorenz. The Impact of Rising Oil Prices of Oil-Importing Developing Countries and the Scope for Adjustment. *Weltwirtsch. Arch.*, 1983, *119*(2), pp. 297–316. **[G: India; Brazil; Kenya]**

Holopainen, Kari. The System of Payment between Finland and the Soviet Union. **In** *Möttölä, K.; Bykov, O. N. and Korolev, I. S., eds.*, 1983, pp. 173–80. **[G: U.S.S.R.; Finland]**

Hood, William C. The Current World Economic Situation and the Problem of Global Payments Imbalances. **In** *Hooke, A. W., ed.*, 1983, pp. 56–70.

Huguel, Catherine. La balance des paiements: baromètre des difficultés françaises. (With English summary.) *Revue Écon. Polit.*, September–October 1983, *93*(5), pp. 740–50. **[G: France]**

Iglesias, Enrique V. Reflections on the Latin American Economy in 1982. *Cepal Rev.*, April 1983, (19), pp. 7–49. **[G: Latin America]**

Kanniainen, Vesa and Tornberg, Pertti. Inflation in an Open Economy: Tests with Finnish Data 1960(I)–1981(IV). *Weltwirtsch. Arch.*, 1983, *119*(2), pp. 317–28. **[G: Finland]**

Katseli, Louka T. Macroeconomic Adjustment and Exchange-Rate Policy in Middle-Income Countries: Greece, Portugal and Spain in the 1970s. **In** *de Cecco, M., ed.*, 1983, pp. 189–211. **[G: Greece; Portugal; Spain]**

Keating, Maryann O'Hagan and Keating, Barry P. A Test of the Federal Reserve's Degree of Domestic Money Stock Control, Given International Capital Flows and Fixed Exchange Rates. *Quart. Rev. Econ. Bus.*, Spring 1983, *23*(1), pp. 46–57. **[G: U.S.]**

Kelly, Margaret. Fiscal Deficits and Fund-Supported Programs. *Finance Develop.*, September 1983, *20*(3), pp. 37–39.

Khan, Mohsin S. Policy Interdependence from a Latin American Perspective: Comment. *Int. Monet. Fund Staff Pap.*, March 1983, *30*(1), pp. 153–59.

Khan, Mohsin S. and Knight, Malcolm D. Determinants of Current Account Balances of Non-Oil Developing Countries in the 1970s. *Int. Monet. Fund Staff Pap.*, December 1983, *30*(4), pp. 819–42. **[G: Non-Oil LDCs]**

Khan, Mohsin S. and Knight, Malcolm D. Sources of Payments Problems in LDCs. *Finance Develop.*, December 1983, *20*(4), pp. 2–5. **[G: LDCs]**

Killick, Tony. Kenya, the IMF, and the Unsuccessful Quest for Stabilization. **In** *Williamson, J., ed.*, 1983, pp. 381–413. **[G: Kenya]**

Kincaid, G. Russell. Korea's Major Adjustment Effort. *Finance Develop.*, December 1983, *20*(4), pp. 20–23. **[G: S. Korea]**

Kjaer, Jørn H. International Adjustment, the EMS and Small European Countries: The Danish Experience. **In** *de Cecco, M., ed.*, 1983, pp. 65–73. **[G: Denmark]**

Komiya, Ryutaro. International Liquidity and Monetary Control: Comment. **In** *von Furstenberg, G. M., ed.*, 1983, pp. 110–15.

Kröger, Jürgen. Devisenkurse, Leistungsbilanz und interne Anpassungsprozesse. (Exchange Rates, the Current Account Balance, and Internal Adjustment Processes. With English summary.) *Konjunkturpolitik*, 1983, *29*(1), pp. 1–20. **[G: W. Germany]**

Langoni, Carlos Geraldo and Haddad, Claudio Luiz da Silva. The Implementation of Monetary Policy in Brazil in 1981. **In** *Meek, P., ed.*, 1983, pp. 86–99. **[G: Brazil]**

Longstreth, Bevis. Toward Neutral Principles of International Securities Regulation. *Wirtsch. Recht*, 1983, *35*(2/3), pp. 164–81.

de Macedo, Jorge Braga. A Portfolio Model of an Inconvertible Currency: The Recent Experience of Portugal. **In** *de Cecco, M., ed.*, 1983, pp. 212–49. **[G: Portugal]**

Makepeace, G. H. and Pikoulakis, E. A Saving-Investment Approach to the Current Account of the Balance of Payments: Some Preliminary Empirical Estimates for the U.K. (1960–1980). *Greek Econ. Rev.*, December 1983, *5*(3), pp. 223–47. **[G: U.K.]**

Mancera, Miguel. Stories of the 1930s for the 1980s: Comment. **In** *Armella, P. A.; Dornbusch, R. and Obstfeld, M., eds.*, 1983, pp. 36–40. **[G: Latin America]**

Marshall S., Jorge; Mardones S., José Luis and Marshall L., Isabel. IMF Conditionality: The Experiences of Argentina, Brazil, and Chile. **In** *Williamson, J., ed.*, 1983, pp. 275–321. **[G: Chile; Brazil; Argentina]**

Masera, Rainer S. International Liquidity and Monetary Control: Comment. **In** *von Furstenberg, G. M., ed.*, 1983, pp. 123–28.

Mawuli, Agogo. Balance of Payments Problem as a Consequence of Rapid Capital Accumulation in Developing Countries. *Indian Econ. J.*, January–March 1983, *30*(3), pp. 39–64. **[G: LDCs]**

McAleese, Dermot. Competitiveness and Economic Performance: The Irish Experience. **In** *Black, J. and Winters, L. A., eds.*, 1983, pp. 65–91. **[G: Ireland; OECD]**

McGuirk, Anne K. Oil Price Changes and Real Exchange Rate Movements among Industrial Countries. *Int. Monet. Fund Staff Pap.*, December 1983, *30*(4), pp. 843–84. **[G: Selected OECD]**

Medio, Alfredo. Worldwide Inflation and Its Impact on Less Developed Countries. *Econ. Forum*, Summer 1983, *14*(1), pp. 1–26. **[G: Global]**

Moore, Geoffrey H. Will the "Real" Trade Balance Please Stand Up? *J. Int. Bus. Stud.*, Spring/Summer 1983, *14*(1), pp. 155–59. **[G: U.S.]**

Mukherjee, Amitabha. Effects of Terms of Trade on Trade Balance with Emphasis on Devaluation: General & Sectoral Cases. *Indian Econ. J.*, January–March 1983, *30*(3), pp. 25–38. **[G: India]**

Nielsen, Peter Erling. Behov og begrænsninger i 1980'ernes pengepolitik. (Recent Developments in Danish Monetary Policy. With English summary.) *Nationaløkon. Tidsskr.*, 1983, *121*(1), pp. 61–73. **[G: Denmark]**

Okyar, Osman. Turkey and the IMF: A Review of Relations, 1978–82. **In** *Williamson, J., ed.*, 1983, pp. 533–61. **[G: Turkey]**

Paish, F. W. Inflation and the Balance of Payments in the United Kingdom 1952–1967. **In** *Feinstein, C., ed.*, 1983, *1968*, pp. 133–46. **[G: U.K.]**

Panayotopoulos, Dimitris. The "Vicious Circle" Hypothesis: The Greek Case. *Kredit Kapital*, 1983, *16*(3), pp. 394–404. **[G: Greece]**

Please, Stanley. IMF Conditionality: Country Studies: Comments, Chapters 15–16. **In** *Williamson, J., ed.*, 1983, pp. 415–20.

Posthumus, Godert. The Netherlands: Financial-Economic Adjustment Policies in the 1970s. **In** *de Cecco, M., ed.*, 1983, pp. 74–98. **[G: Netherlands]**

Purvis, Douglas D. International Liquidity and Monetary Control: Comment. **In** *von Furstenberg, G. M., ed.*, 1983, pp. 115–23.

Radke, Detlef and Taake, Hans-Helmut. Financial Crisis Management in Egypt and Turkey. *J. World Trade Law*, July–August 1983, *17*(4), pp. 325–36. **[G: Turkey; Egypt]**

Sachs, Jeffrey D. Aspects of the Current Account Behavior of OECD Economies. **In** *Claassen, E. and Salin, P., eds.*, 1983, pp. 101–22. **[G: OECD]**

Sachs, Jeffrey D. IMF Conditionality: County Studies: Comments, Chapters 17–19. **In** *Williamson, J., ed.*, 1983, pp. 505–10. **[G: Italy; U.K.; Portugal]**

Saulnier, Raymond J. The President's Economic Report: A Critique. *J. Portfol. Manage.*, Summer 1983, *9*(4), pp. 58–59. **[G: U.S.]**

Schröder, Jürgen. Exchange Rates, Real Economic Activity and the Balance of Payments: Evidence from the 1960s: Comment. **In** *Claassen, E. and Salin, P., eds.*, 1983, pp. 144–48. **[G: Selected Countries]**

Sharpley, Jennifer. Economic Management and IMF Conditionality in Jamaica. **In** *Williamson, J., ed.*, 1983, pp. 233–62. **[G: Jamaica]**

Sheffer, Eliezer. The Role of International Banking in the 'Oil Surplus' Adjustment Process: Comment. *J. Banking Finance*, 1983, *7*(4), pp. 519–20. **[G: Global]**

Shneerson, Dan. The Profitability of Investment in Shipping: The Balance of Payments Criterion. *J. Transp. Econ. Policy*, September 1983, *17*(3), pp. 285–98. **[G: Israel]**

da Silva Lopes, Jose. IMF Conditionality: The Stand-by Arrangement with Portugal, 1978. **In** *Williamson, J., ed.*, 1983, pp. 475–504. **[G: Portugal]**

Sørensen, Peter Birch. Devaluering og finanspolitik under alternative pengepolitiske regimer. (Fiscal and Exchange Rate Policies under Different Monetary Policies Regimes. With English summary.) *Nationaløkon. Tidsskr.*, 1983, *121*(1), pp. 83–101. **[G: Denmark]**

Spinelli, Franco. Fixed Exchange Rates and Adaptive Expectations Monetarism: The Italian Case. *Rev. Econ. Cond. Italy*, February 1983, (1), pp. 97–124. **[G: Italy]**

Swoba, Alexander K. Exchange Rate Regimes and European–U.S. Policy Interdependence. *Int. Monet. Fund Staff Pap.*, March 1983, *30*(1), pp. 75–102. **[G: U.S.; W. Europe]**

Szegö, Giorgio P. The role of International Banking in the 'Oil Surplus' Adjustment Process. *J. Banking Finance*, 1983, *7*(4), pp. 497–518. **[G: Global]**

Teck, Alan and Johns, William B. Portfolio Decisions of Central Banks. **In** *George, A. M. and Giddy, I. H., eds., Vol. 2*, 1983, pp. 8.4:1–16.

Van Arkadie, Brian. The IMF Prescription for Structural Adjustment in Tanzania: A Comment. **In** *Jansen, K., ed.*, 1983, pp. 127–48. **[G: Tanzania]**

Verde, Antimo. Some Considerations about Italy's Foreign Debts (1977–1982). *Rivista Polit. Econ.*, Supplement Dec. 1983, *73*(12), pp. 147–87. **[G: Italy]**

Wallich, Henry C. Statement to the U.S. House Subcommittee on Domestic Monetary Policy of the Committee on Banking, Finance and Urban Affairs, October 5, 1983. *Fed. Res. Bull.*, October 1983, *69*(10), pp. 776–81. **[G: U.S.]**

Wangwe, Samuel M. Industrialization and Resource Allocation in a Developing Country: The Case of Recent Experiences in Tanzania. *World Devel.*, June 1983, *11*(6), pp. 483–92. **[G: Tanzania]**

Wyplosz, Charles A. Aspects of the Current Account Behavior of OECD Economies: Comment. **In** *Claassen, E. and Salin, P., eds.*, 1983, pp. 123–28. **[G: OECD]**

4314 Exchange Rates and Markets: Theory and Studies

Abele, Hanns. A Model of Trade and Exchange Rates: Comment. **In** *Hickman, B. G., ed.*, 1983, pp. 311–13. **[G: OECD; Global]**

Adam, Marie-Christine. The Relation between the Current Account and the Exchange Rate: A Survey of the Recent Literature: Comment. **In** *De Grauwe, P. and Peeters, T., eds.*, 1983, pp. 100–102. **[G: OECD]**

Adler, Michael. Designing Spreads in Forward Exchange Contracts and Foreign Exchange Futures. *J. Futures Markets,* Winter 1983, *3*(4), pp. 355–68.

Adler, Michael and Dumas, Bernard. International Portfolio Choice and Corporation Finance: A Synthesis. *J. Finance,* June 1983, *38*(3), pp. 925–84.

Adler, Michael and Lehmann, Bruce. Deviations from Purchasing Power Parity in the Long Run. *J. Finance,* December 1983, *38*(5), pp. 1471–87. **[G: OECD; LDCs]**

Agmon, Tamir and Arad, Ruth. Currency-Related Risk and Risk Premium in the World's Currency Market. *Europ. Econ. Rev.*, August 1983, *22*(3), pp. 257–64.

d'Alcantara, Gonzales. Exchange Rates in Project LINK: Comment. **In** *De Grauwe, P. and Peeters, T., eds.*, 1983, pp. 134–38. **[G: OECD]**

Aliber, Robert Z. Exchange-Rate Intervention: Arbitrage and Market Efficiency. **In** *[Giersch, H.],* 1983, pp. 171–87. **[G: U.S.]**

Amano, Akihiro. A Structural Approach to Capital Flows and Exchange Rates. *Z. Nationalökon.*, Supplement 3, 1983, *43,* pp. 3–28. **[G: Selected OECD]**

Amano, Akihiro. Exchange-Rate Modelling in the EPA World Economic Model. **In** *De Grauwe, P. and Peeters, T., eds.*, 1983, pp. 139–71. **[G: Japan; W. Germany; U.K.; U.S.]**

Argy, Victor. France's Experience with Monetary and Exchange Rate Management: March 1973 to End-1981. *Banca Naz. Lavoro Quart. Rev.*, December 1983, (147), pp. 387–411. **[G: France]**

Artus, Jacques R. Toward a More Orderly Exchange Rate System. *Finance Develop.*, March 1983, *20*(1), pp. 10–13. **[G: U.K.; U.S.; France; Japan; W. Germany]**

Aschauer, David and Greenwood, Jeremy. A Further Exploration in the Theory of Exchange Rate Regimes. *J. Polit. Econ.*, October 1983, *91*(5), pp. 868–75.

Babbel, David F. Determining the Optimum Strategy for Hedging Currency Exposure. *J. Int. Bus. Stud.*, Spring/Summer 1983, *14*(1), pp. 133–39.

Baillie, Richard T.; Lippens, Robert E. and McMahon, Patrick C. Testing Rational Expectations and Efficiency in the Foreign Exchange Market. *Econometrica,* May, 1983, *51*(3), pp. 553–63. **[G: U.S.]**

Banaian, King; Laney, Leroy O. and Willett, Thomas D. Central Bank Independence: An International Comparison. *Fed. Res. Bank Dallas Econ. Rev.*, March 1983, pp. 1–13. **[G: OECD]**

Batten, Dallas S. and Ott, Mack. Five Common Myths about Floating Exchange Rates. *Fed. Res. Bank St. Louis Rev.*, November 1983, *65*(9), pp. 5–15. **[G: U.S.]**

Beckers, Stan and Soenen, Luc A. Gold Options, an Attractive Investment Instrument for the Non–U.S. Investor—The Case of the Belgian and Dutch Investor. *De Economist,* 1983, *131*(1), pp. 80–87. **[G: Belgium; Netherlands]**

Bedoni, Marisa. Il modello a cuspide della teoria delle catastrofi per i mercati valutari: un'applicazione empirica al cambio lira/dollaro. (The Catastrophe Cusp Model for Currencies Markets: An Empirical Application to the Lira/Dollar Rate. With English summary.) *Rivista Int. Sci. Econ. Com.*, October–November 1983, *30*(10–11), pp. 957–70. **[G: Italy; U.S.]**

Beenstock, Michael. Rational Expectations and the Effect of Exchange-Rate Intervention on the Exchange Rate. *J. Int. Money Finance,* December 1983, *2*(3), pp. 319–31.

Beers, David T.; Sargent, Thomas J. and Wallace, Neil. Speculations about the Speculation against the Hong Kong Dollar. *Fed. Res. Bank Minn. Rev.*, Fall 1983, *7*(4), pp. 14–22. **[G: Hong Kong]**

Béguelin, Jean-Pierre; Büttler, Hans-Jürg and Schiltknecht, Kurt. A First Look at Entropy, Monetary Policy, and Expected Inflation Rates in the Determination of Exchange Rates. *Z. Nationalökon.*, Supplement 3, 1983, *43*, pp. 205–20. **[G: Switzerland; Germany; U.S.]**

Beidleman, Carl R.; Hilley, John L. and Greenleaf, James A. Alternatives in Hedging Long-Date Contractual Foreign Exchange Exposure. *Sloan Manage. Rev.*, Summer 1983, *24*(4), pp. 45–54. **[G: U.S.]**

Bennett, Karl M. Exchange Rate Policy and External Imbalance: The Jamaican Experience, 1973–1982. *Soc. Econ. Stud.*, December 1983, *32*(4), pp. 51–72. **[G: Jamaica]**

Bergsten, C. Fred. The Villain Is an Overvalued Dollar. **In** *Bergsten, C. F.*, 1983, *1982,* pp. 79–91. **[G: U.S.]**

Bergsten, C. Fred. What to Do about Japan. **In** *Bergsten, C. F.*, 1983, *1982,* pp. 145–59. **[G: U.S.; Japan]**

Bergsten, C. Fred and Williamson, John. Exchange Rates and Trade Policy. **In** *Cline W. R., ed.*, 1983, pp. 99–120. **[G: U.S.; EEC; Japan]**

Bergstrand, Jeffrey H. Is Exchange Rate Volatility "Excessive"? *New Eng. Econ. Rev.*, September/October 1983, pp. 5–14. **[G: Selected OECD]**

Bergstrand, Jeffrey H. Selected Views of Exchange Rate Determination after a Decade of "Floating." *New Eng. Econ. Rev.*, May/June 1983, pp. 14–29. **[G: U.S.; Japan; W. Germany; Switzerland; U.K.]**

Bhagwati, Jagdish N. Devaluation in a Small Economy with Flexible and Rigid, Real and Nominal, Prices. **In** *Bhagwati, J. N., Vol. 2,* 1983, *1978,* pp. 517–35.

Bhandari, Jagdeep S. Aggregate Dynamics in an Open Economy. *Manchester Sch. Econ. Soc. Stud.*, June 1983, *51* (2), pp. 129–51.

Bhandari, Jagdeep S. An Alternative Theory of Exchange Rate Dynamics. *Quart. J. Econ.*, May 1983, *98* (2), pp. 337–48.

Bhaskar, V. Exchange Rate Fluctuations under a Free Floating Regime. *Indian Econ. Rev.*, January–June 1983, *18* (1), pp. 47–59. **[G: U.S.; Germany; Japan]**

Bigman, David. Exchange Rate Determination: Some Old Myths and New Paradigms. **In** *Bigman, D. and Taya, T., eds.*, 1983, pp. 73–102.

Bigman, David and Lee, Chee Sung. Variability of Exchange and Interest Rates: The Floating Experience. **In** *Bigman, D. and Taya, T., eds.*, 1983, pp. 29–41. **[G: U.K.; W. Germany; Switzerland]**

Bilson, John F. O. The Evaluation and Use of Foreign Exchange Rate Forecasting Services. **In** *Herring, R. J., ed.*, 1983, pp. 149–79. **[G: OECD]**

Bilson, John F. O. and Hooke, A. W. Conference on Exchange Rate Regimes and Policy Interdependence: Overview. *Int. Monet. Fund Staff Pap.*, March 1983, *30* (1), pp. 185–207.

Bisignano, Joseph. Monetary Policy Regimes and International Term Structures of Interest Rates. *Fed. Res. Bank San Francisco Econ. Rev.*, Fall 1983, (4), pp. 7–26. **[G: U.S.; Canada; W. Germany]**

Blackaby, F. Post-mortem on British Economic Policy 1960–76. **In** *[Saunders, C. T.]*, 1983, pp. 259–70. **[G: U.K.]**

Blackhurst, Richard. The Relation between the Current Account and the Exchange Rate: A Survey of the Recent Literature. **In** *De Grauwe, P. and Peeters, T., eds.*, 1983, pp. 58–99. **[G: OECD]**

Blankmeyer, Eric. A Welfare Gain from a Stable Exchange Rate. *Atlantic Econ. J.*, December 1983, *11* (4), pp. 74–75.

Blejer, Mario I. and Khan, Mohsin S. The Foreign Exchange Market in a Highly-Open Developing Economy: The Case of Singapore. *J. Devel. Econ.*, February/April 1983, *12* (1/2), pp. 237–49. **[G: Singapore]**

Bomhoff, Edward J. and Korteweg, Pieter. Exchange Rate Variability and Monetary Policy under Rational Expectations: Some Euro–American Experience, 1973–1979. *J. Monet. Econ.*, March 1983, *11* (2), pp. 169–206. **[G: U.S.; EEC]**

Boothe, Paul M. Speculative Profit Opportunities in the Canadaian Foreign Exchange Market, 1974–78. *Can. J. Econ.*, November 1983, *16* (4), pp. 603–11. **[G: Canada; U.S.]**

Boughton, James M. Alternatives to Intervention: Domestic Instruments and External Objectives. **In** *Hodgman, D. R., ed.*, 1983, pp. 313–30.

Branson, William H. Macroeconomic Determinants of Real Exchange Risk. **In** *Herring, R. J., ed.*, 1983, pp. 33–74. **[G: Japan; U.K.; U.S.; W. Germany]**

Brewer, Thomas L. Political Sources of Risk in the International Money Markets: Conceptual, Methodological, and Interpretive Refinements. *J. Int. Bus. Stud.*, Spring/Summer 1983, *14* (1), pp. 161–64.

Brittan, Samuel. Breaking the Mould. **In** *Brittan, S.*, 1983, pp. 239–63. **[G: U.K.]**

Brodsky, David A. Exchange Rate Changes and the Measurement of Export Instability. *Oxford Bull. Econ. Statist.*, August 1983, *45* (3), pp. 289–96.

Brodsky, David A. and Sampson, Gary P. Exchange Rate Variations Facing Individual Industries in Developing Countries. *J. Devel. Stud.*, April 1983, *19* (3), pp. 349–67. **[G: India; S. Korea; Ivory Coast; Tunisia]**

Browne, F. X. Departures from Interest Rate Parity: Further Evidence. *J. Banking Finance,* June 1983, *7* (2), pp. 253–72. **[G: U.S.; U.K.; Ireland; W. Germany]**

Bruni, Franco. Interest and Exchange Rate Volatility: Implications for Bank Management. *Giorn. Econ.*, July–August 1983, *42* (7–8), pp. 431–58. **[G: OECD]**

Buiter, Willem H. and Miller, Marcus H. Real Exchange Rate Overshooting and the Output Cost of Bringing Down Inflation: Some Further Results. **In** *Frenkel, J. A., ed.*, 1983, pp. 317–58.

Buiter, Willem H. and Purvis, Douglas D. Oil, Disinflation, and Export Competitiveness: A Model of the "Dutch Disease." **In** *Bhandari, J. S. and Putnam, B. H., eds.*, 1983, pp. 221–47.

Burton, David. Flexible Exchange Rates and Perfect Foresight: The Implications of Domestic Monetary Policy for Foreign Prices and Stabilization Policy. *Weltwirtsch. Arch.*, 1983, *119* (2), pp. 201–13.

Buzelay, A. Variation des taux de change, structure des prix relatifs et balance commerciale. (Variations in Exchange Rates, the Structure of Relative Prices and the Trade Balance. With English summary.) *Écon. Soc.*, July-August 1983, *17* (7–8), pp. 1233–57. **[G: W. Germany; U.K.; France]**

Cachin, Antoine. Change et intérêt en flexibilité. (Exchange and Interest in Flexibility. With English summary.) *Écon. Soc.*, July-August 1983, *17* (7–8), pp. 1213–31.

Cachin, Antoine. La politique française de déconnexion des taux d'intérêt. (With English summary.) *Revue Écon. Polit.*, September–October 1983, *93* (5), pp. 732–39. **[G: France]**

Calvo, Guillermo A. Staggered Contracts and Exchange Rate Policy. **In** *Frenkel, J. A., ed.*, 1983, pp. 235–52.

Calvo, Guillermo A. Trying to Stabilize: Some Theoretical Reflections Based on the Case of Argentina. **In** *Armella, P. A.; Dornbusch, R. and Obstfeld, M., eds.*, 1983, pp. 199–216. **[G: Argentina]**

Campfield, Thomas M. and O'Brien, John G. Foreign Exchange Trading Practices: The Interbank Market. **In** *George, A. M. and Giddy, I. H., eds., Vol. 1,* 1983, pp. 2.4:1–25. **[G: Selected Countries]**

Canto, Victor A. and Miles, Marc A. Exchange Rates in a Global Monetary Model with Currency Substitution and Rational Expectations. **In** *Bhandari, J. S. and Putnam, B. H., eds.*, 1983, pp. 157–75.

Caprio, Jerry and Clark, Peter B. Oil Price Shocks in a Portfolio-Balance Model. *J. Econ. Bus.*, June 1983, *35* (2), pp. 221–33. **[G: U.S.]**

Cardoso, Eliana A. Exchange Rates in Nineteenth-Century Brazil: An Econometric Model. *J. Devel. Stud.*, January 1983, *19*(2), pp. 170–78. **[G: Brazil]**

Carlozzi, Nicholas. Exchange Rate Systems and Linkages. **In** *George, A. M. and Giddy, I. H., eds., Vol. 1,* 1983, pp. 2.1:1–31.

Casas, F. R. Stabilité des marchés de change au comptant et à terme: une approche d'équilibre simultané. (Stability of the Spot and Forward Exchange Markets: A Simultaneous Equilibrium Approach. With English summary.) *L'Actual. Econ.*, June 1983, *59*(2), pp. 240–65.

de Cecco, Marcello. The Vicious/Virtuous Circle Debate in the Twenties and the Seventies. *Banca Naz. Lavoro Quart. Rev.*, September 1983, (146), pp. 285–303. **[G: Europe]**

Chen, Chau-nan and Tsaur, Tien-wang. Currency Substitution and Foreign Inflation. *Quart. J. Econ.*, February 1983, *98*(1), pp. 177–84.

Choudhri, Ehsan U. The Transmission of Inflation in a Small Economy: An Empirical Analysis of the Influence of U.S. Monetary Disturbances on Canadian Inflation, 1962–80. *J. Int. Money Finance,* August 1983, *2*(2), pp. 167–78. **[G: Canada]**

Chrystal, K. Alec; Wilson, Nigel D. and Quinn, Philip. Demand for International Money, 1962–1977. *Europ. Econ. Rev.*, May 1983, *21*(3), pp. 287–98.

Chung, Jae Wan. Substitutability between Currencies: The Dollar versus the Mark and the Yen. *Quart. Rev. Econ. Bus.*, Autumn 1983, *23*(3), pp. 19–28. **[G: U.S.; Japan; W. Germany]**

Claassen, Emil-Maria. Aspects of the Optimal Management of Exchange Rates. **In** *Claassen, E. and Salin, P., eds.*, 1983, pp. 226–30.

Claassen, Emil-Maria. The Keynesian and Classical Determination of the Exchange Rate. *Weltwirtsch. Arch.*, 1983, *119*(1), pp. 19–35.

Claassen, Emil-Maria. The Nominal and Real Exchange Rate in a Quantity-Theoretical Two-Country Model. **In** *Claassen, E. and Salin, P., eds.*, 1983, pp. 57–68.

Claassen, Emil-Maria. What Are the Scope and Limits of Fruitful International Monetary Cooperation in the 1980s? Comment. **In** *von Furstenberg, G. M., ed.*, 1983, pp. 409–19.

Coes, Donald V. Exchange Market Intervention in Four European Countries. **In** *Hodgman, D. R., ed.*, 1983, pp. 206–22. **[G: France; W. Germany; U.K.; Italy]**

Connolly, Michael B. Exchange Rates, Real Economic Activity and the Balance of Payments: Evidence from the 1960s. **In** *Claassen, E. and Salin, P., eds.*, 1983, pp. 129–43. **[G: Selected Countries]**

Connolly, Michael B. Optimum Currency Pegs for Latin America. *J. Money, Credit, Banking,* February 1983, *15*(1), pp. 56–72. **[G: Latin America]**

Corden, Warner Max. The Logic of the International Monetary Non-system. **In** *[Giersch, H.],* 1983, pp. 59–74. **[G: OECD]**

Cortés Douglas, Hernán. Políticas de estabilización en Chile: inflación, desempleo y depresión 1975–1982. (With English summary.) *Cuadernos Econ.*, August 1983, *20*(60), pp. 149–75. **[G: Chile]**

Cross, Sam Y. Treasury and Federal Reserve Foreign Exchange Operations: Interim Report. *Fed. Res. Bull.*, December 1983, *69*(12), pp. 893–95. **[G: U.S.]**

Cross, Sam Y. Treasury and Federal Reserve Foreign Exchange Operations: Interim Report. *Fed. Res. Bull.*, June 1983, *69*(6), pp. 404–08. **[G: U.S.]**

Cross, Sam Y. Treasury and Federal Reserve Foreign Exchange Operations. *Fed. Res. Bull.*, September 1983, *69*(9), pp. 672–92. **[G: U.S.]**

Cross, Sam Y. Treasury and Federal Reserve Foreign Exchange Operations. *Fed. Res. Bull.*, March 1983, *69*(3), pp. 141–63. **[G: U.S.]**

Cross, Sam Y. Treasury and Federal Reserve Foreign Exchange Operations. *Fed. Res. Bank New York Quart. Rev.*, Spring 1983, *8*(1), pp. 55–78. **[G: U.S.]**

Cross, Sam Y. Treasury and Federal Reserve Foreign Exchange Operations. *Fed. Res. Bank New York Quart. Rev.*, Autumn 1983, *8*(3), pp. 48–68. **[G: U.S.]**

Cross, Sam Y. Treasury and Federal Reserve Foreign Exchange Operations. *Fed. Res. Bank New York Quart. Rev.*, Winter 1983-84, *8*(4), pp. 71–74. **[G: U.S.]**

Cross, Sam Y. Treasury and Federal Reserve Foreign Exchange Operations. *Fed. Res. Bank New York Quart. Rev.*, Summer 1983, *8*(2), pp. 45–49. **[G: U.S.]**

Cuddington, John T. Currency Substitution, Capital Mobility and Money Demand. *J. Int. Money Finance,* August 1983, *2*(2), pp. 111–33. **[G: Canada; W. Germany; U.K.; U.S.]**

Cushman, David O. The Effects of Real Exchange Rate Risk on International Trade. *J. Int. Econ.*, August 1983, *15*(1/2), pp. 45–63. **[G: N. America; Japan; U.K.; France; W. Germany]**

Daněček, Jiří. The Basic Relationships between Foreign Exchange Instruments, Prices, and the Plan. *Soviet E. Europ. Foreign Trade,* Fall 1983, *19*(3), pp. 50–79. **[G: Czechoslovakia]**

Daniel, Betty C. and Fried, Harold O. Currency Substitution, Postal Strikes, and Canadian Money Demand. *Can. J. Econ.*, November 1983, *16*(4), pp. 612–24. **[G: Canada]**

Darby, Michael R. International Transmission under Pegged and Floating Exchange Rates: An Empirical Comparison. **In** *Bhandari, J. S. and Putnam, B. H., eds.*, 1983, pp. 427–71. **[G: OECD]**

Darby, Michael R. International Transmission of Monetary and Fiscal Shocks under Pegged and Floating Exchange Rates: Simulation Experiments. **In** *Darby, M. P. and Lothian, J. R., et al.*, 1983, pp. 162–231. **[G: OECD]**

Darby, Michael R. Movements in Purchasing Power Parity: The Short and Long Runs. **In** *Darby, M. P. and Lothian, J. R., et al.*, 1983, pp. 462–77. **[G: OECD]**

De Grauwe, Paul. Exchange Rate Oscillations and Catastrophe Theory. **In** *Claassen, E. and Salin, P., eds.*, 1983, pp. 181–93.

De Grauwe, Paul. Symptoms of an Overvalued Currency: The Case of the Belgian Franc. **In** *de Cecco, M., ed.*, 1983, pp. 99–116. **[G: Belgium]**

De Grauwe, Paul. What Are the Scope and Limits of Fruitful International Monetary Cooperation in the 1980s? **In** *von Furstenberg, G. M., ed.,* 1983, pp. 375–408. **[G: OECD]**

Deardorff, Alan V. and Stern, Robert M. Tariff and Exchange Rate Protection under Fixed and Flexible Exchange Rates in the Major Industrialized Countries. **In** *Bhandari, J. S. and Putnam, B. H., eds.,* 1983, pp. 472–99. **[G: OECD]**

Dell, Sidney. Stabilization: The Political Economy of Overkill. **In** *Williamson, J., ed.,* 1983, pp. 17–45.

Desai, Padma and Bhagwati, Jagdish N. Three Alternative Concepts of Foreign Exchange Difficulties in Centrally Planned Economies. **In** *Bhagwati, J. N., Vol. 2,* 1983, *1979,* pp. 536–46.

Díaz Alejandro, Carlos F. Stories of the 1930s for the 1980s. **In** *Armella, P. A.; Dornbusch, R. and Obstfeld, M., eds.,* 1983, pp. 5–35. **[G: Latin America]**

Djajić, Slobodan. Intermediate Inputs and International Trade: An Analysis of the Real and Monetary Aspects of a Change in the Price of Oil. *J. Int. Money Finance,* August 1983, *2*(2), pp. 179–95.

Dombrecht, Michel. Exchange-Rate Modelling in the EPA World Economic Model: Comment. **In** *De Grauwe, P. and Peeters, T., eds.,* 1983, pp. 172–74. **[G: Japan; U.S.; U.K.; W. Germany]**

Dooley, Michael P. and Isard, Peter. The Portfolio-Balance Model of Exchange Rates and Some Structural Estimates of the Risk Premium. *Int. Monet. Fund Staff Pap.,* December 1983, *30*(4), pp. 683–702. **[G: U.S.; W. Germany]**

Dooley, Michael P. and Shafer, Jeffrey R. Analysis of Short-run Exchange Rate Behavior: March 1973 to November 1981. **In** *Bigman, D. and Taya, T., eds.,* 1983, pp. 43–69. **[G: OECD]**

Dornbusch, Rudiger. Exchange Rate Economics: Where Do We Stand? **In** *Bhandari, J. S. and Putnam, B. H., eds.,* 1983, pp. 45–83.

Dornbusch, Rudiger. Exchange Rate Risk and the Macroeconomics of Exchange Rate Determination. **In** *Hawkins, R. G.; Levich, R. M. and Wihlborg, C. G., eds.,* 1983, pp. 3–27.

Dornbusch, Rudiger. Tassi di cambio di equilibrio e di disequilibrio. (Equilibrium and Disequilibrium Exchange Rates. With English summary.) *Bancaria,* May–June 1983, *39*(5–6), pp. 455–70.

Dornbusch, Rudiger, et al. The Black Market for Dollars in Brazil. *Quart. J. Econ.,* February 1983, *98*(1), pp. 25–40. **[G: Brazil]**

Dramais, André. A Portfolio Approach to the Determination of Exchange Rates within a Multicountry Model: Comment. **In** *De Grauwe, P. and Peeters, T., eds.,* 1983, pp. 208–09.

Dudley, Leonard. A Non-Linear Model of Import Demand under Price Uncertainty and Adjustment Costs. *Can. J. Econ.,* November 1983, *16*(4), pp. 625–40. **[G: OECD]**

Dumas, Bernard and Poncet, Patrice. La demande de dollars des agents économiques ne résidant pas aux U.S.A. (The Dollar Demand of Non-Resident Economic Agents in the U.S.A. With English summary.) *Écon. Soc.,* July-August 1983, *17*(7–8), pp. 1185–1212.

Edwards, Sebastian. An Accounting Framework and Some Issues for Modeling How Exchange Rates Respond to the News: Comment. **In** *Frenkel, J. A., ed.,* 1983, pp. 56–61. **[G: OECD]**

Edwards, Sebastian. Floating Exchange Rates in Less-Developed Countries: A Monetary Analysis of the Peruvian Experience, 1950–54. *J. Money, Credit, Banking,* February 1983, *15*(1), pp. 73–81. **[G: Peru]**

Edwards, Sebastian. Floating Exchange Rates, Expectations and New Information. *J. Monet. Econ.,* May 1983, *11*(3), pp. 321–36.

Edwards, Sebastian. La relacion entre las tasas de interes y el tipo de cambio bajo un sistema de cambio flotante. (With English summary.) *Cuadernos Econ.,* April 1983, *20*(59), pp. 65–74.

Edwards, Sebastian. The Demand for International Reserves and Exchange Rate Adjustments: The Case of LDCs, 1964–1972. *Economica,* August 1983, *50*(199), pp. 269–80. **[G: LDCs]**

Eichengreen, Barry J. Effective Projection and Exchange-Rate Determination. *J. Int. Money Finance,* April 1983, *2*(1), pp. 1–15.

Einzig, Robert S. Comments on "Techniques and Success in Forecasting Exchange Rates: Should It Be Done? Does It Matter? The Long and the Short of It." **In** *Hawkins, R. G.; Levich, R. M. and Wihlborg, C. G., eds.,* 1983, pp. 187–91.

Eisenmenger, Robert W. Alternatives to Intervention: Domestic Instruments and External Objectives: Discussion. **In** *Hodgman, D. R., ed.,* 1983, pp. 331–35.

Ffrench-Davis, Ricardo. Trying to Stabilize: Some Theoretical Reflections Based on the Case of Argentina: Comment. **In** *Armella, P. A.; Dornbusch, R. and Obstfeld, M., eds.,* 1983, pp. 217–20. **[G: Argentina]**

Fieleke, Norman S. Exchange Market Intervention in Four European Countries: Discussion. **In** *Hodgman, D. R., ed.,* 1983, pp. 223–27. **[G: France; U.K.; W. Germany; Italy]**

Filc, Wolfgang. Internationale Wirschaft- und Währungsprobleme: Floating, Arbeitslosigkeit und Geldpolitik. (International Economic and Monetary Problems: Floating, Unemployment and Monetary Policy. With English summary.) *Kredit Kapital,* 1983, *16*(1), pp. 81–97. **[G: W. Germany]**

Fischer, Stanley. Comments on "The Effect of Risk on Interest Rates: A Synthesis of the Macroeconomic and Financial Views." **In** *Hawkins, R. G.; Levich, R. M. and Wihlborg, C. G., eds.,* 1983, pp. 321–25.

Fischer, Stanley. Optimal Stabilization and the Proper Exercise of the Monetary-Policy Instruments under Flexible Exchange Rates: Comment. **In** *Claassen, E. and Salin, P., eds.,* 1983, pp. 256–59.

Flassbeck, Heiner. Das Leistungsbilanzrätsel. Eine kritische Betrachtung zum Stand der Wechselkurstheorie. (The Riddle of the German Balance of Payments—A Critical Assessment of the State of Exchange Rate Theory. With English summary.) *Konjunkturpolitik,* 1983, *29*(5), pp. 261–84. **[G: W. Germany]**

Flood, Robert P. Real Exchange Rate Overshooting

and the Output Cost of Bringing Down Inflation: Some Further Results: Comment. **In** *Frenkel, J. A., ed.*, 1983, pp. 359–65.

Flood, Robert P. and Marion, Nancy P. Exchange-Rate Regimes in Transition: Italy 1974. *J. Int. Money Finance,* December 1983, *2*(3), pp. 279–94. **[G: Italy]**

Ford, Robert P. Contracts, the Trade Account, and Deviations from Purchasing Power Parity in Equilibrium. *Southern Econ. J.*, April 1983, *49*(4), pp. 1066–76.

Frank, Isaiah. Trade Policy in the 1980s: The Setting: Comment. **In** *Cline W. R., ed.*, 1983, pp. 210–15.

Frankel, Jeffrey A. An Accounting Framework and Some Issues for Modeling How Exchange Rates Respond to the News: Comment. **In** *Frenkel, J. A., ed.*, 1983, pp. 61–65. **[G: OECD]**

Frankel, Jeffrey A. Monetary and Portfolio-Balance Models of Exchange Rate Determination. **In** *Bhandari, J. S. and Putnam, B. H., eds.*, 1983, pp. 84–115. **[G: U.S.; W. Germany]**

Frankel, Jeffrey A. The Effect of Excessively Elastic Expectations on Exchange-Rate Volatility in the Dornbusch Overshooting Model. *J. Int. Money Finance,* April 1983, *2*(1), pp. 39–46.

Frenkel, Jacob A. Comments on "Exchange Rate Risk and the Macroeconomics of Exchange Rate Determination." **In** *Hawkins, R. G.; Levich, R. M. and Wihlborg, C. G., eds.*, 1983, pp. 29–34.

Frenkel, Jacob A. Flexible Exchange Rates, Prices, and the Role of "News": Lessons from the 1970s. **In** *Bhandari, J. S. and Putnam, B. H., eds.*, 1983, pp. 3–41. **[G: U.S.]**

Frenkel, Jacob A. International Liquidity and Monetary Control. **In** *Kaushik, S. K., ed.*, 1983, pp. 31–72. **[G: LDCs; MDCs]**

Frenkel, Jacob A. International Liquidity and Monetary Control. **In** *von Furstenberg, G. M., ed.*, 1983, pp. 65–109. **[G: Selected Countries]**

Frenkel, Jacob A. Turbulence in the Foreign Exchange Markets and Macroeconomic Policies. **In** *Bigman, D. and Taya, T., eds.*, 1983, pp. 3–27. **[G: U.S.; France; U.K.; W. Germany]**

Frenkel, Jacob A. and Aizenman, Joshua. Aspects of the Optimal Management of Exchange Rates. **In** *Claassen, E. and Salin, P., eds.*, 1983, pp. 201–25.

Frisch, Helmut. Stabilization Policy in Austria, 1970–80. **In** *de Cecco, M., ed.*, 1983, pp. 117–40. **[G: Austria]**

Fukao, Mitsuhiro. The Risk Premium in the Foreign Exchange Market. *Z. Nationalökon.*, Supplement 3, 1983, *43,* pp. 99–125. **[G: Japan; U.S.]**

von Furstenberg, George M. Changes in U.S. Interest Rates and Their Effects on European Interest and Exchange Rates. **In** *Bigman, D. and Taya, T., eds.*, 1983, pp. 257–82. **[G: U.S.; U.K.; W. Germany; France]**

Galambert, Patrice. La valutazione del rischio di cambio: teoria e practica. (Evaluation of Exchange Risks: Theory and Practice. With English summary.) *Mondo Aperto,* January–February 1983, *37*(1), pp. 1–9.

Gardner, Grant W. The Choice of Monetary Policy Instruments in an Open Economy. *J. Int. Money Finance,* December 1983, *2*(3), pp. 347–54.

Garman, Mark B. and Kohlhagen, Steven W. Foreign Currency Option Values. *J. Int. Money Finance,* December 1983, *2*(3), pp. 231–37.

Gärtner, Manfred and Heri, Erwin W. Konjunktur und realer Wechselkurs. Eine Kausalitätsanalyse für neum OECD-Länder. (The Trade Cycle and Real Exchange Rates: A Causality Analysis for Nine OECD Countries. With English summary.) *Kredit Kapital,* 1983, *16*(1), pp. 98–116. **[G: OECD]**

George, Abraham M. Currency Exposure Management. **In** *George, A. M. and Giddy, I. H., eds., Vol. 2,* 1983, pp. 8.8:1–33.

Gewalt, Staffan. Quanto durerá la forza del dollaro? (How Long Will the Dollar Strength Last? With English summary.) *Mondo Aperto,* January–February 1983, *37*(1), pp. 11–14. **[G: U.S.]**

Gidday, Ian H. Foreign Exchange Options. *J. Futures Markets,* Summer 1983, *3*(2), pp. 143–66.

Giddy, Ian H. and Ho, Sang Kang. Mathematics of International Finance. **In** *George, A. M. and Giddy, I. H., eds., Vol. 2,* 1983, pp. A1–51. **[G: OECD]**

Giovannini, Alberto. An Alternative Test of the Rational Expectations-Perfect Substitutability Hypothesis: Deutsche Mark and Pound Sterling. *Empirical Econ.*, 1983, *8*(1), pp. 59–62. **[G: U.S.; U.K.; W. Germany]**

Glassman, Debra. Rational Expectations and the Foreign Exchange Market: Comment. **In** *Frenkel, J. A., ed.*, 1983, pp. 177–80. **[G: U.K.; U.S.; W. Germany]**

Golub, Stephen S. Oil Prices and Exchange Rates. *Econ. J.*, September 1983, *93*(371), pp. 576–93.

Grabbe, J. Orlin. The Pricing of Call and Put Options on Foreign Exchange. *J. Int. Money Finance,* December 1983, *2*(3), pp. 239–53.

Grammatikos, Theoharry and Saunders, Anthony. Stability and the Hedging Performance of Foreign Currency Futures. *J. Futures Markets,* Fall 1983, *3*(3), pp. 295–305. **[G: Canada; U.K.; Japan; W. Germany; Switzerland]**

Grissa, Abdessatar. The French Monetary and Exchange Rate Experience in the 1920s. **In** *Claassen, E. and Salin, P., eds.*, 1983, pp. 261–80. **[G: France]**

Gruben, William C. and Lawler, Patrick J. Currency Substitution: The Use of Dollar Coin and Currency in the Texas Border Area of Mexico. *Fed. Res. Bank Dallas Econ. Rev.*, July 1983, pp. 10–20. **[G: Mexico; U.S.]**

Gutierrez-Camara, José L. and Huss, Hans-Joachim. The Interaction between Floating Exchange Rates, Money, and Prices—An Empirical Analysis. *Weltwirtsch. Arch.*, 1983, *119*(3), pp. 401–28. **[G: U.S.; Japan; Canada; W. Europe]**

Guy, James R. F. Comments on "A Simple Approach to the Pricing of Risky Assets with Uncertain Exchange Rates." **In** *Hawkins, R. G.; Levich, R. M. and Wihlborg, C. G., eds.*, 1983, pp. 61–67.

Haberler, Gottfried. Trade Policy in the 1980s: The Setting: Comment. **In** *Cline W. R., ed.*, 1983, pp. 203–09.

Hacche, Graham and Townend, John C. Some Problems in Exchange Rate Modelling: The Case of Sterling. Z. *Nationalökon.*, Supplement 3, 1983, *43*, pp. 127–62. **[G: U.S.; U.K.]**

Hagemann, Helmut. Anticipate Your Long-term Foreign Exchange Risks. **In** *Dickson, D. N., ed.*, 1983, pp. 515–26.

Hakkio, Craig S. Risk Averse Speculation in the Forward Foreign Exchange Market: An Econometric Analysis of Linear Models: Comment. **In** *Frenkel, J. A., ed.*, 1983, pp. 142–46. **[G: OECD]**

Hall, S. The Exchange Rate. **In** *Britton, A., ed.*, 1983, pp. 79–90. **[G: U.K.]**

Halttunen, Hannu and Korkman, Sixten. External Shocks and Adjustment Policies in Finland, 1973–80. **In** *de Cecco, M., ed.*, 1983, pp. 7–33. **[G: Finland]**

Hamaui, Rony. Regolarità ed anomalie nel comportamento del tasso di cambio della lira durante gli anni '70: l'ipotesi di "random walk." (Regularities and Anomolies of the Behaviour of the Lira Exchange Rate during the '70s: The Random Walk Hypothesis. With English summary.) *Rivista Int. Sci. Econ. Com.*, October–November 1983, *30*(10–11), pp. 935–56. **[G: Italy]**

Hansen, Lars Peter and Hodrick, Robert J. Risk Averse Speculation in the Forward Foreign Exchange Market: An Econometric Analysis of Linear Models. **In** *Frenkel, J. A., ed.*, 1983, pp. 113–42. **[G: OECD]**

Hartley, Peter R. Rational Expectations and the Foreign Exchange Market. **In** *Frenkel, J. A., ed.*, 1983, pp. 153–77. **[G: U.K.; U.S.; W. Germany]**

Helliwell, John F. and Boothe, Paul M. Macroeconomic Implications of Alternative Exchange-Rate Models. **In** *De Grauwe, P. and Peeters, T., eds.*, 1983, pp. 21–53. **[G: Canada]**

Henner, Henri-François and Yvernault, Jean-Jacques. Les dévaluations du franc depuis 1981. (With English summary.) *Revue Écon. Polit.*, September–October 1983, *93*(5), pp. 751–60. **[G: France]**

Herring, Richard J. Managing Foreign Exchange Risk: Introduction and Overview. **In** *Herring, R. J., ed.*, 1983, pp. 1–31.

Heymann, H. G. and Venkataraman, V. K. An Empirical Study of the Marginal Reserve Requirements and the Exchange Value of the Dollar. *Bus. Econ.*, May 1983, *18*(3), pp. 55–61. **[G: U.S.]**

Hickman, Bert G. Exchange Rates in Project LINK. **In** *De Grauwe, P. and Peeters, T., eds.*, 1983, pp. 103–33. **[G: OECD]**

Holtfrerich, Carl-Ludwig. Wechselkurssystem und Philipps-Kurve: Erwiderung und Kommentar. (Exchange Rate System and Philipps Curve: Reply and Comment. With English summary.) *Kredit Kapital*, 1983, *16*(2), pp. 242–52.

Honohan, Patrick. Measures of Exchange Rate Variability for One Hundred Countries. *Appl. Econ.*, October 1983, *15*(5), pp. 583–602. **[G: Global]**

Hool, Bryce and Richardson, J. David. International Trade, Indebtedness, and Welfare Repercussions among Supply-constrained Economies under Floating Exchange Rates. **In** *Bhandari, J. S. and Putnam, B. H., eds.*, 1983, pp. 402–24. **[G: U.S.]**

Hooper, Peter; Haas, Richard D. and Symansky, Steven A. Revision of Exchange-Rate Determination in the MCM. **In** *De Grauwe, P. and Peeters, T., eds.*, 1983, pp. 210–35. **[G: U.S.]**

Hooper, Peter, et al. Alternative Approaches to General Equilibrium Modeling of Exchange Rates and Capital Flows: The MCM Experience. Z. *Nationalökon.*, Supplement 3, 1983, *43*, pp. 29–60. **[G: N. America; Germany; Japan; U.K.; OPEC]**

Horne, Jocelyn. The Asset Market Model of the Balance of Payments and the Exchange Rate: A Survey of Empirical Evidence. *J. Int. Money Finance*, August 1983, *2*(2), pp. 89–109. **[G: Italy; Australia; Netherlands; W. Germany; U.K.]**

Hughes, M. The Consequences of the Removal of Exchange Controls on Portfolios and the Flow of Funds in the U.K. **In** *Corner, D. and Mayes, D. G., eds.*, 1983, pp. 181–206. **[G: U.K.]**

Igawa, Kazuhiro. Some Evidences between Foreign Direct Investments and Foreign Exchange Rates: A Preliminary Note. *Kobe Econ. Bus. Rev.*, 1983, (29), pp. 21–32. **[G: U.K.; W. Germany; U.S.; Japan]**

Ijiri, Yuji. Foreign Currency Accounting and Its Transition. **In** *Herring, R. J., ed.*, 1983, pp. 181–212. **[G: U.S.]**

Isachsen, Arne Jon. Norwegian Economic Policy in the Past Decade and Some Thoughts on Policy in the Present One. **In** *de Cecco, M., ed.*, 1983, pp. 49–64. **[G: Norway]**

Isard, Peter. An Accounting Framework and Some Issues for Modeling How Exchange Rates Respond to the News. **In** *Frenkel, J. A., ed.*, 1983, pp. 19–56.

Islam, Shafiqul. Currency Misalignments: The Case of the Dollar and the Yen. *Fed. Res. Bank New York Quart. Rev.*, Winter 1983-84, *8*(4), pp. 49–60. **[G: Japan; U.S.]**

Johnson, Mark J. U.S. Foreign Trade Prices in 1982: Import Index Falls, Export Indexes Mixed. *Mon. Lab. Rev.*, May 1983, *106*(5), pp. 20–29. **[G: U.S.]**

Jones, Ronald W. and Purvis, Douglas D. International Differences in Response to Common External Shocks: The Role of Purchasing Power Parity. **In** *Claassen, E. and Salin, P., eds.*, 1983, pp. 33–55.

Kafka, Alexandre. Gold and International Monetary Stability. *Cato J.*, Spring 1983, *3*(1), pp. 277–80. **[G: Global]**

Kaldor, Nicholas. Devaluation and Adjustment in Developing Countries. *Finance Develop.*, June 1983, *20*(2), pp. 35–37.

Kapur, Basant K. Optimal Financial and Foreign-Exchange Liberalization of Less Developed Economies. *Quart. J. Econ.*, February 1983, *98*(1), pp. 41–62.

Karlik, John R. Comments on "Exchange Rate Risk and the Macroeconomics of Exchange Rate Determination." **In** *Hawkins, R. G.; Levich, R. M. and Wihlborg, C. G., eds.*, 1983, pp. 35–37.

Kästli, René. The New Economic Environment in the 1970s: Market and Policy Response in Switzerland. **In** *de Cecco, M., ed.*, 1983, pp. 141–59. **[G: Switzerland]**

Katseli, Louka T. Devaluation: A Critical Appraisal of the IMF's Policy Prescriptions. *Amer. Econ. Rev.*, May 1983, *73*(2), pp. 359–63.

Katseli, Louka T. Exchange Rates and Food in the European Community. *Europ. Econ. Rev.*, January 1983, *20*(1–3), pp. 319–32. **[G: EEC]**

Katseli, Louka T. Macroeconomic Adjustment and Exchange-Rate Policy in Middle-Income Countries: Greece, Portugal and Spain in the 1970s. **In** *de Cecco, M., ed.*, 1983, pp. 189–211. **[G: Greece; Portugal; Spain]**

Kaufmann, Hugo M. Two Decades of Inflation in Western Industrialized Countries under Fixed and Flexible Exchange Rates. **In** *Schmukler, N. and Marcus, E., eds.*, 1983, pp. 707–20. **[G: OECD]**

Kawai, Masahiro. Exchange Rate Volatility and Balance-of-Payments Instability in a Rational Expectations Model of Forward Exchange. **In** *Bigman, D. and Taya, T., eds.*, 1983, pp. 167–94.

Kenen, Peter B. Perspective: Problems in Modeling International Risks [Modeling Exchange Rate Fluctuations and International Disturbances]. **In** *Herring, R. J., ed.*, 1983, pp. 109–13. **[G: Global]**

Kimbrough, Kent P. Exchange-Rate Policy and Monetary Information. *J. Int. Money Finance*, December 1983, *2*(3), pp. 333–46.

Kimbrough, Kent P. The Information Content of the Exchange Rate and the Stability of Real Output under Alternative Exchange-Rate Regimes. *J. Int. Money Finance*, April 1983, *2*(1), pp. 27–38.

King, David T. Uncertainty and Exchange Rate Stability. **In** *Kaushik, S. K., ed.*, 1983, pp. 73–90.

Kitching, Beverly. Don't Blame the Arabs: World Wide Inflation Built In before the Oil Crisis. *Rivista Int. Sci. Econ. Com.*, June 1983, *30*(6), pp. 561–65. **[G: U.S.]**

Klein Haneveld, Henk A. Perspective: International Portfolio Diversification: A Practitioner's Point of View. **In** *Herring, R. J., ed.*, 1983, pp. 143–47. **[G: OECD]**

Klein, Lawrence R. Modeling Exchange Rate Fluctuations and International Disturbances. **In** *Herring, R. J., ed.*, 1983, pp. 85–109. **[G: Global]**

Knight, Malcolm D. and Mathieson, Donald J. Economic Change and Policy Response in Canada under Fixed and Flexible Exchange Rates. **In** *Bhandari, J. S. and Putnam, B. H., eds.*, 1983, pp. 500–529. **[G: Canada]**

Komiya, Ryutaro. International Liquidity and Monetary Control: Comment. **In** *von Furstenberg, G. M., ed.*, 1983, pp. 110–15.

Kouri, Pentti J. K. Balance of Payments and the Foreign Exchange Market: A Dynamic Partial Equilibrium Model. **In** *Bhandari, J. S. and Putnam, B. H., eds.*, 1983, pp. 116–56.

Kouri, Pentti J. K. Macroeconomic Adjustment to Interest Rate Disturbances: Real and Monetary Aspects. **In** *Claassen, E. and Salin, P., eds.*, 1983, pp. 73–97.

Kouri, Pentti J. K. Oil Shocks and Exchange Rate Dynamics: Comment. **In** *Frenkel, J. A., ed.*, 1983, pp. 272–80.

Kouri, Pentti J. K. The Effect of Risk on Interest Rates: A Synthesis of the Macroeconomic and Financial Views. **In** *Hawkins, R. G.; Levich, R. M. and Wihlborg, C. G., eds.*, 1983, pp. 301–20.

Krelle, Wilhelm E. and Sarrazin, Hermann T. Capital Flows and the Exchange Rate in the Bonn Model 11. *Z. Nationalökon.*, Supplement 3, 1983, *43*, pp. 163–201. **[G: Germany]**

Kröger, Jürgen. Devisenkurse, Leistungsbilanz und interne Anpassungsprozesse. (Exchange Rates, the Current Account Balance, and Internal Adjustment Processes. With English summary.) *Konjunkturpolitik*, 1983, *29*(1), pp. 1–20. **[G: W. Germany]**

Krugman, Paul R. Oil and the Dollar. **In** *Bhandari, J. S. and Putnam, B. H., eds.*, 1983, pp. 179–90.

Krugman, Paul R. Oil Shocks and Exchange Rate Dynamics. **In** *Frenkel, J. A., ed.*, 1983, pp. 259–71.

Kurabayashi, Yoshimasa and Sakuma, Itsuo. Alternative Matrix Consistent Methods of Multilateral Comparisons for Real Product and Prices. **In** *[Yamada, I.]*, 1983, pp. 127–41. **[G: Selected LDCs; Selected MDCs]**

Lamfalussy, Alexandre. Implications of Monetary Targeting for Exchange-rate Policy: Exchange-rate Management and the Conduct of Monetary Policy: Comment. **In** *Meek, P., ed.*, 1983, pp. 132–33. **[G: W. Germany; Japan]**

Lamfalussy, Alexandre. Investment and the International Monetary and Financial Environment. **In** *Heertje, A., ed.*, 1983, pp. 56–71. **[G: U.S.; EEC]**

Lang, Peter and Ohr, Renate. Wechselkurssystem und Philipps-Kurve—Neue ökonometrisch fundierte Thesen zuar aktuellen Diskussion um die "beste" Währungsordnung. (Exchange Rate System and Philipps Curve—New Econometrically Founded Theses to the Actual Discussion on the "Best" Currency System. With English summary.) *Kredit Kapital*, 1983, *16*(2), pp. 231–41.

Laskar, Daniel M. Short-run Independence of Monetary Policy under a Pegged Exchange-Rates System: An Econometric Approach. **In** *Darby, M. P. and Lothian, J. R., et al.*, 1983, pp. 314–48. **[G: OECD]**

Lee, Dan. Effects of Open Market Operations and Foreign Exchange Market Operations under Flexible Exchange Rates. **In** *Darby, M. P. and Lothian, J. R., et al.*, 1983, pp. 349–79.

Leone, Alfonso. Some Preliminary Remarks on the Study of Foreign Currency Exchange in the Medieval Period. *J. Europ. Econ. Hist.*, Winter 1983, *12*(3), pp. 619–29.

Levich, Richard M. Comments on "Techniques and Success in Forecasting Exchange Rates: Should It Be Done? Does It Matter? The Long and the Short of It." **In** *Hawkins, R. G.; Levich, R. M. and Wihlborg, C. G., eds.*, 1983, pp. 181–86.

Levich, Richard M. Exchange Rate Forecasting Techniques. **In** *George, A. M. and Giddy, I. H., eds., Vol. 2*, 1983, pp. 8.1:1–30.

Levy, Haim and Sarnat, Marshall. International Portfolio Diversification. **In** *Herring, R. J., ed.*, 1983, pp. 115–42. **[G: OECD]**

Lewis, W. Arthur. The Less Developed Countries and Stable Exchange Rates. **In** *Lewis, W. A.*, 1983, *1978*, pp. 707–18.

Lizondo, José Saúl. Foreign Exchange Futures Prices under Fixed Exchange Rates. *J. Int. Econ.*, February 1983, *14*(1/2), pp. 69–84. **[G: Mexico]**

Lizondo, José Saúl. Interest Differential and Covered Arbitrage. **In** *Armella, P. A.; Dornbusch,*

R. and Obstfeld, M., eds., 1983, pp. 221–40. [G: Mexico; U.S.]

Llewellyn, David T. EC Monetary Arrangements: Britain's Strategy. **In** *El-Agraa, A. M., ed.*, 1983, pp. 251–70. [G: EEC; U.K.]

MacDonald, Ronald. Some Tests of the Rational Expectations Hypothesis in the Foreign Exchange Market. *Scot. J. Polit. Econ.*, November 1983, *30*(3), pp. 235–50. [G: Canada; W. Europe]

MacDonald, Ronald. Tests of Efficiency and the Impact of 'News' in Three Foreign Exchange Markets: The Experience of the 1920's. *Bull. Econ. Res.*, November 1983, *35*(2), pp. 123–44. [G: France; U.K.; U.S.]

de Macedo, Jorge Braga. A Portfolio Model of an Inconvertible Currency: The Recent Experience of Portugal. **In** *de Cecco, M., ed.*, 1983, pp. 212–49. [G: Portugal]

Maciejewski, Edouard B. "Real" Effective Exchange Rate Indices: A Re-Examination of the Major Conceptual and Methodological Issues. *Int. Monet. Fund Staff Pap.*, September 1983, *30*(3), pp. 491–541.

Madura, Jeff. Empirical Measurement of Exchange Rate Betas. *J. Portfol. Manage.*, Summer 1983, *9*(4), pp. 43–46. [G: Switzerland; EEC; U.S.; Canada; Japan]

Madura, Jeff and Nosari, E. Joe. Speculation in International Money Markets. *Atlantic Econ. J.*, July 1983, *11*(2), pp. 87–90.

Makin, John H. Techniques and Success in Forecasting Exchange Rates: Should It Be Done? Does It Matter? The Long and the Short of It. **In** *Hawkins, R. G.; Levich, R. M. and Wihlborg, C. G., eds.*, 1983, pp. 149–80.

Mancera, Miguel. Stories of the 1930s for the 1980s: Comment. **In** *Armella, P. A.; Dornbusch, R. and Obstfeld, M., eds.*, 1983, pp. 36–40. [G: Latin America]

Mansur, Ahsan H. Determining the Appropriate Levels of Exchange Rates for Developing Economies: Some Methods and Issues. *Int. Monet. Fund Staff Pap.*, December 1983, *30*(4), pp. 784–818. [G: LDCs]

Marcus, Mildred Rendl. The Monetary Implications of a Fixed Exchange Rate System. **In** *Schmukler, N. and Marcus, E., eds.*, 1983, pp. 301–11.

Marquez, Jaime R. A Proposition on Short-Run Departures from the Law-of-One-Price: An Extension. *Europ. Econ. Rev.*, September 1983, *23*(1), pp. 99–101.

Marsden, John S. and Hollander, G. Floating Exchange Rates, Inflation and Selective Protectionism: Their Effects on the Competitiveness of Australian Industry. **In** *Black, J. and Winters, L. A., eds.*, 1983, pp. 92–129. [G: Australia]

Martin, John P. Nominal and Real Exchange Rates: Issues and Some Evidence: Comment. **In** *Claassen, E. and Salin, P., eds.*, 1983, pp. 28–31. [G: Selected OECD]

Marwah, Kanta and Klein, Lawrence R. A Model of Foreign Exchange Markets: Endogenising Capital Flows and Exchange Rates. *Z. Nationalökon.*, Supplement 3, 1983, *43*, pp. 61–95. [G: Canada; Germany; France; U.K.; U.S.]

Masera, Rainer S. International Liquidity and Monetary Control: Comment. **In** *von Furstenberg, G. M., ed.*, 1983, pp. 123–28.

McDermott, John. Exchange-Rate Indexation in a Monetary Model: Theory and Evidence. *J. Int. Money Finance*, August 1983, *2*(2), pp. 197–213. [G: Brazil]

McGuirk, Anne K. Oil Price Changes and Real Exchange Rate Movements among Industrial Countries. *Int. Monet. Fund Staff Pap.*, December 1983, *30*(4), pp. 843–84. [G: Selected OECD]

McKinnon, Ronald I. Dollar Overvaluation against the Yen and Mark in 1983: How to Coordinate Central Bank Policies. *Aussenwirtschaft*, December 1983, *38*(4), pp. 357–72. [G: Selected OECD; U.S.; Japan]

McKinnon, Ronald I. The J-Curve, Stabilizing Speculation, and Capital Constraints on Foreign Exchange Dealers. **In** *Bigman, D. and Taya, T., eds.*, 1983, pp. 103–27.

McNelis, Paul D. and Condon, Timothy J. The Stability of Exchange Rate Instabilities: Testing Stock/Flow Specification with Time-varying Parameters. **In** *Bigman, D. and Taya, T., eds.*, 1983, pp. 129–46. [G: U.S.; Switzerland; U.K.]

Meese, Richard A. and Rogoff, Kenneth S. Empirical Exchange Rate Models of the Seventies: Do They Fit Out of Sample? *J. Int. Econ.*, February 1983, *14*(1/2), pp. 3–24. [G: U.S.]

Meese, Richard A. and Rogoff, Kenneth S. The Out-of-Sample Failure of Empirical Exchange Rate Models: Sampling Error or Misspecification? **In** *Frenkel, J. A., ed.*, 1983, pp. 67–105. [G: Japan; U.K.; U.S.; W. Germany]

Meese, Richard A. and Singleton, Kenneth J. Rational Expectations and the Volatility of Floating Exchange Rates. *Int. Econ. Rev.*, October 1983, *24*(3), pp. 721–33.

Meiselman, David I. Is Gold the Question? [Gold Standards: True and False]. *Cato J.*, Spring 1983, *3*(1), pp. 269–75. [G: U.S.]

Melitz, Jacques. Optimal Stabilization and the Proper Exercise of the Monetary-Policy Instruments under Flexible Exchange Rates. **In** *Claassen, E. and Salin, P., eds.*, 1983, pp. 231–55.

Michaely, Michael. The Floating Exchange Rate in Israel: 1977–1980. **In** *Bigman, D. and Taya, T., eds.*, 1983, pp. 283–309. [G: Israel]

Minford, Patrick. Equilibrium Price-Output and the (Non)Insulating Properties of Fixed Exchange Rates: A Comment. *J. Int. Money Finance*, December 1983, *2*(3), pp. 355–56.

Minford, Patrick; Ioannidis, Christos and Marwaha, Satwant. Rational Expectations in a Multilateral Macro-Model. **In** *De Grauwe, P. and Peeters, T., eds.*, 1983, pp. 239–66.

Moffitt, Michael. Floating Has Failed: A Response to Herb Stein. *Challenge*, November/December 1983, *26*(5), pp. 51–53. [G: U.S.]

Mundell, Robert A. International Monetary Options. *Cato J.*, Spring 1983, *3*(1), pp. 189–210. [G: Global]

Mussa, Michael. Empirical Regularities in the Behavior of Exchange Rates and Theories of the Foreign Exchange Market. **In** *Brunner, K. and Meltzer, A. H., eds.*, 1983, *1979*, pp. 165–213.

Mussa, Michael. Staggered Contracts and Exchange

Rate Policy: Comment. In *Frenkel, J. A., ed.*, 1983, pp. 255–58.

Nabli, Mustapha K. Revision of Exchange-Rate Determination in the MCM: Comment. In *De Grauwe, P. and Peeters, T., eds.*, 1983, pp. 236–38. **[G: U.S.]**

Nashashibi, Karim. Devaluation in Developing Countries: The Difficult Choices. *Finance Develop.*, March 1983, *20*(1), pp. 14–17. **[G: LDCs]**

Niehans, Jürg. Real Exchange Rate Overshooting and the Output Cost of Bringing Down Inflation: Some Further Results: Comment. In *Frenkel, J. A., ed.*, 1983, pp. 365–68.

Nogués, Julio J. Tipos de cambio de paridad: algunas estimaciones para la economía Argentina. (Parity Exchange Rates: Some Estimation for the Argentine Economy. With English summary.) *Económica*, January–April 1983, *29*(1), pp. 45–82. **[G: Argentina]**

O'Connell, Joan. Exchange Rate Expectations and the Short-Run Effectiveness of Monetary Policy. *J. Econ. Stud.*, 1983, *10*(2), pp. 21–28.

Obstfeld, Maurice. Rational Expectations and the Foreign Exchange Market: Comment. In *Frenkel, J. A., ed.*, 1983, pp. 180–87. **[G: U.K.; U.S.; W. Germany]**

Officer, Lawrence H. Dollar–Sterling Mint Parity and Exchange Rates, 1791-1834. *J. Econ. Hist.*, September 1983, *43*(3), pp. 579–616. **[G: U.K.; U.S.]**

Ohta, Takeshi. Exchange-rate Management and the Conduct of Monetary Policy. In *Meek, P., ed.*, 1983, pp. 126–31. **[G: Japan]**

Olivera, Julio H. G. Dinero pasivo internacional y hegemonia monetaria. (With English summary.) *Desarrollo Econ.*, April–June 1983, *23*(89), pp. 3–9.

Olsen, Leif H. The Bretton Woods Nostalgia. In *Kaushik, S. K., ed.*, 1983, pp. 19–26. **[G: OECD; U.S.; LDCs]**

Ondrácek, Mojmír. The Attitudes of Economists in the Socialist Countries to the Question of a CMEA Collective Currency. *Soviet E. Europ. Foreign Trade*, Winter 1983–84, *19*(4), pp. 3–25. **[G: CMEA]**

Ortiz, Guillermo. Dollarization in Mexico: Causes and Consequences. In *Armella, P. A.; Dornbusch, R. and Obstfeld, M., eds.*, 1983, pp. 71–95. **[G: Mexico]**

Otani, Ichiro. Exchange Rate Instability and Capital Controls: The Japanese Experience, 1978–1981. In *Bigman, D. and Taya, T., eds.*, 1983, pp. 311–37. **[G: Japan]**

Pala, Gianfranco. Money, Course of Exchanges and Rate of Exploitation. An Introductory Marxian Reading. *Econ. Notes*, 1983, (3), pp. 122–51. **[G: OECD]**

Panayotopoulos, Dimitris. The "Vicious Circle" Hypothesis: The Greek Case. *Kredit Kapital*, 1983, *16*(3), pp. 394–404. **[G: Greece]**

Partee, J. Charles. Statement to the Subcommittee on Domestic Monetary Policy, U.S. House Committee on Banking, Finance, and Urban Affairs, March 10, 1983. *Fed. Res. Bull.*, March 1983, *69*(3), pp. 193–96. **[G: U.S.]**

Pearce, Douglas K. The Transmission of Inflation between the United States and Canada: An Empirical Analysis. *J. Macroecon.*, Summer 1983, *5*(3), pp. 265–79. **[G: Canada; U.S.]**

Phaup, E. Dwight. The Role of Expectations in the Forward Exchange Market: Some Reduced-Form Estimates. *Quart. Rev. Econ. Bus.*, Summer 1983, *23*(2), pp. 45–52. **[G: Selected OECD]**

Poniachek, Harvey A. The Determination of Exchange Rates. In *George, A. M. and Giddy, I. H., eds., Vol. 1*, 1983, pp. 2.3:1–44.

Posthumus, Godert. The Netherlands: Financial-Economic Adjustment Policies in the 1970s. In *de Cecco, M., ed.*, 1983, pp. 74–98. **[G: Netherlands]**

Prasada Rao, D. S. and Shepherd, W. F. A Comparison of Pound Sterling–Australian Dollar Purchasing Power Parities for Selected Population Subgroups in Australia and the United Kingdom. *Rev. Income Wealth*, December 1983, *29*(4), pp. 445–55. **[G: U.K.; Australia]**

Protopapadakis, Aris. Expectations, Exchange Rates and Monetary Theory: The Case of the German Hyperinflation. *J. Int. Money Finance*, April 1983, *2*(1), pp. 47–65. **[G: W. Germany]**

Protopapadakis, Aris and Stoll, Hans R. Spot and Futures Prices and the Law of One Price. *J. Finance*, December 1983, *38*(5), pp. 1431–55. **[G: U.S.; U.K.]**

Puchon, Gilles. Defining and Measuring Currency Exposure. In *George, A. M. and Giddy, I. H., eds., Vol. 2*, 1983, pp. 8.7:1–18.

Purvis, Douglas D. International Liquidity and Monetary Control: Comment. In *von Furstenberg, G. M., ed.*, 1983, pp. 115–23.

Ranuzzi, Paolo. A Portfolio Approach to the Determination of Exchange Rates within a Multicountry Model. In *De Grauwe, P. and Peeters, T., eds.*, 1983, pp. 175–207. **[G: U.K.; W. Germany; France; Italy]**

Rapanos, Vassilis. Exchange Rate Dynamics with Price and Output Adjustment. *Greek Econ. Rev.*, December 1983, *5*(3), pp. 264–77.

Rodríguez Castellanos, A. Empresas multinacionales, gestion de cambios y crisis monetarias. (Multination Businesses, Change of Money, Management and Monetary Crisis. With English summary.) *Écon. Soc.*, September–October–November 1983, *17*(9–10–11), pp. 1451–86.

Rogoff, Kenneth S. Interest Differential and Covered Arbitrage: Comment. In *Armella, P. A.; Dornbusch, R. and Obstfeld, M., eds.*, 1983, pp. 241–43. **[G: Mexico; U.S.]**

Rosenberg, Michael R. Foreign Exchange Controls: An International Comparison. In *George, A. M. and Giddy, I. H., eds., Vol. 1*, 1983, pp. 2.2:1–66.

Ross, Stephen A. and Walsh, Michael M. A Simple Approach to the Pricing of Risky Assets with Uncertain Exchange Rates. In *Hawkins, R. G.; Levich, R. M. and Wihlborg, C. G., eds.*, 1983, pp. 39–54.

Rotberg, Eugene H. Perspective: Some Informal Remarks on Debt Management and Liquidity. In *Herring, R. J., ed.*, 1983, pp. 212–19.

Sacerdoti, Emilio. Componenti attese ed inattese della variazione dei tassi di cambio: una rassegna di contributi empirici. (Expected and Unexpected Components of Exchange Rate Changes: A Review of Empirical Contribution. With English summary.) *Giorn. Econ.*, January–February 1983, *42*(1–2), pp. 27–54.

Sachs, Jeffrey D. Aspects of the Current Account Behavior of OECD Economies. **In** *Claassen, E. and Salin, P., eds.*, 1983, pp. 101–22. **[G: OECD]**

Sachs, Jeffrey D. Energy and Growth under Flexible Exchange Rates: A Simulation Study. **In** *Bhandari, J. S. and Putnam, B. H., eds.*, 1983, pp. 191–220. **[G: OPEC]**

Saïdi, Nasser. The Out-of-Sample Failure of Empirical Exchange Rate Models: Sampling Error or Misspecification? Comment. **In** *Frenkel, J. A., ed.*, 1983, pp. 105–09. **[G: Japan; U.K.; U.S.; W. Germany]**

Saïdi, Nasser and Swoboda, Alexander. Nominal and Real Exchange Rates: Issues and Some Evidence. **In** *Claassen, E. and Salin, P., eds.*, 1983, pp. 3–27. **[G: Selected OECD]**

Salemi, Michael K. The Out-of-Sample Failure of Empirical Exchange Rate Models: Sampling Error or Misspecification? Comment. **In** *Frenkel, J. A., ed.*, 1983, pp. 110–12. **[G: Japan; U.K.; U.S.; W. Germany]**

Salerno, Joseph T. Gold Standards: True and False. *Cato J.*, Spring 1983, *3*(1), pp. 239–67. **[G: U.S.]**

Salin, Pascal. Exchange Rate Oscillations and Catastrophe Theory: Comment. **In** *Claassen, E. and Salin, P., eds.*, 1983, pp. 194–97.

Sargent, Thomas J. Dollarization in Mexico: Causes and Consequences: Comment. **In** *Armella, P. A.; Dornbusch, R. and Obstfeld, M., eds.*, 1983, pp. 95–106.

Scholl, Franz. Implications of Monetary Targeting for Exchange-rate Policy. **In** *Meek, P., ed.*, 1983, pp. 118–25. **[G: W. Germany]**

Schröder, Jürgen. Exchange Rates, Real Economic Activity and the Balance of Payments: Evidence from the 1960s: Comment. **In** *Claassen, E. and Salin, P., eds.*, 1983, pp. 144–48. **[G: Selected Countries]**

Schwartz, Anna J. The Postwar Institutional Evolution of the International Monetary System. **In** *Darby, M. P. and Lothian, J. R., et al.*, 1983, pp. 14–45. **[G: OECD]**

Shapiro, Alan C. What Does Purchasing Power Parity Mean? *J. Int. Money Finance*, December 1983, *2*(3), pp. 295–318.

Sievert, Olaf. Disillusionment in the Conduct of Exchange-Rate Policies. **In** *[Giersch, H.]*, 1983, pp. 188–208. **[G: OECD; W. Germany]**

Singleton, Kenneth J. Risk Averse Speculation in the Forward Foreign Exchange Market: An Econometric Analysis of Linear Models: Comment. **In** *Frenkel, J. A., ed.*, 1983, pp. 147–52. **[G: OECD]**

Skony, Marilyn P. The Foreign Exchange Futures Market. **In** *George, A. M. and Giddy, I. H., eds., Vol. 1*, 1983, pp. 2.5:1–21.

Sørensen, Peter Birch. Devaluering og finanspolitik under alternative pengepolitiske regimer. (Fiscal and Exchange Rate Policies under Different Monetary Policies Regimes. With English summary.) *Nationaløkon. Tidsskr.*, 1983, *121*(1), pp. 83–101. **[G: Denmark]**

Spaventa, Luigi. Feedbacks between Exchange-Rate Movements and Domestic Inflation: Vicious and Not So Virtuous Cycles, Old and New. *Int. Soc. Sci. J.*, 1983, *35*(3), pp. 517–34. **[G: Europe]**

Spinelli, Franco. Fixed Exchange Rates and Adaptive Expectations Monetarism: The Italian Case. *Rev. Econ. Cond. Italy*, February 1983, (1), pp. 97–124. **[G: Italy]**

Startz, Richard. Testing Rational Expectations by the Use of Overidentifying Restrictions. *J. Econometrics*, December 1983, *23*(3), pp. 343–51. **[G: U.S.; W. Germany]**

Stockman, Alan C. Real Exchange Rates under Alternative Nominal Exchange-Rate Systems. *J. Int. Money Finance*, August 1983, *2*(2), pp. 147–66. **[G: Global]**

Strauss, Robert. Economic Effects of Monetary Compensatory Amounts. *J. Common Market Stud.*, March 1983, *21*(3), pp. 261–81. **[G: EEC]**

Subrahmanyam, Marti G. Comments on "A Simple Approach to the Pricing of Risky Assets with Uncertain Exchange Rates." **In** *Hawkins, R. G.; Levich, R. M. and Wihlborg, C. G., eds.*, 1983, pp. 55–59.

Swanson, Peggy E. Compensating Balances and Foreigners' Dollar Deposits in United States Banks. *J. Finan. Res.*, Fall 1983, *6*(3), pp. 257–63. **[G: U.S.]**

Swanson, Peggy E. U.S. Dollar Demand of Private Nonbank Foreigners. *J. Int. Bus. Stud.*, Winter 1983, *14*(3), pp. 107–20. **[G: U.S.]**

Taya, Teizo. Effectiveness of Exchange Market Intervention in Moderating the Speed of Exchange Rate Movements: An Empirical Study of the Case of Japan. **In** *Bigman, D. and Taya, T., eds.*, 1983, pp. 217–55. **[G: Japan]**

Taylor, Harry. Perspective: Managing Foreign Exchange Exposure. **In** *Herring, R. J., ed.*, 1983, pp. 219–25.

Taylor, John B. Staggered Contracts and Exchange Rate Policy: Comment. **In** *Frenkel, J. A., ed.*, 1983, pp. 252–55.

Thygesen, Niels. What Are the Scope and Limits of Fruitful International Monetary Cooperation in the 1980s? Comment. **In** *von Furstenberg, G. M., ed.*, 1983, pp. 419–28.

Tronzano, Marco. Testing the Efficiency of the Spot Foreign-Exchange Market: Some Preliminary Results for the Italian Lira. *Econ. Int.*, May–August–November 1983, *36*(2–3–4), pp. 262–77. **[G: Italy]**

Turnovsky, Stephen J. Exchange Market Intervention Policies in a Small Open Economy. **In** *Bhandari, J. S. and Putnam, B. H., eds.*, 1983, pp. 286–311.

Turnovsky, Stephen J. and Ball, Katrina M. Covered Interest Parity and Speculative Efficiency: Some Empirical Evidence for Australia. *Econ. Rec.*, September 1983, *59*(166), pp. 271–80. **[G: Australia]**

Tutino, Franco. Le quotazioni dello SME. (The EMS

Quotations. With English summary.) *Bancaria,* July 1983, *39*(7), pp. 593–604. **[G: EEC]**

Twomey, Michael J. Devaluations and Income Distribution in Latin America. *Southern Econ. J.,* January 1983, *49*(3), pp. 804–21. **[G: Latin America]**

Ueda, Kazuo. Trade Balance Adjustment with Imported Intermediate Goods: The Japanese Case. *Rev. Econ. Statist.,* November 1983, *65*(4), pp. 618–25. **[G: Japan]**

Vaciago, Giacomo. Re dollaro contro tutti. (King Dollar: One against Everybody. With English summary.) *L'Impresa,* 1983, *25*(6), pp. 59–62. **[G: Italy; U.S.]**

Vander Kraats, Ronald H. and Booth, Laurence D. Empirical Tests of the Monetary Approach to Exchange-Rate Determination. *J. Int. Money Finance,* December 1983, *2*(3), pp. 255–78. **[G: W. Europe; Canada; Japan]**

van Veen, P. Trends in World Trade. *S. Afr. J. Econ.,* December 1983, *51*(4), pp. 486–506. **[G: Global]**

Vencovský, František. Improvement of the Monetary Mechanism in the Process of the International Socialist Economic Integration. *Czech. Econ. Digest.,* March 1983, (2), pp. 3–15. **[G: CMEA]**

Vuchelen, Jozef. Macroeconomic Implications of Alternative Exchange-Rate Models: Comment. **In** *De Grauwe, P. and Peeters, T., eds.,* 1983, pp. 54–57. **[G: Canada]**

Walker, Townsend. The Mechanics of Covering Foreign Exchange Exposures. **In** *George, A. M. and Giddy, I. H., eds., Vol. 2,* 1983, pp. 8.9:1–58.

Wallich, Henry C. Statement to the U.S. House Subcommittee on Domestic Monetary Policy of the Committee on Banking, Finance and Urban Affairs, October 5, 1983. *Fed. Res. Bull.,* October 1983, *69*(10), pp. 776–81. **[G: U.S.]**

Walmsley, Julian. Eurocurrency Dealing. **In** *George, A. M. and Giddy, I. H., eds., Vol. 1,* 1983, pp. 3.2:1–30.

Walsh, Brendan M. Ireland in the European Monetary System: The Effects of a Change in Exchange Rate Regime. **In** *de Cecco, M., ed.,* 1983, pp. 160–88. **[G: Ireland]**

Warner, Dennis L. A Model of Trade and Exchange Rates. **In** *Hickman, B. G., ed.,* 1983, pp. 297–311. **[G: OECD; Global]**

Warner, Dennis L. and Kreinin, Mordechai E. Determinants of International Trade Flows. *Rev. Econ. Statist.,* February 1983, *65*(1), pp. 96–104.

Whitman, Marina v. N. Perspective: On Exchange Rate Analysis and Foreign Exchange Risk. **In** *Herring, R. J., ed.,* 1983, pp. 75–83.

Willett, Thomas D. and Wolf, Matthias. The Vicious Circle Debate: Some Conceptual Distinctions. *Kyklos,* 1983, *36*(2), pp. 231–48.

Wilson, Charles. Oil Shocks and Exchange Rate Dynamics: Comment. **In** *Frenkel, J. A., ed.,* 1983, pp. 281–83.

Witte, Willard E. Policy Interdependence under Flexible Exchange Rates: A Dynamic Analysis of Price Interactions. **In** *Bhandari, J. S. and Putnam, B. H., eds.,* 1983, pp. 312–28.

Witter, Michael. Exchange Rate Policy in Jamaica: A Critical Assessment. *Soc. Econ. Stud.,* December 1983, *32*(4), pp. 1–50. **[G: Jamaica]**

Wyplosz, Charles A. Aspects of the Current Account Behavior of OECD Economies: Comment. **In** *Claassen, E. and Salin, P., eds.,* 1983, pp. 123–28. **[G: OECD]**

Zis, George. Exchange-Rate Fluctuations: 1973–82. *Nat. Westminster Bank Quart. Rev.,* August 1983, pp. 2–13. **[G: France; W. Germany; U.K.; Japan]**

432 International Monetary Arrangements

4320 International Monetary Arrangements

Adams, Richard H., Jr. The Role of Research in Policy Development: The Creation of the IMF Cereal Import Facility. *World Devel.,* July 1983, *11*(7), pp. 549–63. **[G: LDCs]**

van Agtmael, Antoine W. Issuance of Eurobonds: Syndication and Underwriting Techniques and Costs. **In** *George, A. M. and Giddy, I. H., eds., Vol. 1,* 1983, pp. 5.2:1–24. **[G: OECD]**

Allen, Polly Reynolds. Policies to Correct Cyclical Imbalance within a Monetary Union. *J. Common Market Stud.,* March 1983, *21*(3), pp. 313–27.

Anikin, A. V. L'or dans le système monétaire international. (With English summary.) *Écon. Soc.,* January 1983, *17*(1), pp. 1–42.

Ariovich, G. The Impact of Political Tension on the Price of Gold. *J. Stud. Econ. Econometrics,* July 1983, (16), pp. 17–37.

Armstrong, Harvey W. The Assignment of Regional Policy Powers within the EC. **In** *El-Agraa, A. M., ed.,* 1983, pp. 271–98. **[G: EEC; U.K.]**

Avramović, Dragoslav. Development Policies for Today. *J. World Trade Law,* May–June 1983, *17*(3), pp. 189–206. **[G: LDCs]**

Avramović, Dragoslav. Financial Cooperation among Developing Countries: Issues and Opportunities. **In** *Gauhar, A., ed. (I),* 1983, pp. 205–25.

Avramović, Dragoslav. The Role of the International Monetary Fund: The Disputes, Qualifications, and Future. **In** *Williamson, J., ed.,* 1983, pp. 595–603.

Bacha, Edmar L. Vicissitudes of Recent Stabilization Attempts in Brazil and the IMF Alternative. **In** *Williamson, J., ed.,* 1983, pp. 323–40. **[G: Brazil]**

Baneth, Jean. The Role of the World Bank as an International Institution: Comment on the Krueger Paper. *Carnegie-Rochester Conf. Ser. Public Policy,* Spring 1983, *18,* pp. 313–23.

Basevi, Giorgio and Calzolari, Michele. Monetary Authorities' Reaction Functions in a Model of Exchange-Rate Determination for the European Monetary System. **In** *De Grauwe, P. and Peeters, T., eds.,* 1983, pp. 267–82. **[G: EEC]**

Basevi, Giorgio; Calzolari, Michele and Colombo, Caterina. Monetary Authorities' Reaction Functions and the European Monetary System. **In** *Hodgman, D. R., ed.,* 1983, pp. 228–44. **[G: France; Netherlands; W. Germany; Italy; Belgium]**

Berchesi, Nilo. Internal Economic Policies and International Cooperation to Attain International Stability. *Econ. Notes,* 1983, (2), pp. 99–119.

Bergsten, C. Fred. The Evolution and Management

of the Multiple Reserve Currency System. **In** *Bergsten, C. F.,* 1983, *1981,* pp. 111–37. **[G: OECD]**

Bergsten, C. Fred. The International Monetary System: Problems and Policy Needs. **In** *Bergsten, C. F.,* 1983, pp. 73–78.

Bernauer, Kenneth. The Asian Dollar Market. *Fed. Res. Bank San Francisco Econ. Rev.,* Winter 1983, (1), pp. 47–63. **[G: Hong Kong; Singapore]**

Beza, Sterie T. IMF Conditionality: Panel Discussion. **In** *Williamson, J., ed.,* 1983, pp. 589–93.

Bilson, John F. O. The Choice of an Invoice Currency in International Transactions. **In** *Bhandari, J. S. and Putnam, B. H., eds.,* 1983, pp. 384–401.

Bird, Graham. Interest Rate Subsidies on International Finance as a Means of Assisting Low-Income Countries. *World Devel.,* June 1983, *11* (6), pp. 515–25. **[G: LDCs]**

Bird, Graham. Low Income Countries as a Special Case in the International Financial System: An Analysis of Some Proposals for Reform. *Econ. Notes,* 1983, (2), pp. 5–22. **[G: Selected LDCs]**

Bird, Graham. Low-Income Countries and International Financial Reform. *J. Devel. Areas,* October 1983, *18* (1), pp. 53–75. **[G: LDCs]**

Bird, Graham. The Banks and the IMF—Division of Labour. *Lloyds Bank Rev.,* October 1983, (150), pp. 19–33.

Bird, Graham. The International Monetary Fund and Developing Countries: Retrospect and Prospect. *De Economist,* 1983, *131* (2), pp. 161–95. **[G: LDCs]**

Bogdanowicz-Bindert, Christine A. Portugal, Turkey and Peru: Three Successful Stabilization Programmes under the Auspices of the IMF. *World Devel.,* January 1983, *11* (1), pp. 65–70. **[G: Portugal; Turkey; Peru]**

van den Boogaerde, Pierre R. The SDR as a Means of Payment: A Comment. *Int. Monet. Fund Staff Pap.,* September 1983, *30*(3), pp. 650–53.

Boyd, John H.; Dahl, David S. and Line, Carolyn P. A Primer on the International Monetary Fund. *Fed. Res. Bank Minn. Rev.,* Summer 1983, *7*(3), pp. 6–15.

Bruno, Michael. Issues Related to Conditionality: Comments, Chapters 4–6. **In** *Williamson, J., ed.,* 1983, pp. 125–28.

Bryant, Ralph C. Eurocurrency Banking: Alarmist Concerns and Genuine Issues. *OECD Econ. Stud.,* Autumn 1983, (1), pp. 7–41. **[G: W. Europe]**

Buira, Ariel. IMF Financial Programs and Conditionality. *J. Devel. Econ.,* February/April 1983, *12*(1/2), pp. 111–36.

Byler, Ezra U. and Baker, James C. S.W.I.F.T.: A Fast Method to Facilitate International Financial Transactions. *J. World Trade Law,* September–October 1983, *17*(5), pp. 458–65.

Callier, Philippe. Eurobanks and Liquidity Creation: A Broader Perspective. *Weltwirtsch. Arch.,* 1983, *119*(2), pp. 214–25.

Callier, Philippe. The SDR as a Means of Payment: A Comment. *Int. Monet. Fund Staff Pap.,* September 1983, *30*(3), pp. 654–55.

Carlozzi, Nicholas. Exchange Rate Systems and Linkages. **In** *George, A. M. and Giddy, I. H., eds., Vol. 1,* 1983, pp. 2.1:1–31.

de Cecco, Marcello. International Economic Adjustment: Small Countries and the European Monetary System: Introduction. **In** *de Cecco, M., ed.,* 1983, pp. 1–6. **[G: W. Europe]**

Chrystal, K. Alec; Wilson, Nigel D. and Quinn, Philip. Demand for International Money, 1962–1977. *Europ. Econ. Rev.,* May 1983, *21* (3), pp. 287–98.

Claassen, Emil-Maria. What Are the Scope and Limits of Fruitful International Monetary Cooperation in the 1980s? Comment. **In** *von Furstenberg, G. M., ed.,* 1983, pp. 409–19.

Clausen, Alden W. and de Larosière, J. Adjustment and Growth. *Finance Develop.,* June 1983, *20*(2), pp. 13–14.

Cline, William R. Economic Stabilization in Developing Countries: Theory and Stylized Facts. **In** *Williamson, J., ed.,* 1983, *1981,* pp. 175–208.

Coats, Warren L., Jr. SDRs and Their Role in the International Financial System. **In** *Kaushik, S. K., ed.,* 1983, pp. 97–107. **[G: Global]**

Coats, Warren L., Jr. The SDR as a Means of Payment: Reply. *Int. Monet. Fund Staff Pap.,* September 1983, *30*(3), pp. 662–69.

Colombatto, Enrico. CMEA, Money and Ruble Convertibility. *Appl. Econ.,* August 1983, *15*(4), pp. 479–506. **[G: CMEA]**

Connolly, Michael B. Optimum Currency Pegs for Latin America. *J. Money, Credit, Banking,* February 1983, *15*(1), pp. 56–72. **[G: Latin America]**

Cooper, Richard N. IMF Conditionality: Panel Discussion. **In** *Williamson, J., ed.,* 1983, pp. 569–77.

Cooper, Richard N. Use of the SDR to Supplement or Substitute for Other Means of Finance: Comment. **In** *von Furstenberg, G. M., ed.,* 1983, pp. 361–67.

Corden, Warner Max. Is There an Important Role for an International Reserve Asset Such as the SDR? **In** *von Furstenberg, G. M., ed.,* 1983, pp. 213–47.

Corden, Warner Max. The Logic of the International Monetary Non-system. **In** *[Giersch, H.],* 1983, pp. 59–74. **[G: OECD]**

Crane, Dwight B. and Hayes, Samuel L., III. The Evolution of International Banking Competition and Its Implications for Regulation. *J. Bank Res.,* Spring 1983, *14*(1), pp. 39–53. **[G: U.S.; OECD; Selected LDCs]**

Crawford, Malcolm. High-Conditionality Lending: The United Kingdom. **In** *Williamson, J., ed.,* 1983, pp. 421–39. **[G: U.K.]**

Csaba, László. The Transferable Rouble and Convertibility in the CMEA. **In** *Saunders, C. T., ed.,* 1983, pp. 237–56. **[G: CMEA]**

Csikós-Nagy, Béla. Monetary Issues: Comment. **In** *Saunders, C. T., ed.,* 1983, pp. 215–17. **[G: EEC; CMEA]**

Cumby, Robert E. Special Drawing Rights and Plans for Reform of the International Monetary System: A Survey. **In** *von Furstenberg, G. M., ed.,* 1983, pp. 435–73.

Dale, Richard S. International Banking Is Out of Control. *Challenge,* January/February 1983, *25*(6), pp. 14–19.

Dale, William B. Financing and Adjustment of Payments Imbalances. **In** *Williamson, J., ed.,* 1983,

pp. 3–16.

Darby, Michael R. The United States as an Exogenous Source of World Inflation under the Bretton Woods System. **In** *Darby, M. P. and Lothian, J. R., et al.*, 1983, pp. 478–90. **[G: U.S.]**

Davidson, Paul. International Money and International Economic Relations. **In** *Kregel, J. A., ed.*, 1983, pp. 156–72. **[G: Selected Countries]**

De Grauwe, Paul. What Are the Scope and Limits of Fruitful International Monetary Cooperation in the 1980s? **In** *von Furstenberg, G. M., ed.*, 1983, pp. 375–408. **[G: OECD]**

Dell, Sidney. Keynes and the International Economic Order: Comment. **In** *Worswick, D. and Trevithick, J., eds.*, 1983, pp. 119–27.

Dell, Sidney. Stabilization: The Political Economy of Overkill. **In** *Williamson, J., ed.*, 1983, pp. 17–45.

Diaz-Alejandro, Carlos F. IMF Conditionality: Country Studies: Comments, Chapters 11–14. **In** *Williamson, J., ed.*, 1983, pp. 341–46.

Dini, Lamberto. Foreign Debt, Economic Recovery, and the International Monetary System. **In** *Basagni, F., ed.*, 1983, pp. 13–23. **[G: LDCs; E. Europe; OECD]**

Diz, Adolfo. Economic Performance under Three Stand-by Arrangements: Peru, 1977–80. **In** *Williamson, J., ed.*, 1983, pp. 263–73. **[G: Peru]**

Dornbusch, Rudiger. Functioning of the Current International Financial System: Strengths, Weaknesses, and Criteria for Evaluation: Comment. **In** *von Furstenberg, G. M., ed.*, 1983, pp. 45–51. **[G: Japan; U.S.; W. Germany]**

Dornbusch, Rudiger. Issues Related to Conditionality: Comments, Chapters 7–10. **In** *Williamson, J., ed.*, 1983, pp. 223–30.

Dornbusch, Rudiger. Keynes and the International Economic Order: Comment. **In** *Worswick, D. and Trevithick, J., eds.*, 1983, pp. 113–19.

Eng, Maximo and Lees, Francis A. Eurocurrency Centers. **In** *George, A. M. and Giddy, I. H., eds., Vol. 1*, 1983, pp. 3.6:1–29. **[G: Selected Countries]**

Famílton, R. J. The SDR—Its Evolution and Prospects. **In** *Hooke, A. W., ed.*, 1983, pp. 146–60.

Fekete, János. Functioning of the Current International Financial System: Strengths, Weaknesses, and Criteria for Evaluation: Comment. **In** *von Furstenberg, G. M., ed.*, 1983, pp. 51–56.

Fellner, William. Gold and the Uneasy Case for Responsibly Managed Fiat Money. **In** *[Giersch, H.]*, 1983, pp. 91–116. **[G: U.S.; OECD]**

Finch, C. David. Adjustment Policies and Conditionality. **In** *Williamson, J., ed.*, 1983, pp. 75–86.

Fischer, Stanley. The SDR and the IMF: Toward a World Central Bank? **In** *von Furstenberg, G. M., ed.*, 1983, pp. 179–99.

Fratianni, Michele. La crisi dell'indebitamento internazionale: come è sorta e come si può superare. (The International Debt Crisis: Causes and Policy Prescriptions. With English summary.) *Bancaria*, February 1983, *39*(2), pp. 139–46. **[G: LDCs]**

Frenkel, Jacob A. International Liquidity and Monetary Control. **In** *von Furstenberg, G. M., ed.*, 1983, pp. 65–109. **[G: Selected Countries]**

Friedli, Georg. Statements on International Legal Assistance from the Viewpoint of One of the Large Swiss Banks. *Wirtsch. Recht*, 1983, *35*(2/3), pp. 245–47. **[G: Switzerland]**

von Furstenberg, George M. Internationally Managed Moneys. *Amer. Econ. Rev.*, May 1983, *73*(2), pp. 54–58.

von Furstenberg, George M. Summary of Findings. **In** *von Furstenberg, G. M., ed.*, 1983, pp. 429–34.

Garrison, Roger W. Gold: A Standard and an Institution [Why Gold?]. *Cato J.*, Spring 1983, *3*(1), pp. 233–38. **[G: U.S.; U.K.]**

Gerakis, A. S. and Roncesvalles, O. Bahrain's Offshore Banking Center. *Econ. Develop. Cult. Change*, January 1983, *31*(2), pp. 271–93. **[G: Bahrain]**

Giddy, Ian H. Eurocurrency Interest Rates and Their Linkages. **In** *George, A. M. and Giddy, I. H., eds., Vol. 1*, 1983, pp. 3.3:1–28. **[G: OECD]**

Giddy, Ian H. Interbank Arbitrage in the European Market. **In** *Kaushik, S. K., ed.*, 1983, pp. 131–45. **[G: Global]**

Giddy, Ian H. The Eurocurrency Market. **In** *George, A. M. and Giddy, I. H., eds., Vol. 1*, 1983, pp. 3.1:1–37. **[G: OECD]**

Giddy, Ian H. The International Financial Markets. **In** *George, A. M. and Giddy, I. H., eds., Vol. 1*, 1983, pp. 1.1:1–14.

Giddy, Ian H. and Ho, Sang Kang. Mathematics of International Finance. **In** *George, A. M. and Giddy, I. H., eds., Vol. 2*, 1983, pp. A1–51. **[G: OECD]**

Goodman, Laurie S. Syndicated Eurolending: Pricing and Practice. **In** *George, A. M. and Giddy, I. H., eds., Vol. 1*, 1983, pp. 3.4:1–29. **[G: OECD]**

Grassman, Sven. Is There an Important Role for an International Reserve Asset Such as the SDR? Comment. **In** *von Furstenberg, G. M., ed.*, 1983, pp. 248–52.

Green, Christopher. Insulating Countries against Fluctuations in Domestic Production and Exports: An Analysis of Compensatory Financing Schemes. *J. Devel. Econ.*, June 1983, *12*(3), pp. 303–25.

Green, Reginald Herbold. Political–Economic Adjustment and IMF Conditionality: Tanzania 1974–81. **In** *Williamson, J., ed.*, 1983, pp. 347–80.

Grubel, Herbert G. Interest Payments on Commercial Bank Reserves to Curb Euro-money Markets. **In** *[Giersch, H.]*, 1983, pp. 117–35. **[G: OECD]**

Grubel, Herbert G. Is There an Important Role for an International Reserve Asset Such as the SDR? Comment. **In** *von Furstenberg, G. M., ed.*, 1983, pp. 252–59.

Gruben, William C. and Lawler, Patrick J. Currency Substitution: The Use of Dollar Coin and Currency in the Texas Border Area of Mexico. *Fed. Res. Bank Dallas Econ. Rev.*, July 1983, pp. 10–20. **[G: Mexico; U.S.]**

Guitián, Manuel. Fund Programs for Economic Adjustment. **In** *Hooke, A. W., ed.*, 1983, pp. 96–114.

Gupta, Sanjeev. India and the Second OPEC Oil

Price Shock—An Economy-Wide Analysis. *Weltwirtsch. Arch.*, 1983, *119*(1), pp. 122–37. **[G: India]**

Gwin, Catherine. Financing India's Structural Adjustment: The Role of the Fund. **In** *Williamson, J., ed.*, 1983, pp. 511–31. **[G: India]**

Hain, Ferdinand. The European Monetary System (EMS). **In** *Saunders, C. T., ed.*, 1983, pp. 219–35. **[G: EEC]**

Harberger, Arnold C. IMF Conditionality: Panel Discussion. **In** *Williamson, J., ed.*, 1983, pp. 578–80.

Harris, Donald J. The Adjustment Process and the Monetary System: Comment [International Money and International Economic Relations]. **In** *Kregel, J. A., ed.*, 1983, pp. 173–75. **[G: Selected Countries]**

Hekman, Christine R. The International Financial System. **In** *George, A. M. and Giddy, I. H., eds., Vol. 1*, 1983, pp. 1.2:1–19.

Helleiner, Gerald K. IMF Conditionality: Panel Discussion. **In** *Williamson, J., ed.*, 1983, pp. 581–88.

Helleiner, Gerald K. Lender of Early Resort: The IMF and the Poorest. *Amer. Econ. Rev.*, May 1983, *73*(2), pp. 349–53.

Henderson, Dale W. and Waldo, Douglas G. Reserve Requirements on Eurocurrency Deposits: Implications for the Stabilization of Real Outputs. **In** *Bhandari, J. S. and Putnam, B. H., eds.*, 1983, pp. 350–83.

Heymann, H. G. and Venkataraman, V. K. An Empirical Study of the Marginal Reserve Requirements and the Exchange Value of the Dollar. *Bus. Econ.*, May 1983, *18*(3), pp. 55–61. **[G: U.S.]**

Hood, William C. International Money, Credit, and the SDR. *Finance Develop.*, September 1983, *20*(3), pp. 6–9.

Hood, William C. The Current World Economic Situation and the Problem of Global Payments Imbalances. **In** *Hooke, A. W., ed.*, 1983, pp. 56–70.

Hood, William C. The SDR—An Introduction. **In** *Hooke, A. W., ed.*, 1983, pp. 138–45.

Hooke, A. W. The Role of the Fund in Developing Countries. **In** *Hooke, A. W., ed.*, 1983, pp. 163–80.

Israel, Arturo. Management and Institutional Development. *Finance Develop.*, September 1983, *20*(3), pp. 15–18. **[G: LDCs]**

Jamal, Amir M. Man at the Centre of Economic Purpose. **In** *Gauhar, A., ed. (II)*, 1983, pp. 24–29.

Jones, Michael. International Liquidity: A Welfare Analysis. *Quart. J. Econ.*, February 1983, *98*(1), pp. 1–23.

Kaen, Fred R. and Hachey, George A. Eurocurrency and National Money Market Interest Rates: An Empirical Investigation of Causality. *J. Money, Credit, Banking*, August 1983, *15*(3), pp. 327–38. **[G: U.K.; U.S.]**

Kaen, Fred R.; Helms, Billy P. and Booth, G. Geoffrey. The Integration of Eurodollar and U.S. Money Market Interest Rates in the Futures Market. *Weltwirtsch. Arch.*, 1983, *119*(4), pp. 601–15. **[G: U.S.; W. Europe]**

Kafka, Alexandre. Gold and International Monetary Stability. *Cato J.*, Spring 1983, *3*(1), pp. 277–80. **[G: Global]**

Katseli, Louka T. Devaluation: A Critical Appraisal of the IMF's Policy Prescriptions. *Amer. Econ. Rev.*, May 1983, *73*(2), pp. 359–63.

Kelly, Margaret. Fiscal Deficits and Fund-Supported Programs. *Finance Develop.*, September 1983, *20*(3), pp. 37–39.

Kenen, Peter B. The SDR as a Means of Payment: A Comment. *Int. Monet. Fund Staff Pap.*, September 1983, *30*(3), pp. 656–61.

Kenen, Peter B. Use of the SDR to Supplement or Substitute for Other Means of Finance. **In** *von Furstenberg, G. M., ed.*, 1983, pp. 327–60.

Keyzer, Marinus W. International Moneys and Monetary Arrangements in Private Markets: Comment. **In** *von Furstenberg, G. M., ed.*, 1983, pp. 319–22.

Killick, Tony. Kenya, the IMF, and the Unsuccessful Quest for Stabilization. **In** *Williamson, J., ed.*, 1983, pp. 381–413. **[G: Kenya]**

Kincaid, G. Russell. What Are Credit Ceilings? *Finance Develop.*, March 1983, *20*(1), pp. 28–29.

Kindleberger, Charles P. Key Currencies and Financial Centres. **In** *[Giersch, H.]*, 1983, pp. 75–90. **[G: OECD]**

Komiya, Ryutaro. International Liquidity and Monetary Control: Comment. **In** *von Furstenberg, G. M., ed.*, 1983, pp. 110–15.

Konstantinov, Iu. The Transferable Ruble: The Currency of the Socialist Community. *Prob. Econ.*, October 1983, *26*(6), pp. 71–93. **[G: U.S.S.R.; CMEA]**

Kouri, Pentti J. K. International Monetary Reform: The Optimal Mix in Big Countries: Comment. **In** *Tobin, J., ed.*, 1983, pp. 293–95.

Krueger, Anne O. The Role of the World Bank as an International Institution. *Carnegie-Rochester Conf. Ser. Public Policy*, Spring 1983, *18*, pp. 281–311.

Krul, Nicolas. The Debt Problem: Some Observations on the Search for a New Financial Balance (abridged). **In** *Basagni, F., ed.*, 1983, pp. 55–60. **[G: LDCs; OECD]**

Lamfalussy, Alexandre. Investment and the International Monetary and Financial Environment. **In** *Heertje, A., ed.*, 1983, pp. 56–71. **[G: U.S.; EEC]**

Landell-Mills, Joslin. The World Bank and the Training and Visit System. *Finance Develop.*, June 1983, *20*(2), pp. 41–42.

Larsen, Flemming; Llewellyn, John and Potter, Stephen. International Economic Linkages. *OECD Econ. Stud.*, Autumn 1983, (1), pp. 43–91. **[G: OECD]**

Lichtensztejn, Samuel. IMF—Developing Countries: Conditionality and Strategy. **In** *Williamson, J., ed.*, 1983, pp. 209–22.

Little, Jane Sneddon. Eurobank Maturity Transformation and LDC Debts. *New Eng. Econ. Rev.*, September/October 1983, pp. 15–19. **[G: LDCs; MDCs]**

Llewellyn, David T. EC Monetary Arrangements: Britain's Strategy. **In** *El-Agraa, A. M., ed.*, 1983, pp. 251–70. **[G: EEC; U.K.]**

Logue, Dennis E. and Senbet, Lemma W. External Currency Market Equilibrium and Its Implications for Regulation of the Eurocurrency Market. *J. Finance*, May 1983, *38*(2), pp. 435–47.

Lomax, David F. International Moneys and Monetary Arrangements in Private Markets. In *von Furstenberg, G. M., ed.*, 1983, pp. 261–318. [G: U.S.; EEC]

Lomax, David F. Prospects for the European Monetary System. *Nat. Westminster Bank Quart. Rev.*, May 1983, pp. 33–50. [G: EEC]

Magnifico, Giovanni. Problems of the World Economy Today. *Econ. Notes*, 1983, (2), pp. 49–64. [G: Global]

Magraw, Daniel. Legal Aspects of International Bonds. In *George, A. M. and Giddy, I. H., eds., Vol. 1*, 1983, pp. 5.3:1–30. [G: EEC; U.S.]

Marcus, Mildred Rendl. The Monetary Implications of a Fixed Exchange Rate System. In *Schmukler, N. and Marcus, E., eds.*, 1983, pp. 301–11.

Marshall S., Jorge; Mardones S., José Luis and Marshall L., Isabel. IMF Conditionality: The Experiences of Argentina, Brazil, and Chile. In *Williamson, J., ed.*, 1983, pp. 275–321. [G: Chile; Brazil; Argentina]

Masera, Rainer S. International Liquidity and Monetary Control: Comment. In *von Furstenberg, G. M., ed.*, 1983, pp. 123–28.

Massari, Andrea. I diritti speciali di prelievo: un'occasione perduta? (Special Drawing Rights: A Lost Opportunity? With English summary.) *Bancaria*, August 1983, *39*(8), pp. 741–49.

McKenzie, George and Thomas, Stephen. Liquidity, Credit Creation and International Banking: An Econometric Investigation. *J. Banking Finance*, 1983, *7*(4), pp. 467–80. [G: U.K.]

McLeod, A. N. Reforming the International Monetary System. *Int. J. Soc. Econ.*, 1983, *10*(2), pp. 44–61.

McMahon, C. W. Financial Aspects of the International Economic Situation. *Nationaløkon. Tidsskr.*, 1983, *121*(1), pp. 74–82. [G: OECD]

Medio, Alfredo. Worldwide Inflation and Its Impact on Less Developed Countries. *Econ. Forum*, Summer 1983, *14*(1), pp. 1–26. [G: Global]

Meiselman, David I. Is Gold the Question? [Gold Standards: True and False]. *Cato J.*, Spring 1983, *3*(1), pp. 269–75. [G: U.S.]

Metghalchi, Massoud. European Monetary Union: Potential Costs and Benefits. *Rivista Int. Sci. Econ. Com.*, October–November 1983, *30*(10–11), pp. 1002–21. [G: W. Europe]

Mikesell, Raymond F. Appraising IMF Conditionality: Too Loose, Too Tight, or Just Right? In *Williamson, J., ed.*, 1983, pp. 47–62.

Mohammed, Azizali F. IMF and the International Banks. In *Kaushik, S. K., ed.*, 1983, pp. 93–96. [G: LDCs; OECD]

Mohammed, Azizali F. The Evolution of the International Monetary System and the Changing Role of the Fund. In *Hooke, A. W., ed.*, 1983, pp. 4–20.

Muldoon, Robert D. Rethinking the Ground Rules for an Open World Economy: An Opportunity for American Political Leadership. *Foreign Aff.*, Summer 1983, *61*(5), pp. 1078–98. [G: New Zealand; U.S.]

Mundell, Robert A. International Monetary Options. *Cato J.*, Spring 1983, *3*(1), pp. 189–210. [G: Global]

Mundell, Robert A. International Monetary Reform: The Optimal Mix in Big Countries. In *Tobin, J., ed.*, 1983, pp. 285–93.

Mundell, Robert A. The Origins and Evolution of Monetarism. In *Jansen, K., ed.*, 1983, pp. 43–54.

Narvekar, P. R. Collaboration between the Fund and the World Bank. In *Hooke, A. W., ed.*, 1983, pp. 119–34.

Nême, Colette. La politique économique et monétaire de la communauté économique européenne. (With English summary.) *Revue Écon. Polit.*, September–October 1983, *93*(5), pp. 761–71. [G: EEC]

Neufeld, Edward P. International Financial Stability in the New Oil Price Scenarios. *Can. Public Policy*, September 1983, *9*(3), pp. 304–13. [G: OPEC; LDCs]

Neumann, Manfred J. M. International Moneys and Monetary Arrangments in Private Markets: Comment. In *von Furstenberg, G. M., ed.*, 1983, pp. 322–26.

Niehans, Jürg. Financial Innovation, Multinational Banking, and Monetary Policy. *J. Banking Finance*, 1983, *7*(4), pp. 537–51.

Okyar, Osman. Turkey and the IMF: A Review of Relations, 1978–82. In *Williamson, J., ed.*, 1983, pp. 533–61. [G: Turkey]

Olsen, Leif H. The Bretton Woods Nostalgia. In *Kaushik, S. K., ed.*, 1983, pp. 19–26. [G: OECD; U.S.; LDCs]

Ortiz, Guillermo. Currency Substitution in Mexico: The Dollarization Problem. *J. Money, Credit, Banking*, May 1983, *15*(2), pp. 174–85. [G: Mexico]

Parkin, Michael. The SDR and the IMF: Toward a World Central Bank? Comment. In *von Furstenberg, G. M., ed.*, 1983, pp. 200–208.

Partee, J. Charles. Statement to the Subcommittee on Financial Institutions Supervision, Regulation and Insurance of the U.S. House Committee on Banking, Finance, and Urban Affairs, April 21, 1983. *Fed. Res. Bull.*, May 1983, *69*(5), pp. 341–45. [G: U.S.]

Pekshev, V. A. Soviet–Finnish Interbanking Cooperation. In *Möttölä, K.; Bykov, O. N. and Korolev, I. S., eds.*, 1983, pp. 181–87. [G: U.S.S.R.; Finland]

Phillips, Ronnie J. The Role of the International Monetary Fund in the Post-Bretton Woods Era. *Rev. Radical Polit. Econ.*, Summer 1983, *15*(2), pp. 59–81. [G: Global]

Pindyck, Robert S. Liquidity, Credit Creation and International Banking: An Econometric Investigation: Comment. *J. Banking Finance*, 1983, *7*(4), pp. 481–82. [G: U.K.]

Pirzio-Biroli, Corrado. Making Sense of the IMF Conditionality Debate. *J. World Trade Law*, March–April 1983, *17*(2), pp. 115–53.

Please, Stanley. IMF Conditionality: Country Studies: Comments, Chapters 15–16. In *Williamson, J., ed.*, 1983, pp. 415–20.

Polak, Jacques J. Monetarist Policies on a World Scale. In *Jansen, K., ed.*, 1983, pp. 175–88.

Prebisch, Raúl. The Crisis of Capitalism and International Trade. *Cepal Rev.*, August 1983, (20), pp. 51–74. [G: Latin America]

Purvis, Douglas D. International Liquidity and Monetary Control: Comment. **In** *von Furstenberg, G. M., ed.,* 1983, pp. 115–23.

Rambure, Dominique. L'utilizzazione privata dell'Ecu. (The Private Utilization of Ecu. With English summary.) *Mondo Aperto,* November–December 1983, *37*(6), pp. 355–68. **[G: EEC]**

Ranuzzi, Paolo. Some Evidence for European Monetary Union from Eurolink Simulations. *Econ. Notes,* 1983, (2), pp. 23–48. **[G: EEC]**

Reed, Howard Curtis. International Financial Center Preeminence in MNC and Nation–State Interaction. **In** *Goldberg, W. H., ed.,* 1983, pp. 128–58. **[G: Global]**

Reynolds, Alan. Why Gold? *Cato J.,* Spring 1983, *3*(1), pp. 211–32. **[G: U.S.; U.K.]**

Roll, Eric. Financing Investment. **In** *Heertje, A., ed.,* 1983, pp. 188–218. **[G: W. Europe]**

Roper, Don. The SDR and the IMF: Toward a World Central Bank? Comment. **In** *von Furstenberg, G. M., ed.,* 1983, pp. 208–12.

von Rosen, Rüdiger. Gedämpfter Optimismus auf der IWF-Jahresversammlung 1983. (Moderate Optimism at the 1983 IMF-Annual Meeting. With English summary.) *Kredit Kapital,* 1983, *16*(4), pp. 587–99.

Ruggie, John Gerard. Political Structure and Change in the International Economic Order: The North–South Dimension. **In** *Ruggie, J. G., ed.,* 1983, pp. 423–87. **[G: LDCs; MDCs]**

Sacchetti, Ugo. Conditionality in International Finance and the Crisis of the International Monetary System. *Econ. Notes,* 1983, (2), pp. 120–44.

Sachs, Jeffrey D. IMF Conditionality: County Studies: Comments, Chapters 17–19. **In** *Williamson, J., ed.,* 1983, pp. 505–10. **[G: Italy; U.K.; Portugal]**

Sakbani, M. M. A Critique of Bretton Woods: Principal Themes of a Reformed System. **In** *Gauhar, A., ed. (II),* 1983, pp. 121–33.

Salerno, Joseph T. Gold Standards: True and False. *Cato J.,* Spring 1983, *3*(1), pp. 239–67. **[G: U.S.]**

Schefold, Bertram. Political, Natural and Economic Influences: Comment [International Money and International Economic Relations]. **In** *Kregel, J. A., ed.,* 1983, pp. 176–81. **[G: Selected Countries]**

Schnitzel, Paul. Causality in the Euro-Dollar Growth Process. *Nebr. J. Econ. Bus.,* Summer 1983, *22*(3), pp. 66–77.

Schnitzel, Paul. Testing for the Direction of Causation between the Domestic Monetary Base and the Eurodollar System. *Weltwirtsch. Arch.,* 1983, *119*(4), pp. 616–29.

Schwartz, Anna J. The Postwar Institutional Evolution of the International Monetary System. **In** *Darby, M. P. and Lothian, J. R., et al.,* 1983, pp. 14–45. **[G: OECD]**

Sharpley, Jennifer. Economic Management and IMF Conditionality in Jamaica. **In** *Williamson, J., ed.,* 1983, pp. 233–62. **[G: Jamaica]**

Sheffer, Eliezer. The Role of International Banking in the 'Oil Surplus' Adjustment Process: Comment. *J. Banking Finance,* 1983, *7*(4), pp. 519–20. **[G: Global]**

Sievert, Olaf. Disillusionment in the Conduct of Exchange-Rate Policies. **In** *[Giersch, H.],* 1983, pp. 188–208. **[G: OECD; W. Germany]**

Sihag, Balbir S. Precautionary Demand for International Reserves. *Indian Econ. J.,* January-March 1983, *30*(3), pp. 65–74. **[G: Selected Countries]**

da Silva Lopes, Jose. IMF Conditionality: The Stand-by Arrangement with Portugal, 1978. **In** *Williamson, J., ed.,* 1983, pp. 475–504. **[G: Portugal]**

Sitzia, Bruno. Monetary Authorities' Reaction Functions and the European Monetary System: Discussion. **In** *Hodgman, D. R., ed.,* 1983, pp. 245.

Solomon, Anthony M. Toward a More Resilient International Financial System. *Fed. Res. Bank New York Quart. Rev.,* Autumn 1983, *8*(3), pp. 1–5. **[G: LDCs]**

Spaventa, Luigi. Two Letters of Intent: External Crises and Stabilization Policy, Italy, 1973–77. **In** *Williamson, J., ed.,* 1983, pp. 441–73. **[G: Italy]**

Spinelli, Franco. Currency Substitution, Flexible Exchange Rates, and the Case for International Monetary Cooperation: Discussion of a Recent Proposal. *Int. Monet. Fund Staff Pap.,* December 1983, *30*(4), pp. 755–83.

Stansbury, Philip R. Legal Aspects of Syndicated Eurocurrency Lending. **In** *George, A. M. and Giddy, I. H., eds., Vol. 1,* 1983, pp. 3.5:1–20.

Stern, Ernest. The Challenge of Development Today. *Finance Develop.,* September 1983, *20*(3), pp. 2–5. **[G: LDCs]**

Studýnka, Bohumil. The Position of Gold Today. *Soviet E. Europ. Foreign Trade,* Fall 1983, *19*(3), pp. 32–49.

Swoboda, Alexander K. Functioning of the Current International Financial System: Strengths, Weaknesses, and Criteria for Evaluation: Comment. **In** *von Furstenberg, G. M., ed.,* 1983, pp. 56–63.

Szabo Pelsoczi, Miklos. Inflation and the International Monetary Order. **In** *Schmukler, N. and Marcus, E., eds.,* 1983, pp. 340–49.

Szegö, Giorgio P. The role of International Banking in the 'Oil Surplus' Adjustment Process. *J. Banking Finance,* 1983, *7*(4), pp. 497–518. **[G: Global]**

Terrell, Henry S. and Mills, Rodney H. International Banking Facilities and the Eurodollar Market. *Fed. Res. Bull.,* August 1983, *69*(8), pp. 591. **[G: U.S.]**

Tharakan, P. K. M. Some Lessons from the "Mexico Syndrome." *Tijdschrift Econ. Manage.,* 1983, *28*(1), pp. 93–100. **[G: Latin America]**

Thygesen, Niels. What Are the Scope and Limits of Fruitful International Monetary Cooperation in the 1980s? Comment. **In** *von Furstenberg, G. M., ed.,* 1983, pp. 419–28.

Thys-Clement, Françoise. Monetary Authorities' Reaction Functions in a Model of Exchange-Rate Determination for the European Monetary System: Comment. **In** *De Grauwe, P. and Peeters, T., eds.,* 1983, pp. 283–84. **[G: EEC]**

Tumlir, Jan. International Economic Order and Democratic Constitutionalism. **In** *Lenel, H. O.; Willgerodt, H. and Molsberger, J.,* 1983, pp. 71–83.

Ungerer, Horst. Main Developments in the European Monetary System. *Finance Develop.,* June 1983, *20*(2), pp. 16–19. **[G: EEC]**

Van Arkadie, Brian. The IMF Prescription for Structural Adjustment in Tanzania: A Comment. **In** *Jansen, K., ed.*, 1983, pp. 127–48. **[G: Tanzania]**

Van Houtven, Leo. The Framework for Policymaking in the Fund. **In** *Hooke, A. W., ed.*, 1983, pp. 24–52.

Vencovský, František. Improvement of the Monetary Mechanism in the Process of the International Socialist Economic Integration. *Czech. Econ. Digest.*, March 1983, (2), pp. 3–15. **[G: CMEA]**

Vicarelli, Fausto. Incomes Policy and International Money: Comment [International Money and International Economic Relations]. **In** *Kregel, J. A., ed.*, 1983, pp. 182–85. **[G: Selected Countries]**

Volcker, Paul A. Remarks to the Subcommittee on International Finance and Monetary Policy, U.S. Senate, Committee on Banking, Housing, and Urban Affairs, February 17, 1983. *Fed. Res. Bull.*, March 1983, *69*(3), pp. 175–77.

Volcker, Paul A. Statement to the U.S. Senate Committee on Banking, Housing, and Urban Affairs, April 11, 1983. *Fed. Res. Bull.*, April 1983, *69*(4), pp. 273–80. **[G: U.S.]**

Volcker, Paul A. Statement to U.S. House Committee on Banking, Finance and Urban Affairs, February 2, 1983. *Fed. Res. Bull.*, February 1983, *69*(2), pp. 80–89. **[G: U.S.; Argentina; OPEC; Brazil; Mexico]**

de Vries, Rimmer and Porzecanski, Arturo C. IMF Conditionality: Role of the Fund: Comments, Chapters 1–3. **In** *Williamson, J., ed.*, 1983, pp. 63–71. **[G: LDCs; MDCs]**

Wallich, Henry C. Statement to the Subcommittee on International Trade, Investment and Monetary Policy, U.S. House Committee on Banking, Finance, and Urban Affairs, April 7, 1983. *Fed. Res. Bull.*, April 1983, *69*(4), pp. 266–73. **[G: U.S.; Global]**

Walmsley, Julian. Eurocurrency Dealing. **In** *George, A. M. and Giddy, I. H., eds., Vol. 1*, 1983, pp. 3.2:1–30.

Walsh, Brendan M. Ireland in the European Monetary System: The Effects of a Change in Exchange Rate Regime. **In** *de Cecco, M., ed.*, 1983, pp. 160–88. **[G: Ireland]**

Walter, Ingo. The Evolution of International Banking Competition and Its Implications for Regulation: Discussant's Comments. *J. Bank Res.*, Spring 1983, *14*(1), pp. 53–54. **[G: U.S.; OECD; Selected LDCs]**

Walter, Judith A. The Evolution of International Banking Competition and Its Implications for Regulation: Discussant's Comments. *J. Bank Res.*, Spring 1983, *14*(1), pp. 55–58. **[G: U.S.; OECD; Selected LDCs]**

Willett, Thomas D. Functioning of the Current International Financial System: Strengths, Weaknesses, and Criteria for Evaluation. **In** *von Furstenberg, G. M., ed.*, 1983, pp. 5–44.

Willett, Thomas D. U.S. Monetary Policy and World Liquidity. *Amer. Econ. Rev.*, May 1983, *73*(2), pp. 43–47. **[G: U.S.]**

Williamson, John. Keynes and the International Economic Order. **In** *Worswick, D. and Trevithick, J., eds.*, 1983, pp. 87–113.

Williamson, John. On Judging the Success of IMF Policy Advice. **In** *Williamson, J., ed.*, 1983, pp. 129–43.

Williamson, John. On Seeking to Improve the IMF Conditionality. *Amer. Econ. Rev.*, May 1983, *73*(2), pp. 354–58.

Williamson, John. The Lending Policies of the International Monetary Fund. **In** *Williamson, J., ed.*, 1983, pp. 605–60.

Williamson, John. Use of the SDR to Supplement or Substitute for Other Means of Finance: Comment. **In** *von Furstenberg, G. M., ed.*, 1983, pp. 367–73.

Zis, George. Exchange-Rate Fluctuations: 1973–82. *Nat. Westminster Bank Quart. Rev.*, August 1983, pp. 2–13. **[G: France; W. Germany; U.K.; Japan]**

433 Private International Lending

4330 Private International Lending

Adams, F. Gerard; Sanchez, Enrique P. and Adams, Mark E. Can Latin America Carry Its International Debt? A Prospective Analysis Using the Wharton Latin American Debt Simulation Model. *J. Policy Modeling*, November 1983, *5*(3), pp. 419–41. **[G: Latin America]**

Agmon, Tamir and Deitrich, J. KImball. International Lending and Income Redistribution: An Alternative View of Country Risk. *J. Banking Finance*, 1983, *7*(4), pp. 483–95. **[G: LDCs]**

Aliber, Robert Z. A Perspective on the External Debt of Latin America. **In** *Jorge, A.; Salazar-Carillo, J. and Higonnet, R. P., eds.*, 1983, pp. 37–39. **[G: Latin America]**

Basagni, Fabio. International Debt, Financial Stability and Growth. **In** *Basagni, F., ed.*, 1983, pp. 5–12. **[G: LDCs; OECD]**

Beauvoir, Raymond. External Financing and Debt of the Latin American Countries. **In** *Jorge, A.; Salazar-Carillo, J. and Higonnet, R. P., eds.*, 1983, pp. 41–54. **[G: Latin America]**

Bernal, Richard L. Economic Growth and External Debt of Jamaica. **In** *Jorge, A.; Salazar-Carillo, J. and Higonnet, R. P., eds.*, 1983, pp. 89–108. **[G: Jamaica]**

Bird, Graham. Low-Income Countries and International Financial Reform. *J. Devel. Areas*, October 1983, *18*(1), pp. 53–75. **[G: LDCs]**

Bird, Graham. The Banks and the IMF—Division of Labour. *Lloyds Bank Rev.*, October 1983, (150), pp. 19–33.

Bogdanowicz-Bindert, Christine A. Financial Crisis of 1982: A Debtor's Perspective. **In** *Kaushik, S. K., ed.*, 1983, pp. 203–06. **[G: LDCs]**

Bruni, Franco. Interest and Exchange Rate Volatility: Implications for Bank Management. *Giorn. Econ.*, July–August 1983, *42*(7–8), pp. 431–58. **[G: OECD]**

Buiter, Willem H. Implications for the Adjustment Process of International Asset Risks: Exchange Controls, Intervention and Policy Risk, and Sovereign Risk. **In** *Hawkins, R. G.; Levich, R. M. and Wihlborg, C. G., eds.*, 1983, pp. 69–102.

Clifton, Eric V. The Effects of Increased Interest-Rate Volatility on LDCs. *J. Int. Money Finance*,

April 1983, *2*(1), pp. 67–74.

Cohen, Benjamin J. Balance-of-Payments Financing: Evolution of a Regime. **In** *Krasner, S. D., ed.*, 1983, *1982*, pp. 315–36. **[G: Global]**

Coppé, Philippe. The Impact of the International Crisis on Management. *Ann. Sci. Écon. Appl.*, 1983, *39*(3), pp. 173–85. **[G: Global]**

Cullen, Andrew. Structural Economic Domination and World Trade with Reference to Latin America: A Marxist Approach. *Soc. Econ. Stud.*, September 1983, *32*(3), pp. 35–81. **[G: Latin America]**

Delgado, Enrique. Problems of Economic Growth and External Indebtedness in Central America. **In** *Jorge, A.; Salazar-Carillo, J. and Higonnet, R. P., eds.*, 1983, pp. 117–24. **[G: Central America]**

Dennis, Geoffrey E. J. The Growth of International Bank Lending, 1972–1982: Concepts, Measurement and Causes. *Aussenwirtschaft*, September 1983, *38*(3), pp. 263–83. **[G: Global]**

Devlin, Robert T. Renegotiation of Latin America's Debt: An Analysis of the Monopoly Power of Private Banks. *Cepal Rev.*, August 1983, (20), pp. 101–12. **[G: Latin America]**

Dini, Lamberto. Financial Strains in the World Economy. *Banca Naz. Lavoro Quart. Rev.*, March 1983, (144), pp. 51–67. **[G: Global]**

Fieleke, Norman S. International Lending on Trial. *New Eng. Econ. Rev.*, May/June 1983, pp. 5–13. **[G: U.S.; Non-OPEC; LDCs]**

Flanders, M. June. The Effects of Political Economic and Institutional Developments on International Banks: Comment. *J. Banking Finance*, 1983, *7*(4), pp. 623–24. **[G: LDCs]**

Fratianni, Michele. La crisi dell'indebitamento internazionale: come è sorta e come si può superare. (The International Debt Crisis: Causes and Policy Prescriptions. With English summary.) *Bancaria*, February 1983, *39*(2), pp. 139–46. **[G: LDCs]**

Friedman, Irving S. Latin American External Debt and Economic Growth: The Role of Debt Rescheduling. **In** *Jorge, A.; Salazar-Carillo, J. and Higonnet, R. P., eds.*, 1983, pp. 55–60. **[G: Latin America; Zaire]**

Friedman, Irving S. Private Bank Conditionality: Comparison with the IMF and the World Bank. **In** *Williamson, J., ed.*, 1983, pp. 109–24.

Gollas, Manuel. External Debt and Economic Growth: Mexico. **In** *Jorge, A.; Salazar-Carillo, J. and Higonnet, R. P., eds.*, 1983, pp. 139–53. **[G: Mexico]**

Goodman, Laurie S. Syndicated Eurolending: Pricing and Practice. **In** *George, A. M. and Giddy, I. H., eds., Vol. 1*, 1983, pp. 3.4:1–29. **[G: OECD]**

Greene, James. Bank Lending to Third World Countries in the 1980's. *J. Banking Finance*, 1983, *7*(4), pp. 553–58. **[G: LDCs]**

Griffith-Jones, Stephany. Information Access to International Finance: What Problems for Developing Countries? **In** *O'Brien, R. C., ed.*, 1983, pp. 70–77.

Griffiths, Brian. Banking on Crisis. *Policy Rev.*, Summer 1983, (25), pp. 28–35. **[G: U.S.; LDCs]**

Guth, Wilfried. Challenges to the International Financial System. **In** *Basagni, F., ed.*, 1983, pp. 24–32. **[G: LDCs; E. Europe; OECD]**

Guttentag, Jack and Herring, Richard J. What Happens when Countries Cannot Repay Their Bank Loans? The Renegotiation Process. **In** *Kaushik, S. K., ed.*, 1983, pp. 207–27. **[G: LDCs]**

Hankel, Wilhelm. The Global Financial Crisis—A Case Study in Modern Alchemy—Facts, Legends and Realities. **In** *Kaushik, S. K., ed.*, 1983, pp. 191–97. **[G: Global]**

Heimann, John G. The Effects of Political, Economic and Institutional Development on International Banks. *J. Banking Finance*, 1983, *7*(4), pp. 615–21. **[G: LDCs]**

Higonnet, Rene P. Latin American Debt: More Rescheduling? **In** *Jorge, A.; Salazar-Carillo, J. and Higonnet, R. P., eds.*, 1983, pp. 61–76. **[G: Latin America]**

Holbik, Karel. International Interdependence, Financial Intermediation and Multinational Banking. **In** *Kaushik, S. K., ed.*, 1983, pp. 121–30. **[G: LDCs; OECD]**

Johnson, Willene A. Bank Size and U.S. Bank Lending to Latin America. *Fed. Res. Bank New York Quart. Rev.*, Autumn 1983, *8*(3), pp. 20–21. **[G: U.S.; Latin America]**

Jorge, Antonio and Salazar-Carrillo, Jorge. External Debt and Development in Latin America: A Background Paper. **In** *Jorge, A.; Salazar-Carillo, J. and Higonnet, R. P., eds.*, 1983, pp. 1–35. **[G: Latin America]**

Keyzer, Marinus W. International Moneys and Monetary Arrangements in Private Markets: Comment. **In** *von Furstenberg, G. M., ed.*, 1983, pp. 319–22.

Kindleberger, Charles P. International Banks as Leaders or Followers of International Business: An Historical Perspective. *J. Banking Finance*, 1983, *7*(4), pp. 583–95. **[G: Europe; U.S.; Latin America]**

Krul, Nicolas. The Debt Problem: Some Observations on the Search for a New Financial Balance (abridged). **In** *Basagni, F., ed.*, 1983, pp. 55–60. **[G: LDCs; OECD]**

Kubarych, Roger. Responding to International Financial Crisis. **In** *Kaushik, S. K., ed.*, 1983, pp. 199–201. **[G: LDCs]**

Kuczynski, Pedro-Pablo. Why the Music Stopped [Interview]. *Challenge*, January/February 1983, *25*(6), pp. 20–29. **[G: U.S.; Latin America]**

Kwack, Sung Y. Developments in and Prospects for External Debt Position and Burden of Developing Countries: The Case of Korea. *J. Policy Modeling*, November 1983, *5*(3), pp. 443–59. **[G: S. Korea]**

Lessard, Donald R. Comments on "Implications for the Adjustment Process of International Asset Risks: Exchange Controls, Intervention and Policy Risk, and Sovereign Risk." **In** *Hawkins, R. G.; Levich, R. M. and Wihlborg, C. G., eds.*, 1983, pp. 107–10.

Lessard, Donald R. North–South: The Implications for Multinational Banking. *J. Banking Finance*, 1983, *7*(4), pp. 521–36. **[G: Global]**

Lewis, John P. The United States and the Third World, 1983: Can We Escape the Path of Mutual

Injury? In *Lewis, J. P. and Kallab, V., eds.*, 1983, pp. 7–48. **[G: LDCs; OECD; U.S.]**

Little, Jane Sneddon. Eurobank Maturity Transformation and LDC Debts. *New Eng. Econ. Rev.*, September/October 1983, pp. 15–19. **[G: LDCs; MDCs]**

Logue, Dennis E. Comments on "International Capital Allocation: Country Risk, Portfolio Decisions, and Regulation in International Banking." In *Hawkins, R. G.; Levich, R. M. and Wihlborg, C. G., eds.*, 1983, pp. 293–97. **[G: Selected Countries]**

Logue, Dennis E. and Senbet, Lemma W. External Currency Market Equilibrium and Its Implications for Regulation of the Eurocurrency Market. *J. Finance*, May 1983, *38*(2), pp. 435–47.

Lomax, David F. International Moneys and Monetary Arrangements in Private Markets. In *von Furstenberg, G. M., ed.*, 1983, pp. 261–318. **[G: U.S.; EEC]**

Looney, Robert E. and Frederiksen, P. C. The Feasibility of Alternative IMF-Type Stabilization Programs in Mexico, 1983–87. *J. Policy Modeling*, November 1983, *5*(3), pp. 461–70. **[G: Mexico]**

Marini, Luigi. La crisi finanziaria di alcuni paesi in via di sviluppo. Riflessi sul sistema bancario americano e possibili soluzioni. (The Financial Crisis of Several LDCs: Repercussions on the United States Banking System and Consideration of Possible Solutions. With English summary.) *Bancaria*, May–June 1983, *39*(5–6), pp. 489–97. **[G: U.S.; LDCs]**

Meier, Gerald M. Analyzing the Risk of Lending to Developing Countries. In *Kaushik, S. K., ed.*, 1983, pp. 153–60. **[G: LDCs]**

Melnik, Arie. The Role of Banks in the International Financial System: Comment. *J. Banking Finance*, 1983, *7*(4), pp. 465–66. **[G: OECD; LDCs]**

Messer, Oded. Bank Lending to Third World Countries in the 1980's: Comment. *J. Banking Finance*, 1983, *7*(4), pp. 559–60. **[G: LDCs]**

Mizrahi, David. Arab Investment and Banking in the U.S. In *Kaushik, S. K., ed.*, 1983, pp. 147–49. **[G: U.S.]**

Mohammed, Azizali F. IMF and the International Banks. In *Kaushik, S. K., ed.*, 1983, pp. 93–96. **[G: LDCs; OECD]**

Mohl, Andrew and Sobol, Dorothy. Currency Diversification and LDC Debt. *Fed. Res. Bank New York Quart. Rev.*, Autumn 1983, *8*(3), pp. 19–20. **[G: LDCs]**

Morse, Joel N. Banking in a Volatile World: Setting Country Lending Limits. In *Hansen, P., ed.*, 1983, pp. 269–79.

Munroe, Tapan. The Third World Debt Problem. *J. Energy Devel.*, Autumn 1983, *9*(1), pp. 63–67. **[G: LDCs]**

Neufeld, Edward P. International Debt, the Viability of the International Financial System, and World Economic Recovery. In *Basagni, F., ed.*, 1983, pp. 42–54. **[G: LDCs; E. Europe; OECD]**

Neumann, Manfred J. M. International Moneys and Monetary Arrangments in Private Markets: Comment. In *von Furstenberg, G. M., ed.*, 1983, pp. 322–26.

Nölling, Wilhelm. Internationale Verschuldung—Wege aus der Krise. (International Debt—Ways Out of the Crisis. With English summary.) *Kredit Kapital*, 1983, *16*(4), pp. 441–57.

Olsen, Leif H. The Bretton Woods Nostalgia. In *Kaushik, S. K., ed.*, 1983, pp. 19–26. **[G: OECD; U.S.; LDCs]**

Partee, J. Charles. Statement to the Subcommittee on Financial Institutions Supervision, Regulation and Insurance of the U.S. House Committee on Banking, Finance, and Urban Affairs, April 21, 1983. *Fed. Res. Bull.*, May 1983, *69*(5), pp. 341–45. **[G: U.S.]**

Quinn, Gerard. The International Debt Crisis. *Irish Banking Rev.*, December 1983, pp. 36–44.

Ragazzi, Giorgio. La crisi dei PVS colpisce l'export italiano. (The Crisis in the Developing Countries Hits Italian Ports. With English summary.) *L'Impresa*, 1983, *25*(6), pp. 47–50. **[G: Italy]**

Rambure, Dominique. L'utilizzazione privata dell'Ecu. (The Private Utilization of Ecu. With English summary.) *Mondo Aperto*, November-December 1983, *37*(6), pp. 355–68. **[G: EEC]**

Schmidt, Wilson E. The Role of Private Capital in Developing the Third World. In *Thompson, W. S., ed.*, 1983, pp. 267–83.

Sheffer, Eliezer. The Role of International Banking in the 'Oil Surplus' Adjustment Process: Comment. *J. Banking Finance*, 1983, *7*(4), pp. 519–20. **[G: Global]**

Solomon, Anthony M. Toward a More Resilient International Financial System. *Fed. Res. Bank Minn. Rev.*, Summer 1983, *7*(3), pp. 2–5. **[G: LDCs; MDCs]**

Stallings, Barbara. International Capitalism and the Peruvian Military Government. In *McClintock, C. and Lowenthal, A. F., eds.*, 1983, pp. 144–80. **[G: Peru]**

Stansbury, Philip R. Legal Aspects of Syndicated Eurocurrency Lending. In *George, A. M. and Giddy, I. H., eds., Vol. 1*, 1983, pp. 3.5:1–20.

Stern, Robert M. Comments on "Implications for the Adjustment Process of International Asset Risks: Exchange Controls, Intervention and Policy Risk, and Sovereign Risk." In *Hawkins, R. G.; Levich, R. M. and Wihlborg, C. G., eds.*, 1983, pp. 103–06.

Szegö, Giorgio P. The role of International Banking in the 'Oil Surplus' Adjustment Process. *J. Banking Finance*, 1983, *7*(4), pp. 497–518. **[G: Global]**

Teeters, Nancy H. The Role of Banks in the International Financial System. *J. Banking Finance*, 1983, *7*(4), pp. 453–63. **[G: OECD; LDCs]**

Tharakan, P. K. M. Some Lessons from the "Mexico Syndrome." *Tijdschrift Econ. Manage.*, 1983, *28*(1), pp. 93–100. **[G: Latin America]**

Tozaki, Seiki. International Debt Issues and Global Business and Trade: A Japanese Perspective. In *Basagni, F., ed.*, 1983, pp. 33–41. **[G: Japan; LDCs; OECD]**

Verde, Antimo. Some Considerations about Italy's Foreign Debts (1977–1982). *Rivista Polit. Econ.*, Supplement Dec. 1983, *73*(12), pp. 147–87. **[G: Italy]**

Volcker, Paul A. How Serious Is U.S. Bank Exposure? *Challenge*, May/June 1983, *26*(2), pp. 11–19. **[G: Mexico; Non-Oil LDCs; U.S.]**

Wallich, Henry C. LDC Credit Risk and Bank Regulation. **In** *Jorge, A.; Salazar-Carillo, J. and Higonnet, R. P., eds.,* 1983, pp. 85–88. **[G: LDCs]**

Walter, Ingo. International Capital Allocation: Country Risk, Portfolio Decisions, and Regulation in International Banking. **In** *Hawkins, R. G.; Levich, R. M. and Wihlborg, C. G., eds.,* 1983, pp. 245–92. **[G: Selected Countries]**

Williams, David. Opportunities and Constraints in International Lending. *Finance Develop.,* March 1983, *20*(1), pp. 24–27.

Wynant, Larry. International Project Finance. **In** *George, A. M. and Giddy, I. H., eds., Vol. 2,* 1983, pp. 7.3:1–26.

Zecher, J. Richard. The Effects of the Current Turbulent Times on American Multinational Banking: An Overview. *J. Banking Finance,* 1983, *7*(4), pp. 625–37. **[G: U.S.; LDCs]**

440 International Investment and Foreign Aid

441 International Investment and Long-term Capital Movements

4410 Theory of International Investment and Long-Term Capital Movements

Äijö, Toivo S. The Theory of the Special Advantage of the International Firm—A Comprehensive Theory of the International Expansion of the Business Enterprise. *Liiketaloudellinen Aikak.,* 1983, *32*(4), pp. 334–44.

Aliber, Robert Z. Money, Multinationals, and Sovereigns. **In** *Kindleberger, C. P. and Audretsch, D. B., eds.,* 1983, pp. 245–59. **[G: OECD]**

Bhagwati, Jagdish N. and Grinols, Earl. Foreign Capital, Dependence, Destabilisation and Feasibility of Transition to Socialism. **In** *Bhagwati, J. N., Vol. 2,* 1983, *1975,* pp. 479–92. **[G: Ghana; Israel; S. Korea; Philippines; India]**

Bhagwati, Jagdish N. and Tironi, Ernesto. Tariff Change, Foreign Capital and Immiserization. **In** *Bhagwati, J. N., Vol. 2,* 1983, *1980,* pp. 199–211.

Boddewyn, Jean J. Foreign Direct Divestment Theory: Is It the Reverse of FDI Theory? *Weltwirtsch. Arch.,* 1983, *119*(2), pp. 345–55.

Brecher, Richard A. and Bhagwati, Jagdish N. Immiserizing Transfers from Abroad. **In** *Bhagwati, J. N., Vol. 2,* 1983, *1982,* pp. 505–16.

Brecher, Richard A. and Feenstra, Robert C. International Trade and Capital Mobility between Diversified Economies. *J. Int. Econ.,* May 1983, *14*(3/4), pp. 321–39.

Brecher, Richard A. and Findlay, Ronald. Tariffs, Foreign Capital and National Welfare with Sector-Specific Factors. *J. Int. Econ.,* May 1983, *14*(3/4), pp. 277–88.

Buckley, Peter J. Macroeconomic versus International Business Approach to Direct Foreign Investment: A Comment on Professor Kojima's Interpretation. *Hitotsubashi J. Econ.,* June 1983, *24*(1), pp. 95–100. **[G: Japan]**

Buiter, Willem H. Implications for the Adjustment Process of International Asset Risks: Exchange Controls, Intervention and Policy Risk, and Sovereign Risk. **In** *Hawkins, R. G.; Levich, R. M. and Wihlborg, C. G., eds.,* 1983, pp. 69–102.

Carter, E. Eugene and Rodriguez, Rita M. International Capital Budgeting. **In** *George, A. M. and Giddy, I. H., eds., Vol. 2,* 1983, pp. 8.5:1–33.

Feldstein, Martin S. Domestic Saving and International Capital Movements in the Long Run and the Short Run. *Europ. Econ. Rev.,* March/April 1983, *21*(1/2), pp. 129–51. **[G: OECD]**

Gehrels, Franz. Foreign Investment and Technology Transfer: Optimal Policies. *Weltwirtsch. Arch.,* 1983, *119*(4), pp. 663–85.

Grinols, Earl and Bhagwati, Jagdish N. Foreign Capital, Savings and Dependence. **In** *Bhagwati, J. N., Vol. 2,* 1983, *1976,* pp. 493–501.

Grinols, Earl and Bhagwati, Jagdish N. Foreign Capital, Savings and Dependence: A Reply. **In** *Bhagwati, J. N., Vol. 2,* 1983, *1979,* pp. 502–04.

Hamilton, Carl and Svensson, Lars E. O. On the Choice between Capital Import and Labor Export. *Europ. Econ. Rev.,* January 1983, *20*(1–3), pp. 167–92.

Helpman, Elhanan and Razin, Assaf. Increasing Returns, Monopolistic Competition, and Factor Movements: A Welfare Analysis. *J. Int. Econ.,* May 1983, *14*(3/4), pp. 263–76.

Jones, Ronald W. and Dei, Fumio. International Trade and Foreign Investment: A Simple Model. *Econ. Inquiry,* October 1983, *21*(4), pp. 449–64.

Jones, Ronald W.; Neary, J. Peter and Ruane, Frances P. Two-Way Capital Flows: Cross-Hauling in a Model of Foreign Investment. *J. Int. Econ.,* May 1983, *14*(3/4), pp. 357–66.

Kogut, Bruce. Foreign Direct Investment as a Sequential Process. **In** *Kindleberger, C. P. and Audretsch, D. B., eds.,* 1983, pp. 38–56.

Kohlhagen, Steven W. Overlapping National Investment Portfolios: Evidence and Implications of International Integration of Secondary Markets for Financial Assets. **In** *Hawkins, R. G.; Levich, R. M. and Wihlborg, C. G., eds.,* 1983, pp. 113–37. **[G: OECD]**

Krugman, Paul R. The "New Theories" of International Trade and the Multinational Enterprise. **In** *Kindleberger, C. P. and Audretsch, D. B., eds.,* 1983, pp. 57–73.

Lessard, Donald R. Comments on "Implications for the Adjustment Process of International Asset Risks: Exchange Controls, Intervention and Policy Risk, and Sovereign Risk." **In** *Hawkins, R. G.; Levich, R. M. and Wihlborg, C. G., eds.,* 1983, pp. 107–10.

Lipton, David and Sachs, Jeffrey D. Accumulation and Growth in a Two-Country Model: A Simulation Approach. *J. Int. Econ.,* August 1983, *15*(1/2), pp. 135–59.

Logue, Dennis E. Comments on "International Capital Allocation: Country Risk, Portfolio Decisions, and Regulation in International Banking." **In** *Hawkins, R. G.; Levich, R. M. and Wihlborg, C. G., eds.,* 1983, pp. 293–97. **[G: Selected Countries]**

Madeuf, Bernadette and Ominami, Carlos. Crise et investissement international. (Crisis and International Investment. With English summary.) *Revue Écon.*, September 1983, *34*(5), pp. 926–70. [G: OECD]

Magee, Stephen P. and Young, Leslie. Multinationals, Tariffs, and Capital Flows with Endogenous Politicians. In *Kindleberger, C. P. and Audretsch, D. B., eds.*, 1983, pp. 21–37.

Marston, Richard C. Comments on "Overlapping National Investment Portfolios: Evidence and Implications of International Integration of Secondary Markets for Financial Assets." In *Hawkins, R. G.; Levich, R. M. and Wihlborg, C. G., eds.*, 1983, pp. 139–43. [G: OECD]

de Meza, David. The Transfer Problem in a Many-Country World: Is It Better to Give than Receive? *Manchester Sch. Econ. Soc. Stud.*, September 1983, *51*(3), pp. 266–75.

Minabe, Nobuo. Tariffs, Capital Export and Immiserizing Growth: A Reply. *J. Int. Econ.*, November 1983, *15*(3/4), pp. 389–92.

Momigliano, Franco and Balcet, Giovanni. New Trends in Internationalization: Processes and Theories. Diversified Patterns of Multinational Enterprise and Old and New Forms of Foreign Involvement of the Firm. *Econ. Notes*, 1983, (3), pp. 42–68. [G: U.S.; Germany; Japan]

Mutti, John H. and Gerking, Shelby D. Multinational Corporations and Discriminatory Investment Controls. *Weltwirtsch. Arch.*, 1983, *119*(4), pp. 649–62.

Ossola, Rinaldo. Compiti e responsabilità delle banche nei finanziamenti internazionali. (Tasks and Responsibilities of Banks in International Lending. With English summary.) *Bancaria*, August 1983, *39*(8), pp. 690–94.

Putnam, Bluford H. Comments on "Overlapping National Investment Portfolios: Evidence and Implications of International Integration of Secondary Markets of Financial Assets." In *Hawkins, R. G.; Levich, R. M. and Wihlborg, C. G., eds.*, 1983, pp. 145–48. [G: OECD]

Reed, Howard Curtis. Appraising Corporate Investment Policy: A Financial Center Theory of Foreign Direct Investment. In *Kindleberger, C. P. and Audretsch, D. B., eds.*, 1983, pp. 219–44. [G: Global]

Roemer, John E. Unequal Exchange, Labor Migration, and International Capital Flows: A Theoretical Synthesis. In *[Erlich, A.]*, 1983, pp. 34–60.

Roosa, Robert V. The Gap between Trade Theory and Capital Flows. *Challenge*, March/April 1983, *26*(1), pp. 54–57.

Srinivasan, T. N. International Factor Movements, Commodity Trade and Commercial Policy in a Specific Factor Model. *J. Int. Econ.*, May 1983, *14*(3/4), pp. 289–312.

Stern, Robert M. Comments on "Implications for the Adjustment Process of International Asset Risks: Exchange Controls, Intervention and Policy Risk, and Sovereign Risk." In *Hawkins, R. G.; Levich, R. M. and Wihlborg, C. G., eds.*, 1983, pp. 103–06.

Stulz, René M. On the Determinants of Net Foreign Investment. *J. Finance*, May 1983, *38*(2), pp. 459–68.

Tobin, James. 'Domestic Saving and International Capital Movements in the Long Run and the Short Run' by M. Feldstein: Comment. *Europ. Econ. Rev.*, March/April 1983, *21*(1/2), pp. 153–56. [G: OECD]

Vicary, Simon J. R. Endogenous Population Growth in an Overlapping Generations Model with International Lending and Borrowing. *Bull. Econ. Res.*, May 1983, *35*(1), pp. 1–24. [G: LDCs]

Walter, Ingo. International Capital Allocation: Country Risk, Portfolio Decisions, and Regulation in International Banking. In *Hawkins, R. G.; Levich, R. M. and Wihlborg, C. G., eds.*, 1983, pp. 245–92. [G: Selected Countries]

Westphal, Uwe. 'Domestic Saving and International Capital Movements in the Long Run and the Short Run' by M. Feldstein: Comment. *Europ. Econ. Rev.*, March/April 1983, *21*(1/2), pp. 157–59. [G: OECD]

Woodland, Alan D. Stability, Capital Mobility and Trade. *Int. Econ. Rev.*, June 1983, *24*(2), pp. 475–83.

Yeh, Yeong-Her. Tariffs, Capital Export and Immiserizing Growth: A Comment. *J. Int. Econ.*, November 1983, *15*(3/4), pp. 387–88.

4412 International Investment and Long-Term Capital Movements: Studies

Akao, Nobutoshi. Japan's Search for Economic Security. In *Akao, N., ed.*, 1983, pp. 245–72. [G: U.S.; Selected Countries]

Alburo, Florian A. Philippine–Japanese Investment Relations: A Tentative Assessment. *Philippine Econ. J.*, 198, *22*(1), pp. 29–45. [G: Philippines; Japan]

Allen, Polly Reynolds. Gains from Foreign Investment: A Comment [Foreign Investment: A Host Country Perspective Using Australian Experience]. *J. Post Keynesian Econ.*, Winter 1982–83, *5*(2), pp. 318–22.

Alzamora, Carlos and Iglesias, Enrique V. Bases for a Latin American Response to the International Economic Crisis. *Cepal Rev.*, August 1983, (20), pp. 17–46. [G: Latin America]

Artisien, Patrick F. R. and Buckley, Peter J. Investment Legislation in Greece, Portugal and Spain: The Background to Foreign Investment in Mediterranean Europe. *J. World Trade Law*, November–December 1983, *17*(6), pp. 513–23. [G: Greece; Portugal; Spain; EEC]

Beauvoir, Raymond. External Financing and Debt of the Latin American Countries. In *Jorge, A.; Salazar-Carillo, J. and Higonnet, R. P., eds.*, 1983, pp. 41–54. [G: Latin America]

Belli, R. David. Foreign Direct Investment in the United States: Highlights from the 1980 Benchmark Survey. *Surv. Curr. Bus.*, October 1983, *63*(10), pp. 25–35. [G: U.S.]

Bellin, R. David. U.S. Business Enterprises Acquired or Established by Foreign Direct Investors in 1982. *Surv. Curr. Bus.*, June 1983, *63*(6), pp. 27–32. [G: U.S.]

Berend, Iván T. German Capital in Silesian Industry in Poland between the Two World Wars: Commentary. In *Teichova, A. and Cottrell, P. L., eds.*, 1983, pp. 251. [G: Poland; Selected Countries]

Bergsten, C. Fred. International Investment: The Need for a New U.S. Policy. **In** *Bergsten, C. F.*, 1983, pp. 187–97. **[G: U.S.]**

Bergsten, C. Fred. The Future of the Overseas Private Investment Corporation (OPIC). **In** *Bergsten, C. F.*, 1983, pp. 199–205. **[G: U.S.]**

Bhagwati, Jagdish N. and Grinols, Earl. Foreign Capital, Dependence, Destabilisation and Feasibility of Transition to Socialism. **In** *Bhagwati, J. N., Vol. 2*, 1983, *1975*, pp. 479–92. **[G: Ghana; Israel; S. Korea; Philippines; India]**

Bhagwati, Jagdish N. and Srinivasan, T. N. On the Choice between Capital and Labour Mobility. **In** *Bhagwati, J. N., Vol. 2*, 1983, pp. 31–43.

Breimyer, Harold F. Foreign Investment in the U.S. Food-Marketing System: Discussion. *Amer. J. Agr. Econ.*, May 1983, *65*(2), pp. 421–22. **[G: U.S.]**

Bussière, Eric. The Interests of the Banque de l'Union Parisienne in Czechoslovakia, Hungary and the Balkans, 1919–30. **In** *Teichova, A. and Cottrell, P. L., eds.*, 1983, pp. 399–410. **[G: France; Central Europe]**

Cannon, Terry. Foreign Investment and Trade; Origins of the Modernization Policy. **In** *Feuchtwang, S. and Hussain, A., eds.*, 1983, pp. 288–324. **[G: China]**

Chia, Siow Yue. Singapore—EEC Economic Relations. **In** *Chen, P. S. J., ed.*, 1983, pp. 301–34. **[G: Singapore; EEC]**

Chung, William K. and Fouch, Gregory G. Foreign Direct Investment in the United States in 1982. *Surv. Curr. Bus.*, August 1983, *63*(8), pp. 31–41. **[G: U.S.]**

Connor, John M. Determinants of Foreign Direct Investment by Food and Tobacco Manufacturers. *Amer. J. Agr. Econ.*, May 1983, *65*(2), pp. 395–404. **[G: U.S.]**

Cottrell, P. L. Aspects of Western Equity Investment in the Banking Systems of East Central Europe. **In** *Teichova, A. and Cottrell, P. L., eds.*, 1983, pp. 309–47. **[G: Austria; Czechoslovakia; Hungary]**

Coughlin, Cletus C. An Economic Analysis of Yugoslav Joint Ventures. *J. World Trade Law*, January–February 1983, *17*(1), pp. 12–33. **[G: Yugoslavia]**

Crouzet, François. Comment [The Interests of the Union Européenne in Central Europe] [The Interests of the Banque de l'Union Parisienne in Czechoslovakia, Hungary and the Balkans, 1919–30]. **In** *Teichova, A. and Cottrell, P. L., eds.*, 1983, pp. 411–13. **[G: Central Europe; France]**

Dennis, Geoffrey E. J. The Growth of International Bank Lending, 1972–1982: Concepts, Measurement and Causes. *Aussenwirtschaft*, September 1983, *38*(3), pp. 263–83. **[G: Global]**

Devlin, Robert T. Renegotiation of Latin America's Debt: An Analysis of the Monopoly Power of Private Banks. *Cepal Rev.*, August 1983, (20), pp. 101–12. **[G: Latin America]**

Dini, Lamberto. Financial Strains in the World Economy. *Banca Naz. Lavoro Quart. Rev.*, March 1983, (144), pp. 51–67. **[G: Global]**

Dtugorborski, Waclaw. German Capital in Silesian Industry in Poland between the Two World Wars: Commentary. **In** *Teichova, A. and Cottrell, P. L., eds.*, 1983, pp. 247–50. **[G: Poland; Selected Countries]**

Dullum, Kåre B. and Stonehill, Arthur. Towards an International Cost of Capital. *Nationaløkon. Tidsskr.*, 1983, *121*(1), pp. 43–60. **[G: Denmark]**

Dunning, John H. Changes in the Level and Structure of International Production: The Last One Hundred Years. **In** *Casson, M., ed.*, 1983, pp. 84–139. **[G: Global]**

Ehrlich, Edna E. Foreign Pension Fund Investments in the United States. *Fed. Res. Bank New York Quart. Rev.*, Spring 1983, *8*(1), pp. 1–12. **[G: Canada; Netherlands; Japan; U.K.; U.S.]**

von Furstenberg, George M. Domestic Determinants of the Current Account Balance of the United States. *Quart. J. Econ.*, August 1983, *98*(3), pp. 401–25. **[G: U.S.]**

Galenson, Walter. Capitalists and Commissars. *Policy Rev.*, Spring 1983, (24), pp. 9. **[G: E. Europe; W. Europe; U.S.]**

George, Abraham M. and Ittoop, Vinita M. International Portfolio Diversification: Risks and Returns. **In** *George, A. M. and Giddy, I. H., eds., Vol. 2*, 1983, pp. 8.3:1–53. **[G: U.S.; U.K.; Japan; W. Germany]**

Godano, Giuseppe. L'internazionalizzazione del mercato finanziario giapponese. (The Internationalization of the Japanese Financial Market. With English summary.) *Bancaria*, October 1983, *39*(10), pp. 986–94. **[G: Japan]**

Grant, John. Foreign Investment: Turning Off and Turning On. *Can. Public Policy*, March 1983, *9*(1), pp. 32–36. **[G: Canada]**

Gray, H. Peter. A Negotiating Strategy for Trade in Services. *J. World Trade Law*, September–October 1983, *17*(5), pp. 377–88.

Habib, Fawzi. Commentary: Need and Rationale for a Near East Development Fund. **In** *Starr, J. R., ed.*, 1983, pp. 115–20. **[G: Middle East]**

Hansen, Bent. Interest Rates and Foreign Capital in Egypt under British Occupation. *J. Econ. Hist.*, December 1983, *43*(4), pp. 867–84. **[G: Egypt]**

Herold, Marc W. Finanzkapital in El Salvador, 1900–1980. *Econ. Forum*, Summer 1983, *14*(1), pp. 79–94. **[G: El Salvador]**

Houpt, James V. Foreign Ownership of U.S. Banks: Trends and Effects. *J. Bank Res.*, Summer 1983, *14*(2), pp. 144–56. **[G: U.S.]**

Hunter, Shireen T. Middle East Development Funds and Banks: An Overview. **In** *Starr, J. R., ed.*, 1983, pp. 71–102. **[G: Middle East; Africa; OPEC]**

Hussey, C. E., II and Berkson, Stuart M. Tax Policy and International Capital Flows. **In** *Walker, C. E. and Bloomfield, M. E., eds.*, 1983, pp. 346–53. **[G: U.S.]**

Igawa, Kazuhiro. Some Evidences between Foreign Direct Investments and Foreign Exchange Rates: A Preliminary Note. *Kobe Econ. Bus. Rev.*, 1983, (29), pp. 21–32. **[G: U.K.; W. Germany; U.S.; Japan]**

Jao, Y. C. Hong Kong's Role in Financing China's Modernization. **In** *Youngson, A. J., ed.*, 1983, pp. 12–76. **[G: Hong Kong; China]**

Kojima, Kiyoshi. Japanese Direct Foreign Investment in Asian Developing Countries. **In** *Fodella, G., ed.*, 1983, pp. 113–24. **[G: Japan]**

Kozlow, Ralph. Capital Expenditures by Majority-Owned Foreign Affiliates of U.S. Companies, 1983 and 1984. *Surv. Curr. Bus.*, September 1983, *63*(9), pp. 27–33. **[G: U.S.]**

Kozlow, Ralph. Capital Expenditures by Majority-Owned Foreign Affiliates of U.S. Companies, 1983. *Surv. Curr. Bus.*, March 1983, *63*(3), pp. 25–30. **[G: U.S.]**

Lall, Sanjaya and Mohammad, Sharif. Multinationals in Indian Big Business: Industrial Characteristics of Foreign Investments in a Heavily Regulated Economy. *J. Devel. Econ.*, Aug.–Oct. 1983, *13*(1–2), pp. 143–57. **[G: India]**

Lamfalussy, Alexandre. Investment and the International Monetary and Financial Environment. **In** *Heertje, A., ed.*, 1983, pp. 56–71. **[G: U.S.; EEC]**

Lapping, Mark B. and Lecko, Margaret. Foreign Investment in U.S. Agricultural Land: An Overview of the National Issue and a Case Study of Vermont. *Amer. J. Econ. Soc.*, July 1983, *42*(3), pp. 291–304. **[G: U.S.]**

Lee, Chung H. International Production of the United States and Japan in Korean Manufacturing Industries: A Comparative Study. *Weltwirtsch. Arch.*, 1983, *119*(4), pp. 744–53. **[G: Japan; S. Korea; U.S.]**

Lee, Lai To. Singapore and East Asia. **In** *Chen, P. S. J., ed.*, 1983, pp. 335–59. **[G: Singapore; E. Asia]**

Lessard, Donald R. Principles of International Portfolio Selection. **In** *George, A. M. and Giddy, I. H., eds., Vol. 2*, 1983, pp. 8.2:1–19. **[G: Selected Countries]**

Lévy-Leboyer, M. Aspects of Western Equity Investment in the Banking Systems of East Central Europe: Commentary. **In** *Teichova, A. and Cottrell, P. L., eds.*, 1983, pp. 347–49. **[G: Austria; Czechoslovakia; Hungary]**

Lévy, Philippe. The OECD Declaration on International Investment and Multinational Enterprises. **In** *Rubin, S. J. and Hufbauer, G. C., eds.*, 1983, pp. 47–62. **[G: OECD]**

Little, Jane Sneddon. Foreign Investors' Locational Choices: An Update. *New Eng. Econ. Rev.*, January/February 1983, pp. 28–31. **[G: U.S.]**

Lunn, John. Determinants of U.S. Direct Investment in the E.E.C.: Revisited Again. *Europ. Econ. Rev.*, May 1983, *21*(3), pp. 391–93. **[G: U.S.; EEC]**

Marini, Luigi. La crisi finanziaria di alcuni paesi in via di sviluppo. Riflessi sul sistema bancario americano e possibili soluzioni. (The Financial Crisis of Several LDCs: Repercussions on the United States Banking System and Consideration of Possible Solutions. With English summary.) *Bancaria*, May–June 1983, *39*(5–6), pp. 489–97. **[G: U.S.; LDCs]**

Marion, Bruce W. and Nash, Howard J. Foreign Investment in U.S. Food-Retailing Industry. *Amer. J. Agr. Econ.*, May 1983, *65*(2), pp. 413–20. **[G: U.S.]**

Mayes, David G. EC Trade Effects and Factor Mobility. **In** *El-Agraa, A. M., ed.*, 1983, pp. 88–121. **[G: EEC; U.K.]**

McClain, David. Foreign Direct Investment in the United States: Old Currents, "New Waves," and the Theory of Direct Investment. **In** *Kindleberger, C. P. and Audretsch, D. B., eds.*, 1983, pp. 278–333. **[G: U.S.]**

McConnell, James E. The International Location of Manufacturing Investments: Recent Behaviour of Foreign-owned Corporations in the United States. **In** *Hamilton, F. E. I. and Linge, G. J. R., eds.*, 1983, pp. 337–58. **[G: U.S.]**

McCulloch, Rachel and Owen, Robert F. Linking Negotiations on Trade and Foreign Direct Investment. **In** *Kindleberger, C. P. and Audretsch, D. B., eds.*, 1983, pp. 334–58. **[G: Canada]**

Michel, B. Aspects of Western Equity Investment in the Banking Systems of East Central Europe: Commentary. **In** *Teichova, A. and Cottrell, P. L., eds.*, 1983, pp. 350–53. **[G: Austria; Czechoslovakia; Hungary]**

Mytelka, Lynn Krieger. The Limits of Export-led Development: The Ivory Coast's Experience with Manufactures. **In** *Ruggie, J. G., ed.*, 1983, pp. 239–70. **[G: Ivory Coast; Sub-Saharan Africa]**

Nathan, Robert R. and Levinson, Jerome I. A Development Fund for the Near East. **In** *Starr, J. R., ed.*, 1983, pp. 103–13. **[G: Middle East]**

Newfarmer, Richard S. Multinationals and Marketplace Magic in the 1980s. **In** *Kindleberger, C. P. and Audretsch, D. B., eds.*, 1983, pp. 162–97. **[G: Global]**

Pagoulatos, Emilio. Foreign Direct Investment in U.S. Food and Tobacco Manufacturing and Domestic Economic Performance. *Amer. J. Agr. Econ.*, May 1983, *65*(2), pp. 405–12. **[G: U.S.]**

Piper, Don C. Foreign Direct Investment in the United States: The Balance of Foreign and Domestic Policy. **In** *Piper, D. C. and Terchek, R. J., eds.*, 1983, pp. 118–45. **[G: U.S.]**

Pugel, Thomas A. Foreign Investment in the U.S. Food-Marketing System: Discussion. *Amer. J. Agr. Econ.*, May 1983, *65*(2), pp. 423–25.

Ragazzi, Giorgio. Il ruolo del finanziamento estero nello sviluppo economico e la problematica attuale dell'indebitamento. (The Role of Foreign Financing in Economic Development and the Current Debt Problem. With English summary.) *Bancaria*, May–June 1983, *39*(5–6), pp. 477–88. **[G: LDCs]**

Richardson, David R. Foreign Investment: A Rejoinder [Foreign Investment: A Host Country Perspective Using Australian Experience]. *J. Post Keynesian Econ.*, Winter 1982–83, *5*(2), pp. 323–26. **[G: Australia]**

Rosenberg, Michael R. Foreign Exchange Controls: An International Comparison. **In** *George, A. M. and Giddy, I. H., eds., Vol. 1*, 1983, pp. 2.2:1–66.

Rubin, Seymour J. and Hufbauer, Gary Clyde. Emerging Standards of International Trade and Investment: Lessons from the Codes. **In** *Rubin, S. J. and Hufbauer, G. C., eds.*, 1983, pp. 175–96. **[G: Global]**

Rugman, Alan M. Canada: FIRA Updated [The Regulation of Foreign Investment in Canada]. *J. World Trade Law*, July–August 1983, *17*(4), pp. 352–55. **[G: Canada]**

Safarian, A. E. Trade-related Investment Issues. **In** *Cline W. R., ed.*, 1983, pp. 611–37.

Scaperlanda, Anthony and Balough, Robert S. Determinants of U.S. Direct Investment in the E.E.C.: Revisited. *Europ. Econ. Rev.*, May 1983, *21*(3), pp. 381–90. **[G: U.S.; EEC]**

Scholl, Russell B. The International Investment Position of the United States in 1982. *Surv. Curr. Bus.*, August 1983, *63*(8), pp. 42–48. **[G: U.S.]**

Shiriaev, P. Cooperation in Investments: A Factor in the Intensification of Production in CMEA Member Nations. *Prob. Econ.*, May 1983, *26*(1), pp. 74–89.

Stefani, Giorgio. Special Economic Zones and Economic Policy in China. *Ann. Pub. Co-op. Econ.*, July–September 1983, *54*(3), pp. 289–312. **[G: China]**

Thrall, Grant Ian and Erol, Cengiz. A Dynamic Equilibrium Model of Regional Capital Investment with Supporting Evidence from Canada and the United States. *Econ. Geogr.*, July 1983, *59*(3), pp. 272–81. **[G: Canada; U.S.]**

Tomaszewski, Jerzy. German Capital in Silesian Industry in Poland between the Two World Wars. **In** *Teichova, A. and Cottrell, P. L., eds.*, 1983, pp. 227–47. **[G: Poland; Selected Countries]**

Vahlne, Jan-Erik. Foreign Direct Investments: A Swedish Policy Problem. **In** *Goldberg, W. H., ed.*, 1983, pp. 207–18. **[G: Sweden]**

Válek, Vratislav. Selected Questions Concerning the Effectiveness of Joint Investment Activity by CMEA Members. *Soviet E. Europ. Foreign Trade*, Winter 1983–84, *19*(4), pp. 45–61. **[G: CMEA]**

Volcker, Paul A. How Serious Is U.S. Bank Exposure? *Challenge*, May/June 1983, *26*(2), pp. 11–19. **[G: Mexico; Non-Oil LDCs; U.S.]**

Vukmanic, Frank G. Performance Requirements: The General Debate and a Review of Latin American Practices. **In** *Czinkota, M. R., ed. (II)*, 1983, pp. 48–84. **[G: Latin America]**

Whichard, Obie G. U.S. Direct Investment Abroad in 1982. *Surv. Curr. Bus.*, August 1983, *63*(8), pp. 14–30. **[G: U.S.]**

Yu, Xiaosong and Lin, Zhongshu. Utilization of Foreign Capital to Renovate Enterprises Produces Good Results. *Chinese Econ. Stud.*, Spring 1983, *16*(3), pp. 40–47. **[G: China]**

442 International Business and Multinational Enterprises

4420 International Business and Multinational Enterprises

Adelman, Morris A. The Multinationals in the World Oil Market: The 1970s and the 1980s. **In** *Kindleberger, C. P. and Audretsch, D. B., eds.*, 1983, pp. 123–35. **[G: OECD; OPEC]**

Äijö, Toivo S. The Theory of the Special Advantage of the International Firm—A Comprehensive Theory of the International Expansion of the Business Enterprise. *Liiketaloudellinen Aikak.*, 1983, *32*(4), pp. 334–44.

Akinsanya, Adeoye A. State Strategies toward Nigerian and Foreign Business. **In** *Zartman, I. W., ed.*, 1983, pp. 145–84. **[G: Nigeria]**

Akrasanee, Narongchai. ASEAN–Japan Trade and Development: A Synthesis. **In** *Akrasanee, N., ed.*, 1983, pp. 1–35. **[G: ASEAN; Japan]**

Alburo, Florian A. Philippine–Japanese Investment Relations: A Tentative Assessment. *Philippine Econ. J.*, 198, *22*(1), pp. 29–45. **[G: Philippines; Japan]**

Aliber, Robert Z. Money, Multinationals, and Sovereigns. **In** *Kindleberger, C. P. and Audretsch, D. B., eds.*, 1983, pp. 245–59. **[G: OECD]**

Artisien, Patrick F. R. and Buckley, Peter J. Investment Legislation in Greece, Portugal and Spain: The Background to Foreign Investment in Mediterranean Europe. *J. World Trade Law*, November–December 1983, *17*(6), pp. 513–23. **[G: Greece; Portugal; Spain; EEC]**

Atamer, Tugrul. Le processus d'acquisition technologique par les entreprises d'un pays semi-industrialisé. Deux études de cas. (With English summary.) *Rev. Econ. Ind.*, 4th Trimester 1983, (26), pp. 24–33. **[G: France; Turkey]**

Auty, R. M. Multinational Corporations and Regional Revenue Retention in a Vertically Integrated Industry: Bauxite/Aluminium in the Caribbean. *Reg. Stud.*, February 1983, *17*(1), pp. 3–17. **[G: Caribbean; U.S.; Brazil; Australia]**

Babbel, David F. Determining the Optimum Strategy for Hedging Currency Exposure. *J. Int. Bus. Stud.*, Spring/Summer 1983, *14*(1), pp. 133–39.

Balasubramaniam, Kumariah. The Main Lines of Cooperation among Developing Countries in Pharmaceuticals. *World Devel.*, March 1983, *11*(3), pp. 281–87. **[G: LDCs]**

Balasubramanyam, V. N. Transnational Corporations: Choice of Techniques and Employment in Developing Countries. **In** *Weisbrod, B. and Hughes, H., eds.*, 1983, pp. 527–46. **[G: Selected LDCs]**

Baliga, B. R. U.S. Multinational Corporations: A Lesson in the Failure of Success. **In** *Goldberg, W. H., ed.*, 1983, pp. 42–56. **[G: U.S.]**

Barry, Mary. Latin American Exports of Textiles and Apparel—Background Report. **In** *Czinkota, M. R., ed. (II)*, 1983, pp. 126–40. **[G: Latin America; E. Asia]**

Bates, Timothy. The Impact of Multinational Corporations on Power Relations in South Africa. *Rev. Black Polit. Econ.*, Winter 1983, *12*(2), pp. 133–43. **[G: S. Africa]**

Beaud, C. The Interests of the Union Européenne in Central Europe. **In** *Teichova, A. and Cottrell, P. L., eds.*, 1983, pp. 375–97. **[G: Central Europe]**

Beidleman, Carl R.; Hilley, John L. and Greenleaf, James A. Alternatives in Hedging Long-Date Contractual Foreign Exchange Exposure. *Sloan Manage. Rev.*, Summer 1983, *24*(4), pp. 45–54. **[G: U.S.]**

Belli, R. David. Foreign Direct Investment in the United States: Highlights from the 1980 Benchmark Survey. *Surv. Curr. Bus.*, October 1983, *63*(10), pp. 25–35. **[G: U.S.]**

Bellin, R. David. U.S. Business Enterprises Acquired or Established by Foreign Direct Investors in 1982. *Surv. Curr. Bus.*, June 1983, *63*(6), pp. 27–32. **[G: U.S.]**

Berend, Iván T. German Capital in Silesian Industry in Poland between the Two World Wars: Commentary. **In** *Teichova, A. and Cottrell, P. L., eds.*,

1983, pp. 251. **[G: Poland; Selected Countries]**

Bernal, Richard L. Economic Growth and External Debt of Jamaica. **In** *Jorge, A.; Salazar-Carillo, J. and Higonnet, R. P., eds.*, 1983, pp. 89–108. **[G: Jamaica]**

Betsch, Philip A. and Wright, Kevin P. The Practice of Currency Exposure Management. **In** *George, A. M. and Giddy, I. H., eds., Vol. 2*, 1983, pp. 8.10:1–15.

Bhagwati, Jagdish N. and Grinols, Earl. Foreign Capital, Dependence, Destabilisation and Feasibility of Transition to Socialism. **In** *Bhagwati, J. N., Vol. 2*, 1983, *1975*, pp. 479–92. **[G: Ghana; Israel; S. Korea; Philippines; India]**

Biersteker, Thomas J. Indigenization in Nigeria: Renationalization or Denationalization? **In** *Zartman, I. W., ed.*, 1983, pp. 185–206. **[G: Nigeria]**

Bilson, John F. O. The Choice of an Invoice Currency in International Transactions. **In** *Bhandari, J. S. and Putnam, B. H., eds.*, 1983, pp. 384–401.

Blair, Andrew R. The Relationship of MNC Direct Investment to Host Country Trade and Trade Policy: Some Preliminary Evidence. **In** *Goldberg, W. H., ed.*, 1983, pp. 270–301. **[G: Latin America]**

Blomström, Magnus and Persson, Håkan. Foreign Investment and Spillover Efficiency in an Underdeveloped Economy: Evidence from the Mexican Manufacturing Industry. *World Devel.*, June 1983, *11*(6), pp. 493–501. **[G: Mexico]**

Boddewyn, Jean J. Foreign and Domestic Divestment and Investment Decisions: Like or Unlike? *J. Int. Bus. Stud.*, Winter 1983, *14*(3), pp. 23–35.

Boddewyn, Jean J. Foreign Direct Divestment Theory: Is It the Reverse of FDI Theory? *Weltwirtsch. Arch.*, 1983, *119*(2), pp. 345–55.

ter Borg, Frank. The Impact of Cooperation with Western Firms on the Hungarian Clothing Industry. *ACES Bull. (See Comp. Econ. Stud. after 8/85)*, Summer 1983, *25*(2), pp. 105–20. **[G: Hungary]**

Bornschier, Volker. Dependent Reproduction in the World System: A Study on the Incidence of Dependency Reversal. **In** *Doran, C. F.; Modelski, G. and Clark, C., eds.*, 1983, pp. 97–116.

Bosson, Rex and Varon, Bension. Problems of Mineral Development in Developing Countries. **In** *Glassner, M. I., ed.*, 1983, *1977*, pp. 381–95. **[G: LDCs; MDCs]**

Brewer, Thomas L. The Instability of Governments and the Instability of Controls on Funds Transfers by Multinational Enterprises: Implications for Political Risk Analysis. *J. Int. Bus. Stud.*, Winter 1983, *14*(3), pp. 147–57. **[G: Selected Countries]**

Buckley, Peter J. New Forms of International Industrial Cooperation: A Survey of the Literature with Special Reference to North–South Technology Transfer. *Aussenwirtschaft*, June 1983, *38*(2), pp. 195–222. **[G: LDCs; MDCs]**

Buckley, Peter J. New Theories of International Business: Some Unresolved Issues. **In** *Casson, M., ed.*, 1983, pp. 34–50.

Buckley, Peter J. and Enderwick, Peter. Comparative Pay Levels in Domestically-Owned and Foreign-Owned Plants in U.K.: Manufacturing-Evidence from the 1980 Workplace Industrial Relations Survey. *Brit. J. Ind. Relat.*, November 1983, *21*(3), pp. 395–400. **[G: U.K.]**

van den Bulcke, Daniel. Belgian Industrial Policy and Foreign Multinational Corporations: Objectives versus Performance. **In** *Goldberg, W. H., ed.*, 1983, pp. 219–48. **[G: Belgium]**

Burton, F. N. and Saelens, F. H. Direct Investment by Sogo-Shosha in Europe. *J. World Trade Law*, May–June 1983, *17*(3), pp. 249–58. **[G: N. Europe; Japan]**

Buzzell, Robert D. Can You Standardize Multinational Marketing? **In** *Dickson, D. N., ed.*, 1983, pp. 273–92. **[G: France; Italy; W. Germany; Netherlands]**

Cannon, Terry. Foreign Investment and Trade; Origins of the Modernization Policy. **In** *Feuchtwang, S. and Hussain, A., eds.*, 1983, pp. 288–324. **[G: China]**

Carstensen, Fred V. Foreign Participation in Russian Economic Life: Notes on British Enterprise, 1865–1914. **In** *Guroff, G. and Carstensen, F. V., eds.*, 1983, pp. 140–58. **[G: U.S.S.R.]**

Carstensen, Fred V. and Werking, Richard Hume. International Harvester in Russia: The Washington–St. Petersburg Connection? *Bus. Hist. Rev.*, Autumn 1983, *57*(3), pp. 347–66. **[G: U.S.; U.S.S.R.]**

Carter, E. Eugene and Rodriguez, Rita M. International Capital Budgeting. **In** *George, A. M. and Giddy, I. H., eds., Vol. 2*, 1983, pp. 8.5:1–33.

Casson, Mark. The Growth of International Business: Introduction: The Conceptual Framework. **In** *Casson, M., ed.*, 1983, pp. 1–33.

Casson, Mark and Norman, George. Pricing and Sourcing Strategies in a Multinational Oligopoly. **In** *Casson, M., ed.*, 1983, pp. 63–83.

Chai, Joseph. Industrial Co-operation between China and Hong Kong. **In** *Youngson, A. J., ed.*, 1983, pp. 104–55. **[G: China; Hong Kong]**

Chaudhuri, Adhip. American Multinationals and American Employment. **In** *Kindleberger, C. P. and Audretsch, D. B., eds.*, 1983, pp. 263–77. **[G: U.S.]**

Chen, Edward K. Y. Factor Proportions of Foreign and Local Firms in Developing Countries: A Theoretical and Empirical Note. *J. Devel. Econ.*, February/April 1983, *12*(1/2), pp. 267–74.

Chen, Edward K. Y. Multinational Corporations and Technology Diffusion in Hong Kong Manufacturing. *Appl. Econ.*, June 1983, *15*(3), pp. 309–21. **[G: Hong Kong]**

Chen, Edward K. Y. Multinationals from Hong Kong. **In** *Lall, S.*, 1983, pp. 88–136. **[G: Hong Kong]**

Chen, Edward K. Y. The Impact of China's Four Modernizations on Hong Kong's Economic Development. **In** *Youngson, A. J., ed.*, 1983, pp. 77–103. **[G: China; Hong Kong]**

Cherol, Rachelle L. and Nuñez del Arco, José. Andean Multinational Enterprises: A New Approach to Multinational Investment in the Andean Group. *J. Common Market Stud.*, June 1983, *21*(4), pp. 409–28. **[G: Bolivia; Colombia; Ecuador; Peru; Venezuela]**

Chudnovsky, Daniel. Patents and Trademarks in Pharmaceuticals. *World Devel.*, March 1983, *11*(3), pp. 187–93. **[G: LDCs; MDCs]**

Clee, Gilbert H. and di Scipio, Alfred. Creating a World Enterprise. **In** *Dickson, D. N., ed.*, 1983, pp. 93–113.

Contractor, Farok J. Technology Importation Policies in Developing Countries: Some Implications of Recent Theoretical and Empirical Evidence. *J. Devel. Areas,* July 1983, *17*(4), pp. 499–519. **[G: LDCs]**

Corley, T. A. B. Strategic Factors in the Growth of a Multinational Enterprise: The Burmah Oil Company 1886–1928. **In** *Casson, M., ed.*, 1983, pp. 214–35. **[G: U.K.]**

da Costa Pinto, Humberto, Jr. Trading Companies: The Brazilian Experience. **In** *Czinkota, M. R., ed. (II)*, 1983, pp. 244–52. **[G: Brazil]**

Coughlin, Cletus C. An Economic Analysis of Yugoslav Joint Ventures. *J. World Trade Law,* January–February 1983, *17*(1), pp. 12–33. **[G: Yugoslavia]**

Coughlin, Cletus C. The Relationship between Foreign Ownership and Technology Transfer. *J. Compar. Econ.*, December 1983, *7*(4), pp. 400–414. **[G: Europe]**

Cowhey, Peter F. The Engineers and the Price System Revisited: The Future of the International Oil Corporations. **In** *Aronson, J. D. and Cowhey, P. F., eds.*, 1983, pp. 9–52. **[G: U.S.]**

Crane, Dwight B. and Hayes, Samuel L., III. The Evolution of International Banking Competition and Its Implications for Regulation. *J. Bank Res.*, Spring 1983, *14*(1), pp. 39–53. **[G: U.S.; OECD; Selected LDCs]**

Crouzet, François. Comment [The Interests of the Union Européenne in Central Europe] [The Interests of the Banque de I'Union Parisienne in Czechoslovakia, Hungary and the Balkans, 1919–30]. **In** *Teichova, A. and Cottrell, P. L., eds.*, 1983, pp. 411–13. **[G: Central Europe; France]**

Czinkota, Michael R. and Johnston, Wesley J. Exporting: Does Sales Volume Make a Difference? *J. Int. Bus. Stud.*, Spring/Summer 1983, *14*(1), pp. 147–53. **[G: U.S.]**

Dale, Richard S. International Banking Is Out of Control. *Challenge,* January/February 1983, *25*(6), pp. 14–19.

Daly, Maurice T. The Mobility of Manufacturing and Capital: Implications for Regional Development. **In** *Hamilton, F. E. I. and Linge, G. J. R., eds.*, 1983, pp. 399–421. **[G: Australia]**

Darling, John R. and Brownlee, Leonard J., Jr. Management and Leadership in the Multinational Corporation. *Liiketaloudellinen Aikak.*, 1983, *32*(2), pp. 124–34.

Das, Satya P. Multinational Enterprise under Uncertainty. *Can. J. Econ.*, August 1983, *16*(3), pp. 420–28.

Davidow, Joel. The Implementation of International Antitrust Principles. **In** *Rubin, S. J. and Hufbauer, G. C., eds.*, 1983, pp. 119–38. **[G: Global]**

Davidson, William H. and Haspeslagh, Philippe. Shaping a Global Product Organization. **In** *Dickson, D. N., ed.*, 1983, pp. 114–27.

De Meza, David. Multinational Companies and National Welfare. *Australian Econ. Pap.*, December 1983, *22*(41), pp. 491–94.

Derksen, Richard. Forminiere in the Kasai, 1906–1939. *African Econ. Hist.*, 1983, (12), pp. 49–65. **[G: Congo]**

Dickson, Douglas N. Managing Effectively in the World Marketplace: Introduction. **In** *Dickson, D. N., ed.*, 1983, pp. 1–13.

Donnenfeld, Shabtai. Domestic Regulation and the Preservation of Monopoly Power in Foreign Markets. *Southern Econ. J.*, April 1983, *49*(4), pp. 954–65.

Douglas, Susan P. and Craig, C. Samuel. Examining Performance of U.S. Multinationals in Foreign Markets. *J. Int. Bus. Stud.*, Winter 1983, *14*(3), pp. 51–62. **[G: U.S.]**

Doz, Yves L. International Industries, Multinational Companies, and Host Government Control: A Framework. **In** *Goldberg, W. H., ed.*, 1983, pp. 302–31. **[G: W. Europe]**

Doz, Yves L. and Prahalad, C. K. How MNCs Cope with Host Government Intervention. **In** *Dickson, D. N., ed.*, 1983, pp. 412–25.

Droucopoulos, Vassilis. International Big Business Revisited: On the Size and Growth of the World's Largest Firms. *Managerial Dec. Econ.*, December 1983, *4*(4), pp. 244–52. **[G: Global]**

Dtugorborski, Waclaw. German Capital in Silesian Industry in Poland between the Two World Wars: Commentary. **In** *Teichova, A. and Cottrell, P. L., eds.*, 1983, pp. 247–50. **[G: Poland; Selected Countries]**

Dtugorborski, Waclaw. Göring's 'Multi-national Empire': Commentary. **In** *Teichova, A. and Cottrell, P. L., eds.*, 1983, pp. 298–302. **[G: Germany; Europe]**

Dufey, Gunter. International Financial Management: The Overall Investment and Financing Plan. **In** *George, A. M. and Giddy, I. H., eds., Vol. 2*, 1983, pp. 8.12:1–17.

Dunning, John H. Changes in the Level and Structure of International Production: The Last One Hundred Years. **In** *Casson, M., ed.*, 1983, pp. 84–139. **[G: Global]**

Dunning, John H. Market Power of the Firm and International Transfer of Technology: A Historical Excursion. *Int. J. Ind. Organ.*, December 1983, *1*(4), pp. 333–51. **[G: U.S.; Europe; LDCs]**

Dyment, John J. International Cash Management. **In** *Dickson, D. N., ed.*, 1983, pp. 553–65.

Eden, Lorraine. Transfer Pricing Policies under Tariff Barriers. *Can. J. Econ.*, November 1983, *16*(4), pp. 669–85. **[G: Canada]**

Emmanuel, A. The Transfer of Technology and the Multinationals: A Reply [*Appropriate or Underdeveloped Technology*]. *Greek Econ. Rev.*, April 1983, *5*(1), pp. 89–95.

Enderwick, Peter and Buckley, Peter J. The Determinants of Strike Activity in Foreign-Owned Plants: Inter-Industry Evidence from British Manufacturing Industry 1971–1973. *Managerial Dec. Econ.*, June 1983, *4*(2), pp. 83–88. **[G: U.K.]**

Etherington, Norman. The Capitalist Theory of Capitalist Imperialism. *Hist. Polit. Econ.*, Spring 1983, *15*(1), pp. 38–62.

Fallenbuchl, Zbigniew M. The Multinationals' Part in Integration: Comment. **In** *Saunders, C. T., ed.*, 1983, pp. 173–78. **[G: CMEA; EEC]**

Fatouros, A. A. The UN Code of Conduct of Transnational Corporations: Problems of Interpretation and Implementation. **In** *Rubin, S. J. and Hufbauer, G. C., eds.*, 1983, pp. 101–18. **[G: Global]**

Fischer, P. G. The Österreichisch-Alpine Montangesellschaft, 1918–38. **In** *Teichova, A. and Cottrell, P. L., eds.*, 1983, pp. 253–67. **[G: Austria]**

Fong, Chan Onn. Appropriate Technology: An Empirical Study of Bicycle Manufacturing in Malaysia. **In** *Lim, D., ed.*, 1983, *1980*, pp. 181–95. **[G: Malaysia]**

Foote, Marion R. Controlling the Cost of International Compensation. **In** *Dickson, D. N., ed.*, 1983, pp. 539–52. **[G: U.S.]**

Ford, David and Djeflat, Kader. Export Marketing of Industrial Products: Buyer–Seller Relationships between Developed and Developing Countries. **In** *Czinkota, M. R., ed. (I)*, 1983, pp. 262–82. **[G: Algeria; France; U.K.; U.S.]**

Frisch, Daniel J. Issues in the Taxation of Foreign Source Income. **In** *Feldstein, M., ed.*, 1983, pp. 289–330. **[G: U.S.]**

Gaspari, K. Celeste. Foreign Market Operations and Domestic Market Power. **In** *Kindleberger, C. P. and Audretsch, D. B., eds.*, 1983, pp. 77–102. **[G: U.S.]**

Gattiker, Heinrich. Foreign Policy Objectives and the Extraterritorial Application of Law. *Wirtsch. Recht*, 1983, *35*(2/3), pp. 154–61. **[G: U.S.; Switzerland]**

Gausti, Laura. The Peruvian Military Government and the International Corporations. **In** *McClintock, C. and Lowenthal, A. F., eds.*, 1983, pp. 181–205. **[G: Peru]**

Gehrels, Franz. Foreign Investment and Technology Transfer: Optimal Policies. *Weltwirtsch. Arch.*, 1983, *119*(4), pp. 663–85.

Gentry, James. Global Rationalization and MNCs' Trade Credit Policies: Policy Issues. **In** *Goldberg, W. H., ed.*, 1983, pp. 107–27. **[G: U.S.]**

George, Abraham M. Currency Exposure Management. **In** *George, A. M. and Giddy, I. H., eds., Vol. 2*, 1983, pp. 8.8:1–33.

Gerbier, B. Le thatcherisme: vers une économie mondiale anglo-américaine? (Thatcherism: Towards an Anglo-Saxon World Economy. With English summary.) *Écon. Soc.*, September–October–November 1983, *17*(9–10–11), pp. 1763–95. **[G: U.K.]**

Gernon, Helen. The Effect of Translation on Multinational Corporations' Internal Performance Evaluation. *J. Int. Bus. Stud.*, Spring/Summer 1983, *14*(1), pp. 103–12. **[G: U.S.]**

Gestetner, David. Strategy in Managing International Sales. **In** *Dickson, D. N., ed.*, 1983, pp. 293–300.

Giddy, Ian H. and Ho, Sang Kang. Mathematics of International Finance. **In** *George, A. M. and Giddy, I. H., eds., Vol. 2*, 1983, pp. A1–51. **[G: OECD]**

Glade, William. The Levantines in Latin America. *Amer. Econ. Rev.*, May 1983, *73*(2), pp. 118–22. **[G: Latin America]**

Gladwin, Thomas N. and Walter, Ingo. How Multinationals Can Manage Social Conflict. **In** *Goldberg, W. H., ed.*, 1983, pp. 78–101.

Goldberg, Walter H. Introduction: Global Rationalization versus Adaptation to National Interest. **In** *Goldberg, W. H., ed.*, 1983, pp. 1–11.

Gordon, Myron J. and Fowler, David J. Performance of the Multinational Drug Industry in Home and Host Countries: A Canadian Case Study. **In** *Kindleberger, C. P. and Audretsch, D. B., eds.*, 1983, pp. 139–61. **[G: Canada]**

Gray, H. Peter and Walter, Ingo. Investment-Related Trade Distortions in Petrochemicals. *J. World Trade Law*, July–August 1983, *17*(4), pp. 283–307. **[G: U.S.; W. Europe; Japan; Selected LDCs]**

Grosse, Robert. The Andean Foreign Investment Code's Impact on Multinational Enterprises. *J. Int. Bus. Stud.*, Winter 1983, *14*(3), pp. 121–33. **[G: Bolivia; Colombia; Ecuador; Peru; Venezuela]**

Grubel, Herbert G. The New International Banking. *Banca Naz. Lavoro Quart. Rev.*, September 1983, (146), pp. 263–84. **[G: Canada]**

Hagemann, Helmut. Anticipate Your Long-term Foreign Exchange Risks. **In** *Dickson, D. N., ed.*, 1983, pp. 515–26.

Håkanson, Lars. R&D in Foreign-owned Subsidiaries in Sweden. **In** *Goldberg, W. H., ed.*, 1983, pp. 163–76. **[G: Sweden]**

Hancock, R. Kelly. The Social Life of the Modern Corporation: Changing Resources and Forms. **In** *Littrell, W. B.; Sjoberg, G. and Zurcher, L. A., eds.*, 1983, pp. 19–36. **[G: U.S.]**

Hannah, L. German Concerns in Eastern Europe: Commentary. **In** *Teichova, A. and Cottrell, P. L., eds.*, 1983, pp. 192–96. **[G: Europe]**

Harms, Robert. The World Abir Made: The Maringa–Lopori Basin, 1885–1903. *African Econ. Hist.*, 1983, (12), pp. 125–39. **[G: Congo]**

Haug, P.; Hood, N. and Young, S. Mark. R & D Intensity in the Affiliates of U.S. Owned Electronics Companies Manufacturing in Scotland. *Reg. Stud.*, December 1983, *17*(6), pp. 383–92. **[G: U.K.]**

Hawkins, Robert. Una comunità che si espande: il leasing. (The Leasing Community Expands. With English summary.) *Mondo Aperto*, March-April 1983, *37*(2), pp. 83–92.

Heinzen, Barbara J. The United Fruit Company in the 1950s: Trusteeships of the Cameroons. *African Econ. Hist.*, 1983, (12), pp. 141–56. **[G: Cameroons]**

Henley, John. Corporate Strategy and Employment Relations in Multinational Corporations: Some Evidence from Kenya and Malaysia. **In** *Thurley, K. and Wood, S., eds.*, 1983, pp. 111–30. **[G: Malaysia; Kenya]**

Heyzer, Noeleen. International Production and Social Change: An Analysis of the State, Employment, and Trade Unions in Singapore. **In** *Chen, P. S. J., ed.*, 1983, pp. 105–28. **[G: Singapore]**

Hirschman, Charles. Foreign Investment in Malaysia, Once Again. **In** *Lim, D., ed.*, 1983, pp. 235–37. **[G: Malaysia]**

Hirschman, Charles. Foreign Investment, Employment Generation and the Profit–Wage Ratio in the Manufacturing Sector of West Malaysia: Comment. **In** *Lim, D., ed.*, 1983, *1978*, pp. 228–29. **[G: Malaysia]**

Hirschman, Charles. Ownership and Control in the

Manufacturing Sector of West Malaysia: Reply. In *Lim, D., ed.*, 1983, pp. 222–24. **[G: Malaysia]**

Hirschman, Charles. Ownership and Control in the Manufacturing Sector of West Malaysia. **In** *Lim, D., ed.*, 1983, *1971*, pp. 209–20. **[G: Malaysia]**

Horst, Thomas. Issues in the Taxation of Foreign Source Income: Comment. **In** *Feldstein, M., ed.*, 1983, pp. 331–32. **[G: U.S.]**

Hout, Thomas M.; Porter, Michael E. and Rudden, Eileen. How Global Companies Win Out. **In** *Dickson, D. N., ed.*, 1983, pp. 185–200.

Howenstine, Ned G. Gross Product of U.S. Multinational Companies, 1977. *Surv. Curr. Bus.*, February 1983, *63*(2), pp. 24–29. **[G: U.S.]**

Howenstine, Ned G. U.S. Affiliates of Foreign Companies: Operations in 1981. *Surv. Curr. Bus.*, November 1983, *63*(11), pp. 19–34. **[G: U.S.]**

Ihamuotila, Jaakko. Cooperation from the Company Viewpoint. **In** *Möttölä, K.; Bykov, O. N. and Korolev, I. S., eds.*, 1983, pp. 110–21. **[G: U.S.S.R.; Finland]**

Ingham, Keith P. D. Understanding the Scottish Economy: Foreign Firms. **In** *Ingham, K. P. D. and Love, J., eds.*, 1983, pp. 215–26. **[G: U.K.]**

Islam, Nurul. Economic Interdependence between Rich and Poor Nations. **In** *Gauhar, A., ed. (II)*, 1983, pp. 173–93. **[G: LDCs; MDCs]**

Itagaki, Takao. Multinational Firms and the Theory of Effective Protection. *Oxford Econ. Pap.*, November 1983, *35*(3), pp. 447–62.

Jaeger, Alfred M. The Transfer of Organizational Culture Overseas: An Approach to Control in the Multinational Corporation. *J. Int. Bus. Stud.*, Fall 1983, *14*(2), pp. 91–114. **[G: Japan; U.S.]**

Jung, Ku-Hyun. The Sogo Shosha: Can It Be Exported (Imported)? **In** *Czinkota, M. R., ed. (I)*, 1983, pp. 66–88. **[G: Japan; S. Korea]**

Jussawalla, Meheroo. Trade, Technology Transfer, and Development. **In** *Macdonald, S.; Lamberton, D. M. and Mandeville, T., eds.*, 1983, pp. 134–54. **[G: LDCs; MDCs]**

Katrak, Homi. Global Profit Maximization and the Export Performance of Foreign Subsidiaries in India. *Oxford Bull. Econ. Statist.*, May 1983, *45*(2), pp. 205–22. **[G: India]**

Katrak, Homi. Multinational Firms' Global Strategies, Host Country Indigenisation of Ownership and Welfare. *J. Devel. Econ.*, December 1983, *13*(3), pp. 331–48. **[G: LDCs]**

Katz, Jorge and Kosacoff, Bernardo. Multinationals from Argentina. **In** *Lall, S.*, 1983, pp. 137–219. **[G: Argentina]**

Kick, Edward L. and Conaty, Joseph. African Economic Development: The Effects of East, West, and Chinese Penetration. **In** *Bergesen, A., ed.*, 1983, pp. 263–86. **[G: Africa]**

Kierans, Eric W. The Community and the Corporation. **In** *Kindleberger, C. P. and Audretsch, D. B., eds.*, 1983, pp. 198–215. **[G: Global]**

Kilby, Peter. An Entrepreneurial Problem. *Amer. Econ. Rev.*, May 1983, *73*(2), pp. 107–11. **[G: LDCs]**

Killing, J. Peter. How to Make a Joint Global Venture Work. **In** *Dickson, D. N., ed.*, 1983, pp. 426–35.

Killough, James. Improved Payoffs from Transnational Advertising. **In** *Dickson, D. N., ed.*, 1983, pp. 343–57.

Kiser, John W., III. Tapping Eastern Bloc Technology. **In** *Dickson, D. N., ed.*, 1983, pp. 485–500. **[G: COMECON; W. Europe]**

Kogels, H. A. Unitary Taxation: An International Approach. *Bull. Int. Fiscal Doc.*, February 1983, *37*(2), pp. 65–68. **[G: U.S.]**

Kogut, Bruce. Foreign Direct Investment as a Sequential Process. **In** *Kindleberger, C. P. and Audretsch, D. B., eds.*, 1983, pp. 38–56.

Kooiman, K. Article 16: The U.S. Attitude to Treaty Shopping. *Bull. Int. Fiscal Doc.*, May 1983, *37*(5), pp. 195–200. **[G: U.S.; Australia; Argentina; Jamaica; New Zealand]**

Kothari, Vinay. Researching for Export Marketing. **In** *Czinkota, M. R., ed. (I)*, 1983, pp. 154–76. **[G: U.S.]**

Kramer, R. D. Attempts to Curb Treaty Shopping in U.S.–Dutch Treaty Negotiations. *Bull. Int. Fiscal Doc.*, March 1983, *37*(3), pp. 107–09. **[G: U.S.; Netherlands]**

Krugman, Paul R. The "New Theories" of International Trade and the Multinational Enterprise. **In** *Kindleberger, C. P. and Audretsch, D. B., eds.*, 1983, pp. 57–73.

Kujawa, Duane. Technology Strategy and Industrial Relations: Case Studies of Japanese Multinationals in the United States. *J. Int. Bus. Stud.*, Winter 1983, *14*(3), pp. 9–22. **[G: Japan; U.S.]**

Kulev, I. A. Soviet–Finnish Cooperation for Joint Construction of Industrial Objects. **In** *Möttölä, K.; Bykov, O. N. and Korolev, I. S., eds.*, 1983, pp. 122–36. **[G: U.S.S.R.; Finland]**

van der Laan, H. Laurens. A Swiss Family Firm in West Africa: A. Brunnschweiler & Co., 1929–1959. *African Econ. Hist.*, 1983, (12), pp. 287–97. **[G: W. Africa]**

van der Laan, H. Laurens. Trading in the Congo: The NAHV from 1918 to 1955. *African Econ. Hist.*, 1983, (12), pp. 241–59. **[G: Congo]**

Lall, Sanjaya. Brandt on 'Transnational Corporations Investment and the Sharing of Technology.' **In** *Gauhar, A., ed. (II)*, 1983, pp. 149–53.

Lall, Sanjaya. Multinationals and Market Structure in an Open Developing Economy: The Case of Malaysia. **In** *Lim, D., ed.*, 1983, *1979*, pp. 238–54. **[G: Malaysia]**

Lall, Sanjaya. Multinationals from India. **In** *Lall, S.*, 1983, pp. 21–87. **[G: India]**

Lall, Sanjaya. Prospects for Automotive Transnationals in the Third World. *Nat. Westminster Bank Quart. Rev.*, February 1983, pp. 13–20. **[G: LDCs]**

Lall, Sanjaya. The New Multinationals: Synthesis and Conclusions. **In** *Lall, S.*, 1983, pp. 250–68.

Lall, Sanjaya. The New Multinationals: The Theoretical Background. **In** *Lall, S.*, 1983, pp. 1–20.

Lall, Sanjaya and Mohammad, Sharif. Foreign Ownership and Export Performance in the Large Corporate Sector of India. *J. Devel. Stud.*, October 1983, *20*(1), pp. 56–67. **[G: India]**

Lall, Sanjaya and Mohammad, Sharif. Multinationals in Indian Big Business: Industrial Characteristics of Foreign Investments in a Heavily Regulated Economy. *J. Devel. Econ.*, Aug.–Oct. 1983, *13*(1–

2), pp. 143–57. **[G: India]**

Lall, Sanjaya and Mohammed, Sharif. Technological Effort and Disembodied Technology Exports: An Econometric Analysis of Inter-Industry Variations in India. *World Devel.*, June 1983, *11*(6), pp. 527–35. **[G: India]**

Lecraw, Donald J. Performance of Transnational Corporations in Less Developed Countries. *J. Int. Bus. Stud.*, Spring/Summer 1983, *14*(1), pp. 15–33. **[G: ASEAN]**

Lee, Chung H. International Production of the United States and Japan in Korean Manufacturing Industries: A Comparative Study. *Weltwirtsch. Arch.*, 1983, *119*(4), pp. 744–53. **[G: Japan; S. Korea; U.S.]**

Leibrenz, Marylyn L. and Ryans, John K., Jr. Doing Business in Key Latin American Markets: U.S. International Executive Perceptions. **In** *Czinkota, M. R., ed. (II),* 1983, pp. 155–71. **[G: Latin America; U.S.]**

Lévy, Philippe. The OECD Declaration on International Investment and Multinational Enterprises. **In** *Rubin, S. J. and Hufbauer, G. C., eds.*, 1983, pp. 47–62. **[G: OECD]**

Lim, David. Fiscal Incentives and Direct Foreign Investment in Less Developed Countries. *J. Devel. Stud.*, January 1983, *19*(2), pp. 207–12. **[G: LDCs]**

Lim, David. Wages and Work Conditions, and the Effects of Foreign Investment and the Separation of Ownership from Management on Them: A Study of Malaysian Manufacturing. **In** *Lim, D., ed.*, 1983, pp. 162–80. **[G: Malaysia]**

Lim, Linda Y. C. Chinese Business, Multinationals and the State: Manufacturing for Export in Malaysia and Singapore. **In** *Lim, L. Y. C. and Gosling, L. A. P., eds.*, 1983, pp. 245–74. **[G: Malaysia; Singapore]**

Magee, Stephen P. and Young, Leslie. Multinationals, Tariffs, and Capital Flows with Endogenous Politicians. **In** *Kindleberger, C. P. and Audretsch, D. B., eds.*, 1983, pp. 21–37.

Maisonrouge, Jacques G. The Education of a Modern International Manager. *J. Int. Bus. Stud.*, Spring/Summer 1983, *14*(1), pp. 141–46.

Manca, Gavino. L'impresa multinazionale di fronte alla rivoluzione tecnologica. (The Multinational Company and the Technological Revolution. With English summary.) *L'Impresa,* 1983, *25*(6), pp. 37–39.

Marcati, Alberto. Quando l'impresa diventa multinazionale: il problema del controllo. (Problems of Control When the Company Becomes a Multinational One. With English summary.) *L'Impresa,* 1983, *25*(2), pp. 35–41.

Marchetti, Piergaetano. Quale *joint-venture* per una maggiore competitività. (Which *Joint-Venture* for Better Competition. With English summary.) *L'Impresa,* 1983, *25*(1), pp. 55–62. **[G: Italy]**

van Marion, M. F. The Multinational and Integration: The Human Side of Economics. **In** *Saunders, C. T., ed.*, 1983, pp. 151–60. **[G: EEC]**

Marz, Edward. The Österreichisch-Alpine Montangeselleschaft, 1918–38: Commentary. **In** *Teichova, A. and Cottrell, P. L., eds.*, 1983, pp. 267–68. **[G: Austria]**

Mathur, Ike and Hanagan, Kyran. Are Multinational Corporations Superior Investment Vehicles for Achieving International Diversification? *J. Int. Bus. Stud.*, Winter 1983, *14*(3), pp. 135–46.

Matis, Herbert. Disintegration and Multi-national Enterprises in Central Europe during the Postwar Years (1918–23). **In** *Teichova, A. and Cottrell, P. L., eds.*, 1983, pp. 72–96. **[G: Central Europe]**

McConnell, James E. The International Location of Manufacturing Investments: Recent Behaviour of Foreign-owned Corporations in the United States. **In** *Hamilton, F. E. I. and Linge, G. J. R., eds.*, 1983, pp. 337–58. **[G: U.S.]**

McCulloch, Rachel and Owen, Robert F. Linking Negotiations on Trade and Foreign Direct Investment. **In** *Kindleberger, C. P. and Audretsch, D. B., eds.*, 1983, pp. 334–58. **[G: Canada]**

McQueen, Matthew. Appropriate Policies towards Multinational Hotel Corporations in Developing Countries. *World Devel.*, February 1983, *11*(2), pp. 141–52.

Meissner, Frank. Mexican Border and Free Zone Areas: Implications for Development. **In** *Czinkota, M. R., ed. (II),* 1983, pp. 253–78. **[G: Mexico; U.S.]**

Méndez, José A. Immiserisation and the Emergence of Multinational Firms in a Less Developed Country: A General Equilibrium Analysis. *J. Devel. Stud.*, October 1983, *20*(1), pp. 22–23.

Mizrahi, David. Arab Investment and Banking in the U.S. **In** *Kaushik, S. K., ed.*, 1983, pp. 147–49. **[G: U.S.]**

Momigliano, Franco and Balcet, Giovanni. New Trends in Internationalization: Processes and Theories. Diversified Patterns of Multinational Enterprise and Old and New Forms of Foreign Involvement of the Firm. *Econ. Notes,* 1983, (3), pp. 42–68. **[G: U.S.; Germany; Japan]**

Moreira Alves, Maria Helena. Mechanisms of Social Control of the Military Governments in Brazil, 1964–80. **In** *Ritter, A. R. M. and Pollock, D. H., eds.*, 1983, pp. 240–303. **[G: Brazil]**

Mutti, John H. and Gerking, Shelby D. Multinational Corporations and Discriminatory Investment Controls. *Weltwirtsch. Arch.*, 1983, *119*(4), pp. 649–62.

Naor, Jacob. International Orientation of Exporters: Some North–South Trade Implications. **In** *Czinkota, M. R., ed. (I),* 1983, pp. 241–61. **[G: Canada; S. Korea; U.S.]**

Negandhi, Anant R. External and Internal Functioning of American, German, and Japanese Multinational Corporations: Decisionmaking and Policy Issues. **In** *Goldberg, W. H., ed.*, 1983, pp. 21–41. **[G: U.S.; Japan; W. Germany]**

Newfarmer, Richard S. Multinationals and Marketplace Magic in the 1980s. **In** *Kindleberger, C. P. and Audretsch, D. B., eds.*, 1983, pp. 162–97. **[G: Global]**

Nicholas, Stephen J. Agency Contracts, Institutional Modes, and the Transition to Foreign Direct Investment by British Manufacturing Multinationals before 1939. *J. Econ. Hist.*, September 1983, *43*(3), pp. 675–86. **[G: U.K.]**

Nielsen, Richard P. Should a Country Move toward International Strategic Market Planning? *Calif.*

Manage. Rev., January 1983, 25(2), pp. 34–44. [G: U.S.]

Nye, Joseph S., Jr. The Multinational Corporation in the 1980s. **In** *Kindleberger, C. P. and Audretsch, D. B., eds.*, 1983, pp. 1–17. [G: U.S.]

O'Callaghan, John. Ownership and Control in the Manufacturing Sector of West Malaysia: A Note. **In** *Lim, D., ed.*, 1983, *1971*, pp. 221–22. [G: Malaysia]

Ondrack, Daniel A. Responses to Government Industrial Research Policy: A Comparison of Foreign-owned and Canadian-owned Firms. **In** *Goldberg, W. H., ed.*, 1983, pp. 177–200. [G: Canada]

Oshima, Harry T. On the Transferability of Institutions from Abroad: Lessons from the Japanese and Philippine Experience. *Philippine Econ. J.*, 198, *22*(1), pp. 82–98. [G: Philippine; Japan]

Overy, R. F. Göring's 'Multi-national Empire.' **In** *Teichova, A. and Cottrell, P. L., eds.*, 1983, pp. 269–98. [G: Germany; Europe]

Pappas, I. A. Problems in Formalizing Production Planning in a Threshold Country. **In** *Wilson, B.; Berg, C. C. and French, D., eds.*, 1983, pp. 305–11.

Patrick, Robert J., Jr. Tax Treaty Shopping. *Bull. Int. Fiscal Doc.*, March 1983, *37*(3), pp. 105–06. [G: U.S.; OECD]

Pearce, Robert D. Industrial Diversification amongst the World's Leading Multinational Enterprises. **In** *Casson, M., ed.*, 1983, pp. 140–79. [G: OECD]

Perlmutter, Howard V. and Heenan, David A. How Multinational Should Your Top Managers Be? **In** *Dickson, D. N., ed.*, 1983, pp. 69–87.

Pohl, Hans. German Concerns in Eastern Europe: Commentary. **In** *Teichova, A. and Cottrell, P. L., eds.*, 1983, pp. 203–06. [G: Europe]

Puchon, Gilles. Defining and Measuring Currency Exposure. **In** *George, A. M. and Giddy, I. H., eds., Vol. 2*, 1983, pp. 8.7:1–18.

Radebaugh, Lee H. International Accounting. **In** *George, A. M. and Giddy, I. H., eds., Vol. 2*, 1983, pp. 8.6:1–24.

Read, Robert. The Growth and Structure of Multinationals in the Banana Export Trade. **In** *Casson, M., ed.*, 1983, pp. 180–213. [G: Caribbean; Central America; U.S.]

Reed, Howard Curtis. Appraising Corporate Investment Policy: A Financial Center Theory of Foreign Direct Investment. **In** *Kindleberger, C. P. and Audretsch, D. B., eds.*, 1983, pp. 219–44. [G: Global]

Reed, Howard Curtis. International Financial Center Preeminence in MNC and Nation–State Interaction. **In** *Goldberg, W. H., ed.*, 1983, pp. 128–58. [G: Global]

Rege, Udayan P. A Cross Sectional Study of Relative Take-Over Activity. *Appl. Econ.*, April 1983, *15*(2), pp. 235–42. [G: Canada]

Reiners, Gernot H. Leasing in an International Context. **In** *George, A. M. and Giddy, I. H., eds., Vol. 2*, 1983, pp. 7.4:1–28. [G: OECD]

Rejtö, Gábor. A Debate in Hungary on the Possibilities of Cooperation with Western Firms (1982–83): Review Article. *Acta Oecon.*, 1983, *31*(3–4), pp. 327–39. [G: Hungary]

Richardson, Neil R. Foreign Policy Costs of Economic Nationalism: Poisoning the Well? **In** *Doran, C. F.; Modelski, G. and Clark, C., eds.*, 1983, pp. 117–27. [G: Selected Countries]

Robbins, Sidney M. and Stobaugh, Robert B., Jr. The Bent Measuring Stick for Foreign Subsidiaries. **In** *Dickson, D. N., ed.*, 1983, pp. 503–14.

Rodríguez Castellanos, A. Empresas multinacionales, gestion de cambios y crisis monetarias. (Multination Businesses, Change of Money, Management and Monetary Crisis. With English summary.) *Écon. Soc.*, September–October–November 1983, *17*(9–10–11), pp. 1451–86.

Roehl, Thomas. A Transactions Cost Approach to International Trading Structures: The Case of the Japanese General Trading Companies. *Hitotsubashi J. Econ.*, December 1983, *24*(2), pp. 119–35. [G: Japan]

Ronstadt, Robert and Kramer, Robert J. Getting the Most Out of Innovation Abroad. **In** *Dickson, D. N., ed.*, 1983, pp. 477–84. [G: U.S.]

Rousslang, Don and Pelzman, Joseph. The Benefits and Costs of the Deferral of U.S. Taxes on Retained Earnings of Controlled Foreign Corporations. *Europ. Econ. Rev.*, January 1983, *20*(1–3), pp. 79–94. [G: U.S.]

Rubin, Seymour J. and Hufbauer, Gary Clyde. Emerging Standards of International Trade and Investment: Lessons from the Codes. **In** *Rubin, S. J. and Hufbauer, G. C., eds.*, 1983, pp. 175–96. [G: Global]

Rugman, Alan M. Canada: FIRA Updated [The Regulation of Foreign Investment in Canada]. *J. World Trade Law*, July–August 1983, *17*(4), pp. 352–55. [G: Canada]

Rummel, Randolph J. and Heenan, David A. How Multinationals Analyze Political Risk. **In** *Dickson, D. N., ed.*, 1983, pp. 381–97. [G: Indonesia]

Sabolo, Yves. Trade between Developing Countries, Technology Transfers and Employment. *Int. Lab. Rev.*, Sept.–Oct. 1983, *122*(5), pp. 593–608. [G: LDCs]

Safarian, A. E. Trade-related Investment Issues. **In** *Cline W. R., ed.*, 1983, pp. 611–37.

Salita, Domingo C. and Juanico, Meliton B. Export Processing Zones: New Catalysts for Economic Development. **In** *Hamilton, F. E. I. and Linge, G. J. R., eds.*, 1983, pp. 441–61. [G: Selected LDCs]

Sarathy, Ravi. Export Activity and Realized Profit: Some Japanese Evidence. **In** *Czinkota, M. R., ed. (I)*, 1983, pp. 210–26. [G: Japan]

Schröter, Harm. Siemens and Central and South–East Europe between the Two World Wars. **In** *Teichova, A. and Cottrell, P. L., eds.*, 1983, pp. 173–92. [G: Europe]

Schröter, Verena. The IG Farbenindustrie AG in Central and South–East Europe, 1926–38. **In** *Teichova, A. and Cottrell, P. L., eds.*, 1983, pp. 139–72. [G: Europe]

Seidman, Ann. Debt and the Development Options in Central Southern Africa: The Case of Zambia and Zimbabwe. **In** *Carlsson, J., ed.*, 1983, pp. 80–107. [G: Zambia; Zimbabwe]

Shapiro, Daniel M. Entry, Exit, and the Theory of

the Multinational Corporation. In *Kindleberger, C. P. and Audretsch, D. B., eds.*, 1983, pp. 103–22. [G: Canada]

Shapiro, Daniel M. The Comparative Profitability of Canadian- and Foreign-Controlled Firms. *Managerial Dec. Econ.*, June 1983, *4*(2), pp. 97–106.

Shih, Anne and Au-Yeung, P. K. Revenue Law and Practice in the People's Republic of China. *Bull. Int. Fiscal Doc.*, March 1983, *37*(3), pp. 99–104. [G: China]

Sievers, Manfred. The Worsening Financial State of the Multinational Tractor Industry. *Europ. Rev. Agr. Econ.*, 1983, *10*(2), pp. 165–73. [G: Canada; Italy; Japan; U.S.]

Singh, Naunihal. Communication and Competence in Private Sector Involvement in International Trade Policy. In *Czinkota, M. R., ed. (I)*, 1983, pp. 110–26. [G: India]

Skinner, C. Wickham. Management of International Production. In *Dickson, D. N., ed.*, 1983, pp. 224–44.

Skouras, Th. The Transfer of Technology and the Multinationals: A Rejoinder. *Greek Econ. Rev.*, August 1983, *5*(2), pp. 193–96.

Smelyakov, N. N. Industrial Cooperation and Joint Production in Soviet–Finnish Economic Ties. In *Möttölä, K.; Bykov, O. N. and Korolev, I. S., eds.*, 1983, pp. 100–109. [G: U.S.S.R.; Finland]

Smith, Tim. South Africa: The Churches vs. the Corporations. In *Snoeyenbos, M.; Almeder, R. and Humber, J., eds.*, 1983, *1975*, pp. 495–502. [G: U.S.]

Soos, Piroska E. United States: Controlled Foreign Corporations—A Victory for Taxpayers. *Bull. Int. Fiscal Doc.*, May 1983, *37*(5), pp. 201–06. [G: U.S.]

Sorenson, Ralph Z. and Wiechmann, Ulrich E. How Multinationals View Marketing Standardization. In *Dickson, D. N., ed.*, 1983, pp. 301–16.

de Souza, Linda-Mar P.; Schmidt, Angela and Colaiácovo, Juan Luis. Pre-export Behavior: An Analysis of the Variables Influencing the Decision Process. In *Czinkota, M. R., ed. (I)*, 1983, pp. 227–40. [G: Brazil]

Stefani, Giorgio. Special Economic Zones and Economic Policy in China. *Ann. Pub. Co-op. Econ.*, July–September 1983, *54*(3), pp. 289–312. [G: China]

Stein, Leslie. Multinational Corporations in World Trade. *Singapore Econ. Rev.*, April 1983, *28*(1), pp. 34–52. [G: Global]

Stobaugh, Robert B., Jr. How to Analyze Foreign Investment Climates. In *Dickson, D. N., ed.*, 1983, pp. 365–80.

Stobaugh, Robert B., Jr. Where in the World Should We Put That Plant? In *Dickson, D. N., ed.*, 1983, pp. 245–59. [G: Selected Countries]

Stone, Carl. Patterns of Insertion into the World Economy: Historical Profile and Contemporary Options. *Soc. Econ. Stud.*, September 1983, *32*(3), pp. 1–34. [G: Caribbean]

Stout, D. K. Technical Advance and Trade Advantage. In *Macdonald, S.; Lamberton, D. M. and Mandeville, T., eds.*, 1983, pp. 122–33.

Sugden, Roger. The Degree of Monopoly, International Trade, and Transnational Corporations. *Int. J. Ind. Organ.*, June 1983, *1*(2), pp. 165–87.

Susman, Paul and Schutz, Eric. Monopoly and Competitive Firm Relations and Regional Development in Global Capitalism. *Econ. Geogr.*, April 1983, *59*(2), pp. 161–77. [G: U.S.]

Tan, Gerald. Foreign Investment, Employment Generation and the Profit–Wage Ratio in the Manufacturing Sector of West Malaysia. In *Lim, D., ed.*, 1983, *1978*, pp. 225–28. [G: Malaysia]

Tan, Gerald. Foreign Investment, Employment Generation and the Profit–Wage Ration in the Manufacturing Sector of West Malaysia: A Reply to Professor Hirschman. In *Lim, D., ed.*, 1983, *1979*, pp. 230–34. [G: Malaysia]

Tarrant, James R. Stewardship across National Borders (II). In *Martin, T. R., ed.*, 1983, pp. 89–95. [G: U.S.]

Tavis, Lee A. Stewardship across National Borders (I). In *Martin, T. R., ed.*, 1983, pp. 74–88. [G: Selected Countries]

Teece, David J. Technological and Organisational Factors in the Theory of the Multinational Enterprise. In *Casson, M., ed.*, 1983, pp. 51–62.

Teeters, Nancy H. and Terrell, Henry S. The Role of Banks in the International Financial System. *Fed. Res. Bull.*, September 1983, *69*(9), pp. 663–71. [G: OECD; Non-OPEC LDCs]

Teichova, Alice. The Mannesmann Concern in East Central Europe in the Inter-war Period. In *Teichova, A. and Cottrell, P. L., eds.*, 1983, pp. 103–37. [G: Austria]

Tempest, Paul. The International Energy Investment Dilemma. In *Tempest, P., ed.*, 1983, pp. 247–58. [G: OECD]

Terpstra, Vern. Suggestions for Research Themes and Publications: International Marketing. *J. Int. Bus. Stud.*, Spring/Summer 1983, *14*(1), pp. 9–10.

Thunell, Lars H. and Skydel, Jack R. International Cash Management. In *George, A. M. and Giddy, I. H., eds., Vol. 2*, 1983, pp. 8.11A:1–10.

Tironi, Ernesto. Distribution of Benefits from Regional Trade Liberalisation among Country Partners in the Presence of Transnational Corporations. In *Weisbrod, B. and Hughes, H., eds.*, 1983, pp. 547–62.

Tomaszewski, Jerzy. German Capital in Silesian Industry in Poland between the Two World Wars. In *Teichova, A. and Cottrell, P. L., eds.*, 1983, pp. 227–47. [G: Poland; Selected Countries]

Tomita, Teruhiko. Philippine Responses to Japanese Affiliated Enterprises. *Philippine Econ. J.*, 198, *22*(1), pp. 53–81. [G: Philippine; Japan]

Toyne, Brian and Kühne, Robert J. The Management of the International Executive Compensation and Benefits Process. *J. Int. Bus. Stud.*, Winter 1983, *14*(3), pp. 37–50. [G: U.S.]

Trebilcock, C. Comment [Concentration and the Finance of Austrian Industrial Combines, 1880–1914] [Disintegration and Multi-national Enterprises in Central Europe during the Post-war Years (1918–23)]. In *Teichova, A. and Cottrell, P. L., eds.*, 1983, pp. 96–100. [G: Central Europe; Austria]

Tschoegl, Adrian E. Size, Growth, and Transnationality among the World's Largest Banks. *J. Bus.*, April 1983, *56*(2), pp. 187–201.

Vahlne, Jan-Erik. Foreign Direct Investments: A Swedish Policy Problem. In *Goldberg, W. H., ed.*, 1983, pp. 207–18. **[G: Sweden]**

Vastrup, Claus. Economic Motives for Foreign Banking: The Danish Case. *Kredit Kapital*, 1983, *16*(1), pp. 117–25. **[G: Denmark]**

Vernon, Raymond. Gone Are the Cash Cows of Yesteryear. In *Dickson, D. N., ed.*, 1983, pp. 467–76. **[G: U.S.]**

Villela, Annibal V. Multinationals from Brazil. In *Lall, S.*, 1983, pp. 220–49. **[G: Brazil]**

Vukmanic, Frank G. Performance Requirements: The General Debate and a Review of Latin American Practices. In *Czinkota, M. R., ed. (II)*, 1983, pp. 48–84. **[G: Latin America]**

Walker, Townsend. The Mechanics of Covering Foreign Exchange Exposures. In *George, A. M. and Giddy, I. H., eds., Vol. 2*, 1983, pp. 8.9:1–58.

Waller, Robert. Göring's 'Multi-national Empire': Commentary. In *Teichova, A. and Cottrell, P. L., eds.*, 1983, pp. 302–06. **[G: Europe; Germany]**

Walter, Ingo. The Evolution of International Banking Competition and Its Implications for Regulation: Discussant's Comments. *J. Bank Res.*, Spring 1983, *14*(1), pp. 53–54. **[G: U.S.; OECD; Selected LDCs]**

Walter, Judith A. The Evolution of International Banking Competition and Its Implications for Regulation: Discussant's Comments. *J. Bank Res.*, Spring 1983, *14*(1), pp. 55–58. **[G: U.S.; OECD; Selected LDCs]**

Warr, Peter G. The Jakarta Export Processing Zone: Benefits and Costs. *Bull. Indonesian Econ. Stud.*, December 1983, *19*(3), pp. 28–49. **[G: Indonesia]**

Welch, Lawrence R. and Wiedersheim-Paul, Finn. MNCs and the Australian Government: Some Emerging Policy Issues. In *Goldberg, W. H., ed.*, 1983, pp. 249–69. **[G: Australia]**

Welch, Lawrence S. Licensing Strategy and Policy for Internationalization and Technology Transfer. In *Czinkota, M. R., ed. (I)*, 1983, pp. 5–23. **[G: Latin America; Selected Countries]**

Welch, Lawrence S. The Technology Transfer Process in Foreign Licensing Arrangements. In *Macdonald, S.; Lamberton, D. M. and Mandeville, T., eds.*, 1983, pp. 155–68. **[G: LDCs; MDCs]**

Welge, Martin K. Decisionmaking in German Multinationals and Its Impact on External Relationships. In *Goldberg, W. H., ed.*, 1983, pp. 57–77. **[G: Mexico; W. Germany]**

Wells, Louis T., Jr. Don't Overautomate Your Foreign Plant. In *Dickson, D. N., ed.*, 1983, pp. 260–70.

Wells, Louis T., Jr. Negotiating with Third World Governments. In *Dickson, D. N., ed.*, 1983, pp. 453–64. **[G: LDCs]**

Wells, Louis T., Jr. Social Cost/Benefit Analysis for MNCs. In *Dickson, D. N., ed.*, 1983, pp. 398–411.

Wendt, Bernd-Jürgen. German Concerns in Eastern Europe: Commentary. In *Teichova, A. and Cottrell, P. L., eds.*, 1983, pp. 196–203. **[G: Europe]**

White, Eduardo. Cooperation among National Drug Manufacturers: Asociación Latinoamericana de Industrias Farmacéuticas (ALIFAR). *World Devel.*, March 1983, *11*(3), pp. 271–79. **[G: Latin America]**

Wiechmann, Ulrich E. and Pringle, Lewis G. Problems That Plague Multinational Marketers. In *Dickson, D. N., ed.*, 1983, pp. 317–30.

Wikander, Ulla. The Swedish Match Company in Central Europe between the Wars: 'Internal Power Struggle' between Former Competitors—Solo v. Swedish Match. In *Teichova, A. and Cottrell, P. L., eds.*, 1983, pp. 209–25. **[G: Sweden; Europe]**

Wionczek, Miguel S. Research and Development in Pharmaceuticals: Mexico. *World Devel.*, March 1983, *11*(3), pp. 243–50. **[G: Mexico]**

Wright, Peter. Systematic Approach to Finding Export Opportunities. In *Dickson, D. N., ed.*, 1983, pp. 331–42.

Wu, Yuan-li. Chinese Entrepreneurs in Southeast Asia. *Amer. Econ. Rev.*, May 1983, *73*(2), pp. 112–17. **[G: S.E. Asia]**

Wynant, Larry. International Project Finance. In *George, A. M. and Giddy, I. H., eds., Vol. 2*, 1983, pp. 7.3:1–26.

Yannopoulos, George N. The Growth of Transnational Banking. In *Casson, M., ed.*, 1983, pp. 236–57. **[G: LDCs; OECD]**

Zurawicki, Leon. Multinationals in the European Integration Areas. In *Saunders, C. T., ed.*, 1983, pp. 161–72. **[G: CMEA; EEC]**

443 International Lending and Aid (Public)

4430 International Lending and Aid (Public)

Abbott, Philip C. and McCarthy, F. Desmond. Potential Welfare Losses Due to Tied Food Aid. *Can. J. Agr. Econ.*, March 1983, *31*(1), pp. 45–58.

Adams, F. Gerard; Sanchez, Enrique P. and Adams, Mark E. Can Latin America Carry Its International Debt? A Prospective Analysis Using the Wharton Latin American Debt Simulation Model. *J. Policy Modeling*, November 1983, *5*(3), pp. 419–41. **[G: Latin America]**

Aissi, Said. The OPEC Fund and Africa—A Geographical Perspective. In *Shihata, I. F. I., et al.*, 1983, pp. 72–96. **[G: OPEC; Africa]**

Ali, Mehdi. Agriculture and Energy in the OPEC Fund's Activities—A Sectoral Perspective. In *Shihata, I. F. I., et al.*, 1983, pp. 50–71. **[G: OPEC]**

Aliber, Robert Z. A Perspective on the External Debt of Latin America. In *Jorge, A.; Salazar-Carillo, J. and Higonnet, R. P., eds.*, 1983, pp. 37–39. **[G: Latin America]**

Argyle, D. Brian. Development Assistance, National Policies, and Lender Type and Performance. In *Von Pischke, J. D.; Adams, D. W. and Donald, G., eds.*, 1983, pp. 330–35. **[G: World Bank]**

Armstrong, Harvey W. The Assignment of Regional Policy Powers within the EC. In *El-Agraa, A. M., ed.*, 1983, pp. 271–98. **[G: EEC; U.K.]**

Arnesen, Arne. Perspectives of Norwegian Development Aid in the 1980s. In *Parkinson, J. R., ed.*, 1983, pp. 125–38. **[G: Norway]**

Avramović, Dragoslav. Development Policies for Today. *J. World Trade Law,* May–June 1983, *17*(3), pp. 189–206. [G: LDCs]

Avramović, Dragoslav. The Debt Problem of Developing Countries at End-1982. *Aussenwirtschaft,* March 1983, *38*(1), pp. 65–86. [G: LDCs]

Azar, Edward E. Development Diplomacy. **In** *Starr, J. R., ed.,* 1983, pp. 137–48. [G: U.S.; Middle East]

Baneth, Jean. The Role of the World Bank as an International Institution: Comment on the Krueger Paper. *Carnegie-Rochester Conf. Ser. Public Policy,* Spring 1983, *18,* pp. 313–23.

Basagni, Fabio. International Debt, Financial Stability and Growth. **In** *Basagni, F., ed.,* 1983, pp. 5–12. [G: LDCs; OECD]

Bauer, Peter T. and Yamey, Basil S. Foreign Aid: What Is at Stake? **In** *Thompson, W. S., ed.,* 1983, *1982,* pp. 115–35.

Beauvoir, Raymond. External Financing and Debt of the Latin American Countries. **In** *Jorge, A.; Salazar-Carillo, J. and Higonnet, R. P., eds.,* 1983, pp. 41–54. [G: Latin America]

Benamara, Abdelkader. The OPEC Fund and the Least Developed Countries: An Orientation towards the Poor. **In** *Shihata, I. F. I., et al.,* 1983, pp. 97–112. [G: OPEC; LDCs]

Bergsten, C. Fred. The Case for Multilateral Aid. **In** *Bergsten, C. F.,* 1983, pp. 225–27.

Bergsten, C. Fred. U.S. Policy toward the Multilateral Development Bank: The Fatal Flaws of the Treasury Assessment. **In** *Bergsten, C. F.,* 1983, *1982,* pp. 219–33. [G: U.S.]

Bernal, Richard L. Economic Growth and External Debt of Jamaica. **In** *Jorge, A.; Salazar-Carillo, J. and Higonnet, R. P., eds.,* 1983, pp. 89–108. [G: Jamaica]

Bhagwati, Jagdish N. and Grinols, Earl. Foreign Capital, Dependence, Destabilisation and Feasibility of Transition to Socialism. **In** *Bhagwati, J. N., Vol. 2,* 1983, *1975,* pp. 479–92. [G: Ghana; Israel; S. Korea; Philippines; India]

Bienen, Henry S. Broadening Our Foreign Policy Goals: The United States and Sub-Saharan Africa. **In** *Lewis, J. P. and Kallab, V., eds.,* 1983, pp. 66–85. [G: Sub-Saharan Africa; U.S.]

Bird, Graham. Interest Rate Subsidies on International Finance as a Means of Assisting Low-Income Countries. *World Devel.,* June 1983, *11*(6), pp. 515–25. [G: LDCs]

Bird, Graham. Low Income Countries as a Special Case in the International Financial System: An Analysis of Some Proposals for Reform. *Econ. Notes,* 1983, (2), pp. 5–22. [G: Selected LDCs]

Bird, Graham. Low-Income Countries and International Financial Reform. *J. Devel. Areas,* October 1983, *18*(1), pp. 53–75. [G: LDCs]

Bird, Graham. The Banks and the IMF—Division of Labour. *Lloyds Bank Rev.,* October 1983, (150), pp. 19–33.

Bogdanowicz-Bindert, Christine A. Financial Crisis of 1982: A Debtor's Perspective. **In** *Kaushik, S. K., ed.,* 1983, pp. 203–06. [G: LDCs]

Bolin, William H. and Del Canto, Jorge. LDC Debt: Beyond Crisis Management. *Foreign Aff.,* Summer 1983, *61*(5), pp. 1099–1112. [G: LDCs]

Bosson, Rex and Varon, Bension. Problems of Mineral Development in Developing Countries. **In** *Glassner, M. I., ed.,* 1983, *1977,* pp. 381–95. [G: LDCs; MDCs]

Bourne, Compton. External Debt and Economic Growth in the Commonwealth Caribbean. **In** *Jorge, A.; Salazar-Carillo, J. and Higonnet, R. P., eds.,* 1983, pp. 109–12. [G: Caribbean]

Brecher, Richard A. and Bhagwati, Jagdish N. Immiserizing Transfers from Abroad. **In** *Bhagwati, J. N., Vol. 2,* 1983, *1982,* pp. 505–16.

Buira, Ariel. IMF Financial Programs and Conditionality. *J. Devel. Econ.,* February/April 1983, *12*(1/2), pp. 111–36.

Canela-Bueno, Luis A. The Dominican Republic External Debt: An Assessment of Its Evolution over the Last Six Years. **In** *Jorge, A.; Salazar-Carillo, J. and Higonnet, R. P., eds.,* 1983, pp. 113–16. [G: Dominican Republic]

Chichilnisky, Graciela. The Transfer Problem with Three Agents Once Again: Characterization, Uniqueness and Stability [Basic Goods, the Effects of Commodity Transfers and the International Economic Order]. *J. Devel. Econ.,* Aug.–Oct. 1983, *13*(1–2), pp. 237–47.

Clausen, Alden W. Third World Debt and Global Recovery. *Aussenwirtschaft,* September 1983, *38*(3), pp. 249–61. [G: LDCs]

Clay, Edward J. and Mitchell, Mark. Is European Community Food Aid in Dairy Products Cost-Effective? *Europ. Rev. Agr. Econ.,* 1983, *10*(2), pp. 97–121. [G: EEC]

Clunies Ross, Anthony. Scotland and the Third World. **In** *Ingham, K. P. D. and Love, J., eds.,* 1983, pp. 255–70. [G: U.K.]

Cohen, Benjamin J. Balance-of-Payments Financing: Evolution of a Regime. **In** *Krasner, S. D., ed.,* 1983, *1982,* pp. 315–36. [G: Global]

Cooper, Richard N. Some Aspects of the 1982–83 Brazilian Payments Crisis: Comments and Discussion. *Brookings Pap. Econ. Act.,* 1983, (2), pp. 543–47. [G: Brazil]

Coppé, Philippe. The Impact of the International Crisis on Management. *Ann. Sci. Écon. Appl.,* 1983, *39*(3), pp. 173–85. [G: Global]

Cox, Thomas S. Northern Actors in a South–South Setting: External Aid and East African Integration. *J. Common Market Stud.,* March 1983, *21*(3), pp. 283–312. [G: E. Africa]

Crawford, Malcolm. High-Conditionality Lending: The United Kingdom. **In** *Williamson, J., ed.,* 1983, pp. 421–39. [G: U.K.]

Cullen, Andrew. Structural Economic Domination and World Trade with Reference to Latin America: A Marxist Approach. *Soc. Econ. Stud.,* September 1983, *32*(3), pp. 35–81. [G: Latin America]

Deese, David A. The Vulnerability of Modern Nations: Economic Diplomacy in East–West Relations. **In** *Nincic, M. and Wallensteen, P., eds.,* 1983, pp. 155–81. [G: OECD; CMEA]

Delgado, Enrique. Problems of Economic Growth and External Indebtedness in Central America. **In** *Jorge, A.; Salazar-Carillo, J. and Higonnet, R. P., eds.,* 1983, pp. 117–24. [G: Central America]

Díaz-Alejandro, Carlos F. Some Aspects of the 1982–

83 Brazilian Payments Crisis. *Brookings Pap. Econ. Act.*, 1983, (2), pp. 515–42. **[G: Brazil]**

Díaz-Alejandro, Carlos F. Stories of the 1930s for the 1980s. **In** *Armella, P. A.; Dornbusch, R. and Obstfeld, M., eds.*, 1983, pp. 5–35. **[G: Latin America]**

Dini, Lamberto. Foreign Debt, Economic Recovery, and the International Monetary System. **In** *Basagni, F., ed.*, 1983, pp. 13–23. **[G: LDCs; E. Europe; OECD]**

Diz, Adolfo. Economic Performance under Three Stand-by Arrangements: Peru, 1977–80. **In** *Williamson, J., ed.*, 1983, pp. 263–73. **[G: Peru]**

Dornbusch, Rudiger. Some Aspects of the 1982–83 Brazilian Payments Crisis: Comments and Discussion. *Brookings Pap. Econ. Act.*, 1983, (2), pp. 547–52. **[G: Brazil]**

Dos Santos, Theotonio. The Structure of Dependence. **In** *Todaro, M. P., ed.*, 1983, *1970*, pp. 68–75.

Ebinger, Charles K. and Luzius, Harry. The Energy Crisis and the Third World: An Opportunity for the West. **In** *Tempest, P., ed.*, 1983, pp. 217–27. **[G: LDCs]**

Eckaus, Richard S. IMF Conditionality: Country Studies: Comments, Chapters 20–21. **In** *Williamson, J., ed.*, 1983, pp. 4320. **[G: Turkey; India]**

Feinberg, Richard E. Bridging the Crisis: The World Bank and U.S. Interests in the 1980s. **In** *Lewis, J. P. and Kallab, V., eds.*, 1983, pp. 139–61. **[G: LDCs; U.S.]**

Fendt, Robert, Jr. Growth and Debt: Issues and Prospects for the Brazilian Economy in the Eighties. **In** *Jorge, A.; Salazar-Carillo, J. and Higonnet, R. P., eds.*, 1983, pp. 125–37. **[G: Brazil]**

Fieleke, Norman S. International Lending on Trial. *New Eng. Econ. Rev.*, May/June 1983, pp. 5–13. **[G: U.S.; Non-OPEC; LDCs]**

Flanders, M. June. The Effects of Political Economic and Institutional Developments on International Banks: Comment. *J. Banking Finance*, 1983, *7*(4), pp. 623–24. **[G: LDCs]**

Fratianni, Michele. La crisi dell'indebitamento internazionale: come è sorta e come si può superare. (The International Debt Crisis: Causes and Policy Prescriptions. With English summary.) *Bancaria*, February 1983, *39*(2), pp. 139–46. **[G: LDCs]**

Friedman, Irving S. Latin American External Debt and Economic Growth: The Role of Debt Rescheduling. **In** *Jorge, A.; Salazar-Carillo, J. and Higonnet, R. P., eds.*, 1983, pp. 55–60. **[G: Latin America; Zaire]**

Friedman, Irving S. Private Bank Conditionality: Comparison with the IMF and the World Bank. **In** *Williamson, J., ed.*, 1983, pp. 109–24.

Fries, Timothy. The Possibility of an Immiserizing Transfer under Uncertainty. *J. Int. Econ.*, November 1983, *15*(3/4), pp. 297–311.

Garcia-Thoumi, Ines. ODA from Developed Countries. *Finance Develop.*, June 1983, *20*(2), pp. 28–31. **[G: OPEC; OECD]**

Geanakoplos, John and Heal, Geoffrey M. A Geometric Explanation of the Transfer Paradox in a Stable Economy [Basic Goods, the Effects of Commodity Transfers and the International Economic Order]. *J. Devel. Econ.*, Aug.–Oct. 1983, *13*(1–2), pp. 223–36.

Giddy, Ian H. The Theory and Industrial Organization of International Banking. **In** *Hawkins, R. G.; Levich, R. M. and Wihlborg, C. G., eds.*, 1983, pp. 195–243. **[G: U.S.]**

Gollas, Manuel. External Debt and Economic Growth: Mexico. **In** *Jorge, A.; Salazar-Carillo, J. and Higonnet, R. P., eds.*, 1983, pp. 139–53. **[G: Mexico]**

Gottheil, Fred M. Establishing the Preconditions to Long-run Development: Egypt after the Treaty. **In** *Starr, J. R., ed.*, 1983, pp. 35–45. **[G: Egypt]**

Gotur, Padma. Interest Rates and the Developing World. *Finance Develop.*, December 1983, *20*(4), pp. 33–36. **[G: LDCs]**

Gray, Clive and Martens, André. The Political Economy of the 'Recurrent Cost Problem' in the West African Sahel. *World Devel.*, February 1983, *11*(2), pp. 101–17. **[G: Sahel]**

Green, Christopher. Insulating Countries against Fluctuations in Domestic Production and Exports: An Analysis of Compensatory Financing Schemes. *J. Devel. Econ.*, June 1983, *12*(3), pp. 303–25.

Griffith-Jones, Stephany. Information Access to International Finance: What Problems for Developing Countries? **In** *O'Brien, R. C., ed.*, 1983, pp. 70–77.

Grinols, Earl and Bhagwati, Jagdish N. Foreign Capital, Savings and Dependence. **In** *Bhagwati, J. N., Vol. 2*, 1983, *1976*, pp. 493–501.

Grinols, Earl and Bhagwati, Jagdish N. Foreign Capital, Savings and Dependence: A Reply. **In** *Bhagwati, J. N., Vol. 2*, 1983, *1979*, pp. 502–04.

Gunning, Jan Willem. Basic Goods, the Effects of Commodity Transfers and the International Economic Order: Comment. *J. Devel. Econ.*, Aug.–Oct. 1983, *13*(1–2), pp. 197–203.

Gunning, Jan Willem. The Transfer Problem: A Rejoinder [Basic Goods, the Effects of Commodity Transfers and the International Economic Order]. *J. Devel. Econ.*, Aug.–Oct. 1983, *13*(1–2), pp. 249–50.

Guth, Wilfried. Challenges to the International Financial System. **In** *Basagni, F., ed.*, 1983, pp. 24–32. **[G: LDCs; E. Europe; OECD]**

Gwin, Catherine. Financing India's Structural Adjustment: The Role of the Fund. **In** *Williamson, J., ed.*, 1983, pp. 511–31. **[G: India]**

Habib, Fawzi. Commentary: Need and Rationale for a Near East Development Fund. **In** *Starr, J. R., ed.*, 1983, pp. 115–20. **[G: Middle East]**

Havnevik, Kjell J. and Skarstein, Rune. Some Notes on Agricultural Backwardness in Tanzania. **In** *Parkinson, J. R., ed.*, 1983, pp. 151–62. **[G: Tanzania]**

Heimann, John G. The Effects of Political, Economic and Institutional Development on International Banks. *J. Banking Finance*, 1983, *7*(4), pp. 615–21. **[G: LDCs]**

Hewitt, Adrian. Stabex: An Evaluation of the Economic Impact over the First Five Years. *World Devel.*, December 1983, *11*(12), pp. 1005–27. **[G: LDCs; EEC]**

Higonnet, Rene P. Latin American Debt: More Rescheduling? **In** *Jorge, A.; Salazar-Carillo, J. and*

Higonnet, R. P., eds., 1983, pp. 61–76. **[G: Latin America]**

Hittmair, Hans C. The World Bank as a Financial Intermediary. **In** *Kaushik, S. K., ed.*, 1983, pp. 161–66.

Hoffmann, Thomas and Johnson, Brian. Breaking the Logjam. **In** *Glassner, M. I., ed.*, 1983, *1981*, pp. 318–32. **[G: LDCs; MDCs]**

Hope, Nicholas and Klein, Thomas. Issues in External Debt Management. *Finance Develop.*, September 1983, *20*(3), pp. 23–25.

Hunter, Shireen T. Middle East Development Funds and Banks: An Overview. **In** *Starr, J. R., ed.*, 1983, pp. 71–102. **[G: Middle East; Africa; OPEC]**

Ince, Basil A. Coping with Oil Wealth: The Case of Trinidad/Tobago and the Commonwealth Caribbean. **In** *Ritter, A. R. M. and Pollock, D. H., eds.*, 1983, pp. 111–34. **[G: Caribbean; Trinidad/Tobago]**

Ingram, James C. Food for Employment: 20 Years of the World Food Programme. *Int. Lab. Rev.*, Sept.–Oct. 1983, *122*(5), pp. 549–62. **[G: LDCs]**

Iqbal, Zubair. Arab Concessional Assistance, 1975–81. *Finance Develop.*, June 1983, *20*(2), pp. 31–33. **[G: OAPEC]**

Jayawardena, Lal. International Keynesianism—A Solution to the World Crisis? **In** *Jansen, K., ed.*, 1983, pp. 149–74.

Jennings, Anthony. The Recurrent Cost Problem in the Least Developed Countries. *J. Devel. Stud.*, July 1983, *19*(4), pp. 504–21. **[G: LDCs; OECD]**

Jorge, Antonio and Salazar-Carrillo, Jorge. External Debt and Development in Latin America: A Background Paper. **In** *Jorge, A.; Salazar-Carillo, J. and Higonnet, R. P., eds.*, 1983, pp. 1–35. **[G: Latin America]**

Kafka, Alexandre. Comments on Dragoslav Avramovic's "Debt Problem of Developing Countries." *Aussenwirtschaft*, June 1983, *38*(2), pp. 223–28. **[G: LDCs]**

Karadawi, Ahmed. Constraints on Assistance to Refugees: Some Observations from the Sudan. *World Devel.*, June 1983, *11*(6), pp. 537–47. **[G: Sudan]**

Khan, Mohsin S. and Knight, Malcolm D. Sources of Payments Problems in LDCs. *Finance Develop.*, December 1983, *20*(4), pp. 2–5. **[G: LDCs]**

Kick, Edward L. and Conaty, Joseph. African Economic Development: The Effects of East, West, and Chinese Penetration. **In** *Bergesen, A., ed.*, 1983, pp. 263–86. **[G: Africa]**

Killick, Tony. Kenya, the IMF, and the Unsuccessful Quest for Stabilization. **In** *Williamson, J., ed.*, 1983, pp. 381–413. **[G: Kenya]**

Krueger, Anne O. The Role of the World Bank as an International Institution. *Carnegie-Rochester Conf. Ser. Public Policy*, Spring 1983, *18*, pp. 281–311.

Krul, Nicolas. The Debt Problem: Some Observations on the Search for a New Financial Balance (abridged). **In** *Basagni, F., ed.*, 1983, pp. 55–60. **[G: LDCs; OECD]**

Kubarych, Roger. Responding to International Financial Crisis. **In** *Kaushik, S. K., ed.*, 1983, pp. 199–201. **[G: LDCs]**

Kuczynski, Pedro-Pablo. Latin American Debt. *Foreign Aff.*, Winter 1982/83, *61*(2), pp. 344–64. **[G: Latin America]**

Kuczynski, Pedro-Pablo. Latin American Debt: Act Two. *Foreign Aff.*, Fall 1983, *62*(1), pp. 17–38. **[G: Latin America]**

Kwack, Sung Y. Developments in and Prospects for External Debt Position and Burden of Developing Countries: The Case of Korea. *J. Policy Modeling*, November 1983, *5*(3), pp. 443–59. **[G: S. Korea]**

Kwon, Jene K. Toward Incentive Transfers, Global Tax and Welfare Indices. *J. Econ. Devel.*, December 1983, *8*(2), pp. 71–87. **[G: LDCs; MDCs]**

Latortue, Paul R. The External Debt Situation of Haiti. **In** *Jorge, A.; Salazar-Carillo, J. and Higonnet, R. P., eds.*, 1983, pp. 155–61. **[G: Haiti]**

Leipziger, Danny M. Lending versus Giving: The Economics of Foreign Assistance. *World Devel.*, April 1983, *11*(4), pp. 329–35. **[G: OECD]**

Lewis, John P. The United States and the Third World, 1983: Can We Escape the Path of Mutual Injury? **In** *Lewis, J. P. and Kallab, V., eds.*, 1983, pp. 7–48. **[G: LDCs; OECD; U.S.]**

Lewis, W. Arthur. The Evolution of Foreign Aid. **In** *Lewis, W. A.*, 1983, *1972*, pp. 683–96.

Looney, Robert E. and Frederiksen, P. C. The Feasibility of Alternative IMF-Type Stabilization Programs in Mexico, 1983–87. *J. Policy Modeling*, November 1983, *5*(3), pp. 461–70. **[G: Mexico]**

Maasry, Nadeem G. Near East Economic Development: The Marshall Plan Revisited. **In** *Starr, J. R., ed.*, 1983, pp. 27–34. **[G: Middle East; Europe]**

Magnifico, Giovanni. L'economia mondiale ad una svolta: qualche proposta. (The World Economy at a Turning-Point: Some Proposals. With English summary.) *Bancaria*, March 1983, *39*(3), pp. 242–48.

Mancera, Miguel. Stories of the 1930s for the 1980s: Comment. **In** *Armella, P. A.; Dornbusch, R. and Obstfeld, M., eds.*, 1983, pp. 36–40. **[G: Latin America]**

Marini, Luigi. La crisi finanziaria di alcuni paesi in via di sviluppo. Riflessi sul sistema bancario americano e possibili soluzioni. (The Financial Crisis of Several LDCs: Repercussions on the United States Banking System and Consideration of Possible Solutions. With English summary.) *Bancaria*, May–June 1983, *39*(5–6), pp. 489–97. **[G: U.S.; LDCs]**

Maroni, Yves. How to Borrow Reasonably. **In** *Jorge, A.; Salazar-Carillo, J. and Higonnet, R. P., eds.*, 1983, pp. 77–84. **[G: Peru; Brazil]**

Marshall S., Jorge; Mardones S., José Luis and Marshall L., Isabel. IMF Conditionality: The Experiences of Argentina, Brazil, and Chile. **In** *Williamson, J., ed.*, 1983, pp. 275–321. **[G: Chile; Brazil; Argentina]**

Massad, Carlos. The External Debt and the Financial Problems of Latin America. *Cepal Rev.*, August 1983, (20), pp. 149–63. **[G: Latin America]**

Massad, Carlos. The Real Cost of the External Debt for the Creditor and for the Debtor. *Cepal Rev.*, April 1983, (19), pp. 183–95. **[G: Latin America]**

Meerman, Jacob. Cost Recovery in a Project Context: Some World Bank Experience in Tropical Africa. *World Devel.*, June 1983, *11*(6), pp. 503–14. **[G: Tropical Africa]**

Meerman, Jacob. Minimizing the Burden of Recurrent Costs. *Finance Develop.*, December 1983, *20*(4), pp. 41–43. **[G: Africa]**

Melnik, Arie. The Role of Banks in the International Financial System: Comment. *J. Banking Finance*, 1983, *7*(4), pp. 465–66. **[G: OECD; LDCs]**

Munroe, Tapan. The Third World Debt Problem. *J. Energy Devel.*, Autumn 1983, *9*(1), pp. 63–67. **[G: LDCs]**

Narvekar, P. R. Collaboration between the Fund and the World Bank. **In** *Hooke, A. W., ed.*, 1983, pp. 119–34.

Nathan, Robert R. and Levinson, Jerome I. A Development Fund for the Near East. **In** *Starr, J. R., ed.*, 1983, pp. 103–13. **[G: Middle East]**

Neufeld, Edward P. International Debt, the Viability of the International Financial System, and World Economic Recovery. **In** *Basagni, F., ed.*, 1983, pp. 42–54. **[G: LDCs; E. Europe; OECD]**

Newfarmer, Richard S. A Look at Reagan's Revolution in Development Policy. *Challenge*, Sept.–Oct. 1983, *26*(4), pp. 34–43. **[G: U.S.; LDCs]**

Newfarmer, Richard S. The Private Sector and Development. **In** *Lewis, J. P. and Kallab, V., eds.*, 1983, pp. 117–38. **[G: LDCs; U.S.]**

Ofstad, Arve. Some Notes on Aid Policies and Practices in Mozambique. **In** *Parkinson, J. R., ed.*, 1983, pp. 145–50. **[G: Mozambique]**

Okyar, Osman. Turkey and the IMF: A Review of Relations, 1978–82. **In** *Williamson, J., ed.*, 1983, pp. 533–61. **[G: Turkey]**

Owen, Henry. Changing Public Attitudes toward Aid. *Finance Develop.*, December 1983, *20*(4), pp. 39–40. **[G: U.S.]**

Palma, Pedro A. Venezuela's Foreign Public Debt. **In** *Jorge, A.; Salazar-Carillo, J. and Higonnet, R. P., eds.*, 1983, pp. 163–68. **[G: Venezuela]**

Papanek, Gustav F. Aid, Growth and Equity in Southern Asia. **In** *Parkinson, J. R., ed.*, 1983, pp. 169–82. **[G: S. Asia]**

Phillips, Ronnie J. The Role of the International Monetary Fund in the Post-Bretton Woods Era. *Rev. Radical Polit. Econ.*, Summer 1983, *15*(2), pp. 59–81. **[G: Global]**

Please, Stanley. IMF Conditionality: Country Studies: Comments, Chapters 15–16. **In** *Williamson, J., ed.*, 1983, pp. 415–20.

Purcell, Susan Kaufman. War and Debt in South America. *Foreign Aff.*, 1982, *61*(3), pp. 660–74. **[G: S. America]**

Radke, Detlef and Taake, Hans-Helmut. Financial Crisis Management in Egypt and Turkey. *J. World Trade Law*, July–August 1983, *17*(4), pp. 325–36. **[G: Turkey; Egypt]**

Ragazzi, Giorgio. Il ruolo del finanziamento estero nello sviluppo economico e la problematica attuale dell'indebitamento. (The Role of Foreign Financing in Economic Development and the Current Debt Problem. With English summary.) *Bancaria*, May–June 1983, *39*(5–6), pp. 477–88. **[G: LDCs]**

Ravallion, Martin. Commodity Transfers and the International Economic Order: A Comment [Basic Goods, the Effects of Commodity Transfers and the International Economic Order]. *J. Devel. Econ.*, Aug.–Oct. 1983, *13*(1–2), pp. 205–12.

Rice, Gerard; Corr, James and Fennell, Susan. Maintaining Financing for Adjustment and Development. *Finance Develop.*, December 1983, *20*(4), pp. 44–47. **[G: LDCs]**

Rotberg, Eugene H. Perspective: Some Informal Remarks on Debt Management and Liquidity. **In** *Herring, R. J., ed.*, 1983, pp. 212–19.

Rudolph, Lloyd I. and Rudolph, Susanne Hoeber. Broadening Our Foreign Policy Goals: The United States, India, and South Asia. **In** *Lewis, J. P. and Kallab, V., eds.*, 1983, pp. 86–113. **[G: India; S. Asia; U.S.]**

Ruggie, John Gerard. Political Structure and Change in the International Economic Order: The North–South Dimension. **In** *Ruggie, J. G., ed.*, 1983, pp. 423–87. **[G: LDCs; MDCs]**

Sacchetti, Ugo. Conditionality in International Finance and the Crisis of the International Monetary System. *Econ. Notes*, 1983, (2), pp. 120–44.

Sachs, Jeffrey D. IMF Conditionality: County Studies: Comments, Chapters 17–19. **In** *Williamson, J., ed.*, 1983, pp. 505–10. **[G: Italy; U.K.; Portugal]**

Saghafi, Massoud Mokhtari and Nugent, Jeffrey B. Foreign Aid in the Form of Commodity Transfers That Increase the Income Gap between Rich and Poor Countries: The Chichilnisky Theorems Revisited. *J. Devel. Econ.*, Aug.–Oct. 1983, *13*(1–2), pp. 213–16.

Seidman, Ann. Debt and the Development Options in Central Southern Africa: The Case of Zambia and Zimbabwe. **In** *Carlsson, J., ed.*, 1983, pp. 80–107. **[G: Zambia; Zimbabwe]**

Sharpley, Jennifer. Economic Management and IMF Conditionality in Jamaica. **In** *Williamson, J., ed.*, 1983, pp. 233–62. **[G: Jamaica]**

Shihata, Ibrahim F. I. OPEC as a Donor Group. **In** *Gauhar, A., ed. (II)*, 1983, pp. 30–47. **[G: OPEC]**

Shihata, Ibrahim F. I. The OPEC Fund and the North–South Dialogue—Some Personal Reflections. **In** *Shihata, I. F. I., et al.*, 1983, pp. 138–64. **[G: OPEC]**

Shihata, Ibrahim F. I. The OPEC Fund's Experience (Mid-1976 to Mid-1983): Its Approaches and Procedures, the Magnitude of Its Assistance, and Its Impact on Development. **In** *Shihata, I. F. I., et al.*, 1983, pp. 40–49. **[G: OPEC]**

Shihata, Ibrahim F. I. The Role of the OPEC Member Countries in Financing Third-World Development. **In** *Shihata, I. F. I., et al.*, 1983, pp. 1–11. **[G: OPEC]**

Shihata, Ibrahim F. I. and Parra, Antonio R. The Establishment and Evolution of the OPEC Fund. **In** *Shihata, I. F. I., et al.*, 1983, pp. 13–39. **[G: OPEC]**

Shihata, Ibrahim F. I. and Wohlers-Scharf, T. Innovative Forms of Cooperation: The OPEC Fund's Approach. **In** *Shihata, I. F. I., et al.*, 1983, pp. 113–37. **[G: OPEC]**

da Silva Lopes, Jose. IMF Conditionality: The Stand-by Arrangement with Portugal, 1978. **In** *Wil-*

liamson, J., ed., 1983, pp. 475–504. **[G: Portugal]**

Solomon, Anthony M. Toward a More Resilient International Financial System. *Fed. Res. Bank New York Quart. Rev.*, Autumn 1983, *8*(3), pp. 1–5. **[G: LDCs]**

Solomon, Anthony M. Toward a More Resilient International Financial System. *Fed. Res. Bank Minn. Rev.*, Summer 1983, *7*(3), pp. 2–5. **[G: LDCs; MDCs]**

Spaventa, Luigi. Two Letters of Intent: External Crises and Stabilization Policy, Italy, 1973–77. **In** *Williamson, J., ed.*, 1983, pp. 441–73. **[G: Italy]**

Srinivasan, T. N. and Bhagwati, Jagdish N. On Transfer Paradoxes and Immiserizing Growth: Part 1: Comment [Basic Goods, the Effects of Commodity Transfers and the International Economic Order]. *J. Devel. Econ.*, Aug.–Oct. 1983, *13*(1–2), pp. 217–22.

Srinivasan, T. N. and Bhagwati, Jagdish N. Postscript [Basic Goods, the Effects of Commodity Transfers and the International Economic Order]. *J. Devel. Econ.*, Aug.–Oct. 1983, *13*(1–2), pp. 251–52.

Stahl, Heinz-Michael. Brasiliens Finanzierungskrise: Ursachen—Anpassungsmassnahmen—Perspektiven. (Brazil's Current Financial Crisis—Causes and Perspectives. With English summary.) *Konjunkturpolitik*, 1983, *29*(3), pp. 187–98. **[G: Brazil]**

Stallings, Barbara. International Capitalism and the Peruvian Military Government. **In** *McClintock, C. and Lowenthal, A. F., eds.*, 1983, pp. 144–80. **[G: Peru]**

Stern, Ernest. World Bank Financing of Structural Adjustment. **In** *Williamson, J., ed.*, 1983, *1981*, pp. 87–107. **[G: LDCs]**

Streeten, Paul. Why Development Aid? *Banca Naz. Lavoro Quart. Rev.*, December 1983, (147), pp. 379–85. **[G: LDCs]**

Svendsen, Knud Erik. Danish Development Assistance and Its Conditionality. **In** *Parkinson, J. R., ed.*, 1983, pp. 139–44. **[G: Denmark]**

Taslim, Mohammad Ali. Aid-Elasticity of Demand for Money in Bangladesh. *Indian Econ. Rev.*, July–December 1983, *18*(2), pp. 285–91. **[G: Bangladesh]**

Teeters, Nancy H. The Role of Banks in the International Financial System. *J. Banking Finance*, 1983, *7*(4), pp. 453–63. **[G: OECD; LDCs]**

Thirlwall, Anthony P. Confusion over Measuring the Relative Worth of Trade and Aid. *World Devel.*, January 1983, *11*(1), pp. 71–72. **[G: Sudan]**

Thompson, Robert L. The Role of Trade in Food Security and Agricultural Development. **In** *Johnson, D. G. and Schuh, G. E., eds.*, 1983, pp. 227–57.

Tozaki, Seiki. International Debt Issues and Global Business and Trade: A Japanese Perspective. **In** *Basagni, F., ed.*, 1983, pp. 33–41. **[G: Japan; LDCs; OECD]**

Trebat, Thomas J. Latin American External Debt in the Eighties: A Case Study of Brazil. **In** *Jorge, A.; Salazar-Carillo, J. and Higonnet, R. P., eds.*, 1983, pp. 169–74. **[G: Brazil]**

Tremblay, Rodrigue. L'endettement international et les problèmes d'adjustement: une perspective générale. (International Indebtedness and Adjustment Problems: A Review. With English summary.) *L'Actual. Econ.*, June 1983, *59*(2), pp. 283–324. **[G: LDCs]**

Tumlir, Jan. The World Economy Today: Crisis or a New Beginning? *Nat. Westminster Bank Quart. Rev.*, August 1983, pp. 26–44.

Valdés, Alberto. The Role of Trade in Food Security and Agricultural Development: Discussion. **In** *Johnson, D. G. and Schuh, G. E., eds.*, 1983, pp. 258–68.

Villasuso, Juan Manuel. Foreign Debt and Economic Development: The Case of Costa Rica. **In** *Jorge, A.; Salazar-Carillo, J. and Higonnet, R. P., eds.*, 1983, pp. 175–83. **[G: Costa Rica]**

Volcker, Paul A. Statement to U.S. House Committee on Banking, Finance and Urban Affairs, February 2, 1983. *Fed. Res. Bull.*, February 1983, *69*(2), pp. 80–89. **[G: U.S.; Argentina; OPEC; Brazil; Mexico]**

Warley, T. K. The Role of Trade in Food Security and Agricultural Development: Discussion. **In** *Johnson, D. G. and Schuh, G. E., eds.*, 1983, pp. 269–75. **[G: LDCs]**

Weiss, Thomas G. and Jennings, Anthony. What Are the Least Developed Countries and What Benefits May Result from the Paris Conference? *World Devel.*, April 1983, *11*(4), pp. 337–57. **[G: MDCs; LDCs]**

Williamson, John. The Lending Policies of the International Monetary Fund. **In** *Williamson, J., ed.*, 1983, pp. 605–60.

Yano, Makoto. Welfare Aspects of the Transfer Problem. *J. Int. Econ.*, November 1983, *15*(3/4), pp. 277–89.

Zakariya, Hasan S. The Petroleum Lending Programme of the World Bank: The First Five Years. *J. World Trade Law*, November–December 1983, *17*(6), pp. 471–95. **[G: LDCs]**

500 Administration; Business Finance; Marketing; Accounting

5000 General

Duncan, Joseph W. Private Sector Data on Business Failures. *Rev. Public Data Use (See J. Econ. Soc. Meas. after 4/85)*, March 1983, *11*(1), pp. 29–35. **[G: U.S.]**

510 Administration

511 Organization and Decision Theory

5110 Organization and Decision Theory

Aaker, David A. Organizing a Strategic Information Scanning System. *Calif. Manage. Rev.*, January 1983, *25*(2), pp. 76–83.

Adler, Nancy J. A Typology of Management Studies Involving Culture. *J. Int. Bus. Stud.*, Fall 1983, *14*(2), pp. 29–47.

Anderson, Gary M.; McCormick, Robert E. and Tollison, Robert D. The Economic Organization of the English East India Company. *J. Econ. Behav.*

Organ., June–September 1983, 4(2–3), pp. 221–38. [G: U.K.]

Argote, Linda; Goodman, Paul S. and Schkade, David. The Human Side of Robotics: How Workers React to a Robot. *Sloan Manage. Rev.*, Spring 1983, *24*(3), pp. 31–41. [G: U.S.]

Babb, Emerson M. and Lang, Mahlon G. Intrafirm Decision Making: Private and Public Consequences. **In** *Farris, P. L., ed.*, 1983, pp. 38–53. [G: U.S.]

Baiman, Stanley and Evans, John H., III. Pre-Decision Information and Participative Management Control Systems. *J. Acc. Res.*, Autumn 1983, *21* (2), pp. 371–95.

Baliga, B. R. U.S. Multinational Corporations: A Lesson in the Failure of Success. **In** *Goldberg, W. H., ed.*, 1983, pp. 42–56. [G: U.S.]

Bauer, Michael and Cohen, Elie. The Invisibility of Power in Economics: Beyond Markets and Hierarchies. **In** *Francis, A.; Turk, J. and Willman, P., eds.*, 1983, pp. 81–104.

Beckhard, Richard and Dyer, W. Gibb, Jr. Managing Change in the Family Firm—Issues and Strategies. *Sloan Manage. Rev.*, Spring 1983, *24*(3), pp. 59–65. [G: U.S.]

Benson, J. Kenneth. Paradigm and Praxis in Organizational Analysis. **In** *Cummings, L. L. and Staw, B. M., eds.*, 1983, pp. 33–56.

Blaylock, Bruce K. and Karaphillis, George. A Selection Technique for Capital Investment Decisions: An Industrial Application of Stochastic Dominance. *Rev. Bus. Econ. Res.*, Winter, 1983, *18*(2), pp. 1–12.

Braendgaard, Asger. Market, Hierarchy and Technology: Some Implications of Economic Internationalism for Labour. **In** *Francis, A.; Turk, J. and Willman, P., eds.*, 1983, pp. 159–79.

Bronsema, Gloria S. and Keen, Peter G. W. Education Intervention and Implementation in MIS. *Sloan Manage. Rev.*, Summer 1983, *24*(4), pp. 35–43.

Brownell, Peter. The Motivational Impact of Management-by-Exception in a Budgetary Context. *J. Acc. Res.*, Autumn 1983, *21* (2), pp. 456–72. [G: U.S.]

Butler, Richard J. Control through Markets, Hierarchies and Communes: A Transactional Approach to Organisational Analysis. **In** *Francis, A.; Turk, J. and Willman, P., eds.*, 1983, pp. 137–58.

Casson, Mark. The Growth of International Business: Introduction: The Conceptual Framework. **In** *Casson, M., ed.*, 1983, pp. 1–33.

Ciborra, Claudio U. Markets, Bureaucracies, and Groups in the Information Society: An Institutional Appraisal of the Impacts of Information Technology. *Info. Econ. Policy*, 1983, *1* (2), pp. 145–60. [G: Italy]

Correa, Hector. The Firm's Administrative Structure: Theory, Measurement and Applications to Growth Accounting and Income Distribution. *Empirical Econ.*, 1983, *8*(2), pp. 93–109. [G: U.S.]

Daems, Herman. The Determinants of the Hierarchical Organisation of Industry. **In** *Francis, A.; Turk, J. and Willman, P., eds.*, 1983, pp. 35–53.

Demsetz, Harold. The Structure of Ownership and the Theory of the Firm. *J. Law Econ.*, June 1983, *26*(2), pp. 375–90.

Demski, Joel S. Comments on Wilson and Jensen [Auditing: Perspectives from Multi-person Decision Theory] [Organization Theory and Methodology]. *Accounting Rev.*, April 1983, *58*(2), pp. 347–49.

Dye, Ronald A. Communication and Post-Decision Information. *J. Acc. Res.*, Autumn 1983, *21* (2), pp. 514–33.

Earl, Michael J. Perspectives on Management. **In** *Earl, M. J., ed.*, 1983, pp. 234–48.

England, George W. and Harpaz, Itzhak. Some Methodological and Analytic Considerations in Cross-National Comparative Research. *J. Int. Bus. Stud.*, Fall 1983, *14*(2), pp. 49–59.

Fama, Eugene F. and Jensen, Michael C. Agency Problems and Residual Claims. *J. Law Econ.*, June 1983, *26*(2), pp. 327–49.

Fama, Eugene F. and Jensen, Michael C. Separation of Ownership and Control. *J. Law Econ.*, June 1983, *26*(2), pp. 301–25.

Farquhar, Peter H. Research Directions in Multiattribute Utility Analysis. **In** *Hansen, P., ed.*, 1983, pp. 63–85.

Fazekas, Károly. Intensive Product Change and Expansion. *Eastern Europ. Econ.*, Spring–Summer 1983, *21* (3–4), pp. 67–84. [G: Hungary]

Francis, Arthur. Markets and Hierarchies: Efficiency of Domination? **In** *Francis, A.; Turk, J. and Willman, P., eds.*, 1983, pp. 105–16.

Francis, Arthur; Turk, Jeremy and Willman, Paul. Power, Efficiency & Institutions: Introduction. **In** *Francis, A.; Turk, J. and Willman, P., eds.*, 1983, pp. 1–12.

Gal, Tomas. On Efficient Sets in Vector Maximum Problems—A Brief Survey. **In** *Hansen, P., ed.*, 1983, pp. 94–114.

Galambos, Louis. Technology, Political Economy, and Professionalization: Central Themes of the Organizational Synthesis. *Bus. Hist. Rev.*, Winter 1983, *57*(4), pp. 471–93. [G: U.S.]

Gershon, Mark and Duckstein, Lucien. An Algorithm for Choosing a Multiobjective Technique. **In** *Hansen, P., ed.*, 1983, pp. 53–62.

Golabi, Kamal. A Markov Decision Modeling Approach to a Multi-objective Maintenance Problem. **In** *Hansen, P., ed.*, 1983, pp. 115–25.

Gold, Bela. On the Adoption of Technological Innovations in Industry: Superficial Models and Complex Decision Processes. **In** *Macdonald, S.; Lamberton, D. M. and Mandeville, T., eds.*, 1983, pp. 104–21.

Golembiewski, Robert T. Social Desirability and Change in Organizations: Some Surprising Results and Conceptual Musings. *Rev. Bus. Econ. Res.*, Spring 1983, *18*(3), pp. 9–20. [G: U.S.]

Gottinger, Hans W. The Economics of Organizational Design. **In** *Stigum, B. P. and Wenstøp, F., eds.*, 1983, pp. 423–42.

Greenhalgh, Leonard. Organizational Decline. **In** *Bacharach, S. B., ed.*, 1983, pp. 231–76.

Grout, Paul. Welfare Aspects of Naive and Sophisticated Decision-making. **In** *Pattanaik, P. K. and Salles, M., eds.*, 1983, pp. 207–24.

Harari, Oren; Crawford, Kent S. and Rhode, John

Grant. Organization Size and Member Attitudes: An Empirical Study. *Ind. Relat.*, Winter 1983, *22*(1), pp. 94–104.

Hay, Donald. Management and Economic Performance. **In** *Earl, M. J., ed.*, 1983, pp. 55–81.

Heilman, Madeline E. Sex Bias in Work Settings: The Lack of Fit Model. **In** *Cummings, L. L. and Staw, B. M., eds.*, 1983, pp. 269–98.

Hinloopen, Edwin; Nijkamp, Peter and Rietveld, Piet. Qualitative Discrete Multiple Criteria Choice Models in Regional Planning. *Reg. Sci. Urban Econ.*, February 1983, *13*(1), pp. 77–102. **[G: Belgium; Netherlands]**

Hinloopen, Edwin; Nijkamp, Peter and Rietveld, Piet. The Regime Method: A New Multicriteria Technique. **In** *Hansen, P., ed.*, 1983, pp. 146–55. **[G: Netherlands]**

Hofstede, Geert. The Cultural Relativity of Organizational Practices and Theories. *J. Int. Bus. Stud.*, Fall 1983, *14*(2), pp. 75–89.

Holin, S. and Prevot, M. An Application of the Multiobjective Programming to the French Industry. **In** *Hansen, P., ed.*, 1983, pp. 167–76. **[G: France]**

Holtmann, Alphonse G. Uncertainty, Organizational Form, and X-Efficiency. *J. Econ. Bus.*, 1983, *35*(1), pp. 131–37.

Ilgen, Daniel R. and Feldman, Jack M. Performance Appraisal: A Process Focus. **In** *Cummings, L. L. and Staw, B. M., eds.*, 1983, pp. 141–97.

Ivanovic, Branislav. The Selections of Elements from a Given Set Relative to One Criterion. *Econ. Anal. Worker's Manage.*, 1983, *17*(4), pp. 341–60.

Jaeger, Alfred M. The Transfer of Organizational Culture Overseas: An Approach to Control in the Multinational Corporation. *J. Int. Bus. Stud.*, Fall 1983, *14*(2), pp. 91–114. **[G: Japan; U.S.]**

Jensen, Michael C. Organization Theory and Methodology. *Accounting Rev.*, April 1983, *58*(2), pp. 319–39.

Jones, S. R. H. Technology and the Organization of Work: A Reply. *J. Econ. Behav. Organ.*, March 1983, *4*(1), pp. 63–66.

Junnelius, Christian. Strukturförändringar i mogna branscher. (Structural Change in Mature Industries. With English summary.) *Ekon. Samfundets Tidskr.*, 1983, *36*(4), pp. 133–37.

Kaplan, Robert S. Comments on Wilson and Jensen [Auditing: Perspectives from Multi-person Decision Theory] [Organization Theory and Methodology]. *Accounting Rev.*, April 1983, *58*(2), pp. 340–46.

Kaplan, Robert S. Measuring Manufacturing Performance: A New Challenge for Managerial Accounting Research. *Accounting Rev.*, October 1983, *58*(4), pp. 686–705. **[G: U.S.; Japan]**

Karni, Edi; Schmeidler, David and Vind, Karl. On State Dependent Preferences and Subjective Probabilities. *Econometrica*, July 1983, *51*(4), pp. 1021–31.

Kastrinakis, C. A Systems Approach Used in Defining Higher Management Information Needs in a Manufacturing Company: Principles and Methodology. **In** *Wilson, B.; Berg, C. C. and French, D., eds.*, 1983, pp. 313–21.

Keren, Michael and Levhari, David. The Internal Organization of the Firm and the Shape of Average Costs. *Bell J. Econ. (See Rand J. Econ. after 4/85)*, Autumn 1983, *14*(2), pp. 474–86.

Koch, Donald L. Changing the Corporate Culture through Information Systems. **In** *Federal Reserve Bank of Atlanta*, 1983, pp. 87–100. **[G: U.S.]**

Korhonen, Pekka and Wallenius, Jyrki. Principles for Solving Sequential Multiple Criteria Decision Problems. **In** *Hansen, P., ed.*, 1983, pp. 195–203.

Kuhn, James W.; Lewin, David and McNulty, Paul J. Neil W. Chamberlain: A Retrospective Analysis of His Scholarly Work and Influence. *Brit. J. Ind. Relat.*, July 1983, *21*(2), pp. 143–60.

Lehto, Sakari T. Yritysten uudistumisesta. (Regenerating the Enterprise. With English summary.) *Liiketaloudellinen Aikak.*, 1983, *32*(4), pp. 345–57. **[G: Finland]**

Leung, Yee. A Value-based Approach to Conflict Resolution Involving Multiple Objectives and Multiple Decision-making Units. **In** *Isard, W. and Nagao, Y., eds.*, 1983, pp. 55–71.

Lewis, Barry; Shields, Michael D. and Young, S. Mark. Evaluating Human Judgments and Decision Aids. *J. Acc. Res.*, Spring 1983, *21*(1), pp. 271–85.

Lockett, A. G. and Hetherington, B. Subjective Data and MCDM. **In** *Hansen, P., ed.*, 1983, pp. 247–59.

Lower, Milton D. Comments on R. S. Thompson's "The Spread of an Institutional Innovation." *J. Econ. Issues*, June 1983, *17*(2), pp. 539–42. **[G: U.K.]**

Mackinnon, Andrew J. and Wearing, Alexander J. Decision Making in Dynamic Environments. **In** *Stigum, B. P. and Wenstøp, F., eds.*, 1983, pp. 399–422.

Marcati, Alberto. Quando l'impresa diventa multinazionale: il problema del controllo. (Problems of Control When the Company Becomes a Multinational One. With English summary.) *L'Impresa*, 1983, *25*(2), pp. 35–41.

Martin, Patricia Yancey, et al. The Concept of "Integrated" Services Reconsidered. *Soc. Sci. Quart.*, December 1983, *64*(4), pp. 747–63. **[G: U.S.]**

McGuinness, Tony. Markets and Hierarchies: A Suitable Framework for an Evaluation of Organisational Change? **In** *Francis, A.; Turk, J. and Willman, P., eds.*, 1983, pp. 180–88.

Minkes, A. L. and Nuttall, C. S. Business Behaviour and Management Structure—2: A Case Study Comparison of Managerial Initiative and Control in Four Industrial Enterprises. *Managerial Dec. Econ.*, March 1983, *4*(1), pp. 16–34. **[G: U.K.]**

Minkes, A. L. and Nuttall, C. S. Business Behaviour and Management Structure—1: A Case Study Comparison of Managerial Initiative and Control in Four Industrial Enterprises. *Managerial Dec. Econ.*, March 1983, *4*(1), pp. 1–15. **[G: U.K.]**

Nakayama, H.; Takeguchi, T. and Sano, M. Interactive Graphics for Portfolio Selection. **In** *Hansen, P., ed.*, 1983, pp. 280–89. **[G: Japan]**

Narula, Subhash C. and Nwosu, Adiele D. Two-Level Hierarchical Programming Problem. **In** *Hansen, P., ed.*, 1983, pp. 290–99.

Negandhi, Anant R. Cross-Cultural Management Research: Trend and Future Directions. *J. Int. Bus. Stud.*, Fall 1983, *14*(2), pp. 17–28.

Negandhi, Anant R. External and Internal Functioning of American, German, and Japanese Multinational Corporations: Decisionmaking and Policy Issues. **In** *Goldberg, W. H., ed.*, 1983, pp. 21–41. **[G: U.S.; Japan; W. Germany]**

Niitamo, Olavi E. Systeemitarkastelun eräistä juurista ja latvuksista. (Systems Approach Now and Tomorrow. With English summary.) *Liiketaloudellinen Aikak.*, 1983, *32*(1), pp. 42–48.

Nijkamp, Peter and Rietveld, Piet. Multiobjective Decision Analysis in a Regional Context: Introduction. *Reg. Sci. Urban Econ.*, February 1983, *13*(1), pp. 1–3.

Nykowski, Ireneusz and Zólkiewski, Zbigniew. On Some Connections between Bicriteria and Fractional Programming Problems. **In** *Hansen, P., ed.*, 1983, pp. 300–309.

O'Reilly, Charles A., III. The Use of Information in Organizational Decision Making: A Model and Some Propositions. **In** *Cummings, L. L. and Staw, B. M., eds.*, 1983, pp. 103–39.

Parsons, Gregory L. Information Technology: A New Competitive Weapon. *Sloan Manage. Rev.*, Fall 1983, *25*(1), pp. 3–14.

Pfeffer, Jeffrey. Organizational Demography. **In** *Cummings, L. L. and Staw, B. M., eds.*, 1983, pp. 299–357.

Poensgen, Otto H. Between Market and Hierarchy. **In** *Francis, A.; Turk, J. and Willman, P., eds.*, 1983, pp. 54–80. **[G: W. Germany]**

Reeves, Gary R. and Franz, Lori S. A Simplified Approach to Interactive MOLP. **In** *Hansen, P., ed.*, 1983, pp. 310–16.

Ricardo-Campbell, Rita. Comments on the Structure of Ownership and the Theory of the Firm. *J. Law Econ.*, June 1983, *26*(2), pp. 391–93.

Rietveld, Piet. Analysis of Conflicts and Compromises, Using Qualitative Data. *Conflict Manage. Peace Sci.*, Fall 1983, *7*(1), pp. 39–63. **[G: Netherlands; Belgium]**

Robbins, Stephen P. The Theory Z Organization from a Power-Control Perspective. *Calif. Manage. Rev.*, January 1983, *25*(2), pp. 67–75.

Saaty, Thomas L. Priority Setting in Complex Problems. **In** *Hansen, P., ed.*, 1983, pp. 326–36.

Sahlin, Nils-Eric. On Second Order Probabilities and the Notion of Epistemic Risk. **In** *Stigum, B. P. and Wenstøp, F., eds.*, 1983, pp. 95–104.

Sarin, Rakesh Kumar. Measurable Value Function Theory: Survey and Open Problems. **In** *Hansen, P., ed.*, 1983, pp. 337–46.

Sekaran, Uma. Methodological and Theoretical Issues and Advancements in Cross-Cultural Research. *J. Int. Bus. Stud.*, Fall 1983, *14*(2), pp. 61–73.

Shields, Michael D. Effects on Information Supply and Demand on Judgment Accuracy: Evidence from Corporate Managers. *Accounting Rev.*, April 1983, *58*(2), pp. 284–303.

Shubik, Martin. The Strategic Audit: A Game Theoretic Approach to Corporate Competitive Strategy. *Managerial Dec. Econ.*, September 1983, *4*(3), pp. 160–71.

Simon, Herbert A. Rational Decision Making in Business Organizations. **In** *Marr, W. L. and Raj, B., eds.*, 1983, *1978*, pp. 281–315.

Stewart, Rosemary. Managerial Behaviour: How Research Has Changed the Traditional Picture. **In** *Earl, M. J., ed.*, 1983, pp. 82–98.

Strange, J. Leland. Microcomputer Enhancement: Challenges in an Exploding Industry. **In** *Federal Reserve Bank of Atlanta*, 1983, pp. 111–17. **[G: U.S.]**

Suojanen, Waino W. and Keiller, James B. General Management: A Triune Brain Approach. *Liiketaloudellinen Aikak.*, 1983, *32*(1), pp. 3–18.

Taylor, Michael and Kissling, Chris. Resource Dependence, Power Networks and the Airline System of the South Pacific. *Reg. Stud.*, August 1983, *17*(4), pp. 237–50. **[G: South Pacific]**

Taylor, Michael and Thrift, Nigel. Business Organization, Segmentation and Location. *Reg. Stud.*, December 1983, *17*(6), pp. 445–65.

Thompson, R. S. The Spread of an Institutional Innovation: The Multidivisional Corporation in the U.K. *J. Econ. Issues*, June 1983, *17*(2), pp. 529–38. **[G: U.K.]**

Tiller, Mikel G. The Dissonance Model of Participative Budgeting: An Empirical Exploration. *J. Acc. Res.*, Autumn 1983, *21*(2), pp. 581–95. **[G: U.S.]**

Turk, Jeremy. Conclusion: Power, Efficiency and Institutions: Some Implications of the Debate for the Scope of Economics. **In** *Francis, A.; Turk, J. and Willman, P., eds.*, 1983, pp. 189–204.

Viallet, Claude. Resolution of Conflicts of Interest in the Ownership of a Firm: The Case of Mixed Firms. *Ann. Pub. Co-op. Econ.*, July–September 1983, *54*(3), pp. 255–69.

Warmington, Alan. The Nature of Action Research. **In** *Wilson, B.; Berg, C. C. and French, D., eds.*, 1983, pp. 51–60.

Waterman, Robert H., Jr. Management Excellence and Growth. **In** *Federal Reserve Bank of Atlanta*, 1983, pp. 45–59. **[G: U.S.]**

Weber, M. O. An Empirical Investigation on Multiattribute Decision Making. **In** *Hansen, P., ed.*, 1983, pp. 379–88.

Welge, Martin K. Decisionmaking in German Multinationals and Its Impact on External Relationships. **In** *Goldberg, W. H., ed.*, 1983, pp. 57–77. **[G: Mexico; W. Germany]**

Werczberger, Elia. Multiperson Multitarget Decision Making, Using the Versatility Criterion. *Reg. Sci. Urban Econ.*, February 1983, *13*(1), pp. 103–13.

White, Chelsea C., III and El Deib, Hany K. Multistage Decisionmaking with Imprecise Utilities. **In** *Hansen, P., ed.*, 1983, pp. 400–405.

White, D. J. The Foundations of Multi-objective Interactive Programming—Some Questions. **In** *Hansen, P., ed.*, 1983, pp. 406–15.

Wierzbicki, Andrzej P. Critical Essay on the Methodology of Multiobjective Analysis. *Reg. Sci. Urban Econ.*, February 1983, *13*(1), pp. 5–29.

Williamson, Oliver E. Organization Form, Residual Claimants, and Corporate Control. *J. Law Econ.*, June 1983, *26*(2), pp. 351–66.

Williamson, Oliver E. Technology and the Organization of Work: A Rejoinder. *J. Econ. Behav. Organ.*, March 1983, *4*(1), pp. 67–68.

Williamson, Oliver E. Technology and the Organization of Work: A Reply. *J. Econ. Behav. Organ.*, March 1983, *4*(1), pp. 57–62.

Williamson, Oliver E. and Ouchi, William G. The Markets and Hierarchies Programme of Research: Origins, Implications, Prospects. **In** *Francis, A.; Turk, J. and Willman, P., eds.*, 1983, *1981*, pp. 13–34.

Willman, Paul. The Organisational Failures Framework and Industrial Sociology. **In** *Francis, A.; Turk, J. and Willman, P., eds.*, 1983, pp. 117–35.

Wilson, Brian. Methodology Related to Integrated Production Systems. **In** *Wilson, B.; Berg, C. C. and French, D., eds.*, 1983, pp. 61–99.

Wortman, Max S., Jr. Reintegrating and Reconceptualizing Management: A Challenge for the Future. *Rev. Bus. Econ. Res.*, Spring 1983, *18*(3), pp. 1–8.

Wright, Vic. Some Bounds to the Relevance of Decision Theory. *Australian J. Agr. Econ.*, December 1983, *27*(3), pp. 221–30.

Yilmaz, Mustafa R. The Use of Risk and Return Models for Multiattribute Decisions with Decomposable Utilities. *J. Finan. Quant. Anal.*, September 1983, *18*(3), pp. 279–85.

Zif, Jehiel. Explanatory Concepts of Managerial Strategic Behavior in State-Owned Enterprises: A Multinational Study. *J. Int. Bus. Stud.*, Spring/Summer 1983, *14*(1), pp. 35–46. **[G: Selected LDCs]**

Zionts, Stanley. A Report on a Project on Multiple Criteria Decision Making, 1982. **In** *Hansen, P., ed.*, 1983, pp. 416–30.

Zucker, Lynne G. Organizations as Institutions. **In** *Bacharach, S. B., ed.*, 1983, pp. 1–47. **[G: U.S.]**

512 Managerial Economics

5120 Managerial Economics

Abernathy, William J. and Wayne, Kenneth. Limits of the Learning Curve. **In** *Kantrow, A. M., ed.*, 1983, pp. 114–31. **[G: U.S.]**

Alic, J. A. Manufacturing Management: Effects on Productivity and Quality. **In** *Wilson, B.; Berg, C. C. and French, D., eds.*, 1983, pp. 281–92. **[G: Japan; U.S.]**

Anderson, John. Some Impacts of Computer Technology upon Management and Organizations. **In** *Hill, S. and Johnston, R., eds.*, 1983, pp. 115–36. **[G: Australia]**

Aoki, Masahiko. Managerialism Revisited in the Light of Bargaining-Game Theory. *Int. J. Ind. Organ.*, 1983, *1*(1), pp. 1–21.

Austin, Mark. The Theory of the Firm. **In** *Gowland, D. H., ed.*, 1983, pp. 157–70.

Balloni, Valeriano. Origini, moi e tempi di evoluzione delle strutture organizzativo–imprenditoriali. (Origins, Ways and Phases in the Evolution of Organizational–Entrepreneurial Structures. With English summary.) *Giorn. Econ.*, November–December 1983, *42*(11–12), pp. 795–808. **[G: Italy]**

Banerjee, Avijit. An Application of Stochastic Programming in Steel Production. *Rev. Bus. Econ. Res.*, Spring 1983, *18*(3), pp. 58–70. **[G: U.S.]**

Banks, Robert L. and Wheelwright, Steven C. Operations versus Strategy: Trading Tomorrow for Today. **In** *Kantrow, A. M., ed.*, 1983, pp. 159–73. **[G: U.S.]**

Battaglia, Loretta and Savorgnani, Glauco T. Marketing d'acquisto, perché. (Input Marketing and Why. With English summary.) *L'Impresa*, 1983, *25*(2), pp. 19–24.

Beckmann, Martin J. Production Functions in the Analysis of Organizational Structure. **In** *[Yamada, I.]*, 1983, pp. 2–14.

Bertrand, J. W. M. On the Design and Monitoring of a Master Production Scheduling Function in a Manufacturing Resource Planning Environment. **In** *Wilson, B.; Berg, C. C. and French, D., eds.*, 1983, pp. 111–29.

Bishop, John E. Integrating Critical Elements of Production Planning. **In** *Kantrow, A. M., ed.*, 1983, pp. 289–302.

Boucher, T. O. and Muckstadt, J. A. The Inventory Cost Effectiveness of Group Technology Production Systems. *Ann. Sci. Écon. Appl.*, 1983, *39*(1), pp. 27–41. **[G: U.S.]**

Bronsema, Gloria S. and Keen, Peter G. W. Education Intervention and Implementation in MIS. *Sloan Manage. Rev.*, Summer 1983, *24*(4), pp. 35–43.

Brown, Clifton. Effects of Dynamic Task Environment on the Learning of Standard Cost Variance Significance. *J. Acc. Res.*, Autumn 1983, *21*(2), pp. 413–31. **[G: U.S.]**

Brown, Lawrence D. Accounting Changes and the Accuracy of Analysts' Earnings Forecasts. *J. Acc. Res.*, Autumn 1983, *21*(2), pp. 432–43. **[G: U.S.]**

Brownell, Peter. The Motivational Impact of Management-by-Exception in a Budgetary Context. *J. Acc. Res.*, Autumn 1983, *21*(2), pp. 456–72. **[G: U.S.]**

Bruno, Giorgio and Canuto, Enrico. Simulation of Production Systems with DESFOR. **In** *Wilson, B.; Berg, C. C. and French, D., eds.*, 1983, pp. 203–16.

Buck, Trevor and Chiplin, Brian. Risk Bearing and Self Management. *Kyklos*, 1983, *36*(2), pp. 270–84.

Canuto, Enrico; Menga, Giuseppe and Bruno, Giorgio. Analysis of Flexible Manufacturing Systems. **In** *Wilson, B.; Berg, C. C. and French, D., eds.*, 1983, pp. 189–201.

Chaudry, A. Net Income and Productivity Analysis (NIPA) as a Planning Model. **In** *Courville, L.; de Fontenay, A. and Dobell, R., eds.*, 1983, pp. 145–66.

Checkland, P. B. Systems Concepts Relevant to the Problem of Integrated Production Systems. **In** *Wilson, B.; Berg, C. C. and French, D., eds.*, 1983, pp. 35–49.

Chen, Joyce T. Cost Allocation and External Acquisition of Services When Self-services Exist. *Accounting Rev.*, July 1983, *58*(3), pp. 600–605.

Chen, Joyce T. The Effect of Chance Variation on Revenue and Cost Estimations for Breakeven Analysis: A Comment. *Accounting Rev.*, October 1983, *58*(4), pp. 813–19.

Chow, Chee W. The Effects of Job Standard Tightness and Compensation Scheme on Performance: An Exploration of Linkages. *Accounting Rev.*, October 1983, *58*(4), pp. 667–85.

Creedy, John and Johnson, P. S. Firm Formation in Manufacturing Industry. *Appl. Econ.*, April 1983, *15*(2), pp. 177–85. **[G: U.K.]**

Cubbin, John S. and Hall, Graham. Directors' Remuneration in the Theory of the Firm: Specification and Testing of the Null Hypothesis. *Europ. Econ. Rev.*, January 1983, *20*(1–3), pp. 333–48. **[G: U.K.]**

Delporte, Christian M. and Keymolen, G. De l'intérêt des techniques quantitatives: application à un problème de livraisons. *Ann. Sci. Écon. Appl.*, 1983, *39*(1), pp. 87–110. **[G: W. Germany]**

Delporte, Christian M. and Thomas, L. Joseph. Gestion des opérations et productivité: Quelques leçons de l'exemple japonais. *Ann. Sci. Écon. Appl.*, 1983, *39*(1), pp. 9–26. **[G: Japan]**

Demski, Joel S. Comments on Wilson and Jensen [Auditing: Perspectives from Multi-person Decision Theory] [Organization Theory and Methodology]. *Accounting Rev.*, April 1983, *58*(2), pp. 347–49.

Denny, Michael G. S.; de Fontenay, A. and Werner, M. Total Factor Productivity for Management: The Post-mortem and Planning Frameworks. **In** *Courville, L.; de Fontenay, A. and Dobell, R., eds.*, 1983, pp. 167–78.

Dichtl, Erwin; Raffée, Hans and Wellenreuther, Hans. Public Policy towards Small and Medium-Sized Retail Businesses in the Federal Republic of Germany. *Rivista Int. Sci. Econ. Com.*, April-May 1983, *30*(4–5), pp. 424–39. **[G: W. Germany]**

Dollery, Brian Edward. Some Evidence on the Goals of Firms in South African Manufacturing Industry. *J. Stud. Econ. Econometrics,* July 1983, (17), pp. 5–13. **[G: S. Africa]**

Engelhardt, Werner Wilhelm. Zum Situations- und Problembezug von Entscheidungsmodellen bei Johann Heinrich von Thünen. (Relevance of Decision-Oriented Models by Johann Heinrich von Thünen. With English summary.) *Z. Wirtschaft. Sozialwissen.*, 1983, *103*(6), pp. 561–88.

Evans, Kaye D.; Siegfried, John J. and Sweeney, George H. The Economic Cost of Suboptimal Manufacturing Capacity. *J. Bus.*, January 1983, *56*(1), pp. 55–76. **[G: U.S.]**

Fama, Eugene F. Agency Problems and the Theory of the Firm. **In** *Archer, S. H. and D'Ambrosia, C. A.*, 1983, *1980*, pp. 535–54.

Fayolle, Jacky. Emploi et prix: Un Modèle de court terme construit sur des variables d'opinion. (Manpower and Prices: A Short Term Model Based on Business Surveys. With English summary.) *Ann. INSEE,* October–December 1983, (52), pp. 87–121.

Feuer, K. Le calcul de rentabilité des enterprises de financement. (How to Calculate the Probability of Financial Companies. With English summary.) *Ann. Sci. Écon. Appl.*, 1983, *39*(2), pp. 95–112.

Forker, J. J. Managerial Quality, Financial Structure and Signalling: A Test of Pricing Efficiency in the UK Equity Securities Market. *Managerial Dec. Econ.*, December 1983, *4*(4), pp. 266–77. **[G: U.K.]**

Forrester, Jay W. System Dynamics. **In** *Migliaro, A. and Jain, C. L., eds.*, 1983, pp. 66–68.

French, D. A Cluster Algorithm for Process Layout. **In** *Wilson, B.; Berg, C. C. and French, D., eds.*, 1983, pp. 161–73.

Gerwin, Donald. Do's and Don'ts of Computerized Manufacturing. **In** *Kantrow, A. M., ed.*, 1983, pp. 349–62.

Gui, Benedetto. Struttura finanziaria e "Moral Risk" in imprese non quotate nel mercato azionario. (Financial Structure and Moral Risk When Firms' Shares Are Not Traded. With English summary.) *Rivista Int. Sci. Econ. Com.*, February 1983, *30*(2), pp. 125–42.

Guy, Charles E.; Brown, George F., Jr. and O'Hara, Donald J. A Deterministic Profit Attribution Model: The Postal Service, a Case Study. *Managerial Dec. Econ.*, September 1983, *4*(3), pp. 208–13. **[G: U.S.]**

Haahti, Antti and Yavas, Ugur. Taitotiedon välittymisestä kehitysmaihin. (Transfer of Know-How to Underdeveloped Countries. With English summary.) *Liiketaloudellinen Aikak.*, 1983, *32*(4), pp. 399–411. **[G: LDCs]**

Harrington, David H. Costs and Returns: Economic and Accounting Concepts. *Agr. Econ. Res.*, October 1983, *35*(4), pp. 1–8.

Hart, Oliver D. The Market Mechanism as an Incentive Scheme. *Bell J. Econ. (See Rand J. Econ. after 4/85),* Autumn 1983, *14*(2), pp. 366–82.

Hartulari, Carmen and Popescu, Angela. A Cybernetic Mode for Solving the Assembly Line-Balancing Problem. *Econ. Computat. Cybern. Stud. Res.*, 1983, *18*(1), pp. 43–50.

Hayes, Robert H. Why Japanese Factories Work. **In** *Kantrow, A. M., ed.*, 1983, pp. 231–47. **[G: Japan]**

Hayes, Robert H. and Abernathy, William J. Managing Our Way to Economic Decline. **In** *Kantrow, A. M., ed.*, 1983, pp. 15–35. **[G: U.S.]**

Hayes, Robert H. and Garvin, David A. Managing as if Tomorrow Mattered. **In** *Kantrow, A. M., ed.*, 1983, pp. 36–51. **[G: U.S.]**

Hayes, Robert H. and Schmenner, Roger W. How Should You Organize Manufacturing? **In** *Kantrow, A. M., ed.*, 1983, pp. 193–214.

Hayes, Robert H. and Wheelwright, Steven C. Link Manufacturing Process and Product Life Cycles. **In** *Kantrow, A. M., ed.*, 1983, pp. 132–43. **[G: U.S.]**

Hayes, Robert H. and Wheelwright, Steven C. The Dynamics of Process–Product Life Cycles. **In** *Kantrow, A. M., ed.*, 1983, pp. 144–58. **[G: U.S.]**

Herroelen, Willy and Lambrecht, Marc R. Management Aspects of Computerized Manufacturing. *Econ. Soc. Tijdschr.*, December 1983, *37*(6), pp. 723–43.

Hertz, David B. and Thomas, Howard. Decision and Risk Analysis in a New Product and Facilities Planning Problem. *Sloan Manage. Rev.*, Winter 1983, *24*(2), pp. 17–31.

Heskett, James L. Logistics—Essential to Strategy. **In** *Kantrow, A. M., ed.*, 1983, pp. 269–88.

Hicks, John. Limited Liability: Pros and Cons. **In** *Hicks, J.*, 1983, *1982*, pp. 179–88.

Hicks, John. The Concept of Business Income. **In** *Hicks, J.*, 1983, *1979*, pp. 189–203.

Hirst, Mark K. Reliance on Accounting Performance Measures, Task Uncertainty, and Dysfunctional

Behavior: Some Extensions. *J. Acc. Res.*, Autumn 1983, *21* (2), pp. 596–605. **[G: U.S.]**

Hodgson, Thom J.; Lambrecht, Marc R. and Vander Eecken, J. Production Lot Sizing and the Power of 2. *Ann. Sci. Écon. Appl.*, 1983, *39* (1), pp. 43–58.

Hoffman, George and Gustafson, Cole. A New Approach to Estimating Agricultural Costs of Production. *Agr. Econ. Res.*, October 1983, *35* (4), pp. 9–14. **[G: U.S.]**

Holstein, William K. Production Planning and Control Integrated. **In** *Kantrow, A. M., ed.*, 1983, pp. 303–33.

Holt, Knut. Need Assessment—A Tool for Improving Manufacturing System Design. **In** *Wilson, B.; Berg, C. C. and French, D., eds.*, 1983, pp. 255–69.

Hotvedt, James E. Application of Linear Goal Programming to Forest Harvest Scheduling. *Southern J. Agr. Econ.*, July 1983, *15* (1), pp. 103–08. **[G: U.S.]**

Huang, Philip Y. and Clayton, Edward R. A Q-Gert Network Simulation Model for the Selection of Job Shop Scheduling Rules. *Rev. Bus. Econ. Res.*, Fall 1983, *19* (1), pp. 1–12.

Huge, Ernest C. Managing Manufacturing Lead Times. **In** *Kantrow, A. M., ed.*, 1983, pp. 396–408.

Jefferson, Michael. Economic Uncertainty and Business Decision-making. **In** *Wiseman, J., ed.*, 1983, pp. 122–59.

Jensen, Michael C. Organization Theory and Methodology. *Accounting Rev.*, April 1983, *58* (2), pp. 319–39.

Jensen, Michael C. and Meckling, William H. Theory of the Firm: Managerial Behavior, Agency Costs and Ownership Structure. **In** *Archer, S. H. and D'Ambrosia, C. A.*, 1983, *1976*, pp. 479–534.

Kaplan, Robert S. Comments on Wilson and Jensen [Auditing: Perspectives from Multi-person Decision Theory] [Organization Theory and Methodology]. *Accounting Rev.*, April 1983, *58* (2), pp. 340–46.

Kaplan, Robert S. Measuring Manufacturing Performance: A New Challenge for Managerial Accounting Research. *Accounting Rev.*, October 1983, *58* (4), pp. 686–705. **[G: U.S.; Japan]**

Kastrinakis, C. A Systems Approach Used in Defining Higher Management Information Needs in a Manufacturing Company: Principles and Methodology. **In** *Wilson, B.; Berg, C. C. and French, D., eds.*, 1983, pp. 313–21.

Keren, Michael and Levhari, David. The Internal Organization of the Firm and the Shape of Average Costs. *Bell J. Econ. (See Rand J. Econ. after 4/85)*, Autumn 1983, *14* (2), pp. 474–86.

Koshal, Manjulika and Koshal, Rajindar K. Cash Management Economies in the Production of Food. *Managerial Dec. Econ.*, December 1983, *4* (4), pp. 253–57. **[G: U.S.]**

Laitinen, Erkki K. A Life-Cycle Approach to Retail Pricing. *Liiketaloudellinen Aikak.*, 1983, *32* (3), pp. 251–60. **[G: Finland]**

Lange, Oscar and Lerner, Abba P. Strengthening the Economic Foundations of Democracy. **In** *Lerner, A. P.*, 1983, *1944*, pp. 171–86. **[G: U.S.]**

Larcker, David F. The Association between Performance Plan Adoption and Corporate Capital Investment. *J. Acc. Econ.*, April 1983, *5* (1), pp. 3–30. **[G: U.S.]**

Larcker, David F. and Lessig, V. Parker. An Examination of the Linear and Retrospective Process Tracing Approaches to Judgment Modeling. *Accounting Rev.*, January 1983, *58* (1), pp. 58–77.

Laughhunn, Dan J.; Crum, Roy L. and Payne, John W. Risk Attitudes in the Telecommunications Industry. *Bell J. Econ. (See Rand J. Econ. after 4/85)*, Autumn 1983, *14* (2), pp. 517–21. **[G: U.S.; Canada]**

Lawrence, Kenneth Donald; Marose, Robert A. and Lawrence, Sheila M. A Multiple Goal Portfolio Analysis Model for the Selection of MIS Projects. **In** *Hansen, P., ed.*, 1983, pp. 229–37.

Lee, Sang M.; Snyder, Charles A. and Gen, Mitsuo. The Microcomputer: Experience and Implications for the Future of Multiple Criteria Decision Making. **In** *Hansen, P., ed.*, 1983, pp. 238–46.

Leonard, Frank S. and Sasser, W. Earl, Jr. The Incline of Quality. **In** *Kantrow, A. M., ed.*, 1983, pp. 248–61.

Levy, Haim. Economic Evaluation of Voting Power of Common Stock. *J. Finance*, March 1983, *38* (1), pp. 79–93. **[G: U.S.]**

Lockett, A. G. and Hetherington, B. Subjective Data and MCDM. **In** *Hansen, P., ed.*, 1983, pp. 247–59.

Loury, Glenn C. The Welfare Effects of Intermittent Interruptions of Trade. *Amer. Econ. Rev.*, May 1983, *73* (2), pp. 272–77.

Lowenthal, Franklin. Product Warranty Period: A Markovian Approach to Estimation and Analysis of Repair and Replacement Costs—A Comment. *Accounting Rev.*, October 1983, *58* (4), pp. 837–38.

Madsen, Oli B. G. Production Planning in a Small Firm in the Glass Industry. **In** *Wilson, B.; Berg, C. C. and French, D., eds.*, 1983, pp. 245–53.

Maloney, Michael T. and McCormick, Robert E. A Theory of Cost and Intermittent Production. *J. Bus.*, April 1983, *56* (2), pp. 139–53.

Manes, Rene P. Demand Elasticities: Supplements to Sales Budget Variance Reports. *Accounting Rev.*, January 1983, *58* (1), pp. 143–56.

Marchand, M.; Proost, S. and Wilberz, E. A Model of District Heating Using a CHP Plant. *Energy Econ.*, October 1983, *5* (4), pp. 247–57. **[G: Belgium]**

Martin, John P. and Page, John M., Jr. The Impact of Subsidies on *X*-Efficiency in LDC Industry: Theory and an Empirical Test. *Rev. Econ. Statist.*, November 1983, *65* (4), pp. 608–17. **[G: Ghana]**

Michałowski, W. and Żółkiewski, Zbigniew. An Interactive Approach to the Solution of a Linear Production Planning Problem with Multiple Objectives. **In** *Hansen, P., ed.*, 1983, pp. 260–68.

Miller, Jeffrey G. Fit Production Systems to the Task. **In** *Kantrow, A. M., ed.*, 1983, pp. 334–48.

Miller, Jeffrey G. and Gilmour, Peter. Materials Managers: Who Needs Them? **In** *Kantrow, A. M., ed.*, 1983, pp. 377–95.

Miller, Jeffrey G. and Sprague, Linda G. Behind the Growth in Materials Requirements Planning. **In**

Kantrow, A. M., ed., 1983, pp. 365–76.

Minkes, A. L. and Nuttall, C. S. Business Behaviour and Management Structure—2: A Case Study Comparison of Managerial Initiative and Control in Four Industrial Enterprises. *Managerial Dec. Econ.,* March 1983, *4*(1), pp. 16–34. **[G: U.K.]**

Minkes, A. L. and Nuttall, C. S. Business Behaviour and Management Structure—1: A Case Study Comparison of Managerial Initiative and Control in Four Industrial Enterprises. *Managerial Dec. Econ.,* March 1983, *4*(1), pp. 1–15. **[G: U.K.]**

Moore, Geoffrey H. Inflation and Profits. **In** *Moore, G. H.,* 1983, *1977,* pp. 281–85. **[G: U.S.]**

Nakayama, H.; Takeguchi, T. and Sano, M. Interactive Graphics for Portfolio Selection. **In** *Hansen, P., ed.,* 1983, pp. 280–89. **[G: Japan]**

Narula, Subhash C. and Nwosu, Adiele D. Two-Level Hierarchical Programming Problem. **In** *Hansen, P., ed.,* 1983, pp. 290–99.

Naylor, Thomas H. and Thomas, Celia. Microeconomic Foundations of Corporate Strategy. *Managerial Dec. Econ.,* September 1983, *4*(3), pp. 127–35. **[G: U.S.]**

Nerlove, Marc. Expectations, Plans, and Realizations in Theory and Practice. *Econometrica,* September 1983, *51*(5), pp. 1251–79. **[G: France; W. Germany]**

Niho, Yoshio and Mussachio, Robert A. Revenue Maximization and Optimal Capital Policies of a Regulated Firm. **In** *[Yamada, I.],* 1983, pp. 15–26.

Nişanci, Ibrahim. Use of Group Technology Concepts in Integrated Production Planning. **In** *Wilson, B.; Berg, C. C. and French, D., eds.,* 1983, pp. 149–59.

Okun, Arthur M. The Predictive Value of Surveys of Business Intentions. **In** *Okun, A. M.,* 1983, *1962,* pp. 553–61. **[G: U.S.]**

Palfrey, Thomas R. and Romer, Thomas. Warranties, Performance, and the Resolution of Buyer–Seller Disputes. *Bell J. Econ. (See Rand J. Econ. after 4/85),* Spring 1983, *14*(1), pp. 97–117.

Pepe, Federico. Le moderne funzioni gestionali nella banca per un incremento di efficienza e di produttività. (Modern Banking-Management Functions for Greater Efficiency and Productivity. With English summary.) *Bancaria,* April 1983, *39*(4), pp. 357–70. **[G: Italy]**

Pickering, J. F. The Causes and Consequences of Abandoned Mergers. *J. Ind. Econ.,* March 1983, *31*(3), pp. 267–81. **[G: U.K.]**

Porter, Michael E. Industrial Organization and the Evolution of Concepts for Strategic Planning: The New Learning. *Managerial Dec. Econ.,* September 1983, *4*(3), pp. 172–80.

Prašnikar, Janez. The Yugoslav Self-Managed Enterprise and Factors of Its Efficiency. *Econ. Anal. Worker's Manage.,* 1983, *17*(1), pp. 27–42. **[G: Yugoslavia]**

Qureshi, Zia M. Determinants of Corporate Saving in Pakistan: A Macro-econometric Analysis. *Pakistan Devel. Rev.,* Summer 1983, *22*(2), pp. 73–96. **[G: Pakistan]**

Randell, Daniel. Automation in Perspective—An Overview. **In** *Wilson, B.; Berg, C. C. and French, D., eds.,* 1983, pp. 217–32. **[G: U.S.]**

Rhodes, D. J.; Wright, D. M. and Jarrett, M. G. Integration and the Definition of Responsibilities. **In** *Wilson, B.; Berg, C. C. and French, D., eds.,* 1983, pp. 233–43.

Riley, John G. and Zeckhauser, Richard J. Optimal Selling Strategies: When to Haggle, When to Hold Firm. *Quart. J. Econ.,* May 1983, *98*(2), pp. 267–89.

Roehl, Thomas. A Transactions Cost Approach to International Trading Structures: The Case of the Japanese General Trading Companies. *Hitotsubashi J. Econ.,* December 1983, *24*(2), pp. 119–35. **[G: Japan]**

Rooney, Patrick M. Worker Control: Greater Efficiency and Job Satisfaction. *Econ. Forum,* Winter 1983-84, *14*(2), pp. 97–123. **[G: U.S.]**

Ross, Stephen A. The Determination of Financial Structure: The Incentive-signalling Approach. **In** *Archer, S. H. and D'Ambrosia, C. A.,* 1983, *1977,* pp. 555–75.

Rothkopf, Michael H. Bidding Theory: The Phenomena to Be Modeled. **In** *Engelbrecht-Wiggans, R.; Shubik, M. and Stark, R. M., eds.,* 1983, pp. 105–20.

Schmenner, Roger W. Look beyond the Obvious in Plant Location. **In** *Kantrow, A. M., ed.,* 1983, pp. 409–20.

Scott, Charles E. and Breeden, Charles H. Behavioral Style and Group Performance: An Empirical Study. *J. Behav. Econ.,* Summer 1983, *12*(1), pp. 99–119. **[G: U.S.]**

Shapiro, Nina. An Economic Theory of Business Strategy: A Review Article. *J. Post Keynesian Econ.,* Spring 1983, *5*(3), pp. 483–88.

Shipley, David D. Pricing Flexibility in British Manufacturing Industry. *Managerial Dec. Econ.,* December 1983, *4*(4), pp. 224–33. **[G: U.K.]**

Shubik, Martin. The Strategic Audit: A Game Theoretic Approach to Corporate Competitive Strategy. *Managerial Dec. Econ.,* September 1983, *4*(3), pp. 160–71.

Skinner, C. Wickham. Manufacturing: Missing Link in Corporate Strategy. **In** *Kantrow, A. M., ed.,* 1983, *1969,* pp. 99–113.

Skinner, C. Wickham. The Focused Factory. **In** *Kantrow, A. M., ed.,* 1983, *1974,* pp. 179–92. **[G: U.S.]**

Solberg, James J. Mathematical Design Tools for Integrated Production Systems. **In** *Wilson, B.; Berg, C. C. and French, D., eds.,* 1983, pp. 175–87.

Stoica, M. Stochastic Splitors Used in Scheduling. *Econ. Computat. Cybern. Stud. Res.,* 1983, *18*(1), pp. 63–71.

Storey, D. J. Indigenising a Regional Economy: The Importance of Management Buyouts. *Reg. Stud.,* December 1983, *17*(6), pp. 471–75. **[G: U.K.]**

Sufrin, Sidney C. and Odiorne, George. The Strategic Planning Boom: Hope for the Future or a Bureaucratic Exercise? *Rivista Int. Sci. Econ. Com.,* February 1983, *30*(2), pp. 105–24.

Sutton, Clive J. Does Strategy Pay? *Managerial Dec. Econ.,* September 1983, *4*(3), pp. 153–59.

Switzer, Brian C.; Simunek, Vladimir J. and Mathews, H. Lee. Sociometrics. **In** *Migliaro, A. and Jain, C. L., eds.,* 1983, pp. 55–65. **[G: U.S.]**

Tancredi, Mario. Un modello per verificare l'efficienza aziendale. (A Model to Control Management Efficiency. With English summary.) *L'Impresa,* 1983, *25*(2), pp. 43–50.

Tannenbaum, Arnold S. Employee-owned Companies. **In** *Cummings, L. L. and Staw, B. M., eds.,* 1983, pp. 235–68. **[G: U.S.]**

Tapon, Francis. CAPM as a Strategic Planning Tool. *Managerial Dec. Econ.,* September 1983, *4*(3), pp. 181–84.

Tatsiopoulos, I. P. Manufacturing Lead-Times: A Key Control Factor for the Production/Marketing Integration in Small Component-manufacturing Firms. **In** *Wilson, B.; Berg, C. C. and French, D., eds.,* 1983, pp. 271–80.

Thomas, L. Joseph. Incorporating Marketing Considerations into Capacity Planning and Detailed Scheduling. *Ann. Sci. Écon. Appl.,* 1983, *39*(1), pp. 59–86.

Thompson, R. S. Diversifying Mergers and Risk: Some Empirical Tests. *J. Econ. Stud.,* 1983, *10*(3), pp. 12–21. **[G: U.K.]**

Thomson, Arthur R. Integrated Design and Production Systems for Strategic Production. **In** *Wilson, B.; Berg, C. C. and French, D., eds.,* 1983, pp. 293–303. **[G: U.S.; U.S.S.R.]**

Thurston, Philip H. The Concept of a Production System. **In** *Kantrow, A. M., ed.,* 1983, pp. 265–68.

Tiller, Mikel G. The Dissonance Model of Participative Budgeting: An Empirical Exploration. *J. Acc. Res.,* Autumn 1983, *21*(2), pp. 581–95. **[G: U.S.]**

Tokarev, I. P. Co-Ordination in Problems of Optimal Management of Crude-Oil Processing. *Econ. Computat. Cybern. Stud. Res.,* 1983, *18*(2), pp. 73–82.

Trueman, Brett. Motivating Management to Reveal Inside Information. *J. Finance,* September 1983, *38*(4), pp. 1253–69. **[G: U.S.]**

Verrecchia, Robert E. Discretionary Disclosure. *J. Acc. Econ.,* December 1983, *5*(3), pp. 179–94.

Vogelsang, Ingo. Effort Rewarding Incentive Mechanisms for Public Enterprise Managers. *Int. J. Ind. Organ.,* September 1983, *1*(3), pp. 253–73.

Waldraff, Andreas. Improving Manufacturing Efficiency with Better Logistical Control. **In** *Wilson, B.; Berg, C. C. and French, D., eds.,* 1983, pp. 131–48. **[G: W. Germany]**

Waterlow, J. G. Manufacturing Systems Research: Impressions of a Research Programme. **In** *Wilson, B.; Berg, C. C. and French, D., eds.,* 1983, pp. 323–30.

White, Michelle J. Bankruptcy Costs and the New Bankruptcy Code. *J. Finance,* May 1983, *38*(2), pp. 477–88. **[G: U.S.]**

Williamson, Oliver E. and Ouchi, William G. The Markets and Hierarchies Programme of Research: Origins, Implications, Prospects. **In** *Francis, A.; Turk, J. and Willman, P., eds.,* 1983, *1981,* pp. 13–34.

Wilson, Brian. Methodology Related to Integrated Production Systems. **In** *Wilson, B.; Berg, C. C. and French, D., eds.,* 1983, pp. 61–99.

Wilson, Robert. On Competitive Bidding Applied. **In** *Engelbrecht-Wiggans, R.; Shubik, M. and Stark, R. M., eds.,* 1983, pp. 363–68.

Womer, N. Keith and Patterson, J. Wayne. Estimation and Testing of Learning Curves. *J. Bus. Econ. Statist.,* October 1983, *1*(4), pp. 265–72. **[G: U.S.]**

Wortmann, J. C. A Classification Scheme for Master Production Scheduling. **In** *Wilson, B.; Berg, C. C. and French, D., eds.,* 1983, pp. 101–09.

Wright, Roger L. Measuring the Precision of Statistical Cost Allocations. *J. Bus. Econ. Statist.,* April 1983, *1*(2), pp. 93–100.

Young, David W. and Saltman, Richard B. Prospective Reimbursement and the Hospital Power Equilibrium: A Matrix-Based Management Control system. *Inquiry,* Spring 1983, *20*(1), pp. 20–33. **[G: U.S.]**

Zuscovitch, Ehud. Informatisation, flexibilité et division du travail. (With English summary.) *Rev. Econ. Ind.,* 3rd Trimester 1983, (25), pp. 50–61. **[G: France]**

513 Business and Public Administration

5130 General

Benson, J. Kenneth. Paradigm and Praxis in Organizational Analysis. **In** *Cummings, L. L. and Staw, B. M., eds.,* 1983, pp. 33–56.

Bisesi, Michael. SMR Forum: Strategies for Successful Leadership in Changing Times. *Sloan Manage. Rev.,* Fall 1983, *25*(1), pp. 61–64.

Bradley, Keith and Hill, Stephen. 'After Japan': The Quality Circle Transplant and Productive Efficiency. *Brit. J. Ind. Relat.,* November 1983, *21*(3), pp. 291–311. **[G: U.K.; U.S.]**

Fazekas, Károly. Intensive Product Change and Expansion. *Eastern Europ. Econ.,* Spring–Summer 1983, *21*(3–4), pp. 67–84. **[G: Hungary]**

French, J. Lawrence; Hayashi, Paul M. and Gray, David A. The Compensation of National Union Presidents: Moderating Effects of Union Size. *J. Lab. Res.,* Summer 1983, *4*(3), pp. 225–37. **[G: U.S.]**

Golembiewski, Robert T. Social Desirability and Change in Organizations: Some Surprising Results and Conceptual Musings. *Rev. Bus. Econ. Res.,* Spring 1983, *18*(3), pp. 9–20. **[G: U.S.]**

Goonatilake, P. C. L. Production Management—The Forgotten Factor in the Industrialization Policy in Developing Countries. *World Devel.,* September 1983, *11*(9), pp. 845–50. **[G: Commonwealth Nations]**

Gowler, Dan and Legge, Karen. The Meaning of Management and the Management of Meaning: A View from Social Anthropology. **In** *Earl, M. J., ed.,* 1983, pp. 197–233.

Harries-Jenkins, Gwyn. Bureaucracy in Great Britain. **In** *Littrell, W. B.; Sjoberg, G. and Zurcher, L. A., eds.,* 1983, pp. 73–89. **[G: U.K.]**

Ilgen, Daniel R. and Feldman, Jack M. Performance Appraisal: A Process Focus. **In** *Cummings, L. L. and Staw, B. M., eds.,* 1983, pp. 141–97.

Israel, Arturo. Management and Institutional Development. *Finance Develop.,* September 1983, *20*(3), pp. 15–18. **[G: LDCs]**

Laki, Mihály. Growth and Flexibility: The Case of a Transformer-Manufacturing Cooperative. *Eastern Europ. Econ.,* Spring–Summer 1983, *21*(3–4), pp. 170–87. **[G: Hungary]**

Landell-Mills, Pierre. Management: A Limiting Factor in Development. *Finance Develop.*, September 1983, *20*(3), pp. 11–15. **[G: LDCs]**

Lockett, Martin and Littler, Craig R. Trends in Chinese Enterprise Management, 1978–1982. *World Devel.*, August 1983, *11*(8), pp. 683–704. **[G: China]**

Maisonrouge, Jacques G. The Education of a Modern International Manager. *J. Int. Bus. Stud.*, Spring/Summer 1983, *14*(1), pp. 141–46.

McCann, Joseph E. and Gilmore, Thomas N. Diagnosing Organizational Decision Making through Responsibility Charting. *Sloan Manage. Rev.*, Winter 1983, *24*(2), pp. 3–15.

Myers, Charles A. SMR Forum: Top Management Featherbedding? *Sloan Manage. Rev.*, Summer 1983, *24*(4), pp. 55–58. **[G: U.S.]**

Negandhi, Anant R. Cross-Cultural Management Research: Trend and Future Directions. *J. Int. Bus. Stud.*, Fall 1983, *14*(2), pp. 17–28.

Oshima, Harry T. On the Transferability of Institutions from Abroad: Lessons from the Japanese and Philippine Experience. *Philippine Econ. J.*, 198, *22*(1), pp. 82–98. **[G: Philippine; Japan]**

Pfeffer, Jeffrey. Organizational Demography. **In** *Cummings, L. L. and Staw, B. M., eds.*, 1983, pp. 299–357.

Poza, Ernesto J. Twelve Actions to Build Strong U.S. Factories. *Sloan Manage. Rev.*, Fall 1983, *25*(1), pp. 27–38. **[G: U.S.]**

Purcell, John. The Management of Industrial Relations in the Modern Corporation: Agenda for Research. *Brit. J. Ind. Relat.*, March 1983, *21*(1), pp. 1–16. **[G: U.K.]**

Scott, K. Dow and Cook, Brian. The Relationship between Employee Age and Interpersonal Trust within an Organizational Context. *Rev. Bus. Econ. Res.*, Spring 1983, *18*(3), pp. 71–82. **[G: U.S.]**

Tancredi, Mario. Un modello per verificare l'efficienza aziendale. (A Model to Control Management Efficiency. With English summary.) *L'Impresa*, 1983, *25*(2), pp. 43–50.

Weinberg, Martha Wagner. Public Management and Private Management: A Diminishing Gap? *J. Policy Anal. Manage.*, Fall 1983, *3*(1), pp. 106–15. **[G: U.S.]**

Wortman, Max S., Jr. Reintegrating and Reconceptualizing Management: A Challenge for the Future. *Rev. Bus. Econ. Res.*, Spring 1983, *18*(3), pp. 1–8.

5131 Business Administration

Al-Jafary, Abdulrahman and Hollingsworth, A. T. An Exploratory Study of Managerial Practices in the Arabian Gulf Region. *J. Int. Bus. Stud.*, Fall 1983, *14*(2), pp. 143–52. **[G: Arabian Gulf; U.S.]**

Amihud, Yakov; Kamin, Jacob Y. and Ronen, Joshua. 'Managerialism,' 'Ownerism,' and Risk. *J. Banking Finance,* June 1983, *7*(2), pp. 189–96.

Bardwick, Judith M. Plateauing and Productivity. *Sloan Manage. Rev.*, Spring 1983, *24*(3), pp. 67–73. **[G: U.S.]**

Beckhard, Richard and Dyer, W. Gibb, Jr. Managing Change in the Family Firm—Issues and Strategies. *Sloan Manage. Rev.*, Spring 1983, *24*(3), pp. 59–65. **[G: U.S.]**

Danielsson, Christer. Koncernstyrning och divisionsstrategi. (Corporate Management and Division Strategy. With English summary.) *Ekon. Samfundets Tidskr.*, 1983, *36*(2), pp. 71–75.

Darling, John R. and Brownlee, Leonard J., Jr. Management and Leadership in the Multinational Corporation. *Liiketaloudellinen Aikak.*, 1983, *32*(2), pp. 124–34.

Dearden, John. SMR Forum: Will the Computer Change the Job of Top Management? *Sloan Manage. Rev.*, Fall 1983, *25*(1), pp. 57–60.

Eaton, Jonathan and Rosen, Harvey S. Agency, Delayed Compensation, and the Structure of Executive Remuneration. *J. Finance,* December 1983, *38*(5), pp. 1489–1505. **[G: U.S.]**

Elbaum, Bernard. The Internalization of Labor Markets: Causes and Consequences. *Amer. Econ. Rev.*, May 1983, *73*(2), pp. 260–65. **[G: U.S.]**

England, George W. Japanese and American Management: Theory Z and Beyond. *J. Int. Bus. Stud.*, Fall 1983, *14*(2), pp. 131–42. **[G: Japan; U.S.]**

Foote, Marion R. Controlling the Cost of International Compensation. **In** *Dickson, D. N., ed.*, 1983, pp. 539–52. **[G: U.S.]**

Gerstein, Marc and Reisman, Heather. Strategic Selection: Matching Executives to Business Conditions. *Sloan Manage. Rev.*, Winter 1983, *24*(2), pp. 33–49.

Hayes, Robert H. and Abernathy, William J. Managing Our Way to Economic Decline. **In** *Dickson, D. N., ed.*, 1983, pp. 203–23. **[G: U.S.; OECD]**

Hayes, Robert H. and Abernathy, William J. Managing Our Way to Economic Decline. **In** *Kantrow, A. M., ed.*, 1983, pp. 15–35. **[G: U.S.]**

Howard, Robert H. Performance Improvement in a WPPR Program. *Rev. Bus. Econ. Res.*, Spring 1983, *18*(3), pp. 48–57. **[G: U.S.]**

Kanungo, Rabindra N. and Wright, Richard W. A Cross-Cultural Comparative Study of Managerial Job Attitudes. *J. Int. Bus. Stud.*, Fall 1983, *14*(2), pp. 115–29. **[G: Canada; France; Japan; U.K.]**

Larcker, David F. The Association between Performance Plan Adoption and Corporate Capital Investment. *J. Acc. Econ.*, April 1983, *5*(1), pp. 3–30. **[G: U.S.]**

Laughhunn, Dan J.; Crum, Roy L. and Payne, John W. Risk Attitudes in the Telecommunications Industry. *Bell J. Econ. (See Rand J. Econ. after 4/85)*, Autumn 1983, *14*(2), pp. 517–21. **[G: U.S.; Canada]**

Maccoby, Michael. The Managerial Work Ethic in America. **In** *Barbash, J., et al., eds.*, 1983, pp. 183–96. **[G: U.S.]**

Meyer, N. Dean. The Office Automation Cookbook: Management Strategies for Getting Office Automation Moving. *Sloan Manage. Rev.*, Winter 1983, *24*(2), pp. 51–60. **[G: U.S.; Canada]**

Minkes, A. L. and Nuttall, C. S. Business Behaviour and Management Structure—1: A Case Study Comparison of Managerial Initiative and Control in Four Industrial Enterprises. *Managerial Dec. Econ.*, March 1983, *4*(1), pp. 1–15. **[G: U.K.]**

Minkes, A. L. and Nuttall, C. S. Business Behaviour

and Management Structure—2: A Case Study Comparison of Managerial Initiative and Control in Four Industrial Enterprises. *Managerial Dec. Econ.*, March 1983, *4*(1), pp. 16–34. **[G: U.K.]**

Naor, Jacob. International Orientation of Exporters: Some North–South Trade Implications. **In** *Czinkota, M. R., ed. (I),* 1983, pp. 241–61. **[G: Canada; S. Korea; U.S.]**

Oi, Walter Y. Heterogeneous Firms and the Organization of Production. *Econ. Inquiry,* April 1983, *21*(2), pp. 147–71.

Perlmutter, Howard V. and Heenan, David A. How Multinational Should Your Top Managers Be? **In** *Dickson, D. N., ed.*, 1983, pp. 69–87.

Rabby, Rami. Employment of the Disabled in Large Corporations. *Int. Lab. Rev.*, January–February 1983, *122*(1), pp. 23–36. **[G: U.S.]**

Ruozi, Roberto. Personnel-Management in Banking. *Bancaria,* April 1983, *39*(4), pp. 377–88. **[G: Italy]**

Sasser, W. Earl, Jr. and Leonard, Frank S. Let First-level Supervisors Do Their Jobs. **In** *Kantrow, A. M., ed.*, 1983, pp. 563–78.

Schürer, Wolfgang. Una-leadership per il futuro. (A Leadership for the Future. With English summary.) *Mondo Aperto,* June-August 1983, *37*(3–4), pp. 165–71.

Tamminen, Rauno. Positiivisesti korreloivien indeksien ongelma eli selittääkö yrittäjän persoonallisuus yrityksen menestyksen. (Asymmetry of Theory, Additive Indexes, and Correlation Coefficient. With English summary.) *Liiketaloudellinen Aikak.*, 1983, *32*(2), pp. 193–205.

Tomita, Teruhiko. Philippine Responses to Japanese Affiliated Enterprises. *Philippine Econ. J.*, 198, *22*(1), pp. 53–81. **[G: Philippine; Japan]**

Toyne, Brian and Kühne, Robert J. The Management of the International Executive Compensation and Benefits Process. *J. Int. Bus. Stud.*, Winter 1983, *14*(3), pp. 37–50. **[G: U.S.]**

Tyson, Shaun. Personnel Management in Its Organizational Context. **In** *Thurley, K. and Wood, S., eds.*, 1983, pp. 146–56. **[G: U.K.]**

White, Richard A. Employee Preferences for Nontaxable Compensation Offered in a Cafeteria Compensation Plan: An Empirical Study. *Accounting Rev.*, July 1983, *58*(3), pp. 539–61. **[G: U.S.]**

Womer, N. Keith and Patterson, J. Wayne. Estimation and Testing of Learning Curves. *J. Bus. Econ. Statist.*, October 1983, *1*(4), pp. 265–72. **[G: U.S.]**

Zoltners, Andris A. A Manpower Sizing and Resource Allocation Model for Commercial Lending. *J. Bank Res.*, Summer 1983, *14*(2), pp. 134–43. **[G: U.S.]**

5132 Public Administration

Baber, William R. Toward Understanding the Role of Auditing in the Public Sector. *J. Acc. Econ.*, December 1983, *5*(3), pp. 213–27. **[G: U.S.]**

Behn, Robert D. The Fundamentals of Cutback Management. **In** *Zeckhauser, R. J. and Leebaert, D., eds.*, 1983, pp. 310–22.

Bird, Richard M. Income Tax Reform in Developing Countries: The Administrative Dimension. *Bull. Int. Fiscal Doc.*, January 1983, *37*(1), pp. 3–14. **[G: LDCs]**

Cubbin, John S. and Hall, Graham. Directors' Remuneration in the Theory of the Firm: Specification and Testing of the Null Hypothesis. *Europ. Econ. Rev.*, January 1983, *20*(1–3), pp. 333–48. **[G: U.K.]**

Edwards, Ward. Evaluation, Thaumaturgy, and Multiattribute Utility Measurement. *J. Policy Anal. Manage.*, Fall 1983, *3*(1), pp. 115–20. **[G: U.S.]**

Hamilton, William L. The Great Housing Experiment: The Administrative Agency Experiment. **In** *Friedman, J. and Weinberg, D. H., eds.*, 1983, pp. 56–69. **[G: U.S.]**

Johnson, Nevil. Management in Government. **In** *Earl, M. J., ed.*, 1983, pp. 170–96. **[G: U.K.]**

Kuespert, Edward F. Limitations on Moving Ahead, While Cutting Back. *Public Budg. Finance,* Summer 1983, *3*(2), pp. 79–82. **[G: U.S.]**

Martin, Patricia Yancey, et al. The Concept of "Integrated" Services Reconsidered. *Soc. Sci. Quart.*, December 1983, *64*(4), pp. 747–63. **[G: U.S.]**

Mushkat, Miron. Deficiencies in Identifying and Assessing Training Needs in the Public Sector. *Rivista Int. Sci. Econ. Com.*, February 1983, *30*(2), pp. 163–75.

Nacht, Michael. Public Management: Does It Exist? How Do You Do It? **In** *[Yamada, I.],* 1983, pp. 41–50.

Quah, Jon S. T. Public Bureaucracy, Social Change and National Development. **In** *Chen, P. S. J., ed.*, 1983, pp. 197–223. **[G: Singapore]**

Schmidt, Richard E. Evaluability Assessment and Cost Analysis. **In** *Alkin, M. C. and Solmon, L. C., eds.*, 1983, pp. 171–88. **[G: U.S.]**

Sexty, Robert W. The Accountability Dilemma in Canadian Public Enterprises: Social versus Commercial Responsiveness. *Ann. Pub. Co-op. Econ.*, March 1983, *54*(1), pp. 19–33. **[G: Canada]**

Stoffaës, Christian. Objectifs économiques et critères de gestion du secteur public industriel. (Economic Objectives and Management Criteria of the Manufacturing Public Sector. With English summary.) *Revue Écon.*, May 1983, *34*(3), pp. 577–611. **[G: France]**

Viscusi, W. Kip. Presidential Oversight: Controlling the Regulators. *J. Policy Anal. Manage.*, Winter 1983, *2*(2), pp. 157–73. **[G: U.S.]**

Young, Robert A. Business and Budgeting: Recent Proposals for Reforming the Revenue Budgetary Process. *Can. Public Policy,* September 1983, *9*(3), pp. 347–61. **[G: Canada]**

514 Goals and Objectives of Firms

5140 Goals and Objectives of Firms

Almeder, Robert. Morality and Gift-giving. **In** *Snoeyenbos, M.; Almeder, R. and Humber, J., eds.*, 1983, pp. 131–34.

Almeder, Robert. Morality in the Marketplace. **In** *Snoeyenbos, M.; Almeder, R. and Humber, J., eds.*, 1983, pp. 84–93.

Amihud, Yakov; Kamin, Jacob Y. and Ronen, Joshua. 'Managerialism,' 'Ownerism,' and Risk. *J. Bank-*

ing Finance, June 1983, *7*(2), pp. 189–96.

Asquith, K. Paul; Bruner, Robert F. and Mullins, David W., Jr. The Gains to Bidding Firms from Merger. *J. Finan. Econ.,* April 1983, *11* (1–4), pp. 121–39. **[G: U.S.]**

Barnea, Amir; Haugen, Robert A. and Senbet, Lemma W. Market Imperfections, Agency Problems, and Capital Structure: A Review. **In** *Archer, S. H. and D'Ambrosia, C. A.,* 1983, *1981,* pp. 594–619.

Bateman, D. I.; Edwards, J. R. and LeVay, Clare. Agricultural Co-operatives and the Theory of the Firm. **In** *Kennedy, L., ed.,* 1983, *1979,* pp. 77–93.

Boswell, Jonathan. The Informal Social Control of Business in Britain: 1880–1939. *Bus. Hist. Rev.,* Summer 1983, *57* (2), pp. 237–57. **[G: U.K.]**

Bradley, Michael and Wakeman, L. Macdonald. The Wealth Effects of Targeted Share Repurchases. *J. Finan. Econ.,* April 1983, *11* (1–4), pp. 301–28. **[G: U.S.]**

Campsey, B. J. and DeMong, R. F. The Influence of Control on Financial Management: Further Evidence. *Rev. Bus. Econ. Res.,* Winter, 1983, *18* (2), pp. 60–70. **[G: U.S.]**

Crew, Michael A. and Kleindorfer, Paul R. Regulatory Influences on Managerial Incentives: Comment. *Southern Econ. J.,* July 1983, *50* (1), pp. 265–66. **[G: U.S.]**

Dann, Larry Y. and DeAngelo, Harry. Standstill Agreements, Privately Negotiated Stock Repurchases, and the Market for Corporate Control. *J. Finan. Econ.,* April 1983, *11* (1–4), pp. 275–300. **[G: U.S.]**

DeAngelo, Harry and Rice, Edward M. Antitakeover Charter Amendments and Stockholder Wealth. *J. Finan. Econ.,* April 1983, *11* (1–4), pp. 329–59. **[G: U.S.]**

Demsetz, Harold. The Structure of Ownership and the Theory of the Firm. *J. Law Econ.,* June 1983, *26* (2), pp. 375–90.

Dodd, Peter and Warner, Jerold B. On Corporate Governance: A Study of Proxy Contests. *J. Finan. Econ.,* April 1983, *11* (1–4), pp. 401–38. **[G: U.S.]**

Easterbrook, Frank H. and Fischel, Daniel R. Voting in Corporate Law. *J. Law Econ.,* June 1983, *26* (2), pp. 395–427. **[G: U.S.]**

Fama, Eugene F. Agency Problems and the Theory of the Firm. **In** *Archer, S. H. and D'Ambrosia, C. A.,* 1983, *1980,* pp. 535–54.

Fama, Eugene F. and Jensen, Michael C. Agency Problems and Residual Claims. *J. Law Econ.,* June 1983, *26* (2), pp. 327–49.

Fama, Eugene F. and Jensen, Michael C. Separation of Ownership and Control. *J. Law Econ.,* June 1983, *26* (2), pp. 301–25.

Fatemi, Ali M.; Ang, James S. and Chua, Jess H. Evidence Supporting Shareholder Wealth Maximization in Management Controlled Firms. *Appl. Econ.,* February 1983, *15* (1), pp. 49–60. **[G: U.S.]**

Frederick, Robert E. Conflict of Interest. **In** *Snoeyenbos, M.; Almeder, R. and Humber, J., eds.,* 1983, pp. 125–30.

Friedman, Milton. The Social Responsibility of Business Is to Increase Its Profits. **In** *Snoeyenbos, M.; Almeder, R. and Humber, J., eds.,* 1983, *1970,* pp. 73–79.

Gill, Roger W. T. and Leinbach, Lisa J. Corporate Social Responsibility in Hong Kong. *Calif. Manage. Rev.,* January 1983, *25* (2), pp. 107–23. **[G: Hong Kong]**

Gladwin, Thomas N. and Walter, Ingo. How Multinationals Can Manage Social Conflict. **In** *Goldberg, W. H., ed.,* 1983, pp. 78–101.

Gluck, Frederick W.; Kaufman, Stephen P. and Walleck, A. Steven. Strategic Management for Competitive Advantage. **In** *Dickson, D. N., ed.,* 1983, pp. 171–84.

Govind, Har. Political Contributions by Companies in India: Legal Limitations and Tax Traps. *Bull. Int. Fiscal Doc.,* January 1983, *37* (1), pp. 21–24. **[G: India]**

Griffith, Robert. The Selling of America: The Advertising Council and American Politics, 1942–1960. *Bus. Hist. Rev.,* Autumn 1983, *57* (3), pp. 388–412. **[G: U.S.]**

Hancock, R. Kelly. The Social Life of the Modern Corporation: Changing Resources and Forms. **In** *Littrell, W. B.; Sjoberg, G. and Zurcher, L. A., eds.,* 1983, pp. 19–36. **[G: U.S.]**

Hay, Donald. Management and Economic Performance. **In** *Earl, M. J., ed.,* 1983, pp. 55–81.

Hayes, Robert H. and Abernathy, William J. Managing Our Way to Economic Decline. **In** *Kantrow, A. M., ed.,* 1983, pp. 15–35. **[G: U.S.]**

Hessen, Robert. The Modern Corporation and Private Property: A Reappraisal. *J. Law Econ.,* June 1983, *26* (2), pp. 273–89.

Hicks, John. Limited Liability: Pros and Cons. **In** *Hicks, J.,* 1983, *1982,* pp. 179–88.

Hirschey, Mark and Pappas, James L. Regulatory Influences on Managerial Incentives: Reply. *Southern Econ. J.,* July 1983, *50* (1), pp. 267–69. **[G: U.S.]**

Jensen, Michael C. and Meckling, William H. Theory of the Firm: Managerial Behavior, Agency Costs and Ownership Structure. **In** *Archer, S. H. and D'Ambrosia, C. A.,* 1983, *1976,* pp. 479–534.

de Kadt, Maarten. Energy Corporation Propaganda: A Weapon against Public Policy. *Rev. Radical Polit. Econ.,* Fall 1983, *15* (3), pp. 35–50. **[G: U.S.]**

Kierans, Eric W. The Community and the Corporation. **In** *Kindleberger, C. P. and Audretsch, D. B., eds.,* 1983, pp. 198–215. **[G: Global]**

Klein, Benjamin. Contracting Costs and Residual Claims: The Separation of Ownership and Control. *J. Law Econ.,* June 1983, *26* (2), pp. 367–74.

Kristol, Irving. On Corporate Capitalism in America. **In** *Kristol, I.,* 1983, *1976,* pp. 202–18. **[G: U.S.]**

Ladd, John. Morality and the Ideal of Rationality in Formal Organizations. **In** *Snoeyenbos, M.; Almeder, R. and Humber, J., eds.,* 1983, *1970,* pp. 47–60.

Laki, Mihály. Growth and Flexibility: The Case of a Transformer-Manufacturing Cooperative. *Eastern Europ. Econ.,* Spring–Summer 1983, *21* (3–4), pp. 170–87. **[G: Hungary]**

Lease, Ronald C.; McConnell, John J. and Mikkelson, Wayne H. The Market Value of Control in Publicly-Traded Corporations. *J. Finan. Econ.,* April 1983, *11* (1–4), pp. 439–71. **[G: U.S.]**

Linn, Scott C. and McConnell, John J. An Empirical Investigation of the Impact of 'Antitakeover' Amendments on Common Stock Prices. *J. Finan. Econ.*, April 1983, *11*(1–4), pp. 361–99. **[G: U.S.]**

Lipset, Seymour Martin and Schneider, William. The Decline of Confidence in American Institutions. *Polit. Sci. Quart.*, Fall 1983, *98*(3), pp. 379–402. **[G: U.S.]**

Long, C. Richard and Snoeyenbos, Milton. Ladd on Morality and Formal Organizations. **In** *Snoeyenbos, M.; Almeder, R. and Humber, J., eds.*, 1983, pp. 61–68.

Luckhardt, C. G. Duties of Agent to Principal. **In** *Snoeyenbos, M.; Almeder, R. and Humber, J., eds.*, 1983, pp. 115–21.

Martin, T. R. Introduction: Some Thoughts on Stewardship. **In** *Martin, T. R., ed.*, 1983, pp. 1–7.

Means, Gardiner C. Hessen's "Reappraisal" [The Modern Corporation and Private Property: A Reappraisal]. *J. Law Econ.*, June 1983, *26*(2), pp. 297–300.

Nash, John F. and Hermanson, Roger H. Ethics and Management Accountants. **In** *Snoeyenbos, M.; Almeder, R. and Humber, J., eds.*, 1983, pp. 366–71.

North, Douglass C. Comment on Stigler and Friedland, "The Literature of Economics: The Case of Berle and Means." *J. Law Econ.*, June 1983, *26*(2), pp. 269–71. **[G: U.S.]**

Pastin, Mark and Hooker, Michael. Ethics and the Foreign Corrupt Practices Act. **In** *Snoeyenbos, M.; Almeder, R. and Humber, J., eds.*, 1983, *1980*, pp. 150–55. **[G: U.S.]**

Raab, Raymond L. Market Structure and Corporate Power Investment: An Empirical Investigation of Campaign Contributions of the 1972 Federal Elections. *Nebr. J. Econ. Bus.*, Winter, 1983, *22*(1), pp. 59–65. **[G: U.S.]**

Ricardo-Campbell, Rita. Comments on the Structure of Ownership and the Theory of the Firm. *J. Law Econ.*, June 1983, *26*(2), pp. 391–93.

Rosenberg, Nathan. Comments on Robert Hessen, "The Modern Corporation and Private Property: A Reappraisal." *J. Law Econ.*, June 1983, *26*(2), pp. 291–96.

Seoka, Yoshihiko. Steady State Growth of the Long-Run Sales-Maximizing Firm: Comment. *Quart. J. Econ.*, November 1983, *98*(4), pp. 713–19.

Sexty, Robert W. The Accountability Dilemma in Canadian Public Enterprises: Social versus Commercial Responsiveness. *Ann. Pub. Co-op. Econ.*, March 1983, *54*(1), pp. 19–33. **[G: Canada]**

Shane, Philip B. and Spicer, Barry H. Market Response to Environmental Information Produced Outside the Firm. *Accounting Rev.*, July 1983, *58*(3), pp. 521–38. **[G: U.S.]**

Shapiro, Nina. An Economic Theory of Business Strategy: A Review Article. *J. Post Keynesian Econ.*, Spring 1983, *5*(3), pp. 483–88.

Shieh, Yeung-nan and Mai, Chao-cheng. A Firm's Bid Price Curve and the Neoclassical Theory of Production: A Correction and Further Analysis. *Southern Econ. J.*, July 1983, *50*(1), pp. 230–33.

Smirlock, Michael L. and Marshall, William J. Monopoly Power and Expense-Preference Behavior: Theory and Evidence to the Contrary. *Bell J. Econ. (See Rand J. Econ. after 4/85)*, Spring 1983, *14*(1), pp. 166–78. **[G: U.S.]**

Snoeyenbos, Milton; Almeder, Robert and Humber, James. Business Ethics: Introduction. **In** *Snoeyenbos, M.; Almeder, R. and Humber, J., eds.*, 1983, pp. 13–39.

Snoeyenbos, Milton and Dillon, Ray D. Independence and the AICPA Code of Professional Ethics. **In** *Snoeyenbos, M.; Almeder, R. and Humber, J., eds.*, 1983, pp. 356–65.

Snoeyenbos, Milton and Jewell, Donald. Morals and Management. **In** *Snoeyenbos, M.; Almeder, R. and Humber, J., eds.*, 1983, pp. 97–108. **[G: U.S.]**

Stewart, Frances. Macro–Policies for Appropriate Technology: An Introductory Classification. *Int. Lab. Rev.*, May–June 1983, *122*(3), pp. 279–93. **[G: LDCs]**

Stigler, George J. and Friedland, Claire. The Literature of Economics: The Case of Berle and Means. *J. Law Econ.*, June 1983, *26*(2), pp. 237–68. **[G: U.S.]**

Stoffaës, Christian. Objectifs économiques et critères de gestion du secteur public industriel. (Economic Objectives and Management Criteria of the Manufacturing Public Sector. With English summary.) *Revue Écon.*, May 1983, *34*(3), pp. 577–611. **[G: France]**

Tavis, Lee A. Stewardship across National Borders (I). **In** *Martin, T. R., ed.*, 1983, pp. 74–88. **[G: Selected Countries]**

Tricker, R. I. Perspectives on Corporate Governance: Intellectual Influences in the Exercise of Corporate Governance. **In** *Earl, M. J., ed.*, 1983, pp. 143–69.

Tunstall, W. Brooke. Cultural Transition at AT&T. *Sloan Manage. Rev.*, Fall 1983, *25*(1), pp. 15–26. **[G: U.S.]**

Zif, Jehiel. Explanatory Concepts of Managerial Strategic Behavior in State-Owned Enterprises: A Multinational Study. *J. Int. Bus. Stud.*, Spring/Summer 1983, *14*(1), pp. 35–46. **[G: Selected LDCs]**

520 Business Finance and Investment

5200 Business Finance and Investment

Asimakopulos, A. Kalecki and Keynes on Finance, Investment and Saving. *Cambridge J. Econ.*, September/December 1983, *7*(3/4), pp. 221–33.

Bey, Roger P. Capital Budgeting Decisions When Cash Flows and Project Lives Are Stochastic and Dependent. *J. Finan. Res.*, Fall 1983, *6*(3), pp. 175–85.

Cacciafesta, Fabrizio. Un criterio matematico-finanziario per la valutazione di convenienza tra acquisto con mezzi propri, "leasing" e indebitamento. (A Mathematical Criterion for Estimation of the Relative Economic Advantages of Direct-Purchasing, Leasing and Borrowing. With English summary.) *Bancaria,* November 1983, *39*(11), pp. 1109–119.

Chan, Yuk-Shee. On the Positive Role of Financial Intermediation in Allocation of Venture Capital in a Market with Imperfect Information. *J. Finance,* December 1983, *38*(5), pp. 1543–68.

Cooper, Ian and Franks, Julian R. The Interaction of Financing and Investment Decisions When the Firm Has Unused Tax Credits. *J. Finance,* May 1983, *38*(2), pp. 571–83.

Ezzell, John R. and Miles, James A. Capital Project Analysis and the Debt Transaction Plan. *J. Finan. Res.,* Spring 1983, *6*(1), pp. 25–31.

Fabozzi, Frank J. and Yaari, Uzi. Valuation of Safe Harbor Tax Benefit Transfer Leases. *J. Finance,* May 1983, *38*(2), pp. 595–606. **[G: U.S.]**

Fama, Eugene F. The Effects of a Firm's Investment and Financing Decisions on the Welfare of Its Security Holders. **In** *Archer, S. H. and D'Ambrosia, C. A.,* 1983, *1978,* pp. 576–93.

Feldstein, Martin S. and Frisch, Daniel J. Corporate Tax Integration: The Estimated Effects on Capital Accumulation and Tax Distribution of Two Integration Proposals. **In** *Feldstein, M. (I),* 1983, *1977,* pp. 156–79. **[G: U.S.]**

Hamada, Robert S. Portfolio Analysis, Market Equilibrium and Corporation Finance. **In** *Archer, S. H. and D'Ambrosia, C. A.,* 1983, *1969,* pp. 441–61.

Hansen, Derek. Banking and Small Business. **In** *Barker, M., ed. (I),* 1983, pp. 359–473.

Harris, Robert S. and Pringle, John J. Implications of Miller's Argument for Capital Budgeting. *J. Finan. Res.,* Spring 1983, *6*(1), pp. 13–23.

Hochman, Shalom J. and Palmon, Oded. The Irrelevance of Capital Structure for the Impact of Inflation on Investment. *J. Finance,* June 1983, *38*(3), pp. 785–94.

Lee, Cheng Few and Junkus, Joan C. Financial Analysis and Planning: An Overview. *J. Econ. Bus.,* August 1983, *35*(3/4), pp. 259–83.

Miles, James A. Taxes and the Fisher Effect: A Clarifying Analysis. *J. Finance,* March 1983, *38*(1), pp. 67–77.

Modigliani, Franco. Debt, Dividend Policy, Taxes, Inflation, and Market Valuation: Erratum. *J. Finance,* June 1983, *38*(3), pp. 1041–42.

Peterson, Pamela P. and Benesh, Gary A. A Reexamination of the Empirical Relationship between Investment and Financing Decisions. *J. Finan. Quant. Anal.,* December 1983, *18*(4), pp. 439–53. **[G: U.S.]**

521 Business Finance

5210 Business Finance

Abel, Andrew B. Financing Private Business in an Inflationary Context: The Experience of Argentina between 1967 and 1980: Comment. **In** *Armella, P. A.; Dornbusch, R. and Obstfeld, M., eds.,* 1983, pp. 183–85. **[G: Argentina]**

Adler, Michael and Dumas, Bernard. International Portfolio Choice and Corporation Finance: A Synthesis. *J. Finance,* June 1983, *38*(3), pp. 925–84.

Aivazian, Varouj A. and Callen, Jeffrey L. Reorganization in Bankruptcy and the Issue of Strategic Risk. *J. Banking Finance,* March 1983, *7*(1), pp. 119–33.

Akkina, Krishna R. The Effects of Carrying Cost Uncertainty and Expected Price Changes on Inventories in the United States during 1959–1979. *Nebr. J. Econ. Bus.,* Spring 1983, *22*(2), pp. 49–64.

Alam, Kazi Firoz. The Dividend Behavior of Companies in the U.K. Manufacturing Industry. *METU,* 1983, *10*(2), pp. 155–77. **[G: U.K.]**

Alberts, William W. and Hite, Gailen L. The Modigliani–Miller Leverage Equation Considered in a Product Market Context. *J. Finan. Quant. Anal.,* December 1983, *18*(4), pp. 425–37.

Allen, Franklin. Credit Rationing and Payment Incentives. *Rev. Econ. Stud.,* October 1983, *50*(4), pp. 639–46.

Altman, Edward I. Multidimensional Graphics and Bankruptcy Prediction: A Comment [Communicating Financial Information through Multidimensional Graphics]. *J. Acc. Res.,* Spring 1983, *21*(1), pp. 297–99.

Anderson, Gordon J. The Internal Financing Decisions of the Industrial and Commercial Sector: A Reappraisal of the Lintner Model of Dividend Disbursements. *Economica,* August 1983, *50*(199), pp. 235–48. **[G: U.K.]**

Asquith, K. Paul; Bruner, Robert F. and Mullins, David W., Jr. The Gains to Bidding Firms from Merger. *J. Finan. Econ.,* April 1983, *11*(1–4), pp. 121–39. **[G: U.S.]**

Asquith, K. Paul and Mullins, David W., Jr. The Impact of Initiating Dividend Payments on Shareholders' Wealth. *J. Bus.,* January 1983, *56*(1), pp. 77–96.

Auerbach, Alan J. Inflation and the Choice of Asset Life. **In** *Auerbach, A. J.,* 1983, *1979,* pp. 100–117.

Auerbach, Alan J. Inflation and the Tax Treatment of Firm Behavior. **In** *Auerbach, A. J.,* 1983, *1981,* pp. 95–99.

Auerbach, Alan J. Share Valuation and Corporate Equity Policy. **In** *Auerbach, A. J.,* 1983, *1979,* pp. 63–77.

Auerbach, Alan J. Wealth Maximization and the Cost of Capital. **In** *Auerbach, A. J.,* 1983, *1979,* pp. 78–91.

Baldwin, Carliss Y. and Mason, Scott P. The Resolution of Claims in Financial Distress: The Case of Massey Ferguson. *J. Finance,* May 1983, *38*(2), pp. 505–16. **[G: U.S.]**

Barnea, Amir; Haugen, Robert A. and Senbet, Lemma W. Market Imperfections, Agency Problems, and Capital Structure: A Review. **In** *Archer, S. H. and D'Ambrosia, C. A.,* 1983, *1981,* pp. 594–619.

Baron, David P. Tender Offers and Management Resistance. *J. Finance,* May 1983, *38*(2), pp. 331–43.

Beidleman, Carl R.; Hilley, John L. and Greenleaf, James A. Alternatives in Hedging Long-Date Contractual Foreign Exchange Exposure. *Sloan Manage. Rev.,* Summer 1983, *24*(4), pp. 45–54. **[G: U.S.]**

Benninga, Simon. Nonlinear Pricing Systems in Finance. **In** *Levy, H., ed.,* 1983, pp. 21–42.

Bergson, Abram. Entrepreneurship under Labor Participation: The Yugoslav Case. **In** *Ronen, J., ed.,* 1983, pp. 177–233. **[G: Yugoslavia]**

Bhagat, Sanjai. The Effect of Pre-Emptive Right

Amendments on Shareholder Wealth. *J. Finan. Econ.*, November 1983, *12*(3), pp. 289–310. **[G: U.S.]**

Bilson, John F. O. The Evaluation and Use of Foreign Exchange Rate Forecasting Services. **In** *Herring, R. J., ed.*, 1983, pp. 149–79. **[G: OECD]**

Boadway, Robin W.; Bruce, Neil and Mintz, Jack M. On the Neutrality of Flow-of-Funds Corporate Taxation. *Economica*, February 1983, *50*(197), pp. 49–61.

Braswell, Ronald C.; Sumners, Dewitt L. and Reinhart, Walter J. The Effect of the Tax Act of 1982 on the Appropriate Coupon Rate Strategy for Issuing Corporate Bonds. *Nat. Tax J.*, June 1983, *36*(2), pp. 255–56. **[G: U.S.]**

Brealey, Richard A.; Hodges, Stewart D. and Selby, Michael J. P. The Risk of Bank-Loan Portfolios. **In** *Brenner, M., ed.*, 1983, pp. 153–82. **[G: U.S.]**

Brick, Ivan E., et al. Mohl, Murray. Optimal Capital Structure: A Multi-period Programming Model for Use in Financial Planning. *J. Banking Finance*, March 1983, *7*(1), pp. 45–67.

Brickley, James A. Shareholder Wealth, Information Signaling and the Specially Designated Dividend: An Empirical Study. *J. Finan. Econ.*, August 1983, *12*(2), pp. 187–209. **[G: U.S.]**

Brief, Richard P. Yield Approximations: A Historical Perspective: A Correction. *J. Finance*, June 1983, *38*(3), pp. 1039.

Bruch, Mathias. Sources of Financing of Small-Scale Manufacturers: A Micro-Analysis for Malaysia. *Singapore Econ. Rev.*, April 1983, *28*(1), pp. 21–33. **[G: Malaysia]**

Bulow, Jeremy I. and Scholes, Myron S. Who Owns the Assets in a Defined-Benefit Pension Plan? **In** *Bodie, Z. and Shoven, J. B., eds.*, 1983, pp. 17–32, 34–36. **[G: U.S.]**

Butler, Donald T. Why Doesn't Business Float Indexed Bonds? *Bus. Econ.*, January 1983, *18*(1), pp. 57–58. **[G: U.S.]**

Campsey, B. J. and DeMong, R. F. The Influence of Control on Financial Management: Further Evidence. *Rev. Bus. Econ. Res.*, Winter, 1983, *18*(2), pp. 60–70. **[G: U.S.]**

Carleton, Willard T., et al. An Empirical Analysis of the Role of the Medium of Exchange in Mergers. *J. Finance*, June 1983, *38*(3), pp. 813–26. **[G: U.S.]**

Carter, Donald D. Termination and Severance Pay in Ontario: Are the Protections Adequate in the Event of Employer Insolvency? **In** *Queen's Univ. Indust. Relat. Centre*, 1983, pp. 24–31. **[G: Canada]**

Casey, Cornelius J. Prior Probability Disclosure and Loan Officers' Judgments: Some Evidence of the Impact. *J. Acc. Res.*, Spring 1983, *21*(1), pp. 300–307.

Castanias, Richard P. Bankruptcy Risk and Optimal Capital Structure. *J. Finance*, December 1983, *38*(5), pp. 1617–35. **[G: U.S.]**

Cavallo, Domingo F. and Petrei, A. Humberto. Financing Private Business in an Inflationary Context: The Experience of Argentina between 1967 and 1980. **In** *Armella, P. A.; Dornbusch, R. and Obstfeld, M., eds.*, 1983, pp. 153–80. **[G: Argentina]**

Cho, Dongsae. Integrated Risk Management Decision-Making: A Workers' Compensation Loss Exposure Case Study. *J. Risk Ins.*, June 1983, *50*(2), pp. 281–300.

Chow, Chee W. The Impacts of Accounting Regulation on Bondholder and Shareholder Wealth: The Case of the Securities Acts. *Accounting Rev.*, July 1983, *58*(3), pp. 485–520. **[G: U.S.]**

Corcoran, Patrick J. The Cost of Capital: An Update. *Fed. Res. Bank New York Quart. Rev.*, Autumn 1983, *8*(3), pp. 23–24. **[G: U.S.]**

Cordes, Joseph J. and Sheffrin, Steven M. Estimating the Tax Advantage of Corporate Debt. *J. Finance*, March 1983, *38*(1), pp. 95–105. **[G: U.S.]**

Cornell, Bradford and French, Kenneth R. The Pricing of Stock Index Futures. *J. Futures Markets*, Spring 1983, *3*(1), pp. 1–14. **[G: U.S.]**

Cross, Michael. The Small Firm: The United Kingdom. **In** *Storey, D. J., ed.*, 1983, pp. 84–119. **[G: U.K.]**

Crum, Roy L.; Klingman, Darwin D. and Tavis, Lee A. An Operational Approach to Integrated Working Capital Planning. *J. Econ. Bus.*, August 1983, *35*(3/4), pp. 343–78.

Cubbin, John S. and Leech, Dennis. The Effect of Shareholding Dispersion on the Degree of Control in British Companies: Theory and Measurement. *Econ. J.*, June 1983, *93*(370), pp. 351–69. **[G: U.K.]**

Cucinotta, Giovanni. Bank Corporate Lending in Italy, Germany, United Kingdom during the Decade 1968–1978: A Comparative Study. *Econ. Notes*, 1983, (1), pp. 153–72. **[G: Italy; Germany; U.K.]**

Daley, Lane A. and Vigeland, Robert L. The Effects of Debt Covenants and Political Costs on the Choice of Accounting Methods: The Case of Accounting for R&D Costs. *J. Acc. Econ.*, December 1983, *5*(3), pp. 195–211. **[G: U.S.]**

Davis, E. G. and Mokkelbost, P. B. The Recapitalization of Crown Corporations. *Can. Public Policy*, June 1983, *9*(2), pp. 181–88. **[G: Canada]**

De Luca, Amedeo. Una metodologia di calcolo dei rapporti di partecipazione indiretta nei raggruppamenti societari. (A Methodology for Calculation of the Weight of Indirect Holdings in Corporate Groups. With English summary.) *Bancaria*, January 1983, *39*(1), pp. 53–59.

De Marchi, Gianluigi. La polizza di credito commerciale, versione italiana del commercial paper. (Commercial Credit Policies, the Italian Version of Commercial Paper. With English summary.) *L'Impresa*, 1983, *25*(2), pp. 65–68. **[G: Italy]**

Defourny, Jacques. L'autofinancement des coopératives de travailleurs et la théorie économique. (Self-Financing in Workers' Cooperatives and Economic Theory. With English summary.) *Ann. Pub. Co-op. Econ.*, April–June 1983, *54*(2), pp. 201–24.

Dharan, Bala G. Empirical Identification Procedures for Earnings Models. *J. Acc. Res.*, Spring 1983, *21*(1), pp. 256–70. **[G: U.S.]**

Dharan, Bala G. Identification and Estimation Issues for a Causal Earnings Model. *J. Acc. Res.*, Spring 1983, *21*(1), pp. 18–41.

Divecha, Arjun and Morse, Dale. Market Responses

to Dividend Increases and Changes in Payout Ratios. *J. Finan. Quant. Anal.*, June 1983, *18*(2), pp. 163–73. **[G: U.S.]**

Dufey, Gunter. International Financial Management: The Overall Investment and Financing Plan. **In** *George, A. M. and Giddy, I. H., eds., Vol. 2,* 1983, pp. 8.12:1–17.

Duhaime, Irene M. and Thomas, Howard. Financial Analysis and Strategic Management. *J. Econ. Bus.*, August 1983, *35*(3/4), pp. 413–40.

Dullum, Kåre B. and Stonehill, Arthur. Towards an International Cost of Capital. *Nationaløkon. Tidsskr.*, 1983, *121*(1), pp. 43–60. **[G: Denmark]**

Durand, David. The Cost of Capital, Corporation Finance, and the Theory of Investment: Comment. **In** *Archer, S. H. and D'Ambrosia, C. A.*, 1983, *1959,* pp. 386–402.

Dyl, Edward A. and Spahr, Ronald W. Taxes and the Refunding of Discount Bonds. *J. Finan. Res.*, Winter 1983, *6*(4), pp. 265–73. **[G: U.S.]**

Dyment, John J. International Cash Management. **In** *Dickson, D. N., ed.*, 1983, pp. 553–65.

Ebrill, Liam P. and Hartman, David G. The Corporate Income Tax, Entrepreneurship, and the Noncorporate Sector. *Public Finance Quart.*, October 1983, *11*(4), pp. 419–36.

Eger, Carol Ellen. An Empirical Test of the Redistribution Effect in Pure Exchange Mergers. *J. Finan. Quant. Anal.*, December 1983, *18*(4), pp. 547–72. **[G: U.S.]**

Eidman, Vernon R. Cash Flow, Price Risk, and Production Uncertainty Considerations. **In** *Baum, K. H. and Schertz, L. P., eds.*, 1983, pp. 159–80.

Emanuel, David C. Warrant Valuation and Exercise Strategy. *J. Finan. Econ.*, August 1983, *12*(2), pp. 211–35.

Evans, David S. and Rothschild, Michael. The Impact of Divestiture on the Cost of Capital to the Bell System. **In** *Evans, D. S., ed.*, 1983, pp. 157–89. **[G: U.S.]**

Fama, Eugene F. and Jensen, Michael C. Agency Problems and Residual Claims. *J. Law Econ.*, June 1983, *26*(2), pp. 327–49.

Farber, André. A qui profitent les mesures d'encouragement du capital à risque? (With English summary.) *Cah. Écon. Bruxelles,* 1983, *97*(1), pp. 3–13. **[G: Belgium]**

Feldstein, Martin S. Corporate Taxation and Dividend Behavior. **In** *Feldstein, M. (I),* 1983, *1970,* pp. 90–113.

Feldstein, Martin S. Corporate Taxation and Dividend Behavior: A Reply and Extension. **In** *Feldstein, M. (I),* 1983, *1972,* pp. 114–22.

Feldstein, Martin S. and Fane, George. Taxes, Corporate Dividend Policy, and Personal Savings: The British Postwar Experience. **In** *Feldstein, M. (I),* 1983, *1973,* pp. 135–55. **[G: U.K.]**

Feldstein, Martin S. and Green, Jerry R. Why Do Companies Pay Dividends? **In** *Feldstein, M. (I),* 1983, *1983,* pp. 68–69.

Feldstein, Martin S. and Green, Jerry R. Why Do Companies Pay Dividends? *Amer. Econ. Rev.*, March 1983, *73*(1), pp. 17–30.

Feldstein, Martin S.; Green, Jerry R. and Sheshinski, Eytan. Corporate Financial Policy and Taxation in a Growing Economy. **In** *Feldstein, M. (I),* 1983, *1979,* pp. 427–47. **[G: U.S.]**

Feldstein, Martin S.; Green, Jerry R. and Sheshinski, Eytan. Inflation and Taxes in a Growing Economy with Debt and Equity Finance. **In** *Feldstein, M. (II),* 1983, *1978,* pp. 44–60. **[G: U.S.]**

Feldstein, Martin S. and Mørck, Randall. Pension Funding Decisions, Interest Rate Assumptions, and Share Prices. **In** *Bodie, Z. and Shoven, J. B., eds.*, 1983, pp. 177–207, 209–10. **[G: U.S.]**

Feldstein, Martin S. and Summers, Lawrence. Inflation and the Taxation of Capital Income in the Corporate Sector. **In** *Feldstein, M. (II),* 1983, *1979,* pp. 116–50. **[G: U.S.]**

Floyd, Robert H. Government Relationships with Public Enterprise in Papua New Guinea. **In** *[Ramanadham, V. V.],* 1983, pp. 220–48. **[G: Papua New Guinea]**

Francis, Jack Clark. Financial Planning and Forecasting Models: An Overview. *J. Econ. Bus.*, August 1983, *35*(3/4), pp. 285–300.

Francis, Jack Clark; Hastings, Harold M. and Fabozzi, Frank J. Bankruptcy as a Mathematical Catastrophe. **In** *Levy, H., ed.*, 1983, pp. 63–89.

Frecka, Thomas J. and Hopwood, William S. The Effects of Outliers on the Cross-sectional Distributional Properties of Financial Ratios. *Accounting Rev.*, January 1983, *58*(1), pp. 115–28. **[G: U.S.]**

Frecka, Thomas J. and Lee, Cheng Few. A Seemingly Unrelated Regressions Approach to Analyzing and Forecasting Financial Ratios. *J. Econ. Bus.*, August 1983, *35*(3/4), pp. 379–88. **[G: U.S.]**

Frecka, Thomas J. and Lee, Cheng Few. Generalized Financial Ratio Adjustment Processes and Their Implications. *J. Acc. Res.*, Spring 1983, *21*(1), pp. 308–16.

Friedman, Benjamin M. Pension Funding, Pension Asset Allocation, and Corporate Finance: Evidence from Individual Company Data. **In** *Bodie, Z. and Shoven, J. B., eds.*, 1983, pp. 107–47, 152. **[G: U.S.]**

Fullerton, Don and Gordon, Roger H. A Reexamination of Tax Distortions in General Equilibrium Models. **In** *Feldstein, M., ed.*, 1983, pp. 369–420. **[G: U.S.]**

Galper, Harvey and Toder, Eric. Owning or Leasing: Bennington College, and the U.S. Tax System. *Nat. Tax J.*, June 1983, *36*(2), pp. 257–61. **[G: U.S.]**

Gentry, James. Global Rationalization and MNCs' Trade Credit Policies: Policy Issues. **In** *Goldberg, W. H., ed.*, 1983, pp. 107–27. **[G: U.S.]**

George, Abraham M. Currency Exposure Management. **In** *George, A. M. and Giddy, I. H., eds., Vol. 2,* 1983, pp. 8.8:1–33.

Giroux, Gary; Shearon, Winston and Grossman, Steven. How Does Inflation Affect a BHC's Rate of Return? *J. Bank Res.*, Summer 1983, *14*(2), pp. 164–69. **[G: U.S.]**

Gnes, Paolo. The Financial Structure and Financing of Firms: Developments and Prospects. *Rev. Econ. Cond. Italy,* June 1983, (2), pp. 301–23. **[G: Italy]**

Gombola, Michael J. and Ketz, J. Edward. A Note on Cash Flow and Classification Patterns of Financial Ratios. *Accounting Rev.*, January 1983, *58*(1), pp. 105–14.

Gordon, Myron J. Optimal Investment and Financing Policy. **In** *Archer, S. H. and D'Ambrosia, C. A.*, 1983, *1963*, pp. 622–29.

Gordon, Myron J. The Impact of Real Factors and Inflation on the Performance of the U.S. Stock Market from 1960 to 1980. *J. Finance,* May 1983, *38*(2), pp. 553–63. **[G: U.S.]**

Granados, Luis L. The Effect of Employee Stock Ownership Plans on Corporate Profits—Additional Comment. *J. Risk Ins.*, September 1983, *50*(3), pp. 495–97. **[G: U.S.]**

Green, Jerry R. Who Owns the Assets in a Defined-Benefit Pension Plan? Comment. **In** *Bodie, Z. and Shoven, J. B., eds.*, 1983, pp. 32–34. **[G: U.S.]**

Green, Jerry R. and Shoven, John B. The Effects of Financing Opportunities and Bankruptcy on Entrepreneurial Risk Bearing. **In** *Ronen, J., ed.*, 1983, pp. 49–74.

Greenberg, Edward; Marshall, William J. and Yawitz, Jess B. Firm Behavior under Conditions of Uncertainty and the Theory of Finance. *Quart. Rev. Econ. Bus.*, Summer 1983, *23*(2), pp. 6–22.

Greene, Benjamin B., Jr. A Note on Relevant Comparisons of Corporations and Countries. *Amer. J. Econ. Soc.*, January 1983, *42*(1), pp. 39–43.

Grier, Paul and Strebel, Paul J. An Implicit Clientele Test of the Relationship between Taxation and Capital Structure. *J. Finan. Res.*, Summer 1983, *6*(2), pp. 163–74. **[G: U.S.]**

Gui, Benedetto. Struttura finanziaria e "Moral Risk" in imprese non quotate nel mercato azionario. (Financial Structure and Moral Risk When Firms' Shares Are Not Traded. With English summary.) *Rivista Int. Sci. Econ. Com.*, February 1983, *30*(2), pp. 125–42.

Hall, William K. Survival Strategies in a Hostile Environment. **In** *Kantrow, A. M., ed.*, 1983, pp. 52–71. **[G: U.S.]**

Halpern, Paul. Corporate Acquisitions: A Theory of Special Cases? A Review of Event Studies Applied to Acquisitions. *J. Finance,* May 1983, *38*(2), pp. 297–317.

Hamada, Robert S. Portfolio Analysis, Market Equilibrium and Corporation Finance. **In** *Archer, S. H. and D'Ambrosia, C. A.*, 1983, *1969*, pp. 441–61.

Hannan, Timothy H. Bank Profitability and the Threat of Entry. *J. Bank Res.*, Summer 1983, *14*(2), pp. 157–63. **[G: U.S.]**

Harris, John M., Jr.; Roenfeldt, Rodney L. and Cooley, Philip L. Evidence of Financial Leverage Clienteles. *J. Finance,* September 1983, *38*(4), pp. 1125–32. **[G: U.S.]**

Harrison, J. Michael and Sharpe, William F. Optimal Funding and Asset Allocation Rules for Defined-Benefit Pension Plans. **In** *Bodie, Z. and Shoven, J. B., eds.*, 1983, pp. 91–103, 105. **[G: U.S.]**

Helmers, Glenn A. Risk Management in Models of the Farm: Modeling Farm Decisionmaking to Account for Risk: Discussion. **In** *Baum, K. H. and Schertz, L. P., eds.*, 1983, pp. 195–99.

Hirschman, Charles. Foreign Investment in Malaysia, Once Again. **In** *Lim, D., ed.*, 1983, pp. 235–37. **[G: Malaysia]**

Hirschman, Charles. Foreign Investment, Employment Generation and the Profit–Wage Ratio in the Manufacturing Sector of West Malaysia: Comment. **In** *Lim, D., ed.*, 1983, *1978*, pp. 228–29. **[G: Malaysia]**

Hite, Gailen L. and Owers, James E. Security Price Reactions around Corporate Spin-Off Announcements. *J. Finan. Econ.*, December 1983, *12*(4), pp. 409–36. **[G: U.S.]**

Holthausen, Robert W. and Leftwich, Richard W. The Economic Consequences of Accounting Choice: Implications of Costly Contracting and Monitoring. *J. Acc. Econ.*, August 1983, *5*(2), pp. 77–117.

Hsia, Chi-Cheng. On Binomial Option Pricing. *J. Finan. Res.*, Spring 1983, *6*(1), pp. 41–46.

Huffman, Lucy T. Operating Leverage, Financial Leverage, and Equity Risk. *J. Banking Finance,* June 1983, *7*(2), pp. 197–212.

Hunter, John E. and Coggin, T. Daniel. Measuring Stability and Growth in Annual EPS. *J. Portfol. Manage.*, Winter 1983, *9*(2), pp. 75–78. **[G: U.S.]**

Ijiri, Yuji. Foreign Currency Accounting and Its Transition. **In** *Herring, R. J., ed.*, 1983, pp. 181–212. **[G: U.S.]**

James, Christopher M. Pricing Alternatives for Loan Commitments: A Note. *J. Bank Res.*, Winter 1983, *13*(4), pp. 300–303. **[G: U.S.]**

Jensen, Michael C. and Meckling, William H. Theory of the Firm: Managerial Behavior, Agency Costs and Ownership Structure. **In** *Archer, S. H. and D'Ambrosia, C. A.*, 1983, *1976*, pp. 479–534.

Johnson, W. Bruce. "Representativeness" in Judgmental Predictions of Corporate Bankruptcy. *Accounting Rev.*, January 1983, *58*(1), pp. 78–97. **[G: U.S.]**

Jones, J. C. H. and Laudadio, L. Risk, Profitability, and Market Structure: Some Canadian Evidence on Structural and Behavioral Approaches to Antitrust. *Antitrust Bull.*, Summer 1983, *28*(2), pp. 349–79. **[G: Canada]**

Karna, Adi S. and Graddy, Duane B. Bank Holding Company Leverage, Risk Perception, and Cost of Capital. *Rev. Bus. Econ. Res.*, Fall 1983, *19*(1), pp. 99–109. **[G: U.S.]**

Koshal, Manjulika and Koshal, Rajindar K. Cash Management Economies in the Production of Food. *Managerial Dec. Econ.*, December 1983, *4*(4), pp. 253–57. **[G: U.S.]**

Laitinen, Erkki K. A Multivariate Model of the Financial Relationships in the Firm. *Liiketaloudellinen Aikak.*, 1983, *32*(4), pp. 317–33. **[G: Finland]**

Larcker, David F.; Reder, Renee E. and Simon, Daniel T. Trades by Insiders and Mandated Accounting Standards. *Accounting Rev.*, July 1983, *58*(3), pp. 606–20. **[G: U.S.]**

Lawrence, Edward C. Reporting Delays for Failed Firms [Financial Ratios and the Probabilistic Prediction of Bankruptcy]. *J. Acc. Res.*, Autumn 1983, *21*(2), pp. 606–10. **[G: U.S.]**

Ledford, Manfred H. and Sugrue, Paul K. Ratio Analysis: Application to U.S. Motor Common Carriers. *Bus. Econ.*, September 1983, *18*(4), pp. 46–54. **[G: U.S.]**

Lee, Cheng Few and Junkus, Joan C. Financial Analysis and Planning: An Overview. *J. Econ. Bus.*, August 1983, *35*(3/4), pp. 259–83.

Lee, Wayne L.; Thakor, Anjan V. and Vora, Gautam. Screening, Market Signalling, and Capital Structure Theory. *J. Finance,* December 1983, *38*(5), pp. 1507–18.

Leftwich, Richard W. Accounting Information in Private Markets: Evidence from Private Lending Agreements. *Accounting Rev.*, January 1983, *58*(1), pp. 23–42. **[G: U.S.]**

Leray, Catherine. L'appréhension de l'efficacité dans les entreprises publiques industrielles et commerciales. (An Efficiency Assessment of Industrial and Commercial Enterprise both Public and Private. With English summary.) *Revue Écon.*, May 1983, *34*(3), pp. 612–54. **[G: France]**

Levy, Haim. Economic Evaluation of Voting Power of Common Stock. *J. Finance,* March 1983, *38*(1), pp. 79–93. **[G: U.S.]**

Lewis, W. Arthur. Depreciation and Obsolescence as Factors in Costing. **In** *Lewis, W. A.*, 1983, *1952*, pp. 149–72.

Light, Jay O. Pension Funding, Pension Asset Allocation, and Corporate Finance: Evidence from Individual Company Data: Comment. **In** *Bodie, Z. and Shoven, J. B., eds.*, 1983, pp. 147–51. **[G: U.S.]**

Linke, Charles M. and Whitford, David T. A Multiobjective Financial Planning Model for Electric Utility Rate Regulation. *J. Econ. Bus.*, August 1983, *35*(3/4), pp. 313–30. **[G: U.S.]**

Litzenberger, Robert H. and Ramaswamy, Krishna. The Effect of Personal Taxes and Dividends on Capital Asset Prices: Theory and Empirical Evidence. **In** *Archer, S. H. and D'Ambrosia, C. A.*, 1983, *1979*, pp. 690–722. **[G: U.S.]**

Livingston, D. T. and Henry, James B. The Effect of Employee Stock Ownership Plans on Corporate Profits—Reply. *J. Risk Ins.*, September 1983, *50*(3), pp. 498–99. **[G: U.S.]**

Lorie, James H. and Savage, Leonard J. Three Problems in Rationing Capital. **In** *Archer, S. H. and D'Ambrosia, C. A.*, 1983, *1955*, pp. 308–21.

Maher, Michael W. and Nantell, Timothy J. The Tax Effects of Inflation: Depreciation, Debt, and Miller's Equilibrium Tax Rates. *J. Acc. Res.*, Spring 1983, *21*(1), pp. 329–40.

Maier, Steven F. and Vander Weide, James H. What Lockbox and Disbursement Models Really Do. *J. Finance,* May 1983, *38*(2), pp. 361–71.

Main, Brian G. M. Why Large Corporations Purchase Property/Liability Insurance. *Calif. Manage. Rev.*, January 1983, *25*(2), pp. 84–95. **[G: U.S.]**

Maloney, Kevin J.; Marshall, William J. and Yawitz, Jess B. The Effect of Risk on the Firm's Optimal Capital Stock: A Note. *J. Finance,* September 1983, *38*(4), pp. 1279–84.

Mancera, Miguel. Panel Discussion: The Capital Market under Conditions of High and Variable Inflation. **In** *Armella, P. A.; Dornbusch, R. and Obstfeld, M., eds.*, 1983, pp. 279–81.

Marks, Barry R. Calculating the Rate of Return on a Leveraged Lease—A Constant Leverage Approach. *J. Bank Res.*, Winter 1983, *13*(4), pp. 297–99. **[G: U.S.]**

Masulis, Ronald W. The Impact of Capital Structure Change on Firm Value: Some Estimates. *J. Finance,* March 1983, *38*(1), pp. 107–26. **[G: U.S.]**

McConnell, John J. and Schallheim, James S. Valuation of Asset Leasing Contracts. *J. Finan. Econ.*, August 1983, *12*(2), pp. 237–61.

McDaniel, William R. Convertible Bonds in Perfect and Imperfect Markets. *J. Finan. Res.*, Spring 1983, *6*(1), pp. 51–65.

McDonald, Robert L. Government Debt and Private Leverage: An Extension of the Miller Theorem. *J. Public Econ.*, December 1983, *22*(3), pp. 303–25. **[G: U.S.]**

McLure, Charles E., Jr. A Reexamination of Tax Distortions in General Equilibrium Models: Comment. **In** *Feldstein, M., ed.*, 1983, pp. 421–26. **[G: U.S.]**

McLure, Charles E., Jr. Financing Private Business in an Inflationary Context: The Experience of Argentina between 1967 and 1980: Comment. **In** *Armella, P. A.; Dornbusch, R. and Obstfeld, M., eds.*, 1983, pp. 180–83. **[G: Argentina]**

McLure, Charles E., Jr. State Corporate Income Taxes. **In** *Break, G. F., ed.*, 1983, pp. 29–52. **[G: U.S.]**

Mees, Philip. International Cash Management. **In** *George, A. M. and Giddy, I. H., eds., Vol. 2,* 1983, pp. 8.11B:1–25.

Mensah, Yaw M. The Differential Bankruptcy Predictive Ability of Specific Price Level Adjustments: Some Empirical Evidence. *Accounting Rev.*, April 1983, *58*(2), pp. 228–46. **[G: U.S.]**

Mieszkowski, Peter. A General Equilibrium Model of Taxation with Endogenous Financial Behavior: Comment. **In** *Feldstein, M., ed.*, 1983, pp. 455–58. **[G: U.S.]**

Miller, Merton H. Debt and Taxes. **In** *Archer, S. H. and D'Ambrosia, C. A.*, 1983, *1977*, pp. 462–78.

Miller, Merton H. and Modigliani, Franco. Dividend Policy, Growth, and the Valuation of Shares. **In** *Archer, S. H. and D'Ambrosia, C. A.*, 1983, *1961*, pp. 630–57.

Miller, Merton H. and Scholes, Myron S. Dividends and Taxes. **In** *Archer, S. H. and D'Ambrosia, C. A.*, 1983, *1978*, pp. 658–89.

Modigliani, Franco and Miller, Merton H. Corporate Income Taxes and the Cost of Capital: A Correction. **In** *Archer, S. H. and D'Ambrosia, C. A.*, 1983, *1963*, pp. 418–28.

Modigliani, Franco and Miller, Merton H. The Cost of Capital, Corporation Finance, and the Theory of Investment: Reply. **In** *Archer, S. H. and D'Ambrosia, C. A.*, 1983, *1959*, pp. 403–17.

Modigliani, Franco and Miller, Merton H. The Cost of Capital, Corporation Finance, and the Theory of Investment. **In** *Archer, S. H. and D'Ambrosia, C. A.*, 1983, *1958*, pp. 351–85.

Morris, James R. The Role of Cash Balances in Firm Valuation. *J. Finan. Quant. Anal.*, December 1983, *18*(4), pp. 533–45.

Mosser, A. Concentration and the Finance of Austrian Industrial Combines, 1880-1914. **In** *Teichova, A. and Cottrell, P. L., eds.*, 1983, pp. 57–71. **[G: Austria]**

Moyer, R. Charles and Chatfield, Robert. Market Power and Systematic Risk. *J. Econ. Bus.*, 1983, *35*(1), pp. 123–30. **[G: U.S.]**

Myers, Stewart C. Pension Funding Decisions, Interest Rate Assumptions, and Share Prices: Comment. **In** *Bodie, Z. and Shoven, J. B., eds.*, 1983, pp. 207–09. **[G: U.S.]**

Nissen, David. The Economic Accounts of the Resource Firm. **In** *Lev, B., ed.*, 1983, pp. 135–61.

Ohlson, James A. Price–Earnings Ratios and Earnings Capitalization under Uncertainty. *J. Acc. Res.*, Spring 1983, *21* (1), pp. 141–54.

Ooghe, Hubert and De Groote, Wilfried. Bepaling van de sectoriële invloed op de financiële structuur van ondernemingen bij middel van clusteranalyse. (With English summary.) *Cah. Écon. Bruxelles,* 1983, *97* (1), pp. 61–74. **[G: Belgium]**

Ooghe, Hubert and Derycke, G. Financial Structures in Private and Governmental Firms in Belgium: A Comparison. *Tijdschrift Econ. Manage.*, 1983, *28* (4), pp. 489–507. **[G: Belgium]**

Paroush, Jacob and Sokoler, Meir. The Firm's Trade Credit under Uncertainty and Some Macro Implication. **In** *Levy, H., ed.*, 1983, pp. 153–64.

Penman, Stephen H. The Predictive Content of Earnings Forecasts and Dividends. *J. Finance,* September 1983, *38* (4), pp. 1181–99. **[G: U.S.]**

Perrakis, Stylianos. The Value of the Firm under Regulation and the Theory of the Firm under Uncertainty: An Integrated Approach. **In** *Courville, L.; de Fontenay, A. and Dobell, R., eds.*, 1983, pp. 397–413.

Pettway, Richard H. and Jordan, Bradford D. Diversification, Double Leverage, and the Cost of Capital. *J. Finan. Res.*, Winter 1983, *6* (4), pp. 289–300. **[G: U.S.]**

Pick, J. F. Erratum: Introduction of an Inflation-Adjusted Tax Base in Israel. *Bull. Int. Fiscal Doc.*, November 1983, *37* (11), pp. 496. **[G: Israel]**

Pick, J. F. Introduction of an Inflation-Adjusted Tax Base in Israel. *Bull. Int. Fiscal Doc.*, 1983, *37* (6), pp. 259–63. **[G: Israel]**

Pitts, C. G. C. and Selby, Michael J. P. The Pricing of Corporate Debt: A Further Note. *J. Finance,* September 1983, *38* (4), pp. 1311–13.

Pozdena, Randall J. and Iben, Ben. Pricing Debt Instruments: The Options Approach. *Fed. Res. Bank San Francisco Econ. Rev.*, Summer 1983, (3), pp. 19–30. **[G: U.S.]**

Qureshi, Zia M. Determinants of Corporate Saving in Pakistan: A Macro-econometric Analysis. *Pakistan Devel. Rev.*, Summer 1983, *22* (2), pp. 73–96. **[G: Pakistan]**

Rodríguez Castellanos, A. Empresas multinacionales, gestion de cambios y crisis monetarias. (Multination Businesses, Change of Money, Management and Monetary Crisis. With English summary.) *Écon. Soc.*, September–October–November 1983, *17* (9–10–11), pp. 1451–86.

Rosen, Corey M. The Effect of Employee Stock Ownership Plans on Corporate Profits—Comment. *J. Risk Ins.*, September 1983, *50* (3), pp. 493–94. **[G: U.S.]**

Ross, Stephen A. The Determination of Financial Structure: The Incentive-signalling Approach. **In** *Archer, S. H. and D'Ambrosia, C. A.*, 1983, *1977*, pp. 555–75.

Rousseau, Henri-Paul. The Dome Syndrome: The Debt Overhanging Canadian Government and Business. *Can. Public Policy,* March 1983, *9* (1), pp. 37–52. **[G: Canada]**

Roy, S. Paul. Analyst Forecasts and Dividend Information. *J. Econ. Stud.*, 1983, *10* (2), pp. 3–20. **[G: U.S.]**

Rushinek, Avi, et al. The Construction of an International Investor's Perception Model for Corporate Published Forecasted Financial Reports for the USA, the UK and New Zealand. *Managerial Dec. Econ.*, December 1983, *4* (4), pp. 258–65. **[G: New Zealand; U.K.; U.S.]**

Saitow, Seiichiro. The Characteristics of Japanese Enterprises and Their Financing. **In** *[Yamada, I.]*, 1983, pp. 27–40. **[G: Japan]**

Salmi, Timo, et al. Extracting and Analyzing the Time Series for Profitability Measurement from Published Financial Statements: With Results on Publicly Traded Finnish Metal Industry Firms. *Liiketaloudellinen Aikak.*, 1983, *32* (2), pp. 135–74. **[G: Finland]**

Sarathy, Ravi. Export Activity and Realized Profit: Some Japanese Evidence. **In** *Czinkota, M. R., ed. (I)*, 1983, pp. 210–26. **[G: Japan]**

Sartoris, William L. and Hill, Ned C. A Generalized Cash Flow Approach to Short-Term Financial Decisions. *J. Finance,* May 1983, *38* (2), pp. 349–60.

Scherr, Frederick C. Some Evidence on Asset Liquidation Losses: The Case of W. T. Grant. *Nebr. J. Econ. Bus.*, Summer 1983, *22* (3), pp. 3–23. **[G: U.S.]**

Schipper, Katherine and Smith, Abbie. Effects of Recontracting on Shareholder Wealth: The Case of Voluntary Spin-Offs. *J. Finan. Econ.*, December 1983, *12* (4), pp. 437–67. **[G: U.S.]**

Schipper, Katherine and Thompson, Rex. Evidence on the Capitalized Value of Merger Activity for Acquiring Firms. *J. Finan. Econ.*, April 1983, *11* (1–4), pp. 85–119. **[G: U.S.]**

Sealey, C. W., Jr. Valuation, Capital Structure, and Shareholder Unanimity for Depository Financial Intermediaries. *J. Finance,* June 1983, *38* (3), pp. 857–71.

Shapiro, Alan C. Nominal Contracting in a World of Uncertainty. *J. Banking Finance,* March 1983, *7* (1), pp. 69–82.

Shapiro, Daniel M.; Sims, William A. and Hughes, Gwenn. The Efficiency Implications of Earnings Retentions: An Extension. *Rev. Econ. Statist.*, May 1983, *65* (2), pp. 327–31. **[G: Canada]**

Shiller, Robert J. Tax Reform and Corporate Investment: A Microeconometric Simulation Study: Comment. **In** *Feldstein, M., ed.*, 1983, pp. 281–87. **[G: U.S.]**

Sinkey, Joseph F., Jr. The Performance of First Pennsylvania Bank Prior to Its Bail Out. *J. Bank Res.*, Summer 1983, *14* (2), pp. 119–33. **[G: U.S.]**

Skelton, Jeffrey L. Banks, Firms and the Relative Pricing of Tax-Exempt and Taxable Bonds. *J. Finan. Econ.*, November 1983, *12* (3), pp. 343–55. **[G: U.S.]**

Slemrod, Joel. A General Equilibrium Model of Taxation with Endogenous Financial Behavior. **In** *Feldstein, M., ed.*, 1983, pp. 427–54. **[G: U.S.]**

Slovin, Myron B. and Sushka, Marie Elizabeth. The Stability of the Demand for Money: The Case of the Corporate Sector. *J. Macroecon.*, Summer 1983, *5*(3), pp. 361–72. [G: U.S.]

Smirlock, Michael L. and Marshall, William J. An Examination of the Empirical Relationship between the Dividend and Investment Decisions: A Note. *J. Finance,* December 1983, *38*(5), pp. 1659–67. [G: U.S.]

Sonka, Steven T. Risk Management in Models of the Farm: Thoughts on Modeling Risk Management on the Farm: Discussion. **In** *Baum, K. H. and Schertz, L. P., eds.*, 1983, pp. 200–203.

Sprecher, C. Ronald and Pertl, Mars A. Large Losses, Risk Management and Stock Prices. *J. Risk Ins.*, March 1983, *50*(1), pp. 107–17.

Stiegler, Harald. Assessment of the Expedience of Subsidies for the Restoration of Financial Soundness under Operational Analysis Aspects. *Rivista Int. Sci. Econ. Com.*, June 1983, *30*(6), pp. 531–39.

Stiglitz, Joseph E. A Re-examination of the Modigliani–Miller Theorem. **In** *Archer, S. H. and D'Ambrosia, C. A.*, 1983, *1969*, pp. 428–40.

Stone, Bernell K. The Design of a Company's Banking System. *J. Finance,* May 1983, *38*(2), pp. 373–85.

Tan, Gerald. Foreign Investment, Employment Generation and the Profit–Wage Ration in the Manufacturing Sector of West Malaysia: A Reply to Professor Hirschman. **In** *Lim, D., ed.*, 1983, *1979,* pp. 230–34. [G: Malaysia]

Tan, Gerald. Foreign Investment, Employment Generation and the Profit–Wage Ratio in the Manufacturing Sector of West Malaysia. **In** *Lim, D., ed.*, 1983, *1978,* pp. 225–28. [G: Malaysia]

Taylor, Harry. Perspective: Managing Foreign Exchange Exposure. **In** *Herring, R. J., ed.*, 1983, pp. 219–25.

Tepper, Irwin. Optimal Funding and Asset Allocation Rules for Defined-Benefit Pension Plans: Comment. **In** *Bodie, Z. and Shoven, J. B., eds.*, 1983, pp. 104–05. [G: U.S.]

Thunell, Lars H. and Skydel, Jack R. International Cash Management. **In** *George, A. M. and Giddy, I. H., eds., Vol. 2,* 1983, pp. 8.11A:1–10.

Trapp, James N. Risk Management in Models of the Farm: The Need for Prescriptive Risk-Management Models: A Suggested Methodological Approach: Discussion. **In** *Baum, K. H. and Schertz, L. P., eds.*, 1983, pp. 204–09.

Tyson, Laura D'Andrea and Zysman, John. American Industry in International Competition. **In** *Zysman, J. and Tyson, L., eds.*, 1983, pp. 15–59. [G: U.S.]

Wansley, James W. and Lane, William R. A Financial Profile of Merged Firms. *Rev. Bus. Econ. Res.*, Fall 1983, *19*(1), pp. 87–98. [G: U.S.]

Webb, David C. Contingent Claims, Personal Loans and the Irrelevance of Corporate Financial Structure. *Econ. J.*, December 1983, *93*(372), pp. 832–46.

Weiss, Nitzan. Leverage, Risk-Adjusted Discount Rate and Industry Equilibrium. *Amer. Econ.*, Spring 1983, *27*(1), pp. 5–12.

White, Michelle J. Bankruptcy Costs and the New Bankruptcy Code. *J. Finance,* May 1983, *38*(2), pp. 477–88. [G: U.S.]

Wilkins, Trevor and Zimmer, Ian. The Effect of Leasing and Different Methods of Accounting for Leases on Credit Evaluations. *Accounting Rev.*, October 1983, *58*(4), pp. 749–64.

Wilks, Stephen and Dyson, Kenneth. The Character and Economic Context of Industrial Crises. **In** *Dyson, K. and Wilks, S., eds.*, 1983, pp. 1–25. [G: U.S.; W. Europe]

Woolridge, J. Randall. Dividend Changes and Security Prices. *J. Finance,* December 1983, *38*(5), pp. 1607–15. [G: U.S.]

Woolridge, J. Randall. Stock Dividends as Signals. *J. Finan. Res.*, Spring 1983, *6*(1), pp. 1–12. [G: U.S.]

522 Business Investment

5220 Business Investment

Abel, Andrew B. Optimal Investment under Uncertainty. *Amer. Econ. Rev.*, March 1983, *73*(1), pp. 228–33.

Agell, Jonas. Subsidy to Capital through Tax Incentives in the ASEAN Countries: An Application of the Cost of Capital Approach under Inflationary Situations. *Singapore Econ. Rev.*, October 1983, *28*(2), pp. 98–128. [G: ASEAN]

Akhtar, M. A. Effects of Interest Rates and Inflation on Aggregate Inventory Investment in the United States. *Amer. Econ. Rev.*, June 1983, *73*(3), pp. 319–28. [G: U.S.]

Akkina, Krishna R. The Effects of Carrying Cost Uncertainty and Expected Price Changes on Inventories in the United States during 1959–1979. *Nebr. J. Econ. Bus.*, Spring 1983, *22*(2), pp. 49–64.

Albrecht, James W. and Hart, Albert G. A Putty-Clay Model of Demand Uncertainty and Investment. *Scand. J. Econ.*, 1983, *85*(3), pp. 393–402.

Amihud, Yakov and Mendelson, Haim. Price Smoothing and Inventory. *Rev. Econ. Stud.*, January 1983, *50*(1), pp. 87–98.

Anderson, Gordon J. The Internal Financing Decisions of the Industrial and Commercial Sector: A Reappraisal of the Lintner Model of Dividend Disbursements. *Economica,* August 1983, *50*(199), pp. 235–48. [G: U.K.]

Angel, Michael G. and Nitsch, Thomas O. Inflation and the Rationality of Investing in Projects with Negative Net Present Values. *Amer. Econ.*, Fall 1983, *27*(2), pp. 58–66.

Artto, Eero. Kansainvälinen kilpailukyky yritys- ja toimialatasolla—II. (International Competitiveness at Enterprise and Industry Level—II. With English summary.) *Liiketaloudellinen Aikak.*, 1983, *32*(4), pp. 358–88.

Arzac, Enrique R. A Mechanism for the Allocation of Corporate Investment. *J. Finan. Quant. Anal.*, June 1983, *18*(2), pp. 175–88.

Arzac, Enrique R. and Marcus, Matityahu. Flotation Cost Allowance in Rate of Return Regulation: A Reply. *J. Finance,* September 1983, *38*(4), pp. 1339–41.

Auerbach, Alan J. Corporate Taxation in the United States. *Brookings Pap. Econ. Act.*, 1983, (2), pp. 451–513. [G: U.S.]

Auerbach, Alan J. Does ACRS Foster Efficient Capital Allocation? In *Walker, C. E. and Bloomfield, M. E., eds.*, 1983, pp. 77–78. **[G: U.S.]**

Auerbach, Alan J. Efficient Design of Investment Incentives. In *Auerbach, A. J.*, 1983, *1981*, pp. 51–57.

Auerbach, Alan J. Inflation and the Choice of Asset Life. In *Auerbach, A. J.*, 1983, *1979*, pp. 100–117.

Auerbach, Alan J. Taxation, Corporate Financial Policy and the Cost of Capital. *J. Econ. Lit.*, September 1983, *21* (3), pp. 905–40.

Auerbach, Alan J. Wealth Maximization and the Cost of Capital. In *Auerbach, A. J.*, 1983, *1979*, pp. 78–91.

Auten, Gerald E. Capital Gains: An Evaluation of the 1978 and 1981 Tax Cuts. In *Walker, C. E. and Bloomfield, M. E., eds.*, 1983, pp. 121–48. **[G: U.S.]**

Baltas, N. C. Modelling Credit and Private Investment in Greek Agriculture. *Europ. Rev. Agr. Econ.*, 1983, *10*(4), pp. 389–402. **[G: Greece]**

Berend, Iván T. The Renewal Cycle of Fixed Assets under the Conditions of the 1980s in Hungary. *Acta Oecon.*, 1983, *30*(3–4), pp. 401–11. **[G: Hungary]**

Berkowitz, M. K. and Cosgrove, E. G. Financing and Investment Behaviour of the Regulated Firm. In *Courville, L.; de Fontenay, A. and Dobell, R., eds.*, 1983, pp. 383–96.

Bernanke, Ben S. Irreversibility, Uncertainty, and Cyclical Investment. *Quart. J. Econ.*, February 1983, *98*(1), pp. 85–106.

Bernanke, Ben S. The Determinants of Investment: Another Look. *Amer. Econ. Rev.*, May 1983, *73*(2), pp. 71–75. **[G: U.S.]**

Bernstein, Jeffrey I. Taxes, Financing and Investment for a Regulated Firm. In *Courville, L.; de Fontenay, A. and Dobell, R., eds.*, 1983, pp. 367–82.

Bernstein, Peter L. Capital Stock and Management Decisions. *J. Post Keynesian Econ.*, Fall 1983, *6*(1), pp. 20–38. **[G: U.S.]**

Blaylock, Bruce K. and Karaphillis, George. A Selection Technique for Capital Investment Decisions: An Industrial Application of Stochastic Dominance. *Rev. Bus. Econ. Res.*, Winter, 1983, *18*(2), pp. 1–12.

Boddewyn, Jean J. Foreign and Domestic Divestment and Investment Decisions: Like or Unlike? *J. Int. Bus. Stud.*, Winter 1983, *14*(3), pp. 23–35.

Brenner, Menachem and Venezia, Itzhak. The Effects of Inflation and Taxes on Growth Investments and Replacement Policies. *J. Finance*, December 1983, *38*(5), pp. 1519–28.

Cantor, David G. and Lippman, Steven A. Investment Selection with Imperfect Capital Markets. *Econometrica*, July 1983, *51* (4), pp. 1121–44.

Carré, Denis. Une mesure "hédonistique" du stock de capital de l'entreprise: le cas la sidérurgie. (With English summary.) *Rev. Econ. Ind.*, 4th Trimester 1983, (26), pp. 52–67. **[G: France]**

Carter, E. Eugene and Rodriguez, Rita M. International Capital Budgeting. In *George, A. M. and Giddy, I. H., eds., Vol. 2*, 1983, pp. 8.5:1–33.

Chauveau, Thierry. L'inflation et les entreprises. (About Firms and Inflation. With English summary.) *Revue Écon.*, September 1983, *34*(5), pp. 897–925. **[G: France]**

Chesshire, John H. and Robson, Michael J. Capital Stock Rotation, Conservation and Fuel Substitution in the UK Industrial Steam-Raising Market. *Energy Econ.*, October 1983, *5*(4), pp. 218–31. **[G: U.K.]**

Chew, I. Keong and Ferri, Michael G. An Approach to Capital Budgeting When Projects Differ by Risk. *Rev. Bus. Econ. Res.*, Fall 1983, *19*(1), pp. 67–74.

Chirinko, Robert S. and Eisner, Robert. Tax Policy and Investment in Major U.S. Macroeconomic Econometric Models. *J. Public Econ.*, March 1983, *20*(2), pp. 139–66. **[G: U.S.]**

Cohen, Wesley M. Investment and Industrial Expansion: A Corporate Variables Framework. *J. Econ. Behav. Organ.*, June–September 1983, *4*(2–3), pp. 91–111.

Cohodes, Donald R. Which Will Survive? The $150 Billion Capital Question. *Inquiry*, Spring 1983, *20*(1), pp. 5–11. **[G: U.S.]**

Corcoran, Patrick J. The Cost of Capital: An Update. *Fed. Res. Bank New York Quart. Rev.*, Autumn 1983, *8*(3), pp. 23–24. **[G: U.S.]**

Courant, Paul N. On the Effects of Federal Capital Taxation on Growing and Declining Areas. *J. Urban Econ.*, September 1983, *14*(2), pp. 242–61. **[G: U.S.]**

Cox, Samuel H., Jr. and Martin, John D. Abandonment Value and Capital Budgeting under Uncertainty. *J. Econ. Bus.*, August 1983, *35*(3/4), pp. 331–41.

Cranston, Alan. The Option of a Tax Deferred Rollover on Capital Gains. In *Walker, C. E. and Bloomfield, M. E., eds.*, 1983, pp. 149–50. **[G: U.S.]**

Cummins, J. David. Risk Management and the Theory of the Firm: Author's Reply. *J. Risk Ins.*, March 1983, *50*(1), pp. 145–50.

Dajani, Mazen K. Taxation and Investment in Jordan. *Bull. Int. Fiscal Doc.*, January 1983, *37*(1), pp. 31–34. **[G: Jordan]**

Durand, David. The Cost of Capital, Corporation Finance, and the Theory of Investment: Comment. In *Archer, S. H. and D'Ambrosia, C. A.*, 1983, *1959*, pp. 386–402.

Dybvig, Philip H. Duality, Interest Rates, and the Theory of Present Value. *J. Econ. Theory*, June 1983, *30*(1), pp. 98–114.

Eisner, Robert. Government Policy, Saving and Investment. *J. Econ. Educ.*, Spring 1983, *14*(2), pp. 38–49. **[G: U.S.]**

Elliott, J. Walter. Advertising and R&D Investments in the Wealth-Maximizing Firm. *J. Econ. Bus.*, August 1983, *35*(3/4), pp. 389–97.

Epstein, Larry G. and Denny, Michael G. S. The Multivariate Flexible Accelerator Model: Its Empirical Restrictions and an Application to U.S. Manufacturing. *Econometrica*, May, 1983, *51* (3), pp. 647–74. **[G: U.S.]**

Espinosa, Juan Guillermo. Worker Participation in the Management of Enterprises and the Ownership and Financing of the Means of Production: A Transition Strategy. *Econ. Anal. Worker's Manage.*, 1983, *17*(2), pp. 99–121.

Farkas, Katalin. The Changing Role of Enterprise Inventories. *Eastern Europ. Econ.*, Spring–Summer 1983, *21* (3–4), pp. 49–66. [G: Hungary]

Feldman, Stanley J. Industry Analysis and Investment Decision-Making under Conditions of Uncertainty. *Managerial Dec. Econ.*, September 1983, *4* (3), pp. 193–207. [G: U.S.]

Feldstein, Martin S. Domestic Saving and International Capital Movements in the Long Run and the Short Run. *Europ. Econ. Rev.*, March/April 1983, *21* (1/2), pp. 129–51. [G: OECD]

Feldstein, Martin S. Has the Rate of Investment Fallen? *Rev. Econ. Statist.*, February 1983, *65* (1), pp. 144–49. [G: U.S.]

Feldstein, Martin S. Inflation, Tax Rules, and Capital Formation: A Summary of the Theoretical Models. In *Feldstein, M. (II)*, 1983, pp. 17–27.

Feldstein, Martin S. Inflation, Tax Rules, and Investment: Some Econometric Evidence. In *Feldstein, M. (II)*, 1983, *1982*, pp. 243–85. [G: U.S.]

Feldstein, Martin S. Inflation, Tax Rules, and Investment: Some Econometric Evidence. In *Feldstein, M. (I)*, 1983, *1982*, pp. 331–73. [G: U.S.]

Feldstein, Martin S. Inflation, Tax Rules, and Capital Formation: An Introductory Overview. In *Feldstein, M. (II)*, 1983, pp. 1–14. [G: U.S.]

Feldstein, Martin S.; Dicks-Mireaux, Louis-David L. and Poterba, James M. The Effective Tax Rate and the Pretax Rate of Return. *J. Public Econ.*, July 1983, *21* (2), pp. 129–58. [G: U.S.]

Feldstein, Martin S. and Flemming, John. Tax Policy, Corporate Saving, and Investment Behavior in Britain. In *Feldstein, M. (I)*, 1983, *1971*, pp. 269–94. [G: U.K.]

Feldstein, Martin S.; Poterba, James M. and Dicks-Mireaux, Louis-David L. The Effective Tax Rate and the Pretax Rate of Return. In *Feldstein, M. (I)*, 1983, *1982*, pp. 36–68. [G: U.S.]

Feldstein, Martin S. and Rothschild, Michael. Toward an Economic Theory of Replacement Investment. In *Feldstein, M. (I)*, 1983, *1974*, pp. 295–330.

Fisher, Franklin M. and McGowan, John J. On the Misuse of Accounting Rates of Return to Infer Monopoly Profits. *Amer. Econ. Rev.*, March 1983, *73* (1), pp. 82–97.

Fortune, J. N. Expectations, Capital Formation, Sales and Capacity Utilization. *Empirical Econ.*, 1983, *8* (3–4), pp. 177–86.

Fraser, R. W. and Van Noorden, R. J. Extraction of an Exhaustible Resource: The Effects on Investment of Several Parameters Being Subject to Uncertainty. *Econ. Rec.*, December 1983, *59* (167), pp. 365–74.

Fullerton, Don and Gordon, Roger H. A Reexamination of Tax Distortions in General Equilibrium Models. In *Feldstein, M., ed.*, 1983, pp. 369–420. [G: U.S.]

Fullerton, Don and Hamdan, Lawrence A. The Aborted Phase-In of Marginal Effective Corporate Tax Rates. *Public Finance Quart.*, October 1983, *11* (4), pp. 437–64. [G: U.S.]

Gaspard, Michel and Tahar, Gabriel. Investissement et baisse de la durée hebdomadaire du travail: réflexions autour d'un modèle sectoriel. (With English summary.) *Rev. Econ. Ind.*, 3rd Trimester 1983, (25), pp. 1–20. [G: France]

Giddy, Ian H. and Ho, Sang Kang. Mathematics of International Finance. In *George, A. M. and Giddy, I. H., eds., Vol. 2*, 1983, pp. A1–51. [G: OECD]

Giersch, Herbert and Wolter, Frank. Towards an Explanation of the Productivity Slowdown: An Acceleration-Deceleration Hypothesis. *Econ. J.*, March 1983, *93* (369), pp. 35–55. [G: OECD]

Gordon, Myron J. Optimal Investment and Financing Policy. In *Archer, S. H. and D'Ambrosia, C. A.*, 1983, *1963*, pp. 622–29.

Gravelle, Jane G. Capital Income Taxation and Efficiency in the Allocation of Investment. *Nat. Tax J.*, September 1983, *36* (3), pp. 297–306. [G: U.S.]

Gupta, B. R. S. and Agarwal, A. K. Study Group on Corporate Sector. *Econ. Aff.*, April–June 1983, *28* (2), pp. 724–27. [G: India]

Gupta, Vinod K. Labor Productivity, Establishment Size, and Scale Economies [The Extent of Economies of Scale: The Effects of Firm Size on Labor Productivity and Wage Rates]. *Southern Econ. J.*, January 1983, *49* (3), pp. 853–59. [G: U.S.]

Harber, Richard Paul, Jr. Brazil's Fiscal Incentive System and the Northeast: An Econometric Analysis. *J. Econ. Devel.*, July 1983, *8* (1), pp. 131–59. [G: Brazil]

Hartl, Richard. Optimal Maintenance and Production Rates for a Machine: A Nonlinear Economic Control Problem. *J. Econ. Dynam. Control*, November 1983, *6* (3), pp. 281–306.

Hatsopoulos, George N. The Effects of ERTA and TEFRA on the Cost of Capital. In *Walker, C. E. and Bloomfield, M. E., eds.*, 1983, pp. 79–88. [G: U.S.]

Hayes, Robert H. and Garvin, David A. Managing as if Tomorrow Mattered. In *Kantrow, A. M., ed.*, 1983, pp. 36–51. [G: U.S.]

Hendershott, Patric H. and Hu, Sheng Cheng. The Allocation of Capital between Residential and Nonresidential Uses: Taxes, Inflation and Capital Market Constraints. *J. Finance*, June 1983, *38* (3), pp. 795–812. [G: U.S.]

Herroelen, Willy and Lambrecht, Marc R. Management Aspects of Computerized Manufacturing. *Econ. Soc. Tijdschr.*, December 1983, *37* (6), pp. 723–43.

Hertz, David B. and Thomas, Howard. Decision and Risk Analysis in a New Product and Facilities Planning Problem. *Sloan Manage. Rev.*, Winter 1983, *24* (2), pp. 17–31.

Hickman, Frederic W. Changes in Capital Cost Recovery Policies: Costs and Benefits. In *Walker, C. E. and Bloomfield, M. E., eds.*, 1983, pp. 89–91. [G: U.S.]

Hirshleifer, Jack. Investment Decision under Uncertainty: Choice—Theoretic Approaches. In *Archer, S. H. and D'Ambrosia, C. A.*, 1983, *1965*, pp. 61–85.

Hirshleifer, Jack. On the Theory of Optimal Investment Decision. In *Archer, S. H. and D'Ambrosia, C. A.*, 1983, *1958*, pp. 321–50.

Honko, Jaakko. Virheinvestointien anatomiaa: Yrityksen investointiprosessin kriittiset kohdat. (An Anatomy of Capital Investment Failures. With

English summary.) *Liiketaloudellinen Aikak.*, 1983, *32*(2), pp. 99–123. **[G: Finland]**

Howe, Keith M. and McCabe, George M. On Optimal Asset Abandonment and Replacement. *J. Finan. Quant. Anal.*, September 1983, *18*(3), pp. 295–305.

Irvine, F. Owen, Jr. The Real Rate of Interest, for Whom? *Appl. Econ.*, October 1983, *15*(5), pp. 635–48. **[G: U.S.]**

Izenson, Mark Steven. A Brief Note on the Relationship between Investment and the Interest Rate in the United States, 1970–1979. *Econ. Notes*, 1983, (1), pp. 135–39. **[G: U.S.]**

de Kadt, Maarten. Energy Corporation Propaganda: A Weapon against Public Policy. *Rev. Radical Polit. Econ.*, Fall 1983, *15*(3), pp. 35–50. **[G: U.S.]**

Kawasaki, Seiichi; McMillan, John and Zimmermann, Klaus F. Inventories and Price Inflexibility. *Econometrica*, May, 1983, *51*(3), pp. 599–610. **[G: W. Germany]**

Klutznick, Philip M. The Effects of Property Taxation on Investment Decisions. **In** *Harriss, C. L., ed.*, 1983, pp. 72–85. **[G: U.S.]**

Kozlow, Ralph. Capital Expenditures by Majority-Owned Foreign Affiliates of U.S. Companies, 1983 and 1984. *Surv. Curr. Bus.*, September 1983, *63*(9), pp. 27–33. **[G: U.S.]**

Kuhbier, Peter and Sauer, Andreas. Die im Konjunkturtest erfassten Einschätzungen der Wirtschafts- und Geschäftslage als Indikatoren der Investitionstätigkeit: Eine empirische Untersuchung. (Evaluations of the Economic Situation Obtained from the Business Test as an Indicator of Investment Activity: An Empirical Study. With English summary.) *Jahr. Nationalökon. Statist.*, May 1983, *198*(3), pp. 193–210. **[G: W. Germany]**

Kwon, O. Yul. The Neutral, Pure Profit, and Rate-of-Return Taxes: Their Equivalence and Differences. *Public Finance*, 1983, *38*(1), pp. 81–97.

Landefeld, J. Steven and Seskin, Eugene P. Plant and Equipment Expenditures, the Four Quarters of 1983. *Surv. Curr. Bus.*, June 1983, *63*(6), pp. 19–23. **[G: U.S.]**

Landefeld, J. Steven and Seskin, Eugene P. Plant and Equipment Expenditures, Quarters of 1983 and First and Second Quarters of 1984. *Surv. Curr. Bus.*, December 1983, *63*(12), pp. 19–24. **[G: U.S.]**

Lawrence, Kenneth Donald; Marose, Robert A. and Lawrence, Sheila M. A Multiple Goal Portfolio Analysis Model for the Selection of MIS Projects. **In** *Hansen, P., ed.*, 1983, pp. 229–37.

Lerner, Abba P. On the Marginal Product of Capital and the Marginal Efficiency of Investment. **In** *Lerner, A. P.*, 1983, *1953*, pp. 531–44.

Lindbeck, Assar. The Recent Slowdowns of Productivity Growth. *Econ. J.*, March 1983, *93*(369), pp. 13–34. **[G: OECD]**

Lioukas, Spyros K. Investment Behaviour in a Nationalised Industry. *Appl. Econ.*, October 1983, *15*(5), pp. 665–79. **[G: U.K.]**

von der Lippe, Peter and Westerhoff, Horst-Dieter. Ein ökonometrisches Modell des Investitionsprozesses in der Volksrepublik Polen—Empirische Ergebnnisse und wirtschaftspolitische Folgerungen. (An Econometric Model of the Investment Process in Poland. With English summary.) *Jahr. Nationalökon. Statist.*, May 1983, *198*(3), pp. 211–36. **[G: Poland]**

Lorie, James H. and Savage, Leonard J. Three Problems in Rationing Capital. **In** *Archer, S. H. and D'Ambrosia, C. A.*, 1983, *1955*, pp. 308–21.

Lowenthal, Franklin. An Iterative Method for Determining the Internal Rate of Return. *Managerial Dec. Econ.*, March 1983, *4*(1), pp. 35–39.

Main, Brian G. M. Risk Management and the Theory of the Firm: Comment. *J. Risk Ins.*, March 1983, *50*(1), pp. 140–44.

Matluck, Edward. Business Strategy and Investment Behavior. *Managerial Dec. Econ.*, September 1983, *4*(3), pp. 185–92. **[G: U.S.]**

McGreevy, T. E. and Thomson, A. W. J. Regional Policy and Company Investment Behaviour. *Reg. Stud.*, October 1983, *17*(5), pp. 347–57. **[G: U.K.]**

McLure, Charles E., Jr. A Reexamination of Tax Distortions in General Equilibrium Models: Comment. **In** *Feldstein, M., ed.*, 1983, pp. 421–26. **[G: U.S.]**

Mead, Walter J.; Moseidjord, Asbjorn and Sorensen, Philip E. The Rate of Return Earned by Lessees under Cash Bonus Bidding for OCS Oil and Gas Leases. *Energy J.*, October 1983, *4*(4), pp. 37–52. **[G: U.S.]**

Milanovic, Branko. The Investment Behaviour of the Labour-Managed Firm: A Property-Rights Approach. *Econ. Anal. Worker's Manage.*, 1983, *17*(4), pp. 327–40. **[G: Yugoslavia]**

Miller, Edward M. Capital Aggregation in the Presence of Obsolescence-Inducing Technical Change. *Rev. Income Wealth*, September 1983, *29*(3), pp. 283–96.

Modigliani, Franco and Miller, Merton H. Corporate Income Taxes and the Cost of Capital: A Correction. **In** *Archer, S. H. and D'Ambrosia, C. A.*, 1983, *1963*, pp. 418–28.

Modigliani, Franco and Miller, Merton H. The Cost of Capital, Corporation Finance, and the Theory of Investment. **In** *Archer, S. H. and D'Ambrosia, C. A.*, 1983, *1958*, pp. 351–85.

Modigliani, Franco and Miller, Merton H. The Cost of Capital, Corporation Finance, and the Theory of Investment: Reply. **In** *Archer, S. H. and D'Ambrosia, C. A.*, 1983, *1959*, pp. 403–17.

Morris, Derek J. Comment on the Paper by Professor Lindbeck [The Recent Slowdowns of Productivity Growth]. *Econ. J.*, March 1983, *93*(369), pp. 78–83. **[G: OECD]**

Naggl, Walter. Prediction of Inventory Investment with the Use of Business Survey Data. *Konjunkturpolitik*, 1983, *29*(2), pp. 89–99. **[G: W. Germany]**

Nielsen, Peter Bøegh. Aspects of Industrial Financing in Denmark 1890–1914. *Scand. Econ. Hist. Rev.*, 1983, *31*(2), pp. 79–108. **[G: Denmark]**

Niho, Yoshio and Mussachio, Robert A. Revenue Maximization and Optimal Capital Policies of a Regulated Firm. **In** *[Yamada, I.]*, 1983, pp. 15–26.

Nissen, David. The Economic Accounts of the Resource Firm. **In** *Lev, B., ed.*, 1983, pp. 135–61.

Okun, Arthur M. The Predictive Value of Surveys

of Business Intentions. **In** *Okun, A. M.,* 1983, *1962,* pp. 553–61. **[G: U.S.]**

Östermark, Ralf. Poistokelpoisen käyttöomaisuusinvestoinnin nykyarvomalli. (An Investment Model for Depreciable Fixed Assets. With English summary.) *Liiketaloudellinen Aikak.,* 1983, *32* (1), pp. 81–93.

Pagan, A. R. and Gray, M. R. Inflation and Investment: An Historical Overview. **In** *Pagan, A. R. and Trivedi, P. K., eds.,* 1983, pp. 262–81. **[G: Australia]**

Pandit, B. L. A Note on Inflation and Corporate Investment. *Indian Econ. Rev.,* July–December 1983, *18* (2), pp. 273–84. **[G: India]**

Patterson, Cleveland S. Flotation Cost Allowance in Rate of Return Regulation: Comment. *J. Finance,* September 1983, *38* (4), pp. 1335–38.

Paul, Chris W., II. Rate-Base Determination, Inflation, and Realized Rates of Return to Electric Utilities. **In** *[Bonbright, J. C.],* 1983, pp. 219–26. **[G: U.S.]**

Pearce, Douglas K. and Wisley, Thomas O. Sales Expectations and Inventory Changes in Retail Trade. *J. Econ. Bus.,* 1983, *35* (1), pp. 109–21. **[G: U.S.]**

Perazzèlli, P. A. and Perrin, J. R. Investment—Inflation Linkages in the NIF-10 Model. **In** *Pagan, A. R. and Trivedi, P. K., eds.,* 1983, pp. 283–310. **[G: Australia]**

Poterba, James M. and Summers, Lawrence H. Dividend Taxes, Corporate Investment, and '*Q*.'. *J. Public Econ.,* November 1983, *22* (2), pp. 135–67. **[G: U.K.]**

Prais, S. J. Comment on the Paper by Professor Giersch and Dr. Wolter [Towards an Explanation of the Productivity Slowdown: An Acceleration-Deceleration Hypothesis]. *Econ. J.,* March 1983, *93* (369), pp. 84–88.

Raboy, David G. Capital Composition Changes: Effects of Changing Haig–Simons Income Tax Rates. *Public Finance Quart.,* January 1983, *11* (1), pp. 67–78.

Reid, Donald W. and Bradford, Garnett L. On Optimal Replacement of Farm Tractors. *Amer. J. Agr. Econ.,* May 1983, *65* (2), pp. 326–31. **[G: U.S.]**

Resnick, Steven R. Lower Capital Gains Tax Rates and the Stock Market. **In** *Walker, C. E. and Bloomfield, M. E., eds.,* 1983, pp. 150–53. **[G: U.S.]**

Russo, William J., Jr. and Rutledge, Gary L. Plant and Equipment Expenditures by Business for Pollution Abatement, 1982 and Planned 1983. *Surv. Curr. Bus.,* June 1983, *63* (6), pp. 24–26. **[G: U.S.]**

Saitow, Seiichiro. The Characteristics of Japanese Enterprises and Their Financing. **In** *[Yamada, I.],* 1983, pp. 27–40. **[G: Japan]**

Salinger, Michael A. and Summers, Lawrence H. Tax Reform and Corporate Investment: A Microeconometric Simulation Study. **In** *Feldstein, M., ed.,* 1983, pp. 247–81. **[G: U.S.]**

Salmi, Timo, et al. Extracting and Analyzing the Time Series for Profitability Measurement from Published Financial Statements: With Results on Publicly Traded Finnish Metal Industry Firms: Part II. *Liiketaloudellinen Aikak.,* 1983, *32* (3), pp. 209–41. **[G: Finland]**

Schiantarelli, Fabio. Investment Models and Expectations: Some Estimates for the Italian Industrial Sector. *Int. Econ. Rev.,* June 1983, *24* (2), pp. 291–312. **[G: Italy]**

Schinasi, Garry J. Business Fixed Investment: Recent Developments and Outlook. *Fed. Res. Bull.,* January 1983, *69* (1), pp. 1–10. **[G: U.S.]**

Seskin, Eugene P. and Landefeld, J. Steven. Plant and Equipment Expenditures, First and Second Quarters and Second Half of 1983. *Surv. Curr. Bus.,* March 1983, *63* (3), pp. 19–24. **[G: U.S.]**

Seskin, Eugene P. and Landefeld, J. Steven. Plant and Equipment Expenditures, the Four Quarters of 1983. *Surv. Curr. Bus.,* September 1983, *63* (9), pp. 19–26. **[G: U.S.]**

Shiller, Robert J. Tax Reform and Corporate Investment: A Microeconometric Simulation Study: Comment. **In** *Feldstein, M., ed.,* 1983, pp. 281–87. **[G: U.S.]**

Shiriaev, P. Cooperation in Investments: A Factor in the Intensification of Production in CMEA Member Nations. *Prob. Econ.,* May 1983, *26* (1), pp. 74–89.

Shneerson, Dan. The Profitability of Investment in Shipping: The Balance of Payments Criterion. *J. Transp. Econ. Policy,* September 1983, *17* (3), pp. 285–98. **[G: Israel]**

Šik, Ota. Zwei Wirtschaftskrisen in der Bundesrepublik Deutschland. (Two Economic Crises in the Federal Republic of Germany. With English summary.) *Jahr. Nationalökon. Statist.,* September 1983, *198* (5), pp. 385–408. **[G: W. Germany]**

Sinai, Allen and Eckstein, Otto. Tax Policy and Business Fixed Investment Revisited. *J. Econ. Behav. Organ.,* June–September 1983, *4* (2–3), pp. 131–62. **[G: U.S.]**

Sinai, Allen; Lin, Andrew and Robins, Russell. Taxes, Saving, and Investment: Some Empirical Evidence. *Nat. Tax J.,* September 1983, *36* (3), pp. 321–45. **[G: U.S.]**

Smirlock, Michael L. and Marshall, William J. An Examination of the Empirical Relationship between the Dividend and Investment Decisions: A Note. *J. Finance,* December 1983, *38* (5), pp. 1659–67. **[G: U.S.]**

Sprecher, C. Ronald and Pertl, Mars A. Large Losses, Risk Management and Stock Prices. *J. Risk Ins.,* March 1983, *50* (1), pp. 107–17.

Steigum, Erling, Jr. A Financial Theory of Investment Behavior. *Econometrica,* May, 1983, *51* (3), pp. 637–45.

Steuerle, Eugene. Building New Wealth by Preserving Old Wealth: Savings and Investment Tax Incentives in the Postwar Era. *Nat. Tax J.,* September 1983, *36* (3), pp. 307–19. **[G: U.S.]**

Stiglitz, Joseph E. A Re-examination of the Modigliani–Miller Theorem. **In** *Archer, S. H. and D'Ambrosia, C. A.,* 1983, *1969,* pp. 428–40.

Stobaugh, Robert B., Jr. How to Analyze Foreign Investment Climates. **In** *Dickson, D. N., ed.,* 1983, pp. 365–80.

Tannenwald, Robert. The Outlook for Business Fixed Investment. *New Eng. Econ. Rev.,* July–August 1983, pp. 31–35. **[G: U.S.]**

Tapon, Francis. CAPM as a Strategic Planning Tool.

Managerial Dec. Econ., September 1983, *4*(3), pp. 181–84.

Tassey, Gregory. Competitive Strategies and Performance in Technology-Based Industries. *J. Econ. Bus.*, 1983, *35*(1), pp. 21–40. [G: U.S.]

Tatom, John A. The Effect of Energy Prices on the Retirement of Capital Equipment: A Comment. *Bus. Econ.*, January 1983, *18*(1), pp. 54–56. [G: U.S.]

Tobin, James. 'Domestic Saving and International Capital Movements in the Long Run and the Short Run' by M. Feldstein: Comment. *Europ. Econ. Rev.*, March/April 1983, *21*(1/2), pp. 153–56. [G: OECD]

Tonks, Ian. Bayesian Learning and the Optimal Investment Decision of the Firm. *Econ. J.*, Supplement March 1983, pp. 87–98.

Trivedi, P. K. Investment—Inflation Linkages in the NIF-10 Model: Discussion. **In** *Pagan, A. R. and Trivedi, P. K., eds.*, 1983, pp. 311–17. [G: Australia]

Trubac, Edward R. Fluctuations in Non-Electrical Machinery "Unfinished Goods" Inventories during Recent Recessions. *Bus. Econ.*, May 1983, *18*(3), pp. 13–21. [G: U.S.]

Ture, Norman B. The Accelerated Cost Recovery System: An Evaluation of the 1981 and 1982 Cost Recovery Provisions. **In** *Walker, C. E. and Bloomfield, M. E., eds.*, 1983, pp. 47–76. [G: U.S.]

Tybout, James R. Credit Rationing and Investment Behavior in a Developing Country. *Rev. Econ. Statist.*, November 1983, *65*(4), pp. 598–607. [G: Colombia]

Valentine, T. J. Investment—Inflation Linkages in the NIF-10 Model: Discussion. **In** *Pagan, A. R. and Trivedi, P. K., eds.*, 1983, pp. 318–20. [G: Australia]

Venezia, Itzhak. A Bayesian Approach to the Optimal Growth Period Problem: A Note. *J. Finance*, March 1983, *38*(1), pp. 237–46.

Viscusi, W. Kip. Frameworks for Analyzing the Effects of Risk and Environmental Regulations on Productivity. *Amer. Econ. Rev.*, September 1983, *73*(4), pp. 793–801.

Vislie, Jon. On the Dynamics of Production under Cost Uncertainty. *Scand. J. Econ.*, 1983, *85*(2), pp. 249–66.

Westphal, Uwe. 'Domestic Saving and International Capital Movements in the Long Run and the Short Run' by M. Feldstein: Comment. *Europ. Econ. Rev.*, March/April 1983, *21*(1/2), pp. 157–59. [G: OECD]

Wetzel, William E., Jr. Angels and Informal Risk Capital. *Sloan Manage. Rev.*, Summer 1983, *24*(4), pp. 23–34. [G: U.S.]

Wetzler, James W. Proposals to Index Capital Gains. **In** *Walker, C. E. and Bloomfield, M. E., eds.*, 1983, pp. 154–57. [G: U.S.]

Wheaton, William C. Interstate Differences in the Level of Business Taxation. *Nat. Tax J.*, March, 1983, *36*(1), pp. 83–94. [G: U.S.]

Wheaton, William C. Interstate Differences in the Level of Business Taxation: A Correction. *Nat. Tax J.*, December 1983, *36*(4), pp. 543. [G: U.S.]

Woodward, John T.; Seskin, Eugene P. and Landefeld, J. Steven. Plant and Equipment Expenditures, 1983. *Surv. Curr. Bus.*, January 1983, *63*(1), pp. 31–33. [G: U.S.]

Xepapadeas, A. and Kanellopoulos, A. The Dynamic Behavior of the Rates of Return in U.K. Manufacturing Industries. *Greek Econ. Rev.*, December 1983, *5*(3), pp. 248–63. [G: U.K.]

Zotov, M. Financial Problems in Managing the Investment Process. *Prob. Econ.*, September 1983, *26*(5), pp. 25–42. [G: U.S.S.R.]

Zschau, Ed. Was the 1978 Capital Gains Tax Cut Successful? **In** *Walker, C. E. and Bloomfield, M. E., eds.*, 1983, pp. 157–59. [G: U.S.]

530 Marketing

531 Marketing and Advertising

5310 Marketing and Advertising

Ahtomies, Matti; Lehtinen, Uolevi and Näsi, Juha. Kokeellinen tutkimos kilpailukeinojen vaikutuksesta vähittäiskaupassa. (An Evaluation of Experimental Research: A Case Study Concerning the Effects of Marketing Mix on Retail Level. With English summary.) *Liiketaloudellinen Aikak.*, 1983, *32*(1), pp. 49–80. [G: Finland]

Alpert, Leon. Estimating a Multi-Attribute Model for Different Music Styles. *J. Cult. Econ.*, June 1983, *7*(1), pp. 63–81. [G: U.S.]

Archibald, Robert B.; Haulman, Clyde A. and Moody, Carlisle E., Jr. Quality, Price, Advertising, and Published Quality Ratings. *J. Cons. Res.*, March 1983, *9*(4), pp. 347–56. [G: U.S.]

Armbruster, Walter J. Advertising Farm Commodities. **In** *Connor, J. M. and Ward, R. W., eds.*, 1983, pp. 165–77. [G: U.S.]

Arndt, Johan. Towards Ecologically Relevant Concepts of Marketing and Productivity. **In** *Uusitalo, L., ed.*, 1983, pp. 88–102.

Arndt, Johan and Simon, Julian L. Advertising and Economies of Scale: Critical Comments on the Evidence. *J. Ind. Econ.*, December 1983, *32*(2), pp. 229–42.

Arrington, Robert L. Advertising and Behavior Control. **In** *Snoeyenbos, M.; Almeder, R. and Humber, J., eds.*, 1983, *1982*, pp. 431–45.

Aspelin, Arnold. Comments [Advertising Farm Commodities] [Florida Department of Citrus Advertising Research Programs]. **In** *Connor, J. M. and Ward, R. W., eds.*, 1983, pp. 199–200. [G: U.S.]

Ayanian, Robert. The Advertising Capital Controversy. *J. Bus.*, July 1983, *56*(3), pp. 349–64. [G: U.S.]

Barnes, David W. The Significance of Quantitative Evidence in Federal Trade Commission Deceptive Advertising Cases. *Law Contemp. Probl.*, Autumn 1983, *46*(4), pp. 25–47. [G: U.S.]

Barnett, Allen M. Solar Energy Commercialization Strategies. **In** *Rich, D., et al., eds.*, 1983, pp. 145–62.

Battaglia, Loretta and Savorgnani, Glauco T. Marketing d'acquisto, perché. (Input Marketing and Why. With English summary.) *L'Impresa*, 1983, *25*(2), pp. 19–24.

Baye, Michael R. Optimal Adjustments to Restrictions on Advertising: Some Further Comments. *J. Ind. Econ.*, December 1983, *32*(2), pp. 249–51.

Berenson, Conrad. The Product Liability Revolution. **In** *Snoeyenbos, M.; Almeder, R. and Humber, J., eds.*, 1983, *1972*, pp. 379–90.

Biehal, Gabriel and Chakravarti, Dipankar. Information Accessibility as a Moderator of Consumer Choice. *J. Cons. Res.*, June 1983, *10*(1), pp. 1–14. **[G: U.S.]**

Bittlingmayer, George. A Model of Vertical Restriction and Equilibrium in Retailing. *J. Bus.*, October 1983, *56*(4), pp. 477–96.

Bob, C. A. A Modality of Approaching Marketing Selective Researches. *Econ. Computat. Cybern. Stud. Res.*, 1983, *18*(2), pp. 41–54. **[G: Romania]**

Bourgo, Donald G. Forecasting Crest Sales [Advertising and Sales Relationships for Toothpaste]. *Bus. Econ.*, January 1983, *18*(1), pp. 48–50. **[G: U.S.]**

Boynton, Robert D.; McCracken, Vicki and Irwin, Scott. Food Advertising as a Source of Consumer Information: A Case Study of Newspaper Advertising and Its Relationship to Public Price Reports. **In** *Connor, J. M. and Ward, R. W., eds.*, 1983, pp. 371–83. **[G: U.S.]**

Boynton, Robert D. and Schwendiman, Larry. Theoretical Approaches to the Economics of Advertising. **In** *Connor, J. M. and Ward, R. W., eds.*, 1983, pp. 11–46.

Brack, John and Cowling, Keith. Advertising and Labour Supply: Workweek and Workyear in U.S. Manufacturing Industries, 1919–76. *Kyklos*, 1983, *36*(2), pp. 285–303. **[G: U.S.]**

Brezzo, Roberto and Perkal, Isaac. The Role of Marketing Incentives in Export Promotion: The Uruguayan Case. **In** *Czinkota, M. R., ed. (I)*, 1983, pp. 51–65. **[G: Uruguay]**

Brinberg, David and Wood, Ronald. A Resource Exchange Theory Analysis of Consumer Behavior. *J. Cons. Res.*, December 1983, *10*(3), pp. 330–38.

Buzzell, Robert D. Can You Standardize Multinational Marketing? **In** *Dickson, D. N., ed.*, 1983, pp. 273–92. **[G: France; Italy; W. Germany; Netherlands]**

Carli, Carlo. La qualità della pubblicità: sua misura e sua efficacia. (Advertising Quality: Its Measure and Effectiveness. With English summary.) *Rivista Int. Sci. Econ. Com.*, September 1983, *30*(9), pp. 886–98. **[G: Italy]**

Clancy, Katherine L. Voluntary Approaches to Increasing Nutrition Information in the Mass Media. **In** *Connor, J. M. and Ward, R. W., eds.*, 1983, pp. 397–402. **[G: U.S.]**

Clarke, R. and Else, P. K. Optimal Adjustments to Restrictions on Advertising: A Comment. *J. Ind. Econ.*, December 1983, *32*(2), pp. 243–48.

Coleman, Richard P. The Continuing Significance of Social Class to Marketing. *J. Cons. Res.*, December 1983, *10*(3), pp. 265–80. **[G: U.S.]**

Comanor, William. Comment [Advertising and Concentration Change in U.S. Food and Tobacco Product Classes, 1958–1972] [The Causes of Concentration in the U.S. Brewing Industry]. **In** *Connor, J. M. and Ward, R. W., eds.*, 1983, pp. 317–19. **[G: U.S.]**

Comanor, William. Commentary [Theoretical Approaches to the Economics of Advertising] [Advertising and Brand Loyalty as Barriers to Entry]. **In** *Connor, J. M. and Ward, R. W., eds.*, 1983, pp. 71–73.

Connor, John M. The Regulation of Advertising. *Agr. Econ. Res.*, January 1983, *35*(1), pp. 35–43.

Connor, John M. and Ward, Ronald W. Advertising and the Food System: Introduction and Overview. **In** *Connor, J. M. and Ward, R. W., eds.*, 1983, pp. 1–10.

Cotterill, Ronald. Changing Structure of Mass Media Markets: Relevance for Policy Initiatives on Advertising in the Food System. **In** *Connor, J. M. and Ward, R. W., eds.*, 1983, pp. 437–59. **[G: U.S.]**

Culbertson, John. The Effect of Advertising on Price Change for Food Manufacturing Product Classes: Comment. **In** *Connor, J. M. and Ward, R. W., eds.*, 1983, pp. 276–78. **[G: U.S.]**

Curry, David J. and Manasco, Michael B. On the Separability of Weights and Brand Values: Issues and Empirical Results. *J. Cons. Res.*, June 1983, *10*(1), pp. 83–95. **[G: U.S.]**

Demirdjian, Z. S. Sales Effectiveness of Comparative Advertising: An Experimental Field Investigation. *J. Cons. Res.*, December 1983, *10*(3), pp. 362–64.

Dorward, Neil; Pokorny, Mike and Bayldon, Ray. The UK Truck Market: An Investigation into Truck Purchasing Behavior and Changing Market Shares. *J. Ind. Econ.*, September 1983, *32*(1), pp. 73–95. **[G: U.K.]**

Douglas, Susan P. and Craig, C. Samuel. Examining Performance of U.S. Multinationals in Foreign Markets. *J. Int. Bus. Stud.*, Winter 1983, *14*(3), pp. 51–62. **[G: U.S.]**

Edell, Julie E. and Staelin, Richard. The Information Processing of Pictures in Print Advertisements. *J. Cons. Res.*, June 1983, *10*(1), pp. 45–61. **[G: U.S.]**

Elliott, J. Walter. Advertising and R&D Investments in the Wealth–Maximizing Firm. *J. Econ. Bus.*, August 1983, *35*(3/4), pp. 389–97.

Folsom, Roger Nils and Greer, Douglas F. Advertising and Brand Loyalty as Barriers to Entry. **In** *Connor, J. M. and Ward, R. W., eds.*, 1983, pp. 47–70.

Ford, David and Djeflat, Kader. Export Marketing of Industrial Products: Buyer–Seller Relationships between Developed and Developing Countries. **In** *Czinkota, M. R., ed. (I)*, 1983, pp. 262–82. **[G: Algeria; France; U.K.; U.S.]**

Fournier, Gary M. and Martin, Donald L. Does Government-restricted Entry Produce Market Power? New Evidence from the Market for Television Advertising. *Bell J. Econ. (See Rand J. Econ. after 4/85)*, Spring 1983, *14*(1), pp. 44–56. **[G: U.S.]**

Fraser, Cynthia and Bradford, John W. Competitive Market Structure Analysis: Principal Partitioning of Revealed Substitutabilities. *J. Cons. Res.*, June 1983, *10*(1), pp. 15–30. **[G: U.S.]**

Friedman, James W. Advertising and Oligopolistic Equilibrium. *Bell J. Econ. (See Rand J. Econ. after*

4/85), Autumn 1983, *14*(2), pp. 464–73.

Galbraith, John Kenneth. The Dependence Effect. In *Snoeyenbos, M.; Almeder, R. and Humber, J., eds.*, 1983, *1958*, pp. 425–30.

Gardner, Meryl Paula. Advertising Effects on Attributes Recalled and Criteria Used for Brand Evaluations. *J. Cons. Res.*, December 1983, *10*(3), pp. 310–18.

Gestetner, David. Strategy in Managing International Sales. In *Dickson, D. N., ed.*, 1983, pp. 293–300.

Graham, John L. Brazilian, Japanese, and American Business Negotiations. *J. Int. Bus. Stud.*, Spring/Summer 1983, *14*(1), pp. 47–61. **[G: Japan; Brazil; U.S.]**

Grant, Robert M. Transaction Costs to Retailers of Different Methods of Payment: Results of a Pilot Study. *Managerial Dec. Econ.*, June 1983, *4*(2), pp. 89–96. **[G: U.K.]**

Greer, Douglas F. The Causes of Concentration in the U.S. Brewing Industry. In *Connor, J. M. and Ward, R. W., eds.*, 1983, pp. 295–314. **[G: U.S.]**

Grevers, Lawrence H. and Ronkainen, Ilkka A. Marketing-Crisis Management: Coping with Disaster. *Liiketaloudellinen Aikak.*, 1983, *32*(3), pp. 242–50. **[G: U.S.]**

Griffith, Robert. The Selling of America: The Advertising Council and American Politics, 1942–1960. *Bus. Hist. Rev.*, Autumn 1983, *57*(3), pp. 388–412. **[G: U.S.]**

Hallagan, William and Joerding, Wayne. Polymorphic Equilibrium in Advertising. *Bell J. Econ. (See Rand J. Econ. after 4/85)*, Spring 1983, *14*(1), pp. 191–201.

Hamm, Larry G. The Interactions of Food Manufacturer Advertising and Food Retailer Buying Practices: Some Implications for Food System Organizations. In *Connor, J. M. and Ward, R. W., eds.*, 1983, pp. 215–33. **[G: U.S.]**

Hashimoto, Isao. Selling Process and Marketing Process. *Kyoto Univ. Econ. Rev.*, April–October 1983, *53*(1–2), pp. 1–15.

Hayes, Robert H. and Wheelwright, Steven C. Link Manufacturing Process and Product Life Cycles. In *Kantrow, A. M., ed.*, 1983, pp. 132–43. **[G: U.S.]**

Hayes, Robert H. and Wheelwright, Steven C. The Dynamics of Process–Product Life Cycles. In *Kantrow, A. M., ed.*, 1983, pp. 144–58. **[G: U.S.]**

Hisrich, Robert D. Executive Advertisers' Views of Comparison Advertising. *Sloan Manage. Rev.*, Fall 1983, *25*(1), pp. 39–50. **[G: U.S.]**

Hoffman, Oscar. The Interactions of Food Manufacturer Advertising and Food Retailer Buying Practices: Some Implications for Food System Organizations: Commentary. In *Connor, J. M. and Ward, R. W., eds.*, 1983, pp. 235–36. **[G: U.S.]**

Kawashima, Yasuo. Product Differentiation, Prices, and Market Structure. *Europ. Econ. Rev.*, June 1983, *22*(1), pp. 75–96.

Kelton, Christina M. L. The Effect of Advertising on Price Change for Food Manufacturing Product Classes. In *Connor, J. M. and Ward, R. W., eds.*, 1983, pp. 257–73. **[G: U.S.]**

Killough, James. Improved Payoffs from Transnational Advertising. In *Dickson, D. N., ed.*, 1983, pp. 343–57.

Kirkpatrick, Jerry. Theory and History in Marketing. *Managerial Dec. Econ.*, March 1983, *4*(1), pp. 44–49.

Kothari, Vinay. Researching for Export Marketing. In *Czinkota, M. R., ed. (I)*, 1983, pp. 154–76. **[G: U.S.]**

Laitinen, Erkki K. A Life-Cycle Approach to Retail Pricing. *Liiketaloudellinen Aikak.*, 1983, *32*(3), pp. 251–60. **[G: Finland]**

Lambin, J. J. La gestion marketing dans un développement turbulent et hautement concurrentiel. (The New Marketing Priorities in the Present Economic Environment. With English summary.) *Ann. Sci. Écon. Appl.*, 1983, *39*(2), pp. 81–94.

Lamm, R. McFall, Jr. Commentary [Advertising and Concentration Change in U.S. Food and Tobacco Product Classes, 1958–1972] [The Causes of Concentration in the U.S. Brewing Industry]. In *Connor, J. M. and Ward, R. W., eds.*, 1983, pp. 315–17. **[G: U.S.]**

Lee, Jonq-Ying. Florida Department of Citrus Advertising Research Programs. In *Connor, J. M. and Ward, R. W., eds.*, 1983, pp. 179–96. **[G: U.S.]**

Lehtinen, Jarmo R. and Lehtinen, Uolevi. Development of Services Research. *Liiketaloudellinen Aikak.*, 1983, *32*(3), pp. 261–66.

Lesser, William H. Information in Food Advertising: Comment. In *Connor, J. M. and Ward, R. W., eds.*, 1983, pp. 387–92. **[G: U.S.]**

Lindqvist, Lars-Johan. Dagligvarumnarknaden i Finland: Koncentrationen sedd ur konsumenternas, detaljisternas och samhällets synvinkel. (The Market for Convenience Goods in Finland. Concentration from the Point of View of Consumers, Retailers and Society. With English summary.) *Ekon. Samfundets Tidskr.*, 1983, *36*(4), pp. 157–61. **[G: Finland]**

MacDonald, James M.; Scheffman, David T. and Whitten, Ira Taylor. Advertising and Quality in Food Products: Some New Evidence on the Nelson Hypothesis. In *Connor, J. M. and Ward, R. W., eds.*, 1983, pp. 137–47. **[G: U.S.]**

Manchester, Alden C. The Role and Dimensions of Food Advertising for 100 Years. In *Connor, J. M. and Ward, R. W., eds.*, 1983, pp. 105–30. **[G: U.S.]**

Mann, Michael. Advertising and Quality in Food Products: Some New Evidence on the Nelson Hypothesis: Commentary. In *Connor, J. M. and Ward, R. W., eds.*, 1983, pp. 159–60. **[G: U.S.]**

Mann, Michael. The Competitive Impact of Advertising in U.S. Food Processing Industries: A Simultaneous Equation Approach: Commentary. In *Connor, J. M. and Ward, R. W., eds.*, 1983, pp. 275–76. **[G: U.S.]**

Marion, Bruce W. Information in Food Advertising: Commentary. In *Connor, J. M. and Ward, R. W., eds.*, 1983, pp. 385–87.

Mather, Loys L. and Tucker, Laurel I. Conglomerate Mergers, Food Advertising, and the Cross Subsidization Hypothesis. In *Connor, J. M. and Ward, R. W., eds.*, 1983, pp. 201–13. **[G: U.S.]**

Mathewson, G. Frank and Winter, Ralph A. Vertical

Integration by Contractual Restraints in Spatial Markets. *J. Bus.*, October 1983, *56*(4), pp. 497–517.

Metzger, Margaret Ann. Televised Food Advertising Directed to Children: The Constitutionality of Restrictions. **In** *Connor, J. M. and Ward, R. W., eds.*, 1983, pp. 423–36. **[G: U.S.]**

Mihăiţă, N. V. Onicescu Informational Statistics in a Multiple Marketing Data Processing Methodology. *Econ. Computat. Cybern. Stud. Res.*, 1983, *18*(2), pp. 29–39.

Moore, Beverly C., Jr. Product Safety: Who Should Absorb the Cost? **In** *Snoeyenbos, M.; Almeder, R. and Humber, J., eds.*, 1983, *1972*, pp. 391–95.

Muller, Eitan. Trial/Awareness Advertising Decisions: A Control Problem with Phase Diagrams with Non-Stationary Boundaries. *J. Econ. Dynam. Control*, December 1983, *6*(4), pp. 333–50.

Nelson, Phillip. Advertising and Ethics. **In** *Snoeyenbos, M.; Almeder, R. and Humber, J., eds.*, 1983, *1978*, pp. 410–20.

Netter, Jeffry M. Political Competition and Advertising as a Barrier to Entry. *Southern Econ. J.*, October 1983, *50*(2), pp. 510–20. **[G: U.S.]**

Pagoulatos, Emilio and Sorensen, Robert. The Competitive Impact of Advertising in U.S. Food Processing Industries: A Simultaneous Equation Approach. **In** *Connor, J. M. and Ward, R. W., eds.*, 1983, pp. 241–56. **[G: U.S.]**

Parker, Russell. Commentary [Food Advertising, 1954 to 1979] [The Role and Dimensions of Food Advertising for 100 Years]. **In** *Connor, J. M. and Ward, R. W., eds.*, 1983, pp. 131–33. **[G: U.S.]**

Parker, Russell. Comments [Conglomerate Mergers, Food Advertising, and the Cross Subsidization Hypothesis] [The Interactions of Food Manufacturer Advertising and Food Retailer Buying Practices: Some Implications for Food System Organizations]. **In** *Connor, J. M. and Ward, R. W., eds.*, 1983, pp. 236–37. **[G: U.S.]**

Peterson, Rodney D. and Soma, John T. Advertising, Imperfect Competition, and the Market for Legal Services. *J. Behav. Econ.*, Winter 1983, *12*(2), pp. 57–66. **[G: U.S.]**

Petty, Richard E.; Cacioppo, John T. and Schumann, David. Central and Peripheral Routes to Advertising Effectiveness: The Moderating Role of Involvement. *J. Cons. Res.*, September 1983, *10*(2), pp. 135–46. **[G: U.S.]**

Punj, Girish N. and Stewart, David W. An Interaction Framework of Consumer Decision Making. *J. Cons. Res.*, September 1983, *10*(2), pp. 181–96.

Reid, Stanley. Export Research in a Crisis. **In** *Czinkota, M. R., ed. (I)*, 1983, pp. 129–53.

Rogers, Richard T. Advertising and Concentration Change in U.S. Food and Tobacco Product Classes, 1958–1972. **In** *Connor, J. M. and Ward, R. W., eds.*, 1983, pp. 283–94. **[G: U.S.]**

Rogers, Richard T. and Mather, Loys L. Food Advertising, 1954 to 1979. **In** *Connor, J. M. and Ward, R. W., eds.*, 1983, pp. 75–103. **[G: U.S.]**

Rogerson, William P. Reputation and Product Quality. *Bell J. Econ. (See Rand J. Econ. after 4/85)*, Autumn 1983, *14*(2), pp. 508–16.

Round, David K. Advertising and Profitability in Australian Manufacturing. *Australian Econ. Pap.*, December 1983, *22*(41), pp. 345–55. **[G: Australia]**

Rudd, Joel and Kohout, Frank J. Individual and Group Consumer Information Acquisition in Brand Choice Situations. *J. Cons. Res.*, December 1983, *10*(3), pp. 303–09.

Sandy, Robert. Low Price Claims and Market Penetration in the Grocery Industry: The Case of the Kroger Price Patrol. **In** *Connor, J. M. and Ward, R. W., eds.*, 1983, pp. 363–70. **[G: U.S.]**

Schmalensee, Richard. Advertising and Entry Deterrence: An Exploratory Model. *J. Polit. Econ.*, August 1983, *91*(4), pp. 636–53.

Schmalensee, Richard; Silk, Alvin J. and Bojanek, Robert. The Impact of Scale and Media Mix on Advertising Agency Costs. *J. Bus.*, October 1983, *56*(4), pp. 453–75. **[G: U.S.]**

Schmittlein, David C. and Morrison, Donald G. Measuring Miscomprehension for Televised Communications Using True–False Questions. *J. Cons. Res.*, September 1983, *10*(2), pp. 147–56. **[G: U.S.]**

Sekulović, Slobodan. Segmentiranje tržišta lične potrošnje funkcijom jakosti preferiranja jedne marke nad drugom. (Segmentation of the Market of Consumer Goods by the Function of the Strength of Preferences for One Brand over the Other. With English summary.) *Econ. Anal. Worker's Manage.*, 1983, *17*(4), pp. 383–402.

Shapiro, Benson P. Can Marketing and Manufacturing Coexist? **In** *Kantrow, A. M., ed.*, 1983, pp. 215–30.

Sorenson, Ralph Z. and Wiechmann, Ulrich E. How Multinationals View Marketing Standardization. **In** *Dickson, D. N., ed.*, 1983, pp. 301–16.

Soutar, Geoffrey N. and Clarke, Yvonne M. Life Style and Radio Listening Patterns in Perth, Western Australia. *Australian J. Manage.*, June 1983, *8*(1), pp. 71–81. **[G: Australia]**

Stanton, Tom. Commentary [Televised Food Advertising Directed to Children: The Constitutionality of Restrictions] [Changing Structure of Mass Media Markets: Relevance for Policy Initiatives on Advertising in the Food System]. **In** *Connor, J. M. and Ward, R. W., eds.*, 1983, pp. 461–64. **[G: U.S.]**

Stecco, Maurizio. Come entrare nel mercato nordamericano. (How to Enter the North-American Market. With English summary.) *L'Impresa*, 1983, *25*(1), pp. 63–68. **[G: France; U.S.; Canada]**

Talamona, Mario. In tema di esperienze e prospettive del "marketing" bancario: Uno strumento per migliorare l'efficienza produttiva e allocativa del sistema creditizio. (Experience and Prospects of Marketing in Banking: A Tool for Improving Productivity and Efficiency of Resources-Allocation in the Banking System. With English summary.) *Bancaria*, April 1983, *39*(4), pp. 371–76. **[G: Italy]**

Terpstra, Vern. Suggestions for Research Themes and Publications: International Marketing. *J. Int. Bus. Stud.*, Spring/Summer 1983, *14*(1), pp. 9–10.

Thépot, Jacques. Marketing and Investment Policies

of Duopolists in a Growing Industry. *J. Econ. Dynam. Control,* July 1983, *5*(4), pp. 387–404.

Thompson, Stanley R. Commentary [Advertising Farm Commodities] [Florida Department of Citrus Advertising Research Programs]. **In** *Connor, J. M. and Ward, R. W., eds.,* 1983, pp. 197–99. [G: U.S.]

Uhl, Joseph N. Advertising Effects on Food Purchasing Behavior: Comment. **In** *Connor, J. M. and Ward, R. W., eds.,* 1983, pp. 160–61.

Weiss, Leonard W.; Pascoe, George and Martin, Stephen. The Size of Selling Costs. *Rev. Econ. Statist.,* November 1983, *65*(4), pp. 668–72. [G: U.S.]

Westgren, Randall E. Advertising Effects on Food Purchasing Behavior. **In** *Connor, J. M. and Ward, R. W., eds.,* 1983, pp. 149–58.

Wiechmann, Ulrich E. and Pringle, Lewis G. Problems That Plague Multinational Marketers. **In** *Dickson, D. N., ed.,* 1983, pp. 317–30.

Wiggins, Steven N. and Lane, W. J. Quality Uncertainty, Search, and Advertising. *Amer. Econ. Rev.,* December 1983, *73*(5), pp. 881–94.

Wildt, Albert R. and Winer, Russell S. Modeling and Estimation in Changing Market Environments. *J. Bus.,* July 1983, *56*(3), pp. 365–88.

Wright, Peter. Systematic Approach to Finding Export Opportunities. **In** *Dickson, D. N., ed.,* 1983, pp. 331–42.

Zou, Siyi. The Problem of Export Strategy. *Chinese Econ. Stud.,* Spring 1983, *16*(3), pp. 10–23. [G: China]

540 ACCOUNTING

541 Accounting

5410 Accounting

Abdel-khalik, A. Rashad. Overfitting Bias in the Models Assessing the Predictive Power of Quarterly Reports [Expectations Data and the Predictive Value of Interim Reports]. *J. Acc. Res.,* Spring 1983, *21*(1), pp. 293–96. [G: U.S.]

Abdel-khalik, A. Rashad; Snowball, Doug and Wragge, John H. The Effects of Certain Internal Audit Variables on the Planning of External Audit Programs. *Accounting Rev.,* April 1983, *58*(2), pp. 215–27.

Aharoni, Yair. Comprehensive Audit of Management Performance in U.S. State Owned Enterprises. *Ann. Pub. Co-op. Econ.,* March 1983, *54*(1), pp. 73–92. [G: U.S.]

Aho, Teemu and Virtanen, Ilkka. JHH-poistojen ja EVL-poistojen välisistä suhteista. (Analysing Relationships between Straight Line Depreciations and Declining Balance Depreciations under Inflation. With English summary.) *Liiketaloudellinen Aikak.,* 1983, *32*(3), pp. 286–303.

d'Almeida, Raphael Bernardo, Jr. New Brazilian Accounting Principles and Practices. **In** *de Ulhôa Canto, G.; da Silva Martins, I. G. and van Hoorn, J., Jr., eds.,* 1983, pp. 17–31. [G: Brazil]

Anderson, James A. and St. Pierre, Kent E. Market Efficiency and Legal Liability: A Reply [The Potential Impact of Knowledge of Market Efficiency on the Legal Liability of Auditors]. *Accounting Rev.,* October 1983, *58*(4), pp. 833–36. [G: U.S.]

Ang, James S.; Chua, Jess H. and Fatemi, Ali M. A Comparison of Econometric, Times Series, and Composite Forecasting Methods in Predicting Accounting Variables. *J. Econ. Bus.,* August 1983, *35*(3/4), pp. 301–11. [G: U.S.]

Artto, Eero. Kansainvälinen kilpailukyky yritys- ja toimialatasolla—II. (International Competitiveness at Enterprise and Industry Level—II. With English summary.) *Liiketaloudellinen Aikak.,* 1983, *32*(4), pp. 358–88.

Auerbach, Alan J. Does ACRS Foster Efficient Capital Allocation? **In** *Walker, C. E. and Bloomfield, M. E., eds.,* 1983, pp. 77–78. [G: U.S.]

Baber, William R. Toward Understanding the Role of Auditing in the Public Sector. *J. Acc. Econ.,* December 1983, *5*(3), pp. 213–27. [G: U.S.]

Bailey, K. E., III; Bylinski, Joseph H. and Shields, Michael D. Effects of Audit Report Wording Changes on the Perceived Message. *J. Acc. Res.,* Autumn 1983, *21*(2), pp. 355–70. [G: U.S.]

Baiman, Stanley and Evans, John H., III. Pre-Decision Information and Participative Management Control Systems. *J. Acc. Res.,* Autumn 1983, *21*(2), pp. 371–95.

Bamber, E. Michael. Expert Judgment in the Audit Team: A Source Reliability Approach. *J. Acc. Res.,* Autumn 1983, *21*(2), pp. 396–412. [G: U.S.]

Barlev, Benzion. Contingent Equity and the Dilutive Effect on EPS. *Accounting Rev.,* April 1983, *58*(2), pp. 385–93.

Bell, Timothy Barnes. Market Reaction to Reserve Recognition Accounting. *J. Acc. Res.,* Spring 1983, *21*(1), pp. 1–17. [G: U.S.]

Biggs, Stanley F. and Mock, Theodore J. An Investigation of Auditor Decision Processes in the Evaluation of Internal Controls and Audit Scope Decisions. *J. Acc. Res.,* Spring 1983, *21*(1), pp. 234–55. [G: U.S.]

Boidman, Nathan. Tax Evasion: The Present State of Non-Compliance. *Bull. Int. Fiscal Doc.,* Sept.–Oct. 1983, *37*(9–10), pp. 451–79. [G: Selected Countries]

Brown, Clifton. Effects of Dynamic Task Environment on the Learning of Standard Cost Variance Significance. *J. Acc. Res.,* Autumn 1983, *21*(2), pp. 413–31. [G: U.S.]

Brown, Lawrence D. Accounting Changes and the Accuracy of Analysts' Earnings Forecasts. *J. Acc. Res.,* Autumn 1983, *21*(2), pp. 432–43. [G: U.S.]

Brown, Paul R. Independent Auditor Judgment in the Evaluation of Internal Audit Functions. *J. Acc. Res.,* Autumn 1983, *21*(2), pp. 444–55. [G: U.S.]

Brownell, Peter. The Motivational Impact of Management-by-Exception in a Budgetary Context. *J. Acc. Res.,* Autumn 1983, *21*(2), pp. 456–72. [G: U.S.]

Casey, Cornelius J. Prior Probability Disclosure and Loan Officers' Judgments: Some Evidence of the Impact. *J. Acc. Res.,* Spring 1983, *21*(1), pp. 300–307.

Chang, Lucia S.; Most, Kenneth S. and Brain, Carlos W. The Utility of Annual Reports: An International Study. *J. Int. Bus. Stud.,* Spring/Summer 1983, *14*(1), pp. 63–84. [G: New Zealand; U.S.; U.K.]

Chen, Joyce T. Cost Allocation and External Acquisition of Services When Self-services Exist. *Accounting Rev.*, July 1983, *58*(3), pp. 600–605.

Chen, Joyce T. The Effect of Chance Variation on Revenue and Cost Estimations for Breakeven Analysis: A Comment. *Accounting Rev.*, October 1983, *58*(4), pp. 813–19.

Choi, Frederick D. S., et al. Analyzing Foreign Financial Statements: The Use and Misuse of International Ratio Analysis. *J. Int. Bus. Stud.*, Spring/Summer 1983, *14*(1), pp. 113–31. **[G: Japan; Korea]**

Chow, Chee W. The Effects of Job Standard Tightness and Compensation Scheme on Performance: An Exploration of Linkages. *Accounting Rev.*, October 1983, *58*(4), pp. 667–85.

Chow, Chee W. The Impacts of Accounting Regulation on Bondholder and Shareholder Wealth: The Case of the Securities Acts. *Accounting Rev.*, July 1983, *58*(3), pp. 485–520. **[G: U.S.]**

Christenson, Charles. The Methodology of Positive Accounting. *Accounting Rev.*, January 1983, *58*(1), pp. 1–22.

Daley, Lane A. and Vigeland, Robert L. The Effects of Debt Covenants and Political Costs on the Choice of Accounting Methods: The Case of Accounting for R&D Costs. *J. Acc. Econ.*, December 1983, *5*(3), pp. 195–211. **[G: U.S.]**

Danos, Paul and Imhoff, Eugene A., Jr. Factors Affecting Auditors' Evaluation of Forecasts. *J. Acc. Res.*, Autumn 1983, *21*(2), pp. 473–94. **[G: U.S.]**

De Luca, Amedeo. Una metodologia di calcolo dei rapporti di partecipazione indiretta nei raggruppamenti societari. (A Methodology for Calculation of the Weight of Indirect Holdings in Corporate Groups. With English summary.) *Bancaria*, January 1983, *39*(1), pp. 53–59.

Demski, Joel S. Comments on Wilson and Jensen [Auditing: Perspectives from Multi-person Decision Theory] [Organization Theory and Methodology]. *Accounting Rev.*, April 1983, *58*(2), pp. 347–49.

Dharan, Bala G. Empirical Identification Procedures for Earnings Models. *J. Acc. Res.*, Spring 1983, *21*(1), pp. 256–70. **[G: U.S.]**

Dharan, Bala G. Identification and Estimation Issues for a Causal Earnings Model. *J. Acc. Res.*, Spring 1983, *21*(1), pp. 18–41.

DiBlasi, Paolo. Prifili giuridici delle tecniche di valutazione dei crediti nei bilanci bancari. (Legal Aspects of Loans Valuation in the Banks' Balance-Sheets. With English summary.) *Bancaria*, April 1983, *39*(4), pp. 402–09. **[G: Italy]**

Dickhaut, John W. and Lere, John C. Comparison of Accounting Systems and Heuristics in Selecting Economic Optima. *J. Acc. Res.*, Autumn 1983, *21*(2), pp. 495–513.

Dillard, Jessee F. and Jensen, Daniel L. The Auditor's Report: An Analysis of Opinion. *Accounting Rev.*, October 1983, *58*(4), pp. 787–98. **[G: U.S.]**

Dilley, Steven C.; Hayes, Randall B. and Steinbart, Paul. Development of a Paradigm for Applied Accounting Research: A Way of Coping with Subject-Matter Complexity. *Accounting Rev.*, April 1983, *58*(2), pp. 405–16.

Donna, Giorgio and Zamprogna, Luciana. Sistemi di controllo direzionale e dinamismo ambientale. (Management and Control Systems and Company Dynamism. With English summary.) *L'Impresa*, 1983, *25*(5), pp. 13–26.

Earl, Michael J. Accounting and Management. **In** *Earl, M. J., ed.*, 1983, pp. 99–142.

Evans, John H., III and Patton, James M. An Economic Analysis of Participation in the Municipal Finance Officers Association Certificate of Conformance Program. *J. Acc. Econ.*, August 1983, *5*(2), pp. 151–75. **[G: U.S.]**

Fabozzi, Frank J. and Fonfeder, Robert. Have You Seen Any Good Quarterly Statements Lately? *J. Portfol. Manage.*, Winter 1983, *9*(2), pp. 71–74. **[G: U.S.]**

Filios, Vassilios P. Accounting Standards for Corporate Social Performance. *Rivista Int. Sci. Econ. Com.*, December 1983, *30*(12), pp. 1187–95.

Fisher, Franklin M. and McGowan, John J. On the Misuse of Accounting Rates of Return to Infer Monopoly Profits. *Amer. Econ. Rev.*, March 1983, *73*(1), pp. 82–97.

Frecka, Thomas J. and Hopwood, William S. The Effects of Outliers on the Cross-sectional Distributional Properties of Financial Ratios. *Accounting Rev.*, January 1983, *58*(1), pp. 115–28. **[G: U.S.]**

Frecka, Thomas J. and Lee, Cheng Few. A Seemingly Unrelated Regressions Approach to Analyzing and Forecasting Financial Ratios. *J. Econ. Bus.*, August 1983, *35*(3/4), pp. 379–88. **[G: U.S.]**

Frecka, Thomas J. and Lee, Cheng Few. Generalized Financial Ratio Adjustment Processes and Their Implications. *J. Acc. Res.*, Spring 1983, *21*(1), pp. 308–16.

Freeman, Robert N. Alternative Measures of Profit Margin: An Empirical Study of the Potential Information Content of Current Cost Accounting. *J. Acc. Res.*, Spring 1983, *21*(1), pp. 42–64. **[G: U.S.]**

Gernon, Helen. The Effect of Translation on Multinational Corporations' Internal Performance Evaluation. *J. Int. Bus. Stud.*, Spring/Summer 1983, *14*(1), pp. 103–12. **[G: U.S.]**

Gombola, Michael J. and Ketz, J. Edward. A Note on Cash Flow and Classification Patterns of Financial Ratios. *Accounting Rev.*, January 1983, *58*(1), pp. 105–14.

Goodman, Laurie S. and Langer, Martha J. Accounting for Interest Rate Futures in Bank Asset–Liability Management. *J. Futures Markets*, Winter 1983, *3*(4), pp. 415–27. **[G: U.S.]**

Gordon, Lawrence A. and Hamer, Michelle. GASB's Survival Potential: An Agency Theory Perspective. *Public Budg. Finance*, Spring 1983, *3*(1), pp. 103–12. **[G: U.S.]**

Grua, Claudio and Varetto, Franco. Un'analisi "reale" della crisi della grande industria negli anni '70. (Profits and Cash Flows in Big Business during the Seventies. With English summary.) *L'Impresa*, 1983, *25*(5), pp. 43–51. **[G: Italy]**

Hakansson, Nils H. Accounting and Economics: Comment. *Accounting Rev.*, April 1983, *58*(2), pp. 381–84.

Harrington, David H. Costs and Returns: Economic and Accounting Concepts. *Agr. Econ. Res.*, October 1983, *35*(4), pp. 1–8.

Harrison, Walter T., Jr.; Tomassini, Lawrence A. and Dietrich, J. Richard. The Use of Control Groups in Capital Market Research. *J. Acc. Res.*, Spring 1983, *21*(1), pp. 65–77. [G: U.S.]

Hatsopoulos, George N. The Effects of ERTA and TEFRA on the Cost of Capital. **In** *Walker, C. E. and Bloomfield, M. E., eds.*, 1983, pp. 79–88. [G: U.S.]

Hickman, Frederic W. Changes in Capital Cost Recovery Policies: Costs and Benefits. **In** *Walker, C. E. and Bloomfield, M. E., eds.*, 1983, pp. 89–91. [G: U.S.]

Hicks, John. The Concept of Business Income. **In** *Hicks, J.*, 1983, *1979*, pp. 189–203.

Hirst, Mark K. Reliance on Accounting Performance Measures, Task Uncertainty, and Dysfunctional Behavior: Some Extensions. *J. Acc. Res.*, Autumn 1983, *21*(2), pp. 596–605. [G: U.S.]

Hoffman, George and Gustafson, Cole. A New Approach to Estimating Agricultural Costs of Production. *Agr. Econ. Res.*, October 1983, *35*(4), pp. 9–14. [G: U.S.]

Holthausen, Robert W. and Leftwich, Richard W. The Economic Consequences of Accounting Choice: Implications of Costly Contracting and Monitoring. *J. Acc. Econ.*, August 1983, *5*(2), pp. 77–117.

Hoskin, Robert E. Opportunity Cost and Behavior. *J. Acc. Res.*, Spring 1983, *21*(1), pp. 78–95. [G: U.S.]

Howard, Thomas P. and Nikolai, Loren A. Attitude Measurement and Perceptions of Accounting Faculty Publication Outlets. *Accounting Rev.*, October 1983, *58*(4), pp. 765–76. [G: U.S.]

Ijiri, Yuji. Foreign Currency Accounting and Its Transition. **In** *Herring, R. J., ed.*, 1983, pp. 181–212. [G: U.S.]

Jain, Prem C. The Impact of Accounting Regulation on the Stock Market: The Case of Oil and Gas Companies—Some Additional Results. *Accounting Rev.*, July 1983, *58*(3), pp. 633–38. [G: U.S.]

Jensen, Michael C. Organization Theory and Methodology. *Accounting Rev.*, April 1983, *58*(2), pp. 319–39.

Johnson, W. Bruce. "Representativeness" in Judgmental Predictions of Corporate Bankruptcy. *Accounting Rev.*, January 1983, *58*(1), pp. 78–97. [G: U.S.]

Kaplan, Robert S. Comments on Wilson and Jensen [Auditing: Perspectives from Multi-person Decision Theory] [Organization Theory and Methodology]. *Accounting Rev.*, April 1983, *58*(2), pp. 340–46.

Kaplan, Robert S. Measuring Manufacturing Performance: A New Challenge for Managerial Accounting Research. *Accounting Rev.*, October 1983, *58*(4), pp. 686–705. [G: U.S.; Japan]

Kellens, Jean-Pierre. The Consequences of a Real Life Approach to Business Accounting. *Cah. Écon. Bruxelles,* Third Trimestre 1983, (99), pp. 417–58.

Larcker, David F. and Lessig, V. Parker. An Examination of the Linear and Retrospective Process Tracing Approaches to Judgment Modeling. *Accounting Rev.*, January 1983, *58*(1), pp. 58–77.

Larcker, David F.; Reder, Renee E. and Simon, Daniel T. Trades by Insiders and Mandated Accounting Standards. *Accounting Rev.*, July 1983, *58*(3), pp. 606–20. [G: U.S.]

Larcker, David F. and Revsine, Lawrence. The Oil and Gas Accounting Controversy: An Analysis of Economic Consequences. *Accounting Rev.*, October 1983, *58*(4), pp. 706–32. [G: U.S.]

Largay, James A., III and Paul, Jack W. Market Efficiency and the Legal Liability of Auditors: Comment. *Accounting Rev.*, October 1983, *58*(4), pp. 820–32. [G: U.S.]

Lawrence, Edward C. Reporting Delays for Failed Firms [Financial Ratios and the Probabilistic Prediction of Bankruptcy]. *J. Acc. Res.*, Autumn 1983, *21*(2), pp. 606–10. [G: U.S.]

Lee, Cheng Few and Junkus, Joan C. Financial Analysis and Planning: An Overview. *J. Econ. Bus.*, August 1983, *35*(3/4), pp. 259–83.

Leftwich, Richard W. Accounting Information in Private Markets: Evidence from Private Lending Agreements. *Accounting Rev.*, January 1983, *58*(1), pp. 23–42. [G: U.S.]

Lev, Baruch. Some Economic Determinants of Time-Series Properties of Earnings. *J. Acc. Econ.*, April 1983, *5*(1), pp. 31–48. [G: U.S.]

Lewis, Barry; Shields, Michael D. and Young, S. Mark. Evaluating Human Judgments and Decision Aids. *J. Acc. Res.*, Spring 1983, *21*(1), pp. 271–85.

Lorek, Kenneth S.; Icerman, Joe D. and Abdulkader, Abdullah A. Further Descriptive and Predictive Evidence on Alternative Time-Series Models for Quarterly Earnings. *J. Acc. Res.*, Spring 1983, *21*(1), pp. 317–28. [G: U.S.]

Lowenthal, Franklin. Product Warranty Period: A Markovian Approach to Estimation and Analysis of Repair and Replacement Costs—A Comment. *Accounting Rev.*, October 1983, *58*(4), pp. 837–38.

Lusa, Erna. Inflazione e bilanci delle imprese. (Inflation and Businesses' Financial Statement. With English summary.) *Bancaria,* October 1983, *39*(10), pp. 968–85. [G: Italy]

Maher, Michael W. and Nantell, Timothy J. The Tax Effects of Inflation: Depreciation, Debt, and Miller's Equilibrium Tax Rates. *J. Acc. Res.*, Spring 1983, *21*(1), pp. 329–40.

Manes, Rene P. Demand Elasticities: Supplements to Sales Budget Variance Reports. *Accounting Rev.*, January 1983, *58*(1), pp. 143–56.

McNichols, Maureen and Manegold, James G. The Effect of the Information Environment on the Relationship between Financial Disclosure and Security Price Variability. *J. Acc. Econ.*, April 1983, *5*(1), pp. 49–74. [G: U.S.]

Mensah, Yaw M. The Differential Bankruptcy Predictive Ability of Specific Price Level Adjustments: Some Empirical Evidence. *Accounting Rev.*, April 1983, *58*(2), pp. 228–46. [G: U.S.]

Menzefricke, Ulrich. On Sampling Plan Selection with Dollar-Unit Sampling. *J. Acc. Res.*, Spring

1983, *21*(1), pp. 96–105.

Mepham, Michael J. Robert Hamilton's Contribution to Accounting. *Accounting Rev.*, January 1983, *58*(1), pp. 43–57.

Merrilees, William J. Anatomy of a Price Leadership Challenge: An Evaluation of Pricing Strategies in the Australian Newspaper Industry. *J. Ind. Econ.*, March 1983, *31*(3), pp. 291–311. **[G: Australia]**

Messier, William F., Jr. The Effect of Experience and Firm Type on Materiality/Disclosure Judgments. *J. Acc. Res.*, Autumn 1983, *21*(2), pp. 611–18. **[G: U.S.]**

Morse, Dale and Richardson, Gordon. The LIFO/FIFO Decision. *J. Acc. Res.*, Spring 1983, *21*(1), pp. 106–27. **[G: U.S.]**

Murray, Dennis. The Effect of Certain Research Design Choices on the Assessment of the Market's Reaction to LIFO Changes: A Methodological Study. *J. Acc. Res.*, Spring 1983, *21*(1), pp. 128–40. **[G: U.S.]**

Mushkat, Miron. The Societal Accounting Movement: A Critical Appraisal. *METU*, 1983, *10*(2), pp. 199–216.

Nakamura, Nobuichiro. Determination of Business Income and Business Entity Concept. *Osaka Econ. Pap.*, September 1983, *33*(1–2), pp. 19–29.

Nakano, Isao. An Interpretation of Conventional Accounting Income Information. *Kobe Econ. Bus. Rev.*, 1983, (29), pp. 1–8.

Nichols, Donald R. and Smith, David B. Auditor Credibility and Auditor Changes. *J. Acc. Res.*, Autumn 1983, *21*(2), pp. 534–44. **[G: U.S.]**

Nistri, Giuseppe. Strumenti contabili per l'inflazione. (Inflation: Accounting and Financial Systems. With English summary.) *L'Impresa*, 1983, *25*(5), pp. 35–41.

Nurnberg, Hugo. Issues in Funds Statement Presentation. *Accounting Rev.*, October 1983, *58*(4), pp. 799–812. **[G: U.S.]**

Ohlson, James A. Price–Earnings Ratios and Earnings Capitalization under Uncertainty. *J. Acc. Res.*, Spring 1983, *21*(1), pp. 141–54.

Peragallo, Edward. Development of the Compound Entry in the 15th Century Ledger of Jachomo Badoer, a Venetian Merchant. *Accounting Rev.*, January 1983, *58*(1), pp. 98–104.

Pesando, James E. and Clarke, Carol K. Economic Models of the Labor Market and Pension Accounting: An Exploratory Analysis. *Accounting Rev.*, October 1983, *58*(4), pp. 733–48.

Poiani, Mario. Gli antidoti al degrado nell impresa. (Antidotes for Break-Down in Companies. With English summary.) *L'Impresa*, 1983, *25*(4), pp. 67–76.

Puntillo, Tito. Per calcolare la redditività aziendale. (For the Calculation of Company Profitability. With English summary.) *L'Impresa*, 1983, *25*(2), pp. 51–55.

Radebaugh, Lee H. International Accounting. **In** *George, A. M. and Giddy, I. H., eds., Vol. 2*, 1983, pp. 8.6:1–24.

Reeve, James M. Loan Evaluations under Accounting Disclosure Alternatives. *J. Bank Res.*, Autumn 1983, *14*(3), pp. 234–36.

Ross, Stephen A. Accounting and Economics. *Accounting Rev.*, April 1983, *58*(2), pp. 375–80.

Salmi, Timo, et al. Extracting and Analyzing the Time Series for Profitability Measurement from Published Financial Statements: With Results on Publicly Traded Finnish Metal Industry Firms: Part II. *Liiketaloudellinen Aikak.*, 1983, *32*(3), pp. 209–41. **[G: Finland]**

Salmi, Timo, et al. Extracting and Analyzing the Time Series for Profitability Measurement from Published Financial Statements: With Results on Publicly Traded Finnish Metal Industry Firms. *Liiketaloudellinen Aikak.*, 1983, *32*(2), pp. 135–74. **[G: Finland]**

Schepanski, Albert. Tests of Theories of Information Processing Behavior in Credit Judgment. *Accounting Rev.*, July 1983, *58*(3), pp. 581–99.

Schepanski, Albert and Uecker, Wilfred. Toward a Positive Theory of Information Evaluation. *Accounting Rev.*, April 1983, *58*(2), pp. 259–83.

Selto, Frank H. and Grove, Hugh D. The Predictive Power of Voting Power Indices: FASB Voting on Statements of Financial Accounting Standards Nos. 45–69. *J. Acc. Res.*, Autumn 1983, *21*(2), pp. 619–22.

Shane, Philip B. and Spicer, Barry H. Market Response to Environmental Information Produced Outside the Firm. *Accounting Rev.*, July 1983, *58*(3), pp. 521–38. **[G: U.S.]**

Shields, Michael D. Effects on Information Supply and Demand on Judgment Accuracy: Evidence from Corporate Managers. *Accounting Rev.*, April 1983, *58*(2), pp. 284–303.

Shockley, Randolph A. and Holt, Robert N. A Behavioral Investigation of Supplier Differentiation in the Market for Audit Services. *J. Acc. Res.*, Autumn 1983, *21*(2), pp. 545–64. **[G: U.S.]**

Shubik, Martin. The Strategic Audit: A Game Theoretic Approach to Corporate Competitive Strategy. *Managerial Dec. Econ.*, September 1983, *4*(3), pp. 160–71.

Silhan, Peter A. The Effects of Segmenting Quarterly Sales and Margins on Extrapolative Forecasts of Conglomerate Earnings: Extension and Replication. *J. Acc. Res.*, Spring 1983, *21*(1), pp. 341–47. **[G: U.S.]**

Sterner, Julie A. An Empirical Evaluation of SFAS No. 55. *J. Acc. Res.*, Autumn 1983, *21*(2), pp. 623–28. **[G: U.S.]**

Stevens, William P.; Stevens, Kathleen C. and Raabe, William, Jr. Communication in Accounting: Readability of F.A.S.B. Statements. *Rev. Bus. Econ. Res.*, Fall 1983, *19*(1), pp. 110–18. **[G: U.S.]**

Stickney, Clyde P.; Weil, Roman L. and Wolfson, Mark A. Income Taxes and Tax-Transfer Leases: General Electric's Accounting for a Molotov Cocktail. *Accounting Rev.*, April 1983, *58*(2), pp. 439–59.

Sunder, Shyam. Simpson's Reversal Paradox and Cost Allocation. *J. Acc. Res.*, Spring 1983, *21*(1), pp. 222–33. **[G: U.S.]**

Sunder, Shyam and Waymire, Gregory. Marginal Gains in Accuracy of Valuation from Increasingly

Specific Price Indexes: Empirical Evidence for the U.S. Economy. *J. Acc. Res.*, Autumn 1983, *21* (2), pp. 565–80. **[G: U.S.]**

Tabor, Richard H. Internal Control Evaluations and Audit Program Revisions: Some Additional Evidence. *J. Acc. Res.*, Spring 1983, *21* (1), pp. 348–54. **[G: U.S.]**

Taylor, Harry. Perspective: Managing Foreign Exchange Exposure. **In** *Herring, R. J., ed.*, 1983, pp. 219–25.

Thomas, Arthur L. Use of Microcomputer Spreadsheet Software in Preparing and Grading Complex Accounting Problems. *Accounting Rev.*, October 1983, *58* (4), pp. 777–86.

Tiller, Mikel G. The Dissonance Model of Participative Budgeting: An Empirical Exploration. *J. Acc. Res.*, Autumn 1983, *21* (2), pp. 581–95. **[G: U.S.]**

Trotman, Ken T.; Yetton, Philip W. and Zimmer, Ian R. Individual and Group Judgments of Internal Control Systems. *J. Acc. Res.*, Spring 1983, *21* (1), pp. 286–92.

Ture, Norman B. The Accelerated Cost Recovery System: An Evaluation of the 1981 and 1982 Cost Recovery Provisions. **In** *Walker, C. E. and Bloomfield, M. E., eds.*, 1983, pp. 47–76. **[G: U.S.]**

Urbancic, Frank R. University Library Collections of Accounting Periodicals. *Accounting Rev.*, April 1983, *58* (2), pp. 417–27.

Varetto, Franco. Flussi finanziari e flussi di potere d'acquisto. (Cash Flows and Fluctuating Purchasing Power. With English summary.) *L'Impresa*, 1983, *25* (5), pp. 27–33.

Wallin, Jan. En datormodell för planering av interna kontrollsystem. (Computer-Assisted Internal Control Design: A Multicriteria Approach. With English summary.) *Liiketaloudellinen Aikak.*, 1983, *32* (2), pp. 175–92.

Watts, Ross L. and Zimmerman, Jerold L. Agency Problems, Auditing, and the Theory of the Firm: Some Evidence. *J. Law Econ.*, October 1983, *26* (3), pp. 613–33. **[G: U.S.; U.K.]**

Waymire, Gregory and Pownall, Grace. Some Evidence on Potential Effects of Contemporaneous Earnings Disclosures in Tests of Capital Market Effects Associated with FASB Exposure Draft No. 19. *J. Acc. Res.*, Autumn 1983, *21* (2), pp. 629–43. **[G: U.S.]**

Wilkins, Trevor and Zimmer, Ian. The Effect of Leasing and Different Methods of Accounting for Leases on Credit Evaluations. *Accounting Rev.*, October 1983, *58* (4), pp. 749–64.

Williams, David J. and Kennedy, John O. S. A Unique Procedure for Allocating Joint Costs from a Production Process? *J. Acc. Res.*, Autumn 1983, *21* (2), pp. 644–45.

Wilson, Robert. Auditing: Perspectives from Multiperson Decision Theory. *Accounting Rev.*, April 1983, *58* (2), pp. 305–18.

Wright, Arnold. the Impact of CPA-Firm Size on Auditor Disclosure Preferences. *Accounting Rev.*, July 1983, *58* (3), pp. 621–32. **[G: U.S.]**

Wright, Roger L. Measuring the Precision of Statistical Cost Allocations. *J. Bus. Econ. Statist.*, April 1983, *1* (2), pp. 93–100.

Zimmerman, Jerold L. Taxes and Firm Size. *J. Acc. Econ.*, August 1983, *5* (2), pp. 119–49. **[G: U.S.]**

600 Industrial Organization; Technological Change; Industry Studies

610 Industrial Organization and Public Policy

611 Market Structure: Industrial Organization and Corporate Strategy

6110 Market Structure: Industrial Organization and Corporate Strategy

Abbey, David S. and Kolstad, Charles D. The Structure of International Steam Coal Markets. *Natural Res. J.*, October 1983, *23* (4), pp. 859–91. **[G: Selected Countries]**

Aivazian, Varouj A. and Callen, Jeffrey L. Reorganization in Bankruptcy and the Issue of Strategic Risk. *J. Banking Finance*, March 1983, *7* (1), pp. 119–33.

Aksoy, M. Ataman. Türkiye Özel Imalat Sanayiinde Yugunlaşma, Karlilik ve Ücret Ilişkileri. (With English summary.) *METU*, 1983, *10* (4), pp. 367–86. **[G: Turkey]**

Albert, Alain and Crener, Maxime A. Organisation industrielle du secteur des télécommunications: une perspective internationale. (With English summary.) *Rev. Econ. Ind.*, 2nd Trimester 1983, (24), pp. 1–8. **[G: U.S.; Canada; Europe]**

Albin, Peter S. Policy Failure, Growth Failure, and Inflation. **In** *Schmukler, N. and Marcus, E., eds.*, 1983, pp. 278–90. **[G: U.S.]**

Allaya, M.; Ghersi, G. and Padilla, M. Évolution des prix alimentaires et structures de marché. (With English summary.) *Écon. Soc.*, May 1983, *17* (5), pp. 785–822. **[G: France]**

Allen, Bruce T. Concentration, Scale Economies, and the Size Distribution of Plants. *Quart. Rev. Econ. Bus.*, Winter 1983, *23* (4), pp. 6–27. **[G: U.S.]**

Allen, P. T. and Stephenson, G. M. Inter-Group Understanding and Size of Organisation. *Brit. J. Ind. Relat.*, November 1983, *21* (3), pp. 312–29. **[G: U.K.]**

Allen, Robert F. Efficiency, Market Power, and Profitability in American Manufacturing. *Southern Econ. J.*, April 1983, *49* (4), pp. 933–40. **[G: U.S.]**

Anthony, Douglas. The Small Firm: Japan. **In** *Storey, D. J., ed.*, 1983, pp. 46–83. **[G: Japan]**

Aoki, Masahiko. Managerialism Revisited in the Light of Bargaining-Game Theory. *Int. J. Ind. Organ.*, 1983, *1* (1), pp. 1–21.

Arrow, Kenneth J. Innovation in Large and Small Firms. **In** *Ronen, J., ed.*, 1983, pp. 15–28.

Asquith, K. Paul. Merger Bids, Uncertainty, and Stockholder Returns. *J. Finan. Econ.*, April 1983, *11* (1–4), pp. 51–83. **[G: U.S.]**

Asquith, K. Paul; Bruner, Robert F. and Mullins, David W., Jr. The Gains to Bidding Firms from Merger. *J. Finan. Econ.*, April 1983, *11* (1–4), pp. 121–39. **[G: U.S.]**

Audretsch, David B. An Evaluation of Horizontal Merger Enforcement. **In** *Craven, J. V., ed.*, 1983, pp. 69–88. **[G: U.S.]**

Austin, Mark. The Theory of the Firm. **In** *Gowland, D. H., ed.*, 1983, pp. 157–70.

Babb, Emerson M. and Lang, Mahlon G. Intrafirm Decision Making: Private and Public Consequences. **In** *Farris, P. L., ed.*, 1983, pp. 38–53. **[G: U.S.]**

Bade, Franz-Josef. Large Corporations and Regional Development. *Reg. Stud.*, October 1983, *17*(5), pp. 315–25. **[G: W. Germany]**

Baden Fuller, Charles. The Implications of the 'Learning Curve' for Firm Strategy and Public Policy. *Appl. Econ.*, August 1983, *15*(4), pp. 541–51. **[G: U.K.]**

Baldwin, Carliss Y. Administered Prices Fifty Years Later: A Comment of Gardiner C. Means: Corporate Power in the Marketplace. *J. Law Econ.*, June 1983, *26*(2), pp. 487–96. **[G: U.S.]**

Balloni, Valeriano. Origini, moi e tempi di evoluzione delle strutture organizzativo–imprenditoriali. (Origins, Ways and Phases in the Evolution of Organizational–Entrepreneurial Structures. With English summary.) *Giorn. Econ.*, November–December 1983, *42*(11–12), pp. 795–808. **[G: Italy]**

Baron, David P. Tender Offers and Management Resistance. *J. Finance,* May 1983, *38*(2), pp. 331–43.

Bauer, Michael and Cohen, Elie. The Invisibility of Power in Economics: Beyond Markets and Hierarchies. **In** *Francis, A.; Turk, J. and Willman, P., eds.*, 1983, pp. 81–104.

Bauer, Tamás and Soós, Károly Attila. Interfirm Relations and Technological Change: The Case of the Motor Industry. *Eastern Europ. Econ.*, Spring–Summer 1983, *21* (3–4), pp. 85–104. **[G: Hungary]**

Baumol, William J.; Panzar, John C. and Willig, Robert D. Contestable Markets: An Uprising in the Theory of Industry Structure: Reply. *Amer. Econ. Rev.*, June 1983, *73*(3), pp. 491–96.

Beaud, C. The Interests of the Union Européenne in Central Europe. **In** *Teichova, A. and Cottrell, P. L., eds.*, 1983, pp. 375–97. **[G: Central Europe]**

Belinfante, Alexander and Johnson, Richard L. An Economic Analysis of the U.S. Recorded Music Industry. **In** *Hendon, W. S. and Shanahan, J. L., eds.*, 1983, pp. 132–42. **[G: U.S.]**

Benson, Bruce L. and Hartigan, James C. Tariffs Which Lower Price in the Restricting Country: An Analysis of Spatial Markets. *J. Int. Econ.*, August 1983, *15*(1/2), pp. 117–33.

Berend, Iván T. German Capital in Silesian Industry in Poland between the Two World Wars: Commentary. **In** *Teichova, A. and Cottrell, P. L., eds.*, 1983, pp. 251. **[G: Poland; Selected Countries]**

Besen, Stanley M. and Woodbury, John R. Regulation, Deregulation, and Antitrust in the Telecommunications Industry. *Antitrust Bull.*, Spring 1983, *28*(1), pp. 39–68. **[G: U.S.]**

Billings, R. Bruce. Revenue Effects from Changes in a Declining Block Pricing Structure: Comment. *Land Econ.*, August 1983, *59*(3), pp. 355–39. **[G: U.S.]**

Boisjoly, Russell P. and Corsi, Thomas M. The Changing Nature of the Motor Carrier Acquisition Market. *Quarterly Journal of Business and Economics,* Autumn 1983, *22*(4), pp. 25–39. **[G: U.S.]**

Bond, Eric W. Trade in Used Equipment with Heterogeneous Firms. *J. Polit. Econ.*, August 1983, *91*(4), pp. 688–705. **[G: U.S.]**

Bradburd, Ralph M. and Over, A. Mead, Jr. The Notion of a Critical Region of Concentration: Theory and Evidence. **In** *Craven, J. V., ed.*, 1983, pp. 109–28.

Bradley, Michael; Desai, Anand and Kim, E. Han. The Rationale behind Interfirm Tender Offers: Information or Synergy? *J. Finan. Econ.*, April 1983, *11*(1–4), pp. 183–206. **[G: U.S.]**

Bradley, Michael and Wakeman, L. Macdonald. The Wealth Effects of Targeted Share Repurchases. *J. Finan. Econ.*, April 1983, *11*(1–4), pp. 301–28. **[G: U.S.]**

Braendgaard, Asger. Market, Hierarchy and Technology: Some Implications of Economic Internationalism for Labour. **In** *Francis, A.; Turk, J. and Willman, P., eds.*, 1983, pp. 159–79.

Breen, Denis A. Antitrust and Price Competition in the Trucking Industry. *Antitrust Bull.*, Spring 1983, *28*(1), pp. 201–25. **[G: U.S.]**

Brock, William A. Contestable Markets and the Theory of Industry Structure: A Review Article. *J. Polit. Econ.*, December 1983, *91*(6), pp. 1055–66.

Brock, William A. and Scheinkman, José A. Free Entry and the Sustainability of Natural Monopoly: Bertrand Revisited by Cournot. **In** *Evans, D. S., ed.*, 1983, pp. 231–52.

Bruch, Mathias. Sources of Financing of Small-Scale Manufacturers: A Micro-Analysis for Malaysia. *Singapore Econ. Rev.*, April 1983, *28*(1), pp. 21–33. **[G: Malaysia]**

Buckley, Peter J. New Theories of International Business: Some Unresolved Issues. **In** *Casson, M., ed.*, 1983, pp. 34–50.

van den Bulcke, Daniel. Belgian Industrial Policy and Foreign Multinational Corporations: Objectives versus Performance. **In** *Goldberg, W. H., ed.*, 1983, pp. 219–48. **[G: Belgium]**

Bulow, Jeremy I. and Pfleiderer, Paul. A Note on the Effect of Cost Changes on Prices [Measurement of Monopoly Behavior: An Application to the Cigarette Industry]. *J. Polit. Econ.*, February 1983, *91*(1), pp. 182–85. **[G: U.S.]**

Burns, Malcolm R. Economies of Scale in Tobacco Manufacture, 1897–1910. *J. Econ. Hist.*, June 1983, *43*(2), pp. 461–74. **[G: U.S.]**

Butler, Richard J. Control through Markets, Hierarchies and Communes: A Transactional Approach to Organisational Analysis. **In** *Francis, A.; Turk, J. and Willman, P., eds.*, 1983, pp. 137–58.

Cable, John and Dirrheimer, Manfred J. Hierarchies and Markets: An Empirical Test of the Multidivisional Hypothesis in West Germany. *Int. J. Ind. Organ.*, 1983, *1*(1), pp. 43–62. **[G: W. Germany]**

Carleton, Willard T., et al. An Empirical Analysis of the Role of the Medium of Exchange in Mergers. *J. Finance,* June 1983, *38*(3), pp. 813–26. **[G: U.S.]**

Carlson, John A. and McAfee, R. Preston. Discrete Equilibrium Price Dispersion. *J. Polit. Econ.*, June

1983, *91*(3), pp. 480–93.

Carlton, Dennis W. Equilibrium Fluctuations When Price and Delivery Lag Clear the Market. *Bell J. Econ. (See Rand J. Econ. after 4/85)*, Autumn 1983, *14*(2), pp. 562–72. **[G: U.S.]**

Carlton, Dennis W. Futures Trading, Market Interrelationships, and Industry Structure. *Amer. J. Agr. Econ.*, May 1983, *65*(2), pp. 380–87. **[G: U.S.]**

Casson, Mark. The Growth of International Business: Introduction: The Conceptual Framework. **In** *Casson, M., ed.*, 1983, pp. 1–33.

Casson, Mark and Norman, George. Pricing and Sourcing Strategies in a Multinational Oligopoly. **In** *Casson, M., ed.*, 1983, pp. 63–83.

Chakrabarti, Alok K. and Burton, Jonathan. Technological Characteristics of Mergers and Acquisitions in the 1970s in Manufacturing Industries in the U.S. *Quart. Rev. Econ. Bus.*, Autumn 1983, *23*(3), pp. 81–90. **[G: U.S.]**

Chamley, Christophe. Entrepreneurial Abilities and Liabilities in a Model of Self-Selection. *Bell J. Econ. (See Rand J. Econ. after 4/85)*, Spring 1983, *14*(1), pp. 70–80.

Chandler, Alfred D., Jr. The Place of the Modern Industrial Enterprise in Three Economies. **In** *Teichova, A. and Cottrell, P. L., eds.*, 1983, pp. 3–29. **[G: U.S.; U.K.; Germany]**

Chappell, Henry W., Jr. and Addison, John T. Relative Prices, Concentration, and Money Growth. *Amer. Econ. Rev.*, December 1983, *73*(5), pp. 1122–26. **[G: U.S.]**

Chappell, Henry W., Jr.; Marks, William H. and Park, Imkoo. Measuring Entry Barriers Using a Switching Regression Model of Industry Profitability. *Southern Econ. J.*, April 1983, *49*(4), pp. 991–1001. **[G: U.S.]**

Cheung, Steven N. S. The Contractual Nature of the Firm. *J. Law Econ.*, April 1983, *26*(1), pp. 1–21. **[G: Hong Kong]**

Choi, Dosoung and Philippatos, George C. An Examination of Merger Synergism. *J. Finan. Res.*, Fall 1983, *6*(3), pp. 239–56.

Ciborra, Claudio U. Markets, Bureaucracies, and Groups in the Information Society: An Institutional Appraisal of the Impacts of Information Technology. *Info. Econ. Policy*, 1983, *1*(2), pp. 145–60. **[G: Italy]**

Ciscel, David H. and Tuckman, Howard P. Plant Scale and Multiplant Production as Determinants of Industrial Concentration. *J. Behav. Econ.*, Winter 1983, *12*(2), pp. 1–16. **[G: U.S.]**

Clarke, R. On the Specification of Structure–Performance Relationships: A Comment. *Europ. Econ. Rev.*, November 1983, *23*(2), pp. 253–56.

Clarke, R. and Davies, S. W. Aggregate Concentration, Market Concentration and Diversification. *Econ. J.*, March 1983, *93*(369), pp. 182–92. **[G: U.K.]**

Cohen, Wesley M. Investment and Industrial Expansion: A Corporate Variables Framework. *J. Econ. Behav. Organ.*, June–September 1983, *4*(2–3), pp. 91–111.

Comanor, William. Comment [Advertising and Concentration Change in U.S. Food and Tobacco Product Classes, 1958–1972] [The Causes of Concentration in the U.S. Brewing Industry]. **In** *Connor, J. M. and Ward, R. W., eds.*, 1983, pp. 317–19. **[G: U.S.]**

Comanor, William. Commentary [Theoretical Approaches to the Economics of Advertising] [Advertising and Brand Loyalty as Barriers to Entry]. **In** *Connor, J. M. and Ward, R. W., eds.*, 1983, pp. 71–73.

Conrad, Cecilia A. The Advantage of Being First and Competition between Firms. *Int. J. Ind. Organ.*, December 1983, *1*(4), pp. 353–64.

Cowling, Keith. Excess Capacity and the Degree of Collusion: Oligopoly Behaviour in the Slump. *Manchester Sch. Econ. Soc. Stud.*, December 1983, *51*(4), pp. 341–59. **[G: U.K.]**

Crew, Michael A. and Kleindorfer, Paul R. Regulatory Influences on Managerial Incentives: Comment. *Southern Econ. J.*, July 1983, *50*(1), pp. 265–66. **[G: U.S.]**

Crocker, Keith J. Vertical Integration and the Strategic Use of Private Information. *Bell J. Econ. (See Rand J. Econ. after 4/85)*, Spring 1983, *14*(1), pp. 236–48.

Crouzet, François. Comment [The Interests of the Union Européenne in Central Europe] [The Interests of the Banque de I'Union Parisienne in Czechoslovakia, Hungary and the Balkans, 1919–30]. **In** *Teichova, A. and Cottrell, P. L., eds.*, 1983, pp. 411–13. **[G: Central Europe; France]**

Cubbin, John S. and Leech, Dennis. The Effect of Shareholding Dispersion on the Degree of Control in British Companies: Theory and Measurement. *Econ. J.*, June 1983, *93*(370), pp. 351–69. **[G: U.K.]**

Culbertson, John. The Effect of Advertising on Price Change for Food Manufacturing Product Classes: Comment. **In** *Connor, J. M. and Ward, R. W., eds.*, 1983, pp. 276–78. **[G: U.S.]**

Curry, B. and George, K. D. Industrial Concentration: A Survey. *J. Ind. Econ.*, March 1983, *31*(3), pp. 203–55.

Curry, Timothy J. and Rose, John T. Multibank Holding Companies: Recent Evidence on Competition and Performance in Banking Markets. *J. Bank Res.*, Autumn 1983, *14*(3), pp. 212–20. **[G: U.S.]**

Czinkota, Michael R. and Johnston, Wesley J. Exporting: Does Sales Volume Make a Difference? *J. Int. Bus. Stud.*, Spring/Summer 1983, *14*(1), pp. 147–53. **[G: U.S.]**

Daems, Herman. The Determinants of the Hierarchical Organisation of Industry. **In** *Francis, A.; Turk, J. and Willman, P., eds.*, 1983, pp. 35–53.

Danielsson, Christer. Koncernstyrning och divisionsstrategi. (Corporate Management and Division Strategy. With English summary.) *Ekon. Samfundets Tidskr.*, 1983, *36*(2), pp. 71–75.

Dann, Larry Y. and DeAngelo, Harry. Standstill Agreements, Privately Negotiated Stock Repurchases, and the Market for Corporate Control. *J. Finan. Econ.*, April 1983, *11*(1–4), pp. 275–300. **[G: U.S.]**

Dansby, Robert E. R&D Cost Allocation with Endogenous Technology Adoption. **In** *Finsinger, J., ed.*, 1983, pp. 117–47.

DeAngelo, Harry and Rice, Edward M. Antitakeover Charter Amendments and Stockholder Wealth.

J. Finan. Econ., April 1983, *11* (1–4), pp. 329–59. **[G: U.S.]**

Di Gregorio, Renato. Mercato, strutture organizzative, tecnologia: interpretazione di alcune linee evolutive. (Market, Organisation Structures and Technology: An Interpretation of Some Developing Trends. With English summary.) *L'Impresa,* 1983, *25* (2), pp. 25–33. **[G: Italy]**

Dickson, V. A. and McFetridge, D. G. Concentration, Unionization and the Distribution of Income in Canadian Manufacturing Industry: Comment. *Managerial Dec. Econ.*, December 1983, *4* (4), pp. 278–80. **[G: Canada]**

Diewert, W. Erwin. The Measurement of Waste within the Production Sector of an Open Economy. *Scand. J. Econ.*, 1983, *85* (2), pp. 159–79.

Dixit, Avinash. Vertical Integration in a Monopolistically Competitive Industry. *Int. J. Ind. Organ.*, 1983, *1* (1), pp. 63–78.

Dixon, Robert J. Industry Structure and the Speed of Price Adjustment. *J. Ind. Econ.*, September 1983, *32* (1), pp. 25–37. **[G: Australia]**

Dorward, Neil; Pokorny, Mike and Bayldon, Ray. The UK Truck Market: An Investigation into Truck Purchasing Behavior and Changing Market Shares. *J. Ind. Econ.*, September 1983, *32* (1), pp. 73–95. **[G: U.K.]**

Doz, Yves L. International Industries, Multinational Companies, and Host Government Control: A Framework. **In** *Goldberg, W. H., ed.*, 1983, pp. 302–31. **[G: W. Europe]**

Droucopoulos, Vassilis. International Big Business Revisited: On the Size and Growth of the World's Largest Firms. *Managerial Dec. Econ.*, December 1983, *4* (4), pp. 244–52. **[G: Global]**

Dtugorborski, Waclaw. German Capital in Silesian Industry in Poland between the Two World Wars: Commentary. **In** *Teichova, A. and Cottrell, P. L., eds.*, 1983, pp. 247–50. **[G: Poland; Selected Countries]**

Dtugorborski, Waclaw. Göring's 'Multi-national Empire': Commentary. **In** *Teichova, A. and Cottrell, P. L., eds.*, 1983, pp. 298–302. **[G: Germany; Europe]**

Dugger, William M. The Transaction Cost Analysis of Oliver E. Williamson: A New Synthesis? *J. Econ. Issues*, March 1983, *17* (1), pp. 95–114.

Duhaime, Irene M. and Thomas, Howard. Financial Analysis and Strategic Management. *J. Econ. Bus.*, August 1983, *35* (3/4), pp. 413–40.

Dunning, John H. Changes in the Level and Structure of International Production: The Last One Hundred Years. **In** *Casson, M., ed.*, 1983, pp. 84–139. **[G: Global]**

Dunning, John H. Market Power of the Firm and International Transfer of Technology: A Historical Excursion. *Int. J. Ind. Organ.*, December 1983, *1* (4), pp. 333–51. **[G: U.S.; Europe; LDCs]**

Dye, Thomas R. Who Owns America: Strategic Ownership Positions in Industrial Corporations. *Soc. Sci. Quart.*, December 1983, *64* (4), pp. 862–70. **[G: U.S.]**

Eads, George C. Airline Competitive Conduct in a Less Regulated Environment: Implications for Antitrust. *Antitrust Bull.*, Spring 1983, *28* (1), pp. 159–84. **[G: U.S.]**

Eckbo, B. Espen. Horizontal Mergers, Collusion, and Stockholder Wealth. *J. Finan. Econ.*, April 1983, *11* (1–4), pp. 241–73. **[G: U.S.]**

Eger, Carol Ellen. An Empirical Test of the Redistribution Effect in Pure Exchange Mergers. *J. Finan. Quant. Anal.*, December 1983, *18* (4), pp. 547–72. **[G: U.S.]**

Eichner, Alfred S. The Micro Foundations of the Corporate Economy. *Managerial Dec. Econ.*, September 1983, *4* (3), pp. 136–52.

Elliott, Ralph D.; Hawkins, Benjamin M. and Hughes, Woodrow W., Jr. Does Government Spending Affect Industrial Concentration? *Nebr. J. Econ. Bus.*, Summer 1983, *22* (3), pp. 44–52. **[G: U.S.]**

Ericson, Richard E. and Winston, Clifford E. Predatory Capacity Expansion in a Deregulated Motor Carrier Industry. **In** *Keeler, T. E., ed.*, 1983, pp. 185–235.

Esty, Daniel C. and Caves, Richard E. Market Structure and Political Influence: New Data on Political Expenditures, Activity, and Success. *Econ. Inquiry,* January 1983, *21* (1), pp. 24–38. **[G: U.S.]**

Evans, David S. and Heckman, James J. Natural Monopoly. **In** *Evans, D. S., ed.*, 1983, pp. 127–56. **[G: U.S.]**

Fama, Eugene F. Agency Problems and the Theory of the Firm. **In** *Archer, S. H. and D'Ambrosia, C. A.*, 1983, *1980*, pp. 535–54.

Fatemi, Ali M.; Ang, James S. and Chua, Jess H. Evidence Supporting Shareholder Wealth Maximization in Management Controlled Firms. *Appl. Econ.*, February 1983, *15* (1), pp. 49–60. **[G: U.S.]**

Ferguson, James M. Daily Newspaper Advertising Rates, Local Media Cross-Ownership, Newspaper Chains, and Media Competition. *J. Law Econ.*, October 1983, *26* (3), pp. 635–54. **[G: U.S.]**

Fichtenbaum, Rudy. Variations in Hospital Cost by Types of Ownership. *J. Behav. Econ.*, Winter 1983, *12* (2), pp. 17–35. **[G: U.S.]**

Fisher, Franklin M. and McGowan, John J. On the Misuse of Accounting Rates of Return to Infer Monopoly Profits. *Amer. Econ. Rev.*, March 1983, *73* (1), pp. 82–97.

Fixler, Dennis J. Uncertainty, Market Structure and the Incentive to Invent. *Economica*, November 1983, *50* (200), pp. 407–23.

Flexner, Donald L. The Effects of Deregulation in the Motor Carrier Industry. *Antitrust Bull.*, Spring 1983, *28* (1), pp. 185–200. **[G: U.S.]**

Folsom, Roger Nils and Greer, Douglas F. Advertising and Brand Loyalty as Barriers to Entry. **In** *Connor, J. M. and Ward, R. W., eds.*, 1983, pp. 47–70.

Fornell, Claes and Robinson, William T. Industrial Organization and Consumer Satisfaction/Dissatisfaction. *J. Cons. Res.*, March 1983, *9* (4), pp. 403–12. **[G: U.S.]**

Francis, Arthur. Markets and Hierarchies: Efficiency of Domination? **In** *Francis, A.; Turk, J. and Willman, P., eds.*, 1983, pp. 105–16.

Frank, Robert H. When Are Price Differentials Discriminatory? *J. Policy Anal. Manage.*, Winter 1983, *2* (2), pp. 238–55. **[G: U.S.]**

Freeman, Christopher; Walsh, V. and Townsend, J. The Determinants of Technical Change in the Chemical Industry: Demand-pull or Technology-push? **In** *[Saunders, C. T.],* 1983, pp. 83–108. **[G: Italy; U.K.; U.S.; W. Germany]**

Fudenberg, Drew and Tirole, Jean. Learning-by-Doing and Market Performance. *Bell J. Econ. (See Rand J. Econ. after 4/85),* Autumn 1983, *14*(2), pp. 522–30.

Gabel, H. Landis. The Role of Buyer Power in Oligopoly Models: An Empirical Study. *J. Econ. Bus.,* 1983, *35*(1), pp. 95–108. **[G: U.S.]**

Gal-Or, Esther. Quality and Quantity Competition. *Bell J. Econ. (See Rand J. Econ. after 4/85),* Autumn 1983, *14*(2), pp. 590–600.

Gallini, Nancy T. and Winter, Ralph A. On Vertical Control in Monopolistic Competition. *Int. J. Ind. Organ.,* September 1983, *1*(3), pp. 275–86.

Gan, Wee Beng. The Relationship between Market Concentration and Profitability in Malaysian Manufacturing Industries. **In** *Lim, D., ed.,* 1983, *1978,* pp. 89–98. **[G: Malaysia]**

Gaspari, K. Celeste. Foreign Market Operations and Domestic Market Power. **In** *Kindleberger, C. P. and Audretsch, D. B., eds.,* 1983, pp. 77–102. **[G: U.S.]**

Gelman, Judith R. and Salop, Steven C. Judo Economics: Capacity Limitation and Coupon Competition. *Bell J. Econ. (See Rand J. Econ. after 4/85),* Autumn 1983, *14*(2), pp. 315–25.

Geroski, P. A. Some Reflections on the Theory and Application of Concentration Indices. *Int. J. Ind. Organ.,* 1983, *1*(1), pp. 79–94. **[G: U.S.]**

Geroski, P. A. and Knight, K. G. Wages, Strikes and Market Structure: Some Further Evidence. *Oxford Econ. Pap.,* March 1983, *35*(1), pp. 146–52. **[G: U.K.]**

Goddard, John B. Industrial Innovation and Regional Economic Development in Great Britain. **In** *Hamilton, F. E. I. and Linge, G. J. R., eds.,* 1983, pp. 255–77. **[G: U.K.]**

Gort, Michael and Swanson, Eric V. Conglomerate Size and Competition between Large and Small Firms. *Antitrust Bull.,* Summer 1983, *28*(2), pp. 337–48. **[G: U.S.]**

Gospel, Howard F. The Development of Management Organization in Industrial Relations: A Historical Perspective. **In** *Thurley, K. and Wood, S., eds.,* 1983, pp. 91–110. **[G: U.K.]**

Graham, David R.; Kaplan, Daniel P. and Sibley, David S. Efficiency and Competition in the Airline Industry. *Bell J. Econ. (See Rand J. Econ. after 4/85),* Spring 1983, *14*(1), pp. 118–38. **[G: U.S.]**

Greer, Douglas F. The Causes of Concentration in the U.S. Brewing Industry. **In** *Connor, J. M. and Ward, R. W., eds.,* 1983, pp. 295–314. **[G: U.S.]**

Gupta, Vinod K. A Simultaneous Determination of Structure, Conduct and Performance in Canadian Manufacturing. *Oxford Econ. Pap.,* July 1983, *35*(2), pp. 281–301. **[G: Canada]**

Gupta, Vinod K. Labor Productivity, Establishment Size, and Scale Economies [The Extent of Economies of Scale: The Effects of Firm Size on Labor Productivity and Wage Rates]. *Southern Econ. J.,* January 1983, *49*(3), pp. 853–59. **[G: U.S.]**

Hall, William K. Survival Strategies in a Hostile Environment. **In** *Kantrow, A. M., ed.,* 1983, pp. 52–71. **[G: U.S.]**

Hallagan, William and Joerding, Wayne. Polymorphic Equilibrium in Advertising. *Bell J. Econ. (See Rand J. Econ. after 4/85),* Spring 1983, *14*(1), pp. 191–201.

Halpern, Paul. Corporate Acquisitions: A Theory of Special Cases? A Review of Event Studies Applied to Acquisitions. *J. Finance,* May 1983, *38*(2), pp. 297–317.

Hannan, Timothy H. Bank Profitability and the Threat of Entry. *J. Bank Res.,* Summer 1983, *14*(2), pp. 157–63. **[G: U.S.]**

Hannan, Timothy H. Prices, Capacity, and the Entry Decision: A Conditional Logit Analysis. *Southern Econ. J.,* October 1983, *50*(2), pp. 539–50. **[G: U.S.]**

Harris, Robert G. and Winston, Clifford M. Potential Benefits of Rail Mergers: An Econometric Analysis of Network Effects on Service Quality. *Rev. Econ. Statist.,* February 1983, *65*(1), pp. 32–40. **[G: U.S.]**

Hart, Oliver D. The Market Mechanism as an Incentive Scheme. *Bell J. Econ. (See Rand J. Econ. after 4/85),* Autumn 1983, *14*(2), pp. 366–82.

Hart, Peter E. Experience Curves and Industrial Policy. *Int. J. Ind. Organ.,* 1983, *1*(1), pp. 95–106. **[G: U.S.; U.K.]**

Hay, Donald. Management and Economic Performance. **In** *Earl, M. J., ed.,* 1983, pp. 55–81.

Hayes, Robert H. and Wheelwright, Steven C. Link Manufacturing Process and Product Life Cycles. **In** *Kantrow, A. M., ed.,* 1983, pp. 132–43. **[G: U.S.]**

Healey, Michael. Components of Locational Change in Multi-Plant Enterprises. *Urban Stud.,* August 1983, *20*(3), pp. 327–42. **[G: U.K.]**

Hessen, Robert. The Modern Corporation and Private Property: A Reappraisal. *J. Law Econ.,* June 1983, *26*(2), pp. 273–89.

Hetherington, Norriss S. Taking the Risk Out of Risk Arbitrage. *J. Portfol. Manage.,* Summer 1983, *9*(4), pp. 24–25. **[G: U.S.]**

Hill, C. W. L. Conglomerate Performance over the Economic Cycle. *J. Ind. Econ.,* December 1983, *32*(2), pp. 197–211. **[G: U.K.]**

Hirschey, Mark and Pappas, James L. Regulatory Influences on Managerial Incentives: Reply. *Southern Econ. J.,* July 1983, *50*(1), pp. 267–69. **[G: U.S.]**

Hirschey, Mark and Wichern, Dean W. Indicators and Causes of Size Advantages in Industry. *Managerial Dec. Econ.,* June 1983, *4*(2), pp. 64–72. **[G: U.S.]**

Hirschman, Charles. Ownership and Control in the Manufacturing Sector of West Malaysia: Reply. **In** *Lim, D., ed.,* 1983, pp. 222–24. **[G: Malaysia]**

Hirschman, Charles. Ownership and Control in the Manufacturing Sector of West Malaysia. **In** *Lim, D., ed.,* 1983, *1971,* pp. 209–20. **[G: Malaysia]**

Hollander, Abraham. Concentration, Unionization and the Distribution of Income in Canadian Manufacturing Industry: Reply. *Managerial Dec. Econ.,* December 1983, *4*(4), pp. 281–82. **[G: Canada]**

Houston, Douglas A. Revenue Effects from Changes in a Declining Block Pricing Structure: Reply. *Land Econ.*, August 1983, *59*(3), pp. 360–64. **[G: U.S.]**

Ikeda, Katsuhiko and Doi, Noriyuki. The Performances of Merging Firms in Japanese Manufacturing Industry: 1964–75. *J. Ind. Econ.*, March 1983, *31*(3), pp. 257–66. **[G: Japan]**

Ireland, Norman J. A Note on Conglomerate Merger and Behavioural Response to Risk. *J. Ind. Econ.*, March 1983, *31*(3), pp. 283–89.

Ireland, Norman J. Monopolistic Competition and a Firm's Product Range. *Int. J. Ind. Organ.*, September 1983, *1*(3), pp. 239–52.

Jain, Asha and Barthwal, R. R. A Review of Empirical Studies on Price–Cost Margin. *Indian Econ. J.*, October–December 1983, *31*(2), pp. 43–52. **[G: U.S.; U.K.; Canada; Australia; India]**

James, John A. Structural Change in American Manufacturing, 1850–1890. *J. Econ. Hist.*, June 1983, *43*(2), pp. 433–59. **[G: U.S.]**

Jarrell, Stephen. Research and Development and Firm Size in the Pharmaceutical Industry. *Bus. Econ.*, September 1983, *18*(4), pp. 26–39. **[G: U.S.]**

Jensen, Michael C. and Ruback, Richard S. The Market for Corporate Control: The Scientific Evidence. *J. Finan. Econ.*, April 1983, *11*(1–4), pp. 5–50. **[G: U.S.]**

Johns, Brian. The Small Firm: Australia. **In** *Storey, D. J., ed.*, 1983, pp. 120–52. **[G: Australia]**

Johnson, Frederick I. On the Stability of Commodity Cartels. *Amer. Econ.*, Fall 1983, *27*(2), pp. 34–36. **[G: LDCs]**

Johnson, Ronald N. and Parkman, Allen. Spatial Monopoly, Non-Zero Profits and Entry Deterrence: The Case of Cement. *Rev. Econ. Statist.*, August 1983, *65*(3), pp. 431–39. **[G: U.S.]**

Jones, J. C. H. and Laudadio, L. Risk, Profitability, and Market Structure: Some Canadian Evidence on Structural and Behavioral Approaches to Antitrust. *Antitrust Bull.*, Summer 1983, *28*(2), pp. 349–79. **[G: Canada]**

Jones, S. R. H. Technology and the Organization of Work: A Reply. *J. Econ. Behav. Organ.*, March 1983, *4*(1), pp. 63–66.

Joyce, Patrick. Information and Behavior in Experimental Markets. *J. Econ. Behav. Organ.*, December 1983, *4*(4), pp. 411–24.

Juzzawalla, Meheroo and Cheah, Chee-Wah. Towards an Information Economy: The Case of Singapore. *Info. Econ. Policy*, 1983, *1*(2), pp. 161–76. **[G: Singapore]**

Kahn, Alfred E. The Relevance of Industrial Organization. **In** *Craven, J. V., ed.*, 1983, pp. 3–17.

Kamien, Morton I. and Schwartz, Nancy L. Conjectural Variations. *Can. J. Econ.*, May 1983, *16*(2), pp. 191–211.

Kaplinsky, Raphael. Firm Size and Technical Change in a Dynamic Context. *J. Ind. Econ.*, September 1983, *32*(1), pp. 39–59. **[G: U.S.]**

Kay, J. A. A General Equilibrium Approach to the Measurement of Monopoly Welfare Loss. *Int. J. Ind. Organ.*, December 1983, *1*(4), pp. 317–31.

Kellner, S. and Mathewson, G. Frank. Entry, Size Distribution, Scale, and Scope Economies in the Life Insurance Industry. *J. Bus.*, January 1983, *56*(1), pp. 25–44. **[G: Canada]**

Kelton, Christina M. L. The Effect of Advertising on Price Change for Food Manufacturing Product Classes. **In** *Connor, J. M. and Ward, R. W., eds.*, 1983, pp. 257–73. **[G: U.S.]**

Keren, Michael and Levhari, David. The Internal Organization of the Firm and the Shape of Average Costs. *Bell J. Econ. (See Rand J. Econ. after 4/85)*, Autumn 1983, *14*(2), pp. 474–86.

Klein, Benjamin. Contracting Costs and Residual Claims: The Separation of Ownership and Control. *J. Law Econ.*, June 1983, *26*(2), pp. 367–74.

Kovács, Mátyás János. Bargaining—Assimilation—Bargaining: A Fragment of an Economic Drama in Four Acts. *Eastern Europ. Econ.*, Fall 1983, *22*(1), pp. 38–77. **[G: Hungary]**

Kudla, Ronald J. and McInish, Thomas H. Valuation Consequences of Corporate Spin-Offs. *Rev. Bus. Econ. Res.*, Winter, 1983, *18*(2), pp. 71–77. **[G: U.S.]**

Kwoka, John E., Jr. Monopoly, Plant, and Union Effects on Worker Wages. *Ind. Lab. Relat. Rev.*, January 1983, *36*(2), pp. 251–57. **[G: U.S.]**

Lall, Sanjaya. Multinationals and Market Structure in an Open Developing Economy: The Case of Malaysia. **In** *Lim, D., ed.*, 1983, *1979*, pp. 238–54. **[G: Malaysia]**

Lall, Sanjaya and Mohammad, Sharif. Foreign Ownership and Export Performance in the Large Corporate Sector of India. *J. Devel. Stud.*, October 1983, *20*(1), pp. 56–67. **[G: India]**

Lamm, R. McFall, Jr. Commentary [Advertising and Concentration Change in U.S. Food and Tobacco Product Classes, 1958–1972] [The Causes of Concentration in the U.S. Brewing Industry]. **In** *Connor, J. M. and Ward, R. W., eds.*, 1983, pp. 315–17. **[G: U.S.]**

Landon, John H. Theories of Vertical Integration and Their Application to the Electric Utility Industry. *Antitrust Bull.*, Spring 1983, *28*(1), pp. 101–30. **[G: U.S.]**

Lane, Sylvai and Papathanasis, Anastasios. Certification and Industry Concentration Ratios. *Antitrust Bull.*, Summer 1983, *28*(2), pp. 381–95. **[G: U.S.]**

Lazonick, William. Industrial Organization and Technological Change: The Decline of the British Cotton Industry. *Bus. Hist. Rev.*, Summer 1983, *57*(2), pp. 195–236. **[G: U.K.]**

Lecraw, Donald J. Performance of Transnational Corporations in Less Developed Countries. *J. Int. Bus. Stud.*, Spring/Summer 1983, *14*(1), pp. 15–33. **[G: ASEAN]**

Leitzinger, Jeffrey J. and Tamor, Kenneth. Foreign Competition in Antitrust Law. *J. Law Econ.*, April 1983, *26*(1), pp. 87–102.

Lenel, Hans Otto. A Review of the Third Report of the Monopolies Commission of West Germany. *Antitrust Bull.*, Fall 1983, *28*(3), pp. 757–81. **[G: W. Germany]**

Lev, Baruch. Some Economic Determinants of Time-Series Properties of Earnings. *J. Acc. Econ.*, April 1983, *5*(1), pp. 31–48. **[G: U.S.]**

Lewis, Tracy R. Preemption, Divestiture, and Forward Contracting in a Market Dominated by a

Single Firm. *Amer. Econ. Rev.*, December 1983, *73*(5), pp. 1092–1101.

Lewis, W. Arthur. Competition in Retail Trade. **In** *Lewis, W. A.*, 1983, *1946*, pp. 71–111.

Lewis, W. Arthur. Fixed Costs. **In** *Lewis, W. A.*, 1983, *1961*, pp. 113–47.

Lewis, W. Arthur. The Economics of Loyalty. **In** *Lewis, W. A.*, 1983, *1942*, pp. 27–46.

Liebermann, Yehoshua and Syrquin, M. On the Use and Abuse of Rights: An Economic View. *J. Econ. Behav. Organ.*, March 1983, *4*(1), pp. 25–40.

Lim, Linda Y. C. Chinese Economic Activity in Southeast Asia: An Introductory Review. **In** *Lim, L. Y. C. and Gosling, L. A. P., eds.*, 1983, pp. 1–29. **[G: S. E. Asia]**

Lim, Mah Hui. The Ownership and Control of Large Corporations in Malaysia: The Role of Chinese Businessmen. **In** *Lim, L. Y. C. and Gosling, L. A. P., eds.*, 1983, pp. 275–315. **[G: Malaysia]**

Linda, Remo. Morphologie des marchés d'après le pouvoir quantitatif des firmes (Théorie quantitative du pouvoir de marché). (With English summary.) *Rev. Econ. Ind.*, 4th Trimester 1983, (26), pp. 68–81.

Lindmark, Leif. The Small Firm: Sweden. **In** *Storey, D. J., ed.*, 1983, pp. 179–212. **[G: Sweden]**

Link, Albert N. Alternative Sources of Technology: An Analysis of Induced Innovations. *Managerial Dec. Econ.*, March 1983, *4*(1), pp. 40–43. **[G: U.S.]**

Link, Albert N. Market Structure and Voluntary Product Standards. *Appl. Econ.*, June 1983, *15*(3), pp. 393–401. **[G: U.S.]**

Linn, Scott C. and McConnell, John J. An Empirical Investigation of the Impact of 'Antitakeover' Amendments on Common Stock Prices. *J. Finan. Econ.*, April 1983, *11*(1–4), pp. 361–99. **[G: U.S.]**

Littlechild, S. C. The Structure of Telephone Tariffs. *Int. J. Ind. Organ.*, December 1983, *1*(4), pp. 365–77. **[G: Selected Countries]**

Lockett, Martin and Littler, Craig R. Trends in Chinese Enterprise Management, 1978–1982. *World Devel.*, August 1983, *11*(8), pp. 683–704. **[G: China]**

Lofthouse, Stephen. Monopolies and Mergers Commission Reports: A Note. *Managerial Dec. Econ.*, December 1983, *4*(4), pp. 221–23. **[G: U.K.]**

Long, James E. and Link, Albert N. The Impact of Market Structure on Wages, Fringe Benefits, and Turnover. *Ind. Lab. Relat. Rev.*, January 1983, *36*(2), pp. 239–50. **[G: U.S.]**

Lower, Milton D. Comments on R. S. Thompson's "The Spread of an Institutional Innovation." *J. Econ. Issues*, June 1983, *17*(2), pp. 539–42. **[G: U.K.]**

Lundahl, Mats. Imperfect Competition in Haitian Coffee Marketing. **In** *Lundahl, M.*, 1983, pp. 171–89. **[G: Haiti]**

Lunn, John. Market Structure and the Incentive to Invent. *Eastern Econ. J.*, October–December 1983, *9*(4), pp. 333–36.

MacAvoy, Paul W. and Robinson, Kenneth. Winning by Losing: The AT&T Settlement and Its Impact on Telecommunications. *Yale J. Regul.*, 1983, *1*(1), pp. 1–42. **[G: U.S.]**

MacDonald, James M. Merger Statistics Revisited: A Comment [Mergers, External Growth, and Finance in the Development of Large-Scale Enterprise in Germany, 1880–1913]. *J. Econ. Hist.*, June 1983, *43*(2), pp. 483–85. **[G: U.S.; U.K.]**

Malatesta, Paul H. The Wealth Effect of Merger Activity and the Objective Functions of Merging Firms. *J. Finan. Econ.*, April 1983, *11*(1–4), pp. 155–81. **[G: U.S.]**

Mangan, John and Regan, Philip. A Note on Organisational Slack and Market Power in Australian Manufacturing. *Australian Econ. Pap.*, December 1983, *22*(41), pp. 356–63. **[G: Australia]**

Mann, Michael. The Competitive Impact of Advertising in U.S. Food Processing Industries: A Simultaneous Equation Approach: Commentary. **In** *Connor, J. M. and Ward, R. W., eds.*, 1983, pp. 275–76. **[G: U.S.]**

Manove, Michael. Provider Insurance. *Bell J. Econ. (See Rand J. Econ. after 4/85)*, Autumn 1983, *14*(2), pp. 489–96.

Mansfield, Edwin. Industrial Organizational and Technological Change: Recent Econometric Findings. **In** *Craven, J. V., ed.*, 1983, pp. 129–43. **[G: U.S.]**

Mansfield, Edwin. Technological Change and Market Structure: An Empirical Study. *Amer. Econ. Rev.*, May 1983, *73*(2), pp. 205–09. **[G: U.S.]**

Marion, Bruce W. and Mueller, Willard F. Industrial Organization, Economic Power, and the Food System. **In** *Farris, P. L., ed.*, 1983, pp. 16–37. **[G: U.S.]**

Mariti, P. and Smiley, Robert H. Co-Operative Agreements and the Organization of Industry. *J. Ind. Econ.*, June 1983, *31*(4), pp. 437–51.

Marlow, Michael L. Entry and Performance in Financial Markets. *J. Bank Res.*, Autumn 1983, *14*(3), pp. 227–30. **[G: U.S.]**

Martin, Stephen. Vertical Relationships and Industrial Performance. *Quart. Rev. Econ. Bus.*, Spring 1983, *23*(1), pp. 6–18. **[G: U.S.]**

Mather, Loys L. and Tucker, Laurel I. Conglomerate Mergers, Food Advertising, and the Cross Subsidization Hypothesis. **In** *Connor, J. M. and Ward, R. W., eds.*, 1983, pp. 201–13. **[G: U.S.]**

Mathewson, G. Frank and Winter, Ralph A. The Incentives for Resale Price Maintenance under Imperfect Information. *Econ. Inquiry*, July 1983, *21*(3), pp. 337–48.

Matluck, Edward. Business Strategy and Investment Behavior. *Managerial Dec. Econ.*, September 1983, *4*(3), pp. 185–92. **[G: U.S.]**

Matthews, Steven A. and Mirman, Leonard J. Equilibrium Limit Pricing: The Effects of Private Information and Stochastic Demand. *Econometrica*, July 1983, *51*(4), pp. 981–96.

Matthews, Trevor V. Business Associations and the State, 1850–1979. **In** *Head, B. W., ed.*, 1983, pp. 115–49. **[G: Australia]**

McBride, Mark E. Spatial Competition and Vertical Integration: Cement and Concrete Revisited. *Amer. Econ. Rev.*, December 1983, *73*(5), pp. 1011–22. **[G: U.S.]**

McGee, John S. Professor Weiss on Concentration [The Extent and Effects of Aggregate Concentration]. *J. Law Econ.*, June 1983, *26*(2), pp. 457–65. **[G: U.S.]**

McGuinness, Tony. Efficiency and Industrial Organisation. **In** *Shepherd, D.; Turk, J. and Silberston, A., eds.*, 1983, pp. 8–29.

McGuinness, Tony. Markets and Hierarchies: A Suitable Framework for an Evaluation of Organisational Change? **In** *Francis, A.; Turk, J. and Willman, P., eds.*, 1983, pp. 180–88.

Means, Gardiner C. Corporate Power in the Marketplace. *J. Law Econ.*, June 1983, *26*(2), pp. 467–85. **[G: U.S.]**

Means, Gardiner C. Hessen's "Reappraisal" [The Modern Corporation and Private Property: A Reappraisal]. *J. Law Econ.*, June 1983, *26*(2), pp. 297–300.

Meisel, John B. and Lin, Steven A. Y. The Impact of Market Structure on the Firm's Allocation of Resources to Research and Development. *Quart. Rev. Econ. Bus.*, Winter 1983, *23*(4), pp. 28–43. **[G: U.S.]**

Melicher, Ronald W.; Ledolter, Johannes and D'Antonio, Louis J. A Time Series Analysis of Aggregate Merger Activity. *Rev. Econ. Statist.*, August 1983, *65*(3), pp. 423–30. **[G: U.S.]**

Mellow, Wesley. Employer Size, Unionism, and Wages. **In** *Reid, J. D., Jr., ed.*, 1983, pp. 253–82. **[G: U.S.]**

Merrilees, William J. Anatomy of a Price Leadership Challenge: An Evaluation of Pricing Strategies in the Australian Newspaper Industry. *J. Ind. Econ.*, March 1983, *31*(3), pp. 291–311. **[G: Australia]**

Meyer, John R. and Tye, William B. Rational Policies for Development of International Air Transportation. **In** *Khachaturov, T. S. and Goodwin, P. B., eds.*, 1983, pp. 245–64. **[G: Global; U.S.]**

Meyer, Peter J. Concentration and Performance in Local Retail Markets. **In** *Craven, J. V., ed.*, 1983, pp. 145–61. **[G: U.S.]**

Millner, Edward L. Concentration, Mergers and Public Policy. *Atlantic Econ. J.*, December 1983, *11*(4), pp. 89–90.

Mincer, Jacob. George Stigler's Contributions to Economics. *Scand. J. Econ.*, 1983, *85*(1), pp. 65–75.

Mosser, A. Concentration and the Finance of Austrian Industrial Combines, 1880-1914. **In** *Teichova, A. and Cottrell, P. L., eds.*, 1983, pp. 57–71. **[G: Austria]**

Moyer, R. Charles and Chatfield, Robert. Market Power and Systematic Risk. *J. Econ. Bus.*, 1983, *35*(1), pp. 123–30. **[G: U.S.]**

Mueller, Willard F. Market Power and Its Control in the Food System. *Amer. J. Agr. Econ.*, December 1983, *65*(5), pp. 855–63. **[G: U.S.]**

Mulligan, James G. The Economies of Massed Reserves. *Amer. Econ. Rev.*, September 1983, *73*(4), pp. 725–34.

Munkirs, John R. Centralized Private Sector Planning: An Institutionalist's Perspective on the Contemporary U.S. Economy. *J. Econ. Issues*, December 1983, *17*(4), pp. 931–67. **[G: U.S.]**

Munkirs, John R. and Ayers, Michael. Political and Policy Implications of Centralized Private Sector Planning. *J. Econ. Issues*, December 1983, *17*(4), pp. 969–84.

Murrell, Peter. The Economics of Sharing: A Transactions Cost Analysis of Contractual Choice in Farming. *Bell J. Econ. (See Rand J. Econ. after 4/85)*, Spring 1983, *14*(1), pp. 283–93.

Nakao, Takeo. Profitability, Market Share, Product Quality, and Advertising in Oligopoly. *J. Econ. Dynam. Control*, September 1983, *6*(1/2), pp. 153–71.

Nalebuff, Barry J. and Stiglitz, Joseph E. Prizes and Incentives: Towards a General Theory of Compensation and Competition. *Bell J. Econ. (See Rand J. Econ. after 4/85)*, Spring 1983, *14*(1), pp. 21–43.

Naylor, Thomas H. and Thomas, Celia. Microeconomic Foundations of Corporate Strategy. *Managerial Dec. Econ.*, September 1983, *4*(3), pp. 127–35. **[G: U.S.]**

Neck, Philip. The Small Firm: Africa. **In** *Storey, D. J., ed.*, 1983, pp. 248–71. **[G: Africa]**

Nelson, James C. Coming Organizational Change in Transportation. **In** *Nelson, J. C.*, 1983, *1967*, pp. 25–50.

Nelson, James C. Dynamic Competitive Forces in Freight Transport. **In** *Nelson, J. C.*, 1983, *1977*, pp. 51–77. **[G: Canada]**

Nelson, James C. Patterns of Competition and Monopoly in Present-Day Transport and Implications for Public Policy. **In** *Nelson, J. C.*, 1983, *1950*, pp. 2–20.

Nermuth, Manfred. Insolvencies and the Business Cycle in Austria. *Empirica*, 1983, (2), pp. 159–82. **[G: Austria]**

Netter, Jeffry M. Political Competition and Advertising as a Barrier to Entry. *Southern Econ. J.*, October 1983, *50*(2), pp. 510–20. **[G: U.S.]**

Neumann, Manfred; Böbel, Ingo and Haid, Alfred. Business Cycle and Industrial Market Power: An Empirical Investigation for West German Industries, 1965–1977. *J. Ind. Econ.*, December 1983, *32*(2), pp. 187–96. **[G: W. Germany]**

Newfarmer, Richard S. Multinationals and Marketplace Magic in the 1980s. **In** *Kindleberger, C. P. and Audretsch, D. B., eds.*, 1983, pp. 162–97. **[G: Global]**

North, Douglass C. Comment on Stigler and Friedland, "The Literature of Economics: The Case of Berle and Means." *J. Law Econ.*, June 1983, *26*(2), pp. 269–71. **[G: U.S.]**

O'Callaghan, John. Ownership and Control in the Manufacturing Sector of West Malaysia: A Note. **In** *Lim, D., ed.*, 1983, *1971*, pp. 221–22. **[G: Malaysia]**

O'Farrell, P. N. and Crouchley, R. Industrial Closures in Ireland 1973–1981: Analysis and Implications. *Reg. Stud.*, December 1983, *17*(6), pp. 411–27. **[G: Ireland]**

Oi, Walter Y. Heterogeneous Firms and the Organization of Production. *Econ. Inquiry*, April 1983, *21*(2), pp. 147–71.

Overy, R. F. Göring's 'Multi-national Empire.' **In** *Teichova, A. and Cottrell, P. L., eds.*, 1983, pp. 269–98. **[G: Germany; Europe]**

Pagoulatos, Emilio and Sorensen, Robert. The Competitive Impact of Advertising in U.S. Food Processing Industries: A Simultaneous Equation Approach. **In** *Connor, J. M. and Ward, R. W., eds.*, 1983, pp. 241–56. **[G: U.S.]**

Parker, Russell. Comments [Conglomerate Mergers, Food Advertising, and the Cross Subsidization Hypothesis] [The Interactions of Food Manufacturer Advertising and Food Retailer Buying Practices: Some Implications for Food System Organizations]. **In** *Connor, J. M. and Ward, R. W., eds.*, 1983, pp. 236–37. **[G: U.S.]**

Pautler, Paul A. A Review of the Economic Basis for Broad-Based Horizontal-Merger Policy. *Antitrust Bull.*, Fall 1983, *28*(3), pp. 571–651. **[G: U.S.]**

Pearce, Robert D. Industrial Diversification amongst the World's Leading Multinational Enterprises. **In** *Casson, M., ed.*, 1983, pp. 140–79. **[G: OECD]**

Perrakis, Stylianos and Warskett, George. Capacity and Entry under Demand Uncertainty. *Rev. Econ. Stud.*, July 1983, *50*(3), pp. 495–511.

Peterson, Rodney D. and Soma, John T. Advertising, Imperfect Competition, and the Market for Legal Services. *J. Behav. Econ.*, Winter 1983, *12*(2), pp. 57–66. **[G: U.S.]**

Pickering, J. F. The Causes and Consequences of Abandoned Mergers. *J. Ind. Econ.*, March 1983, *31*(3), pp. 267–81. **[G: U.K.]**

Pickford, Michael. The Determinants of Seller Concentration in New Zealand Manufacturing Industry. *Australian Econ. Pap.*, December 1983, *22*(41), pp. 374–83. **[G: New Zealand]**

Poensgen, Otto H. Between Market and Hierarchy. **In** *Francis, A.; Turk, J. and Willman, P., eds.*, 1983, pp. 54–80. **[G: W. Germany]**

Polinsky, A. Mitchell and Rogerson, William P. Products Liability, Consumer Misperceptions, and Market Power. *Bell J. Econ. (See Rand J. Econ. after 4/85)*, Autumn 1983, *14*(2), pp. 581–89.

Porter, Michael E. How Competitive Forces Shape Strategy. **In** *Dickson, D. N., ed.*, 1983, pp. 156–70.

Porter, Michael E. Industrial Organization and the Evolution of Concepts for Strategic Planning: The New Learning. *Managerial Dec. Econ.*, September 1983, *4*(3), pp. 172–80.

Porter, Robert H. A Study of Cartel Stability: The Joint Executive Committee, 1880–1886. *Bell J. Econ. (See Rand J. Econ. after 4/85)*, Autumn 1983, *14*(2), pp. 301–14. **[G: U.S.]**

Prašnikar, Janez. The Yugoslav Self-Managed Enterprise and Factors of Its Efficiency. *Econ. Anal. Worker's Manage.*, 1983, *17*(1), pp. 27–42. **[G: Yugoslavia]**

Puccinelli, Pietro. A Cyclical Model of Large Firms. *Econ. Notes*, 1983, (2), pp. 65–83.

Raab, Raymond L. Market Structure and Corporate Power Investment: An Empirical Investigation of Campaign Contributions of the 1972 Federal Elections. *Nebr. J. Econ. Bus.*, Winter, 1983, *22*(1), pp. 59–65. **[G: U.S.]**

Rafati, M. Reza. Price Determination in Monopolistic Markets with Inventory Adjustments: The Case of Nickel. *Weltwirtsch. Arch.*, 1983, *119*(1), pp. 152–68.

Raimondo, Henry J. Free Agents' Impact on the Labor Market for Baseball Players. *J. Lab. Res.*, Spring 1983, *4*(2), pp. 183–93. **[G: U.S.]**

Ravenscraft, David J. Structure–Profit Relationships at the Line of Business and Industry Level. *Rev. Econ. Statist.*, February 1983, *65*(1), pp. 22–31. **[G: U.S.]**

Read, Robert. The Growth and Structure of Multinationals in the Banana Export Trade. **In** *Casson, M., ed.*, 1983, pp. 180–213. **[G: Caribbean; Central America; U.S.]**

Rege, Udayan P. A Cross Sectional Study of Relative Take-Over Activity. *Appl. Econ.*, April 1983, *15*(2), pp. 235–42. **[G: Canada]**

Reinganum, Jennifer F. Uncertain Innovation and the Persistence of Monopoly. *Amer. Econ. Rev.*, September 1983, *73*(4), pp. 741–48.

Reinganum, Marc R. and Smith, Janet Kiholm. Investor Preference for Large Firms: New Evidence on Economies of Size. *J. Ind. Econ.*, December 1983, *32*(2), pp. 213–27. **[G: U.S.]**

Rhoades, Stephen A. Concentration of World Banking and the role of U.S. Banks among the 100 Largest, 1956–1980. *J. Banking Finance*, September 1983, *7*(3), pp. 427–37. **[G: Selected Countries; U.S.]**

Richards, Daniel J. Wages and the Dominant Firm. *J. Lab. Res.*, Spring 1983, *4*(2), pp. 177–82. **[G: U.S.]**

Riordan, Michael H. Contracting in an Idiosyncratic Market. *Bell J. Econ. (See Rand J. Econ. after 4/85)*, Autumn 1983, *14*(2), pp. 338–50.

Rockwood, Alan. The Impact of Joint Ventures on the Market for OCS Oil and Gas Leases. *J. Ind. Econ.*, June 1983, *31*(4), pp. 453–68. **[G: U.S.]**

Roehl, Thomas. A Transactions Cost Approach to International Trading Structures: The Case of the Japanese General Trading Companies. *Hitotsubashi J. Econ.*, December 1983, *24*(2), pp. 119–35. **[G: Japan]**

Rogers, Richard T. Advertising and Concentration Change in U.S. Food and Tobacco Product Classes, 1958–1972. **In** *Connor, J. M. and Ward, R. W., eds.*, 1983, pp. 283–94. **[G: U.S.]**

Rogerson, William P. Reputation and Product Quality. *Bell J. Econ. (See Rand J. Econ. after 4/85)*, Autumn 1983, *14*(2), pp. 508–16.

Rose, John T. and Savage, Donald T. Bank Holding Company *De Novo* Entry, Bank Performance, and Holding Company Size. *Quart. Rev. Econ. Bus.*, Winter 1983, *23*(4), pp. 54–62. **[G: U.S.]**

Rosen, Corey M. and Klein, Katherine. Job-Creating Performance of Employee-Owned Firms. *Mon. Lab. Rev.*, August 1983, *106*(8), pp. 15–19. **[G: U.S.]**

Rosenberg, Nathan. Comments on Robert Hessen, "The Modern Corporation and Private Property: A Reappraisal." *J. Law Econ.*, June 1983, *26*(2), pp. 291–96.

Round, David K. Intertemporal Profit Margin Variability and Market Structure in Australian Manufacturing. *Int. J. Ind. Organ.*, June 1983, *1*(2), pp. 189–209. **[G: Australia]**

Ruback, Richard S. Assessing Competition in the Market for Corporate Acquisitions. *J. Finan. Econ.*, April 1983, *11*(1–4), pp. 141–53. **[G: U.S.]**

Ruback, Richard S. The Cities Service Takeover: A Case Study. *J. Finance*, May 1983, *38*(2), pp. 319–30. **[G: U.S.]**

Salant, Stephen W.; Switzer, Sheldon and Reynolds,

Robert J. Losses from Horizontal Merger: The Effects of an Exogenous Change in Industry Structure on Cournot–Nash Equilibrium. *Quart. J. Econ.*, May 1983, *98*(2), pp. 185–99.

Salop, Steven C. and Scheffman, David T. Raising Rivals' Costs. *Amer. Econ. Rev.*, May 1983, *73*(2), pp. 267–71.

Sawyer, Malcolm. On the Specification of Structure–Performance Relationships: A Reply. *Europ. Econ. Rev.*, November 1983, *23*(2), pp. 257–59.

Scherer, F. M. Concentration, R&D, and Productivity Change. *Southern Econ. J.*, July 1983, *50*(1), pp. 221–25. [G: U.S.]

Schiller, Bradley R. Small Business Training: A Negative-Sum Game. *Challenge,* Sept.–Oct. 1983, *26*(4), pp. 57–60. [G: U.S.]

Schipper, Katherine and Thompson, Rex. Evidence on the Capitalized Value of Merger Activity for Acquiring Firms. *J. Finan. Econ.*, April 1983, *11*(1–4), pp. 85–119. [G: U.S.]

Schipper, Katherine and Thompson, Rex. The Impact of Merger-Related Regulations on the Shareholders of Acquiring Firms. *J. Acc. Res.*, Spring 1983, *21*(1), pp. 184–221. [G: U.S.]

Schmalensee, Richard. George Stigler's Contributions to Economics. *Scand. J. Econ.*, 1983, *85*(1), pp. 77–86.

Schmalensee, Richard. Product Differentiation Advantages of Pioneering Brands: Errata. *Amer. Econ. Rev.*, March 1983, *73*(1), pp. 250.

Schmalensee, Richard; Silk, Alvin J. and Bojanek, Robert. The Impact of Scale and Media Mix on Advertising Agency Costs. *J. Bus.*, October 1983, *56*(4), pp. 453–75. [G: U.S.]

Schmenner, Roger W. Look beyond the Obvious in Plant Location. **In** *Kantrow, A. M., ed.*, 1983, pp. 409–20.

Schmidt, Hartmut. Marktorganisationsbestimmte Kosten und Transaktionskosten als börsenpolitische Kategorien—Grundsätzliche Überlegungen zur Weiterentwicklung des Anlegerschutzes aus ökonomischer Sicht. (Costs and Transaction Costs Determined by Market Organization as Categories in Stock Exchange Policy. With English summary.) *Kredit Kapital,* 1983, *16*(2), pp. 184–204.

Schönwitz, Dietrich. Ansatzpunkte einer erweiterten Erfassung der Unternehmenskonzentration. (Aspects for an Extended Measurement of Economic Concentration. With English summary.) *Jahr. Nationalökon. Statist.*, January 1983, *198*(1), pp. 21–35.

Schvarzer, Jorge. Cambios en el liderazgo industrial argentino en el período de Martínez de Hoz. (With English summary.) *Desarrollo Econ.*, October-December 1983, *23*(91), pp. 395–422. [G: Argentina]

Schwartz, Marius and Reynolds, Robert J. Contestable Markets: An Uprising in the Theory of Industry Structure: Comment. *Amer. Econ. Rev.*, June 1983, *73*(3), pp. 488–90.

Schwartz, Steven. Micro Determinants of Conglomerate Mergers. **In** *Craven, J. V., ed.*, 1983, pp. 207–41. [G: U.S.]

Scott, A. J. Industrial Organization and the Logic of Intra-Metropolitan Location, II: A Case Study of the Printed Circuits Industry in the Greater Los Angeles Region. *Econ. Geogr.*, October 1983, *59*(4), pp. 343–67. [G: U.S.]

Scott, A. J. Industrial Organization and the Logic of Intra-Metropolitan Location: I. Theoretical Considerations. *Econ. Geogr.*, July 1983, *59*(3), pp. 233–50.

Semmler, Willi. Competition, Monopoly, and Differentials of Profit Rates: A Reply. *Rev. Radical Polit. Econ.*, Winter 1983, *15*(4), pp. 92–99. [G: U.S.]

Sengupta, Jati K.; Leonard, John E. and Vanyo, James P. A Limit Pricing Model for U.S. Computer Industry: An Application. *Appl. Econ.*, June 1983, *15*(3), pp. 297–308. [G: U.S.]

Shapiro, Carl. Optimal Pricing of Experience Goods. *Bell J. Econ. (See Rand J. Econ. after 4/85)*, Autumn 1983, *14*(2), pp. 497–507.

Shapiro, Daniel M. Entry, Exit, and the Theory of the Multinational Corporation. **In** *Kindleberger, C. P. and Audretsch, D. B., eds.*, 1983, pp. 103–22. [G: Canada]

Shapiro, Daniel M. The Comparative Profitability of Canadian- and Foreign-Controlled Firms. *Managerial Dec. Econ.*, June 1983, *4*(2), pp. 97–106.

Shepherd, William G. Economies of Scale and Monopoly Profits. **In** *Craven, J. V., ed.*, 1983, pp. 165–204. [G: U.S.]

Sherman, Howard J. Monopoly Power and Profit Rates [Competition, Monopoly and Differentials of Profit Rates: Theoretical Considerations and Empirical Evidence]. *Rev. Radical Polit. Econ.*, Summer 1983, *15*(2), pp. 125–33. [G: U.S.]

Shipley, David D. Pricing Flexibility in British Manufacturing Industry. *Managerial Dec. Econ.*, December 1983, *4*(4), pp. 224–33. [G: U.K.]

da Silva, Amado and Santos, Aníbal. Uma digressão pela economia industrial: de Harvard a Chicago passando pela Europa. *Economia,* January 1983, *7*(1), pp. 87–110.

Smirlock, Michael L. and Marshall, William J. Monopoly Power and Expense-Preference Behavior: Theory and Evidence to the Contrary. *Bell J. Econ. (See Rand J. Econ. after 4/85)*, Spring 1983, *14*(1), pp. 166–78. [G: U.S.]

Smith, James L. Joint Bidding, Collusion, and Bid Clustering in Competitive Auctions. *Southern Econ. J.*, October 1983, *50*(2), pp. 355–68.

Smith, L. Douglas, et al. A System for Analysing Competition in Distribution of Petroleum Products. **In** *Lev, B., ed.*, 1983, pp. 309–24. [G: U.S.]

Spence, A. Michael. *Contestable Markets and the Theory of Industry Structure:* A Review Article. *J. Econ. Lit.*, September 1983, *21*(3), pp. 981–90.

Stevens, Jerry L. Bank Market Concentration and Costs: Is There X-Inefficiency in Banking? *Bus. Econ.*, May 1983, *18*(3), pp. 36–44. [G: U.S.]

Stigler, George J. and Friedland, Claire. The Literature of Economics: The Case of Berle and Means. *J. Law Econ.*, June 1983, *26*(2), pp. 237–68. [G: U.S.]

Storey, D. J. Indigenising a Regional Economy: The Importance of Management Buyouts. *Reg. Stud.*, December 1983, *17*(6), pp. 471–75. [G: U.K.]

Sturgeon, James I. Micro–Macro Literature and the Implications of Centralized Private Sector Planning. *J. Econ. Issues,* December 1983, *17*(4), pp. 985–1009. [G: U.S.]

Sugden, Roger. The Degree of Monopoly, International Trade, and Transnational Corporations. *Int. J. Ind. Organ.,* June 1983, *1*(2), pp. 165–87.

Sutton, Clive J. Does Strategy Pay? *Managerial Dec. Econ.,* September 1983, *4*(3), pp. 153–59.

Tarantelli, Ezio. The Regulation of Inflation in Western Countries and the Degree of Neocorporatism. *Economia,* May 1983, *7*(2), pp. 199–238. [G: OECD]

Tardos, Márton. The Increasing Role and Ambivalent Reception of Small Enterprises in Hungary. *J. Compar. Econ.,* September 1983, *7*(3), pp. 277–87. [G: Hungary]

Taylor, A. The Expansion of Worker Co-Operatives: the Role of Local Authorities. *Reg. Stud.,* August 1983, *17*(4), pp. 276–81. [G: U.K.]

Taylor, Michael and Thrift, Nigel. Business Organization, Segmentation and Location. *Reg. Stud.,* December 1983, *17*(6), pp. 445–65.

Teece, David J. Technological and Organisational Factors in the Theory of the Multinational Enterprise. **In** *Casson, M., ed.,* 1983, pp. 51–62.

Teichova, Alice and Cottrell, P. L. Industrial Structures in West and East Central Europe during the Inter-war Period. **In** *Teichova, A. and Cottrell, P. L., eds.,* 1983, pp. 31–55. [G: Austria; Hungary; U.K.; Czechoslovakia]

Thompson, R. S. Diffusion of the M-Form Structure in the U.K.: Rate of Imitation, Inter-firm and Inter-industry Differences. *Int. J. Ind. Organ.,* September 1983, *1*(3), pp. 297–315. [G: U.K.]

Thompson, R. S. Diversifying Mergers and Risk: Some Empirical Tests. *J. Econ. Stud.,* 1983, *10*(3), pp. 12–21. [G: U.K.]

Thompson, R. S. The Spread of an Institutional Innovation: The Multidivisional Corporation in the U.K. *J. Econ. Issues,* June 1983, *17*(2), pp. 529–38. [G: U.K.]

Tilly, Richard. Reply [Mergers, External Growth, and Finance in the Development of Large-Scale Enterprises in Germany, 1880–1913]. *J. Econ. Hist.,* June 1983, *43*(2), pp. 486. [G: U.S.; U.K.]

Tomaszewski, Jerzy. German Capital in Silesian Industry in Poland between the Two World Wars. **In** *Teichova, A. and Cottrell, P. L., eds.,* 1983, pp. 227–47. [G: Poland; Selected Countries]

Torgerson, Randall E. Alternative Ownership and Control Mechanisms within the Food System. **In** *Farris, P. L., ed.,* 1983, pp. 184–223. [G: U.S.]

Trebilcock, C. Comment [Concentration and the Finance of Austrian Industrial Combines, 1880–1914] [Disintegration and Multi-national Enterprises in Central Europe during the Post-war Years (1918–23)]. **In** *Teichova, A. and Cottrell, P. L., eds.,* 1983, pp. 96–100. [G: Central Europe; Austria]

Turk, Jeremy. Conclusion: Power, Efficiency and Institutions: Some Implications of the Debate for the Scope of Economics. **In** *Francis, A.; Turk, J. and Willman, P., eds.,* 1983, pp. 189–204.

Vogel, Ronald J. The Industrial Organization of the Nursing Home Industry. **In** *Vogel, R. J. and Palmer, H. C., eds.,* 1983, pp. 579–624. [G: U.S.]

Wahlroos, Björn. Regulation of "Administered" Prices: An Empirical Analysis of the Microeconomics of Price Movement in Finland, 1972–77. *J. Ind. Econ.,* June 1983, *31*(4), pp. 363–81. [G: Finland]

Waldman, Don E. The Impact of Conglomerate Mergers on Acquired Firms' Growth Rates. *Nebr. J. Econ. Bus.,* Summer 1983, *22*(3), pp. 24–43. [G: U.S.]

Waller, Robert. Göring's 'Multi-national Empire': Commentary. **In** *Teichova, A. and Cottrell, P. L., eds.,* 1983, pp. 302–06. [G: Europe; Germany]

Wansley, James W. and Lane, William R. A Financial Profile of Merged Firms. *Rev. Bus. Econ. Res.,* Fall 1983, *19*(1), pp. 87–98. [G: U.S.]

Wansley, James W.; Roenfeldt, Rodney L. and Cooley, Philip L. Abnormal Returns from Merger Profiles. *J. Finan. Quant. Anal.,* June 1983, *18*(2), pp. 149–62. [G: U.S.]

Waterson, Michael. Economies of Scope within Market Frameworks. *Int. J. Ind. Organ.,* June 1983, *1*(2), pp. 223–37.

Waterson, Michael and Lopez, Arcesio. The Determinants of Research and Development Intensity in the U.K. *Appl. Econ.,* June 1983, *15*(3), pp. 379–91. [G: U.K.]

Weiss, Leonard W. The Extent and Effects of Aggregate Concentration. *J. Law Econ.,* June 1983, *26*(2), pp. 429–55. [G: U.S.]

Weitzman, Martin L. Contestable Markets: An Uprising in the Theory of Industry Structure: Comment. *Amer. Econ. Rev.,* June 1983, *73*(3), pp. 486–87.

Whyatt, A. Developments in the Structure and Organization of the Co-Operative Movement: Some Policy Considerations. *Reg. Stud.,* August 1983, *17*(4), pp. 273–76. [G: U.K.]

Wikander, Ulla. The Swedish Match Company in Central Europe between the Wars: 'Internal Power Struggle' between Former Competitors—Solo v. Swedish Match. **In** *Teichova, A. and Cottrell, P. L., eds.,* 1983, pp. 209–25. [G: Sweden; Europe]

Williamson, Oliver E. Credible Commitments: Using Hostages to Support Exchange. *Amer. Econ. Rev.,* September 1983, *73*(4), pp. 519–40.

Williamson, Oliver E. Organization Form, Residual Claimants, and Corporate Control. *J. Law Econ.,* June 1983, *26*(2), pp. 351–66.

Williamson, Oliver E. Organizational Innovation: The Transaction-Cost Approach. **In** *Ronen, J., ed.,* 1983, pp. 101–33.

Williamson, Oliver E. Technology and the Organization of Work: A Rejoinder. *J. Econ. Behav. Organ.,* March 1983, *4*(1), pp. 67–68.

Williamson, Oliver E. Technology and the Organization of Work: A Reply. *J. Econ. Behav. Organ.,* March 1983, *4*(1), pp. 57–62.

Williamson, Oliver E. and Ouchi, William G. The Markets and Hierarchies Programme of Research: Origins, Implications, Prospects. **In** *Francis, A.; Turk, J. and Willman, P., eds.,* 1983, *1981,* pp. 13–34.

Willman, Paul. The Organisational Failures Framework and Industrial Sociology. **In** *Francis, A.; Turk, J. and Willman, P., eds.,* 1983, pp. 117–35.

Wiriyawit, Chandraleka and Veendorp, E. C. H. Concentration Measures as Indicators of Market Performance. *Quart. Rev. Econ. Bus.*, Autumn 1983, *23*(3), pp. 44–53.

Wright, Brian Davern. The Economics of Invention Incentives: Patents, Prizes, and Research Contracts. *Amer. Econ. Rev.*, September 1983, *73*(4), pp. 691–707.

Xepapadeas, A. and Kanellopoulos, A. The Dynamic Behavior of the Rates of Return in U.K. Manufacturing Industries. *Greek Econ. Rev.*, December 1983, *5*(3), pp. 248–63. **[G: U.K.]**

Yon, B. Structures des filières et stratégies des firmes. (With English summary.) *Écon. Soc.*, May 1983, *17*(5), pp. 823–37. **[G: France]**

Zimmerman, Jerold L. Taxes and Firm Size. *J. Acc. Econ.*, August 1983, *5*(2), pp. 119–49. **[G: U.S.]**

Zuscovitch, Ehud. Informatisation, flexibilité et division du travail. (With English summary.) *Rev. Econ. Ind.*, 3rd Trimester 1983, (25), pp. 50–61. **[G: France]**

612 Public Policy Towards Monopoly and Competition

6120 Public Policy Towards Monopoly and Competition

Albon, Robert P. and Kirby, Michael G. Cost-Padding in Profit-Regulated Firms. *Econ. Rec.*, March 1983, *59*(164), pp. 16–27. **[G: U.S.]**

Audretsch, David B. An Evaluation of Horizontal Merger Enforcement. **In** *Craven, J. V., ed.*, 1983, pp. 69–88. **[G: U.S.]**

Baker, Donald I. and Baker, Beverly G. Antitrust and Communications Deregulation. *Antitrust Bull.*, Spring 1983, *28*(1), pp. 1–38. **[G: U.S.]**

Beesley, Michael E. and Littlechild, Stephen. Privatization: Principles, Problems and Priorities. *Lloyds Bank Rev.*, July 1983, (149), pp. 1–20. **[G: U.K.]**

Besen, Stanley M. and Woodbury, John R. Regulation, Deregulation, and Antitrust in the Telecommunications Industry. *Antitrust Bull.*, Spring 1983, *28*(1), pp. 39–68. **[G: U.S.]**

Bornholz, Robert and Evans, David S. The Early History of Competition in the Telephone Industry. **In** *Evans, D. S., ed.*, 1983, pp. 7–40. **[G: U.S.]**

Brock, William A. and Evans, David S. Creamskimming. **In** *Evans, D. S., ed.*, 1983, pp. 61–94. **[G: U.S.]**

Brock, William A. and Evans, David S. Predation: A Critique of the Government's Case in *U.S.* v. *AT&T.* **In** *Evans, D. S., ed.*, 1983, pp. 41–59. **[G: U.S.]**

Brodley, Joseph F. The Goals of Antitrust—Pretrial Hearing No. 1: A Verbatim Account of an Imagined Proceeding. *Antitrust Bull.*, Winter 1983, *28*(4), pp. 823–38.

Brusick, Philippe. UN Control of Restrictive Business Practices: A Decisive First Step. *J. World Trade Law*, July–August 1983, *17*(4), pp. 337–51.

Burns, Malcolm R. An Empirical Analysis of Stockholder Injury under § 2 of the Sherman Act. *J. Ind. Econ.*, June 1983, *31*(4), pp. 333–62. **[G: U.S.]**

Cabanellas, Guillermo and Etzrodt, Wolf. The New Argentine Antitrust Law: Competition as an Economic Policy Instrument. *J. World Trade Law*, January–February 1983, *17*(1), pp. 34–53. **[G: Argentina]**

Carlton, Dennis W. A Reexamination of Delivered Pricing Systems. *J. Law Econ.*, April 1983, *26*(1), pp. 51–70. **[G: U.S.]**

Choi, Dosoung and Philippatos, George C. Financial Consequences of Antitrust Enforcement. *Rev. Econ. Statist.*, August 1983, *65*(3), pp. 501–06. **[G: U.S.]**

Crandall, Robert W. Deregulation: The U.S. Experience. *Z. ges. Staatswiss.*, October 1983, *139*(3), pp. 419–34. **[G: U.S.]**

Davidow, Joel. EEC Proposed Competition Rules for Motor Vehicle Distribution: An American Perspective. *Antitrust Bull.*, Winter 1983, *28*(4), pp. 863–82. **[G: U.S.; EEC]**

Davidow, Joel. The Implementation of International Antitrust Principles. **In** *Rubin, S. J. and Hufbauer, G. C., eds.*, 1983, pp. 119–38. **[G: Global]**

Dichtl, Erwin; Raffée, Hans and Wellenreuther, Hans. Public Policy towards Small and Medium-Sized Retail Businesses in the Federal Republic of Germany. *Rivista Int. Sci. Econ. Com.*, April-May 1983, *30*(4–5), pp. 424–39. **[G: W. Germany]**

Dym, Herbert and Sussman, Robert M. Antitrust and Electric Utility Regulation. *Antitrust Bull.*, Spring 1983, *28*(1), pp. 69–99. **[G: U.S.]**

Eads, George C. Airline Competitive Conduct in a Less Regulated Environment: Implications for Antitrust. *Antitrust Bull.*, Spring 1983, *28*(1), pp. 159–84. **[G: U.S.]**

Easterbrook, Frank H. Antitrust and the Economics of Federalism. *J. Law Econ.*, April 1983, *26*(1), pp. 23–50.

Elsener, Ferdinand. Extraterritorial Application of U.S. Antitrust Laws: The Viewpoint of a European Corporate Lawyer. *Wirtsch. Recht*, 1983, *35*(2/3), pp. 130–40. **[G: U.S.]**

Evans, David S. Breaking Up Bell: Introduction. **In** *Evans, D. S., ed.*, 1983, pp. 1–5. **[G: U.S.]**

Faith, Roger L. and Tollison, Robert D. The Supply of Occupational Regulation. *Econ. Inquiry*, April 1983, *21*(2), pp. 232–40. **[G: U.K.; France]**

Ferguson, James M. Daily Newspaper Advertising Rates, Local Media Cross-Ownership, Newspaper Chains, and Media Competition. *J. Law Econ.*, October 1983, *26*(3), pp. 635–54. **[G: U.S.]**

Finkelstein, Michael O. and Levenbach, Hans. Regression Estimates of Damages in Price-Fixing Cases. *Law Contemp. Probl.*, Autumn 1983, *46*(4), pp. 145–69. **[G: U.S.]**

Finsinger, Jörg and Vogelsang, Ingo. Reply to Professor Gravelle's Comments [Alternative Institutional Frameworks for Price Incentive Mechanisms]. *Kyklos*, 1983, *36*(1), pp. 121–22.

Fournier, Gary M. and Martin, Donald L. Does Government-restricted Entry Produce Market Power? New Evidence from the Market for Television Advertising. *Bell J. Econ. (See Rand J. Econ. after 4/85)*, Spring 1983, *14*(1), pp. 44–56. **[G: U.S.]**

Franco, Joseph A. Limiting the Anticompetitive Prerogative of Patent Owners: Predatory Standards in Patent Licensing. *Yale Law J.*, April 1983, *92*(5), pp. 831–61.

Frank, Robert H. When Are Price Differentials Discriminatory? *J. Policy Anal. Manage.*, Winter 1983, *2*(2), pp. 238–55. **[G: U.S.]**

Fuhr, Joseph P., Jr. Competition in the Terminal Equipment Market after *Carterfone. Antitrust Bull.*, Fall 1983, *28*(3), pp. 669–98. **[G: U.S.]**

Gorinson, Stanley M. Depository Institution Regulatory Reform in the 1980s: The Issue of Geographic Restrictions. *Antitrust Bull.*, Spring 1983, *28*(1), pp. 227–54. **[G: U.S.]**

Grauer, Myron C. Recognition of the National Football League as a Single Entity under Section 1 of the Sherman Act: Implications of the Consumer Welfare Model. *Mich. Law Rev.*, October 1983, *82*(1), pp. 1–59. **[G: U.S.]**

Gravelle, H. S. E. Alternative Institutional Frameworks for Price Incentive Mechanisms: Some Comments. *Kyklos*, 1983, *36*(1), pp. 115–20.

Griffin, Joseph P. Antitrust Law Issues in Countertrade. *J. World Trade Law*, May–June 1983, *17*(3), pp. 236–48. **[G: U.S.]**

Gygi, Fritz. Das Unternehmen im Spiegel der Wirtschaftsverfassung und der wirtschaftspolitischen Gesetzgebung. (The Firm in the Mirror of the Economic Constitution and the Economic Legislation. With English summary.) *Schweiz. Z. Volkswirtsch. Statist.*, September 1983, *119*(3), pp. 321–35. **[G: Switzerland]**

Harris, Robert G. and Winston, Clifford M. Potential Benefits of Rail Mergers: An Econometric Analysis of Network Effects on Service Quality. *Rev. Econ. Statist.*, February 1983, *65*(1), pp. 32–40. **[G: U.S.]**

Havighurst, Clark C. The Contributions of Antitrust Law to a Procompetitive Health Policy. **In** *Meyer, J. A., ed.*, 1983, pp. 295–322. **[G: U.S.]**

Hirschey, Mark and Wichern, Dean W. Indicators and Causes of Size Advantages in Industry. *Managerial Dec. Econ.*, June 1983, *4*(2), pp. 64–72. **[G: U.S.]**

Johnson, M. Bruce. Can Economic Analysis Give Better Guidance to Antitrust Policy? *Econ. Inquiry*, January 1983, *21*(1), pp. 1–10. **[G: U.S.]**

Jones, J. C. H. and Laudadio, L. Risk, Profitability, and Market Structure: Some Canadian Evidence on Structural and Behavioral Approaches to Antitrust. *Antitrust Bull.*, Summer 1983, *28*(2), pp. 349–79. **[G: Canada]**

Kaufer, Erich and Blankart, Charles B. Regulation in Western Germany: The State of the Debate. *Z. ges. Staatswiss.*, October 1983, *139*(3), pp. 435–51. **[G: W. Germany; U.S.]**

Kenney, Roy W. and Klein, Benjamin. The Economics of Block Booking. *J. Law Econ.*, October 1983, *26*(3), pp. 497–540. **[G: U.S.]**

Kindleberger, Charles P. Standards as Public, Collective and Private Goods. *Kyklos*, 1983, *36*(3), pp. 377–96.

Klein, Robert M. Meeting Competition by Price Systems Revisited: The *Vanco* Decision. *Antitrust Bull.*, Winter 1983, *28*(4), pp. 795–822. **[G: U.S.]**

Kopit, William G. Health and Antitrust: The Case for Legislative Relief. **In** *Meyer, J. A., ed.*, 1983, pp. 323–31. **[G: U.S.]**

Korah, Valentine. Exclusive Licenses of Patent and Plant Breeders' Rights under EEC Law after *Maize Seed. Antitrust Bull.*, Fall 1983, *28*(3), pp. 699–755. **[G: EEC]**

Langdale, John. Competition in the United States' Long-Distance Telecommunications Industry. *Reg. Stud.*, December 1983, *17*(6), pp. 393–409. **[G: U.S.]**

Leitzinger, Jeffrey J. and Tamor, Kenneth. Foreign Competition in Antitrust Law. *J. Law Econ.*, April 1983, *26*(1), pp. 87–102.

Lenel, Hans Otto. A Review of the Third Report of the Monopolies Commission of West Germany. *Antitrust Bull.*, Fall 1983, *28*(3), pp. 757–81. **[G: W. Germany]**

Lewis, W. Arthur. Competition in Retail Trade. **In** *Lewis, W. A.*, 1983, *1946*, pp. 71–111.

Lewis, W. Arthur. Monopoly and the Law. **In** *Lewis, W. A.*, 1983, *1943*, pp. 47–70. **[G: U.K.]**

Littlechild, Stephen. Some Suggestions for UK Competition Policy. **In** *Seldon, A., et al.*, 1983, pp. 89–110. **[G: U.K.]**

Litvak, I. A. and Maule, C. J. Competition Policy and Newspapers in Canada. *Antitrust Bull.*, Summer 1983, *28*(2), pp. 461–81. **[G: Canada]**

Lofthouse, Stephen. Monopolies and Mergers Commission Reports: A Note. *Managerial Dec. Econ.*, December 1983, *4*(4), pp. 221–23. **[G: U.K.]**

MacAvoy, Paul W. and Robinson, Kenneth. Winning by Losing: The AT&T Settlement and Its Impact on Telecommunications. *Yale J. Regul.*, 1983, *1*(1), pp. 1–42. **[G: U.S.]**

McBride, Mark E. Spatial Competition and Vertical Integration: Cement and Concrete Revisited. *Amer. Econ. Rev.*, December 1983, *73*(5), pp. 1011–22. **[G: U.S.]**

McElroy, Katherine Maddox; Siegfried, John J. and Sweeney, George H. The Incidence of Price Changes in the U.S. Economy. **In** *Craven, J. V., ed.*, 1983, *1982*, pp. 243–66.

Millner, Edward L. Concentration, Mergers and Public Policy. *Atlantic Econ. J.*, December 1983, *11*(4), pp. 89–90.

Mueller, Willard F. Market Power and Its Control in the Food System. *Amer. J. Agr. Econ.*, December 1983, *65*(5), pp. 855–63. **[G: U.S.]**

Mueller, Willard F. The Anti-antitrust Movement. **In** *Craven, J. V., ed.*, 1983, pp. 19–40. **[G: U.S.]**

Nelson, James C. Implications of Evolving Entry and Licensing Policies in Road Freight Transport. **In** *Nelson, J. C.*, 1983, *1974*, pp. 288–97.

Pasour, E. C., Jr. Information: A Neglected Aspect of the Theory of Price Regulation. *Cato J.*, Winter 1983/84, *3*(3), pp. 855–67.

Pautler, Paul A. A Review of the Economic Basis for Broad-Based Horizontal-Merger Policy. *Antitrust Bull.*, Fall 1983, *28*(3), pp. 571–651. **[G: U.S.]**

Pengilley, Warren. Comparative Approaches to the Enforcement of Antitrust Laws against Price-Fixing Arrangements (With Special Emphasis on the Lessons to Be Learned from Antitrust Law and Enforcement in Australia). *Antitrust Bull.*, Winter 1983, *28*(4), pp. 883–939. **[G: Australia; U.K.]**

Pittman, Russell W. and Snapp, Bruce. Folded, Spindled, and Mutilated: Economic Analysis and U.S. v. IBM. *Atlantic Econ. J.*, December 1983, *11*(4), pp. 91–94. **[G: U.S.]**

Rabino, Samuel. Webb-Pomerene and the Construction Industry. *Calif. Manage. Rev.*, January 1983, *25*(2), pp. 21–33. **[G: U.S.]**

Rubinfeld, Daniel L. and Steiner, Peter O. Quantitative Methods in Antitrust Litigation. *Law Contemp. Probl.*, Autumn 1983, *46*(4), pp. 69–141. **[G: U.S.]**

Ryan, John P., Jr. The Export Trading Company Act of 1982: Antitrust Panacea, Placebo, or Pitfall? *Antitrust Bull.*, Fall 1983, *28*(3), pp. 501–69. **[G: U.S.]**

Salop, Steven C. and Scheffman, David T. Raising Rivals' Costs. *Amer. Econ. Rev.*, May 1983, *73*(2), pp. 267–71.

Scherer, F. M. The Propensity to Patent. *Int. J. Ind. Organ.*, 1983, *1*(1), pp. 107–28. **[G: U.S.]**

Schmidt, Ingo. Different Approaches and Problems in Dealing with Control of Market Power: A Comparison of German, European, and U.S. Policy towards Market-Dominating Enterprises. *Antitrust Bull.*, Summer 1983, *28*(2), pp. 417–60. **[G: EEC; W. Germany; U.S.]**

Shenefield, John H. Extraterritorial Application of United States Antitrust Laws: Economic Imperialism or Correcting the Evil at the Source? *Wirtsch. Recht*, 1983, *35*(2/3), pp. 116–29. **[G: U.S.]**

Shull, Bernard. The Separation of Banking and Commerce: Origin, Development, and Implications for Antitrust. *Antitrust Bull.*, Spring 1983, *28*(1), pp. 255–79. **[G: U.S.]**

Smith, Robert E. Toward a Broader Concept of Competition Policy. **In** *Craven, J. V., ed.*, 1983, pp. 89–105.

Stillman, Robert. Examining Antitrust Policy towards Horizontal Mergers. *J. Finan. Econ.*, April 1983, *11*(1–4), pp. 225–40. **[G: U.S.]**

Tollison, Robert D. Antitrust in the Reagan Administration: A Report from the Belly of the Beast. *Int. J. Ind. Organ.*, June 1983, *1*(2), pp. 211–21. **[G: U.S.]**

Trebilcock, Michael J. Regulating Service Quality in Professional Markets. **In** *Dewees, D. N., ed.*, 1983, pp. 83–107. **[G: U.S.]**

Trebilcock, Michael J., et al. Provincially Induced Barriers to Trade in Canada: A Survey. **In** *Trebilcock, M. J., et al., eds.*, 1983, pp. 243–351. **[G: Canada]**

Vagts, Detlev F. The Scope of Application and Enforcement of U.S. Laws. *Wirtsch. Recht*, 1983, *35*(2/3), pp. 72–97. **[G: U.S.]**

Vischer, Frank. The United States Jurisdictional Concepts Viewed from Abroad. *Wirtsch. Recht*, 1983, *35*(2/3), pp. 98–113. **[G: U.S.; Switzerland]**

Webb, Thomas R. Fixing the Price Fixing Confusion: A Rule of Reason Approach. *Yale Law J.*, March 1983, *92*(4), pp. 706–30. **[G: U.S.]**

Wier, Peggy. The Costs of Antimerger Lawsuits: Evidence from the Stock Market. *J. Finan. Econ.*, April 1983, *11*(1–4), pp. 207–24. **[G: U.S.]**

Williams, Harold R. and Baliga, Gurudutt M. The U.S. Export Trading Company Act of 1982: Nature and Evaluation. *J. World Trade Law*, May–June 1983, *17*(3), pp. 224–35. **[G: U.S.]**

Williamson, Oliver E. Antitrust Enforcement: Where It Has Been; Where It Is Going. **In** *Craven, J. V., ed.*, 1983, pp. 41–68. **[G: U.S.]**

Wiriyawit, Chandraleka and Veendorp, E. C. H. Concentration Measures as Indicators of Market Performance. *Quart. Rev. Econ. Bus.*, Autumn 1983, *23*(3), pp. 44–53.

Wright, Brian Davern. The Economics of Invention Incentives: Patents, Prizes, and Research Contracts. *Amer. Econ. Rev.*, September 1983, *73*(4), pp. 691–707.

613 Public Utilities; Costs of Government Regulation of Other Industries in the Private Sector

6130 General

Ahern, William R. Reorganizing without Too Much Pain. *J. Policy Anal. Manage.*, Spring 1983, *2*(3), pp. 462–65. **[G: U.S.]**

Barkenbus, Jack N. Is Self-Regulation Possible? *J. Policy Anal. Manage.*, Summer 1983, *2*(4), pp. 576–88. **[G: U.S.]**

Beesley, Michael E. and Glaister, Stephen G. Information for Regulating: The Case of Taxis. *Econ. J.*, September 1983, *93*(371), pp. 594–615. **[G: U.K.]**

Benson, Bruce L. The Economic Theory of Regulation as an Explanation of Policies toward Bank Mergers and Holding Company Acquisitions. *Antitrust Bull.*, Winter 1983, *28*(4), pp. 839–62. **[G: U.S.]**

Brand, Donald R. Corporatism, the NRA, and the Oil Industry. *Polit. Sci. Quart.*, Spring 1983, *98*(1), pp. 99–118. **[G: U.S.]**

Connellan, Liam. Industrial Policy. *Irish Banking Rev.*, March 1983, pp. 15–28. **[G: Ireland]**

Cornell, Nina W. and Webbink, Douglas W. The Present Direction of the FCC: An Appraisal. *Amer. Econ. Rev.*, May 1983, *73*(2), pp. 194–97. **[G: U.S.]**

Crampes, Claude. Subventions et régulation d'une entreprise privée. (Subsidies and Regulation of a Private Entreprise. With English summary.) *Ann. INSEE*, July–September 1983, (51), pp. 47–64.

Crew, Michael A. and Kleindorfer, Paul R. Regulatory Influences on Managerial Incentives: Comment. *Southern Econ. J.*, July 1983, *50*(1), pp. 265–66. **[G: U.S.]**

DeMuth, Christopher C. What Is Regulation? **In** *Zeckhauser, R. J. and Leebaert, D., eds.*, 1983, pp. 262–78.

Dewees, Donald N.; Mathewson, G. Frank and Trebilcock, Michael J. Policy Alternatives in Quality Regulation. **In** *Dewees, D. N., ed.*, 1983, pp. 27–51.

Dewees, Donald N.; Mathewson, G. Frank and Trebilcock, Michael J. The Rationale for Government Regulation of Quality. **In** *Dewees, D. N., ed.*, 1983, pp. 3–26. **[G: U.S.]**

Dewees, Donald N.; Trebilcock, Michael J. and Tu-

ohy, Carolyn J. The Regulation of Quality: Summary and Conclusions. In *Dewees, D. N., ed.*, 1983, pp. 325–45.

Donnenfeld, Shabtai. Domestic Regulation and the Preservation of Monopoly Power in Foreign Markets. *Southern Econ. J.*, April 1983, *49*(4), pp. 954–65.

Eckert, Ross D. The Reagan Deregulation Program: An Assessment: Response: Regulation and Self-interest. **In** *Stubblebine, Wm. C. and Willett, T. D., eds.*, 1983, pp. 169–71. **[G: U.S.]**

Feigenbaum, Susan. The Reagan Deregulation Program: An Assessment: Response: What Role for Private Initiatives? **In** *Stubblebine, Wm. C. and Willett, T. D., eds.*, 1983, pp. 171–74. **[G: U.S.]**

Finsinger, Jörg and Vogelsang, Ingo. Reply to Professor Gravelle's Comments [Alternative Institutional Frameworks for Price Incentive Mechanisms]. *Kyklos*, 1983, *36*(1), pp. 121–22.

Frug, Gerald E. Why Neutrality? [Regulation in a Liberal State: The Role of Non-commodity Values]. *Yale Law J.*, July 1983, *92*(8), pp. 1591–1601. **[G: U.S.]**

Gibson, Rosemary and Reiss, John B. Health Care Delivery and Financing: Competition, Regulation, and Incentives. **In** *Meyer, J. A., ed.*, 1983, pp. 243–68. **[G: U.S.]**

Gravelle, H. S. E. Alternative Institutional Frameworks for Price Incentive Mechanisms: Some Comments. *Kyklos*, 1983, *36*(1), pp. 115–20.

Gray, C. Boyden. Regulation and Federalism. *Yale J. Regul.*, 1983, *1*(1), pp. 93–110. **[G: U.S.]**

Gygi, Fritz. Das Unternehmen im Spiegel der Wirtschaftsverfassung und der wirtschaftspolitischen Gesetzgebung. (The Firm in the Mirror of the Economic Constitution and the Economic Legislation. With English summary.) *Schweiz. Z. Volkswirtsch. Statist.*, September 1983, *119*(3), pp. 321–35. **[G: Switzerland]**

Hamlen, William A., Jr. and Jen, Frank. An Alternative Model of Interruptible Service Pricing and Rationing. *Southern Econ. J.*, April 1983, *49*(4), pp. 1108–21.

Hirschey, Mark and Pappas, James L. Regulatory Influences on Managerial Incentives: Reply. *Southern Econ. J.*, July 1983, *50*(1), pp. 267–69. **[G: U.S.]**

Johnson, M. Bruce. Regulation and Justice: An Economist's Perspective. **In** *Machan, T. R. and Johnson, M. B., eds.*, 1983, pp. 127–34.

Kaufer, Erich and Blankart, Charles B. Regulation in Western Germany: The State of the Debate. *Z. ges. Staatswiss.*, October 1983, *139*(3), pp. 435–51. **[G: W. Germany; U.S.]**

Kearl, J. R. Rules, Rule Intermediaries and the Complexity and Stability of Regulation. *J. Public Econ.*, November 1983, *22*(2), pp. 215–26.

Kelman, Steven. Regulation and Paternalism. **In** *Machan, T. R. and Johnson, M. B., eds.*, 1983, pp. 217–48.

Koster, Francis P. The Role of Utilities in Promoting Solar Energy: The Case of the TVA. **In** *Rich, D., et al., eds.*, 1983, pp. 103–22. **[G: U.S.]**

Machan, Tibor R. The Petty Tyranny of Government Regulation. **In** *Machan, T. R. and Johnson, M. B., eds.*, 1983, pp. 259–88.

Meerman, Jacob. Cost Recovery in a Project Context: Some World Bank Experience in Tropical Africa. *World Devel.*, June 1983, *11*(6), pp. 503–14. **[G: Tropical Africa]**

Mincer, Jacob. George Stigler's Contributions to Economics. *Scand. J. Econ.*, 1983, *85*(1), pp. 65–75.

Moore, Thomas Gale. The Reagan Deregulation Program: An Assessment. **In** *Stubblebine, Wm. C. and Willett, T. D., eds.*, 1983, pp. 159–68. **[G: U.S.]**

Nadel, Mark V. Making Regulatory Policy. **In** *Schick, A., ed.*, 1983, pp. 221–56. **[G: U.S.]**

Niho, Yoshio and Musacchio, Robert A. Effects of Regulation and Capital Market Imperfections on the Dynamic Behavior of a Firm. *Southern Econ. J.*, January 1983, *49*(3), pp. 625–36.

Niho, Yoshio and Mussachio, Robert A. Revenue Maximization and Optimal Capital Policies of a Regulated Firm. **In** *[Yamada, I.]*, 1983, pp. 15–26.

Noll, Roger G. The Political Foundations of Regulatory Policy. *Z. ges. Staatswiss.*, October 1983, *139*(3), pp. 377–404.

Noll, Roger G. and Owen, Bruce M. Conclusion: Economics, Politics, and Deregulation. **In** *Noll, R. G. and Owen, B. M.*, 1983, pp. 155–62. **[G: U.S.]**

Noll, Roger G. and Owen, Bruce M. The Political Economy of Deregulation: An Overview. **In** *Noll, R. G. and Owen, B. M.*, 1983, pp. 26–52. **[G: U.S.]**

Noll, Roger G. and Owen, Bruce M. The Predictability of Interest Group Arguments. **In** *Noll, R. G. and Owen, B. M.*, 1983, pp. 53–65. **[G: U.S.]**

Panzar, John C. Regulatory Theory and the U.S. Airline Experience. *Z. ges. Staatswiss.*, October 1983, *139*(3), pp. 490–505. **[G: U.S.]**

Pasour, E. C., Jr. Information: A Neglected Aspect of the Theory of Price Regulation. *Cato J.*, Winter 1983/84, *3*(3), pp. 855–67.

Quandt, Richard E. Complexity in Regulation. *J. Public Econ.*, November 1983, *22*(2), pp. 199–214.

Rescher, Nicholas. On the Rationale of Governmental Regulation. **In** *Machan, T. R. and Johnson, M. B., eds.*, 1983, pp. 249–58.

Ricketts, Martin. Local Authority Housing Investment and Finance: A Test of the Theory of Regulation. *Manchester Sch. Econ. Soc. Stud.*, March 1983, *51*(1), pp. 45–62. **[G: U.K.]**

Rolph, Elizabeth S. Government Allocation of Property Rights: Who Gets What? *J. Policy Anal. Manage.*, Fall 1983, *3*(1), pp. 45–61. **[G: U.S.]**

Schmalensee, Richard. George Stigler's Contributions to Economics. *Scand. J. Econ.*, 1983, *85*(1), pp. 77–86.

Schuck, Peter H. Regulation, Non-market Values, and the Administrative State: A Comment [Regulation in a Liberal State: The Role of Non-commodity Values]. *Yale Law J.*, July 1983, *92*(8), pp. 1602–13. **[G: U.S.]**

Smith, J. C. The Processes of Adjudication and Regulation, a Comparison. **In** *Machan, T. R. and Johnson, M. B., eds.*, 1983, pp. 71–96. **[G: U.S.]**

Steiner, Peter O. The Legalization of American Society: Economic Regulation. *Mich. Law Rev.*, April 1983, *81* (5), pp. 1285–1306. [G: U.S.]

Stewart, Richard B. Regulation in a Liberal State: The Role of Non-commodity Values. *Yale Law J.*, July 1983, *92* (8), pp. 1537–90. [G: U.S.]

Thiemeyer, Theo. Deregulation in the Perspective of the German *Gemeinwirtschaftslehre*. *Z. ges. Staatswiss.*, October 1983, *139* (3), pp. 405–18.

Tollison, Robert D. The Reagan Deregulation Program: An Assessment: Response: Difficulties Facing Regulatory Reform. **In** *Stubblebine, Wm. C. and Willett, T. D., eds.*, 1983, pp. 174–76. [G: U.S.]

Toma, Eugenia Froedge. Institutional Structures, Regulation, and Producer Gains in the Education Industry. *J. Law Econ.*, April 1983, *26* (1), pp. 103–16. [G: U.S.]

Tomlinson, Jim D. Regulating the Capitalist Enterprise: The Impossible Dream? *Scot. J. Polit. Econ.*, February 1983, *30* (1), pp. 54–68. [G: U.K.]

Valentiny, Pál. The Role of the State in Influencing the Market for Heavy Electrical Equipment. *Eastern Europ. Econ.*, Fall 1983, *22* (1), pp. 3–18. [G: W. Europe; Hungary]

Vaughan, Michael B. A Note on the Allocative Differences between Contracting and Regulation. *Atlantic Econ. J.*, March 1983, *11* (1), pp. 117.

Veljanovski, C. G. The Market for Regulatory Enforcement. *Econ. J.*, Supplement March 1983, pp. 123–29.

Viscusi, W. Kip. Frameworks for Analyzing the Effects of Risk and Environmental Regulations on Productivity. *Amer. Econ. Rev.*, September 1983, *73* (4), pp. 793–801.

Viscusi, W. Kip. Presidential Oversight: Controlling the Regulators. *J. Policy Anal. Manage.*, Winter 1983, *2* (2), pp. 157–73. [G: U.S.]

Wahlroos, Björn. Regulation and Free-Enterprise Economy. *Ekon. Samfundets Tidskr.*, 1983, *36* (4), pp. 177–84.

Weingast, Barry R. and Moran, Mark J. Bureaucratic Discretion or Congressional Control? Regulatory Policymaking by the Federal Trade Commission. *J. Polit. Econ.*, October 1983, *91* (5), pp. 765–800. [G: U.S.]

Yeager, Leland B. Is There a Bias Toward Overregulation? **In** *Machan, T. R. and Johnson, M. B., eds.*, 1983, pp. 99–126. [G: U.S.]

6131 Regulation of Public Utilities

Abbott, Catherine Good and Watson, Stephen A. Pitfalls on the Road to Decontrol: Lessons from the Natural Gas Policy Act of 1978. **In** *Mitchell, E. J., ed.*, 1983, pp. 53–70. [G: U.S.]

Acton, Jan Paul and Mitchell, Bridger M. Welfare Analysis of Electricity-Rate Changes. **In** *Berg, S. V., ed.*, 1983, pp. 195–225. [G: U.S.]

Anderson, Robert E. and Mead, David E. A Comparison of Original Cost and Trended Original Cost Ratemaking Methods. *Energy J.*, April 1983, *4* (2), pp. 151–58. [G: U.S.]

Arzac, Enrique R. and Marcus, Matityahu. Flotation Cost Allowance in Rate of Return Regulation: A Reply. *J. Finance*, September 1983, *38* (4), pp. 1339–41.

Atkinson, Scott E. The Implications of Homothetic Separability for Share Equation Price Elasticities [The Bias in Price Elasticity Estimates under Homothetic Separability: Implications for Analysis of Peak-Load Electricity Pricing]. *J. Bus. Econ. Statist.*, July 1983, *1* (3), pp. 211–14. [G: U.S.]

Autin, C. and LeBlanc, G. Empirical Evaluation of Cross-Subsidy Tests for Canadian Interregional Telecommunications Network. **In** *Courville, L.; de Fontenay, A. and Dobell, R., eds.*, 1983, pp. 341–64. [G: Canada]

Baker, Donald I. and Baker, Beverly G. Antitrust and Communications Deregulation. *Antitrust Bull.*, Spring 1983, *28* (1), pp. 1–38. [G: U.S.]

Barnett, William A. The Recent Reappearance of the Homotheticity Restriction on Preferences [The Bias in Price Elasticity Estimates under Homothetic Separability: Implications for Analysis of Peak-Load Electricity Pricing]. *J. Bus. Econ. Statist.*, July 1983, *1* (3), pp. 215–18. [G: U.S.]

Baumol, William J. Minimum and Maximum Pricing Principles for Residual Regulation. **In** *[Bonbright, J. C.]*, 1983, pp. 177–96.

Berg, Sanford V. Consumer Responses to Innovative Electric Rates. **In** *Berg, S. V., ed.*, 1983, pp. 55–78. [G: U.S.]

Berg, Sanford V. Directions for Load-Management Research. **In** *Berg, S. V., ed.*, 1983, pp. 283–304. [G: U.S.]

Berg, Sanford V. Innovative Rates and Regulatory Goals. **In** *Berg, S. V., ed.*, 1983, pp. 31–51. [G: U.S.]

Berg, Sanford V. Power Factors and the Efficient Pricing and Production of Reactive Power. *Energy J.*, Supplement 1983, *4*, pp. 93–102.

Berg, Sanford V. and Savvides, Andreas. The Theory of Maximum kW Demand Charges for Electricity. *Energy Econ.*, October 1983, *5* (4), pp. 258–66.

Berg, Sanford V. and Sullivan, Robert L. An Engineering/Economic Model of the Benefits and Costs of Time-of-Use Pricing. **In** *Berg, S. V., ed.*, 1983, pp. 227–48. [G: U.S.]

Berkowitz, M. K. and Cosgrove, E. G. Financing and Investment Behaviour of the Regulated Firm. **In** *Courville, L.; de Fontenay, A. and Dobell, R., eds.*, 1983, pp. 383–96.

Bernstein, Jeffrey I. Taxes, Financing and Investment for a Regulated Firm. **In** *Courville, L.; de Fontenay, A. and Dobell, R., eds.*, 1983, pp. 367–82.

Besen, Stanley M. and Woodbury, John R. Regulation, Deregulation, and Antitrust in the Telecommunications Industry. *Antitrust Bull.*, Spring 1983, *28* (1), pp. 39–68. [G: U.S.]

Bey, Roger P. Market Model Stationarity of Individual Public Utilities. *J. Finan. Quant. Anal.*, March 1983, *18* (1), pp. 67–85. [G: U.S.]

Bjerkholt, Olav and Olsen, Øystein. Firm Power and Uncertainty in Hydroelectric Power Supply. **In** *Av, R., et al., eds.*, 1983, pp. 281–303. [G: Norway]

Blankart, Charles B. The Contribution of Public Choice to Public Utility Economics—A Survey. **In** *Finsinger, J., ed.*, 1983, pp. 151–70.

Bloom, Jeremy A. Optimal Generation Expansion

Planning for Electric Utilities Using Decomposition and Probabilistic Simulation Techniques. In *Lev, B., ed.*, 1983, pp. 495–511.

Borcherding, Thomas E. Toward a Positive Theory of Public Sector Supply Arrangements. In *Prichard, J. R. S., ed.*, 1983, pp. 99–184. **[G: Canada; Selected Countries]**

Bornholz, Robert and Evans, David S. The Early History of Competition in the Telephone Industry. In *Evans, D. S., ed.*, 1983, pp. 7–40. **[G: U.S.]**

Brander, James A. and Spencer, Barbara J. Local Telephone Pricing: Two-Tariffs and Price Discrimination. In *Courville, L.; de Fontenay, A. and Dobell, R., eds.*, 1983, pp. 305–16.

Breslaw, J. A. and Smith, J. Barry. Des observations empiriques encourageantes pour la théorie dualiste. (Some Encouraging Firm Level Evidence for Duality Theory. With English summary.) *L'Actual. Econ.*, June 1983, *59*(2), pp. 230–39. **[G: Canada]**

Brock, William A. Pricing, Predation, and Entry Barriers in Regulated Industries. In *Evans, D. S., ed.*, 1983, pp. 191–229.

Brock, William A. and Evans, David S. Creamskimming. In *Evans, D. S., ed.*, 1983, pp. 61–94. **[G: U.S.]**

Brock, William A. and Evans, David S. Predation: A Critique of the Government's Case in *U.S.* v. *AT&T.* In *Evans, D. S., ed.*, 1983, pp. 41–59. **[G: U.S.]**

Brown, Stephen P. A. Will Deregulating Natural Gas Increase Its Price to Consumers? *Fed. Res. Bank Dallas Econ. Rev.*, July 1983, pp. 1–9. **[G: U.S.]**

Canes, Michael. The Gordian Knot of Natural Gas Prices: Comment. In *Mitchell, E. J., ed.*, 1983, pp. 149–51. **[G: U.S.]**

Caramanis, Michael C. Electricity Generation Expansion Planning in the Eighties: Requirements and Available Analysis Tools. In *Lev, B., ed.*, 1983, pp. 541–62. **[G: U.S.]**

Carleton, Willard T.; Chambers, Donald R. and Lakonishok, Josef. Inflation Risk and Regulatory Lag. *J. Finance*, May 1983, *38*(2), pp. 419–31. **[G: U.S.]**

Caves, Douglas W. and Christensen, Laurits R. The Bias in Price Elasticity Estimates under Homothetic Separability: Implications for Analysis of Peak-Load Electricity Pricing: Discussion. *J. Bus. Econ. Statist.*, July 1983, *1*(3), pp. 219–20. **[G: U.S.]**

Chamberlin, John H. and Dickson, Charles T. Ratemaking by Objective: A Framework for the Systematic Evaluation of Rate-Design Alternatives. In *Berg, S. V., ed.*, 1983, pp. 9–30. **[G: U.S.]**

Chao, Hung-po. Peak Load Pricing and Capacity Planning with Demand and Supply Uncertainty. *Bell J. Econ. (See Rand J. Econ. after 4/85)*, Spring 1983, *14*(1), pp. 179–90.

Cooper, Mark. The Gordian Knot of Natural Gas Prices: Comment. In *Mitchell, E. J., ed.*, 1983, pp. 151–53. **[G: U.S.]**

Cramer, Curtis and Tschirhart, John. Power Pooling: An Exercise in Industrial Coordination. *Land Econ.*, February 1983, *59*(1), pp. 24–34. **[G: U.S.]**

Crano, William D. Cognitive Factors That Influence Consumers' Responses to Innovative Rate Structures. In *Berg, S. V., ed.*, 1983, pp. 95–107. **[G: U.S.]**

Crew, Michael A. and Kleindorfer, Paul R. Peak Load Pricing of Public Utilities: Some Comments. *Energy Econ.*, April 1983, *5*(2), pp. 137.

Dym, Herbert and Sussman, Robert M. Antitrust and Electric Utility Regulation. *Antitrust Bull.*, Spring 1983, *28*(1), pp. 69–99. **[G: U.S.]**

Earnest, Jack. The Intrastate Pipelines and the Natural Gas Policy Act: Comment. In *Mitchell, E. J., ed.*, 1983, pp. 108–09. **[G: U.S.]**

Erickson, Edward W. Overview of Policy Issues: A Preliminary Assessment: Comment. In *Mitchell, E. J., ed.*, 1983, pp. 33–36. **[G: U.S.]**

Evans, David S. and Grossman, Sanford J. Breaking Up Bell: Integration. In *Evans, D. S., ed.*, 1983, pp. 95–126. **[G: U.S.]**

Evans, David S. and Heckman, James J. Natural Monopoly. In *Evans, D. S., ed.*, 1983, pp. 127–56. **[G: U.S.]**

Evans, David S. and Rothschild, Michael. The Impact of Divestiture on the Cost of Capital to the Bell System. In *Evans, D. S., ed.*, 1983, pp. 157–89. **[G: U.S.]**

Faulhaber, Gerald R. A Public Enterprise Pricing Primer. In *Finsinger, J., ed.*, 1983, pp. 11–26. **[G: U.S.]**

Feigenbaum, Susan and Teeples, Ronald. Public versus Private Water Delivery: A Hedonic Cost Approach. *Rev. Econ. Statist.*, November 1983, *65*(4), pp. 672–78. **[G: U.S.]**

Feldman, Jack. A Theoretical Analysis of Energy-Cost Indicator Impacts on Electricity Consumption. In *Berg, S. V., ed.*, 1983, pp. 109–13.

Filer, John E. and Hollas, Daniel R. Empirical Tests for the Effect of Regulation on Firm and Interruptible Gas Service. *Southern Econ. J.*, July 1983, *50*(1), pp. 195–205. **[G: U.S.]**

Finsinger, Jörg. Public Sector Policy Analysis. In *Finsinger, J., ed.*, 1983, pp. 3–8.

Fischhoff, Baruch. "Acceptable Risk": The Case of Nuclear Power. *J. Policy Anal. Manage.*, Summer 1983, *2*(4), pp. 559–75. **[G: U.S.]**

Fishe, Raymond P. H. The Number and Placement of Rating Periods for Time-of-Day Pricing. In *Berg, S. V., ed.*, 1983, pp. 183–92.

Freixas, Xavier and Laffont, Jean-Jacques. Tarification au coût marginal ou équilibre budgétaire? (Pricing Marginal Cost or Budgetary Equilibrium? With English summary.) *Ann. INSEE*, July–September 1983, (51), pp. 65–88.

Giordano, James N. The Changing Impact of Regulation on the U.S. Electric Utility Industry, 1964–1977. *Eastern Econ. J.*, April–June 1983, *9*(2), pp. 91–101. **[G: U.S.]**

Goettle, Richard J., IV and Hudson, Edward A. Macroeconomic Effects of Natural Gas Price Decontrol. In *Lev, B., ed.*, 1983, pp. 183–93. **[G: U.S.]**

Gormley, William; Hoadley, John and Williams, Charles. Potential Responsiveness in the Bureaucracy: Views of Public Utility Regulation. *Amer. Polit. Sci. Rev.*, September 1983, *77*(3), pp. 704–17. **[G: U.S.]**

Hamilton, Neil W. and Hamilton, Peter R. Duopoly in the Distribution of Electricity: A Policy Failure. *Antitrust Bull.*, Summer 1983, *28*(2), pp. 281–309. [G: U.S.]

Harriss, C. Lowell. Taxation and the Economic Health of Regulated Utilities in a World of Inflation: Selected Elements. **In** *[Bonbright, J. C.]*, 1983, pp. 227–33.

Harvey, Hunter E., Jr. Pricing Telephone Service in the 1980s. **In** *[Bonbright, J. C.]*, 1983, pp. 265–76. [G: U.S.]

Henderson, J. Stephen. Costs and Benefits of Residential Time-of-Use Metering: Comment. *Energy J.*, January 1983, *4*(1), pp. 161–65. [G: U.S.]

Henderson, J. Stephen. The Economics of Electricity Demand Charges. *Energy J.*, Supplement 1983, *4*, pp. 127–40. [G: U.S.]

Hill, Daniel H. The Impact of Natural Gas Deregulation on American Families. **In** *Duncan, G. J. and Morgan, J. N., eds.*, 1983, pp. 178–204. [G: U.S.]

Hill, Daniel H., et al. Incentive Payments in Time-of-Day Electricity Pricing Experiments: The Arizona Experience. *Rev. Econ. Statist.*, February 1983, *65*(1), pp. 59–65. [G: U.S.]

Hirschberg, Joseph G. and Aigner, Dennis J. An Analysis of Commercial and Industrial Customer Response to Time-of-Use Rates. *Energy J.*, Supplement 1983, *4*, pp. 103–26. [G: U.S.]

Houston, Douglas A. Deregulating Electric Utilities: A Market-Process Approach. *Cato J.*, Winter 1983/84, *3*(3), pp. 331–53.

Huettner, David A. Restructuring the Electric Utility Industry: A Modest Proposal. **In** *Brown, H. J., ed.*, 1983, pp. 183–97. [G: U.S.]

Huettner, David A.; Kasulis, Jack and Dikeman, Neil. Costs and Benefits of Residential Time-of-Use Metering: Reply. *Energy J.*, January 1983, *4*(1), pp. 166–69. [G: U.S.]

Hughes, William R. Issues in Deregulation of Electric Generation. **In** *[Bonbright, J. C.]*, 1983, pp. 289–318. [G: U.S.]

Jacoby, Henry D. and Wright, Arthur W. The Gordian Knot of Natural Gas Prices. **In** *Mitchell, E. J., ed.*, 1983, pp. 125–48. [G: U.S.]

John, Kose and Saunders, Anthony. Asymmetry of Information, Regulatory Lags and Optimal Incentive Contracts: Theory and Evidence. *J. Finance*, May 1983, *38*(2), pp. 391–404. [G: U.S.]

Johnston, Stephen A. Peak and Off-Peak Electricity Consumption: A Review and Critique of Load Management and Rate Design Demonstration Projects. **In** *Berg, S. V., ed.*, 1983, pp. 115–28. [G: U.S.]

Jordan, W. John. Heterogeneous Users and the Peak Load Pricing Model. *Quart. J. Econ.*, February 1983, *98*(1), pp. 127–38.

Kafoglis, Milton Z. Regulatory Lag in an Inflationary Environment. **In** *[Bonbright, J. C.]*, 1983, pp. 211–18. [G: U.S.]

Kahn, Alfred E. Utility Diversification. *Energy J.*, January 1983, *4*(1), pp. 149–60. [G: U.S.]

Kahn, Alfred E. Utility Regulation Revisited. **In** *[Bonbright, J. C.]*, 1983, pp. 101–15. [G: U.S.]

Kamerschen, David R. and Keenan, Donald C. Caveats on Applying Ramsey Pricing. **In** *[Bonbright, J. C.]*, 1983, pp. 197–208.

Keeney, Ralph L. A Technology Choice for Model Electricity Generation. *Energy J.*, Supplement 1983, *4*, pp. 13–31.

Knieps, Günter. Is Technological Revolution a Sufficient Reason for Changing the System of Regulation? The Case of Telecommunications. *Z. ges. Staatswiss.*, October 1983, *139*(3), pp. 578–97. [G: W. Germany]

Kohler, Daniel F. The Bias in Price Elasticity Estimates under Homothetic Separability: Implications for Analysis of Peak-Load Electricity Pricing. *J. Bus. Econ. Statist.*, July 1983, *1*(3), pp. 202–10. [G: U.S.]

Kohler, Daniel F. The Bias in Price Elasticity Estimates under Homothetic Separability: Implications for Analysis of Peak-Load Electricity Pricing: Response. *J. Bus. Econ. Statist.*, July 1983, *1*(3), pp. 226–28. [G: U.S.]

Kolb, Robert W.; Morin, Roger A. and Gay, Gerald D. Regulation, Regulatory Lag, and the Use of Futures Markets. *J. Finance*, May 1983, *38*(2), pp. 405–18. [G: U.S.]

Kubitz, Kermit R. The Energy Utilities: How to Increase Rewards to Match Increasing Risks. **In** *Aronson, J. D. and Cowhey, P. F., eds.*, 1983, pp. 137–55. [G: U.S.]

Kuo, Eddie C. Y. Communication Policy and National Development. **In** *Chen, P. S. J., ed.*, 1983, pp. 268–81. [G: Singapore]

LaMorte, Michele. Overview of Reports from the Electric-Utility Rate-Design Study. **In** *Berg, S. V., ed.*, 1983, pp. 305–14. [G: U.S.]

LaTour, Stephen A. and Orwin, Robert G. Determining the Effects of Innovative Rates on Customer Response Using Meta-Analysis. **In** *Berg, S. V., ed.*, 1983, pp. 129–50. [G: U.S.]

Levary, Reuven R. and Dean, Burton V. An Adaptive Model for Planning the Purchasing and Storage of Natural Gas. **In** *Lev, B., ed.*, 1983, pp. 387–97. [G: U.S.]

Lewis, W. Arthur. The Two-part Tariff. **In** *Lewis, W. A.*, 1983, *1941*, pp. 1–26.

Linke, Charles M. and Whitford, David T. A Multiobjective Financial Planning Model for Electric Utility Rate Regulation. *J. Econ. Bus.*, August 1983, *35*(3/4), pp. 313–30. [G: U.S.]

Lioukas, Spyros K. Peak Load Pricing under Periodic and Stochastic Supply. *Europ. Econ. Rev.*, January 1983, *20*(1–3), pp. 13–21. [G: U.K.]

MacAvoy, Paul W. and Robinson, Kenneth. Winning by Losing: The AT&T Settlement and Its Impact on Telecommunications. *Yale J. Regul.*, 1983, *1*(1), pp. 1–42. [G: U.S.]

Malko, J. Robert and Enholm, Gregory B. Challenges for Electric Utilities and Regulatory Commissions. **In** *[Bonbright, J. C.]*, 1983, pp. 117–31. [G: U.S.]

Means, Robert C. The Intrastate Pipelines and the Natural Gas Policy Act. **In** *Mitchell, E. J., ed.*, 1983, pp. 71–107. [G: U.S.]

Milon, J. Walter. Welfare Consequences of Marginal-Cost Rate Designs for Cogenerators and Small Power Producers. **In** *Berg, S. V., ed.*, 1983, pp. 249–60. [G: U.S.]

Mitchell, Bridger M. Local Telephone Costs and the Design of Rate Structures. **In** *Courville, L.; de Fontenay, A. and Dobell, R., eds.*, 1983, pp. 293–304.

Monnier, L. La tarification de l'électricité: nouveau débat. (The Electricity Tariff: A New Debate. With English summary.) *Écon. Soc.*, December 1983, *17*(12), pp. 2053–75. [G: France]

Morris, David. The Pendulum Swings Again: A Century of Urban Electric Systems. **In** *Brown, H. J., ed.*, 1983, pp. 37–58. [G: U.S.]

Nelson, Randy A. and Wohar, Mark E. Regulation, Scale Economies, and Productivity in Steam-Electric Generation. *Int. Econ. Rev.*, February 1983, *24*(1), pp. 57–79. [G: U.S.]

Neumann, Karl-Heinz; Schweizer, Urs and von Weizsäcker, C. Christian. Welfare Analysis of Telecommunication Tariffs in Germany. **In** *Finsinger, J., ed.*, 1983, pp. 65–85. [G: W. Germany]

Nusbaum, William R. New Legislation and the Impact on Changing Price Structure of Telephone Service. **In** *[Bonbright, J. C.]*, 1983, pp. 251–57. [G: U.S.]

Pace, Joe D. Deregulating Electric Generation: An Economist's Perspective. **In** *[Bonbright, J. C.]*, 1983, pp. 277–87.

Parks, Richard W. The Bias in Price Elasticity Estimates under Homothetic Separability: Implications for Analysis of Peak-Load Electricity Pricing: Discussion. *J. Bus. Econ. Statist.*, July 1983, *1*(3), pp. 221–25. [G: U.S.]

Patterson, Cleveland S. Flotation Cost Allowance in Rate of Return Regulation: Comment. *J. Finance*, September 1983, *38*(4), pp. 1335–38.

Paul, Chris W., II. Rate-Base Determination, Inflation, and Realized Rates of Return to Electric Utilities. **In** *[Bonbright, J. C.]*, 1983, pp. 219–26. [G: U.S.]

Peck, Stephen C. Electric Utility Capacity Expansion: Its Implications for Customers and Stockholders. *Energy J.*, Supplement 1983, *4*, pp. 1–11.

Peiser, Richard B. The Economics of Municipal Utility Districts for Land Development. *Land Econ.*, February 1983, *59*(1), pp. 43–57. [G: U.S.]

Peles, Yoram C. Peak Load Pricing of Public Utilities: Reply. *Energy Econ.*, April 1983, *5*(2), pp. 138.

Perrakis, Stylianos. The Value of the Firm under Regulation and the Theory of the Firm under Uncertainty: An Integrated Approach. **In** *Courville, L.; de Fontenay, A. and Dobell, R., eds.*, 1983, pp. 397–413.

Perrakis, Stylianos and Silva-Echenique, Julio. The Profitability and Risk of CATV Operations in Canada. *Appl. Econ.*, December 1983, *15*(6), pp. 745–58. [G: Canada]

Pettway, Richard H. and Jordan, Bradford D. Diversification, Double Leverage, and the Cost of Capital. *J. Finan. Res.*, Winter 1983, *6*(4), pp. 289–300. [G: U.S.]

Phillips, Charles F., Jr. The Changing Environment of Public-Utility Regulation: An Overview. **In** *[Bonbright, J. C.]*, 1983, pp. 25–39. [G: U.S.]

Pijawka, D. and Chalmers, J. Impacts of Nuclear Generating Plants on Local Areas. *Econ. Geogr.*, January 1983, *59*(1), pp. 66–80. [G: U.S.]

Rheaume, G. C. Welfare Optimal Subsidy-free Prices under a Regulated Monopoly. **In** *Courville, L.; de Fontenay, A. and Dobell, R., eds.*, 1983, pp. 319–40.

Rødseth, Asbjørn. Optimal Timing and Dimensioning of Hydro Power Projects. **In** *Av, R., et al., eds.*, 1983, pp. 304–23. [G: Norway]

Russell, Milton. Overview of Policy Issues: A Preliminary Assessment. **In** *Mitchell, E. J., ed.*, 1983, pp. 3–32. [G: U.S.]

Savvides, Andreas. Kw Demand Charges: Practical and Theoretical Implications. **In** *Berg, S. V., ed.*, 1983, pp. 79–91.

Schlesinger, Benjamin. Overview of Policy Issues: A Preliminary Assessment: Comment. **In** *Mitchell, E. J., ed.*, 1983, pp. 36–39. [G: U.S.]

Schmidt, Ronald H. Effects of Natural Gas Deregulation on the Distribution of Income. *Fed. Res. Bank Dallas Econ. Rev.*, May 1983, pp. 1–12. [G: U.S.]

Scott, Frank A., Jr. A Note on Uncertain Input Prices, Profit Risk, and the Rate-of-Return Regulated Firm. *Land Econ.*, August 1983, *59*(3), pp. 337–41.

Shakow, Don M. Disequilibrium Processes in the Market for Electricity: The Case of Municipal Ownership. *Energy J.*, April 1983, *4*(2), pp. 159–64. [G: U.S.]

Sharlin, Harold Issadore. New York's Electricity: Establishing a Technological Paradigm. **In** *[Cochran, T. C.]*, 1983, pp. 101–16. [G: U.S.]

Shepherd, William G. Price Structures in Electricity. **In** *[Bonbright, J. C.]*, 1983, pp. 151–67. [G: U.S.]

Sherman, Roger. Is Public-Utility Regulation beyond Hope?. **In** *[Bonbright, J. C.]*, 1983, pp. 41–75. [G: U.S.]

Slater, M. D. E. and Yarrow, G. K. Distortions in Electricity Pricing in the U.K. *Oxford Bull. Econ. Statist.*, November 1983, *45*(4), pp. 317–38. [G: U.K.]

Stevenson, Rodney E. Institutional Objectives, Structural Barriers, and Deregulation in the Electric Utility Industry. *J. Econ. Issues*, June 1983, *17*(2), pp. 443–52. [G: U.S.]

Strøm, Steinar. Optimal Pricing and Investment in Electricity Supply. **In** *Av, R., et al., eds.*, 1983, pp. 260–80. [G: Norway]

Sullivan, Robert L. Evaluating Reliability and Operating-Cost Impacts of TOU Rates. **In** *Berg, S. V., ed.*, 1983, pp. 153–81. [G: U.S.]

Surrey, John and Walker, William. Electrical Power Plant: Market Collapse and Structural Strains. **In** *Shepherd, G.; Duchêne, F. and Saunders, C., eds.*, 1983, pp. 139–66. [G: OECD]

Swan, Peter L. The Marginal Cost of Base-Load Power: An Application to Alcoa's Portland Smelter. *Econ. Rec.*, December 1983, *59*(167), pp. 332–44. [G: Australia]

Thompson, Edward, III. Cogeneration and Small Power Production: Some Intergovernmental Policy Concerns. In *Brown, H. J., ed.*, 1983, pp. 199–212. [G: U.S.]

Tishler, Asher. The Industrial and Commercial Demand for Electricity under Time-of-Use Pricing. *J. Econometrics*, December 1983, *23*(3), pp. 369–84. [G: U.S.]

Tozzi, Jim J. and Clarke, Edward H. On Information and the Regulation of Public Utilities. **In** *[Bonbright, J. C.]*, 1983, pp. 133–47. [G: U.S.]

Trebing, Harry M. James C. Bonbright's Contributions to Public-Utility Economics and Regulation. In *[Bonbright, J. C.]*, 1983, pp. 3–21.

Veall, Michael R. Industrial Electricity Demand and the Hopkinson Rate: An Application of the Extreme Value Distribution. *Bell J. Econ. (See Rand J. Econ. after 4/85)*, Autumn 1983, *14*(2), pp. 427–40. **[G: Canada]**

Wald, Patricia M. Judicial Review of Economic Analysis. *Yale J. Regul.*, 1983, *1*(1), pp. 43–62. **[G: U.S.]**

Weber, Larry R. The Effects of a Competitive Environment on Local-Service Rates. In *[Bonbright, J. C.]*, 1983, pp. 259–64. **[G: U.S.]**

Wilder, Ronald P. Marginal-Cost Pricing: Theory and Practice. In *[Bonbright, J. C.]*, 1983, pp. 169–76. **[G: U.S.]**

Zimmerman, Martin B. The Valuation of Nuclear Power in the Post-Three Mile Island Era. *Energy J.*, April 1983, *4*(2), pp. 15–29. **[G: U.S.]**

6132 Effects of Intervention on Market Structure, Costs, and Efficiency

Albon, Robert P. and Kirby, Michael G. Cost-Padding in Profit-Regulated Firms. *Econ. Rec.*, March 1983, *59*(164), pp. 16–27. **[G: U.S.]**

Ashford, Nicholas A. and Heaton, George R., Jr. Regulation and Technological Innovation in the Chemical Industry. *Law Contemp. Probl.*, Summer 1983, *46*(3), pp. 109–57. **[G: U.S.]**

Backhaus, Jüergen. Competition, Innovation and Regulation in the Pharmaceutical Industry. *Managerial Dec. Econ.*, June 1983, *4*(2), pp. 107–21. **[G: U.S.; W. Europe]**

Bös, Dieter and Tillmann, Georg. Cost-Axiomatic Regulatory Pricing. *J. Public Econ.*, November 1983, *22*(2), pp. 243–56.

Boyd, Roy. Lumber Transport and the Jones Act: A Multicommodity Spatial Equilibrium Analysis. *Bell J. Econ. (See Rand J. Econ. after 4/85)*, Spring 1983, *14*(1), pp. 202–12. **[G: Canada; U.S.]**

Cordes, Joseph J. and Goldfarb, Robert S. Alternate Rationales for Severence Pay Compensation under Airline Deregulation. *Public Choice*, 1983, *41*(3), pp. 351–69. **[G: U.S.]**

Crandall, Robert W. Deregulation: The U.S. Experience. *Z. ges. Staatswiss.*, October 1983, *139*(3), pp. 419–34. **[G: U.S.]**

David, Martin H. and Joeres, Erhard F. Is a Viable Implementation of TDPs Transferable? In *Joeres, E. F. and David, M. H., eds.*, 1983, pp. 233–48. **[G: U.S.]**

Dewees, Donald N. The Control of Diesel Exhaust Pollution. In *Dewees, D. N., ed.*, 1983, pp. 293–322. **[G: U.S.]**

Dewees, Donald N. The Quality of Consumer Durables: Energy Use. In *Dewees, D. N., ed.*, 1983, pp. 207–46. **[G: Canada]**

Edmonds, Martin. Market Ideology and Corporate Power: The United States. In *Dyson, K. and Wilks, S., eds.*, 1983, pp. 67–101. **[G: U.S.]**

Edwards, Franklin R. Futures Markets in Transition: The Uneasy Balance between Government and Self-regulation. *J. Futures Markets*, Summer 1983, *3*(2), pp. 191–206.

Edwards, Franklin R. The Clearing Association in Futures Markets: Guarantor and Regulator. *J. Futures Markets*, Winter 1983, *3*(4), pp. 369–92. **[G: U.S.]**

Färe, Rolf G. and Logan, James. The Rate-of-Return Regulated Firm: Cost and Production Duality. *Bell J. Econ. (See Rand J. Econ. after 4/85)*, Autumn 1983, *14*(2), pp. 405–14.

Flam, Harry; Persson, Torsten and Svensson, Lars E. O. Optimal Subsidies to Declining Industries: Efficiency and Equity Considerations. *J. Public Econ.*, December 1983, *22*(3), pp. 327–45.

Forster, Bruce A. and Rees, Ray. The Optimal Rate of Decline of an Inefficient Industry. *J. Public Econ.*, November 1983, *22*(2), pp. 227–42.

Fried, Joel. Government Loan and Guarantee Programs. *Fed. Res. Bank St. Louis Rev.*, December 1983, *65*(10), pp. 22–30. **[G: U.S.]**

Graham, David R.; Kaplan, Daniel P. and Sibley, David S. Efficiency and Competition in the Airline Industry. *Bell J. Econ. (See Rand J. Econ. after 4/85)*, Spring 1983, *14*(1), pp. 118–38. **[G: U.S.]**

Green, Diana M. Strategic Management and the State: France. In *Dyson, K. and Wilks, S., eds.*, 1983, pp. 161–92. **[G: France]**

Hahn, Robert W. and Noll, Roger G. Barriers to Implementing Tradable Air Pollution Permits: Problems of Regulatory Interactions. *Yale J. Regul.*, 1983, *1*(1), pp. 63–91. **[G: U.S.]**

Hayashi, Paul M. and Trapani, John M. An Analysis of the Objectives of Domestic Airline Firms under CAB Regulation. *Appl. Econ.*, October 1983, *15*(5), pp. 603–17. **[G: U.S.]**

Ingram, Robert W. and Chewning, Eugene G. The Effect of Financial Disclosure Regulation on Security Market Behavior. *Accounting Rev.*, July 1983, *58*(3), pp. 562–80. **[G: U.S.]**

Long, James E. and Link, Albert N. The Impact of Market Structure on Wages, Fringe Benefits, and Turnover. *Ind. Lab. Relat. Rev.*, January 1983, *36*(2), pp. 239–50. **[G: U.S.]**

Lundmark, Kjell. Welfare State and Employment Policy: Sweden. In *Dyson, K. and Wilks, S., eds.*, 1983, pp. 220–44. **[G: Sweden]**

Mathewson, G. Frank. Markets for Insurance: A Selective Survey of Economic Issues. In *Dewees, D. N., ed.*, 1983, pp. 247–74. **[G: Canada]**

McGarity, Thomas O. Media-Quality, Technology, and Cost-Benefit Balancing Strategies for Health and Environmental Regulation. *Law Contemp. Probl.*, Summer 1983, *46*(3), pp. 159–233.

Morgan, Phillip. The Costs and Benefits of the Power Presses Regulations (1965). *Brit. J. Ind. Relat.*, July 1983, *21*(2), pp. 181–96. **[G: U.K.]**

Nelson, James C. A Critique of Governmental Intervention in Transport. In *Nelson, J. C.*, 1983, *1975*, pp. 371–404. **[G: U.S.]**

Nelson, James C. Effects of Public Regulation on Railroad Performance. In *Nelson, J. C.*, 1983, *1960*, pp. 254–60. **[G: U.S.]**

Nelson, James C. Regulatory Performance in Surface Freight Transportation in Australia, Canada, Great Britain and the U.S.A. In *Nelson, J. C.*, 1983, *1980*, pp. 298–340. **[G: U.K.; U.S.; Australia; Canada]**

Nichols, Albert L. The Regulation of Airborne Ben-zene. In *Schelling, T. C., ed.*, 1983, pp. 145–219. [G: U.S.]

Noll, Roger G. and Owen, Bruce M. Introduction: The Agenda for Deregulation. In *Noll, R. G. and Owen, B. M.*, 1983, pp. 3–25. [G: U.S.]

Penny, Michael; Trebilcock, Michael J. and Laskin, John B. Existing and Proposed Constitutional Constraints on Provincially Induced Barriers to Economic Mobility in Canada. In *Trebilcock, M. J., et al., eds.*, 1983, pp. 501–41. [G: Canada]

Piffano, Horacio L. P. La Incidencia de la Imposición Indirecta en un Enfoque de Equilibrio Parcial. (The Incidence of Indirect Taxation in a Partial Equilibrium Approach. With English summary.) *Económica*, May–December 1983, *29*(2–3), pp. 153–216.

Porter, Richard C. A Social Benefit–Cost Analysis of Mandatory Deposits on Beverage Containers: A Correction. *J. Environ. Econ. Manage.*, June 1983, *10*(2), pp. 191–93. [G: U.S.]

Porter, Richard C. Michigan's Experience with Mandatory Deposits on Beverage Containers. *Land Econ.*, May 1983, *59*(2), pp. 177–94. [G: U.S.]

Quinn, Timothy H. Distributive Consequences and Political Concerns: On the Design of Feasible Market Mechanisms for Environmental Control. In *Joeres, E. F. and David, M. H., eds.*, 1983, pp. 39–54. [G: U.S.]

Repetto, Robert. Air Quality under the Clean Air Act. In *Schelling, T. C., ed.*, 1983, pp. 221–90. [G: U.S.]

Rose-Ackerman, Susan. Unintended Consequences: Regulating the Quality of Subsidized Day Care. *J. Policy Anal. Manage.*, Fall 1983, *3*(1), pp. 14–30. [G: U.S.]

Rosen, Jeffrey S. The Impact of the Futures Trading Act of 1982 upon Commodity Regulation. *J. Futures Markets*, Fall 1983, *3*(3), pp. 235–58. [G: U.S.]

Rusin, Michael. Problems in Modeling Crude Oil Price Decontrol and Windfall Profits Tax Proposals: A Case Study. In *Thrall, R. M.; Thompson, R. G. and Holloway, M. L., eds.*, 1983, pp. 29–50. [G: U.S.]

Sappington, David. Optimal Regulation of a Multiproduct Monopoly with Unknown Technological Capabilities. *Bell J. Econ. (See Rand J. Econ. after 4/85)*, Autumn 1983, *14*(2), pp. 453–63.

Schroeter, John R. A Model of Taxi Service under Fare Structure and Fleet Size Regulation. *Bell J. Econ. (See Rand J. Econ. after 4/85)*, Spring 1983, *14*(1), pp. 81–96. [G: U.S.]

Schwarz, John E. The Hidden Truth about Regulation. *Challenge*, November/December 1983, *26*(5), pp. 54–56. [G: U.S.]

Sonstelie, Jon C. and Portney, Paul R. Truth or Consequences: Cost Revelation and Regulation. *J. Policy Anal. Manage.*, Winter 1983, *2*(2), pp. 280–84. [G: U.S.]

Spulber, Daniel F. and Becker, Robert A. Regulatory Lag and Deregulation with Imperfectly Adjustable Capital. *J. Econ. Dynam. Control*, September 1983, *6*(1/2), pp. 137–51.

Tye, William B. The Postal Service: Economics Made Simplistic. *J. Policy Anal. Manage.*, Fall 1983, *3*(1), pp. 62–73. [G: U.S.]

Wilks, Stephen. Liberal State and Party Competition: Britain. In *Dyson, K. and Wilks, S., eds.*, 1983, pp. 128–60. [G: U.K.]

Wood, William C. Putting a Price on Radiation. *J. Policy Anal. Manage.*, Winter 1983, *2*(2), pp. 291–95. [G: U.S.]

Woodbury, John R.; Besen, Stanley M. and Fournier, Gary M. The Determinants of Network Television Program Prices: Implicit Contracts, Regulation, and Bargaining Power. *Bell J. Econ. (See Rand J. Econ. after 4/85)*, Autumn 1983, *14*(2), pp. 351–65. [G: U.S.]

614 Public Enterprises

6140 Public Enterprises

Aharoni, Yair. Comprehensive Audit of Management Performance in U.S. State Owned Enterprises. *Ann. Pub. Co-op. Econ.*, March 1983, *54*(1), pp. 73–92. [G: U.S.]

Akinsanya, Adeoye A. State Strategies toward Nigerian and Foreign Business. In *Zartman, I. W., ed.*, 1983, pp. 145–84. [G: Nigeria]

Asselain, Jean-Charles. La dimension sociale des nationalisations de 1982. (The Social Scheme of the 1982 Nationalizations. With English summary.) *Revue Écon.*, May 1983, *34*(3), pp. 536–76.

Beesley, Michael E. and Littlechild, Stephen. Privatization: Principles, Problems and Priorities. *Lloyds Bank Rev.*, July 1983, (149), pp. 1–20. [G: U.K.]

Biersteker, Thomas J. Indigenization in Nigeria: Renationalization or Denationalization? In *Zartman, I. W., ed.*, 1983, pp. 185–206. [G: Nigeria]

Bizaquet, Armand. L'importance des entreprises publiques dans l'économie française et européenne après les nationalisations de 1982. (The French Public Sector after the 1982 Nationalizations: An Assessment of Its Relative Size in the Context of the French and European Economies. With English summary.) *Revue Écon.*, May 1983, *34*(3), pp. 434–65. [G: France]

Boneo, Horacio. Government and Public Enterprise in Latin America. In *[Ramanadham, V. V.]*, 1983, pp. 157–80. [G: Latin America]

Boodhoo, Martin J. Management Information Systems in Public Enterprise. In *[Ramanadham, V. V.]*, 1983, pp. 113–24.

Borcherding, Thomas E. Toward a Positive Theory of Public Sector Supply Arrangements. In *Prichard, J. R. S., ed.*, 1983, pp. 99–184. [G: Canada; Selected Countries]

Borins, Sandford F. World War II Crown Corporations: Their Functions and Their Fate. In *Prichard, J. R. S., ed.*, 1983, pp. 447–75. [G: Canada]

Byrd, William. Enterprise-Level Reforms in Chinese State-Owned Industry. *Amer. Econ. Rev.*, May 1983, *73*(2), pp. 329–32. [G: China]

Chambers, David. Target-setting and Performance Assessment in Public Enterprises. In *[Ramanadham, V. V.]*, 1983, pp. 48–66.

Chandler, Marsha A. The Politics of Public Enterprise. In *Prichard, J. R. S., ed.*, 1983, pp. 185–218. [G: Canada]

Chiancone, Aldo. Contributions of Regional Public

Enterprises to Regional Economic Development. In *Biehl, D.; Roskamp, K. W. and Stolper, W. F., eds.*, 1983, pp. 315–28.

Courchene, Thomas J. A Constitutional Perspective on Federal–Provincial Sharing of Revenues from Natural Resources: Comments. **In** *McLure, C. E., Jr. and Mieszkowski, P., eds.*, 1983, pp. 237–43. **[G: Canada]**

Dary, Yves and Gilly, Jean-Pierre. Le nouveau secteur public: un outil de politique industrielle régionale? (With English summary.) *Rev. Econ. Ind.*, 2nd Trimester 1983, (24), pp. 35–47. **[G: France]**

Davis, E. G. and Mokkelbost, P. B. The Recapitalization of Crown Corporations. *Can. Public Policy*, June 1983, *9*(2), pp. 181–88. **[G: Canada]**

De Bandt, Jacques. Les nationalisations: la gestion du secteur public et du système productif. (With English summary.) *Revue Écon. Polit.*, September–October 1983, *93*(5), pp. 704–13. **[G: France]**

De Grauwe, Paul and van de Velde, Greet. Belgium: Politics and the Protection of Failing Companies. **In** *Hindley, B., ed.*, 1983, pp. 96–124. **[G: Belgium]**

Diop, Sidy Modibo and Perrault, Jean-Louis. Ruptures ou continuités dans la politque industrielle française en électronique? (With English summary.) *Rev. Econ. Ind.*, 2nd Trimester 1983, (24), pp. 48–61. **[G: France]**

Duvall, Raymond D. and Freeman, John R. The Techno-Bureaucratic Elite and the Entrepreneurial State in Dependent Industrialization. *Amer. Polit. Sci. Rev.*, September 1983, *77*(3), pp. 569–87. **[G: LDCs]**

Eltis, Walter. Policy for the Nationalised Industries: The British Problem. **In** *Giersch, H., ed.*, 1983, pp. 83–113. **[G: U.K.]**

Engels, Wolfram. Policy for the Nationalised Industries: The British Problem: Comment. **In** *Giersch, H., ed.*, 1983, pp. 114–23.

Faulhaber, Gerald R. A Public Enterprise Pricing Primer. **In** *Finsinger, J., ed.*, 1983, pp. 11–26. **[G: U.S.]**

Fisher, Peter S. The Role of the Public Sector in Local Development Finance: Evaluating Alternative Institutional Arrangements. *J. Econ. Issues*, March 1983, *17*(1), pp. 133–53.

Floyd, Robert H. Government Relationships with Public Enterprise in Papua New Guinea. **In** *[Ramanadham, V. V.]*, 1983, pp. 220–48. **[G: Papua New Guinea]**

Fontanella, Giuseppe. The Costs, Revenues and Deficit of the Italian State Railways' Goods Traffic. *Rev. Econ. Cond. Italy*, October 1983, (3), pp. 431–56. **[G: Italy]**

Freixas, Xavier and Laffont, Jean-Jacques. Tarification au coût marginal ou équilibre budgétaire? (Pricing Marginal Cost or Budgetary Equilibrium? With English summary.) *Ann. INSEE*, July–September 1983, (51), pp. 65–88.

Garner, Maurice R. A Final Reckoning. **In** *[Ramanadham, V. V.]*, 1983, pp. 287–99.

Garner, Maurice R. The Relationship between Government and Public Enterprise. **In** *[Ramanadham, V. V.]*, 1983, pp. 3–23. **[G: U.K.]**

Ghai, Yash. Executive Control Over Public Enterprises in Africa. **In** *[Ramanadham, V. V.]*, 1983, pp. 181–219. **[G: Africa]**

Glade, William. The Privatisation and Denationalisation of Public Enterprises. **In** *[Ramanadham, V. V.]*, 1983, pp. 67–97. **[G: Peru]**

Goodermote, Dean and Mancke, Richard B. Nationalizing Oil in the 1970s. *Energy J.*, October 1983, *4*(4), pp. 67–80. **[G: U.S.; Canada; U.K.]**

Greffe, Xaviere. Les entreprises publiques dans la politique de l'État. (Public Enterprises in National Public Policies. With English summary.) *Revue Écon.*, May 1983, *34*(3), pp. 496–535. **[G: France]**

Greytak, David and Diokno, Benjamin. Local Government Public Enterprises. **In** *Bahl, R. and Miller, B. D., eds.*, 1983, pp. 140–87. **[G: Philippines]**

Guy, Charles E.; Brown, George F., Jr. and O'Hara, Donald J. A Deterministic Profit Attribution Model: The Postal Service, a Case Study. *Managerial Dec. Econ.*, September 1983, *4*(3), pp. 208–13. **[G: U.S.]**

Hagen, Kåre P. Optimal Shadow Prices and Discount Rates for Budget-Constrained Public Firms. *J. Public Econ.*, October 1983, *22*(1), pp. 27–48.

Heath, John B. Public Enterprise in Britain Today. **In** *[Ramanadham, V. V.]*, 1983, pp. 127–39. **[G: U.K.]**

Hindley, Brian and Richardson, Ray. United Kingdom: An Experiment in Picking Winners—The Industrial Reorganisation Corporation. **In** *Hindley, B., ed.*, 1983, pp. 125–55. **[G: U.K.]**

Hindley, Brian and Richardson, Ray. United Kingdom: Pulling Dragon's Teeth—The National Enterprise Board. **In** *Hindley, B., ed.*, 1983, pp. 263–81. **[G: U.K.]**

Jones, Leroy P. and Papanek, Gustav F. The Efficiency of Public Enterprise in Less Developed Countries. **In** *[Ramanadham, V. V.]*, 1983, pp. 98–112. **[G: S. Korea; India]**

Kaul, S. N. and Iyer, V. R. Widening Gap between Telephone Demand and Supply—Its Influence on Service Efficiency. *Margin*, July 1983, *15*(4), pp. 34–49. **[G: India]**

Kreile, Michael. Public Enterprise and the Pursuit of Strategic Management: Italy. **In** *Dyson, K. and Wilks, S., eds.*, 1983, pp. 193–219. **[G: Italy]**

Landell-Mills, Pierre. Management: A Limiting Factor in Development. *Finance Develop.*, September 1983, *20*(3), pp. 11–15. **[G: LDCs]**

Lange, Oscar and Lerner, Abba P. Strengthening the Economic Foundations of Democracy. **In** *Lerner, A. P.*, 1983, *1944*, pp. 171–86. **[G: U.S.]**

Langford, John W. and Huffman, Kenneth J. The Uncharted Universe of Federal Public Corporations. **In** *Prichard, J. R. S., ed.*, 1983, pp. 219–301. **[G: Canada]**

Leray, Catherine. L'appréhension de l'efficacité dans les entreprises publiques industrielles et commerciales. (An Efficiency Assessment of Industrial and Commercial Enterprise both Public and Private. With English summary.) *Revue Écon.*, May 1983, *34*(3), pp. 612–54. **[G: France]**

Lioukas, Spyros K. Investment Behaviour in a Nationalised Industry. *Appl. Econ.*, October 1983,

15(5), pp. 665–79. **[G: U.K.]**

Littlechild, S. C. The Structure of Telephone Tariffs. *Int. J. Ind. Organ.*, December 1983, *1*(4), pp. 365–77. **[G: Selected Countries]**

Livingstone, David. Enterprise or Service? Nationalized and State Owned Industries. **In** *Ingham, K. P. D. and Love, J., eds.*, 1983, pp. 203–12. **[G: U.K.]**

Maki, Dennis R. A Note on the Output Effects of Canadian Postal Strikes. *Can. J. Econ.*, February 1983, *16*(1), pp. 149–54. **[G: Canada]**

Meyer, John R. and Tye, William B. Rational Policies for Development of International Air Transportation. **In** *Khachaturov, T. S. and Goodwin, P. B., eds.*, 1983, pp. 245–64. **[G: Global; U.S.]**

Moloney, M. G. Privatisation. *Irish Banking Rev.*, September 1983, pp. 44–52. **[G: Ireland]**

Moreira Alves, Maria Helena. Mechanisms of Social Control of the Military Governments in Brazil, 1964–80. **In** *Ritter, A. R. M. and Pollock, D. H., eds.*, 1983, pp. 240–303. **[G: Brazil]**

Narain, Laxmi. Parliament and Public Enterprise in India. **In** *[Ramanadham, V. V.]*, 1983, pp. 264–84. **[G: India]**

Noortman, H. J. Organisation of Transport Enterprises. **In** *Khachaturov, T. S. and Goodwin, P. B., eds.*, 1983, pp. 312–25. **[G: W. Europe]**

Ooghe, Hubert and Derycke, G. Financial Structures in Private and Governmental Firms in Belgium: A Comparison. *Tijdschrift Econ. Manage.*, 1983, *28*(4), pp. 489–507. **[G: Belgium]**

Palmer, John; Quinn, John and Resendes, Ray. A Case Study of Public Enterprise: Gray Coach Lines Ltd. **In** *Prichard, J. R. S., ed.*, 1983, pp. 369–446. **[G: Canada]**

Panzoni, Erico Emir. Background, Nature and Problems of the Public Sector in Argentine Economy. *Ann. Pub. Co-op. Econ.*, October-December 1983, *54*(4), pp. 377–85. **[G: Argentina]**

Parenteau, Roland. Le cadre historique et institutionnel des societes d'etat au Quebec. (State Enterprise in Quebec: The Historical and Institutional Background. With English summary.) *Ann. Pub. Co-op. Econ.*, March 1983, *54*(1), pp. 57–72. **[G: Canada]**

Pick, Pedro J. Managing State-Owned Enterprises More Effectively: The Venezuelan Case. *Ann. Pub. Co-op. Econ.*, October-December 1983, *54*(4), pp. 387–96. **[G: Venezuela]**

Pontarollo, Enzo. Italy: Effects of Substituting Political Objectives for Business Goals. **In** *Hindley, B., ed.*, 1983, pp. 25–58. **[G: Italy]**

Premchand, A. Government and Public Enterprise: The Budget Link. **In** *[Ramanadham, V. V.]*, 1983, pp. 24–47.

ten Raa, Thijs. Supportability and Anonymous Equity. *J. Econ. Theory*, October 1983, *31*(1), pp. 176–81.

Seah, Linda. Public Enterprise and Economic Development. **In** *Chen, P. S. J., ed.*, 1983, pp. 129–59. **[G: Singapore]**

Seglow, Peter. Organizational Survival as an Act of Faith: The Case of the BBC. **In** *Thurley, K. and Wood, S., eds.*, 1983, pp. 157–69. **[G: U.K.]**

Seidman, Harold. Public Enterprises in the United States. *Ann. Pub. Co-op. Econ.*, March 1983, *54*(1), pp. 3–18. **[G: U.S.]**

Sen, Amartya K. Carrots, Sticks and Economics: Perception Problems in Incentives. *Indian Econ. Rev.*, January–June 1983, *18*(1), pp. 1–16.

Sexty, Robert W. The Accountability Dilemma in Canadian Public Enterprises: Social versus Commercial Responsiveness. *Ann. Pub. Co-op. Econ.*, March 1983, *54*(1), pp. 19–33. **[G: Canada]**

Sherman, Roger. Pricing Behavior of the Budget-constrained Public Enterprise. *J. Econ. Behav. Organ.*, December 1983, *4*(4), pp. 381–93. **[G: U.S.]**

Sobhan, Rehman. Distributive Regimes under Public Enterprise: A Case Study of the Bangladesh Expeience. **In** *Stewart, F., ed.*, 1983, pp. 138–67. **[G: Bangladesh]**

Spencer, Barbara J. and Brander, James A. Second Best Pricing of Publicly Produced Inputs: The Case of Downstream Imperfect Competition. *J. Public Econ.*, February 1983, *20*(1), pp. 113–19.

Stoffaës, Christian. Objectifs économiques et critères de gestion du secteur public industriel. (Economic Objectives and Management Criteria of the Manufacturing Public Sector. With English summary.) *Revue Écon.*, May 1983, *34*(3), pp. 577–611. **[G: France]**

Tan, Chwee-Huat. Public Enterprise and the Government in Singapore. **In** *[Ramanadham, V. V.]*, 1983, pp. 249–63. **[G: Singapore]**

Thiemeyer, Theo. Deregulation in the Perspective of the German *Gemeinwirtschaftslehre*. *Z. ges. Staatswiss.*, October 1983, *139*(3), pp. 405–18.

Trebilcock, M. J. and Prichard, J. Robert S. Crown Corporations: The Calculus of Instrument Choice. **In** *Prichard, J. R. S., ed.*, 1983, pp. 1–97. **[G: Canada]**

Turk, Ivan. Efficiency Analysis through Interrelated Indicators: The Yugoslav Approach. **In** *[Ramanadham, V. V.]*, 1983, pp. 140–56. **[G: Yugoslavia]**

Tye, William B. Economic Analysis of Selected Costing Concepts as Applied to the U.S. Postal Service. *Logist. Transp. Rev.*, June 1983, *19*(2), pp. 123–40. **[G: U.S.]**

Tye, William B. Ironies to the Application of the Inverse Elasticity Rule to the Pricing of U.S. Postal Services. *Logist. Transp. Rev.*, October 1983, *19*(3), pp. 245–60. **[G: U.S.]**

Tye, William B. The Postal Service: Economics Made Simplistic. *J. Policy Anal. Manage.*, Fall 1983, *3*(1), pp. 62–73. **[G: U.S.]**

Vessilier, Elisabeth. Aspects financiers des nationalisations. (Financial Aspects of Nationalisations. With English summary.) *Revue Écon.*, May 1983, *34*(3), pp. 466–95. **[G: France]**

Viallet, Claude. Resolution of Conflicts of Interest in the Ownership of a Firm: The Case of Mixed Firms. *Ann. Pub. Co-op. Econ.*, July–September 1983, *54*(3), pp. 255–69.

Vining, Aidan R. Provincial Ownership of Government Enterprise in Canada. *Ann. Pub. Co-op. Econ.*, March 1983, *54*(1), pp. 35–55. **[G: Canada]**

Vining, Aidan R. and Botterell, Robert. An Overview of the Origins, Growth, Size and Functions of Provincial Crown Corporations. **In** *Prichard,*

J. R. S., ed., 1983, pp. 303–67. **[G: Canada]**

Vogelsang, Ingo. Effort Rewarding Incentive Mechanisms for Public Enterprise Managers. *Int. J. Ind. Organ.*, September 1983, *1* (3), pp. 253–73.

Whyte, John D. A Constitutional Perspective on Federal–Provincial Sharing of Revenues from Natural Resources. **In** *McLure, C. E., Jr. and Mieszkowski, P., eds.*, 1983, pp. 205–35. **[G: Canada]**

615 Economics of Transportation

6150 Economics of Transportation

Achary, K. K. A Branch and Bound Algorithm for Determining Efficient Solution Pairs in a Special Type of Transportation Problem. *Econ. Computat. Cybern. Stud. Res.*, 1983, *18* (4), pp. 83–92.

Alexis, Marcus. The Political Economy of Federal Regulation of Surface Transportation. **In** *Noll, R. G. and Owen, B. M.*, 1983, pp. 115–31. **[G: U.S.]**

Alperovich, Gershon and Katz, Eliakim. Transport Rate Uncertainty and the Optimal Location of the Firm. *J. Reg. Sci.*, August 1983, *23* (3), pp. 389–96.

Anderson, E. J. and Philpott, A. B. An Algorithm for a Continuous Version of the Assignment Problem. **In** *Fiacco, A. V. and Kortanek, K. O., eds.*, 1983, pp. 108–17.

Andruszkiewicz, Witold. Time as a Factor in Increasing the Economic Efficiency of Ports and Sea—Land Transport. **In** *Khachaturov, T. S. and Goodwin, P. B., eds.*, 1983, pp. 267–73. **[G: Global; Poland]**

Antal, G. Principal Problems of the Development of International Relations in the Transport Sector. **In** *Khachaturov, T. S. and Goodwin, P. B., eds.*, 1983, pp. 361–71. **[G: CMEA; W. Europe]**

Antle, John M. Infrastructure and Aggregate Agricultural Productivity: International Evidence. *Econ. Develop. Cult. Change*, April 1983, *31* (3), pp. 609–19.

Atack, Jeremy and Brueckner, Jan K. Steel Rails and American Railroads, 1867–1880: Reply to Harley. *Exploration Econ. Hist.*, July 1983, *20* (3), pp. 258–62. **[G: U.S.]**

Bajusz, Rezso. Mass Transport and Individual Transport: An Optimum Modal Split. **In** *Khachaturov, T. S. and Goodwin, P. B., eds.*, 1983, pp. 167–78. **[G: Hungary; W. Europe]**

Balcer, Yves. F.O.B. Pricing versus Uniform Delivered Pricing: A Welfare Analysis in a Stochastic Environment. *J. Econ. Theory*, June 1983, *30* (1), pp. 54–73.

Beesley, Michael E. and Glaister, Stephen G. Information for Regulating: The Case of Taxis. *Econ. J.*, September 1983, *93* (371), pp. 594–615. **[G: U.K.]**

Beilock, Richard and Freeman, James. Motor Carrier Deregulation in Florida. *Growth Change*, April 1983, *14* (2), pp. 30–41. **[G: U.S.]**

Beilock, Richard and Shonkwiler, J. Scott. Modeling Weekly Truck Rates for Perishables. *Southern J. Agr. Econ.*, July 1983, *15* (1), pp. 83–87. **[G: U.S.]**

Berechman, Joseph. Costs, Economies of Scale and Factor Demand in Bus Transport: An Analysis. *J. Transp. Econ. Policy*, January 1983, *17* (1), pp. 7–24. **[G: Israel]**

Berechman, Joseph and Paaswell, Robert E. Rail Rapid Transit Investment and CBD Revitalisation: Methodology and Results. *Urban Stud.*, November 1983, *20* (4), pp. 471–86. **[G: U.S.]**

Binkley, James K. and Bessler, David A. Expectations in Bulk Ocean Shipping: An Application of Autoregressive Modeling. *Rev. Econ. Statist.*, August 1983, *65* (3), pp. 516–20.

Binkley, James K.; Tyner, Wallace E. and Matthews, Marie E. Evaluating Alternative Energy Policies: An Example Comparing Transportation Energy Investments. *Energy J.*, April 1983, *4* (2), pp. 91–104. **[G: U.S.]**

Blackmur, Douglas. The Railway Strike, 1948. **In** *Murphy, D. J., ed.*, 1983, pp. 235–52. **[G: Australia]**

Boisjoly, Russell P. and Corsi, Thomas M. The Changing Nature of the Motor Carrier Acquisition Market. *Quarterly Journal of Business and Economics*, Autumn 1983, *22* (4), pp. 25–39. **[G: U.S.]**

Bonus, Holger. Deregulating Air Transportation: The U.S. Experience: Comment. **In** *Giersch, H., ed.*, 1983, pp. 287–89. **[G: U.S.]**

Boyd, Roy. Costs and Distortions of U.S. Regulations Policy in Intercoastal Lumber Shipping. *J. Policy Modeling*, June 1983, *5* (2), pp. 293–307. **[G: U.S.]**

Boyd, Roy. Lumber Transport and the Jones Act: A Multicommodity Spatial Equilibrium Analysis. *Bell J. Econ. (See Rand J. Econ. after 4/85)*, Spring 1983, *14* (1), pp. 202–12. **[G: Canada; U.S.]**

Breen, Denis A. Antitrust and Price Competition in the Trucking Industry. *Antitrust Bull.*, Spring 1983, *28* (1), pp. 201–25. **[G: U.S.]**

Burke, Richard. International Transportation Systems. **In** *Khachaturov, T. S. and Goodwin, P. B., eds.*, 1983, pp. 326–42. **[G: EEC]**

Burkhanov, V. Trunk Line Transportation in Less Accessible Regions. **In** *Khachaturov, T. S. and Goodwin, P. B., eds.*, 1983, pp. 106–11. **[G: U.S.S.R.]**

Byington, Russell and Olin, Gary. An Econometric Analysis of Freight Rate Disparities in U.S. Liner Trades. *Appl. Econ.*, June 1983, *15* (3), pp. 403–07. **[G: U.S.]**

Casavant, Kenneth L. and Binkley, James K. Transportation Changes and Agricultural Marketing Research. **In** *Farris, P. L., ed.*, 1983, pp. 98–116. **[G: U.S.]**

Caves, Douglas W.; Christensen, Laurits R. and Tretheway, Michael W. Productivity Performance of U.S. Trunk and Local Service Airlines in the Era of Deregulation. *Econ. Inquiry*, July 1983, *21* (3), pp. 312–24. **[G: U.S.]**

Chow, Garland. An Evaluation of Less-than-Truckload Transport in Small Rural Communities of Western Canada. *Logist. Transp. Rev.*, October 1983, *19* (3), pp. 225–44. **[G: Canada]**

Clapp, John M. A General Model of Equilibrium Locations. *J. Reg. Sci.*, November 1983, *23* (4), pp. 461–78.

Cohen, Marvin S. The Antitrust Implications of Airline Deregulation. *Antitrust Bull.*, Spring 1983, *28*(1), pp. 131–58. **[G: U.S.]**

Cordes, Joseph J. and Goldfarb, Robert S. Alternate Rationales for Severence Pay Compensation under Airline Deregulation. *Public Choice,* 1983, *41*(3), pp. 351–69. **[G: U.S.]**

Crandall, Robert W. Deregulation: The U.S. Experience. *Z. ges. Staatswiss.*, October 1983, *139*(3), pp. 419–34. **[G: U.S.]**

Creager, Stephen E. Airline Deregulation and Airport Regulation. *Yale Law J.*, December 1983, *93*(2), pp. 319–39. **[G: U.S.]**

Davies, J. E. An Analysis of Cost and Supply Conditions in the Liner Shipping Industry. *J. Ind. Econ.*, June 1983, *31*(4), pp. 417–35.

Davis, E. G. and Mokkelbost, P. B. The Recapitalization of Crown Corporations. *Can. Public Policy,* June 1983, *9*(2), pp. 181–88. **[G: Canada]**

Dorman, Gary Jay. A Model of Unregulated Airline Markets. **In** *Keeler, T. E., ed.*, 1983, pp. 131–48. **[G: U.S.]**

Eads, George C. Airline Competitive Conduct in a Less Regulated Environment: Implications for Antitrust. *Antitrust Bull.*, Spring 1983, *28*(1), pp. 159–84. **[G: U.S.]**

Edgar, J. R. U.S. Rail Deregulation—Implications for Canadian Shippers. *Logist. Transp. Rev.*, December 1983, *19*(4), pp. 325–35. **[G: U.S.; Canada]**

Ericson, Richard E. and Winston, Clifford M. Predatory Capacity Expansion in a Deregulated Motor Carrier Industry. **In** *Keeler, T. E., ed.*, 1983, pp. 185–235.

Fernandez, J. Enrique. Optimum Dynamic Investment Policies for Capacity in Transport Facilities. *J. Transp. Econ. Policy,* September 1983, *17*(3), pp. 267–84.

Findlay, Christopher C. Optimal Air Fares and Flight Frequency and Market Results. *J. Transp. Econ. Policy,* January 1983, *17*(1), pp. 49–66.

Flexner, Donald L. The Effects of Deregulation in the Motor Carrier Industry. *Antitrust Bull.*, Spring 1983, *28*(1), pp. 185–200. **[G: U.S.]**

Fontanella, Giuseppe. The Costs, Revenues and Deficit of the Italian State Railways' Goods Traffic. *Rev. Econ. Cond. Italy,* October 1983, (3), pp. 431–56. **[G: Italy]**

Forsskåhl, Per. Merenkulun murrosaika. (Finnish Shipping Is Undergoing Changes. With English summary.) *Kansant. Aikak.*, 1983, *79*(3), pp. 254–61. **[G: Finland]**

Frank, Robert H. When Are Price Differentials Discriminatory? *J. Policy Anal. Manage.*, Winter 1983, *2*(2), pp. 238–55. **[G: U.S.]**

Friedlaender, Ann F. and Chiang, S. Judy Wang. Productivity Growth in the Regulated Trucking Industry. **In** *Keeler, T. E., ed.*, 1983, pp. 149–84. **[G: U.S.]**

Friesz, Terry L. and Harker, Patrick T. Multi-objective Design of Transportation Networks: The Case of Spatial Price Equilibrium. **In** *Hansen, P., ed.*, 1983, pp. 86–93.

Fruin, Jerry E. Impacts on Agriculture of Deregulating the Transportation System: Reply. *Amer. J. Agr. Econ.*, February 1983, *65*(1), pp. 192–93. **[G: U.S.]**

Fuller, Stephen, et al. Modeling an Intermodal Transfer System: The Case of Export Grain Terminals. *Logist. Transp. Rev.*, October 1983, *19*(3), pp. 195–210. **[G: U.S.]**

Gardner, Bernard and Marlow, Peter. An International Comparison of the Fiscal Treatment of Shipping. *J. Ind. Econ.*, June 1983, *31*(4), pp. 397–415. **[G: EEC; Japan; U.S.; Liberia]**

Gemmell, Andrew W.; Uhm, Ihn H. and Shaw, Gordon C. Economics of Canadian Water Carriers on the Great Lakes and St. Lawrence Seaway System. *J. Transp. Econ. Policy,* May 1983, *17*(2), pp. 191–209. **[G: Canada]**

Glaister, Stephen G. Some Characteristics of Rail Commuter Demand. *J. Transp. Econ. Policy,* May 1983, *17*(2), pp. 115–32. **[G: U.K.]**

Golabi, Kamal. A Markov Decision Modeling Approach to a Multi-objective Maintenance Problem. **In** *Hansen, P., ed.*, 1983, pp. 115–25.

Golbe, Devra L. Product Safety in a Regulated Industry: Evidence from the Railroads. *Econ. Inquiry,* January 1983, *21*(1), pp. 39–52. **[G: U.S.]**

Gomez-Ibanez, Jose A.; Oster, Clinton V., Jr. and Pickrell, Don H. Airline Deregulation: What's behind the Recent Losses? *J. Policy Anal. Manage.*, Fall 1983, *3*(1), pp. 74–89. **[G: U.S.]**

Goodman, Allen C. Willingness to Pay for Car Efficiency: A Hedonic Price Approach. *J. Transp. Econ. Policy,* September 1983, *17*(3), pp. 247–66. **[G: U.S.]**

Graham, David R.; Kaplan, Daniel P. and Sibley, David S. Efficiency and Competition in the Airline Industry. *Bell J. Econ. (See Rand J. Econ. after 4/85),* Spring 1983, *14*(1), pp. 118–38. **[G: U.S.]**

Grieson, Ronald E. and Arnott, Richard J. Optimal Tolls with High-peak Travel Demand. **In** *Grieson, R. E., ed.*, 1983, pp. 193–201.

Gwilliam, Kenneth M. The Future of the Common Transport Policy. **In** *El-Agraa, A. M., ed.*, 1983, pp. 167–86. **[G: EEC]**

Harley, C. Knick. Steel Rails and American Railroads 1867–1880: Cost Minimizing Choice: A Comment on the Analysis of Atack and Brueckner. *Exploration Econ. Hist.*, July 1983, *20*(3), pp. 248–57. **[G: U.S.]**

Harris, Robert G. and Winston, Clifford M. Potential Benefits of Rail Mergers: An Econometric Analysis of Network Effects on Service Quality. *Rev. Econ. Statist.*, February 1983, *65*(1), pp. 32–40. **[G: U.S.]**

Harrison, David, Jr. The Regulation of Aircraft Noise. **In** *Schelling, T. C., ed.*, 1983, pp. 41–143. **[G: U.S.]**

Hayashi, Paul M. and Trapani, John M. An Analysis of the Objectives of Domestic Airline Firms under CAB Regulation. *Appl. Econ.*, October 1983, *15*(5), pp. 603–17. **[G: U.S.]**

Haynes, Kingsley E.; Phillips, Fred Y. and Solomon, Barry D. A Coal Industry Distribution Planning Model under Environmental Constraints. *Econ. Geogr.*, January 1983, *59*(1), pp. 52–65.

Hayter, D. M. and Sharp, C. H. Inland Waterways and Long-distance Freight Traffic. **In** *Khachaturov, T. S. and Goodwin, P. B., eds.*, 1983, pp. 286–300. **[G: U.K.]**

Hensher, David A. and Louviere, Jordan J. Identifying Individual Preferences for International Air Fares: An Application of Functional Measurement Theory. *J. Transp. Econ. Policy,* September 1983, *17*(3), pp. 225–45. **[G: Australia; U.S.]**

Hettich, Walter. The Political Economy of Benefit–Cost Analysis: Evaluating STOL Air Transport for Canada. *Can. Public Policy,* December 1983, *9*(4), pp. 487–98. **[G: Canada]**

Hilton, George W. Impediments to the American Railroads' Achieving Their Comparative Advantage for Long-distance Movement. **In** *Khachaturov, T. S. and Goodwin, P. B., eds.,* 1983, pp. 221–31. **[G: U.S.]**

Honko, Jaakko. What Role for Finland and Her Shipping Industry in the World Economy? *Liiketaloudellinen Aikak.,* 1983, *32*(4), pp. 305–16. **[G: Finland]**

Hunter, Holland; Dienes, Leslie and Bettis, Lee. International Implications of Long-distance Transport of Fuels. **In** *Khachaturov, T. S. and Goodwin, P. B., eds.,* 1983, pp. 81–93. **[G: U.S.S.R.]**

Ilan, Amos, et al. The Treatment of Foreign and Domestic Transportation in Regional Input–Output Modeling—An Analytic Framework. **In** *Dutta, M.; Hartline, J. C. and Loeb, P. D., eds.,* 1983, pp. 269–89. **[G: U.S.]**

Ivantsov, O. M. Pipeline Transportation of Natural Gas in the U.S.S.R. **In** *Khachaturov, T. S. and Goodwin, P. B., eds.,* 1983, pp. 134–41. **[G: U.S.S.R.]**

Jansen, Eirik G. The Development of the Mechanized River Transport Sector in Bangladesh: Aid to the Poor? **In** *Parkinson, J. R., ed.,* 1983, pp. 163–68. **[G: Bangladesh]**

Johnson, Marc A. Impacts on Agriculture of Deregulating the Transportation System: Reply. *Amer. J. Agr. Econ.,* February 1983, *65*(1), pp. 190–91. **[G: U.S.]**

Jondrow, James; Bowes, Marianne and Levy, Robert. The Optimal Speed Limit. *Econ. Inquiry,* July 1983, *21*(3), pp. 325–36. **[G: U.S.]**

Jones, Ian S. and Nichols, Alan J. The Demand for Inter-City Rail Travel in the United Kingdom: Some Evidence. *J. Transp. Econ. Policy,* May 1983, *17*(2), pp. 133–53. **[G: U.K.]**

Jordan, W. John. The Theory of Optimal Highway Pricing and Investment. *Southern Econ. J.,* October 1983, *50*(2), pp. 560–64.

Jung, Allen F. Automobile Insurance Rates in Chicago, Illinois—A Correction. *J. Risk Ins.,* June 1983, *50*(2), pp. 330–31. **[G: U.S.]**

Kahn, Alfred E. Deregulation and Vested Interests: The Case of Airlines. **In** *Noll, R. G. and Owen, B. M.,* 1983, pp. 132–51. **[G: U.S.]**

Kakumoto, Ryohei. Motorisation in Japan. **In** *Khachaturov, T. S. and Goodwin, P. B., eds.,* 1983, pp. 187–96. **[G: Japan]**

Kasper, Hirschel. Toward Estimating the Incidence of Journey-to-Work Costs. *Urban Stud.,* May 1983, *20*(2), pp. 197–208. **[G: U.K.]**

Katus, László. Transport Revolution and Economic Growth in Hungary. **In** *Komlos, J., ed.,* 1983, pp. 183–204. **[G: Hungary]**

Kemperman, J. H. B. On the Role of Duality in the Theory of Moments. **In** *Fiacco, A. V. and Kortanek, K. O., eds.,* 1983, pp. 63–92.

Kennedy, K. H. The South Johnstone Strike, 1927. **In** *Murphy, D. J., ed.,* 1983, pp. 174–85. **[G: Australia]**

Khachaturov, T. S. Introductory Address: Transport Development in the USSR. **In** *Khachaturov, T. S. and Goodwin, P. B., eds.,* 1983, pp. xiii–xvi. **[G: U.S.S.R.]**

Koo, Won W. Impacts on Agriculture of Deregulating the Transportation System: Comment. *Amer. J. Agr. Econ.,* February 1983, *65*(1), pp. 187–89. **[G: U.S.]**

Koran, Donald William. The Welfare Effects of Airline Fare Deregulation in the United States. *J. Transp. Econ. Policy,* May 1983, *17*(2), pp. 177–89. **[G: U.S.]**

Kouris, George. Fuel Consumption for Road Transport in the USA. *Energy Econ.,* April 1983, *5*(2), pp. 89–99. **[G: U.S.]**

Kresge, David T.; Ginn, Royce J. and Gray, John T. Transportation System Planning for Alaska Development. **In** *Khachaturov, T. S. and Goodwin, P. B., eds.,* 1983, pp. 112–33. **[G: U.S.]**

Kriebel, Wesley R. and Baumel, C. Phillip. Issues in Freight Transportation Regulation: Reply. *Amer. J. Agr. Econ.,* August 1983, *65*(3), pp. 629–32. **[G: U.S.]**

Krout, John A. Intercountry Commuting in Nonmetropolitan America in 1960 and 1970. *Growth Change,* January 1983, *14*(1), pp. 10–19. **[G: U.S.]**

Lake, R. W.; Boon, C. J. and Schwier, C. Efficient Long-distance Fuel Transportation. **In** *Khachaturov, T. S. and Goodwin, P. B., eds.,* 1983, pp. 142–56. **[G: Canada]**

Lande, Richard. Possible Remedies to Reconcile the Differences between Canada and U.S. Rail Regulation. *Logist. Transp. Rev.,* October 1983, *19*(3), pp. 211–24. **[G: U.S.; Canada]**

Langhammer, Rolf J. The Importance of 'Natural' Barriers to Trade among Developing Countries: Some Evidence from the Transport Cost Content in Brasilian Imports. *World Devel.,* May 1983, *11*(5), pp. 417–25. **[G: Brazil; LDCs]**

Lányi, Kamilla. Enterprise Identity—Interenterprise Relationships: A State Monopoly in a Competitive Position. *Eastern Europ. Econ.,* Spring–Summer 1983, *21*(3–4), pp. 26–48. **[G: Hungary]**

Larsen, Odd I. Marginal Cost Pricing of Scheduled Transport Services. *J. Transp. Econ. Policy,* September 1983, *17*(3), pp. 315–17.

Layton, Allan P. and Weigh, Jeffrey C. The Efficacy of Some Recent Australian Road Safety Policy Initiatives. *Logist. Transp. Rev.,* October 1983, *19*(3), pp. 267–78. **[G: Australia]**

Ledford, Manfred H. and Sugrue, Paul K. Ratio Analysis: Application to U.S. Motor Common Carriers. *Bus. Econ.,* September 1983, *18*(4), pp. 46–54. **[G: U.S.]**

Leinbach, Thomas R. Rural Transport and Population Mobility in Indonesia. *J. Devel. Areas,* April 1983, *17*(3), pp. 349–63. **[G: Indonesia]**

Leonard, William N. Airline Deregulation: Grand Design or Gross Debacle? *J. Econ. Issues,* June 1983, *17*(2), pp. 453–62. **[G: U.S.]**

Lewis, W. Arthur. Fixed Costs. **In** *Lewis, W. A.,* 1983,

1961, pp. 113–47.

Lindner, Werner. The Optimum Ratio between Private and Public Passenger Transport Services in Conurbations: The Experience of the German Democratic Republic. **In** *Khachaturov, T. S. and Goodwin, P. B., eds.*, 1983, pp. 179–86. **[G: E. Germany]**

Lipnowski, Irwin and Shilony, Yuval. The Design of a Tort Law to Control Accidents. *Math. Soc. Sci.*, April 1983, *4*(2), pp. 103–15.

Logsdon, Charles, et al. Estimation of Demand for Truck-Barge Transportation of Pacific Northwest Wheat. *Logist. Transp. Rev.*, March 1983, *19*(1), pp. 81–89. **[G: U.S.]**

Major, Iván. Tensions in Transportation and the Development Level of Transport in Some Socialist Countries. *Acta Oecon.*, 1983, *30*(2), pp. 221–40. **[G: Hungary]**

Makus, Larry D. and Fuller, Stephen. Motor Carrier Regulation and Its Impact on Service: An Analysis of Texas Fresh Fruit and Vegetable Shippers. *Southern J. Agr. Econ.*, December 1983, *15*(2), pp. 21–26. **[G: U.S.]**

Mao, Chi-Kuo and Martland, Carl D. Improving the Utilization of Railroad Motive Power Units. *Logist. Transp. Rev.*, March 1983, *19*(1), pp. 3–29. **[G: U.S.]**

McBride, Mark E. An Evaluation of Various Methods of Estimating Railway Costs. *Logist. Transp. Rev.*, March 1983, *19*(1), pp. 45–66. **[G: U.S.]**

McRae, James J. and Prescott, David M. Second Thoughts on Tariff Bureaus. *Can. Public Policy*, June 1983, *9*(2), pp. 200–209. **[G: Canada]**

Meerman, Jacob. Cost Recovery in a Project Context: Some World Bank Experience in Tropical Africa. *World Devel.*, June 1983, *11*(6), pp. 503–14. **[G: Tropical Africa]**

Mendelsohn, Robert and Brown, Gardner M., Jr. Revealed Preference Approaches to Valuing Outdoor Recreation. *Natural Res. J.*, July 1983, *23*(3), pp. 607–18. **[G: U.S.]**

Mergen, Bernard. The Government as Manager: Emergency Fleet Shipbuilding, 1917–1919. **In** *[Cochran, T. C.]*, 1983, pp. 49–80. **[G: U.S.]**

Meyer, John R. and Tye, William B. Rational Policies for Development of International Air Transportation. **In** *Khachaturov, T. S. and Goodwin, P. B., eds.*, 1983, pp. 245–64. **[G: Global; U.S.]**

Miller, Elbert G. and Hoffer, George E. Pay-at-the-Pump Automobile Liability Insurance: Reply [The Distribution of Automobile Liability Insurance: An Alternative]. *J. Risk Ins.*, September 1983, *50*(3), pp. 487–92. **[G: U.S.]**

Mitaishvili, A. A. Planning and Mode Split of Freight Traffic in the USSR. **In** *Khachaturov, T. S. and Goodwin, P. B., eds.*, 1983, pp. 3–11. **[G: U.S.S.R.]**

Morash, Edward A. and Enis, Charles R. Investor Perceptions of the Impact of Deregulation on Motor Carrier Earnings. *Logist. Transp. Rev.*, December 1983, *19*(4), pp. 309–23. **[G: U.S.]**

Morrison, Steven A. Estimation of Long-Run Prices and Investment Levels for Airport Runways. **In** *Keeler, T. E., ed.*, 1983, pp. 103–30. **[G: U.S.]**

Müller, Jürgen. Air Transport and Its Regulation in West Germany. *Z. ges. Staatswiss.*, October 1983, *139*(3), pp. 506–26. **[G: W. Germany]**

Murphy, D. J. The North Queensland Railway Strike, 1917. **In** *Murphy, D. J., ed.*, 1983, pp. 132–43. **[G: Australia]**

Mwase, Ngila. The Supply of Road Vehicles in Tanzania: The Problem of Suppressed Demand. *J. Transp. Econ. Policy*, January 1983, *17*(1), pp. 77–89. **[G: Tanzania]**

Nagao, Yoshimi; Kuroda, Katsuhiko and Wakai, Ikujiro. Decisionmaking under Conflict in Project Evaluation. **In** *Isard, W. and Nagao, Y., eds.*, 1983, pp. 73–90.

Nelson, James C. A Critique of DOT Transport Policy. **In** *Nelson, J. C.*, 1983, *1972*, pp. 405–23. **[G: U.S.]**

Nelson, James C. A Critique of Governmental Intervention in Transport. **In** *Nelson, J. C.*, 1983, *1975*, pp. 371–404. **[G: U.S.]**

Nelson, James C. British Freight Transport Deregulation and U.S. Transport Policy. **In** *Nelson, J. C.*, 1983, *1981*, pp. 341–51. **[G: U.S.; U.K.]**

Nelson, James C. Coming Organizational Change in Transportation. **In** *Nelson, J. C.*, 1983, *1967*, pp. 25–50.

Nelson, James C. Competitive Issues in Grain Transport in the Pacific Northwest. **In** *Nelson, J. C.*, 1983, *1964*, pp. 121–30. **[G: U.S.]**

Nelson, James C. Cost Standards for Competitive Freight Rates. **In** *Nelson, J. C.*, 1983, *1971*, pp. 131–52.

Nelson, James C. Dynamic Competitive Forces in Freight Transport. **In** *Nelson, J. C.*, 1983, *1977*, pp. 51–77. **[G: Canada]**

Nelson, James C. Economies of Large-Scale Operation in the Trucking Industry. **In** *Nelson, J. C.*, 1983, *1941*, pp. 21–24. **[G: U.S.]**

Nelson, James C. Effects of Public Regulation on Railroad Performance. **In** *Nelson, J. C.*, 1983, *1960*, pp. 254–60. **[G: U.S.]**

Nelson, James C. Federal Regulatory Restrictions Upon Motor and Water Carriers. **In** *Nelson, J. C.*, 1983, *1974*, pp. 231–53. **[G: U.S.]**

Nelson, James C. Implications of Evolving Entry and Licensing Policies in Road Freight Transport. **In** *Nelson, J. C.*, 1983, *1974*, pp. 288–97.

Nelson, James C. New Concepts in Transportation Regulation. **In** *Nelson, J. C.*, 1983, *1942*, pp. 178–230. **[G: U.S.]**

Nelson, James C. Patterns of Competition and Monopoly in Present-Day Transport and Implications for Public Policy. **In** *Nelson, J. C.*, 1983, *1950*, pp. 2–20.

Nelson, James C. Policy Issues and Economic Effects of Public Aids to Domestic Transport. **In** *Nelson, J. C.*, 1983, *1959*, pp. 353–70.

Nelson, James C. Pricing Policies of the Railroads. **In** *Nelson, J. C.*, 1983, *1959*, pp. 88–120. **[G: U.S.]**

Nelson, James C. Regulatory Performance in Surface Freight Transportation in Australia, Canada, Great Britain and the U.S.A. **In** *Nelson, J. C.*, 1983, *1980*, pp. 298–340. **[G: U.K.; U.S.; Australia; Canada]**

Nelson, James C. The Challenge of Transportation. **In** *Nelson, J. C.*, 1983, *1966*, pp. 424–35.

Nelson, James C. The Effects of Entry Control in

Surface Transport. In *Nelson, J. C.*, 1983, *1965*, pp. 261–86. [G: U.S.]

Nelson, James C. The Pricing of Highway, Water, and Airway Facilities. In *Nelson, J. C.*, 1983, *1962*, pp. 79–87.

Nelson, James C. Toward Rational Price Policies. In *Nelson, J. C.*, 1983, *1971*, pp. 153–76. [G: U.S.]

Nonini, Donald M. The Chinese Truck Transport "Industry" of a Peninsular Malaysian Market Town. In *Lim, L. Y. C. and Gosling, L. A. P., eds.*, 1983, pp. 171–206. [G: Malaysia]

Noortman, H. J. Organisation of Transport Enterprises. In *Khachaturov, T. S. and Goodwin, P. B., eds.*, 1983, pp. 312–25. [G: W. Europe]

Norrie, Kenneth H. Not Much to Crow about: A Primer on the Statutory Grain Freight Rate Issue. *Can. Public Policy*, December 1983, *9*(4), pp. 434–45. [G: Canada]

Norrie, Kenneth H. and Percy, Michael B. Freight Rate Reform and Regional Burden: A General Equilibrium Analysis of Western Freight Rate Proposals. *Can. J. Econ.*, May 1983, *16*(2), pp. 325–49.

North, John. Developments in Transport. In *Wild, T., ed.*, 1983, pp. 130–60. [G: W. Germany]

Northrup, Herbert R. The New Employee-Relations Climate in Airlines. *Ind. Lab. Relat. Rev.*, January 1983, *36*(2), pp. 167–81. [G: U.S.]

Obeng, Kofi. Fare Subsidies to Achieve Pareto Optimality—A Benefit Cost Approach. *Logist. Transp. Rev.*, December 1983, *19*(4), pp. 367–84. [G: U.S.]

Okano, Yukihide. Modal Split, Efficiency and Public Policy. In *Khachaturov, T. S. and Goodwin, P. B., eds.*, 1983, pp. 49–64. [G: Japan]

Osleeb, Jeffrey P. and Patrick, Samuel J. The Impact of Coal Conversions on the Ports of New England. *Econ. Geogr.*, January 1983, *59*(1), pp. 35–51. [G: U.S.]

Oster, Clinton V., Jr. and Zorn, C. Kurt. Airline Deregulation, Commuter Safety, and Regional Air Transportation. *Growth Change*, July 1983, *14*(3), pp. 3–11. [G: U.S.]

Pagano, Anthony M. and McKnight, Claire E. Economies of Scale in the Taxicab Industry: Some Empirical Evidence from the United States. *J. Transp. Econ. Policy*, September 1983, *17*(3), pp. 299–313. [G: U.S.]

Palmer, John; Quinn, John and Resendes, Ray. A Case Study of Public Enterprise: Gray Coach Lines Ltd. In *Prichard, J. R. S., ed.*, 1983, pp. 369–446. [G: Canada]

Panzar, John C. Regulatory Theory and the U.S. Airline Experience. *Z. ges. Staatswiss.*, October 1983, *139*(3), pp. 490–505. [G: U.S.]

Pegrum, Dudley, F. Changes in Freight Traffic among the Modes of Transport Past and Future. In *Khachaturov, T. S. and Goodwin, P. B., eds.*, 1983, pp. 22–33. [G: U.S.]

Polus, Abishai. An Economic Evaluation of Large Truck Combination Options. *Logist. Transp. Rev.*, December 1983, *19*(4), pp. 337–50. [G: Canada]

Porter, Robert H. A Study of Cartel Stability: The Joint Executive Committee, 1880–1886. *Bell J. Econ. (See Rand J. Econ. after 4/85)*, Autumn 1983, *14*(2), pp. 301–14. [G: U.S.]

Pucher, John; Markstedt, Anders and Hirschman, Ira. Impacts of Subsidies on the Costs of Urban Public Transport. *J. Transp. Econ. Policy*, May 1983, *17*(2), pp. 155–76. [G: U.S.]

Pustay, Michael W. Deregulating Air Transportation: The U.S. Experience. In *Giersch, H., ed.*, 1983, pp. 265–86. [G: U.S.]

Pustay, Michael W. Intrastate Motor Carrier Regulation in Texas. *Logist. Transp. Rev.*, June 1983, *19*(2), pp. 141–62. [G: U.S.]

Pustay, Michael W. Regulatory Reform and the Allocation of Wealth: An Empirical Analysis. *Quart. Rev. Econ. Bus.*, Spring 1983, *23*(1), pp. 19–28. [G: U.S.]

Rehbein, Gerhard. Spatial Distribution of Productive Powers and Socialist Transport Policy. In *Khachaturov, T. S. and Goodwin, P. B., eds.*, 1983, pp. 305–11.

Reschenthaler, G. B. and Stanbury, W. T. Deregulating Canada's Airlines: Grounded by False Assumptions. *Can. Public Policy*, June 1983, *9*(2), pp. 210–22. [G: U.S.; Canada]

Rietveld, Piet. Analysis of Conflicts and Compromises, Using Qualitative Data. *Conflict Manage. Peace Sci.*, Fall 1983, *7*(1), pp. 39–63. [G: Netherlands; Belgium]

Roach, William L. Pay-at-the Pump Automobile Liability Insurance [The Distribution of Automobile Liability Insurance: An Alternative]. *J. Risk Ins.*, March 1983, *50*(1), pp. 131–39. [G: U.S.]

Ruppenthal, Karl M. and Toh, Rex. Airline Deregulation and the No Show/Overbooking Problem. *Logist. Transp. Rev.*, June 1983, *19*(2), pp. 111–21. [G: U.S.]

Sasaki, Komei. A Household Production Approach to the Evaluation of Transportation System Change. *Reg. Sci. Urban Econ.*, August 1983, *13*(3), pp. 363–82.

Schulze, Gottfried. Application of Control Models in Port Activities. *Econ. Computat. Cybern. Stud. Res.*, 1983, *18*(3), pp. 95–100.

Seah, Linda. Public Enterprise and Economic Development. In *Chen, P. S. J., ed.*, 1983, pp. 129–59. [G: Singapore]

Seidenfus, H. St. Problems in Attaining an Optimum Ratio Between Long-distance Individual and Public Passenger Transport. In *Khachaturov, T. S. and Goodwin, P. B., eds.*, 1983, pp. 197–210. [G: W. Europe]

Sheehan, Michael F. Land Speculation in Southern California: Energy Monopoly, Fiscal Crisis and the Future. *Amer. J. Econ. Soc.*, January 1983, *42*(1), pp. 67–74. [G: U.S.]

Shimojo, Tetsuji. A Production System for Transport Services. *Kobe Econ. Bus. Rev.*, 1983, (29), pp. 9–19.

Shneerson, Dan. The Profitability of Investment in Shipping: The Balance of Payments Criterion. *J. Transp. Econ. Policy*, September 1983, *17*(3), pp. 285–98. [G: Israel]

Simon, Julian L. A Scheme to Improve Air Travel. *J. Policy Anal. Manage.*, Spring 1983, *2*(3), pp. 465–66. [G: U.S.]

Smith, Anne. The Railway Strike, 1925. In *Murphy, D. J., ed.*, 1983, pp. 162–73. [G: Australia]

Smith, V. Kerry; Desvousges, William H. and McGivney, Matthew P. The Opportunity Cost of Travel Time in Recreation Demand Models. *Land Econ.*, August 1983, *59*(3), pp. 259–78. **[G: U.S.]**

Spiller, Pablo T. The Differential Impact of Airline Regulation on Individual Firms and Markets: An Empirical Analysis. *J. Law Econ.*, October 1983, *26*(3), pp. 655–89. **[G: U.S.]**

Spychalski, John C. Progress, Inconsistencies, and Neglect in the Social Control of Railway Freight Transport. *J. Econ. Issues*, June 1983, *17*(2), pp. 433–42. **[G: U.S.]**

Squilbin, R. The Development and Main Problems of International Transport Systems. **In** *Khachaturov, T. S. and Goodwin, P. B., eds.*, 1983, pp. 232–40. **[G: W. Europe]**

Street, Andrew. Local Authority Capital Spending on Roads and Its Financing. *Nat. Westminster Bank Quart. Rev.*, November 1983, pp. 48–57. **[G: U.K.]**

Stromquist, Shelton. Enginemen and Shopmen: Technological Change and the Organization of Labor in an Era of Railroad Expansion. *Labor Hist.*, Fall 1983, *24*(4), pp. 485–99. **[G: U.S.]**

Strong, Elizabeth J. A Note on the Functional Form of Travel Cost Models with Zones of Unequal Populations. *Land Econ.*, August 1983, *59*(3), pp. 342–49. **[G: U.S.]**

Szplett, Elizabeth S. and Sargious, Michael A. The Comparative Energy Efficiency of Intercity Transportation Modes in Canada. *Logist. Transp. Rev.*, June 1983, *19*(2), pp. 163–80. **[G: Canada]**

Taplin, John H. E. Regulation, Deregulation, and the Sustainability of Transport Monopolies. *Logist. Transp. Rev.*, March 1983, *19*(1), pp. 31–44.

Taplin, John H. E. and Gallagher, F. D. Transport Issues. *Australian J. Agr. Econ.*, August 1983, *27*(2), pp. 139–44. **[G: Australia]**

Tauchen, Helen; Fravel, Frederic D. and Gilbert, Gorman. Cost Structure of the Intercity Bus Industry. *J. Transp. Econ. Policy*, January 1983, *17*(1), pp. 25–47. **[G: U.S.]**

Taylor, Michael and Kissling, Chris. Resource Dependence, Power Networks and the Airline System of the South Pacific. *Reg. Stud.*, August 1983, *17*(4), pp. 237–50. **[G: South Pacific]**

Taylor, Scott and Wright, Robert. An Economic Evaluation of Calgary's North-East Light Rail Transit System. *Logist. Transp. Rev.*, December 1983, *19*(4), pp. 351–65. **[G: Canada]**

Teodorovic, Dušan B. and Tošic, Vojin S. Multi Attribute Ranking of Transport Facility's Order of Construction—An Airport Network Development Case. *Logist. Transp. Rev.*, June 1983, *19*(2), pp. 181–89.

Thomas, Steven G. Transportation and Dependency. **In** *Vogel, R. J. and Palmer, H. C., eds.*, 1983, pp. 463–82. **[G: U.S.]**

Tobin, Roger L. and Friesz, Terry L. Formulating and Solving the Spatial Price Equilibrium Problem with Transshipment in Terms of Arc Variables. *J. Reg. Sci.*, May 1983, *23*(2), pp. 187–98.

Tsankov, Stefan. The Importance of Organisational Forms of Integration in the Field of International Transport. **In** *Khachaturov, T. S. and Goodwin, P. B., eds.*, 1983, pp. 348–52. **[G: CMEA]**

Tucci, Ginarocco. Razionalità sostanziale e funzionale nella programmazione regionale dei trasporti in Italia. (Substantial and Functional Rationality in Regional Planning of Transportation in Italy. With English summary.) *Rivista Int. Sci. Econ. Com.*, June 1983, *30*(6), pp. 540–54. **[G: Italy]**

Tulkens, Henry and Kiabantu, Tomasikila Kioni. A Planning Process for the Efficient Allocation of Resources to Transportation Infrastructure. **In** *Thisse, J.-F. and Zoller, H. G., eds.*, 1983, pp. 127–52.

Tye, William B. Financing the Stand-Alone Railroad. *Logist. Transp. Rev.*, December 1983, *19*(4), pp. 291–308. **[G: U.S.]**

Uemura, Masahiro. The Development of the Shipping Business in the Shiwaku Islands under the Ninmyo System. *Osaka Econ. Pap.*, September 1983, *33*(1–2), pp. 50–70. **[G: Japan]**

Van Kooten, G. C. Rail Rationalization Choices in Saskatchewan: An Examination of Public Choice. *Can. J. Agr. Econ.*, November 1983, *31*(3), pp. 413–24. **[G: Canada]**

Vitek, Karel. Material Relations and Transport Policy in the Czechoslovak Socialist Republic. **In** *Khachaturov, T. S. and Goodwin, P. B., eds.*, 1983, pp. 353–60. **[G: Czechoslovakia]**

Voigt, Fritz. Comparing the Efficiency of Western European Rail and Road Services. **In** *Khachaturov, T. S. and Goodwin, P. B., eds.*, 1983, pp. 12–21. **[G: EEC]**

Wagener, Hermann. The Socialist Transport System—Its Management and Planning. **In** *Khachaturov, T. S. and Goodwin, P. B., eds.*, 1983, pp. 34–48. **[G: E. Germany]**

Whitcombe, Elizabeth and Hurd, John M. Irrigation and Railways. **In** *Kumar, D., ed.*, 1983, pp. 677–761. **[G: India]**

Wickham, S. and Phuc, N. Tien. Port Congestion or Port Dysfunction. **In** *Khachaturov, T. S. and Goodwin, P. B., eds.*, 1983, pp. 274–85. **[G: Global]**

Wilson, Hoyt G. A Criticism of "Multiattribute Ranking of Transport Facilities' Order of Construction: An Airport Network Development Case." *Logist. Transp. Rev.*, June 1983, *19*(2), pp. 190–91.

Wilson, John D. Optimal Road Capacity in the Presence of Unpriced Congestion. *J. Urban Econ.*, May 1983, *13*(3), pp. 337–57.

Wright, Charles L. Issues in Freight Transportation Regulation: Comment. *Amer. J. Agr. Econ.*, February 1983, *65*(1), pp. 162–66. **[G: U.S.]**

Wright, Charles L.; Meyer, Richard L. and Walker, Francis E. Modelling Improvements in Transport Infrastructure in Developing Areas: A Brazilian Example. *J. Devel. Econ.*, February/April 1983, *12*(1/2), pp. 153–68. **[G: Brazil]**

Yamaji, Hidetoshi. Two Types of Railroad Regulation by States in the 19th Century of the U.S.—Search for the Social Foundation of Modern Corporate Financial Reporting. *Kobe Econ. Bus. Rev.*, 1983, (29), pp. 33–42. **[G: U.S.]**

Zaleski, Jerzy. The Today and Tomorrow of Arctic Transportation Routes. **In** *Khachaturov, T. S. and Goodwin, P. B., eds.*, 1983, pp. 97–105. **[G: Canada; U.S.; U.S.S.R.]**

Zerby, J. A. and Conlon, R. M. Joint Costs and Intra-Tariff Cross-Subsidies: The Case of Liner Shipping. *J. Ind. Econ.*, June 1983, *31*(4), pp. 383–96. **[G: Australia]**

616 Industrial Policy

6160 Industrial Policy

Adams, F. Gerard. Criteria for U.S. Industrial-Policy Strategies. **In** *Adams, F. G. and Klein, L. R., eds.*, 1983, pp. 393–420. **[G: U.S.]**

Adams, F. Gerard and Bollino, C. Andrea. Meaning of Industrial Policy. **In** *Adams, F. G. and Klein, L. R., eds.*, 1983, pp. 13–20.

Adams, F. Gerard; Cherkes, Martin and Wescott, Robert F. Innovation, Technical Progress, and Industrial Policy: A Survey. **In** *Adams, F. G. and Klein, L. R., eds.*, 1983, pp. 41–47.

Adams, F. Gerard and Ichimura, Shinichi. Industrial Policy in Japan. **In** *Adams, F. G. and Klein, L. R., eds.*, 1983, pp. 307–30. **[G: Japan]**

Adams, F. Gerard and Klein, Lawrence R. Economic Evaluation of Industrial Policies for Growth and Competitiveness: Overview. **In** *Adams, F. G. and Klein, L. R., eds.*, 1983, pp. 3–11. **[G: U.S.]**

Adams, F. Gerard, et al. Developing-Country Experience with Industrial Policy: Korea, Venezuela, India, and Brazil. **In** *Adams, F. G. and Klein, L. R., eds.*, 1983, pp. 359–89. **[G: Korea; Venezuela; India; Brazil]**

Adams, John. Financial Subinfeudation and the Penchant for Real Investment. *J. Econ. Issues*, June 1983, *17*(2), pp. 485–94. **[G: India]**

Akinsanya, Adeoye A. State Strategies toward Nigerian and Foreign Business. **In** *Zartman, I. W., ed.*, 1983, pp. 145–84. **[G: Nigeria]**

Bailey, Richard. Coal in a Changing Market. *Nat. Westminster Bank Quart. Rev.*, August 1983, pp. 14–25. **[G: U.K.]**

Ballantine, John W. Using Labor Market Information to Evaluate Industrial Performance. *J. Econ. Issues*, December 1983, *17*(4), pp. 1011–34. **[G: U.S.]**

Bautista, Romeo M. The "Turbulent World Economy" and Industrial Development Strategy in the Philippines. *Philippine Econ. J.*, 1983, *22*(2), pp. 130–36. **[G: Philippine]**

Behrman, Jere R. Developing-Country Perspective on Industrial Policy. **In** *Adams, F. G. and Klein, L. R., eds.*, 1983, pp. 153–85. **[G: Selected Countries]**

Berberoglu, Berch. Industrialization, Employment, and Class Formation in the Periphery. *Econ. Forum*, Summer 1983, *14*(1), pp. 131–41. **[G: Brazil; S. Korea; Mexico; Taiwan]**

Blackaby, F. Post-mortem on British Economic Policy 1960–76. **In** *[Saunders, C. T.]*, 1983, pp. 259–70. **[G: U.K.]**

Bollino, C. Andrea. Industrial Policy in Italy: A Survey. **In** *Adams, F. G. and Klein, L. R., eds.*, 1983, pp. 263–305. **[G: Italy]**

Bollino, C. Andrea. Industrial Policy: A Review of European Approaches. **In** *Adams, F. G. and Klein, L. R., eds.*, 1983, pp. 49–86. **[G: Europe]**

Bose, Ashish. Migration in India: Trends and Policies. **In** *Oberai, A. S., ed.*, 1983, pp. 137–82. **[G: India]**

Botham, Ron and Lloyd, Greg. The Political Economy of Enterprise Zones. *Nat. Westminster Bank Quart. Rev.*, May 1983, pp. 24–32. **[G: U.K.]**

Boyle, R. M. Linwood: Government and the Motor Car Industry in Scotland. *Reg. Stud.*, February 1983, *17*(1), pp. 49–52. **[G: U.K.]**

van den Bulcke, Daniel. Belgian Industrial Policy and Foreign Multinational Corporations: Objectives versus Performance. **In** *Goldberg, W. H., ed.*, 1983, pp. 219–48. **[G: Belgium]**

Carlsson, Bo A. W. Industrial Subsidies in Sweden: Macro-Economic Effects and an International Comparison. *J. Ind. Econ.*, September 1983, *32*(1), pp. 1–23. **[G: Sweden; W. Germany; U.K.; Norway; Italy]**

Chen, Peter S. J. Singapore's Development Strategies: A Model for Rapid Growth. **In** *Chen, P. S. J., ed.*, 1983, pp. 3–25. **[G: Singapore]**

Chen, Yun. Several Major Issues in Current Capital Construction Work. **In** *Ch'en, Y.*, 1983, *1959*, pp. 88–111. **[G: China]**

Christainsen, Gregory B. and Hogendorn, Jan S. Japanese Productivity: Adapting to Changing Comparative Advantage in the Face of Lifetime Employment Commitments. *Quart. Rev. Econ. Bus.*, Summer 1983, *23*(2), pp. 23–39. **[G: Japan]**

Connellan, Liam. Industrial Policy. *Irish Banking Rev.*, March 1983, pp. 15–28. **[G: Ireland]**

Cross, Michael. The Small Firm: The United Kingdom. **In** *Storey, D. J., ed.*, 1983, pp. 84–119. **[G: U.K.]**

Crossier, Luis Carlos. The Industrial Sector. **In** *Sampedro, J. L. and Payno, J. A., eds.*, 1983, pp. 224–41. **[G: Spain; EEC]**

Dary, Yves and Gilly, Jean-Pierre. Le nouveau secteur public: un outil de politique industrielle régionale? (With English summary.) *Rev. Econ. Ind.*, 2nd Trimester 1983, (24), pp. 35–47. **[G: France]**

Davenport, Michael. Industrial Policy in the United Kingdom. **In** *Adams, F. G. and Klein, L. R., eds.*, 1983, pp. 331–57. **[G: U.K.]**

De Grauwe, Paul and van de Velde, Greet. Belgium: Politics and the Protection of Failing Companies. **In** *Hindley, B., ed.*, 1983, pp. 96–124. **[G: Belgium]**

DeWitt, Francois. French Industrial Policy from 1945–1981: An Assessment. **In** *Adams, F. G. and Klein, L. R., eds.*, 1983, pp. 221–45. **[G: France]**

Diebold, John. The Information Technology Industries: A Case Study of High Technology Trade. **In** *Cline W. R., ed.*, 1983, pp. 639–71. **[G: U.S.; U.K.; France; W. Germany; Japan]**

Driver, Ciaran. Import Substitution and the Work of the Sector Working Parties. *Appl. Econ.*, April 1983, *15*(2), pp. 165–76. **[G: U.K.]**

Dyson, Kenneth. Industrial Crisis: The Cultural, Ideological and Structural Context. **In** *Dyson, K. and Wilks, S., eds.*, 1983, pp. 26–66. **[G: U.S.; W. Europe]**

Dyson, Kenneth and Wilks, Stephen. Industrial Crisis: Conclusions. **In** *Dyson, K. and Wilks, S., eds.*, 1983, pp. 245–72. **[G: U.S.; W. Europe]**

Edmonds, Martin. Market Ideology and Corporate Power: The United States. **In** *Dyson, K. and Wilks, S., eds.*, 1983, pp. 67–101. **[G: U.S.]**

van Eijk, Cornelis J. Possible Policy Implications of

Modern Underemployment Equilibrium Theory. *De Economist,* 1983, *131* (3), pp. 344–72. [G: Netherlands]

Eliasson, Gunnar and Ysander, Bengt-Christer. Sweden: Problems of Maintaining Efficiency under Political Pressure. In *Hindley, B., ed.,* 1983, pp. 156–91. [G: Sweden]

Emminger, Otmar. Investment and Government Policy. In *Heertje, A., ed.,* 1983, pp. 72–99. [G: OECD]

Esser, Josef; Fach, Wolfgang and Dyson, Kenneth. 'Social Market' and Modernization Policy: West Germany. In *Dyson, K. and Wilks, S., eds.,* 1983, pp. 102–27. [G: W. Germany]

Estrin, Saul and Holmes, Peter. How Far Is Mitterrand from Barre? *Challenge,* November/December 1983, *26* (5), pp. 46–50. [G: France]

Eussner, Ansgar. Industrial Policy and Southward Enlargement of the European Community: The Case of Shipbuilding and Repairs. *J. Common Market Stud.,* December 1983, *22* (2), pp. 147–72. [G: EEC]

Follosco, Ceferino L. Philippine Industrial Development Strategies in the Eighties. *Philippine Econ. J.,* 1983, *22* (2), pp. 119–29. [G: Philippine]

Ford, Ramona L. Revitalizing the Distressed Community: GSOC and ESOP Alternatives to Enterprise Zones. *Growth Change,* October 1983, *14* (4), pp. 22–31. [G: U.S.]

Fothergill, Stephen; Kitson, Michael and Monk, Sarah. The Impact of the New and Expanded Town Programmes on Industrial Location in Britain, 1960–78. *Reg. Stud.,* August 1983, *17* (4), pp. 251–60. [G: U.K.]

Gerken, Egbert. Industriepolitik in Mexiko nach dem Ende des Ölbooms. (Industrial Policy in Mexico after the Oil Boom. With English summary.) *Aussenwirtschaft,* December 1983, *38* (4), pp. 399–429. [G: Mexico]

Glade, William. The Privatisation and Denationalisation of Public Enterprises. In *[Ramanadham, V. V.],* 1983, pp. 67–97. [G: Peru]

Goonatilake, P. C. L. Production Management—The Forgotten Factor in the Industrialization Policy in Developing Countries. *World Devel.,* September 1983, *11* (9), pp. 845–50. [G: Commonwealth Nations]

Grant, Wyn. The Political Economy of Industrial Policy. In *Jones, R. J. B., ed.,* 1983, pp. 118–38. [G: Ireland]

Green, Diana M. France: Enlisting the Aid of the Private Sector. In *Hindley, B., ed.,* 1983, pp. 192–226. [G: France]

Green, Diana M. Strategic Management and the State: France. In *Dyson, K. and Wilks, S., eds.,* 1983, pp. 161–92. [G: France]

Green, Robert T. Import/Export Patterns in Manufactured Goods of Four Latin American Nations, 1963–78. In *Czinkota, M. R., ed. (II),* 1983, pp. 26–47. [G: Argentina; Brazil; Colombia; Venezuela; U.S.]

Hadley, Eleanor M. The Secret of Japan's Success. *Challenge,* May/June 1983, *26* (2), pp. 4–10. [G: Japan]

Hare, Paul. China's System of Industrial Economic Planning. In *Feuchtwang, S. and Hussain, A., eds.,* 1983, pp. 185–223. [G: China]

Hart, Peter E. Experience Curves and Industrial Policy. *Int. J. Ind. Organ.,* 1983, *1* (1), pp. 95–106. [G: U.S.; U.K.]

Hausner, V. A. Urban and Regional Policy in the United States: The Approach of the Carter Administration. *Reg. Stud.,* October 1983, *17* (5), pp. 366–69. [G: U.S.]

Hesselman, Linda. Trends in European Industrial Intervention. *Cambridge J. Econ.,* June 1983, *7* (2), pp. 197–208. [G: U.K.; W. Germany; France]

Hindley, Brian. State Investment Companies in Western Europe: Preface. In *Hindley, B., ed.,* 1983, pp. xix–xxii.

Hindley, Brian. What Is the Case for State Investment Companies? In *Hindley, B., ed.,* 1983, pp. 1–24. [G: W. Europe]

Hindley, Brian and Richardson, Ray. United Kingdom: An Experiment in Picking Winners—The Industrial Reorganisation Corporation. In *Hindley, B., ed.,* 1983, pp. 125–55. [G: U.K.]

Hindley, Brian and Richardson, Ray. United Kingdom: Pulling Dragon's Teeth—The National Enterprise Board. In *Hindley, B., ed.,* 1983, pp. 263–81. [G: U.K.]

Hooper, Diana J. and Walker, David F. Innovative and Cooperative Entrepreneurship: Towards a New Thrust in Industrial Development Policy. In *Hamilton, F. E. I. and Linge, G. J. R., eds.,* 1983, pp. 217–32. [G: U.K.; Canada]

Hull, Chris. The Small Firm: Federal Republic of Germany. In *Storey, D. J., ed.,* 1983, pp. 153–78. [G: W. Germany]

Jepson, D. The Coventry Local Economy, the Motor Vehicles Industry and Some Implications for Public Policy. *Reg. Stud.,* February 1983, *17* (1), pp. 56–59. [G: U.K.]

de Jong, H. W. and Spierenburg, Robert Jan. The Netherlands: Maintenance of Employment as a Primary Objective. In *Hindley, B., ed.,* 1983, pp. 59–95. [G: Netherlands]

Jüttemeier, Karl Heinz and Schatz, Klaus-Werner. West Germany: Managing without a State Investment Company. In *Hindley, B., ed.,* 1983, pp. 227–62. [G: W. Germany]

Kádár, Béla. Changes in the World Economic Environment and Hungarian Industry. *Acta Oecon.,* 1983, *30* (1), pp. 111–27.

Kaur, Kulwinder. A Factor Analysis of Inter-Regional Disparities in Industrialisation—The Case of Haryana. *Margin,* October 1983, *16* (1), pp. 84–91. [G: India]

Kikkawa, Mototada. Shipbuilding, Motor Cars and Semiconductors: The Diminishing Role of Industrial Policy in Japan. In *Shepherd, G.; Duchêne, F. and Saunders, C., eds.,* 1983, pp. 236–67. [G: Japan]

Kreile, Michael. Public Enterprise and the Pursuit of Strategic Management: Italy. In *Dyson, K. and Wilks, S., eds.,* 1983, pp. 193–219. [G: Italy]

Ledebur, Larry C. and Rasmussen, David W. Let's Try a Federalist Industry Policy. *Challenge,* November/December 1983, *26* (5), pp. 58–60. [G: U.S.]

Levitt, Arthur, Jr. Why Growth Is Important. In *Fed-*

eral Reserve Bank of Atlanta, 1983, pp. 15–21. [G: U.S.]

Lindmark, Leif. The Small Firm: Sweden. **In** *Storey, D. J., ed.,* 1983, pp. 179–212. [G: Sweden]

Littler, Craig R. Japan and China. **In** *Feuchtwang, S. and Hussain, A., eds.,* 1983, pp. 121–47. [G: China; Japan]

Lockett, Martin and Littler, Craig R. Trends in Chinese Enterprise Management, 1978–1982. *World Devel.,* August 1983, *11* (8), pp. 683–704. [G: China]

Lundine, Stan N. Now Is the Time for a National Industrial Strategy. *Challenge,* July/August 1983, *26* (3), pp. 16–21. [G: U.S.]

Lundmark, Kjell. Welfare State and Employment Policy: Sweden. **In** *Dyson, K. and Wilks, S., eds.,* 1983, pp. 220–44. [G: Sweden]

McGuinness, Tony. Efficiency and Industrial Organisation. **In** *Shepherd, D.; Turk, J. and Silberston, A., eds.,* 1983, pp. 8–29.

McKenzie, Richard B. NIP in the Air: Fashionable Myths of National Industrial Policy. *Policy Rev.,* Fall 1983, (26), pp. 75–87. [G: U.S.]

Miller, D. The Role of the Motor Car Industry in the West Midlands Economy. *Reg. Stud.,* February 1983, *17* (1), pp. 53–56. [G: U.K.]

Milne, William J. Industrial Policy in Canada: A Survey. **In** *Adams, F. G. and Klein, L. R., eds.,* 1983, pp. 205–20. [G: Canada]

Mollenkopf, John. Economic Development. **In** *Brecher, C. and Horton, R. D., eds.,* 1983, pp. 131–57. [G: U.S.]

Munkirs, John R. and Ayers, Michael. Political and Policy Implications of Centralized Private Sector Planning. *J. Econ. Issues,* December 1983, *17* (4), pp. 969–84.

Neck, Philip. The Small Firm: Africa. **In** *Storey, D. J., ed.,* 1983, pp. 248–71. [G: Africa]

Nolan, Sean. The Telesis Report—A Review Essay. *Econ. Soc. Rev.,* July 1983, *14* (4), pp. 281–89. [G: Ireland]

Piel, Gerard. Re-entering Paradise: The Mechanization of Work. *Challenge,* Sept.–Oct. 1983, *26* (4), pp. 4–11.

Piore, Michael J. and Sabel, Charles F. Italian Small Business Development: Lessons for U.S. Industrial Policy. **In** *Zysman, J. and Tyson, L., eds.,* 1983, pp. 391–421. [G: Italy; U.S.]

Price, Victoria Curzon. The European Community—Friend or Foe of the Market Economy? **In** *Lenel, H. O.; Willgerodt, H. and Molsberger, J.,* 1983, pp. 85–95. [G: EEC]

Quinn, James Brian. U.S. Industrial Strategy: What Directions Should It Take? *Sloan Manage. Rev.,* Summer 1983, *24* (4), pp. 3–21. [G: U.S.; EEC; Japan]

Reynolds, R. Larry. Policy Choices and Economies of Scale. *J. Econ. Issues,* December 1983, *17* (4), pp. 1067–74.

Rossen, Stein. Industrial Cooperation within Regional Groupings of Developing Countries. **In** *Parkinson, J. R., ed.,* 1983, pp. 207–28.

Rothwell, Roy. The Difficulties of National Innovation Policies. **In** *Macdonald, S.; Lamberton, D. M. and Mandeville, T., eds.,* 1983, pp. 202–15. [G: OECD]

Seah, Linda. Public Enterprise and Economic Development. **In** *Chen, P. S. J., ed.,* 1983, pp. 129–59. [G: Singapore]

Silberston, Aubrey. Efficiency and the Individual Firm. **In** *Shepherd, D.; Turk, J. and Silberston, A., eds.,* 1983, pp. 30–45.

Spencer, Barbara J. and Brander, James A. International R & D Rivalry and Industrial Strategy. *Rev. Econ. Stud.,* October 1983, *50* (4), pp. 707–22.

Steel, William F. and Takagi, Yasuoki. Small Enterprise Development and the Employment-Output Trade-Off. *Oxford Econ. Pap.,* November 1983, *35* (3), pp. 423–46. [G: LDCs]

Sufrin, Sidney C. Regulation for Amenities. *Challenge,* November/December 1983, *26* (5), pp. 57–58. [G: U.S.]

Swales, J. K. Industrial Policy in Scotland. **In** *Ingham, K. P. D. and Love, J., eds.,* 1983, pp. 188–202. [G: U.K.]

Tan, Thiam Soon. The Small Firm: South East Asia. **In** *Storey, D. J., ed.,* 1983, pp. 218–47. [G: S. E. Asia]

Tomlinson, R. Industrial Decentralization and the Relief of Poverty in the Homelands. *S. Afr. J. Econ.,* December 1983, *51* (4), pp. 544–63. [G: S. Africa]

Ullman, John E. The Arms Race and the Decline of U.S. Technology. *J. Econ. Issues,* June 1983, *17* (2), pp. 565–74. [G: U.S.]

Urban, Peter. Recent Approaches to Industrial Policy in Australia. **In** *Adams, F. G. and Klein, L. R., eds.,* 1983, pp. 189–203. [G: Australia]

Urban, Peter. Theoretical Justifications for Industrial Policy. **In** *Adams, F. G. and Klein, L. R., eds.,* 1983, pp. 21–40.

Varaiya, Pravin and Wiseman, Michael. Reindustrialization and the Outlook for Declining Areas. **In** *Henderson, J. V., ed.,* 1983, pp. 167–90. [G: U.S.]

Wagenhals, Gerhard. Industrial Policy in the Federal Republic of Germany: A Survey. **In** *Adams, F. G. and Klein, L. R., eds.,* 1983, pp. 247–62. [G: W. Germany]

Weidenbaum, Murray L. Industrial Policy Is Not the Answer. *Challenge,* July/August 1983, *26* (3), pp. 22–25. [G: U.S.]

Wescott, Robert F. U.S. Approaches to Industrial Policy. **In** *Adams, F. G. and Klein, L. R., eds.,* 1983, pp. 87–151. [G: U.S.]

Wilkinson, Christopher. European Industrial Policies in an International Context. *Ann. Sci. Écon. Appl.,* 1983, *39* (3), pp. 197–206. [G: EEC]

Wilks, Stephen. Liberal State and Party Competition: Britain. **In** *Dyson, K. and Wilks, S., eds.,* 1983, pp. 128–60. [G: U.K.]

Wilks, Stephen and Dyson, Kenneth. The Character and Economic Context of Industrial Crises. **In** *Dyson, K. and Wilks, S., eds.,* 1983, pp. 1–25. [G: U.S.; W. Europe]

Zanetti, Giovanni. The Industrial Structure and Efficiency of the Italian Economy: Trends and Planning Aspects. *Rev. Econ. Cond. Italy,* June 1983, (2), pp. 249–300. [G: Italy]

Zysman, John and Cohen, Stephen S. Double or Nothing: Open Trade and Competitive Industry. *Foreign Aff.*, Summer 1983, *61* (5), pp. 1113–39. [G: U.S.]

620 Economics of Technological Change

621 Technological Change; Innovation; Research and Development

6210 General

Adams, F. Gerard; Cherkes, Martin and Wescott, Robert F. Innovation, Technical Progress, and Industrial Policy: A Survey. **In** *Adams, F. G. and Klein, L. R., eds.*, 1983, pp. 41–47.

Allen, Robert C. Collective Invention. *J. Econ. Behav. Organ.*, March 1983, *4* (1), pp. 1–24. [G: U.S.; U.K.]

Alston, Julian M. and Scobie, G. M. Distribution of Research Gains in Multistage Production Systems: Comment. *Amer. J. Agr. Econ.*, May 1983, *65* (2), pp. 353–56. [G: U.S.]

Amendola, M. A Change of Perspective in the Analysis of the Process of Innovation. *Metroecon.*, October 1983, *35* (3), pp. 261–74.

Backhaus, Jüergen. Competition, Innovation and Regulation in the Pharmaceutical Industry. *Managerial Dec. Econ.*, June 1983, *4* (2), pp. 107–21. [G: U.S.; W. Europe]

Bhattacharya, Sudipto and Ritter, Jay R. Innovation and Communication: Signalling with Partial Disclosure. *Rev. Econ. Stud.*, April 1983, *50* (2), pp. 331–46.

Bourmeyster, A. Révolution scientifique et technique et société socialiste avancée. (With English summary.) *Écon. Soc.*, January 1983, *17* (1), pp. 179–201. [G: U.S.S.R.]

Braunstein, Philippe. Innovations in Mining and Metal Production in Europe in the Late Middle Ages. *J. Europ. Econ. Hist.*, Winter 1983, *12* (3), pp. 573–91. [G: Europe]

Brhlovič, Gerhard. Technical Progress—Transformations of Labour—Development of Personality. *Czech. Econ. Digest.*, May 1983, (3), pp. 19–31.

Cocks, Paul. Organizing for Technological Innovation in the 1980s. **In** *Guroff, G. and Carstensen, F. V., eds.*, 1983, pp. 306–46. [G: U.S.S.R.]

Cullen, Ross. Pharmaceuticals Inter-Country Diffusion. *Managerial Dec. Econ.*, June 1983, *4* (2), pp. 73–82. [G: Selected Countries]

Dasgupta, Partha; Gilbert, Richard and Stiglitz, Joseph E. Strategic Considerations in Invention and Innovation: The Case of Natural Resources. *Econometrica*, September 1983, *51* (5), pp. 1439–48.

Diebold, John. The Information Technology Industries: A Case Study of High Technology Trade. **In** *Cline W. R., ed.*, 1983, pp. 639–71. [G: U.S.; U.K.; France; W. Germany; Japan]

Donnenfeld, Shabtai. Market Uncertainty and the Monopolist Incentive to Innovate. *Int. J. Ind. Organ.*, December 1983, *1* (4), pp. 379–86.

Faramazjan, Rachik. The Role of the Scientific Community in the Conversion of the Arms Industry. *Int. Soc. Sci. J.*, 1983, *35* (1), pp. 185–99.

Farrell, Kenneth R. and Runge, Carlisle Ford. Institutional Innovation and Technical Change in American Agriculture: The Role of the New Deal. *Amer. J. Agr. Econ.*, December 1983, *65* (5), pp. 1168–73. [G: U.S.]

Fel'zenbaum, V.; Efimova, E. and Farbirovich, V. The Effectiveness of Scientific and Technical Programs. *Prob. Econ.*, June 1983, *26* (2), pp. 41–60. [G: U.S.S.R.]

Fixler, Dennis J. Uncertainty, Market Structure and the Incentive to Invent. *Economica*, November 1983, *50* (200), pp. 407–23.

Freebairn, John W.; Davis, J. S. and Edwards, G. W. Distribution of Research Gains in Multistage Production Systems: Reply. *Amer. J. Agr. Econ.*, May 1983, *65* (2), pp. 357–59. [G: U.S.]

Freeman, Christopher. Technological Change and the New Economic Context. **In** *Hill, S. and Johnston, R., eds.*, 1983, pp. 47–67. [G: OECD]

Fudenberg, Drew, et al. Preemption, Leapfrogging and Competition in Patent Races. *Europ. Econ. Rev.*, June 1983, *22* (1), pp. 3–31.

Galambos, Louis. Technology, Political Economy, and Professionalization: Central Themes of the Organizational Synthesis. *Bus. Hist. Rev.*, Winter 1983, *57* (4), pp. 471–93. [G: U.S.]

Galenson, Walter. Capitalists and Commissars. *Policy Rev.*, Spring 1983, (24), pp. 9. [G: E. Europe; W. Europe; U.S.]

Hill, Stephen and Johnston, Ron. "The Future's Not What It Used to Be." **In** *Hill, S. and Johnston, R., eds.*, 1983, pp. 1–24. [G: Australia]

Hopkin, John A. Moral Responsibility in Agricultural Research: Discussion. *Southern J. Agr. Econ.*, July 1983, *15* (1), pp. 81–82. [G: U.S.]

Jakeš, Miloš. Report of the Presidium of the Central Committee of the Communist Party of Czechoslovakia on Speeding Up the Practical Application of the Results of Scientific and Technical Research. *Czech. Econ. Digest.*, September 1983, (6), pp. 3–57. [G: Czechoslovakia]

James, Dilmus D. and Street, James H. Technology, Institutions, and Public Policy in the Age of Energy Substitution: The Case of Latin America. *J. Econ. Issues*, June 1983, *17* (2), pp. 521–28. [G: Latin America]

Jensen, Richard. Innovation Adoption and Diffusion When There Are Competing Innovations. *J. Econ. Theory*, February 1983, *29* (1), pp. 161–71.

Johnston, Ron. The Control of Technological Change in Australia. **In** *Hill, S. and Johnston, R., eds.*, 1983, pp. 89–112. [G: Australia]

Johnston, Ron and Hill, Stephen. Future Tense? Technology in Australia: Conclusion. **In** *Hill, S. and Johnston, R., eds.*, 1983, pp. 209–15. [G: Australia]

Junker, Louis. The Conflict between the Scientific-Technological Process and Malignant Ceremonialism. *Amer. J. Econ. Soc.*, July 1983, *42* (3), pp. 341–52.

Kaje, Matti and Niitamo, Olavi E. Scientific and Technological Cooperation between a Small Capitalist Country and a Big Socialist Country. **In** *Möttölä, K.; Bykov, O. N. and Korolev, I. S., eds.*, 1983, pp. 139–51. [G: U.S.S.R.; Finland]

Kaplinsky, Raphael. Firm Size and Technical Change in a Dynamic Context. *J. Ind. Econ.*, September 1983, *32* (1), pp. 39–59. [G: U.S.]

Kapp, K. William. Governmental Furtherance of Environmentally Sound Technologies as a Focus of Research and Environmental Policies. **In** *Kapp, K. W.,* 1983, *1974,* pp. 143–207. **[G: Selected Countries]**

Katz, Jorge. Technological Change in the Latin American Metalworking Industry: Results of a Programme of Case Studies. *Cepal Rev.,* April 1983, (19), pp. 85–143. **[G: Latin America]**

Korovkin, V. Scientific and Technical Programs in Commercial Trade. *Prob. Econ.,* October 1983, *26*(6), pp. 55–70. **[G: U.S.S.R.]**

Lall, Sanjaya and Mohammed, Sharif. Technological Effort and Disembodied Technology Exports: An Econometric Analysis of Inter-Industry Variations in India. *World Devel.,* June 1983, *11*(6), pp. 527–35. **[G: India]**

Lamberton, D. McL. Information Economics and Technological Change. **In** *Macdonald, S.; Lamberton, D. M. and Mandeville, T., eds.,* 1983, pp. 75–92.

Lazonick, William. Industrial Organization and Technological Change: The Decline of the British Cotton Industry. *Bus. Hist. Rev.,* Summer 1983, *57*(2), pp. 195–236. **[G: U.K.]**

Lurie, Robert S. R&D, Innovation and Environmental Regulation: The Case of Copper. *Amer. Econ.,* Fall 1983, *27*(2), pp. 13–20. **[G: U.S.]**

Malecki, Edward J. Technology and Regional Development: A Survey. *Int. Reg. Sci. Rev.,* October 1983, *8*(2), pp. 89–125.

Mansfield, Edwin. Long Waves and Technological Innovation. *Amer. Econ. Rev.,* May 1983, *73*(2), pp. 141–45. **[G: U.S.]**

McGinn, Robert E. The Politics of Technology and the Technology of Politics. **In** *Stansky, P., ed.,* 1983, pp. 67–75.

Piel, Gerard. Re-entering Paradise: The Mechanization of Work. *Challenge,* Sept.-Oct. 1983, *26*(4), pp. 4–11.

Reinganum, Jennifer F. Uncertain Innovation and the Persistence of Monopoly. *Amer. Econ. Rev.,* September 1983, *73*(4), pp. 741–48.

Ricker, Harold S.; Anderson, Dale L. and Phillips, Michael J. Technology Adoption in the Agricultural Marketing System. **In** *Farris, P. L., ed.,* 1983, pp. 117–36. **[G: U.S.]**

Romanov, A. K. and Simonyan, R. R. Scientific and Technical Cooperation between the Soviet Union and Finland: Present State and Prospects. **In** *Möttölä, K.; Bykov, O. N. and Korolev, I. S., eds.,* 1983, pp. 152–60. **[G: U.S.S.R.; Finland]**

Rosenberg, Nathan and Frischtak, Claudio R. Long Waves and Economic Growth: A Critical Appraisal. *Amer. Econ. Rev.,* May 1983, *73*(2), pp. 146–51.

Rosenbrock, H. H. Human Resources and Technology. **In** *Streeten, P. and Maier, H., eds.,* 1983, pp. 345–54.

Rothwell, Roy. The Difficulties of National Innovation Policies. **In** *Macdonald, S.; Lamberton, D. M. and Mandeville, T., eds.,* 1983, pp. 202–15. **[G: OECD]**

Rubinger, Bruce. Industrial Innovation: Implementing the Policy Agenda. *Sloan Manage. Rev.,* Spring 1983, *24*(3), pp. 43–57. **[G: U.S.]**

Ruttan, Vernon W. Moral Responsibility in Agricultural Research. *Southern J. Agr. Econ.,* July 1983, *15*(1), pp. 73–80. **[G: U.S.]**

Scherer, F. M. Concentration, R&D, and Productivity Change. *Southern Econ. J.,* July 1983, *50*(1), pp. 221–25. **[G: U.S.]**

Schmalensee, Richard. Product Differentiation Advantages of Pioneering Brands: Errata. *Amer. Econ. Rev.,* March 1983, *73*(1), pp. 250.

Sills, David L. The Utilization of Social Science Knowledge in Studying Technology and Society: The Case of the Accident at Three Mile Island. **In** *Holzner, B.; Knorr, K. D. and Strasser, H., eds.,* 1983, pp. 327–36. **[G: U.S.]**

Soják, Zbyněk. A Line of Direct Causality: Technology, Effectiveness, Standard of Living. *Czech. Econ. Digest.,* September 1983, (6), pp. 68–78. **[G: Czechoslovakia]**

Stamos, Stephen C., Jr. A Critique of James and Street's "Technology, Institutions, and Public Policy in the Age of Energy Substitution: The Case of Latin America." *J. Econ. Issues,* September 1983, *17*(3), pp. 745–50. **[G: Latin America]**

Stewart, Marion B. Noncooperative Oligopoly and Preemptive Innovation without Winner-Take-All. *Quart. J. Econ.,* November 1983, *98*(4), pp. 681–94.

Street, James H. Institutional Reform and Manpower Development in Mexico. *J. Econ. Issues,* March 1983, *17*(1), pp. 17–33. **[G: Mexico]**

Street, James H. Rejoinder to S. C. Stamos's "Critique of 'Technology, Institutions, and Public Policy in the Age of Energy Substitution.'" *J. Econ. Issues,* December 1983, *17*(4), pp. 1120–25. **[G: Latin America]**

Talamona, Mario. Significato e problemi dell'innovazione nelle piccole e medie imprese. (Significance and Problems in Small and Medium Firms. With English summary.) *Giorn. Econ.,* March-April 1983, *42*(3–4), pp. 131–51. **[G: EEC]**

Teece, David J. Technological and Organisational Factors in the Theory of the Multinational Enterprise. **In** *Casson, M., ed.,* 1983, pp. 51–62.

d'Ursel, Laurent. Politiques de "non-prix": équilibre et optimum: essai de synthèse. (Nonprice Competition: Equilibrium and Optimum. With English summary.) *Revue Écon.,* November 1983, *34*(6), pp. 1057–88.

Varas, Augusto and Bustamante, Fernando. The Effect of R&D on the Transfer of Military Technology to the Third World. *Int. Soc. Sci. J.,* 1983, *35*(1), pp. 141–62. **[G: Selected MDCs; Selected LDCs]**

Weisskopf, Thomas E.; Bowles, Samuel and Gordon, David M. Hearts and Minds: A Social Model of U.S. Productivity Growth. *Brookings Pap. Econ. Act.,* 1983, (2), pp. 381–450. **[G: U.S.]**

Wright, Brian Davern. The Economics of Invention Incentives: Patents, Prizes, and Research Contracts. *Amer. Econ. Rev.,* September 1983, *73*(4), pp. 691–707.

6211 Technological Change and Innovation

Adachi, Hideyuki. Innovations under Monopoly and Competition. *Kobe Univ. Econ.,* 1983, (29), pp. 41–50.

Adler, Paul. Trente ans d'automatisation et couts opératoires dans les banques françaises. (Thirty Years of Automation and Operating Costs in French Banks. With English summary.) *Revue Écon.*, September 1983, *34*(5), pp. 987–1020. **[G: France]**

Agarwal, Bina. Diffusion of Rural Innovations: Some Analytical Issues and the Case of Wood-Burning Stoves. *World Devel.*, April 1983, *11*(4), pp. 359–76. **[G: LDCs]**

Aguilar, A. M., et al. Consequences of Small Rice Farm Mechanization in the Philippines: A Summary of Preliminary Analyses. **In** *Internat'l Rice Res. Inst. and Agric. Devel. Council,* 1983, pp. 151–64. **[G: Philippines]**

Ahmed, Iftikhar. Technology and Rural Women in the Third World. *Int. Lab. Rev.*, July–August 1983, *122*(4), pp. 493–505. **[G: LDCs]**

Alexander, Charles P. Dalla tecnologia la "nuova economia" USA. (The New Economy. With English summary.) *Mondo Aperto,* November–December 1983, *37*(6), pp. 341–54. **[G: U.S.]**

Anderson, John. Some Impacts of Computer Technology upon Management and Organizations. **In** *Hill, S. and Johnston, R., eds.*, 1983, pp. 115–36. **[G: Australia]**

Antle, John M. and Aitah, Ali S. Rice Technology, Farmer Rationality, and Agricultural Policy in Egypt. *Amer. J. Agr. Econ.*, November 1983, *65*(4), pp. 667–74. **[G: Egypt]**

Appelbaum, Eileen. Winners and Losers in the High-Tech Workplace. *Challenge,* Sept.–Oct. 1983, *26*(4), pp. 52–55. **[G: U.S.]**

Argote, Linda; Goodman, Paul S. and Schkade, David. The Human Side of Robotics: How Workers React to a Robot. *Sloan Manage. Rev.*, Spring 1983, *24*(3), pp. 31–41. **[G: U.S.]**

Arrow, Kenneth J. Innovation in Large and Small Firms. **In** *Ronen, J., ed.*, 1983, pp. 15–28.

Ashford, Nicholas A. and Heaton, George R., Jr. Regulation and Technological Innovation in the Chemical Industry. *Law Contemp. Probl.*, Summer 1983, *46*(3), pp. 109–57. **[G: U.S.]**

Atamer, Tugrul. Le processus d'acquisition technologique par les entreprises d'un pays semi-industrialisé. Deux études de cas. (With English summary.) *Rev. Econ. Ind.*, 4th Trimester 1983, (26), pp. 24–33. **[G: France; Turkey]**

Bailis, Stanley. Modernization and Habitual Change: A Model Explored through American Autobiography. **In** *[Cochran, T. C.]*, 1983, pp. 117–43. **[G: U.S.]**

Balasubramanyam, V. N. Transnational Corporations: Choice of Techniques and Employment in Developing Countries. **In** *Weisbrod, B. and Hughes, H., eds.*, 1983, pp. 527–46. **[G: Selected LDCs]**

Baldwin, George B. Why Present Value Calculations Should Not Be Used in Choosing Rural Water Supply Technology. *World Devel.*, December 1983, *11*(12), pp. 1075–81. **[G: LDCs]**

Barnett, Allen M. Solar Energy Commercialization Strategies. **In** *Rich, D., et al., eds.*, 1983, pp. 145–62.

Bauer, Tamás and Soós, Károly Attila. Interfirm Relations and Technological Change: The Case of the Motor Industry. *Eastern Europ. Econ.*, Spring–Summer 1983, *21*(3–4), pp. 85–104. **[G: Hungary]**

Benvignati, Anita M. International Technology Transfer Patterns in a Traditional Industry. *J. Int. Bus. Stud.*, Winter 1983, *14*(3), pp. 63–75. **[G: U.S.; Selected OECD]**

Berg, Charles A. A Suggestion Regarding the Nature of Innovation. **In** *Schurr, S. H.; Sonenblum, S. and Wood, D. O., eds.*, 1983, pp. 261–78.

Bergson, Abram. Technological Progress. **In** *Bergson, A. and Levine, H. S., eds.*, 1983, pp. 34–78. **[G: U.S.S.R.]**

Berndt, Ernst R. The Energy Connection to Recent Productivity Behavior: Comment. **In** *Schurr, S. H.; Sonenblum, S. and Wood, D. O., eds.*, 1983, pp. 179–83. **[G: U.S.]**

Blackorby, Charles and Schworm, William E. Aggregating Heterogeneous Capital Goods in Adjustment-Cost Technologies. *Scand. J. Econ.*, 1983, *85*(2), pp. 207–22.

Bogue, Allan G. Changes in Mechanical and Plant Technology: The Corn Belt, 1910–1940. *J. Econ. Hist.*, March 1983, *43*(1), pp. 1–25. **[G: U.S.]**

Bollard, Alan. Technology, Economic Change, and Small Firms. *Lloyds Bank Rev.*, January 1983, (147), pp. 42–56. **[G: U.K.]**

Bonin, John P. Innovation in a Labor-Managed Firm: A Membership Perspective. *J. Ind. Econ.*, March 1983, *31*(3), pp. 313–29.

Boon, Gerard K. Theory and Reality in North–South Trade: Some Explanations. *De Economist,* 1983, *131*(2), pp. 256–72.

Boulding, Kenneth E. Towards Conceptualising the Process of Technological Change. **In** *Macdonald, S.; Lamberton, D. M. and Mandeville, T., eds.*, 1983, pp. 4–10.

Brandt, Jon A. and French, Ben C. Mechanical Harvesting and the California Tomato Industry: A Simulation Analysis. *Amer. J. Agr. Econ.*, May 1983, *65*(2), pp. 265–72. **[G: U.S.]**

Brinson, Geoff. Assessment of New Technologies. **In** *Hill, S. and Johnston, R., eds.*, 1983, pp. 194–208. **[G: Australia]**

Brookes, Leonard G. Energy and Technology: Comment. **In** *Schurr, S. H.; Sonenblum, S. and Wood, D. O., eds.*, 1983, pp. 307–11. **[G: U.S.]**

Brown, Murray and Greenberg, Richard. The Divisia Index of Technological Change, Path Independence and Endogenous Prices. *Scand. J. Econ.*, 1983, *85*(2), pp. 239–47.

Browne, Lynn E. High Technology and Business Services. *New Eng. Econ. Rev.*, July–August 1983, pp. 5–17. **[G: U.S.]**

Buckley, Peter J. New Forms of International Industrial Cooperation: A Survey of the Literature with Special Reference to North–South Technology Transfer. *Aussenwirtschaft,* June 1983, *38*(2), pp. 195–222. **[G: LDCs; MDCs]**

Bultel, Jean. Flexibilité de production et rentabilité des investissements. L'exemple de la robotisation de l'assemblage tôlerie en soudage par points. (With English summary.) *Rev. Econ. Ind.*, 4th Trimester 1983, (26), pp. 1–13.

Byerlee, Derek, et al. Employment-Output Conflicts, Factor-Price Distortions, and Choice of Technique: Empirical Results from Sierra Leone.

Econ. Develop. Cult. Change, January 1983, 31(2), pp. 315–36. [G: Sierra Leone]

Byler, Ezra U. and Baker, James C. S.W.I.F.T.: A Fast Method to Facilitate International Financial Transactions. *J. World Trade Law,* September–October 1983, *17*(5), pp. 458–65.

Capehart, Barney L. and Storin, Michael O. Technological Advances in Metering. In *Berg, S. V., ed.,* 1983, pp. 263–81. [G: U.S.]

Cappellin, Riccardo. Productivity Growth and Technological Change in a Regional Perspective. *Giorn. Econ.,* July–August 1983, *42*(7–8), pp. 459–82. [G: Italy; France]

Carli, Guido. Investment and Technological Competitiveness. In *Heertje, A., ed.,* 1983, pp. 100–116. [G: EEC]

Carter, Anne P. Energy and Technology: Comment. In *Schurr, S. H.; Sonenblum, S. and Wood, D. O., eds.,* 1983, pp. 311–14. [G: U.S.]

Casson, Mark. The Growth of International Business: Introduction: The Conceptual Framework. In *Casson, M., ed.,* 1983, pp. 1–33.

de Castillo, J. Reestructuraciones sectoriales y regionales en la crisis. (Sectorial and Regional Restructurizations on the Crisis. With English summary.) *Écon. Soc.,* September–October–November 1983, *17*(9–10–11), pp. 1551–68.

Caves, Richard E.; Crookell, Harold and Killing, J. Peter. The Imperfect Market for Technology Licenses. *Oxford Bull. Econ. Statist.,* August 1983, *45*(3), pp. 249–67. [G: U.S.; Canada; U.K.]

Chambers, Robert G. Scale and Productivity Measurement under Risk. *Amer. Econ. Rev.,* September 1983, *73*(4), pp. 802–05.

Chan, M. W. Luke and Mountain, Dean C. Economies of Scale and the Tornqvist Discrete Measure of Productivity Growth. *Rev. Econ. Statist.,* November 1983, *65*(4), pp. 663–67. [G: Canada]

Chen, Edward K. Y. Factor Proportions of Foreign and Local Firms in Developing Countries: A Theoretical and Empirical Note. *J. Devel. Econ.,* February/April 1983, *12*(1/2), pp. 267–74.

Chen, Edward K. Y. Multinational Corporations and Technology Diffusion in Hong Kong Manufacturing. *Appl. Econ.,* June 1983, *15*(3), pp. 309–21. [G: Hong Kong]

Ciborra, Claudio U. Markets, Bureaucracies, and Groups in the Information Society: An Institutional Appraisal of the Impacts of Information Technology. *Info. Econ. Policy,* 1983, *1*(2), pp. 145–60. [G: Italy]

Clark, Wilson and Rose, L. Wade. California: Energy Policies and Renewable Energy Strategies In *Rich, D., et al., eds.,* 1983, pp. 77–102. [G: U.S.]

Collins, Glenn S. and Taylor, C. Robert. TECHSIM: A Regional Field Crop and National Livestock Econometric Simulation Model. *Agr. Econ. Res.,* April 1983, *35*(2), pp. 1–18. [G: U.S.]

Contractor, Farok J. Technology Importation Policies in Developing Countries: Some Implications of Recent Theoretical and Empirical Evidence. *J. Devel. Areas,* July 1983, *17*(4), pp. 499–519. [G: LDCs]

Coriat, Benjamin. La robotique à la Régie Renault. (With English summary.) *Rev. Econ. Ind.,* 2nd Trimester 1983, (24), pp. 18–34. [G: France]

Corina, John. Trade Unions and Technological Change. In *Macdonald, S.; Lamberton, D. M. and Mandeville, T., eds.,* 1983, pp. 178–92. [G: OECD]

Coughlin, Cletus C. The Relationship between Foreign Ownership and Technology Transfer. *J. Compar. Econ.,* December 1983, *7*(4), pp. 400–414. [G: Europe]

Craven, John. Input–Output Analysis and Technical Change. *Econometrica,* May, 1983, *51*(3), pp. 585–98.

Cuadrado Roura, J. R. Crisis industrial y cambios technológicos. Consideraciones desde una óptica espacial. (Industrial Crisis and Technological Changes in the Work Division. Its Reasoning from a Spanish Point of View. With English summary.) *Écon. Soc.,* September–October–November 1983, *17*(9–10–11), pp. 1671–99.

Dahlman, Carl and Westphal, Larry. The Transfer of Technology. *Finance Develop.,* December 1983, *20*(4), pp. 6–9. [G: LDCs]

Danthine, Jean-Pierre; Donaldson, John B. and Mehra, Rajnish. On the Impact of Shock Persistence on the Dynamics of a Recursive Economy. *Europ. Econ. Rev.,* July 1983, *22*(2), pp. 147–66.

Davenport, Paul. Embodied Technical Change: A New Approach. *Can. J. Econ.,* February 1983, *16*(1), pp. 139–49.

Deaglio, Mario. L'economia capitalista in mezzo al guado. (The Capitalist Economy in Deep Water. With English summary.) *L'Impresa,* 1983, *25*(6), pp. 41–46. [G: OECD]

Dearden, John. SMR Forum: Will the Computer Change the Job of Top Management? *Sloan Manage. Rev.,* Fall 1983, *25*(1), pp. 57–60.

Denny, Michael G. S. and Fuss, Melvyn A. The Effects of Factor Prices and Technological Change on the Occupational Demand for Labor: Evidence from Canadian Telecommunications. *J. Human Res.,* Spring 1983, *18*(2), pp. 161–76. [G: Canada]

Devine, Warren D., Jr. From Shafts to Wires: Historical Perspective on Electrification. *J. Econ. Hist.,* June 1983, *43*(2), pp. 347–72. [G: U.S.]

Di Gregorio, Renato. Mercato, strutture organizzative, tecnologia: interpretazione di alcune linee evolutive. (Market, Organisation Structures and Technology: An Interpretation of Some Developing Trends. With English summary.) *L'Impresa,* 1983, *25*(2), pp. 25–33. [G: Italy]

Dosi, Giovanni and Soete, L. Technology Gaps and Cost-based Adjustment: Some Explorations on the Determinants of International Competitiveness. *Metroecon.,* October 1983, *35*(3), pp. 197–222. [G: OECD]

Drabek, Zdenek. The Impact of Technological Differences on East–West Trade. *Weltwirtsch. Arch.,* 1983, *119*(4), pp. 630–48. [G: CMEA; OECD]

Dunning, John H. Changes in the Level and Structure of International Production: The Last One Hundred Years. In *Casson, M., ed.,* 1983, pp. 84–139. [G: Global]

Dunning, John H. Market Power of the Firm and International Transfer of Technology: A Historical Excursion. *Int. J. Ind. Organ.,* December

1983, *1* (4), pp. 333–51. **[G: U.S.; Europe; LDCs]**

Dutton, H. I. and Jones, S. R. H. Invention and Innovation in the British Pin Industry, 1790–1850. *Bus. Hist. Rev.*, Summer 1983, *57* (2), pp. 175–93. **[G: U.K.]**

Ellis, Randall P. and Zimmerman, Martin B. What Happened to Nuclear Power: A Discrete Choice Model of Technology Adoption. *Rev. Econ. Statist.*, May 1983, *65* (2), pp. 234–42. **[G: U.S.]**

Emmanuel, A. The Transfer of Technology and the Multinationals: A Reply [*Appropriate or Underdeveloped Technology*]. *Greek Econ. Rev.*, April 1983, *5* (1), pp. 89–95.

Eto, Hajime and Makino, Kyoko. Theoretical and Empirical Analysis of the Differentiation Process in the Technology Gap between Developed and Developing Nations. **In** *Isard, W. and Nagao, Y., eds.*, 1983, pp. 149–59.

Färe, Rolf G. and Grosskopf, Shawna P. Measuring Congestion in Production. *Z. Nationalökon.*, 1983, *43* (3), pp. 257–71.

Färe, Rolf G.; Grosskopf, Shawna P. and Lovell, C. A. Knox. The Structure of Technical Efficiency. *Scand. J. Econ.*, 1983, *85* (2), pp. 181–90.

Fedorenko, N. and L'vov, D. Economic Strategy and Scientific and Technical Progress. *Prob. Econ.*, April 1983, *25* (12), pp. 30–50. **[G: U.S.S.R.]**

Ferdows, K. Technology-Push Strategies for Manufacturing. *Tijdschrift Econ. Manage.*, 1983, *28* (2), pp. 125–37. **[G: EEC; U.S.; Australia]**

Fernandez Arufe, J. E. La actual crisis económica y políticas de empleo: la situación española. (The Economic Crisis and Employment Policies: The Case of Spain. With English summary.) *Écon. Soc.*, September–October–November 1983, *17* (9–10–11), pp. 1517–35. **[G: Spain]**

Fishelson, Gideon. Hotelling Rule, Economic Responses and Oil Prices. *Energy Econ.*, July 1983, *5* (3), pp. 153–56.

Fong, Chan Onn. Appropriate Technology: An Empirical Study of Bicycle Manufacturing in Malaysia. **In** *Lim, D., ed.*, 1983, *1980*, pp. 181–95. **[G: Malaysia]**

Førsund, Finn R. and Hjalmarsson, Lennart. Technical Progress and Structural Change in the Swedish Cement Industry 1955–1979. *Econometrica*, September 1983, *51* (5), pp. 1449–67. **[G: Sweden]**

Førsund, Finn R. and Jansen, Eilev S. Technical Progress and Structural Change in the Norwegian Primary Aluminum Industry. *Scand. J. Econ.*, 1983, *85* (2), pp. 113–26. **[G: Norway]**

Frantzis, Lisa. The Potential for Diversity: The Production Alternative. **In** *Brown, H. J., ed.*, 1983, pp. 61–92. **[G: U.S.]**

Freeman, Christopher; Walsh, V. and Townsend, J. The Determinants of Technical Change in the Chemical Industry: Demand-pull or Technology-push? **In** *[Saunders, C. T.]*, 1983, pp. 83–108. **[G: Italy; U.K.; U.S.; W. Germany]**

Friedlaender, Ann F.; Winston, Clifford M. and Wang, Kung. Costs, Technology, and Productivity in the U.S. Automobile Industry. *Bell J. Econ. (See Rand J. Econ. after 4/85)*, Spring 1983, *14* (1), pp. 1–20. **[G: U.S.]**

Fujimoto, Takao. Inventions and Technical Change: A Curiosum. *Manchester Sch. Econ. Soc. Stud.*, March 1983, *51* (1), pp. 16–20.

Fujimoto, Takao; Herrero, Carmen and Villar, Antonia. Technical Changes and Their Effects on the Price Structure. *Metroecon.*, February–June 1983, *35* (1–2), pp. 123–27.

Garvin, David A. Spin-Offs and the New Firm Formation Process. *Calif. Manage. Rev.*, January 1983, *25* (2), pp. 3–20. **[G: U.S.]**

Gehrels, Franz. Foreign Investment and Technology Transfer: Optimal Policies. *Weltwirtsch. Arch.*, 1983, *119* (4), pp. 663–85.

Gehrels, Franz. Optimal Private and Collective Consumption in a Growing Economy. *Public Finance*, 1983, *38* (2), pp. 202–16.

Gennard, John and Dunn, Steve. The Impact of New Technology on the Structure and Organisation of Craft Unions in the Printing Industry. *Brit. J. Ind. Relat.*, March 1983, *21* (1), pp. 17–32. **[G: U.K.]**

Giersch, Herbert and Wolter, Frank. Towards an Explanation of the Productivity Slowdown: An Acceleration-Deceleration Hypothesis. *Econ. J.*, March 1983, *93* (369), pp. 35–55. **[G: OECD]**

Goddard, John B. Industrial Innovation and Regional Economic Development in Great Britain. **In** *Hamilton, F. E. I. and Linge, G. J. R., eds.*, 1983, pp. 255–77. **[G: U.K.]**

Gold, Bela. On the Adoption of Technological Innovations in Industry: Superficial Models and Complex Decision Processes. **In** *Macdonald, S.; Lamberton, D. M. and Mandeville, T., eds.*, 1983, pp. 104–21.

Haahti, Antti and Yavas, Ugur. Taitotiedon välittymisestä kehitysmaihin. (Transfer of Know-How to Underdeveloped Countries. With English summary.) *Liiketaloudellinen Aikak.*, 1983, *32* (4), pp. 399–411. **[G: LDCs]**

Hafsah, J. and Bernsten, R. H. Economic, Technical, and Social Aspects of Tractor Operation and Use in South Sulawesi, Indonesia. **In** *Internat'l Rice Res. Inst. and Agric. Devel. Council*, 1983, pp. 85–94. **[G: Indonesia]**

Hagan, Jim and Markey, Ray. Technological Change and the Unions. **In** *Hill, S. and Johnston, R., eds.*, 1983, pp. 154–74. **[G: Australia]**

Hamlin, Alan P. and Heathfield, David F. Shiftwork and the Choice of Technique under Alternative Maximands. *Scand. J. Econ.*, 1983, *85* (2), pp. 283–94.

Hanson, Philip. The Role of Trade and Technology Transfer in the Soviet Economy. **In** *Becker, A. S., ed.*, 1983, pp. 23–48. **[G: OECD; U.S.S.R.]**

Hartley, John T., Jr. Electronics: High Technology Is the Wave of the Future. **In** *Federal Reserve Bank of Atlanta*, 1983, pp. 103–10. **[G: U.S.]**

Hartmann, Gert, et al. Computerised Machine-Tools, Manpower Consequences and Skill Utilisation: A Study of British and West German Manufacturing Firms. *Brit. J. Ind. Relat.*, July 1983, *21* (2), pp. 221–31. **[G: U.K.; W. Germany]**

Hayes, Denis. Environmental Benefits of a Solar World. **In** *Rich, D., et al., eds.*, 1983, pp. 13–24. **[G: U.S.]**

Heertje, Arnold. The Economic Theorist's Dilemma. **In** *Macdonald, S.; Lamberton, D. M. and Mande-*

ville, T., eds., 1983, pp. 37–49.

Herdt, Robert W. Mechanization of Rice Production in Developing Asian Countries: Perspective, Evidence, and Issues. **In** *Internat'l Rice Res. Inst. and Agric. Devel. Council*, 1983, pp. 1–13. **[G: Japan; Taiwan; S. Korea]**

Herroelen, W. Automation of Small Batch Production. *Tijdschrift Econ. Manage.*, 1983, *28*(2), pp. 139–63. **[G: U.S.]**

Herroelen, Willy and Lambrecht, Marc R. Management Aspects of Computerized Manufacturing. *Econ. Soc. Tijdschr.*, December 1983, *37*(6), pp. 723–43.

Hill, Hal. Choice of Technique in the Indonesian Weaving Industry. *Econ. Develop. Cult. Change*, January 1983, *31*(2), pp. 337–53. **[G: Indonesia]**

Hill, Stephen. Technology and Society. **In** *Hill, S. and Johnston, R., eds.*, 1983, pp. 27–46.

Hoffman, Allan R. A National Strategy for Solar Energy: The Role of the Domestic Policy Review. **In** *Rich, D., et al., eds.*, 1983, pp. 35–47. **[G: U.S.]**

Hogan, Andrew J. Crop Credit Insurance and Technical Change in Agricultural Development: A Theoretical Analysis. *J. Risk Ins.*, March 1983, *50*(1), pp. 118–30.

Hope, Kempe R. Basic Needs and Technology Transfer Issues in the 'New International Economic Order.' *Amer. J. Econ. Soc.*, October 1983, *42*(4), pp. 393–404. **[G: LDCs]**

Inada, Koji. Economic Growth and Biased Technical Change: The Japanese Experience. **In** *[Yamada, I.]*, 1983, pp. 164–70. **[G: Japan]**

Ironmonger, Duncan. A Conceptual Framework for Modelling the Role of Technological Change. **In** *Macdonald, S.; Lamberton, D. M. and Mandeville, T., eds.*, 1983, pp. 50–55.

Jain, Harish C. Task Force Encourages Diffusion of Microelectronics in Canada. *Mon. Lab. Rev.*, October 1983, *106*(10), pp. 25–29. **[G: Canada]**

James, John A. Structural Change in American Manufacturing, 1850–1890. *J. Econ. Hist.*, June 1983, *43*(2), pp. 433–59. **[G: U.S.]**

Janiszewski, Hubert A. Restrictive Provisions in Licensing Agreements to Poland. *J. World Trade Law*, March–April 1983, *17*(2), pp. 154–58. **[G: Poland; Selected MDCs]**

Jéquier, Nicolas. Intelligence Requirements and Information Management for Developing Countries. **In** *O'Brien, R. C., ed.*, 1983, pp. 122–40.

Jones, Daniel T. Technology and the UK Automobile Industry. *Lloyds Bank Rev.*, April 1983, (148), pp. 14–27. **[G: U.K.]**

Jorgenson, Dale W. Modeling Production for General Equilibrium Analysis. *Scand. J. Econ.*, 1983, *85*(2), pp. 101–12. **[G: U.S.]**

Juarez, F. and Pathnopas, R. Comparative Analysis of Thresher Adoption and Use in Thailand and the Philippines. **In** *Internat'l Rice Res. Inst. and Agric. Devel. Council*, 1983, pp. 119–37. **[G: Thailand; Philippines]**

Jussawalla, Meheroo. Trade, Technology Transfer, and Development. **In** *Macdonald, S.; Lamberton, D. M. and Mandeville, T., eds.*, 1983, pp. 134–54. **[G: LDCs; MDCs]**

Kahn, James Gustave. The Advantages of Integrating Decentralized Renewable Electrical Technologies: A Connecticut Case Study. **In** *Brown, H. J., ed.*, 1983, pp. 163–81. **[G: U.S.]**

Kanygin, Iu. M. and Parfentseva, N. A. How to Plan and Evaluate the Work of Computer Centers. *Prob. Econ.*, December 1983, *26*(8), pp. 32–44. **[G: U.S.S.R.]**

Kau, James B. and Sirmans, C. F. Technological Change and Economic Growth in Housing. *J. Urban Econ.*, May 1983, *13*(3), pp. 283–95. **[G: U.S.]**

Keeney, Ralph L. A Technology Choice for Model Electricity Generation. *Energy J.*, Supplement 1983, *4*, pp. 13–31.

King, Ron. The Relationship between Technological Change and Education. **In** *Hill, S. and Johnston, R., eds.*, 1983, pp. 175–93. **[G: Australia]**

Kinsey, B. H. and Ahmed, Iftikhar. Mechanical Innovations on Small African Farms: Problems of Development and Diffusion. *Int. Lab. Rev.*, March–April 1983, *122*(2), pp. 227–38. **[G: Africa]**

Kiser, John W., III. Tapping Eastern Bloc Technology. **In** *Dickson, D. N., ed.*, 1983, pp. 485–500. **[G: COMECON; W. Europe]**

Knieps, Günter. Is Technological Revolution a Sufficient Reason for Changing the System of Regulation? The Case of Telecommunications. *Z. ges. Staatswiss.*, October 1983, *139*(3), pp. 578–97. **[G: W. Germany]**

Koch, Donald L. Changing the Corporate Culture through Information Systems. **In** *Federal Reserve Bank of Atlanta*, 1983, pp. 87–100. **[G: U.S.]**

Kolk, David X. Regional Employment Impact of Rapidly Escalating Energy Costs. *Energy Econ.*, April 1983, *5*(2), pp. 105–13. **[G: U.S.]**

Kopp, Raymond J. and Smith, V. Kerry. Neoclassical Modeling of Nonneutral Technological Change: An Experimental Appraisal. *Scand. J. Econ.*, 1983, *85*(2), pp. 127–46.

Koster, Francis P. The Role of Utilities in Promoting Solar Energy: The Case of the TVA. **In** *Rich, D., et al., eds.*, 1983, pp. 103–22. **[G: U.S.]**

Kujawa, Duane. Technology Strategy and Industrial Relations: Case Studies of Japanese Multinationals in the United States. *J. Int. Bus. Stud.*, Winter 1983, *14*(3), pp. 9–22. **[G: Japan; U.S.]**

Kulagin, G. On Ways to Intensify (From an Economist's Notebook). *Prob. Econ.*, December 1983, *26*(8), pp. 45–58. **[G: U.S.S.R.]**

Kumar, Raj. Labour Absorption and Technology Choice in Agriculture. *Econ. Aff.*, July-September 1983, *28*(3), pp. 736–41. **[G: India]**

La Ferney, Preston E. An Administrative Perspective on Microcomputers for Agricultural Research and Education. *Southern J. Agr. Econ.*, July 1983, *15*(1), pp. 53–55. **[G: U.S.]**

Lahera, Eugenio and Nochteff, Hugo. Microelectronics and Latin American Development. *Cepal Rev.*, April 1983, (19), pp. 167–81. **[G: Latin America]**

Lahiri, Sajal. Capacity Constraints, Alternative Technologies and Input–Output Analysis. *Europ. Econ. Rev.*, July 1983, *22*(2), pp. 219–26.

Lall, Sanjaya. Brandt on 'Transnational Corporations Investment and the Sharing of Technology.' **In** *Gauhar, A., ed. (II)*, 1983, pp. 149–53.

Lazarus, William. Landsats, Minerals and Development: A Qualitative Notion of the Down-Side Risk. **In** *O'Brien, R. C., ed.,* 1983, pp. 102–21. **[G: U.S.]**

Lee, J. H. The Measurement and Sources of Technological Change Biases, with an Application to Postwar Japanese Agriculture. *Economica,* May 1983, *50*(198), pp. 159–73. **[G: Japan]**

Lee, Thomas H. Energy and Technology: Comment. **In** *Schurr, S. H.; Sonenblum, S. and Wood, D. O., eds.,* 1983, pp. 315–17. **[G: U.S.]**

Leontief, Wassily W. Technological Advance, Economic Growth, and the Distribution of Income. *Population Devel. Rev.,* September 1983, *9*(3), pp. 403–10.

Levins, Richard A. Implications of Microcomputer Technology for Agricultural Economics Programs. *Southern J. Agr. Econ.,* July 1983, *15*(1), pp. 27–29. **[G: U.S.]**

Lim, David. Scale and Technology in Malaysian Manufacturing. **In** *Lim, D., ed.,* 1983, pp. 153–61. **[G: Malaysia]**

Lindbeck, Assar. The Recent Slowdowns of Productivity Growth. *Econ. J.,* March 1983, *93*(369), pp. 13–34. **[G: OECD]**

Lingard, John and Bagyo, Al Sri. The Impact of Agricultural Mechanisation of Production and Employment in Rice Areas of West Java. *Bull. Indonesian Econ. Stud.,* April 1983, *19*(1), pp. 53–67. **[G: Indonesia]**

Littler, Craig R. Japan and China. **In** *Feuchtwang, S. and Hussain, A., eds.,* 1983, pp. 121–47. **[G: China; Japan]**

Lockwood, B., et al. Farm Mechanization in Pakistan: Policy and Practice. **In** *Internat'l Rice Res. Inst. and Agric. Devel. Council,* 1983, pp. 15–30. **[G: Pakistan]**

Longworth, John W. Agricultural Policy and Innovation. *Australian J. Agr. Econ.,* August 1983, *27*(2), pp. 152–56. **[G: Australia]**

Lovins, Amory B. Technology Is the Answer! (But What Was the Question?) **In** *Brown, H. J., ed.,* 1983, pp. 19–35.

Lundahl, Mats. Obstacles to Technological Change in Haitian Peasant Agriculture. **In** *Lundahl, M.,* 1983, *1977,* pp. 237–50. **[G: Haiti]**

Lundahl, Mats. Peasants, Government and Technological Change in Haitian Agriculture. **In** *Lundahl, M.,* 1983, pp. 251–85. **[G: Haiti]**

Lundahl, Mats. Teknologiska förändringar och ekonomisk tillväxt i u-länder. (Technological Change and Economic Growth in the Developing Countries. With English summary.) *Ekon. Samfundets Tidskr.,* 1983, *36*(3), pp. 91–106. **[G: LDCs; MDCs]**

Lutz, James M. and Green, Robert T. The Product Life Cycle and the Export Position of the United States. *J. Int. Bus. Stud.,* Winter 1983, *14*(3), pp. 77–93. **[G: Japan; U.S.; U.K.; W. Germany]**

Macdonald, Stuart. Technology beyond Machines. **In** *Macdonald, S.; Lamberton, D. M. and Mandeville, T., eds.,* 1983, pp. 26–36. **[G: Australia]**

MacKenzie, James J. Planning the Solar Transition. **In** *Rich, D., et al., eds.,* 1983, pp. 25–34.

MacMinn, Richard D. and Holtmann, Alphonse G. Technological Uncertainty and the Theory of the Firm. *Southern Econ. J.,* July 1983, *50*(1), pp. 120–36.

Maier, Harry. Innovation and the Better Use of Human Resources. **In** *Streeten, P. and Maier, H., eds.,* 1983, pp. 253–88. **[G: E. Germany]**

Malecki, Edward J. Towards a Model of Technical Change and Regional Economic Change. *Reg. Sci. Persp.,* 1983, *13*(2), pp. 51–60.

Manca, Gavino. L'impresa multinazionale di fronte alla rivoluzione tecnologica. (The Multinational Company and the Technological Revolution. With English summary.) *L'Impresa,* 1983, *25*(6), pp. 37–39.

Mandeville, Thomas and Macdonald, Stuart. Information Technology and Employment Levels. **In** *Macdonald, S.; Lamberton, D. M. and Mandeville, T., eds.,* 1983, pp. 169–77. **[G: Australia; U.K.]**

Maneschi, Andrea. The Prebisch-Singer Thesis and the 'Widening Gap' between Developed and Developing Countries. *Can. J. Econ.,* February 1983, *16*(1), pp. 104–08.

Mansfield, Edwin. Entrepreneurship and the Management of Innovation. **In** *Backman, J., ed.,* 1983, pp. 81–109. **[G: U.S.]**

Mansfield, Edwin. Technological Change and Market Structure: An Empirical Study. *Amer. Econ. Rev.,* May 1983, *73*(2), pp. 205–09. **[G: U.S.]**

Mathias, Peter. The Machine: Icon of Economic Growth. **In** *Macdonald, S.; Lamberton, D. M. and Mandeville, T., eds.,* 1983, pp. 11–25. **[G: U.K.]**

Maxwell, J. Robert. Industrial Decision-making for Solar Energy Development. **In** *Rich, D., et al., eds.,* 1983, pp. 123–34. **[G: U.S.]**

McGrann, James M. Microcomputer Software Development and Distribution. *Southern J. Agr. Econ.,* July 1983, *15*(1), pp. 21–25. **[G: U.S.]**

McHugh, Richard and Lane, Julia. The Embodiment Hypothesis: An Interregional Test. *Rev. Econ. Statist.,* May 1983, *65*(2), pp. 323–27. **[G: U.S.]**

Metwally, M. M. and Tamaschke, H. U. The Effect of Inflation and Technology on Factor Shares. *Appl. Econ.,* December 1983, *15*(6), pp. 777–91. **[G: Selected Countries]**

Miller, Edward M. A Problem in the Measurement of Capital Embodied Productivity Change. *Eastern Econ. J.,* January–March 1983, *9*(1), pp. 29–36.

Miller, Edward M. Capital Aggregation in the Presence of Obsolescence-Inducing Technical Change. *Rev. Income Wealth,* September 1983, *29*(3), pp. 283–96.

Minami, Ryoshin and Makino, Fumio. Conditions for Technological Diffusion: Case of Power Looms. *Hitotsubashi J. Econ.,* February 1983, *23*(2), pp. 1–20. **[G: Japan]**

Morris, Derek J. Comment on the Paper by Professor Lindbeck [The Recent Slowdowns of Productivity Growth]. *Econ. J.,* March 1983, *93*(369), pp. 78–83. **[G: OECD]**

Morrissey, Mike. Technological Change and Occupational Health. **In** *Hill, S. and Johnston, R., eds.,* 1983, pp. 137–53. **[G: Australia]**

Myers, John G. Energy and Technology: Comment. **In** *Schurr, S. H.; Sonenblum, S. and Wood, D. O., eds.,* 1983, pp. 317–19. **[G: U.S.]**

Nadkarni, M. V. and Deshpande, R. S. Growth and Instability in Crop Yields: A Case Study of Agriculture in Karnataka, South India. *Reg. Stud.*, February 1983, *17*(1), pp. 29–39. **[G: India]**

Nelson, Randy A. and Wohar, Mark E. Regulation, Scale Economies, and Productivity in Steam-Electric Generation. *Int. Econ. Rev.*, February 1983, *24*(1), pp. 57–79. **[G: U.S.]**

Nironen, Erkki. Transfer of Technology between Finland and the Soviet Union. **In** *Möttölä, K.; Bykov, O. N. and Korolev, I. S., eds.*, 1983, pp. 161–70. **[G: Finland; U.S.S.R.]**

Norsworthy, J. R. Energy Prices, Technical Change, and Productivity Growth. **In** *Schurr, S. H.; Sonenblum, S. and Wood, D. O., eds.*, 1983, pp. 155–77. **[G: U.S.]**

Olson, Mancur. Reassessment of Measures of Levels of Living: Discussion. *J. Econ. Hist.*, March 1983, *43*(1), pp. 86–88.

Oppenländer, Karl-Heinrich. Auswirkungen des technischen Wandels auf Beschäftigtenzahl und Beschäftigtenstruktur. (The Effects of Technical Change on Number Employed and on the Structure of Employment. With English summary.) *Ifo-Studien*, 1983, *29*(2), pp. 77–99. **[G: W. Germany]**

Pack, Howard. Policies to Encourage the Use of Intermediate Technology. **In** *Todaro, M. P., ed.*, 1983, *1976*, pp. 181–91. **[G: S. Korea; Taiwan; Pakistan; Mexico]**

Parsons, Gregory L. Information Technology: A New Competitive Weapon. *Sloan Manage. Rev.*, Fall 1983, *25*(1), pp. 3–14.

Perkins, F. C. Technology Choice, Industrialisation and Development Experiences in Tanzania. *J. Devel. Stud.*, January 1983, *19*(2), pp. 213–43. **[G: Tanzania]**

Phillips, Sheena. Cruise Missiles. **In** *Tsipis, K. and Phillips, S.*, 1983, pp. 148–71.

Phillips, Sheena. Laser Weapons. **In** *Tsipis, K. and Phillips, S.*, 1983, pp. 111–47.

Pindyck, Robert S. The Energy Connection to Recent Productivity Behavior: Comment. **In** *Schurr, S. H.; Sonenblum, S. and Wood, D. O., eds.*, 1983, pp. 183–85. **[G: U.S.]**

Pogrow, Stanley. Linking Technology Use to School Improvement: Implications for Research Policy and Practice. **In** *Odden, A. and Webb, L. D., eds.*, 1983, pp. 127–42. **[G: U.S.]**

Pontius, Steven K. The Communication Process of Adoption: Agriculture in Thailand. *J. Devel. Areas*, October 1983, *18*(1), pp. 93–118. **[G: Thailand]**

Prais, S. J. Comment on the Paper by Professor Giersch and Dr. Wolter [Towards an Explanation of the Productivity Slowdown: An Acceleration-Deceleration Hypothesis]. *Econ. J.*, March 1983, *93*(369), pp. 84–88.

Quan, Daniel C. and Kerr, William A. Truncated Estimates for Incomplete Technical Change in the Canadian Cattle Industry. *Amer. J. Agr. Econ.*, August 1983, *65*(3), pp. 581–86. **[G: Canada]**

Randell, Daniel. Automation in Perspective—An Overview. **In** *Wilson, B.; Berg, C. C. and French, D., eds.*, 1983, pp. 217–32. **[G: U.S.]**

Ravid, S. Abraham and Hadar, Y. A Cost Benefit Analysis of Bio-gas Production: An Israeli Experience. **In** *Lev, B., ed.*, 1983, pp. 413–22. **[G: Israel]**

Ray, George F. The Diffusion of Mature Technologies. *Nat. Inst. Econ. Rev.*, November 1983, (106), pp. 56–62. **[G: U.K.]**

Rayudu, C. S. Measurement of Rural Economic Growth. *Econ. Aff.*, October–December 1983, *28*(4), pp. 829–38. **[G: India]**

Redclift, Michael. Production Programs for Small Farmers: Plan Puebla as Myth and Reality. *Econ. Develop. Cult. Change*, April 1983, *31*(3), pp. 551–70. **[G: Mexico]**

Reinganum, Jennifer F. Technology Adoption under Imperfect Information. *Bell J. Econ. (See Rand J. Econ. after 4/85)*, Spring 1983, *14*(1), pp. 57–69.

Rich, Daniel and Byrne, John. The Solar Energy Transition: Introduction. **In** *Rich, D., et al., eds.*, 1983, pp. 1–11.

Riche, Richard W.; Hecker, Daniel E. and Burgan, John U. High Technology Today and Tomorrow: A Small Slice of the Employment Pie. *Mon. Lab. Rev.*, November 1983, *106*(11), pp. 50–58. **[G: U.S.]**

Ridler, Neil B. Labour Force and Land Distributional Effects of Agricultural Technology: A Case Study of Coffee. *World Devel.*, July 1983, *11*(7), pp. 593–99. **[G: Colombia]**

Rosenberg, Nathan. The Effects of Energy Supply Characteristics on Technology and Economic Growth. **In** *Schurr, S. H.; Sonenblum, S. and Wood, D. O., eds.*, 1983, pp. 279–305. **[G: U.S.]**

Rostow, W. W. Technology and Unemployment in the Western World. *Challenge*, March/April 1983, *26*(1), pp. 6–17. **[G: MDCs]**

Roumasset, James and Thapa, Ganesh. Explaining Tractorization in Nepal: An Alternative to the 'Consequences Approach' *J. Devel. Econ.*, June 1983, *12*(3), pp. 377–95. **[G: Nepal]**

Russell, James R. and Purcell, Wayne D. Costs of Operating a Computerized Trading System for Slaughter Lambs. *Southern J. Agr. Econ.*, July 1983, *15*(1), pp. 123–27. **[G: U.S.]**

Rymes, T. K. More on the Measurement of Total Factor Productivity. *Rev. Income Wealth*, September 1983, *29*(3), pp. 297–316.

Sabolo, Yves. Trade between Developing Countries, Technology Transfers and Employment. *Int. Lab. Rev.*, Sept.–Oct. 1983, *122*(5), pp. 593–608. **[G: LDCs]**

Saefudin, Y., et al. Consequences of Small Rice Farm Mechanization in West Java: A Summary of Preliminary Analyses. **In** *Internat'l Rice Res. Inst. and Agric. Devel. Council*, 1983, pp. 165–75. **[G: Indonesia]**

Sain, K. Economics of Agricultural Machinery. *Econ. Aff.*, July-September 1983, *28*(3), pp. 748–59. **[G: India]**

Sayer, Andrew. Theoretical Problems in the Analysis of Technological Change and Regional Development. **In** *Hamilton, F. E. I. and Linge, G. J. R., eds.*, 1983, pp. 59–73.

Sertel, Murat R. Technological Preferences of Capitalist and Workers' Enterprises. *Econ. Anal. Worker's Manage.*, 1983, *17*(3), pp. 273–77.

Shoazhi, Su. Socialism; China's Conditions; Modern Science and Technology; Democratization; Development Strategies: A Tentative Discourse on the Chinese Road to Modernization. *Econ. Notes,* 1983, (1), pp. 24–41. **[G: China]**

Siegel, Jeremy J. Technological Change and the Superneutrality of Money. *J. Money, Credit, Banking,* August 1983, *15*(3), pp. 363–67.

Simon, Julian L. The Present Value of Population Growth in the Western World. *Population Stud.,* March 1983, *37*(1), pp. 5–21.

Sipek, Kira. Eléments de mesure de la rigidité structurelle des secteurs industriels à la diffusion des innovations. (With English summary.) *Rev. Econ. Ind.,* 4th Trimester 1983, (26), pp. 34–51. **[G: France]**

Skinner, C. Wickham. Technology and the Work Environment (I). **In** *Martin, T. R., ed.,* 1983, pp. 43–53. **[G: U.S.]**

Skouras, Th. The Transfer of Technology and the Multinationals: A Rejoinder. *Greek Econ. Rev.,* August 1983, *5*(2), pp. 193–96.

Sláma, Jiři. Gravity Model and Its Estimations for International Flows of Engineering Products, Chemicals and Patent Applications. *Acta Oecon.,* 1983, *30*(2), pp. 241–53. **[G: Yugoslavia; Europe; CMEA]**

Smilga, E. P. Is There a Need for a Plant Concept of Technical Development? *Prob. Econ.,* January 1983, *25*(9), pp. 3–15. **[G: U.S.S.R.]**

de Sola Pool, Ithiel. Communications Technology and Land Use. **In** *Carr, J. H. and Duensing, E. E., eds.,* 1983, *1980,* pp. 291–303. **[G: U.S.]**

Soós, Károly Attila. Technical Level and Economic Efficiency: Investment Decisions within the Framework of a Central Development Program. *Eastern Europ. Econ.,* Spring–Summer 1983, *21*(3–4), pp. 163–69. **[G: Hungary]**

Standing, Guy. The Notion of Structural Unemployment. *Int. Lab. Rev.,* March–April 1983, *122*(2), pp. 137–53.

Stanley, John A. Reasonable EPA Projection Techniques for Estimating Technological Advances Upheld. *Natural Res. J.,* January 1983, *23*(1), pp. 219–24. **[G: U.S.]**

Stewart, Frances. Inequality, Technology and Payments Systems. **In** *Stewart, F., ed.,* 1983, pp. 1–31. **[G: Selected LDCs; Selected MDCs]**

Stewart, Frances. Macro–Policies for Appropriate Technology: An Introductory Classification. *Int. Lab. Rev.,* May–June 1983, *122*(3), pp. 279–93. **[G: LDCs]**

Stoneman, P. Diffusion, Technology Transfer and Trade. **In** *Macdonald, S.; Lamberton, D. M. and Mandeville, T., eds.,* 1983, pp. 93–103.

Stoneman, P. and Ireland, Norman J. The Role of Supply Factors in the Diffusion of New Process Technology. *Econ. J.,* Supplement March 1983, pp. 66–78.

Stout, D. K. Technical Advance and Trade Advantage. **In** *Macdonald, S.; Lamberton, D. M. and Mandeville, T., eds.,* 1983, pp. 122–33.

Sukharomana, S. Domestic Resource Cost of Agricultural Mechanization in Thailand: A Case Study of Small Rice Farms in Supanburi. **In** *Internat'l Rice Res. Inst. and Agric. Devel. Council,* 1983, pp. 61–69. **[G: Thailand]**

Sveikauskas, Leo A. Science and Technology in United States Foreign Trade. *Econ. J.,* September 1983, *93*(371), pp. 542–54. **[G: U.S.]**

Tange, Toshiko. Trade Frictions and Productivity Performance—Technological, Price, and Cost Competitiveness of Japan and U.S. Exports. *J. Policy Modeling,* November 1983, *5*(3), pp. 313–31. **[G: Japan; U.S.]**

Tárnok, Éva. The Limits of Independent Technological Development: Production and Development after Breaking Off a Traditional License Relationship. *Eastern Europ. Econ.,* Fall 1983, *22*(1), pp. 19–37. **[G: Hungary]**

Tell, Björn, V. The Awakening Information Needs of the Developing Countries. **In** *O'Brien, R. C., ed.,* 1983, *1980,* pp. 141–47.

Teubal, M. The Accumulation of Intangibles by High-Technology Firms. **In** *Macdonald, S.; Lamberton, D. M. and Mandeville, T., eds.,* 1983, pp. 56–74. **[G: Selected Countries]**

Thompson, Alexander M., III. Technological Change and the Control of Work: The U.S. Bituminous Coal Industry 1865–1930. *Econ. Forum,* Winter 1983-84, *14*(2), pp. 1–18. **[G: U.S.]**

Thompson, R. S. Diffusion of the M-Form Structure in the U.K.: Rate of Imitation, Inter-firm and Inter-industry Differences. *Int. J. Ind. Organ.,* September 1983, *1*(3), pp. 297–315. **[G: U.K.]**

Tiano, André. The Dialectics of Dependency Reversal: Technology Transfer. **In** *Doran, C. F.; Modelski, G. and Clark, C., eds.,* 1983, pp. 129–55.

Tiano, André. Transfers of Iron and Steel Technology to the Third World: Effects on Employment in the Developed Countries. *Int. Lab. Rev.,* July–August 1983, *122*(4), pp. 429–42. **[G: France; OECD; LDCs]**

Tinsley, W. A. Teaching with the Microcomputer: Adoption of a New Technology. *Southern J. Agr. Econ.,* July 1983, *15*(1), pp. 57–59. **[G: U.S.]**

Todd, Daniel and Simpson, Jamie A. The Appropriate-Technology Question in a Regional Context. *Growth Change,* October 1983, *14*(4), pp. 46–52.

Tomaskovic-Devey, Donald and Miller, S. M. Can High-Tech Provide the Jobs? *Challenge,* May/June 1983, *26*(2), pp. 57–63. **[G: U.S.]**

Treillon, R. Le sens d l'évolution technique et son enjeu. (With English summary.) *Écon. Soc.,* May 1983, *17*(5), pp. 839–76. **[G: France]**

Tsipis, Kosta. Fundamental Technologies with Extensive Military Applications. **In** *Tsipis, K. and Phillips, S.,* 1983, pp. 49–88.

Turner, Steven C.; Epperson, James E. and Fletcher, Stanley M. Producer Attitudes toward Multicommodity Electronic Marketing. *Amer. J. Agr. Econ.,* November 1983, *65*(4), pp. 818–22. **[G: U.S.]**

Ullman, John E. The Arms Race and the Decline of U.S. Technology. *J. Econ. Issues,* June 1983, *17*(2), pp. 565–74. **[G: U.S.]**

Uri, Noel D. Embodied and Disembodied Technical Change Revisited. *Econ. Int.,* May–August–November 1983, *36*(2–3–4), pp. 278–94. **[G: U.S.]**

Valenta, František. Structure of Innovations in the Process of Intensification of the Economy. *Czech.*

Econ. Digest., June 1983, (4), pp. 36–52. [G: Czechoslovakia]

Walker, Charles A. Science and Technology of the Sources and Management of Radioactive Wastes. **In** *Walker, C. A.; Gould, L. C. and Woodhouse, E. J., eds.*, 1983, pp. 27–74. [G: U.S.]

von Wartensleben, Aurelie. Major Issues Concerning Pharmaceutical Policies in the Third World. *World Devel.*, March 1983, *11*(3), pp. 169–75. [G: LDCs; MDCs]

Waverman, Leonard. The Energy Connection to Recent Productivity Behavior: Comment. **In** *Schurr, S. H.; Sonenblum, S. and Wood, D. O., eds.*, 1983, pp. 185–88. [G: U.S.]

Welch, Lawrence S. Licensing Strategy and Policy for Internationalization and Technology Transfer. **In** *Czinkota, M. R., ed. (I)*, 1983, pp. 5–23. [G: Latin America; Selected Countries]

Welch, Lawrence S. The Technology Transfer Process in Foreign Licensing Arrangements. **In** *Macdonald, S.; Lamberton, D. M. and Mandeville, T., eds.*, 1983, pp. 155–68. [G: LDCs; MDCs]

Wells, Louis T., Jr. Don't Overautomate Your Foreign Plant. **In** *Dickson, D. N., ed.*, 1983, pp. 260–70.

Windschuttle, Keith. Technology and Unemployment. **In** *Hill, S. and Johnston, R., eds.*, 1983, pp. 68–88. [G: Australia]

Witholder, Robert E., Jr. Economic Feasibility of Dispersed Solar Electric Technologies. **In** *Brown, H. J., ed.*, 1983, pp. 121–61. [G: U.S.]

Wood, Richard H., Jr. Tractor Mechanisation and Employment on Larger Private Mexican Farms. *Int. Lab. Rev.*, March–April 1983, *122*(2), pp. 211–25. [G: Mexico]

Zuscovitch, Ehud. Informatisation, flexibilité et division du travail. (With English summary.) *Rev. Econ. Ind.*, 3rd Trimester 1983, (25), pp. 50–61. [G: France]

6212 Research and Development

Adar, Zvi and Agmon, Tamir. Financing Synthetic Fuels Investments in the United States: Public Support and Private Investment. **In** *Aronson, J. D. and Cowhey, P. F., eds.*, 1983, pp. 157–78. [G: U.S.]

Albrecht, Ulrich. Military R&D Communities. *Int. Soc. Sci. J.*, 1983, *35*(1), pp. 7–23. [G: Selected MDCs]

Baily, Martin Neil. 'Comparing Productivity Growth: An Exploration of French and U.S. Industrial and Firm Data' by Z. Griliches and J. Mairesse: Comment. *Europ. Econ. Rev.*, March/April 1983, *21*(1/2), pp. 121–23. [G: U.S.; France]

Baumol, William J. and Wolff, Edward N. Feedback from Productivity Growth to R & D. *Scand. J. Econ.*, 1983, *85*(2), pp. 147–57.

Bergson, Abram. Technological Progress. **In** *Bergson, A. and Levine, H. S., eds.*, 1983, pp. 34–78. [G: U.S.S.R.]

Bloch, Erich; Meindl, James D. and Cromie, William. University Industry Cooperation in Microelectronics and Computers. **In** *National Science Foundation*, 1983, pp. 235–53. [G: U.S.]

Bonnen, James T. Historical Sources of U.S. Agricultural Productivity: Implications for R&D Policy and Social Science Research. *Amer. J. Agr. Econ.*, December 1983, *65*(5), pp. 958–66. [G: U.S.]

Brander, James A. and Spencer, Barbara J. Strategic Commitment with R&D: The Symmetric Case. *Bell J. Econ. (See Rand J. Econ. after 4/85)*, Spring 1983, *14*(1), pp. 225–35.

Bruno, Michael. 'Comparing Productivity Growth: An Exploration of French and U.S. Industrial and Firm Data' by Z. Griliches and J. Mairesse: Comment. *Europ. Econ. Rev.*, March/April 1983, *21*(1/2), pp. 125–27. [G: U.S.; France]

Carli, Guido. Investment and Technological Competitiveness. **In** *Heertje, A., ed.*, 1983, pp. 100–116. [G: EEC]

Chakrabarti, Alok K. and Burton, Jonathan. Technological Characteristics of Mergers and Acquisitions in the 1970s in Manufacturing Industries in the U.S. *Quart. Rev. Econ. Bus.*, Autumn 1983, *23*(3), pp. 81–90. [G: U.S.]

Chudnovsky, Daniel. Patents and Trademarks in Pharmaceuticals. *World Devel.*, March 1983, *11*(3), pp. 187–93. [G: LDCs; MDCs]

Collins, Eileen L. R & D and Labor Productivity: Can Tax Incentives Help? **In** *Weintraub, S. and Goodstein, M., eds.*, 1983, pp. 48–58. [G: U.S.]

Daley, Lane A. and Vigeland, Robert L. The Effects of Debt Covenants and Political Costs on the Choice of Accounting Methods: The Case of Accounting for R&D Costs. *J. Acc. Econ.*, December 1983, *5*(3), pp. 195–211. [G: U.S.]

Dansby, Robert E. R&D Cost Allocation with Endogenous Technology Adoption. **In** *Finsinger, J., ed.*, 1983, pp. 117–47.

Darknell, Frank A. and Darknell, Edith Campbell. State College Science and Engineering Faculty: Collaborative Links with Private Business and Industry in California and Other States. **In** *National Science Foundation*, 1983, pp. 163–92. [G: U.S.]

Edwards, Clark. Social Science Implications of Agricultural Science and Technology: Discussion. *Amer. J. Agr. Econ.*, December 1983, *65*(5), pp. 978–80. [G: U.S.]

Elliott, J. Walter. Advertising and R&D Investments in the Wealth-Maximizing Firm. *J. Econ. Bus.*, August 1983, *35*(3/4), pp. 389–97.

Evenson, Robert E. Intellectual Property Rights and Agribusiness Research and Development: Implications for the Public Agricultural Research System. *Amer. J. Agr. Econ.*, December 1983, *65*(5), pp. 967–75. [G: U.S.]

Finsinger, Jörg. Public Sector Policy Analysis. **In** *Finsinger, J., ed.*, 1983, pp. 3–8.

Frederick, Robert E. and Snoeyenbos, Milton. Trade Secrets, Patents, and Morality. **In** *Snoeyenbos, M.; Almeder, R. and Humber, J., eds.*, 1983, pp. 162–69. [G: U.S.]

Gallini, Nancy T. Sequential Development of Correlated Projects: An Application to Coal Liquefaction. *Energy Econ.*, January 1983, *5*(1), pp. 37–48.

Gallini, Nancy T.; Lewis, Tracy R. and Ware, Roger. Strategic Timing and Pricing of a Substitute in a Cartelized Resource Market. *Can. J. Econ.*, August 1983, *16*(3), pp. 429–46.

Greaves, Cameron G. Hong Kong: Tax Treatment of Patent Rights, Etc. *Bull. Int. Fiscal Doc.*, December 1983, *37*(12), pp. 551. **[G: Hong Kong]**

Griliches, Zvi and Mairesse, Jacques. Comparing Productivity Growth: An Exploration of French and U.S. Industrial and Firm Data. *Europ. Econ. Rev.*, March/April 1983, *21*(1/2), pp. 89–119. **[G: U.S.; France]**

Habib, Mohammed Ahsan; Butterfield, David and Mestelman, Stuart. The Allocation of Research Expenditures among Competing Crops: The Application of an *Ex Ante* Model to Bangladesh. *J. Econ. Devel.*, December 1983, *8*(2), pp. 125–48. **[G: Bangladesh]**

Håkanson, Lars. R&D in Foreign-owned Subsidiaries in Sweden. **In** *Goldberg, W. H., ed.*, 1983, pp. 163–76. **[G: Sweden]**

Hansen, Ronald W. International Issues of Drug Regulation. *Z. ges. Staatswiss.*, October 1983, *139*(3), pp. 568–77. **[G: U.S.]**

Haug, P.; Hood, N. and Young, S. Mark. R & D Intensity in the Affiliates of U.S. Owned Electronics Companies Manufacturing in Scotland. *Reg. Stud.*, December 1983, *17*(6), pp. 383–92. **[G: U.K.]**

Hayes, Robert H. and Abernathy, William J. Managing Our Way to Economic Decline. **In** *Dickson, D. N., ed.*, 1983, pp. 203–23. **[G: U.S.; OECD]**

Hveem, Helge. Selective Dissociation in the Technology Sector. **In** *Ruggie, J. G., ed.*, 1983, pp. 273–316. **[G: Algeria; India; LDCs]**

Jarrell, Stephen. Research and Development and Firm Size in the Pharmaceutical Industry. *Bus. Econ.*, September 1983, *18*(4), pp. 26–39. **[G: U.S.]**

Kaldor, Mary. Military R&D: Cause or Consequence of the Arms Race? *Int. Soc. Sci. J.*, 1983, *35*(1), pp. 25–45. **[G: U.S.; U.S.S.R.; Japan; EEC]**

Kane, Michael B. and Kocher, A. Thel. The Dissemination and Use of Educational R & D in the United States: An Analysis of Recent Federal Attempts to Improve Educational Practice. **In** *Holzner, B.; Knorr, K. D. and Strasser, H., eds.*, 1983, pp. 281–94. **[G: U.S.]**

Kawashima, Yasuo. Product Differentiation, Prices, and Market Structure. *Europ. Econ. Rev.*, June 1983, *22*(1), pp. 75–96.

Levy, David M. and Terleckyj, Nestor E. Effects of Government R&D on Private R&D Investment and Productivity: A Macroeconomic Analysis. *Bell J. Econ. (See Rand J. Econ. after 4/85)*, Autumn 1983, *14*(2), pp. 551–61. **[G: U.S.]**

Link, Albert N. Alternative Sources of Technology: An Analysis of Induced Innovations. *Managerial Dec. Econ.*, March 1983, *4*(1), pp. 40–43. **[G: U.S.]**

Loeb, Peter D. Further Evidence of the Detriments of Industrial Research and Development Using Single and Simultaneous Equation Models. *Empirical Econ.*, 1983, *8*(3–4), pp. 203–14. **[G: U.S.]**

Mansfield, Edwin. Entrepreneurship and the Management of Innovation. **In** *Backman, J., ed.*, 1983, pp. 81–109. **[G: U.S.]**

Mansfield, Edwin. Industrial Organizational and Technological Change: Recent Econometric Findings. **In** *Craven, J. V., ed.*, 1983, pp. 129–43. **[G: U.S.]**

Mansfield, Edwin. Science and Technology. **In** *Miller, G. W., ed.*, 1983, pp. 125–50. **[G: U.S.; OECD; U.S.S.R.]**

McDaniel, Bruce A. Solar Energy and the Policies of First and Second Best. *Rev. Soc. Econ.*, April 1983, *41*(1), pp. 12–24. **[G: U.S.]**

Meisel, John B. and Lin, Steven A. Y. The Impact of Market Structure on the Firm's Allocation of Resources to Research and Development. *Quart. Rev. Econ. Bus.*, Winter 1983, *23*(4), pp. 28–43. **[G: U.S.]**

Mikkelsen, K. W. and Langam, N. N. Innovation in the Philippine Agricultural Machinery Industry. **In** *Internat'l Rice Res. Inst. and Agric. Devel. Council*, 1983, pp. 31–37. **[G: Philippines]**

Mowery, David C. Industrial Research and Firm Size, Survival, and Growth in American Manufacturing, 1921–1946: An Assessment. *J. Econ. Hist.*, December 1983, *43*(4), pp. 953–80. **[G: U.S.]**

Mowery, David C. The Relationship between Intrafirm and Contractual Forms of Industrial Research in American Manufacturing, 1900–1940. *Exploration Econ. Hist.*, October 1983, *20*(4), pp. 351–74. **[G: U.S.]**

Nakao, Takeo. Profitability, Market Share, Product Quality, and Advertising in Oligopoly. *J. Econ. Dynam. Control*, September 1983, *6*(1/2), pp. 153–71.

Nelson, Richard R. Government Support of Technical Progress: Lessons from History. *J. Policy Anal. Manage.*, Summer 1983, *2*(4), pp. 499–514. **[G: U.S.]**

Nordhaus, William D. and Van der Heyden, Ludo. Induced Technical Change: A Programming Approach. **In** *Schurr, S. H.; Sonenblum, S. and Wood, D. O., eds.*, 1983, pp. 379–404. **[G: Global]**

Odagiri, Hiroyuki. R & D Expenditures, Royalty Payments, and Sales Growth in Japanese Manufacturing Corporations. *J. Ind. Econ.*, September 1983, *32*(1), pp. 61–71. **[G: Japan]**

Ondrack, Daniel A. Responses to Government Industrial Research Policy: A Comparison of Foreign-owned and Canadian-owned Firms. **In** *Goldberg, W. H., ed.*, 1983, pp. 177–200. **[G: Canada]**

Pakes, Ariél. On Group Effects and Errors in Variables in Aggregation. *Rev. Econ. Statist.*, February 1983, *65*(1), pp. 168–73. **[G: U.S.]**

Pakes, Ariél and Nitzan, Shmuel. Optimum Contracts for Research Personnel, Research Employment, and the Establishment of "Rival" Enterprises. *J. Lab. Econ.*, October 1983, *1*(4), pp. 345–65.

Peters, Lois S., et al. Current U.S. University/Industry Research Connections. **In** *National Science Foundation*, 1983, pp. 1–161. **[G: U.S.]**

Peterson, Rodney D. On the Defense of University Research in Our Business Society. *J. Behav. Econ.*, Summer 1983, *12*(1), pp. 89–97.

Phillips, Michael J. Social Science Implications of Agricultural Science and Technology: Discussion. *Amer. J. Agr. Econ.*, December 1983, *65*(5), pp. 976–77. **[G: U.S.]**

Phillips, Sheena. Trends in U.S. Military R&D Funding. **In** *Tsipis, K. and Phillips, S.,* 1983, pp. 1–48. **[G: U.S.]**

Piekarz, Rolf. R&D and Productivity Growth: Policy Studies and Issues. *Amer. Econ. Rev.,* May 1983, *73*(2), pp. 210–14.

Pray, Carl E. Underinvestment and the Demand for Agricultural Research: A Case Study of the Punjab. *Food Res. Inst. Stud.,* 1983, *19*(1), pp. 51–79. **[G: Pakistan]**

Quinn, James Brian. U.S. Industrial Strategy: What Directions Should It Take? *Sloan Manage. Rev.,* Summer 1983, *24*(4), pp. 3–21. **[G: U.S.; EEC; Japan]**

Regens, James L. and Rycroft, Robert W. Intergovernmental Issues in Managing Sunbelt Growth. **In** *Ballard, S. C. and James, T. E., eds.,* 1983, pp. 162–79. **[G: U.S.]**

Ronstadt, Robert and Kramer, Robert J. Getting the Most Out of Innovation Abroad. **In** *Dickson, D. N., ed.,* 1983, pp. 477–84. **[G: U.S.]**

Sato, Ryuzo and Nôno, Takayuki. Invariance Principle and "G-Neutral" Types of Technical Change. **In** *[Yamada, I.],* 1983, pp. 177–86.

Scherer, F. M. R&D and Declining Productivity Growth. *Amer. Econ. Rev.,* May 1983, *73*(2), pp. 215–18. **[G: U.S.]**

Scherer, F. M. The Propensity to Patent. *Int. J. Ind. Organ.,* 1983, *1*(1), pp. 107–28. **[G: U.S.]**

Smith, Hilary H. Texas Agricultural Productivity: Is Research the Remedy? *Fed. Res. Bank Dallas Econ. Rev.,* November 1983, pp. 15–28. **[G: U.S.]**

Spencer, Barbara J. and Brander, James A. International R & D Rivalry and Industrial Strategy. *Rev. Econ. Stud.,* October 1983, *50*(4), pp. 707–22.

Srivastava, Alok. Techno-Commercial Aspects of Solar Energy in India. *Econ. Aff.,* July-September 1983, *28*(3), pp. 768–73. **[G: India]**

Sylves, Richard T. National Politics and the Solar Energy Transition. **In** *Rich, D., et al., eds.,* 1983, pp. 49–75. **[G: U.S.]**

Tandon, Pankaj. Rivalry and the Excessive Allocation of Resources to Research. *Bell J. Econ. (See Rand J. Econ. after 4/85),* Spring 1983, *14*(1), pp. 152–65.

Tassey, Gregory. Competitive Strategies and Performance in Technology-Based Industries. *J. Econ. Bus.,* 1983, *35*(1), pp. 21–40. **[G: U.S.]**

Teubal, M. The Accumulation of Intangibles by High-Technology Firms. **In** *Macdonald, S.; Lamberton, D. M. and Mandeville, T., eds.,* 1983, pp. 56–74. **[G: Selected Countries]**

Thackray, Arnold. University–Industry Connections and Chemical Research: An Historical Perspective. **In** *National Science Foundation,* 1983, pp. 193–233. **[G: U.S.]**

Trigo, Eduardo; Piñeiro, Martín and Sábato, Jorge F. La cuestión tecnológica y la organización de la investigación agropecuaria en América Latina. (With English summary.) *Desarrollo Econ.,* April–June 1983, *23*(89), pp. 99–119. **[G: Latin America]**

Väyrynen, Raimo. Military R&D and Science Policy. *Int. Soc. Sci. J.,* 1983, *35*(1), pp. 61–79. **[G: U.S.; U.S.S.R.; France]**

Vernon, Raymond. Gone Are the Cash Cows of Yesteryear. **In** *Dickson, D. N., ed.,* 1983, pp. 467–76. **[G: U.S.]**

Wängborg, Manne. Some Problems of Measuring Military R&D. *Int. Soc. Sci. J.,* 1983, *35*(1), pp. 47–59. **[G: Selected MDCs]**

Waterson, Michael and Lopez, Arcesio. The Determinants of Research and Development Intensity in the U.K. *Appl. Econ.,* June 1983, *15*(3), pp. 379–91. **[G: U.K.]**

Whyte, William Foote. The Farming Systems Research Approach: The Rediscovery of Peasant Rationality. **In** *Whyte, W. F. and Boynton, D., eds.,* 1983, pp. 154–63.

Whyte, William Foote. Toward New Systems of Agricultural Research and Development. **In** *Whyte, W. F. and Boynton, D., eds.,* 1983, pp. 164–93. **[G: Guatemala; Honduras]**

Wiggins, Steven N. The Impact of Regulation on Pharmaceutical Research Expenditures: A Dynamic Approach. *Econ. Inquiry,* January 1983, *21*(1), pp. 115–28. **[G: U.S.]**

Wionczek, Miguel S. Research and Development in Pharmaceuticals: Mexico. *World Devel.,* March 1983, *11*(3), pp. 243–50. **[G: Mexico]**

Yon, B. Structures des filières et stratégies des firmes. (With English summary.) *Écon. Soc.,* May 1983, *17*(5), pp. 823–37. **[G: France]**

630 Industry Studies

6300 General

Akrasanee, Narongchai. ASEAN–Japan Trade and Development: A Synthesis. **In** *Akrasanee, N., ed.,* 1983, pp. 1–35. **[G: ASEAN; Japan]**

Alburo, Florian A. Philippine–Japanese Investment Relations: A Tentative Assessment. *Philippine Econ. J.,* 198, *22*(1), pp. 29–45. **[G: Philippines; Japan]**

Anthony, Douglas. The Small Firm: Japan. **In** *Storey, D. J., ed.,* 1983, pp. 46–83. **[G: Japan]**

Attia, N. Le salaire, Miroir de la spécificité industrielle. (The Wage Mirror of the Industrial Specificity. With English summary.) *Écon. Soc.,* March–April 1983, *17*(3–4), pp. 691–718. **[G: France]**

Auerbach, Alan J. Corporate Taxation in the United States. *Brookings Pap. Econ. Act.,* 1983, (2), pp. 451–513. **[G: U.S.]**

Balassa, Bela. Industrial Prospects and Policies in the Developed Countries. **In** *[Giersch, H.],* 1983, pp. 257–78. **[G: OECD; LDCs]**

Balassa, Bela. Trade Policy in the 1980s: New Issues in the 1980s: Comment. **In** *Cline W. R., ed.,* 1983, pp. 711–22.

Ballantine, John W. Using Labor Market Information to Evaluate Industrial Performance. *J. Econ. Issues,* December 1983, *17*(4), pp. 1011–34. **[G: U.S.]**

Barrow, Christine. Ownership and Control of Resources in Barbados: 1834 to the Present. *Soc. Econ. Stud.,* September 1983, *32*(3), pp. 83–120. **[G: Barbados]**

Bates, Timothy. The Potential for Black Business: A Comment. *Rev. Black Polit. Econ.,* Winter 1983, *12*(2), pp. 237–40. **[G: U.S.]**

Beebe, Jack H. and Haltmaier, Jane. Disaggregation and the Labor Productivity Index. *Rev. Econ. Statist.*, August 1983, *65*(3), pp. 487–91.

van den Bosch, Frans A. J. and Petersen, Carel. An Explanation of the Growth of Social Security Disability Transfers. *De Economist*, 1983, *131* (1), pp. 65–79. **[G: Netherlands]**

Buchele, Robert. Economic Dualism and Employment Stability. *Ind. Relat.*, Fall 1983, *22*(3), pp. 410–18. **[G: U.S.]**

Capros, P.; Ladoux, N. and Outrequin, Ph. Prix de l'énergie et comportement des industriels. (Energy Prices and Manufacturers' Behaviour. With English summary.) *Écon. Soc.*, December 1983, *17*(12), pp. 1977–2011. **[G: OECD]**

de Castillo, J. Reestructuraciones sectoriales y regionales en la crisis. (Sectorial and Regional Restructurizations on the Crisis. With English summary.) *Écon. Soc.*, September–October–November 1983, *17*(9–10–11), pp. 1551–68.

Chappell, Henry W., Jr.; Marks, William H. and Park, Imkoo. Measuring Entry Barriers Using a Switching Regression Model of Industry Profitability. *Southern Econ. J.*, April 1983, *49*(4), pp. 991–1001. **[G: U.S.]**

Charmes, Jacques. Comment mesurer la contribution du secteur non structuré à la production nationale dans les pays du tiers monde? (With English summary.) *Rev. Income Wealth*, December 1983, *29*(4), pp. 429–44. **[G: Tunisia; Nigeria]**

Cima, Ján. Step by Step along the Path of Savings. *Czech. Econ. Digest.*, 1983, (8), pp. 69–81. **[G: Czechoslovakia]**

Cohen, Cynthia Fryer. The Impact on Women of Proposed Changes in the Private Pension System: A Simulation. *Ind. Lab. Relat. Rev.*, January 1983, *36*(2), pp. 258–70. **[G: U.S.]**

Colayco, Rufo. Opportunities for new Directions in Philippine–Japanese Trade. *Philippine Econ. J.*, 198, *22*(1), pp. 46–52. **[G: U.S.; W. Germany]**

Cordes, Joseph J. and Sheffrin, Steven M. Estimating the Tax Advantage of Corporate Debt. *J. Finance*, March 1983, *38*(1), pp. 95–105. **[G: U.S.]**

Cotta, Alain. Investissement industriel et croissance de l'économie française. (Industrial Investment and French Economic Growth. With English summary.) *Revue Écon.*, July 1983, *34*(4), pp. 691–731. **[G: France]**

Crespo, M. García and Flores, F. Aspectos espaciales de la crisis. (Spatial Aspects of the Crisis. With English summary.) *Écon. Soc.*, September–October–November 1983, *17*(9–10–11), pp. 1569–93. **[G: Spain]**

Cross, Michael. The Small Firm: The United Kingdom. **In** *Storey, D. J., ed.*, 1983, pp. 84–119. **[G: U.K.]**

Crossier, Luis Carlos. The Industrial Sector. **In** *Sampedro, J. L. and Payno, J. A., eds.*, 1983, pp. 224–41. **[G: Spain; EEC]**

Crowley, P. T.; O'Mara, L. P. and Campbell, R. Inport Quotas, Resource Development and Intersectoral Adjustment. *Australian Econ. Pap.*, December 1983, *22*(41), pp. 384–410. **[G: Australia]**

Cuadrado Roura, J. R. Crisis industrial y cambios technológicos. Consideraciones desde una óptica espacial. (Industrial Crisis and Technological Changes in the Work Division. Its Reasoning from a Spanish Point of View. With English summary.) *Écon. Soc.*, September–October–November 1983, *17*(9–10–11), pp. 1671–99.

Davis, William M. Collective Bargaining in 1983: A Crowded Agenda. *Mon. Lab. Rev.*, January 1983, *106*(1), pp. 3–16. **[G: U.S.]**

Deaglio, Mario. L'economia capitalista in mezzo al guado. (The Capitalist Economy in Deep Water. With English summary.) *L'Impresa*, 1983, *25*(6), pp. 41–46. **[G: OECD]**

Deardorff, Alan V. and Stern, Robert M. The Economic Effects of Complete Elimination of Post-Tokyo Round Tariffs: Reply. **In** *Cline W. R., ed.*, 1983, pp. 724. **[G: Selected Countries]**

Deardorff, Alan V. and Stern, Robert M. The Economic Effects of Complete Elimination of Post-Tokyo Round Tariffs. **In** *Cline W. R., ed.*, 1983, pp. 673–710. **[G: Selected Countries]**

Deardorff, Alan V. and Stern, Robert M. The Effects of Domestic Tax/Subsidies and Import Tariffs on the Structures of Protection in the United States, United Kingdom and Japan. **In** *Black, J. and Winters, L. A., eds.*, 1983, pp. 43–64. **[G: U.K.; U.S.; Japan]**

DeFina, Robert H. Unions, Relative Wages, and Economic Efficiency. *J. Lab. Econ.*, October 1983, *1*(4), pp. 408–29. **[G: U.S.]**

Donges, Juergen B. Re-appraisal of Foreign Trade Strategies for Industrial Development. **In** *[Giersch, H.]*, 1983, pp. 279–301. **[G: LDCs]**

Droucopoulos, Vassilis. International Big Business Revisited: On the Size and Growth of the World's Largest Firms. *Managerial Dec. Econ.*, December 1983, *4*(4), pp. 244–52. **[G: Global]**

Dyson, Kenneth. Industrial Crisis: The Cultural, Ideological and Structural Context. **In** *Dyson, K. and Wilks, S., eds.*, 1983, pp. 26–66. **[G: U.S.; W. Europe]**

Edmonds, Martin. Market Ideology and Corporate Power: The United States. **In** *Dyson, K. and Wilks, S., eds.*, 1983, pp. 67–101. **[G: U.S.]**

Esposito, Richard and Shipp, Kenneth. Industry Diffusion Indexes for Average Weekly Hours. *Mon. Lab. Rev.*, May 1983, *106*(5), pp. 33–36. **[G: U.S.]**

Esser, Josef; Fach, Wolfgang and Dyson, Kenneth. 'Social Market' and Modernization Policy: West Germany. **In** *Dyson, K. and Wilks, S., eds.*, 1983, pp. 102–27. **[G: W. Germany]**

Feldman, Stanley J. Industry Analysis and Investment Decision-Making under Conditions of Uncertainty. *Managerial Dec. Econ.*, September 1983, *4*(3), pp. 193–207. **[G: U.S.]**

Freudenberger, Herman H. An Industrial Momentum Achieved in the Habsburg Monarchy. *J. Europ. Econ. Hist.*, Fall 1983, *12*(2), pp. 339–50. **[G: Austria; E. Europe]**

Frey, Luigi. Census Developments and Labour Market Analyses. *Rev. Econ. Cond. Italy*, June 1983, (2), pp. 223–47. **[G: Italy]**

Fulco, Lawrence J. Recent Productivity Measures Depict Growth Patterns since 1980. *Mon. Lab. Rev.*, December 1983, *106*(12), pp. 45–48. **[G: U.S.]**

Fullerton, Don. Transition Losses of Partially Mobile Industry-Specific Capital. *Quart. J. Econ.*, February 1983, *98*(1), pp. 107–25. **[G: U.S.]**

Gaspard, Michel and Tahar, Gabriel. Investissement et baisse de la durée hebdomadaire du travail: réflexions autour d'un modèle sectoriel. (With English summary.) *Rev. Econ. Ind.*, 3rd Trimester 1983, (25), pp. 1–20. **[G: France]**

Gollop, Frank M. and Jorgenson, Dale W. Sectoral Measures of Labor Cost for the United States, 1948–1978. **In** *Triplett, J. E., ed.*, 1983, pp. 185–235. **[G: U.S.]**

Gomberg, Ia. and Sushkina, L. Basic Directions of Wage Differentiation in Industry. *Prob. Econ.*, March 1983, *25*(11), pp. 36–50. **[G: U.S.S.R.]**

Gorlin, Alice C. and Doane, David P. Plan Fulfillment and Growth in Soviet Ministries. *J. Compar. Econ.*, December 1983, *7*(4), pp. 415–31. **[G: U.S.S.R.]**

Granick, David. The Ministry and the Ratchet: Response to Keren. *J. Compar. Econ.*, December 1983, *7*(4), pp. 432–43. **[G: E. Germany; U.S.S.R.]**

Grilli, Enzo R. Il deficit pubblico spiazza le imprese. (The Public Spending Deficit Wrong Foots Companies. With English summary.) *L'Impresa,* 1983, *25*(6), pp. 25–28. **[G: Italy]**

Guarini, Renato. The Census as a Means for Knowing about Productive Activity: Its Validity and Limits. *Rev. Econ. Cond. Italy,* June 1983, (2), pp. 327–43. **[G: Italy]**

Hamilton, Clive. Capitalist Industrialization in the Four Little Tigers of East Asia. **In** *Limqueco, P. and McFarlane, B., eds.*, 1983, pp. 137–80. **[G: Korea; Taiwan; Hong Kong; Singapore]**

Hare, Paul. China's System of Industrial Economic Planning. **In** *Feuchtwang, S. and Hussain, A., eds.*, 1983, pp. 185–223. **[G: China]**

Hatch, James; Wynant, Larry and Grant, Mary Jane. Federal Lending Programs for Small Business: No Longer Needed? *Can. Public Policy,* September 1983, *9*(3), pp. 362–73. **[G: Canada]**

Hayton, K. Community Business in Scotland. *Reg. Stud.*, June 1983, *17*(3), pp. 204–08. **[G: U.K.]**

Henderson, J. Vernon. Industrial Bases and City Sizes. *Amer. Econ. Rev.*, May 1983, *73*(2), pp. 164–68.

Hirschberg, Joseph G. and Aigner, Dennis J. An Analysis of Commercial and Industrial Customer Response to Time-of-Use Rates. *Energy J.*, Supplement 1983, *4*, pp. 103–26. **[G: U.S.]**

Honko, Jaakko. Virheinvestointien anatomiaa: Yrityksen investointiprosessin kriittiset kohdat. (An Anatomy of Capital Investment Failures. With English summary.) *Liiketaloudellinen Aikak.*, 1983, *32*(2), pp. 99–123. **[G: Finland]**

Hopkins, Michael. Employment Trends in Developing Countries, 1960–80 and Beyond. *Int. Lab. Rev.*, July–August 1983, *122*(4), pp. 461–78. **[G: LDCs]**

House, William J. Occupational Segregation and Discriminatory Pay: The Position of Women in the Cyprus Labour Market. *Int. Lab. Rev.*, January–February 1983, *122*(1), pp. 75–93. **[G: Cyprus]**

Howenstine, Ned G. U.S. Affiliates of Foreign Companies: Operations in 1981. *Surv. Curr. Bus.*, November 1983, *63*(11), pp. 19–34. **[G: U.S.]**

Hull, Chris. The Small Firm: Federal Republic of Germany. **In** *Storey, D. J., ed.*, 1983, pp. 153–78. **[G: W. Germany]**

Inada, Koji. Economic Growth and Biased Technical Change: The Japanese Experience. **In** *[Yamada, I.]*, 1983, pp. 164–70. **[G: Japan]**

Irvine, F. Owen, Jr. The Real Rate of Interest, for Whom? *Appl. Econ.*, October 1983, *15*(5), pp. 635–48. **[G: U.S.]**

Jain, Asha and Barthwal, R. R. A Review of Empirical Studies on Price–Cost Margin. *Indian Econ. J.*, October–December 1983, *31*(2), pp. 43–52. **[G: U.S.; U.K.; Canada; Australia; India]**

Jenny, Frédéric and Weber, André-Paul. Aggregate Welfare Loss Due to Monopoly Power in the French Economy: Some Tentative Estimates. *J. Ind. Econ.*, December 1983, *32*(2), pp. 113–30. **[G: France]**

Jensen, Roger C.; Klein, Bruce P. and Sanderson, Lee M. Motion–Related Wrist Disorders Traced to Industries, Occupational Groups. *Mon. Lab. Rev.*, September 1983, *106*(9), pp. 13–16. **[G: U.S.]**

Johns, Brian. The Small Firm: Australia. **In** *Storey, D. J., ed.*, 1983, pp. 120–52. **[G: Australia]**

Jones, Derek C. Producer Co-operatives in Industrialised Western Economies. **In** *Kennedy, L., ed.*, 1983, *1980,* pp. 31–60. **[G: OECD]**

Jorgenson, Dale W. Modeling Production for General Equilibrium Analysis. *Scand. J. Econ.*, 1983, *85*(2), pp. 101–12. **[G: U.S.]**

Josefsson, Märtha and Örtengren, Johan. Crises, Inflation and Relative Prices: Investigations into Price Structure Stability in Swedish Industry 1913–80. **In** *Eliasson, G.; Sharefkin, M. and Ysander, B.-C., eds.*, 1983, pp. 53–110. **[G: Sweden]**

Junnelius, Christian. Strukturförändringar i mogna branscher. (Structural Change in Mature Industries. With English summary.) *Ekon. Samfundets Tidskr.*, 1983, *36*(4), pp. 133–37.

Juzzawalla, Meheroo and Cheah, Chee-Wah. Towards an Information Economy: The Case of Singapore. *Info. Econ. Policy,* 1983, *1*(2), pp. 161–76. **[G: Singapore]**

Keating, Michael. Relative Wages and the Changing Industrial Distribution of Employment in Australia. *Econ. Rec.*, December 1983, *59*(167), pp. 384–97. **[G: Australia]**

Keren, Michael. The Ministry and the Ratchet: A Rejoinder to Granick. *J. Compar. Econ.*, December 1983, *7*(4), pp. 444–48. **[G: E. Germany; U.S.S.R.]**

Kieschnick, Michael. Venture Capital and Urban Development. **In** *Barker, M., ed. (I)*, 1983, pp. 303–58. **[G: U.S.]**

Kouris, George. Energy Demand Elasticities in Industrialized Countries: A Survey. *Energy J.*, July 1983, *4*(3), pp. 73–94. **[G: OECD]**

Kwoka, John E., Jr. Monopoly, Plant, and Union Effects on Worker Wages. *Ind. Lab. Relat. Rev.*, January 1983, *36*(2), pp. 251–57. **[G: U.S.]**

Landefeld, J. Steven and Seskin, Eugene P. Plant and Equipment Expenditures, Quarters of 1983 and First and Second Quarters of 1984. *Surv.*

Curr. Bus., December 1983, *63*(12), pp. 19–24. [G: U.S.]

Lévy-Garboua, Louis. Les modes de consommation de quelques pays occidentaux: comparaison et lois d'évolution (1960–1980). (The Modes of Consumption of Some Western Countries: Comparison and Evolution (1960–1980). With English summary.) *Consommation*, January/March 1983, *30*(1), pp. 3–52. [G: EEC; U.S.]

Lindsey, N. Fostering New Enterprises: Enterprise Workshops in Birmingham. *Reg. Stud.*, June 1983, *17*(3), pp. 208–10. [G: U.K.]

Littler, Craig R. Japan and China. In *Feuchtwang, S. and Hussain, A., eds.*, 1983, pp. 121–47. [G: China; Japan]

Long, James E. and Link, Albert N. The Impact of Market Structure on Wages, Fringe Benefits, and Turnover. *Ind. Lab. Relat. Rev.*, January 1983, *36*(2), pp. 239–50. [G: U.S.]

Longva, Svein and Olsen, Øystein. Price Sensitivity of Energy Demand in Norwegian Industries. *Scand. J. Econ.*, 1983, *85*(1), pp. 17–36. [G: Norway]

Longva, Svein and Olsen, Øystein. Producer Behaviour in the MSG Model. In *Av, R., et al., eds.*, 1983, pp. 52–83. [G: Norway]

Lovell, C. A. Knox and Sickles, Robin C. Testing Efficiency Hypotheses in Joint Production: A Parametric Approach. *Rev. Econ. Statist.*, February 1983, *65*(1), pp. 51–58. [G: U.S.]

Macon, Janet. Number of Occupational Deaths Remained Essentially Unchanged in 1981. *Mon. Lab. Rev.*, May 1983, *106*(5), pp. 42–44. [G: U.S.]

Maillet, Pierre and Rollet, Philippe. La spécialisation industrielle dans la communauté européenne: des faits observés aux politiques nécessaires. (Industrial Specialization within the European Economic Community: From Observed Facts to Necessary Policies. With English summary.) *Rivista Int. Sci. Econ. Com.*, March 1983, *30*(3), pp. 244–67. [G: EEC]

Maki, Dennis R. The Effects of Unions and Strikes on the Rate of Growth of Total Factor Productivity in Canada. *Appl. Econ.*, February 1983, *15*(1), pp. 29–41. [G: Canada]

Mark, Jerome A. and Waldorf, William H. Multifactor Productivity: A New BLS Measure. *Mon. Lab. Rev.*, December 1983, *106*(12), pp. 3–15. [G: U.S.]

Markwalder, Don. A Response to Timothy Bates' Comment [The Potential for Black Business]. *Rev. Black Polit. Econ.*, Winter 1983, *12*(2), pp. 241–42. [G: U.S.]

Martin, Stephen. Vertical Relationships and Industrial Performance. *Quart. Rev. Econ. Bus.*, Spring 1983, *23*(1), pp. 6–18. [G: U.S.]

Matis, Herbert. Disintegration and Multi-national Enterprises in Central Europe during the Post-war Years (1918–23). In *Teichova, A. and Cottrell, P. L., eds.*, 1983, pp. 72–96. [G: Central Europe]

McElroy, Katherine Maddox; Siegfried, John J. and Sweeney, George H. The Incidence of Price Changes in the U.S. Economy. In *Craven, J. V., ed.*, 1983, *1982*, pp. 243–66.

Mendizabal Gorostiaga, A. La crisis económica: su incidencia en el País Vasco. (The Economic Crisis: Its Incidence in the Basque Country. With English summary.) *Écon. Soc.*, September–October–November 1983, *17*(9–10–11), pp. 1595–1609. [G: Spain]

Millerd, Frank W. Canadian Urban Industrial Growth from 1961 to 1971. *Growth Change*, January 1983, *14*(1), pp. 20–26. [G: Canada]

Moyer, R. Charles and Chatfield, Robert. Market Power and Systematic Risk. *J. Econ. Bus.*, 1983, *35*(1), pp. 123–30. [G: U.S.]

Niemi, Albert W., Jr. Gross State Product and Productivity in the Southeast, 1950–80. *Growth Change*, April 1983, *14*(2), pp. 3–8. [G: U.S.]

Northrup, Herbert R. and Greis, Theresa Diss. The Decline in Average Annual Hours Worked in the United States, 1947–1979. *J. Lab. Res.*, Spring 1983, *4*(2), pp. 95–113. [G: U.S.]

Nyitrai, Vera. Industrial Structure and Structural Change in Hungary. *Acta Oecon.*, 1983, *31*(3–4), pp. 175–95. [G: Hungary]

Oi, Walter Y. Heterogeneous Firms and the Organization of Production. *Econ. Inquiry*, April 1983, *21*(2), pp. 147–71.

Olson, Mancur. The Ideal Environment for Nuturing Growth. In *Federal Reserve Bank of Atlanta*, 1983, pp. 3–13. [G: U.S.]

Ooghe, Hubert and De Groote, Wilfried. Bepaling van de sectoriële invloed op de financiële structuur van ondernemingen bij middel van clusteranalyse. (With English summary.) *Cah. Écon. Bruxelles*, 1983, *97*(1), pp. 61–74. [G: Belgium]

Pearce, Robert D. Industrial Diversification amongst the World's Leading Multinational Enterprises. In *Casson, M., ed.*, 1983, pp. 140–79. [G: OECD]

Personick, Valerie A. The Job Outlook through 1995: Industry Output and Employment Projections. *Mon. Lab. Rev.*, November 1983, *106*(11), pp. 24–36. [G: U.S.]

Petrakov, N. Ia. On Reflecting Relative Planned Inputs in the Price System. *Matekon*, Fall 1983, *20*(1), pp. 3–28. [G: U.S.S.R.]

Phipps, A. J. Australian Unemployment: Some Evidence from Industry Labour Demand Functions. *Australian Econ. Pap.*, December 1983, *22*(41), pp. 333–44. [G: Australia]

Plaut, Steven E. 'Trade Shocks' in Economies Importing Only Intermediate Goods. *Europ. Econ. Rev.*, May 1983, *21*(3), pp. 363–79. [G: Netherlands; Norway; U.K.]

Price, Robert and Bain, George Sayers. Union Growth in Britain: Retrospect and Prospect. *Brit. J. Ind. Relat.*, March 1983, *21*(1), pp. 46–68. [G: U.K.]

Pullen, M. J. and Proops, J. L. R. The North Staffordshire Regional Economy: An Input–Output Assessment. *Reg. Stud.*, June 1983, *17*(3), pp. 191–200. [G: U.K.]

Quinn, James Brian. U.S. Industrial Strategy: What Directions Should It Take? *Sloan Manage. Rev.*, Summer 1983, *24*(4), pp. 3–21. [G: U.S.; EEC; Japan]

v. Rabenau, K. Trade Policies and Industrialization in a Developing Country: The Case of West Malaysia. In *Lim, D., ed.*, 1983, *1976*, pp. 257–76. [G: Malaysia]

Rey, Guido M. Italy of Censuses. *Rev. Econ. Cond. Italy*, June 1983, (2), pp. 193–221. [G: Italy]

Riche, Richard W.; Hecker, Daniel E. and Burgan, John U. High Technology Today and Tomorrow: A Small Slice of the Employment Pie. *Mon. Lab. Rev.*, November 1983, *106*(11), pp. 50–58. [G: U.S.]

Ruben, George. Collective Bargaining in 1982: Results Dictated by Economy. *Mon. Lab. Rev.*, January 1983, *106*(1), pp. 28–37. [G: U.S.]

Ruggie, John Gerard. Political Structure and Change in the International Economic Order: The North–South Dimension. In *Ruggie, J. G., ed.*, 1983, pp. 423–87. [G: LDCs; MDCs]

Semyonov, Moshe and Scott, Richard Ira. Industrial Shifts, Female Employment, and Occupational Differentiation: A Dynamic Model for American Cities, 1960–1970. *Demography*, May 1983, *20*(2), pp. 163–76. [G: U.S.]

Shaffer, Ron E. A Test of the Differences in Export Base Multipliers in Expanding and Contracting Economies. *Reg. Sci. Persp.*, 1983, *13*(2), pp. 61–74. [G: U.S.]

Sipek, Kira. Eléments de mesure de la rigidité structurelle des secteurs industriels à la diffusion des innovations. (With English summary.) *Rev. Econ. Ind.*, 4th Trimester 1983, (26), pp. 34–51. [G: France]

Talamona, Mario. Significato e problemi dell'innovazione nelle piccole e medie imprese. (Significance and Problems in Small and Medium Firms. With English summary.) *Giorn. Econ.*, March-April 1983, *42*(3–4), pp. 131–51. [G: EEC]

Thomspon, James H. and Leyden, Dennis R. The Small Firm: The United States of America. In *Storey, D. J., ed.*, 1983, pp. 7–45. [G: U.S.]

Tishler, Asher. The Industrial and Commercial Demand for Electricity under Time-of-Use Pricing. *J. Econometrics*, December 1983, *23*(3), pp. 369–84. [G: U.S.]

Trebilcock, C. Comment [Concentration and the Finance of Austrian Industrial Combines, 1880–1914] [Disintegration and Multi-national Enterprises in Central Europe during the Post-war Years (1918–23)]. In *Teichova, A. and Cottrell, P. L., eds.*, 1983, pp. 96–100. [G: Central Europe; Austria]

Troncoso, Carlos Morales, et al. Small- and Medium-sized Companies in the Exportation of Manufactured Goods: The Situation in Mexico. In *Czinkota, M. R., ed. (II)*, 1983, pp. 143–54. [G: Mexico]

Urquhart, Michael A. and Hewson, Marillyn A. Unemployment Continued to Rise in 1982 as Recession Deepened. *Mon. Lab. Rev.*, February 1983, *106*(2), pp. 3–12. [G: U.S.]

Veall, Michael R. Industrial Electricity Demand and the Hopkinson Rate: An Application of the Extreme Value Distribution. *Bell J. Econ. (See Rand J. Econ. after 4/85)*, Autumn 1983, *14*(2), pp. 427–40. [G: Canada]

Wabe, J. Stuart and Gutierrez-Camara, José L. Capital Utilisation, Capital Intensity and Factor Productivity: A Comparison of Factories in Developing and Industrialised Countries. *J. Econ. Stud.*, 1983, *10*(3), pp. 3–11. [G: Selected Countries]

Wagner, Adolf. Wirkungen einer Sozialabgabenbemessung nach Wertschöpfungsgrössen statt nach Arbeitskosten. (Effects of Employers' Social Security Contributions if Based Not on Labour Cost but on Value Added. With English summary.) *Ifo-Studien*, 1983, *29*(4), pp. 255–71. [G: W. Germany]

Wilks, Stephen. Liberal State and Party Competition: Britain. In *Dyson, K. and Wilks, S., eds.*, 1983, pp. 128–60. [G: U.K.]

Wilks, Stephen and Dyson, Kenneth. The Character and Economic Context of Industrial Crises. In *Dyson, K. and Wilks, S., eds.*, 1983, pp. 1–25. [G: U.S.; W. Europe]

Williams, Daniel G. Regional Development as Determined by Alternative Regional Goals. *Growth Change*, July 1983, *14*(3), pp. 23–37. [G: U.S.]

Woodward, John T.; Seskin, Eugene P. and Landefeld, J. Steven. Plant and Equipment Expenditures, 1983. *Surv. Curr. Bus.*, January 1983, *63*(1), pp. 31–33. [G: U.S.]

Zanetti, Giovanni. The Industrial Structure and Efficiency of the Italian Economy: Trends and Planning Aspects. *Rev. Econ. Cond. Italy*, June 1983, (2), pp. 249–300. [G: Italy]

631 Industry Studies: Manufacturing

6310 General

Alam, Kazi Firoz. The Dividend Behavior of Companies in the U.K. Manufacturing Industry. *METU*, 1983, *10*(2), pp. 155–77. [G: U.K.]

Alam, M. Shahid. Efficiency Differentials Favouring Resource-Based Industries. *J. Devel. Econ.*, December 1983, *13*(3), pp. 361–66. [G: LDCs]

Allègre, C. Productivité du travail, rendement et facteurs endogénes de rentabilité: la conception du produit: Étude de cas dans les industries de la forme. (Labour Productivity, Time Rates and Endogenous Factors of the Firm's Efficiency: The Design of the Product. With English summary.) *Écon. Soc.*, March–April 1983, *17*(3–4), pp. 549–78. [G: France]

Allen, P. T. and Stephenson, G. M. Inter-Group Understanding and Size of Organisation. *Brit. J. Ind. Relat.*, November 1983, *21*(3), pp. 312–29. [G: U.K.]

Allen, Robert F. Efficiency, Market Power, and Profitability in American Manufacturing. *Southern Econ. J.*, April 1983, *49*(4), pp. 933–40. [G: U.S.]

Alpert, William T. Manufacturing Workers Private Wage Supplements: A Simultaneous Equations Approach. *Appl. Econ.*, June 1983, *15*(3), pp. 363–78. [G: U.S.]

Apte, P. C. Substitution among Energy and Non-energy Inputs in Selected Indian Manufacturing Industries: An Econometric Analysis. *Indian Econ. J.*, October–December 1983, *31*(2), pp. 71–90. [G: India]

Arestis, P.; Karakitsos, Elias and Sarantis, N. Real Money Balances as a Factor of Production in the United Kingdom. *Rivista Int. Sci. Econ. Com.*,

December 1983, *30*(12), pp. 1171–86. [G: U.K.]

Aslam, Naheed. Level of Real Wages and Labour Productivity in the Manufacturing Sector of the Punjab. *Pakistan Devel. Rev.*, Winter 1983, *22*(4), pp. 283–99. [G: Pakistan]

Babu, V. G. and Vani, K. V. Linear Estimation of the C.E.S. Function—Indian Manufacturing Sector, 1949–'58 and 1959–'66. *Indian Econ. J.*, October–December 1983, *31*(2), pp. 91–95. [G: India]

Bade, Franz-Josef. Locational Behaviour and the Mobility of Firms in West Germany. *Urban Stud.*, August 1983, *20*(3), pp. 279–97. [G: W. Germany]

Baily, Martin Neil. 'Comparing Productivity Growth: An Exploration of French and U.S. Industrial and Firm Data' by Z. Griliches and J. Mairesse: Comment. *Europ. Econ. Rev.*, March/April 1983, *21*(1/2), pp. 121–23. [G: U.S.; France]

Baldwin, Michael A.; Hadid, M. and Phillips, G. D. A. The Estimation and Testing of a System of Demand Equations for the UK. *Appl. Econ.*, February 1983, *15*(1), pp. 81–90. [G: U.K.]

Bautista, Romeo M. The "Turbulent World Economy" and Industrial Development Strategy in the Philippines. *Philippine Econ. J.*, 1983, *22*(2), pp. 130–36. [G: Philippine]

Beach, Charles M. and Balfour, Frederick S. Estimated Payroll Tax Incidence and Aggregate Demand for Labour in the United Kingdom. *Economica*, February 1983, *50*(197), pp. 35–48. [G: U.K.]

Bernanke, Ben S. On the Sources of Labor Productivity Variation in U.S. Manufacturing, 1947–1980. *Rev. Econ. Statist.*, May 1983, *65*(2), pp. 214–24.

Bharat-Ram, Vinay. Import Substitution, Exchange Rates and Growth in the Context of a Developing Economy. *Greek Econ. Rev.*, August 1983, *5*(2), pp. 147–57. [G: LDCs; India]

Bird, Peter J. W. N. Tests for a Threshold Effect in the Price–Cost Relationship. *Cambridge J. Econ.*, March 1983, *7*(1), pp. 37–53. [G: U.K.]

Bollard, Alan. Technology, Economic Change, and Small Firms. *Lloyds Bank Rev.*, January 1983, (147), pp. 42–56. [G: U.K.]

Brack, John and Cowling, Keith. Advertising and Labour Supply: Workweek and Workyear in U.S. Manufacturing Industries, 1919–76. *Kyklos*, 1983, *36*(2), pp. 285–303. [G: U.S.]

Browne, Lynn E. Can High Tech Save the Great Lake States? *New Eng. Econ. Rev.*, November/December 1983, pp. 19–33. [G: U.S.]

Bruch, Mathias. Sources of Financing of Small-Scale Manufacturers: A Micro-Analysis for Malaysia. *Singapore Econ. Rev.*, April 1983, *28*(1), pp. 21–33. [G: Malaysia]

Bruno, Michael. 'Comparing Productivity Growth: An Exploration of French and U.S. Industrial and Firm Data' by Z. Griliches and J. Mairesse: Comment. *Europ. Econ. Rev.*, March/April 1983, *21*(1/2), pp. 125–27. [G: U.S.; France]

Brush, Brian C. and Crane, Steven E. Industry Growth, Labor Compensation, and Labor's Share of Value Added in U.S. Manufacturing, 1967–1979. *Quart. Rev. Econ. Bus.*, Winter 1983, *23*(4), pp. 44–53. [G: U.S.]

Buckley, Peter J. and Enderwick, Peter. Comparative Pay Levels in Domestically-Owned and Foreign-Owned Plants in U.K.: Manufacturing-Evidence from the 1980 Workplace Industrial Relations Survey. *Brit. J. Ind. Relat.*, November 1983, *21*(3), pp. 395–400. [G: U.K.]

Cal, Vasco. The Industrial Sector. **In** *Sampedro, J. L. and Payno, J. A., eds.*, 1983, pp. 167–83. [G: Portugal; EEC]

Carlton, Dennis W. Equilibrium Fluctuations When Price and Delivery Lag Clear the Market. *Bell J. Econ. (See Rand J. Econ. after 4/85)*, Autumn 1983, *14*(2), pp. 562–72. [G: U.S.]

Carlton, Dennis W. The Location and Employment Choices of New Firms: An Econometric Model with Discrete and Continuous Endogenous Variables. *Rev. Econ. Statist.*, August 1983, *65*(3), pp. 440–49. [G: U.S.]

Cavoulacos, Panos and Caramanis, Michael C. Energy and Other Factor Input Demand in Greek Manufacturing, 1963–1975. *Greek Econ. Rev.*, August 1983, *5*(2), pp. 158–81. [G: Greece]

Cella, Guido. Politica di sostituzione delle importazioni industriali e competitività dell'economia italiana. (Import Substitution Policy and Competitiveness of the Italian Economy. With English summary.) *Giorn. Econ.*, March-April 1983, *42*(3–4), pp. 215–38. [G: Italy]

Chai, Joseph. Industrial Co-operation between China and Hong Kong. **In** *Youngson, A. J., ed.*, 1983, pp. 104–55. [G: China; Hong Kong]

Chakrabarti, Alok K. and Burton, Jonathan. Technological Characteristics of Mergers and Acquisitions in the 1970s in Manufacturing Industries in the U.S. *Quart. Rev. Econ. Bus.*, Autumn 1983, *23*(3), pp. 81–90. [G: U.S.]

Chandler, Alfred D., Jr. The Place of the Modern Industrial Enterprise in Three Economies. **In** *Teichova, A. and Cottrell, P. L., eds.*, 1983, pp. 3–29. [G: U.S.; U.K.; Germany]

Charney, Alberta H. Intraurban Manufacturing Location Decisions and Local Tax Differentials. *J. Urban Econ.*, September 1983, *14*(2), pp. 184–205. [G: U.S.]

Choi, Dosoung and Philippatos, George C. Financial Consequences of Antitrust Enforcement. *Rev. Econ. Statist.*, August 1983, *65*(3), pp. 501–06. [G: U.S.]

Christensen, Sandra and Maki, Dennis R. The Wage Effect of Compulsory Union Membership. *Ind. Lab. Relat. Rev.*, January 1983, *36*(2), pp. 230–38. [G: U.S.]

Ciborra, Claudio U. Markets, Bureaucracies, and Groups in the Information Society: An Institutional Appraisal of the Impacts of Information Technology. *Info. Econ. Policy*, 1983, *1*(2), pp. 145–60. [G: Italy]

Ciscel, David H. and Tuckman, Howard P. Plant Scale and Multiplant Production as Determinants of Industrial Concentration. *J. Behav. Econ.*, Winter 1983, *12*(2), pp. 1–16. [G: U.S.]

Clarke, R. and Davies, S. W. Aggregate Concentration, Market Concentration and Diversification. *Econ. J.*, March 1983, *93*(369), pp. 182–92. [G: U.K.]

Common, Michael S. The IIED Industrial Energy Conservation Programme: An Order of Magnitude Assessment. *Energy Econ.*, October 1983, *5*(4), pp. 232–36. **[G: U.K.]**

Conrad, Klaus. Cost Prices and Partially Fixed Factor Proportions in Energy Substitution. *Europ. Econ. Rev.*, May 1983, *21*(3), pp. 299–312. **[G: U.S.]**

Cooper, Richard N. Is Trade Deindustrializing America? A Medium-Term Perspective: Comments and Discussion. *Brookings Pap. Econ. Act.*, 1983, (1), pp. 162–71. **[G: U.S.]**

Correa, Hector. The Firm's Administrative Structure: Theory, Measurement and Applications to Growth Accounting and Income Distribution. *Empirical Econ.*, 1983, *8*(2), pp. 93–109. **[G: U.S.]**

Cowling, Keith. Excess Capacity and the Degree of Collusion: Oligopoly Behaviour in the Slump. *Manchester Sch. Econ. Soc. Stud.*, December 1983, *51*(4), pp. 341–59. **[G: U.K.]**

Creedy, John and Johnson, P. S. Firm Formation in Manufacturing Industry. *Appl. Econ.*, April 1983, *15*(2), pp. 177–85. **[G: U.K.]**

Daly, Maurice T. The Mobility of Manufacturing and Capital: Implications for Regional Development. **In** *Hamilton, F. E. I. and Linge, G. J. R., eds.*, 1983, pp. 399–421. **[G: Australia]**

Dargay, Joyce M. Energy Usage and Energy Prices in Swedish Manufacturing. **In** *Ysander, B.-C., ed.*, 1983, pp. 29–53. **[G: Sweden]**

Dargay, Joyce M. The Demand for Energy in Swedish Manufacturing Industries. *Scand. J. Econ.*, 1983, *85*(1), pp. 37–51.

Dargay, Joyce M. The Demand for Energy in Swedish Manufacturing. **In** *Ysander, B.-C., ed.*, 1983, pp. 57–128. **[G: Sweden]**

Desai, Padma and Martin, Ricardo. Efficiency Loss from Resource Misallocation in Soviet Industry. *Quart. J. Econ.*, August 1983, *98*(3), pp. 441–56. **[G: U.S.S.R.]**

Dhillon, Sharanjit Singh. Productivity Trends and Factor Substitutability in Manufacturing Sector in Karnataka. *Margin*, October 1983, *16*(1), pp. 37–46. **[G: India]**

Dickson, V. A. and McFetridge, D. G. Concentration, Unionization and the Distribution of Income in Canadian Manufacturing Industry: Comment. *Managerial Dec. Econ.*, December 1983, *4*(4), pp. 278–80. **[G: Canada]**

Dixon, Robert J. Industry Structure and the Speed of Price Adjustment. *J. Ind. Econ.*, September 1983, *32*(1), pp. 25–37. **[G: Australia]**

Dollery, Brian Edward. Some Evidence on the Goals of Firms in South African Manufacturing Industry. *J. Stud. Econ. Econometrics*, July 1983, (17), pp. 5–13. **[G: S. Africa]**

Dosi, Giovanni and Soete, L. Technology Gaps and Cost-based Adjustment: Some Explorations on the Determinants of International Competitiveness. *Metroecon.*, October 1983, *35*(3), pp. 197–222. **[G: OECD]**

Dragonette, Joseph E. Returns to Scale: Some Time-Series Evidence. *Eastern Econ. J.*, January–March 1983, *9*(1), pp. 23–27. **[G: U.S.]**

Driver, Ciaran. Import Substitution and the Work of the Sector Working Parties. *Appl. Econ.*, April 1983, *15*(2), pp. 165–76. **[G: U.K.]**

Eckstein, Susan and Hagopian, Frances. The Limits of Industrialization in the Less Developed World: Bolivia. *Econ. Develop. Cult. Change*, October 1983, *32*(1), pp. 63–95. **[G: Bolivia]**

Ehrenberg, Ronald G.; Danziger, Leif and San, Gee. Cost-of-Living Adjustment Clauses in Union Contracts: A Summary of Results. *J. Lab. Econ.*, July 1983, *1*(3), pp. 215–45. **[G: U.S.]**

Elliott, Ralph D. and Hawkins, Benjamin M. The Impact of Government Spending on the Level of Private Sector Strike Activity. *Atlantic Econ. J.*, July 1983, *11*(2), pp. 22–28. **[G: U.S.]**

Ellis, Michael. Supply-Side Linkage of Capacity Utilization and Labor Productivity: U.S. Manufacturing, 1954-1980. *Nebr. J. Econ. Bus.*, Winter, 1983, *22*(1), pp. 15–27. **[G: U.S.]**

Ellis, Michael. Supply-Side Linkage of Capacity Utilization and Labor Productivity: U.S. Manufacturing, 1954–1980. *Bus. Econ.*, May 1983, *18*(3), pp. 62–69. **[G: U.S.]**

Enderwick, Peter and Buckley, Peter J. The Determinants of Strike Activity in Foreign-Owned Plants: Inter-Industry Evidence from British Manufacturing Industry 1971–1973. *Managerial Dec. Econ.*, June 1983, *4*(2), pp. 83–88. **[G: U.K.]**

Epstein, Larry G. and Denny, Michael G. S. The Multivariate Flexible Accelerator Model: Its Empirical Restrictions and an Application to U.S. Manufacturing. *Econometrica*, May, 1983, *51*(3), pp. 647–74. **[G: U.S.]**

Esty, Daniel C. and Caves, Richard E. Market Structure and Political Influence: New Data on Political Expenditures, Activity, and Success. *Econ. Inquiry*, January 1983, *21*(1), pp. 24–38. **[G: U.S.]**

Evans, Kaye D.; Siegfried, John J. and Sweeney, George H. The Economic Cost of Suboptimal Manufacturing Capacity. *J. Bus.*, January 1983, *56*(1), pp. 55–76. **[G: U.S.]**

Ezhov, A. Improving the Mechanism of Planned Price Control. *Prob. Econ.*, May 1983, *26*(1), pp. 20–37. **[G: U.S.S.R.]**

Ferdows, K. Technology-Push Strategies for Manufacturing. *Tijdschrift Econ. Manage.*, 1983, *28*(2), pp. 125–37. **[G: EEC; U.S.; Australia]**

Fluet, Claude and Lefebvre, Pierre. Gains de productivité globale, prix relatifs et rémunération des facteurs dans les industries manufacturières au Québec. (Total Factor Productivity Growth, Relative Prices and Earnings in Quebec Manufacturing Industries. With English summary.) *L'Actual. Econ.*, December 1983, *59*(4), pp. 651–68. **[G: Canada]**

Follosco, Ceferino L. Philippine Industrial Development Strategies in the Eighties. *Philippine Econ. J.*, 1983, *22*(2), pp. 119–29. **[G: Philippine]**

Fornell, Claes and Robinson, William T. Industrial Organization and Consumer Satisfaction/Dissatisfaction. *J. Cons. Res.*, March 1983, *9*(4), pp. 403–12. **[G: U.S.]**

Fortune, J. N. Expectations, Capital Formation, Sales and Capacity Utilization. *Empirical Econ.*, 1983, *8*(3–4), pp. 177–86.

Fothergill, Stephen; Kitson, Michael and Monk, Sarah. The Impact of the New and Expanded Town Programmes on Industrial Location in Britain, 1960–78. *Reg. Stud.*, August 1983, *17*(4), pp. 251–60. [G: U.K.]

Fries, Harald. Structural Change and Industry Performance in Four Western European Countries. In *Eliasson, G.; Sharefkin, M. and Ysander, B.-C., eds.*, 1983, pp. 111–67. [G: Netherlands; Sweden; U.K.; W. Germany]

Gabel, H. Landis. The Role of Buyer Power in Oligopoly Models: An Empirical Study. *J. Econ. Bus.*, 1983, *35*(1), pp. 95–108. [G: U.S.]

Gan, Wee Beng. The Relationship between Market Concentration and Profitability in Malaysian Manufacturing Industries. In *Lim, D., ed.*, 1983, *1978*, pp. 89–98. [G: Malaysia]

Gibson, Katherine D. and Horvath, Ronald J. Global Capital and the Restructuring Crisis in Australian Manufacturing. *Econ. Geogr.*, April 1983, *59*(2), pp. 178–94. [G: Australia]

Gnes, Paolo. The Financial Structure and Financing of Firms: Developments and Prospects. *Rev. Econ. Cond. Italy*, June 1983, (2), pp. 301–23. [G: Italy]

Goddard, John B. Industrial Innovation and Regional Economic Development in Great Britain. In *Hamilton, F. E. I. and Linge, G. J. R., eds.*, 1983, pp. 255–77. [G: U.K.]

Goldar, Bishwanath. Productivity Trends in Indian Manufacturing Industry: 1951–1978. *Indian Econ. Rev.*, January–June 1983, *18*(1), pp. 73–99. [G: India]

Gort, Michael and Swanson, Eric V. Conglomerate Size and Competition between Large and Small Firms. *Antitrust Bull.*, Summer 1983, *28*(2), pp. 337–48. [G: U.S.]

Gowdy, John M. Industrial Demand for Natural Gas: Inter-Industry Variation in New York State. *Energy Econ.*, July 1983, *5*(3), pp. 171–77. [G: U.S.]

Gravelle, Jane G. Capital Income Taxation and Efficiency in the Allocation of Investment. *Nat. Tax J.*, September 1983, *36*(3), pp. 297–306. [G: U.S.]

Greenaway, David. Intra-Industry and Inter-Industry Trade in Switzerland. *Weltwirtsch. Arch.*, 1983, *119*(1), pp. 109–21. [G: Switzerland]

Greenaway, David. Patterns of Intra-industry Trade in the United Kingdom. In *Tharakan, P. K. M., ed.*, 1983, pp. 141–60. [G: U.K.]

Griliches, Zvi and Mairesse, Jacques. Comparing Productivity Growth: An Exploration of French and U.S. Industrial and Firm Data. *Europ. Econ. Rev.*, March/April 1983, *21*(1/2), pp. 89–119. [G: U.S.; France]

Grilli, Enzo R. and La Noce, Mauro. The Political Economy of Protection in Italy: Some Empirical Evidence. *Banca Naz. Lavoro Quart. Rev.*, June 1983, (145), pp. 143–61. [G: Italy]

Grua, Claudio and Varetto, Franco. Un'analisi "reale" della crisi della grande industria negli anni '70. (Profits and Cash Flows in Big Business during the Seventies. With English summary.) *L'Impresa*, 1983, *25*(5), pp. 43–51. [G: Italy]

Gupta, Vinod K. A Simultaneous Determination of Structure, Conduct and Performance in Canadian Manufacturing. *Oxford Econ. Pap.*, July 1983, *35*(2), pp. 281–301. [G: Canada]

Gurwitz, Aaron S. New York State's Economic Turnaround: Services or Manufacturing. *Fed. Res. Bank New York Quart. Rev.*, Autumn 1983, *8*(3), pp. 30–34. [G: U.S.]

Haig, Bryan D. and Cain, Neville G. Industrialization and Productivity: Australian Manufacturing in the 1920s and 1950s. *Exploration Econ. Hist.*, April 1983, *20*(2), pp. 183–98. [G: Australia]

Hall, William K. Survival Strategies in a Hostile Environment. In *Kantrow, A. M., ed.*, 1983, pp. 52–71. [G: U.S.]

Hankinson, G. A. and Rhys, J. M. W. Electricity Consumption, Electricity Intensity and Industrial Structure. *Energy Econ.*, July 1983, *5*(3), pp. 146–52. [G: U.S.]

Hannah, L. German Concerns in Eastern Europe: Commentary. In *Teichova, A. and Cottrell, P. L., eds.*, 1983, pp. 192–96. [G: Europe]

Harper, Carolyn and Field, Barry C. Energy Substitution in U.S. Manufacturing: A Regional Approach. *Southern Econ. J.*, October 1983, *50*(2), pp. 385–95. [G: U.S.]

Hartley, Keith and Lynk, Edward L. Labour Demand and Allocation in the U.K. Engineering Industry: Disaggregation, Structural Change and Defence Reviews. *Scot. J. Polit. Econ.*, February 1983, *30*(1), pp. 42–53. [G: U.K.]

Haudeville, Bernard. Echanges extérieurs, emploi et redéploiement industriel en France de 1974 à 1979. (With English summary.) *Rev. Econ. Ind.*, 3rd Trimester 1983, (25), pp. 21–37. [G: France]

Hayes, Robert H. Why Japanese Factories Work. In *Kantrow, A. M., ed.*, 1983, pp. 231–47. [G: Japan]

Heim, Carol E. Industrial Organization and Regional Development in Interwar Britain. *J. Econ. Hist.*, December 1983, *43*(4), pp. 931–52. [G: U.K.]

Hendricks, Wallace E. and Kahn, Lawrence M. Cost-of-Living Clauses in Union Contracts: Determinants and Effects. *Ind. Lab. Relat. Rev.*, April 1983, *36*(3), pp. 447–60. [G: U.S.]

Herroelen, W. Automation of Small Batch Production. *Tijdschrift Econ. Manage.*, 1983, *28*(2), pp. 139–63. [G: U.S.]

Herroelen, Willy and Lambrecht, Marc R. Management Aspects of Computerized Manufacturing. *Econ. Soc. Tijdschr.*, December 1983, *37*(6), pp. 723–43.

Hirschman, Charles. Ownership and Control in the Manufacturing Sector of West Malaysia. In *Lim, D., ed.*, 1983, *1971*, pp. 209–20. [G: Malaysia]

Hirschman, Charles. Ownership and Control in the Manufacturing Sector of West Malaysia: Reply. In *Lim, D., ed.*, 1983, pp. 222–24. [G: Malaysia]

Holin, S. and Prevot, M. An Application of the Multiobjective Programming to the French Industry. In *Hansen, P., ed.*, 1983, pp. 167–76. [G: France]

Hollander, Abraham. Concentration, Unionization and the Distribution of Income in Canadian Manufacturing Industry: Reply. *Managerial Dec.*

Econ., December 1983, *4*(4), pp. 281–82. **[G: Canada]**

Horwitz, Eva Christina. Price Elasticities in Swedish Foreign Trade. **In** *Eliasson, G.; Sharefkin, M. and Ysander, B.-C., eds.*, 1983, pp. 169–97. **[G: Sweden; Selected Countries]**

Hošková, Adéla. Uniform Principles for Evaluating the Economic Effect of International Specialization and Cooperation in Industry. *Soviet E. Europ. Foreign Trade*, Winter 1983–84, *19*(4), pp. 62–72.

Hughes, Helen. Capital Utilization in Manufacturing. *Finance Develop.*, March 1983, *20*(1), pp. 6–9. **[G: Malaysia; Philippines; Israel; Colombia]**

Ihamuotila, Jaakko. Cooperation from the Company Viewpoint. **In** *Möttölä, K.; Bykov, O. N. and Korolev, I. S., eds.*, 1983, pp. 110–21. **[G: U.S.S.R.; Finland]**

Ikeda, Katsuhiko and Doi, Noriyuki. The Performances of Merging Firms in Japanese Manufacturing Industry: 1964–75. *J. Ind. Econ.*, March 1983, *31*(3), pp. 257–66. **[G: Japan]**

James, John A. Structural Change in American Manufacturing, 1850–1890. *J. Econ. Hist.*, June 1983, *43*(2), pp. 433–59. **[G: U.S.]**

Jenne, C. A. and Cattell, R. K. Structural Change and Energy Efficiency in Industry. *Energy Econ.*, April 1983, *5*(2), pp. 114–23. **[G: U.K.]**

Johnson, P. S. New Manufacturing Firms in the U.K. Regions. *Scot. J. Polit. Econ.*, February 1983, *30*(1), pp. 75–79. **[G: U.K.]**

Johnston, Ron. The Control of Technological Change in Australia. **In** *Hill, S. and Johnston, R., eds.*, 1983, pp. 89–112. **[G: Australia]**

Jones, Evan. Industrial Structure and Labor Force Segmentation. *Rev. Radical Polit. Econ.*, Winter 1983, *15*(4), pp. 24–44. **[G: Australia]**

Jüttner, D. Johannes and Murray, John H. Notes and Numbers on Marx's Falling Rate of Profit. *Econ. Rec.*, December 1983, *59*(167), pp. 375–83. **[G: Australia]**

Kaufman, Bruce E. The Determinants of Strikes over Time and across Industries. *J. Lab. Res.*, Spring 1983, *4*(2), pp. 159–75. **[G: U.S.]**

Kawasaki, Seiichi; McMillan, John and Zimmermann, Klaus F. Inventories and Price Inflexibility. *Econometrica*, May, 1983, *51*(3), pp. 599–610. **[G: W. Germany]**

Keeble, David; Owens, Peter L. and Thompson, Chris. The Urban–Rural Manufacturing Shift in the European Community. *Urban Stud.*, November 1983, *20*(4), pp. 405–18. **[G: EEC]**

Kennedy, Charles and Thirlwall, Anthony P. Import and Export Ratios and the Dynamic Harrod Trade Multiplier: A Reply to McGregor and Swales [Import Penetration, Export Performance and Harrod's Trade Multiplier]. *Oxford Econ. Pap.*, March 1983, *35*(1), pp. 125–29.

Kipnis, Baruch A. and Meir, Avinoam. The Kibbutz Industrial System: A Unique Rural-industrial Community in Israel. **In** *Hamilton, F. E. I. and Linge, G. J. R., eds.*, 1983, pp. 463–84. **[G: Israel]**

Kohli, Harinder and Segura, Edilberto. Industrial Energy Conservation in Developing Countries. *Finance Develop.*, December 1983, *20*(4), pp. 28–31. **[G: LDCs]**

Kokkelenberg, Edward C. Interrelated Factor Demands Revisited. *Rev. Econ. Statist.*, May 1983, *65*(2), pp. 342–47. **[G: U.S.]**

Kovach, Kenneth A. and Millspaugh, Peter E. The Plant Closing Issue Arrives at the Bargaining Table. *J. Lab. Res.*, Fall 1983, *4*(4), pp. 367–74. **[G: U.S.]**

Krumm, Ronald J. Regional Wage Differentials, Fluctuations in Labor Demand, and Migration. *Int. Reg. Sci. Rev.*, June 1983, *8*(1), pp. 23–45.

Lall, Sanjaya and Mohammad, Sharif. Multinationals in Indian Big Business: Industrial Characteristics of Foreign Investments in a Heavily Regulated Economy. *J. Devel. Econ.*, Aug.–Oct. 1983, *13*(1–2), pp. 143–57. **[G: India]**

Lall, Sanjaya and Mohammed, Sharif. Technological Effort and Disembodied Technology Exports: An Econometric Analysis of Inter-Industry Variations in India. *World Devel.*, June 1983, *11*(6), pp. 527–35. **[G: India]**

Laumas, Prem S. and Williams, Martin. An Analysis of the Demand for Cash Balances by the Manufacturing Firms in a Developing Economy. *J. Devel. Econ.*, February/April 1983, *12*(1/2), pp. 169–82. **[G: India]**

Lawrence, Robert Z. Is Trade Deindustrializing America? A Medium-Term Perspective. *Brookings Pap. Econ. Act.*, 1983, (1), pp. 129–61. **[G: U.S.]**

Lawrence, Robert Z. The Myth of U.S. Deindustrialization. *Challenge*, November/December 1983, *26*(5), pp. 12–21. **[G: U.S.; OECD]**

Lee, Chung H. International Production of the United States and Japan in Korean Manufacturing Industries: A Comparative Study. *Weltwirtsch. Arch.*, 1983, *119*(4), pp. 744–53. **[G: Japan; S. Korea; U.S.]**

Leigh, J. Paul. Risk Preference and the Interindustry Propensity to Strike. *Ind. Lab. Relat. Rev.*, January 1983, *36*(2), pp. 271–85. **[G: U.S.]**

Lim, David. Actual, Desired and Full Levels of Capital Utilization in Malaysian Manufacturing. **In** *Lim, D., ed.*, 1983, *1977*, pp. 81–88. **[G: Malaysia]**

Lim, David. Scale and Technology in Malaysian Manufacturing. **In** *Lim, D., ed.*, 1983, pp. 153–61. **[G: Malaysia]**

Lim, David. Tax Incentives and Resource Utilization in Peninsular Malaysian Manufacturing. **In** *Lim, D., ed.*, 1983, *1981*, pp. 277–87. **[G: Malaysia]**

Lim, David. Wages and Work Conditions, and the Effects of Foreign Investment and the Separation of Ownership from Management on Them: A Study of Malaysian Manufacturing. **In** *Lim, D., ed.*, 1983, pp. 162–80. **[G: Malaysia]**

Lindmark, Leif. The Small Firm: Sweden. **In** *Storey, D. J., ed.*, 1983, pp. 179–212. **[G: Sweden]**

Link, Albert N. Alternative Sources of Technology: An Analysis of Induced Innovations. *Managerial Dec. Econ.*, March 1983, *4*(1), pp. 40–43. **[G: U.S.]**

Lusa, Erna. Inflazione e bilanci delle imprese. (Inflation and Businesses' Financial Statement. With English summary.) *Bancaria*, October 1983, *39*(10), pp. 968–85. **[G: Italy]**

Lyckeborg, Håkan. A Box-Jenkins Approach to Short-term Energy Consumption Forecasting in Sweden: Univariate Models. **In** *Sohlman, A. M., ed.*, 1983, pp. 98–123. **[G: Sweden]**

Lynk, Edward L. Long-run Constraints to Industrial Development in India: KLEM Substitution/Complementarity. *Indian Econ. J.*, October–December 1983, *31* (2), pp. 27–42. **[G: India]**

Maizels, A. The Industrialisation of the Developing Countries. **In** *[Saunders, C. T.]*, 1983, pp. 29–50. **[G: LDCs]**

Mangan, John and Regan, Philip. A Note on Organisational Slack and Market Power in Australian Manufacturing. *Australian Econ. Pap.*, December 1983, *22* (41), pp. 356–63. **[G: Australia]**

Marsden, John S. and Hollander, G. Floating Exchange Rates, Inflation and Selective Protectionism: Their Effects on the Competitiveness of Australian Industry. **In** *Black, J. and Winters, L. A., eds.*, 1983, pp. 92–129. **[G: Australia]**

Maskus, Keith E. Evidence on Shifts in the Determinants of the Structure of U.S. Manufacturing Foreign Trade, 1958–76. *Rev. Econ. Statist.*, August 1983, *65* (3), pp. 415–22.

Matits, Ágnes and Temesi, József. Changes in Economic Regulators and Enterprise Reactions. *Acta Oecon.*, 1983, *31* (3–4), pp. 197–208. **[G: Hungary]**

Mayes, David G. Industrial Production. *Nat. Inst. Econ. Rev.*, November 1983, (106), pp. 49–55. **[G: U.K.]**

McConnell, James E. The International Location of Manufacturing Investments: Recent Behaviour of Foreign-owned Corporations in the United States. **In** *Hamilton, F. E. I. and Linge, G. J. R., eds.*, 1983, pp. 337–58. **[G: U.S.]**

McGregor, Peter G. and Swales, J. K. Import and Export Ratios and the Dynamic Harrod Trade Multiplier [Import Penetration, Export Performance and Harrod's Trade Multiplier]. *Oxford Econ. Pap.*, March 1983, *35* (1), pp. 110–24.

McLoughlin, P. J. Community Considerations as Location Attraction Variables for Manufacturing Industry. *Urban Stud.*, August 1983, *20* (3), pp. 359–63. **[G: U.K.; U.S.]**

Metcalfe, J. S. and Hall, P. H. The Verdoorn Law and the Salter Mechanism: A Note on Australian Manufacturing Industry. *Australian Econ. Pap.*, December 1983, *22* (41), pp. 364–73. **[G: Australia]**

Mitsos, Achilles G. J. The Industrial Sector. **In** *Sampedro, J. L. and Payno, J. A., eds.*, 1983, pp. 105–27. **[G: Greece; EEC]**

Mizon, Grayham E. and Nickell, S. J. Vintage Production Models of U.K. Manufacturing Industry. *Scand. J. Econ.*, 1983, *85* (2), pp. 295–310. **[G: U.K.]**

Modiano, Pietro and Onida, Fabrizio. Un'analisi disaggregata delle funzioni di domanda di esportazione dell'Italia e dei principali paesi industriali. (Export Functions for Italy and Main Industrial Countries: A Sectorially Disaggregated Analysis. With English summary.) *Giorn. Econ.*, January–February 1983, *42* (1–2), pp. 3–26. **[G: Italy; W. Europe; Japan; U.S.]**

Moomaw, Ronald L. Is Population Scale a Worthless Surrogate for Business Agglomeration Economies? *Reg. Sci. Urban Econ.*, November 1983, *13* (4), pp. 525–45. **[G: U.S.]**

Morris, Morris D. The Growth of Large-Scale Industry to 1947. **In** *Kumar, D., ed.*, 1983, pp. 553–676. **[G: India]**

Mosser, A. Concentration and the Finance of Austrian Industrial Combines, 1880-1914. **In** *Teichova, A. and Cottrell, P. L., eds.*, 1983, pp. 57–71. **[G: Austria]**

Mowery, David C. Industrial Research and Firm Size, Survival, and Growth in American Manufacturing, 1921–1946: An Assessment. *J. Econ. Hist.*, December 1983, *43* (4), pp. 953–80. **[G: U.S.]**

Murrell, Peter. The Comparative Structure of the Growth of the West German and British Manufacturing Industries. **In** *Mueller, D. C., ed.*, 1983, pp. 109–31. **[G: W. Germany; U.K.]**

Mytelka, Lynn Krieger. The Limits of Export-led Development: The Ivory Coast's Experience with Manufactures. **In** *Ruggie, J. G., ed.*, 1983, pp. 239–70. **[G: Ivory Coast; Sub-Saharan Africa]**

Nagovitsin, A. The Management Structure of a Production Association. *Prob. Econ.*, May 1983, *26* (1), pp. 57–73. **[G: U.S.S.R.]**

Naroff, Joel L. and Madden, Thomas J. Using Discriminant Analysis to Predict Regional Shifts. *Growth Change*, April 1983, *14* (2), pp. 24–29. **[G: U.S.]**

Neck, Philip. The Small Firm: Africa. **In** *Storey, D. J., ed.*, 1983, pp. 248–71. **[G: Africa]**

Neumann, Manfred; Böbel, Ingo and Haid, Alfred. Business Cycle and Industrial Market Power: An Empirical Investigation for West German Industries, 1965–1977. *J. Ind. Econ.*, December 1983, *32* (2), pp. 187–96. **[G: W. Germany]**

Newman, Robert J. Industry Migration and Growth in the South. *Rev. Econ. Statist.*, February 1983, *65* (1), pp. 76–86. **[G: U.S.]**

Nogués, Julio J. Alternative Trade Strategies and Employment in the Argentine Manufacturing Sector. *World Devel.*, December 1983, *11* (12), pp. 1029–42. **[G: Argentina]**

Norsworthy, J. R. and Malmquist, David H. Input Measurement and Productivity Growth in Japanese and U.S. Manufacturing. *Amer. Econ. Rev.*, December 1983, *73* (5), pp. 947–67. **[G: Japan; U.S.]**

O'Callaghan, John. Ownership and Control in the Manufacturing Sector of West Malaysia: A Note. **In** *Lim, D., ed.*, 1983, *1971*, pp. 221–22. **[G: Malaysia]**

O'Farrell, P. N. and Crouchley, R. Industrial Closures in Ireland 1973–1981: Analysis and Implications. *Reg. Stud.*, December 1983, *17* (6), pp. 411–27. **[G: Ireland]**

Odagiri, Hiroyuki. R & D Expenditures, Royalty Payments, and Sales Growth in Japanese Manufacturing Corporations. *J. Ind. Econ.*, September 1983, *32* (1), pp. 61–71. **[G: Japan]**

Odaka, Konosuke. Skill Formation in Development: Case Studies of Philippine Manufacturing (I). *Hitotsubashi J. Econ.*, June 1983, *24* (1), pp. 11–24. **[G: Philippines]**

Ohlsson, Lennart. Structural Adaptability of Regions during Swedish Industrial Adjustment, 1965 to

1975. **In** *Hamilton, F. E. I. and Linge, G. J. R., eds.*, 1983, pp. 297–335. **[G: Sweden]**

Okun, Arthur M. Upward Mobility in a High-Pressure Economy. **In** *Okun, A. M.*, 1983, *1973*, pp. 171–220. **[G: U.S.]**

Ortona, Guido and Santagata, Walter. Industrial Mobility in the Turin Metropolitan Area, 1961–77. *Urban Stud.*, February 1983, *20*(1), pp. 59–71. **[G: Italy]**

Pack, Howard. Policies to Encourage the Use of Intermediate Technology. **In** *Todaro, M. P., ed.*, 1983, *1976*, pp. 181–91. **[G: S. Korea; Taiwan; Pakistan; Mexico]**

Pearce, James E. Unionism and the Cyclical Behavior of the Labor Market in U.S. Manufacturing. *Rev. Econ. Statist.*, August 1983, *65*(3), pp. 450–58. **[G: U.S.]**

Peet, Richard. Relations of Production and the Relocation of United States Manufacturing Industry since 1960. *Econ. Geogr.*, April 1983, *59*(2), pp. 112–43. **[G: U.S.]**

Perkins, F. C. Technology Choice, Industrialisation and Development Experiences in Tanzania. *J. Devel. Stud.*, January 1983, *19*(2), pp. 213–43. **[G: Tanzania]**

Peters, Lois S., et al. Current U.S. University/Industry Research Connections. **In** *National Science Foundation*, 1983, pp. 1–161. **[G: U.S.]**

Phelps Brown, Henry. What Is the British Predicament? **In** *Feinstein, C., ed.*, 1983, *1977*, pp. 207–25. **[G: U.K.]**

Pickford, Michael. The Determinants of Seller Concentration in New Zealand Manufacturing Industry. *Australian Econ. Pap.*, December 1983, *22*(41), pp. 374–83. **[G: New Zealand]**

Pindyck, Robert S. and Rotemberg, Julio J. Dynamic Factor Demands and the Effects of Energy Price Shocks. *Amer. Econ. Rev.*, December 1983, *73*(5), pp. 1066–79. **[G: U.S.]**

Pindyck, Robert S. and Rotemberg, Julio J. Dynamic Factor Demands under Rational Expectations. *Scand. J. Econ.*, 1983, *85*(2), pp. 223–38. **[G: U.S.]**

Poensgen, Otto H. Between Market and Hierarchy. **In** *Francis, A.; Turk, J. and Willman, P., eds.*, 1983, pp. 54–80. **[G: W. Germany]**

Poza, Ernesto J. Twelve Actions to Build Strong U.S. Factories. *Sloan Manage. Rev.*, Fall 1983, *25*(1), pp. 27–38. **[G: U.S.]**

Ravenscraft, David J. Structure–Profit Relationships at the Line of Business and Industry Level. *Rev. Econ. Statist.*, February 1983, *65*(1), pp. 22–31. **[G: U.S.]**

Ray, George F. The Diffusion of Mature Technologies. *Nat. Inst. Econ. Rev.*, November 1983, (106), pp. 56–62. **[G: U.K.]**

Reza, Sadrel. Revealed Comparative Advantage in the South Asian Manufacturing Sector: Some Estimates. *Indian Econ. J.*, October–December 1983, *31*(2), pp. 96–106. **[G: Bangladesh; India; Nepal; Pakistan; Sri Lanka]**

Richardson, J. David. Worker Adjustment to U.S. International Trade: Programs and Prospects. **In** *Cline W. R., ed.*, 1983, pp. 393–424. **[G: U.S.]**

Rosefielde, Steven. Disguised Inflation in Soviet Industry: A Reply to James Steiner. *J. Compar. Econ.*, March 1983, *7*(1), pp. 71–76. **[G: U.S.S.R.]**

Ross, Howard N. and Thomadakis, Stavros. Rate of Return, Firm Size and Development Subsidies: The Case of Greece. *J. Devel. Econ.*, February/April 1983, *12*(1/2), pp. 5–18. **[G: Greece]**

Rossana, Robert J. Some Empirical Estimates of the Demand for Hours in U.S. Manufacturing Industries. *Rev. Econ. Statist.*, November 1983, *65*(4), pp. 560–69. **[G: U.S.]**

Round, David K. Advertising and Profitability in Australian Manufacturing. *Australian Econ. Pap.*, December 1983, *22*(41), pp. 345–55. **[G: Australia]**

Round, David K. Intertemporal Profit Margin Variability and Market Structure in Australian Manufacturing. *Int. J. Ind. Organ.*, June 1983, *1*(2), pp. 189–209. **[G: Australia]**

Saunders, Peter. A Disaggregate Study of the Rationality of Australian Producers' Price Expectations. *Manchester Sch. Econ. Soc. Stud.*, December 1983, *51*(4), pp. 380–98. **[G: Australia]**

Scherer, F. M. The Propensity to Patent. *Int. J. Ind. Organ.*, 1983, *1*(1), pp. 107–28. **[G: U.S.]**

Schiantarelli, Fabio. Investment Models and Expectations: Some Estimates for the Italian Industrial Sector. *Int. Econ. Rev.*, June 1983, *24*(2), pp. 291–312. **[G: Italy]**

Schumacher, D. Intra-industry Trade between the Federal Republic of Germany and Developing Countries: Extent and Some Characteristics. **In** *Tharakan, P. K. M., ed.*, 1983, pp. 87–109. **[G: W. Germany; LDCs]**

Schvarzer, Jorge. Cambios en el liderazgo industrial argentino en el período de Martínez de Hoz. (With English summary.) *Desarrollo Econ.*, October–December 1983, *23*(91), pp. 395–422. **[G: Argentina]**

Schydlowsky, Daniel M. The Short-run Potential for Employment Generation of Installed Capacity in Latin America. **In** *Urquidi, V. L. and Reyes, S. T., eds.*, 1983, pp. 311–47. **[G: Latin America]**

Scott, Walter Giorgio. PMI e mercati internationali. (Small and Medium Sized Businesses and Foreign Markets. With English summary.) *L'Impresa*, 1983, *25*(1), pp. 21–28. **[G: Italy]**

Scouller, John. 'Made in Scotland' (Production). **In** *Ingham, K. P. D. and Love, J., eds.*, 1983, pp. 15–27. **[G: U.K.]**

Shapiro, Daniel M. The Comparative Profitability of Canadian- and Foreign-Controlled Firms. *Managerial Dec. Econ.*, June 1983, *4*(2), pp. 97–106.

Shipley, David D. Pricing Flexibility in British Manufacturing Industry. *Managerial Dec. Econ.*, December 1983, *4*(4), pp. 224–33. **[G: U.K.]**

da Silva, Amado and Santos, Aníbal. Uma digressão pela economia industrial: de Harvard a Chicago passando pela Europa. *Economia*, January 1983, *7*(1), pp. 87–110.

Singh, Ajit. U.K. Industry and the World Economy: A Case of De-industrialisation? **In** *Feinstein, C., ed.*, 1983, *1977*, pp. 226–57. **[G: U.K.]**

Smelyakov, N. N. Industrial Cooperation and Joint Production in Soviet–Finnish Economic Ties. **In** *Möttölä, K.; Bykov, O. N. and Korolev, I. S., eds.*,

1983, pp. 100–109. [G: U.S.S.R.; Finland]

Solimano, Andrés. Reducir costos del trabajo: cuánto empleo genera? (With English summary.) *Cuadernos Econ.*, December 1983, *20*(61), pp. 363–81. [G: Chile]

Soltow, James H. Structure and Strategy: The Small Manufacturing Enterprise in the Modern Industrial Economy. **In** *[Cochran, T. C.]*, 1983, pp. 81–99. [G: U.S.]

Steiner, James E. Disguised Inflation in Soviet Industry: A Final Reply to Steven Rosefielde. *J. Compar. Econ.*, December 1983, *7*(4), pp. 449–51. [G: U.S.S.R.]

Stobaugh, Robert B., Jr. Where in the World Should We Put That Plant? **In** *Dickson, D. N., ed.*, 1983, pp. 245–59. [G: Selected Countries]

Strong, John S. Regional Variations in Industrial Performance. *Reg. Stud.*, December 1983, *17*(6), pp. 429–44. [G: U.S.]

Suarez-Villa, Luis. A Note on Dualism, Capital–Labor Ratios, and the Regions of the U.S. *J. Reg. Sci.*, November 1983, *23*(4), pp. 547–52. [G: U.S.]

Susman, Paul and Schutz, Eric. Monopoly and Competitive Firm Relations and Regional Development in Global Capitalism. *Econ. Geogr.*, April 1983, *59*(2), pp. 161–77. [G: U.S.]

Sylos Labini, Paolo. Princes, Costs and Profits in the Manufacturing Industry: Italy and Japan. **In** *Fodella, G., ed.*, 1983, pp. 64–89. [G: Italy; Japan]

Tan, Chwee-Huat. Public Enterprise and the Government in Singapore. **In** *[Ramanadham, V. V.]*. 1983, pp. 249–63. [G: Singapore]

Tan, Siew Ee and Lai, Yew Wah. Protection and Employment in the West Malaysian Manufacturing Industries. *Weltwirtsch. Arch.*, 1983, *119*(2), pp. 329–44. [G: Malaysia]

Tan, Thiam Soon. The Small Firm: South East Asia. **In** *Storey, D. J., ed.*, 1983, pp. 218–47. [G: S. E. Asia]

Tange, Toshiko. Trade Frictions and Productivity Performance—Technological, Price, and Cost Competitiveness of Japan and U.S. Exports. *J. Policy Modeling*, November 1983, *5*(3), pp. 313–31. [G: Japan; U.S.]

Tassey, Gregory. Competitive Strategies and Performance in Technology-Based Industries. *J. Econ. Bus.*, 1983, *35*(1), pp. 21–40. [G: U.S.]

Tavares, Maria De Conceicao and Souza, Paulo Renato. Employment and Wages in Industry: The Case of Brazil. **In** *Urquidi, V. L. and Reyes, S. T., eds.*, 1983, pp. 195–210. [G: Brazil]

Teichova, Alice and Cottrell, P. L. Industrial Structures in West and East Central Europe during the Inter-war Period. **In** *Teichova, A. and Cottrell, P. L., eds.*, 1983, pp. 31–55. [G: Austria; Hungary; U.K.; Czechoslovakia]

Teubal, M. The Accumulation of Intangibles by High-Technology Firms. **In** *Macdonald, S.; Lamberton, D. M. and Mandeville, T., eds.*, 1983, pp. 56–74. [G: Selected Countries]

Tomaskovic-Devey, Donald and Miller, S. M. Can High-Tech Provide the Jobs? *Challenge*, May/June 1983, *26*(2), pp. 57–63. [G: U.S.]

Tompkinson, Paul and Common, Michael S. Evidence on the Rationality of Expectations in the British Manufacturing Sector. *Appl. Econ.*, August 1983, *15*(4), pp. 425–36. [G: U.K.]

Trubac, Edward R. Fluctuations in Non-Electrical Machinery "Unfinished Goods" Inventories during Recent Recessions. *Bus. Econ.*, May 1983, *18*(3), pp. 13–21. [G: U.S.]

Turner, R. E. A Re-examination of Verdoorn's Law and Its Application to the Manufacturing Industries of the UK, West Germany and the USA. *Europ. Econ. Rev.*, September 1983, *23*(1), pp. 141–48. [G: U.K.; U.S.; W. Germany]

Tybout, James R. Credit Rationing and Investment Behavior in a Developing Country. *Rev. Econ. Statist.*, November 1983, *65*(4), pp. 598–607. [G: Colombia]

Tyson, Laura D'Andrea and Zysman, John. American Industry in International Competition. **In** *Zysman, J. and Tyson, L., eds.*, 1983, pp. 15–59. [G: U.S.]

Ueda, Kazuo. Trade Balance Adjustment with Imported Intermediate Goods: The Japanese Case. *Rev. Econ. Statist.*, November 1983, *65*(4), pp. 618–25. [G: Japan]

Val'tukh, K. K. The Investment Complex and the Intensification of Production. *Prob. Econ.*, April 1983, *25*(12), pp. 3–29. [G: U.S.S.R.]

Viljoen, S. P. The Industrial Achievement of South Africa. *S. Afr. J. Econ.*, March 1983, *51*(1), pp. 29–57. [G: S. Africa]

Voos, Paula B. Union Organizing: Costs and Benefits. *Ind. Lab. Relat. Rev.*, July 1983, *36*(4), pp. 576–91. [G: U.S.]

Wangwe, Samuel M. Industrialization and Resource Allocation in a Developing Country: The Case of Recent Experiences in Tanzania. *World Devel.*, June 1983, *11*(6), pp. 483–92. [G: Tanzania]

Warren, Ronald S., Jr. Labor Market Contacts, Unanticipated Wages, and Employment Growth. *Amer. Econ. Rev.*, June 1983, *73*(3), pp. 389–97. [G: U.S.]

Waterson, Michael and Lopez, Arcesio. The Determinants of Research and Development Intensity in the U.K. *Appl. Econ.*, June 1983, *15*(3), pp. 379–91. [G: U.K.]

Weeks, John. The State and Income Redistribution in Peru, 1968–76, with Special Reference to Manufacturing. **In** *Stewart, F., ed.*, 1983, pp. 62–82. [G: Peru]

Weiss, Leonard W.; Pascoe, George and Martin, Stephen. The Size of Selling Costs. *Rev. Econ. Statist.*, November 1983, *65*(4), pp. 668–72. [G: U.S.]

Weitzman, Martin L. Industrial Production. **In** *Bergson, A. and Levine, H. S., eds.*, 1983, pp. 178–90. [G: U.S.S.R.]

Xepapadeas, A. and Kanellopoulos, A. The Dynamic Behavior of the Rates of Return in U.K. Manufacturing Industries. *Greek Econ. Rev.*, December 1983, *5*(3), pp. 248–63. [G: U.K.]

Ysander, Bengt-Christer. Measuring Energy Substitution: An Introduction. **In** *Ysander, B.-C., ed.*, 1983, pp. 9–25. [G: Sweden]

Ysander, Bengt-Christer and Nordström, Tomas. Energy in Swedish Manufacturing 1980–2000. **In** *Ysander, B.-C., ed.*, 1983, pp. 229–60. [G: Sweden]

Zimmerman, Jerold L. Taxes and Firm Size. *J. Acc. Econ.*, August 1983, *5*(2), pp. 119–49. **[G: U.S.]**

6312 Metals (iron, steel, and other)

Allen, Robert C. Collective Invention. *J. Econ. Behav. Organ.*, March 1983, *4*(1), pp. 1–24. **[G: U.S.; U.K.]**

Auty, R. M. Multinational Corporations and Regional Revenue Retention in a Vertically Integrated Industry: Bauxite/Aluminium in the Caribbean. *Reg. Stud.*, February 1983, *17*(1), pp. 3–17. **[G: Caribbean; U.S.; Brazil; Australia]**

Banerjee, Avijit. An Application of Stochastic Programming in Steel Production. *Rev. Bus. Econ. Res.*, Spring 1983, *18*(3), pp. 58–70. **[G: U.S.]**

Borrus, Michael. The Politics of Competitive Erosion in the U.S. Steel Industry. **In** *Zysman, J. and Tyson, L., eds.*, 1983, pp. 60–105. **[G: U.S.]**

Carré, Denis. Une mesure "hédonistique" du stock de capital de l'entreprise: le cas la sidérurgie. (With English summary.) *Rev. Econ. Ind.*, 4th Trimester 1983, (26), pp. 52–67. **[G: France]**

Carter, Robert A. Resource-Related Development and Regional Labour Markets: The Effects of the Alcoa Aluminum Smelter on Portland. *Australian Econ. Rev.*, 1st Quarter 1983, (61), pp. 22–32. **[G: Australia]**

Chen, Yun. The Problem of Making Practicable the Steel Target. **In** *Ch'en, Y.*, 1983, *1959*, pp. 117–26. **[G: China]**

Crowson, Phillip. Non-fuel Mineral Procurement Policies. **In** *Akao, N., ed.*, 1983, pp. 145–67. **[G: Japan; Selected Countries]**

Elbaum, Bernard. The Internalization of Labor Markets: Causes and Consequences. *Amer. Econ. Rev.*, May 1983, *73*(2), pp. 260–65. **[G: U.S.]**

Fischer, P. G. The Österreichisch-Alpine Montangesellschaft, 1918–38. **In** *Teichova, A. and Cottrell, P. L., eds.*, 1983, pp. 253–67. **[G: Austria]**

Førsund, Finn R. and Jansen, Eilev S. Analysis of Energy Intensive Industries—The Case of Norwegian Aluminium Production 1966–1978. **In** *Av, R., et al., eds.*, 1983, pp. 221–59. **[G: Norway]**

Førsund, Finn R. and Jansen, Eilev S. Technical Progress and Structural Change in the Norwegian Primary Aluminum Industry. *Scand. J. Econ.*, 1983, *85*(2), pp. 113–26. **[G: Norway]**

Fortin, Carlos. Marketing, Technical and Legal Information for Copper Producing Countries: The Case of CIPEC. **In** *O'Brien, R. C., ed.*, 1983, pp. 88–101. **[G: Selected Countries]**

Grey, Rodney de C. A Note on U.S. Trade Policy. **In** *Cline W. R., ed.*, 1983, pp. 243–57. **[G: U.S.]**

Hashimoto, Hideo. A World Iron and Steel Economy Model: A Projection for 1980–95. *J. Policy Modeling*, November 1983, *5*(3), pp. 379–96. **[G: Global]**

Ichniowski, Casey. Have Angels Done More? The Steel Industry Consent Decree. *Ind. Lab. Relat. Rev.*, January 1983, *36*(2), pp. 182–98. **[G: U.S.]**

Jansson, Leif. A Vintage Model for the Swedish Iron and Steel Industry. **In** *Ysander, B.-C., ed.*, 1983, pp. 129–69. **[G: Sweden]**

Jung, Ku-Hyun. The Sogo Shosha: Can It Be Exported (Imported)? **In** *Czinkota, M. R., ed. (I)*, 1983, pp. 66–88. **[G: Japan; S. Korea]**

Karlson, Stephen H. Modeling Location and Production: An Application to U.S. Fully-Integrated Steel Plants. *Rev. Econ. Statist.*, February 1983, *65*(1), pp. 41–50. **[G: U.S.]**

Katz, Jorge. Technological Change in the Latin American Metalworking Industry: Results of a Programme of Case Studies. *Cepal Rev.*, April 1983, (19), pp. 85–143. **[G: Latin America]**

Kymn, Kern O. and Palomba, Catherine. Annual Strike Costs in the Steel Industry in the U.S., 1950 to 1972. *Rivista Int. Sci. Econ. Com.*, April-May 1983, *30*(4–5), pp. 440–51. **[G: U.S.]**

Lim, David. Industrial Processing and Location: A Study of Tin. **In** *Lim, D., ed.*, 1983, *1980*, pp. 99–107. **[G: LDCs]**

Lundgren, Stefan. A Model of Energy Demand in the Swedish Iron and Steel Industry. **In** *Ysander, B.-C., ed.*, 1983, pp. 171–208. **[G: Sweden]**

Mandeville, T. D. An Input–Output Framework for Measuring Economic Impacts: A Case Study of the Aluminium Industry at Gladstone, Australia. **In** *Hamilton, F. E. I. and Linge, G. J. R., eds.*, 1983, pp. 203–16. **[G: Australia]**

Marz, Edward. The Österreichisch-Alpine Montangeselleschaft, 1918–38: Commentary. **In** *Teichova, A. and Cottrell, P. L., eds.*, 1983, pp. 267–68. **[G: Austria]**

Mendizabal Gorostiaga, A. La crisis económica: su incidencia en el País Vasco. (The Economic Crisis: Its Incidence in the Basque Country. With English summary.) *Écon. Soc.*, September–October–November 1983, *17*(9–10–11), pp. 1595–1609. **[G: Spain]**

Messerlin, Patrick and Saunders, Christopher. Steel: Too Much Investment Too Late. **In** *Shepherd, G.; Duchêne, F. and Saunders, C., eds.*, 1983, pp. 52–81. **[G: Selected Countries]**

Nielsen, Peter Bøegh. Aspects of Industrial Financing in Denmark 1890–1914. *Scand. Econ. Hist. Rev.*, 1983, *31*(2), pp. 79–108. **[G: Denmark]**

O'Neill, William D. Direct Empirical Estimation of Effeciency in Secondary Materials Markets: The Case of Steel Scrap. *J. Environ. Econ. Manage.*, September 1983, *10*(3), pp. 270–81. **[G: U.S.]**

Rafati, M. Reza. Price Determination in Monopolistic Markets with Inventory Adjustments: The Case of Nickel. *Weltwirtsch. Arch.*, 1983, *119*(1), pp. 152–68.

Rosenberg, Nathan. The Effects of Energy Supply Characteristics on Technology and Economic Growth. **In** *Schurr, S. H.; Sonenblum, S. and Wood, D. O., eds.*, 1983, pp. 279–305. **[G: U.S.]**

Saha, S. K. Industrial Policy and Locational Dynamics of Small-scale Enterprises in India. **In** *Hamilton, F. E. I. and Linge, G. J. R., eds.*, 1983, pp. 509–31. **[G: India]**

Salmi, Timo, et al. Extracting and Analyzing the Time Series for Profitability Measurement from Published Financial Statements: With Results on Publicly Traded Finnish Metal Industry Firms. *Liiketaloudellinen Aikak.*, 1983, *32*(2), pp. 135–74. **[G: Finland]**

Stoica, M. and Şerban, R. Fuzzy Algorithms for Production Programming. *Econ. Computat. Cybern.*

Stud. Res., 1983, *18*(2), pp. 55–59.

Tatsiopoulos, I. P. Manufacturing Lead-Times: A Key Control Factor for the Production/Marketing Integration in Small Component-manufacturing Firms. **In** *Wilson, B.; Berg, C. C. and French, D., eds.*, 1983, pp. 271–80.

Teichova, Alice. The Mannesmann Concern in East Central Europe in the Inter-war Period. **In** *Teichova, A. and Cottrell, P. L., eds.*, 1983, pp. 103–37. **[G: Austria]**

Thomas, Vinod. Welfare Analysis of Pollution Control with Spatial Alternatives. *Urban Stud.*, May 1983, *20*(2), pp. 219–27. **[G: U.S.]**

Tiano, André. Transfers of Iron and Steel Technology to the Third World: Effects on Employment in the Developed Countries. *Int. Lab. Rev.*, July–August 1983, *122*(4), pp. 429–42. **[G: France; OECD; LDCs]**

Walter, Ingo. Structural Adjustment and Trade Policy in the International Steel Industry. **In** *Cline W. R., ed.*, 1983, pp. 483–525. **[G: Selected Countries]**

Welch, Lawrence R. and Wiedersheim-Paul, Finn. MNCs and the Australian Government: Some Emerging Policy Issues. **In** *Goldberg, W. H., ed.*, 1983, pp. 249–69. **[G: Australia]**

6313 Machinery (tools, electrical equipment, computers, and appliances)

Baldwin, Carliss Y. and Mason, Scott P. The Resolution of Claims in Financial Distress: The Case of Massey Ferguson. *J. Finance*, May 1983, *38*(2), pp. 505–16. **[G: U.S.]**

Barna, Tibor. Process Plant Contracting: A Competitive New European Industry. **In** *Shepherd, G.; Duchêne, F. and Saunders, C., eds.*, 1983, pp. 167–85. **[G: W. Europe]**

Bast, James L. Automated Office Equipment: Will Rapid Growth Continue? **In** *Federal Reserve Bank of Atlanta*, 1983, pp. 123–27. **[G: U.S.]**

Benvignati, Anita M. International Technology Transfer Patterns in a Traditional Industry. *J. Int. Bus. Stud.*, Winter 1983, *14*(3), pp. 63–75. **[G: U.S.; Selected OECD]**

Bingham, Barbara. Instruments to Measure Electricity: Industry's Productivity Growth Rises. *Mon. Lab. Rev.*, October 1983, *106*(10), pp. 11–17. **[G: U.S.]**

Bloch, Erich; Meindl, James D. and Cromie, William. University Industry Cooperation in Microelectronics and Computers. **In** *National Science Foundation*, 1983, pp. 235–53. **[G: U.S.]**

Borrus, Michael, et al. Trade and Development in the Semiconductor Industry: Japanese Challenge and American Response. **In** *Zysman, J. and Tyson, L., eds.*, 1983, pp. 142–248. **[G: Japan; U.S.]**

Boucher, T. O. and Muckstadt, J. A. The Inventory Cost Effectiveness of Group Technology Production Systems. *Ann. Sci. Écon. Appl.*, 1983, *39*(1), pp. 27–41. **[G: U.S.]**

Brand, Horst and Huffstutler, Clyde. Productivity Improvements in Two Fabricated Metals Industries. *Mon. Lab. Rev.*, October 1983, *106*(10), pp. 18–24. **[G: U.S.]**

Canto, Victor A. and Laffer, Arthur B. The Effectiveness of Orderly Marketing Agreements: The Color TV Case. *Bus. Econ.*, January 1983, *18*(1), pp. 38–45. **[G: Japan; U.S.]**

Chen, Edward K. Y. Multinational Corporations and Technology Diffusion in Hong Kong Manufacturing. *Appl. Econ.*, June 1983, *15*(3), pp. 309–21. **[G: Hong Kong]**

Dargay, Joyce M. The Demand for Energy in Swedish Engineering: Factor Substitution, Technical Change and Scale Effects. **In** *Sohlman, A. M., ed.*, 1983, pp. 80–96. **[G: Sweden]**

Diop, Sidy Modibo and Perrault, Jean-Louis. Ruptures ou continuités dans la politque industrielle française en électronique? (With English summary.) *Rev. Econ. Ind.*, 2nd Trimester 1983, (24), pp. 48–61. **[G: France]**

Dosi, Giovanni. Semiconductors: Europe's Precarious Survival in High Technology. **In** *Shepherd, G.; Duchêne, F. and Saunders, C., eds.*, 1983, pp. 209–35. **[G: EEC; Japan; U.S.]**

Eyraud, François. The Principles of Union Action in the Engineering Industries in Great Britain and France: Towards a Neo-Institutional Analysis of Industrial Relations. *Brit. J. Ind. Relat.*, November 1983, *21*(3), pp. 358–76. **[G: U.K.; France]**

Hartley, John T., Jr. Electronics: High Technology Is the Wave of the Future. **In** *Federal Reserve Bank of Atlanta*, 1983, pp. 103–10. **[G: U.S.]**

Haug, P.; Hood, N. and Young, S. Mark. R & D Intensity in the Affiliates of U.S. Owned Electronics Companies Manufacturing in Scotland. *Reg. Stud.*, December 1983, *17*(6), pp. 383–92. **[G: U.K.]**

Horsley, A. and Swann, G. M. P. A Time Series of Computer Price Functions. *Oxford Bull. Econ. Statist.*, November 1983, *45*(4), pp. 339–56.

Jones, Daniel T. Machine Tools: Technical Change and a Japanese Challenge. **In** *Shepherd, G.; Duchêne, F. and Saunders, C., eds.*, 1983, pp. 186–208. **[G: OECD]**

Kaplinsky, Raphael. Firm Size and Technical Change in a Dynamic Context. *J. Ind. Econ.*, September 1983, *32*(1), pp. 39–59. **[G: U.S.]**

Kikkawa, Mototada. Shipbuilding, Motor Cars and Semiconductors: The Diminishing Role of Industrial Policy in Japan. **In** *Shepherd, G.; Duchêne, F. and Saunders, C., eds.*, 1983, pp. 236–67. **[G: Japan]**

Kohlmey, G. Structures économiques et division internationale du travail dans la région européenne du C.A.E.M. (With English summary.) *Écon. Soc.*, January 1983, *17*(1), pp. 89–113. **[G: E. Germany; CMEA]**

Lahera, Eugenio and Nochteff, Hugo. Microelectronics and Latin American Development. *Cepal Rev.*, April 1983, (19), pp. 167–81. **[G: Latin America]**

Laki, Mihály. Growth and Flexibility: The Case of a Transformer-Manufacturing Cooperative. *Eastern Europ. Econ.*, Spring–Summer 1983, *21*(3–4), pp. 170–87. **[G: Hungary]**

Lee, Sang M.; Snyder, Charles A. and Gen, Mitsuo. The Microcomputer: Experience and Implications for the Future of Multiple Criteria Decision Making. **In** *Hansen, P., ed.*, 1983, pp. 238–46.

Lim, Linda Y. C. Chinese Business, Multinationals

and the State: Manufacturing for Export in Malaysia and Singapore. In *Lim, L. Y. C. and Gosling, L. A. P., eds.*, 1983, pp. 245–74. **[G: Malaysia; Singapore]**

Lundmark, Kjell. Welfare State and Employment Policy: Sweden. In *Dyson, K. and Wilks, S., eds.*, 1983, pp. 220–44. **[G: Sweden]**

Merrilees, William J. Alternative Models of Apprentice Recruitment: With Special Reference to the British Engineering Industry. *Appl. Econ.*, February 1983, *15*(1), pp. 1–21. **[G: U.K.]**

Mikkelsen, K. W. and Langam, N. N. Innovation in the Philippine Agricultural Machinery Industry. In *Internat'l Rice Res. Inst. and Agric. Devel. Council*, 1983, pp. 31–37. **[G: Philippines]**

Millstein, James E. Decline in an Expanding Industry: Japanese Competition in Color Television. In *Zysman, J. and Tyson, L., eds.*, 1983, pp. 106–41. **[G: U.S.; Japan]**

Oakey, Ray P. High-technology Industry, Industrial Location and Regional Development: The British Case. In *Hamilton, F. E. I. and Linge, G. J. R., eds.*, 1983, pp. 279–95. **[G: U.K.]**

Ondrack, Daniel A. Responses to Government Industrial Research Policy: A Comparison of Foreign-owned and Canadian-owned Firms. In *Goldberg, W. H., ed.*, 1983, pp. 177–200. **[G: Canada]**

Randell, Daniel. Automation in Perspective—An Overview. In *Wilson, B.; Berg, C. C. and French, D., eds.*, 1983, pp. 217–32. **[G: U.S.]**

Schröter, Harm. Siemens and Central and South–East Europe between the Two World Wars. In *Teichova, A. and Cottrell, P. L., eds.*, 1983, pp. 173–92. **[G: Europe]**

Scott, A. J. Industrial Organization and the Logic of Intra-Metropolitan Location, II: A Case Study of the Printed Circuits Industry in the Greater Los Angeles Region. *Econ. Geogr.*, October 1983, *59*(4), pp. 343–67. **[G: U.S.]**

Sengupta, Jati K.; Leonard, John E. and Vanyo, James P. A Limit Pricing Model for U.S. Computer Industry: An Application. *Appl. Econ.*, June 1983, *15*(3), pp. 297–308. **[G: U.S.]**

Sievers, Manfred. The Worsening Financial State of the Multinational Tractor Industry. *Europ. Rev. Agr. Econ.*, 1983, *10*(2), pp. 165–73. **[G: Canada; Italy; Japan; U.S.]**

Spencer, Edson W. Japan: Stimulus or Scapegoat? *Foreign Aff.*, Fall 1983, *62*(1), pp. 123–37. **[G: Japan; U.S.]**

Strange, J. Leland. Microcomputer Enhancement: Challenges in an Exploding Industry. In *Federal Reserve Bank of Atlanta*, 1983, pp. 111–17. **[G: U.S.]**

Takeoka, Yukiharu. A Study on the History of a French Firm of Machine-Tool Industry. (In Japanese. With English summary.) *Osaka Econ. Pap.*, March 1983, *32*(4), pp. 1–10. **[G: France]**

Tárnok, Éva. The Limits of Independent Technological Development: Production and Development after Breaking Off a Traditional License Relationship. *Eastern Europ. Econ.*, Fall 1983, *22*(1), pp. 19–37. **[G: Hungary]**

Valentiny, Pál. The Role of the State in Influencing the Market for Heavy Electrical Equipment. *Eastern Europ. Econ.*, Fall 1983, *22*(1), pp. 3–18. **[G: W. Europe; Hungary]**

Wattanutchariya, S. Economic Analysis of the Farm Machinery Industry and Tractor Contractor Business in Thailand. In *Internat'l Rice Res. Inst. and Agric. Devel. Council*, 1983, pp. 39–49. **[G: Thailand]**

Wiboonchutikula, Paitoon. Productivity Growth of the Agricultural Machinery Industry in Thailand. In *Internat'l Rice Res. Inst. and Agric. Devel. Council*, 1983, pp. 51–59. **[G: Thailand]**

6314 Transportation and Communication Equipment

Abernathy, William J.; Clark, Kim B. and Kantrow, Alan M. The New Industrial Competition. In *Dickson, D. N., ed.*, 1983, pp. 133–55. **[G: U.S.; Japan]**

Abernathy, William J.; Clark, Kim B. and Kantrow, Alan M. The New Industrial Competition. In *Kantrow, A. M., ed.*, 1983, pp. 72–95. **[G: Japan; U.S.]**

Abernathy, William J. and Wayne, Kenneth. Limits of the Learning Curve. In *Kantrow, A. M., ed.*, 1983, pp. 114–31. **[G: U.S.]**

Albert, Alain and Crener, Maxime A. Organisation industrielle du secteur des télécommunications: une perspective internationale. (With English summary.) *Rev. Econ. Ind.*, 2nd Trimester 1983, (24), pp. 1–8. **[G: U.S.; Canada; Europe]**

Bauer, Tamás and Soós, Károly Attila. Interfirm Relations and Technological Change: The Case of the Motor Industry. *Eastern Europ. Econ.*, Spring–Summer 1983, *21*(3–4), pp. 85–104. **[G: Hungary]**

Blanchard, Olivier J. The Production and Inventory Behavior of the American Automobile Industry. *J. Polit. Econ.*, June 1983, *91*(3), pp. 365–400. **[G: U.S.]**

Bond, Eric W. Trade in Used Equipment with Heterogeneous Firms. *J. Polit. Econ.*, August 1983, *91*(4), pp. 688–705. **[G: U.S.]**

Boyle, R. M. Linwood: Government and the Motor Car Industry in Scotland. *Reg. Stud.*, February 1983, *17*(1), pp. 49–52. **[G: U.K.]**

Brinson, Geoff. Assessment of New Technologies. In *Hill, S. and Johnston, R., eds.*, 1983, pp. 194–208. **[G: Australia]**

Bultel, Jean. Flexibilité de production et rentabilité des investissements. L'exemple de la robotisation de l'assemblage tôlerie en soudage par points. (With English summary.) *Rev. Econ. Ind.*, 4th Trimester 1983, (26), pp. 1–13.

Burch, Susan Weller. The Aging U.S. Auto Stock: Implications for Demand. *Bus. Econ.*, May 1983, *18*(3), pp. 22–26. **[G: U.S.]**

Caporale, Susan and Gross, Andrew. The Automotive Aftermarket in Latin America, 1967–1990. In *Czinkota, M. R., ed. (I)*, 1983, pp. 177–209. **[G: Latin America]**

Carbaugh, Robert. The Consequences of Local Content Protection. *Bus. Econ.*, September 1983, *18*(4), pp. 55–62. **[G: U.S.]**

Chang, Julius Chungshi. An Econometric Model of the Short-Run Demand for Workers and Hours in the U.S. Auto Industry. *J. Econometrics*, August 1983, *22*(3), pp. 301–16. **[G: U.S.]**

Cohen, Robert B. The Prospects for Trade and Protectionism in the Auto Industry. **In** *Cline W. R., ed.*, 1983, pp. 527–63. **[G: Selected Countries]**

Connidis, Lilla Arnet. The Effective Rate of Protection for Motor Vehicle Manufacturing in Canada. *Can. J. Econ.*, February 1983, *16*(1), pp. 98–103. **[G: Canada]**

Conway, Richard S., Jr. Applications of the Washington Projection and Simulation Model. **In** *Dutta, M.; Hartline, J. C. and Loeb, P. D., eds.*, 1983, pp. 105–15. **[G: U.S.]**

Coriat, Benjamin. La robotique à la Régie Renault. (With English summary.) *Rev. Econ. Ind.*, 2nd Trimester 1983, (24), pp. 18–34. **[G: France]**

Dargay, Joyce M. The Demand for Energy in Swedish Engineering: Factor Substitution, Technical Change and Scale Effects. **In** *Sohlman, A. M., ed.*, 1983, pp. 80–96. **[G: Sweden]**

Delporte, Christian M. and Keymolen, G. De l'intérêt des techniques quantitatives: application à un problème de livraisons. *Ann. Sci. Écon. Appl.*, 1983, *39*(1), pp. 87–110. **[G: W. Germany]**

Dewees, Donald N. The Control of Diesel Exhaust Pollution. **In** *Dewees, D. N., ed.*, 1983, pp. 293–322. **[G: U.S.]**

Dorward, Neil; Pokorny, Mike and Bayldon, Ray. The UK Truck Market: An Investigation into Truck Purchasing Behavior and Changing Market Shares. *J. Ind. Econ.*, September 1983, *32*(1), pp. 73–95. **[G: U.K.]**

Edwards, Charles E. and Stansell, Stanley R. New Car Sales Data and Automobile Company Stock Prices: A Study of the Causal Relationships. *Bus. Econ.*, May 1983, *18*(3), pp. 27–35. **[G: U.S.]**

Eussner, Ansgar. Industrial Policy and Southward Enlargement of the European Community: The Case of Shipbuilding and Repairs. *J. Common Market Stud.*, December 1983, *22*(2), pp. 147–72. **[G: EEC]**

Fazekas, Károly. Intensive Product Change and Expansion. *Eastern Europ. Econ.*, Spring–Summer 1983, *21*(3–4), pp. 67–84. **[G: Hungary]**

Fong, Chan Onn. Appropriate Technology: An Empirical Study of Bicycle Manufacturing in Malaysia. **In** *Lim, D., ed.*, 1983, *1980*, pp. 181–95. **[G: Malaysia]**

Fox, Douglas R. Motor Vehicles, Model Year 1983. *Surv. Curr. Bus.*, October 1983, *63*(10), pp. 20–24. **[G: U.S.]**

Friedlaender, Ann F.; Winston, Clifford M. and Wang, Kung. Costs, Technology, and Productivity in the U.S. Automobile Industry. *Bell J. Econ. (See Rand J. Econ. after 4/85)*, Spring 1983, *14*(1), pp. 1–20. **[G: U.S.]**

Friedman, David. Beyond the Age of Ford: The Strategic Basis of the Japanese Success in Automobiles. **In** *Zysman, J. and Tyson, L., eds.*, 1983, pp. 350–90. **[G: U.S.; Japan]**

Gallini, Nancy T. Demand for Gasoline in Canada. *Can. J. Econ.*, May 1983, *16*(2), pp. 299–324. **[G: Canada]**

Gomez-Ibanez, Jose A.; Leone, Robert A. and O'Connell, Stephen A. Restraining Auto Imports: Does Anyone Win? *J. Policy Anal. Manage.*, Winter 1983, *2*(2), pp. 196–219. **[G: U.S.; Japan]**

Gordon, Robert J. Energy Efficiency, User-Cost Change, and the Measurement of Durable Goods Prices: Reply. **In** *Foss, M. F., ed.*, 1983, pp. 265–68. **[G: U.S.]**

Gordon, Robert J. Energy Efficiency, User-Cost Change, and the Measurement of Durable Goods Prices. **In** *Foss, M. F., ed.*, 1983, pp. 205–53. **[G: U.S.]**

Grey, Rodney de C. A Note on U.S. Trade Policy. **In** *Cline W. R., ed.*, 1983, pp. 243–57. **[G: U.S.]**

Guest, Robert H. Quality of Work Life: Learning from Tarrytown. **In** *Kantrow, A. M., ed.*, 1983, pp. 545–62. **[G: U.S.]**

Hoffer, George E. and Reilly, Robert J. Auto Recalls and Consumer Recall: Effects on Sales. *Challenge*, Sept.–Oct. 1983, *26*(4), pp. 56–57. **[G: U.S.]**

Holmes, John. Industrial Reorganization, Capital Restructuring and Locational Change: An Analysis of the Canadian Automobile Industry in the 1960s. *Econ. Geogr.*, July 1983, *59*(3), pp. 251–71. **[G: Canada]**

Holmström, Per and Olsson, Ulf. The Structure of the Defense Industry: Sweden. **In** *Ball, N. and Leitenberg, M., eds.*, 1983, pp. 140–80. **[G: Sweden]**

Irvine, F. Owen, Jr. Demand Equations for Individual New Car Models Estimated Using Transaction Prices with Implications for Regulatory Issues. *Southern Econ. J.*, January 1983, *49*(3), pp. 764–82. **[G: U.S.]**

Jepson, D. The Coventry Local Economy, the Motor Vehicles Industry and Some Implications for Public Policy. *Reg. Stud.*, February 1983, *17*(1), pp. 56–59. **[G: U.K.]**

Jones, Daniel T. Motor Cars: A Maturing Industry? **In** *Shepherd, G.; Duchêne, F. and Saunders, C., eds.*, 1983, pp. 110–38. **[G: OECD; Global]**

Jones, Daniel T. Technology and the UK Automobile Industry. *Lloyds Bank Rev.*, April 1983, (148), pp. 14–27. **[G: U.K.]**

Kikkawa, Mototada. Shipbuilding, Motor Cars and Semiconductors: The Diminishing Role of Industrial Policy in Japan. **In** *Shepherd, G.; Duchêne, F. and Saunders, C., eds.*, 1983, pp. 236–67. **[G: Japan]**

Kwoka, John E., Jr. The Limits of Market-Oriented Regulatory Techniques: The Case of Automotive Fuel Economy. *Quart. J. Econ.*, November 1983, *98*(4), pp. 695–704.

Lall, Sanjaya. Prospects for Automotive Transnationals in the Third World. *Nat. Westminster Bank Quart. Rev.*, February 1983, pp. 13–20. **[G: LDCs]**

Lundmark, Kjell. Welfare State and Employment Policy: Sweden. **In** *Dyson, K. and Wilks, S., eds.*, 1983, pp. 220–44. **[G: Sweden]**

Major, Iván. Transformation of the Product Structure in a Changing Economic Environment: License Purchase by a Telecommunications Enterprise. *Eastern Europ. Econ.*, Spring–Summer 1983, *21*(3–4), pp. 144–62. **[G: Hungary]**

McGoldrick, James. Industrial Relations and the Division of Labour in the Shipbuilding Industry since the War. *Brit. J. Ind. Relat.*, July 1983, *21*(2), pp. 197–220. [G: U.K.]

Miller, D. The Role of the Motor Car Industry in the West Midlands Economy. *Reg. Stud.*, February 1983, *17*(1), pp. 53–56. [G: U.K.]

Mottershead, Peter. Shipbuilding: Adjustment-led Intervention or Intervention-led Adjustment? **In** *Shepherd, G.; Duchêne, F. and Saunders, C., eds.*, 1983, pp. 82–109. [G: Selected Countries]

Murfin, Andy and Smith, Ron. Depreciation and the Quality Adjustment of Prices: An Investigation of the UK Car Market, 1980–81. *Brit. Rev. Econ. Issues*, Autumn 1983, *5*(13), pp. 23–38. [G: U.K.]

Reilly, Robert J. and Hoffer, George E. Will Retarding the Information Flow on Automobile Recalls Affect Consumer Demand? *Econ. Inquiry*, July 1983, *21*(3), pp. 444–47. [G: U.S.]

Soós, Károly Attila. Technical Level and Economic Efficiency: Investment Decisions within the Framework of a Central Development Program. *Eastern Europ. Econ.*, Spring–Summer 1983, *21*(3–4), pp. 163–69. [G: Hungary]

Starzec, Krzysztof. L'économie polonaise vue à travers des circuits parallèles. (Polish "Official" and "Unofficial" Economy: An Empirical Approach. With English summary.) *Consommation*, October–December 1983, *30*(4), pp. 55–94. [G: Poland]

Sugden, Roger. The Degree of Monopoly, International Trade, and Transnational Corporations. *Int. J. Ind. Organ.*, June 1983, *1*(2), pp. 165–87.

Switzer, Brian C.; Simunek, Vladimir J. and Mathews, H. Lee. Sociometrics. **In** *Migliaro, A. and Jain, C. L., eds.*, 1983, pp. 55–65. [G: U.S.]

Sziraczki, G. The Development and Functioning of an Enterprise Labour Market in Hungary. *Écon. Soc.*, March–April 1983, *17*(3–4), pp. 517–47. [G: Hungary]

Tárnok, Éva and Vince, Péter. Organized Uncertainty. *Eastern Europ. Econ.*, Spring–Summer 1983, *21*(3–4), pp. 125–43. [G: Hungary]

Tishler, Asher. The Demand for Cars and Gasoline: A Simultaneous Approach. *Europ. Econ. Rev.*, January 1983, *20*(1–3), pp. 271–87. [G: Israel]

Triplett, Jack E. Energy Efficiency, User-Cost Change, and the Measurement of Durable Goods Prices: Comment. **In** *Foss, M. F., ed.*, 1983, pp. 253–65. [G: U.S.]

Tsurumi, Hiroki and Tsurumi, Yoshi. U.S.–Japan Automobile Trade: A Bayesian Test of a Product Life Cycle. *J. Econometrics*, October 1983, *23*(2), pp. 193–210.

6315 Chemicals, Drugs, Plastics, Ceramics, Glass, Cement, and Rubber

Ashford, Nicholas A. and Heaton, George R., Jr. Regulation and Technological Innovation in the Chemical Industry. *Law Contemp. Probl.*, Summer 1983, *46*(3), pp. 109–57. [G: U.S.]

Backhaus, Jüergen. Competition, Innovation and Regulation in the Pharmaceutical Industry. *Managerial Dec. Econ.*, June 1983, *4*(2), pp. 107–21. [G: U.S.; W. Europe]

Balasubramaniam, Kumariah. The Main Lines of Cooperation among Developing Countries in Pharmaceuticals. *World Devel.*, March 1983, *11*(3), pp. 281–87. [G: LDCs]

Bradley, Keith and Hill, Stephen. 'After Japan': The Quality Circle Transplant and Productive Efficiency. *Brit. J. Ind. Relat.*, November 1983, *21*(3), pp. 291–311. [G: U.K.; U.S.]

Chen, Edward K. Y. Multinational Corporations and Technology Diffusion in Hong Kong Manufacturing. *Appl. Econ.*, June 1983, *15*(3), pp. 309–21. [G: Hong Kong]

Chen, Yun. Speed Up Development of the Nitrogenous Chemical Fertilizer Industry. **In** *Ch'en, Y.*, 1983, *1961*, pp. 129–38. [G: China]

Chudnovsky, Daniel. Patents and Trademarks in Pharmaceuticals. *World Devel.*, March 1983, *11*(3), pp. 187–93. [G: LDCs; MDCs]

Cullen, Ross. Pharmaceuticals Inter-Country Diffusion. *Managerial Dec. Econ.*, June 1983, *4*(2), pp. 73–82. [G: Selected Countries]

Danner, Richard A. Federal Regulation of Non-Nuclear Hazardous Wastes: A Research Bibliography. *Law Contemp. Probl.*, Summer 1983, *46*(3), pp. 285–305.

Das, Kumar and Sahoo, B. Efficiency of Cement Manufacturing firms in India. *Econ. Aff.*, October–December 1983, *28*(4), pp. 812–15. [G: India]

Davies, J. Clarence. The Effects of Federal Regulation on Chemical Industry Innovation. *Law Contemp. Probl.*, Summer 1983, *46*(3), pp. 41–58. [G: U.S.]

Fattorusso, Vittorio. Essential Drugs for the Third World. *World Devel.*, March 1983, *11*(3), pp. 177–79. [G: LDCs]

Fazal, Anwar. The Right Pharmaceuticals at the Right Prices: Consumer Perspectives. *World Devel.*, March 1983, *11*(3), pp. 265–69.

Førsund, Finn R. and Hjalmarsson, Lennart. Technical Progress and Structural Change in the Swedish Cement Industry 1955–1979. *Econometrica*, September 1983, *51*(5), pp. 1449–67. [G: Sweden]

Freeman, Christopher; Walsh, V. and Townsend, J. The Determinants of Technical Change in the Chemical Industry: Demand-pull or Technology-push? **In** *[Saunders, C. T.]*, 1983, pp. 83–108. [G: Italy; U.K.; U.S.; W. Germany]

Friesz, Terry L., et al. A Nonlinear Complementarity Formulation and Solution Procedure for the General Derived Demand Network Equilibrium Problem. *J. Reg. Sci.*, August 1983, *23*(3), pp. 337–59.

Galal, Essam E. National Production of Drugs: Egypt. *World Devel.*, March 1983, *11*(3), pp. 237–41. [G: Egypt]

Gordon, Myron J. and Fowler, David J. Performance of the Multinational Drug Industry in Home and Host Countries: A Canadian Case Study. **In** *Kindleberger, C. P. and Audretsch, D. B., eds.*, 1983, pp. 139–61. [G: Canada]

Gothoskar, S. S. Drug Control: India. *World Devel.*, March 1983, *11*(3), pp. 223–28. [G: India]

Gray, H. Peter and Walter, Ingo. Investment-Related Trade Distortions in Petrochemicals. *J. World Trade Law*, July–August 1983, *17*(4), pp. 283–307. [G: U.S.; W. Europe; Japan; Selected LDCs]

Hadden, Susan G. Labeling of Chemicals to Reduce Risk. *Law Contemp. Probl.*, Summer 1983, *46*(3), pp. 235–66.

Hansen, Ronald W. International Issues of Drug Regulation. *Z. ges. Staatswiss.*, October 1983, *139*(3), pp. 568–77. **[G: U.S.]**

Hinloopen, Edwin; Nijkamp, Peter and Rietveld, Piet. The Regime Method: A New Multicriteria Technique. **In** *Hansen, P., ed.*, 1983, pp. 146–55. **[G: Netherlands]**

Hoerger, Fred; Beamer, William H. and Hanson, James S. The Cumulative Impact of Health, Environmental, and Safety Concerns on the Chemical Industry during the Seventies. *Law Contemp. Probl.*, Summer 1983, *46*(3), pp. 59–107. **[G: U.S.]**

Jarrell, Stephen. Research and Development and Firm Size in the Pharmaceutical Industry. *Bus. Econ.*, September 1983, *18*(4), pp. 26–39. **[G: U.S.]**

Johnson, Ronald N. and Parkman, Allen. Spatial Monopoly, Non-Zero Profits and Entry Deterrence: The Case of Cement. *Rev. Econ. Statist.*, August 1983, *65*(3), pp. 431–39. **[G: U.S.]**

Kovács, Mátyás János. Bargaining—Assimilation—Bargaining: A Fragment of an Economic Drama in Four Acts. *Eastern Europ. Econ.*, Fall 1983, *22*(1), pp. 38–77. **[G: Hungary]**

Landa, Janet T. The Political Economy of the Ethnically Homogeneous Chinese Middleman Group in Southeast Asia: Ethnicity and Entrepreneurship in a Plural Society. **In** *Lim, L. Y. C. and Gosling, L. A. P., eds.*, 1983, pp. 86–116. **[G: Malaysia; Singapore]**

Madsen, Oli B. G. Production Planning in a Small Firm in the Glass Industry. **In** *Wilson, B.; Berg, C. C. and French, D., eds.*, 1983, pp. 245–53.

Marzagão, Carlos and Segall, Malcolm. Drug Selection: Mozambique. *World Devel.*, March 1983, *11*(3), pp. 205–16. **[G: Mozambique]**

McGarity, Thomas O. Media-Quality, Technology, and Cost-Benefit Balancing Strategies for Health and Environmental Regulation. *Law Contemp. Probl.*, Summer 1983, *46*(3), pp. 159–233.

Niculescu-Mizil, E. Cybernetic Peculiarities of the Development of Social-Economical Systems. *Econ. Computat. Cybern. Stud. Res.*, 1983, *18*(4), pp. 5–14. **[G: Romania]**

Patel, Mahesh S. Drug Costs in Developing Countries and Policies to Reduce Them. *World Devel.*, March 1983, *11*(3), pp. 195–204. **[G: LDCs]**

Pereira, Armand. Employment Implications of Ethanol Production in Brazil. *Int. Lab. Rev.*, January–February 1983, *122*(1), pp. 111–27. **[G: Brazil]**

Peretz, S. Michael. Pharmaceuticals in the Third World: The Problem from the Suppliers' Point of View. *World Devel.*, March 1983, *11*(3), pp. 259–64. **[G: LDCs]**

Schroeder, Christopher. A Decade of Change in Regulating the Chemical Industry. *Law Contemp. Probl.*, Summer 1983, *46*(3), pp. 1–40. **[G: U.S.]**

Schröter, Verena. The IG Farbenindustrie AG in Central and South-East Europe, 1926–38. **In** *Teichova, A. and Cottrell, P. L., eds.*, 1983, pp. 139–72. **[G: Europe]**

Stoica, M. and Şerban, R. Fuzzy Algorithms for Production Programming. *Econ. Computat. Cybern. Stud. Res.*, 1983, *18*(2), pp. 55–59.

Thackray, Arnold. University–Industry Connections and Chemical Research: An Historical Perspective. **In** *National Science Foundation*, 1983, pp. 193–233. **[G: U.S.]**

von Wartensleben, Aurelie. Major Issues Concerning Pharmaceutical Policies in the Third World. *World Devel.*, March 1983, *11*(3), pp. 169–75. **[G: LDCs; MDCs]**

White, Eduardo. Cooperation among National Drug Manufacturers: Asociación Latinoamericana de Industrias Farmacéuticas (ALIFAR). *World Devel.*, March 1983, *11*(3), pp. 271–79. **[G: Latin America]**

Wiggins, Steven N. The Impact of Regulation on Pharmaceutical Research Expenditures: A Dynamic Approach. *Econ. Inquiry*, January 1983, *21*(1), pp. 115–28. **[G: U.S.]**

Wionczek, Miguel S. Research and Development in Pharmaceuticals: Mexico. *World Devel.*, March 1983, *11*(3), pp. 243–50. **[G: Mexico]**

York, James D. Productivity Growth in Plastics Lower Than All Manufacturing. *Mon. Lab. Rev.*, September 1983, *106*(9), pp. 17–21. **[G: U.S.]**

6316 Textiles, Leather, and Clothing

Aggarwal, Vinod K. and Haggard, Stephan. The Politics of Protection in the U.S. Textile and Apparel Industries. **In** *Zysman, J. and Tyson, L., eds.*, 1983, pp. 249–312. **[G: U.S.]**

Ashoff, Guido. The Textile Policy of the European Community towards the Mediterranean Countries: Effects and Future Options. *J. Common Market Stud.*, September 1983, *22*(1), pp. 17–45. **[G: EEC]**

Ashtor, Eliyahu. The Wool Guild in Medieval Florence. *J. Europ. Econ. Hist.*, Spring 1983, *12*(1), pp. 197–201. **[G: Italy]**

Balassa, Bela. Industrial Prospects and Policies in the Developed Countries. **In** *[Giersch, H.]*, 1983, pp. 257–78. **[G: OECD; LDCs]**

Barry, Mary. Latin American Exports of Textiles and Apparel—Background Report. **In** *Czinkota, M. R., ed. (II)*, 1983, pp. 126–40. **[G: Latin America; E. Asia]**

ter Borg, Frank. The Impact of Cooperation with Western Firms on the Hungarian Clothing Industry. *ACES Bull. (See Comp. Econ. Stud. after 8/85)*, Summer 1983, *25*(2), pp. 105–20. **[G: Hungary]**

Chen, Edward K. Y. Multinational Corporations and Technology Diffusion in Hong Kong Manufacturing. *Appl. Econ.*, June 1983, *15*(3), pp. 309–21. **[G: Hong Kong]**

Edwards, Anthony. The Structure of Industrial Change: Regional Incentives to the Textile Industry of Northeast Brazil. **In** *Hamilton, F. E. I. and Linge, G. J. R., eds.*, 1983, pp. 485–508. **[G: Brazil]**

Farkas, Katalin. The Changing Role of Enterprise Inventories. *Eastern Europ. Econ.*, Spring–Summer 1983, *21*(3–4), pp. 49–66. **[G: Hungary]**

Fraser, Steven. Combined and Uneven Development in the Men's Clothing Industry. *Bus. Hist. Rev.*, Winter 1983, *57*(4), pp. 522–47. **[G: U.S.]**

Freedman, Martin and Stagliano, A. J. Worker Protection against Cotton Dust. *Challenge,* July/August 1983, *26*(3), pp. 57–59. **[G: U.S.]**

Gibbs, David C. The Effect of International and National Developments on the Clothing Industry of the Manchester Conurbation. **In** *Hamilton, F. E. I. and Linge, G. J. R., eds.,* 1983, pp. 233–54. **[G: U.K.; Selected Countries]**

Green, Diana M. Strategic Management and the State: France. **In** *Dyson, K. and Wilks, S., eds.,* 1983, pp. 161–92. **[G: France]**

Grey, Rodney de C. A Note on U.S. Trade Policy. **In** *Cline W. R., ed.,* 1983, pp. 243–57. **[G: U.S.]**

Halaga, Ondrej R. A Mercantilist Initiative to Compete with Venice: Kaschau's Fustian Monopoly (1411). *J. Europ. Econ. Hist.,* Fall 1983, *12*(2), pp. 407–35. **[G: Czechoslovakia]**

Healey, Michael. Components of Locational Change in Multi-Plant Enterprises. *Urban Stud.,* August 1983, *20*(3), pp. 327–42. **[G: U.K.]**

Hill, Hal. Choice of Technique in the Indonesian Weaving Industry. *Econ. Develop. Cult. Change,* January 1983, *31*(2), pp. 337–53. **[G: Indonesia]**

Jung, Ku-Hyun. The Sogo Shosha: Can It Be Exported (Imported)? **In** *Czinkota, M. R., ed. (I),* 1983, pp. 66–88. **[G: Japan; S. Korea]**

Lazonick, William. Industrial Organization and Technological Change: The Decline of the British Cotton Industry. *Bus. Hist. Rev.,* Summer 1983, *57*(2), pp. 195–236. **[G: U.K.]**

Martin, Randolph C. and Pelzman, Joseph. The Regional Welfare Effects of Tariff Reductions on Textile Products. *J. Reg. Sci.,* August 1983, *23*(3), pp. 323–36. **[G: U.S.]**

Minami, Ryoshin and Makino, Fumio. Conditions for Technological Diffusion: Case of Power Looms. *Hitotsubashi J. Econ.,* February 1983, *23*(2), pp. 1–20. **[G: Japan]**

Molteni, Corrado. The Development of the Silk Reeling Industry in the Process of Japanese Industrialization (1868–1930) *Rivista Int. Sci. Econ. Com.,* August 1983, *30*(8), pp. 735–58. **[G: Japan]**

Muysken, Joan. The Distribution Approach to the Aggregation of Putty–Clay Production Functions. *Europ. Econ. Rev.,* August 1983, *22*(3), pp. 351–62. **[G: Japan]**

Pelzman, Joseph. Economic Costs of Tariffs and Quotas on Textile and Apparel Products Imported into the United States: A Survey of the Literature and Implications for Policies. *Weltwirtsch. Arch.,* 1983, *119*(3), pp. 523–42. **[G: U.S.]**

Roboz, Thomas N. Apparel: Innovations That Will Lead to Growth. **In** *Federal Reserve Bank of Atlanta,* 1983, pp. 151–54. **[G: U.S.]**

Shaw, R. W. and Shaw, S. A. Excess Capacity and Rationalisation in the West European Synthetic Fibres Industry. *J. Ind. Econ.,* December 1983, *32*(2), pp. 149–66. **[G: W. Europe]**

Shepherd, Geoffrey. Textiles: New Ways of Surviving in an Old Industry. **In** *Shepherd, G.; Duchêne, F. and Saunders, C., eds.,* 1983, pp. 26–51. **[G: W. Germany; U.K.; France; U.S.; Italy]**

Shiells, Martha and Wright, Gavin. Night Work as a Labor Market Phenomenon: Southern Textiles in the Interwar Period. *Exploration Econ. Hist.,* October 1983, *20*(4), pp. 331–50. **[G: U.S.]**

Sikder, M. F. S. and Banerjee, Biswa Nath. An Economic Analysis of Jute Cultivation in West Bengal. *Econ. Aff.,* January–March 1983, *28*(1), pp. 592–604. **[G: India]**

Stennis, Earl A.; Pinar, Musa and Allen, Albert J. The Futures Market and Price Discovery in the Textile Industry. *Amer. J. Agr. Econ.,* May 1983, *65*(2), pp. 308–10. **[G: U.S.]**

Twomey, Michael J. Employment in Nineteenth Century Indian Textiles. *Exploration Econ. Hist.,* January 1983, *20*(1), pp. 37–57. **[G: India]**

Watkins, G. C. and Berndt, Ernst R. Energy-Output Coefficients: Complex Realities behind Simple Ratios. *Energy J.,* April 1983, *4*(2), pp. 105–20. **[G: Canada]**

Williams, Harry B. Pay Levels in Hosiery Manufacturing. *Mon. Lab. Rev.,* March 1983, *106*(3), pp. 36–37. **[G: U.S.]**

Wolf, Martin. Managed Trade in Practice: Implications of the Textile Arrangements. **In** *Cline W. R., ed.,* 1983, pp. 455–82. **[G: Selected Countries]**

Yamazawa, Ippei. Renewal of the Textile Industry in Developed Countries and World Textile Trade. *Hitotsubashi J. Econ.,* June 1983, *24*(1), pp. 25–41. **[G: Selected Countries]**

Yoffie, David B. Adjustment in the Footwear Industry: The Consequences of Orderly Marketing Agreements. **In** *Zysman, J. and Tyson, L., eds.,* 1983, pp. 313–49. **[G: U.S.]**

6317 Forest Products, Lumber, Paper, Printing and Publishing

Abbott, Philip C. Problems of the Forest Industry: Discussion. *Amer. J. Agr. Econ.,* December 1983, *65*(5), pp. 1019–20. **[G: U.S.]**

Allen, Bruce T. Concentration, Scale Economies, and the Size Distribution of Plants. *Quart. Rev. Econ. Bus.,* Winter 1983, *23*(4), pp. 6–27. **[G: U.S.]**

Anderson, F. J.; Beaudreau, B. C. and Bonsor, N. C. Effective Corporate Tax Rates, Inflation, and Contestability. *Can. J. Econ.,* November 1983, *16*(4), pp. 686–703. **[G: Canada; U.S.]**

Boyd, Roy. Costs and Distortions of U.S. Regulations Policy in Intercoastal Lumber Shipping. *J. Policy Modeling,* June 1983, *5*(2), pp. 293–307. **[G: U.S.]**

Boyd, Roy. Lumber Transport and the Jones Act: A Multicommodity Spatial Equilibrium Analysis. *Bell J. Econ. (See Rand J. Econ. after 4/85),* Spring 1983, *14*(1), pp. 202–12. **[G: Canada; U.S.]**

Fery, John B. America's Forests: Cash Crop or National Monument? **In** *Barnes, C. H., ed.,* 1983, pp. 34–46. **[G: U.S.]**

Gács, János. Planning and Adjustment Policy Changes in the Development of the Building Materials Industry. *Eastern Europ. Econ.,* Spring–Summer 1983, *21*(3–4), pp. 105–24. **[G: Hungary]**

Gennard, John and Dunn, Steve. The Impact of New Technology on the Structure and Organisation of Craft Unions in the Printing Industry. *Brit. J. Ind. Relat.,* March 1983, *21*(1), pp. 17–32. **[G: U.K.]**

Haavisto, Heikki. Finlands skogs- och skogsindustripolitik. (Finland's Forest and Forest Industry Policy. With English summary.) *Ekon. Samfundets*

Tidskr., 1983, *36*(2), pp. 65–70. [G: Finland]

Hardie, Ian W. Problems of the Forest Industry: Discussion. *Amer. J. Agr. Econ.*, December 1983, *65*(5), pp. 1017–18. [G: U.S.]

Haynes, Richard W. and Adams, Darius M. Changing Perceptions of the U.S. Forest Sector: Implications for the RPA Timber Assessment. *Amer. J. Agr. Econ.*, December 1983, *65*(5), pp. 1002–09. [G: U.S.]

Helliwell, John F. and Margolick, Michael. Some Hard Economics of Soft Energy: Optimal Electricity Generation in Pulp and Paper Mills with Seasonal Steam Requirements. **In** *[Klein, L. R.]*, 1983, pp. 219–35. [G: Canada]

Hultkrantz, Lars. Energy Substitution in the Forest Industry. **In** *Ysander, B.-C., ed.*, 1983, pp. 209–26. [G: Sweden]

Martin, John P. and Page, John M., Jr. The Impact of Subsidies on X-Efficiency in LDC Industry: Theory and an Empirical Test. *Rev. Econ. Statist.*, November 1983, *65*(4), pp. 608–17. [G: Ghana]

McBride, Mark E. Spatial Competition and Vertical Integration: Cement and Concrete Revisited. *Amer. Econ. Rev.*, December 1983, *73*(5), pp. 1011–22. [G: U.S.]

Pittman, Russell W. Multilateral Productivity Comparisons with Undesirable Outputs. *Econ. J.*, December 1983, *93*(372), pp. 883–91. [G: U.S.]

Salmi, Timo, et al. Extracting and Analyzing the Time Series for Profitability Measurement from Published Financial Statements: With Results on Publicly Traded Finnish Metal Industry Firms: Part II. *Liiketaloudellinen Aikak.*, 1983, *32*(3), pp. 209–41. [G: Finland]

Scaggs, Mary Beth W. Recent Employment Trends in the Lumber and Wood Products Industry. *Mon. Lab. Rev.*, August 1983, *106*(8), pp. 20–24. [G: U.S.]

Sedjo, Roger A. and Lyon, Kenneth S. Long-Term Forest Resources Trade, Global Timber Supply, and Intertemporal Comparative Advantage. *Amer. J. Agr. Econ.*, December 1983, *65*(5), pp. 1010–16. [G: U.S.]

Turner, R. K. and Deadman, D. The UK Wastepaper Industry and Its Long Term Prospects. *J. Ind. Econ.*, December 1983, *32*(2), pp. 167–85. [G: U.K.]

Wikander, Ulla. The Swedish Match Company in Central Europe between the Wars: 'Internal Power Struggle' between Former Competitors—Solo v. Swedish Match. **In** *Teichova, A. and Cottrell, P. L., eds.*, 1983, pp. 209–25. [G: Sweden; Europe]

6318 Food Processing, Tobacco, and Beverages

Acheson, Keith. The Pricing Practices of the Liquor Control Board of Ontario: Reconsidered. *Can. J. Econ.*, February 1983, *16*(1), pp. 161–66. [G: Canada]

Allaya, M.; Ghersi, G. and Padilla, M. Évolution des prix alimentaires et structures de marché. (With English summary.) *Écon. Soc.*, May 1983, *17*(5), pp. 785–822. [G: France]

Alpine, Robin L. W. The Case of Whisky: Use of Data. **In** *Ingham, K. P. D. and Love, J., eds.*, 1983, pp. 284–96. [G: U.K.]

Babb, Emerson M. and Lang, Mahlon G. Intrafirm Decision Making: Private and Public Consequences. **In** *Farris, P. L., ed.*, 1983, pp. 38–53. [G: U.S.]

Boehm, William T. and Lenahan, Robert J. Health and Safety Regulations and Food System Performance. **In** *Farris, P. L., ed.*, 1983, pp. 264–77. [G: U.S.]

Brandt, Jon A. and French, Ben C. Mechanical Harvesting and the California Tomato Industry: A Simulation Analysis. *Amer. J. Agr. Econ.*, May 1983, *65*(2), pp. 265–72. [G: U.S.]

Breimyer, Harold F. Foreign Investment in the U.S. Food-Marketing System: Discussion. *Amer. J. Agr. Econ.*, May 1983, *65*(2), pp. 421–22. [G: U.S.]

Bulow, Jeremy I. and Pfleiderer, Paul. A Note on the Effect of Cost Changes on Prices [Measurement of Monopoly Behavior: An Application to the Cigarette Industry]. *J. Polit. Econ.*, February 1983, *91*(1), pp. 182–85. [G: U.S.]

Burns, Malcolm R. An Empirical Analysis of Stockholder Injury under § 2 of the Sherman Act. *J. Ind. Econ.*, June 1983, *31*(4), pp. 333–62. [G: U.S.]

Burns, Malcolm R. Economies of Scale in Tobacco Manufacture, 1897–1910. *J. Econ. Hist.*, June 1983, *43*(2), pp. 461–74. [G: U.S.]

Capps, Oral, Jr.; Tedford, John R. and Havlicek, Joseph, Jr. Impacts of Household Composition on Convenience and Nonconvenience Food Expenditures in the South. *Southern J. Agr. Econ.*, December 1983, *15*(2), pp. 111–18. [G: U.S.]

Chambers, Robert G. International Trade, Gross Substitutability and the Domestic Farm–Retail Price Margin. *Europ. Rev. Agr. Econ.*, 1983, *10*(1), pp. 33–53.

Comanor, William. Comment [Advertising and Concentration Change in U.S. Food and Tobacco Product Classes, 1958–1972] [The Causes of Concentration in the U.S. Brewing Industry]. **In** *Connor, J. M. and Ward, R. W., eds.*, 1983, pp. 317–19. [G: U.S.]

Connor, John M. Determinants of Foreign Direct Investment by Food and Tobacco Manufacturers. *Amer. J. Agr. Econ.*, May 1983, *65*(2), pp. 395–404. [G: U.S.]

Cook, Philip J. The Effect of Liquor Taxes on Drinking, Cirrhosis, and Auto Fatalities. **In** *Zeckhauser, R. J. and Leebaert, D., eds.*, 1983, pp. 203–20. [G: U.S.]

Culbertson, John. The Effect of Advertising on Price Change for Food Manufacturing Product Classes: Comment. **In** *Connor, J. M. and Ward, R. W., eds.*, 1983, pp. 276–78. [G: U.S.]

Duffy, M. The Demand for Alcoholic Drink in the United Kingdom, 1963–78. *Appl. Econ.*, February 1983, *15*(1), pp. 125–40. [G: U.K.]

Faminow, M. D. and Sarhan, M. E. The Location of Fed Cattle Slaughtering and Processing in the United States: An Application of Mixed Integer Programming. *Can. J. Agr. Econ.*, November 1983, *31*(3), pp. 425–36. [G: U.S.]

Geroski, P. A. Some Reflections on the Theory and Application of Concentration Indices. *Int. J. Ind. Organ.*, 1983, *1*(1), pp. 79–94. [G: U.S.]

Greer, Douglas F. The Causes of Concentration in the U.S. Brewing Industry. **In** *Connor, J. M. and Ward, R. W., eds.*, 1983, pp. 295–314. **[G: U.S.]**

Hamm, Larry G. The Interactions of Food Manufacturer Advertising and Food Retailer Buying Practices: Some Implications for Food System Organizations. **In** *Connor, J. M. and Ward, R. W., eds.*, 1983, pp. 215–33. **[G: U.S.]**

Heien, Dale M. Productivity in U.S. Food Processing and Distribution. *Amer. J. Agr. Econ.*, May 1983, *65*(2), pp. 297–302. **[G: U.S.]**

Henry, Mark S. The Impact of Natural Gas Price Deregulation on the South Carolina Food-Processing Sectors. *Southern J. Agr. Econ.*, December 1983, *15*(2), pp. 41–48. **[G: U.S.]**

Hiemstra, Stephen J. Marketing Impacts of the Domestic Food Assistance Programs. **In** *Farris, P. L., ed.*, 1983, pp. 278–95. **[G: U.S.]**

Hoffman, Oscar. The Interactions of Food Manufacturer Advertising and Food Retailer Buying Practices: Some Implications for Food System Organizations: Commentary. **In** *Connor, J. M. and Ward, R. W., eds.*, 1983, pp. 235–36. **[G: U.S.]**

Kelton, Christina M. L. The Effect of Advertising on Price Change for Food Manufacturing Product Classes. **In** *Connor, J. M. and Ward, R. W., eds.*, 1983, pp. 257–73. **[G: U.S.]**

Kilmer, Richard L.; Spreen, Thomas H. and Tilley, Daniel S. A Dynamic Plant Location Model: The East Florida Fresh Citrus Packing Industry. *Amer. J. Agr. Econ.*, November 1983, *65*(4), pp. 730–37. **[G: U.S.]**

Kirchner, Emil and Williams, Karen. The Legal, Political and Institutional Implications of the Isoglucose Judgments 1980. *J. Common Market Stud.*, December 1983, *22*(2), pp. 173–90. **[G: EEC]**

Kitchin, Paul Duncan. Socio-Economic Determinants of UK Alcohol Consumption, 1956–79. *Int. J. Soc. Econ.*, 1983, *10*(3), pp. 34–39. **[G: U.K.]**

Koshal, Manjulika and Koshal, Rajindar K. Cash Management Economies in the Production of Food. *Managerial Dec. Econ.*, December 1983, *4*(4), pp. 253–57. **[G: U.S.]**

Lamm, R. McFall, Jr. Commentary [Advertising and Concentration Change in U.S. Food and Tobacco Product Classes, 1958–1972] [The Causes of Concentration in the U.S. Brewing Industry]. **In** *Connor, J. M. and Ward, R. W., eds.*, 1983, pp. 315–17. **[G: U.S.]**

Lee, Jong-Ying and Tilley, Daniel S. Irreversible Import Shares for Frozen Concentrated Orange Juice in Canada. *Southern J. Agr. Econ.*, December 1983, *15*(2), pp. 99–104. **[G: Brazil; Canada; U.S.]**

Liebowitz, S. J. and Bridgeman, Guy A. The Pricing Practices of the Liquor Control Board of Ontario: Revisited. *Can. J. Econ.*, February 1983, *16*(1), pp. 154–61. **[G: Canada]**

MacDonald, James M.; Scheffman, David T. and Whitten, Ira Taylor. Advertising and Quality in Food Products: Some New Evidence on the Nelson Hypothesis. **In** *Connor, J. M. and Ward, R. W., eds.*, 1983, pp. 137–47. **[G: U.S.]**

Malassis, L. Filières et systèmes agro-alimentaires. (With English summary.) *Écon. Soc.*, May 1983, *17*(5), pp. 911–21.

Manchester, Alden C. The Role and Dimensions of Food Advertising for 100 Years. **In** *Connor, J. M. and Ward, R. W., eds.*, 1983, pp. 105–30. **[G: U.S.]**

Mann, Michael. Advertising and Quality in Food Products: Some New Evidence on the Nelson Hypothesis: Commentary. **In** *Connor, J. M. and Ward, R. W., eds.*, 1983, pp. 159–60. **[G: U.S.]**

Mann, Michael. The Competitive Impact of Advertising in U.S. Food Processing Industries: A Simultaneous Equation Approach: Commentary. **In** *Connor, J. M. and Ward, R. W., eds.*, 1983, pp. 275–76. **[G: U.S.]**

Marion, Bruce W. and Mueller, Willard F. Industrial Organization, Economic Power, and the Food System. **In** *Farris, P. L., ed.*, 1983, pp. 16–37. **[G: U.S.]**

Mather, Loys L. and Tucker, Laurel I. Conglomerate Mergers, Food Advertising, and the Cross Subsidization Hypothesis. **In** *Connor, J. M. and Ward, R. W., eds.*, 1983, pp. 201–13. **[G: U.S.]**

McNiel, Douglas W.; Burbee, Clark R. and Wetzel, Howard R., II. Supply Response to Technological Change and Regulation: The Case of Mechanically Deboned Poultry. *Southern J. Agr. Econ.*, December 1983, *15*(2), pp. 133–37. **[G: U.S.]**

Moy, James H. and Nip, Wai K. Taro: Processed Food. **In** *Wang, J.-K., ed.*, 1983, pp. 261–68.

Mueller, Willard F. Market Power and Its Control in the Food System. *Amer. J. Agr. Econ.*, December 1983, *65*(5), pp. 855–63. **[G: U.S.]**

Nielsen, Peter Bøegh. Aspects of Industrial Financing in Denmark 1890–1914. *Scand. Econ. Hist. Rev.*, 1983, *31*(2), pp. 79–108. **[G: Denmark]**

Norton, George W. and Bernat, G. Andrew, Jr. Estimating the Effects of Pesticide Use on Burley and Flue-Cured Tobacco. *Southern J. Agr. Econ.*, December 1983, *15*(2), pp. 93–98. **[G: U.S.]**

Padberg, Daniel I. and Westgren, Randall E. Adaptability of Consumers and Manufacturers to Changes in Cultural Patterns and Socioeconomic Values. **In** *Farris, P. L., ed.*, 1983, pp. 246–63. **[G: U.S.]**

Pagoulatos, Emilio. Foreign Direct Investment in U.S. Food and Tobacco Manufacturing and Domestic Economic Performance. *Amer. J. Agr. Econ.*, May 1983, *65*(2), pp. 405–12. **[G: U.S.]**

Pagoulatos, Emilio and Sorensen, Robert. The Competitive Impact of Advertising in U.S. Food Processing Industries: A Simultaneous Equation Approach. **In** *Connor, J. M. and Ward, R. W., eds.*, 1983, pp. 241–56. **[G: U.S.]**

Parker, Russell. Commentary [Food Advertising, 1954 to 1979] [The Role and Dimensions of Food Advertising for 100 Years]. **In** *Connor, J. M. and Ward, R. W., eds.*, 1983, pp. 131–33. **[G: U.S.]**

Parker, Russell. Comments [Conglomerate Mergers, Food Advertising, and the Cross Subsidization Hypothesis] [The Interactions of Food Manufacturer Advertising and Food Retailer Buying Practices: Some Implications for Food System Organizations]. **In** *Connor, J. M. and Ward, R. W., eds.*, 1983, pp. 236–37. **[G: U.S.]**

Porter, Richard C. A Social Benefit–Cost Analysis of Mandatory Deposits on Beverage Containers: A

Correction. *J. Environ. Econ. Manage.*, June 1983, *10*(2), pp. 191–93. [G: U.S.]

Porter, Richard C. Michigan's Experience with Mandatory Deposits on Beverage Containers. *Land Econ.*, May 1983, *59*(2), pp. 177–94. [G: U.S.]

Pugel, Thomas A. Foreign Investment in the U.S. Food-Marketing System: Discussion. *Amer. J. Agr. Econ.*, May 1983, *65*(2), pp. 423–25.

Ricker, Harold S.; Anderson, Dale L. and Phillips, Michael J. Technology Adoption in the Agricultural Marketing System. **In** *Farris, P. L., ed.*, 1983, pp. 117–36. [G: U.S.]

Rivero, Nicolás and Díaz Franjúl, Manuel. Thoughts on Sugar Diversification: An Inter-American Fuel Alcohol Program. **In** *Czinkota, M. R., ed. (II)*, 1983, pp. 107–25. [G: Latin America; U.S.]

Rogers, Richard T. Advertising and Concentration Change in U.S. Food and Tobacco Product Classes, 1958–1972. **In** *Connor, J. M. and Ward, R. W., eds.*, 1983, pp. 283–94. [G: U.S.]

Rogers, Richard T. and Mather, Loys L. Food Advertising, 1954 to 1979. **In** *Connor, J. M. and Ward, R. W., eds.*, 1983, pp. 75–103. [G: U.S.]

Rouba, Helena. Functions of the Food-processing Industry in Promoting the Development of Agricultural Regions in Poland. *Europ. Rev. Agr. Econ.*, 1983, *10*(3), pp. 249–69. [G: Poland]

Shoup, Carl S. Current Trends in Excise Taxation. **In** *[Goode, R.]*, 1983, pp. 257–75. [G: OECD]

Witt, Stephen F. and Pass, Christopher L. Forecasting Cigarette Consumption: The Causal Model Approach. *Int. J. Soc. Econ.*, 1983, *10*(3), pp. 18–33. [G: U.K.]

6319 Other Industries

Ayres, Ron. Arms Production as a Form of Import-Substituting Industrialization: The Turkish Case. *World Devel.*, September 1983, *11*(9), pp. 813–23. [G: Turkey]

Ball, Nicole. The Structure of the Defense Industry: Appendix 1: The United Kingdom. **In** *Ball, N. and Leitenberg, M., eds.*, 1983, pp. 344–60. [G: U.K.]

Brzoska, Michael. The Structure of the Defense Industry: The Federal Republic of Germany. **In** *Ball, N. and Leitenberg, M., eds.*, 1983, pp. 111–39. [G: W. Germany]

Hodge, Melville H. Small Business Ventures and Solar Energy Development. **In** *Rich, D., et al., eds.*, 1983, pp. 135–44.

Holloway, David. The Structure of the Defense Industry: The Soviet Union. **In** *Ball, N. and Leitenberg, M., eds.*, 1983, pp. 50–80. [G: U.S.S.R.]

Holmström, Per and Olsson, Ulf. The Structure of the Defense Industry: Sweden. **In** *Ball, N. and Leitenberg, M., eds.*, 1983, pp. 140–80. [G: Sweden]

Kolodziej, Edward A. The Structure of the Defense Industry: France. **In** *Ball, N. and Leitenberg, M., eds.*, 1983, pp. 81–110. [G: France]

Reppy, Judith. The Structure of the Defense Industry: The United States. **In** *Ball, N. and Leitenberg, M., eds.*, 1983, pp. 21–49. [G: U.S.]

Rossi, Sergio A. The Structure of the Defense Industry: Italy. **In** *Ball, N. and Leitenberg, M., eds.*, 1983, pp. 214–56. [G: Italy]

Tiedtke, Stephen. The Structure of the Defense Industry: Czechoslovakia. **In** *Ball, N. and Leitenberg, M., eds.*, 1983, pp. 181–213. [G: Czechoslovakia]

Weissbach, Lee Shai. Entrepreneurial Traditionalism in Nineteenth-Century France: A Study of the *Patronage industriel des enfants de l'ébénisterie. Bus. Hist. Rev.*, Winter 1983, *57*(4), pp. 548–65. [G: France]

Wulf, Herbert. The Structure of the Defense Industry: Developing Countries. **In** *Ball, N. and Leitenberg, M., eds.*, 1983, pp. 310–43. [G: LDCs]

632 Industry Studies: Extractive Industries

6320 General

Akao, Nobutoshi. Resources and Japan's Security. **In** *Akao, N., ed.*, 1983, pp. 15–44. [G: Japan]

Fraser, R. W. and Van Noorden, R. J. Extraction of an Exhaustible Resource: The Effects on Investment of Several Parameters Being Subject to Uncertainty. *Econ. Rec.*, December 1983, *59*(167), pp. 365–74.

Khachaturov, Tigran S. Intensification of the Utilization of Material Resources. *Prob. Econ.*, August 1983, *26*(4), pp. 3–23. [G: U.S.S.R.]

Kulev, I. A. Soviet–Finnish Cooperation for Joint Construction of Industrial Objects. **In** *Möttölä, K.; Bykov, O. N. and Korolev, I. S., eds.*, 1983, pp. 122–36. [G: U.S.S.R.; Finland]

Lantzke, Ulf. Investment and Energy. **In** *Heertje, A., ed.*, 1983, pp. 117–51. [G: W. Europe]

Levin, Nissan; Tishler, Asher and Zahavi, Jacob. Perturbation Analysis of Power Generation Expansion Programs Subject to Uncertainty in the Prices of Primary Energy Resources. **In** *Lev, B., ed.*, 1983, pp. 367–85. [G: U.S.]

Lohrenz, John and Waller, Ray A. Federal Mineral-Lease Bidding Data Bases and the Real World. **In** *Engelbrecht-Wiggans, R.; Shubik, M. and Stark, R. M., eds.*, 1983, pp. 335–61. [G: U.S.]

Zimmerman, Martin B. Comparisons, Recommendations, and Conclusions: Resources and Reserves. **In** *Adelman, M. A., et al.*, 1983, pp. 385–93.

6322 Mining (metal, coal, and other nonmetallic minerals)

Abbey, David S. and Kolstad, Charles D. The Structure of International Steam Coal Markets. *Natural Res. J.*, October 1983, *23*(4), pp. 859–91. [G: Selected Countries]

Adelman, M. A. and Houghton, John C. Introduction to Estimation of Reserves and Resources. **In** *Adelman, M. A., et al.*, 1983, pp. 1–25. [G: U.S.]

Alt, Christopher B.; Baumann, Michael G. and Zimmerman, Martin B. The Economics of Western Coal Severance Taxes. *J. Bus.*, October 1983, *56*(4), pp. 519–36. [G: U.S.]

Antrim, Lance N. and Sebenius, James K. Incentives for Ocean Mining under the Convention. **In** *Oxman, B. H.; Caron, D. D. and Buderi, C. L. O., eds.*, 1983, pp. 79–99. [G: U.S.]

Armstrong, Robert. Le développement des droits miniers au Québec à la fin du XIXe siècle. (The Development of Mining Rights in Quebec at the End of the 19th Century. With English summary.) *L'Actual. Econ.*, September 1983, *59*(3), pp. 576–95. **[G: Canada]**

Bailey, John S. The Future of the Exploitation of the Resources of the Deep Seabed and Subsoil. *Law Contemp. Probl.*, Spring 1983, *46*(2), pp. 71–76. **[G: Global]**

Bailey, Richard. Coal in a Changing Market. *Nat. Westminster Bank Quart. Rev.*, August 1983, pp. 14–25. **[G: U.K.]**

Bieniewicz, Donald J. and Nelson, Robert H. Planning a Market for Federal Coal Leasing. *Natural Res. J.*, July 1983, *23*(3), pp. 593–604. **[G: U.S.]**

Bosson, Rex and Varon, Bension. Problems of Mineral Development in Developing Countries. **In** *Glassner, M. I., ed.*, 1983, *1977*, pp. 381–95. **[G: LDCs; MDCs]**

Braunstein, Philippe. Innovations in Mining and Metal Production in Europe in the Late Middle Ages. *J. Europ. Econ. Hist.*, Winter 1983, *12*(3), pp. 573–91. **[G: Europe]**

Brett, Jeanne M. and Goldberg, Stephen B. Grievance Mediation in the Coal Industry: A Field Experiment. *Ind. Lab. Relat. Rev.*, October 1983, *37*(1), pp. 49–69. **[G: U.S.]**

Bruce, Harry J.; Horwitch, Mel and Nueno, Pedro. The Evolution of the International Coal Trade: A Strategic and Decision-Making Perspective. *J. Int. Bus. Stud.*, Spring/Summer 1983, *14*(1), pp. 85–101. **[G: Hong Kong; OECD; S. Korea; Taiwan]**

Chen, Yun. Talk at the Forum on Coal Work. **In** *Ch'en, Y.*, 1983, *1961*, pp. 174–80. **[G: China]**

Cohen, Lewis I. International Cooperation on Seabed Mining. **In** *Oxman, B. H.; Caron, D. D. and Buderi, C. L. O., eds.*, 1983, pp. 101–09. **[G: OECD]**

Crandall, Robert W. Air Pollution, Environmentalists, and the Coal Lobby. **In** *Noll, R. G. and Owen, B. M.*, 1983, pp. 84–96. **[G: U.S.]**

Crowson, Phillip. Non-fuel Mineral Procurement Policies. **In** *Akao, N., ed.*, 1983, pp. 145–67. **[G: Japan; Selected Countries]**

Davies, Mel. Copper and Credit: Commission Agents and the South Australian Mining Association 1845–77. *Australian Econ. Hist. Rev.*, March 1983, *23*(1), pp. 58–77. **[G: Australia]**

Dubs, Marne A. The Future of the Exploitation of the Resources of the Deep Seabed and Subsoil: Comment. *Law Contemp. Probl.*, Spring 1983, *46*(2), pp. 81–85. **[G: Global]**

Emerson, Craig and Lloyd, Peter J. Improving Mineral Taxation Policy in Australia. *Econ. Rec.*, September 1983, *59*(166), pp. 232–44. **[G: Australia]**

Fischer, P. G. The Österreichisch-Alpine Montangesellschaft, 1918–38. **In** *Teichova, A. and Cottrell, P. L., eds.*, 1983, pp. 253–67. **[G: Austria]**

Gaffen, Michael. The World Coal Trade in the 1980s: The Rebirth of a Market. **In** *Aronson, J. D. and Cowhey, P. F., eds.*, 1983, pp. 83–104. **[G: Global]**

Gallini, Nancy T. Sequential Development of Correlated Projects: An Application to Coal Liquefaction. *Energy Econ.*, January 1983, *5*(1), pp. 37–48.

Garnaut, Ross. Energy Policy, Taxation of Natural Resources and Fiscal Federalism: Comment. **In** *McLure, C. E., Jr., ed.*, 1983, pp. 146–47.

Gaudet, Gérard. Investissement optimal et coûts d'adjustement dans la théorie économique de la mine. (Optimal Investment and Adjustment Costs in the Economic Theory of the Mine. With English summary.) *Can. J. Econ.*, February 1983, *16*(1), pp. 39–51.

Gidlow, R. M. Hedging Policies of the South African Gold Mining Industry. *S. Afr. J. Econ.*, June 1983, *51*(2), pp. 270–82. **[G: S. Africa]**

Goldberg, Stephen B. and Brett, Jeanne M. An Experiment in the Mediation of Grievances. *Mon. Lab. Rev.*, March 1983, *106*(3), pp. 23–30. **[G: U.S.]**

Gordon, Richard L. The Evolution of Coal Market Models and Coal Policy Analysis. **In** *Lev, B., ed.*, 1983, pp. 65–84. **[G: U.S.]**

Haynes, Kingsley E.; Phillips, Fred Y. and Solomon, Barry D. A Coal Industry Distribution Planning Model under Environmental Constraints. *Econ. Geogr.*, January 1983, *59*(1), pp. 52–65.

Hirsch, Barry T. and Hausman, William J. Labour Productivity in the British and South Wales Coal Industry, 1874–1914. *Economica*, May 1983, *50*(198), pp. 145–57. **[G: U.K.]**

Jones, R. A. Mechanization, Learning Periods, and Productivity Change in the South African Coal Mining Industry: 1950–80. *S. Afr. J. Econ.*, December 1983, *51*(4), pp. 507–22. **[G: S. Africa]**

Kalt, Joseph P. The Costs and Benefits of Federal Regulation of Coal Strip Mining. *Natural Res. J.*, October 1983, *23*(4), pp. 893–915. **[G: U.S.]**

Kolstad, Charles D. and Wolak, Frank A., Jr. Competition in Interregional Taxation: The Case of Western Coal. *J. Polit. Econ.*, June 1983, *91*(3), pp. 443–60. **[G: U.S.]**

Lasserre, Pierre. L'aide aux mines d'or ou Les silences du fantôme de Bretton Woods. (With English summary.) *Can. Public Policy*, December 1983, *9*(4), pp. 446–57. **[G: Canada]**

Lazarus, William. Landsats, Minerals and Development: A Qualitative Notion of the Down-Side Risk. **In** *O'Brien, R. C., ed.*, 1983, pp. 102–21. **[G: U.S.]**

Lev, Benjamin and Murphy, Frederic H. The Sensitivity of the Shape of the Long-run Supply Curve of Coal to Different Assumptions on Seam Thickness. **In** *Lev, B., ed.*, 1983, pp. 293–307. **[G: U.S.]**

Marsh, James Barney. Keynes on the Supply of Gold: A Statistical Test. *Eastern Econ. J.*, January–March 1983, *9*(1), pp. 7–12. **[G: S. Africa]**

Marz, Edward. The Österreichisch-Alpine Montangesellschaft, 1918–38: Commentary. **In** *Teichova, A. and Cottrell, P. L., eds.*, 1983, pp. 267–68. **[G: Austria]**

McMahon, L. A. and Harris, Stuart. Coal Development: Issues for Japan and Australia. **In** *Akao, N., ed.*, 1983, pp. 71–95. **[G: Japan; Australia]**

Mehring, Joyce S.; Sarkar, Debashish and Shapiro, Jeremy F. Decomposition Methods and Computation of Spatial Equilibria: An Application to Coal Supply and Demand Markets. **In** *Lev, B., ed.*, 1983, pp. 221–33.

Mero, John L. Will Ocean Mining Revolutionize World Industry? **In** *Glassner, M. I., ed.*, 1983, *1977*, pp. 580–88. **[G: Global]**

Mieszkowski, Peter. Energy Policy, Taxation of Natural Resources, and Fiscal Federalism. **In** *McLure, C. E., Jr., ed.*, 1983, pp. 128–45. **[G: U.S.]**

Mutti, John H. and Morgan, William E. Changing Energy Prices and Economic Rents: The Case of Western Coal. *Land Econ.*, May 1983, *59*(2), pp. 163–76. **[G: U.S.]**

Navarro, Peter. Union Bargaining Power in the Coal Industry, 1945–1981. *Ind. Lab. Relat. Rev.*, January 1983, *36*(2), pp. 214–29. **[G: U.S.]**

Osleeb, Jeffrey P. and Patrick, Samuel J. The Impact of Coal Conversions on the Ports of New England. *Econ. Geogr.*, January 1983, *59*(1), pp. 35–51. **[G: U.S.]**

Pachauri, Rajendra K. and Labys, Walter C. Changing Markets for Coal: Opportunities for the Developing Countries. **In** *Tempest, P., ed.*, 1983, pp. 35–41. **[G: LDCs]**

Pollard, Sidney. Capitalism and Rationality: A Study of Measurements in British Coal Mining, ca. 1750–1850. *Exploration Econ. Hist.*, January 1983, *20*(1), pp. 110–29. **[G: U.K.]**

Rasnic, Carol D. Federally Required Restoration of Surface-Mined Property: Impasse between the Coal Industry and the Environmentally Concerned. *Natural Res. J.*, April 1983, *23*(2), pp. 335–49. **[G: U.S.]**

Rosenblum, Jay. The Swank Decision: Economic Interest in Coal Not Dependent on Lease Terminability. *Natural Res. J.*, January 1983, *23*(1), pp. 247–54. **[G: U.S.]**

Sargent, D. Alec. The United States' Role in the International Thermal Coal Market. *Energy J.*, January 1983, *4*(1), pp. 79–96. **[G: U.S.; OECD]**

Sider, Hal. Safety and Productivity in Underground Coal Mining. *Rev. Econ. Statist.*, May 1983, *65*(2), pp. 225–33. **[G: U.S.]**

Simon, Richard M. Hard Times for Organized Labor in Appalachia. *Rev. Radical Polit. Econ.*, Fall 1983, *15*(3), pp. 21–34. **[G: U.S.]**

Stollery, Kenneth R. Mineral Depletion with Cost as the Extraction Limit: A Model Applied to the Behavior of Prices in the Nickel Industry. *J. Environ. Econ. Manage.*, June 1983, *10*(2), pp. 151–65. **[G: U.S.]**

Terray, E. Gold Production, Slave Labor, and State Intervention in Precolonial Akan Societies: A Reply to Raymond Dumett. **In** *Dalton, G., ed.*, 1983, pp. 95–129. **[G: W. Africa]**

Thirsk, Wayne R. Energy Policy, Taxation of Natural Resources and Fiscal Federalism: Comment. **In** *McLure, C. E., Jr., ed.*, 1983, pp. 148–49. **[G: U.S.]**

Thompson, Alexander M., III. Technological Change and the Control of Work: The U.S. Bituminous Coal Industry 1865–1930. *Econ. Forum*, Winter 1983-84, *14*(2), pp. 1–18. **[G: U.S.]**

United Nations. Seabed Mineral Resource Development: Recent Activities of the International Consortia. **In** *Glassner, M. I., ed.*, 1983, *1980*, pp. 589–99. **[G: Global]**

Watson, William D. Drilling Strategies for Federal Coal Leases. **In** *Lev, B., ed.*, 1983, pp. 465–81. **[G: U.S.]**

Welch, Lawrence R. and Wiedersheim-Paul, Finn. MNCs and the Australian Government: Some Emerging Policy Issues. **In** *Goldberg, W. H., ed.*, 1983, pp. 249–69. **[G: Australia]**

Zimmerman, Martin B. Coal: An Economic Interpretation of Reserve Estimates. **In** *Adelman, M. A., et al.*, 1983, pp. 295–332. **[G: U.S.]**

6323 Oil, Gas, and Other Fuels

Abbott, Catherine Good and Watson, Stephen A. Pitfalls on the Road to Decontrol: Lessons from the Natural Gas Policy Act of 1978. **In** *Mitchell, E. J., ed.*, 1983, pp. 53–70. **[G: U.S.]**

Adelman, Morris A. Oil and Gas: Estimation of Discovered Reserves. **In** *Adelman, M. A., et al.*, 1983, pp. 27–81. **[G: U.S.; Canada]**

Adelman, Morris A. The Changing Structure of the Oil and Gas Market. **In** *Tempest, P., ed.*, 1983, pp. 15–25.

Adelman, Morris A. The Multinationals in the World Oil Market: The 1970s and the 1980s. **In** *Kindleberger, C. P. and Audretsch, D. B., eds.*, 1983, pp. 123–35. **[G: OECD; OPEC]**

Allen, Bruce T. Concentration, Scale Economies, and the Size Distribution of Plants. *Quart. Rev. Econ. Bus.*, Winter 1983, *23*(4), pp. 6–27. **[G: U.S.]**

Alt, Christopher B.; Baumann, Michael G. and Zimmerman, Martin B. The Economics of Western Coal Severance Taxes. *J. Bus.*, October 1983, *56*(4), pp. 519–36. **[G: U.S.]**

Amuzegar, Jahangir. Managing Oil Wealth. *Finance Develop.*, September 1983, *20*(3), pp. 19–22. **[G: OPEC; U.K.; Norway]**

Aronson, Jonathan David and Cragg, Christopher. The Natural Gas Trade in the 1980s. **In** *Aronson, J. D. and Cowhey, P. F., eds.*, 1983, pp. 53–82. **[G: Japan; U.S.; W. Europe]**

Bell, Timothy Barnes. Market Reaction to Reserve Recognition Accounting. *J. Acc. Res.*, Spring 1983, *21*(1), pp. 1–17. **[G: U.S.]**

Benzoni, L. and Leveau, C. La formation des prix de l'énergie: Essai sur la dynamique du système énergétique (France 1973–1983). (Formation of the Energy Prices: An Essay on the Dynamics of the Energy System. With English summary.) *Écon. Soc.*, December 1983, *17*(12), pp. 1869–1926. **[G: France]**

Brand, Donald R. Corporatism, the NRA, and the Oil Industry. *Polit. Sci. Quart.*, Spring 1983, *98*(1), pp. 99–118. **[G: U.S.]**

Brown, Peter G. Improving Equity in the Use of Temporary Workers. **In** *Kasperson, R. E., ed.*, 1983, pp. 291–300. **[G: U.S.]**

Brown, Stephen P. A. Will Deregulating Natural Gas Increase Its Price to Consumers? *Fed. Res. Bank Dallas Econ. Rev.*, July 1983, pp. 1–9. **[G: U.S.]**

Canes, Michael. The Gordian Knot of Natural Gas Prices: Comment. **In** *Mitchell, E. J., ed.*, 1983, pp. 149–51. **[G: U.S.]**

Cochrane, Stuart and Struthers, John J. Nigerian Oil Policies: Some Internal Constraints. *J. Energy*

Devel., Spring 1983, *8*(2), pp. 305–17. **[G: Nigeria]**

Cooper, Mark. The Gordian Knot of Natural Gas Prices: Comment. **In** *Mitchell, E. J., ed.*, 1983, pp. 151–53. **[G: U.S.]**

Corley, T. A. B. Strategic Factors in the Growth of a Multinational Enterprise: The Burmah Oil Company 1886–1928. **In** *Casson, M., ed.*, 1983, pp. 214–35. **[G: U.K.]**

Corredor, Jaime. The Economic Significance of Mexican Petroleum from the Perspective of Mexico–United States Relations. **In** *Reynolds, C. W. and Tello, C., eds.*, 1983, pp. 137–65. **[G: Mexico; U.S.]**

Cowhey, Peter F. The Engineers and the Price System Revisited: The Future of the International Oil Corporations. **In** *Aronson, J. D. and Cowhey, P. F., eds.*, 1983, pp. 9–52. **[G: U.S.]**

Culhane, J. H. The Changing Economics of Oil Refining. **In** *Tempest, P., ed.*, 1983, pp. 79–82. **[G: U.S.; W. Europe]**

DeBrock, Larry M. and Smith, James L. Joint Bidding, Information Pooling, and the Performance of Petroleum Lease Auctions. *Bell J. Econ. (See Rand J. Econ. after 4/85)*, Autumn 1983, *14*(2), pp. 395–404.

Dembo, Ron and Zipkin, Paul. Construction and Evaluation of Compact Refinery Models. **In** *Lev, B., ed.*, 1983, pp. 525–40.

Dworin, Lowell and Deakin, Edward B. The Profitability of Outer Continental Shelf Drilling Ventures: An Alternative Approach. *Nat. Tax J.*, March, 1983, *36*(1), pp. 57–63. **[G: U.S.]**

Earney, Fillmore C. F. Petroleum and the Environment. **In** *Glassner, M. I., ed.*, 1983, *1980*, pp. 564–79. **[G: U.S.; Selected Countries]**

Eck, Theodore R. Energy Economics and Taxation. *J. Energy Devel.*, Spring 1983, *8*(2), pp. 293–304. **[G: U.S.]**

Erickson, Edward W. Overview of Policy Issues: A Preliminary Assessment: Comment. **In** *Mitchell, E. J., ed.*, 1983, pp. 33–36. **[G: U.S.]**

Fariña, Ronald F. and Glover, Fred W. The Application of Generalized Networks to Choice of Raw Materials for Fuels and Petrochemicals. **In** *Lev, B., ed.*, 1983, pp. 513–24.

Feick, John E. Prospects for the Development of Mineable Oil Sands. *Can. Public Policy*, September 1983, *9*(3), pp. 297–303. **[G: Canada]**

Fesharaki, Fereidun and Isaak, David T. The Impact of Hydrocarbon Processing in OPEC Countries. **In** *Tempest, P., ed.*, 1983, pp. 205–13. **[G: OPEC]**

Gately, Dermot. OPEC: Retrospective and Prospects, 1973–1990. *Europ. Econ. Rev.*, May 1983, *21*(3), pp. 313–31. **[G: OPEC]**

Gault, John C. Decision Making for Natural Gas Development. *J. Energy Devel.*, Spring 1983, *8*(2), pp. 283–91. **[G: LDCs]**

Goodermote, Dean and Mancke, Richard B. Nationalizing Oil in the 1970s. *Energy J.*, October 1983, *4*(4), pp. 67–80. **[G: U.S.; Canada; U.K.]**

Gray, H. Peter and Walter, Ingo. Investment-Related Trade Distortions in Petrochemicals. *J. World Trade Law*, July–August 1983, *17*(4), pp. 283–307. **[G: U.S.; W. Europe; Japan; Selected LDCs]**

Harris, Carl M. Oil and Gas Supply Modeling under Uncertainty: Putting DOE Midterm Forecasts in Perspective. *Energy J.*, October 1983, *4*(4), pp. 53–65. **[G: U.S.]**

Helliwell, John F.; MacGregor, Mary E. and Plourde, Andre. The National Energy Program Meets Falling World Oil Prices. *Can. Public Policy*, September 1983, *9*(3), pp. 284–96. **[G: Canada]**

Henry, Mark S. The Impact of Natural Gas Price Deregulation on the South Carolina Food-Processing Sectors. *Southern J. Agr. Econ.*, December 1983, *15*(2), pp. 41–48. **[G: U.S.]**

Hirschfeld, David J. A Fundamental Overview of the Energy Futures Market. *J. Futures Markets*, Spring 1983, *3*(1), pp. 75–100. **[G: U.S.]**

Hoffman, Lutz and Jarass, Lorenz. The Scope for Adjustment. **In** *Tempest, P., ed.*, 1983, pp. 229–38. **[G: Brazil; India; Kenya]**

Hotard, Daniel G.; Liu, Cheng Chi and Ristroph, John H. Logistic Function Modeling of Natural Resource Production. **In** *Lev, B., ed.*, 1983, pp. 353–64. **[G: U.S.]**

Hutchinson, Peter M. Refinery Closings and the Regional Distribution of Refining Capacity. *Reg. Sci. Persp.*, 1983, *13*(2), pp. 15–25. **[G: U.S.]**

Inglehart, Ronald. Domestic Political Constraints on an Atlantic Energy Policy. **In** *Lieber, R. J., ed.*, 1983, pp. 193–227. **[G: U.S.; W. Europe]**

Jacoby, Henry D. and Paddock, James L. Establishing an Oil Price Window: The Influence of Policy on Future Oil Prices. **In** *Tempest, P., ed.*, 1983, pp. 63–76. **[G: U.S.; OPEC]**

Jacoby, Henry D. and Wright, Arthur W. The Gordian Knot of Natural Gas Prices. **In** *Mitchell, E. J., ed.*, 1983, pp. 125–48. **[G: U.S.]**

Jain, Prem C. The Impact of Accounting Regulation on the Stock Market: The Case of Oil and Gas Companies—Some Additional Results. *Accounting Rev.*, July 1983, *58*(3), pp. 633–38. **[G: U.S.]**

Jentleson, Bruce W. Khrushchev's Oil and Brezhnev's Natural Gas Pipelines. **In** *Lieber, R. J., ed.*, 1983, pp. 33–69. **[G: U.S.S.R.; U.S.; W. Europe]**

Johnsen, Arve. Norwegian Gas Reserves and Markets. *J. Energy Devel.*, Spring 1983, *8*(2), pp. 191–202. **[G: Norway]**

Jones, Geoffrey. Some Recent Histories of International Oil. *J. Econ. Hist.*, December 1983, *43*(4), pp. 993–96. **[G: France; Latin America; U.K.]**

Jones, Jack William. Applying a Computer-based Enhanced Oil Recovery Simulation Model to Reservoir Economic Analysis. **In** *Lev, B., ed.*, 1983, pp. 255–70. **[G: U.S.]**

de Kadt, Maarten. Energy Corporation Propaganda: A Weapon against Public Policy. *Rev. Radical Polit. Econ.*, Fall 1983, *15*(3), pp. 35–50. **[G: U.S.]**

Kalt, Joseph P. The Creation, Growth, and Entrenchment of Special Interests in Oil Price Policy. **In** *Noll, R. G. and Owen, B. M.*, 1983, pp. 97–114. **[G: U.S.]**

Kaufman, Gordon. Oil and Gas: Estimation of Undiscovered Resources. **In** *Adelman, M. A., et al.*, 1983, pp. 83–294. **[G: U.S.]**

Klapp, Merrie. Policy and Politics of North Sea Oil and Gas Development. **In** *Aronson, J. D. and*

Cowhey, P. F., eds., 1983, pp. 107–36. **[G: Norway; U.K.]**

Kneese, Allen V., et al. Economic Issues in the Legacy Problem. **In** *Kasperson, R. E., ed.*, 1983, pp. 203–26. **[G: U.S.]**

Koo, Anthony Y. C. and Fisher, Ronald C. Natural Gas Price Deregulation and Windfall Profits Taxation. *Southern Econ. J.*, October 1983, *50*(2), pp. 529–38. **[G: U.S.]**

Larcker, David F. and Revsine, Lawrence. The Oil and Gas Accounting Controversy: An Analysis of Economic Consequences. *Accounting Rev.*, October 1983, *58*(4), pp. 706–32. **[G: U.S.]**

Lawrence, George H. and German, Michael I. The Natural Gas Industry in Transition. *Energy J.*, January 1983, *4*(1), pp. 143–48. **[G: U.S.]**

LeBlanc, Michael and Prato, Anthony. Ethanol Production from Grain in the United States: Agricultural Impacts and Economic Feasibility. *Can. J. Agr. Econ.*, July 1983, *31*(2), pp. 223–32. **[G: U.S.]**

Leone, Robert A. Comment [Pitfalls on the Road to Decontrol: Lessons from the Natural Gas Policy Act of 1978] [The Intrastate Pipelines and the Natural Gas Policy Act]. **In** *Mitchell, E. J., ed.*, 1983, pp. 109–11. **[G: U.S.]**

Lillydahl, Jane H. and Moen, Elizabeth W. Planning, Managing, and Financing Growth and Decline in Energy Rosource Communities: A Case Study of Western Colorado. *J. Energy Devel.*, Spring 1983, *8*(2), pp. 211–29. **[G: U.S.]**

Liu, Ben-chieh. Helium Conservation and Supply and Demand Projections in the USA. *Energy Econ.*, January 1983, *5*(1), pp. 58–64. **[G: U.S.]**

Liu, Ben-chieh. Natural Gas Price Elasticities: Variations by Region and by Sector in the USA. *Energy Econ.*, July 1983, *5*(3), pp. 195–201. **[G: U.S.]**

Lyman, Robert. Economic and Political Issues in International Natural Gas Trade: A Canadian View. *J. Energy Devel.*, Autumn 1983, *9*(1), pp. 49–54. **[G: Canada]**

Maksimov, Iu. I. Siberia's Fuel-Energy Complex. *Prob. Econ.*, September 1983, *26*(5), pp. 15–24. **[G: U.S.S.R.]**

McAleese, Dermot and O'Muircheartaigh, Fionan. The Changing Oil Market: Implications and Prospects. *Irish Banking Rev.*, September 1983, pp. 3–20. **[G: OPEC; Non-OPEC; Ireland]**

McNicoll, Iain. North Sea Oil and Gas. **In** *Ingham, K. P. D. and Love, J., eds.*, 1983, pp. 227–34. **[G: U.K.]**

Mead, Walter J.; Moseidjord, Asbjorn and Sorensen, Philip E. Efficiency in Leasing. **In** *Tempest, P., ed.*, 1983, pp. 85–92. **[G: U.S.]**

Mead, Walter J.; Moseidjord, Asbjorn and Sorensen, Philip E. The Rate of Return Earned by Lessees under Cash Bonus Bidding for OCS Oil and Gas Leases. *Energy J.*, October 1983, *4*(4), pp. 37–52. **[G: U.S.]**

Meloe, Tor. The Energy Industry and Federal Tax Policy. **In** *Walker, C. E. and Bloomfield, M. E., eds.*, 1983, pp. 172–76. **[G: U.S.]**

Melville, Mary H. Temporary Workers in the Nuclear Power Industry: Implications for the Waste Management Program. **In** *Kasperson, R. E., ed.*, 1983, pp. 229–58. **[G: U.S.]**

Mitchell, John. Changes in Trade and Investment. **In** *Tempest, P., ed.*, 1983, pp. 127–33.

Mork, Knut Anton. Comment on "Optimal Oil Producer Behavior Considering Macrofeedbacks." *Energy J.*, October 1983, *4*(4), pp. 29–31.

Mossavar-Rahmani, Bijan. Economic Implications for Iran and Iraq. **In** *Tahir-Kheli, S. and Ayubi, S., eds.*, 1983, pp. 51–64. **[G: Iran; Iraq]**

Odell, Peter R. Towards a System of World Oil Regions: The New Geopolitics of International Energy. **In** *Tempest, P., ed.*, 1983, pp. 27–34. **[G: Global]**

Olofin, S. and Iyaniwura, J. O. From Oil Shortage to Oil Glut: Simulation of Growth Prospects in the Nigerian Economy. *J. Policy Modeling*, November 1983, *5*(3), pp. 363–78. **[G: Nigeria]**

Palmer, Keith. Private Sector Petroleum Exploration in Developing Countries. *Finance Develop.*, March 1983, *20*(1), pp. 36–38. **[G: LDCs]**

Rad-Serecht, Farhad. Stratégie des acteurs et destabilisation de l'oligopole pétrolier. *Rev. Econ. Ind.*, 3rd Trimester 1983, (25), pp. 38–49. **[G: OPEC; W. Europe; U.S.]**

Ramsey, James B. Empirical Analysis on Lease Bidding Using Historical Data. **In** *Engelbrecht-Wiggans, R.; Shubik, M. and Stark, R. M., eds.*, 1983, pp. 285–306. **[G: U.S.]**

Ravid, S. Abraham and Hadar, Y. A Cost Benefit Analysis of Bio-gas Production: An Israeli Experience. **In** *Lev, B., ed.*, 1983, pp. 413–22. **[G: Israel]**

Razavi, Hossein. An Analysis of Iran's Oil Production Policy: A Welfare Maximization Approach. *Appl. Econ.*, April 1983, *15*(2), pp. 243–54. **[G: Iran]**

Reining, Robert C. and Tyner, Wallace E. Comparing Liquid Fuel Costs: Grain Alcohol versus Sunflower Oil. *Amer. J. Agr. Econ.*, August 1983, *65*(3), pp. 567–70.

Robinson, J. Nicholas. The Debate on the Macroeconomic Impact of North Sea Oil: A Survey. *Brit. Rev. Econ. Issues*, Spring 1983, *5*(12), pp. 15–31. **[G: U.K.]**

Robson, Arthur J. OPEC versus the West: A Robust Equilibrium. *J. Environ. Econ. Manage.*, March 1983, *10*(1), pp. 18–34.

Rockwood, Alan. The Impact of Joint Ventures on the Market for OCS Oil and Gas Leases. *J. Ind. Econ.*, June 1983, *31*(4), pp. 453–68. **[G: U.S.]**

Roncaglia, Alessandro. The Price of Oil: Main Interpretations and Their Theoretical Blackground. *J. Post Keynesian Econ.*, Summer 1983, *5*(4), pp. 557–78.

Rowe, W. D. Implicit Equity Considerations in Radiation Protection Standards. **In** *Kasperson, R. E., ed.*, 1983, pp. 259–76. **[G: U.S.]**

Russell, Milton. Overview of Policy Issues: A Preliminary Assessment. **In** *Mitchell, E. J., ed.*, 1983, pp. 3–32. **[G: U.S.]**

Sakakibara, Sakura. The Energy Situation in the Asian–Pacific Region and International Cooperation. *J. Energy Devel.*, Autumn 1983, *9*(1), pp. 41–48. **[G: Asia]**

Saunders, Harry D. Optimal Oil Producer Behavior Considering Macrofeedbacks. *Energy J.*, October 1983, *4*(4), pp. 1–27.

Saunders, Harry D. Optimal Oil Producer Behavior

Considering Macrofeedbacks: Reply. *Energy J.*, October 1983, *4*(4), pp. 31–35.

Schlesinger, Benjamin. Overview of Policy Issues: A Preliminary Assessment: Comment. **In** *Mitchell, E. J., ed.*, 1983, pp. 36–39. **[G: U.S.]**

Schramm, Gunter. The Economics of Gas Utilization in a Gas-Rich, Oil-Poor Country: The Case of Bangladesh. *Energy J.*, January 1983, *4*(1), pp. 47–64. **[G: Bangladesh]**

Shakow, Don M. Market Mechanisms for Compensating Hazardous Work: A Critical Analysis. **In** *Kasperson, R. E., ed.*, 1983, pp. 277–90. **[G: U.S.]**

Smith, L. Douglas, et al. A System for Analysing Competition in Distribution of Petroleum Products. **In** *Lev, B., ed.*, 1983, pp. 309–24. **[G: U.S.]**

Tempest, Paul. The International Energy Investment Dilemma. **In** *Tempest, P., ed.*, 1983, pp. 247–58. **[G: OECD]**

Thimrén, Claes. Potential Benefits from Isolating the Domestic Oil Price Level during Short-run Oil Price Booms. **In** *Sohlman, A. M., ed.*, 1983, pp. 234–73. **[G: Sweden]**

Tishler, Asher. The Demand for Cars and Gasoline: A Simultaneous Approach. *Europ. Econ. Rev.*, January 1983, *20*(1–3), pp. 271–87. **[G: Israel]**

Tokarev, I. P. Co-Ordination in Problems of Optimal Management of Crude-Oil Processing. *Econ. Computat. Cybern. Stud. Res.*, 1983, *18*(2), pp. 73–82.

Wahby, Mandy J. Petroleum Taxation and Efficiency: The Canadian System in Question. *J. Energy Devel.*, Autumn 1983, *9*(1), pp. 111–27. **[G: Canada]**

Weidenbaum, Murray L. Energy Development and U.S. Government Policy: Some Recommendations for Using Market Forces to Achieve Optimum National Goals. *Amer. J. Econ. Soc.*, July 1983, *42*(3), pp. 257–74. **[G: U.S.]**

Wijarso, Ir. The Indonesian Energy Scene. *J. Energy Devel.*, Autumn 1983, *9*(1), pp. 1–10. **[G: Indonesia]**

Wilkinson, Jack W. The Supply, Demand, and Average Price of Natural Gas under Free-Market Conditions. *Energy J.*, January 1983, *4*(1), pp. 99–123. **[G: U.S.]**

Willars, Jaime M. The Mexican Oil Sector in the 1980s: Issues and Perspectives. *J. Energy Devel.*, Autumn 1983, *9*(1), pp. 19–40. **[G: Mexico]**

Wonder, Edward F. Mexican Oil and the Western Alliance. **In** *Lieber, R. J., ed.*, 1983, pp. 135–67. **[G: Mexico; Central America; OECD]**

Woods, Thomas J. and Vidas, E. Harry. Projecting Hydrocarbon Production and Costs: An Integrated Approach. *J. Energy Devel.*, Spring 1983, *8*(2), pp. 267–82. **[G: U.S.]**

Wright, Claudia. Neutral or Neutralized? Iraq, Iran, and the Superpowers. **In** *Tahir-Kheli, S. and Ayubi, S., eds.*, 1983, pp. 172–92. **[G: Iraq; Iran]**

Zakariya, Hasan S. The Petroleum Lending Programme of the World Bank: The First Five Years. *J. World Trade Law*, November–December 1983, *17*(6), pp. 471–95. **[G: LDCs]**

Zimmerman, Jerold L. Taxes and Firm Size. *J. Acc. Econ.*, August 1983, *5*(2), pp. 119–49. **[G: U.S.]**

633 Industry Studies: Distributive Trades

6330 General

Davidow, Joel. EEC Proposed Competition Rules for Motor Vehicle Distribution: An American Perspective. *Antitrust Bull.*, Winter 1983, *28*(4), pp. 863–82. **[G: U.S.; EEC]**

Doyle, Peter and Corstjens, Marcel. Optimal Growth Strategies for Service Organizations. *J. Bus.*, July 1983, *56*(3), pp. 389–405. **[G: U.K.]**

Gosling, L. A. Peter. Chinese Crop Dealers in Malaysia and Thailand: The Myth of the Merciless Monopsonistic Middleman. **In** *Lim, L. Y. C. and Gosling, L. A. P., eds.*, 1983, pp. 131–70. **[G: Malaysia; Thailand]**

Korovkin, V. Scientific and Technical Programs in Commercial Trade. *Prob. Econ.*, October 1983, *26*(6), pp. 55–70. **[G: U.S.S.R.]**

Laitinen, Erkki K. A Life-Cycle Approach to Retail Pricing. *Liiketaloudellinen Aikak.*, 1983, *32*(3), pp. 251–60. **[G: Finland]**

6332 Wholesale Trade

Ryan, John P., Jr. The Export Trading Company Act of 1982: Antitrust Panacea, Placebo, or Pitfall? *Antitrust Bull.*, Fall 1983, *28*(3), pp. 501–69. **[G: U.S.]**

Yengoyan, Aram A. The Buying of Futures: Chinese Merchants and the Fishing Industry in Capiz, Philippines. **In** *Lim, L. Y. C. and Gosling, L. A. P., eds.*, 1983, pp. 117–30. **[G: Philippines]**

6333 Retail Trade

Ahtomies, Matti; Lehtinen, Uolevi and Näsi, Juha. Kokeellinen tutkimos kilpailukeinojen vaikutuksesta vähittäiskaupassa. (An Evaluation of Experimental Research: A Case Study Concerning the Effects of Marketing Mix on Retail Level. With English summary.) *Liiketaloudellinen Aikak.*, 1983, *32*(1), pp. 49–80. **[G: Finland]**

Bittlingmayer, George. A Model of Vertical Restriction and Equilibrium in Retailing. *J. Bus.*, October 1983, *56*(4), pp. 477–96.

Boynton, Robert D.; Blake, Brian F. and Uhl, Joseph N. Retail Price Reporting Effects in Local Food Markets. *Amer. J. Agr. Econ.*, February 1983, *65*(1), pp. 20–29. **[G: U.S.]**

Boynton, Robert D.; McCracken, Vicki and Irwin, Scott. Food Advertising as a Source of Consumer Information: A Case Study of Newspaper Advertising and Its Relationship to Public Price Reports. **In** *Connor, J. M. and Ward, R. W., eds.*, 1983, pp. 371–83. **[G: U.S.]**

Breimyer, Harold F. Foreign Investment in the U.S. Food-Marketing System: Discussion. *Amer. J. Agr. Econ.*, May 1983, *65*(2), pp. 421–22. **[G: U.S.]**

Carlson, John A. and Gieseke, Robert J. Price Search in a Product Market. *J. Cons. Res.*, March 1983, *9*(4), pp. 357–65. **[G: U.S.]**

Cotterill, Ronald. Retail Food Cooperatives: Testing the "Small Is Beautiful" Hypothesis. *Amer. J. Agr. Econ.*, February 1983, *65*(1), pp. 125–30. **[G: U.S.]**

Dichtl, Erwin; Raffée, Hans and Wellenreuther, Hans. Public Policy towards Small and Medium-Sized Retail Businesses in the Federal Republic of Germany. *Rivista Int. Sci. Econ. Com.*, April–May 1983, *30*(4–5), pp. 424–39. **[G: W. Germany]**

Eickelman, Dale F. Religion and Trade in Western Morocco. **In** *Dalton, G., ed.*, 1983, pp. 335–48. **[G: Morocco]**

Forbes, Walter A. Retailing: The Impact of Computerized Shopping. **In** *Federal Reserve Bank of Atlanta*, 1983, pp. 63–71. **[G: U.S.]**

Grant, Robert M. Transaction Costs to Retailers of Different Methods of Payment: Results of a Pilot Study. *Managerial Dec. Econ.*, June 1983, *4*(2), pp. 89–96. **[G: U.K.]**

Haining, Robert. Modeling Intraurban Price Competition: An Example of Gasoline Pricing. *J. Reg. Sci.*, November 1983, *23*(4), pp. 517–28. **[G: U.K.]**

Hall, Bruce F. Neighborhood Differences in Retail Food Stores: Income versus Race and Age of Population. *Econ. Geogr.*, July 1983, *59*(3), pp. 282–95.

Halperin, William C., et al. Exploring Entrepreneurial Cognitions of Retail Environments. *Econ. Geogr.*, January 1983, *59*(1), pp. 3–15. **[G: Australia]**

Hamm, Larry G. The Interactions of Food Manufacturer Advertising and Food Retailer Buying Practices: Some Implications for Food System Organizations. **In** *Connor, J. M. and Ward, R. W., eds.*, 1983, pp. 215–33. **[G: U.S.]**

Hoffman, Oscar. The Interactions of Food Manufacturer Advertising and Food Retailer Buying Practices: Some Implications for Food System Organizations: Commentary. **In** *Connor, J. M. and Ward, R. W., eds.*, 1983, pp. 235–36. **[G: U.S.]**

Lesser, William H. Information in Food Advertising: Comment. **In** *Connor, J. M. and Ward, R. W., eds.*, 1983, pp. 387–92. **[G: U.S.]**

Lewis, W. Arthur. Competition in Retail Trade. **In** *Lewis, W. A.*, 1983, *1946*, pp. 71–111.

Lindqvist, Lars-Johan. Dagligvarumnarknaden i Finland: Koncentrationen sedd ur konsumenternas, detaljisternas och samhällets synvinkel. (The Market for Convenience Goods in Finland. Concentration from the Point of View of Consumers, Retailers and Society. With English summary.) *Ekon. Samfundets Tidskr.*, 1983, *36*(4), pp. 157–61. **[G: Finland]**

Loescher, Samuel M. The Effects of Disseminating Comparative Grocery Chain Prices by the Indiana Public Interest Research Group: A Case Study. **In** *Connor, J. M. and Ward, R. W., eds.*, 1983, pp. 345–61. **[G: U.S.]**

Marion, Bruce W. and Nash, Howard J. Foreign Investment in U.S. Food-Retailing Industry. *Amer. J. Agr. Econ.*, May 1983, *65*(2), pp. 413–20. **[G: U.S.]**

Mathewson, G. Frank and Winter, Ralph A. The Incentives for Resale Price Maintenance under Imperfect Information. *Econ. Inquiry*, July 1983, *21*(3), pp. 337–48.

Mathewson, G. Frank and Winter, Ralph A. Vertical Integration by Contractual Restraints in Spatial Markets. *J. Bus.*, October 1983, *56*(4), pp. 497–517.

Metzger, Michael R. Cherries, Lemons, and the FTC: Minimum Quality Standards in the Retail Used Automobile Industry. *Econ. Inquiry*, January 1983, *21*(1), pp. 129–39. **[G: U.S.]**

Meyer, Peter J. Concentration and Performance in Local Retail Markets. **In** *Craven, J. V., ed.*, 1983, pp. 145–61. **[G: U.S.]**

Morrison, Steven A. and Newman, Robert J. Hours of Operation Restrictions and Competition among Retail Firms. *Econ. Inquiry*, January 1983, *21*(1), pp. 107–14. **[G: Canada]**

Nooteboom, B. Productivity Growth in the Grocery Trade. *Appl. Econ.*, October 1983, *15*(5), pp. 649–64. **[G: Netherlands]**

Pearce, Douglas K. and Wisley, Thomas O. Sales Expectations and Inventory Changes in Retail Trade. *J. Econ. Bus.*, 1983, *35*(1), pp. 109–21. **[G: U.S.]**

Porter, Richard C. A Social Benefit–Cost Analysis of Mandatory Deposits on Beverage Containers: A Correction. *J. Environ. Econ. Manage.*, June 1983, *10*(2), pp. 191–93. **[G: U.S.]**

Porter, Richard C. Michigan's Experience with Mandatory Deposits on Beverage Containers. *Land Econ.*, May 1983, *59*(2), pp. 177–94. **[G: U.S.]**

Pugel, Thomas A. Foreign Investment in the U.S. Food-Marketing System: Discussion. *Amer. J. Agr. Econ.*, May 1983, *65*(2), pp. 423–25.

Rijk, F. J. A. and Vorst, A. C. F. Equilibrium Points in an Urban Retail Model and Their Connection with Dynamical Systems. *Reg. Sci. Urban Econ.*, August 1983, *13*(3), pp. 383–99.

Sandy, Robert. Low Price Claims and Market Penetration in the Grocery Industry: The Case of the Kroger Price Patrol. **In** *Connor, J. M. and Ward, R. W., eds.*, 1983, pp. 363–70. **[G: U.S.]**

Schmidt, Charles G. Location Decision-Making within a Retail Corporation. *Reg. Sci. Persp.*, 1983, *13*(1), pp. 60–71. **[G: U.S.]**

Shaw, Gareth. Trends in Consumer Behaviour and Retailing. **In** *Wild, T., ed.*, 1983, pp. 108–29. **[G: W. Germany]**

Smith, A. D. and Hitchens, D. M. W. N. Comparative British and American Productivity in Retailing. *Nat. Inst. Econ. Rev.*, May 1983, (104), pp. 45–60. **[G: U.S.; U.K.]**

Sullivan, Dennis H. and Gerring, Lori F. Cross-Sectional Analysis of CBD Retail Sales: A Research Note. *Land Econ.*, February 1983, *59*(1), pp. 118–22. **[G: U.S.]**

Svensson, Claes. Consumer Co-Operation and the Federative Form of Organization. *Ann. Pub. Co-op. Econ.*, April–June 1983, *54*(2), pp. 185–200. **[G: Sweden]**

Uhl, Joseph N. Public Provision of Comparative Foodstore Price Information: Problems, Potentials, and Issues. **In** *Connor, J. M. and Ward, R. W., eds.*, 1983, pp. 323–44. **[G: U.S.]**

Wolinsky, Asher. Retail Trade Concentration Due to Consumers' Imperfect Information. *Bell J. Econ. (See Rand J. Econ. after 4/85)*, Spring 1983, *14*(1), pp. 275–82.

634 Industry Studies: Construction

6340 Construction

Allen, Steven G. Much Ado about Davis–Bacon: A Critical Review and New Evidence. *J. Law Econ.*, October 1983, *26*(3), pp. 707–36. **[G: U.S.]**

Barna, Tibor. Process Plant Contracting: A Competitive New European Industry. **In** *Shepherd, G.; Duchêne, F. and Saunders, C., eds.*, 1983, pp. 167–85. **[G: W. Europe]**

Bynum, Stanley D. Construction Management and Design–Build/Fast Track Construction from the Perspective of a General Contractor. *Law Contemp. Probl.*, Winter 1983, *46*(1), pp. 25–38. **[G: U.S.]**

Checkoway, Barry. Large Builders, Federal Housing Programmes, and Postwar Suburbanization. **In** *Lake, R. W., ed.*, 1983, *1980*, pp. 173–96. **[G: U.S.]**

Conner, Richard D. Contracting for Construction Management Services. *Law Contemp. Probl.*, Winter 1983, *46*(1), pp. 5–23. **[G: U.S.]**

Coulson, Robert. Dispute Management under Modern Construction Systems. *Law Contemp. Probl.*, Winter 1983, *46*(1), pp. 127–35. **[G: U.S.]**

Dibner, David R. Construction Management and Design–Build: An Owner's Experience in the Public Sector. *Law Contemp. Probl.*, Winter 1983, *46*(1), pp. 137–44. **[G: U.S.]**

Drobny, Andres and Wells, John. Wages, Minimum Wages, and Income Distribution in Brazil: Results from the Construction Industry. *J. Devel. Econ.*, December 1983, *13*(3), pp. 305–30. **[G: Brazil]**

Eichler, Ned. Homebuilding in the 1980s: Crisis or Transition? *Ann. Amer. Acad. Polit. Soc. Sci.*, January 1983, *465*, pp. 35–44. **[G: U.S.]**

Foster, C. Allen. Construction Management and Design–Build/Fast Track Construction: A Solution Which Uncovers a Problem for the Surety. *Law Contemp. Probl.*, Winter 1983, *46*(1), pp. 95–125. **[G: U.S.]**

Green, David Jay. A Logit Model of the Selection of a Space Heating Fuel by Builders of New Single Family Housing. *Rev. Econ. Statist.*, May 1983, *65*(2), pp. 337–42. **[G: U.S.]**

Hageman, Ronda K. An Assesssment of the Value of Natural Hazards Damage Reduction in Dwellings Due to Building Codes: Two Case Studies. *Natural Res. J.*, July 1983, *23*(3), pp. 531–47. **[G: U.S.]**

Harris, June M. and Borooah, Vani K. Distributed Lag Behaviour in the Housing Market: Some Further Evidence. *J. Econ. Stud.*, 1983, *10*(2), pp. 55–65. **[G: U.K.]**

Herzog, Henry W., Jr.; Schlottmann, Alan M. and Schriver, William R. Regional Planning and Interstate Construction Worker Migration. *Growth Change*, April 1983, *14*(2), pp. 50–54. **[G: U.S.]**

Hough, Douglas E. and Kratz, Charles G. Can "Good" Architecture Meet the Market Test? *J. Urban Econ.*, July 1983, *14*(1), pp. 40–54. **[G: U.S.]**

Katz, Howard R. Construction: Changing Family Residences. **In** *Federal Reserve Bank of Atlanta*, 1983, pp. 81–86. **[G: U.S.]**

Kau, James B. and Sirmans, C. F. Technological Change and Economic Growth in Housing. *J. Urban Econ.*, May 1983, *13*(3), pp. 283–95. **[G: U.S.]**

Kulev, I. A. Soviet–Finnish Cooperation for Joint Construction of Industrial Objects. **In** *Möttölä, K.; Bykov, O. N. and Korolev, I. S., eds.*, 1983, pp. 122–36. **[G: U.S.S.R.; Finland]**

Lérová, Irena. Seminar on the Relationship between Housing and the National Economy. *Czech. Econ. Digest.*, March 1983, (2), pp. 61–79. **[G: E. Europe; W. Europe]**

Lunch, Milton F. New Construction Methods and New Roles for Engineers. *Law Contemp. Probl.*, Winter 1983, *46*(1), pp. 83–94. **[G: U.S.]**

Metzger, Michael R. and Goldfarb, Robert S. Do Davis–Bacon Minimum Wages Raise Product Quality? *J. Lab. Res.*, Summer 1983, *4*(3), pp. 265–72. **[G: U.S.]**

Noam, Eli M. The Interaction of Building Codes and Housing Prices. *Amer. Real Estate Urban Econ. Assoc. J.*, Winter 1983, *10*(4), pp. 394–404. **[G: U.S.]**

Rabino, Samuel. Webb-Pomerene and the Construction Industry. *Calif. Manage. Rev.*, January 1983, *25*(2), pp. 21–33. **[G: U.S.]**

Raphaelson, Arnold H. The Davis–Bacon Act. **In** *Zeckhauser, R. J. and Leebaert, D., eds.*, 1983, pp. 124–36. **[G: U.S.]**

Sachs, Abner and Ziemer, Richard C. Implicit Price Deflators for Military Construction. *Surv. Curr. Bus.*, November 1983, *63*(11), pp. 14–18. **[G: U.S.]**

Squires, William R., III and Murphy, Michael J. The Impact of Fast Track Construction and Construction Management on Subcontractors. *Law Contemp. Probl.*, Winter 1983, *46*(1), pp. 55–67. **[G: U.S.]**

Stark, Robert M. and Varley, Thomas C. Bidding, Estimating, and Engineered Construction Contracting. **In** *Engelbrecht-Wiggans, R.; Shubik, M. and Stark, R. M., eds.*, 1983, pp. 121–33.

Stretton, Alan. Circular Migration, Segmented Labour Markets and Efficiency: The Building Industry in Manila and Port Moresby. *Int. Lab. Rev.*, Sept.–Oct. 1983, *122*(5), pp. 623–39. **[G: Philippines]**

Sumichrast, Michael. A Five-Year Housing Forecast. *Ann. Amer. Acad. Polit. Soc. Sci.*, January 1983, *465*, pp. 45–57. **[G: U.S.]**

Tauchen, Helen and Witte, Ann Dryden. Increased Costs of Office Building Operation and Construction: Effects on the Costs of Office Space and the Equilibrium Distribution of Offices. *Land Econ.*, August 1983, *59*(3), pp. 324–36. **[G: U.S.]**

Thomas, R. William and Stekler, H. O. A Regional Forecasting Model for Construction Activity. *Reg. Sci. Urban Econ.*, November 1983, *13*(4), pp. 557–77. **[G: U.S.]**

Tieder, John B., Jr. and Cox, Robert K. Construction Management and the Specialty Trade (Prime) Contractors. *Law Contemp. Probl.*, Winter 1983, *46*(1), pp. 39–54. **[G: U.S.]**

Tschetter, John and Lukasiewicz, John M. Employment Changes in Construction: Secular, Cyclical, and Seasonal. *Mon. Lab. Rev.*, March 1983,

106(3), pp. 11–17. [G: U.S.]

Westerhoff, Horst-Dieter. Wirkungsverzögerungen in der Konjunkturpolitik. Eine empirische Messung für die Bauwirtschaft. (Time-Lags in Trade Cycle Policy: Empirical Measurement for the Building Industry. With English summary.) *Ifo-Studien,* 1983, *29*(1), pp. 31–71. [G: W. Germany]

635 Industry Studies: Services and Related Industries

6350 General

Carlson, Norma W. Hourly Pay of Contract Cleaners Lags but Sweeps Past Weekly Gains. *Mon. Lab. Rev.,* March 1983, *106*(3), pp. 37–40. [G: U.S.]

Coffield, Shirley A. International Services–Trade Issues and the GATT. **In** *Rubin, S. J. and Graham, T. R., eds.,* 1983, pp. 69–108. [G: U.S.; LDCs; OECD]

Czinkota, Michael R. Services Trade: The Negotiation Agenda. **In** *Czinkota, M. R., ed. (I),* 1983, pp. 285–302. [G: U.S.]

Czinkota, Michael R. and LaLonde, Bernard J. An Analysis of Service Delivery in the Latin American Export Activities of U.S. Manufacturers. **In** *Czinkota, M. R., ed. (II),* 1983, pp. 172–82. [G: Latin America; U.S.]

DeVany, Arthur S., et al. Production in a Service Industry Using Customer Inputs: A Stochastic Model. *Rev. Econ. Statist.,* February 1983, *65*(1), pp. 149–53. [G: U.S.]

Diebold, William, Jr. and Stalson, Helena. Negotiating Issues in International Services Transactions. **In** *Cline W. R., ed.,* 1983, pp. 581–609.

Doyle, Peter and Corstjens, Marcel. Optimal Growth Strategies for Service Organizations. *J. Bus.,* July 1983, *56*(3), pp. 389–405. [G: U.K.]

Edwards, Linda N. and Edwards, Franklin R. Wellington–Winter Revisited: The Case of Municipal Sanitation Collection: Reply. *Ind. Lab. Relat. Rev.,* July 1983, *36*(4), pp. 657–59. [G: U.S.]

Falk, Laurence H. The Service Sector vs. the Manufacturing Sector: A New Jersey Perspective. **In** *Dutta, M.; Hartline, J. C. and Loeb, P. D., eds.,* 1983, pp. 205–15. [G: U.S.]

Fendt, Roberto, Jr. Promotion of Trade in Technical Services: The Brazilian Case. **In** *Czinkota, M. R., ed. (I),* 1983, pp. 303–18. [G: Brazil]

Gray, H. Peter. A Negotiating Strategy for Trade in Services. *J. World Trade Law,* September–October 1983, *17*(5), pp. 377–88.

Kutscher, Ronald E. and Mark, Jerome A. The Service-Producing Sector: Some Common Perceptions Reviewed. *Mon. Lab. Rev.,* April 1983, *106*(4), pp. 21–24. [G: U.S.]

Merrilees, William J. Anatomy of a Price Leadership Challenge: An Evaluation of Pricing Strategies in the Australian Newspaper Industry. *J. Ind. Econ.,* March 1983, *31*(3), pp. 291–311. [G: Australia]

Perkinson, Leon B. and Fearn, Robert M. Wellington–Winter Revisited: The Case of Municipal Sanitation Collection: Comment. *Ind. Lab. Relat. Rev.,* July 1983, *36*(4), pp. 655–57. [G: U.S.]

Polèse, Mario. Le commerce interrégional des services: le rôle des relations intra-firme et des facteurs organisationnels. (Interregional Trade in Services: Intra-Firm Transactions and Organizational Factors. With English summary.) *L'Actual. Econ.,* December 1983, *59*(4), pp. 713–28. [G: Canada]

Roy, Pierre. Notes sur l'information culturelle et sur les industries culturelles dans une optique proprement économique. (An Economic Approach to Cultural Industries. With English summary.) *L'Actual. Econ.,* March 1983, *59*(1), pp. 74–88. [G: Canada]

Rutgaizer, V. The Working Person in the Distribution and Consumption Sphere. *Prob. Econ.,* January 1983, *25*(9), pp. 16–35. [G: U.S.S.R.]

Thompson, G. Rodney and Stollar, Andrew J. An Empirical Test of an International Model of Relative Tertiary Employment. *Econ. Develop. Cult. Change,* July 1983, *31*(4), pp. 775–85. [G: Selected LDCs; Selected MDCs]

6352 Electrical, Gas, Communication, and Information Services

Abbott, Catherine Good and Watson, Stephen A. Pitfalls on the Road to Decontrol: Lessons from the Natural Gas Policy Act of 1978. **In** *Mitchell, E. J., ed.,* 1983, pp. 53–70. [G: U.S.]

Acton, Jan Paul and Mitchell, Bridger M. Welfare Analysis of Electricity-Rate Changes. **In** *Berg, S. V., ed.,* 1983, pp. 195–225. [G: U.S.]

Akinc, Umit and Arbel, Avner. A Planning Model for Short Term Energy Crises Management. **In** *Lev, B., ed.,* 1983, pp. 325–37.

Albert, Alain and Crener, Maxime A. Organisation industrielle du secteur des télécommunications: une perspective internationale. (With English summary.) *Rev. Econ. Ind.,* 2nd Trimester 1983, (24), pp. 1–8. [G: U.S.; Canada; Europe]

Autin, C. and LeBlanc, G. Empirical Evaluation of Cross-Subsidy Tests for Canadian Interregional Telecommunications Network. **In** *Courville, L.; de Fontenay, A. and Dobell, R., eds.,* 1983, pp. 341–64. [G: Canada]

Av, Redigert, et al. Analysis of Supply and Demand of Electricity in the Norwegian Economy: Introduction. **In** *Av, R., et al., eds.,* 1983, pp. 14–26. [G: Norway]

Avi-Itzhak, Benjamin; Iusem, Alfredo and Dantzig, George B. The Consumers Energy Services Model of the Pilot System. **In** *Lev, B., ed.,* 1983, pp. 195–220. [G: U.S.]

Bello, Walden; Harris, John and Zarsky, Lyuba. Nuclear Power in the Philippines: The Plague that Poisons Morong! *Rev. Radical Polit. Econ.,* Fall 1983, *15*(3), pp. 51–65. [G: Philippines]

Benson, James W. Energy: Jobs and Values. **In** *Brown, H. J., ed.,* 1983, pp. 229–41. [G: U.S.]

Berg, Sanford V. Consumer Responses to Innovative Electric Rates. **In** *Berg, S. V., ed.,* 1983, pp. 55–78. [G: U.S.]

Berg, Sanford V. Directions for Load-Management Research. **In** *Berg, S. V., ed.,* 1983, pp. 283–304. [G: U.S.]

Berg, Sanford V. Innovative Rates and Regulatory

Goals. In *Berg, S. V., ed.*, 1983, pp. 31–51. [G: U.S.]

Berg, Sanford V. Power Factors and the Efficient Pricing and Production of Reactive Power. *Energy J.*, Supplement 1983, *4*, pp. 93–102.

Berg, Sanford V. and Savvides, Andreas. The Theory of Maximum kW Demand Charges for Electricity. *Energy Econ.*, October 1983, *5*(4), pp. 258–66. [G: U.S.]

Berg, Sanford V. and Sullivan, Robert L. An Engineering/Economic Model of the Benefits and Costs of Time-of-Use Pricing. In *Berg, S. V., ed.*, 1983, pp. 227–48. [G: U.S.]

Billings, R. Bruce. Revenue Effects from Changes in a Declining Block Pricing Structure: Comment. *Land Econ.*, August 1983, *59*(3), pp. 355–39. [G: U.S.]

Bjerkholt, Olav and Olsen, Øystein. Firm Power and Uncertainty in Hydroelectric Power Supply. In *Av, R., et al., eds.*, 1983, pp. 281–303. [G: Norway]

Blattenberger, Gail R.; Taylor, Lester D. and Rennhack, Robert K. Natural Gas Availability and the Residential Demand for Energy. *Energy J.*, January 1983, *4*(1), pp. 23–45. [G: U.S.]

Bloom, Jeremy A. Optimal Generation Expansion Planning for Electric Utilities Using Decomposition and Probabilistic Simulation Techniques. In *Lev, B., ed.*, 1983, pp. 495–511.

Bornholz, Robert and Evans, David S. The Early History of Competition in the Telephone Industry. In *Evans, D. S., ed.*, 1983, pp. 7–40. [G: U.S.]

Bowen, Robert M.; Castanias, Richard P. and Daley, Lane A. Intra-Industry Effects of the Accident at Three Mile Island. *J. Finan. Quant. Anal.*, March 1983, *18*(1), pp. 87–111. [G: U.S.]

Brander, James A. and Spencer, Barbara J. Local Telephone Pricing: Two-Tariffs and Price Discrimination. In *Courville, L.; de Fontenay, A. and Dobell, R., eds.*, 1983, pp. 305–16.

Breslaw, J. A. and Smith, J. Barry. Des observations empiriques encourageantes pour la théorie dualiste. (Some Encouraging Firm Level Evidence for Duality Theory. With English summary.) *L'Actual. Econ.*, June 1983, *59*(2), pp. 230–39. [G: Canada]

Brock, William A. and Evans, David S. Creamskimming. In *Evans, D. S., ed.*, 1983, pp. 61–94. [G: U.S.]

Brock, William A. and Evans, David S. Predation: A Critique of the Government's Case in *U.S.* v. *AT&T.* In *Evans, D. S., ed.*, 1983, pp. 41–59. [G: U.S.]

Brown, Howard J. Problems, Planning, and Possibilities for the Electric Utility Industry. In *Brown, H. J., ed.*, 1983, pp. 3–18.

Browne, Lynn E. Electric Utilities' Finances since the Energy Crisis. *New Eng. Econ. Rev.*, March/April 1983, pp. 28–45. [G: U.S.]

Bunn, Derek W. and Paschentis, Spiros N. Economic Dispatch of Electric Power by Stochastic Linear Programming. In *Lev, B., ed.*, 1983, pp. 399–412. [G: U.K.]

Bunn, Derek W. and Seigal, Jeremy P. Television Peaks in Electricity Demand. *Energy Econ.*, January 1983, *5*(1), pp. 31–36. [G: U.S.; U.K.]

Canes, Michael. The Gordian Knot of Natural Gas Prices: Comment. In *Mitchell, E. J., ed.*, 1983, pp. 149–51. [G: U.S.]

Capehart, Barney L. and Storin, Michael O. Technological Advances in Metering. In *Berg, S. V., ed.*, 1983, pp. 263–81. [G: U.S.]

Caramanis, Michael C. Electricity Generation Expansion Planning in the Eighties: Requirements and Available Analysis Tools. In *Lev, B., ed.*, 1983, pp. 541–62. [G: U.S.]

Carleton, Willard T.; Chambers, Donald R. and Lakonishok, Josef. Inflation Risk and Regulatory Lag. *J. Finance*, May 1983, *38*(2), pp. 419–31. [G: U.S.]

Chao, Hung-po. Peak Load Pricing and Capacity Planning with Demand and Supply Uncertainty. *Bell J. Econ. (See Rand J. Econ. after 4/85)*, Spring 1983, *14*(1), pp. 179–90.

Christensen, Laurits R.; Cummings, D. and Schoech, P. E. Econometric Estimation of Scale Economies in Telecommunications. In *Courville, L.; de Fontenay, A. and Dobell, R., eds.*, 1983, pp. 27–53. [G: U.S.]

Clarke, Harry R. and Shrestha, Ram M. Location and Input Mix Decisions for Energy Facilities. *Reg. Sci. Urban Econ.*, November 1983, *13*(4), pp. 487–504.

Constantopoulos, Panos; Larson, Richard C. and Schweppe, Fred C. Decision Models for Electric Load Management by Consumers Facing a Variable Price of Electricity. In *Lev, B., ed.*, 1983, pp. 273–91.

Cooper, Mark. The Gordian Knot of Natural Gas Prices: Comment. In *Mitchell, E. J., ed.*, 1983, pp. 151–53. [G: U.S.]

Cornell, Nina W. and Webbink, Douglas W. The Present Direction of the FCC: An Appraisal. *Amer. Econ. Rev.*, May 1983, *73*(2), pp. 194–97. [G: U.S.]

Cramer, Curtis and Tschirhart, John. Power Pooling: An Exercise in Industrial Coordination. *Land Econ.*, February 1983, *59*(1), pp. 24–34. [G: U.S.]

Crandall, Robert W. Deregulation: The U.S. Experience. *Z. ges. Staatswiss.*, October 1983, *139*(3), pp. 419–34. [G: U.S.]

Crano, William D. Cognitive Factors That Influence Consumers' Responses to Innovative Rate Structures. In *Berg, S. V., ed.*, 1983, pp. 95–107. [G: U.S.]

Curien, N. and Vilmin, E. Telephone Demand and Usage: A Global Residential Model. In *Courville, L.; de Fontenay, A. and Dobell, R., eds.*, 1983, pp. 231–49. [G: France]

Dansby, R. E. Economic Analysis of a Measured Service Option. In *Courville, L.; de Fontenay, A. and Dobell, R., eds.*, 1983, pp. 279–92.

Denny, Michael G. S.; de Fontenay, A. and Werner, M. Comparing the Efficiency of Firms: Canadian Telecommunications Companies. In *Courville, L.; de Fontenay, A. and Dobell, R., eds.*, 1983, pp. 115–27. [G: Canada]

Devine, Michael D.; Kumin, Hillel J. and Aly, Adel A. A Survey of Optimization and Stochastic Process Techniques Applied to Solar Energy Systems. In *Lev, B., ed.*, 1983, pp. 339–52.

Dias-Bandaranaike, Romesh and Munasinghe, Mohan. The Demand for Electricity Services and the Quality of Supply. *Energy J.*, April 1983, *4*(2), pp. 49–71. **[G: Costa Rica]**

Dietrich, J. Kimball and Heckerman, D. G. Determinants of the Systematic Risk of Electric Utilities: Theory and Estimation. *Appl. Econ.*, October 1983, *15*(5), pp. 619–33. **[G: U.S.]**

Diop, Sidy Modibo and Perrault, Jean-Louis. Ruptures ou continuités dans la politque industrielle française en électronique? (With English summary.) *Rev. Econ. Ind.*, 2nd Trimester 1983, (24), pp. 48–61. **[G: France]**

Drăgănescu, M. Information Economy. *Econ. Computat. Cybern. Stud. Res.*, 1983, *18*(3), pp. 11–21. **[G: Romania; U.S.]**

Earnest, Jack. The Intrastate Pipelines and the Natural Gas Policy Act: Comment. **In** *Mitchell, E. J., ed.*, 1983, pp. 108–09. **[G: U.S.]**

Edelman, Richard B. Telecommunications Betas: Are They Stable and Unique? *J. Portfol. Manage.*, Fall 1983, *10*(1), pp. 46–52. **[G: U.S.]**

Einhorn, Michael. Optimal System Planning with Fuel Shortages and Emissions Constraints. *Energy J.*, April 1983, *4*(2), pp. 73–90.

Ellis, Randall P. and Zimmerman, Martin B. What Happened to Nuclear Power: A Discrete Choice Model of Technology Adoption. *Rev. Econ. Statist.*, May 1983, *65*(2), pp. 234–42. **[G: U.S.]**

Erickson, Edward W. Overview of Policy Issues: A Preliminary Assessment: Comment. **In** *Mitchell, E. J., ed.*, 1983, pp. 33–36. **[G: U.S.]**

Evans, David S. Breaking Up Bell: Introduction. **In** *Evans, D. S., ed.*, 1983, pp. 1–5. **[G: U.S.]**

Evans, David S. and Grossman, Sanford J. Breaking Up Bell: Integration. **In** *Evans, D. S., ed.*, 1983, pp. 95–126. **[G: U.S.]**

Evans, David S. and Heckman, James J. Multiproduct Cost Function Estimates and Natural Monopoly Tests for the Bell System. **In** *Evans, D. S., ed.*, 1983, pp. 253–82. **[G: U.S.]**

Evans, David S. and Heckman, James J. Natural Monopoly. **In** *Evans, D. S., ed.*, 1983, pp. 127–56. **[G: U.S.]**

Evans, David S. and Rothschild, Michael. The Impact of Divestiture on the Cost of Capital to the Bell System. **In** *Evans, D. S., ed.*, 1983, pp. 157–89. **[G: U.S.]**

Ferguson, James M. Daily Newspaper Advertising Rates, Local Media Cross-Ownership, Newspaper Chains, and Media Competition. *J. Law Econ.*, October 1983, *26*(3), pp. 635–54. **[G: U.S.]**

Fischhoff, Baruch. Informed Consent for Nuclear Workers. **In** *Kasperson, R. E., ed.*, 1983, pp. 301–28. **[G: U.S.]**

Fishe, Raymond P. H. The Number and Placement of Rating Periods for Time-of-Day Pricing. **In** *Berg, S. V., ed.*, 1983, pp. 183–92.

Fishe, Raymond P. H. and McAfee, R. Preston. On the Use of Bonus Payments in an Experimental Study of Electricity Demand. *Rev. Econ. Statist.*, August 1983, *65*(3), pp. 506–11. **[G: U.S.]**

de Fontenay, A. and Lee, J. T. Marshall. B.C./Alberta Long Distance Calling. **In** *Courville, L.; de Fontenay, A. and Dobell, R., eds.*, 1983, pp. 199–227. **[G: Canada]**

Frantzis, Lisa. The Potential for Diversity: The Production Alternative. **In** *Brown, H. J., ed.*, 1983, pp. 61–92. **[G: U.S.]**

Fuhr, Joseph P., Jr. Competition in the Terminal Equipment Market after *Carterfone*. *Antitrust Bull.*, Fall 1983, *28*(3), pp. 669–98. **[G: U.S.]**

Fuss, Melvyn A. A Survey of Recent Results in the Analysis of Production Conditions in Telecommunications. **In** *Courville, L.; de Fontenay, A. and Dobell, R., eds.*, 1983, pp. 3–26. **[G: Canada]**

Garbacz, Christopher. Electricity Demand and the Elasticity of Intra-Marginal Price. *Appl. Econ.*, October 1983, *15*(5), pp. 699–701. **[G: U.S.]**

Gault, John C. Decision Making for Natural Gas Development. *J. Energy Devel.*, Spring 1983, *8*(2), pp. 283–91. **[G: LDCs]**

Gilmer, Robert W. and Mack, Richard S. The Cost of Residential Electric Power Outages. *Energy J.*, Supplement 1983, *4*, pp. 55–74. **[G: U.S.]**

Goettle, Richard J., IV and Hudson, Edward A. Macroeconomic Effects of Natural Gas Price Decontrol. **In** *Lev, B., ed.*, 1983, pp. 183–93. **[G: U.S.]**

Gollop, Frank M. and Roberts, Mark J. Environmental Regulations and Productivity Growth: The Case of Fossil-Fueled Electric Power Generation. *J. Polit. Econ.*, August 1983, *91*(4), pp. 654–74. **[G: U.S.]**

Guldmann, Jean-Michel. Modeling the Structure of Gas Distribution Costs in Urban Areas. *Reg. Sci. Urban Econ.*, August 1983, *13*(3), pp. 299–316. **[G: U.S.]**

Hamilton, Neil W. and Hamilton, Peter R. Duopoly in the Distribution of Electricity: A Policy Failure. *Antitrust Bull.*, Summer 1983, *28*(2), pp. 281–309. **[G: U.S.]**

Harvey, Hunter E., Jr. Pricing Telephone Service in the 1980s. **In** *[Bonbright, J. C.]*, 1983, pp. 265–76. **[G: U.S.]**

Helleiner, Gerald K. Uncertainty, Information and the Economic Interests of the Developing Countries. **In** *O'Brien, R. C., ed.*, 1983, pp. 28–42.

Helliwell, John F. and Margolick, Michael. Some Hard Economics of Soft Energy: Optimal Electricity Generation in Pulp and Paper Mills with Seasonal Steam Requirements. **In** *[Klein, L. R.]*, 1983, pp. 219–35. **[G: Canada]**

Henderson, J. Stephen. Costs and Benefits of Residential Time-of-Use Metering: Comment. *Energy J.*, January 1983, *4*(1), pp. 161–65. **[G: U.S.]**

Henderson, J. Stephen. The Economics of Electricity Demand Charges. *Energy J.*, Supplement 1983, *4*, pp. 127–40. **[G: U.S.]**

Hill, Joanne and Schneeweis, Thomas. The Effect of Three Mile Island on Electric Utility Stock Prices: A Note. *J. Finance*, September 1983, *38*(4), pp. 1285–92. **[G: U.S.]**

Hirschberg, Joseph G. and Aigner, Dennis J. An Analysis of Commercial and Industrial Customer Response to Time-of-Use Rates. *Energy J.*, Supplement 1983, *4*, pp. 103–26. **[G: U.S.]**

Hope, Einar; Magnus, Eivind and Matland, Richard. Economic Incentives and Public Firm Behavior: An Econometric Analysis of Energy Economizing Behavior of Norwegian Electric Utilities. *Scand. J. Econ.*, 1983, *85*(3), pp. 339–57. **[G: Norway]**

Houston, Douglas A. Deregulating Electric Utilities:

A Market-Process Approach. *Cato J.*, Winter 1983/84, *3*(3), pp. 831–53.

Houston, Douglas A. Revenue Effects from Changes in a Declining Block Pricing Structure: Reply. *Land Econ.*, August 1983, *59*(3), pp. 360–64. **[G: U.S.]**

Huettner, David A. Diseconomies of Scale. **In** *Brown, H. J., ed.*, 1983, pp. 215–28. **[G: U.S.]**

Huettner, David A. Restructuring the Electric Utility Industry: A Modest Proposal. **In** *Brown, H. J., ed.*, 1983, pp. 183–97. **[G: U.S.]**

Huettner, David A.; Kasulis, Jack and Dikeman, Neil. Costs and Benefits of Residential Time-of-Use Metering: Reply. *Energy J.*, January 1983, *4*(1), pp. 166–69. **[G: U.S.]**

Hunter, Holland; Dienes, Leslie and Bettis, Lee. International Implications of Long-distance Transport of Fuels. **In** *Khachaturov, T. S. and Goodwin, P. B., eds.*, 1983, pp. 81–93. **[G: U.S.S.R.]**

Iqbal, Mahmood. Residential Demand for Electricity and Natural Gas in Pakistan. *Pakistan Devel. Rev.*, Spring 1983, *22*(1), pp. 23–36. **[G: Pakistan]**

Ivantsov, O. M. Pipeline Transportation of Natural Gas in the U.S.S.R. **In** *Khachaturov, T. S. and Goodwin, P. B., eds.*, 1983, pp. 134–41. **[G: U.S.S.R.]**

Jacoby, Henry D. and Wright, Arthur W. The Gordian Knot of Natural Gas Prices. **In** *Mitchell, E. J., ed.*, 1983, pp. 125–48. **[G: U.S.]**

Jéquier, Nicolas. Intelligence Requirements and Information Management for Developing Countries. **In** *O'Brien, R. C., ed.*, 1983, pp. 122–40.

John, Kose and Saunders, Anthony. Asymmetry of Information, Regulatory Lags and Optimal Incentive Contracts: Theory and Evidence. *J. Finance*, May 1983, *38*(2), pp. 391–404. **[G: U.S.]**

Johnston, Stephen A. Peak and Off-Peak Electricity Consumption: A Review and Critique of Load Management and Rate Design Demonstration Projects. **In** *Berg, S. V., ed.*, 1983, pp. 115–28. **[G: U.S.]**

Jonscher, Charles. Information Resources and Economic Productivity. *Info. Econ. Policy*, 1983, *1*(1), pp. 13–35. **[G: U.S.]**

Joskow, Paul L. and Jones, Donald R. The Simple Economics of Industrial Cogeneration. *Energy J.*, January 1983, *4*(1), pp. 1–22.

Juzzawalla, Meheroo and Cheah, Chee-Wah. Towards an Information Economy: The Case of Singapore. *Info. Econ. Policy*, 1983, *1*(2), pp. 161–76. **[G: Singapore]**

Kafoglis, Milton Z. Regulatory Lag in an Inflationary Environment. **In** *[Bonbright, J. C.]*, 1983, pp. 211–18. **[G: U.S.]**

Kahn, Alfred E. Utility Regulation Revisited. **In** *[Bonbright, J. C.]*, 1983, pp. 101–15. **[G: U.S.]**

Kahn, James Gustave. The Advantages of Integrating Decentralized Renewable Electrical Technologies: A Connecticut Case Study. **In** *Brown, H. J., ed.*, 1983, pp. 163–81. **[G: U.S.]**

Kanygin, Iu. M. and Parfentseva, N. A. How to Plan and Evaluate the Work of Computer Centers. *Prob. Econ.*, December 1983, *26*(8), pp. 32–44. **[G: U.S.S.R.]**

Kaul, S. N. and Iyer, V. R. Widening Gap between Telephone Demand and Supply—Its Influence on Service Efficiency. *Margin*, July 1983, *15*(4), pp. 34–49. **[G: India]**

Keeney, Ralph L. A Technology Choice for Model Electricity Generation. *Energy J.*, Supplement 1983, *4*, pp. 13–31.

Kiss, Ferenc. Productivity Gains in Bell Canada. **In** *Courville, L.; de Fontenay, A. and Dobell, R., eds.*, 1983, pp. 85–113. **[G: Canada]**

Kiss, Ferenc; Karabadjian, Seta and Lefebvre, Bernard J. Economies of Scale and Scope in Bell Canada. **In** *Courville, L.; de Fontenay, A. and Dobell, R., eds.*, 1983, pp. 55–82. **[G: Canada]**

Knieps, Günter. Is Technological Revolution a Sufficient Reason for Changing the System of Regulation? The Case of Telecommunications. *Z. ges. Staatswiss.*, October 1983, *139*(3), pp. 578–97. **[G: W. Germany]**

Koster, Francis P. The Role of Utilities in Promoting Solar Energy: The Case of the TVA. **In** *Rich, D., et al., eds.*, 1983, pp. 103–22. **[G: U.S.]**

Kubitz, Kermit R. The Energy Utilities: How to Increase Rewards to Match Increasing Risks. **In** *Aronson, J. D. and Cowhey, P. F., eds.*, 1983, pp. 137–55. **[G: U.S.]**

Kuo, Eddie C. Y. Communication Policy and National Development. **In** *Chen, P. S. J., ed.*, 1983, pp. 268–81. **[G: Singapore]**

Lake, R. W.; Boon, C. J. and Schwier, C. Efficient Long-distance Fuel Transportation. **In** *Khachaturov, T. S. and Goodwin, P. B., eds.*, 1983, pp. 142–56. **[G: Canada]**

LaMorte, Michele. Overview of Reports from the Electric-Utility Rate-Design Study. **In** *Berg, S. V., ed.*, 1983, pp. 305–14. **[G: U.S.]**

Landon, John H. Theories of Vertical Integration and Their Application to the Electric Utility Industry. *Antitrust Bull.*, Spring 1983, *28*(1), pp. 101–30. **[G: U.S.]**

Langdale, John. Competition in the United States' Long-Distance Telecommunications Industry. *Reg. Stud.*, December 1983, *17*(6), pp. 393–409. **[G: U.S.]**

Lantzke, Ulf. Investment and Energy. **In** *Heertje, A., ed.*, 1983, pp. 117–51. **[G: W. Europe]**

LaTour, Stephen A. and Orwin, Robert G. Determining the Effects of Innovative Rates on Customer Response Using Meta-Analysis. **In** *Berg, S. V., ed.*, 1983, pp. 129–50. **[G: U.S.]**

Laughhunn, Dan J.; Crum, Roy L. and Payne, John W. Risk Attitudes in the Telecommunications Industry. *Bell J. Econ. (See Rand J. Econ. after 4/85)*, Autumn 1983, *14*(2), pp. 517–21. **[G: U.S.; Canada]**

Lazarus, William. Landsats, Minerals and Development: A Qualitative Notion of the Down-Side Risk. **In** *O'Brien, R. C., ed.*, 1983, pp. 102–21. **[G: U.S.]**

Leone, Robert A. Comment [Pitfalls on the Road to Decontrol: Lessons from the Natural Gas Policy Act of 1978] [The Intrastate Pipelines and the Natural Gas Policy Act]. **In** *Mitchell, E. J., ed.*, 1983, pp. 109–11. **[G: U.S.]**

Lesáková, Dagmar. Cooperation of CMEA Member Countries in Data Processing Equipment. *Czech. Econ. Digest.*, August 1983, (5), pp. 61–67. **[G: CMEA]**

Levary, Reuven R. and Dean, Burton V. An Adaptive Model for Planning the Purchasing and Storage of Natural Gas. **In** *Lev, B., ed.,* 1983, pp. 387–97. **[G: U.S.]**

Levin, Nissan; Tishler, Asher and Zahavi, Jacob. Perturbation Analysis of Power Generation Expansion Programs Subject to Uncertainty in the Prices of Primary Energy Resources. **In** *Lev, B., ed.,* 1983, pp. 367–85. **[G: U.S.]**

Lewis, W. Arthur. Fixed Costs. **In** *Lewis, W. A.,* 1983, *1961,* pp. 113–47.

Lindsley, E. F. Planning Practically for a Decentralized Electrical System: How Past Experience Can Guide Us. **In** *Brown, H. J., ed.,* 1983, pp. 243–53. **[G: U.S.]**

Lioukas, Spyros K. Investment Behaviour in a Nationalised Industry. *Appl. Econ.,* October 1983, *15*(5), pp. 665–79. **[G: U.K.]**

Littlechild, S. C. The Structure of Telephone Tariffs. *Int. J. Ind. Organ.,* December 1983, *1*(4), pp. 365–77. **[G: Selected Countries]**

Litvak, I. A. and Maule, C. J. Competition Policy and Newspapers in Canada. *Antitrust Bull.,* Summer 1983, *28*(2), pp. 461–81. **[G: Canada]**

Longva, Svein; Lorentsen, Lorents and Olsen, Øystein. Energy in the Multi-sectoral Growth Model MSG. **In** *Av, R., et al., eds.,* 1983, pp. 27–51. **[G: Norway]**

Longva, Svein and Olsen, Øystein. The Specification of Electricity Flows in the MSG Model. **In** *Av, R., et al., eds.,* 1983, pp. 108–33. **[G: Norway]**

Longva, Svein, et al. Use of the MSG Model in Forecasting Electricity Demand. **In** *Av, R., et al., eds.,* 1983, pp. 180–94. **[G: Norway]**

Lovins, Amory B. Technology Is the Answer! (But What Was the Question?) **In** *Brown, H. J., ed.,* 1983, pp. 19–35.

MacAvoy, Paul W. and Robinson, Kenneth. Winning by Losing: The AT&T Settlement and Its Impact on Telecommunications. *Yale J. Regul.,* 1983, *1*(1), pp. 1–42. **[G: U.S.]**

Malko, J. Robert and Enholm, Gregory B. Challenges for Electric Utilities and Regulatory Commissions. **In** *[Bonbright, J. C.],* 1983, pp. 117–31. **[G: U.S.]**

Marchand, M.; Proost, S. and Wilberz, E. A Model of District Heating Using a CHP Plant. *Energy Econ.,* October 1983, *5*(4), pp. 247–57. **[G: Belgium]**

McElwain, Adrienne and Lifson, Dale P. A Comparison and Reconciliation of Full and Partial Price Elasticities. *Appl. Econ.,* June 1983, *15*(3), pp. 353–62. **[G: U.S.]**

McGrann, James M. Microcomputer Software Development and Distribution. *Southern J. Agr. Econ.,* July 1983, *15*(1), pp. 21–25. **[G: U.S.]**

McQueen, David. Alternative Scenarios in Broadcasting. *Can. Public Policy,* March 1983, *9*(1), pp. 129–34. **[G: Canada]**

Means, Robert C. The Intrastate Pipelines and the Natural Gas Policy Act. **In** *Mitchell, E. J., ed.,* 1983, pp. 71–107. **[G: U.S.]**

Metcalfe, J. S., et al. The Economic Development of Cable TV in the UK. *Metroecon.,* October 1983, *35*(3), pp. 235–59. **[G: U.K.]**

Milon, J. Walter. Welfare Consequences of Marginal-Cost Rate Designs for Cogenerators and Small Power Producers. **In** *Berg, S. V., ed.,* 1983, pp. 249–60. **[G: U.S.]**

Mitchell, Bridger M. Local Telephone Costs and the Design of Rate Structures. **In** *Courville, L.; de Fontenay, A. and Dobell, R., eds.,* 1983, pp. 293–304.

Mitchell, Bridger M. and Acton, Jan Paul. Electricity Consumption by Time of Use in a Hybrid Demand System. **In** *Finsinger, J., ed.,* 1983, pp. 27–64. **[G: U.S.]**

Monash, Curt A. Efficient Allocation of a Stochastic Supply: Auction Mechanisms. **In** *Engelbrecht-Wiggans, R.; Shubik, M. and Stark, R. M., eds.,* 1983, pp. 231–54. **[G: U.S.]**

Monnier, L. La tarification de l'électricité: nouveau débat. (The Electricity Tariff: A New Debate. With English summary.) *Écon. Soc.,* December 1983, *17*(12), pp. 2053–75. **[G: France]**

Morris, David. The Pendulum Swings Again: A Century of Urban Electric Systems. **In** *Brown, H. J., ed.,* 1983, pp. 37–58. **[G: U.S.]**

Morris, Robert D. The Electrical Energy Production System in Transition: The Critical Factor of Reliability. **In** *Brown, H. J., ed.,* 1983, pp. 93–107.

Nelson, Randy A. and Wohar, Mark E. Regulation, Scale Economies, and Productivity in Steam–Electric Generation. *Int. Econ. Rev.,* February 1983, *24*(1), pp. 57–79. **[G: U.S.]**

Neumann, Karl-Heinz; Schweizer, Urs and von Weizsäcker, C. Christian. Welfare Analysis of Telecommunication Tariffs in Germany. **In** *Finsinger, J., ed.,* 1983, pp. 65–85. **[G: W. Germany]**

Nusbaum, William R. New Legislation and the Impact on Changing Price Structure of Telephone Service. **In** *[Bonbright, J. C.],* 1983, pp. 251–57. **[G: U.S.]**

O'Brien, Rita Cruise and Helleiner, Gerald K. The Political Economy of Information in a Changing International Economic Order. **In** *O'Brien, R. C., ed.,* 1983, pp. 1–27.

Osbon, Anthony D. The Market Environment for Utility Securities. **In** *[Bonbright, J. C.],* 1983, pp. 235–47. **[G: U.S.]**

Osleeb, Jeffrey P. and Patrick, Samuel J. The Impact of Coal Conversions on the Ports of New England. *Econ. Geogr.,* January 1983, *59*(1), pp. 35–51. **[G: U.S.]**

Pacey, Patricia L. Long Distance Demand: A Point-to-Point Model. *Southern Econ. J.,* April 1983, *49*(4), pp. 1094–1107. **[G: U.S.]**

Park, Rolla Edward; Wetzel, Bruce M. and Mitchell, Bridger M. Price Elasticities for Local Telephone Calls. *Econometrica,* November 1983, *51*(6), pp. 1699–730. **[G: U.S.]**

Park, Rolla Edward, et al. Charging for Local Telephone Calls: How Household Characteristics Affect the Distribution of Calls in the GTE Illinois Experiment. *J. Econometrics,* August 1983, *22*(3), pp. 339–64. **[G: U.S.]**

Paul, Chris W., II. Rate-Base Determination, Inflation, and Realized Rates of Return to Electric Utilities. **In** *[Bonbright, J. C.],* 1983, pp. 219–26. **[G: U.S.]**

Peck, Stephen C. Electric Utility Capacity Expansion: Its Implications for Customers and Stockholders. *Energy J.*, Supplement 1983, *4*, pp. 1–11.

Perrakis, Stylianos and Silva-Echenique, Julio. The Profitability and Risk of CATV Operations in Canada. *Appl. Econ.*, December 1983, *15*(6), pp. 745–58. **[G: Canada]**

Phillips, Charles F., Jr. The Changing Environment of Public-Utility Regulation: An Overview. **In** *[Bonbright, J. C.]*, 1983, pp. 25–39. **[G: U.S.]**

Platt, Harlan D. An Integrated Approach to Electricity Demand Forecasting. *Energy J.*, Supplement 1983, *4*, pp. 75–91. **[G: U.S.]**

Reimeringer, J. N. Global Factor Productivity (GFP) and EDF's Management. **In** *Courville, L.; de Fontenay, A. and Dobell, R., eds.*, 1983, pp. 131–43.

Renas, Stephen M., et al. Toward an Economic Theory of Defamation, Liability, and the Press. *Southern Econ. J.*, October 1983, *50*(2), pp. 451–60.

Rheaume, G. C. Welfare Optimal Subsidy-free Prices under a Regulated Monopoly. **In** *Courville, L.; de Fontenay, A. and Dobell, R., eds.*, 1983, pp. 319–40.

Rinde, Jon and Strøm, Steinar. Cost Structure of Electricity Production. **In** *Av, R., et al., eds.*, 1983, pp. 134–50. **[G: Norway]**

Rødseth, Asbjørn. Optimal Timing and Dimensioning of Hydro Power Projects. **In** *Av, R., et al., eds.*, 1983, pp. 304–23. **[G: Norway]**

Roth, T. P. Electricity Demand Estimation Using Proxy Variables: Some Reservations. *Appl. Econ.*, October 1983, *15*(5), pp. 703–04. **[G: U.S.]**

Russell, Milton. Overview of Policy Issues: A Preliminary Assessment. **In** *Mitchell, E. J., ed.*, 1983, pp. 3–32. **[G: U.S.]**

Saito, Tadao; Inose, Hiroshi and Kageyama, Sei. A Comparative Study of the Mode of Domestic and Transborder Information Flows Including Data. *Info. Econ. Policy*, 1983, *1*(1), pp. 75–92. **[G: Japan]**

Sanghvi, Arun P. Household Welfare Loss Due to Electricity Supply Disruptions. *Energy J.*, Supplement 1983, *4*, pp. 33–54. **[G: U.S.]**

Sanghvi, Arun P. Optimal Electricity Supply Reliability Using Customer Shortage Costs. *Energy Econ.*, April 1983, *5*(2), pp. 129–36. **[G: U.S.]**

Sanghvi, Arun P.; Shavel, Ira H. and Wagner, Michael H. Fuel Diversification, Stockpiling, and System Interconnection Strategies for Minimizing Power System Vulnerability to Energy Shortages. **In** *Lev, B., ed.*, 1983, pp. 235–54. **[G: U.S.]**

Schlesinger, Benjamin. Overview of Policy Issues: A Preliminary Assessment: Comment. **In** *Mitchell, E. J., ed.*, 1983, pp. 36–39. **[G: U.S.]**

Schreiner, Alette and Strøm, Steinar. Transmission and Distribution of Electricity. **In** *Av, R., et al., eds.*, 1983, pp. 151–60. **[G: Norway]**

Sharlin, Harold Issadore. New York's Electricity: Establishing a Technological Paradigm. **In** *[Cochran, T. C.]*, 1983, pp. 101–16. **[G: U.S.]**

Shepherd, William G. Price Structures in Electricity. **In** *[Bonbright, J. C.]*, 1983, pp. 151–67. **[G: U.S.]**

Sherali, Hanif D. and Soyster, Allen L. Analysis of Network Structured Models for Electric Utility Capacity Planning and Marginal Cost Pricing Problems. **In** *Lev, B., ed.*, 1983, pp. 113–34.

Sherman, Roger. Is Public-Utility Regulation beyond Hope?. **In** *[Bonbright, J. C.]*, 1983, pp. 41–75. **[G: U.S.]**

Shubik, Martin; Heim, Peggy and Baumol, William J. On Contracting with Publishers: Author's Information Updated. *Amer. Econ. Rev.*, May 1983, *73*(2), pp. 365–81. **[G: U.S.]**

Smart, Ian. Nuclear Resources: The Dilemmas of Interdependence. **In** *Akao, N., ed.*, 1983, pp. 119–44. **[G: Japan]**

Snyder, Donald C. Cable Television in the Caribbean: The Case of Jamaica. *Atlantic Econ. J.*, September 1983, *11*(3), pp. 56–62. **[G: Jamaica]**

de Sola Pool, Ithiel. Communications Technology and Land Use. **In** *Carr, J. H. and Duensing, E. E., eds.*, 1983, *1980*, pp. 291–303. **[G: U.S.]**

Sørensen, Bent. The Grid as Energy Absorber and Redistributor. **In** *Brown, H. J., ed.*, 1983, pp. 109–20.

Soutar, Geoffrey N. and Clarke, Yvonne M. Life Style and Radio Listening Patterns in Perth, Western Australia. *Australian J. Manage.*, June 1983, *8*(1), pp. 71–81. **[G: Australia]**

Stern, Jonathan P. Natural Gas: The Perfect Answer to Energy Diversification. **In** *Akao, N., ed.*, 1983, pp. 97–117. **[G: Japan]**

Stevenson, Rodney E. Institutional Objectives, Structural Barriers, and Deregulation in the Electric Utility Industry. *J. Econ. Issues*, June 1983, *17*(2), pp. 443–52. **[G: U.S.]**

Strange, J. Leland. Microcomputer Enhancement: Challenges in an Exploding Industry. **In** *Federal Reserve Bank of Atlanta*, 1983, pp. 111–17. **[G: U.S.]**

Strøm, Steinar. Optimal Pricing and Investment in Electricity Supply. **In** *Av, R., et al., eds.*, 1983, pp. 260–80. **[G: Norway]**

Sturgess, Brian. Government Media Policy in Britain and West Germany. *Nat. Westminster Bank Quart. Rev.*, August 1983, pp. 45–59. **[G: U.K.; W. Germany]**

Sullivan, Robert L. Evaluating Reliability and Operating-Cost Impacts of TOU Rates. **In** *Berg, S. V., ed.*, 1983, pp. 153–81. **[G: U.S.]**

Surrey, John and Walker, William. Electrical Power Plant: Market Collapse and Structural Strains. **In** *Shepherd, G.; Duchêne, F. and Saunders, C., eds.*, 1983, pp. 139–66. **[G: OECD]**

Sutherland, Ronald J. Distributed Lags and the Demand for Electricity. *Energy J.*, Supplement 1983, *4*, pp. 141–51. **[G: U.S.]**

Sweeney, James L. Energy Model Comparison: An Overview. **In** *Thrall, R. M.; Thompson, R. G. and Holloway, M. L., eds.*, 1983, pp. 191–217. **[G: U.S.]**

Takasaki, Nozomu and Ozawa, Takahiro. Analysis of Information Flow in Japan. *Info. Econ. Policy*, 1983, *1*(2), pp. 177–93. **[G: Japan]**

Taylor, Lester D. Problems and Issues in Modeling Telecommunications Demand. **In** *Courville, L.; de Fontenay, A. and Dobell, R., eds.*, 1983, pp. 181–98. **[G: U.S.]**

Tell, Björn, V. The Awakening Information Needs of the Developing Countries. **In** *O'Brien, R. C., ed.*, 1983, *1980*, pp. 141–47.

Thompson, Edward, III. Cogeneration and Small

Power Production: Some Intergovernmental Policy Concerns. **In** *Brown, H. J., ed.*, 1983, pp. 199–212. **[G: U.S.]**

Tishler, Asher. The Industrial and Commercial Demand for Electricity under Time-of-Use Pricing. *J. Econometrics,* December 1983, *23*(3), pp. 369–84. **[G: U.S.]**

Tran, Ngoc-Bich and Smith, V. Kerry. The Role of Air and Water Residuals for Steam Electric Power Generation. *J. Environ. Econ. Manage.*, March 1983, *10*(1), pp. 35–49. **[G: U.S.]**

Uhler, Robert G. Electric-Utility Pricing Issues: Old and New. **In** *[Bonbright, J. C.]*, 1983, pp. 77–82. **[G: U.S.]**

Veall, Michael R. Industrial Electricity Demand and the Hopkinson Rate: An Application of the Extreme Value Distribution. *Bell J. Econ. (See Rand J. Econ. after 4/85),* Autumn 1983, *14*(2), pp. 427–40. **[G: Canada]**

Wilder, Ronald P. Marginal-Cost Pricing: Theory and Practice. **In** *[Bonbright, J. C.]*, 1983, pp. 169–76. **[G: U.S.]**

Wilkinson, G. F. The Estimation of Usage Repression under Local Measured Service: Empirical Evidence from the GTE Experiment. **In** *Courville, L.; de Fontenay, A. and Dobell, R., eds.*, 1983, pp. 253–62. **[G: U.S.]**

Wionczek, Miguel S. Some Reflections on Economic Information Gathering and Processing within the Framework of the North–South Conflict. **In** *O'Brien, R. C., ed.*, 1983, pp. 148–53.

Withers, Glenn A. The Cultural Influence of Public Television. **In** *Hendon, W. S. and Shanahan, J. L., eds.*, 1983, pp. 77–92. **[G: Australia]**

Witholder, Robert E., Jr. Economic Feasibility of Dispersed Solar Electric Technologies. **In** *Brown, H. J., ed.*, 1983, pp. 121–61. **[G: U.S.]**

Wong, T. F. Identifying Tariff Induced Shifts in the Subscriber Distribution of Local Telephone Usage. **In** *Courville, L.; de Fontenay, A. and Dobell, R., eds.*, 1983, pp. 263–78. **[G: U.S.]**

Wood, William C. Putting a Price on Radiation. *J. Policy Anal. Manage.*, Winter 1983, *2*(2), pp. 291–95. **[G: U.S.]**

Woodbury, John R.; Besen, Stanley M. and Fournier, Gary M. The Determinants of Network Television Program Prices: Implicit Contracts, Regulation, and Bargaining Power. *Bell J. Econ. (See Rand J. Econ. after 4/85),* Autumn 1983, *14*(2), pp. 351–65. **[G: U.S.]**

Woods, Thomas J. and Vidas, E. Harry. Projecting Hydrocarbon Production and Costs: An Integrated Approach. *J. Energy Devel.*, Spring 1983, *8*(2), pp. 267–82. **[G: U.S.]**

Yakin, M. Zafer. Optimal Operations of Power Systems: A Survey. **In** *Lev, B., ed.*, 1983, pp. 563–84.

Young, Trevor; Stevens, Thomas H. and Willis, Cleve. Asymmetry in the Residential Demand for Electricity. *Energy J.*, Supplement 1983, *4*, pp. 153–62. **[G: U.S.]**

6354 Business and Legal Services

Barcet, André and Bonamy, Joël. Différenciation des prestations de services aux entreprises. (With English summary.) *Rev. Econ. Ind.*, 2nd Trimester 1983, (24), pp. 9–17.

Browne, Lynn E. High Technology and Business Services. *New Eng. Econ. Rev.*, July–August 1983, pp. 5–17. **[G: U.S.]**

Hawkins, Robert. Una comunità che si espande: il leasing. (The Leasing Community Expands. With English summary.) *Mondo Aperto,* March-April 1983, *37*(2), pp. 83–92.

Hough, Douglas E. and Kratz, Charles G. Can "Good" Architecture Meet the Market Test? *J. Urban Econ.*, July 1983, *14*(1), pp. 40–54. **[G: U.S.]**

Mendels, R. P. The Economist as a Consultant: A Note. *Amer. Econ.*, Fall 1983, *27*(2), pp. 86–88.

Mowery, David C. The Relationship between Intrafirm and Contractual Forms of Industrial Research in American Manufacturing, 1900–1940. *Exploration Econ. Hist.*, October 1983, *20*(4), pp. 351–74. **[G: U.S.]**

Nichols, Donald R. and Smith, David B. Auditor Credibility and Auditor Changes. *J. Acc. Res.*, Autumn 1983, *21*(2), pp. 534–44. **[G: U.S.]**

Peterson, Rodney D. and Soma, John T. Advertising, Imperfect Competition, and the Market for Legal Services. *J. Behav. Econ.*, Winter 1983, *12*(2), pp. 57–66. **[G: U.S.]**

Shockley, Randolph A. and Holt, Robert N. A Behavioral Investigation of Supplier Differentiation in the Market for Audit Services. *J. Acc. Res.*, Autumn 1983, *21*(2), pp. 545–64. **[G: U.S.]**

Stager, David. Are There Too Many Lawyers? *Can. Public Policy,* June 1983, *9*(2), pp. 245–49. **[G: Canada]**

Wright, Arnold. the Impact of CPA-Firm Size on Auditor Disclosure Preferences. *Accounting Rev.*, July 1983, *58*(3), pp. 621–32. **[G: U.S.]**

6355 Repair Services

Remeš, Alois. The Function of Small Enterprises in the Economy. *Czech. Econ. Digest.*, March 1983, (2), pp. 16–42. **[G: Czechoslovakia]**

6356 Insurance

Aaron, Henry J. Orange Light for the Competitive Model [Stability in the Federal Employees Health Benefits Program]. *J. Health Econ.*, December 1983, *2*(3), pp. 281–84. **[G: U.S.]**

Achampong, Francis. The Means and Ends of Insurance Regulation—Basic Ideas. *J. Risk Ins.*, June 1983, *50*(2), pp. 301–06.

Adamache, Killard W. and Sloan, Frank A. Competition between Non-Profit and For-Profit Health Insurers. *J. Health Econ.*, December 1983, *2*(3), pp. 225–43. **[G: U.S.]**

Aronson, Jonathan David and Proctor, Charles Rudicel. Insurance, Risk Management, and Energy in Transition. **In** *Aronson, J. D. and Cowhey, P. F., eds.*, 1983, pp. 181–202. **[G: U.S.]**

Babbel, David F. and Staking, Kim B. A Capital Budgeting Analysis of Life Insurance Costs in the United States: 1950–1979. *J. Finance,* March 1983, *38*(1), pp. 149–70. **[G: U.S.]**

Babbel, David F. and Staking, Kim B. An Engel

Curve Analysis of Gambling and Insurance in Brazil. *J. Risk Ins.*, December 1983, *50*(4), pp. 688–96. **[G: Brazil]**

Ben-Horim, Moshe. Discount for Advance Insurance Premium Payment under Conditions of Inflation. *Quart. Rev. Econ. Bus.*, Spring 1983, *23*(1), pp. 29–34. **[G: U.S.]**

Boyer, Marcel and Dionne, Georges. Variations in the Probability and Magnitude of Loss: Their Impact on Risk. *Can. J. Econ.*, August 1983, *16*(3), pp. 411–19.

Boyle, Phelim P. and Mao, Jennifer. An Exact Solution for the Optimal Stop Loss Limit. *J. Risk Ins.*, December 1983, *50*(4), pp. 719–26.

Brockett, Patrick L. On the Misuse of the Central Limit Theorem in Some Risk Calculations. *J. Risk Ins.*, December 1983, *50*(4), pp. 727–31.

Burnett, John J. and Palmer, Bruce A. Reliance on Life Insurance Agents: A Demographic and Psychographic Analysis of Consumers. *J. Risk Ins.*, September 1983, *50*(3), pp. 510–20. **[G: U.S.]**

Cho, Dongsae. Integrated Risk Management Decision-Making: A Workers' Compensation Loss Exposure Case Study. *J. Risk Ins.*, June 1983, *50*(2), pp. 281–300.

Choudhury, Masudul Alam. Insurance and Investment in Islamic Perspective. *Int. J. Soc. Econ.*, 1983, *10*(5), pp. 14–26.

Christiansen, Hanne D. Equality and Equilibrium: Weaknesses of the Overlap Argument for Unisex Pension Plans. *J. Risk Ins.*, December 1983, *50*(4), pp. 670–80. **[G: U.S.]**

Cozzolino, John M. The Evaluation of Loss Control Options. *J. Risk Ins.*, September 1983, *50*(3), pp. 404–16.

Cross, Mark L. and Thornton, John H. The Probable Effect of an Extreme Hurricane on Texas Catastrophe Plan Insurers. *J. Risk Ins.*, September 1983, *50*(3), pp. 417–44. **[G: U.S.]**

Cummins, J. David and Wiltbank, Laurel J. Estimating the Total Claims Distribution Using Multivariate Frequency and Severity Distributions. *J. Risk Ins.*, September 1983, *50*(3), pp. 377–403.

Dahlby, B. G. Adverse Selection and Statistical Discrimination: An Analysis of Canadian Automobile Insurance. *J. Public Econ.*, February 1983, *20*(1), pp. 121–30. **[G: Canada]**

De Jong, Piet and Boyle, Phelim P. Monitoring Mortality: A State-Space Approach. *J. Econometrics*, September 1983, *23*(1), pp. 131–46.

De Vylder, F. Practical Models in Credibility Theory, Including Parameter Estimation. *J. Econometrics*, September 1983, *23*(1), pp. 147–64.

DesHarnais, Susan; Kibe, Neel M. and Barbus, Shirley. Blue Cross and Blue Shield of Michigan Hospital Laboratory On-Site Review Project. *Inquiry*, Winter 1983, *20*(4), pp. 328–33. **[G: U.S.]**

Dillingham, Alan E. The Effect of Labor Force Age Distribution on Workers' Compensation Costs. *J. Risk Ins.*, June 1983, *50*(2), pp. 235–48. **[G: U.S.]**

Doherty, Neil A. Stochastic Choice in Insurance and Risk Sharing: A Reply. *J. Finance*, June 1983, *38*(3), pp. 1037–38.

Doherty, Neil A. The Measurement of Firm and Market Capacity. *J. Risk Ins.*, June 1983, *50*(2), pp. 224–34. **[G: Canada]**

Doherty, Neil A. and Schlesinger, Harris. Optimal Insurance in Incomplete Markets. *J. Polit. Econ.*, December 1983, *91*(6), pp. 1045–54.

Doherty, Neil A. and Schlesinger, Harris. The Optimal Deductible for an Insurance Policy When Initial Wealth Is Random. *J. Bus.*, October 1983, *56*(4), pp. 555–65.

Finsinger, Jörg. The Performance of Property Liability Insurance Firms under the German Regulatory System. *Z. ges. Staatswiss.*, October 1983, *139*(3), pp. 473–89. **[G: W. Germany]**

Freifelder, Leonard R. Collegiate Sports Risk Management. *J. Risk Ins.*, December 1983, *50*(4), pp. 703–18. **[G: U.S.]**

Frost, A. J. and Henderson, I. J. S. Implications of Modern Portfolio Theory for Life Assurance Companies. **In** *Corner, D. and Mayes, D. G., eds.*, 1983, pp. 163–79. **[G: U.K.]**

Gianfrancesco, Frank D. A Proposal for Improving the Efficiency of Medical Insurance. *J. Health Econ.*, August 1983, *2*(2), pp. 176–84. **[G: U.S.]**

Gibson, Rosemary and Reiss, John B. Health Care Delivery and Financing: Competition, Regulation, and Incentives. **In** *Meyer, J. A., ed.*, 1983, pp. 243–68. **[G: U.S.]**

Goddeeris, John H. Theoretical Considerations on the Cost of Illness. *J. Health Econ.*, August 1983, *2*(2), pp. 149–59.

Goldsmith, Art. Household Life Cycle Protection: Human Capital versus Life Insurance. *J. Risk Ins.*, March 1983, *50*(1), pp. 33–43. **[G: U.S.]**

Goldsmith, Art. Household Life Cycle Protection: Human Capital versus Life Insurance. *J. Risk Ins.*, September 1983, *50*(3), pp. 473–86. **[G: U.S.]**

Goovaerts, M. J. and De Vylder, F. Upper and Lower Bounds on Infinite Time Ruin Probabilities in Case of Constraints on Claim Size Distributions. *J. Econometrics*, September 1983, *23*(1), pp. 77–90.

Greenberg, Warren. How Will Increased Competition Affect the Costs of Health Care? **In** *Meyer, J. A., ed.*, 1983, pp. 46–60. **[G: U.S.]**

Griffith, John R. The Role of Blue Cross and Blue Shield in the Future U.S. Health Care System. *Inquiry*, Spring 1983, *20*(1), pp. 12–19. **[G: U.S.]**

Gustavson, Sandra G. and Schultz, Joseph J., Jr. Property-Liability Loss Reserve Certification: Independent or In-House? *J. Risk Ins.*, June 1983, *50*(2), pp. 307–14. **[G: U.S.]**

Harrington, Scott E. The Relationship between Risk and Return: Evidence for Life Insurance Stocks. *J. Risk Ins.*, December 1983, *50*(4), pp. 587–610. **[G: U.S.]**

Harris, William G. Inflation Risk as Determinant of the Discount Rate in Tort Settlements. *J. Risk Ins.*, June 1983, *50*(2), pp. 265–80. **[G: U.S.]**

Hickman, James C. Pensions and Sex. *J. Risk Ins.*, December 1983, *50*(4), pp. 681–87. **[G: U.S.]**

Hogg, Robert V. and Klugman, Stuart A. On the Estimation of Long Tailed Skewed Distributions with Actuarial Applications. *J. Econometrics*, September 1983, *23*(1), pp. 91–102. **[G: U.S.]**

Huberman, Gur; Mayers, David and Smith, Clifford W., Jr. Optimal Insurance Policy Indemnity Schedules. *Bell J. Econ. (See Rand J. Econ. after*

4/85), Autumn 1983, *14*(2), pp. 415–26.
Jennings, Robert M. and Trout, Andrew P. The Irish Tontine (1777) and Fifty Genevans: An Essay on Comparative Mortality. *J. Europ. Econ. Hist.*, Winter 1983, *12*(3), pp. 611–18. **[G: Ireland]**
Joskow, Paul L. Reimbursement Policy, Cost Containment and Non-Price Competition [Competition and Efficiency in the End Stage Renal Disease Program]. *J. Health Econ.*, August 1983, *2*(2), pp. 167–74. **[G: U.S.]**
Jung, Allen F. Automobile Insurance Rates in Chicago, Illinois—A Correction. *J. Risk Ins.*, June 1983, *50*(2), pp. 330–31. **[G: U.S.]**
Karni, Edi. Risk Aversion for State-Dependent Utility Functions: Measurement and Applications. *Int. Econ. Rev.*, October 1983, *24*(3), pp. 637–47.
Karni, Edi. Risk Aversion in the Theory of Health Insurance. **In** *Helpman, E.; Razin, A. and Sadka, E., eds.*, 1983, pp. 97–106.
Kellner, S. and Mathewson, G. Frank. Entry, Size Distribution, Scale, and Scope Economies in the Life Insurance Industry. *J. Bus.*, January 1983, *56*(1), pp. 25–44. **[G: Canada]**
Kirschen, E. S. Les prix des vies humaines. (With English summary.) *Cah. Écon. Bruxelles*, 4th Trimester 1983, (100), pp. 486–533.
Kott, Phillip S. Returns to Scale in the U.S. Life Insurance Industry—Comment. *J. Risk Ins.*, September 1983, *50*(3), pp. 506–07. **[G: U.S.]**
Kroll, Yoram. Stochastic Choice in Insurance and Risk Sharing: A Comment. *J. Finance*, June 1983, *38*(3), pp. 1033–35.
Kunreuther, Howard; Kleindorfer, Paul R. and Pauly, Mark V. Insurance Regulation and Consumer Behavior in the United States: The Property and Liability Industry. *Z. ges. Staatswiss.*, October 1983, *139*(3), pp. 452–72. **[G: U.S.]**
Lahikainen, Pekka. Rahoitusjärjestelmämme kehittäminen vakuutusyhtiöiden näkökulmasta. (Developing the Finnish Financial System—The View of Insurance Companies. With English summary.) *Kansant. Aikak.*, 1983, *79*(2), pp. 160–73. **[G: Finland]**
Leiken, Alan M. and Dusansky, Richard. The Impact of Health Insurance on Hospital Costs: A Multi-Equation Econometric Approach. *Atlantic Econ. J.*, September 1983, *11*(3), pp. 79–85. **[G: U.S.]**
Leone, Alfonso. Maritime Insurance as a Source for the History of International Credit in the Middle Ages. *J. Europ. Econ. Hist.*, Fall 1983, *12*(2), pp. 363–69. **[G: W. Europe]**
Loubergé, Henri. A Portfolio Model of International Reinsurance Operations. *J. Risk Ins.*, March 1983, *50*(1), pp. 44–60.
Main, Brian G. M. Corporate Insurance Purchases and Taxes. *J. Risk Ins.*, June 1983, *50*(2), pp. 197–223. **[G: U.S.]**
Manove, Michael. Provider Insurance. *Bell J. Econ. (See Rand J. Econ. after 4/85)*, Autumn 1983, *14*(2), pp. 489–96.
Mathewson, G. Frank. Information, Search, and Price Variability of Individual Life Insurance Contracts. *J. Ind. Econ.*, December 1983, *32*(2), pp. 131–48. **[G: Canada; U.S.]**
Mathewson, G. Frank. Markets for Insurance: A Selective Survey of Economic Issues. **In** *Dewees, D. N., ed.*, 1983, pp. 247–74. **[G: Canada]**
Mayers, David and Smith, Clifford W., Jr. The Interdependence of Individual Portfolio Decisions and the Demand for Insurance. *J. Polit. Econ.*, April 1983, *91*(2), pp. 304–11.
Meyer, Richard L. and Power, Fred B. The Investment Value of Corporate Insurance. *J. Risk Ins.*, March 1983, *50*(1), pp. 151–56.
de Meza, David. Health Insurance and the Demand for Medical Care. *J. Health Econ.*, March 1983, *2*(1), pp. 47–54.
Miller, Elbert G. and Hoffer, George E. Pay-at-the-Pump Automobile Liability Insurance: Reply [The Distribution of Automobile Liability Insurance: An Alternative]. *J. Risk Ins.*, September 1983, *50*(3), pp. 487–92. **[G: U.S.]**
Myers, Phyllis Schiller and Pritchett, S. Travis. Rate of Return on Differential Premiums for Selected Participating Life Insurance Contracts. *J. Risk Ins.*, December 1983, *50*(4), pp. 569–86. **[G: U.S.]**
O'Neill, Brian. The Irish Insurance Industry. *Irish Banking Rev.*, March 1983, pp. 29–35. **[G: Ireland]**
Oppenheimer, Henry R. and Schlarbaum, Gary G. Investment Policies of Property-Liability Insurers and Pension Plans: A Lesson from Ben Graham. *J. Risk Ins.*, December 1983, *50*(4), pp. 611–30. **[G: U.S.]**
Panjer, Harry H. and Willmot, Gordon E. Compound Poisson Models in Actuarial Risk Theory. *J. Econometrics*, September 1983, *23*(1), pp. 63–76.
Pauly, Mark V. More on Moral Hazard [Health Insurance and the Demand for Medical Care]. *J. Health Econ.*, March 1983, *2*(1), pp. 81–85.
Praetz, Peter. Returns to Scale in the U.S. Life Insurance Industry—Reply. *J. Risk Ins.*, September 1983, *50*(3), pp. 508–09. **[G: U.S.]**
Price, James R.; Mays, James W. and Trapnell, Gordon R. Stability in the Federal Employees Health Benefits Program. *J. Health Econ.*, December 1983, *2*(3), pp. 207–23. **[G: U.S.]**
Riley, John G. Adverse Selection and Statistical Discrimination: Further Remarks. *J. Public Econ.*, February 1983, *20*(1), pp. 131–37. **[G: Canada]**
Roach, William L. Pay-at-the Pump Automobile Liability Insurance [The Distribution of Automobile Liability Insurance: An Alternative]. *J. Risk Ins.*, March 1983, *50*(1), pp. 131–39. **[G: U.S.]**
Rubinstein, Ariel and Yaari, Menahem E. Repeated Insurance Contracts and Moral Hazard. *J. Econ. Theory*, June 1983, *30*(1), pp. 74–97.
Samors, Patricia W. and Sullivan, Sean. Health Care Cost Containment through Private Sector Initiatives. **In** *Meyer, J. A., ed.*, 1983, pp. 144–59. **[G: U.S.]**
Samson, Danny and Thomas, Howard. Reinsurance Decision Making and Expected Utility. *J. Risk Ins.*, June 1983, *50*(2), pp. 249–64.
Schlesinger, Harris. Nonlinear Pricing Strategies for Competitive and Monopolistic Insurance Markets. *J. Risk Ins.*, March 1983, *50*(1), pp. 61–83.
Shapiro, Arnold F. Death and Survival in Employee Populations. *J. Econometrics*, September 1983, *23*(1), pp. 103–17.
Shavell, Steven. On Liability and Insurance. **In** *Ku-*

perberg, M. and Beitz, C., eds., 1983, *1982*, pp. 235–47.

Shome, Parthasarathi and Saito, Katrine W. The Impact of Contractual Savings on Resource Mobilization and Allocation: The Experience of Malaysia. **In** *Lim, D., ed.*, 1983, *1978*, pp. 288–302. **[G: Malaysia]**

Smith, Barry D. A Model for Workers' Compensation Group Self Insurance: The Delaware Valley School Districts Plan. *J. Risk Ins.*, September 1983, *50*(3), pp. 521–32. **[G: U.S.]**

Smith, Barry D. A Note on the Application of the Normal Power Method When Estimating Probable Yearly Aggregate. *J. Risk Ins.*, March 1983, *50*(1), pp. 157–60.

Taylor, Amy K. and Wilensky, Gail R. The Effect of Tax Policies on Expenditures for Private Health Insurance. **In** *Meyer, J. A., ed.*, 1983, pp. 163–84. **[G: U.S.]**

Taylor, G. C. and Ashe, F. R. Second Moments of Estimates of Outstanding Claims. *J. Econometrics*, September 1983, *23*(1), pp. 37–61.

Turnbull, S. M. Additional Aspects of Rational Insurance Purchasing. *J. Bus.*, April 1983, *56*(2), pp. 217–29.

van de Ven, Wynand P. M. M. and van Praag, Bernard M. S. Corrigendum [The Demand for Deductibles in Private Health Insurance: A Probit Model with Sample Selection]. *J. Econometrics*, August 1983, *22*(3), pp. 395.

Venezian, Emilio C. Insurer Capital Needs under Parameter Uncertainty. *J. Risk Ins.*, March 1983, *50*(1), pp. 19–32.

Viscusi, W. Kip. Alternative Approaches to Valuing the Health Impacts of Accidents: Liability Law and Prospective Evaluations. *Law Contemp. Probl.*, Autumn 1983, *46*(4), pp. 49–68. **[G: U.S.]**

Weese, Samuel H. Another Look at "Nuclear Liability after Three Mile Island." *J. Risk Ins.*, June 1983, *50*(2), pp. 323–27. **[G: U.S.]**

Williams, C. Arthur, Jr. Regulating Property and Liability Insurance Rates through Excess Profits Statutes. *J. Risk Ins.*, September 1983, *50*(3), pp. 445–72. **[G: U.S.]**

Witt, Robert C. and Urrutia, Jorge. A Comparative Economic Analysis of Tort Liability and No-Fault Compensation Systems in Automobile Insurance. *J. Risk Ins.*, December 1983, *50*(4), pp. 631–69. **[G: U.S.]**

Wood, William C. "Nuclear Liability after Three Mile Island"—Author's Reply. *J. Risk Ins.*, June 1983, *50*(2), pp. 328–29. **[G: U.S.]**

Zehnwirth, Ben. Hachemeister's Bayesian Regression Model Revisited. *J. Econometrics*, September 1983, *23*(1), pp. 119–29.

6357 Real Estate

Arnott, Richard J.; Davidson, Russell and Pines, David. Housing Quality, Maintenance and Rehabilitation. *Rev. Econ. Stud.*, July 1983, *50*(3), pp. 467–94.

Bradley, Diarmuid. The Irish Office Market. *Irish Banking Rev.*, September 1983, pp. 33–43. **[G: Ireland]**

Colwell, Peter F.; Cannaday, Roger E. and Wu, Chunchi. The Analytical Foundations of Adjustment Grid Methods. *Amer. Real Estate Urban Econ. Assoc. J.*, Spring 1983, *11*(1), pp. 11–29.

Ellson, Richard and Roberts, Blaine. Residential Land Development under Uncertainty. *J. Reg. Sci.*, August 1983, *23*(3), pp. 309–22.

Feldstein, Martin S. Inflation, Tax Rules, and the Prices of Land and Gold. **In** *Feldstein, M. (II)*, 1983, *1980*, pp. 221–28.

Johnson, Linda L. The Impact of Real Estate Political Action Committees on Congressional Voting and Elections. *Amer. Real Estate Urban Econ. Assoc. J.*, Winter 1983, *11*(4), pp. 462–75. **[G: U.S.]**

Jud, G. Donald. Real Estate Brokers and the Market for Residential Housing. *Amer. Real Estate Urban Econ. Assoc. J.*, Spring 1983, *11*(1), pp. 69–82. **[G: U.S.]**

Mills, David E. Real Estate Speculation and Antispeculation Taxes. *Growth Change*, July 1983, *14*(3), pp. 12–22. **[G: U.S.]**

Ward, C. W. R. Methods of Incorporating Risk in the Analysis of Commercial Property Investment: Multi-period Asset Pricing Approach. **In** *Corner, D. and Mayes, D. G., eds.*, 1983, pp. 135–61. **[G: U.K.]**

6358 Entertainment, Recreation, Tourism

Abt, Clark C. The Economics of Cultural Decisions in the New Art of Computer Games. **In** *Hendon, W. S. and Shanahan, J. L., eds.*, 1983, pp. 121–31. **[G: U.S.]**

Allcock, John B. Tourism and Social Change in Dalmatia. *J. Devel. Stud.*, October 1983, *20*(1), pp. 34–55. **[G: Yugoslavia]**

Alpert, Leon. Estimating a Multi-Attribute Model for Different Music Styles. *J. Cult. Econ.*, June 1983, *7*(1), pp. 63–81. **[G: U.S.]**

Anderson, Lee G. The Demand Curve for Recreational Fishing with an Application to Stock Enhancement Activities. *Land Econ.*, August 1983, *59*(3), pp. 279–86. **[G: U.S.]**

Arbel, Avner and Ravid, S. Abraham. An Industry Energy Price Impact Model: The Case of the Hotel Industry. *Appl. Econ.*, December 1983, *15*(6), pp. 705–14. **[G: U.S.]**

Arbel, Avner and Ravid, S. Abraham. The Differential Impact of Gas Shortages and Fuel Price Increases on Demand: The Case of the Hotel Industry in New York State. *Energy J.*, April 1983, *4*(2), pp. 165–71. **[G: U.S.]**

Babbel, David F. and Staking, Kim B. An Engel Curve Analysis of Gambling and Insurance in Brazil. *J. Risk Ins.*, December 1983, *50*(4), pp. 688–96. **[G: Brazil]**

Belinfante, Alexander and Johnson, Richard L. An Economic Analysis of the U.S. Recorded Music Industry. **In** *Hendon, W. S. and Shanahan, J. L., eds.*, 1983, pp. 132–42. **[G: U.S.]**

Blackwell, Roger D. and Johnston, Wesley J. Markets of North America: An Analysis of Opportunities for Latin American Tourism Development. **In** *Czinkota, M. R., ed. (II)*, 1983, pp. 218–43. **[G: Canada; Latin America; U.S.]**

Blaug, Mark. Justifications for Subsidies to the Arts: A Reply to F. F. Ridley, "Cultural Economics and the Culture of Economists." *J. Cult. Econ.*, June 1983, *7*(1), pp. 19–22.

Boucher, Michel. Le marché des joueurs de la Ligue nationale de hockey: une approche économique. (The National Hockey League Players' Labor Market: An Economic Approach. With English summary.) *L'Actual. Econ.,* December 1983, *59*(4), pp. 753–76.

Brown, Gardner M., Jr. Summary of Results of Odes 1979 Survey of Tourists and Residents. **In** *U.S. Dept. Comm., Nat'l Oceanic and Atmos. Admin.,* 1983, pp. 109–10. **[G: France]**

Brown, Gardner M., Jr.; Congar, Richard and Wilman, Elizabeth A. Recreation: Tourists and Residents. **In** *U.S. Dept. Comm., Nat'l Oceanic and Atmos. Admin.,* 1983, pp. 89–108. **[G: France]**

Brownrigg, Mark. Understanding the Scottish Economy: Tourism. **In** *Ingham, K. P. D. and Love, J., eds.,* 1983, pp. 87–93. **[G: U.K.]**

Bunn, Derek W. and Seigal, Jeremy P. Television Peaks in Electricity Demand. *Energy Econ.,* January 1983, *5*(1), pp. 31–36. **[G: U.S.; U.K.]**

Cwi, David. Arts Councils as Public Agencies: The Policy Impact of Mission, Role and Operations. **In** *Hendon, W. S. and Shanahan, J. L., eds.,* 1983, pp. 38–46. **[G: U.S.]**

Cwi, David. Challenging Cultural Institutions to Make a Profit: Emerging Decisions for Nonprofit Providers. **In** *Hendon, W. S. and Shanahan, J. L., eds.,* 1983, pp. 49–56.

Cymrot, Donald J. Migration Trends and Earnings of Free Agents in Major League Baseball, 1976–1979. *Econ. Inquiry,* October 1983, *21*(4), pp. 545–56. **[G: U.S.]**

Diskin, I. Socioeconomic Problems in the Development of the Cultural Infrastructure. *Prob. Econ.,* October 1983, *26*(6), pp. 3–22. **[G: U.S.S.R.]**

Dupuis, Xavier. La surqualité: le spectacle subventionné malade de la bureaucratie? (The Subsidized Performing Arts: Overquality, a Bureaucratic Disease. With English Summary.) *Revue Écon.,* November 1983, *34*(6), pp. 1089–115. **[G: France]**

Edwards, A. R. Decentralization of Arts Subsidy for Orchestra and Theater in the Netherlands. *J. Cult. Econ.,* June 1983, *7*(1), pp. 83–94. **[G: Netherlands]**

Field, Anthony. Experiment and Public Accountability. **In** *Hendon, W. S. and Shanahan, J. L., eds.,* 1983, pp. 31–37. **[G: U.K.]**

Foner, Philip S. A Martyr to His Cause: The Scenario of the First Labor Film in the United States. *Labor Hist.,* Winter 1983, *24*(1), pp. 103–11. **[G: U.S.]**

Freifelder, Leonard R. Collegiate Sports Risk Management. *J. Risk Ins.,* December 1983, *50*(4), pp. 703–18. **[G: U.S.]**

Gardini, Attilio. Formulazione e stima di un modello stocastico di analisi della domanda turistica. (Demand Analysis for Tourist Services: Specification and Estimation of a Stochastic Model. With English summary.) *Statistica,* October–December 1983, *43*(4), pp. 635–60. **[G: Italy]**

Gold, Sonia S. Consumer Sovereignty and the Performing Arts. **In** *Hendon, W. S. and Shanahan, J. L., eds.,* 1983, pp. 207–18. **[G: U.K.; U.S.]**

Grauer, Myron C. Recognition of the National Football League as a Single Entity under Section 1 of the Sherman Act: Implications of the Consumer Welfare Model. *Mich. Law Rev.,* October 1983, *82*(1), pp. 1–59. **[G: U.S.]**

Grigalunas, Thomas A., et al. Assessing the Social Costs of Oil Spills: The AMOCO CADIZ Case Study: The Tourist Industry. **In** *U.S. Dept. Comm., Nat'l Oceanic and Atmos. Admin.,* 1983, pp. 111–25. **[G: France]**

Grigalunas, Thomas A., et al. Econometric Analyses of Lost Wage Payments in the Tourist Industry. **In** *U.S. Dept. Comm., Nat'l Oceanic and Atmos. Admin.,* 1983, pp. 126–29. **[G: France]**

Harrison, Brian R. and Thera, John R. Economic Status of Canadian Freelance Writers. **In** *Hendon, W. S. and Shanahan, J. L., eds.,* 1983, pp. 143–53. **[G: Canada]**

Hendon, William S. Admission Income and Historic Houses. **In** *Hendon, W. S. and Shanahan, J. L., eds.,* 1983, pp. 93–101. **[G: U.K.]**

Hendon, William S. Admission Income and Historic Houses: Higher Revenue Is Associated with Price Policy, More Services and Less Education. *Amer. J. Econ. Soc.,* October 1983, *42*(4), pp. 473–82. **[G: U.K.]**

Hill, James Richard and Spellman, William. Professional Baseball: The Reserve Clause and Salary Structure. *Ind. Relat.,* Winter 1983, *22*(1), pp. 1–19. **[G: U.S.]**

Horowitz, Harold. Work and Earnings of Artists in the Media Fields. *J. Cult. Econ.,* December 1983, *7*(2), pp. 69–89. **[G: U.S.]**

Johnson, Thomas G. Measuring the Cost of Time in Recreation Demand Analysis: Comment. *Amer. J. Agr. Econ.,* February 1983, *65*(1), pp. 169–71. **[G: U.S.]**

Kay, W. D. Toward a Theory of Cultural Policy in Non-Market, Ideological Societies. *J. Cult. Econ.,* December 1983, *7*(2), pp. 1–24. **[G: U.S.S.R.; E. Europe; China; Germany; CMEA]**

Kealy, Walter G., Jr. and Bolyard, Joan E. International Travel and Passenger Fares, 1982. *Surv. Curr. Bus.,* May 1983, *63*(5), pp. 12–17. **[G: U.S.]**

Kenney, Roy W. and Klein, Benjamin. The Economics of Block Booking. *J. Law Econ.,* October 1983, *26*(3), pp. 497–540. **[G: U.S.]**

Koch, James V. Intercollegiate Athletics: An Economic Explanation. *Soc. Sci. Quart.,* June 1983, *64*(2), pp. 360–74. **[G: U.S.]**

Krohn, Gregor A. Measuring the Experience–Productivity Relationship: The Case of Major League Baseball. *J. Bus. Econ. Statist.,* October 1983, *1*(4), pp. 273–79. **[G: U.S.]**

Leonard, John and Prinzinger, Joseph. A Theoretical Exposition of Monopsonistic Exploitation in NCAA Sports. *Atlantic Econ. J.,* December 1983, *11*(4), pp. 80. **[G: U.S.]**

Livengood, Kerry R. Value of Big Game from Markets for Hunting Leases: The Hedonic Approach. *Land Econ.,* August 1983, *59*(3), pp. 287–91. **[G: U.S.]**

McConnell, Kenneth E. and Strand, Ivar E., Jr. Measuring the Cost of Time in Recreation Demand Analysis: Reply. *Amer. J. Agr. Econ.,* February 1983, *65*(1), pp. 172–74. **[G: U.S.]**

McGuigan, Jim. The Death of the Grants to Writers

Program in England. *J. Cult. Econ.*, June 1983, *7*(1), pp. 33–41. [G: U.K.]

McQueen, Matthew. Appropriate Policies towards Multinational Hotel Corporations in Developing Countries. *World Devel.*, February 1983, *11*(2), pp. 141–52.

Metcalfe, J. S., et al. The Economic Development of Cable TV in the UK. *Metroecon.*, October 1983, *35*(3), pp. 235–59. [G: U.K.]

Nelson, Karen. The Evolution of the Financing of Ballet Companies in the United States. *J. Cult. Econ.*, June 1983, *7*(1), pp. 43–62. [G: U.S.]

O'Hagan, John and Mooney, David. Input–Output Multipliers in a Small Open Economy: An Application to Tourism. *Econ. Soc. Rev.*, July 1983, *14*(4), pp. 273–79. [G: Ireland]

Owen, Virginia Lee. Technological Change and Opera Quality. **In** *Hendon, W. S. and Shanahan, J. L., eds.*, 1983, pp. 57–64. [G: U.S.]

Owen, Virginia Lee. The Cultural Economics of Private Producers of Art. **In** *Hendon, W. S. and Shanahan, J. L., eds.*, 1983, pp. 105–09.

Paterson, D. G. and Rosenbluth, G. Culture, Myth, and Fetish. *Can. Public Policy*, March 1983, *9*(1), pp. 134–37. [G: Canada]

Peacock, Alan. Introduction: A Conspectus of Cultural Economics. **In** *Hendon, W. S. and Shanahan, J. L., eds.*, 1983, pp. ix–xv.

Peacock, Alan. The Politics of Culture and the Ignorance of Political Scientists: A Reply to F. F. Ridley. *J. Cult. Econ.*, June 1983, *7*(1), pp. 23–26.

Pen, Jan. A Very Cultural Economist's Ideas about the Locus of Decision-making. **In** *Hendon, W. S. and Shanahan, J. L., eds.*, 1983, pp. 16–30.

Pick, John. The Compulsion towards Inefficiency. **In** *Hendon, W. S. and Shanahan, J. L., eds.*, 1983, pp. 110–20. [G: U.K.]

Raimondo, Henry J. Free Agents' Impact on the Labor Market for Baseball Players. *J. Lab. Res.*, Spring 1983, *4*(2), pp. 183–93. [G: U.S.]

Ridley, F. F. Cultural Economics and the Culture of Economists. *J. Cult. Econ.*, June 1983, *7*(1), pp. 1–18.

Ronkainen, Ilkka A. and McConville, Daniel. Tourism: Contributions to Latin American Development. **In** *Czinkota, M. R., ed. (II)*, 1983, pp. 201–17. [G: Latin America]

Schneider, Friedrich and Pommerehne, Werner W. Analyzing the Market of Works of Contemporary Fine Arts: An Exploratory Study. *J. Cult. Econ.*, December 1983, *7*(2), pp. 41–67. [G: W. Europe; U.S.]

Schneider, Friedrich and Pommerehne, Werner W. Private Demand for Public Subsidies to the Arts: A Study in Voting and Expenditure Theory. **In** *Hendon, W. S. and Shanahan, J. L., eds.*, 1983, pp. 192–206. [G: Switzerland]

Schofield, J. A. The Demand for Cricket: The Case of the John Player League. *Appl. Econ.*, June 1983, *15*(3), pp. 283–96. [G: U.K.]

Schwarz, Samuel. Differential Economies and a Decreasing Share of Artistic Personnel Costs. *J. Cult. Econ.*, June 1983, *7*(1), pp. 27–31. [G: U.S.]

Scitovsky, Tibor. Subsidies for the Arts: The Economic Argument. **In** *Hendon, W. S. and Shanahan, J. L., eds.*, 1983, pp. 6–15.

Scott, Frank A., Jr.; Long, James E. and Somppi, Ken. Free Agency, Owner Incentives, and the National Football League Players Association. *J. Lab. Res.*, Summer 1983, *4*(3), pp. 257–64. [G: U.S.]

Shoesmith, Eddie and Millner, Geoffrey. Cost Inflation and the London Orchestras. **In** *Hendon, W. S. and Shanahan, J. L., eds.*, 1983, pp. 65–76. [G: U.K.]

Sigelman, Lee and Bookheimer, Samuel. Is It Whether You Win or Lose? Monetary Contributions to Big-Time College Athletic Programs. *Soc. Sci. Quart.*, June 1983, *64*(2), pp. 347–59. [G: U.S.]

Snooks, G. D. Determinants of Earnings Inequality amongst Australian Artists. *Australian Econ. Pap.*, December 1983, *22*(41), pp. 322–32. [G: Australia]

Throsby, C. David. Perception of Quality in Demand for the Theatre. **In** *Hendon, W. S. and Shanahan, J. L., eds.*, 1983, pp. 162–76. [G: Australia]

Throsby, C. David and Withers, Glenn A. Measuring the Demand for the Arts as a Public Good: Theory and Empirical Results. **In** *Hendon, W. S. and Shanahan, J. L., eds.*, 1983, pp. 177–91. [G: Australia]

Tisdell, Clem A. Public Finance and the Appropriation of Gains from International Tourists: Some Theory with ASEAN and Australian Illustrations. *Singapore Econ. Rev.*, April 1983, *28*(1), pp. 3–20. [G: Australia; S. E. Asia]

Tomoda, Shizue. Working Conditions in the Hotel, Restaurant and Catering Sector: A Case Study of Japan. *Int. Lab. Rev.*, March–April 1983, *122*(2), pp. 239–52. [G: Japan]

Tuckwell, R. H. The Thoroughbred Gambling Market: Efficiency, Equity and Related Issues. *Australian Econ. Pap.*, June 1983, *22*(40), pp. 106–18. [G: Australia]

Ward, Frank A. Measuring the Cost of Time in Recreation Demand Analysis: Comment. *Amer. J. Agr. Econ.*, February 1983, *65*(1), pp. 167–68. [G: U.S.]

Wiseman, Jack. Public Finance and the Cultural Factor in Economic Growth. **In** *Biehl, D.; Roskamp, K. W. and Stolper, W. F., eds.*, 1983, pp. 419–27.

Withers, Glenn A. The Cultural Influence of Public Television. **In** *Hendon, W. S. and Shanahan, J. L., eds.*, 1983, pp. 77–92. [G: Australia]

Witt, Stephen F. A Binary Choice Model of Foreign Holiday Demand. *J. Econ. Stud.*, 1983, *10*(1), pp. 46–59. [G: U.K.]

636 Nonprofit Industries: Theory and Studies

6360 Nonprofit Industries: Theory and Studies

Atkinson, Anthony B. The Income Tax Treatment of Charitable Contributions. **In** *Atkinson, A. B.*, 1983, *1976*, pp. 357–70.

Badelt, Christoph. The Impact of the Voluntary Nonprofit Sector on Development and Employment. **In** *Weisbrod, B. and Hughes, H., eds.*, 1983, pp. 120–29.

636 Nonprofit Industries: Theory and Studies

Bays, Carson W. Why Most Private Hospitals Are Nonprofit. *J. Policy Anal. Manage.*, Spring 1983, *2*(3), pp. 366–85. **[G: U.S.]**

Crossland, Fred E. Foundations and Higher Education. **In** *Froomkin, J., ed.*, 1983, pp. 48–60. **[G: U.S.]**

Cwi, David. Challenging Cultural Institutions to Make a Profit: Emerging Decisions for Nonprofit Providers. **In** *Hendon, W. S. and Shanahan, J. L., eds.*, 1983, pp. 49–56.

Dobra, John L. Property Rights in Bureaucracies and Bureaucratic Efficiency. *Public Choice*, 1983, *40*(1), pp. 95–99.

Easley, David and O'Hara, Maureen. The Economic Role of the Nonprofit Firm. *Bell J. Econ. (See Rand J. Econ. after 4/85)*, Autumn 1983, *14*(2), pp. 531–38.

Ehrenberg, Ronald G. and Schwarz, Joshua L. The Effect of Unions on Productivity in the Public Sector: The Case of Municipal Libraries. **In** *Hirsch, W. Z., ed.*, 1983, pp. 311–41. **[G: U.S.]**

Fama, Eugene F. and Jensen, Michael C. Agency Problems and Residual Claims. *J. Law Econ.*, June 1983, *26*(2), pp. 327–49.

Feldstein, Martin S. and Lindsey, Lawrence B. Simulating Nonlinear Tax Rules and Nonstandard Behavior: An Application to the Tax Treatment of Charitable Contributions. **In** *Feldstein, M., ed.*, 1983, pp. 139–67. **[G: U.S.]**

Galper, Harvey. Simulating Nonlinear Tax Rules and Nonstandard Behavior: An Application to the Tax Treatment of Charitable Contributions: Comment. **In** *Feldstein, M., ed.*, 1983, pp. 167–72. **[G: U.S.]**

Hendon, William S. Admission Income and Historic Houses. **In** *Hendon, W. S. and Shanahan, J. L., eds.*, 1983, pp. 93–101. **[G: U.K.]**

Holtmann, Alphonse G. A Theory of Non-Profit Firms. *Economica*, November 1983, *50*(200), pp. 439–49.

James, Estelle. How Nonprofits Grow: A Model. *J. Policy Anal. Manage.*, Spring 1983, *2*(3), pp. 350–65. **[G: U.S.]**

Jones, Philip R. Aid to Charities. *Int. J. Soc. Econ.*, 1983, *10*(2), pp. 3–11. **[G: U.K.]**

Mirvis, Philip H. and Hackett, Edward J. Work and Work Force Characteristics in the Nonprofit Sector. *Mon. Lab. Rev.*, April 1983, *106*(4), pp. 3–12. **[G: U.S.]**

Moreau, Jacques. Une doctrine pour l'economie sociale? (A Doctrine for the "Third Sector" in France? With English summary.) *Ann. Pub. Co-op. Econ.*, July–September 1983, *54*(3), pp. 271–88.

Nelson, Karen. The Evolution of the Financing of Ballet Companies in the United States. *J. Cult. Econ.*, June 1983, *7*(1), pp. 43–62. **[G: U.S.]**

Netzer, Dick. Privatization. **In** *Brecher, C. and Horton, R. D., eds.*, 1983, pp. 158–87. **[G: U.S.]**

Owen, Virginia Lee. The Cultural Economics of Private Producers of Art. **In** *Hendon, W. S. and Shanahan, J. L., eds.*, 1983, pp. 105–09.

Silkman, Richard H. and Young, Dennis R. X-Efficiency, State Formula Grants, and Public Library Systems. **In** *Quigley, J. M., ed.*, 1983, pp. 195–222. **[G: U.S.]**

640 Economic Capacity

641 Economic Capacity

6410 Economic Capacity

Artis, M. J. The Capital Constraint on Employment. **In** *[Saunders, C. T.]*, 1983, pp. 109–26. **[G: U.K.]**

Bernstein, Peter L. Capital Stock and Management Decisions. *J. Post Keynesian Econ.*, Fall 1983, *6*(1), pp. 20–38. **[G: U.S.]**

Bulgaru, M. Consideration Concerning the National Economy Potential Reproduction. *Econ. Computat. Cybern. Stud. Res.*, 1983, *18*(3), pp. 23–33.

Cowling, Keith. Excess Capacity and the Degree of Collusion: Oligopoly Behaviour in the Slump. *Manchester Sch. Econ. Soc. Stud.*, December 1983, *51*(4), pp. 341–59. **[G: U.K.]**

Davenport, Paul. Unemployment, Demand Restraint, and Endogenous Capacity. *Eastern Econ. J.*, July–September 1983, *9*(3), pp. 258–71.

Einhorn, Michael. Optimal System Planning with Fuel Shortages and Emissions Constraints. *Energy J.*, April 1983, *4*(2), pp. 73–90.

Ellis, Michael. Supply-Side Linkage of Capacity Utilization and Labor Productivity: U.S. Manufacturing, 1954-1980. *Nebr. J. Econ. Bus.*, Winter, 1983, *22*(1), pp. 15–27. **[G: U.S.]**

Ellis, Michael. Supply-Side Linkage of Capacity Utilization and Labor Productivity: U.S. Manufacturing, 1954–1980. *Bus. Econ.*, May 1983, *18*(3), pp. 62–69. **[G: U.S.]**

Evans, Kaye D.; Siegfried, John J. and Sweeney, George H. The Economic Cost of Suboptimal Manufacturing Capacity. *J. Bus.*, January 1983, *56*(1), pp. 55–76. **[G: U.S.]**

Fernandez, J. Enrique. Optimum Dynamic Investment Policies for Capacity in Transport Facilities. *J. Transp. Econ. Policy*, September 1983, *17*(3), pp. 267–84.

Fortune, J. N. Expectations, Capital Formation, Sales and Capacity Utilization. *Empirical Econ.*, 1983, *8*(3–4), pp. 177–86.

Harris, R. I. D. The Measurement of Capital Services in Production for UK Regions, 1968-78. *Reg. Stud.*, June 1983, *17*(3), pp. 169–80. **[G: U.K.]**

Hughes, Helen. Capital Utilization in Manufacturing. *Finance Develop.*, March 1983, *20*(1), pp. 6–9. **[G: Malaysia; Philippines; Israel; Colombia]**

Leone, Robert A. and Meyer, John R. Capacity Strategies for the 1980s. **In** *Kantrow, A. M., ed.*, 1983, pp. 421–32.

Lim, David. Actual, Desired and Full Levels of Capital Utilization in Malaysian Manufacturing. **In** *Lim, D., ed.*, 1983, *1977*, pp. 81–88. **[G: Malaysia]**

Rost, Ronald F. New Federal Reserve Measures of Capacity and Capacity Utilization. *Fed. Res. Bull.*, July 1983, *69*(7), pp. 515–21. **[G: U.S.]**

Schydlowsky, Daniel M. The Short-run Potential for Employment Generation of Installed Capacity in Latin America. **In** *Urquidi, V. L. and Reyes, S. T., eds.*, 1983, pp. 311–47. **[G: Latin America]**

Shaw, R. W. and Shaw, S. A. Excess Capacity and Rationalisation in the West European Synthetic

Fibres Industry. *J. Ind. Econ.*, December 1983, *32*(2), pp. 149–66. **[G: W. Europe]**

Val'tukh, K. K. The Investment Complex and the Intensification of Production. *Prob. Econ.*, April 1983, *25*(12), pp. 3–29. **[G: U.S.S.R.]**

Wabe, J. Stuart and Gutierrez-Camara, José L. Capital Utilisation, Capital Intensity and Factor Productivity: A Comparison of Factories in Developing and Industrialised Countries. *J. Econ. Stud.*, 1983, *10*(3), pp. 3–11. **[G: Selected Countries]**

700 Agriculture; Natural Resources

710 Agriculture

7100 Agriculture

Armbruster, Walter J.; Helmuth, John W. and Manley, William T. Data Systems in the Food and Fiber Sector. **In** *Farris, P. L., ed.*, 1983, pp. 163–83. **[G: U.S.]**

Bagchi, Bhanudeb. Factor Shares in Indian Agriculture—An Analytical Study. *Econ. Aff.*, October–December 1983, *28*(4), pp. 866–71. **[G: India]**

Bardhan, Pranab K. Labor-Tying in a Poor Agrarian Economy: A Theoretical and Empirical Analysis. *Quart. J. Econ.*, August 1983, *98*(3), pp. 501–14. **[G: India]**

Barker, Randolph and Whyte, William Foote. Reorienting the Social Sciences. **In** *Whyte, W. F. and Boynton, D., eds.*, 1983, pp. 264–94.

Bennett, John W. and Kanel, Don. Agricultural Economics and Economic Anthropology: Confrontation and Accommodation. **In** *Ortiz, S., ed.*, 1983, pp. 201–47.

Blyn, George. Income Distribution among Haryana and Punjab Cultivators, 1968/69–1975/76. *Indian Econ. Rev.*, July–December 1983, *18*(2), pp. 199–224. **[G: India]**

Blyn, George. The Green Revolution Revisited. *Econ. Develop. Cult. Change*, July 1983, *31*(4), pp. 705–25. **[G: India]**

Bonnen, James T. The Dilemma of Agricultural Economists: Discussion. *Amer. J. Agr. Econ.*, December 1983, *65*(5), pp. 889–90. **[G: U.S.]**

Boynton, Damon. Implications for Education. **In** *Whyte, W. F. and Boynton, D., eds.*, 1983, pp. 295–309.

Boynton, Damon. Implications for Plant and Animal Research. **In** *Whyte, W. F. and Boynton, D., eds.*, 1983, pp. 251–63.

Brinkman, George L. Agricultural Economists and Long-Run Challenges Facing Canadian Agriculture. *Can. J. Agr. Econ.*, March 1983, *31*(1), pp. 3–14. **[G: Canada]**

Brown, Lester R. The U.S.–Soviet Food Connection. *Challenge*, January/February 1983, *25*(6), pp. 40–49. **[G: U.S.; U.S.S.R.]**

Buhr, Walter. Mikroökonomische Modelle der von Thünenschen Standorttheorie. (Microeconomic Models of von Thünen's Location Theory. With English summary.) *Z. Wirtschaft. Sozialwissen.*, 1983, *103*(6), pp. 589–627.

Chaudhry, M. Ghaffar. Green Revolution and Redistribution of Rural Incomes: Pakistan's Experience—A Reply. *Pakistan Devel. Rev.*, Summer 1983, *22*(2), pp. 117–23.

Chen, Fu-Sen and Cheung, Tow. On Some Problems of Modelling Chinese Economic Growth. **In** *Youngson, A. J., ed.*, 1983, pp. 226–81. **[G: China]**

Daniel, Raymond. The Dilemma of Agricultural Economists: Discussion. *Amer. J. Agr. Econ.*, December 1983, *65*(5), pp. 891–92. **[G: U.S.]**

Davies, Timothy. Changes in the Structure of the Wheat Trade in Seventeenth-Century Sicily and the Building of New Villages. *J. Europ. Econ. Hist.*, Fall 1983, *12*(2), pp. 371–405. **[G: Italy]**

Dhaliwal, R. S. and Grewal, S. S. Impact of Agricultural Development on Farmer–Labourer Relationships. *Econ. Aff.*, January–March 1983, *28*(1), pp. 644–49. **[G: India]**

Eddie, Scott M. Agriculture as a Source of Supply: Conjectures from the History of Hungary, 1870–1913. **In** *Komlos, J., ed.*, 1983, pp. 101–15. **[G: Hungary]**

Esman, Milton J. Research and Development Organizations: A Reevaluation. **In** *Whyte, W. F. and Boynton, D., eds.*, 1983, pp. 17–30. **[G: U.S.]**

Gardner, Bruce L. Fact and Fiction in the Public Data Budget Crunch. *Amer. J. Agr. Econ.*, December 1983, *65*(5), pp. 882–88. **[G: U.S.]**

Ghosh, Dipak. Planning for Employment in a Developing Economy. *Acta Oecon.*, 1983, *31* (3–4), pp. 287–96. **[G: LDCs]**

Ginting, Meneth. The Seventh National Conference on Agricultural Economics. *Bull. Indonesian Econ. Stud.*, April 1983, *19*(1), pp. 97–99.

Goodell, Grace. What Life after Land Reform? *Policy Rev.*, Spring 1983, (24), pp. 121–48. **[G: Philippines]**

Grabowski, Richard. A Note on Japanese Development. *Econ. Forum*, Summer 1983, *14*(1), pp. 127–30. **[G: Japan]**

Habib, Mohammed Ahsan; Butterfield, David and Mestelman, Stuart. The Allocation of Research Expenditures among Competing Crops: The Application of an *Ex Ante* Model to Bangladesh. *J. Econ. Devel.*, December 1983, *8*(2), pp. 125–48. **[G: Bangladesh]**

Harl, Neil E. Agriculture Economics: Challenges to the Profession. *Amer. J. Agr. Econ.*, December 1983, *65*(5), pp. 845–54.

Heady, Earl O. Models for Agricultural Policy: The CARD Example. *Europ. Rev. Agr. Econ.*, 1983, *10*(1), pp. 1–14. **[G: U.S.]**

Henn, Jeanne Koopman. Feeding the Cities and Feeding the Peasants: What Role for Africa's Women Farmers? *World Devel.*, December 1983, *11*(12), pp. 1043–55. **[G: Cameroon; Tanzania]**

Hollist, W. Ladd. Dependency Transformed: Brazilian Agriculture in Historical Perspective. **In** *Doran, C. F.; Modelski, G. and Clark, C., eds.*, 1983, pp. 157–86. **[G: Brazil]**

Ingram, James C. Food for Employment: 20 Years of the World Food Programme. *Int. Lab. Rev.*, Sept.–Oct. 1983, *122*(5), pp. 549–62. **[G: LDCs]**

Ionescu, V. and Berar, U. Cybernetic Model for Optimizing the Agro-Economic Development Plan of the Irrigated Zone Balikh (Northern Syria).

Econ. Computat. Cybern. Stud. Res., 1983, *18*(4), pp. 15–24. **[G: Syria]**

Johnson, Marc A. Impacts on Agriculture of Deregulating the Transportation System: Reply. *Amer. J. Agr. Econ.*, February 1983, *65*(1), pp. 190–91. **[G: U.S.]**

Johnston, Bruce F. The Design and Redesign of Strategies for Agricultural Development: Mexico's Experience Revisited. **In** *Reynolds, C. W. and Tello, C., eds.*, 1983, pp. 225–50. **[G: Mexico]**

Just, Richard E. The Impact of Less Data on the Agricultural Economy and Society. *Amer. J. Agr. Econ.*, December 1983, *65*(5), pp. 872–81. **[G: U.S.]**

Kelleher, Carmel. Implications of Different Theoretical Development Perspectives for Policy and Interventions: 1. The Relationship between Development Perspectives and Policy Strategy and Intervention. *Irish J. Agr. Econ. Rural Soc.*, 1983, *9*(2), pp. 133–43.

Khan, Mahmood Hasan. "Green Revolution and Redistribution of Rural Incomes: Pakistan's Experience"—A Comment. *Pakistan Devel. Rev.*, Spring 1983, *22*(1), pp. 47–56. **[G: Pakistan]**

Khan, Mahmood Hasan. Classes and Agrarian Transition in Pakistan. *Pakistan Devel. Rev.*, Autumn 1983, *22*(3), pp. 129–62. **[G: Pakistan]**

Kikuchi, Masao and Hayami, Yujiro. New Rice Technology, Intrarural Migration, and Institutional Innovation in the Philippines. *Population Devel. Rev.*, June 1983, *9*(2), pp. 247–57. **[G: Philippines]**

Koo, Won W. Impacts on Agriculture of Deregulating the Transportation System: Comment. *Amer. J. Agr. Econ.*, February 1983, *65*(1), pp. 187–89. **[G: U.S.]**

Korten, David C.; Uphoff, Norman and Whyte, William Foote. Bureaucratic Reorientation for Agricultural Research and Development. **In** *Whyte, W. F. and Boynton, D., eds.*, 1983, pp. 222–47.

Laband, David N. and Lentz, Bernard F. Occupational Inheritance in Agriculture. *Amer. J. Agr. Econ.*, May 1983, *65*(2), pp. 311–14. **[G: U.S.]**

Lewis, W. Arthur. The Shifting Fortunes of Agriculture. **In** *Lewis, W. A.*, 1983, *1960*, pp. 615–22.

Lundahl, Mats. Haiti's Dilemma. **In** *Lundahl, M.*, 1983, *1980*, pp. 23–40. **[G: Haiti]**

Lundahl, Mats. Peasants, Government and Technological Change in Haitian Agriculture. **In** *Lundahl, M.*, 1983, pp. 251–85. **[G: Haiti]**

McDean, Harry C. "Reform" Social Darwinists and Measuring Levels of Living on American Farms, 1920–1926. *J. Econ. Hist.*, March 1983, *43*(1), pp. 79–85. **[G: U.S.]**

Meerman, Jacob. Cost Recovery in a Project Context: Some World Bank Experience in Tropical Africa. *World Devel.*, June 1983, *11*(6), pp. 503–14. **[G: Tropical Africa]**

Mikkelsen, K. W. and Langam, N. N. Innovation in the Philippine Agricultural Machinery Industry. **In** *Internat'l Rice Res. Inst. and Agric. Devel. Council*, 1983, pp. 31–37. **[G: Philippines]**

Mkandawire, P. Thandika. Economic Crisis in Malawi. **In** *Carlsson, J., ed.*, 1983, pp. 28–47. **[G: Malawi]**

Peacock, Frank. Asian Agriculture: A Decade of Failure. **In** *Glassner, M. I., ed.*, 1983, *1980*, pp. 230–36. **[G: Asia]**

Platteau, Jean-Philippe. Classical Economics and Agrarian Reforms in Underdeveloped Areas: The Radical Views of the Two Mills. *J. Devel. Stud.*, July 1983, *19*(4), pp. 435–60.

Pontius, Steven K. The Communication Process of Adoption: Agriculture in Thailand. *J. Devel. Areas*, October 1983, *18*(1), pp. 93–118. **[G: Thailand]**

Prahladachar, M. Income Distribution Effects on the Green Revolution in India: A Review of Empirical Evidence. *World Devel.*, November 1983, *11*(11), pp. 927–44. **[G: India]**

Pray, Carl E. Underinvestment and the Demand for Agricultural Research: A Case Study of the Punjab. *Food Res. Inst. Stud.*, 1983, *19*(1), pp. 51–79. **[G: Pakistan]**

Puchala, Donald J. and Hopkins, Raymond F. International Regimes: Lessons from Inductive Analysis. **In** *Krasner, S. D., ed.*, 1983, *1982*, pp. 61–91.

Ram, Salik. Comparative Study of Cost and Return of Modern and Traditional Varieties of Rice. *Econ. Aff.*, January–March 1983, *28*(1), pp. 624–29. **[G: India]**

Schmitt, Günther. Johann Heinrich von Thünen und die Agrarökonomie heute. (Johann Heinrich von Thünen and the Present State of Agricultural Economics. With English summary.) *Z. Wirtschaft. Sozialwissen.*, 1983, *103*(6), pp. 641–59.

Selden, Mark. Imposed Collectivization and the Crisis of Agrarian Development in the Socialist States. **In** *Bergesen, A., ed.*, 1983, pp. 227–51. **[G: Yugoslavia; China; U.S.S.R.]**

Selden, Mark. The Logic—and Limits—of Chinese Socialist Development. *World Devel.*, August 1983, *11*(8), pp. 631–37. **[G: China]**

Sen, Raj Kumar. An Analysis of Export of a Few Agricultural Products Entering into Mass Consumption. *Indian Econ. J.*, January-March 1983, *30*(3), pp. 103–10. **[G: India]**

Simon, Julian L.; Reisler, William and Gobin, Roy. 'Population Pressure' on the Land: Analysis of Trends Past and Future. *World Devel.*, September 1983, *11*(9), pp. 825–34. **[G: Global]**

Stokes, Eric, et al. Agrarian Relations. **In** *Kumar, D., ed.*, 1983, pp. 36–241. **[G: India]**

Stuart, Robert C. Russian and Soviet Agriculture: The Western Perspective. *ACES Bull. (See Comp. Econ. Stud. after 8/85)*, Fall 1983, *25*(3), pp. 43–52. **[G: U.S.S.R.]**

Thompson, Robert L. The Role of Trade in Food Security and Agricultural Development. **In** *Johnson, D. G. and Schuh, G. E., eds.*, 1983, pp. 227–57.

Tiao, George C. and Tsay, Ruey S. Multiple Time Series Modeling and Extended Sample Cross-Correlations. *J. Bus. Econ. Statist.*, January 1983, *1*(1), pp. 43–56. **[G: U.S.]**

Turgeon, Lynn. A Quarter Century of Non-Soviet East European Agriculture. *ACES Bull. (See Comp. Econ. Stud. after 8/85)*, Fall 1983, *25*(3), pp. 27–41. **[G: E. Europe]**

Valdés, Alberto. The Role of Trade in Food Security

and Agricultural Development: Discussion. In *Johnson, D. G. and Schuh, G. E., eds.*, 1983, pp. 258–68.

Wampach, Jean-Pierre. Productivité, efficacité économique et équité dans le secteur agricole québécois. (Productivity, Economic Efficiency and Equity in Quebec Agriculture. With English summary.) *L'Actual. Econ.*, December 1983, *59*(4), pp. 669–85. **[G: Canada]**

Warley, T. K. The Role of Trade in Food Security and Agricultural Development: Discussion. In *Johnson, D. G. and Schuh, G. E., eds.*, 1983, pp. 269–75. **[G: LDCs]**

Watson, Andrew. Agriculture Looks for 'Shoes That Fit': The Production Responsibility System and Its Implications. *World Devel.*, August 1983, *11*(8), pp. 705–30. **[G: China]**

Wharton, Clifton R., Jr. Risk, Uncertainty, and the Subsistence Farmer. In *Todaro, M. P., ed.*, 1983, *1969*, pp. 234–39.

Whyte, William Foote. Farmer Organization and Participation as Keys to Agricultural Research and Development. In *Whyte, W. F. and Boynton, D., eds.*, 1983, pp. 197–208. **[G: Mexico]**

Whyte, William Foote. Major Agricultural Research and Development Projects: A Reevaluation. In *Whyte, W. F. and Boynton, D., eds.*, 1983, pp. 31–52. **[G: Bangladesh; Ethiopia; Mexico; Colombia]**

Whyte, William Foote. The Farming Systems Research Approach: The Rediscovery of Peasant Rationality. In *Whyte, W. F. and Boynton, D., eds.*, 1983, pp. 154–63.

Whyte, William Foote. Toward New Systems of Agricultural Research and Development. In *Whyte, W. F. and Boynton, D., eds.*, 1983, pp. 164–93. **[G: Guatemala; Honduras]**

Wiboonchutikula, Paitoon. Productivity Growth of the Agricultural Machinery Industry in Thailand. In *Internat'l Rice Res. Inst. and Agric. Devel. Council*, 1983, pp. 51–59. **[G: Thailand]**

von Witzke, Harald. Growth and Equity in Agricultural Development: A Survey of the 18th International Conference of Agricultural Economists, Jakarta, Indonesia, August 24 to September 2, 1982. *Europ. Rev. Agr. Econ.*, 1983, *10*(2), pp. 151–63. **[G: Global]**

711 Agricultural Supply and Demand Analysis

7110 Agricultural Supply and Demand Analysis

Akiyama, T. and Duncan, Ronald C. Coffee and Cocoa Trends: An Unfavorable Outlook for Developing Countries. *Finance Develop.*, March 1983, *20*(1), pp. 30–33. **[G: LDCs]**

Alston, Julian M. and Scobie, G. M. Distribution of Research Gains in Multistage Production Systems: Comment. *Amer. J. Agr. Econ.*, May 1983, *65*(2), pp. 353–56. **[G: U.S.]**

Alston, Julian M. and Smith, Vincent H. Some Economic Implications of Minimum Pricing: The Case of Wine Grapes in Australia: Comment. *Rev. Marketing Agr. Econ.*, August 1983, *51*(2), pp. 179–85. **[G: Australia]**

Anderson, Ronald W. and Wilkinson, Maurice. Consumer Welfare and the Livestock Economy in the United States. *Can. J. Agr. Econ.*, November 1983, *31*(3), pp. 351–70. **[G: U.S.]**

Antle, John M. Infrastructure and Aggregate Agricultural Productivity: International Evidence. *Econ. Develop. Cult. Change*, April 1983, *31*(3), pp. 609–19.

Bale, Malcolm D. Price Policies in Developing Countries: Discussion. In *Johnson, D. G. and Schuh, G. E., eds.*, 1983, pp. 136–42. **[G: LDCs]**

Bale, Malcolm D. and Duncan, Ronald C. Food Prospects in the Developing Countries: A Qualified Optimistic View. *Amer. Econ. Rev.*, May 1983, *73*(2), pp. 244–48. **[G: LDCs]**

Barnett, Richard C.; Bessler, David A. and Thompson, Robert L. The Money Supply and Nominal Agricultural Prices. *Amer. J. Agr. Econ.*, May 1983, *65*(2), pp. 303–07. **[G: U.S.]**

Bassecoulard, E., et al. Consommation et système agro-alimentaire: Quelques approches et quelques résultats. (With English summary.) *Écon. Soc.*, May 1983, *17*(5), pp. 877–909. **[G: France]**

Baum, Kenneth H. Farm Decisions, Adaptive Economics, and Complex Behavior in Agriculture: Some Thoughts on Adaptive Economic Policy and the Behavioral Science of Modeling the Farm Firm/Household: Discussion. In *Baum, K. H. and Schertz, L. P., eds.*, 1983, pp. 50–55.

Belongia, Michael T. Agricultural Price Supports and Cost of Production: Comment. *Amer. J. Agr. Econ.*, August 1983, *65*(3), pp. 620–22.

Bhide, Shashanka, et al. Silage-Concentrate Substitution in Beef Production. In *Heady, E. O. and Bhide, S., eds.*, 1983, pp. 206–33. **[G: U.S.]**

Bhuyan, K. C. and Sikder, M. F. S. Economics of HYV Rice Cultivation in Bangladesh—A Case Study. *Econ. Aff.*, July-September 1983, *28*(3), pp. 791–97. **[G: Bangladesh]**

Blaylock, James R. and Gallo, Anthony E. Modeling the Decision to Produce Vegetables at Home. *Amer. J. Agr. Econ.*, November 1983, *65*(4), pp. 722–29. **[G: U.S.]**

Boggess, William G.; Olson, K. D. and Heady, Earl O. Gain Isoquants and Production Functions for Swine. In *Heady, E. O. and Bhide, S., eds.*, 1983, pp. 267–303. **[G: U.S.]**

Bond, Daniel L. and Green, Donald W. Prospects for Soviet Agriculture in the Eleventh Five-year Plan: Econometric Analysis and Projections. In *Stuart, R. C., ed.*, 1983, pp. 296–319. **[G: U.S.S.R.]**

Bond, Marian E. Agricultural Responses to Prices in Sub-Saharan African Countries. *Int. Monet. Fund Staff Pap.*, December 1983, *30*(4), pp. 703–26. **[G: Sub-Saharan Africa]**

Bonnen, James T. Historical Sources of U.S. Agricultural Productivity: Implications for R&D Policy and Social Science Research. *Amer. J. Agr. Econ.*, December 1983, *65*(5), pp. 958–66. **[G: U.S.]**

Bonnieux, F. and Rainelli, P. Regional Disparities in Western European Agriculture. *Europ. Rev. Agr. Econ.*, 1983, *10*(3), pp. 295–301. **[G: EEC]**

Boynton, Damon. Climate and Ecology. In *Whyte, W. F. and Boynton, D., eds.*, 1983, pp. 55–59.

Boynton, Damon. Cropping Systems. In *Whyte, W. F. and Boynton, D., eds.*, 1983, pp. 75–89.

Boynton, Damon. Fitting the Parts Together. **In** *Whyte, W. F. and Boynton, D., eds.*, 1983, pp. 122–26.

Braschler, Curtis. The Changing Demand Structure for Pork and Beef in the 1970s: Implications for the 1980s. *Southern J. Agr. Econ.*, December 1983, *15*(2), pp. 105–10. **[G: U.S.]**

Brown, Lester R. Global Food Prospects: Shadow of Malthus. **In** *Glassner, M. I., ed.*, 1983, *1982*, pp. 175–87. **[G: Global]**

Bruinsma, Jelle, et al. Crop Production and Input Requirements in Developing Countries. *Europ. Rev. Agr. Econ.*, 1983, *10*(3), pp. 197–222. **[G: LDCs]**

Campbell, Bruce M. S. Agricultural Progress in Medieval England: Some Evidence from Eastern Norfolk. *Econ. Hist. Rev., 2nd Ser.*, February 1983, *36*(1), pp. 26–46. **[G: U.K.]**

Campbell, Bruce M. S. Arable Productivity in Medieval England: Some Evidence from Norfolk. *J. Econ. Hist.*, June 1983, *43*(2), pp. 379–404. **[G: U.K.]**

Campbell, Joseph. Tools and Machines. **In** *Whyte, W. F. and Boynton, D., eds.*, 1983, pp. 111–21.

Carpenter, James R. and Steinke, William E. Taro: Animal Feed. **In** *Wang, J.-K., ed.*, 1983, pp. 269–300.

Chakraborti, Sibaji. Review of Agricultural Growth Pattern in India. *Econ. Aff.*, April–June 1983, *28*(2), pp. 696–700. **[G: India]**

Chambers, Robert G. and Vasavada, Utpal. Testing Asset Fixity for U.S. Agriculture. *Amer. J. Agr. Econ.*, November 1983, *65*(4), pp. 761–69. **[G: U.S.]**

Chan, M. W. Luke and Mountain, Dean C. A Regional Analysis of Productivity Change in Canadian Agriculture, with Special Reference to Energy Prices. *Can. J. Agr. Econ.*, November 1983, *31*(3), pp. 319–30. **[G: Canada]**

Chavas, Jean-Paul. Structural Change in the Demand for Meat. *Amer. J. Agr. Econ.*, February 1983, *65*(1), pp. 148–53. **[G: U.S.]**

Chen, Yun. Methods of Solving the Tensions in Supplies of Pork and Vegetables. **In** *Ch'en, Y.*, 1983, *1956*, pp. 23–29. **[G: China]**

Collins, Glenn S. and Taylor, C. Robert. TECHSIM: A Regional Field Crop and National Livestock Econometric Simulation Model. *Agr. Econ. Res.*, April 1983, *35*(2), pp. 1–18. **[G: U.S.]**

Colman, David. A Review of the Arts of Supply Response Analysis. *Rev. Marketing Agr. Econ.*, December 1983, *51*(3), pp. 201–30.

Csaki, Csaba. Economic Management and Organization of Hungarian Agriculture. *J. Compar. Econ.*, September 1983, *7*(3), pp. 317–28. **[G: Hungary]**

David, Cristina C. Economic Policies and Agricultural Incentives. *Philippine Econ. J.*, 1983, *22*(2), pp. 154–82. **[G: Philippine]**

Davis, Jeffrey M. The Economic Effects of Windfall Gains in Export Earnings, 1975–1978. *World Devel.*, February 1983, *11*(2), pp. 119–39. **[G: Latin American LDCs; African LDCs]**

Day, Richard H. Farm Decisions, Adaptive Economics, and Complex Behavior in Agriculture. **In** *Baum, K. H. and Schertz, L. P., eds.*, 1983, pp. 18–49.

Deolalikar, Anil B. and Vijverberg, Wim P. M. The Heterogeneity of Family and Hired Labor in Agricultural Production: A Test Using District-Level Data from India. *J. Econ. Devel.*, December 1983, *8*(2), pp. 45–69. **[G: India]**

Diamond, Douglas B.; Bettis, Lee W. and Ramsson, Robert E. Agricultural Production. **In** *Bergson, A. and Levine, H. S., eds.*, 1983, pp. 143–77. **[G: U.S.S.R.]**

Dick, Hermann, et al. The Short-Run Impact of Fluctuating Primary Commodity Prices on Three Developing Economies: Colombia, Ivory Coast and Kenya. *World Devel.*, May 1983, *11*(5), pp. 405–16. **[G: Colombia; Ivory Coast; Kenya]**

van Dijk, G. and Mackel, C. Fundamental Changes in Price Relationships: An Investigation of the UK Feed Grain Market, 1971/72 to 1978/79, Using Spectral Analysis. *Europ. Rev. Agr. Econ.*, 1983, *10*(1), pp. 15–31. **[G: U.K.]**

Dixon, Peter B., et al. The Agricultural Sector of Orani 78: Theory, Data, and Application. **In** *Kelley, A. C.; Sanderson, W. C. and Williamson, J. G., eds.*, 1983, pp. 237–74. **[G: Australia]**

Dodgshon, Robert A. Agricultural Change and Its Social Consequences in the Southern Uplands of Scotland, 1600–1780. **In** *Devine, T. M. and Dickson, D., eds.*, 1983, pp. 46–59. **[G: U.K.]**

Drosdoff, Matthew and Levine, Gilbert. Working with Soils and Water. **In** *Whyte, W. F. and Boynton, D., eds.*, 1983, pp. 60–74.

Easter, Christopher D. and Paris, Quirino. Supply Response with Stochastic Technology and Prices in Australia's Rural Export Industries. *Australian J. Agr. Econ.*, April 1983, *27*(1), pp. 12–30. **[G: U.S.; Australia]**

Engerman, Stanley L. Contract Labor, Sugar, and Technology in the Nineteenth Century. *J. Econ. Hist.*, September 1983, *43*(3), pp. 635–59. **[G: Europe; U.S.]**

Epplin, Francis; Bhide, Shashanka and Heady, Earl O. Forage-Concentrate Substitution in Beef Production. **In** *Heady, E. O. and Bhide, S., eds.*, 1983, pp. 179–205. **[G: U.S.]**

Epplin, Francis and Heady, Earl O. Beef Gain Response to Alternative Protein Levels. **In** *Heady, E. O. and Bhide, S., eds.*, 1983, pp. 251–66. **[G: U.S.]**

Evenson, Robert E. Price Policies in Developing Countries: Discussion. **In** *Johnson, D. G. and Schuh, G. E., eds.*, 1983, pp. 143–51. **[G: India]**

Falcon, Walter P. The World Food Economy: Recent Lessons for the United States and Mexico. **In** *Reynolds, C. W. and Tello, C., eds.*, 1983, pp. 251–58. **[G: U.S.; Mexico]**

Field, Alexander James. Land Abundance, Interest/Profit Rates, and Nineteenth-Century American and British Technology. *J. Econ. Hist.*, June 1983, *43*(2), pp. 405–31. **[G: U.K.; U.S.]**

Fisher, Brian S. Rational Expectations in the Australian Wool Industry. *Australian J. Agr. Econ.*, December 1983, *27*(3), pp. 212–20. **[G: Australia]**

Fisher, Brian S. and Munro, Robyn G. Supply Response in the Australian Extensive Livestock and Cropping Industries: A Study of Intentions and Expectations. *Australian J. Agr. Econ.*, April 1983, *27*(1), pp. 1–11. **[G: Australia]**

Fox, Glenn and Ruttan, Vernon W. A Guide to LDC Food Balance Projections. *Europ. Rev. Agr. Econ.*, 1983, *10*(4), pp. 325–56. **[G: Selected Countries; LDCs]**

Freebairn, John W.; Davis, J. S. and Edwards, G. W. Distribution of Research Gains in Multistage Production Systems: Reply. *Amer. J. Agr. Econ.*, May 1983, *65*(2), pp. 357–59. **[G: U.S.]**

Fruin, Jerry E. Impacts on Agriculture of Deregulating the Transportation System: Reply. *Amer. J. Agr. Econ.*, February 1983, *65*(1), pp. 192–93. **[G: U.S.]**

Gargett, D. Industry versus On-Farm Rates of Change: Australian Dairy Farming during the 1970's. *Rev. Marketing Agr. Econ.*, April 1983, *51*(1), pp. 71–84. **[G: Australia]**

Ghatha, I. S. and Singh, Joginder N. Causes of Stagnation in Production of Pulses and Oilseeds in Punjab. *Econ. Aff.*, July-September 1983, *28*(3), pp. 774–83. **[G: India]**

Gibney, S. J. and Furtan, W. Harley. Welfare Effects of New Crop Variety Licensing Regulations: The Case of Canadian Malt Barley. *Amer. J. Agr. Econ.*, February 1983, *65*(1), pp. 142–47. **[G: Canada]**

Gill, Gerard J. Merchanised Land Preparation, Productivity and Employment in Bangladesh. *J. Devel. Stud.*, April 1983, *19*(3), pp. 329–48. **[G: Bangladesh]**

Gilland, Bernard. Considerations on World Population and Food Supply. *Population Devel. Rev.*, June 1983, *9*(2), pp. 203–11. **[G: Global]**

Glenn, Marcia and Lattimore, Ralph. Canadian Acreage Response to Grain Storage Subsidies. *Can. J. Agr. Econ.*, July 1983, *31*(2), pp. 245–48. **[G: Canada]**

Grant, Warren R., et al. Grain Price Interrelationships. *Agr. Econ. Res.*, January 1983, *35*(1), pp. 1–9. **[G: U.S.]**

Gray, Kenneth R. Improved Agricultural Location: Econometric Evidence from the Ukraine. **In** *Stuart, R. C., ed.*, 1983, pp. 199–222. **[G: U.S.S.R.]**

Griffin, Gerald J. L. and Wang, Jaw-Kai. Taro: Industrial Uses. **In** *Wang, J.-K., ed.*, 1983, pp. 301–12.

Griffith, Garry R. and Meilke, Karl D. The Impact on the Canadian Rapeseed Industry of Removing EEC Import Tariffs. *J. Policy Modeling*, March 1983, *5*(1), pp. 37–54. **[G: Canada; EEC]**

Grilli, Enzo R. and Yang, Maw-cheng. Real and Monetary Determinants of Non-oil Primary Commodity Price Movements. **In** *Kregel, J. A., ed.*, 1983, pp. 115–41. **[G: OECD]**

Groenewegen, John R. and Clayton, Kenneth C. Agricultural Price Supports and Cost of Production: Reply. *Amer. J. Agr. Econ.*, August 1983, *65*(3), pp. 626–28. **[G: U.S.]**

Haaland, Gunnar. Dualistic Development: Issues for Aid Policy. **In** *Parkinson, J. R., ed.*, 1983, pp. 63–78. **[G: Portugal; Mozambique; Botswana]**

Haidacher, Richard C. Assessing Structural Change in the Demand for Food Commodities. *Southern J. Agr. Econ.*, July 1983, *15*(1), pp. 31–37. **[G: U.S.]**

Hall, Harry H. Economic Evaluation of Crop Response to Lime. *Amer. J. Agr. Econ.*, November 1983, *65*(4), pp. 811–17. **[G: U.S.]**

Hall, Harry H.; Stulp, Valter J. and Reed, Michael R. Effects of a Fertilizer Subsidy on Brazilian Crop Production and Exports. *Amer. J. Agr. Econ.*, August 1983, *65*(3), pp. 571–75. **[G: Brazil]**

Hanssens, Dominique M. and Liu, Lon-Mu. Lag Specification in Rational Distributed Lag Structural Models. *J. Bus. Econ. Statist.*, October 1983, *1*(4), pp. 316–25. **[G: U.S.]**

Hart, Gillian. Productivity, Poverty, and Population Pressure: Female Labor Deployment in Rice Production in Java and Bangladesh. *Amer. J. Agr. Econ.*, December 1983, *65*(5), pp. 1037–42. **[G: Indonesia; Bangladesh]**

Heady, Earl O.; Askalani, M. H. and Balloun, S. L. Broiler Production Functions. **In** *Heady, E. O. and Bhide, S., eds.*, 1983, pp. 100–122. **[G: U.S.]**

Heady, Earl O. and Bhide, Shashanka. Livestock Response Functions: Overview. **In** *Heady, E. O. and Bhide, S., eds.*, 1983, pp. 7–29.

Heady, Earl O. and Bhide, Shashanka. Setting of Response Surface Estimates. **In** *Heady, E. O. and Bhide, S., eds.*, 1983, pp. 3–6.

Heady, Earl O.; Guinan, J. F. and Balloun, S. L. Egg Production Functions. **In** *Heady, E. O. and Bhide, S., eds.*, 1983, pp. 64–99. **[G: U.S.]**

Heady, Earl O.; Hunter, R. G. and Bhide, Shashanka. Short-run Output Supply and Input Demand Functions. **In** *Heady, E. O. and Bhide, S., eds.*, 1983, pp. 304–27. **[G: U.S]**

Heady, Earl O., et al. Beef Production and Profit Functions for Grain and Soilage. **In** *Heady, E. O. and Bhide, S., eds.*, 1983, pp. 123–78. **[G: U.S.]**

Heady, Earl O., et al. Milk Production Functions. **In** *Heady, E. O. and Bhide, S., eds.*, 1983, pp. 30–63. **[G: U.S.]**

Henderson, Dennis R.; Schrader, Lee F. and Rhodes, V. James. Public Price Reporting. **In** *Armbruster, W. J.; Henderson, D. R. and Knutson, Ronald D., eds.*, 1983, pp. 21–57. **[G: U.S.]**

Herdt, Robert W. Mechanization of Rice Production in Developing Asian Countries: Perspective, Evidence, and Issues. **In** *Internat'l Rice Res. Inst. and Agric. Devel. Council*, 1983, pp. 1–13. **[G: Japan; Taiwan; S. Korea]**

Hertford, Reed. Issues in International Agricultural Development: Discussion. *Amer. J. Agr. Econ.*, May 1983, *65*(2), pp. 455–57.

Hinchy, Mike and Simmons, Phil. An Optimal-Control Approach to Stabilising Australian Wool Prices. *Australian J. Agr. Econ.*, April 1983, *27*(1), pp. 44–72. **[G: Australia]**

Homem de Melo, Fernando. Trade Policy, Technology, and Food Prices in Brazil. *Quart. Rev. Econ. Bus.*, Spring 1983, *23*(1), pp. 58–78. **[G: Brazil]**

Hopkins, Raymond F. The World Food Situation: Recent and Prospective Developments: Discussion. **In** *Johnson, D. G. and Schuh, G. E., eds.*, 1983, pp. 34–40.

Hottel, J. Bruce and Gardner, Bruce L. The Rate of Return to Investment in Agriculture and Measuring Net Farm Income. *Amer. J. Agr. Econ.*, August 1983, *65*(3), pp. 553–57. **[G: U.S.]**

Huang, Chung L. and Raunikar, Robert. Household Fluid Milk Expenditure Patterns in the South and United States. *Southern J. Agr. Econ.*, December 1983, *15*(2), pp. 27–33. **[G: U.S.]**

Huang, Kuo S. and Haidacher, Richard C. Estimation of a Composite Food Demand System for the United States. *J. Bus. Econ. Statist.*, October 1983, *1*(4), pp. 285–91. **[G: U.S.]**

Huang, Yukon. Tenancy Patterns, Productivity, and Rentals in Malaysia. **In** *Lim, D., ed.*, 1983, *1975*, pp. 43–52. **[G: Malaysia]**

Hussain, M. S. and Sikder, M. F. S. A Study on Economic Potentials of Maize Production in Bangladesh. *Econ. Aff.*, October–December 1983, *28*(4), pp. 808–11, 839. **[G: Bangladesh]**

Jamal, Vali. Nomads and Farmers: Incomes and Poverty in Rural Somalia. **In** *Ghai, D. and Radwan, S., eds.*, 1983, pp. 281–311. **[G: Somalia]**

de Janvry, Alain; Siam, Gamal and Gad, Osman. The Impact of Forced Deliveries on Egyptian Agriculture. *Amer. J. Agr. Econ.*, August 1983, *65*(3), pp. 493–501. **[G: Egypt]**

Johnson, D. Gale. The World Food Situation: Recent and Prospective Developments. **In** *Johnson, D. G. and Schuh, G. E., eds.*, 1983, pp. 1–33. **[G: Global]**

Johnson, Frederick I. Sugar in Brazil: Policy and Production. *J. Devel. Areas*, January 1983, *17*(2), pp. 243–56. **[G: Brazil]**

Johnston, Gary and Martin, Philip L. Employment and Wages Reported by California Farmers in 1982. *Mon. Lab. Rev.*, September 1983, *106*(9), pp. 27–31. **[G: U.S.]**

Just, Richard E.; Zilberman, David and Hochman, Eithan. Estimation of Multicrop Production Functions. *Amer. J. Agr. Econ.*, November 1983, *65*(4), pp. 770–80. **[G: Israel]**

Kaldor, Nicholas. The Role of Commodity Prices in Economic Recovery. *Lloyds Bank Rev.*, July 1983, (149), pp. 21–34.

Kalirajan, K. P. Responsiveness of Indian Agriculture to Price Changes. *J. Econ. Devel.*, December 1983, *8*(2), pp. 185–99. **[G: India]**

Kemp, Murray C. and Long, Ngo Van. On the Economics of Forests. *Int. Econ. Rev.*, February 1983, *24*(1), pp. 113–31.

Kennes, Walter. Estimating Demand for Agricultural Commodities in Thailand, Combining Time-Series and Cross-Section Data. *Europ. Rev. Agr. Econ.*, 1983, *10*(4), pp. 357–76. **[G: Thailand]**

Kim, V. Purchase Prices on Agricultural Products. *Prob. Econ.*, June 1983, *26*(2), pp. 22–40. **[G: U.S.S.R.]**

Kinsey, Jean. Working Wives and the Marginal Propensity to Consume Food Away from Home. *Amer. J. Agr. Econ.*, February 1983, *65*(1), pp. 10–19. **[G: U.S.]**

Kitching, Beverly. Don't Blame the Arabs: World Wide Inflation Built In before the Oil Crisis. *Rivista Int. Sci. Econ. Com.*, June 1983, *30*(6), pp. 561–65. **[G: U.S.]**

Klemyshev, P. The Effectiveness of Utilization of Agriculture's Productive Resources. *Prob. Econ.*, March 1983, *25*(11), pp. 51–69. **[G: U.S.S.R.]**

Knipscheer, Henk, et al. The Economic Role of Sheep and Goats in Indonesia: A Case Study of West Java. *Bull. Indonesian Econ. Stud.*, December 1983, *19*(3), pp. 74–93. **[G: Indonesia]**

Langham, Max R. and Ahmad, Ismet. Measuring Productivity in Economic Growth. *Amer. J. Agr. Econ.*, May 1983, *65*(2), pp. 445–51. **[G: Indonesia]**

Latham, A. J. H. and Neal, Larry. The International Market in Rice and Wheat, 1868–1914. *Econ. Hist. Rev., 2nd Ser.*, May 1983, *36*(2), pp. 260–80. **[G: Selected LDCs; Selected MDCs]**

Leaf, Murray J. The Green Revolution and Cultural Change in a Punjab Village, 1965–1978. *Econ. Develop. Cult. Change,* January 1983, *31*(2), pp. 227–70. **[G: India]**

Lee, Eddy. Export-led Rural Development: The Ivory Coast. **In** *Ghai, D. and Radwan, S., eds.*, 1983, pp. 99–127. **[G: Ivory Coast]**

Lee, J. H. The Measurement and Sources of Technological Change Biases, with an Application to Postwar Japanese Agriculture. *Economica,* May 1983, *50*(198), pp. 159–73. **[G: Japan]**

Levy, Victor. The Welfare and Transfer Effects of Cotton Price Policies in Egypt, 1965–78. *Amer. J. Agr. Econ.*, August 1983, *65*(3), pp. 576–80. **[G: Egypt]**

Lezina, M. Structure of the National Economic Agroindustrial Complex. *Prob. Econ.*, November 1983, *26*(7), pp. 65–84. **[G: U.S.S.R.]**

Lombra, Raymond E. and Mehra, Yash P. Aggregate Demand, Food Prices, and the Underlying Rate of Inflation. *J. Macroecon.*, Fall 1983, *5*(4), pp. 383–98.

Lundahl, Mats. Obstacles to Technological Change in Haitian Peasant Agriculture. **In** *Lundahl, M.*, 1983, *1977*, pp. 237–50. **[G: Haiti]**

Lundahl, Mats. Peasants, Government and Technological Change in Haitian Agriculture. **In** *Lundahl, M.*, 1983, pp. 251–85. **[G: Haiti]**

Mănescu, B.; Davidovici, I. and Stroe, R. Agricultural Production—Complex Dynamic System. *Econ. Computat. Cybern. Stud. Res.*, 1983, *18*(2), pp. 19–27.

Marrese, Michael. Agricultural Policy and Performance in Hungary. *J. Compar. Econ.*, September 1983, *7*(3), pp. 329–45. **[G: Hungary]**

Marsh, John M. A Rational Distributed Lag Model of Quarterly Live Cattle Prices. *Amer. J. Agr. Econ.*, August 1983, *65*(3), pp. 539–47. **[G: U.S.]**

Marsh, Lawrence C.; Jameson, Kenneth P. and Phillips, Joseph M. Production Conditions in Guatemala's Key Agriculture Product: Corn. *Land Econ.*, February 1983, *59*(1), pp. 94–106. **[G: Guatemala]**

Martin, Will. A Note on Cost Functions and the Regression Fallacy. *Rev. Marketing Agr. Econ.*, December 1983, *51*(3), pp. 249–57. **[G: Australia]**

McDowell, Robert and Hildebrand, Peter. Farming Systems, Including Animals. **In** *Whyte, W. F. and Boynton, D., eds.*, 1983, pp. 90–110.

McIntire, John. International Farm Prices and the Social Cost of Cheap Food Policies: Comment. *Amer. J. Agr. Econ.*, November 1983, *65*(4), pp. 823–26. **[G: LDCs]**

McKay, Lloyd; Lawrence, Denis and Vlastuin, Chris. Profit, Output Supply, and Input Demand Functions for Multiproduct Firms: The Case of Australian Agriculture. *Int. Econ. Rev.*, June 1983, *24*(2), pp. 323–39. **[G: Australia]**

Meiendorf, A. Socially Necessary Expenditures and Purchase Prices in Agriculture. *Prob. Econ.*, April 1983, *25*(12), pp. 67–80. **[G: U.S.S.R.]**

Mellor, John W. Food Prospects for the Developing Countries. *Amer. Econ. Rev.*, May 1983, *73*(2), pp. 239–43. **[G: LDCs]**

Menz, Kenneth M. and Pardey, Philip. Technology and U.S. Corn Yields: Plateaus and Price Responsiveness. *Amer. J. Agr. Econ.*, August 1983, *65*(3), pp. 558–62. **[G: U.S.]**

Moar, Lyle. Understanding the Scottish Economy: Farming Today. **In** *Ingham, K. P. D. and Love, J., eds.*, 1983, pp. 74–86. **[G: U.K.]**

Mokyr, Joel. Uncertainty and Prefamine Irish Agriculture. **In** *Devine, T. M. and Dickson, D., eds.*, 1983, pp. 89–101. **[G: Ireland]**

Mules, T. J. Input–Output Analysis in Australia: An Agricultural Perspective. *Rev. Marketing Agr. Econ.*, April 1983, *51*(1), pp. 9–30. **[G: Australia]**

Nadkarni, M. V. and Deshpande, R. S. Growth and Instability in Crop Yields: A Case Study of Agriculture in Karnataka, South India. *Reg. Stud.*, February 1983, *17*(1), pp. 29–39. **[G: India]**

Nagy, Joseph G. Estimating the Yield Advantage of High-Yielding Wheat and Maize: The Use of Pakistani On-Farm Yield Constraints Data. *Pakistan Devel. Rev.*, Autumn 1983, *22*(3), pp. 179–90. **[G: Pakistan]**

Naughtin, John. Lot Size and Breed Effects on Cattle Prices Revisited. *Australian J. Agr. Econ.*, December 1983, *27*(3), pp. 240–42. **[G: Australia]**

Nelson, Gerald C. Time for Tapioca, 1970 to 1980: European Demand and World Supply of Dried Cassava. *Food Res. Inst. Stud.*, 1983, *19*(1), pp. 25–49. **[G: EC]**

Niall, D. Jane; Smith, A. W. and Smith, Rhonda L. The Australian Sugar Industry and Its Prospects. *Australian Econ. Rev.*, 1st Quarter 1983, (61), pp. 33–48. **[G: Australia]**

Niall, D. Jane and Smith, Rhonda L. Development of High Fructose Syrup in the U.S. and Its Implications for Australia. *Rev. Marketing Agr. Econ.*, April 1983, *51*(1), pp. 51–70. **[G: U.S.; Australia]**

Niimi, Reiko. The Problem of Food Security. **In** *Akao, N., ed.*, 1983, pp. 169–96. **[G: Japan]**

Nolan, Peter. De-collectivisation of Agriculture in China, 1979–82: A Long-Term Perspective. *Cambridge J. Econ.*, September/December 1983, *7*(3/4), pp. 381–403. **[G: China]**

Norton, George W. and Bernat, G. Andrew, Jr. Estimating the Effects of Pesticide Use on Burley and Flue-Cured Tobacco. *Southern J. Agr. Econ.*, December 1983, *15*(2), pp. 93–98. **[G: U.S.]**

Omirova, Zh. On the Question of the Role of the Personal Household Plot. *Prob. Econ.*, November 1983, *26*(7), pp. 40–46. **[G: U.S.S.R.]**

Pasour, E. C., Jr. Agricultural Price Supports and Cost of Production: Comment. *Amer. J. Agr. Econ.*, August 1983, *65*(3), pp. 623–25. **[G: U.S.]**

Patel, R. K.; Saini, Amrik S. and Singh, Raj Vir. Energy in Agriculture. *Econ. Aff.*, April–June 1983, *28*(2), pp. 715–23. **[G: India]**

Pepelasis, Admantios. The Agricultural Sector: The Implications of the Accession. **In** *Sampedro, J. L. and Payno, J. A., eds.*, 1983, pp. 70–84. **[G: Greece; EEC]**

Peterson, Willis L. International Farm Prices and the Social Cost of Cheap Food Policies: Reply. *Amer. J. Agr. Econ.*, November 1983, *65*(4), pp. 827–28. **[G: LDCs]**

Petřík, Miroslav. Pasture Crops: A Solution to the Grain Problem. *Czech. Econ. Digest.*, November 1983, (7), pp. 33–51. **[G: Czechoslovakia]**

Petzel, Todd E. Empirical Analysis of Soviet Agricultural Production and Policy: Comment. *Amer. J. Agr. Econ.*, February 1983, *65*(1), pp. 175–77. **[G: U.S.S.R.]**

Pitt, Mark M. Farm-Level Fertilizer Demand in Java: A Meta-Production Function Approach. *Amer. J. Agr. Econ.*, August 1983, *65*(3), pp. 502–08. **[G: Indonesia]**

Poleman, Thomas T. World Hunger: Extent, Causes, and Cures. **In** *Johnson, D. G. and Schuh, G. E., eds.*, 1983, pp. 41–75. **[G: LDCs]**

Pollard, Stephen K. and Heffernan, Peter J. Agricultural Productivity and Credit Use of Small Farmers in Jamaica. *Soc. Econ. Stud.*, March 1983, *32*(1), pp. 42–62. **[G: Jamaica]**

Pope, C. Arden, III and Heady, Earl O. Corn Grain-Silage Substitution in Feeding Steer Calves. **In** *Heady, E. O. and Bhide, S., eds.*, 1983, pp. 234–50. **[G: U.S.]**

Pudasaini, Som P. The Effects of Education in Agriculture: Evidence from Nepal. *Amer. J. Agr. Econ.*, August 1983, *65*(3), pp. 509–15. **[G: Nepal]**

Quadrio-Curzio, Alberto. Alternative Explanations: [Real and Monetary Determinants of Non-oil Primary Commodity Price Movements]. **In** *Kregel, J. A., ed.*, 1983, pp. 142–52. **[G: OECD]**

Quiggin, John C. Wool Price Stabilisation and Profit Risk for Wool Users. *Australian J. Agr. Econ.*, April 1983, *27*(1), pp. 31–43. **[G: Australia]**

Radell, Willard W., Jr. Cuban–Soviet Sugar Trade, 1960–1976: How Great Was the Subsidy? *J. Devel. Areas*, April 1983, *17*(3), pp. 365–81. **[G: Cuba]**

Raj, K. N. Prices, Subsidies and Access to Food. *Indian Econ. Rev.*, July–December 1983, *18*(2), pp. 157–67. **[G: India]**

Ram, Salik. Comparative Study of Cost and Return of Modern and Traditional Varieties of Rice. *Econ. Aff.*, January–March 1983, *28*(1), pp. 624–29. **[G: India]**

Rausser, Gordon C. and Carter, Colin A. Futures Market Efficiency in the Soybean Complex. *Rev. Econ. Statist.*, August 1983, *65*(3), pp. 469–78. **[G: U.S.]**

Reca, Lucio G. Price Policies in Developing Countries. **In** *Johnson, D. G. and Schuh, G. E., eds.*, 1983, pp. 115–35. **[G: LDCs]**

del Rey, Eusebio Cleto. Problemas de cómputo de la corrección por sesgo en el caso lognormal. (Computational Problems of the Bias Corrections in the Lognormal Case. With English summary.) *Económica*, January–April 1983, *29*(1), pp. 27–43. **[G: Argentina]**

Ridler, Neil B. Labour Force and Land Distributional Effects of Agricultural Technology: A Case Study of Coffee. *World Devel.*, July 1983, *11*(7), pp. 593–99. **[G: Colombia]**

van Riemsdijk, J. F. Dutch Agriculture Edging in the Eighties. *Europ. Rev. Agr. Econ.*, 1983, *10*(1), pp. 55–68. **[G: Netherlands]**

Rivero, Nicolás and Díaz Franjúl, Manuel. Thoughts on Sugar Diversification: An Inter-American Fuel Alcohol Program. **In** *Czinkota, M. R., ed. (II)*, 1983, pp. 107–25. **[G: Latin America; U.S.]**

Rodríguez, José J. Romero. The Agricultural Sector. **In** *Sampedro, J. L. and Payno, J. A., eds.*, 1983, pp. 210–23. **[G: Spain; EEC]**

Sarup, Shanti; Pandey, R. K. and Verma, Geetam. An Economic Study of Pulse Production in Madhya Pradesh. *Margin*, October 1983, *16*(1), pp. 47–56. **[G: India]**

Scandizzo, Pasquale L.; Hazell, Peter B. R. and Anderson, Jock R. Producers' Price Expectations and the Size of the Welfare Gains from Price Stabilisation. *Rev. Marketing Agr. Econ.*, August 1983, *51*(2), pp. 93–107.

Schaefer, Donald F. The Effect of the 1859 Crop Year upon Relative Productivity in the Antebellum Cotton South. *J. Econ. Hist.*, December 1983, *43*(4), pp. 851–65. **[G: U.S.]**

Schoney, Richard A. and McGuckin, J. Thomas. Economics of the Wet Fractionation System in Alfalfa Harvesting. *Amer. J. Agr. Econ.*, February 1983, *65*(1), pp. 38–44. **[G: U.S.]**

Sengupta, Jati K. and Sfeir, Raymond I. Risk in Supply Response: An Optimal Control Approach. *Appl. Econ.*, April 1983, *15*(2), pp. 255–65. **[G: U.S.]**

Shaikh, A. Hafeez and Zaman, Asad. Forecasting without Theory: Pakistan's Export of Cotton and Rice. *Pakistan J. Appl. Econ.*, Summer 1983, *2*(1), pp. 65–84. **[G: Pakistan]**

Shapiro, Kenneth H. Efficiency Differentials in Peasant Agriculture and Their Implications for Development Policies. *J. Devel. Stud.*, January 1983, *19*(2), pp. 179–90. **[G: Tanzania]**

Shonkwiler, J. Scott and Spreen, Thomas H. Disequilibrium Market Analysis: An Application to the U.S. Fed Beef Sector: Comment. *Amer. J. Agr. Econ.*, May 1983, *65*(2), pp. 360–63. **[G: U.S.]**

Shumway, C. Richard. Supply, Demand, and Technology in a Multiproduct Industry: Texas Field Crops. *Amer. J. Agr. Econ.*, November 1983, *65*(4), pp. 748–60. **[G: U.S.]**

Sikder, M. F. S. and Banerjee, Biswa Nath. An Economic Analysis of Jute Cultivation in West Bengal. *Econ. Aff.*, January–March 1983, *28*(1), pp. 592–604. **[G: India]**

Singh, Inderjit. Issues in International Agricultural Development: Discussion. *Amer. J. Agr. Econ.*, May 1983, *65*(2), pp. 452–54.

Singh, Joginder N.; Sidhu, D. S. and Singh, A. J. Systems Approach to Simulate the Cropping Pattern on Different Categories of Farms in Central Region of the Punjab. *Econ. Aff.*, October–December 1983, *28*(4), pp. 851–59. **[G: India]**

Sipos, Aladár. Relations between Enterprises in the Agro-Industrial Sphere in Hungary. *Acta Oecon.*, 1983, *31*(1–2), pp. 53–69. **[G: Hungary]**

Smith, Hilary H. Texas Agricultural Productivity: Is Research the Remedy? *Fed. Res. Bank Dallas Econ. Rev.*, November 1983, pp. 15–28. **[G: U.S.]**

Solar, Peter M. Agricultural Productivity and Economic Development in Ireland and Scotland in the Early Nineteenth Century. **In** *Devine, T. M. and Dickson, D., eds.*, 1983, pp. 70–88. **[G: Ireland; U.K.]**

Soufflet, J.-F. Ajustement et adaptation sur les filières. (With English summary.) *Écon. Soc.*, May 1983, *17*(5), pp. 741–84. **[G: France]**

Sporleder, Thomas L. Emerging Information Technologies and Agricultural Structure. *Amer. J. Agr. Econ.*, May 1983, *65*(2), pp. 388–94. **[G: U.S.]**

Srinivasan, T. N. Hunger: Defining It, Estimating Its Global Incidence, and Alleviating It. **In** *Johnson, D. G. and Schuh, G. E., eds.*, 1983, pp. 77–108. **[G: LDCs]**

Srivastava, R. K. and Livingstone, I. Growth and Distribution: The Case of Mozambique. **In** *Ghai, D. and Radwan, S., eds.*, 1983, pp. 249–80. **[G: Mozambique]**

Stein, Robert. The State of French Colonial Commerce on the Eve of the Revolution. *J. Europ. Econ. Hist.*, Spring 1983, *12*(1), pp. 105–17. **[G: France]**

Strout, Alan M. How Productive Are the Soils of Java? *Bull. Indonesian Econ. Stud.*, April 1983, *19*(1), pp. 32–52. **[G: Indonesia]**

Stürzinger, Ulrich. The Introduction of Cotton Cultivation in CHAD: The Role of the Administration, 1920–1936. *African Econ. Hist.*, 1983, (12), pp. 213–25. **[G: CHAD]**

Sylos Labini, Paolo. Secular Movements in Primary and Manufactured Goods' Prices: Comment [Real and Monetary Determinants of Non-oil Primary Commodity Price Movements]. **In** *Kregel, J. A., ed.*, 1983, pp. 153–55.

Taylor, C. Robert. Complementarities between Micro- and Macro-Systems Simulation and Analysis. **In** *Baum, K. H. and Schertz, L. P., eds.*, 1983, pp. 63–72.

Taylor, C. Robert, et al. Aggregate Economic Effects of Alternative Boll Weevil Management Strategies. *Agr. Econ. Res.*, April 1983, *35*(2), pp. 19–28. **[G: U.S.]**

Teal, Francis. The Supply of Agricultural Output in Nigeria, 1950–1974. *J. Devel. Stud.*, January 1983, *19*(2), pp. 191–206. **[G: Nigeria]**

Temin, Peter. Patterns of Cotton Agriculture in Post-Bellum Georgia. *J. Econ. Hist.*, September 1983, *43*(3), pp. 661–74. **[G: U.S.]**

Thomas, Vinod. Discussion [World Hunger: Extent, Causes, and Cures] [Hunger: Defining It, Estimating Its Global Incidence, and Alleviating It]. **In** *Johnson, D. G. and Schuh, G. E., eds.*, 1983, pp. 109–14. **[G: LDCs]**

Trigo de Abreu, Armando. The Agricultural Sector. **In** *Sampedro, J. L. and Payno, J. A., eds.*, 1983, pp. 149–66. **[G: Portugal; EEC]**

Tweeten, Luther. Economic Instability in Agriculture: The Contributions of Prices, Government Programs and Exports. *Amer. J. Agr. Econ.*, December 1983, *65*(5), pp. 922–31. **[G: U.S.]**

Vieth, Gary R. and Chang, Fen-Fen. Socio-economic Aspects of Taro as Food. **In** *Wang, J.-K., ed.*, 1983, pp. 346–54. **[G: Ghana; Philippines; Nigeria; Papua New Guinea]**

Waghmare, P. R. Growth and Disparity in Cotton

Area, Production and Productivity at District Levels in Maharashtra State. *Econ. Aff.*, July-September 1983, *28*(3), pp. 760–67. **[G: India]**

Wampach, Jean-Pierre. Productivité, efficacité économique et équité dans le secteur agricole québécois. (Productivity, Economic Efficiency and Equity in Quebec Agriculture. With English summary.) *L'Actual. Econ.*, December 1983, *59*(4), pp. 669–85. **[G: Canada]**

Wang, Jaw-Kai. Taro: Introduction. **In** *Wang, J.-K., ed.*, 1983, pp. 3–13. **[G: Asia; Africa; Oceania]**

Wang, Jaw-Kai and Steinke, William E. Taro: Production Systems Planning. **In** *Wang, J.-K., ed.*, 1983, pp. 314–45.

Warrick, A. W. and Gardner, W. R. Crop Yield as Affected by Spatial Variations of Soil and Irrigation. *Water Resources Res.*, February 1983, *19*(1), pp. 181–86.

Weaver, Robert D. Multiple Input, Multiple Output Production Choices and Technology in the U.S. Wheat Region. *Amer. J. Agr. Econ.*, February 1983, *65*(1), pp. 45–56.

Wells, R. J. G. An Evaluation of Malaysian Agricultural Commodity Protection. *Singapore Econ. Rev.*, April 1983, *28*(1), pp. 59–72. **[G: Malaysia]**

Wheatcroft, S. G. A Reevaluation of Soviet Agricultural Production in the 1920s and the 1930s. **In** *Stuart, R. C., ed.*, 1983, pp. 32–62. **[G: U.S.S.R.]**

White, Fred C. and Ziemer, Rod F. Disequilibrium Prices and Economic Surplus in the U.S. Fed Beef Market. *Can. J. Agr. Econ.*, July 1983, *31*(2), pp. 197–204. **[G: U.S.]**

Wiens, Thomas B. Price Adjustment, the Responsibility System, and Agricultural Productivity. *Amer. Econ. Rev.*, May 1983, *73*(2), pp. 319–24. **[G: China]**

Willett, Keith. Single- and Multi-Commodity Models of Spatial Equilibrium in a Linear Programming Framework. *Can. J. Agr. Econ.*, July 1983, *31*(2), pp. 205–22.

Williams, Joseph E.; Meyer, Steve R. and Bullock, J. Bruce. Interregional Competition in the U.S. Swine–Pork Industry: An Analysis of Oklahoma's and the Southern States' Expansion Potential. *Southern J. Agr. Econ.*, July 1983, *15*(1), pp. 145–53. **[G: U.S.]**

Wohlgenant, Michael K. Assessing Structural Change in the Demand for Food Commodities: Discussion. *Southern J. Agr. Econ.*, July 1983, *15*(1), pp. 39–41. **[G: U.S.]**

Wyzan, Michael L. Empirical Analysis of Soviet Agricultural Production and Policy: Reply. *Amer. J. Agr. Econ.*, February 1983, *65*(1), pp. 178–80. **[G: U.S.S.R.]**

Wyzan, Michael L. The Kolkhoz and the Sovkhoz: Relative Performance as Measured by Productive Technology. **In** *Stuart, R. C., ed.*, 1983, pp. 173–98. **[G: U.S.S.R.]**

Zaleski, Eugène. The Collectivization Drive and Agricultural Planning in the Soviet Union. **In** *Stuart, R. C., ed.*, 1983, pp. 79–106. **[G: U.S.S.R.]**

Ziemer, Rod F. and White, Fred C. Disequilibrium Market Analysis: An Application to the U.S. Fed Beef Sector: Reply. *Amer. J. Agr. Econ.*, May 1983, *65*(2), pp. 364–65. **[G: U.S.]**

Zilberman, David and Rausser, Gordon C. Farm Decisions, Adaptive Economics, and Complex Behavior in Agriculture: A Proper Perspective for Considering Adaptive Economics: Discussion. **In** *Baum, K. H. and Schertz, L. P., eds.*, 1983, pp. 56–60.

712 Agricultural Situation and Outlook

7120 Agricultural Situation and Outlook

Bale, Malcolm D. and Duncan, Ronald C. Food Prospects in the Developing Countries: A Qualified Optimistic View. *Amer. Econ. Rev.*, May 1983, *73*(2), pp. 244–48. **[G: LDCs]**

Belongia, Michael T. Outlook for Agriculture in 1983. *Fed. Res. Bank St. Louis Rev.*, February 1983, *65*(2), pp. 14–24. **[G: U.S.]**

Berry, Wendell. Solving for Pattern: Standards for a Durable Agriculture. **In** *Brewster, D. E.; Rasmussen, W. D. and Youngberg, G., eds.*, 1983, *1981*, pp. 37–45.

Brown, Lester R. Global Food Prospects: Shadow of Malthus. **In** *Glassner, M. I., ed.*, 1983, *1982*, pp. 175–87. **[G: Global]**

Bruinsma, Jelle, et al. Crop Production and Input Requirements in Developing Countries. *Europ. Rev. Agr. Econ.*, 1983, *10*(3), pp. 197–222. **[G: LDCs]**

Choncho, Jacques. World Food: Failure of Productivist Solutions. **In** *Glassner, M. I., ed.*, 1983, *1981*, pp. 219–29. **[G: Global]**

Clayton, Elizabeth. Factor Endowment, Variable Proportions, and Agricultural Modernization: Regional Production Functions for Soviet Agriculture. **In** *Stuart, R. C., ed.*, 1983, pp. 161–72. **[G: U.S.S.R.]**

Csaki, Csaba. Economic Management and Organization of Hungarian Agriculture. *J. Compar. Econ.*, September 1983, *7*(3), pp. 317–28. **[G: Hungary]**

Csizmadia, Magda. New Features of the Enterprise Structure in the Hungarian Agriculture and Food Industry. *Acta Oecon.*, 1983, *31*(3–4), pp. 225–40. **[G: Hungary]**

Fox, Glenn and Ruttan, Vernon W. A Guide to LDC Food Balance Projections. *Europ. Rev. Agr. Econ.*, 1983, *10*(4), pp. 325–56. **[G: Selected Countries; LDCs]**

Gilland, Bernard. Considerations on World Population and Food Supply. *Population Devel. Rev.*, June 1983, *9*(2), pp. 203–11. **[G: Global]**

Heady, Earl O. Economic Policies and Variables: Potentials and Problems for the Future. **In** *Brewster, D. E.; Rasmussen, W. D. and Youngberg, G., eds.*, 1983, pp. 23–35. **[G: U.S.]**

Hopkins, Raymond F. The World Food Situation: Recent and Prospective Developments: Discussion. **In** *Johnson, D. G. and Schuh, G. E., eds.*, 1983, pp. 34–40.

Hotz, M. C. B. Resources and Development: Trying to Close the Gap Responsibly. **In** *Glassner, M. I., ed.*, 1983, *1981*, pp. 108–17. **[G: LDCs]**

Jabbar, M. A.; Bhuiyan, M. S. R. and Bari, A. K. M. Causes and Consequences of Power Tiller Utilization in Two Areas of Bangladesh. **In** *Internat'l Rice Res. Inst. and Agric. Devel. Council*, 1983, pp. 71–83. **[G: Bangladesh]**

Johnson, D. Gale. The World Food Situation: Recent and Prospective Developments. **In** *Johnson, D. G. and Schuh, G. E., eds.*, 1983, pp. 1–33. **[G: Global]**

Larsen, Arne. Landbrugets økonomiske perspektiver. (Long Term Adjustment Problems in Danish Agriculture. With English summary.) *Nationaløkon. Tidsskr.*, 1983, *121* (2), pp. 259–71. **[G: Denmark]**

Lee, John E., Jr. Some Consequences of the New Reality in U.S. Agriculture. **In** *Brewster, D. E.; Rasmussen, W. D. and Youngberg, G., eds.*, 1983, pp. 3–22. **[G: U.S.]**

Maamum, Y., et al. Consequences of Small Rice Farm Mechanization in South Sulawesi: A Summary of Preliminary Analyses. **In** *Internat'l Rice Res. Inst. and Agric. Devel. Council*, 1983, pp. 177–84. **[G: Indonesia]**

Marrese, Michael. Agricultural Policy and Performance in Hungary. *J. Compar. Econ.*, September 1983, *7*(3), pp. 329–45. **[G: Hungary]**

Martin, Michael V. and Brokken, Ray F. The Scarcity Syndrome: Comment. *Amer. J. Agr. Econ.*, February 1983, *65*(1), pp. 158–59. **[G: U.S.]**

Mellor, John W. Food Prospects for the Developing Countries. *Amer. Econ. Rev.*, May 1983, *73* (2), pp. 239–43. **[G: LDCs]**

Niall, D. Jane; Smith, A. W. and Smith, Rhonda L. The Australian Sugar Industry and Its Prospects. *Australian Econ. Rev.*, 1st Quarter 1983, (61), pp. 33–48. **[G: Australia]**

Niimi, Reiko. The Problem of Food Security. **In** *Akao, N., ed.*, 1983, pp. 169–96. **[G: Japan]**

Pearson, Scott R. Economic Doublethink: Food and Politics. **In** *Stansky, P., ed.*, 1983, pp. 56–65.

van Riemsdijk, J. F. Dutch Agriculture Edging in the Eighties. *Europ. Rev. Agr. Econ.*, 1983, *10* (1), pp. 55–68. **[G: Netherlands]**

Sacay, Orlando J. Agricultural Strategy in the 1980s. *Philippine Econ. J.*, 1983, *22* (2), pp. 137–53. **[G: Philippine]**

Schuh, G. Edward. Changing Trends in World Food Production and Trade. *Amer. Econ. Rev.*, May 1983, *73* (2), pp. 235–38.

Simon, Julian L. World Food Supplies. **In** *Glassner, M. I., ed.*, 1983, *1981*, pp. 188–96. **[G: Global]**

Soedjatmoko. Turning Point in Development: The Food–Energy Pivot. **In** *Glassner, M. I., ed.*, 1983, *1981*, pp. 237–43. **[G: Global]**

Warman, Arturo. The Future of a Crisis: Food and Agrarian Reform. **In** *Reynolds, C. W. and Tello, C., eds.*, 1983, pp. 205–24. **[G: Mexico]**

713 Agricultural Policy, Domestic and International

7130 Agricultural Policy, Domestic and International

Adams, Richard H., Jr. The Role of Research in Policy Development: The Creation of the IMF Cereal Import Facility. *World Devel.*, July 1983, *11*(7), pp. 549–63. **[G: LDCs]**

Al-Sudeary, Abdelmuhsin. South–South Cooperation for Food Security. **In** *Gauhar, A., ed. (I)*, 1983, pp. 227–30.

Ali, Mehdi. Agriculture and Energy in the OPEC Fund's Activities—A Sectoral Perspective. **In** *Shihata, I. F. I., et al.*, 1983, pp. 50–71. **[G: OPEC]**

Allen, Roy; Dodge, Claudia and Schmitz, Andrew. Voluntary Export Restraints as Protection Policy: The U.S. Beef Case. *Amer. J. Agr. Econ.*, May 1983, *65*(2), pp. 291–96. **[G: U.S.]**

Alston, Julian M. and Smith, Vincent H. Some Economic Implications of Minimum Pricing: The Case of Wine Grapes in Australia: Comment. *Rev. Marketing Agr. Econ.*, August 1983, *51* (2), pp. 179–85. **[G: Australia]**

Anderson, Kym. The Peculiar Rationality of Beef Import Quotas in Japan. *Amer. J. Agr. Econ.*, February 1983, *65*(1), pp. 108–12.

Anderson, Ronald W. and Wilkinson, Maurice. Consumer Welfare and the Livestock Economy in the United States. *Can. J. Agr. Econ.*, November 1983, *31* (3), pp. 351–70. **[G: U.S.]**

Antle, John M. and Aitah, Ali S. Rice Technology, Farmer Rationality, and Agricultural Policy in Egypt. *Amer. J. Agr. Econ.*, November 1983, *65*(4), pp. 667–74. **[G: Egypt]**

Armbruster, Walter J. Advertising Farm Commodities. **In** *Connor, J. M. and Ward, R. W., eds.*, 1983, pp. 165–77. **[G: U.S.]**

Armbruster, Walter J. and Jesse, Edward V. Fruit and Vegetable Marketing Orders. **In** *Armbruster, W. J.; Henderson, D. R. and Knutson, Ronald D., eds.*, 1983, pp. 121–58. **[G: U.S.]**

Aspelin, Arnold. Comments [Advertising Farm Commodities] [Florida Department of Citrus Advertising Research Programs]. **In** *Connor, J. M. and Ward, R. W., eds.*, 1983, pp. 199–200. **[G: U.S.]**

Attwood, E. A. Financing and Investment in Irish Agriculture. *Irish Banking Rev.*, December 1983, pp. 13–26. **[G: Ireland]**

Babb, Emerson M., et al. Milk Marketing Orders. **In** *Armbruster, W. J.; Henderson, D. R. and Knutson, Ronald D., eds.*, 1983, pp. 159–97. **[G: U.S.]**

Bale, Malcolm D. Price Policies in Developing Countries: Discussion. **In** *Johnson, D. G. and Schuh, G. E., eds.*, 1983, pp. 136–42. **[G: LDCs]**

Bates, Robert H. Governments and Agricultural Markets in Africa. **In** *Johnson, D. G. and Schuh, G. E., eds.*, 1983, pp. 153–83. **[G: Africa]**

Baum, Kenneth H. and Richardson, James W. FLIPCOM: Farm-Level Continuous Optimization Models for Integrated Policy Analysis. **In** *Baum, K. H. and Schertz, L. P., eds.*, 1983, pp. 211–34. **[G: U.S.]**

Begashaw, Girma. Evaluation of a Supervised Credit Project in Jamaica. *Soc. Econ. Stud.*, March 1983, *32*(1), pp. 135–69. **[G: Jamaica]**

Bell, C. L. G. and Hazell, Peter B. R. Measuring the Indirect Effects of an Agricultural Investment Project on Its Surrounding Region. **In** *Lim, D., ed.*, 1983, *1980*, pp. 65–77. **[G: Malaysia]**

Belongia, Michael T. Agricultural Price Supports and Cost of Production: Comment. *Amer. J. Agr. Econ.*, August 1983, *65*(3), pp. 620–22.

Binswanger, Hans P. Agricultural Growth and Rural Nonfarm Activities. *Finance Develop.*, June 1983, *20*(2), pp. 38–40.

Boehlje, Michael and Eidman, Vernon R. Financial

Stress in Agriculture: Implications for Producers. *Amer. J. Agr. Econ.*, December 1983, *65*(5), pp. 937–44. **[G: U.S.]**

Bond, Daniel L. and Green, Donald W. Prospects for Soviet Agriculture in the Eleventh Five-year Plan: Econometric Analysis and Projections. **In** *Stuart, R. C., ed.*, 1983, pp. 296–319. **[G: U.S.S.R.]**

Bond, Marian E. Agricultural Responses to Prices in Sub-Saharan African Countries. *Int. Monet. Fund Staff Pap.*, December 1983, *30*(4), pp. 703–26. **[G: Sub-Saharan Africa]**

Bonnen, James T. Historical Sources of U.S. Agricultural Productivity: Implications for R&D Policy and Social Science Research. *Amer. J. Agr. Econ.*, December 1983, *65*(5), pp. 958–66. **[G: U.S.]**

Bouis, Howarth E. Seasonal Rice Price Variation in the Philippines: Measuring the Effects of Government Intervention. *Food Res. Inst. Stud.*, 1983, *19*(1), pp. 81–92. **[G: Philippines]**

Bourne, Compton. Effects of Subsidized Credit on the Size Distribution of Farm Household Incomes. *Soc. Econ. Stud.*, March 1983, *32*(1), pp. 81–101. **[G: Jamaica]**

Bovard, James. Feeding Everybody: How Federal Food Programs Grew and Grew. *Policy Rev.*, Fall 1983, (26), pp. 42–51. **[G: U.S.]**

Boynton, Damon. Implications for Plant and Animal Research. **In** *Whyte, W. F. and Boynton, D., eds.*, 1983, pp. 251–63.

Brada, Josef C. The Soviet–American Grain Agreement and the National Interest. *Amer. J. Agr. Econ.*, November 1983, *65*(4), pp. 651–56. **[G: U.S.; U.S.S.R.]**

Breimyer, Harold F. Agricultural Marketing Policy in Perspective. **In** *Armbruster, W. J.; Henderson, D. R. and Knutson, Ronald D., eds.*, 1983, pp. 1–20. **[G: U.S.]**

Breimyer, Harold F. Conceptualization and Climate for New Deal Farm Laws of the 1930s. *Amer. J. Agr. Econ.*, December 1983, *65*(5), pp. 1153–57. **[G: U.S.]**

Breimyer, Harold F. The Agricultural Bailout: Payment in Kind. *Challenge*, July/August 1983, *26*(3), pp. 51–53. **[G: U.S.]**

Brown, Gilbert T. Agricultural Pricing Policies in Developing Countries. **In** *Todaro, M. P., ed.*, 1983, *1978*, pp. 239–47. **[G: LDCs]**

Browne, William P. Mobilizing and Activating Group Demands: The American Agriculture Movement. *Soc. Sci. Quart.*, March 1983, *64*(1), pp. 19–34. **[G: U.S.]**

Butler, Nicholas. The Ploughshares War between Europe and America. *Foreign Aff.*, Fall 1983, *62*(1), pp. 105–22. **[G: Europe; America]**

Cahillane, G. and Lucey, D. I. F. An Examination of the Operation and Scope of the Farm Modernisation Scheme up to 1981. *Irish J. Agr. Econ. Rural Soc.*, 1983, *9*(2), pp. 107–20. **[G: Ireland]**

Cahillane, G. and Lucey, D. I. F. An Interim Examination of the Consequences of the Farm Modernisation Scheme on the Distribution of Incomes among Dairy Farms in Cork County. *Irish J. Agr. Econ. Rural Soc.*, 1983, *9*(2), pp. 121–32. **[G: Ireland]**

Caine, Richard J. H. and Stonehouse, D. Peter. Adjusting the Seasonality of Milk Shipments in Canada: Problems, Economic Impacts and Potential Policies. *Can. J. Agr. Econ.*, November 1983, *31*(3), pp. 331–50. **[G: Canada]**

Castle, Emery N. The Role of Markets and Governments in the World Food Economy: Discussion. **In** *Johnson, D. G. and Schuh, G. E., eds.*, 1983, pp. 302–06.

Chambers, Robert G. and Foster, William E. Participation in the Farmer-Owned Reserve Program: A Discrete Choice Model. *Amer. J. Agr. Econ.*, February 1983, *65*(1), pp. 120–24. **[G: U.S.]**

Chau, L. C. Imports of Consumer Goods from China and the Economic Growth of Hong Kong. **In** *Youngson, A. J., ed.*, 1983, pp. 184–225. **[G: China; Hong Kong]**

Chavas, Jean-Paul and Keplinger, Keith O. Impact of Domestic Food Programs on Nutrient Intake of Low-Income Persons in the United States. *Southern J. Agr. Econ.*, July 1983, *15*(1), pp. 155–63. **[G: U.S.]**

Chen, Yun. An Investigation of Rural Qingpu [County]. **In** *Ch'en, Y.*, 1983, *1961*, pp. 155–73. **[G: China]**

Chen, Yun. Methods of Solving the Tensions in Supplies of Pork and Vegetables. **In** *Ch'en, Y.*, 1983, *1956*, pp. 23–29. **[G: China]**

Chen, Yun. Pay Attention to Grain Work. **In** *Ch'en, Y.*, 1983, *1957*, pp. 67–72. **[G: China]**

Chen, Yun. Responses to a Xinhua Correspondent's Questions on Problems of Market Prices of Commodities [Interview]. **In** *Ch'en, Y.*, 1983, *1957*, pp. 58–62. **[G: China]**

Chen, Yun. We Must Solve the Vegetable Supply Problem Well. **In** *Ch'en, Y.*, 1983, *1957*, pp. 63–66. **[G: China]**

Choncho, Jacques. World Food: Failure of Productivist Solutions. **In** *Glassner, M. I., ed.*, 1983, *1981*, pp. 219–29. **[G: Global]**

Clay, Edward J. and Mitchell, Mark. Is European Community Food Aid in Dairy Products Cost-Effective? *Europ. Rev. Agr. Econ.*, 1983, *10*(2), pp. 97–121. **[G: EEC]**

Cochrane, Willard W. The Economic Research Service: 22 Years Later. *Agr. Econ. Res.*, April 1983, *35*(2), pp. 29–38. **[G: U.S.]**

Cottle, Rex L.; Macaulay, Hugh H. and Yandle, T. Bruce. Some Economic Effects of the California Agricultural Labor Relations Act. *J. Lab. Res.*, Fall 1983, *4*(4), pp. 315–24. **[G: U.S.]**

Coughenour, C. Milton and Christenson, James A. Farm Structure, Social Class, and Farmers' Policy Perspectives. **In** *Brewster, D. E.; Rasmussen, W. D. and Youngberg, G., eds.*, 1983, pp. 67–86. **[G: U.S.]**

Crist, Raymond E. Land for the People—A Vital Need Everywhere: In Latin America and the Caribbean, It's Now 'a Prey to Hastening Ills,' and Decay. *Amer. J. Econ. Soc.*, July 1983, *42*(3), pp. 275–90. **[G: Latin America; Caribbean]**

Csaki, Csaba. Economic Management and Organization of Hungarian Agriculture. *J. Compar. Econ.*, September 1983, *7*(3), pp. 317–28. **[G: Hungary]**

David, Cristina C. Economic Policies and Agricultural Incentives. *Philippine Econ. J.*, 1983, *22*(2), pp. 154–82. **[G: Philippine]**

Davis, Jeffrey M. The Economic Effects of Windfall Gains in Export Earnings, 1975–1978. *World Devel.*, February 1983, *11*(2), pp. 119–39. **[G: Latin American LDCs; African LDCs]**

van Dijk, G. and Mackel, C. Fundamental Changes in Price Relationships: An Investigation of the UK Feed Grain Market, 1971/72 to 1978/79, Using Spectral Analysis. *Europ. Rev. Agr. Econ.*, 1983, *10*(1), pp. 15–31. **[G: U.K.]**

DiLorenzo, Thomas J.; Sementilli, Vincent M. and Southwick, Lawrence, Jr. The Lome Sugar Protocol: Increased Dependency for Fiji and Other ACP States. *Rev. Soc. Econ.*, April 1983, *41*(1), pp. 25–38. **[G: Fiji; ACP; EEC]**

Doering, Otto C., III. Specification and Use of Farm Growth and Planning Models in Policy Extension Activities. **In** *Baum, K. H. and Schertz, L. P., eds.*, 1983, pp. 375–84. **[G: U.S.]**

Dumsday, R. G. Agricultural Resource Management. *Australian J. Agr. Econ.*, August 1983, *27*(2), pp. 157–63. **[G: Australia]**

Durgin, Frank A., Jr. The Relationship of the Death of Stalin to the Economic Change of the Post-Stalin Era or Was Stalin's Departure Really Necessary? **In** *Stuart, R. C., ed.*, 1983, pp. 118–42. **[G: U.S.S.R.]**

Easter, Christopher D. and Paris, Quirino. Supply Response with Stochastic Technology and Prices in Australia's Rural Export Industries. *Australian J. Agr. Econ.*, April 1983, *27*(1), pp. 12–30. **[G: U.S.; Australia]**

Echols, Marsha A. The GATT Ministerial and International Trade in Agricultural Products. **In** *Rubin, S. J. and Graham, T. R., eds.*, 1983, pp. 109–33. **[G: Japan; U.S.; EEC]**

Edwards, Clark. Social Science Implications of Agricultural Science and Technology: Discussion. *Amer. J. Agr. Econ.*, December 1983, *65*(5), pp. 978–80. **[G: U.S.]**

Efstratoglou-Todoulou, Sophia. The Impact of the Common Agricultural Policy. **In** *Sampedro, J. L. and Payno, J. A., eds.*, 1983, pp. 85–104. **[G: Greece; EEC]**

El-Agraa, Ali M. The True Cost of the CAP. **In** *El-Agraa, A. M., ed.*, 1983, pp. 147–66. **[G: EEC; U.K.]**

Elliott, Charles. Equity and Growth: An Unresolved Conflict in Zambian Rural Development Policy. **In** *Ghai, D. and Radwan, S., eds.*, 1983, pp. 155–89. **[G: Zambia]**

Evans, Alfred, Jr. Changes in the Soviet Model of Rural Transformation. **In** *Stuart, R. C., ed.*, 1983, pp. 143–58. **[G: U.S.S.R.]**

Evenson, Robert E. Intellectual Property Rights and Agribusiness Research and Development: Implications for the Public Agricultural Research System. *Amer. J. Agr. Econ.*, December 1983, *65*(5), pp. 967–75. **[G: U.S.]**

Evenson, Robert E. Price Policies in Developing Countries: Discussion. **In** *Johnson, D. G. and Schuh, G. E., eds.*, 1983, pp. 143–51. **[G: India]**

Farrell, Kenneth R. Commodity Programs: Discussion. *Amer. J. Agr. Econ.*, December 1983, *65*(5), pp. 935–36. **[G: U.S.]**

Farrell, Kenneth R. Implications of National Agricultural Policies in Modeling Behavior of Farm Firms. **In** *Baum, K. H. and Schertz, L. P., eds.*, 1983, pp. 101–09. **[G: U.S.]**

Farrell, Kenneth R. and Runge, Carlisle Ford. Institutional Innovation and Technical Change in American Agriculture: The Role of the New Deal. *Amer. J. Agr. Econ.*, December 1983, *65*(5), pp. 1168–73. **[G: U.S.]**

Fisher, Brian S. Rational Expectations in the Australian Wool Industry. *Australian J. Agr. Econ.*, December 1983, *27*(3), pp. 212–20. **[G: Australia]**

Flatt, William P. Financing Agricultural Research and Education in a Period of Tight Budgets. *Southern J. Agr. Econ.*, July 1983, *15*(1), pp. 11–17. **[G: U.S.]**

Freebairn, John W. Drought Assistance Policy. *Australian J. Agr. Econ.*, December 1983, *27*(3), pp. 185–99. **[G: Australia]**

Gardner, Bruce L. Discussion [Governments and Agricultural Markets in Africa] [Why Do Governments Do What They Do? The Case of Food Price Policy]. **In** *Johnson, D. G. and Schuh, G. E., eds.*, 1983, pp. 219–26.

Gardner, Bruce L. Efficient Redistribution through Commodity Markets. *Amer. J. Agr. Econ.*, May 1983, *65*(2), pp. 225–34.

Georgakopoulos, Theodore A. and Paschos, Panagiotis G. The Costs and Benefits of the CAP: Greece's Experience in 1981. *Europ. Rev. Agr. Econ.*, 1983, *10*(4), pp. 377–88. **[G: Greece]**

Gerrard, Christopher D. and Roe, Terry. Government Intervention in Food Grain Markets: An Econometric Study of Tanzania. *J. Devel. Econ.*, Aug.–Oct. 1983, *13*(1–2), pp. 109–32. **[G: Tanzania]**

Gibney, S. J. and Furtan, W. Harley. Welfare Effects of New Crop Variety Licensing Regulations: The Case of Canadian Malt Barley. *Amer. J. Agr. Econ.*, February 1983, *65*(1), pp. 142–47. **[G: Canada]**

Glenn, Marcia and Lattimore, Ralph. Canadian Acreage Response to Grain Storage Subsidies. *Can. J. Agr. Econ.*, July 1983, *31*(2), pp. 245–48. **[G: Canada]**

Gowda, M. V. Srinivasa. Monetary and Fiscal Policies for Expansion of Employment in Agriculture. *Econ. Aff.*, April–June 1983, *28*(2), pp. 701–05, 714. **[G: India]**

Graham, Douglas H. and Pollard, Stephen K. The Crop Lien Programme: Implications of a Credit Project Transformed into an Ad Hoc Income Transfer Programme. *Soc. Econ. Stud.*, March 1983, *32*(1), pp. 63–80. **[G: Jamaica]**

Gray, Clive and Martens, André. The Political Economy of the 'Recurrent Cost Problem' in the West African Sahel. *World Devel.*, February 1983, *11*(2), pp. 101–17. **[G: Sahel]**

Gray, Jack and Gray, Maisie. China's New Agricultural Revolution. **In** *Feuchtwang, S. and Hussain, A., eds.*, 1983, pp. 151–84. **[G: China]**

Griffith, Garry R. and Meilke, Karl D. The Impact on the Canadian Rapeseed Industry of Removing EEC Import Tariffs. *J. Policy Modeling*, March 1983, *5*(1), pp. 37–54. **[G: Canada; EEC]**

Groenewegen, John R. and Clayton, Kenneth C. Agricultural Price Supports and Cost of Production: Reply. *Amer. J. Agr. Econ.*, August 1983, *65*(3),

pp. 626–28. [G: U.S.]

Guither, Harold D. Citizen and Consumer Groups in Policies Affecting Farm Structure. In *Brewster, D. E.; Rasmussen, W. D. and Youngberg, G., eds.,* 1983, pp. 87–101. [G: U.S.]

Hagedorn, Konrad. Reflections on the Methodology of Agricultural Policy Research. *Europ. Rev. Agr. Econ.,* 1983, *10*(4), pp. 303–23.

Hardach, Karl. Wheat, Rye, and the Sources of German Protection: A Comment on Webb's Article [Agricultural Protection in Wilhelminian Germany: Forging an Empire with Pork and Rye]. *J. Econ. Hist.,* June 1983, *43*(2), pp. 481. [G: Germany]

Harling, Kenneth F. Agricultural Protectionism in Developed Countries: Analysis of Systems of Intervention. *Europ. Rev. Agr. Econ.,* 1983, *10*(3), pp. 223–47. [G: Canada; U.K.; W. Germany]

Harling, Kenneth F. and Thompson, Robert L. The Economic Effects of Intervention in Canadian Agriculture. *Can. J. Agr. Econ.,* July 1983, *31* (2), pp. 153–76. [G: Canada]

Harris, Harold M., Jr., et al. Cooperatives and Bargaining. In *Armbruster, W. J.; Henderson, D. R. and Knutson, Ronald D., eds.,* 1983, pp. 199–238. [G: U.S.]

Hathaway, Dale E. Agricultural Trade Policy for the 1980s. In *Cline W. R., ed.,* 1983, pp. 435–53.

Havnevik, Kjell J. and Skarstein, Rune. Some Notes on Agricultural Backwardness in Tanzania. In *Parkinson, J. R., ed.,* 1983, pp. 151–62. [G: Tanzania]

Heady, Earl O. Economic Policies and Variables: Potentials and Problems for the Future. In *Brewster, D. E.; Rasmussen, W. D. and Youngberg, G., eds.,* 1983, pp. 23–35. [G: U.S.]

Heady, Earl O. Models for Agricultural Policy: The CARD Example. *Europ. Rev. Agr. Econ.,* 1983, *10*(1), pp. 1–14. [G: U.S.]

Hertford, Reed. Issues in International Agricultural Development: Discussion. *Amer. J. Agr. Econ.,* May 1983, *65*(2), pp. 455–57.

Hildebrand, Marvin D. The Canadian Wheat Board Delivery Quota System: An Economic Analysis. *Can. J. Agr. Econ.,* November 1983, *31* (3), pp. 437–48. [G: Canada]

Hill, Berkeley. Farm Incomes: Myths and Perspectives. *Lloyds Bank Rev.,* July 1983, (149), pp. 35–48. [G: U.K.]

Hinchy, Mike and Simmons, Phil. An Optimal-Control Approach to Stabilising Australian Wool Prices. *Australian J. Agr. Econ.,* April 1983, *27*(1), pp. 44–72. [G: Australia]

Hodge, Ian. Rural Employment and the Quality of Life. *Rev. Marketing Agr. Econ.,* December 1983, *51* (3), pp. 259–70.

Homem de Melo, Fernando. Trade Policy, Technology, and Food Prices in Brazil. *Quart. Rev. Econ. Bus.,* Spring 1983, *23*(1), pp. 58–78. [G: Brazil]

House, William J. and Killick, Tony. Social Justice and Development Policy in Kenya's Rural Economy. In *Ghai, D. and Radwan, S., eds.,* 1983, pp. 31–69. [G: Kenya]

Huang, Wen-yuan; Heady, Earl O. and Weisz, Reuben N. Linkage of a National Recursive Econometric Model and an Interregional Programming Model for Agricultural Policy Analysis. In *Thrall, R. M.; Thompson, R. G. and Holloway, M. L., eds.,* 1983, pp. 77–99. [G: U.S.]

Infanger, Craig L.; Bailey, William C. and Dyer, David R. Agricultural Policy in Austerity: The Making of the 1981 Farm Bill. *Amer. J. Agr. Econ.,* February 1983, *65*(1), pp. 1–9. [G: U.S.]

Jacobs, Everett M. Soviet Agricultural Management and Planning and the 1982 Administrative Reforms. In *Stuart, R. C., ed.,* 1983, pp. 273–95. [G: U.S.S.R.]

Jamal, Vali. Nomads and Farmers: Incomes and Poverty in Rural Somalia. In *Ghai, D. and Radwan, S., eds.,* 1983, pp. 281–311. [G: Somalia]

James, William E. Settler Selection and Land Settlement Alternatives: New Evidence from the Philippines. *Econ. Develop. Cult. Change,* April 1983, *31* (3), pp. 571–86. [G: Philippines]

de Janvry, Alain. Why Do Governments Do What They Do? The Case of Food Price Policy. In *Johnson, D. G. and Schuh, G. E., eds.,* 1983, pp. 185–212. [G: U.S.; India; Colombia; Egypt]

de Janvry, Alain; Siam, Gamal and Gad, Osman. The Impact of Forced Deliveries on Egyptian Agriculture. *Amer. J. Agr. Econ.,* August 1983, *65*(3), pp. 493–501. [G: Egypt]

Jarrett, Frank. The Balderstone Report: An Overview. *Australian J. Agr. Econ.,* August 1983, *27*(2), pp. 117–23. [G: Australia]

Johnson, D. Gale. Agricultural Organization and Management. In *Bergson, A. and Levine, H. S., eds.,* 1983, pp. 112–42. [G: U.S.S.R.]

Johnson, Frederick I. Sugar in Brazil: Policy and Production. *J. Devel. Areas,* January 1983, *17*(2), pp. 243–56. [G: Brazil]

Johnson, James D. and Short, Sara D. Commodity Programs: Who Has Received the Benefits? *Amer. J. Agr. Econ.,* December 1983, *65*(5), pp. 912–21. [G: U.S.]

Johnson, Paul R. and Norton, Daniel T. Social Cost of the Tobacco Program Redux. *Amer. J. Agr. Econ.,* February 1983, *65*(1), pp. 117–19. [G: U.S.]

Johnson, Wallace H. and Quintin, Yves. U.S. Reliability for Grain Deliveries: The Treaty Option. *J. World Trade Law,* September–October 1983, *17*(5), pp. 397–406. [G: U.S.]

Jones, Paul H. *Lamtoro* and the Amarasi Model from Timor. *Bull. Indonesian Econ. Stud.,* December 1983, *19*(3), pp. 106–12. [G: Indonesia]

Junguito, Roberto and Pizano, Diego. The Role of Information in Commodity Negotiations: The Case of Coffee. In *O'Brien, R. C., ed.,* 1983, pp. 78–87. [G: MDCs; LDCs]

Kane, N. Stephan. Reassessing the Bureaucratic Dimension of Foreign Policy Making: A Case Study of the Cuban Sugar Quota Decision, 1954–56. *Soc. Sci. Quart.,* March 1983, *64*(1), pp. 46–65. [G: U.S.]

Katseli, Louka T. Exchange Rates and Food in the European Community. *Europ. Econ. Rev.,* January 1983, *20*(1–3), pp. 319–32. [G: EEC]

Kelleher, Carmel. Implications of Different Theoretical Development Perspectives for Policy and Interventions: 2. Underlying Frameworks of Irish Agricultural Policies and Interventions Relating to Low-Income Farmers. *Irish J. Agr. Econ. Rural Soc.*, 1983, *9*(2), pp. 145–60. **[G: Ireland; EEC]**

Kelleher, Carmel. Implications of Different Theoretical Development Perspectives for Policy and Interventions: 1. The Relationship between Development Perspectives and Policy Strategy and Intervention. *Irish J. Agr. Econ. Rural Soc.*, 1983, *9*(2), pp. 133–43.

Khan, Azizur Rahman and Ghai, Dharam. Collective Agriculture in Soviet Central Asia. **In** *Stewart, F., ed.*, 1983, pp. 279–305. **[G: U.S.S.R.]**

Kim, V. Purchase Prices on Agricultural Products. *Prob. Econ.*, June 1983, *26*(2), pp. 22–40. **[G: U.S.S.R.]**

Kirschke, Dieter. Maximizing Welfare in Customs Unions: The Case of Agricultural Price Policy Within the EEC. *Amer. J. Agr. Econ.*, November 1983, *65*(4), pp. 791–95. **[G: EEC]**

Kirthisingha, P. N. International Commodity Agreements. *Int. J. Soc. Econ.*, 1983, *10*(3), pp. 40–65.

Klemyshev, P. The Effectiveness of Utilization of Agriculture's Productive Resources. *Prob. Econ.*, March 1983, *25*(11), pp. 51–69. **[G: U.S.S.R.]**

Kloppenburg, Jack R., Jr. Group Development in Botswana: The Principles of Collective Farmer Action. **In** *Dalton, G., ed.*, 1983, pp. 311–33. **[G: Botswana]**

Knutson, Ronald D.; Geyer, L. Leon and Helmuth, John W. Trade Practice Regulation. **In** *Armbruster, W. J.; Henderson, D. R. and Knutson, Ronald D., eds.*, 1983, pp. 239–68. **[G: U.S.]**

Kolsen, H. M. Effective Rates of Protection and Hidden Sectoral Transfers by Public Authorities. *Australian J. Agr. Econ.*, August 1983, *27*(2), pp. 104–15. **[G: Australia]**

Korah, Valentine. Exclusive Licenses of Patent and Plant Breeders' Rights under EEC Law after *Maize Seed*. *Antitrust Bull.*, Fall 1983, *28*(3), pp. 699–755. **[G: EEC]**

Korten, David C.; Uphoff, Norman and Whyte, William Foote. Bureaucratic Reorientation for Agricultural Research and Development. **In** *Whyte, W. F. and Boynton, D., eds.*, 1983, pp. 222–47.

Krueger, Anne O. Protectionism, Exchange Rate Distortions, and Agricultural Trading Patterns. *Amer. J. Agr. Econ.*, December 1983, *65*(5), pp. 864–71. **[G: Global]**

Lapping, Mark B. and Lecko, Margaret. Foreign Investment in U.S. Agricultural Land: An Overview of the National Issue and a Case Study of Vermont. *Amer. J. Econ. Soc.*, July 1983, *42*(3), pp. 291–304. **[G: U.S.]**

Larsen, Arne. Landbrugets økonomiske perspektiver. (Long Term Adjustment Problems in Danish Agriculture. With English summary.) *Nationaløkon. Tidsskr.*, 1983, *121* (2), pp. 259–71. **[G: Denmark]**

Leaf, Murray J. The Green Revolution and Cultural Change in a Punjab Village, 1965–1978. *Econ. Develop. Cult. Change*, January 1983, *31* (2), pp. 227–70. **[G: India]**

Lee, Eddy. Export-led Rural Development: The Ivory Coast. **In** *Ghai, D. and Radwan, S., eds.*, 1983, pp. 99–127. **[G: Ivory Coast]**

Lee, John E., Jr. Some Consequences of the New Reality in U.S. Agriculture. **In** *Brewster, D. E.; Rasmussen, W. D. and Youngberg, G., eds.*, 1983, pp. 3–22. **[G: U.S.]**

Levins, Richard A. Implications of Microcomputer Technology for Agricultural Economics Programs. *Southern J. Agr. Econ.*, July 1983, *15*(1), pp. 27–29. **[G: U.S.]**

Levy, Victor. The Welfare and Transfer Effects of Cotton Price Policies in Egypt, 1965–78. *Amer. J. Agr. Econ.*, August 1983, *65*(3), pp. 576–80. **[G: Egypt]**

Lewis, W. Arthur. Aspects of Tropical Trade. **In** *Lewis, W. A.*, 1983, *1969*, pp. 235–81. **[G: OECD; LDCs]**

Lezina, M. Structure of the National Economic Agroindustrial Complex. *Prob. Econ.*, November 1983, *26*(7), pp. 65–84. **[G: U.S.S.R.]**

Litvin, Valentin. Agro-industrial Complexes: Recent Structural Reform in the Rural Economy of the USSR. **In** *Stuart, R. C., ed.*, 1983, pp. 258–72. **[G: U.S.S.R.]**

Lloyd, A. G. Agricultural Trends and General Economic Policy. *Australian J. Agr. Econ.*, August 1983, *27*(2), pp. 129–33. **[G: Australia]**

Lockwood, B., et al. Farm Mechanization in Pakistan: Policy and Practice. **In** *Internat'l Rice Res. Inst. and Agric. Devel. Council*, 1983, pp. 15–30. **[G: Pakistan]**

Longworth, John W. Agricultural Policy and Innovation. *Australian J. Agr. Econ.*, August 1983, *27*(2), pp. 152–56. **[G: Australia]**

Lundahl, Mats. Imperfect Competition in Haitian Coffee Marketing. **In** *Lundahl, M.*, 1983, pp. 171–89. **[G: Haiti]**

Malish, Anton F. Capital Investments in the USSR's Agro-Industrial Complex. *ACES Bull. (See Comp. Econ. Stud. after 8/85)*, Fall 1983, *25*(3), pp. 69–70. **[G: U.S.S.R.]**

Markish, Yuri and Malish, Anton F. The Soviet Food Program: Prospects for the 1980s. *ACES Bull. (See Comp. Econ. Stud. after 8/85)*, Spring 1983, *25*(1), pp. 47–65. **[G: U.S.S.R.]**

Marrese, Michael. Agricultural Policy and Performance in Hungary. *J. Compar. Econ.*, September 1983, *7*(3), pp. 329–45. **[G: Hungary]**

Mathieu, Alain. Soutien des prix et paradoxes de la politique agricole. (With English summary.) *Revue Écon. Polit.*, September–October 1983, *93*(5), pp. 772–80. **[G: France]**

Matthews, Alan. Evaluating Public Spending on Agricultural Development. *Irish Banking Rev.*, March 1983, pp. 36–48. **[G: Ireland]**

Mauldon, R. G. Agricultural Policy: Commonwealth–State Issues. *Australian J. Agr. Econ.*, August 1983, *27*(2), pp. 124–28. **[G: Australia]**

McIntire, John. International Farm Prices and the Social Cost of Cheap Food Policies: Comment. *Amer. J. Agr. Econ.*, November 1983, *65*(4), pp. 823–26. **[G: LDCs]**

Meiendorf, A. Socially Necessary Expenditures and Purchase Prices in Agriculture. *Prob. Econ.*, April 1983, *25*(12), pp. 67–80. **[G: U.S.S.R.]**

Meilke, Karl D. and Griffith, Garry R. Incorporating Policy Variables in a Model of the World Soybean/Rapeseed Market. *Amer. J. Agr. Econ.*, Feb-

ruary 1983, *65*(1), pp. 65–73.
Mellor, John W. Food Prospects for the Developing Countries. *Amer. Econ. Rev.*, May 1983, *73*(2), pp. 239–43. **[G: LDCs]**
Metzner, Joachim. Innovations in Agriculture Incorporating Traditional Production Methods: The Case of Amarasi (Timor). *Bull. Indonesian Econ. Stud.*, December 1983, *19*(3), pp. 94–105. **[G: Indonesia]**
Millar, James R. Views on the Economics of Soviet Collectivization of Agriculture: The State of the Revisionist Debate. **In** *Stuart, R. C., ed.*, 1983, pp. 109–17. **[G: U.S.S.R.]**
Moar, Lyle. Understanding the Scottish Economy: Farming Today. **In** *Ingham, K. P. D. and Love, J., eds.*, 1983, pp. 74–86. **[G: U.K.]**
Monke, Eric. Tariffs, Implementation Costs, and Optimal Policy Choice. *Weltwirtsch. Arch.*, 1983, *119*(2), pp. 281–96. **[G: Ivory Coast; Senegal; Liberia]**
Müller, Ernst. The Common Market for Agricultural Products. **In** *Saunders, C. T., ed.*, 1983, pp. 183–91. **[G: CMEA; EEC]**
Musgrave, Warren. Rural Communities: Some Social Issues. *Australian J. Agr. Econ.*, August 1983, *27*(2), pp. 145–51. **[G: Australia]**
Nelson, Arthur Christian. Reader Response [The Oregon Agricultural Protection Program: A Review and Assessment]. *Natural Res. J.*, January 1983, *23*(1), pp. 1–5. **[G: U.S.]**
Nelson, Glenn L. A Critique of Executive Branch Decision-Making Processes. *Amer. J. Agr. Econ.*, December 1983, *65*(5), pp. 901–07. **[G: U.S.]**
Nichols, John P.; Hill, Lowell D. and Nelson, Kenneth E. Food and Agricultural Commodity Grading. **In** *Armbruster, W. J.; Henderson, D. R. and Knutson, Ronald D., eds.*, 1983, pp. 59–90. **[G: U.S.]**
Niimi, Reiko. The Problem of Food Security. **In** *Akao, N., ed.*, 1983, pp. 169–96. **[G: Japan]**
Noguchi, Yukio. The Failure of Government to Perform Its Proper Task: A Case Study of Japan. **In** *Lenel, H. O.; Willgerodt, H. and Molsberger, J.*, 1983, pp. 59–70. **[G: Japan]**
Nolan, Peter. De-collectivisation of Agriculture in China, 1979–82: A Long-Term Perspective. *Cambridge J. Econ.*, September/December 1983, *7*(3/4), pp. 381–403. **[G: China]**
Nolan, Peter and White, Gordon. Economic Distribution and Rural Development in China: The Legacy of the Maoist Era. **In** *Stewart, F., ed.*, 1983, pp. 243–78. **[G: China]**
Norrie, Kenneth H. Not Much to Crow about: A Primer on the Statutory Grain Freight Rate Issue. *Can. Public Policy*, December 1983, *9*(4), pp. 434–45. **[G: Canada]**
Norton, Roger D.; Santaniello, Vittorio and Echevarria, Julio A. Economic Evaluation of an Agricultural Sector Investment Program: A Case Study for Peru. *J. Policy Modeling*, June 1983, *5*(2), pp. 149–77. **[G: Peru]**
Nyanin, Ohene Owusu. Lending Costs, Institutional Viability and Agricultural Credit Strategies in Jamaica. *Soc. Econ. Stud.*, March 1983, *32*(1), pp. 103–33. **[G: Jamaica]**
Omirova, Zh. On the Question of the Role of the Personal Household Plot. *Prob. Econ.*, November 1983, *26*(7), pp. 40–46. **[G: U.S.S.R.]**
Paarlberg, Don. Effects of New Deal Farm Programs on the Agricultural Agenda a Half Century Later and Prospect for the Future. *Amer. J. Agr. Econ.*, December 1983, *65*(5), pp. 1163–67.
Paarlberg, Robert L. Discussion [Governments and Agricultural Markets in Africa] [Why Do Governments Do What They Do? The Case of Food Price Policy]. **In** *Johnson, D. G. and Schuh, G. E., eds.*, 1983, pp. 213–18. **[G: India; U.S.]**
Paarlberg, Robert L. Shifting and Sharing Adjustment Burdens: The Role of the Industrial Food-importing Nations. **In** *Glassner, M. I., ed.*, 1983, *1978*, pp. 197–218. **[G: EEC; Japan; U.S.S.R.; Global]**
Paarlberg, Robert L. Using Food Power: Opportunities, Appearances, and Damage Control. **In** *Nincic, M. and Wallensteen, P., eds.*, 1983, *1982*, pp. 131–53.
Paddock, Brian. Estimation of Producer Losses Arising from the Partial Embargo of Grain Exports to the USSR. *Can. J. Agr. Econ.*, July 1983, *31* (2), pp. 233–44. **[G: Canada]**
Pang, Chung Min and De Boer, A. John. Management Decentralization on China's State Farms. *Amer. J. Agr. Econ.*, November 1983, *65*(4), pp. 657–66. **[G: China]**
Papanek, Gustav F. and Mujahid, Eshya. Effect of Policies on Agricultural Development: A Comparison of the Bengals and the Punjabs. *Amer. J. Agr. Econ.*, May 1983, *65*(2), pp. 426–37. **[G: Bangladesh; India; Pakistan]**
Pasour, E. C., Jr. Agricultural Price Supports and Cost of Production: Comment. *Amer. J. Agr. Econ.*, August 1983, *65*(3), pp. 623–25. **[G: U.S.]**
Peacock, Frank. Asian Agriculture: A Decade of Failure. **In** *Glassner, M. I., ed.*, 1983, *1980*, pp. 230–36. **[G: Asia]**
Peterson, Willis L. International Farm Prices and the Social Cost of Cheap Food Policies: Reply. *Amer. J. Agr. Econ.*, November 1983, *65*(4), pp. 827–28. **[G: LDCs]**
Petřík, Miroslav. Pasture Crops: A Solution to the Grain Problem. *Czech. Econ. Digest.*, November 1983, (7), pp. 33–51. **[G: Czechoslovakia]**
Petzel, Todd E. Empirical Analysis of Soviet Agricultural Production and Policy: Comment. *Amer. J. Agr. Econ.*, February 1983, *65*(1), pp. 175–77. **[G: U.S.S.R.]**
Phillips, Michael J. Social Science Implications of Agricultural Science and Technology: Discussion. *Amer. J. Agr. Econ.*, December 1983, *65*(5), pp. 976–77. **[G: U.S.]**
Plascasovitis, Ilias. A Critique on the 'Study of the Regional Impact of the CAP.' *Europ. Rev. Agr. Econ.*, 1983, *10*(2), pp. 141–50. **[G: EEC]**
Plato, Gerald and Gordon, Douglas. Dynamic Programming and the Economics of Optimal Grain Storage. *Agr. Econ. Res.*, January 1983, *35*(1), pp. 10–22.
Pollard, Stephen K. and Grewal, Harpal S. Simulating the Impacts of Credit Policy and Fertilizer Subsidy on Central Luzon Rice Farms, the Philip-

pines: Comment. *Amer. J. Agr. Econ.*, May 1983, *65*(2), pp. 349–50. [G: Philippines]

Pontius, Steven K. The Communication Process of Adoption: Agriculture in Thailand. *J. Devel. Areas,* October 1983, *18*(1), pp. 93–118. [G: Thailand]

Putterman, Louis. Incentives and the Kibbutz: Toward an Economics of Communal Work Motivation. *Z. Nationalökon.*, 1983, *43*(2), pp. 157–88.

Quiggin, John C. Underwriting Agricultural Commodity Prices. *Australian J. Agr. Econ.*, December 1983, *27*(3), pp. 200–211. [G: Australia]

Quiggin, John C. Wool Price Stabilisation and Profit Risk for Wool Users. *Australian J. Agr. Econ.*, April 1983, *27*(1), pp. 31–43. [G: Australia]

Raj, K. N. Prices, Subsidies and Access to Food. *Indian Econ. Rev.*, July–December 1983, *18*(2), pp. 157–67. [G: India]

Rasmussen, Wayne D. The New Deal Farm Programs: What They Were and Why They Survived. *Amer. J. Agr. Econ.*, December 1983, *65*(5), pp. 1158–62. [G: U.S.]

van Ravenswaay, Eileen and Wallace, L. Tim. Changing Agricultural Marketing Programs. In *Armbruster, W. J.; Henderson, D. R. and Knutson, Ronald D., eds.*, 1983, pp. 305–26. [G: U.S.]

Ray, C. R. Macro Impacts of Food Subsidy Policies in Developing Countries. *Margin,* July 1983, *15*(4), pp. 50–65. [G: India]

Read, Robert. The Growth and Structure of Multinationals in the Banana Export Trade. In *Casson, M., ed.*, 1983, pp. 180–213. [G: Caribbean; Central America; U.S.]

Reca, Lucio G. Price Policies in Developing Countries. In *Johnson, D. G. and Schuh, G. E., eds.*, 1983, pp. 115–35. [G: LDCs]

Redclift, Michael. Production Programs for Small Farmers: Plan Puebla as Myth and Reality. *Econ. Develop. Cult. Change,* April 1983, *31*(3), pp. 551–70. [G: Mexico]

Rosegrant, Mark W. and Herdt, Robert W. Simulating the Impacts of Credit Policy and Fertilizer Subsidy on Central Luzon Rice Farms, the Philippines: Reply. *Amer. J. Agr. Econ.*, May 1983, *65*(2), pp. 351–52. [G: Philippines]

Rucker, Randal R. and Fishback, Price V. The Federal Reclamation Program: An Analysis of Rent-seeking Behavior. In *Anderson, T. L., ed.*, 1983, pp. 45–81. [G: U.S.]

Sacay, Orlando J. Agricultural Strategy in the 1980s. *Philippine Econ. J.*, 1983, *22*(2), pp. 137–53. [G: Philippine]

Salant, Stephen W. The Vulnerability of Price Stabilization Schemes to Speculative Attack. *J. Polit. Econ.*, February 1983, *91*(1), pp. 1–38.

Salathe, Larry E.; Price, J. Michael and Gadson, Kenneth E. The Food and Agricultural Policy Simulator: The Poultry- and Egg-Sector Submodel. *Agr. Econ. Res.*, January 1983, *35*(1), pp. 23–34. [G: U.S.]

Sarris, Alexander H. and Freebairn, John W. Endogenous Price Policies and International Wheat Prices. *Amer. J. Agr. Econ.*, May 1983, *65*(2), pp. 214–24.

Sauer, Richard J. The Role of Markets and Governments in the World Food Economy: Discussion. In *Johnson, D. G. and Schuh, G. E., eds.*, 1983, pp. 307–10.

Sayad, João. The Impact of Rural Credit on Production and Income Distribution in Brazil. In *Von Pischke, J. D.; Adams, D. W. and Donald, G., eds.*, 1983, pp. 379–86. [G: Brazil]

Scandizzo, Pasquale L.; Hazell, Peter B. R. and Anderson, Jock R. Producers' Price Expectations and the Size of the Welfare Gains from Price Stabilisation. *Rev. Marketing Agr. Econ.*, August 1983, *51*(2), pp. 93–107.

Schmitz, Andrew. Supply Management in Canadian Agriculture: An Assessment of the Economic Effects. *Can. J. Agr. Econ.*, July 1983, *31*(2), pp. 135–52. [G: Canada]

Schug, Walter. Die Bedeutung von internationalen Rohstoffabkommen für die Verbracherländer von agrarischen und mineralischen Grundstoffen. In *Lenel, H. O.; Willgerodt, H. and Molsberger, J.*, 1983, pp. 169–91. [G: LDCs; MDCs]

Schuh, G. Edward. The Role of Markets and Governments in the World Food Economy. In *Johnson, D. G. and Schuh, G. E., eds.*, 1983, pp. 277–301.

Schumacher, August. Agricultural Development and Rural Employment: A Mexican Dilemma. In *Brown, P. G. and Shue, H., eds.*, 1983, pp. 141–61. [G: Mexico]

Sedjo, Roger A. and Wiseman, A. Clark. The Effectiveness of an Export Restriction on Logs. *Amer. J. Agr. Econ.*, February 1983, *65*(1), pp. 113–16. [G: U.S.]

Sen, Amartya K. The Food Problem: Theory and Policy. In *Gauhar, A., ed. (II)*, 1983, pp. 91–103.

Simanis, Joseph G. Farmer's Pensions and the Polish Economic Crisis. *Soc. Sec. Bull.*, April 1983, *46*(4), pp. 13–22. [G: Poland]

Singh, Inderjit. Issues in International Agricultural Development: Discussion. *Amer. J. Agr. Econ.*, May 1983, *65*(2), pp. 452–54.

Smith, Ian. Prospects for a New International Sugar Agreement. *J. World Trade Law,* July–August 1983, *17*(4), pp. 308–24. [G: Selected LDCs; Selected MDCs]

Sorenson, Vernon L. and Peterson, E. Wesley F. International Marketing of Agricultural Commodities and Interrelations with the Domestic System. In *Farris, P. L., ed.*, 1983, pp. 296–314. [G: U.S.; LDCs; MDCs]

Sorenson, Vernon L. and Rossmiller, George E. Future Options for U.S. Agricultural Trade Policy. *Amer. J. Agr. Econ.*, December 1983, *65*(5), pp. 893–900. [G: U.S.]

Soth, Lauren K. Agricultural Trade and Farm Structure. In *Brewster, D. E.; Rasmussen, W. D. and Youngberg, G., eds.*, 1983, pp. 57–65. [G: U.S.]

Soufflet, J.-F. Ajustement et adaptation sur les filières. (With English summary.) *Écon. Soc.*, May 1983, *17*(5), pp. 741–84. [G: France]

Sporleder, Thomas L.; Kramer, Carol S. and Epp, Donald J. Food Safety. In *Armbruster, W. J.; Henderson, D. R. and Knutson, Ronald D., eds.*, 1983, pp. 269–303. [G: U.S.]

Srivastava, R. K. and Livingstone, I. Growth and Distribution: The Case of Mozambique. In *Ghai, D. and Radwan, S., eds.*, 1983, pp. 249–80. [G: Mozambique]

Standen, B. J. Agricultural Policy Formation: The Differing Functions of Independent Analysts and Advisers. *Australian J. Agr. Econ.*, August 1983, *27*(2), pp. 93–103. **[G: Australia]**

Standen, B. J. and Richardson, R. A. Marketing and Trade Policy. *Australian J. Agr. Econ.*, August 1983, *27*(2), pp. 134–38. **[G: Australia]**

Stoevener, Herbert H. Financing Agricultural Research and Education in a Period of Tight Budgets: Discussion. *Southern J. Agr. Econ.*, July 1983, *15*(1), pp. 19–20. **[G: U.S.]**

Strauss, Robert. Economic Effects of Monetary Compensatory Amounts. *J. Common Market Stud.*, March 1983, *21*(3), pp. 261–81. **[G: EEC]**

Sukhatme, Vasant. Farm Prices in India and Abroad: Implications for Production. *Econ. Develop. Cult. Change,* October 1983, *32*(1), pp. 169–82. **[G: India]**

Taplin, John H. E. and Gallagher, F. D. Transport Issues. *Australian J. Agr. Econ.*, August 1983, *27*(2), pp. 139–44. **[G: Australia]**

Thieme, Günter. Agricultural Change and Its Impact in Rural Areas. **In** *Wild, T., ed.*, 1983, pp. 220–47. **[G: W. Germany]**

Thillainathan, R. Discriminatory Allocation of Public Expenditure Benefits for Reducing Inter-racial Inequality in Malaysia—An Evaluation. **In** *Lim, D., ed.*, 1983, *1980*, pp. 23–40. **[G: Malaysia]**

Thompson, Robert L. The Role of Trade in Food Security and Agricultural Development. **In** *Johnson, D. G. and Schuh, G. E., eds.*, 1983, pp. 227–57.

Thompson, Stanley R. Commentary [Advertising Farm Commodities] [Florida Department of Citrus Advertising Research Programs]. **In** *Connor, J. M. and Ward, R. W., eds.*, 1983, pp. 197–99. **[G: U.S.]**

Tikhonov, V. The Soviet Food Programs. *Prob. Econ.*, June 1983, *26*(2), pp. 3–21. **[G: U.S.S.R.]**

Timmer, C. Peter and Reich, Michael R. Japan and the U.S.: Trading Shots over Beef and Oranges. *Challenge,* Sept.–Oct. 1983, *26*(4), pp. 18–24. **[G: U.S.; Japan]**

Titus, Varkey K. India: Revenue Performance of Agricultural Taxes during the Plan Periods. *Bull. Int. Fiscal Doc.*, December 1983, *37*(12), pp. 541–45. **[G: India]**

Togan, Sübidey. The Welfare Costs of the CAP for Developing Countries under Alternative Policy Regimes: The Case of Turkey. *Europ. Rev. Agr. Econ.*, 1983, *10*(2), pp. 123–39. **[G: EEC; Turkey]**

Tosterud, Robert J. Commodity Programs: Discussion. *Amer. J. Agr. Econ.*, December 1983, *65*(5), pp. 932–34. **[G: U.S.]**

Trigo, Eduardo; Piñeiro, Martín and Sábato, Jorge F. La cuestión tecnológica y la organización de la investigación agropecuaria en América Latina. (With English summary.) *Desarrollo Econ.*, April–June 1983, *23*(89), pp. 99–119. **[G: Latin America]**

Turgeon, Lynn. A Quarter Century of Non-Soviet East European Agriculture. *ACES Bull. (See Comp. Econ. Stud. after 8/85),* Fall 1983, *25*(3), pp. 27–41. **[G: E. Europe]**

Tweeten, Luther. Economic Instability in Agriculture: The Contributions of Prices, Government Programs and Exports. *Amer. J. Agr. Econ.*, December 1983, *65*(5), pp. 922–31. **[G: U.S.]**

Uphoff, Norman; Boynton, Damon and Whyte, William Foote. Implications for Government Policy. **In** *Whyte, W. F. and Boynton, D., eds.*, 1983, pp. 310–20.

Valdés, Alberto. The Role of Trade in Food Security and Agricultural Development: Discussion. **In** *Johnson, D. G. and Schuh, G. E., eds.*, 1983, pp. 258–68.

VanSickle, John J. and Alvarado, Guillermo E. Florida Tomato Market Order Restrictions—An Analysis of Their Effects and Implementation. *Southern J. Agr. Econ.*, July 1983, *15*(1), pp. 109–14. **[G: U.S.]**

Vertrees, James G. Agricultural Policy: Discussion. *Amer. J. Agr. Econ.*, December 1983, *65*(5), pp. 910–11. **[G: U.S.]**

Vink, N. and Kassier, W. E. A Paradigm for a Micro-Level Rural Development Strategy. *S. Afr. J. Econ.*, June 1983, *51*(2), pp. 283–96. **[G: S. Africa]**

Ward, Ronald W.; Thompson, Stanley R. and Armbruster, Walter J. Advertising, Promotion and Research. **In** *Armbruster, W. J.; Henderson, D. R. and Knutson, Ronald D., eds.*, 1983, pp. 91–120. **[G: U.S.]**

Warley, T. K. The Role of Trade in Food Security and Agricultural Development: Discussion. **In** *Johnson, D. G. and Schuh, G. E., eds.*, 1983, pp. 269–75. **[G: LDCs]**

Warman, Arturo. The Future of a Crisis: Food and Agrarian Reform. **In** *Reynolds, C. W. and Tello, C., eds.*, 1983, pp. 205–24. **[G: Mexico]**

Wassermann, Ursula. UNCTAD: International Jute Agreement. *J. World Trade Law,* January–February 1983, *17*(1), pp. 65–67.

Watson, Andrew. Agriculture Looks for 'Shoes That Fit': The Production Responsibility System and Its Implications. *World Devel.*, August 1983, *11*(8), pp. 705–30. **[G: China]**

Webb, Steven B. Reply [Agricultural Protection in Wilhelminian Germany: Forging an Empire with Pork and Rye]. *J. Econ. Hist.*, June 1983, *43*(2), pp. 482. **[G: Germany]**

Wells, R. J. G. An Evaluation of Malaysian Agricultural Commodity Protection. *Singapore Econ. Rev.*, April 1983, *28*(1), pp. 59–72. **[G: Malaysia]**

Whatley, Warren C. Labor for the Picking: The New Deal in the South. *J. Econ. Hist.*, December 1983, *43*(4), pp. 905–29. **[G: U.S.]**

Whipple, Glen D. An Analysis of Reconstituted Fluid Milk Pricing Policy. *Amer. J. Agr. Econ.*, May 1983, *65*(2), pp. 207–13. **[G: U.S.]**

Wiens, Thomas B. Price Adjustment, the Responsibility System, and Agricultural Productivity. *Amer. Econ. Rev.*, May 1983, *73*(2), pp. 319–24. **[G: China]**

Wild, Trevor. Urban and Rural Change in West Germany: Conclusion. **In** *Wild, T., ed.*, 1983, pp. 248–50. **[G: W. Germany]**

Willgerodt, Hans. Die Agrarpolitik der Europäischen Gemeinschaft in der Krise. **In** *Lenel, H. O.; Willgerodt, H. and Molsberger, J.*, 1983, pp. 97–139. **[G: EEC]**

Williams, Fred E. The Market Value of Flue-Cured Tobacco Quota. *Southern J. Agr. Econ.*, July 1983, *15*(1), pp. 129–33. **[G: U.S.]**

Womack, Abner W. Agricultural Policy: Discussion. *Amer. J. Agr. Econ.*, December 1983, *65*(5), pp. 908–09. **[G: U.S.]**

Wyzan, Michael L. Empirical Analysis of Soviet Agricultural Production and Policy: Reply. *Amer. J. Agr. Econ.*, February 1983, *65*(1), pp. 178–80. **[G: U.S.S.R.]**

Zaleski, Eugène. The Collectivization Drive and Agricultural Planning in the Soviet Union. **In** *Stuart, R. C., ed.*, 1983, pp. 79–106. **[G: U.S.S.R.]**

714 Agricultural Finance

7140 Agricultural Finance

Alston, Lee J. Farm Foreclosures in the United States during the Interwar Period. *J. Econ. Hist.*, December 1983, *43*(4), pp. 885–903. **[G: U.S.]**

Argyle, D. Brian. Development Assistance, National Policies, and Lender Type and Performance. **In** *Von Pischke, J. D.; Adams, D. W. and Donald, G., eds.*, 1983, pp. 330–35. **[G: World Bank]**

Bagi, Faqir Singh. A Logit Model of Farmers' Decision about Credit. *Southern J. Agr. Econ.*, December 1983, *15*(2), pp. 13–19. **[G: U.S.]**

Baltas, N. C. Modelling Credit and Private Investment in Greek Agriculture. *Europ. Rev. Agr. Econ.*, 1983, *10*(4), pp. 389–402. **[G: Greece]**

Barry, Peter J. Financing Growth and Adjustment of Farm Firms under Risk and Inflation: Implications for Micromodeling. **In** *Baum, K. H. and Schertz, L. P., eds.*, 1983, pp. 111–34. **[G: U.S.]**

Barry, Peter J. and Lee, Warren F. Financial Stress in Agriculture: Implications for Agricultural Lenders. *Amer. J. Agr. Econ.*, December 1983, *65*(5), pp. 945–52. **[G: U.S.]**

Bathrick, David and Gomez Casco, G. Innovative Approaches to Agricultural Credit in the INVIERNO/PROCAMPO Project in Nicaragua. **In** *Von Pischke, J. D.; Adams, D. W. and Donald, G., eds.*, 1983, pp. 206–11. **[G: Nicaragua]**

Begashaw, Girma. Evaluation of a Supervised Credit Project in Jamaica. *Soc. Econ. Stud.*, March 1983, *32*(1), pp. 135–69. **[G: Jamaica]**

Binswanger, Hans P. and Sillers, Donald A. Risk Aversion and Credit Constraints in Farmers' Decision-Making: A Reinterpretation. *J. Devel. Stud.*, October 1983, *20*(1), pp. 5–21. **[G: El Salvador; India; Philippines; Thailand]**

Boehlje, Michael and Eidman, Vernon R. Financial Stress in Agriculture: Implications for Producers. *Amer. J. Agr. Econ.*, December 1983, *65*(5), pp. 937–44. **[G: U.S.]**

Bourne, Compton. Effects of Subsidized Credit on the Size Distribution of Farm Household Incomes. *Soc. Econ. Stud.*, March 1983, *32*(1), pp. 81–101. **[G: Jamaica]**

Bourne, Compton. Structure and Performance of Jamaican Rural Financial Markets. *Soc. Econ. Stud.*, March 1983, *32*(1), pp. 1–21. **[G: Jamaica]**

Bourne, Compton and Graham, Douglas H. Economic Disequilibria and Rural Financial Market Performance in Developing Economies. *Can. J. Agr. Econ.*, March 1983, *31*(1), pp. 59–76. **[G: Jamaica]**

Brake, John R. Financial Crisis in Agriculture: Discussion. *Amer. J. Agr. Econ.*, December 1983, *65*(5), pp. 953–54. **[G: U.S.]**

Collier, Paul. Malfunctioning of African Rural Factor Markets: Theory and a Kenyan Example. *Oxford Bull. Econ. Statist.*, May 1983, *45*(2), pp. 141–72. **[G: Kenya]**

David, Cristina C. Economic Policies and Agricultural Incentives. *Philippine Econ. J.*, 1983, *22*(2), pp. 154–82. **[G: Philippine]**

Desai, B. M. Group Lending in Rural Areas. **In** *Von Pischke, J. D.; Adams, D. W. and Donald, G., eds.*, 1983, pp. 284–88. **[G: Selected LDCs]**

Drabenstott, Mark. Financial Crisis in Agriculture: Discussion. *Amer. J. Agr. Econ.*, December 1983, *65*(5), pp. 955–57. **[G: U.S.]**

Frattini, Mauro. Quadro attuale del credito all'agricoltura: limiti operativi ed esigenze di adeguamento. (Current Framework of Agricultural Credit: Operational Limits and Adjustments Required. With English summary.) *Bancaria*, August 1983, *39*(8), pp. 702–09. **[G: Italy]**

Freebairn, John W. Drought Assistance Policy. *Australian J. Agr. Econ.*, December 1983, *27*(3), pp. 185–99. **[G: Australia]**

Ghatak, Subrata. On Interregional Variations in Rural Interest Rates in India. *J. Devel. Areas*, October 1983, *18*(1), pp. 21–34. **[G: India]**

Gonzalez-Vega, Claudio. Arguments for Interest Rate Reform. **In** *Von Pischke, J. D.; Adams, D. W. and Donald, G., eds.*, 1983, pp. 365–72.

Gosling, L. A. Peter. Chinese Crop Dealers in Malaysia and Thailand: The Myth of the Merciless Monopsonistic Middleman. **In** *Lim, L. Y. C. and Gosling, L. A. P., eds.*, 1983, pp. 131–70. **[G: Malaysia; Thailand]**

Graham, Douglas H. and Pollard, Stephen K. The Crop Lien Programme: Implications of a Credit Project Transformed into an Ad Hoc Income Transfer Programme. *Soc. Econ. Stud.*, March 1983, *32*(1), pp. 63–80. **[G: Jamaica]**

Halbrook, Steve A. Institutions and Implications for Micromodels: Dealing with Institutional and Legal Information in Models of the Farm Firm: Discussion. **In** *Baum, K. H. and Schertz, L. P., eds.*, 1983, pp. 146–48. **[G: U.S.]**

Harris, Duane G. Institutions and Implications for Micromodels: The Role of Financial and Legal Concepts in Micromodel Building: Discussion. **In** *Baum, K. H. and Schertz, L. P., eds.*, 1983, pp. 149–52. **[G: U.S.]**

Harriss, Barbara. Money and Commodities: Their Interaction in a Rural Indian Setting. **In** *Von Pischke, J. D.; Adams, D. W. and Donald, G., eds.*, 1983, *1982*, pp. 233–41. **[G: India]**

Heffernan, Peter J. and Pollard, Stephen K. The Determinants of Credit Use among Small Farmers in Jamaica. *Soc. Econ. Stud.*, March 1983, *32*(1), pp. 23–41. **[G: Jamaica]**

Hogan, Andrew J. Crop Credit Insurance and Technical Change in Agricultural Development: A Theoretical Analysis. *J. Risk Ins.*, March 1983, *50*(1), pp. 118–30.

Iqbal, Farrukh. The Demands for Funds by Agricultural Households: Evidence from Rural India. *J. Devel. Stud.*, October 1983, *20*(1), pp. 68–86. **[G: India]**

Irwin, George D. Institutions and Implications for Micromodels: Institutional Aspects of Firm-Level Models: Discussion. **In** *Baum, K. H. and Schertz, L. P., eds.*, 1983, pp. 153–57. **[G: U.S.]**

Ladman, Jerry R. and Tinnermeier, Ronald L. The Political Economy of Agricultural Credit: The Case of Bolivia. **In** *Von Pischke, J. D.; Adams, D. W. and Donald, G., eds.*, 1983, pp. 337–45. **[G: Bolivia]**

Lee, John E., Jr. Markets for Agricultural Inputs: Current Status and Needed Research. **In** *Farris, P. L., ed.*, 1983, pp. 78–97. **[G: U.S.]**

Lee, Warren F. The Role of Financial Intermediation in the Activities of Rural Firms and Households. **In** *Von Pischke, J. D.; Adams, D. W. and Donald, G., eds.*, 1983, pp. 104–09.

Miller, Calvin J. and Ladman, Jerry R. Factors Impeding Credit Use in Small-Farm Households in Bolivia. *J. Devel. Stud.*, July 1983, *19*(4), pp. 522–38. **[G: Bolivia]**

Mukhopadhyay, Arun Kumar. Rural Credit in India: Structure, Policy and Practice. *Econ. Aff.*, January–March 1983, *28*(1), pp. 605–13. **[G: India]**

Nyanin, Ohene Owusu. Lending Costs, Institutional Viability and Agricultural Credit Strategies in Jamaica. *Soc. Econ. Stud.*, March 1983, *32*(1), pp. 103–33. **[G: Jamaica]**

O'Hara, Maureen. Tax-Exempt Financing: Some Lessons from History. *J. Money, Credit, Banking*, November 1983, *15*(4), pp. 425–41. **[G: U.S.]**

Oludimu, Olufemi. Co-operative Financing in South-West Nigeria. *Can. J. Agr. Econ.*, March 1983, *31*(1), pp. 111–18. **[G: Nigeria]**

Pollard, Stephen K. and Grewal, Harpal S. Simulating the Impacts of Credit Policy and Fertilizer Subsidy on Central Luzon Rice Farms, the Philippines: Comment. *Amer. J. Agr. Econ.*, May 1983, *65*(2), pp. 349–50. **[G: Philippines]**

Pollard, Stephen K. and Heffernan, Peter J. Agricultural Productivity and Credit Use of Small Farmers in Jamaica. *Soc. Econ. Stud.*, March 1983, *32*(1), pp. 42–62. **[G: Jamaica]**

Ray, Edward John. Impact of General Economic Policies on the Performance of Rural Financial Markets. **In** *Von Pischke, J. D.; Adams, D. W. and Donald, G., eds.*, 1983, pp. 67–71.

Romero Chavez, J. Jesus. Centralized Rediscounting and Loan Guarantee Facilities in Mexico. **In** *Von Pischke, J. D.; Adams, D. W. and Donald, G., eds.*, 1983, pp. 162–68. **[G: Mexico]**

Rosegrant, Mark W. and Herdt, Robert W. Simulating the Impacts of Credit Policy and Fertilizer Subsidy on Central Luzon Rice Farms, the Philippines: Reply. *Amer. J. Agr. Econ.*, May 1983, *65*(2), pp. 351–52. **[G: Philippines]**

Sanint, Luis R. and Barry, Peter J. A Programming Analysis of Farmers' Credit Risks. *Amer. J. Agr. Econ.*, May 1983, *65*(2), pp. 321–25. **[G: U.S.]**

Sayad, João. The Impact of Rural Credit on Production and Income Distribution in Brazil. **In** *Von Pischke, J. D.; Adams, D. W. and Donald, G., eds.*, 1983, pp. 379–86. **[G: Brazil]**

Schaefer-Kehnert, Walter. Success with Group Lending in Malawi. **In** *Von Pischke, J. D.; Adams, D. W. and Donald, G., eds.*, 1983, *1980*, pp. 278–83. **[G: Malawi]**

Schertz, Lyle P.; Calvin, Linda and Willett, Lois Schertz. FAHM 1981: A System Dynamics Model of Financial Behavior of Farming-related Households. **In** *Baum, K. H. and Schertz, L. P., eds.*, 1983, pp. 261–78. **[G: U.S.]**

von Stockhausen, Joachim. Guarantee Funds and the Provision of Capital in the Self-help Sphere. **In** *Von Pischke, J. D.; Adams, D. W. and Donald, G., eds.*, 1983, pp. 169–73.

Sundell, Paul A. The Adjustment of Nominal Interest Rates to Inflation: A Review of Recent Literature. *Agr. Econ. Res.*, October 1983, *35*(4), pp. 15–26. **[G: U.S.]**

Tendulkar, Suresh D. Rural Institutional Credit and Rural Development: A Review Article. *Indian Econ. Rev.*, January–June 1983, *18*(1), pp. 101–37. **[G: India]**

Vogel, Robert C. Implementing Interest Rate Reform. **In** *Von Pischke, J. D.; Adams, D. W. and Donald, G., eds.*, 1983, pp. 387–92.

Von Pischke, J. D. A Penny Saved: Kenya's Cooperative Savings Scheme. **In** *Von Pischke, J. D.; Adams, D. W. and Donald, G., eds.*, 1983, pp. 302–07. **[G: Kenya]**

Von Pischke, J. D. and Adams, Dale W. Fungibility and the Design and Evaluation of Agricultural Credit Projects. **In** *Von Pischke, J. D.; Adams, D. W. and Donald, G., eds.*, 1983, *1980*, pp. 74–83. **[G: LDCs]**

Wise, James O. and Brannen, Robert L. The Relationship of Farmer Goals and Other Factors to Credit Use. *Southern J. Agr. Econ.*, December 1983, *15*(2), pp. 49–54. **[G: U.S.]**

Zuberi, Habib A. Institutional Credit and Balanced Growth: A Case Study of Pakistan. *J. Econ. Devel.*, December 1983, *8*(2), pp. 167–84. **[G: Pakistan]**

Zusman, Pinhas. Collective Choice, Pareto Optimality and the Organization of Cooperatives: The Case of Agricultural Credit Associations. *J. Econ. Behav. Organ.*, June–September 1983, *4*(2–3), pp. 185–204.

715 Agricultural Markets and Marketing

7150 Agricultural Markets and Marketing; Cooperatives

Anderson, Kym. Economic Growth, Comparative Advantage and Agricultural Trade of Pacific Rim Countries. *Rev. Marketing Agr. Econ.*, December 1983, *51*(3), pp. 231–48. **[G: OECD; LDCs]**

Armbruster, Walter J. Advertising Farm Commodities. **In** *Connor, J. M. and Ward, R. W., eds.*, 1983, pp. 165–77. **[G: U.S.]**

Armbruster, Walter J. and Jesse, Edward V. Fruit and Vegetable Marketing Orders. **In** *Armbruster, W. J.; Henderson, D. R. and Knutson, Ronald D., eds.*, 1983, pp. 121–58. **[G: U.S.]**

Aspelin, Arnold. Comments [Advertising Farm Commodities] [Florida Department of Citrus Advertising Research Programs]. **In** *Connor, J. M.*

and Ward, R. W., eds., 1983, pp. 199–200. [G: U.S.]

Babb, Emerson M., et al. Milk Marketing Orders. In *Armbruster, W. J.; Henderson, D. R. and Knutson, Ronald D., eds.*, 1983, pp. 159–97. [G: U.S.]

Bassecoulard, E., et al. Consommation et système agro-alimentaire: Quelques approches et quelques résultats. (With English summary.) *Écon. Soc.*, May 1983, *17*(5), pp. 877–909. [G: France]

Bateman, D. I.; Edwards, J. R. and LeVay, Clare. Agricultural Co-operatives and the Theory of the Firm. In *Kennedy, L., ed.*, 1983, *1979*, pp. 77–93.

Beilock, Richard and Shonkwiler, J. Scott. Modeling Weekly Truck Rates for Perishables. *Southern J. Agr. Econ.*, July 1983, *15*(1), pp. 83–87. [G: U.S.]

Belongia, Michael T. and King, Richard A. A Monetary Analysis of Food Price Determination. *Amer. J. Agr. Econ.*, February 1983, *65*(1), pp. 131–35. [G: U.S.]

Belongia, Michael T. Commodity Options: A New Risk Management Tool for Agricultural Markets. *Fed. Res. Bank St. Louis Rev.*, June/July 1983, *65*(6), pp. 5–15. [G: U.S.]

Bigman, David; Goldfarb, David and Schechtman, Edna. Futures Market Efficiency and the Time Content of the Information Sets. *J. Futures Markets*, Fall 1983, *3*(3), pp. 321–34. [G: U.S.]

Binkley, James K. Marketing Costs and Instability in the International Grain Trade. *Amer. J. Agr. Econ.*, February 1983, *65*(1), pp. 57–64.

Bouis, Howarth E. Seasonal Rice Price Variation in the Philippines: Measuring the Effects of Government Intervention. *Food Res. Inst. Stud.*, 1983, *19*(1), pp. 81–92. [G: Philippines]

Boynton, Robert D.; Blake, Brian F. and Uhl, Joseph N. Retail Price Reporting Effects in Local Food Markets. *Amer. J. Agr. Econ.*, February 1983, *65*(1), pp. 20–29. [G: U.S.]

Bredahl, Maury E. and Green, Leonard. Residual Supplier Model of Coarse Grains Trade. *Amer. J. Agr. Econ.*, November 1983, *65*(4), pp. 785–90. [G: Selected Countries]

Breimyer, Harold F. Agricultural Marketing Policy in Perspective. In *Armbruster, W. J.; Henderson, D. R. and Knutson, Ronald D., eds.*, 1983, pp. 1–20. [G: U.S.]

Browne, William P. Mobilizing and Activating Group Demands: The American Agriculture Movement. *Soc. Sci. Quart.*, March 1983, *64*(1), pp. 19–34. [G: U.S.]

Caine, Richard J. H. and Stonehouse, D. Peter. Adjusting the Seasonality of Milk Shipments in Canada: Problems, Economic Impacts and Potential Policies. *Can. J. Agr. Econ.*, November 1983, *31*(3), pp. 331–50. [G: Canada]

Caldwell, J.; Copeland, J. and Hawkins, M. Alternative Hedging Strategies for an Alberta Feedlot Operator: Reply. *Can. J. Agr. Econ.*, July 1983, *31*(2), pp. 258. [G: U.S.; Canada]

Carl, Ella; Kilmer, Richard L. and Kenny, Lawrence W. Evaluating Implicit Prices of Intermediate Products. *Amer. J. Agr. Econ.*, August 1983, *65*(3), pp. 592–95. [G: U.S.]

Carter, Colin A. and Loyns, R. M. A. Alternative Hedging Strategies for an Alberta Feedlot Operator: A Comment. *Can. J. Agr. Econ.*, July 1983, *31*(2), pp. 257. [G: U.S.; Canada]

Casavant, Kenneth L. and Binkley, James K. Transportation Changes and Agricultural Marketing Research. In *Farris, P. L., ed.*, 1983, pp. 98–116. [G: U.S.]

Chambers, Robert G. International Trade, Gross Substitutability and the Domestic Farm–Retail Price Margin. *Europ. Rev. Agr. Econ.*, 1983, *10*(1), pp. 33–53.

Chambers, Robert G. and Foster, William E. Participation in the Farmer-Owned Reserve Program: A Discrete Choice Model. *Amer. J. Agr. Econ.*, February 1983, *65*(1), pp. 120–24. [G: U.S.]

Conroy, Robert M. and Rendleman, Richard J., Jr. Pricing Commodities When Both Price and Output Are Uncertain. *J. Futures Markets*, Winter 1983, *3*(4), pp. 439–50.

Cotterill, Ronald. Retail Food Cooperatives: Testing the "Small Is Beautiful" Hypothesis. *Amer. J. Agr. Econ.*, February 1983, *65*(1), pp. 125–30. [G: U.S.]

Cuddy, Michael and Curtin, Chris. Commercialisation in West of Ireland Agriculture in the 1890s. *Econ. Soc. Rev.*, April 1983, *14*(3), pp. 173–84. [G: Ireland]

Deere, Carmen Diana. Cooperative Development and Women's Participation in the Nicaraguan Agrarian Reform. *Amer. J. Agr. Econ.*, December 1983, *65*(5), pp. 1043–48. [G: Nicaragua]

Duncan, Ronald C. and Lutz, Ernst. Penetration of Industrial Country Markets by Agricultural Products from Developing Countries. *World Devel.*, September 1983, *11*(9), pp. 771–86. [G: LDCs; MDCs]

Farris, Paul L. Agricultural Marketing Research in Perspective. In *Farris, P. L., ed.*, 1983, pp. 3–15. [G: U.S.]

French, Ben C. and Carman, Hoy F. Production Agriculture as a Force Affecting the Food System. In *Farris, P. L., ed.*, 1983, pp. 54–77. [G: U.S.]

Furtan, W. Harley; Nagy, Joseph G. and Storey, Gary G. The Impact on the Canadian Rapeseed Industry from Changes in Transport and Tariff Rates: Reply. *Amer. J. Agr. Econ.*, August 1983, *65*(3), pp. 618–19. [G: Canada]

Garbade, Kenneth D. and Silber, William L. Price Movements and Price Discovery in Futures and Cash Markets. *Rev. Econ. Statist.*, May 1983, *65*(2), pp. 289–97. [G: U.S.]

Garoyan, Leon. Developments in the Theory of Farmer Cooperatives: Discussion. *Amer. J. Agr. Econ.*, December 1983, *65*(5), pp. 1096–98.

Gerrard, Christopher D. and Roe, Terry. Government Intervention in Food Grain Markets: An Econometric Study of Tanzania. *J. Devel. Econ.*, Aug.–Oct. 1983, *13*(1–2), pp. 109–32. [G: Tanzania]

Gosling, L. A. Peter. Chinese Crop Dealers in Malaysia and Thailand: The Myth of the Merciless Monopsonistic Middleman. In *Lim, L. Y. C. and Gosling, L. A. P., eds.*, 1983, pp. 131–70. [G: Malaysia; Thailand]

Grant, Warren R., et al. Grain Price Interrelationships. *Agr. Econ. Res.*, January 1983, *35*(1), pp. 1–9. **[G: U.S.]**

Griffith, Garry R. and Meilke, Karl D. The Impact on the Canadian Rapeseed Industry from Changes in Transport and Tariff Rates: Comment. *Amer. J. Agr. Econ.*, August 1983, *65*(3), pp. 615–17. **[G: Canada]**

Hamm, Larry G. and Grinnell, Gerald. Evolving Relationships between Food Manufacturers and Retailers: Implications for Food System Organization and Performance. *Amer. J. Agr. Econ.*, December 1983, *65*(5), pp. 1065–72. **[G: U.S.]**

Harling, Kenneth F. and Thompson, Robert L. The Economic Effects of Intervention in Canadian Agriculture. *Can. J. Agr. Econ.*, July 1983, *31*(2), pp. 153–76. **[G: Canada]**

Harris, Harold M., Jr., et al. Cooperatives and Bargaining. **In** *Armbruster, W. J.; Henderson, D. R. and Knutson, Ronald D., eds.*, 1983, pp. 199–238. **[G: U.S.]**

Hathaway, Dale E. Agricultural Trade Policy for the 1980s. **In** *Cline W. R., ed.*, 1983, pp. 435–53.

Helmers, Glenn A. Risk Management in Models of the Farm: Modeling Farm Decisionmaking to Account for Risk: Discussion. **In** *Baum, K. H. and Schertz, L. P., eds.*, 1983, pp. 195–99.

Henderson, Dennis R.; Schrader, Lee F. and Rhodes, V. James. Public Price Reporting. **In** *Armbruster, W. J.; Henderson, D. R. and Knutson, Ronald D., eds.*, 1983, pp. 21–57. **[G: U.S.]**

Herlihy, P. and Cowan, C. Trade in Live Pigs between Northern Ireland and the Republic of Ireland. *Irish J. Agr. Econ. Rural Soc.*, 1983, *9*(2), pp. 173–92. **[G: Ireland; U.K.]**

Hiemstra, Stephen J. Marketing Impacts of the Domestic Food Assistance Programs. **In** *Farris, P. L., ed.*, 1983, pp. 278–95. **[G: U.S.]**

Hildebrand, Marvin D. The Canadian Wheat Board Delivery Quota System: An Economic Analysis. *Can. J. Agr. Econ.*, November 1983, *31*(3), pp. 437–48. **[G: Canada]**

Kahl, Kandice H. Determination of the Recommended Hedging Ratio. *Amer. J. Agr. Econ.*, August 1983, *65*(3), pp. 603–05.

Karp, Larry S. and McCalla, Alex F. Dynamic Games and International Trade: An Application to the World Corn Market. *Amer. J. Agr. Econ.*, November 1983, *65*(4), pp. 641–50.

Kim, V. Purchase Prices on Agricultural Products. *Prob. Econ.*, June 1983, *26*(2), pp. 22–40. **[G: U.S.S.R.]**

Knoeber, Charles R. and Baumer, David L. Understanding Retained Patronage Refunds in Agricultural Cooperatives. *Amer. J. Agr. Econ.*, February 1983, *65*(1), pp. 30–37. **[G: U.S.]**

Kolb, Robert W. and Gay, Gerald D. The Performance of Live Cattle Futures as Predictors of Subsequent Spot Prices. *J. Futures Markets*, Spring 1983, *3*(1), pp. 55–63. **[G: U.S.]**

Krueger, Anne O. Protectionism, Exchange Rate Distortions, and Agricultural Trading Patterns. *Amer. J. Agr. Econ.*, December 1983, *65*(5), pp. 864–71. **[G: Global]**

Lamm, R. McFall, Jr. Agribusiness Management and Food Marketing: Discussion. *Amer. J. Agr. Econ.*, December 1983, *65*(5), pp. 1075–77. **[G: U.S.]**

Leavitt, S.; Hawkins, M. and Veeman, M. Improvements to Market Efficiency through the Operation of the Alberta Pork Producers' Marketing Board. *Can. J. Agr. Econ.*, November 1983, *31*(3), pp. 371–88. **[G: Canada; U.S.]**

Lee, Jonq-Ying. Florida Department of Citrus Advertising Research Programs. **In** *Connor, J. M. and Ward, R. W., eds.*, 1983, pp. 179–96. **[G: U.S.]**

LeVay, Clare. Some Problems of Agricultural Marketing Co-operatives' Price/Output Determination in Imperfect Competition. *Can. J. Agr. Econ.*, March 1983, *31*(1), pp. 105–10.

Lipartito, Kenneth J. The New York Cotton Exchange and the Development of the Cotton Futures Market. *Bus. Hist. Rev.*, Spring 1983, *57*(1), pp. 50–72. **[G: U.S.]**

Lundahl, Mats. Imperfect Competition in Haitian Coffee Marketing. **In** *Lundahl, M.*, 1983, pp. 171–89. **[G: Haiti]**

Lundahl, Mats. The State of Spatial Economic Research on Haiti: A Selective Survey. **In** *Lundahl, M.*, 1983, *1980*, pp. 153–70. **[G: Haiti]**

Lundahl, Mats and Petersson, Erling. Price Series Correlation and Market Integration: Some Evidence from Haiti. **In** *Lundahl, M.*, 1983, *1983*, pp. 190–208. **[G: Haiti]**

Malassis, L. Filières et systèmes agro-alimentaires. (With English summary.) *Écon. Soc.*, May 1983, *17*(5), pp. 911–21.

McLemore, Dan L.; Whipple, Glen D. and Spielman, Kimberly. OLS and Frontier Function Estimates of Long-Run Average Cost for Tennessee Livestock Auction Markets. *Southern J. Agr. Econ.*, December 1983, *15*(2), pp. 79–83. **[G: U.S.]**

Meilke, Karl D. and Griffith, Garry R. Incorporating Policy Variables in a Model of the World Soybean/Rapeseed Market. *Amer. J. Agr. Econ.*, February 1983, *65*(1), pp. 65–73.

Mueller, Willard F. Market Power and Its Control in the Food System. *Amer. J. Agr. Econ.*, December 1983, *65*(5), pp. 855–63. **[G: U.S.]**

Naughtin, John. Lot Size and Breed Effects on Cattle Prices Revisited. *Australian J. Agr. Econ.*, December 1983, *27*(3), pp. 240–42. **[G: Australia]**

Nichols, John P.; Hill, Lowell D. and Nelson, Kenneth E. Food and Agricultural Commodity Grading. **In** *Armbruster, W. J.; Henderson, D. R. and Knutson, Ronald D., eds.*, 1983, pp. 59–90. **[G: U.S.]**

Perloff, Jeffrey M. and Rausser, Gordon C. The Effect of Asymmetrically Held Information and Market Power in Agricultural Markets. *Amer. J. Agr. Econ.*, May 1983, *65*(2), pp. 366–72.

Purcell, Wayne D. Hedging Procedures and Other Marketing Considerations. **In** *Baum, K. H. and Schertz, L. P., eds.*, 1983, pp. 181–94.

van Ravenswaay, Eileen and Wallace, L. Tim. Changing Agricultural Marketing Programs. **In** *Armbruster, W. J.; Henderson, D. R. and Knutson, Ronald D., eds.*, 1983, pp. 305–26. **[G: U.S.]**

Rhodes, V. James. The Large Agricultural Cooperative as a Competitor. *Amer. J. Agr. Econ.*, December 1983, *65*(5), pp. 1090–95.

Ricker, Harold S.; Anderson, Dale L. and Phillips, Michael J. Technology Adoption in the Agricultural Marketing System. **In** *Farris, P. L., ed.*, 1983, pp. 117–36. **[G: U.S.]**

Riley, Harold M. and Weber, Michael T. Marketing in Developing Countries. **In** *Farris, P. L., ed.*, 1983, pp. 315–31. **[G: LDCs]**

Russell, James R. and Dickey, Matthew C. Using Dual Objectives as Decision Guides to Hedge Oklahoma Feeder Cattle—An Economic Evaluation. *Southern J. Agr. Econ.*, December 1983, *15*(2), pp. 35–39. **[G: U.S.]**

Russell, James R. and Purcell, Wayne D. Costs of Operating a Computerized Trading System for Slaughter Lambs. *Southern J. Agr. Econ.*, July 1983, *15*(1), pp. 123–27. **[G: U.S.]**

Sarris, Alexander H. European Community Enlargement and World Trade in Fruits and Vegetables. *Amer. J. Agr. Econ.*, May 1983, *65*(2), pp. 235–46. **[G: EEC]**

Scherr, Bruce A. and Madsen, Howard C. Observations on the Relationship between Agricultural Commodity Prices and Real Interest Rates. *J. Futures Markets*, Spring 1983, *3*(1), pp. 47–54. **[G: U.S.]**

Schmitz, Andrew. Supply Management in Canadian Agriculture: An Assessment of the Economic Effects. *Can. J. Agr. Econ.*, July 1983, *31*(2), pp. 135–52. **[G: Canada]**

Shaffer, James D. Preference Articulation and Food System Performance. **In** *Farris, P. L., ed.*, 1983, pp. 224–45. **[G: U.S.]**

Singhal, R. C. Marketing and Manpower Planning vis-a-vis Product Development in Rural India. *Econ. Aff.*, April–June 1983, *28*(2), pp. 688–94. **[G: India]**

Smith, Louis P. Economists, Economic Theory, and Co-operatives. **In** *Kennedy, L., ed.*, 1983, pp. 95–121. **[G: Selected Countries]**

Song, Dae Hee and Hallberg, M. C. An Analytic Model of the Imperfect World Trade Market: A Case Study of World Wheat Cartels. *Can. J. Agr. Econ.*, November 1983, *31*(3), pp. 389–400. **[G: Global]**

Sonka, Steven T. Risk Management in Models of the Farm: Thoughts on Modeling Risk Management on the Farm: Discussion. **In** *Baum, K. H. and Schertz, L. P., eds.*, 1983, pp. 200–203.

Sorenson, Vernon L. and Peterson, E. Wesley F. International Marketing of Agricultural Commodities and Interrelations with the Domestic System. **In** *Farris, P. L., ed.*, 1983, pp. 296–314. **[G: U.S.; LDCs; MDCs]**

Soufflet, J.-F. Ajustement et adaptation sur les filières. (With English summary.) *Écon. Soc.*, May 1983, *17*(5), pp. 741–84. **[G: France]**

Sporleder, Thomas L. Emerging Information Technologies and Agricultural Structure. *Amer. J. Agr. Econ.*, May 1983, *65*(2), pp. 388–94. **[G: U.S.]**

Sporleder, Thomas L.; Kramer, Carol S. and Epp, Donald J. Food Safety. **In** *Armbruster, W. J.; Henderson, D. R. and Knutson, Ronald D., eds.*, 1983, pp. 269–303. **[G: U.S.]**

Staatz, John M. The Cooperative as a Coalition: A Game-Theoretic Approach. *Amer. J. Agr. Econ.*, December 1983, *65*(5), pp. 1084–89.

Standen, B. J. and Richardson, R. A. Marketing and Trade Policy. *Australian J. Agr. Econ.*, August 1983, *27*(2), pp. 134–38. **[G: Australia]**

Sukhatme, Vasant. Farm Prices in India and Abroad: Implications for Production. *Econ. Develop. Cult. Change*, October 1983, *32*(1), pp. 169–82. **[G: India]**

de Swardt, S. J. J. Agricultural Marketing Problems in the Nineteen Thirties. *S. Afr. J. Econ.*, March 1983, *51*(1), pp. 1–28. **[G: S. Africa]**

Taylor, Stephen J. Price Trends in Wool Prices when Sydney Futures Are Actively Traded. *Australian Econ. Pap.*, June 1983, *22*(40), pp. 99–105. **[G: Australia]**

Thompson, Stanley R. Commentary [Advertising Farm Commodities] [Florida Department of Citrus Advertising Research Programs]. **In** *Connor, J. M. and Ward, R. W., eds.*, 1983, pp. 197–99. **[G: U.S.]**

Tomek, William G. Alternative Pricing Mechanisms in Agriculture. **In** *Farris, P. L., ed.*, 1983, pp. 137–62. **[G: U.S.]**

Trapp, James N. Risk Management in Models of the Farm: The Need for Prescriptive Risk-Management Models: A Suggested Methodological Approach: Discussion. **In** *Baum, K. H. and Schertz, L. P., eds.*, 1983, pp. 204–09.

Treillon, R. Le sens d l'évolution technique et son enjeu. (With English summary.) *Écon. Soc.*, May 1983, *17*(5), pp. 839–76. **[G: France]**

Turner, Steven C.; Epperson, James E. and Fletcher, Stanley M. Producer Attitudes toward Multicommodity Electronic Marketing. *Amer. J. Agr. Econ.*, November 1983, *65*(4), pp. 818–22. **[G: U.S.]**

VanSickle, John J. and Alvarado, Guillermo E. Florida Tomato Market Order Restrictions—An Analysis of Their Effects and Implementation. *Southern J. Agr. Econ.*, July 1983, *15*(1), pp. 109–14. **[G: U.S.]**

VanSickle, John J. and Ladd, George W. A Model of Cooperative Finance. *Amer. J. Agr. Econ.*, May 1983, *65*(2), pp. 273–81.

Vitaliano, Peter. Cooperative Enterprise: An Alternative Conceptual Basis for Analyzing a Complex Institution. *Amer. J. Agr. Econ.*, December 1983, *65*(5), pp. 1078–83.

Ward, Ronald W.; Thompson, Stanley R. and Armbruster, Walter J. Advertising, Promotion and Research. **In** *Armbruster, W. J.; Henderson, D. R. and Knutson, Ronald D., eds.*, 1983, pp. 91–120. **[G: U.S.]**

Whipple, Glen D. An Analysis of Reconstituted Fluid Milk Pricing Policy. *Amer. J. Agr. Econ.*, May 1983, *65*(2), pp. 207–13. **[G: U.S.]**

Yengoyan, Aram A. The Buying of Futures: Chinese Merchants and the Fishing Industry in Capiz, Philippines. **In** *Lim, L. Y. C. and Gosling, L. A. P., eds.*, 1983, pp. 117–30. **[G: Philippines]**

Yon, B. Structures des filières et stratégies des firmes. (With English summary.) *Écon. Soc.*, May 1983, *17*(5), pp. 823–37. **[G: France]**

Zarfaty, Joseph. The Moshav in Israel: Possibilities for Its Application in Developing Countries. **In**

Stewart, F., ed., 1983, pp. 189–214. **[G: Israel]**

Zusman, Pinhas. Collective Choice, Pareto Optimality and the Organization of Cooperatives: The Case of Agricultural Credit Associations. *J. Econ. Behav. Organ.*, June–September 1983, *4*(2–3), pp. 185–204.

7151 Corporate Agriculture

Broussolle, C. Concurrence spatiale en univers aléatoire: le cas de l'industrie laitière et de ses marchés. *Revue Écon. Polit.*, January–February 1983, *93*(1), pp. 113–38. **[G: France]**

French, Ben C. and Carman, Hoy F. Production Agriculture as a Force Affecting the Food System. **In** *Farris, P. L., ed.*, 1983, pp. 54–77. **[G: U.S.]**

Halbrook, Steve A. Institutions and Implications for Micromodels: Dealing with Institutional and Legal Information in Models of the Farm Firm: Discussion. **In** *Baum, K. H. and Schertz, L. P., eds.*, 1983, pp. 146–48. **[G: U.S.]**

Harris, Duane G. Institutions and Implications for Micromodels: The Role of Financial and Legal Concepts in Micromodel Building: Discussion. **In** *Baum, K. H. and Schertz, L. P., eds.*, 1983, pp. 149–52. **[G: U.S.]**

Irwin, George D. Institutions and Implications for Micromodels: Institutional Aspects of Firm-Level Models: Discussion. **In** *Baum, K. H. and Schertz, L. P., eds.*, 1983, pp. 153–57. **[G: U.S.]**

Knutson, Ronald D.; Geyer, L. Leon and Helmuth, John W. Trade Practice Regulation. **In** *Armbruster, W. J.; Henderson, D. R. and Knutson, Ronald D., eds.*, 1983, pp. 239–68. **[G: U.S.]**

Koppenhaver, G. D. The Forward Pricing Efficiency of the Live Cattle Futures Market. *J. Futures Markets*, Fall 1983, *3*(3), pp. 307–19. **[G: U.S.]**

Lamm, R. McFall, Jr. Agribusiness Management and Food Marketing: Discussion. *Amer. J. Agr. Econ.*, December 1983, *65*(5), pp. 1075–77. **[G: U.S.]**

Lauret, F. Sur les études de filières agro-alimentaires. (With English summary.) *Écon. Soc.*, May 1983, *17*(5), pp. 721–40.

Leuthold, Raymond M. Commercial Use and Speculative Measures of the Livestock Commodity Futures Markets. *J. Futures Markets*, Summer 1983, *3*(2), pp. 113–35. **[G: U.S.]**

Lezina, M. Structure of the National Economic Agroindustrial Complex. *Prob. Econ.*, November 1983, *26*(7), pp. 65–84. **[G: U.S.S.R.]**

Litzenberg, Kerry K.; Gorman, William D. and Schneider, Vernon E. Academic and Professional Programs in Agribusiness. *Amer. J. Agr. Econ.*, December 1983, *65*(5), pp. 1060–64. **[G: U.S.]**

Looney, J. W. Tax and Other Legal Considerations in the Organization of the Farm Firm. **In** *Baum, K. H. and Schertz, L. P., eds.*, 1983, pp. 135–45. **[G: U.S.]**

Lundahl, Mats. Co-operative Structures in the Haitian Economy. **In** *Lundahl, M.*, 1983, pp. 211–36. **[G: Haiti]**

Mathieu, Alain. Soutien des prix et paradoxes de la politique agricole. (With English summary.) *Revue Écon. Polit.*, September–October 1983, *93*(5), pp. 772–80. **[G: France]**

Richards, J. F. and McAlpin, Michelle B. Cotton Cultivating and Land Clearing in the Bombay Deccan and Karnatak: 1818–1920. **In** *Tucker, R. P. and Richards, J. F., eds.*, 1983, pp. 68–94. **[G: India]**

Sipos, Aladár. Relations between Enterprises in the Agro-Industrial Sphere in Hungary. *Acta Oecon.*, 1983, *31*(1–2), pp. 53–69. **[G: Hungary]**

Spilka, Walter, Jr. An Overview of the USDA Crop and Livestock Information System. *J. Futures Markets*, Summer 1983, *3*(2), pp. 167–76. **[G: U.S.]**

Stone, Kenneth E. Agribusiness Management and Food Marketing: Discussion. *Amer. J. Agr. Econ.*, December 1983, *65*(5), pp. 1073–74. **[G: U.S.]**

Torgerson, Randall E. Alternative Ownership and Control Mechanisms within the Food System. **In** *Farris, P. L., ed.*, 1983, pp. 184–223. **[G: U.S.]**

716 Farm Management

7160 Farm Management; Allocative Efficiency

Aguilar, A. M., et al. Consequences of Small Rice Farm Mechanization in the Philippines: A Summary of Preliminary Analyses. **In** *Internat'l Rice Res. Inst. and Agric. Devel. Council*, 1983, pp. 151–64. **[G: Philippines]**

Ahammed, Chowdhury S. and Herdt, Robert W. Farm Mechanization in a Semiclosed Input–Output Model: The Philippines. *Amer. J. Agr. Econ.*, August 1983, *65*(3), pp. 516–25. **[G: Philippines]**

Ahmed, J. U. Labor Use Patterns and Mechanization of Rice Postharvest Processing in Bangladesh. **In** *Internat'l Rice Res. Inst. and Agric. Devel. Council*, 1983, pp. 139–49. **[G: Bangladesh]**

Akder, Halis. Türkiye'de Hayvancilik Sorunlarina Ekonomik Açidan Bakiş *METU*, 1983, *10*(1), pp. 97–106. **[G: Turkey]**

Albisu, Luis M. and Blandford, David. An Area Response Model for Perennial Plants and Its Application to Spanish Oranges and Mandarins. *Europ. Rev. Agr. Econ.*, 1983, *10*(2), pp. 175–84. **[G: Spain]**

Alston, Lee J. Farm Foreclosures in the United States during the Interwar Period. *J. Econ. Hist.*, December 1983, *43*(4), pp. 885–903. **[G: U.S.]**

Antle, John M. Incorporating Risk in Production Analysis. *Amer. J. Agr. Econ.*, December 1983, *65*(5), pp. 1099–1106.

Antle, John M. Sequential Decision Making in Production Models. *Amer. J. Agr. Econ.*, May 1983, *65*(2), pp. 282–90.

Antle, John M. and Aitah, Ali S. Rice Technology, Farmer Rationality, and Agricultural Policy in Egypt. *Amer. J. Agr. Econ.*, November 1983, *65*(4), pp. 667–74. **[G: Egypt]**

Attwood, E. A. Financing and Investment in Irish Agriculture. *Irish Banking Rev.*, December 1983, pp. 13–26. **[G: Ireland]**

Bagi, Faqir Singh and Huang, Cliff J. Estimating Production Technical Efficiency for Individual Farms in Tennessee. *Can. J. Agr. Econ.*, July 1983, *31*(2), pp. 249–56. **[G: U.S.]**

Barnum, Howard N. and Squire, Lyn. Technology and Relative Economic Efficiency. **In** *Lim, D., ed.*, 1983, *1978*, pp. 53–64. **[G: Malaysia]**

Baron, Donald. The Status of Farmland Leasing in the United States. **In** *DeBraal, J. P. and Wunderlich, G., eds.,* 1983, pp. 73–91. **[G: U.S.]**

Barry, Peter J. Financing Growth and Adjustment of Farm Firms under Risk and Inflation: Implications for Micromodeling. **In** *Baum, K. H. and Schertz, L. P., eds.,* 1983, pp. 111–34. **[G: U.S.]**

Baum, Kenneth H. Farm Decisions, Adaptive Economics, and Complex Behavior in Agriculture: Some Thoughts on Adaptive Economic Policy and the Behavioral Science of Modeling the Farm Firm/Household: Discussion. **In** *Baum, K. H. and Schertz, L. P., eds.,* 1983, pp. 50–55.

Baum, Kenneth H. and Richardson, James W. FLIPCOM: Farm-Level Continuous Optimization Models for Integrated Policy Analysis. **In** *Baum, K. H. and Schertz, L. P., eds.,* 1983, pp. 211–34. **[G: U.S.]**

Begashaw, Girma. Evaluation of a Supervised Credit Project in Jamaica. *Soc. Econ. Stud.,* March 1983, *32*(1), pp. 135–69. **[G: Jamaica]**

Berry, Wendell. Solving for Pattern: Standards for a Durable Agriculture. **In** *Brewster, D. E.; Rasmussen, W. D. and Youngberg, G., eds.,* 1983, *1981,* pp. 37–45.

Binswanger, Hans P. and Sillers, Donald A. Risk Aversion and Credit Constraints in Farmers' Decision-Making: A Reinterpretation. *J. Devel. Stud.,* October 1983, *20*(1), pp. 5–21. **[G: El Salvador; India; Philippines; Thailand]**

Boehlje, Michael and Eidman, Vernon R. Financial Stress in Agriculture: Implications for Producers. *Amer. J. Agr. Econ.,* December 1983, *65*(5), pp. 937–44. **[G: U.S.]**

Bogue, Allan G. Changes in Mechanical and Plant Technology: The Corn Belt, 1910–1940. *J. Econ. Hist.,* March 1983, *43*(1), pp. 1–25. **[G: U.S.]**

Bose, Pinaki Sankar. Determination of Rent under Share Tenancy—An Analytical Exercise. *Indian Econ. Rev.,* January–June 1983, *18*(1), pp. 35–45.

Boynton, Damon. Implications for Plant and Animal Research. **In** *Whyte, W. F. and Boynton, D., eds.,* 1983, pp. 251–63.

Bradford, Garnett L. Optimizing Models: Some Observations and Opinions on the State of Progress: Discussion. **In** *Baum, K. H. and Schertz, L. P., eds.,* 1983, pp. 358–63.

Brandt, Jon A. and French, Ben C. Mechanical Harvesting and the California Tomato Industry: A Simulation Analysis. *Amer. J. Agr. Econ.,* May 1983, *65*(2), pp. 265–72. **[G: U.S.]**

Brorsen, B. Wade, et al. A Stocker Cattle Growth Simulation Model. *Southern J. Agr. Econ.,* July 1983, *15*(1), pp. 115–22. **[G: U.S.]**

Burrows, Thomas M. Pesticide Demand and Integrated Pest Management: A Limited Dependent Variable Analysis. *Amer. J. Agr. Econ.,* November 1983, *65*(4), pp. 806–10. **[G: U.S.]**

Buttel, Frederick H. Farm Structure and Rural Development. **In** *Brewster, D. E.; Rasmussen, W. D. and Youngberg, G., eds.,* 1983, pp. 103–24. **[G: U.S.]**

Caballero, Jose Maria. Casual Labor in Peruvian Agrarian Co-operatives. **In** *Stewart, F., ed.,* 1983, pp. 168–88. **[G: Peru]**

Cahillane, G. and Lucey, D. I. F. An Interim Examination of the Consequences of the Farm Modernisation Scheme on the Distribution of Incomes among Dairy Farms in Cork County. *Irish J. Agr. Econ. Rural Soc.,* 1983, *9*(2), pp. 121–32. **[G: Ireland]**

Caine, Richard J. H. and Stonehouse, D. Peter. Adjusting the Seasonality of Milk Shipments in Canada: Problems, Economic Impacts and Potential Policies. *Can. J. Agr. Econ.,* November 1983, *31*(3), pp. 331–50. **[G: Canada]**

Caldwell, J.; Copeland, J. and Hawkins, M. Alternative Hedging Strategies for an Alberta Feedlot Operator: Reply. *Can. J. Agr. Econ.,* July 1983, *31*(2), pp. 258. **[G: U.S.; Canada]**

Campbell, Joseph. Tools and Machines. **In** *Whyte, W. F. and Boynton, D., eds.,* 1983, pp. 111–21.

Carter, Colin A. and Loyns, R. M. A. Alternative Hedging Strategies for an Alberta Feedlot Operator: A Comment. *Can. J. Agr. Econ.,* July 1983, *31*(2), pp. 257. **[G: U.S.; Canada]**

Chambers, Robert G. Impact of Federal Fiscal–Monetary Policy on Farm Structure: Discussion. *Southern J. Agr. Econ.,* July 1983, *15*(1), pp. 69–71. **[G: U.S.]**

Chambers, Robert G. Risk in Agricultural Production: Discussion. *Amer. J. Agr. Econ.,* December 1983, *65*(5), pp. 1114–15.

Chandler, Clark. The Effects of the Private Sector on the Labor Behavior of Soviet Collective Farmers. **In** *Stuart, R. C., ed.,* 1983, pp. 224–37. **[G: U.S.S.R.]**

Chen, Yun. An Investigation of Rural Qingpu [County]. **In** *Ch'en, Y.,* 1983, *1961,* pp. 155–73. **[G: China]**

Clayton, Elizabeth. Factor Endowment, Variable Proportions, and Agricultural Modernization: Regional Production Functions for Soviet Agriculture. **In** *Stuart, R. C., ed.,* 1983, pp. 161–72. **[G: U.S.S.R.]**

Condra, Gary D. and Richardson, James W. Farm Size Evaluation in the El Paso Valley: Reply. *Amer. J. Agr. Econ.,* May 1983, *65*(2), pp. 344–48. **[G: U.S.]**

Coughenour, C. Milton and Christenson, James A. Farm Structure, Social Class, and Farmers' Policy Perspectives. **In** *Brewster, D. E.; Rasmussen, W. D. and Youngberg, G., eds.,* 1983, pp. 67–86. **[G: U.S.]**

Crist, Raymond E. Land for the People—A Vital Need Everywhere: In Latin America and the Caribbean, It's Now 'a Prey to Hastening Ills,' and Decay. *Amer. J. Econ. Soc.,* July 1983, *42*(3), pp. 275–90. **[G: Latin America; Caribbean]**

Datta, Samar K. Sharecropping as "Second-Best" Form of Tenancy in Traditional Agriculture. *Indian Econ. J.,* April-June 1983, *30*(4), pp. 71–90.

Day, Richard H. Farm Decisions, Adaptive Economics, and Complex Behavior in Agriculture. **In** *Baum, K. H. and Schertz, L. P., eds.,* 1983, pp. 18–49.

Dobbins, Craig L. and Mapp, Harry P., Jr. A Recursive Goal Programming Model of Intergenerational Transfers by Farm Firms. **In** *Baum, K. H. and Schertz, L. P., eds.,* 1983, pp. 310–31. **[G: U.S.]**

Doering, Otto C., III. Specification and Use of Farm Growth and Planning Models in Policy Extension Activities. **In** *Baum, K. H. and Schertz, L. P., eds.,* 1983, pp. 375–84. **[G: U.S.]**

Dumsday, R. G. Agricultural Resource Management. *Australian J. Agr. Econ.,* August 1983, *27*(2), pp. 157–63. **[G: Australia]**

Duncan, Marvin. Macro–Micro Relationships: Modeling and Evaluating Policy and Institutional Impacts on Farm Firms: Discussion. **In** *Baum, K. H. and Schertz, L. P., eds.,* 1983, pp. 96–99. **[G: U.S.]**

Eddleman, B. R. Micromodeling in Perspective. **In** *Baum, K. H. and Schertz, L. P., eds.,* 1983, pp. 399–402.

Eidman, Vernon R. Cash Flow, Price Risk, and Production Uncertainty Considerations. **In** *Baum, K. H. and Schertz, L. P., eds.,* 1983, pp. 159–80.

Farrell, Kenneth R. Implications of National Agricultural Policies in Modeling Behavior of Farm Firms. **In** *Baum, K. H. and Schertz, L. P., eds.,* 1983, pp. 101–09. **[G: U.S.]**

Farrell, Kenneth R. and Runge, Carlisle Ford. Institutional Innovation and Technical Change in American Agriculture: The Role of the New Deal. *Amer. J. Agr. Econ.,* December 1983, *65*(5), pp. 1168–73. **[G: U.S.]**

Feinerman, Eli and Yaron, D. The Value of Information on the Response Function of Crops to Soil Salinity. *J. Environ. Econ. Manage.,* March 1983, *10*(1), pp. 72–85. **[G: Israel]**

French, Ben C. and Carman, Hoy F. Production Agriculture as a Force Affecting the Food System. **In** *Farris, P. L., ed.,* 1983, pp. 54–77. **[G: U.S.]**

Garcia, Philip; Sonka, Steven T. and Mazzacco, Michael A. A Multivariate Logit Analysis of Farmers' Use of Financial Information. *Amer. J. Agr. Econ.,* February 1983, *65*(1), pp. 136–41. **[G: U.S.]**

Gargett, D. Industry versus On-Farm Rates of Change: Australian Dairy Farming during the 1970's. *Rev. Marketing Agr. Econ.,* April 1983, *51*(1), pp. 71–84. **[G: Australia]**

Garoyan, Leon. Developments in the Theory of Farmer Cooperatives: Discussion. *Amer. J. Agr. Econ.,* December 1983, *65*(5), pp. 1096–98.

Gill, Gerard J. Merchanised Land Preparation, Productivity and Employment in Bangladesh. *J. Devel. Stud.,* April 1983, *19*(3), pp. 329–48. **[G: Bangladesh]**

Gönczi, Iván. Division of Labour and Work Organization in the Hungarian Large-Scale Agricultural Production. *Acta Oecon.,* 1983, *31*(1–2), pp. 71–86. **[G: Hungary]**

Gowda, M. V. Srinivasa. Monetary and Fiscal Policies for Expansion of Employment in Agriculture. *Econ. Aff.,* April–June 1983, *28*(2), pp. 701–05, 714. **[G: India]**

Grisley, William and Kellogg, Earl D. Farmers' Subjective Probabilities in Northern Thailand: An Elicitation Analysis. *Amer. J. Agr. Econ.,* February 1983, *65*(1), pp. 74–82. **[G: Thailand]**

Guither, Harold D. Citizen and Consumer Groups in Policies Affecting Farm Structure. **In** *Brewster, D. E.; Rasmussen, W. D. and Youngberg, G., eds.,* 1983, pp. 87-101. **[G: U.S.]**

Haaland, Gunnar. Dualistic Development: Issues for Aid Policy. **In** *Parkinson, J. R., ed.,* 1983, pp. 63–78. **[G: Portugal; Mozambique; Botswana]**

Hafsah, J. and Bernsten, R. H. Economic, Technical, and Social Aspects of Tractor Operation and Use in South Sulawesi, Indonesia. **In** *Internat'l Rice Res. Inst. and Agric. Devel. Council,* 1983, pp. 85–94. **[G: Indonesia]**

Halbrook, Steve A. Institutions and Implications for Micromodels: Dealing with Institutional and Legal Information in Models of the Farm Firm: Discussion. **In** *Baum, K. H. and Schertz, L. P., eds.,* 1983, pp. 146–48. **[G: U.S.]**

Hanson, Gregory D. and Eidman, Vernon R. Farm Size Evaluation in the El Paso Valley: Comment. *Amer. J. Agr. Econ.,* May 1983, *65*(2), pp. 340–43. **[G: U.S.]**

Hardy, William E., Jr.; Clark, Joy M. and White, Morris. Planning Solar Heating for Poultry—A Linear Programming Approach. *Southern J. Agr. Econ.,* December 1983, *15*(2), pp. 7–11. **[G: U.S.]**

Harrington, David H. Costs and Returns: Economic and Accounting Concepts. *Agr. Econ. Res.,* October 1983, *35*(4), pp. 1–8.

Harris, Duane G. Institutions and Implications for Micromodels: The Role of Financial and Legal Concepts in Micromodel Building: Discussion. **In** *Baum, K. H. and Schertz, L. P., eds.,* 1983, pp. 149–52. **[G: U.S.]**

Helmers, Glenn A. Risk Management in Models of the Farm: Modeling Farm Decisionmaking to Account for Risk: Discussion. **In** *Baum, K. H. and Schertz, L. P., eds.,* 1983, pp. 195–99.

Hildreth, R. J. The Use of Micromodels. **In** *Baum, K. H. and Schertz, L. P., eds.,* 1983, pp. 403–08.

Hoffman, George and Gustafson, Cole. A New Approach to Estimating Agricultural Costs of Production. *Agr. Econ. Res.,* October 1983, *35*(4), pp. 9–14. **[G: U.S.]**

Holt, John. Risk in Agricultural Production: Discussion. *Amer. J. Agr. Econ.,* December 1983, *65*(5), pp. 1116–17.

Hottel, J. Bruce and Gardner, Bruce L. The Rate of Return to Investment in Agriculture and Measuring Net Farm Income. *Amer. J. Agr. Econ.,* August 1983, *65*(3), pp. 553–57. **[G: U.S.]**

House, Robert. Optimizing Models: A Comparison of Optimizing Modeling Methodologies: Discussion. **In** *Baum, K. H. and Schertz, L. P., eds.,* 1983, pp. 351–57.

Hurt, Verner G. Optimizing Farm Models: Some Concerns: Discussion. **In** *Baum, K. H. and Schertz, L. P., eds.,* 1983, pp. 364–66.

Irwin, George D. Institutions and Implications for Micromodels: Institutional Aspects of Firm-Level Models: Discussion. **In** *Baum, K. H. and Schertz, L. P., eds.,* 1983, pp. 153–57. **[G: U.S.]**

Jabbar, M. A.; Bhuiyan, M. S. R. and Bari, A. K. M. Causes and Consequences of Power Tiller Utilization in Two Areas of Bangladesh. **In** *Internat'l Rice Res. Inst. and Agric. Devel. Council,* 1983, pp. 71–83. **[G: Bangladesh]**

Jacobs, Everett M. Soviet Agricultural Management and Planning and the 1982 Administrative Reforms. **In** *Stuart, R. C., ed.,* 1983, pp. 273–95. **[G: U.S.S.R.]**

Johnson, D. Gale. Agricultural Organization and Management. **In** *Bergson, A. and Levine, H. S., eds.,* 1983, pp. 112–42. **[G: U.S.S.R.]**

Jolly, Robert W. Risk Management in Agricultural Production. *Amer. J. Agr. Econ.,* December 1983, *65*(5), pp. 1107–13.

Jones, Paul H. *Lamtoro* and the Amarasi Model from Timor. *Bull. Indonesian Econ. Stud.,* December 1983, *19*(3), pp. 106–12. **[G: Indonesia]**

Juarez, F. and Pathnopas, R. Comparative Analysis of Thresher Adoption and Use in Thailand and the Philippines. **In** *Internat'l Rice Res. Inst. and Agric. Devel. Council,* 1983, pp. 119–37. **[G: Thailand; Philippines]**

Just, Richard E. and Zilberman, David. Stochastic Structure, Farm Size and Technology Adoption in Developing Agriculture. *Oxford Econ. Pap.,* July 1983, *35*(2), pp. 307–28.

Just, Richard E.; Zilberman, David and Hochman, Eithan. Estimation of Multicrop Production Functions. *Amer. J. Agr. Econ.,* November 1983, *65*(4), pp. 770–80. **[G: Israel]**

Kanamori, Hisao. Economic Growth and Interindustry Labour Mobility in Japan. **In** *Weisbrod, B. and Hughes, H., eds.,* 1983, pp. 31–47. **[G: Japan]**

King, Robert P. and Oamek, George E. Generalized Risk-Efficient Monte Carlo Programming: A Technique for Farm Planning under Uncertainty. **In** *Baum, K. H. and Schertz, L. P., eds.,* 1983, pp. 332–50. **[G: U.S.]**

King, Robert P. and Oamek, George E. Risk Management by Colorado Dryland Wheat Farmers and the Elimination of the Disaster Assistance Program. *Amer. J. Agr. Econ.,* May 1983, *65*(2), pp. 247–55. **[G: U.S.]**

Kinsey, B. H. and Ahmed, Iftikhar. Mechanical Innovations on Small African Farms: Problems of Development and Diffusion. *Int. Lab. Rev.,* March–April 1983, *122*(2), pp. 227–38. **[G: Africa]**

Kliebenstein, James B. and McCamley, Francis P. Energy-Related Input Demand by Crop Producers. *Southern J. Agr. Econ.,* December 1983, *15*(2), pp. 63–69. **[G: U.S.]**

Kloppenburg, Jack R., Jr. Group Development in Botswana: The Principles of Collective Farmer Action. **In** *Dalton, G., ed.,* 1983, pp. 311–33. **[G: Botswana]**

Kontos, A. and Young, Trevor. An Analysis of Technical Efficiency on a Sample of Greek Farms. *Europ. Rev. Agr. Econ.,* 1983, *10*(3), pp. 271–80. **[G: Greece]**

Kumar, Raj. Labour Absorption and Technology Choice in Agriculture. *Econ. Aff.,* July-September 1983, *28*(3), pp. 736–41. **[G: India]**

Laird, Roy D. and Laird, Betty A. The Soviet Farm Manager as an Entrepreneur. **In** *Guroff, G. and Carstensen, F. V., eds.,* 1983, pp. 258–83. **[G: U.S.S.R.]**

Lazarus, William F. and Swanson, Earl R. Insecticide Use and Crop Rotation under Risk: Rootworm Control in Corn. *Amer. J. Agr. Econ.,* November 1983, *65*(4), pp. 738–47. **[G: U.S.]**

Lee, John E., Jr. A Perspective on the Evolution and Status of Micromodeling in Agricultural Economics. **In** *Baum, K. H. and Schertz, L. P., eds.,* 1983, pp. 1–9. **[G: U.S.]**

Lee, John E., Jr. Markets for Agricultural Inputs: Current Status and Needed Research. **In** *Farris, P. L., ed.,* 1983, pp. 78–97. **[G: U.S.]**

Lee, John E., Jr. Some Consequences of the New Reality in U.S. Agriculture. **In** *Brewster, D. E.; Rasmussen, W. D. and Youngberg, G., eds.,* 1983, pp. 3–22. **[G: U.S.]**

Lee, Linda K. and Stewart, William H. Landownership and the Adoption of Minimum Tillage. *Amer. J. Agr. Econ.,* May 1983, *65*(2), pp. 256–64. **[G: U.S.]**

Lee, Warren F. The Role of Financial Intermediation in the Activities of Rural Firms and Households. **In** *Von Pischke, J. D.; Adams, D. W. and Donald, G., eds.,* 1983, pp. 104–09.

Liapis, Peter S. and Moffitt, L. Joe. Economic Analysis of Cotton Integrated Pest Management Strategies. *Southern J. Agr. Econ.,* July 1983, *15*(1), pp. 97–102. **[G: U.S.]**

Lingard, John and Bagyo, Al Sri. The Impact of Agricultural Mechanisation of Production and Employment in Rice Areas of West Java. *Bull. Indonesian Econ. Stud.,* April 1983, *19*(1), pp. 53–67. **[G: Indonesia]**

Lockwood, B., et al. Farm Mechanization in Pakistan: Policy and Practice. **In** *Internat'l Rice Res. Inst. and Agric. Devel. Council,* 1983, pp. 15–30. **[G: Pakistan]**

Looney, J. W. Tax and Other Legal Considerations in the Organization of the Farm Firm. **In** *Baum, K. H. and Schertz, L. P., eds.,* 1983, pp. 135–45. **[G: U.S.]**

Lundahl, Mats. Obstacles to Technological Change in Haitian Peasant Agriculture. **In** *Lundahl, M.,* 1983, *1977,* pp. 237–50. **[G: Haiti]**

Maamum, Y., et al. Consequences of Small Rice Farm Mechanization in South Sulawesi: A Summary of Preliminary Analyses. **In** *Internat'l Rice Res. Inst. and Agric. Devel. Council,* 1983, pp. 177–84. **[G: Indonesia]**

Manos, B. and Papanagiotou, E. Fruit-Tree Replacement in Discrete Time: An Application in Central Macedonia. *Europ. Rev. Agr. Econ.,* 1983, *10*(1), pp. 69–78. **[G: Greece]**

Marsh, Lawrence C.; Jameson, Kenneth P. and Phillips, Joseph M. Production Conditions in Guatemala's Key Agriculture Product: Corn. *Land Econ.,* February 1983, *59*(1), pp. 94–106. **[G: Guatemala]**

Massoli, Bruno. Indagini strutturali sulle aziende agricole: il volume del lavoro agricolo in Italia. (Surveys on the Structure of Agricultural Farms. With English summary.) *Rivista Int. Sci. Econ. Com.,* January 1983, *30*(1), pp. 57–72. **[G: Italy]**

Mathieu, Alain. Soutien des prix et paradoxes de la politique agricole. (With English summary.) *Revue Écon. Polit.,* September–October 1983, *93*(5), pp. 772–80. **[G: France]**

McCarl, Bruce A. and Blake, Brian F. Goal Programming via Multidimensional Scaling Applied to Senegalese Subsistence Farming: Reply. *Amer. J. Agr. Econ.,* November 1983, *65*(4), pp. 832–33.

McDowell, Robert and Hildebrand, Peter. Farming Systems, Including Animals. **In** *Whyte, W. F. and Boynton, D., eds.,* 1983, pp. 90–110.

McGrann, James M. Microcomputer Software Development and Distribution. *Southern J. Agr. Econ.*, July 1983, *15*(1), pp. 21–25. **[G: U.S.]**

Meier, Kenneth J. and Browne, William P. Interest Groups and Farm Structure. **In** *Brewster, D. E.; Rasmussen, W. D. and Youngberg, G., eds.*, 1983, pp. 47–56. **[G: U.S.]**

Metzner, Joachim. Innovations in Agriculture Incorporating Traditional Production Methods: The Case of Amarasi (Timor). *Bull. Indonesian Econ. Stud.*, December 1983, *19*(3), pp. 94–105. **[G: Indonesia]**

Miller, Thomas A. Macro–Micro Relationships: Understanding and Human Capital as Outputs of the Modeling Process: Discussion. **In** *Baum, K. H. and Schertz, L. P., eds.*, 1983, pp. 91–95.

Miranowski, John A. Simulation Models: Micromodeling: A Systems Approach at the National Level: Discussion. **In** *Baum, K. H. and Schertz, L. P., eds.*, 1983, pp. 286–88. **[G: U.S.]**

Mitchell, Donald O. and Black, J. Roy. Incorporating Aggregate Forecasts into Farm Firm Decision Models. **In** *Baum, K. H. and Schertz, L. P., eds.*, 1983, pp. 73–87. **[G: U.S.]**

Murrell, Peter. The Economics of Sharing: A Transactions Cost Analysis of Contractual Choice in Farming. *Bell J. Econ. (See Rand J. Econ. after 4/85)*, Spring 1983, *14*(1), pp. 283–93.

Musser, Wesley N.; Martin, Neil R., Jr. and Reid, Donald W. A Polyperiodic Firm Model of Swine Enterprises. **In** *Baum, K. H. and Schertz, L. P., eds.*, 1983, pp. 289–309. **[G: U.S.]**

Nelson, Ted R. Specification and Use of Farm Growth and Planning Models in Farm Management Extension Activities. **In** *Baum, K. H. and Schertz, L. P., eds.*, 1983, pp. 367–74. **[G: U.S.]**

Palanisami, K. and Subramanian, S. R. Determinants of Farm Water Supply in the Lower Bhavani Project, Coimbatore, South India. *Water Resources Res.*, December 1983, *19*(6), pp. 1403–09. **[G: India]**

Pang, Chung Min and De Boer, A. John. Management Decentralization on China's State Farms. *Amer. J. Agr. Econ.*, November 1983, *65*(4), pp. 657–66. **[G: China]**

Pant, Chandrashekar. Tenancy and Family Resources: A Model and Some Empirical Analysis. *J. Devel. Econ.*, February/April 1983, *12*(1/2), pp. 27–39. **[G: India]**

Patrick, George F.; Blake, Brian F. and Whitaker, Suzanne H. Farmers' Goals: Uni- or Multi-Dimensional? *Amer. J. Agr. Econ.*, May 1983, *65*(2), pp. 315–20. **[G: U.S.]**

Perkins, Gerald. Use of Farm Models in Extension Activities: Computer Software Needs in Farm Management Extension Activities: Discussion. **In** *Baum, K. H. and Schertz, L. P., eds.*, 1983, pp. 389–92. **[G: U.S.; LDCs]**

Perloff, Jeffrey M. and Rausser, Gordon C. The Effect of Asymmetrically Held Information and Market Power in Agricultural Markets. *Amer. J. Agr. Econ.*, May 1983, *65*(2), pp. 366–72.

Pitt, Mark M. Farm-Level Fertilizer Demand in Java: A Meta-Production Function Approach. *Amer. J. Agr. Econ.*, August 1983, *65*(3), pp. 502–08. **[G: Indonesia]**

Pollard, Stephen K. and Grewal, Harpal S. Simulating the Impacts of Credit Policy and Fertilizer Subsidy on Central Luzon Rice Farms, the Philippines: Comment. *Amer. J. Agr. Econ.*, May 1983, *65*(2), pp. 349–50. **[G: Philippines]**

Pope, Rulon; Chavas, Jean-Paul and Just, Richard E. Economic Welfare Evaluations for Producers under Uncertainty. *Amer. J. Agr. Econ.*, February 1983, *65*(1), pp. 98–107.

Purcell, Wayne D. Hedging Procedures and Other Marketing Considerations. **In** *Baum, K. H. and Schertz, L. P., eds.*, 1983, pp. 181–94.

Putterman, Louis. A Modified Collective Agriculture in Rural Growth-with-Equity: Reconsidering the Private, Unimodal Solution. *World Devel.*, February 1983, *11*(2), pp. 77–100. **[G: China; Tanzania]**

Quan, Daniel C. and Kerr, William A. Truncated Estimates for Incomplete Technical Change in the Canadian Cattle Industry. *Amer. J. Agr. Econ.*, August 1983, *65*(3), pp. 581–86. **[G: Canada]**

Redclift, Michael. Production Programs for Small Farmers: Plan Puebla as Myth and Reality. *Econ. Develop. Cult. Change*, April 1983, *31*(3), pp. 551–70. **[G: Mexico]**

Regev, Uri; Shalit, Haim and Gutierrez, A. P. On the Optimal Allocation of Pesticides with Increasing Resistance: The Case of Alfalfa Weevil. *J. Environ. Econ. Manage.*, March 1983, *10*(1), pp. 86–100.

Reichelderfer, Katherine H. Simulation Models: Positive Farm Models: A Comment on Aesthetic versus Functional Value: Discussion. **In** *Baum, K. H. and Schertz, L. P., eds.*, 1983, pp. 281–85. **[G: U.S.]**

Reid, Donald W. and Bradford, Garnett L. On Optimal Replacement of Farm Tractors. *Amer. J. Agr. Econ.*, May 1983, *65*(2), pp. 326–31. **[G: U.S.]**

Rhodes, V. James. The Large Agricultural Cooperative as a Competitor. *Amer. J. Agr. Econ.*, December 1983, *65*(5), pp. 1090–95.

Richardson, James W. Complementarities between Micro- and Macro-Simulation Models: Comment. **In** *Baum, K. H. and Schertz, L. P., eds.*, 1983, pp. 88–90.

Richardson, James W.; Lemieux, Catharine M. and Nixon, Clair J. Entry into Farming: The Effects of Leasing and Leverage on Firm Survival. *Southern J. Agr. Econ.*, December 1983, *15*(2), pp. 139–45. **[G: U.S.]**

van Riemsdijk, J. F. Dutch Agriculture Edging in the Eighties. *Europ. Rev. Agr. Econ.*, 1983, *10*(1), pp. 55–68. **[G: Netherlands]**

Robinson, B. H. Use of Farm Models in Extension Activities: An Old Concept with New Techniques: Discussion. **In** *Baum, K. H. and Schertz, L. P., eds.*, 1983, pp. 393–97. **[G: U.S.]**

Romero, Carlos and Rehman, Tahir. Goal Programming via Multidimensional Scaling Applied to Senegalese Subsistence Farming: Comment. *Amer. J. Agr. Econ.*, November 1983, *65*(4), pp. 829–31.

Rosegrant, Mark W. and Herdt, Robert W. Simulating the Impacts of Credit Policy and Fertilizer Subsidy on Central Luzon Rice Farms, the Philippines: Reply. *Amer. J. Agr. Econ.*, May 1983,

65(2), pp. 351–52. [G: Philippines]

Roumasset, James and Thapa, Ganesh. Explaining Tractorization in Nepal: An Alternative to the 'Consequences Approach' *J. Devel. Econ.*, June 1983, *12*(3), pp. 377–95. [G: Nepal]

Saefudin, Y., et al. Consequences of Small Rice Farm Mechanization in West Java: A Summary of Preliminary Analyses. **In** *Internat'l Rice Res. Inst. and Agric. Devel. Council,* 1983, pp. 165–75. [G: Indonesia]

Sain, K. Economics of Agricultural Machinery. *Econ. Aff.*, July-September 1983, *28*(3), pp. 748–59. [G: India]

Schaller, Neill. A Perspective on the Evolution and Status of Micromodeling in Agricultural Economics: Current Perspectives of a Former ERS Model Builder: Discussion. **In** *Baum, K. H. and Schertz, L. P., eds.*, 1983, pp. 15–17. [G: U.S.]

Schertz, Lyle P.; Calvin, Linda and Willett, Lois Schertz. FAHM 1981: A System Dynamics Model of Financial Behavior of Farming-related Households. **In** *Baum, K. H. and Schertz, L. P., eds.*, 1983, pp. 261–78. [G: U.S.]

Schoney, Richard A. and McGuckin, J. Thomas. Economics of the Wet Fractionation System in Alfalfa Harvesting. *Amer. J. Agr. Econ.*, February 1983, *65*(1), pp. 38–44. [G: U.S.]

Scott, John T., Jr. How to Determine the Cost of Land by Observing Rents. **In** *DeBraal, J. P. and Wunderlich, G., eds.*, 1983, pp. 93–115. [G: U.S.]

Sengupta, Jati K. and Sfeir, Raymond I. Risk in Supply Response: An Optimal Control Approach. *Appl. Econ.*, April 1983, *15*(2), pp. 255–65. [G: U.S.]

Shapiro, Kenneth H. Efficiency Differentials in Peasant Agriculture and Their Implications for Development Policies. *J. Devel. Stud.*, January 1983, *19*(2), pp. 179–90. [G: Tanzania]

Siebert, John W. An Early Warning Model for Grain Elevator Bankruptcy. *Amer. J. Agr. Econ.*, August 1983, *65*(3), pp. 563–66. [G: U.S.]

Simpson, Wayne and Kapitany, Marilyn. The Off-Farm Work Behavior of Farm Operators. *Amer. J. Agr. Econ.*, November 1983, *65*(4), pp. 801–05. [G: Canada]

Singh, Joginder N.; Sidhu, D. S. and Singh, A. J. Systems Approach to Simulate the Cropping Pattern on Different Categories of Farms in Central Region of the Punjab. *Econ. Aff.*, October–December 1983, *28*(4), pp. 851–59. [G: India]

Singh, R. K.; Singh, R. P. and Singh, N. K. Resource Productivity on Dryland Farms of Ranchi District, Bihar. *Econ. Aff.*, January–March 1983, *28*(1), pp. 650–55. [G: India]

Skees, Jerry R. FLOSSIM: A Multiple-Farm Opportunity Set Simulation Model. **In** *Baum, K. H. and Schertz, L. P., eds.*, 1983, pp. 235–60. [G: U.S.]

Sonka, Steven T. Risk Management in Models of the Farm: Thoughts on Modeling Risk Management on the Farm: Discussion. **In** *Baum, K. H. and Schertz, L. P., eds.*, 1983, pp. 200–203.

Staatz, John M. The Cooperative as a Coalition: A Game-Theoretic Approach. *Amer. J. Agr. Econ.*, December 1983, *65*(5), pp. 1084–89.

Strickland, Roger P. The Negative Income of Small Farms. *Agr. Econ. Res.*, January 1983, *35*(1), pp. 52–55. [G: U.S.]

Sukharomana, S. Domestic Resource Cost of Agricultural Mechanization in Thailand: A Case Study of Small Rice Farms in Supanburi. **In** *Internat'l Rice Res. Inst. and Agric. Devel. Council,* 1983, pp. 61–69. [G: Thailand]

Sutherland, Alister. The Taxation of Agricultural Wealth: Northfield and After. **In** *Field, F., ed.*, 1983, pp. 88–117. [G: U.K.]

Taylor, C. Robert. Complementarities between Micro- and Macro-Systems Simulation and Analysis. **In** *Baum, K. H. and Schertz, L. P., eds.*, 1983, pp. 63–72.

Thieme, Günter. Agricultural Change and Its Impact in Rural Areas. **In** *Wild, T., ed.*, 1983, pp. 220–47. [G: W. Germany]

Tisdell, Clem A. and De Silva, N. T. M. H. The Economic Spacing of Trees and Other Crops. *Europ. Rev. Agr. Econ.*, 1983, *10*(3), pp. 281–93.

Tomek, William G. Alternative Pricing Mechanisms in Agriculture. **In** *Farris, P. L., ed.*, 1983, pp. 137–62. [G: U.S.]

Trapp, James N. Risk Management in Models of the Farm: The Need for Prescriptive Risk-Management Models: A Suggested Methodological Approach: Discussion. **In** *Baum, K. H. and Schertz, L. P., eds.*, 1983, pp. 204–09.

Turner, Steven C.; Epperson, James E. and Fletcher, Stanley M. Producer Attitudes toward Multicommodity Electronic Marketing. *Amer. J. Agr. Econ.*, November 1983, *65*(4), pp. 818–22. [G: U.S.]

Tweeten, Luther. Economic Instability in Agriculture: The Contributions of Prices, Government Programs and Exports. *Amer. J. Agr. Econ.*, December 1983, *65*(5), pp. 922–31. [G: U.S.]

Tweeten, Luther. Impact of Federal Fiscal–Monetary Policy on Farm Structure. *Southern J. Agr. Econ.*, July 1983, *15*(1), pp. 61–68. [G: U.S.]

Vitaliano, Peter. Cooperative Enterprise: An Alternative Conceptual Basis for Analyzing a Complex Institution. *Amer. J. Agr. Econ.*, December 1983, *65*(5), pp. 1078–83.

Walker, Harold W. Use of Farm Models in Extension Activities: A Conceptual Micromodel for Extension Farm Management and Policy: Discussion. **In** *Baum, K. H. and Schertz, L. P., eds.*, 1983, pp. 385–88. [G: U.S.]

Wang, Jaw-Kai. Taro: Production Management Considerations. **In** *Wang, J.-K., ed.*, 1983, pp. 355–58.

Wattanutchariya, S. Economic Analysis of the Farm Machinery Industry and Tractor Contractor Business in Thailand. **In** *Internat'l Rice Res. Inst. and Agric. Devel. Council,* 1983, pp. 39–49. [G: Thailand]

Weaver, Robert D. Multiple Input, Multiple Output Production Choices and Technology in the U.S. Wheat Region. *Amer. J. Agr. Econ.*, February 1983, *65*(1), pp. 45–56.

Weeks, Eldon E. A Perspective on the Evolution and Status of Micromodeling in Agricultural Economics: Farm Modeling: An Overview: Discussion. **In** *Baum, K. H. and Schertz, L. P., eds.*, 1983, pp. 10–14. [G: U.S.]

Whatley, Warren C. Labor for the Picking: The New Deal in the South. *J. Econ. Hist.*, December 1983, *43*(4), pp. 905–29. [G: U.S.]

Whyte, William Foote. Farmer Organization and Participation as Keys to Agricultural Research and Development. **In** *Whyte, W. F. and Boynton, D., eds.*, 1983, pp. 197–208. [G: Mexico]

Whyte, William Foote. Farmer, Family, Household, and Community. **In** *Whyte, W. F. and Boynton, D., eds.*, 1983, pp. 136–53. [G: Peru; Nepal]

Whyte, William Foote. Systems Thinking for Understanding the Small Farm Enterprise. **In** *Whyte, W. F. and Boynton, D., eds.*, 1983, pp. 129–35.

Whyte, William Foote. The Farming Systems Research Approach: The Rediscovery of Peasant Rationality. **In** *Whyte, W. F. and Boynton, D., eds.*, 1983, pp. 154–63.

Wild, Trevor. Social Fallow and Its Impact on the Rural Landscape. **In** *Wild, T., ed.*, 1983, pp. 200–219. [G: W. Germany]

Wills, I. R. Changes in Rural Land Use and Part-Time Farming, Central Victoria, 1974 to 1978. *Rev. Marketing Agr. Econ.*, August 1983, *51*(2), pp. 109–30. [G: Australia]

Wyzan, Michael L. The Kolkhoz and the Sovkhoz: Relative Performance as Measured by Productive Technology. **In** *Stuart, R. C., ed.*, 1983, pp. 173–98. [G: U.S.S.R.]

Zilberman, David and Rausser, Gordon C. Farm Decisions, Adaptive Economics, and Complex Behavior in Agriculture: A Proper Perspective for Considering Adaptive Economics: Discussion. **In** *Baum, K. H. and Schertz, L. P., eds.*, 1983, pp. 56–60.

717 Land Reform and Land Use

7170 General

Auster, Richard. Privatization, Justice, and Markets [The Privatization Debate: An Insider's View]. *Cato J.*, Winter 1983/84, *3*(3), pp. 869–71. [G: U.S.]

Cain, Mead. Landlessness in India and Bangladesh: A Critical Review of National Data Sources. *Econ. Develop. Cult. Change*, October 1983, *32*(1), pp. 149–67. [G: India; Bangladesh]

Hanke, Steve H. "Privatization, Justice, and Markets": A Reply [The Privatization Debate: An Insider's View]. *Cato J.*, Winter 1983/84, *3*(3), pp. 873–74.

Lee, John E., Jr. Markets for Agricultural Inputs: Current Status and Needed Research. **In** *Farris, P. L., ed.*, 1983, pp. 78–97. [G: U.S.]

Lee, Linda K. and Stewart, William H. Landownership and the Adoption of Minimum Tillage. *Amer. J. Agr. Econ.*, May 1983, *65*(2), pp. 256–64. [G: U.S.]

Metzner, Joachim. Innovations in Agriculture Incorporating Traditional Production Methods: The Case of Amarasi (Timor). *Bull. Indonesian Econ. Stud.*, December 1983, *19*(3), pp. 94–105. [G: Indonesia]

Reiss, Franklin J. The Future of Farmland Leasing. **In** *DeBraal, J. P. and Wunderlich, G., eds.*, 1983, pp. 117–26. [G: U.S.]

Scott, John T., Jr. Factors Affecting Land Price Decline. *Amer. J. Agr. Econ.*, November 1983, *65*(4), pp. 769–800. [G: U.S.]

Sen, Raj Kumar. An Analysis of Export of a Few Agricultural Products Entering into Mass Consumption. *Indian Econ. J.*, January-March 1983, *30*(3), pp. 103–10. [G: India]

7171 Land Ownership and Tenure; Land Reform

Baron, Donald. The Status of Farmland Leasing in the United States. **In** *DeBraal, J. P. and Wunderlich, G., eds.*, 1983, pp. 73–91. [G: U.S.]

Barrow, Christine. Ownership and Control of Resources in Barbados: 1834 to the Present. *Soc. Econ. Stud.*, September 1983, *32*(3), pp. 83–120. [G: Barbados]

Bitney, Larry L. Leasing Practices: An Extension Viewpoint. **In** *DeBraal, J. P. and Wunderlich, G., eds.*, 1983, pp. 133–35. [G: U.S.]

Bose, Pinaki Sankar. Determination of Rent under Share Tenancy—An Analytical Exercise. *Indian Econ. Rev.*, January–June 1983, *18*(1), pp. 35–45.

Bradley, Michael E. Mill on Proprietorship, Productivity, and Population: A Theoretical Reappraisal. *Hist. Polit. Econ.*, Fall 1983, *15*(3), pp. 423–49.

Brass, Tom. Agrarian Reform and the Struggle for Labour-Power: A Peruvian Case Study. *J. Devel. Stud.*, April 1983, *19*(3), pp. 368–89. [G: Peru]

Chao, Kang. Tenure Systems in Traditional China. *Econ. Develop. Cult. Change*, January 1983, *31*(2), pp. 295–314. [G: China]

Collier, Paul. Malfunctioning of African Rural Factor Markets: Theory and a Kenyan Example. *Oxford Bull. Econ. Statist.*, May 1983, *45*(2), pp. 141–72. [G: Kenya]

Collier, Paul. Oil and Inequality in Rural Nigeria. **In** *Ghai, D. and Radwan, S., eds.*, 1983, pp. 191–217. [G: Nigeria]

Crist, Raymond E. Land for the People—A Vital Need Everywhere: In Latin America and the Caribbean, It's Now 'a Prey to Hastening Ills,' and Decay. *Amer. J. Econ. Soc.*, July 1983, *42*(3), pp. 275–90. [G: Latin America; Caribbean]

Datta, Samar K. Sharecropping as "Second-Best" Form of Tenancy in Traditional Agriculture. *Indian Econ. J.*, April-June 1983, *30*(4), pp. 71–90.

Deere, Carmen Diana. Cooperative Development and Women's Participation in the Nicaraguan Agrarian Reform. *Amer. J. Agr. Econ.*, December 1983, *65*(5), pp. 1043–48. [G: Nicaragua]

Doebele, William A. Concepts of Urban Land Tenure. **In** *Dunkerley, H. B., ed.*, 1983, pp. 63–107.

Ehlers, Eckart. Rent-Capitalism and Unequal Development in the Middle East: The Case of Iran. **In** *Stewart, F., ed.*, 1983, pp. 32–61. [G: Iran]

Gluckman, Max. Essays on Lozi Land and Royal Property. **In** *Dalton, G., ed.*, 1983, *1943*, pp. 1–94. [G: S. Africa]

Goodell, Grace. What Life after Land Reform? *Policy Rev.*, Spring 1983, (24), pp. 121–48. [G: Philippines]

Herlitz, Lars. Landlords' Agrarian Reforms? *Scand. Econ. Hist. Rev.*, 1983, *31*(1), pp. 68–73. [G: Denmark]

Heston, Alan W. and Kumar, Dharma. The Persistence of Land Fragmentation in Peasant Agriculture: An Analysis of South Asian Cases. *Exploration Econ. Hist.*, April 1983, *20*(2), pp. 199–220. **[G: India]**

House, William J. and Killick, Tony. Social Justice and Development Policy in Kenya's Rural Economy. **In** *Ghai, D. and Radwan, S., eds.*, 1983, pp. 31–69. **[G: Kenya]**

Huang, Yukon. Tenancy Patterns, Productivity, and Rentals in Malaysia. **In** *Lim, D., ed.*, 1983, *1975*, pp. 43–52. **[G: Malaysia]**

Islam, Rizwanul. Poverty and Income Distribution in Rural Nepal. **In** *Khan, A. R. and Lee, E., eds.*, 1983, pp. 165–83. **[G: Nepal]**

Islam, Rizwanul. Poverty, Income Distribution and Growth in Rural Thailand. **In** *Khan, A. R. and Lee, E., eds.*, 1983, pp. 205–29. **[G: Thailand]**

Jose, A. V. Poverty and Income Distribution: The Case of West Bengal. **In** *Khan, A. R. and Lee, E., eds.*, 1983, pp. 137–63. **[G: India]**

Jose, A. V. Poverty and Inequality—The Case of Kerala. **In** *Khan, A. R. and Lee, E., eds.*, 1983, pp. 107–36. **[G: India]**

Kelly, P. W. Farmland Transfer in the Republic of Ireland. *Irish J. Agr. Econ. Rural Soc.*, 1983, *9*(2), pp. 161–72. **[G: Ireland]**

Khoju, M. R. Economics of Pump Irrigation in Eastern Nepal. **In** *Internat'l Rice Res. Inst. and Agric. Devel. Council*, 1983, pp. 95–105. **[G: Nepal]**

Lapping, Mark B. and Lecko, Margaret. Foreign Investment in U.S. Agricultural Land: An Overview of the National Issue and a Case Study of Vermont. *Amer. J. Econ. Soc.*, July 1983, *42*(3), pp. 291–304. **[G: U.S.]**

Lee, Eddy. Export-led Rural Development: The Ivory Coast. **In** *Ghai, D. and Radwan, S., eds.*, 1983, pp. 99–127. **[G: Ivory Coast]**

Leite, J. Costa. A Portuguese Contrast: Agrarian System and Common Lands in Two Freguesias. *Economia*, January 1983, *7*(1), pp. 1–50. **[G: Portugal]**

Lewis, W. Arthur. Thoughts on Land Settlement. **In** *Lewis, W. A.*, 1983, *1954*, pp. 563–71.

Looney, J. W. Overview of the Legal Aspects of Leasing. **In** *DeBraal, J. P. and Wunderlich, G., eds.*, 1983, pp. 55–72. **[G: U.S.]**

Lundahl, Mats. Intergenerational Sharecropping in Haiti: A Re-interpretation of the Murray Thesis. **In** *Lundahl, M.*, 1983, *1982*, pp. 83–93. **[G: Haiti]**

Lundahl, Mats. Population Pressure and Agrarian Property Rights in Haiti. **In** *Lundahl, M.*, 1983, *1980*, pp. 67–82. **[G: Haiti]**

MacAndrews, Colin and Yamamoto, Kazumi. Induced and Voluntary Migration in Malaysia: The Federal Land Development Authority Role in Migration since 1957. **In** *Lim, D., ed.*, 1983, *1975*, pp. 125–39. **[G: Malaysia]**

Mitra, Pradeep K. A Theory of Interlinked Rural Transactions. *J. Public Econ.*, March 1983, *20*(2), pp. 167–91.

Mundle, Sudipto. Land, Labour and the Level of Living in Rural Punjab. **In** *Khan, A. R. and Lee, E., eds.*, 1983, pp. 81–106. **[G: India]**

Mundle, Sudipto. Land, Labour and the Level of Living in Rural Bihar. **In** *Khan, A. R. and Lee, E., eds.*, 1983, pp. 49–80. **[G: India]**

Murrell, Peter. The Economics of Sharing: A Transactions Cost Analysis of Contractual Choice in Farming. *Bell J. Econ. (See Rand J. Econ. after 4/85)*, Spring 1983, *14*(1), pp. 283–93.

Neale, Walter C. and Edwards, Rex M. Progress and Insecurity, Class and Conflict in Rural India. *J. Econ. Issues*, June 1983, *17*(2), pp. 397–404. **[G: India]**

Newbery, David M. The State of Leasing Theory: Conflicts among Different Models of Decision Making under Uncertainty. **In** *DeBraal, J. P. and Wunderlich, G., eds.*, 1983, pp. 31–38. **[G: India]**

Oppenheimer, H. L. Nobody Loves a Landlord. **In** *DeBraal, J. P. and Wunderlich, G., eds.*, 1983, pp. 127–32.

Pant, Chandrashekar. Tenancy and Family Resources: A Model and Some Empirical Analysis. *J. Devel. Econ.*, February/April 1983, *12*(1/2), pp. 27–39. **[G: India]**

Pretzer, Don D. Leasing Practices: Discussion. **In** *DeBraal, J. P. and Wunderlich, G., eds.*, 1983, pp. 137–39.

Rahman, M. Mustafizur; Rahman, A. K. M. Fazlur and Islam, M. Mafizul. Land Redistribution Programme in Bangladesh. *Econ. Aff.*, April–June 1983, *28*(2), pp. 675–87. **[G: Bangladesh]**

Reid, Joseph D., Jr. Notes toward a Geography of Farm Tenure Choice. **In** *DeBraal, J. P. and Wunderlich, G., eds.*, 1983, pp. 19–30.

Schutjer, Wayne A.; Stokes, C. Shannon and Poindexter, John R. Farm Size, Land Ownership, and Fertility in Rural Egypt. *Land Econ.*, November 1983, *59*(4), pp. 393–403. **[G: Egypt]**

Scott, Anthony. Property Rights and Property Wrongs. *Can. J. Econ.*, November 1983, *16*(4), pp. 555–73.

Scott, John T., Jr. How to Determine the Cost of Land by Observing Rents. **In** *DeBraal, J. P. and Wunderlich, G., eds.*, 1983, pp. 93–115. **[G: U.S.]**

Soltow, Lee. Land Fragmentation as an Index of History in the Virginia Military District of Ohio. *Exploration Econ. Hist.*, July 1983, *20*(3), pp. 263–73. **[G: U.S.]**

Soltow, Lee. Long-Run Wealth Inequality in Malaysia. *Singapore Econ. Rev.*, October 1983, *28*(2), pp. 79–97. **[G: Malaysia]**

Strauch, Judith. The Political Economy of a Chinese-Malaysian New Village: Highly Diversified Insecurity. **In** *Lim, L. Y. C. and Gosling, L. A. P., eds.*, 1983, pp. 207–31. **[G: Malaysia]**

Sturgess, N. H. and Wijaya, Hesti. Rice Havesting: A View from the Theory of Common Property. *Bull. Indonesian Econ. Stud.*, August 1983, *19*(2), pp. 27–45. **[G: Indonesia]**

Sudaryanto, T. Effect of Tubewells on Income and Employment: A Case Study in Three Villages in Kediri, East Java, Indonesia. **In** *Internat'l Rice Res. Inst. and Agric. Devel. Council*, 1983, pp. 107–18. **[G: Indonesia]**

Sutinen, J. G. Agricultural Share Contracts and Risk. **In** *DeBraal, J. P. and Wunderlich, G., eds.*, 1983, pp. 1–17.

Warman, Arturo. The Future of a Crisis: Food and Agrarian Reform. **In** *Reynolds, C. W. and Tello, C., eds.*, 1983, pp. 205–24. **[G: Mexico]**

Wordie, J. R. The Chronology of English Enclosure, 1500–1914. *Econ. Hist. Rev., 2nd Ser.*, November 1983, *36*(4), pp. 483–505. **[G: U.K.]**

Wunderlich, Gene. The Facts of Agricultural Leasing. **In** *DeBraal, J. P. and Wunderlich, G., eds.*, 1983, pp. 39–54. **[G: U.S.]**

7172 Land Development; Land Use; Irrigation Policy

Adams, Martin E. Nile Water: A Crisis Postponed? Review Article. *Econ. Develop. Cult. Change*, April 1983, *31*(3), pp. 639–43. **[G: Egypt; Sudan]**

Amos, Orley M., Jr. and Timmons, John F. Iowa Crop Production and Soil Erosion with Cropland Expansion. *Amer. J. Agr. Econ.*, August 1983, *65*(3), pp. 486–92. **[G: U.S.]**

Benbrook, Charles. Structural Implications of Soil and Water Conservation Policy Alternatives. **In** *Brewster, D. E.; Rasmussen, W. D. and Youngberg, G., eds.*, 1983, pp. 135–47. **[G: U.S.]**

Berger, Curtis J. Controlling Urban Growth via Tax Policy. **In** *Carr, J. H. and Duensing, E. E., eds.*, 1983, *1979*, pp. 254–74. **[G: U.S.]**

Bhattacharyya, Kalyan and Mukhopadhyay, Arunendu. Financial Analysis of Alternative Lift Irrigation Projects—A Case Study in Nadia District of West Bengal. *Econ. Aff.*, January–March 1983, *28*(1), pp. 614–23. **[G: India]**

Boggess, William G. and Amerling, C. B. A Bioeconomic Simulation Analysis of Irrigation Investments. *Southern J. Agr. Econ.*, December 1983, *15*(2), pp. 85–91. **[G: U.S.]**

Boggess, William G., et al. Risk–Return Assessment of Irrigation Decisions in Humid Regions. *Southern J. Agr. Econ.*, July 1983, *15*(1), pp. 135–43. **[G: U.S.]**

Choudhury, Masudul Alam. Towards an Evaluative Study of Joint Venture Projects with Socio-economic Indicators. *Singapore Econ. Rev.*, October 1983, *28*(2), pp. 59–78. **[G: Mauritania]**

Clark, J. S. and Furtan, W. Harley. An Economic Model of Soil Conservation/Depletion. *J. Environ. Econ. Manage.*, December 1983, *10*(4), pp. 356–70. **[G: Canada]**

Clifton, Ivery D. and Spurlock, Stan B. Analysis of Variations in Farm Real Estate Prices over Homogeneous Market Areas in the Southeast. *Southern J. Agr. Econ.*, July 1983, *15*(1), pp. 89–96. **[G: U.S.]**

Collins, Robert A. and Headley, J. C. Optimal Investment to Reduce the Decay Rate of an Income Stream: The Case of Soil Conservation. *J. Environ. Econ. Manage.*, March 1983, *10*(1), pp. 60–71.

Conard, Rebecca. Suburban Encroachment on the Old North 40: The Search for Effective Measures to Preserve Agricultural Land. *Amer. J. Econ. Soc.*, April 1983, *42*(2), pp. 193–208. **[G: U.S.]**

Council on Development Choices for the '80s. Factors Shaping Development in the '80s. **In** *Carr, J. H. and Duensing, E. E., eds.*, 1983, *1981*, pp. 3–17. **[G: U.S.]**

Coward, E. Walter, Jr. New Directions in Irrigation Research and Development. **In** *Whyte, W. F. and Boynton, D., eds.*, 1983, pp. 209–21. **[G: Sri Lanka]**

Deolalikar, Anil B. and Vijverberg, Wim P. M. The Heterogeneity of Family and Hired Labor in Agricultural Production: A Test Using District-Level Data from India. *J. Econ. Devel.*, December 1983, *8*(2), pp. 45–69. **[G: India]**

Doll, John P.; Widdows, Richard and Velde, Paul D. The Value of Agricultural Land in the United States: A Report on Research. *Agr. Econ. Res.*, April 1983, *35*(2), pp. 39–44. **[G: U.S.]**

Dourojeanni, A. and Molina, M. The Andean Peasant, Water and the Role of the State. *Cepal Rev.*, April 1983, (19), pp. 145–66. **[G: Latin America]**

Drosdoff, Matthew and Levine, Gilbert. Working with Soils and Water. **In** *Whyte, W. F. and Boynton, D., eds.*, 1983, pp. 60–74.

Evans, Alan W. Errata [The Determination of the Price of Land]. *Urban Stud.*, November 1983, *20*(4), pp. 391.

Evans, Alan W. The Determination of the Price of Land. *Urban Stud.*, May 1983, *20*(2), pp. 119–29.

Feeny, David H. Extensive versus Intensive Agricultural Development: Induced Public Investment in Southeast Asia, 1900–1940. *J. Econ. Hist.*, September 1983, *43*(3), pp. 687–704. **[G: Asian LDCs]**

Feinerman, Eli; Letey, J. and Vaux, H. J., Jr. The Economics of Irrigation with Nonuniform Infiltration. *Water Resources Res.*, December 1983, *19*(6), pp. 1410–14.

Feinerman, Eli and Yaron, D. Economics of Irrigation Water Mixing within a Farm Framework. *Water Resources Res.*, April 1983, *19*(2), pp. 337–45. **[G: Israel]**

Feinerman, Eli and Yaron, D. The Value of Information on the Response Function of Crops to Soil Salinity. *J. Environ. Econ. Manage.*, March 1983, *10*(1), pp. 72–85. **[G: Israel]**

Ferrett, Robert L. and Ward, Robert M. Agricultural Land Use Planning and Groundwater Quality. *Growth Change*, January 1983, *14*(1), pp. 32–39. **[G: U.S.]**

Gardner, B. Delworth. Water Pricing and Rent Seeking in California Agriculture. **In** *Anderson, T. L., ed.*, 1983, pp. 83–113. **[G: U.S.]**

Goulter, I. C. and Kiely, D. A. Comment on 'Analyzing Floodplain Policies Using an Interdependent Land Use Allocation Model' by L. D. Hopkins, E. D. Brill, Jr., K. B. Kurtz, and H. G. Wenzel, Jr. *Water Resources Res.*, April 1983, *19*(2), pp. 585–87. **[G: U.S.]**

Hafner, James A. Market Gardening in Thailand: The Origins of an Ethnic Chinese Monopoly. **In** *Lim, L. Y. C. and Gosling, L. A. P., eds.*, 1983, pp. 30–45. **[G: Thailand]**

Hess, David E. Institutionalizing the Revolution: Judicial Reaction to State Land Use Laws. **In** *Carr, J. H. and Duensing, E. E., eds.*, 1983, *1981*, pp. 99–112. **[G: U.S.]**

Hopkins, L. D., et al. Reply [Analyzing Floodplain Policies Using an Interdependent Land Use Allocation Model]. *Water Resources Res.*, April 1983,

19(2), pp. 588. [G: U.S.]

Hyde, William F. The Federal Preserve in the West: Environmental Champion or Economic Despoiler. *J. Policy Anal. Manage.*, Summer 1983, *2*(4), pp. 605–14. [G: U.S.]

Jackson, Richard H. Land Use in America: The Dilemma of Changing Values. **In** *Carr, J. H. and Duensing, E. E., eds.*, 1983, *1981*, pp. 18–29. [G: U.S.]

Jackson, Richard H. The Federal Government and Land Use. **In** *Carr, J. H. and Duensing, E. E., eds.*, 1983, *1981*, pp. 113–27. [G: U.S.]

James, William E. Settler Selection and Land Settlement Alternatives: New Evidence from the Philippines. *Econ. Develop. Cult. Change*, April 1983, *31*(3), pp. 571–86. [G: Philippines]

Kmiec, Douglas W. The Role of the Planner in a Deregulated World. **In** *Carr, J. H. and Duensing, E. E., eds.*, 1983, *1982*, pp. 229–41. [G: U.S.]

Korsching, Peter F. and Nowak, Peter J. Flexibility in Conservation Policy. **In** *Brewster, D. E.; Rasmussen, W. D. and Youngberg, G., eds.*, 1983, pp. 149–59. [G: U.S.]

Kramer, Randall A.; McSweeny, William T. and Stavros, Robert W. Soil Conservation with Uncertain Revenues and Input Supplies. *Amer. J. Agr. Econ.*, November 1983, *65*(4), pp. 694–702.

Krutilla, John V., et al. Public versus Private Ownership: The Federal Lands Case. *J. Policy Anal. Manage.*, Summer 1983, *2*(4), pp. 548–58. [G: U.S.]

Kusler, Jon A. Regulating Sensitive Lands: An Overview of Programs. **In** *Carr, J. H. and Duensing, E. E., eds.*, 1983, *1980*, pp. 128–53. [G: U.S.]

Lefcoe, George. The Market's Place in Land Policy. **In** *Carr, J. H. and Duensing, E. E., eds.*, 1983, *1980*, pp. 242–53. [G: U.S.]

Lotterman, Edward D. and Waelti, John J. Efficiency and Equity Implications of Alternative Well Interference Policies in Semi-Arid Regions. *Natural Res. J.*, April 1983, *23*(2), pp. 323–34. [G: U.S.]

MacAndrews, Colin and Yamamoto, Kazumi. Induced and Voluntary Migration in Malaysia: The Federal Land Development Authority Role in Migration since 1957. **In** *Lim, D., ed.*, 1983, *1975*, pp. 125–39. [G: Malaysia]

McConnell, Kenneth E. A Economic Model of Soil Conservation. *Amer. J. Agr. Econ.*, February 1983, *65*(1), pp. 83–89.

Montgomery, John D. When Local Participation Helps. *J. Policy Anal. Manage.*, Fall 1983, *3*(1), pp. 90–105. [G: Selected LDCs]

Moore, Victor. The Public Control of Land Use: An Anglophile's View. **In** *Carr, J. H. and Duensing, E. E., eds.*, 1983, *1981*, pp. 85–98. [G: U.K.; U.S.]

Nelson, Arthur Christian. Reader Response [The Oregon Agricultural Protection Program: A Review and Assessment]. *Natural Res. J.*, January 1983, *23*(1), pp. 1–5. [G: U.S.]

Norton, Roger D.; Santaniello, Vittorio and Echevarria, Julio A. Economic Evaluation of an Agricultural Sector Investment Program: A Case Study for Peru. *J. Policy Modeling*, June 1983, *5*(2), pp. 149–77. [G: Peru]

Oron, Gideon, et al. Economic Evaluation of Water Harvesting in Microcatchments. *Water Resources Res.*, October 1983, *19*(5), pp. 1099–105. [G: Israel]

Pal, Malay Chandan and Banerjee, Biswa Nath. Economics of Alternative Irrigation Devices and Effect of Distance from the Source to the Plot on the Production in Village Barasatpara, Nadia, West Bengal. *Econ. Aff.*, April–June 1983, *28*(2), pp. 706–14. [G: India]

Palanisami, K. and Subramanian, S. R. Determinants of Farm Water Supply in the Lower Bhavani Project, Coimbatore, South India. *Water Resources Res.*, December 1983, *19*(6), pp. 1403–09. [G: India]

Richards, J. F. and McAlpin, Michelle B. Cotton Cultivating and Land Clearing in the Bombay Deccan and Karnatak: 1818–1920. **In** *Tucker, R. P. and Richards, J. F., eds.*, 1983, pp. 68–94. [G: India]

Ridler, Neil B. Labour Force and Land Distributional Effects of Agricultural Technology: A Case Study of Coffee. *World Devel.*, July 1983, *11*(7), pp. 593–99. [G: Colombia]

Rucker, Randal R. and Fishback, Price V. The Federal Reclamation Program: An Analysis of Rent-seeking Behavior. **In** *Anderson, T. L., ed.*, 1983, pp. 45–81. [G: U.S.]

Sampath, Rajan K. Returns to Public Irrigation Development. *Amer. J. Agr. Econ.*, May 1983, *65*(2), pp. 337–39.

van Schilfgaarde, Jan. Earth and Water. **In** *Glassner, M. I., ed.*, 1983, *1980*, pp. 455–67. [G: U.S.]

Sheehan, Michael F. Land Speculation in Southern California: Energy Monopoly, Fiscal Crisis and the Future. *Amer. J. Econ. Soc.*, January 1983, *42*(1), pp. 67–74. [G: U.S.]

Sheldon, Sam. Folk Economy and Impoverishment in Mexico's Zona Ixtlera. *J. Devel. Areas*, July 1983, *17*(4), pp. 453–72. [G: Mexico]

Singh, R. K.; Singh, R. P. and Singh, N. K. Resource Productivity on Dryland Farms of Ranchi District, Bihar. *Econ. Aff.*, January–March 1983, *28*(1), pp. 650–55. [G: India]

Skees, Jerry R. FLOSSIM: A Multiple-Farm Opportunity Set Simulation Model. **In** *Baum, K. H. and Schertz, L. P., eds.*, 1983, pp. 235–60. [G: U.S.]

Smith, Rodney T. The Economic Determinants and Consequences of Private and Public Ownership of Local Irrigation Facilities. **In** *Anderson, T. L., ed.*, 1983, pp. 167–217. [G: U.S.]

Strout, Alan M. How Productive Are the Soils of Java? *Bull. Indonesian Econ. Stud.*, April 1983, *19*(1), pp. 32–52. [G: Indonesia]

Tregarthen, Timothy D. Water in Colorado: Fear and Loathing of the Marketplace. **In** *Anderson, T. L., ed.*, 1983, pp. 119–36. [G: U.S.]

Vars, R. Charles, Jr. Informational Problems in Land-Use Planning and Natural Resource Management. **In** *Break, G. F., ed.*, 1983, pp. 109–31. [G: U.S.]

Whitcombe, Elizabeth and Hurd, John M. Irrigation and Railways. **In** *Kumar, D., ed.*, 1983, pp. 677–761. [G: India]

Wild, Trevor. Social Fallow and Its Impact on the Rural Landscape. **In** *Wild, T., ed.*, 1983, pp. 200–219. [G: W. Germany]

Williams, Jack F.; Chang, Ch'ang-yi and Wang, Ch'iu-yuan. Land Settlement and Development: A Case Study from Taiwan. *J. Devel. Areas,* October 1983, *18*(1), pp. 35–52. **[G: Taiwan]**

Wills, I. R. Changes in Rural Land Use and Part-Time Farming, Central Victoria, 1974 to 1978. *Rev. Marketing Agr. Econ.,* August 1983, *51*(2), pp. 109–30. **[G: Australia]**

718 Rural Economics

7180 Rural Economics

Adepoju, Aderanti. Issues in the Study of Migration and Urbanization in Africa South of the Sahara. **In** *Morrison, P. A., ed.,* 1983, pp. 115–49. **[G: Sub-Saharan Africa]**

Agarwal, Bina. Diffusion of Rural Innovations: Some Analytical Issues and the Case of Wood-Burning Stoves. *World Devel.,* April 1983, *11*(4), pp. 359–76. **[G: LDCs]**

Aguilar, A. M., et al. Consequences of Small Rice Farm Mechanization in the Philippines: A Summary of Preliminary Analyses. **In** *Internat'l Rice Res. Inst. and Agric. Devel. Council,* 1983, pp. 151–64. **[G: Philippines]**

Ahammed, Chowdhury S. and Herdt, Robert W. Farm Mechanization in a Semiclosed Input–Output Model: The Philippines. *Amer. J. Agr. Econ.,* August 1983, *65*(3), pp. 516–25. **[G: Philippines]**

Ahmed, Iftikhar. Technology and Rural Women in the Third World. *Int. Lab. Rev.,* July–August 1983, *122*(4), pp. 493–505. **[G: LDCs]**

Ahmed, J. U. Labor Use Patterns and Mechanization of Rice Postharvest Processing in Bangladesh. **In** *Internat'l Rice Res. Inst. and Agric. Devel. Council,* 1983, pp. 139–49. **[G: Bangladesh]**

Arizpe, Lourdes. The Rural Exodus in Mexico and Mexican Migration to the United States. **In** *Brown, P. G. and Shue, H., eds.,* 1983, pp. 162–83. **[G: Mexico; U.S.]**

Askew, Ian. The Location of Service Facilities in Rural Areas: A Model for Generating and Evaluating Alternative Solutions. *Reg. Stud.,* October 1983, *17*(5), pp. 305–13. **[G: U.K.]**

Bajracharya, Deepak. Fuel, Food or Forest? Dilemmas in a Nepali Village. *World Devel.,* December 1983, *11*(12), pp. 1057–74. **[G: Nepal]**

Basu, Kaushik. The Emergence of Isolation and Interlinkage in Rural Markets. *Oxford Econ. Pap.,* July 1983, *35*(2), pp. 262–80.

Bequele, Assefa. Stagnation and Inequality in Ghana. **In** *Ghai, D. and Radwan, S., eds.,* 1983, pp. 219–47. **[G: Ghana]**

Berry, Albert. Agrarian Structure, Rural Labour Markets and Trends in Rural Incomes in Latin America. **In** *Urquidi, V. L. and Reyes, S. T., eds.,* 1983, pp. 174–94. **[G: Brazil; Colombia; Mexico]**

Bhatia, Kul B. Rural–Urban Migration and Surplus Labour: Rejoinder to Stark. *Oxford Econ. Pap.,* March 1983, *35*(1), pp. 143–45.

Binswanger, Hans P. Agricultural Growth and Rural Nonfarm Activities. *Finance Develop.,* June 1983, *20*(2), pp. 38–40.

Blecher, Marc. Peasant Labour for Urban Industry: Temporary Contract Labour, Urban–Rural Balance and Class Relations in a Chinese County. *World Devel.,* August 1983, *11*(8), pp. 731–45. **[G: China]**

Blyn, George. Income Distribution among Haryana and Punjab Cultivators, 1968/69–1975/76. *Indian Econ. Rev.,* July–December 1983, *18*(2), pp. 199–224. **[G: India]**

Bordes, Ary, et al. Household Distribution of Contraceptives in Rural Haiti: The Results and Costs of the Division of Family Hygiene's Experimental Project. **In** *Sirageldin, I.; Salkever, D. and Osborn, R. W., eds.,* 1983, pp. 476–96. **[G: Haiti]**

Borsotti, Carlos A. Development and Education in Rural Areas. *Cepal Rev.,* December 1983, (21), pp. 113–32. **[G: Latin America]**

Bose, Ashish. Migration in India: Trends and Policies. **In** *Oberai, A. S., ed.,* 1983, pp. 137–82. **[G: India]**

Bourne, Compton. Effects of Subsidized Credit on the Size Distribution of Farm Household Incomes. *Soc. Econ. Stud.,* March 1983, *32*(1), pp. 81–101. **[G: Jamaica]**

Bourne, Compton and Graham, Douglas H. Economic Disequilibria and Rural Financial Market Performance in Developing Economies. *Can. J. Agr. Econ.,* March 1983, *31*(1), pp. 59–76. **[G: Jamaica]**

Bruce, C. J. and Kerr, William A. The Determination of Wages and Working Conditions in the Agricultural Sector: Three Alternatives. *Can. J. Agr. Econ.,* July 1983, *31*(2), pp. 177–96. **[G: Canada]**

Buttel, Frederick H. Farm Structure and Rural Development. **In** *Brewster, D. E.; Rasmussen, W. D. and Youngberg, G., eds.,* 1983, pp. 103–24. **[G: U.S.]**

Caballero, Jose Maria. Casual Labor in Peruvian Agrarian Co-operatives. **In** *Stewart, F., ed.,* 1983, pp. 168 88. **[G: Peru]**

Chakravarti, Anand. Some Aspects of Inequality in Rural India: A Sociological Perspective. **In** *Béteille, A., ed.,* 1983, pp. 129–81. **[G: India]**

Chan, Paul. Population Distribution and Development Strategies in Peninsular Malaysia. **In** *Oberai, A. S., ed.,* 1983, pp. 27–78. **[G: Malaysia]**

Chaudhry, M. Ghaffar. Green Revolution and Redistribution of Rural Incomes: Pakistan's Experience—A Reply. *Pakistan Devel. Rev.,* Summer 1983, *22*(2), pp. 117–23.

Colclough, Christopher and Fallon, Peter. Rural Poverty in Botswana: Dimensions, Causes and Constraints. **In** *Ghai, D. and Radwan, S., eds.,* 1983, pp. 129–53. **[G: Botswana]**

Cole, William E. and Sanders, Richard D. Interstate Migration in Mexico: Variations on the Todaro Theme. *J. Devel. Econ.,* June 1983, *12*(3), pp. 341–54. **[G: Mexico]**

Collier, Paul. Malfunctioning of African Rural Factor Markets: Theory and a Kenyan Example. *Oxford Bull. Econ. Statist.,* May 1983, *45*(2), pp. 141–72. **[G: Kenya]**

Collier, Paul. Oil and Inequality in Rural Nigeria. **In** *Ghai, D. and Radwan, S., eds.,* 1983, pp. 191–217. **[G: Nigeria]**

Coughenour, C. Milton and Christenson, James A. Farm Structure, Social Class, and Farmers' Policy

Perspectives. **In** *Brewster, D. E.; Rasmussen, W. D. and Youngberg, G., eds.*, 1983, pp. 67–86. **[G: U.S.]**

Cuddy, Michael and Curtin, Chris. Commercialisation in West of Ireland Agriculture in the 1890s. *Econ. Soc. Rev.*, April 1983, *14*(3), pp. 173–84. **[G: Ireland]**

Dow, Thomas E., Jr. and Werner, Linda H. Prospects for Fertility Decline in Rural Kenya. *Population Devel. Rev.*, March 1983, *9*(1), pp. 77–97. **[G: Kenya]**

Edmundson, Wade C. and Edmundson, Stella A. A Decade of Village Development in East Java. *Bull. Indonesian Econ. Stud.*, August 1983, *19*(2), pp. 46–59. **[G: Indonesia]**

Ehlers, Eckart. Rent-Capitalism and Unequal Development in the Middle East: The Case of Iran. **In** *Stewart, F., ed.*, 1983, pp. 32–61. **[G: Iran]**

Elliott, Charles. Equity and Growth: An Unresolved Conflict in Zambian Rural Development Policy. **In** *Ghai, D. and Radwan, S., eds.*, 1983, pp. 155–89. **[G: Zambia]**

Evans, Alfred, Jr. Changes in the Soviet Model of Rural Transformation. **In** *Stuart, R. C., ed.*, 1983, pp. 143–58. **[G: U.S.S.R.]**

Freudenberger, Herman H. Levels of Living of European Peasantry: Discussion. *J. Econ. Hist.*, March 1983, *43*(1), pp. 146–47. **[G: Czechoslovakia; U.S.S.R.]**

Fuà, Giorgio. Rural Industralization in Later Developed Countries: The Case of Northeast and Central Italy. *Banca Naz. Lavoro Quart. Rev.*, December 1983, (147), pp. 351–77. **[G: Italy]**

Ganapathy, R. S. The Political Economy of Rural Energy Planning in the Third World. *Rev. Radical Polit. Econ.*, Fall 1983, *15*(3), pp. 83–95. **[G: LDCs]**

Ghai, Dharam and Radwan, Samir. Agrarian Change, Differentiation and Rural Poverty in Africa: A General Survey. **In** *Ghai, D. and Radwan, S., eds.*, 1983, pp. 1–29. **[G: Sub-Saharan Africa]**

Ghai, Dharam and Radwan, Samir. Growth and Inequality: Rural Development in Malawi, 1964–78. **In** *Ghai, D. and Radwan, S., eds.*, 1983, pp. 71–97. **[G: Malawi]**

Ghatak, Subrata. On Interregional Variations in Rural Interest Rates in India. *J. Devel. Areas*, October 1983, *18*(1), pp. 21–34. **[G: India]**

Gomez, Fernando. Rural Household Delivery of Contraceptives in Colombia. **In** *Sirageldin, I.; Salkever, D. and Osborn, R. W., eds.*, 1983, pp. 421–33. **[G: Colombia]**

Gooneratne, W. and Gunawardena, P. J. Poverty and Inequality in Rural Sri Lanka. **In** *Khan, A. R. and Lee, E., eds.*, 1983, pp. 247–71. **[G: Sri Lanka]**

Gow, David D. and VanSant, Jerry. Beyond the Rhetoric of Rural Development Participation: How Can It Be Done? *World Devel.*, May 1983, *11*(5), pp. 427–46. **[G: Guatemala; Indonesia]**

Gregory, Paul R. The Russian Agrarian Crisis Revisited. **In** *Stuart, R. C., ed.*, 1983, pp. 21–31. **[G: U.S.S.R.]**

Griffin, Keith and Griffin, Kimberley. Institutional Change and Income Distribution in the Chinese Countryside. *Oxford Bull. Econ. Statist.*, August 1983, *45*(3), pp. 223–48. **[G: China]**

Gullickson, Gay L. Agriculture and Cottage Industry: Redefining the Causes of Proto-Industrialization. *J. Econ. Hist.*, December 1983, *43*(4), pp. 831–50. **[G: France]**

Gupta, R. P. Rural Women and Economic Development. *Econ. Aff.*, July-September 1983, *28*(3), pp. 784–90. **[G: India]**

Hafsah, J. and Bernsten, R. H. Economic, Technical, and Social Aspects of Tractor Operation and Use in South Sulawesi, Indonesia. **In** *Internat'l Rice Res. Inst. and Agric. Devel. Council*, 1983, pp. 85–94. **[G: Indonesia]**

Havnevik, Kjell J. and Skarstein, Rune. Some Notes on Agricultural Backwardness in Tanzania. **In** *Parkinson, J. R., ed.*, 1983, pp. 151–62. **[G: Tanzania]**

Herring, Ronald J. and Edwards, Rex M. Guaranteeing Employment to the Rural Poor: Social Functions and Class Interests in the Employment Guarantee Scheme in Western India. *World Devel.*, July 1983, *11*(7), pp. 575–92. **[G: India]**

Hill, Berkeley. Farm Incomes: Myths and Perspectives. *Lloyds Bank Rev.*, July 1983, (149), pp. 35–48. **[G: U.K.]**

Hodge, Ian. Rural Employment and the Quality of Life. *Rev. Marketing Agr. Econ.*, December 1983, *51*(3), pp. 259–70.

Hodsdon, Dennis F. Problems of Rural Workers' Organisation: The Cameroonian Experience. *Int. Lab. Rev.*, November–December 1983, *122*(6), pp. 747–59. **[G: Cameroon]**

House, William J. and Killick, Tony. Social Justice and Development Policy in Kenya's Rural Economy. **In** *Ghai, D. and Radwan, S., eds.*, 1983, pp. 31–69. **[G: Kenya]**

Indraratna, A. D. V. de S., et al. Migration-related Policies: A Study of the Sri Lanka Experience. **In** *Oberai, A. S., ed.*, 1983, pp. 79–135. **[G: Sri Lanka]**

Irfan, M. and Amjad, Rashid. Poverty in Rural Pakistan. **In** *Khan, A. R. and Lee, E., eds.*, 1983, pp. 19–47. **[G: Pakistan]**

Isaksen, Jan. Constraints on Rural Production: A Field Impression from Botswana. **In** *Parkinson, J. R., ed.*, 1983, pp. 52–62. **[G: Botswana]**

Islam, Rizwanul. Poverty and Income Distribution in Rural Nepal. **In** *Khan, A. R. and Lee, E., eds.*, 1983, pp. 165–83. **[G: Nepal]**

Islam, Rizwanul. Poverty, Income Distribution and Growth in Rural Thailand. **In** *Khan, A. R. and Lee, E., eds.*, 1983, pp. 205–29. **[G: Thailand]**

Jabbar, M. A.; Bhuiyan, M. S. R. and Bari, A. K. M. Causes and Consequences of Power Tiller Utilization in Two Areas of Bangladesh. **In** *Internat'l Rice Res. Inst. and Agric. Devel. Council*, 1983, pp. 71–83. **[G: Bangladesh]**

Jamal, Vali. Nomads and Farmers: Incomes and Poverty in Rural Somalia. **In** *Ghai, D. and Radwan, S., eds.*, 1983, pp. 281–311. **[G: Somalia]**

Johnston, Bruce F. The Design and Redesign of Strategies for Agricultural Development: Mexico's Experience Revisited. **In** *Reynolds, C. W. and Tello, C., eds.*, 1983, pp. 225–50. **[G: Mexico]**

Jose, A. V. Poverty and Income Distribution: The

Case of West Bengal. In *Khan, A. R. and Lee, E., eds.*, 1983, pp. 137–63. [G: India]

Jose, A. V. Poverty and Inequality—The Case of Kerala. In *Khan, A. R. and Lee, E., eds.*, 1983, pp. 107–36. [G: India]

Katzir, Yael. Yemenite Jewish Women in Israeli Rural Development: Female Power versus Male Authority. *Econ. Develop. Cult. Change*, October 1983, *32*(1), pp. 45–61. [G: Israel]

Khan, Azizur Rahman. Real Wages of Agricultural Workers in Bangladesh. In *Khan, A. R. and Lee, E., eds.*, 1983, pp. 185–203. [G: Bangladesh]

Khan, Azizur Rahman and Ghai, Dharam. Collective Agriculture in Soviet Central Asia. In *Stewart, F., ed.*, 1983, pp. 279–305. [G: U.S.S.R.]

Khan, Azizur Rahman and Lee, Eddy. Poverty in Rural Asia: Introduction. In *Khan, A. R. and Lee, E., eds.*, 1983, pp. 1–18. [G: Asia]

Khan, Mahmood Hasan. "Green Revolution and Redistribution of Rural Incomes: Pakistan's Experience"—A Comment. *Pakistan Devel. Rev.*, Spring 1983, *22*(1), pp. 47–56. [G: Pakistan]

Kipnis, Baruch A. and Meir, Avinoam. The Kibbutz Industrial System: A Unique Rural-industrial Community in Israel. In *Hamilton, F. E. I. and Linge, G. J. R., eds.*, 1983, pp. 463–84. [G: Israel]

Klein, Emilio. Determinants of Manpower Underutilisation and Availability. *Int. Lab. Rev.*, March–April 1983, *122*(2), pp. 183–95.

Klein, Emilio. Problemas metodológicos de una encuesta rural en Chile y estructura del empleo. (With English summary.) *Cuadernos Econ.*, December 1983, *20*(61), pp. 345–61. [G: Chile]

Kloppenburg, Jack R., Jr. Group Development in Botswana: The Principles of Collective Farmer Action. In *Dalton, G., ed.*, 1983, pp. 311–33. [G: Botswana]

Kossoudji, Sherrie and Mueller, Eva. The Economic and Demographic Status of Female-Headed Households in Rural Botswana. *Econ. Develop. Cult. Change*, July 1983, *31*(4), pp. 831–59. [G: Botswana]

Krout, John A. Intercountry Commuting in Nonmetropolitan America in 1960 and 1970. *Growth Change*, January 1983, *14*(1), pp. 10–19. [G: U.S.]

Leaf, Murray J. The Green Revolution and Cultural Change in a Punjab Village, 1965–1978. *Econ. Develop. Cult. Change*, January 1983, *31*(2), pp. 227–70. [G: India]

Lee, Eddy. Agrarian Change and Poverty in Rural Java. In *Khan, A. R. and Lee, E., eds.*, 1983, pp. 231–46. [G: Indonesia]

Lee, Eddy. Export-led Rural Development: The Ivory Coast. In *Ghai, D. and Radwan, S., eds.*, 1983, pp. 99–127. [G: Ivory Coast]

Leinbach, Thomas R. Rural Transport and Population Mobility in Indonesia. *J. Devel. Areas*, April 1983, *17*(3), pp. 349–63. [G: Indonesia]

Lingard, John and Bagyo, Al Sri. The Impact of Agricultural Mechanisation of Production and Employment in Rice Areas of West Java. *Bull. Indonesian Econ. Stud.*, April 1983, *19*(1), pp. 53–67. [G: Indonesia]

Litvin, Valentin. Agro-industrial Complexes: Recent Structural Reform in the Rural Economy of the USSR. In *Stuart, R. C., ed.*, 1983, pp. 258–72. [G: U.S.S.R.]

Lockhart, D. G. Planned Village Development in Scotland and Ireland, 1700–1850. In *Devine, T. M. and Dickson, D., eds.*, 1983, pp. 132–45. [G: Ireland; U.K.]

Lundahl, Mats. Peasants, Government and Technological Change in Haitian Agriculture. In *Lundahl, M.*, 1983, pp. 251–85. [G: Haiti]

Mehmet, Ozay. Growth and Impoverishment in a Dual Economy with Capital Imports. *Australian Econ. Pap.*, June 1983, *22*(40), pp. 221–32.

Mehretu, Assefa; Wittick, Robert I. and Pigozzi, Bruce W. Spatial Design for Basic Needs in Eastern Upper Volta. *J. Devel. Areas*, April 1983, *17*(3), pp. 383–94. [G: Upper Volta]

Minocha, A. C. Rural Employment in Household Industries in Madhya Pradesh. *Margin*, April 1983, *15*(3), pp. 79–90. [G: India]

Mitra, Pradeep K. A Theory of Interlinked Rural Transactions. *J. Public Econ.*, March 1983, *20*(2), pp. 167–91.

Morawetz, David. The Kibbutz as a Model for Developing Countries: On Maintaining Full Economic Equality in Practice. In *Stewart, F., ed.*, 1983, pp. 215–42. [G: Israel]

Mundle, Sudipto. Land, Labour and the Level of Living in Rural Bihar. In *Khan, A. R. and Lee, E., eds.*, 1983, pp. 49–80. [G: India]

Mundle, Sudipto. Land, Labour and the Level of Living in Rural Punjab. In *Khan, A. R. and Lee, E., eds.*, 1983, pp. 81–106. [G: India]

Musgrave, Warren. Rural Communities: Some Social Issues. *Australian J. Agr. Econ.*, August 1983, *27*(2), pp. 145–51. [G: Australia]

Neale, Walter C. and Edwards, Rex M. Progress and Insecurity, Class and Conflict in Rural India. *J. Econ. Issues*, June 1983, *17*(2), pp. 397–404. [G: India]

Nolan, Peter. De-collectivisation of Agriculture in China, 1979–82: A Long-Term Perspective. *Cambridge J. Econ.*, September/December 1983, *7*(3/4), pp. 381–403. [G: China]

Nolan, Peter and White, Gordon. Economic Distribution and Rural Development in China: The Legacy of the Maoist Era. In *Stewart, F., ed.*, 1983, pp. 243–78. [G: China]

Norcliffe, Glen B. Operating Characteristics of Rural Non-farm Enterprises in Central Province, Kenya. *World Devel.*, November 1983, *11*(11), pp. 981–94. [G: Kenya]

Oberai, A. S. An Overview of Migration-influencing Policies and Programmes. In *Oberai, A. S., ed.*, 1983, pp. 11–26.

Oberai, A. S. State Policies and Internal Migration: Introduction. In *Oberai, A. S., ed.*, 1983, pp. 1–10.

Ong, Marcia L.; Adams, Dale W. and Singh, Inderjit. J. Voluntary Rural Savings Capacities in Taiwan, 1960–70. In *Von Pischke, J. D.; Adams, D. W. and Donald, G., eds.*, 1983, pp. 126–33. [G: Taiwan]

Prahladachar, M. Income Distribution Effects on the Green Revolution in India: A Review of Empirical Evidence. *World Devel.*, November 1983,

11(11), pp. 927–44. **[G: India]**

Putterman, Louis. A Modified Collective Agriculture in Rural Growth-with-Equity: Reconsidering the Private, Unimodal Solution. *World Devel.*, February 1983, *11*(2), pp. 77–100. **[G: China; Tanzania]**

Quizon, Jaime B. and Binswanger, Hans P. Income Distribution in Agriculture: A Unified Approach. *Amer. J. Agr. Econ.*, August 1983, *65*(3), pp. 526–38.

Rayudu, C. S. Measurement of Rural Economic Growth. *Econ. Aff.*, October–December 1983, *28*(4), pp. 829–38. **[G: India]**

Reinhardt, Nola. Commercialization of Agriculture and Rural Living Standards: El Palmar, Colombia, 1960–1979. *J. Econ. Hist.*, March 1983, *43*(1), pp. 251–59. **[G: Colombia]**

Rouba, Helena. Functions of the Food-processing Industry in Promoting the Development of Agricultural Regions in Poland. *Europ. Rev. Agr. Econ.*, 1983, *10*(3), pp. 249–69. **[G: Poland]**

Saefudin, Y., et al. Consequences of Small Rice Farm Mechanization in West Java: A Summary of Preliminary Analyses. **In** *Internat'l Rice Res. Inst. and Agric. Devel. Council*, 1983, pp. 165–75. **[G: Indonesia]**

Sarkar, B. N. Disparities in Inter-State Consumer Expenditure, 1957–58 to 1973–74. *Margin*, July 1983, *15*(4), pp. 66–77. **[G: India]**

Sathyamurthy, T. V. The Political Economy of Poverty: The Case of India. **In** *Parkinson, J. R., ed.*, 1983, pp. 90–113. **[G: India]**

Schroeder, Gertrude E. Rural Living Standards in the Soviet Union. **In** *Stuart, R. C., ed.*, 1983, pp. 241–57. **[G: U.S.S.R.]**

Schumacher, August. Agricultural Development and Rural Employment: A Mexican Dilemma. **In** *Brown, P. G. and Shue, H., eds.*, 1983, pp. 141–61. **[G: Mexico]**

Sen, Chandra. A New Approach for Multiobjective Rural Development Planning. *Indian Econ. J.*, April–June 1983, *30*(4), pp. 91–96. **[G: India]**

Sen, Chandra and Shah, S. L. Employment, Unemployment and Underemployment among Landless Agricultural Labourers—A Case Study. *Econ. Aff.*, April–June 1983, *28*(2), pp. 662–63, 695. **[G: India]**

Sheldon, Sam. Folk Economy and Impoverishment in Mexico's Zona Ixtlera. *J. Devel. Areas*, July 1983, *17*(4), pp. 453–72. **[G: Mexico]**

Shlomowitz, Ralph. New and Old Views on the Rural Economy of the Postbellum South: A Review Article. *Australian Econ. Hist. Rev.*, September 1983, *23*(2), pp. 258–75. **[G: U.S.]**

Silvers, Arthur L. and Crosson, Pierre. Urban Bound Migration and Rural Investment: The Case of Mexico. *J. Reg. Sci.*, February 1983, *23*(1), pp. 33–47. **[G: Mexico]**

Simpson, Wayne and Kapitany, Marilyn. The Off-Farm Work Behavior of Farm Operators. *Amer. J. Agr. Econ.*, November 1983, *65*(4), pp. 801–05. **[G: Canada]**

Singh, A. J.; Joshi, A. S. and Sain, Inder. Changing Economic Condition of Agricultural Labour Households in Punjab. *Econ. Aff.*, October-December 1983, *28*(4), pp. 840–43. **[G: India]**

Singh, R. P.; Sahay, S. N. and Pandey, R. K. Income, Savings and Consumption Behaviour of Marginal and Small Farmers, Palamau, Bihar. *Econ. Aff.*, July-September 1983, *28*(3), pp. 733–35. **[G: India]**

Sofranko, Andrew J. and Fliegel, Frederick C. Rural-to-Rural Migrants: The Neglected Component of Rural Population Growth. *Growth Change*, April 1983, *14*(2), pp. 42–49. **[G: U.S.]**

Soltow, Lee. Long-Run Wealth Inequality in Malaysia. *Singapore Econ. Rev.*, October 1983, *28*(2), pp. 79–97. **[G: Malaysia]**

Srivastava, R. K. and Livingstone, I. Growth and Distribution: The Case of Mozambique. **In** *Ghai, D. and Radwan, S., eds.*, 1983, pp. 249–80. **[G: Mozambique]**

Stokes, Eric, et al. Agrarian Relations. **In** *Kumar, D., ed.*, 1983, pp. 36–241. **[G: India]**

Strauch, Judith. The Political Economy of a Chinese-Malaysian New Village: Highly Diversified Insecurity. **In** *Lim, L. Y. C. and Gosling, L. A. P., eds.*, 1983, pp. 207–31. **[G: Malaysia]**

Strickland, Roger P. The Negative Income of Small Farms. *Agr. Econ. Res.*, January 1983, *35*(1), pp. 52–55. **[G: U.S.]**

Stuart, Robert C. Perspectives on the Russian and Soviet Rural Economy. **In** *Stuart, R. C., ed.*, 1983, pp. 1–17. **[G: U.S.S.R.]**

Sudaryanto, T. Effect of Tubewells on Income and Employment: A Case Study in Three Villages in Kediri, East Java, Indonesia. **In** *Internat'l Rice Res. Inst. and Agric. Devel. Council*, 1983, pp. 107–18. **[G: Indonesia]**

Tassinari, Franco. Sviluppo dell'agricoltura e mutamenti sociali in Emilia-Romagna. (Agricultural Development and Social Changes in Emilia Romagna. With English summary.) *Statistica*, July–September 1983, *43*(3), pp. 425–32. **[G: Italy]**

Tendulkar, Suresh D. Rural Institutional Credit and Rural Development: A Review Article. *Indian Econ. Rev.*, January–June 1983, *18*(1), pp. 101–37. **[G: India]**

Thieme, Günter. Agricultural Change and Its Impact in Rural Areas. **In** *Wild, T., ed.*, 1983, pp. 220–47. **[G: W. Germany]**

Tricker, M. and Bozeat, N. Encouraging the Development of Small Businesses in Rural Areas: Recent Local Authority Initiatives in England. *Reg. Stud.*, June 1983, *17*(3), pp. 201–04. **[G: U.K.]**

Tuckman, Howard U.; Nas, Tevfik F. and Caldwell, Jamie S. The Effectiveness of Instructional Radio in a Developing Country Context. *METU*, 1983, *10*(1), pp. 45–64. **[G: Colombia]**

Vink, N. and Kassier, W. E. A Paradigm for a Micro-Level Rural Development Strategy. *S. Afr. J. Econ.*, June 1983, *51*(2), pp. 283–96. **[G: S. Africa]**

Wampach, Jean-Pierre. Productivité, efficacité économique et équité dans le secteur agricole québécois. (Productivity, Economic Efficiency and Equity in Quebec Agriculture. With English summary.) *L'Actual. Econ.*, December 1983, *59*(4), pp. 669–85. **[G: Canada]**

Watts, Michael and Lubeck, Paul. The Popular Classes and the Oil Boom: A Political Economy of Rural and Urban Poverty. **In** *Zartman, I. W.*, *ed.*, 1983, pp. 105–44. [G: Nigeria]

Wharton, Clifton R., Jr. Risk, Uncertainty, and the Subsistence Farmer. In *Todaro, M. P., ed.*, 1983, *1969*, pp. 234–39.

Whyte, I. D. and Whyte, K. A. Some Aspects of the Structure of Rural Society in Seventeenth-Century Lowland Scotland. In *Devine, T. M. and Dickson, D., eds.*, 1983, pp. 32–45. [G: U.K.]

Whyte, Robert Orr. Rural Industrialization in Monsoonal and Equatorial Asia. In *Hamilton, F. E. I. and Linge, G. J. R., eds.*, 1983, pp. 533–49. [G: Asia]

Whyte, William Foote. Farmer, Family, Household, and Community. In *Whyte, W. F. and Boynton, D., eds.*, 1983, pp. 136–53. [G: Peru; Nepal]

Wilbur, Elvira M. Was Russian Peasant Agriculture Really That Impoverished? New Evidence from a Case Study from the "Impoverished Center" at the End of the Nineteenth Century. *J. Econ. Hist.*, March 1983, *43*(1), pp. 137–44. [G: U.S.S.R.]

Wills, I. R. Changes in Rural Land Use and Part-Time Farming, Central Victoria, 1974 to 1978. *Rev. Marketing Agr. Econ.*, August 1983, *51*(2), pp. 109–30. [G: Australia]

Woods, Mike D.; Doeksen, Gerald A. and Nelson, James R. Community Economics: A Simulation Model for Rural Development Planners. *Southern J. Agr. Econ.*, December 1983, *15*(2), pp. 71–77. [G: U.S.]

Yotopoulos, Pan A. A Micro Economic-Demographic Model of the Agricultural Household in the Philippines. *Food Res. Inst. Stud.*, 1983, *19*(1), pp. 1–24. [G: Philippines]

Zarfaty, Joseph. The Moshav in Israel: Possibilities for Its Application in Developing Countries. In *Stewart, F., ed.*, 1983, pp. 189–214. [G: Israel]

720 Natural Resources

7200 General

Khachaturov, Tigran S. Intensification of the Utilization of Material Resources. *Prob. Econ.*, August 1983, *26*(4), pp. 3–23. [G: U.S.S.R.]

Polfeldt, Thomas. Statistics of the Natural Environment—Aims and Methods. *Statist. J.*, October 1983, *1*(4), pp. 407–17. [G: Sweden]

Schroyer, Trent. Critique of the Instrumental Interest in Nature. *Soc. Res.*, Spring 1983, *50*(1), pp. 158–84.

Weber, J.-L. The French Natural Patrimony Accounts. *Statist. J.*, October 1983, *1*(4), pp. 419–44. [G: France]

721 Natural Resources

7210 General

Abbott, Philip C. Problems of the Forest Industry: Discussion. *Amer. J. Agr. Econ.*, December 1983, *65*(5), pp. 1019–20. [G: U.S.]

Ackefors, Hans. Production of Fish and Other Animals in the Sea. In *Glassner, M. I., ed.*, 1983, *1977*, pp. 535–50. [G: Global]

Adams, Martin E. Nile Water: A Crisis Postponed? Review Article. *Econ. Develop. Cult. Change*, April 1983, *31*(3), pp. 639–43. [G: Egypt; Sudan]

Adas, Michael. Colonization, Commercial Agriculture, and the Destruction of the Deltaic Rainforests of British Burma in the Late Nineteenth Century. In *Tucker, R. P. and Richards, J. F., eds.*, 1983, pp. 95–110. [G: Burma]

Adelman, M. A. and Houghton, John C. Introduction to Estimation of Reserves and Resources. In *Adelman, M. A., et al.*, 1983, pp. 1–25. [G: U.S.]

AFL–CIO. Recommendations for a National Materials Policy. In *Glassner, M. I., ed.*, 1983, *1977*, pp. 362–68. [G: U.S.]

Akao, Nobutoshi. Resources and Japan's Security. In *Akao, N., ed.*, 1983, pp. 15–44. [G: Japan]

Allam, Mohamed N. and Marks, David H. Comment on "Robustness of Water Resource Systems." *Water Resources Res.*, October 1983, *19*(5), pp. 1327–28. [G: Sweden]

Alley, William M. Comment on 'Multiobjective River Basin Planning with Qualitative Criteria' by M. Gershon, L. Duckstein, and R. McAniff. *Water Resources Res.*, February 1983, *19*(1), pp. 293–94. [G: U.S.]

Andersen, Peder. 'On Rent of Fishing Grounds': A Translation of Jens Warming's 1911 Article, with an Introduction. *Hist. Polit. Econ.*, Fall 1983, *15*(3), pp. 391–96.

Anderson, A. W. and Manning, T. W. The Use of Input–Output Analysis in Evaluating Water Resource Development. *Can. J. Agr. Econ.*, March 1983, *31*(1), pp. 15–26. [G: Canada]

Anderson, Lee G. Exploitation of the Lobster Fishery: Comment. *J. Environ. Econ. Manage.*, June 1983, *10*(2), pp. 180–83. [G: Canada]

Anderson, Raymond L. Ethical Issues in Resource Economics: Discussion. *Amer. J. Agr. Econ.*, December 1983, *65*(5), pp. 1035–36.

Anderson, Terry L. Introduction: The Water Crisis and the New Resource Economics. In *Anderson, T. L., ed.*, 1983, pp. 1–9. [G: U.S.]

Anderson, Terry L.; Burt, Oscar R. and Fractor, David T. Privatizing Groundwater Basins: A Model and Its Application. In *Anderson, T. L., ed.*, 1983, pp. 223–48. [G: U.S.]

Antrim, Lance N. and Sebenius, James K. Incentives for Ocean Mining under the Convention. In *Oxman, B. H.; Caron, D. D. and Buderi, C. L. O., eds.*, 1983, pp. 79–99. [G: U.S.]

Aronson, Jonathan David and Cragg, Christopher. The Natural Gas Trade in the 1980s. In *Aronson, J. D. and Cowhey, P. F., eds.*, 1983, pp. 53–82. [G: Japan; U.S.; W. Europe]

Bailey, John S. The Future of the Exploitation of the Resources of the Deep Seabed and Subsoil. *Law Contemp. Probl.*, Spring 1983, *46*(2), pp. 71–76. [G: Global]

Bajracharya, Deepak. Fuel, Food or Forest? Dilemmas in a Nepali Village. *World Devel.*, December 1983, *11*(12), pp. 1057–74. [G: Nepal]

Baldwin, George B. Why Present Value Calculations Should Not Be Used in Choosing Rural Water Supply Technology. *World Devel.*, December 1983, *11*(12), pp. 1075–81. [G: LDCs]

Barbet, P. La théorie des prix de l'énergie dans la pensée économique: une recension. (Energy

Prices in the Economic Theory: A General Outlook. With English summary.) *Écon. Soc.*, December 1983, *17*(12), pp. 1809–834.

Barston, R. P. The Law of the Sea: The Conference and After. *J. World Trade Law*, May–June 1983, *17*(3), pp. 207–23.

Berry, Brian J. L. and Horton, Frank E. Assurance of Municipal Water Supplies. **In** *Glassner, M. I., ed.*, 1983, *1974*, pp. 507–22. **[G: U.S.]**

Boadway, Robin; Flatters, F. and Leblanc, A. Revenue Sharing and the Equlization of Natural Resource Revenues. *Can. Public Policy*, June 1983, *9*(2), pp. 174–80. **[G: Canada]**

Bockstael, Nancy E. and Opaluch, James J. Discrete Modelling of Supply Response under Uncertainty: The Case of the Fishery. *J. Environ. Econ. Manage.*, June 1983, *10*(2), pp. 125–37. **[G: U.S.]**

Bosson, Rex and Varon, Bension. Problems of Mineral Development in Developing Countries. **In** *Glassner, M. I., ed.*, 1983, *1977*, pp. 381–95. **[G: LDCs; MDCs]**

Boynton, Damon. Fitting the Parts Together. **In** *Whyte, W. F. and Boynton, D., eds.*, 1983, pp. 122–26.

Brander, James A. and Djajić, Slobodan. Rent-Extracting Tariffs and the Management of Exhaustible Resources. *Can. J. Econ.*, May 1983, *16*(2), pp. 288–98.

Brookshire, David S.; Eubanks, Larry S. and Randall, Alan. Estimating Option Prices and Existence Values for Wildlife Resources. *Land Econ.*, February 1983, *59*(1), pp. 1–15. **[G: U.S.]**

Brookshire, David S.; Merrill, James L. and Watts, Gary L. Economics and the Determination of Indian Reserved Water Rights. *Natural Res. J.*, October 1983, *23*(4), pp. 749–65. **[G: U.S.]**

Burness, H. Stuart; Gorman, William D. and Lansford, Robert L. Economics, Ethics, and the Quantification of Indian Water Rights. *Amer. J. Agr. Econ.*, December 1983, *65*(5), pp. 1027–32. **[G: U.S.]**

Burness, H. Stuart, et al. Practicably Irrigable Acreage and Economic Feasibility: The Role of Time, Ethics, and Discounting. *Natural Res. J.*, April 1983, *23*(2), pp. 289–303. **[G: U.S.]**

Caelleigh, Addeane S. Middle East Water: Vital Resource, Conflict, and Cooperation. **In** *Starr, J. R., ed.*, 1983, pp. 121–35. **[G: Middle East]**

Caron, David D. Reconciling Domestic Principles and International Cooperation. **In** *Oxman, B. H.; Caron, D. D. and Buderi, C. L. O., eds.*, 1983, pp. 3–10. **[G: U.S.]**

Castagne, Maurice; Guidat, Claudine and Voinson, Philippe. Proposition d'une méthodologie de sélection des precédés valorisant la biomasse lignocellulosique. (With English summary.) *Rev. Econ. Ind.*, 4th Trimester 1983, (26), pp. 14–23. **[G: France]**

Cawley, Leo. Scarcity, Distribution and Growth: Notes on Classical Rent Theory. *Rev. Radical Polit. Econ.*, Fall 1983, *15*(3), pp. 143–58.

Charney, Jonathan I. The United States and the Law of the Sea after UNCLOS III—The Impact of General International Law. *Law Contemp. Probl.*, Spring 1983, *46*(2), pp. 37–54. **[G: U.S.]**

Chew, Sing C. Capital in Crisis: Stagnation and Timber Company Operations, Canada, 1873–1896. **In** *Bergesen, A., ed.*, 1983, pp. 287–308. **[G: Canada]**

Clark, J. S. and Furtan, W. Harley. An Economic Model of Soil Conservation/Depletion. *J. Environ. Econ. Manage.*, December 1983, *10*(4), pp. 356–70. **[G: Canada]**

Clawson, Marion. Forests for Whom and for What? **In** *Glassner, M. I., ed.*, 1983, *1977*, pp. 415–28. **[G: U.S.]**

Cohen, Lewis I. International Cooperation on Seabed Mining. **In** *Oxman, B. H.; Caron, D. D. and Buderi, C. L. O., eds.*, 1983, pp. 101–09. **[G: OECD]**

Corden, Warner Max. The Economic Effects of a Booming Sector. *Int. Soc. Sci. J.*, 1983, *35*(3), pp. 441–54.

Council on Environ. Quality and the Dept. of State. The Global 2000 Report to the President: Entering the 21st Century. **In** *Glassner, M. I., ed.*, 1983, *1980*, pp. 647–75. **[G: Global]**

Cox, Thomas R. Trade, Development, and Environmental Change: The Utilization of North America's Pacific Coast Forests to 1914 and Its Consequences. **In** *Tucker, R. P. and Richards, J. F., eds.*, 1983, pp. 14–29. **[G: U.S.]**

Crabbé, Philippe J. The Contribution of L. C. Gray to the Economic Theory of Exhaustible Natural Resources and Its Roots in the History of Economic Thought. *J. Environ. Econ. Manage.*, September 1983, *10*(3), pp. 195–220.

Crowley, P. T.; O'Mara, L. P. and Campbell, R. Inport Quotas, Resource Development and Intersectoral Adjustment. *Australian Econ. Pap.*, December 1983, *22*(41), pp. 384–410. **[G: Australia]**

Crutchfield, Stephen R. A Bioeconomic Model of an International Fishery. *J. Environ. Econ. Manage.*, December 1983, *10*(4), pp. 310–28.

Crutchfield, Stephen R. Estimation of Foreign Willingness to Pay for United States Fishery Resources: Japanese Demand for Alaska Pollock. *Land Econ.*, February 1983, *59*(1), pp. 16–23. **[G: Japan; U.S.]**

Cunningham, Stephen and Young, James A. The EEC Common Fisheries Policy: Retrospect and Prospect. *Nat. Westminster Bank Quart. Rev.*, May 1983, pp. 2–14. **[G: EEC]**

Cuzán, Alfred G. Appropriators versus Expropriators: The Political Economy of Water in the West. **In** *Anderson, T. L., ed.*, 1983, pp. 13–43. **[G: U.S.]**

Dasgupta, Partha; Gilbert, Richard and Stiglitz, Joseph E. Strategic Considerations in Invention and Innovation: The Case of Natural Resources. *Econometrica*, September 1983, *51*(5), pp. 1439–48.

Dasgupta, Swapan and Mitra, Tapan. Intergenerational Equity and Efficient Allocation of Exhaustible Resources. *Int. Econ. Rev.*, February 1983, *24*(1), pp. 133–53.

Dean, Warren. Deforestation in Southeastern Brazil. **In** *Tucker, R. P. and Richards, J. F., eds.*, 1983, pp. 50–67. **[G: Brazil]**

Deshmukh, Sudhakar D. and Pliska, Stanley R. Optimal Consumption of a Nonrenewable Resource with Stochastic Discoveries and a Random Environment. *Rev. Econ. Stud.*, July 1983, *50*(3), pp. 543–54.

Dodds, Daniel and Bishop, Richard C. On the Role of Information in Mineral Exploration. *Land Econ.*, November 1983, *59*(4), pp. 411–19.

Dourojeanni, A. and Molina, M. The Andean Peasant, Water and the Role of the State. *Cepal Rev.*, April 1983, (19), pp. 145–66. **[G: Latin America]**

Dubs, Marne A. The Future of the Exploitation of the Resources of the Deep Seabed and Subsoil: Comment. *Law Contemp. Probl.*, Spring 1983, *46*(2), pp. 81–85. **[G: Global]**

Eckholm, Erik. Planting for the Future: Forestry for Human Needs. **In** *Glassner, M. I., ed.*, 1983, *1979*, pp. 444–52. **[G: Global]**

Eheart, J. Wayland and Lyon, Randolph M. Alternative Structures for Water Rights Markets. *Water Resources Res.*, August 1983, *19*(4), pp. 887–94. **[G: U.S.]**

Emerson, Craig and Lloyd, Peter J. Improving Mineral Taxation Policy in Australia. *Econ. Rec.*, September 1983, *59*(166), pp. 232–44. **[G: Australia]**

Epstein, Larry G. Decreasing Absolute Risk Aversion and Utility Indices Derived from Cake-Eating Problems. *J. Econ. Theory*, April 1983, *29*(2), pp. 245–64.

Eswaran, Mukesh; Lewis, Tracy R. and Heaps, Terry. On the Nonexistence of Market Equilibria in Exhaustible Resource Markets with Decreasing Costs. *J. Polit. Econ.*, February 1983, *91*(1), pp. 154–67.

Falkenmark, M. Main Problems of Water Use and Transfer of Technology. **In** *Glassner, M. I., ed.*, 1983, *1979*, pp. 468–78. **[G: Global]**

Feigenbaum, Susan and Teeples, Ronald. Public versus Private Water Delivery: A Hedonic Cost Approach. *Rev. Econ. Statist.*, November 1983, *65*(4), pp. 672–78. **[G: U.S.]**

Feinerman, Eli and Knapp, Keith C. Benefits from Groundwater Management: Magnitude, Sensitivity, and Distribution. *Amer. J. Agr. Econ.*, November 1983, *65*(4), pp. 703–10. **[G: U.S.]**

Ferrett, Robert L. and Ward, Robert M. Agricultural Land Use Planning and Groundwater Quality. *Growth Change*, January 1983, *14*(1), pp. 32–39. **[G: U.S.]**

Fery, John B. America's Forests: Cash Crop or National Monument? **In** *Barnes, C. H., ed.*, 1983, pp. 34–46. **[G: U.S.]**

Flaaten, Ola. The Optimal Harvesting of a Natural Resource with Seasonal Growth. *Can. J. Econ.*, August 1983, *16*(3), pp. 447–62.

Fodella, Gianni. Technology Transfer in the Energy Field for Water and Soil Conservation. *Rivista Int. Sci. Econ. Com.*, July 1983, *30*(7), pp. 667–77. **[G: LDCs]**

Foreign Policy Association. Protecting World Resources: Is Time Running Out? **In** *Glassner, M. I., ed.*, 1983, *1982*, pp. 53–71.

Fraser, R. W. and Van Noorden, R. J. Extraction of an Exhaustible Resource: The Effects on Investment of Several Parameters Being Subject to Uncertainty. *Econ. Rec.*, December 1983, *59*(167), pp. 365–74.

Frye, Richard. Climatic Change and Fisheries Management. *Natural Res. J.*, January 1983, *23*(1), pp. 77–96. **[G: U.S.]**

Gaffney, Mason. Tax Exporting and the Commerce Clause: Comments. **In** *McLure, C. E., Jr. and Mieszkowski, P., eds.*, 1983, pp. 199–203. **[G: U.S.]**

Gallastegui, Carmen. An Economic Analysis of Sardine Fishing in the Gulf of Valencia (Spain). *J. Environ. Econ. Manage.*, June 1983, *10*(2), pp. 138–50. **[G: Spain]**

Gallini, Nancy T.; Lewis, Tracy R. and Ware, Roger. Strategic Timing and Pricing of a Substitute in a Cartelized Resource Market. *Can. J. Econ.*, August 1983, *16*(3), pp. 429–46.

Gardner, B. Delworth. Water Pricing and Rent Seeking in California Agriculture. **In** *Anderson, T. L., ed.*, 1983, pp. 83–113. **[G: U.S.]**

Garnaut, Ross. Energy Policy, Taxation of Natural Resources and Fiscal Federalism: Comment. **In** *McLure, C. E., Jr., ed.*, 1983, pp. 146–47.

Gaudet, Gérard. Investissement optimal et coûts d'adjustement dans la théorie économique de la mine. (Optimal Investment and Adjustment Costs in the Economic Theory of the Mine. With English summary.) *Can. J. Econ.*, February 1983, *16*(1), pp. 39–51.

Gershon, Mark and Duckstein, Lucien. Reply [Multiobjective River Basin Planning with Qualitative Criteria]. *Water Resources Res.*, February 1983, *19*(1), pp. 295–96. **[G: U.S.]**

Gisser, Micha. Groundwater: Focusing on the Real Issue. *J. Polit. Econ.*, December 1983, *91*(6), pp. 1001–27. **[G: U.S.]**

Gisser, Micha and Johnson, Ronald N. Institutional Restrictions on the Transfer of Water Rights and the Survival of an Agency. **In** *Anderson, T. L., ed.*, 1983, pp. 137–65. **[G: U.S.]**

Goicoechea, A.; Krouse, M. R. and Antle, L. G. An Approach to Risk and Uncertainty in Benefit–Cost Analysis of Water Resources Projects: Reply. *Water Resources Res.*, October 1983, *19*(5), pp. 1333. **[G: U.S.]**

Goldman, Jonathon C. Comment on "An Approach to Risk and Uncertainty in Benefit–Cost Analysis of Water Resources Projects." *Water Resources Res.*, October 1983, *19*(5), pp. 1331–32. **[G: U.S.]**

Goldwin, Robert A. Common Sense vs. "The Common Heritage." **In** *Oxman, B. H.; Caron, D. D. and Buderi, C. L. O., eds.*, 1983, pp. 59–75. **[G: U.S.]**

Goss, Barry A. The Semi-Strong Form Efficiency of the London Metal Exchange. *Appl. Econ.*, October 1983, *15*(5), pp. 681–98. **[G: U.K.]**

Grant, Douglas L. Reasonable Groundwater Pumping Levels under the Appropriation Doctrine: Underlying Social Goals. *Natural Res. J.*, January 1983, *23*(1), pp. 53–75. **[G: U.S.]**

Greider, Thomas. Instream Flows, the State, and Voluntary Action. *Cato J.*, Winter 1983/84, *3*(3), pp. 811–30. **[G: U.S.]**

Greis, Noel P.; Wood, Eric F. and Steuer, Ralph E. Multicriteria Analysis of Water Allocation in a River Basin: The Tchebycheff Approach. *Water Resources Res.*, August 1983, *19*(4), pp. 865–75. **[G: U.S.]**

Haavisto, Heikki. Finlands skogs- och skogsindustripolitik. (Finland's Forest and Forest Industry Policy. With English summary.) *Ekon. Samfundets Tidskr.*, 1983, *36*(2), pp. 65–70. **[G: Finland]**

Hannesson, Rögnvaldur. A Note on Socially Optimal versus Monopolistic Exploitation of a Renewable Resource. *Z. Nationalökon.*, 1983, *43*(1), pp. 63–70.

Hannesson, Rögnvaldur. Optimal Harvesting of Ecologically Interdependent Fish Species. *J. Environ. Econ. Manage.*, December 1983, *10*(4), pp. 329–45.

Hardie, Ian W. Problems of the Forest Industry: Discussion. *Amer. J. Agr. Econ.*, December 1983, *65*(5), pp. 1017–18. **[G: U.S.]**

Hartwick, John M. Learning about and Exploiting Exhaustible Resource Deposits of Uncertain Size. *Can. J. Econ.*, August 1983, *16*(3), pp. 391–410.

Hashimoto, T.; Loucks, D. P. and Stedinger, J. R. Robustness of Water Resource Systems: Reply. *Water Resources Res.*, October 1983, *19*(5), pp. 1329–30. **[G: Sweden]**

Haynes, Richard W. and Adams, Darius M. Changing Perceptions of the U.S. Forest Sector: Implications for the RPA Timber Assessment. *Amer. J. Agr. Econ.*, December 1983, *65*(5), pp. 1002–09. **[G: U.S.]**

Hellerstein, Walter. Legal Constraints on State Taxation of Natural Resources. **In** *McLure, C. E., Jr. and Mieszkowski, P., eds.*, 1983, pp. 135–66. **[G: U.S.]**

Henry, Claude. Some Inconsistencies in Public Land-Use Choices. **In** *Thisse, J.-F. and Zoller, H. G., eds.*, 1983, pp. 183–205.

Henze, Arno. Nutzen–kosten–theoretische Überlegungen zur Sicherstellung der Versorgung für Krisenzeiten. (Theoretical Cost–Benefit–Considerations on Supply Security for Times of Crisis. With English summary.) *Z. Wirtschaft. Sozialwissen.*, 1983, *103*(2), pp. 129–42.

Hillman, Arye L. and Long, Ngo Van. Pricing and Depletion of an Exhaustible Resource When There Is Anticipation of Trade Disruption. *Quart. J. Econ.*, May 1983, *98*(2), pp. 215–33.

Hoel, Michael. Monopoly Resource Extractions under the Presence of Predetermined Substitute Production. *J. Econ. Theory*, June 1983, *30*(1), pp. 201–12.

Hoggan, Daniel H.; Bagley, Jay M. and Kimball, Kirk R. Inadvertent Income Redistribution Effects of State Water Development Financing. *Growth Change*, October 1983, *14*(4), pp. 32–36. **[G: U.S.]**

Hopkin, John A. Moral Responsibility in Agricultural Research: Discussion. *Southern J. Agr. Econ.*, July 1983, *15*(1), pp. 81–82. **[G: U.S.]**

Hotvedt, James E. Application of Linear Goal Programming to Forest Harvest Scheduling. *Southern J. Agr. Econ.*, July 1983, *15*(1), pp. 103–08. **[G: U.S.]**

Houthakker, Hendrik S. Whatever Happened to the Energy Crisis? *Energy J.*, April 1983, *4*(2), pp. 1–8.

Huffman, James. Instream Water Use: Public and Private Alternatives. **In** *Anderson, T. L., ed.*, 1983, pp. 249–82. **[G: U.S.]**

Idyll, C. P. Global Resources: Challenges of Interdependence: The Realities. **In** *Glassner, M. I., ed.*, 1983, *1970*, pp. 551–55.

Islam, Nurul. Economic Interdependence between Rich and Poor Nations. **In** *Gauhar, A., ed. (II)*, 1983, pp. 173–93. **[G: LDCs; MDCs]**

Jackson, Richard H. Land Use in America: The Dilemma of Changing Values. **In** *Carr, J. H. and Duensing, E. E., eds.*, 1983, *1981*, pp. 18–29. **[G: U.S.]**

Jha, Raghbendra and Lächler, Ulrich. Inflation and Economic Growth in a Competitive Economy with Exhaustible Resources. *J. Econ. Behav. Organ.*, June–September 1983, *4*(2–3), pp. 113–29.

Jónsson, Sigfús. The Icelandic Fisheries in the Pre-Mechanization Era, c. 1800–1905: Spatial and Economic Implications of Growth. *Scand. Econ. Hist. Rev.*, 1983, *31*(2), pp. 132–50. **[G: Iceland]**

Kaldor, Nicholas. The Role of Commodity Prices in Economic Recovery. *Lloyds Bank Rev.*, July 1983, (149), pp. 21–34.

Kapp, K. William. Environmental Dangers, National Economy and Forestry. **In** *Kapp, K. W.*, 1983, *1971*, pp. 71–88.

Kemp, Murray C. and Long, Ngo Van. On the Economics of Forests. *Int. Econ. Rev.*, February 1983, *24*(1), pp. 113–31.

Keyes, Dale L. Reagan Energy and Environmental Programs: Implications for State and Local Governments. **In** *Lefcoe, G., ed.*, 1983, pp. 77–89. **[G: U.S.]**

Keyfitz, Nathan. Population and the Struggle for the World Product. **In** *Streeten, P. and Maier, H., eds.*, 1983, pp. 235–52.

Kim, Chungsoo. Optimal Management of Multi-Species North Sea Fishery Resources. *Weltwirtsch. Arch.*, 1983, *119*(1), pp. 138–51. **[G: N. Europe]**

Kim, Dae K. Energy Substitution in the Gulf of Mexico Shrimp Fishery. *Southern J. Agr. Econ.*, December 1983, *15*(2), pp. 1–6. **[G: U.S.]**

Kirthisingha, P. N. International Commodity Agreements. *Int. J. Soc. Econ.*, 1983, *10*(3), pp. 40–65.

Knapp, Keith C. Steady-State Solutions to Dynamic Optimization Models with Inequality Constraints. *Land Econ.*, August 1983, *59*(3), pp. 300–04.

Koh, Tommy T. B. The Third United Nations Conference on the Law of the Sea: What Was Accomplished? *Law Contemp. Probl.*, Spring 1983, *46*(2), pp. 5–9. **[G: Global]**

Kristensen, Gustav. Dansk fiskeri i europæisk belysning. (Development of Danish Fishery and Danish Fishery Policy in Recent Years. With English summary.) *Nationaløkon. Tidsskr.*, 1983, *121*(2), pp. 272–89. **[G: Denmark]**

Kwon, O. Yul. Neutral Taxation and Provincial Mineral Royalties: The Manitoba Metallic Minerals and Saskatchewan Uranium Royalties. *Can. Public Policy*, June 1983, *9*(2), pp. 189–99. **[G: Canada]**

La Duque, Winona. Native America: The Economics of Radioactive Colonization. *Rev. Radical Polit. Econ.*, Fall 1983, *15*(3), pp. 9–19. **[G: U.S.]**

Labys, Walter C. and Afrasiabi, A. Cyclical Disequilibrium in the U.S. Copper Market. *Appl. Econ.*, August 1983, *15*(4), pp. 437–49. **[G: U.S.]**

Lamm, Richard D. Urban Land Policy for the 1980s: Public Resource Management under the Reagan Administration. **In** *Lefcoe, G., ed.*, 1983, pp. 91–100. **[G: U.S.]**

Larkin, Robert P.; Peters, Gary L. and Exline, Christopher H. Natural Resources: The Basis for Economic Development. **In** *Glassner, M. I., ed.*, 1983, *1981*, pp. 3–23. **[G: Selected Countries; U.S.]**

Lee, Tom K. Bilateral Trade, Dynamic Bargaining and Nonrenewable Resources. *J. Int. Econ.*, February 1983, *14*(1/2), pp. 169–78.

Löfgren, Karl G. The Faustmann–Ohlin Theorem: A Historical Note. *Hist. Polit. Econ.*, Summer 1983, *15*(2), pp. 261–64. **[G: Sweden]**

Lotterman, Edward D. and Waelti, John J. Efficiency and Equity Implications of Alternative Well Interference Policies in Semi-Arid Regions. *Natural Res. J.*, April 1983, *23*(2), pp. 323–34. **[G: U.S.]**

Malone, James L. The United States and the Law of the Sea after UNCLOS III. *Law Contemp. Probl.*, Spring 1983, *46*(2), pp. 29–36. **[G: U.S.]**

Mangone, Gerard J. American Politics and the Law of the Sea. **In** *Piper, D. C. and Terchek, R. J., eds.*, 1983, pp. 146–77. **[G: Global; U.S.]**

Martin, Geoffrey J. Global Resources in Historical Perspective. **In** *Glassner, M. I., ed.*, 1983, pp. 35–50. **[G: Global]**

Mather, Kirtley F. The Age of Interdependence. **In** *Glassner, M. I., ed.*, 1983, *1944*, pp. 72–79. **[G: Selected Countries]**

Maw, Carlyle E. The United States and the Law of the Sea after UNCLOS III: Comment. *Law Contemp. Probl.*, Spring 1983, *46*(2), pp. 55–60. **[G: U.S.]**

McConnell, Kenneth E.; Daberkow, J. N. and Hardie, Ian W. Planning Timber Production with Evolving Prices and Costs. *Land Econ.*, August 1983, *59*(3), pp. 292–99. **[G: U.S.]**

McEvoy, Arthur F. Law, Public Policy, and Industrialization in the California Fisheries, 1900–1925. *Bus. Hist. Rev.*, Winter 1983, *57*(4), pp. 494–521. **[G: U.S.]**

McGaw, Richard L. and Cook, Beverly A. Optimum Effort and Rent Distribution in the Gulf of Mexico Shrimp Fishery: Comment. *Amer. J. Agr. Econ.*, February 1983, *65*(1), pp. 160–61. **[G: U.S.]**

McKelvey, Robert. The Fishery in a Fluctuating Environment: Coexistence of Specialist and Generalist Fishing Vessels in a Multipurpose Fleet. *J. Environ. Econ. Manage.*, December 1983, *10*(4), pp. 287–309.

McLure, Charles E., Jr. Fiscal Federalism and the Taxation of Economic Rents. **In** *Break, G. F., ed.*, 1983, pp. 133–60.

McLure, Charles E., Jr. Tax Exporting and the Commerce Clause. **In** *McLure, C. E., Jr. and Mieszkowski, P., eds.*, 1983, pp. 169–92. **[G: U.S.]**

McLure, Charles E., Jr. and Mieszkowski, Peter. Taxation of Mineral Wealth and Interregional Conflicts. **In** *McLure, C. E., Jr. and Mieszkowski, P., eds.*, 1983, pp. 1–10. **[G: U.S.; Canada]**

Mehrez, Abraham and Sinuany-Stern, Zilla. Resource Allocation to Interrelated Projects. *Water Resources Res.*, August 1983, *19*(4), pp. 876–80. **[G: Israel]**

Mero, John L. Will Ocean Mining Revolutionize World Industry? **In** *Glassner, M. I., ed.*, 1983, *1977*, pp. 580–88. **[G: Global]**

Meuriot, Eric and Gates, John M. Fishing Allocations and Optimal Fees: A Single- and Multilevel Programming Analysis. *Amer. J. Agr. Econ.*, November 1983, *65*(4), pp. 711–21.

Mieszkowski, Peter. Energy Policy, Taxation of Natural Resources, and Fiscal Federalism. **In** *McLure, C. E., Jr., ed.*, 1983, pp. 128–45. **[G: U.S.]**

Miller, Robert A. and Voltaire, Karl. A Stochastic Analysis of the Tree Paradigm. *J. Econ. Dynam. Control*, December 1983, *6*(4), pp. 371–86.

Mitchell, Barbara. Resources in Antarctica: Potential for Conflict. **In** *Glassner, M. I., ed.*, 1983, *1977*, pp. 136–46. **[G: Antarctica]**

Mitra, Tapan. Limits on Population Growth under Exhaustible Resource Constraints. *Int. Econ. Rev.*, February 1983, *24*(1), pp. 155–68.

Mori, Nobuhiro. On the Optimal Depletion of Exhaustible Resources: A Survey. (In Japanese. With English summary.) *Osaka Econ. Pap.*, March 1983, *32*(4), pp. 47–60.

Mueller, Michael J. Optimal Groundwater Depletion with Interdependent Nonrenewable and Renewable Resources. *Water Resources Res.*, October 1983, *19*(5), pp. 1091–98. **[G: U.S.]**

Muraoka, Dennis D. and Watson, Richard B. Improving the Efficiency of Federal Timber Sales Procedures. *Natural Res. J.*, October 1983, *23*(4), pp. 815–25. **[G: U.S.]**

Murphey, Rhoads. Deforestation in Modern China. **In** *Tucker, R. P. and Richards, J. F., eds.*, 1983, pp. 111–28. **[G: China]**

National Academy of Sciences. Energy in Transition 1985–2010. **In** *Glassner, M. I., ed.*, 1983, *1980*, pp. 289–310. **[G: U.S.]**

Nobuhara, Naotake and Akao, Nobutoshi. The Politics of Siberian Development. **In** *Akao, N., ed.*, 1983, pp. 197–215. **[G: Japan; U.S.S.R.]**

Ogawa, Haruo. The Behavior of Resource Exploratng Firm under Stochastic World. **In** *[Yamada, I.]*, 1983, pp. 115–21.

Ogg, Clayton W.; Pionke, Harry B. and Heimlich, Ralph E. A Linear Programming Economic Analysis of Lake Quality Improvements Using Phosphorus Buffer Curves. *Water Resources Res.*, February 1983, *19*(1), pp. 21–31. **[G: U.S.]**

Olson, Kent W. Economics of Transferring Water to the High Plains. *Quarterly Journal of Business and Economics*, Autumn 1983, *22*(4), pp. 63–80. **[G: U.S.]**

Oron, Gideon, et al. Economic Evaluation of Water Harvesting in Microcatchments. *Water Resources Res.*, October 1983, *19*(5), pp. 1099–105. **[G: Israel]**

Osaka, Masako M. Forest Preservation in Tokugawa Japan. **In** *Tucker, R. P. and Richards, J. F., eds.*, 1983, pp. 129–45. **[G: Japan]**

Oxman, Bernard H. Law of the Sea and the Future of the International Order: The Two Conferences. **In** *Oxman, B. H.; Caron, D. D. and Buderi, C. L. O., eds.*, 1983, pp. 127–44.

Oxman, Bernard H. Summary of the Law of the Sea Convention. **In** *Oxman, B. H.; Caron, D. D. and Buderi, C. L. O., eds.*, 1983, pp. 147–61.

Palanisami, K. and Subramanian, S. R. Determinants

of Farm Water Supply in the Lower Bhavani Project, Coimbatore, South India. *Water Resources Res.*, December 1983, *19*(6), pp. 1403–09. [G: India]

Parrinello, Sergio. Exhaustible Natural Resources and the Classical Method of Long-Period Equilibrium. In *Kregel, J. A., ed.*, 1983, pp. 186–99.

Pereira, Pedro Telhado. Developing Countries and the Economics of Irrversible Changes in Natural Environments. *Economia*, January 1983, *7*(1), pp. 71–85. [G: LDCs]

Pinto, M. C. W. The Developing Countries and the Exploitation of the Deep Seabed. In *Glassner, M. I., ed.*, 1983, *1980*, pp. 600–614. [G: Global]

Ray, George F. Industrial Materials: Past, Present and Future. In *[Saunders, C. T.]*, 1983, pp. 61–82. [G: Global]

Razavi, Hossein. Effect of Uncertainty on Oil Extraction Decisions. *J. Econ. Dynam. Control*, July 1983, *5*(4), pp. 359–70. [G: Iran]

Repetto, Robert and Holmes, Thomas. The Role of Population in Resource Depletion in Developing Countries. *Population Devel. Rev.*, December 1983, *9*(4), pp. 609–32. [G: LDCs]

Rhodes, John J. Developing a National Water Policy: Problems and Perspectives on Reform. In *Carr, J. H. and Duensing, E. E., eds.*, 1983, *1981*, pp. 154–69. [G: U.S.]

Richardson, James A. and Scott, Loren C. Resource Location Patterns and State Severance Taxes: Some Empirical Evidence. *Natural Res. J.*, April 1983, *23*(2), pp. 351–64. [G: U.S.]

Riesenfeld, Stefan A. The Third United Nations Conference on the Law of the Sea: What Was Accomplished?: Comment. *Law Contemp. Probl.*, Spring 1983, *46*(2), pp. 11–15. [G: Global]

Roth, Dennis M. Philippine Forests and Forestry: 1565–1920. In *Tucker, R. P. and Richards, J. F., eds.*, 1983, pp. 30–49. [G: Philippine]

Roumasset, James; Isaak, David T. and Fesharaki, Fereidun. Oil Prices without OPEC: A Walk on the Supply-Side. *Energy Econ.*, July 1983, *5*(3), pp. 164–70.

Rowe, Robert D. and Chestnut, Lauraine G. Valuing Environmental Commodities: Revisited. *Land Econ.*, November 1983, *59*(4), pp. 404–10.

Ruttan, Vernon W. Moral Responsibility in Agricultural Research. *Southern J. Agr. Econ.*, July 1983, *15*(1), pp. 73–80. [G: U.S.]

Sakhovaler, T. A. and Eskin, V. I. A Nonlinear Scheme for Calculating the Monetary Value of Oil and Gas Deposits. *Matekon*, Fall 1983, *20*(1), pp. 78–92.

Salant, Stephen W.; Eswaran, Mukesh and Lewis, Tracy R. The Length of Optimal Extraction Programs When Depletion Affects Extraction Costs. *J. Econ. Theory*, December 1983, *31*(2), pp. 364–74.

Sander, William. Federal Water Resources Policy and Decision-Making: Their Formulation Is Essentially a Political Process Conditioned by Government Structure and Needs. *Amer. J. Econ. Soc.*, January 1983, *42*(1), pp. 1–12. [G: U.S.]

Scafuri, Allen J. An Overlapping Generations Model of Exhaustible Natural Resources. *Reg. Sci. Persp.*, 1983, *13*(1), pp. 55–59.

Schaab, William C. Prior Appropriation, Impairment, Replacements, Models and Markets. *Natural Res. J.*, January 1983, *23*(1), pp. 25–51. [G: U.S.]

Schachter, Oscar. International Equity and Its Dilemmas. In *Glassner, M. I., ed.*, 1983, *1977*, pp. 122–26. [G: Global]

Schug, Walter. Die Bedeutung von internationalen Rohstoffabkommen für die Verbracherländer von agrarischen und mineralischen Grundstoffen. In *Lenel, H. O.; Willgerodt, H. and Molsberger, J.*, 1983, pp. 169–91. [G: LDCs; MDCs]

Schworm, William E. Monopsonistic Control of a Common Property Renewable Resource. *Can. J. Econ.*, May 1983, *16*(2), pp. 275–87.

Scott, Anthony. Property Rights and Property Wrongs. *Can. J. Econ.*, November 1983, *16*(4), pp. 555–73.

Sedjo, Roger A. and Lyon, Kenneth S. Long-Term Forest Resources Trade, Global Timber Supply, and Intertemporal Comparative Advantage. *Amer. J. Agr. Econ.*, December 1983, *65*(5), pp. 1010–16. [G: U.S.]

Seierstad, Atle and Sydsæter, Knut. Sufficient Conditions Applied to an Optimal Control Problem of Resource Management. *J. Econ. Theory*, December 1983, *31*(2), pp. 375–82.

Shimomura, Kazuo. On the Optimal Order of Exploitation of Deposits of a Renewable Resource. *Z. ges. Staatswiss.*, June 1983, *139*(2), pp. 319–22.

Siebert, Horst. Extraction, Fixed Costs and the Hotelling Rule. *Z. ges. Staatswiss.*, June 1983, *139*(2), pp. 259–68.

Smith, Paul E. and Wisley, Thomas O. On a Model of Economic Growth Using Factors of Production to Extract an Exhaustible Resource. *Southern Econ. J.*, April 1983, *49*(4), pp. 966–74.

Smith, V. Kerry. Option Value: A Conceptual Overview. *Southern Econ. J.*, January 1983, *49*(3), pp. 654–68.

Sorensen, Philip E. Correcting for Autocorrelation Problems in Regression Equations Used to Estimate Losses in Fisheries Catch. In *U.S. Dept. Comm., Nat'l Oceanic and Atmos. Admin.*, 1983, pp. 86–87. [G: France]

Sorensen, Philip E. Marine Resources. In *U.S. Dept. Comm., Nat'l Oceanic and Atmos. Admin.*, 1983, pp. 57–80. [G: France]

Spulber, Daniel F. Pulse-Fishing and Stochastic Equilibrium in the Multicohort Fishery. *J. Econ. Dynam. Control*, December 1983, *6*(4), pp. 309–32.

Stollery, Kenneth R. Mineral Depletion with Cost as the Extraction Limit: A Model Applied to the Behavior of Prices in the Nickel Industry. *J. Environ. Econ. Manage.*, June 1983, *10*(2), pp. 151–65. [G: U.S.]

Strang, William J. On the Optimal Forest Harvesting Decision. *Econ. Inquiry*, October 1983, *21*(4), pp. 576–83.

Szuprowicz, Bohdan O. What Are Strategic Materials? In *Glassner, M. I., ed.*, 1983, *1981*, pp. 335–61. [G: Global]

Takekuma, Shin-ichi. On Existence of Optimal Programs of Capital Accumulation with Exhaustible Resources. *Hitotsubashi J. Econ.*, December

1983, *24*(2), pp. 109–18.

The World Bank. Forestry and Development. **In** *Glassner, M. I., ed.*, 1983, *1978*, pp. 429–38. **[G: LDCs]**

Thirsk, Wayne R. Energy Policy, Taxation of Natural Resources and Fiscal Federalism: Comment. **In** *McLure, C. E., Jr., ed.*, 1983, pp. 148–49. **[G: U.S.]**

Thomson, James T. The Precolonial Woodstock in Sahelien West Africa: The Example of Central Niger (Damagaram, Damergu, Aïr). **In** *Tucker, R. P. and Richards, J. F., eds.*, 1983, pp. 167–77. **[G: W. Africa]**

Trainer, F. E. Potentially Recoverable Resources: How Recoverable? **In** *Glassner, M. I., ed.*, 1983, *1982*, pp. 396–412. **[G: Global]**

Tregarthen, Timothy D. Water in Colorado: Fear and Loathing of the Marketplace. **In** *Anderson, T. L., ed.*, 1983, pp. 119–36. **[G: U.S.]**

Tucker, Richard P. The British Colonial System and the Forests of the Western Himalayas, 1815–1914. **In** *Tucker, R. P. and Richards, J. F., eds.*, 1983, pp. 146–66. **[G: India]**

United Nations. Seabed Mineral Resource Development: Recent Activities of the International Consortia. **In** *Glassner, M. I., ed.*, 1983, *1980*, pp. 589–99. **[G: Global]**

Vars, R. Charles, Jr. Informational Problems in Land-Use Planning and Natural Resource Management. **In** *Break, G. F., ed.*, 1983, pp. 109–31. **[G: U.S.]**

Wallace, Michael B. Managing Resources That Arc Common Property: From Kathmandu to Capitol Hill. *J. Policy Anal. Manage.*, Winter 1983, *2*(2), pp. 220–37. **[G: Nepal; U.S.]**

Wallop, Malcolm. Energy Development and Water: Dilemma for the Western United States. *J. Energy Devel.*, Spring 1983, *8*(2), pp. 203–09. **[G: U.S.]**

Warner, Langdon S. Conservation Aspects of the Fishery Conservation and Management Act and the Protection of Critical Marine Habitat. *Natural Res. J.*, January 1983, *23*(1), pp. 97–130. **[G: U.S.]**

Wassermann, Ursula. World Bank: Report on Fishery. *J. World Trade Law*, May–June 1983, *17*(3), pp. 272–75.

Webb, Kempton E. Global Interdependence. **In** *Glassner, M. I., ed.*, 1983, pp. 629–43. **[G: Global]**

White, Gilbert F.; Bradley, David J. and White, Anne U. Water, Community Well-being, and Public Policy. **In** *Glassner, M. I., ed.*, 1983, *1972*, pp. 479–506. **[G: E. Africa]**

Williams, Michael. Ohio: Microcosm of Agricultural Clearing in the Midwest. **In** *Tucker, R. P. and Richards, J. F., eds.*, 1983, pp. 3–13. **[G: U.S.]**

Williams, Stephen F. The Requirement of Beneficial Use as a Cause of Waste in Water Resource Development. *Natural Res. J.*, January 1983, *23*(1), pp. 7–23. **[G: U.S.]**

Withagen, Cees. The Optimal Exploitation of a Natural Resource When There Is Full Complementarity. *J. Econ. Dynam. Control*, November 1983, *6*(3), pp. 239–52.

Wong, Benedict D. C. and Eheart, J. Wayland. Market Simulations for Irrigation Water Rights: A Hypothetical Case Study. *Water Resources Res.*, October 1983, *19*(5), pp. 1127–38. **[G: U.S.]**

Wright, Jeffrey; ReVelle, Charles and Cohon, Jared. A Multiobjective Integer Programming Model for the Land Acquisition Problem. *Reg. Sci. Urban Econ.*, February 1983, *13*(1), pp. 31–53.

Yamauchi, Hiroshi and Onoe, Hisao. Analytical Concepts and Framework for Environmental Conservation. *Rivista Int. Sci. Econ. Com.*, August 1983, *30*(8), pp. 759–78.

Zimmerman, Martin B. Tax Exporting and the Commerce Clause: Comments. **In** *McLure, C. E., Jr. and Mieszkowski, P., eds.*, 1983, pp. 193–95. **[G: U.S.]**

7211 Recreational Aspects of Natural Resources

Adamowicz, W. L. and Phillips, W. E. A Comparison of Extra Market Benefit Evaluation Techniques. *Can. J. Agr. Econ.*, November 1983, *31*(3), pp. 401–12. **[G: Canada]**

Anderson, Lee G. The Demand Curve for Recreational Fishing with an Application to Stock Enhancement Activities. *Land Econ.*, August 1983, *59*(3), pp. 279–86. **[G: U.S.]**

Bishop, Richard C.; Heberlein, Thomas A. and Kealy, Mary Jo. Contingent Valuation of Environmental Assets: Comparisons with a Simulated Market. *Natural Res. J.*, July 1983, *23*(3), pp. 619–33. **[G: U.S.]**

Brown, William G., et al. Using Individual Observations to Estimate Recreation Demand Functions: A Caution. *Amer. J. Agr. Econ.*, February 1983, *65*(1), pp. 154–57. **[G: U.S.]**

Clawson, Marion. Forests for Whom and for What? **In** *Glassner, M. I., ed.*, 1983, *1977*, pp. 415–28. **[G: U.S.]**

Dickenson, Russell E. Public Parks: Exploration and Preservation—Is There a Middle Way? **In** *Barnes, C. H., ed.*, 1983, pp. 47–57. **[G: U.S.]**

Downing, Paul B. and Frank, James E. Recreational Impact Fees: Characteristics and Current Usage. *Nat. Tax J.*, December 1983, *36*(4), pp. 477–90. **[G: U.S.]**

Flink, James J. The National Parks: The Business of the Environment. **In** *[Cochran, T. C.]*, 1983, pp. 23–48. **[G: U.S.]**

Greig, Peter J. Recreation Evaluation Using a Characteristics Theory of Consumer Behavior. *Amer. J. Agr. Econ.*, February 1983, *65*(1), pp. 90–97. **[G: Australia]**

Hof, John G. and King, David A. On the Necessity of Simultaneous Recreation Demand Equation Estimation: Reply. *Land Econ.*, November 1983, *59*(4), pp. 459–60.

Jackson, Richard H. The Federal Government and Land Use. **In** *Carr, J. H. and Duensing, E. E., eds.*, 1983, *1981*, pp. 113–27. **[G: U.S.]**

Johnson, F. Reed and Haspel, Abraham E. Economic Valuation of Potential Scenic Degradation at Bryce Canyon National Park. **In** *Rowe, R. D. and Chestnut, L. G., eds.*, 1983, pp. 235–45. **[G: U.S.]**

Johnson, Thomas G. Measuring the Cost of Time in Recreation Demand Analysis: Comment. *Amer. J. Agr. Econ.*, February 1983, *65*(1), pp.

169–71. [G: U.S.]

Kusler, Jon A. Regulating Sensitive Lands: An Overview of Programs. **In** *Carr, J. H. and Duensing, E. E., eds.*, 1983, *1980*, pp. 128–53. [G: U.S.]

Livengood, Kerry R. Value of Big Game from Markets for Hunting Leases: The Hedonic Approach. *Land Econ.*, August 1983, *59*(3), pp. 287–91. [G: U.S.]

MacFarland, Karen Kelley; Malm, William and Molenar, John. An Examination of Methodologies for Assessing the Value of Visibility. **In** *Rowe, R. D. and Chestnut, L. G., eds.*, 1983, pp. 151–72. [G: U.S.]

Majid, I.; Sinden, J. A. and Randall, Alan. Benefit Evaluation of Increments to Existing Systems of Public Facilities. *Land Econ.*, November 1983, *59*(4), pp. 377–92. [G: Australia]

McConnell, Kenneth E. Existence and Bequest Value. **In** *Rowe, R. D. and Chestnut, L. G., eds.*, 1983, pp. 254–64.

McConnell, Kenneth E. and Strand, Ivar E., Jr. Measuring the Cost of Time in Recreation Demand Analysis: Reply. *Amer. J. Agr. Econ.*, February 1983, *65*(1), pp. 172–74. [G: U.S.]

Mendelsohn, Robert and Brown, Gardner M., Jr. Revealed Preference Approaches to Valuing Outdoor Recreation. *Natural Res. J.*, July 1983, *23*(3), pp. 607–18. [G: U.S.]

Menz, Fredric C. and Wilton, Donald P. Alternative Ways to Measure Recreation Values by the Travel Cost Method. *Amer. J. Agr. Econ.*, May 1983, *65*(2), pp. 332–36. [G: U.S.]

Rae, Douglas A. The Value to Visitors of Improving Visibility at Mesa Verde and Great Smoky National Parks. **In** *Rowe, R. D. and Chestnut, L. G., eds.*, 1983, pp. 217–34. [G: U.S.]

Randall, Alan; Hoehn, John P. and Brookshire, David S. Contingent Valuation Surveys for Evaluating Environmental Assets. *Natural Res. J.*, July 1983, *23*(3), pp. 635–48. [G: U.S.]

Randall, Alan and Stoll, John R. Existence Value in a Total Valuation Framework. **In** *Rowe, R. D. and Chestnut, L. G., eds.*, 1983, pp. 265–74. [G: U.S.]

Rowe, Robert D. and Chestnut, Lauraine G. Priorities for Economic Analysis of Visibility Values. **In** *Rowe, R. D. and Chestnut, L. G., eds.*, 1983, pp. 246–53. [G: U.S.]

Sandrey, Ronald A.; Buccola, Steven T. and Brown, William G. Pricing Policies for Antlerless Elk Hunting Permits. *Land Econ.*, November 1983, *59*(4), pp. 432–43. [G: U.S.]

Smith, V. Kerry; Desvousges, William H. and McGivney, Matthew P. Estimating Water Quality Benefits: An Econometric Analysis. *Southern Econ. J.*, October 1983, *50*(2), pp. 422–37. [G: U.S.]

Stoll, John R. Recreational Activities and Nonmarket Valuation: The Conceptualization Issue. *Southern J. Agr. Econ.*, December 1983, *15*(2), pp. 119–25.

Talhelm, Daniel R. Unrevealed Extramarket Values: Values Outside the Normal Range of Consumer Choices. **In** *Rowe, R. D. and Chestnut, L. G., eds.*, 1983, pp. 275–86.

Taylor, John A. Managing Our Visual Resources. **In** *Rowe, R. D. and Chestnut, L. G., eds.*, 1983, pp. 289–95. [G: U.S.]

Walsh, Richard G.; Miller, Nicole P. and Gilliam, Lynde O. Congestion and Willingness to Pay for Expansion of Skiing Capacity. *Land Econ.*, May 1983, *59*(2), pp. 195–210. [G: U.S.]

Ward, Frank A. Measuring the Cost of Time in Recreation Demand Analysis: Comment. *Amer. J. Agr. Econ.*, February 1983, *65*(1), pp. 167–68. [G: U.S.]

Ward, Frank A. On the Necessity of Simultaneous Recreation Demand Equation Estimation: Comment. *Land Econ.*, November 1983, *59*(4), pp. 455–58.

722 Conservation and Pollution

7220 Conservation and Pollution

Adas, Michael. Colonization, Commercial Agriculture, and the Destruction of the Deltaic Rainforests of British Burma in the Late Nineteenth Century. **In** *Tucker, R. P. and Richards, J. F., eds.*, 1983, pp. 95–110. [G: Burma]

Alley, William M. Comment on 'Multiobjective River Basin Planning with Qualitative Criteria' by M. Gershon, L. Duckstein, and R. McAniff. *Water Resources Res.*, February 1983, *19*(1), pp. 293–94. [G: U.S.]

Amos, Orley M., Jr. and Timmons, John F. Iowa Crop Production and Soil Erosion with Cropland Expansion. *Amer. J. Agr. Econ.*, August 1983, *65*(3), pp. 486–92. [G: U.S.]

Anderson, Robert C.; Congar, Richard and Meade, Norman F. Emergency Response, Cleanup, and Restoration. **In** *U.S. Dept. Comm., Nat'l Oceanic and Atmos. Admin.*, 1983, pp. 37–56. [G: France]

Anderson, Robert C. and Ostro, Bart D. Benefits Analysis and Air Quality Standards. *Natural Res. J.*, July 1983, *23*(3), pp. 565–75. [G: U.S.]

Andrus, Cecil D. Energy Development without Destruction: An Attainable Goal. **In** *Barnes, C. H., ed.*, 1983, pp. 1–14. [G: U.S.]

Arrington, Robert L. The Economy/Environment Debate: A Wilderness of Questions. **In** *Snoeyenbos, M.; Almeder, R. and Humber, J., eds.*, 1983, pp. 466–78.

Atkinson, Scott E. Marketable Pollution Permits and Acid Rain Externalities. *Can. J. Econ.*, November 1983, *16*(4), pp. 704–22. [G: U.S.; Canada]

Atkinson, Scott E. Nonoptimal Solutions Using Transferable Discharge Permits: The Implications of Acid Rain Deposition. **In** *Joeres, E. F. and David, M. H., eds.*, 1983, pp. 55–69. [G: U.S.]

Ballard, Steven C. and Gunn, Elizabeth M. State Government Capacity for Managing Sunbelt Growth. **In** *Ballard, S. C. and James, T. E., eds.*, 1983, pp. 107–31. [G: U.S.]

Bamford, Shaun C. and Hughes, Joseph P. The Uncertain Case for Controlling Pollution by Taxes on Emissions. **In** *Dutta, M.; Hartline, J. C. and Loeb, P. D., eds.*, 1983, pp. 259–68.

Barnes, David W. Back Door Cost-Benefit Analysis under a Safety-First Clean Air Act. *Natural Res. J.*, October 1983, *23*(4), pp. 827–57. [G: U.S.]

Beavis, Brian and Walker, Martin. Achieving Environmental Standards with Stochastic Discharges. *J. Environ. Econ. Manage.*, June 1983, *10*(2), pp. 103–11.

Beavis, Brian and Walker, Martin. Random Wastes, Imperfect Monitoring and Environmental Quality Standards. *J. Public Econ.*, August 1983, *21* (3), pp. 377–87.

Beckerman, Wilfred. The Case for Economic Growth. In *Snoeyenbos, M.; Almeder, R. and Humber, J., eds.*, 1983, *1974*, pp. 453–60.

Benbrook, Charles. Structural Implications of Soil and Water Conservation Policy Alternatives. In *Brewster, D. E.; Rasmussen, W. D. and Youngberg, G., eds.*, 1983, pp. 135–47. **[G: U.S.]**

Bingham, Tayler H.; Youngblood, Curtis E. and Cooley, Philip C. Conditionally Predictive Supply Elasticity Estimates: Secondary Materials Obtained from Municipal Residuals. *J. Environ. Econ. Manage.*, June 1983, *10*(2), pp. 166–79. **[G: U.S.]**

Bogárdi, István; Bárdossy, András and Duckstein, Lucien. Regional Management of an Aquifer for Mining under Fuzzy Environmental Objectives. *Water Resources Res.*, December 1983, *19*(6), pp. 1394–1402. **[G: Hungary]**

Boland, John J. The Social Value of Tradable Permits: The Application of an Asset Utilization Model. In *Joeres, E. F. and David, M. H., eds.*, 1983, pp. 149–62.

Boulding, Kenneth E. Towards Conceptualising the Process of Technological Change. In *Macdonald, S.; Lamberton, D. M. and Mandeville, T., eds.*, 1983, pp. 4–10.

Braulke, Michael. On the Effectiveness of Effluent Charges. *Z. ges. Staatswiss.*, March 1983, *139*(1), pp. 122–30.

Broder, Ivy E. and Morrall, John F., III. The Economic Basis for OSHA's and EPA's Generic Carcinogen Regulations. In *Zeckhauser, R. J. and Leebaert, D., eds.*, 1983, pp. 242–54. **[G: U.S.]**

Bromley, Daniel W. Economics and Public Policy on Pollution: Some General Observations. In *Joeres, E. F. and David, M. H., eds.*, 1983, pp. 249–52.

Brown, Gardner M., Jr. Noncommercial Marine Biomass and Sea Birds. In *U.S. Dept. Comm., Nat'l Oceanic and Atmos. Admin.*, 1983, pp. 81–85. **[G: France]**

Brown, Gardner M., Jr. Summary of Results of Odes 1979 Survey of Tourists and Residents. In *U.S. Dept. Comm., Nat'l Oceanic and Atmos. Admin.*, 1983, pp. 109–10. **[G: France]**

Brown, Gardner M., Jr.; Congar, Richard and Wilman, Elizabeth A. Recreation: Tourists and Residents. In *U.S. Dept. Comm., Nat'l Oceanic and Atmos. Admin.*, 1983, pp. 89–108. **[G: France]**

Brown, Gardner M., Jr., et al. Assessing the Social Costs of Oil Spills: The AMOCO CADIZ Case Study: Other Costs. In *U.S. Dept. Comm., Nat'l Oceanic and Atmos. Admin.*, 1983, pp. 131–36. **[G: France]**

Brown, Stephen P. A. A Note on Environmental Risk and the Rate of Discount [Environmental Externalities and the Arrow–Lind Public Investment Theorem]. *J. Environ. Econ. Manage.*, September 1983, *10*(3), pp. 282–86.

Brown, William S. and Shaw, W. Doug, Jr. Neoclassical and Post Keynesian Environmental Economics: An Addendum. *J. Post Keynesian Econ.*, Fall 1983, *6*(1), pp. 140–42.

Buc, Lawrence G. and Haymore, Curtis. Regulating Hazardous Waste Incinerators under the Resource Conservation and Recovery Act. *Natural Res. J.*, July 1983, *23*(3), pp. 549–64. **[G: U.S.]**

Burness, H. Stuart, et al. Valuing Policies Which Reduce Environmental Risk. *Natural Res. J.*, July 1983, *23*(3), pp. 675–82. **[G: U.S.]**

Cain, Jonathan T. Routes and Roadblocks: State Controls on Hazardous Waste Imports. *Natural Res. J.*, October 1983, *23*(4), pp. 767–93. **[G: U.S.]**

Calabresi, Guido and Melamed, A. Douglas. Property Rules, Liability Rules, and Inalienability: One View of the Cathedral. In *Kuperberg, M. and Beitz, C., eds.*, 1983, *1972*, pp. 41–80.

Carter, Stephen L. Separatism and Skepticism. *Yale Law J.*, June 1983, *92*(7), pp. 1334–41.

Chesshire, John H. and Robson, Michael J. Capital Stock Rotation, Conservation and Fuel Substitution in the UK Industrial Steam-Raising Market. *Energy Econ.*, October 1983, *5*(4), pp. 218–31. **[G: U.K.]**

Collinge, Robert A. and Bailey, Martin J. Optimal Quasi-Market Choice in the Presence of Pollution Externalities. *J. Environ. Econ. Manage.*, September 1983, *10*(3), pp. 221–32.

Collins, Robert A. and Headley, J. C. Optimal Investment to Reduce the Decay Rate of an Income Stream: The Case of Soil Conservation. *J. Environ. Econ. Manage.*, March 1983, *10*(1), pp. 60–71.

Condominas, S. La crisis economica contemporanea: algunas consideraciones generales. (The Present Economic Crisis. With English summary.) *Écon. Soc.*, September–October–November 1983, *17*(9–10–11), pp. 1383–1401.

Cox, Thomas R. Trade, Development, and Environmental Change: The Utilization of North America's Pacific Coast Forests to 1914 and Its Consequences. In *Tucker, R. P. and Richards, J. F., eds.*, 1983, pp. 14–29. **[G: U.S.]**

Crandall, Robert W. Air Pollution, Environmentalists, and the Coal Lobby. In *Noll, R. G. and Owen, B. M.*, 1983, pp. 84–96. **[G: U.S.]**

Crone, Theodore M. Transferable Discharge Permits and the Control of Stationary Source Air Pollution: Comment. *Land Econ.*, February 1983, *59*(1), pp. 123–25. **[G: U.S.]**

Cross, Mark L. and Thornton, John H. The Probable Effect of an Extreme Hurricane on Texas Catastrophe Plan Insurers. *J. Risk Ins.*, September 1983, *50*(3), pp. 417–44. **[G: U.S.]**

Danner, Richard A. Federal Regulation of Non-Nuclear Hazardous Wastes: A Research Bibliography. *Law Contemp. Probl.*, Summer 1983, *46*(3), pp. 285–305.

David, Martin H. and Joeres, Erhard F. Is a Viable Implementation of TDPs Transferable? In *Joeres, E. F. and David, M. H., eds.*, 1983, pp. 233–48. **[G: U.S.]**

Dean, Warren. Deforestation in Southeastern Brazil. In *Tucker, R. P. and Richards, J. F., eds.*, 1983, pp. 50–67. **[G: Brazil]**

Deshmukh, Sudhakar D. and Pliska, Stanley R. Optimal Consumption of a Nonrenewable Resource with Stochastic Discoveries and a Random Environment. *Rev. Econ. Stud.*, July 1983, *50*(3), pp. 543–54.

Dewees, Donald N. Instrument Choice in Environmental Policy. *Econ. Inquiry,* January 1983, *21*(1), pp. 53–71.

Dewees, Donald N. Regulating Environmental Quality. **In** *Dewees, D. N., ed.*, 1983, pp. 141–72. **[G: Canada; U.S.]**

Dewees, Donald N. The Control of Diesel Exhaust Pollution. **In** *Dewees, D. N., ed.*, 1983, pp. 293–322. **[G: U.S.]**

Dickenson, Russell E. Public Parks: Exploration and Preservation—Is There a Middle Way? **In** *Barnes, C. H., ed.*, 1983, pp. 47–57. **[G: U.S.]**

Drezner, Z. and Wesolowsky, G. O. The Location of an Obnoxious Facility with Rectangular Distances. *J. Reg. Sci.*, May 1983, *23*(2), pp. 241–48.

Dunlap, Riley E. Ecologist versus Exemptionalist: The Ehrlich-Simon Debate. *Soc. Sci. Quart.*, March 1983, *64*(1), pp. 200–203.

Earl, Anthony S. Achieving Environmental Quality in the Face of Social, Economic and Political Constraints. **In** *Joeres, E. F. and David, M. H., eds.*, 1983, pp. 1–5. **[G: U.S.]**

Earney, Fillmore C. F. Petroleum and the Environment. **In** *Glassner, M. I., ed.*, 1983, *1980*, pp. 564–79. **[G: U.S.; Selected Countries]**

Edmonds, Jae A. and Reilly, John M. A Long-Term Global Energy-Economic Model of Carbon Dioxide Release from Fossil Fuel Use. *Energy Econ.*, April 1983, *5*(2), pp. 74–88. **[G: Global]**

Edmonds, Jae A. and Reilly, John M. Global Energy and CO_2 to the Year 2050. *Energy J.*, July 1983, *4*(3), pp. 21–47. **[G: Global]**

Eheart, J. Wayland; Brill, E. Downey, Jr. and Lyon, Randolph M. Transferable Discharge Permits for Control of BOD: An Overview. **In** *Joeres, E. F. and David, M. H., eds.*, 1983, pp. 163–95. **[G: U.S.]**

Ehrlich, Paul R. and Ehrlich, Anne H. 1984: Population and Environment. **In** *Stansky, P., ed.*, 1983, pp. 49–55.

Endres, Alfred. Do Effluent Charges (Always) Reduce Environmental Damage? *Oxford Econ. Pap.*, July 1983, *35*(2), pp. 254–61.

Falcke, Caj O. Water Quality and Property Prices: An Econometric Analysis of Environmental Benefits. *Kansant. Aikak.*, 1983, *79*(1), pp. 94–102. **[G: U.S.]**

Feinerman, Eli and Knapp, Keith C. Benefits from Groundwater Management: Magnitude, Sensitivity, and Distribution. *Amer. J. Agr. Econ.*, November 1983, *65*(4), pp. 703–10. **[G: U.S.]**

Ferrett, Robert L. and Ward, Robert M. Agricultural Land Use Planning and Groundwater Quality. *Growth Change*, January 1983, *14*(1), pp. 32–39. **[G: U.S.]**

Fischhoff, Baruch. "Acceptable Risk": The Case of Nuclear Power. *J. Policy Anal. Manage.*, Summer 1983, *2*(4), pp. 559–75. **[G: U.S.]**

Fodella, Gianni. Technology Transfer in the Energy Field for Water and Soil Conservation. *Rivista Int. Sci. Econ. Com.*, July 1983, *30*(7), pp. 667–77. **[G: LDCs]**

Foster, David. Planning for the Development of Economic Incentives under Institutional Constraints: The Role for Guided Incrementalism. **In** *Joeres, E. F. and David, M. H., eds.*, 1983, pp. 71–81.

Frye, Richard. Climatic Change and Fisheries Management. *Natural Res. J.*, January 1983, *23*(1), pp. 77–96. **[G: U.S.]**

Gershon, Mark and Duckstein, Lucien. Reply [Multiobjective River Basin Planning with Qualitative Criteria]. *Water Resources Res.*, February 1983, *19*(1), pp. 295–96. **[G: U.S.]**

Goble, Robert L. Time Scales and the Problem of Radioactive Waste. **In** *Kasperson, R. E., ed.*, 1983, pp. 139–74. **[G: U.S.]**

Gollop, Frank M. and Roberts, Mark J. Environmental Regulations and Productivity Growth: The Case of Fossil-Fueled Electric Power Generation. *J. Polit. Econ.*, August 1983, *91*(4), pp. 654–74. **[G: U.S.]**

Goodisman, Leonard D. Budgeting and Field Discretion in Disaster Relief. *Public Budg. Finance*, Spring 1983, *3*(1), pp. 89–102. **[G: U.S.]**

Gould, Leroy C. The Radioactive Waste Management Problem. **In** *Walker, C. A.; Gould, L. C. and Woodhouse, E. J., eds.*, 1983, pp. 1–26. **[G: U.S.]**

Graham, John D. and Vaupel, James W. The Value of Life: What Difference Does It Make? **In** *Zeckhauser, R. J. and Leebaert, D., eds.*, 1983, pp. 176–86. **[G: U.S.]**

Grieson, Ronald E. and Wittman, Donald A. Regulation May Be No Worse Than Its Alternatives. **In** *Grieson, R. E., ed.*, 1983, pp. 171–91.

Grigalunas, Thomas A. Distribution of Costs to Brittany, France, and the Rest of the World. **In** *U.S. Dept. Comm., Nat'l Oceanic and Atmos. Admin.*, 1983, pp. 137–44. **[G: France]**

Grigalunas, Thomas A., et al. Assessing the Social Costs of Oil Spills: The AMOCO CADIZ Case Study: The Tourist Industry. **In** *U.S. Dept. Comm., Nat'l Oceanic and Atmos. Admin.*, 1983, pp. 111–25. **[G: France]**

Guruswamy, L. D.; Papps, I. and Storey, D. J. The Development and Impact of an EEC Directive: The Control of Discharges of Mercury to the Aquatic Environment. *J. Common Market Stud.*, September 1983, *22*(1), pp. 71–100. **[G: EEC; U.K.]**

Hafkamp, Wim and Nijkamp, Peter. Conflict Analysis and Compromise Strategies in Integrated Spatial Systems. *Reg. Sci. Urban Econ.*, February 1983, *13*(1), pp. 115–40.

Hageman, Ronda K. An Assesssment of the Value of Natural Hazards Damage Reduction in Dwellings Due to Building Codes: Two Case Studies. *Natural Res. J.*, July 1983, *23*(3), pp. 531–47. **[G: U.S.]**

Hahn, Robert W. Designing Markets in Transferable Property Rights: A Practitioner's Guide. **In** *Joeres, E. F. and David, M. H., eds.*, 1983, pp. 83–97.

Hahn, Robert W. and Noll, Roger G. Barriers to Implementing Tradable Air Pollution Permits: Problems of Regulatory Interactions. *Yale J. Regul.*, 1983, *1*(1), pp. 63–91. **[G: U.S.]**

Harford, Jon D. and Karp, Gordon. The Effects and Efficiencies of Different Pollution Standards. *Eastern Econ. J.*, April–June 1983, *9*(2), pp. 79–89. **[G: U.S.]**

Harford, Jon D. and Ogura, S. Pollution Taxes and Standards: A Continuum of Quasi-Optimal Solutions. *J. Environ. Econ. Manage.*, March 1983, *10*(1), pp. 1–17.

Harrison, David, Jr. The Regulation of Aircraft Noise. In *Schelling, T. C., ed.*, 1983, pp. 41–143. **[G: U.S.]**

Haynes, Kingsley E.; Phillips, Fred Y. and Solomon, Barry D. A Coal Industry Distribution Planning Model under Environmental Constraints. *Econ. Geogr.*, January 1983, *59*(1), pp. 52–65.

Heaney, James P. Coalition Formation and the Size of Regional Pollution Control Systems. In *Joeres, E. F. and David, M. H., eds.*, 1983, pp. 99–120. **[G: U.S.]**

Herbay, Jean-Pierre; Smeers, Yves and Tyteca, Daniel. Water Quality Management with Time Varying River Flow and Discharger Control. *Water Resources Res.*, December 1983, *19*(6), pp. 1481–87.

Hirshfield, D.S. and Rapoport, L. A. Evaluation of U.S. Energy Policy Impacts on Energy Supplies and Costs. In *Lev, B., ed.*, 1983, pp. 445–63. **[G: U.S.]**

Hoerger, Fred; Beamer, William H. and Hanson, James S. The Cumulative Impact of Health, Environmental, and Safety Concerns on the Chemical Industry during the Seventies. *Law Contemp. Probl.*, Summer 1983, *46*(3), pp. 59–107. **[G: U.S.]**

Hotz, M. C. B. Resources and Development: Trying to Close the Gap Responsibly. In *Glassner, M. I., ed.*, 1983, *1981*, pp. 108–17. **[G: LDCs]**

Howe, Charles W. and Lee, Dwight R. Organising the Receptor Side of Pollution Rights Markets. *Australian Econ. Pap.*, December 1983, *22*(41), pp. 280–89. **[G: U.S.]**

Howe, Charles W. and Lee, Dwight R. Priority Pollution Rights: Adapting Pollution Control to a Variable Environment. *Land Econ.*, May 1983, *59*(2), pp. 141–49. **[G: U.S.]**

Howe, Charles W. and Lee, Dwight R. Priority Pollution Rights: An Adaptation of Western Water Law to Pollution Control Problems. In *Joeres, E. F. and David, M. H., eds.*, 1983, pp. 121–29.

Hughes, Joseph P. Controlling a Firm's Emission of a Pollutant from Many Sources. In *Dutta, M.; Hartline, J. C. and Loeb, P. D., eds.*, 1983, pp. 253–58.

Hyde, William F. The Federal Preserve in the West: Environmental Champion or Economic Despoiler. *J. Policy Anal. Manage.*, Summer 1983, *2*(4), pp. 605–14. **[G: U.S.]**

d'Iribarne, Philippe. What Kinds of Alternative Ways of Life Are Possible? In *Uusitalo, L., ed.*, 1983, pp. 27–37.

Isakson, Hans R. Residential Space Heating: An Analysis of Energy Conservation. *Energy Econ.*, January 1983, *5*(1), pp. 49–57. **[G: U.S.]**

Jackson, Richard H. The Federal Government and Land Use. In *Carr, J. H. and Duensing, E. E., eds.*, 1983, *1981*, pp. 113–27. **[G: U.S.]**

Johnson, F. Reed and Haspel, Abraham E. Economic Valuation of Potential Scenic Degradation at Bryce Canyon National Park. In *Rowe, R. D. and Chestnut, L. G., eds.*, 1983, pp. 235–45. **[G: U.S.]**

Kapp, K. William. 'Recycling' in Contemporary China. In *Kapp, K. W.*, 1983, *1974*, pp. 89–97. **[G: China]**

Kapp, K. William. Environmental Dangers, National Economy and Forestry. In *Kapp, K. W.*, 1983, *1971*, pp. 71–88.

Kapp, K. William. Environmental Disruption as an Economic and Political Problem. In *Kapp, K. W.*, 1983, *1972*, pp. 57–69.

Kapp, K. William. Environmental Disruption: General Issues and Methodological Problems. In *Kapp, K. W.*, 1983, *1970*, pp. 39–56.

Kapp, K. William. Governmental Furtherance of Environmentally Sound Technologies as a Focus of Research and Environmental Policies. In *Kapp, K. W.*, 1983, *1974*, pp. 143–207. **[G: Selected Countries]**

Kapp, K. William. Implementation of Environmental Policies. In *Kapp, K. W.*, 1983, *1971*, pp. 111–42. **[G: LDCs]**

Kapp, K. William. Social Costs in Economic Development. In *Kapp, K. W.*, 1983, *1965*, pp. 1–38. **[G: LDCs; Philippines]**

Kasperson, Roger E. Social Issues in Radioactive Waste Management: The National Experience. In *Kasperson, R. E., ed.*, 1983, pp. 24–65. **[G: U.S.]**

Kasperson, Roger E.; Derr, Patrick and Kates, Robert W. Confronting Equity in Radioactive Waste Management: Modest Proposals for a Socially Just and Acceptable Program. In *Kasperson, R. E., ed.*, 1983, pp. 331–68. **[G: U.S.]**

Kasperson, Roger E. and Rubin, Barry L. Siting a Radioactive Waste Repository: What Role for Equity? In *Kasperson, R. E., ed.*, 1983, pp. 118–36. **[G: U.S.]**

Kates, Robert W. and Braine, Bonnie. Locus, Equity, and the West Valley Nuclear Wastes. In *Kasperson, R. E., ed.*, 1983, pp. 94–117. **[G: U.S.]**

Kelman, Steven. Economic Incentives and Environmental Policy: Politics, Ideology, and Philosophy. In *Schelling, T. C., ed.*, 1983, pp. 291–331. **[G: U.S.]**

Ketkar, Kusum W. Pollution Control and Inputs to Production. *J. Environ. Econ. Manage.*, March 1983, *10*(1), pp. 50–59. **[G: U.S.]**

Keyes, Dale L. Reagan Energy and Environmental Programs: Implications for State and Local Governments. In *Lefcoe, G., ed.*, 1983, pp. 77–89. **[G: U.S.]**

Kim, Il-Chung. Financing the Environmental Capacity through Income Tax. *Reg. Sci. Persp.*, 1983, *13*(2), pp. 26–38.

Kneese, Allen V., et al. Economic Issues in the Legacy Problem. In *Kasperson, R. E., ed.*, 1983, pp. 203–26. **[G: U.S.]**

Korsching, Peter F. and Nowak, Peter J. Flexibility in Conservation Policy. In *Brewster, D. E.; Rasmussen, W. D. and Youngberg, G., eds.*, 1983, pp. 149–59. **[G: U.S.]**

Kramer, Randall A.; McSweeny, William T. and Stav-

ros, **Robert W.** Soil Conservation with Uncertain Revenues and Input Supplies. *Amer. J. Agr. Econ.*, November 1983, *65*(4), pp. 694–702.

Krupnick, Alan J.; Oates, Wallace E. and Van De Verg, Eric. On Marketable Air Pollution Permits: The Case for a System of Pollution Offsets. **In** *Joeres, E. F. and David, M. H., eds.*, 1983, pp. 7–23.

Krupnick, Alan J.; Oates, Wallace E. and Van De Verg, Eric. On Marketable Air-Pollution Permits: The Case for a System of Pollution Offsets. *J. Environ. Econ. Manage.*, September 1983, *10*(3), pp. 233–47.

Krzysztofowicz, Roman and Davis, Donald R. A Methodology for Evaluation of Flood Forecast–Response Systems, 1. Analyses and Concepts. *Water Resources Res.*, December 1983, *19*(6), pp. 1423–29.

Krzysztofowicz, Roman and Davis, Donald R. A Methodology for Evaluation of Flood Forecast–Response Systems, 2. Theory. *Water Resources Res.*, December 1983, *19*(6), pp. 1431–40.

Krzysztofowicz, Roman and Davis, Donald R. A Methodology for Evaluation of Flood Forecast–Response Systems, 3. Case Studies. *Water Resources Res.*, December 1983, *19*(6), pp. 1441–54. **[G: U.S.]**

Kusler, Jon A. Regulating Sensitive Lands: An Overview of Programs. **In** *Carr, J. H. and Duensing, E. E., eds.*, 1983, *1980*, pp. 128–53. **[G: U.S.]**

Lake, Laura M. The Environmental Mandate: Activists and the Electorate. *Polit. Sci. Quart.*, Summer 1983, *98*(2), pp. 215–33. **[G: U.S.]**

Lamm, Richard D. Urban Land Policy for the 1980s: Public Resource Management under the Reagan Administration. **In** *Lefcoe, G., ed.*, 1983, pp. 91–100. **[G: U.S.]**

Lee, Dwight R. Monitoring and Budget Maximization on the Control of Pollution. *Econ. Inquiry*, October 1983, *21*(4), pp. 565–75.

Lee, Joon Koo and Lim, Gill Chin. Environmental Policies in Developing Countries: A Case of International Movements of Polluting Industries. *J. Devel. Econ.*, Aug.–Oct. 1983, *13*(1–2), pp. 159–73. **[G: LDCs]**

Lees, Susan H. Environmental Hazards and Decision Making: Another Perspective from Human Ecology. **In** *Ortiz, S., ed.*, 1983, pp. 183–91.

Lipfert, Frederick W. Comment to Robert Mendelsohn and Guy Orcutt Regarding: "An Empirical Analysis of Air Pollution Dose—Response Curves." *J. Environ. Econ. Manage.*, June 1983, *10*(2), pp. 184–86. **[G: U.S.]**

Liu, Ben-chieh. Helium Conservation and Supply and Demand Projections in the USA. *Energy Econ.*, January 1983, *5*(1), pp. 58–64. **[G: U.S.]**

Lott, John R. A Note on Law, Property Rights, and Air Pollution. *Cato J.*, Winter 1983/84, *3*(3), pp. 875–78.

Lurie, Robert S. R&D, Innovation and Environmental Regulation: The Case of Copper. *Amer. Econ.*, Fall 1983, *27*(2), pp. 13–20. **[G: U.S.]**

MacFarland, Karen Kelley; Malm, William and Molenar, John. An Examination of Methodologies for Assessing the Value of Visibility. **In** *Rowe, R. D. and Chestnut, L. G., eds.*, 1983, pp. 151–72. **[G: U.S.]**

MacLean, Douglas. Radioactive Wastes: A Problem of Morality between Generations. **In** *Kasperson, R. E., ed.*, 1983, pp. 175–88.

Majone, Giandomenico. Reforming Standard-Setting. *J. Policy Anal. Manage.*, Winter 1983, *2*(2), pp. 285–90. **[G: W. Europe; U.S.S.R.; U.S.; U.K.]**

Maloney, M. T. and Yandle, T. Bruce. Building Markets for Tradable Pollution Rights. **In** *Anderson, T. L., ed.*, 1983, pp. 283–320. **[G: U.S.]**

McConnell, Kenneth E. A Economic Model of Soil Conservation. *Amer. J. Agr. Econ.*, February 1983, *65*(1), pp. 83–89.

McEvoy, Arthur F. Law, Public Policy, and Industrialization in the California Fisheries, 1900–1925. *Bus. Hist. Rev.*, Winter 1983, *57*(4), pp. 494–521. **[G: U.S.]**

McGarity, Thomas O. Media-Quality, Technology, and Cost–Benefit Balancing Strategies for Health and Environmental Regulation. *Law Contemp. Probl.*, Summer 1983, *46*(3), pp. 159–233.

Meier, Richard L. Redefining Urban Ecosystems. **In** *Glassner, M. I., ed.*, 1983, *1974*, pp. 127–35.

Melville, Mary H. Temporary Workers in the Nuclear Power Industry: Implications for the Waste Management Program. **In** *Kasperson, R. E., ed.*, 1983, pp. 229–58. **[G: U.S.]**

Mendelsohn, Robert. Emission Transfer Markets: How Large Should Each Market Be? **In** *Joeres, E. F. and David, M. H., eds.*, 1983, pp. 25–38. **[G: U.S.]**

Mendelsohn, Robert and Orcutt, Guy. A Reply to a Comment on Estimating Air Pollution Dose—Response Curves. *J. Environ. Econ. Manage.*, June 1983, *10*(2), pp. 187–90. **[G: U.S.]**

Menz, Fredric C. and Driscoll, Charles T. An Estimate of the Costs of Liming to Neutralize Acidic Adirondack Surface Waters. *Water Resources Res.*, October 1983, *19*(5), pp. 1139–49. **[G: U.S.]**

Morgan, Peter J. Alternative Policy Instruments under Uncertainty: A Programming Model of Toxic Pollution Control. *J. Environ. Econ. Manage.*, September 1983, *10*(3), pp. 248–69.

Morgan, Peter J. Alternative Policy Instruments under Uncertainty: A Programming Model of Toxic Pollution Control. **In** *Joeres, E. F. and David, M. H., eds.*, 1983, pp. 197–217.

Murphey, Rhoads. Deforestation in Modern China. **In** *Tucker, R. P. and Richards, J. F., eds.*, 1983, pp. 111–28. **[G: China]**

Nafziger, Richard and Wustner, Michael F. The Energy War on the American West. *Rev. Radical Polit. Econ.*, Fall 1983, *15*(3), pp. 5–8. **[G: U.S.]**

National Academy of Sciences. Energy in Transition 1985–2010. **In** *Glassner, M. I., ed.*, 1983, *1980*, pp. 289–310. **[G: U.S.]**

Nealey, Stanley M. and Hebert, John A. Public Attitudes toward Radioactive Wastes. **In** *Walker, C. A.; Gould, L. C. and Woodhouse, E. J., eds.*, 1983, pp. 94–111. **[G: U.S.]**

Newman, Pixie A. B. and Rosenthal, Stuart S. Buying a Better Environment: Cost-Effective Regulation through Permit Trading: Summary. **In** *Joeres, E. F. and David, M. H., eds.*, 1983, pp. 257–62.

Nichols, Albert L. The Regulation of Airborne Ben-zene. In *Schelling, T. C., ed.*, 1983, pp. 145–219. [G: U.S.]

Noll, Roger G. The Feasibility of Marketable Emissions Permits in the United States. **In** *Finsinger, J., ed.*, 1983, pp. 189–225. [G: U.S.]

O'Neil, William B. The Regulation of Water Pollution Permit Trading under Conditions of Varying Streamflow and Temperature. **In** *Joeres, E. F. and David, M. H., eds.*, 1983, pp. 219–31. [G: U.S.]

O'Neil, William B. Transferable Discharge Permit Trading under Varying Stream Conditions: A Simulation of Multiperiod Permit Market Performance on the Fox River, Wisconsin. *Water Resources Res.*, June 1983, *19*(3), pp. 608–12. [G: U.S.]

O'Neil, William B., et al. Transferable Discharge Permits and Economic Efficiency: The Fox River. *J. Environ. Econ. Manage.*, December 1983, *10*(4), pp. 346–55. [G: U.S.]

O'Neill, William D. Direct Empirical Estimation of Effeciency in Secondary Materials Markets: The Case of Steel Scrap. *J. Environ. Econ. Manage.*, September 1983, *10*(3), pp. 270–81. [G: U.S.]

Odell, Rice. Global Resources: Challenges of Interdependence: Values. **In** *Glassner, M. I., ed.*, 1983, *1980*, pp. 147–57. [G: U.S.]

Ogg, Clayton W.; Pionke, Harry B. and Heimlich, Ralph E. A Linear Programming Economic Analysis of Lake Quality Improvements Using Phosphorus Buffer Curves. *Water Resources Res.*, February 1983, *19*(1), pp. 21–31. [G: U.S.]

Oppenheimer, Joe A. and Russell, Clifford. A Tempest in a Teapot: The Analysis and Evaluation of Environmental Groups Trading in Markets for Pollution Permits. **In** *Joeres, E. F. and David, M. H., eds.*, 1983, pp. 131–48.

Osaka, Masako M. Forest Preservation in Tokugawa Japan. **In** *Tucker, R. P. and Richards, J. F., eds.*, 1983, pp. 129–45. [G: Japan]

Ostro, Bart D. The Effects of Air Pollution on Work Loss and Morbidity. *J. Environ. Econ. Manage.*, December 1983, *10*(4), pp. 371–82. [G: U.S.]

Ostro, Bart D. Urban Air Pollution and Morbidity: A Retrospective Approach. *Urban Stud.*, August 1983, *20*(3), pp. 343–51. [G: U.S.]

Pearce, David W. The Limits of Cost-Benefit Analysis as a Guide to Environmental Policy: A Reply to Professor Cooper. *Kyklos*, 1983, *36*(1), pp. 112–14.

Pereira, Pedro Telhado. Developing Countries and the Economics of Irrversible Changes in Natural Environments. *Economia*, January 1983, *7*(1), pp. 71–85. [G: LDCs]

Peterson, Russell W. Energy Policies and the Quality of Life. **In** *Barnes, C. H., ed.*, 1983, pp. 25–33. [G: U.S.]

Pittman, Russell W. Multilateral Productivity Comparisons with Undesirable Outputs. *Econ. J.*, December 1983, *93*(372), pp. 883–91. [G: U.S.]

Plott, Charles R. Externalities and Corrective Policies in Experimental Markets. *Econ. J.*, March 1983, *93*(369), pp. 106–27.

Porter, Richard C. A Social Benefit-Cost Analysis of Mandatory Deposits on Beverage Containers: A Correction. *J. Environ. Econ. Manage.*, June 1983, *10*(2), pp. 191–93. [G: U.S.]

Porter, Richard C. Michigan's Experience with Mandatory Deposits on Beverage Containers. *Land Econ.*, May 1983, *59*(2), pp. 177–94. [G: U.S.]

Povileiko, R. P. Ecology and Economics (A Survey of Ideas and the Literature). *Prob. Econ.*, September 1983, *26*(5), pp. 3–14. [G: U.S.S.R.]

Prud'homme, Rémy. Le Rôle de la Fiscalité dans la Lutte contre les Encombrements et les Pollutions. **In** *Biehl, D.; Roskamp, K. W. and Stolper, W. F., eds.*, 1983, pp. 387–98.

Quinn, Timothy H. Distributive Consequences and Political Concerns: On the Design of Feasible Market Mechanisms for Environmental Control. **In** *Joeres, E. F. and David, M. H., eds.*, 1983, pp. 39–54. [G: U.S.]

Rae, Douglas A. The Value to Visitors of Improving Visibility at Mesa Verde and Great Smoky National Parks. **In** *Rowe, R. D. and Chestnut, L. G., eds.*, 1983, pp. 217–34. [G: U.S.]

Rapport, D. J. The Stress-Response Environmental Statistical System and Its Applicability to the Laurentian Lower Great Lakes. *Statist. J.*, October 1983, *1*(4), pp. 377–405. [G: Canada]

Rasnic, Carol D. Federally Required Restoration of Surface-Mined Property: Impasse between the Coal Industry and the Environmentally Concerned. *Natural Res. J.*, April 1983, *23*(2), pp. 335–49. [G: U.S.]

Ratick, Samuel J. Multiobjective Programming with Related Bargaining Games: An Application to Utility Coal Conversions. *Reg. Sci. Urban Econ.*, February 1983, *13*(1), pp. 55–76. [G: U.S.]

Raucher, Robert L. A Conceptual Framework for Measuring the Benefits of Groundwater Protection. *Water Resources Res.*, April 1983, *19*(2), pp. 320–26.

Reed, Krista S. and Young, C. Edwin. Impact of Regulatory Delays on the Cost of Wastewater Treatment Plants. *Land Econ.*, February 1983, *59*(1), pp. 35–42. [G: U.S.]

Regev, Uri; Shalit, Haim and Gutierrez, A. P. On the Optimal Allocation of Pesticides with Increasing Resistance: The Case of Alfalfa Weevil. *J. Environ. Econ. Manage.*, March 1983, *10*(1), pp. 86–100.

Repetto, Robert. Air Quality under the Clean Air Act. **In** *Schelling, T. C., ed.*, 1983, pp. 221–90. [G: U.S.]

Roberts, Manley W. A Remedy for the Victims of Pollution Permit Markets. *Yale Law J.*, May 1983, *92*(6), pp. 1022–40.

Rolph, Elizabeth S. Government Allocation of Property Rights: Who Gets What? *J. Policy Anal. Manage.*, Fall 1983, *3*(1), pp. 45–61. [G: U.S.]

Rose, Adam. Modeling the Macroeconomic Impact of Air Pollution Abatement. *J. Reg. Sci.*, November 1983, *23*(4), pp. 441–59. [G: U.S.]

Roth, Dennis M. Philippine Forests and Forestry: 1565–1920. **In** *Tucker, R. P. and Richards, J. F., eds.*, 1983, pp. 30–49. [G: Philippine]

Rowe, Robert D. and Chestnut, Lauraine G. Priorities for Economic Analysis of Visibility Values. **In** *Rowe, R. D. and Chestnut, L. G., eds.*, 1983, pp. 246–53. [G: U.S.]

Rowe, W. D. Implicit Equity Considerations in Radiation Protection Standards. **In** *Kasperson, R. E., ed.*, 1983, pp. 259–76. [G: U.S.]

Ruiz, G.; Narvaez, A. and Gallego, J.-A. Crisis económica, desarrollo y medio ambiente. (Economic Crisis, Development and Environment. With English summary.) *Écon. Soc.*, September–October–November 1983, *17*(–10–11), pp. 1647–69.

Runge, Carlisle Ford. Risk Assessment and Environmental Benefits Analysis. *Natural Res. J.*, July 1983, *23*(3), pp. 683–96. **[G: U.S.]**

Russo, William J., Jr. and Rutledge, Gary L. Plant and Equipment Expenditures by Business for Pollution Abatement, 1982 and Planned 1983. *Surv. Curr. Bus.*, June 1983, *63*(6), pp. 24–26. **[G: U.S.]**

Rutledge, Gary L. and Lease-Trevathan, Susan. Pollution Abatement and Control Expenditures, 1972–81. *Surv. Curr. Bus.*, February 1983, *63*(2), pp. 15–23. **[G: U.S.]**

Ryan, Donald R. Transferable Discharge Permits and the Control of Stationary Source Air Pollution: Reply. *Land Econ.*, February 1983, *59*(1), pp. 126–27. **[G: U.S.]**

Samuels, Warren J. The Distributional Problem in Risk Policy: A Note. *Land Econ.*, February 1983, *59*(1), pp. 114–17. **[G: U.S.]**

Schatz, Klaus-Werner. Market Approaches to Environmental Protection: Comment. **In** *Giersch, H., ed.*, 1983, pp. 259–63.

Schelling, Thomas C. Incentives for Environmental Protection. **In** *Schelling, T. C., ed.*, 1983, pp. ix–xix.

Schelling, Thomas C. Prices as Regulatory Instruments. **In** *Schelling, T. C., ed.*, 1983, pp. 1–40.

Schroeder, Christopher. A Decade of Change in Regulating the Chemical Industry. *Law Contemp. Probl.*, Summer 1983, *46*(3), pp. 1–40. **[G: U.S.]**

Schulze, William D., et al. The Economic Benefits of Preserving Visibility in the National Parklands of the Southwest. *Natural Res. J.*, January 1983, *23*(1), pp. 149–73. **[G: U.S.]**

Seley, John E. and Wolpert, Julian. Equity and Location. **In** *Kasperson, R. E., ed.*, 1983, pp. 69–93. **[G: U.S.]**

Seskin, Eugene P.; Anderson, Robert J., Jr. and Reid, Robert O. An Empirical Analysis of Economic Strategies for Controlling Air Pollution. *J. Environ. Econ. Manage.*, June 1983, *10*(2), pp. 112–24. **[G: U.S.]**

Shane, Philip B. and Spicer, Barry H. Market Response to Environmental Information Produced Outside the Firm. *Accounting Rev.*, July 1983, *58*(3), pp. 521–38. **[G: U.S.]**

Shapiro, Michael and Warhit, Ellen. Marketable Permits: The Case of Chlorofluorocarbons. *Natural Res. J.*, July 1983, *23*(3), pp. 577–91. **[G: U.S.]**

Shibata, Hirofumi. Fiscal Measures against Pollution: Are Effluent Taxes and Abatement Subsidies Equivalent? **In** *Biehl, D.; Roskamp, K. W. and Stolper, W. F., eds.*, 1983, pp. 399–418.

Shibata, Hirofumi and Winrich, J. Steven. Control of Pollution when the Offended Defend Themselves. *Economica*, November 1983, *50*(200), pp. 425–37.

Sills, David L. The Utilization of Social Science Knowledge in Studying Technology and Society: The Case of the Accident at Three Mile Island. **In** *Holzner, B.; Knorr, K. D. and Strasser, H., eds.*, 1983, pp. 327–36. **[G: U.S.]**

Silver, Melinda. Nuclear Power Plant Licensing—Jurisdiction to Consider Foreign Impacts. *Natural Res. J.*, January 1983, *23*(1), pp. 225–37. **[G: U.S.; Philippines]**

Slovic, Paul and Fischhoff, Baruch. How Safe Is Safe Enough? Determinants of Perceived and Acceptable Risk. **In** *Walker, C. A.; Gould, L. C. and Woodhouse, E. J., eds.*, 1983, pp. 112–50.

Smeers, Yves and Tyteca, Daniel. On the Optimal Location of Wastewater Treatment Plants. **In** *Thisse, J.-F. and Zoller, H. G., eds.*, 1983, pp. 395–412.

Smith, J. C. The Processes of Adjudication and Regulation, a Comparison. **In** *Machan, T. R. and Johnson, M. B., eds.*, 1983, pp. 71–96. **[G: U.S.]**

Smith, V. Kerry; Desvousges, William H. and McGivney, Matthew P. Estimating Water Quality Benefits: An Econometric Analysis. *Southern Econ. J.*, October 1983, *50*(2), pp. 422–37. **[G: U.S.]**

Sonstelie, Jon C. and Portney, Paul R. Truth or Consequences: Cost Revelation and Regulation. *J. Policy Anal. Manage.*, Winter 1983, *2*(2), pp. 280–84. **[G: U.S.]**

Sorensen, Philip E. Correcting for Autocorrelation Problems in Regression Equations Used to Estimate Losses in Fisheries Catch. **In** *U.S. Dept. Comm., Nat'l Oceanic and Atmos. Admin.*, 1983, pp. 86–87. **[G: France]**

Sorensen, Philip E. Marine Resources. **In** *U.S. Dept. Comm., Nat'l Oceanic and Atmos. Admin.*, 1983, pp. 57–80. **[G: France]**

Spronk, Jaap and Veeneklaas, Frank. A Feasibility Study of Economic and Environmental Scenarios by Means of Interactive Multiple Goal Programming. *Reg. Sci. Urban Econ.*, February 1983, *13*(1), pp. 141–60. **[G: Netherlands]**

Stanley, John A. Reasonable EPA Projection Techniques for Estimating Technological Advances Upheld. *Natural Res. J.*, January 1983, *23*(1), pp. 219–24. **[G: U.S.]**

Stolwijk, Jan A. J. Nuclear Waste Management and Risks to Human Health. **In** *Walker, C. A.; Gould, L. C. and Woodhouse, E. J., eds.*, 1983, pp. 75–93. **[G: U.S.]**

Strudler, Michael and Strand, Ivar E., Jr. Pricing as a Policy to Reduce Sewage Costs. *Water Resources Res.*, February 1983, *19*(1), pp. 53–56. **[G: U.S.]**

Sullivan, Arthur M. Second-Best Policies for Congestion Externalities. *J. Urban Econ.*, July 1983, *14*(1), pp. 105–23.

Taylor, C. Robert, et al. Aggregate Economic Effects of Alternative Boll Weevil Management Strategies. *Agr. Econ. Res.*, April 1983, *35*(2), pp. 19–28. **[G: U.S.]**

Taylor, John A. Managing Our Visual Resources. **In** *Rowe, R. D. and Chestnut, L. G., eds.*, 1983, pp. 289–95. **[G: U.S.]**

The Georgia Conservancy. The Wolfcreek Statement: Toward a Sustainable Energy Society. **In** *Glassner, M. I., ed.*, 1983, *1976*, pp. 311–17. **[G: U.S.]**

Theiler, Donald. Transferable Discharge Permits: An Implementor's View. **In** *Joeres, E. F. and David, M. H., eds.*, 1983, pp. 253–56.

Thomas, Vinod. Welfare Analysis of Pollution Control with Spatial Alternatives. *Urban Stud.*, May 1983, *20*(2), pp. 219–27. [G: U.S.]

Tietenberg, Thomas H. Market Approaches to Environmental Protection. **In** *Giersch, H., ed.*, 1983, pp. 233–58.

Tietenberg, Thomas H. Transferable Discharge Permits and the Control of Stationary Source Air Pollution: Reply. *Land Econ.*, February 1983, *59*(1), pp. 128–30. [G: U.S.]

Tran, Ngoc-Bich and Smith, V. Kerry. The Role of Air and Water Residuals for Steam Electric Power Generation. *J. Environ. Econ. Manage.*, March 1983, *10*(1), pp. 35–49. [G: U.S.]

Tucker, Richard P. The British Colonial System and the Forests of the Western Himalayas, 1815–1914. **In** *Tucker, R. P. and Richards, J. F., eds.*, 1983, pp. 146–66. [G: India]

United Nations. United Nations Conference on Desertification: Round-up of the Conference. **In** *Glassner, M. I., ed.*, 1983, *1978*, pp. 523–31. [G: Global]

U.S. Department of Commerce. The Social Costs of the Amoco Cadiz Oil Spill: Introduction and Summary. **In** *U.S. Dept. Comm., Nat'l Oceanic and Atmos. Admin.*, 1983, pp. 1–36. [G: France]

Uusitalo, Liisa. Environmental Impacts of Changes in Consumption Style. **In** *Uusitalo, L., ed.*, 1983, pp. 123–42. [G: OECD]

Vallarta, Jose Luis. Protection and Preservation of the Marine Environment and Marine Scientific Research at the Third United Nations Conference on the Law of the Sea. *Law Contemp. Probl.*, Spring 1983, *46*(2), pp. 147–54. [G: Global]

Viscusi, W. Kip. Frameworks for Analyzing the Effects of Risk and Environmental Regulations on Productivity. *Amer. Econ. Rev.*, September 1983, *73*(4), pp. 793–801.

Walker, Charles A. Science and Technology of the Sources and Management of Radioactive Wastes. **In** *Walker, C. A.; Gould, L. C. and Woodhouse, E. J., eds.*, 1983, pp. 27–74. [G: U.S.]

Walker, Charles A.; Gould, Leroy C. and Woodhouse, Edward J. Value Issues in Radioactive Waste Management. **In** *Walker, C. A.; Gould, L. C. and Woodhouse, E. J., eds.*, 1983, pp. 184–206.

Warner, Langdon S. Conservation Aspects of the Fishery Conservation and Management Act and the Protection of Critical Marine Habitat. *Natural Res. J.*, January 1983, *23*(1), pp. 97–130. [G: U.S.]

Wassermann, Ursula. Economic Commission for Europe: Air Pollutants. *J. World Trade Law*, November–December 1983, *17*(6), pp. 533–35. [G: Europe]

Wassermann, Ursula. IMO: Prevention of Ocean Pollution. *J. World Trade Law*, January–February 1983, *17*(1), pp. 81–83.

Wassermann, Ursula. UNEP: Protection of the Ozone Layer. *J. World Trade Law*, March–April 1983, *17*(2), pp. 182–83. [G: Global]

Weinstein, Milton C. and Quinn, Robert J. Psychological Considerations in Valuing Health Risk Reductions. *Natural Res. J.*, July 1983, *23*(3), pp. 659–73. [G: U.S.]

Wenstøp, Fred. Evaluation of Oil Spill Combat Plans by Means of Multi-criteria Decision Analysis. **In** *Stigum, B. P. and Wenstøp, F., eds.*, 1983, pp. 461–82. [G: Norway]

Westing, Arthur H. The Environmental Aftermath of Warfare in Viet Nam. *Natural Res. J.*, April 1983, *23*(2), pp. 365–89. [G: Viet Nam]

Woodhouse, Edward J. The Politics of Nuclear Waste Management. **In** *Walker, C. A.; Gould, L. C. and Woodhouse, E. J., eds.*, 1983, pp. 151–83. [G: U.S.]

Yamauchi, Hiroshi and Onoe, Hisao. Analytical Concepts and Framework for Environmental Conservation. *Rivista Int. Sci. Econ. Com.*, August 1983, *30*(8), pp. 759–78.

Yandle, T. Bruce. Economic Agents and the Level of Pollution Control. *Public Choice*, 1983, *40*(1), pp. 105–09.

Yellin, Joel. Science, Technology, and Administrative Government: Institutional Designs for Environmental Decisionmaking. *Yale Law J.*, June 1983, *92*(7), pp. 1300–1333.

Zimmermann, Klaus. Ansatzpunkte einer verteilungsorientierten Umweltpolitik. (Areas for Applying a Distribution-Oriented Environmental Policy. With English summary.) *Kyklos*, 1983, *36*(3), pp. 420–49.

723 Energy

7230 Energy

Abbey, David S. and Kolstad, Charles D. The Structure of International Steam Coal Markets. *Natural Res. J.*, October 1983, *23*(4), pp. 859–91. [G: Selected Countries]

Abel, Andrew B. Energy Price Uncertainty and Optimal Factor Intensity: A Mean-Variance Analysis. *Econometrica*, November 1983, *51*(6), pp. 1839–45.

Adams, F. Gerard and Marquez, Jaime R. A Global Model of Oil-Price Impacts. **In** *[Klein, L. R.]*, 1983, pp. 317–39. [G: Global]

Adams, F. Gerard and Marquez, Jaime R. The Impact of Petroleum and Commodity Prices in a Model of the World Economy. **In** *Hickman, B. G., ed.*, 1983, pp. 203–16. [G: LDCs; MDCs]

Adar, Zvi and Agmon, Tamir. Financing Synthetic Fuels Investments in the United States: Public Support and Private Investment. **In** *Aronson, J. D. and Cowhey, P. F., eds.*, 1983, pp. 157–78. [G: U.S.]

Adelman, Morris A. Oil and Gas: Estimation of Discovered Reserves. **In** *Adelman, M. A., et al.*, 1983, pp. 27–81. [G: U.S.; Canada]

Adelman, Morris A. The Changing Structure of the Oil and Gas Market. **In** *Tempest, P., ed.*, 1983, pp. 15–25.

Adelman, Morris A. The Multinationals in the World Oil Market: The 1970s and the 1980s. **In** *Kindleberger, C. P. and Audretsch, D. B., eds.*, 1983, pp. 123–35. [G: OECD; OPEC]

Adelman, Morris A. and Houghton, John C. Introduction to Estimation of Reserves and Resources. **In** *Adelman, M. A., et al.*, 1983, pp. 1–25. [G: U.S.]

Akao, Nobutoshi. Resources and Japan's Security. **In**

Akao, N., ed., 1983, pp. 15–44. **[G: Japan]**

Akinc, Umit and Arbel, Avner. A Planning Model for Short Term Energy Crises Management. **In** *Lev, B., ed.*, 1983, pp. 325–37.

Al-Shaikhly, Salah. Some Popular Myths about Energy. **In** *Glassner, M. I., ed.*, 1983, *1981*, pp. 247–54. **[G: LDCs; MDCs; OPEC]**

Ali, Mehdi. Agriculture and Energy in the OPEC Fund's Activities—A Sectoral Perspective. **In** *Shihata, I. F. I., et al.*, 1983, pp. 50–71. **[G: OPEC]**

Almark, Barry and Alvarado, S. S. Dependent Development in the Third World in the Decade of Oil. *Rev. Radical Polit. Econ.*, Fall 1983, *15*(3), pp. 97–114. **[G: LDCs]**

Alt, Christopher B.; Baumann, Michael G. and Zimmerman, Martin B. The Economics of Western Coal Severance Taxes. *J. Bus.*, October 1983, *56*(4), pp. 519–36. **[G: U.S.]**

Anderson, Robert E. and Mead, David E. A Comparison of Original Cost and Trended Original Cost Ratemaking Methods. *Energy J.*, April 1983, *4*(2), pp. 151–58. **[G: U.S.]**

Andrén, Nils. Energy and Soviet Foreign Policy. **In** *Lieber, R. J., ed.*, 1983, pp. 105–21. **[G: U.S.S.R.]**

Andrews, Donald R.; Murdock, Steve H. and Jones, Lonnie L. Private and Public Sector Economies of Lignite-Energy Resource Development in Rural Central Texas. *Southern J. Agr. Econ.*, December 1983, *15*(2), pp. 55–61. **[G: U.S.]**

Andrus, Cecil D. Energy Development without Destruction: An Attainable Goal. **In** *Barnes, C. H., ed.*, 1983, pp. 1–14. **[G: U.S.]**

Angelier, J.-P. Problématique pour un système de prix de l'énergie dans un pays en voie de développement: l'exemple du Nicaragua. (Questions about a Price System of Energy in a Developing Country: The Example of Nicaragua. With English summary.) *Écon. Soc.*, December 1983, *17*(12), pp. 2033–51. **[G: Nicaragua]**

Apte, P. C. Substitution among Energy and Nonenergy Inputs in Selected Indian Manufacturing Industries: An Econometric Analysis. *Indian Econ. J.*, October–December 1983, *31*(2), pp. 71–90. **[G: India]**

Arbel, Avner and Ravid, S. Abraham. An Industry Energy Price Impact Model: The Case of the Hotel Industry. *Appl. Econ.*, December 1983, *15*(6), pp. 705–14. **[G: U.S.]**

Arbel, Avner and Ravid, S. Abraham. The Differential Impact of Gas Shortages and Fuel Price Increases on Demand: The Case of the Hotel Industry in New York State. *Energy J.*, April 1983, *4*(2), pp. 165–71. **[G: U.S.]**

Archibald, Robert and Gillingham, Robert. An Analysis of the Short-Run Consumer Demand for Gasoline Using Household Survey Data: A Reply. *Rev. Econ. Statist.*, August 1983, *65*(3), pp. 533–34. **[G: U.S.]**

Aronson, Jonathan David and Proctor, Charles Rudicel. Insurance, Risk Management, and Energy in Transition. **In** *Aronson, J. D. and Cowhey, P. F., eds.*, 1983, pp. 181–202. **[G: U.S.]**

Artus, Patrick. Formation conjointe des prix et des salaires dans cinq grands pays industriels: Peut-on comprendre les écarts entre les taux d'inflation? (The Joint Determination of Prices and Wages in Five Large Industrial Countries: Can We Explain the Differentials in Inflation? With English summary.) *Ann. INSEE*, Jan.–Mar. 1983, (49), pp. 5–52. **[G: U.S.; France; Japan; W. Germany; U.K.]**

Atkinson, F. J.; Brooks, Simon J. and Hall, S. G. F. The Economic Effects of North Sea Oil. *Nat. Inst. Econ. Rev.*, May 1983, (104), pp. 38–44. **[G: U.K.]**

Attiga, Ali A. The Role of Energy in South–South Cooperation. **In** *Gauhar, A., ed. (I)*, 1983, pp. 159–204. **[G: Global]**

Attiga, Ali Ahmed. Global Energy Transition and the Third World. **In** *Gauhar, A., ed. (II)*, 1983, pp. 48–65. **[G: LDCs]**

Av, Redigert, et al. Analysis of Supply and Demand of Electricity in the Norwegian Economy: Introduction. **In** *Av, R., et al., eds.*, 1983, pp. 14–26. **[G: Norway]**

Avi-Itzhak, Benjamin; Iusem, Alfredo and Dantzig, George B. The Consumers Energy Services Model of the Pilot System. **In** *Lev, B., ed.*, 1983, pp. 195–220. **[G: U.S.]**

Bahl, Roy W. State Energy Revenues: Comments. **In** *McLure, C. E., Jr. and Mieszkowski, P., eds.*, 1983, pp. 61–63. **[G: U.S.]**

Bailey, Richard. Coal in a Changing Market. *Nat. Westminster Bank Quart. Rev.*, August 1983, pp. 14–25. **[G: U.K.]**

Bajracharya, Deepak. Fuel, Food or Forest? Dilemmas in a Nepali Village. *World Devel.*, December 1983, *11*(12), pp. 1057–74. **[G: Nepal]**

Bakke, Dennis. The Least-Cost Energy Strategy. **In** *Schurr, S. H.; Sonenblum, S. and Wood, D. O., eds.*, 1983, pp. 191–202. **[G: U.S.]**

Baltagi, Badi H. and Griffin, James M. Gasoline Demand in the OECD: An Application of Pooling and Testing Procedures. *Europ. Econ. Rev.*, July 1983, *22*(2), pp. 117–37. **[G: OECD]**

Banks, Ferdinand E. European Reliance on Soviet Gas Exports. *Energy J.*, July 1983, *4*(3), pp. 95–96. **[G: Europe]**

Banks, Ferdinand E. Why Europe Needs Siberian Gas. **In** *Tempest, P., ed.*, 1983, pp. 191–96. **[G: W. Europe; U.S.S.R.]**

Barbet, P. La théorie des prix de l'énergie dans la pensée économique: une recension. (Energy Prices in the Economic Theory: A General Outlook. With English summary.) *Écon. Soc.*, December 1983, *17*(12), pp. 1809–834.

Barkenbus, Jack N. Is Self-Regulation Possible? *J. Policy Anal. Manage.*, Summer 1983, *2*(4), pp. 576–88. **[G: U.S.]**

Barkenbus, Jack N. Southern State Energy Data Needs. *Rev. Public Data Use (See J. Econ. Soc. Meas. after 4/85)*, March 1983, *11*(1), pp. 49–55. **[G: U.S.]**

Barnard, Jerald R. Gasohol/Ethanol: A Review of National and Regional Policy and Feasibility Issues. *Reg. Sci. Persp.*, 1983, *13*(2), pp. 3–14. **[G: U.S.]**

Barnett, Allen M. Solar Energy Commercialization Strategies. **In** *Rich, D., et al., eds.*, 1983, pp. 145–62.

Bauerschmidt, Rolf. Die Investitionserfordernisse

verschiedener Energiestrategien. Eine Vergleichsrechnung für die Pfade 2 und 3 der Enquete-Kommission des Deutschen Bundestages. (The Investment Requirements of Different Energy Strategies. With English summary.) *Konjunkturpolitik*, 1983, *29*(6), pp. 367–97. [G: W. Germany]

Baxendell, Sir Peter. International Energy Markets: Forces and Forecasts. **In** *Tempest, P., ed.*, 1983, pp. 5–12.

Beenstock, Michael and Willcocks, Patrick. Energy and Economic Activity: A Reply to Kouris. *Energy Econ.*, July 1983, *5*(3), pp. 212. [G: MDCs]

Bello, Walden; Harris, John and Zarsky, Lyuba. Nuclear Power in the Philippines: The Plague that Poisons Morong! *Rev. Radical Polit. Econ.*, Fall 1983, *15*(3), pp. 51–65. [G: Philippines]

Benzoni, L. and Leveau, C. La formation des prix de l'énergie: Essai sur la dynamique du système énergétique (France 1973–1983). (Formation of the Energy Prices: An Essay on the Dynamics of the Energy System. With English summary.) *Écon. Soc.*, December 1983, *17*(12), pp. 1869–1926. [G: France]

Bergendahl, Per Anders. Energy and the Economy—A Vintage Approach to the Analysis of Adaptation Inertia. **In** *Sohlman, A. M., ed.*, 1983, pp. 221–33.

Bergman, Lars. Intercountry Comparisons of Energy Consumption Patterns: Methodology and Usefulness. **In** *Uusitalo, L., ed.*, 1983, pp. 103–22. [G: W. Germany; France; Netherlands]

Berndt, Ernst R. The Energy Connection to Recent Productivity Behavior: Comment. **In** *Schurr, S. H.; Sonenblum, S. and Wood, D. O., eds.*, 1983, pp. 179–83. [G: U.S.]

Binkley, James K.; Tyner, Wallace E. and Matthews, Marie E. Evaluating Alternative Energy Policies: An Example Comparing Transportation Energy Investments. *Energy J.*, April 1983, *4*(2), pp. 91–104. [G: U.S.]

Bjerkholt, Olav and Rinde, Jon. Consumption Demand in the MSG Model. **In** *Av, R., et al., eds.*, 1983, pp. 84–107. [G: Norway]

Blattenberger, Gail R.; Taylor, Lester D. and Rennhack, Robert K. Natural Gas Availability and the Residential Demand for Energy. *Energy J.*, January 1983, *4*(1), pp. 23–45. [G: U.S.]

Boadway, Robin and Flatters, Frank. Efficiency, Equity, and the Allocation of Resource Rents. **In** *McLure, C. E., Jr. and Mieszkowski, P., eds.*, 1983, pp. 99–123. [G: Canada]

Bowman, John H. and Mikesell, John L. Recent Changes in State Gasoline Taxation: An Analysis of Structure and Rates. *Nat. Tax J.*, June 1983, *36*(2), pp. 163–82. [G: U.S.]

Brillet, Jean-Louis and d'Hose, Claire. The Mini-DMS Energy Model: Some Simulation Results. **In** *Sohlman, A. M., ed.*, 1983, pp. 274–305. [G: France]

Brookes, Leonard G. Energy and Technology: Comment. **In** *Schurr, S. H.; Sonenblum, S. and Wood, D. O., eds.*, 1983, pp. 307–11. [G: U.S.]

Brown, Scott B. An Aggregate Petroleum Consumption Model. *Energy Econ.*, January 1983, *5*(1), pp. 27–30. [G: U.S.]

Bruce, Harry J.; Horwitch, Mel and Nueno, Pedro. The Evolution of the International Coal Trade: A Strategic and Decision-Making Perspective. *J. Int. Bus. Stud.*, Spring/Summer 1983, *14*(1), pp. 85–101. [G: Hong Kong; OECD; S. Korea; Taiwan]

Buiter, Willem H. and Purvis, Douglas D. Oil, Disinflation, and Export Competitiveness: A Model of the "Dutch Disease." **In** *Bhandari, J. S. and Putnam, B. H., eds.*, 1983, pp. 221–47.

Bunn, Derek W. and Paschentis, Spiros N. Economic Dispatch of Electric Power by Stochastic Linear Programming. **In** *Lev, B., ed.*, 1983, pp. 399–412. [G: U.K.]

Byrne, John and Rich, Daniel. The Solar Energy Transition as a Problem of Political Economy. **In** *Rich, D., et al., eds.*, 1983, pp. 163–86.

Campbell, Robert W. Energy. **In** *Bergson, A. and Levine, H. S., eds.*, 1983, pp. 191–217. [G: U.S.S.R.]

Campbell, Robert W. Energy Prices and Decisions on Energy Use in the U.S.S.R. **In** *[Erlich, A.]*, 1983, pp. 249–74. [G: U.S.S.R.]

Caprio, Jerry and Clark, Peter B. Oil Price Shocks in a Portfolio-Balance Model. *J. Econ. Bus.*, June 1983, *35*(2), pp. 221–33. [G: U.S.]

Capros, P.; Ladoux, N. and Outrequin, Ph. Prix de l'énergie et comportement des industriels. (Energy Prices and Manufacturers' Behaviour. With English summary.) *Écon. Soc.*, December 1983, *17*(12), pp. 1977–2011. [G: OECD]

Caramanis, Michael C. Electricity Generation Expansion Planning in the Eighties: Requirements and Available Analysis Tools. **In** *Lev, B., ed.*, 1983, pp. 541–62. [G: U.S.]

Carlevaro, Fabrizio and Spierer, Charles. Dynamic Energy Demand Models with Latent Equipment. *Europ. Econ. Rev.*, November 1983, *23*(2), pp. 161–94. [G: Switzerland]

de Carmoy, Guy. Oil and Security in the Middle East: The French–Iraqi Case. **In** *Lieber, R. J., ed.*, 1983, pp. 123–33. [G: France; Iraq]

Carpentier, M. The Response of the European Community. **In** *Tempest, P., ed.*, 1983, pp. 118–23. [G: EEC]

Carter, Anne P. Energy and Technology: Comment. **In** *Schurr, S. H.; Sonenblum, S. and Wood, D. O., eds.*, 1983, pp. 311–14. [G: U.S.]

Castagne, Maurice; Guidat, Claudine and Voinson, Philippe. Proposition d'une méthodologie de sélection des precédés valorisant la biomasse lignocellulosique. (With English summary.) *Rev. Econ. Ind.*, 4th Trimester 1983, (26), pp. 14–23. [G: France]

Cavoulacos, Panos and Caramanis, Michael C. Energy and Other Factor Input Demand in Greek Manufacturing, 1963–1975. *Greek Econ. Rev.*, August 1983, *5*(2), pp. 158–81. [G: Greece]

Cecchetti, Stephen G., et al. OPEC II and the Wage-Price Spiral. **In** *Zeckhauser, R. J. and Leebaert, D., eds.*, 1983, pp. 137–54. [G: U.S.]

Chan, M. W. Luke and Mountain, Dean C. A Regional Analysis of Productivity Change in Canadian Agriculture, with Special Reference to Energy Prices. *Can. J. Agr. Econ.*, November 1983, *31*(3), pp. 319–30. [G: Canada]

Chaouat, Alfred. Les effets des deux chocs pétroliers sur les entreprises et les ménages. (With English summary.) *Revue Écon. Polit.,* September-October 1983, *93*(5), pp. 714–19. **[G: France]**

Cherif, M'hamed. Sensibilité du bilan énergétique belge par rapport à une tarification optimale. (With English summary.) *Cah. Écon. Bruxelles,* 1983, *97*(1), pp. 38–60. **[G: Belgium]**

Chernoff, Harry. Individual Purchase Criteria for Energy-Related Durables: The Misuse of Life Cycle Cost. *Energy J.,* October 1983, *4*(4), pp. 81–86. **[G: U.S.]**

Chesshire, John H. and Robson, Michael J. Capital Stock Rotation, Conservation and Fuel Substitution in the UK Industrial Steam-Raising Market. *Energy Econ.,* October 1983, *5*(4), pp. 218–31. **[G: U.K.]**

Chevalier, J.-M. Les prix de l'énergie au futur. (The Energy Prices in the Future. With English summary.) *Écon. Soc.,* December 1983, *17*(12), pp. 2089–2107.

Christ, Carl F. An Evaluation of the Economic Policy Proposals of the Joint Economic Committee of the 92nd and 93rd Congresses. **In** *Brunner, K. and Meltzer, A. H., eds.,* 1983, *1977,* pp. 349–83. **[G: U.S.]**

Church, Albert M. Taxation of Energy Resources: Comments. **In** *McLure, C. E., Jr. and Mieszkowski, P., eds.,* 1983, pp. 93–98. **[G: U.S.]**

Churchman, C. West. The Case against Central Planning Research. **In** *Thrall, R. M.; Thompson, R. G. and Holloway, M. L., eds.,* 1983, pp. 25–27.

Clark, Wilson and Rose, L. Wade. California: Energy Policies and Renewable Energy Strategies **In** *Rich, D., et al., eds.,* 1983, pp. 77–102. **[G: U.S.]**

Cochrane, Stuart and Struthers, John J. Nigerian Oil Policies: Some Internal Constraints. *J. Energy Devel.,* Spring 1983, *8*(2), pp. 305–17. **[G: Nigeria]**

Collier, Paul. Oil and Inequality in Rural Nigeria. **In** *Ghai, D. and Radwan, S., eds.,* 1983, pp. 191–217. **[G: Nigeria]**

Collins, Robert A. and Gray, Joan K. Derivation of a Theoretical Form of a Production Function for Home Temperature: A Comment [The Economics of House Heating]. *Energy Econ.,* October 1983, *5*(4), pp. 273–75. **[G: U.K.]**

Common, Michael S. The IIED Industrial Energy Conservation Programme: An Order of Magnitude Assessment. *Energy Econ.,* October 1983, *5*(4), pp. 232–36. **[G: U.K.]**

Commoner, Barry. Energy and the Economy. **In** *Barnes, C. H., ed.,* 1983, pp. 58–69. **[G: U.S.]**

Conant, Melvin A. An Opportunity for Gulf Gas. **In** *Tempest, P., ed.,* 1983, pp. 197–201. **[G: W. Europe; Middle East]**

Conrad, Klaus. Cost Prices and Partially Fixed Factor Proportions in Energy Substitution. *Europ. Econ. Rev.,* May 1983, *21*(3), pp. 299–312. **[G: U.S.]**

Corredor, Jaime. The Economic Significance of Mexican Petroleum from the Perspective of Mexico–United States Relations. **In** *Reynolds, C. W. and Tello, C., eds.,* 1983, pp. 137–65. **[G: Mexico; U.S.]**

Courchene, Thomas J. A Constitutional Perspective on Federal–Provincial Sharing of Revenues from Natural Resources: Comments. **In** *McLure, C. E., Jr. and Mieszkowski, P., eds.,* 1983, pp. 237–43. **[G: Canada]**

Courchene, Thomas J. Efficiency, Equity, and the Allocation of Resource Rents: Comments. **In** *McLure, C. E., Jr. and Mieszkowski, P., eds.,* 1983, pp. 125–33. **[G: Canada]**

Cowhey, Peter F. The Engineers and the Price System Revisited: The Future of the International Oil Corporations. **In** *Aronson, J. D. and Cowhey, P. F., eds.,* 1983, pp. 9–52. **[G: U.S.]**

Cowhey, Peter F. The Problems of Opportunistic Behavior and the Future of Energy Investments. **In** *Aronson, J. D. and Cowhey, P. F., eds.,* 1983, pp. 203–18. **[G: U.S.]**

Craig, C. Samuel. How Predispositions and Discretion Influence Electricity Consumption. *J. Energy Devel.,* Spring 1983, *8*(2), pp. 247–65. **[G: U.S.]**

Criqui, P. Impacts of the First Oil Crisis, International Comparisons from the Sibilin Data Base. **In** *Sohlman, A. M., ed.,* 1983, pp. 13–37. **[G: France; U.K.; U.S.; Japan; W. Germany]**

Criqui, P. Price Effects and Demand Forecasting. The Sibilin Model. **In** *Sohlman, A. M., ed.,* 1983, pp. 149–71. **[G: U.K.; France; Japan; U.S.; W. Germany]**

Criqui, P. Prix du pétrole, prix des énergies finales et consommations d'énergie dans les cinq grandes économies de l'O.C.D.E. (Petroleum Price, Final Energies Prices and Energy Consumption in the Five Bigger Economies of O.E.C.D. With English summary.) *Écon. Soc.,* December 1983, *17*(12), pp. 1927–947. **[G: U.S.; Japan; France; U.K.; Germany]**

Csikós-Nagy, Béla. Hungary's Adjustment to the New World Market Relations. *Acta Oecon.,* 1983, *30*(1), pp. 77–88. **[G: Hungary]**

Cuciti, Peggy; Galper, Harvey and Lucke, Robert. State Energy Revenues. **In** *McLure, C. E., Jr. and Mieszkowski, P., eds.,* 1983, pp. 11–60. **[G: U.S.]**

Dahl, Carol A. An Analysis of the Short-Run Consumer Demand for Gasoline Using Household Survey Data: A Comment. *Rev. Econ. Statist.,* August 1983, *65*(3), pp. 532–33. **[G: U.S.]**

Dailami, Mansoor. Cyclical Economic Fluctuations and Oil Consumption Behavior. *Energy Econ.,* July 1983, *5*(3), pp. 157–63. **[G: OECD]**

Daly, George G.; Griffin, James M. and Steele, Henry B. The Future of OPEC: Price Level and Cartel Stability. *Energy J.,* January 1983, *4*(1), pp. 65–77. **[G: OPEC]**

Daly, George G. and Mayor, Thomas H. Reason and Rationality during Energy Crises. *J. Polit. Econ.,* February 1983, *91*(1), pp. 168–81. **[G: U.S.]**

van Dam, André. Energy Transition: Plenty of Opportunities. *Rivista Int. Sci. Econ. Com.,* April-May 1983, *30*(4–5), pp. 415–23. **[G: LDCs]**

Daniel, Terrence E. and Goldberg, Henry M. Modeling Key Canadian Energy Policy Issues. **In** *Lev, B., ed.,* 1983, pp. 483–91. **[G: Canada]**

Dantzig, George B. Concerns about Large-scale Models. **In** *Thrall, R. M.; Thompson, R. G. and Holloway, M. L., eds.,* 1983, pp. 15–20.

Dantzig, George B. and Iusem, Alfredo. Analyzing

Labor Productivity Growth with the PILOT Model. **In** *Schurr, S. H.; Sonenblum, S. and Wood, D. O., eds.*, 1983, pp. 347–66. **[G: U.S.]**

Darby, Michael R. The Importance of Oil Price Changes in the 1970s World Inflation. **In** *Darby, M. P. and Lothian, J. R., et al.*, 1983, pp. 232–72. **[G: OECD]**

Dargay, Joyce M. Energy Usage and Energy Prices in Swedish Manufacturing. **In** *Ysander, B.-C., ed.*, 1983, pp. 29–53. **[G: Sweden]**

Dargay, Joyce M. The Demand for Energy in Swedish Manufacturing Industries. *Scand. J. Econ.*, 1983, *85*(1), pp. 37–51.

Dargay, Joyce M. The Demand for Energy in Swedish Engineering: Factor Substitution, Technical Change and Scale Effects. **In** *Sohlman, A. M., ed.*, 1983, pp. 80–96. **[G: Sweden]**

Dargay, Joyce M. The Demand for Energy in Swedish Manufacturing. **In** *Ysander, B.-C., ed.*, 1983, pp. 57–128. **[G: Sweden]**

Dasgupta, Partha; Gilbert, Richard and Stiglitz, Joseph E. Strategic Considerations in Invention and Innovation: The Case of Natural Resources. *Econometrica*, September 1983, *51*(5), pp. 1439–48.

Davis, Russell; Wilen, James E. and Jergovic, Rosemarie. Oil and Gas Royalty Recovery Policy on Federal and Indian Lands. *Natural Res. J.*, April 1983, *23*(2), pp. 391–416. **[G: U.S.]**

Davis, Russell; Wilen, James E. and Jergovic, Rosemarie. Royalty Management in the New Minerals Management Service: A Reply to Sant, Haspel, and Boldt. *Natural Res. J.*, April 1983, *23*(2), pp. 435–39. **[G: U.S.]**

DeBrock, Larry M. and Smith, James L. Joint Bidding, Information Pooling, and the Performance of Petroleum Lease Auctions. *Bell J. Econ. (See Rand J. Econ. after 4/85)*, Autumn 1983, *14*(2), pp. 395–404.

Denton, Harold R. Nuclear Power: Epilogue or Prologue? *Energy J.*, January 1983, *4*(1), pp. 125–41. **[G: U.S.]**

Devine, Michael D.; Kumin, Hillel J. and Aly, Adel A. A Survey of Optimization and Stochastic Process Techniques Applied to Solar Energy Systems. **In** *Lev, B., ed.*, 1983, pp. 339–52.

Devine, Warren D., Jr. From Shafts to Wires: Historical Perspective on Electrification. *J. Econ. Hist.*, June 1983, *43*(2), pp. 347–72. **[G: U.S.]**

Dewees, Donald N. The Quality of Consumer Durables: Energy Use. **In** *Dewees, D. N., ed.*, 1983, pp. 207–46. **[G: Canada]**

Dickens, Paul F., III, et al. Net Effects of Government Intervention in Energy Markets. *Energy J.*, April 1983, *4*(2), pp. 135–49. **[G: U.S.]**

Doane, E. David. The Federal Government: Help or Hindrance? **In** *Barnes, C. H., ed.*, 1983, pp. 15–24. **[G: U.S.]**

Ebinger, Charles K. and Luzius, Harry. The Energy Crisis and the Third World: An Opportunity for the West. **In** *Tempest, P., ed.*, 1983, pp. 217–27. **[G: LDCs]**

Eck, Theodore R. Energy Economics and Taxation. *J. Energy Devel.*, Spring 1983, *8*(2), pp. 293–304. **[G: U.S.]**

Edel, Matthew. Energy and the Long Swing. *Rev. Radical Polit. Econ.*, Fall 1983, *15*(3), pp. 115–30. **[G: U.S.]**

Edmonds, Jae A. and Reilly, John M. A Long-Term Global Energy-Economic Model of Carbon Dioxide Release from Fossil Fuel Use. *Energy Econ.*, April 1983, *5*(2), pp. 74–88. **[G: Global]**

Edmonds, Jae A. and Reilly, John M. Global Energy and CO_2 to the Year 2050. *Energy J.*, July 1983, *4*(3), pp. 21–47. **[G: Global]**

Edwards, James B. United States Energy Policy. **In** *Tempest, P., ed.*, 1983, pp. 97–104. **[G: U.S.]**

Ellis, Randall P. and Zimmerman, Martin B. What Happened to Nuclear Power: A Discrete Choice Model of Technology Adoption. *Rev. Econ. Statist.*, May 1983, *65*(2), pp. 234–42. **[G: U.S.]**

Evans, A. C. EEC Oil Policy. *J. World Trade Law*, January–February 1983, *17*(1), pp. 54–65. **[G: EEC]**

Evans, Richard D. An Exercise in OPEC Taxonomy. *Antitrust Bull.*, Fall 1983, *28*(3), pp. 653–67. **[G: OPEC; U.S.]**

Fariña, Ronald F. and Glover, Fred W. The Application of Generalized Networks to Choice of Raw Materials for Fuels and Petrochemicals. **In** *Lev, B., ed.*, 1983, pp. 513–24.

Feick, John E. Prospects for the Development of Mineable Oil Sands. *Can. Public Policy*, September 1983, *9*(3), pp. 297–303. **[G: Canada]**

Fesharaki, Fereidun and Isaak, David T. The Impact of Hydrocarbon Processing in OPEC Countries. **In** *Tempest, P., ed.*, 1983, pp. 205–13. **[G: OPEC]**

Fishe, Raymond P. H. and McAfee, R. Preston. On the Use of Bonus Payments in an Experimental Study of Electricity Demand. *Rev. Econ. Statist.*, August 1983, *65*(3), pp. 506–11. **[G: U.S.]**

Fishelson, Gideon. Hotelling Rule, Economic Responses and Oil Prices. *Energy Econ.*, July 1983, *5*(3), pp. 153–56.

Fitzsimmons, Allan. State Energy Policymaking. *Natural Res. J.*, April 1983, *23*(2), pp. 305–22. **[G: U.S.]**

Fodella, Gianni. Technology Transfer in the Energy Field for Water and Soil Conservation. *Rivista Int. Sci. Econ. Com.*, July 1983, *30*(7), pp. 667–77. **[G: LDCs]**

Fourgeaud, Claude; Lenclup, Bernard and Michel, Pierre. Taux d'actualisation et prix de l'énergie. (On the Social Rate of Discount and the Energy Price. With English summary.) *Revue Écon.*, March 1983, *34*(2), pp. 253–76. **[G: France]**

Frantzis, Lisa. The Potential for Diversity: The Production Alternative. **In** *Brown, H. J., ed.*, 1983, pp. 61–92. **[G: U.S.]**

Freedman, David; Rothenberg, Thomas and Sutch, Richard. On Energy Policy Models. *J. Bus. Econ. Statist.*, January 1983, *1*(1), pp. 24–32. **[G: U.S.]**

Freedman, David; Rothenberg, Thomas and Sutch, Richard. On Energy Policy Models: Rejoinder. *J. Bus. Econ. Statist.*, January 1983, *1*(1), pp. 36. **[G: U.S.]**

Freeman, S. David. Still a Time to Choose . . . Ten Years Later. *Energy J.*, April 1983, *4*(2), pp. 9–14. **[G: U.S.]**

Frieden, Bernard J. and Baker, Kermit. The Market Needs Help: The Disappointing Record of Home Energy Conservation. *J. Policy Anal. Manage.*,

Spring 1983, *2*(3), pp. 432–48. **[G: U.S.]**

Gaffen, Michael. The World Coal Trade in the 1980s: The Rebirth of a Market. **In** *Aronson, J. D. and Cowhey, P. F., eds.*, 1983, pp. 83–104. **[G: Global]**

Gallini, Nancy T. Demand for Gasoline in Canada. *Can. J. Econ.*, May 1983, *16*(2), pp. 299–324. **[G: Canada]**

Ganapathy, R. S. The Political Economy of Rural Energy Planning in the Third World. *Rev. Radical Polit. Econ.*, Fall 1983, *15*(3), pp. 83–95. **[G: LDCs]**

Garbacz, Christopher. A Model of Residential Demand for Electricity Using a National Household Sample. *Energy Econ.*, April 1983, *5*(2), pp. 124–28. **[G: U.S.]**

Garbacz, Christopher. Electricity Demand and the Elasticity of Intra-Marginal Price. *Appl. Econ.*, October 1983, *15*(5), pp. 699–701. **[G: U.S.]**

Garnaut, Ross. Energy Policy, Taxation of Natural Resources and Fiscal Federalism: Comment. **In** *McLure, C. E., Jr., ed.*, 1983, pp. 146–47.

Gass, Saul I. and Parikh, Shailendra C. Credible Analysis for Public Policy Studies. **In** *Lev, B., ed.*, 1983, pp. 85–98.

Gately, Dermot. OPEC: Retrospective and Prospects, 1973–1990. *Europ. Econ. Rev.*, May 1983, *21*(3), pp. 313–31. **[G: OPEC]**

Gault, John C. Decision Making for Natural Gas Development. *J. Energy Devel.*, Spring 1983, *8*(2), pp. 283–91. **[G: LDCs]**

Girod, J. L'élasticité-prix dans les modèles économétriques. (Elasticity Price in the Econometric Models. With English summary.) *Écon. Soc.*, December 1983, *17*(12), pp. 1847–868.

Glassey, C. Roger. Large-scale Model Transplants from the Donor's Point of View. **In** *Thrall, R. M.; Thompson, R. G. and Holloway, M. L., eds.*, 1983, pp. 165–71. **[G: U.S.]**

Goble, Robert L. Time Scales and the Problem of Radioactive Waste. **In** *Kasperson, R. E., ed.*, 1983, pp. 139–74. **[G: U.S.]**

Goettle, Richard J., IV and Hudson, Edward A. Macroeconomic Effects of Natural Gas Price Decontrol. **In** *Lev, B., ed.*, 1983, pp. 183–93. **[G: U.S.]**

Goldstein, Walter. Economic Nationalism and the Disruption of World Trade: The Impact of the Third Oil Shock. **In** *Lieber, R. J., ed.*, 1983, pp. 169–92. **[G: LDCs; OECD; OPEC]**

Goodermote, Dean and Mancke, Richard B. Nationalizing Oil in the 1970s. *Energy J.*, October 1983, *4*(4), pp. 67–80. **[G: U.S.; Canada; U.K.]**

Goodman, Allen C. Willingness to Pay for Car Efficiency: A Hedonic Price Approach. *J. Transp. Econ. Policy*, September 1983, *17*(3), pp. 247–66. **[G: U.S.]**

Gorbet, Frederick W. The Energy Outlook. **In** *Lieber, R. J., ed.*, 1983, pp. 17–32. **[G: OECD]**

Gordon, Richard L. The Evolution of Coal Market Models and Coal Policy Analysis. **In** *Lev, B., ed.*, 1983, pp. 65–84. **[G: U.S.]**

Gordon, Robert B. Cost and Use of Water Power during Industrialization in New England and Great Britain: A Geological Interpretation. *Econ. Hist. Rev., 2nd Ser.*, May 1983, *36*(2), pp. 240–59. **[G: U.K.; U.S.]**

Gordon, Robert J. Energy Efficiency, User-Cost Change, and the Measurement of Durable Goods Prices. **In** *Foss, M. F., ed.*, 1983, pp. 205–53. **[G: U.S.]**

Gordon, Robert J. Energy Efficiency, User-Cost Change, and the Measurement of Durable Goods Prices: Reply. **In** *Foss, M. F., ed.*, 1983, pp. 265–68. **[G: U.S.]**

Gould, Leroy C. The Radioactive Waste Management Problem. **In** *Walker, C. A.; Gould, L. C. and Woodhouse, E. J., eds.*, 1983, pp. 1–26. **[G: U.S.]**

Gowdy, John M. Industrial Demand for Natural Gas: Inter-Industry Variation in New York State. *Energy Econ.*, July 1983, *5*(3), pp. 171–77. **[G: U.S.]**

Gowdy, John M. The Economics of Entropy: Reply to Stehle [Radical Economics and Resource Scarcity]. *Rev. Soc. Econ.*, October 1983, *41*(2), pp. 183–85.

Gowdy, John M. Toward a Sustainable Radical Economy: Reply to Stanfield [Radical Economics and Resource Scarcity]. *Rev. Soc. Econ.*, April 1983, *41*(1), pp. 72–73.

Green, David Jay. A Logit Model of the Selection of a Space Heating Fuel by Builders of New Single Family Housing. *Rev. Econ. Statist.*, May 1983, *65*(2), pp. 337–42. **[G: U.S.]**

Gupta, Sanjeev. India and the Second OPEC Oil Price Shock—An Economy-Wide Analysis. *Weltwirtsch. Arch.*, 1983, *119*(1), pp. 122–37. **[G: India]**

Hall, S. G. E. North Sea Oil. **In** *Britton, A., ed.*, 1983, pp. 91–97. **[G: U.K.]**

Hall, Timothy A. Energy Management and Economic Development in Mississippi. **In** *Ballard, S. C. and James, T. E., eds.*, 1983, pp. 180–96. **[G: U.S.]**

Hamilton, James D. Oil and the Macroeconomy since World War II. *J. Polit. Econ.*, April 1983, *91*(2), pp. 228–48. **[G: U.S.]**

Hankinson, G. A. and Rhys, J. M. W. Electricity Consumption, Electricity Intensity and Industrial Structure. *Energy Econ.*, July 1983, *5*(3), pp. 146–52. **[G: U.S.]**

Hardy, William E., Jr.; Clark, Joy M. and White, Morris. Planning Solar Heating for Poultry—A Linear Programming Approach. *Southern J. Agr. Econ.*, December 1983, *15*(2), pp. 7–11. **[G: U.S.]**

Harper, Carolyn and Field, Barry C. Energy Substitution in U.S. Manufacturing: A Regional Approach. *Southern Econ. J.*, October 1983, *50*(2), pp. 385–95. **[G: U.S.]**

Harris, Carl M. Oil and Gas Supply Modeling under Uncertainty: Putting DOE Midterm Forecasts in Perspective. *Energy J.*, October 1983, *4*(4), pp. 53–65. **[G: U.S.]**

Hartman, Raymond S. The Estimation of Short-run Household Electricity Demand Using Pooled Aggregate Data. *J. Bus. Econ. Statist.*, April 1983, *1*(2), pp. 127–35. **[G: U.S.]**

Hayes, Denis. Environmental Benefits of a Solar World. **In** *Rich, D., et al., eds.*, 1983, pp. 13–24. **[G: U.S.]**

Helliwell, John F.; MacGregor, Mary E. and Plourde, Andre. The National Energy Program Meets Falling World Oil Prices. *Can. Public Pol-*

icy, September 1983, 9(3), pp. 284–96. [G: Canada]

Helliwell, John F. and Margolick, Michael. Some Hard Economics of Soft Energy: Optimal Electricity Generation in Pulp and Paper Mills with Seasonal Steam Requirements. **In** *[Klein, L. R.]*, 1983, pp. 219–35. [G: Canada]

Hénin, Pierre-Yves. L'impact macro-économique d'un choc pétrolier. (The Macroeconomic Impact of an Oil Shock. With English summary.) *Revue Écon.*, September 1983, *34*(5), pp. 865–96.

Henry, Mark S. The Impact of Natural Gas Price Deregulation on the South Carolina Food-Processing Sectors. *Southern J. Agr. Econ.*, December 1983, *15*(2), pp. 41–48. [G: U.S.]

Hentilä, Kalervo. Energy within the Trade between Finland and the Soviet Union. **In** *Möttölä, K.; Bykov, O. N. and Korolev, I. S., eds.*, 1983, pp. 93–99. [G: U.S.S.R.; Finland]

Hewett, Ed. A. Soviet Energy Prospects and Their Implications for East–West Trade. **In** *Becker, A. S., ed.*, 1983, pp. 49–75. [G: OECD; U.S.S.R.]

Hill, Lewis E. The Energy Crisis: Requiem for the Growth-Oriented Economy. *Rev. Soc. Econ.*, October 1983, *41*(2), pp. 97–108. [G: MDCs]

Hirschfeld, David J. A Fundamental Overview of the Energy Futures Market. *J. Futures Markets*, Spring 1983, *3*(1), pp. 75–100. [G: U.S.]

Hirshfield, D.S. and Rapoport, L. A. Evaluation of U.S. Energy Policy Impacts on Energy Supplies and Costs. **In** *Lev, B., ed.*, 1983, pp. 445–63. [G: U.S.]

Hodge, Melville H. Small Business Ventures and Solar Energy Development. **In** *Rich, D., et al., eds.*, 1983, pp. 135–44.

Hoffman, Allan R. A National Strategy for Solar Energy: The Role of the Domestic Policy Review. **In** *Rich, D., et al., eds.*, 1983, pp. 35–47. [G: U.S.]

Hoffman, Kenneth C. Utilizing Available Technical Information for Energy Analyses. **In** *Schurr, S. H.; Sonenblum, S. and Wood, D. O., eds.*, 1983, pp. 366–71.

Hoffman, Lutz and Jarass, Lorenz. The Scope for Adjustment. **In** *Tempest, P., ed.*, 1983, pp. 229–38. [G: Brazil; India; Kenya]

Hoffmann, Lutz. Impact of the Energy Crisis on the Third World and the Prospects for Adjustment. **In** *[Giersch, H.]*, 1983, pp. 302–24. [G: LDCs]

Hoffmann, Lutz and Jarass, Lorenz. The Impact of Rising Oil Prices of Oil-Importing Developing Countries and the Scope for Adjustment. *Weltwirtsch. Arch.*, 1983, *119*(2), pp. 297–316. [G: India; Brazil; Kenya]

Hoffmann, Thomas and Johnson, Brian. Breaking the Logjam. **In** *Glassner, M. I., ed.*, 1983, *1981*, pp. 318–32. [G: LDCs; MDCs]

Hogan, William W. Alternatives to Transfer of Large-scale Models. **In** *Thrall, R. M.; Thompson, R. G. and Holloway, M. L., eds.*, 1983, pp. 173–89.

Hogan, William W. Oil Stockpiling: Help Thy Neighbor. *Energy J.*, July 1983, *4*(3), pp. 49–71. [G: U.S.; OECD]

Hogan, William W. On Energy Policy Models: Comment. *J. Bus. Econ. Statist.*, January 1983, *1*(1), pp. 33. [G: U.S.]

Hogan, William W. and Weyant, John P. Methods and Algorithms for Energy Model Composition: Optimization in a Network of Process Models. **In** *Lev, B., ed.*, 1983, pp. 3–43.

Holaday, Bart. Conditions for Effective Model Utilization in Policy Decision-making. **In** *Thrall, R. M.; Thompson, R. G. and Holloway, M. L., eds.*, 1983, pp. 21–24.

Holloway, Milton L. The Importance of Transfer in Understanding Large-scale Models. **In** *Thrall, R. M.; Thompson, R. G. and Holloway, M. L., eds.*, 1983, pp. 145–63. [G: U.S.]

Holt, Charles C. Quantitative Modeling: Needs and Shortfalls for Energy Analysis. **In** *Thrall, R. M.; Thompson, R. G. and Holloway, M. L., eds.*, 1983, pp. 219–30.

Hong, Nguyen V. Two Measures of Aggregate Energy Production Elasticities. *Energy J.*, April 1983, *4*(2), pp. 172–77. [G: U.S.]

Hope, Einar; Magnus, Eivind and Matland, Richard. Economic Incentives and Public Firm Behavior: An Econometric Analysis of Energy Economizing Behavior of Norwegian Electric Utilities. *Scand. J. Econ.*, 1983, *85*(3), pp. 339–57. [G: Norway]

Hotard, Daniel G.; Liu, Cheng Chi and Ristroph, John H. Logistic Function Modeling of Natural Resource Production. **In** *Lev, B., ed.*, 1983, pp. 353–64. [G: U.S.]

Houghton, John C. Uranium: Estimates of U.S. Reserves and Resources. **In** *Adelman, M. A., et al.*, 1983, pp. 333–84. [G: U.S.]

Houston, Douglas A. Implicit Discount Rates and the Purchase of Untried, Energy-Saving Durable Goods. *J. Cons. Res.*, September 1983, *10*(2), pp. 236–46. [G: U.S.]

Houthakker, Hendrik S. Whatever Happened to the Energy Crisis? *Energy J.*, April 1983, *4*(2), pp. 1–8.

Hubbard, R. Glenn and Weiner, Robert. The 'Sub-Trigger' Crisis: An Economic Analysis of Flexible Stock Policies. *Energy Econ.*, July 1983, *5*(3), pp. 178–89. [G: U.S.]

Hubbard, R. Glenn and Weiner, Robert. When the Oil Spigot Is Suddenly Turned Off: Some Further Thoughts. *J. Policy Anal. Manage.*, Winter 1983, *2*(2), pp. 299–302. [G: U.S.]

Hultkrantz, Lars. Energy Substitution in the Forest Industry. **In** *Ysander, B.-C., ed.*, 1983, pp. 209–26. [G: Sweden]

Hunter, Holland; Dienes, Leslie and Bettis, Lee. International Implications of Long-distance Transport of Fuels. **In** *Khachaturov, T. S. and Goodwin, P. B., eds.*, 1983, pp. 81–93. [G: U.S.S.R.]

Ihamuotila, Jaakko. Energia ja ulkomaankuppa. (Energy and Foreign Trade in Finland. With English summary.) *Kansant. Aikak.*, 1983, *79*(1), pp. 54–67. [G: OECD; Finland]

Ilzkovitz, Fabienne. L'information des consommateurs . . . Une condition de l'efficacité des primes à l'isolation? (With English summary.) *Cah. Écon. Bruxelles*, 4th Trimester 1983, (100), pp. 534–60. [G: Belgium]

Ince, Basil A. Coping with Oil Wealth: The Case of Trinidad/Tobago and the Commonwealth Caribbean. **In** *Ritter, A. R. M. and Pollock, D. H., eds.*, 1983, pp. 111–34. [G: Caribbean; Trinidad/Tobago]

Inglehart, Ronald. Domestic Political Constraints on an Atlantic Energy Policy. **In** *Lieber, R. J., ed.,* 1983, pp. 193–227. **[G: U.S.; W. Europe]**

Isachsen, Arne Jon. Norwegian Economic Policy in the Past Decade and Some Thoughts on Policy in the Present One. **In** *de Cecco, M., ed.,* 1983, pp. 49–64. **[G: Norway]**

Isakson, Hans R. Residential Space Heating: An Analysis of Energy Conservation. *Energy Econ.,* January 1983, *5*(1), pp. 49–57. **[G: U.S.]**

Jacoby, Henry D. and Paddock, James L. Establishing an Oil Price Window: The Influence of Policy on Future Oil Prices. **In** *Tempest, P., ed.,* 1983, pp. 63–76. **[G: U.S.; OPEC]**

Jacoby, Henry D. and Paddock, James L. World Oil Prices and Economic Growth in the 1980s. *Energy J.,* April 1983, *4*(2), pp. 31–47. **[G: U.S.]**

James, Dilmus D. and Street, James H. Technology, Institutions, and Public Policy in the Age of Energy Substitution: The Case of Latin America. *J. Econ. Issues,* June 1983, *17*(2), pp. 521–28. **[G: Latin America]**

Jefferson, Michael. Economic Uncertainty and Business Decision-making. **In** *Wiseman, J., ed.,* 1983, pp. 122–59.

Jenne, C. A. and Cattell, R. K. Structural Change and Energy Efficiency in Industry. *Energy Econ.,* April 1983, *5*(2), pp. 114–23. **[G: U.K.]**

Jennings, Karen L. Supreme Court Opens Door to More State Revenues from Mined Resources. *Natural Res. J.,* January 1983, *23*(1), pp. 213–18. **[G: U.S.]**

Jentleson, Bruce W. Khrushchev's Oil and Brezhnev's Natural Gas Pipelines. **In** *Lieber, R. J., ed.,* 1983, pp. 33–69. **[G: U.S.S.R.; U.S.; W. Europe]**

Johnsen, Arve. Norwegian Gas Reserves and Markets. *J. Energy Devel.,* Spring 1983, *8*(2), pp. 191–202. **[G: Norway]**

Johnson, Ruth C. and Kaserman, David L. Housing Market Capitalization of Energy-Saving Durable Goods Investments. *Econ. Inquiry,* July 1983, *21*(3), pp. 374–86. **[G: U.S.]**

Jones, Geoffrey. Some Recent Histories of International Oil. *J. Econ. Hist.,* December 1983, *43*(4), pp. 993–96. **[G: France; Latin America; U.K.]**

Jones, Jack William. Applying a Computer-based Enhanced Oil Recovery Simulation Model to Reservoir Economic Analysis. **In** *Lev, B., ed.,* 1983, pp. 255–70. **[G: U.S.]**

Jorgenson, Dale W. Energy Prices and Productivity Growth. **In** *Schurr, S. H.; Sonenblum, S. and Wood, D. O., eds.,* 1983, pp. 133–53. **[G: U.S.]**

Jorgenson, Dale W. Engineering and Economic Approaches to Analyzing Energy Policy. **In** *Schurr, S. H.; Sonenblum, S. and Wood, D. O., eds.,* 1983, pp. 372–75.

Joskow, Paul L. and Jones, Donald R. The Simple Economics of Industrial Cogeneration. *Energy J.,* January 1983, *4*(1), pp. 1–22.

de Kadt, Maarten. Energy Corporation Propaganda: A Weapon against Public Policy. *Rev. Radical Polit. Econ.,* Fall 1983, *15*(3), pp. 35–50. **[G: U.S.]**

Kain, John F. Impacts of Higher Petroleum Prices on Transportation Patterns and Urban Development. **In** *Keeler, T. E., ed.,* 1983, pp. 1–26. **[G: U.S.]**

Kalt, Joseph P. The Costs and Benefits of Federal Regulation of Coal Strip Mining. *Natural Res. J.,* October 1983, *23*(4), pp. 893–915. **[G: U.S.]**

Kalt, Joseph P. The Creation, Growth, and Entrenchment of Special Interests in Oil Price Policy. **In** *Noll, R. G. and Owen, B. M.,* 1983, pp. 97–114. **[G: U.S.]**

Kasperson, Roger E.; Derr, Patrick and Kates, Robert W. Confronting Equity in Radioactive Waste Management: Modest Proposals for a Socially Just and Acceptable Program. **In** *Kasperson, R. E., ed.,* 1983, pp. 331–68. **[G: U.S.]**

Kasperson, Roger E. and Rubin, Barry L. Siting a Radioactive Waste Repository: What Role for Equity? **In** *Kasperson, R. E., ed.,* 1983, pp. 118–36. **[G: U.S.]**

Kates, Robert W. and Braine, Bonnie. Locus, Equity, and the West Valley Nuclear Wastes. **In** *Kasperson, R. E., ed.,* 1983, pp. 94–117. **[G: U.S.]**

Kaufman, Gordon. Oil and Gas: Estimation of Undiscovered Resources. **In** *Adelman, M. A., et al.,* 1983, pp. 83–294. **[G: U.S.]**

Kenen, Peter B. Perspective: Problems in Modeling International Risks [Modeling Exchange Rate Fluctuations and International Disturbances]. **In** *Herring, R. J., ed.,* 1983, pp. 109–13. **[G: Global]**

Keyes, Dale L. Reagan Energy and Environmental Programs: Implications for State and Local Governments. **In** *Lefcoe, G., ed.,* 1983, pp. 77–89. **[G: U.S.]**

Kim, Dae K. Energy Substitution in the Gulf of Mexico Shrimp Fishery. *Southern J. Agr. Econ.,* December 1983, *15*(2), pp. 1–6. **[G: U.S.]**

Kim, Inchul. Energy and Growth in an Open Economy: The Korean Case. *J. Energy Devel.,* Autumn 1983, *9*(1), pp. 69–92. **[G: Korea]**

Kjaer, Jørn H. International Adjustment, the EMS and Small European Countries: The Danish Experience. **In** *de Cecco, M., ed.,* 1983, pp. 65–73. **[G: Denmark]**

Klapp, Merrie. Policy and Politics of North Sea Oil and Gas Development. **In** *Aronson, J. D. and Cowhey, P. F., eds.,* 1983, pp. 107–36. **[G: Norway; U.K.]**

Klein, Lawrence R. Modeling Exchange Rate Fluctuations and International Disturbances. **In** *Herring, R. J., ed.,* 1983, pp. 85–109. **[G: Global]**

Kliebenstein, James B. and McCamley, Francis P. Energy-Related Input Demand by Crop Producers. *Southern J. Agr. Econ.,* December 1983, *15*(2), pp. 63–69. **[G: U.S.]**

Kline, David M. and Weyant, John P. Comment on International Energy Agency's World Energy Outlook. *Energy J.,* October 1983, *4*(4), pp. 91–94.

van de Klundert, Theo. The Energy Problem in a Small Open Economy. *J. Macroecon.,* Spring 1983, *5*(2), pp. 211–22.

Kneese, Allen V., et al. Economic Issues in the Legacy Problem. **In** *Kasperson, R. E., ed.,* 1983, pp. 203–26. **[G: U.S.]**

Kohli, Harinder and Segura, Edilberto. Industrial Energy Conservation in Developing Countries.

Finance Develop., December 1983, *20*(4), pp. 28–31. **[G: LDCs]**

Koo, Anthony Y. C. and Fisher, Ronald C. Natural Gas Price Deregulation and Windfall Profits Taxation. *Southern Econ. J.*, October 1983, *50*(2), pp. 529–38. **[G: U.S.]**

Koster, Francis P. The Role of Utilities in Promoting Solar Energy: The Case of the TVA. **In** *Rich, D., et al., eds.*, 1983, pp. 103–22. **[G: U.S.]**

Kouri, Pentti J. K. Oil Shocks and Exchange Rate Dynamics: Comment. **In** *Frenkel, J. A., ed.*, 1983, pp. 272–80.

Kouris, George. Energy Consumption and Economic Activity in Industrialized Economies—A Note. *Energy Econ.*, July 1983, *5*(3), pp. 207–12. **[G: MDCs]**

Kouris, George. Energy Demand Elasticities in Industrialized Countries: A Survey. *Energy J.*, July 1983, *4*(3), pp. 73–94. **[G: OECD]**

Kouris, George. Fuel Consumption for Road Transport in the USA. *Energy Econ.*, April 1983, *5*(2), pp. 89–99. **[G: U.S.]**

Kreutzer, David. Subsidies to New Energy Sources: Do They Add to Energy Stocks? A Comment. *J. Polit. Econ.*, April 1983, *91*(2), pp. 316–18.

Krugman, Paul R. Oil and the Dollar. **In** *Bhandari, J. S. and Putnam, B. H., eds.*, 1983, pp. 179–90.

Krugman, Paul R. Oil Shocks and Exchange Rate Dynamics. **In** *Frenkel, J. A., ed.*, 1983, pp. 259–71.

Kuenne, Robert E. Lessons and Conjectures on OPEC. **In** *Weintraub, S. and Goodstein, M., eds.*, 1983, pp. 164–74. **[G: OPEC]**

Kurihara, Shiro. Macroeconomic Policy Alternatives for Higher Oil Prices in the Japanese Economy. *Econ. Stud. Quart.*, April 1983, *34*(1), pp. 44–69. **[G: Japan]**

Kwoka, John E., Jr. The Limits of Market-Oriented Regulatory Techniques: The Case of Automotive Fuel Economy. *Quart. J. Econ.*, November 1983, *98*(4), pp. 695–704.

Kydes, Andy S. An Energy Case Study Using the Brookhaven National Laboratory Time-stepped Energy System Optimization Model (TESOM) **In** *Lev, B., ed.*, 1983, pp. 425–43. **[G: U.S.]**

La Duque, Winona. Native America: The Economics of Radioactive Colonization. *Rev. Radical Polit. Econ.*, Fall 1983, *15*(3), pp. 9–19. **[G: U.S.]**

Ladoux, N. and Outrequin, Ph. Prix de l'énergie et comportement des ménages. (Energy Prices and Households' Behaviour. With English summary.) *Écon. Soc.*, December 1983, *17*(12), pp. 1949–976.

Lake, R. W.; Boon, C. J. and Schwier, C. Efficient Long-distance Fuel Transportation. **In** *Khachaturov, T. S. and Goodwin, P. B., eds.*, 1983, pp. 142–56. **[G: Canada]**

Lakshmanan, T. R. A Multiregional Model of the Economy, Environment, and Energy Demand in the United States. *Econ. Geogr.*, July 1983, *59*(3), pp. 296–320. **[G: U.S.]**

Lamm, Richard D. Urban Land Policy for the 1980s: Public Resource Management under the Reagan Administration. **In** *Lefcoe, G., ed.*, 1983, pp. 91–100. **[G: U.S.]**

Lantzke, Ulf. Achieving Structural Change: The Policies Required. **In** *Tempest, P., ed.*, 1983, pp. 111–17. **[G: OECD]**

Lantzke, Ulf. Energy Policies in Industrialized Countries: An Evaluation of the Past Decade. *J. Energy Devel.*, Autumn 1983, *9*(1), pp. 11–17. **[G: OECD]**

Lantzke, Ulf. Investment and Energy. **In** *Heertje, A., ed.*, 1983, pp. 117–51. **[G: W. Europe]**

Lapillonne, B. Changes in the Energy Consumption in France: The Role of Energy Savings. **In** *Sohlman, A. M., ed.*, 1983, pp. 57–64. **[G: France]**

Lapillonne, B. and Château, B. The Medee 3 Model. **In** *Sohlman, A. M., ed.*, 1983, pp. 124–48.

Lawson, Nigel. The United Kingdom Energy Framework. **In** *Tempest, P., ed.*, 1983, pp. 105–10. **[G: U.K.]**

LeBlanc, Michael and Prato, Anthony. Ethanol Production from Grain in the United States: Agricultural Impacts and Economic Feasibility. *Can. J. Agr. Econ.*, July 1983, *31*(2), pp. 223–32. **[G: U.S.]**

Leclercq, Claudie. Le demande d'énergie de l'industrie pour les principaux pays de la CEE. (With English summary.) *Cah. Écon. Bruxelles*, 1983, *97*(1), pp. 14–37. **[G: EEC]**

Lee, Thomas H. Energy and Technology: Comment. **In** *Schurr, S. H.; Sonenblum, S. and Wood, D. O., eds.*, 1983, pp. 315–17. **[G: U.S.]**

Leone, Robert A. Comment [Pitfalls on the Road to Decontrol: Lessons from the Natural Gas Policy Act of 1978] [The Intrastate Pipelines and the Natural Gas Policy Act]. **In** *Mitchell, E. J., ed.*, 1983, pp. 109–11. **[G: U.S.]**

Leontief, Wassily W. and Sohn, Ira. Population, Food, Energy and Growth. **In** *Tempest, P., ed.*, 1983, pp. 241–46. **[G: LDCs; MDCs]**

Lerner, Abba P. OPEC—A Plan—If You Can't Beat Them, Join Them. **In** *Lerner, A. P.*, 1983, *1980*, pp. 125–27.

Lev, Benjamin and Murphy, Frederic H. The Sensitivity of the Shape of the Long-run Supply Curve of Coal to Different Assumptions on Seam Thickness. **In** *Lev, B., ed.*, 1983, pp. 293–307. **[G: U.S.]**

Levary, Reuven R. and Dean, Burton V. An Adaptive Model for Planning the Purchasing and Storage of Natural Gas. **In** *Lev, B., ed.*, 1983, pp. 387–97. **[G: U.S.]**

Levin, Nissan; Tishler, Asher and Zahavi, Jacob. Perturbation Analysis of Power Generation Expansion Programs Subject to Uncertainty in the Prices of Primary Energy Resources. **In** *Lev, B., ed.*, 1983, pp. 367–85. **[G: U.S.]**

Lieber, Robert J. Must Europe Fight for Oil? Energy and Atlantic Security. **In** *Lieber, R. J., ed.*, 1983, pp. 1–16. **[G: OECD]**

Lillydahl, Jane H. and Moen, Elizabeth W. Planning, Managing, and Financing Growth and Decline in Energy Rosource Communities: A Case Study of Western Colorado. *J. Energy Devel.*, Spring 1983, *8*(2), pp. 211–29. **[G: U.S.]**

Llewellyn, John. Resource Prices and Macroeconomic Policies: Lessons from Two Oil Price Shocks. *OECD Econ. Stud.*, Autumn 1983, (1), pp. 197–212. **[G: OECD]**

Longva, Svein; Lorentsen, Lorents and Olsen, Øy-

stein. Energy in the Multi-sectoral Growth Model MSG. **In** *Av, R., et al., eds.*, 1983, pp. 27–51. **[G: Norway]**

Longva, Svein and Olsen, Øystein. Price Sensitivity of Energy Demand in Norwegian Industries. *Scand. J. Econ.*, 1983, *85*(1), pp. 17–36. **[G: Norway]**

Longva, Svein and Olsen, Øystein. Producer Behaviour in the MSG Model. **In** *Av, R., et al., eds.*, 1983, pp. 52–83. **[G: Norway]**

Longva, Svein and Olsen, Øystein. The Specification of Electricity Flows in the MSG Model. **In** *Av, R., et al., eds.*, 1983, pp. 108–33. **[G: Norway]**

Longva, Svein; Olsen, Øystein and Rinde, Jon. Energy Price Sensitivity of the Norwegian Economy. **In** *Av, R., et al., eds.*, 1983, pp. 161–79. **[G: Norway]**

Longva, Svein, et al. Use of the MSG Model in Forecasting Electricity Demand. **In** *Av, R., et al., eds.*, 1983, pp. 180–94. **[G: Norway]**

Looney, Robert E. Absorptive Capacity of the Prerevolutionary Iranian Economy. *J. Energy Devel.*, Spring 1983, *8*(2), pp. 319–40. **[G: Iran]**

Lower, Ann K. Natural Gas Pricing: Market Outcome or Industrial Policy? *J. Econ. Issues,* June 1983, *17*(2), pp. 423–32. **[G: U.S.]**

Lücke, Fritz. Recent Developments in Nuclear Energy: A West German Perspective. **In** *Tempest, P., ed.*, 1983, pp. 43–47. **[G: W. Germany]**

Lundgren, Stefan. A Model of Energy Demand in the Swedish Iron and Steel Industry. **In** *Ysander, B.-C., ed.*, 1983, pp. 171–208. **[G: Sweden]**

Luria, Dan and Price, Lee. Solar Energy, Jobs, and Labor: Some Analytical Issues. *Rev. Radical Polit. Econ.*, Fall 1983, *15*(3), pp. 131–42.

Lyckeborg, Håkan. A Box–Jenkins Approach to Short-term Energy Consumption Forecasting in Sweden: Univariate Models. **In** *Sohlman, A. M., ed.*, 1983, pp. 98–123. **[G: Sweden]**

Lyman, Robert. Economic and Political Issues in International Natural Gas Trade: A Canadian View. *J. Energy Devel.*, Autumn 1983, *9*(1), pp. 49–54. **[G: Canada]**

MacKenzie, James J. Planning the Solar Transition. **In** *Rich, D., et al., eds.*, 1983, pp. 25–34.

MacLean, Douglas. Radioactive Wastes: A Problem of Morality between Generations. **In** *Kasperson, R. E., ed.*, 1983, pp. 175–88.

Maddigan, Ruth J.; Chern, Wen S. and Rizy, Colleen Gallagher. Rural Residential Demand for Electricity. *Land Econ.*, May 1983, *59*(2), pp. 150–62. **[G: U.S.]**

Maillard, D. L'élasticité énergie P.I.B. sophisme ou panacée. (Elasticity Energy–G.N.P.: A Fallacy or a Panacea. With English summary.) *Écon. Soc.*, December 1983, *17*(12), pp. 1835–846.

Maksimov, Iu. I. Siberia's Fuel-Energy Complex. *Prob. Econ.*, September 1983, *26*(5), pp. 15–24. **[G: U.S.S.R.]**

Manne, Alan S. A Three-Region Model of Energy, International Trade, and Economic Growth. **In** *Hickman, B. G., ed.*, 1983, pp. 141–62. **[G: LDCs; OECD; OPEC]**

Manne, Alan S. Energy and Productivity: Do Any of the Old Ideas Make Sense? **In** *Schurr, S. H.; Sonenblum, S. and Wood, D. O., eds.*, 1983, pp. 376–79. **[G: U.S.]**

Marston, Geoffrey. The Aminoil-Kuwait Arbitration. *J. World Trade Law,* March–April 1983, *17*(2), pp. 177–82. **[G: Kuwait]**

Martin, J.-M. Prix des énergies et perspectives énergétiques de la France à l'horizon 1990 et 2000. (Energy Prices and Energy Prospects in France in 1990 and 2000. With English summary.) *Écon. Soc.*, December 1983, *17*(12), pp. 2013–31. **[G: France]**

Martin, Robert E. Petrol Supplies and Consumer Expectations. *Energy Econ.*, January 1983, *5*(1), pp. 16–26.

Mattadeen, Al C. Reflections after a Decade of OPEC Pricing Policies. *Nat. Westminster Bank Quart. Rev.*, May 1983, pp. 15–23. **[G: OPEC; OECD]**

Maxwell, J. Robert. Industrial Decision-making for Solar Energy Development. **In** *Rich, D., et al., eds.*, 1983, pp. 123–34. **[G: U.S.]**

McAleese, Dermot and O'Muircheartaigh, Fionan. The Changing Oil Market: Implications and Prospects. *Irish Banking Rev.*, September 1983, pp. 3–20. **[G: OPEC; Non-OPEC; Ireland]**

McColl, G. D. and Gallagher, D. R. Market Price and Resource Cost in Australia. **In** *Tempest, P., ed.*, 1983, pp. 179–87. **[G: Australia]**

McDaniel, Bruce A. Solar Energy and the Policies of First and Second Best. *Rev. Soc. Econ.*, April 1983, *41*(1), pp. 12–24. **[G: U.S.]**

McGuirk, Anne K. Oil Price Changes and Real Exchange Rate Movements among Industrial Countries. *Int. Monet. Fund Staff Pap.*, December 1983, *30*(4), pp. 843–84. **[G: Selected OECD]**

McMahon, L. A. and Harris, Stuart. Coal Development: Issues for Japan and Australia. **In** *Akao, N., ed.*, 1983, pp. 71–95. **[G: Japan; Australia]**

McNicoll, Iain. North Sea Oil and Gas. **In** *Ingham, K. P. D. and Love, J., eds.*, 1983, pp. 227–34. **[G: U.K.]**

Mead, Walter J.; Moseidjord, Asbjorn and Sorensen, Philip E. The Rate of Return Earned by Lessees under Cash Bonus Bidding for OCS Oil and Gas Leases. *Energy J.*, October 1983, *4*(4), pp. 37–52. **[G: U.S.]**

Mehring, Joyce S.; Sarkar, Debashish and Shapiro, Jeremy F. Decomposition Methods and Computation of Spatial Equilibria: An Application to Coal Supply and Demand Markets. **In** *Lev, B., ed.*, 1983, pp. 221–33.

Metzger, Michael R. and Goldfarb, Robert S. The Effectiveness of Odd–Even Gasoline Rationing. *Atlantic Econ. J.*, December 1983, *11*(4), pp. 49–58. **[G: U.S.]**

Mieszkowski, Peter. Energy Policy, Taxation of Natural Resources, and Fiscal Federalism. **In** *McLure, C. E., Jr., ed.*, 1983, pp. 128–45. **[G: U.S.]**

Mieszkowski, Peter and Toder, Eric. Taxation of Energy Resources. **In** *McLure, C. E., Jr. and Mieszkowski, P., eds.*, 1983, pp. 65–91. **[G: U.S.]**

Mills, Donald and Parra, Francisco. Consumer–Producer Potential for a Global Compact? **In** *Glassner, M. I., ed.*, 1983, *1981*, pp. 255–60. **[G: LDCs; MDCs; OPEC]**

Mitchell, Bridger M. and Acton, Jan Paul. Electricity

Consumption by Time of Use in a Hybrid Demand System. **In** *Finsinger, J., ed.*, 1983, pp. 27–64. **[G: U.S.]**

Mitchell, John. Changes in Trade and Investment. **In** *Tempest, P., ed.*, 1983, pp. 127–33.

Monnier, L. La tarification de l'électricité: nouveau débat. (The Electricity Tariff: A New Debate. With English summary.) *Écon. Soc.*, December 1983, *17*(12), pp. 2053–75. **[G: France]**

Mork, Knut Anton. Comment on "Optimal Oil Producer Behavior Considering Macrofeedbacks." *Energy J.*, October 1983, *4*(4), pp. 29–31.

Moses, Lincoln E. Energy Models: Complexity, Documentation, and Simplicity. **In** *Thrall, R. M.; Thompson, R. G. and Holloway, M. L., eds.*, 1983, pp. 5–14.

Mossavar-Rahmani, Bijan. Economic Implications for Iran and Iraq. **In** *Tahir-Kheli, S. and Ayubi, S., eds.*, 1983, pp. 51–64. **[G: Iran; Iraq]**

Motaman, H. Macroeconomic Planning of Oil Revenue in Industrialised Countries: The British Case. **In** *[Saunders, C. T.]*, 1983, pp. 231–57. **[G: U.K.]**

Murphy, Frederic H. Design Strategies for Energy Market Models. **In** *Lev, B., ed.*, 1983, pp. 45–64.

Mutti, John H. and Morgan, William E. Changing Energy Prices and Economic Rents: The Case of Western Coal. *Land Econ.*, May 1983, *59*(2), pp. 163–76. **[G: U.S.]**

Myers, John G. Energy and Technology: Comment. **In** *Schurr, S. H.; Sonenblum, S. and Wood, D. O., eds.*, 1983, pp. 317–19. **[G: U.S.]**

Nafziger, Richard and Wustner, Michael F. The Energy War on the American West. *Rev. Radical Polit. Econ.*, Fall 1983, *15*(3), pp. 5–8. **[G: U.S.]**

Narasimham, Gorti V. L. A Comparison of Three Methods of Modelling Energy Outlooks in a Global Setting. **In** *Lev, B., ed.*, 1983, pp. 99–110.

National Academy of Sciences. Energy in Transition 1985–2010. **In** *Glassner, M. I., ed.*, 1983, *1980*, pp. 289–310. **[G: U.S.]**

Nelson, Paul. The Effect of Deregulating Crude Oil Prices on the Pump Price of Gasoline: A Comment. *Amer. Econ.*, Fall 1983, *27*(2), pp. 74–76.

Neufeld, Edward P. International Financial Stability in the New Oil Price Scenarios. *Can. Public Policy*, September 1983, *9*(3), pp. 304–13. **[G: OPEC; LDCs]**

Nordhaus, William D. Energy Productivity and Total Productivity: Comment. **In** *Schurr, S. H.; Sonenblum, S. and Wood, D. O., eds.*, 1983, pp. 215–19. **[G: U.S.]**

Nordhaus, William D. and Van der Heyden, Ludo. Induced Technical Change: A Programming Approach. **In** *Schurr, S. H.; Sonenblum, S. and Wood, D. O., eds.*, 1983, pp. 379–404. **[G: Global]**

Norsworthy, J. R. Energy Prices, Technical Change, and Productivity Growth. **In** *Schurr, S. H.; Sonenblum, S. and Wood, D. O., eds.*, 1983, pp. 155–77. **[G: U.S.]**

O'Leary, John F. Price Reactive versus Price Active Energy Policy. **In** *Tempest, P., ed.*, 1983, pp. 163–75. **[G: U.S.]**

O'Neill Adams, Margaret and Ross, Frances E. The Energy Data Base within the Kentucky Economic Information System. *Rev. Public Data Use (See J. Econ. Soc. Meas. after 4/85)*, March 1983, *11*(1), pp. 75–78. **[G: U.S.]**

Odell, Peter R. Towards a System of World Oil Regions: The New Geopolitics of International Energy. **In** *Tempest, P., ed.*, 1983, pp. 27–34. **[G: Global]**

Oettinger, Christina. Long-term Simulation of the Effects of Different Energy Policy Measures. **In** *Sohlman, A. M., ed.*, 1983, pp. 190–220. **[G: Sweden]**

Onida, Fabrizio and Perasso, Giancarlo. Oil Export and Economic Development: OPEC Strategies and Opportunities for Western Economic Cooperation. *Rivista Int. Sci. Econ. Com.*, March 1983, *30*(3), pp. 293–303. **[G: OPEC; OECD]**

Östblom, Göran. Price Elasticities Implied in Some Swedish Energy Projections for the 1980's. **In** *Sohlman, A. M., ed.*, 1983, pp. 65–79. **[G: Sweden]**

Pachauri, Rajendra K. and Labys, Walter C. Changing Markets for Coal: Opportunities for the Developing Countries. **In** *Tempest, P., ed.*, 1983, pp. 35–41. **[G: LDCs]**

Palmer, Keith. Private Sector Petroleum Exploration in Developing Countries. *Finance Develop.*, March 1983, *20*(1), pp. 36–38. **[G: LDCs]**

Park, Se-Hark. The Plight of Oil-Importing Developing Countries and South–South Cooperation on Energy. *J. Energy Devel.*, Autumn 1983, *9*(1), pp. 93–110. **[G: LDCs]**

Park, Se-Hark and Kubursi, Atif A. The Energy Constraint and Development: Consistency and Optimality over Time. *Energy Econ.*, January 1983, *5*(1), pp. 9–15. **[G: LDCs]**

Pasqualetti, M. J. The Site Specific Nature of Geothermal Energy: The Primary Role of Land Use Planning in Nonelectric Development. *Natural Res. J.*, October 1983, *23*(4), pp. 795–814. **[G: U.S.]**

Patel, R. K.; Saini, Amrik S. and Singh, Raj Vir. Energy in Agriculture. *Econ. Aff.*, April–June 1983, *28*(2), pp. 715–23. **[G: India]**

Pearce-Batten, Anthony. The Future of Renewable Energy. **In** *Glassner, M. I., ed.*, 1983, *1979*, pp. 261–88. **[G: Global]**

Pearce, David W. and Westoby, Richard. Energy and the EC. **In** *El-Agraa, A. M., ed.*, 1983, pp. 187–212. **[G: EEC]**

Peterson, Russell W. Energy Policies and the Quality of Life. **In** *Barnes, C. H., ed.*, 1983, pp. 25–33. **[G: U.S.]**

Pfister, Richard L. Dire Predictions Reexamined: Regional Impacts of Rising Energy Prices. *Growth Change*, April 1983, *14*(2), pp. 9–16. **[G: U.S.]**

Pindyck, Robert S. The Energy Connection to Recent Productivity Behavior: Comment. **In** *Schurr, S. H.; Sonenblum, S. and Wood, D. O., eds.*, 1983, pp. 183–85. **[G: U.S.]**

Pindyck, Robert S. and Rotemberg, Julio J. Dynamic Factor Demands and the Effects of Energy Price Shocks. *Amer. Econ. Rev.*, December 1983, *73*(5), pp. 1066–79. **[G: U.S.]**

Platt, Harlan D. An Integrated Approach to Electricity Demand Forecasting. *Energy J.*, Supplement 1983, *4*, pp. 75–91. **[G: U.S.]**

Posthumus, Godert. The Netherlands: Financial-Economic Adjustment Policies in the 1970s. **In** *de Cecco, M., ed.*, 1983, pp. 74–98. **[G: Netherlands]**

Prot, B. and Rolland, P. La fiscalité comme outil de la politique de la demande. (The Tax System as a Tool of the Demand Policy. With English summary.) *Écon. Soc.*, December 1983, *17*(12), pp. 2077–88.

Rad-Serecht, Farhad. Stratégie des acteurs et destabilisation de l'oligopole pétrolier. *Rev. Econ. Ind.*, 3rd Trimester 1983, (25), pp. 38–49. **[G: OPEC; W. Europe; U.S.]**

Randall, Stephen J. Harold Ickes and United States Foreign Petroleum Policy Planning, 1939–1945. *Bus. Hist. Rev.*, Autumn 1983, *57*(3), pp. 367–87. **[G: U.S.]**

Ratick, Samuel J. Multiobjective Programming with Related Bargaining Games: An Application to Utility Coal Conversions. *Reg. Sci. Urban Econ.*, February 1983, *13*(1), pp. 55–76. **[G: U.S.]**

Ravid, S. Abraham and Hadar, Y. A Cost Benefit Analysis of Bio-gas Production: An Israeli Experience. **In** *Lev, B., ed.*, 1983, pp. 413–22. **[G: Israel]**

Ray, George F. Energy and the Long Cycles. *Energy Econ.*, January 1983, *5*(1), pp. 3–8. **[G: Austro-Hungary; Sweden; EEC]**

Razavi, Hossein. Effect of Uncertainty on Oil Extraction Decisions. *J. Econ. Dynam. Control,* July 1983, *5*(4), pp. 359–70. **[G: Iran]**

Reining, Robert C. and Tyner, Wallace E. Comparing Liquid Fuel Costs: Grain Alcohol versus Sunflower Oil. *Amer. J. Agr. Econ.*, August 1983, *65*(3), pp. 567–70.

Rich, Daniel and Byrne, John. The Solar Energy Transition: Introduction. **In** *Rich, D., et al., eds.*, 1983, pp. 1–11.

Rigby, Donald E. and Scott, Charles. Low-Income Energy Assistance Program. *Soc. Sec. Bull.*, January 1983, *46*(1), pp. 11–32. **[G: U.S.]**

Rivero, Nicolás and Díaz Franjúl, Manuel. Thoughts on Sugar Diversification: An Inter-American Fuel Alcohol Program. **In** *Czinkota, M. R., ed. (II)*, 1983, pp. 107–25. **[G: Latin America; U.S.]**

Robinson, J. Nicholas. The Debate on the Macroeconomic Impact of North Sea Oil: A Survey. *Brit. Rev. Econ. Issues,* Spring 1983, *5*(12), pp. 15–31. **[G: U.K.]**

Robson, Arthur J. OPEC versus the West: A Robust Equilibrium. *J. Environ. Econ. Manage.*, March 1983, *10*(1), pp. 18–34.

Rødseth, Asbjørn. An Expenditure System for Energy Planning. **In** *Av, R., et al., eds.*, 1983, pp. 195–220. **[G: Norway]**

Roncaglia, Alessandro. The Price of Oil: Main Interpretations and Their Theoretical Blackground. *J. Post Keynesian Econ.*, Summer 1983, *5*(4), pp. 557–78.

Rosenberg, Nathan. The Effects of Energy Supply Characteristics on Technology and Economic Growth. **In** *Schurr, S. H.; Sonenblum, S. and Wood, D. O., eds.*, 1983, pp. 279–305. **[G: U.S.]**

Roth, T. P. Electricity Demand Estimation Using Proxy Variables: Some Reservations. *Appl. Econ.*, October 1983, *15*(5), pp. 703–04. **[G: U.S.]**

Roumasset, James; Isaak, David T. and Fesharaki, Fereidun. Oil Prices without OPEC: A Walk on the Supply-Side. *Energy Econ.*, July 1983, *5*(3), pp. 164–70.

Rovani, Yves. Energy Transition in Developing Countries. *Finance Develop.*, December 1983, *20*(4), pp. 24–27. **[G: LDCs]**

Ruggeri, G. C. A Note on the Energy–GNP Relationship in Canada, 1961–1980. *J. Energy Devel.*, Spring 1983, *8*(2), pp. 341–46. **[G: Canada]**

Ruggeri, G. C. Market Conditions and Future Oil Prices. *Energy Econ.*, July 1983, *5*(3), pp. 190–94. **[G: OPEC; Global]**

Rusin, Michael. Problems in Modeling Crude Oil Price Decontrol and Windfall Profits Tax Proposals: A Case Study. **In** *Thrall, R. M.; Thompson, R. G. and Holloway, M. L., eds.*, 1983, pp. 29–50. **[G: U.S.]**

Sachs, Jeffrey D. Energy and Growth under Flexible Exchange Rates: A Simulation Study. **In** *Bhandari, J. S. and Putnam, B. H., eds.*, 1983, pp. 191–220. **[G: OPEC]**

Sakakibara, Sakura. The Energy Situation in the Asian-Pacific Region and International Cooperation. *J. Energy Devel.*, Autumn 1983, *9*(1), pp. 41–48. **[G: Asia]**

Sakhovaler, T. A. and Eskin, V. I. A Nonlinear Scheme for Calculating the Monetary Value of Oil and Gas Deposits. *Matekon*, Fall 1983, *20*(1), pp. 78–92.

Salib, Anis B. Energy, GDP, and the Structure of Demand: An International Comparison Using Input–Output Techniques. *J. Energy Devel.*, Autumn 1983, *9*(1), pp. 55–61. **[G: U.S.; U.K.; Japan; France; Italy]**

Samouilidis, J-Emmanuel and Mitropoulos, Costas S. Energy Investment and Economic Growth: A Simplified Approach. *Energy Econ.*, October 1983, *5*(4), pp. 237–46. **[G: U.K.]**

Sanghvi, Arun P. Optimal Electricity Supply Reliability Using Customer Shortage Costs. *Energy Econ.*, April 1983, *5*(2), pp. 129–36. **[G: U.S.]**

Sanghvi, Arun P.; Shavel, Ira H. and Wagner, Michael H. Fuel Diversification, Stockpiling, and System Interconnection Strategies for Minimizing Power System Vulnerability to Energy Shortages. **In** *Lev, B., ed.*, 1983, pp. 235–54. **[G: U.S.]**

Sant, Donald T.; Haspel, Abraham E. and Boldt, Robert E. Oil and Gas Royalty Recovery Policy on Federal and Indian Lands: A Response. *Natural Res. J.*, April 1983, *23*(2), pp. 417–33. **[G: U.S.]**

Sargent, D. Alec. The United States' Role in the International Thermal Coal Market. *Energy J.*, January 1983, *4*(1), pp. 79–96. **[G: U.S.; OECD]**

Sarma, K. S. An Examination of the Impact of Changes in the Prices of Fuels and Primary Metals on Nordic Countries Using a World Econometric Model. **In** *Eliasson, G.; Sharefkin, M. and Ysander, B.-C., eds.*, 1983, pp. 245–68. **[G: Nordic Countries; OECD]**

Sathaye, Jayant and Ruderman, Henry. The Role of Renewables in Hawaii's Energy Future. *Energy J.*, April 1983, *4*(2), pp. 121–34. **[G: U.S.]**

Saunders, Harry D. Optimal Oil Producer Behavior Considering Macrofeedbacks. *Energy J.*, October

1983, *4*(4), pp. 1–27.

Saunders, Harry D. Optimal Oil Producer Behavior Considering Macrofeedbacks: Reply. *Energy J.*, October 1983, *4*(4), pp. 31–35.

Scanlan, A. F. G. Communist Bloc Energy Supply and Demand. In *Tempest, P., ed.*, 1983, pp. 149–59. **[G: CMEA]**

Schmidt, Ronald H. Effects of Natural Gas Deregulation on the Distribution of Income. *Fed. Res. Bank Dallas Econ. Rev.*, May 1983, pp. 1–12. **[G: U.S.]**

Schramm, Gunter. The Economics of Gas Utilization in a Gas-Rich, Oil-Poor Country: The Case of Bangladesh. *Energy J.*, January 1983, *4*(1), pp. 47–64. **[G: Bangladesh]**

Schurr, Sam H. Energy Efficiency and Economic Efficiency: An Historical Perspective. In *Schurr, S. H.; Sonenblum, S. and Wood, D. O., eds.*, 1983, pp. 203–14. **[G: U.S.]**

Schurr, Sam H. Energy Efficiency and Production Efficiency: Some Thoughts Based on American Experience. In *Tempest, P., ed.*, 1983, pp. 51–60. **[G: U.S.]**

Scott, Alex and Capper, Graham. Production Functions for House Temperatures: Problems and Issues: A Reply [The Economics of House Heating]. *Energy Econ.*, October 1983, *5*(4), pp. 275–78. **[G: U.K.]**

Seidelmann, Reimund. Energy Trade Relations between the Federal Republic of Germany and the USSR. In *Lieber, R. J., ed.*, 1983, pp. 71–103. **[G: U.S.S.R.; W. Germany]**

Sharefkin, Mark. Stabilization and Growth Policy with Uncertain Oil Prices: Some Rules of Thumb. In *Eliasson, G.; Sharefkin, M. and Ysander, B.-C., eds.*, 1983, pp. 327–74.

Sheehan, Michael F. Land Speculation in Southern California: Energy Monopoly, Fiscal Crisis and the Future. *Amer. J. Econ. Soc.*, January 1983, *42*(1), pp. 67–74. **[G: U.S.]**

Sheehan, Richard G. and Kelly, Neil. Oil Prices and World Inflation. *J. Econ. Bus.*, June 1983, *35*(2), pp. 235–38. **[G: U.S.]**

Sherali, Hanif D. and Soyster, Allen L. Analysis of Network Structured Models for Electric Utility Capacity Planning and Marginal Cost Pricing Problems. In *Lev, B., ed.*, 1983, pp. 113–34.

Simos, Evangelos O. and Triantis, John E. Do Energy Prices and Productivity Developments Affect Inflation Expectations? *Rivista Int. Sci. Econ. Com.*, October–November 1983, *30*(10–11), pp. 923–34. **[G: U.S.]**

Sinclair, P. J. N. How Does an Energy Price Shock Affect Aggregate Output and Employment? *Greek Econ. Rev.*, August 1983, *5*(2), pp. 123–46.

Smart, Ian. Nuclear Resources: The Dilemmas of Interdependence. In *Akao, N., ed.*, 1983, pp. 119–44. **[G: Japan]**

Smith, Wray. On Energy Policy Models: Comment. *J. Bus. Econ. Statist.*, January 1983, *1*(1), pp. 34–35. **[G: U.S.]**

Soedjatmoko. Turning Point in Development: The Food–Energy Pivot. In *Glassner, M. I., ed.*, 1983, *1981*, pp. 237–43. **[G: Global]**

Sohlman, Asa. Energy Use in Sweden 1965–80. In *Sohlman, A. M., ed.*, 1983, pp. 38–56. **[G: Sweden]**

Sohlman, Asa. Using Quantified General Equilibrium Models for Cost-benefit Analysis of Alternative Energy Policies. In *Sohlman, A. M., ed.*, 1983, pp. 306–27. **[G: Sweden]**

Sohlman, Asa and Launay, Didier. Energy Demand Analysis: A Survey and Introduction. In *Sohlman, A. M., ed.*, 1983, pp. 1–12.

Sonenblum, Sidney. Energy Productivity and Total Productivity: Comment. In *Schurr, S. H.; Sonenblum, S. and Wood, D. O., eds.*, 1983, pp. 219–45. **[G: U.S.]**

Sonenblum, Sidney. Energy, Productivity, and Economic Growth: Overview and Commentary. In *Schurr, S. H.; Sonenblum, S. and Wood, D. O., eds.*, 1983, pp. 3–43. **[G: U.S.; Selected Countries]**

Sotomayor Torres, Clivia M. and Rudig, Wolfgang. Nuclear Power in Argentina and Brazil. *Rev. Radical Polit. Econ.*, Fall 1983, *15*(3), pp. 67–82. **[G: Argentina; Brazil]**

Spronk, Jaap and Veeneklaas, Frank. A Feasibility Study of Economic and Environmental Scenarios by Means of Interactive Multiple Goal Programming. *Reg. Sci. Urban Econ.*, February 1983, *13*(1), pp. 141–60. **[G: Netherlands]**

Srivastava, Alok. Techno-Commercial Aspects of Solar Energy in India. *Econ. Aff.*, July-September 1983, *28*(3), pp. 768–73. **[G: India]**

Stanfield, J. Ron. Radical Economics and Resource Scarcity: A Comment. *Rev. Soc. Econ.*, April 1983, *41*(1), pp. 68–71.

Stehle, John F. The Economics of Entropy [Radical Economics and Resource Scarcity]. *Rev. Soc. Econ.*, October 1983, *41*(2), pp. 179–82.

Stern, Jonathan P. Natural Gas: The Perfect Answer to Energy Diversification. In *Akao, N., ed.*, 1983, pp. 97–117. **[G: Japan]**

Street, James H. Rejoinder to S. C. Stamos's "Critique of 'Technology, Institutions, and Public Policy in the Age of Energy Substitution.'" *J. Econ. Issues*, December 1983, *17*(4), pp. 1120–25. **[G: Latin America]**

Surrey, John and Walker, William. Electrical Power Plant: Market Collapse and Structural Strains. In *Shepherd, G.; Duchêne, F. and Saunders, C., eds.*, 1983, pp. 139–66. **[G: OECD]**

Sutherland, Ronald J. Distributed Lags and the Demand for Electricity. *Energy J.*, Supplement 1983, *4*, pp. 141–51. **[G: U.S.]**

Sutherland, Ronald J. Instability of Electricity Demand Functions in the Post-Oil-Embargo Period. *Energy Econ.*, October 1983, *5*(4), pp. 267–72. **[G: U.S.]**

Swan, Peter L. The Marginal Cost of Base-Load Power: An Application to Alcoa's Portland Smelter. *Econ. Rec.*, December 1983, *59*(167), pp. 332–44. **[G: Australia]**

Sweeney, James L. Energy Model Comparison: An Overview. In *Thrall, R. M.; Thompson, R. G. and Holloway, M. L., eds.*, 1983, pp. 191–217. **[G: U.S.]**

Sylves, Richard T. National Politics and the Solar Energy Transition. In *Rich, D., et al., eds.*, 1983, pp. 49–75. **[G: U.S.]**

Szplett, Elizabeth S. and Sargious, Michael A. The Comparative Energy Efficiency of Intercity Transportation Modes in Canada. *Logist. Transp. Rev.*, June 1983, *19*(2), pp. 163–80. **[G: Canada]**

Szuprowicz, Bohdan O. What Are Strategic Materials? **In** *Glassner, M. I., ed.*, 1983, *1981*, pp. 335–61. **[G: Global]**

Tatom, John A. The Effect of Energy Prices on the Retirement of Capital Equipment: A Comment. *Bus. Econ.*, January 1983, *18*(1), pp. 54–56. **[G: U.S.]**

Teller, Edward. Energy—A Society Reacting to Scarcity. **In** *Martin, T. R., ed.*, 1983, pp. 64–73. **[G: U.S.]**

Tempest, Paul. The International Energy Investment Dilemma. **In** *Tempest, P., ed.*, 1983, pp. 247–58. **[G: OECD]**

Tempest, Paul. The International Energy Investment Dilemma. *Energy J.*, July 1983, *4*(3), pp. 1–10.

The American Petroleum Institute. Oil and Gas from Under the Sea. **In** *Glassner, M. I., ed.*, 1983, *1982*, pp. 556–63. **[G: U.S.]**

The Georgia Conservancy. The Wolfcreek Statement: Toward a Sustainable Energy Society. **In** *Glassner, M. I., ed.*, 1983, *1976*, pp. 311–17. **[G: U.S.]**

Thimrén, Claes. Potential Benefits from Isolating the Domestic Oil Price Level during Short-run Oil Price Booms. **In** *Sohlman, A. M., ed.*, 1983, pp. 234–73. **[G: Sweden]**

Thirsk, Wayne R. Energy Policy, Taxation of Natural Resources and Fiscal Federalism: Comment. **In** *McLure, C. E., Jr., ed.*, 1983, pp. 148–49. **[G: U.S.]**

Thompson, Russell G., et al. Input–Output Modeling from the Bottom Up Rather Than from the Top Down. **In** *Thrall, R. M.; Thompson, R. G. and Holloway, M. L., eds.*, 1983, pp. 101–40. **[G: U.S.]**

Thoreson, Per E. Inflation Controlled by Energy Prices. *Energy Econ.*, July 1983, *5*(3), pp. 202–06. **[G: Global]**

Tishler, Asher. The Industrial and Commercial Demand for Electricity under Time-of-Use Pricing. *J. Econometrics*, December 1983, *23*(3), pp. 369–84. **[G: U.S.]**

Trainer, F. E. Potentially Recoverable Resources: How Recoverable? **In** *Glassner, M. I., ed.*, 1983, *1982*, pp. 396–412. **[G: Global]**

Trimble, John and Hirst, Eric. Energy Use in Institutional Buildings: Estimates from State Energy-Audit Surveys. *J. Bus. Econ. Statist.*, October 1983, *1*(4), pp. 337–47. **[G: U.S.]**

Triplett, Jack E. Energy Efficiency, User-Cost Change, and the Measurement of Durable Goods Prices: Comment. **In** *Foss, M. F., ed.*, 1983, pp. 253–65. **[G: U.S.]**

Vanous, Jan. The Impact of the Oil Price Decline on the Soviet Union and Eastern Europe. *Energy J.*, July 1983, *4*(3), pp. 11–19. **[G: E. Europe; U.S.S.R.]**

Verleger, Philip K., Jr. Some Rational Strategies for Supply Disruption. **In** *Tempest, P., ed.*, 1983, pp. 137–44.

Viscio, Albert J., Jr. United States Energy Demand: Conservation and Recession Effects, 1973 to 1982. *J. Energy Devel.*, Spring 1983, *8*(2), pp. 231–46. **[G: U.S.]**

Wallop, Malcolm. Energy Development and Water: Dilemma for the Western United States. *J. Energy Devel.*, Spring 1983, *8*(2), pp. 203–09. **[G: U.S.]**

Wang, George C. Issues in China's International Trade: Editor's Introduction. *Chinese Econ. Stud.*, Spring 1983, *16*(3), pp. 6–9. **[G: China; U.S.]**

Watkins, G. C. and Berndt, Ernst R. Energy-Output Coefficients: Complex Realities behind Simple Ratios. *Energy J.*, April 1983, *4*(2), pp. 105–20. **[G: Canada]**

Watson, William D. Drilling Strategies for Federal Coal Leases. **In** *Lev, B., ed.*, 1983, pp. 465–81. **[G: U.S.]**

Watts, Michael and Lubeck, Paul. The Popular Classes and the Oil Boom: A Political Economy of Rural and Urban Poverty. **In** *Zartman, I. W., ed.*, 1983, pp. 105–44. **[G: Nigeria]**

Waverman, Leonard. The Energy Connection to Recent Productivity Behavior: Comment. **In** *Schurr, S. H.; Sonenblum, S. and Wood, D. O., eds.*, 1983, pp. 185–88. **[G: U.S.]**

Weidenbaum, Murray L. Energy Development and U.S. Government Policy: Some Recommendations for Using Market Forces to Achieve Optimum National Goals. *Amer. J. Econ. Soc.*, July 1983, *42*(3), pp. 257–74. **[G: U.S.]**

Werbos, Paul J. Solving and Optimizing Complex Systems: Lessons from the EIA Long-term Energy Model. **In** *Lev, B., ed.*, 1983, pp. 163–80.

Weyant, John P. The Energy Crisis Is Over . . . Again. *Challenge*, Sept.–Oct. 1983, *26*(4), pp. 12–17. **[G: OPEC; OECD]**

Whalley, John. The Impact of Federal Policies on Interprovincial Activity. **In** *Trebilcock, M. J., et al., eds.*, 1983, pp. 201–42. **[G: Canada]**

Whyte, John D. A Constitutional Perspective on Federal–Provincial Sharing of Revenues from Natural Resources. **In** *McLure, C. E., Jr. and Mieszkowski, P., eds.*, 1983, pp. 205–35. **[G: Canada]**

Wijarso, Ir. The Indonesian Energy Scene. *J. Energy Devel.*, Autumn 1983, *9*(1), pp. 1–10. **[G: Indonesia]**

Wilkinson, Jack W. The Supply, Demand, and Average Price of Natural Gas under Free-Market Conditions. *Energy J.*, January 1983, *4*(1), pp. 99–123. **[G: U.S.]**

Willars, Jaime M. The Mexican Oil Sector in the 1980s: Issues and Perspectives. *J. Energy Devel.*, Autumn 1983, *9*(1), pp. 19–40. **[G: Mexico]**

Williams, Larry J. Energy Productivity and Total Productivity: Comment. **In** *Schurr, S. H.; Sonenblum, S. and Wood, D. O., eds.*, 1983, pp. 245–53. **[G: U.S.]**

Wilson, Charles. Oil Shocks and Exchange Rate Dynamics: Comment. **In** *Frenkel, J. A., ed.*, 1983, pp. 281–83.

Wionczek, Miguel S. Algunas reflexiones sobre la futura política petrolera de México. (With English summary.) *Desarrollo Econ.*, April–June 1983, *23*(89), pp. 59–78. **[G: Mexico]**

Wonder, Edward F. Mexican Oil and the Western

Alliance. **In** *Lieber, R. J., ed.*, 1983, pp. 135–67. **[G: Mexico; Central America; OECD]**

Woods, Thomas J. Energy Productivity and Total Productivity: Comment. **In** *Schurr, S. H.; Sonenblum, S. and Wood, D. O., eds.*, 1983, pp. 253–57. **[G: U.S.]**

Wright, Claudia. Neutral or Neutralized? Iraq, Iran, and the Superpowers. **In** *Tahir-Kheli, S. and Ayubi, S., eds.*, 1983, pp. 172–92. **[G: Iraq; Iran]**

Yorke, Valerie. Oil, the Middle East and Japan's Search for Security. **In** *Akao, N., ed.*, 1983, pp. 45–70. **[G: Middle East; Japan]**

Ysander, Bengt-Christer. Measuring Energy Substitution: An Introduction. **In** *Ysander, B.-C., ed.*, 1983, pp. 9–25. **[G: Sweden]**

Ysander, Bengt-Christer. Oil Prices and Economic Stability: The Macroeconomic Impact of Oil Price Shocks on the Swedish Economy. **In** *Eliasson, G.; Sharefkin, M. and Ysander, B.-C., eds.*, 1983, pp. 225–44. **[G: Sweden]**

Ysander, Bengt-Christer and Nordström, Tomas. Energy in Swedish Manufacturing 1980–2000. **In** *Ysander, B.-C., ed.*, 1983, pp. 229–60. **[G: Sweden]**

Zakariya, Hasan S. The Petroleum Lending Programme of the World Bank: The First Five Years. *J. World Trade Law*, November–December 1983, *17*(6), pp. 471–95. **[G: LDCs]**

Zaki, Ahmed S. and Isakson, Hans R. The Impact of Energy Prices: A Housing Market Analysis. *Energy Econ.*, April 1983, *5*(2), pp. 100–104. **[G: U.S.]**

Zimmerman, Martin B. Coal: An Economic Interpretation of Reserve Estimates. **In** *Adelman, M. A., et al.*, 1983, pp. 295–332. **[G: U.S.]**

Zimmerman, Martin B. Comparisons, Recommendations, and Conclusions: Resources and Reserves. **In** *Adelman, M. A., et al.*, 1983, pp. 385–93.

Zimmerman, Martin B. The Valuation of Nuclear Power in the Post-Three Mile Island Era. *Energy J.*, April 1983, *4*(2), pp. 15–29. **[G: U.S.]**

730 Economic Geography

731 Economic Geography

7310 Economic Geography

Black, William. A Generalization of Destination Effects in Spatial Interaction Modeling. *Econ. Geogr.*, January 1983, *59*(1), pp. 16–34. **[G: U.S.]**

Buhr, Walter. Mikroökonomische Modelle der von Thünenschen Standorttheorie. (Microeconomic Models of von Thünen's Location Theory. With English summary.) *Z. Wirtschaft. Sozialwissen.*, 1983, *103*(6), pp. 589–627.

Carlton, Dennis W. The Location and Employment Choices of New Firms: An Econometric Model with Discrete and Continuous Endogenous Variables. *Rev. Econ. Statist.*, August 1983, *65*(3), pp. 440–49. **[G: U.S.]**

Chalmet, Luc G. Efficiency in Minisum Rectilinear Distance Location Problems. **In** *Thisse, J.-F. and Zoller, H. G., eds.*, 1983, pp. 431–45.

Charney, Alberta H. Intraurban Manufacturing Location Decisions and Local Tax Differentials. *J. Urban Econ.*, September 1983, *14*(2), pp. 184–205. **[G: U.S.]**

Clark, William A. V. and Onaka, Jun L. Life Cycle and Housing Adjustment as Explanations of Residential Mobility. *Urban Stud.*, February 1983, *20*(1), pp. 47–57. **[G: New Zealand; Canada; U.S.; U.K.]**

Clark, William A. V. and Onaka, Jun L. Errata [Life Cycle and Housing Adjustment as Explanations of Residential Mobility]. *Urban Stud.*, November 1983, *20*(4), pp. 391. **[G: U.S.; U.K.; Canada; New Zealand]**

Clarke, M. and Wilson, A. G. The Dynamics of Urban Spatial Structure: Progress and Problems. *J. Reg. Sci.*, February 1983, *23*(1), pp. 1–18.

Cooke, Timothy W. Testing a Model of Intraurban Firm Relocation. *J. Urban Econ.*, May 1983, *13*(3), pp. 257–82. **[G: U.S.]**

Doyle, Peter and Corstjens, Marcel. Optimal Growth Strategies for Service Organizations. *J. Bus.*, July 1983, *56*(3), pp. 389–405. **[G: U.K.]**

Elliott, Harold M. Surrounding Larger Neighbors and the Atlantic Coast Cardinal Neighbor Gradient. *Econ. Geogr.*, October 1983, *59*(4), pp. 426–44. **[G: U.S.]**

Erlenkotter, Donald. On the Choice of Models for Public Facility Location. **In** *Thisse, J.-F. and Zoller, H. G., eds.*, 1983, pp. 385–93.

Faminow, M. D. and Sarhan, M. E. The Location of Fed Cattle Slaughtering and Processing in the United States: An Application of Mixed Integer Programming. *Can. J. Agr. Econ.*, November 1983, *31*(3), pp. 425–36. **[G: U.S.]**

Friedmann, John. Life Space and Economic Space: Contradictions in Regional Development. **In** *Seers, D. and Öström, K., eds.*, 1983, pp. 148–62.

Gibson, Katherine D. and Horvath, Ronald J. Global Capital and the Restructuring Crisis in Australian Manufacturing. *Econ. Geogr.*, April 1983, *59*(2), pp. 178–94. **[G: Australia]**

Hadjimichalis, Costis. Regional Crisis: The State and Regional Social Movements in Southern Europe. **In** *Seers, D. and Öström, K., eds.*, 1983, pp. 127–47. **[G: S. Europe]**

Hall, Bruce F. Neighborhood Differences in Retail Food Stores: Income versus Race and Age of Population. *Econ. Geogr.*, July 1983, *59*(3), pp. 282–95.

Halperin, William C., et al. Exploring Entrepreneurial Cognitions of Retail Environments. *Econ. Geogr.*, January 1983, *59*(1), pp. 3–15. **[G: Australia]**

Halpern, Jonathan and Maimon, Oded. Accord and Conflict among Several Objectives in Locational Decisions on Tree Networks. **In** *Thisse, J.-F. and Zoller, H. G., eds.*, 1983, pp. 301–14.

Hansen, Pierre; Peeters, D. and Thisse, Jacques-François. Public Facility Location Models: A Selective Survey. **In** *Thisse, J.-F. and Zoller, H. G., eds.*, 1983, pp. 223–62.

Holmes, John. Industrial Reorganization, Capital Restructuring and Locational Change: An Analysis of the Canadian Automobile Industry in the 1960s. *Econ. Geogr.*, July 1983, *59*(3), pp. 251–71. **[G: Canada]**

Hsu, Song-ken. Pricing in an Urban Spatial Monopoly: A General Analysis. *J. Reg. Sci.*, May 1983, *23*(2), pp. 165–75.

Hsu, Song-ken. Social Optimal Pricing in a Spatial Market. *Reg. Sci. Urban Econ.*, August 1983, *13*(3), pp. 401–10.

Janelle, Donald and Goodchild, Michael. Diurnal Patterns of Social Group Distributions in a Canadian City. *Econ. Geogr.*, October 1983, *59*(4), pp. 403–25. **[G: Canada]**

Johnson, P. S. New Manufacturing Firms in the U.K. Regions. *Scot. J. Polit. Econ.*, February 1983, *30*(1), pp. 75–79. **[G: U.K.]**

Karlson, Stephen H. Modeling Location and Production: An Application to U.S. Fully-Integrated Steel Plants. *Rev. Econ. Statist.*, February 1983, *65*(1), pp. 41–50. **[G: U.S.]**

Kilmer, Richard L.; Spreen, Thomas H. and Tilley, Daniel S. A Dynamic Plant Location Model: The East Florida Fresh Citrus Packing Industry. *Amer. J. Agr. Econ.*, November 1983, *65*(4), pp. 730–37. **[G: U.S.]**

Lea, Anthony C. Some Lessons from the Theory of Public and Impure Goods for Public Facility Location-Allocation Models. **In** *Thisse, J.-F. and Zoller, H. G., eds.*, 1983, pp. 263–300.

Lesage, Jean-Luc. Comments on 'Regional Development in Portugal.' **In** *Seers, D. and Öström, K., eds.*, 1983, pp. 83–85. **[G: Portugal]**

Ley, David and Mercer, John. Locational Conflict and the Politics of Consumption. **In** *Lake, R. W., ed.*, 1983, *1980*, pp. 118–42.

Lundahl, Mats. The State of Spatial Economic Research on Haiti: A Selective Survey. **In** *Lundahl, M.*, 1983, *1980*, pp. 153–70. **[G: Haiti]**

Mathur, Vijay K. Location Theory of the Firm under Price Uncertainty. *Reg. Sci. Urban Econ.*, August 1983, *13*(3), pp. 411–28.

McGuire, Therese. Firm Location in a Tiebout World. *J. Reg. Sci.*, May 1983, *23*(2), pp. 211–22.

Mehretu, Assefa; Wittick, Robert I. and Pigozzi, Bruce W. Spatial Design for Basic Needs in Eastern Upper Volta. *J. Devel. Areas*, April 1983, *17*(3), pp. 383–94. **[G: Upper Volta]**

Mehrez, Abraham. A Note on the Linear Integer Formulation of the Maximal Covering Location Problem with Facility Placement on the Entire Plane. *J. Reg. Sci.*, November 1983, *23*(4), pp. 553–55.

Mehrez, Abraham; Sinuany-Stern, Zilla and Stulman, Alan. The One-Dimensional Single Facility Maximin Distance Location Problem. *J. Reg. Sci.*, May 1983, *23*(2), pp. 233–39.

Osleeb, Jeffrey P. and Patrick, Samuel J. The Impact of Coal Conversions on the Ports of New England. *Econ. Geogr.*, January 1983, *59*(1), pp. 35–51. **[G: U.S.]**

Peet, Richard. Relations of Production and the Relocation of United States Manufacturing Industry since 1960. *Econ. Geogr.*, April 1983, *59*(2), pp. 112–43. **[G: U.S.]**

Schmidt, Charles G. Location Decision-Making within a Retail Corporation. *Reg. Sci. Persp.*, 1983, *13*(1), pp. 60–71. **[G: U.S.]**

Schöler, Klaus. Alternative Preistechniken im räumlichen Monopol: Ein einzelwirtschaftlicher und wohlfahrtstheoretischer Vergleich. (Alternative Pricing Techniques in Spatial Monopoly. With English summary.) *Z. ges. Staatswiss.*, June 1983, *139*(2), pp. 289–305.

Scott, A. J. Industrial Organization and the Logic of Intra-Metropolitan Location: I. Theoretical Considerations. *Econ. Geogr.*, July 1983, *59*(3), pp. 233–50.

Sheldon, Sam. Folk Economy and Impoverishment in Mexico's Zona Ixtlera. *J. Devel. Areas,* July 1983, *17*(4), pp. 453–72. **[G: Mexico]**

Smith, Christopher J. Locating Alcoholism Treatment Facilities. *Econ. Geogr.*, October 1983, *59*(4), pp. 368–85. **[G: U.S.]**

Soja, Edward; Morales, Rebecca and Wolff, Goetz. Urban Restructuring: An Analysis of Social and Spatial Change in Los Angeles. *Econ. Geogr.*, April 1983, *59*(2), pp. 195–230. **[G: U.S.]**

Stöhr, Walter B. Alternative Strategies for Integrated Regional Development of Peripheral Areas. **In** *Seers, D. and Öström, K., eds.*, 1983, pp. 6–14. **[G: Austria]**

Tobin, Roger L. and Friesz, Terry L. Formulating and Solving the Spatial Price Equilibrium Problem with Transshipment in Terms of Arc Variables. *J. Reg. Sci.*, May 1983, *23*(2), pp. 187–98.

Tuppen, J. N. The Development of French New Towns: An Assessment of Progress. *Urban Stud.*, February 1983, *20*(1), pp. 11–30. **[G: France]**

Valente de Oliveira, Luís F. Regional Development in Portugal. **In** *Seers, D. and Öström, K., eds.*, 1983, pp. 68–82. **[G: Portugal]**

Webber, M. J. Location of Manufacturing and Operational Urban Models. **In** *Hamilton, F. E. I. and Linge, G. J. R., eds.*, 1983, pp. 141–202. **[G: U.S.; U.K.; Australia; Netherlands]**

Wild, Trevor. The Patterning of Cities and Rural Areas in West Germany. **In** *Wild, T., ed.*, 1983, pp. 5–15. **[G: W. Germany]**

800 Manpower; Labor; Population

8000 General

Daymont, Thomas N. and Andrisani, Paul J. The Research Uses of the National Longitudinal Surveys: An Update. *Rev. Public Data Use (See J. Econ. Soc. Meas. after 4/85),* October 1983, *11*(3), pp. 203–310. **[G: U.S.]**

810 Manpower Training and Allocation; Labor Force and Supply

811 Manpower Training and Development

8110 Manpower Training and Development

Ash, J. Colin K.; Udis, Bernard and McNown, Robert F. Enlistments in the All-Volunteer Force: A Military Personnel Supply Model and Its Forecasts. *Amer. Econ. Rev.*, March 1983, *73*(1), pp. 145–55. **[G: U.S.]**

Barker, Michael. State Employment Policy in Hard Times: Introduction. **In** *Barker, M., ed. (II)*, 1983, pp. xi–xxix. [G: U.S.]

Bassi, Laurie J. The Effect of CETA on the Postprogram Earnings of Participants. *J. Human Res.*, Fall 1983, *18* (4), pp. 539–56. [G: U.S.]

Becker, Brian E. and Hills, Stephen M. The Long-Run Effects of Job Changes and Unemployment among Male Teenagers. *J. Human Res.*, Spring 1983, *18* (2), pp. 197–212. [G: U.S.]

Björklund, Anders and Persson-Tanimura, Inga. Youth Employment in Sweden. In *Reubens, B. G., ed.*, 1983, pp. 232–68. [G: Sweden]

Blakemore, Arthur E. and Low, Stuart A. Race and the Acquisition of and Returns to OJT for Youth. *Ind. Relat.*, Fall 1983, *22* (3), pp. 374–86. [G: U.S.]

Bovard, James. Busy Doing Nothing: The Story of Government Job Creation. *Policy Rev.*, Spring 1983, (24), pp. 87–102. [G: U.S.]

Brandao, Antonio Salazar P. The U.S. Graduate Training in Agricultural Economics: The Perspective of a Former Foreign Student. *Amer. J. Agr. Econ.*, December 1983, *65* (5), pp. 1149–52. [G: U.S.]

Caspar, Pierre. French Law on Continuing Vocational Training. In *Levin, H. M. and Schütze, H. G., eds.*, 1983, pp. 257–72. [G: France]

Celestin, Jean-Bernard. Manpower Planning and Labour Market Information in French-Speaking Africa. *Int. Lab. Rev.*, July–August 1983, *122* (4), pp. 507–22. [G: LDCs]

Cherevan', V. Coordinating the Reproduction of Workplaces with Labor Resources. *Prob. Econ.*, May 1983, *26* (1), pp. 38–56. [G: U.S.S.R.]

Choudhury, Masudul Alam. How Effective Is Human Resource Planning in Developing the Third World? *METU*, 1983, *10* (3), pp. 249–69. [G: Libya; Ghana; Gambia]

Christensen, Jens P. From Social Demand to Manpower Approach in Higher Education Planning—The Danish Case. *METU*, 1983, *10* (3), pp. 225–48. [G: Denmark]

Corvalán-Vásquez, Oscar. Vocational Training of Disadvantaged Youth in the Developing Countries. *Int. Lab. Rev.*, May–June 1983, *122* (3), pp. 367–81. [G: LDCs]

Crowley, Joan E.; Pollard, Tom K. and Rumberger, Russell W. Education and Training. In *Borus, M. E., ed.*, 1983, pp. 103–48. [G: U.S.]

Dawson, Peter. Labour Market Imbalances and Occupational Training in Canada: Issues and Implications for Vocational Education Policies: Comment. In *Queen's Univ. Indust. Relat. Centre and John Deutsch Mem.*, 1983, pp. 165–68. [G: Canada]

Dodge, David. Labour Market Policy Concerns: An Evaluation of Current Federal Policies and Priorities. In *Queen's Univ. Indust. Relat. Centre and John Deutsch Mem.*, 1983, pp. 135–43. [G: Canada]

Doyle, Peter S. Labour Market Policy Concerns: An Evaluation of Current Federal Policies and Priorities: Comment. In *Queen's Univ. Indust. Relat. Centre and John Deutsch Mem.*, 1983, pp. 148–50. [G: Canada]

Emmerij, Louis. Paid Educational Leave: A Proposal Based on the Dutch Case. In *Levin, H. M. and Schütze, H. G., eds.*, 1983, pp. 297–316. [G: Netherlands; OECD]

Englander, Frederick. Helping Ex-Offenders Enter the Labor Market. *Mon. Lab. Rev.*, July 1983, *106* (7), pp. 25–30. [G: U.S.]

Fairley, J. Training Policy—The Local Perspective. *Reg. Stud.*, April 1983, *17* (2), pp. 140–43. [G: U.K.]

Farkas, George; Smith, D. Alton and Stromsdorfer, Ernst W. The Youth Entitlement Demonstration: Subsidized Employment with a Schooling Requirement. *J. Human Res.*, Fall 1983, *18* (4), pp. 557–73. [G: U.S.]

Goonatilake, P. C. L. Production Management—The Forgotten Factor in the Industrialization Policy in Developing Countries. *World Devel.*, September 1983, *11* (9), pp. 845–50. [G: Commonwealth Nations]

Guttman, Robert. Job Training Partnership Act: New Help for the Unemployed. *Mon. Lab. Rev.*, March 1983, *106* (3), pp. 3–10. [G: U.S.]

Hartmann, Gert, et al. Computerised Machine-Tools, Manpower Consequences and Skill Utilisation: A Study of British and West German Manufacturing Firms. *Brit. J. Ind. Relat.*, July 1983, *21* (2), pp. 221–31. [G: U.K.; W. Germany]

Hills, Stephen M. and Reubens, Beatrice G. Youth Employment in the United States. In *Reubens, B. G., ed.*, 1983, pp. 269–318. [G: U.S.]

Hunter, Kenneth E. Labour Market Imbalances and Occupational Training in Canada: Issues and Implications for Vocational Education Policies: Comment. In *Queen's Univ. Indust. Relat. Centre and John Deutsch Mem.*, 1983, pp. 163–65. [G: Canada]

Jain, Harish C. Task Force Encourages Diffusion of Microelectronics in Canada. *Mon. Lab. Rev.*, October 1983, *106* (10), pp. 25–29. [G: Canada]

Johnson, George E. Potentials of Labor Market Policy: A View from the Eighties. *Ind. Relat.*, Spring 1983, *22* (2), pp. 283–97. [G: U.S.]

Johnson, Glenn L. The Relevance of U.S. Graduate Curricula in Agricultural Economics for the Training of Foreign Students. *Amer. J. Agr. Econ.*, December 1983, *65* (5), pp. 1142–48. [G: U.S.]

Kapustin, Evgeni. Manpower in the USSR: Development and Utilisation Trends. In *Streeten, P. and Maier, H., eds.*, 1983, pp. 355–69. [G: U.S.S.R.]

Klitgaard, Robert E., et al. The Economics of Teacher Training: An Exploratory Data Analysis. *Pakistan J. Appl. Econ.*, Summer 1983, *2* (1), pp. 13–38. [G: Pakistan]

Lang, Ron. Labour Market Policy Concerns: An Evaluation of Current Federal Policies and Priorities: Comment. In *Queen's Univ. Indust. Relat. Centre and John Deutsch Mem.*, 1983, pp. 143–45. [G: Canada]

Levin, Henry M. Comprehensive Models for Financing Recurrent Education: Individual Entitlements. In *Levin, H. M. and Schütze, H. G., eds.*, 1983, pp. 39–66. [G: OECD]

Levin, Henry M. and Schütze, Hans G. Economic and Political Dimensions of Recurrent Education. In *Levin, H. M. and Schütze, H. G., eds.*, 1983, pp. 9–36. [G: OECD]

Mamalakis, Markos. Overall Employment and Income Strategies. **In** *Urquidi, V. L. and Reyes, S. T., eds.*, 1983, pp. 111–30.

Medoff, James L. The Importance of Employer-sponsored Job-related Training. **In** *Queen's Univ. Indust. Relat. Centre and John Deutsch Mem.*, 1983, pp. 192–220. **[G: U.S.]**

Merrilees, William J. Alternative Models of Apprentice Recruitment: With Special Reference to the British Engineering Industry. *Appl. Econ.*, February 1983, *15*(1), pp. 1–21. **[G: U.K.]**

Metcalf, David and Richards, John. Youth Employment in Great Britain. **In** *Reubens, B. G., ed.*, 1983, pp. 149–84. **[G: U.K.]**

Murtagh, Gregg. Labour Market Imbalances and Occupational Training in Canada: Issues and Implications for Vocational Education Policies: Comment. **In** *Queen's Univ. Indust. Relat. Centre and John Deutsch Mem.*, 1983, pp. 168–70. **[G: Canada]**

Mushkat, Miron. Deficiencies in Identifying and Assessing Training Needs in the Public Sector. *Rivista Int. Sci. Econ. Com.*, February 1983, *30*(2), pp. 163–75.

Newton, Keith and Ostry, Sylvia. The Structure and Evolution of Canadian Manpower Policy: An Overview. **In** *Weisbrod, B. and Hughes, H., eds.*, 1983, pp. 16–30. **[G: Canada]**

Ohashi, Isao. Wage Profiles, Layoffs and Specific Training. *Int. Econ. Rev.*, February 1983, *24*(1), pp. 169–81.

Owen, Wyn F. and Cross, Larry R. Foreign Students in Agricultural Economics from the Perspective of the Economics Institute. *Amer. J. Agr. Econ.*, December 1983, *65*(5), pp. 1136–41. **[G: U.S.]**

Pal, Leslie A. The Fall and Rise of Developmental Uses of UI Funds. *Can. Public Policy*, March 1983, *9*(1), pp. 81–93. **[G: Canada]**

Prais, S. J. and Wagner, Karin. Some Practical Aspects of Human Capital Investment: Training Standards in Five Occupations in Britain and Germany. *Nat. Inst. Econ. Rev.*, August 1983, (105), pp. 46–65. **[G: U.K.; W. Germany]**

Rabby, Rami. Employment of the Disabled in Large Corporations. *Int. Lab. Rev.*, January–February 1983, *122*(1), pp. 23–36. **[G: U.S.]**

Raffa, Frederick A. and Haulman, Clyde A. The Impact of a PSE Program on Employment and Participants. *Growth Change*, October 1983, *14*(4), pp. 14–21. **[G: U.S.]**

Razavi, Hossein. Optimal Adjustment of Manpower-Requirement Forecasts: A Case Study of Iran. *Math. Soc. Sci.*, December 1983, *6*(3), pp. 315–23. **[G: Iran]**

Rogovskii, N. The Effectiveness of Labor under the Eleventh Five-Year Plan. *Prob. Econ.*, April 1983, *25*(12), pp. 51–66. **[G: U.S.S.R.]**

Rubenson, Kjell. Financing Paid Educational Leave: The Swedish Model. **In** *Levin, H. M. and Schütze, H. G., eds.*, 1983, pp. 237–55. **[G: Sweden]**

Saks, Daniel H. Jobs and Training. **In** *Pechman, J. A., ed.*, 1983, pp. 145–72. **[G: U.S.]**

Sawhill, Isabel V. Human Resources. **In** *Miller, G. W., ed.*, 1983, pp. 100–24. **[G: U.S.]**

Schiller, Bradley R. Small Business Training: A Negative-Sum Game. *Challenge*, Sept.–Oct. 1983, *26*(4), pp. 57–60. **[G: U.S.]**

Schober, Karen. Youth Employment in West Germany. **In** *Reubens, B. G., ed.*, 1983, pp. 113–48. **[G: W. Germany]**

Schütze, Hans G. Financing Paid Educational Leave: The Federal Republic of Germany. **In** *Levin, H. M. and Schütze, H. G., eds.*, 1983, pp. 273–95. **[G: W. Germany]**

Seguret, Marie-Claire. Women and Working Conditions: Prospects for Improvement? *Int. Lab. Rev.*, May–June 1983, *122*(3), pp. 295–311. **[G: Global]**

Selleck, Laura. Jobs for University Graduates: Planning or Choice? *Can. Public Policy*, March 1983, *9*(1), pp. 94–104. **[G: Canada]**

Smith, Gregory P. Employer-sponsored Programs. **In** *Levin, H. M. and Schütze, H. G., eds.*, 1983, pp. 159–87. **[G: U.S.]**

Standing, Guy. The Notion of Structural Unemployment. *Int. Lab. Rev.*, March–April 1983, *122*(2), pp. 137–53.

Street, James H. Institutional Reform and Manpower Development in Mexico. *J. Econ. Issues*, March 1983, *17*(1), pp. 17–33. **[G: Mexico]**

Tannen, Michael B. Vocational Education and Earnings for White Males: New Evidence from Longitudinal Data. *Southern Econ. J.*, October 1983, *50*(2), pp. 369–84. **[G: U.S.]**

Umetani, Shun'ichiro and Reubens, Beatrice G. Youth Employment in Japan. **In** *Reubens, B. G., ed.*, 1983, pp. 185–231. **[G: Japan]**

Wagner, Alan P. An Inventory of Programs and Sources of Support. **In** *Levin, H. M. and Schütze, H. G., eds.*, 1983, pp. 133–58. **[G: U.S.]**

Weiermair, Klaus. Labour Market Imbalances and Occupational Training in Canada: Issues and Implications for Vocational Education Policies. **In** *Queen's Univ. Indust. Relat. Centre and John Deutsch Mem.*, 1983, pp. 151–63. **[G: Canada]**

Wolfson, Alan. Labour Market Policy Concerns: An Evaluation of Current Federal Policies and Priorities: Comment. **In** *Queen's Univ. Indust. Relat. Centre and John Deutsch Mem.*, 1983, pp. 145–47. **[G: Canada]**

Woodward, M. On Forecasting Grade, Age and Length of Service Distributions in Manpower Systems. *J. Roy. Statist. Soc.*, 1983, *146*(1), pp. 74–84. **[G: U.K.]**

812 Occupation

8120 Occupation

Al-Jafary, Abdulrahman and Hollingsworth, A. T. An Exploratory Study of Managerial Practices in the Arabian Gulf Region. *J. Int. Bus. Stud.*, Fall 1983, *14*(2), pp. 143–52. **[G: Arabian Gulf; U.S.]**

Allie, Émile and Lefebvre, Pierre. L'aide sociale et le supplément au revenu de travail: une simulation économique des revenus (salaires) de réserve. (A Simulation of the Impact of the Quebec Minimum Income System on Reservation Wages (Income). With English summary.) *L'Actual. Econ.*, June 1983, *59*(2), pp. 190–207. **[G: Canada]**

Almquist, Eric L. Labour Specialization and the Irish Economy in 1841: An Aggregate Occupational

Analysis. *Econ. Hist. Rev., 2nd Ser.,* November 1983, *36*(4), pp. 506–17. **[G: Ireland]**

Ayal, Eliezer B. and Chiswick, Barry R. The Economics of the Diaspora Revisited. *Econ. Develop. Cult. Change,* July 1983, *31*(4), pp. 861–75. **[G: U.S.; Middle East]**

Ballantine, John W. Using Labor Market Information to Evaluate Industrial Performance. *J. Econ. Issues,* December 1983, *17*(4), pp. 1011–34. **[G: U.S.]**

Barrère-Maurisson, Marie-Agnès; Battagliola, Françoise and Duane-Richard, Anne-Marie. Trajectoires professionnelles des femmes et vie familiale. (Women's Career Course and Their Home Life. With English summary.) *Consommation,* October–December 1983, *30*(4), pp. 23–53. **[G: France]**

Bonnell, Sheila M. and Dixon, Peter B. A Measure of the Incidence of the Costs of Structural Change: The Experience of Birthplace Groups in the Australian Labour Force during the Seventies. *Econ. Rec.,* December 1983, *59*(167), pp. 398–406. **[G: Australia]**

Bowie, Robert D. The Peripheral Labour Force. **In** *Easton, B., ed.,* 1983, pp. 49–70. **[G: New Zealand]**

Brenner, Reuven. The Economics of the Diaspora Revisited: A Reply. *Econ. Develop. Cult. Change,* July 1983, *31*(4), pp. 877–78. **[G: U.S.; Middle East]**

Chiswick, Barry R. Illegal Aliens in the United States Labour Market. **In** *Weisbrod, B. and Hughes, H., eds.,* 1983, pp. 346–67. **[G: U.S.]**

Coleman, James S. Equality of Opportunity and Equality of Results. **In** *Letwin, W., ed.,* 1983, *1973,* pp. 189–98. **[G: U.S.]**

Cooter, Robert D. The Objectives of Private and Public Judges. *Public Choice,* 1983, *41*(1), pp. 107–32.

Corcoran, Mary; Duncan, Greg J. and Ponza, Michael. Work Experience and Wage Growth of Women Workers. **In** *Duncan, G. J. and Morgan, J. N., eds.,* 1983, pp. 249–323. **[G: U.S.]**

Corneil, Jim. Labour Market Projections in Canada: A Progress Report: Comment. **In** *Queen's Univ. Indust. Relat. Centre and John Deutsch Mem.,* 1983, pp. 106–09. **[G: Canada]**

Crowley, Joan E.; Pollard, Tom K. and Rumberger, Russell W. Education and Training. **In** *Borus, M. E., ed.,* 1983, pp. 103–48. **[G: U.S.]**

Davis, Carlton G. and Allen, Joyce E. Black Agricultural Economists in the Labor Market: Theoretical and Empirical Issues. *Amer. J. Agr. Econ.,* December 1983, *65*(5), pp. 981–87. **[G: U.S.]**

Daymont, Thomas N. and Statham, Anne. Occupational Atypicality: Changes, Causes, and Consequences. **In** *Shaw, L. B., ed.,* 1983, pp. 61–75. **[G: U.S.]**

Delaney, John Thomas. Strikes, Arbitration, and Teacher Salaries: A Behavioral Analysis. *Ind. Lab. Relat. Rev.,* April 1983, *36*(3), pp. 431–46. **[G: U.S.]**

Denny, Michael G. S. and Fuss, Melvyn A. The Effects of Factor Prices and Technological Change on the Occupational Demand for Labor: Evidence from Canadian Telecommunications. *J. Human Res.,* Spring 1983, *18*(2), pp. 161–76. **[G: Canada]**

Devi, D. Radha and Ravindran, M. Women's Work in India. *Int. Soc. Sci. J.,* 1983, *35*(4), pp. 683–701. **[G: India]**

Faith, Roger L. and Tollison, Robert D. The Supply of Occupational Regulation. *Econ. Inquiry,* April 1983, *21*(2), pp. 232–40. **[G: U.K.; France]**

Goldfarb, Robert S.; Yezer, Anthony M. J. and Crewe, Sebastian. Some New Evidence: Have Regional Wage Differentials Really Disappeared? *Growth Change,* January 1983, *14*(1), pp. 48–51. **[G: U.S.]**

Haber, Sheldon E. Wage Structure in Internal Labor Markets and Marginal Productivity Theory. *Atlantic Econ. J.,* December 1983, *11*(4), pp. 66–70. **[G: U.S.]**

Hauser, Robert M. and Massagli, Michael P. Some Models of Agreement and Disagreement in Repeated Measurements of Occupation. *Demography,* November 1983, *20*(4), pp. 449–60. **[G: U.S.]**

Hirschman, Charles. Labor Markets and Ethnic Inequality in Peninsular Malaysia, 1970. *J. Devel. Areas,* October 1983, *18*(1), pp. 1–20. **[G: Malaysia]**

Hoffman, Dennis L. and Low, Stuart A. Rationality and the Decision to Invest in Economics. *J. Human Res.,* Fall 1983, *18*(4), pp. 480–96. **[G: U.S.]**

Horowitz, Harold. Work and Earnings of Artists in the Media Fields. *J. Cult. Econ.,* December 1983, 7(2), pp. 69–89. **[G: U.S.]**

Jensen, Roger C.; Klein, Bruce P. and Sanderson, Lee M. Motion-Related Wrist Disorders Traced to Industries, Occupational Groups. *Mon. Lab. Rev.,* September 1983, *106*(9), pp. 13–16. **[G: U.S.]**

Jones, Dewitt; Nelson, Mack and Parks, Alfred L. Demand and Supply Factors of Black Agricultural Economists. *Amer. J. Agr. Econ.,* December 1983, *65*(5), pp. 988–92. **[G: U.S.]**

Jura, Michel and Kaminski, Philippe. Mobilité sociale des ménages et évolution économique. *Consommation,* January/March 1983, *30*(1), pp. 93–123. **[G: France]**

Kaliski, Steve F. Labour Market Projections in Canada: A Progress Report: Comment. **In** *Queen's Univ. Indust. Relat. Centre and John Deutsch Mem.,* 1983, pp. 105–06. **[G: Canada]**

Kanungo, Rabindra N. and Wright, Richard W. A Cross-Cultural Comparative Study of Managerial Job Attitudes. *J. Int. Bus. Stud.,* Fall 1983, *14*(2), pp. 115–29. **[G: Canada; France; Japan; U.K.]**

Klitgaard, Robert E., et al. The Economics of Teacher Training: An Exploratory Data Analysis. *Pakistan J. Appl. Econ.,* Summer 1983, *2*(1), pp. 13–38. **[G: Pakistan]**

Krishnamurty, J. The Occupational Structure. **In** *Kumar, D., ed.,* 1983, pp. 533–50. **[G: India]**

Laband, David N. and Lentz, Bernard F. Like Father, Like Son: Toward an Economic Theory of Occupational Following. *Southern Econ. J.,* October 1983, *50*(2), pp. 474–93.

Laband, David N. and Lentz, Bernard F. Occupational Inheritance in Agriculture. *Amer. J. Agr. Econ.,* May 1983, *65*(2), pp. 311–14. **[G: U.S.]**

Levitan, Sar A. and Johnson, Clifford M. The Survival of Work. **In** *Barbash, J., et al., eds.*, 1983, pp. 1–25. **[G: U.S.]**

Litzenberg, Kerry K.; Gorman, William D. and Schneider, Vernon E. Academic and Professional Programs in Agribusiness. *Amer. J. Agr. Econ.*, December 1983, *65*(5), pp. 1060–64. **[G: U.S.]**

Low, Stuart A. and McPheters, Lee R. Wage Differentials and Risk of Death: An Empirical Analysis. *Econ. Inquiry*, April 1983, *21*(2), pp. 271–80. **[G: U.S.]**

Maccoby, Michael. The Managerial Work Ethic in America. **In** *Barbash, J., et al., eds.*, 1983, pp. 183–96. **[G: U.S.]**

Margolis, Stephen E. The Pricing of Physicians' Services. *J. Human Res.*, Fall 1983, *18*(4), pp. 592–608. **[G: U.S.]**

May, Doug. Labour Market Projections in Canada: A Progress Report: Comment. **In** *Queen's Univ. Indust. Relat. Centre and John Deutsch Mem.*, 1983, pp. 109–11. **[G: Canada]**

McPherson, Michael S. and Winston, Gordon C. The Economics of Academic Tenure: A Relational Perspective. *J. Econ. Behav. Organ.*, June–September 1983, *4*(2–3), pp. 163–84.

Mendels, R. P. The Economist as a Consultant: A Note. *Amer. Econ.*, Fall 1983, *27*(2), pp. 86–88.

Meyer, Peter J. and Maes, Patricia L. The Reproduction of Occupational Segregation among Young Women. *Ind. Relat.*, Winter 1983, *22*(1), pp. 115–24. **[G: U.S.]**

Mulvey, Charles. Restrictive Practices, Training and the Legal Profession in Scotland: A Reply [Rates of Return to the Legal Profession in Scotland]. *Scot. J. Polit. Econ.*, November 1983, *30*(3), pp. 302–03. **[G: U.K.]**

Nakanishi, Tamako. Equality or Protection? Protective Legislation for Women in Japan. *Int. Lab. Rev.*, Sept.–Oct. 1983, *122*(5), pp. 609–21. **[G: Japan]**

Needleman, L. The Structure of Industrial Earnings in Seven West European Countries. **In** *[Saunders, C. T.]*, 1983, pp. 175–92. **[G: W. Europe]**

Nolan, Peter and Brown, William. Competition and Workplace Wage Determination. *Oxford Bull. Econ. Statist.*, August 1983, *45*(3), pp. 269–87. **[G: U.K.]**

Olsen, Robert A. The Impact of Inflation on Human Capital as a Diversifiable Asset. *Rev. Bus. Econ. Res.*, Fall 1983, *19*(1), pp. 13–25. **[G: U.S.]**

Oppenlander, Karl-Heinrich. The Impact of Technical and Structural Change on the Structure and Employment of Manpower. **In** *Streeten, P. and Maier, H., eds.*, 1983, pp. 370–94. **[G: W. Germany]**

Pang, Eng Fong. Race, Income Distribution, and Development in Malaysia and Singapore. **In** *Lim, L. Y. C. and Gosling, L. A. P., eds.*, 1983, pp. 316–35. **[G: Malaysia; Singapore]**

Payne, Geoff and Ford, Graeme. Inequality and the Occupational Structure. **In** *Brown, G. and Cook, R., eds.*, 1983, pp. 76–90. **[G: U.K.]**

Pérez-Sainz, J. P. Transmigration and Accumulation in Indonesia. **In** *Oberai, A. S., ed.*, 1983, pp. 183–250. **[G: Indonesia]**

Peterson, Rodney D. On the Defense of University Research in Our Business Society. *J. Behav. Econ.*, Summer 1983, *12*(1), pp. 89–97.

Prais, S. J. and Wagner, Karin. Some Practical Aspects of Human Capital Investment: Training Standards in Five Occupations in Britain and Germany. *Nat. Inst. Econ. Rev.*, August 1983, (105), pp. 46–65. **[G: U.K.; W. Germany]**

Reeve, James M. The Five-Year Accounting Program as a Quality Signal. *Accounting Rev.*, July 1983, *58*(3), pp. 639–46. **[G: U.S.]**

Reichelderfer, Katherine H. Rank and Salary of Federally Employed Agricultural Economists. *Agr. Econ. Res.*, January 1983, *35*(1), pp. 44–51. **[G: U.S.]**

Reubens, Beatrice G. and Harrisson, John A. C. Occupational Dissimilarity by Age and Sex. **In** *Reubens, B. G., ed.*, 1983, pp. 39–85. **[G: Japan; Sweden; U.K.; U.S.]**

Richardson, Sue. Inflation and the Dispersion of Pay. **In** *Blandy, R. and Covick, O., eds.*, 1983, pp. 37–60. **[G: Australia]**

Rochon, Michel. Labour Market Projections in Canada: A Progress Report. **In** *Queen's Univ. Indust. Relat. Centre and John Deutsch Mem.*, 1983, pp. 81–104. **[G: Canada]**

Rosenberg, Sam. Reagan Social Policy and Labour Force Restructuring. *Cambridge J. Econ.*, June 1983, *7*(2), pp. 179–96. **[G: U.S.]**

Rubin, Paul H. The Objectives of Private and Public Judges: A Comment. *Public Choice*, 1983, *41*(1), pp. 133–37.

Semyonov, Moshe and Scott, Richard Ira. Industrial Shifts, Female Employment, and Occupational Differentiation: A Dynamic Model for American Cities, 1960–1970. *Demography*, May 1983, *20*(2), pp. 163–76. **[G: U.S.]**

Shapiro, David. Working Youth. **In** *Borus, M. E., ed.*, 1983, pp. 23–58. **[G: U.S.]**

Shapiro, David and Crowley, Joan E. Hopes and Plans: Education, Work Activity, and Fertility. **In** *Borus, M. E., ed.*, 1983, pp. 149–71. **[G: U.S.]**

Siebert, W. S. and Young, A. Sex and Family Status Differentials in Professional Earnings: The Case of Librarians. *Scot. J. Polit. Econ.*, February 1983, *30*(1), pp. 18–41. **[G: U.K.]**

Silvestri, George T.; Lukasiewicz, John M. and Einstein, Marcus E. Occupational Employment Projections through 1995. *Mon. Lab. Rev.*, November 1983, *106*(11), pp. 37–49. **[G: U.S.]**

Snooks, G. D. Determinants of Earnings Inequality amongst Australian Artists. *Australian Econ. Pap.*, December 1983, *22*(41), pp. 322–32. **[G: Australia]**

Sofer, Catherine. Emplois "féminins" et emplois "masculins": Mesure de la ségrégation et évolution de la féminisation des emplois. ("Female" Jobs and "Male" Jobs: A Measure of Segregation by Sex and the Evolution of the Feminization of Jobs. With English summary.) *Ann. INSEE*, October–December 1983, (52), pp. 55–85. **[G: France]**

Spatt, Chester S. The Objectives of Private and Public Judges: A Comment. *Public Choice*, 1983, *41*(1), pp. 139–43.

Stephan, Paula E. and Levin, Sharon G. Sex Segregation in Education: The Case of Doctorate Recipients. *J. Behav. Econ.*, Winter 1983, *12*(2), pp. 67–94. **[G: U.S.]**

Stewart, Mark B. Racial Discrimination and Occupational Attainment in Britain. *Econ. J.*, September 1983, *93*(371), pp. 521–41. **[G: U.K.]**

Stone, Kenneth E. Agribusiness Management and Food Marketing: Discussion. *Amer. J. Agr. Econ.*, December 1983, *65*(5), pp. 1073–74. **[G: U.S.]**

Thangamuthu, C. and Iyyampillai, S. A Social Profile of Entrepreneurship. *Indian Econ. J.*, October–December 1983, *31*(2), pp. 107–15. **[G: India]**

Weisbrod, Burton A. Nonprofit and Proprietary Sector Behavior: Wage Differentials among Lawyers. *J. Lab. Econ.*, July 1983, *1*(3), pp. 246–63. **[G: U.S.]**

Wilensky, Gail R. and Rossiter, Louis F. Economic Advantages of Board Certification. *J. Health Econ.*, March 1983, *2*(1), pp. 87–94. **[G: U.S.]**

Williams, Harry B. Wages of Appliance Repair Technicians Vary Widely among Metropolitan Areas. *Mon. Lab. Rev.*, December 1983, *106*(12), pp. 52–53. **[G: U.S.]**

Williams, Lynne S. Occupational Mobility in Australia: A Quantitative Approach. *Europ. Econ. Rev.*, January 1983, *20*(1–3), pp. 143–66. **[G: Australia]**

Wilson, Robert A. Rates of Return: Some Further Results. *Scot. J. Polit. Econ.*, June 1983, *30*(2), pp. 114–27. **[G: U.K.]**

Ziderman, Adrian. Restrictive Practices, Training and the Legal Profession in Scotland [Returns to the Legal Profession in Scotland]. *Scot. J. Polit. Econ.*, November 1983, *30*(3), pp. 295–301. **[G: U.K.]**

813 Labor Force

8130 General

Andrisani, Paul J. and Parnes, Herbert S. Commitment to the Work Ethic and Success in the Labor Market: A Review of Research Findings. **In** *Barbash, J., et al., eds.*, 1983, pp. 101–20. **[G: U.S.]**

Anker, Richard. Female Labour Force Participation in Developing Countries: A Critique of Current Definitions and Data Collection Methods. *Int. Lab. Rev.*, November–December 1983, *122*(6), pp. 709–23. **[G: India]**

Appelbaum, Eileen. Women in the Stagflation Economy. **In** *Weintraub, S. and Goodstein, M., eds.*, 1983, pp. 34–47. **[G: U.S.]**

Askanas, B. and Levcik, F. The Dispersion of Wages in the CMEA Countries (Including a Comparison with Austria). **In** *[Saunders, C. T.]*, 1983, pp. 193–230. **[G: CMEA; Austria]**

Ballantine, John W. Using Labor Market Information to Evaluate Industrial Performance. *J. Econ. Issues*, December 1983, *17*(4), pp. 1011–34. **[G: U.S.]**

Barrère-Maurisson, Marie-Agnès; Battagliola, Françoise and Duane-Richard, Anne-Marie. Trajectoires professionnelles des femmes et vie familiale. (Women's Career Course and Their Home Life. With English summary.) *Consommation*, October–December 1983, *30*(4), pp. 23–53. **[G: France]**

Behrman, Jere R. and Wolfe, Barbara L. Women's Labour Force Participation and Earnings Determinants in a Developing Country. **In** *Urquidi, V. L. and Reyes, S. T., eds.*, 1983, pp. 266–76. **[G: Nicaragua]**

Bell, David. The Labour Market in Scotland. **In** *Ingham, K. P. D. and Love, J., eds.*, 1983, pp. 65–73. **[G: U.K.]**

Berberoglu, Berch. Industrialization, Employment, and Class Formation in the Periphery. *Econ. Forum*, Summer 1983, *14*(1), pp. 131–41. **[G: Brazil; S. Korea; Mexico; Taiwan]**

Berger, Mark C. Labor Supply and Spouse's Health: The Effects of Illness, Disability, and Mortality. *Soc. Sci. Quart.*, September 1983, *64*(3), pp. 494–509. **[G: U.S.]**

Berliner, Joseph S. Education, Labor-Force Participation, and Fertility in the USSR. *J. Compar. Econ.*, June 1983, *7*(2), pp. 131–57. **[G: U.S.S.R.]**

Blakemore, Arthur E. and Low, Stuart A. A Simultaneous Determination of Post-High School Education Choice and Labor Supply. *Quart. Rev. Econ. Bus.*, Winter 1983, *23*(4), pp. 81–92. **[G: U.S.]**

Blomquist, N. Sören. The Effect of Income Taxation on the Labor Supply of Married Men in Sweden. *J. Public Econ.*, November 1983, *22*(2), pp. 169–97. **[G: Sweden]**

Boudreaux, Kenneth J. A Further Adjustment Needed to Estimate Lost Earning Capacity [The Use of Worklife Tables in Estimates of Lost Earning Capacity]. *Mon. Lab. Rev.*, October 1983, *106*(10), pp. 30–31. **[G: U.S.]**

Bowman, Mary Jean. Women and the Japanese Economic Performance. **In** *Weisbrod, B. and Hughes, H., eds.*, 1983, *1981*, pp. 250–73. **[G: Japan]**

Braae, Richard. Establishing Comparability between the 1976 and 1981 Census Labour Force Definitions. **In** *Easton, B., ed.*, 1983, pp. 203–06. **[G: New Zealand]**

Braae, Richard and Gallacher, John. Labour Supply in New Zealand, 1976 to 1981: New and Familiar Problems for Descriptive and Empirical Analysis. **In** *Easton, B., ed.*, 1983, pp. 15–48. **[G: New Zealand]**

Burkhauser, Richard V. and Quinn, Joseph F. Is Mandatory Retirement Overrated? Evidence from the 1970s. *J. Human Res.*, Summer 1983, *18*(3), pp. 337–58. **[G: U.S.]**

Chall, Daniel E. New York City's Low Labor Force Participation. *Fed. Res. Bank New York Quart. Rev.*, Autumn 1983, *8*(3), pp. 27–29. **[G: U.S.]**

Cherunalim, Francis. Urbanisation Without Labour Absorption. *Econ. Aff.*, October–December 1983, *28*(4), pp. 844–50. **[G: LDCs]**

Chiew, Seen-Kong. Ethnicity and National Integration: The Evolution of a Multi-ethnic Society. **In** *Chen, P. S. J., ed.*, 1983, pp. 29–64. **[G: Singapore]**

Chirikos, Thomas N. and Nastel, Gilbert. Economic Consequences of Poor Health in Mature Women. **In** *Shaw, L. B., ed.*, 1983, pp. 93–108. **[G: U.S.]**

Clarke, Oliver. The Work Ethic: An International Perspective. **In** *Barbash, J., et al., eds.*, 1983, pp. 121–50. **[G: OECD]**

Coates, Mary Lou. Human Resources and Labour Markets: Summary Outline. **In** *Wood, W. D. and*

Kumar, P., eds., 1983, pp. 31–83. **[G: Canada; OECD]**

Cobbe, James H. The Educational System, Wage and Salary Structures, and Income Distribution: Lesotho as a Case Study, Circa 1975. *J. Devel. Areas*, January 1983, *17*(2), pp. 227–41. **[G: Lesotho]**

Cooney, Rosemary Santana and Ortiz, Vilma. Nativity, National Origin, and Hispanic Female Participation in the Labor Force. *Soc. Sci. Quart.*, September 1983, *64*(3), pp. 510–23. **[G: U.S.]**

Corcoran, Mary; Duncan, Greg J. and Ponza, Michael. A Longitudinal Analysis of White Women's Wages. *J. Human Res.*, Fall 1983, *18*(4), pp. 497–520. **[G: U.S.]**

Denton, Frank T. Participation Rate Changes in Canada in the Early 1980s: Comment. **In** *Queen's Univ. Indust. Relat. Centre and John Deutsch Mem.*, 1983, pp. 76–78. **[G: Canada]**

Devaney, Barbara. An Analysis of Variations in U.S. Fertility and Female Labor Force Participation Trends. *Demography*, May 1983, *20*(2), pp. 147–61. **[G: U.S.]**

Devaney, Barbara. Total Work Effort under a Negative Income Tax. *J. Policy Anal. Manage.*, Summer 1983, *2*(4), pp. 625–27. **[G: U.S.]**

Devi, D. Radha and Ravindran, M. Women's Work in India. *Int. Soc. Sci. J.*, 1983, *35*(4), pp. 683–701. **[G: India]**

Dymond, W. R. European Labour Markets and Policies: Retrospect and Prospect. **In** *Queen's Univ. Indust. Relat. Centre and John Deutsch Mem.*, 1983, pp. 221–42. **[G: W. Europe]**

Eaton, Jonathan and Quandt, Richard E. A Model of Rationing and Labour Supply: Theory and Estimation. *Economica*, August 1983, *50*(199), pp. 221–33. **[G: U.S.]**

Ecevit, Zafer H. Labour Imports/Exports for Economic Development: The Middle East Experience. **In** *Weisbrod, B. and Hughes, H., eds.*, 1983, pp. 331–45. **[G: Middle East]**

Ehrenhalt, Samuel M. No Golden Age for College Graduates. *Challenge*, July/August 1983, *26*(3), pp. 42–50. **[G: U.S.]**

Endres, Anthony M. and Cook, Malcolm. Concepts in Australian Unemployment Statistics to 1940. *Australian Econ. Pap.*, June 1983, *22*(40), pp. 68–82. **[G: Australia]**

Ferber, Marianne A. and Greene, Carole A. Housework vs. Marketwork: Some Evidence How the Decision Is Made. *Rev. Income Wealth*, June 1983, *29*(2), pp. 147–59. **[G: U.S.]**

Ferleger, Lou. Explaining Away Black Poverty: The Structural Determinants of Black Employment. **In** *Goldstein, R. and Sachs, S. M., eds.*, 1983, pp. 148–74. **[G: U.S.]**

Finch, John L. Worklife Estimates Should Be Consistent with Known Labor Force Participation. *Mon. Lab. Rev.*, June 1983, *106*(6), pp. 34–36. **[G: U.S.]**

Flinn, Christopher J. and Heckman, James J. Are Unemployment and Out of the Labor Force Behaviorally Distinct Labor Force States? *J. Lab. Econ.*, January 1983, *1*(1), pp. 28–42. **[G: U.S.]**

Foot, David K. The Impacts of Population Growth and Aging on the Future Canadian Labour Force. **In** *Queen's Univ. Indust. Relat. Centre and John Deutsch Mem.*, 1983, pp. 50–64. **[G: Canada]**

Frankman, Myron J. Employment and the Unperceived Advantages of Being a Latecomer. **In** *Ritter, A. R. M. and Pollock, D. H., eds.*, 1983, pp. 135–46. **[G: Latin America]**

Frenkel, I. Socio-economic Development and Rural–Urban Migration in Poland. **In** *Oberai, A. S., ed.*, 1983, pp. 251–310. **[G: Poland]**

Frey, Luigi. Census Developments and Labour Market Analyses. *Rev. Econ. Cond. Italy*, June 1983, (2), pp. 223–47. **[G: Italy]**

Fullerton, Howard N., Jr. and Tschetter, John. The 1995 Labor Force: A Second Look. *Mon. Lab. Rev.*, November 1983, *106*(11), pp. 3–10. **[G: U.S.]**

Gallacher, John and Bowie, Robert D. Employment and Unemployment. **In** *Easton, B., ed.*, 1983, pp. 158–64. **[G: New Zealand]**

Gay, Robert S. and Hedlund, Jeffrey D. The Labor Market in Recession and Recovery. *Fed. Res. Bull.*, July 1983, *69*(7), pp. 477–88. **[G: U.S.]**

Genosko, Joachim. Erwerbsbeteiligung und gesetzliche Rentenversicherung—Der Fall der 60- bis 65jährigen Männer. (Labor Force Participation and Old Age Insurance—The Case of the 60–65 Year-Old Men. With English summary.) *Z. ges. Staatswiss.*, December 1983, *139*(4), pp. 625–42. **[G: W. Germany]**

Gilbert, Neil. In Support of Domesticity: A Neglected Family Policy Option. *J. Policy Anal. Manage.*, Summer 1983, *2*(4), pp. 628–32. **[G: U.S.]**

Goldfarb, Robert S. and Yezer, Anthony M. J. A Model of Teenage Labor Supply. *J. Econ. Bus.*, June 1983, *35*(2), pp. 245–55. **[G: U.S.]**

Gollop, Frank M. and Jorgenson, Dale W. Sectoral Labor Input. **In** *Triplett, J. E., ed.*, 1983, pp. 503–20. **[G: U.S.]**

Gollop, Frank M. and Jorgenson, Dale W. Sectoral Measures of Labor Cost for the United States, 1948–1978. **In** *Triplett, J. E., ed.*, 1983, pp. 185–235. **[G: U.S.]**

Gordon, Roger H. Social Security and Labor Supply Incentives. *Contemp. Policy Issue*, April 1983, (3), pp. 16–22. **[G: U.S.]**

Grant, E. Kenneth and Vanderkamp, John. Regional Demand–Supply Projections and Migration. **In** *Queen's Univ. Indust. Relat. Centre and John Deutsch Mem.*, 1983, pp. 112–27. **[G: Canada]**

Greenberg, David and Halsey, Harlan. Systematic Misreporting and Effects of Income Maintenance Experiments on Work Effort: Evidence from the Seattle–Denver Experiment. *J. Lab. Econ.*, October 1983, *1*(4), pp. 380–407. **[G: U.S.]**

Gustafsson, Siv. Lifetime Patterns of Labour Force Participation. **In** *Weisbrod, B. and Hughes, H., eds.*, 1983, pp. 231–49. **[G: Sweden; U.S.]**

Hamermesh, Daniel S. Labor Cost Series, Manufacturing and Private Business, 1953–1980. **In** *Triplett, J. E., ed.*, 1983, pp. 521–27. **[G: U.S.]**

Hamermesh, Daniel S. New Measures of Labor Cost: Implications for Demand Elasticities and Nominal Wage Growth. **In** *Triplett, J. E., ed.*, 1983, pp. 287–306. **[G: U.S.]**

Hanoch, Giora and Honig, Marjorie. Retirement, Wages, and Labor Supply of the Elderly. *J. Lab.*

Econ., April 1983, *1*(2), pp. 131–51. **[G: U.S.]**

Hasan, Abrar. Labour Market Imbalances in the 1980s: A Review of Three Perspectives: Comment. **In** *Queen's Univ. Indust. Relat. Centre and John Deutsch Mem.*, 1983, pp. 42–44. **[G: Canada]**

Hauser, Robert M. and Massagli, Michael P. Some Models of Agreement and Disagreement in Repeated Measurements of Occupation. *Demography*, November 1983, *20*(4), pp. 449–60. **[G: U.S.]**

Hill, M. Anne. Female Labor Force Participation in Developing and Developed Countries—Consideration of the Informal Sector. *Rev. Econ. Statist.*, August 1983, *65*(3), pp. 459–68. **[G: Japan]**

Hirschman, Charles. Labor Markets and Ethnic Inequality in Peninsular Malaysia, 1970. *J. Devel. Areas*, October 1983, *18*(1), pp. 1–20. **[G: Malaysia]**

Hopkins, Michael. Employment Trends in Developing Countries, 1960–80 and Beyond. *Int. Lab. Rev.*, July–August 1983, *122*(4), pp. 461–78. **[G: LDCs]**

Iliev, Ivan and Naoumov, Nicolas. Human Resources and Employment in the Peoples' Republic of Bulgaria. **In** *Weisbrod, B. and Hughes, H., eds.*, 1983, pp. 48–54. **[G: Bulgaria]**

Jacobsen, Grethe. Women's Work and Women's Role: Ideology and Reality in Danish Urban Society, 1300–1550. *Scand. Econ. Hist. Rev.*, 1983, *31*(1), pp. 3–20. **[G: Denmark]**

Johnson, Beverly L. and Waldman, Elizabeth. Most Women Who Maintain Families Receive Poor Labor Market Returns. *Mon. Lab. Rev.*, December 1983, *106*(12), pp. 30–34. **[G: U.S.]**

Jura, Michel and Kaminski, Philippe. Mobilité sociale des ménages et évolution économique. *Consommation*, January/March 1983, *30*(1), pp. 93–123. **[G: France]**

Kabaj, Mieczyslaw. Economic Factors Determining Long-term Labour Supply: A Case-study of the Polish Economy, 1950–1978. **In** *Streeten, P. and Maier, H., eds.*, 1983, pp. 457–72. **[G: Poland]**

Kamerman, Sheila B. Child-Care Services: A National Picture. *Mon. Lab. Rev.*, December 1983, *106*(12), pp. 35–39. **[G: U.S.]**

Kanamori, Hisao. Economic Growth and Interindustry Labour Mobility in Japan. **In** *Weisbrod, B. and Hughes, H., eds.*, 1983, pp. 31–47. **[G: Japan]**

Kapustin, Evgeni. Manpower in the USSR: Development and Utilisation Trends. **In** *Streeten, P. and Maier, H., eds.*, 1983, pp. 355–69. **[G: U.S.S.R.]**

Kaser, Michael and Notel, Rudolf. The Development of Human Resources for Development: The East European Experience, 1953–75. **In** *Weisbrod, B. and Hughes, H., eds.*, 1983, pp. 74–83. **[G: E. Europe]**

Kay, Linda B. A Survey of New Zealand Labour Market Data. **In** *Easton, B., ed.*, 1983, pp. 171–202. **[G: New Zealand]**

Kenward, Lloyd. Unemployment in the Major Industrial Countries. *Finance Develop.*, June 1983, *20*(2), pp. 24–27. **[G: U.S.; Canada; Europe; Japan]**

Keyfitz, Nathan. Age Effects in Work and Consumption. *Econ. Notes*, 1983, (3), pp. 86–121. **[G: Global]**

Knight, Ester. Women and the UK Tax System: The Case for Reform? *Cambridge J. Econ.*, June 1983, *7*(2), pp. 151–65. **[G: U.K.]**

Krishnamurty, J. The Occupational Structure. **In** *Kumar, D., ed.*, 1983, pp. 533–50. **[G: India]**

Kuniansky, Anna. Soviet Fertility, Labor-Force Participation, and Marital Instability. *J. Compar. Econ.*, June 1983, *7*(2), pp. 114–30. **[G: U.S.S.R.]**

Lackman, Conway Lee. Gallaway's Labor Force Participation Studies Revisited. *Econ. Notes*, 1983, (1), pp. 140–52. **[G: U.S.]**

Lampman, Robert J. How Has the Labor Supply Changed in Response to Recent Increases in Social Welfare Expenditures and the Taxes to Pay for Them? **In** *Barbash, J., et al., eds.*, 1983, pp. 61–85. **[G: U.S.]**

Lazear, Edward P. New Measures of Labor Cost: Implications for Demand Elasticities and Nominal Wage Growth: Comment. **In** *Triplett, J. E., ed.*, 1983, pp. 306–08. **[G: U.S.]**

Lehrer, Evelyn and Nerlove, Marc. The Impact of Female Life-cycle Time-allocation Decisions on Income Distribution among Families. **In** *Weisbrod, B. and Hughes, H., eds.*, 1983, pp. 274–89. **[G: U.S.]**

Levitan, Sar A. and Johnson, Clifford M. The Survival of Work. **In** *Barbash, J., et al., eds.*, 1983, pp. 1–25. **[G: U.S.]**

Lewis, W. Arthur. Secondary Education and Economic Structure. **In** *Lewis, W. A.*, 1983, *1964*, pp. 509–22. **[G: LDCs]**

MaCurdy, Thomas E. A Simple Scheme for Estimating an Intertemporal Model of Labor Supply and Consumption in the Presence of Taxes and Uncertainty. *Int. Econ. Rev.*, June 1983, *24*(2), pp. 265–89. **[G: U.S.]**

Maslova, I. Improving the Manpower Redistribution Mechanism. *Prob. Econ.*, July 1983, *26*(3), pp. 72–93. **[G: U.S.S.R.]**

Mazumdar, Dipak. Segmented Labor Markets in LDCs. *Amer. Econ. Rev.*, May 1983, *73*(2), pp. 254–59. **[G: LDCs]**

Mellow, Wesley and Sider, Hal. Accuracy of Response in Labor Market Surveys: Evidence and Implications. *J. Lab. Econ.*, October 1983, *1*(4), pp. 331–44. **[G: U.S.]**

Merrilees, William J. Pension Benefits and the Decline in Elderly Male Labour Force Participation. *Econ. Rec.*, September 1983, *59*(166), pp. 260–70. **[G: Australia]**

Miller, Paul W. and Volker, Paul A. A Cross-Section Analysis of the Labour Force Participation of Married Women in Australia. *Econ. Rec.*, March 1983, *59*(164), pp. 28–42. **[G: Australia]**

de Miranda, Glaura Vasques. Human Resource Development and Female Labour Force Participation in Brazil. **In** *Streeten, P. and Maier, H., eds.*, 1983, pp. 420–42. **[G: Brazil]**

Molho, I. I. A Regional Analysis of the Distribution of Married Women's Labour Force Participation Rates in the UK. *Reg. Stud.*, April 1983, *17*(2), pp. 125–33. **[G: U.K.]**

Mott, Frank L. and Shapiro, David. Complementarity of Work and Fertility among Young American

Mothers. *Population Stud.*, July 1983, *37*(2), pp. 239–52. [G: U.S.]

Nelson, David M. The Use of Worklife Tables in Estimates of Lost Earning Capacity. *Mon. Lab. Rev.*, April 1983, *106*(4), pp. 30–31. [G: U.S.]

Nestel, Gilbert; Mercier, Jacqueline and Shaw, Lois B. Economic Consequences of Midlife Change in Marital Status. **In** *Shaw, L. B., ed.*, 1983, pp. 109–25. [G: U.S.]

Nickols, Sharon Y. and Fox, Karen D. Buying Time and Saving Time: Strategies for Managing Household Production. *J. Cons. Res.*, September 1983, *10*(2), pp. 197–208. [G: U.S.]

Niemi, Beth T. and Lloyd, Cynthia B. Inflation and Female Labor Force Participation. **In** *Schmukler, N. and Marcus, E., eds.*, 1983, pp. 820–37. [G: U.S.]

Norwood, Janet L. Labor Market Contrasts: United States and Europe: Errata. *Mon. Lab. Rev.*, September 1983, *106*(9), pp. 21. [G: U.S.; W. Europe]

Norwood, Janet L. Labor Market Contrasts: United States and Europe. *Mon. Lab. Rev.*, August 1983, *106*(8), pp. 3–7. [G: U.S.; W. Europe]

Oblomskaia, I.; Strakhov, A. and Umanets, L. The Social and Economic Homogeneity of Labor. *Prob. Econ.*, December 1983, *26*(8), pp. 75–94. [G: U.S.S.R.]

Ofer, Gur and Vinokur, Aaron. The Labor-Force Participation of Married Women in the Soviet Union: A Household Cross-Section Analysis. *J. Compar. Econ.*, June 1983, *7*(2), pp. 158–76. [G: U.S.S.R.]

Okun, Arthur M. Upward Mobility in a High-Pressure Economy. **In** *Okun, A. M.*, 1983, *1973*, pp. 171–220. [G: U.S.]

Osberg, Lars. Regional Demand–Supply Projections and Migration: Comment. **In** *Queen's Univ. Indust. Relat. Centre and John Deutsch Mem.*, 1983, pp. 128–31. [G: Canada]

Pang, Eng Fong and Seow, Greg. Labour, Employment and Wage Structure. **In** *Chen, P. S. J., ed.*, 1983, pp. 160–70. [G: Singapore]

Piel, Gerard. Re-entering Paradise: The Mechanization of Work. *Challenge,* Sept.–Oct. 1983, *26*(4), pp. 4–11.

Pike, Maureen. A Simulation of the Impact of Introducing Equality for Males and Females into Social Security. *Economica,* August 1983, *50*(199), pp. 351–60. [G: U.K.]

Piore, Michael J. Labor Market Segmentation: To What Paradigm Does It Belong? *Amer. Econ. Rev.*, May 1983, *73*(2), pp. 249–53.

Powell, Alan A. Aspects of the Design of Bachuroo, an Economic–Demographic Model of Labor Supply. **In** *Kelley, A. C.; Sanderson, W. C. and Williamson, J. G., eds.*, 1983, pp. 277–300. [G: Australia]

Powell, Alan A. Aspects of Labour Market Theory and Behaviour Highlighted by IMPACT Project Studies. **In** *Blandy, R. and Covick, O., eds.*, 1983, pp. 137–65. [G: Australia]

Power, Marilyn. From Home Production to Wage Labor: Women as a Reserve Army of Labor. *Rev. Radical Polit. Econ.*, Spring 1983, *15*(1), pp. 71–91. [G: U.S.]

Quinn, Joseph F. The Work Ethic and Retirement. **In** *Barbash, J., et al., eds.*, 1983, pp. 87–100. [G: U.S.]

Ramachandran, P. and Shastri, P. P. Intercensal Urban Indian Female Participation Rates and Their Variations, 1961–71: A Census Analysis. *Econ. Aff.*, October–December 1983, *28*(4), pp. 816–28. [G: India]

Rey, Guido M. Italy of Censuses. *Rev. Econ. Cond. Italy,* June 1983, (2), pp. 193–221. [G: Italy]

Reyes, Alvaro. Economic-demographic Determinants of Labour Supply in Latin America: Some Preliminary Findings. **In** *Urquidi, V. L. and Reyes, S. T., eds.*, 1983, pp. 3–24. [G: Latin America]

Robb, Roberta. Participation Rate Changes in Canada in the Early 1980s: Comment. **In** *Queen's Univ. Indust. Relat. Centre and John Deutsch Mem.*, 1983, pp. 78–80. [G: Canada]

Rogovskii, N. The Effectiveness of Labor under the Eleventh Five-Year Plan. *Prob. Econ.*, April 1983, *25*(12), pp. 51–66. [G: U.S.S.R.]

Selleck, Laura. Jobs for University Graduates: Planning or Choice? *Can. Public Policy,* March 1983, *9*(1), pp. 94–104. [G: Canada]

Shapiro, David. Working Youth. **In** *Borus, M. E., ed.*, 1983, pp. 23–58. [G: U.S.]

Shapiro, David and Mott, Frank L. Effects of Selected Variables on Work Hours of Young Women. *Mon. Lab. Rev.*, July 1983, *106*(7), pp. 31–34. [G: U.S.]

Shapiro, David and Shaw, Lois B. Growth in the Labor Force Attachment of Married Women: Accounting for Changes in the 1970s. *Southern Econ. J.*, October 1983, *50*(2), pp. 461–73. [G: U.S.]

Shaw, Lois B. Causes of Irregular Employment Patterns. **In** *Shaw, L. B., ed.*, 1983, pp. 45–59. [G: U.S.]

Shaw, Lois B. Problems of Labor-Market Reentry. **In** *Shaw, L. B., ed.*, 1983, pp. 33–44. [G: U.S.]

Shaw, Lois B. Unplanned Careers: The Working Lives of Middle-aged Women: Summary and Conclusions. **In** *Shaw, L. B., ed.*, 1983, pp. 127–34. [G: U.S.]

Shaw, Lois B. and O'Brien, Theresa. Unplanned Careers: The Working Lives of Middle-aged Women: Introduction and Overview. **In** *Shaw, L. B., ed.*, 1983, pp. 1–31. [G: U.S.]

Sims, Harvey. Participation Rate Changes in Canada in the Early 1980s. **In** *Queen's Univ. Indust. Relat. Centre and John Deutsch Mem.*, 1983, pp. 65–75. [G: Canada]

Smith, David C. Labour Market Imbalances in the 1980s: A Review of Three Perspectives. **In** *Queen's Univ. Indust. Relat. Centre and John Deutsch Mem.*, 1983, pp. 17–39. [G: Canada]

Smith, Shirley J. Estimating Annual Hours of Labor Force Activity. *Mon. Lab. Rev.*, February 1983, *106*(2), pp. 13–22. [G: U.S.]

Smith, Shirley J. Labor Force Participation Rates Are Not the Relevant Factor. *Mon. Lab. Rev.*, June 1983, *106*(6), pp. 36–38. [G: U.S.]

Smith, Shirley J. Using the Appropriate Worklife Estimate in Court Proceedings [The Use of Worklife Tables in Estimates of Lost Earning Capacity]. *Mon. Lab. Rev.*, October 1983, *106*(10),

pp. 31–32. [G: U.S.]

Sorrentino, Constance. International Comparisons of Labor Force Participation, 1960–81. *Mon. Lab. Rev.*, February 1983, *106*(2), pp. 23–36. [G: OECD]

Staroverov, O. V. On the Allocation of Graduates as a Means of Regulating the Structure of the Labor Force. *Matekon*, Spring 1983, *19*(3), pp. 36–51. [G: Hungary]

Statham, Anne and Rhoton, Patricia. Attitudes toward Women Working: Changes over Time and Implications for the Labor-Force Behaviors of Husbands and Wives. **In** *Shaw, L. B., ed.*, 1983, pp. 77–92. [G: U.S.]

Stokes, C. Shannon and Hsieh, Yeu-Sheng. Female Employment and Reproductive Behavior in Taiwan, 1980. *Demography*, August 1983, *20*(3), pp. 313–31. [G: Taiwan]

Swan, Neil. Regional Demand–Supply Projections and Migration: Comment. **In** *Queen's Univ. Indust. Relat. Centre and John Deutsch Mem.*, 1983, pp. 132–34. [G: Canada]

Swartz, Gerald S. Labour Market Imbalances in the 1980s: A Review of Three Perspectives: Comment. **In** *Queen's Univ. Indust. Relat. Centre and John Deutsch Mem.*, 1983, pp. 44–49. [G: Canada]

Swidinsky, Robert. Working Wives, Income Distribution and Poverty. *Can. Public Policy*, March 1983, *9*(1), pp. 71–80. [G: Canada]

Tate, Donald G. Labour Market Imbalances in the 1980s: A Review of Three Perspectives: Comment. **In** *Queen's Univ. Indust. Relat. Centre and John Deutsch Mem.*, 1983, pp. 39–42. [G: Canada]

Twine, Fred. The Low Paid. **In** *Brown, G. and Cook, R., eds.*, 1983, pp. 107–35. [G: U.K.]

Valli, Vittorio. The Rise of Unemployment and Employment Adjustment Policies in Japan, Italy and West Germany. *Rivista Int. Sci. Econ. Com.*, August 1983, *30*(8), pp. 716–34. [G: Italy; Japan; W. Germany]

Waldman, Elizabeth. Labor Force Statistics from a Family Perspective. *Mon. Lab. Rev.*, December 1983, *106*(12), pp. 16–20. [G: U.S.]

Ward, Kathryn B. The Economic Status of Women in the World-System: A Hidden Crisis in Development. **In** *Bergesen, A., ed.*, 1983, pp. 117–39. [G: Global]

Weinberg, Charles B. and Winer, Russell S. Working Wives and Major Family Expenditures: Replication and Extension. *J. Cons. Res.*, September 1983, *10*(2), pp. 259–63. [G: U.S.]

Weitzman, Martin L. Industrial Production. **In** *Bergson, A. and Levine, H. S., eds.*, 1983, pp. 178–90. [G: U.S.S.R.]

Withers, Glenn A. and Freebairn, John W. Structural Change and Labour Market Adjustment. **In** *Weisbrod, B. and Hughes, H., eds.*, 1983, pp. 113–19. [G: Australia]

Woodward, M. On Forecasting Grade, Age and Length of Service Distributions in Manpower Systems. *J. Roy. Statist. Soc.*, 1983, *146*(1), pp. 74–84. [G: U.K.]

Yanz, Lynda and Smith, David. Women as a Reserve Army of Labour: A Critique. *Rev. Radical Polit. Econ.*, Spring 1983, *15*(1), pp. 92–106. [G: U.K.]

Young, Anne McDougall. Youth Labor Force Marked Turning Point in 1982. *Mon. Lab. Rev.*, August 1983, *106*(8), pp. 29–34. [G: U.S.]

Zabalza, Antoni. The CES Utility Function, Non-Linear Budget Constraints and Labour Supply: Results on Female Participation and Hours. *Econ. J.*, June 1983, *93*(370), pp. 312–30. [G: U.K.]

8131 Agriculture

Ahmed, J. U. Labor Use Patterns and Mechanization of Rice Postharvest Processing in Bangladesh. **In** *Internat'l Rice Res. Inst. and Agric. Devel. Council*, 1983, pp. 139–49. [G: Bangladesh]

Balán, Jorge. Agrarian Structures and Internal Migration in a Historical Perspective: Latin American Case Studies. **In** *Morrison, P. A., ed.*, 1983, pp. 151–85. [G: Latin America]

Berry, Albert. Agrarian Structure, Rural Labour Markets and Trends in Rural Incomes in Latin America. **In** *Urquidi, V. L. and Reyes, S. T., eds.*, 1983, pp. 174–94. [G: Brazil; Colombia; Mexico]

Caballero, Jose Maria. Casual Labor in Peruvian Agrarian Co-operatives. **In** *Stewart, F., ed.*, 1983, pp. 168–88. [G: Peru]

Chandler, Clark. The Effects of the Private Sector on the Labor Behavior of Soviet Collective Farmers. **In** *Stuart, R. C., ed.*, 1983, pp. 224–37. [G: U.S.S.R.]

Deolalikar, Anil B. and Vijverberg, Wim P. M. The Heterogeneity of Family and Hired Labor in Agricultural Production: A Test Using District-Level Data from India. *J. Econ. Devel.*, December 1983, *8*(2), pp. 45–69. [G: India]

Eddie, Scott M. Agriculture as a Source of Supply: Conjectures from the History of Hungary, 1870–1913. **In** *Komlos, J., ed.*, 1983, pp. 101–15. [G: Hungary]

Fulton, Ralph Thomas. Workers in the Fields: Historical Perspectives on U.S. Farm Structure and Agricultural Labor. **In** *Brewster, D. E.; Rasmussen, W. D. and Youngberg, G., eds.*, 1983, pp. 125–33. [G: U.S.]

Gladwin, Christina H. and Staudt, Kathleen. Women's Employment Issues: Discussion. *Amer. J. Agr. Econ.*, December 1983, *65*(5), pp. 1055–57.

Gupta, R. P. Rural Women and Economic Development. *Econ. Aff.*, July-September 1983, *28*(3), pp. 784–90. [G: India]

Hart, Gillian. Productivity, Poverty, and Population Pressure: Female Labor Deployment in Rice Production in Java and Bangladesh. *Amer. J. Agr. Econ.*, December 1983, *65*(5), pp. 1037–42. [G: Indonesia; Bangladesh]

Hodge, Ian. Rural Employment and the Quality of Life. *Rev. Marketing Agr. Econ.*, December 1983, *51*(3), pp. 259–70.

Huffman, Wallace E. Women's Employment Issues: Discussion. *Amer. J. Agr. Econ.*, December 1983, *65*(5), pp. 1058–59.

Jones, Christine. The Mobilization of Women's Labor for Cash Crop Production: A Game Theoretic Approach. *Amer. J. Agr. Econ.*, December 1983, *65*(5), pp. 1049–54. [G: Cameroon]

813 Labor Force

Khan, Azizur Rahman. Real Wages of Agricultural Workers in Bangladesh. **In** *Khan, A. R. and Lee, E., eds.*, 1983, pp. 185–203. **[G: Bangladesh]**

Klein, Emilio. Problemas metodológicos de una encuesta rural en Chile y estructura del empleo. (With English summary.) *Cuadernos Econ.*, December 1983, *20*(61), pp. 345–61. **[G: Chile]**

Rayudu, C. S. Measurement of Rural Economic Growth. *Econ. Aff.*, October–December 1983, *28*(4), pp. 829–38. **[G: India]**

Simon, Julian L.; Reisler, William and Gobin, Roy. 'Population Pressure' on the Land: Analysis of Trends Past and Future. *World Devel.*, September 1983, *11*(9), pp. 825–34. **[G: Global]**

Singh, A. J.; Joshi, A. S. and Sain, Inder. Changing Economic Condition of Agricultural Labour Households in Punjab. *Econ. Aff.*, October–December 1983, *28*(4), pp. 840–43. **[G: India]**

Wood, Richard H., Jr. Tractor Mechanisation and Employment on Larger Private Mexican Farms. *Int. Lab. Rev.*, March–April 1983, *122*(2), pp. 211–25. **[G: Mexico]**

8132 Manufacturing

Askanas, B. and Levcik, F. The Dispersion of Wages in the CMEA Countries (Including a Comparison with Austria). **In** *[Saunders, C. T.]*, 1983, pp. 193–230. **[G: CMEA; Austria]**

Brown, Peter G. Improving Equity in the Use of Temporary Workers. **In** *Kasperson, R. E., ed.*, 1983, pp. 291–300. **[G: U.S.]**

Carter, Robert A. Resource-Related Development and Regional Labour Markets: The Effects of the Alcoa Aluminum Smelter on Portland. *Australian Econ. Rev.*, 1st Quarter 1983, (61), pp. 22–32. **[G: Australia]**

Fischhoff, Baruch. Informed Consent for Nuclear Workers. **In** *Kasperson, R. E., ed.*, 1983, pp. 301–28. **[G: U.S.]**

Kasperson, Roger E.; Derr, Patrick and Kates, Robert W. Confronting Equity in Radioactive Waste Management: Modest Proposals for a Socially Just and Acceptable Program. **In** *Kasperson, R. E., ed.*, 1983, pp. 331–68. **[G: U.S.]**

Melville, Mary H. Temporary Workers in the Nuclear Power Industry: Implications for the Waste Management Program. **In** *Kasperson, R. E., ed.*, 1983, pp. 229–58. **[G: U.S.]**

Needleman, L. The Structure of Industrial Earnings in Seven West European Countries. **In** *[Saunders, C. T.]*, 1983, pp. 175–92. **[G: W. Europe]**

Richardson, J. David. Worker Adjustment to U.S. International Trade: Programs and Prospects. **In** *Cline W. R., ed.*, 1983, pp. 393–424. **[G: U.S.]**

Shakow, Don M. Market Mechanisms for Compensating Hazardous Work: A Critical Analysis. **In** *Kasperson, R. E., ed.*, 1983, pp. 277–90. **[G: U.S.]**

Skinner, C. Wickham. The Anachronistic Factory. **In** *Kantrow, A. M., ed.*, 1983, *1971*, pp. 435–51.

8133 Service

Kutscher, Ronald E. and Mark, Jerome A. The Service-Producing Sector: Some Common Perceptions Reviewed. *Mon. Lab. Rev.*, April 1983, *106*(4), pp. 21–24. **[G: U.S.]**

Thompson, G. Rodney and Stollar, Andrew J. An Empirical Test of an International Model of Relative Tertiary Employment. *Econ. Develop. Cult. Change*, July 1983, *31*(4), pp. 775–85. **[G: Selected LDCs; Selected MDCs]**

8134 Professional

Bhagwati, Jagdish N. and Hamada, Koichi. The Brain Drain, International Integration of Markets for Professionals and Unemployment: A Theoretical Analysis. **In** *Bhagwati, J. N., Vol. 2*, 1983, *1974*, pp. 103–26.

Cooke, William N. and Cobern, Morris. Part-time Post-school Investments in Education and Their Impact on Earnings Growth for Engineers. **In** *Weisbrod, B. and Hughes, H., eds.*, 1983, pp. 178–86. **[G: U.S.]**

Finn, Michael G. Understanding the Higher Unemployment Rate of Women Scientists and Engineers. *Amer. Econ. Rev.*, December 1983, *73*(5), pp. 1137–40. **[G: U.S.]**

Harrison, Brian R. and Thera, John R. Economic Status of Canadian Freelance Writers. **In** *Hendon, W. S. and Shanahan, J. L., eds.*, 1983, pp. 143–53. **[G: Canada]**

Horen, Jeffrey H. The Labor Supply Question. **In** *Vogel, R. J. and Palmer, H. C., eds.*, 1983, pp. 723–42. **[G: U.S.]**

LaCroix, Sumner J. and Getzen, Tom. The Supply of Physician Services: A Comment. *Econ. Inquiry*, July 1983, *21*(3), pp. 441–43. **[G: U.S.]**

Muzondo, Timothy R. and Pazderka, Bohumir. Income-Enhancing Effects of Professional Licensing Restrictions: A Cross-Section Study of Canadian Data. *Antitrust Bull.*, Summer 1983, *28*(2), pp. 397–415. **[G: Canada]**

Scheffler, Richard M. and Rossiter, Louis F. Compensation Schemes and the Labor Supply of Dentists. *Quart. Rev. Econ. Bus.*, Autumn 1983, *23*(3), pp. 29–43. **[G: U.S.]**

Schlechty, Phillip C. and Vance, Victor S. The Promotion of Quality in Teaching. **In** *Odden, A. and Webb, L. D., eds.*, 1983, pp. 144–52. **[G: U.S.]**

Shah, Anup R. K. Professional Earnings in the United Kingdom. *Economica*, November 1983, *50*(200), pp. 451–62. **[G: U.K.]**

Simpson, David. Managers in Workers' Trade Unions: The Case of the NUJ. **In** *Thurley, K. and Wood, S., eds.*, 1983, pp. 19–26.

Smith, J. C. The Processes of Adjudication and Regulation, a Comparison. **In** *Machan, T. R. and Johnson, M. B., eds.*, 1983, pp. 71–96. **[G: U.S.]**

Stager, David. Are There Too Many Lawyers? *Can. Public Policy*, June 1983, *9*(2), pp. 245–49. **[G: Canada]**

Trebilcock, Michael J. Regulating Service Quality in Professional Markets. **In** *Dewees, D. N., ed.*, 1983, pp. 83–107. **[G: U.S.]**

Trebilcock, Michael J. and Shaul, Jeffrey. Regulating the Quality of Psychotherapeutic Services. **In** *Dewees, D. N., ed.*, 1983, pp. 275–91. **[G: Canada]**

Ward, James Gordon. On Teacher Quality. **In** *Od-*

den, A. and Webb, L. D., eds., 1983, pp. 163–68. [G: U.S.]

8135 Government Employees

Ehrenberg, Ronald G. and Schwarz, Joshua L. The Effect of Unions on Productivity in the Public Sector: The Case of Municipal Libraries. **In** *Hirsch, W. Z., ed.,* 1983, pp. 311–41. **[G: U.S.]**

Fisk, Donald M. Modest Productivity Gains in State Unemployment Insurance Service. *Mon. Lab. Rev.,* January 1983, *106*(1), pp. 24–27. **[G: U.S.]**

Ginsberg, Leon H. Changing Public Attitudes about Public Welfare Clients and Services through Research. **In** *Goldstein, R. and Sachs, S. M., eds.,* 1983, pp. 241–52. **[G: U.S.]**

Hall, Arden R. and Smith, William D. The Financial Condition of Public Employee Pension Plans. **In** *Hirsch, W. Z., ed.,* 1983, pp. 247–73. **[G: U.S.]**

Heller, Peter and Tait, Alan A. Government Employment and Pay: Some International Comparisons. *Finance Develop.,* September 1983, *20*(3), pp. 44–47. **[G: OECD; LDCs]**

Hirsch, Werner Z. and Rufolo, Anthony M. Shirking, Monitoring Costs, and Municipal Labor Productivity. **In** *Hirsch, W. Z., ed.,* 1983, pp. 277–310.

Hirsch, Werner Z.; Rufolo, Anthony M. and Mengle, David L. Recent Trends in Municipal Labor Market Research. **In** *Hirsch, W. Z., ed.,* 1983, pp. 13–58. **[G: U.S.]**

Jump, Bernard, Jr. State and Local Government Pension Benefits: Just Desserts or Just Rip-offs? **In** *Hirsch, W. Z., ed.,* 1983, pp. 212–46. **[G: U.S.]**

Lewin, David and Katz, Harry C. Payment Determination in Municipal Building Departments under Unionism and Civil Service. **In** *Hirsch, W. Z., ed.,* 1983, pp. 90–121. **[G: U.S.]**

Mumy, Gene E. Pension Underfunding, Municipal Debt, and the Compensation of Municipal Employees. **In** *Hirsch, W. Z., ed.,* 1983, pp. 161–87.

Noam, Eli M. The Effect of Unionization and Civil Service on the Salaries and Productivity of Regulators. **In** *Reid, J. D., Jr., ed.,* 1983, pp. 157–70. **[G: U.S.]**

Pierson, David A. Labor Market Influences on Entry vs. Nonentry Wages: Evidence from Minnesota Public School Districts. *Nebr. J. Econ. Bus.,* Spring 1983, *22*(2), pp. 33–48. **[G: U.S.]**

Prieser, Carl. Skill Level Differences in White-Collar Pay. *Mon. Lab. Rev.,* December 1983, *106*(12), pp. 49–52. **[G: U.S.]**

Smith, Robert S. Salaries and Pension Funding: Are Public Safety Officers Given Preference over Taxpayers? **In** *Hirsch, W. Z., ed.,* 1983, pp. 188–211. **[G: U.S.]**

Smith, Sharon P. Are State and Local Government Workers Overpaid? **In** *Hirsch, W. Z., ed.,* 1983, pp. 59–89. **[G: U.S.]**

8136 Construction

Stretton, Alan. Circular Migration, Segmented Labour Markets and Efficiency: The Building Industry in Manila and Port Moresby. *Int. Lab. Rev.,* Sept.–Oct. 1983, *122*(5), pp. 623–39. **[G: Philippines]**

820 Labor Markets; Public Policy

8200 General

Bellante, Don. A Subjectivist Essay on Modern Labor Economics. *Managerial Dec. Econ.,* December 1983, *4*(4), pp. 234–43.

Smith, Shirley J. Labor Force Participation Rates Are Not the Relevant Factor. *Mon. Lab. Rev.,* June 1983, *106*(6), pp. 36–38. **[G: U.S.]**

821 Labor Economics

8210 Labor Economics: Theory and Empirical Studies Illustrating Theory

Akerlof, George A. and Main, Brian G. M. Measures of Unemployment Duration as Guides to Research and Policy: Reply [An Experience-Weighted Measure of Employment and Unemployment Duration]. *Amer. Econ. Rev.,* December 1983, *73*(5), pp. 1151–52. **[G: U.S.]**

Alchian, Armen. Research in Labor Economics: Discussion. **In** *Reid, J. D., Jr., ed.,* 1983, pp. 97–98.

Alogoskoufis, George S. The Labour Market in an Equilibrium Business Cycle Model. *J. Monet. Econ.,* January 1983, *11*(1), pp. 117–28.

Amano, Masanori. On the Harris–Todaro Model with Intersectoral Migration of Labour. *Economica,* August 1983, *50*(199), pp. 311–23. **[G: LDCs]**

Aoki, Masahiko. Managerialism Revisited in the Light of Bargaining-Game Theory. *Int. J. Ind. Organ.,* 1983, *1*(1), pp. 1–21.

Arnould, Richard J. and Nichols, Len M. Wage-Risk Premiums and Workers' Compensation: A Refinement of Estimates of Compensating Wage Differential. *J. Polit. Econ.,* April 1983, *91*(2), pp. 332–40. **[G: U.S.]**

Arthur, W. B. Age and Earnings in the Labour Market: Implications of the 1980s Labour Bulge. **In** *Streeten, P. and Maier, H., eds.,* 1983, pp. 405–19.

Artis, M. J. The Capital Constraint on Employment. **In** *[Saunders, C. T.],* 1983, pp. 109–26. **[G: U.K.]**

Ashenfelter, Orley. The Withering away of a Full Employment Goal. *Can. Public Policy,* March 1983, *9*(1), pp. 114–25. **[G: Canada]**

Atesoglu, H. Sonmez. Inflation and Unemployment Models. *Nebr. J. Econ. Bus.,* Summer 1983, *22*(3), pp. 53–65. **[G: U.S.]**

Atkinson, Anthony B. How Progressive Should Income Tax Be? **In** *Atkinson, A. B.,* 1983, *1973,* pp. 295–314.

Atkinson, Anthony B., et al. Durée du chômage et incitations: Résultats d'une enquête sur les dépenses des ménages au Royaume-Uni. (Unemployment Duration and Incentives: Evidence from the Family Expenditure Survey in the United Kingdom. With English summary.) *Ann. INSEE,* October–December 1983, (52), pp. 3–21. **[G: U.K.]**

Azariadis, Costas. Employment with Asymmetric Information. *Quart. J. Econ.*, Supplement 1983, *98*(3), pp. 157–72.

Azariadis, Costas and Stiglitz, Joseph E. Implicit Contracts and Fixed Price Equilibria. *Quart. J. Econ.*, Supplement 1983, *98*(3), pp. 1–22.

Baily, Martin Neil. The Labor Market in the 1930's. **In** *Tobin, J., ed.*, 1983, pp. 21–61. **[G: U.S.]**

Baldwin, Carliss Y. Productivity and Labor Unions: An Application of the Theory of Self-Enforcing Contracts. *J. Bus.*, April 1983, *56*(2), pp. 155–85.

Bardhan, Pranab K. Labor-Tying in a Poor Agrarian Economy: A Theoretical and Empirical Analysis. *Quart. J. Econ.*, August 1983, *98*(3), pp. 501–14. **[G: India]**

Bartlett, William. On the Dynamic Instability of Induced-Migration Unemployment in a Dual Economy. *J. Devel. Econ.*, Aug.–Oct. 1983, *13*(1–2), pp. 85–96.

Baumann, Johann H. A Disaggregate Short Run Phillips Curve for Austria: The Effects of Regional Unemployment Dispersion and Spatial Wage Transfer on the National Wage Rate. *Z. Nationalökon.*, 1983, *43*(2), pp. 189–211. **[G: Austria]**

Baumol, William J. Marx and the Iron Law of Wages. *Amer. Econ. Rev.*, May 1983, *73*(2), pp. 303–08.

Beach, Charles M. and Balfour, Frederick S. Estimated Payroll Tax Incidence and Aggregate Demand for Labour in the United Kingdom. *Economica*, February 1983, *50*(197), pp. 35–48. **[G: U.K.]**

Beaumont, Paul M. Wage Rate Specification in Regional and Interregional Econometric Models. *Int. Reg. Sci. Rev.*, June 1983, *8*(1), pp. 75–83. **[G: U.S.]**

Behrman, Jere R. and Taubman, Paul. Redistribution of Earnings by Unemployment and Inflation. **In** *[Klein, L. R.]*, 1983, pp. 262–81. **[G: U.S.]**

Benhabib, Jess and Bull, Clive. Job Search: The Choice of Intensity. *J. Polit. Econ.*, October 1983, *91*(5), pp. 747–64.

Benham, Harry C. UI Effects on Unemployment: Some Data on Competing Theories. *Ind. Relat.*, Fall 1983, *22*(3), pp. 403–09. **[G: U.S.]**

Bennett, John and Phelps, Michael. A Model of Employment Creation in an Open Developing Economy. *Oxford Econ. Pap.*, November 1983, *35*(3), pp. 373–98.

Berkowitz, Monroe; Fenn, Paul and Lambrinos, James. The Optimal Stock of Health with Endogenous Wages: Application to Partial Disability Compensation. *J. Health Econ.*, August 1983, *2*(2), pp. 139–47. **[G: U.S.]**

Berndt, Ernst R. The Fixed Employment Costs of Specialized Labor: Comment. **In** *Triplett, J. E., ed.*, 1983, pp. 116–22. **[G: U.S.]**

Bernstein, Jeffrey I. Investment, Labour Skills, and Variable Factor Utilization in the Theory of the Firm. *Can. J. Econ.*, August 1983, *16*(3), pp. 463–79.

Berry, Albert and Sabot, Richard H. Unemployment and Economic Development. **In** *Streeten, P. and Maier, H., eds.*, 1983, pp. 147–66.

Bhaduri, Amit. Multimarket Classification of Unemployment: A Sceptical Note. *Cambridge J. Econ.*, September/December 1983, *7*(3/4), pp. 235–41.

Bhagwati, Jagdish N. and Hamada, Koichi. The Brain Drain, International Integration of Markets for Professionals and Unemployment: A Theoretical Analysis. **In** *Bhagwati, J. N., Vol. 2*, 1983, *1974*, pp. 103–26.

Bhagwati, Jagdish N. and Srinivasan, T. N. Education in a 'Job Ladder' Model and the Fairness-in-Hiring Rule. **In** *Bhagwati, J. N., Vol. 2*, 1983, *1977*, pp. 142–63.

Bhandari, Jagdeep S. Indexation, Deficit Finance and the Inflationary Process. *Southern Econ. J.*, April 1983, *49*(4), pp. 1077–93.

Bismut, Claude. 'Wage Rigidity and Unemployment in OECD Countries' by D. Grubb et al.: Comment. *Europ. Econ. Rev.*, March/April 1983, *21*(1/2), pp. 41–44. **[G: OECD]**

Björklund, Anders. Measuring the Duration of Unemployment: A Note. *Scot. J. Polit. Econ.*, June 1983, *30*(2), pp. 175–80. **[G: Sweden; U.S.]**

Blandy, Richard and Richardson, Sue. How Labour Markets Adjust. **In** *Blandy, R. and Covick, O., eds.*, 1983, pp. 1–15. **[G: Australia; U.S.]**

Blomquist, N. Sören. The Effect of Income Taxation on the Labor Supply of Married Men in Sweden. *J. Public Econ.*, November 1983, *22*(2), pp. 169–97. **[G: Sweden]**

Bosworth, Barry P. A Century of Evidence on Wage and Price Stickiness in the United States, the United Kingdom and Japan: Comment. **In** *Tobin, J., ed.*, 1983, pp. 121–24. **[G: U.S.; U.K.; Japan]**

Bowbrick, Peter. The Economics of Superstars: Comment. *Amer. Econ. Rev.*, June 1983, *73*(3), pp. 459.

Bowie, Robert D. The Dual Labour Market. **In** *Easton, B., ed.*, 1983, pp. 71–94. **[G: New Zealand]**

Brandsma, Andries S. and Van Der Windt, Nico. Wage Bargaining and the Phillips Curve: A Macroeconomic View. *Appl. Econ.*, February 1983, *15*(1), pp. 61–71. **[G: Netherlands]**

Braulke, Michael. Anwerbungsstop und Preiselastizität des Angebots. (Recruitment Stop and the Price Elasticity of Supply. With English summary.) *Jahr. Nationalökon. Statist.*, July 1983, *198*(4), pp. 334–40.

Brittan, Samuel. Jobs, Output and Prices. **In** *Brittan, S.*, 1983, pp. 105–24. **[G: U.K.; U.S.]**

Brittan, Samuel. Unemployment and Pay. **In** *Brittan, S.*, 1983, pp. 159–85. **[G: U.K.; OECD]**

Brown, Clair. Unemployment Theory and Policy, 1946–1980. *Ind. Relat.*, Spring 1983, *22*(2), pp. 164–85. **[G: U.S.]**

Brown, James N. Structural Estimation in Implicit Markets. **In** *Triplett, J. E., ed.*, 1983, pp. 123–51. **[G: U.S.]**

Browne, Lynn E. Wages and Inflation. *New Eng. Econ. Rev.*, May/June 1983, pp. 63–66. **[G: U.S.]**

Buchele, Robert. Economic Dualism and Employment Stability. *Ind. Relat.*, Fall 1983, *22*(3), pp. 410–18. **[G: U.S.]**

Bull, Clive. Implicit Contracts in the Absence of Enforcement and Risk Aversion. *Amer. Econ. Rev.*, September 1983, *73*(4), pp. 658–71.

Bull, Clive and Frydman, Roman. The Derivation and Interpretation of the Lucas Supply Function. *J. Money, Credit, Banking*, February 1983, *15*(1), pp. 82–95.

Burdett, Kenneth and Hool, Bryce. Layoffs, Wages

and Unemployment Insurance. *J. Public Econ.*, August 1983, *21* (3), pp. 325–57.

Carlson, John A. and Horrigan, Michael W. Measures of Unemployment Duration as Guides to Research and Policy: Comment [An Experience-Weighted Measure of Employment and Unemployment Duration]. *Amer. Econ. Rev.*, December 1983, *73* (5), pp. 1143–50. **[G: U.S.]**

Carmichael, H. Lorne. The Agent–Agents Problem: Payment by Relative Output. *J. Lab. Econ.*, January 1983, *1* (1), pp. 50–65.

Carmichael, H. Lorne. Does Rising Productivity Explain Seniority Rules for Layoffs? *Amer. Econ. Rev.*, December 1983, *73* (5), pp. 1127–31.

Carmichael, H. Lorne. Firm-Specific Human Capital and Promotion Ladders. *Bell J. Econ. (See Rand J. Econ. after 4/85)*, Spring 1983, *14* (1), pp. 251–58.

Casprini, Flavio. Productivity Changes and Employment in Small Open Economies. *Econ. Notes*, 1983, (1), pp. 42–58.

Cassim, F. Labour Market Segmentation: The Theoretical Case—Reply. *S. Afr. J. Econ.*, December 1983, *51* (4), pp. 574–78.

Cassim, F. Labour Market Segmentation: The Theoretical Case—Rejoinder. *S. Afr. J. Econ.*, December 1983, *51* (4), pp. 580.

Cave, George. Job Rationing, Unemployment, and Discouraged Workers. *J. Lab. Econ.*, July 1983, *1* (3), pp. 286–307.

Cebula, Richard J. A Methodological Note on the Phillips Curve for the United States. *Rivista Int. Sci. Econ. Com.*, January 1983, *30* (1), pp. 91–95. **[G: U.S.]**

Cecchetti, Stephen G., et al. OPEC II and the Wage-Price Spiral. **In** *Zeckhauser, R. J. and Leebaert, D., eds.*, 1983, pp. 137–54. **[G: U.S.]**

Chandler, Clark. The Effects of the Private Sector on the Labor Behavior of Soviet Collective Farmers. **In** *Stuart, R. C., ed.*, 1983, pp. 224–37. **[G: U.S.S.R.]**

Chari, V. V. Involuntary Unemployment and Implicit Contracts. *Quart. J. Econ.*, Supplement 1983, *98* (3), pp. 107–22.

Cherry, Robert. A Marxist Critique of Natural Unemployment Rate Theories. **In** *Schmukler, N. and Marcus, E., eds.*, 1983, pp. 133–43.

Chesher, Andrew and Lancaster, Tony. The Estimation of Models of Labour Market Behavior. *Rev. Econ. Stud.*, October 1983, *50* (4), pp. 609–24.

Chiesa, Gabriella. Disturbi di offerta, natura della disoccupazione ed interventi di riassorbimento in un'economia aperta. (Supply Shocks, the Nature of Unemployment and Policies for Internal and External Balance in an Open Economy. With English summary.) *Giorn. Econ.*, September–October 1983, *42* (9–10), pp. 617–41.

Chow, Chee W. The Effects of Job Standard Tightness and Compensation Scheme on Performance: An Exploration of Linkages. *Accounting Rev.*, October 1983, *58* (4), pp. 667–85.

Chowdhury, Anisuzzaman. The Decentralized Labor Market and the Nonmarket Consideration of Wage Change. *J. Post Keynesian Econ.*, Summer 1983, *5* (4), pp. 648–63.

Christofides, L. N. and Wilton, D. A. The Determinants of Contract Length: An Empirical Analysis Based on Canadian Micro Data. *J. Monet. Econ.*, August 1983, *12* (2), pp. 309–19. **[G: Canada]**

Clark, Kim B. and Freeman, Richard. How Elastic Is the Demand for Labor? A Reply. *Rev. Econ. Statist.*, November 1983, *65* (4), pp. 694. **[G: U.S.]**

Clarke, Frank H. and Darrough, Masako N. Optimal Employment Contracts in a Principal–Agent Relationship. *J. Econ. Behav. Organ.*, June–September 1983, *4* (2–3), pp. 69–90.

Cogoy, Mario. Lavoro eterogeneo, sovrappiù e crescita nel modello di von Neumann. (Heterogeneous Labour, Surplus and Growth in the von Neumann Model. With English summary.) *Giorn. Econ.*, May-June 1983, *42* (5–6), pp. 295–306.

Colombatto, Enrico. Aspetti dinamici dell'indennità di contingenza. (Dynamic Issues in the Wage-Indexation Mechanism. With English summary.) *Giorn. Econ.*, March-April 1983, *42* (3–4), pp. 239–54.

Colombino, Ugo. Variabili dipendenti limitate e selezione non casuale delle osservazioni: una applicazione alla stima della funzione di salario e di offerta di lavoro delle donne sposate in Italia. (Limited Dependent Variables and Non-Random Sample Selection: An Application to the Wage and Labour Supply Function of Married Women in Italy. With English summary.) *Giorn. Econ.*, May-June 1983, *42* (5–6), pp. 369–85. **[G: Italy]**

Copeland, Laurence S. Public Sector Prices and the Real Exchange-Rate in the UK Recession. *Bull. Econ. Res.*, November 1983, *35* (2), pp. 97–121. **[G: U.K.]**

Cothren, Richard D. Job Search and Implicit Contracts. *J. Polit. Econ.*, June 1983, *91* (3), pp. 494–504.

Cothren, Richard D. Monetary Shocks and Labor Market Equilibrium. *Southern Econ. J.*, October 1983, *50* (2), pp. 346–54.

Cothren, Richard D. On a Trigger Mechanism for Indexing Wages: A Note. *J. Money, Credit, Banking*, May 1983, *15* (2), pp. 233–36.

Cousineau, Jean-Michel; Lacroix, Robert and Bilodeau, Danielle. The Determination of Escalator Clauses in Collective Agreements. *Rev. Econ. Statist.*, May 1983, *65* (2), pp. 196–202. **[G: U.S.]**

Danziger, Leif. On the Frequency of Wage Indexation. *Europ. Econ. Rev.*, August 1983, *22* (3), pp. 297–304.

Darity, William A., Jr. and Horn, Bobbie L. Involuntary Unemployment Reconsidered. *Southern Econ. J.*, January 1983, *49* (3), pp. 717–33.

Datcher, Linda. The Impact of Informal Networks of Quit Behavior. *Rev. Econ. Statist.*, August 1983, *65* (3), pp. 491–95. **[G: U.S.]**

Davenport, Paul. Unemployment, Demand Restraint, and Endogenous Capacity. *Eastern Econ. J.*, July–September 1983, *9* (3), pp. 258–71.

Davidson, Paul. The Dubious Labor Market Analysis in Meltzer's Restatement of Keynes' *Theory. J. Econ. Lit.*, March 1983, *21* (1), pp. 52–56.

Davidson, Paul. The Marginal Product Curve Is Not the Demand Curve for Labor and Lucas's Labor Supply Function Is Not the Supply Curve for Labor in the Real World. *J. Post Keynesian Econ.*,

Fall 1983, *6*(1), pp. 105–17.

Dawson, Alistair. The Performance of Three Wage Equations in Postwar Britain. *Appl. Econ.*, February 1983, *15*(1), pp. 91–105. **[G: U.K.]**

Deville, Hervé. Théorie et estimation de modèles mixtes pour le marché belge du travail. (With English summary.) *Cah. Écon. Bruxelles*, 1983, *98*(2), pp. 208–32. **[G: Belgium]**

Diamond, Peter A. The Labor Market in the 1930's: Comment. **In** *Tobin, J., ed.*, 1983, pp. 61–62. **[G: U.S.]**

Dilnot, A. W. and Morris, Carl N. Private Costs and Benefits of Unemployment: Measuring Replacement Rates. *Oxford Econ. Pap.*, Supplement November 1983, *35*, pp. 321–40. **[G: U.K.]**

Dorsey, Stuart and Walzer, Norman. Workers' Compensation, Job Hazards, and Wages. *Ind. Lab. Relat. Rev.*, July 1983, *36*(4), pp. 642–54. **[G: U.S.]**

Driscoll, Michael J., et al. Testing of the Rational Expectations and Structural Neutrality Hypotheses. *J. Macroecon.*, Summer 1983, *5*(3), pp. 353–60. **[G: U.S.]**

Eaton, Curtis and White, William D. The Economy of High Wages: An Agency Problem. *Economica*, May 1983, *50*(198), pp. 175–81.

Eaton, Jonathan and Quandt, Richard E. A Model of Rationing and Labour Supply: Theory and Estimation. *Economica*, August 1983, *50*(199), pp. 221–33. **[G: U.S.]**

Eatwell, John. The Long-Period Theory of Employment. *Cambridge J. Econ.*, September/December 1983, *7*(3/4), pp. 269–85.

Ehrenberg, Ronald G.; Danziger, Leif and San, Gee. Cost-of-Living Adjustment Clauses in Union Contracts: A Summary of Results. *J. Lab. Econ.*, July 1983, *1*(3), pp. 215–45. **[G: U.S.]**

Eichenbaum, Martin. A Rational Expectations Equilibrium Model of Inventories of Finished Goods and Employment. *J. Monet. Econ.*, August 1983, *12*(2), pp. 259–77.

Eichengreen, Barry J. Protection, Real Wage Resistance and Employment. *Weltwirtsch. Arch.*, 1983, *119*(3), pp. 429–52.

van Eijk, Cornelis J. Possible Policy Implications of Modern Underemployment Equilibrium Theory. *De Economist*, 1983, *131*(3), pp. 344–72. **[G: Netherlands]**

Elbaum, Bernard. The Internalization of Labor Markets: Causes and Consequences. *Amer. Econ. Rev.*, May 1983, *73*(2), pp. 260–65. **[G: U.S.]**

Faith, Roger L. and Reid, Joseph D., Jr. The Labor Union as Its Members' Agent. **In** *Reid, J. D., Jr., ed.*, 1983, pp. 3–25.

Feenberg, Daniel R. and Rosen, Harvey S. Alternative Tax Treatments of the Family: Simulation Methodology and Results. **In** *Feldstein, M., ed.*, 1983, pp. 7–41. **[G: U.S.]**

Filippini, Luigi; Scanlon, J. and Tarantelli, Ezio. Towards a Linear Model of Non-homogeneous Labour. **In** *Streeten, P. and Maier, H., eds.*, 1983, pp. 91–105.

Fischhoff, Baruch. Informed Consent for Nuclear Workers. **In** *Kasperson, R. E., ed.*, 1983, pp. 301–28. **[G: U.S.]**

Flaschel, Peter. Actual Labor Values in a General Model of Production. *Econometrica*, March 1983, *51*(2), pp. 435–54.

Flinn, Christopher J. and Heckman, James J. Are Unemployment and Out of the Labor Force Behaviorally Distinct Labor Force States? *J. Lab. Econ.*, January 1983, *1*(1), pp. 28–42. **[G: U.S.]**

Frank, Jeff L. Uncertain Vacancies and Unemployment Equilibria. *J. Econ. Theory*, June 1983, *30*(1), pp. 115–38.

Franz, Wolfgang. The Past Decade's Natural Rate and the Dynamics of German Unemployment: A Case against Demand Policy? *Europ. Econ. Rev.*, March/April 1983, *21*(1/2), pp. 51–76. **[G: W. Germany]**

Fujimoto, Takao and Leslie, Derek. A Two-class Model of Keynesian Unemployment. *Metroecon.*, February–June 1983, *35*(1–2), pp. 53–71.

Garegnani, Pierangelo. The Classical Theory of Wages and the Role of Demand Schedules in the Determination of Relative Prices. *Amer. Econ. Rev.*, May 1983, *73*(2), pp. 309–13.

Garonna, Paolo. On the Heterogeneity and Instability of Italian Segmentation Classification Criteria. *Rivista Int. Sci. Econ. Com.*, December 1983, *30*(12), pp. 1132–49. **[G: Italy]**

Gerfin, Harald. 'The Past Decade's Natural Rate and the Dynamics of German Unemployment: A Case against Demand Policy?' by W. Franz: Comment. *Europ. Econ. Rev.*, March/April 1983, *21*(1/2), pp. 77–82. **[G: W. Germany]**

Giran, Jean-Pierre. Production d-information et accumulation de capital. (Information Production and Capital Accumulation. With English summary.) *Écon. Appl.*, 1983, *36*(2–3), pp. 389–409.

Gleting, Jørgen H. Om fastprismodellernes forklaring af arbejdsløsheden. (Some Critical Comments on Macroeconomic Fixprice Models. With English summary.) *Nationaløkon. Tidsskr.*, 1983, *121*(1), pp. 17–19.

Gordon, Robert J. 'The Past Decade's Natural Rate and the Dynamics of German Unemployment: A Case against Demand Policy?' by W. Franz: Comment. *Europ. Econ. Rev.*, March/April 1983, *21*(1/2), pp. 83–87. **[G: W. Germany]**

Gordon, Robert J. A Century of Evidence on Wage and Price Stickiness in the United States, the United Kingdom, and Japan. **In** *Tobin, J., ed.*, 1983, pp. 85–121. **[G: U.S.; Japan; U.K.]**

Gordon, Robert J. Unemployment and Insurance: A Comment. *Carnegie-Rochester Conf. Ser. Public Policy*, Autumn 1983, *19*, pp. 51–60. **[G: U.S.]**

Gourlaouen, Jean-Pierre. Une analyse économétrique des liens entre l'inflation, le chomage et la nature des anticipations. (An Econometric Analysis of Inflation, Unemployment and the Nature of Expectations. With English summary.) *Revue Écon.*, September 1983, *34*(5), pp. 971–86. **[G: France]**

Gray, Jo Anna. Wage Indexation, Incomplete Information, and the Aggregate Supply Curve. **In** *Dornbusch, R. and Simonsen, M. H., eds.*, 1983, pp. 25–45.

Green, Jerry R. and Kahn, Charles M. Wage–Employment Contracts. *Quart. J. Econ.*, Supplement 1983, *98*(3), pp. 173–87.

Gregory, Paul R. Soviet Theories of Economic Demography: A Survey. *J. Compar. Econ.*, June 1983, *7*(2), pp. 105–13. **[G: U.S.S.R.]**

Gregory, R. G. and Duncan, Ronald C. Equal Pay for Women: A Reply [Segmented Labour Market Theories and the Australian Experience of Equal Pay for Women]. *Australian Econ. Pap.*, June 1983, *22*(40), pp. 60–64. **[G: Australia]**

Gregory, R. G. and Duncan, Ronald C. Reply [Segmented Labor Market Theories and the Australian Experience of Equal Pay for Women]. *J. Post Keynesian Econ.*, Summer 1983, *5*(4), pp. 673–75. **[G: Australia]**

Grossman, Gene M. Union Wages, Temporary Layoffs, and Seniority. *Amer. Econ. Rev.*, June 1983, *73*(3), pp. 277–90.

Grossman, Jean Baldwin. The Impact of the Minimum Wage on Other Wages. *J. Human Res.*, Summer 1983, *18*(3), pp. 359–78. **[G: U.S.]**

Grossman, Sanford J. and Hart, Oliver D. Implicit Contracts under Asymmetric Information. *Quart. J. Econ.*, Supplement 1983, *98*(3), pp. 123–56.

Grossman, Sanford J.; Hart, Oliver D. and Maskin, Eric S. Unemployment with Observable Aggregate Shocks. *J. Polit. Econ.*, December 1983, *91*(6), pp. 907–28.

Grubb, Dennis; Jackman, Richard and Layard, Richard. Wage Rigidity and Unemployment in OECD Countries. *Europ. Econ. Rev.*, March/April 1983, *21*(1/2), pp. 11–39. **[G: OECD]**

Gruen, Fred H. Understanding Labour Markets in Australia: Concluding Comments. **In** *Blandy, R. and Covick, O., eds.*, 1983, pp. 246–50.

Guasch, J. Luis and Sobel, Joel. Breeding and Raiding: A Theory of Strategic Production of Skills. *Europ. Econ. Rev.*, June 1983, *22*(1), pp. 97–115.

Guilhon, Bernard and Roos, Jean-Louis. L'ajustement a court terme de l'emploi a la production: des relations techniques aux fonctions de comportement. (Short Term Employment Adjustment to the Level of Production: From Technical Relations to Behavioural Functions. With English summary.) *Revue Écon.*, July 1983, *34*(4), pp. 732–55. **[G: France]**

Gustman, Alan L. and Steinmeier, Thomas L. Minimum-hours Constraints and Retirement Behavior. *Contemp. Policy Issue*, April 1983, (3), pp. 77–91. **[G: U.S.]**

Gwartney, James and Stroup, Richard. Labor Supply and Tax Rates: A Correction of the Record. *Amer. Econ. Rev.*, June 1983, *73*(3), pp. 446–51.

Haber, Sheldon E. Wage Structure in Internal Labor Markets and Marginal Productivity Theory. *Atlantic Econ. J.*, December 1983, *11*(4), pp. 66–70. **[G: U.S.]**

Haber, Sheldon E. and Lamas, Enrique J. Pay, Training Costs, Turnover and Hiring and Retention Decisions. *J. Behav. Econ.*, Summer 1983, *12*(1), pp. 1–21. **[G: U.S.]**

Hall, Robert E. Is Unemployment a Macroeconomic Problem? *Amer. Econ. Rev.*, May 1983, *73*(2), pp. 219–22. **[G: U.S.]**

Hall, Robert E. Rational Expectations and the Invisible Handshake: Comment. **In** *Tobin, J., ed.*, 1983, pp. 77–79.

Haltiwanger, John C. On the Relationship between Risk Aversion and the Development of Long Term Worker–Firm Attachments. *Southern Econ. J.*, October 1983, *50*(2), pp. 572–77.

Hamada, Koichi and Bhagwati, Jagdish N. Domestic Distortions, Imperfect Information and the Brain Drain. **In** *Bhagwati, J. N., Vol. 2*, 1983, *1976*, pp. 127–41.

Hancock, Keith. The Arbitration Tribunals and the Labour Market. **In** *Blandy, R. and Covick, O., eds.*, 1983, pp. 183–99.

Hannah, Stephen Paul. Cyclical and Structural Determinants of the *uv* Relation. *Appl. Econ.*, April 1983, *15*(2), pp. 141–51. **[G: U.K.]**

Hannah, Stephen Paul. Unemployment and Real Wage Speculation: Empirical Tests for Great Britain 1967–1980. *Scot. J. Polit. Econ.*, June 1983, *30*(2), pp. 128–41. **[G: U.K.]**

Hansen, Bent. LDC Labor Markets: Applications of Internal Labor Market Theory. *Ind. Relat.*, Spring 1983, *22*(2), pp. 238–60. **[G: Egypt; LDCs]**

Hansson, Bjorn. Wicksell's Critique of Ricardo's Chapter "On Machinery." *J. Econ. Stud.*, 1983, *10*(3), pp. 49–55.

Hansson, Ingemar and Stuart, Charles. Taxation, Government Spending, and Labor Supply: A Diagrammatic Exposition. *Econ. Inquiry*, October 1983, *21*(4), pp. 584–87.

Harris, Milton and Holmstrom, Bengt. Microeconomic Developments and Macroeconomics. *Amer. Econ. Rev.*, May 1983, *73*(2), pp. 223–27.

Harris, R. I. D. Specification of Factor Demand Models and Shiftworking—An Extension to the CES Case. *Scot. J. Polit. Econ.*, June 1983, *30*(2), pp. 170–74.

Harrison, Alan J. and Hart, Robert A. Unemployment Benefits and Labor Supply: A Note [The Effects of Unemployment Benefits on U.S. Unemployment Rates]. *Weltwirtsch. Arch.*, 1983, *119*(1), pp. 169–72. **[G: U.S.]**

Hart, Oliver D. Optimal Labour Contracts under Asymmetric Information: An Introduction. *Rev. Econ. Stud.*, January 1983, *50*(1), pp. 3–35.

Hart, Robert A. The Phillips Curve and Cyclical Manhour Variation. *Oxford Econ. Pap.*, July 1983, *35*(2), pp. 186–201. **[G: U.K.]**

Hausman, Jerry A. Stochastic Problems in the Simulation of Labor Supply. **In** *Feldstein, M., ed.*, 1983, pp. 47–69. **[G: U.S.]**

Hawley, Clifford B. The Effects of Labor Market Distortions on Real Wage Rates: A General Equilibrium Analysis. *Southern Econ. J.*, April 1983, *49*(4), pp. 1018–29.

Heckman, James J. A Life-cycle Model of Family Labour Supply. **In** *Weisbrod, B. and Hughes, H., eds.*, 1983, pp. 213–30.

Heckman, James J. Stochastic Problems in the Simulation of Labor Supply: Comment. **In** *Feldstein, M., ed.*, 1983, pp. 70–82. **[G: U.S.]**

Hibbs, Douglas A. Comment on Beck [Parties, Administrations, and American Macroeconomic Outcomes]. *Amer. Polit. Sci. Rev.*, June 1983, *77*(2), pp. 447–51. **[G: U.S.]**

Hicks, John. Edgeworth, Marshall and the 'Indeterminateness' of Wages. **In** *Hicks, J.*, 1983, *1930*, pp. 71–84.

Hirsch, Werner Z. and Rufolo, Anthony M. Shirking, Monitoring Costs, and Municipal Labor Productivity. **In** *Hirsch, W. Z., ed.*, 1983, pp. 277–310.

Hodgson, Geoffrey M. Worker Participation and Macroeconomic Efficiency. *J. Post Keynesian Econ.*, Winter 1982–83, *5*(2), pp. 266–75.

Hojman, David E. Wages, Unemployment and Expectations in Developing Countries: The Labour Market and the Augmented Phillips Curve for Chile. *J. Econ. Stud.*, 1983, *10*(1), pp. 3–16. **[G: Chile]**

Holmlund, Bertil. Payroll Taxes and Wage Inflation: The Swedish Experience. *Scand. J. Econ.*, 1983, *85*(1), pp. 1–15. **[G: Sweden]**

Holmström, Bengt. Equilibrium Long-Term Labor Contracts. *Quart. J. Econ.*, Supplement 1983, *98*(3), pp. 23–54.

Holtfrerich, Carl-Ludwig. Wechselkurssystem und Philipps-Kurve: Erwiderung und Kommentar. (Exchange Rate System and Philipps Curve: Reply and Comment. With English summary.) *Kredit Kapital*, 1983, *16*(2), pp. 242–52.

Homma, Masaaki and Osano, Hiroshi. The Structural Stability of an Implicit Labor Contract System. (In Japanese. With English summary.) *Econ. Stud. Quart.*, August 1983, *34*(2), pp. 133–46.

Hübler, Olaf. Lohn- und Beschäftigungsstrukturbewegungen unter Unsicherheit. (Uncertainty and Changes of Wage and Employment Structure. With English summary.) *Konjunkturpolitik*, 1983, *29*(2), pp. 67–88.

Hughes, Gerard and Walsh, Brendan M. Unemployment Duration, Aggregate Demand and Unemployment Insurance: A Study of Irish Live Register Survival Probabilities, 1967–1978. *Econ. Soc. Rev.*, January 1983, *14*(2), pp. 93–117. **[G: Ireland]**

Hutchens, Robert M. Layoffs and Labor supply. *Int. Econ. Rev.*, February 1983, *24*(1), pp. 37–55. **[G: U.S.]**

Ioannides, Yannis M. and Pissarides, Christopher A. Wages and Employment with Firm-Specific Seniority. *Bell J. Econ. (See Rand J. Econ. after 4/85)*, Autumn 1983, *14*(2), pp. 573–80.

Jennett, N. The Economics of Industrial Relations and Strikes. **In** *Gowland, D. H., ed.*, 1983, pp. 141–56. **[G: U.K.]**

Johnson, Janet L. Unemployment as a Household Labor Supply Decision. *Quart. Rev. Econ. Bus.*, Summer 1983, *23*(2), pp. 71–88. **[G: U.S.]**

Johnson, William R. and Browning, Edgar K. The Distributional and Efficiency Effects of Increasing the Minimum Wage: A Simulation. *Amer. Econ. Rev.*, March 1983, *73*(1), pp. 204–11. **[G: U.S.]**

Jones, Evan. Industrial Structure and Labor Force Segmentation. *Rev. Radical Polit. Econ.*, Winter 1983, *15*(4), pp. 24–44. **[G: Australia]**

Jovanovic, Boyan. A Welfare Analysis of Unemployment Insurance: Variations on Second-Best Themes: A Comment. *Carnegie-Rochester Conf. Ser. Public Policy*, Autumn 1983, *19*, pp. 99–102.

Kahn, Richard F. Malinvaud on Keynes. **In** *Eatwell, J. and Milgate, M., eds.*, 1983, *1977*, pp. 214–28.

Kanbur, S. M. Ravi. Labour Supply under Uncertainty with Piecewise Linear Tax Regimes. *Economica*, November 1983, *50*(200), pp. 379–94.

Kapp, K. William. Socio-economic Effects of Low and High Employment. **In** *Kapp, K. W.*, 1983, *1975*, pp. 99–110. **[G: U.S.]**

Karni, Edi. On Optimal Wage Indexation. *J. Polit. Econ.*, April 1983, *91*(2), pp. 282–92.

Katz, Eliakim and Rosenberg, Jacob. Inflation Variability, Real-Wage Variability and Production Inefficiency. *Economica*, November 1983, *50*(200), pp. 469–75.

Kaufman, Roger T. and Woglom, Geoffrey. Estimating Models with Rational Expectations. *J. Money, Credit, Banking*, August 1983, *15*(3), pp. 275–85.

Kerr, Clark. The Intellectual Role of the Neorealists in Labor Economics. *Ind. Relat.*, Spring 1983, *22*(2), pp. 298–318. **[G: U.S.]**

Kihlstrom, Richard E. and Laffont, Jean-Jacques. Implicit Labor Contracts and Free Entry. *Quart. J. Econ.*, Supplement 1983, *98*(3), pp. 55–105.

Klein, Emilio. Determinants of Manpower Underutilisation and Availability. *Int. Lab. Rev.*, March–April 1983, *122*(2), pp. 183–95.

Kooreman, Peter and Ridder, Geert. The Effects of Age and Unemployment Percentage on the Duration of Unemployment: Evidence from Aggregate Data. *Europ. Econ. Rev.*, January 1983, *20*(1–3), pp. 41–57. **[G: Netherlands]**

Kregel, J. A. The Microfoundations of the 'Generalisation of *The General Theory*' and 'Bastard Keynesianism': Keynes's Theory of Employment in the Long and the Short Period. *Cambridge J. Econ.*, September/December 1983, *7*(3/4), pp. 343–61.

Krueger, Anne O. Alternative Trade Strategies and Employment. **In** *Weisbrod, B. and Hughes, H., eds.*, 1983, pp. 387–404. **[G: LDCs]**

Kubin, Ingrid. Zur Bedeutung der Phillips-Phänomene. (On the Interpretation of the Phillips Phenomena. With English summary.) *Jahr. Nationalökon. Statist.*, July 1983, *198*(4), pp. 318–33.

Lackman, Conway Lee. Gallaway's Labor Force Participation Studies Revisited. *Econ. Notes*, 1983, (1), pp. 140–52. **[G: U.S.]**

Lampman, Robert J. How Has the Labor Supply Changed in Response to Recent Increases in Social Welfare Expenditures and the Taxes to Pay for Them? **In** *Barbash, J., et al., eds.*, 1983, pp. 61–85. **[G: U.S.]**

Lancaster, Tony and Chesher, Andrew. An Econometric Analysis of Reservation Wages. *Econometrica*, November 1983, *51*(6), pp. 1661–76. **[G: U.K.]**

Lang, Peter and Ohr, Renate. Wechselkurssystem und Philipps-Kurve—Neue ökonometrisch fundierte Thesen zuar aktuellen Diskussion um die "beste" Währungsordnung. (Exchange Rate System and Philipps Curve—New Econometrically Founded Theses to the Actual Discussion on the "Best" Currency System. With English summary.) *Kredit Kapital*, 1983, *16*(2), pp. 231–41.

Lazear, Edward P. A Competitive Theory of Monopoly Unionism. *Amer. Econ. Rev.*, September 1983, *73*(4), pp. 631–43.

Lazear, Edward P. A Microeconomic Theory of Labor Unions. In *Reid, J. D., Jr., ed.*, 1983, pp. 53–96.

Lazear, Edward P. Pensions as Severance Pay. In *Bodie, Z. and Shoven, J. B., eds.*, 1983, pp. 57–85, 88–89. **[G: U.S.]**

Leibenstein, Harvey. Notes on the X-efficiency Approach to Inflation, Productivity and Unemployment. In *Weisbrod, B. and Hughes, H., eds.*, 1983, pp. 84–96.

Leigh, J. Paul. Job Choice across Industries when Earnings Are Uncertain. *Quart. Rev. Econ. Bus.*, Autumn 1983, *23*(3), pp. 54–69. **[G: U.S.]**

Leigh, J. Paul. Sex Differences in Absenteeism. *Ind. Relat.*, Fall 1983, *22*(3), pp. 349–61. **[G: U.S.]**

Leontief, Wassily W. Technological Advance, Economic Growth, and the Distribution of Income. *Population Devel. Rev.*, September 1983, *9*(3), pp. 403–10.

Lerner, Abba P. Employment Theory and Employment Policy. In *Lerner, A. P.*, 1983, *1967*, pp. 375–92.

Lerner, Abba P. From Pre-Keynes to Post-Keynes. In *Lerner, A. P.*, 1983, *1977*, pp. 399–427.

Lerner, Abba P. High Full Employment and Low Full Employment. In *Lerner, A. P.*, 1983, *1951*, pp. 279–96.

Lerner, Abba P. On Keynes, Policy, and Theory—A Grumble. In *Lerner, A. P.*, 1983, pp. 441–51.

Lesourne, Jacques and Dominguez, A. Employment Policy of a Self-Financing Firm Facing a Risk of Bankruptcy. *J. Econ. Dynam. Control*, July 1983, *5*(4), pp. 325–58.

Lewis, W. Arthur. Reflections on Unlimited Labor. In *Lewis, W. A.*, 1983, *1972*, pp. 421–42.

Lewis, W. Arthur. The Dual Economy Revisited. In *Lewis, W. A.*, 1983, *1979*, pp. 461–79.

Lim, Chin. Employment Insurance and Competitive Equilibrium Labour Contracts. *Economica*, August 1983, *50*(199), pp. 337–49.

Linde, Robert. Beschäftigungseffekte von Arbeitszeitverkürzungen mit Lohnausgleich. (Employment Effects of Reducing Working Time with Wage Compensation. With English summary.) *Jahr. Nationalökon. Statist.*, September 1983, *198*(5), pp. 425–36.

Linde, Robert. Prämienlohn und Grenzproduktivitätstheorie der Einkommensverteilung. (Premium Pay and Marginal Productivity Theory of Income Distribution. With English summary.) *Z. Wirtschaft. Sozialwissen.*, 1983, *103*(4), pp. 351–68.

Liviatan, Nissan. On the Interaction between Wage and Asset Indexation. In *Dornbusch, R. and Simonsen, M. H., eds.*, 1983, pp. 267–80.

Liviatan, Nissan. On Equilibrium Wage Indexation and Neutrality of Indexation Policy. In *Armella, P. A.; Dornbusch, R. and Obstfeld, M., eds.*, 1983, pp. 107–24.

Long, Ngo Van and Siebert, Horst. Lay-Off Restraints and the Demand for Labor. *Z. ges. Staatswiss.*, December 1983, *139*(4), pp. 612–24.

Lowenstein, Mark A. Worker Heterogeneity, Hours Restrictions, and Temporary Layoffs. *Econometrica*, January 1983, *51*(1), pp. 69–78.

Lundberg, Shelly J. and Startz, Richard. Private Discrimination and Social Intervention in Competitive Labor Markets. *Amer. Econ. Rev.*, June 1983, *73*(3), pp. 340–47.

Maani, Sholeh. La duracion del desempleo y el salario de reserva de varones desempleados: el caso chileno. (With English summary.) *Cuadernos Econ.*, April 1983, *20*(59), pp. 101–11. **[G: Chile]**

MaCurdy, Thomas E. A Simple Scheme for Estimating an Intertemporal Model of Labor Supply and Consumption in the Presence of Taxes and Uncertainty. *Int. Econ. Rev.*, June 1983, *24*(2), pp. 265–89. **[G: U.S.]**

Malcomson, James M. Trade Unions and Economic Efficiency. *Econ. J.*, Supplement March 1983, pp. 51–65.

Markham, Steven E.; Dansereau, Fred, Jr. and Alutto, Joseph A. Absenteeism Rates as Measures in Organizational Experiments: Hidden Cyclical and Structural Variation. *Rev. Bus. Econ. Res.*, Spring 1983, *18*(3), pp. 21–31. **[G: U.S.]**

Martin, Jack K. and Lichter, Daniel T. Geographic Mobility and Satisfaction with Life and Work. *Soc. Sci. Quart.*, September 1983, *64*(3), pp. 524–35. **[G: U.S.]**

Masson, André. Estimation du risque à terme de chômage. (Estimation of the Individual Risk of Future Unemployment. With English summary.) *Ann. INSEE*, October–December 1983, (52), pp. 23–53.

Mazumdar, Dipak. Segmented Labor Markets in LDCs. *Amer. Econ. Rev.*, May 1983, *73*(2), pp. 254–59. **[G: LDCs]**

McCabe, Peter J. Optimal Leisure-Effort Choice with Endogenously Determined Earnings. *J. Lab. Econ.*, July 1983, *1*(3), pp. 308–29.

McCallum, John. Stabilization Policy and Endogenous Wage Stickiness. *Amer. Econ. Rev.*, June 1983, *73*(3), pp. 414–19.

McGavin, P. A. Equal Pay for Women: A Postscript [Segmented Labour Market Theories and the Australian Experience of Equal Pay for Women]. *Australian Econ. Pap.*, June 1983, *22*(40), pp. 65–67. **[G: Australia]**

McGavin, P. A. Equal Pay for Women: A Re-Assessment of the Australian Experience. *Australian Econ. Pap.*, June 1983, *22*(40), pp. 48–59. **[G: Australia]**

McGregor, Alan. Neighbourhood Influence on Job Search and Job Finding Methods. *Brit. J. Ind. Relat.*, March 1983, *21*(1), pp. 91–99. **[G: U.K.]**

McGuire, Timothy W. Price Change Expectations and the Phillips Curve. In *Brunner, K. and Meltzer, A. H., eds.*, 1983, *1976*, pp. 81–127. **[G: U.S.]**

McKenna, Chris. Optimal Search for Overtime Work. *Bull. Econ. Res.*, November 1983, *35*(2), pp. 87–95.

McPherson, Michael S. and Winston, Gordon C. The Economics of Academic Tenure: A Relational Perspective. *J. Econ. Behav. Organ.*, June–September 1983, *4*(2–3), pp. 163–84.

Meade, James. A New Keynesian Approach to Full Employment. *Lloyds Bank Rev.*, October 1983, (150), pp. 1–18.

Medio, Alfredo and Muso, Ignazio. Changes in Money Wages and Employment in a Keynesian

Analysis. *Econ. Notes,* 1983, (1), pp. 5–23.

Meinander, Nils. Huru angripa stagflationen? (How Should We Tackle Stagflation? With English Summary.) *Ekon. Samfundets Tidskr.,* 1983, *36* (1), pp. 9–14.

Michel, Philippe and Padoa Schioppa, Fiorella. A Dynamic Macroeconomic Model with Monopolistic Behavior in the Labor Market. *Europ. Econ. Rev.,* August 1983, *22* (3), pp. 331–50.

Michon, F. Une lecture des hypothèses de dualisme du marché du travail. (An Examination of the Dual Labour Market. With English summary.) *Écon. Soc.,* March–April 1983, *17* (3–4), pp. 579–627. **[G: France]**

Milgate, Murray and Eatwell, John. Unemployment and the Market Mechanism. **In** *Eatwell, J. and Milgate, M., eds.,* 1983, pp. 260–80.

Minford, Patrick. Labour Market Equilibrium in an Open Economy. *Oxford Econ. Pap.,* Supplement November 1983, *35,* pp. 207–44. **[G: U.K.]**

Mitchell, Olivia S. Fringe Benefits and the Cost of Changing Jobs. *Ind. Lab. Relat. Rev.,* October 1983, *37* (1), pp. 70–78. **[G: U.S.]**

Mitchell, William F. Equal Pay for Women: A Reply [Segmented Labor Market Theories and the Australian Experience of Equal Pay for Women]. *J. Post Keynesian Econ.,* Summer 1983, *5* (4), pp. 669–72. **[G: Australia]**

Miyazaki, Hajime and Neary, Hugh M. The Illyrian Firm Revisited. *Bell J. Econ. (See Rand J. Econ. after 4/85),* Spring 1983, *14* (1), pp. 259–70.

Moffitt, Robert A. The Individual Work Incentives and Labor Market Impacts of Transfer Programs with a Work Requirement: The Static Theory. *Quart. Rev. Econ. Bus.,* Spring 1983, *23* (1), pp. 35–45.

Mortensen, Dale T. A Welfare Analysis of Unemployment Insurance: Variations on Second-Best Themes. *Carnegie-Rochester Conf. Ser. Public Policy,* Autumn 1983, *19,* pp. 67–97.

Musalem, Alberto Roque. Déficit operational en la producción de bienes no-comerciables en un modelo de equilibrio general: el caso argentino. (With English summary.) *Cuadernos Econ.,* August 1983, *20* (60), pp. 133–48. **[G: Argentina]**

Mutti, John H. and Gerking, Shelby D. Changes in Income Distribution and Welfare from Greater Immigration of Unskilled Workers. *Europ. Econ. Rev.,* September 1983, *23* (1), pp. 103–16.

Nakamura, Jiro. The Role of the Labor Market for Solving the Problem of Stagflation. *Econ. Stud. Quart.,* August 1983, *34* (2), pp. 147–55. **[G: Japan]**

Neary, J. Peter and Stiglitz, Joseph E. Toward a Reconstruction of Keynesian Economics: Expectations and Constrained Equilibria. *Quart. J. Econ.,* Supplement 1983, *98* (3), pp. 199–228.

Newton, Keith. Labour Market Policies for Australian Stagflation: A Canadian Viewpoint. *Australian Bull. Lab.,* December 1983, *10* (1), pp. 24–35. **[G: Canada; Australia]**

Nickell, S. J. and Andrews, M. Unions, Real Wages and Employment in Britain 1951–79. *Oxford Econ. Pap.,* Supplement November 1983, *35,* pp. 183–206. **[G: U.K.]**

Nohara, Hiroatsu. Dualité et unité du marché du travail industriel: le cas du Japon. (Dualism and Unity in the Industrial Labor Market: The Case of Japan. With English summary.) *Revue Écon.,* November 1983, *34* (6), pp. 1188–212. **[G: Japan]**

Nolan, Peter and Brown, William. Competition and Workplace Wage Determination. *Oxford Bull. Econ. Statist.,* August 1983, *45* (3), pp. 269–87. **[G: U.K.]**

O'Mahony, Mary. The Length of Spells of Unemployment in Ireland. *Econ. Soc. Rev.,* January 1983, *14* (2), pp. 119–35. **[G: Ireland]**

Oest, Wolfgang. National Models as a Tool for Analysing Future Manpower Demand and Supply. **In** *Streeten, P. and Maier, H., eds.,* 1983, pp. 443–56. **[G: W. Germany]**

Ohashi, Isao. Wage Profiles, Layoffs and Specific Training. *Int. Econ. Rev.,* February 1983, *24* (1), pp. 169–81.

Oi, Walter Y. The Fixed Employment Costs of Specialized Labor. **In** *Triplett, J. E., ed.,* 1983, pp. 63–116. **[G: U.S.]**

Okun, Arthur M. Upward Mobility in a High-Pressure Economy. **In** *Okun, A. M.,* 1983, *1973,* pp. 171–220. **[G: U.S.]**

Oulton, Nicholas. Persistence of Wages, Prices and Output under Rational Expectations When the Labour Market Is Dominated by Workplace Bargaining. *Manchester Sch. Econ. Soc. Stud.,* June 1983, *51* (2), pp. 111–28. **[G: U.K.]**

Pagano, U. Profit Maximization, Industrial Democracy and the Allocation of Labour. *Manchester Sch. Econ. Soc. Stud.,* June 1983, *51* (2), pp. 159–83.

Pakes, Ariél and Nitzan, Shmuel. Optimum Contracts for Research Personnel, Research Employment, and the Establishment of "Rival" Enterprises. *J. Lab. Econ.,* October 1983, *1* (4), pp. 345–65.

Pechman, Joseph A. and Carr, Julie A. Macroeconomics Prices & Quantities. **In** *Tobin, J., ed.,* 1983, pp. 1–18.

Pedersen, Peder J. Lønudviklingen i Danmark 1911–1976—stabilitet og specifikation. (Phillips Curves Investigations of Danish Data Covering the Period 1911 to 1976. With English summary.) *Nationaløkon. Tidsskr.,* 1983, *121* (1), pp. 102–29. **[G: Denmark]**

Pedersen, Peder J. Nyere arbejdsmarkedsteori og -empiri—en oversigt. (Recent Trends in Labour Market Theory—A Survey Article. With English summary.) *Nationaløkon. Tidsskr.,* 1983, *121* (2), pp. 141–59.

Perri, Timothy J. Explicit Labor Contracts, Shirking, and Turnover Costs. *Atlantic Econ. J.,* December 1983, *11* (4), pp. 59–65.

Perry, George L. Rational Expectations and the Invisible Handshake: Comment. **In** *Tobin, J., ed.,* 1983, pp. 79–82.

Persson, Mats. The Distribution of Abilities and the Progressive Income Tax. *J. Public Econ.,* October 1983, *22* (1), pp. 73–88.

Pesando, James E. and Clarke, Carol K. Economic Models of the Labor Market and Pension Accounting: An Exploratory Analysis. *Accounting Rev.,* October 1983, *58* (4), pp. 733–48.

Peters, Michael. Labour Contracts in a Stock Market Economy. *J. Econ. Theory,* August 1983, *30*(2), pp. 296–314.

Petrovich, Giuliano. A Contribution to the Labour Reserve Theory and Youth Unemployment. *Rivista Int. Sci. Econ. Com.,* February 1983, *30*(2), pp. 143–62.

Phelps, Edmund S. Implicit Contracts and the Social Contract: Toward a Welfare Economics without Costless Mobility. **In** *Dornbusch, R. and Simonsen, M. H., eds.,* 1983, pp. 46–53.

Pike, Maureen. A Simulation of the Impact of Introducing Equality for Males and Females into Social Security. *Economica,* August 1983, *50*(199), pp. 351–60. **[G: U.K.]**

Piore, Michael J. Labor Market Segmentation: To What Paradigm Does It Belong? *Amer. Econ. Rev.,* May 1983, *73*(2), pp. 249–53.

Piore, Michael J. Understanding Unemployment in Developed Industrial Economies. **In** *Streeten, P. and Maier, H., eds.,* 1983, pp. 106–16.

Pissarides, Christopher A. Efficiency Aspects of the Financing of Unemployment Insurance and Other Government Expenditure. *Rev. Econ. Stud.,* January 1983, *50*(1), pp. 57–69.

Plessner, Yakir and Yitzhaki, Shlomo. Unemployment and Wage Rigidity: The Demand Side. *Oxford Econ. Pap.,* July 1983, *35*(2), pp. 202–12.

van der Ploeg, Frederick. Economic Growth and Conflict over the Distribution of Income. *J. Econ. Dynam. Control,* November 1983, *6*(3), pp. 253–79.

van Praag, Bernard M. S. and Emanuel, Han. On the Concept of Non-employability with Respect to a Non-homogeneous Labor Force. **In** *Söderström, L., ed.,* 1983, pp. 159–75.

Quandt, Richard E. Switching between Equilibrium and Disequilibrium. *Rev. Econ. Statist.,* November 1983, *65*(4), pp. 684–87. **[G: U.S.]**

Rabeau, Yves. Les services et l'inflation: Le cas Canadien. (With English summary.) *Revue Écon. Polit.,* May–June 1983, *93*(3), pp. 421–36. **[G: Canada]**

Raisian, John. Contracts, Job Experience, and Cyclical Labor Market Adjustments. *J. Lab. Econ.,* April 1983, *1*(2), pp. 152–70. **[G: U.S.]**

Ramaswami, Chitra. Equilibrium Unemployment and the Efficient Job-Finding Rate. *J. Lab. Econ.,* April 1983, *1*(2), pp. 171–96.

Ramb, Bernd-Thomas. Die horizontale Phillips-Kurve: Die Quasineutralität der Arbeitslosenquote bezüglich der Inflationsrate. (The Horizontal Phillips-Curve. The Quasi-Neutrality of the Unemployment Rate in Reference to the Inflation Rate. With English summary.) *Z. Wirtschaft. Sozialwissen.,* 1983, *103*(5), pp. 419–36. **[G: W. Germany]**

Rea, John D. The Explanatory Power of Alternative Theories of Inflation and Unemployment, 1895–1979. *Rev. Econ. Statist.,* May 1983, *65*(2), pp. 183–95. **[G: U.S.]**

Reder, M. W. Unionism, Wages, and Contract Enforcement. **In** *Reid, J. D., Jr., ed.,* 1983, pp. 27–51.

Regini, Marino. The Crisis of Representation in Class-oriented Unions: Some Reflections Based on the Italian Case. **In** *Clegg, S.; Dow, G. and Boreham, P., eds.,* 1983, pp. 239–56. **[G: Italy]**

Reinganum, Jennifer F. Nash Equilibrium Search for the Best Alternative. *J. Econ. Theory,* June 1983, *30*(1), pp. 139–52.

Reyes, Saúl Trejo. Urban Labour Markets in Developing Countries. **In** *Urquidi, V. L. and Reyes, S. T., eds.,* 1983, pp. 41–54.

Richards, Daniel J. Wages and the Dominant Firm. *J. Lab. Res.,* Spring 1983, *4*(2), pp. 177–82. **[G: U.S.]**

Richardson, Sue. Inflation and the Dispersion of Pay. **In** *Blandy, R. and Covick, O., eds.,* 1983, pp. 37–60. **[G: Australia]**

Riese, Martin. Eine Rehabilitation des Konzeptes der "bisherigen Dauer der Arbeitslosigkeit." (A Rehabilitation of the Concept of "Interrupted Spell Length of Unemployment." With English summary.) *Jahr. Nationalökon. Statist.,* November 1983, *198*(6), pp. 505–10. **[G: W. Germany]**

Robins, Philip K.; West, Richard W. and Stieger, Gary L. Labor Supply Response to a Negative Income Tax. **In** *Zeckhauser, R. J. and Leebaert, D., eds.,* 1983, pp. 78–96. **[G: U.S.]**

Rosen, Sherwin. The Economics of Superstars: Reply. *Amer. Econ. Rev.,* June 1983, *73*(3), pp. 460–62.

Rosen, Sherwin. Unemployment and Insurance. *Carnegie-Rochester Conf. Ser. Public Policy,* Autumn 1983, *19,* pp. 5–49. **[G: U.S.]**

Rosen, Sherwin. Unemployment and Insurance: Reply to Robert Gordon. *Carnegie-Rochester Conf. Ser. Public Policy,* Autumn 1983, *19,* pp. 61–66. **[G: U.S.]**

Rossana, Robert J. Some Empirical Estimates of the Demand for Hours in U.S. Manufacturing Industries. *Rev. Econ. Statist.,* November 1983, *65*(4), pp. 560–69. **[G: U.S.]**

Rowley, Charles K. and Wiseman, Jack. Inflation versus Unemployment: Is the Government Impotent? *Nat. Westminster Bank Quart. Rev.,* February 1983, pp. 2–12.

Salop, Steven C. A Century of Evidence on Wage and Price Stickiness in the United States, the United Kingdom, and Japan: Comment. **In** *Tobin, J., ed.,* 1983, pp. 124–33. **[G: U.S.; U.K.; Japan]**

Sampson, Anthony A. Employment Policy in a Model with a Rational Trade Union. *Econ. J.,* June 1983, *93*(370), pp. 297–311.

Sandmo, Agnar. Progressive Taxation, Redistribution, and Labor Supply. *Scand. J. Econ.,* 1983, *85*(3), pp. 311–23.

Scarth, William M. Tax-Related Incomes Policies and Macroeconomic Stability. *J. Macroecon.,* Winter 1983, *5*(1), pp. 91–103.

Schefold, Bertram. Kahn on Malinvaud. **In** *Eatwell, J. and Milgate, M., eds.,* 1983, pp. 229–46.

Schneider, H. Mitbestimmung, unvollständige Information und Leistungsanreize: Überlegungen zu einer funktionsfähigen Unternehmensverfassung. (Codetermination, Incomplete Information, and Incentives. With English summary.) *Schweiz. Z. Volkswirtsch. Statist.,* September 1983, *119*(3), pp. 337–55.

von der Schulenberg, J.-Mattias Graf. A Note on Activity-Level and Uncertainty. *Z. Wirtschaft. Sozialwissen.,* 1983, *103*(5), pp. 485–96.

Seton, Francis. A "Phillipsoid" Wage–Push Flation:

"In–," "Stag–," or "Slump–." *J. Post Keynesian Econ.*, Spring 1983, *5*(3), pp. 440–53.

Shah, Anup R. K. Rational Expectations Macro Models with Possible Steady-State Inflation and Unemployment. *J. Macroecon.*, Fall 1983, *5*(4), pp. 461–71.

Shakow, Don M. Market Mechanisms for Compensating Hazardous Work: A Critical Analysis. **In** *Kasperson, R. E., ed.*, 1983, pp. 277–90. **[G: U.S.]**

Shapiro, Edward. Leisure–Income Indifference Curves and the Laffer Curve. *Amer. Econ.*, Spring 1983, *27*(1), pp. 37–39.

Sheshinski, Eytan. Wage Policy in the Public Sector and Income Distribution. **In** *Helpman, E.; Razin, A. and Sadka, E., eds.*, 1983, pp. 299–309.

Simonsen, Mario Henrique. On Equilibrium Wage Indexation and Neutrality of Indexation Policy: Comment. **In** *Armella, P. A.; Dornbusch, R. and Obstfeld, M., eds.*, 1983, pp. 124–30.

Smith, V. Kerry. The Role of Site and Job Characteristics in Hedonic Wage Models. *J. Urban Econ.*, May 1983, *13*(3), pp. 296–321. **[G: U.S.]**

Solimano, Andrés. Reducir costos del trabajo: cuánto empleo genera? (With English summary.) *Cuadernos Econ.*, December 1983, *20*(61), pp. 363–81. **[G: Chile]**

Soskice, David. Economic Theory and Unemployment: Progress and Regress since 1936? *Ind. Relat.*, Spring 1983, *22*(2), pp. 319–33.

Srinivasan, T. N. and Bhagwati, Jagdish N. Alternative Policy Rankings in a Large, Open Economy with Sector-specific, Minimum Wages. **In** *Bhagwati, J. N., Vol. 1*, 1983, *1975*, pp. 505–20.

Standing, Guy. The Notion of Structural Unemployment. *Int. Lab. Rev.*, March–April 1983, *122*(2), pp. 137–53.

Stapleton, David C. How Elastic Is the Demand for Labor? A Comment. *Rev. Econ. Statist.*, November 1983, *65*(4), pp. 692–93. **[G: U.S.]**

Staroverov, O. V. On the Allocation of Graduates as a Means of Regulating the Structure of the Labor Force. *Matekon*, Spring 1983, *19*(3), pp. 36–51. **[G: Hungary]**

Steel, William F. and Takagi, Yasuoki. Small Enterprise Development and the Employment-Output Trade-Off. *Oxford Econ. Pap.*, November 1983, *35*(3), pp. 423–46. **[G: LDCs]**

Stiglitz, Joseph E. and Weiss, Andrew. Alternative Approaches to Analyzing Markets with Asymmetric Information: Reply [The Theory of 'Screening,' Education, and the Distribution of Income]. *Amer. Econ. Rev.*, March 1983, *73*(1), pp. 246–49.

Stiglitz, Joseph E. and Weiss, Andrew. Incentive Effects of Terminations: Applications to the Credit and Labor Markets. *Amer. Econ. Rev.*, December 1983, *73*(5), pp. 912–27.

Strebel, Paul J. Contract Revision and Price Quantity Adjustment: A Catastrophe Model. *Atlantic Econ. J.*, March 1983, *11*(1), pp. 24–35.

Stretton, Alan. Circular Migration, Segmented Labour Markets and Efficiency: The Building Industry in Manila and Port Moresby. *Int. Lab. Rev.*, Sept.–Oct. 1983, *122*(5), pp. 623–39. **[G: Philippines]**

Sumner, M. T. and Ward, R. The Reappearing Phillips Curve. *Oxford Econ. Pap.*, Supplement November 1983, *35*, pp. 306–20. **[G: U.K.]**

Tanaka, Osamu. A Theory of the Supplies of Labor and Homemakers' Services. *Kobe Univ. Econ.*, 1983, (29), pp. 1–14.

Tannery, Frederick J. Search Effort and Unemployment Insurance Reconsidered. *J. Human Res.*, Summer 1983, *18*(3), pp. 432–40. **[G: U.S.]**

Tanskanen, Antti. Työllisyys pienessä avoimessa taloudessa. (Employment in a Small Open Economy. With English summary.) *Kansant. Aikak.*, 1983, *79*(3), pp. 278–83. **[G: Finland]**

Tarantelli, Ezio. Foundations of a Likelihood Theory of Employment and Inflation. **In** *Fitoussi, J.-P., ed.*, 1983, pp. 185–203.

Tarantelli, Ezio. The Regulation of Inflation in Western Countries and the Degree of Neocorporatism. *Economia*, May 1983, *7*(2), pp. 199–238. **[G: OECD]**

Taylor, John B. 'Wage Rigidity and Unemployment in OECD Countries' by D. Grubb et al.: Comment. *Europ. Econ. Rev.*, March/April 1983, *21*(1/2), pp. 45–49. **[G: OECD]**

Taylor, John B. Rational Expectations and the Invisible Handshake. **In** *Tobin, J., ed.*, 1983, pp. 63–77.

Taylor, John B. Union Wage Settlements during a Disinflation. *Amer. Econ. Rev.*, December 1983, *73*(5), pp. 981–93. **[G: U.S.]**

Thirlwall, Anthony P. What Are Estimates of the Natural Rate of Unemployment Measuring? *Oxford Bull. Econ. Statist.*, May 1983, *45*(2), pp. 173–79.

Tolley, George S. and Krumm, Ronald J. On the Regional Labor-Supply Relation. **In** *Grieson, R. E., ed.*, 1983, pp. 203–37. **[G: U.S.]**

Triplett, Jack E. Introduction: An Essay on Labor Cost. **In** *Triplett, J. E., ed.*, 1983, pp. 1–60.

Truu, M. L. Labour Market Segmentation: The Theoretical Case—Comment. *S. Afr. J. Econ.*, December 1983, *51*(4), pp. 567–73.

Truu, M. L. Labour Market Segmentation: The Theoretical Case—Final Comment. *S. Afr. J. Econ.*, December 1983, *51*(4), pp. 579.

Turk, Jeremy. Work and Unemployment. **In** *Shepherd, D.; Turk, J. and Silberston, A., eds.*, 1983, pp. 46–76. **[G: U.K.]**

Ueda, Kazuo and Hamada, Koichi. Migration, Alternative Tax Regimes and Capital Accumulation. **In** *Weisbrod, B. and Hughes, H., eds.*, 1983, pp. 368–84.

Velupillai, Kumaraswamy. A Neo-Cambridge Model of Income Distribution and Unemployment. *J. Post Keynesian Econ.*, Spring 1983, *5*(3), pp. 454–73.

Venables, Anthony J. Random Job Prospects and the Distribution of Income. *Quart. J. Econ.*, November 1983, *98*(4), pp. 637–57.

Viscusi, W. Kip. Employment Relationships with Joint Employer and Worker Experimentation. *Int. Econ. Rev.*, June 1983, *24*(2), pp. 313–22.

Viscusi, W. Kip. The Political Economy of Wage and Price Regulation: The Case of the Carter Pay-Price Standards. **In** *Zeckhauser, R. J. and Leebaert, D., eds.*, 1983, pp. 155–74. **[G: U.S.]**

Waelbroeck, Jean. Protection, Employment and Welfare in a 'Stagflating' Economy. **In** *Weisbrod, B. and Hughes, H., eds.*, 1983, pp. 475–96.

Ward, William A. On Estimating Shadow Wage Rates for Portugal. *Economia*, October 1983, *7*(3), pp. 543–54. **[G: Portugal]**

Warren, Ronald S., Jr. Labor Market Contacts, Unanticipated Wages, and Employment Growth. *Amer. Econ. Rev.*, June 1983, *73*(3), pp. 389–97. **[G: U.S.]**

Warren, Ronald S., Jr. Labor Market Differentials and the Expected Gain from Search. *J. Econ. Bus.*, 1983, *35*(1), pp. 35–59. **[G: U.S.]**

Watanabe, Ken-ichi. An Adaptation of Weintraub's Model. *J. Post Keynesian Econ.*, Winter 1982–83, *5*(2), pp. 228–44.

Watson, Harry. A Note on Pensions in a Neoclassical Model of the Firm. *J. Econ. Dynam. Control*, September 1983, *6*(1/2), pp. 41–54.

Watson, Mark W. Imperfect Information and Wage Inertia in the Business Cycle: A Comment. *J. Polit. Econ.*, October 1983, *91*(5), pp. 876–79.

Weitzman, Martin L. Some Macroeconomic Implications of Alternative Compensation Systems. *Econ. J.*, December 1983, *93*(372), pp. 763–83.

West, Edwin G. Marx's Hypotheses on the Length of the Working Day. *J. Polit. Econ.*, April 1983, *91*(2), pp. 266–81.

Westergård-Nielsen, Niels. En søgemodel for overgangen fra uddannelse til erhverv: Teori og empiri. (A Search Model of the Transition from Education to Work: Theory and Empirical Findings. With English summary.) *Nationaløkon. Tidsskr.*, 1983, *121*(2), pp. 181–99. **[G: Denmark]**

Whinston, Michael D. Moral Hazard, Adverse Selection, and the Optimal Provision of Social Insurance. *J. Public Econ.*, October 1983, *22*(1), pp. 49–71.

White, Barbara Ann. Optimal Strategies for Workers on Temporary Layoff. *Econ. Inquiry*, October 1983, *21*(4), pp. 520–44.

Williamson, Oliver E. Organizational Innovation: The Transaction-Cost Approach. **In** *Ronen, J., ed.*, 1983, pp. 101–33.

Wise, David A. Alternative Tax Treatments of the Family: Simulation Methodology and Results: Comment. **In** *Feldstein, M., ed.*, 1983, pp. 41–46. **[G: U.S.]**

Wise, David A. Pensions as Severance Pay: Comment. **In** *Bodie, Z. and Shoven, J. B., eds.*, 1983, pp. 86–88. **[G: U.S.]**

Withers, Glenn A. and Freebairn, John W. Structural Change and Labour Market Adjustment. **In** *Weisbrod, B. and Hughes, H., eds.*, 1983, pp. 113–19. **[G: Australia]**

Woodbury, Stephen A. Substitution between Wage and Nonwage Benefits. *Amer. Econ. Rev.*, March 1983, *73*(1), pp. 166–82. **[G: U.S.]**

Wörgötter, Andreas. A Note on the Stable Phillips Curve in Austria. *Empirica*, 1983, (1), pp. 29–40. **[G: Austria]**

Wren-Lewis, Simon. Labour Supply and Wealth: Some Macroeconomic Policy Implications. *Manchester Sch. Econ. Soc. Stud.*, March 1983, *51*(1), pp. 1–15. **[G: U.K.]**

Yabushita, Shiro. Theory of Screening and the Behavior of the Firm: Comment. *Amer. Econ. Rev.*, March 1983, *73*(1), pp. 242–45.

Zabalza, Antoni. The CES Utility Function, Non-Linear Budget Constraints and Labour Supply: Results on Female Participation and Hours. *Econ. J.*, June 1983, *93*(370), pp. 312–30. **[G: U.K.]**

Zweifel, Peter. Identifizierung kommt vor Optimierung: Eine Kritik neuerer Entwicklungen in der mikroökonomischen Theorie. (Identification Precedes Optimization: A Critique of Recent Developments in Microeconomics. With English summary.) *Z. Wirtschaft. Sozialwissen.*, 1983, *103*(1), pp. 1–26.

822 Public Policy; Role of Government

8220 General

Barros, Cassio Mesquita, Jr. Monetary Correction in Labor Legislation. **In** *de Ulhôa Canto, G.; da Silva Martins, I. G. and van Hoorn, J., Jr., eds.*, 1983, pp. 152–86. **[G: Brazil]**

Bequela, Assefa and Freedman, David H. Employment and Basic Needs: An Overview. **In** *Todaro, M. P., ed.*, 1983, *1979*, pp. 153–64.

Briggs, Vernon M., Jr. Non-Immigrant Labor Policy in the United States. *J. Econ. Issues*, September 1983, *17*(3), pp. 609–30. **[G: U.S.]**

Bulow, Jeremy I.; Scholes, Myron S. and Menell, Peter. Economic Implications of ERISA. **In** *Bodie, Z. and Shoven, J. B., eds.*, 1983, pp. 37–53, 56. **[G: U.S.]**

Carr, Shirley G. E. Sex-Based Discrimination in Employment: Problems and Progress in Canada. *Int. Lab. Rev.*, November–December 1983, *122*(6), pp. 761–70. **[G: Canada]**

Carroll, Thomas M. Right to Work Laws Do Matter. *Southern Econ. J.*, October 1983, *50*(2), pp. 494–509. **[G: U.S.]**

Chen, Peter S. J. Singapore's Development Strategies: A Model for Rapid Growth. **In** *Chen, P. S. J., ed.*, 1983, pp. 3–25. **[G: Singapore]**

Chen, Yun. An Important Work That Relates to the Overall Situation. **In** *Ch'en, Y.*, 1983, *1961*, pp. 144–54. **[G: China]**

Collins, Doreen. The Impact of Social Policy in the United Kingdom. **In** *El-Agraa, A. M., ed.*, 1983, pp. 213–33. **[G: EEC; U.K.]**

Dodge, David. Labour Market Policy Concerns: An Evaluation of Current Federal Policies and Priorities. **In** *Queen's Univ. Indust. Relat. Centre and John Deutsch Mem.*, 1983, pp. 135–43. **[G: Canada]**

Doyle, Peter S. Labour Market Policy Concerns: An Evaluation of Current Federal Policies and Priorities: Comment. **In** *Queen's Univ. Indust. Relat. Centre and John Deutsch Mem.*, 1983, pp. 148–50. **[G: Canada]**

Dymond, W. R. European Labour Markets and Policies: Retrospect and Prospect. **In** *Queen's Univ. Indust. Relat. Centre and John Deutsch Mem.*, 1983, pp. 221–42. **[G: W. Europe]**

Emmerij, Louis. Paid Educational Leave: A Proposal Based on the Dutch Case. **In** *Levin, H. M. and*

Schütze, H. G., eds., 1983, pp. 297–316. [G: Netherlands; OECD]

Getman, Julius G. and Kohler, Thomas C. The Common Law, Labor Law, and Reality: A Response [A Common Law for Labor Relations: A Critique of the New Deal Labor Legislation]. *Yale Law J.*, July 1983, *92*(8), pp. 1415–34. [G: U.S.]

Hasan, Abrar. Labour Market Imbalances in the 1980s: A Review of Three Perspectives: Comment. **In** *Queen's Univ. Indust. Relat. Centre and John Deutsch Mem.*, 1983, pp. 42–44. [G: Canada]

Jessua, Claude. Les perspectives de l'emploi. (With English summary.) *Revue Écon. Polit.*, September–October 1983, *93*(5), pp. 669–81. [G: France]

Lang, Ron. Labour Market Policy Concerns: An Evaluation of Current Federal Policies and Priorities: Comment. **In** *Queen's Univ. Indust. Relat. Centre and John Deutsch Mem.*, 1983, pp. 143–45. [G: Canada]

Levin, Henry M. Comprehensive Models for Financing Recurrent Education: Individual Entitlements. **In** *Levin, H. M. and Schütze, H. G., eds.*, 1983, pp. 39–66. [G: OECD]

Linhart, Sepp. Social Security versus Family Ideology. The State's Reaction to the Consequences of Early Industrialization in Japan. *Rivista Int. Sci. Econ. Com.*, August 1983, *30*(8), pp. 703–15. [G: Japan]

McMurray, David. The Current Industrial Relations Scene in Canada, 1983: Labour Legislation and Policy: Summary Outline. **In** *Wood, W. D. and Kumar, P., eds.*, 1983, pp. 87–205. [G: Canada]

Nelson, Richard R. State Labor Legislation Enacted in 1982. *Mon. Lab. Rev.*, January 1983, *106*(1), pp. 44–56. [G: U.S.]

Rehn, Gösta. Comprehensive Models for Financing Recurrent Education: Individual Drawing Rights. **In** *Levin, H. M. and Schütze, H. G., eds.*, 1983, pp. 67–79.

Robinson, Derek. Pay Policies for the Future: Indirect and Partial Measures. **In** *Robinson, D. and Mayhew, K., eds.*, 1983, pp. 105–25. [G: U.K.]

Rose-Ackerman, Susan. Unintended Consequences: Regulating the Quality of Subsidized Day Care. *J. Policy Anal. Manage.*, Fall 1983, *3*(1), pp. 14–30. [G: U.S.]

Sanderson, Warren C. The Problems of Planning for the Expected: Demographic Shocks and Policy Paralysis. **In** *Reynolds, C. W. and Tello, C., eds.*, 1983, pp. 277–98. [G: U.S.; Mexico]

Seguret, Marie-Claire. Women and Working Conditions: Prospects for Improvement? *Int. Lab. Rev.*, May–June 1983, *122*(3), pp. 295–311. [G: Global]

Simmons, C. Gordon. The Experience of the Unjust Dismissal Section under Section 61.5 in the Canada Labour Code, 1978–1981. **In** *Queen's Univ. Indust. Relat. Centre*, 1983, pp. 59–67. [G: Canada]

Smith, David C. Labour Market Imbalances in the 1980s: A Review of Three Perspectives. **In** *Queen's Univ. Indust. Relat. Centre and John Deutsch Mem.*, 1983, pp. 17–39. [G: Canada]

Steenkamp, W. F. J. Labour Problems and Policies of Half a Century. *S. Afr. J. Econ.*, March 1983, *51*(1), pp. 58–87. [G: S. Africa]

Swartz, Gerald S. Labour Market Imbalances in the 1980s: A Review of Three Perspectives: Comment. **In** *Queen's Univ. Indust. Relat. Centre and John Deutsch Mem.*, 1983, pp. 44–49. [G: Canada]

Tate, Donald G. Labour Market Imbalances in the 1980s: A Review of Three Perspectives: Comment. **In** *Queen's Univ. Indust. Relat. Centre and John Deutsch Mem.*, 1983, pp. 39–42. [G: Canada]

Timmermann, Dieter. Financing Mechanisms: Their Impact on Postcompulsory Education. **In** *Levin, H. M. and Schütze, H. G., eds.*, 1983, pp. 99–129.

Weis, Peter. Zur arbeitsmarktpolitischen Problematik von Kündigungs- und Besitzstandsregelungen für ältere Arbeitnehmer. (The Problematic Nature of Protection against Dismissal and Earnings Guaranties for Elderly Workers. With English summary.) *Z. Wirtschaft. Sozialwissen.*, 1983, *103*(3), pp. 255–81. [G: W. Germany]

Whalley, John. The Impact of Federal Policies on Interprovincial Activity. **In** *Trebilcock, M. J., et al., eds.*, 1983, pp. 201–42. [G: Canada]

White, Gordon. Urban Employment and Labour Allocation Policies. **In** *Feuchtwang, S. and Hussain, A., eds.*, 1983, pp. 257–87. [G: China]

Wolfson, Alan. Labour Market Policy Concerns: An Evaluation of Current Federal Policies and Priorities: Comment. **In** *Queen's Univ. Indust. Relat. Centre and John Deutsch Mem.*, 1983, pp. 145–47. [G: Canada]

Zeckhauser, Richard J. Economic Implications of ERISA: Comment. **In** *Bodie, Z. and Shoven, J. B., eds.*, 1983, pp. 53–55. [G: U.S.]

8221 Wages and Hours

Adell, Bernard. Termination of Employment on the Initiative of the Employer and Income Security of the Worker Concerned. **In** *Queen's Univ. Indust. Relat. Centre*, 1983, pp. 82–92. [G: Canada]

Allen, Steven G. Much Ado about Davis–Bacon: A Critical Review and New Evidence. *J. Law Econ.*, October 1983, *26*(3), pp. 707–36. [G: U.S.]

Behrman, Jere R.; Sickles, Robin C. and Taubman, Paul. The Impact of Minimum Wages on the Distributions of Earnings for Major Race–Sex Groups: A Dynamic Analysis. *Amer. Econ. Rev.*, September 1983, *73*(4), pp. 766–78. [G: U.S.]

Brand, Horst. The Evolution of Fair Labor Standards: A Study in Class Conflict. *Mon. Lab. Rev.*, August 1983, *106*(8), pp. 25–28. [G: U.S.]

Brown, Charles; Gilroy, Curtis and Kohen, Andrew. Time-Series Evidence of the Effect of the Minimum Wage on Youth Employment and Unemployment. *J. Human Res.*, Winter 1983, *18*(1), pp. 3–31. [G: U.S.]

Bruce, C. J. and Kerr, William A. The Determination of Wages and Working Conditions in the Agricultural Sector: Three Alternatives. *Can. J. Agr. Econ.*, July 1983, *31*(2), pp. 177–96. [G: Canada]

Casteñeda, Tarsicio. Salarios mínimos y empleo en el Gran Santiago: 1978 y 1981. *Cuadernos Econ.*,

December 1983, *20*(61), pp. 279–93. **[G: Chile]**

Cave, George. Job Rationing, Unemployment, and Discouraged Workers. *J. Lab. Econ.*, July 1983, *1*(3), pp. 286–307.

Cortázar, René. Chile: Resultados distributivos 1973–82. (With English summary.) *Desarrollo Econ.*, October-December 1983, *23*(91), pp. 369–94. **[G: Chile]**

Drobny, Andres and Wells, John. Wages, Minimum Wages, and Income Distribution in Brazil: Results from the Construction Industry. *J. Devel. Econ.*, December 1983, *13*(3), pp. 305–30. **[G: Brazil]**

Dublin, Thomas. A Personal Perspective on the Ten Hour Movement in New England. *Labor Hist.*, Summer 1983, *24*(3), pp. 398–403. **[G: U.S.]**

Gagnon, Jean Denis. Le Recours a l'Arbitrage dans les Cas de Congediement Injuste (Arbitration of Unjust Dismissals. With English Summary.) **In** *Queen's Univ. Indust. Relat. Centre,* 1983, pp. 76–81. **[G: Canada]**

Grossman, Jean Baldwin. The Impact of the Minimum Wage on Other Wages. *J. Human Res.*, Summer 1983, *18*(3), pp. 359–78. **[G: U.S.]**

Gustman, Alan L. and Steinmeier, Thomas L. Minimum-hours Constraints and Retirement Behavior. *Contemp. Policy Issue,* April 1983, (3), pp. 77–91. **[G: U.S.]**

Haggard, Thomas R. Government Regulation of the Employment Relationship. **In** *Machan, T. R. and Johnson, M. B., eds.*, 1983, pp. 13–41. **[G: U.S.]**

Hirsch, Werner Z. and Rufolo, Anthony M. Effects of Prevailing Wage Laws on Municipal Government Wages. *J. Urban Econ.*, January 1983, *13*(1), pp. 112–26. **[G: U.S.]**

Johnson, William R. and Browning, Edgar K. The Distributional and Efficiency Effects of Increasing the Minimum Wage: A Simulation. *Amer. Econ. Rev.*, March 1983, *73*(1), pp. 204–11. **[G: U.S.]**

Kaufman, Roger T. Nepotism and the Minimum Wage. *J. Lab. Res.*, Winter 1983, *4*(1), pp. 81–89. **[G: U.S.]**

Kessler, Sid. Comparability. *Oxford Bull. Econ. Statist.*, February 1983, *45*(1), pp. 85–104. **[G: U.K.]**

Kjærsgaard, Kaj. Nogle hovedtendenser i arbejdsmarkedspolitikken. (Recent Trends in Danish Labor Market Policy. With English summary.) *Nationaløkon. Tidsskr.*, 1983, *121*(2), pp. 200–214. **[G: Denmark]**

Metzger, Michael R. and Goldfarb, Robert S. Do Davis–Bacon Minimum Wages Raise Product Quality? *J. Lab. Res.*, Summer 1983, *4*(3), pp. 265–72. **[G: U.S.]**

Meyer, Robert H. and Wise, David A. Discontinuous Distributions and Missing Persons: The Minimum Wage and Unemployed Youth. *Econometrica*, November 1983, *51*(6), pp. 1677–98. **[G: U.S.]**

Meyer, Robert H. and Wise, David A. The Effects of the Minimum Wage on the Employment and Earnings of Youth. *J. Lab. Econ.*, January 1983, *1*(1), pp. 66–100. **[G: U.S.]**

Raphaelson, Arnold H. The Davis–Bacon Act. **In** *Zeckhauser, R. J. and Leebaert, D., eds.*, 1983, pp. 124–36. **[G: U.S.]**

Robinson, Derek and Mayhew, Ken. Pay Policies for the Future: Introduction. **In** *Robinson, D. and Mayhew, K., eds.*, 1983, pp. 3–13. **[G: U.K.]**

Rolph, H. P. Notice Requirements, Termination and Severance Pay under Ontario's Employment Standards Act. **In** *Queen's Univ. Indust. Relat. Centre,* 1983, pp. 32–48. **[G: Canada]**

Rottenberg, Simon. National Commissions: Preaching the Garb of Analysis. *Policy Rev.*, Winter 1983, (23), pp. 217–41. **[G: U.S.]**

Schaafsma, Joseph and Walsh, William D. Employment and Labour Supply Effects of the Minimum Wage: Some Pooled Time-Series Estimates from Canadian Provincial Data. *Can. J. Econ.*, February 1983, *16*(1), pp. 86–97. **[G: Canada]**

Sellekaerts, Brigitte and Sellekaerts, Willy. Methods to Index the National Wage Floor: A Choice among Alternatives. *Atlantic Econ. J.*, July 1983, *11*(2), pp. 1–11. **[G: U.S.]**

Sheshinski, Eytan. Wage Policy in the Public Sector and Income Distribution. **In** *Helpman, E.; Razin, A. and Sadka, E., eds.*, 1983, pp. 299–309.

Twine, Fred. The Low Paid. **In** *Brown, G. and Cook, R., eds.*, 1983, pp. 107–35. **[G: U.K.]**

8222 Workmen's Compensation and Vocational Rehabilitation

Asher, Robert. Failure and Fulfillment: Agitation for Employers' Liability Legislation and the Origins of Workmen's Compensation in New York State, 1876–1910. *Labor Hist.*, Spring 1983, *24*(2), pp. 198–222. **[G: U.S.]**

van den Bosch, Frans A. J. and Petersen, Carel. Disability as an Economic Phenomenon: A First Approach to Estimate Hidden Unemployment among Disability Beneficiaries. **In** *Söderström, L., ed.*, 1983, pp. 177–85. **[G: Netherlands; OECD]**

Butler, Richard J. and Worrall, John D. Workers' Compensation: Benefit and Injury Claims Rates in the Seventies. *Rev. Econ. Statist.*, November 1983, *65*(4), pp. 580–89. **[G: U.S.]**

Dillingham, Alan E. The Effect of Labor Force Age Distribution on Workers' Compensation Costs. *J. Risk Ins.*, June 1983, *50*(2), pp. 235–48. **[G: U.S.]**

Edelbalk, Per Gunnar and Elmér, Åke. Social Insurance in Sweden. **In** *Söderström, L., ed.*, 1983, pp. 53–69. **[G: Sweden]**

Haggard, Thomas R. Government Regulation of the Employment Relationship. **In** *Machan, T. R. and Johnson, M. B., eds.*, 1983, pp. 13–41. **[G: U.S.]**

Haveman, Robert H. and Wolfe, Barbara L. Disability and Work Effort: A Probabilistic Choice Analysis of the Labor Supply Decisions of Older Men. **In** *Söderström, L., ed.*, 1983, pp. 187–205. **[G: U.S.; OECD]**

Jensen, Roger C.; Klein, Bruce P. and Sanderson, Lee M. Motion-Related Wrist Disorders Traced to Industries, Occupational Groups. *Mon. Lab. Rev.*, September 1983, *106*(9), pp. 13–16. **[G: U.S.]**

Nowak, Laura. "A Cost Effectiveness Evaluation of the Federal/State Vocational Rehabilitation Program—Using a Comparison Group." *Amer. Econ.*, Spring 1983, *27*(1), pp. 23–29. **[G: U.S.]**

Price, Daniel N. Workers' Compensation: Coverage, Benefits, and Costs, 1980. *Soc. Sec. Bull.*, May

1983, *46*(5), pp. 14–19. [G: U.S.]

Tinsley, LaVerne C. Workers' Compensation in 1982: Significant Legislation Enacted. *Mon. Lab. Rev.*, January 1983, *106*(1), pp. 57–63. [G: U.S.]

Whinston, Michael D. Moral Hazard, Adverse Selection, and the Optimal Provision of Social Insurance. *J. Public Econ.*, October 1983, *22*(1), pp. 49–71.

8223 Factory Act and Safety Legislation

Ahonen, Guy. Arbetarskyddspolitikens innehåll och olycksfallsförsäkringens utformning. (Labour Protection Policy and Industrial Injuries Insurance. With English summary.) *Ekon. Samfundets Tidskr.*, 1983, *36*(4), pp. 151–56. [G: Finland]

Broder, Ivy E. and Morrall, John F., III. The Economic Basis for OSHA's and EPA's Generic Carcinogen Regulations. **In** *Zeckhauser, R. J. and Leebaert, D., eds.*, 1983, pp. 242–54. [G: U.S.]

Brown, Peter G. Improving Equity in the Use of Temporary Workers. **In** *Kasperson, R. E., ed.*, 1983, pp. 291–300. [G: U.S.]

Freedman, Martin and Stagliano, A. J. Worker Protection against Cotton Dust. *Challenge*, July/August 1983, *26*(3), pp. 57–59. [G: U.S.]

Gevers, J. K. M. Worker Participation in Health and Safety in the EEC: The Role of Representative Institutions. *Int. Lab. Rev.*, July–August 1983, *122*(4), pp. 411–28. [G: EEC]

Macon, Janet. Number of Occupational Deaths Remained Essentially Unchanged in 1981. *Mon. Lab. Rev.*, May 1983, *106*(5), pp. 42–44. [G: U.S.]

Majone, Giandomenico. Reforming Standard-Setting. *J. Policy Anal. Manage.*, Winter 1983, *2*(2), pp. 285–90. [G: W. Europe; U.S.S.R.; U.S.; U.K.]

McCaffrey, David P. An Assessment of OSHA's Recent Effects on Injury Rates. *J. Human Res.*, Winter 1983, *18*(1), pp. 131–46. [G: U.S.]

Melville, Mary H. Temporary Workers in the Nuclear Power Industry: Implications for the Waste Management Program. **In** *Kasperson, R. E., ed.*, 1983, pp. 229–58. [G: U.S.]

Morgan, Phillip. The Costs and Benefits of the Power Presses Regulations (1965). *Brit. J. Ind. Relat.*, July 1983, *21*(2), pp. 181–96. [G: U.K.]

Morrissey, Mike. Technological Change and Occupational Health. **In** *Hill, S. and Johnston, R., eds.*, 1983, pp. 137–53. [G: Australia]

Nakanishi, Tamako. Equality or Protection? Protective Legislation for Women in Japan. *Int. Lab. Rev.*, Sept.–Oct. 1983, *122*(5), pp. 609–21. [G: Japan]

Oi, Walter Y. On a Standards Path to the Regulation of Workplace Safety. **In** *Helpman, E.; Razin, A. and Sadka, E., eds.*, 1983, pp. 67–96. [G: U.S.]

Rea, Samuel A., Jr. Regulating Occupational Health and Safety. **In** *Dewees, D. N., ed.*, 1983, pp. 109–40. [G: U.S.; Canada]

Roustang, Guy. Worker Participation in Occupational Safety and Health Matters in France. *Int. Lab. Rev.*, March–April 1983, *122*(2), pp. 169–82. [G: France]

Rowe, W. D. Implicit Equity Considerations in Radiation Protection Standards. **In** *Kasperson, R. E., ed.*, 1983, pp. 259–76. [G: U.S.]

Semenov, A. Workers' Participation in Occupational Safety and Health Matters in the USSR. *Int. Lab. Rev.*, May–June 1983, *122*(3), pp. 355–66. [G: U.S.S.R.]

Sider, Hal. Safety and Productivity in Underground Coal Mining. *Rev. Econ. Statist.*, May 1983, *65*(2), pp. 225–33. [G: U.S.]

Singleton, W. T. Occupational Safety and Health Systems: A Three-Country Comparison. *Int. Lab. Rev.*, March–April 1983, *122*(2), pp. 155–68. [G: Switzerland; U.K.; U.S.]

Smith, J. C. The Processes of Adjudication and Regulation, a Comparison. **In** *Machan, T. R. and Johnson, M. B., eds.*, 1983, pp. 71–96. [G: U.S.]

Tripp, Joseph F. Progressive Jurisprudence in the West: The Washington Supreme Court, Labor Law, and the Problem of Industrial Accidents. *Labor Hist.*, Summer 1983, *24*(3), pp. 342–65. [G: U.S.]

Worrall, John D. and Butler, Richard J. Health Conditions and Job Hazards: Union and Nonunion Jobs. *J. Lab. Res.*, Fall 1983, *4*(4), pp. 339–47. [G: U.S.]

8224 Unemployment Insurance

Albeck, Hermann. Reassessing the Cost of Social Insurance Programs: Comment. **In** *Giersch, H., ed.*, 1983, pp. 163–71. [G: W. Germany]

Atkinson, Anthony B. Unemployment Benefits and Incentives in Britain. **In** *Atkinson, A. B.*, 1983, pp. 419–35. [G: U.K.]

Atkinson, Anthony B., et al. Durée du chômage et incitations: Résultats d'une enquête sur les dépenses des ménages au Royaume-Uni. (Unemployment Duration and Incentives: Evidence from the Family Expenditure Survey in the United Kingdom. With English summary.) *Ann. INSEE*, October–December 1983, (52), pp. 3–21. [G: U.K.]

Beach, Charles M. and Kaliski, Steve F. The Impact of the 1979 Unemployment Insurance Amendments. *Can. Public Policy*, June 1983, *9*(2), pp. 164–73. [G: Canada]

Becker, Joseph M. National Commission on Unemployment Compensation: A Critique. *Int. J. Soc. Econ.*, 1983, *10*(6/7), pp. 29–44. [G: U.S.]

Benham, Harry C. Unemployment Insurance Incentives and Unemployment Duration Distributions. *Rev. Econ. Statist.*, February 1983, *65*(1), pp. 139–43. [G: U.S.]

Benham, Harry C. UI Effects on Unemployment: Some Data on Competing Theories. *Ind. Relat.*, Fall 1983, *22*(3), pp. 403–09. [G: U.S.]

Boadway, Robin W. and Oswald, Andrew J. Unemployment Insurance and Redistributive Taxation. *J. Public Econ.*, March 1983, *20*(2), pp. 193–210.

Burdett, Kenneth and Hool, Bryce. Layoffs, Wages and Unemployment Insurance. *J. Public Econ.*, August 1983, *21*(3), pp. 325–57.

Burtless, Gary T. Why Is Insured Unemployment So Low? *Brookings Pap. Econ. Act.*, 1983, (1), pp. 225–49. [G: U.S.]

Coates, Mary Lou. Human Resources and Labour Markets: Summary Outline. **In** *Wood, W. D. and*

Kumar, P., eds., 1983, pp. 31–83. **[G: Canada; OECD]**

Decoster, André and Vleminckx, Anne. De financiële situatie van werklozen. (With English summary.) *Cah. Écon. Bruxelles,* 1983, *98*(2), pp. 167–93. **[G: Belgium]**

Dilnot, A. W. and Morris, Carl N. Private Costs and Benefits of Unemployment: Measuring Replacement Rates. *Oxford Econ. Pap.*, Supplement November 1983, *35*, pp. 321–40. **[G: U.K.]**

Edelbalk, Per Gunnar and Elmér, Åke. Social Insurance in Sweden. **In** *Söderström, L., ed.*, 1983, pp. 53–69. **[G: Sweden]**

Gordon, Robert J. Unemployment and Insurance: A Comment. *Carnegie-Rochester Conf. Ser. Public Policy,* Autumn 1983, *19*, pp. 51–60. **[G: U.S.]**

Harrison, Alan J. and Hart, Robert A. Unemployment Benefits and Labor Supply: A Note [The Effects of Unemployment Benefits on U.S. Unemployment Rates]. *Weltwirtsch. Arch.*, 1983, *119*(1), pp. 169–72. **[G: U.S.]**

Hatton, T. J. Unemployment Benefits and the Macroeconomics of the Interwar Labour Market: A Further Analysis. *Oxford Econ. Pap.*, November 1983, *35*(3), pp. 486–505. **[G: U.K.]**

Hughes, Gerard and Walsh, Brendan M. Unemployment Duration, Aggregate Demand and Unemployment Insurance: A Study of Irish Live Register Survival Probabilities, 1967–1978. *Econ. Soc. Rev.*, January 1983, *14*(2), pp. 93–117. **[G: Ireland]**

Johnson, Janet L. Unemployment as a Household Labor Supply Decision. *Quart. Rev. Econ. Bus.*, Summer 1983, *23*(2), pp. 71–88. **[G: U.S.]**

Jovanovic, Boyan. A Welfare Analysis of Unemployment Insurance: Variations on Second-Best Themes: A Comment. *Carnegie-Rochester Conf. Ser. Public Policy,* Autumn 1983, *19*, pp. 99–102.

Lampman, Robert J. How Has the Labor Supply Changed in Response to Recent Increases in Social Welfare Expenditures and the Taxes to Pay for Them? **In** *Barbash, J., et al., eds.*, 1983, pp. 61–85. **[G: U.S.]**

Lynch, Lisa M. Job Search and Youth Unemployment. *Oxford Econ. Pap.*, Supplement November 1983, *35*, pp. 271–82. **[G: U.K.]**

Minford, Patrick. Labour Market Equilibrium in an Open Economy. *Oxford Econ. Pap.*, Supplement November 1983, *35*, pp. 207–44. **[G: U.K.]**

Mortensen, Dale T. A Welfare Analysis of Unemployment Insurance: Variations on Second-Best Themes. *Carnegie-Rochester Conf. Ser. Public Policy,* Autumn 1983, *19*, pp. 67–97.

O'Mahony, Donal P. A Study of Replacement Ratios among a Sample of Unemployed Workers. *Econ. Soc. Rev.*, January 1983, *14*(2), pp. 77–91. **[G: Ireland]**

Pal, Leslie A. The Fall and Rise of Developmental Uses of UI Funds. *Can. Public Policy,* March 1983, *9*(1), pp. 81–93. **[G: Canada]**

Pedersen, Peder J. Inflationary Effects of Unemployment Insurance—An International Survey. **In** *Söderström, L., ed.*, 1983, pp. 225–49. **[G: OECD]**

Pissarides, Christopher A. Efficiency Aspects of the Financing of Unemployment Insurance and Other Government Expenditure. *Rev. Econ. Stud.*, January 1983, *50*(1), pp. 57–69.

Price, Daniel N. 1981 and 1982 Changes in the Unemployment Insurance Program. *Soc. Sec. Bull.*, May 1983, *46*(5), pp. 10–14. **[G: U.S.]**

Rosen, Sherwin. Unemployment and Insurance: Reply to Robert Gordon. *Carnegie-Rochester Conf. Ser. Public Policy,* Autumn 1983, *19*, pp. 61–66. **[G: U.S.]**

Rosen, Sherwin. Unemployment and Insurance. *Carnegie-Rochester Conf. Ser. Public Policy,* Autumn 1983, *19*, pp. 5–49. **[G: U.S.]**

Rosenberg, Sam. Reagan Social Policy and Labour Force Restructuring. *Cambridge J. Econ.*, June 1983, *7*(2), pp. 179–96. **[G: U.S.]**

Runner, Diana. Unemployment Insurance Laws: Legislative Revisions in 1982. *Mon. Lab. Rev.*, January 1983, *106*(1), pp. 38–43. **[G: U.S.]**

Saffer, Henry. The Effects of Unemployment Insurance on Temporary and Permanent Layoffs. *Rev. Econ. Statist.*, November 1983, *65*(4), pp. 647–52. **[G: U.S.]**

Saks, Daniel H. Jobs and Training. **In** *Pechman, J. A., ed.*, 1983, pp. 145–72. **[G: U.S.]**

Seehan, Peter J. and Stricker, Peter P. Welfare Benefits and the Labour Market. **In** *Blandy, R. and Covick, O., eds.*, 1983, pp. 200–221. **[G: Australia]**

Stein, Leslie. General Measures to Assist Workers and Firms in Adjusting to Injury from Freer Trade: Issues Raised by Various European Approaches and Some ad hoc Industry Measures Adopted Elsewhere. *Amer. J. Econ. Soc.*, July 1983, *42*(3), pp. 315–27. **[G: W. Europe; Canada; U.S.; Australia]**

Summers, Lawrence H. Why Is Insured Unemployment So Low? Comments and Discussion. *Brookings Pap. Econ. Act.*, 1983, (1), pp. 250–53. **[G: U.S.]**

Tannery, Frederick J. Search Effort and Unemployment Insurance Reconsidered. *J. Human Res.*, Summer 1983, *18*(3), pp. 432–40. **[G: U.S.]**

Topel, Robert H. On Layoffs and Unemployment Insurance. *Amer. Econ. Rev.*, September 1983, *73*(4), pp. 541–59. **[G: U.S.]**

Trinder, Chris. Income in Work and When Unemployed: Some Problems in Calculating Replacement Ratios. *Nat. Inst. Econ. Rev.*, February 1983, (103), pp. 56–61. **[G: U.K.]**

Walsh, Brendan M. Unemployment and the Labour Market in Ireland. *Econ. Soc. Rev.*, January 1983, *14*(2), pp. 73–76. **[G: Ireland]**

8225 Government Employment Policies (including Employment Services)

Adams, Charles F., Jr.; Cook, Robert F. and Maurice, Arthur J. A Pooled Time-Series Analysis of the Job-Creation Impact of Public Service Employment Grants to Large Cities. *J. Human Res.*, Spring 1983, *18*(2), pp. 283–94. **[G: U.S.]**

Arestis, P. and Driver, Ciaran. U.K. Unemployment and Post-Keynesian Remedies. *Metroecon.*, October 1983, *35*(3), pp. 275–91. **[G: U.K.]**

Barker, Michael. State Employment Policy in Hard Times: Introduction. **In** *Barker, M., ed. (II)*, 1983, pp. xi–xxix. [G: U.S.]

Bovard, James. Busy Doing Nothing: The Story of Government Job Creation. *Policy Rev.*, Spring 1983, (24), pp. 87–102. [G: U.S.]

Briggs, Vernon M., Jr. Foreign Labor Programs as an Alternative to Illegal Immigration: A Dissenting View. **In** *Brown, P. G. and Shue, H., eds.*, 1983, pp. 223–45. [G: Mexico; U.S.]

Buck, Trevor and Atkins, Martin. Regional Policies in Retrospect: An Application of Analysis and Variance. *Reg. Stud.*, June 1983, *17*(3), pp. 181–89. [G: U.K.]

Dodge, David. Labour Market Policy Concerns: An Evaluation of Current Federal Policies and Priorities. **In** *Queen's Univ. Indust. Relat. Centre and John Deutsch Mem.*, 1983, pp. 135–43. [G: Canada]

Doyle, Peter S. Labour Market Policy Concerns: An Evaluation of Current Federal Policies and Priorities: Comment. **In** *Queen's Univ. Indust. Relat. Centre and John Deutsch Mem.*, 1983, pp. 148–50. [G: Canada]

Ford, Ramona L. Revitalizing the Distressed Community: GSOC and ESOP Alternatives to Enterprise Zones. *Growth Change*, October 1983, *14*(4), pp. 22–31. [G: U.S.]

Fremont-Smith, Lee Bowes. Employment Demonstrations: A Strategy for Policy Formulation. **In** *Goldstein, R. and Sachs, S. M., eds.*, 1983, pp. 260–68. [G: U.S.]

Gordon, David M. The Working Poor towards a State Agenda. **In** *Barker, M., ed. (II)*, 1983, pp. 1–91. [G: U.S.]

Guttman, Robert. Job Training Partnership Act: New Help for the Unemployed. *Mon. Lab. Rev.*, March 1983, *106*(3), pp. 3–10. [G: U.S.]

Guzda, Henry P. The U.S. Employment Service at 50: It Too Had to Wait Its Turn. *Mon. Lab. Rev.*, June 1983, *106*(6), pp. 12–19. [G: U.S.]

Herring, Ronald J. and Edwards, Rex M. Guaranteeing Employment to the Rural Poor: Social Functions and Class Interests in the Employment Guarantee Scheme in Western India. *World Devel.*, July 1983, *11*(7), pp. 575–92. [G: India]

de Jong, H. W. and Spierenburg, Robert Jan. The Netherlands: Maintenance of Employment as a Primary Objective. **In** *Hindley, B., ed.*, 1983, pp. 59–95. [G: Netherlands]

Lang, Ron. Labour Market Policy Concerns: An Evaluation of Current Federal Policies and Priorities: Comment. **In** *Queen's Univ. Indust. Relat. Centre and John Deutsch Mem.*, 1983, pp. 143–45. [G: Canada]

Layard, Richard and Nickell, S. J. Marginal Employment Subsidies Again: A Brief Response to Whitely and Wilson. *Econ. J.*, December 1983, *93*(372), pp. 881–82.

Nathan, Richard P. Research Issues in the Evaluation of Broad-gauged and Multipurpose Grants-in-Aid. **In** *Break, G. F., ed.*, 1983, pp. 93–105. [G: U.S.]

Perles, Susan P. Impact of CETA-PSE on Local Public Sector Employment Expenditures. **In** *Hirsch, W. Z., ed.*, 1983, pp. 122–57. [G: U.S.]

Pola, Giorgio and Brosio, Giancarlo. The Role of Public Employment in a Dualistic Economy: The Italian Case. *Econ. Notes*, 1983, (1), pp. 80–97. [G: Italy]

Posner, Richard A. Economic Justice and the Economist. **In** *Letwin, W., ed.*, 1983, *1973*, pp. 345–59. [G: U.S.]

Raffa, Frederick A. and Haulman, Clyde A. The Impact of a PSE Program on Employment and Participants. *Growth Change*, October 1983, *14*(4), pp. 14–21. [G: U.S.]

Richardson, J. David. Worker Adjustment to U.S. International Trade: Programs and Prospects. **In** *Cline W. R., ed.*, 1983, pp. 393–424. [G: U.S.]

Rist, Ray C. Beyond the Quantitative Cul-de-Sac: A Qualitative Perspective on Youth Employment Programs. **In** *Goldstein, R. and Sachs, S. M., eds.*, 1983, pp. 123–37. [G: U.S.]

Ruane, Frances P. Government Financial and Tax Incentives and Industrial Employment. *Irish Banking Rev.*, June 1983, pp. 20–28. [G: Ireland]

Sautter, Udo. North American Government Labor Agencies before World War One: A Cure for Unemployment? *Labor Hist.*, Summer 1983, *24*(3), pp. 366–93. [G: Canada; U.S.]

Slater, David W. Employment Policies in the 1980s: An International Perspective. **In** *Queen's Univ. Indust. Relat. Centre and John Deutsch Mem.*, 1983, pp. 186–91. [G: OECD]

Whitley, J. D. and Wilson, Robert A. The Macroeconomic Merits of a Marginal Employment Subsidy. *Econ. J.*, December 1983, *93*(372), pp. 862–80.

Wolfson, Alan. Labour Market Policy Concerns: An Evaluation of Current Federal Policies and Priorities: Comment. **In** *Queen's Univ. Indust. Relat. Centre and John Deutsch Mem.*, 1983, pp. 145–47. [G: Canada]

Wulwick, Nancy J. Can Keynesian Economics Be Scientific? An Historical Reconstruction. *Eastern Econ. J.*, July–September 1983, *9*(3), pp. 190–204. [G: U.K.]

8226 Employment in the Public Sector

Aaron, Henry J. Orange Light for the Competitive Model [Stability in the Federal Employees Health Benefits Program]. *J. Health Econ.*, December 1983, *2*(3), pp. 281–84. [G: U.S.]

Adams, Charles F., Jr.; Cook, Robert F. and Maurice, Arthur J. A Pooled Time-Series Analysis of the Job-Creation Impact of Public Service Employment Grants to Large Cities. *J. Human Res.*, Spring 1983, *18*(2), pp. 283–94. [G: U.S.]

Aitkin, D. A. Where Does Australia Stand? **In** *Withers, G., ed.*, 1983, pp. 13–31. [G: OECD; Australia]

Cappelli, Peter. Comparability and the British Civil Service. *Brit. J. Ind. Relat.*, March 1983, *21*(1), pp. 33–45. [G: U.K.]

Frey, Luigi. Census Developments and Labour Market Analyses. *Rev. Econ. Cond. Italy,* June 1983, (2), pp. 223–47. [G: Italy]

Grosskopf, Shawna P.; Hayes, Kathy and Sivan, David. Municipal Pensions, Funding and Wage Capitalization. *Nat. Tax J.*, March, 1983, *36*(1), pp. 115–21. [G: U.S.]

Hartley, Keith and Lynk, Edward L. Budget Cuts and Public Sector Employment: The Case of Defence. *Appl. Econ.*, August 1983, *15*(4), pp. 531–40. [G: U.K.]

Hirsch, Werner Z.; Rufolo, Anthony M. and Mengle, David L. Recent Trends in Municipal Labor Market Research. **In** *Hirsch, W. Z., ed.*, 1983, pp. 13–58. **[G: U.S.]**

Kessler, Sid. Pay Policies for the Future: Comparability. **In** *Robinson, D. and Mayhew, K., eds.*, 1983, pp. 85–104. **[G: U.K.]**

Killingsworth, Mark R. and Reimers, Cordelia W. Race, Ranking, Promotions, and Pay at a Federal Facility: A Logit Analysis. *Ind. Lab. Relat. Rev.*, October 1983, *37*(1), pp. 92–107. **[G: U.S.]**

Lewin, David and Katz, Harry C. Payment Determination in Municipal Building Departments under Unionism and Civil Service. **In** *Hirsch, W. Z., ed.*, 1983, pp. 90–121. **[G: U.S.]**

Perles, Susan P. Impact of CETA-PSE on Local Public Sector Employment Expenditures. **In** *Hirsch, W. Z., ed.*, 1983, pp. 122–57. **[G: U.S.]**

Perry, Huey L. The Impact of Black Political Participation on Public Sector Employment and Representation on Municipal Boards and Commissions. *Rev. Black Polit. Econ.*, Winter 1983, *12*(2), pp. 203–17. **[G: U.S.]**

Price, James R.; Mays, James W. and Trapnell, Gordon R. Stability in the Federal Employees Health Benefits Program. *J. Health Econ.*, December 1983, *2*(3), pp. 207–23. **[G: U.S.]**

Ricciuti, James R. Federal Personnel Cuts: A Blessing Still Disguised. *J. Policy Anal. Manage.*, Spring 1983, *2*(3), pp. 457–61. **[G: U.S.]**

Robinson, Derek. Pay Policies for the Future: Indirect and Partial Measures. **In** *Robinson, D. and Mayhew, K., eds.*, 1983, pp. 105–25. **[G: U.K.]**

Rosenberg, Sam. Reagan Social Policy and Labour Force Restructuring. *Cambridge J. Econ.*, June 1983, *7*(2), pp. 179–96. **[G: U.S.]**

Saks, Daniel H. Jobs and Training. **In** *Pechman, J. A., ed.*, 1983, pp. 145–72. **[G: U.S.]**

Saltzstein, Grace Hall. Personnel Directors and Female Employment Representation: A New Addition to Models of Equal Employment Opportunity Policy? *Soc. Sci. Quart.*, December 1983, *64*(4), pp. 734–46. **[G: U.S.]**

Stretton, Hugh. Where Does Australia Stand? Discussion. **In** *Withers, G., ed.*, 1983, pp. 32–36.

823 Labor Mobility; National and International Migration

8230 Labor Mobility; National and International Migration

Althaus, Paul G. and Schachter, Joseph. Interstate Migration and the New Federalism. *Soc. Sci. Quart.*, March 1983, *64*(1), pp. 35–45. **[G: U.S.]**

Amano, Masanori. On the Harris–Todaro Model with Intersectoral Migration of Labour. *Economica*, August 1983, *50*(199), pp. 311–23. **[G: LDCs]**

Arizpe, Lourdes. The Rural Exodus in Mexico and Mexican Migration to the United States. **In** *Brown, P. G. and Shue, H., eds.*, 1983, pp. 162–83. **[G: Mexico; U.S.]**

Arroyo, Jesús and Velázquez, Luis A. Internal Migration and the Formation of Labour Markets in Mexico. **In** *Urquidi, V. L. and Reyes, S. T., eds.*, 1983, pp. 91–107. **[G: Mexico]**

Balán, Jorge. Agrarian Structures and Internal Migration in a Historical Perspective: Latin American Case Studies. **In** *Morrison, P. A., ed.*, 1983, pp. 151–85. **[G: Latin America]**

Banerjee, Biswajit. The Role of the Informal Sector in the Migration Process: A Test of Probabilistic Migration Models and Labour Market Segmentation for India. *Oxford Econ. Pap.*, November 1983, *35*(3), pp. 399–422. **[G: India]**

Bhagwati, Jagdish N. International Migration of the Highly Skilled: Economics, Ethics and Taxes. **In** *Bhagwati, J. N., Vol. 2*, 1983, *1979*, pp. 57–71.

Bhagwati, Jagdish N. The Economic Analysis of International Migration. **In** *Bhagwati, J. N., Vol. 2*, 1983, pp. 44–56.

Bhagwati, Jagdish N. and Hamada, Koichi. Tax Policy in the Presence of Emigration. **In** *Bhagwati, J. N., Vol. 2*, 1983, *1982*, pp. 169–95.

Bhagwati, Jagdish N. and Hamada, Koichi. The Brain Drain, International Integration of Markets for Professionals and Unemployment: A Theoretical Analysis. **In** *Bhagwati, J. N., Vol. 2*, 1983, *1974*, pp. 103–26.

Bhagwati, Jagdish N. and Rodriguez, Carlos. Welfare-Theoretical Analyses of the Brain Drain. **In** *Bhagwati, J. N., Vol. 2*, 1983, *1975*, pp. 75–102.

Bhagwati, Jagdish N. and Srinivasan, T. N. On the Choice between Capital and Labour Mobility. **In** *Bhagwati, J. N., Vol. 2*, 1983, pp. 31–43.

Bhagwati, Jagdish N. and Srinivasan, T. N. On Reanalyzing the Harris–Todaro Model: Policy Rankings in the Case of Sector-specific Sticky Wages. **In** *Bhagwati, J. N., Vol. 1*, 1983, *1974*, pp. 498–504.

Bhatia, Kul B. Rural–Urban Migration and Surplus Labour: Rejoinder to Stark. *Oxford Econ. Pap.*, March 1983, *35*(1), pp. 143–45.

Blecher, Marc. Peasant Labour for Urban Industry: Temporary Contract Labour, Urban–Rural Balance and Class Relations in a Chinese County. *World Devel.*, August 1983, *11*(8), pp. 731–45. **[G: China]**

Böhning, W. R. Guestworker Employment in Selected European Countries—Lessons for the United States? **In** *Brown, P. G. and Shue, H., eds.*, 1983, pp. 99–138. **[G: France; Switzerland; U.S.; W. Germany]**

Bose, Ashish. Migration in India: Trends and Policies. **In** *Oberai, A. S., ed.*, 1983, pp. 137–82. **[G: India]**

Briggs, Vernon M., Jr. Foreign Labor Programs as an Alternative to Illegal Immigration: A Dissenting View. **In** *Brown, P. G. and Shue, H., eds.*, 1983, pp. 223–45. **[G: Mexico; U.S.]**

Briggs, Vernon M., Jr. Non-Immigrant Labor Policy in the United States. *J. Econ. Issues*, September 1983, *17*(3), pp. 609–30. **[G: U.S.]**

Bustamante, Jorge A. Mexican Migration: The Political Dynamic of Perceptions. **In** *Reynolds, C. W. and Tello, C., eds.*, 1983, pp. 259–76. **[G: U.S.; Mexico]**

Chiswick, Barry R. Illegal Aliens in the United States Labour Market. **In** *Weisbrod, B. and Hughes, H., eds.*, 1983, pp. 346–67. **[G: U.S.]**

Clark, M. Gardner. The Swiss Experience with Foreign Workers: Lessons for the United States. *Ind. Lab. Relat. Rev.*, July 1983, *36*(4), pp. 606–23. **[G: Switzerland; U.S.]**

Coeymans, Juan Eduardo. Determinantes de la migracion rural–urbana en chile, segun origen y destino. (With English summary.) *Cuadernos Econ.*, April 1983, *20*(59), pp. 43–64. [G: Chile]

Collins, Doreen. The Impact of Social Policy in the United Kingdom. **In** *El-Agraa, A. M., ed.*, 1983, pp. 213–33. [G: EEC; U.K.]

Cymrot, Donald J. Migration Trends and Earnings of Free Agents in Major League Baseball, 1976–1979. *Econ. Inquiry*, October 1983, *21*(4), pp. 545–56. [G: U.S.]

DaVanzo, Julie. Repeat Migration in the United States: Who Moves Back and Who Moves On? *Rev. Econ. Statist.*, November 1983, *65*(4), pp. 552–59. [G: U.S.]

Davila, Alberto E. Economic Determinants of Illegal Mexican Immigration to the U.S. *Fed. Res. Bank Dallas Econ. Rev.*, May 1983, pp. 13–23. [G: U.S.]

Devoretz, Don and Maki, Dennis R. The Immigration of Third World Professionals to Canada: 1968–1973. *World Devel.*, January 1983, *11*(1), pp. 55–64. [G: Selected LDCs; Canada]

Dinopoulos, Elias. Import Competition, International Factor Mobility and Lobbying Responses: The Schumpeterian Industry Case. *J. Int. Econ.*, May 1983, *14*(3/4), pp. 395–410.

Dixon, Marlene; Jonas, Susanne and McCaughan, Ed. Changes in the International Division of Labor and Low-Wage Labor in the United States. **In** *Bergesen, A., ed.*, 1983, pp. 173–92. [G: U.S.]

Dunlevy, James A. and Bellante, Don. Net Migration, Endogenous Incomes and the Speed of Adjustment to the North-South Differential. *Rev. Econ. Statist.*, February 1983, *65*(1), pp. 66–75. [G: U.S.]

Ecevit, Zafer H. Labour Imports/Exports for Economic Development: The Middle East Experience. **In** *Weisbrod, B. and Hughes, H., eds.*, 1983, pp. 331–45. [G: Middle East]

Engerman, Stanley L. Contract Labor, Sugar, and Technology in the Nineteenth Century. *J. Econ. Hist.*, September 1983, *43*(3), pp. 635–59. [G: Europe; U.S.]

Farber, Stephen C. Post-Migration Earnings Profiles: An Application of Human Capital and Job Search Models. *Southern Econ. J.*, January 1983, *49*(3), pp. 693–705. [G: U.S.]

García y Griego, Manuel. Comments [Mexican Migration: The Political Dynamic Perceptions] [The Problems of Planning for the Expected: Demographic Shocks and Policy Paralysis]. **In** *Reynolds, C. W. and Tello, C., eds.*, 1983, pp. 299–314. [G: U.S.; Mexico]

García y Griego, Manuel. The Importation of Mexican Contract Laborers to the United States, 1942–1964: Antecedents, Operation, and Legacy. **In** *Brown, P. G. and Shue, H., eds.*, 1983, pp. 49–98. [G: Mexico; U.S.]

Gerking, Shelby D. and Mutti, John H. Factor Rewards and the International Migration of Unskilled Labor: A Model with Capital Mobility. *J. Int. Econ.*, May 1983, *14*(3/4), pp. 367–80.

Ghai, Dharam and Radwan, Samir. Growth and Inequality: Rural Development in Malawi, 1964–78. **In** *Ghai, D. and Radwan, S., eds.*, 1983, pp. 71–97. [G: Malawi]

Godfrey, Martin. Surplus Labour as a Source of Foreign Exchange? *World Devel.*, November 1983, *11*(11), pp. 945–56. [G: LDCs]

Grant, E. Kenneth and Vanderkamp, John. Regional Demand–Supply Projections and Migration. **In** *Queen's Univ. Indust. Relat. Centre and John Deutsch Mem.*, 1983, pp. 112–27. [G: Canada]

Graves, Philip E. Migration with a Composite Amenity: The Role of Rents. *J. Reg. Sci.*, November 1983, *23*(4), pp. 541–46. [G: U.S.]

Greenwood, Michael J. Leading Issues of Fact and Theory. *Amer. Econ. Rev.*, May 1983, *73*(2), pp. 173–77. [G: U.S.]

Hamada, Koichi and Bhagwati, Jagdish N. Domestic Distortions, Imperfect Information and the Brain Drain. **In** *Bhagwati, J. N., Vol. 2*, 1983, *1976*, pp. 127–41.

Herzog, Henry W., Jr. and Schlottmann, Alan M. Migrant Information, Job Search and the Remigration Decision. *Southern Econ. J.*, July 1983, *50*(1), pp. 43–56. [G: U.S.]

Herzog, Henry W., Jr.; Schlottmann, Alan M. and Schriver, William R. Regional Planning and Interstate Construction Worker Migration. *Growth Change*, April 1983, *14*(2), pp. 50–54. [G: U.S.]

Horiba, Yukata and Kirkpatrick, Rickey C. U.S. North-South Labor Migration and Trade. *J. Reg. Sci.*, February 1983, *23*(1), pp. 93–103. [G: U.S.]

Hughes, Helen. The International Economy and Employment: Introduction. **In** *Weisbrod, B. and Hughes, H., eds.*, 1983, pp. 319–28.

Hugo, Graeme J. Interstate Migration in Australia, 1976–1981. *Australian Bull. Lab.*, March 1983, *9*(2), pp. 102–30. [G: Australia]

Indraratna, A. D. V. de S., et al. Migration-related Policies: A Study of the Sri Lanka Experience. **In** *Oberai, A. S., ed.*, 1983, pp. 79–135. [G: Sri Lanka]

Islam, Muhammed N. The Efficiency of Interprovincial Migration in Canada, 1961–1978. *Reg. Sci. Urban Econ.*, May 1983, *13*(2), pp. 231–49. [G: Canada]

Jacoby, Sanford M. Industrial Labor Mobility in Historical Perspective. *Ind. Relat.*, Spring 1983, *22*(2), pp. 261–82. [G: U.S.]

Jones, Philip. Guestworkers and Their Spatial Distribution. **In** *Wild, T., ed.*, 1983, pp. 71–107. [G: W. Germany]

Kikuchi, Masao and Hayami, Yujiro. New Rice Technology, Intrarural Migration, and Institutional Innovation in the Philippines. *Population Devel. Rev.*, June 1983, *9*(2), pp. 247–57. [G: Philippines]

Kim, Joochul. Factors Affecting Urban-to-Rural Migration. *Growth Change*, July 1983, *14*(3), pp. 38–43. [G: U.S.]

Krumm, Ronald J. Regional Labor Markets and the Household Migration Decision. *J. Reg. Sci.*, August 1983, *23*(3), pp. 361–76. [G: U.S.]

Krumm, Ronald J. Regional Wage Differentials, Fluctuations in Labor Demand, and Migration. *Int. Reg. Sci. Rev.*, June 1983, *8*(1), pp. 23–45.

Laskin, John B. Personal Mobility in the United States and the EEC. **In** *Trebilcock, M. J., et al., eds.*, 1983, pp. 456–98. [G: U.S.; EEC; Canada]

Leinbach, Thomas R. Rural Transport and Population Mobility in Indonesia. *J. Devel. Areas*, April 1983, *17*(3), pp. 349–63. [G: Indonesia]

Lichtenberg, Judith. Mexican Migration and U.S. Policy: A Guide for the Perplexed. In *Brown, P. G. and Shue, H., eds.*, 1983, pp. 13–30. [G: Mexico; U.S.]

Linneman, Peter and Graves, Philip E. Migration and Job Change: A Multinomial Logit Approach. *J. Urban Econ.*, November 1983, *14*(3), pp. 263–79. [G: U.S.]

Lundahl, Mats. A Note on Haitian Migration to Cuba, 1890–1934. In *Lundahl, M.*, 1983, *1982*, pp. 94–110. [G: Cuba; Haiti]

Lundahl, Mats and Vargas, Rosemary. Haitian Migration to the Dominican Republic. In *Lundahl, M.*, 1983, pp. 111–150. [G: Dominican Republic; Haiti]

Marshall, Adriana and Orlansky, Dora. Inmigración de países limítrofes y demanda de mano de obra en la Argentina, 1940–1980. (With English summary.) *Desarrollo Econ.*, April-June 1983, *23*(89), pp. 35–58. [G: Argentina]

Martin, Jack K. and Lichter, Daniel T. Geographic Mobility and Satisfaction with Life and Work. *Soc. Sci. Quart.*, September 1983, *64*(3), pp. 524–35. [G: U.S.]

Mayes, David G. EC Trade Effects and Factor Mobility. In *El-Agraa, A. M., ed.*, 1983, pp. 88–121. [G: EEC; U.K.]

Mazumdar, Dipak. The Rural–Urban Wage Gap Migration and the Working of Urban Labor Market: An Interpretation Based on a Study of the Workers of Bombay City. *Indian Econ. Rev.*, July–December 1983, *18*(2), pp. 169–98. [G: India]

Menadue, J. L. Immigration and Australia's Development: With Particular Reference to the Labour Market. *Australian Bull. Lab.*, March 1983, *9*(2), pp. 93–101. [G: Australia]

Mutti, John H. and Gerking, Shelby D. Changes in Income Distribution and Welfare from Greater Immigration of Unskilled Workers. *Europ. Econ. Rev.*, September 1983, *23*(1), pp. 103–16.

Nickel, James W. Human Rights and the Rights of Aliens. In *Brown, P. G. and Shue, H., eds.*, 1983, pp. 31–45. [G: Mexico; U.S.]

Ortega, P. A. Reyes; Barrera, S. Zúñiga and Adalid, J. M. Anchondo. Interstate Population Expulsion and Policies for Its Reorientation in Mexico: A Preliminary Study. In *Urquidi, V. L. and Reyes, S. T., eds.*, 1983, pp. 79–90. [G: Mexico]

Osberg, Lars. Regional Demand–Supply Projections and Migration: Comment. In *Queen's Univ. Indust. Relat. Centre and John Deutsch Mem.*, 1983, pp. 128–31. [G: Canada]

Papademetriou, Demetrios G. United States Immigration Policy at the Crossroads. In *Piper, D. C. and Terchek, R. J., eds.*, 1983, pp. 97–117. [G: U.S.]

Pérez-Sainz, J. P. Transmigration and Accumulation in Indonesia. In *Oberai, A. S., ed.*, 1983, pp. 183–250. [G: Indonesia]

Ranney, Susan and Kossoudji, Sherrie. Profiles of Temporary Mexican Labor Migrants to the United States. *Population Devel. Rev.*, September 1983, *9*(3), pp. 475–93. [G: U.S.; Mexico]

Reubens, Edwin P. Immigration Problems, Limited-Visa Programs, and Other Options. In *Brown, P. G. and Shue, H., eds.*, 1983, pp. 187–222. [G: Mexico; U.S.]

Reubens, Edwin P. International Migration Models and Policies. *Amer. Econ. Rev.*, May 1983, *73*(2), pp. 178–82.

Reynolds, Clark W. Mexican–U.S. Interdependence: Economic and Social Perspectives. In *Reynolds, C. W. and Tello, C., eds.*, 1983, pp. 21–45. [G: Mexico; U.S.]

Ribe, Helena. The Relative Economic Position of Migrants and Natives in Colombia: An Economic Analysis of the 1973 Census Sample. In *Urquidi, V. L. and Reyes, S. T., eds.*, 1983, pp. 55–78. [G: Colombia]

Richards, Alan and Martin, Philip L. The Laissez–Faire Approach to International Labor Migration: The Case of the Arab Middle East. *Econ. Develop. Cult. Change*, April 1983, *31*(3), pp. 455–74. [G: Middle East]

Rivera-Batiz, Francisco L. The Economics of the "To and Fro" Migrant: Some Welfare-Theoretical Considerations. *Scand. J. Econ.*, 1983, *85*(3), pp. 403–13.

Sanderson, Warren C. The Problems of Planning for the Expected: Demographic Shocks and Policy Paralysis. In *Reynolds, C. W. and Tello, C., eds.*, 1983, pp. 277–98. [G: U.S.; Mexico]

Sapir, André. Foreign Competition, Immigration and Structural Adjustment. *J. Int. Econ.*, May 1983, *14*(3/4), pp. 381–94.

Savey, Suzane. Organization of Production and the New Spatial Division of Labour in France. In *Hamilton, F. E. I. and Linge, G. J. R., eds.*, 1983, pp. 103–20. [G: France]

Silvers, Arthur L. and Crosson, Pierre. Urban Bound Migration and Rural Investment: The Case of Mexico. *J. Reg. Sci.*, February 1983, *23*(1), pp. 33–47. [G: Mexico]

Simmons, Alan B. A Review and Evaluation of Attempts to Constrain Migration to Selected Urban Centres and Regions. In *Todaro, M. P., ed.*, 1983, *1981*, pp. 213–33. [G: Selected Countries]

Soon, Lee-Ying. Migrant-Native Socio-economic Differences in a Major Metropolitan Area of Peninsular Malaysia: Its Implications on Migration Policy in a Multi-ethnic Society. In *Lim, D., ed.*, 1983, *1978*, pp. 140–50. [G: Malaysia]

Stark, Oded. A Note on Modelling Labour Migration in LDCs. *J. Devel. Stud.*, July 1983, *19*(4), pp. 539–43.

Strachan, A. J. Return Migration to Guyana. *Soc. Econ. Stud.*, September 1983, *32*(3), pp. 121–42. [G: Guyana]

Stretton, Alan. Circular Migration, Segmented Labour Markets and Efficiency: The Building Industry in Manila and Port Moresby. *Int. Lab. Rev.*, Sept.–Oct. 1983, *122*(5), pp. 623–39. [G: Philippines]

Swan, Neil. Regional Demand–Supply Projections and Migration: Comment. In *Queen's Univ. Indust. Relat. Centre and John Deutsch Mem.*, 1983, pp. 132–34. [G: Canada]

Tímár, János and Ehrlich, Eva. Manpower and Industrialisation in Hungary. In *Weisbrod, B. and*

Hughes, H., eds., 1983, pp. 55–73. [G: U.S.; U.K; Japan; Hungary]

Ueda, Kazuo and Hamada, Koichi. Migration, Alternative Tax Regimes and Capital Accumulation. In *Weisbrod, B. and Hughes, H., eds.*, 1983, pp. 368–84.

Voirin, M. Social Security for Migrant Workers in Africa. *Int. Lab. Rev.*, May–June 1983, *122*(3), pp. 329–42. [G: Africa]

Williams, Lynne S. Occupational Mobility in Australia: A Quantitative Approach. *Europ. Econ. Rev.*, January 1983, *20*(1–3), pp. 143–66. [G: Australia]

824 Labor Market Studies, Wages, Employment

8240 General

Adams, Charles F., Jr.; Cook, Robert F. and Maurice, Arthur J. A Pooled Time-Series Analysis of the Job-Creation Impact of Public Service Employment Grants to Large Cities. *J. Human Res.*, Spring 1983, *18*(2), pp. 283–94. [G: U.S.]

Baily, Martin Neil. The Labor Market in the 1930's. In *Tobin, J., ed.*, 1983, pp. 21–61. [G: U.S.]

Ball, R. M. Spatial and Structural Characteristics of Recent Unemployment Change: Some Policy Considerations. *Reg. Stud.*, April 1983, *17*(2), pp. 135–40. [G: U.K.]

Banerjee, Biswajit. The Role of the Informal Sector in the Migration Process: A Test of Probabilistic Migration Models and Labour Market Segmentation for India. *Oxford Econ. Pap.*, November 1983, *35*(3), pp. 399–422. [G: India]

Beach, Charles M. and Balfour, Frederick S. Estimated Payroll Tax Incidence and Aggregate Demand for Labour in the United Kingdom. *Economica*, February 1983, *50*(197), pp. 35–48. [G: U.K.]

Bell, David. The Labour Market in Scotland. In *Ingham, K. P. D. and Love, J., eds.*, 1983, pp. 65–73. [G: U.K.]

Bequela, Assefa and Freedman, David H. Employment and Basic Needs: An Overview. In *Todaro, M. P., ed.*, 1983, *1979*, pp. 153–64.

Bismut, Claude. 'Wage Rigidity and Unemployment in OECD Countries' by D. Grubb et al.: Comment. *Europ. Econ. Rev.*, March/April 1983, *21*(1/2), pp. 41–44. [G: OECD]

Blandy, Richard and Creigh, Stephen. The Australian Labour Market, June 1983. *Australian Bull. Lab.*, June 1983, *9*(3), pp. 159–89. [G: Australia]

Blandy, Richard and Harrison, David. The Australian Labour Market, March 1983. *Australian Bull. Lab.*, March 1983, *9*(2), pp. 75–92. [G: Australia]

Blandy, Richard and Richardson, Sue. How Labour Markets Adjust. In *Blandy, R. and Covick, O., eds.*, 1983, pp. 1–15. [G: Australia; U.S.]

Boucher, Michel. Le marché des joueurs de la Ligue nationale de hockey: une approche économique. (The National Hockey League Players' Labor Market: An Economic Approach. With English summary.) *L'Actual. Econ.*, December 1983, *59*(4), pp. 753–76.

Chang, Julius Chungshi. An Econometric Model of the Short-Run Demand for Workers and Hours in the U.S. Auto Industry. *J. Econometrics*, August 1983, *22*(3), pp. 301–16. [G: U.S.]

Chesher, Andrew and Lancaster, Tony. The Estimation of Models of Labour Market Behavior. *Rev. Econ. Stud.*, October 1983, *50*(4), pp. 609–24.

Clark, M. Gardner. The Swiss Experience with Foreign Workers: Lessons for the United States. *Ind. Lab. Relat. Rev.*, July 1983, *36*(4), pp. 606–23. [G: Switzerland; U.S.]

Clarke, Oliver. The Work Ethic: An International Perspective. In *Barbash, J., et al., eds.*, 1983, pp. 121–50. [G: OECD]

Colombino, Ugo. Variabili dipendenti limitate e selezione non casuale delle osservazioni: una applicazione alla stima della funzione di salario e di offerta di lavoro delle donne sposate in Italia. (Limited Dependent Variables and Non-Random Sample Selection: An Application to the Wage and Labour Supply Function of Married Women in Italy. With English summary.) *Giorn. Econ.*, May-June 1983, *42*(5–6), pp. 369–85. [G: Italy]

Contini, Bruno. Economic Development and Human Resources: Japan's Experience: Comments. In *Tsuru, S., ed.*, 1983, pp. 124–28. [G: MDCs; LDCs]

Diamond, Peter A. The Labor Market in the 1930's: Comment. In *Tobin, J., ed.*, 1983, pp. 61–62. [G: U.S.]

Dixon, Marlene; Jonas, Susanne and McCaughan, Ed. Changes in the International Division of Labor and Low-Wage Labor in the United States. In *Bergesen, A., ed.*, 1983, pp. 173–92. [G: U.S.]

Fougstedt, Gunnar. Ekonomisk stagnation och arbetslöshet. (Economic Stagnation and Unemployment. With English summary.) *Ekon. Samfundets Tidskr.*, 1983, *36*(1), pp. 15–17. [G: Finland]

Garonna, Paolo. On the Heterogeneity and Instability of Italian Segmentation Classification Criteria. *Rivista Int. Sci. Econ. Com.*, December 1983, *30*(12), pp. 1132–49. [G: Italy]

Geroski, P. A. and Knight, K. G. Wages, Strikes and Market Structure: Some Further Evidence. *Oxford Econ. Pap.*, March 1983, *35*(1), pp. 146–52. [G: U.K.]

Gooneratne, W. and Gunawardena, P. J. Poverty and Inequality in Rural Sri Lanka. In *Khan, A. R. and Lee, E., eds.*, 1983, pp. 247–71. [G: Sri Lanka]

Gordon, Robert J. Real Wages and Unemployment in the OECD Countries: Comments and Discussion. *Brookings Pap. Econ. Act.*, 1983, (1), pp. 290–304. [G: OECD]

Grubb, Dennis; Jackman, Richard and Layard, Richard. Wage Rigidity and Unemployment in OECD Countries. *Europ. Econ. Rev.*, March/April 1983, *21*(1/2), pp. 11–39. [G: OECD]

Gruen, Fred H. Understanding Labour Markets in Australia: Concluding Comments. In *Blandy, R. and Covick, O., eds.*, 1983, pp. 246–50.

Hall, Robert E. U.S. Labor Markets: Imbalance, Wage Growth, and Productivity in the 1970s: Comments and Discussion. *Brookings Pap. Econ. Act.*, 1983, (1), pp. 121–23. [G: U.S.]

Hannah, Stephen Paul. Unemployment and Real Wage Speculation: Empirical Tests for Great Britain 1967–1980. *Scot. J. Polit. Econ.*, June 1983, *30*(2), pp. 128–41. **[G: U.K.]**

Harris, R. I. D. Specification of Factor Demand Models and Shiftworking—An Extension to the CES Case. *Scot. J. Polit. Econ.*, June 1983, *30*(2), pp. 170–74.

Hasan, Abrar. Labour Market Imbalances in the 1980s: A Review of Three Perspectives: Comment. **In** *Queen's Univ. Indust. Relat. Centre and John Deutsch Mem.*, 1983, pp. 42–44. **[G: Canada]**

Hedges, Janice Neipert. Job Commitment in America: Is It Waxing or Waning? *Mon. Lab. Rev.*, July 1983, *106*(7), pp. 17–24. **[G: U.S.]**

Hedges, Janice Neipert. Job Commitment. **In** *Barbash, J., et al., eds.*, 1983, pp. 43–60. **[G: U.S.]**

Heyzer, Noeleen. International Production and Social Change: An Analysis of the State, Employment, and Trade Unions in Singapore. **In** *Chen, P. S. J., ed.*, 1983, pp. 105–28. **[G: Singapore]**

Hirsch, Werner Z.; Rufolo, Anthony M. and Mengle, David L. Recent Trends in Municipal Labor Market Research. **In** *Hirsch, W. Z., ed.*, 1983, pp. 13–58. **[G: U.S.]**

Hirschman, Charles. Foreign Investment in Malaysia, Once Again. **In** *Lim, D., ed.*, 1983, pp. 235–37. **[G: Malaysia]**

Hirschman, Charles. Foreign Investment, Employment Generation and the Profit–Wage Ratio in the Manufacturing Sector of West Malaysia: Comment. **In** *Lim, D., ed.*, 1983, *1978*, pp. 228–29. **[G: Malaysia]**

Johnson, George E. Potentials of Labor Market Policy: A View from the Eighties. *Ind. Relat.*, Spring 1983, *22*(2), pp. 283–97. **[G: U.S.]**

Johnston, Gary and Martin, Philip L. Employment and Wages Reported by California Farmers in 1982. *Mon. Lab. Rev.*, September 1983, *106*(9), pp. 27–31. **[G: U.S.]**

Jones, Evan. Industrial Structure and Labor Force Segmentation. *Rev. Radical Polit. Econ.*, Winter 1983, *15*(4), pp. 24–44. **[G: Australia]**

Killingsworth, Mark R. and Reimers, Cordelia W. Race, Ranking, Promotions, and Pay at a Federal Facility: A Logit Analysis. *Ind. Lab. Relat. Rev.*, October 1983, *37*(1), pp. 92–107. **[G: U.S.]**

Kumar, Pradeep. The Current Industrial Relations Scene in Canada, 1983: Technical Notes. **In** *Wood, W. D. and Kumar, P., eds.*, 1983, pp. 479–92. **[G: Canada]**

Maital, Shlomo; Maital, Sharone and Schwartz, Aba. Job Attitudes As Intervening Variables between Situational Factors and Economic Behavior. *J. Behav. Econ.*, Summer 1983, *12*(1), pp. 43–70. **[G: U.S.]**

Mamalakis, Markos. Overall Employment and Income Strategies. **In** *Urquidi, V. L. and Reyes, S. T., eds.*, 1983, pp. 111–30.

Marelli, Enrico. Empirical Estimation of Intersectoral and Interregional Transfers of Surplus Value: The Case of Italy. *J. Reg. Sci.*, February 1983, *23*(1), pp. 49–70.

Marsden, David. Chronicle: Industrial Relations in the United Kingdom, April–July 1983. *Brit. J. Ind. Relat.*, November 1983, *21*(3), pp. 401–12. **[G: U.K.]**

Mazumdar, Dipak. The Rural–Urban Wage Gap Migration and the Working of Urban Labor Market: An Interpretation Based on a Study of the Workers of Bombay City. *Indian Econ. Rev.*, July–December 1983, *18*(2), pp. 169–98. **[G: India]**

Medoff, James L. U.S. Labor Markets: Imbalance, Wage Growth, and Productivity in the 1970s. *Brookings Pap. Econ. Act.*, 1983, (1), pp. 87–120. **[G: U.S.]**

Mellow, Wesley and Sider, Hal. Accuracy of Response in Labor Market Surveys: Evidence and Implications. *J. Lab. Econ.*, October 1983, *1*(4), pp. 331–44. **[G: U.S.]**

Meyer, Robert H. and Wise, David A. Discontinuous Distributions and Missing Persons: The Minimum Wage and Unemployed Youth. *Econometrica*, November 1983, *51*(6), pp. 1677–98. **[G: U.S.]**

Morris, Morris D. The Growth of Large-Scale Industry to 1947. **In** *Kumar, D., ed.*, 1983, pp. 553–676. **[G: India]**

Mundle, Sudipto. Land, Labour and the Level of Living in Rural Punjab. **In** *Khan, A. R. and Lee, E., eds.*, 1983, pp. 81–106. **[G: India]**

Mundle, Sudipto. Land, Labour and the Level of Living in Rural Bihar. **In** *Khan, A. R. and Lee, E., eds.*, 1983, pp. 49–80. **[G: India]**

Napier, Ron. Interrelationships of the Economic and Social Systems in Japan. **In** *Finn, J., ed.*, 1983, pp. 179–94. **[G: Japan]**

Onitiri, H. M. A. Economic Development and Human Resources: Japan's Experience: Comments. **In** *Tsuru, S., ed.*, 1983, pp. 120–23. **[G: Japan]**

Ostro, Bart D. Urban Air Pollution and Morbidity: A Retrospective Approach. *Urban Stud.*, August 1983, *20*(3), pp. 343–51. **[G: U.S.]**

von Otter, Casten. Sweden: Labor Reformism Reshapes the System. **In** *Barkin, S., ed.*, 1983, pp. 187–227. **[G: Sweden]**

Payne, Geoff and Ford, Graeme. Inequality and the Occupational Structure. **In** *Brown, G. and Cook, R., eds.*, 1983, pp. 76–90. **[G: U.K.]**

Pearce, James E. Unionism and the Cyclical Behavior of the Labor Market in U.S. Manufacturing. *Rev. Econ. Statist.*, August 1983, *65*(3), pp. 450–58. **[G: U.S.]**

Peden, G. C. Sir Richard Hopkins and the "Keynesian Revolution" in Employment Policy, 1929–1945. *Econ. Hist. Rev., 2nd Ser.*, May 1983, *36*(2), pp. 281–96. **[G: U.K.]**

Perry, George L. What Have We Learned about Disinflation? *Brookings Pap. Econ. Act.*, 1983, (2), pp. 587–602. **[G: U.S.]**

Piore, Michael J. Labor Market Segmentation: To What Paradigm Does It Belong? *Amer. Econ. Rev.*, May 1983, *73*(2), pp. 249–53.

Pitchford, J. D. Unemployment, Real Wages and the Money Supply in Australia. *Econ. Rec.*, June 1983, *59*(165), pp. 118–31. **[G: Australia]**

Quinn, Joseph F. The Work Ethic and Retirement. **In** *Barbash, J., et al., eds.*, 1983, pp. 87–100. **[G: U.S.]**

Rosen, Sherwin. A Note on Aggregation of Skills and Labor Quality [Linear Synthesis of Skill Distribution]. *J. Human Res.*, Summer 1983, *18*(3), pp.

425–31. [G: U.S.]

Sachs, Jeffrey D. Real Wages and Unemployment in the OECD Countries. *Brookings Pap. Econ. Act.*, 1983, (1), pp. 255–89. [G: OECD]

Schaafsma, Joseph and Walsh, William D. Employment and Labour Supply Effects of the Minimum Wage: Some Pooled Time-Series Estimates from Canadian Provincial Data. *Can. J. Econ.*, February 1983, *16*(1), pp. 86–97. [G: Canada]

Smith, David C. Labour Market Imbalances in the 1980s: A Review of Three Perspectives. **In** *Queen's Univ. Indust. Relat. Centre and John Deutsch Mem.*, 1983, pp. 17–39. [G: Canada]

Smyth, David J. The British Labor Market in Disequilibrium: Did the Dole Reduce Employment in Interwar Britain? *J. Macroecon.*, Winter 1983, *5*(1), pp. 41–51. [G: U.K.]

Solow, Robert M. U.S. Labor Markets: Imbalance, Wage Growth, and Productivity in the 1970s: Comments and Discussion. *Brookings Pap. Econ. Act.*, 1983, (1), pp. 123–28. [G: U.S.]

Steenkamp, W. F. J. Labour Problems and Policies of Half a Century. *S. Afr. J. Econ.*, March 1983, *51*(1), pp. 58–87. [G: S. Africa]

Swartz, Gerald S. Labour Market Imbalances in the 1980s: A Review of Three Perspectives: Comment. **In** *Queen's Univ. Indust. Relat. Centre and John Deutsch Mem.*, 1983, pp. 44–49. [G: Canada]

Tan, Gerald. Foreign Investment, Employment Generation and the Profit–Wage Ratio in the Manufacturing Sector of West Malaysia. **In** *Lim, D., ed.*, 1983, *1978*, pp. 225–28. [G: Malaysia]

Tan, Gerald. Foreign Investment, Employment Generation and the Profit–Wage Ration in the Manufacturing Sector of West Malaysia: A Reply to Professor Hirschman. **In** *Lim, D., ed.*, 1983, *1979*, pp. 230–34. [G: Malaysia]

Tate, Donald G. Labour Market Imbalances in the 1980s: A Review of Three Perspectives: Comment. **In** *Queen's Univ. Indust. Relat. Centre and John Deutsch Mem.*, 1983, pp. 39–42. [G: Canada]

Taylor, John B. 'Wage Rigidity and Unemployment in OECD Countries' by D. Grubb et al.: Comment. *Europ. Econ. Rev.*, March/April 1983, *21*(1/2), pp. 45–49. [G: OECD]

Tokman, Victor E. Wages and Employment in International Recessions: Recent Latin American Experience. *Cepal Rev.*, August 1983, (20), pp. 113–26. [G: Latin America]

Tsuru, Shigeto. Economic Development and Human Resources: Japan's Experience. **In** *Tsuru, S., ed.*, 1983, pp. 95–119. [G: Japan]

Vaughan, Roger J. Inflation and Unemployment Surviving the 1980s. **In** *Barker, M., ed. (II)*, 1983, pp. 93–247. [G: U.S.]

Walton, John. Marx for the Late Twentieth Century: Transnational Capital and Disenfranchised Labor. *Soc. Sci. Quart.*, December 1983, *64*(4), pp. 786–809. [G: U.S.]

Whitley, J. D. and Wilson, Robert A. The Macroeconomic Merits of a Marginal Employment Subsidy. *Econ. J.*, December 1983, *93*(372), pp. 862–80.

Wood, Geoffrey E. Inflation and the Labour Market. **In** *Seldon, A., et al.*, 1983, pp. 35–46. [G: U.K.]

8241 Geographic Labor Market Studies

Armstrong, Harvey W. and Taylor, Jim. Unemployment Stocks and Flows in the Travel-to-Work Areas of the North-West Region. *Urban Stud.*, August 1983, *20*(3), pp. 311–25. [G: U.K.]

Beed, Clive; Singell, Larry D. and Wyatt, Ray. The Dynamics of Intra-City Unemployment Patterns. *Australian Bull. Lab.*, December 1983, *10*(1), pp. 36–46. [G: Australia]

Carter, Robert A. Resource-Related Development and Regional Labour Markets: The Effects of the Alcoa Aluminum Smelter on Portland. *Australian Econ. Rev.*, 1st Quarter 1983, (61), pp. 22–32. [G: Australia]

Cogan, John F. Labor Supply and Negative Income Taxation: New Evidence from the New Jersey–Pennsylvania Experiment. *Econ. Inquiry*, October 1983, *21*(4), pp. 465–84. [G: U.S.]

Kolk, David X. Regional Employment Impact of Rapidly Escalating Energy Costs. *Energy Econ.*, April 1983, *5*(2), pp. 105–13. [G: U.S.]

Ricq, Charles. Frontier Workers in Europe. **In** *Anderson, M., ed.*, 1983, pp. 98–108. [G: Europe]

Savey, Suzane. Organization of Production and the New Spatial Division of Labour in France. **In** *Hamilton, F. E. I. and Linge, G. J. R., eds.*, 1983, pp. 103–20. [G: France]

Simpson, Wayne. On the Appropriate Spatial Unit for Labour Market Analysis and Policy Design. *Urban Stud.*, November 1983, *20*(4), pp. 487–89. [G: U.K.]

Wells, John. Industrial Accumulation and Living Standards in the Long-Run: The São Paulo Industrial Working Class, 1930–75, Part II. *J. Devel. Stud.*, April 1983, *19*(3), pp. 297–328. [G: Brazil]

Wells, John. Industrial Accumulation and Living Standards in the Long-Run: The São Paulo Industrial Working Class, 1930–75, Part I. *J. Devel. Stud.*, January 1983, *19*(2), pp. 145–69. [G: Brazil]

8242 Wage and Fringe Benefit Studies

Abowd, John M. and Killingsworth, Mark R. Sex, Discrimination, Atrophy, and the Male–Female Wage Differential. *Ind. Relat.*, Fall 1983, *22*(3), pp. 387–402. [G: U.S.]

Adamy, Wilhelm and Koeppinghoff, Sigrid. Zur Krisenanfälligkeit der Rentenversicherung. Arbeitsmarktbedingte Finanzierungsprobleme in theoretischer und empirischer Sicht. (Pension Funds: Vulnerability to Crises—Deficits Caused by Unemployment, Viewed from a Theoretical and Empirical Perspective. With English summary.) *Konjunkturpolitik*, 1983, *29*(5), pp. 285–313. [G: W. Germany]

Akaoka, Isao. Motivation of Employees in Japan. *Kyoto Univ. Econ. Rev.*, April–October 1983, *53*(1–2), pp. 25–50. [G: Japan]

Aksoy, M. Ataman. Türkiye Özel Imalat Sanayiinde Yugunlaşma, Karlilik ve Ücret Ilişkileri. (With English summary.) *METU*, 1983, *10*(4), pp. 367–86. [G: Turkey]

Albæk, Karsten and Madsen, Erik Strøjer. Lønspredningen på det danske arbejdsmarked. (Inequality of Pay on the Danish Labour Market. (With English summary.) *Nationaløkon. Tidsskr.*, 1983, *121*(2), pp. 230–44. **[G: Denmark]**

Alpert, William T. Manufacturing Workers Private Wage Supplements: A Simultaneous Equations Approach. *Appl. Econ.*, June 1983, *15*(3), pp. 363–78. **[G: U.S.]**

Angle, John and Wissmann, David A. Work Experience, Age, and Gender Discrimination. *Soc. Sci. Quart.*, March 1983, *64*(1), pp. 66–84. **[G: U.S.]**

Antonelli, Gilberto. Income Distribution and Labour Factor Quality: Models and Applications at a Regional Level. **In** *Weisbrod, B. and Hughes, H., eds.*, 1983, pp. 167–77. **[G: Italy]**

Antos, Joseph R. Analysis of Labor Cost: Data Concepts and Sources. **In** *Triplett, J. E., ed.*, 1983, pp. 153–72. **[G: U.S.]**

Antos, Joseph R. Current and Historical Availability of BLS Wage, Price, and Productivity Series by SIC Industries. **In** *Triplett, J. E., ed.*, 1983, pp. 465–502. **[G: U.S.]**

Antos, Joseph R. Union Effects on White-Collar Compensation. *Ind. Lab. Relat. Rev.*, April 1983, *36*(3), pp. 461–79. **[G: U.S.]**

Arnould, Richard J. and Nichols, Len M. Wage-Risk Premiums and Workers' Compensation: A Refinement of Estimates of Compensating Wage Differential. *J. Polit. Econ.*, April 1983, *91*(2), pp. 332–40. **[G: U.S.]**

Arthur, W. B. Age and Earnings in the Labour Market: Implications of the 1980s Labour Bulge. **In** *Streeten, P. and Maier, H., eds.*, 1983, pp. 405–19.

Ashenfelter, Orley and Layard, Richard. Incomes Policy and Wage Differentials. *Economica*, May 1983, *50*(198), pp. 127–43. **[G: U.K.]**

Askanas, B. and Levcik, F. The Dispersion of Wages in the CMEA Countries (Including a Comparison with Austria). **In** *[Saunders, C. T.]*, 1983, pp. 193–230. **[G: CMEA; Austria]**

Aslam, Naheed. Level of Real Wages and Labour Productivity in the Manufacturing Sector of the Punjab. *Pakistan Devel. Rev.*, Winter 1983, *22*(4), pp. 283–99. **[G: Pakistan]**

Asselain, Jean-Charles. La répartition des revenus en Hongrie: Deuxième partie: les incertitudes des années 70. (With English summary.) *Écon. Soc.*, January 1983, *17*(1), pp. 43–88. **[G: Hungary]**

Atkinson, Anthony B. and Flemming, J. S. Unemployment, Social Security and Incentives in Britain. **In** *Atkinson, A. B.*, 1983, *1978*, pp. 397–418. **[G: U.K.]**

Atrostic, B. K. Fringe Benefits in Employee Compensation: Comment. **In** *Triplett, J. E., ed.*, 1983, pp. 389–94. **[G: U.S.]**

Attia, N. Le salaire, Miroir de la spécificité industrielle. (The Wage Mirror of the Industrial Specificity. With English summary.) *Écon. Soc.*, March–April 1983, *17*(3–4), pp. 691–718. **[G: France]**

Auerbach, Alan J. Portfolio Composition and Pension Wealth: An Econometric Study: Comment. **In** *Bodie, Z. and Shoven, J. B., eds.*, 1983, pp. 436–37. **[G: Canada]**

Bailey, William R. Compensation Cost Increases: Slowdown Continues in 1982. *Mon. Lab. Rev.*, June 1983, *106*(6), pp. 39–41. **[G: U.S.]**

Bassi, Laurie J. The Effect of CETA on the Postprogram Earnings of Participants. *J. Human Res.*, Fall 1983, *18*(4), pp. 539–56. **[G: U.S.]**

Baumann, Johann H. A Disaggregate Short Run Phillips Curve for Austria: The Effects of Regional Unemployment Dispersion and Spatial Wage Transfer on the National Wage Rate. *Z. Nationalökon.*, 1983, *43*(2), pp. 189–211. **[G: Austria]**

Beaumont, Paul M. Wage Rate Specification in Regional and Interregional Econometric Models. *Int. Reg. Sci. Rev.*, June 1983, *8*(1), pp. 75–83. **[G: U.S.]**

Bednarzik, Robert W. Short Workweeks during Economic Downturns. *Mon. Lab. Rev.*, June 1983, *106*(6), pp. 3–11. **[G: U.S.]**

Behrman, Jere R. and Birdsall, Nancy. The Quality of Schooling: Quantity Alone is Misleading. *Amer. Econ. Rev.*, December 1983, *73*(5), pp. 928–46. **[G: Brazil]**

Behrman, Jere R.; Sickles, Robin C. and Taubman, Paul. The Impact of Minimum Wages on the Distributions of Earnings for Major Race–Sex Groups: A Dynamic Analysis. *Amer. Econ. Rev.*, September 1983, *73*(4), pp. 766–78. **[G: U.S.]**

Behrman, Jere R. and Wolfe, Barbara L. Women's Labour Force Participation and Earnings Determinants in a Developing Country. **In** *Urquidi, V. L. and Reyes, S. T., eds.*, 1983, pp. 266–76. **[G: Nicaragua]**

Bequele, Assefa. Stagnation and Inequality in Ghana. **In** *Ghai, D. and Radwan, S., eds.*, 1983, pp. 219–47. **[G: Ghana]**

Berger, Mark C. Changes in Labor Force Composition and Male Earnings: A Production Approach. *J. Human Res.*, Spring 1983, *18*(2), pp. 177–96. **[G: U.S.]**

Berger, Mark C. and Hirsch, Barry T. The Civilian Earnings Experience of Vietnam-Era Veterans. *J. Human Res.*, Fall 1983, *18*(4), pp. 455–79. **[G: U.S.]**

Berkowitz, Monroe; Fenn, Paul and Lambrinos, James. The Optimal Stock of Health with Endogenous Wages: Application to Partial Disability Compensation. *J. Health Econ.*, August 1983, *2*(2), pp. 139–47. **[G: U.S.]**

Berndt, Ernst R. The Fixed Employment Costs of Specialized Labor: Comment. **In** *Triplett, J. E., ed.*, 1983, pp. 116–22. **[G: U.S.]**

Berry, Albert. Predicting Income Distribution in Latin America during the 1980s. **In** *Ritter, A. R. M. and Pollock, D. H., eds.*, 1983, pp. 57–84. **[G: Latin America]**

Björklund, Anders and Persson-Tanimura, Inga. Youth Employment in Sweden. **In** *Reubens, B. G., ed.*, 1983, pp. 232–68. **[G: Sweden]**

Blakemore, Arthur E. and Low, Stuart A. Race and the Acquisition of and Returns to OJT for Youth. *Ind. Relat.*, Fall 1983, *22*(3), pp. 374–86. **[G: U.S.]**

Blostin, Allan and Marclay, William. HMOs and Other Health Plans: Coverage and Employee Premiums. *Mon. Lab. Rev.*, June 1983, *106*(6), pp. 28–33. **[G: U.S.]**

Bodie, Zvi and Pesando, James E. Retirement Annuity Design in an Inflationary Climate. **In** *Bodie,*

Z. *and Shoven, J. B., eds.*, 1983, pp. 291–316, 322–23. [G: U.S.]

Bodie, Zvi and Shoven, John B. Financial Aspects of the United States Pension System: Introduction. **In** *Bodie, Z. and Shoven, J. B., eds.*, 1983, pp. 1–16. [G: U.S.]

Borjas, George J. The Measurement of Race and Gender Wage Differentials: Evidence from the Federal Sector. *Ind. Lab. Relat. Rev.*, October 1983, *37*(1), pp. 79–91. [G: U.S.]

Borjas, George J.; Frech, H. E., III and Ginsburg, Paul B. Property Rights and Wages: The Case of Nursing Homes. *J. Human Res.*, Spring 1983, *18*(2), pp. 231–46. [G: U.S.]

Borus, Michael E., et al. Youth Looking for Work. **In** *Borus, M. E., ed.*, 1983, pp. 59–102. [G: U.S.]

Bossons, John. Observations on the Indexation of Old Age Pensions: Comment. **In** *Bodie, Z. and Shoven, J. B., eds.*, 1983, pp. 252–57. [G: U.S.]

Bosworth, Barry P. A Century of Evidence on Wage and Price Stickiness in the United States, the United Kingdom and Japan: Comment. **In** *Tobin, J., ed.*, 1983, pp. 121–24. [G: U.S.; U.K.; Japan]

Bourguignon, François. The Role of Education in the Urban Labour Market in Developing Countries: The Case of Colombia. **In** *Urquidi, V. L. and Reyes, S. T., eds.*, 1983, pp. 211–35. [G: Colombia]

Bowie, Robert D. The Peripheral Labour Force. **In** *Easton, B., ed.*, 1983, pp. 49–70. [G: New Zealand]

Brack, John and Cowling, Keith. Advertising and Labour Supply: Workweek and Workyear in U.S. Manufacturing Industries, 1919–76. *Kyklos*, 1983, *36*(2), pp. 285–303. [G: U.S.]

Bretzfelder, Robert and Friedenberg, Howard. Regional and State Nonfarm Wages and Salaries Thus Far in the 1980's. *Surv. Curr. Bus.*, January 1983, *63*(1), pp. 23–26. [G: U.S.]

Brinker, Paul A. Labor Union Coercion of Employees: The Use of Fringe Benefits. *J. Lab. Res.*, Summer 1983, *4*(3), pp. 249–55. [G: U.S.]

Brown, Charles. Estimating Wage-fringe Trade-offs: Some Data Problems: Comment. **In** *Triplett, J. E., ed.*, 1983, pp. 367–69. [G: U.S.]

Browne, Lynn E. Wages and Inflation. *New Eng. Econ. Rev.*, May/June 1983, pp. 63–66. [G: U.S.]

Bruce, C. J. and Kerr, William A. The Determination of Wages and Working Conditions in the Agricultural Sector: Three Alternatives. *Can. J. Agr. Econ.*, July 1983, *31*(2), pp. 177–96. [G: Canada]

Brush, Brian C. and Crane, Steven E. Industry Growth, Labor Compensation, and Labor's Share of Value Added in U.S. Manufacturing, 1967–1979. *Quart. Rev. Econ. Bus.*, Winter 1983, *23*(4), pp. 44–53. [G: U.S.]

Buckley, Peter J. and Enderwick, Peter. Comparative Pay Levels in Domestically-Owned and Foreign-Owned Plants in U.K.: Manufacturing-Evidence from the 1980 Workplace Industrial Relations Survey. *Brit. J. Ind. Relat.*, November 1983, *21*(3), pp. 395–400. [G: U.K.]

Bulow, Jeremy I. and Scholes, Myron S. Who Owns the Assets in a Defined-Benefit Pension Plan? **In** *Bodie, Z. and Shoven, J. B., eds.*, 1983, pp. 17–32, 34–36. [G: U.S.]

Bulow, Jeremy I.; Scholes, Myron S. and Menell, Peter. Economic Implications of ERISA. **In** *Bodie, Z. and Shoven, J. B., eds.*, 1983, pp. 37–53, 56. [G: U.S.]

Burkhauser, Richard V. and Quinn, Joseph F. Financial Incentives and Retirement in the United States. **In** *Söderström, L., ed.*, 1983, pp. 207–24. [G: U.S.]

Burkhauser, Richard V. and Quinn, Joseph F. Is Mandatory Retirement Overrated? Evidence from the 1970s. *J. Human Res.*, Summer 1983, *18*(3), pp. 337–58. [G: U.S.]

Burkhauser, Richard V. and Quinn, Joseph F. The Effect of Pension Plans on the Pattern of Life Cycle Compensation. **In** *Triplett, J. E., ed.*, 1983, pp. 395–415. [G: U.S.]

Burtless, Gary T. and Greenberg, David. Measuring the Impact of NIT Experiments on Work Effort. *Ind. Lab. Relat. Rev.*, July 1983, *36*(4), pp. 592–605. [G: U.S.]

Cagan, Phillip and Fellner, William. Tentative Lessons from the Recent Disinflationary Effort. *Brookings Pap. Econ. Act.*, 1983, (2), pp. 603–08. [G: U.S.]

Cappelli, Peter. Comparability and the British Civil Service. *Brit. J. Ind. Relat.*, March 1983, *21*(1), pp. 33–45. [G: U.K.]

Card, David. Cost-of-Living Escalators in Major Union Contracts. *Ind. Lab. Relat. Rev.*, October 1983, *37*(1), pp. 34–48. [G: Canada]

Carlson, Norma W. Hourly Pay of Contract Cleaners Lags but Sweeps Past Weekly Gains. *Mon. Lab. Rev.*, March 1983, *106*(3), pp. 37–40. [G: U.S.]

Carter, Donald D. Termination and Severance Pay in Ontario: Are the Protections Adequate in the Event of Employer Insolvency? **In** *Queen's Univ. Indust. Relat. Centre*, 1983, pp. 24–31. [G: Canada]

Carter, Gene. Private Pensions: 1982 Legislation. *Soc. Sec. Bull.*, August 1983, *46*(8), pp. 3–8. [G: U.S.]

Carter, Michael and Maddock, Rodney. Working Hours in Australia: Some Issues. **In** *Blandy, R. and Covick, O., eds.*, 1983, pp. 222–45. [G: Australia]

Carvalho, Jose L. and Haddad, Claudio Luiz da Silva. Trade and Factor Market Distortions: Effects on Employment in Brazil. **In** *Weisbrod, B. and Hughes, H., eds.*, 1983, pp. 405–28. [G: Brazil]

Caspar, Pierre. French Law on Continuing Vocational Training. **In** *Levin, H. M. and Schütze, H. G., eds.*, 1983, pp. 257–72. [G: France]

Cecchetti, Stephen G., et al. OPEC II and the Wage-Price Spiral. **In** *Zeckhauser, R. J. and Leebaert, D., eds.*, 1983, pp. 137–54. [G: U.S.]

Chamberlin, John R. Pension Plan Equity: The Case against a Gender Classification. *J. Policy Anal. Manage.*, Fall 1983, *3*(1), pp. 126–29. [G: U.S.]

Chau, L. C. Imports of Consumer Goods from China and the Economic Growth of Hong Kong. **In** *Youngson, A. J., ed.*, 1983, pp. 184–225. [G: China; Hong Kong]

Chen, Yung-Ping. Employee Benefits and Social Security. *Contemp. Policy Issue*, April 1983, (3), pp.

23–32. [G: U.S.]

Chick, Victoria. A Question of Relevance: The *General Theory* in Keynes's Time and Ours. *S. Afr. J. Econ.*, September 1983, *51* (3), pp. 380–406. [G: U.K.]

Chiswick, Barry R. An Analysis of the Earnings and Employment of Asian-American Men. *J. Lab. Econ.*, April 1983, *1* (2), pp. 197–214. [G: U.S.]

Chiswick, Carmel U. Analysis of Earnings from Household Enterprises: Methodology and Application to Thailand. *Rev. Econ. Statist.*, November 1983, *65* (4), pp. 658–62. [G: Thailand]

Christensen, Sandra and Maki, Dennis R. The Wage Effect of Compulsory Union Membership. *Ind. Lab. Relat. Rev.*, January 1983, *36* (2), pp. 230–38. [G: U.S.]

Christiansen, Hanne D. Equality and Equilibrium: Weaknesses of the Overlap Argument for Unisex Pension Plans. *J. Risk Ins.*, December 1983, *50* (4), pp. 670–80. [G: U.S.]

Christofides, L. N. and Wilton, D. A. Incomes Policy Reconsidered. *J. Macroecon.*, Winter 1983, *5* (1), pp. 119–34. [G: Canada]

Cobbe, James H. The Educational System, Wage and Salary Structures, and Income Distribution: Lesotho as a Case Study, Circa 1975. *J. Devel. Areas*, January 1983, *17* (2), pp. 227–41. [G: Lesotho]

Cogan, John F. Labor Supply and Negative Income Taxation: New Evidence from the New Jersey–Pennsylvania Experiment. *Econ. Inquiry*, October 1983, *21* (4), pp. 465–84. [G: U.S.]

Cohen, Cynthia Fryer. The Impact on Women of Proposed Changes in the Private Pension System: A Simulation. *Ind. Lab. Relat. Rev.*, January 1983, *36* (2), pp. 258–70. [G: U.S.]

Cohen, Edwin S. Family Issues in Taxation: Commentary. **In** *Penner, R. G., ed.*, 1983, pp. 27–30. [G: U.S.]

Collier, Paul. Oil and Inequality in Rural Nigeria. **In** *Ghai, D. and Radwan, S., eds.*, 1983, pp. 191–217. [G: Nigeria]

Conway, Delores A. and Roberts, Harry V. Reverse Regression, Fairness, and Employment Discrimination. *J. Bus. Econ. Statist.*, January 1983, *1* (1), pp. 75–85. [G: U.S.]

Corbo, Vittorio and Stelcner, Morton. Earnings Determination and Labour Markets: Gran Santiago, Chile—1978. *J. Devel. Econ.*, February/April 1983, *12* (1/2), pp. 251–66. [G: Chile]

Corcoran, Mary; Duncan, Greg J. and Ponza, Michael. A Longitudinal Analysis of White Women's Wages. *J. Human Res.*, Fall 1983, *18* (4), pp. 497–520. [G: U.S.]

Corcoran, Mary; Duncan, Greg J. and Ponza, Michael. Work Experience and Wage Growth of Women Workers. **In** *Duncan, G. J. and Morgan, J. N., eds.*, 1983, pp. 249–323. [G: U.S.]

Cottle, Rex L.; Macaulay, Hugh H. and Yandle, T. Bruce. Some Economic Effects of the California Agricultural Labor Relations Act. *J. Lab. Res.*, Fall 1983, *4* (4), pp. 315–24. [G: U.S.]

Cousineau, Jean-Michel and Lacroix, Robert. 'Effet de structure' et 'effet de marché régional' dans les disparités interrégionales de salaire: une application au cas de Montréal et Toronto. *Can. J. Econ.*, November 1983, *16* (4), pp. 655–68. [G: Canada]

Covick, Owen. Self-employment Growth in Australia. **In** *Blandy, R. and Covick, O., eds.*, 1983, pp. 84–110. [G: Australia]

Cymrot, Donald J. Migration Trends and Earnings of Free Agents in Major League Baseball, 1976–1979. *Econ. Inquiry*, October 1983, *21* (4), pp. 545–56. [G: U.S.]

Dalrymple, Robert; Grad, Susan and Wilson, Duke. Civil Service Retirement System Annuitants and Social Security. *Soc. Sec. Bull.*, February 1983, *46* (2), pp. 39–59. [G: U.S.]

Dalton, Amy H. and Snellings, Eleanor C. A Note on Salary Variations in an Academic Internal Labor Market. *Atlantic Econ. J.*, September 1983, *11* (3), pp. 70–78. [G: U.S.]

Datcher, Linda. Racial Differences in the Persistence of Affluence. **In** *Duncan, G. J. and Morgan, J. N., eds.*, 1983, pp. 205–17. [G: U.S.]

David, Martin H. The Size Distribution of Wage and Nonwage Compensation: Employer Cost versus Employee Value: Comment. **In** *Triplett, J. E., ed.*, 1983, pp. 278–85. [G: U.S.]

DeFina, Robert H. Unions, Relative Wages, and Economic Efficiency. *J. Lab. Econ.*, October 1983, *1* (4), pp. 408–29. [G: U.S.]

Delaney, John Thomas. Strikes, Arbitration, and Teacher Salaries: A Behavioral Analysis. *Ind. Lab. Relat. Rev.*, April 1983, *36* (3), pp. 431–46. [G: U.S.]

Dhaliwal, R. S. and Grewal, S. S. Impact of Agricultural Development on Farmer–Labourer Relationships. *Econ. Aff.*, January–March 1983, *28* (1), pp. 644–49. [G: India]

Dicks-Mireaux, Louis-David L. and King, Mervyn A. Portfolio Composition and Pension Wealth: An Econometric Study. **In** *Bodie, Z. and Shoven, J. B., eds.*, 1983, pp. 399–435, 438–39. [G: Canada]

Dolde, Walter and Tobin, James. Mandatory Retirement Saving and Capital Formation. **In** *Modigliani, F. and Hemming, R., eds.*, 1983, pp. 56–88. [G: U.S.]

Dorsey, Stuart and Walzer, Norman. Workers' Compensation, Job Hazards, and Wages. *Ind. Lab. Relat. Rev.*, July 1983, *36* (4), pp. 642–54. [G: U.S.]

Drobny, Andres and Wells, John. Wages, Minimum Wages, and Income Distribution in Brazil: Results from the Construction Industry. *J. Devel. Econ.*, December 1983, *13* (3), pp. 305–30. [G: Brazil]

Duncan, Greg J. and Hoffman, Saul D. A New Look at the Causes of the Improved Economic Status of Black Workers. *J. Human Res.*, Spring 1983, *18* (2), pp. 268–82. [G: U.S.]

Duncan, Greg J. and Holmlund, Bertil. Was Adam Smith Right after All? Another Test of the Theory of Compensating Wage Differentials. *J. Lab. Econ.*, October 1983, *1* (4), pp. 366–79. [G: Sweden]

Duncan, Greg J. and Liker, Jeffrey. Disentangling the Efficacy–Earnings Relationship among White Men. **In** *Duncan, G. J. and Morgan, J. N., eds.*, 1983, pp. 218–48. [G: U.S.]

Eddie, Scott M. Agriculture as a Source of Supply:

Conjectures from the History of Hungary, 1870–1913. In *Komlos, J., ed.*, 1983, pp. 101–15. **[G: Hungary]**

Eden, Benjamin and Pakes, Ariél. Measuring the Variance-Age Profile of Lifetime Earnings. In *Helpman, E.; Razin, A. and Sadka, E., eds.*, 1983, pp. 109–21. **[G: Israel]**

Edwards, Linda N. and Edwards, Franklin R. Wellington–Winter Revisited: The Case of Municipal Sanitation Collection: Reply. *Ind. Lab. Relat. Rev.*, July 1983, *36*(4), pp. 657–59. **[G: U.S.]**

Ehrlich, Edna E. Foreign Pension Fund Investments in the United States. *Fed. Res. Bank New York Quart. Rev.*, Spring 1983, *8*(1), pp. 1–12. **[G: Canada; Netherlands; Japan; U.K.; U.S.]**

Elbaum, Bernard. The Internalization of Labor Markets: Causes and Consequences. *Amer. Econ. Rev.*, May 1983, *73*(2), pp. 260–65. **[G: U.S.]**

Englander, A. Steven and Chandoha, Marie. Will Wage Givebacks Be Reversed? *Fed. Res. Bank New York Quart. Rev.*, Autumn 1983, *8*(3), pp. 24–25. **[G: U.S.]**

Englander, A. Steven and Los, Cornelis A. Recovery without Accelerating Inflation? *Fed. Res. Bank New York Quart. Rev.*, Summer 1983, *8*(2), pp. 19–28. **[G: U.S.]**

Espinguet, Patrice and Terraza, Michel. Essai d'extrapolation des distributions de salaires français. (An Attempt to Extrapolate the Distribution of French Wages. With English summary.) *Écon. Appl.*, 1983, *36*(2–3), pp. 535–61. **[G: France]**

Esposito, Richard and Shipp, Kenneth. Industry Diffusion Indexes for Average Weekly Hours. *Mon. Lab. Rev.*, May 1983, *106*(5), pp. 33–36. **[G: U.S.]**

Farber, Stephen C. Post-Migration Earnings Profiles: An Application of Human Capital and Job Search Models. *Southern Econ. J.*, January 1983, *49*(3), pp. 693–705. **[G: U.S.]**

Feenberg, Daniel R. The Tax Treatment of Married Couples and the 1981 Tax Law. In *Penner, R. G., ed.*, 1983, pp. 32–63. **[G: U.S.]**

Feldstein, Martin S. Should Private Pensions Be Indexed? In *Bodie, Z. and Shoven, J. B., eds.*, 1983, pp. 211–30.

Ferber, Marianne A. and Greene, Carole A. Housework vs. Marketwork: Some Evidence How the Decision Is Made. *Rev. Income Wealth*, June 1983, *29*(2), pp. 147–59. **[G: U.S.]**

Ferleger, Lou. Explaining Away Black Poverty: The Structural Determinants of Black Employment. In *Goldstein, R. and Sachs, S. M., eds.*, 1983, pp. 148–74. **[G: U.S.]**

Fernandez Arufe, J. E. La actual crisis económica y políticas de empleo: la situación española. (The Economic Crisis and Employment Policies: The Case of Spain. With English summary.) *Écon. Soc.*, September–October–November 1983, *17*(9-10-11), pp. 1517–35. **[G: Spain]**

Filc, Wolfgang. Internationale Wirschaft- und Währungsprobleme: Floating, Arbeitslosigkeit und Geldpolitik. (International Economic and Monetary Problems: Floating, Unemployment and Monetary Policy. With English summary.) *Kredit Kapital*, 1983, *16*(1), pp. 81–97. **[G: W. Germany]**

Filer, Randall K. Sexual Differences in Earnings: The Role of Individual Personalities and Tastes. *J. Human Res.*, Winter 1983, *18*(1), pp. 82–99. **[G: U.S.]**

Fischhoff, Baruch. Informed Consent for Nuclear Workers. In *Kasperson, R. E., ed.*, 1983, pp. 301–28. **[G: U.S.]**

Forster, C. and Harris, P. A Note on Engineering Wages in Melbourne 1892–1929. *Australian Econ. Hist. Rev.*, March 1983, *23*(1), pp. 50–57. **[G: Australia]**

Fosu, Augustin Kwasi. Impact of Unionism on Pension Fringes. *Ind. Relat.*, Fall 1983, *22*(3), pp. 419–25. **[G: U.S.]**

Frenkel, I. Socio-economic Development and Rural–Urban Migration in Poland. In *Oberai, A. S., ed.*, 1983, pp. 251–310. **[G: Poland]**

Friedman, Benjamin M. Pension Funding, Pension Asset Allocation, and Corporate Finance: Evidence from Individual Company Data. In *Bodie, Z. and Shoven, J. B., eds.*, 1983, pp. 107–47, 152. **[G: U.S.]**

Fujii, Edwin T. and Mak, James. On the Specification of the Income Equation for Immigrants. *Southern Econ. J.*, April 1983, *49*(4), pp. 1141–46. **[G: U.S.]**

Fujii, Edwin T. and Mak, James. The Determinants of Income of Native- and Foreign-Born Men in a Multiracial Society. *Appl. Econ.*, December 1983, *15*(6), pp. 759–76. **[G: U.S.]**

Gafni, Amiram, et al. Is There a Trade-Off between Income and Health? The Case of Hypertensive Steelworkers in Canada. *Inquiry*, Winter 1983, *20*(4), pp. 343–49. **[G: Canada]**

Gahin, Fikry S. The Financial Feasibility of Tax-Sheltered Individual Retirement Plans. *J. Risk Ins.*, March 1983, *50*(1), pp. 84–106. **[G: U.S.]**

Garofalo, Gasper A. and Fogarty, Michael S. A Note on the Measurement of Agglomeration Economies with Compensation for Urban Disamenities. *J. Environ. Econ. Manage.*, December 1983, *10*(4), pp. 383–87. **[G: U.S.]**

Gärtner, Manfred. Causality Patterns in Aggregate Labor Markets: A Statistical Analysis of West German Data. *Empirical Econ.*, 1983, *8*(3–4), pp. 229–45. **[G: W. Germany]**

Gaspard, Michel and Tahar, Gabriel. Investissement et baisse de la durée hebdomadaire du travail: réflexions autour d'un modèle sectoriel. (With English summary.) *Rev. Econ. Ind.*, 3rd Trimester 1983, (25), pp. 1–20. **[G: France]**

Gerking, Shelby D. and Weirick, William N. Compensating Differences and Interregional Wage Differentials. *Rev. Econ. Statist.*, August 1983, *65*(3), pp. 483–87. **[G: U.S.]**

Goldfarb, Robert S.; Yezer, Anthony M. J. and Crewe, Sebastian. Some New Evidence: Have Regional Wage Differentials Really Disappeared? *Growth Change*, January 1983, *14*(1), pp. 48–51. **[G: U.S.]**

Gollier, J. J. Tendances à long terme du régime de pensions légales. Une solution alternative? (An Alternative Solution to Cover the Pension Costs in Belgium. With English summary.) *Ann. Sci. Écon. Appl.*, 1983, *39*(2), pp. 7–52. **[G: Belgium]**

Gollop, Frank M. and Jorgenson, Dale W. Sectoral

Labor Input. **In** *Triplett, J. E., ed.*, 1983, pp. 503–20. **[G: U.S.]**

Gollop, Frank M. and Jorgenson, Dale W. Sectoral Measures of Labor Cost for the United States, 1948–1978. **In** *Triplett, J. E., ed.*, 1983, pp. 185–235. **[G: U.S.]**

Gomberg, Ia. and Sushkina, L. Basic Directions of Wage Differentiation in Industry. *Prob. Econ.*, March 1983, *25*(11), pp. 36–50. **[G: U.S.S.R.]**

Gordon, Robert J. A Century of Evidence on Wage and Price Stickiness in the United States, the United Kingdom, and Japan. **In** *Tobin, J., ed.*, 1983, pp. 85–121. **[G: U.S.; Japan; U.K.]**

Granados, Luis L. The Effect of Employee Stock Ownership Plans on Corporate Profits—Additional Comment. *J. Risk Ins.*, September 1983, *50*(3), pp. 495–97. **[G: U.S.]**

Green, Jerry R. Who Owns the Assets in a Defined-Benefit Pension Plan? Comment. **In** *Bodie, Z. and Shoven, J. B., eds.*, 1983, pp. 32–34. **[G: U.S.]**

Greene, William H. Estimation of Limited Dependent Variable Models by Ordinary Least Squares and the Method of Moments. *J. Econometrics*, February 1983, *21*(2), pp. 195–212. **[G: U.S.]**

Gregory, R. G. and Duncan, Ronald C. Equal Pay for Women: A Reply [Segmented Labour Market Theories and the Australian Experience of Equal Pay for Women]. *Australian Econ. Pap.*, June 1983, *22*(40), pp. 60–64. **[G: Australia]**

Gregory, R. G. and Duncan, Ronald C. Reply [Segmented Labor Market Theories and the Australian Experience of Equal Pay for Women]. *J. Post Keynesian Econ.*, Summer 1983, *5*(4), pp. 673–75. **[G: Australia]**

Grigalunas, Thomas A., et al. Econometric Analyses of Lost Wage Payments in the Tourist Industry. **In** *U.S. Dept. Comm., Nat'l Oceanic and Atmos. Admin.*, 1983, pp. 126–29. **[G: France]**

Grosskopf, Shawna P.; Hayes, Kathy and Sivan, David. Municipal Pensions, Funding and Wage Capitalization. *Nat. Tax J.*, March, 1983, *36*(1), pp. 115–21. **[G: U.S.]**

Grossman, Jean Baldwin. The Impact of the Minimum Wage on Other Wages. *J. Human Res.*, Summer 1983, *18*(3), pp. 359–78. **[G: U.S.]**

Gupta, Vinod K. Labor Productivity, Establishment Size, and Scale Economies [The Extent of Economies of Scale: The Effects of Firm Size on Labor Productivity and Wage Rates]. *Southern Econ. J.*, January 1983, *49*(3), pp. 853–59. **[G: U.S.]**

Haber, Sheldon E. Wage Structure in Internal Labor Markets and Marginal Productivity Theory. *Atlantic Econ. J.*, December 1983, *11*(4), pp. 66–70. **[G: U.S.]**

Haber, Sheldon E. and Lamas, Enrique J. Pay, Training Costs, Turnover and Hiring and Retention Decisions. *J. Behav. Econ.*, Summer 1983, *12*(1), pp. 1–21. **[G: U.S.]**

Hall, Arden R. and Smith, William D. The Financial Condition of Public Employee Pension Plans. **In** *Hirsch, W. Z., ed.*, 1983, pp. 247–73. **[G: U.S.]**

Hall, S.; Henry, S. G. B. and Trinder, Chris. Wages and Prices. **In** *Britton, A., ed.*, 1983, pp. 65–78. **[G: U.K.]**

Hamermesh, Daniel S. Labor Cost Series, Manufacturing and Private Business, 1953–1980. **In** *Triplett, J. E., ed.*, 1983, pp. 521–27. **[G: U.S.]**

Hamermesh, Daniel S. New Measures of Labor Cost: Implications for Demand Elasticities and Nominal Wage Growth. **In** *Triplett, J. E., ed.*, 1983, pp. 287–306. **[G: U.S.]**

Hanoch, Giora and Honig, Marjorie. Retirement, Wages, and Labor Supply of the Elderly. *J. Lab. Econ.*, April 1983, *1*(2), pp. 131–51. **[G: U.S.]**

Harrison, Brian R. and Thera, John R. Economic Status of Canadian Freelance Writers. **In** *Hendon, W. S. and Shanahan, J. L., eds.*, 1983, pp. 143–53. **[G: Canada]**

Harrison, J. Michael and Sharpe, William F. Optimal Funding and Asset Allocation Rules for Defined-Benefit Pension Plans. **In** *Bodie, Z. and Shoven, J. B., eds.*, 1983, pp. 91–103, 105. **[G: U.S.]**

Hart, Peter E. The Size Mobility of Earnings. *Oxford Bull. Econ. Statist.*, May 1983, *45*(2), pp. 181–93. **[G: U.K.]**

Hayghe, Howard. Married Couples: Work and Income Patterns. *Mon. Lab. Rev.*, December 1983, *106*(12), pp. 26–29. **[G: U.S.]**

Hedger, Douglas and Schmitt, Donald. Trends in Major Medical Coverage during a Period of Rising Costs. *Mon. Lab. Rev.*, July 1983, *106*(7), pp. 11–16. **[G: U.S.]**

Heller, Peter and Tait, Alan A. Government Employment and Pay: Some International Comparisons. *Finance Develop.*, September 1983, *20*(3), pp. 44–47. **[G: OECD; LDCs]**

Hemming, Richard and Harvey, Russell. Occupational Pension Scheme Membership and Retirement Saving. *Econ. J.*, March 1983, *93*(369), pp. 128–44. **[G: U.K.]**

Henderson, James W. Earnings Functions for the Self-Employed: Comment. *J. Devel. Econ.*, Aug.–Oct. 1983, *13*(1–2), pp. 97–102. **[G: Iran]**

Hendricks, Wallace E. and Kahn, Lawrence M. Cost-of-Living Clauses in Union Contracts: Determinants and Effects. *Ind. Lab. Relat. Rev.*, April 1983, *36*(3), pp. 447–60. **[G: U.S.]**

Hickman, James C. Pensions and Sex. *J. Risk Ins.*, December 1983, *50*(4), pp. 681–87. **[G: U.S.]**

Hill, James Richard and Spellman, William. Professional Baseball: The Reserve Clause and Salary Structure. *Ind. Relat.*, Winter 1983, *22*(1), pp. 1–19. **[G: U.S.]**

Hills, Stephen M. and Reubens, Beatrice G. Youth Employment in the United States. **In** *Reubens, B. G., ed.*, 1983, pp. 269–318. **[G: U.S.]**

Hirsch, Werner Z. and Rufolo, Anthony M. Effects of Prevailing Wage Laws on Municipal Government Wages. *J. Urban Econ.*, January 1983, *13*(1), pp. 112–26. **[G: U.S.]**

Holmlund, Bertil. Payroll Taxes and Wage Inflation: The Swedish Experience. *Scand. J. Econ.*, 1983, *85*(1), pp. 1–15. **[G: Sweden]**

Horowitz, Harold. Work and Earnings of Artists in the Media Fields. *J. Cult. Econ.*, December 1983, *7*(2), pp. 69–89. **[G: U.S.]**

House, William J. Occupational Segregation and Discriminatory Pay: The Position of Women in the Cyprus Labour Market. *Int. Lab. Rev.*, January–February 1983, *122*(1), pp. 75–93. **[G: Cyprus]**

Ihnen, Loren A. Black Agricultural Economists: Discussion. *Amer. J. Agr. Econ.*, December 1983, *65*(5), pp. 999–1001. **[G: U.S.]**

Ippolito, Richard A. Public Policy towards Private Pensions. *Contemp. Policy Issue*, April 1983, (3), pp. 53–76. **[G: U.S.]**

Izraeli, Oded. The Effect of Variations in Cost of Living and City Size on the Rate of Return to Schooling. *Quart. Rev. Econ. Bus.*, Winter 1983, *23*(4), pp. 93–108. **[G: U.S.]**

Johnson, George E. Intermetropolitan Wage Differentials in the United States. **In** *Triplett, J. E., ed.*, 1983, pp. 309–30. **[G: U.S.]**

Johnson, William R. and Browning, Edgar K. The Distributional and Efficiency Effects of Increasing the Minimum Wage: A Simulation. *Amer. Econ. Rev.*, March 1983, *73*(1), pp. 204–11. **[G: U.S.]**

Jones, F. L. On Decomposing the Wage Gap: A Critical Comment on Blinder's Method [Wage Discrimination: Reduced Form and Structural Estimates]. *J. Human Res.*, Winter 1983, *18*(1), pp. 126–30. **[G: U.S.]**

Jose, A. V. Poverty and Income Distribution: The Case of West Bengal. **In** *Khan, A. R. and Lee, E., eds.*, 1983, pp. 137–63. **[G: India]**

Jose, A. V. Poverty and Inequality—The Case of Kerala. **In** *Khan, A. R. and Lee, E., eds.*, 1983, pp. 107–36. **[G: India]**

Jump, Bernard, Jr. State and Local Government Pension Benefits: Just Desserts or Just Rip-offs? **In** *Hirsch, W. Z., ed.*, 1983, pp. 212–46. **[G: U.S.]**

Juster, F. Thomas. Analysis of Labor Cost: Data Concepts and Sources: Comment. **In** *Triplett, J. E., ed.*, 1983, pp. 173–81. **[G: U.S.]**

Kasnakoğlu, Zehra and Kiliç, Atilla. Ankara'da gelir farkliliklarini belirleyen etmenler (1977). (Determinants of Income Differentials in Ankara [1977]. With English summary.) *METU*, 1983, *10*(2), pp. 179–98. **[G: Turkey]**

Kasper, Hirschel. Toward Estimating the Incidence of Journey-to-Work Costs. *Urban Stud.*, May 1983, *20*(2), pp. 197–208. **[G: U.K.]**

Kaufman, Roger T. Nepotism and the Minimum Wage. *J. Lab. Res.*, Winter 1983, *4*(1), pp. 81–89. **[G: U.S.]**

Kay, Linda B. A Survey of New Zealand Labour Market Data. **In** *Easton, B., ed.*, 1983, pp. 171–202. **[G: New Zealand]**

Keating, Michael. Relative Wages and the Changing Industrial Distribution of Employment in Australia. *Econ. Rec.*, December 1983, *59*(167), pp. 384–97. **[G: Australia]**

Kenny, Lawrence W. The Accumulation of Human Capital during Marriage by Males. *Econ. Inquiry*, April 1983, *21*(2), pp. 223–31. **[G: U.S.]**

Kessler, Sid. Comparability. *Oxford Bull. Econ. Statist.*, February 1983, *45*(1), pp. 85–104. **[G: U.K.]**

Kessler, Sid. Pay Policies for the Future: Comparability. **In** *Robinson, D. and Mayhew, K., eds.*, 1983, pp. 85–104. **[G: U.K.]**

Khan, Azizur Rahman. Real Wages of Agricultural Workers in Bangladesh. **In** *Khan, A. R. and Lee, E., eds.*, 1983, pp. 185–203. **[G: Bangladesh]**

Kheifets, L. State Regulation of Wages. *Prob. Econ.*, July 1983, *26*(3), pp. 39–52. **[G: U.S.S.R.]**

Killingsworth, Mark R. Union–Nonunion Wage Gaps and Wage Gains: New Estimates from an Industry Cross-Section. *Rev. Econ. Statist.*, May 1983, *65*(2), pp. 332–36. **[G: U.S.]**

Klitgaard, Robert E., et al. The Economics of Teacher Training: An Exploratory Data Analysis. *Pakistan J. Appl. Econ.*, Summer 1983, *2*(1), pp. 13–38. **[G: Pakistan]**

Knight, John B. and Sabot, Richard H. Educational Expansion and the Kuznets Effect. *Amer. Econ. Rev.*, December 1983, *73*(5), pp. 1132–36. **[G: Kenya; Tanzania]**

Knight, John B. and Sabot, Richard H. The Role of the Firm in Wage Determination: An African Case Study. *Oxford Econ. Pap.*, March 1983, *35*(1), pp. 45–66. **[G: Tanzania]**

Koskie, Raymond. Recent Developments in the Law of Pensions. **In** *Queen's Univ. Indust. Relat. Centre*, 1983, pp. 68–75. **[G: Canada]**

Krengel, Jochen. Der Beschäftigungseffekt von Arbeitszeitverkürzungen im sekundären Sektor Deutschlands 1871 bis 1913—ein historisches Beispiel. (The Effect of Shorter Working Hours on Employment within the Secondary Sector of the German Economy between 1871 and 1913—An Historical Example. With English summary.) *Konjunkturpolitik*, 1983, *29*(5), pp. 314–28. **[G: W. Germany]**

Krumm, Ronald J. Regional Wage Differentials, Fluctuations in Labor Demand, and Migration. *Int. Reg. Sci. Rev.*, June 1983, *8*(1), pp. 23–45.

Kulash, Marjorie M. Pension Plan Equity: The Unintended Consequences. *J. Policy Anal. Manage.*, Fall 1983, *3*(1), pp. 129–34. **[G: U.S.]**

Kumar, Pradeep. The Current Industrial Relations Scene in Canada, 1983: Wages, Productivity and Labour Costs: Summary Outline. **In** *Wood, W. D. and Kumar, P., eds.*, 1983, pp. 405–76. **[G: Canada; OECD]**

Kwoka, John E., Jr. Monopoly, Plant, and Union Effects on Worker Wages. *Ind. Lab. Relat. Rev.*, January 1983, *36*(2), pp. 251–57. **[G: U.S.]**

Lancaster, Tony and Chesher, Andrew. An Econometric Analysis of Reservation Wages. *Econometrica*, November 1983, *51*(6), pp. 1661–76. **[G: U.K.]**

Lazear, Edward P. New Measures of Labor Cost: Implications for Demand Elasticities and Nominal Wage Growth: Comment. **In** *Triplett, J. E., ed.*, 1983, pp. 306–08. **[G: U.S.]**

Lazear, Edward P. Pensions as Severance Pay. **In** *Bodie, Z. and Shoven, J. B., eds.*, 1983, pp. 57–85, 88–89. **[G: U.S.]**

Leibowitz, Arleen. Fringe Benefits in Employee Compensation. **In** *Triplett, J. E., ed.*, 1983, pp. 371–89. **[G: U.S.]**

Leiderman, Leonardo. The Response of Real Wages to Unanticipated Money Growth. *J. Monet. Econ.*, January 1983, *11*(1), pp. 73–88. **[G: U.S.]**

Leigh, J. Paul. Job Choice across Industries when Earnings Are Uncertain. *Quart. Rev. Econ. Bus.*, Autumn 1983, *23*(3), pp. 54–69. **[G: U.S.]**

Lewin, David and Katz, Harry C. Payment Determination in Municipal Building Departments under Unionism and Civil Service. **In** *Hirsch, W. Z., ed.*, 1983, pp. 90–121. **[G: U.S.]**

Lewis, H. Gregg. Comments [Union Effects: Wages,

Turnover, and Job Training] [Employer Size, Unionism, and Wages]. **In** *Reid, J. D., Jr., ed.*, 1983, pp. 283–90. **[G: U.S.]**

Lewis, H. Gregg. Union Relative Wage Effects: A Survey of Macro Estimates. *J. Lab. Econ.*, January 1983, *1*(1), pp. 1–27. **[G: U.S.]**

Light, Jay O. Pension Funding, Pension Asset Allocation, and Corporate Finance: Evidence from Individual Company Data: Comment. **In** *Bodie, Z. and Shoven, J. B., eds.*, 1983, pp. 147–51. **[G: U.S.]**

Lim, David. Wages and Work Conditions, and the Effects of Foreign Investment and the Separation of Ownership from Management on Them: A Study of Malaysian Manufacturing. **In** *Lim, D., ed.*, 1983, pp. 162–80. **[G: Malaysia]**

Lindauer, David L. and Sabot, Richard H. The Public/Private Wage Differential in a Poor Urban Economy. *J. Devel. Econ.*, February/April 1983, *12*(1/2), pp. 137–52. **[G: Tanzania]**

Livingston, D. T. and Henry, James B. The Effect of Employee Stock Ownership Plans on Corporate Profits—Reply. *J. Risk Ins.*, September 1983, *50*(3), pp. 498–99. **[G: U.S.]**

Llach, Juan J. Economically Active Population, Unemployment Rates and Aggregate Demand: Recent Argentine Experience in Pursuit of a Theory. **In** *Urquidi, V. L. and Reyes, S. T., eds.*, 1983, pp. 387–405. **[G: Argentina]**

Long, James E. and Link, Albert N. The Impact of Market Structure on Wages, Fringe Benefits, and Turnover. *Ind. Lab. Relat. Rev.*, January 1983, *36*(2), pp. 239–50. **[G: U.S.]**

MacDonald, Glenn M. The Size and Structure of Union–Non-Union Wage Differentials in Canadian Industry: Corroboration, Refinement, and Extension. *Can. J. Econ.*, August 1983, *16*(3), pp. 480–85. **[G: Canada]**

Maddison, Angus. Measuring Labour Slack. **In** *Weisbrod, B. and Hughes, H., eds.*, 1983, pp. 97–112. **[G: U.K.; W. Germany]**

Martínez, Manuel Silos. Returns to Schooling in the Metropolitan Area of Monterrey: An Analysis of Its Behaviour over Time, 1975–79. **In** *Urquidi, V. L. and Reyes, S. T., eds.*, 1983, pp. 252–65. **[G: Mexico]**

Martino, Antonio. Tales from the Public Sector: Red Tape all'Italiana. *Policy Rev.*, Fall 1983, (26), pp. 93. **[G: Italy]**

McGavin, P. A. Equal Pay for Women: A Postscript [Segmented Labour Market Theories and the Australian Experience of Equal Pay for Women]. *Australian Econ. Pap.*, June 1983, *22*(40), pp. 65–67. **[G: Australia]**

McGavin, P. A. Equal Pay for Women: A Re-Assessment of the Australian Experience. *Australian Econ. Pap.*, June 1983, *22*(40), pp. 48–59. **[G: Australia]**

McKenna, Chris. Optimal Search for Overtime Work. *Bull. Econ. Res.*, November 1983, *35*(2), pp. 87–95.

McMenamin, J. Stuart and Russell, R. Robert. Measuring Labor Compensation in Controls Programs. **In** *Triplett, J. E., ed.*, 1983, pp. 423–48. **[G: U.S.]**

Mellow, Wesley. Employer Size, Unionism, and Wages. **In** *Reid, J. D., Jr., ed.*, 1983, pp. 253–82. **[G: U.S.]**

Mennemeyer, Stephen T. and Gaumer, Gary. Nursing Wages and the Value of Educational Credentials. *J. Human Res.*, Winter 1983, *18*(1), pp. 32–48. **[G: U.S.]**

Merrilees, William J. Pension Benefits and the Decline in Elderly Male Labour Force Participation. *Econ. Rec.*, September 1983, *59*(166), pp. 260–70. **[G: Australia]**

Merton, Robert C. On Consumption Indexed Public Pension Plans. **In** *Bodie, Z. and Shoven, J. B., eds.*, 1983, pp. 259–76, 287–89. **[G: U.S.]**

Metcalf, David and Richards, John. Youth Employment in Great Britain. **In** *Reubens, B. G., ed.*, 1983, pp. 149–84. **[G: U.K.]**

Mieszkowski, Peter. The Tax Treatment of Married Couples and the 1981 Tax Law: Commentary. **In** *Penner, R. G., ed.*, 1983, pp. 69–70. **[G: U.S.]**

Miller, Paul W. Education and the Distribution of Earned Income. **In** *Blandy, R. and Covick, O., eds.*, 1983, pp. 16–36. **[G: Australia]**

Minarik, Joseph J. Family Issues in Taxation: Commentary. **In** *Penner, R. G., ed.*, 1983, pp. 23–27. **[G: U.S.]**

Mincer, Jacob. Union Effects: Wages, Turnover, and Job Training. **In** *Reid, J. D., Jr., ed.*, 1983, pp. 217–52. **[G: U.S.]**

Mitchell, Olivia S. Fringe Benefits and the Cost of Changing Jobs. *Ind. Lab. Relat. Rev.*, October 1983, *37*(1), pp. 70–78. **[G: U.S.]**

Mitchell, William F. Equal Pay for Women: A Reply [Segmented Labor Market Theories and the Australian Experience of Equal Pay for Women]. *J. Post Keynesian Econ.*, Summer 1983, *5*(4), pp. 669–72. **[G: Australia]**

Mizon, Grayham E. and Nickell, S. J. Vintage Production Models of U.K. Manufacturing Industry. *Scand. J. Econ.*, 1983, *85*(2), pp. 295–310. **[G: U.K.]**

Modigliani, Franco. Retirement Annuity Design in an Inflationary Climate: Comment. **In** *Bodie, Z. and Shoven, J. B., eds.*, 1983, pp. 316–22. **[G: U.S.]**

Moore, Geoffrey H. Inflation and Statistics. **In** *Moore, G. H.*, 1983, *1980*, pp. 287–311. **[G: U.S.]**

Moore, Robert L. Employer Discrimination: Evidence from Self-Employed Workers. *Rev. Econ. Statist.*, August 1983, *65*(3), pp. 496–501. **[G: U.S.]**

Moore, William J. and Raisian, John. The Level and Growth of Union/Nonunion Relative Wage Effects, 1967–1977. *J. Lab. Res.*, Winter 1983, *4*(1), pp. 65–79. **[G: U.S.]**

Moschos, D. Aggregate Price Responses to Wage and Productivity Changes: Evidence from the U.S. *Empirical Econ.*, 1983, *8*(3–4), pp. 169–75. **[G: U.S.]**

Mukasa, R. Les conditions de travail au Japon: Leur aspect global après la Seconde Guerre mondiale. (Labour Conditions in Japan: The Overall Post-War Picture. With English summary.) *Écon. Soc.*, March–April 1983, *17*(3–4), pp. 481–516. **[G: Japan]**

Mumy, Gene E. and Manson, William D. Payroll Taxes, Social Security, and the Unique Tax Advantage of Company Pensions. *J. Risk Ins.*, March 1983, *50*(1), pp. 161–65.

Munnell, Alicia H. Financing Options for Social Security. **In** *Parnes, H. S., ed.*, 1983, pp. 197–240. **[G: U.S.]**

Munnell, Alicia H. Who Should Manage the Assets of Collectively Bargained Pension Plans? *New Eng. Econ. Rev.*, July–August 1983, pp. 18–30. **[G: U.S.]**

Muth, Richard F. Intermetropolitan Wage Differentials in the United States: Comment. **In** *Triplett, J. E., ed.*, 1983, pp. 330–32. **[G: U.S.]**

Nakamura, Alice and Nakamura, Masao. Part-Time and Full-Time Work Behaviour of Married Women: A Model with a Doubly Truncated Dependent Variable. *Can. J. Econ.*, May 1983, *16*(2), pp. 229–57. **[G: U.S.; Canada]**

Needleman, L. The Structure of Industrial Earnings in Seven West European Countries. **In** *[Saunders, C. T.]*, 1983, pp. 175–92. **[G: W. Europe]**

Nestel, Gilbert; Mercier, Jacqueline and Shaw, Lois B. Economic Consequences of Midlife Change in Marital Status. **In** *Shaw, L. B., ed.*, 1983, pp. 109–25. **[G: U.S.]**

Nichols, Donald A. Macroeconomic Determinants of Wage Adjustments in White-Collar Occupations. *Rev. Econ. Statist.*, May 1983, *65*(2), pp. 203–13. **[G: U.S.]**

Nichols, Donald A. Wage Measurement Questions Raised by an Incomes Policy. **In** *Triplett, J. E., ed.*, 1983, pp. 449–62. **[G: U.S.]**

Nickell, S. J. and Andrews, M. Unions, Real Wages and Employment in Britain 1951–79. *Oxford Econ. Pap.*, Supplement November 1983, *35*, pp. 183–206. **[G: U.K.]**

Noam, Eli M. The Effect of Unionization and Civil Service on the Salaries and Productivity of Regulators. **In** *Reid, J. D., Jr., ed.*, 1983, pp. 157–70. **[G: U.S.]**

Nohara, Hiroatsu. Dualité et unité du marché du travail industriel: le cas du Japon. (Dualism and Unity in the Industrial Labor Market: The Case of Japan. With English summary.) *Revue Écon.*, November 1983, *34*(6), pp. 1188–212. **[G: Japan]**

Nolan, Peter and Brown, William. Competition and Workplace Wage Determination. *Oxford Bull. Econ. Statist.*, August 1983, *45*(3), pp. 269–87. **[G: U.K.]**

Northrup, Herbert R. and Greis, Theresa Diss. The Decline in Average Annual Hours Worked in the United States, 1947–1979. *J. Lab. Res.*, Spring 1983, *4*(2), pp. 95–113. **[G: U.S.]**

Nowak, Margaret J. and Crockett, Geoffrey V. Education, Training & Earnings of Managers: Some Western Australian Evidence. *Australian Bull. Lab.*, March 1983, *9*(2), pp. 131–51. **[G: Australia]**

O'Neill, June. Family Issues in Taxation. **In** *Penner, R. G., ed.*, 1983, pp. 1–22. **[G: U.S.]**

Oi, Walter Y. The Fixed Employment Costs of Specialized Labor. **In** *Triplett, J. E., ed.*, 1983, pp. 63–116. **[G: U.S.]**

Olmsted, Barney. Changing Times: The Use of Reduced Work Time Options in the United States. *Int. Lab. Rev.*, July–August 1983, *122*(4), pp. 479–92. **[G: U.S.]**

Olson, Craig A. and Becker, Brian E. Sex Discrimination in the Promotion Process. *Ind. Lab. Relat. Rev.*, July 1983, *36*(4), pp. 624–41. **[G: U.S.]**

Orsatti, Alvaro. La nueva distribución funcional del ingreso en la Argentina. (With English summary.) *Desarrollo Econ.*, October-December 1983, *23*(91), pp. 315–37. **[G: Argentina]**

Paldam, Martin. Industrial Conflicts and Economic Conditions: A Comparative Empirical Investigation. *Europ. Econ. Rev.*, January 1983, *20*(1–3), pp. 231–56.

Pang, Eng Fong and Seow, Greg. Labour, Employment and Wage Structure. **In** *Chen, P. S. J., ed.*, 1983, pp. 160–70. **[G: Singapore]**

Pankert, Alfred. Government Influence on Wage Bargaining: The Limits Set by International Labour Standards. *Int. Lab. Rev.*, Sept.–Oct. 1983, *122*(5), pp. 579–91. **[G: ILO]**

Pedersen, Peder J. Inflationary Effects of Unemployment Insurance—An International Survey. **In** *Söderström, L., ed.*, 1983, pp. 225–49. **[G: OECD]**

Penn, Roger. The Course of Wage Differentials between Skilled and Nonskilled Manual Workers in Britain between 1856 and 1964. *Brit. J. Ind. Relat.*, March 1983, *21*(1), pp. 69–90. **[G: U.K.]**

Perkinson, Leon B. and Fearn, Robert M. Wellington–Winter Revisited: The Case of Municipal Sanitation Collection: Comment. *Ind. Lab. Relat. Rev.*, July 1983, *36*(4), pp. 655–57. **[G: U.S.]**

Perles, Susan P. Impact of CETA-PSE on Local Public Sector Employment Expenditures. **In** *Hirsch, W. Z., ed.*, 1983, pp. 122–57. **[G: U.S.]**

Peterson, Paul and Mackay, Keith. Youth Employment in Australia. **In** *Reubens, B. G., ed.*, 1983, pp. 86–112. **[G: Australia]**

Pierson, David A. Labor Market Influences on Entry vs. Nonentry Wages: Evidence from Minnesota Public School Districts. *Nebr. J. Econ. Bus.*, Spring 1983, *22*(2), pp. 33–48. **[G: U.S.]**

Playford, Clive and Pond, Chris. The Right to Be Unequal: Inequality in Incomes. **In** *Field, F., ed.*, 1983, pp. 34–55. **[G: U.K.]**

Podgursky, Michael. Unions and Family Income Inequality. *J. Human Res.*, Fall 1983, *18*(4), pp. 574–91. **[G: U.S.]**

Poirier, Dale J. and Ruud, Paul A. Diagnostic Testing in Missing Data Models. *Int. Econ. Rev.*, October 1983, *24*(3), pp. 537–46.

Powell, Alan A. Aspects of Labour Market Theory and Behaviour Highlighted by IMPACT Project Studies. **In** *Blandy, R. and Covick, O., eds.*, 1983, pp. 137–65. **[G: Australia]**

Prieser, Carl. Skill Level Differences in White-Collar Pay. *Mon. Lab. Rev.*, December 1983, *106*(12), pp. 49–52. **[G: U.S.]**

Quinn, Joseph F. and Burkhauser, Richard V. Influencing Retirement Behavior: A Key Issue for Social Security. *J. Policy Anal. Manage.*, Fall 1983, *3*(1), pp. 1–13. **[G: U.S.]**

Raisian, John. Contracts, Job Experience, and Cyclical Labor Market Adjustments. *J. Lab. Econ.*, April 1983, *1*(2), pp. 152–70. **[G: U.S.]**

Raisian, John. Union Dues and Wage Premiums. *J. Lab. Res.*, Winter 1983, *4*(1), pp. 1–18. **[G: U.S.]**

Rath, B. Estimation of SWR: An Empirical Verification from a Multi-Purpose Project in Orissa. *Indian Econ. J.*, April-June 1983, *30*(4), pp. 97–102. **[G: India]**

Reddin, Mike. Pensions, Wealth and the Extension of Inequality. **In** *Field, F., ed.*, 1983, pp. 138–58. **[G: U.K.]**

Reichelderfer, Katherine H. Rank and Salary of Federally Employed Agricultural Economists. *Agr. Econ. Res.*, January 1983, *35*(1), pp. 44–51. **[G: U.S.]**

Reimers, Cordelia W. Labor Market Discrimination against Hispanic and Black Men. *Rev. Econ. Statist.*, November 1983, *65*(4), pp. 570–79. **[G: U.S.]**

Reimers, Cordelia W. The Effect of Pension Plans on the Pattern of Life Cycle Compensation: Comment. **In** *Triplett, J. E., ed.*, 1983, pp. 416–20. **[G: U.S.]**

Rein, Martin. The Social Policy of the Firm. **In** *Rein, M.*, 1983, *1982*, pp. 3–22. **[G: OECD]**

Remus, William E. and Kelley, Lane. Evidence of Sex Discrimination: In Similar Populations, Men Are Paid Better Than Women. *Amer. J. Econ. Soc.*, April 1983, *42*(2), pp. 149–52. **[G: U.S.]**

Ribe, Helena. The Relative Economic Position of Migrants and Natives in Colombia: An Economic Analysis of the 1973 Census Sample. **In** *Urquidi, V. L. and Reyes, S. T., eds.*, 1983, pp. 55–78. **[G: Colombia]**

Rice, G. Randolph. The Variance of Expected Inflation and the Rate of Inflation: Implications from Inter-Industry Wage Equations. *Appl. Econ.*, August 1983, *15*(4), pp. 553–61. **[G: U.K.]**

Richards, Daniel J. Wages and the Dominant Firm. *J. Lab. Res.*, Spring 1983, *4*(2), pp. 177–82. **[G: U.S.]**

Richardson, Sue. Inflation and the Dispersion of Pay. **In** *Blandy, R. and Covick, O., eds.*, 1983, pp. 37–60. **[G: Australia]**

Riddell, W. Craig. The Responsiveness of Wage Settlements in Canada and Economic Policy. *Can. Public Policy*, March 1983, *9*(1), pp. 9–23. **[G: Canada; U.S.]**

Robbins, Richard D. and Evans, Sidney H. Characteristics of Black Agricultural Economists. *Amer. J. Agr. Econ.*, December 1983, *65*(5), pp. 993–98. **[G: U.S.]**

Robinson, Derek. Indirect and Partial Measures. *Oxford Bull. Econ. Statist.*, February 1983, *45*(1), pp. 105–25. **[G: U.K.]**

Robinson, Derek. Pay Policies for the Future: Indirect and Partial Measures. **In** *Robinson, D. and Mayhew, K., eds.*, 1983, pp. 105–25. **[G: U.K.]**

Roman, Paul M. Medicalization and Social Control in the Workplace. **In** *Littrell, W. B.; Sjoberg, G. and Zurcher, L. A., eds.*, 1983, pp. 115–29. **[G: U.S.]**

Rosen, Corey M. The Effect of Employee Stock Ownership Plans on Corporate Profits—Comment. *J. Risk Ins.*, September 1983, *50*(3), pp. 493–94. **[G: U.S.]**

Rossana, Robert J. Some Empirical Estimates of the Demand for Hours in U.S. Manufacturing Industries. *Rev. Econ. Statist.*, November 1983, *65*(4), pp. 560–69. **[G: U.S.]**

Rubenson, Kjell. Financing Paid Educational Leave: The Swedish Model. **In** *Levin, H. M. and Schütze, H. G., eds.*, 1983, pp. 237–55. **[G: Sweden]**

Rubin, Donald B. Imputing Income in the CPS: Comments on "Measures of Aggregate Labor Cost in the United States." **In** *Triplett, J. E., ed.*, 1983, pp. 333–43. **[G: U.S.]**

Ruggles, Nancy D. and Ruggles, Richard. The Treatment of Pensions and Insurance in National Accounts. *Rev. Income Wealth*, December 1983, *29*(4), pp. 371–404. **[G: U.S.]**

Rytina, Nancy. Comparing Annual and Weekly Earnings from the Current Population Survey. *Mon. Lab. Rev.*, April 1983, *106*(4), pp. 32–36. **[G: U.S.]**

Saffran, Bernard. The Tax Treatment of Married Couples and the 1981 Tax Law: Commentary. **In** *Penner, R. G., ed.*, 1983, pp. 64–68. **[G: U.S.]**

Sahling, Leonard G. and Smith, Sharon P. Regional Wage Differentials: Has the South Risen Again? *Rev. Econ. Statist.*, February 1983, *65*(1), pp. 131–35. **[G: U.S.]**

Salop, Steven C. A Century of Evidence on Wage and Price Stickiness in the United States, the United Kingdom, and Japan: Comment. **In** *Tobin, J., ed.*, 1983, pp. 124–33. **[G: U.S.; U.K.; Japan]**

Samuelson, Paul A. On Consumption Indexed Public Pension Plans: Comment. **In** *Bodie, Z. and Shoven, J. B., eds.*, 1983, pp. 276–87. **[G: U.S.]**

Schaefer, Gordon. Escalation Measures: What Is the Answer? What Is the Question? Comment. **In** *Diewert, W. E. and Montmarquette, C., eds.*, 1983, pp. 483–87.

Schapper, Paul R. Hospital Cost Inflation: The Case of Australia. *Inquiry*, Fall 1983, *20*(3), pp. 276–81. **[G: Australia]**

Scheffler, Richard M. and Rossiter, Louis F. Compensation Schemes and the Labor Supply of Dentists. *Quart. Rev. Econ. Bus.*, Autumn 1983, *23*(3), pp. 29–43. **[G: U.S.]**

Scheiber, Sylvester J. Providing Income Security to the Elderly: The Role of Programs Other than Social Security. *Contemp. Policy Issue*, April 1983, (3), pp. 33–52. **[G: U.S.]**

Schober, Karen. Youth Employment in West Germany. **In** *Reubens, B. G., ed.*, 1983, pp. 113–48. **[G: W. Germany]**

Schulz, James H. Private Pensions, Inflation, and Employment. **In** *Parnes, H. S., ed.*, 1983, pp. 241–64. **[G: U.S.]**

Schütze, Hans G. Financing Paid Educational Leave: The Federal Republic of Germany. **In** *Levin, H. M. and Schütze, H. G., eds.*, 1983, pp. 273–95. **[G: W. Germany]**

Scott, Frank A., Jr.; Long, James E. and Somppi, Ken. Free Agency, Owner Incentives, and the National Football League Players Association. *J. Lab. Res.*, Summer 1983, *4*(3), pp. 257–64. **[G: U.S.]**

Seguret, Marie-Claire. Women and Working Conditions: Prospects for Improvement? *Int. Lab. Rev.*, May-June 1983, *122*(3), pp. 295–311. **[G: Global]**

Seidman, Bert. Discussion [Financing Options for Social Security] [Private Pensions, Inflation, and Employment]. **In** *Parnes, H. S., ed.*, 1983, pp. 265–69. **[G: U.S.]**

Shah, Anup R. K. Professional Earnings in the United Kingdom. *Economica,* November 1983, *50*(200), pp. 451–62. [G: U.K.]

Shah, Anup R. K. and Walker, Martin. The Distribution of Regional Earnings in the UK. *Appl. Econ.,* August 1983, *15*(4), pp. 507–19. [G: U.K.]

Shahidsaless, Shahin; Gillis, William and Shaffer, Ron. Community Characteristics and Employment Multipliers in Nonmetropolitan Counties, 1950–1970. *Land Econ.,* February 1983, *59*(1), pp. 84–93. [G: U.S.]

Shakow, Don M. Market Mechanisms for Compensating Hazardous Work: A Critical Analysis. **In** *Kasperson, R. E., ed.,* 1983, pp. 277–90. [G: U.S.]

Shapiro, David. Working Youth. **In** *Borus, M. E., ed.,* 1983, pp. 23–58. [G: U.S.]

Shaw, Lois B. and O'Brien, Theresa. Unplanned Careers: The Working Lives of Middle-aged Women: Introduction and Overview. **In** *Shaw, L. B., ed.,* 1983, pp. 1–31. [G: U.S.]

Shiells, Martha and Wright, Gavin. Night Work as a Labor Market Phenomenon: Southern Textiles in the Interwar Period. *Exploration Econ. Hist.,* October 1983, *20*(4), pp. 331–50. [G: U.S.]

Shome, Parthasarathi and Saito, Katrine W. The Impact of Contractual Savings on Resource Mobilization and Allocation: The Experience of Malaysia. **In** *Lim, D., ed.,* 1983, *1978,* pp. 288–302. [G: Malaysia]

Siebert, W. S. and Young, A. Sex and Family Status Differentials in Professional Earnings: The Case of Librarians. *Scot. J. Polit. Econ.,* February 1983, *30*(1), pp. 18–41. [G: U.K.]

Singh, Harbhajan. Inequality in Labour-Market Rewards and Education in India (A Case Study of Delhi). *Indian Econ. Rev.,* July–December 1983, *18*(2), pp. 245–72. [G: India]

Sirén, Pekka. Terveydenhuollon menot, rakenne ja rahoitus. (Health Care Expenditure, Structure and Financing in Finland. With English summary.) *Kansant. Aikak.,* 1983, *79*(4), pp. 418–35. [G: Finland]

Smeeding, Timothy M. The Size Distribution of Wage and Nonwage Compensation: Employer Cost versus Employee Value. **In** *Triplett, J. E., ed.,* 1983, pp. 237–77. [G: U.S.]

Smith, Gregory P. Employer-sponsored Programs. **In** *Levin, H. M. and Schütze, H. G., eds.,* 1983, pp. 159–87. [G: U.S.]

Smith, Robert S. Salaries and Pension Funding: Are Public Safety Officers Given Preference over Taxpayers? **In** *Hirsch, W. Z., ed.,* 1983, pp. 188–211. [G: U.S.]

Smith, Robert S. and Ehrenberg, Ronald G. Estimating Wage-fringe Trade-offs: Some Data Problems. **In** *Triplett, J. E., ed.,* 1983, pp. 347–67. [G: U.S.]

Smith, Sharon P. Are State and Local Government Workers Overpaid? **In** *Hirsch, W. Z., ed.,* 1983, pp. 59–89. [G: U.S.]

Smith, Shirley J. Estimating Annual Hours of Labor Force Activity. *Mon. Lab. Rev.,* February 1983, *106*(2), pp. 13–22. [G: U.S.]

Smith, V. Kerry. The Role of Site and Job Characteristics in Hedonic Wage Models. *J. Urban Econ.,* May 1983, *13*(3), pp. 296–321. [G: U.S.]

Snooks, G. D. Determinants of Earnings Inequality amongst Australian Artists. *Australian Econ. Pap.,* December 1983, *22*(41), pp. 322–32. [G: Australia]

Sobhan, Rehman. Distributive Regimes under Public Enterprise: A Case Study of the Bangladesh Experience. **In** *Stewart, F., ed.,* 1983, pp. 138–67. [G: Bangladesh]

Stewart, Mark B. Relative Earnings and Individual Union Membership in the United Kingdom. *Economica,* May 1983, *50*(198), pp. 111–25. [G: U.K.]

Sturgess, N. H. and Wijaya, Hesti. Rice Havesting: A View from the Theory of Common Property. *Bull. Indonesian Econ. Stud.,* August 1983, *19*(2), pp. 27–45. [G: Indonesia]

Summers, Lawrence H. Observations on the Indexation of Old Age Pensions. **In** *Bodie, Z. and Shoven, J. B., eds.,* 1983, pp. 231–51, 257–58. [G: U.S.]

Swenson, James R. Discussion [Financing Options for Social Security] [Private Pensions, Inflation, and Employment]. **In** *Parnes, H. S., ed.,* 1983, pp. 271–79. [G: U.S.]

Tannen, Michael B. Vocational Education and Earnings for White Males: New Evidence from Longitudinal Data. *Southern Econ. J.,* October 1983, *50*(2), pp. 369–84. [G: U.S.]

Tanskanen, Antti. Työllisyys pienessä avoimessa taloudessa. (Employment in a Small Open Economy. With English summary.) *Kansant. Aikak.,* 1983, *79*(3), pp. 278–83. [G: Finland]

Taussig, Michael K. Discussion [Financing Options for Social Security] [Private Pensions, Inflation, and Employment]. **In** *Parnes, H. S., ed.,* 1983, pp. 281–86. [G: U.S.]

Tavares, Maria De Conceicao and Souza, Paulo Renato. Employment and Wages in Industry: The Case of Brazil. **In** *Urquidi, V. L. and Reyes, S. T., eds.,* 1983, pp. 195–210. [G: Brazil]

Taylor, John B. Union Wage Settlements during a Disinflation. *Amer. Econ. Rev.,* December 1983, *73*(5), pp. 981–93. [G: U.S.]

Teilhet-Waldorf, Saral and Waldorf, William H. Earnings of Self-Employed in an Informal Sector: A Case Study of Bangkok. *Econ. Develop. Cult. Change,* April 1983, *31*(3), pp. 587–607. [G: Thailand]

Tepper, Irwin. Optimal Funding and Asset Allocation Rules for Defined-Benefit Pension Plans: Comment. **In** *Bodie, Z. and Shoven, J. B., eds.,* 1983, pp. 104–05. [G: U.S.]

Terry, Sylvia Lazos. Work Experience, Earnings, and Family Income in 1981. *Mon. Lab. Rev.,* April 1983, *106*(4), pp. 13–20. [G: U.S.]

Thoris, Gérard. Les limites de la redistribution des revenus: perspective macroéconomique. (With English summary.) *Revue Écon. Polit.,* September–October 1983, *93*(5), pp. 682–92. [G: France]

Tinbergen, Jan and Wegner, Eckhard. Zu einem makroökonomischen Modell der Einkommensbildung. (A Macro-Economic Model of Income Formation. With English summary.) *Schweiz. Z. Volkswirtsch. Statist.,* March 1983, *119*(1), pp. 69–78. [G: Switzerland]

Tokman, Victor E. Labour Market Dynamics and Income Distribution in Latin America. **In** *Urquidi, V. L. and Reyes, S. T., eds.*, 1983, pp. 151–73. **[G: Latin America]**

Tomoda, Shizue. Working Conditions in the Hotel, Restaurant and Catering Sector: A Case Study of Japan. *Int. Lab. Rev.*, March–April 1983, *122*(2), pp. 239–52. **[G: Japan]**

Treble, John G. and McGrady, Diane. Geometric versus Arithmetic Mean in the Measurement of the Union/Non-Union Wage Differential. *Appl. Econ.*, February 1983, *15*(1), pp. 43–48. **[G: U.K.]**

Treyz, George I. and Duguay, Gerry E. Endogenous Wage Determination: Its Significance for State Policy Analysis Models. **In** *Dutta, M.; Hartline, J. C. and Loeb, P. D., eds.*, 1983, pp. 116–30. **[G: U.S.]**

Trinder, Chris. Income in Work and When Unemployed: Some Problems in Calculating Replacement Ratios. *Nat. Inst. Econ. Rev.*, February 1983, (103), pp. 56–61. **[G: U.K.]**

Triplett, Jack E. Escalation Measures: What Is the Answer? What Is the Question? **In** *Diewert, W. E. and Montmarquette, C., eds.*, 1983, pp. 457–82.

Triplett, Jack E. Introduction: An Essay on Labor Cost. **In** *Triplett, J. E., ed.*, 1983, pp. 1–60.

Twine, Fred. The Low Paid. **In** *Brown, G. and Cook, R., eds.*, 1983, pp. 107–35. **[G: U.K.]**

Umetani, Shun'ichiro and Reubens, Beatrice G. Youth Employment in Japan. **In** *Reubens, B. G., ed.*, 1983, pp. 185–231. **[G: Japan]**

Utgoff, Kathleen Classen. Compensation Levels and Quit Rates in the Public Sector. *J. Human Res.*, Summer 1983, *18*(3), pp. 394–406. **[G: U.S.]**

Voos, Paula B. Union Organizing: Costs and Benefits. *Ind. Lab. Relat. Rev.*, July 1983, *36*(4), pp. 576–91. **[G: U.S.]**

Ward, James Gordon. On Teacher Quality. **In** *Odden, A. and Webb, L. D., eds.*, 1983, pp. 163–68. **[G: U.S.]**

Ward, William A. On Estimating Shadow Wage Rates for Portugal. *Economia*, October 1983, *7*(3), pp. 543–54. **[G: Portugal]**

Watson, Mark W. and Engle, Robert F. Alternative Algorithms for the Estimation of Dynamic Factor, MIMIC and Varying Coefficient Regression Models. *J. Econometrics*, December 1983, *23*(3), pp. 385–400. **[G: U.S.]**

Weeks, John. The State and Income Redistribution in Peru, 1968–76, with Special Reference to Manufacturing. **In** *Stewart, F., ed.*, 1983, pp. 62–82. **[G: Peru]**

Weisbrod, Burton A. Nonprofit and Proprietary Sector Behavior: Wage Differentials among Lawyers. *J. Lab. Econ.*, July 1983, *1*(3), pp. 246–63. **[G: U.S.]**

White, Richard A. Employee Preferences for Nontaxable Compensation Offered in a Cafeteria Compensation Plan: An Empirical Study. *Accounting Rev.*, July 1983, *58*(3), pp. 539–61. **[G: U.S.]**

Wilensky, Gail R. and Rossiter, Louis F. Economic Advantages of Board Certification. *J. Health Econ.*, March 1983, *2*(1), pp. 87–94. **[G: U.S.]**

Williams, Harry B. Pay Levels in Hosiery Manufacturing. *Mon. Lab. Rev.*, March 1983, *106*(3), pp. 36–37. **[G: U.S.]**

Williams, Harry B. Wages of Appliance Repair Technicians Vary Widely among Metropolitan Areas. *Mon. Lab. Rev.*, December 1983, *106*(12), pp. 52–53. **[G: U.S.]**

Wise, David A. Pensions as Severance Pay: Comment. **In** *Bodie, Z. and Shoven, J. B., eds.*, 1983, pp. 86–88. **[G: U.S.]**

Woodbury, Stephen A. Substitution between Wage and Nonwage Benefits. *Amer. Econ. Rev.*, March 1983, *73*(1), pp. 166–82. **[G: U.S.]**

Zabalza, Antoni. The CES Utility Function, Non-Linear Budget Constraints and Labour Supply: Results on Female Participation and Hours. *Econ. J.*, June 1983, *93*(370), pp. 312–30. **[G: U.K.]**

Zeckhauser, Richard J. Economic Implications of ERISA: Comment. **In** *Bodie, Z. and Shoven, J. B., eds.*, 1983, pp. 53–55. **[G: U.S.]**

8243 Employment Studies, Unemployment and Vacancies; Retirements and Quits

Abbott, Walter F. and Leasure, J. W. Income Level and Inflation in the United States: 1947–1977. **In** *Schmukler, N. and Marcus, E., eds.*, 1983, pp. 804–19. **[G: U.S.]**

Abraham, Katharine G. Structural/Frictional vs. Deficient Demand Unemployment: Some New Evidence. *Amer. Econ. Rev.*, September 1983, *73*(4), pp. 708–24. **[G: U.S.]**

Adams, Charles F., Jr.; Cook, Robert F. and Maurice, Arthur J. A Pooled Time-Series Analysis of the Job-Creation Impact of Public Service Employment Grants to Large Cities. *J. Human Res.*, Spring 1983, *18*(2), pp. 283–94. **[G: U.S.]**

Adell, Bernard. Termination of Employment on the Initiative of the Employer and Income Security of the Worker Concerned. **In** *Queen's Univ. Indust. Relat. Centre*, 1983, pp. 82–92. **[G: Canada]**

Aislabie, C. J. The Australian Tariff as a Selective Employment Policy Instrument: An Empirical Study. *Australian Econ. Pap.*, June 1983, *22*(40), pp. 119–31. **[G: Australia]**

Akerlof, George A. and Main, Brian G. M. Measures of Unemployment Duration as Guides to Research and Policy: Reply [An Experience-Weighted Measure of Employment and Unemployment Duration]. *Amer. Econ. Rev.*, December 1983, *73*(5), pp. 1151–52. **[G: U.S.]**

Albert, Michel. Growth, Investment and Employment in Europe in the 1980s. **In** *Heertje, A., ed.*, 1983, pp. 41–55. **[G: EEC]**

Alejo, Francisco Javier. Employment and the Allocation of Resources: Mexico. **In** *Urquidi, V. L. and Reyes, S. T., eds.*, 1983, pp. 348–61. **[G: Mexico]**

Allen, Steven G. How Much Does Absenteeism Cost? *J. Human Res.*, Summer 1983, *18*(3), pp. 379–93. **[G: U.S.]**

Andreassen, Arthur J.; Saunders, Norman C. and Su, Betty W. Economic Outlook for the 1990's: Three Scenarios for Economic Growth. *Mon. Lab. Rev.*, November 1983, *106*(11), pp. 11–23. **[G: U.S.]**

Anthony, Douglas. The Small Firm: Japan. **In** *Storey,*

D. J., ed., 1983, pp. 46–83. **[G: Japan]**

Appelbaum, Eileen. Winners and Losers in the High-Tech Workplace. *Challenge*, Sept.–Oct. 1983, *26*(4), pp. 52–55. **[G: U.S.]**

Arestis, P. and Driver, Ciaran. U.K. Unemployment and Post-Keynesian Remedies. *Metroecon.*, October 1983, *35*(3), pp. 275–91. **[G: U.K.]**

Armstrong, Harvey and Taylor, Jim. Unemployment Stocks and Flows in the Travel-to-Work Areas of the North-West Region. *Urban Stud.*, August 1983, *20*(3), pp. 311–25. **[G: U.K.]**

Artis, M. J. The Capital Constraint on Employment. **In** *[Saunders, C. T.]*, 1983, pp. 109–26. **[G: U.K.]**

Ashcroft, Brian. The Scottish Region and the Regions of Scotland. **In** *Ingham, K. P. D. and Love, J., eds.*, 1983, pp. 173–87. **[G: U.K.]**

Ashenfelter, Orley. The Withering away of a Full Employment Goal. *Can. Public Policy*, March 1983, *9*(1), pp. 114–25. **[G: Canada]**

Atkinson, Anthony B. Unemployment Benefits and Incentives in Britain. **In** *Atkinson, A. B.*, 1983, pp. 419–35. **[G: U.K.]**

Atkinson, Anthony B. and Flemming, J. S. Unemployment, Social Security and Incentives in Britain. **In** *Atkinson, A. B.*, 1983, *1978*, pp. 397–418. **[G: U.K.]**

Atkinson, Anthony B., et al. Durée du chômage et incitations: Résultats d'une enquête sur les dépenses des ménages au Royaume-Uni. (Unemployment Duration and Incentives: Evidence from the Family Expenditure Survey in the United Kingdom. With English summary.) *Ann. INSEE*, October–December 1983, (52), pp. 3–21. **[G: U.K.]**

Ball, R. J. Economic Management and Aggregate Supply. **In** *[Klein, L. R.]*, 1983, pp. 239–61. **[G: OECD]**

Ball, R. M. Spatial and Structural Characteristics of Recent Unemployment Change: Some Policy Considerations. *Reg. Stud.*, April 1983, *17*(2), pp. 135–40. **[G: U.K.]**

Barnes, David W. The Problem of Multiple Components or Divisions in Title VII Litigation: A Comment [Testing for Discrimination in Employment Practices]. *Law Contemp. Probl.*, Autumn 1983, *46*(4), pp. 185–88. **[G: U.S.]**

Barrett, Nancy S. Perspectives on Unemployment and Policy. *Rev. Black Polit. Econ.*, Spring 1983, *12*(3), pp. 55–61. **[G: U.S.]**

Baumann, Johann H. A Disaggregate Short Run Phillips Curve for Austria: The Effects of Regional Unemployment Dispersion and Spatial Wage Transfer on the National Wage Rate. *Z. Nationalökon.*, 1983, *43*(2), pp. 189–211. **[G: Austria]**

Beach, Charles M. and Kaliski, Steve F. Measuring the Duration of Unemployment from Gross Flow Data. *Can. J. Econ.*, May 1983, *16*(2), pp. 258–63. **[G: Canada]**

Beach, Charles M. and Kaliski, Steve F. The Impact of the 1979 Unemployment Insurance Amendments. *Can. Public Policy*, June 1983, *9*(2), pp. 164–73. **[G: Canada]**

Becker, Brian E. and Hills, Stephen M. The Long-Run Effects of Job Changes and Unemployment among Male Teenagers. *J. Human Res.*, Spring 1983, *18*(2), pp. 197–212. **[G: U.S.]**

Bednarzik, Robert W. Layoffs and Permanent Job Losses: Workers' Traits and Cyclical Patterns. *Mon. Lab. Rev.*, September 1983, *106*(9), pp. 3–12. **[G: U.S.]**

Bednarzik, Robert W. Short Workweeks during Economic Downturns. *Mon. Lab. Rev.*, June 1983, *106*(6), pp. 3–11. **[G: U.S.]**

Behrman, Jere R. and Taubman, Paul. Redistribution of Earnings by Unemployment and Inflation. **In** *[Klein, L. R.]*, 1983, pp. 262–81. **[G: U.S.]**

Bell, Carolyn Shaw. On DeGrasse and Military Spending [Military Spending and Jobs]. *Challenge*, Sept.–Oct. 1983, *26*(4), pp. 49–51. **[G: U.S.]**

Bender, Lloyd D. and Parcels, Larry C. Structural Differences and the Time Pattern of Basic Employment. *Land Econ.*, May 1983, *59*(2), pp. 220–34. **[G: U.S.]**

Benham, Harry C. Unemployment Insurance Incentives and Unemployment Duration Distributions. *Rev. Econ. Statist.*, February 1983, *65*(1), pp. 139–43. **[G: U.S.]**

Benham, Harry C. UI Effects on Unemployment: Some Data on Competing Theories. *Ind. Relat.*, Fall 1983, *22*(3), pp. 403–09. **[G: U.S.]**

Benson, James W. Energy: Jobs and Values. **In** *Brown, H. J., ed.*, 1983, pp. 229–41. **[G: U.S.]**

Berberoglu, Berch. Industrialization, Employment, and Class Formation in the Periphery. *Econ. Forum*, Summer 1983, *14*(1), pp. 131–41. **[G: Brazil; S. Korea; Mexico; Taiwan]**

Berlin, Ira and Gutman, Herbert G. Natives and Immigrants, Free Men and Slaves: Urban Workingmen in the Antebellum American South. *Amer. Hist. Rev.*, December 1983, *88*(5), pp. 1175–1200. **[G: U.S.]**

Berndt, Ernst R. The Fixed Employment Costs of Specialized Labor: Comment. **In** *Triplett, J. E., ed.*, 1983, pp. 116–22. **[G: U.S.]**

Berry, Albert. Agrarian Structure, Rural Labour Markets and Trends in Rural Incomes in Latin America. **In** *Urquidi, V. L. and Reyes, S. T., eds.*, 1983, pp. 174–94. **[G: Brazil; Colombia; Mexico]**

Berry, Albert and Sabot, Richard H. Unemployment and Economic Development. **In** *Streeten, P. and Maier, H., eds.*, 1983, pp. 147–66.

Björklund, Anders. Measuring the Duration of Unemployment: A Note. *Scot. J. Polit. Econ.*, June 1983, *30*(2), pp. 175–80. **[G: Sweden; U.S.]**

Björklund, Anders and Persson-Tanimura, Inga. Youth Employment in Sweden. **In** *Reubens, B. G., ed.*, 1983, pp. 232–68. **[G: Sweden]**

Blakemore, Arthur E. and Low, Stuart A. A Simultaneous Determination of Post-High School Education Choice and Labor Supply. *Quart. Rev. Econ. Bus.*, Winter 1983, *23*(4), pp. 81–92. **[G: U.S.]**

Blandy, Richard and Sloan, Judy. The Australian Labour Market, September 1983. *Australian Bull. Lab.*, September 1983, *9*(4), pp. 223–46. **[G: Australia]**

Blau, Francine D. and Kahn, Lawrence M. Job Search and Unionized Employment. *Econ. Inquiry*, July 1983, *21*(3), pp. 412–30. **[G: U.S.]**

Blau, Francine D. and Kahn, Lawrence M. Unionism, Seniority, and Turnover. *Ind. Relat.*, Fall 1983, *22*(3), pp. 362–73. **[G: U.S.]**

Bluestone, Barry. Deindustrialization and Unemployment in America. *Rev. Black Polit. Econ.*, Spring 1983, *12*(3), pp. 27–42. **[G: U.S.]**

Boardman, Anthony E. and Vining, Aidan R. The Role of Probative Statistics in Employment Discrimination Cases. *Law Contemp. Probl.*, Autumn 1983, *46*(4), pp. 189–218. **[G: U.S.]**

Böhning, W. R. Guestworker Employment in Selected European Countries—Lessons for the United States? **In** *Brown, P. G. and Shue, H., eds.*, 1983, pp. 99–138. **[G: France; Switzerland; U.S.; W. Germany]**

Booth, G. Geoffrey and Koveos, Peter E. Employment Fluctuations: An R/S Analysis. *J. Reg. Sci.*, February 1983, *23*(1), pp. 19–31. **[G: U.S.]**

Borjas, George J. The Substitutability of Black, Hispanic, and White Labor. *Econ. Inquiry*, January 1983, *21*(1), pp. 93–106. **[G: U.S.]**

Borus, Michael E. and Santos, Richard. The Youth Population. **In** *Borus, M. E., ed.*, 1983, pp. 1–21. **[G: U.S.]**

Borus, Michael E., et al. Youth Looking for Work. **In** *Borus, M. E., ed.*, 1983, pp. 59–102. **[G: U.S.]**

Bowers, Norman. Employment on the Rise in the First Half of 1983. *Mon. Lab. Rev.*, August 1983, *106*(8), pp. 8–14. **[G: U.S.]**

Bowie, Robert D. The Dual Labour Market. **In** *Easton, B., ed.*, 1983, pp. 71–94. **[G: New Zealand]**

Bowie, Robert D. The Peripheral Labour Force. **In** *Easton, B., ed.*, 1983, pp. 49–70. **[G: New Zealand]**

Boyle, R. M. Linwood: Government and the Motor Car Industry in Scotland. *Reg. Stud.*, February 1983, *17*(1), pp. 49–52. **[G: U.K.]**

Braae, Richard and Gallacher, John. Labour Supply in New Zealand, 1976 to 1981: New and Familiar Problems for Descriptive and Empirical Analysis. **In** *Easton, B., ed.*, 1983, pp. 15–48. **[G: New Zealand]**

Broadberry, S. N. Unemployment in Interwar Britain: A Disequilibrium Approach. *Oxford Econ. Pap.*, November 1983, *35*(3), pp. 463–85. **[G: U.K.]**

Brown, Charles; Gilroy, Curtis and Kohen, Andrew. Time-Series Evidence of the Effect of the Minimum Wage on Youth Employment and Unemployment. *J. Human Res.*, Winter 1983, *18*(1), pp. 3–31. **[G: U.S.]**

Brown, Peter G. Improving Equity in the Use of Temporary Workers. **In** *Kasperson, R. E., ed.*, 1983, pp. 291–300. **[G: U.S.]**

Brzoska, Michael. The Structure of the Defense Industry: The Federal Republic of Germany. **In** *Ball, N. and Leitenberg, M., eds.*, 1983, pp. 111–39. **[G: W. Germany]**

Buchele, Robert. Economic Achievement and the Power of Positive Thinking. *J. Human Res.*, Summer 1983, *18*(3), pp. 441–49. **[G: U.S.]**

Buchele, Robert. Economic Dualism and Employment Stability. *Ind. Relat.*, Fall 1983, *22*(3), pp. 410–18. **[G: U.S.]**

Buiter, Willem H. and Miller, Marcus H. Changing the Rules: Economic Consequences of the Thatcher Regime. *Brookings Pap. Econ. Act.*, 1983, (2), pp. 305–79. **[G: U.K.]**

Burkhauser, Richard V. and Quinn, Joseph F. Financial Incentives and Retirement in the United States. **In** *Söderström, L., ed.*, 1983, pp. 207–24. **[G: U.S.]**

Burkhauser, Richard V. and Quinn, Joseph F. The Effect of Pension Plans on the Pattern of Life Cycle Compensation. **In** *Triplett, J. E., ed.*, 1983, pp. 395–415. **[G: U.S.]**

Burtless, Gary T. Why Is Insured Unemployment So Low? *Brookings Pap. Econ. Act.*, 1983, (1), pp. 225–49. **[G: U.S.]**

Butcher, Geoff. Employment Multipliers from Input/Output Tables. **In** *Easton, B., ed.*, 1983, pp. 141–57. **[G: New Zealand]**

Carbaugh, Robert. The Consequences of Local Content Protection. *Bus. Econ.*, September 1983, *18*(4), pp. 55–62. **[G: U.S.]**

Carlson, John A. and Horrigan, Michael W. Measures of Unemployment Duration as Guides to Research and Policy: Comment [An Experience-Weighted Measure of Employment and Unemployment Duration]. *Amer. Econ. Rev.*, December 1983, *73*(5), pp. 1143–50. **[G: U.S.]**

Carter, Donald D. Termination and Severance Pay in Ontario: Are the Protections Adequate in the Event of Employer Insolvency? **In** *Queen's Univ. Indust. Relat. Centre*, 1983, pp. 24–31. **[G: Canada]**

Carvalho, Jose L. and Haddad, Claudio Luiz da Silva. Trade and Factor Market Distortions: Effects on Employment in Brazil. **In** *Weisbrod, B. and Hughes, H., eds.*, 1983, pp. 405–28. **[G: Brazil]**

Casteñeda, Tarsicio. Salarios mínimos y empleo en el Gran Santiago: 1978 y 1981. *Cuadernos Econ.*, December 1983, *20*(61), pp. 279–93. **[G: Chile]**

Cave, George. Job Rationing, Unemployment, and Discouraged Workers. *J. Lab. Econ.*, July 1983, *1*(3), pp. 286–307.

Chakravarty, S. P.; Jones, D. R. and Mackay, R. R. United Kingdom Manpower Policy against a Background of National Economic Decline: The Welsh Example. *Reg. Stud.*, April 1983, *17*(2), pp. 91–104. **[G: U.K.]**

Chandler, Alfred D., Jr. The Place of the Modern Industrial Enterprise in Three Economies. **In** *Teichova, A. and Cottrell, P. L., eds.*, 1983, pp. 3–29. **[G: U.S.; U.K.; Germany]**

Chaudhuri, Adhip. American Multinationals and American Employment. **In** *Kindleberger, C. P. and Audretsch, D. B., eds.*, 1983, pp. 263–77. **[G: U.S.]**

Chick, Victoria. A Question of Relevance: The *General Theory* in Keynes's Time and Ours. *S. Afr. J. Econ.*, September 1983, *51*(3), pp. 380–406. **[G: U.K.]**

Chiswick, Barry R. An Analysis of the Earnings and Employment of Asian-American Men. *J. Lab. Econ.*, April 1983, *1*(2), pp. 197–214. **[G: U.S.]**

Christie, Innis. Termination of Employment: Trends and Overview. **In** *Queen's Univ. Indust. Relat. Centre*, 1983, pp. 1–17. **[G: Canada]**

Coates, Mary Lou. Human Resources and Labour Markets: Summary Outline. **In** *Wood, W. D. and Kumar, P., eds.*, 1983, pp. 31–83. **[G: Canada; OECD]**

Congdon, Peter. A Model for the Interaction of Migration and Commuting. *Urban Stud.*, May 1983, *20*(2), pp. 185–95. [G: U.K.]

Conway, Richard S., Jr. Applications of the Washington Projection and Simulation Model. In *Dutta, M.; Hartline, J. C. and Loeb, P. D., eds.*, 1983, pp. 105–15. [G: U.S.]

Corneil, Jim. Labour Market Projections in Canada: A Progress Report: Comment. In *Queen's Univ. Indust. Relat. Centre and John Deutsch Mem.*, 1983, pp. 106–09. [G: Canada]

Corvalán-Vásquez, Oscar. Vocational Training of Disadvantaged Youth in the Developing Countries. *Int. Lab. Rev.*, May–June 1983, *122*(3), pp. 367–81. [G: LDCs]

Covick, Owen. Self-employment Growth in Australia. In *Blandy, R. and Covick, O., eds.*, 1983, pp. 84–110. [G: Australia]

Cross, Michael. The Small Firm: The United Kingdom. In *Storey, D. J., ed.*, 1983, pp. 84–119. [G: U.K.]

Dalton, Dan R.; Krackhardt, David M. and Porter, Lyman W. The Impact of Teller Turnover in Banking: First Appearances Are Deceiving. *J. Bank Res.*, Autumn 1983, *14*(3), pp. 184–92. [G: U.S.]

Datcher, Linda. The Impact of Informal Networks of Quit Behavior. *Rev. Econ. Statist.*, August 1983, *65*(3), pp. 491–95. [G: U.S.]

Davies, Trevor and Sinfield, Adrian. The Unemployed. In *Brown, G. and Cook, R., eds.*, 1983, pp. 91–106. [G: U.K.]

Davis, Carlton G. and Allen, Joyce E. Black Agricultural Economists in the Labor Market: Theoretical and Empirical Issues. *Amer. J. Agr. Econ.*, December 1983, *65*(5), pp. 981–87. [G: U.S.]

De Wolff, P. Income Policy Developments in the Netherlands. *Ind. Relat.*, Spring 1983, *22*(2), pp. 203–23. [G: Netherlands]

Deardorff, Alan V. and Stern, Robert M. Changes in Trade and Employment in the Major Industrial Countries, 1970–76. In *Weisbrod, B. and Hughes, H., eds.*, 1983, pp. 447–74. [G: MDCs; LDCs]

Decoster, André and Vleminckx, Anne. De financiële situatie van werklozen. (With English summary.) *Cah. Écon. Bruxelles*, 1983, *98*(2), pp. 167–93. [G: Belgium]

DeGrasse, Robert W., Jr. Helping Those Who Need It Least [Military Spending and Jobs]. *Challenge*, Sept.–Oct. 1983, *26*(4), pp. 51–52. [G: U.S.]

DeGrasse, Robert W., Jr. Military Spending and Jobs. *Challenge*, July/August 1983, *26*(3), pp. 4–15. [G: U.S.]

Denny, Michael G. S. and Fuss, Melvyn A. The Effects of Factor Prices and Technological Change on the Occupational Demand for Labor: Evidence from Canadian Telecommunications. *J. Human Res.*, Spring 1983, *18*(2), pp. 161–76. [G: Canada]

Dilnot, A. W. and Morris, Carl N. Private Costs and Benefits of Unemployment: Measuring Replacement Rates. *Oxford Econ. Pap.*, Supplement November 1983, *35*, pp. 321–40. [G: U.K.]

Dodge, David. Labour Market Policy Concerns: An Evaluation of Current Federal Policies and Priorities. In *Queen's Univ. Indust. Relat. Centre and John Deutsch Mem.*, 1983, pp. 135–43. [G: Canada]

Doyle, Peter S. Labour Market Policy Concerns: An Evaluation of Current Federal Policies and Priorities: Comment. In *Queen's Univ. Indust. Relat. Centre and John Deutsch Mem.*, 1983, pp. 148–50. [G: Canada]

Dymond, W. R. European Labour Markets and Policies: Retrospect and Prospect. In *Queen's Univ. Indust. Relat. Centre and John Deutsch Mem.*, 1983, pp. 221–42. [G: W. Europe]

Ehrenhalt, Samuel M. No Golden Age for College Graduates. *Challenge*, July/August 1983, *26*(3), pp. 42–50. [G: U.S.]

Elton, C. J. The Impact of the Rayner Review on Unemployment and Employment Statistics. *Reg. Stud.*, April 1983, *17*(2), pp. 143–46. [G: U.K.]

Endres, Anthony M. and Cook, Malcolm. Concepts in Australian Unemployment Statistics to 1940. *Australian Econ. Pap.*, June 1983, *22*(40), pp. 68–82. [G: Australia]

Falk, Laurence H. The Service Sector vs. the Manufacturing Sector: A New Jersey Perspective. In *Dutta, M.; Hartline, J. C. and Loeb, P. D., eds.*, 1983, pp. 205–15. [G: U.S.]

Fallon, Peter R. Education and the Duration of Job Search and Unemployment in Urban India: An Empirical Analysis Based on a Survey of Delhi Jobseekers. *J. Devel. Econ.*, June 1983, *12*(3), pp. 327–40. [G: India]

Farkas, George; Smith, D. Alton and Stromsdorfer, Ernst W. The Youth Entitlement Demonstration: Subsidized Employment with a Schooling Requirement. *J. Human Res.*, Fall 1983, *18*(4), pp. 557–73. [G: U.S.]

Ferleger, Lou. Explaining Away Black Poverty: The Structural Determinants of Black Employment. In *Goldstein, R. and Sachs, S. M., eds.*, 1983, pp. 148–74. [G: U.S.]

Fernandez Arufe, J. E. La actual crisis económica y políticas de empleo: la situación española. (The Economic Crisis and Employment Policies: The Case of Spain. With English summary.) *Écon. Soc.*, September–October–November 1983, *17*(9–10–11), pp. 1517–35. [G: Spain]

Finn, Michael G. Understanding the Higher Unemployment Rate of Women Scientists and Engineers. *Amer. Econ. Rev.*, December 1983, *73*(5), pp. 1137–40. [G: U.S.]

Flinn, Christopher J. and Heckman, James J. Are Unemployment and Out of the Labor Force Behaviorally Distinct Labor Force States? *J. Lab. Econ.*, January 1983, *1*(1), pp. 28–42. [G: U.S.]

Follett, Robert and Welch, Finis. Testing for Discrimination in Employment Practices. *Law Contemp. Probl.*, Autumn 1983, *46*(4), pp. 171–84. [G: U.S.]

Foot, David K. The Impacts of Population Growth and Aging on the Future Canadian Labour Force. In *Queen's Univ. Indust. Relat. Centre and John Deutsch Mem.*, 1983, pp. 50–64. [G: Canada]

Foster, Will F. and Gregory, R. G. A Flow Analysis of the Labour Market in Australia. In *Blandy, R. and Covick, O., eds.*, 1983, pp. 111–36. [G: U.S.; Canada]

Fothergill, Stephen; Kitson, Michael and Monk,

Sarah. The Impact of the New and Expanded Town Programmes on Industrial Location in Britain, 1960–78. *Reg. Stud.*, August 1983, *17*(4), pp. 251–60. **[G: U.K.]**

Frankman, Myron J. Employment and the Unperceived Advantages of Being a Latecomer. **In** *Ritter, A. R. M. and Pollock, D. H., eds.*, 1983, pp. 135–46. **[G: Latin America]**

Franz, Wolfgang. The Past Decade's Natural Rate and the Dynamics of German Unemployment: A Case against Demand Policy? *Europ. Econ. Rev.*, March/April 1983, *21*(1/2), pp. 51–76. **[G: W. Germany]**

Frey, Luigi. Census Developments and Labour Market Analyses. *Rev. Econ. Cond. Italy,* June 1983, (2), pp. 223–47. **[G: Italy]**

Fries, Harald. Structural Change and Industry Performance in Four Western European Countries. **In** *Eliasson, G.; Sharefkin, M. and Ysander, B.-C., eds.*, 1983, pp. 111–67. **[G: Netherlands; Sweden; U.K.; W. Germany]**

Gallacher, John and Bowie, Robert D. Employment and Unemployment. **In** *Easton, B., ed.*, 1983, pp. 158–64. **[G: New Zealand]**

Gay, Robert S. and Hedlund, Jeffrey D. The Labor Market in Recession and Recovery. *Fed. Res. Bull.*, July 1983, *69*(7), pp. 477–88. **[G: U.S.]**

Gemmell, Norman. International Comparisons of the Effects of Nonmarket-Sector Growth. *J. Compar. Econ.*, December 1983, *7*(4), pp. 368–81. **[G: Selected MDCs; Selected LDCs]**

Gerfin, Harald. 'The Past Decade's Natural Rate and the Dynamics of German Unemployment: A Case against Demand Policy?' by W. Franz: Comment. *Europ. Econ. Rev.*, March/April 1983, *21*(1/2), pp. 77–82. **[G: W. Germany]**

Gill, Gerard J. Merchanised Land Preparation, Productivity and Employment in Bangladesh. *J. Devel. Stud.*, April 1983, *19*(3), pp. 329–48. **[G: Bangladesh]**

Glynn, Sean and Booth, Alan. Unemployment in Interwar Britain: A Case for Re-learning the Lessons of the 1930s? *Econ. Hist. Rev., 2nd Ser.*, August 1983, *36*(3), pp. 329–48. **[G: U.K.]**

Gollop, Frank M. and Jorgenson, Dale W. Sectoral Measures of Labor Cost for the United States, 1948–1978. **In** *Triplett, J. E., ed.*, 1983, pp. 185–235. **[G: U.S.]**

Gordon, David M. The Working Poor towards a State Agenda. **In** *Barker, M., ed. (II)*, 1983, pp. 1–91. **[G: U.S.]**

Gordon, Robert J. 'The Past Decade's Natural Rate and the Dynamics of German Unemployment: A Case against Demand Policy?' by W. Franz: Comment. *Europ. Econ. Rev.*, March/April 1983, *21*(1/2), pp. 83–87. **[G: W. Germany]**

Gordon, Robert J. Unemployment and Insurance: A Comment. *Carnegie-Rochester Conf. Ser. Public Policy,* Autumn 1983, *19*, pp. 51–60. **[G: U.S.]**

Gowda, M. V. Srinivasa. Monetary and Fiscal Policies for Expansion of Employment in Agriculture. *Econ. Aff.*, April–June 1983, *28*(2), pp. 701–05, 714. **[G: India]**

Grant, E. Kenneth and Vanderkamp, John. Regional Demand–Supply Projections and Migration. **In** *Queen's Univ. Indust. Relat. Centre and John Deutsch Mem.*, 1983, pp. 112–27. **[G: Canada]**

Guarini, Renato. The Census as a Means for Knowing about Productive Activity: Its Validity and Limits. *Rev. Econ. Cond. Italy,* June 1983, (2), pp. 327–43. **[G: Italy]**

Gurwitz, Aaron S. New York State's Economic Turnaround: Services or Manufacturing. *Fed. Res. Bank New York Quart. Rev.*, Autumn 1983, *8*(3), pp. 30–34. **[G: U.S.]**

Gustman, Alan L. and Steinmeier, Thomas L. Minimum-hours Constraints and Retirement Behavior. *Contemp. Policy Issue,* April 1983, (3), pp. 77–91. **[G: U.S.]**

Guttman, Robert. Job Training Partnership Act: New Help for the Unemployed. *Mon. Lab. Rev.*, March 1983, *106*(3), pp. 3–10. **[G: U.S.]**

Haber, Sheldon E.; Lamas, Enrique J. and Green, Gordon. A New Method for Estimating Job Separations by Sex and Race. *Mon. Lab. Rev.*, June 1983, *106*(6), pp. 20–27. **[G: U.S.]**

Hall, Robert E. Is Unemployment a Macroeconomic Problem? *Amer. Econ. Rev.*, May 1983, *73*(2), pp. 219–22. **[G: U.S.]**

Hannah, Stephen Paul. Cyclical and Structural Determinants of the *uv* Relation. *Appl. Econ.*, April 1983, *15*(2), pp. 141–51. **[G: U.K.]**

Hannah, Stephen Paul. The Dynamics of the U.S. Unemployment/Help-Wanted Index Relation, 1965–80. *Appl. Econ.*, December 1983, *15*(6), pp. 831–41. **[G: U.S.]**

Hanoch, Giora and Honig, Marjorie. Retirement, Wages, and Labor Supply of the Elderly. *J. Lab. Econ.*, April 1983, *1*(2), pp. 131–51. **[G: U.S.]**

Harrison, Alan J. and Hart, Robert A. Unemployment Benefits and Labor Supply: A Note [The Effects of Unemployment Benefits on U.S. Unemployment Rates]. *Weltwirtsch. Arch.*, 1983, *119*(1), pp. 169–72. **[G: U.S.]**

Harrisson, John A. C.; Reubens, Beatrice G. and Sparr, Pamela. Trends in Numbers Employed 1960–1980. **In** *Reubens, B. G., ed.*, 1983, pp. 17–38. **[G: Selected OECD]**

Hartley, Keith and Lynk, Edward L. Labour Demand and Allocation in the U.K. Engineering Industry: Disaggregation, Structural Change and Defence Reviews. *Scot. J. Polit. Econ.*, February 1983, *30*(1), pp. 42–53. **[G: U.K.]**

Hartmann, Gert, et al. Computerised Machine-Tools, Manpower Consequences and Skill Utilisation: A Study of British and West German Manufacturing Firms. *Brit. J. Ind. Relat.*, July 1983, *21*(2), pp. 221–31. **[G: U.K.; W. Germany]**

Hatton, T. J. Unemployment Benefits and the Macroeconomics of the Interwar Labour Market: A Further Analysis. *Oxford Econ. Pap.*, November 1983, *35*(3), pp. 486–505. **[G: U.K.]**

Haudeville, Bernard. Echanges extérieurs, emploi et redéploiement industriel en France de 1974 à 1979. (With English summary.) *Rev. Econ. Ind.*, 3rd Trimester 1983, (25), pp. 21–37. **[G: France]**

Haveman, Robert H. and Wolfe, Barbara L. Disability and Work Effort: A Probabilistic Choice Analysis of the Labor Supply Decisions of Older Men. **In** *Söderström, L., ed.*, 1983, pp.

187–205. [G: U.S.; OECD]

Hawley, Amos H.; Fernandez, Dorothy and Singh, Harbans. Migration and Employment in Peninsular Malaysia, 1970. **In** *Lim, D., ed.*, 1983, *1979*, pp. 196–206. [G: Malaysia]

Hayghe, Howard. Married Couples: Work and Income Patterns. *Mon. Lab. Rev.*, December 1983, *106*(12), pp. 26–29. [G: U.S.]

Healey, Michael. Components of Locational Change in Multi-Plant Enterprises. *Urban Stud.*, August 1983, *20*(3), pp. 327–42. [G: U.K.]

Hills, Stephen M. and Reubens, Beatrice G. Youth Employment in the United States. **In** *Reubens, B. G., ed.*, 1983, pp. 269–318. [G: U.S.]

Hopkins, Michael. Employment Trends in Developing Countries, 1960–80 and Beyond. *Int. Lab. Rev.*, July–August 1983, *122*(4), pp. 461–78. [G: LDCs]

Howenstine, Ned G. U.S. Affiliates of Foreign Companies: Operations in 1981. *Surv. Curr. Bus.*, November 1983, *63*(11), pp. 19–34. [G: U.S.]

Hughes, Gerard and Walsh, Brendan M. Unemployment Duration, Aggregate Demand and Unemployment Insurance: A Study of Irish Live Register Survival Probabilities, 1967–1978. *Econ. Soc. Rev.*, January 1983, *14*(2), pp. 93–117. [G: Ireland]

Hughes, Helen. The International Economy and Employment: Introduction. **In** *Weisbrod, B. and Hughes, H., eds.*, 1983, pp. 319–28.

Hull, Chris. The Small Firm: Federal Republic of Germany. **In** *Storey, D. J., ed.*, 1983, pp. 153–78. [G: W. Germany]

Hull, Everson. Money Growth and the Employment Aspirations of Black Americans. *Rev. Black Polit. Econ.*, Spring 1983, *12*(3), pp. 63–74. [G: U.S.]

Hutchens, Robert M. Layoffs and Labor supply. *Int. Econ. Rev.*, February 1983, *24*(1), pp. 37–55. [G: U.S.]

Ingram, James C. Food for Employment: 20 Years of the World Food Programme. *Int. Lab. Rev.*, Sept.–Oct. 1983, *122*(5), pp. 549–62. [G: LDCs]

Jessua, Claude. Les perspectives de l'emploi. (With English summary.) *Revue Écon. Polit.*, September–October 1983, *93*(5), pp. 669–81. [G: France]

Johns, Brian. The Small Firm: Australia. **In** *Storey, D. J., ed.*, 1983, pp. 120–52. [G: Australia]

Johnson, Beverly L. and Waldman, Elizabeth. Most Women Who Maintain Families Receive Poor Labor Market Returns. *Mon. Lab. Rev.*, December 1983, *106*(12), pp. 30–34. [G: U.S.]

Johnson, George E. Potentials of Labor Market Policy: A View from the Eighties. *Ind. Relat.*, Spring 1983, *22*(2), pp. 283–97. [G: U.S.]

Johnson, Janet L. Sex Differentials in Unemployment Rates: A Case for No Concern. *J. Polit. Econ.*, April 1983, *91*(2), pp. 293–303. [G: U.S.]

Johnson, Janet L. Unemployment as a Household Labor Supply Decision. *Quart. Rev. Econ. Bus.*, Summer 1983, *23*(2), pp. 71–88. [G: U.S.]

Johnston, R. J. On the Symmetry of Leads and Lags in Studies of Regional Unemployment. *Reg. Stud.*, April 1983, *17*(2), pp. 105–12. [G: New Zealand]

Jones, Dewitt; Nelson, Mack and Parks, Alfred L. Demand and Supply Factors of Black Agricultural Economists. *Amer. J. Agr. Econ.*, December 1983, *65*(5), pp. 988–92. [G: U.S.]

de Jong, H. W. and Spierenburg, Robert Jan. The Netherlands: Maintenance of Employment as a Primary Objective. **In** *Hindley, B., ed.*, 1983, pp. 59–95. [G: Netherlands]

Kabaj, Mieczyslaw. Economic Factors Determining Long-term Labour Supply: A Case-study of the Polish Economy, 1950–1978. **In** *Streeten, P. and Maier, H., eds.*, 1983, pp. 457–72. [G: Poland]

Kaliski, Steve F. Labour Market Projections in Canada: A Progress Report: Comment. **In** *Queen's Univ. Indust. Relat. Centre and John Deutsch Mem.*, 1983, pp. 105–06. [G: Canada]

Kanamori, Hisao. Economic Growth and Interindustry Labour Mobility in Japan. **In** *Weisbrod, B. and Hughes, H., eds.*, 1983, pp. 31–47. [G: Japan]

Kapp, K. William. Socio-economic Effects of Low and High Employment. **In** *Kapp, K. W.*, 1983, *1975*, pp. 99–110. [G: U.S.]

Kaser, Michael and Notel, Rudolf. The Development of Human Resources for Development: The East European Experience, 1953–75. **In** *Weisbrod, B. and Hughes, H., eds.*, 1983, pp. 74–83. [G: E. Europe]

Kay, Linda B. A Survey of New Zealand Labour Market Data. **In** *Easton, B., ed.*, 1983, pp. 171–202. [G: New Zealand]

Keating, Giles. The Effect of Answering Practices on the Relationship between CBI Survey Data and Official Data: Erratum. *Appl. Econ.*, June 1983, *15*(3), pp. 424. [G: U.K.]

Keating, Giles. The Effect of Answering Practices on the Relationship between CBI Survey Data and Official Data. *Appl. Econ.*, April 1983, *15*(2), pp. 213–24. [G: U.K.]

Keating, Michael. Relative Wages and the Changing Industrial Distribution of Employment in Australia. *Econ. Rec.*, December 1983, *59*(167), pp. 384–97. [G: Australia]

Keeble, David; Owens, Peter L. and Thompson, Chris. The Urban–Rural Manufacturing Shift in the European Community. *Urban Stud.*, November 1983, *20*(4), pp. 405–18. [G: EEC]

Kehoe, Timothy J. and Serra-Puche, Jaime. A Computational General Equilibrium Model with Endogenous Unemployment: An Analysis of the 1980 Fiscal Reform in Mexico. *J. Public Econ.*, October 1983, *22*(1), pp. 1–26. [G: Mexico]

Kendrick, Stephen. Social Change in Scotland. **In** *Brown, G. and Cook, R., eds.*, 1983, pp. 40–65. [G: U.K.]

Kenney, Patrick J. The Effect of State Economic Conditions on the Vote for Governor. *Soc. Sci. Quart.*, March 1983, *64*(1), pp. 154–62. [G: U.S.]

Kenward, Lloyd. Unemployment in the Major Industrial Countries. *Finance Develop.*, June 1983, *20*(2), pp. 24–27. [G: U.S.; Canada; Europe; Japan]

Kieschnick, Michael. Venture Capital and Urban Development. **In** *Barker, M., ed. (I)*, 1983, pp. 303–58. [G: U.S.]

Kjæersgaard, Kaj. Nogle hovedtendenser i arbejdsmarkedspolitikken. (Recent Trends in Danish Labor Market Policy. With English summary.)

Nationaløkon. Tidsskr., 1983, *121*(2), pp. 200–214. **[G: Denmark]**

Klein, Deborah Pisetzner. Trends in Employment and Unemployment in Families. *Mon. Lab. Rev.*, December 1983, *106*(12), pp. 21–25. **[G: U.S.]**

Klein, Emilio. Determinants of Manpower Underutilisation and Availability. *Int. Lab. Rev.*, March–April 1983, *122*(2), pp. 183–95.

Klein, Emilio. Problemas metodológicos de una encuesta rural en Chile y estructura del empleo. (With English summary.) *Cuadernos Econ.*, December 1983, *20*(61), pp. 345–61. **[G: Chile]**

Kooreman, Peter and Ridder, Geert. The Effects of Age and Unemployment Percentage on the Duration of Unemployment: Evidence from Aggregate Data. *Europ. Econ. Rev.*, January 1983, *20*(1–3), pp. 41–57. **[G: Netherlands]**

Kovach, Kenneth A. and Millspaugh, Peter E. The Plant Closing Issue Arrives at the Bargaining Table. *J. Lab. Res.*, Fall 1983, *4*(4), pp. 367–74. **[G: U.S.]**

Krengel, Jochen. Der Beschäftigungseffekt von Arbeitszeitverkürzungen im sekundären Sektor Deutschlands 1871 bis 1913—ein historisches Beispiel. (The Effect of Shorter Working Hours on Employment within the Secondary Sector of the German Economy between 1871 and 1913—An Historical Example. With English summary.) *Konjunkturpolitik*, 1983, *29*(5), pp. 314–28. **[G: W. Germany]**

Lang, Ron. Labour Market Policy Concerns: An Evaluation of Current Federal Policies and Priorities: Comment. **In** *Queen's Univ. Indust. Relat. Centre and John Deutsch Mem.*, 1983, pp. 143–45. **[G: Canada]**

Lawrence, Robert Z. The Myth of U.S. Deindustrialization. *Challenge*, November/December 1983, *26*(5), pp. 12–21. **[G: U.S.; OECD]**

Lee, Eddy. Agrarian Change and Poverty in Rural Java. **In** *Khan, A. R. and Lee, E., eds.*, 1983, pp. 231–46. **[G: Indonesia]**

Leigh, J. Paul. Sex Differences in Absenteeism. *Ind. Relat.*, Fall 1983, *22*(3), pp. 349–61. **[G: U.S.]**

Levin, Bruce and Robbins, Herbert. Urn Models for Regression Analysis, with Applications to Employment Discrimination Studies. *Law Contemp. Probl.*, Autumn 1983, *46*(4), pp. 247–67. **[G: U.S.]**

Levin, Henry M. Raising Employment and Productivity with Producer Co-operatives. **In** *Streeten, P. and Maier, H., eds.*, 1983, pp. 310–28. **[G: Spain]**

Levitan, Sar A. and Taggart, Robert. The Bitter Fruits of Labor. *Challenge*, March/April 1983, *26*(1), pp. 18–22. **[G: U.S.]**

Lewis, W. Arthur. Employment Policy in an Underdeveloped Area. **In** *Lewis, W. A.*, 1983, *1958*, pp. 397–409. **[G: Caribbean]**

Lewis, W. Arthur. Unemployment in Developing Countries. **In** *Lewis, W. A.*, 1983, *1967*, pp. 411–20.

Lim, David. The Political Economy of the New Economic Policy in Malaysia. **In** *Lim, D., ed.*, 1983, pp. 3–22. **[G: Malaysia]**

Lindmark, Leif. The Small Firm: Sweden. **In** *Storey, D. J., ed.*, 1983, pp. 179–212. **[G: Sweden]**

Littler, Craig R. Japan and China. **In** *Feuchtwang, S. and Hussain, A., eds.*, 1983, pp. 121–47. **[G: China; Japan]**

Llach, Juan J. Economically Active Population, Unemployment Rates and Aggregate Demand: Recent Argentine Experience in Pursuit of a Theory. **In** *Urquidi, V. L. and Reyes, S. T., eds.*, 1983, pp. 387–405. **[G: Argentina]**

Lobue, Marie. Adjustment to Labor Productivity: An Application to the Economics of Discrimination. *Southern Econ. J.*, July 1983, *50*(1), pp. 151–59.

Loeb, Peter D. Leading and Coincident Indicators of Recession and Recovery in New Jersey. **In** *Dutta, M.; Hartline, J. C. and Loeb, P. D., eds.*, 1983, pp. 151–72. **[G: U.S.]**

Long, James E. and Link, Albert N. The Impact of Market Structure on Wages, Fringe Benefits, and Turnover. *Ind. Lab. Relat. Rev.*, January 1983, *36*(2), pp. 239–50. **[G: U.S.]**

Luria, Dan and Price, Lee. Solar Energy, Jobs, and Labor: Some Analytical Issues. *Rev. Radical Polit. Econ.*, Fall 1983, *15*(3), pp. 131–42.

Lynch, Lisa M. Job Search and Youth Unemployment. *Oxford Econ. Pap.*, Supplement November 1983, *35*, pp. 271–82. **[G: U.K.]**

Maani, Sholeh. El desempleo en Chile: una estimación de la probabilidad de empleo para varones. (With English summary.) *Cuadernos Econ.*, August 1983, *20*(60), pp. 229–41. **[G: Chile]**

Maddison, Angus. Measuring Labour Slack. **In** *Weisbrod, B. and Hughes, H., eds.*, 1983, pp. 97–112. **[G: U.K.; W. Germany]**

Magun, Sunder. Unemployment Experience in Canada: A 5-Year Longitudinal Analysis. *Mon. Lab. Rev.*, April 1983, *106*(4), pp. 36–38. **[G: Canada]**

Main, Brian G. M. and Raffe, David. Determinants of Employment and Unemployment among School Leavers: Evidence from the 1979 Survey of Scottish School Leavers. *Scot. J. Polit. Econ.*, February 1983, *30*(1), pp. 1–17. **[G: U.K.]**

Maldonado, I. and Mercier, D. Chômage des jeunes et répartition du revenu: une problématique. (Unemployment among Youth and Income Distribution: The Problem-Setting. With English summary.) *Écon. Soc.*, March–April 1983, *17*(3–4), pp. 629–54. **[G: Canada]**

Mandeville, Thomas and Macdonald, Stuart. Information Technology and Employment Levels. **In** *Macdonald, S.; Lamberton, D. M. and Mandeville, T., eds.*, 1983, pp. 169–77. **[G: Australia; U.K.]**

Mangan, John and Regan, Philip. A Note on Organisational Slack and Market Power in Australian Manufacturing. *Australian Econ. Pap.*, December 1983, *22*(41), pp. 356–63. **[G: Australia]**

Markham, Steven E.; Dansereau, Fred, Jr. and Alutto, Joseph A. Absenteeism Rates as Measures in Organizational Experiments: Hidden Cyclical and Structural Variation. *Rev. Bus. Econ. Res.*, Spring 1983, *18*(3), pp. 21–31. **[G: U.S.]**

Martin, Preston. Statement to the Subcommittee on Domestic Monetary Policy, U.S. House Committee on Banking, Finance, and Urban Affairs, June 1, 1983. *Fed. Res. Bull.*, June 1983, *69*(6), pp. 411–15. **[G: U.S.]**

Masson, André. Estimation du risque à terme de chômage. (Estimation of the Individual Risk of Future Unemployment. With English summary.) *Ann. INSEE,* October–December 1983, (52), pp. 23–53.

Matthews, R. C. O. Why Has Britain Had Full Employment since the War? **In** *Feinstein, C., ed.,* 1983, *1968,* pp. 118–32. **[G: U.K.]**

May, Doug. Labour Market Projections in Canada: A Progress Report: Comment. **In** *Queen's Univ. Indust. Relat. Centre and John Deutsch Mem.,* 1983, pp. 109–11. **[G: Canada]**

McConnell, Stephen R. Age Discrimination in Employment. **In** *Parnes, H. S., ed.,* 1983, pp. 159–96. **[G: U.S.]**

McCormick, Barry. Housing and Unemployment in Great Britain. *Oxford Econ. Pap.,* Supplement November 1983, *35,* pp. 283–305. **[G: U.K.]**

McGregor, Alan. Neighbourhood Influence on Job Search and Job Finding Methods. *Brit. J. Ind. Relat.,* March 1983, *21* (1), pp. 91–99. **[G: U.K.]**

McManus, Walter; Gould, William and Welch, Finis. Earnings of Hispanic Men: The Role of English Language Proficiency. *J. Lab. Econ.,* April 1983, *1* (2), pp. 101–30. **[G: U.S.]**

Medoff, James L. The Importance of Employer-sponsored Job-related Training. **In** *Queen's Univ. Indust. Relat. Centre and John Deutsch Mem.,* 1983, pp. 192–220. **[G: U.S.]**

Metcalf, David and Richards, John. Youth Employment in Great Britain. **In** *Reubens, B. G., ed.,* 1983, pp. 149–84. **[G: U.K.]**

Metcalfe, J. S. and Hall, P. H. The Verdoorn Law and the Salter Mechanism: A Note on Australian Manufacturing Industry. *Australian Econ. Pap.,* December 1983, *22* (41), pp. 364–73. **[G: Australia]**

Meyer, Peter J. and Maes, Patricia L. The Reproduction of Occupational Segregation among Young Women. *Ind. Relat.,* Winter 1983, *22* (1), pp. 115–24. **[G: U.S.]**

Meyer, Robert H. and Wise, David A. The Effects of the Minimum Wage on the Employment and Earnings of Youth. *J. Lab. Econ.,* January 1983, *1* (1), pp. 66–100. **[G: U.S.]**

Miller, D. The Role of the Motor Car Industry in the West Midlands Economy. *Reg. Stud.,* February 1983, *17* (1), pp. 53–56. **[G: U.K.]**

Mincer, Jacob. Union Effects: Wages, Turnover, and Job Training. **In** *Reid, J. D., Jr., ed.,* 1983, pp. 217–52. **[G: U.S.]**

Minford, Patrick. Labour Market Equilibrium in an Open Economy. *Oxford Econ. Pap.,* Supplement November 1983, *35,* pp. 207–44. **[G: U.K.]**

Minocha, A. C. Rural Employment in Household Industries in Madhya Pradesh. *Margin,* April 1983, *15* (3), pp. 79–90. **[G: India]**

Mitchell, Olivia S. Fringe Benefits and the Cost of Changing Jobs. *Ind. Lab. Relat. Rev.,* October 1983, *37* (1), pp. 70–78. **[G: U.S.]**

Moir, Hazel V. J. and Robinson, Chris. Labour Market Measurement: A Review of Some Popular Labour Market Measures. **In** *Blandy, R. and Covick, O., eds.,* 1983, pp. 61–83.

Moore, Geoffrey H. A New Leading Index of Employment and Unemployment. **In** *Moore, G. H.,* 1983, *1981,* pp. 353–60. **[G: U.S.]**

Moore, Geoffrey H. Employment, Unemployment, and the Inflation–Recession Dilemma. **In** *Moore, G. H.,* 1983, *1976,* pp. 211–32. **[G: U.S.]**

Moore, Geoffrey H. Presenting Employment and Unemployment Statistics in a Business Cycle Context. **In** *Moore, G. H.,* 1983, *1978,* pp. 93–125. **[G: U.S.]**

Moore, Geoffrey H. Some Secular Changes in Business Cycles. **In** *Moore, G. H.,* 1983, *1974,* pp. 161–68. **[G: U.S.]**

Moore, Geoffrey H. Using a Leading Employment Index to Forecast Unemployment in 1983. *Mon. Lab. Rev.,* May 1983, *106* (5), pp. 30–32. **[G: U.S.]**

Moore, William J., et al. A Quality-Adjustment Model of the Academic Labor Market: The Case of Economists. *Econ. Inquiry,* April 1983, *21* (2), pp. 241–54. **[G: U.S.]**

Mukasa, R. Les conditions de travail au Japon: Leur aspect global après la Seconde Guerre mondiale. (Labour Conditions in Japan: The Overall Post-War Picture. With English summary.) *Écon. Soc.,* March–April 1983, *17* (3–4), pp. 481–516. **[G: Japan]**

Myers, Samuel L., Jr. Racial Differences in Postprison Employment. *Soc. Sci. Quart.,* September 1983, *64* (3), pp. 655–69. **[G: U.S.]**

Neffa, Julio César. Development and Employment Models in Argentina: A Long-term View of Their Relations. **In** *Urquidi, V. L. and Reyes, S. T., eds.,* 1983, pp. 362–86. **[G: Argentina]**

Newton, Keith and Vella, Frank. The UV Relationship in Labour Market Analysis. *Australian Bull. Lab.,* September 1983, *9* (4), pp. 290–306. **[G: Australia]**

Nickell, S. J. and Andrews, M. Unions, Real Wages and Employment in Britain 1951–79. *Oxford Econ. Pap.,* Supplement November 1983, *35,* pp. 183–206. **[G: U.K.]**

Nogués, Julio J. Alternative Trade Strategies and Employment in the Argentine Manufacturing Sector. *World Devel.,* December 1983, *11* (12), pp. 1029–42. **[G: Argentina]**

Norwood, Janet L. Labor Market Contrasts: United States and Europe: Errata. *Mon. Lab. Rev.,* September 1983, *106* (9), pp. 21. **[G: U.S.; W. Europe]**

Norwood, Janet L. Labor Market Contrasts: United States and Europe. *Mon. Lab. Rev.,* August 1983, *106* (8), pp. 3–7. **[G: U.S.; W. Europe]**

O'Mahony, Donal P. A Study of Replacement Ratios among a Sample of Unemployed Workers. *Econ. Soc. Rev.,* January 1983, *14* (2), pp. 77–91. **[G: Ireland]**

O'Mahony, Mary. The Length of Spells of Unemployment in Ireland. *Econ. Soc. Rev.,* January 1983, *14* (2), pp. 119–35. **[G: Ireland]**

O'Neill, Dave M. Racial Differentials in Teenage Unemployment: A Note on Trends. *J. Human Res.,* Spring 1983, *18* (2), pp. 295–306. **[G: U.S.]**

Ogawa, Naohiro and Suits, Daniel B. Retirement Policy and Japanese Workers: Some Results of an Opinion Survey. *Int. Lab. Rev.,* November–December 1983, *122* (6), pp. 733–46. **[G: Japan; France]**

Ohlsson, Lennart. Structural Adaptability of Regions

during Swedish Industrial Adjustment, 1965 to 1975. **In** *Hamilton, F. E. I. and Linge, G. J. R., eds.,* 1983, pp. 297–335. **[G: Sweden]**

Oi, Walter Y. The Fixed Employment Costs of Specialized Labor. **In** *Triplett, J. E., ed.,* 1983, pp. 63–116. **[G: U.S.]**

Okun, Arthur M. Conflicting National Goals. **In** *Okun, A. M.,* 1983, *1976,* pp. 221–49. **[G: U.S.]**

Okun, Arthur M. The Role of Aggregate Demand in Alleviating Unemployment. **In** *Okun, A. M.,* 1983, *1965,* pp. 159–70. **[G: U.S.]**

Okun, Arthur M. Upward Mobility in a High-Pressure Economy. **In** *Okun, A. M.,* 1983, *1973,* pp. 171–220. **[G: U.S.]**

Olmsted, Barney. Changing Times: The Use of Reduced Work Time Options in the United States. *Int. Lab. Rev.,* July–August 1983, *122* (4), pp. 479–92. **[G: U.S.]**

Oppenländer, Karl-Heinrich. Auswirkungen des technischen Wandels auf Beschäftigtenzahl und Beschäftigtenstruktur. (The Effects of Technical Change on Number Employed and on the Structure of Employment. With English summary.) *Ifo-Studien,* 1983, *29* (2), pp. 77–99. **[G: W. Germany]**

Oppenländer, Karl-Heinrich. The Impact of Technical and Structural Change on the Structure and Employment of Manpower. **In** *Streeten, P. and Maier, H., eds.,* 1983, pp. 370–94. **[G: W. Germany]**

Osberg, Lars. Regional Demand–Supply Projections and Migration: Comment. **In** *Queen's Univ. Indust. Relat. Centre and John Deutsch Mem.,* 1983, pp. 128–31. **[G: Canada]**

Pang, Eng Fong. Race, Income Distribution, and Development in Malaysia and Singapore. **In** *Lim, L. Y. C. and Gosling, L. A. P., eds.,* 1983, pp. 316–35. **[G: Malaysia; Singapore]**

Passmore, Davin Lynn, et al. Health and Youth Employment. *Appl. Econ.,* December 1983, *15* (6), pp. 715–29. **[G: U.S.]**

Pereira, Armand. Employment Implications of Ethanol Production in Brazil. *Int. Lab. Rev.,* January–February 1983, *122* (1), pp. 111–27. **[G: Brazil]**

Pérez-Sainz, J. P. Transmigration and Accumulation in Indonesia. **In** *Oberai, A. S., ed.,* 1983, pp. 183–250. **[G: Indonesia]**

Perles, Susan P. Impact of CETA-PSE on Local Public Sector Employment Expenditures. **In** *Hirsch, W. Z., ed.,* 1983, pp. 122–57. **[G: U.S.]**

Perlman, Mark. Human Resources and Population Growth. **In** *Streeten, P. and Maier, H., eds.,* 1983, pp. 167–80. **[G: OECD]**

Personick, Valerie A. The Job Outlook through 1995: Industry Output and Employment Projections. *Mon. Lab. Rev.,* November 1983, *106* (11), pp. 24–36. **[G: U.S.]**

Peterson, Paul and Mackay, Keith. Youth Employment in Australia. **In** *Reubens, B. G., ed.,* 1983, pp. 86–112. **[G: Australia]**

Phipps, A. J. Australian Unemployment: Some Evidence from Industry Labour Demand Functions. *Australian Econ. Pap.,* December 1983, *22* (41), pp. 333–44. **[G: Australia]**

Piore, Michael J. Understanding Unemployment in Developed Industrial Economies. **In** *Streeten, P. and Maier, H., eds.,* 1983, pp. 106–16.

Pola, Giorgio and Brosio, Giancarlo. The Role of Public Employment in a Dualistic Economy: The Italian Case. *Econ. Notes,* 1983, (1), pp. 80–97. **[G: Italy]**

Polachek, Solomon W. and McCutcheon, Ernest P. Union Effects of Employment Stability: A Comparison of Panel versus Cross-Sectional Data. *J. Lab. Res.,* Summer 1983, *4* (3), pp. 273–87. **[G: U.S.]**

Quiñones, Fernando Gonzáles. Employment and Development in Latin America. **In** *Urquidi, V. L. and Reyes, S. T., eds.,* 1983, pp. 406–23. **[G: Latin America]**

Rabby, Rami. Employment of the Disabled in Large Corporations. *Int. Lab. Rev.,* January–February 1983, *122* (1), pp. 23–36. **[G: U.S.]**

Raffe, David. Education and Class Inequality in Scotland. **In** *Brown, G. and Cook, R., eds.,* 1983, pp. 190–205. **[G: U.K.]**

Reeve, James M. The Five-Year Accounting Program as a Quality Signal. *Accounting Rev.,* July 1983, *58* (3), pp. 639–46. **[G: U.S.]**

Reimers, Cordelia W. The Effect of Pension Plans on the Pattern of Life Cycle Compensation: Comment. **In** *Triplett, J. E., ed.,* 1983, pp. 416–20. **[G: U.S.]**

Reppy, Judith. The Structure of the Defense Industry: The United States. **In** *Ball, N. and Leitenberg, M., eds.,* 1983, pp. 21–49. **[G: U.S.]**

Reubens, Beatrice G. Youth at Work: An International Survey: Perspectives and Problems. **In** *Reubens, B. G., ed.,* 1983, pp. 1–16. **[G: Selected OECD]**

Reubens, Beatrice G. Youth at Work: An International Survey: Overview and Implications. **In** *Reubens, B. G., ed.,* 1983, pp. 319–41. **[G: Selected OECD]**

Rey, Guido M. Italy of Censuses. *Rev. Econ. Cond. Italy,* June 1983, (2), pp. 193–221. **[G: Italy]**

Reynolds, Clark W. Mexican–U.S. Interdependence: Economic and Social Perspectives. **In** *Reynolds, C. W. and Tello, C., eds.,* 1983, pp. 21–45. **[G: Mexico; U.S.]**

Ricciuti, James R. Federal Personnel Cuts: A Blessing Still Disguised. *J. Policy Anal. Manage.,* Spring 1983, *2* (3), pp. 457–61. **[G: U.S.]**

Riche, Richard W.; Hecker, Daniel E. and Burgan, John U. High Technology Today and Tomorrow: A Small Slice of the Employment Pie. *Mon. Lab. Rev.,* November 1983, *106* (11), pp. 50–58. **[G: U.S.]**

Riese, Martin. Eine Rehabilitation des Konzeptes der "bisherigen Dauer der Arbeitslosigkeit." (A Rehabilitation of the Concept of "Interrupted Spell Length of Unemployment." With English summary.) *Jahr. Nationalökon. Statist.,* November 1983, *198* (6), pp. 505–10. **[G: W. Germany]**

Rochon, Michel. Labour Market Projections in Canada: A Progress Report. **In** *Queen's Univ. Indust. Relat. Centre and John Deutsch Mem.,* 1983, pp. 81–104. **[G: Canada]**

Rolph, H. P. Notice Requirements, Termination and Severance Pay under Ontario's Employment Standards Act. **In** *Queen's Univ. Indust. Relat. Centre,* 1983, pp. 32–48. **[G: Canada]**

Rones, Philip L. The Labor Market Problems of Older Workers. *Mon. Lab. Rev.*, May 1983, *106*(5), pp. 3–12. **[G: U.S.]**

Rosen, Corey M. and Klein, Katherine. Job-Creating Performance of Employee-Owned Firms. *Mon. Lab. Rev.*, August 1983, *106*(8), pp. 15–19. **[G: U.S.]**

Rosen, Sherwin. Unemployment and Insurance: Reply to Robert Gordon. *Carnegie-Rochester Conf. Ser. Public Policy*, Autumn 1983, *19*, pp. 61–66. **[G: U.S.]**

Rosen, Sherwin. Unemployment and Insurance. *Carnegie-Rochester Conf. Ser. Public Policy*, Autumn 1983, *19*, pp. 5–49. **[G: U.S.]**

Rosenberg, Sam. Reagan Social Policy and Labour Force Restructuring. *Cambridge J. Econ.*, June 1983, *7*(2), pp. 179–96. **[G: U.S.]**

Rostow, W. W. Technology and Unemployment in the Western World. *Challenge*, March/April 1983, *26*(1), pp. 6–17. **[G: MDCs]**

Rothstein, Mark A. Employee Selection Based on Susceptibility to Occupational Illness. *Mich. Law Rev.*, May 1983, *81*(6), pp. 1379–496. **[G: U.S.]**

Sääski, Niilo. Työttömyyden kestosta Suomessa. (Durations of Unemployment in Finland. With English summary.) *Kansant. Aikak.*, 1983, *79*(1), pp. 72–83. **[G: Finland]**

Sabolo, Yves. Disarmament and Employment: Background for a Research Programme. *Int. Lab. Rev.*, May–June 1983, *122*(3), pp. 263–77. **[G: Selected MDCs; Selected LDCs]**

Sabolo, Yves. Trade between Developing Countries, Technology Transfers and Employment. *Int. Lab. Rev.*, Sept.–Oct. 1983, *122*(5), pp. 593–608. **[G: LDCs]**

Saffer, Henry. The Effects of Unemployment Insurance on Temporary and Permanent Layoffs. *Rev. Econ. Statist.*, November 1983, *65*(4), pp. 647–52. **[G: U.S.]**

Saltzstein, Grace Hall. Personnel Directors and Female Employment Representation: A New Addition to Models of Equal Employment Opportunity Policy? *Soc. Sci. Quart.*, December 1983, *64*(4), pp. 734–46. **[G: U.S.]**

Sawhill, Isabel V. Human Resources. **In** *Miller, G. W., ed.*, 1983, pp. 100–24. **[G: U.S.]**

Scaggs, Mary Beth W. Recent Employment Trends in the Lumber and Wood Products Industry. *Mon. Lab. Rev.*, August 1983, *106*(8), pp. 20–24. **[G: U.S.]**

Scarpat, Orlando. Un tentativo di analisi costi–benefici dell'inserimento dei disabili nel mercato del lavoro. (A Tentative Cost–Benefit Analysis of the Employment of Disabled Workers. With English summary.) *Rivista Int. Sci. Econ. Com.*, September 1983, *30*(9), pp. 849–60. **[G: Italy]**

Schapiro, Morton Owen and Ahlburg, Dennis A. Suicide: The Ultimate Cost of Unemployment. *J. Post Keynesian Econ.*, Winter 1982–83, *5*(2), pp. 276–80. **[G: U.S.]**

Schober, Karen. Youth Employment in West Germany. **In** *Reubens, B. G., ed.*, 1983, pp. 113–48. **[G: W. Germany]**

Schumacher, August. Agricultural Development and Rural Employment: A Mexican Dilemma. **In** *Brown, P. G. and Shue, H., eds.*, 1983, pp. 141–61. **[G: Mexico]**

Schuster, Michael. The Impact of Union-Management Cooperation on Productivity and Employment. *Ind. Lab. Relat. Rev.*, April 1983, *36*(3), pp. 415–30. **[G: U.S.]**

Schydlowsky, Daniel M. The Short-run Potential for Employment Generation of Installed Capacity in Latin America. **In** *Urquidi, V. L. and Reyes, S. T., eds.*, 1983, pp. 311–47. **[G: Latin America]**

Seidman, Laurence S. A "Third Way" for Feldstein: TIP. *Challenge*, Sept.–Oct. 1983, *26*(4), pp. 44–48. **[G: U.S.]**

Selleck, Laura. Jobs for University Graduates: Planning or Choice? *Can. Public Policy*, March 1983, *9*(1), pp. 94–104. **[G: Canada]**

Sen, C. and Shah, S. L. Employment, Unemployment and Underemployment among Landless Agricultural Labourers—A Case Study. *Econ. Aff.*, April–June 1983, *28*(2), pp. 662–63, 695. **[G: India]**

Shaffer, Ron E. A Test of the Differences in Export Base Multipliers in Expanding and Contracting Economies. *Reg. Sci. Persp.*, 1983, *13*(2), pp. 61–74. **[G: U.S.]**

Shapiro, David. Working Youth. **In** *Borus, M. E., ed.*, 1983, pp. 23–58. **[G: U.S.]**

Shaw, Lois B. Causes of Irregular Employment Patterns. **In** *Shaw, L. B., ed.*, 1983, pp. 45–59. **[G: U.S.]**

Shaw, Lois B. and O'Brien, Theresa. Unplanned Careers: The Working Lives of Middle-aged Women: Introduction and Overview. **In** *Shaw, L. B., ed.*, 1983, pp. 1–31. **[G: U.S.]**

Shoben, Elaine W. The Use of Statistics to Prove Intentional Employment Discrimination. *Law Contemp. Probl.*, Autumn 1983, *46*(4), pp. 219–45. **[G: U.S.]**

Silvestri, George T.; Lukasiewicz, John M. and Einstein, Marcus E. Occupational Employment Projections through 1995. *Mon. Lab. Rev.*, November 1983, *106*(11), pp. 37–49. **[G: U.S.]**

Simmons, C. Gordon. The Experience of the Unjust Dismissal Section under Section 61.5 in the Canada Labour Code, 1978–1981. **In** *Queen's Univ. Indust. Relat. Centre*, 1983, pp. 59–67. **[G: Canada]**

Singell, Larry D. Youth Unemployment in Australia: Some Comparative Observations. *Australian Econ. Rev.*, 3rd Quarter 1983, (63), pp. 46–55. **[G: Australia; OECD]**

Singh, Ajit. U.K. Industry and the World Economy: A Case of De-industrialisation? **In** *Feinstein, C., ed.*, 1983, *1977*, pp. 226–57. **[G: U.K.]**

Slater, David W. Employment Policies in the 1980s: An International Perspective. **In** *Queen's Univ. Indust. Relat. Centre and John Deutsch Mem.*, 1983, pp. 186–91. **[G: OECD]**

Smiley, Gene. Recent Unemployment Rate Estimates for the 1920s and 1930s. *J. Econ. Hist.*, June 1983, *43*(2), pp. 487–93. **[G: U.S.]**

Smith, Nina. Varighed af ledighed og indstrømning til arbejdsløshed. (Duration of and Inflow to Unemployment in the Danish Labour Market. With English summary.) *Nationaløkon. Tidsskr.*, 1983, *121*(2), pp. 160–80. **[G: Denmark]**

Sofer, Catherine. Emplois "féminins" et emplois "masculins": Mesure de la ségrégation et évolution de la féminisation des emplois. ("Female" Jobs and "Male" Jobs: A Measure of Segregation by Sex and the Evolution of the Feminization of Jobs. With English summary.) *Ann. INSEE*, October–December 1983, (52), pp. 55–85. **[G: France]**

Solimano, Andrés. Reducir costos del trabajo: cuánto empleo genera? (With English summary.) *Cuadernos Econ.*, December 1983, *20*(61), pp. 363–81. **[G: Chile]**

Solttila, Heikki. Työttömyyden kohdistuminen eri työntekijäryhmiin. (The Incidence of Unemployment among Different Groups of Population in Finland. With English summary.) *Kansant. Aikak.*, 1983, *79*(4), pp. 436–47. **[G: Finland]**

Standing, Guy. The Notion of Structural Unemployment. *Int. Lab. Rev.*, March–April 1983, *122*(2), pp. 137–53.

Steel, William F. and Takagi, Yasuoki. Small Enterprise Development and the Employment-Output Trade-Off. *Oxford Econ. Pap.*, November 1983, *35*(3), pp. 423–46. **[G: LDCs]**

Stern, J. The Relationship between Unemployment, Morbidity and Mortality in Britain. *Population Stud.*, March 1983, *37*(1), pp. 61–74. **[G: U.K.]**

Storey, D. J. Regional Policy in a Recession. *Nat. Westminster Bank Quart. Rev.*, November 1983, pp. 39–47. **[G: U.K.]**

Sudaryanto, T. Effect of Tubewells on Income and Employment: A Case Study in Three Villages in Kediri, East Java, Indonesia. **In** *Internat'l Rice Res. Inst. and Agric. Devel. Council*, 1983, pp. 107–18. **[G: Indonesia]**

Summers, Lawrence H. Why Is Insured Unemployment So Low? Comments and Discussion. *Brookings Pap. Econ. Act.*, 1983, (1), pp. 250–53. **[G: U.S.]**

Swan, Kenneth P. Protections against Discriminatory Dismissal. **In** *Queen's Univ. Indust. Relat. Centre*, 1983, pp. 49–58. **[G: Canada]**

Swan, Neil. Regional Demand–Supply Projections and Migration: Comment. **In** *Queen's Univ. Indust. Relat. Centre and John Deutsch Mem.*, 1983, pp. 132–34. **[G: Canada]**

Swinton, David H. Orthodox and Systemic Explanations for Unemployment and Racial Inequality: Implications for Policy. *Rev. Black Polit. Econ.*, Spring 1983, *12*(3), pp. 9–25. **[G: U.S.]**

Sziraczki, G. The Development and Functioning of an Enterprise Labour Market in Hungary. *Écon. Soc.*, March–April 1983, *17*(3–4), pp. 517–47. **[G: Hungary]**

Taira, Koji. Japan's Low Unemployment: Economic Miracle or Statistical Artifact? *Mon. Lab. Rev.*, July 1983, *106*(7), pp. 3–10. **[G: Japan]**

Tan, Siew Ee and Lai, Yew Wah. Protection and Employment in the West Malaysian Manufacturing Industries. *Weltwirtsch. Arch.*, 1983, *119*(2), pp. 329–44. **[G: Malaysia]**

Tan, Thiam Soon. The Small Firm: South East Asia. **In** *Storey, D. J., ed.*, 1983, pp. 218–47. **[G: S. E. Asia]**

Tavares, Maria De Conceicao and Souza, Paulo Renato. Employment and Wages in Industry: The Case of Brazil. **In** *Urquidi, V. L. and Reyes, S. T., eds.*, 1983, pp. 195–210. **[G: Brazil]**

Taylor, Jim and Bradley, Steven. Spatial Variations in the Unemployment Rate: A Case Study of North West England. *Reg. Stud.*, April 1983, *17*(2), pp. 113–24. **[G: U.K.]**

Terra, Juan Pablo. The Role of Education in Relation to Employment Problems. *Cepal Rev.*, December 1983, (21), pp. 81–111. **[G: Latin America]**

Terry, Sylvia Lazos. Work Experience, Earnings, and Family Income in 1981. *Mon. Lab. Rev.*, April 1983, *106*(4), pp. 13–20. **[G: U.S.]**

Thompson, G. Rodney and Stollar, Andrew J. An Empirical Test of an International Model of Relative Tertiary Employment. *Econ. Develop. Cult. Change*, July 1983, *31*(4), pp. 775–85. **[G: Selected LDCs; Selected MDCs]**

Thompson, John Scott. Patterns of Employment Multipliers in a Central Place System: An Alternative to Economic Base Estimation. *J. Reg. Sci.*, February 1983, *23*(1), pp. 71–82. **[G: Philippines]**

Thomspon, James H. and Leyden, Dennis R. The Small Firm: The United States of America. **In** *Storey, D. J., ed.*, 1983, pp. 7–45. **[G: U.S.]**

Tiano, André. Transfers of Iron and Steel Technology to the Third World: Effects on Employment in the Developed Countries. *Int. Lab. Rev.*, July–August 1983, *122*(4), pp. 429–42. **[G: France; OECD; LDCs]**

Tiller, Richard B. and Bednarzik, Robert W. The Behavior of Regional Unemployment Rates over Time: Effects on Dispersion and National Unemployment. *J. Reg. Sci.*, November 1983, *23*(4), pp. 479–99. **[G: U.S.]**

Tímár, János. Problems of Full Employment. *Acta Oecon.*, 1983, *31*(3–4), pp. 209–24. **[G: Hungary]**

Tímár, János and Ehrlich, Eva. Manpower and Industrialisation in Hungary. **In** *Weisbrod, B. and Hughes, H., eds.*, 1983, pp. 55–73. **[G: U.S.; U.K; Japan; Hungary]**

Tokman, Victor E. Labour Market Dynamics and Income Distribution in Latin America. **In** *Urquidi, V. L. and Reyes, S. T., eds.*, 1983, pp. 151–73. **[G: Latin America]**

Tomaskovic-Devey, Donald and Miller, S. M. Can High-Tech Provide the Jobs? *Challenge*, May/June 1983, *26*(2), pp. 57–63. **[G: U.S.]**

Tomlinson, Jim D. Does Mass Unemployment Matter? *Nat. Westminster Bank Quart. Rev.*, February 1983, pp. 35–45. **[G: U.K.]**

Topel, Robert H. On Layoffs and Unemployment Insurance. *Amer. Econ. Rev.*, September 1983, *73*(4), pp. 541–59. **[G: U.S.]**

Treyz, George I. and Duguay, Gerry E. Endogenous Wage Determination: Its Significance for State Policy Analysis Models. **In** *Dutta, M.; Hartline, J. C. and Loeb, P. D., eds.*, 1983, pp. 116–30. **[G: U.S.]**

Trinder, Chris. Income in Work and When Unemployed: Some Problems in Calculating Replacement Ratios. *Nat. Inst. Econ. Rev.*, February 1983, (103), pp. 56–61. **[G: U.K.]**

Trivedi, P. K. and Baker, G. M. Unemployment in Australia: Duration and Recurrent Spells. *Econ. Rec.*, June 1983, *59*(165), pp. 132–48. **[G: Australia]**

Tschetter, John and Lukasiewicz, John M. Employment Changes in Construction: Secular, Cyclical, and Seasonal. *Mon. Lab. Rev.*, March 1983, *106*(3), pp. 11–17. **[G: U.S.]**

Turk, Jeremy. Work and Unemployment. **In** *Shepherd, D.; Turk, J. and Silberston, A., eds.*, 1983, pp. 46–76. **[G: U.K.]**

Twomey, Michael J. Employment in Nineteenth Century Indian Textiles. *Exploration Econ. Hist.*, January 1983, *20*(1), pp. 37–57. **[G: India]**

Umetani, Shun'ichiro and Reubens, Beatrice G. Youth Employment in Japan. **In** *Reubens, B. G., ed.*, 1983, pp. 185–231. **[G: Japan]**

Urquhart, Michael A. and Hewson, Marillyn A. Unemployment Continued to Rise in 1982 as Recession Deepened. *Mon. Lab. Rev.*, February 1983, *106*(2), pp. 3–12. **[G: U.S.]**

Utgoff, Kathleen Classen. Compensation Levels and Quit Rates in the Public Sector. *J. Human Res.*, Summer 1983, *18*(3), pp. 394–406. **[G: U.S.]**

Valli, Vittorio. The Rise of Unemployment and Employment Adjustment Policies in Japan, Italy and West Germany. *Rivista Int. Sci. Econ. Com.*, August 1983, *30*(8), pp. 716–34. **[G: Italy; Japan; W. Germany]**

Varaiya, Pravin and Wiseman, Michael. Reindustrialization and the Outlook for Declining Areas. **In** *Henderson, J. V., ed.*, 1983, pp. 167–90. **[G: U.S.]**

Walsh, Brendan M. Unemployment and the Labour Market in Ireland. *Econ. Soc. Rev.*, January 1983, *14*(2), pp. 73–76. **[G: Ireland]**

Warren, Ronald S., Jr. Labor Market Contacts, Unanticipated Wages, and Employment Growth. *Amer. Econ. Rev.*, June 1983, *73*(3), pp. 389–97. **[G: U.S.]**

Wegner, Manfred. Erklärungen für das Arbeitsplatzwunder in den USA und für die stagnierende Beschäftigung in der EG. (Employment Creation in the U.S.A. and the European Community. With English summary.) *Ifo-Studien*, 1983, *29*(2), pp. 101–37. **[G: U.S.; EEC]**

Weis, Peter. Zur arbeitsmarktpolitischen Problematik von Kündigungs- und Besitzstandsregelungen für ältere Arbeitnehmer. (The Problematic Nature of Protection against Dismissal and Earnings Guaranties for Elderly Workers. With English summary.) *Z. Wirtschaft. Sozialwissen.*, 1983, *103*(3), pp. 255–81. **[G: W. Germany]**

Weller, Barry R. The Political Business Cycle: A Discriminating Analysis. *Soc. Sci. Quart.*, June 1983, *64*(2), pp. 398–403. **[G: U.S.]**

Westergård-Nielsen, Niels. En søgemodel for overgangen fra uddannelse til erhverv: Teori og empiri. (A Search Model of the Transition from Education to Work: Theory and Empirical Findings. With English summary.) *Nationaløkon. Tidsskr.*, 1983, *121*(2), pp. 181–99. **[G: Denmark]**

White, Gordon. Urban Employment and Labour Allocation Policies. **In** *Feuchtwang, S. and Hussain, A., eds.*, 1983, pp. 257–87. **[G: China]**

White, W. R. The Ontario Budget Deficit: A Cause for Concern? Comment. **In** *Conklin, D. W. and Courchene, T. J., eds.*, 1983, pp. 107–13. **[G: Canada]**

Windschuttle, Keith. Technology and Unemployment. **In** *Hill, S. and Johnston, R., eds.*, 1983, pp. 68–88. **[G: Australia]**

Wolfson, Alan. Labour Market Policy Concerns: An Evaluation of Current Federal Policies and Priorities: Comment. **In** *Queen's Univ. Indust. Relat. Centre and John Deutsch Mem.*, 1983, pp. 145–47. **[G: Canada]**

Wood, Richard H., Jr. Tractor Mechanisation and Employment on Larger Private Mexican Farms. *Int. Lab. Rev.*, March–April 1983, *122*(2), pp. 211–25. **[G: Mexico]**

Wren-Lewis, S. Employment. **In** *Britton, A., ed.*, 1983, pp. 52–64. **[G: U.K.]**

Yanz, Lynda and Smith, David. Women as a Reserve Army of Labour: A Critique. *Rev. Radical Polit. Econ.*, Spring 1983, *15*(1), pp. 92–106. **[G: U.K.]**

You, Jong Keun. Intrastate Shifts in a Regional Economy. **In** *Dutta, M.; Hartline, J. C. and Loeb, P. D., eds.*, 1983, pp. 216–29. **[G: U.S.]**

825 Productivity Studies: Labor, Capital, and Total Factor

8250 Productivity Studies: Labor, Capital, and Total Factor

Abramovitz, Moses. Notes on International Differences in Productivity Growth Rates. **In** *Mueller, D. C., ed.*, 1983, pp. 79–89. **[G: OECD]**

Addison, John T. Comment [The Effect of Unionization and Civil Service on the Salaries and Productivity of Regulators] [Worker Preferences for Union Representation]. **In** *Reid, J. D., Jr., ed.*, 1983, pp. 207–15.

Addison, John T. and Gerlach, Knut. Gewerkschaften und Produktivität: Fehlallokation von Ressourcen oder Produktivitätssteigerung? (Trade Unions and Productivity: Misallocation of Resources or Productivity Enhancement? With English Summary.) *Z. ges. Staatswiss.*, June 1983, *139*(2), pp. 215–28.

Adler, Paul. Trente ans d'automatisation et couts opératoires dans les banques françaises. (Thirty Years of Automation and Operating Costs in French Banks. With English summary.) *Revue Écon.*, September 1983, *34*(5), pp. 987–1020. **[G: France]**

Alam, M. Shahid. Efficiency Differentials Favouring Resource-Based Industries. *J. Devel. Econ.*, December 1983, *13*(3), pp. 361–66. **[G: LDCs]**

Allègre, C. Productivité du travail, rendement et facteurs endogénes de rentabilité: la conception du produit: Étude de cas dans les industries de la forme. (Labour Productivity, Time Rates and Endogenous Factors of the Firm's Efficiency: The Design of the Product. With English summary.) *Écon. Soc.*, March–April 1983, *17*(3–4), pp. 549–78. **[G: France]**

Allen, Steven G. How Much Does Absenteeism Cost? *J. Human Res.*, Summer 1983, *18*(3), pp. 379–93. **[G: U.S.]**

Andrisani, Paul J. and Parnes, Herbert S. Commitment to the Work Ethic and Success in the Labor Market: A Review of Research Findings. **In** *Barbash, J., et al., eds.*, 1983, pp. 101–20. **[G: U.S.]**

Antos, Joseph R. Current and Historical Availability of BLS Wage, Price, and Productivity Series by SIC Industries. **In** *Triplett, J. E., ed.*, 1983, pp. 465–502. **[G: U.S.]**

Arndt, Johan. Towards Ecologically Relevant Concepts of Marketing and Productivity. **In** *Uusitalo, L., ed.*, 1983, pp. 88–102.

Aslam, Naheed. Level of Real Wages and Labour Productivity in the Manufacturing Sector of the Punjab. *Pakistan Devel. Rev.*, Winter 1983, *22*(4), pp. 283–99. **[G: Pakistan]**

Baily, Martin Neil. 'Comparing Productivity Growth: An Exploration of French and U.S. Industrial and Firm Data' by Z. Griliches and J. Mairesse: Comment. *Europ. Econ. Rev.*, March/April 1983, *21*(1/2), pp. 121–23. **[G: U.S.; France]**

Baily, Martin Neil. Productivity Trends: Comment. **In** *Schurr, S. H.; Sonenblum, S. and Wood, D. O., eds.*, 1983, pp. 121–26. **[G: OECD; U.S.]**

Baily, Martin Neil. The Labor Market in the 1930's. **In** *Tobin, J., ed.*, 1983, pp. 21–61. **[G: U.S.]**

Baldwin, Carliss Y. Productivity and Labor Unions: An Application of the Theory of Self-Enforcing Contracts. *J. Bus.*, April 1983, *56*(2), pp. 155–85.

Baumol, William J. and Wolff, Edward N. Feedback from Productivity Growth to R & D. *Scand. J. Econ.*, 1983, *85*(2), pp. 147–57.

Beebe, Jack H. and Haltmaier, Jane. Disaggregation and the Labor Productivity Index. *Rev. Econ. Statist.*, August 1983, *65*(3), pp. 487–91.

Berndt, Ernst R. The Fixed Employment Costs of Specialized Labor: Comment. **In** *Triplett, J. E., ed.*, 1983, pp. 116–22. **[G: U.S.]**

Bingham, Barbara. Instruments to Measure Electricity: Industry's Productivity Growth Rises. *Mon. Lab. Rev.*, October 1983, *106*(10), pp. 11–17. **[G: U.S.]**

Blakemore, Arthur E. and Schlagenhauf, Don E. Estimation of the Trend Rate of Growth of Productivity. *Appl. Econ.*, December 1983, *15*(6), pp. 807–14. **[G: U.S.]**

Blomström, Magnus and Persson, Håkan. Foreign Investment and Spillover Efficiency in an Underdeveloped Economy: Evidence from the Mexican Manufacturing Industry. *World Devel.*, June 1983, *11*(6), pp. 493–501. **[G: Mexico]**

Böhm, Bernhard and Clemenz, Gerhard. The Development of Factor Productivity in an International Comparison. *Empirica*, 1983, (1), pp. 41–66. **[G: Selected OECD]**

Bradley, Keith and Hill, Stephen. 'After Japan': The Quality Circle Transplant and Productive Efficiency. *Brit. J. Ind. Relat.*, November 1983, *21*(3), pp. 291–311. **[G: U.K.; U.S.]**

Brand, Horst and Huffstutler, Clyde. Productivity Improvements in Two Fabricated Metals Industries. *Mon. Lab. Rev.*, October 1983, *106*(10), pp. 18–24. **[G: U.S.]**

Broner, Adam. Regional Comparisons of Labor Productivity. **In** *Dutta, M.; Hartline, J. C. and Loeb, P. D., eds.*, 1983, pp. 190–204. **[G: U.S.]**

Bruno, Michael. 'Comparing Productivity Growth: An Exploration of French and U.S. Industrial and Firm Data' by Z. Griliches and J. Mairesse: Comment. *Europ. Econ. Rev.*, March/April 1983, *21*(1/2), pp. 125–27. **[G: U.S.; France]**

Chambers, Robert G. Scale and Productivity Measurement under Risk. *Amer. Econ. Rev.*, September 1983, *73*(4), pp. 802–05.

Chaudry, A. Net Income and Productivity Analysis (NIPA) as a Planning Model. **In** *Courville, L.; de Fontenay, A. and Dobell, R., eds.*, 1983, pp. 145–66.

Cherevan', V. Coordinating the Reproduction of Workplaces with Labor Resources. *Prob. Econ.*, May 1983, *26*(1), pp. 38–56. **[G: U.S.S.R.]**

Christainsen, Gregory B. and Hogendorn, Jan S. Japanese Productivity: Adapting to Changing Comparative Advantage in the Face of Lifetime Employment Commitments. *Quart. Rev. Econ. Bus.*, Summer 1983, *23*(2), pp. 23–39. **[G: Japan]**

Collins, Eileen L. R & D and Labor Productivity: Can Tax Incentives Help? **In** *Weintraub, S. and Goodstein, M., eds.*, 1983, pp. 48–58. **[G: U.S.]**

Cravioglio, Antonio. Come si può misurare la produttività. (How to Measure Productivity. With English summary.) *L'Impresa*, 1983, *25*(2), pp. 59–64.

Dantzig, George B. and Iusem, Alfredo. Analyzing Labor Productivity Growth with the PILOT Model. **In** *Schurr, S. H.; Sonenblum, S. and Wood, D. O., eds.*, 1983, pp. 347–66. **[G: U.S.]**

Delporte, Christian M. and Thomas, L. Joseph. Gestion des opérations et productivité: Quelques leçons de l'exemple japonais. *Ann. Sci. Écon. Appl.*, 1983, *39*(1), pp. 9–26. **[G: Japan]**

Denny, Michael G. S.; de Fontenay, A. and Werner, M. Comparing the Efficiency of Firms: Canadian Telecommunications Companies. **In** *Courville, L.; de Fontenay, A. and Dobell, R., eds.*, 1983, pp. 115–27. **[G: Canada]**

Denny, Michael G. S.; de Fontenay, A. and Werner, M. Total Factor Productivity for Management: The Post-mortem and Planning Frameworks. **In** *Courville, L.; de Fontenay, A. and Dobell, R., eds.*, 1983, pp. 167–78.

Dirksen, Erik. Chinese Industrial Productivity in an International Context. *World Devel.*, April 1983, *11*(4), pp. 381–87. **[G: China]**

Drach, Marcel and Revuz, Christine. La brigade de travail sous contrat dans l'industrie soviétique et la réforme de juillet 1979. (With English summary.) *Écon. Soc.*, January 1983, *17*(1), pp. 115–78. **[G: U.S.S.R.]**

Duncan, Greg J. and Holmlund, Bertil. Was Adam Smith Right after All? Another Test of the Theory of Compensating Wage Differentials. *J. Lab. Econ.*, October 1983, *1*(4), pp. 366–79. **[G: Sweden]**

Ehrenberg, Ronald G. and Schwarz, Joshua L. The Effect of Unions on Productivity in the Public Sector: The Case of Municipal Libraries. **In** *Hirsch, W. Z., ed.*, 1983, pp. 311–41. **[G: U.S.]**

Ehrenberg, Ronald G.; Sherman, Daniel R. and Schwarz, Joshua L. Unions and Productivity in the Public Sector: A Study of Municipal Libraries. *Ind. Lab. Relat. Rev.*, January 1983, *36*(2), pp. 199–213. **[G: U.S.]**

Ellis, Michael. Supply-Side Linkage of Capacity Utilization and Labor Productivity: U.S. Manufacturing, 1954-1980. *Nebr. J. Econ. Bus.*, Winter, 1983, *22*(1), pp. 15–27. **[G: U.S.]**

English, Jon and Marchione, Anthony R. Productivity: A New Perspective. *Calif. Manage. Rev.*, January 1983, *25*(2), pp. 57–66. **[G: U.S.]**

Fabricant, Solomon. The Productivity-Growth Slowdown—A Review of the "Facts." **In** *Schurr, S. H.; Sonenblum, S. and Wood, D. O., eds.*, 1983, pp. 47–70. **[G: U.S.]**

Fisk, Donald M. Modest Productivity Gains in State Unemployment Insurance Service. *Mon. Lab. Rev.*, January 1983, *106*(1), pp. 24–27. **[G: U.S.]**

Fulco, Lawrence J. Recent Productivity Measures Depict Growth Patterns since 1980. *Mon. Lab. Rev.*, December 1983, *106*(12), pp. 45–48. **[G: U.S.]**

Gavrilov, R. Rates, Factors, and New Indicators of the Growth of Labor Productivity. *Prob. Econ.*, March 1983, *25*(11), pp. 3–18. **[G: U.S.S.R.]**

Gay, Robert S. and Hedlund, Jeffrey D. The Labor Market in Recession and Recovery. *Fed. Res. Bull.*, July 1983, *69*(7), pp. 477–88. **[G: U.S.]**

Giersch, Herbert and Wolter, Frank. Towards an Explanation of the Productivity Slowdown: An Acceleration-Deceleration Hypothesis. *Econ. J.*, March 1983, *93*(369), pp. 35–55. **[G: OECD]**

Gollop, Frank M. and Jorgenson, Dale W. Sectoral Labor Input. **In** *Triplett, J. E., ed.*, 1983, pp. 503–20. **[G: U.S.]**

Griliches, Zvi. Productivity Trends: Comment. **In** *Schurr, S. H.; Sonenblum, S. and Wood, D. O., eds.*, 1983, pp. 127–30. **[G: OECD; U.S.]**

Griliches, Zvi and Mairesse, Jacques. Comparing Productivity Growth: An Exploration of French and U.S. Industrial and Firm Data. *Europ. Econ. Rev.*, March/April 1983, *21*(1/2), pp. 89–119. **[G: U.S.; France]**

Gupta, Vinod K. Labor Productivity, Establishment Size, and Scale Economies [The Extent of Economies of Scale: The Effects of Firm Size on Labor Productivity and Wage Rates]. *Southern Econ. J.*, January 1983, *49*(3), pp. 853–59. **[G: U.S.]**

Hajpál, Gyula. Valuation of the Economic Role of the Human Factor. *Acta Oecon.*, 1983, *31*(1–2), pp. 23–36.

Hall, Robert E. U.S. Labor Markets: Imbalance, Wage Growth, and Productivity in the 1970s: Comments and Discussion. *Brookings Pap. Econ. Act.*, 1983, (1), pp. 121–23. **[G: U.S.]**

Harvey, Leonard. Technology and the Work Environment (II): Technology and Productivity—What Is The Relationship? **In** *Martin, T. R., ed.*, 1983, pp. 54–63. **[G: U.S.]**

Hayes, Robert H. and Abernathy, William J. Managing Our Way to Economic Decline. **In** *Dickson, D. N., ed.*, 1983, pp. 203–23. **[G: U.S.; OECD]**

Heien, Dale M. Productivity in U.S. Food Processing and Distribution. *Amer. J. Agr. Econ.*, May 1983, *65*(2), pp. 297–302. **[G: U.S.]**

Hildred, William M. Some Methodological and Political Issues Surrounding Productivity. *J. Econ. Issues*, December 1983, *17*(4), pp. 1075–86.

Hirsch, Barry T. and Hausman, William J. Labour Productivity in the British and South Wales Coal Industry, 1874–1914. *Economica*, May 1983, *50*(198), pp. 145–57. **[G: U.K.]**

Hirsch, Werner Z. and Rufolo, Anthony M. Shirking, Monitoring Costs, and Municipal Labor Productivity. **In** *Hirsch, W. Z., ed.*, 1983, pp. 277–310.

Hulten, Charles R. and Robertson, James W. Labor Productivity in the Local Public Sector. **In** *Hirsch, W. Z., ed.*, 1983, pp. 342–88. **[G: U.S.]**

Kendrick, John W. Entrepreneurship, Productivity, and Economic Growth. **In** *Backman, J., ed.*, 1983, pp. 111–48. **[G: OECD]**

Kendrick, John W. International Comparisons of Recent Productivity Trends. **In** *Schurr, S. H.; Sonenblum, S. and Wood, D. O., eds.*, 1983, pp. 71–120. **[G: OECD]**

Keyfitz, Nathan. Age and Productivity. *J. Policy Anal. Manage.*, Summer 1983, *2*(4), pp. 632–37. **[G: U.S.]**

Kiss, Ferenc. Productivity Gains in Bell Canada. **In** *Courville, L.; de Fontenay, A. and Dobell, R., eds.*, 1983, pp. 85–113. **[G: Canada]**

Koriagin, A. Socialist Reproduction and the Comparison of Labor Inputs. *Prob. Econ.*, July 1983, *26*(3), pp. 53–71. **[G: U.S.S.R.]**

Krohn, Gregor A. Measuring the Experience–Productivity Relationship: The Case of Major League Baseball. *J. Bus. Econ. Statist.*, October 1983, *1*(4), pp. 273–79. **[G: U.S.]**

Kumar, Pradeep. The Current Industrial Relations Scene in Canada, 1983: Wages, Productivity and Labour Costs: Summary Outline. **In** *Wood, W. D. and Kumar, P., eds.*, 1983, pp. 405–76. **[G: Canada; OECD]**

Ledebur, Larry C. and Moomaw, Ronald L. A Shift-Share Analysis of Regional Labor Productivity in Manufacturing. *Growth Change*, January 1983, *14*(1), pp. 2–9. **[G: U.S.]**

Leibenstein, Harvey. Notes on the X-efficiency Approach to Inflation, Productivity and Unemployment. **In** *Weisbrod, B. and Hughes, H., eds.*, 1983, pp. 84–96.

Levin, Henry M. Raising Employment and Productivity with Producer Co-operatives. **In** *Streeten, P. and Maier, H., eds.*, 1983, pp. 310–28. **[G: Spain]**

Lindbeck, Assar. The Recent Slowdowns of Productivity Growth. *Econ. J.*, March 1983, *93*(369), pp. 13–34. **[G: OECD]**

Lobue, Marie. Adjustment to Labor Productivity: An Application to the Economics of Discrimination. *Southern Econ. J.*, July 1983, *50*(1), pp. 151–59.

Maki, Dennis R. The Effects of Unions and Strikes on the Rate of Growth of Total Factor Productivity in Canada. *Appl. Econ.*, February 1983, *15*(1), pp. 29–41. **[G: Canada]**

Mansfield, Edwin. Science and Technology. **In** *Miller, G. W., ed.*, 1983, pp. 125–50. **[G: U.S.; OECD; U.S.S.R.]**

Mark, Jerome A. and Waldorf, William H. Multifactor Productivity: A New BLS Measure. *Mon. Lab. Rev.*, December 1983, *106*(12), pp. 3–15. **[G: U.S.]**

Marks, Phillipa. The Slowdown in Labour Productivity Growth Rates in New Zealand in the 1970s. **In** *Easton, B., ed.*, 1983, pp. 95–140. **[G: New Zealand]**

Mayer, Jean. Workers' Well-Being and Productivity:

The Role of Bargaining. *Int. Lab. Rev.*, May–June 1983, *122*(3), pp. 343–53.

Medoff, James L. U.S. Labor Markets: Imbalance, Wage Growth, and Productivity in the 1970s. *Brookings Pap. Econ. Act.*, 1983, (1), pp. 87–120. **[G: U.S.]**

Metcalfe, J. S. and Hall, P. H. The Verdoorn Law and the Salter Mechanism: A Note on Australian Manufacturing Industry. *Australian Econ. Pap.*, December 1983, *22*(41), pp. 364–73. **[G: Australia]**

Metzger, Michael R. and Goldfarb, Robert S. Do Davis–Bacon Minimum Wages Raise Product Quality? *J. Lab. Res.*, Summer 1983, *4*(3), pp. 265–72. **[G: U.S.]**

Miller, Edward M. A Difficulty in Measuring Productivity with a Perpetual Inventory Capital Stock Measure. *Oxford Bull. Econ. Statist.*, August 1983, *45*(3), pp. 297–306.

Miller, Edward M. Productive Efficiency and Region: Comment. *Southern Econ. J.*, July 1983, *50*(1), pp. 257–60. **[G: U.S.]**

Moomaw, Ronald L. Productive Efficiency and Region: Reply. *Southern Econ. J.*, July 1983, *50*(1), pp. 261–64. **[G: U.S.]**

Moomaw, Ronald L. Spatial Productivity Variations in Manufacturing: A Critical Survey of Cross-Sectional Analyses. *Int. Reg. Sci. Rev.*, June 1983, *8*(1), pp. 1–22. **[G: U.S.]**

Morris, Derek J. Comment on the Paper by Professor Lindbeck [The Recent Slowdowns of Productivity Growth]. *Econ. J.*, March 1983, *93*(369), pp. 78–83. **[G: OECD]**

Moseley, Fred. Marx's Concepts of Productive Labor and Unproductive Labor: An Application to the Postwar U.S. Economy. *Eastern Econ. J.*, July–September 1983, *9*(3), pp. 180–89. **[G: U.S.]**

Nevis, Edwin C. Cultural Assumptions and Productivity: The United States and China. *Sloan Manage. Rev.*, Spring 1983, *24*(3), pp. 17–29. **[G: China; U.S.]**

Niemi, Albert W., Jr. Gross State Product and Productivity in the Southeast, 1950–80. *Growth Change*, April 1983, *14*(2), pp. 3–8. **[G: U.S.]**

Noam, Eli M. The Effect of Unionization and Civil Service on the Salaries and Productivity of Regulators. **In** *Reid, J. D., Jr., ed.*, 1983, pp. 157–70. **[G: U.S.]**

Nooteboom, B. Productivity Growth in the Grocery Trade. *Appl. Econ.*, October 1983, *15*(5), pp. 649–64. **[G: Netherlands]**

Norsworthy, J. R. and Malmquist, David H. Input Measurement and Productivity Growth in Japanese and U.S. Manufacturing. *Amer. Econ. Rev.*, December 1983, *73*(5), pp. 947–67. **[G: Japan; U.S.]**

Odaka, Konosuke. Skill Formation in Development: Case Studies of Philippine Manufacturing (I). *Hitotsubashi J. Econ.*, June 1983, *24*(1), pp. 11–24. **[G: Philippines]**

Oi, Walter Y. The Fixed Employment Costs of Specialized Labor. **In** *Triplett, J. E., ed.*, 1983, pp. 63–116. **[G: U.S.]**

Oppenlander, Karl-Heinrich. The Impact of Technical and Structural Change on the Structure and Employment of Manpower. **In** *Streeten, P. and Maier, H., eds.*, 1983, pp. 370–94. **[G: W. Germany]**

Perlman, Mark. Human Resources and Population Growth. **In** *Streeten, P. and Maier, H., eds.*, 1983, pp. 167–80. **[G: OECD]**

Poza, Ernesto J. Twelve Actions to Build Strong U.S. Factories. *Sloan Manage. Rev.*, Fall 1983, *25*(1), pp. 27–38. **[G: U.S.]**

Prais, S. J. Comment on the Paper by Professor Giersch and Dr. Wolter [Towards an Explanation of the Productivity Slowdown: An Acceleration-Deceleration Hypothesis]. *Econ. J.*, March 1983, *93*(369), pp. 84–88.

Putterman, Louis. Incentives and the Kibbutz: Toward an Economics of Communal Work Motivation. *Z. Nationalökon.*, 1983, *43*(2), pp. 157–88.

Reimeringer, J. N. Global Factor Productivity (GFP) and EDF's Management. **In** *Courville, L.; de Fontenay, A. and Dobell, R., eds.*, 1983, pp. 131–43.

Rogovskii, N. The Effectiveness of Labor under the Eleventh Five-Year Plan. *Prob. Econ.*, April 1983, *25*(12), pp. 51–66. **[G: U.S.S.R.]**

Rooney, Patrick M. Worker Control: Greater Efficiency and Job Satisfaction. *Econ. Forum*, Winter 1983-84, *14*(2), pp. 97–123. **[G: U.S.]**

Scherer, F. M. Concentration, R&D, and Productivity Change. *Southern Econ. J.*, July 1983, *50*(1), pp. 221–25. **[G: U.S.]**

Scherer, F. M. R&D and Declining Productivity Growth. *Amer. Econ. Rev.*, May 1983, *73*(2), pp. 215–18. **[G: U.S.]**

Schuster, Michael. The Impact of Union-Management Cooperation on Productivity and Employment. *Ind. Lab. Relat. Rev.*, April 1983, *36*(3), pp. 415–30. **[G: U.S.]**

Schydlowsky, Daniel M. The Short-run Potential for Employment Generation of Installed Capacity in Latin America. **In** *Urquidi, V. L. and Reyes, S. T., eds.*, 1983, pp. 311–47. **[G: Latin America]**

Sider, Hal. Safety and Productivity in Underground Coal Mining. *Rev. Econ. Statist.*, May 1983, *65*(2), pp. 225–33. **[G: U.S.]**

Siegel, Irving H. Work Ethic and Productivity. **In** *Barbash, J., et al., eds.*, 1983, pp. 27–42. **[G: U.S.]**

Simos, Evangelos O. and Triantis, John E. Do Energy Prices and Productivity Developments Affect Inflation Expectations? *Rivista Int. Sci. Econ. Com.*, October–November 1983, *30*(10–11), pp. 923–34. **[G: U.S.]**

Smith, A. D. and Hitchens, D. M. W. N. Comparative British and American Productivity in Retailing. *Nat. Inst. Econ. Rev.*, May 1983, (104), pp. 45–60. **[G: U.S.; U.K.]**

Solow, Robert M. U.S. Labor Markets: Imbalance, Wage Growth, and Productivity in the 1970s: Comments and Discussion. *Brookings Pap. Econ. Act.*, 1983, (1), pp. 123–28. **[G: U.S.]**

Sonenblum, Sidney. Energy, Productivity, and Economic Growth: Overview and Commentary. **In** *Schurr, S. H.; Sonenblum, S. and Wood, D. O., eds.*, 1983, pp. 3–43. **[G: U.S.; Selected Countries]**

Sorokin, G. Patterns of Socialist Intensification. *Prob. Econ.*, July 1983, *26*(3), pp. 3–21. **[G: U.S.S.R.]**

Steedman, Ian. On the Measurement and Aggregation of Productivity Increase. *Metroecon.*, October 1983, *35*(3), pp. 223–33.

Stretton, Alan. Circular Migration, Segmented Labour Markets and Efficiency: The Building Industry in Manila and Port Moresby. *Int. Lab. Rev.*, Sept.–Oct. 1983, *122*(5), pp. 623–39. **[G: Philippines]**

Teitel, Simon. Technology and Labour Productivity Patterns in the Manufacturing Industries of Less Industrialised Countries. **In** *Urquidi, V. L. and Reyes, S. T., eds.*, 1983, pp. 25–40.

Triplett, Jack E. Introduction: An Essay on Labor Cost. **In** *Triplett, J. E., ed.*, 1983, pp. 1–60.

Wabe, J. Stuart and Gutierrez-Camara, José L. Capital Utilisation, Capital Intensity and Factor Productivity: A Comparison of Factories in Developing and Industrialised Countries. *J. Econ. Stud.*, 1983, *10*(3), pp. 3–11. **[G: Selected Countries]**

Weisskopf, Thomas E.; Bowles, Samuel and Gordon, David M. Hearts and Minds: A Social Model of U.S. Productivity Growth. *Brookings Pap. Econ. Act.*, 1983, (2), pp. 381–450. **[G: U.S.]**

Wiboonchutikula, Paitoon. Productivity Growth of the Agricultural Machinery Industry in Thailand. **In** *Internat'l Rice Res. Inst. and Agric. Devel. Council*, 1983, pp. 51–59. **[G: Thailand]**

York, James D. Productivity Growth in Plastics Lower Than All Manufacturing. *Mon. Lab. Rev.*, September 1983, *106*(9), pp. 17–21. **[G: U.S.]**

826 Labor Markets: Demographic Characteristics

8260 Labor Markets: Demographic Characteristics

Anker, Richard. Female Labour Force Participation in Developing Countries: A Critique of Current Definitions and Data Collection Methods. *Int. Lab. Rev.*, November–December 1983, *122*(6), pp. 709–23. **[G: India]**

Arthur, W. B. Age and Earnings in the Labour Market: Implications of the 1980s Labour Bulge. **In** *Streeten, P. and Maier, H., eds.*, 1983, pp. 405–19.

Becker, Brian E. and Hills, Stephen M. The Long-Run Effects of Job Changes and Unemployment among Male Teenagers. *J. Human Res.*, Spring 1983, *18*(2), pp. 197–212. **[G: U.S.]**

Bergmann, Barbara R. Women's Plight: Bad and Getting Worse. *Challenge*, March/April 1983, *26*(1), pp. 22–26. **[G: U.S.]**

Björklund, Anders and Persson-Tanimura, Inga. Youth Employment in Sweden. **In** *Reubens, B. G., ed.*, 1983, pp. 232–68. **[G: Sweden]**

Bonnell, Sheila M. and Dixon, Peter B. A Measure of the Incidence of the Costs of Structural Change: The Experience of Birthplace Groups in the Australian Labour Force during the Seventies. *Econ. Rec.*, December 1983, *59*(167), pp. 398–406. **[G: Australia]**

Borus, Michael E. Tomorrow's Workers: Summary and Policy Implications. **In** *Borus, M. E., ed.*, 1983, pp. 173–80. **[G: U.S.]**

Borus, Michael E. and Santos, Richard. The Youth Population. **In** *Borus, M. E., ed.*, 1983, pp. 1–21. **[G: U.S.]**

Borus, Michael E., et al. Youth Looking for Work. **In** *Borus, M. E., ed.*, 1983, pp. 59–102. **[G: U.S.]**

Boudreaux, Kenneth J. A Further Adjustment Needed to Estimate Lost Earning Capacity [The Use of Worklife Tables in Estimates of Lost Earning Capacity]. *Mon. Lab. Rev.*, October 1983, *106*(10), pp. 30–31. **[G: U.S.]**

Bowie, Robert D. The Dual Labour Market. **In** *Easton, B., ed.*, 1983, pp. 71–94. **[G: New Zealand]**

Bowie, Robert D. The Peripheral Labour Force. **In** *Easton, B., ed.*, 1983, pp. 49–70. **[G: New Zealand]**

Braae, Richard and Gallacher, John. Labour Supply in New Zealand, 1976 to 1981: New and Familiar Problems for Descriptive and Empirical Analysis. **In** *Easton, B., ed.*, 1983, pp. 15–48. **[G: New Zealand]**

Brown, Charles; Gilroy, Curtis and Kohen, Andrew. Time-Series Evidence of the Effect of the Minimum Wage on Youth Employment and Unemployment. *J. Human Res.*, Winter 1983, *18*(1), pp. 3–31. **[G: U.S.]**

Buchele, Robert. Economic Achievement and the Power of Positive Thinking. *J. Human Res.*, Summer 1983, *18*(3), pp. 441–49. **[G: U.S.]**

Chiswick, Barry R. An Analysis of the Earnings and Employment of Asian-American Men. *J. Lab. Econ.*, April 1983, *1*(2), pp. 197–214. **[G: U.S.]**

Coates, Mary Lou. Human Resources and Labour Markets: Summary Outline. **In** *Wood, W. D. and Kumar, P., eds.*, 1983, pp. 31–83. **[G: Canada; OECD]**

Corvalán-Vásquez, Oscar. Vocational Training of Disadvantaged Youth in the Developing Countries. *Int. Lab. Rev.*, May–June 1983, *122*(3), pp. 367–81. **[G: LDCs]**

Darden, Joe T. Racial Differences in Unemployment: A Spatial Perspective. *Rev. Black Polit. Econ.*, Spring 1983, *12*(3), pp. 93–105. **[G: U.S.]**

Davis, Carlton G. and Allen, Joyce E. Black Agricultural Economists in the Labor Market: Theoretical and Empirical Issues. *Amer. J. Agr. Econ.*, December 1983, *65*(5), pp. 981–87. **[G: U.S.]**

De Tray, Dennis. Children's Work Activities in Malaysia. *Population Devel. Rev.*, September 1983, *9*(3), pp. 437–55. **[G: Malaysia]**

Devaney, Barbara. An Analysis of Variations in U.S. Fertility and Female Labor Force Participation Trends. *Demography*, May 1983, *20*(2), pp. 147–61. **[G: U.S.]**

Devaney, Barbara. Total Work Effort under a Negative Income Tax. *J. Policy Anal. Manage.*, Summer 1983, *2*(4), pp. 625–27. **[G: U.S.]**

Feshbach, Murray. Population and Labor Force. **In** *Bergson, A. and Levine, H. S., eds.*, 1983, pp. 79–111. **[G: U.S.S.R.]**

Finch, John L. Worklife Estimates Should Be Consistent with Known Labor Force Participation. *Mon. Lab. Rev.*, June 1983, *106*(6), pp. 34–36. **[G: U.S.]**

Foot, David K. The Impacts of Population Growth and Aging on the Future Canadian Labour Force. **In** *Queen's Univ. Indust. Relat. Centre and John Deutsch Mem.*, 1983, pp. 50–64. **[G: Canada]**

Foster, Will F. and Gregory, R. G. A Flow Analysis of the Labour Market in Australia. **In** *Blandy, R. and Covick, O., eds.*, 1983, pp. 111–36. **[G: U.S.; Canada]**

Fujii, Edwin T. and Mak, James. The Determinants of Income of Native- and Foreign-Born Men in a Multiracial Society. *Appl. Econ.*, December 1983, *15*(6), pp. 759–76. **[G: U.S.]**

Fullerton, Howard N., Jr. and Tschetter, John. The 1995 Labor Force: A Second Look. *Mon. Lab. Rev.*, November 1983, *106*(11), pp. 3–10. **[G: U.S.]**

Genosko, Joachim. Erwerbsbeteiligung und gesetzliche Rentenversicherung—Der Fall der 60- bis 65jährigen Männer. (Labor Force Participation and Old Age Insurance—The Case of the 60–65 Year-Old Men. With English summary.) *Z. ges. Staatswiss.*, December 1983, *139*(4), pp. 625–42. **[G: W. Germany]**

Gilbert, Neil. In Support of Domesticity: A Neglected Family Policy Option. *J. Policy Anal. Manage.*, Summer 1983, *2*(4), pp. 628–32. **[G: U.S.]**

Gladwin, Christina H. and Staudt, Kathleen. Women's Employment Issues: Discussion. *Amer. J. Agr. Econ.*, December 1983, *65*(5), pp. 1055–57.

Goldfarb, Robert S. and Yezer, Anthony M. J. A Model of Teenage Labor Supply. *J. Econ. Bus.*, June 1983, *35*(2), pp. 245–55. **[G: U.S.]**

Haber, Sheldon E.; Lamas, Enrique J. and Green, Gordon. A New Method for Estimating Job Separations by Sex and Race. *Mon. Lab. Rev.*, June 1983, *106*(6), pp. 20–27. **[G: U.S.]**

Hanoch, Giora and Honig, Marjorie. Retirement, Wages, and Labor Supply of the Elderly. *J. Lab. Econ.*, April 1983, *1*(2), pp. 131–51. **[G: U.S.]**

Harrisson, John A. C.; Reubens, Beatrice G. and Sparr, Pamela. Trends in Numbers Employed 1960–1980. **In** *Reubens, B. G., ed.*, 1983, pp. 17–38. **[G: Selected OECD]**

Hart, Gillian. Productivity, Poverty, and Population Pressure: Female Labor Deployment in Rice Production in Java and Bangladesh. *Amer. J. Agr. Econ.*, December 1983, *65*(5), pp. 1037–42. **[G: Indonesia; Bangladesh]**

Hayghe, Howard. Married Couples: Work and Income Patterns. *Mon. Lab. Rev.*, December 1983, *106*(12), pp. 26–29. **[G: U.S.]**

Hill, M. Anne. Female Labor Force Participation in Developing and Developed Countries—Consideration of the Informal Sector. *Rev. Econ. Statist.*, August 1983, *65*(3), pp. 459–68. **[G: Japan]**

Hills, Stephen M. and Reubens, Beatrice G. Youth Employment in the United States. **In** *Reubens, B. G., ed.*, 1983, pp. 269–318. **[G: U.S.]**

Hirschman, Charles. Labor Markets and Ethnic Inequality in Peninsular Malaysia, 1970. *J. Devel. Areas*, October 1983, *18*(1), pp. 1–20. **[G: Malaysia]**

Huffman, Wallace E. Women's Employment Issues: Discussion. *Amer. J. Agr. Econ.*, December 1983, *65*(5), pp. 1058–59.

Ihnen, Loren A. Black Agricultural Economists: Discussion. *Amer. J. Agr. Econ.*, December 1983, *65*(5), pp. 999–1001. **[G: U.S.]**

Johnson, Beverly L. and Waldman, Elizabeth. Most Women Who Maintain Families Receive Poor Labor Market Returns. *Mon. Lab. Rev.*, December 1983, *106*(12), pp. 30–34. **[G: U.S.]**

Jones, Dewitt; Nelson, Mack and Parks, Alfred L. Demand and Supply Factors of Black Agricultural Economists. *Amer. J. Agr. Econ.*, December 1983, *65*(5), pp. 988–92. **[G: U.S.]**

Kabaj, Mieczyslaw. Economic Factors Determining Long-term Labour Supply: A Case-study of the Polish Economy, 1950–1978. **In** *Streeten, P. and Maier, H., eds.*, 1983, pp. 457–72. **[G: Poland]**

Keyfitz, Nathan. Age Effects in Work and Consumption. *Econ. Notes*, 1983, (3), pp. 86–121. **[G: Global]**

Lampman, Robert J. How Has the Labor Supply Changed in Response to Recent Increases in Social Welfare Expenditures and the Taxes to Pay for Them? **In** *Barbash, J., et al., eds.*, 1983, pp. 61–85. **[G: U.S.]**

Maddison, Angus. Measuring Labour Slack. **In** *Weisbrod, B. and Hughes, H., eds.*, 1983, pp. 97–112. **[G: U.K.; W. Germany]**

Maldonado, I. and Mercier, D. Chômage des jeunes et répartition du revenu: une problématique. (Unemployment among Youth and Income Distribution: The Problem-Setting. With English summary.) *Écon. Soc.*, March–April 1983, *17*(3–4), pp. 629–54. **[G: Canada]**

Mazumdar, Dipak. Segmented Labor Markets in LDCs. *Amer. Econ. Rev.*, May 1983, *73*(2), pp. 254–59. **[G: LDCs]**

McManus, Walter; Gould, William and Welch, Finis. Earnings of Hispanic Men: The Role of English Language Proficiency. *J. Lab. Econ.*, April 1983, *1*(2), pp. 101–30. **[G: U.S.]**

Metcalf, David and Richards, John. Youth Employment in Great Britain. **In** *Reubens, B. G., ed.*, 1983, pp. 149–84. **[G: U.K.]**

Meyer, Peter J. and Maes, Patricia L. The Reproduction of Occupational Segregation among Young Women. *Ind. Relat.*, Winter 1983, *22*(1), pp. 115–24. **[G: U.S.]**

Miller, Paul W. and Volker, Paul A. A Cross-Section Analysis of the Labour Force Participation of Married Women in Australia. *Econ. Rec.*, March 1983, *59*(164), pp. 28–42. **[G: Australia]**

Molho, I. I. A Regional Analysis of the Distribution of Married Women's Labour Force Participation Rates in the UK. *Reg. Stud.*, April 1983, *17*(2), pp. 125–33. **[G: U.K.]**

Morrison, Malcolm H. The Aging of the U.S. Population: Human Resource Implications. *Mon. Lab. Rev.*, May 1983, *106*(5), pp. 13–19. **[G: U.S.]**

Nakamura, Jiro. The Role of the Labor Market for Solving the Problem of Stagflation. *Econ. Stud. Quart.*, August 1983, *34*(2), pp. 147–55. **[G: Japan]**

Nelson, David M. The Use of Worklife Tables in Estimates of Lost Earning Capacity. *Mon. Lab. Rev.*, April 1983, *106*(4), pp. 30–31. **[G: U.S.]**

Norwood, Janet L. Labor Market Contrasts: United States and Europe: Errata. *Mon. Lab. Rev.*, September 1983, *106*(9), pp. 21. **[G: U.S.; W. Europe]**

Norwood, Janet L. Labor Market Contrasts: United States and Europe. *Mon. Lab. Rev.*, August 1983, *106*(8), pp. 3–7. **[G: U.S.; W. Europe]**

O'Neill, Dave M. Racial Differentials in Teenage Unemployment: A Note on Trends. *J. Human Res.*, Spring 1983, *18*(2), pp. 295–306. [G: U.S.]

Okun, Arthur M. Conflicting National Goals. **In** *Okun, A. M.*, 1983, *1976*, pp. 221–49. [G: U.S.]

Paringer, Lynn. Women and Absenteeism: Health or Economics? *Amer. Econ. Rev.*, May 1983, *73*(2), pp. 123–27. [G: U.S.]

Passmore, Davin Lynn, et al. Health and Youth Employment. *Appl. Econ.*, December 1983, *15*(6), pp. 715–29. [G: U.S.]

Peterson, Paul and Mackay, Keith. Youth Employment in Australia. **In** *Reubens, B. G., ed.*, 1983, pp. 86–112. [G: Australia]

Piore, Michael J. Labor Market Segmentation: To What Paradigm Does It Belong? *Amer. Econ. Rev.*, May 1983, *73*(2), pp. 249–53.

Ramachandran, P. and Shastri, P. P. Intercensal Urban Indian Female Participation Rates and Their Variations, 1961–71: A Census Analysis. *Econ. Aff.*, October–December 1983, *28*(4), pp. 816–28. [G: India]

Reimers, Cordelia W. Labor Market Discrimination against Hispanic and Black Men. *Rev. Econ. Statist.*, November 1983, *65*(4), pp. 570–79. [G: U.S.]

Reubens, Beatrice G. Youth at Work: An International Survey: Overview and Implications. **In** *Reubens, B. G., ed.*, 1983, pp. 319–41. [G: Selected OECD]

Reubens, Beatrice G. Youth at Work: An International Survey: Perspectives and Problems. **In** *Reubens, B. G., ed.*, 1983, pp. 1–16. [G: Selected OECD]

Reubens, Beatrice G. and Harrisson, John A. C. Occupational Dissimilarity by Age and Sex. **In** *Reubens, B. G., ed.*, 1983, pp. 39–85. [G: Japan; Sweden; U.K.; U.S.]

Reyes, Alvaro. Economic-demographic Determinants of Labour Supply in Latin America: Some Preliminary Findings. **In** *Urquidi, V. L. and Reyes, S. T., eds.*, 1983, pp. 3–24. [G: Latin America]

Robbins, Richard D. and Evans, Sidney H. Characteristics of Black Agricultural Economists. *Amer. J. Agr. Econ.*, December 1983, *65*(5), pp. 993–98. [G: U.S.]

Rones, Philip L. The Labor Market Problems of Older Workers. *Mon. Lab. Rev.*, May 1983, *106*(5), pp. 3–12. [G: U.S.]

Schober, Karen. Youth Employment in West Germany. **In** *Reubens, B. G., ed.*, 1983, pp. 113–48. [G: W. Germany]

Shapiro, David. Working Youth. **In** *Borus, M. E., ed.*, 1983, pp. 23–58. [G: U.S.]

Shapiro, David and Crowley, Joan E. Hopes and Plans: Education, Work Activity, and Fertility. **In** *Borus, M. E., ed.*, 1983, pp. 149–71. [G: U.S.]

Shapiro, David and Shaw, Lois B. Growth in the Labor Force Attachment of Married Women: Accounting for Changes in the 1970s. *Southern Econ. J.*, October 1983, *50*(2), pp. 461–73. [G: U.S.]

Shorey, John. An Analysis of Sex Differences in Quits. *Oxford Econ. Pap.*, July 1983, *35*(2), pp. 213–27. [G: U.K.]

Siegers, Jacques J. An Economic–Demographic Ten-Equation Model. *De Economist*, 1983, *131*(3), pp. 400–443. [G: Netherlands]

Singell, Larry D. Youth Unemployment in Australia: Some Comparative Observations. *Australian Econ. Rev.*, 3rd Quarter 1983, (63), pp. 46–55. [G: Australia; OECD]

Sirageldin, Ismail. Some Issues in Middle Eastern International Migration. *Pakistan Devel. Rev.*, Winter 1983, *22*(4), pp. 217–37. [G: Middle East; Kuwait; Egypt]

Smith, Sharon P. Are State and Local Government Workers Overpaid? **In** *Hirsch, W. Z., ed.*, 1983, pp. 59–89. [G: U.S.]

Smith, Shirley J. Estimating Annual Hours of Labor Force Activity. *Mon. Lab. Rev.*, February 1983, *106*(2), pp. 13–22. [G: U.S.]

Smith, Shirley J. Using the Appropriate Worklife Estimate in Court Proceedings [The Use of Worklife Tables in Estimates of Lost Earning Capacity]. *Mon. Lab. Rev.*, October 1983, *106*(10), pp. 31–32. [G: U.S.]

Sofer, Catherine. Emplois "féminins" et emplois "masculins": Mesure de la ségrégation et évolution de la féminisation des emplois. ("Female" Jobs and "Male" Jobs: A Measure of Segregation by Sex and the Evolution of the Feminization of Jobs. With English summary.) *Ann. INSEE*, October–December 1983, (52), pp. 55–85. [G: France]

Solttila, Heikki. Työttömyyden kohdistuminen eri työntekijäryhmiin. (The Incidence of Unemployment among Different Groups of Population in Finland. With English summary.) *Kansant. Aikak.*, 1983, *79*(4), pp. 436–47. [G: Finland]

Sorrentino, Constance. International Comparisons of Labor Force Participation, 1960–81. *Mon. Lab. Rev.*, February 1983, *106*(2), pp. 23–36. [G: OECD]

Swidinsky, Robert. Working Wives, Income Distribution and Poverty. *Can. Public Policy*, March 1983, *9*(1), pp. 71–80. [G: Canada]

Swinton, David H. Orthodox and Systemic Explanations for Unemployment and Racial Inequality: Implications for Policy. *Rev. Black Polit. Econ.*, Spring 1983, *12*(3), pp. 9–25. [G: U.S.]

Terry, Sylvia Lazos. Work Experience, Earnings, and Family Income in 1981. *Mon. Lab. Rev.*, April 1983, *106*(4), pp. 13–20. [G: U.S.]

Trivedi, P. K. and Baker, G. M. Unemployment in Australia: Duration and Recurrent Spells. *Econ. Rec.*, June 1983, *59*(165), pp. 132–48. [G: Australia]

Umetani, Shun'ichiro and Reubens, Beatrice G. Youth Employment in Japan. **In** *Reubens, B. G., ed.*, 1983, pp. 185–231. [G: Japan]

Wolfe, Barbara L. and Haveman, Robert H. Time Allocation, Market Work, and Changes in Female Health. *Amer. Econ. Rev.*, May 1983, *73*(2), pp. 134–39. [G: U.S.]

Young, Anne McDougall. Recent Trends in Higher Education and Labor Force Activity. *Mon. Lab. Rev.*, February 1983, *106*(2), pp. 39–41. [G: U.S.]

Young, Anne McDougall. Youth Labor Force Marked Turning Point in 1982. *Mon. Lab. Rev.*, August 1983, *106*(8), pp. 29–34. [G: U.S.]

830 Trade Unions; Collective Bargaining; Labor–Management Relations

8300 General

Barkin, Solomon. The Postwar Decades: Growth and Activism Followed by Stagnancy and Malaise. **In** *Barkin, S., ed.,* 1983, pp. 1–38. **[G: OECD]**

Dunning, Harold. The Origins of an International Labour Convention. *Int. Lab. Rev.,* November–December 1983, *122* (6), pp. 725–31.

Forster, C. and Harris, P. A Note on Engineering Wages in Melbourne 1892–1929. *Australian Econ. Hist. Rev.,* March 1983, *23* (1), pp. 50–57. **[G: Australia]**

Hodsdon, Dennis F. Problems of Rural Workers' Organisation: The Cameroonian Experience. *Int. Lab. Rev.,* November–December 1983, *122* (6), pp. 747–59. **[G: Cameroon]**

Lilja, Kari. Yrityksen teoria, työpaikan työelämän suhteet ja työntekijöiden työpaikkaorganisaation käsite. (The Theory of the Firm, Workplace Industrial Relations, and the Concept of Workers' Workplace Organisation. With English summary.) *Liiketaloudellinen Aikak.,* 1983, *32* (4), pp. 389–98.

Marsden, David. Chronicle: Industrial Relations in the United Kingdom, April–July 1983. *Brit. J. Ind. Relat.,* November 1983, *21* (3), pp. 401–12. **[G: U.K.]**

Mayhew, Ken. Traditional Incomes Policies. *Oxford Bull. Econ. Statist.,* February 1983, *45* (1), pp. 15–32. **[G: U.K.]**

Pang, Eng Fong and Tan, Chwee Huat. Trade Unions and Industrial Relations. **In** *Chen, P. S. J., ed.,* 1983, pp. 227–39. **[G: Singapore]**

Rawson, D. W. British and Australian Labour Law: The Background to the 1982 Bills. *Brit. J. Ind. Relat.,* July 1983, *21* (2), pp. 161–80. **[G: U.K.; Australia]**

Robinson, Derek. Indirect and Partial Measures. *Oxford Bull. Econ. Statist.,* February 1983, *45* (1), pp. 105–25. **[G: U.K.]**

Schmitz, Wolfgang. Economic and Social Partnership and Incomes Policy and the Social Doctrine of the Church. *Economia,* May 1983, *7* (2), pp. 307–29.

Swanson, Dorothy. Annual Bibliography on American Labor History 1982: Periodicals, Dissertations, and Research in Progress. *Labor Hist.,* Fall 1983, *24* (4), pp. 526–45. **[G: U.S.]**

Winchester, David. Industrial Relations Research in Britain. *Brit. J. Ind. Relat.,* March 1983, *21* (1), pp. 100–114. **[G: U.K.]**

Zieger, Robert H. Industrial Relations and Labor History in the Eighties. *Ind. Relat.,* Winter 1983, *22* (1), pp. 58–70. **[G: U.S.]**

831 Trade Unions

8310 Trade Unions

Addison, John T. Comment [The Effect of Unionization and Civil Service on the Salaries and Productivity of Regulators] [Worker Preferences for Union Representation]. **In** *Reid, J. D., Jr., ed.,* 1983, pp. 207–15.

Addison, John T. and Gerlach, Knut. Gewerkschaften und Produktivität: Fehlallokation von Ressourcen oder Produktivitätssteigerung? (Trade Unions and Productivity: Misallocation of Resources or Productivity Enhancement? With English Summary.) *Z. ges. Staatswiss.,* June 1983, *139* (2), pp. 215–28.

Alchian, Armen. Research in Labor Economics: Discussion. **In** *Reid, J. D., Jr., ed.,* 1983, pp. 97–98.

Alpert, William T. Manufacturing Workers Private Wage Supplements: A Simultaneous Equations Approach. *Appl. Econ.,* June 1983, *15* (3), pp. 363–78. **[G: U.S.]**

Antos, Joseph R. Union Effects on White-Collar Compensation. *Ind. Lab. Relat. Rev.,* April 1983, *36* (3), pp. 461–79. **[G: U.S.]**

Armstrong, John. The Sugar Strike, 1911. **In** *Murphy, D. J., ed.,* 1983, pp. 100–116. **[G: Australia]**

Arthurs, A. J. Management and Managerial Unionism. **In** *Thurley, K. and Wood, S., eds.,* 1983, pp. 13–18. **[G: U.K.]**

Baldwin, Carliss Y. Productivity and Labor Unions: An Application of the Theory of Self-Enforcing Contracts. *J. Bus.,* April 1983, *56* (2), pp. 155–85.

Barkin, Solomon. Summary and Conclusion: Redesigned Collective Bargaining Systems in Eras of Prosperity and Stagnancy. **In** *Barkin, S., ed.,* 1983, pp. 379–426. **[G: OECD]**

Beaupain, Thérèse. Belgium: Collective Bargaining and Concertation System Inhibited by Economic Crisis and Government. **In** *Barkin, S., ed.,* 1983, pp. 147–86. **[G: Belgium]**

Bellace, Janice R. and Gospel, Howard F. Disclosure of Information to Trade Unions: A Comparative Perspective. *Int. Lab. Rev.,* January–February 1983, *122* (1), pp. 57–74. **[G: U.S.; U.K.; Sweden]**

Bennett, James T. and DiLorenzo, Thomas J. Public Employee Unions and the Privatization of "Public" Services. *J. Lab. Res.,* Winter 1983, *4* (1), pp. 33–45. **[G: U.S.]**

Bennett, James T. and Johnson, Manuel H. Private Sector Unions in the Political Arena: Public Policy versus Employee Preference. **In** *Zeckhauser, R. J. and Leebaert, D., eds.,* 1983, pp. 116–22. **[G: U.S.]**

Bergmann, Joachim and Müller-Jentsch, Walther. The Federal Republic of Germany: Cooperative Unionism and Dual Bargaining System Challenged. **In** *Barkin, S., ed.,* 1983, pp. 229–77. **[G: W. Germany]**

Blackmur, Douglas. The Meat Industry Strike, 1946. **In** *Murphy, D. J., ed.,* 1983, pp. 217–34. **[G: Australia]**

Blackmur, Douglas. The Railway Strike, 1948. **In** *Murphy, D. J., ed.,* 1983, pp. 235–52. **[G: Australia]**

Blau, Francine D. and Kahn, Lawrence M. Job Search and Unionized Employment. *Econ. Inquiry,* July 1983, *21* (3), pp. 412–30. **[G: U.S.]**

Blau, Francine D. and Kahn, Lawrence M. Unionism, Seniority, and Turnover. *Ind. Relat.,* Fall 1983, *22* (3), pp. 362–73. **[G: U.S.]**

Booth, Alison. A Reconsideration of Trade Union Growth in the United Kingdom. *Brit. J. Ind.*

Relat., November 1983, *21* (3), pp. 377–91. **[G: U.K.]**

Brandini, Pietro Merli. Italy: A New Industrial Relations System Moving from Accommodation to Edge of Confrontation. **In** *Barkin, S., ed.*, 1983, pp. 81–110. **[G: Italy]**

Breviere, Chr. Communicating Information to Workers in Belgian Undertakings. *Int. Lab. Rev.*, March–April 1983, *122* (2), pp. 197–210. **[G: Belgium]**

Brinker, Paul A. Labor Union Coercion of Employees: The Use of Fringe Benefits. *J. Lab. Res.*, Summer 1983, *4* (3), pp. 249–55. **[G: U.S.]**

Brody, David. On the Failure of U.S. Radical Politics: A Farmer-Labor Analysis. *Ind. Relat.*, Spring 1983, *22* (2), pp. 141–63. **[G: U.S.]**

Brown, W. J. and Rowe, L. G. Industrial Relations in Australia: The Need for Change. *Australian Bull. Lab.*, September 1983, *9* (4), pp. 247–87. **[G: Australia]**

Brown, William. Central Co-ordination. **In** *Robinson, D. and Mayhew, K., eds.*, 1983, pp. 51–62. **[G: U.K.]**

Burton, John and Tullock, Gordon. Research in Labor Economics: Concluding Comments. **In** *Reid, J. D., Jr., ed.*, 1983, pp. 347–53.

Carroll, Thomas M. Right to Work Laws Do Matter. *Southern Econ. J.*, October 1983, *50* (2), pp. 494–509. **[G: U.S.]**

Cebula, Richard J. Right-to-Work Laws and Geographic Differences in Living Costs: An Analysis of Effects of the 'Union Shop' Ban for the Years 1974, 1976, and 1978. *Amer. J. Econ. Soc.*, July 1983, *42* (3), pp. 329–40. **[G: U.S.]**

Chaison, Gary N. Local Union Mergers: Frequency, Forms, and National Union Policy. *J. Lab. Res.*, Fall 1983, *4* (4), pp. 325–38. **[G: U.S.]**

Christensen, Sandra and Maki, Dennis R. The Wage Effect of Compulsory Union Membership. *Ind. Lab. Relat. Rev.*, January 1983, *36* (2), pp. 230–38. **[G: U.S.]**

Cooke, William N. Determinants of the Outcomes of Union Certification Elections. *Ind. Lab. Relat. Rev.*, April 1983, *36* (3), pp. 402–14. **[G: U.S.]**

Corina, John. Trade Unions and Technological Change. **In** *Macdonald, S.; Lamberton, D. M. and Mandeville, T., eds.*, 1983, pp. 178–92. **[G: OECD]**

Costar, Brian. Two Depression Strikes, 1931. **In** *Murphy, D. J., ed.*, 1983, pp. 186–201. **[G: Australia]**

Cottle, Rex L.; Macaulay, Hugh H. and Yandlc, T. Bruce. Some Economic Effects of the California Agricultural Labor Relations Act. *J. Lab. Res.*, Fall 1983, *4* (4), pp. 315–24. **[G: U.S.]**

Cottle, Rex L.; Macaulay, Hugh H. and Yandle, T. Bruce. Codetermination: Union Style. *J. Lab. Res.*, Spring 1983, *4* (2), pp. 125–35. **[G: U.S.]**

Craft, James A. and Abboushi, Suhail. The Union Image: Concept, Programs and Analysis. *J. Lab. Res.*, Fall 1983, *4* (4), pp. 299–314. **[G: U.S.]**

Craft, James A. and Extejt, Marian M. New Strategies in Union Organizing. *J. Lab. Res.*, Winter 1983, *4* (1), pp. 19–32. **[G: U.S.]**

Cribb, Margaret Bridson. The Mount Isa Strikes, 1961, 1964. **In** *Murphy, D. J., ed.*, 1983, pp. 270–97. **[G: Australia]**

Deery, Stephen. Trade Union Amalgamations and Government Policy in Australia. *Australian Bull. Lab.*, June 1983, *9* (3), pp. 190–207. **[G: Australia]**

DeFina, Robert H. Unions, Relative Wages, and Economic Efficiency. *J. Lab. Econ.*, October 1983, *1* (4), pp. 408–29. **[G: U.S.]**

Deitsch, Clarence R. and Dilts, David A. *NLRB v. Yeshiva University:* A Positive Perspective. *Mon. Lab. Rev.*, July 1983, *106* (7), pp. 34–37. **[G: U.S.]**

Delorme, Charles D., Jr.; Hill, R. Carter and Wood, Norman J. The Determinants of Voting by Workers in NLRB Representation Elections. *Atlantic Econ. J.*, March 1983, *11* (1), pp. 58–63. **[G: U.S.]**

Dickens, William T. The Effect of Company Campaigns on Certification Elections: *Law and Reality* Once Again. *Ind. Lab. Relat. Rev.*, July 1983, *36* (4), pp. 560–75. **[G: U.S.]**

Dickson, V. A. and McFetridge, D. G. Concentration, Unionization and the Distribution of Income in Canadian Manufacturing Industry: Comment. *Managerial Dec. Econ.*, December 1983, *4* (4), pp. 278–80. **[G: Canada]**

Dorfman, Gerald A. The Proles of Airstrip One. **In** *Stansky, P., ed.*, 1983, pp. 170–76. **[G: U.K.]**

Dorsey, Stuart and Walzer, Norman. Workers' Compensation, Job Hazards, and Wages. *Ind. Lab. Relat. Rev.*, July 1983, *36* (4), pp. 642–54. **[G: U.S.]**

Dow, M. Bradley. The Current Industrial Relations Scene in Canada, 1983: The Labour Movement and Trade Unionism: Summary Outline. **In** *Wood, W. D. and Kumar, P., eds.*, 1983, pp. 209–85. **[G: Canada]**

Eberts, Randall W. How Unions Affect Management Decisions: Evidence from Public Schools. *J. Lab. Res.*, Summer 1983, *4* (3), pp. 239–47. **[G: U.S.]**

Edwards, Linda N. and Edwards, Franklin R. Wellington–Winter Revisited: The Case of Municipal Sanitation Collection: Reply. *Ind. Lab. Relat. Rev.*, July 1983, *36* (4), pp. 657–59. **[G: U.S.]**

Edwards, P. K. The End of American Strike Statistics. *Brit. J. Ind. Relat.*, November 1983, *21* (3), pp. 392–94. **[G: U.S.]**

Ehrenberg, Ronald G. and Schwarz, Joshua L. The Effect of Unions on Productivity in the Public Sector: The Case of Municipal Libraries. **In** *Hirsch, W. Z., ed.*, 1983, pp. 311–41. **[G: U.S.]**

Ehrenberg, Ronald G.; Sherman, Daniel R. and Schwarz, Joshua L. Unions and Productivity in the Public Sector: A Study of Municipal Libraries. *Ind. Lab. Relat. Rev.*, January 1983, *36* (2), pp. 199–213. **[G: U.S.]**

Epstein, Richard A. A Common Law for Labor Relations: A Critique of the New Deal Labor Legislation. *Yale Law J.*, July 1983, *92* (8), pp. 1357–1408. **[G: U.S.]**

Epstein, Richard A. Common Law, Labor Law, and Reality: A Rejoinder [A Common Law for Labor Relations: A Critique of the New Deal Labor Legislation]. *Yale Law J.*, July 1983, *92* (8), pp. 1435–41. **[G: U.S.]**

Erlich, Mark. Peter J. McGuire's Trade Unionism: Socialism of a Trades Union Kind? *Labor Hist.*, Spring 1983, *24* (2), pp. 165–97. **[G: U.S.]**

Ewing, A. F. OECD: Trade Unions and International Trade. *J. World Trade Law,* January–February 1983, *17*(1), pp. 87–89.

Eyraud, François. The Principles of Union Action in the Engineering Industries in Great Britain and France: Towards a Neo-Institutional Analysis of Industrial Relations. *Brit. J. Ind. Relat.,* November 1983, *21* (3), pp. 358–76. **[G: U.K.; France]**

Faith, Roger L. and Reid, Joseph D., Jr. The Labor Union as Its Members' Agent. **In** *Reid, J. D., Jr., ed.,* 1983, pp. 3–25.

Farber, Henry S. The Determination of the Union Status of Workers. *Econometrica,* September 1983, *51* (5), pp. 1417–37. **[G: U.S.]**

Farber, Henry S. Worker Preferences for Union Representation. **In** *Reid, J. D., Jr., ed.,* 1983, pp. 171–205. **[G: U.S.]**

Fiorito, Jack and Greer, Charles R. Reply to Professor Voos [Determinants of U.S. Unionism: Past Research and Future Needs]. *Ind. Relat.,* Fall 1983, *22*(3), pp. 451–53. **[G: U.S.]**

Flaherty, Sean. Contract Status and the Economic Determinants of Strike Activity. *Ind. Relat.,* Winter 1983, *22*(1), pp. 20–33. **[G: U.S.]**

Flanagan, Robert J. Workplace Public Goods and Union Organizations. *Ind. Relat.,* Spring 1983, *22*(2), pp. 224–37.

Foner, Philip S. A Martyr to His Cause: The Scenario of the First Labor Film in the United States. *Labor Hist.,* Winter 1983, *24*(1), pp. 103–11. **[G: U.S.]**

Fosu, Augustin Kwasi. Impact of Unionism on Pension Fringes. *Ind. Relat.,* Fall 1983, *22*(3), pp. 419–25. **[G: U.S.]**

Freeman, R. B. and Medoff, James L. The Impact of Collective Bargaining: Can the New Facts be Explained by Monopoly Unionism? **In** *Reid, J. D., Jr., ed.,* 1983, pp. 293–332. **[G: U.S.]**

French, J. Lawrence; Hayashi, Paul M. and Gray, David A. The Compensation of National Union Presidents: Moderating Effects of Union Size. *J. Lab. Res.,* Summer 1983, *4*(3), pp. 225–37. **[G: U.S.]**

Gaudio, Ricardo and Pilone, Jorge. El desarrollo de la negociación colectiva durante la etapa de modernización industrial en la Argentina. 1935–1943. (With English summary.) *Desarrollo Econ.,* July–September 1983, *23*(90), pp. 255–86. **[G: Argentina]**

Gennard, John and Dunn, Steve. The Impact of New Technology on the Structure and Organisation of Craft Unions in the Printing Industry. *Brit. J. Ind. Relat.,* March 1983, *21* (1), pp. 17–32. **[G: U.K.]**

Glick, Jean H. An Economic Implication of Right-to-Work Laws. *Atlantic Econ. J.,* July 1983, *11* (2), pp. 100. **[G: U.S.]**

Golin, Steve. Defeat Becomes Disaster: The Paterson Strike of 1913 and the Decline of the IWW. *Labor Hist.,* Spring 1983, *24*(2), pp. 223–48. **[G: U.S.]**

Goodman, John F. B. Great Britain: Labor Moves from Power to Constraint. **In** *Barkin, S., ed.,* 1983, pp. 39–80. **[G: U.K.]**

Gospel, Howard F. Trade Unions and the Legal Obligation to Bargain: An American, Swedish and British Comparison. *Brit. J. Ind. Relat.,* November 1983, *21* (3), pp. 343–57. **[G: U.S.; Sweden; U.K.]**

Grossman, Gene M. Union Wages, Temporary Layoffs, and Seniority. *Amer. Econ. Rev.,* June 1983, *73*(3), pp. 277–90.

Hagan, Jim and Markey, Ray. Technological Change and the Unions. **In** *Hill, S. and Johnston, R., eds.,* 1983, pp. 154–74. **[G: Australia]**

Halevi, Joseph. Italy's Labour Movement: Growth and Decline. **In** *Groenewegen, P. and Halevi, J., eds.,* 1983, pp. 167–82. **[G: Italy]**

Harnett, Donald L. and Wall, James A., Jr. Aspiration/Competitive Effects on the Mediation of Bargaining. **In** *Tietz, R., ed.,* 1983, pp. 8–21.

Haythorne, George Vickers. Canada: Industrial Relations—Internal and External Pressures. **In** *Barkin, S., ed.,* 1983, pp. 325–57. **[G: Canada]**

Hendricks, Wallace E. and Kahn, Lawrence M. Cost-of-Living Clauses in Union Contracts: Determinants and Effects. *Ind. Lab. Relat. Rev.,* April 1983, *36*(3), pp. 447–60. **[G: U.S.]**

Heneman, Herbert G., III and Sandver, Marcus Hart. Predicting the Outcome of Union Certification Elections: A Review of the Literature. *Ind. Lab. Relat. Rev.,* July 1983, *36*(4), pp. 537–59. **[G: U.S.]**

Heyzer, Noeleen. International Production and Social Change: An Analysis of the State, Employment, and Trade Unions in Singapore. **In** *Chen, P. S. J., ed.,* 1983, pp. 105–28. **[G: Singapore]**

Hirsch, Werner Z.; Rufolo, Anthony M. and Mengle, David L. Recent Trends in Municipal Labor Market Research. **In** *Hirsch, W. Z., ed.,* 1983, pp. 13–58. **[G: U.S.]**

Hollander, Abraham. Concentration, Unionization and the Distribution of Income in Canadian Manufacturing Industry: Reply. *Managerial Dec. Econ.,* December 1983, *4*(4), pp. 281–82. **[G: Canada]**

Howard, William A. Trade Unions and the Arbitration System. **In** *Head, B. W., ed.,* 1983, pp. 238–51. **[G: Australia]**

Howells, J. M. For or against Compulsory Unionism? Recent Ballots in New Zealand. *Int. Lab. Rev.,* January–February 1983, *122*(1), pp. 95–110. **[G: New Zealand]**

Hunt, Doug. The Townsville Meatworkers' Strike, 1919. **In** *Murphy, D. J., ed.,* 1983, pp. 144–61. **[G: Australia]**

Hunt, Janet C. and White, Rudolph A. The Effects of Right-to-Work Legislation on Union Outcomes: Additional Evidence. *J. Lab. Res.,* Winter 1983, *4*(1), pp. 47–63. **[G: U.S.]**

Huszczo, Gregory E. Attitudinal and Behavioral Variables Related to Participation in Union Activities. *J. Lab. Res.,* Summer 1983, *4*(3), pp. 289–97. **[G: U.S.]**

Hutt, W. H. The Face and Mask of Unionism. *J. Lab. Res.,* Summer 1983, *4*(3), pp. 197–211. **[G: U.S.]**

Jacoby, Sanford M. Union–Management Cooperation in the United States: Lessons from the 1920s. *Ind. Lab. Relat. Rev.,* October 1983, *37*(1), pp. 18–33. **[G: U.S.]**

Kahn-Freund, Otto. Labour Law and Industrial Relations in Great Britain and West Germany. **In** *Wedderburn of Charlton [Lord]; Lewis, R. and*

Clark, J., eds., 1983, pp. 1–13. [G: U.K.; W. Germany]

Kaufman, Bruce E. Interindustry Trends in Strike Activity. *Ind. Relat.*, Winter 1983, *22*(1), pp. 45–57. [G: U.S.]

Kaufman, Bruce E. The Determinants of Strikes over Time and across Industries. *J. Lab. Res.*, Spring 1983, *4*(2), pp. 159–75. [G: U.S.]

Kennedy, K. H. The South Johnstone Strike, 1927. In *Murphy, D. J., ed.*, 1983, pp. 174–85. [G: Australia]

Killingsworth, Mark R. Union–Nonunion Wage Gaps and Wage Gains: New Estimates from an Industry Cross-Section. *Rev. Econ. Statist.*, May 1983, *65*(2), pp. 332–36. [G: U.S.]

Klehr, Harvey. American Communism and the United Auto Workers: New Evidence on an Old Controversy. *Labor Hist.*, Summer 1983, *24*(3), pp. 404–13. [G: U.S.]

Kurth, Michael M. Public Employee Organizations as Political Firms. In *Reid, J. D., Jr., ed.*, 1983, pp. 101–25. [G: U.S.]

Kwoka, John E., Jr. Monopoly, Plant, and Union Effects on Worker Wages. *Ind. Lab. Relat. Rev.*, January 1983, *36*(2), pp. 251–57. [G: U.S.]

Lawler, John J. and Hundley, Greg. Determinants of Certification and Decertification Activity. *Ind. Relat.*, Fall 1983, *22*(3), pp. 335–48. [G: U.S.]

Lazear, Edward P. A Competitive Theory of Monopoly Unionism. *Amer. Econ. Rev.*, September 1983, *73*(4), pp. 631–43.

Lazear, Edward P. A Microeconomic Theory of Labor Unions. In *Reid, J. D., Jr., ed.*, 1983, pp. 53–96.

Leigh, J. Paul. Risk Preference and the Interindustry Propensity to Strike. *Ind. Lab. Relat. Rev.*, January 1983, *36*(2), pp. 271–85. [G: U.S.]

Lentz, Bernard F. Research in Labor Economics: Discussion. In *Reid, J. D., Jr., ed.*, 1983, pp. 149–53.

Lewin, David. Theoretical Perspectives on the Modern Grievance Procedure. In *Reid, J. D., Jr., ed.*, 1983, pp. 127–47.

Lewin, David and Feuille, Peter. Behavioral Research in Industrial Relations. *Ind. Lab. Relat. Rev.*, April 1983, *36*(3), pp. 341–60. [G: U.K.; U.S.]

Lewin, David and Katz, Harry C. Payment Determination in Municipal Building Departments under Unionism and Civil Service. In *Hirsch, W. Z., ed.*, 1983, pp. 90–121. [G: U.S.]

Lewis, H. Gregg. Comments [Union Effects: Wages, Turnover, and Job Training] [Employer Size, Unionism, and Wages]. In *Reid, J. D., Jr., ed.*, 1983, pp. 283–90. [G: U.S.]

Lewis, H. Gregg. Union Relative Wage Effects: A Survey of Macro Estimates. *J. Lab. Econ.*, January 1983, *1*(1), pp. 1–27. [G: U.S.]

Lockett, Martin. Enterprise Management—Moves towards Democracy? In *Feuchtwang, S. and Hussain, A., eds.*, 1983, pp. 224–56. [G: China]

Lundh, Per-Erik. Arbetsmarknadspolitik—nuläget och framtiden. (The Central Organization of the Finnish Labor Unions. With English summary.) *Ekon. Samfundets Tidskr.*, 1983, *36*(3), pp. 115–18. [G: Finland]

MacDonald, Glenn M. The Size and Structure of Union–Non-Union Wage Differentials in Canadian Industry: Corroboration, Refinement, and Extension. *Can. J. Econ.*, August 1983, *16*(3), pp. 480–85. [G: Canada]

Maki, Dennis R. The Effects of Unions and Strikes on the Rate of Growth of Total Factor Productivity in Canada. *Appl. Econ.*, February 1983, *15*(1), pp. 29–41. [G: Canada]

Maki, Dennis R. Unions as 'Gatekeepers' of Occupational Sex Discrimination: Canadian Evidence. *Appl. Econ.*, August 1983, *15*(4), pp. 469–77. [G: Canada]

Malcomson, James M. Trade Unions and Economic Efficiency. *Econ. J.*, Supplement March 1983, pp. 51–65.

Marsh, A. I. and Gillies, J. G. The Involvement of Line and Staff Managers in Industrial Relations. In *Thurley, K. and Wood, S., eds.*, 1983, pp. 27–38. [G: U.K.]

McMurchy, Anne. The Pastoral Strike, 1956. In *Murphy, D. J., ed.*, 1983, pp. 253–69. [G: Australia]

Mellow, Wesley. Employer Size, Unionism, and Wages. In *Reid, J. D., Jr., ed.*, 1983, pp. 253–82. [G: U.S.]

Menghetti, Diane. The Weil's Disease Strike, 1935. In *Murphy, D. J., ed.*, 1983, pp. 201–16. [G: Australia]

Michel, Philippe and Padoa Schioppa, Fiorella. A Dynamic Macroeconomic Model with Monopolistic Behavior in the Labor Market. *Europ. Econ. Rev.*, August 1983, *22*(3), pp. 331–50.

Mincer, Jacob. Union Effects: Wages, Turnover, and Job Training. In *Reid, J. D., Jr., ed.*, 1983, pp. 217–52. [G: U.S.]

Minford, Patrick. Labour Market Equilibrium in an Open Economy. *Oxford Econ. Pap.*, Supplement November 1983, *35*, pp. 207–44. [G: U.K.]

Moore, William J. and Raisian, John. The Level and Growth of Union/Nonunion Relative Wage Effects, 1967–1977. *J. Lab. Res.*, Winter 1983, *4*(1), pp. 65–79. [G: U.S.]

Murphy, D. J. The Big Strikes: Queensland 1889–1965: Trade Unions. In *Murphy, D. J., ed.*, 1983, pp. 33–44. [G: Australia]

Murphy, D. J. The North Queensland Railway Strike, 1917. In *Murphy, D. J., ed.*, 1983, pp. 132–43. [G: Australia]

Murphy, D. J. The Tramway and General Strike, 1912. In *Murphy, D. J., ed.*, 1983, pp. 117–31. [G: Australia]

Navrátil, Oldřich and Pudík, Vladimír. Economic Management and Trade Union Bodies. *Czech. Econ. Digest.*, February 1983, (1), pp. 47–108. [G: Czechoslovakia]

Nickell, S. J. and Andrews, M. Unions, Real Wages and Employment in Britain 1951–79. *Oxford Econ. Pap.*, Supplement November 1983, *35*, pp. 183–206. [G: U.K.]

Noam, Eli M. The Effect of Unionization and Civil Service on the Salaries and Productivity of Regulators. In *Reid, J. D., Jr., ed.*, 1983, pp. 157–70. [G: U.S.]

Northrup, Herbert R. The New Employee-Relations Climate in Airlines. *Ind. Lab. Relat. Rev.*, January 1983, *36*(2), pp. 167–81. [G: U.S.]

Olson, Mancur. The South Will Fall Again: The South as Leader and Laggard in Economic Growth. *Southern Econ. J.*, April 1983, *49*(4), pp. 917–32. [G: U.S.]

von Otter, Casten. Sweden: Labor Reformism Reshapes the System. In *Barkin, S., ed.*, 1983, pp. 187–227. [G: Sweden]

Pearce, James E. Unionism and the Cyclical Behavior of the Labor Market in U.S. Manufacturing. *Rev. Econ. Statist.*, August 1983, *65*(3), pp. 450–58. [G: U.S.]

Peper, Bram and van Kooten, Gerrit. The Netherlands: From an Ordered Harmonic to a Bargaining Relationship. In *Barkin, S., ed.*, 1983, pp. 111–45. [G: Netherlands]

Perkinson, Leon B. and Fearn, Robert M. Wellington–Winter Revisited: The Case of Municipal Sanitation Collection: Comment. *Ind. Lab. Relat. Rev.*, July 1983, *36*(4), pp. 655–57. [G: U.S.]

Podgursky, Michael. Unions and Family Income Inequality. *J. Human Res.*, Fall 1983, *18*(4), pp. 574–91. [G: U.S.]

Polachek, Solomon W. and McCutcheon, Ernest P. Union Effects of Employment Stability: A Comparison of Panel versus Cross-Sectional Data. *J. Lab. Res.*, Summer 1983, *4*(3), pp. 273–87. [G: U.S.]

Poole, Michael, et al. Why Managers Join Unions: Evidence from Britain. *Ind. Relat.*, Fall 1983, *22*(3), pp. 426–44. [G: U.K.]

Poulson, Barry W. Is Collective Bargaining a Collective Good? *J. Lab. Res.*, Fall 1983, *4*(4), pp. 349–65. [G: U.S.]

Price, Robert and Bain, George Sayers. Union Growth in Britain: Retrospect and Prospect. *Brit. J. Ind. Relat.*, March 1983, *21*(1), pp. 46–68. [G: U.K.]

Raisian, John. Union Dues and Wage Premiums. *J. Lab. Res.*, Winter 1983, *4*(1), pp. 1–18. [G: U.S.]

Raynaud, Jean-Daniel. France: Elitist Society Inhibits Articulated Bargaining. In *Barkin, S., ed.*, 1983, pp. 279–311. [G: France]

Reder, M. W. Unionism, Wages, and Contract Enforcement. In *Reid, J. D., Jr., ed.*, 1983, pp. 27–51.

Rojot, Jacques. A New Chapter in French Industrial Relations. In *Barkin, S., ed.*, 1983, pp. 312–23. [G: France]

Rose, Joseph B. Some Notes on the Building Trades–Canadian Labour Congress Dispute. *Ind. Relat.*, Winter 1983, *22*(1), pp. 87–93. [G: Canada]

Rosen, Sumner M. The United States: American Industrial Relations System in Jeopardy? In *Barkin, S., ed.*, 1983, pp. 359–77. [G: U.S.]

Rosenzweig, Roy. "United Action Means Victory": Militant Americanism on Film. *Labor Hist.*, Spring 1983, *24*(2), pp. 274–88. [G: U.S.]

Rubenson, Kjell. Financing Paid Educational Leave: The Swedish Model. In *Levin, H. M. and Schütze, H. G., eds.*, 1983, pp. 237–55. [G: Sweden]

Sampson, Anthony A. Employment Policy in a Model with a Rational Trade Union. *Econ. J.*, June 1983, *93*(370), pp. 297–311.

Sandver, Marcus Hart. Reply to Becker and Delaney [South/Non-South Differentials in National Labor Relations Board Certification Election Outcomes]. *J. Lab. Res.*, Fall 1983, *4*(4), pp. 385–91. [G: U.S.]

Schuller, Tom and Robertson, Don. How Representatives Allocate Their Time: Shop Steward Activity and Membership Contact. *Brit. J. Ind. Relat.*, November 1983, *21*(3), pp. 330–42. [G: U.K.]

Scott, Frank A., Jr.; Long, James E. and Somppi, Ken. Free Agency, Owner Incentives, and the National Football League Players Association. *J. Lab. Res.*, Summer 1983, *4*(3), pp. 257–64. [G: U.S.]

Seeber, Ronald L. and Cooke, William N. The Decline in Union Success in NLRB Representation Elections. *Ind. Relat.*, Winter 1983, *22*(1), pp. 34–44. [G: U.S.]

Shafto, Tony. The Growth of Shop Steward 'Managerial Functions.' In *Thurley, K. and Wood, S., eds.*, 1983, pp. 45–52. [G: U.K.]

Sheflin, Neil and Troy, Leo. Finances of American Unions in the 1970s. *J. Lab. Res.*, Spring 1983, *4*(2), pp. 149–57. [G: U.S.]

Simon, Richard M. Hard Times for Organized Labor in Appalachia. *Rev. Radical Polit. Econ.*, Fall 1983, *15*(3), pp. 21–34. [G: U.S.]

Simpson, David. Managers in Workers' Trade Unions: The Case of the NUJ. In *Thurley, K. and Wood, S., eds.*, 1983, pp. 19–26.

Smith, Anne. The Railway Strike, 1925. In *Murphy, D. J., ed.*, 1983, pp. 162–73. [G: Australia]

Smith, Robin. Work Control and Managerial Prerogatives. In *Thurley, K. and Wood, S., eds.*, 1983, pp. 39–44.

Stacey, Nevzer and Charner, Ivan. Unions and Postsecondary Education. In *Levin, H. M. and Schütze, H. G., eds.*, 1983, pp. 189–201. [G: U.S.]

Stewart, Mark B. Relative Earnings and Individual Union Membership in the United Kingdom. *Economica*, May 1983, *50*(198), pp. 111–25. [G: U.K.]

Stromquist, Shelton. Enginemen and Shopmen: Technological Change and the Organization of Labor in an Era of Railroad Expansion. *Labor Hist.*, Fall 1983, *24*(4), pp. 485–99. [G: U.S.]

Sullivan, Rodney J. The Maritime Strike, 1890. In *Murphy, D. J., ed.*, 1983, pp. 65–79. [G: Australia]

Sullivan, Rodney J. and Sullivan, Robyn A. The London Dock Strike, the Jondaryan Strike and the Brisbane Bootmakers' Strike, 1889–1890. In *Murphy, D. J., ed.*, 1983, pp. 47–64. [G: Australia; U.K.]

Sullivan, Rodney J. and Sullivan, Robyn A. The Pastoral Strikes, 1891 and 1894. In *Murphy, D. J., ed.*, 1983, pp. 80–99. [G: Australia]

Synder, Donald W. The Decision to Join a Union. *Nebr. J. Econ. Bus.*, Spring 1983, *22*(2), pp. 3–21. [G: U.S.]

Thee, Marek. Swords into Ploughshares: The Quest for Peace and Human Development. *Int. Lab. Rev.*, Sept.–Oct. 1983, *122*(5), pp. 535–48. [G: W. Europe]

Thompson, Mark and Blum, Albert A. International Unionism in Canada: The Move to Local Control. *Ind. Relat.*, Winter 1983, *22*(1), pp. 71–86. [G: Canada]

Treble, John G. and McGrady, Diane. Geometric versus Arithmetic Mean in the Measurement of the Union/Non-Union Wage Differential. *Appl. Econ.*, February 1983, *15*(1), pp. 43–48. **[G: U.K.]**

Tyler, Gus. The Work Ethic: A Union View. **In** *Barbash, J., et al., eds.*, 1983, pp. 197–210. **[G: U.S.]**

Valenzuela, J. Samuel. Movimientos obreros y sistemas políticos: un análisis conceptual y tipológico. (With English summary.) *Desarrollo Econ.*, October-December 1983, *23*(91), pp. 339–68.

Verkuil, Paul R. Whose Common Law for Labor Relations? [A Common Law for Labor Relations: A Critique of the New Deal Labor Legislation]. *Yale Law J.*, July 1983, *92*(8), pp. 1409–14. **[G: U.S.]**

Vogelsang, Ingo. Public Interest Firms as Leaders in Oligopolistic Industries. **In** *Finsinger, J., ed.*, 1983, pp. 86–99. **[G: W. Germany]**

Voos, Paula B. Determinants of U.S. Unionism: Past Research and Future Needs. *Ind. Relat.*, Fall 1983, *22*(3), pp. 445–50. **[G: U.S.]**

Voos, Paula B. Union Organizing: Costs and Benefits. *Ind. Lab. Relat. Rev.*, July 1983, *36*(4), pp. 576–91. **[G: U.S.]**

Wedderburn [Lord]. Otto Kahn-Freund and British Labour Law. **In** *Wedderburn of Charlton [Lord]; Lewis, R. and Clark, J., eds.*, 1983, pp. 29–80. **[G: U.K.]**

Wilentz, Sean. Conspiracy, Power, and the Early Labor Movement: *The People v. James Melvin, et al*, 1811. *Labor Hist.*, Fall 1983, *24*(4), pp. 572–79. **[G: U.S.]**

Worrall, John D. and Butler, Richard J. Health Conditions and Job Hazards: Union and Nonunion Jobs. *J. Lab. Res.*, Fall 1983, *4*(4), pp. 339–47. **[G: U.S.]**

832 Collective Bargaining

8320 General

Adell, Bernard. Termination of Employment on the Initiative of the Employer and Income Security of the Worker Concerned. **In** *Queen's Univ. Indust. Relat. Centre,* 1983, pp. 82–92. **[G: Canada]**

Barkin, Solomon. Summary and Conclusion: Redesigned Collective Bargaining Systems in Eras of Prosperity and Stagnancy. **In** *Barkin, S., ed.*, 1983, pp. 379–426. **[G: OECD]**

Becker, Edmund R. and Delaney, John Thomas. South/Non-South Differentials in National Labor Relations Board Certification Election Outcomes: Comment. *J. Lab. Res.*, Fall 1983, *4*(4), pp. 375–84. **[G: U.S.]**

Bednar, David A. and Curington, William P. Interaction Analysis: A Tool for Understanding Negotiations. *Ind. Lab. Relat. Rev.*, April 1983, *36*(3), pp. 389–401. **[G: U.S.]**

Bellace, Janice R. and Gospel, Howard F. Disclosure of Information to Trade Unions: A Comparative Perspective. *Int. Lab. Rev.*, January–February 1983, *122*(1), pp. 57–74. **[G: U.S.; U.K.; Sweden]**

Bergmann, Joachim and Müller-Jentsch, Walther. The Federal Republic of Germany: Cooperative Unionism and Dual Bargaining System Challenged. **In** *Barkin, S., ed.*, 1983, pp. 229–77. **[G: W. Germany]**

Bigoness, William J. and Grigsby, David W. The Effects of Need for Achievement and Alternative Forms of Arbitration upon Bargaining Behavior. **In** *Tietz, R., ed.*, 1983, pp. 122–35.

Brown, W. J. and Rowe, L. G. Industrial Relations in Australia: The Need for Change. *Australian Bull. Lab.*, September 1983, *9*(4), pp. 247–87. **[G: Australia]**

Brown, William. Central Co-ordination. **In** *Robinson, D. and Mayhew, K., eds.*, 1983, pp. 51–62. **[G: U.K.]**

Brown, William. Central Co-ordination. *Oxford Bull. Econ. Statist.*, February 1983, *45*(1), pp. 51–62. **[G: U.K.]**

Clark, Jon. Towards a Sociology of Labour Law: An Analysis of the German Writings of Otto Kahn-Freund. **In** *Wedderburn of Charlton [Lord]; Lewis, R. and Clark, J., eds.*, 1983, pp. 81–106.

Clark, Jon and Wedderburn [Lord]. Modern Labour Law: Problems, Functions, and Policies. **In** *Wedderburn of Charlton [Lord]; Lewis, R. and Clark, J., eds.*, 1983, pp. 127–242. **[G: U.K.]**

Clegg, Hugh Armstrong. Otto Kahn-Freund and British Industrial Relations. **In** *Wedderburn of Charlton [Lord]; Lewis, R. and Clark, J., eds.*, 1983, pp. 14–28. **[G: U.K.]**

Craft, James A. and Extejt, Marian M. New Strategies in Union Organizing. *J. Lab. Res.*, Winter 1983, *4*(1), pp. 19–32. **[G: U.S.]**

Creigh, Stephen; Robertson, Frances and Wooden, Mark. Research Note: Inter-State Variations in Strike-Proneness. *Australian Bull. Lab.*, June 1983, *9*(3), pp. 208–16. **[G: Australia]**

Cribb, Margaret Bridson. Causes and Catalysts of Strikes. **In** *Murphy, D. J., ed.*, 1983, pp. 3–14. **[G: Australia]**

Crouch, Colin. Corporative Industrial Relations and the Welfare State. **In** *Jones, R. J. B., ed.*, 1983, pp. 139–66. **[G: OECD]**

Davis, William M. Collective Bargaining in 1983: A Crowded Agenda. *Mon. Lab. Rev.*, January 1983, *106*(1), pp. 3–16. **[G: U.S.]**

Edwards, P. K. The End of American Strike Statistics. *Brit. J. Ind. Relat.*, November 1983, *21*(3), pp. 392–94. **[G: U.S.]**

Epstein, Richard A. A Common Law for Labor Relations: A Critique of the New Deal Labor Legislation. *Yale Law J.*, July 1983, *92*(8), pp. 1357–1408. **[G: U.S.]**

Epstein, Richard A. Common Law, Labor Law, and Reality: A Rejoinder [A Common Law for Labor Relations: A Critique of the New Deal Labor Legislation]. *Yale Law J.*, July 1983, *92*(8), pp. 1435–41. **[G: U.S.]**

Fosu, Augustin Kwasi. Impact of Unionism on Pension Fringes. *Ind. Relat.*, Fall 1983, *22*(3), pp. 419–25. **[G: U.S.]**

Gagnon, Jean Denis. Le Recours a l'Arbitrage dans les Cas de Congediement Injuste (Arbitration of Unjust Dismissals. With English Summary.) **In** *Queen's Univ. Indust. Relat. Centre,* 1983, pp. 76–81. **[G: Canada]**

Geroski, P. A. and Knight, K. G. Wages, Strikes and

Market Structure: Some Further Evidence. *Oxford Econ. Pap.*, March 1983, *35*(1), pp. 146–52. **[G: U.K.]**

Grossman, Gene M. Union Wages, Temporary Layoffs, and Seniority. *Amer. Econ. Rev.*, June 1983, *73*(3), pp. 277–90.

Hall, D. R. Strike Law in Queensland. **In** *Murphy, D. J., ed.*, 1983, pp. 15–32. **[G: Australia]**

Hancock, Keith. The Arbitration Tribunals and the Labour Market. **In** *Blandy, R. and Covick, O., eds.*, 1983, pp. 183–99.

Harnett, Donald L. and Wall, James A., Jr. Aspiration/Competitive Effects on the Mediation of Bargaining. **In** *Tietz, R., ed.*, 1983, pp. 8–21.

Harris, Ralph. The Mould to Be Broken. **In** *Seldon, A., et al.*, 1983, pp. 15–31. **[G: U.K.]**

Haythorne, George Vickers. Canada: Industrial Relations—Internal and External Pressures. **In** *Barkin, S., ed.*, 1983, pp. 325–57. **[G: Canada]**

Hendricks, Wallace E. and Kahn, Lawrence M. Cost-of-Living Clauses in Union Contracts: Determinants and Effects. *Ind. Lab. Relat. Rev.*, April 1983, *36*(3), pp. 447–60. **[G: U.S.]**

Heneman, Herbert G., III and Sandver, Marcus Hart. Arbitrators' Backgrounds and Behavior. *J. Lab. Res.*, Spring 1983, *4*(2), pp. 115–24. **[G: U.S.]**

Hoyman, Michele M. and Stallworth, Lamont E. Arbitrating Discrimination Grievances in the Wake of *Gardner-Denver. Mon. Lab. Rev.*, October 1983, *106*(10), pp. 3–10. **[G: U.S.]**

Hunt, Janet C. and White, Rudolph A. The Effects of Right-to-Work Legislation on Union Outcomes: Additional Evidence. *J. Lab. Res.*, Winter 1983, *4*(1), pp. 47–63. **[G: U.S.]**

Hunter, L. C. Arbitration. *Oxford Bull. Econ. Statist.*, February 1983, *45*(1), pp. 63–83. **[G: U.K.]**

Kahn-Freund, Otto. Labour Law and Industrial Relations in Great Britain and West Germany. **In** *Wedderburn of Charlton [Lord]; Lewis, R. and Clark, J., eds.*, 1983, pp. 1–13. **[G: U.K.; W. Germany]**

Karim, Ahmad and Pegnetter, Richard. Mediator Strategies and Qualities and Mediation Effectiveness. *Ind. Relat.*, Winter 1983, *22*(1), pp. 105–14. **[G: U.S.]**

Kochan, Thomas A. and McKersie, Robert B. SMR Forum: Collective Bargaining—Pressures for Change. *Sloan Manage. Rev.*, Summer 1983, *24*(4), pp. 59–65. **[G: U.S.]**

Kuhn, James W.; Lewin, David and McNulty, Paul J. Neil W. Chamberlain: A Retrospective Analysis of His Scholarly Work and Influence. *Brit. J. Ind. Relat.*, July 1983, *21*(2), pp. 143–60.

Lewin, David and Feuille, Peter. Behavioral Research in Industrial Relations. *Ind. Lab. Relat. Rev.*, April 1983, *36*(3), pp. 341–60. **[G: U.K.; U.S.]**

Lewis, Roy. Method and Ideology in the Labour Law Writings of Otto Kahn-Freund. **In** *Wedderburn of Charlton [Lord]; Lewis, R. and Clark, J., eds.*, 1983, pp. 107–26.

Lundh, Per-Erik. Arbetsmarknadspolitik—nuläget och framtiden. (The Central Organization of the Finnish Labor Unions. With English summary.) *Ekon. Samfundets Tidskr.*, 1983, *36*(3), pp. 115–18. **[G: Finland]**

Magenau, John M. The Impact of Alternative Impasse Procedures on Bargaining: A Laboratory Experiment. *Ind. Lab. Relat. Rev.*, April 1983, *36*(3), pp. 361–77. **[G: U.S.]**

Maki, Dennis R. The Effects of Unions and Strikes on the Rate of Growth of Total Factor Productivity in Canada. *Appl. Econ.*, February 1983, *15*(1), pp. 29–41. **[G: Canada]**

Mayer, Jean. Workers' Well-Being and Productivity: The Role of Bargaining. *Int. Lab. Rev.*, May–June 1983, *122*(3), pp. 343–53.

McMurray, David. The Current Industrial Relations Scene in Canada, 1983: Labour Legislation and Policy: Summary Outline. **In** *Wood, W. D. and Kumar, P., eds.*, 1983, pp. 87–205. **[G: Canada]**

Michel, Philippe and Padoa Schioppa, Fiorella. A Dynamic Macroeconomic Model with Monopolistic Behavior in the Labor Market. *Europ. Econ. Rev.*, August 1983, *22*(3), pp. 331–50.

Mills, D. Quinn. Reforming the U.S. System of Collective Bargaining. *Mon. Lab. Rev.*, March 1983, *106*(3), pp. 18–22. **[G: U.S.]**

Navarro, Peter. Union Bargaining Power in the Coal Industry, 1945–1981. *Ind. Lab. Relat. Rev.*, January 1983, *36*(2), pp. 214–29. **[G: U.S.]**

Neale, Margaret A. and Bazerman, Max H. The Role of Perspective-Taking Ability in Negotiating under Different Forms of Arbitration. *Ind. Lab. Relat. Rev.*, April 1983, *36*(3), pp. 378–88. **[G: U.S.]**

Newby, Martin and Winterton, Jonathan. The Duration of Industrial Stoppages. *J. Roy. Statist. Soc.*, 1983, *146*(1), pp. 62–70. **[G: U.K.]**

Niland, John R. A Comparative Assessment of Labour Market Regulation through Collective Bargaining and Compulsory Arbitration. **In** *Blandy, R. and Covick, O., eds.*, 1983, pp. 166–82. **[G: Australia]**

von Otter, Casten. Sweden: Labor Reformism Reshapes the System. **In** *Barkin, S., ed.*, 1983, pp. 187–227. **[G: Sweden]**

Paldam, Martin. Industrial Conflicts and Economic Conditions: A Comparative Empirical Investigation. *Europ. Econ. Rev.*, January 1983, *20*(1–3), pp. 231–56.

Pankert, Alfred. Government Influence on Wage Bargaining: The Limits Set by International Labour Standards. *Int. Lab. Rev.*, Sept.–Oct. 1983, *122*(5), pp. 579–91. **[G: ILO]**

Poulson, Barry W. Is Collective Bargaining a Collective Good? *J. Lab. Res.*, Fall 1983, *4*(4), pp. 349–65. **[G: U.S.]**

Pruitt, Dean G., et al. Incentives for Cooperation in Integrative Bargaining. **In** *Tietz, R., ed.*, 1983, pp. 22–34.

Riddell, W. Craig. The Responsiveness of Wage Settlements in Canada and Economic Policy. *Can. Public Policy*, March 1983, *9*(1), pp. 9–23. **[G: Canada; U.S.]**

Robinson, Derek. Pay Policies for the Future: Indirect and Partial Measures. **In** *Robinson, D. and Mayhew, K., eds.*, 1983, pp. 105–25. **[G: U.K.]**

Robinson, Derek and Mayhew, Ken. Pay Policies for the Future: Introduction. **In** *Robinson, D. and Mayhew, K., eds.*, 1983, pp. 3–13. **[G: U.K.]**

Rojot, Jacques. A New Chapter in French Industrial

Relations. **In** *Barkin, S., ed.*, 1983, pp. 312–23. **[G: France]**

Rose, Joseph B. Some Notes on the Building Trades–Canadian Labour Congress Dispute. *Ind. Relat.*, Winter 1983, *22*(1), pp. 87–93. **[G: Canada]**

Ruben, George. Collective Bargaining in 1982: Results Dictated by Economy. *Mon. Lab. Rev.*, January 1983, *106*(1), pp. 28–37. **[G: U.S.]**

Taylor, John B. Union Wage Settlements during a Disinflation. *Amer. Econ. Rev.*, December 1983, *73*(5), pp. 981–93. **[G: U.S.]**

Verkuil, Paul R. Whose Common Law for Labor Relations? [A Common Law for Labor Relations: A Critique of the New Deal Labor Legislation]. *Yale Law J.*, July 1983, *92*(8), pp. 1409–14. **[G: U.S.]**

Wedderburn [Lord]. Otto Kahn-Freund and British Labour Law. **In** *Wedderburn of Charlton [Lord]; Lewis, R. and Clark, J., eds.*, 1983, pp. 29–80. **[G: U.K.]**

Weis, Peter. Zur arbeitsmarktpolitischen Problematik von Kündigungs- und Besitzstandsregelungen für ältere Arbeitnehmer. (The Problematic Nature of Protection against Dismissal and Earnings Guaranties for Elderly Workers. With English summary.) *Z. Wirtschaft. Sozialwissen.*, 1983, *103*(3), pp. 255–81. **[G: W. Germany]**

Wood, W. D., et al. The Current Industrial Relations Scene in Canada, 1983: Collective Bargaining: Summary Outline. **In** *Wood, W. D. and Kumar, P., eds.*, 1983, pp. 289–402. **[G: Canada; U.S.]**

Zara, Stefano. Sindacato: meno ideologia, più pragmatismo. (The Unions: Less Ideology, More Pragmatism. With English summary.) *L'Impresa*, 1983, *25*(6), pp. 67–71. **[G: Italy]**

8321 Collective Bargaining in the Private Sector

Armstrong, John. The Sugar Strike, 1911. **In** *Murphy, D. J., ed.*, 1983, pp. 100–116. **[G: Australia]**

Beaupain, Thérèse. Belgium: Collective Bargaining and Concertation System Inhibited by Economic Crisis and Government. **In** *Barkin, S., ed.*, 1983, pp. 147–86. **[G: Belgium]**

Blackmur, Douglas. The Meat Industry Strike, 1946. **In** *Murphy, D. J., ed.*, 1983, pp. 217–34. **[G: Australia]**

Brandini, Pietro Merli. Italy: A New Industrial Relations System Moving from Accommodation to Edge of Confrontation. **In** *Barkin, S., ed.*, 1983, pp. 81–110. **[G: Italy]**

Brannick, Teresa and Kelly, Aidan. The Reliability and Validity of Irish Strike Data and Statistics. *Econ. Soc. Rev.*, July 1983, *14*(4), pp. 249–58. **[G: Ireland]**

Brett, Jeanne M. and Goldberg, Stephen B. Grievance Mediation in the Coal Industry: A Field Experiment. *Ind. Lab. Relat. Rev.*, October 1983, *37*(1), pp. 49–69. **[G: U.S.]**

Card, David. Cost-of-Living Escalators in Major Union Contracts. *Ind. Lab. Relat. Rev.*, October 1983, *37*(1), pp. 34–48. **[G: Canada]**

Christie, Innis. Termination of Employment: Trends and Overview. **In** *Queen's Univ. Indust. Relat. Centre*, 1983, pp. 1–17. **[G: Canada]**

Costar, Brian. Two Depression Strikes, 1931. **In** *Murphy, D. J., ed.*, 1983, pp. 186–201. **[G: Australia]**

Cousineau, Jean-Michel; Lacroix, Robert and Bilodeau, Danielle. The Determination of Escalator Clauses in Collective Agreements. *Rev. Econ. Statist.*, May 1983, *65*(2), pp. 196–202. **[G: U.S.]**

Cribb, Margaret Bridson. The Mount Isa Strikes, 1961, 1964. **In** *Murphy, D. J., ed.*, 1983, pp. 270–97. **[G: Australia]**

Deitsch, Clarence R. and Dilts, David A. *NLRB v. Yeshiva University:* A Positive Perspective. *Mon. Lab. Rev.*, July 1983, *106*(7), pp. 34–37. **[G: U.S.]**

Ehrenberg, Ronald G.; Danziger, Leif and San, Gee. Cost-of-Living Adjustment Clauses in Union Contracts: A Summary of Results. *J. Lab. Econ.*, July 1983, *1*(3), pp. 215–45. **[G: U.S.]**

Elliott, Ralph D. and Hawkins, Benjamin M. The Impact of Government Spending on the Level of Private Sector Strike Activity. *Atlantic Econ. J.*, July 1983, *11*(2), pp. 22–28. **[G: U.S.]**

Enderwick, Peter and Buckley, Peter J. The Determinants of Strike Activity in Foreign-Owned Plants: Inter-Industry Evidence from British Manufacturing Industry 1971–1973. *Managerial Dec. Econ.*, June 1983, *4*(2), pp. 83–88. **[G: U.K.]**

Englander, A. Steven and Chandoha, Marie. Will Wage Givebacks Be Reversed? *Fed. Res. Bank New York Quart. Rev.*, Autumn 1983, *8*(3), pp. 24–25. **[G: U.S.]**

Ephlin, Donald F. The UAW–Ford Agreement—Joint Problem Solving. *Sloan Manage. Rev.*, Winter 1983, *24*(2), pp. 61–65. **[G: U.S.]**

Ficken, Robert E. The Wobbly Horrors: Pacific Northwest Lumbermen and the Industrial Workers of the World, 1917–1918. *Labor Hist.*, Summer 1983, *24*(3), pp. 325–41. **[G: U.S.]**

Flaherty, Sean. Contract Status and the Economic Determinants of Strike Activity. *Ind. Relat.*, Winter 1983, *22*(1), pp. 20–33. **[G: U.S.]**

Freeman, R. B. and Medoff, James L. The Impact of Collective Bargaining: Can the New Facts be Explained by Monopoly Unionism? **In** *Reid, J. D., Jr., ed.*, 1983, pp. 293–332. **[G: U.S.]**

Friedman, Debra. Why Workers Strike: Individual Decisions and Structural Constraints. **In** *Hechter, M., ed.*, 1983, pp. 250–83.

Gärtner, Manfred. Causality Patterns in Aggregate Labor Markets: A Statistical Analysis of West German Data. *Empirical Econ.*, 1983, *8*(3–4), pp. 229–45. **[G: W. Germany]**

Gaudio, Ricardo and Pilonc, Jorge. El desarrollo de la negociación colectiva durante la etapa de modernización industrial en la Argentina. 1935–1943. (With English summary.) *Desarrollo Econ.*, July–September 1983, *23*(90), pp. 255–86. **[G: Argentina]**

Goldberg, Stephen B. and Brett, Jeanne M. An Experiment in the Mediation of Grievances. *Mon. Lab. Rev.*, March 1983, *106*(3), pp. 23–30. **[G: U.S.]**

Golin, Steve. Defeat Becomes Disaster: The Paterson Strike of 1913 and the Decline of the IWW. *Labor Hist.*, Spring 1983, *24*(2), pp. 223–48. **[G: U.S.]**

Goodman, John F. B. Great Britain: Labor Moves from Power to Constraint. **In** *Barkin, S., ed.*, 1983, pp. 39–80. **[G: U.K.]**

Gospel, Howard F. Trade Unions and the Legal Obligation to Bargain: An American, Swedish and

British Comparison. *Brit. J. Ind. Relat.*, November 1983, *21* (3), pp. 343–57. **[G: U.S.; Sweden; U.K.]**

Hall, P. H. Strikes and Their Repercussions. *Greek Econ. Rev.*, August 1983, *5* (2), pp. 182–92.

Howard, William A. Trade Unions and the Arbitration System. **In** *Head, B. W., ed.*, 1983, pp. 238–51. **[G: Australia]**

Hunt, Doug. The Townsville Meatworkers' Strike, 1919. **In** *Murphy, D. J., ed.*, 1983, pp. 144–61. **[G: Australia]**

Hunter, L. C. Pay Policies for the Future: Arbitration. **In** *Robinson, D. and Mayhew, K., eds.*, 1983, pp. 68–83. **[G: U.K.]**

Jacoby, Sanford M. Union–Management Cooperation in the United States: Lessons from the 1920s. *Ind. Lab. Relat. Rev.*, October 1983, *37* (1), pp. 18–33. **[G: U.S.]**

Jennett, N. The Economics of Industrial Relations and Strikes. **In** *Gowland, D. H., ed.*, 1983, pp. 141–56. **[G: U.K.]**

Katz, Harry C.; Kochan, Thomas A. and Gobeille, Kenneth R. Industrial Relations Performance, Economic Performance, and QWL Programs: An Interplant Analysis. *Ind. Lab. Relat. Rev.*, October 1983, *37* (1), pp. 3–17. **[G: U.S.]**

Kaufman, Bruce E. Interindustry Trends in Strike Activity. *Ind. Relat.*, Winter 1983, *22* (1), pp. 45–57. **[G: U.S.]**

Kaufman, Bruce E. The Determinants of Strikes over Time and across Industries. *J. Lab. Res.*, Spring 1983, *4* (2), pp. 159–75. **[G: U.S.]**

Kennedy, K. H. The South Johnstone Strike, 1927. **In** *Murphy, D. J., ed.*, 1983, pp. 174–85. **[G: Australia]**

Killingsworth, Mark R. Union–Nonunion Wage Gaps and Wage Gains: New Estimates from an Industry Cross-Section. *Rev. Econ. Statist.*, May 1983, *65* (2), pp. 332–36. **[G: U.S.]**

Kovach, Kenneth A. and Millspaugh, Peter E. The Plant Closing Issue Arrives at the Bargaining Table. *J. Lab. Res.*, Fall 1983, *4* (4), pp. 367–74. **[G: U.S.]**

Kujawa, Duane. Technology Strategy and Industrial Relations: Case Studies of Japanese Multinationals in the United States. *J. Int. Bus. Stud.*, Winter 1983, *14* (3), pp. 9–22. **[G: Japan; U.S.]**

Kwoka, John E., Jr. Monopoly, Plant, and Union Effects on Worker Wages. *Ind. Lab. Relat. Rev.*, January 1983, *36* (2), pp. 251–57. **[G: U.S.]**

Kymn, Kern O. and Palomba, Catherine. Annual Strike Costs in the Steel Industry in the U.S., 1950 to 1972. *Rivista Int. Sci. Econ. Com.*, April-May 1983, *30* (4–5), pp. 440–51. **[G: U.S.]**

Leigh, J. Paul. Risk Preference and the Interindustry Propensity to Strike. *Ind. Lab. Relat. Rev.*, January 1983, *36* (2), pp. 271–85. **[G: U.S.]**

Lewis, Paul. A Note on Applicants' Choice of Remedies in Unfair Dismissal Cases [An Analysis of Why Legislation Has Failed to Provide Employment Protection for Unfairly Dismissed Employees]. *Brit. J. Ind. Relat.*, July 1983, *21* (2), pp. 232–33. **[G: U.K.]**

Macintyre, Stuart F. Labour, Capital and Arbitration, 1890–1920. **In** *Head, B. W., ed.*, 1983, pp. 98–114. **[G: Australia]**

McCallum, John. Inflation and Social Consensus in the Seventies. *Econ. J.*, December 1983, *93* (372), pp. 784–805. **[G: Selected OECD]**

McMurchy, Anne. The Pastoral Strike, 1956. **In** *Murphy, D. J., ed.*, 1983, pp. 253–69. **[G: Australia]**

Menghetti, Diane. The Weil's Disease Strike, 1935. **In** *Murphy, D. J., ed.*, 1983, pp. 201–16. **[G: Australia]**

Munnell, Alicia H. Who Should Manage the Assets of Collectively Bargained Pension Plans? *New Eng. Econ. Rev.*, July–August 1983, pp. 18–30. **[G: U.S.]**

Murphy, D. J. The Tramway and General Strike, 1912. **In** *Murphy, D. J., ed.*, 1983, pp. 117–31. **[G: Australia]**

Peper, Bram and van Kooten, Gerrit. The Netherlands: From an Ordered Harmonic to a Bargaining Relationship. **In** *Barkin, S., ed.*, 1983, pp. 111–45. **[G: Netherlands]**

Purcell, John. Management Control through Collective Bargaining: A Future Strategy. **In** *Thurley, K. and Wood, S., eds.*, 1983, pp. 53–61.

Purcell, John. The Management of Industrial Relations in the Modern Corporation: Agenda for Research. *Brit. J. Ind. Relat.*, March 1983, *21* (1), pp. 1–16. **[G: U.K.]**

Raynaud, Jean-Daniel. France: Elitist Society Inhibits Articulated Bargaining. **In** *Barkin, S., ed.*, 1983, pp. 279–311. **[G: France]**

Richards, Daniel J. Wages and the Dominant Firm. *J. Lab. Res.*, Spring 1983, *4* (2), pp. 177–82. **[G: U.S.]**

Rosen, Sumner M. The United States: American Industrial Relations System in Jeopardy? **In** *Barkin, S., ed.*, 1983, pp. 359–77. **[G: U.S.]**

Rosenzweig, Roy. "United Action Means Victory": Militant Americanism on Film. *Labor Hist.*, Spring 1983, *24* (2), pp. 274–88. **[G: U.S.]**

Saxe, Stewart D. Recent Developments in Wrongful Dismissal Law. **In** *Queen's Univ. Indust. Relat. Centre*, 1983, pp. 18–23. **[G: Canada]**

Shafto, Tony. The Growth of Shop Steward 'Managerial Functions.' **In** *Thurley, K. and Wood, S., eds.*, 1983, pp. 45–52. **[G: U.K.]**

Simon, Richard M. Hard Times for Organized Labor in Appalachia. *Rev. Radical Polit. Econ.*, Fall 1983, *15* (3), pp. 21–34. **[G: U.S.]**

Sullivan, Rodney J. The Maritime Strike, 1890. **In** *Murphy, D. J., ed.*, 1983, pp. 65–79. **[G: Australia]**

Sullivan, Rodney J. and Sullivan, Robyn A. The London Dock Strike, the Jondaryan Strike and the Brisbane Bootmakers' Strike, 1889–1890. **In** *Murphy, D. J., ed.*, 1983, pp. 47–64. **[G: Australia; U.K.]**

Sullivan, Rodney J. and Sullivan, Robyn A. The Pastoral Strikes, 1891 and 1894. **In** *Murphy, D. J., ed.*, 1983, pp. 80–99. **[G: Australia]**

Weintraub, Sidney. Collective Bargaining *Is* Obsolete: On Revising the Practice to Escape the Stagflation Madness. **In** *Weintraub, S. and Goodstein, M., eds.*, 1983, pp. 151–63. **[G: U.S.]**

8322 Collective Bargaining in the Public Sector

Black, Rebecca R. W. Impacts on Public Sector Labor Relations. **In** *Susskind, L. E. and Serio, J. F., eds.*, 1983, pp. 325–49. **[G: U.S.]**

Blackmur, Douglas. The Railway Strike, 1948. **In** *Murphy, D. J., ed.*, 1983, pp. 235–52. **[G: Australia]**

Brandini, Pietro Merli. Italy: A New Industrial Relations System Moving from Accommodation to Edge of Confrontation. **In** *Barkin, S., ed.*, 1983, pp. 81–110. **[G: Italy]**

Delaney, John Thomas. Strikes, Arbitration, and Teacher Salaries: A Behavioral Analysis. *Ind. Lab. Relat. Rev.*, April 1983, *36*(3), pp. 431–46. **[G: U.S.]**

Edwards, Linda N. and Edwards, Franklin R. Wellington–Winter Revisited: The Case of Municipal Sanitation Collection: Reply. *Ind. Lab. Relat. Rev.*, July 1983, *36*(4), pp. 657–59. **[G: U.S.]**

Goodman, John F. B. Great Britain: Labor Moves from Power to Constraint. **In** *Barkin, S., ed.*, 1983, pp. 39–80. **[G: U.K.]**

Hunt, Janet C. and White, Rudolph A. The Legal Status of Collective Bargaining by Public School Teachers. *J. Lab. Res.*, Summer 1983, *4*(3), pp. 213–24. **[G: U.S.]**

Kessler, Sid. Pay Policies for the Future: Comparability. **In** *Robinson, D. and Mayhew, K., eds.*, 1983, pp. 85–104. **[G: U.K.]**

Lewin, David and Katz, Harry C. Payment Determination in Municipal Building Departments under Unionism and Civil Service. **In** *Hirsch, W. Z., ed.*, 1983, pp. 90–121. **[G: U.S.]**

Maki, Dennis R. A Note on the Output Effects of Canadian Postal Strikes. *Can. J. Econ.*, February 1983, *16*(1), pp. 149–54. **[G: Canada]**

Murphy, D. J. The North Queensland Railway Strike, 1917. **In** *Murphy, D. J., ed.*, 1983, pp. 132–43. **[G: Australia]**

Perkinson, Leon B. and Fearn, Robert M. Wellington–Winter Revisited: The Case of Municipal Sanitation Collection: Comment. *Ind. Lab. Relat. Rev.*, July 1983, *36*(4), pp. 655–57. **[G: U.S.]**

Raynaud, Jean-Daniel. France: Elitist Society Inhibits Articulated Bargaining. **In** *Barkin, S., ed.*, 1983, pp. 279–311. **[G: France]**

Seglow, Peter. Organizational Survival as an Act of Faith: The Case of the BBC. **In** *Thurley, K. and Wood, S., eds.*, 1983, pp. 157–69. **[G: U.K.]**

Smith, Anne. The Railway Strike, 1925. **In** *Murphy, D. J., ed.*, 1983, pp. 162–73. **[G: Australia]**

Vanderporten, Bruce and Hall, W. Clayton. Conditions Leading to Collective Negotiations among Police. *J. Lab. Res.*, Spring 1983, *4*(2), pp. 137–48. **[G: U.S.]**

833 Labor–Management Relations

8330 General

Albrecht, Sandra L. Politics, Bureaucracy, and Worker Participation: The Swedish Case. **In** *Littrell, W. B.; Sjoberg, G. and Zurcher, L. A., eds.*, 1983, pp. 55–71. **[G: Sweden]**

Andrisani, Paul J. and Parnes, Herbert S. Commitment to the Work Ethic and Success in the Labor Market: A Review of Research Findings. **In** *Barbash, J., et al., eds.*, 1983, pp. 101–20. **[G: U.S.]**

Barbash, Jack. Which Work Ethic? **In** *Barbash, J., et al., eds.*, 1983, pp. 231–61.

Barkin, Solomon. Summary and Conclusion: Redesigned Collective Bargaining Systems in Eras of Prosperity and Stagnancy. **In** *Barkin, S., ed.*, 1983, pp. 379–426. **[G: OECD]**

Bellace, Janice R. and Gospel, Howard F. Disclosure of Information to Trade Unions: A Comparative Perspective. *Int. Lab. Rev.*, January–February 1983, *122*(1), pp. 57–74. **[G: U.S.; U.K.; Sweden]**

Brand, Horst. The Evolution of Fair Labor Standards: A Study in Class Conflict. *Mon. Lab. Rev.*, August 1983, *106*(8), pp. 25–28. **[G: U.S.]**

Brewster, C. J.; Gill, C. G. and Richbell, S. Industrial Relations Policy: A Framework for Analysis. **In** *Thurley, K. and Wood, S., eds.*, 1983, pp. 62–72.

Changrong, Chen. An Experiment Attracting World-Wide Attention. *Econ. Anal. Worker's Manage.*, 1983, *17*(1), pp. 43–54. **[G: China]**

Clarke, Frank H. and Darrough, Masako N. Optimal Employment Contracts in a Principal–Agent Relationship. *J. Econ. Behav. Organ.*, June–September 1983, *4*(2–3), pp. 69–90.

Clarke, Oliver. The Work Ethic: An International Perspective. **In** *Barbash, J., et al., eds.*, 1983, pp. 121–50. **[G: OECD]**

Dore, Ronald P. Quality Circles and Their Transferability to Britain. *Rivista Int. Sci. Econ. Com.*, August 1983, *30*(8), pp. 696–702. **[G: Japan; U.K.]**

Drach, Marcel and Revuz, Christine. La brigade de travail sous contrat dans l'industrie soviétique et la réforme de juillet 1979. (With English summary.) *Écon. Soc.*, January 1983, *17*(1), pp. 115–78. **[G: U.S.S.R.]**

Dumas, André. Economic Systems and Participation: An Essay on the Practical Experiences of Participation. *Econ. Anal. Worker's Manage.*, 1983, *17*(2), pp. 177–200. **[G: Yugoslavia; France; W. Germany]**

Edwards, Linda N. and Edwards, Franklin R. Wellington–Winter Revisited: The Case of Municipal Sanitation Collection: Reply. *Ind. Lab. Relat. Rev.*, July 1983, *36*(4), pp. 657–59. **[G: U.S.]**

Epstein, Richard A. A Common Law for Labor Relations: A Critique of the New Deal Labor Legislation. *Yale Law J.*, July 1983, *92*(8), pp. 1357–1408. **[G: U.S.]**

Epstein, Richard A. Common Law, Labor Law, and Reality: A Rejoinder [A Common Law for Labor Relations: A Critique of the New Deal Labor Legislation]. *Yale Law J.*, July 1983, *92*(8), pp. 1435–41. **[G: U.S.]**

Fanning, Connell and O'Mahony, David. The Worker Co-operative. **In** *Kennedy, L., ed.*, 1983, pp. 11–29.

Ferman, Louis A. The Work Ethic in the World of Informal Work. **In** *Barbash, J., et al., eds.*, 1983, pp. 211–29.

Fox, Alan. British Management and Industrial Relations: The Social Origins of a System. **In** *Earl, M. J., ed.*, 1983, pp. 6–39. **[G: U.K.]**

Getman, Julius G. and Kohler, Thomas C. The Common Law, Labor Law, and Reality: A Response [A Common Law for Labor Relations: A Critique of the New Deal Labor Legislation]. *Yale Law J.*, July 1983, *92*(8), pp. 1415–34. **[G: U.S.]**

Gevers, J. K. M. Worker Participation in Health and Safety in the EEC: The Role of Representative

Institutions. *Int. Lab. Rev.*, July–August 1983, *122*(4), pp. 411–28. **[G: EEC]**

Goodman, John F. B. Great Britain: Labor Moves from Power to Constraint. **In** *Barkin, S., ed.*, 1983, pp. 39–80. **[G: U.K.]**

Gospel, Howard. The Development of Management Organization in Industrial Relations: A Historical Perspective. **In** *Thurley, K. and Wood, S., eds.*, 1983, pp. 91–110. **[G: U.K.]**

Haltiwanger, John C. On the Relationship between Risk Aversion and the Development of Long Term Worker–Firm Attachments. *Southern Econ. J.*, October 1983, *50*(2), pp. 572–77.

Hunter, L. C. Arbitration. *Oxford Bull. Econ. Statist.*, February 1983, *45*(1), pp. 63–83. **[G: U.K.]**

Jain, Harish C. Task Force Encourages Diffusion of Microelectronics in Canada. *Mon. Lab. Rev.*, October 1983, *106*(10), pp. 25–29. **[G: Canada]**

Jones, Derek C. Producer Co-operatives in Industrialised Western Economies. **In** *Kennedy, L., ed.*, 1983, *1980*, pp. 31–60. **[G: OECD]**

Kesselman, Mark. From State Theory to Class Struggle and Compromise: Contemporary Marxist Political Study. *Soc. Sci. Quart.*, December 1983, *64*(4), pp. 826–45.

Lentz, Bernard F. Research in Labor Economics: Discussion. **In** *Reid, J. D., Jr., ed.*, 1983, pp. 149–53.

Levitan, Sar A. and Johnson, Clifford M. The Survival of Work. **In** *Barbash, J., et al., eds.*, 1983, pp. 1–25. **[G: U.S.]**

Lewin, David. Theoretical Perspectives on the Modern Grievance Procedure. **In** *Reid, J. D., Jr., ed.*, 1983, pp. 127–47.

Lewin, David and Feuille, Peter. Behavioral Research in Industrial Relations. *Ind. Lab. Relat. Rev.*, April 1983, *36*(3), pp. 341–60. **[G: U.K.; U.S.]**

Maital, Shlomo; Maital, Sharone and Schwartz, Aba. Job Attitudes As Intervening Variables between Situational Factors and Economic Behavior. *J. Behav. Econ.*, Summer 1983, *12*(1), pp. 43–70. **[G: U.S.]**

Martin, Jack K. and Lichter, Daniel T. Geographic Mobility and Satisfaction with Life and Work. *Soc. Sci. Quart.*, September 1983, *64*(3), pp. 524–35. **[G: U.S.]**

McGoldrick, James. Industrial Relations and the Division of Labour in the Shipbuilding Industry since the War. *Brit. J. Ind. Relat.*, July 1983, *21*(2), pp. 197–220. **[G: U.K.]**

Mirvis, Philip H. and Hackett, Edward J. Work and Work Force Characteristics in the Nonprofit Sector. *Mon. Lab. Rev.*, April 1983, *106*(4), pp. 3–12. **[G: U.S.]**

Mukasa, R. Les conditions de travail au Japon: Leur aspect global après la Seconde Guerre mondiale. (Labour Conditions in Japan: The Overall Post-War Picture. With English summary.) *Écon. Soc.*, March–April 1983, *17*(3–4), pp. 481–516. **[G: Japan]**

Nelson, Richard R. State Labor Legislation Enacted in 1982. *Mon. Lab. Rev.*, January 1983, *106*(1), pp. 44–56. **[G: U.S.]**

Norton, David L. Good Government, Justice, and Self-fulfilling Individuality. **In** *Skurski, R., ed.*, 1983, pp. 33–52.

Pakes, Ariél and Nitzan, Shmuel. Optimum Contracts for Research Personnel, Research Employment, and the Establishment of "Rival" Enterprises. *J. Lab. Econ.*, October 1983, *1*(4), pp. 345–65.

Pelinka, Anton. The Austrian Experience of Social and Economic Cooperation. *Economia*, May 1983, *7*(2), pp. 239–53. **[G: Austria]**

Peper, Bram and van Kooten, Gerrit. The Netherlands: From an Ordered Harmonic to a Bargaining Relationship. **In** *Barkin, S., ed.*, 1983, pp. 111–45. **[G: Netherlands]**

Poniedzialek, C. When the King Went on Strike. *Rev. Radical Polit. Econ.*, Spring 1983, *15*(1), pp. 161–70.

Poole, Michael, et al. Why Managers Join Unions: Evidence from Britain. *Ind. Relat.*, Fall 1983, *22*(3), pp. 426–44. **[G: U.K.]**

Rabinowitz, William, et al. Worker Motivation: Unsolved Problem or Untapped Resource? *Calif. Manage. Rev.*, January 1983, *25*(2), pp. 45–56. **[G: U.S.]**

Ramsay, Harvie. An International Participation Cycle: Variations on a Recurring Theme. **In** *Clegg, S.; Dow, G. and Boreham, P., eds.*, 1983, pp. 257–317. **[G: W. Europe]**

Raynaud, Jean-Daniel. France: Elitist Society Inhibits Articulated Bargaining. **In** *Barkin, S., ed.*, 1983, pp. 279–311. **[G: France]**

Rojot, Jacques. A New Chapter in French Industrial Relations. **In** *Barkin, S., ed.*, 1983, pp. 312–23. **[G: France]**

Roman, Paul M. Medicalization and Social Control in the Workplace. **In** *Littrell, W. B.; Sjoberg, G. and Zurcher, L. A., eds.*, 1983, pp. 115–29. **[G: U.S.]**

Rosen, Sumner M. The United States: American Industrial Relations System in Jeopardy? **In** *Barkin, S., ed.*, 1983, pp. 359–77. **[G: U.S.]**

Roustang, Guy. Worker Participation in Occupational Safety and Health Matters in France. *Int. Lab. Rev.*, March–April 1983, *122*(2), pp. 169–82. **[G: France]**

Siegel, Irving H. Work Ethic and Productivity. **In** *Barbash, J., et al., eds.*, 1983, pp. 27–42. **[G: U.S.]**

Simon, Herbert A. What Is Industrial Democracy? *Challenge*, January/February 1983, *25*(6), pp. 30–39. **[G: U.S.]**

Smith, Louis P. Economists, Economic Theory, and Co-operatives. **In** *Kennedy, L., ed.*, 1983, pp. 95–121. **[G: Selected Countries]**

Stein, Barry A. and Kanter, Rosabeth Moss. Building the Parallel Organization: Creating Mechanisms for Permanent Quality of Work Life. **In** *Littrell, W. B.; Sjoberg, G. and Zurcher, L. A., eds.*, 1983, pp. 97–114.

Stewart, Frances. Work and Welfare. **In** *Streeten, P. and Maier, H., eds.*, 1983, pp. 209–26.

Tarantelli, Ezio. The Regulation of Inflation in Western Countries and the Degree of Neocorporatism. *Economia*, May 1983, *7*(2), pp. 199–238. **[G: OECD]**

Thomson, A. W. J. The Contexts of Management Behaviour in Industrial Relations in the Public and Private Sectors. **In** *Thurley, K. and Wood, S., eds.*, 1983, pp. 131–45. **[G: U.K.]**

Verkuil, Paul R. Whose Common Law for Labor Relations? [A Common Law for Labor Relations: A Critique of the New Deal Labor Legislation]. *Yale Law J.*, July 1983, *92*(8), pp. 1409–14. **[G: U.S.]**

Walton, John. Marx for the Late Twentieth Century: Transnational Capital and Disenfranchised Labor. *Soc. Sci. Quart.*, December 1983, *64*(4), pp. 786–809. **[G: U.S.]**

Worrall, John D. and Butler, Richard J. Health Conditions and Job Hazards: Union and Nonunion Jobs. *J. Lab. Res.*, Fall 1983, *4*(4), pp. 339–47. **[G: U.S.]**

Zara, Stefano. Sindacato: meno ideologia, più pragmatismo. (The Unions: Less Ideology, More Pragmatism. With English summary.) *L'Impresa*, 1983, *25*(6), pp. 67–71. **[G: Italy]**

8331 Labor–Management Relations in Private Sector

Akaoka, Isao. Motivation of Employees in Japan. *Kyoto Univ. Econ. Rev.*, April–October 1983, *53*(1–2), pp. 25–50. **[G: Japan]**

Allen, P. T. and Stephenson, G. M. Inter-Group Understanding and Size of Organisation. *Brit. J. Ind. Relat.*, November 1983, *21*(3), pp. 312–29. **[G: U.K.]**

Beaupain, Thérèse. Belgium: Collective Bargaining and Concertation System Inhibited by Economic Crisis and Government. **In** *Barkin, S., ed.*, 1983, pp. 147–86. **[G: Belgium]**

Bergmann, Joachim and Müller-Jentsch, Walther. The Federal Republic of Germany: Cooperative Unionism and Dual Bargaining System Challenged. **In** *Barkin, S., ed.*, 1983, pp. 229–77. **[G: W. Germany]**

Bradley, Keith and Hill, Stephen. 'After Japan': The Quality Circle Transplant and Productive Efficiency. *Brit. J. Ind. Relat.*, November 1983, *21*(3), pp. 291–311. **[G: U.K.; U.S.]**

Breviere, Chr. Communicating Information to Workers in Belgian Undertakings. *Int. Lab. Rev.*, March–April 1983, *122*(2), pp. 197–210. **[G: Belgium]**

Brown, Peter G. Improving Equity in the Use of Temporary Workers. **In** *Kasperson, R. E., ed.*, 1983, pp. 291–300. **[G: U.S.]**

Christainsen, Gregory B. and Hogendorn, Jan S. Japanese Productivity: Adapting to Changing Comparative Advantage in the Face of Lifetime Employment Commitments. *Quart. Rev. Econ. Bus.*, Summer 1983, *23*(2), pp. 23–39. **[G: Japan]**

Christie, Innis. Termination of Employment: Trends and Overview. **In** *Queen's Univ. Indust. Relat. Centre*, 1983, pp. 1–17. **[G: Canada]**

Cottle, Rex L.; Macaulay, Hugh H. and Yandle, T. Bruce. Codetermination: Union Style. *J. Lab. Res.*, Spring 1983, *4*(2), pp. 125–35. **[G: U.S.]**

Delporte, Christian M. and Thomas, L. Joseph. Gestion des opérations et productivité: Quelques leçons de l'exemple japonais. *Ann. Sci. Écon. Appl.*, 1983, *39*(1), pp. 9–26. **[G: Japan]**

Devine, James N. and Reich, Michael. The Microeconomics of Conflict and Hierarchy under Capitalist Production: A Reply. *Rev. Radical Polit. Econ.*, Summer 1983, *15*(2), pp. 133–35.

Dhaliwal, R. S. and Grewal, S. S. Impact of Agricultural Development on Farmer–Labourer Relationships. *Econ. Aff.*, January–March 1983, *28*(1), pp. 644–49. **[G: India]**

England, George W. Japanese and American Management: Theory Z and Beyond. *J. Int. Bus. Stud.*, Fall 1983, *14*(2), pp. 131–42. **[G: Japan; U.S.]**

Espinosa, Juan Guillermo. Worker Participation in the Management of Enterprises and the Ownership and Financing of the Means of Production: A Transition Strategy. *Econ. Anal. Worker's Manage.*, 1983, *17*(2), pp. 99–121.

Eyraud, François. The Principles of Union Action in the Engineering Industries in Great Britain and France: Towards a Neo-Institutional Analysis of Industrial Relations. *Brit. J. Ind. Relat.*, November 1983, *21*(3), pp. 358–76. **[G: U.K.; France]**

Fanning, Connell and McCarthy, Thomas. Hypotheses Concerning the Non-Viability of Labour-Directed Firms in Capitalist Economies. *Econ. Anal. Worker's Manage.*, 1983, *17*(2), pp. 123–54.

Fischhoff, Baruch. Informed Consent for Nuclear Workers. **In** *Kasperson, R. E., ed.*, 1983, pp. 301–28. **[G: U.S.]**

Goldman, Paul. The Labor Process and the Sociology of Organizations. **In** *Bacharach, S. B., ed.*, 1983, pp. 49–81. **[G: U.S.]**

Guest, Robert H. Quality of Work Life: Learning from Tarrytown. **In** *Kantrow, A. M., ed.*, 1983, pp. 545–62. **[G: U.S.]**

Harvey, Leonard. Technology and the Work Environment (II): Technology and Productivity—What Is The Relationship? **In** *Martin, T. R., ed.*, 1983, pp. 54–63. **[G: U.S.]**

Hedges, Janice Neipert. Job Commitment. **In** *Barbash, J., et al., eds.*, 1983, pp. 43–60. **[G: U.S.]**

Henley, John. Corporate Strategy and Employment Relations in Multinational Corporations: Some Evidence from Kenya and Malaysia. **In** *Thurley, K. and Wood, S., eds.*, 1983, pp. 111–30. **[G: Malaysia; Kenya]**

Hunter, L. C. Pay Policies for the Future: Arbitration. **In** *Robinson, D. and Mayhew, K., eds.*, 1983, pp. 68–83. **[G: U.K.]**

Jacoby, Sanford M. Union–Management Cooperation in the United States: Lessons from the 1920s. *Ind. Lab. Relat. Rev.*, October 1983, *37*(1), pp. 18–33. **[G: U.S.]**

Katz, Harry C.; Kochan, Thomas A. and Gobeille, Kenneth R. Industrial Relations Performance, Economic Performance, and QWL Programs: An Interplant Analysis. *Ind. Lab. Relat. Rev.*, October 1983, *37*(1), pp. 3–17. **[G: U.S.]**

Kujawa, Duane. Technology Strategy and Industrial Relations: Case Studies of Japanese Multinationals in the United States. *J. Int. Bus. Stud.*, Winter 1983, *14*(3), pp. 9–22. **[G: Japan; U.S.]**

Leone, Richard D. and Eleey, Michael F. The Origins and Operations of Area Labor–Management Committees. *Mon. Lab. Rev.*, May 1983, *106*(5), pp. 37–41. **[G: U.S.]**

Loveridge, Ray. Centralism versus Federalism: Corporate Models in Industrial Relations. In *Thurley, K. and Wood, S., eds.*, 1983, pp. 170–93. [G: U.K.]

Maccoby, Michael. The Managerial Work Ethic in America. In *Barbash, J., et al., eds.*, 1983, pp. 183–96. [G: U.S.]

Marchington, Mick and Loveridge, Ray. Management Decision-making and Shop Floor Participation. In *Thurley, K. and Wood, S., eds.*, 1983, pp. 73–82.

Marsh, A. I. and Gillies, J. G. The Involvement of Line and Staff Managers in Industrial Relations. In *Thurley, K. and Wood, S., eds.*, 1983, pp. 27–38. [G: U.K.]

Melville, Mary H. Temporary Workers in the Nuclear Power Industry: Implications for the Waste Management Program. In *Kasperson, R. E., ed.*, 1983, pp. 229–58. [G: U.S.]

Menghetti, Diane. The Weil's Disease Strike, 1935. In *Murphy, D. J., ed.*, 1983, pp. 201–16. [G: Australia]

Nevis, Edwin C. Cultural Assumptions and Productivity: The United States and China. *Sloan Manage. Rev.*, Spring 1983, *24*(3), pp. 17–29. [G: China; U.S.]

Northrup, Herbert R. The New Employee-Relations Climate in Airlines. *Ind. Lab. Relat. Rev.*, January 1983, *36*(2), pp. 167–81. [G: U.S.]

Nutzinger, Hans G. Empirical Research into German Codetermination: Problems and Perspectives. *Econ. Anal. Worker's Manage.*, 1983, *17*(4), pp. 361–82. [G: Germany]

Pejovich, Svetozar. Codetermination in the West: The Case of Germany. In *Pejovich, S., ed.*, 1983, pp. 101–17. [G: W. Germany]

Purcell, John. Management Control through Collective Bargaining: A Future Strategy. In *Thurley, K. and Wood, S., eds.*, 1983, pp. 53–61.

Purcell, John. The Management of Industrial Relations in the Modern Corporation: Agenda for Research. *Brit. J. Ind. Relat.*, March 1983, *21*(1), pp. 1–16. [G: U.K.]

Reid, Donald W. The Origins of Industrial Labor Management in France: The Case of the Decazeville Ironworks during the July Monarchy. *Bus. Hist. Rev.*, Spring 1983, *57*(1), pp. 1–19. [G: France]

Remus, Jean. Financial Participation of Employees: An Attempted Classification and Major Trends. *Int. Lab. Rev.*, January–February 1983, *122*(1), pp. 1–21. [G: Selected MDCs]

Rooney, Patrick M. Worker Control: Greater Efficiency and Job Satisfaction. *Econ. Forum*, Winter 1983-84, *14*(2), pp. 97–123. [G: U.S.]

Runcie, John F. "By Days I Make the Cars." In *Kantrow, A. M., ed.*, 1983, pp. 474–89.

Sasser, W. Earl, Jr. and Leonard, Frank S. Let First-level Supervisors Do Their Jobs. In *Kantrow, A. M., ed.*, 1983, pp. 563–78.

Schappe, Robert H. Twenty-two Arguments against Job Enrichment. In *Snoeyenbos, M.; Almeder, R. and Humber, J., eds.*, 1983, *1974*, pp. 310–20.

Schuster, Michael. The Impact of Union-Management Cooperation on Productivity and Employment. *Ind. Lab. Relat. Rev.*, April 1983, *36*(3), pp. 415–30. [G: U.S.]

Scobel, Donald N. Doing Away with the Factory Blues. In *Kantrow, A. M., ed.*, 1983, pp. 510–25.

Shakow, Don M. Market Mechanisms for Compensating Hazardous Work: A Critical Analysis. In *Kasperson, R. E., ed.*, 1983, pp. 277–90. [G: U.S.]

Simmons, C. Gordon. The Experience of the Unjust Dismissal Section under Section 61.5 in the Canada Labour Code, 1978–1981. In *Queen's Univ. Indust. Relat. Centre*, 1983, pp. 59–67. [G: Canada]

Skinner, C. Wickham. The Anachronistic Factory. In *Kantrow, A. M., ed.*, 1983, *1971*, pp. 435–51.

Smith, Robin. Work Control and Managerial Prerogatives. In *Thurley, K. and Wood, S., eds.*, 1983, pp. 39–44.

Stephen, Frank H. Understanding the Scottish Economy: Producers' Cooperatives. In *Ingham, K. P. D. and Love, J., eds.*, 1983, pp. 94–104. [G: U.K.]

Stromquist, Shelton. Enginemen and Shopmen: Technological Change and the Organization of Labor in an Era of Railroad Expansion. *Labor Hist.*, Fall 1983, *24*(4), pp. 485–99. [G: U.S.]

Swan, Kenneth P. Protections against Discriminatory Dismissal. In *Queen's Univ. Indust. Relat. Centre*, 1983, pp. 49–58. [G: Canada]

Takagi, Tadao. Labour Relations in Japan and Italy. In *Fodella, G., ed.*, 1983, pp. 158–78. [G: Japan; Italy]

Tannenbaum, Arnold S. Employee-owned Companies. In *Cummings, L. L. and Staw, B. M., eds.*, 1983, pp. 235–68. [G: U.S.]

Thompson, Alexander M., III. Technological Change and the Control of Work: The U.S. Bituminous Coal Industry 1865–1930. *Econ. Forum*, Winter 1983-84, *14*(2), pp. 1–18. [G: U.S.]

Thurley, Keith and Wood, Stephen. Business Strategy and Industrial Relations Strategy. In *Thurley, K. and Wood, S., eds.*, 1983, pp. 197–224. [G: U.K.; France; Japan]

Thurley, Keith and Wood, Stephen. Industrial Relations and Management Strategy: Introduction. In *Thurley, K. and Wood, S., eds.*, 1983, pp. 1–6.

Tyler, Gus. The Work Ethic: A Union View. In *Barbash, J., et al., eds.*, 1983, pp. 197–210. [G: U.S.]

Tyson, Shaun. Personnel Management in Its Organizational Context. In *Thurley, K. and Wood, S., eds.*, 1983, pp. 146–56. [G: U.K.]

Vogelsang, Ingo. Public Interest Firms as Leaders in Oligopolistic Industries. In *Finsinger, J., ed.*, 1983, pp. 86–99. [G: W. Germany]

Walker, Charles R. and Guest, Robert H. The Man on the Assembly Line. In *Kantrow, A. M., ed.*, 1983, pp. 452–73.

Walton, Richard E. How to Counter Alienation in the Plant. In *Kantrow, A. M., ed.*, 1983, *1972*, pp. 490–509.

Walton, Richard E. Work Innovations in the United States. In *Kantrow, A. M., ed.*, 1983, pp. 526–44. [G: U.S.]

Watts, Martin J. Microeconomic Theory: Should Radicals Steal the Neoclassicals' Clothes? [The Microeconomics of Conflict and Hierarchy under

Capitalist Production: A Reply to Watts]. *Rev. Radical Polit. Econ.*, Winter 1983, *15*(4), pp. 100–103.

Wrege, Charles D. Medical Men and Scientific Management: A Forgotten Chapter in Management History. *Rev. Bus. Econ. Res.*, Spring 1983, *18*(3), pp. 32–47. **[G: U.S.]**

Zanjani, Sally Springmeyer. The Mike Smith Case: A Note on High Grading in Goldfield, Nevada, 1910. *Labor Hist.*, Fall 1983, *24*(4), pp. 580–87. **[G: U.S.]**

Zuboff, Shoshana. The Work Ethic and Work Organization. **In** *Barbash, J., et al., eds.*, 1983, pp. 153–81. **[G: U.S.]**

8332 Labor–Management Relations in Public Sector

Arthurs, A. J. Management and Managerial Unionism. **In** *Thurley, K. and Wood, S., eds.*, 1983, pp. 13–18. **[G: U.K.]**

Asselain, Jean-Charles. La dimension sociale des nationalisations de 1982. (The Social Scheme of the 1982 Nationalizations. With English summary.) *Revue Écon.*, May 1983, *34*(3), pp. 536–76.

Black, Rebecca R. W. Impacts on Public Sector Labor Relations. **In** *Susskind, L. E. and Serio, J. F., eds.*, 1983, pp. 325–49. **[G: U.S.]**

Eberts, Randall W. How Unions Affect Management Decisions: Evidence from Public Schools. *J. Lab. Res.*, Summer 1983, *4*(3), pp. 239–47. **[G: U.S.]**

Estrin, Saul and Connock, Michael. Ideas of Industrial Democracy in Eastern Europe: A Comment from the Yugoslav Perspective. *ACES Bull. (See Comp. Econ. Stud. after 8/85)*, Spring 1983, *25*(1), pp. 67–74.

Karim, Ahmad and Pegnetter, Richard. Mediator Strategies and Qualities and Mediation Effectiveness. *Ind. Relat.*, Winter 1983, *22*(1), pp. 105–14. **[G: U.S.]**

Kurth, Michael M. Public Employee Organizations as Political Firms. **In** *Reid, J. D., Jr., ed.*, 1983, pp. 101–25. **[G: U.S.]**

Lockett, Martin. Enterprise Management—Moves towards Democracy? **In** *Feuchtwang, S. and Hussain, A., eds.*, 1983, pp. 224–56. **[G: China]**

Mergen, Bernard. The Government as Manager: Emergency Fleet Shipbuilding, 1917–1919. **In** *[Cochran, T. C.]*, 1983, pp. 49–80. **[G: U.S.]**

Navrátil, Oldřich and Pudík, Vladimír. Economic Management and Trade Union Bodies. *Czech. Econ. Digest.*, February 1983, (1), pp. 47–108. **[G: Czechoslovakia]**

Pryor, Frederic L. The Economics of Production Cooperatives: A Reader's Guide. *Ann. Pub. Co-op. Econ.*, April–June 1983, *54*(2), pp. 133–72.

Seglow, Peter. Organizational Survival as an Act of Faith: The Case of the BBC. **In** *Thurley, K. and Wood, S., eds.*, 1983, pp. 157–69. **[G: U.K.]**

Semenov, A. Workers' Participation in Occupational Safety and Health Matters in the USSR. *Int. Lab. Rev.*, May–June 1983, *122*(3), pp. 355–66. **[G: U.S.S.R.]**

Sirc, Ljubo. Employee Participation and the Promotion of Employee Ownership. **In** *Seldon, A., et al.*, 1983, pp. 113–27. **[G: W. Germany; Yugoslavia]**

Sziraczki, G. The Development and Functioning of an Enterprise Labour Market in Hungary. *Écon. Soc.*, March–April 1983, *17*(3–4), pp. 517–47. **[G: Hungary]**

Turk, Ivan. Efficiency Analysis through Interrelated Indicators: The Yugoslav Approach. **In** *[Ramanadham, V. V.]*, 1983, pp. 140–56. **[G: Yugoslavia]**

Whitehorn, Alan. Alienation and Socialism: An Analysis of Yugoslav Workers' Self-Management. *Econ. Anal. Worker's Manage.*, 1983, *17*(3), pp. 245–71. **[G: Yugoslavia; Canada]**

Ziegler, Charles E. Worker Participation and Worker Discontent in the Soviet Union. *Polit. Sci. Quart.*, Summer 1983, *98*(2), pp. 235–53. **[G: U.S.S.R.]**

840 Demographic Economics

841 Demographic Economics

8410 Demographic Economics

Adepoju, Aderanti. Issues in the Study of Migration and Urbanization in Africa South of the Sahara. **In** *Morrison, P. A., ed.*, 1983, pp. 115–49. **[G: Sub-Saharan Africa]**

Alonso, William. The Demographic Factor in Housing for the Balance of This Century. **In** *Gau, G. W. and Goldberg, M. A., eds.*, 1983, pp. 33–50.

Alperovich, Gershon. An Empirical Study of Population Density Gradients and Their Determinants. *J. Reg. Sci.*, November 1983, *23*(4), pp. 529–40. **[G: Israel]**

Alperovich, Gershon. Determinants of Urban Population Density Functions: A Procedure for Efficient Estimates. *Reg. Sci. Urban Econ.*, May 1983, *13*(2), pp. 287–95. **[G: Israel]**

Alperovich, Gershon. Economic Analysis of Intraurban Migration in Tel-Aviv. *J. Urban Econ.*, November 1983, *14*(3), pp. 280–92. **[G: Israel]**

Alperovich, Gershon. Lagged Response in Intra-Urban Migration of Home Owners. *Reg. Stud.*, October 1983, *17*(5), pp. 297–304. **[G: Israel]**

Alter, G. Plague and the Amsterdam Annuitant: A New Look at Life Annuities as a Source for Historial Demography. *Population Stud.*, March 1983, *37*(1), pp. 23–41. **[G: Netherlands]**

Althaus, Paul G. and Schachter, Joseph. Interstate Migration and the New Federalism. *Soc. Sci. Quart.*, March 1983, *64*(1), pp. 35–45. **[G: U.S.]**

Anderson, Barbara A. and Silver, Brian D. Estimating Russification of Ethnic Identity among Non-Russians in the USSR. *Demography*, November 1983, *20*(4), pp. 461–89. **[G: U.S.S.R.]**

Anderson, Kathryn H. The Determination of Fertility, Schooling, and Child Survival in Guatemala. *Int. Econ. Rev.*, October 1983, *24*(3), pp. 567–89. **[G: Guatemala]**

Anderson, Kathryn H. and Hill, M. Anne. Marriage and Labor Market Discrimination in Japan. *Southern Econ. J.*, April 1983, *49*(4), pp. 941–53. **[G: Japan]**

Anderton, Douglas L.; Conaty, Joseph and Pullum, Thomas W. Population Estimates from Longitudinal Records in Otherwise Data-Deficient Settings. *Demography,* August 1983, *20*(3), pp. 273–84. **[G: U.S.]**

Angeli, Aurora. Strutture familiari nella pianura e nella montagna bolognesi a meta' del XIX secolo. Confronti territoriali. (The Family Structures in the Plain and Mountain of Bologna's Area in the XIX Century. With English summary.) *Statistica,* October–December 1983, *43*(4), pp. 727–41. **[G: Italy]**

Arab-Ogly, E. Twentieth-Century Demographic Processes and Social Problems. *Prob. Econ.,* February 1983, *25*(10), pp. 3–33.

Arndt, H. W. Transmigration: Achievements, Problems, Prospects. *Bull. Indonesian Econ. Stud.,* December 1983, *19*(3), pp. 50–73. **[G: Indonesia]**

Arthur, W. B. and Stoto, Michael A. An Analysis of Indirect Mortality Estimation. *Population Stud.,* July 1983, *37*(2), pp. 301–14.

Asabere, Paul K. and Owusu-Banahene, K. Population Density Function For Ghanaian (African) Cities: An Empirical Note. *J. Urban Econ.,* November 1983, *14*(3), pp. 370–79. **[G: Ghana]**

Baily, Samuel L. The Adjustment of Italian Immigrants in Buenos Aires and New York, 1870–1914. *Amer. Hist. Rev.,* April 1983, *88*(2), pp. 281–305. **[G: U.S.; Argentina]**

Balán, Jorge. Agrarian Structures and Internal Migration in a Historical Perspective: Latin American Case Studies. **In** *Morrison, P. A., ed.,* 1983, pp. 151–85. **[G: Latin America]**

Balán, Jorge. Comment [The Integration of Italian Immigrants into the United States and Argentina: A Comparative Analysis]. *Amer. Hist. Rev.,* April 1983, *88*(2), pp. 330–34. **[G: U.S.; Argentina]**

Banerjee, Biswajit. Social Networks in the Migration Process: Empirical Evidence on Chain Migration in India. *J. Devel. Areas,* January 1983, *17*(2), pp. 185–96. **[G: India]**

Bartlett, William. On the Dynamic Instability of Induced-Migration Unemployment in a Dual Economy. *J. Devel. Econ.,* Aug.–Oct. 1983, *13*(1–2), pp. 85–96.

Batty, Michael and Karmeshu. A Strategy for Generating and Testing Models of Migration and Urban Growth. *Reg. Stud.,* August 1983, *17*(4), pp. 223–36.

Bean, Frank D.; King, Allan G. and Passel, Jeffrey S. The Number of Illegal Migrants of Mexican Origin in the United States: Sex Ratio-Based Estimates for 1980. *Demography,* February 1983, *20*(1), pp. 99–109. **[G: U.S.]**

Beckman, Linda J., et al. A Theoretical Analysis of Antecedents of Young Couples' Fertility Decisions and Outcomes. *Demography,* November 1983, *20*(4), pp. 519–33. **[G: U.S.]**

Bennett, Neil G. and Garson, Lea Keil. The Centenarian Question and Old-Age Mortaility in the Soviet Union, 1959–1970. *Demography,* November 1983, *20*(4), pp. 587–606. **[G: U.S.S.R.]**

Bentzel, Ragnar and Berg, Lennart. The Role of Demographic Factors as a Determinant of Savings in Sweden. **In** *Modigliani, F. and Hemming, R., eds.,* 1983, pp. 152–79. **[G: Sweden]**

Berliner, Joseph S. Culture, Social Structure, and Fertility in the U.S.S.R. **In** *[Erlich, A.],* 1983, pp. 217–48. **[G: U.S.S.R.]**

Berliner, Joseph S. Education, Labor-Force Participation, and Fertility in the USSR. *J. Compar. Econ.,* June 1983, *7*(2), pp. 131–57. **[G: U.S.S.R.]**

Bertrand, Jane T.; Bertrand, W. E. and Malonga, Maitudila. The Use of Traditional and Modern Methods of Fertility Control in Kinshasa, Zaire. *Population Stud.,* March 1983, *37*(1), pp. 129–36. **[G: Zaire]**

Bertrand, Jane T. and Mangani, Nlandu. Operations Research Project Experience: The Zaire Family Planning Project. **In** *Sirageldin, I.; Salkever, D. and Osborn, R. W., eds.,* 1983, pp. 245–63. **[G: Zaire]**

Bhatia, Kul B. Rural–Urban Migration and Surplus Labour: Rejoinder to Stark. *Oxford Econ. Pap.,* March 1983, *35*(1), pp. 143–45.

Bialkovskaia, V. and Novikov, V. Urbanization and the Problem of Restricting the Growth of Very Large Cities. *Prob. Econ.,* October 1983, *26*(6), pp. 23–39. **[G: U.S.S.R.]**

Bilsborrow, Richard E. and Akin, John S. U.S. and Canadian Migration Data: Reply to Robert Nakosteen. *Rev. Public Data Use (See J. Econ. Soc. Meas. after 4/85),* March 1983, *11*(1), pp. 73–74. **[G: U.S.; Canada]**

Bingham, T. R. G. The Implications of Demographic Change for Economic Growth. **In** *Weisbrod, B. and Hughes, H., eds.,* 1983, pp. 309–16.

Birdsall, Nancy. Fertility and Economic Change in Eighteenth and Nineteenth Century Europe: A Comment [Fertility, Economy, and Household Formation in England over Three Centuries]. *Population Devel. Rev.,* March 1983, *9*(1), pp. 111–23. **[G: U.K.]**

Birdsall, Nancy and Jamison, Dean T. Income and Other Factors Influencing Fertility in China. *Population Devel. Rev.,* December 1983, *9*(4), pp. 651–75. **[G: China]**

Blumenfeld, Stewart N. Cost Analysis of the Danfa (Ghana) Project Family Planning Component. **In** *Sirageldin, I.; Salkever, D. and Osborn, R. W., eds.,* 1983, pp. 228–44. **[G: Ghana]**

Bollen, Kenneth A. Temporal Variations in Mortality: A Comparison of U.S. Suicides and Motor Vehicle Fatalities, 1972–1976. *Demography,* February 1983, *20*(1), pp. 45–59. **[G: U.S.]**

Bongaarts, John. The Proximate Determinants of Natural Marital Fertility. **In** *Bulatao, R. A. and Lee, R. D., eds., Vol. 1,* 1983, pp. 103–38. **[G: LDCs; MDCs]**

Bongaarts, John and Menken, Jane. The Supply of Children: A Critical Essay. **In** *Bulatao, R. A. and Lee, R. D., eds., Vol. 1,* 1983, pp. 27–60.

Bordes, Ary, et al. Household Distribution of Contraceptives in Rural Haiti: The Results and Costs of the Division of Family Hygiene's Experimental Project. **In** *Sirageldin, I.; Salkever, D. and Osborn, R. W., eds.,* 1983, pp. 476–96. **[G: Haiti]**

Bose, Ashish. Migration in India: Trends and Policies. **In** *Oberai, A. S., ed.,* 1983, pp. 137–82. **[G: India]**

Bourne, Larry S. Living with Uncertainty: The Changing Spatial Components of Urban Growth and Housing Demand in Canada. **In** *Gau, G. W.*

and Goldberg, M. A., eds., 1983, pp. 51–72. [G: Canada]

Brown, Philip W. The Demographic Future: Impacts on the Demand for Housing in Canada, 1981–2001. **In** *Gau, G. W. and Goldberg, M. A., eds.*, 1983, pp. 5–31. [G: Canada]

Bulatao, Rodolfo A. and Lee, Ronald D. A Framework for the Study of Fertility Determinants. **In** *Bulatao, R. A. and Lee, R. D., eds., Vol. 1,* 1983, pp. 1–25.

Bulatao, Rodolfo A. and Lee, Ronald D. An Overview of Fertility Determinants in Developing Countries. **In** *Bulatao, R. A. and Lee, R. D., eds., Vol. 2,* 1983, pp. 757–87. [G: LDCs]

Cain, Mead. Fertility as an Adjustment to Risk. *Population Devel. Rev.*, December 1983, *9*(4), pp. 688–702. [G: LDCs]

Caldwell, John C. Direct Economic Costs and Benefits of Children. **In** *Bulatao, R. A. and Lee, R. D., eds., Vol. 1,* 1983, pp. 458–92.

Caldwell, John C.; Reddy, P. H. and Caldwell, Pat. The Causes of Marriage Change in South India. *Population Stud.*, November 1983, *37*(3), pp. 343–61. [G: India]

Caldwell, John C.; Reddy, P. H. and Caldwell, Pat. The Social Component of Mortality Decline: An Investigation in South India Employing Alternative Methodologies. *Population Stud.*, July 1983, *37*(2), pp. 185–205. [G: India]

Cerone, P. The Long-Term Effects of Time-Dependent Maternity Behavior. *Demography,* February 1983, *20*(1), pp. 79–86.

Chall, Daniel E. Neighborhood Changes in New York City during the 1970s: Are the "Gentry" Returning? *Fed. Res. Bank New York Quart. Rev.*, Winter 1983-84, *8*(4), pp. 38–48. [G: U.S.]

Chamberlin, John R. Pension Plan Equity: The Case against a Gender Classification. *J. Policy Anal. Manage.*, Fall 1983, *3*(1), pp. 126–29. [G: U.S.]

Chan, Paul. Population Distribution and Development Strategies in Peninsular Malaysia. **In** *Oberai, A. S., ed.*, 1983, pp. 27–78. [G: Malaysia]

Chaudhry, Mahinder D. The Demographic Transition in India: Review Article. *Econ. Develop. Cult. Change,* January 1983, *31*(2), pp. 397–404. [G: India]

Chen, Kwan-Hwa Marnie. The Cost-effectiveness of a Community-based Social Marketing Project in Thailand: The Family Planning Health and Hygiene Project. **In** *Sirageldin, I.; Salkever, D. and Osborn, R. W., eds.*, 1983, pp. 391–405. [G: Thailand]

Chen, Lincoln C. Child Survival: Levels, Trends, and Determinants. **In** *Bulatao, R. A. and Lee, R. D., eds., Vol. 1,* 1983, pp. 199–231. [G: LDCs]

Cheng, Siok Hwa. Demographic Trends. **In** *Chen, P. S. J., ed.*, 1983, pp. 65–86. [G: Singapore]

Chengrui, Li. On the Results of the Chinese Census. *Population Devel. Rev.*, June 1983, *9*(2), pp. 326–44. [G: China]

Cherlin, Andrew; Griffith, Jeanne and McCarthy, James. A Note on Maritally-Disrupted Men's Reports of Child Support in the June 1980 Current Population Survey. *Demography,* August 1983, *20*(3), pp. 385–89. [G: U.S.]

Chiew, Seen-Kong. Ethnicity and National Integration: The Evolution of a Multi-ethnic Society. **In** *Chen, P. S. J., ed.*, 1983, pp. 29–64. [G: Singapore]

Cigno, Alessandro. Corrigendum [On Optimal Family Allowances]. *Oxford Econ. Pap.,* July 1983, *35*(2), pp. 329.

Cigno, Alessandro. On Optimal Family Allowances. *Oxford Econ. Pap.,* March 1983, *35*(1), pp. 13–22.

Clark, M. Gardner. The Swiss Experience with Foreign Workers: Lessons for the United States. *Ind. Lab. Relat. Rev.*, July 1983, *36*(4), pp. 606–23. [G: Switzerland; U.S.]

Clark, William A. V. and Onaka, Jun L. Life Cycle and Housing Adjustment as Explanations of Residential Mobility. *Urban Stud.*, February 1983, *20*(1), pp. 47–57. [G: New Zealand; Canada; U.S.; U.K.]

Clark, William A. V. and Onaka, Jun L. Errata [Life Cycle and Housing Adjustment as Explanations of Residential Mobility]. *Urban Stud.*, November 1983, *20*(4), pp. 391. [G: U.S.; U.K.; Canada; New Zealand]

Cochrane, Susan H. Effects of Education and Urbanization on Fertility. **In** *Bulatao, R. A. and Lee, R. D., eds., Vol. 2,* 1983, pp. 587–626. [G: LDCs]

Coeymans, Juan Eduardo. Determinantes de la migracion rural–urbana en chile, segun origen y destino. (With English summary.) *Cuadernos Econ.*, April 1983, *20*(59), pp. 43–64. [G: Chile]

Cole, William E. and Sanders, Richard D. Interstate Migration in Mexico: Variations on the Todaro Theme. *J. Devel. Econ.*, June 1983, *12*(3), pp. 341–54. [G: Mexico]

Collins, Jane L. Fertility Determinants in a High Andes Community. *Population Devel. Rev.*, March 1983, *9*(1), pp. 61–75. [G: Peru]

Courtois, Claude. Ricardo et la population. (With English summary.) *Revue Écon. Polit.*, March–April 1983, *93*(2), pp. 197–210.

Craine, Roger. The Baby Boom, the Housing Market and the Stock Market. *Fed. Res. Bank San Francisco Econ. Rev.*, Spring 1983, (2), pp. 6–11. [G: U.S.]

Crimmins, Eileen M. Implications of Recent Mortality Trends for the Size and Composition of the Population over 65. *Rev. Public Data Use (See J. Econ. Soc. Meas. after 4/85),* March 1983, *11*(1), pp. 37–48. [G: U.S.]

Croll, Elisabeth J. Production versus Reproduction: A Threat to China's Developing Strategy. *World Devel.*, June 1983, *11*(6), pp. 467–81. [G: China]

Dales, John H. Distortions and Dissipations. *Can. Public Policy,* June 1983, *9*(2), pp. 257–63. [G: Canada]

Darity, William A., Jr. and Myers, Samuel L., Jr. Changes in Black Family Structure: Implications for Welfare Dependency. *Amer. Econ. Rev.*, May 1983, *73*(2), pp. 59–64. [G: U.S.]

DaVanzo, Julie. Repeat Migration in the United States: Who Moves Back and Who Moves On? *Rev. Econ. Statist.*, November 1983, *65*(4), pp. 552–59. [G: U.S.]

DaVanzo, Julie; Butz, W. P. and Habicht, J.-P. How

Biological and Behavioural Influences on Mortality in Malaysia Vary during the First Year of Life. *Population Stud.*, November 1983, *37*(3), pp. 381–402. **[G: Malaysia]**

Davies, Richard B. and Davies, Sheila. The Retired Migrant: A Study in North Wales. *Urban Stud.*, May 1983, *20*(2), pp. 209–17. **[G: U.K.]**

De Jong, Piet and Boyle, Phelim P. Monitoring Mortality: A State-Space Approach. *J. Econometrics*, September 1983, *23*(1), pp. 131–46.

De Tray, Dennis. Children's Work Activities in Malaysia. *Population Devel. Rev.*, September 1983, *9*(3), pp. 437–55. **[G: Malaysia]**

Denton, Frank T. and Spencer, Byron G. Population Aging and Future Health Costs in Canada. *Can. Public Policy*, June 1983, *9*(2), pp. 155–63. **[G: Canada]**

Desai, Meghnad J. and Shah, Anup R. K. Bequest and Inheritance in Nuclear Families and Joint Families. *Economica*, May 1983, *50*(198), pp. 193–202.

Devaney, Barbara. An Analysis of Variations in U.S. Fertility and Female Labor Force Participation Trends. *Demography*, May 1983, *20*(2), pp. 147–61. **[G: U.S.]**

Devoretz, Don and Maki, Dennis R. The Immigration of Third World Professionals to Canada: 1968–1973. *World Devel.*, January 1983, *11*(1), pp. 55–64. **[G: Selected LDCs; Canada]**

Di Comite, Luigi. L'emigrazione italiana nella prima fase dell processo transizionale. (Italian Migrations in the First Phase of the Transitional Process. With English summary.) *Giorn. Econ.*, July–August 1983, *42*(7–8), pp. 507–17. **[G: Italy]**

Dow, Thomas E., Jr. and Werner, Linda H. Prospects for Fertility Decline in Rural Kenya. *Population Devel. Rev.*, March 1983, *9*(1), pp. 77–97. **[G: Kenya]**

Dyson, Tim and Moore, Mick. On Kinship Structure, Female Autonomy, and Demographic Behavior in India. *Population Devel. Rev.*, March 1983, *9*(1), pp. 35–60. **[G: India]**

Easterlin, Richard A. Modernization and Fertility: A Critical Essay. **In** *Bulatao, R. A. and Lee, R. D., eds., Vol. 2*, 1983, pp. 562–86.

Eastwood, David A. Reality or Delusion: Migrant Perception of Levels of Living and Opportunity in Venezuela, 1961–1971. *J. Devel. Areas*, July 1983, *17*(4), pp. 491–97. **[G: Venezuela]**

Edmonston, Barry. Community Variations in Infant and Child Mortality in Rural Jordan. *J. Devel. Areas*, July 1983, *17*(4), pp. 473–89. **[G: Jordan]**

Ehrlich, Paul R. and Ehrlich, Anne H. 1984: Population and Environment. **In** *Stansky, P., ed.*, 1983, pp. 49–55.

Elkins, Henry and Macias, Luis Fernando. Component Cost-effectiveness Analysis of the Mexican New Strategies Project. **In** *Sirageldin, I.; Salkever, D. and Osborn, R. W., eds.*, 1983, pp. 497–508. **[G: Mexico]**

Eltis, David. Free and Coerced Transatlantic Migrations: Some Comparisons. *Amer. Hist. Rev.*, April 1983, *88*(2), pp. 251–80. **[G: U.S.; S. America]**

Ewbank, Douglas C.; Gómez de León, José C. and Stoto, Michael A. A Reducible Four-Parameter System of Model Life Tables. *Population Stud.*, March 1983, *37*(1), pp. 105–27. **[G: Selected Countries]**

Faruqee, Rashid. Family Planning and Health: The Narangwal Experiment. *Finance Develop.*, June 1983, *20*(2), pp. 43–46. **[G: India]**

Faruqee, Rashid and Sarma, R. S. S. Determinants of Fertility and Its Decline. **In** *Taylor, C. E., et al.*, 1983, pp. 155–90. **[G: India]**

Fawcett, James T. Perceptions of the Value of Children: Satisfaction and Costs. **In** *Bulatao, R. A. and Lee, R. D., eds., Vol. 1*, 1983, pp. 429–56.

Feeney, G. Population Dynamics Based on Birth Intervals and Parity Progression. *Population Stud.*, March 1983, *37*(1), pp. 75–89. **[G: U.S.; Costa Rica]**

Feshbach, Murray. Population and Labor Force. **In** *Bergson, A. and Levine, H. S., eds.*, 1983, pp. 79–111. **[G: U.S.S.R.]**

Fetter, Bruce. The Union Miniere and its Hinterland: A Demographic Reconstruction. *African Econ. Hist.*, 1983, (12), pp. 67–81. **[G: Congo]**

Flagle, Charles D. National Experiences in Analysis of Costs, Benefits and Effectiveness of Family Planning. **In** *Sirageldin, I.; Salkever, D. and Osborn, R. W., eds.*, 1983, pp. 197–201.

Flegg, A. T. On the Determinants of Infant Mortality in Underdeveloped Countries. *Int. J. Soc. Econ.*, 1983, *10*(5), pp. 38–51. **[G: LDCs]**

Foreit, James R., et al. A Cost-effectiveness Comparison of Service Delivery Systems and Geographic Areas in Piaui State, Brazil. **In** *Sirageldin, I.; Salkever, D. and Osborn, R. W., eds.*, 1983, pp. 405–20. **[G: Brazil]**

Frank, Odile. Infertility in Sub-Saharan Africa: Estimates and Implications. *Population Devel. Rev.*, March 1983, *9*(1), pp. 137–44. **[G: Selected LDCs]**

Frauenthal, James C. and Swick, Kenneth E. Limit Cycle Oscillations of the Human Population. *Demography*, August 1983, *20*(3), pp. 285–98. **[G: U.S.]**

Frejka, Tomas. Induced Abortion and Fertility: A Quarter Century of Experience in Eastern Europe. *Population Devel. Rev.*, September 1983, *9*(3), pp. 494–520. **[G: E. Europe]**

Frenkel, I. Socio-economic Development and Rural–Urban Migration in Poland. **In** *Oberai, A. S., ed.*, 1983, pp. 251–310. **[G: Poland]**

Friedlander, Dov. Demographic Responses and Socioeconomic Structure: Population Processes in England and Wales in the Nineteenth Century. *Demography*, August 1983, *20*(3), pp. 249–72. **[G: U.K.]**

Fujii, Edwin T. and Mak, James. On the Specification of the Income Equation for Immigrants. *Southern Econ. J.*, April 1983, *49*(4), pp. 1141–46. **[G: U.S.]**

Fujii, Edwin T. and Mak, James. The Determinants of Income of Native- and Foreign-Born Men in a Multiracial Society. *Appl. Econ.*, December 1983, *15*(6), pp. 759–76. **[G: U.S.]**

Fullerton, Howard N., Jr. and Tschetter, John. The 1995 Labor Force: A Second Look. *Mon. Lab. Rev.*, November 1983, *106*(11), pp. 3–10. **[G: U.S.]**

Fure, Eli. Are Children Poor Men's Riches? *Scand.*

Econ. Hist. Rev., 1983, *31* (3), pp. 161–77. **[G: Norway]**

Garnick, Daniel H. U.S. Population Distribution into the Twenty-First Century. **In** *Gau, G. W. and Goldberg, M. A., eds.*, 1983, pp. 73–88. **[G: U.S.]**

Ghoshal, Animesh and Crowley, Thomas M. Political versus Economic Refugees. *Rev. Soc. Econ.*, October 1983, *41* (2), pp. 124–36. **[G: U.S.]**

Gigliotti, Gary Anthony. Total Utility, Overlapping Generations and Optimal Population. *Rev. Econ. Stud.*, January 1983, *50* (1), pp. 71–86.

Giles, David E. A. and Hampton, Peter. Urban Migration in New Zealand: Dummy Variable Interpretations. *J. Urban Econ.*, July 1983, *14* (1), pp. 124–25. **[G: New Zealand]**

Gilland, Bernard. Considerations on World Population and Food Supply. *Population Devel. Rev.*, June 1983, *9* (2), pp. 203–11. **[G: Global]**

Gillespie, Duff G.; Mamlouk, Maria E. and Chen, Kwan-Hwa Marnie. Cost-effectiveness of Family Planning: Overview of the Literature. **In** *Sirageldin, I.; Salkever, D. and Osborn, R. W., eds.*, 1983, pp. 103–40. **[G: Selected Countries]**

Gillespie, Fran. Comprehending the Slow Pace of Urbanization in Paraguay between 1950 and 1972. *Econ. Develop. Cult. Change*, January 1983, *31* (2), pp. 355–75. **[G: Paraguay]**

Glazier, Ira A. Levels of Living of European Peasantry: Discussion. *J. Econ. Hist.*, March 1983, *43* (1), pp. 145–46. **[G: U.S.S.R.; France]**

Goldman, Noreen and Lord, Graham. Sex Differences in Life Cycle Measures of Widowhood. *Demography*, May 1983, *20* (2), pp. 177–95. **[G: U.S.]**

Goldscheider, Calvin. Modernization, Migration, and Urbanization. **In** *Morrison, P. A., ed.*, 1983, pp. 47–66. **[G: LDCs; MDCs]**

Golini, Antonio. Present Relationships between Migration and Urbanization: The Italian Case. **In** *Morrison, P. A., ed.*, 1983, pp. 187–209. **[G: Italy]**

Gomez, Fernando. Rural Household Delivery of Contraceptives in Colombia. **In** *Sirageldin, I.; Salkever, D. and Osborn, R. W., eds.*, 1983, pp. 421–33. **[G: Colombia]**

Goss, Ernest and Chang, Hui S. Changes in Elasticities of Interstate Migration: Implication of Alternative Functional Forms. *J. Reg. Sci.*, May 1983, *23* (2), pp. 223–32. **[G: U.S.]**

Gould, John D. Comment [The Integration of Italian Immigrants into the United States and Argentina: A Comparative Analysis]. *Amer. Hist. Rev.*, April 1983, *88* (2), pp. 334–38. **[G: U.S.; Argentina]**

Graves, Philip E. Migration with a Composite Amenity: The Role of Rents. *J. Reg. Sci.*, November 1983, *23* (4), pp. 541–46. **[G: U.S.]**

Graves, Philip E.; Sexton, Robert L. and Vedder, Richard K. Slavery, Amenities, and Factor Price Equilization: A Note on Migration and Freedom. *Exploration Econ. Hist.*, April 1983, *20* (2), pp. 156–62. **[G: U.S.]**

Gray, Malcolm. Migration in the Rural Lowlands of Scotland, 1750–1850. **In** *Devine, T. M. and Dickson, D., eds.*, 1983, pp. 104–17. **[G: U.K.]**

Gray, Ronald. The Impact of Health and Nutrition on Natural Fertility. **In** *Bulatao, R. A. and Lee, R. D., eds., Vol. 1*, 1983, pp. 139–62.

Greenberg, Michael R. Urbanization and Cancer: Changing Mortality Patterns? *Int. Reg. Sci. Rev.*, October 1983, *8* (2), pp. 127–45. **[G: U.S.]**

Greenfield, C. C. On Estimators for Dual Record Systems. *J. Roy. Statist. Soc.*, 1983, *146* (3), pp. 273–80. **[G: Indonesia]**

Greenwood, Michael J. Leading Issues of Fact and Theory. *Amer. Econ. Rev.*, May 1983, *73* (2), pp. 173–77. **[G: U.S.]**

Gregory, Paul R. Soviet Theories of Economic Demography: A Survey. *J. Compar. Econ.*, June 1983, *7* (2), pp. 105–13. **[G: U.S.S.R.]**

Grosse, Robert N. and Perry, Barbara H. Correlates of Life Expectancy in Less Developed Countries. **In** *Salkever, D.; Sirageldin, I. and Sorkin, A., eds.*, 1983, pp. 217–53. **[G: LDCs]**

Haberman, Steven; Kosmin, Barry A. and Levy, Caren. Mortality Patterns of British Jews 1975–79: Insights and Applications for the Size and Structure of British Jewry. *J. Roy. Statist. Soc.*, 1983, *146* (3), pp. 294–310. **[G: U.K.]**

Haines, Michael R.; Avery, Roger C. and Strong, Michael E. Differentials in Infant and Child Mortality and Their Change over Time: Guatemala, 1959–1973. *Demography*, November 1983, *20* (4), pp. 607–21. **[G: Guatemala]**

Halperin-Donghi, Tulio. Comment [The Integration of Italian Immigrants into the United States and Argentina: A Comparative Analysis]. *Amer. Hist. Rev.*, April 1983, *88* (2), pp. 338–42. **[G: U.S.; Argentina]**

Hanley, Susan B. Economic Growth and Population Control in Preindustrial Japan. **In** *Dalton, G., ed.*, 1983, pp. 185–223. **[G: Japan]**

Harvey, David. Population, Resources, and the Ideology of Science. **In** *Glassner, M. I., ed.*, 1983, *1974*, pp. 97–103.

Hatchuel, Georges. Les ressources des familles et l'impact des prestations familiales. (Families' Income and the Impact of Social Benefits. With English summary.) *Consommation*, January/March 1983, *30* (1), pp. 53–92. **[G: France]**

Hauser, Robert M. and Massagli, Michael P. Some Models of Agreement and Disagreement in Repeated Measurements of Occupation. *Demography*, November 1983, *20* (4), pp. 449–60. **[G: U.S.]**

Hawley, Amos H.; Fernandez, Dorothy and Singh, Harbans. Migration and Employment in Peninsular Malaysia, 1970. **In** *Lim, D., ed.*, 1983, *1979*, pp. 196–206. **[G: Malaysia]**

Haynes, Stephen E. The Subtle Danger of Symmetry Restrictions in Time Series Regressions, with Application to Fertility Models. *Southern Econ. J.*, October 1983, *50* (2), pp. 521–28. **[G: Finland]**

Heer, David M. Infant and Child Mortality and the Demand for Children. **In** *Bulatao, R. A. and Lee, R. D., eds., Vol. 1*, 1983, pp. 369–86.

Hermalin, Albert I. Fertility Regulation and Its Costs: A Critical Essay. **In** *Bulatao, R. A. and Lee, R. D., eds., Vol. 2*, 1983, pp. 1–53. **[G: LDCs]**

Hill, Allan G. The Palestinian Population of the Middle East. *Population Devel. Rev.*, June 1983, *9* (2), pp. 293–316. **[G: Middle East]**

Hill, Martha S. Female Household Headship and the

Poverty of Children. In *Duncan, G. J. and Morgan, J. N., eds.*, 1983, pp. 324–76. **[G: U.S.]**

Hirschman, Charles. Recent Urbanization Trends in Peninsular Malaysia. In *Lim, D., ed.*, 1983, *1976*, pp. 111–24. **[G: Malaysia]**

Hodge, Gerald. Canadian Small Town Renaissance: Implications for Settlement System Concepts. *Reg. Stud.*, February 1983, *17*(1), pp. 19–28. **[G: Canada]**

Hodgson, Dennis. Demography as Social Science and Policy Science. *Population Devel. Rev.*, March 1983, *9*(1), pp. 1–34. **[G: Global]**

Hoem, Jan M. Distortions Caused by Nonobservation of Periods of Cohabitation before the Latest. *Demography*, November 1983, *20*(4), pp. 491–506. **[G: U.S.]**

Hollerbach, Paula E. Fertility Decision-making Processes: A Critical Essay. In *Bulatao, R. A. and Lee, R. D., eds., Vol. 2*, 1983, pp. 340–80.

Horlacher, David E. Application of Cost Analysis to Fertility: Conceptual and Methodological Issues. In *Sirageldin, I.; Salkever, D. and Osborn, R. W., eds.*, 1983, pp. 166–75.

Hsieh, Chang-tseh and Liu, Ben-chieh. The Pursuance of Better Quality of Life: In the Long Run, Better Quality of Social Life Is the Most Important Factor in Migration. *Amer. J. Econ. Soc.*, October 1983, *42*(4), pp. 431–40. **[G: U.S.]**

Hugo, Graeme J. Interstate Migration in Australia, 1976–1981. *Australian Bull. Lab.*, March 1983, *9*(2), pp. 102–30. **[G: Australia]**

Hugo, Graeme J. New Conceptual Approaches to Migration in the Context of Urbanization: A Discussion Based on the Indonesian Experience. In *Morrison, P. A., ed.*, 1983, pp. 69–113. **[G: Indonesia]**

Hull, Terence H. Cultural Influences on Fertility Decision Styles. In *Bulatao, R. A. and Lee, R. D., eds., Vol. 2*, 1983, pp. 381–414.

Indraratna, A. D. V. de S., et al. Migration-related Policies: A Study of the Sri Lanka Experience. In *Oberai, A. S., ed.*, 1983, pp. 79–135. **[G: Sri Lanka]**

Inoue, Shunichi. Stagnant Growth of Japanese Major Metropolitan Regions in the Era of Post-industrial Development. In *Morrison, P. A., ed.*, 1983, pp. 211–37. **[G: Japan]**

Islam, Muhammed N. The Efficiency of Interprovincial Migration in Canada, 1961–1978. *Reg. Sci. Urban Econ.*, May 1983, *13*(2), pp. 231–49. **[G: Canada]**

Jacobesen, Christian Wells. A Correction to Whitney and Boots' 'An Examination of Residential Mobility through the Use of the Log-Linear Model: Part II.' *Reg. Sci. Urban Econ.*, May 1983, *13*(2), pp. 173–76. **[G: Canada]**

Jones, Ellen and Grupp, Fred W. Infant Mortality Trends in the Soviet Union. *Population Devel. Rev.*, June 1983, *9*(2), pp. 213–46. **[G: U.S.S.R.]**

Jones, Gavin. Population Projections and Planning Decisions in Developed and Developing Countries. In *Morrison, P. A., ed.*, 1983, pp. 313–24. **[G: LDCs; MDCs]**

Jones, Philip. Guestworkers and Their Spatial Distribution. In *Wild, T., ed.*, 1983, pp. 71–107. **[G: W. Germany]**

Jura, Michel and Kaminski, Philippe. Mobilité sociale des ménages et évolution économique. *Consommation*, January/March 1983, *30*(1), pp. 93–123. **[G: France]**

Karadawi, Ahmed. Constraints on Assistance to Refugees: Some Observations from the Sudan. *World Devel.*, June 1983, *11*(6), pp. 537–47. **[G: Sudan]**

Kendrick, Stephen. Social Change in Scotland. In *Brown, G. and Cook, R., eds.*, 1983, pp. 40–65. **[G: U.K.]**

Keyfitz, Nathan. Age and Productivity. *J. Policy Anal. Manage.*, Summer 1983, *2*(4), pp. 632–37. **[G: U.S.]**

Keyfitz, Nathan. Age Effects in Work and Consumption. *Econ. Notes*, 1983, (3), pp. 86–121. **[G: Global]**

Keyfitz, Nathan. Population and the Struggle for the World Product. In *Streeten, P. and Maier, H., eds.*, 1983, pp. 235–52.

Khan, M. Ali and Sirageldin, Ismail. How Meaningful Are Statements about the Desired Number of Additional Children? An Analysis of 1968 Pakistani Data. *Pakistan Devel. Rev.*, Spring 1983, *22*(1), pp. 1–22. **[G: Pakistan]**

Kielmann, Arnfried A., et al. Child and Maternal Health Services in Rural India: Analysis of Morbidity and Mortality. In *Kielmann, A. A., et al.*, 1983, pp. 172–214. **[G: India]**

Kim, Joochul. Factors Affecting Urban-to-Rural Migration. *Growth Change*, July 1983, *14*(3), pp. 38–43. **[G: U.S.]**

Kirk, Dudley. Recent Demographic Trends and Present Population Prospects for Mexico. *Food Res. Inst. Stud.*, 1983, *19*(1), pp. 93–111. **[G: Mexico]**

Klein, Herbert S. Reply [The Integration of Italian Immigrants into the United States and Argentina: A Comparative Analysis]. *Amer. Hist. Rev.*, April 1983, *88*(2), pp. 343–46. **[G: U.S.; Argentina]**

Klein, Herbert S. The Integration of Italian Immigrants into the United States and Argentina: A Comparative Analysis. *Amer. Hist. Rev.*, April 1983, *88*(2), pp. 306–29. **[G: U.S.; Argentina]**

Knodel, John. Natural Fertility: Age Patterns, Levels, and Trends. In *Bulatao, R. A. and Lee, R. D., eds., Vol. 1*, 1983, pp. 61–102. **[G: LDCs; MDCs]**

Koo, Helen P. and Janowitz, Barbara K. Interrelationships between Fertility and Marital Dissolution: Results of a Simultaneous Logit Model. *Demography*, May 1983, *20*(2), pp. 129–45. **[G: U.S.]**

Krumm, Ronald J. Regional Labor Markets and the Household Migration Decision. *J. Reg. Sci.*, August 1983, *23*(3), pp. 361–76. **[G: U.S.]**

Kulash, Marjorie M. Pension Plan Equity: The Unintended Consequences. *J. Policy Anal. Manage.*, Fall 1983, *3*(1), pp. 129–34. **[G: U.S.]**

Kuniansky, Anna. Soviet Fertility, Labor-Force Participation, and Marital Instability. *J. Compar. Econ.*, June 1983, *7*(2), pp. 114–30. **[G: U.S.S.R.]**

Kunitz, Stephen J. Speculations on the European Mortality Decline. *Econ. Hist. Rev., 2nd Ser.*, August 1983, *36*(3), pp. 349–64. **[G: Europe]**

Kvasha, A. and Kaliniuk, I. Long-Term Trends in the Reproduction of the Population. *Prob. Econ.*,

June 1983, *26*(2), pp. 78–92. **[G: U.S.S.R.]**

Kynch, Jocelyn and Sen, Amartya K. Indian Women: Well-Being and Survival. *Cambridge J. Econ.*, September/December 1983, 7(3/4), pp. 363–80. **[G: India]**

Labbok, M.; Nichols, D. and Zarouf, M. A Limited Cost-effectiveness Analysis of Household Distribution of Contraceptives (VDMS) in Marrakech, Morocco. **In** *Sirageldin, I.; Salkever, D. and Osborn, R. W., eds.*, 1983, pp. 264–68. **[G: Morocco]**

Land, Kenneth C. and Cantor, David. ARIMA Models of Seasonal Variation in U.S. Birth and Death Rates. *Demography*, November 1983, *20*(4), pp. 541–68. **[G: U.S.]**

Lapham, Robert J. Notes on Issues in Data Collection and Evaluation. **In** *Sirageldin, I.; Salkever, D. and Osborn, R. W., eds.*, 1983, pp. 202–16.

Laskin, John B. Personal Mobility in the United States and the EEC. **In** *Trebilcock, M. J., et al., eds.*, 1983, pp. 456–98. **[G: U.S.; EEC; Canada]**

Layton, Brent. British Migration to New Zealand after World War II. *Australian Econ. Hist. Rev.*, September 1983, *23*(2), pp. 219–37. **[G: U.K.; New Zealand]**

Lee, R. and Lam, D. Age Distribution Adjustments for English Censuses, 1821 to 1931. *Population Stud.*, November 1983, *37*(3), pp. 445–64. **[G: U.K.]**

Lee, Ronald D. and Bulatao, Rodolfo A. The Demand for Children: A Critical Essay. **In** *Bulatao, R. A. and Lee, R. D., eds., Vol. 1*, 1983, pp. 233–86.

Leppel, Karen. Market and Household Sectors: Is Dual Participation Optimal? *Atlantic Econ. J.*, December 1983, *11*(4), pp. 81–82.

Lesthaeghe, Ron. A Century of Demographic and Cultural Change in Western Europe: An Exploration of Underlying Dimensions. *Population Devel. Rev.*, September 1983, *9*(3), pp. 411–35. **[G: W. Europe]**

Leven, Charles L. Reversing Metropolitan Concentration as an Economic Issue. *J. Econ. Educ.*, Spring 1983, *14*(2), pp. 50–64. **[G: U.S.]**

Lewis, Frank D. Fertility and Savings in the United States: 1830–1900. *J. Polit. Econ.*, October 1983, *91*(5), pp. 825–40. **[G: U.S.]**

Liebermann, Yehoshua. The Economics of *Kethubah* Valuation. *Hist. Polit. Econ.*, Winter 1983, *15*(4), pp. 519–28.

Lindert, Peter H. English Living Standards, Population Growth, and Wrigley-Schofield. *Exploration Econ. Hist.*, April 1983, *20*(2), pp. 131–55. **[G: U.K.]**

Lindert, Peter H. The Changing Economic Costs and Benefits of Having Children. **In** *Bulatao, R. A. and Lee, R. D., eds., Vol. 1*, 1983, pp. 494–516.

Linhart, Sepp. Social Security versus Family Ideology. The State's Reaction to the Consequences of Early Industrialization in Japan. *Rivista Int. Sci. Econ. Com.*, August 1983, *30*(8), pp. 703–15. **[G: Japan]**

Linneman, Peter and Graves, Philip E. Migration and Job Change: A Multinomial Logit Approach. *J. Urban Econ.*, November 1983, *14*(3), pp. 263–79. **[G: U.S.]**

Lundahl, Mats. A Note on Haitian Migration to Cuba, 1890–1934. **In** *Lundahl, M.*, 1983, *1982*, pp. 94–110. **[G: Cuba; Haiti]**

Lundahl, Mats. The State of Spatial Economic Research on Haiti: A Selective Survey. **In** *Lundahl, M.*, 1983, *1980*, pp. 153–70. **[G: Haiti]**

Lundahl, Mats and Vargas, Rosemary. Haitian Migration to the Dominican Republic. **In** *Lundahl, M.*, 1983, pp. 111–150. **[G: Dominican Republic; Haiti]**

MacAndrews, Colin and Yamamoto, Kazumi. Induced and Voluntary Migration in Malaysia: The Federal Land Development Authority Role in Migration since 1957. **In** *Lim, D., ed.*, 1983, *1975*, pp. 125–39. **[G: Malaysia]**

Madden, M. and Batey, P. W. J. Linked Population and Economic Models: Some Methodological Issues in Forecasting, Analysis, and Policy Optimization. *J. Reg. Sci.*, May 1983, *23*(2), pp. 141–64.

Markandya, Anil. Headship Rates and the Household Formation Process in Great Britain. *Appl. Econ.*, December 1983, *15*(6), pp. 821–30. **[G: U.K.]**

Marshall, Adriana and Orlansky, Dora. Inmigración de países limítrofes y demanda de mano de obra en la Argentina, 1940–1980. (With English summary.) *Desarrollo Econ.*, April–June 1983, *23*(89), pp. 35–58. **[G: Argentina]**

Martin, Linda G. and Culter, Suzanne. Mortality Decline and Japanese Family Structure. *Population Devel. Rev.*, December 1983, *9*(4), pp. 633–49. **[G: Japan]**

Martin, Linda G., et al. Co-variates of Child Mortality in the Philippines, Indonesia, and Pakistan: An Analysis Based on Hazard Models. *Population Stud.*, November 1983, *37*(3), pp. 417–32. **[G: Philippines; Indonesia; Pakistan]**

Mason, Karen Oppenheim. Norms Relating to the Desire for Children. **In** *Bulatao, R. A. and Lee, R. D., eds., Vol. 1*, 1983, pp. 388–428. **[G: LDCs; U.S.]**

Masser, Ian. Planning and Migration Research. **In** *Morrison, P. A., ed.*, 1983, pp. 241–60. **[G: Netherlands]**

Matthiessen, Poul Christian. Befolkningssituationen i Europa. (The Demographic Situation in Europe. With English summary.) *Nationaløkon. Tidsskr.*, 1983, *121*(2), pp. 215–29. **[G: W. Europe]**

Mattioli, Elvio and Merlini, Augusto. Alcuni aspetti metodologici nello studio delle migrazioni interne: L'esperienza italiana 1969–1979. (Some Methodological Aspects in the Study of Internal Migrations: The Italian Experience 1969–1979. With English summary.) *Statistica*, April–June 1983, *43*(2), pp. 275–88. **[G: Italy]**

Mauldin, W. Parker. Population Programs and Fertility Regulation. **In** *Bulatao, R. A. and Lee, R. D., eds., Vol. 2*, 1983, pp. 267–94. **[G: LDCs]**

Mauskopf, Josephine. Reproductive Response to Child Mortality: A Maximum Likelihood Estimation Model. *J. Amer. Statist. Assoc.*, June 1983, *78*(382), pp. 238–48. **[G: Brazil]**

McCarthy, Kevin F. California: Ellis Island of the '80s. *Challenge*, July/August 1983, *26*(3), pp. 59–63. **[G: U.S.]**

McClelland, Gary H. Family-Size Desires as Measures of Demand. **In** *Bulatao, R. A. and Lee, R. D., eds.; Vol. 1,* 1983, pp. 288–342. **[G: LDCs; U.S.; Japan]**

McDonald, John. The Emergence of Countercyclical U.S. Fertility: A Reassessment of the Evidence. *J. Macroecon.,* Fall 1983, *5* (4), pp. 421–36. **[G: U.S.]**

McIntosh, James. Reproductive Behaviour in Peasant Societies: A Theoretical and Empirical Analysis. *Rev. Econ. Stud.,* January 1983, *50* (1), pp. 133–42. **[G: Bangladesh]**

McNicoll, Geoffrey and Nag, Moni. Population Growth: Current Issues and Strategies. **In** *Todaro, M. P., ed.,* 1983, *1982,* pp. 121–35. **[G: Global]**

Ménard, Claude. Régulation et direction le projet économique de Malthus. (With English summary.) *Revue Écon. Polit.,* March–April 1983, *93* (2), pp. 233–47.

Meyering, Anne C. Did Capitalism Lead to the Decline of the Peasantry? The Case of the French Combraille. *J. Econ. Hist.,* March 1983, *43* (1), pp. 121–28. **[G: France]**

Micheli, Giuseppe A. Le trappole del controllo ottimo parametrico della popolazione. (The Pitfalls of the Optimal Control of Population. With English summary.) *Giorn. Econ.,* May-June 1983, *42* (5–6), pp. 321–46. **[G: Italy]**

Miranda, Armindo. The Demographic Perspective. **In** *Parkinson, J. R., ed.,* 1983, pp. 40–51. **[G: Selected Countries]**

Mitra, S. A Simple Model for Linking Life Tables by Survival–Mortality Ratios. *Demography,* May 1983, *20* (2), pp. 227–34. **[G: U.S.]**

Mitra, S. Generalization of the Immigration and the Stable Population Model. *Demography,* February 1983, *20* (1), pp. 111–15. **[G: U.S.]**

Mitra, Tapan. Limits on Population Growth under Exhaustible Resource Constraints. *Int. Econ. Rev.,* February 1983, *24* (1), pp. 155–68.

Mokyr, Joel. Three Centuries of Population Change. *Econ. Develop. Cult. Change,* October 1983, *32* (1), pp. 183–92. **[G: U.K.]**

Morrill, Richard L. Migration Data: A Comment [Data Availability versus Data Needs for Analyzing the Determinants and Consequences of Internal Migration: An Evaluation of U.S. Survey Data] [Internal Migration in the United States: An Evaluation of Federal Data]. *Rev. Public Data Use (See J. Econ. Soc. Meas. after 4/85),* December 1983, *11* (4), pp. 345–47. **[G: U.S.]**

Morrison, Malcolm H. The Aging of the U.S. Population: Human Resource Implications. *Mon. Lab. Rev.,* May 1983, *106* (5), pp. 13–19. **[G: U.S.]**

Mott, Frank L. and Shapiro, David. Complementarity of Work and Fertility among Young American Mothers. *Population Stud.,* July 1983, *37* (2), pp. 239–52. **[G: U.S.]**

Mueller, Eva and Short, Kathleen. Effects of Income and Wealth on the Demand for Children. **In** *Bulatao, R. A. and Lee, R. D., eds., Vol. 1,* 1983, pp. 590–642.

Muthiah, A. and Jones, G. W. Fertility Trends among Overseas Indian Populations. *Population Stud.,* July 1983, *37* (2), pp. 273–99. **[G: India]**

Nadarajah, T. The Transition from Higher Female to Higher Male Mortality in Sri Lanka. *Population Devel. Rev.,* June 1983, *9* (2), pp. 317–25. **[G: Sri Lanka]**

Nag, Moni. The Impact of Sociocultural Factors on Breastfeeding and Sexual Behavior. **In** *Bulatao, R. A. and Lee, R. D., eds., Vol. 1,* 1983, pp. 163–98. **[G: LDCs]**

Nakosteen, Robert A. U.S. and Canadian Migration Data: A Comment. *Rev. Public Data Use (See J. Econ. Soc. Meas. after 4/85),* March 1983, *11* (1), pp. 69–71. **[G: U.S.; Canada]**

Namboodiri, N. Krishnan. Sequential Fertility Decision Making and the Life Course. **In** *Bulatao, R. A. and Lee, R. D., eds., Vol. 2,* 1983, pp. 444–72.

Nelson, Joan M. Population Redistribution Policies and Migrants' Choices. **In** *Morrison, P. A., ed.,* 1983, pp. 281–312. **[G: LDCs]**

Newman, John L. Economic Analyses of the Spacing of Births. *Amer. Econ. Rev.,* May 1983, *73* (2), pp. 33–37.

Norris, Douglas. New Sources of Canadian Small Area Migration Data. *Rev. Public Data Use (See J. Econ. Soc. Meas. after 4/85),* March 1983, *11* (1), pp. 11–25. **[G: Canada]**

Nour, El-Sayed. On the Estimation of the Distribution of Desired Family Size for a Synthetic Cohort. *Population Stud.,* July 1983, *37* (2), pp. 315–22.

Nugent, Jeffrey B. and Gillaspy, R. Thomas. Old Age Pensions and Fertility in Rural Areas of Less Developed Countries: Some Evidence from Mexico. *Econ. Develop. Cult. Change,* July 1983, *31* (4), pp. 809–29. **[G: Mexico]**

O'Connell, Martin and Rogers, Carolyn C. Assessing Cohort Birth Expectations Data from the Current Population Survey, 1971–1981. *Demography,* August 1983, *20* (3), pp. 369–84. **[G: U.S.]**

Ó Gráda, Cormac. Across the Briny Ocean: Some Thoughts on Irish Emigration to America, 1800–1850. **In** *Devine, T. M. and Dickson, D., eds.,* 1983, pp. 118–30. **[G: U.S.; Ireland]**

Oberai, A. S. An Overview of Migration-influencing Policies and Programmes. **In** *Oberai, A. S., ed.,* 1983, pp. 11–26.

Oberai, A. S. State Policies and Internal Migration: Introduction. **In** *Oberai, A. S., ed.,* 1983, pp. 1–10.

Oest, Wolfgang. National Models as a Tool for Analysing Future Manpower Demand and Supply. **In** *Streeten, P. and Maier, H., eds.,* 1983, pp. 443–56. **[G: W. Germany]**

Ofer, Gur and Vinokur, Aaron. The Labor-Force Participation of Married Women in the Soviet Union: A Household Cross-Section Analysis. *J. Compar. Econ.,* June 1983, *7* (2), pp. 158–76. **[G: U.S.S.R.]**

Ojeda, Gabriel C., et al. A Comparison of the Cost-effectiveness of Profamilia's Service Programs in Colombia, 1977–80. **In** *Sirageldin, I.; Salkever, D. and Osborn, R. W., eds.,* 1983, pp. 434–57. **[G: Colombia]**

Olney, Martha L. Fertility and the Standard of Living in Early Modern England: In Consideration of Wrigley and Schofield. *J. Econ. Hist.,* March 1983, *43* (1), pp. 71–77. **[G: U.K.]**

Olsen, Randall J. Mortality Rates, Mortality Events,

and the Number of Births. *Amer. Econ. Rev.*, May 1983, *73*(2), pp. 29–32. **[G: Malaysia]**

Olsen, Randall J. and Wolpin, Kenneth I. The Impact of Exogenous Child Mortality on Fertility: A Waiting Time Regression with Dynamic Regressors. *Econometrica*, May, 1983, *51*(3), pp. 731–49. **[G: Malaysia]**

Oppong, Christine. Women's Roles, Opportunity Costs, and Fertility. **In** *Bulatao, R. A. and Lee, R. D., eds., Vol. 1,* 1983, pp. 547–89.

Oshima, Harry T. The Industrial and Demographic Transitions in East Asia. *Population Devel. Rev.*, December 1983, *9*(4), pp. 583–607. **[G: E. Asia]**

Ouellet, Fernand. L'accroissement naturel de la population catholique québécoise avant 1850: aperçus historiographiques et quantitatifs. (The Natural Increase of the Roman Catholic Quebec Population before 1850: Historiographical and Quantitative Snapshots. With English summary.) *L'Actual. Econ.*, September 1983, *59*(3), pp. 402–22. **[G: Canada]**

Pampel, Fred C. Changes in the Propensity to Live Alone: Evidence from Consecutive Cross-Sectional Surveys, 1960–1976. *Demography*, November 1983, *20*(4), pp. 433–47. **[G: U.S.]**

Pantelides, Edith Alejandra. La transición demográfica argentina: un modelo no ortodoxo. (With English summary.) *Desarrollo Econ.*, January–March 1983, *22*(88), pp. 511–34. **[G: Argentina]**

Papademetriou, Demetrios G. United States Immigration Policy at the Crossroads. **In** *Piper, D. C. and Terchek, R. J., eds.,* 1983, pp. 97–117. **[G: U.S.]**

Paquet, Gilles and Smith, Wayne R. L'émigration des Canadiens français vers les États-Unis, 1790–1940; problématique et coups de sonde. (The Emigration of French Canadians to the United States, 1790–1940: A Conceptual Framework and Some Quantitative Guesstimates. With English summary.) *L'Actual. Econ.*, September 1983, *59*(3), pp. 423–53. **[G: Canada; U.S.]**

Park, Chai Bin. Preference for Sons, Family Size, and Sex Ratio: An Empirical Study in Korea. *Demography*, August 1983, *20*(3), pp. 333–52. **[G: S. Korea]**

Parker, Robert L. and Sarma, R. S. S. Efficiency and Equity of Project Services. **In** *Taylor, C. E., et al.,* 1983, pp. 191–213. **[G: India]**

Parker, Robert L., et al. Determinants of the Use of Family Planning. **In** *Taylor, C. E., et al.,* 1983, pp. 129–53. **[G: India]**

Parlange, J. Y.; Guilfoyle, M. J. and Rickson, R. E. Mortality Levels and Family Fertility Goals. *Demography*, November 1983, *20*(4), pp. 535–40.

Parr, John B. and Jones, Colin. City Size Distributions and Urban Density Functions: Some Interrelationships. *J. Reg. Sci.*, August 1983, *23*(3), pp. 283–307. **[G: Selected MDCs]**

Pérez-Sainz, J. P. Transmigration and Accumulation in Indonesia. **In** *Oberai, A. S., ed.,* 1983, pp. 183–250. **[G: Indonesia]**

Perlman, Mark. Human Resources and Population Growth. **In** *Streeten, P. and Maier, H., eds.,* 1983, pp. 167–80. **[G: OECD]**

Petersen, William. Thoughts on Writing a Dictionary of Demography. *Population Devel. Rev.*, December 1983, *9*(4), pp. 677–87.

Pickles, Andrew R. The Analysis of Residence Histories and Other Longitudinal Panel Data: A Continuous Time Mixed Markov Renewal Model Incorporating Exogeneous Variables. *Reg. Sci. Urban Econ.*, May 1983, *13*(2), pp. 271–85. **[G: U.K.]**

Plaut, Steven E. The Economics of Population Dispersal Policy. *Urban Stud.*, August 1983, *20*(3), pp. 353–57. **[G: Israel]**

Poffenberger, Mark. Toward a New Understanding of Population Change in Bali. *Population Stud.*, March 1983, *37*(1), pp. 43–59. **[G: Indonesia]**

Potter, Joseph E. Effects of Societal and Community Institutions on Fertility. **In** *Bulatao, R. A. and Lee, R. D., eds., Vol. 2,* 1983, pp. 627–65.

Powell, Alan A. Aspects of the Design of Bachuroo, an Economic–Demographic Model of Labor Supply. **In** *Kelley, A. C.; Sanderson, W. C. and Williamson, J. G., eds.,* 1983, pp. 277–300. **[G: Australia]**

Preston, Samuel H. An Integrated System for Demographic Estimation from Two Age Distributions. *Demography*, May 1983, *20*(2), pp. 213–26. **[G: India; S. Korea]**

Preston, Samuel H. and Bennett, N. G. A Census-based Method for Estimating Adult Mortality. *Population Stud.*, March 1983, *37*(1), pp. 91–104. **[G: Sweden; India; S. Korea]**

Pullum, Thomas W. Correlates of Family-Size Desires. **In** *Bulatao, R. A. and Lee, R. D., eds., Vol. 1,* 1983, pp. 344–68. **[G: LDCs]**

Ranney, Susan and Kossoudji, Sherrie. Profiles of Temporary Mexican Labor Migrants to the United States. *Population Devel. Rev.*, September 1983, *9*(3), pp. 475–93. **[G: U.S.; Mexico]**

Ray, Ranjan. Measuring the Costs of Children: An Alternative Approach. *J. Public Econ.*, October 1983, *22*(1), pp. 89–102. **[G: U.K.]**

Reaume, David M. Migration and the Dynamic Stability of Regional Econometric Models. *Econ. Inquiry*, April 1983, *21*(2), pp. 281–93. **[G: U.S.]**

Reinke, William A. Cost-effectiveness with Equity: A Review of Narangwal (India) Project Experiences. **In** *Sirageldin, I.; Salkever, D. and Osborn, R. W., eds.,* 1983, pp. 319–50. **[G: India]**

Reinke, William A. The Lampang (Thailand) Health Development Project: Proposed Methodology for Integrated Cost/Task Analysis. **In** *Sirageldin, I.; Salkever, D. and Osborn, R. W., eds.,* 1983, pp. 351–90. **[G: Thailand]**

Reinke, William A. and Parker, Robert L. Relations between the Use of Health Services and Family Planning. **In** *Taylor, C. E., et al.,* 1983, pp. 109–28. **[G: India]**

Repetto, Robert and Holmes, Thomas. The Role of Population in Resource Depletion in Developing Countries. *Population Devel. Rev.*, December 1983, *9*(4), pp. 609–32. **[G: LDCs]**

Retherford, Robert D. and Palmore, James A. Diffusion Process Affecting Fertility Regulation. **In** *Bulatao, R. A. and Lee, R. D., eds., Vol. 2,* 1983, pp. 295–339.

Reubens, Edwin P. International Migration Models and Policies. *Amer. Econ. Rev.*, May 1983, *73*(2), pp. 178–82.

Rey, Guido M. Italy of Censuses. *Rev. Econ. Cond. Italy,* June 1983, (2), pp. 193–221. **[G: Italy]**

Riabushkin, T. and Galetskaia, R. The Dynamics and Structure of the Population of the U.S.S.R. over the Last Sixty Years. *Prob. Econ.,* June 1983, *26*(2), pp. 61–77. **[G: U.S.S.R.]**

Ricci, Renzo. Le esigenze di informazioni dal censimento demografico per la politica della casa. (Information's Requirement in the Census of Population for a Policy of Housing. With English summary.) *Statistica,* April–June 1983, *43*(2), pp. 251–58. **[G: Italy]**

Richards, Toni. Statistical Studies of Aggregate Fertility Change: Time Series of Cross Sections. **In** *Bulatao, R. A. and Lee, R. D., eds., Vol. 2,* 1983, pp. 696–736. **[G: Taiwan]**

Richards, Toni. Weather, Nutrition, and the Economy: Short-Run Fluctuations in Births, Deaths, and Marriages, France, 1740–1909. *Demography,* May 1983, *20*(2), pp. 197–212. **[G: France]**

Rider, Rowland V. and Tayback, Matthew. A Note Concerning the Couple-Years-Protection (CYP) Index Adjusted for Age. **In** *Sirageldin, I.; Salkever, D. and Osborn, R. W., eds.,* 1983, pp. 217–22.

Rindfuss, Ronald R. and Morgan, S. Philip. Marriage, Sex, and the First Birth Interval: The Quiet Revolution in Asia. *Population Devel. Rev.,* June 1983, *9*(2), pp. 259–78. **[G: S. Korea; Malaysia; Taiwan]**

Rindfuss, Ronald R.; Parnell, A. and Hirschman, Charles. The Timing of Entry into Motherhood in Asia: A Comparative Perspective. *Population Stud.,* July 1983, *37*(2), pp. 253–72. **[G: Asia]**

Rivera-Batiz, Francisco L. The Economics of the "To and Fro" Migrant: Some Welfare-Theoretical Considerations. *Scand. J. Econ.,* 1983, *85*(3), pp. 403–13.

Rivera-Batiz, Francisco L. Trade Theory, Distribution of Income, and Immigration. *Amer. Econ. Rev.,* May 1983, *73*(2), pp. 183–87.

Rodgers, Gerry. Population Growth, Inequality and Poverty. *Int. Lab. Rev.,* July–August 1983, *122*(4), pp. 443–60. **[G: LDCs]**

Rosenhouse-Persson, Sandra and Sabagh, Georges. Attitudes toward Abortion among Catholic Mexican-American Women: The Effect of Religiosity and Education. *Demography,* February 1983, *20*(1), pp. 87–98.

Rosenwaike, Ira. Mortality among the Puerto Rican Born in New York City. *Soc. Sci. Quart.,* June 1983, *64*(2), pp. 375–85. **[G: U.S.]**

Rosenwaike, Ira and Logue, Barbara. Accuracy of Death Certificate Ages for the Extreme Aged. *Demography,* November 1983, *20*(4), pp. 569–85. **[G: U.S.]**

Rosenzweig, Mark R. and Schultz, T. Paul. Consumer Demand and Household Production: The Relationship between Fertility and Child Mortality. *Amer. Econ. Rev.,* May 1983, *73*(2), pp. 38–42. **[G: U.S.]**

Rosenzweig, Mark R. and Schultz, T. Paul. Estimating a Household Production Function: Heterogeneity, the Demand for Health Inputs, and Their Effects on Birth Weight. *J. Polit. Econ.,* October 1983, *91*(5), pp. 723–46. **[G: U.S.]**

Ross, John A. Birth Control Methods and Their Effects on Fertility. **In** *Bulatao, R. A. and Lee, R. D., eds., Vol. 2,* 1983, pp. 54–88. **[G: LDCs]**

Rossi, Fiorenzo. Il controllo dei dati nel censimento della popolazione del 1981 in Italia. (The Post-Enumeration Surveys of the 1981 Population Census of Italy. With English summary.) *Statistica,* October–December 1983, *43*(4), pp. 661–72. **[G: Italy]**

Ryder, Norman B. Cohort and Period Measures of Changing Fertility. **In** *Bulatao, R. A. and Lee, R. D., eds., Vol. 2,* 1983, pp. 737–56. **[G: U.S.; Colombia]**

Sain, Gustavo E.; Martin, Philip L. and Paris, Quirino. A Regional Analysis of Illegal Aliens. *Growth Change,* January 1983, *14*(1), pp. 27–31. **[G: U.S.]**

Salkever, David S. and Sirageldin, Ismail. Cost-benefit and Cost-effectiveness Analysis in Population Programs: Its Role in Program Planning and Management. **In** *Sirageldin, I.; Salkever, D. and Osborn, R. W., eds.,* 1983, pp. 3–102.

Sanderson, Warren C. A Two-Sex General Equilibrium Marriage Model. **In** *Kelley, A. C.; Sanderson, W. C. and Williamson, J. G., eds.,* 1983, pp. 301–16. **[G: Austria]**

Sarma, R. S. S. and Faruqee, Rashid. The Use of Family Planning. **In** *Taylor, C. E., et al.,* 1983, pp. 59–84. **[G: India]**

Satia, J. K. Experiences in the Indian Family Planning Program with Cost-benefit and Cost-effectiveness Analysis. **In** *Sirageldin, I.; Salkever, D. and Osborn, R. W., eds.,* 1983, pp. 269–318. **[G: India]**

Schearer, S. Bruce. Monetary and Health Costs of Contraception. **In** *Bulatao, R. A. and Lee, R. D., eds., Vol. 2,* 1983, pp. 89–150. **[G: LDCs]**

Schmähl, Winfried. Auswirkungen von Veränderungen der Altersstruktur der Bevölkerung auf die Finanzsituation der gesetzlichen Krankenversicherung im Vergleich zur gesetzlichen Rentenversicherung—Eine modelltheoretische Analyse. (A Comparison of the Effects of a Changing Age Structure on the Financing of Social Health Insurance and on That of the Social Retirement System—A Theoretical Analysis. With English summary.) *Konjunkturpolitik,* 1983, *29*(2), pp. 100–20. **[G: W. Germany]**

Schmidt, Robert M. Incorporating Demography into General Equilibrium Modeling. **In** *Kelley, A. C.; Sanderson, W. C. and Williamson, J. G., eds.,* 1983, pp. 317–37.

Schoen, Robert. Measuring the Tightness of a Marriage Squeeze. *Demography,* February 1983, *20*(1), pp. 61–78. **[G: U.S.]**

Schroeder, Esther C. and Pittenger, Donald B. Improving the Accuracy of Migration Age Detail in Multiple-Area Population Forecasts. *Demography,* May 1983, *20*(2), pp. 235–48. **[G: U.S.]**

Schutjer, Wayne A.; Stokes, C. Shannon and Poindexter, John R. Farm Size, Land Ownership, and Fertility in Rural Egypt. *Land Econ.,* November 1983, *59*(4), pp. 393–403. **[G: Egypt]**

Schweitzer, Walter. Analyse und Prognose der Binnenwanderungen in der Bundesrepublik Deutschland mit Markov-Modellen. (Analysis and Forecast of Internal Migrations within the Federal Republic of Germany Using Markov Models. With English summary.) *Ifo-Studien*, 1983, *29*(3), pp. 217–41. **[G: W. Germany]**

Seidman, Laurence S. Social Security and Demographics in a Life Cycle Growth Model. *Nat. Tax J.*, June 1983, *36*(2), pp. 213–24. **[G: U.S.]**

Sell, Ralph R. Analyzing Migration Decisions: The First Step—Whose Decision? *Demography*, August 1983, *20*(3), pp. 299–311. **[G: U.S.]**

Shields, Michael P. and Tsui, Steve W. The Probability of Another Child in Costa Rica. *Econ. Develop. Cult. Change*, July 1983, *31*(4), pp. 787–807. **[G: Costa Rica]**

Shoup, Carl S. Collective Goods and Population Growth. **In** *Biehl, D.; Roskamp, K. W. and Stolper, W. F., eds.*, 1983, pp. 55–68.

Siegers, Jacques J. An Economic–Demographic Ten-Equation Model. *De Economist*, 1983, *131* (3), pp. 400–443. **[G: Netherlands]**

Silvers, Arthur L. and Crosson, Pierre. Urban Bound Migration and Rural Investment: The Case of Mexico. *J. Reg. Sci.*, February 1983, *23*(1), pp. 33–47. **[G: Mexico]**

Simmons, Alan B. A Review and Evaluation of Attempts to Constrain Migration to Selected Urban Centres and Regions. **In** *Todaro, M. P., ed.*, 1983, *1981*, pp. 213–33. **[G: Selected Countries]**

Simmons, Alan B. Social Inequality and the Demographic Transition. **In** *Ritter, A. R. M. and Pollock, D. H., eds.*, 1983, pp. 85–110. **[G: Latin America; Sweden]**

Simmons, George B. On Family Planning Program Efficiency and Management. **In** *Sirageldin, I.; Salkever, D. and Osborn, R. W., eds.*, 1983, pp. 141–65.

Simmons, Ruth; Ness, Gayl D. and Simmons, George B. On the Institutional Analysis of Population Programs. *Population Devel. Rev.*, September 1983, *9*(3), pp. 457–74.

Simon, Julian L. The Present Value of Population Growth in the Western World. *Population Stud.*, March 1983, *37*(1), pp. 5–21.

Simon, Julian L.; Reisler, William and Gobin, Roy. 'Population Pressure' on the Land: Analysis of Trends Past and Future. *World Devel.*, September 1983, *11*(9), pp. 825–34. **[G: Global]**

Sirageldin, Ismail. Some Issues in Middle Eastern International Migration. *Pakistan Devel. Rev.*, Winter 1983, *22*(4), pp. 217–37. **[G: Middle East; Kuwait; Egypt]**

Sirageldin, Ismail; Salkever, David S. and Osborn, Richard W. Evaluating Population Programs: Introduction and Summary. **In** *Sirageldin, I.; Salkever, D. and Osborn, R. W., eds.*, 1983, pp. xiii–xxxi.

Sloane, Douglas M. and Lee, Che-Fu. Sex of Previous Children and Intentions for Further Births in the United States, 1965–1976. *Demography*, August 1983, *20*(3), pp. 353–67. **[G: U.S.]**

Smith, Peter C. The Impact of Age at Marriage and Proportions Marrying on Fertility. **In** *Bulatao, R. A. and Lee, R. D., eds., Vol. 2*, 1983, pp. 473–531.

Smith, Richard M. On Putting the Child before the Marriage: Reply to Birdsall [Fertility, Economy, and Household Formation in England over Three Centuries]. *Population Devel. Rev.*, March 1983, *9*(1), pp. 124–35. **[G: U.K.]**

Smith, Stanley K. and Lewis, Bart B. Some New Techniques for Applying the Housing Unit Method of Local Population Estimation: Further Evidence. *Demography*, August 1983, *20*(3), pp. 407–13. **[G: U.S.]**

Sofranko, Andrew J. and Fliegel, Frederick C. Rural-to-Rural Migrants: The Neglected Component of Rural Population Growth. *Growth Change*, April 1983, *14*(2), pp. 42–49. **[G: U.S.]**

Soon, Lee-Ying. Migrant-Native Socio-economic Differences in a Major Metropolitan Area of Peninsular Malaysia: Its Implications on Migration Policy in a Multi-ethnic Society. **In** *Lim, D., ed.*, 1983, *1978*, pp. 140–50. **[G: Malaysia]**

Speare, Alden, Jr. Methods of Projecting Rural-to-Urban Migration, with Reference to Southeast Asia. **In** *Morrison, P. A., ed.*, 1983, pp. 261–78. **[G: Southeast Asia]**

Speidel, J. Joseph. Cost Implications of Population Stabilization. **In** *Sirageldin, I.; Salkever, D. and Osborn, R. W., eds.*, 1983, pp. 176–96. **[G: Selected Countries]**

Spengler, Joseph. Knut Wicksell, Father of the Optimum. *Atlantic Econ. J.*, December 1983, *11*(4), pp. 1–5.

Stahl, Konrad. A Note on the Microeconomics of Migration. *J. Urban Econ.*, November 1983, *14*(3), pp. 318–26.

Standing, Guy. Women's Work Activity and Fertility. **In** *Bulatao, R. A. and Lee, R. D., eds., Vol. 1*, 1983, pp. 517–46.

Stark, Oded. A Note on Modelling Labour Migration in LDCs. *J. Devel. Stud.*, July 1983, *19*(4), pp. 539–43.

Steckel, Richard H. The Economic Foundations of East-West Migration during the 19th Century. *Exploration Econ. Hist.*, January 1983, *20*(1), pp. 14–36. **[G: U.S.]**

Sternlieb, George and Hughes, James W. Energy Constraints and Development Patterns in the 1980s. **In** *Carr, J. H. and Duensing, E. E., eds.*, 1983, *1982*, pp. 51–66. **[G: U.S.]**

Stokes, C. Shannon and Hsieh, Yeu-Sheng. Female Employment and Reproductive Behavior in Taiwan, 1980. *Demography*, August 1983, *20*(3), pp. 313–31. **[G: Taiwan]**

Stolnitz, George J. Three to Five Main Challenges to Demographic Research. *Demography*, November 1983, *20*(4), pp. 415–32.

Stoto, Michael A. The Accuracy of Population Projections. *J. Amer. Statist. Assoc.*, March 1983, *78*(381), pp. 13–20. **[G: U.S.]**

Strachan, A. J. Return Migration to Guyana. *Soc. Econ. Stud.*, September 1983, *32*(3), pp. 121–42. **[G: Guyana]**

Stycos, J. Mayone. The Timing of Spanish Marriages: A Socio-Statistical Study. *Population Stud.*, July 1983, *37*(2), pp. 227–38. **[G: Spain]**

Süssmilch, Johann Peter. On Removing Obstacles to Population Growth. *Population Devel. Rev.*, September 1983, *9*(3), pp. 521–29. **[G: Germany]**

Swidler, Steve. An Empirical Test of the Effect of Social Security on Fertility in the United States.

Amer. Econ., Fall 1983, *27*(2), pp. 50–57. **[G: U.S.]**

Taylor, Carl E. Background, Design, and Policy Issues. **In** *Taylor, C. E., et al.*, 1983, pp. 3–32. **[G: India]**

Taylor, Carl E., et al. Main Research Findings on Policy Issues. **In** *Taylor, C. E., et al.*, 1983, pp. 33–56. **[G: India]**

Thomas, Albert. On the International Control of Migration. *Population Devel. Rev.*, December 1983, *9*(4), pp. 703–11. **[G: Global]**

Thomson, Elizabeth. Individual and Couple Utility of Children. *Demography*, November 1983, *20*(4), pp. 507–18. **[G: U.S.]**

Townsend, John, et al. Cost-effectiveness of Family Planning Services in the Sinaps Primary Health Care Program in Guatemala. **In** *Sirageldin, I.; Salkever, D. and Osborn, R. W., eds.*, 1983, pp. 458–75. **[G: Guatemala]**

Trebici, Vl. The Stable Population: Mathematical Model and Applications to the Population of Romania. *Econ. Computat. Cybern. Stud. Res.*, 1983, *18*(4), pp. 67–78. **[G: Romania]**

Trussell, James and Bloom, David E. Estimating the Co-variates of Age at Marriage and First Birth. *Population Stud.*, November 1983, *37*(3), pp. 403–16. **[G: Colombia]**

Trussell, James and Hammerslough, Charles. A Hazards-Model Analysis of the Covariates of Infant and Child Mortality in Sri Lanka. *Demography*, February 1983, *20*(1), pp. 1–26. **[G: Sri Lanka]**

Trussell, James and Olsen, Randall J. Evaluation of the Olson Technique for Estimating the Fertility Response to Child Mortality. *Demography*, August 1983, *20*(3), pp. 391–405. **[G: U.S.]**

Udry, J. Richard. Do Couples Make Fertility Plans One Birth at a Time? *Demography*, May 1983, *20*(2), pp. 117–28. **[G: U.S.]**

Vicary, Simon J. R. Endogenous Population Growth in an Overlapping Generations Model with International Lending and Borrowing. *Bull. Econ. Res.*, May 1983, *35*(1), pp. 1–24. **[G: LDCs]**

Vining, Daniel R., Jr. Illegitimacy and Public Policy. *Population Devel. Rev.*, March 1983, *9*(1), pp. 105–10. **[G: U.S.]**

Visaria, Leela and Visaria, Pravin. Population (1757–1947). **In** *Kumar, D., ed.*, 1983, pp. 463–532. **[G: India]**

Volsky, Victor. Latin America: Demographic Problems and Socio-economic Development. **In** *Urquidi, V. L. and Reyes, S. T., eds.*, 1983, pp. 299–310. **[G: Latin America]**

Wagner, Janet and Hanna, Sherman. The Effectiveness of Family Life Cycle Variables in Consumer Expenditure Research. *J. Cons. Res.*, December 1983, *10*(3), pp. 281–91. **[G: U.S.]**

Weatherby, Norman L.; Nam, Charles B. and Isaac, Larry W. Development, Inequality, Health Care, and Mortality at the Older Ages: A Cross-National Analysis. *Demography*, February 1983, *20*(1), pp. 27–43. **[G: Selected MDCs; Selected LDCs]**

Westoff, Charles F. Fertility Decline in the West: Causes and Prospects. *Population Devel. Rev.*, March 1983, *9*(1), pp. 99–104. **[G: U.S.; Europe]**

Whitney, Vincent Heath. Planning for Migration and Urbanization: Some Issues and Options for Policymakers and Planners. **In** *Morrison, P. A., ed.*, 1983, pp. 325–38. **[G: LDCs]**

Wilensky, Gail R. and Cafferata, Gail Lee. Women and the Use of Health Services. *Amer. Econ. Rev.*, May 1983, *73*(2), pp. 128–33. **[G: U.S.]**

Wolfe, John R. Perceived Longevity and Early Retirement. *Rev. Econ. Statist.*, November 1983, *65*(4), pp. 544–51. **[G: U.S.]**

Woods, R. and Smith, C. W. The Decline of Marital Fertility in the Late Nineteenth Century: The Case of England and Wales. *Population Stud.*, July 1983, *37*(2), pp. 207–25. **[G: U.K.]**

Wrigley, E. A. and Schofield, R. S. English Population History from Family Reconstitution: Summary Results 1600–1799. *Population Stud.*, July 1983, *37*(2), pp. 157–84. **[G: U.K.]**

Yotopoulos, Pan A. A Micro Economic-Demographic Model of the Agricultural Household in the Philippines. *Food Res. Inst. Stud.*, 1983, *19*(1), pp. 1–24. **[G: Philippines]**

Zelinsky, Wilbur. The Impasse in Migration Theory: A Sketch Map for Potential Escapees. **In** *Morrison, P. A., ed.*, 1983, pp. 19–46. **[G: LDCs; MDCs]**

850 Human Capital; Value of Human Life

851 Human Capital; Value of Human Life

8510 Human Capital; Value of Human Life

Adelman, Irma and Hihn, Jairus M. The Political Economy of Investment in Human Capital. **In** *Streeten, P. and Maier, H., eds.*, 1983, pp. 117–46. **[G: LDCs]**

Antonelli, Gilberto. Income Distribution and Labour Factor Quality: Models and Applications at a Regional Level. **In** *Weisbrod, B. and Hughes, H., eds.*, 1983, pp. 167–77. **[G: Italy]**

Barrett, Nancy S. How the Study of Women has Restructured the Discipline of Economics. **In** *Langland, E. and Gove, W., eds.*, 1983, pp. 101–09.

Bassett, W. Bruce. Does It Pay to Learn? *Labor Hist.*, Spring 1983, *24*(2), pp. 254–58. **[G: U.S.]**

Beckerman, Wilfred. Human Resources: Are They Worth Preserving? **In** *Streeten, P. and Maier, H., eds.*, 1983, pp. 8–28.

Behrman, Jere R. and Birdsall, Nancy. The Quality of Schooling: Quantity Alone is Misleading. *Amer. Econ. Rev.*, December 1983, *73*(5), pp. 928–46. **[G: Brazil]**

Behrman, Jere R. and Wolfe, Barbara L. Women's Labour Force Participation and Earnings Determinants in a Developing Country. **In** *Urquidi, V. L. and Reyes, S. T., eds.*, 1983, pp. 266–76. **[G: Nicaragua]**

Bellante, Don. A Subjectivist Essay on Modern Labor Economics. *Managerial Dec. Econ.*, December 1983, *4*(4), pp. 234–43.

Berger, Mark C. Changes in Labor Force Composition and Male Earnings: A Production Approach. *J. Human Res.*, Spring 1983, *18*(2), pp. 177–96. **[G: U.S.]**

Berry, Albert. Predicting Income Distribution in

Latin America during the 1980s. **In** *Ritter, A. R. M. and Pollock, D. H., eds.*, 1983, pp. 57–84. **[G: Latin America]**

Bhagwati, Jagdish N. and Srinivasan, T. N. Education in a 'Job Ladder' Model and the Fairness-in-Hiring Rule. **In** *Bhagwati, J. N., Vol. 2*, 1983, *1977*, pp. 142–63.

Blakemore, Arthur E. and Low, Stuart A. A Simultaneous Determination of Post-High School Education Choice and Labor Supply. *Quart. Rev. Econ. Bus.*, Winter 1983, *23*(4), pp. 81–92. **[G: U.S.]**

Bourguignon, François. The Role of Education in the Urban Labour Market in Developing Countries: The Case of Colombia. **In** *Urquidi, V. L. and Reyes, S. T., eds.*, 1983, pp. 211–35. **[G: Colombia]**

Caire, Guy. Plaidoyer et agenda pour la prise en compte des ressources humaines dans la recherche relative aux pays sous-développés. (Defense and Agenda for Taking Human Resources into Account in Research Regarding Underdeveloped Countries. With English summary.) *Consommation*, October–December 1983, *30*(4), pp. 3–21.

Carmichael, H. Lorne. Does Rising Productivity Explain Seniority Rules for Layoffs? *Amer. Econ. Rev.*, December 1983, *73*(5), pp. 1127–31.

Carmichael, H. Lorne. Firm-Specific Human Capital and Promotion Ladders. *Bell J. Econ. (See Rand J. Econ. after 4/85)*, Spring 1983, *14*(1), pp. 251–58.

Cervinka, Antonín. Investments That Are Certain to Return. *Czech. Econ. Digest.*, August 1983, (5), pp. 54–60. **[G: Czechoslovakia]**

Chiswick, Barry R. The Earnings and Human Capital of American Jews. *J. Human Res.*, Summer 1983, *18*(3), pp. 313–36. **[G: U.S.]**

Chiswick, Carmel U. Analysis of Earnings from Household Enterprises: Methodology and Application to Thailand. *Rev. Econ. Statist.*, November 1983, *65*(4), pp. 658–62. **[G: Thailand]**

Choudhury, Masudul Alam. How Effective Is Human Resource Planning in Developing the Third World? *METU*, 1983, *10*(3), pp. 249–69. **[G: Libya; Ghana; Gambia]**

Clement, W. From the Human-capital Approach to a Political Economy of Human Resources. **In** *Streeten, P. and Maier, H., eds.*, 1983, pp. 329–44.

Contini, Bruno. Economic Development and Human Resources: Japan's Experience: Comments. **In** *Tsuru, S., ed.*, 1983, pp. 124–28. **[G: MDCs; LDCs]**

Cooke, William N. and Cobern, Morris. Part-time Post-school Investments in Education and Their Impact on Earnings Growth for Engineers. **In** *Weisbrod, B. and Hughes, H., eds.*, 1983, pp. 178–86. **[G: U.S.]**

Corbo, Vittorio and Stelcner, Morton. Earnings Determination and Labour Markets: Gran Santiago, Chile—1978. *J. Devel. Econ.*, February/April 1983, *12*(1/2), pp. 251–66. **[G: Chile]**

Corcoran, Mary; Duncan, Greg J. and Ponza, Michael. A Longitudinal Analysis of White Women's Wages. *J. Human Res.*, Fall 1983, *18*(4), pp. 497–520. **[G: U.S.]**

Corman, Hope. Postsecondary Education Enrollment Responses by Recent High School Graduates and Older Adults. *J. Human Res.*, Spring 1983, *18*(2), pp. 247–67. **[G: U.S.]**

DaVanzo, Julie. Repeat Migration in the United States: Who Moves Back and Who Moves On? *Rev. Econ. Statist.*, November 1983, *65*(4), pp. 552–59. **[G: U.S.]**

Dresch, Stephen P. Education and Lifetime Earnings: The Census Bureau's Misguided Misrepresentations. *Rev. Public Data Use (See J. Econ. Soc. Meas. after 4/85)*, December 1983, *11*(4), pp. 357–60. **[G: U.S.]**

Duncan, Greg J. and Holmlund, Bertil. Was Adam Smith Right after All? Another Test of the Theory of Compensating Wage Differentials. *J. Lab. Econ.*, October 1983, *1*(4), pp. 366–79. **[G: Sweden]**

Eden, Benjamin and Pakes, Ariél. Measuring the Variance-Age Profile of Lifetime Earnings. **In** *Helpman, E.; Razin, A. and Sadka, E., eds.*, 1983, pp. 109–21. **[G: Israel]**

Ehrenhalt, Samuel M. No Golden Age for College Graduates. *Challenge*, July/August 1983, *26*(3), pp. 42–50. **[G: U.S.]**

Filippini, Luigi; Scanlon, J. and Tarantelli, E. Towards a Linear Model of Non-homogeneous Labour. **In** *Streeten, P. and Maier, H., eds.*, 1983, pp. 91–105.

Findlay, Ronald and Kierzkowski, Henryk. International Trade and Human Capital: A Simple General Equilibrium Model. *J. Polit. Econ.*, December 1983, *91*(6), pp. 957–78.

Goldsmith, Art. Short-Run Macroeconomic Consequences of Government-Financed Human Capital Expenditures. *Quart. Rev. Econ. Bus.*, Summer 1983, *23*(2), pp. 89–107. **[G: U.S.]**

Graham, John D. and Vaupel, James W. The Value of Life: What Difference Does It Make? **In** *Zeckhauser, R. J. and Leebaert, D., eds.*, 1983, pp. 176–86. **[G: U.S.]**

Guasch, J. Luis and Sobel, Joel. Breeding and Raiding: A Theory of Strategic Production of Skills. *Europ. Econ. Rev.*, June 1983, *22*(1), pp. 97–115.

Hajpál, Gyula. Valuation of the Economic Role of the Human Factor. *Acta Oecon.*, 1983, *31*(1–2), pp. 23–36.

Heyneman, Stephen P. Improving the Quality of Education in Developing Countries. *Finance Develop.*, March 1983, *20*(1), pp. 18–21. **[G: LDCs]**

Hoffman, Dennis L. and Low, Stuart A. Rationality and the Decision to Invest in Economics. *J. Human Res.*, Fall 1983, *18*(4), pp. 480–96. **[G: U.S.]**

Izraeli, Oded. The Effect of Variations in Cost of Living and City Size on the Rate of Return to Schooling. *Quart. Rev. Econ. Bus.*, Winter 1983, *23*(4), pp. 93–108. **[G: U.S.]**

Jallade, Jean-Pierre. Financing Education for Income Distribution. **In** *Todaro, M. P., ed.*, 1983, *1979*, pp. 276–85. **[G: Brazil; Colombia]**

Jha, S. M. Human Resource Management: Anatomy of Operation. *Econ. Aff.*, July-September 1983, *28*(3), pp. 742–47.

Jorgenson, Dale W. and Pachon, Alvaro. Lifetime Income and Human Capital. **In** *Streeten, P. and Maier, H., eds.*, 1983, pp. 29–90. **[G: U.S.]**

Jorgenson, Dale W. and Pachon, Alvaro. The Accumulation of Human and Non-human Capital. **In** *Modigliani, F. and Hemming, R., eds.*, 1983, pp. 302–50. **[G: U.S.]**

Kasnakoğlu, Zehra and Kiliç, Atilla. Ankara'da gelir farkliliklarini belirleyen etmenler (1977). (Determinants of Income Differentials in Ankara [1977]. With English summary.) *METU*, 1983, *10*(2), pp. 179–98. **[G: Turkey]**

Kenny, Lawrence W. The Accumulation of Human Capital during Marriage by Males. *Econ. Inquiry*, April 1983, *21*(2), pp. 223–31. **[G: U.S.]**

Kovács, János. Labour Planning and Economic Development Strategy. **In** *Streeten, P. and Maier, H., eds.*, 1983, pp. 395–404.

Kubinski, Z. M. Non-growth Paths of Human-capital Accumulation. **In** *Weisbrod, B. and Hughes, H., eds.*, 1983, pp. 187–96.

Lazear, Edward P. Intergenerational Externalities. *Can. J. Econ.*, May 1983, *16*(2), pp. 212–28. **[G: U.S.]**

Leppel, Karen. Market and Household Sectors: Is Dual Participation Optimal? *Atlantic Econ. J.*, December 1983, *11*(4), pp. 81–82.

Levin, Henry M. and Schütze, Hans G. Economic and Political Dimensions of Recurrent Education. **In** *Levin, H. M. and Schütze, H. G., eds.*, 1983, pp. 9–36. **[G: OECD]**

Lewis, W. Arthur. Economic Aspects of Quality in Education. **In** *Lewis, W. A.*, 1983, *1969*, pp. 523–40.

Lewis, W. Arthur. Education and Economic Development. **In** *Lewis, W. A.*, 1983, *1961*, pp. 483–97. **[G: LDCs]**

Lewis, W. Arthur. Education for Scientific Professions in the Poor Countries. **In** *Lewis, W. A.*, 1983, *1962*, pp. 499–507.

Lewis, W. Arthur. Secondary Education and Economic Structure. **In** *Lewis, W. A.*, 1983, *1964*, pp. 509–22. **[G: LDCs]**

Low, Stuart A. and McPheters, Lee R. Wage Differentials and Risk of Death: An Empirical Analysis. *Econ. Inquiry*, April 1983, *21*(2), pp. 271–80. **[G: U.S.]**

Maani, Sholeh. El desempleo en Chile: una estimación de la probabilidad de empleo para varones. (With English summary.) *Cuadernos Econ.*, August 1983, *20*(60), pp. 229–41. **[G: Chile]**

Maier, Harry. Human Resources: Long-run Perspectives: Introduction. **In** *Streeten, P. and Maier, H., eds.*, 1983, pp. 229–34.

Maier, Harry. Innovation and the Better Use of Human Resources. **In** *Streeten, P. and Maier, H., eds.*, 1983, pp. 253–88. **[G: E. Germany]**

Marder, William D. and Hough, Douglas E. Medical Residency as Investment in Human Capital. *J. Human Res.*, Winter 1983, *18*(1), pp. 49–64. **[G: U.S.]**

Martínez, Manuel Silos. Returns to Schooling in the Metropolitan Area of Monterrey: An Analysis of Its Behaviour over Time, 1975–79. **In** *Urquidi, V. L. and Reyes, S. T., eds.*, 1983, pp. 252–65. **[G: Mexico]**

McCabe, Peter J. Optimal Leisure–Effort Choice with Endogenously Determined Earnings. *J. Lab. Econ.*, July 1983, *1*(3), pp. 308–29.

Menchik, Paul L. and David, Martin H. Income Distribution, Lifetime Savings, and Bequests. *Amer. Econ. Rev.*, September 1983, *73*(4), pp. 672–90. **[G: U.S.]**

Mennemeyer, Stephen T. and Gaumer, Gary. Nursing Wages and the Value of Educational Credentials. *J. Human Res.*, Winter 1983, *18*(1), pp. 32–48. **[G: U.S.]**

Merrilees, William J. Alternative Models of Apprentice Recruitment: With Special Reference to the British Engineering Industry. *Appl. Econ.*, February 1983, *15*(1), pp. 1–21. **[G: U.K.]**

Merton, Robert C. On the Role of Social Security as a Means for Efficient Risk Sharing in an Economy Where Human Capital Is Not Tradable. **In** *Bodie, Z. and Shoven, J. B., eds.*, 1983, pp. 325–58. **[G: U.S.]**

Miller, Paul W. Education and the Distribution of Earned Income. **In** *Blandy, R. and Covick, O., eds.*, 1983, pp. 16–36. **[G: Australia]**

Miller, Robert A. and Voltaire, Karl. A Stochastic Analysis of the Tree Paradigm. *J. Econ. Dynam. Control*, December 1983, *6*(4), pp. 371–86.

Mingat, Alain and Eicher, J. C. The Higher Education and Employment Markets in France. **In** *Weisbrod, B. and Hughes, H., eds.*, 1983, pp. 133–46. **[G: France]**

Mulvey, Charles. Restrictive Practices, Training and the Legal Profession in Scotland: A Reply [Rates of Return to the Legal Profession in Scotland]. *Scot. J. Polit. Econ.*, November 1983, *30*(3), pp. 302–03. **[G: U.K.]**

Muzondo, Timothy R. and Pazderka, Bohumir. Income-Enhancing Effects of Professional Licensing Restrictions: A Cross-Section Study of Canadian Data. *Antitrust Bull.*, Summer 1983, *28*(2), pp. 397–415. **[G: Canada]**

Nicholson, J. L. The Whys and Wherefores of Human Resources. **In** *Streeten, P. and Maier, H., eds.*, 1983, pp. 198–208.

Nowak, Margaret J. and Crockett, Geoffrey V. Education, Training & Earnings of Managers: Some Western Australian Evidence. *Australian Bull. Lab.*, March 1983, *9*(2), pp. 131–51. **[G: Australia]**

Olsen, Robert A. The Impact of Inflation on Human Capital as a Diversifiable Asset. *Rev. Bus. Econ. Res.*, Fall 1983, *19*(1), pp. 13–25. **[G: U.S.]**

Onitiri, H. M. A. Economic Development and Human Resources: Japan's Experience: Comments. **In** *Tsuru, S., ed.*, 1983, pp. 120–23. **[G: Japan]**

Prais, S. J. and Wagner, Karin. Some Practical Aspects of Human Capital Investment: Training Standards in Five Occupations in Britain and Germany. *Nat. Inst. Econ. Rev.*, August 1983, (105), pp. 46–65. **[G: U.K.; W. Germany]**

Pudasaini, Som P. The Effects of Education in Agriculture: Evidence from Nepal. *Amer. J. Agr. Econ.*, August 1983, *65*(3), pp. 509–15. **[G: Nepal]**

Quadrio-Curzio, Alberto. Planning Manpower Education and Economic Growth. **In** *Weisbrod, B. and Hughes, H., eds.*, 1983, pp. 197–209.

Raffe, David. Education and Class Inequality in Scotland. **In** *Brown, G. and Cook, R., eds.*, 1983, pp. 190–205. **[G: U.K.]**

Ramos, Joseph. Inversión en capital humano y la oferta de trabajo. (With English summary.) *Cuadernos Econ.*, August 1983, *20*(60), pp. 243–50. **[G: Chile]**

Raymond, Richard and Sesnowitz, Michael. Labor Market Discrimination against Mexican American College Graduates. *Southern Econ. J.*, April 1983, *49*(4), pp. 1122–36. **[G: U.S.]**

Raymond, Richard and Sesnowitz, Michael. The Rate of Return to Mexican Americans and Anglos on an Investment in a College Education. *Econ. Inquiry*, July 1983, *21*(3), pp. 400–411. **[G: U.S.]**

Razavi, Hossein. Optimal Adjustment of Manpower-Requirement Forecasts: A Case Study of Iran. *Math. Soc. Sci.*, December 1983, *6*(3), pp. 315–23. **[G: Iran]**

Ribe, Helena. The Relative Economic Position of Migrants and Natives in Colombia: An Economic Analysis of the 1973 Census Sample. **In** *Urquidi, V. L. and Reyes, S. T., eds.*, 1983, pp. 55–78. **[G: Colombia]**

Riveros, Luis A. El retorno privado y social de la educación en Chile. (With English summary.) *Cuadernos Econ.*, August 1983, *20*(60), pp. 191–210. **[G: Chile]**

Robinson, Warren C. Educational Disinvestment: Who Benefits from Subsidies? Does Anyone? *Policy Rev.*, Fall 1983, (26), pp. 59–64. **[G: U.S.]**

Rosen, Sherwin. A Note on Aggregation of Skills and Labor Quality [Linear Synthesis of Skill Distribution]. *J. Human Res.*, Summer 1983, *18*(3), pp. 425–31. **[G: U.S.]**

Rosen, Sherwin. Specialization and Human Capital. *J. Lab. Econ.*, January 1983, *1*(1), pp. 43–49.

Rosenbrock, H. H. Human Resources and Technology. **In** *Streeten, P. and Maier, H., eds.*, 1983, pp. 345–54.

Roskamp, Karl W. and Neumann, Manfred. Human Capital Formation and Public Finance: A Dynamic Model. **In** *Biehl, D.; Roskamp, K. W. and Stolper, W. F., eds.*, 1983, pp. 207–16.

Sawhill, Isabel V. Human Resources. **In** *Miller, G. W., ed.*, 1983, pp. 100–24. **[G: U.S.]**

Selleck, Laura. Jobs for University Graduates: Planning or Choice? *Can. Public Policy*, March 1983, *9*(1), pp. 94–104. **[G: Canada]**

Selowsky, Marcelo. Nutrition, Health and Education: The Economic Significance of Complementarities at Early Ages. **In** *Streeten, P. and Maier, H., eds.*, 1983, pp. 181–97. **[G: Columbia]**

Sheshinski, Eytan and Weiss, Yoram. Inequality within and between Families. **In** *Helpman, E.; Razin, A. and Sadka, E., eds.*, 1983, pp. 255–77.

Simmons, John. Education for Development, Reconsidered. **In** *Todaro, M. P., ed.*, 1983, *1979*, pp. 262–76. **[G: Sri Lanka; Colombia; China; Pakistan]**

Singer, Hans W. The Role of Human Capital in Development. *Pakistan J. Appl. Econ.*, Summer 1983, *2*(1), pp. 1–11. **[G: S. Korea]**

Singh, Harbhajan. Inequality in Labour-Market Rewards and Education in India (A Case Study of Delhi). *Indian Econ. Rev.*, July–December 1983, *18*(2), pp. 245–72. **[G: India]**

Snooks, G. D. Determinants of Earnings Inequality amongst Australian Artists. *Australian Econ. Pap.*, December 1983, *22*(41), pp. 322–32. **[G: Australia]**

Solmon, Lewis C. Economic Issues in Considering the Costs of Evaluation. **In** *Alkin, M. C. and Solmon, L. C., eds.*, 1983, pp. 15–26. **[G: U.S.]**

Stiglitz, Joseph E. and Weiss, Andrew. Alternative Approaches to Analyzing Markets with Asymmetric Information: Reply [The Theory of 'Screening,' Education, and the Distribution of Income]. *Amer. Econ. Rev.*, March 1983, *73*(1), pp. 246–49.

Streeten, Paul. Human Resources: Concepts and Measurement: Introduction. **In** *Streeten, P. and Maier, H., eds.*, 1983, pp. 3–7.

Tannen, Michael B. Vocational Education and Earnings for White Males: New Evidence from Longitudinal Data. *Southern Econ. J.*, October 1983, *50*(2), pp. 369–84. **[G: U.S.]**

Tinbergen, Jan and Wegner, Eckhard. Zu einem makroökonomischen Modell der Einkommensbildung. (A Macro-Economic Model of Income Formation. With English summary.) *Schweiz. Z. Volkswirtsch. Statist.*, March 1983, *119*(1), pp. 69–78. **[G: Switzerland]**

Tomes, Nigel. Religion and the Rate of Return on Human Capital: Evidence from Canada. *Can. J. Econ.*, February 1983, *16*(1), pp. 122–38. **[G: Canada]**

Tsuru, Shigeto. Economic Development and Human Resources: Japan's Experience. **In** *Tsuru, S., ed.*, 1983, pp. 95–119. **[G: Japan]**

Venti, Steven F. and Wise, David A. Individual Attributes and Self-Selection of Higher Education: College Attendance versus College Completion. *J. Public Econ.*, June 1983, *21*(1), pp. 1–32. **[G: U.S.]**

Viscusi, W. Kip. Alternative Approaches to Valuing the Health Impacts of Accidents: Liability Law and Prospective Evaluations. *Law Contemp. Probl.*, Autumn 1983, *46*(4), pp. 49–68. **[G: U.S.]**

Weisbrod, Burton A. Human Resources and Employment in Developed Countries: Introduction. **In** *Weisbrod, B. and Hughes, H., eds.*, 1983, pp. 3–13.

Weiss, Andrew. A Sorting-cum-Learning Model of Education. *J. Polit. Econ.*, June 1983, *91*(3), pp. 420–42.

Widmaier, Hans Peter. Human Resources and Social Policy. **In** *Streeten, P. and Maier, H., eds.*, 1983, pp. 295–309.

Wilcox-Gök, Virginia L. The Determination of Child Health: An Application of Sibling and Adoption Data. *Rev. Econ. Statist.*, May 1983, *65*(2), pp. 266–73.

Wilson, Robert A. Rates of Return: Some Further Results. *Scot. J. Polit. Econ.*, June 1983, *30*(2), pp. 114–27. **[G: U.K.]**

Yabushita, Shiro. Theory of Screening and the Behavior of the Firm: Comment. *Amer. Econ. Rev.*, March 1983, *73*(1), pp. 242–45.

Young, Anne McDougall. Recent Trends in Higher Education and Labor Force Activity. *Mon. Lab. Rev.*, February 1983, *106*(2), pp. 39–41. **[G: U.S.]**

Ziderman, Adrian. Restrictive Practices, Training and the Legal Profession in Scotland [Returns to the Legal Profession in Scotland]. *Scot. J. Polit. Econ.*, November 1983, *30*(3), pp. 295–301. [G: U.K.]

900 Welfare Programs; Consumer Economics; Urban and Regional Economics

910 Welfare, Health, and Education

9100 General

Aaron, Henry J. Cutting Back the Social Welfare State. **In** *[Goode, R.]*, 1983, pp. 199–213. [G: U.S.]

Aaron, Henry J. Distributional Effects of the Reagan Program: Response: Raising Some Doubts. **In** *Stubblebine, Wm. C. and Willett, T. D., eds.*, 1983, pp. 199–202. [G: U.S.]

Aitkin, D. A. Where Does Australia Stand? **In** *Withers, G., ed.*, 1983, pp. 13–31. [G: OECD; Australia]

Alexander, John K. The Functions of Public Welfare in Late-Eighteenth-Century Philadelphia: Regulating the Poor? **In** *Trattner, W. I., ed.*., 1983, pp. 15–34. [G: U.S.]

Alperovitz, Gar. Social Justice and the New Inflation. **In** *Skurski, R., ed.*, 1983, pp. 159–97. [G: U.S.]

Beenstock, Michael. Social Policy for Social Democracy. **In** *Seldon, A., et al.*, 1983, pp. 73–86. [G: U.K.]

Bixby, Ann Kallman. Social Welfare Expenditures, Fiscal Year 1980. *Soc. Sec. Bull.*, August 1983, *46*(8), pp. 9–17. [G: U.S.]

Boskin, Michael J. Distributional Effects of the Reagan Program. **In** *Stubblebine, Wm. C. and Willett, T. D., eds.*, 1983, pp. 179–98. [G: U.S.]

Collins, Doreen. The Impact of Social Policy in the United Kingdom. **In** *El-Agraa, A. M., ed.*, 1983, pp. 213–33. [G: EEC; U.K.]

Domke, William K.; Eichenberg, Richard C. and Kelleher, Catherine M. The Illusion of Choice: Defense and Welfare in Advanced Industrial Democracies, 1948–1978. *Amer. Polit. Sci. Rev.*, March 1983, *77*(1), pp. 19–35. [G: U.S.; U.K.; W. Germany; France]

Ferejohn, John. Congress and Redistribution. **In** *Schick, A., ed.*, 1983, pp. 131–57. [G: U.S.]

Frank, Charles R., Jr. and Webb, Richard. Policy Choices and Income Distributions in Less Developed Countries. **In** *Todaro, M. P., ed.*, 1983, *1978*, pp. 102–18. [G: LDCs]

Kakabadse, Andrew. Bureaucracy and the Social Services: A Comparative Study of English Social Service Departments. *Int. J. Soc. Econ.*, 1983, *10*(5), pp. 3–13. [G: U.K.]

Lampman, Robert J. How Has the Labor Supply Changed in Response to Recent Increases in Social Welfare Expenditures and the Taxes to Pay for Them? **In** *Barbash, J., et al., eds.*, 1983, pp. 61–85. [G: U.S.]

Lampman, Robert J. and Smeeding, Timothy M. Interfamily Transfers as Alternatives to Government Transfers to Persons. *Rev. Income Wealth*, March 1983, *29*(1), pp. 45–66. [G: U.S.]

Nice, David C. Representation in the States: Policymaking and Ideology. *Soc. Sci. Quart.*, June 1983, *64*(2), pp. 404–11. [G: U.S.]

Oates, Wallace E. The Economics of the New Federalism: Response: Strengths and Weaknesses of the New Federalism. **In** *Stubblebine, Wm. C. and Willett, T. D., eds.*, 1983, pp. 153–57. [G: U.S.]

Rodgers, Harrell R., Jr. Social Welfare Programs: Lessons from Europe, the Need for Comparative Analysis. **In** *Goldstein, R. and Sachs, S. M., eds.*, 1983, pp. 269–83. [G: Sweden; W. Europe]

Stretton, Hugh. Where Does Australia Stand? Discussion. **In** *Withers, G., ed.*, 1983, pp. 32–36.

Stubblebine, Wm. Craig. The Economics of the New Federalism. **In** *Stubblebine, Wm. C. and Willett, T. D., eds.*, 1983, pp. 143–51. [G: U.S.]

Tolley, George S.; Krumm, Ronald J. and Sanders, Jeffrey. On the Effects of Federal Aid. *Amer. Econ. Rev.*, May 1983, *73*(2), pp. 159–63. [G: U.S.]

Trebilcock, Michael J., et al. Provincially Induced Barriers to Trade in Canada: A Survey. **In** *Trebilcock, M. J., et al., eds.*, 1983, pp. 243–351. [G: Canada]

Whinston, Michael D. Moral Hazard, Adverse Selection, and the Optimal Provision of Social Insurance. *J. Public Econ.*, October 1983, *22*(1), pp. 49–71.

911 General Welfare Programs

9110 General Welfare Programs

Aaron, Henry J. Cutting Back the Welfare State. **In** *Helpman, E.; Razin, A. and Sadka, E., eds.*, 1983, pp. 147–60. [G: U.S.]

Akin, John S., et al. The Demand for School Lunches: An Analysis of Individual Participation in the School Lunch Program. *J. Human Res.*, Spring 1983, *18*(2), pp. 213–30. [G: U.S.]

Allie, Émile and Lefebvre, Pierre. L'aide sociale et le supplément au revenu de travail: une simulation économique des revenus (salaires) de réserve. (A Simulation of the Impact of the Quebec Minimum Income System on Reservation Wages (Income). With English summary.) *L'Actual. Econ.*, June 1983, *59*(2), pp. 190–207. [G: Canada]

Ashenfelter, Orley. Determining Participation in Income-Tested Social Programs. *J. Amer. Statist. Assoc.*, September 1983, *78*(383), pp. 517–25. [G: U.S.]

Asselain, Jean-Charles. La répartition des revenus en Hongrie: Deuxième partie: les incertitudes des années 70. (With English summary.) *Écon. Soc.*, January 1983, *17*(1), pp. 43–88. [G: Hungary]

Barnes, Fred. TV News: The Shock Horror Welfare Cut Show. *Policy Rev.*, Spring 1983, (24), pp. 58–73. [G: U.S.]

Basiotis, Peter, et al. Nutrient Availability, Food Costs, and Food Stamps. *Amer. J. Agr. Econ.*, November 1983, *65*(4), pp. 685–93. [G: U.S.]

Bellemare, D. and Poulin Simon, L. La tendance à la sélectivité ou les tensions difficiles entre les stratégies d'assurance et d'assistance. (Tendencies towards Selectivity or Tensions between Insurance and Assistance Strategies. With English summary.) *Écon. Soc.*, March–April 1983, *17*(3–4), pp. 655–89. **[G: Canada]**

Betson, David M. Complementary Strategies for Policy Analysis: Combining Microeconomic and Regional Simulation Models. *Reg. Sci. Urban Econ.*, May 1983, *13*(2), pp. 213–29. **[G: U.S.]**

Betson, David M. and Greenberg, David. Uses of Microsimulation in Applied Poverty Research. **In** *Goldstein, R. and Sachs, S. M., eds.*, 1983, pp. 175–90. **[G: U.S.]**

Bovard, James. Feeding Everybody: How Federal Food Programs Grew and Grew. *Policy Rev.*, Fall 1983, (26), pp. 42–51. **[G: U.S.]**

Burtless, Gary T. and Greenberg, David. Measuring the Impact of NIT Experiments on Work Effort. *Ind. Lab. Relat. Rev.*, July 1983, *36*(4), pp. 592–605. **[G: U.S.]**

Carter, Grace M.; Coleman, Sinclair B. and Wendt, James C. The Great Housing Experiment: Participation under Open Enrollment. **In** *Friedman, J. and Weinberg, D. H., eds.*, 1983, pp. 73–90. **[G: U.S.]**

Chavas, Jean-Paul and Keplinger, Keith O. Impact of Domestic Food Programs on Nutrient Intake of Low-Income Persons in the United States. *Southern J. Agr. Econ.*, July 1983, *15*(1), pp. 155–63. **[G: U.S.]**

Chisholm, Nancy S. A Future for Public Housing. *Amer. Real Estate Urban Econ. Assoc. J.*, Summer 1983, *11*(2), pp. 203–20. **[G: U.S.]**

Christ, Carl F. An Evaluation of the Economic Policy Proposals of the Joint Economic Committee of the 92nd and 93rd Congresses. **In** *Brunner, K. and Meltzer, A. H., eds.*, 1983, *1977*, pp. 349–83. **[G: U.S.]**

Cigno, Alessandro. Corrigendum [On Optimal Family Allowances]. *Oxford Econ. Pap.*, July 1983, *35*(2), pp. 329.

Cigno, Alessandro. On Optimal Family Allowances. *Oxford Econ. Pap.*, March 1983, *35*(1), pp. 13–22.

Coe, Richard D. Nonparticipation in Welfare Programs by Eligible Households: The Case of the Food Stamp Program. *J. Econ. Issues*, December 1983, *17*(4), pp. 1035–56. **[G: U.S.]**

Coe, Richard D. Participation in the Food Stamp Program, 1979. **In** *Duncan, G. J. and Morgan, J. N., eds.*, 1983, pp. 121–77. **[G: U.S.]**

Cogan, John F. Labor Supply and Negative Income Taxation: New Evidence from the New Jersey–Pennsylvania Experiment. *Econ. Inquiry*, October 1983, *21*(4), pp. 465–84. **[G: U.S.]**

Cronin, Francis J. The Efficiency of Demand-Oriented Housing Programs: Generalizing from Experimental Findings. *J. Human Res.*, Winter 1983, *18*(1), pp. 100–125. **[G: U.S.]**

Crouch, Colin. Corporative Industrial Relations and the Welfare State. **In** *Jones, R. J. B., ed.*, 1983, pp. 139–66. **[G: OECD]**

Danziger, Sheldon. Budget Cuts as Welfare Reform. *Amer. Econ. Rev.*, May 1983, *73*(2), pp. 65–70. **[G: U.S.]**

Darity, William A., Jr. and Myers, Samuel L., Jr. Changes in Black Family Structure: Implications for Welfare Dependency. *Amer. Econ. Rev.*, May 1983, *73*(2), pp. 59–64. **[G: U.S.]**

Devaney, Barbara. Total Work Effort under a Negative Income Tax. *J. Policy Anal. Manage.*, Summer 1983, *2*(4), pp. 625–27. **[G: U.S.]**

Downs, Anthony. The President's Housing Commission and Two Tests of Realistic Recommendations. *Amer. Real Estate Urban Econ. Assoc. J.*, Summer 1983, *11*(2), pp. 182–91. **[G: U.S.]**

Duvall, Henrietta J. Utilization of Medicaid Services by AFDC Recipients. *Soc. Sec. Bull.*, June 1983, *46*(6), pp. 16–18. **[G: U.S.]**

Eekhoff, Johann. The Role of Government in the Housing Sector: Comment. **In** *Giersch, H., ed.*, 1983, pp. 225–31. **[G: U.S.]**

Friedman, Joseph and Weinberg, Daniel H. The Great Housing Experiment: History and Overview. **In** *Friedman, J. and Weinberg, D. H., eds.*, 1983, pp. 11–22. **[G: U.S.]**

Ginsberg, Leon H. Changing Public Attitudes about Public Welfare Clients and Services through Research. **In** *Goldstein, R. and Sachs, S. M., eds.*, 1983, pp. 241–52. **[G: U.S.]**

Green, Cynthia B. and Sanger, Mary Bryna. Aiding the Poor. **In** *Brecher, C. and Horton, R. D., eds.*, 1983, pp. 99–130. **[G: U.S.]**

Greenberg, David and Halsey, Harlan. Systematic Misreporting and Effects of Income Maintenance Experiments on Work Effort: Evidence from the Seattle–Denver Experiment. *J. Lab. Econ.*, October 1983, *1*(4), pp. 380–407. **[G: U.S.]**

Grubel, Herbert G. Reassessing the Cost of Social Insurance Programs. **In** *Giersch, H., ed.*, 1983, pp. 145–62. **[G: Canada]**

Hamilton, William L. The Great Housing Experiment: The Administrative Agency Experiment. **In** *Friedman, J. and Weinberg, D. H., eds.*, 1983, pp. 56–69. **[G: U.S.]**

Hiemstra, Stephen J. Food Stamps, Program Parameters and Standards of Living for Low-Income Households: Discussion. *Southern J. Agr. Econ.*, July 1983, *15*(1), pp. 51–52. **[G: U.S.]**

Hiemstra, Stephen J. Marketing Impacts of the Domestic Food Assistance Programs. **In** *Farris, P. L., ed.*, 1983, pp. 278–95. **[G: U.S.]**

Hill, Martha S. Female Household Headship and the Poverty of Children. **In** *Duncan, G. J. and Morgan, J. N., eds.*, 1983, pp. 324–76. **[G: U.S.]**

Holshouser, William L., Jr. The Great Housing Experiment: The Role of Supportive Services. **In** *Friedman, J. and Weinberg, D. H., eds.*, 1983, pp. 112–24. **[G: U.S.]**

Kamerman, Sheila B. Child-Care Services: A National Picture. *Mon. Lab. Rev.*, December 1983, *106*(12), pp. 35–39. **[G: U.S.]**

Kasten, Richard A. and Todd, John E. Transfer Recipients and the Poor during the 1970s. **In** *Zeckhauser, R. J. and Leebaert, D., eds.*, 1983, pp. 60–77. **[G: U.S.]**

Kennedy, Stephen D. The Great Housing Experiment: The Demand Experiment. **In** *Friedman, J. and Weinberg, D. H., eds.*, 1983, pp. 37–55. **[G: U.S.]**

Kennedy, Stephen D. and MacMillan, Jean E. The Great Housing Experiment: Participation under Random Assignment. **In** *Friedman, J. and Wein-*

berg, D. H., eds., 1983, pp. 91–111. [G: U.S.]

Leiby, James. Social Control and Historical Explanation: Historians View the Piven and Cloward Thesis. **In** *Trattner, W. I., ed..,* 1983, pp. 90–113.

Levitt, Ian. Scottish Poverty: The Historical Background. **In** *Brown, G. and Cook, R., eds.,* 1983, pp. 66–75. **[G: U.K.]**

Lewis, Gordon H. The Day Care Tangle: Unexpected Outcomes When Programs Interact. *J. Policy Anal. Manage.,* Summer 1983, *2*(4), pp. 531–47. **[G: U.S.]**

Linhart, Sepp. Social Security versus Family Ideology. The State's Reaction to the Consequences of Early Industrialization in Japan. *Rivista Int. Sci. Econ. Com.,* August 1983, *30*(8), pp. 703–15. **[G: Japan]**

Lowry, Ira S. The Great Housing Experiment: The Supply Experiment. **In** *Friedman, J. and Weinberg, D. H., eds.,* 1983, pp. 23–36. **[G: U.S.]**

Mayo, Stephen K. Benefits from Subsidized Housing. **In** *Friedman, J. and Weinberg, D. H., eds.,* 1983, pp. 235–57. **[G: U.S.]**

Moffitt, Robert A. An Economic Model of Welfare Stigma. *Amer. Econ. Rev.,* December 1983, *73*(5), pp. 1023–35. **[G: U.S.]**

Moffitt, Robert A. The Individual Work Incentives and Labor Market Impacts of Transfer Programs with a Work Requirement: The Static Theory. *Quart. Rev. Econ. Bus.,* Spring 1983, *23*(1), pp. 35–45.

Mohl, Raymond A. The Abolition of Public Outdoor Relief, 1870–1900: A Critique of the Piven and Cloward Thesis. **In** *Trattner, W. I., ed..,* 1983, pp. 35–50. **[G: U.S.]**

Mulberg, Ruthellen. AFDC: Good Cause Claims for Refusing to Cooperate in Establishing Paternity or Securing Child Support. *Soc. Sec. Bull.,* May 1983, *46*(5), pp. 7–10. **[G: U.S.]**

Mulford, John E. The Great Housing Experiment: Earmarked Income Supplements. **In** *Friedman, J. and Weinberg, D. H., eds.,* 1983, pp. 163–74. **[G: U.S.]**

Neubeck, Kenneth J. Income Maintenance Experimentation: Cui Bono. **In** *Goldstein, R. and Sachs, S. M., eds.,* 1983, pp. 253–59. **[G: U.S.]**

Okun, Arthur M. Equal Rights but Unequal Incomes. **In** *Okun, A. M.,* 1983, *1976,* pp. 595–605. **[G: U.S.]**

Olsen, Edgar O. The Great Housing Experiment: Implications for Housing Policy. **In** *Friedman, J. and Weinberg, D. H., eds.,* 1983, pp. 266–75. **[G: U.S.]**

Olsen, Edgar O. The Role of Government in the Housing Sector. **In** *Giersch, H., ed.,* 1983, pp. 199–224. **[G: U.S.]**

Olsen, Edgar O. and Barton, David M. The Benefits and Costs of Public Housing in New York City. *J. Public Econ.,* April 1983, *20*(3), pp. 299–332. **[G: U.S.]**

Owens, Jeffery P. Tax Expenditures and Direct Expenditures as Instruments of Social Policy. **In** *[Goode, R.],* 1983, pp. 171–97. **[G: OECD]**

Piven, Frances Fox and Cloward, Richard A. Humanitarianism in History: A Response to the Critics. **In** *Trattner, W. I., ed..,* 1983, pp. 114–48.

Playford, Clive and Pond, Chris. The Right to Be Unequal: Inequality in Incomes. **In** *Field, F., ed.,* 1983, pp. 34–55. **[G: U.K.]**

Plotnick, Robert. Turnover in the AFDC Population: An Event History Analysis. *J. Human Res.,* Winter 1983, *18*(1), pp. 65–81. **[G: U.S.]**

Pumphrey, Muriel W. and Pumphrey, Ralph E. The Widows' Pension Movement, 1900–1930: Preventive Child-saving or Social Control? **In** *Trattner, W. I., ed..,* 1983, pp. 51–66. **[G: U.S.]**

Ray, C. R. Macro Impacts of Food Subsidy Policies in Developing Countries. *Margin,* July 1983, *15*(4), pp. 50–65. **[G: India]**

Rein, Martin. Social Services: Purpose and Form. **In** *Rein, M.,* 1983, *1972,* pp. 40–58.

Rein, Martin. The Design of In-kind Benefits. **In** *Rein, M.,* 1983, pp. 78–95.

Rein, Martin. The Social Policy of the Firm. **In** *Rein, M.,* 1983, *1982,* pp. 3–22. **[G: OECD]**

Rein, Martin. Value Tensions in Program Design. **In** *Rein, M.,* 1983, pp. 96–112. **[G: U.S.]**

Rigby, Donald E. and Scott, Charles. Low-Income Energy Assistance Program. *Soc. Sec. Bull.,* January 1983, *46*(1), pp. 11–32. **[G: U.S.]**

Robins, Philip K.; West, Richard W. and Stieger, Gary L. Labor Supply Response to a Negative Income Tax. **In** *Zeckhauser, R. J. and Leebaert, D., eds.,* 1983, pp. 78–96. **[G: U.S.]**

Rose-Ackerman, Susan. Unintended Consequences: Regulating the Quality of Subsidized Day Care. *J. Policy Anal. Manage.,* Fall 1983, *3*(1), pp. 14–30. **[G: U.S.]**

Rosenberg, Sam. Reagan Social Policy and Labour Force Restructuring. *Cambridge J. Econ.,* June 1983, *7*(2), pp. 179–96. **[G: U.S.]**

Sawyer, Darwin O. Pharmaceutical Reimbursement and Drug Cost Control: The MAC Experience in Maryland. *Inquiry,* Spring 1983, *20*(1), pp. 76–87. **[G: U.S.]**

Seah, Linda. Public Enterprise and Economic Development. **In** *Chen, P. S. J., ed.,* 1983, pp. 129–59. **[G: Singapore]**

Seehan, Peter J. and Stricker, Peter P. Welfare Benefits and the Labour Market. **In** *Blandy, R. and Covick, O., eds.,* 1983, pp. 200–221. **[G: Australia]**

Smeeding, Timothy M. The Anti-poverty Effect of In-Kind Transfers: A "Good Idea" Gone Too Far? **In** *Goldstein, R. and Sachs, S. M., eds.,* 1983, pp. 77–101. **[G: U.S.]**

Solano, Paul L. Institutional Explanations of Public Expenditures among High Income Democracies. *Public Finance,* 1983, *38*(3), pp. 440–58. **[G: OECD]**

Tulloch, Patricia. The Welfare State and Social Policy. **In** *Head, B. W., ed.,* 1983, pp. 252–71. **[G: Australia]**

Vedlitz, Arnold and Alston, Jon. Welfare Terminations and Benefit Reductions: What Program Recipients Can Tell Policy Planners. **In** *Goldstein, R. and Sachs, S. M., eds.,* 1983, pp. 138–47. **[G: U.S.]**

Vining, Daniel R., Jr. Illegitimacy and Public Policy. *Population Devel. Rev.,* March 1983, *9*(1), pp. 105–10. **[G: U.S.]**

Wallace, James E. Direct Household Assistance and Block Grants. *Amer. Real Estate Urban Econ. As-*

soc. J., Summer 1983, *11* (2), pp. 192–202. [G: U.S.]

Weicher, John C. The Report of the President's Commission on Housing: Policy Proposals for Subsidized Housing. *Amer. Real Estate Urban Econ. Assoc. J.*, Summer 1983, *11* (2), pp. 117–32. [G: U.S.]

Weiss, Janet A.; Rein, Martin and White, Sheldon. The Plea for Coordination of Services. **In** *Rein, M.*, 1983, *1981*, pp. 59–77.

Young, Ronald. A Little Local Inequality. **In** *Brown, G. and Cook, R., eds.*, 1983, pp. 223–51. [G: U.K.]

912 Economics of Education

9120 Economics of Education

Agarwal, Vinod B. Foreign Students' Demand for United States Higher Education. *Eastern Econ. J.*, October–December 1983, *9* (4), pp. 309–22. [G: U.S.; Latin America]

Alkin, Marvin C. and Solmon, Lewis C. Conducting Benefit–Cost Analysis of Program Evaluation. **In** *Alkin, M. C. and Solmon, L. C., eds.*, 1983, pp. 137–47.

Alkin, Marvin C. and Stecher, Brian. A Study of Evaluation Costs. **In** *Alkin, M. C. and Solmon, L. C., eds.*, 1983, pp. 119–32.

Andersen, David F. Disentangling Statistical Artifacts from Hard Conclusions. *J. Policy Anal. Manage.*, Winter 1983, *2* (2), pp. 296–99. [G: U.S.]

Anderson, R. D. Education and the State in Nineteenth-Century Scotland. *Econ. Hist. Rev., 2nd Ser.*, November 1983, *36* (4), pp. 518–34. [G: Scotland]

Balderston, Frederick E. Strategic Management Approaches for the 1980s: Navigating in the Trough. **In** *Froomkin, J., ed.*, 1983, pp. 146–56. [G: U.S.]

Bandeen, Robert. Higher Education: Policies and Priorities: Comment. **In** *Queen's Univ. Indust. Relat. Centre and John Deutsch Mem.*, 1983, pp. 182–85. [G: Canada]

Bassett, W. Bruce. Cost Control in Higher Education. **In** *Froomkin, J., ed.*, 1983, pp. 135–45. [G: U.S.]

Behrman, Jere R. and Birdsall, Nancy. The Quality of Schooling: Quantity Alone is Misleading. *Amer. Econ. Rev.*, December 1983, *73* (5), pp. 928–46. [G: Brazil]

Berglas, Eitan, et al. A Threshold Fund. **In** *Helpman, E.; Razin, A. and Sadka, E., eds.*, 1983, pp. 181–205. [G: Israel]

Berliner, Joseph S. Education, Labor-Force Participation, and Fertility in the USSR. *J. Compar. Econ.*, June 1983, *7* (2), pp. 131–57. [G: U.S.S.R.]

Bhagwati, Jagdish N. and Srinivasan, T. N. Education in a 'Job Ladder' Model and the Fairness-in-Hiring Rule. **In** *Bhagwati, J. N., Vol. 2*, 1983, *1977*, pp. 142–63.

Blackwell, J. Lloyd. A Statistical Interpretation of Student Evaluation Feedback: A Comment. *J. Econ. Educ.*, Summer 1983, *14* (3), pp. 28–31. [G: U.S.]

Blakemore, Arthur E. and Low, Stuart A. A Simultaneous Determination of Post-High School Education Choice and Labor Supply. *Quart. Rev. Econ. Bus.*, Winter 1983, *23* (4), pp. 81–92. [G: U.S.]

Blakemore, Arthur E. and Low, Stuart A. Scholarship Policy and Race–Sex Differences in the Demand for Higher Education. *Econ. Inquiry*, October 1983, *21* (4), pp. 504–19.

Blaug, Mark. Declining Subsidies to Higher Education: An Economic Analysis. **In** *Giersch, H., ed.*, 1983, pp. 125–43. [G: OECD]

Bloch, Erich; Meindl, James D. and Cromie, William. University Industry Cooperation in Microelectronics and Computers. **In** *National Science Foundation*, 1983, pp. 235–53. [G: U.S.]

Borcherding, Thomas E. Toward a Positive Theory of Public Sector Supply Arrangements. **In** *Prichard, J. R. S., ed.*, 1983, pp. 99–184. [G: Canada; Selected Countries]

Borsotti, Carlos A. Development and Education in Rural Areas. *Cepal Rev.*, December 1983, (21), pp. 113–32. [G: Latin America]

Boynton, Damon. Implications for Education. **In** *Whyte, W. F. and Boynton, D., eds.*, 1983, pp. 295–309.

Breneman, David W. Where Would Tuition Tax Credits Take Us? Should We Agree to Go? **In** *James, T. and Levin, H. M., eds.*, 1983, pp. 101–14. [G: U.S.]

Brown, Byron W. and Saks, Daniel H. Spending for Local Public Education: Income Distribution and the Aggregation of Private Demands. *Public Finance Quart.*, January 1983, *11* (1), pp. 21–45. [G: U.S.]

Burke, Gerald. Public Educational Expenditure in the 1970s and 1980s. *Australian Econ. Rev.*, 3rd Quarter 1983, (63), pp. 34–45. [G: Australia]

Caldwell, John C.; Reddy, P. H. and Caldwell, Pat. The Social Component of Mortality Decline: An Investigation in South India Employing Alternative Methodologies. *Population Stud.*, July 1983, *37* (2), pp. 185–205. [G: India]

Catterall, James S. A Theoretical Model for Examining the Costs of Testing. **In** *Alkin, M. C. and Solmon, L. C., eds.*, 1983, pp. 45–51.

Catterall, James S. Fundamental Issues in the Costing of Testing Programs. **In** *Alkin, M. C. and Solmon, L. C., eds.*, 1983, pp. 71–80.

Catterall, James S. Tuition Tax Credits: Issues of Equity. **In** *James, T. and Levin, H. M., eds.*, 1983, pp. 130–50. [G: U.S.]

Chen, Peter S. J. Singapore's Development Strategies: A Model for Rapid Growth. **In** *Chen, P. S. J., ed.*, 1983, pp. 3–25. [G: Singapore]

Chizmar, John F. and Zak, Thomas A. Modeling Multiple Outputs in Educational Production Functions. *Amer. Econ. Rev.*, May 1983, *73* (2), pp. 17–22. [G: U.S.]

Christensen, Jens P. From Social Demand to Manpower Approach in Higher Education Planning—The Danish Case. *METU*, 1983, *10* (3), pp. 225–48. [G: Denmark]

Christoffel, Pamela H. An Opportunity Deferred: Lifelong Learning in the United States. **In** *Levin, H. M. and Schütze, H. G., eds.*, 1983, pp. 225–34. [G: U.S.]

Clement, Werner. Comprehensive Models for Financing Recurrent Education: Intermediate ("Parafiscal") Financing Schemes. **In** *Levin,*

H. M. and Schütze, H. G., eds., 1983, pp. 81–98.

Cobbe, James H. The Educational System, Wage and Salary Structures, and Income Distribution: Lesotho as a Case Study, Circa 1975. *J. Devel. Areas*, January 1983, *17*(2), pp. 227–41. **[G: Lesotho]**

Corman, Hope. Postsecondary Education Enrollment Responses by Recent High School Graduates and Older Adults. *J. Human Res.*, Spring 1983, *18*(2), pp. 247–67. **[G: U.S.]**

Crispin, Alan. National Interests and Local Government: The Case of Education: Comment. **In** *Young, K., ed.*, 1983, pp. 75–81. **[G: U.K.]**

Crossland, Fred E. Foundations and Higher Education. **In** *Froomkin, J., ed.*, 1983, pp. 48–60. **[G: U.S.]**

Crowley, Joan E.; Pollard, Tom K. and Rumberger, Russell W. Education and Training. **In** *Borus, M. E., ed.*, 1983, pp. 103–48. **[G: U.S.]**

Dalton, Amy H. and Snellings, Eleanor C. A Note on Salary Variations in an Academic Internal Labor Market. *Atlantic Econ. J.*, September 1983, *11*(3), pp. 70–78. **[G: U.S.]**

Darknell, Frank A. and Darknell, Edith Campbell. State College Science and Engineering Faculty: Collaborative Links with Private Business and Industry in California and Other States. **In** *National Science Foundation*, 1983, pp. 163–92. **[G: U.S.]**

David, Jane L. School Improvement and Programs for Special Populations: Finance and Governance Linkages. **In** *Odden, A. and Webb, L. D., eds.*, 1983, pp. 109–25. **[G: U.S.]**

Deaton, Brady J. New Institutional Arrangements for Supplying Local Public Services under New Federalism with Special Reference to Education. *Amer. J. Agr. Econ.*, December 1983, *65*(5), pp. 1124–30. **[G: U.S.]**

Demo, Pedro. Education and Culture: A Political Perspective. Hypotheses on the Importance of Education for Development. *Cepal Rev.*, December 1983, (21), pp. 147–56. **[G: Brazil]**

Dolton, Peter J. and Makepeace, G. H. A Regression Analysis of the UGC's Financial Recommendations for Universities. *Appl. Econ.*, February 1983, *15*(1), pp. 107–19. **[G: U.K.]**

Dresch, Stephen P. College Enrollment. **In** *Froomkin, J., ed.*, 1983, pp. 108–18. **[G: U.S.]**

Dresch, Stephen P. Education and Lifetime Earnings: The Census Bureau's Misguided Misrepresentations. *Rev. Public Data Use (See J. Econ. Soc. Meas. after 4/85)*, December 1983, *11*(4), pp. 357–60. **[G: U.S.]**

Eden, Benjamin and Pakes, Ariél. Measuring the Variance-Age Profile of Lifetime Earnings. **In** *Helpman, E.; Razin, A. and Sadka, E., eds.*, 1983, pp. 109–21. **[G: Israel]**

Edwards, Ward. Evaluation, Thaumaturgy, and Multiattribute Utility Measurement. *J. Policy Anal. Manage.*, Fall 1983, *3*(1), pp. 115–20. **[G: U.S.]**

Emmerij, Louis. Paid Educational Leave: A Proposal Based on the Dutch Case. **In** *Levin, H. M. and Schütze, H. G., eds.*, 1983, pp. 297–316. **[G: Netherlands; OECD]**

Encarnation, Dennis J. Public Finance and Regulation of Nonpublic Education: Retrospect and Prospect. **In** *James, T. and Levin, H. M., eds.*, 1983, pp. 175–95. **[G: U.S.]**

Fallon, Peter R. Education and the Duration of Job Search and Unemployment in Urban India: An Empirical Analysis Based on a Survey of Delhi Jobseekers. *J. Devel. Econ.*, June 1983, *12*(3), pp. 327–40. **[G: India]**

Filgueira, Carlos H. To Educate or Not to Educate: Is That the Question? *Cepal Rev.*, December 1983, (21), pp. 57–80. **[G: Latin America]**

Froomkin, Joseph. Financing Graduate Students. **In** *Froomkin, J., ed.*, 1983, pp. 97–107. **[G: U.S.]**

Froomkin, Joseph. The Research Universities. **In** *Froomkin, J., ed.*, 1983, pp. 34–47. **[G: U.S.]**

Fuller, Winship C.; Manski, Charles F. and Wise, David A. The Impact of the Basic Educational Opportunity Grant Program on College Enrollments. **In** *Helpman, E.; Razin, A. and Sadka, E., eds.*, 1983, pp. 123–42. **[G: U.S.]**

Geiogue, Harold E. Tax Limitation Measures: Their Impact in California. **In** *Levin, H. M. and Schütze, H. G., eds.*, 1983, pp. 203–24. **[G: U.S.]**

Gemello, John M. and Osman, Jack W. The Choice for Public and Private Education: An Economist's View. **In** *James, T. and Levin, H. M., eds.*, 1983, pp. 196–209. **[G: U.S.]**

Gladieux, Lawrence E. The Issue of Equity in College Finance. **In** *Froomkin, J., ed.*, 1983, pp. 72–83. **[G: U.S.]**

Glazer, Nathan. The Future under Tuition Tax Credits. **In** *James, T. and Levin, H. M., eds.*, 1983, pp. 87–100. **[G: U.S.]**

Grout, Paul. Education Finance and Imperfections in Information. *Econ. Soc. Rev.*, October 1983, *15*(1), pp. 25–33.

Grout, Paul. Imperfect Information, Markets and Public Provision of Education. *J. Public Econ.*, October 1983, *22*(1), pp. 113–21.

Hadley, Jack. Teaching and Hospital Costs. *J. Health Econ.*, March 1983, *2*(1), pp. 75–79. **[G: U.S.]**

Haggart, Sue A. Determining the Resource Requirements and Cost of Evaluation. **In** *Alkin, M. C. and Solmon, L. C., eds.*, 1983, pp. 59–70.

Hamilton, Bruce W. The Flypaper Effect and Other Anomalies. *J. Public Econ.*, December 1983, *22*(3), pp. 347–61.

Hansen, W. Lee. Impact of Student Financial Aid on Access. **In** *Froomkin, J., ed.*, 1983, pp. 84–96. **[G: U.S.]**

Heyneman, Stephen P. Improving the Quality of Education in Developing Countries. *Finance Develop.*, March 1983, *20*(1), pp. 18–21. **[G: LDCs]**

Hilley, John L. The Distributive Impact of Education Finance Reform. *Nat. Tax J.*, December 1983, *36*(4), pp. 503–09. **[G: U.S.]**

Hoachlander, E. Gareth. Financing Public Education in the Wake of Federal and State Spending Cuts: Crisis and Opportunities. **In** *Lefcoe, G., ed.*, 1983, pp. 125–45. **[G: U.S.]**

Hosek, James R. and Palmer, Adele R. Teaching and Hospital Costs: The Case of Radiology. *J. Health Econ.*, March 1983, *2*(1), pp. 29–46. **[G: U.S.]**

Jallade, Jean-Pierre. Financing Education for Income Distribution. **In** *Todaro, M. P., ed.*, 1983, *1979*, pp. 276–85. **[G: Brazil; Colombia]**

James, Thomas. Questions about Educational Choice: An Argument from History. **In** *James,*

T. and Levin, H. M., eds., 1983, pp. 55–70. [G: U.S.]

James, Thomas and Levin, Henry M. Public Dollars for Private Schools: Introduction. **In** *James, T. and Levin, H. M., eds.*, 1983, pp. 3–13. [G: U.S.]

Jensen, Donald N. Constitutional and Legal Implications of Tuition Tax Credits. **In** *James, T. and Levin, H. M., eds.*, 1983, pp. 151–72. [G: U.S.]

Johnson, Glenn L. The Relevance of U.S. Graduate Curricula in Agricultural Economics for the Training of Foreign Students. *Amer. J. Agr. Econ.*, December 1983, *65*(5), pp. 1142–48. [G: U.S.]

Jud, G. Donald. School Quality and Intra-Metropolitan Mobility: A Further Test of the Tiebout Hypothesis. *J. Behav. Econ.*, Winter 1983, *12*(2), pp. 37–55. [G: U.S.]

Jud, G. Donald. Schools and Housing Values: Reply. *Land Econ.*, February 1983, *59*(1), pp. 135–37. [G: U.S.]

Kane, Michael B. and Kocher, A. Thel. The Dissemination and Use of Educational R & D in the United States: An Analysis of Recent Federal Attempts to Improve Educational Practice. **In** *Holzner, B.; Knorr, K. D. and Strasser, H., eds.*, 1983, pp. 281–94. [G: U.S.]

Karlekar, Malavika. Education and Inequality. **In** *Béteille, A., ed.*, 1983, pp. 182–242. [G: India]

Kiesling, H. J. Nineteenth-Century Education According to West: A Comment [Resource Allocation and Growth in Early Nineteenth-Century British Education]. *Econ. Hist. Rev., 2nd Ser.*, August 1983, *36*(3), pp. 416–25. [G: U.K.]

King, Ron. The Relationship between Technological Change and Education. **In** *Hill, S. and Johnston, R., eds.*, 1983, pp. 175–93. [G: Australia]

Kirst, Michael W. A New School Finance for a New Era of Fiscal Constraint. **In** *Odden, A. and Webb, L. D., eds.*, 1983, pp. 1–15. [G: U.S.]

Klitgaard, Robert E., et al. The Economics of Teacher Training: An Exploratory Data Analysis. *Pakistan J. Appl. Econ.*, Summer 1983, *2*(1), pp. 13–38. [G: Pakistan]

Knight, J. B. and Sabot, Richard H. Educational Expansion and the Kuznets Effect. *Amer. Econ. Rev.*, December 1983, *73*(5), pp. 1132–36. [G: Kenya; Tanzania]

Koch, James V. Intercollegiate Athletics: An Economic Explanation. *Soc. Sci. Quart.*, June 1983, *64*(2), pp. 360–74. [G: U.S.]

Kogan, Maurice. National Interests and Local Government: The Case of Education. **In** *Young, K., ed.*, 1983, pp. 58–75. [G: U.K.]

Kramer, Martin. A Decade of Growth in Student Assistance. **In** *Froomkin, J., ed.*, 1983, pp. 61–71. [G: U.S.]

Kumar, Ramesh C. Economies of Scale in School Operation: Evidence from Canada. *Appl. Econ.*, June 1983, *15*(3), pp. 323–40. [G: Canada]

Lemelin, André. Un modèle de production et une méthode d'analyse des coûts de l'enseignement universitaire. (A Production Model and a University Cost Analysis Method. With English summary.) *L'Actual. Econ.*, December 1983, *59*(4), pp. 686–712.

Levin, Henry M. Comprehensive Models for Financing Recurrent Education: Individual Entitlements. **In** *Levin, H. M. and Schütze, H. G., eds.*, 1983, pp. 39–66. [G: OECD]

Levin, Henry M. Educational Choice and the Pains of Democracy. **In** *James, T. and Levin, H. M., eds.*, 1983, pp. 17–38. [G: U.S.]

Levin, Henry M. and Schütze, Hans G. Economic and Political Dimensions of Recurrent Education. **In** *Levin, H. M. and Schütze, H. G., eds.*, 1983, pp. 9–36. [G: OECD]

Levitan, Sar A. and Johnson, Clifford M. The Survival of Work. **In** *Barbash, J., et al., eds.*, 1983, pp. 1–25. [G: U.S.]

Lewis, W. Arthur. Aspects of Economic Development. **In** *Dalton, G., ed.*, 1983, *1969*, pp. 247–310. [G: LDCs]

Lewis, W. Arthur. Economic Aspects of Quality in Education. **In** *Lewis, W. A.*, 1983, *1969*, pp. 523–40.

Lewis, W. Arthur. Education and Economic Development. **In** *Lewis, W. A.*, 1983, *1961*, pp. 483–97. [G: LDCs]

Lewis, W. Arthur. Education for Scientific Professions in the Poor Countries. **In** *Lewis, W. A.*, 1983, *1962*, pp. 499–507.

Lewis, W. Arthur. Secondary Education and Economic Structure. **In** *Lewis, W. A.*, 1983, *1964*, pp. 509–22. [G: LDCs]

Lewis, W. Arthur. The University in Less Developed Countries. **In** *Lewis, W. A.*, 1983, *1974*, pp. 541–60. [G: LDCs]

Longanecker, David A. The Public Cost of Tuition Tax Credits. **In** *James, T. and Levin, H. M., eds.*, 1983, pp. 115–29. [G: U.S.]

Maier, Harry. Innovation and the Better Use of Human Resources. **In** *Streeten, P. and Maier, H., eds.*, 1983, pp. 253–88. [G: E. Germany]

Maynard, Alan K. The Economics of Education. **In** *Gowland, D. H., ed.*, 1983, pp. 237–52. [G: U.K.]

McDowell, George R. Local Services in the New Federalism: Discussion. *Amer. J. Agr. Econ.*, December 1983, *65*(5), pp. 1133–35. [G: U.S.]

McPherson, Michael S. and Winston, Gordon C. The Economics of Academic Tenure: A Relational Perspective. *J. Econ. Behav. Organ.*, June–September 1983, *4*(2–3), pp. 163–84.

Meerman, Jacob. Cost Recovery in a Project Context: Some World Bank Experience in Tropical Africa. *World Devel.*, June 1983, *11*(6), pp. 503–14. [G: Tropical Africa]

Megdal, Sharon Bernstein. Equalization of Expenditures and the Demand for Local Public Education: The Case of New Jersey. *Public Finance Quart.*, July 1983, *11*(3), pp. 365–76. [G: U.S.]

Miller, Paul W. The Determinants of School Participation Rates: A Cross-Sectional Analysis for New South Wales and Victoria. *Econ. Rec.*, March 1983, *59*(164), pp. 43–56. [G: Australia]

Moore, Peter G. Higher Education: The Next Decade. *J. Roy. Statist. Soc.*, 1983, *146*(3), pp. 213–29. [G: U.K.]

Muller, Carol Blue. The Social and Political Consequences of Increased Public Support for Private Schools. **In** *James, T. and Levin, H. M., eds.*, 1983, pp. 39–54. [G: U.S.]

Murnane, Richard J. How Clients' Characteristics

Affect Organization Performance: Lessons from Education. *J. Policy Anal. Manage.*, Spring 1983, *2*(3), pp. 403–17. **[G: U.S.]**

Murnane, Richard J. The Uncertain Consequences of Tuition Tax Credits: An Analysis of Student Achievement and Economic Incentives. **In** *James, T. and Levin, H. M., eds.*, 1983, pp. 210–22. **[G: U.S.]**

Murphy, Joseph S. The Public Urban University and the Costs of Equality. **In** *Froomkin, J., ed.*, 1983, pp. 14–22. **[G: U.S.]**

Nord, Stephen. On the Determinants of Public Education Expenditures. *Amer. Econ.*, Fall 1983, *27*(2), pp. 21–28. **[G: U.S.]**

Nord, Stephen. On the Determinants of Public Education Expenditures. *Rivista Int. Sci. Econ. Com.*, April-May 1983, *30*(4–5), pp. 401–14. **[G: U.S.]**

Peters, Lois S., et al. Current U.S. University/Industry Research Connections. **In** *National Science Foundation*, 1983, pp. 1–161. **[G: U.S.]**

Pissarides, Christopher A. An Overview of the Demand for Post-compulsory Education by British Men, 1955–77. **In** *Weisbrod, B. and Hughes, H., eds.*, 1983, pp. 147–56. **[G: U.K.]**

Pogrow, Stanley. Linking Technology Use to School Improvement: Implications for Research Policy and Practice. **In** *Odden, A. and Webb, L. D., eds.*, 1983, pp. 127–42. **[G: U.S.]**

Quadrio-Curzio, Alberto. Planning Manpower Education and Economic Growth. **In** *Weisbrod, B. and Hughes, H., eds.*, 1983, pp. 197–209.

Raffe, David. Education and Class Inequality in Scotland. **In** *Brown, G. and Cook, R., eds.*, 1983, pp. 190–205. **[G: U.K.]**

Rama, Germán W. Education in Latin America. Exclusion or Participation. *Cepal Rev.*, December 1983, (21), pp. 13–38. **[G: Latin America]**

Rehn, Gösta. Comprehensive Models for Financing Recurrent Education: Individual Drawing Rights. **In** *Levin, H. M. and Schütze, H. G., eds.*, 1983, pp. 67–79.

Reuber, Grant L. Higher Education: Policies and Priorities. **In** *Queen's Univ. Indust. Relat. Centre and John Deutsch Mem.*, 1983, pp. 171–80. **[G: Canada]**

Robinson, Warren C. Educational Disinvestment: Who Benefits from Subsidies? Does Anyone? *Policy Rev.*, Fall 1983, (26), pp. 59–64. **[G: U.S.]**

Rubenson, Kjell. Financing Paid Educational Leave: The Swedish Model. **In** *Levin, H. M. and Schütze, H. G., eds.*, 1983, pp. 237–55. **[G: Sweden]**

Sanders, James R. Cost Implications of the *Standards*. **In** *Alkin, M. C. and Solmon, L. C., eds.*, 1983, pp. 101–17.

Saunders, Charles B., Jr. Reshaping Federal Aid to Higher Education. **In** *Froomkin, J., ed.*, 1983, pp. 119–34. **[G: U.S.]**

Schaffer, William A. The Financial Impact of a University: A Case Study—The Impact of Georgia Tech on Georgia State Economy. **In** *Dutta, M.; Hartline, J. C. and Loeb, P. D., eds.*, 1983, pp. 131–50. **[G: U.S.]**

Schlechty, Phillip C. and Vance, Victor S. The Promotion of Quality in Teaching. **In** *Odden, A. and Webb, L. D., eds.*, 1983, pp. 144–52. **[G: U.S.]**

Schmidt, Robert M. Who Maximizes What? A Study in Student Time Allocation. *Amer. Econ. Rev.*, May 1983, *73*(2), pp. 23–28. **[G: U.S.]**

Schütze, Hans G. Financing Paid Educational Leave: The Federal Republic of Germany. **In** *Levin, H. M. and Schütze, H. G., eds.*, 1983, pp. 273–95. **[G: W. Germany]**

Seah, Chee Meow and Seah, Linda. Education Reform and National Integration. **In** *Chen, P. S. J., ed.*, 1983, pp. 240–67. **[G: Singapore]**

Seiver, Daniel A. Evaluations and Grades: A Simultaneous Framework. *J. Econ. Educ.*, Summer 1983, *14*(3), pp. 32–38. **[G: U.S.]**

Selowsky, Marcelo. Nutrition, Health and Education: The Economic Significance of Complementarities at Early Ages. **In** *Streeten, P. and Maier, H., eds.*, 1983, pp. 181–97. **[G: Columbia]**

Sherman, Joel D. Public Finance of Private Schools: Observations from Abroad. **In** *James, T. and Levin, H. M., eds.*, 1983, pp. 71–83. **[G: Canada; Australia]**

Sigelman, Lee and Bookheimer, Samuel. Is It Whether You Win or Lose? Monetary Contributions to Big-Time College Athletic Programs. *Soc. Sci. Quart.*, June 1983, *64*(2), pp. 347–59. **[G: U.S.]**

Simmons, John. Education for Development, Reconsidered. **In** *Todaro, M. P., ed.*, 1983, *1979*, pp. 262–76. **[G: Sri Lanka; Colombia; China; Pakistan]**

Singh, Vijai P. Use of Social Science Knowledge and Data in Public Policy Making: The Deliberations on the Compensatory Educational Policy by U.S. Congress. **In** *Holzner, B.; Knorr, K. D. and Strasser, H., eds.*, 1983, pp. 295–305.

Sloan, Frank A.; Feldman, Roger D. and Steinwald, A. Bruce. Effects of Teaching on Hospital Costs. *J. Health Econ.*, March 1983, *2*(1), pp. 1–28. **[G: U.S.]**

Smith, Gregory P. Employer-sponsored Programs. **In** *Levin, H. M. and Schütze, H. G., eds.*, 1983, pp. 159–87. **[G: U.S.]**

Smith, Hayden W. The Outlook for Corporate Financial Aid to Higher Education. **In** *Froomkin, J., ed.*, 1983, pp. 157–72. **[G: U.S.]**

Solmon, Lewis C. Economic Issues in Considering the Costs of Evaluation. **In** *Alkin, M. C. and Solmon, L. C., eds.*, 1983, pp. 15–26. **[G: U.S.]**

Sonstelie, Jon C. The Public Finance of Education: Subsidy versus Supply. **In** *Break, G. F., ed.*, 1983, pp. 161–82. **[G: U.S.]**

Stacey, Nevzer and Charner, Ivan. Unions and Postsecondary Education. **In** *Levin, H. M. and Schütze, H. G., eds.*, 1983, pp. 189–201. **[G: U.S.]**

Stefani, Giorgio. Allocative and Redistributive Aspects of Financing Higher Education with Special Regard to Italy. **In** *Weisbrod, B. and Hughes, H., eds.*, 1983, pp. 157–66. **[G: Italy]**

Street, James H. Institutional Reform and Manpower Development in Mexico. *J. Econ. Issues*, March 1983, *17*(1), pp. 17–33. **[G: Mexico]**

Street, James H. The Reality of Power and the Poverty of Economic Doctrine. *J. Econ. Issues*, June 1983, *17*(2), pp. 294–313. **[G: Chile; Argentina; Paraguay; Uraguay]**

Sunley, Emil M. A Note on the Proposed Higher

Education Tax Incentive. *Nat. Tax J.*, March, 1983, *36*(1), pp. 123–24. **[G: U.S.]**

Tedesco, Juan Carlos. Pedagogical Model and School Failure. *Cepal Rev.*, December 1983, (21), pp. 133–46. **[G: Latin America]**

Terny, Guy. Finances Publiques et Formation du Capital Humain: Elements d'une Strategie alternative de Financement de l'Enseignement superieur. **In** *Biehl, D.; Roskamp, K. W. and Stolper, W. F., eds.*, 1983, pp. 217–50.

Terra, Juan Pablo. The Role of Education in Relation to Employment Problems. *Cepal Rev.*, December 1983, (21), pp. 81–111. **[G: Latin America]**

Thackray, Arnold. University–Industry Connections and Chemical Research: An Historical Perspective. **In** *National Science Foundation*, 1983, pp. 193–233. **[G: U.S.]**

Tilak, Jandhyala B. G. On Allocating Plan Resources for Education in India. *Margin*, October 1983, *16*(1), pp. 92–102. **[G: India]**

Timmermann, Dieter. Financing Mechanisms: Their Impact on Postcompulsory Education. **In** *Levin, H. M. and Schütze, H. G., eds.*, 1983, pp. 99–129.

Toma, Eugenia Froedge. Institutional Structures, Regulation, and Producer Gains in the Education Industry. *J. Law Econ.*, April 1983, *26*(1), pp. 103–16. **[G: U.S.]**

Tuckman, Howard U.; Nas, Tevfik F. and Caldwell, Jamie S. The Effectiveness of Instructional Radio in a Developing Country Context. *METU*, 1983, *10*(1), pp. 45–64. **[G: Colombia]**

Venti, Steven F. and Wise, David A. Individual Attributes and Self-Selection of Higher Education: College Attendance versus College Completion. *J. Public Econ.*, June 1983, *21*(1), pp. 1–32. **[G: U.S.]**

Verner, Joel G. Budgetary Trade-Offs between Education and Defense in Latin America: A Research Note. *J. Devel. Areas*, October 1983, *18*(1), pp. 77–91. **[G: Latin America]**

Wagner, Alan P. An Inventory of Programs and Sources of Support. **In** *Levin, H. M. and Schütze, H. G., eds.*, 1983, pp. 133–58. **[G: U.S.]**

Wallace, Catherine. Higher Education: Policies and Priorities: Comment. **In** *Queen's Univ. Indust. Relat. Centre and John Deutsch Mem.*, 1983, pp. 180–82. **[G: Canada]**

Ward, James Gordon. On Teacher Quality. **In** *Odden, A. and Webb, L. D., eds.*, 1983, pp. 163–68. **[G: U.S.]**

Weathersby, George B. State Colleges in Transition. **In** *Froomkin, J., ed.*, 1983, pp. 23–33. **[G: U.S.]**

Weinberg, Gregorio. A Historical Perspective of Latin American Education. *Cepal Rev.*, December 1983, (21), pp. 39–55. **[G: Latin America]**

Weiss, Andrew. A Sorting-cum-Learning Model of Education. *J. Polit. Econ.*, June 1983, *91*(3), pp. 420–42.

Wenzlau, Thomas E. The Outlook for Liberal-Arts Colleges. **In** *Froomkin, J., ed.*, 1983, pp. 1–13. **[G: U.S.]**

West, Edwin G. Nineteenth-Century Educational History: The Kiesling Critique [Resource Allocation and Growth in Early Nineteenth-Century British Education]. *Econ. Hist. Rev., 2nd Ser.*, August 1983, *36*(3), pp. 426–34. **[G: U.K.]**

West, Edwin G. and McKee, Michael. De Gustibus *Est* Disputandum: The Phenomenon of "Merit Wants" Revisited. *Amer. Econ. Rev.*, December 1983, *73*(5), pp. 1110–21. **[G: U.K.]**

Wetzel, James N. Schools and Housing Values: Comment. *Land Econ.*, February 1983, *59*(1), pp. 131–34. **[G: U.S.]**

Williams, T. D. Education in Scotland. **In** *Ingham, K. P. D. and Love, J., eds.*, 1983, pp. 139–50. **[G: U.K.]**

Willms, J. Douglas. Do Private Schools Produce Higher Levels of Academic Achievement? New Evidence for the Tuition Tax Credit Debate. **In** *James, T. and Levin, H. M., eds.*, 1983, pp. 223–31. **[G: U.S.]**

Wolfe, Marshall. Styles of Development and Education: A Stocktaking of Myths, Prescriptions and Potentialities. *Cepal Rev.*, December 1983, (21), pp. 157–73. **[G: Latin America]**

Wren, Daniel A. American Business Philanthropy and Higher Education in the Nineteenth Century. *Bus. Hist. Rev.*, Autumn 1983, *57*(3), pp. 321–46. **[G: U.S.]**

913 Economics of Health (including medical subsidy programs)

9130 Economics of Health (including medical subsidy programs)

Aaron, Henry J. Orange Light for the Competitive Model [Stability in the Federal Employees Health Benefits Program]. *J. Health Econ.*, December 1983, *2*(3), pp. 281–84. **[G: U.S.]**

Adamache, Killard W. and Sloan, Frank A. Competition between Non-Profit and For-Profit Health Insurers. *J. Health Econ.*, December 1983, *2*(3), pp. 225–43. **[G: U.S.]**

Almore, Mary G. and Richardson, Frances. Urban Health Care Delivery in the Sunbelt. **In** *Ballard, S. C. and James, T. E., eds.*, 1983, pp. 93–106. **[G: U.S.]**

Alter, G. Plague and the Amsterdam Annuitant: A New Look at Life Annuities as a Source for Historial Demography. *Population Stud.*, March 1983, *37*(1), pp. 23–41. **[G: Netherlands]**

Anderson, Gerard F.; Boardman, Anthony E. and Inman, Robert P. The Formation of Health-related Habits. **In** *Zeckhauser, R. J. and Leebaert, D., eds.*, 1983, pp. 187–202. **[G: U.S.]**

Aptekar, Lewis S. Suggestions for Providing Services to the Handicapped in Latin America. *World Devel.*, November 1983, *11*(11), pp. 995–1004. **[G: Latin America]**

Atkinson, Anthony B. Smoking and the Economics of Government Intervention. **In** *Atkinson, A. B.*, 1983, *1974*, pp. 371–82. **[G: U.K.; U.S.]**

Barer, Morris L. and Evans, Robert G. Prices, Proxies and Productivity: An Historical Analysis of Hospital and Medical Care in Canada. **In** *Diewert, W. E. and Montmarquette, C., eds.*, 1983, pp. 705–77. **[G: Canada]**

Basiotis, Peter, et al. Nutrient Availability, Food Costs, and Food Stamps. *Amer. J. Agr. Econ.*, November 1983, *65*(4), pp. 685–93. **[G: U.S.]**

Bays, Carson W. Why Most Private Hospitals Are

Nonprofit. *J. Policy Anal. Manage.*, Spring 1983, *2*(3), pp. 366–85. **[G: U.S.]**

Becker, Edmund R. and Sloan, Frank A. Utilization of Hospital Services: The Roles of Teaching, Case Mix, and Reimbursement. *Inquiry,* Fall 1983, *20*(3), pp. 248–57. **[G: U.S.]**

Ben-Zion, Uri and Gafni, Amiram. Evaluation of Public Investment in Health Care: Is the Risk Irrelevant? *J. Health Econ.*, August 1983, *2*(2), pp. 161–65.

Berger, Mark C. Labor Supply and Spouse's Health: The Effects of Illness, Disability, and Mortality. *Soc. Sci. Quart.*, September 1983, *64*(3), pp. 494–509. **[G: U.S.]**

Berk, Marc L.; Bernstein, Amy B. and Taylor, Amy K. The Use and Availability of Medical Care in Health Manpower Shortage Areas. *Inquiry,* Winter 1983, *20*(4), pp. 369–80. **[G: U.S.]**

Berkowitz, Monroe; Fenn, Paul and Lambrinos, James. The Optimal Stock of Health with Endogenous Wages: Application to Partial Disability Compensation. *J. Health Econ.*, August 1983, *2*(2), pp. 139–47. **[G: U.S.]**

Blostin, Allan and Marclay, William. HMOs and Other Health Plans: Coverage and Employee Premiums. *Mon. Lab. Rev.*, June 1983, *106*(6), pp. 28–33. **[G: U.S.]**

Boardman, Anthony E. and Inman, Robert P. Early Life Environments and Adult Health: A Policy Perspective. **In** *Salkever, D.; Sirageldin, I. and Sorkin, A., eds.*, 1983, pp. 183–207. **[G: U.S.]**

Boardman, Anthony E., et al. A Model of Physicians' Practice Attributes Determination. *J. Health Econ.*, December 1983, *2*(3), pp. 259–68. **[G: U.S.]**

Borjas, George J.; Frech, H. E., III and Ginsburg, Paul B. Property Rights and Wages: The Case of Nursing Homes. *J. Human Res.*, Spring 1983, *18*(2), pp. 231–46. **[G: U.S.]**

van den Bosch, Frans A. J. and Petersen, Carel. An Explanation of the Growth of Social Security Disability Transfers. *De Economist,* 1983, *131*(1), pp. 65–79. **[G: Netherlands]**

Brambilla, Francesco. Un modello economico della professione medica. (An Economic Model of the Physician's Profession. With English summary.) *Giorn. Econ.*, May-June 1983, *42*(5–6), pp. 289–94.

Brooks, Richard G. Scotland's Health. **In** *Ingham, K. P. D. and Love, J., eds.*, 1983, pp. 107–16. **[G: U.K.]**

Buchanan, Robert J. Medicaid Cost Containment: Prospective Reimbursement for Long-Term Care. *Inquiry,* Winter 1983, *20*(4), pp. 334–42. **[G: U.S.]**

Butler, Richard J. and Worrall, John D. Workers' Compensation: Benefit and Injury Claims Rates in the Seventies. *Rev. Econ. Statist.*, November 1983, *65*(4), pp. 580–89. **[G: U.S.]**

Caldwell, John C.; Reddy, P. H. and Caldwell, Pat. The Social Component of Mortality Decline: An Investigation in South India Employing Alternative Methodologies. *Population Stud.*, July 1983, *37*(2), pp. 185–205. **[G: India]**

Capó, Luis R. International Drug Procurement and Market Intelligence: Cuba. *World Devel.*, March 1983, *11*(3), pp. 217–22. **[G: Cuba]**

Chavas, Jean-Paul and Keplinger, Keith O. Impact of Domestic Food Programs on Nutrient Intake of Low-Income Persons in the United States. *Southern J. Agr. Econ.*, July 1983, *15*(1), pp. 155–63. **[G: U.S.]**

Chen, Kwan-Hwa Marnie. The Cost-effectiveness of a Community-based Social Marketing Project in Thailand: The Family Planning Health and Hygiene Project. **In** *Sirageldin, I.; Salkever, D. and Osborn, R. W., eds.*, 1983, pp. 391–405. **[G: Thailand]**

Chernichovsky, Dov and Coate, Douglas. An Economic Analysis of the Diet, Growth and Health of Young Children in the United States. **In** *Salkever, D.; Sirageldin, I. and Sorkin, A., eds.*, 1983, pp. 111–25. **[G: U.S.]**

Chirikos, Thomas N. and Nastel, Gilbert. Economic Consequences of Poor Health in Mature Women. **In** *Shaw, L. B., ed.*, 1983, pp. 93–108. **[G: U.S.]**

Church, Richard and Stimson, Robert. Modelling Spatial Allocation–Location Solutions for General Practitioner Medical Services in Cities: The Equity-Revenue Maximizing Conflict Case. *Reg. Sci. Urban Econ.*, May 1983, *13*(2), pp. 161–72.

Coffey, Rosanna M. The Effect of Time Price on the Demand for Medical-Care Services. *J. Human Res.*, Summer 1983, *18*(3), pp. 407–24. **[G: U.S.]**

Cohen, David R. Health Education as a Demand Concept. *Int. J. Soc. Econ.*, 1983, *10*(5), pp. 52–62.

Cohodes, Donald R. Which Will Survive? The $150 Billion Capital Question. *Inquiry,* Spring 1983, *20*(1), pp. 5–11. **[G: U.S.]**

Connor, Michael J. and Greene, Sandra B. Should Extended Care Following Hospitalization Be Encouraged? *Inquiry,* Fall 1983, *20*(3), pp. 258–63. **[G: U.S.]**

Conrad, Robert F. and Strauss, Robert P. A Multiple–Output Multiple–Input Model of the Hospital Industry in North Carolina. *Appl. Econ.*, June 1983, *15*(3), pp. 341–52. **[G: U.S.]**

Contandriopoulos, A. P.; Dionne, Georges and Tessier, G. La mobilité des patients et les modèles de création de demande: le cas du Québec. (The Effect of Patients' Mobility on a Private Market of Chirurgical Services: The Case of Quebec. With English summary.) *L'Actual. Econ.*, December 1983, *59*(4), pp. 729–52. **[G: Canada]**

Correa, Hector. A Conceptual Model of Health. **In** *Salkever, D.; Sirageldin, I. and Sorkin, A., eds.*, 1983, pp. 3–28.

Cotterill, Philip G. Provider Incentives under Alternative Reimbursement Systems. **In** *Vogel, R. J. and Palmer, H. C., eds.*, 1983, pp. 625–64.

Cowing, Thomas G. and Holtmann, Alphonse G. Multiproduct Short-Run Hospital Cost Functions: Empirical Evidence and Policy Implications from Cross-Section Data. *Southern Econ. J.*, January 1983, *49*(3), pp. 637–53. **[G: U.S.]**

Coyte, Peter C. The Economics of Medicare: Equilibrium within the Medical Community. *J. Lab. Econ.*, July 1983, *1*(3), pp. 264–85.

Craig, John E., Jr. Cost Containment in the Voluntary Sector: Introduction. *Inquiry,* Summer 1983, *20*(2), pp. 101–02. **[G: U.S.]**

913 Economics of Health (including medical subsidy programs)

Cullen, Ross. Pharmaceuticals Inter-Country Diffusion. *Managerial Dec. Econ.*, June 1983, *4*(2), pp. 73–82. **[G: Selected Countries]**

Culyer, A. J. Health Indicators: Conclusions and Recommendations. **In** *Culyer, A. J., ed.*, 1983, pp. 186–93.

Culyer, A. J. Health Indicators: Introduction. **In** *Culyer, A. J., ed.*, 1983, pp. 1–22.

Culyer, A. J. Public or Private Health Services? A Skeptic's View. *J. Policy Anal. Manage.*, Spring 1983, *2*(3), pp. 386–402. **[G: U.S.]**

Cyr, A. Bruce. Proxy Case Mix Measures for Nursing Homes. *Inquiry*, Winter 1983, *20*(4), pp. 350–60. **[G: U.S.]**

Danziger, Sheldon. Budget Cuts as Welfare Reform. *Amer. Econ. Rev.*, May 1983, *73*(2), pp. 65–70. **[G: U.S.]**

Davis, Carolyne K. and Schieber, George J. Reforming the U.S. Health Care Financing System. *Atlantic Econ. J.*, September 1983, *11*(3), pp. 1–8. **[G: U.S.]**

Denton, Frank T. and Spencer, Byron G. Population Aging and Future Health Costs in Canada. *Can. Public Policy*, June 1983, *9*(2), pp. 155–63. **[G: Canada]**

DesHarnais, Susan; Kibe, Neel M. and Barbus, Shirley. Blue Cross and Blue Shield of Michigan Hospital Laboratory On-Site Review Project. *Inquiry*, Winter 1983, *20*(4), pp. 328–33. **[G: U.S.]**

DeSweemer, Cecile, et al. Child and Maternal Health Services in Rural India: Research Objectives, Design, and Methodology. **In** *Kielmann, A. A., et al.*, 1983, pp. 35–61. **[G: India]**

DeVany, Arthur S.; House, Donald R. and Saving, Thomas R. The Role of Patient Time in the Pricing of Dental Services: The Fee-Provider Density Relation Explained. *Southern Econ. J.*, January 1983, *49*(3), pp. 669–80. **[G: U.S.]**

DeVany, Arthur S., et al. Production in a Service Industry Using Customer Inputs: A Stochastic Model. *Rev. Econ. Statist.*, February 1983, *65*(1), pp. 149–53. **[G: U.S.]**

DeVries, Robert A. Hospice Care in the United States: Quest for Quality. *Inquiry*, Fall 1983, *20*(3), pp. 223–26. **[G: U.S.]**

Digby, Anne. Changes in the Asylum: The Case of York, 1777–1815. *Econ. Hist. Rev., 2nd Ser.*, May 1983, *36*(2), pp. 218–39. **[G: U.K.]**

Donabedian, Avedis. The Quality of Care in a Health Maintenance Organization: A Personal View. *Inquiry*, Fall 1983, *20*(3), pp. 218–22. **[G: U.S.]**

Duan, Naihua, et al. A Comparison of Alternative Models for the Demand for Medical Care. *J. Bus. Econ. Statist.*, April 1983, *1*(2), pp. 115–26. **[G: U.S.]**

Dunkelberg, John S.; Furst, Richard W. and Roenfeldt, Rodney L. State Rate Review and the Relationship between Capital Expenditures and Operating Costs. *Inquiry*, Fall 1983, *20*(3), pp. 240–47. **[G: U.S.]**

Duvall, Henrietta J. Utilization of Medicaid Services by AFDC Recipients. *Soc. Sec. Bull.*, June 1983, *46*(6), pp. 16–18. **[G: U.S.]**

Edwards, Linda N. and Grossman, Michael. Adolescent Health, Family Background, and Preventive Medical Care. **In** *Salkever, D.; Sirageldin, I. and Sorkin, A., eds.*, 1983, pp. 77–109. **[G: U.S.]**

Elliott, William B., et al. The Hospital Capitation Payment Project: New Incentives and Tools for Cost Containment. *Inquiry*, Summer 1983, *20*(2), pp. 114–20. **[G: U.S.]**

Emi, Koichi. Increasing Medical Expenses and the Social Insurance System. *Hitotsubashi J. Econ.*, June 1983, *24*(1), pp. 1–10. **[G: Japan]**

Erickson, Pennifer; Henke, Klaus-Dirk and Brittain, Roger Dean. A Health Statistics Framework: U.S. Data Systems as a Model for European Health Information? **In** *Culyer, A. J., ed.*, 1983, pp. 117–38. **[G: U.S.]**

Evans, R. G. The Welfare Economics of Public Health Insurance: Theory and Canadian Practice. **In** *Söderström, L., ed.*, 1983, pp. 71–103. **[G: Canada]**

Farley, Dean E. Evaluating a Hospital Cost-Containment Program in a Paired Experiment: Comment. *J. Amer. Statist. Assoc.*, June 1983, *78*(382), pp. 256–57.

Faruqee, Rashid. Family Planning and Health: The Narangwal Experiment. *Finance Develop.*, June 1983, *20*(2), pp. 43–46. **[G: India]**

Fattorusso, Vittorio. Essential Drugs for the Third World. *World Devel.*, March 1983, *11*(3), pp. 177–79. **[G: LDCs]**

Fichtenbaum, Rudy. Variations in Hospital Cost by Types of Ownership. *J. Behav. Econ.*, Winter 1983, *12*(2), pp. 17–35. **[G: U.S.]**

Folland, Sherman T. Predicting Hospital Market Shares. *Inquiry*, Spring 1983, *20*(1), pp. 34–44. **[G: U.S.]**

Fox, A. J. Health Monitoring in England and Wales. **In** *Culyer, A. J., ed.*, 1983, pp. 139–49. **[G: U.K.]**

Fülöp, T. and Reinke, William A. Health Manpower in Relation to Socioeconomic Development and Health Status. **In** *Salkever, D.; Sirageldin, I. and Sorkin, A., eds.*, 1983, pp. 392–52. **[G: Global]**

Gadreau, M. La régulation des dépenses de santé: Un choix de société sous contrainte de croissance économique. (The Regulation of Health Expenditure: A Collective Choice under the Constraint of Economic Growth. With English summary.) *Schweiz. Z. Volkswirtsch. Statist.*, September 1983, *119*(3), pp. 285–305. **[G: France]**

Gafni, Amiram, et al. Is There a Trade-Off between Income and Health? The Case of Hypertensive Steelworkers in Canada. *Inquiry*, Winter 1983, *20*(4), pp. 343–49. **[G: Canada]**

George, C. F. and Hands, D. E. Drug and Therapeutics Committees and Information Pharmacy Services: The United Kingdom. *World Devel.*, March 1983, *11*(3), pp. 229–36. **[G: U.K.]**

Gerber, Donna L. Community Programs for Affordable Health Care. *Inquiry*, Summer 1983, *20*(2), pp. 127–33. **[G: U.S.]**

Gianfrancesco, Frank D. A Proposal for Improving the Efficiency of Medical Insurance. *J. Health Econ.*, August 1983, *2*(2), pp. 176–84. **[G: U.S.]**

Gibson, Rosemary. Quiet Revolutions in Medicaid. **In** *Meyer, J. A., ed.*, 1983, pp. 75–102. **[G: U.S.]**

Gibson, Rosemary and Reiss, John B. Health Care Delivery and Financing: Competition, Regulation, and Incentives. **In** *Meyer, J. A., ed.*, 1983, pp. 243–68. **[G: U.S.]**

Ginsburg, Paul B. Market-oriented Options in Medicare and Medicaid. **In** *Meyer, J. A., ed.*, 1983, pp. 103–18. **[G: U.S.]**

Ginzberg, Eli. The Delivery of Health Care: What Lies Ahead? *Inquiry,* Fall 1983, *20*(3), pp. 201–17. **[G: U.S.]**

Gish, Oscar. Health Development: A Discussion of Some Issues. **In** *Salkever, D.; Sirageldin, I. and Sorkin, A., eds.*, 1983, pp. 57–74. **[G: LDCs]**

Goddeeris, John H. Theoretical Considerations on the Cost of Illness. *J. Health Econ.*, August 1983, *2*(2), pp. 149–59.

Goss, Simon. Cost–Benefit Analysis of the Detection and Treatment of Phenylketonuria (PKU) in Newly-Born Babies, in Belgium. *Cah. Écon. Bruxelles,* Third Trimestre 1983, (99), pp. 459–68. **[G: Belgium]**

Gothoskar, S. S. Drug Control: India. *World Devel.*, March 1983, *11*(3), pp. 223–28. **[G: India]**

Gray, Ronald. The Impact of Health and Nutrition on Natural Fertility. **In** *Bulatao, R. A. and Lee, R. D., eds., Vol. 1,* 1983, pp. 139–62.

Greenberg, Michael R. Urbanization and Cancer: Changing Mortality Patterns? *Int. Reg. Sci. Rev.*, October 1983, *8*(2), pp. 127–45. **[G: U.S.]**

Greenberg, Warren. How Will Increased Competition Affect the Costs of Health Care? **In** *Meyer, J. A., ed.*, 1983, pp. 46–60. **[G: U.S.]**

Greenlees, John S. and Manser, Marilyn E. Prices, Proxies and Productivity: An Historical Analysis of Hospital and Medical Care in Canada: Comment. **In** *Diewert, W. E. and Montmarquette, C., eds.*, 1983, pp. 778–81. **[G: Canada]**

Griffith, John R. The Role of Blue Cross and Blue Shield in the Future U.S. Health Care System. *Inquiry,* Spring 1983, *20*(1), pp. 12–19. **[G: U.S.]**

Grosse, Robert N. and Perry, Barbara H. Correlates of Life Expectancy in Less Developed Countries. **In** *Salkever, D.; Sirageldin, I. and Sorkin, A., eds.*, 1983, pp. 217–53. **[G: LDCs]**

Hadley, Jack. Teaching and Hospital Costs. *J. Health Econ.*, March 1983, *2*(1), pp. 75–79. **[G: U.S.]**

Hall, Marni J. Mental Illness and the Elderly. **In** *Vogel, R. J. and Palmer, H. C., eds.*, 1983, pp. 483–505. **[G: U.S.]**

Hamm, Linda V.; Kickham, Thomas M. and Curler, Dolores A. Research, Demonstrations, and Evaluations. **In** *Vogel, R. J. and Palmer, H. C., eds.*, 1983, pp. 167–253. **[G: U.S.]**

Havighurst, Clark C. Decentralizing Decision Making: Private Contract versus Professional Norms. **In** *Meyer, J. A., ed.*, 1983, pp. 22–45. **[G: U.S.]**

Havighurst, Clark C. The Contributions of Antitrust Law to a Procompetitive Health Policy. **In** *Meyer, J. A., ed.*, 1983, pp. 295–322. **[G: U.S.]**

Hedger, Douglas and Schmitt, Donald. Trends in Major Medical Coverage during a Period of Rising Costs. *Mon. Lab. Rev.*, July 1983, *106*(7), pp. 11–16. **[G: U.S.]**

Held, Philip J. and Pauly, Mark V. Charging the Victim: An Evaluation of Reimbursement Policy in the U.S. End-Stage Renal Disease Program. **In** *Helpman, E.; Razin, A. and Sadka, E., eds.*, 1983, pp. 43–65. **[G: U.S.]**

Held, Philip J. and Pauly, Mark V. Competition and Efficiency in the End Stage Renal Disease Program. *J. Health Econ.*, August 1983, *2*(2), pp. 95–118. **[G: U.S.]**

Hey, John D. and Patel, Mahesh S. Prevention and Cure? Or: Is an Ounce of Prevention Worth a Pound of Cure? *J. Health Econ.*, August 1983, *2*(2), pp. 119–38.

Horen, Jeffrey H. Operations Research. **In** *Vogel, R. J. and Palmer, H. C., eds.*, 1983, pp. 63–79.

Horen, Jeffrey H. The Labor Supply Question. **In** *Vogel, R. J. and Palmer, H. C., eds.*, 1983, pp. 723–42. **[G: U.S.]**

Horn, Susan D. and Sharkey, Phoebe D. Measuring Severity of Illness to Predict Patient Resource Use within DRGs. *Inquiry,* Winter 1983, *20*(4), pp. 314–21. **[G: U.S.]**

Hosek, James R. and Palmer, Adele R. Teaching and Hospital Costs: The Case of Radiology. *J. Health Econ.*, March 1983, *2*(1), pp. 29–46. **[G: U.S.]**

Hubley, John. Poverty and Health in Scotland. **In** *Brown, G. and Cook, R., eds.*, 1983, pp. 206–22. **[G: U.K.]**

Hunter, David J. Centre–Periphery Relations in the National Health Service: Facilitators or Inhibitors of Innovation? **In** *Young, K., ed.*, 1983, pp. 133–61. **[G: U.K.]**

Hurst, J. W. and Mooney, G. H. Implicit Values in Administrative Decisions. **In** *Culyer, A. J., ed.*, 1983, pp. 174–85. **[G: U.K.]**

Hynes, Kevin and Givner, Nathaniel. Physician Distribution in a Predominantly Rural State: Predictors and Trends. *Inquiry,* Summer 1983, *20*(2), pp. 185–90. **[G: U.S.]**

Joseph, Hyman, et al. Pharmacy Costs: Capitation versus Fee-for-Service. *Quarterly Journal of Business and Economics,* Autumn 1983, *22*(4), pp. 41–51. **[G: U.S.]**

Joskow, Paul L. Reimbursement Policy, Cost Containment and Non-Price Competition [Competition and Efficiency in the End Stage Renal Disease Program]. *J. Health Econ.*, August 1983, *2*(2), pp. 167–74. **[G: U.S.]**

Kalirajan, K. P. Analysis of Nutritional Adequacy in the Philippines: A Suggested Methodology. *Singapore Econ. Rev.*, October 1983, *28*(2), pp. 46–58. **[G: Philippines]**

Karni, Edi. Risk Aversion in the Theory of Health Insurance. **In** *Helpman, E.; Razin, A. and Sadka, E., eds.*, 1983, pp. 97–106.

Kehrer, Barbara H. and Woolridge, Judith. An Evaluation of Criteria to Designate Urban Health Manpower Shortage Areas. *Inquiry,* Fall 1983, *20*(3), pp. 264–75. **[G: Canada]**

Kielmann, Arnfried A., et al. Child and Maternal Health Services in Rural India: Analysis of Morbidity and Mortality. **In** *Kielmann, A. A., et al.*, 1983, pp. 172–214. **[G: India]**

King, Roland E. Actuarial Status of the Hospital Insurance and Supplementary Medical Insurance Trust Funds. *Soc. Sec. Bull.*, October 1983, *46*(10), pp. 9–15. **[G: U.S.]**

Kirschen, E. S. Les prix des vies humaines. (With English summary.) *Cah. Écon. Bruxelles,* 4th Trimester 1983, (100), pp. 486–533.

Klein, Rudolf. Centre–Periphery Relations in the National Health Service: Facilitators or Inhibitors of Innovation? Comment. **In** *Young, K., ed.*, 1983, pp. 161–67. [G: U.K.]

Kmiec, Douglas W. The Role of the Planner in a Deregulated World. **In** *Carr, J. H. and Duensing, E. E., eds.*, 1983, *1982*, pp. 229–41. [G: U.S.]

Kopit, William G. Health and Antitrust: The Case for Legislative Relief. **In** *Meyer, J. A., ed.*, 1983, pp. 323–31. [G: U.S.]

Korchagin, Iu. The Economic Health Fund. *Prob. Econ.*, September 1983, *26*(5), pp. 77–90. [G: U.S.S.R.]

Kritzer, Barbara E. Chile Changes Its Health Care System. *Soc. Sec. Bull.*, December 1983, *46*(12), pp. 16–18. [G: Chile]

Kurowski, Bettina D. and Shaughnessy, Peter W. The Measurement and Assurance of Quality. **In** *Vogel, R. J. and Palmer, H. C., eds.*, 1983, pp. 103–32. [G: U.S.]

LaCroix, Sumner J. and Getzen, Tom. The Supply of Physician Services: A Comment. *Econ. Inquiry*, July 1983, *21*(3), pp. 441–43. [G: U.S.]

Leiken, Alan M. and Dusansky, Richard. The Impact of Health Insurance on Hospital Costs: A Multi-Equation Econometric Approach. *Atlantic Econ. J.*, September 1983, *11*(3), pp. 79–85. [G: U.S.]

Leiken, Alan M.; Stern, Eve and Baines, Ruth E. The Effect of Clinical Education Programs on Hospital Production. *Inquiry*, Spring 1983, *20*(1), pp. 88–92. [G: U.S.]

Lerner, Monroe; Salkever, David S. and Newman, John F. The Decline in the Blue Cross Plan Admission Rate: Four Explanations. *Inquiry*, Summer 1983, *20*(2), pp. 103–13. [G: U.S.]

Lévy, Emile. La mesure de l'efficacité dans l'évaluation des politiques sociales: L'exemple de la santé. (With English summary.) *Revue Écon. Polit.*, May–June 1983, *93*(3), pp. 377–87. [G: France]

Lewit, Eugene. The Demand for Prenatal Care and the Production of Healthy Infants. **In** *Salkever, D.; Sirageldin, I. and Sorkin, A., eds.*, 1983, pp. 127–81. [G: U.S.]

Lipfert, Frederick W. Comment to Robert Mendelsohn and Guy Orcutt Regarding: "An Empirical Analysis of Air Pollution Dose—Response Curves." *J. Environ. Econ. Manage.*, June 1983, *10*(2), pp. 184–86. [G: U.S.]

Littrell, W. Boyd. Competition, Bureaucracy, and Hospital Care: Costs in a Midwestern City. **In** *Littrell, W. B.; Sjoberg, G. and Zurcher, L. A., eds.*, 1983, pp. 251–69.

Liu, Ben-chieh. Evaluating a Hospital Cost-Containment Program in a Paired Experiment. *J. Amer. Statist. Assoc.*, June 1983, *78*(382), pp. 249–56. [G: U.S.]

Liu, Korbin; Manton, Kenneth and Alliston, Wiley. Demographic and Epidemiologic Determinants of Expenditures. **In** *Vogel, R. J. and Palmer, H. C., eds.*, 1983, pp. 81–102. [G: U.S.]

Lloyd, Susan and Greenspan, Nancy T. Nursing Homes, Home Health Services, and Adult Day Care. **In** *Vogel, R. J. and Palmer, H. C., eds.*, 1983, pp. 133–66. [G: U.S.]

Logsdon, Donald N.; Rosen, Matthew A. and Demak, Michele M. The INSURE Project on Life-cycle Preventive Health Services: Cost Containment Issues. *Inquiry*, Summer 1983, *20*(2), pp. 121–26. [G: U.S.]

Majone, Giandomenico. Reforming Standard-Setting. *J. Policy Anal. Manage.*, Winter 1983, *2*(2), pp. 285–90. [G: W. Europe; U.S.S.R.; U.S.; U.K.]

Malenbaum, Wilfred. The Power of Health. **In** *Salkever, D.; Sirageldin, I. and Sorkin, A., eds.*, 1983, pp. 255–70. [G: LDCs]

Manser, Marilyn E. and Fineman, Elisabeth A. The Impact of the NHSC on the Utilization of Physician Services and on Health Status in Rural Areas. *J. Human Res.*, Fall 1983, *18*(4), pp. 521–38. [G: U.S.]

Marder, William D. and Hough, Douglas E. Medical Residency as Investment in Human Capital. *J. Human Res.*, Winter 1983, *18*(1), pp. 49–64. [G: U.S.]

Margolis, Stephen E. The Pricing of Physicians' Services. *J. Human Res.*, Fall 1983, *18*(4), pp. 592–608. [G: U.S.]

Martin, Patricia Yancey, et al. The Concept of "Integrated" Services Reconsidered. *Soc. Sci. Quart.*, December 1983, *64*(4), pp. 747–63. [G: U.S.]

Marx, Thomas G. The Cost of Living: Life, Liberty, and Cost–Benefit Analysis. *Policy Rev.*, Summer 1983, (25), pp. 53–58. [G: U.S.]

Marzagão, Carlos and Segall, Malcolm. Drug Selection: Mozambique. *World Devel.*, March 1983, *11*(3), pp. 205–16. [G: Mozambique]

Maynard, Alan K. Privatizing the National Health Service. *Lloyds Bank Rev.*, April 1983, (148), pp. 28–41. [G: U.K.]

Maynard, Alan K. The Production of Health and Health Care. *J. Econ. Stud.*, 1983, *10*(1), pp. 31–45. [G: Selected MDCs]

McGrath, M. D. Health Expenditure in a Racially Segregated Society: A Case Study of South Africa. **In** *Salkever, D.; Sirageldin, I. and Sorkin, A., eds.*, 1983, pp. 311–28. [G: S. Africa]

McGuire, Thomas G. Patients' Trust and the Quality of Physicians. *Econ. Inquiry*, April 1983, *21*(2), pp. 203–22.

Melrose, Dianna. Double Deprivation: Public and Private Drug Distribution from the Perspective of the Third World Poor. *World Devel.*, March 1983, *11*(3), pp. 181–86. [G: LDCs]

Mendelsohn, Robert and Orcutt, Guy. A Reply to a Comment on Estimating Air Pollution Dose—Response Curves. *J. Environ. Econ. Manage.*, June 1983, *10*(2), pp. 187–90. [G: U.S.]

Mennemeyer, Stephen T. and Gaumer, Gary. Nursing Wages and the Value of Educational Credentials. *J. Human Res.*, Winter 1983, *18*(1), pp. 32–48. [G: U.S.]

Meyer, Jack A. Market Reforms in Health Care: Introduction. **In** *Meyer, J. A., ed.*, 1983, pp. 1–11. [G: U.S.]

de Meza, David. Health Insurance and the Demand for Medical Care. *J. Health Econ.*, March 1983, *2*(1), pp. 47–54.

Morell, Jonathan A. and Weirich, Thomas W. Determining the Costs of Evaluation. **In** *Alkin, M. C. and Solmon, L. C., eds.*, 1983, pp. 81–100.

Mossé, Philippe. Multidimensionality of Health Indicators: The French Discussion. **In** *Culyer, A. J., ed.*, 1983, pp. 82–90.

Mullner, Ross M. and Byre, Calvin S. Toward an Inventory of U.S. Health Care Data Bases. *Rev.*

Public Data Use (See J. Econ. Soc. Meas. after 4/85), March 1983, *11*(1), pp. 57–65. **[G: U.S.]**

Mullner, Ross M.; Byre, Calvin S. and Killingsworth, Cleve L. An Inventory of U.S. Health Care Data Bases. *Rev. Public Data Use (See J. Econ. Soc. Meas. after 4/85)*, June 1983, *11*(2), pp. 85–192. **[G: U.S.]**

Musgrove, Philip. Family Health Care Spending in Latin America. *J. Health Econ.*, December 1983, *2*(3), pp. 245–57. **[G: Latin America]**

Newhouse, Joseph P. Two Prospective Difficulties with Prospective Payment of Hospitals, or, It's Better to Be a Resident than a Patient with a Complex Problem. *J. Health Econ.*, December 1983, *2*(3), pp. 269–74. **[G: U.S.]**

Newman, John F.; Schreiber, Mark and Gibbs, James O. The Providence Plan: Prepaid Health Care for a Voluntary Enrolled Population. *Inquiry*, Summer 1983, *20*(2), pp. 134–41. **[G: U.S.]**

Newman, Peter. Conceptual Framework for the Planning of Medicine in Developing Countries. **In** *Salkever, D.; Sirageldin, I. and Sorkin, A., eds.*, 1983, pp. 29–56. **[G: LDCs]**

Nord-Larsen, Mogens. What Kind of Health Measure for What Kind of Purpose? **In** *Culyer, A. J., ed.*, 1983, pp. 101–09.

Nord, Stephen. Urban Size and the Quality of Human Health: A Social Indicator Approach. *Atlantic Econ. J.*, July 1983, *11*(2), pp. 35–43. **[G: U.S.]**

O'Brien-Place, P. M. and Tomek, William G. Inflation in Food Prices as Measured by Least-Cost Diets. *Amer. J. Agr. Econ.*, November 1983, *65*(4), pp. 781–84. **[G: U.S.]**

Ostro, Bart D. The Effects of Air Pollution on Work Loss and Morbidity. *J. Environ. Econ. Manage.*, December 1983, *10*(4), pp. 371–82. **[G: U.S.]**

Ostro, Bart D. Urban Air Pollution and Morbidity: A Retrospective Approach. *Urban Stud.*, August 1983, *20*(3), pp. 343–51. **[G: U.S.]**

Palley, Howard A.; Yishai, Yael and Ever-Hadani-Pnina. Pluralist Social Constraints on the Development of a Health Care System: The Case of Israel. *Inquiry*, Spring 1983, *20*(1), pp. 65–75. **[G: Israel]**

Palmer, Hans C. Adult Day Care. **In** *Vogel, R. J. and Palmer, H. C., eds.*, 1983, pp. 415–36. **[G: U.S.]**

Palmer, Hans C. Domiciliary Care: A Semantic Tangle. **In** *Vogel, R. J. and Palmer, H. C., eds.*, 1983, pp. 437–61. **[G: U.S.]**

Palmer, Hans C. Home Care. **In** *Vogel, R. J. and Palmer, H. C., eds.*, 1983, pp. 337–90. **[G: U.S.]**

Palmer, Hans C. The Alternatives Question. **In** *Vogel, R. J. and Palmer, H. C., eds.*, 1983, pp. 255–305. **[G: U.S.]**

Palmer, Hans C. The System of Provision. **In** *Vogel, R. J. and Palmer, H. C., eds.*, 1983, pp. 1–62. **[G: U.S.]**

Palmer, Hans C. and Cotterill, Philip G. Studies of Nursing Home Costs. **In** *Vogel, R. J. and Palmer, H. C., eds.*, 1983, pp. 665–721. **[G: U.S.]**

Palmer, Hans C. and Vogel, Ronald J. Models of the Nursing Home. **In** *Vogel, R. J. and Palmer, H. C., eds.*, 1983, pp. 537–78.

Paringer, Lynn. Economic Incentives in the Provision of Long-term Care. **In** *Meyer, J. A., ed.*, 1983, pp. 119–43. **[G: U.S.]**

Paringer, Lynn. Women and Absenteeism: Health or Economics? *Amer. Econ. Rev.*, May 1983, *73*(2), pp. 123–27. **[G: U.S.]**

Parker, Robert L. and Reinke, William A. The Use of Health Services. **In** *Taylor, C. E., et al.*, 1983, pp. 85–108. **[G: India]**

Parker, Robert L. and Sarma, R. S. S. Efficiency and Equity of Project Services. **In** *Taylor, C. E., et al.*, 1983, pp. 191–213. **[G: India]**

Parker, Robert L., et al. Evaluation of Program Utilization and Cost Effectiveness. **In** *Kielmann, A. A., et al.*, 1983, pp. 228–56. **[G: India]**

Passmore, Davin Lynn, et al. Health and Youth Employment. *Appl. Econ.*, December 1983, *15*(6), pp. 715–29. **[G: U.S.]**

Patel, Mahesh S. Drug Costs in Developing Countries and Policies to Reduce Them. *World Devel.*, March 1983, *11*(3), pp. 195–204. **[G: LDCs]**

Paterson, Morton L. Cost–Benefit Evaluation of a New Technology for Treatment of Peptic Ulcer Disease. *Managerial Dec. Econ.*, March 1983, *4*(1), pp. 50–62. **[G: U.S.; W. Europe]**

Patrick, Donald and Guttmacher, Sally. Socio-political Issues in the Use of Health Indicators. **In** *Culyer, A. J., ed.*, 1983, pp. 165–73.

Pauly, Mark V. More on Moral Hazard [Health Insurance and the Demand for Medical Care]. *J. Health Econ.*, March 1983, *2*(1), pp. 81–85.

Pauly, Mark V. and Langwell, Kathryn M. Research on Competition in the Market for Health Services: Problems and Prospects. *Inquiry*, Summer 1983, *20*(2), pp. 142–61. **[G: U.S.]**

Phelps, Charles E. Tax Policy, Health Insurance, and Health Care. **In** *Meyer, J. A., ed.*, 1983, pp. 198–224. **[G: U.S.]**

Pitt, Mark M. Food Preferences and Nutrition in Rural Bangladesh. *Rev. Econ. Statist.*, February 1983, *65*(1), pp. 105–14. **[G: Bangladesh]**

Poleman, Thomas T. World Hunger: Extent, Causes, and Cures. **In** *Johnson, D. G. and Schuh, G. E., eds.*, 1983, pp. 41–75. **[G: LDCs]**

Price, James R.; Mays, James W. and Trapnell, Gordon R. Stability in the Federal Employees Health Benefits Program. *J. Health Econ.*, December 1983, *2*(3), pp. 207–23. **[G: U.S.]**

Reinke, William A. The Lampang (Thailand) Health Development Project: Proposed Methodology for Integrated Cost/Task Analysis. **In** *Sirageldin, I.; Salkever, D. and Osborn, R. W., eds.*, 1983, pp. 351–90. **[G: Thailand]**

Reinke, William A. and Parker, Robert L. Relations between the Use of Health Services and Family Planning. **In** *Taylor, C. E., et al.*, 1983, pp. 109–28. **[G: India]**

Rice, Dorothy P. Health Care Data in the United States. *Rev. Public Data Use (See J. Econ. Soc. Meas. after 4/85)*, June 1983, *11*(2), pp. 79–84. **[G: U.S.]**

Rice, Thomas and McCall, Nelda. Factors Influencing Physician Assignment Decisions under Medicare. *Inquiry*, Spring 1983, *20*(1), pp. 45–56. **[G: U.S.]**

Rodgers, James F. and Musacchio, Robert A. Physician Acceptance of Medicare Patients on Assignment. *J. Health Econ.*, March 1983, *2*(1), pp. 55–73. [G: U.S.]

Rosenzweig, Mark R. and Schultz, T. Paul. Consumer Demand and Household Production: The Relationship between Fertility and Child Mortality. *Amer. Econ. Rev.*, May 1983, *73*(2), pp. 38–42. [G: U.S.]

Rosser, Rachel. Issues of Measurement in the Design of Health Indicators: A Review. **In** *Culyer, A. J., ed.*, 1983, pp. 34–81.

Rossiter, Louis F. and Wilensky, Gail R. A Reexamination of the Use of Physician Services: The Role of Physician-Initiated Demand. *Inquiry*, Summer 1983, *20*(2), pp. 162–72. [G: U.S.]

Rothstein, Mark A. Employee Selection Based on Susceptibility to Occupational Illness. *Mich. Law Rev.*, May 1983, *81*(6), pp. 1379–496. [G: U.S.]

Roustang, Guy. Worker Participation in Occupational Safety and Health Matters in France. *Int. Lab. Rev.*, March–April 1983, *122*(2), pp. 169–82. [G: France]

Runge, Carlisle Ford. Risk Assessment and Environmental Benefits Analysis. *Natural Res. J.*, July 1983, *23*(3), pp. 683–96. [G: U.S.]

Russell, Louise B. Medical Care. **In** *Pechman, J. A., ed.*, 1983, pp. 111–44. [G: U.S.]

Salkever, David S. Health in Human Capital Formation: Comment. **In** *Salkever, D.; Sirageldin, I. and Sorkin, A., eds.*, 1983, pp. 209–14. [G: U.S.]

Samors, Patricia W. and Sullivan, Sean. Health Care Cost Containment through Private Sector Initiatives. **In** *Meyer, J. A., ed.*, 1983, pp. 144–59. [G: U.S.]

Sangl, Judith. The Family Support System of the Elderly. **In** *Vogel, R. J. and Palmer, H. C., eds.*, 1983, pp. 307–36. [G: U.S.]

Sawyer, Darwin O. Pharmaceutical Reimbursement and Drug Cost Control: The MAC Experience in Maryland. *Inquiry*, Spring 1983, *20*(1), pp. 76–87. [G: U.S.]

Scarpat, Orlando. Un tentativo di analisi costi–benefici dell'inserimento dei disabili nel mercato del lavoro. (A Tentative Cost–Benefit Analysis of the Employment of Disabled Workers. With English summary.) *Rivista Int. Sci. Econ. Com.*, September 1983, *30*(9), pp. 849–60. [G: Italy]

Schapper, Paul R. Hospital Cost Inflation: The Case of Australia. *Inquiry*, Fall 1983, *20*(3), pp. 276–81. [G: Australia]

Schearer, S. Bruce. Monetary and Health Costs of Contraception. **In** *Bulatao, R. A. and Lee, R. D., eds., Vol. 2*, 1983, pp. 89–150. [G: LDCs]

Scheffler, Richard M. and Rossiter, Louis F. Compensation Schemes and the Labor Supply of Dentists. *Quart. Rev. Econ. Bus.*, Autumn 1983, *23*(3), pp. 29–43. [G: U.S.]

Schlenker, Robert; Shaughnessy, Peter W. and Yslas, Inez. The Effect of Case Mix and Quality on Cost Differences between Hospital-Based and Freestanding Nursing Homes. *Inquiry*, Winter 1983, *20*(4), pp. 361–68. [G: U.S.]

Schlesinger, Harris. A Theoretical Model of Medical Malpractice and the Quality of Care. *J. Econ. Bus.*, 1983, *35*(1), pp. 83–94.

Schmähl, Winfried. Auswirkungen von Veränderungen der Altersstruktur der Bevölkerung auf die Finanzsituation der gesetzlichen Krankenversicherung im Vergleich zur gesetzlichen Rentenversicherung—Eine modelltheoretische Analyse. (A Comparison of the Effects of a Changing Age Structure on the Financing of Social Health Insurance and on That of the Social Retirement System—A Theoretical Analysis. With English summary.) *Konjunkturpolitik*, 1983, *29*(2), pp. 100–20. [G: W. Germany]

Schneider, Karen C. and Dove, Henry G. High Users of VA Emergency Room Facilities: Are Outpatients Abusing the System or Is the System Abusing Them? *Inquiry*, Spring 1983, *20*(1), pp. 57–64. [G: U.S.]

Schroeder, Ernst. Concepts of Health and Illness. **In** *Culyer, A. J., ed.*, 1983, pp. 23–33.

Schwartz, William B. The Competitive Strategy: Will It Affect Quality of Care? **In** *Meyer, J. A., ed.*, 1983, pp. 15–21. [G: U.S.]

Selowsky, Marcelo. Nutrition, Health and Education: The Economic Significance of Complementarities at Early Ages. **In** *Streeten, P. and Maier, H., eds.*, 1983, pp. 181–97. [G: Columbia]

Sen, Amartya K. Economic Development: Some Strategic Issues. **In** *Gauhar, A., ed. (I)*, 1983, pp. 43–54. [G: LDCs]

Shah, C. H. Food Preference, Poverty, and the Nutrition Gap. *Econ. Develop. Cult. Change*, October 1983, *32*(1), pp. 121–48. [G: India]

Shapiro, Lynn E. Legal Issues Arising under the Consumer Choice Proposals. **In** *Meyer, J. A., ed.*, 1983, pp. 269–94. [G: U.S.]

Shukla, Ramesh K. All-RN Model of Nursing Care Delivery: A Cost-Benefit Evaluation. *Inquiry*, Summer 1983, *20*(2), pp. 173–84. [G: U.S.]

Shukla, Ramesh K. Technical and Structural Support Systems and Nurse Utilization: Systems Model. *Inquiry*, Winter 1983, *20*(4), pp. 381–89. [G: U.S.]

Singleton, W. T. Occupational Safety and Health Systems: A Three-Country Comparison. *Int. Lab. Rev.*, March–April 1983, *122*(2), pp. 155–68. [G: Switzerland; U.K.; U.S.]

Sirén, Pekka. Terveydenhuollon menot, rakenne ja rahoitus. (Health Care Expenditure, Structure and Financing in Finland. With English summary.) *Kansant. Aikak.*, 1983, *79*(4), pp. 418–35. [G: Finland]

Sloan, Frank A.; Feldman, Roger D. and Steinwald, A. Bruce. Effects of Teaching on Hospital Costs. *J. Health Econ.*, March 1983, *2*(1), pp. 1–28. [G: U.S.]

Smith, Christopher J. Locating Alcoholism Treatment Facilities. *Econ. Geogr.*, October 1983, *59*(4), pp. 368–85. [G: U.S.]

Somers, Anne R. And Who Shall Be the Gatekeeper? The Role of the Primary Physician in the Health Care Delivery System. *Inquiry*, Winter 1983, *20*(4), pp. 301–13. [G: U.S.]

Sommers, Paul M. and Thomas, Laura S. Restricting Federal Funds for Abortion: Another Look. *Soc. Sci. Quart.*, June 1983, *64*(2), pp. 340–46. [G: U.S.]

Sorkin, Alan L. Health in Development: Comment. **In** *Salkever, D.; Sirageldin, I. and Sorkin, A., eds.*, 1983, pp. 353–58. [G: Selected Countries]

Southwick, Lawrence, Jr. and Cadigan, John F., Jr. The Medical Expense Deduction and Income Levels: Progressive or Regressive? *J. Econ. Bus.*, 1983, *35*(1), pp. 61–70. **[G: U.S.]**

Srinivasan, T. N. Hunger: Defining It, Estimating Its Global Incidence, and Alleviating It. **In** *Johnson, D. G. and Schuh, G. E., eds.*, 1983, pp. 77–108. **[G: LDCs]**

Stern, J. The Relationship between Unemployment, Morbidity and Mortality in Britain. *Population Stud.*, March 1983, *37*(1), pp. 61–74. **[G: U.K.]**

Stevenson, Ray. Medical Services: Contributions to Growth. **In** *Federal Reserve Bank of Atlanta*, 1983, pp. 73–80. **[G: U.S.]**

Stolwijk, Jan A. J. Nuclear Waste Management and Risks to Human Health. **In** *Walker, C. A.; Gould, L. C. and Woodhouse, E. J., eds.*, 1983, pp. 75–93. **[G: U.S.]**

Stoto, Michael A. Estimating Distribution Functions for Small Groups: Postoperative Hospital Stay. **In** *Zeckhauser, R. J. and Leebaert, D., eds.*, 1983, pp. 221–40. **[G: U.S.]**

Sullivan, Sean and Gibson, Rosemary. Tax-related Issues in Health Care Market Reform. **In** *Meyer, J. A., ed.*, 1983, pp. 185–97. **[G: U.S.]**

Sullivan, Sean and Samors, Patricia W. Administrative Problems with Proposals for Health Care Reform. **In** *Meyer, J. A., ed.*, 1983, pp. 225–40. **[G: U.S.]**

Taylor, Amy K. and Wilensky, Gail R. The Effect of Tax Policies on Expenditures for Private Health Insurance. **In** *Meyer, J. A., ed.*, 1983, pp. 163–84. **[G: U.S.]**

Taylor, Carl E. Background, Design, and Policy Issues. **In** *Taylor, C. E., et al.*, 1983, pp. 3–32. **[G: India]**

Taylor, Carl E., et al. Child and Maternal Health Services in Rural India: Main Research Findings on Policy Issues. **In** *Kielmann, A. A., et al.*, 1983, pp. 62–92. **[G: India]**

Taylor, Carl E., et al. Child and Maternal Health Services in Rural India: Background and Summary of Findings. **In** *Kielmann, A. A., et al.*, 1983, pp. 3–34. **[G: India]**

Taylor, Carl E., et al. Main Research Findings on Policy Issues. **In** *Taylor, C. E., et al.*, 1983, pp. 33–56. **[G: India]**

Temin, Peter. Costs and Benefits in Switching Drugs from Rx to OTC. *J. Health Econ.*, December 1983, *2*(3), pp. 187–205. **[G: U.S.]**

Teres, Daniel, et al. A Comparison of Mortality and Charges in Two Differently Staffed Intensive Care Units. *Inquiry*, Fall 1983, *20*(3), pp. 282–89. **[G: U.S.]**

Thomas, J. William, et al. Increasing Medicare Enrollment in HMOs: The Need for Capitation Rates Adjusted for Health Status. *Inquiry*, Fall 1983, *20*(3), pp. 227–39. **[G: U.S.]**

Thomas, Steven G. The Significance of Housing as a Resource. **In** *Vogel, R. J. and Palmer, H. C., eds.*, 1983, pp. 391–414. **[G: U.S.]**

Thomas, Steven G. Transportation and Dependency. **In** *Vogel, R. J. and Palmer, H. C., eds.*, 1983, pp. 463–82. **[G: U.S.]**

Thomas, Vinod. Discussion [World Hunger: Extent, Causes, and Cures] [Hunger: Defining It, Estimating Its Global Incidence, and Alleviating It]. **In** *Johnson, D. G. and Schuh, G. E., eds.*, 1983, pp. 109–14. **[G: LDCs]**

Townsend, John, et al. Cost-effectiveness of Family Planning Services in the Sinaps Primary Health Care Program in Guatemala. **In** *Sirageldin, I.; Salkever, D. and Osborn, R. W., eds.*, 1983, pp. 458–75. **[G: Guatemala]**

Trebilcock, Michael J. and Shaul, Jeffrey. Regulating the Quality of Psychotherapeutic Services. **In** *Dewees, D. N., ed.*, 1983, pp. 275–91. **[G: Canada]**

Tresnowski, Bernard R. Cost Containment: Short Steps in a Long Journey. *Inquiry*, Summer 1983, *20*(2), pp. 99–100. **[G: U.S.]**

Tussing, A. Dale. Physician-Induced Demand for Medical Care: Irish General Practitioners. *Econ. Soc. Rev.*, April 1983, *14*(3), pp. 225–47. **[G: Ireland]**

Uhde, Aina. The Need for Health Indicators. **In** *Culyer, A. J., ed.*, 1983, pp. 110–16.

Van Regemorter, Denise. Les effectifs et les revenus de la catégorie des invalides en Belgique. (With English summary.) *Cah. Écon. Bruxelles*, 1983, *97*(1), pp. 104–14. **[G: Belgium]**

van de Ven, Wynand P. M. M. and van Praag, Bernard M. S. Corrigendum [The Demand for Deductibles in Private Health Insurance: A Probit Model with Sample Selection]. *J. Econometrics*, August 1983, *22*(3), pp. 395.

Virts, John R. and Wilson, George W. Inflation and the Behavior of Sectoral Prices. *Bus. Econ.*, May 1983, *18*(3), pp. 45–54. **[G: U.S.]**

Viscusi, W. Kip. Alternative Approaches to Valuing the Health Impacts of Accidents: Liability Law and Prospective Evaluations. *Law Contemp. Probl.*, Autumn 1983, *46*(4), pp. 49–68. **[G: U.S.]**

Vogel, Ronald J. The Industrial Organization of the Nursing Home Industry. **In** *Vogel, R. J. and Palmer, H. C., eds.*, 1983, pp. 579–624. **[G: U.S.]**

Vogel, Ronald J. and Greenspan, Nancy T. Health Planning in the Sudan. **In** *Salkever, D.; Sirageldin, I. and Sorkin, A., eds.*, 1983, pp. 271–309. **[G: Sudan]**

Waldman, Saul. A Legislative History of Nursing Home Care. **In** *Vogel, R. J. and Palmer, H. C., eds.*, 1983, pp. 507–35. **[G: U.S.]**

Walter, John P. and Leahy, William H. Demand for Medical Services by Deprived Urban Youth in North and South America. *Amer. Econ.*, Fall 1983, *27*(2), pp. 29–33. **[G: U.S.; Peru]**

Wardell, William M. Economic or Medical Criteria, or Both, in Policy Decisions about Medicines? [Costs and Benefits in Switching Drugs from Rx to OTC]. *J. Health Econ.*, December 1983, *2*(3), pp. 275–79. **[G: U.S.]**

von Wartensleben, Aurelie. Major Issues Concerning Pharmaceutical Policies in the Third World. *World Devel.*, March 1983, *11*(3), pp. 169–75. **[G: LDCs; MDCs]**

Wassermann, Ursula. National Legislation on Hormones and Antibiotics. *J. World Trade Law*, March–April 1983, *17*(2), pp. 158–69. **[G: Selected Countries]**

Weatherby, Norman L.; Nam, Charles B. and Isaac,

Larry W. Development, Inequality, Health Care, and Mortality at the Older Ages: A Cross-National Analysis. *Demography*, February 1983, *20*(1), pp. 27–43. **[G: Selected MDCs; Selected LDCs]**

Weehuizen, J. W. and Klaassen, H. L. Uses and Users of Information in Health Care. **In** *Culyer, A. J., ed.*, 1983, pp. 91–100.

Weese, Samuel H. Another Look at "Nuclear Liability after Three Mile Island." *J. Risk Ins.*, June 1983, *50*(2), pp. 323–27. **[G: U.S.]**

Weinstein, Milton C. and Quinn, Robert J. Psychological Considerations in Valuing Health Risk Reductions. *Natural Res. J.*, July 1983, *23*(3), pp. 659–73. **[G: U.S.]**

Weisbrod, Burton A. A Guide to Benefit–Cost Analysis, as Seen through a Controlled Experiment in Treating the Mentally Ill. **In** *Helpman, E.; Razin, A. and Sadka, E., eds.*, 1983, pp. 5–42. **[G: U.S.]**

Weisbrod, Burton A. Competition in Health Care: A Cautionary View. **In** *Meyer, J. A., ed.*, 1983, pp. 61–71. **[G: U.S.]**

Wilcox-Gök, Virginia L. The Determination of Child Health: An Application of Sibling and Adoption Data. *Rev. Econ. Statist.*, May 1983, *65*(2), pp. 266–73.

Wilensky, Gail R. and Cafferata, Gail Lee. Women and the Use of Health Services. *Amer. Econ. Rev.*, May 1983, *73*(2), pp. 128–33. **[G: U.S.]**

Wilensky, Gail R. and Rossiter, Louis F. Economic Advantages of Board Certification. *J. Health Econ.*, March 1983, *2*(1), pp. 87–94. **[G: U.S.]**

Williams, Alan. The Economics of Health. **In** *Gowland, D. H., ed.*, 1983, pp. 201–22. **[G: U.K.]**

Williams, Rory. Disability as a Health Indicator. **In** *Culyer, A. J., ed.*, 1983, pp. 150–64.

Wilson, Barry P., et al. Hospice Care: Perspectives on a Blue Cross Plan's Community Pilot Program. *Inquiry*, Winter 1983, *20*(4), pp. 322–27. **[G: U.S.]**

Wlodkowski, Bonita A. Caveat Emptor in Health Care. *Polit. Sci. Quart.*, Spring 1983, *98*(1), pp. 35–45. **[G: U.S.]**

Wolfe, Barbara L. and Behrman, Jere R. Is Income Overrated in Determining Adequate Nutrition? *Econ. Develop. Cult. Change*, April 1983, *31*(3), pp. 525–49. **[G: Managua]**

Wolfe, Barbara L. and Haveman, Robert H. Time Allocation, Market Work, and Changes in Female Health. *Amer. Econ. Rev.*, May 1983, *73*(2), pp. 134–39. **[G: U.S.]**

Wood, William C. "Nuclear Liability after Three Mile Island"—Author's Reply. *J. Risk Ins.*, June 1983, *50*(2), pp. 328–29. **[G: U.S.]**

Wrege, Charles D. Medical Men and Scientific Management: A Forgotten Chapter in Management History. *Rev. Bus. Econ. Res.*, Spring 1983, *18*(3), pp. 32–47. **[G: U.S.]**

Young, David W. and Saltman, Richard B. Prospective Reimbursement and the Hospital Power Equilibrium: A Matrix-Based Management Control system. *Inquiry*, Spring 1983, *20*(1), pp. 20–33. **[G: U.S.]**

Zweifel, Peter. Inflation in the Health Care Sector and the Demand for Insurance: A Micro Study. **In** *Söderström, L., ed.*, 1983, pp. 105–35. **[G: Switzerland]**

914 Economics of Poverty

9140 Economics of Poverty

Akin, John S.; Guilkey, David K. and Popkin, Barry M. The School Lunch Program and Nutrient Intake: A Switching Regression Analysis. *Amer. J. Agr. Econ.*, August 1983, *65*(3), pp. 477–85. **[G: U.S.]**

Alam, M. Shahid. The Nature of Mass Poverty: A Review Article. *Pakistan J. Appl. Econ.*, Summer 1983, *2*(1), pp. 85–92.

Altimir, Oscar. Poverty in Latin America: An Examination of the Evidence. **In** *Urquidi, V. L. and Reyes, S. T., eds.*, 1983, pp. 279–98. **[G: Latin America]**

Bequele, Assefa. Stagnation and Inequality in Ghana. **In** *Ghai, D. and Radwan, S., eds.*, 1983, pp. 219–47. **[G: Ghana]**

Betson, David M. and Greenberg, David. Uses of Microsimulation in Applied Poverty Research. **In** *Goldstein, R. and Sachs, S. M., eds.*, 1983, pp. 175–90. **[G: U.S.]**

Brown, Gordon. Scotland: The Real Divide: Poverty and Deprivation in Scotland: Introduction. **In** *Brown, G. and Cook, R., eds.*, 1983, pp. 9–22. **[G: U.K.]**

Burkhauser, Richard V. and Wilkinson, James T. The Effect of Retirement on Income Distribution: A Comprehensive Income Approach. *Rev. Econ. Statist.*, November 1983, *65*(4), pp. 653–58. **[G: U.S.]**

Carmichael, Kay. Family Poverty. **In** *Brown, G. and Cook, R., eds.*, 1983, pp. 145–51. **[G: U.K.]**

Chakravarti, Anand. Some Aspects of Inequality in Rural India: A Sociological Perspective. **In** *Béteille, A., ed.*, 1983, pp. 129–81. **[G: India]**

Chakravarty, Satya Ranjan. A New Index of Poverty. *Math. Soc. Sci.*, December 1983, *6*(3), pp. 307–13.

Chakravarty, Satya Ranjan. Ethically Flexible Measures of Poverty. *Can. J. Econ.*, February 1983, *16*(1), pp. 74–85.

Chenery, Hollis B. Poverty and Progress—Choices for the Developing World. **In** *Todaro, M. P., ed.*, 1983, *1980*, pp. 86–94.

Clark, Bill and Casserly, John. The Disabled. **In** *Brown, G. and Cook, R., eds.*, 1983, pp. 162–71. **[G: U.K.]**

Coe, Richard D. Nonparticipation in Welfare Programs by Eligible Households: The Case of the Food Stamp Program. *J. Econ. Issues*, December 1983, *17*(4), pp. 1035–56. **[G: U.S.]**

Colclough, Christopher and Fallon, Peter. Rural Poverty in Botswana: Dimensions, Causes and Constraints. **In** *Ghai, D. and Radwan, S., eds.*, 1983, pp. 129–53. **[G: Botswana]**

Condominas, S. La crisis economica contemporanea: algunas consideraciones generales. (The Present Economic Crisis. With English summary.) *Écon. Soc.*, September–October–November 1983, *17*(9-10-11), pp. 1383–1401.

Cook, Robin. Housing and Deprivation. **In** *Brown, G. and Cook, R., eds.*, 1983, pp. 172–89. **[G: U.K.]**

Corvalán-Vásquez, Oscar. Vocational Training of

Disadvantaged Youth in the Developing Countries. *Int. Lab. Rev.*, May–June 1983, *122*(3), pp. 367–81. **[G: LDCs]**

Datcher, Linda. Racial Differences in the Persistence of Affluence. **In** *Duncan, G. J. and Morgan, J. N., eds.*, 1983, pp. 205–17. **[G: U.S.]**

Davies, Trevor and Sinfield, Adrian. The Unemployed. **In** *Brown, G. and Cook, R., eds.*, 1983, pp. 91–106. **[G: U.K.]**

Dixon, John; Nagorcka, Barry and Cutt, James. Evaluating Poverty Programs: The Usefulness of Dynamic Continuous Simulation Modelling. **In** *Goldstein, R. and Sachs, S. M., eds.*, 1983, pp. 191–208. **[G: Australia]**

Downs, Anthony. The President's Housing Commission and Two Tests of Realistic Recommendations. *Amer. Real Estate Urban Econ. Assoc. J.*, Summer 1983, *11*(2), pp. 182–91. **[G: U.S.]**

Elliott, Charles. Equity and Growth: An Unresolved Conflict in Zambian Rural Development Policy. **In** *Ghai, D. and Radwan, S., eds.*, 1983, pp. 155–89. **[G: Zambia]**

Field, Frank. Breaking the Mould: The Thatcher Government's Fiscal Policies. **In** *Field, F., ed.*, 1983, pp. 56–68. **[G: U.K.]**

Fox, M. Louise. Income Distribution in Post-1964 Brazil: New Results. *J. Econ. Hist.*, March 1983, *43*(1), pp. 261–71. **[G: Brazil]**

Freudenberger, Herman H. Levels of Living of European Peasantry: Discussion. *J. Econ. Hist.*, March 1983, *43*(1), pp. 146–47. **[G: Czechoslovakia; U.S.S.R.]**

Ghai, Dharam and Radwan, Samir. Agrarian Change, Differentiation and Rural Poverty in Africa: A General Survey. **In** *Ghai, D. and Radwan, S., eds.*, 1983, pp. 1–29. **[G: Sub-Saharan Africa]**

Ginsberg, Leon H. Changing Public Attitudes about Public Welfare Clients and Services through Research. **In** *Goldstein, R. and Sachs, S. M., eds.*, 1983, pp. 241–52. **[G: U.S.]**

Girshick, Lori B. and Williamson, John B. The Politics of Measuring Poverty among the Elderly. **In** *Goldstein, R. and Sachs, S. M., eds.*, 1983, pp. 64–76. **[G: U.S.]**

Goldstein, Richard. Who Really Benefits from Applied Poverty Research? Opening Up a Question. **In** *Goldstein, R. and Sachs, S. M., eds.*, 1983, pp. 29–39. **[G: U.S.]**

Goldstein, Richard and Sachs, Stephen M. Applied Poverty Research: Introduction. **In** *Goldstein, R. and Sachs, S. M., eds.*, 1983, pp. 3–13. **[G: U.S.; Europe]**

Goldstein, Richard and Sachs, Stephen M. Applied Poverty Research: Alternative Research Perspectives: Introduction. **In** *Goldstein, R. and Sachs, S. M., eds.*, 1983, pp. 117–22. **[G: U.S.]**

Goldstein, Richard and Sachs, Stephen M. Measuring Poverty: Introduction. **In** *Goldstein, R. and Sachs, S. M., eds.*, 1983, pp. 43–48. **[G: U.S.]**

Gooneratne, W. and Gunawardena, P. J. Poverty and Inequality in Rural Sri Lanka. **In** *Khan, A. R. and Lee, E., eds.*, 1983, pp. 247–71. **[G: Sri Lanka]**

Green, Cynthia B. and Sanger, Mary Bryna. Aiding the Poor. **In** *Brecher, C. and Horton, R. D., eds.*, 1983, pp. 99–130. **[G: U.S.]**

Greenberg, David and Halsey, Harlan. Systematic Misreporting and Effects of Income Maintenance Experiments on Work Effort: Evidence from the Seattle–Denver Experiment. *J. Lab. Econ.*, October 1983, *1*(4), pp. 380–407. **[G: U.S.]**

Grimes, Alistair. Pensioners in Poverty. **In** *Brown, G. and Cook, R., eds.*, 1983, pp. 136–44. **[G: U.K.]**

Guinness, Patrick. The Gelandangan of Yogyakarta. *Bull. Indonesian Econ. Stud.*, April 1983, *19*(1), pp. 68–82. **[G: Indonesia]**

Harvey, Russell and Hemming, Richard. Inflation, Pensioner Living Standards and Poverty. *Oxford Bull. Econ. Statist.*, May 1983, *45*(2), pp. 195–204. **[G: U.K.]**

Hicks, Norman L. Is There a Tradeoff between Growth and Basic Needs? **In** *Todaro, M. P., ed.*, 1983, *1980*, pp. 95–101.

Hill, Martha S. Female Household Headship and the Poverty of Children. **In** *Duncan, G. J. and Morgan, J. N., eds.*, 1983, pp. 324–76. **[G: U.S.]**

House, William J. and Killick, Tony. Social Justice and Development Policy in Kenya's Rural Economy. **In** *Ghai, D. and Radwan, S., eds.*, 1983, pp. 31–69. **[G: Kenya]**

Hubley, John. Poverty and Health in Scotland. **In** *Brown, G. and Cook, R., eds.*, 1983, pp. 206–22. **[G: U.K.]**

Hunter, Eveline. Women and Poverty. **In** *Brown, G. and Cook, R., eds.*, 1983, pp. 152–61. **[G: U.K.]**

Irfan, M. and Amjad, Rashid. Poverty in Rural Pakistan. **In** *Khan, A. R. and Lee, E., eds.*, 1983, pp. 19–47. **[G: Pakistan]**

Islam, Rizwanul. Poverty and Income Distribution in Rural Nepal. **In** *Khan, A. R. and Lee, E., eds.*, 1983, pp. 165–83. **[G: Nepal]**

Islam, Rizwanul. Poverty, Income Distribution and Growth in Rural Thailand. **In** *Khan, A. R. and Lee, E., eds.*, 1983, pp. 205–29. **[G: Thailand]**

Jamal, Vali. Nomads and Farmers: Incomes and Poverty in Rural Somalia. **In** *Ghai, D. and Radwan, S., eds.*, 1983, pp. 281–311. **[G: Somalia]**

Jose, A. V. Poverty and Income Distribution: The Case of West Bengal. **In** *Khan, A. R. and Lee, E., eds.*, 1983, pp. 137–63. **[G: India]**

Jose, A. V. Poverty and Inequality—The Case of Kerala. **In** *Khan, A. R. and Lee, E., eds.*, 1983, pp. 107–36. **[G: India]**

Khan, Azizur Rahman and Lee, Eddy. Poverty in Rural Asia: Introduction. **In** *Khan, A. R. and Lee, E., eds.*, 1983, pp. 1–18. **[G: Asia]**

Komlos, John H. Poverty and Industrialization at the End of the "Phase-Transition" in the Czech Crown Lands. *J. Econ. Hist.*, March 1983, *43*(1), pp. 129–35. **[G: Czechoslovakia]**

Kundu, Amitabh and Smith, Tony E. An Impossibility Theorem on Poverty Indices. *Int. Econ. Rev.*, June 1983, *24*(2), pp. 423–34.

Kynch, Jocelyn and Sen, Amartya K. Indian Women: Well-Being and Survival. *Cambridge J. Econ.*, September/December 1983, 7(3/4), pp. 363–80. **[G: India]**

Lee, Eddy. Agrarian Change and Poverty in Rural Java. **In** *Khan, A. R. and Lee, E., eds.*, 1983, pp. 231–46. **[G: Indonesia]**

Levitan, Sar A. and Taggart, Robert. The Bitter Fruits of Labor. *Challenge,* March/April 1983, *26*(1), pp. 18–22. **[G: U.S.]**

Levitt, Ian. Scottish Poverty: The Historical Background. **In** *Brown, G. and Cook, R., eds.,* 1983, pp. 66–75. **[G: U.K.]**

Lim, David. The Political Economy of the New Economic Policy in Malaysia. **In** *Lim, D., ed.,* 1983, pp. 3–22. **[G: Malaysia]**

McIlvanney, William. Being Poor. **In** *Brown, G. and Cook, R., eds.,* 1983, pp. 23–26. **[G: U.K.]**

Mehretu, Assefa; Wittick, Robert I. and Pigozzi, Bruce W. Spatial Design for Basic Needs in Eastern Upper Volta. *J. Devel. Areas,* April 1983, *17*(3), pp. 383–94. **[G: Upper Volta]**

Mesa-Lago, Carmelo. Social Security and Extreme Poverty in Latin America. *J. Devel. Econ.,* February/April 1983, *12*(1/2), pp. 83–110. **[G: Latin America]**

Moffitt, Robert A. An Economic Model of Welfare Stigma. *Amer. Econ. Rev.,* December 1983, *73*(5), pp. 1023–35. **[G: U.S.]**

Mohl, Raymond A. The Abolition of Public Outdoor Relief, 1870–1900: A Critique of the Piven and Cloward Thesis. **In** *Trattner, W. I., ed..,* 1983, pp. 35–50. **[G: U.S.]**

Mondal, S. K. Balanced Diet, Availability of Food, Cereal Consumption and Poverty. *Margin,* July 1983, *15*(4), pp. 92–102. **[G: India]**

Morris, Cynthia Taft and Adelman, Irma. Institutional Influences on Poverty in the Nineteenth Century: A Quantitative Comparative Study: Reply to Williamson. *J. Econ. Hist.,* March 1983, *43*(1), pp. 61–62. **[G: MDCs; LDCs]**

Morris, Cynthia Taft and Adelman, Irma. Institutional Influences on Poverty in the Nineteenth Century: A Quantitative Comparative Study. *J. Econ. Hist.,* March 1983, *43*(1), pp. 43–55. **[G: MDCs; LDCs]**

Mundle, Sudipto. Land, Labour and the Level of Living in Rural Bihar. **In** *Khan, A. R. and Lee, E., eds.,* 1983, pp. 49–80. **[G: India]**

Mundle, Sudipto. Land, Labour and the Level of Living in Rural Punjab. **In** *Khan, A. R. and Lee, E., eds.,* 1983, pp. 81–106. **[G: India]**

Neubeck, Kenneth J. Income Maintenance Experimentation: Cui Bono. **In** *Goldstein, R. and Sachs, S. M., eds.,* 1983, pp. 253–59. **[G: U.S.]**

Newman, Sandra J. and Struyk, Raymond J. Housing and Poverty. *Rev. Econ. Statist.,* May 1983, *65*(2), pp. 243–53. **[G: U.S.]**

Norbye, O. D. Koht. Mass Poverty and International Income Transfers. **In** *Parkinson, J. R., ed.,* 1983, pp. 15–39.

Norris, G. M. Poverty in Scotland, 1979–83. **In** *Brown, G. and Cook, R., eds.,* 1983, pp. 27–39. **[G: U.K.]**

Nugent, Jeffrey B. and Tarawneh, Fayez A. The Anatomy of Changes in Income Distribution and Poverty among Mexico's Economically Active Population between 1950 and 1970. *J. Devel. Areas,* January 1983, *17*(2), pp. 197–226. **[G: Mexico]**

Olson, Mancur. Reassessment of Measures of Levels of Living: Discussion. *J. Econ. Hist.,* March 1983, *43*(1), pp. 86–88.

Othick, John. Development Indicators and the Historical Study of Human Welfare: Towards a New Perspective. *J. Econ. Hist.,* March 1983, *43*(1), pp. 63–70.

Panning, William H. Inequality, Social Comparison, and Relative Deprivation. *Amer. Polit. Sci. Rev.,* June 1983, *77*(2), pp. 323–29.

Parkinson, J. R. Poverty and Aid: Introduction: A Window on the World. **In** *Parkinson, J. R., ed.,* 1983, pp. 1–11.

Payne, Geoff and Ford, Graeme. Inequality and the Occupational Structure. **In** *Brown, G. and Cook, R., eds.,* 1983, pp. 76–90. **[G: U.K.]**

Pfeffermann, Guy and Webb, Richard. Poverty and Income Distribution in Brazil. *Rev. Income Wealth,* June 1983, *29*(2), pp. 101–24. **[G: Brazil]**

van Praag, Bernard M. S.; Hagenaars, Aldi J. M. and van Weeren, Hans. Poverty in Europe: Errata. *Rev. Income Wealth,* June 1983, *29*(2), pp. 215. **[G: EEC]**

Rodgers, Harrell R., Jr. Limiting Poverty by Design: The Official Measure of Poverty. **In** *Goldstein, R. and Sachs, S. M., eds.,* 1983, pp. 49–63. **[G: U.S.]**

Rodgers, Harrell R., Jr. Social Welfare Programs: Lessons from Europe, the Need for Comparative Analysis. **In** *Goldstein, R. and Sachs, S. M., eds.,* 1983, pp. 269–83. **[G: Sweden; W. Europe]**

Sachs, Stephen M. Toward a Political Economy of Poverty Research: A Critique from Right to Left. **In** *Goldstein, R. and Sachs, S. M., eds.,* 1983, pp. 14–28. **[G: U.S.]**

Sachs, Stephen M. and Goldstein, Richard. Politics, Ethics, and Poverty Research. **In** *Goldstein, R. and Sachs, S. M., eds.,* 1983, pp. 287–93. **[G: U.S.]**

Sathyamurthy, T. V. The Political Economy of Poverty: The Case of India. **In** *Parkinson, J. R., ed.,* 1983, pp. 90–113. **[G: India]**

Sen, Amartya K. Poor, Relatively Speaking. *Oxford Econ. Pap.,* July 1983, *35*(2), pp. 153–69.

Shah, C. H. Food Preference, Poverty, and the Nutrition Gap. *Econ. Develop. Cult. Change,* October 1983, *32*(1), pp. 121–48. **[G: India]**

Smeeding, Timothy M. The Anti-poverty Effect of In-Kind Transfers: A "Good Idea" Gone Too Far? **In** *Goldstein, R. and Sachs, S. M., eds.,* 1983, pp. 77–101. **[G: U.S.]**

Sternlieb, George and Hughes, James W. Housing the Poor in a Postshelter Society. *Ann. Amer. Acad. Polit. Soc. Sci.,* January 1983, *465,* pp. 109–22. **[G: U.S.]**

Stinson, Thomas F. and Larson, Ronald B. A Poverty of Government Services: Estimates 1962, 1972, 1977. **In** *Goldstein, R. and Sachs, S. M., eds.,* 1983, pp. 102–14. **[G: U.S.]**

Swidinsky, Robert. Working Wives, Income Distribution and Poverty. *Can. Public Policy,* March 1983, *9*(1), pp. 71–80. **[G: Canada]**

Teckenberg, Wolfgang. Economic Well-being in the Soviet Union Inflation and the Distribution of Resources. **In** *Schmukler, N. and Marcus, E., eds.,* 1983, pp. 659–76. **[G: U.S.S.R.]**

Tendulkar, Suresh D. Economic Inequality in an Indian Perspective. **In** *Béteille, A., ed.,* 1983, pp.

71–128. [G: India]

Thon, Dominique. A Note on a Troublesome Axiom for Poverty Indices [On Indices for the Measurement of Poverty]. *Econ. J.*, March 1983, *93*(369), pp. 199–200.

Thon, Dominique. A Poverty Measure. *Indian Econ. J.*, April-June 1983, *30*(4), pp. 55–70. **[G: India]**

Thoris, Gérard. Les limites de la redistribution des revenus: perspective macroéconomique. (With English summary.) *Revue Écon. Polit.*, September–October 1983, *93*(5), pp. 682–92. **[G: France]**

Tomlinson, R. Industrial Decentralization and the Relief of Poverty in the Homelands. *S. Afr. J. Econ.*, December 1983, *51*(4), pp. 544–63. **[G: S. Africa]**

Trattner, Walter I. Social Welfare or Social Control? Some Historical Reflections: Introduction. **In** *Trattner, W. I., ed..*, 1983, pp. 3–14.

Wallace, James E. Direct Household Assistance and Block Grants. *Amer. Real Estate Urban Econ. Assoc. J.*, Summer 1983, *11*(2), pp. 192–202. **[G: U.S.]**

Walter, John P. and Leahy, William H. Demand for Medical Services by Deprived Urban Youth in North and South America. *Amer. Econ.*, Fall 1983, *27*(2), pp. 29–33. **[G: U.S.; Peru]**

Watts, Michael and Lubeck, Paul. The Popular Classes and the Oil Boom: A Political Economy of Rural and Urban Poverty. **In** *Zartman, I. W., ed.*, 1983, pp. 105–44. **[G: Nigeria]**

Wedderburn, Dorothy. Policy Issues in the Distribution of Income and Wealth: Some Lessons from the Diamond Commission. **In** *Field, F., ed.*, 1983, pp. 69–87. **[G: U.K.]**

Weicher, John C. The Report of the President's Commission on Housing: Policy Proposals for Subsidized Housing. *Amer. Real Estate Urban Econ. Assoc. J.*, Summer 1983, *11*(2), pp. 117–32. **[G: U.S.]**

Wilbur, Elvira M. Was Russian Peasant Agriculture Really That Impoverished? New Evidence from a Case Study from the "Impoverished Center" at the End of the Nineteenth Century. *J. Econ. Hist.*, March 1983, *43*(1), pp. 137–44. **[G: U.S.S.R.]**

Williamson, Jeffrey G. Institutional Influences on Poverty in the Nineteenth Century: A Quantitative Comparative Study: Discussion. *J. Econ. Hist.*, March 1983, *43*(1), pp. 56–60. **[G: MDCs; LDCs]**

Young, Ronald. A Little Local Inequality. **In** *Brown, G. and Cook, R., eds.*, 1983, pp. 223–51. **[G: U.K.]**

915 Social Security

9150 Social Security

Aaron, Henry J. Cutting Back the Social Welfare State. **In** *[Goode, R.]*, 1983, pp. 199–213. **[G: U.S.]**

Aaron, Henry J. Cutting Back the Welfare State. **In** *Helpman, E.; Razin, A. and Sadka, E., eds.*, 1983, pp. 147–60. **[G: U.S.]**

Aaron, Henry J. Modeling Alternative Solutions to the Long-run Social Security Funding Problem: Comment. **In** *Feldstein, M., ed.*, 1983, pp. 237–46. **[G: U.S.]**

Abbott, Julian. Knowledge of Social Security: Survivor Families with Young Children. *Soc. Sec. Bull.*, December 1983, *46*(12), pp. 3–13. **[G: U.S.]**

Achenbaum, W. Andrew. The Formative Years of Social Security: A Test Case of the Piven and Cloward Thesis. **In** *Trattner, W. I., ed..*, 1983, pp. 67–89. **[G: U.S.]**

Adamy, Wilhelm and Koeppinghoff, Sigrid. Zur Krisenanfälligkeit der Rentenversicherung. Arbeitsmarktbedingte Finanzierungsprobleme in theoretischer und empirischer Sicht. (Pension Funds: Vulnerability to Crises—Deficits Caused by Unemployment, Viewed from a Theoretical and Empirical Perspective. With English summary.) *Konjunkturpolitik*, 1983, *29*(5), pp. 285–313. **[G: W. Germany]**

Aldrich, Jonathan; Fox, Alan and Lopez, Eduard. Purchasing Power of U.S. Social Security Benefits Abroad, 1970–82. *Soc. Sec. Bull.*, September 1983, *46*(9), pp. 3–9. **[G: U.S.; Europe; Philippines; Mexico]**

Asimakopulos, A. Public Pensions, the Federal Budget, and Discrimination. *Can. Public Policy*, March 1983, *9*(1), pp. 105–13. **[G: Canada]**

Asimakopulos, A. Social Security and Economists. *J. Post Keynesian Econ.*, Summer 1983, *5*(4), pp. 679–82. **[G: U.S.]**

Atkinson, Anthony B. and Flemming, J. S. Unemployment, Social Security and Incentives in Britain. **In** *Atkinson, A. B.*, 1983, *1978*, pp. 397–418. **[G: U.K.]**

Atkinson, Anthony B.; King, Mervyn A. and Sutherland, H. The Analysis of Personal Taxation and Social Security. *Nat. Inst. Econ. Rev.*, November 1983, (106), pp. 63–74. **[G: U.K.]**

Auerbach, Alan J. and Kotlikoff, Laurence J. An Examination of Empirical Tests of Social Security and Savings. **In** *Helpman, E.; Razin, A. and Sadka, E., eds.*, 1983, pp. 161–79. **[G: U.S.]**

Ballantyne, Harry C. Actuarial Status of the Old-Age and Survivors Insurance and Disability Insurance Trust Funds. *Soc. Sec. Bull.*, October 1983, *46*(10), pp. 3–8. **[G: U.S.]**

Becker, Irene. Umverteilungswirkungen monetärer Transfers—Eine empirische Analyse von Steuern, Sozialabgaben und Sozialleistungen. (Redistributive Effects of Monetary Transfers—An Empirical Analysis of Taxes, Payroll Taxes and Social Transfers in the Federal Republic of Germany. With English summary.) *Ifo-Studien*, 1983, *29*(4), pp. 273–98. **[G: W. Germany]**

Bellante, Don. Breaking the Political Barriers to Privatization [Private Alternatives to Social Security: The Experience of Other Countries]. *Cato J.*, Fall 1983, *3*(2), pp. 575–80. **[G: U.K.; Chile; U.S.]**

Bentzel, Ragnar and Berg, Lennart. The Role of Demographic Factors as a Determinant of Savings in Sweden. **In** *Modigliani, F. and Hemming, R., eds.*, 1983, pp. 152–79. **[G: Sweden]**

Blinder, Alan S.; Gordon, Roger H. and Wise, Donald E. Social Security, Bequests and the Life Cycle Theory of Saving: Cross-sectional Tests. **In** *Modi-*

gliani, F. and Hemming, R., eds., 1983, pp. 89–122. [G: U.S.]

van den Bosch, Frans A. J. and Petersen, Carel. An Explanation of the Growth of Social Security Disability Transfers. *De Economist,* 1983, *131* (1), pp. 65–79. [G: Netherlands]

Boskin, Michael J.; Avrin, Marcy and Cone, Kenneth. Modeling Alternative Solutions to the Long-run Social Security Funding Problem. In *Feldstein, M., ed.,* 1983, pp. 211–37. [G: U.S.]

Browning, Edgar K. "The Economics and Politics of the Emergence of Social Security": A Comment. *Cato J.,* Fall 1983, *3* (2), pp. 381–84. [G: U.S.]

Buchanan, James M. Social Security Survival: A Public-Choice Perspective. *Cato J.,* Fall 1983, *3* (2), pp. 339–53. [G: U.S.]

Burbridge, John B. Social Security and Savings Plans in Overlapping-Generations Models. *J. Public Econ.,* June 1983, *21* (1), pp. 79–92. [G: U.S.]

Burkhauser, Richard V. Social Security and the Family: Commentary. In *Penner, R. G., ed.,* 1983, pp. 167–72. [G: U.S.]

Burkhauser, Richard V. and Quinn, Joseph F. Financial Incentives and Retirement in the United States. In *Söderström, L., ed.,* 1983, pp. 207–24. [G: U.S.]

Burkhauser, Richard V. and Quinn, Joseph F. Is Mandatory Retirement Overrated? Evidence from the 1970s. *J. Human Res.,* Summer 1983, *18* (3), pp. 337–58. [G: U.S.]

Burkhauser, Richard V. and Quinn, Joseph F. The Effect of Pension Plans on the Pattern of Life Cycle Compensation. In *Triplett, J. E., ed.,* 1983, pp. 395–415. [G: U.S.]

Burtless, Gary T. "Misdirection of Labor and Capital under Social Security": A Comment. *Cato J.,* Fall 1983, *3* (2), pp. 531–36. [G: U.S.]

Butler, Stuart and Germanis, Peter. Achieving a "Leninist" Strategy. *Cato J.,* Fall 1983, *3* (2), pp. 547–56. [G: U.S.]

Campbell, Colin D. Alternative Constraints on Social Security [Social Security: The Absence of Lasting Reform]. *Cato J.,* Fall 1983, *3* (2), pp. 483–87. [G: U.S.]

Carvalho, Jose L. and Haddad, Claudio Luiz da Silva. Trade and Factor Market Distortions: Effects on Employment in Brazil. In *Weisbrod, B. and Hughes, H., eds.,* 1983, pp. 405–28. [G: Brazil]

Chen, Yung-Ping. Employee Benefits and Social Security. *Contemp. Policy Issue,* April 1983, (3), pp. 23–32. [G: U.S.]

Clark, Robert L. and Gohmann, Stephan F. Retirement and the Acceptance of Social Security Benefits. *Nat. Tax J.,* December 1983, *36* (4), pp. 529–34. [G: U.S.]

Coe, Richard D. Participation in the Supplemental Security Income Program by the Eligible Elderly. In *Duncan, G. J. and Morgan, J. N., eds.,* 1983, pp. 93–120. [G: U.S.]

Cumming, Christine. Social Security in Germany and the United Kingdom. *Fed. Res. Bank New York Quart. Rev.,* Spring 1983, *8* (1), pp. 13–25. [G: U.K.; W. Germany; U.S.]

Dalrymple, Robert; Grad, Susan and Wilson, Duke. Civil Service Retirement System Annuitants and Social Security. *Soc. Sec. Bull.,* February 1983, *46* (2), pp. 39–59. [G: U.S.]

Daly, Michael J. Some Microeconometric Evidence Concerning the Effect of the Canada Pension Plan on Personal Saving. *Economica,* February 1983, *50* (197), pp. 63–69. [G: Canada]

Daly, Michael J. and Macnaughton, Alan. Reverse Annuity Mortgages and Recent Tax Changes. *Can. Public Policy,* September 1983, *9* (3), pp. 398. [G: Canada]

Darbon, Sébastien. Assurance maladie et redistribution du revenu: Une question de méthodes. (With English summary.) *Revue Écon. Polit.,* May–June 1983, *93* (3), pp. 397–420. [G: France]

DiLorenzo, Thomas J. A Constitutionalist Approach to Social Security Reform. *Cato J.,* Fall 1983, *3* (2), pp. 443–59. [G: U.S.]

Dolde, Walter and Tobin, James. Mandatory Retirement Saving and Capital Formation. In *Modigliani, F. and Hemming, R., eds.,* 1983, pp. 56–88. [G: U.S.]

Dorn, James A. Social Security: Continuing Crisis or Real Reform? *Cato J.,* Fall 1983, *3* (2), pp. 335–38. [G: U.S.]

Edelbalk, Per Gunnar and Elmér, Åke. Social Insurance in Sweden. In *Söderström, L., ed.,* 1983, pp. 53–69. [G: Sweden]

Eisner, Robert. Social Security, Saving, and Macroeconomics. *J. Macroecon.,* Winter 1983, *5* (1), pp. 1–19. [G: U.S.]

Evans, Owen J. Social Security and Household Saving in the United States: A Re-Examination. *Int. Monet. Fund Staff Pap.,* September 1983, *30* (3), pp. 601–18. [G: U.S.]

de Falleur, Richard. Les perspectives de la sécurité sociale dans les projections à moyen terme du Bureau du Plan. (With English summary.) *Cah. Écon. Bruxelles,* 1983, *97* (1), pp. 115–60. [G: Belgium]

Feldstein, Martin S. Social Security Benefits and the Accumulation of Pre-retirement Wealth. In *Modigliani, F. and Hemming, R., eds.,* 1983, pp. 3–23. [G: U.S.]

Ferrara, Peter J. The Prospect of Real Reform. *Cato J.,* Fall 1983, *3* (2), pp. 609–21. [G: U.S.]

Flowers, Marilyn R. The Political Feasibility of Privatizing Social Security [Achieving a "Leninist" Strategy]. *Cato J.,* Fall 1983, *3* (2), pp. 557–61. [G: U.S.]

Garfinkel, Irv. The Role of Universal Demogrants and Child Support in Social Security Reform. *Int. J. Soc. Econ.,* 1983, *10* (6/7), pp. 12–20.

Garrison, Roger W. Misdirection of Labor and Capital under Social Security. *Cato J.,* Fall 1983, *3* (2), pp. 513–29. [G: U.S.]

Genosko, Joachim. Erwerbsbeteiligung und gesetzliche Rentenversicherung—Der Fall der 60- bis 65jährigen Männer. (Labor Force Participation and Old Age Insurance—The Case of the 60–65 Year-Old Men. With English summary.) *Z. ges. Staatswiss.,* December 1983, *139* (4), pp. 625–42. [G: W. Germany]

Gollier, J. J. Tendances à long terme du régime de pensions légales. Une solution alternative? (An Alternative Solution to Cover the Pension Costs in Belgium. With English summary.) *Ann. Sci. Écon. Appl.*, 1983, *39*(2), pp. 7–52. **[G: Belgium]**

Goodman, John C. Private Alternatives to Social Security: The Experience of Other Countries. *Cato J.*, Fall 1983, *3*(2), pp. 563–73. **[G: Chile; U.K.; U.S.]**

Gordon, Roger H. Social Security and Labor Supply Incentives. *Contemp. Policy Issue*, April 1983, (3), pp. 16–22. **[G: U.S.]**

Grimes, Alistair. Pensioners in Poverty. **In** *Brown, G. and Cook, R., eds.*, 1983, pp. 136–44. **[G: U.K.]**

Grubel, Herbert G. Reassessing the Cost of Social Insurance Programs. **In** *Giersch, H., ed.*, 1983, pp. 145–62. **[G: Canada]**

Haber, William. Social Security in the United States—An Ongoing Debate. *Int. J. Soc. Econ.*, 1983, *10*(6/7), pp. 21–28. **[G: U.S.]**

Harpham, Edward J. Social Security: Political History and Prospects for Reform [The Economics and Politics of the Emergence of Social Security: Some Implications for Reform]. *Cato J.*, Fall 1983, *3*(2), pp. 385–91. **[G: U.S.]**

Harvey, Russell and Hemming, Richard. Inflation, Pensioner Living Standards and Poverty. *Oxford Bull. Econ. Statist.*, May 1983, *45*(2), pp. 195–204. **[G: U.K.]**

Hauser, Mark; Meyer, Peter and Oberhänsli, Urs. Die obligatorische Altervorsorge in der Schweiz: Rentabilitätsüberlegungen und Einkommensumverteilungsaspekte. (The Obligatory Provision for Old Age in Switzerland: Rentability and Aspects of Income Redistribution. With English summary.) *Schweiz. Z. Volkswirtsch. Statist.*, June 1983, *119*(2), pp. 147–70. **[G: Switzerland]**

Hauser, Richard. Zur Diskussion um die Witwenrenten Ökonomische und sozialpolitische Aspekte der "Rentenreform '84." (Widow's Pensions: Economic and Social-Policy Aspects of the "1984 Reform." With English summary.) *Ifo-Studien*, 1983, *29*(2), pp. 139–61. **[G: W. Germany]**

Hawkins, Sue C. SSI: Characteristics of Persons Receiving Federally Administered State Supplementation Only. *Soc. Sec. Bull.*, April 1983, *46*(4), pp. 3–12. **[G: U.S.]**

Hawkins, Sue C. SSI: Trends in State Supplementation, 1979–81. *Soc. Sec. Bull.*, June 1983, *46*(6), pp. 3–8. **[G: U.S.]**

Hemming, Richard and Harvey, Russell. Occupational Pension Scheme Membership and Retirement Saving. *Econ. J.*, March 1983, *93*(369), pp. 128–44. **[G: U.K.]**

Hu, Sheng Cheng. Value-Added Tax as a Source of Social Security Financing. *Public Finance Quart.*, April 1983, *11*(2), pp. 154–80. **[G: U.S.]**

Janssen, Martin and Müller, Heinz. Die Substitutionswirkungen zwischen kollektiver Vorsorge und privatem Sparen in der Schweiz. (The Rates of Substitution between Collective Provision and Private Saving in Switzerland. With English summary.) *Schweiz. Z. Volkswirtsch. Statist.*, June 1983, *119*(2), pp. 139–45. **[G: Switzerland]**

Kennedy, Lenna D. Unearned Income of Supplemental Security Income Recipients, May 1982. *Soc. Sec. Bull.*, May 1983, *46*(5), pp. 3–6. **[G: U.S.]**

Kessler, Denis. Les politiques sociales modifient-elles le comportement des individus? Le cas du système de retraite. (With English summary.) *Revue Écon. Polit.*, May–June 1983, *93*(3), pp. 328–44.

Keyfitz, Nathan. Age Effects in Work and Consumption. *Econ. Notes*, 1983, (3), pp. 86–121. **[G: Global]**

King, Roland E. Actuarial Status of the Hospital Insurance and Supplementary Medical Insurance Trust Funds. *Soc. Sec. Bull.*, October 1983, *46*(10), pp. 9–15. **[G: U.S.]**

Koskela, Erkki and Virén, Matti. Social Security and Household Saving in an International Cross Section. *Amer. Econ. Rev.*, March 1983, *73*(1), pp. 212–17.

Koskie, Raymond. Recent Developments in the Law of Pensions. **In** *Queen's Univ. Indust. Relat. Centre*, 1983, pp. 68–75. **[G: Canada]**

Kuné, Jan B. Studies on the Relationship between Social Security and Personal Saving: A Tabular Survey. *Kredit Kapital*, 1983, *16*(3), pp. 371–80. **[G: U.S.; Canada; W. Europe]**

Kunz, Peter. Solidarität und Beitragsäquivalenz in der Altersversicherung. (Solidarity and Old-Age Pension. With English summary.) *Schweiz. Z. Volkswirtsch. Statist.*, June 1983, *119*(2), pp. 171–93. **[G: Switzerland]**

Lévy, Emile. La mesure de l'efficacité dans l'évaluation des politiques sociales: L'exemple de la santé. (With English summary.) *Revue Écon. Polit.*, May–June 1983, *93*(3), pp. 377–87. **[G: France]**

Levy, Mickey. Social Security and the Family: Commentary. **In** *Penner, R. G., ed.*, 1983, pp. 165–67. **[G: U.S.]**

Lingg, Barbara A. Beneficiaries Affected by the Annual Earnings Test in 1978. *Soc. Sec. Bull.*, April 1983, *46*(4), pp. 23–34. **[G: U.S.]**

Lingg, Barbara A. Female Social Security Beneficiaries Aged 62 or Older, 1960–82. *Soc. Sec. Bull.*, September 1983, *46*(9), pp. 10–12. **[G: U.S.]**

Lundahl, Mats. Insuring against Risk in Primitive Economies: The Role of Prestige Goods. **In** *Söderström, L., ed.*, 1983, pp. 35–51.

Maxfield, Linda Drazga. The 1982 New Beneficiary Survey: An Introduction. *Soc. Sec. Bull.*, November 1983, *46*(11), pp. 3–11. **[G: U.S.]**

McKenzie, Richard B. Social Security: The Absence of Lasting Reform. *Cato J.*, Fall 1983, *3*(2), pp. 467–78. **[G: U.S.]**

McMurray, David. The Current Industrial Relations Scene in Canada, 1983: Labour Legislation and Policy: Summary Outline. **In** *Wood, W. D. and Kumar, P., eds.*, 1983, pp. 87–205. **[G: Canada]**

Merton, Robert C. On the Role of Social Security as a Means for Efficient Risk Sharing in an Economy Where Human Capital Is Not Tradable. **In** *Bodie, Z. and Shoven, J. B., eds.*, 1983, pp. 325–58. **[G: U.S.]**

Merton, Robert C. On Consumption Indexed Public Pension Plans. **In** *Bodie, Z. and Shoven, J. B., eds.*, 1983, pp. 259–76, 287–89. **[G: U.S.]**

Mesa-Lago, Carmelo. Social Security and Extreme Poverty in Latin America. *J. Devel. Econ.*, February/April 1983, *12*(1/2), pp. 83–110. **[G: Latin America]**

Modigliani, Franco and Sterling, Arlie. Determinants

of Private Saving with Special Reference to the Role of Social Security—Cross-country Tests. **In** *Modigliani, F. and Hemming, R., eds.*, 1983, pp. 24–55. **[G: Selected OECD]**

Müller-Groeling, Hubertus. Reforming Social Security for Old Age: Comment. **In** *Giersch, H., ed.*, 1983, pp. 191–97.

Munnell, Alicia H. Financing Options for Social Security. **In** *Parnes, H. S., ed.*, 1983, pp. 197–240. **[G: U.S.]**

Munnell, Alicia H. Social Security. **In** *Pechman, J. A., ed.*, 1983, pp. 81–110. **[G: U.S.]**

Munnell, Alicia H. The Current Status of Social Security Financing. *New Eng. Econ. Rev.*, May/June 1983, pp. 46–62. **[G: U.S.]**

Munnell, Alicia H. The Pitfalls of Social Investing: The Case of Public Pensions and Housing. *New Eng. Econ. Rev.*, September/October 1983, pp. 20–41. **[G: U.S.]**

Myers, Robert J. Financial Status of the Social Security Program. *Soc. Sec. Bull.*, March 1983, *46*(3), pp. 3–13. **[G: U.S.]**

Myers, Robert J. The Significance and Use of Long-range Actuarial Cost Estimates for the Social Security System. *Contemp. Policy Issue*, April 1983, (3), pp. 9–15. **[G: U.S.]**

Noguchi, Yukio. Problems of Public Pensions in Japan. *Hitotsubashi J. Econ.*, June 1983, *24*(1), pp. 43–68. **[G: Japan]**

Noguchi, Yukio. The Failure of Government to Perform Its Proper Task: A Case Study of Japan. **In** *Lenel, H. O.; Willgerodt, H. and Molsberger, J.*, 1983, pp. 59–70. **[G: Japan]**

Oberhänsli, Urs. Substitutionswirkungen zwischen persönlichen Ersparnissen und der kollecktiven Altersvorsorge in der Schwiez. (Rates of Substitution between Personal Saving and the Collective Provision for Old Age in Switzerland. With English summary.) *Schweiz. Z. Volkswirtsch. Statist.*, June 1983, *119*(2), pp. 117–37. **[G: Switzerland]**

Olson, Mancur. "Social Security Survival": A Comment [Social Security Survival: A Public-Choice Perspective]. *Cato J.*, Fall 1983, *3*(2), pp. 355–59. **[G: U.S.]**

Owens, Jeffery P. Tax Expenditures and Direct Expenditures as Instruments of Social Policy. **In** *[Goode, R.]*, 1983, pp. 171–97. **[G: OECD]**

Pechman, Joseph A. "Absence of Lasting Reform": A Comment. *Cato J.*, Fall 1983, *3*(2), pp. 479–81. **[G: U.S.]**

Pellechio, Anthony and Goodfellow, Gordon. Individual Gains and Losses from Social Security before and after the 1983 Amendments. *Cato J.*, Fall 1983, *3*(2), pp. 417–42. **[G: U.S.]**

Penner, Rudolph G. Explaining Social Security Growth [A Constitutionalist Approach to Social Security Reform]. *Cato J.*, Fall 1983, *3*(2), pp. 461–65. **[G: U.S.]**

Pilon, Roger. Beyond Efficiency: A Comment [Funded Social Security: Collective and Private Options]. *Cato J.*, Fall 1983, *3*(2), pp. 603–08. **[G: U.S.]**

van Praag, Bernard M. S. and Emanuel, Han. On the Concept of Non-employability with Respect to a Non-homogeneous Labor Force. **In** *Söderström, L., ed.*, 1983, pp. 159–75.

van Praag, Bernard M. S. and Konijn, Peter A. B. Solidarity and Social Security. *Challenge*, July/August 1983, *26*(3), pp. 54–56. **[G: U.S.]**

Quinn, Joseph F. and Burkhauser, Richard V. Influencing Retirement Behavior: A Key Issue for Social Security. *J. Policy Anal. Manage.*, Fall 1983, *3*(1), pp. 1–13. **[G: U.S.]**

Ranson, David. Criteria for Reforming Social Security. *Cato J.*, Fall 1983, *3*(2), pp. 489–505. **[G: U.S.]**

Reddin, Mike. Pensions, Wealth and the Extension of Inequality. **In** *Field, F., ed.*, 1983, pp. 138–58. **[G: U.K.]**

Reimers, Cordelia W. The Effect of Pension Plans on the Pattern of Life Cycle Compensation: Comment. **In** *Triplett, J. E., ed.*, 1983, pp. 416–20. **[G: U.S.]**

Reno, Virginia P. and Upp, Melinda M. Social Security and the Family. **In** *Penner, R. G., ed.*, 1983, pp. 139–64. **[G: U.S.]**

Rice, Thomas and McCall, Nelda. Factors Influencing Physician Assignment Decisions under Medicare. *Inquiry*, Spring 1983, *20*(1), pp. 45–56. **[G: U.S.]**

Roberts, Paul Craig. Social Security: Myths and Realities. *Cato J.*, Fall 1983, *3*(2), pp. 393–401. **[G: U.S.]**

Robertson, A. Haeworth. "Criteria for Reforming Social Security": A Comment. *Cato J.*, Fall 1983, *3*(2), pp. 507–12. **[G: U.S.]**

Robertson, A. Haeworth. The National Commission's Failure to Achieve Real Form. *Cato J.*, Fall 1983, *3*(2), pp. 403–16. **[G: U.S.]**

Ruggles, Nancy D. and Ruggles, Richard. The Treatment of Pensions and Insurance in National Accounts. *Rev. Income Wealth*, December 1983, *29*(4), pp. 371–404. **[G: U.S.]**

Samuelson, Paul A. On Consumption Indexed Public Pension Plans: Comment. **In** *Bodie, Z. and Shoven, J. B., eds.*, 1983, pp. 276–87. **[G: U.S.]**

Schmähl, Winfried. Auswirkungen von Veränderungen der Altersstruktur der Bevölkerung auf die Finanzsituation der gesetzlichen Krankenversicherung im Vergleich zur gesetzlichen Rentenversicherung—Eine modelltheoretische Analyse. (A Comparison of the Effects of a Changing Age Structure on the Financing of Social Health Insurance and on That of the Social Retirement System—A Theoretical Analysis. With English summary.) *Konjunkturpolitik*, 1983, *29*(2), pp. 100–20. **[G: W. Germany]**

Schobel, Bruce D. Interfund Borrowing under the Social Security Act. *Soc. Sec. Bull.*, September 1983, *46*(9), pp. 13–14. **[G: U.S.]**

Schobel, Bruce D. Special Age-72 Social Security Benefits Awarded in 1981. *Soc. Sec. Bull.*, January 1983, *46*(1), pp. 33–35. **[G: U.S.]**

Schröder, Jürgen. Social Security and the Macroeconomic Saving-Income Ratio. *Weltwirtsch. Arch.*, 1983, *119*(3), pp. 554–68.

Seehan, Peter J. and Stricker, Peter P. Welfare Benefits and the Labour Market. **In** *Blandy, R. and Covick, O., eds.*, 1983, pp. 200–221. **[G: Australia]**

Seidman, Bert. Discussion [Financing Options for Social Security] [Private Pensions, Inflation, and Employment]. In *Parnes, H. S., ed.*, 1983, pp. 265–69. **[G: U.S.]**

Seidman, Laurence S. Social Security and Demographics in a Life Cycle Growth Model. *Nat. Tax J.*, June 1983, *36*(2), pp. 213–24. **[G: U.S.]**

Simanis, Joseph G. Farmer's Pensions and the Polish Economic Crisis. *Soc. Sec. Bull.*, April 1983, *46*(4), pp. 13–22. **[G: Poland]**

Ståhlberg, Ann-Charlotte. Public Pensions and Private Saving: A Brief Review of the Swedish System. In *Söderström, L., ed.*, 1983, pp. 137–58. **[G: Sweden]**

Summers, Lawrence H. Observations on the Indexation of Old Age Pensions. In *Bodie, Z. and Shoven, J. B., eds.*, 1983, pp. 231–51, 257–58. **[G: U.S.]**

Svahn, John A. and Ross, Mary. Social Security Amendments of 1983: Legislative History and Summary of Provisions. *Soc. Sec. Bull.*, July 1983, *46*(7), pp. 3–48. **[G: U.S.]**

Swenson, James R. Discussion [Financing Options for Social Security] [Private Pensions, Inflation, and Employment]. In *Parnes, H. S., ed.*, 1983, pp. 271–79. **[G: U.S.]**

Swidler, Steve. An Empirical Test of the Effect of Social Security on Fertility in the United States. *Amer. Econ.*, Fall 1983, *27*(2), pp. 50–57. **[G: U.S.]**

Tamburi, G. Escalation of State Pension Costs: The Reasons and the Issues. *Int. Lab. Rev.*, May–June 1983, *122*(3), pp. 313–27. **[G: Japan; U.S.; France; W. Germany]**

Taussig, Michael K. Discussion [Financing Options for Social Security] [Private Pensions, Inflation, and Employment]. In *Parnes, H. S., ed.*, 1983, pp. 281–86. **[G: U.S.]**

Thomas, J. William, et al. Increasing Medicare Enrollment in HMOs: The Need for Capitation Rates Adjusted for Health Status. *Inquiry*, Fall 1983, *20*(3), pp. 227–39. **[G: U.S.]**

Thompson, Lawrence H. The Social Security Reform Debate. *J. Econ. Lit.*, December 1983, *21*(4), pp. 1425–67. **[G: U.S.]**

Tresnowski, Bernard R. Cost Containment: Short Steps in a Long Journey. *Inquiry*, Summer 1983, *20*(2), pp. 99–100. **[G: U.S.]**

Ture, Norman B. Supply-Side Effects of Social Insurance. *Cato J.*, Fall 1983, *3*(2), pp. 537–46. **[G: U.S.]**

Vaubel, Roland. Reforming Social Security for Old Age. In *Giersch, H., ed.*, 1983, pp. 173–90.

Voirin, M. Social Security for Migrant Workers in Africa. *Int. Lab. Rev.*, May–June 1983, *122*(3), pp. 329–42. **[G: Africa]**

Wagner, Adolf. Wirkungen einer Sozialabgabenbemessung nach Wertschöpfungsgrössen statt nach Arbeitskosten. (Effects of Employers' Social Security Contributions if Based Not on Labour Cost but on Value Added. With English summary.) *Ifo-Studien*, 1983, *29*(4), pp. 255–71. **[G: W. Germany]**

Wagner, Richard E. Funded Social Security: Collective and Private Options. *Cato J.*, Fall 1983, *3*(2), pp. 581–602. **[G: U.S.]**

Wartonick, Daniel and Packard, Michael. Slowing Down Pension Indexing: The Foreign Experience. *Soc. Sec. Bull.*, June 1983, *46*(6), pp. 9–15. **[G: Canada; Finland; Sweden; U.K.; W. Germany]**

Weaver, Carolyn L. On the Lack of a Political Market for Compulsory Old-Age Insurance Prior to the Great Depression: Insights from Economic Theories of Government. *Exploration Econ. Hist.*, July 1983, *20*(3), pp. 294–328. **[G: U.S.]**

Weaver, Carolyn L. The Economics and Politics of the Emergence of Social Security: Some Implications for Reform. *Cato J.*, Fall 1983, *3*(2), pp. 361–79. **[G: U.S.]**

Wickström, Bengt-Arne. Income Redistribution and the Demand for Social Insurance. In *Söderström, L., ed.*, 1983, pp. 21–33.

Williamson, Samuel H. and Jones, Warren L. Computing the Impact of Social Security Using the Life Cycle Consumption Function. *Amer. Econ. Rev.*, December 1983, *73*(5), pp. 1036–52. **[G: U.S.]**

Wolfe, John R. Perceived Longevity and Early Retirement. *Rev. Econ. Statist.*, November 1983, *65*(4), pp. 544–51. **[G: U.S.]**

Worcester, Dean A., Jr. Social Security: Overview and Options. *Contemp. Policy Issue*, April 1983, (3), pp. 1–8. **[G: U.S.]**

Zeitzer, Illene R. Social Security Trends and Developments in Industrialized Countries. *Soc. Sec. Bull.*, March 1983, *46*(3), pp. 52–62. **[G: Selected MDCs]**

916 Economics of Law and Crime

9160 Economics of Law and Crime

Ackerman, Bruce A. Forward: Law in an Activist State. *Yale Law J.*, June 1983, *92*(7), pp. 1083–1128.

Bawly, Dan and Lapidoth, Arye. Tax Avoidance/Tax Evasion: Israel. In *International Fiscal Association (II)*, 1983, pp. 431–47. **[G: Israel]**

Bergström, Sture. Tax Avoidance/Tax Evasion: Sweden. In *International Fiscal Association (II)*, 1983, pp. 601–16. **[G: Sweden]**

Berk, Richard A. and Rauma, David. Capitalizing on Nonrandom Assignment to Treatments: A Regression-Discontinuity Evaluation of a Crime-Control Program. *J. Amer. Statist. Assoc.*, March 1983, *78*(381), pp. 21–27. **[G: U.S.]**

Bhagwati, Jagdish N. Alternative Theories of Illegal Trade: Economic Consequences and Statistical Detection. In *Bhagwati, J. N., Vol. 1*, 1983, *1981*, pp. 325–42.

Bhagwati, Jagdish N. and Hansen, Bent. A Theoretical Analysis of Smuggling. In *Bhagwati, J. N., Vol. 1*, 1983, *1973*, pp. 286–301.

Bhagwati, Jagdish N. and Srinivasan, T. N. Smuggling and Trade Policy. In *Bhagwati, J. N., Vol. 1*, 1983, *1973*, pp. 302–14.

Bischel, Jon E.; Gann, Pamela B. and Klein, Susan F. Tax Avoidance/Tax Evasion: United States. In *International Fiscal Association (II)*, 1983, pp. 333–55. **[G: U.S.]**

Bloom, David H. and Sweeney, Charles A. Tax Avoidance/Tax Evasion: Australia. In *Interna-*

tional Fiscal Association (II), 1983, pp. 227–44. [G: Australia]

Blum, Walter J. Dissenting Opinions by Supreme Court Justices in Federal Income Tax Controversies. *Mich. Law Rev.*, December 1983, *82*(3), pp. 431–60. [G: U.S.]

Boidman, Nathan. Tax Evasion: The Present State of Non-Compliance. *Bull. Int. Fiscal Doc.*, Sept.–Oct. 1983, *37*(9–10), pp. 451–79. [G: Selected Countries]

Brown, John Prather. Toward an Economic Theory of Liability. **In** *Kuperberg, M. and Beitz, C., eds.*, 1983, *1973*, pp. 185–209.

Buck, Andrew J., et al. The Deterrence Hypothesis Revisited. *Reg. Sci. Urban Econ.*, November 1983, *13*(4), pp. 471–86. [G: U.S.]

Bullard, Peter D. and Resnik, Alan J. SMR Forum: Too Many Hands in the Corporate Cookie Jar. *Sloan Manage. Rev.*, Fall 1983, *25*(1), pp. 51–56. [G: U.S.]

Calabresi, Guido and Hirschoff, Jon T. Toward A Test for Strict Liability in Torts. **In** *Kuperberg, M. and Beitz, C., eds.*, 1983, *1981*, pp. 154–84.

Calabresi, Guido and Melamed, A. Douglas. Property Rules, Liability Rules, and Inalienability: One View of the Cathedral. **In** *Kuperberg, M. and Beitz, C., eds.*, 1983, *1972*, pp. 41–80.

Capriglione, Francesco. Segreto della banca, segreto delle banche, segreto bancario. (Banking Confidentiality. With English summary.) *Bancaria*, March 1983, *39*(3), pp. 249–58. [G: Italy]

Chiswick, Barry R. Illegal Aliens in the United States Labour Market. **In** *Weisbrod, B. and Hughes, H., eds.*, 1983, pp. 346–67. [G: U.S.]

Clotfelter, Charles T. Tax Evasion and Tax Rates: An Analysis of Individual Returns. *Rev. Econ. Statist.*, August 1983, *65*(3), pp. 363–73. [G: U.S.]

Coase, R. H. The Problem of Social Cost. **In** *Kuperberg, M. and Beitz, C., eds.*, 1983, *1960*, pp. 13–40.

Coleman, Jules L. The Economic Analysis of Law. **In** *Kuperberg, M. and Beitz, C., eds.*, 1983, *1982*, pp. 102–22.

Courchene, Thomas J. A Constitutional Perspective on Federal–Provincial Sharing of Revenues from Natural Resources: Comments. **In** *McLure, C. E., Jr. and Mieszkowski, P., eds.*, 1983, pp. 237–43. [G: Canada]

Damaška, Mirjan. Activism in Perspective. *Yale Law J.*, June 1983, *92*(7), pp. 1189–197.

Danzon, Patricia Munch. Contingent Fees for Personal Injury Litigation. *Bell J. Econ. (See Rand J. Econ. after 4/85)*, Spring 1983, *14*(1), pp. 213–24. [G: U.S.]

Datt, Ruddar. The Parallel Economy in India. *Indian Econ. J.*, April-June 1983, *30*(4), pp. 19–54. [G: India]

Davila, Alberto E. Economic Determinants of Illegal Mexican Immigration to the U.S. *Fed. Res. Bank Dallas Econ. Rev.*, May 1983, pp. 13–23. [G: U.S.]

Dezza, Marcello Cogliati. Tax Avoidance/Tax Evasion: Italy. **In** *International Fiscal Association (II)*, 1983, pp. 449–68. [G: Italy]

Dornbusch, Rudiger, et al. The Black Market for Dollars in Brazil. *Quart. J. Econ.*, February 1983, *98*(1), pp. 25–40. [G: Brazil]

Dworkin, Ronald. Why Efficiency? **In** *Kuperberg, M. and Beitz, C., eds.*, 1983, *1980*, pp. 123–40.

Elvinger, André and Kremer, Claude. Evasion fiscale/Fraude fiscale: Luxembourg. (With English summary.) **In** *International Fiscal Association (II)*, 1983, pp. 491–510. [G: Luxembourg]

Englander, Frederick. Helping Ex-Offenders Enter the Labor Market. *Mon. Lab. Rev.*, July 1983, *106*(7), pp. 25–30. [G: U.S.]

Epstein, Richard A. A Common Law for Labor Relations: A Critique of the New Deal Labor Legislation. *Yale Law J.*, July 1983, *92*(8), pp. 1357–1408. [G: U.S.]

Epstein, Richard A. Common Law, Labor Law, and Reality: A Rejoinder [A Common Law for Labor Relations: A Critique of the New Deal Labor Legislation]. *Yale Law J.*, July 1983, *92*(8), pp. 1435–41. [G: U.S.]

Filho, Olimpio Guernieri. Tax Avoidance/Tax Evasion: Brazil. **In** *International Fiscal Association (II)*, 1983, pp. 285–93. [G: Brazil]

Fletcher, George P. Fairness and Utility in Tort Theory. **In** *Kuperberg, M. and Beitz, C., eds.*, 1983, *1972*, pp. 248–84.

Frederick, Robert E. Conflict of Interest. **In** *Snoeyenbos, M.; Almeder, R. and Humber, J., eds.*, 1983, pp. 125–30.

Frederick, Robert E. and Snoeyenbos, Milton. Trade Secrets, Patents, and Morality. **In** *Snoeyenbos, M.; Almeder, R. and Humber, J., eds.*, 1983, pp. 162–69. [G: U.S.]

Frey, Bruno S. and Weck, Hannelore. Estimating the Shadow Economy: A 'Naive' Approach. *Oxford Econ. Pap.*, March 1983, *35*(1), pp. 23–44. [G: OECD]

Frug, Gerald E. Why Neutrality? [Regulation in a Liberal State: The Role of Non-commodity Values]. *Yale Law J.*, July 1983, *92*(8), pp. 1591–1601. [G: U.S.]

Gaffney, Mason. Tax Exporting and the Commerce Clause: Comments. **In** *McLure, C. E., Jr. and Mieszkowski, P., eds.*, 1983, pp. 199–203. [G: U.S.]

Gassner, Wolfgang. Steuervermeidung/Steuerhinterziehung: Osterreich. (With English summary.) **In** *International Fiscal Association (II)*, 1983, pp. 245–63. [G: Austria]

Getman, Julius G. and Kohler, Thomas C. The Common Law, Labor Law, and Reality: A Response [A Common Law for Labor Relations: A Critique of the New Deal Labor Legislation]. *Yale Law J.*, July 1983, *92*(8), pp. 1415–34. [G: U.S.]

Ghali, Moheb, et al. Economic Factors and the Composition of Juvenile Property Crimes. *Appl. Econ.*, April 1983, *15*(2), pp. 267–81. [G: U.S.]

Ginger, Ann Fagan. Workers' Self-Defense in the Courts. *Sci. Soc.*, Fall 1983, *47*(3), pp. 257–84. [G: U.S.]

Gjesti, Per O. Tax Avoidance/Tax Evasion: Norway. **In** *International Fiscal Association (II)*, 1983, pp. 525–32. [G: Norway]

González de Rechter, Beatriz S. Tax Avoidance/Tax Evasion: Argentina. **In** *International Fiscal Association (II)*, 1983, pp. 211–25. [G: Argentina]

Grady, Mark F. A New Positive Economic Theory of Negligence. *Yale Law J.*, April 1983, *92*(5),

pp. 799–829.

Green, Harold P. Legal Aspects of Intergenerational Equity Issues. In *Kasperson, R. E., ed.*, 1983, pp. 189–202. **[G: U.S.]**

Grinover, Ada Pellegrini. Monetary Correction in the Law Courts. In *de Ulhôa Canto, G.; da Silva Martins, I. G. and van Hoorn, J., Jr., eds.*, 1983, pp. 187–91. **[G: Brazil]**

Grossman, Gene M. and Katz, Michael L. Plea Bargaining and Social Welfare. *Amer. Econ. Rev.*, September 1983, *73*(4), pp. 749–57.

van den Haag, Ernest. How Not to Cut Crime: Rehabilitating Criminals Cannot Cut Crime. *Policy Rev.*, Fall 1983, (26), pp. 53–58.

Hall, D. R. Strike Law in Queensland. In *Murphy, D. J., ed.*, 1983, pp. 15–32. **[G: Australia]**

Handler, Joel F. Discretion in Social Welfare: The Uneasy Position in the Rule of Law. *Yale Law J.*, June 1983, *92*(7), pp. 1270–286.

Harris, I. W. Tax Avoidance/Tax Evasion: Hong Kong. In *International Fiscal Association (II)*, 1983, pp. 419–29. **[G: Hong Kong]**

Heineman, Ben W., Jr. The Law Schools' Failing Grade on Federalism. *Yale Law J.*, June 1983, *92*(7), pp. 1349–56.

Hellerstein, Walter. Legal Constraints on State Taxation of Natural Resources. In *McLure, C. E., Jr. and Mieszkowski, P., eds.*, 1983, pp. 135–66. **[G: U.S.]**

Ishi, Hiromitsu. Tax Avoidance/Tax Evasion: Japan. In *International Fiscal Association (II)*, 1983, pp. 477–89. **[G: Japan]**

Jenkin, Peter J. H. Tax Avoidance/Tax Evasion: New Zealand. In *International Fiscal Association (II)*, 1983, pp. 533–44. **[G: New Zealand]**

Karlin, Norman. Substantive Due Process: A Doctrine for Regulatory Control. In *Machan, T. R. and Johnson, M. B., eds.*, 1983, pp. 43–70. **[G: U.S.]**

Kennedy, Peter E. On an Inappropriate Means of Reducing Multicollinearity. *Reg. Sci. Urban Econ.*, November 1983, *13*(4), pp. 579–81.

Kirchgässner, Gebhard. Size and Development of the West German Shadow Economy, 1955–1980. *Z. ges. Staatswiss.*, June 1983, *139*(2), pp. 197–214. **[G: W. Germany]**

Kirk, Richard M. Political Terrorism and the Size of Government: A Positive Institutional Analysis of Violent Political Activity. *Public Choice*, 1983, *40*(1), pp. 41–52.

Koch-Nielsen, Robert and Schmith, Esther. Tax Avoidance/Tax Evasion: Denmark. In *International Fiscal Association (II)*, 1983, pp. 317–31. **[G: Denmark]**

Kornhauser, Lewis A. Reliance, Reputation, and Breach of Contract. *J. Law Econ.*, October 1983, *26*(3), pp. 691–706.

Koskela, Erkki. A Note on Progression, Penalty Schemes and Tax Evasion. *J. Public Econ.*, October 1983, *22*(1), pp. 127–33.

Kronman, Anthony T. Paternalism and the Law of Contracts. *Yale Law J.*, April 1983, *92*(5), pp. 763–98.

Kuperberg, Mark and Beitz, Charles. Theoretical Foundations of the Economic Analysis of Law: Introduction. In *Kuperberg, M. and Beitz, C., eds.*, 1983, pp. 3–12.

Layson, Stephen K. Homicide and Deterrence: Another View of the Canadian Time-Series Evidence. *Can. J. Econ.*, February 1983, *16*(1), pp. 52–73. **[G: Canada]**

Layton, Allan P. The Impact of Increased Penalties on Australian Drink/Driving Behaviour. *Logist. Transp. Rev.*, October 1983, *19*(3), pp. 261–66. **[G: Australia]**

Leamer, Edward E. Let's Take the Con Out of Econometrics. *Amer. Econ. Rev.*, March 1983, *73*(1), pp. 31–43. **[G: U.S.]**

Lehner, Moris. Steuervermeidung/Steuerhinterziehung: Deutschland. (With English summary.) In *International Fiscal Association (II)*, 1983, pp. 193–210. **[G: W. Germany]**

Lewis, Donald E. Economic Aspects of the Parole Decision. *Australian Econ. Pap.*, December 1983, *22*(41), pp. 259–79. **[G: Australia]**

Liebermann, Yehoshua and Syrquin, M. On the Use and Abuse of Rights: An Economic View. *J. Econ. Behav. Organ.*, March 1983, *4*(1), pp. 25–40.

Lipnowski, Irwin and Shilony, Yuval. The Design of a Tort Law to Control Accidents. *Math. Soc. Sci.*, April 1983, *4*(2), pp. 103–15.

Liu, Yih-wu and Bee, Richard H. Modeling Criminal Activity in an Area in Economic Decline: Local Economic Conditions Are a Major Factor in Local Property Crimes. *Amer. J. Econ. Soc.*, October 1983, *42*(4), pp. 385–92. **[G: U.S.]**

Lopes, Mauro Brandão. Updating of Unindexed Pecuniary Liabilities. In *de Ulhôa Canto, G.; da Silva Martins, I. G. and van Hoorn, J., Jr., eds.*, 1983, pp. 192–201. **[G: Brazil]**

Mashaw, Jerry L. "Rights" in the Federal Administrative State. *Yale Law J.*, June 1983, *92*(7), pp. 1129–173.

McDonald, John F. and Balkin, Steven. Citizen Demand for Exposure to Street Crime. *Urban Stud.*, November 1983, *20*(4), pp. 419–29. **[G: U.S.]**

McLure, Charles E., Jr. Tax Exporting and the Commerce Clause. In *McLure, C. E., Jr. and Mieszkowski, P., eds.*, 1983, pp. 169–92. **[G: U.S.]**

Meyers, Samuel L., Jr. Estimating the Economic Model of Crime: Employment versus Punishment Effects. *Quart. J. Econ.*, February 1983, *98*(1), pp. 157–66. **[G: U.S.]**

Moreira, Raul. Tax Avoidance/Tax Evasion: Mexico. In *International Fiscal Association (II)*, 1983, pp. 511–23. **[G: Mexico]**

Myers, Samuel L., Jr. Racial Differences in Postprison Employment. *Soc. Sci. Quart.*, September 1983, *64*(3), pp. 655–69. **[G: U.S.]**

Nickel, James W. Human Rights and the Rights of Aliens. In *Brown, P. G. and Shue, H., eds.*, 1983, pp. 31–45. **[G: Mexico; U.S.]**

Nickerson, Gary W. Analytical Problems in Explaining Criminal Behavior: Neoclassical and Radical Economic Theories and an Alternative Formulation. *Rev. Radical Polit. Econ.*, Winter 1983, *15*(4), pp. 1–23.

Nooteboom, A. Tax Avoidance/Tax Evasion: Netherlands. In *International Fiscal Association (II)*, 1983, pp. 545–66. **[G: Netherlands]**

Norton, Eleanor Holmes. Public Assistance, Post-New Deal Bureaucracy, and the Law: Learning from Negative Models. *Yale Law J.*, June 1983, *92*(7), pp. 1287–99.

P'ng, I. P. L. Strategic Behavior in Suit, Settlement, and Trial. *Bell J. Econ. (See Rand J. Econ. after 4/85)*, Autumn 1983, *14*(2), pp. 539–50. **[G: U.S.]**

Page, Talbot. On the Meaning of the Preponderance Test in Judicial Regulation of Chemical Hazard. *Law Contemp. Probl.*, Summer 1983, *46*(3), pp. 267–83.

Parsons, Wese. The Inefficient Common Law. *Yale Law J.*, April 1983, *92*(5), pp. 862–87.

Pommerehne, Werner W. Steuerhinterziehung und Schwarzarbeit als Grenzen der Staatstätigkeit. (Tax Evasion and Underground Activities as Limits of Government's Growth. With English summary.) *Schweiz. Z. Volkswirtsch. Statist.*, September 1983, *119*(3), pp. 261–84. **[G: Switzerland]**

Posner, Richard A. The Ethical and Political Basis of the Efficiency Norm in Common Law Adjudication. **In** *Kuperberg, M. and Beitz, C., eds.*, 1983, *1980*, pp. 81–101.

Rabin, Robert L. Legitimacy, Discretion, and the Concept of Rights. *Yale Law J.*, June 1983, *92*(7), pp. 1174–188.

Reubens, Edwin P. Immigration Problems, Limited-Visa Programs, and Other Options. **In** *Brown, P. G. and Shue, H., eds.*, 1983, pp. 187–222. **[G: Mexico; U.S.]**

Reynolds, B. J. Tax Avoidance/Tax Evasion: United Kingdom. **In** *International Fiscal Association (II)*, 1983, pp. 581–99. **[G: U.K.]**

Rodrigues Pardal, Francisco. Evasion fiscale/Fraude fiscale: Portugal. (With English summary.) **In** *International Fiscal Association (II)*, 1983, pp. 567–79. **[G: Portugal]**

Roneck, Dennis W. and Lobosco, Antoinette. The Effect of High Schools on Crime in Their Neighborhoods. *Soc. Sci. Quart.*, September 1983, *64*(3), pp. 598–613. **[G: U.S.]**

Rubin, Seymour J. and Hufbauer, Gary Clyde. Emerging Standards of International Trade and Investment: Lessons from the Codes. **In** *Rubin, S. J. and Hufbauer, G. C., eds.*, 1983, pp. 175–96. **[G: Global]**

Ryan, John E. Statement to U.S. House Commerce, Consumer, and Monetary Affairs Subcommittee of the Committee on Government Operations, June 28, 1983. *Fed. Res. Bull.*, July 1983, *69*(7), pp. 535–37. **[G: U.S.]**

Sartorius, Rolf. Government Regulation and Intergenerational Justice. **In** *Machan, T. R. and Johnson, M. B., eds.*, 1983, pp. 177–201.

Schuck, Peter H. Regulation, Non-market Values, and the Administrative State: A Comment [Regulation in a Liberal State: The Role of Non-commodity Values]. *Yale Law J.*, July 1983, *92*(8), pp. 1602–13. **[G: U.S.]**

Shafer, Joel and Solursh, John M. Tax Avoidance/Tax Evasion: Canada. **In** *International Fiscal Association (II)*, 1983, pp. 295–315. **[G: Canada]**

Shavell, Steven. On Liability and Insurance. **In** *Kuperberg, M. and Beitz, C., eds.*, 1983, *1982*, pp. 235–47.

Shavell, Steven. Strict Liability versus Negligence. **In** *Kuperberg, M. and Beitz, C., eds.*, 1983, *1980*, pp. 210–34.

Siembos, Tryfon. Tax Avoidance/Tax Evasion: Greece. **In** *International Fiscal Association (II)*, 1983, pp. 401–18. **[G: Greece]**

Simon, William H. Legality, Bureaucracy, and Class in the Welfare System. *Yale Law J.*, June 1983, *92*(7), pp. 1198–1269.

Singh, A. J. and Singh, Tirath. Black Money—Genesis, Estimation, Causes and Remedies. *Econ. Aff.*, January–March 1983, *28*(1), pp. 632–43. **[G: India]**

Smith, J. C. The Processes of Adjudication and Regulation, a Comparison. **In** *Machan, T. R. and Johnson, M. B., eds.*, 1983, pp. 71–96. **[G: U.S.]**

Smith, Susan J. Public Policy and the Effects of Crime in the Inner City: A British Example. *Urban Stud.*, May 1983, *20*(2), pp. 229–39. **[G: U.K.]**

Snyder, Donald C. and Schiller, Bradley R. The Effect of Inflation on the Elderly. **In** *Schmukler, N. and Marcus, E., eds.*, 1983, pp. 867–81. **[G: U.S.]**

Solomon, R.; Single, E. and Erickson, P. Legal Considerations in Canadian Cannabis Policy. *Can. Public Policy*, December 1983, *9*(4), pp. 419–33. **[G: Canada]**

Starzec, Krzysztof. L'économie polonaise vue à travers des circuits parallèles. (Polish "Official" and "Unofficial" Economy: An Empirical Approach. With English summary.) *Consommation*, October–December 1983, *30*(4), pp. 55–94. **[G: Poland]**

Stein, Bruno and Wenig, Alois. The Economics of the Shadow Economy: A Conference Report. *Z. ges. Staatswiss.*, December 1983, *139*(4), pp. 690–707.

Stewart, Richard B. Regulation in a Liberal State: The Role of Non-commodity Values. *Yale Law J.*, July 1983, *92*(8), pp. 1537–90. **[G: U.S.]**

Sufrin, Sidney C. The Ethics of Administration. *Rivista Int. Sci. Econ. Com.*, September 1983, *30*(9), pp. 829–39. **[G: U.S.]**

Sukarya, Sutadi and Sutomo. Tax Avoidance/Tax Evasion: Indonesia. **In** *International Fiscal Association (II)*, 1983, pp. 469–75. **[G: Indonesia]**

Tanzi, Vito. The Underground Economy. *Finance Develop.*, December 1983, *20*(4), pp. 10–13. **[G: Selected Countries]**

Tanzi, Vito. The Underground Economy in the United States: Annual Estimates, 1930–80. *Int. Monet. Fund Staff Pap.*, June 1983, *30*(2), pp. 283–305. **[G: U.S.]**

Thomson, Judith Jarvis. Some Questions about Government Regulation of Behavior. **In** *Machan, T. R. and Johnson, M. B., eds.*, 1983, pp. 137–56.

Tikka, Kari S. Tax Avoidance/Tax Evasion: Finland. **In** *International Fiscal Association (II)*, 1983, pp. 357–71. **[G: Finland]**

Tisdell, Clem A. Law, Economics and Risk-Taking. *Kyklos*, 1983, *36*(1), pp. 3–20.

Tumlir, Jan. International Economic Order and Democratic Constitutionalism. **In** *Lenel, H. O.; Willgerodt, H. and Molsberger, J.*, 1983, pp. 71–83.

Uckmar, V. Tax Avoidance/Tax Evasion: General Report. In *International Fiscal Association (II)*, 1983, pp. 15–53. **[G: OECD]**

de Ulhôa Canto, Gilberto. Monetary Correction and the Legal Tender of the Cruzeiro. In *de Ulhôa Canto, G.; da Silva Martins, I. G. and van Hoorn, J., Jr., eds.*, 1983, pp. 13–16. **[G: Brazil]**

Verkuil, Paul R. Whose Common Law for Labor Relations? [A Common Law for Labor Relations: A Critique of the New Deal Labor Legislation]. *Yale Law J.*, July 1983, *92*(8), pp. 1409–14. **[G: U.S.]**

Wald, Patricia M. Judicial Review of Economic Analysis. *Yale J. Regul.*, 1983, *1*(1), pp. 43–62. **[G: U.S.]**

Walker, Monica A. Some Problems in Interpreting Statistics Relating to Crime. *J. Roy. Statist. Soc.*, 1983, *146*(3), pp. 281–93. **[G: U.K.]**

Weinblatt, J., et al. Crime Prevention Policies and Externalities: A Theoretical Analysis. *Public Finance*, 1983, *38*(1), pp. 110–31.

White, Michael D. and Luksetich, William A. Heroin: Price Elasticity and Enforcement Strategies. *Econ. Inquiry*, October 1983, *21*(4), pp. 557–64.

Whyte, John D. A Constitutional Perspective on Federal–Provincial Sharing of Revenues from Natural Resources. In *McLure, C. E., Jr. and Mieszkowski, P., eds.*, 1983, pp. 205–35. **[G: Canada]**

Williamson, Oliver E. Credible Commitments: Using Hostages to Support Exchange. *Amer. Econ. Rev.*, September 1983, *73*(4), pp. 519–40.

Willis, K. G. Spatial Variations in Crime in England and Wales: Testing an Economic Model. *Reg. Stud.*, August 1983, *17*(4), pp. 261–72. **[G: U.K.]**

Witte, Ann Dryden. Estimating the Economic Model of Crime: Reply. *Quart. J. Econ.*, February 1983, *98*(1), pp. 167–75. **[G: U.S.]**

Zanjani, Sally Springmeyer. The Mike Smith Case: A Note on High Grading in Goldfield, Nevada, 1910. *Labor Hist.*, Fall 1983, *24*(4), pp. 580–87. **[G: U.S.]**

Zimmerman, Martin B. Tax Exporting and the Commerce Clause: Comments. In *McLure, C. E., Jr. and Mieszkowski, P., eds.*, 1983, pp. 193–95. **[G: U.S.]**

917 Economics of Minorities; Economics of Discrimination

9170 Economics of Minorities; Economics of Discrimination

Abowd, John M. and Killingsworth, Mark R. Sex, Discrimination, Atrophy, and the Male–Female Wage Differential. *Ind. Relat.*, Fall 1983, *22*(3), pp. 387–402. **[G: U.S.]**

Ahmed, Iftikhar. Technology and Rural Women in the Third World. *Int. Lab. Rev.*, July–August 1983, *122*(4), pp. 493–505. **[G: LDCs]**

Anderson, Kathryn H. and Hill, M. Anne. Marriage and Labor Market Discrimination in Japan. *Southern Econ. J.*, April 1983, *49*(4), pp. 941–53. **[G: Japan]**

Anderson, Raymond L. Ethical Issues in Resource Economics: Discussion. *Amer. J. Agr. Econ.*, December 1983, *65*(5), pp. 1035–36.

Angle, John and Wissmann, David A. Work Experience, Age, and Gender Discrimination. *Soc. Sci. Quart.*, March 1983, *64*(1), pp. 66–84. **[G: U.S.]**

Applebaum, Eileen. Women in the Stagflation Economy. In *Weintraub, S. and Goodstein, M., eds.*, 1983, pp. 34–47. **[G: U.S.]**

Asimakopulos, A. Public Pensions, the Federal Budget, and Discrimination. *Can. Public Policy*, March 1983, *9*(1), pp. 105–13. **[G: Canada]**

Ayal, Eliezer B. and Chiswick, Barry R. The Economics of the Diaspora Revisited. *Econ. Develop. Cult. Change*, July 1983, *31*(4), pp. 861–75. **[G: U.S.; Middle East]**

Barnes, David W. The Problem of Multiple Components or Divisions in Title VII Litigation: A Comment [Testing for Discrimination in Employment Practices]. *Law Contemp. Probl.*, Autumn 1983, *46*(4), pp. 185–88. **[G: U.S.]**

Barrère-Maurisson, Marie-Agnès; Battagliola, Françoise and Duane-Richard, Anne-Marie. Trajectoires professionnelles des femmes et vie familiale. (Women's Career Course and Their Home Life. With English summary.) *Consommation*, October–December 1983, *30*(4), pp. 23–53. **[G: France]**

Barrett, Nancy S. How the Study of Women has Restructured the Discipline of Economics. In *Langland, E. and Gove, W., eds.*, 1983, pp. 101–09.

Bates, Timothy. The Declining Relative Incomes of Urban Black Households. *Challenge*, May/June 1983, *26*(2), pp. 48–49. **[G: U.S.]**

Bates, Timothy. The Impact of Multinational Corporations on Power Relations in South Africa. *Rev. Black Polit. Econ.*, Winter 1983, *12*(2), pp. 133–43. **[G: S. Africa]**

Bates, Timothy. The Potential for Black Business: A Comment. *Rev. Black Polit. Econ.*, Winter 1983, *12*(2), pp. 237–40. **[G: U.S.]**

Becker, Brian E. and Hills, Stephen M. The Long-Run Effects of Job Changes and Unemployment among Male Teenagers. *J. Human Res.*, Spring 1983, *18*(2), pp. 197–212. **[G: U.S.]**

Behrman, Jere R. and Wolfe, Barbara L. Women's Labour Force Participation and Earnings Determinants in a Developing Country. In *Urquidi, V. L. and Reyes, S. T., eds.*, 1983, pp. 266–76. **[G: Nicaragua]**

Bergmann, Barbara R. Women's Plight: Bad and Getting Worse. *Challenge*, March/April 1983, *26*(1), pp. 22–26. **[G: U.S.]**

Blakemore, Arthur E. and Low, Stuart A. Race and the Acquisition of and Returns to OJT for Youth. *Ind. Relat.*, Fall 1983, *22*(3), pp. 374–86. **[G: U.S.]**

Blakemore, Arthur E. and Low, Stuart A. Scholarship Policy and Race–Sex Differences in the Demand for Higher Education. *Econ. Inquiry*, October 1983, *21*(4), pp. 504–19.

Bloom, David E.; Preiss, Beth and Trussell, James. Mortgage Lending Discrimination and the Decision to Apply: A Methodological Note. *Amer. Real Estate Urban Econ. Assoc. J.*, Spring 1983, *11*(1), pp. 97–103. **[G: U.S.]**

Boardman, Anthony E. and Vining, Aidan R. The Role of Probative Statistics in Employment Discrimination Cases. *Law Contemp. Probl.*, Autumn 1983, *46*(4), pp. 189–218. **[G: U.S.]**

Borjas, George J. The Measurement of Race and Gender Wage Differentials: Evidence from the Federal Sector. *Ind. Lab. Relat. Rev.*, October 1983, *37*(1), pp. 79–91. **[G: U.S.]**

Borjas, George J. The Substitutability of Black, Hispanic, and White Labor. *Econ. Inquiry*, January 1983, *21*(1), pp. 93–106. **[G: U.S.]**

Borus, Michael E., et al. Youth Looking for Work. **In** *Borus, M. E., ed.*, 1983, pp. 59–102. **[G: U.S.]**

Bowman, Mary Jean. Women and the Japanese Economic Performance. **In** *Weisbrod, B. and Hughes, H., eds.*, 1983, *1981*, pp. 250–73. **[G: Japan]**

Brenner, Reuven. The Economics of the Diaspora Revisited: A Reply. *Econ. Develop. Cult. Change*, July 1983, *31*(4), pp. 877–78. **[G: U.S.; Middle East]**

Brookshire, David S.; Merrill, James L. and Watts, Gary L. Economics and the Determination of Indian Reserved Water Rights. *Natural Res. J.*, October 1983, *23*(4), pp. 749–65. **[G: U.S.]**

Burness, H. Stuart; Gorman, William D. and Lansford, Robert L. Economics, Ethics, and the Quantification of Indian Water Rights. *Amer. J. Agr. Econ.*, December 1983, *65*(5), pp. 1027–32. **[G: U.S.]**

Burris, Val. Who Opposed the ERA? An Analysis of the Social Bases of Antifeminism. *Soc. Sci. Quart.*, June 1983, *64*(2), pp. 305–17. **[G: U.S.]**

Butler, Richard J. Direct Estimates of the Demand for Race and Sex Discrimination. *Southern Econ. J.*, April 1983, *49*(4), pp. 975–90. **[G: U.S.]**

Carr, Shirley G. E. Sex-Based Discrimination in Employment: Problems and Progress in Canada. *Int. Lab. Rev.*, November–December 1983, *122*(6), pp. 761–70. **[G: Canada]**

Cassim, F. Labour Market Segmentation: The Theoretical Case—Rejoinder. *S. Afr. J. Econ.*, December 1983, *51*(4), pp. 580.

Cassim, F. Labour Market Segmentation: The Theoretical Case—Reply. *S. Afr. J. Econ.*, December 1983, *51*(4), pp. 574–78.

Cebula, Richard J. and Avery, K. Leslie. The Tiebout Hypothesis in the United States: An Analysis of Black Consumer-Voters, 1970–75. *Public Choice*, 1983, *41*(2), pp. 307–10. **[G: U.S.]**

Chachere, Bernadette P. The Economics of Thomas Sowell: A Critique of *Markets and Minorities*. *Rev. Black Polit. Econ.*, Winter 1983, *12*(2), pp. 163–77. **[G: U.S.]**

Chakravarti, Anand. Some Aspects of Inequality in Rural India: A Sociological Perspective. **In** *Béteille, A., ed.*, 1983, pp. 129–81. **[G: India]**

Chirikos, Thomas N. and Nastel, Gilbert. Economic Consequences of Poor Health in Mature Women. **In** *Shaw, L. B., ed.*, 1983, pp. 93–108. **[G: U.S.]**

Chiswick, Barry R. An Analysis of the Earnings and Employment of Asian-American Men. *J. Lab. Econ.*, April 1983, *1*(2), pp. 197–214. **[G: U.S.]**

Chiswick, Barry R. The Earnings and Human Capital of American Jews. *J. Human Res.*, Summer 1983, *18*(3), pp. 313–36. **[G: U.S.]**

Christiansen, Hanne D. Equality and Equilibrium: Weaknesses of the Overlap Argument for Unisex Pension Plans. *J. Risk Ins.*, December 1983, *50*(4), pp. 670–80. **[G: U.S.]**

Clark, Bill and Casserly, John. The Disabled. **In** *Brown, G. and Cook, R., eds.*, 1983, pp. 162–71. **[G: U.K.]**

Cohen, Cynthia Fryer. The Impact on Women of Proposed Changes in the Private Pension System: A Simulation. *Ind. Lab. Relat. Rev.*, January 1983, *36*(2), pp. 258–70. **[G: U.S.]**

Cohen, Edwin S. Family Issues in Taxation: Commentary. **In** *Penner, R. G., ed.*, 1983, pp. 27–30. **[G: U.S.]**

Collins, Doreen. The Impact of Social Policy in the United Kingdom. **In** *El-Agraa, A. M., ed.*, 1983, pp. 213–33. **[G: EEC; U.K.]**

Conway, Delores A. and Roberts, Harry V. Reverse Regression, Fairness, and Employment Discrimination. *J. Bus. Econ. Statist.*, January 1983, *1*(1), pp. 75–85. **[G: U.S.]**

Cooney, Rosemary Santana and Ortiz, Vilma. Nativity, National Origin, and Hispanic Female Participation in the Labor Force. *Soc. Sci. Quart.*, September 1983, *64*(3), pp. 510–23. **[G: U.S.]**

Corcoran, Mary; Duncan, Greg J. and Ponza, Michael. A Longitudinal Analysis of White Women's Wages. *J. Human Res.*, Fall 1983, *18*(4), pp. 497–520. **[G: U.S.]**

Corcoran, Mary; Duncan, Greg J. and Ponza, Michael. Work Experience and Wage Growth of Women Workers. **In** *Duncan, G. J. and Morgan, J. N., eds.*, 1983, pp. 249–323. **[G: U.S.]**

Crowley, Joan E.; Pollard, Tom K. and Rumberger, Russell W. Education and Training. **In** *Borus, M. E., ed.*, 1983, pp. 103–48. **[G: U.S.]**

Darden, Joe T. Racial Differences in Unemployment: A Spatial Perspective. *Rev. Black Polit. Econ.*, Spring 1983, *12*(3), pp. 93–105. **[G: U.S.]**

Darity, William A., Jr. Reaganomics and the Black Community. **In** *Weintraub, S. and Goodstein, M., eds.*, 1983, pp. 59–77. **[G: U.S.]**

Darity, William A., Jr. and Myers, Samuel L., Jr. Changes in Black Family Structure: Implications for Welfare Dependency. *Amer. Econ. Rev.*, May 1983, *73*(2), pp. 59–64. **[G: U.S.]**

Datcher, Linda. Racial Differences in the Persistence of Affluence. **In** *Duncan, G. J. and Morgan, J. N., eds.*, 1983, pp. 205–17. **[G: U.S.]**

DaVanzo, Julie and Kusnic, Michael W. Ethnic Differences in Income in Peninsular Malaysia: Their Sensitivity to the Definition and Measurement of Income. *Singapore Econ. Rev.*, October 1983, *28*(2), pp. 22–45. **[G: Malaysia]**

Davis, Carlton G. and Allen, Joyce E. Black Agricultural Economists in the Labor Market: Theoretical and Empirical Issues. *Amer. J. Agr. Econ.*, December 1983, *65*(5), pp. 981–87. **[G: U.S.]**

Daymont, Thomas N. and Statham, Anne. Occupational Atypicality: Changes, Causes, and Consequences. **In** *Shaw, L. B., ed.*, 1983, pp. 61–75. **[G: U.S.]**

Deere, Carmen Diana. Cooperative Development and Women's Participation in the Nicaraguan Agrarian Reform. *Amer. J. Agr. Econ.*, December 1983, *65*(5), pp. 1043–48. **[G: Nicaragua]**

Denton, Frank T. Participation Rate Changes in Canada in the Early 1980s: Comment. **In** *Queen's Univ. Indust. Relat. Centre and John Deutsch*

Mem., 1983, pp. 76–78. **[G: Canada]**

Devi, D. Radha and Ravindran, M. Women's Work in India. *Int. Soc. Sci. J.*, 1983, *35*(4), pp. 683–701. **[G: India]**

Duncan, Greg J. and Hoffman, Saul D. A New Look at the Causes of the Improved Economic Status of Black Workers. *J. Human Res.*, Spring 1983, *18*(2), pp. 268–82. **[G: U.S.]**

Feenberg, Daniel R. The Tax Treatment of Married Couples and the 1981 Tax Law. **In** *Penner, R. G., ed.*, 1983, pp. 32–63. **[G: U.S.]**

Ferber, Marianne A. Are Women Economists at a Disadvantage in Publishing Journal Articles? Reply. *Eastern Econ. J.*, April–June 1983, *9*(2), pp. 139–40. **[G: U.S.]**

Ferleger, Lou. Explaining Away Black Poverty: The Structural Determinants of Black Employment. **In** *Goldstein, R. and Sachs, S. M., eds.*, 1983, pp. 148–74. **[G: U.S.]**

Filer, Randall K. Sexual Differences in Earnings: The Role of Individual Personalities and Tastes. *J. Human Res.*, Winter 1983, *18*(1), pp. 82–99. **[G: U.S.]**

Finn, Michael G. Understanding the Higher Unemployment Rate of Women Scientists and Engineers. *Amer. Econ. Rev.*, December 1983, *73*(5), pp. 1137–40. **[G: U.S.]**

Follett, Robert and Welch, Finis. Testing for Discrimination in Employment Practices. *Law Contemp. Probl.*, Autumn 1983, *46*(4), pp. 171–84. **[G: U.S.]**

Freedman, Ann E. Sex Equality, Sex Differences, and the Supreme Court. *Yale Law J.*, May 1983, *92*(6), pp. 913–68.

Fujii, Edwin T. and Mak, James. On the Specification of the Income Equation for Immigrants. *Southern Econ. J.*, April 1983, *49*(4), pp. 1141–46. **[G: U.S.]**

Fujii, Edwin T. and Mak, James. The Determinants of Income of Native- and Foreign-Born Men in a Multiracial Society. *Appl. Econ.*, December 1983, *15*(6), pp. 759–76. **[G: U.S.]**

Garabaghi, Ninou K. A New Approach to Women's Participation in the Economy. *Int. Soc. Sci. J.*, 1983, *35*(4), pp. 659–82. **[G: OECD]**

Gersovitz, Mark. Savings and Nutrition at Low Incomes. *J. Polit. Econ.*, October 1983, *91*(5), pp. 841–55.

Gilbert, Neil. In Support of Domesticity: A Neglected Family Policy Option. *J. Policy Anal. Manage.*, Summer 1983, *2*(4), pp. 628–32. **[G: U.S.]**

Gill, H. Leroy. Changes in City and Suburban House Prices during a Period of Expected School Desegregation. *Southern Econ. J.*, July 1983, *50*(1), pp. 169–84. **[G: U.S.]**

Gladwin, Christina H. and Staudt, Kathleen. Women's Employment Issues: Discussion. *Amer. J. Agr. Econ.*, December 1983, *65*(5), pp. 1055–57.

Gray, Thomas A. Student Housing and Discrimination: An Empirical Approach. *Amer. Econ.*, Spring 1983, *27*(1), pp. 61–68. **[G: U.S.]**

Gregory, R. G. and Duncan, Ronald C. Equal Pay for Women: A Reply [Segmented Labour Market Theories and the Australian Experience of Equal Pay for Women]. *Australian Econ. Pap.*, June 1983, *22*(40), pp. 60–64. **[G: Australia]**

Gregory, R. G. and Duncan, Ronald C. Reply [Segmented Labor Market Theories and the Australian Experience of Equal Pay for Women]. *J. Post Keynesian Econ.*, Summer 1983, *5*(4), pp. 673–75. **[G: Australia]**

Gupta, R. P. Rural Women and Economic Development. *Econ. Aff.*, July-September 1983, *28*(3), pp. 784–90. **[G: India]**

Gustafsson, Siv. Lifetime Patterns of Labour Force Participation. **In** *Weisbrod, B. and Hughes, H., eds.*, 1983, pp. 231–49. **[G: Sweden; U.S.]**

Haber, Sheldon E.; Lamas, Enrique J. and Green, Gordon. A New Method for Estimating Job Separations by Sex and Race. *Mon. Lab. Rev.*, June 1983, *106*(6), pp. 20–27. **[G: U.S.]**

Hamilton, William L. The Great Housing Experiment: Economic and Racial/Ethnic Concentration. **In** *Friedman, J. and Weinberg, D. H., eds.*, 1983, pp. 210–19. **[G: U.S.]**

Harris, Donald J. Economic Growth, Structural Change, and the Relative Income Status of Blacks in the U.S. Economy, 1947–78. *Rev. Black Polit. Econ.*, Spring 1983, *12*(3), pp. 75–92. **[G: U.S.]**

Hart, Gillian. Productivity, Poverty, and Population Pressure: Female Labor Deployment in Rice Production in Java and Bangladesh. *Amer. J. Agr. Econ.*, December 1983, *65*(5), pp. 1037–42. **[G: Indonesia; Bangladesh]**

Hayghe, Howard. Married Couples: Work and Income Patterns. *Mon. Lab. Rev.*, December 1983, *106*(12), pp. 26–29. **[G: U.S.]**

Heilman, Madeline E. Sex Bias in Work Settings: The Lack of Fit Model. **In** *Cummings, L. L. and Staw, B. M., eds.*, 1983, pp. 269–98.

Henn, Jeanne Koopman. Feeding the Cities and Feeding the Peasants: What Role for Africa's Women Farmers? *World Devel.*, December 1983, *11*(12), pp. 1043–55. **[G: Cameroon; Tanzania]**

Hickman, James C. Pensions and Sex. *J. Risk Ins.*, December 1983, *50*(4), pp. 681–87. **[G: U.S.]**

Hill, David B. Women State Legislators and Party Voting on the ERA. *Soc. Sci. Quart.*, June 1983, *64*(2), pp. 318–26. **[G: U.S.]**

Hill, M. Anne. Female Labor Force Participation in Developing and Developed Countries—Consideration of the Informal Sector. *Rev. Econ. Statist.*, August 1983, *65*(3), pp. 459–68. **[G: Japan]**

Hill, Martha S. Female Household Headship and the Poverty of Children. **In** *Duncan, G. J. and Morgan, J. N., eds.*, 1983, pp. 324–76. **[G: U.S.]**

Hirschman, Charles. Labor Markets and Ethnic Inequality in Peninsular Malaysia, 1970. *J. Devel. Areas*, October 1983, *18*(1), pp. 1–20. **[G: Malaysia]**

Hogan, Lloyd L. The Political Economy of Black Americans: Perspectives on Curriculum Development. *Rev. Black Polit. Econ.*, Winter 1983, *12*(2), pp. 145–61. **[G: U.S.]**

House, William J. Occupational Segregation and Discriminatory Pay: The Position of Women in the Cyprus Labour Market. *Int. Lab. Rev.*, January–February 1983, *122*(1), pp. 75–93. **[G: Cyprus]**

Hoyman, Michele M. and Stallworth, Lamont E. Arbitrating Discrimination Grievances in the Wake of *Gardner-Denver. Mon. Lab. Rev.*, October 1983, *106*(10), pp. 3–10. **[G: U.S.]**

Huffman, Wallace E. Women's Employment Issues: Discussion. *Amer. J. Agr. Econ.*, December 1983, *65*(5), pp. 1058–59.

Hull, Everson. Money Growth and the Employment Aspirations of Black Americans. *Rev. Black Polit. Econ.*, Spring 1983, *12*(3), pp. 63–74. **[G: U.S.]**

Hunt, Janet C. Discrimination in ERA States? [The Equal Rights Amendment: An Empirical Analysis of Sex Discrimination]. *Econ. Inquiry*, January 1983, *21*(1), pp. 140–45. **[G: U.S.]**

Hunter, Eveline. Women and Poverty. **In** *Brown, G. and Cook, R., eds.*, 1983, pp. 152–61. **[G: U.K.]**

Ichniowski, Casey. Have Angels Done More? The Steel Industry Consent Decree. *Ind. Lab. Relat. Rev.*, January 1983, *36*(2), pp. 182–98. **[G: U.S.]**

Ihnen, Loren A. Black Agricultural Economists: Discussion. *Amer. J. Agr. Econ.*, December 1983, *65*(5), pp. 999–1001. **[G: U.S.]**

Jacobsen, Grethe. Women's Work and Women's Role: Ideology and Reality in Danish Urban Society, 1300–1550. *Scand. Econ. Hist. Rev.*, 1983, *31*(1), pp. 3–20. **[G: Denmark]**

Johnson, Beverly L. and Waldman, Elizabeth. Most Women Who Maintain Families Receive Poor Labor Market Returns. *Mon. Lab. Rev.*, December 1983, *106*(12), pp. 30–34. **[G: U.S.]**

Johnson, Janet L. Sex Differentials in Unemployment Rates: A Case for No Concern. *J. Polit. Econ.*, April 1983, *91*(2), pp. 293–303. **[G: U.S.]**

Jones, Christine. The Mobilization of Women's Labor for Cash Crop Production: A Game Theoretic Approach. *Amer. J. Agr. Econ.*, December 1983, *65*(5), pp. 1049–54. **[G: Cameroon]**

Jones, Dewitt; Nelson, Mack and Parks, Alfred L. Demand and Supply Factors of Black Agricultural Economists. *Amer. J. Agr. Econ.*, December 1983, *65*(5), pp. 988–92. **[G: U.S.]**

Jones, F. L. On Decomposing the Wage Gap: A Critical Comment on Blinder's Method [Wage Discrimination: Reduced Form and Structural Estimates]. *J. Human Res.*, Winter 1983, *18*(1), pp. 126–30. **[G: U.S.]**

Kahan, Arcadius. Notes on Jewish Entrepreneurship in Tsarist Russia. **In** *Guroff, G. and Carstensen, F. V., eds.*, 1983, pp. 104–24. **[G: U.S.S.R.]**

Katzir, Yael. Yemenite Jewish Women in Israeli Rural Development: Female Power versus Male Authority. *Econ. Develop. Cult. Change*, October 1983, *32*(1), pp. 45–61. **[G: Israel]**

Kendrick, Stephen. Social Change in Scotland. **In** *Brown, G. and Cook, R., eds.*, 1983, pp. 40–65. **[G: U.K.]**

Kessler-Harris, Alice. "Rosie the Riveter": Who Was She? *Labor Hist.*, Spring 1983, *24*(2), pp. 249–53. **[G: U.S.]**

Killingsworth, Mark R. and Reimers, Cordelia W. Race, Ranking, Promotions, and Pay at a Federal Facility: A Logit Analysis. *Ind. Lab. Relat. Rev.*, October 1983, *37*(1), pp. 92–107. **[G: U.S.]**

Klitgaard, Robert E. and Katz, Ruth. Overcoming Ethnic Inequalities: Lessons from Malaysia. *J. Policy Anal. Manage.*, Spring 1983, *2*(3), pp. 333–49. **[G: Malaysia]**

Knight, Ester. Women and the UK Tax System: The Case for Reform? *Cambridge J. Econ.*, June 1983, *7*(2), pp. 151–65. **[G: U.K.]**

Knowles, Daniel E. Keeping Older Workers on the Job: Methods and Inducements. **In** *Parnes, H. S., ed.*, 1983, pp. 99–108. **[G: U.S.]**

Kossoudji, Sherrie and Mueller, Eva. The Economic and Demographic Status of Female-Headed Households in Rural Botswana. *Econ. Develop. Cult. Change*, July 1983, *31*(4), pp. 831–59. **[G: Botswana]**

Kwast, Myron L. and Black, Harold A. An Analysis of the Behavior of Mature Black-Owned Commercial Banks. *J. Econ. Bus.*, 1983, *35*(1), pp. 41–54. **[G: U.S.]**

Kynch, Jocelyn and Sen, Amartya K. Indian Women: Well-Being and Survival. *Cambridge J. Econ.*, September/December 1983, *7*(3/4), pp. 363–80. **[G: India]**

La Duque, Winona. Native America: The Economics of Radioactive Colonization. *Rev. Radical Polit. Econ.*, Fall 1983, *15*(3), pp. 9–19. **[G: U.S.]**

Landa, Janet T. The Political Economy of the Ethnically Homogeneous Chinese Middleman Group in Southeast Asia: Ethnicity and Entrepreneurship in a Plural Society. **In** *Lim, L. Y. C. and Gosling, L. A. P., eds.*, 1983, pp. 86–116. **[G: Malaysia; Singapore]**

Lehrer, Evelyn and Nerlove, Marc. The Impact of Female Life-cycle Time-allocation Decisions on Income Distribution among Families. **In** *Weisbrod, B. and Hughes, H., eds.*, 1983, pp. 274–89. **[G: U.S.]**

Leigh, J. Paul. Sex Differences in Absenteeism. *Ind. Relat.*, Fall 1983, *22*(3), pp. 349–61. **[G: U.S.]**

Leigh, Wilhelmina A. The Impact of Inflation upon Homeownership Affordability: Comparisons by Race and Sex for the South. **In** *Schmukler, N. and Marcus, E., eds.*, 1983, pp. 838–59. **[G: U.S.]**

Levin, Bruce and Robbins, Herbert. Urn Models for Regression Analysis, with Applications to Employment Discrimination Studies. *Law Contemp. Probl.*, Autumn 1983, *46*(4), pp. 247–67. **[G: U.S.]**

Lim, David. The Political Economy of the New Economic Policy in Malaysia. **In** *Lim, D., ed.*, 1983, pp. 3–22. **[G: Malaysia]**

Lobue, Marie. Adjustment to Labor Productivity: An Application to the Economics of Discrimination. *Southern Econ. J.*, July 1983, *50*(1), pp. 151–59.

Lott, William F. Are Women Economists at a Disadvantage in Publishing Journal Articles? A Methodological Comment. *Eastern Econ. J.*, April–June 1983, *9*(2), pp. 133–38. **[G: U.S.]**

Loury, Glenn C. Economics, Politics, and Blacks. *Rev. Black Polit. Econ.*, Spring 1983, *12*(3), pp. 43–54. **[G: U.S.]**

Lundberg, Shelly J. and Startz, Richard. Private Discrimination and Social Intervention in Competitive Labor Markets. *Amer. Econ. Rev.*, June 1983, *73*(3), pp. 340–47.

Maki, Dennis R. Unions as 'Gatekeepers' of Occupational Sex Discrimination: Canadian Evidence. *Appl. Econ.*, August 1983, *15*(4), pp. 469–77. **[G: Canada]**

Markwalder, Don. A Response to Timothy Bates' Comment [The Potential for Black Business]. *Rev. Black Polit. Econ.*, Winter 1983, *12*(2), pp.

241–42. [G: U.S.]

Massey, Doreen. Industrial Restructuring as Class Restructuring: Production Decentralization and Local Uniqueness. *Reg. Stud.*, April 1983, *17*(2), pp. 73–89. [G: U.K.]

McCarthy, Kevin F. Housing Search and Residential Mobility. **In** *Friedman, J. and Weinberg, D. H., eds.*, 1983, pp. 191–209. [G: U.S.]

McConnell, Stephen R. Age Discrimination in Employment. **In** *Parnes, H. S., ed.*, 1983, pp. 159–96. [G: U.S.]

McGavin, P. A. Equal Pay for Women: A Postscript [Segmented Labour Market Theories and the Australian Experience of Equal Pay for Women]. *Australian Econ. Pap.*, June 1983, *22*(40), pp. 65–67. [G: Australia]

McGavin, P. A. Equal Pay for Women: A Re-Assessment of the Australian Experience. *Australian Econ. Pap.*, June 1983, *22*(40), pp. 48–59. [G: Australia]

McGrath, M. D. Health Expenditure in a Racially Segregated Society: A Case Study of South Africa. **In** *Salkever, D.; Sirageldin, I. and Sorkin, A., eds.*, 1983, pp. 311–28. [G: S. Africa]

McManus, Walter; Gould, William and Welch, Finis. Earnings of Hispanic Men: The Role of English Language Proficiency. *J. Lab. Econ.*, April 1983, *1*(2), pp. 101–30. [G: U.S.]

Meyer, Peter J. and Maes, Patricia L. The Reproduction of Occupational Segregation among Young Women. *Ind. Relat.*, Winter 1983, *22*(1), pp. 115–24. [G: U.S.]

Mieszkowski, Peter. The Tax Treatment of Married Couples and the 1981 Tax Law: Commentary. **In** *Penner, R. G., ed.*, 1983, pp. 69–70. [G: U.S.]

Minarik, Joseph J. Family Issues in Taxation: Commentary. **In** *Penner, R. G., ed.*, 1983, pp. 23–27. [G: U.S.]

de Miranda, Glaura Vasques. Human Resource Development and Female Labour Force Participation in Brazil. **In** *Streeten, P. and Maier, H., eds.*, 1983, pp. 420–42. [G: Brazil]

Mitchell, William F. Equal Pay for Women: A Reply [Segmented Labor Market Theories and the Australian Experience of Equal Pay for Women]. *J. Post Keynesian Econ.*, Summer 1983, *5*(4), pp. 669–72. [G: Australia]

Moore, Robert L. Employer Discrimination: Evidence from Self-Employed Workers. *Rev. Econ. Statist.*, August 1983, *65*(3), pp. 496–501. [G: U.S.]

Motroshilova, Nelya V. Soviet Women in the Life of Society: Achievements and Problems. *Int. Soc. Sci. J.*, 1983, *35*(4), pp. 733–46. [G: U.S.S.R.]

Mott, Frank L. and Shapiro, David. Complementarity of Work and Fertility among Young American Mothers. *Population Stud.*, July 1983, *37*(2), pp. 239–52. [G: U.S.]

Myers, Samuel L., Jr. Racial Differences in Postprison Employment. *Soc. Sci. Quart.*, September 1983, *64*(3), pp. 655–69. [G: U.S.]

Nakanishi, Tamako. Equality or Protection? Protective Legislation for Women in Japan. *Int. Lab. Rev.*, Sept.–Oct. 1983, *122*(5), pp. 609–21. [G: Japan]

Nestel, Gilbert; Mercier, Jacqueline and Shaw, Lois B. Economic Consequences of Midlife Change in Marital Status. **In** *Shaw, L. B., ed.*, 1983, pp. 109–25. [G: U.S.]

Niemi, Beth T. and Lloyd, Cynthia B. Inflation and Female Labor Force Participation. **In** *Schmukler, N. and Marcus, E., eds.*, 1983, pp. 820–37. [G: U.S.]

Nord, Stephen. An Interstate Analysis of Changes in Nonwhite and White Family Incomes 1960 to 1970. *Eastern Econ. J.*, January–March 1983, *9*(1), pp. 13–21. [G: U.S.]

O'Neill, Dave M. Racial Differentials in Teenage Unemployment: A Note on Trends. *J. Human Res.*, Spring 1983, *18*(2), pp. 295–306. [G: U.S.]

O'Neill, June. Family Issues in Taxation. **In** *Penner, R. G., ed.*, 1983, pp. 1–22. [G: U.S.]

Olson, Craig A. and Becker, Brian E. Sex Discrimination in the Promotion Process. *Ind. Lab. Relat. Rev.*, July 1983, *36*(4), pp. 624–41. [G: U.S.]

Oppong, Christine. Women's Roles, Opportunity Costs, and Fertility. **In** *Bulatao, R. A. and Lee, R. D., eds., Vol. 1*, 1983, pp. 547–89.

Pang, Eng Fong. Race, Income Distribution, and Development in Malaysia and Singapore. **In** *Lim, L. Y. C. and Gosling, L. A. P., eds.*, 1983, pp. 316–35. [G: Malaysia; Singapore]

Paringer, Lynn. Women and Absenteeism: Health or Economics? *Amer. Econ. Rev.*, May 1983, *73*(2), pp. 123–27. [G: U.S.]

Pastin, Mark and Hooker, Michael. Ethics and the Foreign Corrupt Practices Act. **In** *Snoeyenbos, M.; Almeder, R. and Humber, J., eds.*, 1983, *1980*, pp. 150–55. [G: U.S.]

Perry, Huey L. The Impact of Black Political Participation on Public Sector Employment and Representation on Municipal Boards and Commissions. *Rev. Black Polit. Econ.*, Winter 1983, *12*(2), pp. 203–17. [G: U.S.]

Pike, Maureen. A Simulation of the Impact of Introducing Equality for Males and Females into Social Security. *Economica*, August 1983, *50*(199), pp. 351–60. [G: U.K.]

Pinderhughes, Dianne M. Collective Goods and Black Interest Groups. *Rev. Black Polit. Econ.*, Winter 1983, *12*(2), pp. 219–36. [G: U.S.]

Power, Marilyn. From Home Production to Wage Labor: Women as a Reserve Army of Labor. *Rev. Radical Polit. Econ.*, Spring 1983, *15*(1), pp. 71–91. [G: U.S.]

Raimondo, Henry J. Free Agents' Impact on the Labor Market for Baseball Players. *J. Lab. Res.*, Spring 1983, *4*(2), pp. 183–93. [G: U.S.]

Raymond, Richard and Sesnowitz, Michael. Labor Market Discrimination against Mexican American College Graduates. *Southern Econ. J.*, April 1983, *49*(4), pp. 1122–36. [G: U.S.]

Raymond, Richard and Sesnowitz, Michael. The Rate of Return to Mexican Americans and Anglos on an Investment in a College Education. *Econ. Inquiry*, July 1983, *21*(3), pp. 400–411. [G: U.S.]

Reimers, Cordelia W. Labor Market Discrimination against Hispanic and Black Men. *Rev. Econ. Statist.*, November 1983, *65*(4), pp. 570–79. [G: U.S.]

Remus, William E. and Kelley, Lane. Evidence of Sex Discrimination: In Similar Populations, Men Are Paid Better Than Women. *Amer. J. Econ. Soc.*, April 1983, *42*(2), pp. 149–52. [G: U.S.]

Robb, Roberta. Participation Rate Changes in Canada in the Early 1980s: Comment. **In** *Queen's Univ. Indust. Relat. Centre and John Deutsch Mem.*, 1983, pp. 78–80. **[G: Canada]**

Robbins, Richard D. and Evans, Sidney H. Characteristics of Black Agricultural Economists. *Amer. J. Agr. Econ.*, December 1983, *65*(5), pp. 993–98. **[G: U.S.]**

Rosenzweig, Mark R. and Schultz, T. Paul. Estimating a Household Production Function: Heterogeneity, the Demand for Health Inputs, and Their Effects on Birth Weight. *J. Polit. Econ.*, October 1983, *91*(5), pp. 723–46. **[G: U.S.]**

Rytina, Nancy. Comparing Annual and Weekly Earnings from the Current Population Survey. *Mon. Lab. Rev.*, April 1983, *106*(4), pp. 32–36. **[G: U.S.]**

Saffran, Bernard. The Tax Treatment of Married Couples and the 1981 Tax Law: Commentary. **In** *Penner, R. G., ed.*, 1983, pp. 64–68. **[G: U.S.]**

Sagalyn, Lynne Beyer. Mortgage Lending in Older Urban Neighborhoods: Lessons from Past Experience. *Ann. Amer. Acad. Polit. Soc. Sci.*, January 1983, *465*, pp. 98–108. **[G: U.S.]**

Saltzstein, Grace Hall. Personnel Directors and Female Employment Representation: A New Addition to Models of Equal Employment Opportunity Policy? *Soc. Sci. Quart.*, December 1983, *64*(4), pp. 734–46. **[G: U.S.]**

Seguret, Marie-Claire. Women and Working Conditions: Prospects for Improvement? *Int. Lab. Rev.*, May–June 1983, *122*(3), pp. 295–311. **[G: Global]**

Shapiro, David and Mott, Frank L. Effects of Selected Variables on Work Hours of Young Women. *Mon. Lab. Rev.*, July 1983, *106*(7), pp. 31–34. **[G: U.S.]**

Shaw, Lois B. Causes of Irregular Employment Patterns. **In** *Shaw, L. B., ed.*, 1983, pp. 45–59. **[G: U.S.]**

Shaw, Lois B. Problems of Labor-Market Reentry. **In** *Shaw, L. B., ed.*, 1983, pp. 33–44. **[G: U.S.]**

Shaw, Lois B. Unplanned Careers: The Working Lives of Middle-aged Women: Summary and Conclusions. **In** *Shaw, L. B., ed.*, 1983, pp. 127–34. **[G: U.S.]**

Shaw, Lois B. and O'Brien, Theresa. Unplanned Careers: The Working Lives of Middle-aged Women: Introduction and Overview. **In** *Shaw, L. B., ed.*, 1983, pp. 1–31. **[G: U.S.]**

Shear, William B. and Yezer, Anthony M. J. An Indirect Test for Differential Treatment of Borrowers in Mortgage Markets. *Amer. Real Estate Urban Econ. Assoc. J.*, Winter 1983, *10*(4), pp. 405–20. **[G: U.S.]**

Shoben, Elaine W. The Use of Statistics to Prove Intentional Employment Discrimination. *Law Contemp. Probl.*, Autumn 1983, *46*(4), pp. 219–45. **[G: U.S.]**

Shorey, John. An Analysis of Sex Differences in Quits. *Oxford Econ. Pap.*, July 1983, *35*(2), pp. 213–27. **[G: U.K.]**

Siebert, W. S. and Young, A. Sex and Family Status Differentials in Professional Earnings: The Case of Librarians. *Scot. J. Polit. Econ.*, February 1983, *30*(1), pp. 18–41. **[G: U.K.]**

Siegers, Jacques J. An Economic–Demographic Ten-Equation Model. *De Economist*, 1983, *131*(3), pp. 400–443. **[G: Netherlands]**

Sims, Harvey. Participation Rate Changes in Canada in the Early 1980s. **In** *Queen's Univ. Indust. Relat. Centre and John Deutsch Mem.*, 1983, pp. 65–75. **[G: Canada]**

Singh, Harbhajan. Inequality in Labour-Market Rewards and Education in India (A Case Study of Delhi). *Indian Econ. Rev.*, July–December 1983, *18*(2), pp. 245–72. **[G: India]**

Smith, Neil. Toward a Theory of Gentrification: A Back to the City Movement by Capital, Not People. **In** *Lake, R. W., ed.*, 1983, *1979*, pp. 278–98. **[G: U.S.]**

Smith, Sharon P. Are State and Local Government Workers Overpaid? **In** *Hirsch, W. Z., ed.*, 1983, pp. 59–89. **[G: U.S.]**

Smith, Tim. South Africa: The Churches vs. the Corporations. **In** *Snoeyenbos, M.; Almeder, R. and Humber, J., eds.*, 1983, *1975*, pp. 495–502. **[G: U.S.]**

Sofer, Catherine. Emplois "féminins" et emplois "masculins": Mesure de la ségrégation et évolution de la féminisation des emplois. ("Female" Jobs and "Male" Jobs: A Measure of Segregation by Sex and the Evolution of the Feminization of Jobs. With English summary.) *Ann. INSEE*, October–December 1983, (52), pp. 55–85. **[G: France]**

Sommers, Paul M. and Thomas, Laura S. Restricting Federal Funds for Abortion: Another Look. *Soc. Sci. Quart.*, June 1983, *64*(2), pp. 340–46. **[G: U.S.]**

Spalter-Roth, Roberta M. Differentiating between the Living Standards of Husbands and Wives in Two-Wage-Earner Families, 1968 and 1979. *J. Econ. Hist.*, March 1983, *43*(1), pp. 231–40. **[G: U.S.]**

Standing, Guy. Women's Work Activity and Fertility. **In** *Bulatao, R. A. and Lee, R. D., eds., Vol. 1*, 1983, pp. 517–46.

Statham, Anne and Rhoton, Patricia. Attitudes toward Women Working: Changes over Time and Implications for the Labor-Force Behaviors of Husbands and Wives. **In** *Shaw, L. B., ed.*, 1983, pp. 77–92. **[G: U.S.]**

Stephan, Paula E. and Levin, Sharon G. Sex Segregation in Education: The Case of Doctorate Recipients. *J. Behav. Econ.*, Winter 1983, *12*(2), pp. 67–94. **[G: U.S.]**

Stewart, Mark B. Racial Discrimination and Occupational Attainment in Britain. *Econ. J.*, September 1983, *93*(371), pp. 521–41. **[G: U.K.]**

Swan, Kenneth P. Protections against Discriminatory Dismissal. **In** *Queen's Univ. Indust. Relat. Centre*, 1983, pp. 49–58. **[G: Canada]**

Swinton, David H. Orthodox and Systemic Explanations for Unemployment and Racial Inequality: Implications for Policy. *Rev. Black Polit. Econ.*, Spring 1983, *12*(3), pp. 9–25. **[G: U.S.]**

Thillainathan, R. Discriminatory Allocation of Public Expenditure Benefits for Reducing Inter-racial Inequality in Malaysia—An Evaluation. **In** *Lim, D., ed.*, 1983, *1980*, pp. 23–40. **[G: Malaysia]**

Tomlinson, R. Industrial Decentralization and the

Relief of Poverty in the Homelands. *S. Afr. J. Econ.*, December 1983, *51* (4), pp. 544–63. **[G: S. Africa]**

Truu, M. L. Labour Market Segmentation: The Theoretical Case—Comment. *S. Afr. J. Econ.*, December 1983, *51* (4), pp. 567–73.

Truu, M. L. Labour Market Segmentation: The Theoretical Case—Final Comment. *S. Afr. J. Econ.*, December 1983, *51* (4), pp. 579.

Wallendorf, Melanie and Reilly, Michael D. Ethnic Migration, Assimilation, and Consumption. *J. Cons. Res.*, December 1983, *10* (3), pp. 292–302. **[G: Mexico; U.S.]**

Ward, Kathryn B. The Economic Status of Women in the World-System: A Hidden Crisis in Development. **In** *Bergesen, A., ed.*, 1983, pp. 117–39. **[G: Global]**

Weicher, John C. Re-Evaluating Housing Policy Alternatives: What Do We Really Know? *Amer. Real Estate Urban Econ. Assoc. J.*, Spring 1983, *11* (1), pp. 1–10. **[G: U.S.]**

Willingham, Alex. Sowell's *Knowledge and Decisions:* Can Black Conservatism Establish Its Intellectual Credibility? *Rev. Black Polit. Econ.*, Winter 1983, *12* (2), pp. 179–87. **[G: U.S.]**

Winsberg, Morton D. Ethnic Competition for Residential Space in Miami, Florida, 1970–80. *Amer. J. Econ. Soc.*, July 1983, *42* (3), pp. 305–14. **[G: U.S.]**

Yanz, Lynda and Smith, David. Women as a Reserve Army of Labour: A Critique. *Rev. Radical Polit. Econ.*, Spring 1983, *15* (1), pp. 92–106. **[G: U.K.]**

918 Economics of Aging

9180 Economics of Aging

Asimakopulos, A. Public Pensions, the Federal Budget, and Discrimination. *Can. Public Policy*, March 1983, *9* (1), pp. 105–13. **[G: Canada]**

Bernstein, Theodore. Discussion [Aging, Health, and Work] [Health and Retirement, Retirement and Health: Background and Future Directions]. **In** *Parnes, H. S., ed.*, 1983, pp. 75–82. **[G: U.S.]**

Buchmann, Anna Marie. Maximizing Post-retirement Labor Market Opportunities. **In** *Parnes, H. S., ed.*, 1983, pp. 109–29. **[G: U.S.]**

Burkhauser, Richard V. and Quinn, Joseph F. Is Mandatory Retirement Overrated? Evidence from the 1970s. *J. Human Res.*, Summer 1983, *18* (3), pp. 337–58. **[G: U.S.]**

Burkhauser, Richard V. and Wilkinson, James T. The Effect of Retirement on Income Distribution: A Comprehensive Income Approach. *Rev. Econ. Statist.*, November 1983, *65* (4), pp. 653–58. **[G: U.S.]**

Chen, Alexander. Alternative Reverse Mortgages: A Simulation Analysis of Initial Benefits in Baltimore. *Housing Finance Rev.*, Oct 1983, *2* (4), pp. 295–308. **[G: U.S.]**

Clark, Robert L. and Gohmann, Stephan F. Retirement and the Acceptance of Social Security Benefits. *Nat. Tax J.*, December 1983, *36* (4), pp. 529–34. **[G: U.S.]**

Coe, Richard D. Participation in the Supplemental Security Income Program by the Eligible Elderly. **In** *Duncan, G. J. and Morgan, J. N., eds.*, 1983, pp. 93–120. **[G: U.S.]**

Cremer, Helmuth. Epargne et consommation des personnes âgées. (With English summary.) *Cah. Écon. Bruxelles*, 1983, *97* (1), pp. 75–103. **[G: Belgium]**

Crimmins, Eileen M. Implications of Recent Mortality Trends for the Size and Composition of the Population over 65. *Rev. Public Data Use (See J. Econ. Soc. Meas. after 4/85)*, March 1983, *11* (1), pp. 37–48. **[G: U.S.]**

Danziger, Sheldon, et al. The Life-Cycle Hypothesis and the Consumption Behavior of the Elderly. *J. Post Keynesian Econ.*, Winter 1982–83, *5* (2), pp. 208–27. **[G: U.S.]**

Davies, Richard B. and Davies, Sheila. The Retired Migrant: A Study in North Wales. *Urban Stud.*, May 1983, *20* (2), pp. 209–17. **[G: U.K.]**

Denton, Frank T. and Spencer, Byron G. Population Aging and Future Health Costs in Canada. *Can. Public Policy*, June 1983, *9* (2), pp. 155–63. **[G: Canada]**

Eisdorfer, Carl and Cohen, Donna. Health and Retirement, Retirement and Health: Background and Future Directions. **In** *Parnes, H. S., ed.*, 1983, pp. 57–73. **[G: U.S.]**

Feenberg, Daniel R. The Economic Status of the Elderly: Comment. **In** *Bodie, Z. and Shoven, J. B., eds.*, 1983, pp. 393–96. **[G: U.S.]**

Foner, Anne. Discussion [Aging, Health, and Work] [Health and Retirement, Retirement and Health: Background and Future Directions]. **In** *Parnes, H. S., ed.*, 1983, pp. 83–89. **[G: U.S.]**

Garbacz, Christopher and Thayer, Mark A. An Experiment in Valuing Senior Companion Program Services. *J. Human Res.*, Winter 1983, *18* (1), pp. 147–53. **[G: U.S.]**

Ginzberg, Eli. Life without Work: Does It Make Sense? **In** *Parnes, H. S., ed.*, 1983, pp. 29–37. **[G: U.S.]**

Girshick, Lori B. and Williamson, John B. The Politics of Measuring Poverty among the Elderly. **In** *Goldstein, R. and Sachs, S. M., eds.*, 1983, pp. 64–76. **[G: U.S.]**

Grimes, Alistair. Pensioners in Poverty. **In** *Brown, G. and Cook, R., eds.*, 1983, pp. 136–44. **[G: U.K.]**

Hall, Marni J. Mental Illness and the Elderly. **In** *Vogel, R. J. and Palmer, H. C., eds.*, 1983, pp. 483–505. **[G: U.S.]**

Hanoch, Giora and Honig, Marjorie. Retirement, Wages, and Labor Supply of the Elderly. *J. Lab. Econ.*, April 1983, *1* (2), pp. 131–51. **[G: U.S.]**

Harris, William T. Property Tax Circuit-Breakers: Good Causes but Bad Economics. *Amer. J. Econ. Soc.*, April 1983, *42* (2), pp. 209–16. **[G: U.S.]**

Haveman, Robert H. and Wolfe, Barbara L. Disability and Work Effort: A Probabilistic Choice Analysis of the Labor Supply Decisions of Older Men. **In** *Söderström, L., ed.*, 1983, pp. 187–205. **[G: U.S.; OECD]**

Hurd, Michael D. and Shoven, John B. The Economic Status of the Elderly. **In** *Bodie, Z. and Shoven, J. B., eds.*, 1983, pp. 359–93, 396–97. **[G: U.S.]**

Jump, Bernard, Jr. State and Local Government Pension Benefits: Just Desserts or Just Rip-offs? **In** *Hirsch, W. Z., ed.*, 1983, pp. 212–46. **[G: U.S.]**

Knowles, Daniel E. Keeping Older Workers on the Job: Methods and Inducements. **In** *Parnes, H. S., ed.*, 1983, pp. 99–108. **[G: U.S.]**

Koyl, Leon F. Aging, Health, and Work. **In** *Parnes, H. S., ed.*, 1983, pp. 39–56. **[G: U.S.]**

Kuhns, E. Douglas. Discussion [Keeping Older Workers on the Job: Methods and Inducements] [Maximizing Post-retirement Labor Market Opportunities]. **In** *Parnes, H. S., ed.*, 1983, pp. 131–38. **[G: U.S.]**

Liebow, Elliot. Discussion [Aging, Health, and Work] [Health and Retirement, Retirement and Health: Background and Future Directions]. **In** *Parnes, H. S., ed.*, 1983, pp. 91–97.

Lingg, Barbara A. Beneficiaries Affected by the Annual Earnings Test in 1978. *Soc. Sec. Bull.*, April 1983, *46*(4), pp. 23–34. **[G: U.S.]**

Liu, Korbin; Manton, Kenneth and Alliston, Wiley. Demographic and Epidemiologic Determinants of Expenditures. **In** *Vogel, R. J. and Palmer, H. C., eds.*, 1983, pp. 81–102. **[G: U.S.]**

McConnell, Stephen R. Age Discrimination in Employment. **In** *Parnes, H. S., ed.*, 1983, pp. 159–96. **[G: U.S.]**

McIntosh, Barbara L. Discussion [Keeping Older Workers on the Job: Methods and Inducements] [Maximizing Post-retirement Labor Market Opportunities]. **In** *Parnes, H. S., ed.*, 1983, pp. 151–58. **[G: U.S.]**

Merrilees, William J. Pension Benefits and the Decline in Elderly Male Labour Force Participation. *Econ. Rec.*, September 1983, *59*(166), pp. 260–70. **[G: Australia]**

Morrison, Malcolm H. The Aging of the U.S. Population: Human Resource Implications. *Mon. Lab. Rev.*, May 1983, *106*(5), pp. 13–19. **[G: U.S.]**

Ogawa, Naohiro and Suits, Daniel B. Retirement Policy and Japanese Workers: Some Results of an Opinion Survey. *Int. Lab. Rev.*, November–December 1983, *122*(6), pp. 733–46. **[G: Japan; France]**

Palmer, Hans C. Adult Day Care. **In** *Vogel, R. J. and Palmer, H. C., eds.*, 1983, pp. 415–36. **[G: U.S.]**

Palmer, Hans C. Domiciliary Care: A Semantic Tangle. **In** *Vogel, R. J. and Palmer, H. C., eds.*, 1983, pp. 437–61. **[G: U.S.]**

Parnes, Herbert S. Policy Issues in Work and Retirement: Introduction and Overview. **In** *Parnes, H. S., ed.*, 1983, pp. 1–27. **[G: U.S.]**

Price, Karl. Discussion [Keeping Older Workers on the Job: Methods and Inducements] [Maximizing Post-retirement Labor Market Opportunities]. **In** *Parnes, H. S., ed.*, 1983, pp. 139–44. **[G: U.S.]**

Quinn, Joseph F. The Work Ethic and Retirement. **In** *Barbash, J., et al., eds.*, 1983, pp. 87–100. **[G: U.S.]**

Quinn, Joseph F. and Burkhauser, Richard V. Influencing Retirement Behavior: A Key Issue for Social Security. *J. Policy Anal. Manage.*, Fall 1983, *3*(1), pp. 1–13. **[G: U.S.]**

Reddin, Mike. Pensions, Wealth and the Extension of Inequality. **In** *Field, F., ed.*, 1983, pp. 138–58. **[G: U.K.]**

Rones, Philip L. The Labor Market Problems of Older Workers. *Mon. Lab. Rev.*, May 1983, *106*(5), pp. 3–12. **[G: U.S.]**

Sangl, Judith. The Family Support System of the Elderly. **In** *Vogel, R. J. and Palmer, H. C., eds.*, 1983, pp. 307–36. **[G: U.S.]**

Scheiber, Sylvester J. Providing Income Security to the Elderly: The Role of Programs Other than Social Security. *Contemp. Policy Issue*, April 1983, (3), pp. 33–52. **[G: U.S.]**

Sheppard, Harold L. Discussion [Keeping Older Workers on the Job: Methods and Inducements] [Maximizing Post-retirement Labor Market Opportunities]. **In** *Parnes, H. S., ed.*, 1983, pp. 145–49. **[G: U.S.]**

Sproat, Kezia. How Do Families Fare When the Breadwinner Retires? *Mon. Lab. Rev.*, December 1983, *106*(12), pp. 40–44. **[G: U.S.]**

Thomas, Steven G. The Significance of Housing as a Resource. **In** *Vogel, R. J. and Palmer, H. C., eds.*, 1983, pp. 391–414. **[G: U.S.]**

Thomas, Steven G. Transportation and Dependency. **In** *Vogel, R. J. and Palmer, H. C., eds.*, 1983, pp. 463–82. **[G: U.S.]**

Upp, Melinda M. Relative Importance of Various Income Sources of the Aged, 1980. *Soc. Sec. Bull.*, January 1983, *46*(1), pp. 3–10. **[G: U.S.]**

Weaver, Carolyn L. On the Lack of a Political Market for Compulsory Old-Age Insurance Prior to the Great Depression: Insights from Economic Theories of Government. *Exploration Econ. Hist.*, July 1983, *20*(3), pp. 294–328. **[G: U.S.]**

Weis, Peter. Zur arbeitsmarktpolitischen Problematik von Kündigungs- und Besitzstandsregelungen für ältere Arbeitnehmer. (The Problematic Nature of Protection against Dismissal and Earnings Guaranties for Elderly Workers. With English summary.) *Z. Wirtschaft. Sozialwissen.*, 1983, *103*(3), pp. 255–81. **[G: W. Germany]**

Wolfe, John R. Perceived Longevity and Early Retirement. *Rev. Econ. Statist.*, November 1983, *65*(4), pp. 544–51. **[G: U.S.]**

920 CONSUMER ECONOMICS

921 Consumer Economics; Levels and Standards of Living

9210 General

Adamowicz, W. L. and Phillips, W. E. A Comparison of Extra Market Benefit Evaluation Techniques. *Can. J. Agr. Econ.*, November 1983, *31*(3), pp. 401–12. **[G: Canada]**

Addison, John T. and Burton, John. The Sociopolitical Analysis of Global Inflation: A Theoretical and Empirical Examination of an Influential Basic Explanation. *Amer. J. Econ. Soc.*, January 1983, *42*(1), pp. 13–28. **[G: OECD; Selected LDCs]**

Arnould, Richard J. and Nichols, Len M. Wage-Risk Premiums and Workers' Compensation: A Refinement of Estimates of Compensating Wage Differential. *J. Polit. Econ.*, April 1983, *91*(2), pp. 332–40. **[G: U.S.]**

Atkinson, Anthony B. The Distribution of Wealth and the Individual Life-Cycle. **In** *Atkinson, A. B.*, 1983, *1971*, pp. 131–45. **[G: U.K.]**

Atkinson, Anthony B. and Micklewright, J. On the Reliability of Income Data in the Family Expenditure Survey 1970–1977. *J. Roy. Statist. Soc.*, 1983, *146*(1), pp. 33–53. **[G: U.K.]**

Bagozzi, Richard P. Issues in the Application of Covariance Structure Analysis: A Further Comment. *J. Cons. Res.*, March 1983, *9*(4), pp. 449–50.

Baranova, L. Shaping the Population's Needs. *Prob. Econ.*, August 1983, *26*(4), pp. 57–72. **[G: U.S.S.R.]**

Biehal, Gabriel and Chakravarti, Dipankar. Information Accessibility as a Moderator of Consumer Choice. *J. Cons. Res.*, June 1983, *10*(1), pp. 1–14. **[G: U.S.]**

Bishop, Richard C.; Heberlein, Thomas A. and Kealy, Mary Jo. Contingent Valuation of Environmental Assets: Comparisons with a Simulated Market. *Natural Res. J.*, July 1983, *23*(3), pp. 619–33. **[G: U.S.]**

Bossons, John. Leisure Time and the Measurement of Economic Welfare: Comment. **In** *Diewert, W. E. and Montmarquette, C., eds.*, 1983, pp. 368–72. **[G: Canada]**

Bradbury, Katharine L. Revenues and Expenditures in New England's Largest Cities and Towns. *New Eng. Econ. Rev.*, July–August 1983, pp. 42–53. **[G: U.S.]**

Brinberg, David and Wood, Ronald. A Resource Exchange Theory Analysis of Consumer Behavior. *J. Cons. Res.*, December 1983, *10*(3), pp. 330–38.

Calder, Bobby J.; Philips, Lynn W. and Tybout, Alice M. Beyond External Validity. *J. Cons. Res.*, June 1983, *10*(1), pp. 112–24.

Chauveau, Thierry and Frochen, Patrick. Étude du comportement de l'épargnant français vis-à-vis des liquidités 1971–1981. (French Households and Liquid Assets (1971–1981). With English summary.) *Revue Écon.*, January 1983, *34*(1), pp. 152–81. **[G: France]**

Cohen, David R. Health Education as a Demand Concept. *Int. J. Soc. Econ.*, 1983, *10*(5), pp. 52–62.

Coleman, Richard P. The Continuing Significance of Social Class to Marketing. *J. Cons. Res.*, December 1983, *10*(3), pp. 265–80. **[G: U.S.]**

Cooper, Lee G. and Nakanishi, Masao. Standardizing Variables in Multiplicative Choice Models. *J. Cons. Res.*, June 1983, *10*(1), pp. 96–108.

Curry, David J. and Manasco, Michael B. On the Separability of Weights and Brand Values: Issues and Empirical Results. *J. Cons. Res.*, June 1983, *10*(1), pp. 83–95. **[G: U.S.]**

Dahmann, Donald C. Subjective Assessments of Neighborhood Quality by Size of Place. *Urban Stud.*, February 1983, *20*(1), pp. 31–45. **[G: U.S.]**

Dickerson, Mary Dee and Gentry, James W. Characteristics of Adopters and Non-Adopters of Home Computers. *J. Cons. Res.*, September 1983, *10*(2), pp. 225–35. **[G: U.S.]**

Didow, Nicholas M., Jr.; Perreault, William D., Jr. and Williamson, Nicholas C. A Cross-Sectional Optimal Scaling Analysis of the Index of Consumer Sentiment. *J. Cons. Res.*, December 1983, *10*(3), pp. 339–47. **[G: U.S.]**

Dybvig, Philip H. Recovering Additive Utility Functions. *Int. Econ. Rev.*, June 1983, *24*(2), pp. 379–96.

Edell, Julie E. and Staelin, Richard. The Information Processing of Pictures in Print Advertisements. *J. Cons. Res.*, June 1983, *10*(1), pp. 45–61. **[G: U.S.]**

Edmonds, Radcliffe G., Jr. Travel Time Valuation through Hedonic Regression. *Southern Econ. J.*, July 1983, *50*(1), pp. 83–98. **[G: Japan]**

Elbadawi, Ibrahim; Gallant, A. Ronald and Souza, Geraldo. An Elasticity Can Be Estimated Consistently without A Priori Knowledge of Functional Form. *Econometrica*, November 1983, *51*(6), pp. 1731–51.

Ferri, Piero. The Consumption–Wage Gap. *J. Post Keynesian Econ.*, Summer 1983, *5*(4), pp. 579–89. **[G: Developed Countries]**

Ferris, James M. Demands for Public Spending: An Attitudinal Approach. *Public Choice*, 1983, *40*(2), pp. 135–54. **[G: U.S.]**

Fornell, Claes. Issues in the Application of Covariance Structure Analysis: A Comment. *J. Cons. Res.*, March 1983, *9*(4), pp. 443–48.

Fraser, Cynthia and Bradford, John W. Competitive Market Structure Analysis: Principal Partitioning of Revealed Substitutabilities. *J. Cons. Res.*, June 1983, *10*(1), pp. 15–30. **[G: U.S.]**

Gahin, Fikry S. The Financial Feasibility of Tax-Sheltered Individual Retirement Plans. *J. Risk Ins.*, March 1983, *50*(1), pp. 84–106. **[G: U.S.]**

Gardner, Meryl Paula. Advertising Effects on Attributes Recalled and Criteria Used for Brand Evaluations. *J. Cons. Res.*, December 1983, *10*(3), pp. 310–18.

Genser, Bernd. Household Outlay Index: A Measure of Real Purchasing Power and Tax Progressivity. *Empirica*, 1983, (2), pp. 205–14. **[G: Austria]**

Goldsmith, Art. Household Life Cycle Protection: Human Capital versus Life Insurance. *J. Risk Ins.*, September 1983, *50*(3), pp. 473–86. **[G: U.S.]**

Green, Robert T., et al. Societal Development and Family Purchasing Roles: A Cross-National Study. *J. Cons. Res.*, March 1983, *9*(4), pp. 436–42. **[G: Venezuela; U.S.; France; Gabon; Netherlands]**

Grootaert, Christiaan. The Conceptual Basis of Measures of Household Welfare and Their Implied Survey Data Requirements. *Rev. Income Wealth*, March 1983, *29*(1), pp. 1–21.

Hondrich, Karl Otto. How Do Needs Change? **In** *Uusitalo, L., ed.*, 1983, pp. 56–73.

Hsieh, Chang-tseh and Liu, Ben-chieh. The Pursuance of Better Quality of Life: In the Long Run, Better Quality of Social Life Is the Most Important Factor in Migration. *Amer. J. Econ. Soc.*, October 1983, *42*(4), pp. 431–40. **[G: U.S.]**

Huang, Kuo S. The Family of Inverse Demand Systems. *Europ. Econ. Rev.*, December 1983, *23*(3), pp. 329–37.

Huber, Joel and Puto, Christopher. Market Boundaries and Product Choice: Illustrating Attraction and Substitution Effects. *J. Cons. Res.*, June 1983, *10*(1), pp. 31–44. **[G: U.S.]**

d'Iribarne, Philippe. What Kinds of Alternative Ways of Life Are Possible? **In** *Uusitalo, L., ed.*, 1983, pp. 27–37.

Jagodzinski, Wolfgang. Materialism in Japan Reconsidered: Toward a Synthesis of Generational and Life-Cycle Explanations. *Amer. Polit. Sci. Rev.*, December 1983, *77*(4), pp. 887–94. **[G: Japan]**

James, Jeffrey. The New Household Economics, General X-Efficiency Theory, and Developing Countries. *J. Devel. Stud.*, July 1983, *19*(4), pp. 485–503.

Kesenne, Stefan. Substitution in Consumption: An Application to the Allocation of Time. *Europ. Econ. Rev.*, November 1983, *23*(2), pp. 231–39. **[G: Belgium]**

Krishnamurthi, Lakshman. The Salience of Relevant Others and Its Effect on Individual and Joint Preferences: An Experimental Investigation. *J. Cons. Res.*, June 1983, *10*(1), pp. 62–72. **[G: U.S.]**

Kristol, Irving. Some Personal Reflections on Economic Well-being and Income Distribution. **In** *Kristol, I.*, 1983, *1980*, pp. 194–201.

Lampman, Robert J. and Smeeding, Timothy M. Interfamily Transfers as Alternatives to Government Transfers to Persons. *Rev. Income Wealth*, March 1983, *29*(1), pp. 45–66. **[G: U.S.]**

Laumas, Prem S. and Williams, Martin. Household Demand for Money in an Underdeveloped Economy: A Case Study of India. *Pakistan Devel. Rev.*, Spring 1983, *22*(1), pp. 37–46. **[G: India]**

Liebermann, Yehoshua. The Economics of *Kethubah* Valuation. *Hist. Polit. Econ.*, Winter 1983, *15*(4), pp. 519–28.

Lindqvist, Lars-Johan. Dagligvarumnarknaden i Finland: Koncentrationen sedd ur konsumenternas, detaljisternas och samhällets synvinkel. (The Market for Convenience Goods in Finland. Concentration from the Point of View of Consumers, Retailers and Society. With English summary.) *Ekon. Samfundets Tidskr.*, 1983, *36*(4), pp. 157–61. **[G: Finland]**

Livengood, Kerry R. Value of Big Game from Markets for Hunting Leases: The Hedonic Approach. *Land Econ.*, August 1983, *59*(3), pp. 287–91. **[G: U.S.]**

Lynch, John G., Jr. The Role of External Validity in Theoretical Research. *J. Cons. Res.*, June 1983, *10*(1), pp. 109–11.

MacManus, Susan A. Managing Urban Growth: Citizen Perceptions and Preferences. **In** *Ballard, S. C. and James, T. E., eds.*, 1983, pp. 132–61.

Markandya, Anil. Headship Rates and the Household Formation Process in Great Britain. *Appl. Econ.*, December 1983, *15*(6), pp. 821–30. **[G: U.K.]**

Mayers, David and Smith, Clifford W., Jr. The Interdependence of Individual Portfolio Decisions and the Demand for Insurance. *J. Polit. Econ.*, April 1983, *91*(2), pp. 304–11.

McElroy, Katherine Maddox; Siegfried, John J. and Sweeney, George H. The Incidence of Price Changes in the U.S. Economy. **In** *Craven, J. V., ed.*, 1983, *1982*, pp. 243–66.

McGrath, Joseph E. and Brinberg, David. External Validity and the Research Process: A Comment on the Calder/Lynch Dialogue. *J. Cons. Res.*, June 1983, *10*(1), pp. 115–24.

Mendelsohn, Robert and Brown, Gardner M., Jr. Revealed Preference Approaches to Valuing Outdoor Recreation. *Natural Res. J.*, July 1983, *23*(3), pp. 607–18. **[G: U.S.]**

Metzger, Michael R. and Goldfarb, Robert S. The Effectiveness of Odd–Even Gasoline Rationing. *Atlantic Econ. J.*, December 1983, *11*(4), pp. 49–58. **[G: U.S.]**

Miniard, Paul W. and Cohen, Joel B. Modeling Personal and Normative Influences on Behavior. *J. Cons. Res.*, September 1983, *10*(2), pp. 169–80. **[G: U.S.]**

Nelson, Glenn L. A Critique of Executive Branch Decision-Making Processes. *Amer. J. Agr. Econ.*, December 1983, *65*(5), pp. 901–07. **[G: U.S.]**

Nickols, Sharon Y. and Fox, Karen D. Buying Time and Saving Time: Strategies for Managing Household Production. *J. Cons. Res.*, September 1983, *10*(2), pp. 197–208. **[G: U.S.]**

Orlov, A. V. Assigning Top Priority to Demand and Coordination. *Prob. Econ.*, January 1983, *25*(9), pp. 36–51. **[G: U.S.S.R.]**

Punj, Girish N. and Stewart, David W. An Interaction Framework of Consumer Decision Making. *J. Cons. Res.*, September 1983, *10*(2), pp. 181–96.

Richins, Marsha L. An Analysis of Consumer Interaction Styles in the Marketplace. *J. Cons. Res.*, June 1983, *10*(1), pp. 73–82. **[G: U.S.]**

Riddell, W. Craig. Leisure Time and the Measurement of Economic Welfare. **In** *Diewert, W. E. and Montmarquette, C., eds.*, 1983, pp. 337–67. **[G: Canada]**

Rosenzweig, Mark R. and Schultz, T. Paul. Estimating a Household Production Function: Heterogeneity, the Demand for Health Inputs, and Their Effects on Birth Weight. *J. Polit. Econ.*, October 1983, *91*(5), pp. 723–46. **[G: U.S.]**

Rudd, Joel and Kohout, Frank J. Individual and Group Consumer Information Acquisition in Brand Choice Situations. *J. Cons. Res.*, December 1983, *10*(3), pp. 303–09.

Sandrey, Ronald A.; Buccola, Steven T. and Brown, William G. Pricing Policies for Antlerless Elk Hunting Permits. *Land Econ.*, November 1983, *59*(4), pp. 432–43. **[G: U.S.]**

Shah, C. H. Food Preference, Poverty, and the Nutrition Gap. *Econ. Develop. Cult. Change*, October 1983, *32*(1), pp. 121–48. **[G: India]**

Sherry, John F., Jr. Gift Giving in Anthropological Perspective. *J. Cons. Res.*, September 1983, *10*(2), pp. 157–68.

Smirnov, V. The Plan and the Increase in the Consumer's Influence on Production. *Prob. Econ.*, July 1983, *26*(3), pp. 22–38. **[G: U.S.S.R.]**

Smith, V. Kerry; Desvousges, William H. and McGivney, Matthew P. The Opportunity Cost of Travel Time in Recreation Demand Models. *Land Econ.*, August 1983, *59*(3), pp. 259–78. **[G: U.S.]**

Solomon, Michael R. The Role of Products as Social Stimuli: A Symbolic Interactionism Perspective. *J. Cons. Res.*, December 1983, *10*(3), pp. 319–29.

Spiro, Rosann L. Persuasion in Family Decision-Making. *J. Cons. Res.*, March 1983, *9*(4), pp. 393–402.

Stoll, John R. Recreational Activities and Nonmarket Valuation: The Conceptualization Issue. *Southern*

J. Agr. Econ., December 1983, *15*(2), pp. 119–25.

Strong, Elizabeth J. A Note on the Functional Form of Travel Cost Models with Zones of Unequal Populations. *Land Econ.*, August 1983, *59*(3), pp. 342–49. **[G: U.S.]**

Strümpel, Burkhard. Postmaterial Values and Their Institutional Inertia. In *Uusitalo, L., ed.*, 1983, pp. 74–87.

Ulbrich, Holley and Wallace, Myles S. Church Attendance, Age, and Belief in the Afterlife: Some Additional Evidence. *Atlantic Econ. J.*, July 1983, *11*(2), pp. 44–51. **[G: U.S.]**

Unger, Lynette S. and Kernan, Jerome B. On the Meaning of Leisure: An Investigation of Some Determinants of the Subjective Experience. *J. Cons. Res.*, March 1983, *9*(4), pp. 381–92. **[G: U.S.]**

Volker, Paul A. A Note on Factors Influencing the Utilization of Bankcard. *Econ. Rec.*, September 1983, *59*(166), pp. 281–89. **[G: Australia]**

Wolf, Charles and Pohlman, Larry. The Recovery of Risk Preferences from Actual Choices. *Econometrica*, May, 1983, *51*(3), pp. 843–50. **[G: U.S.]**

Wu, Mickey T. C. and Monahan, Dennis. An Experimental Study of Consumer Demand Using Rats. *J. Behav. Econ.*, Summer 1983, *12*(1), pp. 121–38.

9211 Living Standards, Composition of Overall Expenditures, and Empirical Consumption and Savings Studies

Aasness, Jørgen and Rødseth, Asbjørn. Engel Curves and Systems of Demand Functions. *Europ. Econ. Rev.*, January 1983, *20*(1–3), pp. 95–121. **[G: Norway]**

Abbott, Walter F. and Leasure, J. W. Income Level and Inflation in the United States: 1947–1977. In *Schmukler, N. and Marcus, E., eds.*, 1983, pp. 804–19. **[G: U.S.]**

Akin, John S.; Guilkey, David K. and Popkin, Barry M. The School Lunch Program and Nutrient Intake: A Switching Regression Analysis. *Amer. J. Agr. Econ.*, August 1983, *65*(3), pp. 477–85. **[G: U.S.]**

Aldrich, Jonathan; Fox, Alan and Lopez, Eduard. Purchasing Power of U.S. Social Security Benefits Abroad, 1970–82. *Soc. Sec. Bull.*, September 1983, *46*(9), pp. 3–9. **[G: U.S.; Europe; Philippines; Mexico]**

Anderson, Gordon J. and Blundell, Richard. Testing Restrictions in a Flexible Dynamic Demand System: An Application to Consumers' Expenditure in Canada. *Rev. Econ. Stud.*, July 1983, *50*(3), pp. 397–410. **[G: Canada]**

Andrikopoulos, Andreas A. and Brox, James A. Short-Run Forecasts of Consumer Expenditures Based on the Linear Expenditure Systems. *Atlantic Econ. J.*, December 1983, *11*(4), pp. 20–33. **[G: Canada]**

Anstie, Roslyn K.; Gray, M. R. and Pagan, A. R. Inflation and the Consumption Ratio. In *Pagan, A. R. and Trivedi, P. K., eds.*, 1983, pp. 322–49. **[G: Australia]**

Anyadike-Danes, Michael. A 'Comment' on Chrystal [The 'New Cambridge' Aggregate Expenditure Function]. *J. Monet. Econ.*, January 1983, *11*(1), pp. 133–35. **[G: U.K.]**

Atkinson, A. B.; Maynard, Alan K. and Trinder, C. G. Evidence on Intergenerational Income Mobility in Britain: Some Further Preliminary Results. In *Weisbrod, B. and Hughes, H., eds.*, 1983, pp. 290–308. **[G: U.K.]**

Auerbach, Alan J. Portfolio Composition and Pension Wealth: An Econometric Study: Comment. In *Bodie, Z. and Shoven, J. B., eds.*, 1983, pp. 436–37. **[G: Canada]**

Auerbach, Alan J. and Kotlikoff, Laurence J. An Examination of Empirical Tests of Social Security and Savings. In *Helpman, E.; Razin, A. and Sadka, E., eds.*, 1983, pp. 161–79. **[G: U.S.]**

Auerbach, Alan J. and Kotlikoff, Laurence J. National Savings, Economic Welfare, and the Structure of Taxation. In *Feldstein, M., ed.*, 1983, pp. 459–93. **[G: U.S.]**

Babeau, André. Le rapport macro-économique du patrimoine au revenu des ménages. (The Macro-Economic Wealth-Income Ration of Households. With English summary.) *Revue Écon.*, January 1983, *34*(1), pp. 64–123. **[G: France; U.S.]**

Babeau, André. The Macro-Economic Wealth–Income Ratio of Households. *Rev. Income Wealth*, December 1983, *29*(4), pp. 347–70. **[G: France; U.S.]**

Bailey, Martin J. Alternative Tax Rules and Personal Saving Incentives: Microeconomic Data and Behavioral Simulations: Comment. In *Feldstein, M., ed.*, 1983, pp. 209–10. **[G: U.S.]**

Baldwin, Michael A.; Hadid, M. and Phillips, G. D. A. The Estimation and Testing of a System of Demand Equations for the UK. *Appl. Econ.*, February 1983, *15*(1), pp. 81–90. **[G: U.K.]**

Bentzel, Ragnar and Berg, Lennart. The Role of Demographic Factors as a Determinant of Savings in Sweden. In *Modigliani, F. and Hemming, R., eds.*, 1983, pp. 152–79. **[G: Sweden]**

Berch, Bettina. The Inflation of Housework. In *Schmukler, N. and Marcus, E., eds.*, 1983, pp. 860–66.

Berry, Albert; Bourguignon, François and Morrisson, Christian. The Level of World Inequality: How Much Can One Say? *Rev. Income Wealth*, September 1983, *29*(3), pp. 217–41. **[G: Global]**

Bewley, R. A. Tests of Restrictions in Large Demand Systems. *Europ. Econ. Rev.*, January 1983, *20*(1–3), pp. 257–69.

Biørn, Erik and Jansen, Eilev S. Individual Effects in a System of Demand Functions. *Scand. J. Econ.*, 1983, *85*(4), pp. 461–83. **[G: Norway]**

Bladen-Hovell, R. C. and Richards, G. M. Inflation and Australian Savings Behaviour, 1959–1981. *Australian Econ. Pap.*, December 1983, *22*(41), pp. 290–301. **[G: Australia]**

Blinder, Alan S.; Gordon, Roger H. and Wise, Donald E. Social Security, Bequests and the Life Cycle Theory of Saving: Cross-sectional Tests. In *Modigliani, F. and Hemming, R., eds.*, 1983, pp. 89–122. **[G: U.S.]**

Bloch, Laurence. Le Modèle de cycle de vie. Application aux données individuelles tirées de l'enquête épargne 1973–1975, INSEE. (The Life-

Cycle Hypothesis. An Application to a Cross-Section Drawn from the INSEE 1973–1975 Survey of Households Savings. With English summary.) *Ann. INSEE,* October–December 1983, (52), pp. 123–61. **[G: France]**

Boniver, Véronique; Laguesse, Yvette and Thiry, Bernard. Le "Nouveau Consommateur": mythe ou réalité? (With English summary.) *Cah. Écon. Bruxelles,* Third Trimestre 1983, (99), pp. 361–86. **[G: Belgium]**

Boren, David L. Policies, Problems, and Politics of the Consumption Based Tax. **In** *Walker, C. E. and Bloomfield, M. E., eds.,* 1983, pp. 253–56.

Boskin, Michael J. Saving Incentives: The Role of Tax Policy. **In** *Walker, C. E. and Bloomfield, M. E., eds.,* 1983, pp. 93–111. **[G: U.S.]**

Bradford, David F. The Choice Between Income and Consumption Taxes. **In** *Walker, C. E. and Bloomfield, M. E., eds.,* 1983, pp. 229–52.

Brown, Mark and Johnson, Stanley R. Food Stamps: Program Parameters and Standards of Living for Low-Income Households. *Southern J. Agr. Econ.,* July 1983, *15*(1), pp. 43–49. **[G: U.S.]**

Burbridge, John B. Social Security and Savings Plans in Overlapping-Generations Models. *J. Public Econ.,* June 1983, *21*(1), pp. 79–92. **[G: U.S.]**

Cage, R. A. The Standard of Living Debate: Glasgow, 1800–1850. *J. Econ. Hist.,* March 1983, *43*(1), pp. 175–82. **[G: U.K.]**

Cain, Louis P. Incomes in the Twentieth Century United States: Discussion. *J. Econ. Hist.,* March 1983, *43*(1), pp. 241–42. **[G: U.S.]**

Cebula, Richard J. Determinants of Geographic Living-Cost Differentials in the United States: Reply. *Land Econ.,* August 1983, *59*(3), pp. 353–54. **[G: U.S.]**

Cebula, Richard J. and Smith, Lisa K. On the Determinants of Inter-Regional Living-Cost Differentials in the United States, 1970 and 1975: Reply. *Reg. Sci. Urban Econ.,* November 1983, *13*(4), pp. 587–89. **[G: U.S.]**

Chakrabarty, Gurupada. Studies on Size Distribution of Income and Consumption—A Review. *Margin,* October 1983, *16*(1), pp. 57–83. **[G: India]**

Chatterji, Monojit. On Forecasting U.K. Consumption. *Appl. Econ.,* June 1983, *15*(3), pp. 417–23. **[G: U.K.]**

Chrystal, K. Alec. The New Cambridge Aggregate Expenditure Function: Reply. *J. Monet. Econ.,* January 1983, *11*(1), pp. 137–38. **[G: U.K.]**

Clemens, Paul G. E. Levels of Living in Colonial America: Discussion. *J. Econ. Hist.,* March 1983, *43*(1), pp. 118–19. **[G: U.S.]**

Cobas, José A. Estimating the Urban Family Budget with a Pooled Cross-Section/Times-Series Model: A Reply to Hogan [A Method to Estimate the Bureau of Labor Statistics Family Budgets for All Standard Metropolitan Statistical Areas]. *Soc. Sci. Quart.,* June 1983, *64*(2), pp. 416–17. **[G: U.S.]**

Cohen, Edwin S. Expanding Saving Incentives: Practical and Political Problems. **In** *Walker, C. E. and Bloomfield, M. E., eds.,* 1983, pp. 112–15. **[G: U.S.]**

Cooper, Russel J. and McLaren, Keith R. Modelling Price Expectations in Intertemporal Consumer Demand Systems: Theory and Application. *Rev. Econ. Statist.,* May 1983, *65*(2), pp. 282–88. **[G: Australia]**

Cremer, Helmuth. Epargne et consommation des personnes âgées. (With English summary.) *Cah. Écon. Bruxelles,* 1983, *97*(1), pp. 75–103. **[G: Belgium]**

Cuthbertson, K. Consumer Spending. **In** *Britton, A., ed.,* 1983, pp. 16–27. **[G: U.K.]**

Dániel, Zsuzsa. Public Housing, Personal Income and Central Redistribution in Hungary. *Acta Oecon.,* 1983, *31*(1–2), pp. 87–104. **[G: Hungary]**

Danziger, Sheldon, et al. The Life-Cycle Hypothesis and the Consumption Behavior of the Elderly. *J. Post Keynesian Econ.,* Winter 1982–83, *5*(2), pp. 208–27. **[G: U.S.]**

Davidson, Russell and MacKinnon, James G. Inflation and the Savings Rate. *Appl. Econ.,* December 1983, *15*(6), pp. 731–43. **[G: U.S.; Canada]**

Deaton, Angus. Savings and Inflation: Theory and British Evidence. **In** *Modigliani, F. and Hemming, R., eds.,* 1983, pp. 125–39. **[G: U.K.]**

Denny, Michael G. S. and Fuss, Melvyn A. Regional Price Indexes: The Canadian Practice and Some Potential Extensions. **In** *Diewert, W. E. and Montmarquette, C., eds.,* 1983, pp. 783–816. **[G: Canada]**

Dicks-Mireaux, Louis-David L. and King, Mervyn A. Portfolio Composition and Pension Wealth: An Econometric Study. **In** *Bodie, Z. and Shoven, J. B., eds.,* 1983, pp. 399–435, 438–39. **[G: Canada]**

Dodgson, John S. Expenditure Function Estimates of the Efficiency and Distributive Impact of Indirect Taxes in the United Kingdom. *Europ. Econ. Rev.,* January 1983, *20*(1–3), pp. 59–78. **[G: U.K.]**

Dolde, Walter and Tobin, James. Mandatory Retirement Saving and Capital Formation. **In** *Modigliani, F. and Hemming, R., eds.,* 1983, pp. 56–88. **[G: U.S.]**

Duncan, Greg J. and Liker, Jeffrey. Disentangling the Efficacy–Earnings Relationship among White Men. **In** *Duncan, G. J. and Morgan, J. N., eds.,* 1983, pp. 218–48. **[G: U.S.]**

Eastwood, David A. Reality or Delusion: Migrant Perception of Levels of Living and Opportunity in Venezuela, 1961–1971. *J. Devel. Areas,* July 1983, *17*(4), pp. 491–97. **[G: Venezuela]**

Eisner, Robert. Social Security, Saving, and Macroeconomics. *J. Macroecon.,* Winter 1983, *5*(1), pp. 1–19. **[G: U.S.]**

Evans, Owen J. Social Security and Household Saving in the United States: A Re-Examination. *Int. Monet. Fund Staff Pap.,* September 1983, *30*(3), pp. 601–18. **[G: U.S.]**

Fancher, Susan K.; Palash, Carl J. and Stoddard, Robert B. Why Consumption Surged in the First Half of 1983. *Fed. Res. Bank New York Quart. Rev.,* Autumn 1983, *8*(3), pp. 21–23. **[G: U.S.]**

Feldstein, Martin S. Social Security Benefits and the Accumulation of Pre-retirement Wealth. **In** *Modigliani, F. and Hemming, R., eds.,* 1983, pp. 3–23. **[G: U.S.]**

Feldstein, Martin S. and Fane, George. Taxes, Corporate Dividend Policy, and Personal Savings: The British Postwar Experience. **In** *Feldstein, M. (I),* 1983, *1973,* pp. 135–55. **[G: U.K.]**

Feldstein, Martin S. and Feenberg, Daniel R. Alternative Tax Rules and Personal Saving Incentives: Microeconomic Data and Behavioral Simulations. In *Feldstein, M., ed.*, 1983, pp. 173–209. [G: U.S.]

Fellner, William. The Effect of Government Absorption of Savings on Capital Formation. In *Walker, C. E. and Bloomfield, M. E., eds.*, 1983, pp. 116–18. [G: U.S.]

Ferri, Piero and Szego, Giorgio P. Saving in a Stagflation Process. In *Modigliani, F. and Hemming, R., eds.*, 1983, pp. 219–32. [G: Selected OECD]

Ferson, Wayne E. Expectations of Real Interest Rates and Aggregate Consumption: Empirical Tests. *J. Finan. Quant. Anal.*, December 1983, *18*(4), pp. 477–97. [G: U.S.]

Field, Frank. Introduction: The Politics of Wealth. In *Field, F., ed.*, 1983, pp. 1–8. [G: U.K.]

Friend, Irwin and Hasbrouck, Joel. Saving and After-Tax Rates of Return. *Rev. Econ. Statist.*, November 1983, *65*(4), pp. 537–43. [G: U.S.]

Gardes, François. L'évolution de la consommation marchande en Europe et aux U.S.A. depuis 1960. (The Change of Consumption in Europe and in the U.S.A. since 1960. With English summary.) *Consommation*, April–June 1983, *30*(2), pp. 3–32. [G: France; Netherlands; W. Germany; U.K.; U.S.]

Gazioglou, Şhaziye. Consumption and Wealth Effect in Turkey. *METU*, 1983, *10*(2), pp. 131–53. [G: Turkey]

Gersovitz, Mark. Savings and Nutrition at Low Incomes. *J. Polit. Econ.*, October 1983, *91*(5), pp. 841–55.

Gilmer, Robert W. and Mack, Richard S. The Cost of Residential Electric Power Outages. *Energy J.*, Supplement 1983, *4*, pp. 55–74. [G: U.S.]

Giovannini, Alberto. The Interest Elasticity of Savings in Developing Countries: The Existing Evidence. *World Devel.*, July 1983, *11*(7), pp. 601–07. [G: Selected LDCs]

Goddard, Dean. An Analysis of Canadian Aggregate Demand for Food at Home and Away from Home. *Can. J. Agr. Econ.*, November 1983, *31*(3), pp. 289–318. [G: Canada]

Goldsmith, Raymond W. Saving and Changes in National and Sectoral Balance Sheets. In *Modigliani, F. and Hemming, R., eds.*, 1983, pp. 289–301. [G: Selected Countries]

Gottschalk, Peter and Maloney, Tim. What Averages Don't Reveal about Real Income Growth. *J. Policy Anal. Manage.*, Fall 1983, *3*(1), pp. 120–25. [G: U.S.]

Goux, Jean-François. La dynamique de l'accumulation réelle des ménages. (The Dynamics of Household Real Estate Accumulation. With English summary.) *Revue Écon.*, January 1983, *34*(1), pp. 182–235. [G: France]

Grassini, Maurizio. A System of Demand Equations for Medium-to-Long-Term Forecasting with Input–Output Econometric Models. *Econ. Notes*, 1983, (2), pp. 84–98. [G: Italy]

Hanley, Susan B. A High Standard of Living in Nineteenth-Century Japan: Fact or Fantasy? *J. Econ. Hist.*, March 1983, *43*(1), pp. 183–92. [G: Japan]

Hartwell, R. M. Growth and Equity: Discussion. *J. Econ. Hist.*, March 1983, *43*(1), pp. 203–06. [G: U.K.; Australia]

Hemming, Richard and Harvey, Russell. Occupational Pension Scheme Membership and Retirement Saving. *Econ. J.*, March 1983, *93*(369), pp. 128–44. [G: U.K.]

Hiemstra, Stephen J. Food Stamps, Program Parameters and Standards of Living for Low-Income Households: Discussion. *Southern J. Agr. Econ.*, July 1983, *15*(1), pp. 51–52. [G: U.S.]

Hjorth-Anderson, Christian. Lancaster's Principle of Efficient Choice: An Empirical Note. *Int. J. Ind. Organ.*, September 1983, *1*(3), pp. 287–95. [G: U.S.]

Hogan, Timothy D. Estimating the Urban Family Budget with a Pooled Cross-Section/Time-Series Model [A Method to Estimate the Bureau of Labor Statistics Family Budgets for All Standard Metropolitan Statistical Areas]. *Soc. Sci. Quart.*, June 1983, *64*(2), pp. 413–16. [G: U.S.]

Huber, Paul B. Pensions and Inflation: A Comment [Inflation and the Standard of Living of Pensioners: A Case Study]. *Can. Public Policy*, June 1983, *9*(2), pp. 250–55. [G: Canada]

Ioannidis, Christos and Peel, David A. Involuntary Saving through Unanticipated Inflation: Some Further Empirical Evidence. *Empirical Econ.*, 1983, *8*(2), pp. 87–92. [G: Canada; Japan; U.K.; U.S.]

Janssen, Martin and Müller, Heinz. Die Substitutionswirkungen zwischen kollektiver Vorsorge und privatem Sparen in der Schweiz. (The Rates of Substitution between Collective Provision and Private Saving in Switzerland. With English summary.) *Schweiz. Z. Volkswirtsch. Statist.*, June 1983, *119*(2), pp. 139–45. [G: Switzerland]

Johnson, Paul. Life-Cycle Consumption under Rational Expectations: Some Australian Evidence. *Econ. Rec.*, December 1983, *59*(167), pp. 345–50. [G: Australia]

Jorgenson, Dale W. and Slesnick, Daniel T. Individual and Social Cost-of-Living Indexes. In *Diewert, W. E. and Montmarquette, C., eds.*, 1983, pp. 241–323. [G: U.S.]

Jose, A. V. Poverty and Income Distribution: The Case of West Bengal. In *Khan, A. R. and Lee, E., eds.*, 1983, pp. 137–63. [G: India]

Jose, A. V. Poverty and Inequality—The Case of Kerala. In *Khan, A. R. and Lee, E., eds.*, 1983, pp. 107–36. [G: India]

Kalirajan, K. P. Analysis of Nutritional Adequacy in the Philippines: A Suggested Methodology. *Singapore Econ. Rev.*, October 1983, *28*(2), pp. 46–58. [G: Philippines]

Keyfitz, Nathan. Age Effects in Work and Consumption. *Econ. Notes*, 1983, (3), pp. 86–121. [G: Global]

Kormendi, Roger C. Government Debt, Government Spending, and Private Sector Behavior. *Amer. Econ. Rev.*, December 1983, *73*(5), pp. 994–1010. [G: U.S.]

Koskela, Erkki and Virén, Matti. Social Security and Household Saving in an International Cross Section. *Amer. Econ. Rev.*, March 1983, *73*(1), pp. 212–17.

Kosonen, Katri. Suomalaisten kotitalouksien säästämisestä poikkileikkausaineiston valossa. (Cross-Section Analysis of Saving Behaviour of Finnish Households. With English summary.) *Kansant. Aikak.*, 1983, *79*(1), pp. 4–20. **[G: Finland]**

Kotlikoff, Laurence J. National Savings and Economic Policy: The Efficacy of Investment vs. Savings Incentives. *Amer. Econ. Rev.*, May 1983, *73*(2), pp. 82–87. **[G: U.S.]**

Kuné, Jan B. Studies on the Relationship between Social Security and Personal Saving: A Tabular Survey. *Kredit Kapital,* 1983, *16*(3), pp. 371–80. **[G: U.S.; Canada; W. Europe]**

Laumas, Prem S. and Bausch, James. On the Proper Specification of the Permanent Income Hypothesis. *Econ. Notes,* 1983, (2), pp. 152–60. **[G: U.S.]**

Lévy-Garboua, Louis. Les modes de consommation de quelques pays occidentaux: comparaison et lois d'évolution (1960–1980). (The Modes of Consumption of Some Western Countries: Comparison and Evolution (1960–1980). With English summary.) *Consommation,* January/March 1983, *30*(1), pp. 3–52. **[G: EEC; U.S.]**

Lewis, Frank D. Fertility and Savings in the United States: 1830–1900. *J. Polit. Econ.*, October 1983, *91*(5), pp. 825–40. **[G: U.S.]**

Liang, Ming-Yih. Savings in Taiwan: An Empirical Investigation. *J. Econ. Devel.*, July 1983, *8*(1), pp. 109–29. **[G: Taiwan]**

Lindert, Peter H. and Williamson, Jeffrey G. English Workers' Living Standards during the Industrial Revolution: A New Look. *Econ. Hist. Rev., 2nd Ser.*, February 1983, *36*(1), pp. 1–25. **[G: U.K.]**

Lukaszewicz, Aleksander. The Determinants and Role of Private Saving in Poland. **In** *Modigliani, F. and Hemming, R., eds.*, 1983, pp. 255–71. **[G: Poland]**

Lustig, Nora. Distribution of Income and Patterns of Consumption in Mexico: Empirical Testing of Some Latin American Structuralist Hypotheses. **In** *Urquidi, V. L. and Reyes, S. T., eds.*, 1983, pp. 236–51. **[G: Mexico]**

MaCurdy, Thomas E. A Simple Scheme for Estimating an Intertemporal Model of Labor Supply and Consumption in the Presence of Taxes and Uncertainty. *Int. Econ. Rev.*, June 1983, *24*(2), pp. 265–89. **[G: U.S.]**

Main, Gloria L. The Standard of Living in Colonial Massachusetts. *J. Econ. Hist.*, March 1983, *43*(1), pp. 101–08. **[G: U.S.]**

Main, Jackson Turner. Standards of Living and the Life Cycle in Colonial Connecticut. *J. Econ. Hist.*, March 1983, *43*(1), pp. 159–65. **[G: U.S.]**

Masson, André. Profils d'accumulation patrimoniale et modèles de cycle de vie. (Wealth Accumulation Profiles and Life-Cycle Models. With English summary.) *Revue Écon.*, January 1983, *34*(1), pp. 10–63. **[G: France]**

McCarthy, D. M. P. Measurement of Levels of Living in the People's Republic of the Congo since 1950: Discussion. *J. Econ. Hist.*, March 1983, *43*(1), pp. 272–73. **[G: Congo]**

McCormick, Ken. Duesenberry and Veblen: The Demonstration Effect Revisited. *J. Econ. Issues,* December 1983, *17*(4), pp. 1125–29.

McDean, Harry C. "Reform" Social Darwinists and Measuring Levels of Living on American Farms, 1920–1926. *J. Econ. Hist.*, March 1983, *43*(1), pp. 79–85. **[G: U.S.]**

McLean, Ian W. and Pincus, Jonathan J. Did Australian Living Standards Stagnate between 1890 and 1940? *J. Econ. Hist.*, March 1983, *43*(1), pp. 193–202. **[G: Australia]**

Mellin, Ilkka and Virén, Matti. Real Wages, Inflation and Household Consumption Behavior. *Liiketaloudellinen Aikak.*, 1983, *32*(3), pp. 267–85. **[G: Finland]**

Menchik, Paul L. and David, Martin H. Income Distribution, Lifetime Savings, and Bequests. *Amer. Econ. Rev.*, September 1983, *73*(4), pp. 672–90. **[G: U.S.]**

Modest, David M. and Smith, Bruce D. The Standard of Living Debate, Rational Expectations, and Neutrality: Some Evidence from the Industrial Revolution. *J. Monet. Econ.*, November 1983, *12*(4), pp. 571–93. **[G: U.K.]**

Modigliani, Franco and Sterling, Arlie. Determinants of Private Saving with Special Reference to the Role of Social Security—Cross-country Tests. **In** *Modigliani, F. and Hemming, R., eds.*, 1983, pp. 24–55. **[G: Selected OECD]**

Moore, W. Henson. The Congressional Outlook for Increased Saving Incentives. **In** *Walker, C. E. and Bloomfield, M. E., eds.*, 1983, pp. 119–20. **[G: U.S.]**

Morgan, James N. Effects of Inflation on Attitudes, Status, and Behavior. **In** *Duncan, G. J. and Morgan, J. N., eds.*, 1983, pp. 60–92. **[G: U.S.]**

Morgan, James N. The Redistribution of Income by Families and Institutions and Emergency Help Patterns. **In** *Duncan, G. J. and Morgan, J. N., eds.*, 1983, pp. 1–59. **[G: U.S.]**

Muellbauer, John. Surprises in the Consumption Function. *Econ. J.*, Supplement March 1983, pp. 34–50. **[G: U.K.]**

Nakamura, James I. Growth and Equity: Discussion. *J. Econ. Hist.*, March 1983, *43*(1), pp. 206–08. **[G: Japan; Australia]**

Nellor, David C. L. The Size of Government, Capital Accumulation, and the Tax Base. *Public Finance Quart.*, July 1983, *11*(3), pp. 321–45. **[G: U.S.]**

Nevile, J. W. Inflation and the Consumption Ratio: Discussion. **In** *Pagan, A. R. and Trivedi, P. K., eds.*, 1983, pp. 356–61. **[G: Australia]**

Oberhänsli, Urs. Substitutionswirkungen zwischen persönlichen Ersparnissen und der kollecktiven Altersvorsorge in der Schwiez. (Rates of Substitution between Personal Saving and the Collective Provision for Old Age in Switzerland. With English summary.) *Schweiz. Z. Volkswirtsch. Statist.*, June 1983, *119*(2), pp. 117–37. **[G: Switzerland]**

Okun, Arthur M. Measuring the Impact of the 1964 Tax Reduction. **In** *Okun, A. M.*, 1983, *1968*, pp. 405–23. **[G: U.S.]**

Okun, Arthur M. The Personal Tax Surcharge and Consumer Demand, 1968–70. **In** *Okun, A. M.*, 1983, *1971*, pp. 338–74. **[G: U.S.]**

Olney, Martha L. Fertility and the Standard of Living in Early Modern England: In Consideration of Wrigley and Schofield. *J. Econ. Hist.*, March 1983, *43*(1), pp. 71–77. **[G: U.K.]**

Olson, Mancur. Reassessment of Measures of Levels

of Living: Discussion. *J. Econ. Hist.*, March 1983, *43*(1), pp. 86–88.

Ostrosky, Anthony L. An Exploratory Note on Determinants of Inter-Regional Living-Cost Differentials in the United States, 1970 and 1975: Comment. *Reg. Sci. Urban Econ.*, November 1983, *13*(4), pp. 583–85. **[G: U.S.]**

Ostrosky, Anthony L. Determinants of Geographic Living-Cost Differentials in the United States: Comment. *Land Econ.*, August 1983, *59*(3), pp. 350–52. **[G: U.S.]**

Paltschik, Mikael and Strandvik, Tore. Konsumentperspektiv på aktiesparandet. (A Consumer Perspective on Company Shares as a Form of Savings. With English summary.) *Ekon. Samfundets Tidskr.*, 1983, *36*(1), pp. 25–36. **[G: Finland]**

Peek, Joe. Capital Gains and Personal Saving Behavior. *J. Money, Credit, Banking*, February 1983, *15*(1), pp. 1–23. **[G: U.S.]**

Pickersgill, Joyce. Household Saving in the USSR. **In** *Modigliani, F. and Hemming, R., eds.*, 1983, pp. 272–85. **[G: U.S.S.R.]**

Pitt, Mark M. Food Preferences and Nutrition in Rural Bangladesh. *Rev. Econ. Statist.*, February 1983, *65*(1), pp. 105–14. **[G: Bangladesh]**

Pollak, Robert A. The Theory of the Cost-of-Living Index. **In** *Diewert, W. E. and Montmarquette, C., eds.*, 1983, pp. 87–161.

Pollak, Robert A. The Treatment of 'Quality' in the Cost of Living Index. *J. Public Econ.*, February 1983, *20*(1), pp. 25–53.

Prasada Rao, D. S. and Shepherd, W. F. A Comparison of Pound Sterling–Australian Dollar Purchasing Power Parities for Selected Population Subgroups in Australia and the United Kingdom. *Rev. Income Wealth*, December 1983, *29*(4), pp. 445–55. **[G: U.K.; Australia]**

Quick, Perry D. The Consumption Based Tax: Prospects for Reform. **In** *Walker, C. E. and Bloomfield, M. E., eds.*, 1983, pp. 261–64.

Ram, Rati. Some Direct Estimates of "Discount Rates" and Consumer "Horizon" from Kendrick's Data. *Southern Econ. J.*, January 1983, *49*(3), pp. 860–66. **[G: U.S.]**

Ramsaran, Ramesh F. The Retail Price Index of Trinidad and Tobago and Its Relevance as a Measure of Changes in the Cost of Living. *Soc. Econ. Stud.*, December 1983, *32*(4), pp. 73–106. **[G: Trinidad and Tobago]**

Ray, Ranjan. Measuring the Costs of Children: An Alternative Approach. *J. Public Econ.*, October 1983, *22*(1), pp. 89–102. **[G: U.K.]**

Rettig, Rudi. Ein vollständiges Nachfragesystem für den privaten Verbrauch. (A Complete Demand System for Private Consumption. With English summary.) *Z. Wirtschaft. Sozialwissen.*, 1983, *103*(3), pp. 205–24. **[G: W. Germany]**

Rock, Steven M. The Incidence of Household-Based Taxes: Evidence from the Consumer Expenditure Survey. *Amer. Econ.*, Fall 1983, *27*(2), pp. 37–41. **[G: U.S.]**

Rossi, Nicola; Tarantelli, Ezio and Tresoldi, Carlo. The Consumption Function in Italy: A Critical Survey. **In** *Modigliani, F. and Hemming, R., eds.*, 1983, pp. 140–51. **[G: Italy]**

Roy, Siddarth. Demand for Industrial Consumer Goods—Some Pertinent Issues. *Indian Econ. J.*, October–December 1983, *31*(2), pp. 116–20. **[G: India]**

Russell, R. Robert. Individual and Social Cost-of-Living Indexes: Comments. **In** *Diewert, W. E. and Montmarquette, C., eds.*, 1983, pp. 324–36. **[G: U.S.]**

Saito, Mitsuo. Finance and Economic Growth: The Japanese Experience. **In** *[Klein, L. R.]*, 1983, pp. 296–313. **[G: Japan]**

Sanders, Margaret. Measurement of Levels of Living in the People's Republic of the Congo since 1950. *J. Econ. Hist.*, March 1983, *43*(1), pp. 243–50. **[G: Congo]**

Sanghvi, Arun P. Household Welfare Loss Due to Electricity Supply Disruptions. *Energy J.*, Supplement 1983, *4*, pp. 33–54. **[G: U.S.]**

Sarma, I. R. K. Capital Formation and Saving in India, 1950–51 to 1979–80, Report of the Working Group on Savings, Some Observations. *Margin*, July 1983, *15*(4), pp. 29–33. **[G: India]**

Schaafsma, Joseph. A Response [Inflation and the Standard of Living of Pensioners: A Case Study]. *Can. Public Policy*, June 1983, *9*(2), pp. 255–56. **[G: Canada]**

Schaefer, Gordon. Escalation Measures: What Is the Answer? What Is the Question? Comment. **In** *Diewert, W. E. and Montmarquette, C., eds.*, 1983, pp. 483–87.

Schokkaert, Erik. The Introduction of Sociological Variables in Engle Curve Analysis. *Tijdschrift Econ. Manage.*, 1983, *28*(4), pp. 409–36. **[G: Belgium]**

Schroeder, Gertrude E. Consumption. **In** *Bergson, A. and Levine, H. S., eds.*, 1983, pp. 311–49. **[G: U.S.S.R.]**

Schroeder, Gertrude E. Rural Living Standards in the Soviet Union. **In** *Stuart, R. C., ed.*, 1983, pp. 241–57. **[G: U.S.S.R.]**

Shaw, Gareth. Trends in Consumer Behaviour and Retailing. **In** *Wild, T., ed.*, 1983, pp. 108–29. **[G: W. Germany]**

Shinohara, Miyohei. The Determinants of Post-war Savings Behaviour in Japan. **In** *Modigliani, F. and Hemming, R., eds.*, 1983, pp. 201–18. **[G: Japan]**

Sinai, Allen; Lin, Andrew and Robins, Russell. Taxes, Saving, and Investment: Some Empirical Evidence. *Nat. Tax J.*, September 1983, *36*(3), pp. 321–45. **[G: U.S.]**

Singh, R. P.; Sahay, S. N. and Pandey, R. K. Income, Savings and Consumption Behaviour of Marginal and Small Farmers, Palamau, Bihar. *Econ. Aff.*, July-September 1983, *28*(3), pp. 733–35. **[G: India]**

Spalter-Roth, Roberta M. Differentiating between the Living Standards of Husbands and Wives in Two-Wage-Earner Families, 1968 and 1979. *J. Econ. Hist.*, March 1983, *43*(1), pp. 231–40. **[G: U.S.]**

Sproat, Kezia. How Do Families Fare When the Breadwinner Retires? *Mon. Lab. Rev.*, December 1983, *106*(12), pp. 40–44. **[G: U.S.]**

Ståhlberg, Ann-Charlotte. Public Pensions and Private Saving: A Brief Review of the Swedish System. In *Söderström, L., ed.*, 1983, pp. 137–58. [G: Sweden]

Steuerle, Eugene. Building New Wealth by Preserving Old Wealth: Savings and Investment Tax Incentives in the Postwar Era. *Nat. Tax J.*, September 1983, *36*(3), pp. 307–19. [G: U.S.]

Stigler, George J. The Early History of Empirical Studies of Consumer Behavior. In *Stigler, G. J.*, 1983, *1954*, pp. 198–233. [G: U.K.; U.S.; Belgium]

Stiglitz, Joseph E. National Savings, Economic Welfare, and the Structure of Taxation: Comment. In *Feldstein, M., ed.*, 1983, pp. 493–98. [G: U.S.]

Strauss-Kahn, Dominique. Explaining the Composition of Household Saving Flows and Their Relationship to Aggregate Saving in France. In *Modigliani, F. and Hemming, R., eds.*, 1983, pp. 180–200. [G: France]

Sturm, Peter H. Determinants of Saving: Theory and Evidence. *OECD Econ. Stud.*, Autumn 1983, (1), pp. 147–96. [G: OECD]

Summers, Lawrence H. An Equity Case for Consumption Taxation. In *Walker, C. E. and Bloomfield, M. E., eds.*, 1983, pp. 257–60.

Swamy, Paravastu A. V. B. and Mehta, Jatinder S. Ridge Regression Estimation of the Rotterdam Model. *J. Econometrics*, August 1983, *22*(3), pp. 365–90.

Tannenwald, Robert. Redistribution of Wealth in Conversion to a Flat Rate Tax. *New Eng. Econ. Rev.*, January/February 1983, pp. 5–17. [G: U.S.]

Teckenberg, Wolfgang. Economic Well-being in the Soviet Union Inflation and the Distribution of Resources. In *Schmukler, N. and Marcus, E., eds.*, 1983, pp. 659–76. [G: U.S.S.R.]

Tedeschi, Jardena. La stabilizzazione del reddito reale come obiettivo di politica economica, con un'applicazione all'economia egiziana. (The Stabilization of Real Income as a Goal of Economic Policy with an Application to the Egyptian Economy. With English summary.) *Rivista Int. Sci. Econ. Com.*, December 1983, *30*(12), pp. 1161–70. [G: Egypt]

Thys-Clement, Françoise; Van Regemorter, Denise and Vuchelen, Josef. La consommation privée: Cycle de vie et rationalité, une analyse empirique. (With English summary.) *Cah. Écon. Bruxelles*, Third Trimestre 1983, (99), pp. 327–60. [G: Belgium]

Triplett, Jack E. Escalation Measures: What Is the Answer? What Is the Question? In *Diewert, W. E. and Montmarquette, C., eds.*, 1983, pp. 457–82.

Uusitalo, Liisa. Environmental Impacts of Changes in Consumption Style. In *Uusitalo, L., ed.*, 1983, pp. 123–42. [G: OECD]

Val'toukh, K. K. Dynamique des dépenses privées des consommateurs français: Analyse avec utilisation d'une fonction théorique d'utilité. (Dynamics of Private Consumer Expenditures in France: An Analysis Using a Theoretical Utility Function. With English summary.) *Ann. INSEE*, Jan.–Mar. 1983, (49), pp. 89–112. [G: France]

Walsh, Lorena S. Urban Amenities and Rural Sufficiency: Living Standards and Consumer Behavior in the Colonial Chesapeake, 1643–1777. *J. Econ. Hist.*, March 1983, *43*(1), pp. 109–17. [G: U.S.]

Wansbeek, Tom and Kapteyn, Arie. Tackling Hard Questions by Means of Soft Methods: The Use of Individual Welfare Functions in Socio–Economic Policy. *Kyklos*, 1983, *36*(2), pp. 249–69.

Wells, John. Industrial Accumulation and Living Standards in the Long-Run: The São Paulo Industrial Working Class, 1930–75, Part II. *J. Devel. Stud.*, April 1983, *19*(3), pp. 297–328. [G: Brazil]

Wells, John. Industrial Accumulation and Living Standards in the Long-Run: The São Paulo Industrial Working Class, 1930–75, Part I. *J. Devel. Stud.*, January 1983, *19*(2), pp. 145–69. [G: Brazil]

Williams, Ross A. and Ouliaris, Sam. Inflation and the Consumption Ratio: Comments. In *Pagan, A. R. and Trivedi, P. K., eds.*, 1983, pp. 350–55. [G: Australia]

Williamson, Samuel H. and Jones, Warren L. Computing the Impact of Social Security Using the Life Cycle Consumption Function. *Amer. Econ. Rev.*, December 1983, *73*(5), pp. 1036–52. [G: U.S.]

Wittman, Donald. The Peak Income Hypothesis: An Econometric Reinvestigation. *Rev. Econ. Statist.*, May 1983, *65*(2), pp. 358–60. [G: U.S.]

Wolff, Edward N. The Size Distribution of Household Disposable Wealth in the United States. *Rev. Income Wealth*, June 1983, *29*(2), pp. 125–46. [G: U.S.]

Yitzhaki, Shlomo. On Two Proposals to Promote Saving. *Public Finance Quart.*, July 1983, *11*(3), pp. 299–319. [G: U.S.]

Zartman, William and Schatz, Sayre P. The Political Economy of Nigeria: Introduction. In *Zartman, I. W., ed.*, 1983, pp. 1–24.

9212 Expenditure Patterns and Consumption of Expenditure on Specific Items

Acton, Jan Paul and Mitchell, Bridger M. Welfare Analysis of Electricity-Rate Changes. In *Berg, S. V., ed.*, 1983, pp. 195–225. [G: U.S.]

Alpert, Leon. Estimating a Multi-Attribute Model for Different Music Styles. *J. Cult. Econ.*, June 1983, *7*(1), pp. 63–81. [G: U.S.]

Anderson, Ronald W. and Wilkinson, Maurice. Consumer Welfare and the Livestock Economy in the United States. *Can. J. Agr. Econ.*, November 1983, *31*(3), pp. 351–70. [G: U.S.]

Archibald, Robert and Gillingham, Robert. An Analysis of the Short-Run Consumer Demand for Gasoline Using Household Survey Data: A Reply. *Rev. Econ. Statist.*, August 1983, *65*(3), pp. 533–34. [G: U.S.]

Atkinson, Scott E. The Implications of Homothetic Separability for Share Equation Price Elasticities [The Bias in Price Elasticity Estimates under Homothetic Separability: Implications for Analysis of Peak-Load Electricity Pricing]. *J. Bus. Econ. Statist.*, July 1983, *1*(3), pp. 211–14. [G: U.S.]

Avi-Itzhak, Benjamin; Iusem, Alfredo and Dantzig, George B. The Consumers Energy Services Model of the Pilot System. In *Lev, B., ed.*, 1983,

pp. 195–220. [G: U.S.]

Babbel, David F. and Staking, Kim B. An Engel Curve Analysis of Gambling and Insurance in Brazil. *J. Risk Ins.*, December 1983, *50*(4), pp. 688–96. [G: Brazil]

Bajusz, Rezso. Mass Transport and Individual Transport: An Optimum Modal Split. **In** *Khachaturov, T. S. and Goodwin, P. B., eds.*, 1983, pp. 167–78. [G: Hungary; W. Europe]

Baltagi, Badi H. and Griffin, James M. Gasoline Demand in the OECD: An Application of Pooling and Testing Procedures. *Europ. Econ. Rev.*, July 1983, *22*(2), pp. 117–37. [G: OECD]

Barnett, William A. The Recent Reappearance of the Homotheticity Restriction on Preferences [The Bias in Price Elasticity Estimates under Homothetic Separability: Implications for Analysis of Peak-Load Electricity Pricing]. *J. Bus. Econ. Statist.*, July 1983, *1*(3), pp. 215–18. [G: U.S.]

Barr, G. D. I. Estimating a Consumer Demand Function for South Africa. *S. Afr. J. Econ.*, December 1983, *51*(4), pp. 523–29. [G: S. Africa]

Basiotis, Peter, et al. Nutrient Availability, Food Costs, and Food Stamps. *Amer. J. Agr. Econ.*, November 1983, *65*(4), pp. 685–93. [G: U.S.]

Beenstock, Michael and Willcocks, Patrick. Energy and Economic Activity: A Reply to Kouris. *Energy Econ.*, July 1983, *5*(3), pp. 212. [G: MDCs]

Bello, Walden; Harris, John and Zarsky, Lyuba. Nuclear Power in the Philippines: The Plague that Poisons Morong! *Rev. Radical Polit. Econ.*, Fall 1983, *15*(3), pp. 51–65. [G: Philippines]

Berg, Sanford V. Consumer Responses to Innovative Electric Rates. **In** *Berg, S. V., ed.*, 1983, pp. 55–78. [G: U.S.]

Berg, Sanford V. and Savvides, Andreas. The Theory of Maximum kW Demand Charges for Electricity. *Energy Econ.*, October 1983, *5*(4), pp. 258–66. [G: U.S.]

Billings, R. Bruce. Revenue Effects from Changes in a Declining Block Pricing Structure: Comment. *Land Econ.*, August 1983, *59*(3), pp. 355–39. [G: U.S.]

Billings, R. Bruce. Specification of Block Rate Price Variables in Demand Models: Reply. *Land Econ.*, August 1983, *59*(3), pp. 370–71. [G: U.S.]

Bjerkholt, Olav and Rinde, Jon. Consumption Demand in the MSG Model. **In** *Av, R., et al., eds.*, 1983, pp. 84–107. [G: Norway]

Blanciforti, Laura and Green, Richard. An Almost Ideal Demand System Incorporating Habits: An Analysis of Expenditures on Food and Aggregate Commodity Groups. *Rev. Econ. Statist.*, August 1983, *65*(3), pp. 511–15. [G: U.S.]

Blanciforti, Laura and Green, Richard. The Almost Ideal Demand System: A Comparison and Application to Food Groups. *Agr. Econ. Res.*, July 1983, *35*(3), pp. 1–10. [G: U.S.]

Blattenberger, Gail R.; Taylor, Lester D. and Rennhack, Robert K. Natural Gas Availability and the Residential Demand for Energy. *Energy J.*, January 1983, *4*(1), pp. 23–45. [G: U.S.]

Bopp, Anthony E. The Demand for Kerosene: A Modern Giffen Good. *Appl. Econ.*, August 1983, *15*(4), pp. 459–67. [G: U.S.]

Bourgo, Donald G. Forecasting Crest Sales [Advertising and Sales Relationships for Toothpaste]. *Bus. Econ.*, January 1983, *18*(1), pp. 48–50. [G: U.S.]

Boynton, Robert D.; Blake, Brian F. and Uhl, Joseph N. Retail Price Reporting Effects in Local Food Markets. *Amer. J. Agr. Econ.*, February 1983, *65*(1), pp. 20–29. [G: U.S.]

Braschler, Curtis. The Changing Demand Structure for Pork and Beef in the 1970s: Implications for the 1980s. *Southern J. Agr. Econ.*, December 1983, *15*(2), pp. 105–10. [G: U.S.]

Brown, Philip W. The Demographic Future: Impacts on the Demand for Housing in Canada, 1981–2001. **In** *Gau, G. W. and Goldberg, M. A., eds.*, 1983, pp. 5–31. [G: Canada]

Brown, Scott B. An Aggregate Petroleum Consumption Model. *Energy Econ.*, January 1983, *5*(1), pp. 27–30. [G: U.S.]

Burch, Susan Weller. The Aging U.S. Auto Stock: Implications for Demand. *Bus. Econ.*, May 1983, *18*(3), pp. 22–26. [G: U.S.]

Burnett, John J. and Palmer, Bruce A. Reliance on Life Insurance Agents: A Demographic and Psychographic Analysis of Consumers. *J. Risk Ins.*, September 1983, *50*(3), pp. 510–20. [G: U.S.]

Capps, Oral, Jr. and Love, John M. Determinants of Household Expenditure on Fresh Vegetables. *Southern J. Agr. Econ.*, December 1983, *15*(2), pp. 127–32. [G: U.S.]

Capps, Oral, Jr.; Tedford, John R. and Havlicek, Joseph, Jr. Impacts of Household Composition on Convenience and Nonconvenience Food Expenditures in the South. *Southern J. Agr. Econ.*, December 1983, *15*(2), pp. 111–18. [G: U.S.]

Carlson, John A. and Gieseke, Robert J. Price Search in a Product Market. *J. Cons. Res.*, March 1983, *9*(4), pp. 357–65. [G: U.S.]

Caves, Douglas W. and Christensen, Laurits R. The Bias in Price Elasticity Estimates under Homothetic Separability: Implications for Analysis of Peak-Load Electricity Pricing: Discussion. *J. Bus. Econ. Statist.*, July 1983, *1*(3), pp. 219–20. [G: U.S.]

Chambers, Robert G. and McConnell, Kenneth E. Decomposition and Additivity in Price-Dependent Demand Systems. *Amer. J. Agr. Econ.*, August 1983, *65*(3), pp. 596–602. [G: U.S.]

Chavas, Jean-Paul. Structural Change in the Demand for Meat. *Amer. J. Agr. Econ.*, February 1983, *65*(1), pp. 148–53. [G: U.S.]

Chernoff, Harry. Individual Purchase Criteria for Energy-Related Durables: The Misuse of Life Cycle Cost. *Energy J.*, October 1983, *4*(4), pp. 81–86. [G: U.S.]

Clements, Kenneth W. and Johnson, Lester W. The Demand for Beer, Wine, and Spirits: A Systemwide Analysis. *J. Bus.*, July 1983, *56*(3), pp. 273–304. [G: Australia]

Coffey, Rosanna M. The Effect of Time Price on the Demand for Medical-Care Services. *J. Human Res.*, Summer 1983, *18*(3), pp. 407–24. [G: U.S.]

Collins, Robert A. and Gray, Joan K. Derivation of a Theoretical Form of a Production Function for Home Temperature: A Comment [The Economics of House Heating]. *Energy Econ.*, October 1983, *5*(4), pp. 273–75. [G: U.K.]

Cook, Philip J. The Effect of Liquor Taxes on Drinking, Cirrhosis, and Auto Fatalities. **In** *Zeckhauser, R. J. and Leebaert, D., eds.*, 1983, pp. 203–20. **[G: U.S.]**

Craig, C. Samuel. How Predispositions and Discretion Influence Electricity Consumption. *J. Energy Devel.*, Spring 1983, *8*(2), pp. 247–65. **[G: U.S.]**

Crano, William D. Cognitive Factors That Influence Consumers' Responses to Innovative Rate Structures. **In** *Berg, S. V., ed.*, 1983, pp. 95–107. **[G: U.S.]**

Criqui, P. Prix du pétrole, prix des énergies finales et consommations d'énergie dans les cinq grandes économies de l'O.C.D.E. (Petroleum Price, Final Energies Prices and Energy Consumption in the Five Bigger Economies of O.E.C.D. With English summary.) *Écon. Soc.*, December 1983, *17*(12), pp. 1927–947. **[G: U.S.; Japan; France; U.K.; Germany]**

Curien, N. and Vilmin, E. Telephone Demand and Usage: A Global Residential Model. **In** *Courville, L.; de Fontenay, A. and Dobell, R., eds.*, 1983, pp. 231–49. **[G: France]**

Dahl, Carol A. An Analysis of the Short-Run Consumer Demand for Gasoline Using Household Survey Data: A Comment. *Rev. Econ. Statist.*, August 1983, *65*(3), pp. 532–33. **[G: U.S.]**

Daly, George G. and Mayor, Thomas H. Reason and Rationality during Energy Crises. *J. Polit. Econ.*, February 1983, *91*(1), pp. 168–81. **[G: U.S.]**

Darrough, Masako N.; Pollak, Robert A. and Wales, Terence J. Dynamic and Stochastic Structure: An Analysis of Three Time Series of Household Budget Studies. *Rev. Econ. Statist.*, May 1983, *65*(2), pp. 274–81. **[G: Japan; U.K.]**

Dias-Bandaranaike, Romesh and Munasinghe, Mohan. The Demand for Electricity Services and the Quality of Supply. *Energy J.*, April 1983, *4*(2), pp. 49–71. **[G: Costa Rica]**

Dickerson, Mary Dee and Gentry, James W. Characteristics of Adopters and Non-Adopters of Home Computers. *J. Cons. Res.*, September 1983, *10*(2), pp. 225–35. **[G: U.S.]**

Dickson, Peter R.; Lusch, Robert F. and Wilkie, William L. Consumer Acquisition Priorities for Home Appliances: A Replication and Re-evaluation. *J. Cons. Res.*, March 1983, *9*(4), pp. 432–35. **[G: U.S.]**

Duffy, M. The Demand for Alcoholic Drink in the United Kingdom, 1963–78. *Appl. Econ.*, February 1983, *15*(1), pp. 125–40. **[G: U.K.]**

Feldman, Jack. A Theoretical Analysis of Energy-Cost Indicator Impacts on Electricity Consumption. **In** *Berg, S. V., ed.*, 1983, pp. 109–13.

Fishe, Raymond P. H. and McAfee, R. Preston. On the Use of Bonus Payments in an Experimental Study of Electricity Demand. *Rev. Econ. Statist.*, August 1983, *65*(3), pp. 506–11. **[G: U.S.]**

de Fontenay, A. and Lee, J. T. Marshall. B.C./Alberta Long Distance Calling. **In** *Courville, L.; de Fontenay, A. and Dobell, R., eds.*, 1983, pp. 199–227. **[G: Canada]**

Fornell, Claes and Robinson, William T. Industrial Organization and Consumer Satisfaction/Dissatisfaction. *J. Cons. Res.*, March 1983, *9*(4), pp. 403–12. **[G: U.S.]**

Frieden, Bernard J. and Baker, Kermit. The Market Needs Help: The Disappointing Record of Home Energy Conservation. *J. Policy Anal. Manage.*, Spring 1983, *2*(3), pp. 432–48. **[G: U.S.]**

Friedman, Joseph and Weinberg, Daniel H. Rent Rebates and Housing Standards. **In** *Friedman, J. and Weinberg, D. H., eds.*, 1983, pp. 127–43. **[G: U.S.]**

Gallini, Nancy T. Demand for Gasoline in Canada. *Can. J. Econ.*, May 1983, *16*(2), pp. 299–324. **[G: Canada]**

Garbacz, Christopher. A Model of Residential Demand for Electricity Using a National Household Sample. *Energy Econ.*, April 1983, *5*(2), pp. 124–28. **[G: U.S.]**

Gardini, Attilio. Formulazione e stima di un modello stocastico di analisi della domanda turistica. (Demand Analysis for Tourist Services: Specification and Estimation of a Stochastic Model. With English summary.) *Statistica*, October–December 1983, *43*(4), pp. 635–60. **[G: Italy]**

Gemello, John M. and Osman, Jack W. The Choice for Public and Private Education: An Economist's View. **In** *James, T. and Levin, H. M., eds.*, 1983, pp. 196–209. **[G: U.S.]**

Goddard, Dean. An Analysis of Canadian Aggregate Demand for Food at Home and Away from Home. *Can. J. Agr. Econ.*, November 1983, *31*(3), pp. 289–318. **[G: Canada]**

Gold, Sonia S. Consumer Sovereignty and the Performing Arts. **In** *Hendon, W. S. and Shanahan, J. L., eds.*, 1983, pp. 207–18. **[G: U.K.; U.S.]**

Goodman, Allen C. Willingness to Pay for Car Efficiency: A Hedonic Price Approach. *J. Transp. Econ. Policy*, September 1983, *17*(3), pp. 247–66. **[G: U.S.]**

Grieves, Robin. The Demand for Consumer Durables. *J. Money, Credit, Banking*, August 1983, *15*(3), pp. 316–26. **[G: U.S.]**

Haidacher, Richard C. Assessing Structural Change in the Demand for Food Commodities. *Southern J. Agr. Econ.*, July 1983, *15*(1), pp. 31–37. **[G: U.S.]**

Hartman, Raymond S. The Estimation of Short-run Household Electricity Demand Using Pooled Aggregate Data. *J. Bus. Econ. Statist.*, April 1983, *1*(2), pp. 127–35. **[G: U.S.]**

Hassan, Zuhair A. and Johnson, Stanley R. Quarterly Demands for Meat in Canada with Alternative Seasonality Hypotheses. *Can. J. Agr. Econ.*, March 1983, *31*(1), pp. 77–94. **[G: Canada]**

Heien, Dale M. Seasonality in U.S. Consumer Demand. *J. Bus. Econ. Statist.*, October 1983, *1*(4), pp. 280–84. **[G: U.S.]**

Hiemstra, Stephen J. Marketing Impacts of the Domestic Food Assistance Programs. **In** *Farris, P. L., ed.*, 1983, pp. 278–95. **[G: U.S.]**

Hill, Daniel H. The Impact of Natural Gas Deregulation on American Families. **In** *Duncan, G. J. and Morgan, J. N., eds.*, 1983, pp. 178–204. **[G: U.S.]**

Hill, Daniel H., et al. Incentive Payments in Time-of-Day Electricity Pricing Experiments: The Arizona Experience. *Rev. Econ. Statist.*, February 1983, *65*(1), pp. 59–65. **[G: U.S.]**

Ho, James K. Multiple Criteria Optimization Using Analytic Hierarchies and Holistic Preferences. **In**

Hansen, P., ed., 1983, pp. 156–66.

Houston, Douglas A. Implicit Discount Rates and the Purchase of Untried, Energy-Saving Durable Goods. *J. Cons. Res.*, September 1983, *10*(2), pp. 236–46. **[G: U.S.]**

Houston, Douglas A. Revenue Effects from Changes in a Declining Block Pricing Structure: Reply. *Land Econ.*, August 1983, *59*(3), pp. 360–64. **[G: U.S.]**

Huang, Chung L. and Raunikar, Robert. Household Fluid Milk Expenditure Patterns in the South and United States. *Southern J. Agr. Econ.*, December 1983, *15*(2), pp. 27–33. **[G: U.S.]**

Huang, Kuo S. and Haidacher, Richard C. Estimation of a Composite Food Demand System for the United States. *J. Bus. Econ. Statist.*, October 1983, *1*(4), pp. 285–91. **[G: U.S.]**

Ilzkovitz, Fabienne. L'information des consommateurs . . . Une condition de l'efficacité des primes à l'isolation? (With English summary.) *Cah. Écon. Bruxelles*, 4th Trimester 1983, (100), pp. 534–60. **[G: Belgium]**

Iqbal, Mahmood. Residential Demand for Electricity and Natural Gas in Pakistan. *Pakistan Devel. Rev.*, Spring 1983, *22*(1), pp. 23–36. **[G: Pakistan]**

Irvine, F. Owen, Jr. Demand Equations for Individual New Car Models Estimated Using Transaction Prices with Implications for Regulatory Issues. *Southern Econ. J.*, January 1983, *49*(3), pp. 764–82. **[G: U.S.]**

Johnston, Stephen A. Peak and Off-Peak Electricity Consumption: A Review and Critique of Load Management and Rate Design Demonstration Projects. **In** *Berg, S. V., ed.*, 1983, pp. 115–28. **[G: U.S.]**

Jones, Philip R. Aid to Charities. *Int. J. Soc. Econ.*, 1983, *10*(2), pp. 3–11. **[G: U.K.]**

Katz, Arnold J. Valuing the Services of Consumer Durables. *Rev. Income Wealth*, December 1983, *29*(4), pp. 405–27. **[G: U.S.]**

Keller, Wouter J. and Wansbeek, Tom. Private Consumption Expenditures and Price Index Numbers for the Netherlands 1951–1977. *Rev. Public Data Use (See J. Econ. Soc. Meas. after 4/85)*, December 1983, *11*(4), pp. 311–13. **[G: Netherlands]**

Kinsey, Jean. Working Wives and the Marginal Propensity to Consume Food Away from Home. *Amer. J. Agr. Econ.*, February 1983, *65*(1), pp. 10–19. **[G: U.S.]**

Kitchin, Paul Duncan. Socio-Economic Determinants of UK Alcohol Consumption, 1956–79. *Int. J. Soc. Econ.*, 1983, *10*(3), pp. 34–39. **[G: U.K.]**

Kohler, Daniel F. The Bias in Price Elasticity Estimates under Homothetic Separability: Implications for Analysis of Peak-Load Electricity Pricing. *J. Bus. Econ. Statist.*, July 1983, *1*(3), pp. 202–10. **[G: U.S.]**

Kohler, Daniel F. The Bias in Price Elasticity Estimates under Homothetic Separability: Implications for Analysis of Peak-Load Electricity Pricing: Response. *J. Bus. Econ. Statist.*, July 1983, *1*(3), pp. 226–28. **[G: U.S.]**

Kolk, David X. Regional Employment Impact of Rapidly Escalating Energy Costs. *Energy Econ.*, April 1983, *5*(2), pp. 105–13. **[G: U.S.]**

Kouris, George. Energy Consumption and Economic Activity in Industrialized Economies—A Note. *Energy Econ.*, July 1983, *5*(3), pp. 207–12. **[G: MDCs]**

Kouris, George. Energy Demand Elasticities in Industrialized Countries: A Survey. *Energy J.*, July 1983, *4*(3), pp. 73–94. **[G: OECD]**

Kouris, George. Fuel Consumption for Road Transport in the USA. *Energy Econ.*, April 1983, *5*(2), pp. 89–99. **[G: U.S.]**

Ladoux, N. and Outrequin, Ph. Prix de l'énergie et comportement des ménages. (Energy Prices and Households' Behaviour. With English summary.) *Écon. Soc.*, December 1983, *17*(12), pp. 1949–976.

LaTour, Stephen A. and Orwin, Robert G. Determining the Effects of Innovative Rates on Customer Response Using Meta-Analysis. **In** *Berg, S. V., ed.*, 1983, pp. 129–50. **[G: U.S.]**

Lehmann, Donald R. and Moore, William L. On Hypotheses, Measurements, and the Extension of Knowledge. *J. Cons. Res.*, June 1983, *10*(1), pp. 132–33. **[G: U.S.]**

Leigh, Wilhelmina A. The Impact of Inflation upon Homeownership Affordability: Comparisons by Race and Sex for the South. **In** *Schmukler, N. and Marcus, E., eds.*, 1983, pp. 838–59. **[G: U.S.]**

Longva, Svein, et al. Use of the MSG Model in Forecasting Electricity Demand. **In** *Av, R., et al., eds.*, 1983, pp. 180–94. **[G: Norway]**

Louviere, Jordan J. and Hensher, David A. Using Discrete Choice Models with Experimental Design Data to Forecast Consumer Demand for a Unique Cultural Event. *J. Cons. Res.*, December 1983, *10*(3), pp. 348–61. **[G: Australia]**

Lyckeborg, Håkan. A Box-Jenkins Approach to Short-term Energy Consumption Forecasting in Sweden: Univariate Models. **In** *Sohlman, A. M., ed.*, 1983, pp. 98–123. **[G: Sweden]**

Maddigan, Ruth J.; Chern, Wen S. and Rizy, Colleen Gallagher. Rural Residential Demand for Electricity. *Land Econ.*, May 1983, *59*(2), pp. 150–62. **[G: U.S.]**

Maillard, D. L'élasticité énergie P.I.B. sophisme ou panacée. (Elasticity Energy–G.N.P.: A Fallacy or a Panacea. With English summary.) *Écon. Soc.*, December 1983, *17*(12), pp. 1835–846.

Malhotra, Naresh K. On 'Individual Differences in Search Behavior for a Nondurable.' *J. Cons. Res.*, June 1983, *10*(1), pp. 125–31. **[G: U.S.]**

Manes, Rene P. Demand Elasticities: Supplements to Sales Budget Variance Reports. *Accounting Rev.*, January 1983, *58*(1), pp. 143–56.

McElwain, Adrienne and Lifson, Dale P. A Comparison and Reconciliation of Full and Partial Price Elasticities. *Appl. Econ.*, June 1983, *15*(3), pp. 353–62. **[G: U.S.]**

Merrill, Sally R. The Great Housing Experiment: The Use of Hedonic Indices. **In** *Friedman, J. and Weinberg, D. H., eds.*, 1983, pp. 144–62. **[G: U.S.]**

Merz, Joachim. Der Einfluss sozioökonomischer Grössen auf die individuelle private Nachfrage nach dauerhaften Konsumgütern: Eine Anwendung der diskreten Entscheidungsmodelle LOGIT und TOBIT. (Socioeconomic Influence on Individual Private Demand for Durable Goods.

An Application of the Discrete Choice Models LOGIT and TOBIT. With English summary.) *Z. Wirtschaft. Sozialwissen.*, 1983, *103*(3), pp. 225–53. **[G: W. Germany]**

Merz, Joachim. FELES: The Functionalized Extended Linear Expenditure System: Theory, Estimation Procedures and Application to Individual Household Consumption Expenditures Involving Socioeconomic and Sociodemographic Characteristics. *Europ. Econ. Rev.*, December 1983, *23*(3), pp. 359–94. **[G: W. Germany]**

Mitchell, Bridger M. and Acton, Jan Paul. Electricity Consumption by Time of Use in a Hybrid Demand System. **In** *Finsinger, J., ed.*, 1983, pp. 27–64. **[G: U.S.]**

Mondal, S. K. Balanced Diet, Availability of Food, Cereal Consumption and Poverty. *Margin*, July 1983, *15*(4), pp. 92–102. **[G: India]**

Moriizumi, Yoko and Takagi, Shintaro. The Income Elasticity of Housing Demand in Japan. *Econ. Stud. Quart.*, April 1983, *34*(1), pp. 70–86. **[G: Japan]**

Morin, Roger A. and Fernandez Suarez, Antonio. Risk Aversion Revisited. *J. Finance*, September 1983, *38*(4), pp. 1201–16. **[G: Canada]**

Mulford, John E. The Great Housing Experiment: Earmarked Income Supplements. **In** *Friedman, J. and Weinberg, D. H., eds.*, 1983, pp. 163–74. **[G: U.S.]**

Murfin, Andy and Smith, Ron. Depreciation and the Quality Adjustment of Prices: An Investigation of the UK Car Market, 1980–81. *Brit. Rev. Econ. Issues*, Autumn 1983, *5*(13), pp. 23–38. **[G: U.K.]**

Musgrove, Philip. Family Health Care Spending in Latin America. *J. Health Econ.*, December 1983, *2*(3), pp. 245–57. **[G: Latin America]**

O'Brien-Place, P. M. and Tomek, William G. Inflation in Food Prices as Measured by Least-Cost Diets. *Amer. J. Agr. Econ.*, November 1983, *65*(4), pp. 781–84. **[G: U.S.]**

Ohsfeldt, Robert L. Specification of Block Rate Price Variables in Demand Models: Comment. *Land Econ.*, August 1983, *59*(3), pp. 365–69. **[G: U.S.]**

Okamura, Minoru. Estimating Taste Changes: Impacts of the U.S. Soybean Embargo on the Japanese Demand for Meat. *Southern Econ. J.*, April 1983, *49*(4), pp. 1053–65. **[G: Japan]**

Okun, Arthur M. The Personal Tax Surcharge and Consumer Demand, 1968–70. **In** *Okun, A. M.*, 1983, *1971*, pp. 338–74. **[G: U.S.]**

Pacey, Patricia L. Long Distance Demand: A Point-to-Point Model. *Southern Econ. J.*, April 1983, *49*(4), pp. 1094–1107. **[G: U.S.]**

Padberg, Daniel I. and Westgren, Randall E. Adaptability of Consumers and Manufacturers to Changes in Cultural Patterns and Socioeconomic Values. **In** *Farris, P. L., ed.*, 1983, pp. 246–63. **[G: U.S.]**

Park, Rolla Edward; Wetzel, Bruce M. and Mitchell, Bridger M. Price Elasticities for Local Telephone Calls. *Econometrica*, November 1983, *51*(6), pp. 1699–730. **[G: U.S.]**

Park, Rolla Edward, et al. Charging for Local Telephone Calls: How Household Characteristics Affect the Distribution of Calls in the GTE Illinois Experiment. *J. Econometrics*, August 1983, *22*(3), pp. 339–64. **[G: U.S.]**

Parks, Richard W. The Bias in Price Elasticity Estimates under Homothetic Separability: Implications for Analysis of Peak-Load Electricity Pricing: Discussion. *J. Bus. Econ. Statist.*, July 1983, *1*(3), pp. 221–25. **[G: U.S.]**

Podkaminer, Leon. Estimates of the Disequilibria in Poland's Consumer Markets (1965–1978). **In** *Kelley, A. C.; Sanderson, W. C. and Williamson, J. G., eds.*, 1983, pp. 167–84. **[G: Poland; Italy; Ireland]**

Prot, B. and Rolland, P. La fiscalité comme outil de la politique de la demande. (The Tax System as a Tool of the Demand Policy. With English summary.) *Écon. Soc.*, December 1983, *17*(12), pp. 2077–88.

Punj, Girish N. and Staelin, Richard. A Model of Consumer Information Search Behavior for New Automobiles. *J. Cons. Res.*, March 1983, *9*(4), pp. 366–80. **[G: U.S.]**

Ray, C. R. Macro Impacts of Food Subsidy Policies in Developing Countries. *Margin*, July 1983, *15*(4), pp. 50–65. **[G: India]**

Reilly, Robert J. and Hoffer, George E. Will Retarding the Information Flow on Automobile Recalls Affect Consumer Demand? *Econ. Inquiry*, July 1983, *21*(3), pp. 444–47. **[G: U.S.]**

Rødseth, Asbjørn. An Expenditure System for Energy Planning. **In** *Av, R., et al., eds.*, 1983, pp. 195–220. **[G: Norway]**

Rosen, Dennis L. and Granbois, Donald H. Determinants of Role Structure in Family Financial Management. *J. Cons. Res.*, September 1983, *10*(2), pp. 253–58. **[G: U.S.]**

Rowe, Robert D. and Chestnut, Lauraine G. Valuing Environmental Commodities: Revisited. *Land Econ.*, November 1983, *59*(4), pp. 404–10.

Rutgaizer, V. The Working Person in the Distribution and Consumption Sphere. *Prob. Econ.*, January 1983, *25*(9), pp. 16–35. **[G: U.S.S.R.]**

Rutgaizer, V.; Bokov, A. and Orlov, V. Forecasting the Population's Monetary Savings. *Prob. Econ.*, January 1983, *25*(9), pp. 52–70. **[G: U.S.S.R.; E. Germany]**

Rydell, C. Peter and Barnett, C. Lance. Price Effects of Housing Allowances. **In** *Friedman, J. and Weinberg, D. H., eds.*, 1983, pp. 175–88. **[G: U.S.]**

Sarkar, B. N. Disparities in Inter-State Consumer Expenditure, 1957–58 to 1973–74. *Margin*, July 1983, *15*(4), pp. 66–77. **[G: India]**

Schmidt, Ronald H. Effects of Natural Gas Deregulation on the Distribution of Income. *Fed. Res. Bank Dallas Econ. Rev.*, May 1983, pp. 1–12. **[G: U.S.]**

Schofield, J. A. The Demand for Cricket: The Case of the John Player League. *Appl. Econ.*, June 1983, *15*(3), pp. 283–96. **[G: U.K.]**

Schulze, William D., et al. The Economic Benefits of Preserving Visibility in the National Parklands of the Southwest. *Natural Res. J.*, January 1983, *23*(1), pp. 149–73. **[G: U.S.]**

Scott, Alex and Capper, Graham. Production Functions for House Temperatures: Problems and Issues: A Reply [The Economics of House Heating].

Energy Econ., October 1983, *5*(4), pp. 275–78. [G: U.K.]

Seek, N. H. Adjusting Housing Consumption: Improve or Move. *Urban Stud.*, November 1983, *20*(4), pp. 455–69. [G: Australia]

Shammas, Carole. Food Expenditures and Economic Well-Being in Early Modern England. *J. Econ. Hist.*, March 1983, *43*(1), pp. 89–100. [G: U.K.]

Sohlman, Asa. Energy Use in Sweden 1965–80. **In** *Sohlman, A. M., ed.*, 1983, pp. 38–56. [G: Sweden]

Soutar, Geoffrey N. and Clarke, Yvonne M. Life Style and Radio Listening Patterns in Perth, Western Australia. *Australian J. Manage.*, June 1983, *8*(1), pp. 71–81. [G: Australia]

Starzec, Krzysztof. L'économie polonaise vue à travers des circuits parallèles. (Polish "Official" and "Unofficial" Economy: An Empirical Approach. With English summary.) *Consommation*, October–December 1983, *30*(4), pp. 55–94. [G: Poland]

Sullivan, Robert L. Evaluating Reliability and Operating-Cost Impacts of TOU Rates. **In** *Berg, S. V., ed.*, 1983, pp. 153–81. [G: U.S.]

Swamy, Gurushri and Binswanger, Hans P. Flexible Consumer Demand Systems and Linear Estimation: Food in India. *Amer. J. Agr. Econ.*, November 1983, *65*(4), pp. 675–84. [G: India]

Taylor, Lester D. Problems and Issues in Modeling Telecommunications Demand. **In** *Courville, L.; de Fontenay, A. and Dobell, R., eds.*, 1983, pp. 181–98. [G: U.S.]

Thatcher, L. P. and Couchman, R. C. Determining Consumer Requirements for Lamb Loin Chops—A Preliminary Study. *Rev. Marketing Agr. Econ.*, August 1983, *51*(2), pp. 167–77. [G: Australia]

Theil, Henri and Finke, Renate. The Consumer's Demand for Diversity. *Europ. Econ. Rev.*, December 1983, *23*(3), pp. 395–400. [G: Selected Countries]

Throsby, C. David. Perception of Quality in Demand for the Theatre. **In** *Hendon, W. S. and Shanahan, J. L., eds.*, 1983, pp. 162–76. [G: Australia]

Throsby, C. David and Withers, Glenn A. Measuring the Demand for the Arts as a Public Good: Theory and Empirical Results. **In** *Hendon, W. S. and Shanahan, J. L., eds.*, 1983, pp. 177–91. [G: Australia]

Tishler, Asher. The Demand for Cars and Gasoline: A Simultaneous Approach. *Europ. Econ. Rev.*, January 1983, *20*(1–3), pp. 271–87. [G: Israel]

Tsolakis, D. Taxation and Consumption of Wine. *Rev. Marketing Agr. Econ.*, August 1983, *51*(2), pp. 155–65. [G: Australia]

Tsolakis, D.; Riethmuller, P. and Watts, G. The Demand for Wine and Beer. *Rev. Marketing Agr. Econ.*, August 1983, *51*(2), pp. 131–53. [G: Australia]

Tuccillo, John A. Inflation, Housing Prices, and Investment: A U.S. Perspective. **In** *Gau, G. W. and Goldberg, M. A., eds.*, 1983, pp. 259–88. [G: U.S.]

Uhl, Joseph N. Advertising Effects on Food Purchasing Behavior: Comment. **In** *Connor, J. M. and Ward, R. W., eds.*, 1983, pp. 160–61.

Uhl, Joseph N. Public Provision of Comparative Foodstore Price Information: Problems, Potentials, and Issues. **In** *Connor, J. M. and Ward, R. W., eds.*, 1983, pp. 323–44. [G: U.S.]

Wagner, Janet and Hanna, Sherman. The Effectiveness of Family Life Cycle Variables in Consumer Expenditure Research. *J. Cons. Res.*, December 1983, *10*(3), pp. 281–91. [G: U.S.]

Wales, Terence J. and Woodland, Alan D. Estimation of Consumer Demand Systems with Binding Non-Negativity Constraints. *J. Econometrics*, April 1983, *21*(3), pp. 263–85. [G: Australia]

Wallendorf, Melanie and Reilly, Michael D. Ethnic Migration, Assimilation, and Consumption. *J. Cons. Res.*, December 1983, *10*(3), pp. 292–302. [G: Mexico; U.S.]

Weinberg, Charles B. and Winer, Russell S. Working Wives and Major Family Expenditures: Replication and Extension. *J. Cons. Res.*, September 1983, *10*(2), pp. 259–63. [G: U.S.]

Westgren, Randall E. Advertising Effects on Food Purchasing Behavior. **In** *Connor, J. M. and Ward, R. W., eds.*, 1983, pp. 149–58.

Wilkinson, G. F. The Estimation of Usage Repression under Local Measured Service: Empirical Evidence from the GTE Experiment. **In** *Courville, L.; de Fontenay, A. and Dobell, R., eds.*, 1983, pp. 253–62. [G: U.S.]

Witt, Stephen F. A Binary Choice Model of Foreign Holiday Demand. *J. Econ. Stud.*, 1983, *10*(1), pp. 46–59. [G: U.K.]

Witt, Stephen F. and Pass, Christopher L. Forecasting Cigarette Consumption: The Causal Model Approach. *Int. J. Soc. Econ.*, 1983, *10*(3), pp. 18–33. [G: U.K.]

Wohlgenant, Michael K. Assessing Structural Change in the Demand for Food Commodities: Discussion. *Southern J. Agr. Econ.*, July 1983, *15*(1), pp. 39–41. [G: U.S.]

Wong, T. F. Identifying Tariff Induced Shifts in the Subscriber Distribution of Local Telephone Usage. **In** *Courville, L.; de Fontenay, A. and Dobell, R., eds.*, 1983, pp. 263–78. [G: U.S.]

Young, Trevor. The Demand for Cigarettes: Alternative Specifications of Fujii's Model. *Appl. Econ.*, April 1983, *15*(2), pp. 203–11. [G: U.S.]

Young, Trevor; Stevens, Thomas H. and Willis, Cleve. Asymmetry in the Residential Demand for Electricity. *Energy J.*, Supplement 1983, *4*, pp. 153–62. [G: U.S.]

9213 Consumer Protection

Berenson, Conrad. The Product Liability Revolution. **In** *Snoeyenbos, M.; Almeder, R. and Humber, J., eds.*, 1983, *1972*, pp. 379–90.

Boehm, William T. Commentary [Voluntary Approaches to Increasing Nutrition Information in the Mass Media] [Consumer Organizations as a Source of Information in Food Markets]. **In** *Connor, J. M. and Ward, R. W., eds.*, 1983, pp. 419–20. [G: U.S.]

Boehm, William T. and Lenahan, Robert J. Health and Safety Regulations and Food System Performance. **In** *Farris, P. L., ed.*, 1983, pp. 264–77. [G: U.S.]

Boynton, Robert D.; McCracken, Vicki and Irwin,

Scott. Food Advertising as a Source of Consumer Information: A Case Study of Newspaper Advertising and Its Relationship to Public Price Reports. In *Connor, J. M. and Ward, R. W., eds.*, 1983, pp. 371–83. [G: U.S.]

Calabresi, Guido and Hirschoff, Jon T. Toward A Test for Strict Liability in Torts. In *Kuperberg, M. and Beitz, C., eds.*, 1983, *1981*, pp. 154–84.

Clancy, Katherine L. Voluntary Approaches to Increasing Nutrition Information in the Mass Media. In *Connor, J. M. and Ward, R. W., eds.*, 1983, pp. 397–402. [G: U.S.]

Connor, John M. and Ward, Ronald W. Advertising and the Food System: Introduction and Overview. In *Connor, J. M. and Ward, R. W., eds.*, 1983, pp. 1–10.

Dewees, Donald N. The Quality of Consumer Durables: Energy Use. In *Dewees, D. N., ed.*, 1983, pp. 207–46. [G: Canada]

Dewees, Donald N.; Mathewson, G. Frank and Trebilcock, Michael J. Policy Alternatives in Quality Regulation. In *Dewees, D. N., ed.*, 1983, pp. 27–51.

Dewees, Donald N.; Mathewson, G. Frank and Trebilcock, Michael J. The Rationale for Government Regulation of Quality. In *Dewees, D. N., ed.*, 1983, pp. 3–26. [G: U.S.]

Eisman, Deborah E. Product Liability: Who Should Bear the Burden? *Amer. Econ.*, Spring 1983, *27*(1), pp. 54–57.

Fazal, Anwar. The Right Pharmaceuticals at the Right Prices: Consumer Perspectives. *World Devel.*, March 1983, *11*(3), pp. 265–69.

Fletcher, George P. Fairness and Utility in Tort Theory. In *Kuperberg, M. and Beitz, C., eds.*, 1983, *1972*, pp. 248–84.

Golbe, Devra L. Product Safety in a Regulated Industry: Evidence from the Railroads. *Econ. Inquiry*, January 1983, *21*(1), pp. 39–52. [G: U.S.]

Gothoskar, S. S. Drug Control: India. *World Devel.*, March 1983, *11*(3), pp. 223–28. [G: India]

Graham, John D. and Vaupel, James W. The Value of Life: What Difference Does It Make? In *Zeckhauser, R. J. and Leebaert, D., eds.*, 1983, pp. 176–86. [G: U.S.]

Grether, David M. and Wilde, Louis L. Consumer Choice and Information: New Experimental Evidence. *Info. Econ. Policy*, 1983, *1*(2), pp. 115–44. [G: U.S.]

Guither, Harold D. Citizen and Consumer Groups in Policies Affecting Farm Structure. In *Brewster, D. E.; Rasmussen, W. D. and Youngberg, G., eds.*, 1983, pp. 87–101. [G: U.S.]

Hirshhorn, Ronald. Regulating Quality in Product Markets. In *Dewees, D. N., ed.*, 1983, pp. 55–81. [G: Canada]

Hirshhorn, Ronald. The Administration of the *Hazardous Products Act*. In *Dewees, D. N., ed.*, 1983, pp. 175–206. [G: Canada]

Hoffer, George E. and Reilly, Robert J. Auto Recalls and Consumer Recall: Effects on Sales. *Challenge*, Sept.–Oct. 1983, *26*(4), pp. 56–57. [G: U.S.]

Kelman, Steven. Regulation and Paternalism. In *Machan, T. R. and Johnson, M. B., eds.*, 1983, pp. 217–48.

Kunreuther, Howard; Kleindorfer, Paul R. and Pauly, Mark V. Insurance Regulation and Consumer Behavior in the United States: The Property and Liability Industry. *Z. ges. Staatswiss.*, October 1983, *139*(3), pp. 452–72. [G: U.S.]

Lane, Sylvai and Papathanasis, Anastasios. Certification and Industry Concentration Ratios. *Antitrust Bull.*, Summer 1983, *28*(2), pp. 381–95. [G: U.S.]

Layton, Allan P. The Impact of Increased Penalties on Australian Drink/Driving Behaviour. *Logist. Transp. Rev.*, October 1983, *19*(3), pp. 261–66. [G: Australia]

Layton, Allan P. and Weigh, Jeffrey C. The Efficacy of Some Recent Australian Road Safety Policy Initiatives. *Logist. Transp. Rev.*, October 1983, *19*(3), pp. 267–78. [G: Australia]

Lehert, Ph. and De Wasch, A. Representation of Best Buys for a Heterogeneous Population. In *Hansen, P., ed.*, 1983, pp. 221–28.

Lesser, William H. Information in Food Advertising: Comment. In *Connor, J. M. and Ward, R. W., eds.*, 1983, pp. 387–92. [G: U.S.]

Loescher, Samuel M. The Effects of Disseminating Comparative Grocery Chain Prices by the Indiana Public Interest Research Group: A Case Study. In *Connor, J. M. and Ward, R. W., eds.*, 1983, pp. 345–61. [G: U.S.]

Lowenthal, Franklin. Product Warranty Period: A Markovian Approach to Estimation and Analysis of Repair and Replacement Costs—A Comment. *Accounting Rev.*, October 1983, *58*(4), pp. 837–38.

MacDonald, James M.; Scheffman, David T. and Whitten, Ira Taylor. Advertising and Quality in Food Products: Some New Evidence on the Nelson Hypothesis. In *Connor, J. M. and Ward, R. W., eds.*, 1983, pp. 137–47. [G: U.S.]

Mann, Michael. Advertising and Quality in Food Products: Some New Evidence on the Nelson Hypothesis: Commentary. In *Connor, J. M. and Ward, R. W., eds.*, 1983, pp. 159–60. [G: U.S.]

Metzger, Margaret Ann. Televised Food Advertising Directed to Children: The Constitutionality of Restrictions. In *Connor, J. M. and Ward, R. W., eds.*, 1983, pp. 423–36. [G: U.S.]

Metzger, Michael R. Cherries, Lemons, and the FTC: Minimum Quality Standards in the Retail Used Automobile Industry. *Econ. Inquiry*, January 1983, *21*(1), pp. 129–39. [G: U.S.]

Moore, Beverly C., Jr. Product Safety: Who Should Absorb the Cost? In *Snoeyenbos, M.; Almeder, R. and Humber, J., eds.*, 1983, *1972*, pp. 391–95.

Noll, Roger G. and Owen, Bruce M. The Predictability of Interest Group Arguments. In *Noll, R. G. and Owen, B. M.*, 1983, pp. 53–65. [G: U.S.]

Palfrey, Thomas R. and Romer, Thomas. Warranties, Performance, and the Resolution of Buyer–Seller Disputes. *Bell J. Econ. (See Rand J. Econ. after 4/85)*, Spring 1983, *14*(1), pp. 97–117.

Peterson, Richard L. Consumer Finance. In *Benston, G. J., ed.*, 1983, pp. 185–212. [G: U.S.]

Polinsky, A. Mitchell and Rogerson, William P. Products Liability, Consumer Misperceptions, and Market Power. *Bell J. Econ. (See Rand J. Econ. after 4/85)*, Autumn 1983, *14*(2), pp. 581–89.

Reilly, Robert J. and Hoffer, George E. Will Retarding the Information Flow on Automobile Recalls

Affect Consumer Demand? *Econ. Inquiry*, July 1983, *21*(3), pp. 444–47. **[G: U.S.]**

Rens, Lawrence A. Consumer Organizations as a Source of Information in Food Markets. **In** *Connor, J. M. and Ward, R. W., eds.*, 1983, pp. 403–18. **[G: U.S.]**

Schöppe, Günter. Consumer Protection by Law and Information: A View of Western German Practice and Experience. *Z. ges. Staatswiss.*, October 1983, *139*(3), pp. 545–67. **[G: W. Germany]**

Schwartz, Alan. The Enforceability of Security Interests in Consumer Goods. *J. Law Econ.*, April 1983, *26*(1), pp. 117–62. **[G: U.S.]**

Schwartz, Alan and Wilde, Louis L. Warranty Markets and Public Policy. *Info. Econ. Policy*, 1983, *1*(1), pp. 55–67.

Shapiro, Carl. Consumer Protection Policy in the United States. *Z. ges. Staatswiss.*, October 1983, *139*(3), pp. 527–44. **[G: U.S.]**

Shapiro, Lynn E. Legal Issues Arising under the Consumer Choice Proposals. **In** *Meyer, J. A., ed.*, 1983, pp. 269–94. **[G: U.S.]**

Silver, Rugenia. Federal and State Laws on Consumer Financial Services: The Doctrine of Preemption. *Fed. Res. Bull.*, November 1983, *69*(11), pp. 823–29. **[G: U.S.]**

Sporleder, Thomas L.; Kramer, Carol S. and Epp, Donald J. Food Safety. **In** *Armbruster, W. J.; Henderson, D. R. and Knutson, Ronald D., eds.*, 1983, pp. 269–303. **[G: U.S.]**

Stanton, Tom. Commentary [Televised Food Advertising Directed to Children: The Constitutionality of Restrictions] [Changing Structure of Mass Media Markets: Relevance for Policy Initiatives on Advertising in the Food System]. **In** *Connor, J. M. and Ward, R. W., eds.*, 1983, pp. 461–64. **[G: U.S.]**

Teeters, Nancy H. Statement to U.S. Senate Subcommittee on Consumer Affairs of the Committee on Banking, Housing, and Urban Affairs, July 19, 1983. *Fed. Res. Bull.*, August 1983, *69*(8), pp. 599–601. **[G: U.S.]**

Temin, Peter. Costs and Benefits in Switching Drugs from Rx to OTC. *J. Health Econ.*, December 1983, *2*(3), pp. 187–205. **[G: U.S.]**

Trebilcock, Michael J. Regulating Service Quality in Professional Markets. **In** *Dewees, D. N., ed.*, 1983, pp. 83–107. **[G: U.S.]**

Trebilcock, Michael J. and Shaul, Jeffrey. Regulating the Quality of Psychotherapeutic Services. **In** *Dewees, D. N., ed.*, 1983, pp. 275–91. **[G: Canada]**

Wardell, William M. Economic or Medical Criteria, or Both, in Policy Decisions about Medicines? [Costs and Benefits in Switching Drugs from Rx to OTC]. *J. Health Econ.*, December 1983, *2*(3), pp. 275–79. **[G: U.S.]**

Wassermann, Ursula. National Legislation on Hormones and Antibiotics. *J. World Trade Law*, March–April 1983, *17*(2), pp. 158–69. **[G: Selected Countries]**

Werthan, Susan M. Alternative Mortgages and Truth in Lending. *Fed. Res. Bull.*, May 1983, *69*(5), pp. 327–32. **[G: U.S.]**

Witt, Robert C. and Urrutia, Jorge. A Comparative Economic Analysis of Tort Liability and No-Fault Compensation Systems in Automobile Insurance. *J. Risk Ins.*, December 1983, *50*(4), pp. 631–69. **[G: U.S.]**

Young, Trevor. The Demand for Cigarettes: Alternative Specifications of Fujii's Model. *Appl. Econ.*, April 1983, *15*(2), pp. 203–11. **[G: U.S.]**

Zussman, David. Consumer Complaint Behavior and Third Party Mediation. *Can. Public Policy*, June 1983, *9*(2), pp. 223–35. **[G: Canada]**

Graham, John D. and Vaupel, James W. The Value of Life: What Difference Does It Make? **In** *Zeckhauser, R. J. and Leebaert, D., eds.*, 1983, pp. 176–86. **[G: U.S.]**

930 Urban Economics

9300 General

Butt, John. Belfast and Glasgow: Connections and Comparisons, 1790–1850. **In** *Devine, T. M. and Dickson, D., eds.*, 1983, pp. 193–203. **[G: U.K.; Ireland]**

Congdon, Peter. A Model for the Interaction of Migration and Commuting. *Urban Stud.*, May 1983, *20*(2), pp. 185–95. **[G: U.K.]**

Dickson, David. The Place of Dublin in the Eighteenth-Century Irish Economy. **In** *Devine, T. M. and Dickson, D., eds.*, 1983, pp. 177–92. **[G: Ireland]**

Hochman, Harold M. and Nitzan, Shmuel. Tiebout and Sympathy. *Math. Soc. Sci.*, November 1983, *6*(2), pp. 195–214.

Janelle, Donald and Goodchild, Michael. Diurnal Patterns of Social Group Distributions in a Canadian City. *Econ. Geogr.*, October 1983, *59*(4), pp. 403–25. **[G: Canada]**

Kennedy, Peter E. On an Inappropriate Means of Reducing Multicollinearity. *Reg. Sci. Urban Econ.*, November 1983, *13*(4), pp. 579–81.

Lake, Robert W. Readings in Urban Analysis: Introduction. **In** *Lake, R. W., ed.*, 1983, pp. ix–xxv.

LeRoy, Stephen F. and Sonstelie, Jon C. Paradise Lost and Regained: Transportation Innovation, Income, and Residential Location. *J. Urban Econ.*, January 1983, *13*(1), pp. 67–89. **[G: U.S.]**

Molotch, Harvey L. Toward a More Human Human Ecology: An Urban Research Strategy. **In** *Lake, R. W., ed.*, 1983, *1967*, pp. 65–72.

Shaw, Denis J. B. The Soviet Urban General Plan and Recent Advances in Soviet Urban Planning. *Urban Stud.*, November 1983, *20*(4), pp. 393–403. **[G: U.S.S.R.]**

Sullivan, Arthur M. Second-Best Policies for Congestion Externalities. *J. Urban Econ.*, July 1983, *14*(1), pp. 105–23.

Sullivan, Arthur M. The General Equilibrium Effects of Congestion Externalities. *J. Urban Econ.*, July 1983, *14*(1), pp. 80–104.

Wyrobisz, Andrej. Functional Types of Polish Towns in the XVI–XVIIIth Centuries. *J. Europ. Econ. Hist.*, Spring 1983, *12*(1), pp. 69–103. **[G: Poland]**

931 Urban Economics and Public Policy

9310 Urban Economics and Public Policy

Adepoju, Aderanti. Issues in the Study of Migration and Urbanization in Africa South of the Sahara.

In *Morrison, P. A., ed.*, 1983, pp. 115–49. [G: Sub-Saharan Africa]

Almore, Mary G. and Richardson, Frances. Urban Health Care Delivery in the Sunbelt. **In** *Ballard, S. C. and James, T. E., eds.*, 1983, pp. 93–106. [G: U.S.]

Alonso, William. A Theory of the Urban Land Market. **In** *Lake, R. W., ed.*, 1983, *1960*, pp. 1–10.

Alperovich, Gershon. An Empirical Study of Population Density Gradients and Their Determinants. *J. Reg. Sci.*, November 1983, *23*(4), pp. 529–40. [G: Israel]

Alperovich, Gershon. Determinants of Urban Population Density Functions: A Procedure for Efficient Estimates. *Reg. Sci. Urban Econ.*, May 1983, *13*(2), pp. 287–95. [G: Israel]

Alperovich, Gershon. Economic Analysis of Intraurban Migration in Tel-Aviv. *J. Urban Econ.*, November 1983, *14*(3), pp. 280–92. [G: Israel]

Alperovich, Gershon. Lagged Response in Intra-Urban Migration of Home Owners. *Reg. Stud.*, October 1983, *17*(5), pp. 297–304. [G: Israel]

Asabere, Paul K. and Owusu-Banahene, K. Population Density Function For Ghanaian (African) Cities: An Empirical Note. *J. Urban Econ.*, November 1983, *14*(3), pp. 370–79. [G: Ghana]

Ashcroft, Brian. The Scottish Region and the Regions of Scotland. **In** *Ingham, K. P. D. and Love, J., eds.*, 1983, pp. 173–87. [G: U.K.]

Bahl, Roy and Schroeder, Larry. The Business License Tax. **In** *Bahl, R. and Miller, B. D., eds.*, 1983, pp. 82–99. [G: Philippines]

Banerjee, Biswajit. The Role of the Informal Sector in the Migration Process: A Test of Probabilistic Migration Models and Labour Market Segmentation for India. *Oxford Econ. Pap.*, November 1983, *35*(3), pp. 399–422. [G: India]

Barr, Brenton M. Industrial Parks as Locational Environments: A Research Challenge. **In** *Hamilton, F. E. I. and Linge, G. J. R., eds.*, 1983, pp. 423–40.

Barrese, James T. Efficiency and Equity Considerations in the Operation of Transfer of Development Rights Plans. *Land Econ.*, May 1983, *59*(2), pp. 235–41.

Bates, Timothy. The Declining Relative Incomes of Urban Black Households. *Challenge*, May/June 1983, *26*(2), pp. 48–49. [G: U.S.]

Beck, John H. Tax Competition, Uniform Assessment, and the Benefit Principle. *J. Urban Econ.*, March 1983, *13*(2), pp. 127–46.

Beed, Clive; Singell, Larry D. and Wyatt, Ray. The Dynamics of Intra-City Unemployment Patterns. *Australian Bull. Lab.*, December 1983, *10*(1), pp. 36–46. [G: Australia]

Bentham, C. G. Urban Problems and Public Dissatisfaction in the Metropolitan Areas of England. *Reg. Stud.*, October 1983, *17*(5), pp. 339–46. [G: U.K.]

Berechman, Joseph and Paaswell, Robert E. Rail Rapid Transit Investment and CBD Revitalisation: Methodology and Results. *Urban Stud.*, November 1983, *20*(4), pp. 471–86. [G: U.S.]

Berger, Curtis J. Controlling Urban Growth via Tax Policy. **In** *Carr, J. H. and Duensing, E. E., eds.*, 1983, *1979*, pp. 254–74. [G: U.S.]

Berry, Brian J. L. and Horton, Frank E. Assurance of Municipal Water Supplies. **In** *Glassner, M. I., ed.*, 1983, *1974*, pp. 507–22. [G: U.S.]

Bialkovskaia, V. and Novikov, V. Urbanization and the Problem of Restricting the Growth of Very Large Cities. *Prob. Econ.*, October 1983, *26*(6), pp. 23–39. [G: U.S.S.R.]

Bird, Richard M. and Slack, N. Enid. Urban Finance and User Charges. **In** *Break, G. F., ed.*, 1983, pp. 211–37. [G: U.S.; Canada]

Blewett, Robert A. Fiscal Externalities and Residential Growth Controls: A Theory-of-Clubs Perspective. *Public Finance Quart.*, January 1983, *11*(1), pp. 3–20.

Bradbury, Katharine L. Structural Fiscal Distress in Cities—Causes and Consequences. *New Eng. Econ. Rev.*, January/February 1983, pp. 32–43. [G: U.S.]

Bradbury, Katharine L. and Small, Kenneth A. Central City Decline: The Case for Attacking the Symptoms. **In** *Henderson, J. V., ed.*, 1983, pp. 191–216. [G: U.S.]

Brecher, Charles and Horton, Raymond D. Expenditures. **In** *Brecher, C. and Horton, R. D., eds.*, 1983, pp. 68–96. [G: U.S.]

Brueckner, Jan K. Central-City Income Redistribution and the Flight to the Suburbs: A Stylized Model. *Reg. Sci. Urban Econ.*, May 1983, *13*(2), pp. 177–93.

Brueckner, Jan K. Property Value Maximization and Public Sector Efficiency. *J. Urban Econ.*, July 1983, *14*(1), pp. 1–15.

Brueckner, Jan K. and Fansler, David A. The Economics of Urban Sprawl: Theory and Evidence on the Spatial Sizes of Cities. *Rev. Econ. Statist.*, August 1983, *65*(3), pp. 479–82. [G: U.S.]

Buhr, Walter. Mikroökonomische Modelle der von Thünenschen Standorttheorie. (Microeconomic Models of von Thünen's Location Theory. With English summary.) *Z. Wirtschaft. Sozialwissen.*, 1983, *103*(6), pp. 589–627.

Bularzik, Mary J. The Bonds of Belonging: Leonora O'Reilly and Social Reform. *Labor Hist.*, Winter 1983, *24*(1), pp. 60–83. [G: U.S.]

Cain, Louis P. To Annex or Not? A Tale of Two Towns: Evanston and Hyde Park. *Exploration Econ. Hist.*, January 1983, *20*(1), pp. 58–72. [G: U.S.]

Cason, Forrest M. Land-Use Concomitants of Urban Fiscal Squeeze. **In** *Carr, J. H. and Duensing, E. E., eds.*, 1983, *1981*, pp. 67–81. [G: U.S.]

Chall, Daniel E. Neighborhood Changes in New York City during the 1970s: Are the "Gentry" Returning? *Fed. Res. Bank New York Quart. Rev.*, Winter 1983-84, *8*(4), pp. 38–48. [G: U.S.]

Chan, Paul. Population Distribution and Development Strategies in Peninsular Malaysia. **In** *Oberai, A. S., ed.*, 1983, pp. 27–78. [G: Malaysia]

Chan, Paul. The Political Economy of Urban Chinese Squatters in Metropolitan Kuala Lumpur. **In** *Lim, L. Y. C. and Gosling, L. A. P., eds.*, 1983, pp. 232–44. [G: Malaysia]

Charney, Alberta H. Intraurban Manufacturing Location Decisions and Local Tax Differentials. *J. Urban Econ.*, September 1983, *14*(2), pp. 184–205. [G: U.S.]

Cherunalim, Francis. Urbanisation Without Labour Absorption. *Econ. Aff.*, October–December 1983, *28*(4), pp. 844–50. **[G: LDCs]**

Church, Richard and Stimson, Robert. Modelling Spatial Allocation–Location Solutions for General Practitioner Medical Services in Cities: The Equity-Revenue Maximizing Conflict Case. *Reg. Sci. Urban Econ.*, May 1983, *13*(2), pp. 161–72.

Clapp, John M. A General Model of Equilibrium Locations. *J. Reg. Sci.*, November 1983, *23*(4), pp. 461–78.

Clarke, M. and Wilson, A. G. The Dynamics of Urban Spatial Structure: Progress and Problems. *J. Reg. Sci.*, February 1983, *23*(1), pp. 1–18.

Coffin, Donald A. and Nelson, Michael A. An Empirical Test: The Economic Effects of Land Value Taxation—Comment. *Growth Change,* July 1983, *14*(3), pp. 44–46. **[G: U.S.]**

Cooke, Timothy W. Testing a Model of Intraurban Firm Relocation. *J. Urban Econ.*, May 1983, *13*(3), pp. 257–82. **[G: U.S.]**

Cord, Steven B. Taxing Land More Than Buildings: The Record in Pennsylvania. **In** *Harriss, C. L., ed.*, 1983, pp. 172–79. **[G: U.S.]**

Council on Development Choices for the '80s. Factors Shaping Development in the '80s. **In** *Carr, J. H. and Duensing, E. E., eds.*, 1983, *1981*, pp. 3–17. **[G: U.S.]**

Courtney, John M. Intervention through Land Use Regulation. **In** *Dunkerley, H. B., ed.*, 1983, pp. 153–70.

Crone, Theodore M. Elements of an Economic Justification for Municipal Zoning. *J. Urban Econ.*, September 1983, *14*(2), pp. 168–83. **[G: U.S.]**

Cushing, Brian J. and Straszheim, Mahlon R. Agglomeration Economies in the Public and Private Sector: Urban Spatial and Fiscal Structure. **In** *Quigley, J. M., ed.*, 1983, pp. 223–42. **[G: U.S.]**

Dahmann, Donald C. Subjective Assessments of Neighborhood Quality by Size of Place. *Urban Stud.*, February 1983, *20*(1), pp. 31–45. **[G: U.S.]**

Denman, Donald R. Lessons from Experience: A Review of Britain's Land Policies. **In** *Lefcoe, G., ed.*, 1983, pp. 59–69. **[G: U.K.]**

Donnithorne, Audrey. Hong Kong as an Economic Model for the Great Cities of China. **In** *Youngson, A. J., ed.*, 1983, pp. 282–310. **[G: Hong Kong]**

Doolittle, Frederick C. Federal Grants for Urban Economic Development. **In** *Break, G. F., ed.*, 1983, pp. 75–91. **[G: U.S.]**

Dowall, David E. Reducing the Cost Effects of Local Land Use Controls. **In** *Carr, J. H. and Duensing, E. E., eds.*, 1983, *1981*, pp. 173–89. **[G: U.S.]**

Dowall, David E. The Effects of Tax and Expenditure Limitations on Local Land Use Policies. **In** *Quigley, J. M., ed.*, 1983, pp. 69–87. **[G: U.S.]**

Drennan, Matthew. The Local Economy and Local Revenues. **In** *Brecher, C. and Horton, R. D., eds.*, 1983, pp. 19–44. **[G: U.S.]**

Eckart, Wolfgang. Land Speculation and the Rental Price of Housing. *J. Urban Econ.*, January 1983, *13*(1), pp. 1–21.

Eckart, Wolfgang. The Neutrality of Land Taxation in an Uncertain World. *Nat. Tax J.*, June 1983, *36*(2), pp. 237–41.

Ehrenberg, Ronald G.; Sherman, Daniel R. and Schwarz, Joshua L. Unions and Productivity in the Public Sector: A Study of Municipal Libraries. *Ind. Lab. Relat. Rev.*, January 1983, *36*(2), pp. 199–213. **[G: U.S.]**

Eisinger, Peter K. Municipal Residency Requirements and the Local Economy. *Soc. Sci. Quart.*, March 1983, *64*(1), pp. 85–96. **[G: U.S.]**

Elliott, Harold M. Surrounding Larger Neighbors and the Atlantic Coast Cardinal Neighbor Gradient. *Econ. Geogr.*, October 1983, *59*(4), pp. 426–44. **[G: U.S.]**

Evans, Alan W. Errata [The Determination of the Price of Land]. *Urban Stud.*, November 1983, *20*(4), pp. 391.

Evans, Alan W. The Determination of the Price of Land. *Urban Stud.*, May 1983, *20*(2), pp. 119–29.

Farr, Cheryl. Modifying Land Use Regulations for Economic Development. **In** *Carr, J. H. and Duensing, E. E., eds.*, 1983, *1980*, pp. 207–28. **[G: U.S.]**

Fogarty, Michael S. Decline of the Metropolitan Economy: A New Interpretation. *Urban Stud.*, November 1983, *20*(4), pp. 495–97.

Ford, Ramona L. Revitalizing the Distressed Community: GSOC and ESOP Alternatives to Enterprise Zones. *Growth Change,* October 1983, *14*(4), pp. 22–31. **[G: U.S.]**

Frieden, Bernard J. The Exclusionary Effect of Growth Controls. *Ann. Amer. Acad. Polit. Soc. Sci.*, January 1983, *465*, pp. 123–35. **[G: U.S.]**

Garnick, Daniel H. Shifting Patterns in the Growth of Metropolitan and Nonmetropolitan Areas. *Surv. Curr. Bus.*, May 1983, *63*(5), pp. 39–44. **[G: U.S.]**

Garofalo, Gasper A. and Fogarty, Michael S. A Note on the Measurement of Agglomeration Economies with Compensation for Urban Disamenities. *J. Environ. Econ. Manage.*, December 1983, *10*(4), pp. 383–87. **[G: U.S.]**

Gibbs, David C. The Effect of International and National Developments on the Clothing Industry of the Manchester Conurbation. **In** *Hamilton, F. E. I. and Linge, G. J. R., eds.*, 1983, pp. 233–54. **[G: U.K.; Selected Countries]**

Giles, David E. A. and Hampton, Peter. Urban Migration in New Zealand: Dummy Variable Interpretations. *J. Urban Econ.*, July 1983, *14*(1), pp. 124–25. **[G: New Zealand]**

Gillen, William J. and Guccione, Antonio. The Relevance of Wage Differentials in Neoclassical Urban Growth. *Reg. Sci. Urban Econ.*, November 1983, *13*(4), pp. 547–55. **[G: Canada]**

Gillespie, Fran. Comprehending the Slow Pace of Urbanization in Paraguay between 1950 and 1972. *Econ. Develop. Cult. Change,* January 1983, *31*(2), pp. 355–75. **[G: Paraguay]**

Goldman, Ellis G. and Field, Charles G. Summary of an Article on Reforming Land-Use Regulations. *Amer. Real Estate Urban Econ. Assoc. J.*, Summer 1983, *11*(2), pp. 300–319. **[G: U.S.]**

Goldscheider, Calvin. Modernization, Migration, and Urbanization. **In** *Morrison, P. A., ed.*, 1983, pp. 47–66. **[G: LDCs; MDCs]**

Goldsmith, Mike. The Role of Central Government

in Local Economic Development: Comment. **In** *Young, K., ed.*, 1983, pp. 129–32. **[G: U.K.]**

Golini, Antonio. Present Relationships between Migration and Urbanization: The Italian Case. **In** *Morrison, P. A., ed.*, 1983, pp. 187–209. **[G: Italy]**

Gottdiener, Mark. Understanding Metropolitan Deconcentration: A Clash of Paradigms. *Soc. Sci. Quart.*, June 1983, *64*(2), pp. 227–46.

Green, Cynthia B. and Sanger, Mary Bryna. Aiding the Poor. **In** *Brecher, C. and Horton, R. D., eds.*, 1983, pp. 99–130. **[G: U.S.]**

Greenberg, Michael R. Urbanization and Cancer: Changing Mortality Patterns? *Int. Reg. Sci. Rev.*, October 1983, *8*(2), pp. 127–45. **[G: U.S.]**

Grieson, Ronald E. and Wittman, Donald A. Regulation May Be No Worse Than Its Alternatives. **In** *Grieson, R. E., ed.*, 1983, pp. 171–91.

Guinness, Patrick. The Gelandangan of Yogyakarta. *Bull. Indonesian Econ. Stud.*, April 1983, *19*(1), pp. 68–82. **[G: Indonesia]**

Guldmann, Jean-Michel. Modeling the Structure of Gas Distribution Costs in Urban Areas. *Reg. Sci. Urban Econ.*, August 1983, *13*(3), pp. 299–316. **[G: U.S.]**

Haining, Robert. Modeling Intraurban Price Competition: An Example of Gasoline Pricing. *J. Reg. Sci.*, November 1983, *23*(4), pp. 517–28. **[G: U.K.]**

Hajdu, Joe. Postwar Development and Planning of West German Cities. **In** *Wild, T., ed.*, 1983, pp. 16–39. **[G: W. Germany]**

Hall, Peter. Housing, Planning, Land, and Local Finance: The British Experience. **In** *Lefcoe, G., ed.*, 1983, pp. 47–58. **[G: U.K.]**

Halpin, Michael C. New Land Use Economics and Opportunities for the 1980s. **In** *Carr, J. H. and Duensing, E. E., eds.*, 1983, *1980*, pp. 277–90. **[G: U.S.]**

Harvey, David. The Urban Process under Capitalism: A Framework for Analysis. **In** *Lake, R. W., ed.*, 1983, *1978*, pp. 197–227. **[G: U.S.; U.K.]**

Hatta, Tatsuo. Competition and Nationally Optimum Resource Allocation under the Presence of Urban Traffic Congestion. *J. Urban Econ.*, September 1983, *14*(2), pp. 145–67.

Haurin, Donald R. The Effect of Reimbursement of Worker's Transport Costs: The Case of Urban Areas in Japan. *J. Urban Econ.*, March 1983, *13*(2), pp. 205–15.

Hayton, K. Community Business in Scotland. *Reg. Stud.*, June 1983, *17*(3), pp. 204–08. **[G: U.K.]**

Henderson, J. Vernon. Industrial Bases and City Sizes. *Amer. Econ. Rev.*, May 1983, *73*(2), pp. 164–68.

Hendon, William S. Admission Income and Historic Houses: Higher Revenue Is Associated with Price Policy, More Services and Less Education. *Amer. J. Econ. Soc.*, October 1983, *42*(4), pp. 473–82. **[G: U.K.]**

Hicks, Donald A. National Urban Land Policy: Facing the Inevitability of City and Regional Evolution. **In** *Lefcoe, G., ed.*, 1983, pp. 21–39. **[G: U.S.]**

Hill, Richard Child. Capital Accumulation and Urbanization in the United States. **In** *Lake, R. W., ed.*, 1983, *1977*, pp. 228–49. **[G: U.S.]**

Hirschman, Charles. Recent Urbanization Trends in Peninsular Malaysia. **In** *Lim, D., ed.*, 1983, *1976*, pp. 111–24. **[G: Malaysia]**

Hodge, Gerald. Canadian Small Town Renaissance: Implications for Settlement System Concepts. *Reg. Stud.*, February 1983, *17*(1), pp. 19–28. **[G: Canada]**

Hoffman, Joan. Urban Squeeze Plays: New York City Crises of the 1930s and 1970s. *Rev. Radical Polit. Econ.*, Summer 1983, *15*(2), pp. 29–57. **[G: U.S.]**

Holland, Daniel M. and McCarney, Patricia L. User Fees and Charges. **In** *Susskind, L. E. and Serio, J. F., eds.*, 1983, pp. 81–103. **[G: U.S.]**

Hooper, Diana J. and Walker, David F. Innovative and Cooperative Entrepreneurship: Towards a New Thrust in Industrial Development Policy. **In** *Hamilton, F. E. I. and Linge, G. J. R., eds.*, 1983, pp. 217–32. **[G: U.K.; Canada]**

Hsu, Song-ken. Pricing in an Urban Spatial Monopoly: A General Analysis. *J. Reg. Sci.*, May 1983, *23*(2), pp. 165–75.

Hugo, Graeme J. New Conceptual Approaches to Migration in the Context of Urbanization: A Discussion Based on the Indonesian Experience. **In** *Morrison, P. A., ed.*, 1983, pp. 69–113. **[G: Indonesia]**

Inoue, Shunichi. Stagnant Growth of Japanese Major Metropolitan Regions in the Era of Post-industrial Development. **In** *Morrison, P. A., ed.*, 1983, pp. 211–37. **[G: Japan]**

Izraeli, Oded. Federal Individual Income Tax and Allocation of Labor between SMSA's. *J. Reg. Sci.*, February 1983, *23*(1), pp. 105–13. **[G: U.S.]**

Izraeli, Oded. The Effect of Variations in Cost of Living and City Size on the Rate of Return to Schooling. *Quart. Rev. Econ. Bus.*, Winter 1983, *23*(4), pp. 93–108. **[G: U.S.]**

Jackson, Peter M. Urban Fiscal Stress in U.K. Cities. **In** *Biehl, D.; Roskamp, K. W. and Stolper, W. F., eds.*, 1983, pp. 329–47. **[G: U.K.]**

Jacobesen, Christian Wells. A Correction to Whitney and Boots' 'An Examination of Residential Mobility through the Use of the Log-Linear Model: Part II.' *Reg. Sci. Urban Econ.*, May 1983, *13*(2), pp. 173–76. **[G: Canada]**

Johnson, George E. Intermetropolitan Wage Differentials in the United States. **In** *Triplett, J. E., ed.*, 1983, pp. 309–30. **[G: U.S.]**

Jud, G. Donald. School Quality and Intra-Metropolitan Mobility: A Further Test of the Tiebout Hypothesis. *J. Behav. Econ.*, Winter 1983, *12*(2), pp. 37–55. **[G: U.S.]**

Kasper, Hirschel. Toward Estimating the Incidence of Journey-to-Work Costs. *Urban Stud.*, May 1983, *20*(2), pp. 197–208. **[G: U.K.]**

Kau, James B.; Lee, Cheng Few and Chen, Rong C. Structural Shifts in Urban Population Density Gradients: An Empirical Investigation. *J. Urban Econ.*, May 1983, *13*(3), pp. 364–77. **[G: U.S.]**

Kelley, Allen C. and Williamson, Jeffrey G. A Computable General Equilibrium Model of Third-World Urbanization and City Growth: Preliminary Comparative Statics. **In** *Kelley, A. C.; Sanderson, W. C. and Williamson, J. G., eds.*, 1983, pp. 3–41. **[G: LDCs]**

Kiel, Lisa J. and McKenzie, Richard B. The Impact of Tenure on the Flow of Federal Benefits to SMSA's. *Public Choice,* 1983, *41* (2), pp. 285–93. **[G: U.S.]**

Kieschnick, Michael. Venture Capital and Urban Development. **In** *Barker, M., ed. (I),* 1983, pp. 303–58. **[G: U.S.]**

Kim, Joochul. Factors Affecting Urban-to-Rural Migration. *Growth Change,* July 1983, *14* (3), pp. 38–43. **[G: U.S.]**

Lahiri, Kajal and Numrich, Richard P. An Econometric Study on the Dynamics of Urban Spatial Structure. *J. Urban Econ.,* July 1983, *14* (1), pp. 55–79. **[G: U.S.]**

Lamb, Richard F. The Extent and Form of Exurban Sprawl. *Growth Change,* January 1983, *14* (1), pp. 40–47. **[G: U.S.]**

Lefcoe, George. The Market's Place in Land Policy. **In** *Carr, J. H. and Duensing, E. E., eds.,* 1983, *1980,* pp. 242–53. **[G: U.S.]**

Leven, Charles L. Reversing Metropolitan Concentration as an Economic Issue. *J. Econ. Educ.,* Spring 1983, *14* (2), pp. 50–64. **[G: U.S.]**

Levine, Charles H.; Rubin, Irene S. and Wolohojian, George C. Fiscal Stress and Local Government Adaptations: Toward a Multi-stage Theory of Retrenchment. **In** *Henderson, J. V., ed.,* 1983, pp. 253–303. **[G: U.S.]**

Lewis, W. Arthur. Unemployment in Developing Countries. **In** *Lewis, W. A.,* 1983, *1967,* pp. 411–20.

Ley, David and Mercer, John. Locational Conflict and the Politics of Consumption. **In** *Lake, R. W., ed.,* 1983, *1980,* pp. 118–42.

Lindsey, N. Fostering New Enterprises: Enterprise Workshops in Birmingham. *Reg. Stud.,* June 1983, *17* (3), pp. 208–10. **[G: U.K.]**

Liu, Yih-wu and Stocks, Anthony H. A Labor-Oriented Quarterly Econometric Forecasting Model of the Youngstown–Warren SMSA. *Reg. Sci. Urban Econ.,* August 1983, *13* (3), pp. 317–40. **[G: U.S.]**

MacManus, Susan A. Managing Urban Growth: Citizen Perceptions and Preferences. **In** *Ballard, S. C. and James, T. E., eds.,* 1983, pp. 132–61.

Martin, Dolores Tremewan and Schmidt, James R. Expenditure Effects of Metropolitan Tax Base Sharing: A Public Choice Analysis. *Public Choice,* 1983, *40* (2), pp. 175–86.

Masser, Ian. Planning and Migration Research. **In** *Morrison, P. A., ed.,* 1983, pp. 241–60. **[G: Netherlands]**

Mathis, Edward J. and Zech, Charles E. An Empirical Test: The Economic Effects of Land Value Taxation—Reply. *Growth Change,* July 1983, *14* (3), pp. 47–48. **[G: U.S.]**

McDonald, John F. An Economic Analysis of Local Inducements for Business. *J. Urban Econ.,* May 1983, *13* (3), pp. 322–36. **[G: U.S.]**

McGregor, Alan. Neighbourhood Influence on Job Search and Job Finding Methods. *Brit. J. Ind. Relat.,* March 1983, *21* (1), pp. 91–99. **[G: U.K.]**

Meier, Richard L. Redefining Urban Ecosystems. **In** *Glassner, M. I., ed.,* 1983, *1974,* pp. 127–35.

Millerd, Frank W. Canadian Urban Industrial Growth from 1961 to 1971. *Growth Change,* January 1983, *14* (1), pp. 20–26. **[G: Canada]**

Mollenkopf, John. Economic Development. **In** *Brecher, C. and Horton, R. D., eds.,* 1983, pp. 131–57. **[G: U.S.]**

Moomaw, Ronald L. Is Population Scale a Worthless Surrogate for Business Agglomeration Economies? *Reg. Sci. Urban Econ.,* November 1983, *13* (4), pp. 525–45. **[G: U.S.]**

Morris, David. The Pendulum Swings Again: A Century of Urban Electric Systems. **In** *Brown, H. J., ed.,* 1983, pp. 37–58. **[G: U.S.]**

Mulligan, Gordon F. Central Place Populations: A Microeconomic Consideration. *J. Reg. Sci.,* February 1983, *23* (1), pp. 83–92.

Murphy, Joseph S. The Public Urban University and the Costs of Equality. **In** *Froomkin, J., ed.,* 1983, pp. 14–22. **[G: U.S.]**

Muth, Richard F. Intermetropolitan Wage Differentials in the United States: Comment. **In** *Triplett, J. E., ed.,* 1983, pp. 330–32. **[G: U.S.]**

Nelson, Joan M. Population Redistribution Policies and Migrants' Choices. **In** *Morrison, P. A., ed.,* 1983, pp. 281–312. **[G: LDCs]**

Netzer, Dick. Privatization. **In** *Brecher, C. and Horton, R. D., eds.,* 1983, pp. 158–87. **[G: U.S.]**

Nice, David C. An Intergovernmental Perspective on Urban Fragmentation. *Soc. Sci. Quart.,* March 1983, *64* (1), pp. 111–18. **[G: U.S.]**

Nord, Stephen. Urban Size and the Quality of Human Health: A Social Indicator Approach. *Atlantic Econ. J.,* July 1983, *11* (2), pp. 35–43. **[G: U.S.]**

Oberai, A. S. An Overview of Migration-influencing Policies and Programmes. **In** *Oberai, A. S., ed.,* 1983, pp. 11–26.

Okabe, Atsuyuki and Kume, Yoshiaki. A Dynamic von Thünen Model with a Demand Function. *J. Urban Econ.,* November 1983, *14* (3), pp. 355–69.

Ortona, Guido and Santagata, Walter. Industrial Mobility in the Turin Metropolitan Area, 1961–77. *Urban Stud.,* February 1983, *20* (1), pp. 59–71. **[G: Italy]**

Palumbo, George. City Government Expenditures and City Government Reality: A Comment on Sjoquist. *Nat. Tax J.,* June 1983, *36* (2), pp. 249–51. **[G: U.S.]**

Papageorgiou, Yorgo Y. and Smith, Terrence R. Agglomeration as Local Instability of Spatially Uniform Steady-States. *Econometrica,* July 1983, *51* (4), pp. 1109–19.

Parr, John B. and Jones, Colin. City Size Distributions and Urban Density Functions: Some Interrelationships. *J. Reg. Sci.,* August 1983, *23* (3), pp. 283–307. **[G: Selected MDCs]**

Parry, Robert W., Jr. Moody's Analytical Overview of 25 Leading U.S. Cities—Revisited. *Public Finance Quart.,* January 1983, *11* (1), pp. 79–93. **[G: U.S.]**

Peiser, Richard B. The Economics of Municipal Utility Districts for Land Development. *Land Econ.,* February 1983, *59* (1), pp. 43–57. **[G: U.S.]**

Peterson, George E. Rebuilding Public Infrastructure: The Institutional Choices. **In** *Lefcoe, G., ed.,* 1983, pp. 109–23. **[G: U.S.]**

Plaut, Steven E. The Economics of Population Dispersal Policy. *Urban Stud.,* August 1983, *20* (3), pp. 353–57. [G: Israel]

Pogue, Thomas F. The Incidence of Property Tax Relief via State Aid to Local Governments. *Land Econ.*, November 1983, *59*(4), pp. 420–31. [G: U.S.]

Raimondo, Henry J. Municipal Hardship in New Jersey and the Distribution of Intergovernmental Grants, 1961–1977. **In** *Dutta, M.; Hartline, J. C. and Loeb, P. D., eds.*, 1983, pp. 173–89. [G: U.S.]

Reyes, Saúl Trejo. Urban Labour Markets in Developing Countries. **In** *Urquidi, V. L. and Reyes, S. T., eds.*, 1983, pp. 41–54.

Rijk, F. J. A. and Vorst, A. C. F. Equilibrium Points in an Urban Retail Model and Their Connection with Dynamical Systems. *Reg. Sci. Urban Econ.*, August 1983, *13*(3), pp. 383–99.

Roy, John R. and Lesse, Paul F. Planning Models for Non-Cooperative Situations: A Two-Player Game Approach. *Reg. Sci. Urban Econ.*, May 1983, *13*(2), pp. 195–211.

Sardy, Hyman. The Economic Impact of Inflation on Urban Areas. **In** *Schmukler, N. and Marcus, E., eds.*, 1983, pp. 312–25. [G: U.S.]

Shaw, Gareth. Trends in Consumer Behaviour and Retailing. **In** *Wild, T., ed.*, 1983, pp. 108–29. [G: W. Germany]

Shieh, Yeung-nan. Location and Bid Price Curves of the Urban Firm. *Urban Stud.*, November 1983, *20*(4), pp. 491–94.

Shieh, Yeung-nan and Mai, Chao-cheng. A Firm's Bid Price Curve and the Neoclassical Theory of Production: A Correction and Further Analysis. *Southern Econ. J.*, July 1983, *50*(1), pp. 230–33.

Simmons, Alan B. A Review and Evaluation of Attempts to Constrain Migration to Selected Urban Centres and Regions. **In** *Todaro, M. P., ed.*, 1983, *1981*, pp. 213–33. [G: Selected Countries]

Simpson, Wayne. On the Appropriate Spatial Unit for Labour Market Analysis and Policy Design. *Urban Stud.*, November 1983, *20*(4), pp. 487–89. [G: U.K.]

Sjoquist, David L. Reply and Comment on Palumbo [The Effect of the Number of Local Governments on Central City Expenditures]. *Nat. Tax J.*, June 1983, *36*(2), pp. 253–54. [G: U.S.]

Smith, Susan J. Public Policy and the Effects of Crime in the Inner City: A British Example. *Urban Stud.*, May 1983, *20*(2), pp. 229–39. [G: U.K.]

Soja, Edward; Morales, Rebecca and Wolff, Goetz. Urban Restructuring: An Analysis of Social and Spatial Change in Los Angeles. *Econ. Geogr.*, April 1983, *59*(2), pp. 195–230. [G: U.S.]

de Sola Pool, Ithiel. Communications Technology and Land Use. **In** *Carr, J. H. and Duensing, E. E., eds.*, 1983, *1980*, pp. 291–303. [G: U.S.]

Sternlieb, George and Hughes, James W. Energy Constraints and Development Patterns in the 1980s. **In** *Carr, J. H. and Duensing, E. E., eds.*, 1983, *1982*, pp. 51–66. [G: U.S.]

Stewart, Murray. The Role of Central Government in Local Economic Development. **In** *Young, K., ed.*, 1983, pp. 105–29. [G: U.K.]

Stilwell, Frank J. B. State and Capital in Urban and Regional Development. **In** *Head, B. W., ed.*, 1983, pp. 199–218. [G: Australia]

Sullivan, Arthur M. A General Equilibrium Model with External Scale Economies in Production. *J. Urban Econ.*, March 1983, *13*(2), pp. 235–55.

Sullivan, Dennis H. and Gerring, Lori F. Cross-Sectional Analysis of CBD Retail Sales: A Research Note. *Land Econ.*, February 1983, *59*(1), pp. 118–22. [G: U.S.]

Susskind, Lawrence and Horan, Cynthia. Proposition 2½: The Response to Tax Restrictions in Massachusetts. **In** *Harriss, C. L., ed.*, 1983, pp. 158–71. [G: U.S.]

Tauchen, Helen and Witte, Ann Dryden. Increased Costs of Office Building Operation and Construction: Effects on the Costs of Office Space and the Equilibrium Distribution of Offices. *Land Econ.*, August 1983, *59*(3), pp. 324–36. [G: U.S.]

To, Minh Chau; Lapointe, Alain and Kryzanowski, Lawrence. Externalities, Preferences, and Urban Residential Location: Some Empirical Evidence. *J. Urban Econ.*, November 1983, *14*(3), pp. 338–54. [G: Canada]

Tokman, Victor E. The Influence of the Urban Informal Sector on Economic Inequality. **In** *Stewart, F., ed.*, 1983, pp. 108–37. [G: Mexico; Chile]

Tuppen, J. N. The Development of French New Towns: An Assessment of Progress. *Urban Stud.*, February 1983, *20*(1), pp. 11–30. [G: France]

Varaiya, Pravin and Wiseman, Michael. Reindustrialization and the Outlook for Declining Areas. **In** *Henderson, J. V., ed.*, 1983, pp. 167–90. [G: U.S.]

Ward, J. E. and Wendell, R. E. Characterizing Efficient Points in Location Problems under the One-Infinity Norm. **In** *Thisse, J.-F. and Zoller, H. G., eds.*, 1983, pp. 413–29.

Waste, Robert J. The Early Years in the Life Cycle of City Councils: A Downsian Analysis. *Urban Stud.*, February 1983, *20*(1), pp. 73–81. [G: U.S.]

Webber, M. J. Location of Manufacturing and Operational Urban Models. **In** *Hamilton, F. E. I. and Linge, G. J. R., eds.*, 1983, pp. 141–202. [G: U.S.; U.K.; Australia; Netherlands]

Werczberger, Elia. Multiperson Multitarget Decision Making, Using the Versatility Criterion. *Reg. Sci. Urban Econ.*, February 1983, *13*(1), pp. 103–13.

Wheaton, William C. Theories of Urban Growth and Metropolitan Spatial Development. **In** *Henderson, J. V., ed.*, 1983, pp. 3–36.

White, Gordon. Urban Employment and Labour Allocation Policies. **In** *Feuchtwang, S. and Hussain, A., eds.*, 1983, pp. 257–87. [G: China]

Whitehead, Christine M. E. The Rationale for Government Intervention. **In** *Dunkerley, H. B., ed.*, 1983, pp. 108–31.

Whitney, Vincent Heath. Planning for Migration and Urbanization: Some Issues and Options for Policymakers and Planners. **In** *Morrison, P. A., ed.*, 1983, pp. 325–38. [G: LDCs]

Wild, Trevor. Urban and Rural Change in West Germany: Conclusion. **In** *Wild, T., ed.*, 1983, pp. 248–50. [G: W. Germany]

Young, Ronald. A Little Local Inequality. **In** *Brown, G. and Cook, R., eds.*, 1983, pp. 223–51. [G: U.K.]

932 Housing Economics

9320 Housing Economics (including nonurban housing)

Agarwal, Vinod B. and Phillips, Richard A. The Effect of Mortgage Rate Buydowns on Housing Prices: Recent Evidence from FHA-VA Transactions. *Amer. Real Estate Urban Econ. Assoc. J.*, Winter 1983, *11*(4), pp. 491–503. **[G: U.S.]**

Albon, Robert P. and Piggott, John. Housing Interest Rate Deregulation and the Campbell Report. *Econ. Rec.*, March 1983, *59*(164), pp. 80–87. **[G: Australia]**

Alonso, William. The Demographic Factor in Housing for the Balance of This Century. **In** *Gau, G. W. and Goldberg, M. A., eds.*, 1983, pp. 33–50.

Alperovich, Gershon. Lagged Response in Intra-Urban Migration of Home Owners. *Reg. Stud.*, October 1983, *17*(5), pp. 297–304. **[G: Israel]**

Anstie, Roslyn K.; Findlay, Christopher C. and Harper, Ian. The Impact of Inflation and Taxation on Tenure Choice and the Redistributive Effects of Home-Mortgage Interest Rate Regulation. *Econ. Rec.*, June 1983, *59*(165), pp. 105–10. **[G: Australia]**

Atkinson, Anthony B. Housing Allowances, Income Maintenance and Income Taxation. **In** *Atkinson, A. B.*, 1983, *1977*, pp. 323–35.

Atkinson, Anthony B. Introduction to Part IV: Issues of Public Policy. **In** *Atkinson, A. B.*, 1983, pp. 317–22.

Atkinson, Anthony B. and King, Mervyn A. Housing Policy, Taxation and Reform. **In** *Atkinson, A. B.*, 1983, *1980*, pp. 337–56. **[G: U.K.]**

Bajic, Vladimir. The Effects of a New Subway Line on Housing Prices in Metropolitan Toronto. *Urban Stud.*, May 1983, *20*(2), pp. 147–58. **[G: Canada]**

Bajic, Vladimir. Urban Housing Markets Modelling: Short-Run Equilibrium Implications. *Amer. Real Estate Urban Econ. Assoc. J.*, Fall 1983, *11*(3), pp. 416–38. **[G: Canada]**

Bendick, Marc, Jr. and Struyk, Raymond J. The Great Housing Experiment: Lessons for Future Social Experiments. **In** *Friedman, J. and Weinberg, D. H., eds.*, 1983, pp. 258–65. **[G: U.S.]**

Bentham, C. G. Urban Problems and Public Dissatisfaction in the Metropolitan Areas of England. *Reg. Stud.*, October 1983, *17*(5), pp. 339–46. **[G: U.K.]**

Berger, Curtis J. Controlling Urban Growth via Tax Policy. **In** *Carr, J. H. and Duensing, E. E., eds.*, 1983, *1979*, pp. 254–74. **[G: U.S.]**

Berglas, Eitan, et al. A Threshold Fund. **In** *Helpman, E.; Razin, A. and Sadka, E., eds.*, 1983, pp. 181–205. **[G: Israel]**

Blackley, Dixie and Follain, James R. Inflation, Tax Advantages to Homeownership and the Locational Choices of Households. *Reg. Sci. Urban Econ.*, November 1983, *13*(4), pp. 505–16. **[G: U.S.]**

Bloom, David E.; Preiss, Beth and Trussell, James. Mortgage Lending Discrimination and the Decision to Apply: A Methodological Note. *Amer. Real Estate Urban Econ. Assoc. J.*, Spring 1983, *11*(1), pp. 97–103. **[G: U.S.]**

Bloom, Howard S.; Ladd, Helen F. and Yinger, John. Are Property Taxes Capitalized into House Values? **In** *Zodrow, G. R., ed.*, 1983, pp. 145–63. **[G: U.S.]**

Boehm, Thomas P. and McKenzie, Joseph A. The Affordability of Alternative Mortgage Instruments: A Household Analysis. *Housing Finance Rev.*, Oct 1983, *2*(4), pp. 287–94. **[G: U.S.]**

Bone, Robert M. and Green, Milford B. Housing Assistance and Maintenance for the Métis in Northern Saskatchewan. *Can. Public Policy,* December 1983, *9*(4), pp. 476–86. **[G: Canada]**

Bourne, Larry S. Living with Uncertainty: The Changing Spatial Components of Urban Growth and Housing Demand in Canada. **In** *Gau, G. W. and Goldberg, M. A., eds.*, 1983, pp. 51–72. **[G: Canada]**

Brown, Philip W. The Demographic Future: Impacts on the Demand for Housing in Canada, 1981–2001. **In** *Gau, G. W. and Goldberg, M. A., eds.*, 1983, pp. 5–31. **[G: Canada]**

Brueckner, Jan K. Property Value Maximization and Public Sector Efficiency. *J. Urban Econ.*, July 1983, *14*(1), pp. 1–15.

Brueckner, Jan K. The Economics of Urban Yard Space: An "Implicit-Market" Model for Housing Attributes. *J. Urban Econ.*, March 1983, *13*(2), pp. 216–34.

Brueckner, Jan K. and Colwell, Peter F. A Spatial Model of Housing Attributes: Theory and Evidence. *Land Econ.*, February 1983, *59*(1), pp. 58–69. **[G: U.S.]**

Buckley, Robert M. Inflation, Homeownership Tax Subsidies, and Fiscal Illusion [The Interaction of Inflation and the U.S. Tax Subsidies of Housing]. *Nat. Tax J.*, December 1983, *36*(4), pp. 521–23. **[G: U.S.]**

Buckley, Robert M. and Ermisch, John. Theory and Empiricism in the Econometric Modelling of House Prices. *Urban Stud.*, February 1983, *20*(1), pp. 83–90. **[G: U.K.]**

Buckley, Robert M. and Van Order, Robert A. Housing and the Economy: Popular Myths. *Amer. Real Estate Urban Econ. Assoc. J.*, Winter 1983, *10*(4), pp. 421–41. **[G: U.S.]**

Burns, Leland S. Self-Help Housing: An Evaluation of Outcomes. *Urban Stud.*, August 1983, *20*(3), pp. 299–309. **[G: El Salvador]**

Buser, Stephen A. and Sanders, Anthony B. Tenure Decisions under a Progressive Tax Structure. *Amer. Real Estate Urban Econ. Assoc. J.*, Fall 1983, *11*(3), pp. 371–81.

Capozza, Dennis R. and Gau, George W. Optimal Mortgage Instrument Designs. **In** *Gau, G. W. and Goldberg, M. A., eds.*, 1983, pp. 233–58. **[G: U.S.; Canada]**

Carr, Jack L. and Smith, Lawrence B. Inflation, Uncertainty and Future Mortgage Instruments. **In** *Gau, G. W. and Goldberg, M. A., eds.*, 1983, pp. 203–31. **[G: Canada]**

Carter, Grace M.; Coleman, Sinclair B. and Wendt, James C. The Great Housing Experiment: Participation under Open Enrollment. **In** *Friedman, J.*

and Weinberg, D. H., eds., 1983, pp. 73–90. [G: U.S.]

Chambers, Edward J. Recent Comparative Trends in the Canadian and U.S. CPIS: The Treatment of Homeownership. *Can. Public Policy,* June 1983, *9*(2), pp. 236–44. [G: U.S.; Canada]

Checkoway, Barry. Large Builders, Federal Housing Programmes, and Postwar Suburbanization. **In** *Lake, R. W., ed.*, 1983, *1980,* pp. 173–96. [G: U.S.]

Chen, Alexander. Alternative Reverse Mortgages: A Simulation Analysis of Initial Benefits in Baltimore. *Housing Finance Rev.*, Oct 1983, *2*(4), pp. 295–308. [G: U.S.]

Chen, Peter S. J. Singapore's Development Strategies: A Model for Rapid Growth. **In** *Chen, P. S. J., ed.*, 1983, pp. 3–25. [G: Singapore]

Chernick, Howard and Reschovsky, Andrew. Tax Policies for Managing Urban Decline: A Microsimulation Approach. **In** *Henderson, J. V., ed.*, 1983, pp. 217–51. [G: U.S.]

Chernick, Howard and Reschovsky, Andrew. The Consequences of Limitations on Growth in the Property Tax Base. **In** *Quigley, J. M., ed.*, 1983, pp. 89–107. [G: U.S.]

Chinloy, Peter. Housing Repair and Housing Stocks. **In** *Gau, G. W. and Goldberg, M. A., eds.*, 1983, pp. 139–58. [G: Canada]

Chisholm, Nancy S. A Future for Public Housing. *Amer. Real Estate Urban Econ. Assoc. J.*, Summer 1983, *11*(2), pp. 203–20. [G: U.S.]

Clark, William A. V. and Onaka, Jun L. Life Cycle and Housing Adjustment as Explanations of Residential Mobility. *Urban Stud.*, February 1983, *20*(1), pp. 47–57. [G: New Zealand; Canada; U.S.; U.K.]

Clark, William A. V. and Onaka, Jun L. Errata [Life Cycle and Housing Adjustment as Explanations of Residential Mobility]. *Urban Stud.*, November 1983, *20*(4), pp. 391. [G: U.S.; U.K.; Canada; New Zealand]

Clauretie, Terrence M. A Note on the Bias in House Price Capitalization Models. *Amer. Real Estate Urban Econ. Assoc. J.*, Winter 1983, *11*(4), pp. 521–24.

Clayton, Frank and Hobart, Robert. The Supply of New Housing in Canada into the Twenty-First Century. **In** *Gau, G. W. and Goldberg, M. A., eds.*, 1983, pp. 127–38. [G: Canada]

Clemmer, Richard B. and Simonson, John C. Trends in Substandard Housing, 1940–1980. *Amer. Real Estate Urban Econ. Assoc. J.*, Winter 1983, *10*(4), pp. 442–64. [G: U.S.]

Clemmer, Richard B. and Weicher, John C. The Individual Housing Account. *Amer. Real Estate Urban Econ. Assoc. J.*, Summer 1983, *11*(2), pp. 221–36. [G: U.S.; Canada]

Colton, Kent W. The Report of the President's Commission on Housing: The Nation's System of Housing Finance. *Amer. Real Estate Urban Econ. Assoc. J.*, Summer 1983, *11*(2), pp. 133–65. [G: U.S.]

Colton, Kent W.; Seiders, David F. and Tuccillo, John A. Perspective on the Work of the President's Commission on Housing: Introduction. *Amer. Real Estate Urban Econ. Assoc. J.*, Summer 1983, *11*(2), pp. 111–16. [G: U.S.]

Cook, Robin. Housing and Deprivation. **In** *Brown, G. and Cook, R., eds.*, 1983, pp. 172–89. [G: U.K.]

Council on Development Choices for the '80s. Factors Shaping Development in the '80s. **In** *Carr, J. H. and Duensing, E. E., eds.*, 1983, *1981*, pp. 3–17. [G: U.S.]

Courtney, John M. Intervention through Land Use Regulation. **In** *Dunkerley, H. B., ed.*, 1983, pp. 153–70.

Craine, Roger. The Baby Boom, the Housing Market and the Stock Market. *Fed. Res. Bank San Francisco Econ. Rev.*, Spring 1983, (2), pp. 6–11. [G: U.S.]

Crawford, Peggy J. and Harper, Charles P. The Effect of the AML Index on the Borrower. *Housing Finance Rev.*, Oct 1983, *2*(4), pp. 309–20. [G: U.S.]

Crone, Theodore M. Elements of an Economic Justification for Municipal Zoning. *J. Urban Econ.*, September 1983, *14*(2), pp. 168–83. [G: U.S.]

Cronin, Francis J. Federal Tax Regulations and the Housing Demands of Owner Occupants. *Land Econ.*, August 1983, *59*(3), pp. 305–14. [G: U.S.]

Cronin, Francis J. Market Structure and the Price of Housing Services. *Urban Stud.*, August 1983, *20*(3), pp. 365–75. [G: U.S.]

Cronin, Francis J. The Efficiency of Demand-Oriented Housing Programs: Generalizing from Experimental Findings. *J. Human Res.*, Winter 1983, *18*(1), pp. 100–125. [G: U.S.]

Dale-Johnson, David. Clientele Effects on the Demand for Housing Price Appreciation. *Amer. Real Estate Urban Econ. Assoc. J.*, Fall 1983, *11*(3), pp. 382–96. [G: U.S.]

Daly, Michael J. and Macnaughton, Alan. Reverse Annuity Mortgages and Recent Tax Changes. *Can. Public Policy,* September 1983, *9*(3), pp. 398. [G: Canada]

Dániel, Zsuzsa. Public Housing, Personal Income and Central Redistribution in Hungary. *Acta Oecon.*, 1983, *31*(1–2), pp. 87–104. [G: Hungary]

Darrough, Masako N. The Treatment of Housing in a Cost-of-Living Index: Rental Equivalence and User Cost. **In** *Diewert, W. E. and Montmarquette, C., eds.*, 1983, pp. 599–618. [G: Canada]

Denny, Michael G. S. and Fuss, Melvyn A. Regional Price Indexes: The Canadian Practice and Some Potential Extensions. **In** *Diewert, W. E. and Montmarquette, C., eds.*, 1983, pp. 783–816. [G: Canada]

Dhrymes, Phoebus J. On the Determinants of the Probability of First-Home Acquisition and Its Relation to Credit Stringency. **In** *Grieson, R. E., ed.*, 1983, pp. 59–103. [G: U.S.]

Doebele, William A. Concepts of Urban Land Tenure. **In** *Dunkerley, H. B., ed.*, 1983, pp. 63–107.

Doling, J. British Housing Policy 1974–1983: A Review. *Reg. Stud.*, December 1983, *17*(6), pp. 475–78. [G: U.K.]

Dowall, David E. Reducing the Cost Effects of Local Land Use Controls. **In** *Carr, J. H. and Duensing, E. E., eds.*, 1983, *1981*, pp. 173–89. [G: U.S.]

Dowall, David E. The Effects of Tax and Expenditure Limitations on Local Land Use Policies. **In**

Quigley, J. M., ed., 1983, pp. 69–87. [G: U.S.]

Downs, Anthony. The Coming Crunch in Rental Housing. *Ann. Amer. Acad. Polit. Soc. Sci.*, January 1983, *465*, pp. 76–85. [G: U.S.]

Downs, Anthony. The President's Housing Commission and Two Tests of Realistic Recommendations. *Amer. Real Estate Urban Econ. Assoc. J.*, Summer 1983, *11*(2), pp. 182–91. [G: U.S.]

Dunkerley, Harold B. Urban Land Policy: Introduction and Overview. **In** *Dunkerley, H. B., ed.*, 1983, pp. 3–39.

Eckart, Wolfgang. Land Speculation and the Rental Price of Housing. *J. Urban Econ.*, January 1983, *13*(1), pp. 1–21.

Edelstein, Robert H. The Production Function for Housing and Its Implications for Future Urban Development. **In** *Gau, G. W. and Goldberg, M. A., eds.*, 1983, pp. 93–125. [G: U.S.]

Edwards, Michael. Residential Mobility in a Changing Housing Market: The Case of Bucaramanga, Colombia. *Urban Stud.*, May 1983, *20*(2), pp. 131–45. [G: Colombia]

Eekhoff, Johann. The Role of Government in the Housing Sector: Comment. **In** *Giersch, H., ed.*, 1983, pp. 225–31. [G: U.S.]

Eichler, Ned. Homebuilding in the 1980s: Crisis or Transition? *Ann. Amer. Acad. Polit. Soc. Sci.*, January 1983, *465*, pp. 35–44. [G: U.S.]

Ellerman, David P. A Model Structure for Cooperatives: Worker Co-ops and Housing Co-ops. *Rev. Soc. Econ.*, April 1983, *41*(1), pp. 52–67.

Ellickson, Bryan. Indivisibility, Housing Markets, and Public Goods. **In** *Henderson, J. V., ed.*, 1983, pp. 91–116.

Ellickson, Bryan. Is a Local Public Good Different from Any Other? **In** *Grieson, R. E., ed.*, 1983, pp. 143–70.

Elliott, Donald S., Jr. and Quinn, Michael A. Concentrated Housing Code Enforcement in St. Louis. *Amer. Real Estate Urban Econ. Assoc. J.*, Fall 1983, *11*(3), pp. 344–70. [G: U.S.]

Ellson, Richard and Roberts, Blaine. Residential Land Development under Uncertainty. *J. Reg. Sci.*, August 1983, *23*(3), pp. 309–22.

Engle, Robert F. and Marshall, Robert C. A Microeconometric Analysis of Vacant Housing Units. **In** *Grieson, R. E., ed.*, 1983, pp. 105–23. [G: U.S.]

Epple, Dennis; Filimon, Radu and Romer, Thomas. Housing, Voting, and Moving: Equilibrium in a Model of Local Public Goods with Multiple Jurisdictions. **In** *Henderson, J. V., ed.*, 1983, pp. 59–90.

Fallis, George B. Housing Tenure in a Model of Consumer Choice: A Simple Diagrammatic Analysis. *Amer. Real Estate Urban Econ. Assoc. J.*, Spring 1983, *11*(1), pp. 30–44.

Fallis, George B. The Normative Basis of Housing Policy. **In** *Gau, G. W. and Goldberg, M. A., eds.*, 1983, pp. 293–310. [G: Canada]

Farr, Cheryl. Modifying Land Use Regulations for Economic Development. **In** *Carr, J. H. and Duensing, E. E., eds.*, 1983, *1980*, pp. 207–28. [G: U.S.]

Farrell, L. M. Le marché immobilier: quelques perspectives à long terme pour la région de Trois-Rivières. (Real Estate Market in the City of Trois-Rivières: Long Term Perspectives. With English summary.) *L'Actual. Econ.*, March 1983, *59*(1), pp. 153–63. [G: Canada]

Feldstein, Martin S. Inflation, Tax Rules, and the Accumulation of Residential and Nonresidential Capital. **In** *Feldstein, M. (II)*, 1983, *1982*, pp. 81–98. [G: U.S.]

Fleming, M. C. and Nellis, Joseph G. A Regional Comparison of House Price Inflation Rates in Britain 1967—A Comment. *Urban Stud.*, February 1983, *20*(1), pp. 91–94. [G: U.K.]

Fox, Derek. Central Control and Local Capacity in the Housing Field. **In** *Young, K., ed.*, 1983, pp. 82–100. [G: U.K.]

Freund, James L. The Housing Market: Recent Developments and Underlying Trends. *Fed. Res. Bull.*, February 1983, *69*(2), pp. 61–69. [G: U.S.]

Frieden, Bernard J. The Exclusionary Effect of Growth Controls. *Ann. Amer. Acad. Polit. Soc. Sci.*, January 1983, *465*, pp. 123–35. [G: U.S.]

Friedman, Joseph and Weinberg, Daniel H. Rent Rebates and Housing Standards. **In** *Friedman, J. and Weinberg, D. H., eds.*, 1983, pp. 127–43. [G: U.S.]

Friedman, Joseph and Weinberg, Daniel H. The Great Housing Experiment: History and Overview. **In** *Friedman, J. and Weinberg, D. H., eds.*, 1983, pp. 11–22. [G: U.S.]

Galster, George C. Empirical Evidence on Cross-Tenure Differences in Home Maintenance and Conditions. *Land Econ.*, February 1983, *59*(1), pp. 107–13. [G: U.S.]

Gau, George W. and Goldberg, Michael A. The Future of North American Housing Markets. **In** *Gau, G. W. and Goldberg, M. A., eds.*, 1983, pp. 353–63. [G: N. America]

Gertcher, Franklin L. Military Family Housing Compared to Private Housing: Alternate Amounts of Housing Service Consumption. *Rev. Soc. Econ.*, October 1983, *41*(2), pp. 163–71. [G: U.S.]

Gill, H. Leroy. Changes in City and Suburban House Prices during a Period of Expected School Desegregation. *Southern Econ. J.*, July 1983, *50*(1), pp. 169–84. [G: U.S.]

Gillingham, Robert. Measuring the Cost of Shelter for Homeowners: Theoretical and Empirical Considerations. *Rev. Econ. Statist.*, May 1983, *65*(2), pp. 254–65. [G: U.S.]

Gillingham, Robert and Greenlees, John S. Estimating Inter-City Differences in the Price of Housing Services: Rejoinder. *Urban Stud.*, February 1983, *20*(1), pp. 95–97.

Gillingham, Robert and Hagemann, Robert. Cross-Sectional Estimation of a Simultaneous Model of Tenure Choice and Housing Services Demand. *J. Urban Econ.*, July 1983, *14*(1), pp. 16–39. [G: U.S.]

Gleeson, Michael E. Rental Vouchers and Homeownership Subsidies: A Dynamic Duo. *J. Policy Anal. Manage.*, Summer 1983, *2*(4), pp. 621–25. [G: U.S.]

Goldberg, Michael A. and Gau, George W. North American Housing Markets into the Twenty-First Century: Introduction. **In** *Gau, G. W. and Gold-*

berg, M. A., eds., 1983, pp. xv–xxv. [G: Canada; U.S.]

Goldman, Ellis G. and Field, Charles G. Summary of an Article on Reforming Land-Use Regulations. *Amer. Real Estate Urban Econ. Assoc. J.*, Summer 1983, *11*(2), pp. 300–319. [G: U.S.]

Goodman, Allen C. Capitalization of Property Tax Differentials within and among Municipalities. *Land Econ.*, May 1983, *59*(2), pp. 211–19. [G: U.S.]

Gray, Thomas A. Student Housing and Discrimination: An Empirical Approach. *Amer. Econ.*, Spring 1983, *27*(1), pp. 61–68. [G: U.S.]

Grebler, Leo. Inflation: A Blessing or a Curse? *Ann. Amer. Acad. Polit. Soc. Sci.*, January 1983, *465*, pp. 21–34. [G: U.S.]

Grebler, Leo. The Commission's Recommendations on Housing Finance. *Amer. Real Estate Urban Econ. Assoc. J.*, Summer 1983, *11*(2), pp. 166–81. [G: U.S.]

Grieson, Ronald E. and Arnott, Richard J. The Supply of Urban Housing. **In** *Grieson, R. E., ed.*, 1983, pp. 3–10. [G: U.S.]

Grigsby, William G.; Baratz, Morton and Maclennan, Duncan. Toward Coherent U.S. Housing Policies. **In** *Gau, G. W. and Goldberg, M. A., eds.*, 1983, pp. 311–38. [G: U.S.]

Grigsby, William G. and Corl, Thomas C. Declining Neighborhoods: Problem or Opportunity? *Ann. Amer. Acad. Polit. Soc. Sci.*, January 1983, *465*, pp. 86–97. [G: U.S.]

Guria, Jagadish C. A Planning Model for Housing: Integrating Sequence of Development, Allocation and Market Operation in Disequilibrium. *Indian Econ. Rev.*, July–December 1983, *18*(2), pp. 225–43. [G: India]

Hall, Peter. Housing, Planning, Land, and Local Finance: The British Experience. **In** *Lefcoe, G., ed.*, 1983, pp. 47–58. [G: U.K.]

Hamilton, William L. The Great Housing Experiment: The Administrative Agency Experiment. **In** *Friedman, J. and Weinberg, D. H., eds.*, 1983, pp. 56–69. [G: U.S.]

Hamilton, William L. The Great Housing Experiment: Economic and Racial/Ethnic Concentration. **In** *Friedman, J. and Weinberg, D. H., eds.*, 1983, pp. 210–19. [G: U.S.]

Harris, June M. and Borooah, Vani K. Distributed Lag Behaviour in the Housing Market: Some Further Evidence. *J. Econ. Stud.*, 1983, *10*(2), pp. 55–65. [G: U.K.]

Harris, William T. Property Tax Circuit-Breakers: Good Causes but Bad Economics. *Amer. J. Econ. Soc.*, April 1983, *42*(2), pp. 209–16. [G: U.S.]

Harvey, David. Class-Monopoly Rent, Finance Capital and the Urban Revolution. **In** *Lake, R. W., ed.*, 1983, *1974*, pp. 250–77. [G: U.S.]

Hendershott, Patric H. The Distribution of Gains and Losses from Changes in the Tax Treatment of Housing: Comment. **In** *Feldstein, M., ed.*, 1983, pp. 133–37. [G: U.K.]

Hendershott, Patric H. and Hu, Sheng Cheng. The Allocation of Capital between Residential and Nonresidential Uses: Taxes, Inflation and Capital Market Constraints. *J. Finance*, June 1983, *38*(3), pp. 795–812. [G: U.S.]

Hendershott, Patric H. and Slemrod, Joel. Taxes and the User Cost of Capital for Owner-Occupied Housing. *Amer. Real Estate Urban Econ. Assoc. J.*, Winter 1983, *10*(4), pp. 375–93. [G: U.S.]

Hendershott, Patric H. and Villani, Kevin E. Housing Finance in America in the Year 2001. **In** *Gau, G. W. and Goldberg, M. A., eds.*, 1983, pp. 181–202. [G: U.S.]

Henderson, J. Vernon and Ioannides, Yannis M. A Model of Housing Tenure Choice. *Amer. Econ. Rev.*, March 1983, *73*(1), pp. 98–113.

Henderson, William J. and Long, Keith. A Comment on 'Planning for Remote Communities: A Case Study of Housing Need Assessment.' *Can. Public Policy*, September 1983, *9*(3), pp. 399–400. [G: Canada]

Hillestad, Carol E. and McDowell, James L. The Great Housing Experiment: Neighborhood Change. **In** *Friedman, J. and Weinberg, D. H., eds.*, 1983, pp. 220–31. [G: U.S.]

Hohm, Charles F. The Reaction of Landlords to Rent Control. *Amer. Real Estate Urban Econ. Assoc. J.*, Winter 1983, *11*(4), pp. 504–20. [G: U.S.]

Holshouser, William L., Jr. The Great Housing Experiment: The Role of Supportive Services. **In** *Friedman, J. and Weinberg, D. H., eds.*, 1983, pp. 112–24. [G: U.S.]

Houstoun, Lawrence O., Jr. Market Trends Reveal Housing Choices for the 1980s. **In** *Carr, J. H. and Duensing, E. E., eds.*, 1983, *1981*, pp. 30–36. [G: U.S.]

Ihlanfeldt, Keith R. and Boehm, Thomas P. Property Taxation and the Demand for Homeownership. *Public Finance Quart.*, January 1983, *11*(1), pp. 47–66. [G: U.S.]

Ioannides, Yannis M. Renting versus Ownership in Housing Markets. *Greek Econ. Rev.*, December 1983, *5*(3), pp. 201–22.

Jenkins, S. P. and Maynard, Alan K. Intergenerational Continuities in Housing. *Urban Stud.*, November 1983, *20*(4), pp. 431–38. [G: U.K.]

Jimenez, Emmanuel. The Magnitude and Determinants of Home Improvement in Self-Help Housing: Manila's Tondo Project. *Land Econ.*, February 1983, *59*(1), pp. 70–83. [G: Philippines]

Johnson, Ruth C. and Kaserman, David L. Housing Market Capitalization of Energy-Saving Durable Goods Investments. *Econ. Inquiry*, July 1983, *21*(3), pp. 374–86. [G: U.S.]

Jones, Philip. Guestworkers and Their Spatial Distribution. **In** *Wild, T., ed.*, 1983, pp. 71–107. [G: W. Germany]

Jud, G. Donald. Real Estate Brokers and the Market for Residential Housing. *Amer. Real Estate Urban Econ. Assoc. J.*, Spring 1983, *11*(1), pp. 69–82. [G: U.S.]

Jud, G. Donald. Schools and Housing Values: Reply. *Land Econ.*, February 1983, *59*(1), pp. 135–37. [G: U.S.]

Kain, John F. America's Persistent Housing Crises: Errors in Analysis and Policy. *Ann. Amer. Acad. Polit. Soc. Sci.*, January 1983, *465*, pp. 136–48. [G: U.S.]

Kain, John F. The Journey-to-Work as a Determinant of Residential Location. **In** *Lake, R. W., ed.*, 1983,

1962, pp. 27–52. [G: U.S.]

Kaneko, Mamoru. Housing Markets with Indivisibilities. *J. Urban Econ.*, January 1983, *13*(1), pp. 22–50.

Kau, James B. and Keenan, Donald C. Inflation, Taxes and Housing: A Theoretical Analysis. *J. Public Econ.*, June 1983, *21*(1), pp. 93–104.

Kau, James B. and Sirmans, C. F. Technological Change and Economic Growth in Housing. *J. Urban Econ.*, May 1983, *13*(3), pp. 283–95. [G: U.S.]

Kennedy, Stephen D. The Great Housing Experiment: The Demand Experiment. **In** *Friedman, J. and Weinberg, D. H., eds.*, 1983, pp. 37–55. [G: U.S.]

Kennedy, Stephen D. and MacMillan, Jean E. The Great Housing Experiment: Participation under Random Assignment. **In** *Friedman, J. and Weinberg, D. H., eds.*, 1983, pp. 91–111. [G: U.S.]

Kent, Richard J. The Relationships between Income and Price Elasticities in Studies of Housing Demand, Tenure Choice, and Household Formation. *J. Urban Econ.*, March 1983, *13*(2), pp. 196–204. [G: U.S.]

Kent, Richard J. The Relationships between Income and Price Elasticities in Studies of Housing Demand, Tenure Choice, and Household Formation: Erratum. *J. Urban Econ.*, July 1983, *14*(1), pp. 126. [G: U.S.]

Kiefer, David. Inflation and Homeownership Tax Subsidies: A Correction. *Nat. Tax J.*, December 1983, *36*(4), pp. 525–27. [G: U.S.]

Kindahl, James K. Tax Limits and Property Values. *Land Econ.*, August 1983, *59*(3), pp. 315–23. [G: U.S.]

King, Mervyn A. The Distribution of Gains and Losses from Changes in the Tax Treatment of Housing. **In** *Feldstein, M., ed.*, 1983, pp. 109–32. [G: U.K.]

Komarov, V. and Ulanovskaia, V. The Effectiveness of Housing and Communal Services. *Prob. Econ.*, December 1983, *26*(8), pp. 18–31. [G: U.S.S.R.]

Kort, John R. A Multiregional Test of the Conway–Howard Housing Construction Model. *J. Reg. Sci.*, August 1983, *23*(3), pp. 413–18. [G: U.S.]

Kosonen, Katri. Suomalaisten kotitalouksien säästämisestä poikkileikkausaineiston valossa. (Cross-Section Analysis of Saving Behaviour of Finnish Households. With English summary.) *Kansant. Aikak.*, 1983, *79*(1), pp. 4–20. [G: Finland]

Krout, John A. Intercountry Commuting in Nonmetropolitan America in 1960 and 1970. *Growth Change*, January 1983, *14*(1), pp. 10–19. [G: U.S.]

Lea, Michael J. and Wasylenko, Michael J. Tenure Choice and Condominium Conversion. *J. Urban Econ.*, September 1983, *14*(2), pp. 127–44. [G: U.S.]

Lefcoe, George. The Market's Place in Land Policy. **In** *Carr, J. H. and Duensing, E. E., eds.*, 1983, *1980*, pp. 242–53. [G: U.S.]

Leigh, Wilhelmina A. The Impact of Inflation upon Homeownership Affordability: Comparisons by Race and Sex for the South. **In** *Schmukler, N. and Marcus, E., eds.*, 1983, pp. 838–59. [G: U.S.]

Lerman, Steven R. and Kern, Clifford R. Hedonic Theory, Bid Rents, and Willingness-to-Pay: Some Extensions of Ellickson's Results. *J. Urban Econ.*, May 1983, *13*(3), pp. 358–63.

Lérová, Irena. Seminar on the Relationship between Housing and the National Economy. *Czech. Econ. Digest.*, March 1983, (2), pp. 61–79. [G: E. Europe; W. Europe]

Linneman, Peter and Graves, Philip E. Migration and Job Change: A Multinomial Logit Approach. *J. Urban Econ.*, November 1983, *14*(3), pp. 263–79. [G: U.S.]

Litvak, Lawrence. Pension Funds and Economic Renewal. **In** *Barker, M., ed. (I)*, 1983, pp. 159–301. [G: U.S.]

Litvak, Lawrence and Daniels, Belden. Innovations in Development Finance. **In** *Barker, M., ed. (I)*, 1983, pp. 1–158. [G: U.S.]

Lowry, Ira S. Managing the Existing Housing Stock: Prospects and Problems. **In** *Gau, G. W. and Goldberg, M. A., eds.*, 1983, pp. 159–76. [G: U.S.]

Lowry, Ira S. Rental Housing: Shortage or Surplus? **In** *Lefcoe, G., ed.*, 1983, pp. 181–91. [G: U.S.]

Lowry, Ira S. The Great Housing Experiment: The Supply Experiment. **In** *Friedman, J. and Weinberg, D. H., eds.*, 1983, pp. 23–36. [G: U.S.]

Mann, Bruce D. and Veseth, Michael. Moderate Rent Controls: A Microeconomic and Public Choice Analysis. *Amer. Real Estate Urban Econ. Assoc. J.*, Fall 1983, *11*(3), pp. 333–43. [G: U.S.]

Mark, Jonathan H. An Empirical Examination of the Stability of Housing Price Equations over Time. *Amer. Real Estate Urban Econ. Assoc. J.*, Fall 1983, *11*(3), pp. 397–415. [G: U.S.]

Marks, Denton. Public Choice and Rent Control. *Atlantic Econ. J.*, September 1983, *11*(3), pp. 63–69. [G: U.S.]

Marshall, Robert C. and Guasch, J. Luis. Occupancy Discounts in the U.S. Rental Housing Market. *Oxford Bull. Econ. Statist.*, November 1983, *45*(4), pp. 357–78. [G: U.S.]

Martin, Preston. Statement to the Subcommittee on Financial Institutions Supervision, Regulation and Insurance, U.S. House Committee on Banking, Finance, and Urban Affairs, February 24, 1983. *Fed. Res. Bull.*, March 1983, *69*(3), pp. 177–81. [G: U.S.]

Martinez-Vazquez, Jorge. Renters' Illusion or Savvy? *Public Finance Quart.*, April 1983, *11*(2), pp. 237–47. [G: U.S.]

Maynard, Alan K. The Economics of Housing. **In** *Gowland, D. H., ed.*, 1983, pp. 223–36. [G: U.K.]

Mayo, Stephen K. Benefits from Subsidized Housing. **In** *Friedman, J. and Weinberg, D. H., eds.*, 1983, pp. 235–57. [G: U.S.]

McCarthy, Kevin F. Housing Search and Residential Mobility. **In** *Friedman, J. and Weinberg, D. H., eds.*, 1983, pp. 191–209. [G: U.S.]

McCormick, Barry. Housing and Unemployment in Great Britain. *Oxford Econ. Pap.*, Supplement November 1983, *35*, pp. 283–305. [G: U.K.]

Merrill, Sally R. The Great Housing Experiment: The Use of Hedonic Indices. **In** *Friedman, J. and Weinberg, D. H., eds.*, 1983, pp. 144–62. [G: U.S.]

Mills, David E. The Timing of Urban Residential

Land Development. In *Henderson, J. V., ed.*, 1983, pp. 37–57.

Moriizumi, Yoko and Takagi, Shintaro. The Income Elasticity of Housing Demand in Japan. *Econ. Stud. Quart.*, April 1983, *34*(1), pp. 70–86. **[G: Japan]**

Mouillart, Michel. Endettement des ménages et rationnement du crédit. (Households Indebtedness and Credit Rationing. With English summary.) *Consommation*, July–Sept. 1983, *30*(3), pp. 23–59. **[G: France]**

Mulford, John E. The Great Housing Experiment: Earmarked Income Supplements. In *Friedman, J. and Weinberg, D. H., eds.*, 1983, pp. 163–74. **[G: U.S.]**

Munnell, Alicia H. The Pitfalls of Social Investing: The Case of Public Pensions and Housing. *New Eng. Econ. Rev.*, September/October 1983, pp. 20–41. **[G: U.S.]**

Murie, Alan. Central Control and Local Capacity in the Housing Field: Comment. In *Young, K., ed.*, 1983, pp. 101–04. **[G: U.K.]**

Murray, Michael P. Subsidized and Unsubsidized Housing Starts: 1961–1977. *Rev. Econ. Statist.*, November 1983, *65*(4), pp. 590–97. **[G: U.S.]**

Muth, Richard F. Effects of the U.S. Tax System on Housing Prices and Consumption. In *Grieson, R. E., ed.*, 1983, pp. 11–27. **[G: U.S.]**

Muth, Richard F. Panel Discussion on Government Housing Policy. In *Gau, G. W. and Goldberg, M. A., eds.*, 1983, pp. 348–51. **[G: U.S.]**

Muth, Richard F. The Spatial Structure of the Housing Market. In *Lake, R. W., ed.*, 1983, *1961*, pp. 11–26. **[G: U.S.]**

Nesslein, Thomas S. Alternative Decision-Making Models for Housing: The Question of Efficiency. *Kyklos*, 1983, *36*(4), pp. 604–33.

Newman, Sandra J. and Struyk, Raymond J. Housing and Poverty. *Rev. Econ. Statist.*, May 1983, *65*(2), pp. 243–53. **[G: U.S.]**

Noam, Eli M. The Interaction of Building Codes and Housing Prices. *Amer. Real Estate Urban Econ. Assoc. J.*, Winter 1983, *10*(4), pp. 394–404. **[G: U.S.]**

Noguchi, Yukio. The Failure of Government to Perform Its Proper Task: A Case Study of Japan. In *Lenel, H. O.; Willgerodt, H. and Molsberger, J.*, 1983, pp. 59–70. **[G: Japan]**

Olsen, Edgar O. The Great Housing Experiment: Implications for Housing Policy. In *Friedman, J. and Weinberg, D. H., eds.*, 1983, pp. 266–75. **[G: U.S.]**

Olsen, Edgar O. The Role of Government in the Housing Sector. In *Giersch, H., ed.*, 1983, pp. 199–224. **[G: U.S.]**

Olsen, Edgar O. and Barton, David M. The Benefits and Costs of Public Housing in New York City. *J. Public Econ.*, April 1983, *20*(3), pp. 299–332. **[G: U.S.]**

Olsen, Edgar O. and Reeder, William J. Misdirected Rental Subsidies. *J. Policy Anal. Manage.*, Summer 1983, *2*(4), pp. 614–20. **[G: U.S.]**

Ozanne, Larry and Thibodeau, Thomas. Explaining Metropolitan Housing Price Differences. *J. Urban Econ.*, January 1983, *13*(1), pp. 51–66. **[G: U.S.]**

Pickles, Andrew R. The Analysis of Residence Histories and Other Longitudinal Panel Data: A Continuous Time Mixed Markov Renewal Model Incorporating Exogeneous Variables. *Reg. Sci. Urban Econ.*, May 1983, *13*(2), pp. 271–85. **[G: U.K.]**

Quah, Jon S. T. Public Bureaucracy, Social Change and National Development. In *Chen, P. S. J., ed.*, 1983, pp. 197–223. **[G: Singapore]**

Quigley, John M. Estimates of a More General Model of Consumer Choice in the Housing Market. In *Grieson, R. E., ed.*, 1983, pp. 125–40. **[G: U.S.]**

Rasmussen, David W. and Struyk, Raymond J. A Housing Strategy for the City of Detroit: Policy Perspectives Based on Economic Analysis. In *Quigley, J. M., ed.*, 1983, pp. 151–93. **[G: U.S.]**

Ricci, Renzo. Le esigenze di informazioni dal censimento demografico per la politica della casa. (Information's Requirement in the Census of Population for a Policy of Housing. With English summary.) *Statistica*, April–June 1983, *43*(2), pp. 251–58. **[G: Italy]**

Ricketts, Martin. Local Authority Housing Investment and Finance: A Test of the Theory of Regulation. *Manchester Sch. Econ. Soc. Stud.*, March 1983, *51*(1), pp. 45–62. **[G: U.K.]**

Riedy, Mark J. Where Will the Money Come From? *Ann. Amer. Acad. Polit. Soc. Sci.*, January 1983, *465*, pp. 14–20. **[G: U.S.]**

Riew, John. Property Taxation and Economic Development: With Focus on Korea. *J. Econ. Devel.*, December 1983, *8*(2), pp. 7–24. **[G: S. Korea]**

Rivkin, Malcolm D. Intervention through Direct Participation. In *Dunkerley, H. B., ed.*, 1983, pp. 171–97.

Rosen, Kenneth T. and Smith, Lawrence B. The Price-Adjustment Process for Rental Housing and the Natural Vacancy Rate. *Amer. Econ. Rev.*, September 1983, *73*(4), pp. 779–86. **[G: U.S.]**

Rothenberg, Jerome. Housing Investment, Housing Consumption, and Tenure Choice. In *Grieson, R. E., ed.*, 1983, pp. 29–55.

Rutgaizer, V. The Working Person in the Distribution and Consumption Sphere. *Prob. Econ.*, January 1983, *25*(9), pp. 16–35. **[G: U.S.S.R.]**

Rydell, C. Peter and Barnett, C. Lance. Price Effects of Housing Allowances. In *Friedman, J. and Weinberg, D. H., eds.*, 1983, pp. 175–88. **[G: U.S.]**

Sagalyn, Lynne Beyer. Mortgage Lending in Older Urban Neighborhoods: Lessons from Past Experience. *Ann. Amer. Acad. Polit. Soc. Sci.*, January 1983, *465*, pp. 98–108. **[G: U.S.]**

Sandilands, Roger J. Understanding the Scottish Economy: Housing Schemes and Schemes for Housing. In *Ingham, K. P. D. and Love, J., eds.*, 1983, pp. 127–38. **[G: U.K.]**

Scaggs, Mary Beth W. Recent Employment Trends in the Lumber and Wood Products Industry. *Mon. Lab. Rev.*, August 1983, *106*(8), pp. 20–24. **[G: U.S.]**

Schlicht, Ekkehart. The Tenant's Decreasing Willingness to Pay and the Rent Abatement Phenomenon. *Z. ges. Staatswiss.*, March 1983, *139*(1), pp. 155–59.

Schwab, Robert M. Expected Inflation and Housing: Tax and Cash Flow Considerations. *Southern*

Econ. J., April 1983, *49*(4), pp. 1162–68.

Schwab, Robert M. Real and Nominal Interest Rates and the Demand for Housing. *J. Urban Econ.*, March 1983, *13*(2), pp. 181–95. **[G: U.S.]**

Seek, N. H. Adjusting Housing Consumption: Improve or Move. *Urban Stud.*, November 1983, *20*(4), pp. 455–69. **[G: Australia]**

Seiders, David F. Managing Mortgage Interest-Rate Risks in Forward, Futures, and Options Markets. *Amer. Real Estate Urban Econ. Assoc. J.*, Summer 1983, *11*(2), pp. 237–63. **[G: U.S.]**

Seiders, David F. Mortgage Pass–Through Securities: Progress and Prospects. *Amer. Real Estate Urban Econ. Assoc. J.*, Summer 1983, *11*(2), pp. 264–87. **[G: U.S.]**

Shear, William B. A Note on Occupancy Turnover in Rental Housing Units. *Amer. Real Estate Urban Econ. Assoc. J.*, Winter 1983, *11*(4), pp. 525–38. **[G: U.S.]**

Shear, William B. Urban Housing Rehabilitation and Move Decisions. *Southern Econ. J.*, April 1983, *49*(4), pp. 1030–52. **[G: U.S.]**

Shear, William B. and Yezer, Anthony M. J. An Indirect Test for Differential Treatment of Borrowers in Mortgage Markets. *Amer. Real Estate Urban Econ. Assoc. J.*, Winter 1983, *10*(4), pp. 405–20. **[G: U.S.]**

Shoup, Donald C. Intervention through Property Taxation and Public Ownership. **In** *Dunkerley, H. B., ed.*, 1983, pp. 132–52.

Sirmans, G. Stacy; Smith, Stanley D. and Sirmans, C. F. Assumption Financing and Selling Price of Single-Family Homes. *J. Finan. Quant. Anal.*, September 1983, *18*(3), pp. 307–17. **[G: U.S.]**

Smith, Lawrence B. Panel Discussion on Government Housing Policy. **In** *Gau, G. W. and Goldberg, M. A., eds.*, 1983, pp. 345–48. **[G: Canada]**

Smith, Lawrence B. The Crisis in Rental Housing: A Canadian Perspective. *Ann. Amer. Acad. Polit. Soc. Sci.*, January 1983, *465*, pp. 58–75. **[G: Canada]**

Smith, Neil. Toward a Theory of Gentrification: A Back to the City Movement by Capital, Not People. **In** *Lake, R. W., ed.*, 1983, *1979*, pp. 278–98. **[G: U.S.]**

Starrett, David A. Welfare Measures Based on Capitalization: A Unified General Treatment. **In** *Henderson, J. V., ed.*, 1983, pp. 117–35.

Sternlieb, George and Hughes, James W. Housing the Poor in a Postshelter Society. *Ann. Amer. Acad. Polit. Soc. Sci.*, January 1983, *465*, pp. 109–22. **[G: U.S.]**

Straszheim, Mahlon R. Public Sector Capitalization Models with Heterogeneous Housing Stocks. **In** *Henderson, J. V., ed.*, 1983, pp. 137–63.

Struyk, Raymond J. and Lynn, Robert. Determinants of Housing Investment in Slum Areas: Tondo and Other Locations in Metro Manila. *Land Econ.*, November 1983, *59*(4), pp. 444–54. **[G: Philippines]**

Struyk, Raymond J. and Tuccillo, John A. Defining the Federal Role in Housing: Back to Basics. *J. Urban Econ.*, September 1983, *14*(2), pp. 206–23. **[G: U.S.]**

Sumichrast, Michael. A Five-Year Housing Forecast. *Ann. Amer. Acad. Polit. Soc. Sci.*, January 1983, *465*, pp. 45–57. **[G: U.S.]**

Thom, D. Rodney. House Prices, Inflation and the Mortgage Market. *Econ. Soc. Rev.*, October 1983, *15*(1), pp. 57–68. **[G: Ireland]**

Thomas, Steven G. The Significance of Housing as a Resource. **In** *Vogel, R. J. and Palmer, H. C., eds.*, 1983, pp. 391–414. **[G: U.S.]**

Thurow, Charles and Vranicar, John. Procedural Reform of Local Land-Use Regulation. **In** *Carr, J. H. and Duensing, E. E., eds.*, 1983, *1979*, pp. 190–206. **[G: U.S.]**

Tuccillo, John A. Inflation, Housing Prices, and Investment: A U.S. Perspective. **In** *Gau, G. W. and Goldberg, M. A., eds.*, 1983, pp. 259–88. **[G: U.S.]**

Tuccillo, John A. The Tax Treatment of Mortgage Investment. *Amer. Real Estate Urban Econ. Assoc. J.*, Summer 1983, *11*(2), pp. 288–99. **[G: U.S.]**

Tucker, S. N. An Analysis of Housing Subsidy Schemes in Australia. *Urban Stud.*, November 1983, *20*(4), pp. 439–53. **[G: Australia]**

Villani, Kevin E. Panel Discussion on Government Housing Policy. **In** *Gau, G. W. and Goldberg, M. A., eds.*, 1983, pp. 342–45.

Vitaliano, Donald F. Public Housing and Slums: Cure or Cause? *Urban Stud.*, May 1983, *20*(2), pp. 173–83. **[G: U.S.]**

Wallace, James E. Direct Household Assistance and Block Grants. *Amer. Real Estate Urban Econ. Assoc. J.*, Summer 1983, *11*(2), pp. 192–202. **[G: U.S.]**

Walters, Alan A. The Value of Land. **In** *Dunkerley, H. B., ed.*, 1983, pp. 40–62.

Weibull, Jörgen W. A Dynamic Model of Trade Frictions and Disequilibrium in the Housing Market. *Scand. J. Econ.*, 1983, *85*(3), pp. 373–92.

Weicher, John C. Re-Evaluating Housing Policy Alternatives: What Do We Really Know? *Amer. Real Estate Urban Econ. Assoc. J.*, Spring 1983, *11*(1), pp. 1–10. **[G: U.S.]**

Weicher, John C. The Report of the President's Commission on Housing: Policy Proposals for Subsidized Housing. *Amer. Real Estate Urban Econ. Assoc. J.*, Summer 1983, *11*(2), pp. 117–32. **[G: U.S.]**

Weinrobe, Maurice D. Home Equity Conversion Instruments with Fixed Term to Maturity: Alternatives to End of Term Pay-Off. *Amer. Real Estate Urban Econ. Assoc. J.*, Spring 1983, *11*(1), pp. 83–96. **[G: U.S.]**

Werczberger, Elia. Multiperson Multitarget Decision Making, Using the Versatility Criterion. *Reg. Sci. Urban Econ.*, February 1983, *13*(1), pp. 103–13.

Wetzel, James N. Schools and Housing Values: Comment. *Land Econ.*, February 1983, *59*(1), pp. 131–34. **[G: U.S.]**

Wheaton, William C. Theories of Urban Growth and Metropolitan Spatial Development. **In** *Henderson, J. V., ed.*, 1983, pp. 3–36.

Whitehead, Christine M. E. The Rationale for Government Intervention. **In** *Dunkerley, H. B., ed.*, 1983, pp. 108–31.

Wieand, Kenneth F. The Performance of Annual Housing Survey Quality Measures in Explaining Dwelling Rentals in 20 Metropolitan Areas.

Amer. Real Estate Urban Econ. Assoc. J., Spring 1983, *11*(1), pp. 45–68. [G: U.S.]

Wild, Trevor. Residential Environments in West German Inner Cities. In *Wild, T., ed.*, 1983, pp. 40–70. [G: W. Germany]

Wild, Trevor. The Residential Dimension to Rural Change. In *Wild, T., ed.*, 1983, pp. 161–99. [G: W. Germany]

Williams, Peter R. The Role of Institutions in the Inner London Housing Market: The Case of Islington. In *Lake, R. W., ed.*, 1983, *1976*, pp. 157–72. [G: U.K.]

Winsberg, Morton D. Ethnic Competition for Residential Space in Miami, Florida, 1970–80. *Amer. J. Econ. Soc.*, July 1983, *42*(3), pp. 305–14. [G: U.S.]

Zaki, Ahmed S. and Isakson, Hans R. The Impact of Energy Prices: A Housing Market Analysis. *Energy Econ.*, April 1983, *5*(2), pp. 100–104. [G: U.S.]

Zarinnia, Abdullah. Non-Mortgage Factors Affecting Housing Sales and Construction: A Case Study of Transactions in 3 Counties of Southeastern Wisconsin, 1974–78. *Amer. J. Econ. Soc.*, January 1983, *42*(1), pp. 29–37. [G: U.S.]

933 Urban Transportation Economics

9330 Urban Transportation Economics

Bajic, Vladimir. The Effects of a New Subway Line on Housing Prices in Metropolitan Toronto. *Urban Stud.*, May 1983, *20*(2), pp. 147–58. [G: Canada]

Bajusz, Rezso. Mass Transport and Individual Transport: An Optimum Modal Split. In *Khachaturov, T. S. and Goodwin, P. B., eds.*, 1983, pp. 167–78. [G: Hungary; W. Europe]

Edmonds, Radcliffe G., Jr. Travel Time Valuation through Hedonic Regression. *Southern Econ. J.*, July 1983, *50*(1), pp. 83–98. [G: Japan]

Frankena, Mark W. The Efficiency of Public Transport Objectives and Subsidy Formulas. *J. Transp. Econ. Policy*, January 1983, *17*(1), pp. 67–76.

Glaister, Stephen G. Some Characteristics of Rail Commuter Demand. *J. Transp. Econ. Policy*, May 1983, *17*(2), pp. 115–32. [G: U.K.]

Grieson, Ronald E. and Arnott, Richard J. Optimal Tolls with High-peak Travel Demand. In *Grieson, R. E., ed.*, 1983, pp. 193–201.

Gunn, H. F. "Generalised Cost" or "Generalised Time": A Note on the Forecasting Implications. *J. Transp. Econ. Policy*, January 1983, *17*(1), pp. 91–94.

Hatta, Tatsuo. Competition and Nationally Optimum Resource Allocation under the Presence of Urban Traffic Congestion. *J. Urban Econ.*, September 1983, *14*(2), pp. 145–67.

Haurin, Donald R. The Effect of Reimbursement of Worker's Transport Costs: The Case of Urban Areas in Japan. *J. Urban Econ.*, March 1983, *13*(2), pp. 205–15.

Jones, Ian S. and Nichols, Alan J. The Demand for Inter-City Rail Travel in the United Kingdom: Some Evidence. *J. Transp. Econ. Policy*, May 1983, *17*(2), pp. 133–53. [G: U.K.]

Kain, John F. Impacts of Higher Petroleum Prices on Transportation Patterns and Urban Development. In *Keeler, T. E., ed.*, 1983, pp. 1–26. [G: U.S.]

Kain, John F. The Journey-to-Work as a Determinant of Residential Location. In *Lake, R. W., ed.*, 1983, *1962*, pp. 27–52. [G: U.S.]

Knight, Robert L. The Impact of Rail Transit on Land Use. In *Carr, J. H. and Duensing, E. E., eds.*, 1983, *1980*, pp. 37–50. [G: Canada; U.S.]

Lindner, Werner. The Optimum Ratio between Private and Public Passenger Transport Services in Conurbations: The Experience of the German Democratic Republic. In *Khachaturov, T. S. and Goodwin, P. B., eds.*, 1983, pp. 179–86. [G: E. Germany]

Madre, Jean-Loup. Construction d'indicateurs de redistribution. (The Construction of Redistribution Indicators. With English summary.) *Consommation*, July–Sept. 1983, *30*(3), pp. 3–22. [G: France]

Mohring, Herbert. Minibuses in Urban Transportation. *J. Urban Econ.*, November 1983, *14*(3), pp. 293–317. [G: U.S.]

Obeng, Kofi. Fare Subsidies to Achieve Pareto Optimality—A Benefit Cost Approach. *Logist. Transp. Rev.*, December 1983, *19*(4), pp. 367–84. [G: U.S.]

Palmer, John; Quinn, John and Resendes, Ray. A Case Study of Public Enterprise: Gray Coach Lines Ltd. In *Prichard, J. R. S., ed.*, 1983, pp. 369–446. [G: Canada]

Pucher, John; Markstedt, Anders and Hirschman, Ira. Impacts of Subsidies on the Costs of Urban Public Transport. *J. Transp. Econ. Policy*, May 1983, *17*(2), pp. 155–76. [G: U.S.]

Quah, Jon S. T. Public Bureaucracy, Social Change and National Development. In *Chen, P. S. J., ed.*, 1983, pp. 197–223. [G: Singapore]

Rivkin, Malcolm D. Intervention through Direct Participation. In *Dunkerley, H. B., ed.*, 1983, pp. 171–97.

Schroeter, John R. A Model of Taxi Service under Fare Structure and Fleet Size Regulation. *Bell J. Econ. (See Rand J. Econ. after 4/85)*, Spring 1983, *14*(1), pp. 81–96. [G: U.S.]

Shilony, Yuval. More Methodological Notes on Welfare Calculus. *J. Transp. Econ. Policy*, January 1983, *17*(1), pp. 95–98.

Small, Kenneth A. Bus Priority and Congestion Pricing on Urban Expressways. In *Keeler, T. E., ed.*, 1983, pp. 27–74. [G: U.S.]

Small, Kenneth A. The Incidence of Congestion Tolls on Urban Highways. *J. Urban Econ.*, January 1983, *13*(1), pp. 90–111.

Soberman, Richard M. Urban Transportation in the U.S. and Canada: A Canadian Perspective. *Logist. Transp. Rev.*, June 1983, *19*(2), pp. 99–109. [G: U.S.; Canada]

de Sola Pool, Ithiel. Communications Technology and Land Use. In *Carr, J. H. and Duensing, E. E., eds.*, 1983, *1980*, pp. 291–303. [G: U.S.]

Southworth, Frank. Temporal versus Other Impacts upon Trip Distribution Model Parameter Values. *Reg. Stud.*, February 1983, *17*(1), pp. 41–47. [G: U.K.]

Stern, Eliahu; Tzelgov, Joseph and Henik, Avishai. Driving Efforts and Urban Route Choice. *Logist.*

Transp. Rev., March 1983, *19*(1), pp. 67–79.

Viton, Philip A. Pareto-Optimal Urban Transportation Equilibria. **In** *Keeler, T. E., ed.*, 1983, pp. 75–101. **[G: U.S.]**

Wilson, John D. Optimal Road Capacity in the Presence of Unpriced Congestion. *J. Urban Econ.*, May 1983, *13*(3), pp. 337–57.

940 Regional Economics

941 Regional Economics

9410 General

Barr, Brenton M. Industrial Parks as Locational Environments: A Research Challenge. **In** *Hamilton, F. E. I. and Linge, G. J. R., eds.*, 1983, pp. 423–40.

Bartoli, Henri. Le problème des régions dans la pensée économique italienne. (The Problem of Regions in the Italian Economic Thought. With English summary.) *Giorn. Econ.*, September–October 1983, *42*(9–10), pp. 561–99. **[G: Italy]**

Courchene, Thomas J. Analytical Perspectives on the Canadian Economic Union. **In** *Trebilcock, M. J., et al., eds.*, 1983, pp. 51–110. **[G: Canada]**

Davis, Dwight F. Policy and Research Needs. **In** *Ballard, S. C. and James, T. E., eds.*, 1983, pp. 212–19. **[G: U.S.]**

Eskelinen, Heikki. Regional Alternatives: The Finnish Case. **In** *Seers, D. and Öström, K., eds.*, 1983, pp. 15–22. **[G: Finland]**

Giorgi, Giovanni Maria. An Analysis of Some Methodological Aspects of a Recent Research Regarding the Classification of Italian Communes. *Econ. Notes*, 1983, (3), pp. 199–206. **[G: Italy]**

Hadjimichalis, Costis. Regional Crisis: The State and Regional Social Movements in Southern Europe. **In** *Seers, D. and Öström, K., eds.*, 1983, pp. 127–47. **[G: S. Europe]**

Hamilton, F. E. Ian and Linge, Godfrey J. R. Regional Economies and Industrial Systems. **In** *Hamilton, F. E. I. and Linge, G. J. R., eds.*, 1983, pp. 1–39.

Hansen, Niles. International Cooperation in Border Regions: An Overview and Research Agenda. *Int. Reg. Sci. Rev.*, December 1983, *8*(3), pp. 255–70. **[G: U.S.; Mexico]**

Hausner, V. A. Urban and Regional Policy in the United States: The Approach of the Carter Administration. *Reg. Stud.*, October 1983, *17*(5), pp. 366–69. **[G: U.S.]**

Henderson, J. Vernon. Industrial Bases and City Sizes. *Amer. Econ. Rev.*, May 1983, *73*(2), pp. 164–68.

Kasperson, Roger E. and Rubin, Barry L. Siting a Radioactive Waste Repository: What Role for Equity? **In** *Kasperson, R. E., ed.*, 1983, pp. 118–36. **[G: U.S.]**

Malecki, Edward J. Technology and Regional Development: A Survey. *Int. Reg. Sci. Rev.*, October 1983, *8*(2), pp. 89–125.

Malecki, Edward J. Towards a Model of Technical Change and Regional Economic Change. *Reg. Sci. Persp.*, 1983, *13*(2), pp. 51–60.

Mathews, Russell. Intergovernmental Fiscal Relations and Regional Growth in a Federal Context. **In** *Biehl, D.; Roskamp, K. W. and Stolper, W. F., eds.*, 1983, pp. 265–96. **[G: Australia]**

Mawson, J. and Miller, D. The Regional Debate in the Labour Party. *Reg. Stud.*, October 1983, *17*(5), pp. 362–66. **[G: U.K.]**

Nekrasov, O.; Rutgaizer, V. and Kovaleva, N. Territorial Planning of Social Development. *Prob. Econ.*, March 1983, *25*(11), pp. 70–88. **[G: U.S.S.R.]**

Olson, Mancur. The South Will Fall Again: The South as Leader and Laggard in Economic Growth. *Southern Econ. J.*, April 1983, *49*(4), pp. 917–32. **[G: U.S.]**

Paelinck, Jean Henri Paul. Investment and the Development of Backward Regions. **In** *Heertje, A., ed.*, 1983, pp. 152–87. **[G: EEC]**

Prichard, J. Robert S. and Benedickson, Jamie. Securing the Canadian Economic Union: Federalism and Internal Barriers to Trade. **In** *Trebilcock, M. J., et al., eds.*, 1983, pp. 3–50. **[G: Canada]**

Rietveld, Piet. Analysis of Conflicts and Compromises, Using Qualitative Data. *Conflict Manage. Peace Sci.*, Fall 1983, *7*(1), pp. 39–63. **[G: Netherlands; Belgium]**

Ross, Robert J. S. Facing Leviathan: Public Policy and Global Capitalism. *Econ. Geogr.*, April 1983, *59*(2), pp. 144–60. **[G: U.S.; U.K.]**

Seley, John E. and Wolpert, Julian. Equity and Location. **In** *Kasperson, R. E., ed.*, 1983, pp. 69–93. **[G: U.S.]**

Stilwell, Frank J. B. State and Capital in Urban and Regional Development. **In** *Head, B. W., ed.*, 1983, pp. 199–218. **[G: Australia]**

Stöhr, Walter B. Alternative Strategies for Integrated Regional Development of Peripheral Areas. **In** *Seers, D. and Öström, K., eds.*, 1983, pp. 6–14. **[G: Austria]**

Storey, D. J. Indigenising a Regional Economy: The Importance of Management Buyouts. *Reg. Stud.*, December 1983, *17*(6), pp. 471–75. **[G: U.K.]**

Todd, Daniel and Simpson, Jamie A. The Appropriate-Technology Question in a Regional Context. *Growth Change*, October 1983, *14*(4), pp. 46–52.

Tolley, George S.; Krumm, Ronald J. and Sanders, Jeffrey. On the Effects of Federal Aid. *Amer. Econ. Rev.*, May 1983, *73*(2), pp. 159–63. **[G: U.S.]**

Trebilcock, Michael J., et al. Federalism and the Canadian Economic Union: Summary and Implications. **In** *Trebilcock, M. J., et al., eds.*, 1983, pp. 542–60. **[G: Canada]**

Waters, N. The Urban and Regional Policies of the Social Democratic Party. *Reg. Stud.*, October 1983, *17*(5), pp. 359–62. **[G: U.K.]**

Wierzbicki, Andrzej P. Critical Essay on the Methodology of Multiobjective Analysis. *Reg. Sci. Urban Econ.*, February 1983, *13*(1), pp. 5–29.

Wray, I. Planning for Declines? An Unconventional Regional Policy for the 1980s and 1990s. *Reg. Stud.*, December 1983, *17*(6), pp. 467–71. **[G: U.K.]**

9411 Theory of Regional Economics

Alperovich, Gershon and Katz, Eliakim. Transport Rate Uncertainty and the Optimal Location of the Firm. *J. Reg. Sci.*, August 1983, *23*(3), pp. 389–96.

941 Regional Economics

Arcangeli, Fabio. Un riesame dell' "ordine spaziale dell'economia" di August Lösch. (Lösch's "Spatial Order of Economics." With English summary.) *Giorn. Econ.*, July–August 1983, *42*(7–8), pp. 483–506.

Aziz, Rashid; Butterfield, David and Kubursi, Atif A. Regional Equity and Efficiency: Some Experiments for Canada. *J. Reg. Sci.*, August 1983, *23*(3), pp. 397–412. **[G: Canada]**

Balcer, Yves. F.O.B. Pricing versus Uniform Delivered Pricing: A Welfare Analysis in a Stochastic Environment. *J. Econ. Theory*, June 1983, *30*(1), pp. 54–73.

Beckmann, Martin J. Der "isolirte Staat" im räumlichen Gleichgewicht. (The "Isolirte Staat" in the General Spatial Equilibrium. With English summary.) *Z. Wirtschaft. Sozialwissen.*, 1983, *103*(6), pp. 629–39.

Beckmann, Martin J. On Optimal Spacing under Exponential Distance Effect. **In** *Thisse, J.-F. and Zoller, H. G., eds.*, 1983, pp. 117–25.

Benson, Bruce L. and Hartigan, James C. Tariffs Which Lower Price in the Restricting Country: An Analysis of Spatial Markets. *J. Int. Econ.*, August 1983, *15*(1/2), pp. 117–33.

Black, William. A Generalization of Destination Effects in Spatial Interaction Modeling. *Econ. Geogr.*, January 1983, *59*(1), pp. 16–34. **[G: U.S.]**

Buhr, Walter. Mikroökonomische Modelle der von Thünenschen Standorttheorie. (Microeconomic Models of von Thünen's Location Theory. With English summary.) *Z. Wirtschaft. Sozialwissen.*, 1983, *103*(6), pp. 589–627.

Carlton, Dennis W. The Location and Employment Choices of New Firms: An Econometric Model with Discrete and Continuous Endogenous Variables. *Rev. Econ. Statist.*, August 1983, *65*(3), pp. 440–49. **[G: U.S.]**

Chalmet, Luc G. Efficiency in Minisum Rectilinear Distance Location Problems. **In** *Thisse, J.-F. and Zoller, H. G., eds.*, 1983, pp. 431–45.

Chiancone, Aldo. Contributions of Regional Public Enterprises to Regional Economic Development. **In** *Biehl, D.; Roskamp, K. W. and Stolper, W. F., eds.*, 1983, pp. 315–28.

Clapp, John M. A General Model of Equilibrium Locations. *J. Reg. Sci.*, November 1983, *23*(4), pp. 461–78.

Clarke, Harry R. and Shrestha, Ram M. Location and Input Mix Decisions for Energy Facilities. *Reg. Sci. Urban Econ.*, November 1983, *13*(4), pp. 487–504.

Clarke, M. and Wilson, A. G. The Dynamics of Urban Spatial Structure: Progress and Problems. *J. Reg. Sci.*, February 1983, *23*(1), pp. 1–18.

Coelho, J. Dias. Formulação em programação matemática do modelo gravitacional e sua interpretação económica. (With English summary.) *Economia*, October 1983, *7*(3), pp. 471–517.

Cooke, Timothy W. Testing a Model of Intraurban Firm Relocation. *J. Urban Econ.*, May 1983, *13*(3), pp. 257–82. **[G: U.S.]**

Corden, Warner Max. The Economic Effects of a Booming Sector. *Int. Soc. Sci. J.*, 1983, *35*(3), pp. 441–54.

Courant, Paul N. On the Effects of Federal Capital Taxation on Growing and Declining Areas. *J. Urban Econ.*, September 1983, *14*(2), pp. 242–61. **[G: U.S.]**

Demange, Gabrielle. Spatial Models of Collective Choice. **In** *Thisse, J.-F. and Zoller, H. G., eds.*, 1983, pp. 153–82.

Drezner, Z. and Wesolowsky, G. O. The Location of an Obnoxious Facility with Rectangular Distances. *J. Reg. Sci.*, May 1983, *23*(2), pp. 241–48.

Ellson, Richard and Roberts, Blaine. Residential Land Development under Uncertainty. *J. Reg. Sci.*, August 1983, *23*(3), pp. 309–22.

Erlenkotter, Donald. On the Choice of Models for Public Facility Location. **In** *Thisse, J.-F. and Zoller, H. G., eds.*, 1983, pp. 385–93.

Friedmann, John. Life Space and Economic Space: Contradictions in Regional Development. **In** *Seers, D. and Öström, K., eds.*, 1983, pp. 148–62.

Friesz, Terry L., et al. A Nonlinear Complementarity Formulation and Solution Procedure for the General Derived Demand Network Equilibrium Problem. *J. Reg. Sci.*, August 1983, *23*(3), pp. 337–59.

Fujita, Masahisa. Efficiency and Equity in Regional Development with Agglomeration Economies. **In** *Isard, W. and Nagao, Y., eds.*, 1983, pp. 187–223.

Fukuchi, Takao. Growth and Stability of Multi-Regional Economy. *Int. Econ. Rev.*, June 1983, *24*(2), pp. 509–20.

Funck, Rolf H. and Blum, Ulrich. Regional Development and Investments in Infrastructure—The Evaluation of Conflicting Impacts. **In** *Isard, W. and Nagao, Y., eds.*, 1983, pp. 91–116. **[G: W. Germany]**

Furlong, William J. and Slotsve, George A. "Will That Be Pickup or Delivery?" An Alternative Spatial Pricing Strategy. *Bell J. Econ. (See Rand J. Econ. after 4/85)*, Spring 1983, *14*(1), pp. 271–74.

Gillen, William J. and Guccione, Antonio. The Relevance of Wage Differentials in Neoclassical Urban Growth. *Reg. Sci. Urban Econ.*, November 1983, *13*(4), pp. 547–55. **[G: Canada]**

Greenberg, Joseph. Local Public Goods with Mobility: Existence and Optimality of a General Equilibrium. *J. Econ. Theory*, June 1983, *30*(1), pp. 17–33.

Griffith, Daniel A. The Boundary Value Problem in Spatial Statistical Analysis. *J. Reg. Sci.*, August 1983, *23*(3), pp. 377–87.

Gunn, H. F. "Generalised Cost" or "Generalised Time": A Note on the Forecasting Implications. *J. Transp. Econ. Policy*, January 1983, *17*(1), pp. 91–94.

Halpern, Jonathan and Maimon, Oded. Accord and Conflict among Several Objectives in Locational Decisions on Tree Networks. **In** *Thisse, J.-F. and Zoller, H. G., eds.*, 1983, pp. 301–14.

Hansen, Pierre; Peeters, D. and Thisse, Jacques-François. Public Facility Location Models: A Selective Survey. **In** *Thisse, J.-F. and Zoller, H. G., eds.*, 1983, pp. 223–62.

Henry, Claude. Some Inconsistencies in Public Land-Use Choices. **In** *Thisse, J.-F. and Zoller, H. G., eds.*, 1983, pp. 183–205.

Hewings, Geoffrey J. D. and O'hUallachain, Breandan. Industrial Factors in the Development of Regional Systems. **In** *Hamilton, F. E. I. and Linge, G. J. R., eds.*, 1983, pp. 41–57.

Higgins, Benjamin. From Growth Poles to Systems of Interactions in Space. *Growth Change*, October 1983, *14*(4), pp. 3–13.

Hsu, Song-ken. Pricing in an Urban Spatial Monopoly: A General Analysis. *J. Reg. Sci.*, May 1983, *23*(2), pp. 165–75.

Hsu, Song-ken. Social Optimal Pricing in a Spatial Market. *Reg. Sci. Urban Econ.*, August 1983, *13*(3), pp. 401–10.

Karaska, Gerald J.; Moore, Craig L. and Susman, Paul. The Regional Industrial System. **In** *Hamilton, F. E. I. and Linge, G. J. R., eds.*, 1983, pp. 387–98.

Kilmer, Richard L.; Spreen, Thomas H. and Tilley, Daniel S. A Dynamic Plant Location Model: The East Florida Fresh Citrus Packing Industry. *Amer. J. Agr. Econ.*, November 1983, *65*(4), pp. 730–37. **[G: U.S.]**

Lea, Anthony C. Some Lessons from the Theory of Public and Impure Goods for Public Facility Location-Allocation Models. **In** *Thisse, J.-F. and Zoller, H. G., eds.*, 1983, pp. 263–300.

Leonardi, Giorgio. The Use of Random-Utility Theory in Building Location-Allocation Models. **In** *Thisse, J.-F. and Zoller, H. G., eds.*, 1983, pp. 357–83.

Martin, Randolph C. and Pelzman, Joseph. The Regional Welfare Effects of Tariff Reductions on Textile Products. *J. Reg. Sci.*, August 1983, *23*(3), pp. 323–36. **[G: U.S.]**

Martynov, G. V. and Pitelin, A. K. A Two-Stage System for Optimizing the Development and Location of a Multibranch Complex Which Uses Variants for the Branch Models. *Matekon*, Winter 1983–84, *20*(2), pp. 55–73.

Mathur, Vijay K. Location Theory of the Firm under Price Uncertainty. *Reg. Sci. Urban Econ.*, August 1983, *13*(3), pp. 411–28.

McGuire, Therese. Firm Location in a Tiebout World. *J. Reg. Sci.*, May 1983, *23*(2), pp. 211–22.

Mehrez, Abraham. A Note on the Linear Integer Formulation of the Maximal Covering Location Problem with Facility Placement on the Entire Plane. *J. Reg. Sci.*, November 1983, *23*(4), pp. 553–55.

Mehrez, Abraham; Sinuany-Stern, Zilla and Stulman, Alan. The One-Dimensional Single Facility Maximin Distance Location Problem. *J. Reg. Sci.*, May 1983, *23*(2), pp. 233–39.

Michel, Philippe; Pestieau, Pierre and Thisse, Jacques-François. Regional Allocation of Investment with Distributive Objectives. *J. Reg. Sci.*, May 1983, *23*(2), pp. 199–209.

Moomaw, Ronald L. Is Population Scale a Worthless Surrogate for Business Agglomeration Economies? *Reg. Sci. Urban Econ.*, November 1983, *13*(4), pp. 525–45. **[G: U.S.]**

Mulligan, Gordon F. Central Place Populations: A Microeconomic Consideration. *J. Reg. Sci.*, February 1983, *23*(1), pp. 83–92.

Norcliffe, Glen B. Using Location Quotients to Estimate the Economic Base and Trade Flows. *Reg. Stud.*, June 1983, *17*(3), pp. 161–68. **[G: Canada]**

Norman, George. Spatial Competition and Spatial Price Discrimination: A Correction. *Rev. Econ. Stud.*, October 1983, *50*(4), pp. 755–56.

Norman, George. Spatial Pricing with Differentiated Products. *Quart. J. Econ.*, May 1983, *98*(2), pp. 291–310.

Okabe, Atsuyuki and Kume, Yoshiaki. A Dynamic von Thünen Model with a Demand Function. *J. Urban Econ.*, November 1983, *14*(3), pp. 355–69.

Rondinelli, Dennis A. and Evans, Hugh. Integrated Regional Development Planning: Linking Urban Centres and Rural Areas in Bolivia. *World Devel.*, January 1983, *11*(1), pp. 31–53. **[G: Bolivia; S. America]**

Round, Jeffrey I. Nonsurvey Techniques: A Critical Review of the Theory and the Evidence. *Int. Reg. Sci. Rev.*, December 1983, *8*(3), pp. 189–212.

Sayer, Andrew. Theoretical Problems in the Analysis of Technological Change and Regional Development. **In** *Hamilton, F. E. I. and Linge, G. J. R., eds.*, 1983, pp. 59–73.

Sayer, Stuart. The Economic Analysis of Frontier Regions. **In** *Anderson, M., ed.*, 1983, pp. 64–80.

Schöler, Klaus. Alternative Preistechniken im räumlichen Monopol: Ein einzelwirtschaftlicher und wohlfahrtstheoretischer Vergleich. (Alternative Pricing Techniques in Spatial Monopoly. With English summary.) *Z. ges. Staatswiss.*, June 1983, *139*(2), pp. 289–305.

Schöler, Klaus. Preisbildung bei räumlichem Wettbewerb. (Pricing under Spatial Competition. With English summary.) *Jahr. Nationalökon. Statist.*, March 1983, *198*(2), pp. 145–60.

Shieh, Yeung-nan. The Moses–Predöhl Pull and the Neoclassical Location Theory: An Alternative Approach. *Reg. Sci. Urban Econ.*, November 1983, *13*(4), pp. 517–24.

Shieh, Yeung-nan. The Space Cost Curve and Variable Transport Costs: A General Production Function Case. *Urban Stud.*, May 1983, *20*(2), pp. 241–45.

Sinclair, M. Thea and Sutcliffe, Charles M. S. Injection Leakages, Trade Repercussions and the Regional Income Multiplier: An Extension. *Scot. J. Polit. Econ.*, November 1983, *30*(3), pp. 275–86. **[G: U.K.]**

Smeers, Yves and Tyteca, Daniel. On the Optimal Location of Wastewater Treatment Plants. **In** *Thisse, J.-F. and Zoller, H. G., eds.*, 1983, pp. 395–412.

Spatt, Chester S. Imperfect Price Discrimination and Variety. *J. Bus.*, April 1983, *56*(2), pp. 203–16.

Stroe, R. National Wealth in National-Territorial Connexion. *Econ. Computat. Cybern. Stud. Res.*, 1983, *18*(1), pp. 15–22.

Tapiero, Charles S. and Desplas, Maurice. Optimal Location of Two Competing Facilities under Uncertainty. **In** *Thisse, J.-F. and Zoller, H. G., eds.*, 1983, pp. 315–30.

Tervo, Hannu and Okko, Paavo. A Note on Shift-Share Analysis as a Method of Estimating the Employment Effects of Regional Economic Policy. *J. Reg. Sci.*, February 1983, *23*(1), pp. 115–21.

Thisse, Jacques-François and Zoller, Henri G. Some

Notes on Public Facility Location. **In** *Thisse, J.-F. and Zoller, H. G., eds.*, 1983, pp. 1–8.

Thrall, Grant Ian and Erol, Cengiz. A Dynamic Equilibrium Model of Regional Capital Investment with Supporting Evidence from Canada and the United States. *Econ. Geogr.*, July 1983, *59*(3), pp. 272–81. **[G: Canada; U.S.]**

Tobin, Roger L. and Friesz, Terry L. Formulating and Solving the Spatial Price Equilibrium Problem with Transshipment in Terms of Arc Variables. *J. Reg. Sci.*, May 1983, *23*(2), pp. 187–98.

Tolley, George S. and Krumm, Ronald J. On the Regional Labor-Supply Relation. **In** *Grieson, R. E., ed.*, 1983, pp. 203–37. **[G: U.S.]**

Tucci, Ginarocco. Razionalità sostanziale e funzionale nella programmazione regionale dei trasporti in Italia. (Substantial and Functional Rationality in Regional Planning of Transportation in Italy. With English summary.) *Rivista Int. Sci. Econ. Com.*, June 1983, *30*(6), pp. 540–54. **[G: Italy]**

Tulkens, Henry and Kiabantu, Tomasikila Kioni. A Planning Process for the Efficient Allocation of Resources to Transportation Infrastructure. **In** *Thisse, J.-F. and Zoller, H. G., eds.*, 1983, pp. 127–52.

Willett, Keith. Single- and Multi-Commodity Models of Spatial Equilibrium in a Linear Programming Framework. *Can. J. Agr. Econ.*, July 1983, *31*(2), pp. 205–22.

Wolinsky, Asher. Retail Trade Concentration Due to Consumers' Imperfect Information. *Bell J. Econ. (See Rand J. Econ. after 4/85)*, Spring 1983, *14*(1), pp. 275–82.

Wolsey, L. A. Fundamental Properties of Certain Discrete Location Problems. **In** *Thisse, J.-F. and Zoller, H. G., eds.*, 1983, pp. 331–55.

Woodfine, William J. Regional Disparities—Once Again [Regional Dependency in Canada]. *Can. Public Policy*, December 1983, *9*(4), pp. 499–505. **[G: Canada]**

9412 Regional Economic Studies

Alley, William M. Comment on 'Multiobjective River Basin Planning with Qualitative Criteria' by M. Gershon, L. Duckstein, and R. McAniff. *Water Resources Res.*, February 1983, *19*(1), pp. 293–94. **[G: U.S.]**

Almore, Mary G. and Richardson, Frances. Urban Health Care Delivery in the Sunbelt. **In** *Ballard, S. C. and James, T. E., eds.*, 1983, pp. 93–106. **[G: U.S.]**

Almquist, Eric L. Labour Specialization and the Irish Economy in 1841: An Aggregate Occupational Analysis. *Econ. Hist. Rev., 2nd Ser.*, November 1983, *36*(4), pp. 506–17. **[G: Ireland]**

Amos, Orley M., Jr. The Relationship between Regional Income Inequality, Personal Income Inequality, and Development. *Reg. Sci. Persp.*, 1983, *13*(1), pp. 3–14. **[G: U.S.]**

Anastasopoulos, Anastasios and Sims, William A. The Regional Impact of the Disintegration of the Canadian Common Market: The Case of Quebec. *Southern Econ. J.*, January 1983, *49*(3), pp. 743–63. **[G: Canada]**

Andrews, Donald R.; Murdock, Steve H. and Jones, Lonnie L. Private and Public Sector Economies of Lignite-Energy Resource Development in Rural Central Texas. *Southern J. Agr. Econ.*, December 1983, *15*(2), pp. 55–61. **[G: U.S.]**

Ansari, M. M. Variations in Plan Expenditure and Physical Achievement among the Indian States: An Empirical Analysis. *Margin*, April 1983, *15*(3), pp. 49–58. **[G: India]**

Anton, Thomas J. The Regional Distribution of Federal Expenditures, 1971–1980. *Nat. Tax J.*, December 1983, *36*(4), pp. 429–42. **[G: U.S.]**

Antonelli, Gilberto. Income Distribution and Labour Factor Quality: Models and Applications at a Regional Level. **In** *Weisbrod, B. and Hughes, H., eds.*, 1983, pp. 167–77. **[G: Italy]**

Armstrong, Harvey and Taylor, Jim. Unemployment Stocks and Flows in the Travel-to-Work Areas of the North-West Region. *Urban Stud.*, August 1983, *20*(3), pp. 311–25. **[G: U.K.]**

Arndt, H. W. Transmigration: Achievements, Problems, Prospects. *Bull. Indonesian Econ. Stud.*, December 1983, *19*(3), pp. 50–73. **[G: Indonesia]**

Arnold, Victor L. Long Range Planning for Managing Growth and Change. **In** *Ballard, S. C. and James, T. E., eds.*, 1983, pp. 197–211. **[G: U.S.]**

Ashcroft, Brian. The Scottish Region and the Regions of Scotland. **In** *Ingham, K. P. D. and Love, J., eds.*, 1983, pp. 173–87. **[G: U.K.]**

Atkinson, Scott E. Marketable Pollution Permits and Acid Rain Externalities. *Can. J. Econ.*, November 1983, *16*(4), pp. 704–22. **[G: U.S.; Canada]**

Atkinson, Scott E. Nonoptimal Solutions Using Transferable Discharge Permits: The Implications of Acid Rain Deposition. **In** *Joeres, E. F. and David, M. H., eds.*, 1983, pp. 55–69. **[G: U.S.]**

Auld, D. A. L. The Ontario Budget Deficit: A Cause for Concern? **In** *Conklin, D. W. and Courchene, T. J., eds.*, 1983, pp. 78–106. **[G: Canada]**

Aziz, Rashid; Butterfield, David and Kubursi, Atif A. Regional Equity and Efficiency: Some Experiments for Canada. *J. Reg. Sci.*, August 1983, *23*(3), pp. 397–412. **[G: Canada]**

Bade, Franz-Josef. Large Corporations and Regional Development. *Reg. Stud.*, October 1983, *17*(5), pp. 315–25. **[G: W. Germany]**

Bade, Franz-Josef. Locational Behaviour and the Mobility of Firms in West Germany. *Urban Stud.*, August 1983, *20*(3), pp. 279–97. **[G: W. Germany]**

Bajec, Jurij. Regional Disparities in Yugoslavia. **In** *Seers, D. and Öström, K., eds.*, 1983, pp. 47–61. **[G: Yugoslavia]**

Ball, R. M. Spatial and Structural Characteristics of Recent Unemployment Change: Some Policy Considerations. *Reg. Stud.*, April 1983, *17*(2), pp. 135–40. **[G: U.K.]**

Ballard, Steven C. and Gunn, Elizabeth M. State Government Capacity for Managing Sunbelt Growth. **In** *Ballard, S. C. and James, T. E., eds.*, 1983, pp. 107–31. **[G: U.S.]**

Baumann, Johann H. A Disaggregate Short Run Phillips Curve for Austria: The Effects of Regional Unemployment Dispersion and Spatial Wage Transfer on the National Wage Rate. *Z. Nationa-*

lökon., 1983, *43*(2), pp. 189–211. [G: Austria]

Becker, Edmund R. and Delaney, John Thomas. South/Non-South Differentials in National Labor Relations Board Certification Election Outcomes: Comment. *J. Lab. Res.*, Fall 1983, *4*(4), pp. 375–84. [G: U.S.]

Bell, C. L. G. and Hazell, Peter B. R. Measuring the Indirect Effects of an Agricultural Investment Project on Its Surrounding Region. In *Lim, D., ed.*, 1983, *1980*, pp. 65–77. [G: Malaysia]

Bender, Lloyd D. and Parcels, Larry C. Structural Differences and the Time Pattern of Basic Employment. *Land Econ.*, May 1983, *59*(2), pp. 220–34. [G: U.S.]

Black, Harold A. Deregulation and Locational Rents in Banking: Discussant's Comments. *J. Bank Res.*, Spring 1983, *14*(1), pp. 107–08. [G: U.S.]

Boos, Xavier. Economic Aspects of a Frontier Situation: The Case of Alsace. In *Anderson, M., ed.*, 1983, pp. 81–97. [G: France]

Booth, G. Geoffrey and Koveos, Peter E. Employment Fluctuations: An R/S Analysis. *J. Reg. Sci.*, February 1983, *23*(1), pp. 19–31. [G: U.S.]

Botham, Ron and Lloyd, Greg. The Political Economy of Enterprise Zones. *Nat. Westminster Bank Quart. Rev.*, May 1983, pp. 24–32. [G: U.K.]

Boyle, R. M. Linwood: Government and the Motor Car Industry in Scotland. *Reg. Stud.*, February 1983, *17*(1), pp. 49–52. [G: U.K.]

Bradbury, Katharine L. Revenues and Expenditures in New England's Largest Cities and Towns. *New Eng. Econ. Rev.*, July–August 1983, pp. 42–53. [G: U.S.]

Broner, Adam. Regional Comparisons of Labor Productivity. In *Dutta, M.; Hartline, J. C. and Loeb, P. D., eds.*, 1983, pp. 190–204. [G: U.S.]

Broussolle, C. Concurrence spatiale en univers aléatoire: le cas de l'industrie laitière et de ses marchés. *Revue Écon. Polit.*, January–February 1983, *93*(1), pp. 113–38. [G: France]

Browne, Lynn E. Can High Tech Save the Great Lake States? *New Eng. Econ. Rev.*, November/December 1983, pp. 19–33. [G: U.S.]

Browne, Lynn E. Electric Utilities' Finances since the Energy Crisis. *New Eng. Econ. Rev.*, March/April 1983, pp. 28–45. [G: U.S.]

Browne, Lynn E. High Technology and Business Services. *New Eng. Econ. Rev.*, July–August 1983, pp. 5–17. [G: U.S.]

Bryden, John M. Comments on 'Regional Development in Sweden.' In *Seers, D. and Öström, K., eds.*, 1983, pp. 41–46. [G: Sweden]

Buck, Andrew J., et al. The Deterrence Hypothesis Revisited. *Reg. Sci. Urban Econ.*, November 1983, *13*(4), pp. 471–86. [G: U.S.]

Buck, Trevor and Atkins, Martin. Regional Policies in Retrospect: An Application of Analysis and Variance. *Reg. Stud.*, June 1983, *17*(3), pp. 181–89. [G: U.K.]

Cappellin, Riccardo. Productivity Growth and Technological Change in a Regional Perspective. *Giorn. Econ.*, July–August 1983, *42*(7–8), pp. 459–82. [G: Italy; France]

Carter, Robert A. Resource-Related Development and Regional Labour Markets: The Effects of the Alcoa Aluminum Smelter on Portland. *Australian Econ. Rev.*, 1st Quarter 1983, (61), pp. 22–32. [G: Australia]

Cebula, Richard J. Determinants of Geographic Living-Cost Differentials in the United States: Reply. *Land Econ.*, August 1983, *59*(3), pp. 353–54. [G: U.S.]

Cebula, Richard J. Right-to-Work Laws and Geographic Differences in Living Costs: An Analysis of Effects of the 'Union Shop' Ban for the Years 1974, 1976, and 1978. *Amer. J. Econ. Soc.*, July 1983, *42*(3), pp. 329–40. [G: U.S.]

Cebula, Richard J. and Smith, Lisa K. On the Determinants of Inter-Regional Living-Cost Differentials in the United States, 1970 and 1975: Reply. *Reg. Sci. Urban Econ.*, November 1983, *13*(4), pp. 587–89. [G: U.S.]

Chakravarty, S. P.; Jones, D. R. and Mackay, R. R. United Kingdom Manpower Policy against a Background of National Economic Decline: The Welsh Example. *Reg. Stud.*, April 1983, *17*(2), pp. 91–104. [G: U.K.]

Chan, M. W. Luke and Mountain, Dean C. A Regional Analysis of Productivity Change in Canadian Agriculture, with Special Reference to Energy Prices. *Can. J. Agr. Econ.*, November 1983, *31*(3), pp. 319–30. [G: Canada]

Clayton, Elizabeth. Factor Endowment, Variable Proportions, and Agricultural Modernization: Regional Production Functions for Soviet Agriculture. In *Stuart, R. C., ed.*, 1983, pp. 161–72. [G: U.S.S.R.]

Clifton, Ivery D. and Spurlock, Stan B. Analysis of Variations in Farm Real Estate Prices over Homogeneous Market Areas in the Southeast. *Southern J. Agr. Econ.*, July 1983, *15*(1), pp. 89–96. [G: U.S.]

Cloutier, Norman R. Growth Centers and the Spatial Distribution of Development Funds: The Case of West Virginia. *Reg. Sci. Persp.*, 1983, *13*(1), pp. 15–24. [G: U.S.]

Cole, William E. and Sanders, Richard D. Interstate Migration in Mexico: Variations on the Todaro Theme. *J. Devel. Econ.*, June 1983, *12*(3), pp. 341–54. [G: Mexico]

Conway, Richard S., Jr. Applications of the Washington Projection and Simulation Model. In *Dutta, M.; Hartline, J. C. and Loeb, P. D., eds.*, 1983, pp. 105–15. [G: U.S.]

Cousineau, Jean-Michel and Lacroix, Robert. 'Effet de structure' et 'effet de marché régional' dans les disparités interrégionales de salaire: une application au cas de Montréal et Toronto. *Can. J. Econ.*, November 1983, *16*(4), pp. 655–68. [G: Canada]

Crespo, M. García and Flores, F. Aspectos espaciales de la crisis. (Spatial Aspects of the Crisis. With English summary.) *Écon. Soc.*, September–October–November 1983, *17*(9–10–11), pp. 1569–93. [G: Spain]

Crist, Raymond E. Westward Thursts the Pioneer Zone in Venezuela: A Half Century of Economic Development along the Llanos-Andes Border. *Amer. J. Econ. Soc.*, October 1983, *42*(4), pp. 451–62. [G: Venezuela]

Cuadrado Roura, J. R. Crisis industrial y cambios technológicos. Consideraciones desde una óptica espacial. (Industrial Crisis and Technological Changes in the Work Division. Its Reasoning from a Spanish Point of View. With English summary.) *Écon. Soc.*, September–October–November 1983, *17*(9–10–11), pp. 1671–99.

Daly, Maurice T. The Mobility of Manufacturing and Capital: Implications for Regional Development. **In** *Hamilton, F. E. I. and Linge, G. J. R., eds.*, 1983, pp. 399–421. **[G: Australia]**

Darden, Joe T. Racial Differences in Unemployment: A Spatial Perspective. *Rev. Black Polit. Econ.*, Spring 1983, *12*(3), pp. 93–105. **[G: U.S.]**

Dary, Yves and Gilly, Jean-Pierre. Le nouveau secteur public: un outil de politique industrielle régionale? (With English summary.) *Rev. Econ. Ind.*, 2nd Trimester 1983, (24), pp. 35–47. **[G: France]**

Deichert, Jerome A. and Dobitz, Clifford P. Inequality in the Distribution of Income: United States, March 1979. *Nebr. J. Econ. Bus.*, Spring 1983, *22*(2), pp. 22–32. **[G: U.S.]**

Denny, Michael G. S. and Fuss, Melvyn A. Regional Price Indexes: The Canadian Practice and Some Potential Extensions. **In** *Diewert, W. E. and Montmarquette, C., eds.*, 1983, pp. 783–816. **[G: Canada]**

Dienes, Leslie. Regional Economic Development. **In** *Bergson, A. and Levine, H. S., eds.*, 1983, pp. 218–68. **[G: U.S.S.R.]**

Doyle, Peter and Corstjens, Marcel. Optimal Growth Strategies for Service Organizations. *J. Bus.*, July 1983, *56*(3), pp. 389–405. **[G: U.K.]**

Dunlevy, James A. and Bellante, Don. Net Migration, Endogenous Incomes and the Speed of Adjustment to the North-South Differential. *Rev. Econ. Statist.*, February 1983, *65*(1), pp. 66–75. **[G: U.S.]**

Dyson, Tim and Moore, Mick. On Kinship Structure, Female Autonomy, and Demographic Behavior in India. *Population Devel. Rev.*, March 1983, *9*(1), pp. 35–60. **[G: India]**

Edmundson, Wade C. and Edmundson, Stella A. A Decade of Village Development in East Java. *Bull. Indonesian Econ. Stud.*, August 1983, *19*(2), pp. 46–59. **[G: Indonesia]**

Edwards, Anthony. The Structure of Industrial Change: Regional Incentives to the Textile Industry of Northeast Brazil. **In** *Hamilton, F. E. I. and Linge, G. J. R., eds.*, 1983, pp. 485–508. **[G: Brazil]**

Faini, Riccardo. Cumulative Processes of De-Industrialisation in an Open Region: The Case of Southern Italy, 1951-1973. *J. Devel. Econ.*, June 1983, *12*(3), pp. 277–301. **[G: Italy]**

Falk, Laurence H. The Service Sector vs. the Manufacturing Sector: A New Jersey Perspective. **In** *Dutta, M.; Hartline, J. C. and Loeb, P. D., eds.*, 1983, pp. 205–15. **[G: U.S.]**

Fothergill, Stephen; Kitson, Michael and Monk, Sarah. The Impact of the New and Expanded Town Programmes on Industrial Location in Britain, 1960–78. *Reg. Stud.*, August 1983, *17*(4), pp. 251–60. **[G: U.K.]**

Fraser, Neil. Scotland in Europe. **In** *Ingham, K. P. D. and Love, J., eds.*, 1983, pp. 245–54. **[G: U.K.]**

Fromm, Daniel W., et al. Determination of Output at the Regional Level: The New York Power Pool and New York Region Econometric Models. **In** *Dutta, M.; Hartline, J. C. and Loeb, P. D., eds.*, 1983, pp. 230–45. **[G: U.S.]**

Fuà, Giorgio. Rural Industralization in Later Developed Countries: The Case of Northeast and Central Italy. *Banca Naz. Lavoro Quart. Rev.*, December 1983, (147), pp. 351–77. **[G: Italy]**

Furuki, Toshiaki. The Post-war Development of Capitalism and Regional Problems: A Comparison of Italy and Japan. **In** *Fodella, G., ed.*, 1983, pp. 179–92. **[G: Italy; Japan]**

Garnick, Daniel H. Shifting Patterns in the Growth of Metropolitan and Nonmetropolitan Areas. *Surv. Curr. Bus.*, May 1983, *63*(5), pp. 39–44. **[G: U.S.]**

Garnick, Daniel H. U.S. Population Distribution into the Twenty-First Century. **In** *Gau, G. W. and Goldberg, M. A., eds.*, 1983, pp. 73–88. **[G: U.S.]**

Garrison, Charles B. and Kort, John R. Regional Impact of Monetary and Fiscal Policy: A Comment. *J. Reg. Sci.*, May 1983, *23*(2), pp. 249–61. **[G: U.S.]**

Gerking, Shelby D. and Weirick, William N. Compensating Differences and Interregional Wage Differentials. *Rev. Econ. Statist.*, August 1983, *65*(3), pp. 483–87. **[G: U.S.]**

Gershon, Mark and Duckstein, Lucien. Reply [Multiobjective River Basin Planning with Qualitative Criteria]. *Water Resources Res.*, February 1983, *19*(1), pp. 295–96. **[G: U.S.]**

Goddard, John B. Industrial Innovation and Regional Economic Development in Great Britain. **In** *Hamilton, F. E. I. and Linge, G. J. R., eds.*, 1983, pp. 255–77. **[G: U.K.]**

Goldfarb, Robert S.; Yezer, Anthony M. J. and Crewe, Sebastian. Some New Evidence: Have Regional Wage Differentials Really Disappeared? *Growth Change*, January 1983, *14*(1), pp. 48–51. **[G: U.S.]**

Good, David F. Economic Union and Uneven Development in the Habsburg Monarchy. **In** *Komlos, J., ed.*, 1983, *1981*, pp. 65–80. **[G: Austria; Hungary]**

Gray, Kenneth R. Improved Agricultural Location: Econometric Evidence from the Ukraine. **In** *Stuart, R. C., ed.*, 1983, pp. 199–222. **[G: U.S.S.R.]**

Gurwitz, Aaron S. New York State's Economic Turnaround: Services or Manufacturing. *Fed. Res. Bank New York Quart. Rev.*, Autumn 1983, *8*(3), pp. 30–34. **[G: U.S.]**

Hall, Timothy A. Energy Management and Economic Development in Mississippi. **In** *Ballard, S. C. and James, T. E., eds.*, 1983, pp. 180–96. **[G: U.S.]**

Halpin, Michael C. New Land Use Economics and Opportunities for the 1980s. **In** *Carr, J. H. and Duensing, E. E., eds.*, 1983, *1980*, pp. 277–90. **[G: U.S.]**

Harber, Richard Paul, Jr. Brazil's Fiscal Incentive System and the Northeast: An Econometric Analysis. *J. Econ. Devel.*, July 1983, *8*(1), pp. 131–59. **[G: Brazil]**

Harper, Carolyn and Field, Barry C. Energy Substitution in U.S. Manufacturing: A Regional Approach. *Southern Econ. J.*, October 1983, *50*(2), pp. 385–95. **[G: U.S.]**

Harris, R. I. D. The Measurement of Capital Services in Production for UK Regions, 1968-78. *Reg. Stud.*, June 1983, *17*(3), pp. 169–80. **[G: U.K.]**

Harrison, Joseph. Heavy Industry, the State, and Economic Development in the Basque Region, 1876–1936. *Econ. Hist. Rev., 2nd Ser.*, November 1983, *36*(4), pp. 535–51. **[G: Spain]**

Haug, P.; Hood, N. and Young, S. Mark. R & D Intensity in the Affiliates of U.S. Owned Electronics Companies Manufacturing in Scotland. *Reg. Stud.*, December 1983, *17*(6), pp. 383–92. **[G: U.K.]**

Healey, Michael. Components of Locational Change in Multi-Plant Enterprises. *Urban Stud.*, August 1983, *20*(3), pp. 327–42. **[G: U.K.]**

Heaney, James P. Coalition Formation and the Size of Regional Pollution Control Systems. **In** *Joeres, E. F. and David, M. H., eds.*, 1983, pp. 99–120. **[G: U.S.]**

Heim, Carol E. Industrial Organization and Regional Development in Interwar Britain. *J. Econ. Hist.*, December 1983, *43*(4), pp. 931–52. **[G: U.K.]**

Herzog, Henry W., Jr.; Schlottmann, Alan M. and Schriver, William R. Regional Planning and Interstate Construction Worker Migration. *Growth Change*, April 1983, *14*(2), pp. 50–54. **[G: U.S.]**

Hester, Donald D. Deregulation and Locational Rents in Banking. *J. Bank Res.*, Spring 1983, *14*(1), pp. 96–107. **[G: U.S.]**

Hodge, Gerald. Canadian Small Town Renaissance: Implications for Settlement System Concepts. *Reg. Stud.*, February 1983, *17*(1), pp. 19–28. **[G: Canada]**

Horiba, Yukata and Kirkpatrick, Rickey C. U.S. North-South Labor Migration and Trade. *J. Reg. Sci.*, February 1983, *23*(1), pp. 93–103. **[G: U.S.]**

Hudson, Ray. Capital Accumulation and Regional Problems: A Study of North East England, 1945 to 1980. **In** *Hamilton, F. E. I. and Linge, G. J. R., eds.*, 1983, pp. 75–101. **[G: U.K.]**

Hutchinson, Peter M. Refinery Closings and the Regional Distribution of Refining Capacity. *Reg. Sci. Persp.*, 1983, *13*(2), pp. 15–25. **[G: U.S.]**

Ingham, Keith P. D. and Love, James. Scotland in the UK Economy. **In** *Ingham, K. P. D. and Love, J., eds.*, 1983, pp. 235–44.

Isakson, Hans R. Residential Space Heating: An Analysis of Energy Conservation. *Energy Econ.*, January 1983, *5*(1), pp. 49–57. **[G: U.S.]**

Islam, Muhammed N. The Efficiency of Interprovincial Migration in Canada, 1961–1978. *Reg. Sci. Urban Econ.*, May 1983, *13*(2), pp. 231–49. **[G: Canada]**

Izraeli, Oded. Federal Individual Income Tax and Allocation of Labor between SMSA's. *J. Reg. Sci.*, February 1983, *23*(1), pp. 105–13. **[G: U.S.]**

James, Thomas E., Jr. Anticipating Future Growth in the Sunbelt. **In** *Ballard, S. C. and James, T. E., eds.*, 1983, pp. 37–62. **[G: U.S.]**

Jepson, D. The Coventry Local Economy, the Motor Vehicles Industry and Some Implications for Public Policy. *Reg. Stud.*, February 1983, *17*(1), pp. 56–59. **[G: U.K.]**

Johnson, Kenneth; Friedenberg, Howard and Downey, George. Tracking the BEA Regional and State Economic Projections. *Surv. Curr. Bus.*, May 1983, *63*(5), pp. 45–52. **[G: U.S.]**

Johnson, P. S. New Manufacturing Firms in the U.K. Regions. *Scot. J. Polit. Econ.*, February 1983, *30*(1), pp. 75–79. **[G: U.K.]**

Karlson, Stephen H. Modeling Location and Production: An Application to U.S. Fully-Integrated Steel Plants. *Rev. Econ. Statist.*, February 1983, *65*(1), pp. 41–50. **[G: U.S.]**

Kaur, Kulwinder. A Factor Analysis of Inter-Regional Disparities in Industrialisation—The Case of Haryana. *Margin*, October 1983, *16*(1), pp. 84–91. **[G: India]**

Keeble, David; Owens, Peter L. and Thompson, Chris. The Urban–Rural Manufacturing Shift in the European Community. *Urban Stud.*, November 1983, *20*(4), pp. 405–18. **[G: EEC]**

Kessinger, Tom G., et al. Regional Economy (1757–1857). **In** *Kumar, D., ed.*, 1983, pp. 242–375. **[G: India]**

Kiljunen, Kimmo. Comments on 'Regional Disparities in Yugoslavia.' **In** *Seers, D. and Öström, K., eds.*, 1983, pp. 62–67. **[G: Yugoslavia; OECD]**

van der Knaap, Gijsbertus A. An Economic Potential Model for the European Economic Community: A Tool for Understanding Industrial Systems. **In** *Hamilton, F. E. I. and Linge, G. J. R., eds.*, 1983, pp. 121–40. **[G: EEC]**

Kolk, David X. Regional Employment Impact of Rapidly Escalating Energy Costs. *Energy Econ.*, April 1983, *5*(2), pp. 105–13. **[G: U.S.]**

Kresge, David T.; Ginn, Royce J. and Gray, John T. Transportation System Planning for Alaska Development. **In** *Khachaturov, T. S. and Goodwin, P. B., eds.*, 1983, pp. 112–33. **[G: U.S.]**

Krumm, Ronald J. Regional Labor Markets and the Household Migration Decision. *J. Reg. Sci.*, August 1983, *23*(3), pp. 361–76. **[G: U.S.]**

Krumm, Ronald J. Regional Wage Differentials, Fluctuations in Labor Demand, and Migration. *Int. Reg. Sci. Rev.*, June 1983, *8*(1), pp. 23–45.

Lamb, Richard F. The Extent and Form of Exurban Sprawl. *Growth Change*, January 1983, *14*(1), pp. 40–47. **[G: U.S.]**

Ledebur, Larry C. and Moomaw, Ronald L. A Shift-Share Analysis of Regional Labor Productivity in Manufacturing. *Growth Change*, January 1983, *14*(1), pp. 2–9. **[G: U.S.]**

Leigh, Wilhelmina A. The Impact of Inflation upon Homeownership Affordability: Comparisons by Race and Sex for the South. **In** *Schmukler, N. and Marcus, E., eds.*, 1983, pp. 838–59. **[G: U.S.]**

Leinbach, Thomas R. Rural Transport and Population Mobility in Indonesia. *J. Devel. Areas*, April 1983, *17*(3), pp. 349–63. **[G: Indonesia]**

Lesage, Jean-Luc. Comments on 'Regional Development in Portugal.' **In** *Seers, D. and Öström, K., eds.*, 1983, pp. 83–85. **[G: Portugal]**

Ley, David and Mercer, John. Locational Conflict and the Politics of Consumption. **In** *Lake, R. W., ed.*, 1983, *1980*, pp. 118–42.

Little, Jane Sneddon. Foreign Investors' Locational Choices: An Update. *New Eng. Econ. Rev.*, January/February 1983, pp. 28–31. [G: U.S.]

Loeb, Peter D. Leading and Coincident Indicators of Recession and Recovery in New Jersey. In *Dutta, M.; Hartline, J. C. and Loeb, P. D., eds.*, 1983, pp. 151–72. [G: U.S.]

Love, James and Stewart, William J. Scottish Trade. In *Ingham, K. P. D. and Love, J., eds.*, 1983, pp. 28–37. [G: U.K.]

Lundahl, Mats. The State of Spatial Economic Research on Haiti: A Selective Survey. In *Lundahl, M.*, 1983, *1980*, pp. 153–70. [G: Haiti]

Madden, J. R.; Challen, D. W. and Hagger, A. J. The Grants Commission's Relativities Proposals: Effects on the State Economies. *Australian Econ. Pap.*, December 1983, *22*(41), pp. 302–21. [G: Australia]

Maddigan, Ruth J.; Chern, Wen S. and Rizy, Colleen Gallagher. Rural Residential Demand for Electricity. *Land Econ.*, May 1983, *59*(2), pp. 150–62. [G: U.S.]

Majmudar, Madhavi G. Government and the Scottish Economic Performance: 1954–1978. *Scot. J. Polit. Econ.*, June 1983, *30*(2), pp. 153–69. [G: U.K.]

Marelli, Enrico. Empirical Estimation of Intersectoral and Interregional Transfers of Surplus Value: The Case of Italy. *J. Reg. Sci.*, February 1983, *23*(1), pp. 49–70.

Marr, William and Whitney, Wayne. The Changing Pattern of Differential Regional Growth in Canada, 1951–61 and 1961–71. *Nebr. J. Econ. Bus.*, Winter, 1983, *22*(1), pp. 29–43. [G: Canada]

Marzano, Ferruccio, et al. The Southern Banking System, the Development of the Mezzogiorno and the Entry of Foreign Banks into Italy. *Rev. Econ. Cond. Italy*, February 1983, (1), pp. 55–96. [G: Italy]

Masser, Ian. Planning and Migration Research. In *Morrison, P. A., ed.*, 1983, pp. 241–60. [G: Netherlands]

Massey, Doreen. Industrial Restructuring as Class Restructuring: Production Decentralization and Local Uniqueness. *Reg. Stud.*, April 1983, *17*(2), pp. 73–89. [G: U.K.]

Mathur, Ashok. Regional Development and Income Disparities in India: A Sectoral Analysis. *Econ. Develop. Cult. Change*, April 1983, *31*(3), pp. 475–505. [G: India]

Mathur, Vijay K. and Stein, Sheldon H. Regional Impact of Monetary and Fiscal Policy: A Reply. *J. Reg. Sci.*, May 1983, *23*(2), pp. 263–65. [G: U.S.]

McConnell, James E. The International Location of Manufacturing Investments: Recent Behaviour of Foreign-owned Corporations in the United States. In *Hamilton, F. E. I. and Linge, G. J. R., eds.*, 1983, pp. 337–58. [G: U.S.]

McGovern, Daniel J. Capital Flight: Anticipating Sunbelt Problems. In *Ballard, S. C. and James, T. E., eds.*, 1983, pp. 63–92. [G: U.S.]

McGreevy, T. E. and Thomson, A. W. J. Regional Policy and Company Investment Behaviour. *Reg. Stud.*, October 1983, *17*(5), pp. 347–57. [G: U.K.]

McGuire, Alistair J. The Regional Income and Employment Impacts of Nuclear Power Stations. *Scot. J. Polit. Econ.*, November 1983, *30*(3), pp. 264–74. [G: U.K.]

McLoughlin, P. J. Community Considerations as Location Attraction Variables for Manufacturing Industry. *Urban Stud.*, August 1983, *20*(3), pp. 359–63. [G: U.K.; U.S.]

McNicoll, Iain. Understanding the Scottish Economy: Structure. In *Ingham, K. P. D. and Love, J., eds.*, 1983, pp. 3–14. [G: U.K.]

Meissner, Frank. Mexican Border and Free Zone Areas: Implications for Development. In *Czinkota, M. R., ed. (II)*, 1983, pp. 253–78. [G: Mexico; U.S.]

Mendizabal Gorostiaga, A. La crisis económica: su incidencia en el País Vasco. (The Economic Crisis: Its Incidence in the Basque Country. With English summary.) *Écon. Soc.*, September–October–November 1983, *17*(9–10–11), pp. 1595–1609. [G: Spain]

Merrifield, John. The Role of Shift-Share in Regional Analysis. *Reg. Sci. Persp.*, 1983, *13*(1), pp. 48–54. [G: U.S.]

Miller, D. The Role of the Motor Car Industry in the West Midlands Economy. *Reg. Stud.*, February 1983, *17*(1), pp. 53–56. [G: U.K.]

Miller, Edward M. Productive Efficiency and Region: Comment. *Southern Econ. J.*, July 1983, *50*(1), pp. 257–60. [G: U.S.]

Montanari, Silvano. La produttività nelle regioni comunitarie europee per branca di attività nel 1970 e nel 1973. (Productivity in European Community Regions for Branches of Activity in 1970 and 1973. With English summary.) *Rivista Int. Sci. Econ. Com.*, July 1983, *30*(7), pp. 654–66. [G: EEC]

Moomaw, Ronald L. Productive Efficiency and Region: Reply. *Southern Econ. J.*, July 1983, *50*(1), pp. 261–64. [G: U.S.]

Moomaw, Ronald L. Spatial Productivity Variations in Manufacturing: A Critical Survey of Cross-Sectional Analyses. *Int. Reg. Sci. Rev.*, June 1983, *8*(1), pp. 1–22. [G: U.S.]

Morrell, Stephen O. and Saba, Richard P. The Effects of Federal Home Loan Mortgage Corporation Secondary Market on Regional Mortgage Yield Differentials. *Quart. Rev. Econ. Bus.*, Spring 1983, *23*(1), pp. 85–97. [G: U.S.]

Musto, Stefan A. Comments on 'Towards a New Regional Policy in Spain.' In *Seers, D. and Öström, K., eds.*, 1983, pp. 121–26. [G: Spain]

Nenonen, Tuomo and Linnainmaa, Hannu T. Regional Effects of the Eastern Trade: An Example from Northern Finland. In *Möttölä, K.; Bykov, O. N. and Korolev, I. S., eds.*, 1983, pp. 213–19. [G: U.S.S.R.; Finland]

Newman, Robert J. Industry Migration and Growth in the South. *Rev. Econ. Statist.*, February 1983, *65*(1), pp. 76–86. [G: U.S.]

Niemi, Albert W., Jr. Gross State Product and Productivity in the Southeast, 1950–80. *Growth Change*, April 1983, *14*(2), pp. 3–8. [G: U.S.]

Norrie, Kenneth H. and Percy, Michael B. Freight Rate Reform and Regional Burden: A General Equilibrium Analysis of Western Freight Rate Proposals. *Can. J. Econ.*, May 1983, *16*(2), pp. 325–49.

O'Farrell, P. N. and Crouchley, R. Industrial Closures in Ireland 1973–1981: Analysis and Implications. *Reg. Stud.*, December 1983, *17*(6), pp. 411–27. **[G: Ireland]**

Oakey, Ray P. High-technology Industry, Industrial Location and Regional Development: The British Case. **In** *Hamilton, F. E. I. and Linge, G. J. R., eds.*, 1983, pp. 279–95. **[G: U.K.]**

Ohlsson, Lennart. Structural Adaptability of Regions during Swedish Industrial Adjustment, 1965 to 1975. **In** *Hamilton, F. E. I. and Linge, G. J. R., eds.*, 1983, pp. 297–335. **[G: Sweden]**

Ortona, Guido and Santagata, Walter. Industrial Mobility in the Turin Metropolitan Area, 1961–77. *Urban Stud.*, February 1983, *20*(1), pp. 59–71. **[G: Italy]**

Osborne, Dale K. Is the Southwest Short of Capital? *Fed. Res. Bank Dallas Econ. Rev.*, January 1983, pp. 1–10. **[G: U.S.]**

Öström, Kjell. Regional Development in the Northern Periphery of Sweden: A Failure? **In** *Seers, D. and Öström, K., eds.*, 1983, pp. 23–40. **[G: Sweden]**

Ostrosky, Anthony L. An Exploratory Note on Determinants of Inter-Regional Living-Cost Differentials in the United States, 1970 and 1975: Comment. *Reg. Sci. Urban Econ.*, November 1983, *13*(4), pp. 583–85. **[G: U.S.]**

Ostrosky, Anthony L. Determinants of Geographic Living-Cost Differentials in the United States: Comment. *Land Econ.*, August 1983, *59*(3), pp. 350–52. **[G: U.S.]**

Parenteau, Roland. Le cadre historique et institutionnel des societes d'etat au Quebec. (State Enterprise in Quebec: The Historical and Institutional Background. With English summary.) *Ann. Pub. Co-op. Econ.*, March 1983, *54*(1), pp. 57–72. **[G: Canada]**

Penny, Michael; Trebilcock, Michael J. and Laskin, John B. Existing and Proposed Constitutional Constraints on Provincially Induced Barriers to Economic Mobility in Canada. **In** *Trebilcock, M. J., et al., eds.*, 1983, pp. 501–41. **[G: Canada]**

Pfister, Richard L. Dire Predictions Reexamined: Regional Impacts of Rising Energy Prices. *Growth Change*, April 1983, *14*(2), pp. 9–16. **[G: U.S.]**

Pijawka, D. and Chalmers, J. Impacts of Nuclear Generating Plants on Local Areas. *Econ. Geogr.*, January 1983, *59*(1), pp. 66–80. **[G: U.S.]**

Plaut, Thomas R. and Pluta, Joseph E. Business Climate, Taxes and Expenditures, and State Industrial Growth in the United States. *Southern Econ. J.*, July 1983, *50*(1), pp. 99–119. **[G: U.S.]**

Pola, Giorgio and Brosio, Giancarlo. The Role of Public Employment in a Dualistic Economy: The Italian Case. *Econ. Notes*, 1983, (1), pp. 80–97. **[G: Italy]**

Polèse, Mario. Le commerce interrégional des services: le rôle des relations intra-firme et des facteurs organisationnels. (Interregional Trade in Services: Intra-Firm Transactions and Organizational Factors. With English summary.) *L'Actual. Econ.*, December 1983, *59*(4), pp. 713–28. **[G: Canada]**

Regens, James L. and Rycroft, Robert W. Intergovernmental Issues in Managing Sunbelt Growth. **In** *Ballard, S. C. and James, T. E., eds.*, 1983, pp. 162–79. **[G: U.S.]**

Reppy, Judith. The Structure of the Defense Industry: The United States. **In** *Ball, N. and Leitenberg, M., eds.*, 1983, pp. 21–49. **[G: U.S.]**

Rice, G. Randolph and Lozada, Gabriel A. The Effects of Unemployment and Inflation on the Income Distribution: A Regional View. *Atlantic Econ. J.*, July 1983, *11*(2), pp. 12–21. **[G: U.S.]**

Ricq, Charles. Frontier Workers in Europe. **In** *Anderson, M., ed.*, 1983, pp. 98–108. **[G: Europe]**

Roberts, Rebecca S. and Butler, Lisa M. The Sunbelt Phenomenon: Causes of Growth. **In** *Ballard, S. C. and James, T. E., eds.*, 1983, pp. 1–36. **[G: U.S.]**

Rose, Adam. Modeling the Macroeconomic Impact of Air Pollution Abatement. *J. Reg. Sci.*, November 1983, *23*(4), pp. 441–59. **[G: U.S.]**

Saenz de Buruaga, Gonzalo. Towards a New Regional Policy in Spain. **In** *Seers, D. and Öström, K., eds.*, 1983, pp. 86–120. **[G: Spain]**

Saha, S. K. Industrial Policy and Locational Dynamics of Small-scale Enterprises in India. **In** *Hamilton, F. E. I. and Linge, G. J. R., eds.*, 1983, pp. 509–31. **[G: India]**

Sahling, Leonard G. and Smith, Sharon P. Regional Wage Differentials: Has the South Risen Again? *Rev. Econ. Statist.*, February 1983, *65*(1), pp. 131–35. **[G: U.S.]**

Sain, Gustavo E.; Martin, Philip L. and Paris, Quirino. A Regional Analysis of Illegal Aliens. *Growth Change*, January 1983, *14*(1), pp. 27–31. **[G: U.S.]**

Sandver, Marcus Hart. Reply to Becker and Delaney [South/Non-South Differentials in National Labor Relations Board Certification Election Outcomes]. *J. Lab. Res.*, Fall 1983, *4*(4), pp. 385–91. **[G: U.S.]**

Santoni, G. J. Business Cycles and the Eighth District. *Fed. Res. Bank St. Louis Rev.*, December 1983, *65*(10), pp. 14–21. **[G: U.S.]**

Sarkar, B. N. Disparities in Inter-State Consumer Expenditure, 1957–58 to 1973–74. *Margin*, July 1983, *15*(4), pp. 66–77. **[G: India]**

Savey, Suzane. Organization of Production and the New Spatial Division of Labour in France. **In** *Hamilton, F. E. I. and Linge, G. J. R., eds.*, 1983, pp. 103–20. **[G: France]**

Schaffer, William A. The Financial Impact of a University: A Case Study—The Impact of Georgia Tech on Georgia State Economy. **In** *Dutta, M.; Hartline, J. C. and Loeb, P. D., eds.*, 1983, pp. 131–50. **[G: U.S.]**

Schmidt, Charles G. Location Decision-Making within a Retail Corporation. *Reg. Sci. Persp.*, 1983, *13*(1), pp. 60–71. **[G: U.S.]**

Scott, A. J. Industrial Organization and the Logic of Intra-Metropolitan Location, II: A Case Study of the Printed Circuits Industry in the Greater Los Angeles Region. *Econ. Geogr.*, October 1983, *59*(4), pp. 343–67. **[G: U.S.]**

Scouller, John. 'Made in Scotland' (Production). **In** *Ingham, K. P. D. and Love, J., eds.*, 1983, pp. 15–27. **[G: U.K.]**

Shaffer, Ron E. A Test of the Differences in Export Base Multipliers in Expanding and Contracting

Economies. *Reg. Sci. Persp.*, 1983, *13*(2), pp. 61–74. [G: U.S.]

Shah, Anup R. K. and Walker, Martin. The Distribution of Regional Earnings in the UK. *Appl. Econ.*, August 1983, *15*(4), pp. 507–19. [G: U.K.]

Shahidsaless, Shahin; Gillis, William and Shaffer, Ron. Community Characteristics and Employment Multipliers in Nonmetropolitan Counties, 1950–1970. *Land Econ.*, February 1983, *59*(1), pp. 84–93. [G: U.S.]

Sit, Victor F. S. The Informal Sector within a Communist Industrial Structure: The Case of the People's Republic of China. In *Hamilton, F. E. I. and Linge, G. J. R., eds.*, 1983, pp. 551–80. [G: China]

Storey, D. J. Regional Policy in a Recession. *Nat. Westminster Bank Quart. Rev.*, November 1983, pp. 39–47. [G: U.K.]

Strong, John S. Regional Variations in Industrial Performance. *Reg. Stud.*, December 1983, *17*(6), pp. 429–44. [G: U.S.]

Suarez-Villa, Luis. A Note on Dualism, Capital–Labor Ratios, and the Regions of the U.S. *J. Reg. Sci.*, November 1983, *23*(4), pp. 547–52. [G: U.S.]

Tassinari, Franco. Sviluppo dell'agricoltura e mutamenti sociali in Emilia-Romagna. (Agricultural Development and Social Changes in Emilia Romagna. With English summary.) *Statistica*, July–September 1983, *43*(3), pp. 425–32. [G: Italy]

Taylor, Jim and Bradley, Steven. Spatial Variations in the Unemployment Rate: A Case Study of North West England. *Reg. Stud.*, April 1983, *17*(2), pp. 113–24. [G: U.K.]

Taylor, Michael and Kissling, Chris. Resource Dependence, Power Networks and the Airline System of the South Pacific. *Reg. Stud.*, August 1983, *17*(4), pp. 237–50. [G: South Pacific]

Taylor, Michael and Thrift, Nigel. The Role of Finance in the Evolution and Functioning of Industrial Systems. In *Hamilton, F. E. I. and Linge, G. J. R., eds.*, 1983, pp. 359–85. [G: U.K.; U.S.]

Thomas, Vinod. Welfare Analysis of Pollution Control with Spatial Alternatives. *Urban Stud.*, May 1983, *20*(2), pp. 219–27. [G: U.S.]

Thompson, John Scott. Patterns of Employment Multipliers in a Central Place System: An Alternative to Economic Base Estimation. *J. Reg. Sci.*, February 1983, *23*(1), pp. 71–82. [G: Philippines]

Tiller, Richard B. and Bednarzik, Robert W. The Behavior of Regional Unemployment Rates over Time: Effects on Dispersion and National Unemployment. *J. Reg. Sci.*, November 1983, *23*(4), pp. 479–99. [G: U.S.]

Tomlinson, R. Industrial Decentralization and the Relief of Poverty in the Homelands. *S. Afr. J. Econ.*, December 1983, *51*(4), pp. 544–63. [G: S. Africa]

Trebilcock, Michael J., et al. Provincially Induced Barriers to Trade in Canada: A Survey. In *Trebilcock, M. J., et al., eds.*, 1983, pp. 243–351. [G: Canada]

Twine, Fred. The Low Paid. In *Brown, G. and Cook, R., eds.*, 1983, pp. 107–35. [G: U.K.]

Valente de Oliveira, Luís F. Regional Development in Portugal. In *Seers, D. and Öström, K., eds.*, 1983, pp. 68–82. [G: Portugal]

Vander Weide, James H. Deregulation and Locational Rents in Banking: Discussant's Comments. *J. Bank Res.*, Spring 1983, *14*(1), pp. 108–09. [G: U.S.]

Whalley, John. Induced Distortions of Interprovincial Activity: An Overview of Issues. In *Trebilcock, M. J., et al., eds.*, 1983, pp. 161–200. [G: Canada]

White, W. R. The Ontario Budget Deficit: A Cause for Concern? Comment. In *Conklin, D. W. and Courchene, T. J., eds.*, 1983, pp. 107–13. [G: Canada]

Wiegersma, Nancy. Regional Differences in Socialist Transformation in Vietnam. *Econ. Forum*, Summer 1983, *14*(1), pp. 95–109. [G: Vietnam]

Williams, Daniel G. Regional Development as Determined by Alternative Regional Goals. *Growth Change*, July 1983, *14*(3), pp. 23–37. [G: U.S.]

Williams, Harry B. Wages of Appliance Repair Technicians Vary Widely among Metropolitan Areas. *Mon. Lab. Rev.*, December 1983, *106*(12), pp. 52–53. [G: U.S.]

Williams, Joseph E.; Meyer, Steve R. and Bullock, J. Bruce. Interregional Competition in the U.S. Swine–Pork Industry: An Analysis of Oklahoma's and the Southern States' Expansion Potential. *Southern J. Agr. Econ.*, July 1983, *15*(1), pp. 145–53. [G: U.S.]

Witholder, Robert E., Jr. Economic Feasibility of Dispersed Solar Electric Technologies. In *Brown, H. J., ed.*, 1983, pp. 121–61. [G: U.S.]

Wulwick, Nancy J. Can Keynesian Economics Be Scientific? An Historical Reconstruction. *Eastern Econ. J.*, July–September 1983, *9*(3), pp. 190–204. [G: U.K.]

You, Jong Keun. Intrastate Shifts in a Regional Economy. In *Dutta, M.; Hartline, J. C. and Loeb, P. D., eds.*, 1983, pp. 216–29. [G: U.S.]

Zimmermann, Horst. Grants to Communities in Their Relation to National Growth. In *Biehl, D.; Roskamp, K. W. and Stolper, W. F., eds.*, 1983, pp. 297–313. [G: W. Germany]

9413 Regional Economic Models and Forecasts

Baird, Catherine Ann. A Multiregional Econometric Model of Ohio. *J. Reg. Sci.*, November 1983, *23*(4), pp. 501–15. [G: U.S.]

Ballard, Kenneth P. The Structure of a Large-Scale Small-Area Multiregional Model of California: Modelling an Integrated System of Urban, Suburban and Rural Growth. *Reg. Stud.*, October 1983, *17*(5), pp. 327–38. [G: U.S.]

Batty, Michael and Karmeshu. A Strategy for Generating and Testing Models of Migration and Urban Growth. *Reg. Stud.*, August 1983, *17*(4), pp. 223–36.

Beaumont, Paul M. Wage Rate Specification in Regional and Interregional Econometric Models. *Int. Reg. Sci. Rev.*, June 1983, *8*(1), pp. 75–83. [G: U.S.]

Betson, David M. Complementary Strategies for Policy Analysis: Combining Microeconomic and Regional Simulation Models. *Reg. Sci. Urban Econ.*, May 1983, *13*(2), pp. 213–29. [G: U.S.]

Beyers, William B. The Interregional Structure of the U.S. Economy. *Int. Reg. Sci. Rev.*, December 1983, *8*(3), pp. 213–31. [G: U.S.]

Blommestein, Hans J. Specification and Estimation of Spatial Econometric Models: A Discussion of Alternative Strategies for Spatial Economic Modelling. *Reg. Sci. Urban Econ.*, May 1983, *13*(2), pp. 251–70.

Charney, Alberta H. and Taylor, Carol A. Consistent Region-Subregion Econometric Models: A Comparison of Multiarea Methods. *Int. Reg. Sci. Rev.*, June 1983, *8*(1), pp. 59–74. [G: U.S.]

Collins, Glenn S. and Taylor, C. Robert. TECHSIM: A Regional Field Crop and National Livestock Econometric Simulation Model. *Agr. Econ. Res.*, April 1983, *35*(2), pp. 1–18. [G: U.S.]

Conway, Richard S., Jr. Applications of the Washington Projection and Simulation Model. **In** *Dutta, M.; Hartline, J. C. and Loeb, P. D., eds.*, 1983, pp. 105–15. [G: U.S.]

Dutta, Manoranjan. Modeling and Intersectoral Analysis of the State Economy—The Rationale. **In** *Dutta, M.; Hartline, J. C. and Loeb, P. D., eds.*, 1983, pp. 51–64.

Emerson, M. Jarvin and Carey, Stephen. Relationships between Regional Economic Development and Regional Economic Structure. **In** *Dutta, M.; Hartline, J. C. and Loeb, P. D., eds.*, 1983, pp. 80–104. [G: U.S.]

Folland, Sherman T. Predicting Hospital Market Shares. *Inquiry*, Spring 1983, *20*(1), pp. 34–44. [G: U.S.]

Fromm, Daniel W., et al. Determination of Output at the Regional Level: The New York Power Pool and New York Region Econometric Models. **In** *Dutta, M.; Hartline, J. C. and Loeb, P. D., eds.*, 1983, pp. 230–45. [G: U.S.]

Ghosh, Dilip K. A Forecasting Framework for the Nascent New Jersey—South: A Mathematical Note. **In** *Dutta, M.; Hartline, J. C. and Loeb, P. D., eds.*, 1983, pp. 246–52.

Grant, E. Kenneth and Vanderkamp, John. Regional Demand–Supply Projections and Migration. **In** *Queen's Univ. Indust. Relat. Centre and John Deutsch Mem.*, 1983, pp. 112–27. [G: Canada]

Gustely, Richard D. and Ireland, Timothy C. Developing a Quarterly Counterpart to an Existing Annual Regional Econometric Model. *Reg. Sci. Persp.*, 1983, *13*(1), pp. 25–47. [G: U.S.]

Hafkamp, Wim and Nijkamp, Peter. Conflict Analysis and Compromise Strategies in Integrated Spatial Systems. *Reg. Sci. Urban Econ.*, February 1983, *13*(1), pp. 115–40.

Heady, Earl O.; Langley, James A. and Huang, Wen-yuan. A Recursive Adaptive Hybrid Model for National and Interregional Analysis. **In** *Gruber, J., ed.*, 1983, pp. 183–220. [G: U.S.]

Henry, Mark S. A Cost Effective Approach to Primary Input–Output Data Collection: Reply. *Rev. Public Data Use (See J. Econ. Soc. Meas. after 4/85)*, October 1983, *11*(3), pp. 193–95.

Hewings, Geoffrey J. D. A Cost Effective Approach to Primary Input–Output Data Collection: Some Comments. *Rev. Public Data Use (See J. Econ. Soc. Meas. after 4/85)*, October 1983, *11*(3), pp. 197–99.

Hinloopen, Edwin; Nijkamp, Peter and Rietveld, Piet. Qualitative Discrete Multiple Criteria Choice Models in Regional Planning. *Reg. Sci. Urban Econ.*, February 1983, *13*(1), pp. 77–102. [G: Belgium; Netherlands]

Ilan, Amos, et al. The Treatment of Foreign and Domestic Transportation in Regional Input–Output Modeling—An Analytic Framework. **In** *Dutta, M.; Hartline, J. C. and Loeb, P. D., eds.*, 1983, pp. 269–89. [G: U.S.]

Johnston, R. J. On the Symmetry of Leads and Lags in Studies of Regional Unemployment. *Reg. Stud.*, April 1983, *17*(2), pp. 105–12. [G: New Zealand]

Kort, John R. A Multiregional Test of the Conway–Howard Housing Construction Model. *J. Reg. Sci.*, August 1983, *23*(3), pp. 413–18. [G: U.S.]

Lakshmanan, T. R. A Multiregional Model of the Economy, Environment, and Energy Demand in the United States. *Econ. Geogr.*, July 1983, *59*(3), pp. 296–320. [G: U.S.]

Liu, Ben-chieh. Natural Gas Price Elasticities: Variations by Region and by Sector in the USA. *Energy Econ.*, July 1983, *5*(3), pp. 195–201. [G: U.S.]

Liu, Yih-wu and Stocks, Anthony H. A Labor–Oriented Quarterly Econometric Forecasting Model of the Youngstown–Warren SMSA. *Reg. Sci. Urban Econ.*, August 1983, *13*(3), pp. 317–40. [G: U.S.]

Maki, Wilbur R.; del Ninno, Carlo and Stenberg, Peter L. Forecasting State Economic Growth in Recession and Recovery. *Reg. Sci. Persp.*, 1983, *13*(2), pp. 39–50. [G: U.S.]

Mandeville, T. D. An Input–Output Framework for Measuring Economic Impacts: A Case Study of the Aluminium Industry at Gladstone, Australia. **In** *Hamilton, F. E. I. and Linge, G. J. R., eds.*, 1983, pp. 203–16. [G: Australia]

Mehretu, Assefa; Wittick, Robert I. and Pigozzi, Bruce W. Spatial Design for Basic Needs in Eastern Upper Volta. *J. Devel. Areas*, April 1983, *17*(3), pp. 383–94. [G: Upper Volta]

Miller, Ronald E. and Blair, Peter. Estimating State-Level Input–Output Relationships from U.S. Multiregional Data. *Int. Reg. Sci. Rev.*, December 1983, *8*(3), pp. 233–54. [G: U.S.]

Molho, I. I. A Regional Analysis of the Distribution of Married Women's Labour Force Participation Rates in the UK. *Reg. Stud.*, April 1983, *17*(2), pp. 125–33. [G: U.K.]

Mueller, Michael J. Optimal Groundwater Depletion with Interdependent Nonrenewable and Renewable Resources. *Water Resources Res.*, October 1983, *19*(5), pp. 1091–98. [G: U.S.]

Naroff, Joel L. and Madden, Thomas J. Using Discriminant Analysis to Predict Regional Shifts. *Growth Change*, April 1983, *14*(2), pp. 24–29. [G: U.S.]

Nijkamp, Peter and Rietveld, Piet. Multiobjective Decision Analysis in a Regional Context: Introduction. *Reg. Sci. Urban Econ.*, February 1983, *13*(1), pp. 1–3.

Osberg, Lars. Regional Demand–Supply Projections and Migration: Comment. **In** *Queen's Univ. Indust. Relat. Centre and John Deutsch Mem.*, 1983, pp. 128–31. **[G: Canada]**

Pullen, M. J. and Proops, J. L. R. The North Staffordshire Regional Economy: An Input–Output Assessment. *Reg. Stud.*, June 1983, *17*(3), pp. 191–200. **[G: U.K.]**

Ratick, Samuel J. Multiobjective Programming with Related Bargaining Games: An Application to Utility Coal Conversions. *Reg. Sci. Urban Econ.*, February 1983, *13*(1), pp. 55–76. **[G: U.S.]**

Reaume, David M. Migration and the Dynamic Stability of Regional Econometric Models. *Econ. Inquiry*, April 1983, *21*(2), pp. 281–93. **[G: U.S.]**

Round, Jeffrey I. Nonsurvey Techniques: A Critical Review of the Theory and the Evidence. *Int. Reg. Sci. Rev.*, December 1983, *8*(3), pp. 189–212.

Schaffer, William A. The Financial Impact of a University: A Case Study—The Impact of Georgia Tech on Georgia State Economy. **In** *Dutta, M.; Hartline, J. C. and Loeb, P. D., eds.*, 1983, pp. 131–50. **[G: U.S.]**

Sinclair, M. Thea and Sutcliffe, Charles M. S. Injection Leakages, Trade Repercussions and the Regional Income Multiplier: An Extension. *Scot. J. Polit. Econ.*, November 1983, *30*(3), pp. 275–86. **[G: U.K.]**

Stevens, Benjamin H., et al. A New Technique for the Construction of Non-survey Regional Input–Output Models. *Int. Reg. Sci. Rev.*, December 1983, *8*(3), pp. 271–86. **[G: U.S.]**

Swan, Neil. Regional Demand–Supply Projections and Migration: Comment. **In** *Queen's Univ. Indust. Relat. Centre and John Deutsch Mem.*, 1983, pp. 132–34. **[G: Canada]**

Takayama, T. and Uri, Noel D. A Note on Spatial and Temporal Price and Allocation Modeling: Quadratic Programming or Linear Complementarity Programming? *Reg. Sci. Urban Econ.*, November 1983, *13*(4), pp. 455–70.

Taylor, Carol A. and Charney, Alberta H. State–Substate Multiarea Modeling: The Case for Nonrigid Aggregation Rules. *Rev. Public Data Use (See J. Econ. Soc. Meas. after 4/85)*, December 1983, *11*(4), pp. 315–29. **[G: U.S.]**

Thomas, R. William and Stekler, H. O. A Regional Forecasting Model for Construction Activity. *Reg. Sci. Urban Econ.*, November 1983, *13*(4), pp. 557–77. **[G: U.S.]**

Treyz, George I. and Duguay, Gerry E. Endogenous Wage Determination: Its Significance for State Policy Analysis Models. **In** *Dutta, M.; Hartline, J. C. and Loeb, P. D., eds.*, 1983, pp. 116–30. **[G: U.S.]**

Webber, M. J. Location of Manufacturing and Operational Urban Models. **In** *Hamilton, F. E. I. and Linge, G. J. R., eds.*, 1983, pp. 141–202. **[G: U.S.; U.K.; Australia; Netherlands]**

Topical Guide
To Classification Schedule

TOPICAL GUIDE TO CLASSIFICATION SCHEDULE

This index refers to the subject index *group, category,* or *subcategory* in which the listed topic may be found. The subject index classifications include, in most cases, related topics as well. The term *category* generally indicates that the topic may be found in all of the *subcategories* of the 3-digit code; the term *group,* indicates that the topics may be found in all of the *subcategories* in the 2-digit code. The classification schedule (p. xxxiv) serves to refer the user to cross references.